CASES AND MATERIALS

CRIMINAL JUSTICE ADMINISTRATION

FIFTH EDITION

by

FRANK W. MILLER
James Carr Professor Emeritus of Criminal Jurisprudence,
Washington University

ROBERT O. DAWSON
Bryant Smith Chair in Law,
University of Texas

GEORGE E. DIX
A. W. Walker Centennial Chair in Law,
University of Texas

RAYMOND I. PARNAS
Professor of Law Emeritus,
University of California, Davis

NEW YORK, NEW YORK
FOUNDATION PRESS
2000

ISBN 1–56662–943–8

TEXT IS PRINTED ON 10% POST
CONSUMER RECYCLED PAPER

PREFACE

Since the first publication of these materials in 1971, the United States Supreme Court has greatly increased the amount of federal constitutional law relevant to criminal justice administration. This edition incorporates that law developing since the last edition was published in 1990 and important new aspects of nonconstitutional law.

As in prior editions, we have been selective in picking cases for use as principal ones. We have chosen for presentation in this manner those decisions that, in our view, constitute the most effective vehicles for classroom discussion. In order to fully present "the law," however, we have continued to make extensive use of introductory textual material and notes following principal cases. In these textual materials and notes, we have discussed many decisions in sufficient detail to permit consideration and discussion of their rationales and implications as well as to inform the students of their holdings.

We have renumbered the footnotes that we retained from opinions. We have deleted footnotes and textual citations to authority from principal opinions without specific indication of the omissions. Editors' footnotes are indicated by letters. We have noted omissions of opinions in principal cases only when, in our view, the existence of such opinions is useful in understanding the procedural or precedential significance of the opinion reprinted.

As was true of earlier editions, this edition is divided into two Parts of roughly equal size. The first deals with investigation of crime and the second with prosecution and adjudication. Part One is reprinted in a paperback titled, The Police Function (Sixth Edition), and Part Two in a paperback titled, Prosecution and Adjudication (Fifth Edition).

We wish to thank our very capable research assistants for the aid they provided in preparing this edition. They are Wenda Ferrell, Alison Holland, Elizabeth Niemeyer and Andrew Walker. Further, we appreciate the editorial assistance of Brenna Ryan.

FRANK W. MILLER
ROBERT O. DAWSON
GEORGE E. DIX
RAYMOND I. PARNAS

December 1999

*

SUMMARY OF CONTENTS

TABLE OF CONTENTS

*

TABLE OF CASES

Principal cases are in bold type. Non-principal cases are in roman type. References are to Pages.

*

CASES AND MATERIALS

CRIMINAL JUSTICE ADMINISTRATION

*

INTRODUCTION: THE CRIMINAL JUSTICE PROCESS

Analysis

NATIONAL ADVISORY COMMISSION ON CRIMINAL JUSTICE STANDARDS AND GOALS, COURTS 11–15 (1973)

* * *

ARREST

The first formal contact of an accused with the criminal justice system is likely to be an arrest by a police officer. In most cases, the arrest will be made upon the police officer's own evaluation that there is sufficient basis for believing that a crime had been committed by the accused. However, the arrest may be made pursuant to a warrant; in this case, the police officer or some other person will have submitted the evidence against the accused to a judicial officer, who determines whether the evidence is sufficient to justify an arrest. In some situations, the accused may have no formal contact with the law until he has been indicted by a grand jury. Following such an indictment, a court order may be issued authorizing police officers to take the accused into custody. But these are exceptional situations. Ordinarily, the arrest is made without any court order and the court's contact with the accused comes only after the arrest.

* * *

INITIAL JUDICIAL APPEARANCE

In all jurisdictions, a police officer or other person making an arrest must bring the arrested person before a judge within a short period of time. It is at this initial appearance that most accused have their first contact with the courts. This initial appearance is usually before a lower court—a justice of the peace or a magistrate. * * * Often by the time of the initial appearance, the prosecution will have prepared a formal document called a complaint, which charges the defendant with a specific crime.

At the initial appearance, several things may occur. First, the defendant will be informed of the charges against him, usually by means of the complaint. Second, he will be informed of his rights, including his constitutional privilege against self-incrimination. Third, if the case is one in which the accused will be provided with an attorney at State expense, the mechanical process of assigning the attorney at least may begin at this stage. Fourth, unless the defendant is convicted of an offense at this point, arrangements may be made concerning the release of the defendant before further proceedings. This may take the traditional form of setting bail, that is, establishment of an amount of security the defendant himself or a professional bondsman whom he may hire must deposit with the court (or

1

assume the obligation to pay) to assure that the defendant does appear for later proceedings. Pre-trial release, in some jurisdictions, also may take the form of being released on one's own recognizance, that is, release simply upon the defendant's promise to appear at a later time. * * *

In addition to these matters collateral to the issue of guilt, it is at the initial appearance that judicial inquiry into the merits of the case begins. If the charge is one the lower court has authority to try, the defendant may be asked how he pleads. If he pleads guilty, he may be convicted at this point. If he pleads not guilty, a trial date may be set and trial held later in this court.

However, if the charge is more serious, the court must give the defendant the opportunity for a judicial evaluation to determine whether there is enough evidence to justify putting him to trial in the higher court. In this type of case, the judge at the initial appearance ordinarily will ask the defendant whether he wants a preliminary hearing. If the defendant does, the matter generally is continued, or postponed to give both the prosecution and the defense time to prepare their cases.

The matter will be taken up again later in the lower court at the preliminary hearing. At this proceeding, the prosecutor introduces evidence to try to prove the defendant's guilt. He need not convince the court of the defendant's guilt beyond a reasonable doubt, but need only establish that there is enough evidence from which an average person (juror) could conclude that the defendant was guilty of the crime charged. If this evidence is produced, the court may find that the prosecution has established probable cause to believe the defendant guilty.

At this preliminary hearing the defendant may cross-examine witnesses produced by the prosecution and present evidence himself. If the court finds at the end of the preliminary hearing that probable cause does not exist, it dismisses the complaint. This does not ordinarily prevent the prosecution from bringing another charge, however. If the court finds that probable cause does exist, it orders that the defendant be bound over to the next step in the prosecution. As a practical matter, the preliminary hearing also serves the function of giving the defendant and his attorney a look at the case the prosecution will produce at trial. It gives a defense attorney the opportunity to cross-examine witnesses he later will have to confront. This informal previewing function may be more valuable to defendants than the theoretical function of the preliminary hearing.

FILING OF FORMAL CRIMINAL CHARGE

Generally, it is following the decision of the lower court to bind over a defendant that the formal criminal charge is made in the court that would try the case if it goes to formal trial. If no grand jury action is to be taken, this is a simple step consisting of the prosecutor's filing a document called an information. But in many jurisdictions the involvement of the grand jury makes the process more complex. There, the decision at the preliminary hearing simply is to bind the defendant over for consideration by the grand jury. In these areas, the prosecutor then must go before the grand jury and again present his evidence. Only if the grand jury determines that there is probable cause does it act. Its action—consisting of issuing a document called an indictment—constitutes the formal charging of the defendant. If it does not find probable cause, it takes no action and the prosecution is dismissed.

In some jurisdictions, it is not necessary to have both a grand jury inquiry and a preliminary hearing. In most Federal jurisdictions, for example, if a defendant has been indicted by a grand jury he no longer has a right to a preliminary hearing, on the theory that he is entitled to only one determination as to whether probable cause exists.

Although the defendant is entitled to participate in the preliminary hearing, he has no right to take part in a grand jury inquiry. Traditionally, he has not been able to ascertain what went on in front of the grand jury, although increasingly the law has given him the right, after the fact, to know.

Following the formal charge—whether it has been by indictment or information—any of a variety of matters that require resolution may arise. The defendant's competency to stand trial may be in issue. This requires the court to resolve the question of whether the defendant is too ill mentally or otherwise impaired to participate meaningfully in his trial. If he is sufficiently impaired, trial must be postponed until he regains his competency.

The defendant also may challenge the validity of the indictment or information or the means by which they were issued. For example, he may assert that those acts with which he is charged do not constitute a crime under the laws of the jurisdiction. Or, if he was indicted by a grand jury, he may assert that the grand jury was selected in a manner not consistent with State or Federal law and, therefore, that the indictment is invalid.

A defendant also may—and in some jurisdictions must—raise, before trial, challenges to the admissibility of certain evidence, especially evidence seized by police officers in a search or statements obtained from him by interrogation. In view of the rapid growth of legal doctrine governing the admissibility of statements of defendants and evidence obtained by police search and seizure, resolution of the issues raised by defendants' challenges to the admissibility of such evidence may be more complex and time-consuming than anything involved in determining guilt or innocence.

* * *

ARRAIGNMENT

In view of the potential complexity of pretrial matters, much of the significant activity in a criminal prosecution already may have occurred at the time the defendant makes his first formal appearance before the court that is to try him. This first appearance—the arraignment—is the point at which he is asked to plead to the charge. He need not plead, in which case a plea of not guilty automatically is entered for him. If he pleads guilty, the law requires that certain precautions be taken to assure that this plea is made validly. Generally, the trial judge accepting the plea first must inquire of the defendant whether he understands the charge against him and the penalties that may be imposed. The judge also must assure himself that there is some reasonable basis in the facts of the case for the plea. This may involve requiring the prosecution to present some of its evidence to assure the court that there is evidence tending to establish guilt.

TRIAL

Unless the defendant enters a guilty plea, the full adversary process is put into motion. The prosecution now must establish to a jury or a judge the guilt of the defendant beyond a reasonable doubt. If the defendant elects to have the case tried by a jury, much effort is expended on the selection of a jury. Prospective jurors are questioned to ascertain whether they might be biased and what their views on numerous matters might be. Both sides have the right to have a potential juror rejected on the ground that he may be biased. In addition, both have the right to reject a limited number of potential jurors without having to state any reason. When the jury has been selected and convened, both sides may make opening statements explaining what they intend to prove or disprove.

The prosecution presents its evidence first, and the defendant has the option of making no case and relying upon the prosecution's inability to establish guilt beyond a reasonable doubt. He also has the option of presenting evidence tending to disprove the prosecution's case or tending to prove additional facts constituting a defense under applicable law. Throughout, however, the burden remains upon the prosecution. Procedurally, this is effectuated by defense motions to dismiss, which often are made after the prosecution's case has been presented and after all of the evidence is in. These motions in effect assert that the prosecution's case is so weak that no reasonable jury could conclude beyond a reasonable doubt that the defendant was guilty. If the judge grants the motion, he is in effect determining that no jury could reasonably return a verdict of guilty. This not only results in a dismissal of the prosecution but also prevents the prosecution from bringing another charge for the same crime.

After the evidence is in and defense motions are disposed of, the jury is instructed on the applicable law. Often both defense and prosecution lawyers submit instructions which they ask the court to read to the jury, and the court chooses from those and others it composes itself. It is in the formulation of these instructions that many issues regarding the definition of the applicable law arise and must be resolved. After—or sometimes before—the instructions are read, both sides present formal arguments to the jury. The jury then retires for its deliberations.

Generally, the jury may return only one of two verdicts: guilty or not guilty. A verdict of not guilty may be misleading; it may mean not that the jury believed that the defendant was not guilty but rather that the jury determined that the prosecution had not established guilt by the criterion—beyond a reasonable doubt—the law imposes. If the insanity defense has been raised, the jury may be told it should specify if insanity is the reason for acquittal; otherwise, there is no need for explanation. If a guilty verdict is returned, the court formally enters a judgment of conviction unless there is a legally sufficient reason for not doing so.

The defendant may attack his conviction, usually by making a motion to set aside the verdict and order a new trial. In his attack, he may argue that evidence was improperly admitted during the trial, that the evidence was so weak that no reasonable jury could have found that it established guilt beyond a reasonable doubt, or that there is newly discovered evidence which, had it been available at the time of trial, would have changed the result. If the court grants a motion raising one of these arguments, the effect generally is not to acquit the defendant but merely to require the holding of a new trial.

SENTENCING

Sentencing then follows. (If the court has accepted a plea of guilty, this step follows acceptance of the plea.) In an increasing number of jurisdictions, an investigation called the presentence report is conducted by professional probation officers. This involves investigation of the offense, the offender and his background, and any other matters of potential value to the sentencing judge. Following submission of the report to the court, the defendant is given the opportunity to comment upon the appropriateness of sentencing. In some jurisdictions, this has developed into a more extensive court hearing on sentencing issues, with the defendant given the opportunity to present evidence as well as argument for leniency. Sentencing itself generally is the responsibility of the judge, although in some jurisdictions juries retain that authority.

APPEAL

Following the conclusion of the proceeding in the trial court, the matter shifts to the appellate courts. In some jurisdictions, a defendant who is convicted of a minor offense in a lower court has the right to a new trial (trial de novo) in a higher court. But in most situations—and in all cases involving serious offenses—the right to appeal is limited to the right to have an appellate court examine the record of the trial proceedings for error. If error is found, the appellate court either may take definitive action—such as ordering that the prosecution be dismissed—or it may set aside the conviction and remand the case for a new trial. The latter gives the prosecution the opportunity to obtain a valid conviction. Generally, a time limit is placed upon the period during which an appeal may be taken.

COLLATERAL ATTACK

Even if no appeal is taken or the conviction is upheld, the courts' participation in the criminal justice process is not necessarily ended. To some extent, a convicted defendant who has either exhausted his appeal rights or declined to exercise them within the appropriate time limits can seek further relief by means of collateral attack upon the conviction. This method involves a procedure collateral to the standard process of conviction and appeal.

Traditionally this relief was sought by applying for a writ of habeas corpus on the ground that the conviction under which the applicant was held was invalid. Many jurisdictions have found this vehicle too cumbersome for modern problems and have developed special procedures for collateral attacks. * * *

A general view of The Criminal Justice System

This chart seeks to present a simple yet comprehensive view of the movement of cases through the criminal justice system. Procedures in individual jurisdictions may vary from the pattern shown here. The differing weights of line indicate the relative volumes of cases disposed of at various points in the system, but this is only suggestive since no nationwide data of this sort exists.

<table>
<tr><td>1 May continue until trial.</td><td>3 Before magistrate, commissioner, or justice of peace. Formal notice of charge, advice of rights. Bail set. Summary trials for petty offenses usually conducted here without further processing.</td><td>5 Charge filed by prosecutor on basis of information submitted by police or citizens. Alternative to grand jury indictment, often used in felonies, almost always in misdemeanors.</td></tr>
<tr><td>2 Administrative record of arrest. First step at which temporary release on bail may be available.</td><td>4 Preliminary testing of evidence against defendant. Charge may be reduced. No separate preliminary hearing for misdemeanors in some systems.</td><td>6 Reviews whether Government evidence sufficient to justify trial. Some States have no grand jury system; others seldom use it.</td></tr>
</table>

Source: The President's Commission on Law Enforcement and Administration of Justice, The Challenge of Crime in a Free Society (1967).

Corrections

7   Appearance for plea; defendant elects trial by judge or jury (if available); counsel for indigent usually appointed here in felonies. Often not at all in other cases.

8   Charge may be reduced at any time prior to trial in return for plea of guilty or for other reasons.

9   Challenge on constitutional grounds to legality of detention. May be sought at any point in process.

10 Police often hold informal hearings, dismiss or adjust many cases without further processing.

11 Probation officer decides desirability of further court action.

12 Welfare agency, social services, counselling, medical care, etc., for cases where adjudicatory handling not needed.

✳

PART ONE

Investigation of Crime

EDITORS' INTRODUCTION: FEDERAL AND STATE
CONSTITUTIONAL PROVISIONS AFFECTING LAW ENFORCEMENT
CONDUCT

Law enforcement conduct, and the admissibility of evidence developed by such conduct, is affected by law emanating from numerous sources other than the United States Constitution. Nevertheless, because of the United States Supreme Court's "constitutionalization" of criminal procedure, several provisions of the federal document—applicable to the states by virtue of the Fourteenth Amendment—have taken on immense significance for law enforcement activity. Much of the material in Part One of this book is devoted to exploring the content of these provisions.

United States Constitution

Amendment IV

The right of the people to be secure in their persons, houses, papers, and effects, against unreasonable searches and seizures, shall not be violated, and no Warrants shall issue, but upon probable cause, supported by Oath or affirmation, and particularly describing the place to be searched, and the persons or things to be seized.

Amendment V

No person * * * shall be compelled in any criminal case to be a witness against himself, nor be deprived of life, liberty, or property, without due process of law * * *.

Amendment VI

In all criminal prosecutions, the accused shall enjoy the right * * * to have the Assistance of Counsel for his defense.

Amendment XIV, Section 1

No State shall * * * deprive any person of life, liberty, or property, without due process of law; nor deny to any person within its jurisdiction the equal protection of the laws.

———

State constitutions usually have provisions analogous and sometimes identical to those provisions. Article 1 of the Utah constitution, for example, contains the following provisions:

Section 12. Right of accused persons

In criminal prosecutions the accused shall have the right to appear and defend in person and by counsel * * *. The accused shall not be compelled to give evidence against himself.

Section 14. Unreasonable searches forbidden—Issuance of warrant

The right of the people to be secure in their persons, houses, papers and effects against unreasonable searches and seizures shall not be violated; and no warrant shall issue but upon probable cause supported by oath or affirmation, particularly describing the place to be searched and the person or thing to be seized.

Other state provisions differ more significantly from their federal counterparts. Article 1, Section 4 of the Washington Constitution, for example, provides:

No person shall be disturbed in his private affairs, or his home invaded, without authority of law.

The state constitutional convention that proposed the Washington provision had been presented with language identical to that used in the Fourth Amendment to the United States Constitution but rejected it in favor of that finally used. See State v. Ringer, 100 Wn.2d 686, 690, 674 P.2d 1240, 1243 (1983).

Obviously, a state cannot—by constitutional provision or otherwise—deprive its citizens of rights which they have by virtue of the United States Constitution. But it is equally obvious that states can—by constitutional provision or otherwise—give their citizens more protection than those citizens are afforded by the federal Constitution. Even if a state constitutional provision is phrased similarly or identically to an analogous federal constitutional provision, the state courts need not construe the state provision as having the same content as the United States Supreme Court has given to the federal provision. State judicial willingness to "independently" construe state constitutional provisions has become widely labeled "new federalism." See, e.g., Wilkes, The New Federalism in Criminal Procedure: State Court Evasion of the Burger Court, 62 Ky.L.J. 421 (1974). The state tribunals may, of course, construe state provisions as conferring no more rights upon citizens, suspects or defendants than the Supreme Court construes the federal provisions as providing, and in fact many state courts do so.

When a state court properly construes a state provision more expansively than the Supreme Court has construed its federal counterpart is a difficult question. The Pennsylvania Supreme Court suggested it would look at four factors: 1) the text of the state constitutional provision; 2) the history of the provision, including state case law. 3) related case-law from other states; and 4) policy considerations unique to the state. Commonwealth v. Edmunds, 526 Pa. 374, 390, 586 A.2d 887, 895 (1991). In State v. Carter, 596 N.W.2d 654, 657 (Minn.1999), the Minnesota Supreme Court reviewed its "new federalism" case law. That case law, it concluded, reflects "we interpreted the Minnesota Constitution as according greater protection than the Supreme Court's interpretation of the Fourth Amendment because we viewed the Supreme Court's decisions as "radical" or "sharp" departures from precedent."

Some state courts have construed state provisions as conferring more rights upon suspects and defendants than their federal counterparts because the state tribunals concluded that the Supreme Court case law reflects inappropriate evaluation of relevant policy considerations. In State v. Mendez, 137 Wash.2d 208, 970 P.2d 722 (1999), for example, the Washington Supreme Court held that during a traffic stop the Washington constitution limits a police officer's authority to order passengers out of the vehicle. Such action is permitted only if the officer has an objective rationale for doing so based specifically on safety concerns regarding officers, vehicle occupants or other persons. As is discussed in Chapter 4, the Supreme Court has held that the Fourth Amendment requires no justification for such action by an officer. The Washington court explained its holding as based primarily upon its longstanding position that the Washington constitutional search and seizure provision recognizes greater privacy in automobiles in general and for passengers in particular than the Supreme Court has read into the Fourth Amendment.

In any case, State courts are in general agreement that a party seeking to have state courts construe state provisions as more protective of suspects and defendants than their federal counterparts must persuade the state courts of the propriety and wisdom of the proposed constructions.

> [A] [state] court should not "cavalierly construe [the state] constitution more expansively than the United States Supreme Court has construed the federal constitution." Minnesota courts will not apply more stringent state standards, absent a compelling reason to do so.

State v. Martin, 595 N.W.2d 214, 217 (Minn.App.1999) review denied. California courts apply a "general rule of deference—that the California Constitution should only be interpreted more broadly when there are cogent reasons, independent state interests requiring additional protection, or strong countervailing policies justifying an independent reliance on a broader construction of the California Constitution." Iraheta v. Superior Court, 70 Cal.App.4th 1500, 1507, 83 Cal.Rptr.2d 471, 476 (1999) review denied. "When the issue of broader state constitutional protections arises," the Washington Supreme Court has explained, "the party seeking that broader protection must discuss reasons for reading the state provision differently from its federal counterpart." State v. Bustamante–Davila, 983 P.2d 590, 597 (Wash.1999).

These materials emphasize the federal constitutional provisions and their construction. But full treatment of these issues in state litigation cannot ignore "new federalism" and state law arguments independent of federal constitutional ones.

CHAPTER 1

THE EXCLUSIONARY SANCTION

Analysis

EDITORS' INTRODUCTION: EXCLUSIONARY RULES

The most dramatic development in American criminal procedure has been its "constitutionalization." To a significant extent, the requirements imposed by local statutes, case law and court rules have been eclipsed by the development of federal constitutional requirements. Constitutionalization of certain evidence matters by federal constitutional exclusionary requirements has been particularly important.

The major federal constitutional requirements affecting law enforcement conduct and the admissibility in a criminal trial of evidence obtained by law enforcement efforts are set out in the Editors' Introduction to Part One of these materials. These are, of course, binding on the states because of the Fourteenth Amendment. This chapter considers the enforcement of these provisions and other legal requirements by rules excluding evidence obtained in violation of their terms. The substance of these provisions is considered throughout much of the remainder of Part One; the basic contours of the Fourth and Fifth Amendments are addressed in Chapter 2.

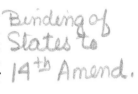

Binding of States to 14th Amend.

Requirements that evidence offered by the prosecution at a criminal trial be rejected because of impropriety in the process of gathering it are often referred to as "exclusionary rules." In one sense, any legal rule resulting in evidence being held inadmissible is "exclusionary." But in common legal usage, the phrase "exclusionary rule" has come to mean a legal requirement mandating exclusion of evidence because of the illegal manner in which it was obtained. Exclusion is usually imposed without regard to whether the illegality affects the reliability of the evidence. The traditional requirement that out-of-court confessions given by defendants be "voluntary" (discussed in Chapter 7) is an exclusionary rule under this definition. But in its original form, the prohibition against the use of involuntary confessions appears to have been based more upon a perception that coercion rendered confessions unreliable than upon the desirability of responding to illegality in the interrogation process by holding the fruits of that illegality inadmissible.

Discussions are often conducted in terms of what is assumed to be "the exclusionary rule," as if only one doctrine or legal requirement is involved. This is simply not the case. "[T]he exclusionary rule" usually describes the requirement—announced in Mapp v. Ohio, reprinted in this chapter—that evidence obtained in violation of the Fourth Amendment be excluded from state criminal trials. But *Mapp* is not the only legal requirement mandating exclusion of evidence because of impropriety in the manner in which it was obtained. Other federal constitutional provisions also require exclusion of evidence obtained in violation of their requirements. Moreover, the exclusionary requirements attaching to the various federal constitutional provisions are not necessarily the same. As is developed later in these materials, for example, the extent to which evidence derived from a violation must be excluded may differ significantly depending upon whether the underlying violation is of the Fourth Amendment's requirements or, instead, of judicially-developed rules based upon the Fifth Amendment.

Evidence obtained by conduct violating state legal requirements but not a federal constitutional provision may be inadmissible as a matter of state law. If state law imposes such a requirement, the details of that requirement—as, for example, the number and scope of exceptions sometime permitting the use of illegally seized evidence—may not be the same as the details of the Fourth Amendment federal constitutional exclusionary rule.

Conceptually, then, it is best to regard exclusionary requirements as consisting of a number of potentially quite different exclusionary demands imposed by various legal requirements. There could be as many exclusionary rules as there are legal requirements that might be violated in the obtaining of evidence.

The Fourth Amendment exclusionary rule announced in Mapp v. Ohio has generated the most controversy. Consequently, these materials emphasize that holding and its development. Showings that evidence was obtained in violation of other legal requirements present distinguishable although related exclusionary rule issues.

Exclusionary rule concerns are presented throughout Part One of these materials. Chapters 2 through 6 address a variety of issues concerning law enforcement authority to make searches and seizures. Action taken beyond this authority may invoke exclusionary sanctions. While exclusionary rule considerations are less pervasive in the material addressed in Chapters 7 through 10, they are nevertheless present and important. Chapter 1 limits itself to the exclusionary sanction and its procedural aspects: When, if ever, is it appropriate? If it applies, when does it require the exclusion of challenged evidence? What exceptions to the general rule of exclusion do and should exist?

A. ADOPTION OF THE FEDERAL CONSTITUTIONAL EXCLUSIONARY SANCTION

Exclusion of evidence resulting from improper law enforcement conduct was not a notion original with the United States Supreme Court. The Vermont court, for example, embraced an exclusionary rule as a matter of state law in State v. Slamon, 50 A. 1097 (Vt.1901). Nevertheless, the Supreme Court's adoption of this sanction for violation of federal constitutional rights is largely responsible for the pervasive impact exclusionary rules have on modern criminal procedure.

The Court's position in the case law culminating in the case reprinted in this part, Mapp v. Ohio, reflects both a break from evidence law tradition and the Court's prior position. In Adams v. New York, 192 U.S. 585, 24 S.Ct. 372, 48 L.Ed. 575 (1904), the Court rejected a state defendant's complaint regarding the use in his trial of evidence seized in violation of the Fourth Amendment. Where such evidence shows the accused's guilt, the Court explained, "the weight of authority as well as reason limits the inquiry to the competency of the proffered testimony, and the courts do not stop to inquire as to the means by which the evidence was obtained." This traditional position—that the manner in which otherwise competent evidence was obtained does not affect its admissibility—was supported by two major consideration: the need to have all available relevant evidence bearing on the important issues posed in criminal litigation, and the inconvenience, disruption, and other costs involved in making the complex and collateral inquiries determining whether challenged evidence was in fact improperly obtained. See generally, McCormick on Evidence § 164 (Fifth edition, J. Strong ed. 1999).

A major issue posed by *Mapp* is the role history should play in construction of those federal constitutional provisions applicable to law enforcement conduct. Some members of the Supreme Court believe many aspects of the Fourth Amendment's contents should be determined or informed by the "intent" or contemplation of the framers as reflected in then-current law. Thus in Wyoming v. Houghton, 526 U.S. 295, ___, 119 S.Ct. 1297, 1300, 143 L.Ed.2d 408, 414 (1999), reprinted in part in Chapter 5, Justice Scalia—writing for the Court—explained that "[i]n determining whether a particular governmental action violates [the Fourth Amendment], we inquire first whether the action was regarded as an unlawful search or seizure under the common law when the amendment was framed." Only if that inquiry provides no answer, he continued, is the Court to balance competing policy considerations in assessing the action's reasonableness. Should the Court have taken a similar approach in *Mapp*, and inquired whether under the common law in effect when the Fourth Amendment was framed a defendant such as *Mapp* was entitled to have excluded evidence improperly obtained?

The major argument against the approach applied by Justice Scalia in *Houghton* is its failure to take into account the vast difference between the common law context and modern criminal justice. In another decision relying heavily upon the common law position, the Supreme Court cautioned against excessive reliance upon this source:

> The significance accorded to [common law] authority * * * must be kept in perspective, for our decisions in this area have not "simply frozen into constitutional law those enforcement practices that existed at the time of the Fourth Amendment's passage." The common-law rules governing searches and arrests evolved in a society far simpler than ours is today. Crime has changed, as have the means of law enforcement, and it would therefore be naive to assume that those actions a constable could take in an English or American village three centuries ago should necessarily govern what we, as a society, now regard as proper. Instead, the Amendment's prohibition against "unreasonable searches and seizures" must be interpreted "in light of contemporary norms and conditions."

Steagald v. United States, 451 U.S. 204, 218 n. 10, 101 S.Ct. 1642, 1651 n. 10, 68 L.Ed.2d 38, 48 n. 10 (1981).

Mapp v. Ohio

Supreme Court of the United States, 1961.
367 U.S. 643, 81 S.Ct. 1684, 6 L.Ed.2d 1081.

■ MR. JUSTICE CLARK delivered the opinion of the Court.

Appellant stands convicted of knowingly having had in her possession and under her control certain lewd and lascivious books, pictures, and photographs * * * though "based primarily upon the introduction in evidence of lewd and lascivious books and pictures unlawfully seized during an unlawful search of defendant's home * * *." * * *

On May 23, 1957, three Cleveland police officers arrived at appellant's residence in that city pursuant to information that "a person [was] hiding out in the home, who was wanted for questioning in connection with a recent bombing, and that there was a large amount of policy paraphernalia being hidden in the home." * * * [B]ut appellant, after telephoning her attorney, refused to admit them without a search warrant. * * *

The officers again sought entrance some three hours later when four or more additional officers arrived on the scene. When Miss Mapp did not come to the door immediately, at least one of the several doors to the house was forcibly opened and the policemen gained admittance. Meanwhile Miss Mapp's attorney arrived, but the officers, having secured their own entry, and continuing in their defiance of the law, would permit him neither to see Miss Mapp nor to enter the house. It appears that Miss Mapp was halfway down the stairs from the upper floor to the front door when the officers, in this highhanded manner, broke into the hall. She demanded to see the search warrant. A paper, claimed to be a warrant, was held up by one of the officers. She grabbed the "warrant" and placed it in her bosom. A struggle ensued in which the officers recovered the piece of paper and as a result of which they handcuffed appellant because she had been "belligerent" in resisting their official rescue of the "warrant" from her person.

* * * The obscene materials for possession of which she was ultimately convicted were discovered in the course of [a] widespread search.

At the trial no search warrant was produced by the prosecution, nor was the failure to produce one explained or accounted for. * * * The Ohio Supreme Court believed a "reasonable argument" could be made that the conviction should be reversed "because the 'methods' employed to obtain the [evidence] were such as to 'offend "a sense of justice,"' " but the court found determinative the fact that the evidence had not been taken 'from defendant's person by the use of brutal or offensive physical force against defendant.' "

* * *

The State says that even if the search were made without authority, or otherwise unreasonably, it is not prevented from using the unconstitutionally seized evidence at trial, citing Wolf v. People of the State of Colorado, 1949, 338 U.S. 25, at page 33, 69 S.Ct. 1359 * * *, in which this Court did indeed hold "that in a prosecution in a State court for a State crime the Fourteenth Amendment does not forbid the admission of evidence obtained by an unreasonable search and seizure." On this appeal * * * it is urged once again that we review that holding.

I.

Seventy-five years ago, in Boyd v. United States, 1886, 116 U.S. 616, 630, 6 S.Ct. 524, 532, 29 L.Ed. 746, considering the Fourth and Fifth Amendments as running "almost into each other" on the facts before it, this Court held that the doctrines of those Amendments

> "apply to all invasions on the part of the government and its employes of the sanctity of a man's home and the privacies of life. It is not the breaking of his doors, and the rummaging of his drawers, that constitutes the essence of the offence; but it is the invasion of his indefeasible right of personal security, personal liberty and private property * * * . Breaking into a house and opening boxes and drawers are circumstances of aggravation; but any forcible and compulsory extortion of a man's own testimony or of his private papers to be used as evidence to convict him of crime or to forfeit his goods, is within the condemnation * * * [of those Amendments]."

* * *

Less than 30 years after *Boyd*, this Court, in Weeks v. United States, 1914, [232 U.S. 383, 393, 34 S.Ct. 341, 344, 58 L.Ed.2d 652,] * * * [s]pecifically dealing with the use of * * * evidence unconstitutionally seized, * * * concluded:

> "If letters and private documents can thus be seized and held and used in evidence against a citizen accused of an offense, the protection of the Fourth Amendment declaring his right to be secure against such searches and seizures is of no value, and, so far as those thus placed are concerned, might as well be stricken from the Constitution. The efforts of the courts and their officials to bring the guilty to punishment, praiseworthy as they are, are not to be aided by the sacrifice of

those great principles established by years of endeavor and suffering which have resulted in their embodiment in the fundamental law of the land."

* * * Thus, in the year 1914, in the *Weeks* case, this Court "for the first time" held that "in a federal prosecution the Fourth Amendment barred the use of evidence secured through an illegal search and seizure."

* * * There are in the cases of this Court some passing references to the *Weeks* rule as being one of evidence. But the plain and unequivocal language of *Weeks* * * * to the effect that the *Weeks* rule is of constitutional origin, remains entirely undisturbed. * * *

II.

In 1949, 35 years after *Weeks* was announced, this Court, in Wolf v. People of the State of Colorado, supra, again for the first time, discussed the effect of the Fourth Amendment upon the States through the operation of the Due Process Clause of the Fourteenth Amendment. It said:

"[W]e have no hesitation in saying that were a State affirmatively to sanction such police incursion into privacy it would run counter to the guaranty of the Fourteenth Amendment." * * *

Nevertheless, after declaring that the "security of one's privacy against arbitrary intrusion by the police" is "implicit in 'the concept of ordered liberty' and as such enforceable against the States through the Due Process Clause," * * * and announcing that it "stoutly adhere[d]" to the *Weeks* decision, the Court decided that the *Weeks* exclusionary rule would not then be imposed upon the States as "an essential ingredient of the right." * * * The Court's reasons for not considering essential to the right to privacy, as a curb imposed upon the States by the Due Process Clause, that which decades before had been posited as part and parcel of the Fourth Amendment's limitation upon federal encroachment of individual privacy, were bottomed on factual considerations.

While they are not basically relevant to a decision that the exclusionary rule is an essential ingredient of the Fourth Amendment as the right it embodies is vouchsafed against the States by the Due Process Clause, we will consider the current validity of the factual grounds upon which *Wolf* was based.

The Court in *Wolf* * * * stated that "[t]he contrariety of views of the States" on the adoption of the exclusionary rule of *Weeks* was "particularly impressive" * * * ; and, in this connection that it could not "brush aside the experience of States which deem the incidence of such conduct by the police too slight to call for a deterrent remedy * * * by overriding the [States'] relevant rules of evidence." * * * While in 1949, prior to the *Wolf* case, almost two-thirds of the States were opposed to the use of the exclusionary rule, now, despite the *Wolf* case, more than half of those since passing upon it, by their own legislative or judicial decision, have wholly or partly adopted or adhered to the *Weeks* rule. * * * Significantly, among those now following the rule is California, which, according to its highest court, was "compelled to reach that conclusion because other remedies have completely failed to secure compliance with the constitutional provisions * * *." People v. Cahan, 1955, 44 Cal.2d 434, 445, 282 P.2d 905, 911. In connection with this California case, we note that the second basis elaborated in *Wolf* in support of its failure to enforce the exclusionary doctrine against the States was that "other means of protection" have been afforded "the right to privacy." The experience of California that such other remedies have been worthless and futile is buttressed by the experience of other States. The obvious futility of relegating the Fourth Amendment to the protection of other remedies has, moreover, been recognized by this Court since *Wolf.*

* * *

It, therefore, plainly appears that the factual considerations supporting the failure of the *Wolf* Court to include the *Weeks* exclusionary rule when it recognized the enforceability of the right to privacy against the States in 1949, while not basically relevant to the constitutional consideration, could not, in any analysis, now be deemed controlling.

III.

Some five years after *Wolf*, in answer to a plea made here Term after Term that we overturn its doctrine on applicability of the *Weeks* exclusionary rule, this Court indicated that such should not be done until the States had "adequate opportunity to adopt or reject the [*Weeks*] rule." Irvine v. People of State of California, [1954, 347 U.S. 128, 134, 74 S.Ct. 381, 384, 98 L.Ed. 561] * * *. Today we once again examine *Wolf's* constitutional documentation of the right to privacy free from unreasonable state intrusion, and, after its dozen years on our books, are led by it to close the only courtroom door remaining open to evidence secured by official lawlessness in flagrant abuse of that basic right, reserved to all persons as a specific guarantee against that very same unlawful conduct. We hold that all evidence obtained by searches and seizures in violation of the Constitution is, by that same authority, inadmissible in a state court.

IV.

Since the Fourth Amendment's right of privacy has been declared enforceable against the States through the Due Process Clause of the Fourteenth, it is enforceable against them by the same sanction of exclusion as is used against the Federal Government. Were it otherwise, then just as without the *Weeks* rule the assurance against unreasonable federal searches and seizures would be "a form of words", valueless and undeserving of mention in a perpetual charter of inestimable human liberties, so too, without that rule the freedom from state invasions of privacy would be so ephemeral and so neatly severed from its conceptual nexus with the freedom from all brutish means of coercing evidence as not to merit this Court's high regard as a freedom "implicit in 'the concept of ordered liberty.' " * * * In short, the admission of the new constitutional right by *Wolf* could not consistently tolerate denial of its most important constitutional privilege, namely, the exclusion of the evidence which an accused had been forced to give by reason of the unlawful seizure. To hold otherwise is to grant the right but in reality to withhold its privilege and enjoyment. Only last year the Court itself recognized that the purpose of the exclusionary rule "is to deter—to compel respect for the constitutional guaranty in the only effectively available way—by removing the incentive to disregard it." Elkins v. United States [1960, 364 U.S. 206, 217, 80 S.Ct. 1437, 1444, 4 L.Ed.2d 1669].

* * *

V.

Moreover, our holding that the exclusionary rule is an essential part of both the Fourth and Fourteenth Amendments is not only the logical dictate of prior cases, but it also makes very good sense. There is no war between the Constitution and common sense. Presently, a federal prosecutor may make no use of evidence illegally seized, but a State's attorney across the street may, although he supposedly is operating under the enforceable prohibitions of the same Amendment. Thus the State, by admitting evidence unlawfully seized, served to encourage disobedience to the Federal Constitution which it is bound to uphold. * * *

Federal-state cooperation in the solution of crime under constitutional standards will be promoted, if only by recognition of their now mutual obligation to respect the same fundamental criteria in their approaches. "However much in a particular case insistence upon such rules may appear as a technicality that inures to the benefit of a guilty person, the history of the criminal law proves that tolerance of shortcut methods in law enforcement impairs its enduring effectiveness." Miller v. United States, 1958, 357 U.S. 301, 313, 78 S.Ct. 1190, 1197, 2 L.Ed.2d 1332. Denying shortcuts to only one of two cooperating law enforcement agencies tends naturally to breed legitimate suspicion of "working arrangements" whose results are equally tainted. * * *

There are those who say, as did Justice (then Judge) Cardozo, that under our constitutional exclusionary doctrine "[t]he criminal is to go free because the constable has blundered." People v. Defore, [1926, 242 N.Y. 13, 21, 150 N.E. 585, 587]. In some cases this will undoubtedly be the result. But, as was said in *Elkins*, "there is another consideration—the imperative of judicial integrity." * * * The criminal goes free, if he must, but it is the law that sets him free. Nothing can destroy a government more quickly than its failure to observe its own laws, or worse, its disregard of the charter of its own existence. As Mr. Justice Brandeis, dissenting, said in Olmstead v. United States, 1928, 277 U.S. 438, 485, 48 S.Ct. 564, 575, 72 L.Ed. 944: "Our government is the potent, the omnipresent teacher. For good or for ill, it teaches the whole people by its example. * * * If the government becomes a lawbreaker, it breeds contempt for law; it invites every man to become a law unto himself; it invites anarchy." Nor can it lightly be assumed that, as a practical matter, adoption of the exclusionary rule fetters law enforcement. Only last year this Court expressly considered that contention and found that "pragmatic evidence of a sort" to the contrary was not wanting. Elkins v. United States, supra. The Court noted that

"The federal courts themselves have operated under the exclusionary rule of *Weeks* for almost half a century; yet it has not been suggested either that the Federal Bureau of Investigation has thereby been rendered ineffective, or that the administration of criminal justice in the federal courts has thereby been disrupted. Moreover, the experience of the states is impressive * * * . The movement towards the rule of exclusion has been halting but seemingly inexorable." * * *

The ignoble shortcut to conviction left open to the State tends to destroy the entire system of constitutional restraints on which the liberties of the people rest. Having once recognized that the right to privacy embodied in the Fourth Amendment is enforceable against the States, and that the right to be secure against rude invasions of privacy by state officers is, therefore, constitutional in origin, we can no longer permit that right to remain an empty promise. Because it is enforceable in the same manner and to like effect as other basic rights secured by the Due Process Clause, we can no longer permit it to be revocable at the whim of any police officer who, in the name of law enforcement itself, chooses to suspend its enjoyment. Our decision, founded on reason and truth, gives to the individual no more than that which the Constitution guarantees him, to the police officer no less than that to which honest law enforcement is entitled, and, to the courts, that judicial integrity so necessary in the true administration of justice.

The judgment of the Supreme Court of Ohio is reversed and the cause remanded for further proceedings not inconsistent with this opinion.

Reversed and remanded.

[The concurring opinions of JUSTICES BLACK and DOUGLAS and the dissenting opinion of JUSTICE HARLAN, joined by JUSTICES FRANKFURTER and WHITTAKER, are omitted.]

NOTES

1. **Exclusionary Sanctions for Fifth and Sixth Amendment Violations.** Following *Mapp,* the Supreme Court virtually without discussion assumed the federal constitution requires exclusion of evidence obtained in violation of the defendant's Fifth Amendment privilege against compelled self-incrimination, Miranda v. Arizona, 384 U.S. 436, 86 S.Ct. 1602, 16 L.Ed.2d 694 (1966), the Sixth Amendment right to counsel, Brewer v. Williams, 430 U.S. 387, 97 S.Ct. 1232, 51 L.Ed.2d 424 (1977), and the Sixth Amendment right to counsel during certain pretrial identification procedures, Gilbert v. California, 388 U.S. 263, 87 S.Ct. 1951, 18 L.Ed.2d 1178 (1967).

2. **Judicial Integrity.** In post-*Mapp* case law, the Supreme Court refined its view as to the policy considerations supporting the Fourth Amendment exclusionary rule developed in that case. *Mapp,* for example, relied in part upon what it called "judicial integrity." This has clearly become considerably less significant. Fifteen years after *Mapp* the Court commented:

Judicial integrity clearly does not mean that the courts must never admit evidence obtained in violation of the Fourth Amendment. * * *

The primary meaning of "judicial integrity" in the context of evidentiary rules is that the courts must not commit or encourage violations of the Constitution. In the Fourth Amendment area, however, * * * the violation is complete by the time the evidence is presented to the court. The focus therefore must be on the question whether the admission of the evidence encourages violations of Fourth Amendment rights. * * * [T]his inquiry is essentially the same as the inquiry into whether exclusion would serve a deterrent purpose.

United States v. Janis, 428 U.S. 433, 458 n. 35, 96 S.Ct. 3021, 3034 n. 35, 49 L.Ed.2d 1046, 1063 n. 35 (1976).

3. **Remedial Function.** Is the *Mapp* exclusionary requirement supportable on the ground it provides an appropriate remedy for the wrong done to the person unreasonably searched or seized? The Court has stated:

> Post-*Mapp* decisions have established that the [exclusionary] rule is not a personal constitutional right. It is not calculated to redress the injury to the privacy of the victim of the search or seizure, for any "[r]eparation comes too late." Linkletter v. Walker, 381 U.S. 618, 637, 85 S.Ct. 1731, 14 L.Ed.2d 601 (1965). * * *

Stone v. Powell, 428 U.S. 465, 484–86, 96 S.Ct. 3037, 3047, 49 L.Ed.2d 1067, 1082–83 (1976).

4. **Systemic Prevention.** Most discussions of the exclusionary sanction assumes it works by consciously deterring particular officers from engaging in conduct they know will violate suspects' Fourth Amendment rights. But the sanction may prevent violations in other ways. In Stone v. Powell, 428 U.S. 465, 96 S.Ct. 3037, 49 L.Ed.2d 1067 (1976), the Court commented:

> [W]e have assumed that the immediate effect of exclusion will be to discourage law enforcement officials from violating the Fourth Amendment by removing the incentive to disregard it. More importantly, over the long term, this demonstration that our society attaches serious consequences to violation of constitutional rights is thought to encourage those who formulate law enforcement policies, and the officers who implement them, to incorporate Fourth Amendment ideals into their value system.

428 U.S. at 492, 96 S.Ct. at 3051, 49 L.Ed.2d 1086–87. Even if exclusion of evidence does not cause law enforcement officials and officers to incorporate Fourth Amendment ideals into their internal value system, it may cause them to encourage compliance with the provision's requirements by the development of specific and practical guidelines and training programs. Some commentators refer to these processes by which exclusion might affect law enforcement behavior as "systemic deterrence." See Christopher Slobogin, Why Liberals Should Chuck the Exclusionary Rule, 1999 Ill.L.Rev. 363, 393 (1999).

5. **Other Uses of Unconstitutionally Obtained Evidence.** In determining whether a federal constitutional exclusionary rule should be expanded beyond a prohibition against using unconstitutionally obtained evidence at trial to prove the defendant's guilt, the Court has utilized a balancing analysis. That analysis asks how much the functions of the rule would be increased by the additional exclusion of evidence that would result from the potential expansion. Addressing this generally involves primarily a consideration of the incremental deterrence that would be accomplished. The Court then weighs against this incremental deterrence the costs of so expanding the rule, and inquires whether the incremental deterrence is worth the cost. See United States v. Calandra, 414 U.S. 338, 349–52, 94 S.Ct. 613, 620–22, 38 L.Ed.2d 561, 572–73 (1974).

In Pennsylvania Board of Probation and Parole v. Scott, 524 U.S. 357, 118 S.Ct. 2014, 141 L.Ed.2d 344 (1998), for example, the Court addressed whether evidence obtained in violation of the Fourth Amendment could be used at a parole violation hearing to prove a convicted and paroled defendant violated the conditions of parole. By a 5–to–4 vote, it held such evidence could be so used. Justice Thomas' opinion first stressed the cost of exclusion:

Because the exclusionary rule precludes consideration of reliable, probative evidence, it imposes significant costs: it undeniably detracts from the truthfinding process and allows many who would otherwise be incarcerated to escape the consequences of their actions . .* * * [O]ur cases have repeatedly emphasized that the rule's "costly toll" upon truth-seeking and law enforcement objectives presents a high obstacle for those urging application of the rule.

524 U.S. at ___, 118 S.Ct. at 2020, 141 L.Ed.2d at 352. These costs are particularly high in the parole context, the Court continued, because states give up the right to continue incarceration of convicted persons on the condition they abide by the terms and conditions of parole release. Therefore, states have an "overwhelming interest" in enforcing these terms and limits, and this interest would be frustrated by application of the exclusionary rule. Further, application of the exclusionary rule would compel the states to transform parole revocation proceedings from "a 'productive and discretionary' effort to promote the best interests of both parolees and society into trial-like proceedings less attuned to the interests of the parolee."

The deterrent effect of applying the exclusionary rule to parole revocation would not, the *Scott* majority added, outweigh these costs. Officers will often be unaware that suspects are parolees, and thus "the remote possibility that the subject is a parolee and that the evidence may be admitted at a parole revocation proceeding surely has little, if any, effect on the officer's incentives."

The state court held the Fourth Amendment exclusionary rule should apply to parole revocation proceedings but only upon proof officers who engaged in the challenged search or seizure were aware of the suspect's status as a parolee. Rejecting this view, *Scott* first indicated this "piecemeal approach" would add to exclusionary rule procedure an undesirable need to inquire into officers' knowledge of parolees' status. Even in these cases, it added, deterrence would be minimal. Police officers aware of a suspect's parolee status will be deterred by the inadmissibility of illegally-seized evidence at criminal trials. Parole officers' relationship with parolees "is more supervisory than adversarial." This means "the harsh deterrent of exclusion [from parole revocation proceedings] is unwarranted," because adequate deterrence can be achieved by "other deterrents as departmental training and discipline and the threat of damages actions."

For these reasons, the *Scott* majority declined "to extend the operation of the exclusionary rule beyond the criminal trial context" as urged by Scott.

Four members of the Court disagreed:

[T]he majority does not see that in the investigation of criminal conduct by someone known to be on parole, Fourth Amendment standards will have very little deterrent sanction unless evidence offered for parole revocation is subject to suppression for unconstitutional conduct. * * * [P]arole revocation will frequently be pursued instead of prosecution as the course of choice * * *. * * * [W]ithout a suppression remedy in revocation proceedings, there will often be no influence capable of deterring Fourth Amendment violations when parole revocation is a possible response to new crime. Suppression in the revocation proceeding cannot be looked upon, then, as furnishing merely incremental or marginal deterrence over and above the effect of exclusion in criminal prosecution. Instead, it will commonly provide the only deterrence to unconstitutional conduct when the incarceration of parolees is sought, and the reasons that support the suppression remedy in prosecution therefore support it in parole revocation.

524 U.S. at ___, 118 S.Ct. at 2027, 141 L.Ed.2d at 361–62 (Souter, J., dissenting).

In *Calandra*, using a similar analysis, the Court held the Fourth Amendment exclusionary rule does not apply before a grand jury. Thus a suspect questioned by a grand jury has no right to avoid questions based on information obtained in violation of his Fourth Amendment rights. Any increase in deterrence resulting from extending the exclusionary rule to grand juries would be "speculative and undoubtedly minimal," the Court reasoned, and applying the exclusionary demand in this area might delay and impede grand jury investigations. 414 U.S. at 351–52, 94 S.Ct. at 621–22, 38 L.Ed.2d 572–73.

The same approach used in *Calandra* and *Scott* was used in Stone v. Powell, 428 U.S. 465, 96 S.Ct. 3037, 49 L.Ed.2d 1067 (1976), to determine whether state criminal defendants who had unsuccessfully sought suppression of evidence in their state trials on Fourth Amendment grounds could seek reconsideration of the matters in federal habeas corpus proceedings. Unless such state defendants were denied in the state trial an opportunity for full and fair litigation of their Fourth Amendment claims, the Court held, the *Mapp* exclusionary requirement did not entitle them to seek federal habeas corpus relief. If permitting state defendants to seek such relief in federal court would increase the deterrent effect of the exclusionary requirement—a matter on which the Court expressed doubt—this increased deterrence would be outweighed by the costs of so expanding the rule.

Much the same approach has been taken in the Court's consideration of proposed exceptions to the general requirements of exclusion. Exceptions in general, and the "good faith" exception in particular, are addressed in Part C of this chapter.

6.   **Actual Effect of Exclusion of Evidence.** Do exclusionary requirements affect law enforcement conduct? If so, how do they do so? What costs are paid for these requirements? These are matters that in theory should be subject to empirical study. Engaging in such study, however, is difficult because there are few opportunities to compare police actions subject to exclusionary sanctions and similar actions not so limited.

Many efforts to conduct such research on the effectiveness of the federal constitutional rules were reviewed in T. Perrin, H. Caldwell, C. Chase, and R. Fagan, It It's Broken, Fix It: Moving Beyond the Exclusionary Rule, 83 Iowa L.Rev. 669, 678–710 (1998). Some involved analysis of statistics regarding arrests, convictions, and suppression motions, others were conducted by direct observation of police officers, and a number undertook to survey police officers and others regarding their knowledge and attitudes. Perrin and his colleagues concluded the research is subject to methodological criticism but in general fails to support the promise that *Mapp* would "dramatically and beneficially impact[ ] police practices." They elaborated:

> The most that can be said is that *Mapp* has probably made officers more aware of the Fourth Amendment, and has increased the number of warrants they obtain, although it is less certain that it has actually affected their performance of their other duties. One costly effect of the exclusionary rule that emerges from the studies in that it has encouraged police officers to falsify their reports and their testimony.
>
> The studies show that *Mapp* has significantly increased the number of suppression motions filed * * *. The filing of these motions has driven up the cost of processing cases, and it beyond dispute that a number of apparently guilty defendants go free as a result of the rule.

83 Iowa L.Rev. at 710–11.

In 1984, the Supreme Court noted the developing research and commented on some interpretations of the leading study of the costs of *Mapp*:

> Researchers have only recently begun to study extensively the effects of the exclusionary rule on the disposition of felony arrests. One study suggests that

the rule results in the nonprosecution or nonconviction of between 0.6% and 2.35% of individuals arrested for felonies. Davies, A Hard Look at What We Know (and Still Need to Learn) About the "Costs" of the Exclusionary Rule: The NIJ Study and Other Studies of "Lost" Arrests, 1983 A.B.F.Res.J. 611, 621. The estimates are higher for particular crimes the prosecution of which depends heavily on physical evidence. Thus, the cumulative loss due to nonprosecution or nonconviction of individuals arrested on felony drug charges is probably in the range of 2.8% to 7.1%. Davies' analysis of California data suggests that screening by police and prosecutors results in the release because of illegal searches or seizures of as many as 1.4% of all felony arrestees, that 0.9% of felony arrestees are released, because of illegal searches or seizures, at the preliminary hearing or after trial, and that roughly 0.5% of all felony arrestees benefit from reversals on appeal because of illegal searches. * * *

Many * * * researchers have concluded that the impact of the exclusionary rule is insubstantial, but the small percentages with which they deal mask a large absolute number of felons who are released because the cases against them were based in part on illegal searches or seizures. * * *

United States v. Leon, 468 U.S 897, 908 n. 6, 104 S.Ct. 3405, 3412 n. 6, 82 L.Ed.2d 677,–688 n. 6 (1984).

Christopher Slobogin, Why Liberals Should Chuck the Exclusionary Rule, 1999 Ill.L.Rev. 363, 369, 394 (1999), agreeing generally with Perrin, Caldwell, Chase, and Fagan, observed "we do not know how much the [exclusionary] rule deters, * * * [and, given the limitations of empirical inquiry, w]e probably never will." With regard to "systemic" deterrence or prevention, he concluded that "the systemic deterrent effect of the exclusionary rule is just not powerful enough to overcome a police culture that is unsympathetic to rules that restrict investigative powers."

7. **Nonconstitutional Illegality.** When evidence is obtained in violation of a nonconstitutional legal requirement—such as a federal or state statute—whether exclusion is possible or required presents a more difficult question. Clearly, there is no federal or state constitutional right to have evidence excluded because of a statutory violation. A few states have statutory provisions or court rules requiring exclusion in many such situations. E.g., Vernon's Ann.Tex.Code Crim.Pro. art. 38.23 (evidence obtained in violation of "any provisions of the Constitution or laws of the State of Texas" must be excluded); Alaska Evid.R. 412 (evidence "illegally obtained" is not to be used in a criminal prosecution). Sometimes statutory requirements explicitly direct exclusion.

Courts differ in their willingness to find unexpressed legislative "intentions" that violations of statutes are to result in exclusion of evidence. The Supreme Court has held without explanation that violation of a federal statute requiring prior announcement before entering premises to execute a warrant required exclusion. Miller v. United States, 357 U.S. 301, 78 S.Ct. 1190, 2 L.Ed.2d 1332 (1958). In addition, the Supreme Court has held it has a "supervisory power" giving it authority to sometimes require exclusion of evidence obtained in violation of nonconstitutional legal requirements. McNabb v. United States, 318 U.S. 332, 63 S.Ct. 608, 87 L.Ed. 819 (1943). State courts may have a similar power. See People v. Dyla, 142 A.D.2d 423, 536 N.Y.S.2d 799 (1988). The Supreme Court has in recent cases been unwilling to exercise its supervisory power to create or develop "new" exclusionary requirements. See United States v. Payner, 447 U.S. 727, 100 S.Ct. 2439, 65 L.Ed.2d 468 (1980); United States v. Caceres, 440 U.S. 741, 99 S.Ct. 1465, 59 L.Ed.2d 733 (1979).

B. SCOPE OF EXCLUSIONARY SANCTIONS: STANDING, FRUIT OF THE POISONOUS TREE, INDEPENDENT SOURCE AND ATTENUATION OF THE TAINT

EDITORS' INTRODUCTORY NOTE: EXCLUSIONARY SANCTION ISSUES, REQUIREMENTS AND EXCEPTIONS

Determinations that law enforcement officers engaged in activity during the preparation of the prosecution's case and that this activity violated the Fourth Amendment or some other legal requirement that triggers an exclusionary sanction does not complete inquiry into the admissibility of evidence obtained by the officers. In fact, the Supreme Court's post-*Mapp* case law has greatly increased the complexity of two subissues needing consideration: (1) what evidence is rendered inadmissible by demonstrated law enforcement misconduct; and (2) what persons are able to invoke the exclusionary remedy?

In considering the issues presented by these cases, it may be useful to first identify those matters a defendant seeking exclusion of evidence must establish to make a basic case for exclusion. These might usefully be distinguished from "exceptions" to the requirement of exclusion triggered by the making of such a basic case. The distinction may be useful in litigation because it may determine which party has the burden of persuasion. Although the Supreme Court has never comprehensively addressed the allocation of the burden[s] of persuasion in litigation under the federal constitutional exclusionary sanction, there is widespread agreement that a defendant seeking to have evidence suppressed must prove (1) illegality sufficient to trigger the exclusionary sanction; (2) the defendant's right to invoke that sanction ("standing"); and (3) that the challenged evidence was obtained as a factual result of the illegality or, as courts often put the matter, that the evidence was "fruit of the poisonous tree." There is also widespread agreement that if the prosecution responds by relying on an "exception" to the general requirement of exclusion, the prosecution bears the burden of persuasion regarding the exception.

Whatever the allocation of the burden[s] of persuasion, those burdens are not high. In general, the Court announced in United States v. Matlock, 415 U.S. 164, 178 n. 14, 94 S.Ct. 988, 996 n. 14, 39 L.Ed.2d 242, 253 n. 14 (1974), the controlling burden of proof at suppression hearings should impose no greater burden than proof by a preponderance of the evidence.

The principal case in this part is an early one, but the opinion demonstrates the interrelationship among the issues presented by many instances of exclusionary sanction litigation. The propriety of the arrests of the defendants was in dispute. Four members of the Supreme Court, in a dissenting opinion by Justice Clark, took the position that neither arrest was constitutionally impermissible. For present purposes, assume the arrests were constitutionally unreasonable and consider what effect those arrests have upon the admissibility of the various evidence offered by the prosecution against each of the defendants.

Wong Sun v. United States

Supreme Court of the United States, 1963.
371 U.S. 471, 83 S.Ct. 407, 9 L.Ed.2d 441.

■ MR. JUSTICE BRENNAN delivered the opinion of the Court.

The petitioners were tried without a jury in the District Court for the Northern District of California under a two-count indictment for violation of the Federal Narcotics Laws * * *. They were acquitted under the first count which charged a conspiracy, but convicted under the second count which charged the substantive offense of fraudulent and knowing transportation and concealment of illegally imported heroin. The Court of Appeals for the Ninth Circuit, one judge dissenting, affirmed the convictions. We granted certiorari. * * *.

About 2 a. m. on the morning of June 4, 1959, federal narcotics agents in San Francisco, after having had one Hom Way under surveillance for six weeks, arrested him and found heroin in his possession. Hom Way, who had not before been an informant, stated after his arrest that he had bought an ounce of heroin the night before from one known to him only as "Blackie Toy," proprietor of a laundry on Leavenworth Street.

About 6 a. m. that morning six or seven federal agents went to a laundry at 1733 Leavenworth Street. The sign above the door of this establishment said "Oye's Laundry." It was operated by the petitioner James Wah Toy. There is, however, nothing in the record which identifies James Wah Toy and "Blackie Toy" as the same person. The other federal officers remained nearby out of sight while Agent Alton Wong, who was of Chinese ancestry, rang the bell. When petitioner Toy appeared and opened the door, Agent Wong told him that he was calling for laundry and dry cleaning. Toy replied that he didn't open until 8 o'clock and told the agent to come back at that time. Toy started to close the door. Agent Wong thereupon took his badge from his pocket and said, "I am a federal narcotics agent." Toy immediately "slammed the door and started running" down the hallway through the laundry to his living quarters at the back where his wife and child were sleeping in a bedroom. Agent Wong and the other federal officers broke open the door and followed Toy down the hallway to the living quarters and into the bedroom. Toy reached into a nightstand drawer. Agent Wong thereupon drew his pistol, pulled Toy's hand out of the drawer, placed him under arrest and handcuffed him. There was nothing in the drawer and a search of the premises uncovered no narcotics.

One of the agents said to Toy " * * * [Hom Way] says he got narcotics from you." Toy responded, "No, I haven't been selling any narcotics at all. However, I do know somebody who has." When asked who that was, Toy said, "I only know him as Johnny. I don't know his last name." However, Toy described a house on Eleventh Avenue where he said Johnny lived; he also described a bedroom in the house where he said "Johnny kept about a piece"[1] of heroin, and where he and Johnny had smoked some of the drug the night before. The agents left immediately for Eleventh Avenue and

---

1. A "piece" is approximately one ounce.

located the house. They entered and found one Johnny Yee in the bedroom. After a discussion with the agents, Yee took from a bureau drawer several tubes containing in all just less than one ounce of heroin, and surrendered them. Within the hour Yee and Toy were taken to the Office of the Bureau of Narcotics. Yee there stated that the heroin had been brought to him some four days earlier by petitioner Toy and another Chinese known to him only as "Sea Dog."

Toy was questioned as to the identity of "Sea Dog" and said that "Sea Dog" was Wong Sun. Some agents, including Agent Alton Wong, took Toy to Wong Sun's neighborhood where Toy pointed out a multifamily dwelling where he said Wong Sun lived. Agent Wong rang a downstairs door bell and a buzzer sounded, opening the door. The officer identified himself as a narcotics agent to a woman on the landing and asked "for Mr. Wong." The woman was the wife of petitioner Wong Sun. She said that Wong Sun was "in the back room sleeping." Alton Wong and some six other officers climbed the stairs and entered the apartment. One of the officers went into the back room and brought petitioner Wong Sun from the bedroom in handcuffs. A thorough search of the apartment followed, but no narcotics were discovered.

Petitioner Toy and Johnny Yee were arraigned before a United States Commissioner on June 4 on a complaint * * *. Later that day, each was released on his own recognizance. Petitioner Wong Sun was arraigned on a similar complaint filed the next day and was also released on his own recognizance. Within a few days, both petitioners and Yee were interrogated at the office of the Narcotics Bureau by Agent William Wong, also of Chinese ancestry. The agent advised each of the three of his right to withhold information which might be used against him, and stated to each that he was entitled to the advice of counsel, though it does not appear that any attorney was present during the questioning of any of the three. The officer also explained to each that no promises or offers of immunity or leniency were being or could be made.

The agent interrogated each of the three separately. After each had been interrogated the agent prepared a statement in English from rough notes. The agent read petitioner Toy's statement to him in English and interpreted certain portions of it for him in Chinese. Toy also read the statement in English aloud to the agent, said there were corrections to be made, and made the corrections in his own hand. Toy would not sign the statement, however; in the agent's words "he wanted to know first if the other persons involved in the case had signed theirs." Wong Sun had considerable difficulty understanding the statement in English and the agent restated its substance in Chinese. Wong Sun refused to sign the statement although he admitted the accuracy of its contents.

Hom Way did not testify at petitioners' trial. The Government offered Johnny Yee as its principal witness but excused him after he invoked the privilege against self-incrimination and flatly repudiated the statement he had given to Agent William Wong. That statement was not offered in evidence nor was any testimony elicited from him identifying either petitioner as the source of the heroin in his possession, or otherwise tending to support the charges against the petitioners.

The statute expressly provides that proof of the accused's possession of the drug will support a conviction under the statute unless the accused satisfactorily explains the possession. The Government's evidence tending to prove the petitioners' possession (the petitioners offered no exculpatory testimony) consisted of four items which the trial court admitted over timely objections that they were inadmissible as "fruits" of unlawful arrests or of attendant searches: (1) the statements made orally by petitioner Toy in his bedroom at the time of his arrest; (2) the heroin surrendered to the agents by Johnny Yee; (3) petitioner Toy's pretrial unsigned statement; and (4) petitioner Wong Sun's similar statement. The dispute below and here has centered around the correctness of the rulings of the trial judge allowing these items in evidence.

The Court of Appeals held that the arrests of both petitioners were illegal because not based on " 'probable cause' within the meaning of the Fourth Amendment" * * * [but] nevertheless [also] held that the four items of proof were not the "fruits" of the illegal arrests and that they were therefore properly admitted in evidence.

The Court of Appeals rejected [an] additional [contention] of the petitioners. [This] was that there was insufficient evidence to corroborate the petitioners' unsigned admissions of possession of narcotics. The court held that the narcotics in evidence surrendered by Johnny Yee, together with Toy's statements in his bedroom at the time of arrest corroborated petitioners' admissions. * * *

We believe that significant differences between the cases of the two petitioners require separate discussion of each. We shall first consider the case of petitioner Toy.

I.

The Court of Appeals found there was [not] probable cause for Toy's arrest. Giving due weight to that finding, we think it is amply justified by the facts clearly shown on this record. * * *

II.

It is conceded that Toy's declarations in his bedroom are to be excluded if they are held to be "fruits" of the agents' unlawful action.

In order to make effective the fundamental constitutional guarantees of sanctity of the home and inviolability of the person, this Court held nearly half a century ago that evidence seized during an unlawful search could not constitute proof against the victim of the search. The exclusionary prohibition extends as well to the indirect as the direct products of such invasions. Silverthorne Lumber Co. v. United States, 251 U.S. 385, 40 S.Ct. 182, 64 L.Ed. 319. Mr. Justice Holmes, speaking for the Court in that case, in holding that the Government might not make use of information obtained during an unlawful search to subpoena from the victims the very documents illegally viewed, expressed succinctly the policy of the broad exclusionary rule:

"The essence of a provision forbidding the acquisition of evidence in a certain way is that not merely evidence so acquired shall not be held before the Court but that it shall not be used at all. Of course this does not mean that the facts thus obtained become sacred and inaccessible. If knowledge of them is gained from an independent source they may be proved like any others, but the knowledge gained by the Government's own wrong cannot be used by it in the way proposed."

The exclusionary rule has traditionally barred from trial physical, tangible materials obtained either during or as a direct result of an unlawful invasion. It follows from our holding in Silverman v. United States, 365 U.S. 505, 81 S.Ct. 679, 5 L.Ed.2d 734, that the Fourth Amendment may protect against the overhearing of verbal statements as well as against the more traditional seizure of "papers and effects." Similarly, testimony as to matters observed during an unlawful invasion has been excluded in order to enforce the basic constitutional policies. Thus, verbal evidence which derives so immediately from an unlawful entry and an unauthorized arrest as the officers' action in the present case is no less the "fruit" of official illegality than the more common tangible fruits of the unwarranted intrusion. Nor do the policies underlying the exclusionary rule invite any logical distinction between physical and verbal evidence. * * * [T]he danger in relaxing the exclusionary rules in the case of verbal evidence would seem too great to warrant introducing such a distinction.

The Government argues that Toy's statements to the officers in his bedroom, although closely consequent upon the invasion which we hold unlawful, were nevertheless admissible because they resulted from "an intervening independent act of a free will." This contention, however, takes insufficient account of the circumstances. Six or seven officers had broken the door and followed on Toy's heels into the bedroom where his wife and child were sleeping. He had been almost immediately handcuffed and arrested. Under such circumstances it is unreasonable to infer that Toy's response was sufficiently an act of free will to purge the primary taint of the unlawful invasion.

* * *

III.

We now consider whether the exclusion of Toy's declarations requires also the exclusion of the narcotics taken from Yee, to which those declarations led the police. The prosecutor candidly told the trial court that "we wouldn't have found those drugs except that Mr. Toy helped us to." Hence this is not the case envisioned by this Court where the exclusionary rule has no application because the Government learned of the evidence "from an independent source," Silverthorne Lumber Co. v. United States, 251 U.S. 385, 392, 40 S.Ct. 182, 183, 64 L.Ed. 319; nor is this a case in which the connection between the lawless conduct of the police and the discovery of the challenged evidence has "become so attenuated as to dissipate the taint." Nardone v. United States, 308 U.S. 338, 341, 60 S.Ct. 266, 268, 84 L.Ed. 307. We need not hold that all evidence is "fruit of the poisonous tree" simply because it would not have come to light but for the illegal actions of the police. Rather, the more apt question in such a case is "whether, granting establishment of the primary illegality, the evidence to which instant objection is made has been come at by exploitation of that illegality or instead by means sufficiently distinguishable to be purged of the primary taint." Maguire, Evidence of Guilt, 221 (1959). We think it clear that the narcotics were "come at by the exploitation of that illegality" and hence that they may not be used against Toy.

[handwritten margin note: Finding of Drugs on Yee]

IV.

It remains only to consider Toy's unsigned statement. We need not decide whether, in light of the fact that Toy was free on his own recognizance when he made the statement, that statement was a fruit of the illegal arrest. Since we have concluded that his declarations in the bedroom and the narcotics surrendered by Yee should not have been admitted in evidence against him, the only proofs remaining to sustain his conviction are his and Wong Sun's unsigned statements. Without scrutinizing the contents of Toy's ambiguous recitals, we conclude that no reference to Toy in Wong Sun's statement constitutes admissible evidence corroborating any admission by Toy. We arrive at this conclusion upon two clear lines of decisions which converge to require it. One line of our decisions establishes that criminal confessions and admissions of guilt require extrinsic corroboration; the other line of precedents holds that an out-of-court declaration made after arrest may not be used at trial against one of the declarant's partners in crime.

It is a settled principle of the administration of criminal justice in the federal courts that a conviction must rest upon firmer ground than the uncorroborated admission or confession of the accused. We observed in Smith v. United States, 348 U.S. 147, 153, 75 S.Ct. 194, 197, 99 L.Ed. 192, that the requirement of corroboration is rooted in "a long history of judicial experience with confessions and in the realization that sound law enforcement requires police investigations which extend beyond the words of the accused." * * * Wong Sun's unsigned confession does not furnish competent corroborative evidence. The second governing principle, likewise well settled in our decisions, is that an out-of-court declaration made after arrest may not be used at trial against one of the declarant's partners in crime. While such a statement is "admissible against the others where it is in furtherance of the criminal undertaking * * * all such responsibility is at an end when the conspiracy ends." Fiswick v. United States, 329 U.S. 211, 217, 67 S.Ct. 224, 227, 91 L.Ed. 196. * * *

V.

We turn now to the case of the other petitioner, Wong Sun. We have no occasion to disagree with the finding of the Court of Appeals that his arrest, also, was without probable cause or reasonable grounds. At all events no evidentiary consequences turn upon that question. For Wong Sun's unsigned confession was not the fruit of that arrest, and was therefore properly admitted at trial. On the evidence that Wong Sun had been released on his own recognizance after a lawful arraignment, and had returned voluntarily several days later to make the statement, we hold that the connection between the arrest and the statement had "become so attenuated as to dissipate the taint." * * *

We must then consider the admissibility of the narcotics surrendered by Yee. Our holding, supra, that this ounce of heroin was inadmissible against Toy does not compel a like result with respect to Wong Sun. The exclusion of the narcotics as to Toy was required solely by their tainted relationship to information unlawfully obtained from Toy, and not by any official impropriety connected with their surrender by Yee. The seizure of this heroin invaded no right of privacy of person or premises which would entitle Wong Sun to object to its use at his trial.

However, for the reasons that Wong Sun's statement was incompetent to corroborate Toy's admissions contained in Toy's own statement, any references to Wong Sun in Toy's statement were incompetent to corroborate Wong Sun's admissions. Thus, the only competent source of corroboration for Wong Sun's statement was the heroin itself. We cannot be certain, however, on this state of the record, that the trial judge may not also have considered the contents of Toy's statement as a source of corroboration. Petitioners raised as one ground of objection to the introduction of the statements the claim that each statement, "even if it were a purported admission or confession or declaration against interest of a defendant * * * would not be binding upon the other defendant." The trial judge, in allowing the statements in, apparently overruled all of petitioners' objections, including this one. Thus we presume that he considered all portions of both statements as bearing upon the guilt of both petitioners.

We intimate no view one way or the other as to whether the trial judge might have found in the narcotics alone sufficient evidence to corroborate Wong Sun's admissions that he delivered heroin to Yee and smoked heroin at Yee's house around the date in question. But because he might, as the factfinder, have found insufficient corroboration from the narcotics alone, we cannot be sure that the scales were not tipped in favor of conviction by reliance upon the inadmissible Toy statement. * * * We therefore hold that petitioner Wong Sun is also entitled to a new trial.

The judgment of the Court of Appeals is reversed and the case is remanded to the District Court for further proceedings consistent with this opinion.

It is so ordered.

Judgment of Court of Appeals reversed and case remanded to the District Court.

[The concurring opinion of Justice Douglas and the dissenting opinion of Justice Clark, joined by Justices Harlan, Stewart and White, are omitted.]

NOTES

1. The requirement that a confession be corroborated is discussed in Chapter 7.

2. **"Standing" Or the "Personal Nature" of Federal Constitutional Rights.** The doctrine which precluded Wong Sun from successfully objecting to the introduction of the heroin on the same grounds as were successful for Toy has traditionally been described as a requirement of "standing." Application of the

requirement to specific search situations is explored further in Part B(3) of Chapter 2.

In Rakas v. Illinois, 439 U.S. 128, 99 S.Ct. 421, 58 L.Ed.2d 387 (1978) (reprinted in part in Chapter 2), however, the Supreme Court appeared to "dispens[e] with the rubric of standing." Cases containing standing discussions, it explained, simply applied the principle that Fourth Amendment rights are personal in nature. Whether particular defendants can challenge particular law enforcement conduct should be discussed in those terms:

> Analyzed in these terms, the question is whether the challenged search or seizure violated the Fourth Amendment rights of a criminal defendant who seeks to exclude the evidence obtained during it. That inquiry in turn requires a determination of whether the disputed search and seizure has infringed an interest of the defendant which the Fourth Amendment was designed to protect. * * * [T]his aspect of the analysis belongs more properly under the heading of substantive Fourth Amendment doctrine rather than under the heading of standing * * *.

439 U.S. at 140, 99 S.Ct. at 429, 58 L.Ed.2d at 399. The majority emphasized the abandonment of standing rubric would not change either the basic inquiry or the outcome of cases. But the shift, it explained, should focus concern on "the extent of a particular defendant's rights under the Fourth Amendment, rather than on any theoretically separate, but invariably intertwined concept of standing." Further, this approach should result in particular decisions resting on "sounder logical footing."

Earlier, the Court had defended the requirement of "standing" on its merits:

> Fourth Amendment rights are personal rights which, like some other constitutional rights, may not be vicariously asserted. * * * There is no necessity to exclude evidence against one defendant in order to protect the rights of another. No rights of the victim of an illegal search are at stake when the evidence is offered against some other party. The victim can and very probably will object for himself when and if it becomes important for him to do so. * * * [None of our cases] hold that anything which deters illegal searches is thereby commanded by the Fourth Amendment. The deterrent values of preventing the incrimination of those whose rights the police have violated have been considered sufficient to justify the suppression of probative evidence even though the case against the defendant is weakened or destroyed. We adhere to that judgment. But we are not convinced that the additional benefits of extending the exclusionary rule to other defendants would justify further encroachment upon the public interest in prosecuting those accused of crime and having them acquitted or convicted on the basis of all the evidence which exposes the truth.

Alderman v. United States, 394 U.S. 165, 174–75, 89 S.Ct. 961, 966–97, 22 L.Ed.2d 176, 187 (1969).

In *Rakas*, the Court rejected a proposal that it permit any criminal defendant at whom a search was "directed" to challenge the admissibility of evidence obtained as a result of that search. It explained it was unwilling to increase the amount of reliable evidence that would be rendered unavailable by the exclusionary rule. It also quoted with approval Justice Harlan's argument in *Alderman* that such a "target" rule would involve excessive administrative costs in the form of lengthy hearings to determine whether or not particular defendants were the "targets" of particular police action.

3. **Fruit of the Poisonous Tree.** In holding Toy's bedroom statements inadmissible, *Wong Sun* applied what is often called the "fruit of the poisonous tree" rule. Once a defendant establishes a violation of his constitutional rights, he is

entitled to suppression of all "fruit of [that] poisonous tree." Nardone v. United States, 308 U.S. 338, 341, 60 S.Ct. 266, 268, 84 L.Ed. 307, 312 (1939). This position is sometimes stated as the "derivative evidence" rule—all evidence derived from a violation of the defendant's rights must be suppressed. The "core rationale" for this rule, the Court has explained, is "that this admittedly drastic and socially costly course is needed to deter police from violations" of the protections involved. Nix v. Williams, 467 U.S. 431, 442–43, 104 S.Ct. 2501, 2508, 81 L.Ed.2d 377, 386–87 (1984).

The "fruits" rule is not applied in some situations where police illegality consists of a violation of *Miranda* requirements. Admissibility of evidence obtained as a result of a *Miranda* violation is developed in subsection B(4) of Chapter 7.

A defendant seeking to invoke the "fruits" doctrine must establish that the challenged evidence was obtained by police as a factual result of a violation of his rights. Murray v. United States, 487 U.S. 533, 108 S.Ct. 2529, 101 L.Ed.2d 472 (1988). Obviously, evidence obtained by law enforcement officers *before* they violated a defendant's rights is not the "fruit" of the violation and hence is not subject to challenge. See Waller v. Georgia, 467 U.S. 39, 104 S.Ct. 2210, 81 L.Ed.2d 31 (1984).

Murray illustrates the difficulty sometimes involved in showing the required factual causation. Federal officers conducting a drug investigation observed several suspicious vehicles enter and leave a warehouse in South Boston. About 2:30 p.m. and without a search warrant, the officers went to the warehouse, forced open the door, and entered. While inside, they observed burlap-wrapped bales. They then, without seizing or disturbing those bales, left the warehouse. Later, the officers applied for a search warrant for the warehouse. The application relied upon other information possessed by the officers at the time of their first entry and did not mention they had already entered the structure. The warrant issued about 10:45 p.m. Pursuant to that warrant, the officers entered the warehouse and seized 270 bales of marijuana—including the bales observed during the earlier entry—as well as other incriminating items. Murray and Carter were charged with conspiracy to possess and distribute the marijuana. Before trial, they moved to suppress the evidence obtained from the warehouse on the ground it was the "fruit" of the officers' first and unreasonable warrantless entry of the warehouse. The Court of Appeals held that this motion should have been granted. By a 4–3 vote, with two justices not participating, the Supreme Court vacated and remanded. Knowledge that the marijuana was in the warehouse, Justice Scalia wrote for the majority, was obtained in the first and presumably-unreasonable search of the warehouse. But such knowledge as well as the marijuana itself were acquired in the second and reasonable search pursuant to the warrant. If the search pursuant to the warrant was "genuinely independent" of the first search, the evidence would be admissible. This "independent source" rule, he explained, is based on the need to limit exclusion of evidence to those situations in which rejecting it is necessary to deter improper police activity. Deterrence is adequately accomplished by placing the police in the position they would have occupied had the illegal search not occurred. It does not require placing them in a *worse* position. Excluding evidence having an independent source would be to unjustifiably place the police in such a worse position; they would be deprived of evidence that they in fact obtained independently of their improper conduct.

But this doctrine requires that the manner in which the evidence was obtained be "genuinely independent" of the illegal search. "This would not have been the case," Justice Scalia explained, "if the agents' decision to seek the warrant was prompted by what they had seen during the initial entry, or if information obtained during that entry was presented to the Magistrate and affected his decision to issue the warrant." The lower courts determined the officers had not revealed to the magistrate issuing the search warrant any information from the illegal entry. But no finding was made as to whether or not the officers would have sought a warrant for the warehouse if they had not earlier entered it. The matter was therefore remanded to the District Court for a determination as to whether the search pursuant to the warrant was an independent source of the challenged evidence in the sense that the opinion defined independent source.

4. **Limits on Fruits Doctrine.** In one search situation, the Supreme Court has refused to apply the general rule that all evidence obtained as a factual result of conduct violating Fourth Amendment standards must be suppressed. In New York v. Harris, 495 U.S. 14, 110 S.Ct. 1640, 109 L.Ed.2d 13 (1990), officers had probable cause to believe Harris committed a homicide but obtained no warrant. They nevertheless entered his home and placed him under arrest. This warrantless entry violated the Fourth Amendment; the warrant requirement in this context is considered in Chapter 4. Harris was warned of his rights and admitted the killing. He was taken to the stationhouse, warned again, and signed a written incriminating statement. Later, ignoring Harris's expressed desire to remain silent, police video-taped an interview with him. The trial court suppressed the oral statement made at his home and the videotaped statement, but admitted the written statement despite the earlier violation of his Fourth Amendment rights.

The Supreme Court held admission of the statement this was proper, applying what the dissenters characterized as a "newly-fashioned *per se* rule." No need existed to inquire whether the taint of the improper entry became attenuated, Justice White reasoned for the majority, because that analysis is necessary only if the challenged evidence is the product or fruit of the Fourth Amendment violation. The illegality of the officers' entry and Harris's arrest in his home, he continued, did not render unlawful Harris's continued custody once he was removed from the house:

> Harris's statement taken at the police station was not the product of being in unlawful custody. Neither was it the fruit of having been arrested in the home rather than someplace else. * * * [T]he police had a justification to question Harris prior to his arrest; therefore, his subsequent statement was not an exploitation of the illegal entry into Harris' home.

495 U.S. at 19, 110 S.Ct. at 1644, 109 L.Ed.2d at 21. Therefore:

> [W]here the police have probable cause to arrest a suspect, the exclusionary rule does not bar the State's use of a statement made by the defendant outside of his home, even though the statement is taken after an arrest made in the home in violation of [the Fourth Amendment].

495 U.S. at 21, 110 S.Ct. at 1644–45, 109 L.Ed.2d at 22.

Its decision, the Court explained further, implemented the principle that penalties, including exclusion of evidence, must bear some relation to the purposes of the legal requirement violated. The underlying rule requiring a warrant for arrests in the home was designed to protect the physical integrity of the home. "[I]t was not intended to grant criminal suspects, like Harris, protection for statements made outside their premises where the police have probable cause to arrest the suspects for committing a crime." Once incriminating evidence gathered from arresting the suspect in his home, the purpose of the rule is vindicated. Moreover, the threat of suppression of such evidence retains the principal incentive for officers to comply with the warrant requirement. Suppression of statements obtained after the suspect is removed would provide only "minimal" incremental deterrence.

5. **Independent Source.** Justice Holmes's discussion in *Silverthorne Lumber Co.*, quoted in *Wong Sun*, referred to evidence gained from "an independent source." If evidence is obtained by police after they violated a defendant's rights,

but not as a consequence of that violation, the evidence is often said to have such an independent source and, as a result, is admissible despite officers' intrusion upon the defendant's rights.

If the prosecution argues challenged evidence is admissible under the independent source doctrine, which side has the burden of persuasion? This may depend upon how the doctrine is conceptualized. If it is an exception to the general rule that all evidence proved fruit of a poisonous tree must be suppressed, the prosecution would most likely have the burden of establishing its applicability. Independent source may, on the other hand, be simply a label for a conclusion that a defendant has failed to establish that the challenged evidence was obtained as a factual result of the official misconduct. A defendant probably has the burden of establishing that challenged evidence was obtained as a factual result of unreasonable law enforcement conduct. Thus independent source would seem to be only a theory on which the prosecution argue that the defendant has failed to meet his burden of persuasion regarding the necessary causal link.

In general, the Supreme Court has not made clear either the nature of independent source or the placement of the burden of persuasion. It has, however, addressed the situation in which a defendant establishes a lineup was conducted in violation of his Sixth Amendment right to counsel, and a witness identified him at that lineup. The prosecution can escape suppression of the witness's in-court identification testimony only if it establishes—by clear and convincing evidence—the in-court testimony of that witness's in-court identification testimony would be based on a source independent of the tainted lineup. United States v. Wade, 388 U.S. 218, 240, 87 S.Ct. 1926, 1939, 18 L.Ed.2d 1149, 1165 (1967) (reprinted in Chapter 10). This holding may rest upon a perception that independent source, as applied in lineup situations, involves such an unusually difficult and speculative inquiry that error can be avoided only by placing the burden of persuasion on the prosecution. Cf., Nix v. Williams. 467 U.S. 431, 444 n. 5, 104 S.Ct. 2501, 2509 n. 5, 81 L.Ed.2d 377, 388 n. 5 (1984). In other situations, the burden of proof may remain on the defendant to show the challenged evidence was discovered as a factual result of the illegality, although only by a preponderance of the evidence.

6. **Defendant's Presence as "Fruit."** The Supreme Court recognized one qualification to the general rule that "fruit of the poisonous tree" must be excluded: the defendant's physical presence for trial and punishment is never the excludable "fruit" of improper law enforcement conduct. Illegal police activity, the Court made clear, affects only the admissibility of evidence; it does not affect the jurisdiction of the trial court or otherwise serve as a basis for dismissing the prosecution. Ker v. Illinois, 119 U.S. 436, 7 S.Ct. 225, 30 L.Ed.2d 421 (1886). In United States v. Blue, 384 U.S. 251, 86 S.Ct. 1416, 16 L.Ed.2d 510 (1966), the Court explained its adherence to this approach despite *Mapp* and the "constitutionalization" of the exclusionary rule:

> So drastic a step [as barring the prosecution altogether] might advance marginally some of the ends served by the exclusionary rules, but it would also increase to an intolerable degree interference with the public interest in having the guilty brought to book.

384 U.S. at 225, 86 S.Ct. at 1419, 16 L.Ed.2d at 515.

7. **Attenuation of the Taint.** As the principal case makes clear, the "fruit of the poisonous tree" doctrine is subject to the qualification that "fruit" of a violation of the defendant's rights becomes admissible if the prosecution establishes the "taint" of the constitutional violation was "attenuated" when the challenged evidence was obtained. Determining whether attenuation has occurred is sometimes difficult. The issue has arisen in a number of post—*Wong Sun* Supreme Court cases, many involving defendants' claims that their confessions were excludable

fruit of an earlier improper arrest or detention. Perhaps the leading case is Brown v. Illinois, 422 U.S. 590, 95 S.Ct. 2254, 45 L.Ed.2d 416 (1975), in which the Court held compliance with Miranda v. Arizona, 384 U.S. 436, 86 S.Ct. 1602, 16 L.Ed.2d 694 (1966) (reprinted in Chapter 7), would not alone attenuate the taint. Moreover, a finding that the statement was "voluntary," while a "threshold requirement" for a finding of attenuation of taint, does not resolve the matter. Taylor v. Alabama, 457 U.S. 687, 690, 102 S.Ct. 2664, 2667, 73 L.Ed.2d 314, 319 (1982). Instead, events intervening between the unlawful detention and the making of the statement determine whether the statement was a sufficient act of free will to purge the taint. In *Brown,* the Court explained:

> No single fact is dispositive. * * * The *Miranda* warnings are an important factor, to be sure, in determining whether the confession is obtained by exploitation of an illegal arrest. But they are not the only factor to be considered. The temporal proximity of the arrest and the confession, the presence of intervening circumstances, and, particularly, the purpose and flagrancy of the official misconduct are all relevant.

422 U.S. at 603–04, 95 S.Ct. at 2261–62, 45 L.Ed.2d at 427.

Application of this approach was illustrated in Rawlings v. Kentucky, 448 U.S. 98, 100 S.Ct. 2556, 65 L.Ed.2d 633 (1980). Six officers arrived at a residence with a warrant for the arrest of one Marquess. Two of the occupants and four guests, including Rawlings and Cox, were present. During the search for Marquess, the officers smelled marihuana smoke and observed marihuana seeds. Two officers left to obtain a search warrant and four officers remained. The officers who remained on the scene permitted any occupant who would submit to a body search to leave; two did. About 45 minutes later, the two officers returned with a search warrant. The warrant and the *Miranda* rights were read to the remaining occupants. One officer then approached Cox and ordered her to empty her purse. 1,800 tablets of LSD and a variety of other controlled substances were among the contents. After pouring these items on a table, Cox turned to Rawlings and told him "to take what was his." Rawlings immediately claimed ownership of the controlled substances. At Rawlings's trial for trafficking in and possession of the controlled substances, his claim of ownership was admitted over his objection that it was the fruit of an illegal detention. ←

The Supreme Court upheld the admission of the statement. Assuming without deciding that the detention was invalid, the Court held the statement not tainted by this detention. Several factors were relevant. First, that the *Miranda* warnings were given was "important" but not "dispositive." Second, the atmosphere during the period of detention was "congenial." This outweighed the short 45 minute period between the detention and the making of the statement which under more "strict" conditions would not be long enough to purge the taint of the detention. Third, the *statements are voluntary* discovery of the drugs in Cox's purse and Rawlings's apparent desire to assume responsibility for them was a "circumstance" which "intervened between the initial detention and the challenged statements." Fourth, the police misconduct "[did] not rise to the level of conscious or flagrant misconduct." Finally, the statement was "voluntary," i.e., it was an act of free will unaffected by any illegality in the detention.

In regard to the motive for the illegal detention, contrast *Taylor* in which the Court found no attenuation of taint. The detention in that case was characterized as "an investigatory arrest without probable cause" followed by the involuntary transportation of the defendant to the station "for interrogation in the hope that something would turn up."

8. **Testimony of Witness as Excludable Fruit.** When, if ever, should the fruits of the poisonous tree doctrine include testimony of a witness whose identity

was discovered in violation of a defendant's constitutional rights? In United States v. Ceccolini, 435 U.S. 268, 98 S.Ct. 1054, 55 L.Ed.2d 268 (1978), Biro, a local police officer, entered Ceccolini's place of business to talk with Lois Hennessey, a friend and an employee of the shop. During the course of the conversation he noticed an envelope with money sticking out of it lying on the drawer of the cash register behind the counter. Biro picked up the envelope and, upon examining its contents, discovered it contained not only money but policy (gambling) slips. He placed the envelope back on the register and, without telling his friend what he had seen, asked her to whom the envelope belonged. She replied the envelope belonged to Ceccolini and that he had instructed her to give it to someone. The officer related what he had observed and been told to local police detectives who, in turn, gave the information to an FBI agent. Ceccolini had already been the subject of an FBI gambling investigation. An agent interviewed Ms. Hennessey at her home and she agreed to provide information about the envelope to the agent. Ceccolini was subpoenaed before a grand jury, where he denied any knowledge of a policy operation run from his shop. Ms. Hennessey testified about the envelope and the grand jury indicted Ceccolini for committing perjury in his grand jury testimony. The District Court and the Court of Appeals concluded that Biro's examination of the envelope was an unreasonable search and that the trial testimony of the store employee was a fruit of that illegality. The Supreme Court disagreed. Writing for the Court, Justice Rehnquist concluded that although there was a causal connection between the initial illegality and the employee's testimony, the taint had been dissipated:

> [W]e hold that the Court of Appeals erred in holding that the degree of attenuation was not sufficient to dissipate the connection between the illegality and the testimony. The evidence indicates overwhelmingly that the testimony given by the witness was an act of her own free will in no way coerced or even induced by official authority as a result of Biro's discovery of the policy slips. Nor were the slips themselves used in questioning Hennessey. Substantial periods of time elapsed between the time of the illegal search and the initial contact with the witness, on the one hand, and between the latter and the testimony at trial on the other. While the particular knowledge to which Hennessey testified at trial can be logically traced back to Biro's discovery of the policy slips both the identity of Hennessey and her relationship with the respondent was well known to those investigating the case. There is in addition, not the slightest evidence to suggest that Biro entered the shop or picked up the envelope with the intent of finding tangible evidence bearing on an illicit gambling operation, much less any suggestion that he entered the shop and searched with the intent of finding a willing and knowledgeable witness to testify against respondent. Application of the exclusionary rule in this situation could not have the slightest deterrent effect on the behavior of an officer such as Biro. The cost of permanently silencing Hennessey is too great for an even-handed system of law enforcement to bear in order to secure such a speculative and very likely negligible deterrent effect.

> Obviously no mathematical weight can be assigned to any of the factors which we have discussed, but just as obviously they all point to the conclusion that the exclusionary rule should be invoked with much greater reluctance where the claim is based on a causal relationship between a constitutional violation and the discovery of a live witness than when a similar claim is advanced to support suppression of an inanimate object.

435 U.S. at 279–80, 98 S.Ct. at 1062, 55 L.Ed.2d at 279. Justices Marshall and Brennan dissented.

C.   EXCEPTIONS TO EXCLUSIONARY REQUIREMENTS

EDITORS' INTRODUCTION: EXCLUSIONARY SANCTION
EXCEPTIONS

The federal constitutional requirement that evidence obtained as a result of a violation of a defendant's Fourth, Fifth, or Sixth Amendment rights be excluded from evidence is subject to exceptions.

Attenuation of Taint and Independent Source

Several of these have already been addressed. The last part of this chapter considered the attenuation of taint doctrine rendering certain evidence admissible.

As the last part similarly developed, the independent source doctrine also renders challenged evidence admissible at the behest of the prosecution. There is some question, however, whether independent source is properly conceptualized as an exception to the general requirement of exclusion. It may be a description of certain situations in which defendants failed to carry the burden of proving challenged evidence was obtained as factual results of the law enforcement conduct.

Impeachment of Testifying Defendant

Generally, the exceptions permit the use of evidence prove the defendant's guilt. One, however, allows use of evidence only for the limited purpose of impeaching the credibility of a testifying defendant.

Evidence obtained in violation of a defendant's Fourth Amendment rights can be used, if the defendant takes the witness stand at trial, to impeach the defendant's credibility. Harris v. New York, 401 U.S. 222, 91 S.Ct. 643, 28 L.Ed.2d 1 (1971). It may even be used to contradict answers given by a testifying defendant on cross-examination, as long as the testimony is in response to questions "plainly within the scope of the defendant's direct examination." United States v. Havens, 446 U.S. 620, 627, 100 S.Ct. 1912, 1916, 64 L.Ed.2d 559, 566 (1980). The exception applies to other federal constitutional exclusionary requirements. See Michigan v. Harvey, 494 U.S. 344, 350–53, 110 S.Ct. 1176, 1180–81, 108 L.Ed.2d 293, 302–04 (1990) (evidence obtained in violation of the defendant's Sixth Amendment right to counsel could be used to impeach).

In support of the impeachment exception, the Court has stressed the great need for such evidence, as it limits defendants' ability to give possibly perjurious testimony. It has characterized the possibility that the exception will encourage impermissible law enforcement conduct as purely "speculative." Thus:

> Assuming that the exclusionary rule has a deterrent effect on proscribed police conduct, sufficient deterrence flows when the evidence in question is made unavailable to the prosecution in its case in chief.

Harris v. New York, 401 U.S. at 225, 91 S.Ct. at 645, 28 L.Ed.2d at 4, "reaffirmed" in United States v. Havens, supra, 446 U.S. at 627, 100 S.Ct.

at 1916–17, 64 L.Ed.2d at 566. Dissenters argued impeachment exception "will seriously undermine the achievement of [the exclusionary rule's deterrent] objective," and is inconsistent with the exclusionary rule's objective of preserving the courts from the taint of aiding and abetting the law-breaking police officer. Harris v. New York, 401 U.S. at 232, 91 S.Ct. at 649, 28 L.Ed.2d at 8–9 (Brennan, J., dissenting).

In *Harris*, the Court made clear the exception would apply only if "the trustworthiness of the evidence satisfies legal standards." A confession obtained in a manner rendering it involuntary therefore cannot be used to impeach the defendant if he testifies at trial. Mincey v. Arizona, 437 U.S. 385, 402, 98 S.Ct. 2408, 2418, 57 L.Ed.2d 290, 306 (1978).

The Supreme Court—by a close 5-to-4 vote—refused to expand the *Harris* impeachment exception into a broader rule permitting the use of unconstitutionally obtained evidence to rebut *any* evidence offered by the defense. James v. Illinois, 493 U.S. 307, 110 S.Ct. 648, 107 L.Ed.2d 676 (1990). The balancing approach used in *Harris*, the *James* majority reasoned, did not support this narrowing of the exclusionary sanction. Permitting such rebuttal use of unconstitutionally obtained evidence, the Court acknowledged, might deter some perjurious testimony. It would also, however, discourage defendants from producing even legitimate defenses. Nondefendant witnesses cannot be "controlled" by defense counsel as effectively as defendant witnesses, so calling such witnesses might often result in accidentally rendering improperly obtained evidence admissible. Defendants would with some frequency, then, refrain from presenting defense witnesses. Moreover, once law enforcement officers learned of the expanded exception they would have significant incentive to proceed in violation of suspects' rights because the more extensive use that could be made of the fruits of their action would make such activity worthwhile. Thus expansion of the exception would significantly weaken the exclusionary sanction's deterrent effect.

* * *

The principal case that follows develops what is often—but perhaps improperly—called the "good faith" exception. One other exception is considered in the notes after the decision.

United States v. Leon

Supreme Court of the United States, 1984.
468 U.S. 897, 104 S.Ct. 3405, 82 L.Ed.2d 677.

■ JUSTICE WHITE delivered the opinion of the Court.

This case presents the question whether the Fourth Amendment exclusionary rule should be modified so as not to bar the use in the prosecution's case-in-chief of evidence obtained by officers acting in reasonable reliance on a search warrant issued by a detached and neutral magistrate but ultimately found to be unsupported by probable cause. * * *

I

In August 1981, a confidential informant of unproven reliability informed an officer of the Burbank Police Department that two persons known to him as "Armando" and "Patsy" were selling large quantities of cocaine and methaqualone from their residence at 620 Price Drive in Burbank, Cal. The informant also indicated that he had witnessed a sale of methaqualone by "Patsy" at the residence approximately five months earlier and had observed at that time a shoebox containing a large amount of cash that belonged to "Patsy." He further declared that "Armando" and "Patsy" generally kept only small quantities of drugs at their residence and stored the remainder at another location in Burbank.

On the basis of this information, the Burbank police initiated an extensive investigation focusing first on the Price Drive residence and later on two other residences as well. Cars parked at the Price Drive residence were determined to belong to respondents Armando Sanchez, who had previously been arrested for possession of marihuana, and Patsy Stewart, who had no criminal record. During the course of the investigation, officers observed an automobile belonging to respondent Ricardo Del Castillo, who had previously been arrested for possession of 50 pounds of marihuana, arrive at the Price Drive residence. The driver of that car entered the house, exited shortly thereafter carrying a small paper sack, and drove away. A check of Del Castillo's probation records led the officers to respondent Alberto Leon, whose telephone number Del Castillo had listed as his employer's. Leon had been arrested in 1980 on drug charges, and a companion had informed the police at that time that Leon was heavily involved in the importation of drugs into this country. Before the current investigation began, the Burbank officers had learned that an informant had told a Glendale police officer that Leon stored a large quantity of methaqualone at his residence in Glendale. During the course of this investigation, the Burbank officers learned that Leon was living at 716 South Sunset Canyon in Burbank.

Subsequently, the officers observed several persons, at least one of whom had prior drug involvement, arriving at the Price Drive residence and leaving with small packages; observed a variety of other material activity at the two residences as well as at a condominium at 7902 Via Magdalena; and witnessed a variety of relevant activity involving respondents' automobiles. The officers also observed respondents Sanchez and Stewart board separate flights for Miami. The pair later returned to Los Angeles together, consented to a search of their luggage that revealed only a small amount of marihuana, and left the airport. Based on these and other observations summarized in the affidavit, Officer Cyril Rombach of the Burbank Police Department, an experienced and well-trained narcotics investigator, prepared an application for a warrant to search 620 Price Drive, 716 South Sunset Canyon, 7902 Via Magdalena, and automobiles registered to each of the respondents for an extensive list of items believed to be related to respondents' drug-trafficking activities. Officer Rombach's extensive application was reviewed by several Deputy District Attorneys.

A facially valid search warrant was issued in September 1981 by a state superior court judge. The ensuing searches produced large quantities of drugs at the Via Magdalena and Sunset Canyon addresses and a small quantity at the Price Drive residence. Other evidence was discovered at each of the residences and in Stewart's and Del Castillo's automobiles. Respondents were indicted by a grand jury in the District Court for the Central District of California and charged with conspiracy to possess and distribute cocaine and a variety of substantive counts.

The respondents then filed motions to suppress the evidence seized pursuant to the warrant. The District Court held an evidentiary hearing and, while recognizing that the case was a close one, granted the motions to suppress in part. It concluded that the affidavit was insufficient to establish probable cause, but did not suppress all of the evidence as to all of the respondents because none of the respondents had standing to challenge all of the searches. In response to a request from the Government, the court made clear that Officer Rombach had acted in good faith, but it rejected the Government's suggestion that the Fourth Amendment exclusionary rule should not apply where evidence is seized in reasonable, good-faith reliance on a search warrant.

[A] divided panel of the Court of Appeals for the Ninth Circuit affirmed. * * *

The Government's petition for certiorari expressly declined to seek review of the lower courts' determinations that the search warrant was unsupported by probable cause and presented only the question "[w]hether the Fourth Amendment exclusionary rule should be modified so as not to bar the admission of evidence seized in reasonable, good-faith reliance on a search warrant that is subsequently held to be defective." We granted certiorari to consider the propriety of such a modification. * * *

We have concluded that, in the Fourth Amendment context, the exclusionary rule can be modified somewhat without jeopardizing its ability to perform its intended functions. Accordingly, we reverse the judgment of the Court of Appeals.

II

Language in opinions of this Court and of individual Justices has sometimes implied that the exclusionary rule is a necessary corollary of the Fourth Amendment. * * * These implications need not detain us long. The * * * Fourth Amendment "has never been interpreted to proscribe the introduction of illegally seized evidence in all proceedings or against all persons."

A

The Fourth Amendment contains no provision expressly precluding the use of evidence obtained in violation of its commands * * *. The [exclusionary] rule * * * operates as "a judicially created remedy designed to safeguard Fourth Amendment rights generally through its deterrent effect, rather than a personal constitutional right of the person aggrieved."

Whether the exclusionary sanction is appropriately imposed in a particular case, our decisions make clear, is "an issue separate from the question whether the Fourth Amendment rights of the party seeking to invoke the rule were violated by police conduct." Only the former question is currently before us, and it must be resolved by weighing the costs and benefits of preventing the use in the prosecution's case-in-chief of inherently trustworthy tangible evidence obtained in reliance on a search warrant issued by a detached and neutral magistrate that ultimately is found to be defective.

The substantial social costs exacted by the exclusionary rule for the vindication of Fourth Amendment rights have long been a source of concern. "Our cases have consistently recognized that unbending application of the exclusionary sanction to enforce ideals of governmental rectitude would impede unacceptably the truth-finding functions of judge and jury." United States v. Payner, 447 U.S. 727, 734, 100 S.Ct. 2439, 2445, 65 L.Ed.2d 468 (1980). An objectionable collateral consequence of this interference with the criminal justice system's truth-finding function is that some guilty defendants may go free or receive reduced sentences as a result of favorable plea bargains. Particularly when law enforcement officers have acted in objective good faith or their transgressions have been minor, the magnitude of the benefit conferred on such guilty defendants offends basic concepts of the criminal justice system. Indiscriminate application of the exclusionary rule, therefore, may well "generat[e] disrespect for the law and the administration of justice." Accordingly, "[a]s with any remedial device, the application of the rule has been restricted to those areas where its remedial objectives are thought most efficaciously served."

B

Close attention to those remedial objectives has characterized our recent decisions concerning the scope of the Fourth Amendment exclusionary rule. * * * [T]he balancing approach that has evolved in various contexts—including criminal trials—"forcefully suggest[s] that the exclusionary rule be more generally modified to permit the introduction of evidence obtained in the reasonable good-faith belief that a search or seizure was in accord with the Fourth Amendment."

* * *

As yet, we have not recognized any form of good-faith exception to the Fourth Amendment exclusionary rule. But the balancing approach that has evolved during the years of experience with the rule provides strong support for the modification currently urged upon us. As we discuss below, our evaluation of the costs and benefits of suppressing reliable physical evidence seized by officers reasonably relying on a warrant issued by a detached and neutral magistrate leads to the conclusion that such evidence should be admissible in the prosecution's case-in-chief.

III

A

Because a search warrant "provides the detached scrutiny of a neutral magistrate, which is a more reliable safeguard against improper searches than the hurried judgment of a law enforcement officer 'engaged in the often competitive enterprise of ferreting out crime,'" we have expressed a strong preference for warrants and declared that "in a doubtful or marginal case a search under a warrant may be sustainable where without one it would fail." Reasonable minds frequently may differ on the question whether a particular affidavit establishes probable cause, and we have thus concluded that the preference for warrants is most appropriately effectuated by according "great deference" to a magistrate's determination.

[Seldom], however, has the Court set forth a rationale for suppressing evidence obtained pursuant to a search warrant; * * * it has [frequently] simply excluded such evidence without considering whether Fourth Amendment interests will be advanced. To the extent that proponents of exclusion rely on its behavioral effects on judges and magistrates in these areas, their reliance is misplaced. First, the exclusionary rule is designed to deter police misconduct rather than to punish the errors of judges and magistrates. Second, there exists no evidence suggesting that judges and magistrates are inclined to ignore or subvert the Fourth Amendment or that lawlessness among these actors requires application of the extreme sanction of exclusion.[2]

Third, and most important, we discern no basis, and are offered none, for believing that exclusion of evidence seized pursuant to a warrant will have a significant deterrent effect on the issuing judge or magistrate. Many of the factors that indicate that the exclusionary rule cannot provide an effective "special" or "general" deterrent for individual offending law enforcement officers apply as well to judges or magistrates. And, to the extent that the rule is thought to operate as a "systemic" deterrent on a wider audience, it clearly can have no such effect on individuals empowered to issue search warrants. Judges and magistrates are not adjuncts to the law enforcement team; as neutral judicial officers, they have no stake in the outcome of particular criminal prosecutions. The threat of exclusion thus cannot be expected significantly to deter them. Imposition of the exclusionary sanction is not necessary meaningfully to inform judicial officers of their errors, and we cannot conclude that admitting evidence obtained pursuant to a warrant while at the same time declaring that the warrant was somehow defective will in any way reduce judicial officers' professional incentives to comply with the Fourth Amendment, encourage them to repeat their mistakes, or lead to the granting of all colorable warrant requests.[3]

B

If exclusion of evidence obtained pursuant to a subsequently invalidated warrant is to have any deterrent effect, therefore, it must alter the

2. Although there are assertions that some magistrates become rubber stamps for the police and others may be unable effectively to screen police, * * * we are not convinced that this is a problem of major proportions. * * *

3. Limiting the application of the exclusionary sanction may well increase the care with which magistrates scrutinize warrant applications. We doubt that magistrates are more desirous of avoiding the exclusion of evidence obtained pursuant to warrants they have issued than of avoiding invasions of privacy.

Federal magistrates, moreover, are subject to the direct supervision of district courts. They may be removed for "incompetency, misconduct, neglect of duty, or physical or mental disability." 28 U.S.C. § 631(i). If a magistrate serves merely as a "rubber stamp" for the police or is unable to exercise mature judgment, closer supervision or removal provides a more effective remedy than the exclusionary rule.

behavior of individual law enforcement officers or the policies of their departments. One could argue that applying the exclusionary rule in cases where the police failed to demonstrate probable cause in the warrant application deters future inadequate presentations or "magistrate shopping" and thus promotes the ends of the Fourth Amendment. Suppressing evidence obtained pursuant to a technically defective warrant supported by probable cause also might encourage officers to scrutinize more closely the form of the warrant and to point out suspected judicial errors. We find such arguments speculative and conclude that suppression of evidence obtained pursuant to a warrant should be ordered only on a case-by-case basis and only in those unusual cases in which exclusion will further the purposes of the exclusionary rule.

We have frequently questioned whether the exclusionary rule can have any deterrent effect when the offending officers acted in the objectively reasonable belief that their conduct did not violate the Fourth Amendment. * * *[4]

This is particularly true, we believe, when an officer acting with objective good faith has obtained a search warrant from a judge or magistrate and acted within its scope. In most such cases, there is no police illegality and thus nothing to deter. It is the magistrate's responsibility to determine whether the officer's allegations establish probable cause and, if so, to issue a warrant comporting in form with the requirements of the Fourth Amendment. In the ordinary case, an officer cannot be expected to question the magistrate's probable-cause determination or his judgment that the form of the warrant is technically sufficient. "[O]nce the warrant issues, there is literally nothing more the policeman can do in seeking to comply with the law." Penalizing the officer for the magistrate's error, rather than his own, cannot logically contribute to the deterrence of Fourth Amendment violations.[5]

C

We conclude that the marginal or nonexistent benefits produced by suppressing evidence obtained in objectively reasonable reliance on a subse-

---

4. We emphasize that the standard of reasonableness we adopt is an objective one. Many objections to a good-faith exception assume that the exception will turn on the subjective good faith of individual officers. * * * The objective standard we adopt, moreover, requires officers to have a reasonable knowledge of what the law prohibits.

5. [Considerations relating to the integrity of the courts do not support exclusion in these situations.] Our cases establish that the question whether the use of illegally obtained evidence in judicial proceedings represents judicial participation in a Fourth Amendment violation and offends the integrity of the courts

"is essentially the same as the inquiry into whether exclusion would serve a deterrent purpose. * * * The analysis

showing that exclusion in this case has no demonstrated deterrent effect and is unlikely to have any significant such effect shows, by the same reasoning, that the admission of the evidence is unlikely to encourage violations of the Fourth Amendment." United States v. Janis, [428 U.S. 433, 459, n. 35, 96 S.Ct. 3021, 3034, n. 35, 49 L.Ed.2d 1046 (1976)].

Absent unusual circumstances, when a Fourth Amendment violation has occurred because the police have reasonably relied on a warrant issued by a detached and neutral magistrate but ultimately found to be defective, "the integrity of the courts is not implicated." Illinois v. Gates, [462 U.S. 213 245, n. 14, 103 S.Ct. 2317, 2343, n. 14, 76 L.Ed.2d 527 (1983)] (White, J., concurring in the judgment).

quently invalidated search warrant cannot justify the substantial costs of exclusion. We do not suggest, however, that exclusion is always inappropriate in cases where an officer has obtained a warrant and abided by its terms. * * * [T]he officer's reliance on the magistrate's probable-cause determination and on the technical sufficiency of the warrant he issues must be objectively reasonable,[6] and it is clear that in some circumstances the officer[7] will have no reasonable grounds for believing that the warrant was properly issued.

Suppression therefore remains an appropriate remedy if the magistrate or judge in issuing a warrant was misled by information in an affidavit that the affiant knew was false or would have known was false except for his reckless disregard of the truth. Franks v. Delaware, 438 U.S. 154, 98 S.Ct. 2674, 57 L.Ed.2d 667 (1978). The exception we recognize today will also not apply in cases where the issuing magistrate wholly abandoned his judicial role in the manner condemned in Lo–Ji Sales, Inc. v. New York, 442 U.S. 319, 99 S.Ct. 2319, 60 L.Ed.2d 920 (1979); in such circumstances, no reasonably well-trained officer should rely on the warrant. Nor would an officer manifest objective good faith in relying on a warrant based on an affidavit "so lacking in indicia of probable cause as to render official belief in its existence entirely unreasonable." Brown v. Illinois, [422 U.S. 590, 610–611, 95 S.Ct. 2254, 2265, 45 L.Ed.2d 416 (1975)] (Powell, J., concurring in part). Finally, depending on the circumstances of the particular case, a warrant may be so facially deficient—i.e., in failing to particularize the place to be searched or the things to be seized—that the executing officers cannot reasonably presume it to be valid.

In so limiting the suppression remedy, we leave untouched the probable-cause standard and the various requirements for a valid warrant. Other objections to the modification of the Fourth Amendment exclusionary rule we consider to be insubstantial. The good-faith exception for searches conducted pursuant to warrants is not intended to signal our unwillingness strictly to enforce the requirements of the Fourth Amendment, and we do not believe that it will have this effect. As we have already suggested, the good-faith exception, turning as it does on objective reasonableness, should not be difficult to apply in practice. When officers have acted pursuant to a

---

6. [W]e * * * eschew inquiries into the subjective beliefs of law enforcement officers who seize evidence pursuant to a subsequently invalidated warrant. * * * [W]e believe that "sending state and federal courts on an expedition into the minds of police officers would produce a grave and fruitless misallocation of judicial resources." Massachusetts v. Painten, 389 U.S. 560, 565, 88 S.Ct. 660, 663, 19 L.Ed.2d 770 (1968) (WHITE, J., dissenting). Accordingly, our good-faith inquiry is confined to the objectively ascertainable question whether a reasonably well trained officer would have known that the search was illegal despite the magistrate's authorization. In making this determination, all of the circumstances—including whether the warrant

application had previously been rejected by a different magistrate—may be considered.

7. References to "officer" throughout this opinion should not be read too narrowly. It is necessary to consider the objective reasonableness, not only of the officers who eventually executed a warrant, but also of the officers who originally obtained it or who provided information material to the probable-cause determination. Nothing in our opinion suggests, for example, that an officer could obtain a warrant on the basis of a "bare bones" affidavit and then rely on colleagues who are ignorant of the circumstances under which the warrant was obtained to conduct the search.

warrant, the prosecution should ordinarily be able to establish objective good faith without a substantial expenditure of judicial time.

Nor are we persuaded that application of a good-faith exception to searches conducted pursuant to warrants will preclude review of the constitutionality of the search or seizure, deny needed guidance from the courts, or freeze Fourth Amendment law in its present state. There is no need for courts to adopt the inflexible practice of always deciding whether the officers' conduct manifested objective good faith before turning to the question whether the Fourth Amendment has been violated. * * *

[handwritten: even if in good faith still must review]

If the resolution of a particular Fourth Amendment question is necessary to guide future action by law enforcement officers and magistrates, nothing will prevent reviewing courts from deciding that question before turning to the good-faith issue. Indeed, it frequently will be difficult to determine whether the officers acted reasonably without resolving the Fourth Amendment issue. Even if the Fourth Amendment question is not one of broad import, reviewing courts could decide in particular cases that magistrates under their supervision need to be informed of their errors and so evaluate the officers' good faith only after finding a violation. In other circumstances, those courts could reject suppression motions posing no important Fourth Amendment questions by turning immediately to a consideration of the officers' good faith. We have no reason to believe that our Fourth Amendment jurisprudence would suffer by allowing reviewing courts to exercise an informed discretion in making this choice.

IV

When the principles we have enunciated today are applied to the facts of this case, it is apparent that the judgment of the Court of Appeals cannot stand. * * *

In the absence of an allegation that the magistrate abandoned his detached and neutral role, suppression is appropriate only if the officers were dishonest or reckless in preparing their affidavit or could not have harbored an objectively reasonable belief in the existence of probable cause. * * * Officer Rombach's application for a warrant clearly was supported by much more than a ''bare bones'' affidavit. The affidavit related the results of an extensive investigation and, as the opinions of the divided panel of the Court of Appeals make clear, provided evidence sufficient to create disagreement among thoughtful and competent judges as to the existence of probable cause. Under these circumstances, the officers' reliance on the magistrate's determination of probable cause was objectively reasonable, and application of the extreme sanction of exclusion is inappropriate.

[handwritten: conclusion]

Accordingly, the judgment of the Court of Appeals is reversed.

[The concurring opinion of JUSTICE BLACKMUN is omitted.]

■ JUSTICE BRENNAN, with whom JUSTICE MARSHALL joins, dissenting.

* * * I have witnessed the Court's gradual but determined strangulation of the [exclusionary] rule. It now appears that the Court's victory over the Fourth Amendment is complete. * * *

I

* * *

At bottom, the Court's decision turns on the proposition that the exclusionary rule is merely a " 'judicially created remedy designed to safeguard Fourth Amendment rights generally through its deterrent effect, rather than a personal constitutional right.' " * * * This reading of the Amendment implies that its proscriptions are directed solely at those government agents who may actually invade an individual's constitutionally protected privacy. The courts are not subject to any direct constitutional duty to exclude illegally obtained evidence, because the question of the admissibility of such evidence is not addressed by the Amendment. * * *

Such a reading appears plausible, because * * * the Fourth Amendment makes no express provision for the exclusion of evidence secured in violation of its commands. A short answer to this claim, of course, is that many of the Constitution's most vital imperatives are stated in general terms and the task of giving meaning to these precepts is therefore left to subsequent judicial decision-making in the context of concrete cases. * * *

[T]he Court's decisions over the past decade have made plain that the entire enterprise of attempting to assess the benefits and costs of the exclusionary rule in various contexts is virtually an impossible task for the judiciary to perform honestly or accurately. Although the Court's language in those cases suggests that some specific empirical basis may support its analyses, the reality is that the Court's opinions represent inherently unstable compounds of intuition, hunches, and occasional pieces of partial and often inconclusive data. * * * Rather than seeking to give effect to the liberties secured by the Fourth Amendment through guesswork about deterrence, the Court should restore to its proper place the principle framed 70 years ago in *Weeks* that an individual whose privacy has been invaded in violation of the Fourth Amendment has a right grounded in that Amendment to prevent the government from subsequently making use of any evidence so obtained.

* * *

III

Even if I were to accept the Court's general approach to the exclusionary rule, I could not agree with today's result. * * * [S]uch a result cannot be justified even on the Court's own terms.

At the outset, the Court suggests that society has been asked to pay a high price—in terms either of setting guilty persons free or of impeding the proper functioning of trials—as a result of excluding relevant physical evidence in cases where the police, in conducting searches and seizing evidence, have made only an "objectively reasonable" mistake concerning the constitutionality of their actions. But what evidence is there to support such a claim?

Significantly, the Court points to none, and, indeed, * * * recent studies have demonstrated that the "costs" of the exclusionary rule—

calculated in terms of dropped prosecutions and lost convictions—are quite low. * * *

What then supports the Court's insistence that this evidence be admitted? Apparently, the Court's only answer is that even though the costs of exclusion are not very substantial, the potential deterrent effect in these circumstances is so marginal that exclusion cannot be justified. * * *

The flaw in the Court's argument, however, is that its logic captures only one comparatively minor element of the generally acknowledged deterrent purposes of the exclusionary rule. To be sure, the rule operates to some extent to deter future misconduct by individual officers who have had evidence suppressed in their own cases. But what the Court overlooks is that the deterrence rationale for the rule is not designed to be, nor should it be thought of as, a form of "punishment" of individual police officers for their failures to obey the restraints imposed by the Fourth Amendment. Instead, the chief deterrent function of the rule is its tendency to promote institutional compliance with Fourth Amendment requirements on the part of law enforcement agencies generally. Thus, as the Court has previously recognized, "over the long term, [the] demonstration [provided by the exclusionary rule] that our society attaches serious consequences to violation of constitutional rights is thought to encourage those who formulate law enforcement policies, and the officers who implement them, to incorporate Fourth Amendment ideals into their value system." It is only through such an institution-wide mechanism that information concerning Fourth Amendment standards can be effectively communicated to rank and file officers.

If the overall educational effect of the exclusionary rule is considered, application of the rule to even those situations in which individual police officers have acted on the basis of a reasonable but mistaken belief that their conduct was authorized can still be expected to have a considerable long-term deterrent effect. If evidence is consistently excluded in these circumstances, police departments will surely be prompted to instruct their officers to devote greater care and attention to providing sufficient information to establish probable cause when applying for a warrant, and to review with some attention the form of the warrant that they have been issued, rather than automatically assuming that whatever document the magistrate has signed will necessarily comport with Fourth Amendment requirements.

After today's decision, however, that institutional incentive will be lost. Indeed, the Court's "reasonable mistake" exception to the exclusionary rule will tend to put a premium on police ignorance of the law. Armed with the assurance provided by today's decision that evidence will always be admissible whenever an officer has "reasonably" relied upon a warrant, police departments will be encouraged to train officers that if a warrant has simply been signed, it is reasonable, without more, to rely on it. Since in close cases there will no longer be any incentive to err on the side of constitutional behavior, police would have every reason to adopt a "let's-wait-until-it's-decided" approach in situations in which there is a question about a warrant's validity or the basis for its issuance. * * *

Although the Court brushes these concerns aside, a host of grave consequences can be expected to result from its decision to carve this new exception out of the exclusionary rule. A chief consequence of today's decision will be to convey a clear and unambiguous message to magistrates that their decisions to issue warrants are now insulated from subsequent judicial review. Creation of this new exception for good faith reliance upon a warrant implicitly tells magistrates that they need not take much care in reviewing warrant applications, since their mistakes will from now on have virtually no consequence: If their decision to issue a warrant was correct, the evidence will be admitted; if their decision was incorrect but the police relied in good faith on the warrant, the evidence will also be admitted. Inevitably, the care and attention devoted to such an inconsequential chore will dwindle. Although the Court is correct to note that magistrates do not share the same stake in the outcome of a criminal case as the police, they nevertheless need to appreciate that their role is of some moment in order to continue performing the important task of carefully reviewing warrant applications. Today's decision effectively removes that incentive.

Moreover, the good faith exception will encourage police to provide only the bare minimum of information in future warrant applications. The police will now know that if they can secure a warrant, so long as the circumstances of its issuance are not "entirely unreasonable," all police conduct pursuant to that warrant will be protected from further judicial review. The clear incentive that operated in the past to establish probable cause adequately because reviewing courts would examine the magistrate's judgment carefully, has now been so completely vitiated that the police need only show that it was not "entirely unreasonable" under the circumstances of a particular case for them to believe that the warrant they were issued was valid. The long-run effect unquestionably will be to undermine the integrity of the warrant process.

* * *

IV

[T]he relaxation of Fourth Amendment standards seems a tempting, costless means of meeting the public's demand for better law enforcement. In the long run, however, we as a society pay a heavy price for such expediency, because as Justice Jackson observed, the rights guaranteed in the Fourth Amendment "are not mere second-class rights but belong in the catalog of indispensable freedoms." Brinegar v. United States, 338 U.S. 160, 180, 69 S.Ct. 1302, 1313, 93 L.Ed. 1879 (1949) (dissenting opinion). Once lost, such rights are difficult to recover. There is hope, however, that in time this or some later Court will restore these precious freedoms to their rightful place as a primary protection for our citizens against overreaching officialdom.

I dissent.

■ JUSTICE STEVENS, * * * dissenting.

* * * It is probable, though admittedly not certain, that the Court of Appeals would now conclude that the warrant * * * satisfied the Fourth Amendment if it were given the opportunity to reconsider the issue in the light of [Illinois v.] Gates [462 U.S. 213, 103 S.Ct. 2317, 76 L.Ed.2d 527 (1983), reprinted in Chapter 3]. * * * Yet if the Court's assumption is correct—if there was no probable cause—it must follow that it was "unreasonable" for the authorities to make unheralded entries into and searches of private dwellings and automobiles. The Court's conclusion that such searches undertaken without probable cause can nevertheless be "reasonable" is totally without support in our Fourth Amendment jurisprudence.

[I]f * * * there is no probable cause here, then by definition—as a matter of constitutional law—the officers' conduct was unreasonable. * * *

The majority's contrary conclusion rests on the notion that it might be reasonable for a police officer to rely on a magistrate's finding. Until today that has plainly not been the law; it has been well-settled that even when a magistrate issues a warrant there is no guarantee that the ensuing search and seizure is constitutionally reasonable. * * *

The notion that a police officer's reliance on a magistrate's warrant is automatically appropriate is one the Framers of the Fourth Amendment would have vehemently rejected. The precise problem that the Amendment was intended to address was *the unreasonable issuance of warrants.* * * * The fact that colonial officers had magisterial authorization for their conduct when they engaged in general searches surely did not make their conduct "reasonable." The Court's view that it is consistent with our Constitution to adopt a rule that it is presumptively reasonable to rely on a defective warrant is the product of constitutional amnesia.

* * * I would vacate the judgment * * * and remand the case to the Court of Appeals for reconsideration in light of *Gates.* * * *

NOTES

1. In Massachusetts v. Sheppard, 468 U.S. 981, 104 S.Ct. 3424, 82 L.Ed.2d 737 (1984), a companion case to *Leon,* evidence at issue was also obtained during a search pursuant to a warrant. In *Sheppard,* the judge issuing the warrant incorrectly assured the officer he had modified the warrant form to incorporate by reference a list of items for which the warrant authorized police to search. Although the warrant may have been inadequate for failure to specify the items for which the officers could search, see Part 3 of Chapter 3, the officer reasonably believed it was valid. Thus the evidence was admissible under *Leon.*

2. **Warrantless Activity Authorized by Invalid Statute.** The "good faith" exception was extended to warrantless searches made pursuant to an invalid statute in Illinois v. Krull, 480 U.S. 340, 107 S.Ct. 1160, 94 L.Ed.2d 364 (1987). A Chicago police officer made a warrantless inspection of a junkyard, believing that the Illinois statute authorizing such inspections was valid. But the statute authorizing inspections of this sort was later held invalid. Nevertheless, the Supreme Court held, the evidence was admissible because of the officer's reliance on the statute. *Krull,* therefore, extended *Leon* to at least certain searches conducted without warrants. *Leon's* analysis, Justice Blackmun explained for the *Krull* majority, indicated a *Leon*-like exception covering the facts before it should be recognized:

> The application of the exclusionary rule to suppress evidence obtained by an officer acting in objectively reasonable reliance on a statute would have as little deterrent effect on the officer's actions as would the exclusion of evidence when an officer acts in objectively reasonable reliance on a warrant. Unless a statute

is clearly unconstitutional, an officer cannot be expected to question the judgment of the legislature that passed the law. * * *

Any difference between our holding in *Leon* and our holding in the instant case * * * must rest on a difference between the effect of the exclusion of evidence on judicial officers and the effect of the exclusion on legislators. * * * We noted in *Leon* as an initial matter that the exclusionary rule was aimed at deterring police misconduct. Thus, legislators, like judicial officers, are not the focus of the rule. * * *

There is no evidence suggesting that Congress or state legislatures have enacted a significant number of statutes permitting warrantless administrative searches violative of the Fourth Amendment. * * * Thus, we are given no basis for believing that legislators are inclined to subvert their oaths and the Fourth Amendment and that "lawlessness among these actors requires application of the extreme sanction of exclusion." * * * There is nothing to indicate that applying the exclusionary rule to evidence seized pursuant to [an invalid] statute prior to the declaration of its invalidity will act as a significant, additional deterrent. Moreover, to the extent that application of the exclusionary rule could provide some incremental deterrent, that possible benefit must be weighed against the "substantial social costs exacted by the exclusionary rule." When we indulge in such weighing, we are convinced that applying the exclusionary rule in this context is unjustified.

480 U.S. at 351–53, 107 S.Ct. at 1168–69, 94 L.Ed.2d at 376–77. But, the Court continued, the *Krull* exception is subject to certain constraints:

A statute cannot support objectively reasonable reliance if, in passing the statute, the legislature wholly abandoned its responsibility to enact constitutional laws. Nor can a law enforcement officer be said to have acted in good-faith reliance upon a statute if its provisions are such that a reasonable officer should have known that the statute was unconstitutional. As we emphasized in *Leon,* the standard of reasonableness we adopt is an objective one; the standard does not turn on the subjective good faith of individual officers.

480 U.S. at 355, 107 S.Ct. at 1170, 94 L.Ed.2d at 378–79.

Turning to the case before it, the majority concluded any such defects as existed in the Illinois statute were not so obvious that an objectively reasonable police officer would have realized the statute was unconstitutional. The officer "relied, in objective good faith, on a statute that appeared legitimately to allow a warrantless administrative search of [Krull's] business," and the evidentiary products of his actions were therefore admissible against Krull. The majority assumed the officer acted within the scope of the statute, but indicated this could be explored on remand:

At this juncture, we decline the State's invitation to recognize an exception for an officer who erroneously but in good faith believes he is acting within the scope of a statute. * * * [S]uch a ruling * * * does not follow inexorably from today's decision. As our opinion makes clear, the question whether the exclusionary rule is applicable in a particular context depends significantly upon the actors who are making the relevant decision that the rule is designed to influence. The answer to this question might well be different when police officers act outside the scope of a statute, albeit in good faith. In that context, the relevant actors are not legislators or magistrates, but police officers who concededly are "engaged in the often competitive enterprise of ferreting out crime."

480 U.S. at 360 n. 17, 107 S.Ct. at 1172 n. 17, 94 L.Ed.2d at 382 n. 17. Justice O'Connor, joined by Justices Brennan, Marshall and Stevens, dissented.

3. **Mistaken Perception that Valid Warrant Exists.** Does the *Leon* good faith exception apply if no valid warrant actually exists but an officer reasonably believes it does? The issue was presented in Arizona v. Evans, 514 U.S. 1, 115 S.Ct. 1185, 131 L.Ed.2d 34 (1995), in which Evans was stopped by a Phoenix police officer for a traffic offense. The officer entered Evans's name into a computer terminal located in the patrol car and he received a message in reply indicating there was an outstanding misdemeanor warrant for Evans's arrest. Based on his belief that such a warrant existed, the officer placed Evans under arrest and, in the process, discovered marijuana. In fact, an arrest warrant was issued for Evans but was quashed 17 days before his arrest. When Evans was prosecuted for possession of the marijuana, he sought suppression of the marijuana. Testimony at the hearing on his motion established the warrant had been for nonappearance on traffic tickets. When Evans appeared before a Justice of the Peace, the justice made a notation on the file to "quash warrant." Evidence also showed standard procedure in such a case was for a justice court clerk to telephone the sheriff's office and relay that the warrant had been quashed. The sheriff's office would then remove the warrant from its computer records. Evans's file did not contain the notation usually made when the clerk calls the sheriff's office and the sheriff's office had no record of a call from the clerk. The trial court made no findings regarding whether the court clerk or the sheriff's office erred but suppressed the marijuana. The Arizona Supreme Court upheld this action, indicating it attached no significance to whether the error was made by a court employee or law enforcement personnel.

The Supreme Court reversed. The Arizona Supreme Court's conclusion that suppression was required even if responsibility for the error rested with the clerk of the justice court "is contrary to the reasoning of [*Leon, Sheppard,* and *Krull*]." Chief Justice Rehnquist continued for the Court:

> If court employees were responsible for the erroneous computer record, the exclusion of evidence at trial would not sufficiently deter future errors so as to warrant such a severe sanction. First, as we noted in *Leon,* the exclusionary rule was historically designed as a means of deterring police misconduct, not mistakes by court employees. Second, respondent offers no evidence that court employees are inclined to ignore or subvert the Fourth Amendment or that lawlessness among these actors requires application of the extreme sanction of exclusion. To the contrary, the Chief Clerk of the Justice Court testified at the suppression hearing that this type of error occurred once every three or four years.

> Finally, and most important, there is no basis for believing that application of the exclusionary rule in these circumstances will have a significant effect on court employees responsible for informing the police that a warrant has been quashed. Because court clerks are not adjuncts to the law enforcement team engaged in the often competitive enterprise of ferreting out crime, they have no stake in the outcome of particular criminal prosecutions. The threat of exclusion of evidence could not be expected to deter such individuals from failing to inform police officials that a warrant had been quashed.

> If it were indeed a court clerk who was responsible for the erroneous entry on the police computer, application of the exclusionary rule also could not be expected to alter the behavior of the arresting officer. As the trial court in this case stated: "I think the police officer [was] bound to arrest. I think he would [have been] derelict in his duty if he failed to arrest." The Chief Clerk of the Justice Court testified that this type of error occurred "on[c]e every three or four years." In fact, once the court clerks discovered the error, they immediately corrected it, and then proceeded to search their files to make sure that no similar mistakes had occurred. There is no indication that the arresting officer

was not acting objectively reasonable when he relied upon the police computer record. Application of the *Leon* framework supports a categorical exception to the exclusionary rule for clerical errors of court employees.

514 U.S. at 14–16, 115 S.Ct. at 1193–94, 131 L.Ed.2d at 47. The Court explicitly refused to address whether it would apply a similar analysis to determine whether the evidence would be suppressed if "police personnel" were responsible for the error. It remanded the case to the Arizona Supreme Court for further proceedings not inconsistent with the Supreme Court's opinion.

Justice Stevens dissented on the merits of the basic issue:

> *Leon* stands for the dubious but limited proposition that courts should not look behind the face of a warrant on which police have relied in good faith. The *Leon* Court's exemption of judges and magistrates from the deterrent ambit of the exclusionary rule rested, consistently with the emphasis on the warrant requirement, on those officials' constitutionally determined role in issuing warrants. Taken on its own terms, *Leon's* logic does not extend to the time after the warrant has issued; nor does it extend to court clerks and functionaries, some of whom work in the same building with police officers and may have more regular and direct contact with police than with judges or magistrates.

514 U.S. at 20, 115 S.Ct. at 1196, 131 L.Ed.2d at 50–51 (Stevens, J., dissenting). Justice Ginsburg, joined by Justice Stevens, dissented on the ground that the Arizona court's ruling should be regarded as based on state rather than federal constitutional law.

There have been no further substantive proceedings on remand in *Evans*. The Arizona Supreme Court remanded the case to the trial court for further proceedings. At an appearance before the trial court, the prosecution was informed that, since the original changes were dismissed to render the matter appealable under local procedure, there was no longer any case in which further proceedings could occur. The State refiled the case and the court issued a bench warrant for Evans. Arizona law enforcement agencies are apparently not vigorously searching for Evans given the minor nature of the offense, but the trial prosecutor indicated if Evans is rearrested the case will proceed. Interview with Kim N. Stuart, Deputy Maricopa County Attorney, February 7, 1997.

4. **Statutory "Good Faith" Proposals.** A number of efforts have been made to enact legislation providing for "good faith" exceptions to various exclusionary rules. On the federal level, numerous legislative proposals have been made; none have been enacted. A 1997 proposal for reform, the "Exclusionary Rule Reform Act of 1997," for example, was part of S.B. 3 (105th Congress, Jan. 21, 1997). It would have added the following to Title 18 of the United States Code:

Sec. 3510. Admissibility of evidence obtained by search or seizure

(a) EVIDENCE OBTAINED BY OBJECTIVELY REASONABLE SEARCH OR SEIZURE—

(1) IN GENERAL—Evidence that is obtained as a result of a search or seizure shall not be excluded in a proceeding in a court of the United States on the ground that the search or seizure was in violation of the fourth amendment to the Constitution of the United States, if the search or seizure was carried out in circumstances justifying an objectively reasonable belief that the search or seizure was in conformity with the fourth amendment.

(2) PRIMA FACIE EVIDENCE—The fact that evidence was obtained pursuant to and within the scope of a warrant constitutes prima facie

evidence of the existence of circumstances justifying an objectively reasonable belief that it was in conformity with the fourth amendment.

* * *

The proposal was not enacted. Identical language was introduced in the 1st Session of the 106th Congress. See S.B. 899 (April 28, 1999).

5. **Inevitable Discovery Exception.** Another exception to exclusionary sanctions attaching to violations of federal constitutional rights was recognized in Nix v. Williams, 467 U.S. 431, 104 S.Ct. 2501, 81 L.Ed.2d 377 (1984). Williams was convicted of the murder of a young girl. Following his first trial, the Supreme Court determined he was interrogated in violation of his Sixth and Fourteenth Amendments right to counsel and consequently the statements he made during this interrogation were improperly admitted into evidence at his trial. Brewer v. Williams, 430 U.S. 387, 97 S.Ct. 1232, 51 L.Ed.2d 424 (1977), discussed in Chapter 6(C). In addition, however, Williams revealed to the interrogating officers the location of the victim's body. Using this information, officers found the body. At Williams's second trial, the prosecution did not offer into evidence his incriminating statements nor did it show Williams directed police to the body. It did, however, offer evidence of the condition of the body as found, articles and photographs of clothing found on the body, and the results of medical and chemical tests performed on the body. In support of its offer of this evidence, the prosecution showed that, at the time of Williams' interrogation, a search for the body was underway and that 200 volunteers were involved. This search was called off when Williams began to cooperate with law enforcement officers. But, the state's witness testified, had the search not been called off it would have resulted in discovery of the body after three to five additional hours of searching. The trial judge admitted the evidence on the ground that the prosecution showed that, if Williams had not been improperly interrogated, the victim's body would nevertheless have been found and therefore evidence resulting from the body's discovery was admissible. Williams was again convicted and later sought invalidation of that conviction in federal habeas corpus litigation.

The Supreme Court found no violation of Williams's federal constitutional rights in the use of the evidence. All nine members of the Court agreed the exclusionary sanction attaching to the violation of Williams's Sixth and Fourteenth Amendments right to counsel is subject to an "ultimate or inevitable discovery" exception:

> [W]hen * * * the evidence in question would inevitably have been discovered without reference to the police error or misconduct, there is no nexus [between the error and the evidence] sufficient to provide a taint and the evidence is admissible.

467 U.S. at 448, 104 S.Ct. at 2511, 81 L.Ed.2d at 390. The rationale for this exception, Chief Justice Burger explained for the Court, is the same as that for the "independent source" rule discussed in Part B of this chapter. The need to deter unlawful police conduct is sufficiently met if police engaging in misconduct are put in the same position they would have been in had the misconduct not occurred. This need does not, however, justify putting law enforcement in a worse position than it would have been in had no misconduct taken place. Society's need for reliable evidence of offenders' guilt, on the other hand, strongly argues against any aspect of the exclusionary rules putting a law enforcement agency in a worse position than it would have been in had misconduct not taken place. Both the inevitable discovery exception and the independent source doctrine serve the purpose of assuring that misbehaving law enforcement agencies are not put in any worse position than they would have been in had they avoided the misbehavior. While the case involved the exclusionary penalty for a violation of the Sixth Amendment right to counsel, the

Court's discussion strongly suggests identical exceptions will be recognized with regard to other exclusionary rules, including that adopted in *Mapp* for violations of the Fourth Amendment.

All members of the Court agreed the inevitable discovery exception should not be qualified by requiring the prosecution, as a condition of invoking it, to show the officers acted without "bad faith." Such a condition, the Court reasoned, would in no way further the purpose of the inevitable discovery exception. The members of the Court split, however, on the appropriate burden of proof. Justice Brennan, joined by Justice Marshall, reasoned:

> The inevitable discovery exception necessarily implicates a hypothetical finding that differs in kind from the factual finding that precedes application of the independent source rule. To ensure that this hypothetical finding is narrowly confined to circumstances that are functionally equivalent to an independent source, and to protect fully the fundamental rights served by the exclusionary rule, I would require clear and convincing evidence before concluding that the government had met its burden of proof on this issue.

467 U.S. at 459, 104 S.Ct. at 2517, 81 L.Ed.2d at 397–98 (Brennan, J., dissenting). The Court, however, rejected Justice Brennan's characterization of the analysis and conclusion as to the appropriate burden of proof:

> [I]nevitable discovery involves no speculative elements but focuses on demonstrated historical facts capable of ready verification or impeachment and does not require a departure from the usual burden of proof [by a preponderance of the evidence] at suppression hearings.

467 U.S. at 444 n. 5, 104 S.Ct. at 2509 n. 5, 81 L.Ed.2d at 388 n. 5.

CHAPTER 2

Constitutional Doctrines Relating to Law Enforcement Conduct

Analysis

Exclusionary sanctions of the sort considered in Chapter 1 come into operation only if there has been a violation of underlying legal requirements. In constitutional terms, challenges to law enforcement conduct usually rest on provisions guaranteeing protection from compelled self-incrimination, rights to privacy and freedom from unreasonable searches and seizures, rights to the assistance of counsel, and general rights to due process of law. Major federal provisions and illustrative state provisions are set out in the Editors' Introduction at the beginning of Part One of these materials.

This chapter develops the basic content of the major federal constitutional provisions. Part A provides an opportunity to compare several of these provisions as they apply to the extraction of a sample of a suspect's blood. Part B then focuses on the Fourth Amendment. The Fifth Amendment privilege against compelled self-incrimination applies primarily to law enforcement efforts to obtain confessions and other self-incriminating admissions; this is the subject of Chapter 7, and the Fifth Amendment privilege is considered at length in that chapter.

A.   SCOPE OF THE BASIC DOCTRINES

Before considering in detail the impact of the major doctrines, it is important to consider the framework for analyzing situations under these doctrines. The principal case in this section addresses the relevance of these doctrines to a single police activity—the extraction from a suspect of a sample of blood. It is important to distinguish two matters. First, what are the "threshold" issues determining whether the doctrine applies? Second, *if* the doctrine applies, what requirements does it impose upon law enforcement conduct?

Schmerber v. California

Supreme Court of the United States, 1966.
384 U.S. 757, 86 S.Ct. 1826, 16 L.Ed.2d 908.

■ MR. JUSTICE BRENNAN delivered the opinion of the Court.

Petitioner was convicted in Los Angeles Municipal Court of the criminal offense of driving an automobile while under the influence of intoxicating liquor. He had been arrested at a hospital while receiving treatment for injuries suffered in an accident involving the automobile that he had apparently been driving. At the direction of a police officer, a blood sample was then withdrawn from petitioner's body by a physician at the hospital. The chemical analysis of this sample revealed a percent by weight of alcohol in his blood at the time of the offense which indicated intoxication, and the report of this analysis was admitted in evidence at the trial. Petitioner objected to receipt of this evidence of the analysis on the ground that the blood had been withdrawn despite his refusal, on the advice of his counsel, to consent to the test. He contended that in that circumstance the withdrawal of the blood and the admission of the analysis in evidence denied him due process of law under the Fourteenth Amendment, as well as specific guarantees of the Bill of Rights secured against the States by that Amendment: his privilege against self-incrimination under the Fifth Amendment; * * * and his right not to be subjected to unreasonable searches and seizures in violation of the Fourth Amendment. The Appellate Department of the California Superior Court rejected these contentions and affirmed the conviction. In view of constitutional decisions since we last considered these issues in Breithaupt v. Abram, 352 U.S. 432, 77 S.Ct. 408, 1 L.Ed.2d 448 we granted certiorari. We affirm.

I.

The Due Process Clause Claim

[In Rochin v. California, 342 U.S. 165, 72 S.Ct. 205, 96 L.Ed. 183, officers lacking probable cause had entered Rochin's house through an open door. Forcing open the door to Rochin's second floor room, they found Rochin partly dressed and sitting on a bed, upon which his wife was lying. When they asked about two capsules which were on a night stand next to the bed, Rochin grabbed the capsules and swallowed them despite the efforts of the three officers to prevent this. Rochin was then taken to a hospital, where a doctor forced an emetic solution through a tube into his stomach, causing him to vomit. In the vomited matter were found the two capsules which were used in evidence in his later prosecution for possession of the morphine in the capsules. The Supreme Court held that the resulting conviction violated due process:

> This is conduct that shocks the conscience. Illegally breaking into the privacy of [Rochin], the struggle to open his mouth and remove what was there, the forcible extraction of his stomach contents—this course of proceeding by agents of government to obtain evidence is bound to offend even hardened sensibilities. They are methods too close to the rack and screw to permit of constitutional differentiation.

342 U.S. at 172, 72 S.Ct. at 209–10, 96 L.Ed. at 190. Petitioner argues that *Rochin* controls here. Editors.]

Breithaupt was also a case in which police officers caused blood to be withdrawn from the driver of an automobile involved in an accident, and in which there was ample justification for the officer's conclusion that the driver was under the influence of alcohol. There, as here, the extraction was made by a physician in a simple, medically acceptable manner in a hospital environment. There, however, the driver was unconscious at the time the blood was withdrawn and hence had no opportunity to object to the procedure. We affirmed the conviction there resulting from the use of the test in evidence, holding that under such circumstances the withdrawal did not offend "that 'sense of justice' of which we spoke in *Rochin*." *Breithaupt* thus requires the rejection of petitioner's due process argument, and nothing in the circumstances of this case or in supervening events persuades us that this aspect of *Breithaupt* should be overruled.

II.

The Privilege Against Self-incrimination Claim

Breithaupt summarily rejected an argument that the withdrawal of blood and the admission of the analysis report involved in that state case violated the Fifth Amendment privilege of any person not to "be compelled in any criminal case to be a witness against himself," citing Twining v. State of New Jersey, 211 U.S. 78, 29 S.Ct. 14, 53 L.Ed. 97. But that case, holding that the protections of the Fourteenth Amendment do not embrace this Fifth Amendment privilege, has been succeeded by Malloy v. Hogan, 378 U.S. 1, 8, 84 S.Ct. 1489, 1493, 12 L.Ed.2d 653. We there held that "[t]he Fourteenth Amendment secures against state invasion the same privilege that the Fifth Amendment guarantees against federal infringement—the right of a person to remain silent unless he chooses to speak in the unfettered exercise of his own will, and to suffer no penalty * * * for such silence." We therefore must now decide whether the withdrawal of the blood and admission in evidence of the analysis involved in this case violated petitioner's privilege. We hold that the privilege protects an accused only from being compelled to testify against himself, or otherwise provide the State with evidence of a testimonial or communicative nature,[1] and that the withdrawal of blood and use of the analysis in question in this case did not involve compulsion to these ends.

It could not be denied that in requiring petitioner to submit to the withdrawal and chemical analysis of his blood the State compelled him to submit to an attempt to discover evidence that might be used to prosecute him for a criminal offense. He submitted only after the police officer rejected his objection and directed the physician to proceed. The officer's direction to the physician to administer the test over petitioner's objection constituted compulsion for the purposes of the privilege. The critical question, then, is whether petitioner was thus compelled "to be a witness against himself."

If the scope of the privilege coincided with the complex of values it helps to protect, we might be obliged to conclude that the privilege was violated. In Miranda v. Arizona, 384 U.S. 436, at 460, 86 S.Ct. 1602, at 1620, 16 L.Ed.2d 694, at 715, the Court said of the interests protected by the privilege: "All these policies point to one overriding thought: the constitutional foundation underlying the privilege is the respect a government—state or federal—must accord to the dignity and integrity of its citizens. To maintain a 'fair state-individual balance,' to require the government 'to shoulder the entire load,' * * * to respect the inviolability of the human personality, our accusatory system of criminal justice demands that the government seeking to punish an individual produce the evidence against him by its own independent labors, rather than by the cruel, simple expedient of compelling it from his own mouth." The withdrawal of blood necessarily involves puncturing the skin for extraction, and the percent by weight of alcohol in that blood, as established by chemical analysis, is evidence of criminal guilt. Compelled submission fails on one view to respect the "inviolability of the human personality." Moreover, since it enables the State to rely on evidence forced from the accused, the compulsion violates at least one meaning of the requirement that the State procure the evidence against an accused "by its own independent labors."

As the passage in *Miranda* implicitly recognizes, however, the privilege has never been given the full scope which the values it helps to protect suggest. History and a long line of authorities in lower courts have consistently limited its protection to situations in which the State seeks to submerge those values by obtaining the evidence against an accused through "the cruel, simple expedient of compelling it from his own mouth. * * * In sum, the privilege is fulfilled only when the person is guaranteed

---

1. A dissent suggests that the report of the blood test was "testimonial" or "communicative," because the test was performed in order to obtain the testimony of others, communicating to the jury facts about petitioner's condition. Of course, all evidence received in court is "testimonial" or "communicative" if these words are thus used. But the Fifth Amendment relates only to acts on the part of the person to whom the privilege applies, and we use these words subject to the same limitations. A nod or headshake is as much a "testimonial" or "communicative" act in this sense as are spoken words. But the terms as we use them do not apply to evidence of acts noncommunicative in nature as to the person asserting the privilege, even though, as here, such acts are compelled to obtain the testimony of others.

the right 'to remain silent unless he chooses to speak in the unfettered exercise of his own will.' " The leading case in this Court is Holt v. United States, 218 U.S. 245, 31 S.Ct. 2, 54 L.Ed. 1021. There the question was whether evidence was admissible that the accused, prior to trial and over his protest, put on a blouse that fitted him. It was contended that compelling the accused to submit to the demand that he model the blouse violated the privilege. Mr. Justice Holmes, speaking for the Court, rejected the argument as "based upon an extravagant extension of the 5th Amendment," and went on to say: "[T]he prohibition of compelling a man in a criminal court to be witness against himself is a prohibition of the use of physical or moral compulsion to extort communications from him, not an exclusion of his body as evidence when it may be material. The objection in principle would forbid a jury to look at a prisoner and compare his features with a photograph in proof."

It is clear that the protection of the privilege reaches an accused's communications, whatever form they might take * * *. On the other hand, both federal and state courts have usually held that it offers no protection against compulsion to submit to fingerprinting, photographing, or measurements, to write or speak for identification, to appear in court, to stand, to assume a stance, to walk, or to make a particular gesture. The distinction which has emerged, often expressed in different ways, is that the privilege is a bar against compelling "communications" or "testimony," but that compulsion which makes a suspect or accused the source of "real or physical evidence" does not violate it.

Although we agree that this distinction is a helpful framework for analysis, we are not to be understood to agree with past applications in all instances. There will be many cases in which such a distinction is not readily drawn. Some tests seemingly directed to obtain "physical evidence," for example, lie detector tests measuring changes in body function during interrogation, may actually be directed to eliciting responses which are essentially testimonial. To compel a person to submit to testing in which an effort will be made to determine his guilt or innocence on the basis of physiological responses, whether willed or not, is to evoke the spirit and history of the Fifth Amendment. Such situations call to mind the principle that the protection of the privilege "is as broad as the mischief against which it seeks to guard." Counselman v. Hitchcock, 142 U.S. 547, 562, 12 S.Ct. 195, 198.

In the present case, however, no such problem of application is presented. Not even a shadow of testimonial compulsion upon or enforced communication by the accused was involved either in the extraction or in the chemical analysis. Petitioner's testimonial capacities were in no way implicated; indeed, his participation, except as a donor, was irrelevant to the results of the test, which depend on chemical analysis and on that alone.[2] Since the blood test evidence, although an incriminating product of

self incrim = N/A as blood not testimony / words

---

2. This conclusion would not necessarily govern had the State tried to show that the accused had incriminated himself when told that he would have to be tested. Such incriminating evidence may be an unavoidable by-product of the compulsion to take the test, especially for an individual who fears the extraction or opposes it on religious grounds. If it wishes to compel persons to submit to such attempts to discover evidence, the State compulsion, was neither petitioner's testimony nor evidence relating to some communicative act or writing by the petitioner, it was not inadmissible on privilege grounds.

* * *

IV.

The Search and Seizure Claim

* * *

The values protected by the Fourth Amendment * * * substantially overlap those the Fifth Amendment helps to protect. History and precedent have required that we today reject the claim that the Self–Incrimination Clause of the Fifth Amendment requires the human body in all circumstances to be held inviolate against state expeditions seeking evidence of crime. But if compulsory administration of a blood test does not implicate the Fifth Amendment, it plainly involves the broadly conceived reach of a search and seizure under the Fourth Amendment. That Amendment expressly provides that "[t]he right of the people to be secure in their *persons*, houses, papers, and effects, against unreasonable searches and seizures, shall not be violated * * * ." (Emphasis added.) It could not reasonably be argued, and indeed respondent does not argue, that the administration of the blood test in this case was free of the constraints of the Fourth Amendment. Such testing procedures plainly constitute searches of "persons," and depend antecedently upon seizures of "persons," within the meaning of that Amendment.

Because we are dealing with intrusions into the human body rather than with state interferences with property relationships or private papers—"houses, papers, and effects"—we write on a clean slate. Limitations on the kinds of property which may be seized under warrant, as distinct from the procedures for search and the permissible scope of search, are not instructive in this context. We begin with the assumption that once the privilege against self-incrimination has been found not to bar compelled intrusions into the body for blood to be analyzed for alcohol content, the Fourth Amendment's proper function is to constrain, not against all intrusions as such, but against intrusions which are not justified in the circumstances, or which are made in an improper manner. In other words, the questions we must decide in this case are whether the police were justified in requiring petitioner to submit to the blood test, and whether the means and procedures employed in taking his blood respected relevant Fourth Amendment standards of reasonableness.

[handwritten margin note: human body rather than property]

In this case, as will often be true when charges of driving under the influence of alcohol are pressed, these questions arise in the context of an arrest made by an officer without a warrant. Here, there was plainly

---

may have to forego the advantage of any *testimonial* products of administering the test—products which would fall within the privilege. Indeed, there may be circumstances in which the pain, danger, or severity of an operation would almost inevitably cause a person to prefer confession to undergoing the "search," and nothing we say today should be taken as establishing the permissibility of compulsion in that case. But no such situation is presented in this case. * * *

probable cause for the officer to arrest petitioner and charge him with driving an automobile while under the influence of intoxicating liquor. The police officer who arrived at the scene shortly after the accident smelled liquor on petitioner's breath, and testified that petitioner's eyes were "bloodshot, watery, sort of a glassy appearance." The officer saw petitioner again at the hospital, within two hours of the accident. There he noticed similar symptoms of drunkenness. He thereupon informed petitioner "that he was under arrest and that he was entitled to the services of an attorney, and that he could remain silent, and that anything that he told me would be used against him in evidence."

While early cases suggest that there is an unrestricted "right on the part of the government always recognized under English and American law, to search the person of the accused when legally arrested, to discover and seize the fruits or evidences of crime," the mere fact of a lawful arrest does not end our inquiry. The suggestion of these cases apparently rests on two factors—first, there may be more immediate danger of concealed weapons or of destruction of evidence under the direct control of the accused; second, once a search of the arrested person for weapons is permitted, it would be both impractical and unnecessary to enforcement of the Fourth Amendment's purpose to attempt to confine the search to those objects alone. Whatever the validity of these considerations in general, they have little applicability with respect to searches involving intrusions beyond the body's surface. The interests in human dignity and privacy which the Fourth Amendment protects forbid any such intrusions on the mere chance that desired evidence might be obtained. In the absence of a clear indication that in fact such evidence will be found, these fundamental human interests require law officers to suffer the risk that such evidence may disappear unless there is an immediate search.

Although the facts which established probable cause to arrest in this case also suggested the required relevance and likely success of a test of petitioner's blood for alcohol, the question remains whether the arresting officer was permitted to draw these inferences himself, or was required instead to procure a warrant before proceeding with the test. Search warrants are ordinarily required for searches of dwellings, and absent an emergency, no less could be required where intrusions into the human body are concerned. The requirement that a warrant be obtained is a requirement that inferences to support the search "be drawn by a neutral and detached magistrate instead of being judged by the officer engaged in the often competitive enterprise of ferreting out crime." The importance of informed, detached and deliberate determinations of the issue whether or not to invade another's body in search of evidence of guilt is indisputable and great.

The officer in the present case, however, might reasonably have believed that he was confronted with an emergency, in which the delay necessary to obtain a warrant, under the circumstances, threatened "the destruction of evidence." We are told that the percentage of alcohol in the blood begins to diminish shortly after drinking stops, as the body functions to eliminate it from the system. Particularly in a case such as this, where time had to be taken to bring the accused to a hospital and to investigate the scene of the accident, there was no time to seek out a magistrate and secure a warrant. Given these special facts, we conclude that the attempt to secure evidence of blood-alcohol content in this case was an appropriate incident to petitioner's arrest.

Similarly, we are satisfied that the test chosen to measure petitioner's blood-alcohol level was a reasonable one. Extraction of blood samples for testing is a highly effective means of determining the degree to which a person is under the influence of alcohol. Such tests are a commonplace in these days of periodic physical examinations and experience with them teaches that the quantity of blood extracted is minimal, and that for most people the procedure involves virtually no risk, trauma, or pain. Petitioner is not one of the few who on grounds of fear, concern for health, or religious scruple might prefer some other means of testing, such as the "breathalyzer" test petitioner refused. * * * We need not decide whether such wishes would have to be respected.

Finally, the record shows that the test was performed in a reasonable manner. Petitioner's blood was taken by a physician in a hospital environment according to accepted medical practices. We are thus not presented with the serious questions which would arise if a search involving use of a medical technique, even of the most rudimentary sort, were made by other than medical personnel or in other than a medical environment—for example, if it were administered by police in the privacy of the stationhouse. To tolerate searches under these conditions might be to invite an unjustified element of personal risk of infection and pain.

We thus conclude that the present record shows no violation of petitioner's right under the Fourth and Fourteenth Amendments to be free of unreasonable searches and seizures. It bears repeating, however, that we reach this judgment only on the facts of the present record. The integrity of an individual's person is a cherished value of our society. That we today hold that the Constitution does not forbid the States minor intrusions into an individual's body under stringently limited conditions in no way indicates that it permits more substantial intrusions, or intrusions under other conditions.

Affirmed.

NOTES

1. **Providing Voice Samples as Nontestimonial Activity.** In United States v. Wade, 388 U.S. 218, 87 S.Ct. 1926, 18 L.Ed.2d 1149 (1967), the Court held that police did not violate the Fifth Amendment by requiring Wade to say at a lineup the words uttered by a robber—"put the money in the bag." Wade was required, the Court reasoned, only to use his voice in demonstrating its physical characteristics. See also, United States v. Dionisio, 410 U.S. 1, 93 S.Ct. 764, 35 L.Ed.2d 67 (1973) (Fifth Amendment not implicated by subpoena directing suspect to appear at prosecutor's office and read into a recording device from a transcript); United States v. Mara, 410 U.S. 19, 93 S.Ct. 774, 35 L.Ed.2d 99 (1973) (Fifth Amendment not implicated by compulsion to prepare and provide exemplar of handwriting or printing).

2. **Testimonial Aspects of Field Sobriety Tests.** The Court discussed the Fifth Amendment requirement that a compelled act be "testimonial" and the rationale for this demand in Pennsylvania v. Muniz, 496 U.S. 582, 110 S.Ct. 2638, 110 L.Ed.2d 528 (1990), involving the processing—and videotaping—of a suspect arrested for driving while intoxicated. Requiring the arrestee to speak to demonstrate the slurred nature of his speech, all justices agreed, did not involve compelled testimonial activity. "Requiring a suspect to reveal the physical manner in which he articulates words, like requiring him to reveal the physical properties of the sound produced by his voice ... does not, without more, compel him to provide a 'testimonial' response for purposes of the privilege." Having him perform sobriety tests (the "horizontal gaze nystagus" test, the "walk and turn" test and the "one leg stand" test), eight of the justices also held, did not implicate the Fifth Amendment. But asking him the date of his sixth birthday (apparently to determine if he could calculate that from his date of birth), a 5 to 4 majority concluded, did demand testimonial activity. It rejected the argument, accepted by the four dissenters, that this question simply sought a demonstration of the physiological functioning of the suspect's brain, and thus was no different from requiring him to demonstrate his ability to articulate words. Justice Brennan explained for the majority:

> We recently explained in Doe v. United States, 487 U.S. 201, 108 S.Ct. 2341, 101 L.Ed.2d 184 (1988), that "in order to be testimonial, an accused's communication must itself, explicitly or implicitly, relate a factual assertion or disclose information." We reached this conclusion after addressing our reasoning in *Schmerber,* supra, and its progeny:
>
>> The Court accordingly held that the privilege was not implicated in [the line of cases beginning with *Schmerber*] because the suspect was not required "to disclose any knowledge he might have," or "to speak his guilt." *Wade,* 388 U.S., at 222–223, 87 S.Ct. at 1929–1930. It is the "extortion of information from the accused," the attempt to force him "to disclose the contents of his own mind," that implicates the Self–Incrimination Clause * * * "Unless some attempt is made to secure a communication—written, oral or otherwise—upon which reliance is to be placed as involving (the accused's) consciousness of the facts and the operations of his mind in expressing it, the demand made upon him is not a testimonial one." 8 Wigmore § 2265, p. 386.
>
> 487 U.S., at 210–211, 108 S.Ct. at 2348.
>
> After canvassing the purposes of the privilege recognized in prior cases, we concluded that "[t]hese policies are served when the privilege is asserted to spare the accused from having to reveal, directly or indirectly, his knowledge of facts relating him to the offense or from having to share his thoughts and beliefs with the Government."
>
> This definition of testimonial evidence reflects an awareness of the historical abuses against which the privilege against self-incrimination was aimed. "Historically, the privilege was intended to prevent the use of legal compulsion to extract from the accused a sworn communication of facts which would incriminate him. Such was the process of the ecclesiastical courts and the Star Chamber—the inquisitorial method of putting the accused upon his oath and compelling him to answer questions designed to uncover uncharged offenses, without evidence from another source. The major thrust of the policies undergirding the privilege is to prevent such compulsion." At its core, the privilege reflects our fierce "unwillingness to subject those suspected of crime to the cruel trilemma of self-accusation, perjury or contempt," that defined the operation of the Star Chamber, wherein suspects were forced to choose between

revealing incriminating private thoughts and forsaking their oath by committing perjury. See United States v. Nobles, 422 U.S. 225, 233, 95 S.Ct. 2160, 2167, 45 L.Ed.2d 141 (1975) ("The Fifth Amendment privilege against compulsory self-incrimination ... protects 'a private inner sanctum of individual feeling and thought and proscribes state intrusion to extract self-condemnation' ").

We need not explore the outer boundaries of what is "testimonial" today, for our decision flows from the concept's core meaning. Because the privilege was designed primarily to prevent "a recurrence of the Inquisition and the Star Chamber, even if not in their stark brutality," it is evident that a suspect is "compelled ... to be a witness against himself" at least whenever he must face the modern-day analog of the historic trilemma—either during a criminal trial where a sworn witness faces the identical three choices, or during custodial interrogation where ... the choices are analogous and hence raise similar concerns. Whatever else it may include, therefore, the definition of "testimonial" evidence ... must encompass all responses to questions that, if asked of a sworn suspect during a criminal trial, could place the suspect in the "cruel trilemma." This conclusion is consistent with our recognition in *Doe* that "[t]he vast majority of verbal statements thus will be testimonial" because "[t]here are very few instances in which a verbal statement, either oral or written, will not convey information or assert facts." Whenever a suspect is asked for a response requiring him to communicate an express or implied assertion of fact or belief, the suspect confronts the "trilemma" of truth, falsity, or silence and hence the response (whether based on truth or falsity) contains a testimonial component.

496 U.S. at 594–97, 110 S.Ct. at 2646–48, 110 L.Ed.2d at 547–49.

Turning to the facts of the case, it continued:

When [the officer] asked Muniz if he knew the date of his sixth birthday and Muniz, for whatever reason, could not remember or calculate that date, he was confronted with the trilemma. By hypothesis the inherently coercive environment created by the custodial interrogation precluded the option of remaining silent. Muniz was left with the choice of incriminating himself by admitting that he did not then know the date of his sixth birthday, or answering untruthfully by reporting a date that he did not then believe to be accurate (an incorrect guess would be incriminating as well as untruthful). The content of his truthful answer supported an inference that his mental faculties were impaired, because his assertion (he did not know the date of his sixth birthday) was different from the assertion (he knew the date was (correct date)) that the trier of fact might reasonably have expected a lucid person to provide. Hence, the incriminating inference of impaired mental faculties stemmed, not just from the fact that Muniz slurred his response, but also from a testimonial aspect of that response.

496 U.S. at 599, 110 S.Ct. at 2649, 110 L.Ed.2d at 550. The Court did not reach whether asking Muniz to count out loud while performing the physical sobriety tests involved "testimonial" activity. During one test, he counted accurately and thus his responses were not incriminating. During another, he failed to count and did not argue that his silence had any "independent incriminating significance."

3. **Compulsion Must be "Impermissible."** The Fifth Amendment is violated only if compulsion to engage in testimonial and self-incriminating activity is impermissible. Many states provide under "implied consent" statutes that, under certain circumstances, a person suspected of driving while intoxicated may be "requested" by an officer to provide a blood or breath sample but may not be forced to provide the sample if he refuses. Such a refusal is itself often admissible against

the suspect if he does not provide the requested sample. In South Dakota v. Neville, 459 U.S. 553, 103 S.Ct. 916, 74 L.Ed.2d 748 (1983), the Court held that whether or not such a refusal is "testimonial," the Fifth Amendment does not bar use of such evidence because no "impermissible compulsion" is imposed upon the suspect. *Schmerber*, the Court observed, clearly permits a State under certain circumstances to force a person to submit to a blood test:

> Given * * * that the offer of taking a blood-alcohol test is clearly legitimate, the action becomes no *less* legitimate when the State offers a second option of refusing the test, with the attendant penalties of making that choice.

459 U.S. at 563, 103 S.Ct. at 923, 74 L.Ed.2d at 759 (emphasis in original).

4.   The application of the privilege against compelled self-incrimination to subpoenas requiring the production of documents is considered in Chapter 9. Fifth Amendment self-incrimination principles are examined more fully in the setting of police interrogation in Chapter 7.

5.   **Requirement That Compelled Activity be "Incriminating."** The Fifth Amendment bars law enforcement officers compelling a person to engage in testimonial activity only when that activity is "incriminating." In Minnesota v. Murphy, 465 U.S. 420, 104 S.Ct. 1136, 79 L.Ed.2d 409 (1984), the Supreme Court, in dicta, indicated revocation of probation is not "incrimination" within the meaning of the privilege. Thus, probationers can apparently be compelled, without violation of the privilege, to answer questions that might result in revocation of probation but that pose "no realistic threat of incrimination in a separate criminal proceeding."

6.   **Fourth Amendment Warrant Requirement.** *Schmerber's* Fourth Amendment analysis reflects the Court's controversial conclusion that the Fourth Amendment reasonableness requirement demands—as a general rule subject to exceptions—a search be conducted pursuant to a search warrant. The literal terms of the provision impose no such requirement, and in fact have little to offer concerning when a search warrant is necessary. Would the spirit and purpose of the Fourth Amendment be better served if the Court did not focus upon a need to fit a warrantless search into one of the exceptions to a general rule that a warrant is necessary? The Court might instead scrutinize each search for reasonableness under a more flexible standard.

7.   **Fourth Amendment Probable Cause Requirement.** *Schmerber* appeared to recognize a general Fourth Amendment requirement that a search be based upon "probable cause" to believe that the search would result in discovery of something the officers had a right to seize. The meaning of probable cause is developed in part A(1) of Chapter 3, addressing the showing that must be made for issuance of a search warrant. Generally, however, probable cause means "a fair probability" that seizable material or items will be found in the location at issue. Thus as applied to the *Schmerber* situation, facts establishing probable cause would mean facts establishing a fair probability that seizable material—evidence that Schmerber was guilty of driving while intoxication—would be found if the search were conducted.

Is it clear that *Schmerber* required probable cause for the search at issue in the case—the insertion of a needle into the suspect's arm to seek blood believed to contain alcohol?

8.   **Due Process Prohibition Against Conduct Shocking the Conscience.** *Schmerber* discussed the due process claim based on *Rochin* as an independent potential basis for excluding the evidence obtained from a blood withdrawal. Is the due process prohibition against law enforcement conduct that "shocks the conscience" still a viable independent basis for challenging the admissi-

bility of evidence? County of Sacramento v. Lewis, 523 U.S. 833, 118 S.Ct. 1708, 140 L.Ed.2d 1043 (1998), indicated yes and suggested the requirements for such an attack. In *Lewis*, the Court addressed the civil liability of officers' employing governmental entity for damages based on the Lewis's death, caused by a vehicle collision resulting from a high speed police chase. The plaintiff argued the officers' actions violated suspect Lewis's right to substantive due process. Discussing *Rochin*, the Court commented that the case "today would be treated under the Fourth Amendment, albeit with the same result." This is apparently because the officers' actions in *Rochin* would now constitute unreasonable searches and seizures and the resultant evidence would be inadmissible under *Mapp*.

The law enforcement action in *Lewis*, however, was held at most an *attempted* seizure, and thus not within the Fourth Amendment's prohibition against unreasonable seizures. Nevertheless, *Lewis* indicated a high speed chase could constitute an actionable violation of substantive due process under *Rochin* if the officers acted with "intent to harm [the] suspects physically or to worsen their legal plight * * *." In *Rochin*, it added, "it was not the ultimate purpose of the [officers] to harm the plaintiff, but they apparently acted with full appreciation of what the Court described as the brutality of their acts." This appreciation of the brutality of the conduct apparently sufficed to trigger substantive due process in *Rochin*.

B.   The Fourth Amendment's Prohibition Against Unreasonable Searches and Seizures

Perhaps in part because of the limited applicability of the Fifth Amendment, the Fourth Amendment's prohibition against unreasonable searches and seizures has become the major federal constitutional vehicle for regulating police conduct in gathering evidence. Several threshold issues presented by efforts to invoke this prohibition are considered in this portion of the materials. The first two subsections consider when law enforcement conduct constitutes a "search" or a "seizure" so as to invoke the Fourth Amendment. The third subsection then addresses the effect of the requirement of standing and a narrow conception of what constitutes a search. But first the Introduction discusses the limitation of the Fourth Amendment to official conduct.

EDITORS' INTRODUCTION: PRIVATE PARTY SEARCHES AND SEIZURES

The Fourth Amendment's application is limited by the Supreme Court's position that it constrains only governmental action and does not apply to the conduct of a person acting purely in a private capacity. The leading case on private party searches is Burdeau v. McDowell, 256 U.S. 465, 41 S.Ct. 574, 65 L.Ed. 1048 (1921). The petitioner moved for return of private papers wrongfully taken from his office by private persons and turned over to the government. The Court disposed of his Fourth Amendment claim with the following comments:

> The Fourth Amendment gives protection against unlawful searches and seizures, and * * * its protection applies to governmental action. Its origin and history clearly show that it was intended as a restraint upon the activities of sovereign authority, and was not intended to be a limitation upon other than governmental agencies * * *.

In the present case the record clearly shows that no official of the federal government had anything to do with the wrongful seizure of the petitioner's property, or any knowledge thereof until several months after the property had been taken from him and was in the possession of the Cities Service Company. It is manifest that there was no invasion of the security afforded by the Fourth Amendment against unreasonable searches and seizure, as whatever wrong was done was the act of individuals in taking the property of another. A portion of the property so taken and held was turned over to the prosecuting officers of the federal government. We assume that petitioner has an unquestionable right of redress against those who illegally and wrongfully took his private property under the circumstances here disclosed, but with such remedies we are not now concerned.

256 U.S. at 475, 41 S.Ct. at 576, 65 L.Ed. at 1051.

The Court continued to apply this approach, although leaving open the possibility that involvement of governmental officers in stimulating or conducting a search by a private person might render that search within the scope of the Fourth Amendment. See United States v. Jacobsen, 466 U.S. 109, 113, 104 S.Ct. 1652, 1656, 80 L.Ed.2d 85, 94 (1984); Walter v. United States, 447 U.S. 649, 100 S.Ct. 2395, 65 L.Ed.2d 410 (1980). In Coolidge v. New Hampshire, 403 U.S. 443, 91 S.Ct. 2022, 29 L.Ed.2d 564 (1971), for example, the murder suspect's wife was interviewed at the couple's home while he was in custody. In response to officers' inquiries concerning guns owned by her husband and the clothing he wore the day of the crime, she—apparently on her own initiative—obtained guns and clothing and offered them to the officers. Rejecting Coolidge's argument that this was a search despite Burdeau v. McDowell, the Court explained:

> The question presented here is whether the conduct of the police officers at the Coolidge house was such as to make her actions their actions for purposes of the Fourth and Fourteenth Amendment and their attendant exclusionary rules. The test * * * is whether Mrs. Coolidge, in light of all the circumstances of the case, must be regarded as having acted as an "instrument" or agent of the state when she produced her husband's belongings. * * * Mrs. Coolidge described her own motive as that of clearing her husband, and that she believed that she had nothing to hide. * * * The two officers who questioned her behaved, as her own testimony shows, with perfect courtesy. There is not the slightest implication of an attempt of their part to coerce or dominate her, or, for that matter, to direct her actions by the more subtle techniques of suggestion that are available to officials in circumstances like these.

403 U.S. at 487–89, 91 S.Ct. at 2048–50, 29 L.Ed.2d at 595–96.

1. POLICE ACTIVITY CONSTITUTING A "SEARCH"

EDITORS' INTRODUCTION: THE *KATZ* CRITERION FOR IDENTIFYING SEARCHES AND THE REASONABLENESS OF SEARCHES

Whether law enforcement conduct constitutes a search for purposes of the Fourth Amendment is often determined by application of a standard derived from Katz v. United States, 389 U.S. 347, 88 S.Ct. 507, 19 L.Ed.2d 576 (1967). Whether conduct constituting a search is reasonable is generally determined by whether it is based on probable cause and is either supported by a warrant or within an exception to the general requirement of a warrant.

Katz and the Reasonable Expectation of Privacy Test

Prior to *Katz*, Fourth Amendment case law defining searches focused to some extent upon whether police had intruded in some physical sense into a protected area. In Silverman v. United States, 365 U.S. 505, 81 S.Ct. 679, 5 L.Ed.2d 734 (1961), for example, the Court held that officers engaged in a search when they used a "spike mike" to overhear conversations in an adjacent row house. The discussion suggested that this result was based on the showing officers inserted the microphone into a wall of the suspects house until it touched a heating duct. Thus the police conducted "an unauthorized physical penetration into the premises."

In *Katz*, federal officers attached an electronic listening and recording device to the outside of a public telephone booth that they anticipated Katz would use. Katz did use the booth, and the officers were able to overhear his end of the conversation. Finding the officers engaged in a "search," the Court stressed this conclusion did not turn upon whether the phone booth was a protected area. Instead it explained:

> What a person knowingly exposes to the public, even in his own home or office, is not a subject of Fourth Amendment protection. * * * But what he seeks to preserve as private, even in an area accessible to the public, may be constitutionally protected.

389 U.S. at 351, 88 S.Ct. at 511, 19 L.Ed.2d at 582. Later cases, however, often cite and use language from a concurring opinion by Justice Harlan:

> My understanding of the rule [determining the protection provided by the Fourth Amendment] is that there is a twofold requirement, first that a person have exhibited an actual (subjective) expectation of privacy and, second, that the expectation be one that society is prepared to recognize as "reasonable."

389 U.S. at 361, 88 S.Ct. at 516, 19 L.Ed.2d at 587–88 (Harlan, J., concurring). Thus a search was conducted in *Katz* because when Katz used the telephone booth, he subjectively believed his conversation would be private between him and the other party and that belief was objectively reasonable.

"Plain View" Observations

The definition of law enforcement activity constituting a search is closely related to one use of the term, "plain view." As the Supreme Court noted in Horton v. California, 496 U.S. 128, 133 n. 4, 110 S.Ct. 2301, 2306 n. 4, 110 L.Ed.2d 112, 121 n. 4 (1990), the term sometimes describes a situation in which an officer has merely observed an item "left in plain view." In these situations, characterization of the facts as presenting plain view—what might be best termed a "plain view observation"—means the observation was not a search. This is because the location of the item in

plain view means the owner had no reasonable expectation of privacy in
information obtainable by looking at the item. As *Horton* (reprinted later in
this chapter) makes clear, this use of the term plain view must be
distinguished from its use in describing or justifying a *seizure* of an item.
This use generally reflects a conclusion that an officer's action, although
constituting a seizure, was nevertheless reasonable under the Fourth
Amendment requirements applicable to seizures of items.

[handwritten margin note: plain view = no expectation of privacy]

In the principal cases reprinted in the following two sections of this
chapter, for example, the question is whether the officers engaged in
unreasonable searches by either going on the land or observing a structure
from an aircraft. Suppose Fourth Amendment law established the officers
in the first case engaged in no searches by entering upon the land of the
defendants. In that case, the officers' observations of the marijuana were
plain view observations; neither getting to the place where the observations
were made nor making the observation involved an intrusion upon a
reasonable expectation of privacy harbored by the defendants. Had the
officers also seized the marijuana, the case would present a much different
question—the reasonableness of what was clearly a seizure. This seizure
would probably have been defended by the prosecution as a reasonable—
although warrantless—plain view seizure.

If, because of darkness, an officer cannot see what is in a parked car
but shines his flashlight into the car and observes incriminating items, has
the officer "searched" or has the offer merely exercised the right to engage
in plain view observations? A plurality of the Court, with no disagreement
from other justices, indicated that "the use of artificial means to illuminate
a darkened area," like the use of "a marine glass or a field glass," does not
constitute a search. Texas v. Brown, 460 U.S. 730, 740, 103 S.Ct. 1535,
1542, 75 L.Ed.2d 502, 512 (1983) (opinion of Rehnquist, J., announcing the
judgment of the Court).

Law Enforcement Conduct Revealing Only Criminal Information

Law enforcement conduct may escape characterization as a search if it
can reveal only information which, because of its criminal nature, permits
no reasonable expectation of privacy.

In United States v. Jacobsen, 466 U.S. 109, 104 S.Ct. 1652, 80 L.Ed.2d
85 (1984), federal officers took small amounts of a suspicious substance
found in plastic bags and subjected them to field tests to determine
whether the substance was cocaine. This action was held not to involve a
search, on the assumption that the tests could reveal nothing other than
whether or not the substance was cocaine. Congress criminalized even
private possession of cocaine; "thus governmental conduct that can reveal
whether a substance is cocaine and no other arguably 'private' fact,
compromises no legitimate privacy interest."

Searches Permissible on Less Than Probable Cause

Generally, law enforcement activity constituting a search is reasonable
under the Fourth Amendment only if: (a) it is conducted pursuant to a
search warrant; and (b) it is supported by probable cause to believe it will
result in obtaining information that a crime has been committed or the

identity of a person who has committed a crime. A number of exceptions to the requirement of a warrant have also been developed; these exceptions are addressed in Chapter 5. As Chapter 5 also demonstrates, the Supreme Court has sometimes been willing to hold law enforcement activity constituting a seizure reasonable on less than such probable cause. The Court has been reluctant, however, to characterize searches—at least of items rather than persons—as permissible on such a relaxed standard.

This reluctance was reflected in Arizona v. Hicks, 480 U.S. 321, 107 S.Ct. 1149, 94 L.Ed.2d 347 (1987). An officer, properly present in an apartment to look for someone who had shot through the floor into the apartment below, moved some suspicious stereo equipment slightly to permit him to see serial numbers on the items. This movement of the equipment was a search, because it enabled the officer to obtain information—the serial numbers—otherwise unavailable to them. Justice O'Connor, joined in dissent by the Chief Justice and Justice Powell, characterized the action as not a "full-blown search" but rather a "cursory inspection of an item in view." Since the action intruded upon privacy interests less than a full-blown search, it should be reasonable on less than is required for such a full-blown search. Specifically, Justice O'Connor argued that it should require not probable cause but only "reasonable suspicion." Reasonable suspicion is used in several contexts as the standard for determining the Fourth Amendment reasonableness of relatively-nonintrusive law enforcement activity; its content—as applied to certain nonarrest detentions of suspects—is addressed in Part C(1) of Chapter 4. Reasonable suspicion requires some objective basis for a belief that "seizable" items or information will be found by a search, but it clearly does not demand as firm a basis for this belief as is required for probable cause. Justice O'Connor explained specifically:

> [T]he balance of the governmental and privacy interests strongly supports a reasonable suspicion standard for the cursory examination of items in plain view. The additional intrusion caused by an inspection of an item in plain view for its serial number is minuscule. * * *
>
> Weighed against this * * * are rather major gains in law enforcement. The use of identification numbers in tracing stolen property is a powerful law enforcement tool. Serial numbers are far more helpful and accurate in detecting stolen property than simple police recollection of the evidence. Given the prevalence of mass produced goods in our national economy, a serial number is often the only sure method of detecting stolen property.

480 U.S. at 338–39, 107 S.Ct. at 1159–60 94 L.Ed.2d at 355 (O'Connor, J., dissenting). Justice Scalia's opinion for the Court, however, rejected this approach:

> [A] truly cursory inspection—one that involves merely looking at what is already exposed to view, without disturbing it—is not a "search" for Fourth Amendment purposes, and therefore does not even require reasonable suspicion. We are unwilling to send police and judges into a new thicket of Fourth Amendment law, to seek a creature of uncertain description that is neither a plain-view inspection nor yet a "full-blown search."

480 U.S. at 328–29, 107 S.Ct. at 1154, 94 L.Ed.2d at 356.

Electronic Surveillance as a Search

Katz itself established that mechanical interception of spoken words is sometimes a "search," and thus gave rise to the law dealing with wiretapping and electronic surveillance considered in Chapter 6. But in Smith v. Maryland, 442 U.S. 735, 99 S.Ct. 2577, 61 L.Ed.2d 220 (1979), the Court considered the use of a pen register. Installed at the telephone company's main office, this device records the numbers dialed from a given telephone but does not permit the overhearing of conversations. Under *Katz,* this recording of dialed numbers was not a search, the Court concluded, because telephone users cannot reasonably entertain an expectation of privacy in numbers dialed from telephones:

> All telephone users realize that they must "convey" phone numbers to the telephone company, since it is through telephone company switching equipment that their calls are completed. All subscribers realize, moreover, that the phone company has facilities for making permanent records of the numbers they dial, for they see a list of their long-distance (toll) calls on their monthly bills. * * * Although most people may be oblivious to a pen register's esoteric functions, they presumably have some awareness of one common use: to aid in the identification of persons making annoying or obscene calls.

442 U.S. at 742, 99 S.Ct. at 2581, 61 L.Ed.2d at 228.

Dog Sniffing as a Search

In United States v. Place, 462 U.S. 696, 103 S.Ct. 2637, 77 L.Ed.2d 110 (1983), the Court held that exposure of luggage, located in a public place, to "sniffing" by a drug detecting dog did not amount to a "search." The Court explained:

> A "canine sniff" by a well-trained dog * * * does not require opening the luggage. It does not expose noncontraband items that otherwise would remain hidden from public view, as does, for example, an officer's rummaging through the contents of the luggage. Thus, the manner in which information is obtained through this investigative technique is much less intrusive than a typical search. Moreover, the sniff discloses only the presence or absence of narcotics, a contraband item. Thus, despite the fact that the sniff tells the authorities something about the contents of the luggage, the information obtained is limited. This limited disclosure also ensures that the owner of the property is not subjected to the embarrassment and inconvenience entailed in less discriminate and more intrusive investigative methods.

462 U.S. at 707, 103 S.Ct. at 2644, 77 L.Ed.2d at 121.

Examination of Trash as a Search

Whether law enforcement examination of a suspect's trash constitutes a search was considered in California v. Greenwood, 486 U.S. 35, 108 S.Ct. 1625, 100 L.Ed.2d 30 (1988). Suspicious Greenwood might be involved in drug trafficking, a police officer asked the trash collector to pick up the plastic garbage bags from Greenwood's curb and turn them over to the officer rather than mixing them with other trash. Before going past Greenwood's curb, the garbage collector removed all previously-collected trash from his truck. He then collected the bags from Greenwood's curb and gave them to the officer, who found items indicating that Greenwood used narcotics. Police used this information was used to procure a search warrant for Greenwood's residence. Drugs were found during execution of that warrant. Greenwood and Dyanne Van Houten were arrested at the premises. After their release on bail, officers again inspected their trash and a search pursuant to another warrant disclosed additional drugs. The state courts held the officers' examinations of the trash constituted unreasonable searches under the Fourth Amendment. Reversing, a majority of the Supreme Court found no Fourth Amendment search in the officers' conduct:

> [Respondents] assert * * * that they had, and exhibited, an expectation of privacy with respect to the trash that was searched by the police: The trash, which was placed on the street for collection at a fixed time, was contained in opaque plastic bags, which the garbage collector was expected to pick up, mingle with the trash of others, and deposit at the garbage dump. The trash was only temporarily on the street, and there was little likelihood that it would be inspected by anyone.
>
> It may well be that respondents did not expect that the contents of their garbage bags would become known to the police or any other members of the public. An expectation of privacy does not give rise to Fourth Amendment protection, however, unless society is prepared to accept that expectation as objectively reasonable.
>
> Here, we conclude that respondents exposed their garbage to the public sufficiently to defeat their claim to Fourth Amendment protection. It is common knowledge that plastic garbage bags left on or at the side of a public street are readily accessible to animals, children, scavengers, snoops, and other members of the public. Moreover, respondents placed their refuse at the curb for the express purpose of conveying it to a third party, the trash collector, who might himself have sorted through respondents' trash or permitted others, such as the police, to do so. Accordingly, having deposited their garbage "in an area particularly suited for public inspection, and, in a manner of speaking, public consumption, for the express purpose of having strangers take it," United States v. Reicherter, 647 F.2d 397, 399 (3d Cir.1981), respondents could have had no reasonable expectation of privacy in the inculpatory items that they discarded.

486 U.S. at 39–41, 108 S.Ct. at 1628–29, 100 L.Ed.2d at 36–37.

Justice Brennan, joined by Justice Marshall, dissented. He argued that a trash bag, like other containers, is a repository of personal effects and therefore associated with privacy expectations. Given the nature of trash and what it reveals about "sexual practices, health, and personal hygiene," a sealed trash bag often harbors evidence of private activities closely associated with the sanctity of the home and the privacies of life protected by the Fourth Amendment. He continued:

Had Greenwood flaunted his intimate activity by strewing his trash all over the curb for all to see, or had some nongovernmental intruder invaded his privacy and done the same, I could accept the Court's conclusion that an expectation of privacy would have been unreasonable. Similarly, had police searching the city dump run across incriminating evidence that, despite commingling with the trash of others, still retained its identity as Greenwood's, we would have a different case. * * *

The mere *possibility* that unwelcome meddlers *might* open and rummage through the containers does not negate the expectation of privacy in its contents any more than the possibility of a burglary negates an expectation of privacy in the home * * *.

Nor is it dispositive that "respondents placed their refuse at the curb * * *." In the first place, Greenwood can hardly be faulted for leaving trash on his curb when a county ordinance commanded him to do so * * *. More importantly, even the voluntary relinquishment of possession or control over an effect does not necessarily amount to a relinquishment of a privacy expectation in it. Were it otherwise, a letter or package would lose all Fourth Amendment protection when placed in a mail box * * *.

486 U.S. at 53–55, 108 S.Ct. at 1636–37, 100 L.Ed.2d at 45–46 (Brennan, J., dissenting).

* * *

The two following subsections consider application of the *Katz* standard to two particularly important areas: physical entry of private property and aerial and other surveillance. In each of the principal cases, the police failed to obtain a warrant; if their activity is a search, that search will almost certainly be unreasonable and the evidence unavailable to the prosecution. But on a more general level, characterizing such activity as a search does not mean the Fourth Amendment prohibits police from engaging in the conduct. Rather, the conduct becomes subject to the requirements of Fourth Amendment reasonableness. The Fourth Amendment should be construed as applicable to law enforcement conduct sufficiently intruding upon privacy concerns to justify its *regulation*—not its *prohibition*—by application of the Fourth Amendment's requirement of reasonableness. Does the Court properly follow this approach in the two principal cases?

a.   ENTRY ONTO "OPEN FIELDS"

When officers physically go on real property, do they engage in a search? To what extent does the answer to this question depend upon the efforts the person in possession or control of the property has taken to preserve from others what is or occurs on the property?

Oliver v. United States

Supreme Court of the United States, 1984.
466 U.S. 170, 104 S.Ct. 1735, 80 L.Ed.2d 214.

■ JUSTICE POWELL delivered the opinion of the Court.

The "open fields" doctrine, first enunciated by this Court in Hester v. United States, 265 U.S. 57, 44 S.Ct. 445, 68 L.Ed. 898 (1924), permits *open field* → *doctrine*

↳ *casual*
Intrusion

police officers to enter and search a field without a warrant. We granted certiorari in these cases to clarify confusion that has arisen as to the continued vitality of the doctrine.

I

No. 82–15. Acting on reports that marijuana was being raised on the farm of petitioner Oliver, two narcotics agents of the Kentucky State Police went to the farm to investigate.[3] Arriving at the farm, they drove past petitioner's house to a locked gate with a "No Trespassing" sign. A footpath led around one side of the gate. The agents walked around the gate and along the road for several hundred yards, passing a barn and a parked camper. At that point, someone standing in front of the camper shouted, "No hunting is allowed, come back here." The officers shouted back that they were Kentucky State Police officers, but found no one when they returned to the camper. The officers resumed their investigation of the farm and found a field of marijuana over a mile from petitioner's home.

Petitioner was arrested and indicted for "manufactur[ing]" a "controlled substance." After a pretrial hearing, the District Court suppressed evidence of the discovery of the marijuana fields. Applying Katz v. United States, 389 U.S. 347, 357, 88 S.Ct. 507, 514, 19 L.Ed.2d 576 (1967), the court found that petitioner had a reasonable expectation that the fields would remain private because petitioner "had done all that could be expected of him to assert his privacy in the area of farm that was searched." He had posted no trespassing signs at regular intervals and had locked the gate at the entrance to the center of the farm. Further, the court noted that the fields themselves are highly secluded: they are bounded on all sides by woods, fences and embankments and cannot be seen from any point of public access. The court concluded that this was not an "open" field that invited casual intrusion.

The Court of Appeals for the Sixth Circuit, sitting *en banc,* reversed the district court. The court concluded that *Katz,* upon which the District Court relied, had not impaired the vitality of the open fields doctrine of *Hester.* Rather, the open fields doctrine was entirely compatible with *Katz's* emphasis on privacy. The court reasoned that the "human relations that create the need for privacy do not ordinarily take place" in open fields, and that the property owner's common law right to exclude trespassers is insufficiently linked to privacy to warrant the Fourth Amendment's protection. We granted certiorari.

No. 82–1273. After receiving an anonymous tip that marijuana was being grown in the woods behind respondent Thornton's residence, two police officers entered the woods by a path between this residence and a neighboring house. They followed a footpath through the woods until they reached two marijuana patches fenced with chicken wire. Later, the officers determined that the patches were on the property of respondent, obtained a

---

3. It is conceded that the police did not have a warrant authorizing the search, that there was no probable cause for the search and that no exception to the warrant requirement is applicable.

warrant to search the property and seized the marijuana. On the basis of this evidence, respondent was arrested and indicted.

The trial court granted respondent's motion to suppress the fruits of the second search. The warrant for this search was premised on information that the police had obtained during their previous warrantless search, that the court found to be unreasonable. "No Trespassing" signs and the secluded location of the marijuana patches evinced a reasonable expectation of privacy. Therefore, the court held, the "open fields" doctrine did not apply.

The Maine Supreme Judicial Court affirmed. It agreed with the trial court that the correct question was whether the search "is a violation of privacy on which the individual justifiably relied," and that the search violated respondent's privacy. The court also agreed that the "open fields" doctrine did not justify the search. That doctrine applies, according to the court, only when officers are lawfully present on property and observe "open and patent" activity. In this case, the officers had trespassed upon defendant's property, and the respondent had made every effort to conceal his activity. We granted certiorari.

II

The rule announced in Hester v. United States was founded upon the explicit language of the Fourth Amendment. That Amendment indicates with some precision the places and things encompassed by its protections. As Justice Holmes explained for the Court in his characteristically laconic style: "[T]he special protection accorded by the Fourth Amendment to the people in their 'persons, houses, papers, and effects,' is not extended to the open fields. The distinction between the latter and the house is as old as the common law." Hester v. United States, 265 U.S., at 59, 44 S.Ct., at 446.

Nor are the open fields "effects" within the meaning of the Fourth Amendment. In this respect, it is suggestive that James Madison's proposed draft of what became the Fourth Amendment preserves "[t]he rights of the people to be secured in their persons, their houses, their papers, and their other property, from all unreasonable searches and seizures...." Although Congress' revisions of Madison's proposal broadened the scope of the Amendment in some respects, the term "effects" is less inclusive than "property" and cannot be said to encompass open fields.[4] We conclude, as did the Court in deciding Hester v. United States, that the government's intrusion upon the open fields is not one of those "unreasonable searches" proscribed by the text of the Fourth Amendment.

III

This interpretation of the Fourth Amendment's language is consistent with the understanding of the right to privacy expressed in our Fourth Amendment jurisprudence. Since Katz v. United States, 389 U.S. 347, 88 S.Ct. 507, 19 L.Ed.2d 576 (1967), the touchstone of Amendment analysis

---

4. The Framers would have understood the term "effects" to be limited to personal, rather than real, property. See generally, Doe v. Dring, 2 M. & S. 448, 454 (1814) (discussing prior cases); 2 Blackstone, Commentaries 16, 384–385.

has been the question whether a person has a "constitutionally protected reasonable expectation of privacy." 389 U.S., at 360, 88 S.Ct., at 516 (Harlan, J., concurring). The Amendment does not protect the merely subjective expectation of privacy, but only "those expectations that society is prepared to recognize as 'reasonable.' "

A

No single factor determines whether an individual legitimately may claim under the Fourth Amendment that a place should be free of government intrusion not authorized by warrant. In assessing the degree to which a search infringes upon individual privacy, the Court has given weight to such factors as the intention of the Framers of the Fourth Amendment, the uses to which the individual has put a location, and our societal understanding that certain areas deserve the most scrupulous protection from government invasion. These factors are equally relevant to determining whether the government's intrusion upon open fields without a warrant or probable cause violates reasonable expectations of privacy and is therefore a search proscribed by the Amendment.

In this light, the rule of Hester v. United States, supra, that we reaffirm today, may be understood as providing that an individual may not legitimately demand privacy for activities conducted out of doors in fields, except in the area immediately surrounding the home. This rule is true to the conception of the right to privacy embodied in the Fourth Amendment. The Amendment reflects the recognition of the Founders that certain enclaves should be free from arbitrary government interference. For example, the Court since the enactment of the Fourth Amendment has stressed "the overriding respect for the sanctity of the home that has been embedded in our traditions since the origins of the Republic."

In contrast, open fields do not provide the setting for those intimate activities that the Amendment is intended to shelter from government interference or surveillance. There is no societal interest in protecting the privacy of those activities, such as the cultivation of crops, that occur in open fields. Moreover, as a practical matter these lands usually are accessible to the public and the police in ways that a home, an office or commercial structure would not be. It is not generally true that fences or no trespassing signs effectively bar the public from viewing open fields in rural areas. And both petitioner Oliver and respondent Thornton concede that the public and police lawfully may survey lands from the air.[5] For these reasons, the asserted expectation of privacy in open fields is not an expectation that "society recognizes as reasonable."[6]

5. In practical terms, petitioner Oliver's and respondent Thornton's analysis merely would require law enforcement officers, in most situations, to use aerial surveillance to gather the information necessary to obtain a warrant or to justify warrantless entry onto the property. It is not easy to see how such a requirement would advance legitimate privacy interests.

6. The dissent conceives of open fields as bustling with private activity as diverse as lovers' trysts and worship services. But in most instances police will disturb no one when they enter upon open fields. These fields, by their very character as open and unoccupied, are unlikely to provide the setting for activities whose privacy is sought to be protected by the Fourth Amendment. One

The historical underpinnings of the "open fields" doctrine also demonstrate that the doctrine is consistent with respect for "reasonable expectations of privacy." As Justice Holmes, writing for the Court, observed in *Hester,* the common law distinguished "open fields" from the "curtilage," the land immediately surrounding and associated with the home. The distinction implies that only the curtilage, not the neighboring open fields, warrants the Fourth Amendment protections that attach to the home. At common law, the curtilage is the area to which extends the intimate activity associated with the "sanctity of a man's home and the privacies of life," and therefore has been considered part of home itself for Fourth Amendment purposes. Thus, courts have extended Fourth Amendment protection to the curtilage; and they have defined the curtilage, as did the common law, by reference to the factors that determine whether an individual reasonably may expect that an area immediately adjacent to the home will remain private. Conversely, the common law implies, as we reaffirm today, that no expectation of privacy legitimately attaches to open fields.[7]

We conclude, from the text of the Fourth Amendment and from the historical and contemporary understanding of its purposes, that an individual has no legitimate expectation that open fields will remain free from warrantless intrusion by government officers.

Finding

B

Petitioner Oliver and respondent Thornton contend, to the contrary, that the circumstances of a search sometimes may indicate that reasonable expectations of privacy were violated; and that courts therefore should analyze these circumstances on a case-by-case basis. The language of the Fourth Amendment itself answers their contention.

Nor would a case-by-case approach provide a workable accommodation between the needs of law enforcement and the interests protected by the Fourth Amendment. Under this approach, police officers would have to guess before every search whether landowners had erected fences sufficiently high, posted a sufficient number of warning signs, or located contraband in an area sufficiently secluded to establish a right of privacy. The lawfulness of a search would turn on "[a] highly sophisticated set of

need think only of the vast expanse of some western ranches or of the undeveloped woods of the Northwest to see the unreality of the dissent's conception. Further, the Fourth Amendment provides ample protection to activities in the open fields that might implicate an individual's privacy. An individual who enters a place defined to be "public" for Fourth Amendment analysis does not lose all claims to privacy or personal security. For example, the Fourth Amendment's protections against unreasonable arrest or unreasonable seizure of effects upon the person remain fully applicable.

7. Neither petitioner Oliver nor respondent Thornton has contended that the prop-

erty searched was within the curtilage. Nor is it necessary in this case to consider the scope of the curtilage exception to the open fields doctrine or the degree of Fourth Amendment protection afforded the curtilage, as opposed to the home itself. It is clear, however, that the term "open fields" may include any unoccupied or undeveloped area outside of the curtilage. An open field need be neither "open" nor a "field" as those terms are used in common speech. For example, contrary to respondent Thornton's suggestion, a thickly wooded area nonetheless may be an open field as that term is used in construing the Fourth Amendment.

rules, qualified by all sorts of ifs, ands, and buts and requiring the drawing of subtle nuances and hairline distinctions...." New York v. Belton, 453 U.S. 454, 458, 101 S.Ct. 2860, 2863, 69 L.Ed.2d 768 (1981) (quoting LaFave, "Case–By–Case Adjudication" versus "Standardized Procedures": The Robinson Dilemma, 1974 S.Ct.Rev. 127, 142). This Court repeatedly has acknowledged the difficulties created for courts, police and citizens by an *ad hoc,* case-by-case definition of Fourth Amendment standards to be applied in differing factual circumstances. The *ad hoc* approach not only makes it difficult for the policeman to discern the scope of his authority; it also creates a danger that constitutional rights will be arbitrarily and inequitably enforced.[8]

IV

In any event, while the factors that petitioner Oliver and respondent Thornton urge the courts to consider may be relevant to Fourth Amendment analysis in some contexts, these factors cannot be decisive on the question whether the search of an open field is subject to the Amendment. Initially, we reject the suggestion that steps taken to protect privacy establish that expectations of privacy in an open field are legitimate. It is true, of course, that petitioner Oliver and respondent Thornton, in order to conceal their criminal activities, planted the marijuana upon secluded land and erected fences and no trespassing signs around the property. And it may be that because of such precautions, few members of the public stumbled upon the marijuana crops seized by the police. Neither of these suppositions demonstrates, however, that the expectation of privacy was *legitimate* in the sense required by the Fourth Amendment. The test of legitimacy is not whether the individual chooses to conceal assertedly "private" activity. Rather, the correct inquiry is whether the government's intrusion infringes upon the personal and societal values protected by the Fourth Amendment. As we have explained, we find no basis for concluding that a police inspection of open fields accomplishes such an infringement.

Nor is the government's intrusion upon an open field a "search" in the constitutional sense because that intrusion is a trespass at common law. The existence of a property right is but one element in determining whether expectations of privacy are legitimate. * * *

The common law may guide consideration of what areas are protected by the Fourth Amendment by defining areas whose invasion by others is wrongful. The law of trespass, however, forbids intrusions upon land that the Fourth Amendment would not proscribe. For trespass law extends to instances where the exercise of the right to exclude vindicates no legitimate

8. The clarity of the open fields doctrine that we reaffirm today is not sacrificed, as the dissent suggests, by our recognition that the curtilage remains within the protections of the Fourth Amendment. Most of the many millions of acres that are "open fields" are not close to any structure and so not arguably within the curtilage. And, for most homes, the boundaries of the curtilage will be clearly marked; and the conception defining the curtilage—as the area around the home to which the activity of home life extends—is a familiar one easily understood from our daily experience. The occasional difficulties that courts might have in applying this, like other, legal concepts, do not argue for the unprecedented expansion of the Fourth Amendment advocated by the dissent.

privacy interest.[9] Thus, in the case of open fields, the general rights of property protected by the common law of trespass have little or no relevance to the applicability of the Fourth Amendment.

V

We conclude that the open fields doctrine, as enunciated in *Hester,* is consistent with the plain language of the Fourth Amendment and its historical purposes. Moreover, Justice Holmes' interpretation of the Amendment in *Hester* accords with the "reasonable expectation of privacy" analysis developed in subsequent decisions of this Court. We therefore affirm Oliver v. United States; Maine v. Thornton is reversed and remanded for further proceedings not inconsistent with this opinion.

It is so ordered.

■ JUSTICE WHITE, concurring in part and in the judgment.

I concur in the judgment and join Parts I and II of the Court's opinion. These parts dispose of the issue before us; there is no need to go further and deal with the expectation of privacy matter. However reasonable a landowner's expectations of privacy may be, those expectations cannot convert a field into a "house" or an "effect."

■ JUSTICE MARSHALL, with whom JUSTICE BRENNAN and JUSTICE STEVENS join, dissenting.

* * *

I

The first ground on which the Court rests its decision is that the Fourth Amendment "indicates with some precision the places and things encompassed by its protections," and that real property is not included in the list of protected spaces and possessions. This line of argument has several flaws. Most obviously, it is inconsistent with the results of many of our previous decisions, none of which the Court purports to overrule. For example, neither a public telephone booth nor a conversation conducted therein can fairly be described as a person, house, paper, or effect, yet we have held that the Fourth Amendment forbids the police without a warrant to eavesdrop on such a conversation. Katz v. United States, 389 U.S. 347, 88 S.Ct. 507, 19 L.Ed.2d 576 (1967). * * *

9. The law of trespass recognizes the interest in possession and control of one's property and for that reason permits exclusion of unwanted intruders. But it does not follow that the right to exclude conferred by trespass law embodies a privacy interest also protected by the Fourth Amendment. To the contrary, the common law of trespass furthers a range of interests that have nothing to do with privacy and that would not be served by applying the strictures of trespass law to public officers. Criminal laws against trespass are prophylactic: they protect against intruders who poach, steal livestock and crops or vandalize property. And the civil action of trespass serves the important function of authorizing an owner to defeat claims of prescription by asserting his own title. In any event, unlicensed use of property by others is presumptively unjustified, as anyone who wishes to use the property is free to bargain for the right to do so with the property owner. For these reasons, the law of trespass confers protections from intrusion by others far broader than those required by Fourth Amendment interests.

II

The second ground for the Court's decision is its contention that any interest a landowner might have in the privacy of his woods and fields is not one that "society is prepared to recognize as 'reasonable.' " The mode of analysis that underlies this assertion is certainly more consistent with our prior decisions than that discussed above. But the Court's conclusion cannot withstand scrutiny.

As the Court acknowledges, we have traditionally looked to a variety of factors in determining whether an expectation of privacy asserted in a physical space is "reasonable." Though those factors do not lend themselves to precise taxonomy, they may be roughly grouped into three categories. First, we consider whether the expectation at issue is rooted in entitlements defined by positive law. Second, we consider the nature of the uses to which spaces of the sort in question can be put. Third, we consider whether the person claiming a privacy interest manifested that interest to the public in a way that most people would understand and respect. When the expectations of privacy asserted by petitioner Oliver and respondent Thornton are examined through these lenses, it becomes clear that those expectations are entitled to constitutional protection.

A

We have frequently acknowledged that privacy interests are not coterminous with property rights. However, because "property rights reflect society's explicit recognition of a person's authority to act as he wishes in certain areas, [they] should be considered in determining whether an individual's expectations of privacy are reasonable." * * *

It is undisputed that Oliver and Thornton each owned the land into which the police intruded. That fact alone provides considerable support for their assertion of legitimate privacy interests in their woods and fields. But even more telling is the nature of the sanctions that Oliver and Thornton could invoke, under local law, for violation of their property rights. In Kentucky, a knowing entry upon fenced or otherwise enclosed land, or upon unenclosed land conspicuously posted with signs excluding the public, constitutes criminal trespass. The law in Maine is similar. * * * Thus, positive law not only recognizes the legitimacy of Oliver's and Thornton's insistence that strangers keep off their land, but subjects those who refuse to respect their wishes to the most severe of penalties—criminal liability. Under these circumstances, it is hard to credit the Court's assertion that Oliver's and Thornton's expectations of privacy were not of a sort that society is prepared to recognize as reasonable.

B

The uses to which a place is put are highly relevant to the assessment of a privacy interest asserted therein. If, in light of our shared sensibilities, those activities are of a kind in which people should be able to engage without fear of intrusion by private persons or government officials, we extend the protection of the Fourth Amendment to the space in question, even in the absence of any entitlement derived from positive law.

Privately-owned woods and fields that are not exposed to public view regularly are employed in a variety of ways that society acknowledges deserve privacy. Many landowners like to take solitary walks on their property, confident that they will not be confronted in their rambles by strangers or policemen. Others conduct agricultural businesses on their property. Some landowners use their secluded spaces to meet lovers, others to gather together with fellow worshippers, still others to engage in sustained creative endeavor. Private land is sometimes used as a refuge for wildlife, where flora and fauna are protected from human intervention of any kind. Our respect for the freedom of landowners to use their posted "open fields" in ways such as these partially explains the seriousness with which the positive law regards deliberate invasions of such spaces, and substantially reinforces the landowners' contention that their expectations of privacy are "reasonable."

C

Whether a person "took normal precautions to maintain his privacy" in a given space affects whether his interest is one protected by the Fourth Amendment. The reason why such precautions are relevant is that we do not insist that a person who has a right to exclude others exercise that right. A claim to privacy is therefore strengthened by the fact that the claimant somehow manifested to other people his desire that they keep their distance.

Certain spaces are so presumptively private that signals of this sort are unnecessary; a homeowner need not post a "do not enter" sign on his door in order to deny entrance to uninvited guests. Privacy interests in other spaces are more ambiguous, and the taking of precautions is consequently more important; placing a lock on one's footlocker strengthens one's claim that an examination of its contents is impermissible. Still other spaces are, by positive law and social convention, presumed accessible to members of the public *unless* the owner manifests his intention to exclude them.

Undeveloped land falls into the last-mentioned category. If a person has not marked the boundaries of his fields or woods in a way that informs passersby that they are not welcome, he cannot object if members of the public enter onto the property. There is no reason why he should have any greater rights as against government officials. Accordingly, we have held that an official may, without a warrant, enter private land from which the public is not excluded and make observations from that vantage point. Fairly read, the case on which the majority so heavily relies, Hester v. United States, 265 U.S. 57, 44 S.Ct. 445, 68 L.Ed. 898 (1924), affirms little more than the foregoing unremarkable proposition. From aught that appears in the opinion in that case, the defendants, fleeing from revenue agents who had observed them committing a crime, abandoned incriminating evidence on private land from which the public had not been excluded. Under such circumstances, it is not surprising that the Court was unpersuaded by the defendants' argument that the entry onto their fields by the agents violated the Fourth Amendment.

A very different case is presented when the owner of undeveloped land has taken precautions to exclude the public. As indicated above, a deliberate entry by a private citizen onto private property marked with "no trespassing" signs will expose him to criminal liability. I see no reason why a government official should not be obliged to respect such unequivocal and universally understood manifestations of a landowner's desire for privacy.

In sum, examination of the three principal criteria we have traditionally used for assessing the reasonableness of a person's expectation that a given space would remain private indicates that interests of the sort asserted by Oliver and Thornton are entitled to constitutional protection. An owner's right to insist that others stay off his posted land is firmly grounded in positive law. Many of the uses to which such land may be put deserve privacy. And, by marking the boundaries of the land with warnings that the public should not intrude, the owner has dispelled any ambiguity as to his desires.

The police in these cases proffered no justification for their invasions of Oliver's and Thornton's privacy interests; in neither case was the entry legitimated by a warrant or by one of the established exceptions to the warrant requirement. I conclude, therefore, that the searches of their land violated the Fourth Amendment, and the evidence obtained in the course of those searches should have been suppressed.

III

A clear, easily administrable rule emerges from the analysis set forth above: Private land marked in a fashion sufficient to render entry thereon a criminal trespass under the law of the state in which the land lies is protected by the Fourth Amendment's proscription of unreasonable searches and seizures. One of the advantages of the foregoing rule is that it draws upon a doctrine already familiar to both citizens and government officials. In each jurisdiction, a substantial body of statutory and case law defines the precautions a landowner must take in order to avail himself of the sanctions of the criminal law. The police know that body of law, because they are entrusted with responsibility for enforcing it against the public; it therefore would not be difficult for the police to abide by it themselves.

By contrast, the doctrine announced by the Court today is incapable of determinate application. Police officers, making warrantless entries upon private land, will be obliged in the future to make on-the-spot judgments as to how far the curtilage extends, and to stay outside that zone. In addition, we may expect to see a spate of litigation over the question of how much improvement is necessary to remove private land from the category of "unoccupied or undeveloped area" to which the "open fields exception" is now deemed applicable.

The Court's holding not only ill serves the need to make constitutional doctrine "workable for application by rank and file, trained police officers," it withdraws the shield of the Fourth Amendment from privacy interests that clearly deserve protection. * * *

I dissent.

NOTE: THE PROTECTED CURTILAGE

The role played by the concept of the "curtilage" in defining the scope of Fourth Amendment coverage was confirmed and the definition of curtilage fleshed out in United States v. Dunn, 480 U.S. 294, 107 S.Ct. 1134, 94 L.Ed.2d 326 (1987). Federal officers, suspecting Dunn of manufacturing controlled substances, went to his Texas ranch on the evening of November 5, 1980. The ranch's 198 acres were completely encircled by a "perimeter fence" and contained a number of internal fenced areas. About a half-mile from a public road, one internal fenced enclosure included the ranch house and a greenhouse. Approximately fifty yards from this fence were two barns. The larger of the two was enclosed by a wooden fence; locked waist-high gates prevented entry into the barn and a netting material was stretched from the ceiling of the barn to the top of the fence gates. The officers crossed over the perimeter fence, climbed a barbed wire fence and the fence surrounding the large barn front and approached the barn. They walked under the overhang and up to the locked gates. By shining a flashlight through the netting, they observed a drug laboratory. At no point did the officers physically enter the barn. Using the information obtained by looking into the barn, they obtained a search warrant and by executing the warrant they seized evidence of Dunn's manufacture of controlled substances. This evidence was held inadmissible by the intermediate federal court on the ground it was the product of a warrantless—and therefore unreasonable—search.

The Supreme Court reversed, concluding that under *Oliver* the officers did not engage in a search. Whether the officers' approach to the barn constituted a search, Justice White explained for the Court, depended upon whether the barn was within the protected curtilage. Turning to the meaning of that term, he continued:

> [W]e believe that curtilage questions should be resolved with particular reference to four factors: the proximity of the area claimed to be curtilage to the home, whether the area is included within an enclosure surrounding the home, the nature of the uses to which the area is put, and the steps taken by the resident to protect the area from observation by people passing by. We do not suggest that combining these factors produces a finely tuned formula that, when mechanically applied, yields a "correct" answer to all extent-of-curtilage questions. Rather, these factors are useful analytical tools only to the degree that, in any given case, they bear upon the centrally relevant consideration— whether the area in question is so intimately tied to the home itself that it should be placed under the home's "umbrella" of Fourth Amendment protection.

Rules to curtilage

480 U.S. at 301, 107 S.Ct. at 1139–40, 94 L.Ed.2d at 334–35.

Applying this approach to the facts of *Dunn* led the Court "with little difficulty" to conclude the barn and the area immediately surrounding it lay outside the protected curtilage. First, the 50 yards separating the barn from the house—a "substantial distance"—rendered it "in isolation." Second, the fence surrounding the ranch house demarked "a specific area of land immediately adjacent to the house that is readily identifiable as part and parcel of the house," and the barn was not within it. Third, the officers had substantial information from surveillance and smells emanating from the barn indicating it was used for the manufacture of drugs. This information indicated "the use to which the barn was being put could not fairly be characterized as so associated with the activities and privacies of domestic life that the officers should have deemed the barn as part of [the] home." Finally, Dunn had done little to protect the barn area from observation by those "standing in the open fields." The fences were designed to corral livestock and did not bar observations.

The majority also rejected Dunn's argument that, regardless of whether the barn was within the curtilage of the ranch house, the officers' actions intruded upon a protected privacy interest related to the barn and his use of it. Assuming the barn protected from entry by the Fourth Amendment, the Court stressed it was situated on an "open field." The officers' progression up to the barn involved only entry onto "open fields" and did not constitute a "search," regardless of whether the objects they observed from this vantage point lay within an area that might be protected by the Fourth Amendment.

b.   AERIAL AND OTHER OBSERVATIONS

When officers make observations by use of some aid such as an aircraft or a transmitter or "beeper," have the officers engaged in a search? The principal case reprinted here involves the use of a helicopter.

Florida v. Riley

Supreme Court of the United States, 1989.
488 U.S. 445, 109 S.Ct. 693, 102 L.Ed.2d 835.

■ JUSTICE WHITE announced the judgment of the Court and delivered an opinion, in which THE CHIEF JUSTICE, JUSTICE SCALIA and JUSTICE KENNEDY join.

On certification to it by a lower state court, the Florida Supreme Court addressed the following question: "Whether surveillance of the interior of a partially covered greenhouse in a residential backyard from the vantage point of a helicopter located 400 feet above the greenhouse constitutes a 'search' for which a warrant is required under the Fourth Amendment and Article I, Section 12 of the Florida Constitution." The court answered the question in the affirmative, and we granted the State's petition for certiorari challenging that conclusion.

Respondent Riley lived in a mobile home located on five acres of rural property. A greenhouse was located 10 to 20 feet behind the mobile home. Two sides of the greenhouse were enclosed. The other two sides were not enclosed but the contents of the greenhouse were obscured from view from surrounding property by trees, shrubs and the mobile home. The greenhouse was covered by corrugated roofing panels, some translucent and some opaque. At the time relevant to this case, two of the panels, amounting to approximately 10% of the roof area, were missing. A wire fence surrounded the mobile home and the greenhouse, and the property was posted with a "DO NOT ENTER" sign.

This case originated with an anonymous tip to the Pasco County Sheriff's office that marijuana was being grown on respondent's property. When an investigating officer discovered that he could not see the contents of the greenhouse from the road, he circled twice over respondent's property in a helicopter at the height of 400 feet. With his naked eye, he was able to see through the openings in the roof and one or more of the open sides of the greenhouse and to identify what he thought was marijuana growing in the structure. A warrant was obtained based on these observations, and the ensuing search revealed marijuana growing in the greenhouse. Respondent was charged with possession of marijuana under

Florida law. The trial court granted his motion to suppress; the Florida Court of Appeals reversed but certified the case to the Florida Supreme Court, which quashed the decision of the Court of Appeals and reinstated the trial court's suppression order.

We agree with the State's submission that our decision in California v. Ciraolo, 476 U.S. 207, 106 S.Ct. 1809, 90 L.Ed.2d 210 (1986), controls this case. There, acting on a tip, the police inspected the back yard of a particular house while flying in a fixed-wing aircraft at 1,000 feet. With the naked eye the officers saw what they concluded was marijuana growing in the yard. A search warrant was obtained on the strength of this airborne inspection, and marijuana plants were found. The trial court refused to suppress this evidence, but a state appellate court held that the inspection violated the Fourth and Fourteenth Amendments of the United States Constitution and that the warrant was therefore invalid. We in turn reversed, holding that the inspection was not a search subject to the Fourth Amendment. We recognized that the yard was within the curtilage of the house, that a fence shielded the yard from observation from the street and that the occupant had a subjective expectation of privacy. We held, however, that such an expectation was not reasonable and not one "that society is prepared to honor." Our reasoning was that the home and its curtilage are not necessarily protected from inspection that involves no physical invasion. " 'What a person knowingly exposes to the public, even in his own home or office, is not a subject of Fourth Amendment protection.' "Id., at 213, 106 S.Ct., at 1812, quoting Katz v. United States, 389 U.S. 347, 351, 88 S.Ct. 507, 511, 19 L.Ed.2d 576 (1967). As a general proposition, the police may see what may be seen "from a public vantage point where [they have] a right to be." Thus the police, like the public, would have been free to inspect the backyard garden from the street if their view had been unobstructed. They were likewise, free to inspect the yard from the vantage point of an aircraft flying in the navigable airspace as this plane was. "In an age where private and commercial flight in the public airways is routine, it is unreasonable for respondent to expect that his marijuana plants were constitutionally protected from being observed with the naked eye from an altitude of 1,000 feet. The Fourth Amendment simply does not require the police traveling in the public airways at this altitude to obtain a warrant in order to observe what is visible to the naked eye." *[naked eye]*

We arrive at the same conclusion in the present case. In this case, as in *Ciraolo,* the property surveyed was within the curtilage of respondent's home. Riley no doubt intended and expected that his greenhouse would not be open to public inspection, and the precautions he took protected against ground-level observation. Because the sides and roof of his greenhouse were left partially open, however, what was growing in the greenhouse was subject to viewing from the air. Under the holding in *Ciraolo,* Riley could not reasonably have expected the contents of his greenhouse to be immune from examination by an officer seated in a fixed-wing aircraft flying in navigable airspace at an altitude of 1,000 feet or, as the Florida Supreme Court seemed to recognize, at an altitude of 500 feet, the lower limit of the navigable airspace for such an aircraft. Here, the inspection was made from a helicopter, but as is the case with fixed-wing planes, "private and commercial flight [by helicopter] in the public airways is routine" in this country, and there is no indication that such flights are unheard of in Pasco County, Florida. Riley could not reasonably have expected that his greenhouse was protected from public or official observation from a helicopter had it been flying within the navigable airspace for fixed-wing aircraft.

Nor on the facts before us, does it make a difference for Fourth Amendment purposes that the helicopter was flying at 400 feet when the officer saw what was growing in the greenhouse through the partially open roof and sides of the structure. We would have a different case if flying at that altitude had been contrary to law or regulation. But helicopters are not bound by the lower limits of the navigable airspace allowed to other aircraft.[10] Any member of the public could legally have been flying over Riley's property in a helicopter at the altitude of 400 feet and could have observed Riley's greenhouse. The police officer did no more. This is not to say that an inspection of the curtilage of a house from an aircraft will always pass muster under the Fourth Amendment simply because the plane is within the navigable airspace specified by law. But it is of obvious importance that the helicopter in this case was not violating the law, and there is nothing in the record or before us to suggest that helicopters flying at 400 feet are sufficiently rare in this country to lend substance to respondent's claim that he reasonably anticipated that his greenhouse would not be subject to observation from that altitude. Neither is there any intimation here that the helicopter interfered with respondent's normal use of the greenhouse or of other parts of the curtilage. As far as this record reveals, no intimate details connected with the use of the home or curtilage were observed, and there was no undue noise, no wind, dust, or threat of injury. In these circumstances, there was no violation of the Fourth Amendment.

The judgment of the Florida Supreme Court is accordingly reversed.

SO ORDERED.

■ JUSTICE O'CONNOR, concurring in the judgment.

I concur in the judgment reversing the Supreme Court of Florida because I agree that police observation of the greenhouse in Riley's curtilage from a helicopter passing at an altitude of 400 feet did not violate an expectation of privacy "that society is prepared to recognize as 'reasonable.'" I write separately, however, to clarify the standard I believe follows from California v. Ciraolo, 476 U.S. 207, 106 S.Ct. 1809, 90 L.Ed.2d 210 (1986). In my view, the plurality's approach rests the scope of Fourth Amendment protection too heavily on compliance with FAA regulations whose purpose is to promote air safety not to protect "[t]he right of the people to be secure in their persons, houses, papers, and effects, against unreasonable searches and seizures." U.S. Const., Amdt. 4.

* * *

10. While Federal Aviation Administration regulations permit fixed wing aircraft to be operated at an altitude of 1,000 feet while flying over congested areas and at an altitude of 500 feet above the surface in other than congested areas, helicopters may be operated at less than the minimums for fixed wing aircraft "if the operation is conducted without hazard to persons or property on the surface. In addition, each person operating a helicopter shall comply with routes or altitudes specifically prescribed for helicopters by the [FAA] Administrator." 14 CFR § 91.79 (1988).

Ciraolo's expectation of privacy was unreasonable not because the airplane was operating where it had a "right to be," but because public air travel at 1,000 feet is a sufficiently routine part of modern life that it is unreasonable for persons on the ground to expect that their curtilage will not be observed from the air at that altitude. * * * Because the FAA has decided that helicopters can lawfully operate at virtually any altitude so long as they pose no safety hazard, it does not follow that the expectations of privacy "society is prepared to recognize as 'reasonable' "simply mirror the FAA's safety concerns.

* * *

In determining whether Riley had a reasonable expectation of privacy from aerial observation, the relevant inquiry after *Ciraolo* is not whether the helicopter was where it had a right to be under FAA regulations. Rather, consistent with *Katz,* we must ask whether the helicopter was in the public airways at an altitude at which members of the public travel with sufficient regularity that Riley's expectation of privacy from aerial observation was not "one that society is prepared to recognize as 'reasonable.' " *Katz,* supra, 389 U.S., at 361, 88 S.Ct., at 516. * * * [I]t is not conclusive to observe, as the plurality does, that "[a]ny member of the public could legally have been flying over Riley's property in a helicopter at the altitude of 400 feet and could have observed Riley's greenhouse." Nor is it conclusive that police helicopters may often fly at 400 feet. If the public rarely, if ever, travels overhead at such altitudes, the observation cannot be said to be from a vantage point generally used by the public and Riley cannot be said to have "knowingly expose[d]" his greenhouse to public view. However, if the public can generally be expected to travel over residential backyards at an altitude of 400 feet, Riley cannot reasonably expect his curtilage to be free from such aerial observation.

In my view, the defendant must bear the burden of proving that his expectation of privacy was a reasonable one, and thus that a "search" within the meaning of the Fourth Amendment even took place.

Because there is reason to believe that there is considerable public use of airspace at altitudes of 400 feet and above, and because Riley introduced no evidence to the contrary before the Florida courts, I conclude that Riley's expectation that his curtilage was protected from naked-eye aerial observation from that altitude was not a reasonable one. However, public use of altitudes lower than that—particularly public observations from helicopters circling over the curtilage of a home—may be sufficiently rare that police surveillance from such altitudes would violate reasonable expectations of privacy, despite compliance with FAA air safety regulations.

■ JUSTICE BRENNAN, with whom JUSTICE MARSHALL and JUSTICE STEVENS, join, dissenting.

* * *

The opinion for a plurality of the Court reads almost as if Katz v. United States, 389 U.S. 347, 88 S.Ct. 507, 19 L.Ed.2d 576 (1967), had never been decided. * * *

I agree, of course, that "[w]hat a person knowingly exposes to the public . . . is not a subject of Fourth Amendment protection." But I cannot agree that one "knowingly exposes [an area] to the public" solely because a helicopter may legally fly above it. Under the plurality's exceedingly grudging Fourth Amendment theory, the expectation of privacy is defeated if a single member of the public could conceivably position herself to see into the area in question without doing anything illegal. It is defeated whatever the difficulty a person would have in so positioning herself, and however infrequently anyone would in fact do so. In taking this view the plurality ignores the very essence of *Katz*. The reason why there is no reasonable expectation of privacy in an area that is exposed to the public is that little diminution in "the amount of privacy and freedom remaining to citizens" will result from police surveillance of something that any passerby readily sees. To pretend, as the plurality opinion does, that the same is true when the police use a helicopter to peer over high fences is, at best, disingenuous.
* * *

* * * The question before us must be not whether the police were where they had a right to be, but whether public observation of Riley's curtilage was so commonplace that Riley's expectation of privacy in his backyard could not be considered reasonable. While, as we held in *Ciraolo,* air traffic at elevations of 1000 feet or more may be so common that whatever could be seen with the naked eye from that elevation is unprotected by the Fourth Amendment, it is a large step from there to say that the Amendment offers no protection against low-level helicopter surveillance of enclosed curtilage areas. To take this step is error enough. That the plurality does so with little analysis beyond its determination that the police complied with FAA regulations is particularly unfortunate.

* * *

Equally disconcerting is the lack of any meaningful limit to the plurality's holding. It is worth reiterating that the FAA regulations the plurality relies on as establishing that the officer was where he had a right to be set no minimum flight altitude for helicopters. It is difficult, therefore, to see what, if any, helicopter surveillance would run afoul of the plurality's rule that there exists no reasonable expectation of privacy as long as the helicopter is where it has a right to be.

* * *

Perhaps the most remarkable passage in the plurality opinion is its suggestion that the case might be a different one had any "intimate details connected with the use of the home or curtilage [been] observed." What, one wonders, is meant by "intimate details"? If the police had observed Riley embracing his wife in the backyard greenhouse, would we then say that his reasonable expectation of privacy had been infringed? Where in the Fourth Amendment or in our cases is there any warrant for imposing a requirement that the activity observed must be "intimate" in order to be protected by the Constitution?

It is difficult to avoid the conclusion that the plurality has allowed its analysis of Riley's expectation of privacy to be colored by its distaste for the activity in which he was engaged. It is indeed easy to forget, especially in view of current concern over drug trafficking, that the scope of the Fourth Amendment's protection does not turn on whether the activity disclosed by a search is illegal or innocuous. But we dismiss this as a "drug case" only at the peril of our own liberties. * * *

I find little to disagree with in Justice O'CONNOR's concurrence, apart from its closing paragraphs. A majority of the Court thus agrees that the fundamental inquiry is not whether the police were where they had a right to be under FAA regulations, but rather whether Riley's expectation of privacy was rendered illusory by the extent of public observation of his backyard from aerial traffic at 400 feet.

What separates me from Justice O'CONNOR is essentially an empirical matter concerning the extent of public use of the airspace at that altitude, together with the question of how to resolve that issue. I do not think the constitutional claim should fail simply because "there is reason to believe" that there is "considerable" public flying this close to earth or because Riley "introduced no evidence to the contrary before the Florida courts." * * * I think we could take judicial notice that, while there may be an occasional privately owned helicopter that flies over populated areas at an altitude of 400 feet, such flights are a rarity and are almost entirely limited to approaching or leaving airports or to reporting traffic congestion near major roadways. * * *

If, however, we are to resolve the issue by considering whether the appropriate party carried its burden of proof, I again think that Riley must prevail. Because the State has greater access to information concerning customary flight patterns and because the coercive power of the State ought not be brought to bear in cases in which it is unclear whether the prosecution is a product of an unconstitutional, warrantless search, the burden of proof properly rests with the State and not with the individual defendant. The State quite clearly has not carried this burden.

                                        * * *

    * * * I respectfully dissent.

■ JUSTICE BLACKMUN, dissenting.

The question before the Court is whether the helicopter surveillance over Riley's property constituted a "search" within the meaning of the Fourth Amendment. Like Justice Brennan, Justice Marshall, Justice Stevens, and Justice O'Connor, I believe that answering this question depends upon whether Riley has a "reasonable expectation of privacy" that no such surveillance would occur, and does not depend upon the fact that the helicopter was flying at a lawful altitude under FAA regulations. A majority of this Court thus agrees to at least this much.

The inquiry then becomes how to determine whether Riley's expectation was a reasonable one. Both Justice Brennan, and the two Justices who have joined him, and Justice O'Connor believe that the reasonableness of Riley's expectation depends, in large measure, on the frequency of nonpolice helicopter flights at an altitude of 400 feet. Again, I agree.

How is this factual issue to be decided? Justice Brennan suggests that we may resolve it ourselves without any evidence in the record on this point. I am wary of this approach. While I, too, suspect that for most American communities it is a rare event when nonpolice helicopters fly over one's curtilage at an altitude of 400 feet, I am not convinced that we should establish a *per se* rule for the entire Nation based on judicial suspicion alone.

But we need not abandon our judicial intuition entirely. * * * [I]t is appropriate for us to take into account our estimation of the frequency of nonpolice helicopter flights. * * * [B]ecause I believe that private helicopters rarely fly over curtilages at an altitude of 400 feet, I would impose upon the prosecution the burden of proving contrary facts necessary to show that Riley lacked a reasonable expectation of privacy. * * *

In this case, the prosecution did not meet this burden of proof, as Justice Brennan notes. This failure should compel a finding that a Fourth Amendment search occurred. But because our prior cases gave the parties little guidance on the burden of proof issue, I would remand this case to allow the prosecution an opportunity to meet this burden.

The order of this Court, however, is not to remand the case in this manner. Rather, because Justice O'Connor would impose the burden of proof on Riley and because she would not allow Riley an opportunity to meet this burden, she joins the plurality's view that no Fourth Amendment search occurred. The judgment of the Court, therefore, is to reverse outright on the Fourth Amendment issue. Accordingly, for the reasons set forth above, I respectfully dissent.

NOTES

1. On remand, the Florida Supreme Court concluded, "A majority of the United States Supreme Court agreed that the record below lacked evidentiary development concerning the reasonableness of Riley's expectation of privacy." Therefore, the Florida tribunal directed the case remanded to the trial court "for further proceedings consistent with the opinion of the United States Supreme Court in this cause." Riley v. State, 549 So.2d 673, 674 (Fla.1989). Counsel for Riley construed this as meaning they were entitled to an evidentiary hearing at which to develop further whether helicopter flights in the area of Riley's home were insufficient in number and/or nature that he had a reasonable expectation his greenhouse would not be observed from the vantage provided by such a flight. The trial judge, however, refused to hold such a hearing. Counsel for Riley sought relief from the state appellate courts in action generating no published opinions. When these efforts proved unsuccessful, Riley pleaded guilty and received a sentence of four years probation. Interviews with Craig Vallente and Keith Hammond, Feb. 7, 12, 1997.

2. **Use of Camera in Aerial Surveillance.** In Dow Chemical Company v. United States, 476 U.S. 227, 106 S.Ct. 1819, 90 L.Ed.2d 226 (1986), investigators for the Environmental Protection Agency (EPA) used an airplane equipped with a precision aerial mapping camera to photograph Dow's Midland, Michigan plant from altitudes of 12,000, 3,000 and 1,200 feet. The plant was a 2,000 acre facility surrounded by a fence. Precautions were not taken to conceal all of the manufacturing equipment in the plant from aerial view. Nevertheless, its desire to protect trade secret information caused Dow to remain concerned about aerial photography. Low-flying planes were identified when possible and efforts made to obtain possession of

any photographs taken. A majority of the Court concluded the EPA's actions did not constitute a search for Fourth Amendment purposes:

> Admittedly, Dow's enclosed plant complex, like the area in *Oliver,* does not fall precisely within the "open fields" doctrine. The area at issue here can perhaps be seen as falling somewhere between "open fields" and curtilage, but lacking some of the critical characteristics of both. Dow's inner manufacturing areas are elaborately secured to ensure they are not open or exposed to the public from the ground. Any actual physical entry by EPA into any enclosed area would raise significantly different questions * * *. The narrow issue raised by [Dow] * * * concerns aerial observation of a 2,000 acre outdoor manufacturing facility without physical entry.

> * * *

> It may well be, as the Government concedes, that surveillance of private property by using highly sophisticated surveillance equipment not generally available to the public, such as satellite technology, might be constitutionally proscribed absent a warrant. But the photographs here are not so revealing of intimate details as to raise constitutional concerns. Although they undoubtedly give EPA more detailed information than naked-eye views, they remain limited to an outline of the facility's buildings and equipment. The mere fact that human vision is enhanced somewhat, at least to the degree here, does not give rise to constitutional problems.

476 U.S. at 236–38, 106 S.Ct. at 1826, 90 L.Ed.2d at 236–38.

3. **Surveillance by "Beeper."** Law enforcement's use of "beepers" to conduct surveillance raises issue akin to those presented by aerial surveillance. The Supreme Court addressed these issues in two decisions.

In United States v. Knotts, 460 U.S. 276, 103 S.Ct. 1081, 75 L.Ed.2d 55 (1983), the defendants were under suspicion because of reports they were purchasing chemicals which could be used in the manufacture of illicit drugs. With the consent of the seller, federal agents placed a "beeper" inside a five gallon container of chloroform that was to be sold to one of the defendants, Petschen. This beeper emitted signals that could be picked up by a radio receiver. Petschen, as he drove off with the container, was followed by means of both visual surveillance and a monitor which received signals from the beeper. The surveillance ended after Petschen took evasive maneuvers. About one hour later, a monitoring device in a helicopter located the beeper at a cabin owned by defendant Knotts. On the basis of this and other information obtained during three days of intermittent visual surveillance of the cabin, a search warrant for the cabin was obtained. The resulting search disclosed a fully operable drug laboratory; the container of chloroform containing the beeper was found under a barrel outside the cabin. The Court held the monitoring activities by the officers did not invade any legitimate expectation of privacy and therefore did not constitute a "search" under *Katz:*

> The governmental surveillance conducted by means of the beeper in this case amounted principally to the following of an automobile on public streets and highways. * * *

> A person travelling in an automobile on public thoroughfares has no reasonable expectation of privacy in his movements from one place to another. When Petschen traveled over the public street he voluntarily conveyed to anyone who wanted to look the fact that he was travelling over particular roads in a particular direction, the fact of whatever stops he made, and the fact of his final destination when he exited from public roads onto private property.

> Respondent Knotts, as the owner of the cabin and surrounding premises to which Petschen drove, undoubtedly had the traditional expectation of privacy within a dwelling place insofar as the cabin was concerned * * *. But no such

Beeper / Tracker is okay

expectation of privacy extended to the visual observation of Petschen's automobile arriving on his premises after leaving a public highway, nor to movements of objects such as the drum of chloroform outside the cabin in the "open fields." Hester v. United States, 265 U.S. 57, 44 S.Ct. 445, 68 L.Ed. 898 (1924).

Visual surveillance from public places along Petschen's route or adjoining Knotts' premises would have sufficed to reveal all of these facts to the police. The fact that the officers in this case relied not only on visual surveillance, but on the use of the beeper to signal the presence of Petschen's automobile to the police receiver, does not alter the situation. Nothing in the Fourth Amendment prohibited the police from augmenting the sensory faculties bestowed upon them at birth with such enhancement as science and technology afforded them in this case.

460 U.S. at 281–82, 103 S.Ct. at 1085–86, 75 L.Ed.2d at 62–63. After noting the failure of the visual surveillance, the majority acknowledged the use of the beeper enabled officers to ascertain the destination of the chloroform when they would not have been able to do so by reliance solely by sight. "But scientific enhancement of this sort raises no constitutional issues," the Court commented, "which visual surveillance would not also raise." It also noted the record contained no indication the beeper was used to reveal information concerning the movement of the drum inside the cabin or any other movement of it that would not have been visible to the naked eye from outside the cabin. All members of the Court joined in the result.

The Court noted that the warrantless installation of the beeper had not been challenged and the propriety of this action by the officers was therefore not addressed. Justice Brennan, joined by Justice Marshall, commented that a challenge to the installation of the beeper would have made the case more difficult.

In United States v. Karo, 468 U.S. 705, 104 S.Ct. 3296, 82 L.Ed.2d 530 (1984), the Court returned to beeper issues. A beeper was installed in a can of ether sold to the defendants; this beeper was then used to determine the can was inside a specific house. A majority of the Court held that no Fourth Amendment interest of the defendants was infringed by installation of the beeper. At the time the device was placed in the can, it reasoned, the defendants had neither title to nor possession of the can. Therefore, installing the beeper in the can intruded upon no expectation of privacy.

But the Court found the use of the beeper once installed constituted a search because it enabled the officers to obtain information they could not have obtained by observation from outside the curtilage of the house:

> The beeper tells the agent that a particular article is actually located at a particular time in the private residence and is in the possession of the person or persons whose residence is being surveilled. Even if visual surveillance has revealed that the article to which the beeper is attached has entered the house, the later monitoring not only verifies the officers' observations but also establishes that the article remains on the premises.

468 U.S. at 715, 104 S.Ct. at 3303, 82 L.Ed.2d at 541. The *Karo* beeper, unlike the *Knotts'* beeper, revealed the article to which it was attached was inside the house, a fact that could not have been determined by visual observation of the premises.

2.   Definition and Reasonableness of Activity Constituting a "Seizure" of Property

EDITORS' INTRODUCTION: SEIZURES OF ITEMS UNDER FOURTH AMENDMENT LAW

The Fourth Amendment's application to "seizures" of property was reaffirmed in Soldal v. Cook County, Illinois, 506 U.S. 56, 113 S.Ct. 538,

121 L.Ed.2d 450 (1992), a civil case. Soldal's trailer home was removed from its location in a mobile home park by the park owners, acting illegally under state law but with the active protection of local police. He sued for civil damages under 42 U.S.C.A. § 1983, claiming a conspiracy to unreasonably seize and remove his trailer. The district court granted summary judgment for the defendants; the Court of Appeals affirmed, reasoning the defendants had not seized Soldal's trailer within the meaning of the Fourth Amendment.

A unanimous Supreme Court reversed. The Court of Appeals, Justice White explained, construed the Fourth Amendment as not covering "technical" seizures infringing upon neither privacy nor liberty interests. Therefore, in its view, no seizure occurred since the officers had not invaded Soldal's privacy by entering or rummaging through the house or his liberty by detaining him. *Katz* and its progeny make clear, Justice White responded for the Court, property rights "are not the sole measure of Fourth Amendment violations." That case law did not, however, signal abandonment of the previously recognized protection for property under the Amendment. "[O]ur cases unmistakably hold," he emphasized, "that the [Fourth] Amendment protects property as well as privacy."

The Court of Appeals reasoned that the "plain view" seizure cases—such as the principal case reprinted after this Introduction—reflect that the Fourth Amendment protects against seizures resulting from "searches" but not seizures generally. This reading of the "plain view" cases was faulty, Justice White explained:

> [A]n officer who happens to come across an individual's property in a public area could seize it only if Fourth Amendment standards are satisfied—for example, if the items are evidence of a crime or contraband.

506 U.S. at 68, 113 S.Ct. at 547, 121 L.Ed.2d at 463.

Soldal's complaint, the Court concluded, alleged not simply a " 'garden-variety' landlord-tenant or commercial dispute" below Fourth Amendment recognition. Rather, it alleged a situation plainly implicating the interests protected by the Fourth Amendment and thus constituted a seizure within the meaning of that provision.

A person as well as an item may, of course, be seized. Seizures of persons raise quite different issues, and this topic is addressed in Chapter 4.

Definition of "Seizures." Whether police activity concerning places or items constitutes a "seizure" turns not upon whether that activity intrudes upon privacy interests but rather whether it constitutes a meaningful interference with the suspect's possessory interests. United States v. Jacobsen, 466 U.S. 109, 113, 104 S.Ct. 1652, 1656, 80 L.Ed.2d 85, 94 (1984). In United States v. Karo, 468 U.S. 705, 104 S.Ct. 3296, 82 L.Ed.2d 530 (1984), the defense urged that a seizure occurred when Karo took possession of a can of ether which, unbeknownst to him, contained a beeping device placed there by federal officers. Rejecting this, the Court explained:

> Although the can may have contained an unknown and unwanted foreign object, it cannot be said that anyone's possessory interest was

interfered with in any meaningful way. At most, there was a technical trespass on the space occupied by the beeper.

468 U.S. at 712, 104 S.Ct. at 3302, 82 L.Ed.2d at 540.

Items Subject to Seizure. Officers are clearly entitled—if other requirements are met—to seize items which they have sufficient reason to believe are seizable. Seizable items include stolen property and other "fruits" of criminal conduct, instrumentalities used in the commission of crime, or contraband, i.e., items—such as drugs—the possession of which is prohibited by law. But seizure of items of "mere evidence"—items which are of concern or value to public officers only because they constitute evidence of the commission of a crime or of someone's guilt of a crime—was at one time barred by the Fourth Amendment. Gouled v. United States, 255 U.S. 298, 311, 41 S.Ct. 261, 265, 65 L.Ed. 647, 653 (1921). In Warden v. Hayden, 387 U.S. 294, 87 S.Ct. 1642, 18 L.Ed.2d 2d 782 (1967), the Supreme Court abandoned this rule, holding that the Fourth Amendment did not absolutely bar seizure of mere evidence. No significant objective of the Amendment is served by the distinction, the Court noted, and citizens can be adequately protected from improper searches whether the object of those searches is to find and seize mere evidence or items subject to seizure under traditional doctrines.

The traditional list of items subject to seizure—contraband, instrumentalities and fruits of crime, and evidence—may be incomplete. Law enforcement officers may sometimes have authority to assume possession of items not coming within these categories. For example, an officer who arrests a suspect in or near the suspect's automobile may, under some circumstances, have authority to seize the automobile to protect the suspect's interest or to protect the officer from later claims that by his actions he subjected the automobile to increased risk of vandalism or other harm.

Need for Probable Cause. Does a seizure require probable cause to believe the item seized one to which the officers are entitled to possession, i.e., probable cause to believe that the item is contraband, an instrument or fruit of a crime or evidence? The plurality discussion in Coolidge v. New Hampshire, 403 U.S. 443, 91 S.Ct. 2022, 29 L.Ed.2d 564 (1971), considered at length in the principal case, suggested a "plain view" seizure requires it be "immediately apparent" to the officer that the item is subject to seizure. Whether this meant probable cause is necessary was considered but not resolved in Texas v. Brown, 460 U.S. 730, 103 S.Ct. 1535, 75 L.Ed.2d 502 (1983). The Court returned to the question in Arizona v. Hicks, 480 U.S. 321, 107 S.Ct. 1149, 94 L.Ed.2d 347 (1987), and addressed specifically whether probable cause was necessary for the plain view seizure of an item which officers came upon during a reasonable warrantless search of an apartment:

> We now hold that probable cause is required. To say otherwise would cut the "plain view" doctrine loose from its theoretical and practical moorings. The theory of that doctrine consists of extending to nonpublic places such as the home * * * the police's longstanding authority to make warrantless seizures in public places of such objects as weapons and contraband. And the practical justification for that extension is the desirability of sparing police, whose viewing of the

object in the course of a lawful search is as legitimate as it would have been in a public place, the inconvenience and the risk—to themselves or to preservation of the evidence—of going to obtain a warrant. Dispensing with the need for a warrant is worlds apart from permitting a lesser standard of *cause* for the seizure than a warrant would require, i.e., the standard of probable cause. No reason is apparent why an object should routinely be seizable on lesser grounds, during an unrelated search and seizure, than would have been needed to obtain a warrant for the same object if it had been known to be on the premises.

480 U.S. at 326–27, 107 S.Ct. at 1153, 94 L.Ed.2d at 355.

Searches of Seized Items. If an item is "seized" under the Fourth Amendment and that seizure is "reasonable," what additional is necessary before officers may "search" the seized item?

In United States v. Chadwick, 433 U.S. 1, 97 S.Ct. 2476, 53 L.Ed.2d 538 (1977), officers observed two Amtrak rail passengers arrive in Boston, and suspected the large footlocker they brought contained contraband. A trained dog released near the footlocker signaled it contained a controlled substance. Chadwick met the two passengers and the footlocker was placed in the trunk of Chadwick's car, parked outside the rail station. While the trunk of the car was still open, officers arrested all three and seized the footlocker. The footlocker was taken to the federal building in Boston. An hour and a half after the arrests, the footlocker was opened and searched. It was locked with a padlock and a regular trunk lock; the evidence did not establish how the officers opened it. Marijuana was found inside. Assuming the officers validly seized the footlocker, the Court nevertheless held their search of it unreasonable because they obtained no warrant:

> Once law enforcement authorities have reduced luggage or other personal property not immediately associated with the person of [an] arrestee to their exclusive control, and there is no longer any danger that the arrestee might gain access to the property to seize a weapon or destroy evidence, a search of that property is no longer an incident of the arrest.
>
> Here the search was conducted more than an hour after federal agents had gained exclusive control of the footlocker and long after [the arrestees] were securely in custody; the search therefore cannot be viewed as incidental to the arrest or as justified by any other exigency. Even though on this record the issuance of a warrant by a judicial officer was reasonably predictable, a line must be drawn. In our view, where no exigency is shown to support the need for an immediate search, the Warrant Clause places the line at the point where the property to be searched comes under the exclusive dominion of police authority.

433 U.S. at 15, 97 S.Ct. at 2485–86, 53 L.Ed.2d at 551.

Chadwick has given rise to significant difficulties, especially with regard to "containers" found in automobiles. These issues are considered in Chapters 4 and 5.

* * *

Fourth Amendment discussion, culminating in the principal case, has focused upon when, if ever, the Fourth Amendment requires judicial authorization for a seizure, in the form of a warrant or a specific provision in a warrant authorizing seizure of the property.

Horton v. California

Supreme Court of the United States, 1990.
496 U.S. 128, 110 S.Ct. 2301, 110 L.Ed.2d 112.

Justice STEVENS delivered the opinion of the Court.

In this case we revisit an issue that was considered, but not conclusively resolved, in Coolidge v. New Hampshire, 403 U.S. 443, 91 S.Ct. 2022, 29 L.Ed.2d 564 (1971): Whether the warrantless seizure of evidence of crime in plain view is prohibited by the Fourth Amendment if the discovery of the evidence was not inadvertent. We conclude that even though inadvertence is a characteristic of most legitimate "plain view" seizures, it is not a necessary condition.

I

Petitioner was convicted of the armed robbery of Erwin Wallaker, the treasurer of the San Jose Coin Club. When Wallaker returned to his home after the Club's annual show, he entered his garage and was accosted by two masked men, one armed with a machine gun and the other with an electrical shocking device, sometimes referred to as a "stun gun." The two men shocked Wallaker, bound and handcuffed him, and robbed him of jewelry and cash. During the encounter sufficient conversation took place to enable Wallaker subsequently to identify petitioner's distinctive voice. His identification was partially corroborated by a witness who saw the robbers leaving the scene, and by evidence that petitioner had attended the coin show.

Sergeant LaRault, an experienced police officer, investigated the crime and determined that there was probable cause to search petitioner's home for the proceeds of the robbery and for the weapons used by the robbers. His affidavit for a search warrant referred to police reports that described the weapons as well as the proceeds, but the warrant issued by the Magistrate only authorized a search for the proceeds, including three specifically described rings.

Pursuant to the warrant, LaRault searched petitioner's residence, but he did not find the stolen property. During the course of the search, however, he discovered the weapons in plain view and seized them. Specifically, he seized an Uzi machine gun, a .38 caliber revolver, two stun guns, a handcuff key, a San Jose Coin Club advertising brochure, and a few items of clothing identified by the victim.[11] LaRault testified that while he was searching for the rings, he also was interested in finding other evidence

___

11. Although the officer viewed other handguns and rifles, he did not seize them because there was no probable cause to be-lieve they were associated with criminal activity.

connecting petitioner to the robbery. Thus, the seized evidence was not discovered "inadvertently."

The trial court refused to suppress the evidence found in petitioner's home and, after a jury trial, petitioner was found guilty and sentenced to prison. The California Court of Appeal affirmed. * * * The California Supreme Court denied petitioner's request for review.

* * *

II

* * *

[handwritten margin note: –Search = compromise of privacy – seizure = domain over property / person]

The right to security in person and property protected by the Fourth Amendment may be invaded in quite different ways by searches and seizures. A search compromises the individual interest in privacy; a seizure deprives the individual of dominion over his or her person or property. The "plain view" doctrine is often considered an exception to the general rule that warrantless searches are presumptively unreasonable, but this characterization overlooks the important difference between searches and seizures.[12] If an article is already in plain view, neither its observation nor its seizure would involve any invasion of privacy. A seizure of the article, however, would obviously invade the owner's possessory interest. If "plain view" justifies an exception from an otherwise applicable warrant requirement, therefore, it must be an exception that is addressed to the concerns that are implicated by seizures rather than by searches.

The criteria that generally guide "plain view" seizures were set forth in Coolidge v. New Hampshire, 403 U.S. 443, 91 S.Ct. 2022, 29 L.Ed.2d 564 (1971). The Court held that the seizure of two automobiles parked in plain view on the defendant's driveway in the course of arresting the defendant violated the Fourth Amendment. Accordingly, particles of gun powder that had been subsequently found in vacuum sweepings from one of the cars could not be introduced in evidence against the defendant. The State endeavored to justify the seizure of the automobiles, and their subsequent search at the police station, on four different grounds, including the "plain view" doctrine. The scope of that doctrine as it had developed in earlier cases was fairly summarized in these three paragraphs from Justice Stewart's opinion:

> It is well established that under certain circumstances the police may seize evidence in plain view without a warrant. But it is important to keep in mind that, in the vast majority of cases, ANY evidence seized by the police will be in plain view, at least at the moment of seizure. The problem with the "plain view" doctrine has been to identify the circumstances in which plain view has legal significance rather than being simply the normal concomitant of any search, legal or illegal.

12. It is important to distinguish "plain view," as used in *Coolidge* to justify seizure of an object, from an officer's mere observation of an item left in plain view. Whereas the latter generally involves no Fourth Amendment search, the former generally does implicate the Amendment's limitations upon seizures of personal property.

An example of the applicability of the "plain view" doctrine is the situation in which the police have a warrant to search a given area for specified objects, and in the course of the search come across some other article of incriminating character. Where the initial intrusion that brings the police within plain view of such an article is supported, not by a warrant, but by one of the recognized exceptions to the warrant requirement, the seizure is also legitimate. Thus the police may inadvertently come across evidence while in "hot pursuit" of a fleeing suspect. And an object that comes into view during a search incident to arrest that is appropriately limited in scope under existing law may be seized without a warrant. Finally, the "plain view" doctrine has been applied where a police officer is not searching for evidence against the accused, but nonetheless inadvertently comes across an incriminating object.

What the "plain view" cases have in common is that the police officer in each of them had a prior justification for an intrusion in the course of which he came inadvertently across a piece of evidence incriminating the accused. The doctrine serves to supplement the prior justification—whether it be a warrant for another object, hot pursuit, search incident to lawful arrest, or some other legitimate reason for being present unconnected with a search directed against the accused—and permits the warrantless seizure. Of course, the extension of the original justification is legitimate only where it is immediately apparent to the police that they have evidence before them; the "plain view" doctrine may not be used to extend a general exploratory search from one object to another until something incriminating at last emerges.

Justice Stewart then described the two limitations on the doctrine that he found implicit in its rationale: First, "that plain view ALONE is never enough to justify the warrantless seizure of evidence,"; and second, "that the discovery of evidence in plain view must be inadvertent."

Justice Stewart's analysis of the "plain view" doctrine did not command a majority and a plurality of the Court has since made clear that the discussion is "not a binding precedent." Texas v. Brown, [460 U.S. 730, 737, 103 S.Ct. 1535, 1541, 75 L.Ed.2d 502 (1983)] (opinion of REHNQUIST, J.). Justice Harlan, who concurred in the Court's judgment and in its response to the dissenting opinions, did not join the plurality's discussion of the "plain view" doctrine. The decision nonetheless is a binding precedent. Before discussing the second limitation, which is implicated in this case, it is therefore necessary to explain why the first adequately supports the Court's judgment.

It is, of course, an essential predicate to any valid warrantless seizure of incriminating evidence that the officer did not violate the Fourth Amendment in arriving at the place from which the evidence could be plainly viewed. There are, moreover, two additional conditions that must be satisfied to justify the warrantless seizure. First, not only must the item be in plain view, its incriminating character must also be "immediately apparent." Thus, in *Coolidge,* the cars were obviously in plain view, but their probative value remained uncertain until after the interiors were swept and examined microscopically. Second, not only must the officer be lawfully located in a place from which the object can be plainly seen, but he or she must also have a lawful right of access to the object itself. As the Solicitor General has suggested, Justice Harlan's vote in *Coolidge* may have rested on the fact that the seizure of the cars was accomplished by means of a warrantless trespass on the defendant's property.

In all events, we are satisfied that the absence of inadvertence was not essential to the Court's rejection of the State's "plain view" argument in *Coolidge.*

III

Justice Stewart concluded that the inadvertence requirement was necessary to avoid a violation of the express constitutional requirement that a valid warrant must particularly describe the things to be seized. He explained:

The rationale of the exception to the warrant requirement, as just stated, is that a plain-view seizure will not turn an initially valid (and therefore limited) search into a "general" one, while the inconvenience of procuring a warrant to cover an inadvertent discovery is great. But where the discovery is anticipated, where the police know in advance the location of the evidence and intend to seize it, the situation is altogether different. The requirement of a warrant to seize imposes no inconvenience whatever, or at least none which is constitutionally cognizable in a legal system that regards warrantless searches as "per se unreasonable" in the absence of "exigent circumstances."

If the initial intrusion is bottomed upon a warrant that fails to mention a particular object, though the police know its location and intend to seize it, then there is a violation of the express constitutional requirement of "Warrants ... particularly describing ... [the] things to be seized."

We find two flaws in this reasoning. First, evenhanded law enforcement is best achieved by the application of objective standards of conduct, rather than standards that depend upon the subjective state of mind of the officer. The fact that an officer is interested in an item of evidence and fully expects to find it in the course of a search should not invalidate its seizure if the search is confined in area and duration by the terms of a warrant or a valid exception to the warrant requirement. If the officer has knowledge approaching certainty that the item will be found, we see no reason why he or she would deliberately omit a particular description of the item to be seized from the application for a search warrant. Specification of the additional item could only permit the officer to expand the scope of the search. On the other hand, if he or she has a valid warrant to search for one item and merely a suspicion concerning the second, whether or not it amounts to probable cause, we fail to see why that suspicion should immunize the second item from seizure if it is found during a lawful search for the first. * * *

Second, the suggestion that the inadvertence requirement is necessary to prevent the police from conducting general searches, or from converting specific warrants into general warrants, is not persuasive because that interest is already served by the requirements that no warrant issue unless it "particularly describ[es] the place to be searched and the persons or things to be seized," and that a warrantless search be circumscribed by the exigencies which justify its initiation. Scrupulous adherence to these requirements serves the interests in limiting the area and duration of the search that the inadvertence requirement inadequately protects. Once those commands have been satisfied and the officer has a lawful right of access, however, no additional Fourth Amendment interest is furthered by requiring that the discovery of evidence be inadvertent. If the scope of the search exceeds that permitted by the terms of a validly issued warrant or the character of the relevant exception from the warrant requirement, the subsequent seizure is unconstitutional without more. * * *

In this case, the scope of the search was not enlarged in the slightest by the omission of any reference to the weapons in the warrant. Indeed, if the three rings and other items named in the warrant had been found at the outset—or if petitioner had them in his possession and had responded to the warrant by producing them immediately—no search for weapons could have taken place. * * * Justice White's dissenting opinion in *Coolidge* is instructive:

> Police with a warrant for a rifle may search only places where rifles might be and must terminate the search once the rifle is found; the inadvertence rule will in no way reduce the number of places into which they may lawfully look.

As we have already suggested, by hypothesis the seizure of an object in plain view does not involve an intrusion on privacy.[13] If the interest in privacy has been invaded, the violation must have occurred before the object came into plain view and there is no need for an inadvertence limitation on seizures to condemn it. The prohibition against general searches and general warrants serves primarily as a protection against unjustified intrusions on privacy. But reliance on privacy concerns that support that prohibition is misplaced when the inquiry concerns the scope of an exception that merely authorizes an officer with a lawful right of access to an item to seize it without a warrant.

In this case the items seized from petitioner's home were discovered during a lawful search authorized by a valid warrant. When they were discovered, it was immediately apparent to the officer that they constituted incriminating evidence. He had probable cause, not only to obtain a warrant to search for the stolen property, but also to believe that the weapons and handguns had been used in the crime he was investigating. The search was authorized by the warrant, the seizure was authorized by the "plain view" doctrine. The judgment is affirmed.

It is so ordered.

---

13. Even if the item is a container, its seizure does not compromise the interest in preserving the privacy of its contents because it may only be opened pursuant to either a search warrant, see * * * United States v. Chadwick, 433 U.S. 1, 97 S.Ct. 2476, 53 L.Ed.2d 538 (1977) * * *, or one of the well-delineated exceptions to the warrant requirement.

■ JUSTICE BRENNAN, with whom JUSTICE MARSHALL joins, dissenting.

* * *

The Fourth Amendment * * * protects two distinct interests. The prohibition against unreasonable searches and the requirement that a warrant "particularly describ[e] the place to be searched" protect an interest in privacy. The prohibition against unreasonable seizures and the requirement that a warrant "particularly describ[e] . . . the . . . things to be seized" protect a possessory interest in property. The Fourth Amendment, by its terms, declares the privacy and possessory interests to be equally important. As this Court recently stated, "Although the interest protected by the Fourth Amendment injunction against unreasonable searches is quite different from that protected by its injunction against unreasonable seizures, neither the one nor the other is of inferior worth or necessarily requires only lesser protection." Arizona v. Hicks, 480 U.S. 321, 328, 107 S.Ct. 1149, 1154, 94 L.Ed.2d 347 (1987) (citation omitted).

The Amendment protects these equally important interests in precisely the same manner: by requiring a neutral and detached magistrate to evaluate, before the search or seizure, the government's showing of probable cause and its particular description of the place to be searched and the items to be seized. Accordingly, just as a warrantless search is per se unreasonable absent exigent circumstances, so too a seizure of personal property is "per se unreasonable within the meaning of the Fourth Amendment unless it is accomplished pursuant to a judicial warrant issued upon probable cause and particularly describing the items to be seized." * * *

The plain view doctrine is an exception to the general rule that a seizure of personal property must be authorized by a warrant. As Justice Stewart explained in *Coolidge,* we accept a warrantless seizure when an officer is lawfully in a location and inadvertently sees evidence of a crime because of "the inconvenience of procuring a warrant" to seize this newly discovered piece of evidence. But "where the discovery is anticipated, where the police know in advance the location of the evidence and intend to seize it," the argument that procuring a warrant would be "inconvenient" loses much, if not all, of its force. Barring an exigency, there is no reason why the police officers could not have obtained a warrant to seize this evidence before entering the premises. The rationale behind the inadvertent discovery requirement is simply that we will not excuse officers from the general requirement of a warrant to seize if the officers know the location of evidence, have probable cause to seize it, intend to seize it, and yet do not bother to obtain a warrant particularly describing that evidence. To do so would violate "the express constitutional requirement of 'Warrants . . . particularly describing . . . [the] things to be seized,' and would 'fly in the face of the basic rule that no amount of probable cause can justify a warrantless seizure.' "

* * *

The Court posits two "flaws" in Justice Stewart's reasoning that it believes demonstrate the inappropriateness of the inadvertent discovery requirement. But these flaws are illusory. First, the majority explains that it can see no reason why an officer who "has knowledge approaching certainty" that an item will be found in a particular location "would deliberately omit a particular description of the item to be seized from the application for a search warrant." * * * [T]here are[, however,] a number of instances in which a law enforcement officer might deliberately choose to omit certain items from a warrant application even though he has probable cause to seize them, knows they are on the premises, and intends to seize them when they are discovered in plain view. For example, the warrant application process can often be time-consuming, especially when the police attempt to seize a large number of items. An officer interested in conducting a search as soon as possible might decide to save time by listing only one or two hard-to-find items, such as the stolen rings in this case, confident that he will find in plain view all of the other evidence he is looking for before he discovers the listed items. Because rings could be located almost anywhere inside or outside a house, it is unlikely that a warrant to search for and seize the rings would restrict the scope of the search. An officer might rationally find the risk of immediately discovering the items listed in the warrant—thereby forcing him to conclude the search immediately—outweighed by the time saved in the application process.

The majority also contends that, once an officer is lawfully in a house and the scope of his search is adequately circumscribed by a warrant, "no additional Fourth Amendment interest is furthered by requiring that the discovery of evidence be inadvertent." * * * The majority is correct, but it has asked the wrong question. It is true that the inadvertent discovery requirement furthers no privacy interests. The requirement in no way reduces the scope of a search or the number of places into which officers may look. But it does protect possessory interests. The inadvertent discovery requirement is essential if we are to take seriously the Fourth Amendment's protection of possessory interests as well as privacy interests. The Court today eliminates a rule designed to further possessory interests on the ground that it fails to further privacy interests. I cannot countenance such constitutional legerdemain.

* * *

* * * I respectfully dissent.

NOTE

If officers "secure" premises, as for example pending application for a search warrant, by preventing the owner or residents from entering, have they "seized" those premises? The Court has not resolved this issue. See Segura v. United States, 468 U.S. 796, 104 S.Ct. 3380, 82 L.Ed.2d 599 (1984).

3. APPLYING THE "STANDING" REQUIREMENT

As *Wong Sun* and the material in Part B of Chapter 1 make clear, the Supreme Court has traditionally limited defendants to claims that evidence was obtained in violation of their own federal constitutional rights. Application of this requirement has presented the greatest difficulty in search and seizure cases. Once a court determines officers' activity constituted a "search," a "seizure," or both, it is often faced with a further and sometimes difficult determination as to whose Fourth Amendment interests were infringed upon by the searches and seizures that occurred. These determinations are the subject of the principal case in this subsection.

Rakas v. Illinois

Supreme Court of the United States, 1978.
439 U.S. 128, 99 S.Ct. 421, 58 L.Ed.2d 387.

■ MR. JUSTICE REHNQUIST delivered the opinion of the Court.

Petitioners were convicted of armed robbery in the Circuit Court of Kankakee County, Ill., and their convictions were affirmed on appeal. At their trial, the prosecution offered into evidence a sawed-off rifle and rifle shells that had been seized by police during a search of an automobile in which petitioners had been passengers. Neither petitioner is the owner of the automobile and neither has ever asserted that he owned the rifle or shells seized. The Illinois Appellate Court held that petitioners lacked standing to object to the allegedly unlawful search and seizure and denied their motion to suppress the evidence. We granted certiorari in light of the obvious importance of the issues raised to the administration of criminal justice, and now affirm.

I.

Because we are not here concerned with the issue of probable cause, a brief description of the events leading to the search of the automobile will suffice. A police officer on a routine patrol received a radio call notifying him of a robbery of a clothing store in Bourbonnais, Ill., and describing the getaway car. Shortly thereafter, the officer spotted an automobile which he thought might be the getaway car. After following the car for some time and after the arrival of assistance, he and several other officers stopped the vehicle. The occupants of the automobile, petitioners and two female companions, were ordered out of the car and after the occupants had left the car, two officers searched the interior of the vehicle. They discovered a box of rifle shells in the glove compartment, which had been locked, and a sawed-off rifle under the front passenger seat. After discovering the rifle and the shells, the officer took petitioners to the station and placed them under arrest.

Before trial petitioners moved to suppress the rifle and shells seized from the car on the ground that the search violated the Fourth and Fourteenth Amendments. They conceded that they did not own the automobile and were simply passengers; the owner of the car had been the driver of the vehicle at the time of the search. Nor did they assert that they owned the rifle or the shells seized. The prosecutor challenged petitioners' standing to object to the lawfulness of the search of the car because neither the car, the shells nor the rifle belonged to them. The trial court agreed that petitioners lacked standing and denied the motion to suppress the evidence. In view of this holding, the court did not determine whether there was probable cause for the search and seizure. On appeal after petitioners' conviction, the Appellate Court of Illinois, Third Judicial District, affirmed the trial court's denial of petitioners' motion to suppress because it held that "without a proprietary or other similar interest in an automobile, a mere passenger therein lacks standing to challenge the legality of the search of the vehicle." * * * The Illinois Supreme Court denied petitioners leave to appeal.

II.

* * *

[The Court first rejected petitioners' argument that the traditional standing requirement should be relaxed or broadened. After adhering to its traditional position, the Court further commented, that "the type of standing requirement * * * reaffirmed today is more properly subsumed under substantive Fourth Amendment doctrine." This aspect of the decision is discussed in part B of Chapter 1. Editors.]

Analyzed in these terms, the question is whether the challenged search or seizure violated the Fourth Amendment rights of a criminal defendant who seeks to exclude the evidence obtained during it. That inquiry in turn requires a determination of whether the disputed search and seizure has infringed an interest of the defendant which the Fourth Amendment was designed to protect. We are under no illusion that by dispensing with the rubric of standing * * * we have rendered any simpler the determination of whether the proponent of a motion to suppress is entitled to contest the legality of a search and seizure. But by frankly recognizing that this aspect of the analysis belongs more properly under the heading of substantive Fourth Amendment doctrine than under the heading of standing, we think the decision of this issue will rest on sounder logical footing.

C.

Here petitioners, who were passengers occupying a car which they neither owned nor leased, seek to analogize their position to that of the defendant in Jones v. United States, 362 U.S. 257, 80 S.Ct. 725, 4 L.Ed.2d 697 (1960). In *Jones*, petitioner was present at the time of the search of an apartment which was owned by a friend. The friend had given Jones permission to use the apartment and a key to it, with which Jones had admitted himself on the day of the search. He had a suit and shirt at the apartment and had slept there "maybe a night," but his home was elsewhere. At the time of the search, Jones was the only occupant of the apartment because the lessee was away for a period of several days. Under these circumstances, this Court stated that while one wrongfully on the premises could not move to suppress evidence obtained as a result of searching them, "anyone legitimately on premises where a search occurs may challenge its legality." Petitioners argue that their occupancy of the automobile in question was comparable to that of Jones in the apartment and that they therefore have standing to contest the legality of the search— or as we have rephrased the inquiry, that they, like Jones, had their Fourth Amendment rights violated by the search.

We do not question the conclusion in *Jones* that the defendant in that case suffered a violation of his personal Fourth Amendment rights if the search in question was unlawful. Nonetheless, we believe that the phrase "legitimately on premises" coined in *Jones* creates too broad a gauge for measurement of Fourth Amendment rights. For example, applied literally, this statement would permit a casual visitor who has never seen, or been permitted to visit the basement of another's house to object to a search of the basement if the visitor happened to be in the kitchen of the house at the time of the search. Likewise, a casual visitor who walks into a house one minute before a search of the house commences and leaves one minute after the search ends would be able to contest the legality of the search. The first visitor would have absolutely no interest or legitimate expectation of privacy in the basement, the second would have none in the house, and it advances no purpose served by the Fourth Amendment to permit either of them to object to the lawfulness of the search.

We think that *Jones* on its facts merely stands for the unremarkable proposition that a person can have a legally sufficient interest in a place other than his own home so that the Fourth Amendment protects him from unreasonable governmental intrusion into that place. In defining the scope of that interest, we adhere to the view expressed in *Jones* and echoed in later cases that arcane distinctions developed in property and tort law between guests, licensees, invitees, and the like, ought not to control. But the *Jones* statement that a person need only be "legitimately on premises" in order to challenge the validity of the search of a dwelling place cannot be taken in its full sweep beyond the facts of that case.

* * *

Our BROTHER WHITE in dissent expresses the view that by rejecting the phrase "legitimately on [the] premises" as the appropriate measure of Fourth Amendment rights, we are abandoning a thoroughly workable, "bright line" test in favor of a less certain analysis of whether the facts of a particular case give rise to a legitimate expectation of privacy. If "legitimately on premises" were the successful litmus test of Fourth Amendment rights that he assumes it is, his approach would have at least the merit of easy application, whatever it lacked in fidelity to the history and purposes of the Fourth Amendment. But a reading of lower court cases that have applied the phrase "legitimately on premises," and of the dissent itself, reveals that this expression is not a shorthand summary for a bright line rule which somehow encapsulates the "core" of the Fourth Amendment's protections.

The dissent itself shows that the facile consistency it is striving for is illusory. The dissenters concede that "there comes a point when use of an area is shared with so many that one simply cannot reasonably expect seclusion." But surely the "point" referred to is not one demarcating a line which is black on one side and white on another; it is inevitably a point which separates one shade of gray from another. We are likewise told by the dissent that a person "legitimately on *private* premises * * *, though his privacy is *not absolute*, is entitled to expect that he is sharing it only with those persons and that governmental officials will intrude only with *consent* or by complying with the Fourth Amendment." (emphasis added). This single sentence describing the contours of the supposedly easily applied rule virtually abounds with unanswered questions: What are "private" premises? Indeed, what are the "premises?" It may be easy to describe the "premises" when one is confronted with a one-room apartment, but what of the case of a 10–room house, or of a house with an attached garage that is searched? Also, if one's privacy is not absolute, how is it bounded? If he risks governmental intrusion "with consent," who may give that consent?

Again, we are told by the dissent that the Fourth Amendment assures that "*some* expectations of privacy are justified and will be protected from official intrusion." (emphasis added). But we are not told which of many possible expectations of privacy are embraced within this sentence. And our dissenting Brethren concede that "perhaps the Constitution provides some degree less protection for the personal freedom from unreasonable governmental intrusion when one does not have a possessory interest in the invaded private place." But how much "less" protection is available when one does not have such a possessory interest?

* * *

D.

Judged by the foregoing analysis, petitioners' claims must fail. They asserted neither a property nor a possessory interest in the automobile, nor an interest in the property seized. And as we have previously indicated, the fact that they were "legitimately on [the] premises" in the sense that they were in the car with the permission of its owner is not determinative of whether they had a legitimate expectation of privacy in the particular areas of the automobile searched. It is unnecessary for us to decide here whether the same expectations of privacy are warranted in a car as would be justified in a dwelling place in analogous circumstances. We have on numerous occasions pointed out that cars are not to be treated identically with houses or apartments for Fourth Amendment purposes. But here petitioners' claim is one which would fail even in an analogous situation in a dwelling place since they made no showing that they had any legitimate expectation of privacy in the glove compartment or area under the seat of the car in which they were merely passengers. Like the trunk of an automobile, these are areas in which a passenger *qua* passenger simply would not normally have a legitimate expectation of privacy.

Jones v. United States, 362 U.S. 257, 80 S.Ct. 725, 4 L.Ed.2d 697 (1960), involved significantly different factual circumstances. Jones not only had permission to use the apartment of his friend, but had a key to the apartment with which he admitted himself on the day of the search and kept possessions in the apartment. Except with respect to his friend, Jones had complete dominion and control over the apartment and could exclude others from it. * * *

IV.

The Illinois courts were therefore correct in concluding that it was unnecessary to decide whether the search of the car might have violated the rights secured to someone else by the Fourth and Fourteenth Amendments to the United States Constitution. Since it did not violate any rights of these petitioners, their judgment of conviction is

Affirmed.

■ MR. JUSTICE WHITE, with whom MR. JUSTICE BRENNAN, MR. JUSTICE MARSHALL, and MR. JUSTICE STEVENS, join, dissenting.

The Court today holds that the Fourth Amendment protects property, not people, and specifically that a legitimate occupant of an automobile may not invoke the exclusionary rule and challenge a search of that vehicle unless he happens to own or have a possessory interest in it. * * * If the Court is troubled by the practical impact of the exclusionary rule, it should face the issue of that rule's continued validity squarely instead of distorting other doctrines in an attempt to reach what are perceived as the correct results in specific cases.

* * *

[M]any of our opinions have assumed that a mere passenger in an automobile is entitled to protection against unreasonable searches occurring in his presence. In decisions upholding the validity of automobile searches, we have gone directly to the merits even though some of the petitioners did not own or possess the vehicles in question. * * * The Court's silence on this issue in light of its actions can only mean that, until now, we, like most lower courts, had assumed that *Jones* foreclosed the answer now supplied by the majority. That assumption was perfectly understandable, since all private premises would seem to be the same for the purposes of the analysis set out in *Jones*.

* * * My Brethren in the majority assertedly do not deny that automobiles warrant at least some protection from official interference with privacy. Thus, the next step is to decide who is entitled, vis à vis the State, to enjoy that privacy. The answer to that question must be found by determining "whether petitioner had an interest in connection with the searched premises that gave rise to 'a reasonable expectation [on his part] of freedom from governmental intrusion' upon those premises." Combs v. United States, 408 U.S. 224, 227, 92 S.Ct. 2284, 2286, 33 L.Ed.2d 308 (1972), quoting Mancusi v. DeForte, 392 U.S. 364, 368, 88 S.Ct. 2120, 2123, 20 L.Ed.2d 1154 (1968) (bracketed material in original).

Not only does *Combs* supply the relevant inquiry, it also directs us to the proper answer. We recognized there that *Jones* had held that one of those protected interests is created by legitimate presence on the searched premises, even absent any possessory interest. This makes unquestionable sense. We have concluded on numerous occasions that the entitlement to an expectation of privacy does not hinge on ownership * * *.

* * *

[O]ne consistent theme in our decisions under the Fourth Amendment has been, until now, that "the Amendment does not shield only those who have title to the searched premises." Mancusi v. DeForte, 392 U.S. 364, 367, 88 S.Ct. 2120, 2123, 20 L.Ed.2d 1154 (1968). Though there comes a point when use of an area is shared with so many that one simply cannot reasonably expect seclusion, short of that limit a person legitimately on private premises knows the others allowed there and, though his privacy is not absolute, is entitled to expect that he is sharing it only with those persons and that governmental officials will intrude only with consent or by complying with the Fourth Amendment.

It is true that the Court asserts that it is not limiting the Fourth Amendment bar against unreasonable searches to the protection of property rights, but in reality it is doing exactly that.[14] Petitioners were in a private place with the permission of the owner, but the Court states that that is not sufficient to establish entitlement to a legitimate expectation of privacy. But if that is not sufficient, what would be? We are not told, and it is hard to imagine anything short of a property interest that would satisfy the majority. Insofar as the Court's rationale is concerned, no passenger in an automobile, without an ownership or possessory interest and regardless of his relationship to the owner, may claim Fourth Amendment protection against illegal stops and searches of the automobile in which he is rightfully present. The Court approves the result in *Jones*, but it fails to give any explanation why the facts in *Jones* differ, in a fashion material to the Fourth Amendment, from the facts here.[15] More importantly, how is the Court able to avoid answering the question why presence in a private place with the owner's permission is insufficient? * * *

* * *

* * * If the owner of the car had not only invited petitioners to join her but had said to them, "I give you a temporary possessory interest in my vehicle so that you will share the right to privacy that the Supreme Court says that I own," then apparently the majority would reverse. But people seldom say such things, though they may mean their invitation to encompass them if only they had thought of the problem. If the nonowner were the spouse or child of the owner, would the Court recognize a sufficient interest? If so, would distant relatives somehow have more of an expectation of privacy than close friends? What if the nonowner were driving with the owner's permission? Would nonowning drivers have more of an expectation of privacy than mere passengers? What about a passenger in a taxicab? * * *

* * * The *Jones* rule is relatively easily applied by police and courts; the rule announced today will not provide law enforcement officials with a bright line between the protected and the unprotected. Only rarely will

14. The Court's reliance on property law concepts is additionally shown by its suggestion that visitors could "contest the lawfulness of the seizure of evidence or the search if their own property were seized during the search." What difference should that property interest make to constitutional protection against unreasonable searches, which is concerned with privacy? Contrary to the Court's suggestion, a legitimate passenger in a car expects to enjoy the privacy of the vehicle whether or not he happens to carry some item along for the ride. We have never before limited our concern for a person's privacy to those situations in which he is in possession of personal property. Even a person living in a barren room without possessions is entitled to expect that the police will not intrude without cause.

15. Jones had permission to use the apartment, had slept in it one night, had a key, had left a suit and a shirt there, and was the only occupant at the time of the search. Petitioners here had permission to be in the car and were occupying it at the time of the search. Thus the only distinguishing fact is that Jones could exclude others from the apartment by using his friend's key. But petitioners and their friend the owner had excluded others by entering the automobile and shutting the doors. Petitioners did not need a key because the owner was present. * * *

police know whether one private party has or has not been granted a sufficient possessory or other interest by another private party. Surely in this case the officers had no such knowledge. The Court's rule will ensnare defendants and police in needless litigation over factors that should not be determinative of Fourth Amendment rights.

More importantly, the ruling today undercuts the force of the exclusionary rule in the one area in which its use is most certainly justified—the deterrence of bad-faith violations of the Fourth Amendment. This decision invites police to engage in patently unreasonable searches every time an automobile contains more than one occupant. Should something be found, only the owner of the vehicle, or of the item, will have standing to seek suppression, and the evidence will presumably be usable against the other occupants. The danger of such bad faith is especially high in cases such as this one where the officers are only after the passengers and can usually infer accurately that the driver is the owner. The suppression remedy for those owners in whose vehicles something is found and who are charged with crime is small consolation for all those owners *and* occupants whose privacy will be needlessly invaded by officers following mistaken hunches not rising to the level of probable cause but operated on in the knowledge that someone in a crowded car will probably be unprotected if contraband or incriminating evidence happens to be found. After this decision, police will have little to lose by unreasonably searching vehicles occupied by more than one person.

* * *

NOTES

1. **Privacy in Premises.** Whether a search of premises violates the privacy rights of persons on the premises is, as the Court noted in *Rakas*, potentially a different question than that resolved in *Rakas*. The premises issue was addressed in two post-*Rakas* decisions.

In Minnesota v. Olson, 495 U.S. 91, 110 S.Ct. 1684, 109 L.Ed.2d 85 (1990), Olson was arrested in a duplex unit used as a residence by Luanne and Julie Bergstrom. Olson, with permission of the Bergstroms, spent the previous night in the duplex (sleeping on the floor) and had a change of clothes with him. At issue was whether Olson could contest the reasonableness of police entry of the duplex. The Supreme Court held that he could: "Olson's status as an overnight guest is alone enough to show that he had an expectation of privacy in the home that society is prepared to recognize as reasonable." Jones v. United States, distinguished in *Rakas,* was controlling, Justice White explained, despite the State's argument that Olson, unlike Jones, was never left alone in the unit and was never given a key to it.

> That the guest has a host who has ultimate control of the house is not inconsistent with the guest having a legitimate expectation of privacy. * * * [H]osts will more likely than not respect the privacy interests of their guests, who are entitled to a legitimate expectation of privacy despite the fact that they have no legal interest in the premises and do not have the legal authority to determine who may or may not enter the household.

495 U.S. at 99, 110 S.Ct. at 1689, 109 L.Ed.2d at 95. Chief Justice Rehnquist and Justice Blackmun dissented without opinion.

Olson was developed in Minnesota v. Carter, 525 U.S. 83, 119 S.Ct. 469, 142 L.Ed.2d 373 (1998). The question was whether Carter and Johns had a privacy interest in an apartment located in Eagan, Minnesota, and leased by Kimberly Thompson. Carter and Johns lived in Chicago and came to the apartment for the sole purpose of packaging cocaine for resale. They had never been in the apartment before and were in it for about 2 and 1/2 hours. In return for the brief use of the apartment, Carter and Johns gave Thompson one-eighth of an ounce of the cocaine. At issue in the case was whether Carter and Johns could challenge the admissibility of certain evidence on the ground it was the result of an observation of the packaging process in the apartment that Carter and Johns contended was an unreasonable search. The Court held Carter and Johns had no protected privacy interest in the premises and thus could not challenge any search that might have been involved in the observation:

> The [Fourth] Amendment protects persons against unreasonable searches of "their persons [and] houses" and thus indicates that the Fourth Amendment is a personal right that must be invoked by an individual. See Katz v. United States, 389 U.S. 347, 351, 88 S.Ct. 507, 19 L.Ed.2d 576 (1967). But the extent to which the Fourth Amendment protects people may depend upon where those people are. * * *

> The text of the Amendment suggests that its protections extend only to people in "their" houses. But we have held that in some circumstances a person may have a legitimate expectation of privacy in the house of someone else. In Minnesota v. Olson, 495 U.S. 91, 110 S.Ct. 1684, 109 L.Ed.2d 85 (1990), for example, we decided that an overnight guest in a house had the sort of expectation of privacy that the Fourth Amendment protects. * * *

> Respondents here were obviously not overnight guests, but were essentially present for a business transaction and were only in the home a matter of hours. There is no suggestion that they had a previous relationship with Thompson, or that there was any other purpose to their visit. Nor was there anything similar to the overnight guest relationship in *Olson* to suggest a degree of acceptance into the household. While the apartment was a dwelling place for Thompson, it was for these respondents simply a place to do business.

> Property used for commercial purposes is treated differently for Fourth Amendment purposes than residential property. "An expectation of privacy in commercial premises, however, is different from, and indeed less than, a similar expectation in an individual's home." New York v. Burger, 482 U.S. 691, 700, 107 S.Ct. 2636, 96 L.Ed.2d 601 (1987). And while it was a "home" in which respondents were present, it was not their home. Similarly, the Court has held that in some circumstances a worker can claim Fourth Amendment protection over his own workplace. See, e.g., O'Connor v. Ortega, 480 U.S. 709, 107 S.Ct. 1492, 94 L.Ed.2d 714 (1987). But there is no indication that respondents in this case had nearly as significant a connection to Thompson's apartment as the worker in O'Connor had to his own private office.

> If we regard the overnight guest in Minnesota v. Olson as typifying those who may claim the protection of the Fourth Amendment in the home of another, and one merely "legitimately on the premises" as typifying those who may not do so, the present case is obviously somewhere in between. But the purely commercial nature of the transaction engaged in here, the relatively short period of time on the premises, and the lack of any previous connection between respondents and the householder, all lead us to conclude that respondents' situation is closer to that of one simply permitted on the premises. We therefore hold that any search which may have occurred did not violate their Fourth Amendment rights.

525 U.S. at 88–91, 119 S.Ct. at 470–74, 142 L.Ed.2d at 379–81. Four members of the Court disagreed. They reasoned that "when a homeowner or lessor personally invites a guest into her home to share in a common endeavor, whether it be for conversation, to engage in leisure activities, or for business purposes licit or illicit, that guest should share his host's shelter against unreasonable searches and seizures." 525 U.S. at 106, 119 S.Ct. at 481–82, 142 L.Ed.2d at 390, 392 (Ginsburg, J., dissenting,), 525 U.S. at 103, 119 S.Ct. at 480, 142 L.Ed.2d at 388 (Breyer, J., concurring in the judgment) (agreeing with Justice Ginsburg that the respondents can claim Fourth Amendment protection but concluding further that the challenged observation did not violate that protection).

    2. **Use of a Place for Storage.** Suppose Rakas had testified he owned the rifle and shells and the owner of the automobile permitted him to use the car a repository for his property. Would he have established a protected privacy interest in at least that portion of the car the owner permitted him to use for storage of his property?

    The issue was presented in Rawlings v. Kentucky, 448 U.S. 98, 100 S.Ct. 2556, 65 L.Ed.2d 633 (1980). Rawlings, the petitioner before the Supreme Court, Vannessa Cox and several others were detained by Bowling Green officers while other officers applied for a search warrant. One officer approached Cox and directed her to empty the contents of her purse onto a nearby coffee table. She complied. The contents of her purse included a jar containing 1,800 tablets of LSD and other controlled substances. She turned to Rawlings—standing next to her—and told him "to take what was his." Rawlings claimed ownership of the controlled substances. At his trial for possession of and trafficking in those substances, could he challenge the officer's search of Cox's purse? The Court described the testimony explaining the situation as follows:

> Petitioner testified that he had flown into Bowling Green about a week before his arrest to look for a job and perhaps to attend the local university. He brought with him at that time the drugs later found in Cox's purse. Initially, petitioner stayed in the house where the arrest took place as the guest of Michael Swank, who shared the house with Marquess and Saddler. While at a party at that house, he met Cox and spent at least two nights of the next week on a couch at Cox's house.
>
> On the morning of petitioner's arrest, Cox had dropped him off at Swank's house where he waited for her to return from class. At that time, he was carrying the drugs in a green bank bag. When Cox returned to the house to meet him, petitioner dumped the contents of the bank bag into Cox's purse. Although there is dispute over the discussion that took place, petitioner testified that he "asked her if she would carry this for me, and she said, 'yes'...." Petitioner then left the room to use the bathroom and, by the time he returned, discovered that the police had arrived * * *.

During Rawlings' testimony, the following exchange took place:

> Q: Did you feel that Vanessa Cox's purse would be free from the intrusion of the officers as you sat there [waiting for the warrant?] When you put the pills in her purse, did you feel that they would be free from governmental intrusion?
>
> A: No, sir.

The state court, emphasizing Rawlings' admission he did not believe Cox's purse would be free from governmental intrusion, held Rawlings failed to show that the search of the purse violated his reasonable expectation of privacy.

    The Supreme Court affirmed. It explained:

We believe that the record in this case supports [the state court's] conclusion. Petitioner, of course, bears the burden of proving * * * that he had a legitimate expectation of privacy in [the] purse. At the time petitioner dumped thousands of dollars worth of illegal drugs into Cox's purse, he had known her for only a few days. According to Cox's uncontested testimony, petitioner had never sought or received access to her purse prior to that sudden bailment. Nor did petitioner have any right to exclude other persons from access to Cox's purse. In fact, Cox testified that Bob Stallons, a longtime acquaintance and frequent companion of Cox's, had free access to her purse and on the very morning of the arrest had rummaged through its contents in search of a hairbrush. Moreover, even assuming that petitioner's version of the bailment is correct and that Cox did consent to the transfer of possession, the precipitous nature of the transaction hardly supports a reasonable inference that petitioner took normal precautions to maintain his privacy. * * * [T]he record also contains a frank admission by petitioner that he had no subjective expectation that Cox's purse would remain free from governmental intrusion * * *.

Petitioner contends nevertheless that, because he claimed ownership of the drugs in Cox's purse, he should be entitled to challenge the search regardless of his expectation of privacy. We disagree. While petitioner's ownership of the drugs is undoubtedly one fact to be considered in this case, *Rakas* emphatically rejected the notion that "arcane" concepts of property law ought to control the ability to claim the protections of the Fourth Amendment. * * *

In sum, we find no reason to overturn the lower court's conclusion that petitioner had no legitimate expectation of privacy in Cox's purse at the time of the search.

448 U.S. at 104–06, 100 S.Ct. at 2561–62, 65 L.Ed.2d at 641–42.

CHAPTER 3

ISSUANCE AND EXECUTION OF ARREST AND SEARCH WARRANTS

Analysis

EDITORS' INTRODUCTION: WARRANTS, THEIR USE, AND BASIC FOURTH AMENDMENT REQUIREMENTS

A warrant is a court order authorizing a law enforcement officer to arrest an identified person or search a specified place for and to seize specific items, or for both arrest and search. It also typically commands the officer executing the warrant to bring the person or items seized to the issuing magistrate. For obvious reasons, a judge, or sometimes a clerk, issues a warrant *ex parte*, that is, without notice to the person whose arrest is sought or whose property will be searched. The warrant is issued upon presentation of information believed justifying the arrest or search. When an arrest warrant is sought, that information is presented in a document usually called a complaint. When a search warrant is desired, the document of application is ordinarily called simply an affidavit. The warrant may be executed by any law enforcement officer in the jurisdiction of the issuing

[handwritten margin note: warrant defined]

115

judge; the executing officers are not necessarily the same persons supplying the information upon which issuance was based.

Warrants play an important role in the theory of Fourth Amendment law. The Fourth Amendment itself concludes with the admonition that "no Warrants shall issue, but upon probable cause supported by Oath or affirmation, and particularly describing the place to be searched, and the persons or things to be seized." The Supreme Court has made clear that Fourth Amendment law should encourage law enforcement officers to use arrest and search warrants. Use of warrants is preferred because the warrant process interposes a decision by an impartial official—called a magistrate when performing warrant issuance functions—between the desires of the police to apprehend violators and citizens' privacy and liberty. Whether grounds exist for an arrest or search—whether probable cause exists—is determined by a person with no vested interest in finding that such grounds do exist. This is preferable to litigating the matters in response to a defendant's motion to suppress evidence because the warrant process can prevent unreasonable searches and arrests rather than respond to an after-the-fact demonstration that an unreasonable search or arrest occurred.

The warrant process regulates but does not bar those police actions to which it applies. This point was made by Justice Jackson in language that has been repeated numerous times in Supreme Court opinions:

> The point of the Fourth Amendment, which often is not grasped by zealous officers, is not that it denies law enforcement the support of the usual inferences which reasonable men draw from evidence. Its protection consists in requiring that those inferences be drawn by a neutral and detached magistrate instead of being judged by the officer engaged in the often competitive enterprise of ferreting out crime.

Johnson v. United States, 333 U.S. 10, 13–14, 68 S.Ct. 367, 369, 92 L.Ed. 436, 440 (1948). Warrants involve the judiciary in the investigative process before action is taken by law enforcement. This should often prevent violation of the Fourth Amendment right to be free from unreasonable searches and seizures, which is obviously preferable to efforts after-the-fact to remedy violations that have taken place. Furthermore, use of the warrant process to prevent improper law enforcement actions avoids the difficult task of litigating after-the-fact whether a violation occurred and of then selecting an appropriate remedy if a violation is found. Finally, when an arrest or search warrant has been issued, it gives specific instructions to law enforcement officers as to what they may and may not do in execution of the warrant. It also subjects further investigative effort to supervision of the judiciary by requiring a report of action taken under the warrant in the form of a return (and inventory of items seized) on a search warrant or, with respect to an arrest warrant, the presentation of the arrestee before the court.

In fact, arrest warrants are far less significant than search warrants. This is in part because Fourth Amendment law requires an arrest warrant be used only in very limited situations; the limited Fourth Amendment need for an arrest warrant is addressed in Chapter 4. Fourth Amendment theory generally requires that an arrest warrant be issued and drafted under the same rules applicable to search warrants. Because an arrest warrant is seldom needed, however, courts only rarely reach the validity of arrest warrants.

Use of Search Warrants in Actual Practice

The extent to which the warrant process actually functions in the manner intended by Fourth Amendment theory has been the subject of much speculation. An extensive empirical study of search warrant practices was, however, conducted by the National Center for State Courts. The results are reported in Van Duizend, Sutton and Cater, The Search Warrant Process: Preconceptions, Perceptions, and Practices (National Center for State Courts, undated). Probably the most important part of the study consisted of examining 844 search warrant cases and resulting prosecutions in seven different cities. In addition, interviews with police, judges, prosecutors and defense lawyers were conducted in these seven cities and direct observations of the warrant issuing process were undertaken in one location.

The study confirmed that officers seek search warrants in relatively few investigations and that they conduct the vast majority of searches without warrants. Id., at 20–21. In regard to search warrants issued, an average (or "mean") of 38% involved drug offenses and 29% concerned property crimes. But an average of 21% were used in investigations of violent offenses. Id., at 33. An average of 40% of the warrants were issued in part upon the basis of information received from a confidential informant—that is, an unidentified informant. Id., at 40.

Statistics

Many of the judges issuing warrants perceived themselves as performing a role independent of law enforcement, but a few saw their role as "assisting the police." Id., at 64. Often, officers were able, by "judge shopping," to avoid submitting a request for a warrant to a judge known as particularly demanding. Because of difficulty in locating rejected applications, the study could not address how often warrant applications were rejected. But the authors suggested the rate of "outright rejection" was probably "extremely low." Id., at 32. On the other hand, warrant applications were often reviewed and screened by a superior police official or a prosecutor. While this review apparently led to few "screening outs," the process sometimes resulted in the officer being requested to add further information to the application. Id., at 24–25. Similarly, judicial officers who did not reject applications with some frequency required additional information from applying officers. The judge's review was seldom lengthy. Of the warrant proceedings directly observed, 65% lasted 2.5 minutes or less. Only 11% lasted longer than five minutes. Id., at 31.

In all of the cities studied, searches conducted pursuant to those warrants actually served resulted in the discovery of something which the officers thought worth seizing in at least 90% of the cases. In an average of over one third of the cases, officers seized items not specifically identified in the warrant. Id. at 52.

Motions to suppress evidence were filed in a significant number of the prosecutions arising out of the searches. But they were seldom granted. Of 347 warrant-related prosecutions studied, motions to suppress evidence were granted in only 17. In at least 12 of these 17, convictions were nevertheless obtained.

Interviewed police officers often complained of the delay involved in applying for and getting a search warrant and of the resulting loss of "good cases." But the study found little relationship between the delay and the actual loss of cases. Id., at 96.

In regard to "bottom lines," the study concluded the search warrant requirement has several beneficial effects. First, it requires officers to "at least contemplate" the requirement of probable cause before a search, and this reflection induces a higher standard of care than they would otherwise use. Second, it produces "a multi-layered review that reduces the likelihood that a search will occur in the absence of probable cause." Finally, it provides a clear and tangible record permitting a more objective later evaluation of the search. On the other hand, the study concluded "it was clear in many cases that the review process was largely perfunctory," and that there was "infrequent but significant" evidence of efforts undermining "and sometimes entirely defeat[ing]" the integrity of the review process. But "the most striking and significant—and perhaps the most troubling— discovery," the report concluded, was the infrequency with which the search warrant process was invoked. It is perceived as "burdensome, time-consuming, intimidating, frustrating, and confusing." Many easier methods of obtaining incriminating evidence or of developing a case against a suspect exist. "It is not surprising * * *," the report concluded, "that many officers tend to regard the warrant option as a last resort." Id., at 148–49.

Does the study suggest reason to rethink the central role of warrants in the theory of Fourth Amendment law? Or, to the extent that there are deficiencies in warrant practice, should efforts be focused upon making practice more closely correspond with theory?

The Foundation Requirement—A Neutral and Detached Magistrate

As a basic foundation requirement for an effective search or arrest warrant, the Supreme Court has mandated the issuing person be an individual sufficiently likely to perform the tasks the Fourth Amendment requires—a critical and independent evaluation of the sufficiently of the information offered to justify the warrant

Generally, courts assume the person issuing a warrant must be a "judicial officer" or a "magistrate." In Shadwick v. Tampa, 407 U.S. 345, 92 S.Ct. 2119, 32 L.Ed.2d 783 (1972), however, the Court noted that the constitutional validity of a warrant "does not turn on the labeling of the issuing party." It explained:

> [A]n issuing magistrate must meet two tests. He must be neutral and detached, and he must be capable of determining whether probable cause exists for the requested arrest or search.

407 U.S. at 350, 92 S.Ct. at 2123, 32 L.Ed.2d at 788. In Shadwick itself, the Court held misdemeanor arrest warrants for violations of city ordinance could be issued by clerks of a municipal court, rather than by the judge of the court. No showing had been made, it emphasized, that these clerks

were affiliated with prosecutors or police or that they were partial in any sense. Nor had any demonstration been made that the clerks were incapable of determining probable cause. It was not considering, the Court stressed, whether "someone completely outside the sphere of the judicial branch" could issue warrants. Nor did *Shadwick* address whether court clerks could issue arrest warrants for more serious offenses or search warrants.

Where those issuing warrants were subject to some institutional risk of bias in favor of those applying for warrants, the Court held the resulting warrants unreasonable. An attorney general actively involved in an investigation, then, could not issue a search warrant for that investigation. Coolidge v. New Hampshire, 403 U.S. 443, 450, 91 S.Ct. 2022, 2029, 29 L.Ed.2d 564, 573 (1971). A justice of the peace paid $5.00 for each search warrant issued but nothing for a search warrant application denied was held to have a direct, personal, and substantial pecuniary interest favoring the issuance of warrants. Consequently, a search under a warrant issued by such a judicial officer was unreasonable. Connally v. Georgia, 429 U.S. 245, 97 S.Ct. 546, 50 L.Ed.2d 444 (1977).

Further, the conduct of a judicial officer in the specific case may show the officer lacked the Fourth Amendment capacity to issue an effective warrant. Thus in In Lo–Ji Sales, Inc. v. New York, 442 U.S. 319, 99 S.Ct. 2319, 60 L.Ed.2d 920 (1979), upon a showing two obscene films had been purchased by a police officer at a bookstore, a Town Justice issued a search warrant for other copies of the films. In addition, the warrant authorized the officers to seize the "following" items "that the Court independently [on examination] has determined to be" obscene. No items were listed. But the Justice accompanied the officers to the bookstore and there examined numerous items. Those he found obscene he included in the warrant. The Court held that this violated the Fourth Amendment:

> The Town Justice did not manifest that neutrality and detachment demanded of a judicial officer when presented with a warrant application for a search and seizure. We need not question the subjective belief of the Town Justice in the propriety of his actions, but the objective facts of record manifest an erosion of whatever neutral and detached posture existed at the outset. He allowed himself to become a member, if not the leader, of the search party which was essentially a police operation.

442 U.S. at 326–27, 99 S.Ct. at 2324, 60 L.Ed.2d at 928–29. It continued:

> We do not suggest, of course, that a "neutral and detached magistrate" loses his character as such merely because he leaves his regular office in order to make himself readily available to law enforcement officers who may wish to seek the issuance of warrants by him. * * * But * * * [in] this case * * * the Town Justice undertook not merely to issue a warrant, but to participate with the police and prosecutors in its execution.

442 U.S. at 328 n. 6, 99 S.Ct. 2325 n. 6, 60 L.Ed.2d at 930 n. 6.

* * *

This chapter addresses separately several major aspects of Fourth Amendment "warrant law." First, it considers the requirement that the warrant be issued on a showing of probable cause and several related issues. Second, it addresses limitations on the manner of gaining entry to execute the warrant and some related limits on execution of warrants. Finally, it turns to the terms of the warrant and their role in the warrant's execution.

A.   The Showing of Probable Cause

The essence of the warrant process is the judicial scrutiny of the information submitted as justification for the warrant's issuance. Effective scrutiny requires, of course, the information presented be sufficient and adequately detailed. The information required to support a warrant's issuance is considered in the first subsection. A defendant's later ability to challenge the accuracy of this information is addressed in the next subsection.

1.   The Initial Showing Before the Magistrate

EDITORS' INTRODUCTION: THE "PROBABLE CAUSE" SHOWING

The specific terms of the Fourth Amendment prohibit the issuance of a warrant except "upon probable cause supported by Oath or affirmation." A warrant application often is accompanied by a written and sworn affidavit setting out the facts which the applying officers believe constitute the required probable cause. In many cases, then, the issuing magistrate's function consists largely of reviewing the affidavit to determine if the alleged information rises to this level.

There is probably no federal constitutional requirement that all or even any of the information submitted to the magistrate be written. Statutes and court rules sometimes authorize a warrant's issuance in whole or in part upon oral information. Rule 41(c)(1) of the Federal Rules of Criminal Procedure requires, as a general rule, a search warrant issue on the basis of a sworn affidavit. But it further provides:

> Before ruling on a request for a warrant the federal magistrate * * * may require the affiant to appear personally and may examine under oath the affiant and any witnesses he may produce, provided that such proceedings shall be taken down by a court reporter or recording equipment and made part of the affidavit.

If a magistrate requires such additional information beyond the affidavit, it is quite likely any warrant issued will be based in part upon that additional and oral information. Generally, however, magistrates do not demand further facts. Therefore, the magistrate's task is usually one of reviewing the affidavit "on its face"—probably assuming the correctness of the facts alleged—to determine if those facts establish probable cause. Insofar as this is the process, no critical consideration of whether the facts alleged are correct occurs until and if the defendant later challenges the accuracy of the "face" of the affidavit. The next subsection considers defendants' ability to make such challenges.

Rule 41(c)(2) authorizes a search warrant's issuance "upon sworn oral testimony communicated by telephone or other appropriate means" if "circumstances make it reasonable to dispense with a written affidavit." Where application for a warrant is made by telephone, the applicant prepares a "duplicate original" warrant and reads it to the magistrate. The magistrate then signs the original warrant (which is before the magistrate) and authorizes the applicant to sign the magistrate's name to the duplicate original. If a voice recording device is available, the magistrate records the telephone call, has the recording transcribed, certifies the accuracy of the recording, and files a copy with the court. If no such device is available, a stenographic or longhand verbatim record is made, and a copy signed by the magistrate is filed. Fed.R.Crim.P. 41(D). Interestingly, the rule provides that absent a "finding of bad faith," evidence obtained pursuant to a warrant is not subject to a motion to suppress on the ground the circumstances did not justify dispensing with a written affidavit. Fed.R.Crim.P. 41(G).

The Supreme Court decisions addressing the sufficiency of warrant affidavits involve situations in which the information submitted for a warrant consists in part of information from persons other than the affiant. The leading—or at least the seminal—case is Aguilar v. Texas, 378 U.S. 108, 84 S.Ct. 1509, 12 L.Ed.2d 723 (1964). Two police officers submitted to a Justice of the Peace an application for a search warrant for Aguilar's home. In support, they provided an affidavit which stated:

> Affiants have received reliable information from a credible person and do believe that heroin, marijuana, barbiturates and other narcotics and narcotics paraphernalia are being kept at the above described premises for the purpose of sale and use contrary to the provisions of the law.

The justice issued the warrant; the officers executed it and found drugs. These drugs were admitted into evidence at Aguilar's trial. Finding constitutional error, the Supreme Court reasoned the guiding principles must be that the magistrate must decide for himself whether probable cause exists and not accept without question the officers' "mere conclusion." These principles require an affidavit permitting the magistrate to perform these tasks. Further:

> Although an affidavit may be based on hearsay information and need not reflect the direct personal observations of the affiant, the magistrate must be informed of some of the underlying circumstances from which the informant concluded that the narcotics were where he claimed they were, and some of the underlying circumstances from which the officer concluded that the informant, whose identity need not be disclosed, was "credible" or his information "reliable." Otherwise, "the inferences from the facts which lead to the complaint" will be drawn not "by a neutral and detached magistrate," as the Constitution requires, but instead, by a police officer * * *, or, as in this case, by an unidentified informant.

378 U.S. at 114–15, 84 S.Ct. at 1514, 12 L.Ed.2d at 729.

This approach was developed further in Spinelli v. United States, 393 U.S. 410, 89 S.Ct. 584, 21 L.Ed.2d 637 (1969). Evidence of gambling activities was obtained in a search pursuant to a warrant of an apartment located in St. Louis. The affidavit on which the warrant was issued recited in part:

> The Federal Bureau of Investigation has been informed by a confidential reliable informant that William Spinelli is operating a handbook and accepting wagers and disseminating wagering information by means of the telephones which have been assigned the numbers WYdown 4–0029 and WYdown 4–0136.

In addition, the affidavit recited that telephone company records disclosed the phones to which those numbers were assigned were located in a specific apartment under the name of Grace B. Hagen. Further, the affidavit stated federal agents conducting surveillance had observed Spinelli enter the apartment once, and on several other occasions they observed him in the parking lot of the apartment building or in its vicinity. Holding the warrant invalid, a majority of the Court noted that the tip met neither prong of *Aguilar*. It then suggested a tip was not sufficient under *Aguilar* might nevertheless establish probable cause for either of two reasons. First, the tip might describe the suspect's criminal activity in sufficient detail that a magistrate could infer from this detail that the informant had gained the information in a reliable way. Second, other reliable information might sufficiently corroborate parts of the information in the tip to justify a magistrate in concluding that the tip's ultimate and incriminating assertions could be relied upon. Neither method "cured" the *Spinelli* affidavit, however. The detailed information in the tip concerning the telephones was a "meager report" that "could easily have been obtained from an offhand remark heard at a neighborhood bar." The corroborating evidence gathered by the federal agents "at most * * * indicated that Spinelli could have used the telephones specified by the informant for some purpose."

As the principal case in this subsection makes clear, the *Aguilar–Spinelli* approach has not survived further consideration.

Illinois v. Gates

Supreme Court of the United States, 1983.
462 U.S. 213, 103 S.Ct. 2317, 76 L.Ed.2d 527.

■ JUSTICE REHNQUIST delivered the opinion of the Court.

Respondents Lance and Susan Gates were indicted for violation of state drug laws after police officers, executing a search warrant, discovered marijuana and other contraband in their automobile and home. Prior to trial the Gates moved to suppress evidence seized during this search. The Illinois Supreme Court affirmed the decisions of lower state courts granting the motion. It held that the affidavit submitted in support of the State's application for a warrant to search the Gates' property was inadequate under this Court's decisions in Aguilar v. Texas, 378 U.S. 108, 84 S.Ct.

1509, 12 L.Ed.2d 723 (1964) and Spinelli v. United States, 393 U.S. 410, 89 S.Ct. 584, 21 L.Ed.2d 637 (1969).

* * *

II

* * * A chronological statement of events usefully introduces the issues at stake. Bloomingdale, Ill., is a suburb of Chicago located in DuPage County. On May 3, 1978, the Bloomingdale Police Department received by mail an anonymous handwritten letter which read as follows:

"This letter is to inform you that you have a couple in your town who strictly make their living on selling drugs. They are Sue and Lance Gates, they live on Greenway, off Bloomingdale Rd. in the condominiums. Most of their buys are done in Florida. Sue his wife drives their car to Florida, where she leaves it to be loaded up with drugs, then Lance flys down and drives it back. Sue flys back after she drops the car off in Florida. May 3 she is driving down there again and Lance will be flying down in a few days to drive it back. At the time Lance drives the car back he has the trunk loaded with over $100,000.00 in drugs. Presently they have over $100,000.00 worth of drugs in their basement.

They brag about the fact they never have to work, and make their entire living on pushers.

I guarantee if you watch them carefully you will make a big catch. They are friends with some big drugs dealers, who visit their house often.

Lance & Susan Gates

Greenway

in Condominiums"

The letter was referred by the Chief of Police of the Bloomingdale Police Department to Detective Mader, who decided to pursue the tip. Mader learned, from the office of the Illinois Secretary of State, that an Illinois driver's license had been issued to one Lance Gates, residing at a stated address in Bloomingdale. He contacted a confidential informant, whose examination of certain financial records revealed a more recent address for the Gates, and he also learned from a police officer assigned to O'Hare Airport that "L. Gates" had made a reservation on Eastern Airlines flight 245 to West Palm Beach, Fla., scheduled to depart from Chicago on May 5 at 4:15 p.m.

Mader then made arrangements with an agent of the Drug Enforcement Administration for surveillance of the May 5 Eastern Airlines flight. The agent later reported to Mader that Gates had boarded the flight, and that federal agents in Florida had observed him arrive in West Palm Beach and take a taxi to the nearby Holiday Inn. They also reported that Gates went to a room registered to one Susan Gates and that, at 7:00 a.m. the next morning, Gates and an unidentified woman left the motel in a Mercury bearing Illinois license plates and drove northbound on an interstate frequently used by travelers to the Chicago area. In addition, the DEA agent informed Mader that the license plate number on the Mercury was registered to a Hornet station wagon owned by Gates. The agent also advised Mader that the driving time between West Palm Beach and Bloomingdale was approximately 22 to 24 hours.

Mader signed an affidavit setting forth the foregoing facts, and submitted it to a judge of the Circuit Court of DuPage County, together with a copy of the anonymous letter. The judge of that court thereupon issued a search warrant for the Gates' residence and for their automobile. The judge, in deciding to issue the warrant, could have determined that the *modus operandi* of the Gates had been substantially corroborated. As the anonymous letter predicted, Lance Gates had flown from Chicago to West Palm Beach late in the afternoon of May 5th, had checked into a hotel room registered in the name of his wife, and, at 7:00 a.m. the following morning, had headed north, accompanied by an unidentified woman, out of West Palm Beach on an interstate highway used by travelers from South Florida to Chicago in an automobile bearing a license plate issued to him.

At 5:15 a.m. on May 7th, only 36 hours after he had flown out of Chicago, Lance Gates, and his wife, returned to their home in Bloomingdale, driving the car in which they had left West Palm Beach some 22 hours earlier. The Bloomingdale police were awaiting them, searched the trunk of the Mercury, and uncovered approximately 350 pounds of marijuana. A search of the Gates' home revealed marijuana, weapons, and other contraband. The Illinois Circuit Court ordered suppression of all these items, on the ground that the affidavit submitted to the Circuit Judge failed to support the necessary determination of probable cause to believe that the Gates' automobile and home contained the contraband in question. This decision was affirmed in turn by the Illinois Appellate Court and by a divided vote of the Supreme Court of Illinois.

The Illinois Supreme Court concluded—and we are inclined to agree—that, standing alone, the anonymous letter sent to the Bloomingdale Police Department would not provide the basis for a magistrate's determination that there was probable cause to believe contraband would be found in the Gates' car and home. The letter provides virtually nothing from which one might conclude that its author is either honest or his information reliable; likewise, the letter gives absolutely no indication of the basis for the writer's predictions regarding the Gates' criminal activities. Something more was required, then, before a magistrate could conclude that there was probable cause to believe that contraband would be found in the Gates' home and car.

The Illinois Supreme Court also properly recognized that Detective Mader's affidavit might be capable of supplementing the anonymous letter with information sufficient to permit a determination of probable cause. In holding that the affidavit in fact did not contain sufficient additional information to sustain a determination of probable cause, the Illinois court applied a "two-pronged test," derived from our decision in Spinelli v. United States, 393 U.S. 410, 89 S.Ct. 584, 21 L.Ed.2d 637 (1969). The Illinois Supreme Court, like some others, apparently understood *Spinelli* as requiring that the anonymous letter satisfy each of two independent requirements before it could be relied on. According to this view, the letter, as supplemented by Mader's affidavit, first had to adequately reveal the "basis of knowledge" of the letter writer—the particular means by which he came by the information given in his report. Second, it had to provide facts sufficiently establishing either the "veracity" of the affiant's informant, or, alternatively, the "reliability" of the informant's report in this particular case.

The Illinois court * * * found that the test had not been satisfied. First, the "veracity" prong was not satisfied because, "there was simply no basis [for] * * * conclud[ing] that the anonymous person [who wrote the letter to the Bloomingdale Police Department] was credible." The court indicated that corroboration by police of details contained in the letter might never satisfy the "veracity" prong, and in any event, could not do so if, as in the present case, only "innocent" details are corroborated. In addition, the letter gave no indication of the basis of its writer's knowledge of the Gates' activities. The Illinois court understood *Spinelli* as permitting the detail contained in a tip to be used to infer that the informant had a reliable basis for his statements, but it thought that the anonymous letter failed to provide sufficient detail to permit such an inference. Thus, it concluded that no showing of probable cause had been made.

We agree with the Illinois Supreme Court that an informant's "veracity," "reliability" and "basis of knowledge" are all highly relevant in determining the value of his report. We do not agree, however, that these elements should be understood as entirely separate and independent requirements to be rigidly exacted in every case, which the opinion of the Supreme Court of Illinois would imply. Rather, as detailed below, they should be understood simply as closely intertwined issues that may usefully illuminate the common-sense, practical question whether there is "probable cause" to believe that contraband or evidence is located in a particular place.

III

This totality of the circumstances approach is far more consistent with our prior treatment of probable cause than is any rigid demand that specific "tests" be satisfied by every informant's tip. Perhaps the central teaching of our decisions bearing on the probable cause standard is that it is a "practical, nontechnical conception." * * * [P]robable cause is a fluid concept—turning on the assessment of probabilities in particular factual contexts—not readily, or even usefully, reduced to a neat set of legal rules. Informants' tips doubtless come in many shapes and sizes from many different types of persons. * * * Rigid legal rules are ill-suited to an area of such diversity. * * *

Moreover, the "two-pronged test" directs analysis into two largely independent channels—the informant's "veracity" or "reliability" and his "basis of knowledge." There are persuasive arguments against according these two elements such independent status. Instead, they are better understood as relevant considerations in the totality of circumstances analysis that traditionally has guided probable cause determinations: a deficiency in one may be compensated for, in determining the overall reliability of a tip, by a strong showing as to the other, or by some other indicia of reliability. * * * Unlike a totality of circumstances analysis, which permits a balanced assessment of the relative weights of all the various indicia of reliability (and unreliability) attending an informant's tip, the "two-pronged test" has encouraged an excessively technical dissection of informants' tips, with undue attention being focused on isolated issues that cannot sensibly be divorced from the other facts presented to the magistrate.

* * *

We * * * have recognized that affidavits "are normally drafted by nonlawyers in the midst and haste of a criminal investigation. Technical requirements of elaborate specificity once exacted under common law pleading have no proper place in this area." Likewise, search and arrest warrants long have been issued by persons who are neither lawyers nor judges, and who certainly do not remain abreast of each judicial refinement of the nature of "probable cause." The rigorous inquiry into the *Spinelli* prongs and the complex superstructure of evidentiary and analytical rules that some have seen implicit in our *Spinelli* decision, cannot be reconciled with the fact that many warrants are—quite properly—issued on the basis of nontechnical, commonsense judgments of laymen applying a standard less demanding than those used in more formal legal proceedings. Likewise, given the informal, often hurried context in which it must be applied, the "built-in subtleties," of the "two-pronged test" are particularly unlikely to assist magistrates in determining probable cause.

Similarly, we have repeatedly said that after-the-fact scrutiny by courts of the sufficiency of an affidavit should not take the form of *de novo* review. A magistrate's "determination of probable cause should be paid great deference by reviewing courts."

If the affidavits submitted by police officers are subjected to the type of scrutiny some courts have deemed appropriate, police might well resort to warrantless searches, with the hope of relying on consent or some other exception to the warrant clause that might develop at the time of the search. * * * Reflecting this preference for the warrant process, the traditional standard for review of an issuing magistrate's probable cause determination has been that so long as the magistrate had a "substantial basis for ... conclud[ing]" that a search would uncover evidence of wrongdoing, the Fourth Amendment requires no more. Jones v. United States, 362 U.S. 257, 271, 80 S.Ct. 725, 736, 4 L.Ed.2d 697 (1960). We think reaffirmation of this standard better serves the purpose of encouraging recourse to the warrant procedure and is more consistent with our traditional deference to the probable cause determinations of magistrates than is the "two-pronged test."

Finally, the direction taken by decisions following *Spinelli* poorly serves "the most basic function of any government": "to provide for the security of the individual and of his property." The strictures that inevitably accompany the "two-pronged test" cannot avoid seriously impeding the task of law enforcement. If, as the Illinois Supreme Court apparently thought, that test must be rigorously applied in every case, anonymous tips seldom would be of greatly diminished value in police work. Ordinary citizens, like ordinary witnesses, generally do not provide extensive recitations of the basis of their everyday observations. Likewise, as the Illinois Supreme Court observed in this case, the veracity of persons supplying anonymous tips is by hypothesis largely unknown, and unknowable. As a result, anonymous tips seldom could survive a rigorous application of either of the *Spinelli* prongs. Yet, such tips, particularly when supplemented by independent police investigation, frequently contribute to the solution of otherwise "perfect crimes." While a conscientious assessment of the basis for crediting such tips is required by the Fourth Amendment, a standard that leaves virtually no place for anonymous citizen informants is not.

For all these reasons, we conclude that it is wiser to abandon the "two-pronged test" established by our decisions in *Aguilar* and *Spinelli*.[1] In its place we reaffirm the totality of the circumstances analysis that traditionally has informed probable cause determinations. The task of the issuing magistrate is simply to make a practical, common-sense decision whether, given all the circumstances set forth in the affidavit before him, including the "veracity" and "basis of knowledge" of persons supplying hearsay information, there is a fair probability that contraband or evidence of a crime will be found in a particular place. And the duty of a reviewing court is simply to ensure that the magistrate had a "substantial basis for * * * conclud[ing]" that probable cause existed. We are convinced that this flexible, easily applied standard will better achieve the accommodation of public and private interests that the Fourth Amendment requires than does the approach that has developed from *Aguilar* and *Spinelli*.

Our earlier cases illustrate the limits beyond which a magistrate may not venture in issuing a warrant. A sworn statement of an affiant that "he has cause to suspect and does believe that" liquor illegally brought into the United States is located on certain premises will not do. Nathanson v. United States, 290 U.S. 41, 54 S.Ct. 11, 78 L.Ed. 159 (1933). An affidavit must provide the magistrate with a substantial basis for determining the existence of probable cause, and the wholly conclusory statement at issue in *Nathanson* failed to meet this requirement. An officer's statement that "affiants have received reliable information from a credible person and believe" that heroin is stored in a home, is likewise inadequate. Aguilar v. Texas, 378 U.S. 108, 84 S.Ct. 1509, 12 L.Ed.2d 723 (1964). As in *Nathanson*, this is a mere conclusory statement that gives the magistrate virtually no basis at all for making a judgment regarding probable cause. Sufficient information must be presented to the magistrate to allow that official to determine probable cause; his action cannot be a mere ratification of the bare conclusions of others. In order to ensure that such an abdication of the magistrate's duty does not occur, courts must continue to conscientiously review the sufficiency of affidavits on which warrants are issued. But when

---

1. * * *

Whether the allegations submitted to the magistrate in *Spinelli* would, under the view we now take, have supported a finding of probable cause, we think it would not be profitable to decide. There are so many variables in the probable cause equation that one determination will seldom be a useful "prece-dent" for another. Suffice it to say that while we in no way abandon *Spinelli's* concern for the trustworthiness of informers and for the principle that it is the magistrate who must ultimately make a finding of probable cause, we reject the rigid categorization suggested by some of its language.

we move beyond the "bare bones" affidavits present in cases such as *Nathanson* and *Aguilar,* this area simply does not lend itself to a prescribed set of rules, like that which had developed from *Spinelli.* Instead, the flexible, commonsense standard * * * better serves the purposes of the Fourth Amendment's probable cause requirement.

* * *

IV

Our decisions applying the totality of circumstances analysis outlined above have consistently recognized the value of corroboration of details of an informant's tip by independent police work. * * *

Our decision in Draper v. United States, 358 U.S. 307, 79 S.Ct. 329, 3 L.Ed.2d 327 (1959), however, is the classic case on the value of corroborative efforts of police officials. There, an informant named Hereford reported that Draper would arrive in Denver on a train from Chicago on one of two days, and that he would be carrying a quantity of heroin. The informant also supplied a fairly detailed physical description of Draper, and predicted that he would be wearing a light colored raincoat, brown slacks and black shoes, and would be walking "real fast." Hereford gave no indication of the basis for his information.

On one of the stated dates police officers observed a man matching this description exit a train arriving from Chicago; his attire and luggage matched Hereford's report and he was walking rapidly. We explained in *Draper* that, by this point in his investigation, the arresting officer "had personally verified every facet of the information given him by Hereford except whether petitioner had accomplished his mission and had the three ounces of heroin on his person or in his bag. And surely, with every other bit of Hereford's information being thus personally verified, [the officer] had 'reasonable grounds' to believe that the remaining unverified bit of Hereford's information—that Draper would have the heroin with him—was likewise true."

The showing of probable cause in the present case was fully as compelling as that in *Draper.* Even standing alone, the facts obtained through the independent investigation of Mader and the DEA at least suggested that the Gates were involved in drug trafficking. In addition to being a popular vacation site, Florida is well-known as a source of narcotics and other illegal drugs. Lance Gates' flight to Palm Beach, his brief, overnight stay in a motel, and apparent immediate return north to Chicago in the family car, conveniently awaiting him in West Palm Beach, is as suggestive of a prearranged drug run, as it is of an ordinary vacation trip.

In addition, the magistrate could rely on the anonymous letter, which had been corroborated in major part by Mader's efforts—just as had occurred in *Draper.* The Supreme Court of Illinois reasoned that *Draper* involved an informant who had given reliable information on previous occasions, while the honesty and reliability of the anonymous informant in this case were unknown to the Bloomingdale police. While this distinction might be an apt one at the time the police department received the anonymous letter, it became far less significant after Mader's independent investigative work occurred. The corroboration of the letter's predictions that the Gates' car would be in Florida, that Lance Gates would fly to Florida in the next day or so, and that he would drive the car north toward Bloomingdale all indicated, albeit not with certainty, that the informant's other assertions also were true. "Because an informant is right about some things, he is more probably right about other facts,"—including the claim regarding the Gates' illegal activity. This may well not be the type of "reliability" or "veracity" necessary to satisfy some views of the "veracity prong" of *Spinelli,* but we think it suffices for the practical, commonsense judgment called for in making a probable cause determination. It is enough, for purposes of assessing probable cause, that "corroboration through other sources of information reduced the chances of a reckless or prevaricating tale," thus providing "a substantial basis for crediting the hearsay."

Finally, the anonymous letter contained a range of details relating not just to easily obtained facts and conditions existing at the time of the tip, but to future actions of third parties ordinarily not easily predicted. The letter writer's accurate information as to the travel plans of each of the Gates was of a character likely obtained only from the Gates themselves, or from someone familiar with their not entirely ordinary travel plans. If the informant had access to accurate information of this type a magistrate could properly conclude that it was not unlikely that he also had access to reliable information of the Gates' alleged illegal activities.[2] Of course, the Gates' travel plans might have been learned from a talkative neighbor or travel agent; under the "two-pronged test" developed from *Spinelli,* the character of the details in the anonymous letter might well not permit a sufficiently clear inference regarding the letter writer's "basis of knowledge." But, as discussed previously, probable cause does not demand the certainty we associate with formal trials. It is enough that there was a fair probability that the writer of the anonymous letter had obtained his entire

---

2. The dissent seizes on one inaccuracy in the anonymous informant's letter—its statement that Sue Gates would fly from Florida to Illinois, when in fact she drove—and argues that the probative value of the entire tip was undermined by this allegedly "material mistake." We have never required that informants used by the police be infallible, and can see no reason to impose such a requirement in this case. Probable cause, particularly when police have obtained a warrant, simply does not require the perfection the dissent finds necessary.

Likewise, there is no force to the dissent's argument that the Gates' action in leaving their home unguarded undercut the informant's claim that drugs were hidden there. Indeed, the line-by-line scrutiny that the dissent applies to the anonymous letter is akin to that we find inappropriate in reviewing magistrate's decisions. The dissent apparently attributes to the magistrate who issued the warrant in this case the rather implausible notion that persons dealing in drugs always stay at home, apparently out of fear that to leave might risk intrusion by criminals. If accurate, one could not help sympathizing with the self-imposed isolation of people so situated. In reality, however, it is scarcely likely that the magistrate ever thought that the anonymous tip "kept one spouse" at home, much less that he relied on the theory advanced by the dissent. The letter simply says that Sue would fly from Florida to Illinois, without indicating whether the Gates made the bitter choice of leaving the drugs in their house, or those in their car, unguarded. The magistrate's determination that there might be drugs or evidence of criminal activity in the Gates' home was well-supported by the less speculative theory, noted in text, that if the informant could predict with considerable accuracy the somewhat unusual travel plans of the Gates, he probably also had a reliable basis for his statements that the Gates kept a large quantity of drugs in their home and frequently were visited by other drug traffickers there.

story either from the Gates or someone they trusted. And corroboration of major portions of the letter's predictions provides just this probability. It is apparent, therefore, that the judge issuing the warrant had a "substantial basis for ... conclud[ing]" that probable cause to search the Gates' home and car existed. The judgment of the Supreme Court of Illinois therefore must be

Reversed.

■ JUSTICE BRENNAN, with whom JUSTICE MARSHALL joins, dissenting.

Although I join Justice Stevens' dissenting opinion and agree with him that the warrant is invalid even under the Court's newly announced "totality of the circumstances" test, I write separately to dissent from the Court's unjustified and ill-advised rejection of the two-prong test for evaluating the validity of a warrant based on hearsay announced in Aguilar v. Texas, 378 U.S. 108, 84 S.Ct. 1509, 12 L.Ed.2d 723 (1964), and refined in Spinelli v. United States, 393 U.S. 410, 89 S.Ct. 584, 21 L.Ed.2d 637 (1969).

* * *

Although the rules drawn from the [Aguilar–Spinelli line of cases] are cast in procedural terms, they advance an important underlying substantive value: Findings of probable cause, and attendant intrusions, should not be authorized unless there is some assurance that the information on which they are based has been obtained in a reliable way by an honest or credible person. As applied to police officers, the rules focus on the way in which the information was acquired. As applied to informants, the rules focus both on the honesty or credibility of the informant and on the reliability of the way in which the information was acquired. Insofar as it is more complicated, an evaluation of affidavits based on hearsay involves a more difficult inquiry. This suggests a need to structure the inquiry in an effort to insure greater accuracy. The standards announced in Aguilar, as refined by Spinelli, fulfill that need. The standards inform the police of what information they have to provide and magistrates of what information they should demand. The standards also inform magistrates of the subsidiary findings they must make in order to arrive at an ultimate finding of probable cause. Spinelli, properly understood, directs the magistrate's attention to the possibility that the presence of self-verifying detail might satisfy Aguilar's basis of knowledge prong and that corroboration of the details of a tip might satisfy Aguilar's veracity prong. By requiring police to provide certain crucial information to magistrates and by structuring magistrates' probable cause inquiries, Aguilar and Spinelli assure the magistrate's role as an independent arbiter of probable cause, insure greater accuracy in probable cause determinations, and advance the substantive value identified above.

* * *

■ JUSTICE STEVENS, with whom JUSTICE BRENNAN joins, dissenting.

The fact that Lance and Sue Gates made a 22hour nonstop drive from West Palm Beach, Florida, to Bloomingdale, Illinois, only a few hours after Lance had flown to Florida provided persuasive evidence that they were engaged in illicit activity. That fact, however, was not known to the magistrate when he issued the warrant to search their home.

What the magistrate did know at that time was that the anonymous informant had not been completely accurate in his or her predictions. The informant had indicated that "Sue drives their car to Florida *where she leaves it to be loaded up with drugs. . . . Sue flies back after she drops the car off in Florida.*" (emphasis added). Yet Detective Mader's affidavit reported that she "left the West Palm Beach area driving the Mercury northbound."

The discrepancy between the informant's predictions and the facts known to Detective Mader is significant for three reasons. First, it cast doubt on the informant's hypothesis that the Gates already had "over $100,000 worth of drugs in their basement." The informant had predicted an itinerary that always kept one spouse in Bloomingdale, suggesting that the Gates did not want to leave their home unguarded because something valuable was hidden within. That inference obviously could not be drawn when it was known that the pair was actually together over a thousand miles from home.

Second, the discrepancy made the Gates' conduct seem substantially less unusual than the informant had predicted it would be. It would have been odd if, as predicted, Sue had driven down to Florida on Wednesday, left the car, and flown right back to Illinois. But the mere facts that Sue was in West Palm Beach with the car, that she was joined by her husband at the Holiday Inn on Friday, and that the couple drove north together the next morning are neither unusual nor probative of criminal activity.

Third, the fact that the anonymous letter contained a material mistake undermines the reasonableness of relying on it as a basis for making a forcible entry into a private home.

Of course, the activities in this case did not stop when the magistrate issued the warrant. The Gates drove all night to Bloomingdale, the officers searched the car and found 400 pounds of marijuana, and then they searched the house. However, none of these subsequent events may be considered in evaluating the warrant, and the search of the house was legal only if the warrant was valid. I cannot accept the Court's casual conclusion that, *before the Gates arrived in Bloomingdale,* there was probable cause to justify a valid entry and search of a private home. No one knows who the informant in this case was, or what motivated him or her to write the note. Given that the note's predictions were faulty in one significant respect, and were corroborated by nothing except ordinary innocent activity, I must surmise that the Court's evaluation of the warrant's validity has been colored by subsequent events.

* * *

NOTE: ASSERTIONS OF LAW ENFORCEMENT "KNOWLEDGE"

In *Spinelli,* the affidavit recited the suspect "is known to this affiant and to federal law enforcement agents and local law enforcement agents as a bookmaker, an associate of bookmakers, a gambler, and an associate of gamblers." In considering whether the affidavit supported the magistrate's determination that probable cause existed, the Court commented that his allegation "is but a bald and unilluminating assertion of suspicion that is entitled to no weight in appraising the magistrate's decision."

In United States v. Harris, 403 U.S. 573, 91 S.Ct. 2075, 29 L.Ed.2d 723 (1971), the affidavit recited that the suspect "has had a reputation with me for over four years as being a trafficker of nontax-paid distilled spirits * * *." There was no opinion of the Court; the judgment of the Court was announced in an opinion by the Chief Justice. In a portion of that opinion joined by two other members of the Court, he considered the significance of this allegation in the warrant affidavit:

> We cannot conclude that a policeman's knowledge of a suspect's reputation—something that policemen frequently know * * *—is not a "practical consideration of everyday life" upon which an officer (or a magistrate) may properly rely in assessing the reliability of an informant's tip. To the extent that *Spinelli* prohibits the use of such probative information, it has no support in our prior cases, logic, or experience and we decline to apply it to preclude a magistrate from relying on a law enforcement officer's knowledge of a suspect's reputation.

403 U.S. at 583, 91 S.Ct. at 2081–82, 29 L.Ed.2d at 733 (opinion of Burger, C.J., announcing the judgment of the Court).

2.   CHALLENGING FACTUAL STATEMENTS IN THE AFFIDAVIT

Prior to the principal case in this subsection, many courts took the position that whether there was probable cause for issuance of an arrest or search warrant could be determined only from the face of the affidavit or complaint. The facts alleged were to be accepted as true and the sole question for debate was whether they established probable cause. To some extent, this position—barring defendants from attacking the "face" of a warrant affidavit—was based on the perception that the appropriate inquiry was whether the magistrate had probable cause to issue the warrant. If the magistrate had probable cause, no significance was attached to the fact the officer who applied for the warrant may not have had probable cause justifying a request for a warrant.

The principal case in this subsection requires defendants, to some extent, be permitted to challenge the accuracy of the facts in a warrant affidavit. Consider separately (although not necessarily in this order) what facts a defendant must establish to prevail on a challenge of this sort and what a defendant must do in order to have a factual hearing where he can establish those facts.

Franks v. Delaware

Supreme Court of the United States, 1978.
438 U.S. 154, 98 S.Ct. 2674, 57 L.Ed.2d 667.

■ MR. JUSTICE BLACKMUN delivered the opinion of the Court.

This case presents an important and longstanding issue of Fourth Amendment law. Does a defendant in a criminal proceeding ever have the right, under the Fourth and Fourteenth Amendments, subsequent to the *ex parte* issuance of a search warrant, to challenge the truthfulness of factual statements made in an affidavit supporting the warrant?

In the present case the Supreme Court of Delaware held, as a matter of first impression for it, that a defendant under *no* circumstances may so challenge the veracity of a sworn statement used by police to procure a search warrant. We reverse, and we hold that, where the defendant makes a substantial preliminary showing that a false statement knowingly and intentionally, or with reckless disregard for the truth, was included by the affiant in the warrant affidavit, and if the allegedly false statement is necessary to the finding of probable cause, the Fourth Amendment requires that a hearing be held at the defendant's request. In the event that at that hearing the allegation of perjury or reckless disregard is established by the defendant by a preponderance of the evidence, and, with the affidavit's false material set to one side, the affidavit's remaining content is insufficient to establish probable cause, the search warrant must be voided and the fruits of the search excluded to the same extent as if probable cause was lacking on the face of the affidavit.

I.

The controversy over the veracity of the search warrant affidavit in this case arose in connection with petitioner Jerome Franks' state conviction for rape, kidnapping, and burglary. On Friday, March 5, 1976, Mrs. Cynthia Bailey told police in Dover, Delaware, that she had been confronted in her home earlier that morning by a man with a knife, and that he had sexually assaulted her. She described her assailant's age, race, height, build, and facial hair, and gave a detailed description of his clothing as consisting of a white thermal undershirt, black pants with a silver or gold buckle, a brown leather three-quarter length coat, and a dark knit cap that he wore pulled down around his eyes.

That same day, petitioner Franks coincidentally was taken into custody for an assault involving a 15-year-old girl, Brenda B. _____, six days earlier. After his formal arrest, and while awaiting a bail hearing in Family Court, petitioner allegedly stated to Robert McClements, the youth officer accompanying him, that he was surprised the bail hearing was "about Brenda B. _____. I know her. I thought you said Bailey. I don't know her." At the time of this statement, the police allegedly had not yet recited to petitioner his rights under Miranda v. Arizona, 384 U.S. 436, 86 S.Ct. 1602, 16 L.Ed.2d 694 (1966).

On the following Monday, March 8, officer McClements happened to mention the courthouse incident to a detective, Ronald R. Brooks, who was working on the Bailey case. On March 9, detective Brooks and detective Larry D. Gray submitted a sworn affidavit to a justice of the peace in Dover, in support of a warrant to search petitioner's apartment.[3] In paragraph 8 of the affidavit's "probable cause page" mention was made of petitioner's statement to McClements. In paragraph 10, it was noted that the description of the assailant given to the police by Mrs. Bailey included the abovementioned clothing. Finally, the affidavit also described the

---

3.   The affidavit is reproduced as Appendix A of this opinion.

attempt made by police to confirm that petitioner's typical outfit matched that of the assailant. Paragraph 15 recited: "On Tuesday, 3/9/76, your affiant contacted Mr. James Williams and Mr. Wesley Lucas of the Delaware Youth Center where Jerome Franks is employed and did have personal conversation with both these people." Paragraphs 16 and 17 respectively stated: "Mr. James Williams revealed to your affiant that the normal dress of Jerome Franks does consist of a white knit thermal undershirt and a brown leather jacket," and "Mr. Wesley Lucas revealed to your affiant that in addition to the thermal undershirt and jacket, Jerome Franks often wears a large green knit hat."

The warrant was issued on the basis of this affidavit. Pursuant to the warrant, police searched petitioner's apartment and found a white thermal undershirt, a knit hat, dark pants, and a leather jacket, and, on petitioner's kitchen table, a single-blade knife. All these ultimately were introduced in evidence at trial.

Prior to the trial, however, petitioner's counsel filed a written motion to suppress the clothing and the knife found in the search; this motion alleged that the warrant on its face did not show probable cause and that the search and seizure were in violation of the Fourth and Fourteenth Amendments. At the hearing on the motion to suppress, defense counsel orally amended the challenge to include an attack on the veracity of the warrant affidavit; he also specifically requested the right to call as witnesses detective Brooks, Wesley Lucas of the Youth Center, and James D. Morrison, formerly of the Youth Center.[4] Counsel asserted that Lucas and Morrison would testify that neither had been personally interviewed by the warrant affiants, and that, although they might have talked to another police officer, any information given by them to that officer was "somewhat different" from what was recited in the affidavit. Defense counsel charged that the misstatements were included in the affidavit not inadvertently, but in "bad faith." * * *

In rebuttal, the State's attorney argued in detail (a) that [Delaware law] contemplated that any challenge to a search warrant was to be limited to questions of sufficiency based on the face of the affidavit; [and] (b) that, purportedly, a majority of the States whose practice was not dictated by statute observed such a rule * * *. * * * The State objected to petitioner's "going behind [the warrant affidavit] in any way," and argued that the court must decide petitioner's motion "on the four corners" of the affidavit.

The trial court sustained the State's objection to petitioner's proposed evidence. The motion to suppress was denied, and the clothing and knife were admitted as evidence at the ensuing trial. Petitioner was convicted

---

4. The references in paragraphs 15 and 16 of the warrant affidavit's probable cause page to "James Williams" appear to have been intended as references to James D. Morrison, who was petitioner's supervisor at the Youth Center. This misapprehension on the part of the State continued until shortly before trial. Eleven days prior to trial, the prosecution requested the clerk of the Kent County Superior Court to summon "James Williams, Delaware Youth Center," for petitioner's trial. In his return on the summons, Record Document No. 15, the Kent County sheriff stated that he "[s]erved the within summons upon * * * James Williams (Morrison)." The summons actually delivered was made out in the name of James Morrison.

[and] sentenced to two consecutive terms of 25 years each and an additional consecutive life sentence.

On appeal, the Supreme Court of Delaware affirmed. It agreed with what it deemed to be the "majority rule" that no attack upon the veracity of a warrant affidavit could be made:

> "We agree with the majority rule for two reasons. First, it is the function of the issuing magistrate to determine the reliability of information and credibility of affiants in deciding whether the requirement of probable cause has been met. There has been no need demonstrated for interfering with this function. Second, neither the probable cause nor suppression hearings are adjudications of guilt or innocence; the matters asserted by defendant are more properly considered in a trial on the merits."

Because of this resolution, the Delaware Supreme Court noted that there was no need to consider petitioner's "other contentions, relating to the evidence that would have been introduced for impeachment purposes."

Franks' petition for certiorari presented only the issue whether the trial court had erred in refusing to consider his allegation of misrepresentation in the warrant affidavit. Because of the importance of the question, and because of the conflict among both state and federal courts, we granted certiorari.

II.

* * *

Respondent * * * suggests that any error here was harmless. Assuming, *arguendo*, respondent says, that petitioner's Fourth Amendment claim was valid, and that the warrant should have been tested for veracity and the evidence excluded, it is still clear beyond a reasonable doubt that the evidence complained of did not contribute to petitioner's conviction. This contention falls of its own weight. The sole issue at trial was that of consent. Petitioner admitted that he had engaged in sexual relations with Mrs. Bailey on the day in question. She testified that she had not consented to this, and that petitioner, upon first encountering her in the house, had threatened her with a knife to force her to submit. Petitioner claimed that she had given full consent and that no knife had been present. To corroborate its contention that consent was lacking, the State introduced in evidence a stainless steel wooden-handled kitchen knife found by the detectives on the kitchen table in petitioner's apartment four days after the alleged rape. Defense counsel objected to its admission, arguing that Mrs. Bailey had not given any detailed description of the knife alleged to be involved in the incident and had claimed to have seen the knife only in "pitch blackness." The State obtained its admission, however, as a knife that matched the description contained in the search warrant, and Mrs. Bailey testified that the knife allegedly used was, like the knife in evidence, single-edged and not a pocket knife, and that the knife in evidence was the same length and thickness as the knife used in the crime. The State carefully elicited from detective Brooks the fact that this was the only knife found in petitioner's apartment. Although respondent argues that the knife was presented to the jury as "merely exemplary of the generic class of weapon testimonially described by the victim," the State at trial clearly meant to suggest that this was the knife that had been used against Mrs. Bailey. Had the warrant been quashed, and the knife excluded from the trial as evidence, we cannot say with any assurance that the jury would have reached the same decision on the issue of consent, particularly since there was other countervailing evidence on that issue.

* * *

III.

Whether the Fourth and Fourteenth Amendments, and the derivative exclusionary rule made applicable to the States under Mapp v. Ohio, 367 U.S. 643, 81 S.Ct. 1684, 6 L.Ed.2d 1081 (1961), ever mandate that a defendant be permitted to attack the veracity of a warrant affidavit after the warrant has been issued and executed, is a question that encounters conflicting values. The bulwark of Fourth Amendment protection, of course, is the Warrant Clause, requiring that, absent certain exceptions, police obtain a warrant from a neutral and disinterested magistrate before embarking upon a search. In deciding today, that, in certain circumstances, a challenge to a warrant's veracity must be permitted, we derive our ground from language of the Warrant Clause itself, which surely takes the affiant's good faith as its premise: "[N]o warrants shall issue, but upon probable cause, supported by Oath or affirmation * * * ." Judge Frankel, in United States v. Halsey, 257 F.Supp. 1002, 1005 (S.D.N.Y.1966), aff'd, Docket No. 31369 (CA2, June 12, 1967) (unreported), put the matter simply: "[W]hen the Fourth Amendment demands a factual showing sufficient to comprise 'probable cause,' the obvious assumption is that there will be a *truthful* showing" (emphasis in original). This does not mean "truthful" in the sense that every fact recited in the warrant affidavit is necessarily correct, for probable cause may be founded upon hearsay and upon information received from informants, as well as upon information within the affiant's own knowledge that sometimes must be garnered hastily. But surely it is to be "truthful" in the sense that the information put forth is believed or appropriately accepted by the affiant as true. It is established law that a warrant affidavit must set forth particular facts and circumstances underlying the existence of probable cause, so as to allow the magistrate to make an independent evaluation of the matter. If an informant's tip is the source of information, the affidavit must recite "some of the underlying circumstances from which the informant concluded" that relevant evidence might be discovered, and "some of the underlying circumstances from which the officer concluded that the informant, whose identity need not be disclosed, * * * was 'credible' or his information 'reliable.'" Because it is the magistrate who must determine independently whether there is probable cause, it would be an unthinkable imposition upon his authority if a warrant affidavit, revealed after the fact to contain a deliberately or recklessly false statement, were to stand beyond impeachment.

In saying this, however, one must give cognizance to competing values that lead us to impose limitations. They perhaps can best be addressed by noting the arguments of respondent and others against allowing veracity challenges. The arguments are several:

First, respondent argues that the exclusionary rule is not a personal constitutional right, but only a judicially created remedy extended where its benefit as a deterrent promises to outweigh the societal cost of its use. * * * Respondent argues that applying the exclusionary rule to another situation—the deterrence of deliberate or reckless untruthfulness in a warrant affidavit—is not justified * * * [because] interfering with a criminal conviction in order to deter official misconduct is a burden too great to impose on society.

Second, respondent argues that a citizen's privacy interests are adequately protected by a requirement that applicants for a warrant submit a sworn affidavit and by the magistrate's independent determination of sufficiency based on the face of the affidavit. Applying the exclusionary rule to attacks upon veracity would weed out a minimal number of perjurious government statements, says respondent, but would overlap unnecessarily with existing penalties against perjury, including criminal prosecutions, departmental discipline for misconduct, contempt of court, and civil actions.

Third, it is argued that the magistrate already is equipped to conduct a fairly vigorous inquiry into the accuracy of the factual affidavit supporting a warrant application. He may question the affiant, or summon other persons to give testimony at the warrant proceeding. The incremental gain from a post-search adversary proceeding, it is said, would not be great.

Fourth, it is argued that it would unwisely diminish the solemnity and moment of the magistrate's proceeding to make his inquiry into probable cause reviewable in regard to veracity. The less final, and less deference paid to, the magistrate's determination of veracity, the less initiative will he use in that task. Denigration of the magistrate's function would be imprudent insofar as his scrutiny is the last bulwark preventing any particular invasion of privacy before it happens.

Fifth, it is argued that permitting a post-search evidentiary hearing on issues of veracity would confuse the pressing issue of guilt or innocence with the collateral question as to whether there had been official misconduct in the drafting of the affidavit. The weight of criminal dockets, and the need to prevent diversion of attention from the main issue of guilt or innocence, militate against such an added burden on the trial courts. And if such hearings were conducted routinely, it is said, they would be misused by defendants as a convenient source of discovery. Defendants might even use the hearings in an attempt to force revelation of the identity of informants.

Sixth and finally, it is argued that a post-search veracity challenge is inappropriate because the accuracy of an affidavit in large part is beyond the control of the affiant. An affidavit may properly be based on hearsay, on fleeting observations, and on tips received from unnamed informants whose identity often will be properly protected from revelation under McCray v. Illinois, 386 U.S. 300, 87 S.Ct. 1056, 18 L.Ed.2d 62 (1967).

None of these considerations is trivial. Indeed, because of them, the rule announced today has a limited scope, both in regard to when exclusion of the seized evidence is mandated, and when a hearing on allegations of misstatements must be accorded. But neither do the considerations cited by respondent and others have a fully controlling weight; we conclude that they are insufficient to justify an *absolute* ban on post-search impeachment of veracity. On this side of the balance, also, there are pressing considerations:

First, a flat ban on impeachment of veracity could denude the probable cause requirement of all real meaning. The requirement that a warrant not issue "but upon probable cause, supported by Oath or affirmation," would be reduced to a nullity if a police officer was able to use deliberately falsified allegations to demonstrate probable cause, and, having misled the magistrate, then was able to remain confident that the ploy was worthwhile. It is this specter of intentional falsification that, we think, has evoked such widespread opposition to the flat nonimpeachment rule * * *. On occasion, of course, an instance of deliberate falsity will be exposed and confirmed without a special inquiry either at trial, or at a hearing on the sufficiency of the affidavit. A flat nonimpeachment rule would bar reexamination of the warrant even in these cases.

Second, the hearing before the magistrate not always will suffice to discourage lawless or reckless misconduct. The pre-search proceeding is necessarily *ex parte*, since the subject of the search cannot be tipped off to the application for a warrant lest he destroy or remove evidence. The usual reliance of our legal system on adversary proceedings itself should be an indication that an *ex parte* inquiry is likely to be less vigorous. The magistrate has no acquaintance with the information that may contradict the good faith and reasonable basis of the affiant's allegations. The pre-search proceeding will frequently be marked by haste, because of the understandable desire to act before the evidence disappears; this urgency will not always permit the magistrate to make an extended independent examination of the affiant or other witnesses.

Third, the alternative sanctions of a perjury prosecution, administrative discipline, contempt, or a civil suit are not likely to fill the gap. Mapp v. Ohio, supra, implicitly rejected the adequacy of these alternatives. * * *

Fourth, allowing an evidentiary hearing, after a suitable preliminary proffer of material falsity, would not diminish the importance and solemnity of the warrant-issuing process. It is the *ex parte* nature of the initial hearing, rather than the magistrate's capacity, that is the reason for the review. A magistrate's determination is presently subject to review before trial as to *sufficiency* without any undue interference with the dignity of the magistrate's function. Our reluctance today to extend the rule of exclusion beyond instances of deliberate misstatements, and those of reckless disregard, leaves a broad field where the magistrate is the sole protection of a citizen's Fourth Amendment rights, namely, in instances where police have been merely negligent in checking or recording the facts relevant to a probable cause determination.

Fifth, the claim that a post-search hearing will confuse the issue of the defendant's guilt with the issue of the State's possible misbehavior is footless. The hearing will not be in the presence of the jury. An issue extraneous to guilt already is examined in any probable cause determination or review of probable cause. Nor, if a sensible threshold showing is required and sensible substantive requirements for suppression are maintained, need there be any new large-scale commitment of judicial resources; many claims will wash out at an early stage, and the more substantial ones in any event would require judicial resources for vindication if the suggested alternative sanctions were truly to be effective. The requirement of a substantial preliminary showing should suffice to prevent the misuse of a veracity hearing for purposes of discovery or obstruction. And because we are faced today with only the question of the integrity of the affiant's representations as to his own activities, we need not decide, and we in no way predetermine, the difficult question whether a reviewing court must ever require the revelation of the identity of an informant once a substantial preliminary showing of falsity has been made. McCray v. Illinois, the Court's earlier disquisition in this area, concluded only that the Due Process Clause of the Fourteenth Amendment did not require the State to expose an informant's identity routinely, upon a defendant's mere demand, when there was ample evidence in the probable cause hearing to show that the informant was reliable and his information credible.

Sixth and finally, as to the argument that the exclusionary rule should not be extended to a "new" area, we cannot regard any such extension really to be at issue here. Despite the deep skepticism of Members of this Court as to the wisdom of extending the exclusionary rule to collateral areas, such as civil or grand jury proceedings, the Court has not questioned, in the absence of a more efficacious sanction, the continued application of the rule to suppress evidence from the State's case where a Fourth Amendment violation has been substantial and deliberate. We see no principled basis for distinguishing between the question of the sufficiency of an affidavit, which also is subject to a post-search reexamination, and the question of its integrity.

IV.

In sum, and to repeat with some embellishment what we stated at the beginning of this opinion: There is, of course, a presumption of validity with respect to the affidavit supporting the search warrant. To mandate an evidentiary hearing, the challenger's attack must be more than conclusory and must be supported by more than a mere desire to cross-examine. There must be allegations of deliberate falsehood or of reckless disregard for the truth, and those allegations must be accompanied by an offer of proof. They should point out specifically the portion of the warrant affidavit that is claimed to be false; and they should be accompanied by a statement of supporting reasons. Affidavits or sworn or otherwise reliable statements of witnesses should be furnished, or their absence satisfactorily explained. Allegations of negligence or innocent mistake are insufficient. The deliberate falsity or reckless disregard whose impeachment is permitted today is only that of the affiant, not of any nongovernmental informant. Finally, if these requirements are met, and if, when material that is the subject of the alleged falsity or reckless disregard is set to one side, there remains sufficient content in the warrant affidavit to support a finding of probable cause, no hearing is required. On the other hand, if the remaining content is insufficient, the defendant is entitled, under the Fourth Amendment, to his hearing. Whether he will prevail at that hearing is, of course, another issue.

Because of Delaware's absolute rule, its courts did not have occasion to consider the proffer put forward by petitioner Franks. Since the framing of suitable rules to govern proffers is a matter properly left to the States, we decline ourselves to pass on petitioner's proffer. The judgment of the Supreme Court of Delaware is reversed, and the case is remanded for further proceedings not inconsistent with this opinion.

It is so ordered.

APPENDIX A TO OPINION OF THE COURT

J.P.Court #7

IN THE MATTER OF: Jerome Franks, B/M, DOB: 10/9/54 and 222 S. Governors Ave., Apt. #3, Dover, Delaware. A two room apartment located on the South side, second floor, of a white block building on the west side of S. Governors Avenue, between Loockerman Street and North Street, in the City of Dover. The ground floor of this building houses Wayman's Barber Shop.

STATE OF DELAWARE

ss:

COUNTY OF KENT

Be it remembered that on this 9th day of March A.D. 1976 before me John Green, personally appeared Det. Ronald R. Brooks and Det. Larry Gray of the Dover Police Department who being by me duly sworn depose and say:

That they have reason to believe and do believe that in the 222 S. Governors Avenue, Apartment #3, Dover, Delaware. A two room apartment located on the South side second floor of a white block building on the west side of S. Governors Avenue between Loockerman Street and North Street in the City of Dover. The ground floor of this building houses Wayman's Barber Shop the occupant of which is Jerome Franks. There has been and/or there is now located and/or concealed certain property in said house, place, conveyance and/or on the person or persons of the occupants thereof, consisting of property, papers, articles, or things which are the instruments of criminal offense, and/or obtained in the commission of a crime, and/or designated to be used in the commission of a crime, and not reasonably calculated to be used for any other purpose and/or the possession of which is unlawful, papers, articles, or things which are of an evidentiary nature pertaining to the commission of a crime or crimes specified therein and in particular, a white knit thermal undershirt; a brown ¾ length leather jacket with a tie-belt; a pair of black mens pants; a dark colored knit hat; a long thin bladed knife or other instruments or items relating to the crime.

Articles, or things were, are, or will be possessed and/or used in violation of Title 11, Sub-Chapter D, Section 763, Delaware Code in that [See attached probable cause page].

Wherefore, affiants pray that a search warrant may be issued authorizing a search of the aforesaid 222 S. Governors Avenue, Apartment #3, Dover, Delaware. A two room apartment located on the south side second floor of a white block building on the west side of S. Governors Avenue between Loockerman St. and North Street, in the City of Dover in the manner provided by law.

/s/ Det. Ronald R. Brooks

Affiant

/s/ Det. Larry D. Gray

Affiant

Sworn to (or affirmed) and subscribed before me this 9th day of March A.D. 1976.

/s/ John [illegible] Green

Judge Ct 7

The facts tending to establish probable cause for the issuance of this search warrant are:

1. On Saturday, 2/28/76, Brenda L. B. _____, W/F/15, reported to the Dover Police Department that she had been kidnapped and raped.

2. An investigation of this complaint was conducted by Det. Boyce Failing of the Dover Police Department.

3. Investigation of the aforementioned complaint revealed that Brenda B. _____, while under the influence of drugs, was taken to 222 S. Governors Avenue, Apartment 3, Dover, Delaware.

4. Investigation of the aforementioned complaint revealed that 222 S. Governors Avenue, Apartment #3, Dover, Delaware, is the residence of Jerome Franks, B/M DOB: 10/9/54.

5. Investigation of the aforementioned complaint revealed that on Saturday, 2/29/76, Jerome Franks did have sexual contact with Brenda B. _____ without her consent.

6. On Thursday, 3/4/76 at the Dover Police Department, Brenda B. _____, revealed to Det. Boyce Failing that Jerome Franks was the person who committed the Sexual Assault against her.

7. On Friday, 3/5/76, Jerome Franks was placed under arrest by Cpl. Robert McClements of the Dover Police Department, and charged with Sexual Misconduct.

8. On 3/5/76 at Family Court in Dover, Delaware, Jerome Franks did, after being arrested on the charge of Sexual Misconduct, make a statement of Cpl. Robert McClements, that he thought the charge was concerning Cynthia Bailey not Brenda B. _____.

9.   On Friday, 3/5/76, Cynthia C. Bailey, W/F/21 of 132 North Street, Dover, Delaware, did report to Dover Police Department that she had been raped at her residence during the night.

10.   Investigation conducted by your affiant on Friday, 3/5/76, revealed the perpetrator of the crime to be an unknown black male, approximately 57, 150 lbs., dark complexion, wearing white thermal undershirt, black pants with a belt having a silver or gold buckle, a brown leather ¾ length coat with a tie belt in the front, and a dark knit cap pulled around the eyes.

11.   Your affiant can state, that during the commission of this crime, Cynthia Bailey was forced at knife point and with the threat of death to engage in sexual intercourse with the perpetrator of the crime.

12.   Your affiant can state that entry was gained to the residence of Cynthia Bailey through a window located on the east side of the residence.

13.   Your affiant can state that the residence of Jerome Franks is within a very short distance and direct sight of the residence of Cynthia Bailey.

14.   Your affiant can state that the description given by Cynthia Bailey of the unknown black male does coincide with the description of Jerome Franks.

15.   On Tuesday, 3/9/76, your affiant contacted Mr. James Williams and Mr. Wesley Lucas of the Delaware Youth Center where Jerome Franks is employed and did have personal conversation with both these people.

16.   On Tuesday, 3/9/76, Mr. James Williams revealed to your affiant that the normal dress of Jerome Franks does consist of a white knit thermal undershirt and a brown leather jacket.

17.   On Tuesday, 3/9/76, Mr. Wesley Lucas revealed to your affiant that in addition to the thermal undershirt and jacket, Jerome Franks often wears a dark green knit hat.

18.   Your affiant can state that a check of official records reveals that in 1971 Jerome Franks was arrested for the crime of rape and subsequently convicted with Assault with intent to Rape.

NOTES

1.   On remand in *Franks*, the Delaware Supreme Court held that even if paragraphs 15 through 17 were set aside in their entirety, the remaining allegations were sufficient to establish probable cause. Consequently, Franks' proffer of evidence to contradict the facts alleged in the affidavit was insufficient and the trial judge erred in failing to hold an evidentiary hearing. The conviction was, therefore, again upheld by that court. Franks v. State, 398 A.2d 783 (Del.1979).

2.   **Availability of Informant's Identity.** A defendant's ability to determine whether there is any viable basis for attacking a warrant under *Franks* may depend

upon his ability to determine the identity of the informant whose information was relied upon in the showing of probable cause. But does the Fourth Amendment ever give a defendant a right to that information in order to determine whether a *Franks* challenge is possible?

Defendants' right under the Fourth Amendment to the identity of an informant whose information was used to support law enforcement action challenged on Fourth Amendment grounds was addressed in McCray v. Illinois, 386 U.S. 300, 87 L.Ed.2d 1056, 18 L.Ed.2d 62 (1967), noted several times in the principal case. McCray complained of the trial court's refusal to require officers to disclose the name of the informant on whose tip they made a warrantless arrest of McCray. Roviaro v. United States, 353 U.S. 53, 77 S.Ct. 623, 1 L.Ed.2d 639 (1957), *McCray* suggested, held that federal procedural law and perhaps due process require the disclosure of an informant's identity when the facts show the informant may have information bearing on the accused's guilt or innocence. This obligation to disclose an informant's identity did not apply, the Court continued, to situations such as McCray's, where defendants sought similar information only to challenge the evidence's admissibility on Fourth Amendment exclusionary rule grounds. Thus the trial court's refusal to require disclosure to McCray did not violate his Fourth Amendment rights.

The Court left unclear whether *McCray* simply held that on the facts of the case the defendant failed to make a persuasive enough case for his need for the informant's identity or, rather, that no defendant could ever establish a right to disclosure of an informant's identity for purposes of litigating a Fourth Amendment right to exclusion of evidence. *McCray's* discussion leaves open the possibility that some defendants may, under some quite limited circumstances, have a Fourth Amendment right to disclosure of this information. Perhaps such a right exists only if the trial judge hears all other evidence and determines a reliable resolution of the Fourth Amendment issue is difficult or impossible without further information that might become available if the defendant is permitted to know and perhaps interview the informant.

In at least some warrant situations, it is arguable the *Franks* right to challenge the accuracy of a search warrant affidavit is of no significance unless the defendant has the right to find out the identity of the informant and to inquire of that informant whether the affidavit accurately states what he told officers. Despite *McCray*, then, *Franks* suggests defendants sometimes may have a Fourth Amendment right to an informant's identity to determine whether, on the facts of the case, *Franks* permits a challenge to the affidavit's accuracy and the warrant's validity.

Whatever the constitutional demands, local statutes and court rules sometimes give defendants some right to informants' identities to investigate the validity of possible challenges to evidence's admissibility. The Model Code of Pre-Arraignment Procedure would require disclosure of the identity of an informant where the information relied upon to establish probable cause includes a report of information from that informant unless the judge finds "that the issue of [probable] cause can be fairly determined without such disclosure." Model Code of Pre-Arraignment Procedure § 290.4 (Official Draft, 1975). Disclosure would not be required, however, if (a) the evidence at issue was seized under a search warrant; or (b) the prosecution produced "substantial corroboration of the informant's existence and reliability" consisting of testimony of someone other than the person to whom the informant gave his information. For purposes of deciding whether a "fair" determination can be made without disclosure, the judge is authorized to require the prosecution, *in camera,* to disclose the informant's identity or to produce the informant for questioning by the judge. Is this approach inconsistent with *Roviaro* and *McCray*? Perhaps *McCray* can be read as a case in which the trial judge implicitly found on the facts before him that a "fair" determination of whether the officers had probable cause could be made without requiring disclosure.

B.   ENTERING THE PREMISES AND OTHER LIMITS ON EXECUTION OF WARRANTS

EDITORS' INTRODUCTION: ANNOUNCEMENT DEMANDS AND OTHER REQUIREMENTS FOR EXECUTION OF WARRANTS

Officers' executions of warrants—especially search warrants—are often affected by numerous statutory and perhaps court rule requirements. Those requirements govern matters such as the time of day or night the warrant may be executed, the need to serve the warrant upon, or present it to, those on the premises when the officers arrive, and the making of a "return" to the issuing magistrate indicating the warrant has been executed and, perhaps, in the case of a search warrant specifying the items seized during the search.

These requirements raise two related: First, to what if any extent do the Fourth Amendment or similar state constitutional provisions embody some version of these requirements? Second, what if any is the effect of violating these requirements upon the admissibility of evidence obtained during execution of the warrants.

Announcement Requirements

The most controversial of these execution requirements has been that demanding that before entering premises to execute a warrant, or at least before certain kinds of entry, officers announce their identity and purpose and perhaps comply with other requirements related to entry. Often the issue is posed negatively: when are so-called "no-knock" entries—those involving no such announcement—permitted?

Statutes in many jurisdictions address the matter. A federal statute, 18 U.S.C.A. § 3109, for example, provides:

> The officer may break open any outer or inner door or window of a house, or any part of a house, or anything therein, to execute a search warrant, if, after notice of his authority and purpose, he is refused admittance or when necessary to liberate himself or a person aiding him in the execution of a warrant.

In Miller v. United States, 357 U.S. 301, 78 S.Ct. 1190, 2 L.Ed.2d 1332 (1958), and Sabbath v. United States, 391 U.S. 585, 88 S.Ct. 1755, 20 L.Ed.2d 828 (1968), the Supreme Court held the "validity" of an entry made to effect an arrest without a warrant must comply with criteria identical to those set out in the statute, apparently as a matter of nonconstitutional law applicable to arrests made by federal officers. Evidence obtained in a search related to an entry violating these provisions cannot be used in a federal criminal trial.

Whether the Fourth Amendment ever requires announcement prior to entry remained uncertain until the Supreme Court addressed the issue in Wilson v. Arkansas, 514 U.S. 927, 115 S.Ct. 1914, 131 L.Ed.2d 976 (1995).

Holding that the Arkansas court below erred in concluding the Fourth Amendment imposed no "knock and announce" requirement for execution of a search warrant, Justice Thomas's *Wilson* opinion for the Court reviewed the common law authority requiring announcement and continued:

> Our own cases have acknowledged that the common-law principle of announcement is "embedded in Anglo-American law," but we have never squarely held that this principle is an element of the reasonableness inquiry under the Fourth Amendment. We now so hold. Given the longstanding common-law endorsement of the practice of announcement, we have little doubt that the Framers of the Fourth Amendment thought that the method of an officer's entry into a dwelling was among the factors to be considered in assessing the reasonableness of a search or seizure. Contrary to the decision below, we hold that in some circumstances an officer's unannounced entry into a home might be unreasonable under the Fourth Amendment.
>
> This is not to say, of course, that every entry must be preceded by an announcement. The Fourth Amendment's flexible requirement of reasonableness should not be read to mandate a rigid rule of announcement that ignores countervailing law enforcement interests. * * * [T]he common-law principle of announcement was never stated as an inflexible rule requiring announcement under all circumstances.
>
> Indeed, at the time of the framing, the common-law admonition that an officer "ought to signify the cause of his coming," had not been extended conclusively to the context of felony arrests. The common-law principle gradually was applied to cases involving felonies, but at the same time the courts continued to recognize that under certain circumstances the presumption in favor of announcement necessarily would give way to contrary considerations.
>
> Thus, because the common-law rule was justified in part by the belief that announcement generally would avoid "the destruction or breaking of any house ... by which great damage and inconvenience might ensue," courts acknowledged that the presumption in favor of announcement would yield under circumstances presenting a threat of physical violence. See, e.g., Read v. Case, 4 Conn. 166, 170 (1822) (plaintiff who "had resolved ... to resist even to the shedding of blood ... was not within the reason and spirit of the rule requiring notice"); Mahomed v. The Queen, 4 Moore 239, 247, 13 Eng. Rep. 293, 296 (P.C. 1843) ("While he was firing pistols at them, were they to knock at the door, and to ask him to be pleased to open it for them? The law in its wisdom only requires this ceremony to be observed when it possibly may be attended with some advantage, and may render the breaking open of the outer door unnecessary"). Similarly, courts held that an officer may dispense with announcement in cases where a prisoner escapes from him and retreats to his dwelling. See, e.g., ibid.; Allen v. Martin, 10 Wend. 300, 304 (N.Y.Sup.Ct.1833). Proof of "demand and refusal" was deemed unnecessary in such cases because it would be a "senseless ceremony" to require an officer in pursuit of a recently escaped arrestee to make an announcement prior to breaking the door

[handwritten margin notes:] Wilson = ANNOUNCEMENT REQUIREMENT

Knock + announce = rule but based on situation

to retake him. Finally, courts have indicated that unannounced entry may be justified where police officers have reason to believe that evidence would likely be destroyed if advance notice were given.

We need not attempt a comprehensive catalog of the relevant countervailing factors here. For now, we leave to the lower courts the task of determining the circumstances under which an unannounced entry is reasonable under the Fourth Amendment. We simply hold that although a search or seizure of a dwelling might be constitutionally defective if police officers enter without prior announcement, law enforcement interests may also establish the reasonableness of an unannounced entry.

514 U.S. at 934–36, 115 S.Ct. at 1918–19, 131 L.Ed.2d at 982–84.

Wilson made clear the Fourth Amendment sometimes requires announcement, but it did not address the effect of officers' failure to announce and the admissibility of evidence obtained in the post-entry search. To the contrary, the Court commented:

Respondent * * * ask[s] us to affirm the denial of petitioner's suppression motion on an alternative ground: that exclusion is not a constitutionally compelled remedy where the unreasonableness of a search stems from the failure of announcement. Analogizing to the "independent source" doctrine * * *, and the "inevitable discovery" rule * * *, respondent * * * argue[s] that any evidence seized after an unreasonable, unannounced entry is causally disconnected from the constitutional violation and that exclusion goes beyond the goal of precluding any benefit to the government flowing from the constitutional violation. Because this remedial issue was not addressed by the court below and is not within the narrow question on which we granted certiorari, we decline to address these arguments.

514 U.S. at 937 n. 4, 115 S.Ct. at 1919 n. 4, 131 L.Ed.2d at 984 n. 4.

In *Miller* and *Sabbath*, the Court assumed entry of premises to make an arrest, if made in violation of the federal statute, rendered the arrest "unlawful," and evidence that would otherwise be admissible as seized in a search incident to the defendant's arrest must be suppressed. Perhaps the Fourth Amendment requirement recognized in *Wilson* will not have the same effect on subsequently obtained evidence as the statutory requirement applied in *Miller* and *Sabbath*. Or, perhaps exclusionary sanction developments since *Miller* and *Sabbath* have reduced the effect of an improper no-knock entry on the admissibility of evidence obtained by searching the premises.

The details of *Wilson's* Fourth Amendment announcement requirement are explored in the principal case reprinted in this subsection.

Return of the Warrant and Inventories of Seized Items

Despite *Wilson's* "constitutionalization" of the announcement requirement, the Supreme Court made clear not all traditional procedural requirements for the execution of warrants are imposed as a matter of Fourth Amendment law.

Statutes or court rules often require search warrants be in some sense returned to the issuing magistrate and persons on the searched premises be provided with an inventory of items seized. Fed.R.Crim.P. 41(d), for example, provides in part:

> (d) Execution and Return with Inventory. The officer taking property under the warrant shall give to the person from whom or from whose premises the property was taken a copy of the warrant and a receipt for the property taken or shall leave the copy and receipt at the place from which the property was taken. The return shall be made promptly and shall be accompanied by a written inventory of any property taken. * * *

Are there circumstances in which failure to observe these requirements means the Fourth Amendment is violated? If so, does this demand the exclusion of evidence obtained in the search?

In Cady v. Dombrowski, 413 U.S. 433, 93 S.Ct. 2523, 37 L.Ed.2d 706 (1973), the officers failed to list all items seized on the inventory filed with the court issuing the search warrant. The Court rejected the argument that this failure required the exclusion of the unlisted items:

> As these items were constitutionally seized, we do not deem it constitutionally significant that they were not listed in the return of the warrant. The ramification of that "defect," if such it was, is purely a question of state law.

93 U.S. at 449, 93 S.Ct. at 2532, 37 L.Ed.2d at 719.

Due process—but not Fourth Amendment—requirements were at issue in City of West Covina v. Perkins, 525 U.S. 234, 119 S.Ct. 678, 142 L.Ed.2d 636 (1999). Officers executing a search warrant searched Perkins' home and seized certain personal property. The officers left a notice giving their names, identifying their employing department (the West Covina Police Department) and a telephone number at which they could be contacted. In addition, they attached an inventory of property seized, but the notice did not specify the number of the warrant because it was under seal to preserve the integrity of an ongoing investigation. After unsuccessful efforts to secure return of his property, Perkins and his family members sued the officers and West Covina, arguing the process by which the property was taken and retained violated their federal constitutional rights. The federal district court granted summary judgment for the defendants, but the Court of Appeals reversed on the ground the officers failed to give constitutionally-required notice regarding state law procedures for seeking the return of seized property.

The Supreme Court reversed:

> When the police seize property for a criminal investigation, * * * due process does not require them to provide the owner with notice of state law remedies.
>
> A primary purpose of the notice required by the Due Process Clause is to ensure that the opportunity for a hearing is meaningful. It follows that when law enforcement agents seize property pursuant to warrant, due process requires them to take reasonable steps to give

notice that the property has been taken so the owner can pursue available remedies for its return. Individualized notice that the officers have taken the property is necessary in a case such as the one before us because the property owner would have no other reasonable means of ascertaining who was responsible for his loss.

No similar rationale justifies requiring individualized notice of state-law remedies which, like those at issue here, are established by published, generally available state statutes and case law. Once the property owner is informed that his property has been seized, he can turn to these public sources to learn about the remedial procedures available to him. The City need not take other steps to inform him of his options. * * *

Respondents urge that * * * we should, at least, affirm the Court of Appeals' judgment on the narrower ground that the notice provided respondents was inadequate because it did not provide them with the factual information—specifically, the search warrant number—they needed to invoke their judicial remedies. The District Court, however, made an explicit factual finding that respondents failed to establish that they needed the search warrant number to file a court motion seeking return of their property * * *. This finding undermines the factual predicate for respondents' alternative argument, and we need not discuss it further.

525 U.S. at ___, 119 S.Ct. at 681–83, 142 L.Ed.2d at 642–44. *Perkins* seemed to assume some notice is constitutionally demanded. Would failure to provide such notice serve as a basis for challenging the admissibility of the evidence seized?

Richards v. Wisconsin

Supreme Court of the United States, 1997.
520 U.S. 385, 117 S.Ct. 1416, 137 Ed.2d 615.

■ JUSTICE STEVENS delivered the opinion of the Court.

* * *

In this case, the Wisconsin Supreme Court concluded that police officers are never required to knock and announce their presence when executing a search warrant in a felony drug investigation. In so doing, it reaffirmed a pre-[Wilson v. Arkansas, 514 U.S. 927, 115 S.Ct. 1914, 131 L.Ed.2d 976 (1995)] holding and concluded that *Wilson* did not preclude this *per se* rule. * * *

I

On December 31, 1991, police officers in Madison, Wisconsin obtained a warrant to search Steiney Richards' hotel room for drugs and related paraphernalia. The search warrant was the culmination of an investigation that had uncovered substantial evidence that Richards was one of several individuals dealing drugs out of hotel rooms in Madison. The police requested a warrant that would have given advance authorization for a "no-knock" entry into the hotel room, but the magistrate explicitly deleted those portions of the warrant.

The officers arrived at the hotel room at 3:40 a.m. Officer Pharo, dressed as a maintenance man, led the team. With him were several plainclothes officers and at least one man in uniform. Officer Pharo knocked on Richards' door and, responding to the query from inside the room, stated that he was a maintenance man. With the chain still on the door, Richards cracked it open. Although there is some dispute as to what occurred next, Richards acknowledges that when he opened the door he saw the man in uniform standing behind Officer Pharo. He quickly slammed the door closed and, after waiting two or three seconds, the officers began kicking and ramming the door to gain entry to the locked room. At trial, the officers testified that they identified themselves as police while they were kicking the door in. When they finally did break into the room, the officers caught Richards trying to escape through the window. They also found cash and cocaine hidden in plastic bags above the bathroom ceiling tiles.

Richards sought to have the evidence from his hotel room suppressed on the ground that the officers had failed to knock and announce their presence prior to forcing entry into the room. The trial court denied the motion, concluding that the officers could gather from Richards' strange behavior when they first sought entry that he knew they were police officers and that he might try to destroy evidence or to escape. The judge emphasized that the easily disposable nature of the drugs the police were searching for further justified their decision to identify themselves as they crossed the threshold instead of announcing their presence before seeking entry. Richards appealed the decision to the Wisconsin Supreme Court and that court affirmed.

The Wisconsin Supreme Court did not delve into the events underlying Richards' arrest in any detail, but accepted the following facts: "[O]n December 31, 1991, police executed a search warrant for the motel room of the defendant seeking evidence of the felonious crime of Possession with Intent to Deliver a Controlled Substance * * *. They did not knock and announce prior to their entry. Drugs were seized."

Assuming these facts, the court proceeded to consider whether our decision in *Wilson* required the court to abandon its decision in State v. Stevens, 181 Wis.2d 410, 511 N.W.2d 591 (1994), cert. denied, 515 U.S. 1102, 115 S.Ct. 2245, 132 L.Ed.2d 254 (1995), which held that "when the police have a search warrant, supported by probable cause, to search a residence for evidence of delivery of drugs or evidence of possession with intent to deliver drugs, they necessarily have reasonable cause to believe exigent circumstances exist" to justify a no-knock entry. The court concluded that nothing in *Wilson's* acknowledgment that the knock-and-announce rule was an element of the Fourth Amendment "reasonableness" requirement would prohibit application of a *per se* exception to that rule in a category of cases.

In reaching this conclusion, the Wisconsin court found it reasonable—after considering criminal conduct surveys, newspaper articles, and other judicial opinions—to assume that all felony drug crimes will involve "an extremely high risk of serious if not deadly injury to the police as well as the potential for the disposal of drugs by the occupants prior to entry by the police." Notwithstanding its acknowledgment that in "some cases, police officers will undoubtedly decide that their safety, the safety of others, and the effective execution of the warrant dictate that they knock and announce," the court concluded that exigent circumstances justifying a no-knock entry are always present in felony drug cases. Further, the court reasoned that the violation of privacy that occurs when officers who have a search warrant forcibly enter a residence without first announcing their presence is minimal, given that the residents would ultimately be without authority to refuse the police entry. The principal intrusion on individual privacy interests in such a situation, the court concluded, comes from the issuance of the search warrant, not the manner in which it is executed. Accordingly, the court determined that police in Wisconsin do not need specific information about dangerousness, or the possible destruction of drugs in a particular case, in order to dispense with the knock-and-announce requirement in felony drug cases.

* * *

II

We recognized in *Wilson* that the knock-and-announce requirement could give way "under circumstances presenting a threat of physical violence," or "where police officers have reason to believe that evidence would likely be destroyed if advance notice were given." It is indisputable that felony drug investigations may frequently involve both of these circumstances. The question we must resolve is whether this fact justifies dispensing with case-by-case evaluation of the manner in which a search was executed.

The Wisconsin court explained its blanket exception as necessitated by the special circumstances of today's drug culture, and the State asserted at oral argument that the blanket exception was reasonable in "felony drug cases because of the convergence in a violent and dangerous form of commerce of weapons and the destruction of drugs." But creating exceptions to the knock-and-announce rule based on the "culture" surrounding a general category of criminal behavior presents at least two serious concerns.

First, the exception contains considerable overgeneralization. For example, while drug investigation frequently does pose special risks to officer safety and the preservation of evidence, not every drug investigation will pose these risks to a substantial degree. For example, a search could be conducted at a time when the only individuals present in a residence have no connection with the drug activity and thus will be unlikely to threaten officers or destroy evidence. Or the police could know that the drugs being searched for were of a type or in a location that made them impossible to destroy quickly. In those situations, the asserted governmental interests in preserving evidence and maintaining safety may not outweigh the individual privacy interests intruded upon by a no-knock entry.[5] Wisconsin's blanket rule impermissibly insulates these cases from judicial review.

5. The State asserts that the intrusion on individual interests effectuated by a no- knock entry is minimal because the execution of the warrant itself constitutes the primary

A second difficulty with permitting a criminal-category exception to the knock-and-announce requirement is that the reasons for creating an exception in one category can, relatively easily, be applied to others. Armed bank robbers, for example, are, by definition, likely to have weapons, and the fruits of their crime may be destroyed without too much difficulty. If a *per se* exception were allowed for each category of criminal investigation that included a considerable—albeit hypothetical—risk of danger to officers or destruction of evidence, the knock-and-announce element of the Fourth Amendment's reasonableness requirement would be meaningless.

Thus, the fact that felony drug investigations may frequently present circumstances warranting a no-knock entry cannot remove from the neutral scrutiny of a reviewing court the reasonableness of the police decision not to knock and announce in a particular case. Instead, in each case, it is the duty of a court confronted with the question to determine whether the facts and circumstances of the particular entry justified dispensing with the knock-and-announce requirement.

In order to justify a "no-knock" entry, the police must have a reasonable suspicion that knocking and announcing their presence, under the particular circumstances, would be dangerous or futile, or that it would inhibit the effective investigation of the crime by, for example, allowing the destruction of evidence. This standard—as opposed to a probable cause requirement—strikes the appropriate balance between the legitimate law enforcement concerns at issue in the execution of search warrants and the individual privacy interests affected by no-nock entries. This showing is not high, but the police should be required to make it whenever the reasonableness of a no-knock entry is challenged.

III

Although we reject the Wisconsin court's blanket exception to the knock-and-announce requirement, we conclude that the officers' no-knock entry into Richards' hotel room did not violate the Fourth Amendment. We agree with the trial court * * *, that the circumstances in this case show that the officers had a reasonable suspicion that Richards might destroy evidence if given further opportunity to do so.

The judge who heard testimony at Richards' suppression hearing concluded that it was reasonable for the officers executing the warrant to

intrusion on individual privacy and that the individual privacy interest cannot outweigh the generalized governmental interest in effective and safe law enforcement. While it is true that a no-knock entry is less intrusive than, for example, a warrantless search, the individual interests implicated by an unannounced, forcible entry should not be unduly minimized. As we observed in [*Wilson*], the common law recognized that individuals should have an opportunity to themselves comply with the law and to avoid the destruction of property occasioned by a forcible entry. These interests are not inconsequential.

Additionally, when police enter a residence without announcing their presence, the residents are not given any opportunity to prepare themselves for such an entry. The State pointed out at oral argument that, in Wisconsin, most search warrants are executed during the late night and early morning hours. The brief interlude between announcement and entry with a warrant may be the opportunity that an individual has to pull on clothes or get out of bed.

believe that Richards knew, after opening the door to his hotel room the first time, that the men seeking entry to his room were the police. Once the officers reasonably believed that Richards knew who they were, the court concluded, it was reasonable for them to force entry immediately given the disposable nature of the drugs.

In arguing that the officers' entry was unreasonable, Richards places great emphasis on the fact that the magistrate who signed the search warrant for his hotel room deleted the portions of the proposed warrant that would have given the officers permission to execute a no-knock entry. But this fact does not alter the reasonableness of the officers' decision, which must be evaluated as of the time they entered the hotel room. At the time the officers obtained the warrant, they did not have evidence sufficient, in the judgment of the magistrate, to justify a no-knock warrant. Of course, the magistrate could not have anticipated in every particular the circumstances that would confront the officers when they arrived at Richards' hotel room. These actual circumstances—petitioner's apparent recognition of the officers combined with the easily disposable nature of the drugs—justified the officers' ultimate decision to enter without first announcing their presence and authority.

* * *

Accordingly, although we reject the blanket exception to the knock-and-announce requirement for felony drug investigations, the judgment of the Wisconsin Supreme Court is affirmed.

Courts conclusion

It is so ordered.

NOTES AND QUESTIONS

1. **Entries Requiring Announcement.** What entries require announcement? In Sabbath v. United States 391 U.S. 585, 88 S.Ct. 1755, 20 L.Ed.2d 828 (1968), discussed in the Introductory Note to this part of the present chapter, the entry at issue was made by officers who knocked on the door of the premises and, upon receiving no answer after a few seconds passed, opened the unlocked door and entered. Sabbath argued that the entry violated 18 U.S.C. § 3109, reprinted in the Introductory Note. The Government argued in response that "the use of 'force' is an indispensable element of the statute," and since no force was used on the facts, the entry was not subject to the statute. Rejecting the Government's contention, the Court explained:

> Considering the purposes of § 3109, it would indeed be a "grudging application" to hold, as the Government urges, that the use of "force" is an indispensable element of the statute. To be sure, the statute uses the phrase "break open" and that connotes some use of force. But linguistic analysis seldom is adequate when a statute is designed to incorporate fundamental values and the ongoing development of the common law. * * * [Lower courts have] held that § 3109 applies to entries effected by the use of a passkey, which requires no more force than does the turning of a doorknob. An unannounced intrusion into a dwelling—what § 3109 basically proscribes—is no less an unannounced intrusion whether officers break down a door, force open a chain lock on a partially open door, open a locked door by use of a passkey, or, as here, open a closed but unlocked door. The protection afforded by, and the values inherent in, § 3109 must be "governed by something more than the

fortuitous circumstance of an unlocked door." Keiningham v. United States, 109 U.S.App.D.C. 272, 276, 287 F.2d 126, 130 (1960).

391 U.S. at 589–90, 88 S.Ct. at 1758, 20 L.Ed.2d at 833–34. "We do not deal here with entries obtained by ruse," the Court added, "which have been viewed as involving no 'breaking.' "

Will the Court take the same approach in construing the Fourth Amendment requirement as it took in *Sabbath* with the federal statutory requirement? If *Sabbath* applies the common law position and *Wilson* finds the basic common law requirement embodied in the Fourth Amendment, perhaps that Fourth Amendment requirement applies to those situations *Sabbath* indicated were covered by the federal statute.

2. **Service of the Warrant.** Statutory provisions often require some sort of service of the warrant. For example, Fed.R.Crim.P. 41(d), reprinted in the Editors' Introduction, requires an officer taking property under a search warrant "shall give to the person from whom or from whose premises the property was taken a copy of the warrant * * * or shall leave the copy * * * at the place from which the property was taken." Courts often take the position that violations of these requirements affect the admissibility of evidence obtained only if the violation was "substantial" or intentional or if the complaining defendant was in some sense prejudiced. See Moya v. State, 335 Ark. 193, 205, 981 S.W.2d 521, 527 (1998).

The federal provision, however, was taken with unusual seriousness in United States v. Gantt, 179 F.3d 782 (9th Cir.1999). Federal agents executing a search warrant showed Gantt, the occupant of the premises, "the face of the warrant" but not the incorporated attachment specifying the items for which the agents were authorized to search. The court rejected the Government's contention that Rule 41(d) is complied with if officers leave a copy of the warrant at the scene, even if— as in *Gantt*—the person is arrested and thus has no opportunity to examine that copy. Rule 41(d), the court reasoned, implements important policies flowing from the Fourth Amendment warrant requirement:

> If the warrant is not disclosed until after the completion of the search then * * * [t]he individual [searched] loses the opportunity to point out to the agents that certain items are beyond the scope of the warrant or even that the agents have targeted the wrong residence. Most importantly, until the search is completed, the individual cannot be certain that the officers are acting under valid judicial authority.

179 F.3d at 879. The court found unconvincing the Government's argument that enabling those on the premises to challenge whether the agents exceeded the authority of the warrant would encourage violent confrontation between officers and those searched. Given the nature and importance of the underlying purposes of the Rule 41(d) requirement, the court concluded, those executing a search warrant "should utilize the disfavored alternative of leaving behind a copy of the warrant only when necessary."

The officers' violation of Rule 41(b), *Gantt* further reasoned, required exclusion even if it was only a "technical" or "non-fundamental" violation of the rule. Such a violation should lead to exclusion of the resulting evidence only upon proof that it was a deliberate disregard of the rule or the defendant was prejudiced. Gantt asked to see the warrant; the agents nevertheless failed to show her the full warrant with the attachment and the Government provided no explanation or justification for this failure to comply with her request. Thus, the court concluded, the violation was deliberate. Prejudice, in this context, requires proof the search might not have occurred or would not have been as abrasive had the rule been followed. *Gantt* determined that Gantt had also shown prejudice as so defined:

Had Gantt been provided a copy of the warrant the search would have been less abrasive. She would not have been in doubt as to the authority of the agents, and she might also have been able to point out to the agents that many of the items seized were beyond the scope of the warrant.

179 F.3d at 791.

3. **Destruction of Property in Entering.** The relationship between no-knock entry under *Wilson* and *Richards* and destruction of property was addressed in United States v. Ramirez, 523 U.S. 65, 118 S.Ct. 992, 140 L.Ed.2d 191 (1998). Officers with a search warrant made an unannounced entry into Ramirez's home to locate and arrest Shelby, a violent escaped prison inmate. The officers believed there were weapons in the garage. As they entered, the officers broke a window in the garage and pointed a gun through it to dissuade any occupants from rushing to those weapons. The lower courts held that an unannounced entry involving destruction of property requires a higher degree of exigency than other such entries and that this heightened standard had not been met. The Supreme Court rejected this approach:

> Neither [*Wilson* nor *Richards*] explicitly addressed the question whether the lawfulness of a no-knock entry depends on whether property is damaged in the course of the entry. It is obvious from their holdings, however, that it does not. Under *Richards*, a no-knock entry is justified if police have a "reasonable suspicion" that knocking and announcing would be dangerous, futile, or destructive to the purposes of the investigation. Whether such a "reasonable suspicion" exists depends in no way on whether police must destroy property in order to enter.
>
> This is not to say that the Fourth Amendment speaks not at all to the manner of executing a search warrant. The general touchstone of reasonableness which governs Fourth Amendment analysis governs the method of execution of the warrant. Excessive or unnecessary destruction of property in the course of a search may violate the Fourth Amendment, even though the entry itself is lawful and the fruits of the search not subject to suppression.

523 U.S. at 70–71, 118 S.Ct. at 996, 140 L.Ed.2d at 198. Given what the officers knew about Shelby, it continued, they had reasonable suspicion that announcement might be dangerous required by *Richards* for no-knock entry. The Court then concluded:

> As for the manner in which the entry was accomplished, the police here broke a single window in respondent's garage. They did so because they wished to discourage Shelby, or any other occupant of the house, from rushing to the weapons that the informant had told them respondent might have kept there. Their conduct was clearly reasonable and we conclude that there was no Fourth Amendment violation.

523 U.S. at 71–72, 118 S.Ct. at 997, 140 L.Ed.2d at 198. Since it found no Fourth Amendment violation, the Court added, it was not required to decide whether unreasonable damage to property in the course of an entry to execute a search warrant would require suppression of evidence found in a search conducted after that entry.

4. **Magistrate's Authorization for No–Knock Entry.** What is the constitutionally necessary role of the magistrate issuing a warrant in determining the propriety of no-knock entry? In *Richards*, the police officers applying for the search warrant requested a warrant authorizing no-knock entry and submitted to the magistrate a "proposed" warrant containing such authorization. The magistrate, however, explicitly deleted this authorization from the warrant before issuing it. In arguing that the no-knock entry was unreasonable, Richards emphasized the

magistrate's judgment that such entry was not justified. The Court, however, found this of little or no significance:

> [The magistrate's denial of permission to make a no-knock entry] does not alter the reasonableness of the officers' decision, which must be evaluated as of the time they entered the hotel room. At the time the officers obtained the warrant, they did not have evidence sufficient, in the judgment of the magistrate, to justify a no-knock warrant. Of course, the magistrate could not have anticipated in every particular the circumstances that would confront the officers when they arrived at Richards' hotel room. These actual circumstances * * * justified the officers' ultimate decision to enter without first announcing their presence and authority.

520 U.S. at 395–96, 117 S.Ct. at 1422, 137 L.Ed.2d at 625. Commenting more generally, the Court added:

> A number of States give magistrate judges the authority to issue "no-knock" warrants if the officers demonstrate ahead of time a reasonable suspicion that entry without prior announcement will be appropriate in a particular context.

judge can issue a no Knock warrent

> The practice of allowing magistrates to issue no-knock warrants seems entirely reasonable when sufficient cause to do so can be demonstrated ahead of time. But, as the facts of this case demonstrate, a magistrate's decision not to authorize a no-knock entry should not be interpreted to remove the officers' authority to exercise independent judgment concerning the wisdom of a no-knock entry at the time the warrant is being executed.

520 U.S. at 396 n. 7, 117 S.Ct. at 1422 n. 7, 137 L.Ed.2d at 625 n. 7.

5. **Delay in Execution of a Warrant.** Statutory provisions and court rules often direct that search warrants be executed within specified times of their issuance, and permit the magistrate issuing a warrant to further limit the time for execution. Federal Rule of Criminal Procedure 41(c), for example, mandates that a search warrant "shall command the officer to search, within a specified period of time not to exceed 10 days, the person or place named for the property or person specified."

What is the effect of execution of a warrant beyond such time limits? In Sgro v. United States, 287 U.S. 206, 53 S.Ct. 138, 77 L.Ed.2d 260 (1932), the Supreme Court considered the admissibility of evidence obtained pursuant to a federal search warrant. The warrant was subject to a since-repealed statute directing such warrants be executed within ten days and specifically adding, "[A]fter the expiration of this time the warrant, unless executed, is void." Officers did not execute the warrant within ten days of its initial issuance, but took it back to the issuing magistrate who changed the date on it and "thus reissued [it]." It was executed soon thereafter. An issuing magistrate has no authority to simply and summarily redate a warrant, the Court held, and that was what was done in the case. Thus the redating of the warrant was ineffective. The Court then assumed without discussion execution of the warrant after the expiration of the ten day period required suppression of the evidence obtained.

Does *Sgro* mean the Fourth Amendment somehow incorporates legislatively-mandated timing requirements? Perhaps the language of the statute convinced the Court that Congress intended any evidence obtained by executing a warrant beyond the ten day period be inadmissible—not as a matter of federal constitutional law but as a matter of legislative mandate.

Search warrants may become subject to challenge due to passage of time within generally permissible time periods for execution, such as the ten day window provided for in the federal rule. In United States v. Williams, 10 F.3d 590 (8th

Cir.1993), for example, a warrant for an apartment issued on October 22, 1992, for an apartment. It was based on information from an informant that on that same day the informant saw a kilogram of cocaine, in its original packaging from Colombia, and $25,000.00 in currency inside the apartment. After the warrant was issued, the officer learned from the informant the kilo of cocaine was distributed; the officer therefore did not execute the warrant immediately. On October 29, however, the officer had the informant telephone Williams. The informant learned Williams received another shipment of cocaine. Consequently, the officer executed the warrant at 1:15 a.m. on October 30. Williams contended that the delay in executing the warrant, although within the ten day rule, nevertheless was unreasonable and rendered the search constitutionally unreasonable. By the time of the search, he reasoned, the information on which the warrant was issued was "stale" and failed to establish probable cause to believe that at the time the warrant was executed cocaine was on the premises. "Whether the period of delay between issuance and execution of a warrant is reasonable," the court explained in rejecting this contention, "necessarily depends upon the facts and circumstances of each case." Specifically, a court must consider the nature of the criminal activity involved and the kind of property sought to determine whether the passage of the time so increased the likelihood that the property sought was no longer on the premises. At some point, this likelihood is high enough to destroy the probable cause originally existing. On the facts of *Williams*, the court concluded, the eight day delay did not have this effect:

> [T]he continuing and ongoing nature of cocaine trafficking supports the continued existence of probable cause. It is reasonable for law enforcement officers to conclude that large-scale drug operations continued at the same location for a period of time.

10 F.3d at 595. "[T]he better practice," the court nevertheless acknowledged, would have been for the officer to have obtained a new warrant based on the information obtained on the 29th.

6. **Nighttime Execution.** What if any limits are there upon the time of day or night officers may execute a search warrant, and what are the effects of violating these requirements? Statutes and court rules often require nighttime execution of a warrant be authorized by the issuing magistrate. These provisions sometimes explicitly require any such authorization be supported by information made available to the issuing magistrate. Federal Rule of Criminal Procedure 41(c)(1), for example, provides that "the warrant shall be served in the daytime, unless the issuing authority, by appropriate provision in the warrant, and for reasonable cause shown, authorizes its execution at times other than daytime."

These provisions are construed and applied with varying degrees of vigor. In State v. Richardson, 80 Hawai'i 1, 904 P.2d 886 (1995), the court construed the Hawai'i rule on the assumption that at least a nighttime search of a family-occupied residence might have federal or state constitutional implications. It acknowledged, however, that some courts have indicated to the contrary. Given the importance of limitation on nighttime execution of warrants, the court concluded, judges issuing warrants for nighttime execution must have facts presented to them demonstrating the existence of circumstances justifying a nighttime search before issuing such a warrant. Turning to what might justify a nighttime search, the court explained that one justification might be "reasonable necessity." Such necessity would usually be based upon apprehension that evidence within the place would be removed, hidden or destroyed before morning. It continued:

> [A] nighttime search warrant * * * may also be properly authorized when a nighttime search will not violate the policies that underlie the nighttime search prohibition.

need to justify

One policy underlying the nighttime search prohibition is protection of the greater expectation of privacy that individuals possess in their homes at night. * * *

In addition * * * "ordinarily a nighttime search would pose a heightened safety risk since people may tend to overreact to an entry by force in the dead of night. Darkness may exacerbate the reaction or heighten the confusion inherent in a search[.]" [State v. Rowe, 806 P.2d 730, 734 n. 5 (Utah App. 1991)]. Thus, the rule against nighttime searches also functions "to avoid the possibility of terror and gunplay which may arise from forcible nighttime entries[.]" [State v. Brock, 294 Or. 15, 19, 653 P.2d 543, 545 (1982).].

[handwritten: night searches have heightened safety risk]

Under some circumstances, nighttime searches will not encroach upon either the special privacy interests or the public safety concerns that underlie the nighttime search prohibition. * * *

In the instant case, the affidavit in support of the warrant indicated that sales of crystal methamphetamine were taking place until at least 2:00 a.m., thereby implying that the occupants of the home would neither be asleep nor surprised by a knock at the door until a later hour. * * * Thus, we hold that the authorization for a search until 2:00 a.m. that was given in the instant case was justified because such a search would not conflict with the policies underlying the ordinary prohibition against nighttime searches.

80 Hawai'i at 7–8, 904 P.2d at 892.

In Gooding v. United States, 416 U.S. 430, 94 S.Ct. 1780, 40 L.Ed.2d 250 (1974), the United States Supreme Court took a quite different approach to 21 U.S.C.A. § 879(a), governing execution of certain search warrants for drugs. The statute provides:

> A search warrant relating to offenses involving controlled substances may be served at any time of the day or night if the judge or United States magistrate issuing the warrant is satisfied that there is probable cause to believe that grounds exist for the warrant and for its service at this time.

[handwritten: drug warrents can be served anytime]

Relying on the legislative history of this statute, the Court held that the statute requires for nighttime execution of a warrant only a showing that the contraband is likely to be on the premises at that time. It does *not* require any showing that nighttime execution is necessary, justified in any sense, or even preferable to daytime execution. Although the majority did not explicitly address whether the Fourth Amendment requires a specific justification for nighttime execution of a search warrant, the Court's failure to mention any such possibility suggests it was not receptive to the argument that any special showing is constitutionally required.

If a warrant is executed in violation of nonconstitutional limits on nighttime searches, exclusion of the resulting evidence may not be required. In State v. Moore, 2 Neb.App. 206, 508 N.W.2d 305 (1993) review overruled, for example, the court held that if the search warrant at issue had been issued in violation of state rule requirements, suppression was required only upon "a showing that there was prejudice in the sense that the search might not have occurred, that the search would not have been so abusive if the rule had been followed, or that there was evidence that the rule was deliberately and intentionally disregarded." Turning to the contention that the evidence before it showed prejudice, the court responded:

> [W]e do not find that the search would not have occurred or would not have been so abusive if the search had been during the daytime. There was probable cause for the issuance of a warrant. The warrant was executed at about 9 p.m., not in the middle of the night, but at a time of the year when it is dark before 8 p.m. Moore has not shown that she was prejudiced by the execution of the warrant at approximately 9 p.m. * * *

2 Neb.App. at 212, 508 N.W.2d at 309. Other courts, however, find exclusion required—sometimes with little or no discussion. See State v. Fitch, 255 Neb. 108, 582 N.W.2d 342 (1998), holding that since the affidavit for a search warrant contained no factual basis supporting a nighttime search, issuance of the search warrant authorizing a search "at any time" was "error" and evidence obtained by 10:00 p.m. execution of that warrant had to be suppressed.

C. PARTICULARITY DEMANDED OF WARRANTS AND RELATED LIMITS ON EXECUTION OF WARRANTS

The Fourth Amendment reasonableness of a search or arrest pursuant to a warrant may be affected by the manner in which that search or arrest is carried out as well as by the procedure followed in issuing the warrant. Some, although not all, Fourth Amendment requirements affecting the execution of warrants flow from limits imposed by the terms of the warrants themselves; this is particularly true with regard to search warrants. It is therefore useful to consider together the Fourth Amendment requirements governing what the warrant itself must specify and the often-related requirements applicable to the manner in which officers execute warrants.

In connection with the material in this section, reconsider Horton v. California, 496 U.S. 128, 110 S.Ct. 2301, 110 L.Ed.2d 112 (1990), reprinted in part B(2) of Chapter 2, concerning the right of officers executing a search warrant to seize undescribed items found in "plain view" during the course of the search.

EDITORS' INTRODUCTION: PARTICULARITY AND ITS EFFECT ON EXECUTION OF THE WARRANT

The terms of the Fourth Amendment provide in part that "no Warrants shall issue, but * * * particularly describing the place to be searched, and the persons or things to be seized." Compared to the probable cause requirement for warrant issuance, however, the mandate of particularity in the warrant has received relatively little attention from the Supreme Court. It is clear, however, the particularity requirement is related to the execution of the warrant and is designed to limit the officers' activity under the warrant. Without a warrant describing with precision the place to be searched and the things to be seized, the Court has observed, "officers are free to determine for themselves the extent of their search and the precise objects to be seized." Trupiano v. United States, 334 U.S. 699, 710, 68 S.Ct. 1229, 1235, 92 L.Ed. 1663, 1672 (1948).

The Place to Be Searched. Until the case reprinted in this section, the Supreme Court seldom addressed the requirement that the place to be searched be described with precision. In United States v. Karo, 468 U.S. 705, 104 S.Ct. 3296, 82 L.Ed.2d 530 (1984), however, the Court indirectly considered the scope of this Fourth Amendment demand. The discussion makes clear that the Court regards the precision requirements as having sufficient flexibility to accommodate use of warrants for law enforcement activity other than traditional searches of premises easily described.

In *Karo*, the Government concealed an electronic beeping device in a can of chemicals which was then transferred to Karo; law enforcement officers used the device to trace Karo's movements in his car. Karo contended that the Government's concealment of the device in the car was a search. In response, the Government urged that if this was a search, no valid warrant could be obtained for it because the Government would not be able to describe the "place to be searched" with adequate precision. In fact, it suggested, the very purpose of the use of the beeper was to determine the place to be searched, i.e., the place to which the can of chemicals would be taken. The Court rejected the Government's argument:

> [I]t will still be possible to describe the object into which the beeper is to be placed, the circumstances that led agents to wish to install the beeper, and the length of time for which beeper surveillance is requested. In our view, this information will suffice to permit issuance of a warrant authorizing beeper installation and surveillance.

468 U.S. at 718, 104 S.Ct. at 3305, 82 L.Ed.2d at 543.

Things to Be Seized. As to the purpose of the mandate that "things to be seized" be described with precision in a search warrant, the Court offered:

> The requirement * * * makes general searches under [warrants] impossible and prevents the seizure of one thing under a warrant describing another. As to what is to be taken, nothing is left to the discretion of the officer executing the warrant.

Marron v. United States, 275 U.S. 192, 196, 48 S.Ct. 74, 76, 72 L.Ed. 231, 237 (1927). The Court's comment that officers executing warrants have no discretion as to what is to be seized is, to some extent, incorrect. Under the "plain view seizure rule" (considered in Part B(2) of Chapter 2), officers may sometimes seize items not described in the search warrant if they have probable cause to believe the items are subject to seizure and they come upon the items while searching within the terms of the warrant.

But, as *Marron* suggests, the description of things to be seized may limit the officers' authority to search within the described premises. This is illustrated by Stanley v. Georgia, 394 U.S. 557, 89 S.Ct. 1243, 22 L.Ed.2d 542 (1969). Officers searched Stanley's residence under a warrant authorizing them to search the premises for, and to seize, numerous categories of items related to bookmaking. While searching desk drawers in a bedroom, they discovered three reels of eight millimeter film. Using Stanley's projector and screen, they viewed the films. This screening convinced the officers—apparently with good cause—the films were obscene and, therefore, they seized them. At Stanley's trial for possession of the films, the films were admitted into evidence over his objection. A majority of the Supreme Court reversed Stanley's conviction on other grounds and did not reach the propriety of the officers' actions. Justice Stewart, however, concurred on the ground the officers, by examining the film as they did, had gone beyond their authority to search under the warrant. Consequently, he reasoned, the films had been improperly seized:

> To condone what happened here is to invite a governmental official to use a seemingly precise and legal warrant only as a ticket to get into a man's home, and, once inside, to launch forth upon unconfined searches and indiscriminate seizures as if armed with all the unbridled and illegal power of a general warrant.

394 U.S. at 572, 89 S.Ct. at 1251–52, 22 L.Ed.2d at 553. Under this approach, when did the officers' conduct become improper? Did the warrant authorize them to look into closed desk drawers? Almost certainly so, since the bookmaking items might well have been located there. But did it authorize them to examine the film in such a manner as was necessary to determine its contents? to screen the film as they did? Perhaps this turns upon whether the officers could reasonably have anticipated that this action—examining the film—would enable them to locate and seize those items which the warrant specified.

If the specificity of description of the things to be searched for and seized in a search warrant limits the officers' right to search the premises, this may explain the requirement of specificity. Only a specific warrant can limit the officers to a search of no greater scope or intensity than is necessary to locate the items which the officers have reason to believe are in the premises.

The Court addressed the required specificity in regard to "things." In Stanford v. Texas, 379 U.S. 476, 85 S.Ct. 506, 13 L.Ed.2d 431 (1965), a search warrant was issued listing various materials believed related to the operation of the Communist Party in Texas. The Court invalidated the resulting conviction on the ground the warrant offended the requirement of particularity:

> We need not decide in the present case whether the description of the things to be seized would have been too generalized to pass constitutional muster, had the things been weapons, narcotics or "cases of whiskey." * * * The point is that it was not any contraband of that kind which was ordered to be seized, but literary material—"books, records, pamphlets, cards, receipts, lists, memoranda, pictures, recordings and other written instruments concerning the Communist Party of Texas and the operation of the Communist Party in Texas." The indiscriminate sweep of that language is constitutionally intolerable. To hold otherwise would be false to the terms of the Fourth Amendment, false to its meaning, and false to its history.

379 U.S. at 486, 85 S.Ct. at 512, 13 L.Ed.2d at 437–38.

In Andresen v. Maryland, 427 U.S. 463, 96 S.Ct. 2737, 49 L.Ed.2d 627 (1976), on the other hand, the warrant listed numerous documents believed related to the fraudulent transfer of a specifically described piece of realty. It concluded with authorization to seize "other fruits, instrumentalities and evidence of crime at this [time] unknown." The Court construed this as limited to other evidence relating to the crime committed by transfer of the identified lot. As so construed, it concluded, the warrant did not authorize the officers to conduct a search for evidence of other crimes and, therefore, was sufficiently precise. Andresen did not argue it was constitutionally necessary for the warrant to describe the evidence of the crime more specifically. But he did contend the list of the specified documents constituted a prohibited "general warrant." The Court responded:

> We disagree. Under investigation was a complex real estate scheme whose existence could be proved only by piecing together many bits of evidence. * * * The complexity of an illegal scheme may not be used as a shield to avoid detection when the State has demonstrated probable cause to believe that a crime has been committed and probable cause to believe that evidence of this crime is in the suspect's possession. * * *

427 U.S. at 482 n. 10, 96 S.Ct. at 2749 n. 10, 49 L.Ed.2d at 642–43 n. 10. Apparently, this means that the complexity of a crime under investigation sometimes causes difficulty in predicting in advance of a search what documents would constitute evidence of its commission. *Andresen* seems to hold that this justifies some relaxation of the specificity requirement. The things sought in *Stanford* (or the things that might have been seized under the warrant in that case) were more likely protected by the First Amendment than the items sought in *Andresen*. This may help explain the demand for greater specificity on the facts of *Stanford*.

Persons to Be Seized. The terms of the Fourth Amendment also require that at least certain warrants describe "persons * * * to be seized" with particularity. Presumably, this requirement applies to arrest warrants. When is a person described with sufficient particularity? Is a name sufficient? A name and a date of birth? A physical description without a name? In Visor v. State, 660 S.W.2d 816 (Tex.Crim.App.1983), the arrest warrant described the person to be arrested as an "unknown black female." Holding this aspect of the warrant ineffective, the court observed that to uphold it "would be to approve a general warrant prohibited by the federal constitution."

* * *

The principal case in this section addresses the criterion for determining whether a warrant is sufficiently precise for Fourth Amendment purposes. In addition, however, it considers the demands upon officers who in the process of executing a warrant discover the warrant is not as precise—at least "as applied"—as they previously thought.

Maryland v. Garrison

Supreme Court of the United States, 1987.
480 U.S. 79, 107 S.Ct. 1013, 94 L.Ed.2d 72.

whether a warrant is sufficiently precise.

■ JUSTICE STEVENS delivered the opinion of the Court.

Baltimore police officers obtained and executed a warrant to search the person of Lawrence McWebb and "the premises known as 2036 Park Avenue third floor apartment." When the police applied for the warrant and when they conducted the search pursuant to the warrant, they reasonably believed that there was only one apartment on the premises described in the warrant. In fact, the third floor was divided into two apartments, one occupied by McWebb and one by respondent. Before the officers executing the warrant became aware that they were in a separate apartment occupied by respondent, they had discovered the contraband that provided the basis for respondent's conviction for violating Maryland's Controlled Substances Act. The question presented is whether the seizure of that contraband was prohibited by the Fourth Amendment.

The trial court denied respondent's motion to suppress the evidence seized from his apartment, and the Maryland Special Court of Appeals affirmed. The Court of Appeals of Maryland reversed and remanded with instructions to remand the case for a new trial.

There is no question that the warrant was valid and was supported by probable cause. The trial court found, and the two appellate courts did not dispute, that after making a reasonable investigation, including a verification of information obtained from a reliable informant, an exterior examination of the three-story building at 2036 Park Avenue, and an inquiry of the utility company, the officer who obtained the warrant reasonably concluded that there was only one apartment on the third floor and that it was occupied by McWebb. When six Baltimore police officers executed the warrant, they fortuitously encountered McWebb in front of the building and used his key to gain admittance to the first floor hallway and to the locked door at the top of the stairs to the third floor. As they entered the vestibule on the third floor, they encountered respondent, who was standing in the hallway area. The police could see into the interior of both McWebb's apartment to the left and respondent's to the right, for the doors to both were open. Only after respondent's apartment had been entered and heroin, cash, and drug paraphernalia had been found did any of the officers realize that the third floor contained two apartments. As soon as they became aware of that fact, the search was discontinued. All of the officers reasonably believed that they were searching McWebb's apartment. No further search of respondent's apartment was made.

The matter on which there is a difference of opinion concerns the proper interpretation of the warrant. A literal reading of its plain language, as well as the language used in the application for the warrant, indicates that it was intended to authorize a search of the entire third floor.[6] [T]he Court of Appeals[, however,] concluded that the warrant [authorized a search of McWebb's apartment only and thus] did not authorize the search of respondent's apartment and the police had no justification for making a warrantless entry into his premises.

* * *

In our view, the case presents two separate constitutional issues, one concerning the validity of the warrant and the other concerning the

---

6.   The warrant states:

"Affidavit having been made before me by Detective Albert Marcus, Baltimore Police Department, Narcotic Unit, that he has reason to believe that on the person of Lawrence Meril McWebb ... (and) that on the premises known as 2036 Park Avenue third floor apartment, described as a three story brick dwelling with the numerals 2-0-3-6 affixed

to the front of same in the City of Baltimore, there is now being concealed certain property....

You are therefor commanded, with the necessary and proper assistants, to search forthwith the person/premises hereinabove described for the property specified, executing this warrant and making the search...."

reasonableness of the manner in which it was executed. We shall discuss the questions separately.

I

The Warrant Clause of the Fourth Amendment categorically prohibits the issuance of any warrant except one "particularly describing the place to be searched and the persons or things to be seized." The manifest purpose of this particularity requirement was to prevent general searches. By limiting the authorization to search to the specific areas and things for which there is probable cause to search, the requirement ensures that the search will be carefully tailored to its justifications, and will not take on the character of the wide-ranging exploratory searches the Framers intended to prohibit. Thus, the scope of a lawful search is "defined by the object of the search and the places in which there is probable cause to believe that it may be found. Just as probable cause to believe that a stolen lawnmower may be found in a garage will not support a warrant to search an upstairs bedroom, probable cause to believe that undocumented aliens are being transported in a van will not justify a warrantless search of a suitcase."

In this case there is no claim that the "persons or things to be seized" were inadequately described or that there was no probable cause to believe that those things might be found in "the place to be searched" as it was described in the warrant. With the benefit of hindsight, however, we now know that the description of that place was broader than appropriate because it was based on the mistaken belief that there was only one apartment on the third floor of the building at 2036 Park Avenue. The question is whether that factual mistake invalidated a warrant that undoubtedly would have been valid if it had reflected a completely accurate understanding of the building's floor plan. Plainly, if the officers had known, or even if they should have known, that there were two separate dwelling units on the third floor of 2036 Park Avenue, they would have been obligated to exclude respondent's apartment from the scope of the requested warrant. But we must judge the constitutionality of their conduct in light of the information available to them at the time they acted. Those items of evidence that emerge after the warrant is issued have no bearing on whether or not a warrant was validly issued. Just as the discovery of contraband cannot validate a warrant invalid when issued, so is it equally clear that the discovery of facts demonstrating that a valid warrant was unnecessarily broad does not retroactively invalidate the warrant. The validity of the warrant must be assessed on the basis of the information that the officers disclosed, or had a duty to discover and to disclose, to the issuing magistrate.[7] On the basis of that information, we

---

7. Arguments can certainly be made that the police in this case should have been able to ascertain that there was more than one apartment on the third floor of this building. It contained seven separate dwelling units and it was surely possible that two of them might be on the third floor. But the record also establishes that Officer Marcus made specific inquiries to determine the identity of the occupants of the third floor premises. The officer went to 2036 Park Avenue and found that it matched the description given by the informant: a three-story brick dwelling with the numerals 2–0–3–6 affixed to the front of the premises. The officer "made a check with the Baltimore Gas and Electric Company and discovered that the premises of 2036 Park Ave. third floor was in agree with the conclusion of all three Maryland courts that the warrant, insofar as it authorized a search that turned out to be ambiguous in scope, was valid when it issued.

II

The question whether the execution of the warrant violated respondent's constitutional right to be secure in his home is somewhat less clear. We have no difficulty concluding that the officers' entry into the third-floor common area was legal; they carried a warrant for those premises, and they were accompanied by McWebb, who provided the key that they used to open the door giving access to the thirdfloor common area. If the officers had known, or should have known, that the third floor contained two apartments before they entered the living quarters on the third floor, and thus had been aware of the error in the warrant, they would have been obligated to limit their search to McWebb's apartment. Moreover, as the officers recognized, they were required to discontinue the search of respondent's apartment as soon as they discovered that there were two separate units on the third floor and therefore were put on notice of the risk that they might be in a unit erroneously included within the terms of the warrant. The officers' conduct and the limits of the search were based on the information available as the search proceeded. While the purposes justifying a police search strictly limit the permissible extent of the search, the Court has also recognized the need to allow some latitude for honest mistakes that are made by officers in the dangerous and difficult process of making arrests and executing search warrants.

In Hill v. California, 401 U.S. 797, 91 S.Ct. 1106, 28 L.Ed.2d 484 (1971), we considered the validity of the arrest of a man named Miller based on the mistaken belief that he was Hill. The police had probable cause to arrest Hill and they in good faith believed that Miller was Hill when they found him in Hill's apartment. As we explained:

> "The upshot was that the officers in good faith believed Miller was Hill and arrested him. They were quite wrong as it turned out, and subjective good-faith belief would not in itself justify either the arrest or the subsequent search. But sufficient probability, not certainty, is the touchstone of reasonableness under the Fourth Amendment and on the record before us the officers' mistake was understandable and the arrest a reasonable response to the situation facing them at the time."

While *Hill* involved an arrest without a warrant, its underlying rationale that an officer's reasonable misidentification of a person does not invalidate a valid arrest is equally applicable to an officer's reasonable

the name of Lawrence McWebb." Officer Marcus testified at the suppression hearing that he inquired of the Baltimore Gas and Electric Company in whose name the third floor apartment was listed: "I asked if there is a front or rear or middle room. They told me, one third floor was only listed to Lawrence McWebb." The officer also discovered from a check with the Baltimore police department that the police records of Lawrence McWebb matched the address and physical description given by the informant. The Maryland courts that are presumptively familiar with local conditions were unanimous in concluding that the officer reasonably believed McWebb was the only tenant on that floor. Because the evidence supports their conclusion, we accept that conclusion for the purpose of our decision.

failure to appreciate that a valid warrant describes too broadly the premises to be searched. Under the reasoning in *Hill,* the validity of the search of respondent's apartment pursuant to a warrant authorizing the search of the entire third floor depends on whether the officers' failure to realize the overbreadth of the warrant was objectively understandable and reasonable. Here it unquestionably was. The objective facts available to the officers at the time suggested no distinction between McWebb's apartment and the third-floor premises.[8]

For that reason, the officers properly responded to the command contained in a valid warrant even if the warrant is interpreted as authorizing a search limited to McWebb's apartment rather than the entire third floor. Prior to the officers' discovery of the factual mistake, they perceived McWebb's apartment and the third-floor premises as one and the same; therefore their execution of the warrant reasonably included the entire third floor.[9] Under either interpretation of the warrant, the officers' conduct was consistent with a reasonable effort to ascertain and identify the place intended to be searched within the meaning of the Fourth Amendment.

police in good faith believe warrant was properly served

The judgment of the Court of Appeals is reversed, and the case is remanded for further proceedings not inconsistent with this opinion.

It is so ordered.

■ JUSTICE BLACKMUN, with whom JUSTICE BRENNAN and JUSTICE MARSHALL join, dissenting.

* * *

I

* * *

* * * The words of the warrant were plain and distinctive: the warrant directed the officers to seize marijuana and drug paraphernalia on the person of McWebb and in McWebb's apartment, i.e., "on the premises known as 2036 Park Avenue third floor apartment." * * * Accordingly, * * * the warrant was limited in its description to the third floor apartment of McWebb, then the search of an additional apartment—respondent's—was warrantless and is presumed unreasonable "in the absence of some one of a number of well defined 'exigent circumstances.' " Because the State has not advanced any such exception to the warrant requirement,

---

8. Nothing McWebb did or said after he was detained outside 2036 Park Avenue would have suggested to the police that there were two apartments on the third floor. McWebb provided the key that opened the doors on the first floor and on the third floor. The police could reasonably have believed that McWebb was admitting them to an undivided apartment on the third floor. When the officers entered the foyer on the third floor, neither McWebb nor Garrison informed them that they lived in separate apartments.

9. We expressly distinguish the facts of this case from a situation in which the police know there are two apartments on a certain floor of a building, and have probable cause to believe that drugs are being sold out of that floor, but do not know in which of the two apartments the illegal transactions are taking place. A search pursuant to a warrant authorizing a search of the entire floor under those circumstances would present quite different issues from the ones before us in this case.

the evidence obtained as a result of this search should have been exclud-ed.[10]

II

[T]he Court * * * analyzes the police conduct here in terms of "mis-take." * * * [But even if] there is no Fourth Amendment violation where the officers' mistake is reasonable, it is questionable whether that standard was met in this case. The "place" at issue here is a small multiple-occupancy building. Such forms of habitation are now common in this country, particularly in neighborhoods with changing populations and of declining affluence. Accordingly, any analysis of the "reasonableness" of the officers' behavior here must be done with this context in mind.

The efforts of Detective Marcus, the officer who procured the search warrant, do not meet a standard of reasonableness, particularly considering that the detective knew the search concerned a unit in a multiple-occupan-cy building. Upon learning from his informant that McWebb was selling marijuana in his third floor apartment, Marcus inspected the outside of the building. He did not approach it, however, to gather information about the configuration of the apartments. Had he done so, he would have discovered, as did another officer on the day of executing the warrant, that there were seven separate mailboxes and bells on the porch outside the main entrance to the house. Although there is some dispute over whether names were affixed near these boxes and bells, their existence alone puts a reasonable observer on notice that the three-story structure (with, possibly, a base-ment) had seven individual units. The detective, therefore, should have been aware that further investigation was necessary to eliminate the possibility of more than one unit's being located on the third floor. Moreover, when Detective Marcus' informant told him that he had pur-chased drugs in McWebb's apartment, it appears that the detective never thought to ask the informant whether McWebb's apartment was the only one on the third floor. These efforts, which would have placed a slight burden upon the detective, are necessary in order to render reasonable the officer's behavior in seeking the warrant.

Moreover, even if one believed that Marcus' efforts in providing infor-mation for issuance of the warrant were reasonable, I doubt whether the officers' execution of the warrant could meet such a standard. * * *

In my view, * * * the "objective facts" should have made the officers aware that there were two different apartments on the third floor well

---

10. If the officers were confused about the residence of respondent when they en-countered him in the third floor vestibule * * *, they might have been justified in de-taining him temporarily as an occupant of McWebb's apartment. The officers asserted that, upon entering the vestibule, they ob-served marijuana lying upon a dresser in respondent's bedroom, the door to respon-dent's apartment being open. Although it is not entirely clear that the drug could have been seized immediately under the "plain view" exception to the warrant requirement, for this would depend upon whether the offi-cers' "access to the object has some prior Fourth Amendment justification," the offi-cers probably would have had probable cause to obtain a search warrant and conceivably could have impounded respondent's apart-ment while seeking the warrant. Nothing, however, justified the full-scale search of re-spondent's apartment in which the officers engaged.

before they discovered the incriminating evidence in respondent's apartment. Before McWebb happened to drive up while the search party was preparing to execute the warrant, one of the officers, Detective Shea, somewhat disguised as a construction worker, was already on the porch of the row house and was seeking to gain access to the locked first-floor door that permitted entrance into the building. From this vantage point he had time to observe the seven mailboxes and bells; indeed, he rang all seven bells, apparently in an effort to summon some resident to open the front door to the search party. A reasonable officer in Detective Shea's position, already aware that this was a multiunit building and now armed with further knowledge of the number of units in the structure, would have conducted at that time more investigation to specify the exact location of McWebb's apartment before proceeding further. For example, he might have questioned another resident of the building.

It is surprising, moreover, that the Court places so much emphasis on the failure of McWebb to volunteer information about the exact location of his apartment. * * * [I]t would * * * have been reasonable for the officers, aware of the problem, from Detective Shea's discovery, in the specificity of their warrant, to ask McWebb whether his apartment was the only one on the third floor. As it is, the officers made several requests of and questioned McWebb, * * * and yet failed to ask him the question, obvious in the circumstances, concerning the exact location of his apartment.

Moreover, a reasonable officer would have realized the mistake in the warrant during the moments following the officers' entrance to the third floor. The officers gained access to the vestibule separating McWebb's and respondent's apartments through a locked door for which McWebb supplied the key. There, in the open doorway to his apartment, they encountered respondent, clad in pajamas and wearing a halfbody cast as a result of a recent spinal operation. Although the facts concerning what next occurred are somewhat in dispute, it appears that respondent, together with McWebb and the passenger from McWebb's car, were shepherded into McWebb's apartment across the vestibule from his own. Once again, the officers were curiously silent. The informant had not led the officers to believe that anyone other than McWebb lived in the third-floor apartment; the search party had McWebb, the person targeted by the search warrant, in custody when it gained access to the vestibule; yet when they met respondent on the third floor, they simply asked him who he was but never where he lived. Had they done so, it is likely that they would have discovered the mistake in the warrant before they began their search.

Finally and most importantly, even if the officers had learned nothing from respondent, they should have realized the error in the warrant from their initial security sweep. Once on the third floor, the officers first fanned out through the rooms to conduct a preliminary check for other occupants who might pose a danger to them. * * * [T]he two apartments were almost a mirror image of each other—each had a bathroom, a kitchen, a living room, and a bedroom. Given the somewhat symmetrical layout of the apartments, it is difficult to imagine that, in the initial security sweep, a reasonable officer would not have discerned that two apartments were on the third floor, realized his mistake, and then confined the ensuing search to McWebb's residence.

Accordingly, even if a reasonable error on the part of police officers prevents a Fourth Amendment violation, the mistakes here, both with respect to obtaining and executing the warrant, are not reasonable and could easily have been avoided.

I respectfully dissent.

NOTES

1. **Search of Persons on Premises.** The extent to which a search warrant does and can authorize officers to search persons on the premises to be searched pursuant to a warrant was addressed in Ybarra v. Illinois, 444 U.S. 85, 100 S.Ct. 338, 62 L.Ed.2d 238 (1979). In support of the warrant application, officers recounted an informant's tip that he had observed tinfoil packets on the person of "Greg," bartender at the Aurora Tap Tavern, and behind the bar. He also previously observed such packets in the same places. The informant knew from experience that such tinfoil packets are a common method of packaging heroin. In addition, Greg told the informant that he would have heroin for sale on March 1. A warrant was obtained authorizing the search of "the Aurora Tap Tavern" and "the person of 'Greg,' the bartender," for controlled substances. An Illinois statute purported to authorize officers executing a search warrant to detain and search "any person in the place at the time" either to protect themselves from attack or to prevent disposal or concealment of items described in the warrant. Ill.Rev.Stat., ch. 38, section 108–9. When, on March 1, the warrant was executed, Ybarra was one of about a dozen persons in the bar. He was first "frisked" and then more thoroughly searched. Drugs were found. Addressing the officers' right under the warrant to search Ybarra, the Court first indicated the warrant did not authorize such a search given the specific authorization to search the person of "Greg:"

> Had the issuing judge intended that the warrant would or could authorize a search of every person found within the tavern, he would hardly have specifically authorized the search of "Greg" alone. "Greg" was an employee of the tavern, and the complaint upon which the search warrant was issued gave every indication that he would be present at the tavern on March 1.

444 U.S. at 90 n. 2, 100 S.Ct. at 342 n. 2, 62 L.Ed.2d at 245 n. 2. It then suggested the warrant *could not* constitutionally be read as authorizing such a search. The officers' probable cause, the Court stressed, did not extend to Ybarra and others like him. Moreover:

> The Fourth Amendment directs that "no Warrants shall issue, but upon probable cause ... and particularly describing the place to be searched, and the persons or things to be seized." Thus, "open-ended" or "general" warrants are constitutionally prohibited. It follows that a warrant to search a place cannot normally be construed to authorize a search of each individual in that place. The warrant for the Aurora Tap Tavern provided no basis for departing from this general rule. Consequently, we need not consider situations where the warrant itself authorizes the search of unnamed persons in a place and is supported by probable cause to believe that persons who will be in the place at the time of the search will be in possession of illegal drugs.

444 U.S. at 92 n. 4, 100 S.Ct. at 342 n. 4, 62 L.Ed.2d at 246 n. 4.

Finally, the prosecution asked that the Court recognize a "new" exception to the warrant requirement:

[handwritten margin notes:]
1) warrant pertains to "Greg" in bar
2) Ybarra not "Greg" but searched + drugs found
3) warrant says Greg only therefore search of Ybarra not conform to warrant!

to permit evidence searches of persons who, at the commencement of the search, are on "compact" premises subject to a search warrant, at least where the police have a "reasonable belief" that such persons "are connected with" drug trafficking and "may be concealing or carrying away the contraband."

Rejecting this request, the Court explained the "long-prevailing" standard of probable cause embodies the appropriate compromise between citizens' interests and law enforcement; the Court was unprepared to deviate from that standard in this situation.

The State also defended the first frisk of Ybarra as a permissible weapons search under Terry v. Ohio, 392 U.S. 1, 88 S.Ct. 1868, 20 L.Ed.2d 889 (1968). This aspect of the case is discussed in Chapter 4.

2. **Detention of Persons "Associated With" Premises.** In some situations, a warrant may authorize the detention of persons associated with the searched premises. Should the limitations on searching persons present when a search warrant is executed apply to the occupants of a private residence being searched?

In Michigan v. Summers, 452 U.S. 692, 101 S.Ct. 2587, 69 L.Ed.2d 340 (1981), law officers were approaching Summers' home to execute a search warrant for contraband when they observed him leave the residence. They detained him while the home was searched. When the search revealed narcotics, they arrested Summers, whom they knew owned the premises, and searched his person, finding still more narcotics. He was prosecuted for possession of the drugs found on his person. The state argued the authority to search premises granted by the warrant implicitly included the authority to search persons on those premises, just as that authority included authorization to search furniture and containers in which the particular things described might be concealed. But the Court, in an opinion authored by Justice Stevens, did not rule on that contention because it found the search warrant implicitly authorized the temporary detention of Summers while the search was conducted and that the discovery of the contraband in respondent's home gave the police authority to arrest him for its possession. The search of his person was justified as a search incident to his lawful arrest. Justices Stewart, Brennan and Marshall dissented.

3. **Permitting News Media Coverage.** What if any Fourth Amendment significance arises from officers' permitting media members to accompany them when executing a warrant?

In Wilson v. Layne, 526 U.S. 603, 119 S.Ct. 1692, 143 L.Ed.2d 818 (1999), federal marshals with an arrest warrant for Dominic Wilson entered a residence in Rockville, Maryland listed on a computer as Wilson's home. In fact, this was the residence of Wilson's parents, Charles and Geraldine Wilson. The marshals were accompanied by a reporter and a photographer from the Washington Post, invited by the marshals to accompany them as part of a ride-along program. The Supreme Court described the events:

> At around 6:45 a.m., the officers, with media representatives in tow, entered the dwelling * * *. Petitioners Charles and Geraldine Wilson were still in bed when they heard the officers enter the home. Petitioner Charles Wilson, dressed only in a pair of briefs, ran into the living room to investigate. Discovering at least five men in street clothes with guns in his living room, he angrily demanded that they state their business, and repeatedly cursed the officers. Believing him to be an angry Dominic Wilson, the officers quickly subdued him on the floor. Geraldine Wilson next entered the living room to investigate, wearing only a nightgown. She observed her husband being restrained by the armed officers.

When their protective sweep was completed, the officers learned that Dominic Wilson was not in the house, and they departed. During the time that the officers were in the home, the Washington Post photographer took numerous pictures. The print reporter was also apparently in the living room observing the confrontation between the police and Charles Wilson. At no time, however, were the reporters involved in the execution of the arrest warrant. The Washington Post never published its photographs of the incident.

The Wilsons sued the marshals for money damages, contending the marshals' actions violated their Fourth Amendment rights. The federal District Court denied the defendant marshals' motion for summary judgment. On review, the Supreme Court first considered whether the marshals' actions violated the Wilsons' Fourth Amendment rights:

> [T]he officers had * * * a[n arrest] warrant, and they were undoubtedly entitled to enter the Wilson home in order to execute the arrest warrant for Dominic Wilson. But it does not necessarily follow that they were entitled to bring a newspaper reporter and a photographer with them. In Horton v. California, 496 U.S. 128, 140, 110 S.Ct. 2301, 110 L.Ed.2d 112 (1990), we held "[i]f the scope of the search exceeds that permitted by the terms of a validly issued warrant or the character of the relevant exception from the warrant requirement, the subsequent seizure is unconstitutional without more." While this does not mean that every police action while inside a home must be explicitly authorized by the text of the warrant, the Fourth Amendment does require that police actions in execution of a warrant be related to the objectives of the authorized intrusion.

> Certainly the presence of reporters inside the home was not related to the objectives of the authorized intrusion. Respondents concede that the reporters did not engage in the execution of the warrant, and did not assist the police in their task. The reporters therefore were not present for any reason related to the justification for police entry into the home the apprehension of Dominic Wilson.

* * *

> [I]t is a violation of the Fourth Amendment for police to bring members of the media or other third parties into a home during the execution of a warrant when the presence of the third parties in the home was not in aid of the execution of the warrant.

526 U.S. at ___, 119 S.Ct. at 1697–99, 143 L.Ed.2d at 828–30. It added:

> Even though such actions might violate the Fourth Amendment, if the police are lawfully present, the violation of the Fourth Amendment is the presence of the media and not the presence of the police in the home. We have no occasion here to decide whether the exclusionary rule would apply to any evidence discovered or developed by the media representatives.

526 U.S. at ___ n. 2, 119 S.Ct. at 1699 n. 2, 143 L.Ed.2d at 830 n. 2.

CHAPTER 4

DETENTIONS OF PERSONS AND RELATED SEARCHES

Analysis

EDITORS' INTRODUCTION: DETENTIONS, SEIZURES AND THEIR CHARACTERIZATION

This chapter addresses law enforcement detentions of persons suspected of crime—"seizures" of the person in the language of the Fourth Amendment—and related searches. An lawful detention may, in theory at least, create civil or possibly even criminal liability on the part of the officer. In most circumstances, however, the legality of an arrest or other detention is of practical significance only if it is accompanied by or leads to a search yielding incriminating evidence. Should such evidence be offered against the suspect at trial and challenged, its admissibility is often affected by the validity of the detention.

At one time, all detentions were regarded as indistinguishable from one another and characterized as arrests. This is no longer the case. Case law, much of it involving the Fourth Amendment requirement that "seizures" of the person be "reasonable," distinguishes a variety of detentions. Given the different requirements that have developed for different detentions and the variation in the searches that can be made in relation to different types of detentions, how a detention is characterized is often important. See generally, LaFave, "Seizures" Typology: Classifying Detentions of the Person To Resolve Warrant, Grounds, and Search Issues, 17 U.Mich.J.L.Reform 417 (1984).

This chapter begins with the problem of determining whether any detention at all has occurred. It then considers detentions or seizures constituting "arrests," the benchmark of Fourth Amendment analysis in this area. After this, it addresses field detentions for investigation—so-called *"Terry"* stops—and the right to make weapon searches where no arrest has occurred. Next, the chapter considers certain non-arrest detentions of persons in automobiles. The following section deals with traffic stops, detentions arguably different from both arrests and field detentions. Finally, attention turns to roadblock stops and the "pretext" issue—whether an otherwise proper arrest or detention can be challenged on the basis of the officer's subjective "intent" or on the basis of what a reasonable officer would do in the situation.

A. DETERMINING WHETHER A PERSON IS DETAINED OR SEIZED

EDITORS' INTRODUCTION: DEFINING "SEIZURES" OF THE PERSON

Whether confrontations between police officers and suspects involve "seizures" as that term is used in the Fourth Amendment has long presented a difficult problem. Until the principal case, the Supreme Court's case law appeared to indicate that whether a seizure occurred depended upon how a reasonable person would react to the officer's actions.

In 1984, the Court indicated that "police questioning, by itself" is unlikely to result in a seizure. Only if an officer, "by means of physical force or show of authority," restrains a person's liberty has the person been seized. An officer seizes a person by approaching him and posing questions, therefore, only if "the circumstances of the encounter are so intimidating as to demonstrate that a reasonable person would have believed he was not free to leave if he [did not respond]." Immigration and Naturalization Service v. Delgado, 466 U.S. 210, 216, 104 S.Ct. 1758, 1762, 80 L.Ed.2d 247, 255 (1984).

The standard was applied in Michigan v. Chesternut, 486 U.S. 567, 108 S.Ct. 1975, 100 L.Ed.2d 565 (1988). Four Detroit officers were engaged in routine patrol in a marked police cruiser. As the cruiser came to an intersection, one officer saw a car pull over to the curb and an occupant alight. This person approached Chesternut, standing alone on the corner. Chesternut saw the cruiser as it approached; he immediately turned and ran. The cruiser caught up with him and drove alongside him for a short distance. During this time, the officers observed Chesternut pull several packets from his pocket and discard them. Chesternut then stopped and one officer examined the discarded packets. Concluding that the packets contained codeine, the officers placed Chesternut under arrest. A search revealed other drugs, including heroin. After Chesternut was charged with drug offenses, a magistrate held he had been unlawfully seized before he discarded the codeine. This holding was affirmed on appeal in reliance upon state court holdings that any police pursuit was a seizure. Since the officers did not have reasonable suspicion when their pursuit of Chesternut began, the state courts reasoned, their seizure of him was unreasonable.

A unanimous Supreme Court reversed. Justice Blackmun, writing for the Court, rejected both the position that any pursuit is a seizure and the view that no seizure can occur until and if the officer actually apprehends the person. Instead, he indicated, the Court would continue to apply its traditional "contextual approach." Under this approach, "the police can be said to have seized an individual 'only if, in view of all of the circumstances surrounding the incident, a reasonable person would have believed that he was not free to leave.' "Applying this standard, the Court found no seizure occurred before Chesternut discarded the packets:

no seizure until apprehended by police

> [T]he police conduct involved here would not have communicated to the reasonable person an attempt to capture or otherwise intrude upon [the person's] freedom of movement. The record does not reflect that the police activated a siren or flashers; or that they commanded [Chesternut] to halt, or displayed any weapons; or that they operated the car in an aggressive manner to block [Chesternut's] course or otherwise control the direction or speed of his movement. While the very presence of a police car driving parallel to a running pedestrian could be somewhat intimidating, this kind of police presence does not, standing alone, constitute a seizure.

486 U.S. at 575, 108 S.Ct. at 1980, 100 L.Ed.2d at 573. Consequently, the prosecution was not required to establish the reasonableness of the officers' actions prior to Chesternut's discarding of the packets.

California v. Hodari D.

Supreme Court of the United States, 1991.
499 U.S. 621, 111 S.Ct. 1547, 113 L.Ed.2d 690.

■ JUSTICE SCALIA delivered the opinion of the Court.

Late one evening in April 1988, Officers Brian McColgin and Jerry Pertoso were on patrol in a high-crime area of Oakland, California. They were dressed in street clothes but wearing jackets with "Police" embossed on both front and back. Their unmarked car proceeded west on Foothill Boulevard, and turned south onto 63rd Avenue. As they rounded the corner, they saw four or five youths huddled around a small red car parked at the curb. When the youths saw the officers' car approaching they apparently panicked, and took flight. The respondent here, Hodari D., and one companion ran west through an alley; the others fled south. The red car also headed south, at a high rate of speed.

The officers were suspicious and gave chase. McColgin remained in the car and continued south on 63rd Avenue; Pertoso left the car, ran back north along 63rd, then west on Foothill Boulevard, and turned south on 62nd Avenue. Hodari, meanwhile, emerged from the alley onto 62nd and ran north. Looking behind as he ran, he did not turn and see Pertoso until the officer was almost upon him, whereupon he tossed away what appeared to be a small rock. A moment later, Pertoso tackled Hodari, handcuffed him, and radioed for assistance. Hodari was found to be carrying $130 in cash and a pager; and the rock he had discarded was found to be crack cocaine.

Motion to Suppress

Procedurally
1) denied by trial
2) reversed by Appeals
3) Calif Supreme denied review
4) U.S. Supreme Crt.

In the juvenile proceeding brought against him, Hodari moved to suppress the evidence relating to the cocaine. The court denied the motion without opinion. The California Court of Appeal reversed, holding that Hodari had been "seized" when he saw Officer Pertoso running towards him, that this seizure was unreasonable under the Fourth Amendment, and that the evidence of cocaine had to be suppressed as the fruit of that illegal seizure. The California Supreme Court denied the State's application for review. We granted certiorari.

Issue →

As this case comes to us, the only issue presented is whether, at the time he dropped the drugs, Hodari had been "seized" within the meaning of the Fourth Amendment. If so, respondent argues, the drugs were the fruit of that seizure and the evidence concerning them was properly excluded. If not, the drugs were abandoned by Hodari and lawfully recovered by the police, and the evidence should have been admitted. * * *

seizure =
taking possession

We have long understood that the Fourth Amendment's protection against "unreasonable . . . seizures" includes seizure of the person. From the time of the founding to the present, the word "seizure" has meant a "taking possession," 2 N. Webster, An American Dictionary of the English Language 67 (1828). For most purposes at common law, the word connoted not merely grasping, or applying physical force to, the animate or inanimate object in question, but actually bringing it within physical control. * * * To constitute an arrest, however—the quintessential "seizure of the person" under our Fourth Amendment jurisprudence—the mere grasping or application of physical force with lawful authority, whether or not it succeeded in subduing the arrestee, was sufficient. See, e.g., Whithead v. Keyes, 85 Mass. 495, 501 (1862) ("[A]n officer effects an arrest of a person whom he has authority to arrest, by laying his hand on him for the purpose of arresting him, though he may not succeed in stopping and holding him"). * * *

To say that an arrest is effected by the slightest application of physical force, despite the arrestee's escape, is not to say that for Fourth Amendment purposes there is a continuing arrest during the period of fugitivity. If, for example, Pertoso had laid his hands upon Hodari to arrest him, but Hodari had broken away and had then cast away the cocaine, it would hardly be realistic to say that that disclosure had been made during the course of an arrest. The present case, however, is even one step further removed. It does not involve the application of any physical force; Hodari was untouched by Officer Pertoso at the time he discarded the cocaine. His defense relies instead upon the proposition that a seizure occurs "when the officer, by means of physical force *or show of authority*, has in some way restrained the liberty of a citizen." Terry v. Ohio, 392 U.S. 1, 19, n. 16, 88 S.Ct. 1868, 1879, n. 16, 20 L.Ed.2d 889 (1968) (emphasis added). Hodari contends (and we accept as true for purposes of this decision) that Pertoso's pursuit qualified as a "show of authority" calling upon Hodari to halt. The narrow question before us is whether, with respect to a show of authority as with respect to application of physical force, a seizure occurs even though the subject does not yield. We hold that it does not. [*Hodari says*] [*Supreme Court*]

The language of the Fourth Amendment, of course, cannot sustain respondent's contention. The word "seizure" readily bears the meaning of a laying on of hands or application of physical force to restrain movement, even when it is ultimately unsuccessful. ("She seized the purse-snatcher, but he broke out of her grasp.") It does not remotely apply, however, to the prospect of a policeman yelling "Stop, in the name of the law!" at a fleeing form that continues to flee. That is no seizure. Nor can the result respondent wishes to achieve be produced—indirectly, as it were—by suggesting that Pertoso's uncomplied-with show of authority was a common-law arrest, and then appealing to the principle that all common-law arrests are seizures. An arrest requires either physical force (as described above) or, where that is absent, submission to the assertion of authority.

* * *

We do not think it desirable, even as a policy matter, to stretch the Fourth Amendment beyond its words and beyond the meaning of arrest, as respondent urges. Street pursuits always place the public at some risk, and compliance with police orders to stop should therefore be encouraged. Only a few of those orders, we must presume, will be without adequate basis, and since the addressee has no ready means of identifying the deficient ones it almost invariably is the responsible course to comply. Unlawful orders will not be deterred, moreover, by sanctioning through the exclusionary rule those of them that are not obeyed. Since policemen do not command "Stop!" expecting to be ignored, or give chase hoping to be outrun, it fully suffices to apply the deterrent to their genuine, successful seizures.

Respondent contends that his position is sustained by the so-called *Mendenhall* test, formulated by Justice Stewart's opinion in United States v. Mendenhall, 446 U.S. 544, 554, 100 S.Ct. 1870, 1877, 64 L.Ed.2d 497 (1980), and adopted by the Court in later cases: "[A] person has been 'seized' within the meaning of the Fourth Amendment only if, in view of all the circumstances surrounding the incident, a reasonable person would [*Mendenhall test*] have believed that he was not free to leave." In seeking to rely upon that test here, respondent fails to read it carefully. It says that a person has been seized "only if," not that he has been seized "whenever"; it states a necessary, but not a sufficient, condition for seizure—or, more precisely, for seizure effected through a "show of authority." *Mendenhall* establishes that the test for existence of a "show of authority" is an objective one: not whether the citizen perceived that he was being ordered to restrict his movement, but whether the officer's words and actions would have conveyed that to a reasonable person. Application of this objective test was the basis for our decision in the other case principally relied upon by respondent, [Michigan v. Chesternut, 486 U.S. 567, 108 S.Ct. 1975, 100 L.Ed.2d 565 (1988)], where we concluded that the police cruiser's slow following of the defendant did not convey the message that he was not free to disregard the police and go about his business. We did not address in *Chesternut*, however, the question whether, if the *Mendenhall* test was met—if the message that the defendant was not free to leave had been conveyed—a Fourth Amendment seizure would have occurred.

Quite relevant to the present case, however, was our decision in Brower v. Inyo County, 489 U.S. 593, 596, 109 S.Ct. 1378, 1381, 103 L.Ed.2d 628 (1989). In that case, police cars with flashing lights had chased the decedent for 20 miles—surely an adequate "show of authority"—but he did not stop until his fatal crash into a police-erected blockade. The issue was whether his death could be held to be the consequence of an unreasonable seizure in violation of the Fourth Amendment. We did not even consider the possibility that a seizure could have occurred during the course of the chase because, as we explained, that "show of authority" did not produce his stop. * * *

In sum, assuming that Pertoso's pursuit in the present case constituted a "show of authority" enjoining Hodari to halt, since Hodari did not comply with that injunction he was not seized until he was tackled. The cocaine abandoned while he was running was in this case not the fruit of a seizure, and his motion to exclude evidence of it was properly denied. We reverse the decision of the California Court of Appeal, and remand for further proceedings not inconsistent with this opinion.

It is so ordered.

■ JUSTICE STEVENS, with whom JUSTICE MARSHALL joins, dissenting.

* * *

The first question * * * is whether the common law should define the scope of the outer boundaries of the constitutional protection against unreasonable seizures. Even if, contrary to settled precedent, traditional common-law analysis were controlling, it would still be necessary to decide whether the unlawful attempt to make an arrest should be considered a seizure within the meaning of the Fourth Amendment, and whether the exclusionary rule should apply to unlawful attempts.

* * *

Whatever else one may think of today's decision, it unquestionably represents a departure from earlier Fourth Amendment case law. * * *

[handwritten margin note: show of authority did not produce the stop!]

Because the facts of this case are somewhat unusual, it is appropriate to note that the same issue would arise if the show of force took the form of a command to "freeze," a warning shot, or the sound of sirens accompanied by a patrol car's flashing lights. In any of these situations, there may be a significant time interval between the initiation of the officer's show of force and the complete submission by the citizen. At least on the facts of this case, the Court concludes that the timing of the seizure is governed by the citizen's reaction, rather than by the officer's conduct. One consequence of this conclusion is that the point at which the interaction between citizen and police officer becomes a seizure occurs, not when a reasonable citizen believes he or she is no longer free to go, but, rather, only after the officer exercises control over the citizen.

In my view, our interests in effective law enforcement and in personal liberty would be better served by adhering to a standard that "allows the police to determine in advance whether the conduct contemplated will implicate the Fourth Amendment." The range of possible responses to a police show of force, and the multitude of problems that may arise in determining whether, and at which moment, there has been "submission," can only create uncertainty and generate litigation.

* * *

It seems equally clear to me that the constitutionality of a police officer's show of force should be measured by the conditions that exist at the time of the officer's action. A search must be justified on the basis of the facts available at the time it is initiated; the subsequent discovery of evidence does not retroactively validate an unconstitutional search. The same approach should apply to seizures; the character of the citizen's response should not govern the constitutionality of the officer's conduct.

If an officer effects an arrest by touching a citizen, apparently the Court would accept the fact that a seizure occurred, even if the arrestee should thereafter break loose and flee. In such a case, the constitutionality of the seizure would be evaluated as of the time the officer acted. That category of seizures would then be analyzed in the same way as searches, namely, was the police action justified when it took place? It is anomalous, at best, to fashion a different rule for the subcategory of "show of force" arrests.

In cases within this new subcategory, there will be a period of time during which the citizen's liberty has been restrained, but he or she has not yet completely submitted to the show of force. A motorist pulled over by a highway patrol car cannot come to an immediate stop, even if the motorist intends to obey the patrol car's signal. If an officer decides to make the kind of random stop forbidden by Delaware v. Prouse, 440 U.S. 648, 99 S.Ct. 1391, 59 L.Ed.2d 660 (1979), and, after flashing his lights, but before the vehicle comes to a complete stop, sees that the license plate has expired, can he justify his action on the ground that the seizure became lawful after it was initiated but before it was completed? In an airport setting, may a drug enforcement agent now approach a group of passengers with his gun drawn, announce a "baggage search," and rely on the passengers' reactions to justify his investigative stops? The holding of today's majority fails to recognize the coercive and intimidating nature of such behavior and creates a rule that may allow such behavior to go unchecked.

The deterrent purposes of the exclusionary rule focus on the conduct of law enforcement officers and on discouraging improper behavior on their part, and not on the reaction of the citizen to the show of force. In the present case, if Officer Pertoso had succeeded in tackling respondent before he dropped the rock of cocaine, the rock unquestionably would have been excluded as the fruit of the officer's unlawful seizure. Instead, under the Court's logic-chopping analysis, the exclusionary rule has no application because an attempt to make an unconstitutional seizure is beyond the coverage of the Fourth Amendment, no matter how outrageous or unreasonable the officer's conduct may be.

It is too early to know the consequences of the Court's holding. If carried to its logical conclusion, it will encourage unlawful displays of force that will frighten countless innocent citizens into surrendering whatever privacy rights they may still have. * * *

I respectfully dissent.

NOTE: SEIZURE OF A STATIONARY SUSPECT

Whether a person approached while stationary has been seized presents a somewhat different question. Florida v. Bostick, 501 U.S. 429, 111 S.Ct. 2382, 115 L.Ed.2d 389 (1991), presented the issue in the context of "bus sweeps." Bostick was prosecuted for possession of cocaine found in his luggage; his motion to suppress the cocaine was overruled. The basic facts were as follows:

> Two officers, complete with badges, insignia and one of them holding a recognizable zipper pouch, containing a pistol, boarded a bus bound from Miami to Atlanta during a stopover in Fort Lauderdale. Eyeing the passengers, the officers admittedly without articulable suspicion, picked out the defendant passenger and asked to inspect his ticket and identification. The ticket, from Miami to Atlanta, matched the defendant's identification and both were immediately returned to him as unremarkable. However, the two police officers persisted and explained their presence as narcotics agents on the lookout for illegal drugs. In pursuit of that aim, they then requested the defendant's consent to search his luggage.

Although the testimony was conflicting, the trial court implicitly found the officers advised Bostick that he had a right to refuse the consent and that he nevertheless consented to a search of the bag in which the cocaine was found.

A majority of the Supreme Court construed the Florida Supreme Court's holding below as adopting a *per se* rule that officers who board buses during scheduled stops to question passengers and to seek consent for luggage searches necessarily seize the passengers confronted. If the officers lack reasonable suspicion, the seizure is unreasonable and taints the subsequently-given consent. In so adopting a *per se* rule, the Supreme Court held, the Florida tribunal erred. As in other situations, a seizure does not necessarily occur simply because an officer approaches a bus passenger and asks a few questions. Whether on the facts of *Bostick* a seizure took place, the Court observed, was in "some doubt," and it remanded the case for the state courts to address this under the correct legal standard. That standard, it continued, requires in the context presented the state courts not focus upon whether Bostick felt "free to leave":

When police attempt to question a person who is walking down the street or through an airport lobby, it makes sense to inquire whether a reasonable person would feel free to continue walking. But when the person is seated on a bus and has no desire to leave, the degree to which a reasonable person would feel that he or she could leave is not an accurate measure of the coercive effect of the encounter. * * * In such a situation, the appropriate inquiry is whether a reasonable person would feel free to decline the officers' requests or otherwise terminate the encounter. This formulation follows logically from prior cases and breaks no new ground. We have said before that the crucial test is whether, taking into account all of the circumstances surrounding the encounter, the police conduct would "have communicated to a reasonable person that he was not at liberty to ignore the police presence and go about his business." Where the encounter takes place is one factor, but it is not the only one. And * * * an individual may decline an officer's request without fearing prosecution. We have consistently held that a refusal to cooperate, without more, does not furnish the minimal level of objective justification needed for a detention or seizure.

501 U.S. at 435–37, 111 S.Ct. at 2387, 115 L.Ed.2d at 399–400.

B. ARRESTS AND ASSOCIATED SEARCHES

EDITORS' INTRODUCTION: ARRESTS AND THEIR VALIDITY

The right to search arising by virtue of effectuation of certain "arrests" is quite broad. It is at least broader than the right to search arising when other detentions are made. Among the reasons why it is important to identify those detentions constituting arrests, therefore, is that characterizing detentions will often determine officers' right to search because of those detentions.

Definition of Arrest. The increased complexity of the law relating to detentions makes the definition of arrest more difficult. In part, this is because the definition may be called into play to distinguish arrests from other detentions. One court—with these considerations in mind—offered:

> The classic definition of arrest consists of " ' . . . the apprehending or restraining of one's person, in order to be forthcoming to answer an alleged or suspected crime.' " E. Fisher, *Laws of Arrest* 7 (1967) (quoting 4 W. Blackstone, *Commentaries* 288, 289). The necessary first step in determining whether there has been an arrest is to ask whether the individual was free to leave the presence of the police.
>
> A second element of arrest is the likelihood that the present confinement will be accompanied by future interference with the individual's freedom of movement. This element reflects the common law notion that an arrest is more than a present confinement. To be an arrest, confinement should simply be the initial action in criminal prosecution.

State v. Rupe, 101 Wn.2d 664, 683–84, 683 P.2d 571, 584 (1984). This definition suggest an arrest requires a certain intention on the part of the officer. Discussions of arrest sometimes speak of a necessity for an intent to

[handwritten marginalia: "Arrest Defined" and "? was citizen free to leave"]

effect an arrest. E.g., United States v. Chaffen, 587 F.2d 920, 923 (8th Cir.1978).

"Custodial" and Other Arrests. As the cases discussed in this section and elsewhere in these materials make clear, the Supreme Court's case law sometimes speaks in terms of "custodial" arrests. The Court has never developed precisely what is meant by this term. Perhaps, however, the Court intends to distinguish those arrests that will result in the release of the suspect in the field from those that will result in the suspect's being removed to some other location—a stationhouse or courtroom—for further "processing." The distinction between custodial arrests and other detentions is considered later in this chapter in the material on so-called "traffic stops."

"Formal" Arrests. The Supreme Court's cases also refer to "formal" arrests. Berkemer v. McCarty, 468 U.S. 420, 441, 104 S.Ct. 3138, 3151, 82 L.Ed.2d 317, 336 (1984); Rawlings v. Kentucky, 448 U.S. 98, 111, 100 S.Ct. 2556, 2564, 65 L.Ed.2d 633, 645 (1980). Again, however, the Court has not defined this term. It seems likely, however, the Court regards a "formal" arrest as a detention accompanied by the officer's expressed announcement to the detained person that the officer is making an arrest.

Some jurisdictions require such an announcement. In a number of jurisdictions, for example, an officer is directed to inform the person of the officer's authority and the reason or cause for the arrest. Exceptions are commonly provided for situations in which the suspect's flight or resistance make such action by the officer impractical. E.g., Mich.Code Crim.Pro. § 764.19; N.Y.—McKinney's Crim.Pro.L. § 00140.15(2). Nevertheless, lower courts have held that compliance with provisions such as these is not necessary to the making of a valid arrest under state law. E.g., Williams v. State, 278 Ark. 9, 12, 642 S.W.2d 887, 889 (1982). The Supreme Court has never indicated that the Fourth Amendment requires such an announcement. Nor has an announcement of this sort been required by the lower courts as a matter of federal constitutional law. As one federal court stated, "the determination of whether an arrest has occurred for Fourth Amendment purposes does not depend upon whether the officers announced that they were placing the suspects under arrest." United States v. Rose, 731 F.2d 1337, 1342 (8th Cir.1984).

Warrant Requirements—Arrests. Arrests may be made pursuant to arrest warrants, issued by magistrates on the basis of information found by those magistrates to constitute probable cause to believe the persons guilty of offenses. Rule 4 of the Federal Rules of Criminal Procedure, for example, authorizes issuance of an arrest warrant.

Such warrants are, however, seldom required as a matter of Fourth Amendment law. In United States v. Watson, 423 U.S. 411, 96 S.Ct. 820, 46 L.Ed.2d 598 (1976), the Supreme Court considered whether the Fourth Amendment requires—in the absence of exigent circumstances—that an arrest warrant be procured for an arrest in a public place. The Court noted long and widespread acceptance of the common law rule that a warrantless arrest for a felony was permissible, even if the felony was not committed in the presence of the officer, if the officer had probable cause to believe the suspect guilty. Congressional enactments authorizing such arrests reflected the understanding of that body that the Fourth Amendment did not require more. Thus, the Court concluded:

> Law enforcement officers may find it wise to seek arrest warrants where practicable to do so, and their judgments about probable cause may be more readily accepted where backed by a warrant issued by a magistrate. But we decline to transform this judicial preference into a constitutional rule when the judgment of the Nation and Congress has for so long been to authorize warrantless public arrests on probable cause rather than to encumber criminal prosecutions with endless litigation with respect to the existence of exigent circumstances, whether it was practicable to get a warrant, whether the suspect was about to flee, and the like.

423 U.S. at 423–24, 96 S.Ct. at 827–28, 46 L.Ed.2d at 609.

In regard to misdemeanors, the law is less clear. At common law, a warrantless arrest was permitted for a misdemeanor only if the offense was a breach of the peace and committed in the presence of the officer. See Commonwealth v. Reeves, 223 Pa.Super. 51, 52–53, 297 A.2d 142, 143 (1972). Many American jurisdictions, however, permit warrantless misdemeanor arrests in more circumstances. Warrantless arrests are, for example, often permitted for any misdemeanor committed in the presence of the officer. Sometimes state statutory authority or case law is broader. See State v. Martin, 275 S.C. 141, 268 S.E.2d 105 (1980), construing the South Carolina statutes as permitting an officer to make a warrantless arrest for a misdemeanor when the facts and circumstances observed by the officer give the officer probable cause to believe that a misdemeanor has been "freshly committed."

If a misdemeanor arrest is invalid *under state law* because an arrest warrant was not obtained, does the Fourth Amendment require suppression of evidence obtained in a search incident to that arrest? If not, does state law? Some courts—without much consideration—conclude evidence of this sort cannot be used. See Commonwealth v. Trefry, 249 Pa.Super. 117, 375 A.2d 786 (1977); Commonwealth v. Reeves, supra.

Does the Fourth Amendment impose some version of the traditional requirement of an arrest warrant for certain arrests? *Watson* relied heavily upon acceptance of the common law rule that felony arrests did not require warrants. Perhaps the widespread acceptance of the common law notion that some misdemeanor arrests demand warrants means a warrant requirement for such arrests is incorporated into the Fourth Amendment. The Supreme Court has never addressed the issue.

Warrant Requirements—Search for Person to be Arrested. When an arrest requires entry into premises to find the suspect and arrest him, it is clear the Fourth Amendment's warrant requirement comes into play. In Payton v. New York, 445 U.S. 573, 100 S.Ct. 1371, 63 L.Ed.2d 639 (1980), officers entered the suspects' residences seeking them for purposes of arrest. Such activity, the Court reasoned, breaches the entrance of an individual's home just as does a search for evidence. "Absent exigent circumstance," it concluded, "that threshold may not reasonably be crossed without a warrant." It then continued:

> [W]e note the State's suggestion that only a search warrant based on probable cause to believe the suspect is at home at a given time can adequately protect the privacy interests at stake, and since such a warrant requirement is manifestly impractical, there need be no warrant of any kind. We find this ingenious argument unpersuasive. It is true that an arrest warrant requirement may afford less protection than a search warrant requirement, but it will suffice to interpose the magistrate's determination of probable cause between the zealous officer and the citizen. If there is sufficient evidence of a citizen's participation in a felony to persuade a judicial officer that his arrest is justified, it is constitutionally reasonable to require him to open his doors to the officers of the law. Thus, for Fourth Amendment purposes, an arrest warrant founded on probable cause implicitly carries with it the limited authority to enter a dwelling in which the suspect lives when there is reason to believe the suspect is within.

445 U.S. at 602–03, 100 S.Ct. at 1388, 63 L.Ed.2d at 660–61.

But when the premises entered are not those of the suspect, a different situation arises. In Steagald v. United States, 451 U.S. 204, 101 S.Ct. 1642, 68 L.Ed.2d 38 (1981), federal drug Enforcement Administration agents had a warrant for the arrest of Lyons. Two days after receiving a tip from an informant that Lyons could be found at a particular residence, they searched that residence. They did not find Lyons but discovered a substantial quantity of cocaine. This was admitted at Steagald's trial for possession of that substance. Finding constitutional error, the Supreme Court held the absence of a valid search warrant rendered the search of the premises for Lyons unreasonable:

> [W]hile the [arrest] warrant * * * may have protected Lyons from an unreasonable seizure, it did absolutely nothing to protect [Steagald's] privacy interest in being free from an unreasonable invasion and search of his home. Instead, [Steagald's] only protection from an illegal entry and search was the agent's personal determination of probable cause. In the absence of exigent circumstances, we have consistently held that such judicially untested determinations are not reliable enough to justify an entry into a person's home to arrest him without a warrant, or a search of a home for objects in the absence of a search warrant. We see no reason to depart from this settled course when the search of a home is for a person rather than an object.

451 U.S. at 213–14, 101 S.Ct. at 1648, 68 L.Ed.2d at 46. In *Steagald,* Steagald and one Gaultney were apprehended standing outside the house; Gaultney's wife was inside when it was searched. Before the Supreme Court, the Government urged that Steagald had failed to demonstrate he had an expectation of privacy in the house. The Court, however, concluded the Government had effectively conceded in the lower courts that Steagald had a privacy interest in the premises and that it could therefore not challenge the matter before the Court. In future cases where a suspect is found during a search of a third party's premises, will the suspect be able to show a sufficient privacy interest in those premises to enable him to challenge the absence of the search warrant required by *Steagald*?

The warrant requirement here, just as the general search warrant requirement (see part A of Chapter 5), is subject to an emergency exception. The matter was addressed in Welsh v. Wisconsin, 466 U.S. 740, 104 S.Ct. 2091, 80 L.Ed.2d 732 (1984). Information from a witness led police officers to believe Welsh had, while intoxicated, driven his automobile off the highway into a field, abandoned it, and gone to his nearby residence. Police went to his residence, entered, and—upon finding Welsh lying naked in bed—placed him under arrest for driving a motor vehicle under the influence of an intoxicant. They took him to the station where he refused to submit to a breathalyzer test. Subsequently, authorities began proceedings to revoke his driver's license, based upon his refusal to submit to the breathalyzer test. Under Wisconsin law, if his arrest had been unlawful his refusal to submit to the breathalyzer test would have been reasonable and that refusal could not serve as the basis for revocation. The state courts ultimately rejected Welsh's argument that his arrest violated the Fourth Amendment, despite the officers' failure to obtain a warrant. The officers' actions were reasonable, they reasoned, in view of their "hot pursuit," the risk of harm to the public and Welsh himself, and the need for an immediate arrest and breath test before the alcohol in Welsh's blood disappeared from his system.

The Supreme Court reversed. Justice Brennan, writing for the Court, acknowledged that some "emergency conditions" would sometimes justify warrantless home arrests. But, he continued:

> [A]n important factor to be considered when determining whether any exigency exists is the gravity of the underlying offense for which the arrest is being made. * * * [A]pplication of the exigent-circumstances exception in the context of a home entry should rarely be sanctioned where there is probable cause to believe that only a minor offense, such as the kind at issue in this case, has been committed.

emergency exception & underlying offense

466 U.S. at 753, 104 S.Ct. at 2099, 80 L.Ed.2d at 745. Under Wisconsin law, first offense driving while intoxicated is a noncriminal civil forfeiture offense for which the maximum penalty was, at the time, a $200 fine. Turning to the facts of the case, the Court continued:

> [T]he claim of hot pursuit is unconvincing because there was no immediate or continuous pursuit of the petitioner from the scene of a crime. Moreover, because the petitioner had already arrived home and had abandoned his car at the scene of the accident, there was little remaining threat to the public safety. Hence, the only potential emergency claimed by the State was the need to ascertain the petitioner's blood-alcohol level.
>
> Even assuming, however, that the underlying facts would support a finding of this exigent circumstance, mere similarity to other cases involving the imminent destruction of evidence is not sufficient. [Wisconsin's classification of driving while intoxicated as a civil offense for which no imprisonment is possible] * * * is the best indication of the state's interest in precipitating an arrest, and is one that can easily be identified both by the courts and by officers faced with a decision to arrest. Given this expression of the state's interest, a warrantless home arrest cannot be upheld simply because evidence of the petitioner's

blood-alcohol level might have dissipated while the police obtained a warrant.

466 U.S. at 753–54, 104 S.Ct. at 2099–2100, 80 L.Ed.2d at 745–46.

In view of this conclusion, the Court found "no occasion to consider whether the Fourth Amendment might impose an absolute ban on warrantless home arrests for certain minor offenses."

The Supreme Court had earlier applied a "hot pursuit" sort of exception to the warrant requirement in this context. In United States v. Santana, 427 U.S. 38, 96 S.Ct. 2406, 49 L.Ed.2d 300 (1976), officers in an automobile pulled up in front of Santana's residence. She was standing in the door. When the officers shouted, "Police," displayed their badges and advanced, she "retreated" into the vestibule of her house. The officers— without a warrant—followed her into the vestibule and arrested her. No constitutional defect was found in the officers' actions. While she was in her doorway, the Court reasoned, Santana was in a "public place" and, under *Watson,* no warrant was required. Where the police follow in "true 'hot pursuit,'" a suspect may not, by retreating into a house, "defeat an arrest which has been set in motion in a public place * * *."

Entry to Arrest—Announcement Requirement. Where officers rely upon a search warrant as authority to enter premises and search those premises for a suspect they have grounds to arrest, the propriety of the officers' actions in gaining entry is undoubtedly governed by the rules relating to entry to execute a search warrant, discussed in Chapter 3. In other situations, however, must officers make some sort of preliminary announcements—as, for example, to their purpose—and perhaps also a request for admission before entering?

In Miller v. United States, 357 U.S. 301, 78 S.Ct. 1190, 2 L.Ed.2d 1332 (1958), the Government conceded that the validity of an entry to make an arrest without a warrant was to be tested by criteria identical to those which 18 U.S.C.A. § 3109 (set out in the Editors' Introduction to Part 3 of Chapter 3) imposes upon entry to execute a search warrant. Since the officers in *Miller* failed to give notice of their authority and purpose before breaking to enter to locate and arrest Miller, the entry, Miller's arrest, and the search incident to the arrest were held invalid and the evidence obtained in the search was inadmissible. The Court reached a similar result in Sabbath v. United States, 391 U.S. 585, 88 S.Ct. 1755, 20 L.Ed.2d 828 (1968). *Miller* and *Sabbath* may, of course, reflect only the Court's application of federal statutory law. However, the Supreme Court's Fourth Amendment case law concerning entry to execute a search warrant, covered in Part C of Chapter 3, suggests that entry to make an arrest is subject to similar requirements. Thus, *Miller* and *Sabbath* may reflect a constitutionally-required construction of the federal statute.

State law often imposes a notice requirement and frequently provides for exceptions. Under New York statutory law, for example, an officer must, before entering to effect an arrest, give "or make reasonable effort to give" notice of "his authority and purpose." Notice is not required if the officer has reasonable cause to believe giving the notice would result in the suspect escaping (or attempting to escape), the life or safety of anyone being endangered, or the destruction, damaging or secretion of material evidence. N.Y.—McKinney's Crim.Proc.L. §§ 120.80(4) (arrests under arrest warrants), 140.15(4) (warrantless arrests). See also, West's Ann.Cal.Penal Code § 844 (officer may "break open the door or window" to make an arrest "after having demanded admittance and explained the purpose for which admittance is desired").

Probable Cause Requirement—In General. Although the warrant requirement has relatively little application to the reasonableness of an arrest, the Fourth Amendment's requirement of probable cause has substantial significance:

> Whether [an] arrest was constitutionally valid depends * * * upon whether, at the moment the arrest was made, the officers had probable cause to make it—whether at that moment the facts and circumstances within their knowledge and of which they had reasonably trustworthy information were sufficient to warrant a prudent man in believing that the [suspect] had committed or was committing an offense.

Beck v. Ohio, 379 U.S. 89, 91, 85 S.Ct. 223, 225, 13 L.Ed.2d 142, 145 (1964).

A subaspect of the probable cause issue is the effect of an arrest under a law later determined invalid. In Michigan v. DeFillippo, 443 U.S. 31, 99 S.Ct. 2627, 61 L.Ed.2d 343 (1979), DeFillippo was arrested under a Detroit ordinance. A search incident to that arrest resulted in discovery of controlled substances and DeFillippo was prosecuted for possession of those substances. The state courts held the ordinance under which he was arrested was unconstitutionally vague and therefore the arrest and the incidental search were invalid. The Supreme Court reversed, holding the information indicating DeFillippo violated the ordinance rendered the arrest constitutionally permissible. As to the unconstitutionality of the ordinance, the Court continued:

> Police are charged to enforce laws until and unless they are declared unconstitutional. The enactment of a law forecloses speculation by enforcement officers concerning its constitutionality—with the possible exception of a law so grossly and flagrantly unconstitutional that any person of reasonable prudence would be bound to see its flaws. Society would be ill-served if its police officers took upon themselves to determine which laws are and which are not constitutionally entitled to enforcement.

443 U.S. at 37–38, 99 S.Ct. at 2632, 61 L.Ed.2d at 350.

Probable Cause—Cooperative Action and "Collective" Information. Given the complexity of many criminal offenses and the mobility of many suspects, investigations often involve more than one officer and, in fact, officers of several jurisdictions. Action by law enforcement officers may be taken upon request of other officers, perhaps ones of another jurisdiction. When one officer or agency makes an arrest upon the request of another officer or police agency, what information is to be considered in determining if probable cause exists?

In Whiteley v. Warden, 401 U.S. 560, 91 S.Ct. 1031, 28 L.Ed.2d 306 (1971), a Carbon County, Wyoming sheriff issued a message through a statewide law enforcement radio network describing a suspect and stating an arrest warrant had been issued for him. The information submitted in support of the warrant request was not set out in the message. In response to the message, officers in another Wyoming locality—Laramie—arrested and searched the suspect. During the suspect's prosecution, items found in the search were admitted into evidence over his objection. The State urged, with regard to the Laramie officers, the radio request constituted probable cause on which they could act regardless of the validity of the warrant on which the request was based. After concluding the warrant was invalid because it was issued without probable cause, the Court continued:

> We do not * * * question that the Laramie police were entitled to act on the strength of the radio bulletin. Certainly police officers called upon to aid other officers in executing arrest warrants are entitled to assume that the officers requesting aid offered the magistrate the information requisite to support an independent judicial assessment of probable cause. Where, however, the contrary turns out to be true, an otherwise illegal arrest cannot be insulated from challenge by the decision of the instigating officer to rely on fellow officers to make the arrest.

401 U.S. at 568, 91 S.Ct. at 1037, 28 L.Ed.2d at 313.

In United States v. Hensley, 469 U.S. 221, 105 S.Ct. 675, 83 L.Ed.2d 604 (1985), the Court developed the implications of this holding:

> *Whiteley* supports the proposition that, when evidence is uncovered during a search incident to an arrest in reliance merely on a flyer or bulletin, its admissibility turns on whether the officers who *issued* the flyer possessed probable cause to make the arrest. It does not turn on whether those relying on the flyer were themselves aware of the specific facts which led their colleagues to seek their assistance. In an era when criminal suspects are increasingly mobile and increasingly likely to flee across jurisdictional boundaries, this rule is a matter of common sense: it minimizes the volume of information concerning suspects that must be transmitted to other jurisdictions and enables police in one jurisdiction to act promptly in reliance on information from another jurisdiction.

469 U.S. at 231, 105 S.Ct. at 681, 83 L.Ed.2d at 613–14.

Excessive Force. Traditionally, the amount of force permissible to make an arrest has been a matter of nonconstitutional law. In Tennessee v. Garner, 471 U.S. 1, 105 S.Ct. 1694, 85 L.Ed.2d 1 (1985), however, the Supreme Court held excessive deadly force in making an otherwise proper arrest renders that arrest "unreasonable" under the Fourth Amendment. Such reasonableness, the Court explained, depends not simply upon whether there are grounds for arrest—that is, probable cause—"but also on how [the arrest] is carried out." In Graham v. Connor, 490 U.S. 386, 109 S.Ct. 1865, 104 L.Ed.2d 443 (1989), it held that nondeadly but excessive force could have the same effect.

Traditional law permitted officers to use deadly force whenever they reasonably believed that necessary to make the arrest of a person reasonably believed to have committed a felony. *Garner* defined acceptable deadly

[handwritten margin note: Excessive Force = how arrest was carried out]

force for purposes of the Fourth Amendment rule more narrowly. Use of deadly force, the Court concluded, is unreasonable if used against a nondangerous suspect. Putting the holding affirmatively, it explained:

> Where the officer has probable cause to believe that the suspect poses a threat of serious physical harm, either to the officer or to others, it is not constitutionally unreasonable to prevent escape by using deadly force. Thus, if the suspect threatens the officer with a weapon or there is probable cause to believe that he has committed a crime involving the infliction or threatened infliction of serious physical harm, deadly force may be used if necessary to prevent escape, and if, where feasible, some warning has been given.

471 U.S. at 11–12, 105 S.Ct. at 1701, 85 L.Ed.2d at 10. On the facts of *Garner,* the Court held the officer's reasonable belief the suspect had committed nighttime burglary was *not* sufficient to justify the use of the fatal gunfire there at issue to stop the suspect.

In *Graham,* the Court explained whether nondeadly force was excessive under the Fourth Amendment

> requires careful attention to the facts and circumstances of each particular case, including the severity of the crime at issue, whether the suspect poses an immediate threat to the safety of officers or others, and whether he is actively resisting arrest or attempting to evade arrest by flight.

490 U.S. at 396, 109 S.Ct. at 1872, 104 L.Ed.2d at 454–55. Courts must consider the evidence "from the perspective of a reasonable officer on the scene," rather than with "the 20–20 vision of hindsight," and make allowances for officers' need to make split-second judgments in situations that are tense, uncertain, and rapidly evolving.

Both *Garner* and *Graham* were civil cases in which damages were sought under 42 U.S.C.A. § 1983 on the theory that the officers' use of force had made the arrests unreasonable. When, if ever, will force that is excessive under these cases render evidence inadmissible? Suppose, for example, in *Garner* the officer's gunfire had not killed Garner but had disabled him and thus enabled the officer to arrest him. Suppose further in a search incident to this arrest, items taken from the burglarized premises were found on Garner's person. Would these items be inadmissible because of the excessive force?

1.   SEARCHES INCIDENT TO ARRESTS

EDITORS' INTRODUCTION: SEARCHES INCIDENT TO ARRESTS AND THOSE PART OF STATIONHOUSE PROCESSING

The occurrence of a valid arrest itself brings into play a right to make certain searches. This right to search because of an arrest is the subject of the present subsection.

This right to search a suspect incident to an arrest must be distinguished from what may be done as part of later processing of the suspect. The Supreme Court addressed authorities' right to search at the stationhouse in Illinois v. Lafayette, 462 U.S. 640, 103 S.Ct. 2605, 77 L.Ed.2d 65

(1983). LaFayette was arrested and handcuffed at a theater for disturbing the peace. He carried a "purse-type shoulder bag" with him to the police station. Upon arrival at the station, officers took him to the "booking room" and examined the bag's contents; they found amphetamines. These were admitted into evidence at LaFayette's prosecution for possession of a controlled substance. The Supreme Court found no constitutional error, reasoning "it is not 'unreasonable' for police, as part of the routine procedure incident to incarcerating an arrested person, to search any container or article in his possession, in accordance with established inventory procedures." Characterizing an inventory search as "not an independent legal consent but rather an incidental administrative step following arrest and preceding incarceration," the majority explained its holding:

> At the stationhouse, it is entirely proper for police to remove and list or inventory property found on the person or in the possession of an arrested person who is to be jailed. A range of governmental interests support such an inventory process. It is not unheard of for persons employed in police activities to steal property taken from arrested persons; similarly, arrested persons have been known to make false claims regarding what was taken from their possession at the stationhouse. A standardized procedure for making a list or inventory as soon as reasonable after reaching the stationhouse not only deters false claims but also inhibits theft or careless handling of articles taken from the arrested person. Arrested persons have also been known to injure themselves—or others—with belts, knives, drugs or other items on their persons while being detained. Dangerous instrumentalities— such as razor blades, bombs, or weapons—can be concealed in inno-cent-looking articles taken from the arrestee's possession. The bare recital of these mundane realities justifies reasonable measures by police to limit these risks—either while the items are in police posses-sion or at the time they are returned to the arrestee upon his release. Examining all the items removed from the arrestee's person or posses-sion and listing or inventorying them is an entirely reasonable admin-istrative procedure. It is immaterial whether the police actually fear any particular package or container; the need to protect against such risks arises independent of a particular officer's subjective concerns. Finally, inspection of an arrestee's personal property may assist the police in ascertaining or verifying his identity.

462 U.S. at 646, 103 S.Ct. at 2609–10, 77 L.Ed.2d at 71. These interests, the Court noted, may sometimes be greater than those supporting a search immediately after arrest:

> Consequently, the scope of a stationhouse search will often vary from that made at the time of arrest. Police conduct that would be impracti-cal or unreasonable—or embarrassingly intrusive—on the street can more readily—and privately—be performed at the station. For exam-ple, the interest supporting a search incident to arrest would hardly justify disrobing an arrestee on the street, but the practical necessities of routine jail administration may even justify taking a prisoner's

clothing from him before confining him, although that step would be rare.

462 U.S. at 645, 103 S.Ct. at 2609, 77 L.Ed.2d at 70–71. The majority noted that it was not addressing the circumstances in which a strip search of an arrestee "may or may not be appropriate."

The Illinois court had held the search of LaFayette's shoulder bag unreasonable because the State's interests could be served by less intrusive methods, such as placing the bag in a secured locker or sealing it in a plastic bag. Granting this might have been so, a majority of the Supreme Court rejected the position that the Fourth Amendment required the Illinois police to use such less intrusive methods:

> The reasonableness of any particular governmental activity does not necessarily or invariably turn on the existence of alternative "less intrusive" means. * * * We are hardly in a position to second-guess police departments as to what practical administrative method will best deter theft by and false claims against its employees and preserve the security of the stationhouse. * * *

> Even if less intrusive means existed of protecting some particular types of property, it would be unreasonable to expect police officers in the everyday course of business to make fine and subtle distinctions in deciding which containers or items may be searched and which must be sealed as a unit.

462 U.S. at 647–48, 103 S.Ct. at 2610, 77 L.Ed.2d at 72. But the Court apparently intended to limit inventory inspections to situations in which the suspect was to be more than "booked." It noted uncertainty in the record as to whether LaFayette was to be incarcerated after being booked for disturbing the peace. "That," it offered, "is an appropriate inquiry on remand."

Perhaps the most troublesome aspect of the right to search incident to arrests is defining the scope of the permissible search. This is the subject of the principal case that follows.

Chimel v. California

Supreme Court of the United States, 1969.
395 U.S. 752, 89 S.Ct. 2034, 23 L.Ed.2d 685.

■ MR. JUSTICE STEWART delivered the opinion of the Court.

This case raises basic questions concerning the permissible scope under the Fourth Amendment of a search incident to a lawful arrest.

The relevant facts are essentially undisputed. Late in the afternoon of September 13, 1965, three police officers arrived at the Santa Ana, California, home of the petitioner with a warrant authorizing his arrest for the burglary of a coin shop. The officers knocked on the door, identified themselves to the petitioner's wife, and asked if they might come inside. She ushered them into the house, where they waited 10 or 15 minutes until the petitioner returned home from work. When the petitioner entered the house, one of the officers handed him the arrest warrant and asked for permission to "look around." The petitioner objected, but was advised that "on the basis of the lawful arrest," the officers would nonetheless conduct a search. No search warrant had been issued.

Accompanied by the petitioner's wife, the officers then looked through the entire three-bedroom house, including the attic, the garage, and a small workshop. In some rooms the search was relatively cursory. In the master bedroom and sewing room, however, the officers directed the petitioner's wife to open drawers and "to physically move contents of the drawers from side to side so that [they] might view any items that would have come from [the] burglary." After completing the search, they seized numerous items—primarily coins, but also several medals, tokens, and a few other objects. The entire search took between 45 minutes and an hour.

At the petitioner's subsequent state trial on two charges of burglary, the items taken from his house were admitted into evidence against him, over his objection that they had been unconstitutionally seized. He was convicted, and the judgments of conviction were affirmed by both the California Court of Appeal, and the California Supreme Court. Both courts accepted the petitioner's contention that the arrest warrant was invalid because the supporting affidavit was set out in conclusory terms, but held that since the arresting officers had procured the warrant "in good faith," and since in any event they had had sufficient information to constitute probable cause for the petitioner's arrest, that arrest had been lawful. From this conclusion the appellate courts went on to hold that the search of the petitioner's home had been justified, despite the absence of a search warrant, on the ground that it had been incident to a valid arrest. * * *

Without deciding the question, we proceed on the hypothesis that the California courts were correct in holding that the arrest of the petitioner was valid under the Constitution. This brings us directly to the question whether the warrantless search of the petitioner's entire house can be constitutionally justified as incident to that arrest. The decisions of this Court bearing upon that question have been far from consistent * * *.

Approval of a warrantless search incident to a lawful arrest seems first to have been articulated by the Court in 1914 as dictum in Weeks v. United States, 232 U.S. 383, 34 S.Ct. 341, 58 L.Ed. 652. * * *

That statement made no reference to any right to search the *place* where an arrest occurs, but was limited to a right to search the "person." * * *

In 1950 * * * came United States v. Rabinowitz, 339 U.S. 56, 70 S.Ct. 430, 94 L.Ed. 653, the decision upon which California primarily relies in the case now before us. In *Rabinowitz*, federal authorities had been informed that the defendant was dealing in stamps bearing forged overprints. On the basis of that information they secured a warrant for his arrest, which they executed at his one-room business office. At the time of the arrest, the officers "searched the desk, safe, and file cabinets in the office for about an hour and a half," and seized 573 stamps with forged overprints. The stamps were admitted into evidence at the defendant's trial, and this Court affirmed his conviction, rejecting the contention that the warrantless search had been unlawful. The Court held that the search in its entirety fell within the principle giving law enforcement authorities "[t]he right 'to search the place where the arrest is made in order to find and seize things connected with the crime * * *.' " * * *

Rabinowitz has come to stand for the proposition, *inter alia*, that a warrantless search "incident to a lawful arrest" may generally extend to the area that is considered to be in the "possession" or under the "control" of the person arrested. And it was on the basis of that proposition that the California courts upheld the search of the petitioner's entire house in this case. That doctrine, however, at least in the broad sense in which it was applied by the California courts in this case, can withstand neither historical nor rational analysis.

Even limited to its own facts, the *Rabinowitz* decision was * * * hardly founded on an unimpeachable line of authority. * * * Nor is the rationale by which the State seeks here to sustain the search of the petitioner's house supported by a reasoned view of the background and purpose of the Fourth Amendment.

* * *

Only last Term in Terry v. Ohio, 392 U.S. 1, 88 S.Ct. 1868, 20 L.Ed.2d 889, we emphasized that "the police must, whenever practicable, obtain advance judicial approval of searches and seizures through the warrant procedure," and that "[t]he scope of [a] search must be 'strictly tied to and justified by' the circumstances which rendered its initiation permissible." * * *

A similar analysis underlies the "search incident to arrest" principle, and marks its proper extent. When an arrest is made, it is reasonable for the arresting officer to search the person arrested in order to remove any weapons that the latter might seek to use in order to resist arrest or effect his escape. Otherwise, the officer's safety might well be endangered, and the arrest itself frustrated. In addition, it is entirely reasonable for the arresting officer to search for and seize any evidence on the arrestee's person in order to prevent its concealment or destruction. And the area into which an arrestee might reach in order to grab a weapon or evidentiary items must, of course, be governed by a like rule. A gun on a table or in a drawer in front of one who is arrested can be as dangerous to the arresting officer as one concealed in the clothing of the person arrested. There is ample justification, therefore, for a search of the arrestee's person and the area "within his immediate control" construing that phrase to mean the area from within which he might gain possession of a weapon or destructible evidence.

There is no comparable justification, however, for routinely searching any room other than that in which an arrest occurs—or, for that matter, for searching through all the desk drawers or other closed or concealed areas in that room itself. Such searches, in the absence of well-recognized exceptions, may be made only under the authority of a search warrant. The "adherence to judicial processes" mandated by the Fourth Amendment requires no less.

* * *

It is argued in the present case that it is "reasonable" to search a man's house when he is arrested in it. Under such an unconfined analysis, Fourth Amendment protection in this area would approach the evaporation point. It is not easy to explain why, for instance, it is less subjectively "reasonable" to search a man's house when he is arrested on his front lawn—or just down the street—than it is when he happens to be in the house at the time of arrest.

No consideration relevant to the Fourth Amendment suggests any point of rational limitation, once the search is allowed to go beyond the area from which the person arrested might obtain weapons or evidentiary items. The only reasoned distinction is one between a search of the person arrested and the area within his reach on the one hand and more extensive searches on the other.

The petitioner correctly points out that one result of decisions such as *Rabinowitz* * * * is to give law enforcement officials the opportunity to engage in searches not justified by probable cause, by the simple expedient of arranging to arrest suspects at home rather than elsewhere. We do not suggest that the petitioner is necessarily correct in his assertion that such a strategy was utilized here but the fact remains that had he been arrested earlier in the day, at his place of employment rather than at home, no search of his house could have been made without a search warrant.

* * *

Rabinowitz * * * [has] been the subject of critical commentary for many years, and [has] been relied upon less and less in our own decisions. It is time, for the reasons we have stated, to hold that * * * [it is] no longer to be followed.

Application of sound Fourth Amendment principles to the facts of this case produces a clear result. The search here went far beyond the petitioner's person and the area from within which he might have obtained either a weapon or something that could have been used as evidence against him. There was no constitutional justification, in the absence of a search warrant, for extending the search beyond that area. The scope of the search was, therefore, "unreasonable" under the Fourth and Fourteenth Amendments and the petitioner's conviction cannot stand.

Reversed.

■ MR. JUSTICE WHITE, with whom MR. JUSTICE BLACK joins, dissenting.

* * * The Court has always held, and does not today deny, that when there is probable cause to search and it is "impracticable" for one reason or another to get a search warrant, then a warrantless search may be reasonable.

* * *

* * * An arrest itself may often create an emergency situation making it impracticable to obtain a warrant before embarking on a related search. Again assuming that there is probable cause to search premises at the spot where a suspect is arrested, it seems to me unreasonable to require the police to leave the scene in order to obtain a search warrant when they are

already legally there to make a valid arrest, and when there must almost always be a strong possibility that confederates of the arrested man will in the meanwhile remove the items for which the police have probable cause to search. This must so often be the case that it seems to me as unreasonable to require a warrant for a search of the premises as to require a warrant for search of the person and his very immediate surroundings.

* * *

NOTES

1. **Establishing the Arrest.** Is it important when—or whether—the formal arrest occurs? In Rawlings v. Kentucky, 448 U.S. 98, 100 S.Ct. 2556, 65 L.Ed.2d 633 (1980), Rawlings was present when officers searched his companion's purse; they found 1,800 tablets of LSD and a variety of other controlled substances. When the companion told Rawlings to "take what was his," he claimed ownership of all the substances. One of the officers searched Rawlings and found $4,500 in a shirt pocket and a knife in a sheath at his side. Rawlings was then placed under "formal arrest." Challenging the admissibility of the money and the knife, Rawlings argued the search could not be justified as incident to his arrest since the arrest did not occur until after the search. A majority of the Court experienced "no difficulty" in rejecting this claim:

> Once [Rawlings] admitted ownership of the sizable quantity of drugs found in [the] purse, the police clearly had probable cause to place [him] under arrest. Where the formal arrest followed quickly on the heels of the challenged search of [Rawlings'] person, we do not believe it particularly important that the search preceded the arrest rather than vice versa.

448 U.S. at 111, 100 S.Ct. at 2564, 65 L.Ed.2d at 645–46.

2. **Need for Case Specific Justification.** Do officers need reason to believe a particular search incident to an arrest would be fruitful? In United States v. Robinson, 414 U.S. 218, 94 S.Ct. 467, 38 L.Ed.2d 427 (1973), District of Columbia police officer Jenks stopped Robinson's automobile to arrest him on probable cause to believe Robinson was driving after revocation of his motor vehicle operator's license. Jenks then searched Robinson:

> Jenks felt an object in the left breast pocket of the heavy coat [Robinson] was wearing, but testified that he "couldn't tell what it was" and also that he "couldn't actually tell the size of it." Jenks then reached into the pocket and pulled out the object, which turned out to be a "crumpled up cigarette package." Jenks testified that at this point he still did not know what was in the package:

> > "As I felt the package I could feel objects in the package but I couldn't tell what they were * * *. I knew they weren't cigarettes."

> > The officer then opened the cigarette pack and found 14 gelatin capsules of white powder which he thought to be, and which later analysis proved to be, heroin. Jenks then continued his search of [Robinson] to completion, feeling around his waist and trouser legs, and examining the remaining pockets. The heroin * * * was admitted into evidence at the trial which resulted in his conviction in the District Court.

The Supreme Court, reversing the Court of Appeals, held the search permissible:

> [O]ur * * * fundamental disagreement with the Court of Appeals arises from its suggestion that there must be litigated in each case the issue of whether or

not there was present one of the reasons supporting the authority for a search of the person incident to a lawful arrest. We do not think the long line of authorities of this Court * * *, nor what we can glean from the history of practice in this country and in England, requires such a case by case adjudication. A police officer's determination as to how and where to search the person of a suspect whom he has arrested is necessarily a quick *ad hoc* judgment which the Fourth Amendment does not require to be broken down in each instance into an analysis of each step in the search. The authority to search the person incident to a lawful custodial arrest, while based upon the need to disarm and to discover evidence, does not depend on what a court may later decide was the probability in a particular arrest situation that weapons or evidence would in fact be found upon the person of the suspect. A custodial arrest of a suspect based on probable cause is a reasonable intrusion under the Fourth Amendment; that intrusion being lawful, a search incident to the arrest requires no additional justification. It is the fact of the lawful arrest which establishes the authority to search, and we hold that in the case of a lawful custodial arrest a full search of the person is not only an exception to the warrant requirement of the Fourth Amendment, but is also a "reasonable" search under that Amendment.

414 U.S. at 235, 94 S.Ct. at 477, 38 L.Ed.2d at 440–41. Justices Marshall, Douglas and Brennan dissented.

3. **Moving and Accompanying the Suspect.** May an officer who has arrested a suspect in a public place accompany the suspect into his dwelling or into particular parts of the dwelling as an incident of the arrest? In Washington v. Chrisman, 455 U.S. 1, 102 S.Ct. 812, 70 L.Ed.2d 778 (1982), a campus police officer observed a student, Overdahl, exit a dormitory carrying a half-gallon bottle of gin. Overdahl appeared to be underage. The officer stopped him and asked for identification. He responded that his identification was in his dormitory room and asked whether the officer could wait until he retrieved it. The officer replied he would have to accompany Overdahl to his room, to which Overdahl responded, "O.K." Overdahl's roommate, Chrisman, was in the room when the officer and Overdahl arrived. The officer remained at the doorway while Overdahl entered the room to look for identification. While at the doorway, the officer observed what he believed to be marijuana seeds and a pipe on a desk about 8 to 10 feet away. He entered the room and confirmed his suspicions. After placing the roommates under arrest and obtaining their consent to a search of the room, the officer found additional drugs. Chrisman was prosecuted for possession of controlled substances. His conviction was overturned by the Washington Supreme Court on the ground that, although the officer could have accompanied Overdahl into the room after arresting him, he was not permitted under the Fourth Amendment to enter the room to seize evidence of crime without a warrant or exigent circumstances.

The Supreme Court reversed. The majority reasoned the Fourth Amendment permits the officer "to remain literally at [the arrestee's] elbow at all times":

[I]t is not "unreasonable" under the Fourth Amendment for a police officer, as a matter of routine, to monitor the movements of an arrested person, as his judgment dictates, following the arrest. The officer's need to ensure his own safety—as well as the integrity of the arrest—is compelling. Such surveillance is not an impermissible invasion of the privacy or personal liberty of an individual who has been arrested.

455 U.S. at 7, 102 S.Ct. at 817, 70 L.Ed.2d at 785. The majority also concluded that since the officer could have accompanied Overdahl into the dormitory room, his remaining in the doorway did not make his entry into the room after seeing contraband in plain view a Fourth Amendment violation.

4. **Search for Dangerous Persons.** What action may officers take at the scene of an arrest to protect themselves from persons other than the individual arrested? In Maryland v. Buie, 494 U.S. 325, 334, 110 S.Ct. 1093, 1098, 108 L.Ed.2d 276, 286 (1990), the Court commented that officers making an arrest in a private residence could, "as an incident to the arrest * * *, as a precautionary matter and without probable cause or reasonable suspicion, look in closets and other spaces immediately adjoining the place of arrest from which an attack could be immediately launched."

A more intensive and extensive "protective sweep" of the premises—described by the Court as "a quick and limited search of a premises, incident to an arrest and conducted to protect the safety of officers or others"—requires "articulable facts which, taken together with the rational inferences from those facts, would warrant a reasonably prudent officer in believing that the area to be swept harbors an individual posing a danger to those on the arrest scene." The Court continued:

> We should emphasize that such a protective sweep, aimed at protecting the arresting officers, if justified by the circumstances, is nevertheless not a full search of the premises, but may extend only to a cursory inspection of those spaces where a person may be found. The sweep lasts no longer than is necessary to dispel the reasonable suspicion of danger and in any event no longer than it takes to complete the arrest and depart the premises.

494 U.S. at 335, 110 S.Ct. at 1099, 108 L.Ed.2d at 287.

2. "INCIDENTAL" SEARCHES OF VEHICLES

Searches of vehicles have given rise to particularly difficult problems. The Supreme Court's approach to these problems has been colored by— among other matters—its perception that persons have a less significant privacy interest in their vehicles than in their residences. This is developed further in Part D of Chapter 5, considering the so-called "vehicle exception" to the requirement of a warrant; this exception permits warrantless searches of certain vehicles *if* the officers have probable cause to believe that the vehicles contain items the officers are entitled to seize. As the principal case in this subsection makes clear, however, officers may often search vehicles incident to the arrest of person in and perhaps around those vehicles, regardless of whether those searches would be reasonable under the vehicle exception.

Consider whether in the principal case the Supreme Court is true to the rationale and spirit of *Chimel*.

New York v. Belton

Supreme Court of the United States, 1981.
453 U.S. 454, 101 S.Ct. 2860, 69 L.Ed.2d 768.

■ JUSTICE STEWART delivered the opinion of the Court.

When the occupant of an automobile is subject to a lawful custodial arrest, does the constitutionally permissible scope of a search incident to his arrest include the passenger compartment of the automobile in which he was riding? That is the question at issue in the present case.

Issue = passenger compartment

I.

On April 9, 1978, Trooper Douglas Nicot, a New York State policeman driving an unmarked car on the New York Thruway, was passed by another automobile travelling at an excessive rate of speed. Nicot gave chase, overtook the speeding vehicle, and ordered its driver to pull it over to the side of the road and stop. There were four men in the car, one of whom was Roger Belton, the respondent in this case. The policeman asked to see the driver's license and automobile registration, and discovered that none of the men owned the vehicle or was related to its owner. Meanwhile, the policeman had smelled burnt marihuana and had seen on the floor of the car an envelope marked "Supergold" that he associated with marihuana. He therefore directed the men to get out of the car, and placed them under arrest for the unlawful possession of marihuana. He patted down each of the men and "split them up into four separate areas of the Thruway at this time so they would not be in physical touching area of each other." He then picked up the envelope marked "Supergold" and found that it contained marihuana [and next] searched the passenger compartment of the car. On the back seat he found a black leather jacket belonging to Belton. He unzipped one of the pockets of the jacket and discovered cocaine. Placing the jacket in his automobile, he drove the four arrestees to a nearby police station.

Belton was subsequently indicted for criminal possession of a controlled substance. In the trial court he moved that the cocaine the trooper had seized from the jacket pocket be suppressed. The court denied the motion. * * *

The New York Court of Appeals reversed, holding that "[a] warrantless search of the zippered pockets of an unaccessible jacket may not be upheld as a search incident to a lawful arrest where there is no longer any danger that the arrestee or a confederate might gain access to the article." * * * We granted certiorari to consider the constitutionally permissible scope of a search in circumstances such as these.

II.

It is a first principle of Fourth Amendment jurisprudence that the police may not conduct a search unless they first convince a neutral magistrate that there is probable cause to do so. This Court has recognized, however, that "the exigencies of the situation" may sometimes make exemption from the warrant requirement "imperative." Specifically, the Court held in Chimel v. California, 395 U.S. 752, 89 S.Ct. 2034, 23 L.Ed.2d 685, that a lawful custodial arrest creates a situation which justifies the contemporaneous search without a warrant of the person arrested and of the immediately surrounding area. Such searches have long been considered valid because of the need "to remove any weapons that [the arrestee] might seek to use in order to resist arrest or effect his escape" and the need to prevent the concealment or destruction of evidence.

Chimel Finding

The Court's opinion in *Chimel* emphasized the principle that * * *, "The scope of [a] search must be 'strictly tied to and justified by' the circumstances which rendered its initiation permissible." Thus while the Court in *Chimel* found "ample justification" for a search of "the area from within which [an arrestee] might gain possession of a weapon or destructible evidence," the Court found "no comparable justification . . . for routinely searching any room other than that in which an arrest occurs—or, for that matter, for searching through all the desk drawers or other closed or concealed areas in that room itself."

Although the principle that limits a search incident to a lawful custodial arrest may be stated clearly enough, courts have discovered the principle difficult to apply in specific cases. Yet, as one commentator has pointed out, the protection of the Fourth and Fourteenth Amendments "can only be realized if the police are acting under a set of rules which, in most instances, makes it possible to reach a correct determination beforehand as to whether an invasion of privacy is justified in the interest of law enforcement." LaFave, "Case-by-Case Adjudication" versus "Standardized Procedures": The Robinson Dilemma, 1974 Sup.Ct.Rev. 127, 142. This is because

> "Fourth Amendment doctrine, given force and effect by the exclusionary rule, is primarily intended to regulate the police in their day-to-day activities and thus ought to be expressed in terms that are readily applicable by the police in the context of the law enforcement activities in which they are necessarily engaged. A highly sophisticated set of rules, qualified by all sorts of ifs, ands, and buts and requiring the drawing of subtle nuances and hairline distinctions, may be the sort of heady stuff upon which the facile minds of lawyers and judges eagerly feed, but they may be 'literally impossible of application by the officer in the field.'"

In short, "A single, familiar standard is essential to guide police officers, who have only limited time and expertise to reflect on and balance the social and individual interests involved in the specific circumstances they confront."

* * *

But no straightforward rule has emerged from the litigated cases respecting the question involved here—the question of the proper scope of a search of the interior of an automobile incident to a lawful custodial arrest of its occupants. * * *

When a person cannot know how a court will apply a settled principle to a recurring factual situation, that person cannot know the scope of his constitutional protection, nor can a policeman know the scope of his authority. While the *Chimel* case established that a search incident to an arrest may not stray beyond the area within the immediate control of the arrestee, courts have found no workable definition of "the area within the immediate control of the arrestee" when that area arguably includes the interior of an automobile and the arrestee is its recent occupant. Our reading of the cases suggests the generalization that articles inside the relatively narrow compass of the passenger compartment of an automobile are in fact generally, even if not inevitably, within "the area into which an arrestee might reach in order to grab a weapon or evidentiary item." In order to establish the workable rule this category of cases requires, we read *Chimel's* definition of the limits of the area that may be searched in light of

Finding
Rule
— and contents
too

that generalization. Accordingly, we hold that when a policeman has made a lawful custodial arrest of the occupant of an automobile, he may, as a contemporaneous incident of that arrest, search the passenger compartment of that automobile.[1]

It follows from this conclusion that the police may also examine the contents of any containers found within the passenger compartment, for if the passenger compartment is within reach of the arrestee, so also will containers in it be within his reach.[2] Such a container may, of course, be searched whether it is open or closed, since the justification for the search is not that the arrestee has no privacy interest in the container, but that the lawful custodial arrest justifies the infringement of any privacy interest the arrestee may have. Thus, while the Court in *Chimel* held that the police could not search all the drawers in an arrestee's house simply because the police had arrested him at home, the Court noted that drawers within an arrestee's reach could be searched because of the danger their contents might pose to the police.

It is true, of course, that these containers will sometimes be such that they could hold neither a weapon nor evidence of the criminal conduct for which the suspect was arrested. However, [a custodial arrest of a reasonably arrested suspect is a reasonable intrusion that requires no additional justification in terms of the facts of the specific case].

* * *

III.

It is not questioned that the respondent was the subject of a lawful custodial arrest on a charge of possessing marihuana. The search of the respondent's jacket followed immediately upon that arrest. The jacket was located inside the passenger compartment of the car in which the respondent had been a passenger just before he was arrested. The jacket was thus within the area which we have concluded was "within the arrestee's immediate control" within the meaning of the *Chimel* case.[3] The search of the jacket, therefore, was a search incident to a lawful custodial arrest, and it did not violate the Fourth and Fourteenth Amendments. Accordingly, the judgment is reversed.

It is so ordered.

■ JUSTICE BRENNAN, with whom JUSTICE MARSHALL joins, dissenting.

* * *

1. Our holding today does no more than determine the meaning of *Chimel's* principles in this particular and problematic content. It in no way alters the fundamental principles established in the *Chimel* case regarding the basic scope of searches incident to lawful custodial arrests.

2. "Container" here denotes any object capable of holding another object. It thus includes closed or open glove compartments, consoles, or other receptacles located any-

where within the passenger compartment, as well as luggage, boxes, bags, clothing, and the like. Our holding encompasses only the interior of the passenger compartment of an automobile and does not encompass the trunk.

3. Because of this disposition of the case, there is no need here to consider whether the search and seizure were permissible under the so-called "automobile exception."

The * * * new approach leaves open too many questions and, more important, it provides the police and the courts with too few tools with which to find the answers.

Thus, although the Court concludes that a warrantless search of a car may take place even though the suspect was arrested outside the car, it does not indicate how long after the suspect's arrest that search may validly be conducted. Would a warrantless search incident to arrest be valid if conducted five minutes after the suspect left his car? Thirty minutes? Three hours? Does it matter whether the suspect is standing in close proximity to the car when the search is conducted? Does it matter whether the police formed probable cause to arrest before or after the suspect left his car? And *why* is the rule announced today necessarily limited to searches of cars? What if a suspect is seen walking out of a house where the police, peering in from outside, had formed probable cause to believe a crime was being committed? Could the police then arrest that suspect and enter the house to conduct a search incident to arrest? Even assuming today's rule is limited to searches of the "interior" of cars—an assumption not demanded by logic—what is meant by "interior"? Does it include locked glove compartments, the interior of door panels, or the area under the floorboards? Are special rules necessary for station wagons and hatchbacks, where the luggage compartment may be reached through the interior, or taxicabs, where a glass panel might separate the driver's compartment from the rest of the car? Are the only containers that may be searched those that are large enough to be "capable of holding another object"? Or does the new rule apply to any container, even if it "could hold neither a weapon nor evidence of the criminal conduct for which the suspect was arrested"?

C. FIELD DETENTIONS FOR INVESTIGATION AND RELATED SEARCHES

EDITORS' INTRODUCTION: *TERRY* "STOPS" AND "FRISKS"

Prior to a trilogy of Supreme Court decisions in 1968, the Court's case law could have been read as holding that any seizure of a person challenged under the Fourth Amendment must be supported by at least the probable cause necessary to render reasonable an arrest. In 1968, however, the Court decided Terry v. Ohio, 392 U.S. 1, 88 S.Ct. 1868, 20 L.Ed.2d 889 (1968), and two companion cases, Sibron v. New York and Peters v. New York, 392 U.S. 40, 88 S.Ct. 1889, 20 L.Ed.2d 917 (1968). Those decisions, particularly *Terry*, established that the Fourth Amendment has sufficient flexibility to permit certain law enforcement conduct—often called "stop and frisk"—on less than probable cause.

Terry and its companion cases made clear Fourth Amendment analysis requires a distinction to be drawn between investigatory "stops"—seizures of suspects for purposes of questioning or other investigation—and "frisks"—searches to locate weapons to prevent suspects from harming investigating officers. The two subparts of this section address, first, so-called *Terry* stops and, second, weapon searches permissible in nonarrest situations. The impact of the *Terry* trilogy on Fourth Amendment law in general and the role of stop and frisk in law enforcement general policy, however, deserve preliminary discussion.

The Terry Trilogy: Fourth Amendment Flexibility

Terry noted the exclusionary sanction attaching to Fourth Amendment requirements may be less effective in preventing improper nonarrest field practices than deterring other unacceptable law enforcement conduct:

> [W]e approach the issues in this case mindful of the limitations of the judicial function in controlling the myriad daily situations in which policemen and citizens confront each other on the street. * * * Ever since its inception, the rule excluding evidence seized in violation of the Fourth Amendment has been recognized as a principal mode of discouraging lawless police conduct. * * * The exclusionary rule has its limitations, however, as a tool of judicial control. * * * [I]n some contexts the rule is ineffective as a deterrent. * * * Encounters are initiated by the police for a wide variety of purposes, some of which are wholly unrelated to a desire to prosecute for crime. Doubtless some police "field interrogation" conduct violates the Fourth Amendment. But a stern refusal by this Court to condone such activity does not necessarily render it responsive to the exclusionary rule. Regardless of how effective the rule may be where obtaining convictions is an important objective of the police, it is powerless to deter invasions of constitutionally guaranteed rights where the police either have no interest in prosecuting or are willing to forgo successful prosecution in the interest of serving some other goal.

> Proper adjudication of cases in which the exclusionary rule is invoked demands a constant awareness of these limitations. * * *

392 U.S. at 12–14, 88 S.Ct. at 1875–76, 20 L.Ed.2d at 900–02.

The Fourth Amendment reasonableness of law enforcement conduct, *Terry* continued, must be determined by balancing the extent to which particular kinds of police conduct further governmental interests, such as those in crime detection and prevention, against the nature and extent of the conduct's intrusion on Fourth Amendment interests. The first consideration, it noted, suggests "in dealing with the rapidly unfolding and often dangerous situations on city streets the police are in need of an escalating set of flexible responses, graduated in relation to the amount of information they possess." The safety of officers engaged in legitimate investigations, of course, is an especially important objective of this area's law.

Among the factors bearing on the second consideration, *Terry* suggested, is the risk that power to make nonarrest detentions will be abused and its use or abuse experienced as particularly oppressive by minorities. Nonarrest field practices may be particularly subject to abuse, the Court noted. Further, it cited reason to fear that officers' implementation of the right to make field stops and frisks may be influenced by the race of the suspects:

> The President's Commission on Law Enforcement and Administration of Justice found that "[I]n many communities, field interrogations

are a major source of friction between the police and minority groups."
President's Commission on Law Enforcement and Administration of
Justice, Task Force Report: The Police 183 (1967). It was reported that
the friction caused by "[m]isuse of field interrogations" increases "as
more police departments adopt 'aggressive patrol' in which officers are
encouraged routinely to stop and question persons on the street who
are unknown to them, who are suspicious, or whose purpose for being
abroad is not readily evident." While the frequency with which "frisking" forms a part of field interrogation practice varies tremendously
with the locale, the objective of the interrogation, and the particular
officer, it cannot help but be a severely exacerbating factor in police-
community tensions. This is particularly true in situations where the
"stop and frisk" of youths or minority group members is "motivated
by the officers' perceived need to maintain the power image of the beat
officer, an aim sometimes accomplished by humiliating anyone who
attempts to undermine police control of the streets."

392 U.S. at 15 n. 11, 88 S.Ct. at 1877 n. 11, 20 L.Ed.2d at 902 n. 11.

Much of the Court's discussion in *Terry* and its companion cases was
very broad and obviously applied to fields stops for investigation as well as
weapons searches. Nevertheless, the three 1968 cases actually decided only
the constitutionality of police action, on less than probable cause, constituting weapons searches and seizures of suspects to the extent necessary to
perform those protective searches.

Conducting the balancing analysis identified as necessary, the Court
rejected Terry's argument that no search or seizure was reasonable unless
supported by probable cause as developed in the law of arrest:

[Terry's] argument * * * assumes that the law of arrest has already
worked out the balance between the particular interests involved
here—the neutralization of danger to the policeman in the investigative circumstance and the sanctity of the individual. But this is not so.
An arrest is a wholly different kind of intrusion upon individual
freedom from a limited search for weapons, and the interests each is
designed to serve are likewise quite different. An arrest is the initial
stage of a criminal prosecution. It is intended to vindicate society's
interest in having its laws obeyed, and it is inevitably accompanied by
future interference with the individual's freedom of movement, whether or not trial or conviction ultimately follows. The protective search
for weapons, on the other hand, constitutes a brief, though far from
inconsiderable, intrusion upon the sanctity of the person. It does not
follow that because an officer may lawfully arrest a person only when
he is apprised of facts sufficient to warrant a belief that the person has
committed or is committing a crime, the officer is equally unjustified,
absent that kind of evidence, in making any intrusions short of an
arrest. Moreover, a perfectly reasonable apprehension of danger may
arise long before the officer is possessed of adequate information to
justify taking a person into custody for the purpose of prosecuting him
for a crime. [Terry's] reliance on cases which have worked out standards of reasonableness with regard to "seizures" constituting arrests
and searches incident thereto is thus misplaced. It assumes that the

interests sought to be vindicated and the invasions of personal security may be equated in the two cases, and thereby ignores a vital aspect of the analysis of the reasonableness of particular types of conduct under the Fourth Amendment.

Our evaluation of the proper balance that has to be struck in this type of case leads us to conclude that there must be a narrowly drawn authority to permit a reasonable search for weapons for the protection of the police officer, where he has reason to believe that he is dealing with an armed and dangerous individual, regardless of whether he has probable cause to arrest the individual for a crime.

392 U.S. at 26–27, 88 S.Ct. at 1882, 20 L.Ed.2d at 908–09. The precise contours of the right to search for weapons on less than probable cause is developed in more detail in the material that follows.

In *Terry* and its companion cases, the Court appeared satisfied to set out its general approach to resolving issues in this area and to decide only the narrow question of the propriety of a weapon search and any detention necessary to accomplish that search. "We * * * decide nothing today," it stressed, "concerning the constitutional propriety of an investigative 'seizure' upon less than probable cause for purposes of 'detention' and/or interrogation." *Terry*, 392 U.S. at 19 n. 16, 88 S.Ct. at 1879 n. 16, 20 L.Ed.2d at 95 n. 16. Nevertheless, its general approach strongly suggested that it would be receptive to the argument that such detentions are—at least under certain circumstances—constitutionally reasonable. In fact, the Court subsequently assumed that *Terry* established the permissibility of such stops. Consequently, nonarrest stops for investigation are widely referred to as *Terry* stops.

Statutory provisions in some jurisdictions authorize the sort of law enforcement activity discussed by the Supreme Court in the *Terry* trilogy. Probably the leading example is the New York statute, which provides:

140.50   Temporary questioning of persons in public places; search for weapons

1.   * * * [A] police officer may stop a person in a public place located within the geographical area of such officer's employment when he reasonably suspects that such person is committing, has committed or is about to commit either (a) a felony or (b) a misdemeanor defined in the penal law, and may demand of him his name, address and an explanation of his conduct.

* * *

3.   When upon stopping a person under circumstances prescribed in subdivision[ ] one * * * a police officer * * * reasonably suspects that he is in danger of physical injury, he may search such person for a deadly weapon or any instrument, article or substance readily capable of causing serious physical injury and of a sort not ordinarily carried in public places by law-abiding persons. If he finds such a weapon or instrument, or any other property possession of which he reasonably believes may constitute the commission of a crime, he may take it and keep it until the completion of the questioning, at which time he shall either return it, if lawfully possessed, or arrest such person.

Stop and Frisk in the Context of General Law Enforcement Philosophy

When New York's Attorney General undertook a comprehensive examination of stop and frisk practices in New York City, he began by putting the formal law in conceptual context. See The New York City Police Department's "Stop & Frisk" Practices: A Report to the People of the State of New York from the Office of the Attorney General (1999) ("New York Report"). Stop and frisk, he suggested, can only be fully understood if it is considered not simply as a specific law enforcement technique to prevent, investigate, detect, and solve crime but also as part of an overall crime-fighting philosophy.

Addressing stop and frisk as part of New York City's comprehensive law enforcement approach to crime, the report noted that New York police, like many other modern departments, embrace modern policing philosophies of "community policing" and "order maintenance"/"broken windows" theory.

> "Community policing" holds that effective crime-fighting is based on a "partnership" between police and the residents of the immediate community they serve. The goal of the partnership is to ensure that police "meet the demands" of law-abiding people within their jurisdiction.

New York Report at 47. Implementing community policing, the department discovered that rank-and-file community residents were more concerned about petty crime and disorder problem than the major crimes that had preoccupied police.

> The * * * impact was to increase police presence in the everyday life of the community. The cop on foot patrol—walking the neighborhood, interacting with its residents, learning the complex social dynamics of the area, and responding to low-level disorder complaints—is emblematic of the "community policing" model.

New York Report at 47. In addition, New York police adopted

> a second approach known as "order maintenance" theory (or simply, "broken windows"). Order maintenance theory rests on two fundamental premises * * *.
>
> The first premise holds that low-level disorder in the streets—graffiti, aggressive panhandling, public drunkenness and the like—makes people fearful and weakens neighborhood social controls. In this atmosphere, law-abiding civilians become more fearful and withdrawn from the daily life of the community, effectively ceding the street to the forces of greater disorder and more serious crime. As Kelling and Wilson [Broken Windows: The Police and Neighborhood Safety, Atlantic Monthly, March 1982] put it: "[I]f [one broken window] is left unrepaired, all the rest of the windows will soon be broken."
>
> Only by actively combating low-level disorder, can police and the neighborhood residents signal to the criminal element their resolve that "law breaking of any kind will not be tolerated"—and thus begin to restore standards of behavior which make serious crime untenable.

Second, as a tactical matter, order maintenance theory "advocate[s] close collaboration between police and citizens ... in the development of neighborhood standards" of conduct. Such standards are "to be enforced for the most part though non-arrest approaches—education, persuasion, counseling, and ordering"—so that arrest would only be resorted to when other approaches failed. In this sense, order maintenance theory and "community policing" connect and overlap to a substantial degree.

The results * * * seemed to confirm the order maintenance hypothesis. * * * [Police] discovered that persons arrested for turnstyle-jumping frequently were found to be "carrying weapons or [to] have outstanding warrants." As the progenitor of "broken windows" theory would later describe the key lesson of the * * * experience: "Restoring order reduces crime ... at least in part because restoring order puts police in contact with persons who carry weapons and who commit serious crime." [G.L. Kelling & C.M. Coles, Fixing Broken Windows: Restoring Order and Reducing Crime in Our communities (1996).]

* * *

[T]he role of "stop & frisk" in furthering the Department's goals of order maintenance, deterrence, crime prevention, and a direct attack on gun violence is clear. Given the Department's focus on apprehending violent criminals and preventing more serious crimes by aggressively enforcing laws aimed at low-level criminality, "stop & frisk" serves as an important wedge into the criminal element.

Order maintenance theory encourages officers to intervene in instances of low-level disorder, whether observed or suspected, with approaches which fall short of arrest. A "stop" intervention provides an occasion for the police to have context with persons presumably involved in low-level criminality—without having to effect a formal arrest, and under a lower-constitutional standard (*i.e.*, "reasonable suspicion"). Indeed, because low-level "quality of life" and misdemeanor offenses are more likely to be committed in the open, as a theoretical matter, the "reasonable suspicion" standard may be more readily satisfied as to those sorts of crimes. To the extent that "stop" encounters create points of contact between police and low-level offenders, such contacts can lead to the apprehension of persons already wanted for more serious crimes, or who might be prepared to commit them in the near future.

* * *

Finally, as implemented by the NYPD, "stop & frisk" serves the Department's No. 1 strategic goal—"getting guns off the streets of New York." Notwithstanding its origin as a technique designed to assure officer safety, "stop & frisk" plainly has been used as a method to detect and seize illegal handguns. [During a study period], fully 34% of all documented "stop & frisk" encounters by NYPD officers citywide were for suspected weapons possession.

* * *

Thus, a model which values both proactive police interventions short of arrest and an aggressive approach to low-level disorder is well served by aggressive use of "stop & frisk." More to the point, "stop & frisk" has served as an important tactical resource in promoting the Department's specific strategic crime-fighting goals.

New York Report at 47–59. The specific conclusions of the report concerning stop and frisk practices in New York are discussed later in this subsection.

1. FIELD DETENTIONS

EDITORS' INTRODUCTION: REASONABLE SUSPICION

The Supreme Court's case law after *Terry* and its companion decisions clearly regards law enforcement as constitutionally permitted to seize and briefly detain persons for purposes of investigation on less than the probable cause required for an arrest. What factual basis is required for such action? Post-*Terry* decisions used somewhat different terminology to describe the required basis, but the Court appears to have settled on "reasonable suspicion" as the standard.

What is this required reasonable suspicion? In Alabama v. White, 496 U.S. 325, 110 S.Ct. 2412, 110 L.Ed.2d 301 (1990), the Court explained in general terms:

> Reasonable suspicion is a less demanding standard than probable cause not only in the sense that reasonable suspicion can be established with information that is different in quantity or content than that required to establish probable cause, but also in the sense that reasonable suspicion can arise from information that is less reliable than that required to show probable cause. * * * Reasonable suspicion, like probable cause, is dependent upon both the content of information possessed by police and its degree of reliability. Both factors—quantity and quality—are considered in the "totality of the circumstances—the whole picture," that must be taken into account when evaluating whether there is reasonable suspicion. * * *

496 U.S. at 330, 110 S.Ct. at 2416, 110 L.Ed.2d at 309. The case reprinted in this section presents an interesting application of this standard. Several specific aspects of reasonable suspicion as the standard for nonarrest investigatory field detentions, however, merit preliminary consideration.

Reasonable Suspicion as Applied

What specific facts support valid nonarrest field detentions is obviously a difficult question. The Supreme Court has addressed the problem in a number of contexts.

Several cases involved informant tips. In Adams v. Williams, 407 U.S. 143, 92 S.Ct. 1921, 32 L.Ed.2d 612 (1972), an informant approached a police cruiser and informed the officer a person seated in a nearby vehicle was carrying narcotics and had a gun at his waist. The officer knew the informant and had received information from him in the past. On the other hand, this information involved claims of homosexual activity in a local railroad station and the followup investigation resulted in neither confirmation nor arrests. The officer located the person described by the informant and detained him. Upholding the detention, the Supreme Court rejected the proposition that the necessary reasonable cause must be based upon the officer's personal observation. While the tip may not have amounted to probable cause justifying an arrest, it did support the action taken:

> This is a stronger case than obtains in the case of an anonymous telephone tip. The informant here came forward personally to give information that was immediately verifiable at the scene. Indeed, * * * the informant might have been subject to immediate arrest for making a false complaint had [the] investigation proved the tip incorrect.

407 U.S. at 146–47, 92 S.Ct. at 1923, 32 L.Ed.2d at 617.

An anonymous tip was at issue in Alabama v. White, 496 U.S. 325, 110 S.Ct. 2412, 110 L.Ed.2d 301 (1990). The facts were as follows:

> On April 22, 1987, at approximately 3 p.m., Corporal B.H. Davis of the Montgomery Police Department received a telephone call from an anonymous person, stating that Vanessa White would be leaving 235–C Lynwood Terrace Apartments at a particular time in a brown Plymouth station wagon with the right taillight lens broken, that she would be going to Dobey's Motel, and that she would be in possession of about an ounce of cocaine inside a brown attache case. Corporal Davis and his partner, Corporal P.A. Reynolds, proceeded to the Lynwood Terrace Apartments. The officers saw a brown Plymouth station wagon with a broken right taillight in the parking lot in front of the 235 building. The officers observed [White] leave the 235 building, carrying nothing in her hands, and enter the station wagon. They followed the vehicle as it drove the most direct route to Dobey's Motel. When the vehicle reached the Mobile Highway, on which Dobey's Motel is located, Corporal Reynolds requested a patrol unit to stop the vehicle. The vehicle was stopped at approximately 4:18 p.m., just short of Dobey's Motel.

Relying heavily upon Illinois v. Gates, reprinted in Chapter 3, the Court held *Gates'* totality of the circumstances approach should be taken, with appropriate accommodation for the less demanding standard applicable in field stop situations. It declined to conclude that an anonymous caller's tip alone could never provide reasonable suspicion. Further, the range of detailed assertions in the tip before it suggested that it was reliable. Nevertheless, the Court—after acknowledging the case was a close one—finally concluded the tip lacked sufficient indicia of reliability to itself constitute reasonable suspicion. But the tip and the officers' corroboration of some information in it adequately supported suspicion White was engaged in criminal activity:

> What was important was the caller's ability to predict [White's] *future behavior,* because it demonstrated inside information—a special familiarity with [White's] affairs. The general public would have no way of knowing that [White] would shortly leave the building, get in the described car, and drive the most direct route to Dobey's Motel.

Because only a small number of people are generally privy to an individual's itinerary, it is reasonable for police to believe that a person with access to such information is likely to also have access to reliable information about that individual's illegal activities. When significant aspects of the caller's predictions were verified, there was reason to believe not only that the caller was honest but also that he was well informed, at least well enough to justify the stop.

Key issue

496 U.S. at 332, 110 S.Ct. at 2417, 110 L.Ed.2d at 310 (emphasis in original).

The leading decision finding reasonable suspicion lacking is Brown v. Texas, 443 U.S. 47, 99 S.Ct. 2637, 61 L.Ed.2d 357 (1979). The Court described the facts as follows:

> At 12:45 on the afternoon of December 9, 1977, officers Venegas and Soleto of the El Paso Police Department were cruising in a patrol car. They observed [Brown] and another man walking in opposite directions away from one another in an alley. Although the two men were a few feet apart when they were first seen, officer Venegas later testified that both officers believed the two had been together or were about to meet until the patrol car appeared.

The area had a high incidence of drug traffic. Brown was stopped because, as one officer testified, the situation "looked suspicious" and the officers had never seen Brown in the area before. The Supreme Court held the stop unreasonable:

> Officer Venegas testified at [Brown's] trial that the situation in the alley "looked suspicious," but he was unable to point to any facts supporting that conclusion. There is no indication in the record that it was unusual for people to be in the alley. The fact that [Brown] was in a neighborhood frequented by drug users, standing alone, is not a basis for concluding that [Brown] himself was engaged in criminal conduct. * * * When pressed, Officer Venegas acknowledged that the only reason he stopped [Brown] was to ascertain his identity. The record suggests an understandable desire to assert a police presence; however that purpose does not negate Fourth Amendment guarantees.

443 U.S. at 52, 99 S.Ct. at 2641, 61 L.Ed.2d at 362–63.

Reasonable Suspicion, Airport Stops, and "Profiles"

Investigatory stops at airports have given rise to particular difficulties in determining whether reasonable suspicion was shown. Barebones testimony that a passenger meets a "drug carrier profile" does not constitute reasonable suspicion. Reid v. Georgia, 448 U.S. 438, 100 S.Ct. 2752, 65 L.Ed.2d 890 (1980) (per curiam). But passengers' evasive and objectively suspicious may meet the standard. Florida v. Rodriguez, 469 U.S. 1, 105 S.Ct. 308, 83 L.Ed.2d 165 (1984).

Airport stops—and the significance of profile testimony—were addressed at length in United States v. Sokolow, 490 U.S. 1, 109 S.Ct. 1581, 104 L.Ed.2d 1 (1989). In July of 1984, Andrew Sokolow and a female companion flew from Honolulu to Miami, a 20 hour flight. When they returned after a 48 hour stay in Miami, DEA officers stopped Sokolow for investigative purposes. The officers had the following information: Sokolow was about 25 years old. He paid $2,100 for the tickets with cash from a roll of $20 bills that appeared to contain about $4,000. He was wearing a black jumpsuit and gold jewelry and appeared nervous. His destination was Miami, a "source city for drugs." Neither Sokolow nor his companion checked their luggage. Sokolow gave the ticket agent a home telephone number. Although he gave his name to the agent as "Andrew Kray," the telephone number was listed to "Karl Herman." The agent, however, identified the voice on the answering machine tape at the number as that of the man who purchased the tickets. (Herman, it was later discovered, was Sokolow's roommate.) The majority acknowledged Sokolow's activity was itself "lawful" but held it established reasonable suspicion. It stressed the evidence that Sokolow was traveling under an alias, that he conducted a large-scale purchase in cash, and that his trip to a source city was surprisingly short for the expense involved. After concluding that the facts established reasonable suspicion, the majority noted that one of the agents had testified that Sokolow's behavior "had all the classic aspects of a drug courier." It then commented:

> We do not agree with [Sokolow] that our analysis is somehow changed by the agents' belief that his behavior was consistent with one of the DEA's "drug courier profiles." A court sitting to determine the existence of reasonable suspicion must require the agent to articulate the factors leading to that conclusion, but the fact that these factors may be set forth in a "profile" does not somehow detract from their evidentiary significance as seen by a trained agent.

490 U.S. at 10, 109 S.Ct. at 1587, 104 L.Ed.2d at 12. Justice Marshall, joined by Justice Brennan, dissented.

Possible Limits on Suspected Offenses

Are there any limits on the offenses for which field stops may be made? Stops might, for example, be permitted only on reasonable suspicion that the person is involved in relatively serious criminal behavior. In United States v. Hensley, 469 U.S. 221, 105 S.Ct. 675, 83 L.Ed.2d 604 (1985), discussed in detail later in this Introduction, the Court was careful to limit its approval of investigatory stops to those involving past *serious* offenses—those constituting felonies. "We need not and do not decide today," it commented, "whether *Terry* stops to investigate all past crimes, however serious, are permitted."

The nature of some offenses may suggest too high a risk that *Terry* stops to investigate them might be abused. In Adams v. Williams, 407 U.S. 143, 92 S.Ct. 1921, 32 L.Ed.2d 612 (1972), the officer's suspicion concerned the suspect's possible commission of crimes consisting of possessing items—possession of drugs and possession of a prohibited weapon. One of the judges in the Court of Appeals urged stops not be permitted for such possessory crimes. "There is too much danger," he reasoned, "that, instead of the stop being the object and the protective frisk an incident thereto, the reverse will be true." Williams v. Adams, 436 F.2d 30, 38 (2d Cir.1970) (Friendly, J., dissenting), reversed 441 F.2d 394 (2d Cir.1971) (en banc) (per curiam). Justice Brennan adopted this position in the Supreme Court.

407 U.S. at 151–53, 92 S.Ct. at 1926–27, 32 L.Ed.2d at 620 (Brennan, J., dissenting). The opinion of the Court, written by then-Justice Rehnquist, did not address the matter.

Reasonable Suspicion Concerning Past and Future Offenses

The Court has somewhat offhanded suggested *Terry* and later decisions settled the constitutionality of investigatory stops for past and future offenses as well as those being committed at the time of the stop. "Under the Fourth Amendment [] we have held," the Court commented in Berkemer v. McCarty, 468 U.S. 420, 439, 104 S.Ct. 3138, 3150, 82 L.Ed.2d 317, 334 (1984), "a policeman who lacks probable cause but whose 'observations lead him reasonably to suspect' that a particular person has committed, is committing, or is about to commit a crime, may detain that person briefly in order to 'investigate the circumstances that provoke suspicion.'"

Until United States v. Hensley, 469 U.S. 221, 105 S.Ct. 675, 83 L.Ed.2d 604 (1985), however, the cases decided by the Court—many of which were discussed earlier in this Introduction—all involved situations in which the suspected criminal activity was still in progress when the officers intervened. In *Hensley*, the Court acknowledged it had never actually held a nonarrest *Terry* stop constitutionally permissible on probable cause to believe the suspect had committed an offense in the past. Hensley had been stopped on reasonable suspicion that he had been involved in a robbery committed twelve days earlier. The Court treated the question whether stops for investigation are permissible for completed past offenses as a significant one, and addressed the matter at length. Application of the balancing analysis used to determine the reasonableness of nonarrest stops, it acknowledged, must be somewhat different in past crime situations:

> The factors in the balance may be somewhat different when a stop to investigate past criminal activity is involved rather than a stop to investigate ongoing criminal conduct. * * * [O]ne general interest present in the context of ongoing or imminent criminal activity is "that of effective crime prevention and detention." A stop to investigate an already completed crime does not necessarily promote the interest of crime prevention as directly as a stop to investigate suspected ongoing criminal activity. Similarly, the exigent circumstances which require a police officer to step in before a crime is committed or completed are not necessarily as pressing long afterwards. Public safety may be less threatened by a suspect in a past crime who now appears to be going about his lawful business than it is by a suspect who is currently in the process of violating the law. Finally, officers making a stop to investigate past crimes may have a wider range of opportunity to choose the time and circumstances of the stop.

469 U.S. at 228–29, 105 S.Ct. at 680, 83 L.Ed.2d at 612. Nevertheless, the Court concluded in some situations the law enforcement interests at stake outweigh the interests of individuals in being free of relatively nonintrusive *Terry* stops. Disclaiming a decision on whether its holding would apply to less serious crimes, the Court concluded that "if police have a reasonable suspicion, grounded in specific and articulable facts, that a person they

encounter was involved in or is wanted in connection with a completed felony, then a *Terry* stop may be made to investigate that suspicion."

Neither *Hensley* nor any other of the Court's decisions has actually passed on the reasonableness of an investigatory stop based on reasonable suspicion the person would commit a crime *in the future*. *Hensley* characterized *Terry* itself as a case in which "police stopped or seized a person because they suspected he was about to commit a crime." But *Terry* in fact passed only on the seizure of Terry to the extent necessary to conduct the weapons search. Arguably the Court was careful to avoid, at this early stage in the development of nonarrest detention law, any definitive decision on stops to investigate concern that a person will commit a future crime. In *Terry's* companion cases, the parties sought to have the Court pass on the constitutionality of New York's "stop-and-frisk" law, set out earlier in the Editors' Introduction to Part C of this chapter, which authorized an officer to stop a person "whom [the officer] reasonably suspects is committing, has committed or *is about to commit*" one of the specific offenses. In neither case, however, did the Court address the facial validity of the statute generally or, in particular, the authorization to stop those reasonably suspected of being "about to commit" an offense.

N.Y. stop and Frisk

If officers are permitted by the Fourth Amendment to make investigatory stops regarding future offenses, whether *Terry's* facts justified such a stop arguably presented a quite difficult question. The Supreme Court acknowledged the reasonableness of detentions on less than probable cause only in the 1968 trilogy of decisions. It may have believed that the courts should have more opportunity to address investigatory stop situations before the Supreme Court resolved particularly difficult subquestions concerning the scope of the stop authority. The facts of *Terry* were as follows:

Officer McFadden testified that while he was patrolling in plain clothes in downtown Cleveland at approximately 2:30 in the afternoon of October 31, 1963, his attention was attracted by two men, Chilton and Terry, standing on the corner of Huron Road and Euclid Avenue. He had never seen the two men before, and he was unable to say precisely what first drew his eye to them. However, he testified that he had been a policeman for 39 years and a detective for 35 and that he had been assigned to patrol this vicinity of downtown Cleveland for shoplifters and pickpockets for 30 years. He explained that he had developed routine habits of observation over the years and that he would "stand and watch people or walk and watch people at many intervals of the day." He added: "Now, in this case when I looked over they didn't look right to me at the time."

His interest aroused, Officer McFadden took up a post of observation in the entrance to a store 300 to 400 feet away from the two men. "I get more purpose to watch them when I seen their movements,'" he testified. He saw one of the men leave the other one and walk southwest on Huron Road, past some stores. The man paused for a moment and looked in a store window, then walked on a short distance, turned around and walked back toward the corner, pausing once again to look in the same store window. He rejoined his companion at the corner, and the two conferred briefly. Then the second man went through the same series of motions, strolling down Huron Road, looking in the same window, walking on a short distance, turning back, peering in the store window again, and returning to confer with the first man at the corner. The two men repeated this ritual alternately between five and six times apiece—in all, roughly a dozen trips. At one point, while the two were standing together on the corner, a third man approached them and engaged them briefly in conversation. This man then left the two others and walked west on Euclid Avenue. Chilton and Terry resumed their measured pacing, peering and conferring. After this had gone on for 10 to 12 minutes, the two men walked off together, heading west on Euclid Avenue, following the path taken earlier by the third man. By this time Officer McFadden had become thoroughly suspicious. He testified that after observing their elaborately casual and oft-repeated reconnaissance of the store window on Huron Road, he suspected the two men of "casing a job, a stick-up," and that he considered it his duty as a police officer to investigate further. He added that he feared "they may have a gun." Thus, Officer McFadden followed Chilton and Terry and saw them stop in front of Zucker's store to talk to the same man who had conferred with them earlier on the street corner. Deciding that the situation was ripe for direct action, Officer McFadden approached the three men, identified himself as a police officer and asked for their names. At this point his knowledge was confined to what he had observed. He was not acquainted with any of the three men by name or by sight, and he had received no information concerning them from any other source. When the men "mumbled something" in response to his inquiries, Officer McFadden grabbed petitioner Terry, spun him around so that they were facing the other two, with Terry between McFadden and the others, and patted down the outside of his clothing. In the left breast pocket of Terry's overcoat Officer McFadden felt a pistol. He reached inside the overcoat pocket, but was unable to remove the gun. At this point, keeping Terry between himself and the others, the officer ordered all three men to enter Zucker's store. As they went in, he removed Terry's overcoat completely, removed a .38–caliber revolver from the pocket and ordered all three men to face the wall with their hands raised. Officer McFadden proceeded to pat down the outer clothing of Chilton and the third man, Katz. He discovered another revolver in the outer pocket of Chilton's overcoat, but no weapons were found on Katz. The officer testified that he only patted the men down to see whether they had weapons, and that he did not put his hands beneath the outer garments of either Terry or Chilton until he felt their guns. So far as appears from the record, he never placed his hands beneath Katz' outer garments. Officer McFadden seized Chilton's gun, asked the proprietor of the store to call a police wagon, and took all three men to the station, where Chilton and Terry were formally charged with carrying concealed weapons.

If McFadden seized Terry when he confronted him and his companions in front of Zucker's store and requested their names, was that stop constitutionally permissible? Finding McFadden could constitutionally search the trio for weapons, the Court explained:

[O]n the facts and circumstances Officer McFadden detailed before the trial judge a reasonably prudent man would have been warranted in believing petitioner was armed and thus presented a threat to the officer's safety while he was investigating his suspicious behavior. The actions of Terry and Chilton were consistent with McFadden's hypothesis that these men were contemplating a daylight robbery—which, it is reasonable to assume, would be likely to involve the use of weapons—and nothing in their conduct from the time he first noticed them until the time he confronted them and identified himself as a police officer gave him sufficient reason to negate that hypothesis. Although the trio had departed the original scene, there was nothing to indicate abandonment of an intent to commit a robbery at some point. Thus, when Officer McFadden approached the three men gathered before the display window at Zucker's store he had observed enough to make it quite reasonable to fear that they were armed * * *.

392 U.S. at 28, 88 S.Ct. at 1883, 20 L.Ed.2d at 910. The Court did not, however, reach whether McFadden could seize Terry to question him about any plans he might have had to commit robber.

Perhaps the difficulty of predicting whether suspects will commit future crimes means that stops on reasonable suspicion this will occur are unacceptable. Or, perhaps such stops are acceptable only if an officer has reasonable suspicion the suspect is—in the words of the New York statute—*about to* commit an offense. Arguably predictions concerning whether suspects will quite soon engage in criminal activity are more accurate than other predictions, and therefore only stops for relatively imminent future offenses are reasonable. If investigatory stops are permissible only upon reasonable suspicion that the suspect is about to commit an offense, could McFadden have reasonably suspected that Terry and his companions were *about to* commit the robbery McFadden reasonably suspected the three had in mind?

Stop and Frisk in Practice

The New York Attorney General made an effort to determine how New York City police actually used the authority to make *Terry* stops. The results were reported in New York City. The New York City Police Department's "Stop & Frisk" Practices: A Report to the People of the State of New York from the Office of the Attorney General (1999) ("New York Report").

Under New York departmental policies, an officer is required to file a "UF–250" report on each incident in which a person is stopped and (a) force is used to make the stop; (b) the person stopped is frisked or searched; (c) the person stopped is arrested; or (d) the person stopped refuses to identify himself. If an incident involves a stop but none of the factors mandating a report applies, the officer may file a report. The reports are to include the race of the person stopped and the facts which led the officer to make the stop. The study analyzed 174,919 reports of stops during 1998–1999; 72.5% of the reports reflected incidents in which a report was required, and the remaining 27.5% reflected incidents in which the officer chose to file a report.

The investigators looked at which the facts set out by the officers were sufficient to constitute reasonable suspicion. The results were as follows:

facts sufficient to constitute reasonable suspicion	61.1%
facts not sufficient to constitute reasonable suspicion	15.4%
report insufficient to permit determination	23.5%
	100%

New York Report at xiii–xiv. A form was put into the insufficient to determine category if the situation suggested that additional information "readily hypothesized" might justify the stop. Thus if a form said, "moving furniture/carrying 'out of place objects,'" the investigators assumed other information available but not reported might justify the stop and they treated it as insufficient to permit determination.

Overall, one out of nine stops resulted in an arrest. The study found this "unsurprising, given the purpose of a 'stop' and the lower level of suspicion required to justify a 'stop' as opposed to an arrest." New York Report at viii.

The study provided some support for concern that field stops are made in part on racial grounds. Overall, the results were as follows

	City Population	Stops
Blacks	25.6%	50.6%
Hispanics	23.7%	33.0%
Whites	43.4%	12.9%

The disparity was most pronounced in those precincts in which a majority of the population was white. New York Report at vii–viii.

Precincts in which minorities constituted the majority of the population tended to have more "stop & frisk" activity than precincts in which whites constituted the majority. Some, but not all, of this was accounted for by the higher crime rate in those precincts with a nonwhite majority.

Blacks were less likely to be stopped on suspicion of property crimes than whites or hispanics. But—controlling for other factors—blacks were 2.1 times more often than whites stopped on suspicion of committing a violent crime and 2.4 times more often on suspicion of carrying a weapon. Hispanics were stopped 1.7 times as often as whites on suspicion of committing a violent crime and 2.0 times as often on suspicion of carrying a weapon. New York Report at x–xi.

* * *

Questioning of suspects during a nonarrest detention raises special issues concerning the suspects' right to be free from compelled self-incrimination and related matters. These questioning issues are considered in Chapter 7.

Florida v. Royer

Supreme Court of the United States, 1983.
460 U.S. 491, 103 S.Ct. 1319, 75 L.Ed.2d 229.

■ JUSTICE WHITE announced the judgment of the Court and delivered an opinion in which JUSTICES MARSHALL, POWELL and STEVENS joined.

* * *

I

On January 3, 1978, Royer was observed at Miami International Airport by two plain-clothes detectives of the Dade County, Florida, Public Safety Department assigned to the County's Organized Crime Bureau, Narcotics Investigation Section. Detectives Johnson and Magdalena believed that Royer's appearance, mannerisms, luggage, and actions fit the so-called "drug courier profile." Royer, apparently unaware of the attention he had attracted, purchased a one-way ticket to New York City and checked his two suitcases, placing on each suitcase an identification tag bearing the name "Holt" and the destination, "LaGuardia". As Royer made his way to the concourse which led to the airline boarding area, the two detectives approached him, identified themselves as policemen working out of the sheriff's office, and asked if Royer had a "moment" to speak with them; Royer said "Yes."

Upon request, but without oral consent, Royer produced for the detectives his airline ticket and his driver's license. The airline ticket, like the baggage identification tags, bore the name "Holt," while the driver's license carried respondent's correct name, "Royer." When the detectives asked about the discrepancy, Royer explained that a friend had made the reservation in the name of "Holt." Royer became noticeably more nervous during this conversation, whereupon the detectives informed Royer that they were in fact narcotics investigators and that they had reason to suspect him of transporting narcotics.

The detectives did not return his airline ticket and identification but asked Royer to accompany them to a room, approximately forty feet away, adjacent to the concourse. Royer said nothing in response but went with the officers as he had been asked to do. The room was later described by Detective Johnson as a "large storage closet," located in the stewardesses' lounge and containing a small desk and two chairs. Without Royer's consent or agreement, Detective Johnson, using Royer's baggage check stubs, retrieved the "Holt" luggage from the airline and brought it to the room where respondent and Detective Magdalena were waiting. Royer was asked if he would consent to a search of the suitcases. Without orally responding to this request, Royer produced a key and unlocked one of the suitcases, which the detective then opened without seeking further assent from Royer. Drugs were found in that suitcase. According to Detective Johnson, Royer stated that he did not know the combination to the lock on the second suitcase. When asked if he objected to the detective opening the second suitcase, Royer said "no, go ahead," and did not object when the detective explained that the suitcase might have to be broken open. The suitcase was pried open by the officers and more marihuana was found.

Royer was then told that he was under arrest. Approximately fifteen minutes had elapsed from the time the detectives initially approached respondent until his arrest upon the discovery of the contraband.

Prior to his trial for felony possession of marihuana, Royer made a motion to suppress the evidence obtained in the search of the suitcases. The trial court found that Royer's consent to the search was "freely and voluntarily given," and that, regardless of the consent, the warrantless search was reasonable because "the officer doesn't have the time to run out and get a search warrant because the plane is going to take off." Following the denial of the motion to suppress, Royer * * * was convicted.

The District Court of Appeal, sitting en banc, reversed Royer's conviction. * * * We granted the State's petition for certiorari, and now affirm.

II

* * * The Florida Court of Appeal * * * concluded * * * that Royer had been seized when he gave his consent to search his luggage [and] also that the bounds of an investigative stop had been exceeded. In its view the "confinement" in this case went beyond the limited restraint of a *Terry* investigative stop, and Royer's consent was thus tainted by the illegality, a conclusion that required reversal in the absence of probable cause to arrest. The question before us is whether the record warrants that conclusion. We think that it does.

III

The State proffers three reasons for holding that when Royer consented to the search of his luggage, he was not being illegally detained. First, it is submitted that the entire encounter was consensual and hence Royer was not being held against his will at all. We find this submission untenable. Asking for and examining Royer's ticket and his driver's license were no doubt permissible in themselves, but when the officers identified themselves as narcotics agents, told Royer that he was suspected of transporting narcotics, and asked him to accompany them to the police room, while retaining his ticket and driver's license and without indicating in any way that he was free to depart, Royer was effectively seized for the purposes of the Fourth Amendment. These circumstances surely amount to a show of official authority such that "a reasonable person would have believed he was not free to leave." United States v. Mendenhall, 446 U.S. 544, 554, 100 S.Ct. 1870, 1877, 64 L.Ed.2d 497 (Opinion of Stewart, J.).

Second, the State submits that if Royer was seized, there existed reasonable, articulable suspicion to justify a temporary detention and that the limits of a *Terry*-type stop were never exceeded. We agree with the State that when the officers discovered that Royer was travelling under an assumed name, this fact, and the facts already known to the officers— paying cash for a one-way ticket, the mode of checking the two bags, and Royer's appearance and conduct in general—were adequate grounds for suspecting Royer of carrying drugs and for temporarily detaining him and his luggage while they attempted to verify or dispel their suspicions in a manner that did not exceed the limits of an investigative detention. We also agree that had Royer voluntarily consented to the search of his luggage while he was justifiably being detained on reasonable suspicion, the products of the search would be admissible against him. We have concluded, however, that at the time Royer produced the key to his suitcase, the detention to which he was then subjected was a more serious intrusion on his personal liberty than is allowable on mere suspicion of criminal activity.

By the time Royer was informed that the officers wished to examine his luggage, he had identified himself when approached by the officers and had attempted to explain the discrepancy between the name shown on his identification and the name under which he had purchased his ticket and identified his luggage. The officers were not satisfied, for they informed him they were narcotics agents and had reason to believe that he was carrying illegal drugs. They requested him to accompany them to the police room. Royer went with them. He found himself in a small room—a large closet—equipped with a desk and two chairs. He was alone with two police officers who again told him that they thought he was carrying narcotics. He also found that the officers, without his consent, had retrieved his checked luggage from the airlines. What had begun as a consensual inquiry in a public place had escalated into an investigatory procedure in a police interrogation room, where the police, unsatisfied with previous explanations, sought to confirm their suspicions. The officers had Royer's ticket, they had his identification, and they had seized his luggage. Royer was never informed that he was free to board his plane if he so chose, and he reasonably believed that he was being detained. At least as of that moment, any consensual aspects of the encounter had evaporated, and we cannot fault the Florida Court of Appeal for concluding that Terry v. Ohio and the cases following it did not justify the restraint to which Royer was then subjected. As a practical matter, Royer was under arrest. Consistent with this conclusion, the State conceded in the Florida courts that Royer would not have been free to leave the interrogation room had he asked to do so. Furthermore, the state's brief in this Court interprets the testimony of the officers at the suppression hearing as indicating that had Royer refused to consent to a search of his luggage, the officers would have held the luggage and sought a warrant to authorize the search.

We also think that the officers' conduct was more intrusive than necessary to effectuate an investigative detention otherwise authorized by the *Terry* line of cases. First, by returning his ticket and driver's license, and informing him that he was free to go if he so desired, the officers may have obviated any claim that the encounter was anything but a consensual matter from start to finish. Second, there are undoubtedly reasons of safety and security that would justify moving a suspect from one location to another during an investigatory detention, such as from an airport concourse to a more private area. There is no indication in this case that such reasons prompted the officers to transfer the site of the encounter from the concourse to the interrogation room. It appears, rather, that the primary interest of the officers was not in having an extended conversation with Royer but in the contents of his luggage, a matter which the officers did not pursue orally with Royer until after the encounter was relocated to the police room. The record does not reflect any facts which would support a finding that the legitimate law enforcement purposes which justified the detention in the first instance were furthered by removing Royer to the police room prior to the officer's attempt to gain his consent to a search of his luggage. As we have noted, had Royer consented to a search on the spot, the search could have been conducted with Royer present in the area where the bags were retrieved by Officer Johnson and any evidence recovered would have been admissible against him. If the search proved negative, Royer would have been free to go much earlier and with less likelihood of missing his flight, which in itself can be a very serious matter in a variety of circumstances.

Third, the State has not touched on the question whether it would have been feasible to investigate the contents of Royer's bags in a more expeditious way. The courts are not strangers to the use of trained dogs to detect the presence of controlled substances in luggage. There is no indication here that this means was not feasible and available. If it had been used, Royer and his luggage could have been momentarily detained while this investigative procedure was carried out. Indeed, it may be that no detention at all would have been necessary. A negative result would have freed Royer in short order; a positive result would have resulted in his justifiable arrest on probable cause.

We do not suggest that there is a litmus-paper test for distinguishing a consensual encounter from a seizure or for determining when a seizure exceeds the bounds of an investigative stop. Even in the discrete category of airport encounters, there will be endless variations in the facts and circumstances, so much variation that it is unlikely that the courts can reduce to a sentence or a paragraph a rule that will provide unarguable answers to the question whether there has been an unreasonable search or seizure in violation of the Fourth Amendment. Nevertheless, we must render judgment, and we think that the Florida Court of Appeal cannot be faulted in concluding that the limits of a *Terry*-stop had been exceeded.

IV

The State's third and final argument is that Royer was not being illegally held when he gave his consent because there was probable cause to arrest him at that time. Officer Johnson testified at the suppression hearing and the Florida Court of Appeal held that there was no probable cause to arrest until Royer's bags were opened, but the fact that the officers did not believe there was probable cause and proceeded on a consensual or *Terry*-stop rationale would not foreclose the State from justifying Royer's custody by proving probable cause and hence removing any barrier to relying on Royer's consent to search. We agree with the Florida Court of Appeal, however, that probable cause to arrest Royer did not exist at the time he consented to the search of his luggage. The facts are that a nervous young man with two American Tourister bags paid cash for an airline ticket to a "target city." These facts led to inquiry, which in turn revealed that the ticket had been bought under an assumed name. The proffered explanation did not satisfy the officers. We cannot agree with the State, if this is its position, that every nervous young man paying cash for a ticket to New York City under an assumed name and carrying two heavy American Tourister bags may be arrested and held to answer for a serious felony charge.

V

Because we affirm the Florida Court of Appeal's conclusion that Royer was being illegally detained when he consented to the search of his luggage, we agree that the consent was tainted by the illegality and was ineffective to justify the search. The judgment of the Florida Court of Appeal is accordingly

Affirmed.

■ JUSTICE BRENNAN, concurring in the result.

* * *

To the extent that the plurality endorses the legality of the officers' initial stop of Royer, it was wholly unnecessary to reach that question. For even assuming the legality of the initial stop, the plurality correctly holds, and I agree, that the officers' subsequent actions clearly exceeded the permissible bounds of a *Terry* "investigative" stop. * * *

In any event, I dissent from the plurality's view that the initial stop of Royer was legal. For plainly Royer was "seized" * * *. [The] facts clearly are not sufficient to provide the reasonable suspicion of criminal activity necessary to justify the * * * seizure * * *.

■ JUSTICE REHNQUIST, with whom THE CHIEF JUSTICE and JUSTICE O'CONNOR join, dissenting.

* * *

I think the articulable suspicion which concededly focused upon Royer [after the officers' initial conversation with him] justified the length and nature of his detention.

The reasonableness of the officers' activity in this case did not depend upon Royer's consent to the investigation. Nevertheless, the presence of consent further justifies the action taken. * * * [I]f Royer was legally approached in the first instance and consented to accompany the detectives to the room, it does not follow that his consent went up in smoke and he was "arrested" upon entering the room. * * * [L]ogical analysis would focus on whether the environment in the room rendered the subsequent consent to a search of the luggage involuntary.

[T]here is nothing in the record which would indicate that Royer's resistance was overborne by anything * * *.

NOTES

1. **Movement of the Suspect.** How much may officers who have made a proper nonarrest investigatory detention move the suspect? In Dunaway v. New York, 442 U.S. 200, 99 S.Ct. 2248, 60 L.Ed.2d 824 (1979), officers with information—but less than probable cause—connecting Dunaway with a robbery-murder had Dunaway "picked up" at a neighbor's home. They drove him to police headquarters, placed him in an interrogation room, warned him of his rights, and questioned him. Finding that the officers' actions were "in important respects indistinguishable from an arrest," the Court held the lack of probable cause rendered the detention invalid. The *Dunaway* holding that movement to the

stationhouse is prohibited was confirmed in Hayes v. Florida, 470 U.S. 811, 105 S.Ct. 1643, 84 L.Ed.2d 705 (1985).

2. **Stationhouse Detentions on Reasonable Suspicion.** In Davis v. Mississippi, 394 U.S. 721, 89 S.Ct. 1394, 22 L.Ed.2d 676 (1969), the Court had indicated in dictum that stationhouse detentions for fingerprinting might be permissible upon less than probable cause:

> It is arguable * * * that, because of the unique nature of the fingerprinting process, * * * detentions [for fingerprinting] might, under narrowly defined circumstances, be found to comply with the Fourth Amendment even though there is no probable cause in the traditional sense. Detention for fingerprinting may constitute a much less serious intrusion upon personal security than other types of police searches and detentions. Fingerprinting involves none of the probing into an individual's private life and thoughts that mark an interrogation or search. Nor can fingerprint detention be employed repeatedly to harass any individual, since the police need only one set of each person's prints. Furthermore, fingerprinting is an inherently more reliable and effective crime-stopping tool than eyewitness identification or confessions and is not subject to such abuses as the improper lineup and the "third degree." Finally, because there is no danger of destruction of fingerprints, the limited detention need not come unexpectedly or at an inconvenient time. For this same reason, the general requirement that the authorization of a judicial officer be obtained in advance of detention would seem not to admit of any exception in the fingerprinting context.

394 U.S. at 727–28, 89 S.Ct. at 1397–98, 22 L.Ed.2d at 681. The court reaffirmed this suggestion in Hayes v. Florida, 470 U.S. 811, 817, 105 S.Ct. 1643, 1647, 84 L.Ed.2d 705, 711 (1985), noting a number of jurisdictions, in reliance on the *Davis* suggestion, had enacted provisions for judicial authorizations for fingerprinting detentions.

3. **Length of the Detention.** How long may a non-arrest investigatory detention last? The American Law Institute has proposed such detentions be limited to a "period as is reasonably necessary for the accomplishment of the purposes authorized * * * but in no case for more than twenty minutes * * *". Model Code of Pre-Arraignment Procedure § 110.2(1) (Official Draft 1975). In United States v. Place, 462 U.S. 696, 103 S.Ct. 2637, 77 L.Ed.2d 110 (1983), dealing with detention of luggage as discussed later in these Notes, the Court noted the Institute's proposal but declined "to adopt any outside time limitation for a permissible *Terry* stop:"

[handwritten: ✱ no more than 20 minutes]

> We understand the desirability of providing law enforcement authorities with a clear rule to guide their conduct. Nevertheless, we question the wisdom of a rigid time limitation. Such a limit would undermine the equally important need to allow authorities to graduate their responses to the demands of any particular situation.

462 U.S. at 710 n. 10, 103 S.Ct. at 2646 n. 10, 77 L.Ed.2d at 122 n. 10. But it then continued:

> The [90–minute] length of the detention of [Place's] luggage alone precludes the conclusion that the seizure was reasonable in the absence of probable cause. Although we have recognized the reasonableness of seizures longer than * * * momentary ones * * *, the brevity of the invasion of the individual's Fourth Amendment interests is an important factor in determining whether the seizure is so minimally intrusive as to be justifiable on reasonable suspicion. Moreover, in assessing the effect of the length of the detention, we take into account whether the police diligently pursue their investigation. We note that here the New York agents knew the time of Place's scheduled arrival

at LaGuardia [Airport], had ample time to arrange for their additional investigation at that location, and thereby could have minimized the intrusion on [Place's] Fourth Amendment interests. * * * [W]e have never approved a seizure of the person for the prolonged 90–minute period involved here and cannot do so on the facts presented by this case.

462 U.S. at 709–10, 103 S.Ct. at 2645–46, 77 L.Ed.2d at 122.

The permissible length of investigatory detentions was again addressed in United States v. Sharpe, 470 U.S. 675, 105 S.Ct. 1568, 84 L.Ed.2d 605 (1985). Drug Enforcement Administration agent Cooke was patrolling a coastal road in North Carolina and observed a pickup truck (driven by Savage) and a Pontiac (driven by Sharpe) traveling "in tandem." After observing the pickup truck was heavily loaded, Cooke called for assistance. Highway patrol officer Thrasher, driving a marked patrol car, responded. Within approximately a minute of Thrasher's joining the "procession," the truck and the Pontiac turned off the highway onto a campground road and—despite the 35 mph speed limit—progressed at 55 to 60 mph until the road looped back onto the highway. The officers decided to stop the vehicles and Thrasher pulled aside the Pontiac (which was in the lead), turned on his flashing light, and motioned for the driver to pull over. As the Pontiac pulled over, the pickup truck "cut" between the Pontiac and the patrol car and continued down the highway. Thrasher pursued the truck and Cooke pulled over behind the Pontiac. Cooke obtained identification from Sharpe, the driver of the Pontiac. When he was unable to make radio contact with Thrasher, he called local police, directed them to "maintain the situation," and joined Thrasher.

Thrasher had stopped and secured identification from the driver of the truck, Savage. Savage explained that the truck belonged to a friend (and produced a bill of sale) and that he was taking the truck to have its shock absorbers repaired. Thrasher told Savage that the two would await the arrival of a DEA agent. Savage became nervous and asked for his identification; Thrasher told him that he was not free to leave. Cooke arrived at the scene about 15 minutes after the truck had been stopped. When Cooke stated that he believed the truck contained marihuana and twice asked for permission to search it, Savage twice refused. Cooke stepped on the rear of the truck, noting that it did not sink. He then put his nose against the rear window, reported that he could smell marihuana, and searched the vehicle. Bales of marihuana were found and Savage was placed under arrest. Cooke then returned to the Pontiac and arrested Sharpe; this was about 30 to 40 minutes from the time the Pontiac was stopped. At the trial of Sharpe and Savage for possession of the marihuana, the marihuana was admitted into evidence. On appeal, the Court of Appeals reversed, reasoning that the detentions of Sharpe and Savage were too long to be supported on less than probable cause and that these detentions tainted the discovery and seizure of the marihuana.

The Supreme Court reversed. Writing for the Court, Chief Justice Burger reaffirmed that the Fourth Amendment imposes no "hard-and-fast" time limit upon the duration of a *Terry* stop:

> In assessing whether a detention is too long in duration to be justified as an investigative stop, we consider it appropriate to examine whether the police diligently pursued a means of investigation that was likely to confirm or dispel their suspicions quickly, during which time it was necessary to detain the defendant. A court making this assessment should take care to consider whether the police are acting in a swiftly developing situation, and in such cases the court should not indulge in unrealistic second-guessing. * * * The question is not simply whether some other alternative was available, but whether the police acted unreasonably in failing to recognize or pursue it.

470 U.S. at 686–87, 105 S.Ct. at 1575–76, 84 L.Ed.2d at 615–16.

On the facts before it, the Court concluded, Cooke pursued the investigation with regard to Savage in a diligent and reasonable manner. Most of the delay was attributable to Savage's actions in maneuvering around the Pontiac and Thrasher's patrol car, which required separate stops of the two vehicles. The Court assumed this was a conscious effort by Savage to elude the officers, but commented that Savage's actions would also justify the delay even if they were "innocent." To affirm the decision of the lower court with regard to Savage's 20 minute detention, the majority concluded, would be to "effectively establish a *per se* rule that a 20–minute detention is too long to be justified under the *Terry* doctrine." This, the Court indicated, it was unwilling to do. In regard to Sharpe's detention, the Court found no reason to consider the validity of its 30 to 40 minute duration. The challenged evidence was obtained by searching the truck and was not "fruit" of any improper detention of Sharpe as may have taken place.

4. **Investigatory "Detentions" of Items.** Some seizures of items as well as persons may be made upon less than probable cause. In United States v. Place, 462 U.S. 696, 103 S.Ct. 2637, 77 L.Ed.2d 110 (1983), Drug Enforcement Administration officers approached Place at New York's LaGuardia airport after he aroused suspicion while departing from Miami and upon arrival in New York. Discrepancies were noted concerning the addresses placed on his two pieces of luggage. At both Miami and New York, he volunteered to officers who approached him that he had recognized them as police officers. At New York, he falsely claimed that his baggage had been searched in Miami. He refused to consent to a search of the luggage at the New York airport. One of the agents then informed him that the officers would take the luggage to a federal judge and apply for a search warrant. He added that Place was free to accompany the officers (and the luggage). Place declined the invitation, but obtained a number at which the officers indicated they could be reached. The officers took the bags to another airport where, one hour and thirty minutes later, a trained narcotics detention dog reacted positively to the smaller bag but "ambiguously" to the larger one. As it was late on Friday, the agents retained the bags until Monday, when they obtained a search warrant. The smaller bag was found to contain cocaine. Applying the principles of *Terry*, the Supreme Court concluded certain seizures of personal luggage on the basis of "reasonable, articulable suspicion, premised on objective facts," would be reasonable under the Fourth Amendment. Balancing the relevant interests, the Court noted a substantial governmental interest in a brief seizure of luggage believed to contain drugs. On the other hand, some brief seizures of luggage intrude only minimally upon the owner's Fourth Amendment protected interests:

> In sum, we conclude that when an officer's observations lead him reasonably to believe that a traveler is carrying luggage that contains narcotics, the principles of *Terry* and its progeny would permit the officer to detain the luggage briefly to investigate the circumstances that aroused his suspicion, provided that the investigative detention is properly limited in scope.

462 U.S. at 706, 103 S.Ct. at 2644, 77 L.Ed.2d at 120. But—as discussed earlier in these Notes—the Court further concluded the length of the detention before it exceeded what was permissible on less than probable cause.

2. WEAPON SEARCHES

EDITORS' INTRODUCTION: SEARCHING FOR WEAPONS ON LESS THAN PROBABLE CAUSE

In *Terry*, the Supreme Court held Officer McFadden's search of Terry for weapons was, at its inception, reasonable despite McFadden's lack of probable cause to believe Terry in possession of a weapon. The Court's reasoning was set out in the last subsection. Subsequent decisions have confirmed *Terry* established the reasonableness of such a search on less than probable cause:

> *Terry* * * * held that "[w]hen an officer is justified in believing that the individual whose suspicious behavior he is investigating at close range is armed and presently dangerous to the officer or others," the officer may conduct a patdown search "to determine whether the person is in fact carrying a weapon" * * * [A] protective search [is] permitted without a warrant and on the basis of reasonable suspicion less than probable cause * * *.

Minnesota v. Dickerson, 508 U.S. 366, 373, 113 S.Ct. 2130, 2136, 124 L.Ed.2d 334, 344 (1993).

Terry made clear the Fourth Amendment limits not only when such a search may be conducted but the manner in which it may be made. After concluding that McFadden's search of Terry was reasonable at its inception, the Court in *Terry* turned to whether McFadden's search was reasonable in Fourth Amendment terms "as conducted." It explained:

> The manner in which the seizure and search were conducted is, of course, as vital a part of the inquiry as whether they were warranted at all. * * *
>
> We need not develop at length in this case * * * the limitations which the Fourth Amendment places upon a protective seizure and search for weapons. * * * Suffice it to note that such a search, unlike a search without a warrant incident to a lawful arrest, is not justified by any need to prevent the disappearance or destruction of evidence of crime. The sole justification of the search in the present situation is the protection of the police officer and others nearby, and it must therefore be confined in scope to an intrusion reasonably designed to discover guns, knives, clubs, or other hidden instruments for the assault of the police officer.
>
> The scope of the search in this case presents no serious problem in light of these standards. Officer McFadden patted down the outer clothing of petitioner and his two companions. He did not place his hands in their pockets or under the outer surface of their garments until he had felt weapons, and then he merely reached for and removed the guns. * * * Officer McFadden confined his search strictly to what was minimally necessary to learn whether the men were armed and to disarm them once he discovered the weapons. He did not conduct a general exploratory search for whatever evidence of criminal activity he might find.

392 U.S. at 28–30, 88 S.Ct. at 1883–84, 20 L.Ed.2d at 910–11.

In Sibron v. New York, 392 U.S. 40, 88 S.Ct. 1889, 20 L.Ed.2d 917 (1968), a companion case to *Terry*, the Court further developed limits on weapons searches. The Court stated *Sibron's* facts as follows:

> Sibron * * * was convicted of the unlawful possession of heroin. He moved before trial to suppress the heroin seized from his person by the arresting officer, Brooklyn Patrolman Anthony Martin. * * * At

the hearing on the motion to suppress, Officer Martin testified that while he was patrolling his beat in uniform on March 9, 1965, he observed Sibron "continually from the hours of 4:00 P.M. to 12:00, midnight * * * in the vicinity of 742 Broadway." He stated that during this period of time he saw Sibron in conversation with six or eight persons whom he (Patrolman Martin) knew from past experience to be narcotics addicts. The officer testified that he did not overhear any of these conversations, and that he did not see anything pass between Sibron and any of the others. Late in the evening Sibron entered a restaurant. Patrolman Martin saw Sibron speak with three more known addicts inside the restaurant. Once again, nothing was overheard and nothing was seen to pass between Sibron and the addicts. Sibron sat down and ordered pie and coffee, and, as he was eating Patrolman Martin approached him and told him to come outside. Once outside, the officer said to Sibron, "You know what I am after." According to the officer, Sibron "mumbled something and reached into his pocket." Simultaneously, Patrolman Martin thrust his hand into the same pocket, discovering several glassine envelopes, which, it turned out, contained heroin.

* * * Patrolman Martin * * * [never] seriously suggest[ed] that he was in fear of bodily harm and that he searched Sibron in self-protection to find weapons.

The Court concluded Officer Martin lacked probable cause to arrest until after the heroin was seized. It then turned to the reasonableness of the officer's conduct under *Terry*. As to whether the officer was entitled under *Terry* to frisk Sibron, the Court observed:

The suspect's mere act of talking with a number of known addicts over an eight-hour period no more gives rise to reasonable fear of life or limb on the part of the police officer than it justifies an arrest for committing a crime. Nor did Patrolman Martin urge that when Sibron put his hand in his pocket, he feared that he was going for a weapon and acted in self-defense. His opening statement to Sibron—"You know what I am after"—made it abundantly clear that he sought narcotics, and his testimony at the hearing left no doubt that he thought there were narcotics in Sibron's pocket.

392 U.S. at 64, 88 S.Ct. at 1903, 20 L.Ed.2d at 935. Finally, the Court concluded even if the officer had been authorized to frisk Sibron, the officer's actions did went beyond a self-protective search and constituted a search for evidence:

[handwritten margin note: beyond self protection + a search for evidence]

[W]ith no attempt at an initial limited exploration for arms, Patrolman Martin thrust his hand into Sibron's pocket and took from him envelopes of heroin. His testimony shows that he was looking for narcotics, and he found them. The search was not reasonably limited in scope to the accomplishment of the only goal which might conceivably have justified its inception—the protection of the officer by disarming a potentially dangerous man.

392 U.S. at 65, 88 S.Ct. at 1904, 20 L.Ed.2d at 936.

Minnesota v. Dickerson

Supreme Court of the United States, 1993.
508 U.S. 366, 113 S.Ct. 2130, 124 L.Ed.2d 334.

■ JUSTICE WHITE delivered the opinion of the Court.

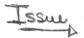

In this case, we consider whether the Fourth Amendment permits the seizure of contraband detected through a police officer's sense of touch during a protective pat-down search.

I

On the evening of November 9, 1989, two Minneapolis police officers were patrolling an area on the city's north side in a marked squad car. At about 8:15 p.m., one of the officers observed respondent leaving a 12–unit apartment building on Morgan Avenue North. The officer, having previously responded to complaints of drug sales in the building's hallways and having executed several search warrants on the premises, considered the building to be a notorious "crack house." According to testimony credited by the trial court, respondent began walking toward the police but, upon spotting the squad car and making eye contact with one of the officers, abruptly halted and began walking in the opposite direction. His suspicion aroused, this officer watched as respondent turned and entered an alley on the other side of the apartment building. Based upon respondent's seemingly evasive actions and the fact that he had just left a building known for cocaine traffic, the officers decided to stop respondent and investigate further.

The officers pulled their squad car into the alley and ordered respondent to stop and submit to a patdown search. The search revealed no weapons, but the officer conducting the search did take an interest in a small lump in respondent's nylon jacket. The officer later testified: "[A]s I pat-searched the front of his body, I felt a lump, a small lump, in the front pocket. I examined it with my fingers and it slid and it felt to be a lump of crack cocaine in cellophane." The officer then reached into respondent's pocket and retrieved a small plastic bag containing one fifth of one gram of crack cocaine. Respondent was arrested and charged in Hennepin County District Court with possession of a controlled substance.

Before trial, respondent moved to suppress the cocaine. The trial court first concluded that the officers were justified under Terry v. Ohio, 392 U.S. 1, 88 S.Ct. 1868, 20 L.Ed.2d 889 (1968), in stopping respondent to investigate whether he might be engaged in criminal activity. The court further found that the officers were justified in frisking respondent to ensure that he was not carrying a weapon. Finally, analogizing to the "plain-view" doctrine, under which officers may make a warrantless seizure of contraband found in plain view during a lawful search for other items, the trial court ruled that the officers' seizure of the cocaine did not violate the Fourth Amendment:

"To this Court there is no distinction as to which sensory perception the officer uses to conclude that the material is contraband. An experienced officer may rely upon his sense of smell in DWI stops or in recognizing the smell of burning marijuana in an automobile. The sound of a shotgun being racked would clearly support certain reactions by an officer. The sense of touch, grounded in experience and training, is as reliable as perceptions drawn from other senses. 'Plain feel,' therefore, is no different than plain view and will equally support the seizure here.''

His suppression motion having failed, respondent proceeded to trial and was found guilty.

On appeal, the Minnesota Supreme Court affirmed [the intermediate court's reversal of the conviction]. * * * [T]he State Supreme Court held that both the stop[a] and the frisk[b] of respondent were valid under *Terry*, but found the seizure of the cocaine to be unconstitutional. The court expressly refused "to extend the plain view doctrine to the sense of touch" on the grounds that "the sense of touch is inherently less immediate and less reliable than the sense of sight" and that "the sense of touch is far more intrusive into the personal privacy that is at the core of the [F]ourth [A]mendment." The court thus appeared to adopt a categorical rule barring the seizure of any contraband detected by an officer through the sense of touch during a patdown search for weapons. The court further noted that "[e]ven if we recognized a 'plain feel' exception, the search in this case would not qualify" because "[t]he pat search of the defendant went far beyond what is permissible under *Terry*." As the State Supreme Court read the record, the officer conducting the search ascertained that the lump in respondent's jacket was contraband only after probing and investigating what he certainly knew was not a weapon.

We granted certiorari to resolve a conflict among the state and federal courts over whether contraband detected through the sense of touch during a patdown search may be admitted into evidence. We now affirm.

II

A

* * *

Terry * * * held that "[w]hen an officer is justified in believing that the individual whose suspicious behavior he is investigating at close range is armed and presently dangerous to the officer or to others," the officer may conduct a patdown search "to determine whether the person is in fact carrying a weapon." * * * [A] protective search * * * must be strictly "limited to that which is necessary for the discovery of weapons which might be used to harm the officer or others nearby." If the protective search goes beyond what is necessary to determine if the suspect is armed,

---

a. The Minnesota court explained that "the defendant's suspicious behavior, the history of drug activity in the immediate vicinity and [the officer's] personal experience in seizing guns from the building the defendant left justified a pat search." State v. Dickerson, 481 N.W.2d 840, 843 (Minn.1992).

b. The Minnesota court explained that Dickerson's "evasive conduct after eye contact with police, combined with his departure from a building with a history of drug activity, justified police in reasonably suspecting criminal activity [and] therefore * * * the stop was valid." State v. Dickerson, 481 N.W.2d 840, 843 (Minn.1992).

it is no longer valid under *Terry* and its fruits will be suppressed. Sibron v. New York, 392 U.S. 40, 65–66, 88 S.Ct. 1889, 1904, 20 L.Ed.2d 917 (1968).

These principles were settled 25 years ago when, on the same day, the Court announced its decisions in *Terry* and *Sibron.* The question presented today is whether police officers may seize nonthreatening contraband detected during a protective patdown search of the sort permitted by *Terry.* We think the answer is clearly that they may, so long as the officer's search stays within the bounds marked by *Terry.*

B

We have already held that police officers, at least under certain circumstances, may seize contraband detected during the lawful execution of a *Terry* search. * * *

The Court in [Michigan v. Long, 463 U.S. 1032, 103 S.Ct. 3469, 77 L.Ed.2d 1201 (1983)] justified this * * * holding by reference to our cases under the "plain-view" doctrine. Under that doctrine, if police are lawfully in a position from which they view an object, if its incriminating character is immediately apparent, and if the officers have a lawful right of access to the object, they may seize it without a warrant. If, however, the police lack probable cause to believe that an object in plain view is contraband without conducting some further search of the object—i.e., if "its incriminating character [is not] 'immediately apparent,' "—the plain-view doctrine cannot justify its seizure.

We think that this doctrine has an obvious application by analogy to cases in which an officer discovers contraband through the sense of touch during an otherwise lawful search. The rationale of the plain view doctrine is that if contraband is left in open view and is observed by a police officer from a lawful vantage point, there has been no invasion of a legitimate expectation of privacy and thus no "search" within the meaning of the Fourth Amendment—or at least no search independent of the initial intrusion that gave the officers their vantage point. The warrantless seizure of contraband that presents itself in this manner is deemed justified by the realization that resort to a neutral magistrate under such circumstances would often be impracticable and would do little to promote the objectives of the Fourth Amendment. The same can be said of tactile discoveries of contraband. If a police officer lawfully pats down a suspect's outer clothing and feels an object whose contour or mass makes its identity immediately apparent, there has been no invasion of the suspect's privacy beyond that already authorized by the officer's search for weapons; if the object is contraband, its warrantless seizure would be justified by the same practical considerations that inhere in the plain view context.

The Minnesota Supreme Court rejected an analogy to the plain-view doctrine on two grounds: first, its belief that "the sense of touch is inherently less immediate and less reliable than the sense of sight," and second, that "the sense of touch is far more intrusive into the personal privacy that is at the core of the [F]ourth [A]mendment." We have a somewhat different view. First, *Terry* itself demonstrates that the sense of touch is capable of revealing the nature of an object with sufficient reliability to support a seizure. The very premise of *Terry,* after all, is that

[handwritten margin note: Touch is less reliable than sight]

officers will be able to detect the presence of weapons through the sense of touch and *Terry* upheld precisely such a seizure. Even if it were true that the sense of touch is generally less reliable than the sense of sight, that only suggests that officers will less often be able to justify seizures of unseen contraband. Regardless of whether the officer detects the contraband by sight or by touch, however, the Fourth Amendment's requirement that the officer have probable cause to believe that the item is contraband before seizing it ensures against excessively speculative seizures. The court's second concern—that touch is more intrusive into privacy than is sight—is inapposite in light of the fact that the intrusion the court fears has already been authorized by the lawful search for weapons. The seizure of an item whose identity is already known occasions no further invasion of privacy. Accordingly, the suspect's privacy interests are not advanced by a categorical rule barring the seizure of contraband plainly detected through the sense of touch.

III

It remains to apply these principles to the facts of this case. Respondent has not challenged the finding made by the trial court and affirmed by both the Court of Appeals and the State Supreme Court that the police were justified under *Terry* in stopping him and frisking him for weapons. Thus, the dispositive question before this Court is whether the officer who conducted the search was acting within the lawful bounds marked by *Terry* at the time he gained probable cause to believe that the lump in respondent's jacket was contraband. The State District Court did not make precise findings on this point, instead finding simply that the officer, after feeling "a small, hard object wrapped in plastic" in respondent's pocket, "formed the opinion that the object . . . was crack . . . cocaine." The District Court also noted that the officer made "no claim that he suspected this object to be a weapon," a finding affirmed on appeal. The Minnesota Supreme Court, after "a close examination of the record," held that the officer's own testimony "belies any notion that he 'immediately' "recognized the lump as crack cocaine. Rather, the court concluded, the officer determined that the lump was contraband only after "squeezing, sliding and otherwise manipulating the contents of the defendant's pocket"—a pocket which the officer already knew contained no weapon.

Under the State Supreme Court's interpretation of the record before it, it is clear that the court was correct in holding that the police officer in this case overstepped the bounds of the "strictly circumscribed" search for weapons allowed under *Terry*. Where, as here, "an officer who is executing a valid search for one item seizes a different item," this Court rightly "has been sensitive to the danger * * * that officers will enlarge a specific authorization, furnished by a warrant or an exigency, into the equivalent of a general warrant to rummage and seize at will." Texas v. Brown, 460 U.S. [730,] 748, 103 S.Ct. [1535,] 1546–47[, 75 L.Ed.2d 502 (1983)] (Stevens, J., concurring in judgment). Here, the officer's continued exploration of respondent's pocket after having concluded that it contained no weapon was unrelated to "[t]he sole justification of the search [under *Terry*:] . . . the protection of the police officer and others nearby." It therefore amounted to the sort of evidentiary search that *Terry* expressly refused to authorize, and that we have condemned in subsequent cases.

* * * Although the officer was lawfully in a position to feel the lump in respondent's pocket, because *Terry* entitled him to place his hands upon respondent's jacket, the court below determined that the incriminating character of the object was not immediately apparent to him. Rather, the officer determined that the item was contraband only after conducting a further search, one not authorized by *Terry* or by any other exception to the warrant requirement. Because this further search of respondent's pocket was constitutionally invalid, the seizure of the cocaine that followed is likewise unconstitutional.

[handwritten margin note: Finding Rule = not immediately apparent]

IV

For these reasons, the judgment of the Minnesota Supreme Court is

Affirmed.

■ CHIEF JUSTICE REHNQUIST, with whom JUSTICE BLACKMUN and JUSTICE THOMAS join, concurring in part and dissenting in part.

I join Parts I and II of the Court's opinion. Unlike the Court, however, I would vacate the judgment of the Supreme Court of Minnesota and remand the case to that court for further proceedings.

The Court, correctly in my view, states that "the dispositive question before this Court is whether the officer who conducted the search was acting within the lawful bounds marked by Terry [v. Ohio, 392 U.S. 1, 88 S.Ct. 1868, 20 L.Ed.2d 889 (1968),] at the time he gained probable cause to believe that the lump in respondent's jacket was contraband." The Court then goes on to point out that the state trial court did not make precise findings on this point, but accepts the appellate findings made by the Supreme Court of Minnesota. I believe that these findings, like those of the trial court, are imprecise and not directed expressly to the question of the officer's probable cause to believe that the lump was contraband. Because the Supreme Court of Minnesota employed a Fourth Amendment analysis which differs significantly from that now adopted by this Court, I would vacate its judgment and remand the case for further proceedings there in the light of this Court's opinion.

NOTES

1. **Grounds for Weapons Search.** What constitutes grounds for a *Terry* weapons search is addressed by the Supreme Court in several additional cases. In Adams v. Williams, 407 U.S. 143, 92 S.Ct. 1921, 32 L.Ed.2d 612 (1972), the officer—Sgt. Connolly—was told the suspect was carrying drugs and had a gun at his waist. It was 2:15 a.m. when the officer approached the suspect seated in a car; the area was known to the officer as a high crime rate area. He tapped on the car window and asked the suspect to open the door. The suspect instead rolled down the window. At that point, the officer reached into the car and "removed" a loaded revolver from the suspect's waistband. The Court upheld the action, explaining:

Sgt. Connolly had ample reason to fear for his safety. When Williams rolled down his window, rather than complying with the policeman's request to step out of the car so that his movements could more easily be seen, the revolver allegedly at Williams' waist became an even greater threat. Under these circumstances the policeman's action in reaching to the spot where the gun was thought to be hidden constituted a limited intrusion designed to insure his safety, and we conclude that it was reasonable.

407 U.S. at 147–48, 92 S.Ct. at 1924, 32 L.Ed.2d at 618.

In Pennsylvania v. Mimms, 434 U.S. 106, 98 S.Ct. 330, 54 L.Ed.2d 331 (1977) (per curiam), an officer stopped a car driven by Mimms to issue him a traffic citation for having an expired license plate. When Mimms stepped out of the car, the officer observed a large bulge under Mimms' sports jacket. Under *Terry*, the Court held, the bulge permitted the officer to conclude Mimms posed a serious and present danger to the officer's safety. Thus, the officer properly conducted a pat down of Mimms. The pat down revealed Mimms was in fact armed.

The matter was again considered in Ybarra v. Illinois, 444 U.S. 85, 100 S.Ct. 338, 62 L.Ed.2d 238 (1979). Officers obtained a valid search warrant authorizing the search of the Aurora Tap Tavern and Greg, the bartender. When the officers entered the tavern in late afternoon, between 9 and 13 customers—including Ybarra—were present. All were "frisked" and the officer felt "a cigarette pack with objects in it" in Ybarra's pocket; he did not at that time remove it. Several minutes later, Ybarra was searched again, this time more thoroughly. Drugs were found in the cigarette package. The State argued the first patdown frisk was permissible under *Terry* and since this revealed probable cause to believe Ybarra was in possession of drugs, the second and thorough search was permissible as an exigent circumstances search made on probable cause. Without addressing whether the frisk gave rise to probable cause, a majority of the Court held the frisk invalid:

> The initial frisk of Ybarra was simply not supported by a reasonable belief that he was armed and presently dangerous, a belief which this Court has invariably held must form the predicate to a patdown of a person for weapons. When the police entered the Aurora Tap Tavern * * *, the lighting was sufficient for them to observe the customers. Upon seeing Ybarra, they neither recognized him as a person with a criminal history nor had any particular reason to believe that he might be inclined to assault them. Moreover, as Police Agent Johnson later testified, Ybarra, whose hands were empty, gave no indication of possessing a weapon, made no gestures or other actions indicative of an intent to commit an assault, and acted generally in a manner that was not threatening. At the suppression hearing, the most Agent Johnson could point to was that Ybarra was wearing a 3/4–length lumber jacket, clothing which the State admits could be expected on almost any tavern patron in Illinois in early March. In short, the State is unable to articulate any specific fact that would have justified a police officer at the scene in even suspecting that Ybarra was armed and dangerous.

> * * * The "narrow scope" of the *Terry* exception does not permit a frisk for weapons on less than reasonable belief or suspicion directed at the person to be frisked, even though that person happens to be on premises where an authorized narcotics search is taking place.

444 U.S. at 92–94, 100 S.Ct. at 343, 62 L.Ed.2d at 246–47.

2. **Need to Begin With Patdown.** Is a weapons search under *Terry* always required to begin with a patdown? In Adams v. Williams, discussed in note 2 above, the officer apparently conducted no patdown but rather reached into the automobile and "removed" a gun from the suspect's waistband. The Court upheld the constitutionality of this action but did not discuss the officer's failure to conduct a preliminary patdown. How might this be justified?

D. TRAFFIC STOPS

EDITORS' INTRODUCTION: TRAFFIC STOPS AS A DISTINGUISHABLE TYPE OF DETENTION

The Supreme Court and lower tribunals have long assumed that traffic stops are a type of detention different from arrests or investigatory field stops. Nevertheless, the case law arguably fails to make clear how, in at least some situations, a traffic stop should be distinguished from an arrest.

The Supreme Court first referred to traffic stops in United States v. Robinson, 414 U.S. 218, 94 S.Ct. 467, 38 L.Ed.2d 427 (1973). In a discussion of search incident to custodial arrest, it noted the court below "discussed its understanding of the law where the police officer makes what the court characterized as 'a routine traffic stop,' i.e., where the officer would simply issue a notice of violation and allow the offender to proceed." Since *Robinson* involved "a full-custody arrest of the violator," the Court did not reach the question discussed by the lower tribunal.

Citations as Alternatives to Custodial Arrest

The major alternative to "a full-custody arrest" as a law enforcement officer's response to observing a traffic offense, of course, is the issuance of what is varyingly called a citation, a "ticket," or in the language of the lower court in *Robinson*, a "notice of violation." A citation directs the cited person to appear, generally in a specified court, at some future time to respond to the official contention that he has committed an offense or violation. Failure to appear is generally a criminal offense. In many jurisdictions—including, as the principal case in this part indicates, Iowa— local nonconstitutional law gives officers considerable discretion whether, in the case of a traffic offense, to issue a citation or rather make a full custody arrest.

Some jurisdictions, however, limit officers' authority to make a full custody arrest for some minor offenses. A Minnesota rule, for example, provides:

> Law enforcement officers acting without a warrant, who have decided to proceed with prosecution, shall issue citations to persons subject to lawful arrest for misdemeanors, unless it reasonably appears to the officer that arrest or detention is necessary to prevent bodily harm to the accused or another or further criminal conduct, or that there is a substantial likelihood that the accused will fail to respond to a citation. The citation may be issued in lieu of an arrest, or if an arrest has been made, in lieu of continued detention.

Minn.R.Crim.Pro. 6.01, subd.1(1)(a).

A full custody arrest for some minor offenses or violations may violate the Fourth Amendment requirement that such seizures be reasonable. The Supreme Court has not addressed the matter, but one member of the tribunal has noted the issue. In Gustafson v. Florida, 414 U.S. 260, 94 S.Ct. 488, 38 L.Ed.2d 456 (1973), a companion case to *Robinson*, the Court upheld a search incident to a custodial arrest for driving without a license. Justice Stewart wrote separately, noting Gustafson had not contested the constitutional validity of his custodial arrest. "[A] persuasive claim might have been made in this case," Justice Stewart commented, "that the custodial arrest * * * for a minor traffic offense violated [Gustafson's] rights under the Fourth and Fourteenth Amendments."

The validity of full custody arrests for minor offenses was explored in State v. Jones, 1999 WL 76817 (Ohio App.) (unpublished), discretionary appeals allowed, 86 Ohio St.3d 1406, 711 N.E.2d 233 (1999), involving an arrest for jaywalking as prohibited by a city ordinance. The offense is a "minor misdemeanor," punishable by only a fine. Under an Ohio statute, an officer is barred from making an arrest for a minor misdemeanor and must issue a citation, unless one of four special circumstances exist. None existed in *Jones*, so the arrest violated Ohio law. The prosecution, however, argued the arrest did not violate the Fourth Amendment and thus evidence obtained by it was not inadmissible. Holding that the arrest did violate the Fourth Amendment, the court noted under Supreme Court case law common law informs the understanding as to what is unreasonable under the Fourth Amendment. At common law a warrantless arrest for a misdemeanor was permissible only if the offense took place in the presence of the officer and was a breach of the peace; this of course suggests warrantless arrests for misdemeanors are unreasonable in other situations.

More functionally, *Jones* reasoned, the Fourth Amendment requires an arrest be justified by some adequate state interest and this requirement is embodied in the constitutional requirement of probable cause. The weight of the underlying state interest is determined, at least in part, by state law. Where a state determines its interest reflected in a crime does not justify custodial arrests for that crime, the state interest is not sufficient to render a custodial arrest for that crime reasonable in Fourth Amendment terms. Probable cause, as required by Fourth Amendment law, means probable cause to believe the suspect has committed an offense for which state law authorizes a custodial arrest. *Jones* noted further:

> For a minor-misdemeanor offender, * * * the power of the police officer to arrest him creates a form of potential punishment that exceeds anything that could be meted out by a judge after a finding of guilt

Multiple Functions of Traffic Law Enforcement

The complexity of the law in this area is undoubtedly affected by the nature of traffic law's role in policing. Certainly, to some extent, law enforcement agencies properly regard traffic laws themselves as deserving of enforcement:

> [T]raffic problems are a quality-of-life issue nearly everywhere. If the essence of community policing is to be sensitive to citizen concerns, we cannot afford to ignore traffic enforcement. Citizens need to feel safe on the streets and highways—not only from careless and drunk drivers, but also from the violent quarrels that sometimes occur when hot-tempered, aggressive individuals act out because another driver "cut them off."

Earl M. Sweeney, Traffic Enforcement: New Uses for an Old Tool, 68 Police Chief 45 (1996). Aggressive traffic law enforcement may—perhaps because of the increase in resulting visibility of police officers—further other law enforcement objectives. Sweeney, for example, added:

> Many cities that are plagued by gang activities, illegal guns, open-air drug markets and drive-by shootings have discovered that saturating an area with traffic patrol shuts down these illegal operations.

In addition, traffic enforcement may be used as a means of investigating suspicions that particular persons are involved in more serious criminal behavior. Sweeney continued:

> [A]n alert police officer who "looks beyond the traffic ticket" and uses the motor vehicle stop to "sniff out" possible criminal behavior may be our most effective tool for interdicting criminals. Serious lawbreakers almost always have aggressive personalities that also show up in their driving behavior. They drive after drinking, speed, cross over solid center lines, run red lights and stop signs, and neglect to register their vehicles or renew their driver's licenses. And they pass through our communities every day on their way to or from holdups and burglaries, or en route in the transport of drugs or illegal loads of hazardous wastes. Many of them are apprehended in routine traffic stops—and still more could be—if we re-emphasized traffic patrol.

If traffic enforcement is a valuable tool for use against serious crime, how is it best used? In 1997, Indianapolis police implemented "directed patrol" programs in two high crime areas. In the first ("east"), officers tended to stop vehicles for any observed violation in order to create a sense of significantly increased police presence. In the second ("north") area, officers again used traffic stops but focused upon those motorists specifically suspected of involvement in nontraffic criminal activity. Officers made more stops in the first area, and every 100 stops resulted in 24.5 citations, 14.5 arrests, 1.1 felony arrests, and 0.34 seizures of illegal guns. In the second area, every 100 stops resulted in 49.2 citations, 30.6 arrests, 2.9 felony arrests and 0.085 seizures of illegal guns. Total gun crimes actually increased somewhat in the first area but dropped 29 percent in the second. Office of Justice Program, U.S. Department of Justice, Promising Strategies to Reduce Gun Violence 53–54, 95–96 (1999). This, of course, suggests that simply vigorous traffic enforcement is less effective than using stops to follow through on suspicions developed by other methods. But the more extensive use of warnings rather than citations in the first area may have muted the "zero tolerance" message the police sought to convey by the increased police presence.

A major issue, of course, is whether the legal rules relating to traffic stops should be affected by the likelihood that traffic stops are sometimes used for purposes other than simply enforcing traffic laws themselves.

Definition and Requirements of Traffic Stops

Judicial discussions—including those in the Supreme Court's case law—often assume traffic stops are self-defining. This, however, is not necessarily the case. Moreover, there is some question as to the basis required for a traffic stop. Further—as the first principal case reprinted here makes clear—there remains considerable question as to what officers may do during a traffic stop.

Implicit in a traffic stop is some particularized information suggesting the driver has committed a violation of a traffic law. As is discussed in the Editors' Introduction to the next part of this chapter, the Supreme Court has held the Fourth Amendment prohibits random or "suspicionless" stops of motorists to determine whether they lack valid driver's licenses or registration documents for the vehicles. Delaware v. Prouse, 440 U.S. 648, 99 S.Ct. 1391, 59 L.Ed.2d 660 (1979), so holding, made clear some focused showing of at least a basis for suspecting a driver of committing an offense is necessary for a traffic stop.

In Whren v. United States, 517 U.S. 806, 116 S.Ct. 1769, 135 L.Ed.2d 89 (1996), reprinted later in this chapter, the Supreme Court observed that an "[a]utomobile stop"—by which the Court apparently meant a routine traffic stop—"is reasonable where the police have probable cause to believe that a traffic violation has occurred." But is a traffic stop reasonable *only* if such probable cause exists? Or would a traffic stop to issue a citation be constitutionally permissible on reasonable suspicion the driver has committed a traffic violation? The issue seldom arises, of course, because traffic stops are nearly always supported by officers' testimony that they observed the drivers commit acts constituting violations of the traffic laws. Since such testimony constitutes probable cause, the cases present no occasion to consider whether less than probable cause might support a traffic stop. In *Whren*, for example, the parties apparently agreed that the officers had probable cause to believe the suspects committed multiple traffic violations.

The principal case reprinted next involved what all members of the Supreme Court apparently agreed was a nonarrest traffic stop. This agreement enabled the Court to address what the Fourth Amendment permits as incident to such a seizure.

Knowles v. Iowa

Supreme Court of the United States, 1998.
525 U.S. 113, 119 S.Ct. 484, 142 L.Ed.2d 492.

■ CHIEF JUSTICE REHNQUIST delivered the opinion of the Court.

An Iowa police officer stopped petitioner Knowles for speeding, but issued him a citation rather than arresting him. The question presented is whether such a procedure authorizes the officer, consistently with the Fourth Amendment, to conduct a full search of the car. We answer this question "no."

Knowles was stopped in Newton, Iowa, after having been clocked driving 43 miles per hour on a road where the speed limit was 25 miles per hour. The police officer issued a citation to Knowles, although under Iowa law he might have arrested him. The officer then conducted a full search of the car, and under the driver's seat he found a bag of marijuana and a "pot pipe." Knowles was then arrested and charged with violation of state laws dealing with controlled substances.

[handwritten margin note: Issue — Traffic stop + ticket = ? authority to search car]

Before trial, Knowles moved to suppress the evidence so obtained. He argued that the search could not be sustained under the "search incident to arrest" exception recognized in United States v. Robinson, 414 U.S. 218, 94 S.Ct. 467, 38 L.Ed.2d 427 (1973), because he had not been placed under arrest. At the hearing on the motion to suppress, the police officer conceded that he had neither Knowles' consent nor probable cause to conduct the search. He relied on Iowa law dealing with such searches.

Iowa Code Ann. § 321.485(1)(a) (West 1997) provides that Iowa peace officers having cause to believe that a person has violated any traffic or motor vehicle equipment law may arrest the person and immediately take the person before a magistrate. Iowa law also authorizes the far more usual practice of issuing a citation in lieu of arrest or in lieu of continued custody after an initial arrest.[4] See Iowa Code Ann. § 805.1(1) (West Supp.1997). Section 805.1(4) provides that the issuance of a citation in lieu of an arrest "does not affect the officer's authority to conduct an otherwise lawful search." The Iowa Supreme Court has interpreted this provision as providing authority to officers to conduct a full-blown search of an automobile and driver in those cases where police elect not to make a custodial arrest and instead issue a citation—that is, a search incident to citation.

Based on this authority, the trial court denied the motion to suppress and found Knowles guilty. The Supreme Court of Iowa, sitting en banc, affirmed by a divided vote. * * * [T]he Iowa Supreme Court upheld the constitutionality of the search under a bright-line "search incident to citation" exception to the Fourth Amendment's warrant requirement, reasoning that so long as the arresting officer had probable cause to make a custodial arrest, there need not in fact have been a custodial arrest. We granted certiorari * * *. * * * Knowles did not argue below, and does not argue here, that the statute could never be lawfully applied. The question we therefore address is whether the search at issue, authorized as it was by state law, nonetheless violates the Fourth Amendment.

In *Robinson*, supra, we noted the two historical rationales for the "search incident to arrest" exception: (1) the need to disarm the suspect in order to take him into custody, and (2) the need to preserve evidence for later use at trial. But neither of these underlying rationales for the search incident to arrest exception is sufficient to justify the search in the present case.

We have recognized that the first rationale—officer safety—is " 'both legitimate and weighty.' " The threat to officer safety from issuing a traffic citation, however, is a good deal less than in the case of a custodial arrest. In *Robinson*, we stated that a custodial arrest involves "danger to an officer" because of "the extended exposure which follows the taking of a suspect into custody and transporting him to the police station." We recognized that "[t]he danger to the police officer flows from the fact of the

---

4. Iowa law permits the issuance of a citation in lieu of arrest for most offenses for which an accused person would be "eligible for bail." See Iowa Code Ann. § 805.1(1) (West Supp.1997). In addition to traffic and motor vehicle equipment violations, this would permit the issuance of a citation in lieu of arrest for such serious felonies as second-degree burglary, and first-degree theft, both bailable offenses under Iowa law. The practice in Iowa of permitting citation in lieu of arrest is consistent with law reform efforts.

arrest, and its attendant proximity, stress, and uncertainty, and not from the grounds for arrest.'' A routine traffic stop, on the other hand, is a relatively brief encounter and ''is more analogous to a so-called '*Terry* stop' . . . than to a formal arrest.'' Berkemer v. McCarty, 468 U.S. 420, 437, 104 S.Ct. 3138, 82 L.Ed.2d 317 (1984). See also Cupp v. Murphy, 412 U.S. 291, 296, 93 S.Ct. 2000, 36 L.Ed.2d 900 (1973) (''Where there is no formal arrest . . . a person might well be less hostile to the police and less likely to take conspicuous, immediate steps to destroy incriminating evidence'').

This is not to say that the concern for officer safety is absent in the case of a routine traffic stop. It plainly is not. But while the concern for officer safety in this context may justify the ''minimal'' additional intrusion of ordering a driver and passengers out of the car, it does not by itself justify the often considerably greater intrusion attending a full field-type search. Even without the search authority Iowa urges, officers have other, independent bases to search for weapons and protect themselves from danger. For example, they may order out of a vehicle both the driver, and any passengers; perform a ''patdown'' of a driver and any passengers upon reasonable suspicion that they may be armed and dangerous; conduct a ''*Terry* patdown'' of the passenger compartment of a vehicle upon reason-able suspicion that an occupant is dangerous and may gain immediate control of a weapon; and even conduct a full search of the passenger compartment, including any containers therein, pursuant to a custodial arrest.

Nor has Iowa shown the second justification for the authority to search incident to arrest—the need to discover and preserve evidence. Once Knowles was stopped for speeding and issued a citation, all the evidence necessary to prosecute that offense had been obtained. No further evidence of excessive speed was going to be found either on the person of the offender or in the passenger compartment of the car.

Iowa nevertheless argues that a ''search incident to citation'' is justi-fied because a suspect who is subject to a routine traffic stop may attempt to hide or destroy evidence related to his identity (e. g., a driver's license or vehicle registration), or destroy evidence of another, as yet undetected crime. As for the destruction of evidence relating to identity, if a police officer is not satisfied with the identification furnished by the driver, this may be a basis for arresting him rather than merely issuing a citation. As for destroying evidence of other crimes, the possibility that an officer would stumble onto evidence wholly unrelated to the speeding offense seems remote.

In *Robinson*, we held that the authority to conduct a full field search as incident to an arrest was a ''bright-line rule,'' which was based on the concern for officer safety and destruction or loss of evidence, but which did not depend in every case upon the existence of either concern. Here we are asked to extend that ''bright-line rule'' to a situation where the concern for officer safety is not present to the same extent and the concern for destruction or loss of evidence is not present at all. We decline to do so. The judgment of the Supreme Court of Iowa is reversed, and the cause remand-ed for further proceedings not inconsistent with this opinion.

It is so ordered.

NOTES

1. **Distinguishing Traffic Stops From Arrests.** Often, as in Iowa, an officer has authority to either issue a motor a citation for a traffic offense or make a full custody arrest. If in such situations the officer searches before actually issuing a citation, how should the courts determine whether the situation is an arrest permitting an incidental search or rather a nonarrest traffic stop that under *Knowles* does not permit such a search? The issue was raised during oral argument in *Knowles*. One member of the Court inquired of counsel for Knowles, Paul Rosenberg:

QUESTION: * * * Suppose the officer had just said, I'm placing you under arrest, and he said those words before he searched the driver and the passenger and the inside of the car. * * *

MR. ROSENBERG: If he had done that, then it would have been a valid search incident to a lawful arrest.

QUESTION: So, the whole thing turns on whether the officer says you're under * * * arrest or here's a ticket.

MR. ROSENBERG: Yes * * *.

During the argument by counsel for Iowa, Bridget A. Chambers, the following exchange took place:

MS. CHAMBERS: * * * [U]nder Iowa law officers can arrest, search, and then subsequently release on citation. * * *

QUESTION: Excuse me. They can arrest, search, and then say never mind the arrest?

MS. CHAMBERS: Yes.

QUESTION: Wow.

(Laughter.)

The questioning of Ms. Chambers continued:

QUESTION: [T]he usual rule is there can be a search incident to an arrest. You want to turn it around and have an arrest incident to a search. And it seems to me that that's an abuse of authority. * * * If the officer arrests not intending really to arrest, that's an abuse of authority. You're not really proposing that this could happen, are you?

MS. CHAMBERS: We're certainly not advocating that that should happen, and we're certainly not * * * not encouraging that. * * * [W]e think it could conceivably happen, and * * * [it is likely that this] wouldn't violate the Fourth Amendment * * *.

2. **Duration of Traffic Stops.** Are there Fourth Amendment limits on the duration of a traffic stop? In Ohio v. Robinette, 519 U.S. 33, 117 S.Ct. 417, 136 L.Ed.2d 347 (1996), Deputy Newsome stopped Robinette for speeding, asked for and received his driver's license, and ran a computer check which indicated that Robinette had no prior violations.

Newsome then asked Robinette to step out of his car, turned on his mounted video camera, issued a verbal warning to Robinette, and returned his license.

At this point, Newsome asked, "One question before you get gone: [A]re you carrying any illegal contraband in your car? Any weapons of any kind, drugs, anything like that?" Robinette answered "no" to these questions, after which Deputy Newsome asked if he could search the car. Robinette consented. In the car, Deputy Newsome discovered a small amount of marijuana and, in a film container, a pill which was later determined to be methylenedioxymeth-amphetamine (MDMA).

The Supreme Court granted review primarily to address the state court's holding that Robinette's consent was ineffective; this aspect of the case is discussed in Chapter 5. Robinette contended, however, the Court should not reach the consent issue because the state court had held the evidence inadmissible on an alternative basis. Before Newsome returned to Robinette's vehicle, he had determined not to give Robinette a ticket but rather to pursue his suspicion that Robinette might be in possession of drugs. "When the motivation behind a police officer's continued detention of a person stopped for a traffic violation is not related to the purpose of the original, constitutional stop, and when that continued detention is not based on articulable facts giving rise to a suspicion of some separate illegal activity justifying an extension of the detention," the state court explained, "the continued detention constitutes an illegal seizure." Thus the consent and search were all the tainted "fruit" of a detention that had become unreasonable. The Supreme Court, however, disagreed:

> We think that under our recent decision in Whren v. United States, 517 U.S. 806, 116 S.Ct. 1769, 135 L.Ed.2d 89 (1996) [reprinted later in this chapter] * * *, the subjective intentions of the officer did not make the continued detention of respondent illegal under the Fourth Amendment. As we made clear in *Whren*, " 'the fact that [an] officer does not have the state of mind which is hypothecated by the reasons which provide the legal justification for the officer's action does not invalidate the action taken as long as the circumstances, viewed objectively, justify that action.' * * * Subjective intentions play no role in ordinary, probable-cause Fourth Amendment analysis." * * *

519 U.S. at 38, 117 S.Ct. at 420–21, 136 L.Ed.2d at 354. It is not clear the Supreme Court intended by this discussion to reject the possibility that Deputy Newsome may have impermissibly extended the traffic stop. *Robinette* appears to reject only the state court's holding that the stop became unreasonable because the officer's subjective motivation had shifted from traffic matters to drug concerns.

On remand in *Robinette*, the Ohio Supreme Court reanalyzed the situation. In recognition of *Whren*, it first held that a continued detention resulting from a traffic stop becomes unreasonable "[w]hen [the] police officer's objective justification to continue detention * * * is not related to the purpose of the original stop," unless it is justified on some other ground. The Fourth Amendment permissibility of brief stops at sobriety checkpoints, the court continued, establishes the weight properly given to the strong policy in favor of quelling the drug trade. This policy also permits an officer who has made a proper traffic stop, pursuant to a drug interdiction policy, to briefly detain the motorist in order to ask him whether he is carrying any illegal drugs or weapons.

If during that continued detention reasonable suspicion develops, the Ohio court added, the officer may detain the motorist for a more in-depth investigation that may include soliciting consent to search. But where, as in *Robinette*, the questioning does not give rise to reasonable suspicion, the officer cannot reasonably continue to detain the motorist "to ask for and execute an intrusive search." State v. Robinette, 80 Ohio St.3d 234, 241, 685 N.E.2d 762, 768 (1997). Thus Robinette's detention became unreasonable, apparently after he responded negatively to Newsome's inquiries about drugs and weapons.

3. **"Frisks" of Automobiles.** Under certain circumstances officers' right to conduct a protective weapons search extends beyond the person of a motorist and includes some parts of the automobile. Such searches are sometimes permissible during traffic stops.

In Michigan v. Long, 463 U.S. 1032, 103 S.Ct. 3469, 77 L.Ed.2d 1201 (1983), two Michigan sheriff's deputies, Howell and Lewis, were on routine patrol in a rural area. Shortly after midnight, they observed a car driven erratically and at excessive speed. When it swerved into a ditch, they stopped to investigate. Long, the only occupant of the vehicle, met the officers at the rear of the car which protruded from the ditch onto the road. Howell asked Long to produce his operator's license; Long did not respond until the request was repeated. When asked to produce the registration for the vehicle, Long again failed to respond. When this request was repeated, Long turned and walked towards the front open door on the driver's side of the vehicle. The officers followed Long and observed a large hunting knife on the floorboard of the vehicle. They then stopped Long and conducted a patdown; they found no weapons. Shining a flashlight into the car, one deputy noticed "something" protruding from under the armrest on the front seat. He entered the car, knelt, and lifted the armrest, revealing an open leather pouch on the seat. The officer then "determined" that the pouch contained marihuana. At issue before the Supreme Court was the propriety of the officers' action leading to the discovery of the marihuana as a *Terry*-type weapons search conducted on less than probable cause.

Neither *Terry's* language nor its rationale, Justice O'Connor concluded for the Court, required the right to search for weapons during a nonarrest detention be restricted to the person of the detained suspect. To the contrary, suspects confronted while in automobiles present special dangers to officers' safety because of their access to weapons that might be in the vehicles. Consequently, during a nonarrest detention of a suspect:

> the search of the passenger compartment of an automobile, limited to those areas in which a weapon might be placed or hidden, is permissible if the police officer possessed a reasonable belief based on "specific and articulable facts which, taken together with the rational inferences from those facts, reasonably warrant" the officers in believing that the suspect is dangerous and the suspect may gain immediate control of weapons. * * * If, while conducting a legitimate *Terry* search of the interior of the automobile, the officer should * * * discover contraband other than weapons, he clearly cannot be required to ignore the contraband, and the Fourth Amendment does not require its suppression in such circumstances.

463 U.S. at 1049–50, 103 S.Ct. at 3480–81, 77 L.Ed.2d at 1220. Turning to the facts before it, the Court held the deputies entertained the requisite reasonable fear for their safety. The rural nature of the area and late time of the stop were relevant. Further, the officers had reason to believe Long intoxicated and their pre-search observations disclosed a knife in the car. Although Long was, in some sense, under the "control" of the officers, he might still have been able to obtain and use weapons in the car. If released after the detention, he would in any event have had access to any such weapons. Even if methods other than the search were available to the officers to assure their safety, in contexts such as this in which quick decisions are crucial, the Court has "not required that officers adopt alternative means to ensure their safety in order to avoid the intrusion involved in a *Terry* encounter." Once begun, the search was properly limited. It was restricted to "those areas to which Long would generally have immediate control, and that could

contain a weapon." Examining the contents of the pouch was permissible, since the trial court determined the pouch "could have contained a weapon."

4. **Removal of Driver and Passengers from Stopped Vehicle.** Some protective action by officers during a traffic stop does not require even the justification demanded by the Court for the search in *Long*. This is the case, for example, with removal of persons from a stopped vehicle.

In Pennsylvania v. Mimms, 434 U.S. 106, 98 S.Ct. 330, 54 L.Ed.2d 331 (1977) (per curiam), an officer stopped Mimms for driving an automobile with an expired license plate, intending to issue a traffic citation. The officer asked Mimms to step out of the car and produce his owner's card and operator's license. When Mimms complied, the officer noticed a large bulge under Mimms' sports jacket. A frisk resulted in discovery of a revolver. The state court held ordering Mimms out of his car was unreasonable because the officer lacked any reason to believe criminal activity was afoot or Mimms posed a danger; the State conceded the officer had no reason to fear Mimms particularly. Reversing, the Supreme Court held the officers' action permissible. Conversing with a driver while standing exposed to traffic, it emphasized, creates a risk of injury to the officer. On the other hand, given the fact that the motorist had already been stopped, the additional intrusion involved in requiring the motorist to get out of the car "can only be described as *de minimis*." Once the officer observed the bulge in Mimms' jacket, the Court continued, *Terry* justified the officer's further action:

> The bulge in the jacket permitted the officer to conclude that Mimms was armed and thus posed a serious and present danger to the safety of the officer. In these circumstances, any man of "reasonable caution" would likely have conducted the "pat-down."

434 U.S. at 112, 98 S.Ct. at 334, 54 L.Ed.2d at 338.

In Maryland v. Wilson, 519 U.S. 408, 117 S.Ct. 882, 137 L.Ed.2d 41 (1997), *Mimms* was extended and the Court held that an officer making a traffic stop may order passengers to get out of a vehicle during the stop. Under *Mimms*, the Court reasoned, the reasonableness of such action depends on a balance between the public interests implicated and individuals' interest in personal security free of arbitrary interference by officers. Passenger removal furthers the same "legitimate and weighty" need for officer safety as was involved in *Mimms*. In fact, the Court added, "the fact that there is more than one occupant of the vehicle increases the possible sources of harm to the officer." That the persons involved are passengers rather than drivers does not significantly reduce the risk:

> It would seem that the possibility of a violent encounter stems not from the ordinary reaction of a motorist stopped for a speeding violation, but from the fact that evidence of a more serious crime might be encountered during the stop. And the motivation of a passenger to employ violence to prevent apprehension of such a crime is every bit as great as that of the driver.

519 U.S. at 413, 117 S.Ct. at 886, 137 L.Ed.2d at 47–48.

Considering the public interest side of the balance, the Court acknowledged the case for suspicionless removal of passengers is "in one sense" weaker than that for removal of drivers. Although there is probable cause to believe the driver has committed an offense, there is no similar basis for stopping or detaining the passengers. Therefore, the passengers' personal liberty interests weigh more heavily against removal than did those of drivers. Nevertheless, the Court found this weightier liberty interest of minimal significance:

> [A]s a practical matter, the passengers are already stopped by virtue of the stop of the vehicle. The only change in their circumstances which will result from

ordering them out of the car is that they will be outside of, rather than inside of, the stopped car.

519 U.S. at 413–14, 117 S.Ct. at 886, 137 L.Ed.2d at 47. Consequently, "the additional intrusion on the passenger is minimal." The risk of harm to those involved "is minimized if the officers routinely exercise unquestioned command of the situation." The Fourth Amendment therefore permits officers making traffic stops to order passengers to get out of the cars pending completion of the stops.

Maryland urged the Court to hold an officer may forcibly detain a passenger for the duration of a stop. Wilson had not been detained after he was directed to get out of the car, the Court responded, and therefore the Court did not reach, and expressly reserved comment on, officers' power to detain passengers.

State v. Soto

Superior Court of New Jersey, 1996.[c]
324 N.J.Super. 66, 734 A.2d 350.

■ FRANCIS, J.S.C.

These are consolidated motions to suppress under the equal protection and due process clauses of the Fourteenth Amendment.[5] Seventeen defendants of African ancestry claim that their arrests on the New Jersey Turnpike south of exit 3 between 1988 and 1991 result from discriminatory enforcement of the traffic laws by the New Jersey State Police. After a lengthy hearing, I find defendants have established a *prima facie* case of selective enforcement which the State has failed to rebut requiring suppression of all contraband and evidence seized.

Defendants base their claim of institutional racism primarily on statistics. During discovery, each side created a database of all stops and arrests by State Police members patrolling the Turnpike between exits 1 and 7A out of the Moorestown Station for thirty-five randomly selected days between April 1988 and May 1991 from arrest reports, patrol charts, radio logs and traffic tickets. The databases are essentially the same. Both sides counted 3060 stops which the State found to include 1212 race identified stops (39.6%), the defense 1146 (37.4%).

To establish a standard against which to compare the stop data, the defense conducted a traffic survey and a violator survey. Dr. John Lamberth, Chairman of the Psychology Department at Temple University * * * designed both surveys.

The traffic survey was conducted over twenty-one randomly selected two and one-half hour sessions between June 11 and June 24, 1993 and between 8:00 a.m. and 8:00 p.m. at four sites, two northbound and two southbound, between exits 1 and 3 of the Turnpike. Teams supervised by Fred Last, Esq., of the Office of the Public Defender observed and recorded

c. The trial court granted the motion to suppress in 1996, and the State appealed. In 1999, the State dropped the appeal. At the request of the New Jersey Supreme Court's Committee on Opinions, the trial judge then submitted this opinion, written three years earlier, for publication.

5. The motions also include claims under the Fourth Amendment, but they were severed before the hearing to await future proceedings if not rendered moot by this decision.

the number of vehicles that passed them except for large trucks, tractor-trailers, buses and government vehicles, how many contained a "black" occupant and the state of origin of each vehicle. Of the 42,706 vehicles counted, 13.5% had a black occupant. * * *

The violator survey was conducted over ten sessions in four days in July 1993 by Mr. Last traveling between exits 1 and 3 in his vehicle at sixty miles per hour on cruise control after the speedometer had been calibrated and observing and recording the number of vehicles that passed him, the number of vehicles he passed and how many had a black occupant. Mr. Last counted a total of 2096 vehicles other than large trucks, tractortrailers, buses and government vehicles of which 2062 or 98.1% passed him going in excess of sixty miles per hour including 306 with a black occupant equaling about 15% of those vehicles clearly speeding. Multiple violators, that is those violating the speed limit and committing some other moving violation like tailgating, also equaled about 15% black. * * *

Using 13.5% as the standard or benchmark against which to compare the stop data, Dr. Lamberth found that 127 or 46.2% of the race identified stops between exits 1 and 3 were of blacks constituting an absolute disparity of 32.7%, a comparative disparity of 242% (32.7% divided by 13.5%) and 16.35 standard deviations. By convention, something is considered statistically significant if it would occur by chance fewer than five times in a hundred (over two standard deviations). * * *

Supposing that the disproportionate stopping of blacks was related to police discretion, the defense studied the traffic tickets issued by State Police members between exits 1 and 7A on the thirty-five randomly selected days broken down by State Police unit.[6] There are 533 racially identified tickets in the databases issued by either the now disbanded Radar Unit, the Tactical Patrol Unit or general road troopers ("Patrol Unit"). The testimony indicates that the Radar Unit focused mainly on speeders using a radar van and chase cars and exercised limited discretion regarding which vehicles to stop. The Tac–Pac concentrates on traffic problems at specific locations and exercises somewhat more discretion as regards which vehicles to stop. Responsible to provide general law enforcement, the Patrol Unit exercises by far the most discretion among the three units. From Mr. Last's count, Dr. Lamberth computed that 18% of the tickets issued by the Radar Unit were to blacks, 23.8% of the tickets issued by the Tac–Pac were to blacks while 34.2% of the tickets issued by the Patrol Unit were to blacks. South of exit 3, Dr. Lamberth computed that 19.4% of the tickets issued by the Radar Unit were to blacks, 0.0% of the tickets issued by the Tac–Pac were to blacks while 43.8% of the tickets issued by the Patrol Unit were to blacks. In his opinion, the Radar Unit percentages are statistically consistent with the standard established by the violator survey, but the differences between the Radar Unit and the Patrol Unit between both exits 1 and 3 and 1 and 7A are statistically significant or well in excess of two standard deviations.

6. Of the 3060 stops in the databases, 1292 are ticketed stops. Hence, no tickets were issued for nearly 60% of the stops.

The State presented the testimony of Dr. Leonard Cupingood to challenge or refute the statistical evidence offered by the defense. I found Dr. Cupingood is qualified to give expert testimony in the field of statistics * * *.

Dr. Cupingood had no genuine criticism of the defense traffic survey. Rather, he centered his criticism of the defense statistical evidence on the violator survey. Throughout his testimony he maintained that the violator survey failed to capture the relevant data which he opined was the racial mix of those speeders most likely to be stopped or the "tail of the distribution." * * * He was unclear, though, how he would design a study to ascertain in a safe way the vehicle going the fastest above the speed limit at a given time at a given location and the race of its occupants without involving the credibility of State Police members. In any event, his supposition that maybe blacks drive faster than whites above the speed limit was repudiated by all State Police members called by the State who were questioned about it. * * *

The defense [also] conducted a profile study * * *. It concentrated on the race identified stops of just blacks issued tickets and found that an adult black male was present in 88% of the cases where the gender of all occupants could be determined and that where gender and age could be determined, a black male 30 or younger was present in 63% of the cases. * * *

The defense did not rest on its statistical evidence alone. Along with the testimony of former troopers Kenneth Ruff and Kenneth Wilson about having been trained and coached to make race based profile stops but whose testimony is weakened by bias related to their not having been reappointed at the end of their terms, the defense elicited evidence through cross-examination of State witnesses and a rebuttal witness, Dr. James Fyfe, that the State Police hierarchy allowed, condoned, cultivated and tolerated discrimination between 1988 and 1991 in its crusade to rid New Jersey of the scourge of drugs.

Conjointly with the passage of the Comprehensive Drug Reform Act of 1987 and to advance the Attorney General's Statewide Action Plan for Narcotics Enforcement issued in January 1988 which "directed that the enforcement of our criminal drug laws shall be the highest priority law enforcement activity", Colonel Pagano formed the Drug Interdiction Training Unit (DITU) in late 1987 consisting of two supervisors and ten other members, two from each Troop selected for their successful seizure statistics, " . . . to actually patrol with junior road personnel and provide critical on-the-job training in recognizing potential violators." According to Colonel Pagano, the DITU program was intended to be one step beyond the existing coach program to impart to newer troopers insight into drug enforcement and the "criminal program" (patrol related arrests) in general. DITU was disbanded in or around July 1992.

[A] glimpse of the work of DITU emerges from * * * the testimony of Sergeants Brian Caffrey and David Cobb. Sergeant Caffrey was the original assistant supervisor of DITU and became the supervisor in 1989. Sergeant Cobb was an original member of DITU and became the assistant supervisor in 1989. Sergeant Caffrey left DITU sometime in 1992, Sergeant Cobb sometime in 1991. Both testified that a major purpose of DITU was to teach trainees tip-offs and techniques about what to look for and do to talk or "dig" their way into a vehicle after, not before, a motor vehicle stop to effectuate patrol related arrests. Both denied teaching or using race as a tip-off either before or after a stop. Nevertheless, Sergeant Caffrey condoned a comment by a DITU trainer during the time he was the supervisor of DITU stating:

> "Trooper Fash previously had DITU training, and it showed in the way he worked. He has become a little reluctant to stop cars in lieu [sic] of the Channel 9 News Report. He was told as long as he uses Title 39 he can stop any car he wants. He enjoys DITU and would like to ride again."

As the defense observes in its closing brief, "Why would a trooper who is acting in a racially neutral fashion become reluctant to stop cars as a result of a news story charging that racial minorities were being targeted [by the New Jersey State Police]?" Even A.A.G. Ronald Susswein, Deputy Director of the Division of Criminal Justice, acknowledged that this comment is incomplete because it fails to add the caveat, "as long as he doesn't also use race or ethnicity." Further, Sergeant Caffrey testified that "ethnicity is something to keep in mind" albeit not a tip-off and that he taught attendees at both the annual State Police in-service training session in March 1987 and the special State Police in-service training sessions in July and August 1987 that Hispanics are mainly involved in drug trafficking and showed them the film Operation Pipeline wherein the ethnicity of those arrested, mostly Hispanics, is prominently depicted. Dr. Fyfe criticized Sergeant Caffrey's teaching Hispanics are mainly involved and his showing Operation Pipeline as well as the showing of the Jamaican Posse film wherein only blacks are depicted as drug traffickers at the 1989 annual State Police in-service training session saying trainers should not teach what they do not intend their trainees to act upon. At a minimum, teaching Hispanics are mainly involved in drug trafficking and showing films depicting mostly Hispanics and blacks trafficking in drugs at training sessions worked at cross-purposes with concomitant instruction pointing out that neither race nor ethnicity may be considered in making traffic stops.

Key corroboration for finding the State Police hierarchy allowed and tolerated discrimination came from Colonel Pagano. Colonel Pagano was Superintendent of the State Police from 1975 to February 1990. He testified there was a noisy demand in the 1980s to get drugs off the streets. In accord, Attorney General Cary Edwards and he made drug interdiction the number one priority of law enforcement. He helped formulate the Attorney General's Statewide Action Plan for Narcotics Enforcement and established DITU within the State Police. He kept an eye on DITU through conversations with staff officers and Sergeants Mastella and Caffrey and review of reports generated under the traditional reporting system * * *. He had no thought DITU would engage in constitutional violations. * * *

More telling, however, is what Colonel Pagano said and did, or did not do, in response to the Channel 9 expose entitled "Without Just Cause" which aired in 1989 and which troubled Trooper Fash and what he did not do in response to complaints of profiling from the NAACP and ACLU and these consolidated motions to suppress and similar motions in Warren and

Middlesex Counties. He said to Joe Collum of Channel 9 that "[violating rights of motorists was] of serious concern [to him], *but no where near* the concern that I think we have got to look to in trying to correct some of the problems we find with the criminal element in this State" and "the bottom line is that those stops were not made on the basis of race *alone*." (emphasis added) Since perhaps these isolated comments were said inadvertently or edited out of context, a truer reflection of his attitude about claims of racism would appear to be his videotaped remarks shown all members of the State Police at roll call in conjunction with the WOR series. Thereon he clearly said that he did not want targeting or discriminatory enforcement and that "[w]hen you put on this uniform, you leave your biases and your prejudices behind." But he also said as regarded the charge of a Trenton school principal named Jones that he had been stopped on the Turnpike and threatened, intimidated and assaulted by a trooper, "We know that the teacher assaulted the trooper. He didn't have a driver's license or a registration *for his fancy new Mercedes*." (emphasis added) And he called Paul McLemore, the first African–American trooper in New Jersey and now a practicing attorney and who spoke of discrimination within the ranks of the State Police, "an ingrate." And he told the members to "keep the heat on" and then assured them: " . . .[H]ere at Division Headquarters we'll make sure that when the wheels start to squeak, we'll do whatever we can to make sure that you're supported out in the field. . . .Anything that goes toward implementing the Drug Reform Act is important. And, we'll handle the squeaky wheels here."

He admitted the Internal Affairs Bureau was not designed to investigate general complaints, so he could not refer the general complaints of discrimination to it for scrutiny. Yet he never requested the Analytical Unit to investigate stop data from radio logs, patrol charts and tickets or search and seizure data from arrest reports, operations reports, investigation reports and consent to search forms, not even after the Analytical Unit informed him in a report on arrests by region, race and crime that he had requested from it for his use in the WOR series that " . . .arrests are not a valid reflection of stops (data relative to stops with respect to race is not compiled)." The databases compiled for these motions attest, of course, to the fact that race identified stop data could have been compiled. He testified he could not launch an investigation into every general complaint because of limited resources and that there was insufficient evidence of discrimination in the Channel 9 series, the NAACP and ACLU complaints and the various motions to suppress for him to spend his "precious" resources. In short, he left the issue of discrimination up to the courts and months of testimony in this and other counties at State expense.

The right to be free from discrimination is firmly supported by the Fourteenth Amendment to the United States Constitution and the protections of Article I, paragraphs 1 and 5 of the New Jersey Constitution of 1947. * * * It is indisputable * * * that the police may not stop a motorist based on race or any other invidious classification.

Generally, however, the inquiry for determining the constitutionality of a stop or a search and seizure is limited to "whether the conduct of the law enforcement officer who undertook the [stop or] search was objectively reasonable, without regard to his or her underlying motives or intent." Thus, it has been said that the courts will not inquire into the motivation of a police officer whose stop of a vehicle was based upon a traffic violation committed in his presence. But where objective evidence establishes "that a police agency has embarked upon an officially sanctioned or *de facto* policy of targeting minorities for investigation and arrest," any evidence seized will be suppressed to deter future insolence in office by those charged with enforcement of the law and to maintain judicial integrity. State v. Kennedy, 247 N.J.Super. 21, 588 A.2d 834 (App.Div.1991).

Rule = cannot target group

Statistics may be used to make out a case of targeting minorities for prosecution of traffic offenses provided the comparison is between the racial composition of the motorist population violating the traffic laws and the racial composition of those arrested for traffic infractions on the relevant roadway patrolled by the police agency. While defendants have the burden of proving "the existence of purposeful discrimination," discriminatory intent may be inferred from statistical proof presenting a stark pattern or an even less extreme pattern in certain limited contexts. * * * [D]iscriminatory intent may be inferred from statistical proof in a traffic stop context probably because only uniform variables (Title 39 violations) are relevant to the challenged stops and the State has an opportunity to explain the statistical disparity. "[A] selection procedure that is susceptible of abuse . . .supports the presumption of discrimination raised by the statistical showing." Castaneda v. Partida, 430 U.S. 482, 494, 97 S.Ct. 1272, 51 L.Ed.2d 498 (1977).

Once defendants expose a *prima facie* case of selective enforcement, the State generally cannot rebut it by merely calling attention to possible flaws or unmeasured variables in defendants' statistics. Rather, the State must introduce specific evidence showing that either there actually are defects which bias the results or the missing factors, when properly organized and accounted for, eliminate or explain the disparity. Nor will mere denials or reliance on the good faith of the officers suffice. Here, defendants have proven at least a *de facto* policy on the part of the State Police out of the Moorestown Station of targeting blacks for investigation and arrest between April 1988 and May 1991 both south of exit 3 and between exits 1 and 7A of the Turnpike. * * * The statistical disparities and standard deviations revealed are indeed stark. The discretion devolved upon general road troopers to stop any car they want as long as Title 39 is used evinces a selection process that is susceptible of abuse. The utter failure of the State Police hierarchy to monitor and control a crackdown program like DITU or investigate the many claims of institutional discrimination manifests its indifference if not acceptance. Against all this, the State submits only denials and * * * conjecture and flawed studies * * *.

The eradication of illegal drugs from our State is an obviously worthy goal, but not at the expense of individual rights. * * *

Motions granted.

E.   SOBRIETY CHECKPOINTS AND RELATED DETENTIONS

EDITORS' INTRODUCTION: SUSPICIONLESS STOPS

Arrests, *Terry* stops for investigation, and traffic stops all involve action based on suspicion focused upon the suspects. The criteria for determining the reasonableness of these seizures impose different standards for judging the adequacy of suspicion, or at least the basis for such suspicion. Those criteria all, however, address the adequacy of the facts to support a belief that the suspect is involved in criminal activity.

Some law enforcement action, in contrast, is permissible without regard to officers' suspicion the suspect is involved in criminal activity or any basis for such suspicion. This action may usefully be regarded as "suspicionless" law enforcement action.

Suspicionless action by officers is considered earlier in these materials. Thus searches incident to custodial arrests, addressed in subsection B(1) of this chapter, are suspicionless in the sense they are permissible regardless of whether the officers have any subjective concern that the suspects have evidence or weapons or whether the officers have any objective information supporting such concern.

This part considers the constitutionality of suspicionless stops of persons in certain situations. Eleven years before the principal case, the Supreme Court had refused to permit suspicionless stops of motorists in a different context. In Delaware v. Prouse, 440 U.S. 648, 99 S.Ct. 1391, 59 L.Ed.2d 660 (1979), the Court considered Delaware's contention that its police officers were permitted by the Fourth Amendment to stop any motorist to determine whether the driver was in possession of a valid driver's license and registration for the vehicle being driven. No suspicion that the driver lacked either was required, the state argued, nor did an officer need facts that would support any such suspicion. Holding that these suspicionless stops were unreasonable, the Court explained:

> We agree that the States have a vital interest in ensuring that only those qualified to do so are permitted to operate motor vehicles, that these vehicles are fit for safe operation, and hence that licensing, registration, and vehicle inspection requirements are being observed.
> * * *
>
> The question remains, however, whether in the service of these important ends the discretionary spot check is a sufficiently productive mechanism to justify the intrusion upon Fourth Amendment interests which such stops entail. On the record before us, that question must be answered in the negative. Given the alternative mechanisms available, both those in use and those that might be adopted, we are unconvinced that the incremental contribution to highway safety of the random spot check justifies the practice under the Fourth Amendment.
>
> The foremost method of enforcing traffic and vehicle safety regulations * * * is acting upon observed violations. Vehicle stops for traffic violations occur countless times each day; and on these occasions, licenses and registration papers are subject to inspection and drivers without them will be ascertained. Furthermore, drivers without licenses are presumably the less safe drivers whose propensities may well exhibit themselves. * * * The contribution to highway safety made by discretionary stops selected from among drivers generally will therefore be marginal at best. Furthermore, and again absent something more than mere assertion to the contrary, we find it difficult to believe

that the unlicensed driver would not be deterred by the possibility of being involved in a traffic violation or having some other experience calling for proof of his entitlement to drive but that he would be deterred by the possibility that he would be one of those chosen for a spot check. In terms of actually discovering unlicensed drivers or deterring them from driving, the spot check does not appear sufficiently productive to qualify as a reasonable law-enforcement practice under the Fourth Amendment.

Much the same can be said about the safety aspects of automobiles as distinguished from drivers. * * *

The marginal contribution to roadway safety possibly resulting from a system of spot checks cannot justify subjecting every occupant of every vehicle on the roads to a seizure—limited in magnitude compared to other intrusions but nonetheless constitutionally cognizable—at the unbridled discretion of law-enforcement officials. * * * This kind of standardless and unconstrained discretion is the evil the Court has discerned when in previous cases it has insisted that the discretion of the official in the field be circumscribed, at least to some extent. * * *

Accordingly, we hold that except in those situations in which there is at least articulable and reasonable suspicion that a motorist is unlicensed or that an automobile is not registered, or that either the vehicle or an occupant is otherwise subject to seizure for violation of law, stopping an automobile and detaining the driver in order to check his driver's license and the registration of the automobile are unreasonable under the Fourth Amendment. This holding does not preclude the State of Delaware or other States from developing methods for spot checks that involve less intrusion or that do not involve the unconstrained exercise of discretion. Questioning of all oncoming traffic at roadblock-type stops is one possible alternative. We hold only that persons in automobiles on public roadways may not for that reason alone have their travel and privacy interfered with at the unbridled discretion of police officers.

440 U.S. at 658–63, 99 S.Ct. at 1398–1401, 59 L.Ed.2d at 670–74. Justice Rehnquist dissented, noting the majority's statement concerning roadblocks "elevates the adage 'misery loves company' to a novel role in Fourth Amendment jurisprudence."

Prouse obviously invited the litigation of stops at "roadblock-type stops," and the issue was presented to the Court in the principal case that follows.

Michigan v. Sitz

Supreme Court of the United States, 1990.
496 U.S. 444, 110 S.Ct. 2481, 110 L.Ed.2d 412.

■ CHIEF JUSTICE REHNQUIST delivered the opinion of the Court.

This case poses the question whether a State's use of highway sobriety checkpoints violates the Fourth and Fourteenth Amendments to the United

States Constitution. We hold that it does not and therefore reverse the contrary holding of the Court of Appeals of Michigan.

Petitioners, the Michigan Department of State Police and its Director, established a sobriety checkpoint pilot program in early 1986. The Director appointed a Sobriety Checkpoint Advisory Committee comprising representatives of the State Police force, local police forces, state prosecutors, and the University of Michigan Transportation Research Institute. Pursuant to its charge, the Advisory Committee created guidelines setting forth procedures governing checkpoint operations, site selection, and publicity.

Under the guidelines, checkpoints would be set up at selected sites along state roads. All vehicles passing through a checkpoint would be stopped and their drivers briefly examined for signs of intoxication. In cases where a checkpoint officer detected signs of intoxication, the motorist would be directed to a location out of the traffic flow where an officer would check the motorist's driver's license and car registration and, if warranted, conduct further sobriety tests. Should the field tests and the officer's observations suggest that the driver was intoxicated, an arrest would be made. All other drivers would be permitted to resume their journey immediately.

average delay = 25 seconds

The first—and to date the only—sobriety checkpoint operated under the program was conducted in Saginaw County with the assistance of the Saginaw County Sheriff's Department. During the hour-and-fifteen-minute duration of the checkpoint's operation, 126 vehicles passed through the checkpoint. The average delay for each vehicle was approximately 25 seconds. Two drivers were detained for field sobriety testing, and one of the two was arrested for driving under the influence of alcohol. A third driver who drove through without stopping was pulled over by an officer in an observation vehicle and arrested for driving under the influence.

On the day before the operation of the Saginaw County checkpoint, respondents filed a complaint in the Circuit Court of Wayne County seeking declaratory and injunctive relief from potential subjection to the checkpoints. * * * During pretrial proceedings, petitioners agreed to delay further implementation of the checkpoint program pending the outcome of this litigation.

After the trial, at which the court heard extensive testimony concerning, inter alia, the "effectiveness" of highway sobriety checkpoint programs, the court ruled that the Michigan program violated the Fourth Amendment and Art. 1, § 11, of the Michigan Constitution. On appeal, the Michigan Court of Appeals affirmed the holding that the program violated the Fourth Amendment and, for that reason, did not consider whether the program violated the Michigan Constitution. After the Michigan Supreme Court denied petitioners' application for leave to appeal, we granted certiorari.

Rule →

To decide this case the [lower courts] performed a balancing test derived from our opinion in Brown v. Texas, 443 U.S. 47, 99 S.Ct. 2637, 61 L.Ed.2d 357 (1979) [which involved] "balancing the state's interest in preventing accidents caused by drunk drivers, the effectiveness of sobriety checkpoints in achieving that goal, and the level of intrusion on an individual's privacy caused by the checkpoints." * * *

As characterized by the Court of Appeals, the trial court's findings with respect to the balancing factors were that the State has "a grave and legitimate" interest in curbing drunken driving; that sobriety checkpoint programs are generally "ineffective" and, therefore, do not significantly further that interest; and that the checkpoints' "subjective intrusion" on individual liberties is substantial. According to the court, the record disclosed no basis for disturbing the trial court's findings, which were made within the context of an analytical framework prescribed by this Court for determining the constitutionality of seizures less intrusive than traditional arrests. * * *

[United States v.] Martinez–Fuerte, [428 U.S. 543, 96 S.Ct. 3074, 49 L.Ed.2d 1116 (1976) (reprinted in Chapter 5)], which utilized a balancing analysis in approving highway checkpoints for detecting illegal aliens, and Brown v. Texas, supra, are the relevant authorities here.

Petitioners concede, correctly in our view, that a Fourth Amendment "seizure" occurs when a vehicle is stopped at a checkpoint. The question thus becomes whether such seizures are "reasonable" under the Fourth Amendment.

It is important to recognize what our inquiry is NOT about. No allegations are before us of unreasonable treatment of any person after an actual detention at a particular checkpoint. As pursued in the lower courts, the instant action challenges only the use of sobriety checkpoints generally. We address only the initial stop of each motorist passing through a checkpoint and the associated preliminary questioning and observation by checkpoint officers. Detention of particular motorists for more extensive field sobriety testing may require satisfaction of an individualized suspicion standard.

No one can seriously dispute the magnitude of the drunken driving problem or the States' interest in eradicating it. * * *

Conversely, the weight bearing on the other scale—the measure of the intrusion on motorists stopped briefly at sobriety checkpoints—is slight. We reached a similar conclusion as to the intrusion on motorists subjected to a brief stop at a highway checkpoint for detecting illegal aliens. See *Martinez–Fuerte,* supra, at 558, 96 S.Ct. at 3083. We see virtually no difference between the levels of intrusion on law-abiding motorists from the brief stops necessary to the effectuation of these two types of checkpoints, which to the average motorist would seem identical save for the nature of the questions the checkpoint officers might ask. The trial court and the Court of Appeals[] thus[] accurately gauged the "objective" intrusion, measured by the duration of the seizure and the intensity of the investigation, as minimal.

With respect to what it perceived to be the "subjective" intrusion on motorists, however, the Court of Appeals found such intrusion substantial. The court first affirmed the trial court's finding that the guidelines governing checkpoint operation minimize the discretion of the officers on the scene. But the court also agreed with the trial court's conclusion that the checkpoints have the potential to generate fear and surprise in motorists. This was so because the record failed to demonstrate that approaching motorists would be aware of their option to make U-turns or turnoffs to avoid the checkpoints. On that basis, the court deemed the subjective intrusion from the checkpoints unreasonable.

We believe the Michigan courts misread our cases concerning the degree of "subjective intrusion" and the potential for generating fear and surprise. The "fear and surprise" to be considered are not the natural fear of one who has been drinking over the prospect of being stopped at a sobriety checkpoint but, rather, the fear and surprise engendered in law abiding motorists by the nature of the stop. * * * Here, checkpoints are selected pursuant to the guidelines, and uniformed police officers stop every approaching vehicle. The intrusion resulting from the brief stop at the sobriety checkpoint is for constitutional purposes indistinguishable from the checkpoint stops we upheld in *Martinez–Fuerte.*

The Court of Appeals went on to consider as part of the balancing analysis the "effectiveness" of the proposed checkpoint program. Based on extensive testimony in the trial record, the court concluded that the checkpoint program failed the "effectiveness" part of the test, and that this failure materially discounted petitioners' strong interest in implementing the program. We think the Court of Appeals was wrong on this point as well.

The actual language from Brown v. Texas, upon which the Michigan courts based their evaluation of "effectiveness," describes the balancing factor as "the degree to which the seizure advances the public interest." This passage from *Brown* was not meant to transfer from politically accountable officials to the courts the decision as to which among reasonable alternative law enforcement techniques should be employed to deal with a serious public danger. Experts in police science might disagree over which of several methods of apprehending drunken drivers is preferable as an ideal. But for purposes of Fourth Amendment analysis, the choice among such reasonable alternatives remains with the governmental officials who have a unique understanding of, and a responsibility for, limited public resources, including a finite number of police officers. * * *

Unlike [Delaware v. Prouse, 440 U.S. 648, 99 S.Ct. 1391, 59 L.Ed.2d 660 (1979)], this case involves neither a complete absence of empirical data nor a challenge to random highway stops. During the operation of the Saginaw County checkpoint, the detention of each of the 126 vehicles that entered the checkpoint resulted in the arrest of two drunken drivers. Stated as a percentage, approximately 1.5 percent of the drivers passing through the checkpoint were arrested for alcohol impairment. In addition, an expert witness testified at the trial that experience in other States demonstrated that, on the whole, sobriety checkpoints resulted in drunken driving arrests of around 1 percent of all motorists stopped. By way of comparison, the record from one of the consolidated cases in *Martinez–Fuerte,* showed that in the associated checkpoint, illegal aliens were found in only 0.12 percent of the vehicles passing through the checkpoint. The ratio of illegal aliens detected to vehicles stopped (considering that on occasion two or more illegal aliens were found in a single vehicle) was approximately 0.5 percent. We concluded that this "record ... provides a rather complete picture of the effectiveness of the San Clemente checkpoint", and we sustained its constitutionality. We see no justification for a different conclusion here.

In sum, the balance of the State's interest in preventing drunken driving, the extent to which this system can reasonably be said to advance that interest, and the degree of intrusion upon individual motorists who are briefly stopped, weighs in favor of the state program. We therefore hold that it is consistent with the Fourth Amendment. The judgment of the Michigan Court of Appeals is accordingly reversed, and the cause is remanded for further proceedings not inconsistent with this opinion.

Reversed.

■ JUSTICE STEVENS, with whom JUSTICE BRENNAN and JUSTICE MARSHALL join * * *, dissenting.

[T]he record in this case makes clear that a decision holding these suspicionless seizures unconstitutional would not impede the law enforcement community's remarkable progress in reducing the death toll on our highways. * * * [I]t seems inconceivable that a higher arrest rate could not have been achieved by more conventional means. * * *

[T]he Court today * * * overvalues the law enforcement interest in using sobriety checkpoints, undervalues the citizen's interest in freedom from random, unannounced investigatory seizures, and mistakenly assumes that there is "virtually no difference" between a routine stop at a permanent, fixed checkpoint and a surprise stop at a sobriety checkpoint. I believe this case is controlled by our * * * precedent[] condemning suspicionless random stops of motorists for investigatory purposes. Delaware v. Prouse, 440 U.S. 648, 99 S.Ct. 1391, 59 L.Ed.2d 660 (1979).

* * *

There is a critical difference between a seizure that is preceded by fair notice and one that is effected by surprise. That is one reason why a border search, or indeed any search at a permanent and fixed checkpoint, is much less intrusive than a random stop. A motorist with advance notice of the location of a permanent checkpoint has an opportunity to avoid the search entirely, or at least to prepare for, and limit, the intrusion on her privacy.

No such opportunity is available in the case of a random stop or a temporary checkpoint, which both depend for their effectiveness on the element of surprise. A driver who discovers an unexpected checkpoint on a familiar local road will be startled and distressed. She may infer, correctly, that the checkpoint is not simply "business as usual," and may likewise infer, again correctly, that the police have made a discretionary decision to focus their law enforcement efforts upon her and others who pass the chosen point.

This element of surprise is the most obvious distinction between the sobriety checkpoints permitted by today's majority and the interior border checkpoints approved by this Court in *Martinez–Fuerte*. The distinction casts immediate doubt upon the majority's argument, for *Martinez–Fuerte* is the only case in which we have upheld suspicionless seizures of motorists. But the difference between notice and surprise is only one of the important reasons for distinguishing between permanent and mobile checkpoints. With respect to the former, there is no room for discretion in either the timing or the location of the stop—it is a permanent part of the landscape. In the latter case, however, although the checkpoint is most frequently employed during the hours of darkness on weekends (because that is when drivers with alcohol in their blood are most apt to be found on the road), the police have extremely broad discretion in determining the exact timing and placement of the roadblock.

There is also a significant difference between the kind of discretion that the officer exercises after the stop is made. A check for a driver's license, or for identification papers at an immigration checkpoint, is far more easily standardized than is a search for evidence of intoxication. * * *

For all these reasons, I do not believe that this case is analogous to *Martinez–Fuerte*. In my opinion, the sobriety checkpoints are instead similar to—and in some respects more intrusive than—the random investigative stops that the Court held unconstitutional in * * * *Prouse*. * * *

I respectfully dissent.

NOTE

On remand, the Michigan courts held the roadblock at issue violated the Michigan Constitution's prohibition against unreasonable searches and seizures. Sitz v. Department of State Police, 443 Mich. 744, 506 N.W.2d 209 (1993), affirming 193 Mich.App. 690, 485 N.W.2d 135 (1992).

F.   PRETEXT MOTIVATION

American courts have long disagreed on whether law enforcement activity objectively within legal limits can be successfully challenged on the basis that the officer's motive rendered it a "pretext" and, hence, invalid. Arrests and other detentions are probably attacked on this basis more frequently than other types of law enforcement activity. In the principal case that follows, the Supreme Court addressed the extent to which the Fourth Amendment provides a basis for this sort of attack.

There is considerable inconsistency in the terminology used in judicial discussions, but this inconsistency may reflect underlying conceptual confusion. Lower courts differ on precisely what constitutes a "pretext arrest." Moreover, there is confusion regarding the need to, or wisdom of, inquiring whether an arrest was made "on" various possible grounds and—to the extent such inquiries are undertaken—how to determine whether a particular arrest was made "on" a particular ground.

In connection with the pretext issue, consider the Supreme Court's willingness in other contexts to tie the validity of law enforcement action to officers' subjective state of mind. Reconsider, for example, the argument that an investigatory stop is invalid if the officer intended to detain the suspect longer than Fourth Amendment law permits; see the discussion in part C(1) of this chapter.

Whren v. United States

Supreme Court of the United States, 1996.
517 U.S. 806, 116 S.Ct. 1769, 135 L.Ed.2d 89.

■ JUSTICE SCALIA delivered the opinion of the Court.

In this case we decide whether the temporary detention of a motorist who the police have probable cause to believe has committed a civil traffic violation is inconsistent with the Fourth Amendment's prohibition against unreasonable seizures unless a reasonable officer would have been motivated to stop the car by a desire to enforce the traffic laws.

[handwritten margin note: temporary detention in violation of 4th Amendment]

I

On the evening of June 10, 1993, plainclothes vice-squad officers of the District of Columbia Metropolitan Police Department were patrolling a "high drug area" of the city in an unmarked car. Their suspicions were aroused when they passed a dark Pathfinder truck with temporary license plates and youthful occupants waiting at a stop sign, the driver looking down into the lap of the passenger at his right. The truck remained stopped at the intersection for what seemed an unusually long time—more than 20 seconds. When the police car executed a U-turn in order to head back toward the truck, the Pathfinder turned suddenly to its right, without signaling, and sped off at an "unreasonable" speed. The policemen followed, and in a short while overtook the Pathfinder when it stopped behind other traffic at a red light. They pulled up alongside, and Officer Ephraim Soto stepped out and approached the driver's door, identifying himself as a police officer and directing the driver, petitioner Brown, to put the vehicle in park. When Soto drew up to the driver's window, he immediately observed two large plastic bags of what appeared to be crack cocaine in petitioner Whren's hands. Petitioners were arrested, and quantities of several types of illegal drugs were retrieved from the vehicle.

Petitioners were charged in a four-count indictment with violating various federal drug laws * * *. At a pretrial suppression hearing, they challenged the legality of the stop and the resulting seizure of the drugs. * * * The District Court denied the suppression motion * * *.

[handwritten margin note: challanged the legality of the stop.]

Petitioners were convicted of the counts at issue here. The Court of Appeals affirmed the convictions. * * * We granted certiorari.

II

The Fourth Amendment guarantees "[t]he right of the people to be secure in their persons, houses, papers, and effects, against unreasonable searches and seizures." Temporary detention of individuals during the stop of an automobile by the police, even if only for a brief period and for a limited purpose, constitutes a "seizure" of "persons" within the meaning of this provision. An automobile stop is thus subject to the constitutional imperative that it not be "unreasonable" under the circumstances. As a general matter, the decision to stop an automobile is reasonable where the police have probable cause to believe that a traffic violation has occurred.

[handwritten margin note: 4th Amendment = unreasonable search + seizure]

Petitioners accept that Officer Soto had probable cause to believe that various provisions of the District of Columbia traffic code had been violated. See 18 D.C. Mun. Regs. §§ 2213.4 (1995) ("An operator shall ... give full time and attention to the operation of the vehicle"); 2204.3 ("No person shall turn any vehicle ... without giving an appropriate signal"); 2200.3 ("No person shall drive a vehicle ... at a speed greater than is reasonable and prudent under the conditions"). They argue, however, that "in the unique context of civil traffic regulations" probable cause is not enough. Since, they contend, the use of automobiles is so heavily and minutely regulated that total compliance with traffic and safety rules is nearly impossible, a police officer will almost invariably be able to catch any given motorist in a technical violation. This creates the temptation to use traffic stops as a means of investigating other law violations, as to which no probable cause or even articulable suspicion exists. Petitioners, who are both black, further contend that police officers might decide which motorists to stop based on decidedly impermissible factors, such as the race of the car's occupants. To avoid this danger, they say, the Fourth Amendment test for traffic stops should be, not the normal one (applied by the Court of Appeals) of whether probable cause existed to justify the stop; but rather, whether a police officer, acting reasonably, would have made the stop for the reason given.

traffic stop as a means to investigate for other crimes

argument of defendants = stop for reason given is: drugs

A

Petitioners contend that the standard they propose is consistent with our past cases' disapproval of police attempts to use valid bases of action against citizens as pretexts for pursuing other investigatory agendas. We are reminded that in Florida v. Wells, 495 U.S. 1, 4, 110 S.Ct. 1632, 1635, 109 L.Ed.2d 1 (1990), we stated that "an inventory search must not be used as a ruse for a general rummaging in order to discover incriminating evidence"; that in Colorado v. Bertine, 479 U.S. 367, 372, 107 S.Ct. 738, 741, 93 L.Ed.2d 739 (1987), in approving an inventory search, we apparently thought it significant that there had been "no showing that the police, who were following standard procedures, acted in bad faith or for the sole purpose of investigation"; and that in New York v. Burger, 482 U.S. 691, 716–717, n. 27, 107 S.Ct. 2636, 2651, n. 27, 96 L.Ed.2d 601 (1987), we observed, in upholding the constitutionality of a warrantless administrative inspection, that the search did not appear to be "a 'pretext' for obtaining evidence of ... violation of ... penal laws." But only an undiscerning reader would regard these cases as endorsing the principle that ulterior motives can invalidate police conduct that is justifiable on the basis of probable cause to believe that a violation of law has occurred. In each case we were addressing the validity of a search conducted in the absence of probable cause. Our quoted statements simply explain that the exemption from the need for probable cause (and warrant), which is accorded to searches made for the purpose of inventory or administrative regulation, is not accorded to searches that are not made for those purposes.

* * *

* * * Petitioners' difficulty is not simply a lack of affirmative support for their position. Not only have we never held, outside the context of inventory search or administrative inspection (discussed above), that an officer's motive invalidates objectively justifiable behavior under the Fourth

Amendment; but we have repeatedly held and asserted the contrary. In United States v. Villamonte–Marquez, 462 U.S. 579, 584, n. 3, 103 S.Ct. 2573, 2577, n. 3, 77 L.Ed.2d 22 (1983), we held that an otherwise valid warrantless boarding of a vessel by customs officials was not rendered invalid "because the customs officers were accompanied by a Louisiana state policeman, and were following an informant's tip that a vessel in the ship channel was thought to be carrying marihuana." We flatly dismissed the idea that an ulterior motive might serve to strip the agents of their legal justification. In United States v. Robinson, 414 U.S. 218, 94 S.Ct. 467, 38 L.Ed.2d 427 (1973), we held that a traffic-violation arrest (of the sort here) would not be rendered invalid by the fact that it was "a mere pretext for a narcotics search;" and that a lawful postarrest search of the person would not be rendered invalid by the fact that it was not motivated by the officer-safety concern that justifies such searches. And in Scott v. United States, 436 U.S. 128, 138, 98 S.Ct. 1717, 1723, 56 L.Ed.2d 168 (1978), in rejecting the contention that wiretap evidence was subject to exclusion because the agents conducting the tap had failed to make any effort to comply with the statutory requirement that unauthorized acquisitions be minimized, we said that "[s]ubjective intent alone ... does not make otherwise lawful conduct illegal or unconstitutional." We described *Robinson* as having established that "the fact that the officer does not have the state of mind which is hypothecated by the reasons which provide the legal justification for the officer's action does not invalidate the action taken as long as the circumstances, viewed objectively, justify that action."

We think these cases foreclose any argument that the constitutional reasonableness of traffic stops depends on the actual motivations of the individual officers involved. We of course agree with petitioners that the Constitution prohibits selective enforcement of the law based on considerations such as race. But the constitutional basis for objecting to intentionally discriminatory application of laws is the Equal Protection Clause, not the Fourth Amendment. Subjective intentions play no role in ordinary, probable-cause Fourth Amendment analysis.

B

Recognizing that we have been unwilling to entertain Fourth Amendment challenges based on the actual motivations of individual officers, petitioners disavow any intention to make the individual officer's subjective good faith the touchstone of "reasonableness." They insist that the standard they have put forward—whether the officer's conduct deviated materially from usual police practices, so that a reasonable officer in the same circumstances would not have made the stop for the reasons given—is an "objective" one.

But although framed in empirical terms, this approach is plainly and indisputably driven by subjective considerations. Its whole purpose is to prevent the police from doing under the guise of enforcing the traffic code what they would like to do for different reasons. Petitioners' proposed standard may not use the word "pretext," but it is designed to combat nothing other than the perceived "danger" of the pretextual stop, albeit only indirectly and over the run of cases. Instead of asking whether the individual officer had the proper state of mind, the petitioners would have us ask, in effect, whether (based on general police practices) it is plausible to believe that the officer had the proper state of mind.

Why one would frame a test designed to combat pretext in such fashion that the court cannot take into account actual and admitted pretext is a curiosity that can only be explained by the fact that our cases have foreclosed the more sensible option. If those cases were based only upon the evidentiary difficulty of establishing subjective intent, petitioners' attempt to root out subjective vices through objective means might make sense. But they were not based only upon that, or indeed even principally upon that. Their principal basis—which applies equally to attempts to reach subjective intent through ostensibly objective means—is simply that the Fourth Amendment's concern with "reasonableness" allows certain actions to be taken in certain circumstances, whatever the subjective intent. But even if our concern had been only an evidentiary one, petitioners' proposal would by no means assuage it. Indeed, it seems to us somewhat easier to figure out the intent of an individual officer than to plumb the collective consciousness of law enforcement in order to determine whether a "reasonable officer" would have been moved to act upon the traffic violation. While police manuals and standard procedures may sometimes provide objective assistance, ordinarily one would be reduced to speculating about the hypothetical reaction of a hypothetical constable—an exercise that might be called virtual subjectivity.

Moreover, police enforcement practices, even if they could be practicably assessed by a judge, vary from place to place and from time to time. We cannot accept that the search and seizure protections of the Fourth Amendment are so variable, and can be made to turn upon such trivialities.
* * *

III

In what would appear to be an elaboration on the "reasonable officer" test, petitioners argue that the balancing inherent in any Fourth Amendment inquiry requires us to weigh the governmental and individual interests implicated in a traffic stop such as we have here. That balancing, petitioners claim, does not support investigation of minor traffic infractions by plainclothes police in unmarked vehicles; such investigation only minimally advances the government's interest in traffic safety, and may indeed retard it by producing motorist confusion and alarm—a view said to be supported by the Metropolitan Police Department's own regulations generally prohibiting this practice. And as for the Fourth Amendment interests of the individuals concerned, petitioners point out that our cases acknowledge that even ordinary traffic stops entail "a possibly unsettling show of authority"; that they at best "interfere with freedom of movement, are inconvenient, and consume time" and at worst "may create substantial anxiety." That anxiety is likely to be even more pronounced when the stop is conducted by plainclothes officers in unmarked cars.

It is of course true that in principle every Fourth Amendment case, since it turns upon a "reasonableness" determination, involves a balancing of all relevant factors. With rare exceptions not applicable here, however, the result of that balancing is not in doubt where the search or seizure is based upon probable cause. * * *

Where probable cause has existed, the only cases in which we have found it necessary actually to perform the "balancing" analysis involved searches or seizures conducted in an extraordinary manner, unusually harmful to an individual's privacy or even physical interests—such as, for example, seizure by means of deadly force, see Tennessee v. Garner, 471 U.S. 1, 105 S.Ct. 1694, 85 L.Ed.2d 1 (1985), unannounced entry into a home, see Wilson v. Arkansas, 514 U.S. 927, 115 S.Ct. 1914, 131 L.Ed.2d 976 (1995), entry into a home without a warrant, see Welsh v. Wisconsin, 466 U.S. 740, 104 S.Ct. 2091, 80 L.Ed.2d 732 (1984), or physical penetration of the body, see Winston v. Lee, 470 U.S. 753, 105 S.Ct. 1611, 84 L.Ed.2d 662 (1985). The making of a traffic stop out-of-uniform does not remotely qualify as such an extreme practice, and so is governed by the usual rule that probable cause to believe the law has been broken "outbalances" private interest in avoiding police contact.

Petitioners urge as an extraordinary factor in this case that the "multitude of applicable traffic and equipment regulations" is so large and so difficult to obey perfectly that virtually everyone is guilty of violation, permitting the police to single out almost whomever they wish for a stop. But we are aware of no principle that would allow us to decide at what point a code of law becomes so expansive and so commonly violated that infraction itself can no longer be the ordinary measure of the lawfulness of enforcement. And even if we could identify such exorbitant codes, we do not know by what standard (or what right) we would decide, as petitioners would have us do, which particular provisions are sufficiently important to merit enforcement.

For the run-of-the-mine case, which this surely is, we think there is no realistic alternative to the traditional common-law rule that probable cause justifies a search and seizure.

* * *

Here the District Court found that the officers had probable cause to believe that petitioners had violated the traffic code. That rendered the stop reasonable under the Fourth Amendment, the evidence thereby discovered admissible, and the upholding of the convictions by the Court of Appeals for the District of Columbia Circuit correct.

Judgment affirmed.

NOTE: PRETEXT MOTIVATION UNDER STATE LAW

Despite *Whren*, state constitutional provisions may provide a basis for challenging law enforcement conduct as a pretext.

The Washington Supreme Court reaffirmed in State v. Ladson, 138 Wash.2d 343, 979 P.2d 833, 842 n. 10 (1999), that pretextual stops are unreasonable under the Washington constitution. Rejecting the Supreme Court's reasoning in *Whren*, the state tribunal explained the state constitution "requires we look beyond the formal justification for the stop to the actual one." It continued:

We note if we were to depart from our holdings and allow pretextual traffic stops, Washington citizens would lose their privacy every time they enter their automobiles. The traffic code is sufficiently extensive in its regulation that "[w]hether it be for failing to signal while changing lanes, driving with a headlight out, or not giving 'full time and attention' to the operation of the vehicle, virtually the entire driving population is in violation of some regulation as soon as they get in their cars, or shortly thereafter." Peter Shakow, Let He Who Never Has Turned Without Signaling Cast the First Stone: An Analysis of Whren v. United States, 24 Am. J.Crim. L. 627, 633 (1997) (footnote omitted). Thus, nearly every citizen would be subject to a *Terry* stop simply because he or she is in his or her car. But we have repeatedly affirmed that Washingtonians retain their privacy while in the automobile and we will do so today.

138 Wash.2d at 358 n. 10, 979 P.2d at 842 n. 10. In determining whether a particular stop is pretextual, the *Ladson* court added, a court "should consider the totality of the circumstances, including both the subjective intent of the officer as well as the objective reasonableness of the officer's behavior." Courts applying the *Ladson* analysis are likely to often give controlling significance to an officer's subjective motive. Thus in State v. DeSantiago, 983 P.2d 1173 (Wash.App.1999), the stop at issue was for a left turn made improperly because DeSantiago did not turn into the left hand lane of the street into which the turn was made. The trial court found the officer followed DeSantiago because he had observed DeSantiago leave a "narcotics hot spot" and "was looking for a basis to stop the vehicle." This established subjective pretext motivation, and for this reason the stop was unreasonable.

CHAPTER 5

"WARRANTLESS" SEARCHES

Analysis

EDITORS' INTRODUCTION: EXCEPTIONS TO BENCHMARK FOURTH AMENDMENT REQUIREMENTS

If law enforcement conduct constitutes a "search," the material in Chapters 2 and 3 made clear—as a general rule—certain benchmark Fourth Amendment requirements apply. Information amounting to "probable cause" to believe that the intrusion is justified must be present. In addition, officers must use the search warrant process and obtained a judicial determination that probable cause exists before the intrusion.

But the Fourth Amendment's reasonableness requirement has significant flexibility. In some situations, either or both of the benchmark demands may be modified or abandoned. Relaxation of these requirements was explored to some extent in Chapter 4, which considered officers' right to conduct certain searches as incidents to arrests or because of nonarrest police-citizen contacts. Other situations in which the Fourth Amendment's demands may deviate from the benchmark requirements are the subject of the present chapter.

Most of these situations involve law enforcement activity investigating whether a criminal offense has been committed and, if so, the offender's identity. But this is not always the case. Part B of this chapter considers the so-called "administrative" searches. These may be conducted by inspectors not law enforcement officers. Inspectors' primary objective may be to end violation of legal but noncriminal requirements by means other than criminal prosecution of those found in noncompliance with the law's demands. Whether a noncriminal objective justifies relaxation of Fourth Amendment requirements, of course, is among the issues raised by such inspections.

Each situation discussed in this chapter presents two categories of issues. The first concerns the requirement of a search warrant. In many situations, the issue is whether this requirement should be abandoned entirely and so-called "warrantless" searches regarded as reasonable. In other situations, however, the question is whether the warrant requirement should be retained but relaxed to accommodate special needs presented by the situation. In still others, the issue is whether Fourth Amendment reasonableness should be retained and modified so as to impose *more* stringent requirements than involved in the traditional warrant process considered in Chapter 3.

These situations are often discussed as if the only question is whether—and when—warrantless searches are reasonable. Many, however, also present issues in a second category, concerning possible changes in the traditional requirement of probable cause. If a decision is made to dispense with the warrant requirement, of course, Fourth Amendment reasonableness might still require that an officer have information amounting to probable cause before beginning the search. But in some situations persuasive arguments can be made for demanding only information meeting a less stringent standard or for dispensing entirely with any requirement that the officer have information indicating that a search is justified. Even if a warrant or court order is necessary, the standard for deciding whether that order or warrant can issue might demand less than traditional probable cause. In some situations involving unusually intrusive law enforcement conduct, the Fourth Amendment might permit a warrant to issue or a warrantless search conducted only under a *more* stringent standard than the traditional probable cause requirement.

The significance of these issues often results from the application of the plain view seizure rule, considered in part B(2) of Chapter 2. If law enforcement officers or other public officials are engaged in a proper, i.e., "reasonable," search and in the course of that search come upon items in plain view, they may often seize those items. Whether the search placing the items in the officers' plain view was proper will, in many cases, determine whether the seizure was permissible. If the officers came upon the items in the course of an unreasonable search, the discovery and seizure of the items is likely to be tainted "fruit" of the improper search.

The case law presented in this chapter consists entirely of United States Supreme Court decisions construing the Fourth Amendment requirement of reasonableness. State constitutional, statutory or case law may here as well as elsewhere impose more stringent requirements upon official activity than is mandated by the federal constitutional provision.

Several subsequent chapters address other areas of official conduct raising issues similar to those considered in this chapter. Electronic surveillance, for example, is considered in Chapter 6 and use of grand jury subpoenas is discussed in Chapter 9. Among the issues raised in Chapter 8 is the extent to which undercover law enforcement activity so intrudes upon privacy as to justify subjecting such activity to Fourth Amendment reasonableness requirements. If the Fourth Amendment were applied to this activity, the courts would have to address the extent and nature of the regulation which Fourth Amendment reasonableness imposes.

A. THE EMERGENCY DOCTRINE

The Supreme Court has upheld certain searches without warrants upon demonstrations that the officers reasonably believed delays necessary to apply for search warrants would result in destruction of the evidence or contraband sought. See Schmerber v. California, 384 U.S. 757, 86 S.Ct. 1826, 16 L.Ed.2d 908 (1966) (reprinted in Chapter 2), upholding a warrantless taking of a blood sample because delaying the process might result in the suspect's body eliminating alcohol from his system. But it remains unclear how great a risk the officer must perceive before a warrantless search becomes permissible.

Exigent circumstances—or "emergencies"—are generally treated by courts as dispensing only with the need for a warrant. The officer must still have probable cause to believe evidence or contraband will be found by the search. Perhaps, however, standards for determining when probable cause exists are relaxed when the officer was required to evaluate facts under the pressure of an emergency situation.

In a sense, the emergency exception is a benchmark for analysis of other situations that may dispense with the need for a warrant and perhaps probable cause. In regard to the warrant requirement, many other exceptions—such as that for certain vehicles—involve situations in which a claim might be made that an emergency exists. Fitting a case within one of the other exceptions, however, dispenses with the need for the prosecution to show that *on the facts of the particular case* delay to apply for a warrant would create sufficient risk of loss of the evidence or contraband. In considering the wisdom of various other more specific exceptions and their scope, the availability of the general emergency exception might usefully be kept in mind. If a case falls without any other exception, the prosecution always has the opportunity to demonstrate that, on the facts of the particular situation, the emergency exception applies.

Vale v. Louisiana

Supreme Court of the United States, 1970.
399 U.S. 30, 90 S.Ct. 1969, 26 L.Ed.2d 409.

■ MR. JUSTICE STEWART delivered the opinion of the Court.

The appellant, Donald Vale, was convicted in a Louisiana court on a charge of possessing heroin and was sentenced as a multiple offender to 15 years' imprisonment at hard labor. The Louisiana Supreme Court affirmed the conviction, rejecting the claim that evidence introduced at the trial was the product of an unlawful search and seizure. * * *

The evidence adduced at the pretrial hearing on a motion to suppress showed that on April 24, 1967, officers possessing two warrants for Vale's arrest and having information that he was residing at a specified address proceeded there in an unmarked car and set up a surveillance of the house. The evidence of what then took place was summarized by the Louisiana Supreme Court as follows:

"After approximately 15 minutes the officers observed a green 1958 Chevrolet drive up and sound the horn and after backing into a parking place, again blew the horn. At this juncture Donald Vale, who was well known to Officer Brady having arrested him twice in the previous month, was seen coming out of the house and walk up to the passenger side of the Chevrolet where he had a close brief conversation with the driver; and after looking up and down the street returned inside of the house. Within a few minutes he reappeared on the porch, and again cautiously looked up and down the street before proceeding to the passenger side of the Chevrolet, leaning through the window. From this the officers were convinced a narcotics sale had taken place. They returned to their car and immediately drove toward Donald Vale, and as they reached within approximately three car lengths from the accused, (Donald Vale) he looked up and, obviously recognizing the officers, turned around, walking quickly toward the house. At the same time the driver of the Chevrolet started to make his get away when the car was blocked by the police vehicle. The three officers promptly alighted from the car, whereupon Officers Soule and Laumann called to Donald Vale to stop as he reached the front steps of the house, telling him he was under arrest. Officer Brady at the same time, seeing the driver of the Chevrolet, Arizzio Saucier, whom the officers knew to be a narcotic addict, place something hurriedly in his mouth, immediately placed him under arrest and joined his co-officers. Because of the transaction they had just observed they, informed Donald Vale they were going to search the house, and thereupon advised him of his constitutional rights. After they all entered the front room, Officer Laumann made a cursory inspection of the house to ascertain if anyone else was present and within about three minutes Mrs. Vale and James Vale, mother and brother of Donald Vale, returned home carrying groceries and were informed of the arrest and impending search."

The search of a rear bedroom revealed a quantity of narcotics.

* * *

The Louisiana Supreme Court thought the search * * * supportable because it involved narcotics, which are easily removed, hidden, or destroyed. It would be unreasonable, the Louisiana court concluded, "to require the officers under the facts of the case to first secure a search warrant before searching the premises, as time is of the essence inasmuch as the officers never know whether there is anyone on the premises to be searched who could very easily destroy the evidence." Such a rationale could not apply to the present case, since by their own account the arresting officers satisfied themselves that no one else was in the house when they first entered the premises. But entirely apart from that point, our past decisions make clear that only in "a few specifically established and well-delineated" situations, may a warrantless search of a dwelling withstand constitutional scrutiny, even though the authorities have probable cause to conduct it. The burden rests on the State to show the existence of such an exceptional situation. And the record before us discloses none.

There is no suggestion that anyone consented to the search. The officers were not responding to an emergency. They were not in hot pursuit of a fleeing felon. Warden v. Hayden, 387 U.S. 294, 298–299, 87 S.Ct. 1642, 1645–1646, 18 L.Ed.2d 782. The goods ultimately seized were not in the process of destruction. Schmerber v. California, 384 U.S. 757, 770–771, 86 S.Ct. 1826, 1835–1836, 16 L.Ed.2d 908. Nor were they about to be removed from the jurisdiction.

The officers were able to procure two warrants for Vale's arrest. They also had information that he was residing at the address where they found him. There is thus no reason, so far as anything before us appears, to suppose that it was impracticable for them to obtain a search warrant as well. * * * We decline to hold that an arrest on the street can provide its own "exigent circumstance" so as to justify a warrantless search of the arrestee's house.

* * *

Reversed and remanded.

■ MR. JUSTICE BLACKMUN took no part in the consideration or decision of this case.

■ MR. JUSTICE BLACK, with whom THE CHIEF JUSTICE joins, dissenting.

* * *

[T]he police had probable cause to believe that Vale was engaged in a narcotics transfer, and that a supply of narcotics would be found in the house, to which Vale had returned after his first conversation, from which he had emerged furtively bearing what the police could readily deduce was a supply of narcotics, and toward which he hurried after seeing the police. But the police did not know then who else might be in the house. Vale's arrest took place near the house, and anyone observing from inside would surely have been alerted to destroy the stocks of contraband which the police believed Vale had left there. The police had already seen Saucier, the narcotics addict, apparently swallow what Vale had given him. Believing that some evidence had already been destroyed and that other evidence might well be, the police were faced with the choice of risking the immediate destruction of evidence or entering the house and conducting a search. I cannot say that their decision to search was unreasonable. Delay in order to obtain a warrant would have given an accomplice just the time he needed.

* * *

[T]he circumstances here were sufficiently exceptional to justify a search * * *. The Court recognizes that searches to prevent the destruction or removal of evidence have long been held reasonable by the Court. * * * It is only necessary to find that, given Vale's arrest in a spot readily visible to anyone in the house and the probable existence of narcotics inside, it was reasonable for the police to conduct an immediate search of the premises.

The Court, however, finds the search here unreasonable. First, the Court suggests that the contraband was not "in the process of destruction." None of the cases cited by the Court supports the proposition that "exceptional circumstances" exist only when the process of destruction has already begun. On the contrary we implied that those circumstances did exist when "evidence or contraband was *threatened* with removal or destruction." Johnson v. United States, [333 U.S. 10, 15, 68 S.Ct. 367, 369, 92 L.Ed. 436 (1948)] (emphasis added).

Second, the Court seems to argue that the search was unreasonable because the police officers had time to obtain a warrant. I agree that the opportunity to obtain a warrant is one of the factors to be weighed in determining reasonableness. But the record conclusively shows that there was no such opportunity here. As I noted above, once the officers had observed Vale's conduct in front of the house they had probable cause to believe that a felony had been committed and that immediate action was necessary. At no time after the events in front of Mrs. Vale's house would it have been prudent for the officers to leave the house in order to secure a warrant.

The Court asserts, however, that because the police obtained two warrants for Vale's arrest there is "no reason * * * to suppose that it was impracticable for them to obtain a search warrant as well." The difficulty is that the two arrest warrants on which the Court seems to rely so heavily were not issued because of any present misconduct of Vale's; they were issued because the bond had been increased for an earlier narcotics charge then pending against Vale. When the police came to arrest Vale, they knew only that his bond had been increased. There is nothing in the record to indicate that, absent the increased bond, there would have been probable cause for an arrest, much less a search. Probable cause for the search arose for the first time when the police observed the activity of Vale and Saucier in and around the house.

* * *

NOTES

1. In Minnesota v. Olson, 495 U.S. 91, 110 S.Ct. 1684, 109 L.Ed.2d 85 (1990), officers investigating a robbery-murder occurring about 6 a.m. on July 18, 1987 developed probable cause to believe Olson the driver of the getaway car. On July 19, they determined Olson was staying in a duplex unit occupied by Louanne and Julie Bergstrom. The occupant of the other duplex unit promised to call when Olson returned; officers were directed to stay away from the duplex in the interim. At 2:45 p.m., the neighbor called and told police Olson had returned. Officers surrounded the unit and telephoned Julie Bergstrom to tell her Olson should come out. The telephoning detective heard a male voice say, "[T]ell them I left." Julie said "Rob" had left. At 3 p.m., police entered and found Olson hiding in a closet. The Minnesota Supreme Court found this warrantless entry of the duplex was not justified by exigent circumstances. In the absence of hot pursuit, it reasoned, officers must have probable cause to believe the situation involved a risk of imminent destruction of evidence, the suspect's escape, or danger to police or persons inside or outside the dwelling. In assessing these risks, it also concluded, the crime's gravity and the likelihood the suspect is armed could be considered. Applying this standard, the state court held that the entry was unjustified. A majority of the Supreme Court held the state tribunal "applied essentially the correct standard in determining whether exigent circumstances existed." Moreover, it declined to disagree with the state court's "fact-specific application" of the standard:

> The [state] court pointed out that although a grave crime was involved, [Olson] "was known not to be the murderer but thought to be the driver of the getaway car," and that the police had already recovered the murder weapon. "The police knew that Louanne and Julie were with the suspect in the upstairs duplex with no suggestion of danger to them. Three or four Minneapolis police squads surrounded the house. The time was 3 p.m., Sunday.... It was evident the suspect was going nowhere. If he came out of the house he would have been promptly apprehended." We do not disturb the state court's judgment that these facts do not add up to exigent circumstances.

495 U.S. at 100–01, 110 S.Ct. at 1690, 109 L.Ed.2d at 96. Justice Kennedy joined with the "understanding" that the Court's discussion was not an endorsement of the state court's application of the standard. Chief Justice Rehnquist and Justice Blackmun dissented without opinion.

2. **"Hot Pursuit" Situations.** In Warden v. Hayden, 387 U.S. 294, 87 S.Ct. 1642, 18 L.Ed.2d 782 (1967), two cab drivers followed the armed robber of the cab company to a residence. A description of the robber and the drivers' information was relayed to police, who arrived at the residence within minutes. They knocked on the door and told the woman who answered they had reason to believe a robber had entered the house. The officers asked to search and the woman did not object. Hayden was found in an upstairs bedroom feigning sleep, and was arrested when no other male was found in the house. One officer was attracted to a bathroom adjoining that in which Hayden was found; in the flush tank of a toilet he found a shotgun and pistol. Another officer searching the cellar for the gun or money looked in a washing machine and found a jacket and trousers resembling what the fleeing robber wore. Under the mattress of Hayden's bed the officers found ammunition for the pistol and a cap. Additional ammunition was found in the drawer of the bedroom dresser. Upholding the admission of these items into evidence, the Su-

[handwritten: plenty of time to get warrant]

preme Court held that the entry of the premises and the search for the robber and his weapons without a warrant was reasonable, because delay might have endangered the officers or others. "[O]nly a thorough search of the house for persons or weapons could have insured that Hayden was the only man present and that the police had control of all weapons which could be used against them or to effect an escape."

Hayden is sometimes—as in the principal case—cited as a "hot pursuit" case. Was it? And how does hot pursuit expand officers' power to search?

3. **"Securing" Premises as Alternative to Searching.** If the officers in *Vale* could not conduct a warrantless search of the premises, could they have prevented Vale's mother and brother from entering the premises until the officers had time to apply for a search warrant? When—and even whether—officers may "secure" a residence pending application for and arrival of a search warrant remains uncertain. See Rawlings v. Kentucky, 448 U.S. 98, 106, 100 S.Ct. 2556, 2562, 65 L.Ed.2d 633, 643 (1980), assuming officers detaining occupants of a house for about an hour pending application for a warrant did so improperly. See also, Segura v. United States, 468 U.S. 796, 104 S.Ct. 3380, 82 L.Ed.2d 599 (1984).

If officers may secure premises pending application for a warrant, does this mean there are two levels of emergency? Perhaps one authorizes a warrantless search while the other permits only the securing of the premises pending application for a warrant.

4. **Crime Scenes.** In Mincey v. Arizona, 437 U.S. 385, 98 S.Ct. 2408, 57 L.Ed.2d 290 (1978), the Supreme Court rejected the proposition that emergency considerations justify a broad exception to the warrant requirement for scenes of even serious offenses such as homicides. Police officers entered Mincey's apartment to arrest him for possession of drugs. A police officer was shot and killed and Mincey was wounded. Officers secured the apartment and arrested Mincey and the other occupants. There then ensued four days of searching the apartment for evidence related to the homicide; two or three hundred items were seized and inventoried. No warrant was obtained. Mincey was convicted of murder and other offenses after a trial in which some of the seized items were introduced. The Arizona Supreme Court affirmed in part, holding the search permissible without a warrant because the place searched was a "murder scene." The Supreme Court reversed. That the premises were a crime scene did not itself dispense with the warrant requirement. Considered under the emergency doctrine, the search exceeded what emergency justification the case presented:

> All the persons in Mincey's apartment had been located before the investigating homicide officers arrived there and began their search. And a fourday search that included opening dresser drawers and ripping up carpets can hardly be rationalized in terms of the legitimate concerns that justify an emergency search.

437 U.S. at 393, 98 S.Ct. at 2414, 57 L.Ed.2d at 300. See also, Flippo v. West Virginia, ___ U.S. ___, 120 S.Ct. 7, 145 L.Ed.2d 16 (1999) (per curiam); Thompson v. Louisiana, 469 U.S. 17, 105 S.Ct. 409, 83 L.Ed.2d 246 (1984) (per curiam).

B. ADMINISTRATIVE INSPECTIONS AND SEARCHES OF LICENSED PREMISES

EDITOR'S' INTRODUCTION: "ADMINISTRATIVE" HOUSING CODE INSPECTIONS

The Fourth Amendment by its terms is not limited to traditional criminal investigation but is potentially applicable to any governmental activity meeting the threshold requirements of a "search" or a "seizure." Supreme Court case law, however, has tended to dilute the requirements of the Amendment when governmental activity has a purpose other than the location of evidence to use in a criminal prosecution.

Such dilution was clearly evidenced in Frank v. Maryland, 359 U.S. 360, 79 S.Ct. 804, 3 L.Ed.2d 877 (1959). The Health Code of the City of Baltimore required all dwellings be kept clean and free from rodent infestation. Health inspectors having "cause to suspect" a violation were authorized to demand entry to premises for purposes of inspection. Frank was convicted and fined $20 for refusing to permit an inspector to enter his premises to look for rats. Finding no federal constitutional defect in this conviction, a majority of the Supreme Court explained:

> The attempted inspection of appellant's home is merely to determine whether conditions exist which the Baltimore Health Code proscribes. If they do appellant is notified to remedy the infringing condition. No evidence for criminal prosecution is sought to be seized. * * * The power of inspection granted by the Baltimore City Code is strictly limited * * *. Valid grounds for suspicion of the existence of a nuisance must exist. * * * The inspection must be made in the day time. * * * Moreover, the inspector has no power to force entry * * *. A fine is imposed for resistance, but officials are not authorized to break past the unwilling occupant.

> Thus, not only does the inspection touch at most upon the periphery of the important interests safeguarded by the Fourteenth Amendment's protection against official intrusion, but it is hedged about with safeguards designed to make the least possible demand on the individual occupant, and to cause only the slightest restriction on his claims of privacy.

359 U.S. at 366–67, 79 S.Ct. at 808–09, 3 L.Ed. at 882. Against this, the Court continued, must be weighed the interests served by inspections:

> Time and experience have forcefully taught that the power to inspect dwelling places, either as a matter of systematic area-by-area search or * * * to treat a specific problem, is of indispensable importance to the maintenance of community health; a power that would be greatly hobbled by the blanket requirement of the safeguards necessary for a search of evidence for criminal acts.

359 U.S. at 372, 79 S.Ct. at 811, 3 L.Ed.2d at 885. In light of this, a five justice majority of the Court held the inspector's entry would not have been an unreasonable search and thus Frank was properly convicted of refusing to permit it.

Franks suggested warrants are unnecessary for administrative inspections. In 1967, however, the Court held that despite *Franks* the Fourth Amendment requires warrants for nonemergency Housing Code inspections of residences. Camara v. Municipal Court, 387 U.S. 523, 87 S.Ct. 1727, 18 L.Ed.2d 930 (1967). But it also held warrants authorizing such inspections need not be based upon probable cause to believe that each building to be inspected contains Code violations. Several considerations justified modification of the probable cause standard for this context. Code violations are a serious problem and so limiting inspectors would render effective enforcement impossible. Moreover, since "the inspections are neither personal in nature nor aimed at the discovery of evidence of crime, they involve a relatively limited invasion of the urban citizen's privacy." Consequently, the warrant process is appropriately modified in this context so as to permit warrants to issue for "area inspections"—inspections of all premises in a particular area based on conditions in the area as a whole rather than on knowledge of conditions in particular buildings. Thus:

> "probable cause" to issue a warrant to inspect must exist if reasonable legislative or administrative standards for conducting an area inspection are satisfied with respect to a particular dwelling. Such standards, which will vary with the municipal program being enforced, may be based upon the passage of time, the nature of the building (e.g., a multifamily apartment house), or the condition of the entire area, but they will not necessarily depend upon specific knowledge of the condition of the particular dwelling.

387 U.S. at 538, 87 S.Ct. at 1736, 18 L.Ed.2d at 941. In a companion case, the Court held the same general Fourth Amendment rules apply to administrative inspections of commercial premises and added that the nature of such premises might make them subject to inspection in more situations than permit inspections of private residence. See v. City of Seattle, 387 U.S. 541, 87 S.Ct. 1737, 18 L.Ed.2d 943 (1967).

The principal case in this section deals with inspections of heavily regulated businesses, which are permitted under even more relaxed Fourth Amendment standards than were applied in *Camara* and *See*.

New York v. Burger

Supreme Court of the United States, 1987.
482 U.S. 691, 107 S.Ct. 2636, 96 L.Ed.2d 601.

■ Justice Blackmun delivered the opinion of the Court.

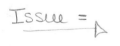

This case presents the question whether the warrantless search of an automobile junkyard, conducted pursuant to a statute authorizing such a search, falls within the exception to the warrant requirement for administrative inspections of pervasively regulated industries. The case also presents the question whether an otherwise proper administrative inspection is unconstitutional because the ultimate purpose of the regulatory statute pursuant to which the search is done—the deterrence of criminal behavior—is the same as that of penal laws, with the result that the inspection may disclose violations not only of the regulatory statute but also of the penal statutes.

I

Respondent Joseph Burger is the owner of a junkyard in Brooklyn, N.Y. His business consists, in part, of the dismantling of automobiles and the selling of their parts. His junkyard is an open lot with no buildings. A high metal fence surrounds it, wherein are located, among other things, vehicles and parts of vehicles. At approximately noon on November 17,

1982, Officer Joseph Vega and four other plainclothes officers, all members of the Auto Crimes Division of the New York City Police Department, entered respondent's junkyard to conduct an inspection pursuant to N.Y.Veh. & Traf.Law § 415–a5 (McKinney 1986). On any given day, the Division conducts from 5 to 10 inspections of vehicle dismantlers, automobile junkyards, and related businesses.

Upon entering the junkyard, the officers asked to see Burger's license[1] and his "police book"—the record of the automobiles and vehicle parts in his possession. Burger replied that he had neither a license nor a police book. The officers then announced their intention to conduct a § 415–a inspection. Burger did not object. In accordance with their practice, the officers copied down the Vehicle Inspection Numbers (VINs) of several vehicles and parts of vehicles that were in the junkyard. After checking these numbers against a police computer, the officers determined that respondent was in possession of stolen vehicles and parts. Accordingly, Burger was arrested and charged with five counts of possession of stolen property and one count of unregistered operation as a vehicle dismantler * * *.

In the Kings County Supreme Court, Burger moved to suppress the evidence obtained as a result of the inspection, primarily on the ground that § 415–a5 was unconstitutional. After a hearing, the court denied the motion. * * *

The New York Court of Appeals, however, reversed. In its view, § 415–a5 violated the Fourth Amendment's prohibition of unreasonable searches and seizures. According to the Court of Appeals, "[t]he fundamental defect [of § 415–a5] * * * is that [it] authorize[s] searches undertaken solely to uncover evidence of criminality and not to enforce a comprehensive regulatory scheme. The asserted 'administrative schem[e]' here [is], in reality, designed simply to give the police an expedient means of enforcing penal sanctions for possession of stolen property." * * * [W]e granted certiorari.

II

A

The Court long has recognized that the Fourth Amendment's prohibition on unreasonable searches and seizures is applicable to commercial premises, as well as to private homes. An owner or operator of a business thus has an expectation of privacy in commercial property, which society is prepared to consider to be reasonable. This expectation exists not only with respect to traditional police searches conducted for the gathering of criminal evidence but also with respect to administrative inspections designed to enforce regulatory statutes. See Marshall v. Barlow's, Inc., 436 U.S. 307,

[handwritten margin note: commercial property = reasonable expectation of privacy]

---

1. An individual operating a vehicle-dismantling business in New York is required to have a license:

"Definition and registration of vehicle dismantlers. A vehicle dismantler is any person who is engaged in the business of acquiring motor vehicles or trailers for the purpose of dismantling the same for parts or reselling such vehicles as scrap. No person shall engage in the business of or operate as a vehicle dismantler unless there shall have been issued to him a registration in accordance with the provisions of this section. A violation of this subdivision shall be a class E felony." N.Y.Veh. & Traf.Laws 415–a1 (McKinney 1986).

[handwritten margin note: certian industries have exception to privacy — "closely regulated business"]

312–313, 98 S.Ct. 1816, 1820–1821, 56 L.Ed.2d 305 (1978). An expectation of privacy in commercial premises, however, is different from, and indeed less than, a similar expectation in an individual's home. See Donovan v. Dewey, 452 U.S. 594, 598–599, 101 S.Ct. 2534, 2537–2538, 69 L.Ed.2d 262 (1981). This expectation is particularly attenuated in commercial property employed in "closely regulated" industries. The Court observed in *Marshall v. Barlow's, Inc.*: "Certain industries have such a history of government oversight that no reasonable expectation of privacy could exist for a proprietor over the stock of such an enterprise."

The Court first examined the "unique" problem of inspections of "closely regulated" businesses in two enterprises that had "a long tradition of close government supervision." In Colonnade Corp. v. United States, 397 U.S. 72, 90 S.Ct. 774, 25 L.Ed.2d 60 (1970), it considered a warrantless search of a catering business pursuant to several federal revenue statutes authorizing the inspection of the premises of liquor dealers. Although the Court disapproved the search because the statute provided that a sanction be imposed when entry was refused, and because it did not authorize entry without a warrant as an alternative in this situation, it recognized that "the liquor industry [was] long subject to close supervision and inspection."

[handwritten margin note: 1) liquor 2) gun dealers are examples]

We returned to this issue in United States v. Biswell, 406 U.S. 311, 92 S.Ct. 1593, 32 L.Ed.2d 87 (1972), which involved a warrantless inspection of the premises of a pawn shop operator, who was federally licensed to sell sporting weapons pursuant to the Gun Control Act of 1968, 82 Stat. 1213, 18 U.S.C. § 921 et seq. While noting that "[f]ederal regulation of the interstate traffic in firearms is not as deeply rooted in history as is governmental control of the liquor industry," we nonetheless concluded that the warrantless inspections authorized by the Gun Control Act would "pose only limited threats to the dealer's justifiable expectations of privacy." We observed: "When a dealer chooses to engage in this pervasively regulated business and to accept a federal license, he does so with the knowledge that his business records, firearms, and ammunition will be subject to effective inspection."

The "*Colonnade–Biswell*" doctrine, stating the reduced expectation of privacy by an owner of commercial premises in a "closely regulated" industry, has received renewed emphasis in more recent decisions. In *Marshall v. Barlow's, Inc.*, we noted its continued vitality but declined to find that warrantless inspections, made pursuant to the Occupational Safety and Health Act of 1970, 84 Stat. 1598, 29 U.S.C. §§ 657(a), of all businesses engaged in interstate commerce fell within the narrow focus of this doctrine. However, we found warrantless inspections made pursuant to the Federal Mine Safety and Health Act of 1977, 91 Stat. 1290, 30 U.S.C. § 801 et seq., proper because they were of a "closely regulated" industry. *Donovan v. Dewey, supra.*

Indeed, in Donovan v. Dewey, we declined to limit our consideration to the length of time during which the business in question—stone quarries— had been subject to federal regulation. We pointed out that the doctrine is essentially defined by "the pervasiveness and regularity of the federal regulation" and the effect of such regulation upon an owner's expectation of privacy. We observed, however, that "the duration of a particular regulatory scheme" would remain an "important factor" in deciding whether a warrantless inspection pursuant to the scheme is permissible.

B

Because the owner or operator of commercial premises in a "closely regulated" industry has a reduced expectation of privacy, the warrant and probable cause requirements, which fulfill the traditional Fourth Amendment standard of reasonableness for a government search, have lessened application in this context. Rather, we conclude that, as in other situations of "special need," where the privacy interests of the owner are weakened and the government interests in regulating particular businesses are concomitantly heightened, a warrantless inspection of commercial premises may well be reasonable within the meaning of the Fourth Amendment.

This warrantless inspection, however, even in the context of a pervasively regulated business, will be deemed to be reasonable only so long as three criteria are met. First, there must be a "substantial" government interest that informs the regulatory scheme pursuant to which the inspection is made. See Donovan v. Dewey, 452 U.S., at 602, 101 S.Ct., at 2540 ("substantial federal interest in improving the health and safety conditions in the Nation's underground and surface mines"); United States v. Biswell, 406 U.S., at 315, 92 S.Ct., at 1596 (regulation of firearms is "of central importance to federal efforts to prevent violent crime and to assist the States in regulating the firearms traffic within their borders"); Colonnade Corp. v. United States, 397 U.S., at 75, 90 S.Ct., at 776 (federal interest "in protecting the revenue against various types of fraud").

① Substantial government interests

Second, the warrantless inspections must be "necessary to further [the] regulatory scheme." For example, in *Dewey* we recognized that forcing mine inspectors to obtain a warrant before every inspection might alert mine owners or operators to the impending inspection, thereby frustrating the purposes of the Mine Safety and Health Act—to detect and thus to deter safety and health violations.

② necessary to regulate

Finally, "the statute's inspection program, in terms of the certainty and regularity of its application, [must] provid[e] a constitutionally adequate substitute for a warrant." In other words, the regulatory statute must perform the two basic functions of a warrant: it must advise the owner of the commercial premises that the search is being made pursuant to the law and has a properly defined scope, and it must limit the discretion of the inspecting officers. To perform this first function, the statute must be "sufficiently comprehensive and defined that the owner of commercial property cannot help but be aware that his property will be subject to periodic inspections undertaken for specific purposes." In addition, in defining how a statute limits the discretion of the inspectors, we have observed that it must be "carefully limited in time, place, and scope."

③ constitutional adequate for a warrant
- search being made per law
- must limit discretion of inspecting officers

III

A

Searches made pursuant to § 415–a, in our view, clearly fall within this established exception to the warrant requirement for administrative inspections in "closely regulated" businesses. First, the nature of the regulatory statute reveals that the operation of a junkyard, part of which is devoted to vehicle dismantling, is a "closely regulated" business in the State of New York. The provisions regulating the activity of vehicle dismantling are extensive. An operator cannot engage in this industry without first obtaining a license, which means that he must meet the registration requirements and must pay a fee. Under § 415–a5(a), the operator must maintain a police book recording the acquisition and disposition of motor vehicles and vehicle parts, and make such records and inventory available for inspection by the police or any agent of the Department of Motor Vehicles. The operator also must display his registration number prominently at his place of business, on business documentation, and on vehicles and parts that pass through his business. Moreover, the person engaged in this activity is subject to criminal penalties, as well as to loss of license or civil fines, for failure to comply with these provisions. That other States besides New York have imposed similarly extensive regulations on automobile junkyards further supports the "closely regulated" status of this industry.

In determining whether vehicle dismantlers constitute a "closely regulated" industry, the "duration of [this] particular regulatory scheme," has some relevancy. Section 415–a could be said to be of fairly recent vintage, and the inspection provision of § 415–a5 was added only in 1979. But because the automobile is a relatively new phenomenon in our society and because its widespread use is even newer, automobile junkyards and vehicle dismantlers have not been in existence very long and thus do not have an ancient history of government oversight. * * *

The automobile junkyard business * * * is simply a new branch of an industry that has existed, and has been closely regulated, for many years. The automobile junkyard is closely akin to the secondhand shop or the general junkyard. Both share the purpose of recycling salvageable articles and components of items no longer usable in their original form. As such, vehicle dismantlers represent a modern, specialized version of a traditional activity.

In New York, general junkyards and secondhand shops long have been subject to regulation. * * * The history of government regulation of junk-related activities argues strongly in favor of the "closely regulated" status of the automobile junkyard.

Accordingly, in light of the regulatory framework governing his business and the history of regulation of related industries, an operator of a junkyard engaging in vehicle dismantling has a reduced expectation of privacy in this "closely regulated" business.

B

The New York regulatory scheme satisfies the three criteria necessary to make reasonable warrantless inspections pursuant to § 415–a5. First, the State has a substantial interest in regulating the vehicle-dismantling and automobile-junkyard industry because motor vehicle theft has increased in the State and because the problem of theft is associated with this industry. In this day, automobile theft has become a significant social problem, placing enormous economic and personal burdens upon the citizens of different States. * * * Because contemporary automobiles are made from standardized parts, the nationwide extent of vehicle theft and concern about it are understandable.

Second, regulation of the vehicle-dismantling industry reasonably serves the State's substantial interest in eradicating automobile theft. It is well established that the theft problem can be addressed effectively by controlling the receiver of, or market in, stolen property. Automobile junkyards and vehicle dismantlers provide the major market for stolen vehicles and vehicle parts. Thus, the State rationally may believe that it will reduce car theft by regulations that prevent automobile junkyards from becoming markets for stolen vehicles and that help trace the origin and destination of vehicle parts.

Moreover, the warrantless administrative inspections pursuant to § 415–a5 "are necessary to further [the] regulatory scheme." In this respect, we see no difference between these inspections and those approved by the Court in United States v. Biswell and Donovan v. Dewey. We explained in *Biswell:*

> "[I]f inspection is to be effective and serve as a credible deterrent, unannounced, even frequent, inspections are essential. In this context, the prerequisite of a warrant could easily frustrate inspection; and if the necessary flexibility as to time, scope, and frequency is to be preserved, the protections afforded by a warrant would be negligible."

effective search = a credible deterrent

Similarly, in the present case, a warrant requirement would interfere with the statute's purpose of deterring automobile theft accomplished by identifying vehicles and parts as stolen and shutting down the market in such items. Because stolen cars and parts often pass quickly through an automobile junkyard, "frequent" and "unannounced" inspections are necessary in order to detect them. In sum, surprise is crucial if the regulatory scheme aimed at remedying this major social problem is to function at all.

Third, § 415–a5 provides a "constitutionally adequate substitute for a warrant." The statute informs the operator of a vehicle dismantling business that inspections will be made on a regular basis. Thus, the vehicle dismantler knows that the inspections to which he is subject do not constitute discretionary acts by a government official but are conducted pursuant to statute. Section 415–a5 also sets forth the scope of the inspection and, accordingly, places the operator on notice as to how to comply with the statute. In addition, it notifies the operator as to who is authorized to conduct an inspection.

Finally, the "time, place, and scope" of the inspection is limited, to place appropriate restraints upon the discretion of the inspecting officers. The officers are allowed to conduct an inspection only "during [the] regular and usual business hours."[2] The inspections can be made only of vehicle-

---

2. Respondent contends that § 415–a5 is unconstitutional because it fails to limit the number of searches that may be conducted of a particular business during any given period. While such limitations, or the absence thereof, are a factor in an analysis of the adequacy of a particular statute, they are not determinative of the result so long as the statute, as a whole, places adequate limits upon the discretion of the inspecting officers. * * *

dismantling and related industries. And the permissible scope of these searches is narrowly defined: the inspectors may examine the records, as well as "any vehicles or parts of vehicles which are subject to the record keeping requirements of this section and which are on the premises."

IV

A search conducted pursuant to § 415–a5, therefore, clearly falls within the well-established exception to the warrant requirement for administrative inspections of "closely regulated" businesses. The Court of Appeals, nevertheless, struck down the statute as violative of the Fourth Amendment because, in its view, the statute had no truly administrative purpose but was "designed simply to give the police an expedient means of enforcing penal sanctions for possession of stolen property." The court rested its conclusion that the administrative goal of the statute was pretextual and that § 415–a5 really "authorize[d] searches undertaken solely to uncover evidence of criminality" particularly on the fact that, even if an operator failed to produce his police book, the inspecting officers could continue their inspection for stolen vehicles and parts. The court also suggested that the identity of the inspectors—police officers—was significant in revealing the true nature of the statutory scheme.

In arriving at this conclusion, the Court of Appeals failed to recognize that a State can address a major social problem both by way of an administrative scheme and through penal sanctions. Administrative statutes and penal laws may have the same ultimate purpose of remedying the social problem, but they have different subsidiary purposes and prescribe different methods of addressing the problem. An administrative statute establishes how a particular business in a "closely regulated" industry should be operated, setting forth rules to guide an operator's conduct of the business and allowing government officials to ensure that those rules are followed. Such a regulatory approach contrasts with that of the penal laws, a major emphasis of which is the punishment of individuals for specific acts of behavior.

* * *

Accordingly, to state that § 415–a5 is "really" designed to gather evidence to enable convictions under the penal laws is to ignore the plain administrative purposes of § 415–a, in general, and § 415–a5, in particular. If the administrative goals of § 415–a5 are recognized, the difficulty the Court of Appeals perceives in allowing inspecting officers to examine vehicles and vehicle parts even in the absence of records evaporates. The regulatory purposes of § 415–a5 certainly are served by having the inspecting officers compare the records of a particular vehicle dismantler with vehicles and vehicle parts in the junkyard. The purposes of maintaining junkyards in the hands of legitimate-business persons and of tracing vehicles that pass through these businesses, however, also are served by having the officers examine the operator's inventory even when the operator, for whatever reason, fails to produce the police book. Forbidding inspecting officers from examining the inventory in this situation would permit an illegitimate vehicle dismantler to thwart the purposes of the administrative scheme and would have the absurd result of subjecting his counterpart who maintained records to a more extensive search.

Nor do we think that this administrative scheme is unconstitutional simply because, in the course of enforcing it, an inspecting officer may discover evidence of crimes, besides violations of the scheme itself. The discovery of evidence of crimes in the course of an otherwise proper administrative inspection does not render that search illegal or the administrative scheme suspect.

Finally, we fail to see any constitutional significance in the fact that police officers, rather than "administrative" agents, are permitted to conduct the § 415–a5 inspection. The significance respondent alleges lies in the role of police officers as enforcers of the penal laws and in the officers' power to arrest for offenses other than violations of the administrative scheme. It is, however, important to note that state police officers, like those in New York, have numerous duties in addition to those associated with traditional police work. As a practical matter, many States do not have the resources to assign the enforcement of a particular administrative scheme to a specialized agency. So long as a regulatory scheme is properly administrative, it is not rendered illegal by the fact that the inspecting officer has the power to arrest individuals for violations other than those created by the scheme itself. In sum, we decline to impose upon the States the burden of requiring the enforcement of their regulatory statutes to be carried out by specialized agents.

V

Accordingly, the judgment of the New York Court of Appeals is reversed and the case is remanded to that court for further proceedings not inconsistent with this opinion.

It is so ordered.

■ JUSTICE BRENNAN, with whom JUSTICE MARSHALL joins, and with whom JUSTICE O'CONNOR joins as to all but Part III, dissenting.

Warrantless inspections of pervasively regulated businesses are valid if necessary to further an urgent state interest, and if authorized by a statute that carefully limits their time, place, and scope. I have no objection to this general rule. Today, however, * * * the Court renders virtually meaningless the general rule that a warrant is required for administrative searches of commercial property.

I

In See v. City of Seattle, 387 U.S. 541, 543, 87 S.Ct. 1737, 1739, 18 L.Ed.2d 943 (1967), we held that an administrative search of commercial property generally must be supported by a warrant. We make an exception to this rule, and dispense with the warrant requirement, in cases involving "closely regulated" industries, where we believe that the commercial operator's privacy interest is adequately protected by detailed regulatory schemes authorizing warrantless inspections. See Donovan v. Dewey, 452 U.S. 594, 599, 101 S.Ct. 2534, 2538, 69 L.Ed.2d 262 (1981). * * *

* * * In *Dewey* * * * we clarified that * * * it is "the pervasiveness and regularity of * * * regulation that ultimately determines whether a warrant is necessary to render an inspection program reasonable under the Fourth Amendment."

The provisions governing vehicle dismantling in New York simply are not extensive. A vehicle dismantler must register and pay a fee, display the registration in various circumstances, maintain a police book, and allow inspections. Of course, the inspections themselves cannot be cited as proof of pervasive regulation justifying elimination of the warrant requirement; that would be obvious bootstrapping. Nor can registration and recordkeeping requirements be characterized as close regulation. New York City, like many States and municipalities, imposes similar, and often more stringent licensing, recordkeeping, and other regulatory requirements on a myriad of trades and businesses. Few substantive qualifications are required of an aspiring vehicle dismantler; no regulation governs the condition of the premises, the method of operation, the hours of operation, the equipment utilized, etc. * * *

In sum, if New York City's administrative scheme renders the vehicle-dismantling business closely regulated, few businesses will escape such a finding. Under these circumstances, the warrant requirement is the exception not the rule * * *.

II

Even if vehicle dismantling were a closely regulated industry, I would nonetheless conclude that this search violated the Fourth Amendment. The warrant requirement protects the owner of a business from the "unbridled discretion [of] executive and administrative officers," by ensuring that "reasonable legislative or administrative standards for conducting an ... inspection are satisfied with respect to a particular [business]." In order to serve as the equivalent of a warrant, an administrative statute must create "a predictable and guided (governmental) presence," *Dewey*, 452 U.S., at 604, 101 S.Ct., at 2541. Section 415–a5 does not approach the level of "certainty and regularity of * * * application" necessary to provide "a constitutionally adequate substitute for a warrant."[3]

The statute does not inform the operator of a vehicle-dismantling business that inspections will be made on a regular basis; in fact, there is no assurance that any inspections at all will occur. There is neither an upper nor a lower limit on the number of searches that may be conducted at any given operator's establishment in any given time period. Neither the statute, nor any regulations, nor any regulatory body, provide limits or guidance on the selection of vehicle dismantlers for inspection. In fact, the State could not explain why Burger's operation was selected for inspection. * * *

---

3. I also dispute the contention that warrantless searches are necessary to further the regulatory scheme, because of the need for unexpected and/or frequent searches. If surprise is essential (as it usually is in a criminal case), a warrant may be obtained *ex parte*. If the State seeks to conduct frequent inspections, then the statute (or some regulatory authority) should somewhere inform the industry of that fact.

The Court also maintains that this statute effectively limits the scope of the search. We have previously found significant that "the standards with which a [business] operator is required to comply are all specifically set forth," reasoning that a clear and complete definition of potential administrative violations constitutes an implied limitation on the scope of any inspection. Plainly, a statute authorizing a search which can uncover no administrative violations is not sufficiently limited in scope to avoid the warrant requirement. This statute fails to tailor the scope of administrative inspection to the particular concerns posed by the regulated business. I conclude that "the frequency and purpose of the inspections [are left] to the unchecked discretion of Government officers." The conduct of the police in this case underscores this point. The police removed identification numbers from a walker and a wheelchair, neither of which fell within the statutory scope of a permissible administrative search.

The Court also finds significant that an operator is on notice as to who is authorized to search the premises; I do not find the statutory limitation—to "any police officer" or "agent of the commissioner"—significant. The sole limitation I see on a police search of the premises of a vehicle dismantler is that it must occur during business hours; otherwise it is open season. The unguided discretion afforded police in this scheme precludes its substitution for a warrant.

III

The fundamental defect in § 415–a5 is that it authorizes searches intended solely to uncover evidence of criminal acts. The New York Court of Appeals correctly found that § 415–a5 authorized a search of Burger's business "solely to discover whether defendant was storing stolen property on his premises." In the law of administrative searches, one principle emerges with unusual clarity and unanimous acceptance: the government may not use an administrative inspection scheme to search for criminal violations. * * *

Here the State has used an administrative scheme as a pretext to search without probable cause for evidence of criminal violations. It thus circumvented the requirements of the Fourth Amendment by altering the label placed on the search. * * *

Moreover, it is factually impossible that the search was intended to discover wrongdoing subject to administrative sanction. Burger stated that he was not registered to dismantle vehicles as required by § 415–a1, and that he did not have a police book, as required by § 415–a5(a). At that point he had violated every requirement of the administrative scheme. There is no administrative provision forbidding possession of stolen automobiles or automobile parts. The inspection became a search for evidence of criminal acts when all possible administrative violations had been uncovered.

The Court * * * implicitly holds that if an administrative scheme has certain goals and if the search serves those goals, it may be upheld even if no concrete administrative consequences could follow from a particular search. This is a dangerous suggestion, for the goals of administrative schemes often overlap with the goals of the criminal law. * * * If the

Fourth Amendment is to retain meaning in the commercial context, it must be applied to searches for evidence of criminal acts even if those searches would also serve an administrative purpose, unless that administrative purpose takes the concrete form of seeking an administrative violation.

IV

The implications of the Court's opinion, if realized, will virtually eliminate Fourth Amendment protection of commercial entities in the context of administrative searches. No State may require, as a condition of doing business, a blanket submission to warrantless searches for any purpose. I respectfully dissent.

NOTES

1. **Inspections and Searches Related to Arson Investigations.** The Supreme Court has explored the relationship among emergency, "administrative" warrant, and traditional searches for criminal evidence in the context of arson investigations. In Michigan v. Tyler, 436 U.S. 499, 98 S.Ct. 1942, 56 L.Ed.2d 486 (1978), firemen arrived at a furniture store ablaze at midnight and extinguished the fire by 4 a.m. Two plastic containers holding flammable liquid were discovered during the course of extinguishing the fire. Investigators were not able to conduct a thorough investigation of the scene when the fire was extinguished because of the darkness and the smoke. The fire chief returned at 9 a.m. the next morning and discovered some suspicious burn marks in the carpeting. Samples of the carpet were seized. Three weeks later a state fire inspector entered the premises several times and seized more items. No warrant was obtained. Tyler was subsequently tried for arson of the store. The items seized in both inspections and evidence derived from them was admitted over defense objection and Tyler was convicted.

The Supreme Court held this constitutional error. Firefighters do not need a warrant to enter a burning building and extinguish the fire, Justice Stewart's opinion for the Court explained. Moreover:

> Prompt determination of the fire's origin may be necessary to prevent its recurrence, as through the detection of continuing dangers such as faulty wiring or a defective furnace. Immediate investigation may also be necessary to preserve evidence from intentional or accidental destruction. * * * For these reasons, officials need no warrant to remain in a building for a reasonable time to investigate the cause of a blaze after it has been extinguished.

436 U.S. at 510, 98 S.Ct. at 1950, 56 L.Ed.2d at 498–99. But other entries require a warrant. Despite the fire, privacy interests may still be implicated. Burned premises are sometimes still used for living or business purposes after the fire. Private effects are often left at the scene of a fire. The court declined, however, to require a traditional search warrant for all post-fire entries. In some situations, an administrative warrant will suffice. Rejecting the argument administrative warrants serve no purpose, Justice Stewart explained for the Court:

> To secure a warrant to investigate the cause of a fire, an official must show more than the bare fact that a fire has occurred. The magistrate's duty is to assure that the proposed search will be reasonable, a determination that requires inquiry into the need for the intrusion on the one hand, and the threat of disruption of the occupant on the other. * * * Even though a fire victim's privacy must normally yield to the vital social objective of ascertaining the cause of the fire, the magistrate can perform the important function of preventing harassment by keeping that invasion to a minimum.

In addition, * * * [another] major function of the warrant is to provide the property owner with sufficient information to reassure him of the entry's legality.

436 U.S. at 507–08, 98 S.Ct. at 1949, 56 L.Ed.2d at 497. But, Justice Stewart continued:

[I]f the investigating officials find probable cause to believe that arson has occurred and require further access to gather evidence for a possible prosecution, they may obtain a warrant only upon a traditional showing of probable cause applicable to searches for evidence of crime.

436 U.S. at 512, 98 S.Ct. at 1951, 56 L.Ed.2d at 500. On the facts of the case, the Court concluded the entry on the morning after the fire was "no more than an actual continuation" of the firefighters' entry the previous night to extinguish the fire and to conduct an immediate investigation into its origin; therefore, no warrant was needed. But the later entries required a warrant. Since none had been secured, evidence obtained from those entries should not have been used against Tyler.

The Fourth Amendment need for a warrant to conduct post-fire inspections was before the Court again in Michigan v. Clifford, 464 U.S. 287, 104 S.Ct. 641, 78 L.Ed.2d 477 (1984). In *Clifford,* a majority of the Court's members appeared to reject *Tyler's* analysis. Justice Rehnquist, joined by the Chief Justice and Justices Blackmun and O'Connor, took the position that no warrant whatsoever is necessary for a post-fire investigation conducted within a reasonable time of a fire. Since the right to enter is contingent upon the happening of an event—a fire—over which authorities have no control, application of the warrant requirement is not necessary to regulate authorities' power to initiate searches. Property owners could be adequately assured of the legality of an inspection by providing inspectors with identification or by efforts to notify the owners before the inspection. 464 U.S. at 309, 104 S.Ct. at 655, 78 L.Ed.2d at 494–95 (Rehnquist, J., dissenting). Justice Stevens construed the Fourth Amendment as requiring a traditional search warrant for an unannounced entry. But an entry without any warrant would be reasonable, he concluded, if the inspector had either given the owner sufficient advance notice to enable him or an agent to be present at the inspection or had made a reasonable effort to provide such notice. 464 U.S. at 303, 104 S.Ct. at 652, 78 L.Ed.2d at 490 (Stevens, J., concurring in the judgment).

2. Administrative-like considerations were held to justify considerable flexibility in the Fourth Amendment as it applies to searches of probationers in Griffin v. Wisconsin, 483 U.S. 868, 107 S.Ct. 3164, 97 L.Ed.2d 709 (1987). Application of Fourth Amendment standards to searches by a public employer of employee workplaces split the Court in O'Connor v. Ortega, 480 U.S. 709, 107 S.Ct. 1492, 94 L.Ed.2d 714 (1987).

C. CONSENT SEARCHES

Evidence obtained by a search need not be excluded if the search was conducted pursuant to effective consent provided by a person with authority to give it. Effective consent means the absence of a warrant will not render evidence inadmissible, even if under general Fourth Amendment requirements a warrant is usually required for similar searches of the sort at issue. In addition, the officers need not have had information rising to the level of probable cause.

Consent searches present three major categories of issues. First are those related to the legal effectiveness of words appearing on their face to constitute consent to search; these are addressed in the first subsection that follows. Second are those related to the authority of the consenting person to consent to the search; these are addressed in the second subsection. Third are questions regarding the scope of authority resulting from particular consents; these are considered in the last subsection.

1.   THE EFFECTIVENESS OF CONSENT

The Supreme Court has long recognized that not all words or actions of consent are effective. In Amos v. United States, 255 U.S. 313, 41 S.Ct. 266, 65 L.Ed. 654 (1921), for example, officers testified that they went to Amos's residence and told the only person there, Amos' wife, they had come to search the premises. She opened the nearby store and the officers entered and searched. The Court held:

> The contention that the constitutional rights of defendant were waived when his wife admitted to his home the governmental officers * * * cannot be entertained. * * * [I]t is perfectly clear that, under the implied coercion here presented, no such waiver was intended or effected.

255 U.S. at 317, 41 S.Ct. at 268, 65 L.Ed. at 656. But under what circumstances will words of consent have full effect? In analyzing this problem, is it necessary or permissible to conceptualize consent as a "waiver" of the right to be free from searches in the absence of compliance with certain requirements, such as a search warrant based on probable cause? To the extent consent operates as a waiver, perhaps it must meet standards developed in other contexts for determining the effectiveness of a waiver of federal constitutional rights. These issues are addressed in the following case.

Schneckloth v. Bustamonte

Supreme Court of the United States, 1973.
412 U.S. 218, 93 S.Ct. 2041, 36 L.Ed.2d 854.

■ MR. JUSTICE STEWART delivered the opinion of the Court.

* * *

I.

The respondent was brought to trial in a California court upon a charge of possessing a check with intent to defraud. He moved to suppress the introduction of certain material as evidence against him on the ground that the material had been acquired through an unconstitutional search and seizure. In response to the motion, the trial judge conducted an evidentiary hearing where it was established that the material in question had been acquired by the State under the following circumstances:

While on routine patrol in Sunnyvale, California, at approximately 2:40 in the morning, Police Officer James Rand stopped an automobile when he observed that one headlight and its license plate light were burned out. Six men were in the vehicle. Joe Alcala and the respondent, Robert Busta-monte, were in the front seat with Joe Gonzales, the driver. Three older men were seated in the rear. When, in response to the policeman's question, Gonzales could not produce a driver's license, Officer Rand asked if any of the other five had any evidence of identification. Only Alcala produced a license, and he explained that the car was his brother's. After the six occupants had stepped out of the car at the officer's request and after two additional policemen had arrived, Officer Rand asked Alcala if he could search the car. Alcala replied, "Sure, go ahead." Prior to the search no one was threatened with arrest and, according to Officer Rand's uncon-tradicted testimony, it "was all very congenial at this time." Gonzales testified that Alcala actually helped in the search of the car, by opening the trunk and glove compartment. In Gonzales' words: " * * * the police officer asked Joe [Alcala], he goes, 'Does the trunk open?' And Joe said, 'Yes.' He went to the car and got the keys and opened up the trunk." Wadded up under the left rear seat, the police officers found three checks that had previously been stolen from a car wash.

[Bustamonte, by means never explained, had come into possession of a checkwriting machine previously stolen from a car wash. He, Alcala, and Gonzales had cashed at least one check from the machine. On the day prior to the stop in Sunnydale, the three had gone to San Jose to find other people willing to use false identification to cash checks written on the machine. The three passengers in the rear seat of the car at the time of the stop had joined the trio for this purpose. By the time Alcala gave his consent to the search, there were four police cars and an undetermined number of officers at the scene. The facts do not suggest that the officers connected the car and its occupants with the theft of the checkwriting machine or the passing of the checks before the search. Two of the older men seated in the rear seat had given inconsistent stories concerning the situation. One officer stated that permission to search the car was sought because things "just didn't fit in right." The search was quite intensive; the officers removed the rear seat from the car. After discovery of the checks, Gonzales "cooperated" with the officers and provided information that linked Bustamonte and the others to the checkwriting machine and the scheme to cash the forged checks. Editors.]

The trial judge denied the motion to suppress, and the checks in question were admitted in evidence at Bustamonte's trial. On the basis of this and other evidence he was convicted, and the California Court of Appeals for the First Appellate District affirmed the conviction. In agreeing that the search and seizure were constitutionally valid, the appellate court applied the standard earlier formulated by the Supreme Court of California in an opinion by then Justice Traynor: "Whether in a particular case an apparent consent was in fact voluntarily given or was in submission to an express or implied assertion of authority, is a question of fact to be determined in the light of all the circumstances." People v. Michael, 45 Cal.2d 751, 753, 290 P.2d 852, 854. The appellate court found that "[i]n the instant case the prosecution met the necessary burden of showing consent * * * since there were clearly circumstances from which the trial court could ascertain that consent had been freely given without coercion or

Key ✱

submission to authority. Not only officer Rand, but Gonzales, the driver of the automobile, testified that Alcala's assent to the search of his brother's automobile was freely, even casually given. At the time of the request to search the automobile the atmosphere, according to Rand, was 'congenial' and there had been no discussion of any crime. As noted, Gonzales said Alcala even attempted to aid in the search." The California Supreme Court denied review.

Thereafter, the respondent sought a writ of habeas corpus in a federal district court. It was denied. On appeal, the Court of Appeals for the Ninth Circuit * * * set aside the District Court's order. The appellate court reasoned that a consent was a waiver of a person's Fourth and Fourteenth Amendment rights, and that the State was under an obligation to demonstrate not only that the consent had been uncoerced, but that it had been given with an understanding that it could be freely and effectively withheld. Consent could not be found, the court held, solely from the absence of coercion and a verbal expression of assent. Since the District Court had not determined that Alcala had *known* that his consent could be withheld and that he could have refused to have his vehicle searched, the Court of Appeals vacated the order denying the writ and remanded the case for further proceedings. We granted the State's petition for certiorari to determine whether the Fourth and Fourteenth Amendments require the showing thought necessary by the Court of Appeals.

II.

It is important to make it clear at the outset what is not involved in this case. The respondent concedes that a search conducted pursuant to a valid consent is constitutionally permissible. * * * And similarly the State concedes that "[w]hen a prosecutor seeks to rely upon consent to justify the lawfulness of a search he has the burden of proving that the consent was, in fact, freely and voluntarily given." Bumper v. North Carolina, 391 U.S. 543, 548, 88 S.Ct. 1788, 1792, 20 L.Ed.2d 797.

The precise question in this case, then, is what must the state prove to demonstrate that a consent was "voluntarily" given. * * *

A.

The most extensive judicial exposition of the meaning of "voluntariness" has been developed in those cases in which the Court has had to determine the "voluntariness" of a defendant's confession for purposes of the Fourteenth Amendment. * * * It is to that body of case law to which we turn for initial guidance on the meaning of "voluntariness" in the present context.

Those cases yield no talismanic definition of "voluntariness," mechanically applicable to the host of situations where the question has arisen. "The notion of 'voluntariness,'" Mr. Justice Frankfurter once wrote, "is itself an amphibian." Culombe v. Connecticut, 367 U.S. 568, 604–605, 81 S.Ct. 1860, 1880–1881, 6 L.Ed.2d 1037. It cannot be taken literally to mean a "knowing" choice. "Except where a person is unconscious or drugged or otherwise lacks capacity for conscious choice, all incriminating statements—even those made under brutal treatment—are 'voluntary' in the sense of representing a choice of alternatives. On the other hand, if 'voluntariness' incorporates notions of 'but-for' cause, the question should be whether the statement would have been made even absent inquiry or other official action. Under such a test, virtually no statement would be voluntary because very few people give incriminating statements in the absence of official action of some kind." It is thus evident that neither linguistics nor epistemology will provide a ready definition of the meaning of "voluntariness."

Rather, "voluntariness" has reflected an accommodation of the complex of values implicated in police questioning of a suspect. At one end of the spectrum is the acknowledged need for police questioning as a tool for the effective enforcement of criminal laws. Without such investigation, those who were innocent might be falsely accused, those who were guilty might wholly escape prosecution, and many crimes would go unsolved. In short, the security of all would be diminished. At the other end of the spectrum, is the set of values reflecting society's deeply felt belief that the criminal law cannot be used as an instrument of unfairness, and that the possibility of unfair and even brutal police tactics poses a real and serious threat to civilized notions of justice. "[I]n cases involving involuntary confessions, this Court enforces the strongly felt attitude of our society that important human values are sacrificed where an agency of the government, in the course of securing a conviction, wrings a confession out of an accused against his will."

This Court's decisions reflect a frank recognition that the Constitution requires the sacrifice of neither security nor liberty. The Due Process Clause does not mandate that the police forego all questioning, nor that they be given carte blanche to extract what they can from a suspect. "The ultimate test remains that which has been the only clearly established test in Anglo–American courts for two hundred years: the test of voluntariness. Is the confession the product of an essentially free and unconstrained choice by its maker? If it is, if he has willed to confess, it may be used against him. If it is not, if his will has been overborne and his capacity for self-determination critically impaired, the use of his confession offends due process." Culombe v. Connecticut, supra, 367 U.S., at 602, 81 S.Ct., at 1879.

In determining whether a defendant's will was overborne in a particular case, the Court has assessed the totality of all the surrounding circumstances—both the characteristics of the accused and the details of the interrogation. Some of the factors taken into account have included the youth of the accused, his lack of education, or his low intelligence, the lack of any advice to the accused of his constitutional rights, the length of detention, the repeated and prolonged nature of the questioning, and the use of physical punishment such as the deprivation of food or sleep. In all of these cases, the Court determined the factual circumstances surrounding the confession, assessed the psychological impact on the accused, and evaluated the legal significance of how the accused reacted.

The significant fact about all of these decisions is that none of them turned on the presence or absence of a single controlling criterion; each reflected a careful scrutiny of all the surrounding circumstances. In none of them did the Court rule that the Due Process Clause required the prosecution to prove as part of its initial burden that the defendant knew he had a right to refuse to answer the questions that were put. While the state of the accused's mind, and the failure of the police to advise the accused of his rights, were certainly factors to be evaluated in assessing the "voluntariness" of an accused's responses, they were not in and of themselves determinative.

B.

Similar considerations lead us to agree with the courts of California that the question whether a consent to a search was in fact "voluntary" or was the product of duress or coercion, express or implied, is a question of fact to be determined from the totality of all the circumstances. While knowledge of the right to refuse consent is one factor to be taken into account, the government need not establish such knowledge as the *sine qua non* of an effective consent. As with police questioning, two competing concerns must be accommodated in determining the meaning of a "voluntary" consent—the legitimate need for such searches and the equally important requirement of assuring the absence of coercion.

In situations where the police have some evidence of illicit activity, but lack probable cause to arrest or search, a search authorized by a valid consent may be the only means of obtaining important and reliable evidence. In the present case for example, while the police had reason to stop the car for traffic violations, the State does not contend that there was probable cause to search the vehicle or that the search was incident to a valid arrest of any of the occupants. Yet, the search yielded tangible evidence that served as a basis for a prosecution, and provided some assurance that others, wholly innocent of the crime, were not mistakenly brought to trial. And in those cases where there is probable cause to arrest or search, but where the police lack a warrant, a consent search may still be valuable. If the search is conducted and proves fruitless, that in itself may convince the police that an arrest with its possible stigma and embarrassment is unnecessary, or that a far more extensive search pursuant to a warrant is not justified. In short, a search pursuant to consent may result in considerably less inconvenience for the subject of the search, and, properly conducted, is a constitutionally permissible and wholly legitimate aspect of effective police activity.

But the Fourth and Fourteenth Amendments require that a consent not be coerced, by explicit or implicit means, by implied threat or covert force. For, no matter how subtly the coercion were applied, the resulting "consent" would be no more than a pretext for the unjustified police intrusion against which the Fourth Amendment is directed. * * *

The problem of reconciling the recognized legitimacy of consent searches with the requirement that they be free from any aspect of official coercion cannot be resolved by any infallible touchstone. To approve such searches without the most careful scrutiny would sanction the possibility of official coercion; to place artificial restrictions upon such searches would jeopardize their basic validity. Just as was true with confessions, the requirement of a "voluntary" consent reflects a fair accommodation of the constitutional requirements involved. In examining all the surrounding circumstances to determine if in fact the consent to search was coerced, account must be taken of subtly coercive police questions, as well as the possibly vulnerable subjective state of the person who consents. Those searches that are the product of police coercion can thus be filtered out without undermining the continuing validity of consent searches. In sum, there is no reason for us to depart in the area of consent searches, from the traditional definition of "voluntariness."

The approach of the Court of Appeals for the Ninth Circuit * * *, that the State must affirmatively prove that the subject of the search knew that he had a right to refuse consent, would, in practice, create serious doubt whether consent searches could continue to be conducted. There might be rare cases where it could be proved from the record that a person in fact affirmatively knew of his right to refuse—such as a case where he announced to the police that if he didn't sign the consent form, "you [police] are going to get a search warrant;" or a case where by prior experience and training a person had clearly and convincingly demonstrated such knowledge. But more commonly where there was no evidence of any coercion, explicit or implicit, the prosecution would nevertheless be unable to demonstrate that the subject of the search in fact had known of his right to refuse consent.

[handwritten margin note: state must prove that subject was aware he had right to refuse consent]

The very object of the inquiry—the nature of a person's subjective understanding—underlines the difficulty of the prosecution's burden under the rule applied by the Court of Appeals in this case. Any defendant who was the subject of a search authorized solely by his consent could effectively frustrate the introduction into evidence of the fruits of that search by simply failing to testify that he in fact knew he could refuse to consent. And the near impossibility of meeting this prosecutorial burden suggests why this Court has never accepted any such litmus-paper test of voluntariness. * * *

One alternative that would go far towards proving that the subject of a search did know he had a right to refuse consent would be to advise him of that right before eliciting his consent. That, however, is a suggestion that has been almost universally repudiated by both federal and state courts, and, we think, rightly so. For it would be thoroughly impractical to impose on the normal consent search the detailed requirements of an effective warning. Consent searches are part of the standard investigatory techniques of law enforcement agencies. They normally occur on the highway, or in a person's home or office, and under informal and unstructured conditions. The circumstances that prompt the initial request to search may develop quickly or be a logical extension of investigative police questioning. The police may seek to investigate further suspicious circumstances or to follow up leads developed in questioning persons at the scene of a crime. These situations are a far cry from the structured atmosphere of a trial where, assisted by counsel if he chooses, a defendant is informed of his trial rights. And, while surely a closer question, these situations are still immeasurably, far removed from "custodial interrogation" where * * * we found that the Constitution required certain now familiar warnings as a prerequisite to police interrogation. * * *

[handwritten margin note: facts will show if consent was gotten voluntarily —]

Consequently, we cannot accept the position of the Court of Appeals in this case that proof of knowledge of the right to refuse consent is a necessary prerequisite to demonstrating a "voluntary" consent. Rather it is only by analyzing all the circumstances of an individual consent that it can be ascertained whether in fact it was voluntary or coerced. It is this careful sifting of the unique facts and circumstances of each case that is evidenced in our prior decisions involving consent searches.

* * *

[I]f under all the circumstances it has appeared that the consent was not given voluntarily—that it was coerced by threats or force, or granted only in submission to a claim of lawful authority—then we have found the consent invalid and the search unreasonable. In *Bumper*, a 66-year-old Negro widow, who lived in a house located in a rural area at the end of an isolated mile-long dirt road, allowed four white law enforcement officials to search her home after they asserted they had a warrant to search the house. We held the alleged consent to be invalid, noting that "[w]hen a law enforcement officer claims authority to search a home under a warrant, he announces in effect that the occupant has no right to resist the search. The situation is instinct with coercion—albeit colorably lawful coercion. Where there is coercion there cannot be consent."

Implicit in all of these cases is the recognition that knowledge of a right to refuse is not a prerequisite of a voluntary consent. If the prosecution were required to demonstrate such knowledge, * * * [the] opinions would surely have focused upon the subjective mental state of the person who consented. Yet they did not.

In short, neither this Court's prior cases, nor the traditional definition of "voluntariness" requires proof of knowledge of a right to refuse as the *sine qua non* of an effective consent to a search.

C.

It is said, however, that a "consent" is a "waiver" of a person's rights under the Fourth and Fourteenth Amendments. The argument is that by allowing the police to conduct a search, a person "waives" whatever right he had to prevent the police from searching. It is argued that under the doctrine of Johnson v. Zerbst, 304 U.S. 458, 464, 58 S.Ct. 1019, 1023, 82 L.Ed. 1461, to establish such a "waiver" the state must demonstrate "an intentional relinquishment or abandonment of a known right or privilege."

But these standards were enunciated in *Johnson* in the context of the safeguards of a fair criminal trial. Our cases do not reflect an uncritical demand for a knowing and intelligent waiver in every situation where a person has failed to invoke a constitutional protection. As Mr. Justice Black once observed for the Court: " 'Waiver' is a vague term used for a great variety of purposes, good and bad, in the law." Green v. United States, 355 U.S. 184, 191, 78 S.Ct. 221, 226, 2 L.Ed.2d 199. * * *

The requirement of a "knowing" and "intelligent" waiver was articulated in a case involving the validity of a defendant's decision to forego a right constitutionally guaranteed to protect a fair trial and the reliability of the truth-determining process. Johnson v. Zerbst, supra, dealt with the denial of counsel in a federal criminal trial. There the Court held that under the Sixth Amendment a criminal defendant is entitled to the assistance of counsel, and that if he lacks sufficient funds to retain counsel, it is the Government's obligation to furnish him with a lawyer. * * * To preserve the fairness of the trial process the Court established an appropriately heavy burden on the government before waiver could be found—"an intentional relinquishment or abandonment of a known right or privilege."

Almost without exception the requirement of a knowing and intelligent waiver has been applied only to those rights which the Constitution guarantees to a criminal defendant in order to preserve a fair trial. Hence, and hardly surprisingly in view of the facts of *Johnson* itself, the standard of a knowing and intelligent waiver has most often been applied to test the validity of a waiver of counsel, either at trial, or upon a guilty plea. And the Court has also applied the *Johnson* criteria to assess the effectiveness of a waiver of other trial rights such as the right to confrontation, to a jury trial and to a speedy trial, and the right to be free from twice being placed in jeopardy. Guilty pleas have been carefully scrutinized to determine whether the accused knew and understood all the rights to which he would be entitled at trial, and that he had intentionally chosen to forego them. And the Court has evaluated the knowing and intelligent nature of the waiver of trial rights in trial-type situations, such as the waiver of the privilege against compulsory self-incrimination before an administrative agency or a congressional committee or the waiver of counsel in a juvenile proceeding.

The guarantees afforded a criminal defendant at trial also protect him at certain stages before the actual trial, and any alleged waiver must meet the strict standard of an intentional relinquishment of a "known" right. But the "trial" guarantees that have been applied to the "pretrial" stage of the criminal process are similarly designed to protect the fairness of the trial itself.

* * *

There is a vast difference between those rights that protect a fair criminal trial and the rights guaranteed under the Fourth Amendment. Nothing, either in the purposes behind requiring a "knowing" and "intelligent" waiver of trial rights, or in the practical application of such a requirement suggests that it ought to be extended to the constitutional guarantee against unreasonable searches and seizures.

A strict standard of waiver has been applied to those rights guaranteed to a criminal defendant to insure that he will be accorded the greatest possible opportunity to utilize every facet of the constitutional model of a fair criminal trial. Any trial conducted in derogation of that model leaves open the possibility that the trial reached an unfair result precisely because all the protections specified in the Constitution were not provided. A prime example is the right to counsel. For without that right, a wholly innocent accused faces the real and substantial danger that simply because of his lack of legal expertise he may be convicted. * * * The Constitution requires that every effort be made to see to it that a defendant in a criminal case has not unknowingly relinquished the basic protections that the Framers thought indispensable to a fair trial.

The protections of the Fourth Amendment are of a wholly different order, and have nothing whatever to do with promoting the fair ascertainment of truth at a criminal trial. Rather, * * * the Fourth Amendment protects the "security of one's privacy against arbitrary intrusion by the police. * * *" * * * The Fourth Amendment "is not an adjunct to the ascertainment of truth." The guarantees of the Fourth Amendment stand "as a protection of quite different constitutional values—values reflecting the concern of our society for the right of each individual to be let alone. To recognize this is no more than to accord those values undiluted respect."

Nor can it even be said that a search, as opposed to an eventual trial, is somehow "unfair" if a person consents to a search. While the Fourth and Fourteenth Amendments limit the circumstances under which the police can conduct a search, there is nothing constitutionally suspect in a person voluntarily allowing a search. The actual conduct of the search may be precisely the same as if the police had obtained a warrant. And, unlike those constitutional guarantees that protect a defendant at trial, it cannot be said every reasonable presumption ought to be indulged against voluntary relinquishment. We have only recently stated: "[I]t is no part of the policy underlying the Fourth and Fourteenth Amendments to discourage citizens from aiding to the utmost of their ability in the apprehension of criminals." Coolidge v. New Hampshire, 403 U.S. 443, 448, 91 S.Ct. 2022, 2049, 29 L.Ed.2d 564. Rather the community has a real interest in encouraging consent, for the resulting search may yield necessary evidence for the solution and prosecution of crime, evidence that may insure that a wholly innocent person is not wrongly charged with a criminal offense.

Those cases that have dealt with the application of the Johnson v. Zerbst rule make clear that it would be next to impossible to apply to a consent search the standard of "an intentional relinquishment or abandonment of a known right or privilege." To be true to *Johnson* and its progeny, there must be examination into the knowing and understanding nature of the waiver, an examination that was designed for a trial judge in the structured atmosphere of a courtroom. * * * It would be unrealistic to expect that in the informal, unstructured context of a consent search a policeman, upon pain of tainting the evidence obtained, could make the detailed type of examination demanded by *Johnson*. And, if for this reason a diluted form of "waiver" were found acceptable, that would itself be ample recognition of the fact that there is no universal standard that must be applied in every situation where a person forgoes a constitutional right.

Similarly, a "waiver" approach to consent searches would be thoroughly inconsistent with our decisions that have approved "third party consents." * * * [I]t is inconceivable that the Constitution could countenance the waiver of a defendant's right to counsel by a third party, or that a waiver could be found because a trial judge reasonably though mistakenly believed a defendant had waived his right to plead not guilty.

In short, there is nothing in the purposes or application of the waiver requirements of Johnson v. Zerbst that justifies, much less compels, the easy equation of a knowing waiver with a consent search. * * *

* * *

E.

Our decision today is a narrow one. We hold only that when the subject of a search is not in custody and the State attempts to justify a search on the basis of his consent, the Fourth and Fourteenth Amendments require that it demonstrate that the consent was in fact voluntarily given, and not the result of duress or coercion, express or implied. Voluntariness is a question of fact to be determined from all the circumstances, and while the subject's knowledge of a right to refuse is a factor to be taken into account, the prosecution is not required to demonstrate such knowledge as a prerequisite to establishing a voluntary consent. Because the California courts followed these principles in affirming the respondent's conviction, and because the Court of Appeals for the Ninth Circuit in remanding for an evidentiary hearing required more, its judgment must be reversed.

It is so ordered.

■ Mr. Justice Marshall, dissenting.

Several years ago, Mr. Justice Stewart reminded us that "[t]he Constitution guarantees * * * a society of free choice. Such a society presupposes the capacity of its members to choose." Ginsberg v. New York, 390 U.S. 629, 649, 88 S.Ct. 1274, 1285, 20 L.Ed.2d 195 (1968) (concurring opinion). I would have thought that the capacity to choose necessarily depends upon knowledge that there is a choice to be made. But today the Court reaches the curious result that one can choose to relinquish a constitutional right—the right to be free of unreasonable searches—without knowing that he has the alternative of refusing to accede to a police request to search. I cannot agree, and therefore dissent.

NOTES

1. **Consent From Person in Custody.** Despite the limitations the Court placed upon its holding in the principal case, the same analysis was soon applied to consent given by an arrested person. United States v. Watson, 423 U.S. 411, 96 S.Ct. 820, 46 L.Ed.2d 598 (1976).

2. **Suspect's Knowledge Search Would be Incriminating.** Does the fact the suspect was likely aware that a search would be fruitful suggest that the suspect's consent to the search was not voluntary? In United States v. Mendenhall, 446 U.S. 544, 100 S.Ct. 1870, 64 L.Ed.2d 497 (1980), Mendenhall was approached by two Drug Enforcement Administration agents at the Detroit Metropolitan Airport and agreed to accompany them to a nearby office. She consented to being searched. When told that the search would require her to remove her clothing, Mendenhall stated she had a plane to catch. The officer, however, assured her that if she were carrying no drugs "there would be no problem." After beginning to disrobe, Mendenhall took two small packages from her undergarments and handed them to the officer. One contained heroin. Upholding a lower court finding that Mendenhall's consent was voluntary, Justice Stewart's plurality opinion rejected the assertion that Mendenhall's consent was involuntary because she would not have voluntarily consented to a search she knew was likely to disclose incriminating narcotics. "[T]he question," he responded, "is not whether [she] acted in her ultimate self-interest, but whether she acted voluntarily." Nevertheless, he also noted the possibility that Mendenhall may have thought she was acting in self-

interest by voluntarily cooperating with the officers in a manner she perceived would result in later more lenient treatment.

3. **Consents During or After Traffic Stops.** Do consents solicited during traffic stops pose special risks justifying special Fourth Amendment requirements? In Ohio v. Robinette, 519 U.S. 33, 117 S.Ct. 417, 136 L.Ed.2d 347 (1996), Deputy Newsome stopped Robinette for speeding, asked for and received his driver's license, and ran a computer check which indicated Robinette had no prior violations.

> Newsome then asked Robinette to step out of his car, turned on his mounted video camera, issued a verbal warning to Robinette, and returned his license.
>
> At this point, Newsome asked, "One question before you get gone: [A]re you carrying any illegal contraband in your car? Any weapons of any kind, drugs, anything like that?" Robinette answered "no" to these questions, after which Deputy Newsome asked if he could search the car. Robinette consented. In the car, Deputy Newsome discovered a small amount of marijuana and, in a film container, a pill which was later determined to be methylenedioxymethamphetamine (MDMA).

The Ohio Supreme Court held the prosecution barred from establishing the consent was "an independent act of free will" by the officer's failure to follow what the court found to be the applicable Fourth Amendment law:

> This case demonstrates the need for this court to draw a bright line between the conclusion of a valid seizure and the beginning of a consensual exchange. * * *
>
> The transition between detention and a consensual exchange can be so seamless that the untrained eye may not notice that it has occurred. The undetectability of that transition may be used by police officers to coerce citizens into answering questions that they need not answer, or to allow a search of a vehicle that they are not legally obligated to allow.
>
> The present case offers an example of the blurring between a legal detention and an attempt at consensual interaction. Even assuming that Newsome's detention of Robinette was legal through the time when Newsome handed back Robinette's driver's license, Newsome then said, "One question *before you get gone*: are you carrying any illegal contraband in your car?" (Emphasis added.) Newsome tells Robinette that before he leaves Newsome wants to know whether Robinette is carrying any contraband. Newsome does not ask if he may ask a question, he simply asks it, implying that Robinette must respond before he may leave. The interrogation then continues. Robinette is never told that he is free to go or that he may answer the question at his option.
>
> Most people believe that they are validly in a police officer's custody as long as the officer continues to interrogate them. The police officer retains the upper hand and the accouterments of authority. That the officer lacks legal license to continue to detain them is unknown to most citizens, and a reasonable person would not feel free to walk away as the officer continues to address him.
>
> We are aware that consensual encounters between police and citizens are an important, and constitutional, investigative tool. However, citizens who have not been detained immediately prior to being encountered and questioned by police are more apt to realize that they need not respond to a police officer's questions. A "consensual encounter" immediately following a detention is likely to be imbued with the authoritative aura of the detention. Without a clear break from the detention, the succeeding encounter is not consensual at all.

Therefore, we are convinced that the right, guaranteed by the federal and Ohio Constitutions, to be secure in one's person and property requires that citizens stopped for traffic offenses be clearly informed by the detaining officer when they are free to go after a valid detention, before an officer attempts to engage in a consensual interrogation. Any attempt at consensual interrogation must be preceded by the phrase "At this time you legally are free to go" or by words of similar import.

73 Ohio St.3d at 654–55, 653 N.E.2d at 698–99.

The United States Supreme Court disagreed:

We have long held that the "touchstone of the Fourth Amendment is reasonableness." Reasonableness, in turn, is measured in objective terms by examining the totality of the circumstances.

In applying this test we have consistently eschewed bright-line rules, instead emphasizing the fact-specific nature of the reasonableness inquiry. * * *

The Fourth Amendment test for a valid consent to search is that the consent be voluntary, and "[v]oluntariness is a question of fact to be determined from all the circumstances." The Supreme Court of Ohio having held otherwise, its judgment is reversed, and the case is remanded for further proceedings not inconsistent with this opinion.

519 U.S. at 39–40, 117 S.Ct. at 421, 136 L.Ed.2d at 354–55.

On remand, the Ohio court assessed the voluntariness of Robinette's consent under *Bustamonte* and *Florida v. Royer* (reprinted in Chapter 4) and concluded that the consent was not voluntary:

Newsome's words did not give Robinette any indication that he was free to go, but rather implied just the opposite—that Robinette was not free to go until he answered Newsome's additional questions. The timing of Newsome's immediate transition from giving Robinette the warning for speeding into questioning regarding contraband and the request to search is troubling. * * *

When these factors are combined with a police officer's superior position of authority, any reasonable person would have felt compelled to submit to the officer's questioning. While Newsome's questioning was not expressly coercive, the circumstances surrounding the request to search made the questioning impliedly coercive. * * * [A]n officer has discretion to issue a ticket rather than a warning to a motorist if the motorist becomes uncooperative. From the totality of the circumstances, it appears that Robinette merely submitted to "a claim of lawful authority" rather than consenting as a voluntary act of free will.

State v. Robinette, 80 Ohio St.3d 234, 244–45, 685 N.E.2d 762, 770–71 (1997).

2. AUTHORITY TO CONSENT: "THIRD PARTY" CONSENTS

EDITORS' INTRODUCTION: CONSENTS GIVEN BY THIRD PARTIES

In a substantial number of cases, law enforcement officers rely on consent provided by persons other than those against whom the discovered evidence is eventually offered at trial. The sufficiency of such consents was addressed in United States v. Matlock, 415 U.S. 164, 94 S.Ct. 988, 39 L.Ed.2d 242 (1974):

This Court left open in Amos v. United States, 255 U.S. 313, 317, 41 S.Ct. 266, 267, 65 L.Ed. 654 (1921), the question whether a wife's permission to search the residence in which she lived with her husband could "waive his constitutional rights," but more recent authority here clearly indicates that the consent of one who possesses common authority over premises or effects is valid as against the absent, nonconsenting person with whom that authority is shared. In Frazier v. Cupp, 394 U.S. 731, 740, 89 S.Ct. 1420, 1425, 22 L.Ed.2d 684 (1969), the Court "dismissed rather quickly" the contention that the consent of the petitioner's cousin to the search of a duffel bag, which was being used jointly by both men and had been left in the cousin's home, would not justify the seizure of petitioner's clothing found inside; joint use of the bag rendered the cousin's authority to consent to the search clear. Indeed, the Court was unwilling to engage in the "metaphysical subtleties" raised by Frazier's claim that his cousin only had permission to use one compartment within the bag. By allowing the cousin the use of the bag, and by leaving it in his house, Frazier was held to have assumed the risk that his cousin would allow someone else to look inside. * * * [W]hen the prosecution seeks to justify a warrantless search by proof of voluntary consent, it is not limited to proof that consent was given by the defendant, but may show that permission to search was obtained from a third party who possessed common authority over or other sufficient relationship to the premises or effect sought to be inspected.

415 U.S. at 170–71, 94 S.Ct. at 993, 39 L.Ed.2d at 249–50. The Court elaborated further:

Common authority is * * * not to be implied from the mere property interest a third party has in the premises. The authority which justifies the third-party consent does not rest upon the law of property, with its attendant historical and legal refinements, see Chapman v. United States, 365 U.S. 610, 81 S.Ct. 776, 5 L.Ed.2d 828 (1961) (landlord could not validly consent to the search of a house he had rented to another), Stoner v. California, 376 U.S. 483, 84 S.Ct. 889, 11 L.Ed.2d 856 (1964) (night hotel clerk could not validly consent to search of customer's room) but rests rather on mutual use of the property by persons generally having joint access or control for most purposes, so that it is reasonable to recognize that any of the cohabitants has the right to permit the inspection in his own right and that the others have assumed the risk that one of their number might permit the common area to be searched.

415 U.S. at 171 n. 7, 94 S.Ct. at 993 n. 7, 39 L.Ed.2d at 250 n. 7.

In *Matlock*, the officers searched a room in a house leased by Mr. and Mrs. Marshall and occupied by Mrs. Marshall, several of her children including Gayle Graff, Graff's three-year old son, and Matlock. Matlock was arrested in the yard. Several officers, without consulting Matlock, went to the door, met Mrs. Graff, and—after telling her they were looking for money and a gun—asked Graff if they could search the house. She consented. While going through an upstairs bedroom occupied by Matlock and Graff, officers found $4,995 in cash concealed in a diaper bag in the only closet in the room. At issue was the admissibility at the hearing on the motion to suppress of Graff's out-of-court statements concerning her joint occupancy of the bedroom and similar statements by both Graff and Matlock representing themselves as husband and wife. After finding the statements were admissible, the Court concluded the Government's evidence was sufficient to prove Graff's consent was "legally sufficient." But since the Court preferred that the trial court first pass on the sufficiency of the evidence in light of the *Matlock* opinion, it remanded the case for such reconsideration.

Suppose, however, the person giving consent lacks authority to give effective authorization for the search? This problem is considered in the following case.

Illinois v. Rodriguez

Supreme Court of the United States, 1990.
497 U.S. 177, 110 S.Ct. 2793, 111 L.Ed.2d 148.

■ JUSTICE SCALIA delivered the opinion of the Court.

In United States v. Matlock, 415 U.S. 164, 94 S.Ct. 988, 39 L.Ed.2d 242 (1974), this Court reaffirmed that a warrantless entry and search by law enforcement officers does not violate the Fourth Amendment's proscription of "unreasonable searches and seizures" if the officers have obtained the consent of a third party who possesses common authority over the premises. The present case presents an issue we expressly reserved in *Matlock*: whether a warrantless entry is valid when based upon the consent of a third party whom the police, at the time of the entry, reasonably believe to possess common authority over the premises, but who in fact does not do so.

I

Respondent Edward Rodriguez was arrested in his apartment by law enforcement officers and charged with possession of illegal drugs. The police gained entry to the apartment with the consent and assistance of Gail Fischer, who had lived there with respondent for several months. The relevant facts leading to the arrest are as follows.

On July 26, 1985, police were summoned to the residence of Dorothy Jackson on South Wolcott in Chicago. They were met by Ms. Jackson's daughter, Gail Fischer, who showed signs of a severe beating. She told the officers that she had been assaulted by respondent Edward Rodriguez earlier that day in an apartment on South California. Fischer stated that Rodriguez was then asleep in the apartment, and she consented to travel there with the police in order to unlock the door with her key so that the officers could enter and arrest him. During this conversation, Fischer several times referred to the apartment on South California as "our" apartment, and said that she had clothes and furniture there. It is unclear whether she indicated that she currently lived at the apartment, or only that she used to live there.

The police officers drove to the apartment on South California, accompanied by Fischer. They did not obtain an arrest warrant for Rodriguez, nor did they seek a search warrant for the apartment. At the apartment, Fischer unlocked the door with her key and gave the officers permission to enter. They moved through the door into the living room, where they observed in plain view drug paraphernalia and containers filled with white powder that they believed (correctly, as later analysis showed) to be cocaine. They proceeded to the bedroom, where they found Rodriguez asleep and discovered additional containers of white powder in two open attache cases. The officers arrested Rodriguez and seized the drugs and related paraphernalia.

Rodriguez was charged with possession of a controlled substance with intent to deliver. He moved to suppress all evidence seized at the time of his arrest, claiming that Fischer had vacated the apartment several weeks earlier and had no authority to consent to the entry. The Cook County Circuit Court granted the motion, holding that at the time she consented to the entry Fischer did not have common authority over the apartment. The Court concluded that Fischer was not a "usual resident" but rather an "infrequent visitor" at the apartment on South California, based upon its findings that Fischer's name was not on the lease, that she did not contribute to the rent, that she was not allowed to invite others to the apartment on her own, that she did not have access to the apartment when respondent was away, and that she had moved some of her possessions from the apartment. The Circuit Court also rejected the State's contention that, even if Fischer did not possess common authority over the premises, there was no Fourth Amendment violation if the police reasonably believed at the time of their entry that Fischer possessed the authority to consent.

The Appellate Court of Illinois affirmed the Circuit Court in all respects. The Illinois Supreme Court denied the State's Petition for Leave to Appeal, and we granted certiorari.

II

The Fourth Amendment generally prohibits the warrantless entry of a person's home, whether to make an arrest or to search for specific objects. The prohibition does not apply, however, to situations in which voluntary consent has been obtained, either from the individual whose property is searched, see Schneckloth v. Bustamonte, 412 U.S. 218, 93 S.Ct. 2041, 36 L.Ed.2d 854 (1973), or from a third party who possesses common authority over the premises. The State of Illinois contends that that exception applies in the present case.

As we stated in *Matlock*, "[c]ommon authority" rests "on mutual use of the property by persons generally having joint access or control for most purposes...." The burden of establishing that common authority rests upon the State. On the basis of this record, it is clear that burden was not sustained. The evidence showed that although Fischer, with her two small children, had lived with Rodriguez beginning in December 1984, she had moved out on July 1, 1985, almost a month before the search at issue here, and had gone to live with her mother. She took her and her children's clothing with her, though leaving behind some furniture and household effects. During the period after July 1 she sometimes spent the night at Rodriguez's apartment, but never invited her friends there, and never went there herself when he was not home. Her name was not on the lease nor did she contribute to the rent. She had a key to the apartment, which she said at trial she had taken without Rodriguez's knowledge (though she testified at the preliminary hearing that Rodriguez had given her the key). On these facts the State has not established that, with respect to the South California apartment, Fischer had "joint access or control for most purposes." To the contrary, the Appellate Court's determination of no common authority over the apartment was obviously correct.

III

A

The State contends that, even if Fischer did not in fact have authority to give consent, it suffices to validate the entry that the law enforcement officers reasonably believed she did. * * *

B

[R]espondent asserts that permitting a reasonable belief of common authority to validate an entry would cause a defendant's Fourth Amendment rights to be "vicariously waived." We disagree. We have been unyielding in our insistence that a defendant's waiver of his trial rights cannot be given effect unless it is "knowing" and "intelligent." We would assuredly not permit, therefore, evidence seized in violation of the Fourth Amendment to be introduced on the basis of a trial court's mere "reasonable belief"—derived from statements by unauthorized persons—that the defendant has waived his objection. But one must make a distinction between, on the one hand, trial rights that derive from the violation of constitutional guarantees and, on the other hand, the nature of those constitutional guarantees themselves. As we said in *Schneckloth*:

> "There is a vast difference between those rights that protect a fair criminal trial and the rights guaranteed under the Fourth Amendment. Nothing, either in the purposes behind requiring a 'knowing' and 'intelligent' waiver of trial rights, or in the practical application of such a requirement suggests that it ought to be extended to the constitutional guarantee against unreasonable searches and seizures."

What Rodriguez is assured by the trial right of the exclusionary rule, where it applies, is that no evidence seized in violation of the Fourth Amendment will be introduced at his trial unless he consents. What he is assured by the Fourth Amendment itself, however, is not that no government search of his house will occur unless he consents; but that no such search will occur that is "unreasonable." U.S. Const., Amdt. 4. There are various elements, of course, that can make a search of a person's house "reasonable"—one of which is the consent of the person or his cotenant. The essence of respondent's argument is that we should impose upon this element a requirement that we have not imposed upon other elements that regularly compel government officers to exercise judgment regarding the facts: namely, the requirement that their judgment be not only responsible but correct.

The fundamental objective that alone validates all unconsented government searches is, of course, the seizure of persons who have committed or are about to commit crimes, or of evidence related to crimes. But "reasonableness," with respect to this necessary element, does not demand that the government be factually correct in its assessment that that is what a search will produce. * * * If a magistrate, based upon seemingly reliable but factually inaccurate information, issues a warrant for the search of a house in which the sought-after felon is not present, has never been present, and was never likely to have been present, the owner of that house suffers one of the inconveniences we all expose ourselves to as the cost of living in a safe society; he does not suffer a violation of the Fourth Amendment.

* * *

It would be superfluous to multiply * * * examples. It is apparent that in order to satisfy the "reasonableness" requirement of the Fourth Amendment, what is generally demanded of the many factual determinations that must regularly be made by agents of the government—whether the magistrate issuing a warrant, the police officer executing a warrant, or the police officer conducting a search or seizure under one of the exceptions to the warrant requirement—is not that they always be correct, but that they always be reasonable. * * *

We see no reason to depart from this general rule with respect to facts bearing upon the authority to consent to a search. Whether the basis for such authority exists is the sort of recurring factual question to which law enforcement officials must be expected to apply their judgment; and all the Fourth Amendment requires is that they answer it reasonably. The Constitution is no more violated when officers enter without a warrant because they reasonably (though erroneously) believe that the person who has consented to their entry is a resident of the premises, than it is violated when they enter without a warrant because they reasonably (though erroneously) believe they are in pursuit of a violent felon who is about to escape.

* * *

[W]hat we hold today does not suggest that law enforcement officers may always accept a person's invitation to enter premises. Even when the invitation is accompanied by an explicit assertion that the person lives there, the surrounding circumstances could conceivably be such that a reasonable person would doubt its truth and not act upon it without further inquiry. As with other factual determinations bearing upon search and seizure, determination of consent to enter must "be judged against an objective standard: would the facts available to the officer at the moment * * * 'warrant a man of reasonable caution in the belief' "that the consenting party had authority over the premises? If not, then warrantless entry without further inquiry is unlawful unless authority actually exists. But if so, the search is valid.

* * *

In the present case, the Appellate Court found it unnecessary to determine whether the officers reasonably believed that Fischer had the authority to consent, because it ruled as a matter of law that a reasonable belief could not validate the entry. Since we find that ruling to be in error, we remand for consideration of that question. The judgment of the Illinois Appellate Court is reversed and remanded for further proceedings not inconsistent with this opinion.

So ordered.

■ JUSTICE MARSHALL, with whom JUSTICE BRENNAN and JUSTICE STEVENS join, dissenting.

* * *

The majority [concludes] that Fischer did not have authority to consent to the officers' entry of Rodriguez's apartment. The Court holds that the warrantless entry into Rodriguez's home was nonetheless valid if the officers reasonably believed that Fischer had authority to consent. The majority's defense of this position rests on a misconception of the basis for third-party consent searches. That such searches do not give rise to claims of constitutional violations rests not on the premise that they are "reasonable" under the Fourth Amendment, but on the premise that a person may voluntarily limit his expectation of privacy by allowing others to exercise authority over his possessions. Thus, an individual's decision to permit another "joint access [to] or control [over the property] for most purposes," United States v. Matlock, 415 U.S. 164, 171, n. 7, 94 S.Ct. 988, 993, n. 7, 39 L.Ed.2d 242 (1974), limits that individual's reasonable expectation of privacy and to that extent limits his Fourth Amendment protections. If an individual has not so limited his expectation of privacy, the police may not dispense with the safeguards established by the Fourth Amendment.

* * *

I

* * * We have * * * held that "a search or seizure carried out on a suspect's premises without a warrant is per se unreasonable, unless the police can show that it falls within one of a carefully defined set of exceptions." Coolidge v. New Hampshire, 403 U.S. 443, 474, 91 S.Ct. 2022, 2042, 29 L.Ed.2d 564 (1971). * * *

The Court has tolerated departures from the warrant requirement only when an exigency makes a warrantless search imperative to the safety of the police and of the community. The Court has often heard, and steadfastly rejected, the invitation to carve out further exceptions to the warrant requirement for searches of the home because of the burdens on police investigation and prosecution of crime. * * *

In the absence of an exigency, then, warrantless home searches and seizures are unreasonable under the Fourth Amendment. The weighty constitutional interest in preventing unauthorized intrusions into the home overrides any law enforcement interest in relying on the reasonable but potentially mistaken belief that a third party has authority to consent to such a search or seizure. Indeed, as the present case illustrates, only the minimal interest in avoiding the inconvenience of obtaining a warrant weighs in on the law enforcement side.

* * *

Unlike searches conducted pursuant to the recognized exceptions to the warrant requirement, third-party consent searches are not based on an exigency and therefore serve no compelling social goal. Police officers, when faced with the choice of relying on consent by a third party or securing a warrant, should secure a warrant, and must therefore accept the risk of error should they instead choose to rely on consent.

II

Our prior cases discussing searches based on third-party consent have never suggested that such searches are "reasonable." * * * As the Court's assumption-of-risk analysis makes clear, third-party consent limits a person's ability to challenge the reasonableness of the search only because that person voluntarily has relinquished some of his expectation of privacy by sharing access or control over his property with another person.

A search conducted pursuant to an officer's reasonable but mistaken belief that a third party had authority to consent is thus on an entirely different constitutional footing from one based on the consent of a third party who in fact has such authority. Even if the officers reasonably believed that Fischer had authority to consent, she did not, and Rodriguez's expectation of privacy was therefore undiminished. Rodriguez accordingly can challenge the warrantless intrusion into his home as a violation of the Fourth Amendment.

* * *

III

Acknowledging that the third party in this case lacked authority to consent, the majority seeks to rely on cases suggesting that reasonable but mistaken factual judgments by police will not invalidate otherwise reasonable searches. The majority reads these cases as establishing a "general rule" that "what is generally demanded of the many factual determinations that must regularly be made by agents of the government—whether the magistrate issuing a warrant, the police officer executing a warrant, or the police officer conducting a search or seizure under one of the exceptions to the warrant requirement—is not that they always be correct, but that they always be reasonable."

The majority's assertion, however, is premised on the erroneous assumption that third-party consent searches are generally reasonable. The cases the majority cites thus provide no support for its holding. * * * Because reasonable factual errors by law enforcement officers will not validate unreasonable searches, the reasonableness of the officer's mistaken belief that the third party had authority to consent is irrelevant.

* * *

IV

* * *

Instead of judging the validity of consent searches, as we have in the past, based on whether a defendant has in fact limited his expectation of privacy, the Court today carves out an additional exception to the warrant requirement for third-party consent searches without pausing to consider whether " 'the exigencies of the situation' make the needs of law enforcement so compelling that the warrantless search is objectively reasonable under the Fourth Amendment." Where this freefloating creation of "reasonable" exceptions to the warrant requirement will end, now that the Court has departed from the balancing approach that has long been part of our Fourth Amendment jurisprudence, is unclear. But by allowing a person to be subjected to a warrantless search in his home without his consent and without exigency, the majority has taken away some of the liberty that the Fourth Amendment was designed to protect.

NOTE

On remand, the Illinois Appellate Court remanded the case to the trial court for a factual hearing. The trial judge noted that Rodriguez had not been in further "trouble," and suggested the State reduce the charge. The State did so and Rodriguez pled guilty. Therefore, the Illinois courts did not further consider admissibility of the evidence seized during the search of the apartment. Interview with James W. Reilly, counsel for Edward Rodriguez.

3. SCOPE OF CONSENT

If effective consent was given by a person with authority to provide it, defining the scope of that consent may present further problems. How extensive and intrusive a search is supported by particular words of consent? How should a court approach the task of construing words constituting consent to a search of some sort? The Supreme Court addressed these issues in the following case.

Florida v. Jimeno

Supreme Court of the United States, 1991.
500 U.S. 248, 111 S.Ct. 1801, 114 L.Ed.2d 297.

■ CHIEF JUSTICE REHNQUIST delivered the opinion of the Court.

* * *

This case began when a Dade County police officer, Frank Trujillo, overheard respondent, Enio Jimeno, arranging what appeared to be a drug transaction over a public telephone. Believing that respondent might be involved in illegal drug trafficking, Officer Trujillo followed his car. The officer observed respondent make a right turn at a red light without stopping. He then pulled respondent over to the side of the road in order to issue him a traffic citation. Officer Trujillo told respondent that he had been stopped for committing a traffic infraction. The officer went on to say that he had reason to believe that respondent was carrying narcotics in his car, and asked permission to search the car. He explained that respondent did not have to consent to a search of the car. Respondent stated that he had nothing to hide, and gave Trujillo permission to search the automobile. After two passengers stepped out of respondent's car, Officer Trujillo went to the passenger side, opened the door, and saw a folded, brown paper bag on the floorboard. The officer picked up the bag, opened it, and found a kilogram of cocaine inside.

Respondent was charged with possession with intent to distribute cocaine in violation of Florida law. Before trial, he moved to suppress the cocaine found in the bag on the ground that his consent to search the car did not extend to the closed paper bag inside of the car. The trial court granted the motion. It found that although respondent "could have assumed that the officer would have searched the bag" at the time he gave his consent, his mere consent to search the car did not carry with it specific consent to open the bag and examine its contents.

The Florida District Court of Appeal affirmed the trial court's decision to suppress the evidence of the cocaine. In doing so, the court established a *per se* rule that "consent to a general search for narcotics does not extend to 'sealed containers within the general area agreed to by the defendant.'" The Florida Supreme Court affirmed, relying upon its decision in State v. Wells, 539 So.2d 464 (1989) aff'd on other grounds, 495 U.S. 1, 110 S.Ct. 1632, 109 L.Ed.2d 1 (1990). We granted certiorari to determine whether consent to search a vehicle may extend to closed containers found inside the vehicle * * * and we now reverse the judgment of the Supreme Court of Florida.

The touchstone of the Fourth Amendment is reasonableness. The Fourth Amendment does not proscribe all state-initiated searches and seizures; it merely proscribes those which are unreasonable. Thus, we have long approved consensual searches because it is no doubt reasonable for the police to conduct a search once they have been permitted to do so. The standard for measuring the scope of a suspect's consent under the Fourth Amendment is that of "objective" reasonableness—what would the typical reasonable person have understood by the exchange between the officer and the suspect? The question before us, then, is whether it is reasonable for an officer to consider a suspect's general consent to a search of his car to include consent to examine a paper bag lying on the floor of the car. We think that it is.

The scope of a search is generally defined by its expressed object. In this case, the terms of the search's authorization were simple. Respondent granted Officer Trujillo permission to search his car, and did not place any explicit limitation on the scope of the search. Trujillo had informed respondent that he believed respondent was carrying narcotics, and that he would be looking for narcotics in the car. We think that it was objectively reasonable for the police to conclude that the general consent to search respondent's car included consent to search containers within that car which might bear drugs. A reasonable person may be expected to know that narcotics are generally carried in some form of a container. "Contraband goods rarely are strewn across the trunk or floor of a car." The authorization to search in this case, therefore, extended beyond the surfaces of the car's interior to the paper bag lying on the car's floor.

The facts of this case are therefore different from those in State v. Wells, supra, on which the Supreme Court of Florida relied in affirming the suppression order in this case. There the Supreme Court of Florida held that consent to search the trunk of a car did not include authorization to pry open a locked briefcase found inside the trunk. It is very likely unreasonable to think that a suspect, by consenting to the search of his trunk, has agreed to the breaking open of a locked briefcase within the trunk, but it is otherwise with respect to a closed paper bag.

Respondent argues, and the Florida trial court agreed with him, that if the police wish to search closed containers within a car they must separately request permission to search each container. But we see no basis for adding this sort of superstructure to the Fourth Amendment's basic test of objective reasonableness. A suspect may of course delimit as he chooses the scope of the search to which he consents. But if his consent would reasonably be understood to extend to a particular container, the Fourth Amendment provides no grounds for requiring a more explicit authorization. * * *

The judgment of the Supreme Court of Florida is accordingly reversed, and the case remanded for further proceedings not inconsistent with this opinion.

It is so ordered.

■ JUSTICE MARSHALL, with whom JUSTICE STEVENS joins, dissenting.

[A]nalysis of this question must start by identifying the differing expectations of privacy that attach to cars and closed containers. It is well established that an individual has but a limited expectation of privacy in the interior of his car. * * * In contrast, it is equally well established that an individual has a heightened expectation of privacy in the contents of a closed container. Luggage, handbags, paper bags, and other containers are common repositories for one's papers and effects, and the protection of these items from state intrusion lies at the heart of the Fourth Amendment. * * *

The distinct privacy expectations that a person has in a car as opposed to a closed container do not merge when the individual uses his car to transport the container. * * *

Because an individual's expectation of privacy in a container is distinct from, and far greater than, his expectation of privacy in the interior of his car, it follows that an individual's consent to a search of the interior of his car cannot necessarily be understood as extending to containers in the car. At the very least, general consent to search the car is ambiguous with respect to containers found inside the car. In my view, the independent and divisible nature of the privacy interests in cars and containers mandates that a police officer who wishes to search a suspicious container found during a consensual automobile search obtain additional consent to search the container. If the driver intended to authorize search of the container, he will say so; if not, then he will say no.[4] The only objection that the police could have to such a rule is that it would prevent them from exploiting the ignorance of a citizen who simply did not anticipate that his consent to search the car would be understood to authorize the police to rummage through his packages.

* * *

I dissent.

D.   SEARCHES AND SEIZURES OF VEHICLES

Searches and seizures of vehicles have probably given rise to more difficulties than any other category of searches. In all of its vehicle search or seizure case law, the Supreme court has assumed citizens' privacy interest in vehicles and their contents is less than their privacy in homes and some other places:

> One has a lesser expectation of privacy in a motor vehicle because its function is transportation and it seldom serves as one's residence or as the repository of personal effects. A car has little capacity for escaping public scrutiny. It travels public thoroughfares where both its occupants and its contents are in plain view.

Cardwell v. Lewis, 417 U.S. 583, 590, 94 S.Ct. 2464, 2469, 41 L.Ed.2d 325, 335 (1974) (opinion of Blackmun, J., announcing the judgment of the Court).

Searches of vehicles may be permissible under several doctrines. The right to search a car "incident to" the arrest of a person in the car was considered in Chapter 4, as was the right to make a weapons search of some cars during nonarrest confrontations between officers and citizens. This chapter addresses two additional aspects of vehicle searches. The first subsection that follows presents the traditional "vehicle exception" to the requirement of a search warrant; the second subsection considers officers' ability to search containers found in vehicles searched under this doctrine.

1.   THE "VEHICLE" EXCEPTION TO THE SEARCH WARRANT REQUIREMENTS

EDITORS' INTRODUCTION: "AUTOMOBILE" OR "VEHICLE" EXCEPTION

In two early cases, the Supreme Court recognized a right on the part of law enforcement officers to conduct warrantless searches of automobiles independent of any right the officers may have to arrest occupants. In Carroll v. United States, 267 U.S. 132, 45 S.Ct. 280, 69 L.Ed. 543 (1925), officers observed a car coming from the direction of Detroit, which they knew to be a location where much illicit liquor entered the United States. Several months earlier the officers, acting undercover, met with two men

---

4. Alternatively, the police could obtain such consent in advance by asking the indi-   vidual for permission to search both the car and any closed containers found inside.

who agreed to sell them illicit liquor; the men came to the meeting in the same automobile. The officers stopped the car and searched it; they found 68 bottles of illicit liquor concealed under the seat upholstery. Finding the search reasonable, the Supreme Court noted there is

> a necessary difference between a search of a store, dwelling house or other structure in respect of which a proper official warrant readily may be obtained, and a search of a ship, motor boat, wagon or automobile for contraband goods, where it is not practicable to secure a warrant because the vehicle can be quickly moved out of the locality or jurisdiction in which the warrant must be sought.

267 U.S. at 153, 45 S.Ct. at 285, 69 L.Ed. at 551. The right of those using public highways to free passage without interruption or search, it continued, is adequately protected by the prohibition against search of vehicles "unless there is known to a competent official authorized to search, probable cause for believing that their vehicles are carrying contraband or illegal merchandise." Transporting the liquor was in violation of the National Prohibition Act. Those transporting it were guilty of a criminal offense; the first two offenses were misdemeanors but a third conviction constituted a felony. Carroll urged that federal law permitted a warrantless arrest for a misdemeanor only if the offense was committed in the officers' presence and consequently that the officers lacked authority to arrest him without a warrant. It followed, he argued, the officers should not be permitted to make a warrantless search related to a crime for which no warrantless arrest was permissible. The Court responded:

> The argument of defendants is based on the theory that the seizure in this case can only be * * * justified [on the ground that it was incident to a lawful arrest]. If their theory were sound, their conclusion would be. The validity of the seizure would turn wholly on the validity of the arrest without a seizure. But the theory is unsound. The right to search and the validity of the seizure are not dependent on the right to arrest. They are dependent on the reasonable cause the seizing officers has for belief that the contents of the automobile offend against the law. The seizure in such a proceeding comes before the arrest * * *. The character of the offense for which, after the contraband liquor is found and seized, the driver can be prosecuted does not affect the validity of the seizure.

267 U.S. at 158–59, 45 S.Ct. at 287, 69 L.Ed. at 553–54. The *Carroll* approach was reaffirmed in the second leading case, Brinegar v. United States, 338 U.S. 160, 69 S.Ct. 1302, 93 L.Ed. 1879 (1949), involving similar facts.

Chief Justice Burger's opinion for the Court in California v. Carney, 471 U.S. 386, 105 S.Ct. 2066, 85 L.Ed.2d 406 (1985), traced the evolution of the rationale for the vehicle exception as follows:

> [A]lthough ready mobility alone was perhaps the original justification for the vehicle exception, our later cases have made clear that ready mobility is not the only basis for the exception. The reasons for the vehicle exception, we have said, are twofold. "Besides the element of mobility, less rigorous warrant requirements govern because the expec-

tation of privacy with respect to one's automobile is significantly less than that relating to one's home or office." [South Dakota v. Opperman, 428 U.S. 364, 367, 96 S.Ct. 3092, 49 L.Ed.2d 1000 (1976)].

* * *

These reduced expectations of privacy derive not from the fact that the area to be searched is in plain view, but from the pervasive regulation of vehicles capable of traveling on the public roadway. As we explained in South Dakota v. Opperman * * * :

> "Automobiles, unlike homes, are subjected to pervasive and continuing governmental regulations and controls, including periodic inspection and licensing requirements. As an everyday occurrence, police stop and examine vehicles when license plates or inspection stickers have expired, or if other violations, such as exhaust fumes or excessive noise, are noted, or if headlights or other safety equipment are not in proper working order."

The public is fully aware that it is accorded less privacy in its automobiles because of this compelling governmental need for regulation. Historically, "individuals always [have] been on notice that movable vessels may be stopped and searched on facts giving rise to probable cause that the vehicle contains contraband, without the protection afforded by a magistrate's prior evaluation of those facts." [United States v.] Ross, [456 U.S. 798, 806 n. 8, 102 S.Ct. 2157, 2163 n. 8, 72 L.Ed.2d 572, 582 n. 8 (1982)].

471 U.S. at 391–92, 105 S.Ct. at 2069–70, 85 L.Ed.2d at 413–14.

[handwritten margin note: * public is aware]

Chambers v. Maroney

Supreme Court of the United States, 1970.
399 U.S. 42, 90 S.Ct. 1975, 26 L.Ed.2d 419.

■ MR. JUSTICE WHITE delivered the opinion of the Court.

[handwritten margin note: Issue →]

The principal question in this case concerns the admissibility of evidence seized from an automobile, in which petitioner was riding at the time of his arrest, after the automobile was taken to a police station and was there thoroughly searched without a warrant.

* * *

I

During the night of May 20, 1963, a Gulf service station in North Braddock, Pennsylvania, was robbed by two men, each of whom carried and displayed a gun. The robbers took the currency from the cash register; the service station attendant, one Stephen Kovacich, was directed to place the coins in his righthand glove, which was then taken by the robbers. Two teenagers, who had earlier noticed a blue compact station wagon circling the block in the vicinity of the Gulf station, then saw the station wagon speed away from a parking lot close to the Gulf station. About the same time, they learned that the Gulf station had been robbed. They reported to police, who arrived immediately, that four men were in the station wagon and one was wearing a green sweater. Kovacich told the police that one of the men who robbed him was wearing a green sweater and the other was wearing a trench coat. A description of the car and the two robbers was broadcast over the police radio. Within an hour, a light blue compact station wagon answering the description and carrying four men was stopped by the police about two miles from the Gulf station. Petitioner was one of the men in the station wagon. He was wearing a green sweater and there was a trench coat in the car. The occupants were arrested and the car was driven to the police station. In the course of a thorough search of the car at the station, the police found concealed in a compartment under the dashboard two .38 caliber revolvers (one loaded with dumdum bullets), a righthand glove containing small change, and certain cards bearing the name of Raymond Havicon, the attendant at a Boron service station in McKeesport, Pennsylvania, who had been robbed at gunpoint on May 13, 1963. * * *

Petitioner was indicted for both robberies. * * * The materials taken from the station wagon were introduced into evidence, Kovacich identifying his glove and Havicon the cards taken in the May 13 robbery. Petitioner was sentenced to a term of four to eight years' imprisonment for the May 13 robbery and to a term of two to seven years' imprisonment for the May 20 robbery, the sentences to run consecutively. Petitioner did not take a direct appeal from these convictions. In 1965, petitioner sought a writ of habeas corpus in the state court, which denied the writ after a brief evidentiary hearing; the denial of the writ was affirmed on appeal in the Pennsylvania appellate courts. Habeas corpus proceedings were then commenced in the United States District Court for the Western District of Pennsylvania. An order to show cause was issued. Based on the State's response and the state court record, the petition for habeas corpus was denied without a hearing. The Court of Appeals for the Third Circuit affirmed and we granted certiorari.

II

We pass quickly the claim that the search of the automobile was the fruit of an unlawful arrest. Both the courts below thought the arresting officers had probable cause to make the arrest. We agree. Having talked to the teenage observers and to the victim Kovacich, the police had ample cause to stop a light blue compact station wagon carrying four men and to arrest the occupants, one of whom was wearing a green sweater and one of whom had a trench coat with him in the car.

Even so, the search that produced the incriminating evidence was made at the police station some time after the arrest and cannot be justified as a search incident to an arrest: "Once an accused is under arrest and in custody, then a search made at another place, without a warrant, is simply not incident to the arrest." Preston v. United States, 376 U.S. 364, 367, 84 S.Ct. 881, 883, 11 L.Ed.2d 777 (1964).

There are, however alternative grounds arguably justifying the search of the car in this case. * * * Here * * * the police had probable cause to believe that the robbers, carrying guns and the fruits of the crime, had fled the scene in a light blue compact station wagon which would be carrying four men, one wearing a green sweater and another wearing a trench coat. As the state courts correctly held, there was probable cause to arrest the occupants of the station wagon that the officers stopped; just as obviously was there probable cause to search the car for guns and stolen money.

In terms of the circumstances justifying a warrantless search, the Court has long distinguished between an automobile and a home or office. In Carroll v. United States, 267 U.S. 132, 45 S.Ct. 280, 69 L.Ed. 543 (1925), the issue was the admissibility in evidence of contraband liquor seized in a warrantless search of a car on the highway. After surveying the law from the time of the adoption of the Fourth Amendment onward, the Court held that automobiles and other conveyances may be searched without a warrant in circumstances that would not justify the search without a warrant of a house or an office, provided that there is probable cause to believe that the car contains articles that the officers are entitled to seize. * * * Finding that there was probable cause for the search and seizure at issue before it, the Court affirmed the convictions.

* * *

Neither *Carroll,* supra, nor other cases in this Court require or suggest that in every conceivable circumstance the search of an auto even with probable cause may be made without the extra protection for privacy that a warrant affords. But the circumstances that furnish probable cause to search a particular auto for particular articles are most often unforeseeable; moreover, the opportunity to search is fleeting since a car is readily movable. Where this is true, as in *Carroll* and the case before us now, if an effective search is to be made at any time, either the search must be made immediately without a warrant or the car itself must be seized and held without a warrant for whatever period is necessary to obtain a warrant for the search.

In enforcing the Fourth Amendment's prohibition against unreasonable searches and seizures, the Court has insisted upon probable cause as a minimum requirement for a reasonable search permitted by the Constitution. As a general rule, it has also required the judgment of a magistrate on the probable-cause issue and the issuance of a warrant before a search is made. Only in exigent circumstances will the judgment of the police as to probable cause serve as a sufficient authorization for a search. *Carroll,* supra, holds a search warrant unnecessary where there is probable cause to search an automobile stopped on the highway; the car is movable, the occupants are alerted, and the car's contents may never be found again if a warrant must be obtained. Hence an immediate search is constitutionally permissible. * * *[5]

* * *

Arguably, because of the preference for a magistrate's judgment, only the immobilization of the car should be permitted until a search warrant is

---

5. Following the car until a warrant can be obtained seems an impractical alternative since, among other things, the car may be taken out of the jurisdiction. Tracing the car and searching it hours or days later would of course permit instruments or fruits of crime to be removed from the car before the search.

obtained; arguably, only the "lesser" intrusion is permissible until the magistrate authorizes the "greater." But which is the "greater" and which the "lesser" intrusion is itself a debatable question and the answer may depend on a variety of circumstances. For constitutional purposes, we see no difference between on the one hand seizing and holding a car before presenting the probable cause issue to a magistrate and on the other hand carrying out an immediate search without a warrant. Given probable cause to search, either course is reasonable under the Fourth Amendment.

On the facts before us, the blue station wagon could have been searched on the spot when it was stopped since there was probable cause to search and it was a fleeting target for a search. The probable cause factor still obtained at the station house and so did the mobility of the car unless the Fourth Amendment permits a warrantless seizure of the car and the denial of its use to anyone until a warrant is secured. In that event there is little to choose in terms of practical consequences between an immediate search without a warrant and the car's immobilization until a warrant is obtained.[6] The same consequences may not follow where there is unforeseeable cause to search a house. But as *Carroll*, supra, held, for the purposes of the Fourth Amendment there is a constitutional difference between houses and cars.

Constitutional Difference between a house + car

* * *

Affirmed.

■ MR. JUSTICE HARLAN, concurring in part and dissenting in part.

* * *

Where officers have probable cause to search a vehicle on a public way, a * * * limited exception to the warrant requirement is reasonable * * * . I agree with the Court that they should be permitted to take the steps necessary to preserve evidence and to make a search possible. The Court holds that those steps include making a warrantless search of the entire vehicle on the highway * * * and indeed appears to go further and to condone the removal of the car to the police station for a warrantless search there at the convenience of the police. I cannot agree that this result is consistent with our insistence in other areas that departures from the warrant requirement strictly conform to the exigency presented.

[I]n the circumstances in which this problem is likely to occur the lesser intrusion will almost always be the simple seizure of the car for the period—perhaps a day—necessary to enable the officers to obtain a search warrant. * * * To be sure, one can conceive of instances in which the occupant, having nothing to hide and lacking concern for the privacy of the automobile, would be more deeply offended by a temporary immobilization of his vehicle than by a prompt search of it. However, such a person always remains free to consent to an immediate search, thus avoiding any delay.

---

6. It was not unreasonable in this case to take the car to the station house. All occupants in the car were arrested in a dark parking lot in the middle of the night. A careful search at that point was impractical and perhaps not safe for the officers, and it would serve the owner's convenience and the safety of his car to have the vehicle and the keys together at the station house.

Where consent is not forthcoming, the occupants of the car have an interest in privacy that is protected by the Fourth Amendment even where the circumstances justify a temporary seizure. * * * The Court's endorsement of a warrantless invasion of that privacy where another course would suffice is simply inconsistent with our repeated stress on the Fourth Amendment's mandate of "adherence to judicial processes."[7]

* * *

NOTES

1. The lower courts' occasional failures to fully grasp the scope of the vehicle exception was made clear in Pennsylvania v. Labron, 518 U.S. 938, 116 S.Ct. 2485, 135 L.Ed.2d 1031 (1996)(per curiam), involving two cases in which the Pennsylvania Supreme Court construed the United States Supreme Court's case law as requiring for the search of an automobile both probable cause and the presence of exigent circumstances. Summarily reversing, the United States Supreme Court majority explained:

> The Supreme Court of Pennsylvania held the rule permitting warrantless searches of automobiles is limited to cases where " 'unforeseen circumstances involving the search of an automobile [are] coupled with the presence of probable cause.' " (emphasis deleted). This was incorrect. * * * If a car is readily mobile and probable cause exists to believe it contains contraband, the Fourth Amendment * * * permits the police to search the vehicle without more.

518 U.S. at 940, 116 S.Ct. at 2487, 135 L.Ed.2d at 1035–36.

On remand, the Pennsylvania Supreme Court reinstated its original order in *Labron*, explaining that this order had in fact been based on article I, section 8 of the Pennsylvania Constitution: "The people shall be secure in their persons, houses, papers and possessions from unreasonable searches and seizures * * *." Case law applying the state provision, the court stressed, has long required both the existence of probable cause and the presence of exigent circumstances to justify a warrantless search of an automobile. Commonwealth v. Labron, 547 Pa. 344, 690 A.2d 228 (1997).

2. **Vehicles Subject to Search.** What vehicles are within the exception? In California v. Carney, 471 U.S. 386, 105 S.Ct. 2066, 85 L.Ed.2d 406 (1985), DEA agents received uncorroborated information that Carney's Dodge Mini Motor Home was being used by someone else for purposes of exchanging marihuana for sex. An agent observed Carney approach a youth in downtown San Diego; the two went to Carney's motor home, parked in a nearby lot. The shades of the motor home were drawn and the youth remained in it for about one and one-quarter hours. After the youth left, the agents stopped him and elicited from him that he had received marihuana in return for allowing Carney sexual contacts. At the agent's request, the youth knocked on the motor home door. Carney came out. An agent immediately entered and observed marihuana and related items. The Supreme Court, in an

---

7. Circumstances might arise in which it would be impracticable to immobilize the car for the time required to obtain a warrant—for example, where a single police officer must take arrested suspects to the station, and has no way of protecting the suspects' car during his absence. In such situations it might be wholly reasonable to perform an on-the-spot search based on probable cause. However, where nothing in the situation makes impracticable the obtaining of a warrant, I cannot join the Court in shunting aside that vital Fourth Amendment safeguard.

opinion by Chief Justice Burger, held the motor home was within the vehicle exception:

> While it is true that [Carney's] vehicle possessed some, if not many of the attributes of a home, it is equally clear that the vehicle falls clearly within the scope of the exception * * *. Like the automobile in *Carroll*, [Carney's] motor home was readily mobile. Absent the prompt search and seizure, it could readily have been moved beyond the reach of the police. Furthermore, the vehicle was licensed to "operate on public streets; [was] serviced in public places; ...and [was] subject to extensive regulation and inspection." Rakas v. Illinois, 439 U.S. 128, 154, n. 2, 99 S.Ct. 421, 436, n. 2, 58 L.Ed.2d 387 (1978) (Powell, J., concurring). And the vehicle was so situated that an objective observer would conclude that it was being used not as a residence, but as a vehicle. * * *
>
> Our application of the vehicle exception has never turned on the other uses to which a vehicle might be put. * * *

471 U.S. at 393–94, 105 S.Ct. at 2070, 85 L.Ed.2d at 414–15. The Court added:

> We need not pass on the application of the vehicle exception to a motor home that is situated in a way or place that objectively indicates that it is being used as a residence. Among the factors that might be relevant in determining whether a warrant would be required in such a circumstance is its location, whether the vehicle is readily mobile or instead, for instance, elevated on blocks, whether the vehicle is licensed, whether it is connected to utilities, and whether it has convenient access to a public road.

471 U.S. at 394 n. 3, 105 S.Ct. at 2071 n. 3, 85 L.Ed.2d at 415 n. 3. The information available to the agents, the Court also concluded, gave them "abundant probable cause" to enter and search the vehicle for evidence of a crime. As a result, the search was "reasonable" for Fourth Amendment purposes.

3. **Vehicles Parked in Public Places.** Does *Carney* also signal another expansion of the exception? Officers did not stop Carney's motor home but instead came upon it parked in an off-the-street lot. The Court's opinion equated "a vehicle * * * being used on the highways"—like those in *Carroll* and *Chambers*—with one—like Carney's motor home—"readily capable of such use and * * * found stationary in a place not regularly used for residential purposes." Justice Stevens commented:

> Until today, * * * the Court has never decided whether the practical justifications that apply to a vehicle stopped in transit on a public way apply with the same force to a vehicle parked in a lot near a court house where it could easily be detained while a warrant is issued.

471 U.S. at 403, 105 S.Ct. at 2075, 85 L.Ed.2d at 421 (Stevens, J., dissenting).

2. SEARCHES OF CONTAINERS FOUND IN VEHICLES

In United States v. Chadwick, 433 U.S. 1, 97 S.Ct. 2476, 53 L.Ed.2d 538 (1977), discussed in subsection B(2) of Chapter 2, the Supreme Court held that in some circumstances officers may seize a "container" but not search it until they obtain a search warrant. Court have had particular difficulty applying *Chadwick* to containers found in vehicles. Issues of this sort have been considered already. New York v. Belton, reprinted in subsection B(2) of Chapter 4 considered an officer's right to search a container found in a vehicle that is being searched incident to a valid custodial arrest. This subsection focuses on containers in vehicles searched pursuant to the doctrine developed in Chambers v. Maroney.

The Supreme Court's struggle to properly develop *Chadwick* in this context, culminating in the principal case in this subsection, was reflected in several major cases decided between *Chadwick* and the principal case. Arkansas v. Sanders, 442 U.S. 753, 99 S.Ct. 2586, 61 L.Ed.2d 235 (1979), illustrates the Court's initial approach.

In *Sanders*, an informant of demonstrated reliability told a Little Rock officer that Sanders—who was known to both the informant and the officer—would arrive at a specific gate at the Municipal Airport that afternoon and would be carrying a green suitcase containing marihuana. During surveillance, the officers observed Sanders's arrival at the designated gate and followed him while he met another man and obtained a green suitcase from the airline baggage. Sanders and the other man hailed a taxi, placed the green suitcase in the trunk, and entered the taxi. Several blocks from the airport, the officers stopped the taxi, retrieved the green suitcase from the trunk, and searched it. They found marihuana. The Supreme Court concluded the officers had probable cause to believe the suitcase contained marihuana and that they acted properly in seizing the suitcase. But, it continued, search of the suitcase without a warrant offended the Fourth Amendment:

> A closed suitcase in the trunk of an automobile may be as mobile as the automobile in which it rides. But * * * the exigencies of mobility must be assessed at the point immediately before the search—after the police have seized the object to be searched and have it securely within their control. Once police have seized a suitcase, as they did here, the extent of its mobility is in no way affected by the place from which it was taken. Accordingly as a general rule there is no greater need for warrantless searches of luggage taken from automobiles than of luggage taken from other places.

442 U.S. at 763–64, 99 S.Ct. at 2593, 61 L.Ed.2d at 244–45. This approach was reconsidered in the principal case that follows.

California v. Acevedo

Supreme Court of the United States, 1991.
500 U.S. 565, 111 S.Ct. 1982, 114 L.Ed.2d 619.

■ JUSTICE BLACKMUN delivered the opinion of the Court.

This case requires us once again to consider the so-called "automobile exception" to the warrant requirement of the Fourth Amendment and its application to the search of a closed container in the trunk of a car.

I

On October 28, 1987, Officer Coleman of the Santa Ana, Cal., Police Department received a telephone call from a federal drug enforcement agent in Hawaii. The agent informed Coleman that he had seized a package containing marijuana which was to have been delivered to the Federal Express Office in Santa Ana and which was addressed to J.R. Daza at 805

West Stevens Avenue in that city. The agent arranged to send the package to Coleman instead. Coleman then was to take the package to the Federal Express office and arrest the person who arrived to claim it.

Coleman received the package on October 29, verified its contents, and took it to the Senior Operations Manager at the Federal Express office. At about 10:30 a.m. on October 30, a man, who identified himself as Jamie Daza, arrived to claim the package. He accepted it and drove to his apartment on West Stevens. He carried the package into the apartment.

At 11:45 a.m., officers observed Daza leave the apartment and drop the box and paper that had contained the marijuana into a trash bin. Coleman at that point left the scene to get a search warrant. About 12:05 p.m., the officers saw Richard St. George leave the apartment carrying a blue knapsack which appeared to be half full. The officers stopped him as he was driving off, searched the knapsack, and found 1½ pounds of marijuana.

At 12:30 p.m., respondent Charles Steven Acevedo arrived. He entered Daza's apartment, stayed for about 10 minutes, and reappeared carrying a brown paper bag that looked full. The officers noticed that the bag was the size of one of the wrapped marijuana packages sent from Hawaii. Acevedo walked to a silver Honda in the parking lot. He placed the bag in the trunk of the car and started to drive away. Fearing the loss of evidence, officers in a marked police car stopped him. They opened the trunk and the bag, and found marijuana.

Respondent was charged in state court with possession of marijuana for sale * * *. He moved to suppress the marijuana found in the car. The motion was denied. He then pleaded guilty but appealed the denial of the suppression motion.

The California Court of Appeal, Fourth District, concluded that the marijuana found in the paper bag in the car's trunk should have been suppressed. * * *

The Supreme Court of California denied the State's petition for review. * * *

We granted certiorari to reexamine the law applicable to a closed container in an automobile, a subject that has troubled courts and law enforcement officers since it was first considered in [United States v. Chadwick, 433 U.S. 1, 97 S.Ct. 2476, 53 L.Ed.2d 538 (1977)].

II

* * *

In United States v. Ross, 456 U.S. 798, 102 S.Ct. 2157, 72 L.Ed.2d 572, decided in 1982, we held that a warrantless search of an automobile under the *Carroll* doctrine could include a search of a container or package found inside the car when such a search was supported by probable cause. The warrantless search of Ross' car occurred after an informant told the police that he had seen Ross complete a drug transaction using drugs stored in the trunk of his car. The police stopped the car, searched it, and discovered in the trunk a brown paper bag containing drugs. We decided that the search of Ross' car was not unreasonable under the Fourth Amendment:

Scope of Search based on probable cause

"The scope of a warrantless search based on probable cause is no narrower—and no broader—than the scope of a search authorized by a warrant supported by probable cause." Thus, "[i]f probable cause justifies the search of a lawfully stopped vehicle, it justifies the search of every part of the vehicle and its contents that may conceal the object of the search." In *Ross*, therefore, we clarified the scope of the *Carroll* doctrine as properly including a "probing search" of compartments and containers within the automobile so long as the search is supported by probable cause.

In addition to this clarification, *Ross* distinguished the *Carroll* doctrine from the separate rule that governed the search of closed containers. The Court had announced this separate rule, unique to luggage and other closed packages, bags, and containers, in United States v. Chadwick. In *Chadwick*, federal narcotics agents had probable cause to believe that a 200–pound double-locked footlocker contained marijuana. The agents tracked the locker as the defendants removed it from a train and carried it through the station to a waiting car. As soon as the defendants lifted the locker into the trunk of the car, the agents arrested them, seized the locker, and searched it. In this Court, the United States did not contend that the locker's brief contact with the automobile's trunk sufficed to make the *Carroll* doctrine applicable. Rather, the United States urged that the search of movable luggage could be considered analogous to the search of an automobile.

The Court rejected this argument because, it reasoned, a person expects more privacy in his luggage and personal effects than he does in his automobile. Moreover, it concluded that as "may often not be the case when automobiles are seized," secure storage facilities are usually available when the police seize luggage.

In Arkansas v. Sanders, 442 U.S. 753, 99 S.Ct. 2586, 61 L.Ed.2d 235 (1979), the Court extended *Chadwick's* rule to apply to a suitcase actually being transported in the trunk of a car. In *Sanders*, the police had probable cause to believe a suitcase contained marijuana. They watched as the defendant placed the suitcase in the trunk of a taxi and was driven away. The police pursued the taxi for several blocks, stopped it, found the suitcase in the trunk, and searched it. Although the Court had applied the *Carroll* doctrine to searches of integral parts of the automobile itself, (indeed, in *Carroll*, contraband whiskey was in the upholstery of the seats), it did not extend the doctrine to the warrantless search of personal luggage "merely because it was located in an automobile lawfully stopped by the police." Again, the *Sanders* majority stressed the heightened privacy expectation in personal luggage and concluded that the presence of luggage in an automobile did not diminish the owner's expectation of privacy in his personal items.

In *Ross*, the Court endeavored to distinguish between *Carroll*, which governed the *Ross* automobile search, and *Chadwick*, which governed the *Sanders* automobile search. It held that the *Carroll* doctrine covered searches of automobiles when the police had probable cause to search an entire vehicle, but that the *Chadwick* doctrine governed searches of luggage when the officers had probable cause to search only a container within the vehicle. Thus, in a *Ross* situation, the police could conduct a reasonable search under the Fourth Amendment without obtaining a warrant, whereas in a *Sanders* situation, the police had to obtain a warrant before they searched.

* * * *Ross* involved the scope of an automobile search [and] held that closed containers encountered by the police during a warrantless search of a car pursuant to the automobile exception could also be searched. Thus, this Court in *Ross* took the critical step of saying that closed containers in cars could be searched without a warrant because of their presence within the automobile. Despite the protection that *Sanders* purported to extend to closed containers, the privacy interest in those closed containers yielded to the broad scope of an automobile search.

III

* * *

* * * We now must decide the question deferred in *Ross*: whether the Fourth Amendment requires the police to obtain a warrant to open the sack in a movable vehicle simply because they lack probable cause to search the entire car. We conclude that it does not.

[handwritten margin note: Finding = need not warrent]

IV

Dissenters in *Ross* asked why the suitcase in *Sanders* was "more private, less difficult for police to seize and store, or in any other relevant respect more properly subject to the warrant requirement, than a container that police discover in a probable-cause search of an entire automobile?" We now agree that a container found after a general search of the automobile and a container found in a car after a limited search for the container are equally easy for the police to store and for the suspect to hide or destroy. In fact, we see no principled distinction in terms of either the privacy expectation or the exigent circumstances between the paper bag found by the police in *Ross* and the paper bag found by the police here. Furthermore, by attempting to distinguish between a container for which the police are specifically searching and a container which they come across in a car, we have provided only minimal protection for privacy and have impeded effective law enforcement.

The line between probable cause to search a vehicle and probable cause to search a package in that vehicle is not always clear, and separate rules that govern the two objects to be searched may enable the police to broaden their power to make warrantless searches and disserve privacy interests. We noted this in *Ross* in the context of a search of an entire vehicle. Recognizing that under Carroll [v. United States, 267 U.S. 132, 45 S.Ct. 280, 69 L.Ed. 543 (1925)], the "entire vehicle itself . . . could be searched without a warrant," we concluded that "prohibiting police from opening immediately a container in which the object of the search is most likely to be found and instead forcing them first to comb the entire vehicle would actually exacerbate the intrusion on privacy interests." At the moment when officers stop an automobile, it may be less than clear whether they suspect with a high degree of certainty that the vehicle contains drugs in a bag or simply contains drugs. If the police know that they may open a bag only if they are actually searching the entire car, they may search more extensively than they otherwise would in order to establish the general probable cause required by *Ross.*

To the extent that the *Chadwick–Sanders* rule protects privacy, its protection is minimal. Law enforcement officers may seize a container and hold it until they obtain a search warrant. "Since the police, by hypothesis, have probable cause to seize the property, we can assume that a warrant will be routinely forthcoming in the overwhelming majority of cases." *Sanders,* 442 U.S., at 770, 99 S.Ct. at 2596 (dissenting opinion). And the police often will be able to search containers without a warrant, despite the *Chadwick–Sanders* rule, as a search incident to a lawful arrest. * * *

Finally, the search of a paper bag intrudes far less on individual privacy than does the incursion sanctioned long ago in *Carroll.* In that case, prohibition agents slashed the upholstery of the automobile. This Court nonetheless found their search to be reasonable under the Fourth Amendment. If destroying the interior of an automobile is not unreasonable, we cannot conclude that looking inside a closed container is. In light of the minimal protection to privacy afforded by the *Chadwick–Sanders* rule, and our serious doubt whether that rule substantially serves privacy interests, we now hold that the Fourth Amendment does not compel separate treatment for an automobile search that extends only to a container within the vehicle.

V

The *Chadwick–Sanders* rule not only has failed to protect privacy but it has also confused courts and police officers and impeded effective law enforcement. The conflict between the *Carroll* doctrine cases and the *Chadwick–Sanders* line has been criticized in academic commentary. * * *

The discrepancy between the two rules has led to confusion for law enforcement officers. For example, when an officer, who has developed probable cause to believe that a vehicle contains drugs, begins to search the vehicle and immediately discovers a closed container, which rule applies? The defendant will argue that the fact that the officer first chose to search the container indicates that his probable cause extended only to the container and that *Chadwick* and *Sanders* therefore require a warrant. On the other hand, the fact that the officer first chose to search in the most obvious location should not restrict the propriety of the search. The *Chadwick* rule, as applied in *Sanders,* has devolved into an anomaly such that the more likely the police are to discover drugs in a container, the less authority they have to search it. We have noted the virtue of providing " 'clear and unequivocal' guidelines to the law enforcement profession." The *Chadwick–Sanders* rule is the antithesis of a " 'clear and unequivocal' guideline."

* * *

VI

The interpretation of the *Carroll* doctrine set forth in *Ross* now applies to all searches of containers found in an automobile. In other words, the

police may search without a warrant if their search is supported by ☐ *Rule*
probable cause. The Court in *Ross* put it this way:

> "The scope of a warrantless search of an automobile ... is not defined
> by the nature of the container in which the contraband is secreted.
> Rather, it is defined by the object of the search and the places in which
> there is probable cause to believe that it may be found."

It went on to note: "Probable cause to believe that a container placed
in the trunk of a taxi contains contraband or evidence does not justify a
search of the entire cab." We reaffirm that principle. In the case before us,
the police had probable cause to believe that the paper bag in the automobile's trunk contained marijuana. That probable cause now allows a warrantless search of the paper bag. The facts in the record reveal that the
police did not have probable cause to believe that contraband was hidden in
any other part of the automobile and a search of the entire vehicle would
have been without probable cause and unreasonable under the Fourth
Amendment.

* * *

Until today, this Court has drawn a curious line between the search of
an automobile that coincidentally turns up a container and the search of a
container that coincidentally turns up in an automobile. The protections of
the Fourth Amendment must not turn on such coincidences. We therefore
interpret *Carroll* as providing one rule to govern all automobile searches.
The police may search an automobile and the containers within it where
they have probable cause to believe contraband or evidence is contained.

The judgment of the California Court of Appeal is reversed and the
case is remanded to that court for further proceedings not inconsistent
with this opinion.

It is so ordered.

■ JUSTICE SCALIA, concurring in the judgment.

* * *

I would reverse the judgment in the present case, not because a closed
container carried inside a car becomes subject to the "automobile" exception to the general warrant requirement, but because the search of a closed
container, outside a privately owned building, with probable cause to
believe that the container contains contraband, and when it in fact does
contain contraband, is not one of those searches whose Fourth Amendment
reasonableness depends upon a warrant. For that reason I concur in the
judgment of the Court.

■ JUSTICE WHITE, dissenting.

Agreeing as I do with most of JUSTICE STEVENS' opinion and with the
result he reaches, I dissent and would affirm the judgment below.

■ JUSTICE STEVENS, with whom JUSTICE MARSHALL joins, dissenting.

* * *

The Court's statement that *Chadwick* and *Sanders* provide only "minimal protection to privacy," is * * * unpersuasive. Every citizen clearly has

an interest in the privacy of the contents of his or her luggage, briefcase, handbag or any other container that conceals private papers and effects from public scrutiny. That privacy interest has been recognized repeatedly in cases spanning more than a century.

Under the Court's holding today, the privacy interest that protects the contents of a suitcase or a briefcase from a warrantless search when it is in public view simply vanishes when its owner climbs into a taxicab. Unquestionably * * * today's decision will result in a significant loss of individual privacy.

* * *

Even if the warrant requirement does inconvenience the police to some extent, that fact does not distinguish this constitutional requirement from any other procedural protection secured by the Bill of Rights. It is merely a part of the price that our society must pay in order to preserve its freedom. * * *

I respectfully dissent.

NOTE: CONTAINERS BELONGING TO PASSENGERS

Is ownership of a container relevant to whether it may be searched during a vehicle search? In Wyoming v. Houghton, 526 U.S. 295, 119 S.Ct. 1297, 143 L.Ed.2d 408 (1999), a Wyoming police officer made a traffic stop of an automobile driven by David Young. Houghton and another woman were passengers; both were sitting in the front seat. During the stop, the officer observed a hypodermic syringe in Young's pocket. When asked, Young reported he used the syringe to take drugs. The officer then, after removing the three occupants, began to search the car. He came upon a purse in the rear seat and, as he began to search it, Houghton claimed it as hers. Nevertheless, the officer continued to search the purse and discovered methamphetamine and drug paraphernalia. The Wyoming court held the drugs and paraphernalia could not be used in Houghton's prosecution. An officer's right to search a vehicle on probable cause to believe it contains contraband, the court reasoned, does not extent to a container the officer knows or should know belongs to a passenger not suspected of criminal activity—unless there was an opportunity for someone to conceal the contraband sought in that container.

The Supreme Court reversed. Justice Scalia's opinion for the Court reasoned the Court's automobile cases, and United States v. Ross, 456 U.S. 798, 806, 102 S.Ct. 2157, 72 L.Ed.2d 572 (1982), in particular, reflect a conclusion that the Framers would have regarded as reasonable a warrantless search of all containers in a vehicle regardless of ownership if those containers might conceal contraband the officer has probable cause to believe is in the vehicle. Reasonableness of a search, it continued, historically does not depend upon whether the owner of property is suspected of a crime but rather whether there is probable cause to believe seizable items are in or on the property. Further:

> Even if the historical evidence * * * were thought to be equivocal, we would find that the balancing of the relative interests weighs decidedly in favor of allowing searches of a passenger's belongings. Passengers, no less than drivers, possess a reduced expectation of privacy with regard to the property that they transport in cars * * *.

> Whereas the passenger's privacy expectations are * * * considerably diminished, the governmental interests at stake are substantial. Effective law

enforcement would be appreciably impaired without the ability to search a passenger's personal belongings when there is reason to believe contraband or evidence of criminal wrongdoing is hidden in the car. As in all car-search cases, the "ready mobility" of an automobile creates a risk that the evidence or contraband will be permanently lost while a warrant is obtained. In addition, a car passenger * * * will often be engaged in a common enterprise with the driver, and have the same interest in concealing the fruits or the evidence of their wrongdoing. A criminal might be able to hide contraband in a passenger's belongings as readily as in other containers in the car perhaps even surreptitiously, without the passenger's knowledge or permission. * * *

To be sure, these factors favoring a search will not always be present, but the balancing of interests must be conducted with an eye to the generality of cases. To require that the investigating officer have positive reason to believe that the passenger and driver were engaged in a common enterprise, or positive reason to believe that the driver had time and occasion to conceal the item in the passenger's belongings, surreptitiously or with friendly permission, is to impose requirements so seldom met that a "passenger's property" rule would dramatically reduce the ability to find and seize contraband and evidence of crime. Of course these requirements would not attach (under the Wyoming Supreme Court's rule) until the police officer knows or has reason to know that the container belongs to a passenger. But once a "passenger's property" exception to car searches became widely known, one would expect passenger-confederates to claim everything as their own. And one would anticipate a bog of litigation in the form of both civil lawsuits and motions to suppress in criminal trials involving such questions as whether the officer should have believed a passenger's claim of ownership, whether he should have inferred ownership from various objective factors, whether he had probable cause to believe that the passenger was a confederate, or to believe that the driver might have introduced the contraband into the package with or without the passenger's knowledge. When balancing the competing interests, our determinations of "reasonableness" under the Fourth Amendment must take account of these practical realities. We think they militate in favor of the needs of law enforcement, and against a personal-privacy interest that is ordinarily weak.

Finally, if we were to invent an exception from the historical practice * * *, it is perplexing why that exception should protect only property belonging to a passenger, rather than (what seems much more logical) property belonging to anyone other than the driver. * * *

526 U.S. at ___, 119 S.Ct. at 1302–03, 143 L.Ed.2d at 416–19. United States v. Di Re, 332 U.S. 581, 68 S.Ct. 222, 92 L.Ed. 210 (1948), the Court added, "held that probable cause to search a car did not justify a body search of a passenger." *Houghton* apparently did not disturb this holding.

Justice Breyer joined the *Houghton* majority opinion but wrote separately to comment on one aspect of the facts:

[It is important, in my view,] that the container here at issue, a woman's purse, was found at a considerable distance from its owner, who did not claim ownership until the officer discovered her identification while looking through it. Purses are special containers. They are repositories of especially personal items that people generally like to keep with them at all times. So I am tempted to say that a search of a purse involves an intrusion so similar to a search of one's person that the same rule should govern both. However, given this Court's prior cases, I cannot argue that the fact that the container was a purse automatically makes a legal difference, for the Court has warned against trying to make that kind of distinction. But I can say that it would matter if a woman's purse, like a man's billfold, were attached to her person. It might then amount to a kind of "outer clothing," which under the Court's cases would properly receive increased protection. In this case, the purse was separate from the person, and no one has claimed that, under those circumstances, the type of container makes a difference. For that reason, I join the Court's opinion.

526 U.S. at ___, 119 S.Ct. at 1304, 143 L.Ed.2d at 420 (Breyer, J., concurring).

Justice Stevens, joined by Justices Souter and Ginsburg, dissented:

In all of our prior cases applying the automobile exception to the Fourth Amendment's warrant requirement, either the defendant was the operator of the vehicle and in custody of the object of the search, or no question was raised as to the defendant's ownership or custody. In the only automobile case confronting the search of a passenger defendant—United States v. Di Re, 332 U.S. 581, 68 S.Ct. 222, 92 L.Ed. 210 (1948)—the Court held that the exception to the warrant requirement did not apply. In *Di Re*, as here, the information prompting the search directly implicated the driver, not the passenger. Today, instead of adhering to the settled distinction between drivers and passengers, the Court fashions a new rule that is based on a distinction between property contained in clothing worn by a passenger and property contained in a passenger's briefcase or purse. In cases on both sides of the Court's newly minted test, the property is in a "container" (whether a pocket or a pouch) located in the vehicle. Moreover, unlike the Court, I think it quite plain that the search of a passenger's purse or briefcase involves an intrusion on privacy that may be just as serious as was the intrusion in *Di Re*.

* * *

[I]n my view, the State's legitimate interest in effective law enforcement does not outweigh the privacy concerns at issue. I am as confident in a police officer's ability to apply a rule requiring a warrant or individualized probable cause to search belongings that areas in this case obviously owned by and in the custody of a passenger as is the Court in a "passenger-confederate[']s" ability to circumvent the rule. Certainly the ostensible clarity of the Court's rule is attractive. But that virtue is insufficient justification for its adoption. Moreover, a rule requiring a warrant or individualized probable cause to search passenger belongings is every bit as simple as the Court's rule; it simply protects more privacy.

* * *

Instead of applying ordinary Fourth Amendment principles to this case, the majority extends the automobile warrant exception to allow searches of passenger belongings based on the driver's misconduct. Thankfully, the Court's automobile-centered analysis limits the scope of its holding. But it does not justify the outcome in this case.

526 U.S. at ___, 119 S.Ct. at 1305–06, 143 L.Ed.2d at 420–23 (Stevens, J., dissenting).

3.   SEIZURE AND INVENTORY OF VEHICLES

EDITORS' INTRODUCTION: IMPOUNDMENT OF VEHICLES AND INVENTORYING OF IMPOUNDED VEHICLES

Two often-related issues frequently arise regarding official exercises of control over vehicles. One is officials' authority to seize or "impound" vehicles. The other is officers' authority to examine the contents of a properly seized vehicle, most often as part of "inventorying" those contents. Unfortunately, the Supreme Court's case law has focused more upon the power to inventory than on the power to seize.

Inventory Inspections of Seized Automobiles. Just as officers may inventory personal possessions of a person to be incarcerated after arrest (see subsection B(1) of Chapter 4), the Supreme Court held that the Fourth Amendment permits some inventory inspections of seized automobiles. The leading case is South Dakota v. Opperman, 428 U.S. 364, 96 S.Ct. 3092, 49 L.Ed.2d 1000 (1976). At 3 A.M., a Vermillion, South Dakota police officer noted Opperman's car parked in a downtown area in violation of an ordinance prohibiting parking in such areas between 2 a.m. and 6 a.m. He issued a citation and placed it on the windshield. After another officer issued a second citation at 10 a.m., the vehicle was "inspected" and towed to the city impound lot. At the lot, an officer noted a watch on the dashboard and other items of personal property on the back seat and floorboard. The locked car doors were opened and "using a standard inventory form, pursuant to police procedures, the officer inventoried the contents of the car * * *." The glove compartment was not locked; upon opening it, the officer discovered marihuana in a plastic bag. All items found in the car were removed to the police department for safekeeping. Opperman was prosecuted for possession of marihuana. His objection to the admissibility of the marihuana was overruled and he was convicted. Finding the police activity reasonable, a majority of the Supreme Court explained:

> When vehicles are impounded, local police departments generally follow a routine practice of securing and inventorying the automobiles' contents. These procedures developed in response to three distinct needs: the protection of the owner's property while it remains in police custody; the protection of the police against claims or disputes over lost or stolen property; and the protection of the police from potential danger. The practice has been viewed as essential to respond to incidents of theft or vandalism. In addition, police frequently attempt to determine whether a vehicle has been stolen and thereafter abandoned. * * *

> The decisions of this Court point unmistakably to the conclusion * * * that inventories pursuant to standard police procedures are reasonable.

> The Vermillion police were indisputably engaged in a caretaking search of a lawfully impounded automobile. The inventory was conducted only after the car had been impounded for multiple parking violations. The owner, having left his car illegally parked for an extended period, and thus subject to impoundment, was not present to make other arrangements for the safekeeping of his belongings. The inventory itself was prompted by the presence in plain view of a number of valuables inside the car. * * * [T]here is no suggestion whatever that this standard procedure * * * was a pretext concealing an investigatory motive.

[Handwritten margin notes: Impound vehicle search (1) protect owner property while in police custody (2) protect police over claim of dispute property (3) protect police from potential danger]

428 U.S. at 369, 372, 375–76, 96 S.Ct. at 3097–99, 3100, 49 L.Ed.2d at 1005, 1007, 1009. Nor, the majority continued, was the inventory unlawful in scope because it extended to items not in plain view from outside the car:

> [O]nce the policeman was lawfully inside the car to secure the personal property in plain view, it was not unreasonable to open the unlocked glove compartment, to which vandals would have had ready and unobstructed access once inside the car.

428 U.S. at 376 n. 10, 96 S.Ct. at 3100 n. 10, 49 L.Ed.2d at 1009 n. 10.

Opperman's holding that certain vehicular inventory examinations are permissible was developed in the principal case in this subsection. An otherwise proper inventory examination is fatally tainted, however, if the vehicle's impoundment was an unreasonable seizure of it. Courts have considerable difficulty determining when impoundments of vehicles are reasonable.

Seizures or Impoundments of Automobiles. Despite the frequency with which police assume control over automobiles, the extent of officers' authority to impound vehicles is not well developed in case law. Police authority to impound in several situations is, however, quite settled. In *Opperman* itself, the Court commented, "The authority of police to seize and remove from the streets vehicles impeding traffic or threatening public safety and convenience is beyond challenge." Statutes in many jurisdictions authorize judicial proceedings for the forfeiture of some vehicles used illegally, such as in the commission of particular criminal offenses. When officers have probable cause to believe a vehicle subject to forfeiture under such provisions, they may seize the vehicle and hold it pending the completion of judicial forfeiture proceedings. Cf. Cooper v. California, 386 U.S. 58, 87 S.Ct. 788, 17 L.Ed.2d 730 (1967).

It has also been suggested that grounds for impoundment exist when— or at least when officers have reason to believe—the automobile has been abandoned or stolen, the automobile constitutes evidence of the commission of a crime or of someone's guilt of a crime, or the driver (as by reason of injury, intoxication or mental incapacitation) is unable to attend to the car. See State v. Singleton, 9 Wn.App. 327, 332–33, 511 P.2d 1396, 1399–1400 (1973).

Courts disagree regarding the propriety of vehicle impoundments made because the driver was arrested. Unfortunately, judicial discussions often do not clearly distinguish between validity of the initial impoundment and inventory inspection of a vehicle properly in official custody. In State v. Duncan, 77 Ohio Misc.2d 7, 665 N.E.2d 767 (Ohio Ct.Common Pleas 1996), however, the distinction was carefully made. Officers arrested Duncan at a hospital where he sought treatment for injuries sustained in an attempted robbery. They learned he had driven to the hospital alone in his mother's automobile which he was parked on the street near the hospital. Without seeking a warrant they searched the automobile and found drugs. When the admissibility of the drugs was challenged, the prosecution defended the search as an inventory inspection of a seized vehicle. The trial court ruled the prosecution had failed to establish the vehicle's seizure was reasonable:

No evidence was offered that the car was illegally parked or that its prolonged presence on the street would violate any parking laws. The police attempted to justify the impoundment on the ground that such action was necessary to protect the car from vandalism or theft.

Merely because the driver of a vehicle is taken into custody does not justify impoundment. The state must show that a law would be violated, that a danger would be posed to others if impoundment did not occur, that no reasonable alternative existed for safeguarding the vehicle, or that the impoundment was made pursuant to a reasonable police regulation. No evidence was presented that the vehicle was illegally parked or obstructed traffic. No evidence was presented that the defendant desired it to be towed for safekeeping or could not have called his mother (the owner of the car) or a friend to move the vehicle. The state has, thus, not sustained its burden of showing the reasonableness of towing this vehicle.

77 Ohio Misc.2d at 9, 665 N.E.2d at 769.

Colorado v. Bertine

Supreme Court of the United States, 1987.
479 U.S. 367, 107 S.Ct. 738, 93 L.Ed.2d 739.

■ CHIEF JUSTICE REHNQUIST delivered the opinion of the Court.

On February 10, 1984, a police officer in Boulder, Colorado, arrested respondent Steven Lee Bertine for driving while under the influence of alcohol. After Bertine was taken into custody and before the arrival of a tow truck to take Bertine's van to an impoundment lot,[8] a backup officer inventoried the contents of the van. The officer opened a closed backpack in which he found controlled substances, cocaine paraphernalia, and a large amount of cash. Bertine was subsequently charged with driving while under the influence of alcohol, unlawful possession of cocaine with intent to dispense, sell, and distribute, and unlawful possession of methaqualone. We are asked to decide whether the Fourth Amendment prohibits the State from proving these charges with the evidence discovered during the inventory of Bertine's van. We hold that it does not.

The backup officer inventoried the van in accordance with local police procedures, which require a detailed inspection and inventory of impounded vehicles. He found the backpack directly behind the frontseat of the van. Inside the pack, the officer observed a nylon bag containing metal canisters. Opening the canisters, the officer discovered that they contained cocaine, methaqualone tablets, cocaine paraphernalia, and $700 in cash. In an outside zippered pouch of the backpack, he also found $210 in cash in a

---

8. Section 772(a)(4) of the Boulder Revised Code authorizes police officers to impound vehicles when drivers are taken into custody. Section 772(a)(4) provides:

"A peace officer is authorized to remove or cause to be removed a vehicle from any street, parking lot, or driveway when:

(4) The driver of a vehicle is taken into custody by the police department." Boulder Rev.Code § 772(a)(4) (1981).

sealed envelope. After completing the inventory of the van, the officer had the van towed to an impound lot and brought the backpack, money, and contraband to the police station.

After Bertine was charged with the offenses described above, he moved to suppress the evidence found during the inventory search on the ground, inter alia, that the search of the closed backpack and containers exceeded the permissible scope of such a search under the Fourth Amendment. The Colorado trial court ruled that probable cause supported Bertine's arrest and that the police officers had made the decisions to impound the vehicle and to conduct a thorough inventory search in good faith. Although noting that the inventory of the vehicle was performed in a "somewhat slipshod" manner, the District Court concluded that "the search of the backpack was done for the purpose of protecting the owner's property, protection of the police from subsequent claims of loss or stolen property, and the protection of the police from dangerous instrumentalities." The court observed that the standard procedures for impounding vehicles mandated a "detailed inventory involving the opening of containers and the listing of [their] contents." Based on these findings, the court determined that the inventory search did not violate Bertine's rights under the Fourth Amendment of the United States Constitution. * * *

On the State's interlocutory appeal, the Supreme Court of Colorado [disagreed]. * * * The court recognized that in South Dakota v. Opperman, 428 U.S. 364, 96 S.Ct. 3092, 49 L.Ed.2d 1000 (1976), we had held inventory searches of automobiles to be consistent with the Fourth Amendment, and that in Illinois v. Lafayette, 462 U.S. 640, 103 S.Ct. 2605, 77 L.Ed.2d 65 (1983), we had held that the inventory search of personal effects of an arrestee at a police station was also permissible under that Amendment. The Supreme Court of Colorado felt, however, that our decisions in Arkansas v. Sanders, 442 U.S. 753, 99 S.Ct. 2586, 61 L.Ed.2d 235 (1979), and United States v. Chadwick, 433 U.S. 1, 97 S.Ct. 2476, 53 L.Ed.2d 538 (1977), holding searches of closed trunks and suitcases to violate the Fourth Amendment, meant that *Opperman* and *Lafayette* did not govern this case.

We granted certiorari to consider the important and recurring question of federal law decided by the Colorado Supreme Court. As that court recognized, inventory searches are now a well-defined exception to the warrant requirement of the Fourth Amendment. The policies behind the warrant requirement are not implicated in an inventory search, nor is the related concept of probable cause:

> "The standard of probable cause is peculiarly related to criminal investigations, not routine, noncriminal procedures.... The probable-cause approach is unhelpful when analysis centers upon the reasonableness of routine administrative caretaking functions, particularly when no claim is made that the protective procedures are a subterfuge for criminal investigations."

For these reasons, the Colorado Supreme Court's reliance on Arkansas v. Sanders, supra, and United States v. Chadwick, supra, was incorrect. Both of these cases concerned searches solely for the purpose of investigating criminal conduct, with the validity of the searches therefore dependent on the application of the probable-cause and warrant requirements of the Fourth Amendment.

By contrast, an inventory search may be "reasonable" under the Fourth Amendment even though it is not conducted pursuant to a warrant based upon probable cause. In *Opperman*, this Court assessed the reasonableness of an inventory search of the glove compartment in an abandoned automobile impounded by the police. We found that inventory procedures serve to protect an owner's property while it is in the custody of the police, to insure against claims of lost, stolen, or vandalized property, and to guard the police from danger. In light of these strong governmental interests and the diminished expectation of privacy in an automobile, we upheld the search. In reaching this decision, we observed that our cases accorded deference to police caretaking procedures designed to secure and protect vehicles and their contents within police custody.

In our more recent decision, *Lafayette*, a police officer conducted an inventory search of the contents of a shoulder bag in the possession of an individual being taken into custody. In deciding whether this search was reasonable, we recognized that the search served legitimate governmental interests similar to those identified in *Opperman*. We determined that those interests outweighed the individual's Fourth Amendment interests and upheld the search.

In the present case, as in *Opperman* and *Lafayette*, there was no showing that the police, who were following standardized procedures, acted in bad faith or for the sole purpose of investigation. In addition, the governmental interests justifying the inventory searches in *Opperman* and *Lafayette* are nearly the same as those which obtain here. In each case, the police were potentially responsible for the property taken into their custody. By securing the property, the police protected the property from unauthorized interference. Knowledge of the precise nature of the property helped guard against claims of theft, vandalism, or negligence. Such knowledge also helped to avert any danger to police or others that may have been posed by the property.

* * *   *Supreme Court of Col. says search was not reasonable*

The Supreme Court of Colorado * * * expressed the view that the search in this case was unreasonable because Bertine's van was towed to a secure, lighted facility and because Bertine himself could have been offered the opportunity to make other arrangements for the safekeeping of his property. But the security of the storage facility does not completely eliminate the need for inventorying; the police may still wish to protect themselves or the owners of the lot against false claims of theft or dangerous instrumentalities. And while giving Bertine an opportunity to make alternative arrangements would undoubtedly have been possible, we said in *Lafayette*:

"[T]he real question is not what 'could have been achieved,' but whether the Fourth Amendment requires such steps . . .

"The reasonableness of any particular governmental activity does not necessarily or invariably turn on the existence of alternative 'less intrusive' means."

We conclude that here, as in *Lafayette*, reasonable police regulations relating to inventory procedures administered in good faith satisfy the Fourth Amendment, even though courts might as a matter of hindsight be able to devise equally reasonable rules requiring a different procedure.[9]

The Supreme Court of Colorado also thought it necessary to require that police, before inventorying a container, weigh the strength of the individual's privacy interest in the container against the possibility that the container might serve as a repository for dangerous or valuable items. We think that such a requirement is contrary to our decisions in *Opperman* and *Lafayette* * * *:

> "Even if less intrusive means existed of protecting some particular types of property, it would be unreasonable to expect police officers in the everyday course of business to make fine and subtle distinctions in deciding which containers or items may be searched and which must be sealed as a unit." *Lafayette*, supra, 462 U.S., at 648, 103 S.Ct., at 2610.

* * *

We reaffirm these principles here: " '[a] single familiar standard is essential to guide police officers, who have only limited time and expertise to reflect on and balance the social and individual interests involved in the specific circumstances they confront.' " *Lafayette*, supra, 462 U.S., at 648, 103 S.Ct., at 2610.

Bertine finally argues that the inventory search of his van was unconstitutional because departmental regulations gave the police officers discretion to choose between impounding his van and parking and locking it in a public parking place. The Supreme Court of Colorado did not rely on this argument in reaching its conclusion, and we reject it. Nothing in *Opperman* or *Lafayette* prohibits the exercise of police discretion so long as that discretion is exercised according to standard criteria and on the basis of something other than suspicion of evidence of criminal activity. Here, the discretion afforded the Boulder police was exercised in light of standardized criteria, related to the feasibility and appropriateness of parking and locking a vehicle rather than impounding it.[10] There was no showing that

9. We emphasize that, in this case, the trial court found that the Police Department's procedures mandated the opening of closed containers and the listing of their contents. Our decisions have always adhered to the requirement that inventories be conducted according to standardized criteria.

[T]he dissent suggests that the inventory here was not authorized by the standard procedures of the Boulder Police Department. Yet that court specifically stated that the procedure followed here was "officially authorized." In addition, the court did not disturb the trial court's finding that the police procedures for impounding vehicles required a detailed inventory of Bertine's van.

10. In arguing that the Boulder Police Department procedures set forth no standardized criteria guiding an officer's decision to impound a vehicle, the dissent selectively quotes from the police directive concerning the care and security of vehicles taken into police custody. The dissent fails to mention that the directive establishes several conditions that must be met before an officer may pursue the park-and-lock alternative. For example, police may not park and lock the vehicle where there is reasonable risk of damage or vandalism to the vehicle or where the approval of the arrestee cannot be obtained. Not only do such conditions circumscribe the discretion of individual officers, but they also protect the vehicle and its contents and minimize claims of property loss.

the police chose to impound Bertine's van in order to investigate suspected criminal activity.

While both *Opperman* and *Lafayette* are distinguishable from the present case on their facts, we think that the principles enunciated in those cases govern the present one. The judgment of the Supreme Court of Colorado is therefore

Reversed.

■ JUSTICE MARSHALL, with whom JUSTICE BRENNAN joins, dissenting.

[The] search [in this case]—it cannot legitimately be labeled an inventory—was unreasonable and violated the Fourth Amendment. * * * [I]t was not conducted according to standardized procedures. * * *

As the Court acknowledges, inventory searches are reasonable only if conducted according to standardized procedures. * * *

The Court today attempts to evade these clear prohibitions on unfettered police discretion by declaring that "the discretion afforded the Boulder police was exercised in light of standardized criteria, related to the feasibility and appropriateness of parking and locking a vehicle rather than impounding it." This vital assertion is flatly contradicted by the record in this case. The officer who conducted the inventory, Officer Reichenbach, testified at the suppression hearing that the decision not to "park and lock" respondent's vehicle was his "own individual discretionary decision." Indeed, application of these supposedly standardized "criteria" upon which the Court so heavily relies would have yielded a different result in this case. Since there was ample public parking adjacent to the intersection where respondent was stopped, consideration of "feasibility" would certainly have militated in favor of the "park and lock" option, not against it. I do not comprehend how consideration of "appropriateness" serves to channel a field officer's discretion; nonetheless, the "park and lock" option would seem particularly appropriate in this case, where respondent was stopped for a traffic offense and was not likely to be in custody for a significant length of time.

Indeed, the record indicates that *no* standardized criteria limit a Boulder police officer's discretion. According to a departmental directive, after placing a driver under arrest, an officer has three options for disposing of the vehicle. First, he can allow a third party to take custody. Second, the officer or the driver (depending on the nature of the arrest) may take the car to the nearest public parking facility, lock it, and take the keys. Finally, the officer can do what was done in this case: impound the vehicle, and search and inventory its contents, including closed containers.

Under the first option, the police have no occasion to search the automobile. Under the "park and lock" option, "[c]losed containers that give no indication of containing either valuables or a weapon *may not be opened and the contents searched* (i.e., inventoried)." Only if the police choose the third option are they entitled to search closed containers in the vehicle. Where the vehicle is not itself evidence of a crime,[11] as in this case,

---

11. Respondent's van was not evidence of a crime within the meaning of the depart- mental directive; Officer Reichenbach testi- fied that it was not his practice to impound the police apparently have totally unbridled discretion as to which procedure to use. Consistent with this conclusion, Officer Reichenbach testified that such decisions were left to the discretion of the officer on the scene.

Once a Boulder police officer has made this initial completely discretionary decision to impound a vehicle, he is given little guidance as to which areas to search and what sort of items to inventory. The arresting officer, Officer Toporek, testified at the suppression hearing as to what items would be inventoried: "That would I think be very individualistic as far as what an officer may or may not go into. I think whatever arouses his suspicious [sic] as far as what may be contained in any type of article in the car." In application, these so-called procedures left the breadth of the "inventory" to the whim of the individual officer. Clearly, "[t]he practical effect of this system is to leave the [owner] subject to the discretion of the official in the field."

Inventory searches are not subject to the warrant requirement because they are conducted by the government as part of a "community caretaking" function, "totally divorced from the detection, investigation, or acquisition of evidence relating to the violation of a criminal statute." Standardized procedures are necessary to ensure that this narrow exception is not improperly used to justify, after the fact, a warrantless investigative foray. Accordingly, to invalidate a search that is conducted without established procedures, it is not necessary to establish that the police actually acted in bad faith, or that the inventory was in fact a "pretext." By allowing the police unfettered discretion, Boulder's discretionary scheme * * * is unreasonable because of the " 'grave danger' of abuse of discretion."

* * *

NOTE: REQUIRED STANDARDIZED PROCEDURES

Bertine's emphasis upon the need for "standardized procedures" was developed in Florida v. Wells, 495 U.S. 1, 110 S.Ct. 1632, 109 L.Ed.2d 1 (1990). Officers examined the contents of a suitcase found in an impounded car. The state court held the search improper because no evidence was produced that the police agency had any policy concerning opening of closed containers found during inventory searches. The Supreme Court affirmed, reasoning that "absent [a policy with respect to the opening of closed containers encountered during an inventory search], the instant search was not sufficiently regulated to satisfy the Fourth Amendment * * *." Chief Justice Rehnquist, writing for the majority, explained:

> Our view that standardized criteria or established routine must regulate the opening of containers found during inventory searches is based on the principle that an inventory search must not be a ruse for a general rummaging in order to discover incriminating evidence. The policy or practice governing inventory searches should be designed to produce an inventory. The individual police officer must not be allowed so much latitude that inventory inspections are

all cars following an arrest for driving while under the influence of alcohol. The Memorandum also requires the "approval of the arrestee" before the police can "park and lock" his car. In this case, however, respondent was never advised of this option and had no opportunity to consent. At the suppression hearing, he indicated that he would have consented to such a procedure.

turned into "a purposeful and general means of discovering evidence of crime," *Bertine,* supra, 479 U.S., at 376, 107 S.Ct., at 744 (Blackmun, J., concurring).

495 U.S. at 4, 110 S.Ct. at 1635, 109 L.Ed.2d at 6. He expressed disagreement, however, with the state court's comment that under *Bertine* the policy must mandate that either all or no containers be opened:

> A police officer may be allowed sufficient latitude whether a particular container should or should not be opened in light of the nature of the search and characteristics of the container itself. Thus, while policies of opening all containers or of opening no containers are unquestionably permissible, it would be equally permissible, for example, to allow the opening of closed containers whose contents officers determine they are unable to ascertain from examining the containers' exteriors. The allowance of the exercise of judgment based on concerns relevant to the purposes of an inventory search does not violate the Fourth Amendment.

495 U.S. at 4, 110 S.Ct. at 1635, 109 L.Ed.2d at 6–7.

Justice Brennan, joined by Justice Marshall, disagreed that the majority's dicta was consistent with *Bertine,* which he read as the Florida court had. Justice Blackmun agreed the Florida court was wrong in reading *Bertine* as requiring all or no containers be opened but complained the majority's dicta permitted too much flexibility:

> A State * * * probably could adopt a policy which requires the opening of all containers that are not locked, or a policy which requires the opening of all containers over or under a certain size, even though these policies do not call for the opening of all or no containers. In other words, a State has the discretion to choose a scheme that lies somewhere between the extremes identified by the Florida Supreme Court.
>
> It is an entirely different matter, however, to say, as this majority does, that an individual policeman may be afforded discretion in conducting an inventory search. The exercise of discretion by an individual officer, especially when it cannot be measured against objective, standard criteria, creates the potential for abuse of Fourth Amendment rights our earlier inventory search cases were designed to guard against.

495 U.S. at 11, 110 S.Ct. at 1639, 109 L.Ed.2d at 11 (Blackmun, J., concurring in the judgment). Justice Stevens agreed. 495 U.S. at 12, 110 S.Ct. at 1639, 109 L.Ed.2d at 11 (Stevens, J., concurring in the judgment).

E. SEARCHES AND SEIZURES AT OR NEAR INTERNATIONAL BORDERS

Searches and other law enforcement activity related to the international border have traditionally given rise to substantial concern. Statutory authority to conduct border-related activity consists of grants of authority to both the Bureau of Customs and the Department of Immigration. Customs officers are authorized in 19 U.S.C.A. § 482 to "stop, search, and examine * * * any vehicle, beast, or person, on which or whom he or they shall suspect there is merchandise which is subject to duty, or shall have been introduced into the United States in any manner contrary to law * * *." Under 19 U.S.C.A. § 1581(a), customs officers are authorized to board any vessel or vehicle and "search the vessel or vehicle and every part thereof and any person, trunk, package or cargo on board * * *." Immigration officers, on the other hand, are authorized by 8 U.S.C.A. § 1357(a)(1) to interrogate any person "believed to be an alien as to his right to be or remain in the United States * * * ". They are also authorized to board any vessel, railway car or conveyance "within a reasonable distance" of any external border to search for persons who have illegally entered the country. 8 U.S.C.A. § 1357(a)(3). "Reasonable distance" is defined by regulation. Border patrol officers, as agents of the Department of Immigration, might be thought by the nature of their duties to have a more limited right to search than customs officials. But the Bureau of Customs has designates border patrol officers as customs agents and, in this latter capacity, they may search for things improperly brought over the border. See United States v. Thompson, 475 F.2d 1359 (5th Cir.1973).

Federal law enforcement activity conducted pursuant to this authority consists of several legally significant types. One, of course, is the process at the international border itself (and at the "functional equivalents" of the border) of searching and questioning persons and things actually then crossing the border. In addition, the Immigration and Naturalization Service conducts "area control" operations in the country's interior. These consist of traffic control operations and factory surveys to identify illegally entered aliens working at those places. See Immigration and Naturalization Service v. Delgado, 466 U.S. 210, 225 n. 1, 104 S.Ct. 1758, 1767 n. 1, 80 L.Ed.2d 247, 261 n. 1 (1984) (Brennan, J., concurring in part and dissenting in part). In regard to the traffic control operations, the Court has noted:

> The Border Patrol conducts three types of surveillance along inland roadways, all in the asserted interest of detecting the illegal importation of aliens. Permanent checkpoints are maintained at certain nodal intersections; temporary checkpoints are established from time to time at various places; and finally, there are roving patrols * * *.

Almeida-Sanchez v. United States, 413 U.S. 266, 268, 93 S.Ct. 2535, 2537, 37 L.Ed.2d 596, 600 (1973). The first subsection of this section deals with law enforcement activity at the border or its functional equivalents. In the second, "area control" operations are considered.

1.   ENFORCEMENT ACTIVITY AT THE INTERNATIONAL BORDER

The Supreme Court did not have occasion, until the following principal case, to definitively address the limits that the federal constitution places upon law enforcement activity at the international border itself. But its basic position was clear in dictum:

> That searches made at the border, pursuant to the longstanding right of the sovereign to protect itself by stopping and examining persons and property crossing into this country, are reasonable simply by virtue of the fact that they occur at the border, should, by now, require no extended demonstration.

United States v. Ramsey, 431 U.S. 606, 616, 97 S.Ct. 1972, 1978, 52 L.Ed.2d 617, 626 (1977). These discussions left significant question as to the additional requirements applicable when the search is nonroutine or extraordinarily intrusive.

The Court has made clear at least some activity permissible at the border may also take place at other locations within the country's borders:

> [R]outine border search[s] * * * may in certain circumstances take place not only at the border itself, but at its functional equivalents as well. For example, searches at an established station near the border, at a point marking the confluence of two or more roads that extend from the border, might be functional equivalents of border searches. For another example, a search of the passengers and cargo of an airplane arriving at a St. Louis airport after a nonstop flight from Mexico City would clearly be the functional equivalent of a border search.

Almeida-Sanchez v. United States, 413 U.S. 266, 272–73, 93 S.Ct. 2535, 2539, 37 L.Ed.2d 596, 602–03 (1973).

United States v. Montoya de Hernandez

Supreme Court of the United States, 1985.
473 U.S. 531, 105 S.Ct. 3304, 87 L.Ed.2d 381.

■ JUSTICE REHNQUIST delivered the opinion of the Court.

Respondent Rosa Elvira Montoya de Hernandez * * * arrived at Los Angeles International Airport shortly after midnight, March 5, 1983, on Avianca Flight 080, a direct 10 hour flight from Bogota, Colombia. Her visa was in order so she was passed through Immigration and proceeded to the customs desk. At the customs desk she encountered Customs Inspector Talamantes, who reviewed her documents and noticed from her passport that she had made at least eight recent trips to either Miami or Los Angeles. Talamantes referred respondent to a secondary customs' desk for further questioning. At this desk Talamantes and another inspector asked respondent general questions concerning herself and the purpose of her trip. Respondent revealed that she spoke no English and had no family or friends in the United States. She explained in Spanish that she had come to the United States to purchase goods for her husband's store in Bogota. The customs inspectors recognized Bogota as a "source city" for narcotics. Respondent possessed $5,000 in cash, mostly $50 bills, but had no billfold. She indicated to the inspectors that she had no appointments with merchandise vendors, but planned to ride around Los Angeles in taxicabs visiting retail stores such as J.C. Penney and K–Mart in order to buy goods for her husband's store with the $5,000.

Respondent admitted that she had no hotel reservations, but stated that she planned to stay at a Holiday Inn. Respondent could not recall how her airline ticket was purchased. When the inspectors opened respondent's one small valise they found about four changes of "cold weather" clothing. Respondent had no shoes other than the highheeled pair she was wearing. Although respondent possessed no checks, waybills, credit cards, or letters of credit, she did produce a Colombian business card and a number of old receipts, waybills, and fabric swatches displayed in a photo album.

At this point Talamantes and the other inspector suspected that respondent was a "balloon swallower," one who attempts to smuggle narcotics into this country hidden in her alimentary canal. Over the years Inspector Talamantes had apprehended dozens of alimentary canal smugglers arriving on Avianca Flight 080.

The inspectors requested a female customs inspector to take respondent to a private area and conduct a patdown and strip search. During the search the female inspector felt respondent's abdomen area and noticed a firm fullness, as if respondent were wearing a girdle. The search revealed no contraband but the inspector noticed that respondent was wearing two pair of elastic underpants with a paper towel lining the crotch area.

When respondent returned to the customs area and the female inspector reported her discoveries, the inspector in charge told respondent that he suspected she was smuggling drugs in her alimentary canal. Respondent agreed to the inspector's request that she be x rayed at a hospital but in answer to the inspector's query stated that she was pregnant. She agreed to a pregnancy test before the x ray. Respondent withdrew the consent for an x ray when she learned that she would have to be handcuffed en route to the hospital. The inspector then gave respondent the option of returning to Colombia on the next available flight, agreeing to an x ray, or remaining in detention until she produced a monitored bowel movement that would confirm or rebut the inspectors' suspicions. Respondent chose the first option and was placed in a customs' office under observation. She was told that if she went to the toilet she would have to use a wastebasket in the women's restroom, in order that female customs inspectors could inspect her stool for balloons or capsules carrying narcotics. The inspectors refused respondent's request to place a telephone call.

Respondent sat in the customs office, under observation, for the remainder of the night. During the night customs officials attempted to place respondent on a Mexican airline that was flying to Bogota via Mexico City in the morning. The airline refused to transport respondent because she lacked a Mexican visa necessary to land in Mexico City. Respondent was not permitted to leave, and was informed that she would be detained until she agreed to an x ray or her bowels moved. She remained detained in the customs office under observation, for most of the time curled up in a chair leaning to one side. She refused all offers of food and drink, and refused to use the toilet facilities. The Court of Appeals noted that she exhibited symptoms of discomfort consistent with "heroic efforts to resist the usual calls of nature."

At the shift change at 4:00 p.m. the next afternoon, almost 16 hours after her flight had landed, respondent still had not defecated or urinated or partaken of food or drink. At that time customs officials sought a court order authorizing a pregnancy test, an x ray, and a rectal examination. The Federal Magistrate issued an order just before midnight that evening, which authorized a rectal examination and involuntary x ray, provided that the physician in charge considered respondent's claim of pregnancy. Respondent was taken to a hospital and given a pregnancy test, which later turned out to be negative. Before the results of the pregnancy test were known, a physician conducted a rectal examination and removed from respondent's rectum a balloon containing a foreign substance. Respondent was then placed formally under arrest. By 4:10 a.m. respondent had passed

6 similar balloons; over the next 4 days she passed 88 balloons containing a total of 528 grams of 80% pure cocaine hydrochloride.

After a suppression hearing the District Court admitted the cocaine in evidence against respondent. She was convicted of possession of cocaine with intent to distribute and unlawful importation of cocaine.

A divided panel of the United States Court of Appeals for the Ninth Circuit reversed respondent's convictions. The court noted that customs inspectors had a "justifiably high level of official skepticism" about respondent's good motives, but the inspectors decided to let nature take its course rather than seek an immediate magistrate's warrant for an x ray. Such a magistrate's warrant required a "clear indication" or "plain suggestion" that the traveler was an alimentary canal smuggler under previous decisions of the Court of Appeals. The court applied this required level of suspicion to respondent's case. The court questioned the "humanity" of the inspectors' decision to hold respondent until her bowels moved, knowing that she would suffer "many hours of humiliating discomfort" if she chose not to submit to the x-ray examination. The court concluded that under a "clear indication" standard "the evidence available to the customs officers when they decided to hold [respondent] for continued observation was insufficient to support the 16-hour detention."

The government contends that the customs inspectors reasonably suspected that respondent was an alimentary canal smuggler, and this suspicion was sufficient to justify the detention. In support of the judgment below respondent argues, *inter alia*, that reasonable suspicion would not support respondent's detention, and in any event the inspectors did not reasonably suspect that respondent was carrying narcotics internally.

The Fourth Amendment commands that searches and seizures be reasonable. What is reasonable depends upon all of the circumstances surrounding the search or seizure and the nature of the search or seizure itself. The permissibility of a particular law enforcement practice is judged by "balancing its intrusion on the individual's Fourth Amendment interests against its promotion of legitimate governmental interests."

Here the seizure of respondent took place at the international border. Since the founding of our Republic, Congress has granted the Executive plenary authority to conduct routine searches and seizures at the border, without probable cause or a warrant, in order to regulate the collection of duties and to prevent the introduction of contraband into this country. This Court has long recognized Congress' power to police entrants at the border. * * * Consistently, therefore, with Congress' power to protect the Nation by stopping and examining persons entering this country, the Fourth Amendment's balance of reasonableness is qualitatively different at the international border than in the interior. Routine searches of the persons and effects of entrants are not subject to any requirement of reasonable suspicion, probable cause, or warrant, and first-class mail may be opened without a warrant on less than probable cause. Automotive travelers may be stopped at fixed check points near the border without individualized suspicion even if the stop is based largely on ethnicity, and boats on inland waters with ready access to the sea may be hailed and boarded with no suspicion whatever.

These cases reflect longstanding concern for the protection of the integrity of the border. This concern is, if anything, heightened by the veritable national crisis in law enforcement caused by smuggling of illicit narcotics, and in particular by the increasing utilization of alimentary canal smuggling. This desperate practice appears to be a relatively recent addition to the smugglers' repertoire of deceptive practices, and it also appears to be exceedingly difficult to detect. * * *

Balanced against the sovereign's interests at the border are the Fourth Amendment rights of respondent. Having presented herself at the border for admission, and having subjected herself to the criminal enforcement powers of the Federal Government, respondent was entitled to be free from unreasonable search and seizure. But not only is the expectation of privacy less at the border than in the interior, but the Fourth Amendment balance between the interests of the Government and the privacy right of the individual is struck much more favorably to the Government at the border.

We have not previously decided what level of suspicion would justify a seizure of an incoming traveler for purposes other than a routine border search. The Court of Appeals held that the initial detention of respondent was permissible only if the inspectors possessed a "clear indication" of alimentary canal smuggling. This "clear indication" language comes from our opinion in Schmerber v. California, 384 U.S. 757, 86 S.Ct. 1826, 16 L.Ed.2d 908 (1966), but we think that the Court of Appeals misapprehended the significance of that phrase in the context in which it was used in *Schmerber*. The Court of Appeals for the Ninth Circuit viewed "clear indication" as an intermediate standard between "reasonable suspicion" and "probable cause." But we think that the words in *Schmerber* were used to indicate the necessity for particularized suspicion that the evidence sought might be found within the body of the individual, rather than as enunciating still a third Fourth Amendment threshold between "reasonable suspicion" and "probable cause."

No other court, including this one, has ever adopted *Schmerber's* "clear indication" language as a Fourth Amendment standard. * * * We do not think that the Fourth Amendment's emphasis upon reasonableness is consistent with the creation of a third verbal standard in addition to "reasonable suspicion" and "probable cause"; we are dealing with a constitutional requirement of reasonableness, * * * and subtle verbal gradations may obscure rather than elucidate the meaning of the provision in question.

We hold that the detention of a traveler at the border, beyond the scope of a routine customs search and inspection, is justified at its inception if customs agents, considering all the facts surrounding the traveler and her trip, reasonably suspect that the traveler is smuggling contraband in her alimentary canal.[12]

12. It is also important to note what we do *not* hold. Because the issues are not presented today we suggest no view on what level of suspicion, if any, is required for nonroutine border searches such as strip, body cavity, or involuntary x-ray searches. Both parties would have us decide the issue of whether aliens possess lesser Fourth Amendment rights at the border; that question was

The "reasonable suspicion" standard has been applied in a number of contexts and effects a needed balance between private and public interests when law enforcement officials must make a limited intrusion on less than probable cause. It thus fits well into the situations involving alimentary canal smuggling at the border: this type of smuggling gives no external signs and inspectors will rarely possess probable cause to arrest or search, yet governmental interests in stopping smuggling at the border are high indeed. Under this standard officials at the border must have a "particularized and objective basis for suspecting the particular person" of alimentary canal smuggling.

The facts, and their rational inferences, known to customs inspectors in this case clearly supported a reasonable suspicion that respondent was an alimentary canal smuggler. We need not belabor the facts, including respondent's implausible story, that supported this suspicion. The trained customs inspectors had encountered many alimentary canal smugglers and certainly had more than an "inchoate and unparticularized suspicion or 'hunch,'" that respondent was smuggling narcotics in her alimentary canal. The inspectors' suspicion was a "'commonsense conclusio[n] about human behavior' upon which 'practical people,'—including government officials, are entitled to rely."

The final issue in this case is whether the detention of respondent was reasonably related in scope to the circumstances which justified it initially. In this regard we have cautioned that courts should not indulge in "unrealistic second-guessing," and we have noted that "creative judge[s], engaged in *post hoc* evaluations of police conduct can almost always imagine some alternative means by which the objectives of the police might have been accomplished." But "[t]he fact that the protection of the public might, in the abstract, have been accomplished by 'less intrusive' means does not, in itself, render the search unreasonable." Authorities must be allowed "to graduate their response to the demands of any particular situation." Here, respondent was detained *incommunicado* for almost 16 hours before inspectors sought a warrant; the warrant then took a number of hours to procure, through no apparent fault of the inspectors. This length of time undoubtedly exceeds any other detention we have approved under reasonable suspicion. But we have also consistently rejected hard-and-fast time limits. Instead, "common sense and ordinary human experience must govern over rigid criteria."

The rudimentary knowledge of the human body which judges possess in common with the rest of humankind tells us that alimentary canal smuggling cannot be detected in the amount of time in which other illegal activity may be investigated through brief *Terry*-type stops. It presents few, if any external signs; a quick frisk will not do, nor will even a strip search. In the case of respondent the inspectors had available, as an alternative to simply awaiting her bowel movement, an x ray. They offered her the alternative of submitting herself to that procedure. But when she refused that alternative, the customs inspectors were left with only two practical alternatives: detain her for such time as necessary to confirm their suspi-

not raised in either court below and we do not consider it today.

cions, a detention which would last much longer than the typical *"Terry"* stop, or turn her loose into the interior carrying the reasonably suspected contraband drugs.

The inspectors in this case followed this former procedure. They no doubt expected that respondent, having recently disembarked from a 10hour direct flight with a full and stiff abdomen, would produce a bowel movement without extended delay. But her visible efforts to resist the call of nature, which the court below labeled "heroic," disappointed this expectation and in turn caused her humiliation and discomfort. Our prior cases have refused to charge police with delays in investigatory detention attributable to the suspect's evasive actions, and that principle applies here as well. Respondent alone was responsible for much of the duration and discomfort of the seizure.

Under these circumstances, we conclude that the detention in this case was not unreasonably long. It occurred at the international border, where the Fourth Amendment balance of interests leans heavily to the Government. At the border, customs officials have more than merely an investigative law enforcement role. They are also charged, along with immigration officials, with protecting this Nation from entrants who may bring anything harmful into this country, whether that be communicable diseases, narcotics, or explosives. In this regard the detention of a suspected alimentary canal smuggler at the border is analogous to the detention of a suspected tuberculosis carrier at the border: both are detained until their bodily processes dispel the suspicion that they will introduce a harmful agent into this country.

Respondent's detention was long, uncomfortable, indeed, humiliating; but both its length and its discomfort resulted solely from the method by which she chose to smuggle illicit drugs into this country. * * * [I]n the presence of articulable suspicion of smuggling in her alimentary canal, the customs officers were not required by the Fourth Amendment to pass respondent and her 88 cocaine-filled balloons into the interior. Her detention for the period of time necessary to either verify or dispel the suspicion was not unreasonable. The judgment of the Court of Appeals is therefore

Reversed.

■ JUSTICE STEVENS, concurring in the judgment.

If a seizure and a search of the person of the kind disclosed by this record may be made on the basis of reasonable suspicion, we must assume that a significant number of innocent persons will be required to undergo similar procedures. The rule announced in this case cannot, therefore, be supported on the ground that respondent's prolonged and humiliating detention "resulted solely from the method by which she chose to smuggle illicit drugs into this country."

The prolonged detention of respondent was, however, justified by a different choice that respondent made; she withdrew her consent to an x-ray examination that would have easily determined whether the reasonable suspicion that she was concealing contraband was justified. I believe that Customs agents may require that a nonpregnant person reasonably sus-

[handwritten margin note: Court says "Serves her right"]

pected of this kind of smuggling submit to an x-ray examination as an incident to a border search. I therefore concur in the judgment.

■ JUSTICE BRENNAN, with whom JUSTICE MARSHALL joins, dissenting.

* * *

I

Travelers at the national border are routinely subjected to questioning, pat-downs, and thorough searches of their belongings. These measures, which involve relatively limited invasions of privacy and which typically are conducted on all incoming travelers, do not violate the Fourth Amendment given the interests of "national self-protection reasonably requiring one entering the country to identify himself as entitled to come in, and his belongings as effects which may lawfully be brought in." Carroll v. United States, 267 U.S. 132, 154, 45 S.Ct. 280, 285, 69 L.Ed. 543 (1925). Individual travelers also may be singled out on "reasonable suspicion" and briefly held for further investigation. Cf. Terry v. Ohio, 392 U.S. 1, 88 S.Ct. 1868, 20 L.Ed.2d 889 (1968). At some point, however, further investigation involves such severe intrusions on the values the Fourth Amendment protects that more stringent safeguards are required. For example, the length and nature of a detention may, at least when conducted for criminal-investigative purposes, ripen into something approximating a full-scale custodial arrest—indeed, the arrestee, unlike the detainee in cases such as this, is at least given such basic rights as a telephone call, *Miranda* warnings, a bed, a prompt hearing before the nearest federal magistrate, an appointed attorney, and consideration of bail. In addition, border detentions may involve the use of such highly intrusive investigative techniques as body-cavity searches, x-ray searches, and stomach-pumping.

I believe that detentions and searches falling into these more intrusive categories are presumptively "reasonable" within the meaning of the Fourth Amendment only if authorized by a judicial officer. * * *

We have, to be sure, held that executive officials need not obtain prior judicial authorization where exigent circumstances would make such authorization impractical and counterproductive. In so holding, however, we have reaffirmed the general rule that "the police must, whenever practicable, obtain advance judicial approval of searches and seizures through the warrant procedure." * * *

The Government contends, however, that because investigative detentions of the sort that occurred in this case need not be supported by probable cause, no warrant is required given the phraseology of the Fourth Amendment's Warrant Clause. * * * Even assuming that border detentions and searches that become lengthy and highly intrusive need not be supported by probable cause, * * * this reasoning runs squarely contrary to the Court's administrative-warrant cases. * * *

Something has gone fundamentally awry in our constitutional jurisprudence when a neutral and detached magistrate's authorization is required before the authorities may inspect "the plumbing, heating, ventilation, gas, and electrical systems" in a person's home, investigate the back rooms of his workplace, or poke through the charred remains of his gutted garage, but *not* before they may hold him in indefinite involuntary isolation at the nation's border to investigate whether he might be engaged in criminal wrongdoing. * * *

The Court argues, however, that the length and "discomfort" of de Hernandez' detention "resulted *solely* from the method by which she chose to smuggle illicit drugs into this country," and it speculates that only her " 'heroic' "efforts prevented the detention from being brief and to the point. Although we now know that de Hernandez was indeed guilty of smuggling drugs internally, such *post hoc* rationalizations have no place in our Fourth Amendment jurisprudence, which demands that we "prevent hindsight from coloring the evaluation of the reasonableness of a search or seizure." At the time the authorities simply had, at most, a reasonable suspicion that de Hernandez might be engaged in such smuggling. * * * [W]ith all respect to the Court, it is not " 'unrealistic second-guessing' " to predict that an innocent traveler, locked away in *incommunicado* detention in unfamiliar surroundings in a foreign land, might well be so frightened and exhausted as to be unable so to "cooperate" with the authorities.

* * *

Finally, I disagree with Justice Stevens that de Hernandez' alternative "choice" of submitting to abdominal x-irradiation at the discretion of customs officials made this detention "justified." * * * [T]he crux of my disagreement is this: We have learned in our lifetimes, time and again, the inherent dangers that result from coupling unchecked "law enforcement" discretion with the tools of medical technology. * * * This should be so whether the intrusion is by incision, by stomach-pumping, or by exposure to x-irradiation. Because no exigent circumstances prevented the authorities from seeking a magistrate's authorization so to probe de Hernandez' abdominal cavity, the proffered alternative "choice" of a warrantless x-ray was just as impermissible as the 27-hour detention that actually occurred.

II

I believe that de Hernandez' detention violated the Fourth Amendment for an additional reason: it was not supported by probable cause. In the domestic context, a detention of the sort that occurred here would be permissible only if there were probable cause at the outset.

To be sure, it is commonly asserted that as a result of the Fourth Amendment's "border exception" there is no requirement of probable cause for such investigations. But the justifications for the border exception necessarily limit its breadth. The exception derives from the unquestioned and paramount interest in "national self-protection reasonably requiring one entering the country to identify himself as entitled to come in, and his belongings as effects which may be lawfully brought in." * * * Subject only to the other applicable guarantees of the Bill of Rights, this interest in "national self-protection" is plenary. Thus, as the Court notes, a suspected tuberculosis carrier may be detained at the border for medical testing and treatment as a condition of entry. As a condition of entry, the traveler may be subjected to exhaustive processing and examinations, and his belongings may be scrutinized with exacting care. I have no doubt as well that, *as a* *condition of entry,* travelers in appropriate circumstances may be required to excrete their bodily wastes for further scrutiny and to submit to diagnostic x-rays.

Contrary to the Court's reasoning, however, the Government in carrying out such immigration and customs functions does not simply have the two stark alternatives of either forcing a traveler to submit to such procedures or allowing him to "pass . . . into the interior." There is a third alternative: to instruct the traveler who refuses to submit to burdensome but reasonable conditions of entry that he is free to turn around and leave the country. In fact, I believe that the "reasonableness" of any burdensome requirement for entry is necessarily conditioned on the potential entrant's freedom to leave the country if he objects to that requirement. Surely the Government's manifest interest in preventing potentially excludable individuals carrying potential contraband from crossing our borders is fully vindicated if those individuals voluntarily decided not to cross the borders.

* * * If the traveler does not wish to consent to prolonged detentions or intrusive examinations, the nation's customs and immigration interests are fully served by sending the traveler on his way elsewhere. If the authorities nevertheless propose to detain the traveler for purposes of subjecting him to criminal investigation and possible arrest and punishment, they may do so only pursuant to constitutional safeguards applicable to everyone else in the country. Chief among those safeguards is the requirement that, except in limited circumstances not present here, custodial detentions occur only on probable cause. * * * That standard obviously is not met, and was not met here, simply by courier profiles, "common rumor or report, suspicion, or even 'strong reason to suspect.' " Because the contraband in this case was the fruit of the authorities' indefinite detention of Rosa de Hernandez without probable cause or a warrant, I would affirm the judgment of the Court of Appeals for the Ninth Circuit reversing her conviction.

2. BORDER-RELATED ENFORCEMENT ACTIVITY

Law enforcement activity conducted in the interior of the country is arguably less directly related to the federal government's interest in protecting the security of its borders. It also may intrude upon privacy and other concerns more significantly than activity occurring at the border. For these and other reasons, the Supreme Court has treated such law enforcement activity differently than law enforcement activity at the border or its functional equivalent. Most of the Court's case law, including the principal case in this subsection, deals with traffic control operations.

In United States v. Ortiz, 422 U.S. 891, 95 S.Ct. 2585, 45 L.Ed.2d 623 (1975), Border Patrol officers stopped Ortiz' automobile at a fixed checkpoint at San Clemente, California; the checkpoint is described and discussed in the principal case in this subsection. A search of the vehicle's trunk revealed three aliens and Ortiz was convicted of knowingly transporting illegal aliens. A unanimous Supreme Court invalidated the search of the automobile because it was conducted without probable cause to believe illegal aliens would be found. The government urged the probable cause requirement be found inapplicable for two reasons. First, careful selection of locations for checkpoints by high-level Border Patrol officials limited officers' discretion in stopping and searching cars. Second, checkpoints provided visible signs of officers' authority and demonstrated to stopped motorists that others were being stopped and searched as well; motorists were, as a result, less likely to be frightened or annoyed by the search and consequently the search was less intrusive upon privacy than other law enforcement activities. Rejecting the government's argument, the Court stressed that a search of a car, even under the conditions at issue, remains a substantial invasion of privacy. Moreover, only a small portion of cars passing through checkpoints were searched; throughout the system, less than 3% were examined. Officers manning the checkpoints exercised a degree of discretion in deciding which cars to search. "This degree of discretion," the Court observed, "is not consistent with the Fourth Amendment."

Evidence showed inspections of cars for illegal aliens typically included examinations of the trunk, under the hood, and beneath the chassis. Enclosed portions of trucks, campers and similar vehicles were also examined. But inspections sometimes became more rigorous. The Court noted in one case previously before it officers removed a back seat cushion because of reports aliens were found seated upright behind seats from which the springs had been removed. Not every aspect of the routine "inspections" necessarily constitutes a "search" for which probable cause is required, the Court commented. It found no occasion in the case "to define the exact limits of an automobile 'search.'"

United States v. Martinez–Fuerte

Supreme Court of the United States, 1976.
428 U.S. 543, 96 S.Ct. 3074, 49 L.Ed.2d 1116.

■ MR. JUSTICE POWELL delivered the opinion of the Court.

These cases involve criminal prosecutions for offenses relating to the transportation of illegal Mexican aliens. Each defendant was arrested at a permanent checkpoint operated by the Border Patrol away from the international border with Mexico, and each sought the exclusion of certain evidence on the ground that the operation of the checkpoint was incompatible with the Fourth Amendment. In each instance whether the Fourth Amendment was violated turns primarily on whether a vehicle may be stopped at a fixed checkpoint for brief questioning of its occupants even though there is no reason to believe the particular vehicle contains illegal aliens. We reserved this question last Term in United States v. Ortiz, 422 U.S. 891, 897 n. 3, 95 S.Ct. 2585, 2589, 45 L.Ed.2d 623 (1975). We hold today that such stops are consistent with the Fourth Amendment. We also hold that the operation of a fixed checkpoint need not be authorized in advance by a judicial warrant.

I

A

The respondents in No. 74–1560 are defendants in three separate prosecutions resulting from arrests made on three different occasions at the permanent immigration checkpoint on Interstate 5 near San Clemente, Cal. Interstate 5 is the principal highway between San Diego and Los Angeles, and the San Clemente checkpoint is 66 road miles north of the Mexican border. We previously have described the checkpoint as follows:

" 'Approximately one mile south of the checkpoint is a large black on yellow sign with flashing yellow lights over the highway stating "ALL VEHICLES, STOP AHEAD, 1 MILE." Three quarters of a mile further north are two black on yellow signs suspended over the highway with flashing lights stating "WATCH FOR BRAKE LIGHTS." At the checkpoint, which is also the location of a State of California weighing station, are two large signs with flashing red lights suspended over the highway. These signs each state "STOP HERE—U.S. OFFI-CERS." Placed on the highway are a number of orange traffic cones funneling traffic into two lanes where a Border Patrol agent in full dress uniform, standing behind a white on red "STOP" sign checks traffic. Blocking traffic in the unused lanes are official U.S. Border Patrol vehicles with flashing red lights. In addition, there is a perma-nent building which houses the Border Patrol office and temporary detention facilities. There are also floodlights for nighttime opera-tion.' "

The "point" agent standing between the two lanes of traffic visually screens all northbound vehicles, which the checkpoint brings to a virtual, if not a complete, halt. Most motorists are allowed to resume their progress without any oral inquiry or close visual examination. In a relatively small number of cases the "point" agent will conclude that further inquiry is in order. He directs these cars to a secondary inspection area, where their occupants are asked about their citizenship and immigration status. The Government informs us that at San Clemente the average length of an investigation in the secondary inspection area is three to five minutes. A direction to stop in the secondary inspection area could be based on something suspicious about a particular car passing through the check-point, but the Government concedes that [the stop] at issue in No. 74–1560 was [not] based on any articulable suspicion. During the period when these stops were made, the checkpoint was operating under a magistrate's "warrant of inspection," which authorized the Border Patrol to conduct a routine-stop operation at the San Clemente location.

general procedure

We turn now to the particulars of the stops involved in No. 74–1560, and the procedural history of the case. Respondent Amado Martinez-Fuerte approached the checkpoint driving a vehicle containing two female passen-gers. The women were illegal Mexican aliens who had entered the United States at the San Ysidro port of entry by using false papers and rendez-voused with Martinez-Fuerte in San Diego to be transported northward. At the checkpoint their car was directed to the secondary inspection area. Martinez-Fuerte produced documents showing him to be a lawful resident alien, but his passengers admitted being present in the country unlawfully. He was charged, *inter alia*, with two counts of illegally transporting aliens in violation of 8 U.S.C. § 1324(a)(2). He moved before trial to suppress all evidence stemming from the stop on the ground that the operation of the checkpoint was in violation of the Fourth Amendment. The motion to suppress was denied, and he was convicted on both counts after a jury trial.

* * *

Martinez-Fuerte appealed his conviction * * *. The Court of Appeals held, with one judge dissenting, that [the stop] violated the Fourth Amendment, concluding that a stop for inquiry is constitutional only if the Border Patrol reasonably suspects the presence of illegal aliens on the basis of articulable facts. It reversed Martinez-Fuerte's conviction * * *. We reverse and remand.

B

Petitioner in No. 75–5387, Rodolfo Sifuentes, was arrested at the permanent immigration checkpoint on U.S. Highway 77 near Sarita, Tex. Highway 77 originates in Brownsville, and it is one of the two major highways running north from the lower Rio Grande valley. The Sarita checkpoint is about 90 miles north of Brownsville, and 65–90 miles from the nearest points of the Mexican border. The physical arrangement of the checkpoint resembles generally that at San Clemente, but the checkpoint is operated differently in that the officers customarily stop all northbound motorists for a brief inquiry. Motorists whom the officers recognize as local inhabitants, however, are waved through the checkpoint without inquiry. Unlike the San Clemente checkpoint the Sarita operation was conducted without a judicial warrant.

Sifuentes drove up to the checkpoint without any visible passengers. When an agent approached the vehicle, however, he observed four passengers, one in the front seat and the other three in the rear, slumped down in the seats. Questioning revealed that each passenger was an illegal alien, although Sifuentes was a United States citizen. The aliens had met Sifuentes in the United States, by prearrangement, after swimming across the Rio Grande.

Sifuentes was indicted on four counts of illegally transporting aliens. He moved on Fourth Amendment grounds to suppress the evidence derived from the stop. The motion was denied and he was convicted after a jury trial. Sifuentes renewed his Fourth Amendment argument on appeal, contending primarily that stops made without reason to believe a car is transporting aliens illegally are unconstitutional. The United States Court of Appeals for the Fifth Circuit affirmed the conviction, * * * rul[ing] that routine checkpoint stops are consistent with the Fourth Amendment. We affirm.

II

The Courts of Appeals for the Ninth and the Fifth Circuits are in conflict on the constitutionality of a law enforcement technique considered important by those charged with policing the Nation's borders. Before turning to the constitutional question, we examine the context in which it arises.

A

It has been national policy for many years to limit immigration into the United States. Since July 1, 1968, the annual quota for immigrants from all independent countries of the Western Hemisphere, including Mexico, has been 120,000 persons. Many more aliens than can be accommodated under the quota want to live and work in the United States. Consequently, large numbers of aliens seek illegally to enter or to remain in the United States. We noted last Term that "[e]stimates of the number of illegal immigrants [already] in the United States vary widely. A conservative estimate in 1972 produced a figure of about one million, but the Immigration and Naturalization Service now suggests there may be as many as 10 or 12 million aliens illegally in the country." United States v. Brignoni-Ponce, 422 U.S. 873, 878, 95 S.Ct. 2574, 2578, 45 L.Ed.2d 607 (1975) (footnote omitted). It is estimated that 85% of the illegal immigrants are from Mexico, drawn by the fact that economic opportunities are significantly greater in the United States than they are in Mexico.

Interdicting the flow of illegal entrants from Mexico poses formidable law enforcement problems. The principal problem arises from surreptitious entries. The United States shares a border with Mexico that is almost 2,000 miles long, and much of the border area is uninhabited desert or thinly populated arid land. Although the Border Patrol maintains personnel, electronic equipment, and fences along portions of the border, it remains relatively easy for individuals to enter the United States without detection. It also is possible for an alien to enter unlawfully at a port of entry by the use of falsified papers or to enter lawfully but violate restrictions of entry in an effort to remain in the country unlawfully. Once within the country, the aliens seek to travel inland to areas where employment is believed to be available, frequently meeting by prearrangement with friends or professional smugglers who transport them in private vehicles.

The Border Patrol conducts three kinds of inland traffic-checking operations in an effort to minimize illegal immigration. Permanent checkpoints, such as those at San Clemente and Sarita, are maintained at or near intersections of important roads leading away from the border. They operate on a coordinated basis designed to avoid circumvention by smugglers and others who transport the illegal aliens. Temporary checkpoints, which operate like permanent ones, occasionally are established in other strategic locations. Finally, roving patrols are maintained to supplement the checkpoint system. See Almeida-Sanchez v. United States, 413 U.S. 266, 268, 93 S.Ct. 2535, 2537, 37 L.Ed.2d 596 (1973). In fiscal 1973, 175,511 deportable aliens were apprehended throughout the Nation by "line watch" agents stationed at the border itself. Traffic-checking operations in the interior apprehended approximately 55,300 more deportable aliens. Most of the traffic-checking apprehensions were at checkpoints, though precise figures are not available.

B

We are concerned here with permanent checkpoints, the locations of which are chosen on the basis of a number of factors. The Border Patrol believes that to assure effectiveness, a checkpoint must be (i) distant enough from the border to avoid interference with traffic in populated areas near the border, (ii) close to the confluence of two or more significant roads leading away from the border, (iii) situated in terrain that restricts vehicle passage around the checkpoint, (iv) on a stretch of highway compatible with safe operation, and (v) beyond the 25 mile zone in which "border passes" are valid.

The record in No. 74–1560 provides a rather complete picture of the effectiveness of the San Clemente checkpoint. Approximately 10 million cars pass the checkpoint location each year, although the checkpoint actually is in operation only about 70% of the time. In calendar year 1973, approximately 17,000 illegal aliens were apprehended there. During an eight-day period in 1974 that included the arrests involved in No. 74–1560, roughly 146,000 vehicles passed through the checkpoint during 124⅙ hours of operation. Of these, 820 vehicles were referred to the secondary inspection area, where Border Patrol agents found 725 deportable aliens in 171 vehicles. In all but two cases, the aliens were discovered without a conventional search of the vehicle. A similar rate of apprehensions throughout the year would have resulted in an annual total of over 33,000, although the Government contends that many illegal aliens pass through the checkpoint undetected. * * *

IV

It is agreed that checkpoint stops are "seizures" within the meaning of the Fourth Amendment. The defendants contend primarily that the routine stopping of vehicles at a checkpoint is invalid because *Brignoni–Ponce* must be read as proscribing any stops in the absence of reasonable suspicion. Sifuentes alternatively contends in No. 75–5387 that routine checkpoint stops are permissible only when the practice has the advance judicial authorization of a warrant. There was a warrant authorizing the stops at San Clemente but none at Sarita. As we reach the issue of a warrant requirement only if reasonable suspicion is not required, we turn first to whether reasonable suspicion is a prerequisite to a valid stop, a question to be resolved by balancing the interests at stake.

A

Our previous cases have recognized that maintenance of a traffic-checking program in the interior is necessary because the flow of illegal aliens cannot be controlled effectively at the border. We note here only the substantiality of the public interest in the practice of routine stops for inquiry at permanent checkpoints, a practice which the Government identifies as the most important of the traffic-checking operations. These checkpoints are located on important highways; in their absence such highways would offer illegal aliens a quick and safe route into the interior. Routine checkpoint inquiries apprehend many smugglers and illegal aliens who succumb to the lure of such highways. And the prospect of such inquiries forces others onto less efficient roads that are less heavily traveled, slowing their movement and making them more vulnerable to detection by roving patrols.

A requirement that stops on major routes inland always be based on reasonable suspicion would be impractical because the flow of traffic tends to be too heavy to allow the particularized study of a given car that would enable it to be identified as a possible carrier of illegal aliens. In particular, such a requirement would largely eliminate any deterrent to the conduct of well-disguised smuggling operations, even though smugglers are known to use these highways regularly.

B

While the need to make routine checkpoint stops is great, the consequent intrusion on Fourth Amendment interests is quite limited. The stop does intrude to a limited extent on motorists' right to "free passage without interruption," and arguably on their right to personal security. But it involves only a brief detention of travelers during which

Brief Detention

> " '[a]ll that is required of the vehicle's occupants is a response to a brief question or two and possibly the production of a document evidencing a right to be in the United States.' "

Neither the vehicle nor its occupants are searched, and visual inspection of the vehicle is limited to what can be seen without a search. This objective intrusion—the stop itself, the questioning, and the visual inspection—also existed in roving-patrol stops. But we view checkpoint stops in a different light because the subjective intrusion—the generating of concern or even fright on the part of lawful travelers—is appreciably less in the case of a checkpoint stop. * * *

In *Brignoni–Ponce,* we recognized that Fourth Amendment analysis in this context also must take into account the overall degree of interference with legitimate traffic. We concluded there that random roving-patrol stops could not be tolerated because they "would subject the residents of * * * [border] areas to potentially unlimited interference with their use of the highways, solely at the discretion of Border Patrol officers. * * * [They] could stop motorists at random for questioning, day or night, anywhere within 100 air miles of the 2,000 mile border, on a city street, a busy highway, or a desert road * * *." There also was a grave danger that such unreviewable discretion would be abused by some officers in the field.

Rule on Stops

Routine checkpoint stops do not intrude similarly on the motoring public. First, the potential interference with legitimate traffic is minimal. Motorists using these highways are not taken by surprise as they know, or may obtain knowledge of, the location of the checkpoints and will not be stopped elsewhere. Second, checkpoint operations both appear to and actually involve less discretionary enforcement activity. The regularized manner in which established checkpoints are operated is visible evidence, reassuring to lawabiding motorists, that the stops are duly authorized and believed to serve the public interest. The location of a fixed checkpoint is not chosen by officers in the field, but by officials responsible for making overall decisions as to the most effective allocation of limited enforcement resources. We may assume that such officials will be unlikely to locate a checkpoint where it bears arbitrarily or oppressively on motorists as a class. And since field officers may stop only those cars passing the checkpoint, there is less room for abusive or harassing stops of individuals than there was in the case of roving-patrol stops. Moreover, a claim that a particular exercise of discretion in locating or operating a checkpoint is unreasonable is subject to post-stop judicial review.

The defendants arrested at the San Clemente checkpoint suggest that its operation involves a significant extra element of intrusiveness in that only a small percentage of cars are referred to the secondary inspection area, thereby "stigmatizing" those diverted and reducing the assurances provided by equal treatment of all motorists. We think defendants overstate the consequences. Referrals are made for the sole purpose of conducting a routine and limited inquiry into residence status that cannot feasibly be made of every motorist where the traffic is heavy. The objective intrusion of the stop and inquiry thus remains minimal. Selective referral may involve some annoyance, but it remains true that the stops should not be frightening or offensive because of their public and relatively routine nature. Moreover, selective referrals—rather than questioning the occupants of every car—tend to advance some Fourth Amendment interests by minimizing the intrusion on the general motoring public.

C

The defendants note correctly that to accommodate public and private interests some quantum of individualized suspicion is usually a prerequisite to a constitutional search or seizure. But the Fourth Amendment imposes no irreducible requirement of such suspicion. * * *

[H]ere * * * we deal neither with searches nor with the sanctity of private dwellings, ordinarily afforded the most stringent Fourth Amendment protection. * * * [O]ne's expectation of privacy in an automobile and of freedom in its operation are significantly different from the traditional expectation of privacy and freedom in one's residence. And the reasonableness of the procedures followed in making these checkpoint stops makes the resulting intrusion on the interests of motorists minimal. On the other hand, the purpose of the stops is legitimate and in the public interest, and the need for this enforcement technique is demonstrated by the records in the cases before us. Accordingly, we hold that the stops and questioning at issue may be made in the absence of any individualized suspicion at reasonably located checkpoints.[13]

13. [W]e deem the argument by the defendants in No. 74–1560 * * * to raise the question whether, even though a warrant is not required, it is unreasonable to locate a checkpoint at San Clemente.

We answer this question in the negative. As indicated above, the choice of checkpoint locations is an administrative decision that must be left largely within the discretion of the Border Patrol. We think the decision to locate a checkpoint at San Clemente was reasonable. The location meets the criteria prescribed by the Border Patrol to assure effectiveness and the evidence supports the view that the needs of law enforcement are furthered by this location. The absolute number of apprehensions at the checkpoint is high confirming Border Patrol judgment that significant numbers of illegal aliens regularly use Interstate 5 at this point. Also, San Clemente was selected as the location where traffic is lightest between San Diego and Los Angeles, thereby minimizing interference with legitimate traffic.

No question has been raised about the reasonableness of the location of the Sarita checkpoint.

We further believe that it is constitutional to refer motorists selectively to the secondary inspection area at the San Clemente checkpoint on the basis of criteria that would not sustain a roving-patrol stop. Thus, even if it be assumed that such referrals are made largely on the basis of apparent Mexican ancestry, we perceive no constitutional violation. As the intrusion here is sufficiently minimal that no particularized reason need exist to justify it, we think it follows that the Border Patrol officers must have wide discretion in selecting the motorists to be diverted for the brief questioning involved.

V

Sifuentes' alternative argument is that routine stops at a checkpoint are permissible only if a warrant has given judicial authorization to the particular checkpoint location and the practice of routine stops. A warrant requirement in these circumstances draws some support from [Camara v. Municipal Court, 387 U.S. 523, 87 S.Ct. 1727, 18 L.Ed.2d 930 (1967) (discussed in part B of this chapter)], where the Court held that, absent consent, an "area" warrant was required to make a building code inspection, even though the search could be conducted absent cause to believe that there were violations in the building searched.

We do not think, however, that *Camara* is an apt model. It involved the search of private residences, for which a warrant traditionally has been required. * * * [T]he strong Fourth Amendment interests that justify the warrant requirement in that context are absent here. The degree of intrusion upon privacy that may be occasioned by a search of a house hardly can be compared with the minor interference with privacy resulting from the mere stop for questioning as to residence. Moreover, the warrant requirement in *Camara* served specific Fourth Amendment interests to which a warrant requirement here would make little contribution. The Court there said:

> "[W]hen [an] inspector [without a warrant] demands entry, the occupant has no way of knowing whether enforcement of the municipal code involved requires inspection of his premises, no way of knowing the lawful limits of the inspector's power to search, and no way of knowing whether the inspector himself is acting under proper authorization."

A warrant provided assurance to the occupant on these scores. We believe that the visible manifestations of the field officers' authority at a checkpoint provide substantially the same assurances in this case.

Other purposes served by the requirement of a warrant also are inapplicable here. One such purpose is to prevent hindsight from coloring the evaluation of the reasonableness of a search or seizure. The reasonableness of checkpoint stops, however, turns on factors such as the location and method of operation of the checkpoint, factors that are not susceptible to the distortion of hindsight, and therefore will be open to post-stop review notwithstanding the absence of a warrant. Another purpose for a warrant requirement is to substitute the judgment of the magistrate for that of the searching or seizing officer. But the need for this is reduced when the decision to "seize" is not entirely in the hands of the officer in the field, and deference is to be given to the administrative decisions of higher ranking officials.

VI

In summary, we hold that stops for brief questioning routinely conducted at permanent checkpoints are consistent with the Fourth Amendment and need not be authorized by warrant. The principal protection of Fourth Amendment rights at checkpoints lies in appropriate limitations on the scope of the stop. We have held that checkpoint searches are constitutional only if justified by consent or probable cause to search. United States v. Ortiz, 422 U.S. 891, 95 S.Ct. 2585, 45 L.Ed.2d 623 (1975). And our holding today is limited to the type of stops described in this opinion. "[A]ny further detention must be based on consent or probable cause." United States v. Brignoni–Ponce, supra, at 882, 95 S.Ct., at 2580. None of the defendants in these cases argues that the stopping officers exceeded these limitations. Consequently, we affirm the judgment of the Court of Appeals for the Fifth Circuit, which had affirmed the conviction of Sifuentes. We reverse the judgment of the Court of Appeals for the Ninth Circuit and remand the case with directions to affirm the conviction of Martinez-Fuerte * * *.

It is so ordered.

■ Mr. Justice Brennan, with whom Mr. Justice Marshall joins, dissenting.

* * *

The Court assumes, and I certainly agree, that persons stopped at fixed checkpoints, whether or not referred to a secondary detention area, are "seized" within the meaning of the Fourth Amendment. Moreover, since the vehicle and its occupants are subjected to a "visual inspection," the intrusion clearly exceeds mere physical restraint, for officers are able to see more in a stopped vehicle than in vehicles traveling at normal speeds down the highway. As the Court concedes, the checkpoint stop involves essentially the same intrusions as a roving-patrol stop, yet the Court provides no principled basis for distinguishing checkpoint stops.

Certainly that basis is not provided in the Court's reasoning that the subjective intrusion here is appreciably less than in the case of a stop by a roving patrol. *Brignoni–Ponce* nowhere bases the requirement of reasonable suspicion upon the subjective nature of the intrusion. In any event, the subjective aspects of checkpoint stops, even if different from the subjective aspects of roving-patrol stops, just as much require some principled restraint on law enforcement conduct. The motorist whose conduct has been nothing but innocent—and this is overwhelmingly the case—surely resents his own detention and inspection. And checkpoints, unlike roving stops, detain thousands of motorists, a dragnet-like procedure offensive to the sensibilities of free citizens. Also, the delay occasioned by stopping hundreds of vehicles on a busy highway is particularly irritating.

In addition to overlooking these dimensions of subjective intrusion, the Court, without explanation, also ignores one major source of vexation. In abandoning any requirement of a minimum of reasonable suspicion, or even articulable suspicion, the Court in every practical sense renders meaningless, as applied to checkpoint stops, the *Brignoni–Ponce* holding that "standing alone [Mexican appearance] does not justify stopping all Mexican-Americans to ask if they are aliens." Since the objective is almost entirely the Mexican illegally in the country, checkpoint officials, uninhibited by any objective standards and therefore free to stop any or all motorists without explanation or excuse, wholly on whim, will perforce target motorists of Mexican appearance. The process will then inescapably discriminate against citizens of Mexican ancestry and Mexican aliens lawfully in this country for no other reason than that they unavoidably possess the same "suspicious" physical and grooming characteristics of illegal Mexican aliens.

* * *

The Court argues * * * that practicalities necessitate [upholding the stops]. * * *

As an initial matter, whatever force this argument may have, it cannot apply to the secondary detentions that occurred in No. 74–1560. Once a vehicle has been slowed and observed at a checkpoint, ample opportunity exists to formulate the reasonable suspicion which, if it actually exists, would justify further detention. * * *

The Court's rationale is also not persuasive because several of the factors upon which officers may rely in establishing reasonable suspicion are readily ascertainable, regardless of the flow of traffic. * * *

Finally, the Court's argument fails for more basic reasons. There is no principle in the jurisprudence of fundamental rights which permits constitutional limitations to be dispensed with merely because they cannot be conveniently satisfied. * * *

NOTES: "ROVING" PATROLS

1. The Supreme Court first addressed the effect of Fourth Amendment considerations upon the technique often described as conducting "roving" border patrols in Almeida–Sanchez v. United States, 413 U.S. 266, 93 S.Ct. 2535, 37 L.Ed.2d 596 (1973). Almeida–Sanchez's car was stopped and searched while traveling on highway 78 in California. Highway 78 runs east-west and although it meanders it does not touch the border; the point of the stop was 25 air miles north of the border. The Immigration and Nationality Act purports to authorize warrantless searches of automobiles or other conveyances for illegally entered aliens "within a reasonable distance from any external boundary of the United States," as authorized by regulations promulgated by the Attorney General. "Reasonable distance" was defined in such regulations as within 100 air miles from any external boundary. 8 C.F.R. § 287.1. Rejecting the argument that extraordinary needs of border enforcement justify searches such as that in the case, the Court held that the absence of probable cause or consent rendered the search unreasonable.

2. In United States v. Brignoni–Ponce, 422 U.S. 873, 95 S.Ct. 2574, 45 L.Ed.2d 607 (1975), the Court returned to roving patrol stops. Border Patrol officers stopped Brignoni–Ponce's car on Interstate Highway 5 in California south of San Clemente. The Government defended the stop on the ground the officers believed the three occupants of the vehicle to be of Mexican decent. When questioned, the occupants acknowledged the two passengers were aliens who had entered the country illegally.

At Brignoni–Ponce's trial for transportation of illegally entered aliens, evidence from the stop and questioning of the occupants was admitted over defense objection. The Supreme Court reversed the resulting conviction. It acknowledged the important need to enforce border security created special problems, but it rejected the argument that this need permitted law enforcement officers to stop motorists at random within 100 air miles of the border. Law enforcement needs are sufficiently met, the Court concluded, by officers' right to conduct brief field stops on reasonable suspicion. On the facts before it, however, the Government failed to show the officers harbored reasonable suspicion that Brignoni–Ponce's vehicle contained illegally entered aliens. In response to the Government's contention that the occupants' apparent Mexican ancestry supported the stop, the Court explained:

> [T]his factor alone would justify neither a reasonable belief that they were aliens, nor a reasonable belief that the car concealed other aliens who were illegally in the country. Large numbers of native-born and naturalized citizens have the physical characteristics identified with Mexican ancestry, and even in the border area a relatively small proportion of them are aliens. The likelihood that any given person of Mexican ancestry is an alien is high enough to make Mexican appearance a relevant factor, but standing alone it does not justify stopping all Mexican-Americans to ask if they are aliens.

422 U.S. at 886–87, 95 S.Ct. at 2583, 45 L.Ed.2d at 619–20. As to what other factors might contribute to the development of reasonable suspicion, the Court offered:

> Officers may consider the characteristics of the area in which they encounter a vehicle. Its proximity to the border, the usual patterns of traffic on the particular road, and previous experience with alien traffic are all relevant. They may also consider information about recent illegal border crossings in the area. The driver's behavior may be relevant, as erratic driving or obvious attempts to evade officers can support a reasonable suspicion. Aspects of the vehicle itself may justify suspicion. For instance, officers say that certain station wagons, with large compartments for fold-down seats or spare tires, are frequently used for transporting concealed aliens. The vehicle may appear to be heavily loaded, it may have an extraordinary number of passengers, or the officers may observe persons trying to hide. The Government also points out that trained officers can recognize the characteristic appearance of persons who live in Mexico, relying on such factors as the mode of dress and haircut. In all situations the officer is entitled to assess the facts in light of his experience in detecting illegal entry and smuggling.

422 U.S. at 884–85, 95 S.Ct. at 2582, 45 L.Ed.2d at 618–19. Where the factors amount to reasonable suspicion, the Court has held that a stop of a vehicle and questioning of the driver is permissible. United States v. Cortez, 449 U.S. 411, 101 S.Ct. 690, 66 L.Ed.2d 621 (1981).

F.   EXTRAORDINARILY INTRUSIVE SEARCHES

In all of the situations covered in the preceding parts of this chapter, attention has focused on whether or to what extent the benchmark requirements of probable cause and a traditional search warrant should be abandoned or diluted. But in other situations, it is at least arguable that those requirements should not only be retained but also tightened so as to impose greater limitations on police ability to search than are imposed in standard situations. One of those situations—surgical removal of evidence from the suspect's body—is covered in this section.

Winston v. Lee

Supreme Court of the United States, 1985.
470 U.S. 753, 105 S.Ct. 1611, 84 L.Ed.2d 662.

■ JUSTICE BRENNAN delivered the opinion of the Court.

* * *

I

A

At approximately 1 a.m. on July 18, 1982, Ralph E. Watkinson was closing his shop for the night. As he was locking the door, he observed someone armed with a gun coming toward him from across the street. Watkinson was also armed and when he drew his gun, the other person told him to freeze. Watkinson then fired at the other person, who returned his fire. Watkinson was hit in the legs, while the other individual, who appeared to be wounded in his left side, ran from the scene. The police arrived on the scene shortly thereafter, and Watkinson was taken by ambulance to the emergency room of the Medical College of Virginia (MCV) Hospital.

Approximately 20 minutes later, police officers responding to another call found respondent eight blocks from where the earlier shooting occurred. Respondent was suffering from a gunshot wound to his left chest area and told the police that he had been shot when two individuals attempted to rob him. An ambulance took respondent to the MCV Hospital. Watkinson was still in the MCV emergency room and, when respondent entered that room, said "[t]hat's the man that shot me." After an investigation, the police decided that respondent's story of having been himself the victim of a robbery was untrue and charged respondent with attempted robbery, malicious wounding, and two counts of using a firearm in the commission of a felony.

B

The Commonwealth shortly thereafter moved in state court for an order directing respondent to undergo surgery to remove an object thought to be a bullet lodged under his left collarbone. The court conducted several evidentiary hearings on the motion. At the first hearing, the Commonwealth's expert testified that the surgical procedure would take 45 minutes and would involve a three to four percent chance of temporary nerve damage, a one percent chance of permanent nerve damage, and a one-tenth of one percent chance of death. At the second hearing, the expert testified that on reexamination of respondent, he discovered that the bullet was not "back inside close to the nerves and arteries," as he originally had thought. Instead, he now believed the bullet to be located "just beneath the skin." He testified that the surgery would require an incision of only one and one-half centimeters (slightly more than one-half inch), could be performed under local anesthesia, and would result in "no danger on the basis that there's no general anesthesia employed."

The state trial judge granted the motion to compel surgery. Respondent petitioned the Virginia Supreme Court for a writ of prohibition and/or a writ of habeas corpus, both of which were denied. Respondent then brought an action in the United States District Court for the Eastern District of Virginia to enjoin the pending operation on Fourth Amendment grounds. The court refused to issue a preliminary injunction, holding that respondent's cause had little likelihood of success on the merits.

On October 18, 1982, just before the surgery was scheduled, the surgeon ordered that X rays be taken of respondent's chest. The X rays revealed that the bullet was in fact lodged two and one-half to three centimeters (approximately one inch) deep in muscular tissue in respondent's chest, substantially deeper than had been thought when the state court granted the motion to compel surgery. The surgeon now believed that a general anesthetic would be desirable for medical reasons.

Respondent moved the state trial court for a rehearing based on the new evidence. After holding an evidentiary hearing, the state trial court denied the rehearing and the Virginia Supreme Court affirmed. Respondent then returned to federal court, where he moved to alter or amend the judgment previously entered against him. After an evidentiary hearing, the District Court enjoined the threatened surgery. A divided panel of the Court of Appeals for the Fourth Circuit affirmed. We granted certiorari to consider whether a State may consistently with the Fourth Amendment compel a suspect to undergo surgery of this kind in a search for evidence of a crime.

II

The Fourth Amendment protects "expectations of privacy," see Katz v. United States, 389 U.S. 347, 88 S.Ct. 507, 19 L.Ed.2d 576 (1967)—the individual's legitimate expectations that in certain places and at certain times he has "the right to be let alone—the most comprehensive of rights and the right most valued by civilized men." Olmstead v. United States, 277 U.S. 438, 478, 48 S.Ct. 564, 572, 72 L.Ed. 944 (1928) (Brandeis, J., dissenting). Putting to one side the procedural protections of the warrant requirement, the Fourth Amendment generally protects the "security" of "persons, houses, papers, and effects" against official intrusions up to the point where the community's need for evidence surmounts a specified standard, ordinarily "probable cause." Beyond this point, it is ordinarily justifiable for the community to demand that the individual give up some part of his interest in privacy and security to advance the community's vital interests in law enforcement; such a search is generally "reasonable" in the Amendment's terms.

A compelled surgical intrusion into an individual's body for evidence, however, implicates expectations of privacy and security of such magnitude that the intrusion may be "unreasonable" even if likely to produce evidence of a crime. In Schmerber v. California, 384 U.S. 757, 86 S.Ct. 1826, 16 L.Ed.2d 908 (1966), we addressed a claim that the State had breached the Fourth Amendment's protection of the "right of the people to be secure in their *persons* ... against unreasonable searches and seizures" (emphasis added) when it compelled an individual suspected of drunken driving to undergo a blood test. Schmerber had been arrested at a hospital while receiving treatment for injuries suffered when the automobile he was driving struck a tree. Despite Schmerber's objection, a police officer at the hospital had directed a physician to take a blood sample from him. Schmerber subsequently objected to the introduction at trial of evidence obtained as a result of the blood test.

The authorities in *Schmerber* clearly had probable cause to believe that he had been driving while intoxicated, and to believe that a blood test would provide evidence that was exceptionally probative in confirming this belief. Because the case fell within the exigent circumstances exception to the warrant requirement, no warrant was necessary. The search was not more intrusive than reasonably necessary to accomplish its goals. Nonetheless, Schmerber argued that the Fourth Amendment prohibited the authorities from intruding into his body to extract the blood that was needed as evidence.

Schmerber noted that "[t]he overriding function of the Fourth Amendment is to protect personal privacy and dignity against unwarranted intrusion by the State." * * * [W]e observed that these values were "basic to a free society." We also noted that "[b]ecause we are dealing with intrusions into the human body rather than with state interferences with property relationships or private papers—'houses, papers, and effects'—we write on a clean slate." The intrusion perhaps implicated Schmerber's most personal and deep-rooted expectations of privacy, and the Court recognized that Fourth Amendment analysis thus required a discerning inquiry into the facts and circumstances to determine whether the intrusion was justifiable. The Fourth Amendment neither forbids nor permits all such intrusions; rather, the Amendment's "proper function is to constrain, not against all intrusions as such, but against intrusions which are not justified in the circumstances, or which are made in an improper manner."

The reasonableness of surgical intrusions beneath the skin depends on a case-by-case approach, in which the individual's interests in privacy and security are weighed against society's interests in conducting the procedure. In a given case, the question whether the community's need for evidence outweighs the substantial privacy interests at stake is a delicate one admitting of few categorical answers. We believe that *Schmerber,* however, provides the appropriate framework of analysis for such cases.

Schmerber recognized that the ordinary requirements of the Fourth Amendment would be the threshold requirements for conducting this kind of surgical search and seizure. We noted the importance of probable cause. And we pointed out: "Search warrants are ordinarily required for searches of dwellings, and, absent an emergency, no less could be required where intrusions into the human body are concerned.... The importance of informed, detached and deliberate determinations of the issue whether or not to invade another's body in search of evidence of guilt is indisputable and great."

Beyond these standards, *Schmerber* 's inquiry considered a number of other factors in determining the "reasonableness" of the blood test. A crucial factor in analyzing the magnitude of the intrusion in *Schmerber* is the extent to which the procedure may threaten the safety or health of the individual. "[F]or most people [a blood test] involves virtually no risk, trauma, or pain." Moreover, all reasonable medical precautions were taken and no unusual or untested procedures were employed in *Schmerber,* the procedure was performed "by a physician in a hospital environment according to accepted medical practices." Notwithstanding the existence of probable cause, a search for evidence of a crime may be unjustifiable if it endangers the life or health of the suspect.

Another factor is the extent of intrusion upon the individual's dignitary interests in personal privacy and bodily integrity. Intruding into an individual's living room, eavesdropping upon an individual's telephone conversations, or forcing an individual to accompany police officers to the police station typically do not injure the physical person of the individual. Such intrusions do, however, damage the individual's sense of personal privacy and security and are thus subject to the Fourth Amendment's dictates. In noting that a blood test was "a commonplace in these days of periodic physical examinations," *Schmerber* recognized society's judgment that blood tests do not constitute an unduly extensive imposition on an individual's personal privacy and bodily integrity.

Weighed against these individual interests is the community's interest in fairly and accurately determining guilt or innocence. This interest is of course of great importance. We noted in *Schmerber* that a blood test is "a highly effective means of determining the degree to which a person is under the influence of alcohol." Moreover, there was "a clear indication that in fact [desired] evidence [would] be found" if the blood test were undertaken. Especially given the difficulty of proving drunkenness by other means, these considerations showed that results of the blood test were of vital importance if the State were to enforce its drunken driving laws. In *Schmerber,* we concluded that this state interest was sufficient to justify the intrusion, and the compelled blood test was thus "reasonable" for Fourth Amendment purposes.

III

Applying the *Schmerber* balancing test in this case, we believe that the Court of Appeals reached the correct result. The Commonwealth plainly had probable cause to conduct the search. In addition, all parties apparently agree that respondent has had a full measure of procedural protections and has been able fully to litigate the difficult medical and legal questions necessarily involved in analyzing the reasonableness of a surgical incision of this magnitude.[14] Our inquiry therefore must focus on the extent of the intrusion on respondent's privacy interests and on the State's need for the evidence.

The threats to the health or safety of respondent posed by the surgery are the subject of sharp dispute between the parties. Before the new revelations of October 18, the District Court found that the procedure could be carried out "with virtually no risk to [respondent]." On rehearing, however, with new evidence before it, the District Court held that "the

---

14. Because the State has afforded respondent the benefit of a full adversary presentation and appellate review, we do not reach the question whether the State may compel a suspect to undergo a surgical search of this magnitude for evidence absent such special procedural protections.

risks previously involved have increased in magnitude even as new risks are being added."

The Court of Appeals examined the medical evidence in the record and found that respondent would suffer some risks associated with the surgical procedure. One surgeon had testified that the difficulty of discovering the exact location of the bullet "could require extensive probing and retracting of the muscle tissue," carrying with it "the concomitant risks of injury to the muscle as well as injury to the nerves, blood vessels and other tissue in the chest and pleural cavity." The court further noted that "the greater intrusion and the larger incisions increase the risks of infection." Moreover, there was conflict in the testimony concerning the nature and the scope of the operation. One surgeon stated that it would take 15–20 minutes, while another predicted the procedure could take up to two and one-half hours. The court properly took the resulting uncertainty about the medical risks into account.

Risk ?

Both lower courts in this case believed that the proposed surgery, which for purely medical reasons required the use of a general anesthetic, would be an "extensive" intrusion on respondent's personal privacy and bodily integrity. When conducted with the consent of the patient, surgery requiring general anesthesia is not necessarily demeaning or intrusive. In such a case, the surgeon is carrying out the patient's own will concerning the patient's body and the patient's right to privacy is therefore preserved. In this case, however, the Court of Appeals noted that the Commonwealth proposes to take control of respondent's body, to "drug this citizen—not yet convicted of a criminal offense—with narcotics and barbiturates into a state of unconsciousness," and then to search beneath his skin for evidence of a crime. This kind of surgery involves a virtually total divestment of respondent's ordinary control over surgical probing beneath his skin.

The other part of the balance concerns the Commonwealth's need to intrude into respondent's body to retrieve the bullet. The Commonwealth claims to need the bullet to demonstrate that it was fired from Watkinson's gun, which in turn would show that respondent was the robber who confronted Watkinson. However, although we recognize the difficulty of making determinations in advance as to the strength of the case against respondent, petitioners' assertions of a compelling need for the bullet are hardly persuasive. The very circumstances relied on in this case to demonstrate probable cause to believe that evidence will be found tend to vitiate the Commonwealth's need to compel respondent to undergo surgery. The Commonwealth has available substantial additional evidence that respondent was the individual who accosted Watkinson on the night of the robbery. No party in this case suggests that Watkinson's entirely spontaneous identification of respondent at the hospital would be inadmissible. In addition, petitioners can no doubt prove that [respondent] was found a few blocks from Watkinson's store shortly after the incident took place. And petitioners can certainly show that the location of the bullet (under respondent's left collarbone) seems to correlate with Watkinson's report that the robber "jerked" to the left. The fact that the Commonwealth has available such substantial evidence of the origin of the bullet restricts the need for the Commonwealth to compel respondent to undergo the contemplated surgery.[15]

In weighing the various factors in this case, we therefore reach the same conclusion as the courts below. The operation sought will intrude substantially on respondent's protected interests. The medical risks of the operation, although apparently not extremely severe, are a subject of considerable dispute: the very uncertainty militates against finding the operation to be "reasonable." In addition, the intrusion on respondent's privacy interests entailed by the operation can only be characterized as severe. On the other hand, although the bullet may turn out to be useful to the Commonwealth in prosecuting respondent, the Commonwealth has failed to demonstrate a compelling need for it. We believe that in these circumstances the Commonwealth has failed to demonstrate that it would be "reasonable" under the terms of the Fourth Amendment to search for evidence of this crime by means of the contemplated surgery.

IV

The Fourth Amendment is a vital safeguard of the right of the citizen to be free from unreasonable governmental intrusions into any area in which he has a reasonable expectation of privacy. Where the Court has found a lesser expectation of privacy, or where the search involves a minimal intrusion on privacy interests, the Court has held that the Fourth Amendment's protections are correspondingly less stringent. Conversely, however, the Fourth Amendment's command that searches be "reasonable" requires that when the State seeks to intrude upon an area in which our society recognizes a significantly heightened privacy interest, a more substantial justification is required to make the search "reasonable." Applying these principles, we hold that the proposed search in this case would be "unreasonable" under the Fourth Amendment.

Affirmed.

■ JUSTICE BLACKMUN and JUSTICE REHNQUIST concur in the judgment.

■ CHIEF JUSTICE BURGER, concurring.

I join because I read the Court's opinion as not preventing detention of an individual if there are reasonable grounds to believe that natural bodily functions will disclose the presence of contraband materials secreted internally.

---

15. There are also some questions concerning the probative value of the bullet, even if it could be retrieved. The evidentiary value of the bullet depends on a comparison between markings, if any, on the bullet in respondent's shoulder and markings, if any, found on a test bullet that the police could fire from Watkinson's gun. However, the record supports some doubt whether this kind of comparison is possible. This is because the bullet's markings may have been corroded in the time that the bullet has been in respondent's shoulder, thus making it useless for comparison purposes. In addition, respondent argues that any given gun may be incapable of firing bullets that have a consistent set of markings. The record is devoid of any evidence that the police have attempted to test-fire Watkinson's gun, and there thus remains the additional possibility that a comparison of bullets is impossible because Watkinson's gun does not consistently fire bullets with the same markings. However, because the courts below made no findings on this point, we hesitate to give it significant weight in our analysis.

CHAPTER 6

ELECTRONIC SURVEILLANCE

Analysis

Modern technology has resulted in the development of very sophisticated devices that can enhance the effectiveness of the human senses, especially sight and hearing. The use of these devices—often referred to as "electronic surveillance"—in criminal investigations is the subject of this chapter. Most attention is devoted to surveillance of the spoken word and this is the focus of the federal statute emphasized in this discussion. But other law enforcement techniques raise similar issues. Norwood, "Available Dark" Photography, Industrial Photography, Nov. 1971, at 24, for example, describes the electronic intensifier, which permits taking of photographs in very low light. This, he claims, permits law enforcement surveillance work to take place in "almost complete darkness." Excellent photographs of narcotics transactions have been taken, he continues, apparently in circumstances in which most persons would believe their actions not subject to "capture" on film or even—given the darkness—to visual observation by others.[1]

---

1. A number of courts have held that use of a light enhancing device to conduct nighttime surveillance does not involve a search under federal or state constitutions. Eg., United States v. Ward, 703 F.2d 1058, 1061 (8th Cir.1983); State v. Wacker, 317 Or. 419, 856 P.2d 1029, 1036 (Or.1993). But the Pennsylvania Supreme Court has commented:

> It is not necessary at this time and in this case to hold that every time a * * * device that "sees" through darkness is used by authorities to obtain evidence without a search warrant the evidence must be suppressed. However, when such a device is used for nine days to observe a private apartment frequented by other than those sought by the police, including two acts of sexual intercourse not involving the person, the subject for detection, for whom the surveillance was established, then the warrantless observation of a third floor apartment in darkness has truly impermissibly invaded privacy to which all citizens * * * are guaranteed by the Fourth Amendment.

Commonwealth v. Williams, 494 Pa. 496, 500, 431 A.2d 964, 966 (1981).

A.   THE CONSTITUTIONAL BACKGROUND

EDITORS' NOTE: BACKGROUND OF FEDERAL AND STATE
ELECTRONIC SURVEILLANCE LAW

Electronic surveillance of communication is pervasively regulated by a
number of federal statutes, most significantly legislation originally enacted
as Title III of the Omnibus Crime Control and Safe Streets Act of 1968. It
was somewhat modified by subsequent congressional action, most importantly 1986 legislation, The Federal Electronic Communications Privacy
Act, codified as 18 U.S.C.A. §§ 2510–2522. The basic statute is still widely
known as "Title III," and will be so described in this discussion. This
statute is the subject of the second portion of this chapter.

Although Title III was based in part on legislation enacted earlier, it
clearly reflected a new approach to the matter. This approach was molded
by two important Supreme Court cases decided shortly before Congress's
1968 action.

In Berger v. New York, 388 U.S. 41, 87 S.Ct. 1873, 18 L.Ed.2d 1040
(1967), the Court considered the validity of New York's eavesdrop statute,
which permitted eavesdropping pursuant to a court order issued under the
statute. Assuming the conduct which the statute authorized constituted a
search under the Fourth Amendment, the Court found several defects in
the New York statute. First, the statute did not require the court order
specify with particularity the crime under investigation, the "place" to be
"searched," or the conversations to be "seized." Although the statute
demanded identification of the persons whose conversations were to be
overheard, this requirement was not sufficient to meet Fourth Amendment
specificity needs. Second, the statute permitted officers serving the court
order to seize all conversations of all persons coming into the area during a
two-month period without regard to their connection to the crime under
investigation. Therefore, the order authorized a series of intrusions pursuant to a single showing of probable cause, which might not constitute an
adequate basis for each of the numerous intrusions authorized by the court
order. Third, the two-month period of eavesdropping which the statute
authorized permitted avoidance of the requirement of prompt execution of
the order. Fourth, two-month extensions of the eavesdropping order could
be obtained upon a showing continued eavesdropping would be "in the
public interest." Such extensions violated the requirement of probable
cause, which demands a showing of present probable cause for the authorized activity. Fifth, there was no provision for termination of the seizure
once the conversation sought was overheard. Sixth, the statute had neither
a requirement of notice to persons whose conversations were seized nor any
reasonable substitute. Finally, the statute provided for no return on the
court order and consequently left the use of conversations overheard and
information obtained completely within the discretion of the officer.

The New York statute permitted the issuance of an eavesdrop order
upon the "oath" of a prosecutor or high police official that "there is
probable cause to believe that evidence of a crime may thus be obtained."

Whether orders issued on this basis complied with the Fourth Amendment's requirement that search warrants be issued only upon an adequate showing of probable cause was described by the Court as a serious question that did not have to be resolved in the case.

The Fourth Amendment requirements which *Berger* applied to the New York statute are significantly more stringent than those which the Court has applied to regular search warrants. Cady v. Dombrowski, 413 U.S. 433, 93 S.Ct. 2523, 37 L.Ed.2d 706 (1973), for example, strongly suggested there is no Fourth Amendment requirement of a return of a standard search warrant. Yet *Berger* indicated that a return may be constitutionally required for electronic surveillance. Of course, *Berger* did not make clear whether each of the defects identified by the Court in the New York statute constituted an application of a separate and independent constitutional requirement or, rather, whether the statute fell because of the totality of the deficiencies.

The second case, Katz v. United States, 389 U.S. 347, 88 S.Ct. 507, 19 L.Ed.2d 576 (1967), resolved the issue left unaddressed in *Berger*—whether electronic interception of the spoken word is a search under the Fourth Amendment.

In Olmstead v. United States, 277 U.S. 438, 48 S.Ct. 564, 72 L.Ed. 944 (1928), the Court found no infringement upon interests protected by the Fourth Amendment in the "tapping" of the defendant's telephone line accomplished without unlawful entry into (or onto) his premises. Section 605 of the Communications Act of 1934, however, barred "interception" of any interstate communication by wire. In Nardone v. United States, 302 U.S. 379, 58 S.Ct. 275, 82 L.Ed. 314 (1937), the Court held that Section 605 required the exclusion in federal criminal trials of the products of wiretaps that, under *Olmstead*, would not have involved searches under the Fourth Amendment. In Goldman v. United States, 316 U.S. 129, 62 S.Ct. 993, 86 L.Ed. 1322 (1942), the Court found no violation of the Fourth Amendment in the use of a "detectaphone" placed against an office wall to hear private conversations in the office next door because there was no "trespass" on the premises under surveillance. *Olmstead* and *Goldman* were generally regarded as establishing that surveillance did not amount to a search and therefore did not have to be reasonable in Fourth Amendment terms unless it involved some physical trespass on or into premises in which the subject had a privacy interest.

Katz, however, held that this trespass requirement was no longer controlling. In *Katz*, FBI agents attached an electronic listening and recording device to the outside of a public telephone booth. This device enabled them to overhear Katz's end of a telephone conversation he carried on in the booth, but involved no physical penetration of, or trespass into, the booth. Nevertheless, the Court held this a search. The Fourth Amendment protects people—and not merely areas—against unreasonable searches and seizures, Justice Stewart explained for the majority, and consequently "the reach of that Amendment cannot turn upon the presence or absence of a physical intrusion into any given enclosure." Since Katz reasonably expected, when he used the booth, that his words would "not be broadcast to the world," he had a privacy interest in the content of those words that was infringed by the agents' use of the recording and listening device. The result of *Katz*, Justice Harlan noted in his concurrence, is that any surveillance resulting in obtaining information the subjects actually and reasonably believed was relatively private constitutes a search and must be scrutinized under Fourth Amendment reasonableness standards. 389 U.S. at 361, 88 S.Ct. at 516–17, 19 L.Ed.2d at 587–88 (Harlan, J., concurring).

The Senate Judiciary Report on Title III noted both *Berger* and *Katz*. It further commented that Title III was drafted to meet the constitutional criteria for electronic surveillance delineated in *Berger* and to "conform with" *Katz*. Senate Report No. 1097, 90th Congress, 2nd Session, 1968, U.S. Code Congressional and Administrative News, 1968, Vol. 2, 2112, at 2153.

The Supreme Court has not addressed the facial validity of the electronic surveillance statute. It has given no indication in its numerous decisions dealing with the statute that the statute suffers from the fatal defects *Berger* found in the New York provision. Lower courts have upheld Title III against constitutional attacks. E.g., United States v. Sklaroff, 506 F.2d 837 (5th Cir.1975), cert. denied 423 U.S. 874, 96 S.Ct. 142, 46 L.Ed.2d 105; United States v. Tortorello, 480 F.2d 764 (2d Cir.1973), cert. denied 414 U.S. 866, 94 S.Ct. 63, 38 L.Ed.2d 86; United States v. Cox, 449 F.2d 679 (8th Cir. 1971), cert. denied 406 U.S. 934, 92 S.Ct. 1783, 32 L.Ed.2d 136 (1972).

B.   The Federal Statute and Its Application

EDITORS' INTRODUCTION: A SUMMARY OF THE FEDERAL
ELECTRONIC COMMUNICATIONS PRIVACY ACT ("TITLE III")

Title III was originally enacted in 1968. It has been amended several times. One federal court commented that another tribunal "might have put the matter too mildly" when that second tribunal noted that the statute "is famous (if not infamous) for its lack of clarity." United States v. Smith, 155 F.3d 1051, 1055 (9th Cir.1998). The following is a summary of the current provisions.

Coverage and Prohibitions

The essence of Title III is its prohibition against the interception of any wire, oral or electronic communication. 18 U.S.C.A. § 2511(1)(a).

Title III distinguishes among "wire communications," "oral communications," and "electronic communications." All three are covered, but in somewhat different ways.

A "wire communication" is defined as an aural transfer that in whole or part uses wire, cable or other "like connection." It must at some point involve the human voice. An "oral communication" is defined as "any oral communication uttered by a person exhibiting an expectation that such communication is not subject to interception under circumstances justifying such expectation."

In 1986, Title III was expanded to protect electronic communications. An "electronic communication" is defined as a transfer of signs, signals, images, data or intelligence by means of wire, radio, or similar means. Thus it includes such innovations as electronic mail, facsimile transmissions, and video teleconferences. 18 U.S.C.A. § 2510.

"Intercept" is defined as "the aural or other acquisition of the contents of any wire, electronic, or oral communication through the use of any electronic, mechanical, or other device." 18 U.S.C.A. § 2510(4). "Electronic, mechanical, or other device" is defined as "any device or apparatus which can be used to intercept a wire or oral communication." Specifically designated as not such devices are telephone or telegraph equipment furnished to a user and used in the ordinary course of business (i.e., an extension phone) and a hearing aid or similar device used to correct subnormal hearing to not better than normal. 18 U.S.C.A. § 2510(5).

Exceptions Permitting Interception

Several exceptions to the statute's general prohibition permit interception of communications covered by Title III. First, a party to the conversation or a person authorized by one of the parties to the communication may intercept the communication. 18 U.S.C.A. § 2511(2)(c), (d).

Second, federal law enforcement officers may intercept communications in certain emergency situations. The situations must be believed to involve "immediate danger of death or serious physical injury" or "conspiratorial activities threatening the national security interest or * * * characteristic of organized crime." Application for a court order approving the interception must be made within 48 hours. 18 U.S.C.A. § 2518(7).

Third—and most important—the statute provides for federal law enforcement agencies to obtain court orders from federal judges authorizing certain interceptions. 18 U.S.C.A. § 2516. Further, the statute authorizes states to enact statutes permitting state law enforcement officers to obtain similar court orders from state judges "in conformity with" the provisions of Title III. 18 U.S.C.A. § 2516(2). In the absence of an order obtained pursuant to a state "enabling" statute, the federal statute bars state law enforcement officers from engaging in the conduct prohibited by the statute.

Interceptions Under Court Order

The process of applying for, obtaining, and serving a court order permitting otherwise prohibited interceptions under the statute is complex and best considered in several steps.

(1) Offenses Involved

An application may be made to a federal court for interception of wire or oral communications only if the surveillance is sought to obtain evidence of certain enumerated offenses. State statutes may authorize court orders only to obtain evidence regarding "murder, kidnapping, gambling, robbery, bribery, extortion, or dealing in narcotic drugs, marihuana or other dangerous drugs, or other crime dangerous to life, limb, or property, and punishable by imprisonment for more than one year * * * or any conspiracy to commit any of the foregoing offenses." 18 U.S.C.A. § 2516(2). An application for authorization to intercept electronic communications may be made for any federal felony.

(2) Authorization

An application for interception of wire or oral communications may be made to a federal court for a surveillance order only if application is authorized by certain high level members of the Attorney General's staff. 18 U.S.C.A. § 2516(1). Any assistant United States Attorney may authorize application for an electronic communications intercept. A state procedure must require authorization by the principal prosecuting attorney of the state or of a political subdivision of the state. 18 U.S.C.A. § 2516(2).

(3) Application Contents

The contents of the application are governed by 18 U.S.C.A. § 2518(1):

Each application for an order authorizing or approving the interception of a wire, oral, or electronic communication * * * shall be made in writing upon oath or affirmation to a judge of competent jurisdiction and shall state the applicant's authority to make such application. Each application shall include the following information:

(a) the identity of the investigative or law enforcement officer making the application, and the officer authorizing the application;

(b) a full and complete statement of the facts and circumstances relied upon by the applicant, to justify his belief that an order should be issued, including (i) details as to the particular offense that has been, is being, or is about to be committed, (ii) * * * a particular description of the nature and location of the facilities from which or the place where the communication is to be intercepted, (iii) a particular description of the type of communications sought to be intercepted, (iv) the identity of the person, if known, committing the offense and whose communications are to be intercepted;

(c) a full and complete statement as to whether or not other investigative procedures have been tried and failed or why they reasonably appear to be unlikely to succeed if tried or to be too dangerous;

(d) a statement of the period of time for which the interception is required to be maintained. If the nature of the investigation is such that the authorization for interception should not automatically terminate when the described type of communication has been first obtained, a particular description of facts establishing probable cause to believe that additional communications of the same type will occur thereafter;

(e) a full and complete statement of the facts concerning all previous applications known to the individual authorizing and making the application, made to any judge for authorization to intercept, or for approval of interceptions of, wire, oral, or electronic communications involving any of the same persons, facilities or places specified in the application, and the action taken by the judge on each such application; and

(f) where the application is for the extension of an order, a statement setting forth the results thus far obtained from the interception, or a reasonable explanation of the failure to obtain such results.

(4) Judicial Function and Issuance of Order

The judge to whom the application is made may require the applicant to furnish additional testimony or evidence in support of the application. 18 U.S.C.A. § 2518(2). An *ex parte* order authorizing interception may be issued:

if the judge determines on the basis of the facts submitted by the applicant that—

(a) there is probable cause for belief that an individual is committing, has committed, or is about to commit [an offense for which an order may be issued];

(b) there is probable cause for belief that particular communications concerning that offense will be obtained through such interception;

(c) normal investigative procedures have been tried and have failed or reasonably appear to be unlikely to succeed if tried or to be too dangerous; [and]

(d) * * * there is probable cause for belief that the facilities from which, or the place where, the wire or oral communications are to be intercepted are being used, or are about to be used, in connection with the commission of such offense, or are leased to, listed in the name of, or commonly used by such person.

18 U.S.C.A. § 2518(3).

(5) Contents of Order

Under 18 U.S.C.A. § 2518(4), each order shall specify:

(a) the identity of the person, if known, whose communications are to be intercepted;

(b) the nature and location of the communications facilities as to which, or the place where, authority to intercept is granted;

(c) a particular description of the type of communication sought to be intercepted, and a statement of the particular offense to which it relates;

(d) the identity of the agency authorized to intercept the communications, and of the person authorizing the application; and

(e) the period of time during which such interception is authorized, including a statement as to whether or not the interception shall automatically terminate when the described communication has been first obtained.

Further, every order must contain a provision "that the authorization to intercept shall be executed as soon as practicable, [and] shall be conducted in such a way as to minimize the interception of communications not otherwise subject to interception under this chapter * * *." 18 U.S.C.A. § 2518(5).

The period of time during which interception may be authorized is only as long as is necessary to achieve the objective of the order, but never longer than thirty days. Each order must contain a directive that the interception "must terminate upon attainment of the authorized objective." 18 U.S.C.A. § 2518(5).

Upon request of the applicant, the judge "shall" include in the order a directive that a communication common carrier, landlord, custodian "or other person" shall furnish the officers with "all information, facilities, and technical assistance necessary to accomplish the interception unobtrusively." Such persons are compensated at prevailing rates. 18 U.S.C.A. § 2518(4).

The judge may also include a requirement the officers submit progress reports at designated intervals. These reports may require a showing as to what progress has been made toward achievement of the authorized objective and the need for continued interception. 18 U.S.C.A. § 2518(6).

(6) Service of the Intercept Order

The statute contains very few provisions relating directly to the manner in which the court order is to be served. Some limits on execution of orders, however, can be read into the provisions discussed above. It is clear, for example, the statute contemplates compliance with the order's provisions that the interception occur as soon as practicable and that it be conducted in such a manner as to minimize the interception of communications not subject to interception. Further, assistance from landlords and other persons may be obtained.

The statute does explicitly direct that the contents of any intercepted communications "shall, if possible, be recorded on tape or wire or other comparable device" and that this be done "in such way as will protect the recording from editing or other alteration." 18 U.S.C.A. § 2518(8)(a).

In Dalia v. United States, 441 U.S. 238, 99 S.Ct. 1682, 60 L.Ed.2d 177 (1979), the Supreme Court upheld covert entry of private premises by agents to install a listening device whose use was authorized by a court order. Such entries are not inherently unreasonable under the Fourth Amendment, it reasoned, and the statute does not prohibit them. Nor is it necessary the court order specifically authorize such covert entry. The precise manner in which search warrants are to be served, Justice Powell noted for the majority, has always been left to the discretion of the officers executing the order, subject to later judicial review for "reasonableness." There is no need, the Court concluded, to depart from this approach in the electronic surveillance area.

(7) Extensions

Extensions of an intercept order may be granted. But an application for such an extension must comply with the requirements for applications for an initial order and an extension may be granted only if the judge makes the determinations required for an initial order. Extensions may be for no longer than is necessary to achieve the purposes for which they are granted and may never exceed thirty days. 18 U.S.C.A. § 2518(5).

(8) Return to Court

The statute does not specifically impose a requirement of a return of the order to the issuing court. But immediately upon the expiration of the order, any recordings made of intercepted communications are to "be made available" to the judge, sealed, and shall be retained in custody as ordered by the court. 18 U.S.C.A. § 2518(8)(a). The provisions for notice (discussed below) assume some communication to the court from the serving agency or officers, if not a formal return.

(9) Notice

The statute contains two provisions for notice to persons whose communications may have been intercepted. Within a reasonable time, but not more than ninety days after denial of an application or the termination of an interception authorized by an order, an inventory is to be served on certain persons. This inventory is to include notice of (a) the fact of the entry of the order or the application; (b) the date of the entry and the period of authorized, approved or disapproved interception, or the denial of the application; and (c) the fact that, during the period, communications were or were not intercepted. An inventory is to be served on persons named in the application or order and "such other parties to the intercepted communications as the judge may determine in his discretion that is in the interest of justice." On an *ex parte* showing of good cause, the service of the inventory may be postponed. 18 U.S.C.A. § 2518(8)(d).

The second provision focuses upon use of results of surveillance. If the contents of an intercepted communication or evidence derived from such communications are to be used or disclosed in any trial, hearing or "other proceeding," each party must be given, no less than ten days before the proceedings, a copy of the court order and the application. 18 U.S.C.A. § 2518(9).

"Roving" Interception Orders

As a result of 1986 legislation, interception orders sometimes need not specify the specific location of the facilities where or from which the communications are to be intercepted. These orders are often called "roving" orders, since they give law enforcement officers considerable flexibility regarding where to intercept the targeted communications.

If the order permits interception of oral communications, the judge must find—on the basis of facts contained in the application—specifying the facilities is not "practical."

If the order is to permit interception of wire or electronic communications, the judge must find—again on the basis of the facts in the application—there is probable cause to believe the actions of the person whose communications are sought "could have the effect of thwarting interception from a specified facility." 18 U.S.C.A. § 2518(11).

Roving Orders

An earlier version of these provisions was found constitutional over arguments they violate the Fourth Amendment requirements established in Berger v. New York, 388 U.S. 41, 87 S.Ct. 1873, 18 L.Ed.2d 1040 (1967). See United States v. Gaytan, 74 F.3d 545, 553 (5th Cir.1996).

Intercepted Communications Concerning Nontarget Offenses

Officers serving a court order authorizing the interception of communications related to a specified offense may overhear communications concerning other offenses. What is required to enable law enforcement officers to use the information obtained by intercepting such nontarget communications depends upon the use the officers seek to make of them.

The statute provides officers may disclose the contents of these communications to other law enforcement officers to the extent that such action is appropriate to the proper performance of the intercepting officer's official duties. Further, the officer may use the contents of these communications in the proper performance of his duties.

An officer may, however, disclose the contents of such communications in testimony given in an official proceeding only:

> when authorized or approved by a judge of competent jurisdiction where such judge finds on subsequent application that the contents were otherwise intercepted in accordance with the provisions of this chapter. Such application shall be made as soon as practicable.

18 U.S.C.A. § 2517(5). One court has explained:

> The danger inherent in disclosure without judicial approval is that the original application may have been a subterfuge, that is, the government, not having probable cause to obtain a wiretap for some crime, might obtain it by purporting to investigate a different crime. We have acknowledged the potential for this kind of abuse. We have therefore held that a court, when faced with evidence of other crimes obtained in the course of a wiretap, may allow its disclosure only if it determines that:
>
>> the original order was lawfully obtained, that it was sought in good faith and not as a subterfuge search, and that the communication was, in fact, incidentally intercepted during the course of a lawfully executed order.

United States v. Barnes, 47 F.3d 963, 964–65 (8th Cir.1995).

But the necessary judicial authorization can be easily obtained. Courts have held, for example, that if, in applying for an extension of the original interception order, the Government discloses it has intercepted communications regarding other offenses, the court's action in granting the extension is authorization to use those communications. United States v. London, 66 F.3d 1227, 1235 (1st Cir.1995). In *Barnes*, the court held that if the Government uses such nontarget communications to obtain an indictment, it may obtain the necessary judicial approval after-the-fact, that is, after it uses the communications in testimony before the grand jury.

Remedies for Violation of the Statute

The statute provides several remedies for a violation of its provisions. "Intentional" violations are punishable as criminal offenses and carry penalties of a fine or imprisonment for not more than five years, or both. 18 U.S.C.A. § 2511. A civil cause of action is also created and provisions are made for recovery of attorney's fees, punitive damages, and actual damages not less than liquidated damages computed at the rate of $100 a day for each day of violation or $10,000, whichever is higher. 18 U.S.C.A. § 2520.

Title III has its own exclusionary sanction in 18 U.S.C.A. § 2515:

> Whenever any wire or oral communication has been intercepted, no part of the contents of such communication and no evidence derived therefrom may be received in evidence in any trial, hearing, or other proceeding in or before any court, grand jury, department, officer, agency, regulatory body, legislative committee, or other authority of the United States, a State, or a political subdivision thereof if the disclosure of that information would be in violation of this chapter.

"Any aggrieved person" may move to suppress the contents of an intercepted communication or evidence derived from it on the following grounds:

> (i) the communication was unlawfully intercepted;

> (ii) the order of authorization or approval under which it was intercepted is insufficient on its face; or

> (iii) the interception was not made in conformity with the order of authorization or approval.

18 U.S.C.A. § 2518(10)(a). "Aggrieved person" is defined as "a person who was a party to any intercepted wire, oral, or electronic communication or a person against whom the interception was directed." 18 U.S.C.A. § 2510(11).

To some extent, this statutory exclusionary remedy is broader than that of the Fourth Amendment. In Gelbard v. United States, 408 U.S. 41, 92 S.Ct. 2357, 33 L.Ed.2d 179 (1972), for example, the Court held that witnesses who had been subpoenaed before a grand jury could invoke 18 U.S.C.A. § 2515. Thus, they could not be cited for contempt for refusal to answer questions based upon information obtained in violation of the statute. It may not follow, however, that an indictment is subject to attack by a defendant on the basis that the grand jury considered or relied upon evidence obtained in violation of the statute.

Perhaps the most perplexing problem is the determination of what noncompliance with the statutory procedures requires suppression of the results of an interception. In United States v. Giordano, 416 U.S. 505, 94 S.Ct. 1820, 40 L.Ed.2d 341 (1974), the Supreme Court held the Congressional intention was to provide for suppression where "there is failure to satisfy any of those statutory requirements that directly and substantially implement the congressional intent to limit the use of intercept procedures to those situations clearly calling for the employment of this extraordinary investigative device." In *Giordano*, the application for the court order recited that it had been approved by a designated Assistant Attorney

General; evidence showed, however, that the Executive Assistant to the Attorney General approved it. Finding the requirement of approval by the Attorney General or a designated Assistant Attorney General was one that directly and substantially implemented the congressional purpose, the Court held the products of the order must be suppressed under 18 U.S.C.A. § 2515. In United States v. Chavez, 416 U.S. 562, 94 S.Ct. 1849, 40 L.Ed.2d 380 (1974), however, the application recited that it had been approved by the Assistant Attorney General although the facts showed the Attorney General himself had approved it. The statute's requirement that the application accurately state which of the several authorized persons approved it, held the Court, was not so directly and substantially related to the Congressional purpose as to require suppression of the products of the surveillance.

If there is a violation of a statutory requirement that brings 18 U.S.C.A. § 2515 into play, does it require suppression of evidence or information obtained *before* that violation took place? In United States v. Donovan, 429 U.S. 413, 97 S.Ct. 658, 50 L.Ed.2d 652 (1977), the defendant did not receive post-interception notice because the government left the defendant's name off the list of persons whose conversations were intercepted. This omission, the Supreme Court held, violated the statute, since the government had exclusive access to this information and thus was obligated to provide a full list. But, it continued, this violation of the notice provision of the statute was not "retroactive" in the sense that it would render the earlier interceptions unlawful and therefore subject to suppression.

Section 2518(8)(a), requiring officers record intercepted conversations and make the recording available to the judge, also directs the recording sealed under the judge's direction. This is to occur "[i]mmediately upon the expiration" of the order or any extensions that are authorized. In United States v. Ojeda Rios, 495 U.S. 257, 110 S.Ct. 1845, 109 L.Ed.2d 224 (1990), no seal was immediately obtained as the statute directs. Section 2518(8)(a) provides the seal "or a satisfactory explanation for the absence thereof, shall be a prerequisite for the use or disclosure" of a communication intercepted under the statute or evidence derived from such a communication. Thus, the Court observed, the statute contains its own "explicit exclusionary remedy." It continued:

> The presence or absence of a seal does not in itself establish the integrity of electronic surveillance tapes [but] is a means of ensuring that subsequent to its placement on a tape, the Government has no opportunity to tamper with, alter, or edit the conversations that have been recorded.

495 U.S. at 263, 110 S.Ct. at 1849, 109 L.Ed.2d at 234. Next, it rejected the Government's argument that evidence was admissible if the Government provided an explanation that was not "satisfactory" but showed the offered recording authentic. Under the language of the statute, proof that no tampering with the recording occurred in the particular case is not an adequate substitute for a "satisfactory explanation" for the failure to have the recording sealed. There was also evidence that the attorney supervising the investigation misconstrued the statute as requiring no effort on the

Government's part to have the recording sealed until there was a "meaningful hiatus" in the investigation as a whole. This interpretation, the Court held, was an objectively reasonable—although ultimately incorrect—reading of the law. If offered to the trial court, it would constitute a "satisfactory explanation" for the absence of a seal timely secured. The case was remanded for a determination as to whether the Government had presented this explanation to the trial court at the suppression hearing.

Determining Whether Surveillance Occurred

Defendants may experience difficulty in determining whether law enforcement investigations leading to their prosecutions involved activity actually or potentially subject to the statutory provisions. Unless defendants can establish that activity of this sort occurred, they are in no position to claim government evidence the "fruit" of impermissible surveillance.

Such defendants can sometimes invoke a federal statute that provides:

upon a claim by a party aggrieved that evidence is admissible because it is the * * * product of an unlawful act * * * the opponent of the claim shall affirm or deny the occurrence of the alleged unlawful act.

18 U.S.C.A. § 3504(a)(1). Thus a defendant can claim illegal surveillance and the government must affirm or deny it.

The specificity which lower courts have required of governmental claims that no such surveillance took place depends upon the specificity of and support for the defendant's assertion it did. Where only a general unsupported claim is made by the defendant, a general denial by the government has been held to suffice. A more specific claim supported by facts indicating surveillance was conducted may require the government to conduct a more comprehensive inquiry of agencies with surveillance capabilities before its denial will be accepted. See Matter of Grand Jury, 529 F.2d 543 (3d Cir.1976).

If it is established illegal surveillance took place and the defendant has "standing" to raise the matter, the defense is entitled to access to records of that surveillance. It is not sufficient for the trial judge to examine the records *in camera* and turn over to the defense those records the judge determines "arguably relevant" to the proceedings. Alderman v. United States, 394 U.S. 165, 89 S.Ct. 961, 22 L.Ed.2d 176 (1969). The Court reached a different result where the defendant did not establish which intercepted conversations he participated in and therefore had standing to challenge. In this situation, the trial judge acted properly in examining the recordings of the intercepted conversations *in camera* and disclosing to the defense only those to which the defendant was a party. Taglianetti v. United States, 394 U.S. 316, 89 S.Ct. 1099, 22 L.Ed.2d 302 (1969).

State Statutes

Section 2516(2) authorizes states to enact legislation permitting state court judges to issue to state law enforcement officers—"in conformity with section 2518 of [the federal statute]"—a court order authorizing interceptions otherwise barred by the federal statute. As of December 31, 1998, forty two states (as well as the District of Columbia and the Virgin Islands) had such legislation. Administrative Office of the United States Courts, Report on Applications for Orders Authorizing or Approving the Interception of Wire or Oral Communications for the Period January 1 Through December 31, 1998. These statutes raise a number of issues, including the extent to which state legislation must embody provisions identical or similar to the federal statute.

States are free to enact legislation providing those subject to investigations with more protection than the federal statute extends. Some states, for example, prohibit the interception of communications even by a party to the conversation if the other party does not consent. The Pennsylvania statute was held to cover the action of a police officer in secretly recording conversations with persons the officer stopped for traffic violations. Commonwealth v. McIvor, 448 Pa.Super. 98, 670 A.2d 697 (1996), appeal denied, 547 Pa. 753, 692 A.2d 564 (1997).

NOTES

1. **Pen Registers and "Trap and Trace" Devices.** In 1986 Congress passed legislation covering devices enabling law enforcement officers to ascertain numbers dialed *from* particular telephones (pen registers) or the numbers from which calls are placed *to* particular telephones ("trap and trace" devices). These devices do not intercept the contents of calls.

Use of these devices would otherwise be free of statutory or constitutional limitation. In United States v. New York Telephone Co., 434 U.S. 159, 98 S.Ct. 364, 54 L.Ed.2d 376 (1977), the Court held that pen registers are not covered by Title III because they do not intercept communications. Two years later, in Smith v. Maryland, 442 U.S. 735, 99 S.Ct. 2577, 61 L.Ed.2d 220 (1979), discussed in Chapter 2, the Court held that use of a pen register does not constitute a search.

As a general rule under the 1986 legislation, use of these devices by law enforcement authorities or private persons is prohibited without a court order. 18 U.S.C.A. § 3121(a). Authorization to use them without an order is provided for certain emergency situations. 18 U.S.C.A. § 3125.

An application for an order authorizing use of one of these devices is required to include "a certification by the applicant that the information likely to be obtained is relevant to an ongoing criminal investigation being conducted by [a law enforcement agency]." 18 U.S.C.A. § 3122(b). States may provide for state officers to obtain similar orders.

The role of the court to which application must be made is minimal. The statute provides that upon finding the applicant has made the required certification, "the court shall issue an ex parte order authorizing [use of the devices]." 18 U.S.C.A. § 3123(a). The order is to state the offense to which the information likely to be obtained relates, the identity of the person who is the subject of the investigation, and the number and location of the telephone line to which the device is to be attached. 18 U.S.C.A. § 3123(b). An agency using an authorized device is to employ "technology reasonably available" that "restricts the recording or decoding of electronic or other impulses to the dialing and signaling information utilized in call processing." 18 U.S.C.A. § 3121(c).

The statute provides that a person who knowingly violates the general prohibition against use of these devices is subject to criminal conviction. 18 U.S.C.A. § 3121(d). It contains no provision for exclusion of evidence resulting from law enforcement activity conducted in violation of its provisions. There is authority for the proposition that such evidence may be used. See United States v. Thompson, 936 F.2d 1249, 1249–50 (11th Cir.1991). State statutes have been similarly construed. Thus in State v. Cain, 670 So.2d 515 (La.App.1996), the court explained:

> We find * * * that there is no statutory or constitutional basis to require exclusion of evidence gathered from a pen register that was authorized without compliance with [the state statute authorizing court orders]. We recognize that there is little incentive for law enforcement officials to comply with the procedural requirements for obtaining authorization for a pen register when there is no sanction for the failure to comply. However, absent a constitutionally protected privacy interest with regard to the numbers dialed from one's home, it is for the legislature to determine what, if any, consequence will flow from the failure to comply with the procedures it has established for obtaining a pen register.

670 So.2d at 520.

2. **Accessing or Intercepting "Stored" Communications.** The Stored Communication Act, 18 U.S.C. §§ 2701–2710, covers wire or electronic communications while in electronic storage. It prohibits any person without authorization from accessing a facility through which an electronic communication service is provided and thereby obtaining access to a stored communication. 18 U.S.C.A. § 2701(a). A governmental agency may obtain a search warrant authorizing the provider of such services to disclose the content of a stored communication. 18 U.S.C.A. § 2703(a).

The statute provides a civil action for damages that may be invoked by any person aggrieved by a violation of the chapter. 18 U.S.C.A. § 2707(a). If a court finds a violation of the statute occurred and the circumstances raise a question as to whether governmental agency's employee willfully or intentionally committed the violation, the agency or department is to initiate a proceeding to determine whether disciplinary action is warranted against the employee. 18 U.S.C.A. § 2707(d). But the statute also provides, "The remedies and sanctions described in this chapter are the only judicial remedies and sanctions for nonconstitutional violations of this chapter." 18 U.S.C.A. § 2708. Thus the statute provides no basis for challenging the admissibility of evidence obtained as a result of violation of its requirements.

The relationship between this statute and Title III is uncertain. In United States v. Smith, 155 F.3d 1051 (9th Cir.1998), the court considered whether in a federal criminal trial the Government was barred from using evidence resulting from a private person's action in obtaining access to the defendant's voice mail system and retrieving a message stored in his "mailbox." If this action violated only The Stored Communication Act, the court held, exclusion would not be required because the Act's provisions bar an exclusionary remedy. But a person who not only accesses the voice mail system in violation of the Act but obtains the contents of a stored communication violates the federal wiretap statute. The private person in *Smith* obtained the contents of a stored communication in a manner violating the wiretap statute. Thus the exclusionary provision of the wiretap statute demanded exclusion of the resulting evidence.

3. **Silent Video Surveillance.** No federal statute covers video surveillance conducted for domestic law enforcement purposes where the device does not record voices. Such surveillance is regulated when conducted for purposes of gathering information for foreign intelligence by the Foreign Intelligence Surveillance Act, 50 U.S.C. §§ 1801–1811. See generally, United States v. Koyomejian, 970 F.2d 536 (9th Cir.1992) (en banc).

United States v. Kahn

Supreme Court of the United States, 1974.
415 U.S. 143, 94 S.Ct. 977, 39 L.Ed.2d 225.

■ MR. JUSTICE STEWART delivered the opinion of the Court.

On March 20, 1970, an attorney from the United States Department of Justice submitted an application for an order authorizing a wiretap interception pursuant to Title III of the Omnibus Crime Control and Safe Streets Act of 1970, 18 U.S.C.A. §§ 2510–2520, to Judge William J. Campbell of the United States District Court for the Northern District of Illinois. The affidavit accompanying the application contained information indicating that the respondent, Irving Kahn, was a bookmaker who operated from his residence and used two home telephones to conduct his business. The affidavit also noted that the Government's informants had stated that they would refuse to testify against Kahn, that telephone company records alone would be insufficient to support a bookmaking conviction, and that physical surveillance or normal search-and-seizure techniques would be unlikely to produce useful evidence. The application therefore concluded that "normal investigative procedures reasonably appear to be unlikely to succeed," and asked for authorization to intercept wire communications of Irving Kahn and "others as yet unknown" over two named telephone lines, in order that information concerning the gambling offenses might be obtained.

Judge Campbell entered an order, pursuant to 18 U.S.C.A. § 2518, approving the application. He specifically found that there was probable cause to believe that Irving Kahn and "others as yet unknown" were using the two telephones to conduct an illegal gambling business, and that normal investigative techniques were unlikely to succeed in providing federal officials with sufficient evidence to successfully prosecute such crimes. The order authorized special agents of the F.B.I. to "intercept wire communications of Irving Kahn and others as yet unknown" to and from the two named telephones concerning gambling activities.

The authorization order further provided that status reports were to be filed with Judge Campbell on the fifth and 10th days following the date of the order, showing what progress had been made towards achievement of the order's objective, and describing any need for further interceptions. The first such report, filed with Judge Campbell on March 25, 1970, indicated that the wiretap had been terminated because its objectives had been attained. The status report gave a summary of the information garnered by the interceptions, stating in part that on March 21, Irving Kahn made two telephone calls from Arizona to his wife at their home in Chicago and discussed gambling wins and losses, and that on the same date Minnie Kahn, Irving's wife, made two telephone calls from the intercepted telephones to a person described in the status report as "a known gambling figure," with whom she discussed various kinds of betting information.

Both Irving and Minnie Kahn were subsequently indicted for using a facility in interstate commerce to promote, manage, and facilitate an illegal gambling business, in violation of 19 U.S.C.A. § 1952. The Government prosecutor notified the Kahns that he intended to introduce into evidence at trial the conversations intercepted under the court order. The Kahns in turn filed motions to suppress the conversations. These motions were heard by Judge Thomas R. McMillen in the Northern District of Illinois, who, in an unreported opinion, granted the motion to suppress. * * * [A]ll * * * conversations in which Minnie Kahn was a participant were suppressed as being outside the scope of Judge Campbell's order, on the ground that Minnie Kahn was not a person "as yet unknown" to the federal authorities at the time of the original application.

[handwritten margin note: evidence suppressed at wife, Minnie Kahn, was "known" to parties and application flawed]

The Government filed an interlocutory appeal from the suppression order. A divided panel of the United States Court of Appeals for the Seventh Circuit affirmed that part of the District Court's order suppressing all conversations of Minnie Kahn, * * *. The court held that under the wiretap order all intercepted conversations had to meet two requirements before they could be admitted into evidence:

> "(1) that Irving Kahn be a party to the conversations, and (2) that his conversations intercepted be with 'others as yet unknown.'"

The court then construed the statutory requirements of 18 U.S.C.A. §§ 2518(1)(b)(iv) and 2518(4)(a) that the person whose communications are to be intercepted is to be identified if known, as excluding from the term "others as yet unknown" any "persons whom careful investigation by the government would disclose were probably using the Kahn telephones in conversations for illegal activities." Since the Government in this case had not shown that further investigation of Irving Kahn's activities would not have implicated Minnie in the gambling business, the Court of Appeals felt that Mrs. Kahn was not a "person as yet unknown" within the purview of Judge Campbell's order.

We granted the Government's petition for certiorari, in order to resolve a seemingly important issue involving the construction of this relatively new federal statute.

At the outset, it is worth noting what issues are not involved in this case. First, we are not presented with an attack upon the constitutionality of any part of Title III of the Omnibus Crime Control and Safe Streets Act of 1970. Secondly, review of this interlocutory order does not involve any questions as to the propriety of the Justice Department's internal procedures in authorizing the application for the wiretap. Finally, no argument is presented that the federal agents failed to conduct the wiretap here in such a manner as to minimize the interception of innocent conversations. The question presented is simply whether the conversations that the Government wishes to introduce into evidence at the respondents' trial are made inadmissible by the "others as yet unknown" language of Judge Campbell's order or by the corresponding statutory requirements of Title III.

[handwritten margin note: — issue]

In deciding that Minnie Kahn was not a person "as yet unknown" within the meaning of the wiretap order, the Court of Appeals relied heavily on an expressed objective of Congress in the enactment of Title III: the protection of the personal privacy of those engaging in wire communications. In light of this clear congressional concern, the Court of Appeals reasoned, the Government could not lightly claim that a person whose conversations were intercepted was "unknown" within the meaning of

Title III. Thus, it was not enough that Mrs. Kahn was not known to be taking part in any illegal gambling business at the time that the Government applied for the wiretap order; in addition, the court held that the Government was required to show that such complicity would not have been discovered had a thorough investigation of Mrs. Kahn been conducted before the wiretap application.

In our view, neither the legislative history nor the specific language of Title III compels this conclusion. To be sure, Congress was concerned with protecting individual privacy when it enacted this statute. But it is also clear that Congress intended to authorize electronic surveillance as a weapon against the operations of organized crime. There is, of course, some tension between these two stated congressional objectives, and the question of how Congress struck the balance in any particular instance cannot be resolved simply through general reference to the statute's expressed concern for the protection of individual privacy. Rather, the starting point, as in all statutory construction, is the precise wording chosen by Congress in enacting Title III.

Section 2518(1) of Title 18, United States Code Annotated, sets out in detail the requirements for the information to be included in an application for an order authorizing the interception of wire communications. The sole provision pertaining to the identification of persons whose communications are to be intercepted is contained in § 2518(1)(b)(iv), which requires that the application state "the identity of the person, if known, *committing the offense* and whose communications are to be intercepted." (Emphasis supplied.) This statutory language would plainly seem to require the naming of a specific person in the wiretap application only when law enforcement officials believe that such an individual is actually committing one of the offenses specified in 18 U.S.C.A. § 2516. Since it is undisputed here that Minnie Kahn was not known to the Government to be engaging in gambling activities at the time the interception order was sought, the failure to include her name in the application would thus seem to comport with the literal language of § 2518(1)(b)(v).

Moreover, there is no reason to conclude that the omission of Minnie Kahn's name from the actual wiretap order was in conflict with any of the provisions of Title III. Section 2518(4)(a) requires that the order specify "the identity of the person, if known, whose communications are to be intercepted." Since the judge who prepares the order can only be expected to learn of the target individual's identity through reference to the original application, it can hardly be inferred that this statutory language imposes any broader requirement than the identification provisions of § 2518(1)(b)(iv).

In effect, the Court of Appeals read these provisions of § 2518 as if they required that the application and order identify "all persons, known or discoverable, who are committing the offense and whose communications are to be intercepted." But that is simply not what the statute says: identification is required only of those "known" to be "committing the offense." Had Congress wished to engraft a separate requirement of "discoverability" onto the provisions of Title III, it surely would have done so in language plainer than that now embodied in § 2518.

Moreover, the Court of Appeals' interpretation of § 2518 would have a broad impact. A requirement that the Government fully investigate the possibility that any likely user of a telephone was engaging in criminal activities before applying for an interception order would greatly subvert the effectiveness of the law enforcement mechanism that Congress constructed. In the case at hand, the Court of Appeals' holding would require the complete investigation not only of Minnie Kahn, but also of the two teenaged Kahn children and other frequenters of the Kahn residence before a wiretap order could be applied for. If the telephone were in a store or an office, the Government might well be required to investigate everyone who had access to it—in some cases, literally hundreds of people—even though there was no reason to suspect that any of them were violating any criminal law. It is thus open to considerable doubt that such a requirement would ultimately serve the interests of individual privacy. In any event, the statute as actually drafted contains no intimation of such total investigative demands.

In arriving at its reading of § 2518, the Court of Appeals seemed to believe that taking the statute at face value would result in a wiretap order amounting to a "virtual general warrant," since the law enforcement authorities would be authorized to intercept communications of anyone who talked on the named telephone line. But neither the statute nor the wiretap order in this case would allow the federal agents such total unfettered discretion. By its own terms, the wiretap order in this case conferred authority to intercept only communications "concerning the above-described [gambling] offenses." Moreover, in accord with the statute the order required the agents to execute the warrant in such a manner as to minimize the interception of any innocent conversations. And the order limited the length of any possible interception to 15 days, while requiring status reports as to the progress of the wiretap to be submitted to the District Judge every five days, so that any possible abuses might be quickly discovered and halted. Thus, the failure of the order to specify that Mrs. Kahn's conversations might be the subject of interception hardly left the executing agents free to seize at will every communication that came over the wire—and there is no indication that such abuses took place in this case.[2]

We conclude, therefore, that Title III requires the naming of a person in the application or interception order only when the law enforcement authorities have probable cause to believe that that individual is "committing the offense" for which the wiretap is sought. Since it is undisputed that the Government had no reason to suspect Minnie Kahn of complicity in the gambling business before the wire interceptions here began, it

probable cause of offense

~no reason to suspect Minnie Kahn

---

2. The fallacy in the Court of Appeals' "general warrant" approach may be illustrated by examination of an analogous conventional search and seizure. If a warrant had been issued, upon a showing of probable cause, to search the Kahn residence for physical records of gambling operations, there could be no question that a subsequent seizure of such records bearing Minnie Kahn's handwriting would be fully lawful, despite the fact that she had not been identified in the warrant nor independently investigated. In fact, as long as the property to be seized is described with sufficient specificity, even a warrant failing to name the owner of the premises at which a search is directed, while not the best practice, has been held to pass muster under the Fourth Amendment. * * *

Minnie falls under "as yet unknown"

follows that under the statute she was among the class of persons "as yet unknown" covered by Judge Campbell's order.

The remaining question is whether, under the actual language of Judge Campbell's order, only those intercepted conversations to which Irving Kahn himself was a party are admissible in evidence at the Kahn's trial, as the Court of Appeals concluded. The effect of such an interpretation of the wiretap order in this case would be to exclude from evidence the intercepted conversations between Minnie Kahn and the "known gambling figure" concerning betting information. Again, we are unable to read either the District Court order or the underlying provisions of Title III as requiring such a result.

The order signed by Judge Campbell in this case authorized the Government to "intercept wire communications of Irving Kahn and others as yet unknown to and from two telephones, subscribed to by Irving Kahn." The order does not refer to conversations *between* Irving Kahn and others; rather, it describes "communications *of* Irving Kahn and others as yet unknown" to and from the target telephones. To read this language as requiring that Irving Kahn be a party to every intercepted conversation would not only involve a substantial feat of verbal gymnastics, but would also render the phrase "and others as yet unknown" quite redundant, since Kahn perforce could not communicate except with others.

Moreover, the interpretation of the wiretap authorization adopted by the Court of Appeals is at odds with one of the stated purposes of Judge Campbell's order. The District Judge specifically found that the wiretap was needed to "reveal the identities of [Irving Kahn's] confederates, their places of operation, and the nature of the conspiracy involved." It is evident that such information might be revealed in conversations to which Irving Kahn was not a party. For example, a confederate might call in Kahn's absence, and leave either a name, a return telephone number, or an incriminating message. Or, one of Kahn's associates might himself come to the family home and employ the target telephones to conduct the gambling business. It would be difficult under any circumstances to believe that a District Judge meant such intercepted conversations to be inadmissible at any future trial; given the specific language employed by Judge Campbell in the wiretap order today before us, such a conclusion is simply untenable.

Nothing in Title III requires that, despite the order's language, it must be read to exclude Minnie Kahn's communications. As already noted, 18 U.S.C.A. §§ 2518(1)(b)(iv) and 2518(4)(a) require identification of the person committing the offense only "if known." The clear implication of this language is that when there is probable cause to believe that a particular telephone is being used to commit an offense but no particular person is identifiable, a wire interception order may, nevertheless, properly issue under the statute. It necessarily follows that Congress could not have intended that the authority to intercept must be limited to those conversations *between* a party named in the order and others, since at least in some cases, the order might not name any specific party at all.

For these reasons, we hold that the Court of Appeals was in error when it interpreted the phrase "others as yet unknown" so as to exclude conversations involving Minnie Kahn from the purview of the wiretap order. We further hold that neither the language of Judge Campbell's order nor that of Title III requires the suppression of legally intercepted conversations to which Irving Kahn was not himself a party.

Accordingly, the judgment of the Court of Appeals is reversed, and the case is remanded to that court for further proceedings consistent with this opinion.

It is so ordered.

NOTES

1. **Need To Name Persons Not Principal Target.** Suppose the investigating officers had information indicating Minnie Kahn was involved in the bookmaking operation. Would the failure to name her in the application have been improper? In United States v. Donovan, 429 U.S. 413, 97 S.Ct. 658, 50 L.Ed.2d 652 (1977), the Court rejected the argument that the statute required the applicant for a surveillance order to identify only the principal target of the surveillance. "[A] wiretap application," held the Court, "must name an individual if the Government has probable cause to believe that the individual is engaged in the criminal activity under investigation and expects to intercept the individual's conversations over the target telephone."

2. **Exclusionary Penalty for Failing to Name Persons.** Suppose the Government had information indicating Minnie Kahn was involved and nevertheless failed to identify her in the application. Would this omission require exclusion of the results of the surveillance? In *Donovan*, the Court held the failure to name such a person did not require exclusion of the results of the surveillance. The majority concluded that § 2518(1)(b)(iv) does not play a "substantive role" with respect to judicial authorization of intercept orders:

> [Despite noncompliance with § 2518(1)(b)(iv)] the statutorily imposed preconditions to judicial authorization were satisfied, and the issuing judge was simply unaware that additional persons might be overheard engaging in incriminating conversations. In no meaningful sense can it be said that the presence of that information as to additional targets would have precluded judicial authorization of the intercept. * * * [T]he instant intercept is lawful because the application provided sufficient information to enable the issuing judge to determine that the statutory preconditions were satisfied.

429 U.S. at 436, 97 S.Ct. at 672, 50 L.Ed.2d at 673. The Court noted, however, there was no suggestion the Government agents "intentionally" failed to identify the person or omitting this person's name resulted in the person's failure to receive the mandatory inventory notice required by § 2518(8)(d).

3. **Proof that Other Investigative Procedures Would Not Suffice.** Under section 2518(3)(c), the judge who issued the intercept order in *Kahn* determined, "on the basis of the facts submitted by the applicant," that "normal investigative procedures have been tried and have failed or reasonably appear to be unlikely to succeed if tried or to be too dangerous." If Kahn challenged the sufficiency of the evidence to support such a determination, should such a challenge have succeeded? The application apparently did not explain why the applicant believed physical surveillance or "normal search and seizure techniques" would not produce useful evidence. Could the issuing judge have made an "independent" determination of the matter required by section 2518(3)(c)? If this determination was not supported by adequate facts submitted by the applicant, would the absence of the supporting facts invalidate the order and require suppression of its "fruits"?

4. **Minimization of Interception of Innocent Communications.** In *Kahn*, the Court noted no argument had been made that the officers failed to conduct the wiretap in such a manner as to minimize the interception of innocent conversations. But suppose such an argument had been made? Were the officers justified in listening to the conversations between Irving and Minnie Kahn? Between Minnie and an unidentified person? Suppose the officers had listened to conversations between the two teenage Kahn children and their friends. Would it make any difference whether all of these conversations were listened to? Whether any effort was made to identify conversations that should not be listened to in the future, at least in their entirety? If the officers violated the "minimization" requirement, what impact would this violation have upon the admissibility of information obtained during interception of conversations clearly within the order's authorization?

The leading Supreme Court decision, Scott v. United States, 436 U.S. 128, 98 S.Ct. 1717, 56 L.Ed.2d 168 (1978), involved an investigation of a conspiracy to distribute heroin. An intercept order was issued and, for the month of the surveillance, the officers intercepted and recorded all conversations over the telephone described in the order. Forty percent of the calls were ultimately determined to relate to the conspiracy under investigation. The agent in charge of the investigation testified that, although he was aware of the minimization requirement, he made no effort to avoid the interception of innocent calls. The Court rejected the argument that this was bad faith which itself violated the statute. Objective circumstances, not the officers' subjective intent, determine the legality of the actions:

> [B]lind reliance on the percentage of nonpertinent calls intercepted is not a sure guide * * * . Such percentages may provide assistance, but there are surely cases * * * where the percentage of nonpertinent calls is relatively high and yet their interception was still reasonable. Many of the nonpertinent calls may have been very short. Others may have been one-time-only calls. Still other calls may have been ambiguous in nature or apparently involved guarded or coded language. In all these circumstances agents can hardly be expected to know that the calls are not pertinent prior to their termination.

> [I]t is also important to consider the circumstances of the wiretap. For example, when the investigation is focusing on what is thought to be a widespread conspiracy more extensive surveillance may be justified in an attempt to determine the precise scope of the enterprise. And it is possible that many more of the conversations will be permissibly interceptable because they will involve one or more of the co-conspirators. The type of use to which the telephone is normally put may also have some bearing on the extent of minimization required. For example, if the agents are permitted to tap a public telephone because one individual is thought to be placing bets over the phone, substantial doubts as to minimization may arise if the agents listen to every call which goes out over that phone regardless of who places the call. On the other hand, if the phone is located in the residence of a person thought to be the head of a major drug ring, a contrary conclusion may be indicated.

> [I]t may be important to determine at exactly what point during the authorized period the investigation was made. During the early stages of surveillance the agents may be forced to intercept all calls to establish categories of nonpertinent calls which will not be intercepted thereafter. Interception of these same types of calls might be unreasonable later on, however, once the nonpertinent categories have been established and it is clear that this particular conversation is of that type. Other situations may arise where patterns of nonpertinent calls do not appear. In these circumstances it may not be

unreasonable to intercept almost every short conversation because the determination of relevancy cannot be made before the call is completed.

436 U.S. at 140–41, 98 S.Ct. at 1724–25, 56 L.Ed.2d at 179–80.

On the facts of the case, the majority found no violation of the minimization requirement despite the high percentage of nonpertinent calls intercepted. Many of the nonpertinent calls were short and many were ambiguous in nature, making characterization impossible until the call was terminated. Further, the agents' conduct must be considered in light of the fact that the crime under investigation was a wide-ranging conspiracy with a large number of participants. The Court noted, but did not reach, the argument that, if the agents violated the minimization requirements, suppression is required only of those conversations improperly intercepted, not of all intercepted conversations.

Justice Brennan, joined by Justice Marshall, dissented. The majority, he suggested, undercut that portion of *Kahn's* reasoning which relied upon the minimization requirement to answer the contention that the holding in *Kahn* would authorize general search warrants.

5. **Actual Use and Effect of Electronic Surveillance Legislation.** The federal statute requires periodic reports by judges and prosecutors concerning applications, orders, and interceptions. These reports are apparently intended to develop and maintain a pool of information useful in evaluating the continued wisdom of making these law enforcement devices available under the limitations and restrictions imposed by present federal and state legislation. The reports are made to the Administrative Office of the United States Courts, which issues yearly reports summarizing information collected for the previous year. See, e.g., Administrative Office of the United States Courts, 1998 Wiretap Report, covering the period from January 1, 1998 through December 31, 1998. Several aspects of this information for recent years are especially useful.

Statutory authorization of electronic surveillance exists in 31 states, the District of Columbia and the federal system.

During 1998, 1,329 applications were granted for authorization of wire, oral, or electronic surveillance—566 were granted by federal judges and 763 by state judges. Only 2 applications were denied in 1998. During the 11 years from 1988 through 1988, a total of only 5 applications were denied by the judiciary; 11,000 applications were granted.

The number of orders issued has been increasing. In 1988, federal judges issued 293 orders and in 1993 they issued 450. In 1988, state judges issues 445 orders and in 1993 they issued 526.

The average number of interceptions per day ranged from zero to 427 for each device. The average number of persons whose conversations were intercepted was 129 per installed intercept and the average number of conversations intercepted was 1,251. About 25 percent of those conversations produced incriminating evidence.

The best measure of the effectiveness of electronic surveillance would be the number of persons arrested and convicted as a result of intercepts who would not otherwise have been arrested and convicted. That information, however, is not available. The Administrative Office does provide the numbers of arrests and convictions reported as resulting from intercept orders. There is often considerable lapse of time from the year in which an intercept occurs to when an arrest or a conviction is obtained. The Administrative Office's 1998 Report provides information on arrests and convictions reported as resulting from intercept orders installed in the years from 1987 through 1997. In 1993, 976 federal and statute intercept orders were issued and 938 resulted in actual installation of intercepts. The results of those 1993 intercepts were reported as follows:

	1993	1994	1995	1996	1997	Total
Arrests Made During Year	2,428	981	390	130	109	4,038
Convictions During Year	413	912	538	233	179	2,275

The 938 intercepts made in 1993, then, resulted in 2,275 convictions.

CHAPTER 7

INTERROGATION AND CONFESSIONS

Analysis

EDITORS' INTRODUCTION: CONFESSIONS AND CONFESSIONS LAW
IN THE CONTEXT OF MODERN LAW ENFORCEMENT

Among traditional law enforcement techniques are the collection and
preservation of suspects' out-of-court statements and, in some situations,
active elicitation or encouragement of such statements. These techniques
and the legal issues they raise are the subjects of this chapter.

Terminology: Confessions, Admissions, and Exculpatory Statements

When prosecutors offer defendants' out-of-court self-incriminating
statements into evidence against them, courts sometimes distinguished
between a "confession"—a statement admitting or acknowledging all facts
necessary for conviction of the crime charged—and an "admission"—an
acknowledgement of one or more facts that tend to establish guilt but not
of all elements of the crime. Moreover, both are sometimes distinguished
from an "exculpatory" statement, a statement which, at the time it was
made, was intended to exculpate rather than incriminate the speaker, but
which later is offered to prove the speaker's guilt. Prosecutors often use
exculpatory statements by of proving that a suspect gave a false explanation of incriminating circumstances; this is offered to prove that the
suspect was conscious of his or her guilt and, therefore, that the suspect is
in fact guilty. It is doubtful that these distinctions have much significance
today.

Basic Issues and Policy Considerations

The legal doctrines related to the admissibility of confessions raise two
basic questions: First, when should a confession be excluded as a means of
discouraging or punishing inappropriate law enforcement behavior? Second, when should a confession be excluded because—without regard to the
existence or nonexistence of any "fault" on the part of law enforcement
personnel—it was given in circumstances that make its use unacceptable?
There is substantial overlap between these two matters, but it is also clear
the admissibility of confessions is sometimes attacked on the basis of
factors which cannot be the fault of law enforcement officers or other
government agents.

In addressing these and other questions raised in this chapter—what
rules should govern the admissibility of confessions and how should these
rules be interpreted and applied—it is important to identify various and
sometimes competing policy considerations involved. The government, of
course, has an obvious interest in being able to use reliable evidence of
defendants' guilt of crimes; confessions are traditionally regarded as exceptionally reliable evidence of guilt. In Hopt v. Utah, 110 U.S. 574, 584–85, 4
S.Ct. 202, 207, 28 L.Ed. 262, 267 (1884), the Court explained:

A confession, if freely and voluntarily made, is evidence of the most
satisfactory character. Such a confession * * * "is deserving of the
highest credit, because it is presumed to flow from the strongest sense
of guilt, and, therefore, it is admitted as proof of the crime to which it
refers." * * * [T]he presumption upon which weight is given to such
evidence [is] * * * that one who is innocent will not imperil his safety
or prejudice his interests by an untrue statement * * * .

How important confessions are to securing convictions is a matter of dispute. It is clear that in some cases, available evidence other than the confession would result in conviction. In others, it seems certain the confession is essential to proof of guilt. Project, Interrogations in New Haven: The Impact of Miranda, 76 Yale L.J. 1519 (1967), studied the investigation of 90 cases. In 49 questioning was successful, i.e., it resulted in a self-incriminating statement. But the researchers concluded that in only 4 cases (8%) was questioning "necessary," in the sense that other evidence available would not have been sufficient to prove guilt. But Seeburger and Wettick, Miranda in Pittsburgh—A Statistical Study, 29 U.Pitt.L.Rev. 1 (1967), studied two samples of cases and concluded that confessions were necessary to conviction in 24.7% and 32.8% of those cases.

Reliability of Confessions

To some extent, legal requirements relating to interrogation and the admissibility of confessions are concerned with confessions' reliability. In this regard, why is *exclusion* of confessions appropriate? Why not simply trust juries to consider the credibility of evidence that defendants confessed and give that evidence the weight it deserves?

Defendants are entitled—as a matter of federal constitutional law—to the opportunity to persuade judges and juries that confessions should not be believed because of the manner in which they were elicited. In Crane v. Kentucky, 476 U.S. 683, 106 S.Ct. 2142, 90 L.Ed.2d 636 (1986), the defense moved before trial to suppress Crane's confession to the murder for which he was to be tried. A pretrial hearing was held on the motion, at which Crane testified he had been detained for questioning in a windowless room for some time, as many as six officers had been present during the questioning, he had unsuccessfully made repeated requests to contact his family and he had been badgered into making a false confession. Several police officers' testimonies contradicted this version of the facts and the trial court held the confession admissible. At trial, the prosecution introduced the confession into evidence. The defense contended in response that contradictions in the confession and the circumstances under which it was given meant the jury should not believe it. In support of this, the defense unsuccessfully attempted to introduce before the jury evidence concerning the interrogation during which the defendant made the confession. The state supreme court affirmed the resulting conviction, reasoning that evidence relating only to the "voluntariness" of a confession is not admissible before the jury. While evidence relating to the "credibility" of the confession is admissible, the court reasoned, all of Crane's offered evidence went only to voluntariness. A unanimous Supreme Court, speaking through Justice O'Connor, reversed:

> Whether rooted directly in the due process clause of the Fourteenth Amendment or in the Compulsory Process or Confrontation clauses of the Sixth Amendment, the Constitution guarantees criminal defendants "a meaningful opportunity to present a complete defense." We break no new ground in observing that an essential component of procedural fairness is an opportunity to be heard. That opportunity would be an empty one if the State were permitted to exclude compe-

tent, reliable evidence bearing on the credibility of a confession when such evidence is central to the defendant's claim of innocence. * * *

Under these principles, the Kentucky courts erred in foreclosing [Crane's] efforts to introduce testimony about the environment in which the police secured his confession. * * * [E]vidence about the manner in which a confession was obtained is often highly relevant to its reliability and credibility.

476 U.S. at 690–91, 106 S.Ct. at 2146–47, 90 L.Ed.2d at 645.

In view of defendants' right to challenge confessions' voluntariness before trial juries, why is exclusion of confessions ever justified on reliability grounds? Are jurors likely to be insensitive to evidence that should cause them to disregard a confession as unreliable? Perhaps the need to discourage police actions that, in general, tend to result in inaccurate confessions requires that the law provide an especially strong disincentive for engaging in such action. Such a disincentive might best be provided by completely excluding confessions rather than giving the prosecution opportunities to convince juries that such confessions ought to be credited.

Should confession law encourage police to elicit self-incriminating admissions from suspects and prosecutors to use them in trying cases? Or, should it attempt to discourage either or both? Courts sometimes assume restrictions on the admissibility of confessions will encourage law enforcement officers to seek out more reliable evidence of accuseds' guilt. Whether such evidence is available and—if so—whether confession law can successfully encourage officers to obtain it is not clear.

The number and significance of inaccurate convictions is a matter of longstanding controversy. Richard A. Leo and Richard J. Ofshe, The Consequences of False Confessions: Deprivations of Liberty and Miscarriages of Justice in the Age of Psychological Interrogation, 88 J.Crim.L. & Crim. 429 (1998), presented 60 cases involving what they characterized as proven false confessions (34 cases), highly probable false confessions (18 cases) and probable false confessions (8 cases). In 29 of the 60 cases the confessing defendant was convicted. Currently used interrogation techniques, they maintained, encourage inaccurate confessions. Further, law enforcement officers are not trained to be sensitive to this risk. Law enforcement officers, prosecutors, and jurors, moreover, "treat confession evidence with such deference that it outweighs strong evidence of a defendant's innocence." Leo and Ofshe concluded that "the problems caused by police-induced false confessions are significant, recurrent, and deeply troubling."

As might be expected, the claims of Leo and Ofshe have not gone unchallenged. Paul G. Cassell, The Guilty and the "Innocent": An Examination of Alleged Cases of Wrongful Conviction From False Confessions, 22 Harv. J. L. & Pub.Policy 523 (1999), maintained that in nine of the cases in which Leo and Ofshe claimed false confessions led to convictions there was substantial evidence supporting the guilt of the accused and that these persons were most likely guilty. Cassell suggested current interrogation techniques pose a worrisome risk of inducing false confessions only if the suspects are mentally retarded.

Nonevidentiary Law Enforcement Objectives

The undeniable fact that interrogation and resulting statements may serve a number of law enforcement objectives other than securing admissible evidence of suspects' guilt of criminal offenses complicates confession law. See Project, Interrogation in New Haven: The Impact of Miranda, 76 Yale L.J. 1519, 1593–96 (1967). For example, confessions may be useful or necessary for identifying accomplices to an offense. While a confession may not be admissible against the accomplice, it may direct law enforcement officers to other information and admissible evidence of the accomplice's guilt. And statements may be used to "clear" crimes for purposes of internal police records. If a case is "cleared"—even if no prosecution results—the police books are closed and no further resources will be expended on it. Further, a law enforcement agency's effectiveness is often judged in part by its clearance rate, so such agencies have a strong incentive to seek information permitting them to close cases even if no criminal prosecutions are possible or likely. Statements elicited by interrogation may serve a variety of other functions. Statements may permit the recovery of stolen property or of weapons that might otherwise be available to persons for future crimes. Or the statements may be used for "intelligence" purposes, to allocate resources most effectively, and to make various decisions as to how to proceed with the "policing" job.

In considering matters raised in this chapter, consider whether the law should be concerned with police techniques serving these functions as well as those designed to secure admissible evidence for courtroom use. Is exclusion of statements offered in criminal trials sufficient response to such problems as exist? Or should the law seek to discourage techniques such as interrogation even when those techniques are not intended to and will not result in the use against the suspect of a self-incriminating statement? If so, how might this be done?

Concerns Unrelated to Reliability

There are almost certainly considerations other than accuracy that should be accommodated in confession law. Suspects may have legitimate interests in being free from use against them of some law enforcement techniques, even if those techniques pose no danger of eliciting inaccurate statements. Encouraging suspects to incriminate themselves in some circumstances and by use of some techniques may be inconsistent with the manner in which human beings—even those believed on adequate grounds to be guilty of crimes—should be treated. There has, of course, been little brief made for the position that suspects should never be permitted to incriminate themselves or that all self-incriminating admissions should be rejected at trial. As then-Justice Rehnquist commented, "[The Supreme Court] has never held that an accused is constitutionally protected from his inability to keep quiet * * * ." United States v. Henry, 447 U.S. 264, 297, 100 S.Ct. 2183, 2201, 65 L.Ed.2d 115, 140 (1980) (Rehnquist, J., dissenting).

But suspects may have a legitimate interest in being encouraged or permitted to incriminate themselves only when they have certain information concerning the consequences of doing so and the alternatives available to them. Dix, Mistake, Ignorance, Expectation of Benefit, and the Modern Law of Confessions, 1975 Wash.U.L.Q. 275, 330–31, argued:

> A major objective of the law of confessions * * * should be * * * assuring that a person who confesses does so with as complete an understanding of his tactical position as possible. This, of course, would require awareness not only of his abstract legal rights, but also of his practical ability to implement those rights in light of his factual situation and of the tactical wisdom of asserting them.

Should this be one of the law's objectives in this area? If the act of making a confession as a practical matter assures conviction, perhaps a confession should be regarded as a "waiver" of the right to trial and the right to have the state prove guilt beyond a reasonable doubt. Waivers of important trial rights must, under prevailing law, be "knowing" and "intelligent" as well as "voluntary." Johnson v. Zerbst, 304 U.S. 458, 58 S.Ct. 1019, 82 L.Ed. 1461 (1938). Arguably, decisions to confess, then, should be given legal effect only if they were "knowing" and "intelligent" in this sense. It may follow that legal rules should discourage interrogation in situations likely to result in confessions failing these requirements. Further, perhaps confessions should be regarded as admissible only if they meet these standards.

The material in this chapter reflects to some extent a progression of developments. The first part develops the requirement that a confession be "voluntary," the traditional doctrine governing admissibility of confessions. Consider the reasons why the Supreme Court may have been dissatisfied with this doctrine as a means for dealing with what the Court perceived to be the problems presented by confessions in general and custodial interrogation in particular. That such dissatisfaction existed is made clear by the Court's 1966 action in Miranda v. Arizona, the subject of Part B of this chapter. Given the nature of the *Miranda* rules and their subsequent development, have they lived up to the Court's 1966 expectations? Do they adequately deal with the problems presented by custodial interrogation? What alternatives should be considered? How should they be evaluated? The third part of this chapter deals with suspects' Sixth Amendment right to counsel. Consider how this meshes with the voluntariness rule and the *Miranda* requirements.

Requirement of Corroboration or "Independent" Proof of the Corpus Delicti.

The doctrines discussed in this chapter relating to the admissibility of confessions must be distinguished from the very different requirement of "corroboration." The requirement of corroboration is often put as a demand that the prosecution, in order to prove guilt beyond a reasonable doubt, produce evidence other than an out-of-court confession by the defendant. This other evidence is often required to show the *corpus delicti,* that is, that the crime charged was committed *by someone.* The evidence independent of the confession need not tend to show that the defendant committed the crime. Nor need it be sufficient in itself to prove commission of the crime beyond a reasonable doubt. The confession can be the only evidence tending to show that the defendant committed the offense; the corroborating evidence can be considered together with the confession in determining whether the prosecution has proven guilt beyond a reasonable doubt. In some states, the requirement has been incorporated into statute. Section 60.50 of New York's Criminal Procedure Law, for example, provides that a conviction is not permitted "solely upon evidence of a confession made by [the defendant] without additional proof that the offense charged has been committed."

The requirement is sometimes stated as one addressing the admissibility of a confession—a confession is not admissible unless the prosecution has first introduced other evidence showing that the charged offense was committed. But trial judges have great discretion over the order of proof. A trial judge is therefore unlikely to commit reversible error even under this formulation of the requirement by admitting a confession, if the prosecution later in the case produces other evidence showing the charged offense was committed. See generally, McCormick on Evidence § 145 (5th ed. 1999).

In some jurisdictions, the requirement is somewhat more flexible than one of independent proof of the *corpus delicti.* In federal litigation, for example, the Supreme Court has held that in order for a conviction to be upheld the Government must have introduced "substantial independent evidence which would tend to establish the trustworthiness of the [defendant's] statement." Opper v. United States, 348 U.S. 84, 93, 75 S.Ct. 158, 164, 99 L.Ed. 101, 109 (1954). This is the requirement applied by the Court in Wong Sun v. United States, 371 U.S. 471, 83 S.Ct. 407, 9 L.Ed.2d 441 (1963), reprinted in Chapter 1. However the requirement is formulated, it is in effect a requirement that a confession be corroborated by some other evidence at trial in order to justify the conviction of the defendant.

Like the voluntariness rule, the requirement of corroboration is based upon concern regarding the accuracy of out-of-court self-incriminating statements. In *Opper* the Court explained:

> [O]ur concept of justice that finds no man guilty until proven has led our state and federal courts generally to refuse conviction on testimony concerning confessions of the accused not made by him at the trial of his case. * * * [T]he doubt persists that the zeal of the agencies of prosecution to protect the peace, the self-interest of the accomplice, the maliciousness of an enemy or the aberration or weakness of the accused under the strain of suspicion may tinge or warp the facts of the confession. Admissions, retold at trial, are much like hearsay, that is, statements not made at the pending trial. They had neither the compulsion of the oath nor the test of cross-examination.

348 U.S. at 89–90, 75 S.Ct. at 162–63, 99 L.Ed. at 106–07. Despite its concern with the accuracy of confessions and trials, however, the requirement of corroboration has not been incorporated into any federal constitutional doctrine and remains exclusively a matter of state or local definition of evidence sufficiency.

Statutory Provisions Related to Confessions

There have been relatively few legislative efforts addressing confession issues. The federal statute set out in part B(6) of this chapter is one of the few such efforts. The American Law Institute's Model Code of Pre-Arraignment Procedure (Official Draft, 1975) offers a more comprehensive effort.

Article 150 deals with Exclusion of Statements and some portions of Article 140, Conditions of Investigation During Custody of an Arrested Person, are also relevant to confession issues.

A. THE REQUIREMENT OF "VOLUNTARINESS"

EDITORS' INTRODUCTION: DEVELOPMENT, CONTENT, AND CURRENT SIGNATURE OF THE VOLUNTARINESS REQUIREMENT

Because of the widespread publicity given the *Miranda* decision, contemporary discussions of "confession law" tend to revolve around the *Miranda* requirements. An adequate understanding of the reasons for the "*Miranda* revolution," however, demands acquaintance with pre-*Miranda* voluntariness law. In addition, the voluntariness requirement is not without current significance. If *Miranda* does not apply to a given situation, the voluntariness requirement is likely to be the major consideration in determining whether a confession can be used in evidence. If a confession is inadmissible to prove a defendant's guilt because of the *Miranda* requirements, its availability to impeach the defendant's credibility—should the defendant testify at trial—apparently depends in part upon the voluntariness of the admission. Even if *Miranda* applies to a situation, there is a high likelihood that the effectiveness of the suspect's waiver of the rights to silence and to counsel will be at issue. Traditional voluntariness law undoubtedly bears upon the appropriate resolution of such matters. Further, if a suspect has given several confessions and *Miranda* was violated only during the elicitation of the first, the admissibility of the later confessions depends largely or entirely upon their voluntariness.

Development of the Federal Constitutional Requirement. In its first confession case, Hopt v. Utah, 110 U.S. 574, 4 S.Ct. 202, 28 L.Ed. 262 (1884), the United States Supreme Court treated the admissibility of an incriminating statement as a matter of federal evidence law. The admissibility of such statements, the Court noted, "so largely depends upon the special circumstances connected with the confession, that it is difficult, if not impossible, to formulate a rule that will comprehend all cases." But, it then held, the case could be resolved by "the weight of authority," which stated a confession is involuntary and inadmissible if

> the confession appears to have been made either in consequence of inducements of a temporal nature, held out by one in authority, touching the charge preferred, or because of a threat or promise by or in the presence of such person, which, operating upon the fears or hopes of the accused, in reference to the charge, deprive him of that freedom of will or self-control essential to make his confession voluntary within the meaning of the law.

110 U.S. at 585, 4 S.Ct. at 207–08, 28 L.Ed. at 266–67.

Thirteen years later, in Bram v. United States, 168 U.S. 532, 18 S.Ct. 183, 42 L.Ed. 568 (1897), the Court commented that "[i]n criminal trials, in the courts of the United States wherever a question arises whether a confession is incompetent because not voluntary, the issue is controlled by that portion of the fifth amendment to the constitution of the United States, commanding that no person 'shall be compelled in any criminal case, to be a witness against himself.' " The Fifth Amendment privilege, the Court continued, was a crystallization of the common law voluntariness rule existing at the time of the adoption of the Constitution. The "principle by which the admissibility of the confession of an accused person is to be determined is expressed in the textbooks," the high tribunal added, and it then cited with approval the following passage from 3 Russell on Crimes 478 (6th ed.):

> [A] confession, in order to be admissible, must be free and voluntary; that is, must not be extracted by any sort of threats or violence, nor obtained by any direct or implied promises, however slight, nor by the exertion of any improper influence.

The Fifth Amendment privilege against compelled self-incrimination was not held binding upon the states until Malloy v. Hogan, 378 U.S. 1, 84 S.Ct. 1489, 12 L.Ed.2d 653 (1964). But, beginning with Brown v. Mississippi, 297 U.S. 278, 56 S.Ct. 461, 80 L.Ed. 682 (1936), the Supreme Court imposed Constitutional limitations upon the use of confessions in state criminal trials through application of the Fourteenth Amendment's general requirement of due process. Although earlier cases suggested some difference between the due process requirement and the *Bram* Fifth Amendment rules, in 1966 the Court commented that "[t]he decisions of this Court have guaranteed the same procedural protection for the defendant whether his confession was used in a federal or state court." Miranda v. Arizona, 384 U.S. 436, 464 n. 33, 86 S.Ct. 1602, 1623 n. 33, 16 L.Ed.2d 694, 717–18 n. 33 (1966).

Not only has the "voluntariness" requirement been imposed as a matter of federal constitutional law, but state courts have universally accepted it as a matter of state constitutional doctrine. It is clear, then, that an appreciation of the need for and significance of subsequent developments in the legal standards governing the admissibility of confessions in American courts requires an understanding of this concept of voluntariness.

voluntary – state courts have accepted as a constitutional doctrine.

Content of the Voluntariness Requirement. In Blackburn v. Alabama, 361 U.S. 199, 80 S.Ct. 274, 4 L.Ed.2d 242 (1960), the Supreme Court observed that "a complex of values underlies the stricture against use by the state of confessions which, by way of convenient shorthand, this Court terms involuntary, and the role played by each in any situation varies according to the particular circumstances of the case." The Court commented further upon these values:

> The abhorrence of society to the use of involuntary confessions does not turn alone on their inherent untrustworthiness. It also turns on the deep-rooted feeling that the police must obey the law while enforcing the law; that in the end life and liberty can be as much endangered from illegal methods used to convict those thought to be criminals as from the actual criminals themselves. Accordingly, the actions of police in obtaining confessions * * * come under scrutiny * * *.

Spano v. New York, 360 U.S. 315, 320–21, 79 S.Ct. 1202, 1205–06, 3 L.Ed.2d 1265, 1270 (1959).

Brown and many early cases involved "coerced" confessions—that is, confessions stimulated by improper violence or the threat of such violence. In *Brown*, for example, police beat the suspects and told them such beatings would continue until the suspects provided confessions of the substance desired by the officers. But in subsequent cases the Court extended the prohibition against involuntary confessions far beyond such coerced statements.

Overbearing of the Will. In Blackburn v. Alabama, the Court noted that "coercion can be mental as well as physical and * * * the blood of the accused is not the only hallmark of an unconstitutional inquisition." In Spano v. New York, the Court observed:

> [A]s * * * the methods used to extract confessions [become] more sophisticated, our duty to enforce federal constitutional protections does not cease. It only becomes more difficult because of the more delicate judgments to be made.

360 U.S. at 321, 79 S.Ct. at 1206, 3 L.Ed.2d at 1271. In cases lacking overt brutality, the Court has applied a "totality of the circumstances" analysis. Justice Frankfurter authored the classic statement of this approach:

> No single litmus-paper test for constitutionally-impermissible interrogation has been evolved: neither extensive cross questioning * * *; nor undue delay in arraignment * * *; nor failure to caution a prisoner * * *; nor refusal to permit communication with friends and legal counsel at stages in the proceeding when the prisoner is still only a suspect * * *.
>
> Each of these factors, in company with all of the surrounding circumstances—the duration and conditions of detention (if the confessor has been detained), the manifest attitude of the police towards him, his physical and mental state, the diverse pressures which sap or sustain his powers of resistance and self-control—is relevant. The ultimate test remains * * *: * * * Is the confession the product of an essentially free and unconstrained choice by its maker? * * * [I]f his will has been overborne and his capacity for self-determination critically impaired, the use of his confession offends due process.

Culombe v. Connecticut, 367 U.S. 568, 601–02, 81 S.Ct. 1860, 1878–79, 6 L.Ed.2d 1037, 1057–58 (1961).

Greenwald v. Wisconsin, 390 U.S. 519, 88 S.Ct. 1152, 20 L.Ed.2d 77 (1968) (per curiam), illustrated application of the test. Although the case was decided by the Supreme Court after *Miranda*, *Miranda's* nonretroactivity meant that it did not govern the admissibility of the confession. The facts were as follows:

> [Greenwald], who has a ninth-grade education, was arrested on suspicion of burglary shortly before 10:45 on the evening of January 20, 1965. He was taken to a police station. He was suffering from high blood pressure, a condition for which he was taking medication twice a day. [He] had last taken food and medication, before his arrest, at 4

p.m. He did not have medication with him at the time of the arrest. At the police station [he] was interrogated from 10:45 until midnight. He was not advised of his constitutional rights. [He] repeatedly denied guilt. No incriminating statements were made at this time.

[He] was booked and fingerprinted and, sometime after 2 a.m., he was taken to a cell in the city jail. A plank fastened to the wall served as his bed. [He] claims he did not sleep. At 6 a.m., [he] was led from the cell to a "bullpen." At 8:30 he was placed in a lineup. At 8:45, his interrogation recommenced. It was conducted by several officers at a time, in a small room. [Greenwald] testified that in the course of the morning he was not offered food and that he continued to be without medication. For an hour or two he refused to answer any questions. When he did speak, it was to deny, once again, his guilt.

Sometime after 10 a.m., [Greenwald] was asked to write out a confession. He refused, stating that "it was against my constitutional rights" and that he was "entitled to have a lawyer." These statements were ignored. No further reference was made to an attorney, by [Greenwald] or by the police officers.

At about 11 a.m. [Greenwald] began a series of oral admissions culminating in a full oral confession at about 11:30. At noon he was offered food. The confession was reduced to writing about 1 p.m. Just before the confession was reduced to writing, [he] was advised of his constitutional rights. According to his testimony, he confessed because "I knew they weren't going to leave me alone until I did."

Considering the totality of these circumstances, a majority of the Court held the Wisconsin Supreme Court had erred in finding that Greenwald's statements "were the product of his free and rational choice." Justice Stewart, joined by two other members of the Court, read the circumstances as adequately supporting the state court's conclusion:

[Greenwald] was nearly 30 years old and was by no means a stranger to the criminal law. He was questioned for little more than an hour one evening and for less than four hours the next morning. He was neither abused nor threatened and was promised no benefit for confessing. * * * [H]e himself testified that, during his interrogation, "he knew he had a constitutional right to refuse to answer any questions, * * * he knew anything he said could be used against him, and * * * he knew he had a constitutional right to retain counsel." Moreover, * * * [he] himself testified that at no time between his arrest and his confession did he express to anyone a desire for food or for medication.

390 U.S. at 521–22, 88 S.Ct. at 1154, 20 L.Ed.2d at 80 (Stewart, J., dissenting).

As applied in cases such as *Greenwald,* does the voluntariness case law provide a meaningful standard for determining the admissibility of confessions? Judge Posner of the Seventh Circuit suggested not:

[W]hether a confession is voluntary is not really a fact, but a characterization. There is indeed no "faculty of will" inside our heads that has two states, on and off, such that through careful reconstruction of events the observer can determine whether the switch was on when the defendant was confessing. * * *

[C]ourts have not been successful in devising a standard that will determine in a consistent fashion when confessions should be excluded on grounds of involuntariness. Of course if the confession is unreliable, it should go out, along with other unreliable evidence. It is on this basis that confessions extracted by torture are excluded. But in most cases in which a confession is sought to be excluded because involuntary, there is little likelihood that the inducements placed before the defendant were so overpowering as to induce an untrue confession. The courts in such cases retreat to the proposition that a confession, to be admissible, must be the product of a free choice. [B]ut [this] is just the faculty of will approach, and, as the courts are beginning to suspect, it leads nowhere. Taken seriously it would require the exclusion of virtually all fruits of custodial interrogation, since few choices to confess can be thought truly "free" when made by a person who is incarcerated and is being questioned by armed officers without the presence of counsel or anyone else to give him moral support. The formula is not taken seriously. * * * [V]ery few incriminating statements, custodial or otherwise, are held to be involuntary, though few are the product of a choice that the interrogators left completely free.

United States v. Rutledge, 900 F.2d 1127, 1128–29 (7th Cir.1990) (Posner, J.).

Promises. The traditional requirement of voluntariness mandated exclusion of a confession obtained as a result of a promise or inducement, made by a person in a position of authority, concerning the criminal charges to which the defendant confessed. See generally, Dix, Mistake, Ignorance, Expectation of Benefit, and the Modern Law of Confessions, 1975 Wash.U.L.Q. 275 (1975). As the language from *Bram* set out above suggests, the Supreme Court appeared to incorporate this traditional requirement into the due process voluntariness standard.

The Supreme Court addressed the modern constitutional significance of promises in Arizona v. Fulminante, 499 U.S. 279, 111 S.Ct. 1246, 113 L.Ed.2d 302 (1991). Fulminante was a prisoner in a federal correctional facility and had begun to receive "rough treatment" from other inmates because of a rumor he had killed a child. Sarivola was a fellow inmate who was also an informant for the Federal Bureau of Investigation. Federal agents encouraged Sarivola to elicit information about the killing from Fulminante. Sarivola then offered to protect Fulminante from other inmates if Fulminante told him about the matter. Fulminante admitted the killing to Sarivola. At Fulminante's trial for the murder of the child, the prosecution successfully offered his confession. On appeal, the Arizona Supreme Court reversed, holding the confession inadmissible. The Supreme Court granted review to consider the State's contention that the Arizona Supreme Court had incorrectly applied a standard under which the confession was involuntary upon proof that "but for" the "promise" by Sarivola, Fulminante would not have made the confession. The Supreme Court noted the *Bram* language but made clear that this 1897 discussion's statement of voluntariness was no longer accurate federal constitutional law:

Although the Court noted in *Bram* that a confession cannot be obtained by " 'any direct or implied promises, however slight, nor by the exertion of any improper influence,' " it is clear this passage from *Bram* * * * does not state the standard for determining the voluntariness of a confession * * *.

499 U.S. at 285, 111 S.Ct. at 1251, 113 L.Ed.2d at 315. But it further found the Arizona court had properly applied a totality of the circumstances analysis. Although the question was a "close one," the majority concluded the Arizona court acceptably found the confession involuntary:

The Arizona Supreme Court found a credible threat of physical violence unless Fulminante confessed. Our cases have made clear that a finding of coercion need not depend upon actual violence by a government agent; a credible threat is sufficient. * * * [T]he Arizona Supreme Court found that it was fear of physical violence, absent protection from his friend (and Government agent) Sarivola, which motivated Fulminante to confess. Accepting the Arizona court's finding, permissible on this record, that there was a credible threat of physical violence, we agree with its conclusion that Fulminante's will was overborne in such a way as to render his confession the product of coercion.

499 U.S. at 287, 111 S.Ct. at 1252–53, 113 L.Ed.2d at 316–17.

Deception. Despite the case law's traditionally rigid prohibition against promises, American courts developed no similar voluntariness rule barring police officers from deceiving suspects during interrogation. Some courts have traditionally held that deception is simply not a basis for regarding a confession involuntary. In Commonwealth v. Graham, 408 Pa. 155, 182 A.2d 727 (1962), for example, a female police employee attended a lineup, pointed to the defendant, and said, "That's the man." The Pennsylvania Supreme Court expressed emphatic disapproval of the action, but held that the deception did not amount to legal duress or coercion rendering the confession inadmissible. Some courts have stated the voluntariness requirement so as to leave open the possibility that at least some deception affects admissibility. In People v. Everett, 10 N.Y.2d 500, 225 N.Y.S.2d 193, 180 N.E.2d 556 (1962), for example, an officer misrepresented to a murder suspect that the victim had only been injured and had identified the suspect as his assailant. "Deception alone will not render a confession invalid," the New York court held, "unless the deceiving acts amount to a deprivation of due process." On the facts before it, the court found no aggravation of the sort necessary to violate due process.

Others courts have indicated that deception would render a confession involuntary only if the deception was likely to induce a false confession. In applying this test, however, the courts have been reluctant to find that particular deception created the required risk of a false statement. E.g., People v. Castello, 194 Cal. 595, 229 P. 855 (1924) (inaccurate statement by officer that defendant had been seen stealing the property was not such as to produce an untrue confession and therefore did not render confession inadmissible).

The Supreme Court did not address the relationship between deception and the federal due process standard until Frazier v. Cupp, 394 U.S. 731,

89 S.Ct. 1420, 22 L.Ed.2d 684 (1969). (Although *Frazier* was decided after *Miranda*, *Miranda's* requirements did not apply to the confession there at issue and therefore its admissibility turned upon its voluntariness.) Police interrogated Frazier; he denied committing the offense and claimed to have been with his cousin, Rawls, on the night of the crime. The officer then falsely told Frazier that Rawls had confessed to the murder. Subsequently, Frazier decided to make a statement. The trial court, over defense objection, admitted the statement at Frazier's trial.

The Supreme Court found no violation of the due process standard. It noted that Frazier had received a "partial warning" of his constitutional rights, the questioning was of short duration, and Frazier was "a mature individual of normal intelligence." Without citation of authority or discussion of the relevant considerations, the Court then commented, "The fact that the police misrepresented the statement that Rawls made is, while relevant, insufficient in our view to make this otherwise voluntary confession inadmissible."

Burden of Proof. If the prosecution offers a confession against a defendant, the prosecution must prove the voluntariness of that confession. In Lego v. Twomey, 404 U.S. 477, 92 S.Ct. 619, 30 L.Ed.2d 618 (1972), however, the Court held that the federal Constitution required only that voluntariness be proved by a preponderance of the evidence. No basis existed, the majority reasoned, to believe that rulings made under the preponderance of the evidence standard have been unreliable or otherwise wanting in quality. Consequently, the prosecution's ability to put confessions before juries need not be further impeded by a need to prove voluntariness beyond a reasonable doubt. States, of course, remain free to impose such a higher standard as a matter of state law.

Harmless Error. Earlier Supreme Court discussions suggested that if on appeal an appellate court determined that the trial judge had erroneously admitted an involuntary confession, reversal of the conviction for a new trial was always necessary. Admission of such a confession, in other words, could not be "harmless error." In Arizona v. Fulminante, discussed earlier in this Introductory Note as addressing promises made to suspects, a bare majority of the Supreme Court held that even admission of an involuntary confession could be harmless error if the appellate court is convinced beyond a reasonable doubt that the confession did not contribute to the defendant's conviction. Trial errors generally are subject to the harmless error rule, the Court concluded, and insufficient reason exists to treat involuntary confessions any differently. Admission of such a confession is not a "structural defect[ ] in the constitution of the trial mechanism, which def[ies] analysis by 'harmless error' standards." Nor is the admission of such a confession a type of error that should always require reversal because it "transcends the criminal process." On the facts of *Fulminante*, however, the State failed to meet its burden of establishing beyond a reasonable doubt that the confession did not contribute to Fulminante's conviction. Therefore, his conviction was reversed.

* * *

The principal case in this section reflects a major conceptual development of the federal constitutional voluntariness doctrine. In addition to the statements raising the due process voluntariness concern discussed in those parts of the opinions reprinted here, the defendant made other statements to which *Miranda* applied. The Supreme Court's holdings on the *Miranda* issues are discussed in Part B of this chapter.

Colorado v. Connelly

Supreme Court of the United States, 1986.
479 U.S. 157, 107 S.Ct. 515, 93 L.Ed.2d 473.

■ CHIEF JUSTICE REHNQUIST delivered the opinion of the Court.

* * *

I

On August 18, 1983, Officer Patrick Anderson of the Denver Police Department was in uniform, working in an off-duty capacity in downtown Denver. Respondent Francis Connelly approached Officer Anderson and, without any prompting, stated that he had murdered someone and wanted to talk about it. Anderson immediately advised respondent that he had the right to remain silent, that anything he said could be used against him in court, and that he had the right to an attorney prior to any police questioning. See Miranda v. Arizona, 384 U.S. 436, 86 S.Ct. 1602, 16 L.Ed.2d 694 (1966). Respondent stated that he understood these rights but he still wanted to talk about the murder. Understandably bewildered by this confession, Officer Anderson asked respondent several questions. Connelly denied that he had been drinking, denied that he had been taking any drugs, and stated that, in the past, he had been a patient in several mental hospitals. Officer Anderson again told Connelly that he was under no obligation to say anything. Connelly replied that it was "all right," and that he would talk to Officer Anderson because his conscience had been bothering him. To Officer Anderson, respondent appeared to understand fully the nature of his acts.

Shortly thereafter, Homicide Detective Stephen Antuna arrived. Respondent was again advised of his rights, and Detective Antuna asked him "what he had on his mind." Respondent answered that he had come all the way from Boston to confess to the murder of Mary Ann Junta, a young girl whom he had killed in Denver sometime during November 1982. Respondent was taken to police headquarters, and a search of police records revealed that the body of an unidentified female had been found in April 1983. Respondent openly detailed his story to Detective Antuna and Sergeant Thomas Haney, and readily agreed to take the officers to the scene of the killing. Under Connelly's sole direction, the two officers and respondent proceeded in a police vehicle to the location of the crime. Respondent pointed out the exact location of the murder. Throughout this episode, Detective Antuna perceived no indication whatsoever that respondent was suffering from any kind of mental illness.

Respondent was held overnight. During an interview with the public defender's office the following morning, he became visibly disoriented. He began giving confused answers to questions, and for the first time, stated that "voices" had told him to come to Denver and that he had followed the directions of these voices in confessing. Respondent was sent to a state hospital for evaluation. He was initially found incompetent to assist in his own defense. By March 1984, however, the doctors evaluating respondent determined that he was competent to proceed to trial.

At a preliminary hearing, respondent moved to suppress all of his statements. Doctor Jeffrey Metzner, a psychiatrist employed by the state hospital, testified that respondent was suffering from chronic schizophrenia and was in a psychotic state at least as of August 17, 1983, the day before he confessed. Metzner's interviews with respondent revealed that respondent was following the "voice of God." This voice instructed respondent to withdraw money from the bank, to buy an airplane ticket, and to fly from Boston to Denver. When respondent arrived from Boston, God's voice became stronger and told respondent either to confess to the killing or to commit suicide. Reluctantly following the command of the voices, respondent approached Officer Anderson and confessed.

Dr. Metzner testified that, in his expert opinion, respondent was experiencing "command hallucinations." This condition interfered with respondent's "volitional abilities; that is, his ability to make free and rational choices." Dr. Metzner further testified that Connelly's illness did not significantly impair his cognitive abilities. Thus, respondent understood the rights he had when Officer Anderson and Detective Antuna advised him that he need not speak. Dr. Metzner admitted that the "voices" could in reality be Connelly's interpretation of his own guilt, but explained that in his opinion, Connelly's psychosis motivated his confession.

On the basis of this evidence the Colorado trial court decided that respondent's statements must be suppressed because they were "involuntary." * * *

The Colorado Supreme Court affirmed. * * *

II

The Due Process Clause of the Fourteenth Amendment provides that no State shall "deprive any person of life, liberty, or property, without due process of law." Just last Term, in Miller v. Fenton, 474 U.S. 104, 109, 106 S.Ct. 445, 449, 88 L.Ed.2d 405 (1985), we held that by virtue of the Due Process Clause "certain interrogation techniques, either in isolation or as applied to the unique characteristics of a particular suspect, are so offensive to a civilized system of justice that they must be condemned." * * * [T]he cases considered by this Court * * * have focused upon the crucial element of police overreaching. While each confession case has turned on its own set of factors justifying the conclusion that police conduct was oppressive, all have contained a substantial element of coercive police conduct. Absent police conduct causally related to the confession, there is simply no basis for concluding that any state actor has deprived a criminal defendant of due process of law. Respondent correctly notes that as interrogators have turned to more subtle forms of psychological persuasion, courts have found the mental condition of the defendant a more significant factor in the "voluntariness" calculus. But this fact does not justify a conclusion that a defendant's mental condition, by itself and apart from its relation to official coercion, should ever dispose of the inquiry into constitutional "voluntariness."

mental condition linked to "voluntariness"

Respondent relies on Blackburn v. Alabama, 361 U.S. 199, 80 S.Ct. 274, 4 L.Ed.2d 242 (1960), and Townsend v. Sain, 372 U.S. 293, 83 S.Ct. 745, 9 L.Ed.2d 770 (1963), for the proposition that the "deficient mental condition of the defendants in those cases was sufficient to render their confessions involuntary." But respondent's reading of *Blackburn* and *Townsend* ignores the integral element of police overreaching present in both cases. In *Blackburn,* the Court found that the petitioner was probably insane at the time of his confession and the police learned during the interrogation that Blackburn had a history of mental problems. The police exploited this weakness with coercive tactics: "the eight- to nine-hour sustained interrogation in a tiny room which was upon occasion literally filled with police officers; the absence of Blackburn's friends, relatives, or legal counsel; [and] the composition of the confession by the Deputy Sheriff rather than by Blackburn." These tactics supported a finding that the confession was involuntary. Indeed, the Court specifically condemned police activity that "wrings a confession out of an accused against his will." *Townsend* presented a similar instance of police wrongdoing. In that case, a police physician had given Townsend a drug with truth-serum properties. The subsequent confession, obtained by officers who knew that Townsend had been given drugs, was held involuntary. These two cases demonstrate that while mental condition is surely relevant to an individual's susceptibility to police coercion, mere examination of the confessant's state of mind can never conclude the due process inquiry.

Our "involuntary confession" jurisprudence is entirely consistent with the settled law requiring some sort of "state action" to support a claim of violation of the Due Process Clause of the Fourteenth Amendment. The Colorado trial court, of course, found that the police committed no wrongful acts, and that finding has been neither challenged by the respondent nor disturbed by the Supreme Court of Colorado. The latter court, however, concluded that sufficient state action was present by virtue of the admission of the confession into evidence in a court of the State.

The difficulty with the approach of the Supreme Court of Colorado is that it fails to recognize the essential link between coercive activity of the State, on the one hand, and a resulting confession by a defendant, on the other. The flaw in respondent's constitutional argument is that it would expand our previous line of "voluntariness" cases into a far-ranging requirement that courts must divine a defendant's motivation for speaking or acting as he did even though there be no claim that governmental conduct coerced his decision.

The most outrageous behavior by a private party seeking to secure evidence against a defendant does not make that evidence inadmissible under the Due Process Clause. * * * Moreover, suppressing respondent's statements would serve absolutely no purpose in enforcing constitutional guarantees. The purpose of excluding evidence seized in violation of the

Constitution is to substantially deter future violations of the Constitution. Only if we were to establish a brand new constitutional right—the right of a criminal defendant to confess to his crime only when totally rational and properly motivated—could respondent's present claim be sustained.

We have previously cautioned against expanding "currently applicable exclusionary rules by erecting additional barriers to placing truthful and probative evidence before state juries." * * * We abide by that counsel now. "[T]he central purpose of a criminal trial is to decide the factual question of the defendant's guilt or innocence," and while we have previously held that exclusion of evidence may be necessary to protect constitutional guarantees, both the necessity for the collateral inquiry and the exclusion of evidence deflect a criminal trial from its basic purpose. Respondent would now have us require sweeping inquiries into the state of mind of a criminal defendant who has confessed, inquiries quite divorced from any coercion brought to bear on the defendant by the State. We think the Constitution rightly leaves this sort of inquiry to be resolved by state laws governing the admission of evidence and erects no standard of its own in this area. A statement rendered by one in the condition of respondent might be proved to be quite unreliable, but this is a matter to be governed by the evidentiary laws of the forum, see, e.g., Fed.Rule Evid. 601, and not by the Due Process Clause of the Fourteenth Amendment. "The aim of the requirement of due process is not to exclude presumptively false evidence, but to prevent fundamental unfairness in the use of evidence, whether true or false." Lisenba v. California, 314 U.S. 219, 236, 62 S.Ct. 280, 290, 86 L.Ed. 166 (1941).

We hold that coercive police activity is a necessary predicate to the finding that a confession is not "voluntary" within the meaning of the Due Process Clause of the Fourteenth Amendment. We also conclude that the taking of respondent's statements, and their admission into evidence, constitute no violation of that Clause.

* * *

IV

The judgment of the Supreme Court of Colorado is accordingly reversed, and the cause remanded for further proceedings not inconsistent with this opinion.

■ JUSTICE BRENNAN, with whom JUSTICE MARSHALL joins, dissenting.

* * * Because I believe that the use of a mentally ill person's involuntary confession is antithetical to the notion of fundamental fairness embodied in the Due Process Clause, I dissent.

* * *

The absence of police wrongdoing should not, by itself, determine the voluntariness of a confession by a mentally ill person. The requirement that a confession be voluntary reflects a recognition of the importance of free will and of reliability in determining the admissibility of a confession, and thus demands an inquiry into the totality of the circumstances surrounding the confession.

* * *

We have never confined our focus to police coercion, because the value of freedom of will has demanded a broader inquiry. The confession cases decided by this Court * * * have focused upon both police overreaching and free will. While it is true that police overreaching has been an element of every confession case to date, it is also true that in every case the Court has made clear that ensuring that a confession is a product of free will is an independent concern. The fact that involuntary confessions have always been excluded in part because of police overreaching signifies only that this is a case of first impression. Until today, we have never upheld the admission of a confession that does not reflect the exercise of free will.

[I]f state action is required, police overreaching is not its only relevant form. The Colorado Supreme Court held that the trial court's admission of the involuntary confession into evidence is also state action. * * *

The instant case starkly highlights the danger of admitting a confession by a person with a severe mental illness. The trial court made no findings concerning the reliability of Mr. Connelly's involuntary confession, since it believed that the confession was excludable on the basis of involuntariness. However, the overwhelming evidence in the record points to the unreliability of Mr. Connelly's delusional mind. * * *

Moreover, the record is barren of any corroboration of the mentally ill defendant's confession. No physical evidence links the defendant to the alleged crime. Police did not identify the alleged victim's body as the woman named by the defendant. Mr. Connelly identified the alleged scene of the crime, but it has not been verified that the unidentified body was found there or that a crime actually occurred there. There is not a shred of competent evidence in this record linking the defendant to the charged homicide. There is only Mr. Connelly's confession.

Minimum standards of due process should require that the trial court find substantial indicia of reliability, on the basis of evidence extrinsic to the confession itself, before admitting the confession of a mentally ill person into evidence. I would require the trial court to make such a finding on remand. To hold otherwise allows the State to imprison and possibly to execute a mentally ill defendant based solely upon an inherently unreliable confession.

dissent = not of free will

* * *

NOTES

1. **Relevance of Accuracy.** While the unreliability of involuntary confessions may be among the rationales for excluding them, the accuracy of a particular confession is irrelevant to its due process voluntariness. In Rogers v. Richmond, 365 U.S. 534, 81 S.Ct. 735, 5 L.Ed.2d 760 (1961), the police misrepresented to defendant that they were about to bring his wife into the stationhouse for questioning. The trial judge held the resulting confession admissible because the police pretense "had

no tendency to produce a confession that was not in accord with the truth." The United States Supreme Court reversed the conviction:

> From a fair reading of * * * [the record] we cannot but conclude that the question whether Rogers' confessions were admissible was answered by reference to a legal standard which took into account the circumstance of probable truth or falsity. And this is not a permissible standard under the Due Process Clause of the Fourteenth Amendment. The attention of the trial court should have been focused * * * on the question whether the behavior of the State's law enforcement officials was such as to overbear petitioner's will to resist and to bring about confessions not freely self-determined—a question to be answered with complete disregard of whether or not petitioner in fact spoke the truth.

365 U.S. at 543–44, 81 S.Ct. at 741, 5 L.Ed.2d at 768.

2. **Violation of "Prompt Presentation" Requirements.** Rule 5(a) of the Federal Rules of Criminal Procedure demands presentation of an arrested person before a judicial officer without "unnecessary delay." Most if not all states have similar requirements of "prompt presentation" of arrested suspects. In part, prompt presentation minimizes the opportunity for coercive or otherwise improper interrogation techniques. At the arrestee's appearance before the magistrate, the arrestee may be given information concerning the charges pending and may be informed by the judge regarding legal rights. Moreover, provision may be made for pretrial release. What is the effect upon the admissibility of a confession of a delay in presenting the accused before a magistrate in accordance with these requirements?

In McNabb v. United States, 318 U.S. 332, 63 S.Ct. 608, 87 L.Ed. 819 (1943), the Supreme Court held that under its supervisory power it would require exclusion of a confession made by a defendant after federal officers who had the defendant in custody failed to comply with a statutory predecessor to Rule 5(a) demanding prompt presentation. The Court later applied the same exclusionary rule to Rule 5(a). Upshaw v. United States, 335 U.S. 410, 69 S.Ct. 170, 93 L.Ed. 100 (1948). In Mallory v. United States, 354 U.S. 449, 77 S.Ct. 1356, 1 L.Ed.2d 1479 (1957), the Court considered the meaning of "unnecessary delay" under Rule 5(a), and made clear this was to be defined so as to minimize the opportunity for custodial interrogation:

> Circumstances may justify a brief delay between arrest and arraignment, as for instance, where the story volunteered by the accused is susceptible of quick verification through third parties. But the delay must not be of a nature to give opportunity for the extraction of a confession.

354 U.S. at 455, 77 S.Ct. at 1360, 1 L.Ed.2d at 1483. The delay in the case before it, the Court held, was "unnecessary" because a magistrate was readily available and the defendant was not presented only because the officers desired the opportunity for interrogation.

The Supreme Court has never held the *McNabb-Mallory* rule in any way binding on the states. Instead, a showing that a confession was obtained during an improper delay in presenting the defendant before a magistrate has always been regarded as merely one factor to consider in determining the confession's due process voluntariness. Of course, this lack of any federal constitutional prompt presentation requirement is no bar to states adopting, as a matter of state law, an exclusionary rule requiring the suppression of confessions made during a period of delay violative of the state's prompt presentation requirement.

As a matter of federal law, Congress has modified the *McNabb-Mallory* rule. Under 18 U.S.C.A. § 3501(c), other portions of which are reprinted later in subsection B(6) of this chapter, a confession offered against a federal criminal defendant is not to be excluded solely because of delay in presenting a defendant before a magistrate if the confession is voluntary and made within six hours following the defendant's taking into custody. Further, a confession obtained after a six-hour period is not to be excluded on delay grounds alone if the delay is found reasonable, considering the distance traveled to a judicial officer and the means of transportation available to the officers.

Precisely what effect flows from the federal statute is unclear. The Supreme Court has, for example, noted but not passed on the contention that the statute mandates suppression of a confession made during improper delay in presenting a suspect before a magistrate if the confession is made after the six hour "safe harbor" period has expired. United States v. Alvarez–Sanchez, 511 U.S. 350, 355–56, 114 S.Ct. 1599, 1602–03, 114 L.Ed.2d 319, 326–27 (1994).

3. **Violation of Fourth Amendment Right to Probable Cause Determination.** Under Gerstein v. Pugh, 420 U.S. 103, 95 S.Ct. 854, 43 L.Ed.2d 54 (1975), an unindicted defendant arrested without a warrant has a Fourth Amendment right to a "prompt" judicial determination of probable cause. County of Riverside v. McLaughlin, 500 U.S. 44, 111 S.Ct. 1661, 114 L.Ed.2d 49 (1991), made clear that promptness generally requires such probable cause determinations be made within 48 hours of arrests. These determinations may—but need not—be made when the defendants go before magistrates pursuant to the statutory provisions discussed in note 2, above. If an arrested defendant is not provided with the probable cause determination required under *Gerstein* and *McLaughlin*, is a confession given during that detention—and after the defendant was entitled to a probable cause determination—inadmissible as the fruit of the Fourth Amendment violation?

The issue was noted but not addressed by the Supreme Court in Powell v. Nevada, 511 U.S. 79, 84–85, 114 S.Ct. 1280, 1283–84, 128 L.Ed.2d 1, 7–8 (1994). Justice Thomas, joined by the Chief Justice, argued in *Powell* that the Court should reach the issue. He further offered an analysis that would render suppression inappropriate in some and perhaps all such cases. Powell was arrested on November 3, 1989 after he brought a badly injured child to a hospital for treatment. On November 7, he made a statement admitting abusing the child. Later on the 7th, a magistrate determined the arrest was supported by probable cause; the magistrate relied upon facts recited in a "declaration of arrest" prepared by officers within an hour of Powell's arrest. On these facts, Justice Thomas reasoned, the November 7th statement need not be suppressed:

> [S]uppression of petitioner's statement would not be appropriate because the statement was not a product of the *McLaughlin* violation.
>
> Our decisions make clear "that evidence will not be excluded as 'fruit' [of an unlawful act] unless the illegality is at least the 'but for' cause of the discovery of the evidence." * * *

a "but for" test

> Contrary to petitioner's arguments, the violation of *McLaughlin* (as opposed to his arrest and custody) bore no causal relationship whatsoever to his November 7 statement. The timing of the probable cause determination would have affected petitioner's statement only if a proper hearing at or before the 48–hour mark would have resulted in a finding of no probable cause. Yet, as the Magistrate found, the police had probable cause to suspect petitioner of child abuse, and there is no suggestion that the delay in securing a determination of probable cause permitted the police to gather additional evidence to be presented to the Magistrate. On the contrary, the Magistrate based his determination on the facts included in the declaration of arrest that was completed within an hour of petitioner's arrest. Thus, if the probable cause determination had been made within 48 hours as required by *McLaughlin,* the same information would

have been presented, the same result would have been obtained, and none of the circumstances of petitioner's custody would have been altered.

Moreover, it cannot be argued that the *McLaughlin* error somehow made petitioner's custody unlawful and thereby rendered the statement the product of unlawful custody. Because the arresting officers had probable cause to arrest petitioner, he was lawfully arrested at the hospital. The presumptively unconstitutional delay in securing a judicial determination of probable cause during a period of lawful custody did not render that custody illegal. We have never suggested that lawful custody becomes unlawful due to a failure to obtain a prompt judicial finding of probable cause—that is, probable cause does not disappear if not judicially determined within 48 hours.

511 U.S. at 89–91 114 S.Ct. at 1286–87, 128 L.Ed.2d at 10–12 (Thomas, J., dissenting). Since the confession was not the product of illegal governmental activity, he added, "conventional attenuation principles are inapplicable in this case * * *."

4. **Adequacy of Voluntariness Requirement.** Was the voluntariness requirement insufficient to protect suspects' interests during custodial interrogation? Schulhofer, Confessions and the Court, 79 Mich.L.Rev. 865, 869–72 (1981), summarized a number of defects which critics found in the due process voluntariness requirement. It failed to provide specific guidance to law enforcement on which questioning tactics were and were not permissible. The "elusive task of balancing" invited trial judges to give weight to their subjective preferences and discouraged appellate review; judicial review of police activity was therefore impaired. Often, the critical issue was one of fact—what happened in the interrogation room—resulting in "swearing matches" between officers and defendants; defendants generally lost. And despite the requirement, considerable pressure was placed on suspects to confess, those with special weaknesses were especially susceptible to such pressure, and even physical brutality was not effectively enough discouraged.

For a general discussion of the voluntariness requirement concluding it is the only constitutional restraint that can justifiably be imposed upon police interrogation, see Grano, Voluntariness, Free Will and the Law of Confessions, 65 Va.L.Rev. 859 (1979).

B. SELF-INCRIMINATION AND *MIRANDA*'S RIGHT TO COUNSEL

Beginning with Escobedo v. Illinois, 378 U.S. 478, 84 S.Ct. 1758, 12 L.Ed.2d 977 (1964), the Supreme Court began to shift away from the voluntariness requirement as the major federal constitutional means of addressing what it perceived to be the continuing problems posed by police questioning of suspects in custody. This shift was completed two years later in Miranda v. Arizona, 384 U.S. 436, 86 S.Ct. 1602, 16 L.Ed.2d 694 (1966).

The *Miranda* decision itself is presented in the first subsection of this section. The second subsection addresses the task of determining those situations to which *Miranda* applies. The next presents one aspect of *Miranda* that has undergone considerable evolution—the right to prevent questioning. Subsection four considers what has become a major problem area in *Miranda* law—the existence and validity of waivers of the *Miranda* rights. In the fifth subsection, attention is turned to a particularly troublesome problem concerning remedy—a defendant's potential right to exclusion of evidence obtained as a factual result of an inadmissible confession.

Finally, the last subsection considers the impact of the *Miranda* requirements and the Congressional effort to "overrule" the decision.

1.   THE *MIRANDA* DECISION

EDITORS' INTRODUCTION: THE *MIRANDA* RIGHTS

Miranda v. Arizona is, of course, one of the most widely-known and
controversial decisions of the "Warren Court." To put the decision in
doctrinal perspective, it is necessary to understand that before *Miranda*
there was substantial support for the proposition that police interrogation
did not—directly, at least—implicate the Fifth Amendment privilege
against compelled self-incrimination. The privilege, it was widely considered, applied only where the suspect could be the subject of "legal compulsion," that is, compulsion authorized by law, to answer questions. In a
courtroom or before a grand jury a witness can be penalized for contempt
of court for refusing to respond to questions; thus the court applies "legal"
compulsion to the witness and consequently the situation implicated the
privilege. Police officers, on the other hand, have no legal right to impose
penalties upon suspects who refuse to answer the officers' questions.
Consequently, although police interrogation could give rise to an involuntary confession, it could not directly violate the Fifth Amendment privilege.

In addition, even where the privilege against compelled self-incrimination applies, it is, as a general rule, violated only if a person first specifically
claims a right under the privilege to refuse to answer a question and then
is nevertheless encouraged to answer. Unless the person first claims the
privilege, he has not been "compelled" to incriminate himself within the
meaning of the privilege. It follows from this, of course, that—again, as a
general rule—the government has no obligation before or during questioning to inform the person of the privilege. The person has the obligation to
assert the privilege. See Minnesota v. Murphy, 465 U.S. 420, 427, 104 S.Ct.
1136, 1142, 79 L.Ed.2d 409, 418–19 (1984).

Miranda first determined that police custodial interrogation of a person implicated interests of the person protected by the Fifth Amendment,
and thus that provision. The Court then proceeded to define the requirements of the Fifth Amendment in this context.

Subsequent judicial discussion and development of *Miranda* sometimes
emphasized the identification of so-called *"per se"* rules. The precise
meaning of this characterization of some *Miranda* requirements is not
always clear. Perhaps, however, it is best considered as describing the
relationship between a legal requirement and the exclusionary remedy. A
per se requirement, then, is one that, when violated, automatically demands
the exclusion of resulting evidence. Police violation of other requirements,
on the other hand, may not require exclusion of resulting evidence unless
other considerations apply. In the *Miranda* context, for example, violation
of some requirements announced in the decision or subsequent case law
might require the exclusion of resulting evidence only if it rendered the
suspect's waiver of the right to remain silent involuntary or otherwise
ineffective.

Whatever the terminology used, it is important in identifying and understanding the *Miranda* rights to separate two matters. One, of course, is the contents of the requirements which case law places upon law enforcement officers. The other, however, is the relationship between violation of these requirements and the admissibility of suspects' self-incriminating statements and other evidence obtained as the result of such statements.

Miranda v. Arizona

Supreme Court of the United States, 1966.
384 U.S. 436, 86 S.Ct. 1602, 16 L.Ed.2d 694.

■ MR. CHIEF JUSTICE WARREN delivered the opinion of the Court.

The cases before us raise questions which go to the roots of our concepts of American criminal jurisprudence: the restraints society must observe consistent with the Federal Constitution in prosecuting individuals for crime. More specifically, we deal with the admissibility of statements obtained from an individual who is subjected to custodial police interrogation and the necessity for procedures which assure that the individual is accorded his privilege under the Fifth Amendment to the Constitution not to be compelled to incriminate himself.

Issue →
statements in
violation of ...
- custodial interrogation

* * *

Our holding will be spelled out with some specificity in the pages which follow but briefly stated it is this: the prosecution may not use statements, whether exculpatory or inculpatory, stemming from custodial interrogation of the defendant unless it demonstrates the use of procedural safeguards effective to secure the privilege against self-incrimination. By custodial interrogation, we mean questioning initiated by law enforcement officers after a person has been taken into custody or otherwise deprived of his freedom of action in any significant way. As for the procedural safeguards to be employed, unless other fully effective means are devised to inform accused persons of their right of silence and to assure a continuous opportunity to exercise it, the following measures are required. Prior to any questioning, the person must be warned that he has a right to remain silent, that any statement he does make may be used as evidence against him, and that he has a right to the presence of an attorney, either retained or appointed. The defendant may waive effectuation of these rights, provided the waiver is made voluntarily, knowingly and intelligently. If, however, he indicates in any manner and at any stage of the process that he wishes to consult with an attorney before speaking there can be no questioning. Likewise, if the individual is alone and indicates in any manner that he does not wish to be interrogated, the police may not question him. The mere fact that he may have answered some questions or volunteered some statements on his own does not deprive him of the right to refrain from answering any further inquiries until he has consulted with an attorney and thereafter consents to be questioned.

I.

* * *

An understanding of the nature and setting of * * * in-custody interrogation is essential to our decisions today. The difficulty in depicting what transpires at such interrogations stems from the fact that in this country they have largely taken place incommunicado. From extensive factual studies undertaken in the early 1930's, including the famous Wickersham Report to Congress by a Presidential Commission, it is clear that police violence and the "third degree" flourished at that time. In a series of cases decided by this Court long after these studies, the police resorted to physical brutality—beatings, hanging, whipping—and to sustained and protracted questioning incommunicado in order to extort confessions. * * *

[Situations involving brutality] are undoubtedly the exception now, but they are sufficiently widespread to be the object of concern. Unless a proper limitation upon custodial interrogation is achieved—such as these decisions will advance—there can be no assurance that practices of this nature will be eradicated in the foreseeable future.

* * *

[T]he modern practice of in-custody interrogation is psychologically rather than physically oriented. * * * "[T]his Court has recognized that coercion can be mental as well as physical, and that the blood of the accused is not the only hallmark of an unconstitutional inquisition." Blackburn v. State of Alabama, 361 U.S. 199, 206, 80 S.Ct. 274, 279, 4 L.Ed.2d 242 (1960). Interrogation still takes place in privacy. Privacy results in secrecy and this in turn results in a gap in our knowledge as to what in fact goes on in the interrogation rooms. A valuable source of information about present police practices, however, may be found in various police manuals and texts which document procedures employed with success in the past, and which recommend various other effective tactics. These texts are used by law enforcement agencies themselves as guides. It should be noted that these texts professedly present the most enlightened and effective means presently used to obtain statements through custodial interrogation. By considering these texts and other data, it is possible to describe procedures observed and noted around the country.

The officers are told by the manuals that the "principal psychological factor contributing to a successful interrogation is privacy—being alone with the person under interrogation." The efficacy of this tactic has been explained as follows:

> "If at all practicable, the interrogation should take place in the investigator's office or at least in a room of his own choice. The subject should be deprived of every psychological advantage. In his own home he may be confident, indignant, or recalcitrant. He is more keenly aware of his rights and more reluctant to tell of his indiscretions or criminal behavior within the walls of his home. Moreover his family and other friends are nearby, their presence lending moral support. In his office, the investigator possesses all the advantages. The atmosphere suggests the invincibility of the forces of the law."

To highlight the isolation and unfamiliar surroundings, the manuals instruct the police to display an air of confidence in the suspect's guilt and from outward appearance to maintain only an interest in confirming certain details. The guilt of the subject is to be posited as a fact. The interrogator should direct his comments toward the reasons why the subject committed the act, rather than court failure by asking the subject whether he did it. Like other men, perhaps the subject has had a bad family life, had an unhappy childhood, had too much to drink, had an unrequited desire for women. The officers are instructed to minimize the moral seriousness of the offense, to cast blame on the victim or on society. These tactics are designed to put the subject in a psychological state where his story is but an elaboration of what the police purport to know already—that he is guilty. Explanations to the contrary are dismissed and discouraged.

The texts thus stress that the major qualities an interrogator should possess are patience and perseverance. One writer describes the efficacy of these characteristics in this manner:

"In the preceding paragraphs emphasis has been placed on kindness and stratagems. The investigator will, however, encounter many situations where the sheer weight of his personality will be the deciding factor. Where emotional appeals and tricks are employed to no avail, he must rely on an oppressive atmosphere of dogged persistence. He must interrogate steadily and without relent, leaving the subject no prospect of surcease. He must dominate his subject and overwhelm him with his inexorable will to obtain the truth. He should interrogate for a spell of several hours pausing only for the subject's necessities in acknowledgment of the need to avoid a charge of duress that can be technically substantiated. In a serious case, the interrogation may continue for days, with the required intervals for food and sleep, but with no respite from the atmosphere of domination. It is possible in this way to induce the subject to talk without resorting to duress or coercion. The method should be used only when the guilt of the subject appears highly probable."

The manuals suggest that the suspect be offered legal excuses for his actions in order to obtain an initial admission of guilt. Where there is a suspected revenge-killing, for example, the interrogator may say:

"Joe, you probably didn't go out looking for this fellow with the purpose of shooting him. My guess is, however, that you expected something from him and that's why you carried a gun—for your own protection. You knew him for what he was, no good. Then when you met him he probably started using foul, abusive language and he gave some indication that he was about to pull a gun on you, and that's when you had to act to save your own life. That's about it, isn't it, Joe?"

Having then obtained the admission of shooting, the interrogator is advised to refer to circumstantial evidence which negates the self-defense explanation. This should enable him to secure the entire story. One text notes that "Even if he fails to do so, the inconsistency between the subject's original denial of the shooting and his present admission of at least doing the shooting will serve to deprive him of a self-defense 'out' at the time of trial."

When the techniques described above prove unavailing, the texts recommend they be alternated with a show of some hostility. One ploy often used has been termed the "friendly-unfriendly" or the "Mutt and Jeff" act:

> " * * * In this technique, two agents are employed. Mutt, the relentless investigator, who knows the subject is guilty and is not going to waste any time. He's sent a dozen men away for this crime and he's going to send the subject away for the full term. Jeff, on the other hand, is obviously a kindhearted man. He has a family himself. He has a brother who was involved in a little scrape like this. He disapproves of Mutt and his tactics and will arrange to get him off the case if the subject will cooperate. He can't hold Mutt off for very long. The subject would be wise to make a quick decision. The technique is applied by having both investigators present while Mutt acts out his role. Jeff may stand by quietly and demur at some of Mutt's tactics. When Jeff makes his plea for cooperation, Mutt is not present in the room."

The interrogators sometimes are instructed to induce a confession out of trickery. The technique here is quite effective in crimes which require identification or which run in series. In the identification situation, the interrogator may take a break in his questioning to place the subject among a group of men in a lineup. "The witness or complainant (previously coached, if necessary) studies the lineup and confidently points out the subject as the guilty party." Then the questioning resumes "as though there were now no doubt about the guilt of the subject." A variation on this technique is called the "reverse lineup":

> "The accused is placed in a lineup, but this time he is identified by several fictitious witnesses or victims who associated him with different offenses. It is expected that the subject will become desperate and confess to the offense under investigation in order to escape from the false accusations."

The manuals also contain instructions for police on how to handle the individual who refuses to discuss the matter entirely or who asks for an attorney or relatives. The examiner is to concede him the right to remain silent. "This usually has a very undermining effect. First of all, he is disappointed in his expectation of an unfavorable reaction on the part of the interrogator. Secondly, a concession of this right to remain silent impresses the subject with the apparent fairness of his interrogator." After this psychological conditioning, however, the officer is told to point out the incriminating significance of the suspect's refusal to talk:

> "Joe, you have a right to remain silent. That's your privilege and I'm the last person in the world who'll try to take it away from you. If that's the way you want to leave this, O. K. But let me ask you this. Suppose you were in my shoes and I were in yours and you called me in to ask me about this and I told you, 'I don't want to answer any of your questions.' You'd think I had something to hide, and you'd probably be right in thinking that. That's exactly what I'll have to

think about you, and so will everybody else. So let's sit here and talk this whole thing over."

Few will persist in their initial refusal to talk, it is said, if this monologue is employed correctly.

In the event that the subject wishes to speak to a relative or an attorney, the following advice is tendered:

"[T]he interrogator should respond by suggesting that the subject first tell the truth to the interrogator himself rather than get anyone else involved in the matter. If the request is for an attorney, the interrogator may suggest that the subject save himself or his family the expense of any such professional service, particularly if he is innocent of the offense under investigation. The interrogator may also add, 'Joe, I'm only looking for the truth, and if you're telling the truth, that's it. You can handle this by yourself.' "

From these representative samples of interrogation techniques, the setting prescribed by the manuals and observed in practice becomes clear. In essence, it is this: To be alone with the subject is essential to prevent distraction and to deprive him of any outside support. The aura of confidence in his guilt undermines his will to resist. He merely confirms the preconceived story the police seek to have him describe. Patience and persistence, at times relentless questioning, are employed. To obtain a confession, the interrogator must "patiently maneuver himself or his quarry into a position from which the desired objective may be attained." When normal procedures fail to produce the needed result, the police may resort to deceptive stratagems such as giving false legal advice. It is important to keep the subject off balance, for example, by trading on his insecurity about himself or his surroundings. The police then persuade, trick, or cajole him out of exercising his constitutional rights.

Even without employing brutality, the "third degree" or the specific stratagems described above, the very fact of custodial interrogation exacts a heavy toll on individual liberty and trades on the weakness of individuals.
* * *

In those cases before us today * * * we might not find the defendants' statements to have been involuntary in traditional terms. * * * The fact remains that in none of these cases did the officers undertake to afford appropriate safeguards at the outset of the interrogation to insure that the statements were truly the product of free choice.

It is obvious that such an interrogation environment is created for no purpose other than to subjugate the individual to the will of his examiner. This atmosphere carries its own badge of intimidation. To be sure, this is not physical intimidation, but it is equally destructive of human dignity. The current practice of incommunicado interrogation is at odds with one of our Nation's most cherished principles—that the individual may not be compelled to incriminate himself. Unless adequate protective devices are employed to dispel the compulsion inherent in custodial surroundings, no statement obtained from the defendant can truly be the product of his free choice.

From the foregoing, we can readily perceive an intimate connection between the privilege against self-incrimination and police custodial questioning. * * *

II.

* * *

The question in these cases is whether the [Fifth Amendment] privilege is fully applicable during a period of custodial interrogation. * * * We are satisfied that all the principles embodied in the privilege apply to informal compulsion exerted by law-enforcement officers during in-custody questioning. An individual swept from familiar surroundings into police custody, surrounded by antagonistic forces, and subjected to the techniques of persuasion described above cannot be otherwise than under compulsion to speak. As a practical matter, the compulsion to speak in the isolated setting of the police station may well be greater than in courts or other official investigations, where there are often impartial observers to guard against intimidation or trickery.

Rule — 5th Amend. applies to interrogation

* * *

III.

* * * We have concluded that without proper safeguards the process of in-custody interrogation of persons suspected or accused of crime contains inherently compelling pressures which work to undermine the individual's will to resist and to compel him to speak where he would not otherwise do so freely. In order to combat these pressures and to permit a full opportunity to exercise the privilege against self-incrimination, the accused must be adequately and effectively apprised of his rights and the exercise of those rights must be fully honored.

It is impossible for us to foresee the potential alternatives for protecting the privilege which might be devised by Congress or the States in the exercise of their creative rulemaking capacities. Therefore we cannot say that the Constitution necessarily requires adherence to any particular solution for the inherent compulsions of the interrogation process as it is presently conducted. Our decision in no way creates a constitutional straitjacket which will handicap sound efforts at reform, nor is it intended to have this effect. We encourage Congress and the States to continue their laudable search for increasingly effective ways of protecting the rights of the individual while promoting efficient enforcement of our criminal laws. However, unless we are shown other procedures which are at least as effective in apprising accused persons of their right of silence and in assuring a continuous opportunity to exercise it, the following safeguards must be observed.

At the outset, if a person in custody is to be subjected to interrogation, he must first be informed in clear and unequivocal terms that he has the right to remain silent. For those unaware of the privilege, the warning is needed simply to make them aware of it—the threshold requirement for an intelligent decision as to its exercise. More important, such a warning is an absolute prerequisite in overcoming the inherent pressures of the interrogation atmosphere. It is not just the subnormal or woefully ignorant who succumb to an interrogator's imprecations, whether implied or expressly stated, that the interrogation will continue until a confession is obtained or that silence in the face of accusation is itself damning and will bode ill when presented to a jury. Further, the warning will show the individual that his interrogators are prepared to recognize his privilege should he choose to exercise it.

The Fifth Amendment privilege is so fundamental to our system of constitutional rule and the expedient of giving an adequate warning as to the availability of the privilege so simple, we will not pause to inquire in individual cases whether the defendant was aware of his rights without a warning being given. Assessments of the knowledge the defendant possessed, based on information as to his age, education, intelligence, or prior contact with authorities, can never be more than speculation; a warning is a clearcut fact. More important, whatever the background of the person interrogated, a warning at the time of the interrogation is indispensable to overcome its pressures and to insure that the individual knows he is free to exercise the privilege at that point in time.

The warning of the right to remain silent must be accompanied by the explanation that anything said can and will be used against the individual in court. This warning is needed in order to make him aware not only of the privilege, but also of the consequences of forgoing it. It is only through an awareness of these consequences that there can be any assurance of real understanding and intelligent exercise of the privilege. Moreover, this warning may serve to make the individual more acutely aware that he is faced with a phase of the adversary system—that he is not in the presence of persons acting solely in his interest.

The circumstances surrounding in-custody interrogation can operate very quickly to overbear the will of one merely made aware of his privilege by his interrogators. Therefore, the right to have counsel present at the interrogation is indispensable to the protection of the Fifth Amendment privilege under the system we delineate today. Our aim is to assure that the individual's right to choose between silence and speech remains unfettered throughout the interrogation process. A once-stated warning, delivered by those who will conduct the interrogation, cannot itself suffice to that end among those who most require knowledge of their rights. A mere warning given by the interrogators is not alone sufficient to accomplish that end. * * * Even preliminary advice given to the accused by his own attorney can be swiftly overcome by the secret interrogation process. * * * Thus, the need for counsel to protect the Fifth Amendment privilege comprehends not merely a right to consult with counsel prior to questioning, but also to have counsel present during any questioning if the defendant so desires.

The presence of counsel at the interrogation may serve several significant subsidiary functions as well. If the accused decides to talk to his interrogators, the assistance of counsel can mitigate the dangers of untrustworthiness. With a lawyer present the likelihood that the police will practice coercion is reduced, and if coercion is nevertheless exercised the lawyer can testify to it in court. The presence of a lawyer can also help to guarantee that the accused gives a fully accurate statement to the police and that the statement is rightly reported by the prosecution at trial.

An individual need not make a preinterrogation request for a lawyer. While such request affirmatively secures his right to have one, his failure to ask for a lawyer does not constitute a waiver. No effective waiver of the right to counsel during interrogation can be recognized unless specifically made after the warnings we here delineate have been given. The accused who does not know his rights and therefore does not make a request may be the person who most needs counsel. * * *

Accordingly we hold that an individual held for interrogation must be clearly informed that he has the right to consult with a lawyer and to have the lawyer with him during interrogation under the system for protecting the privilege we delineate today. As with the warnings of the right to remain silent and that anything stated can be used in evidence against him, this warning is an absolute prerequisite to interrogation. No amount of circumstantial evidence that the person may have been aware of this right will suffice to stand in its stead. Only through such a warning is there ascertainable assurance that the accused was aware of this right.

If an individual indicates that he wishes the assistance of counsel before any interrogation occurs, the authorities cannot rationally ignore or deny his request on the basis that the individual does not have or cannot afford a retained attorney. The financial ability of the individual has no relationship to the scope of the rights involved here. The privilege against self-incrimination secured by the Constitution applies to all individuals. The need for counsel in order to protect the privilege exists for the indigent as well as the affluent. In fact, were we to limit these constitutional rights to those who can retain an attorney, our decisions today would be of little significance. The cases before us as well as the vast majority of confession cases with which we have dealt in the past involve those unable to retain counsel. While authorities are not required to relieve the accused of his poverty, they have the obligation not to take advantage of indigence in the administration of justice. * * *

In order fully to apprise a person interrogated of the extent of his rights under this system then, it is necessary to warn him not only that he has the right to consult with an attorney, but also that if he is indigent a lawyer will be appointed to represent him. Without this additional warning, the admonition of the right to consult with counsel would often be understood as meaning only that he can consult with a lawyer if he has one or has the funds to obtain one. The warning of a right to counsel would be hollow if not couched in terms that would convey to the indigent—the person most often subjected to interrogation—the knowledge that he too has a right to have counsel present. As with the warnings of the right to remain silent and of the general right to counsel, only by effective and express explanation to the indigent of this right can there be assurance that he was truly in a position to exercise it.[1]

---

1. While a warning that the indigent may have counsel appointed need not be given to the person who is known to have an attorney or is known to have ample funds to secure one, the expedient of giving a warning is too simple and the rights involved too

Once warnings have been given, the subsequent procedure is clear. If the individual indicates in any manner, at any time prior to or during questioning, that he wishes to remain silent, the interrogation must cease.[2] At this point he has shown that he intends to exercise his Fifth Amendment privilege; any statement taken after the person invokes his privilege cannot be other than the product of compulsion, subtle or otherwise. Without the right to cut off questioning, the setting of in-custody interrogation operates on the individual to overcome free choice in producing a statement after the privilege has been once invoked. If the individual states that he wants an attorney, the interrogation must cease until an attorney is present. At that time, the individual must have an opportunity to confer with the attorney and to have him present during any subsequent questioning. If the individual cannot obtain an attorney and he indicates that he wants one before speaking to police, they must respect his decision to remain silent.

* * *

If the interrogation continues without the presence of an attorney and a statement is taken, a heavy burden rests on the government to demonstrate that the defendant knowingly and intelligently waived his privilege against self-incrimination and his right to retained or appointed counsel. * * * This Court has always set high standards of proof for the waiver of constitutional rights, Johnson v. Zerbst, 304 U.S. 458, 58 S.Ct. 1019, 82 L.Ed. 1461 (1938), and we reassert these standards as applied to in-custody interrogation. Since the State is responsible for establishing the isolated circumstances under which the interrogation takes place and has the only means of making available corroborated evidence of warnings given during incommunicado interrogation, the burden is rightly on its shoulders.

An express statement that the individual is willing to make a statement and does not want an attorney followed closely by a statement could constitute a waiver. But a valid waiver will not be presumed simply from the silence of the accused after warnings are given or simply from the fact that a confession was in fact eventually obtained. * * * Moreover, where in-custody interrogation is involved, there is no room for the contention that the privilege is waived if the individual answers some questions or gives some information on his own prior to invoking his right to remain silent when interrogated.

Whatever the testimony of the authorities as to waiver of rights by an accused, the fact of lengthy interrogation or incommunicado incarceration before a statement is made is strong evidence that the accused did not validly waive his rights. In these circumstances the fact that the individual eventually made a statement is consistent with the conclusion that the compelling influence of the interrogation finally forced him to do so. It is

important to engage in *ex post facto* inquiries into financial ability when there is any doubt at all on that score.

2. If an individual indicates his desire to remain silent, but has an attorney present, there may be some circumstances in which further questioning would be permissible. In the absence of evidence of overbearing, statements then made in the presence of counsel might be free of the compelling influence of the interrogation process and might fairly be construed as a waiver of the privilege for purposes of these statements.

inconsistent with any notion of a voluntary relinquishment of the privilege. Moreover, any evidence that the accused was threatened, tricked, or cajoled into a waiver will, of course, show that the defendant did not voluntarily waive his privilege. The requirement of warnings and waiver of rights is a fundamental with respect to the Fifth Amendment privilege and not simply a preliminary ritual to existing methods of interrogation.

The warnings required and the waiver necessary in accordance with our opinion today are, in the absence of a fully effective equivalent, prerequisites to the admissibility of any statement made by a defendant. * * *

Our decision is not intended to hamper the traditional function of police officers in investigating crime. When an individual is in custody on probable cause, the police may, of course, seek out evidence in the field to be used at trial against him. Such investigation may include inquiry of persons not under restraint. General on-the-scene questioning as to facts surrounding a crime or other general questioning of citizens in the factfinding process is not affected by our holding. It is an act of responsible citizenship for individuals to give whatever information they may have to aid in law enforcement. In such situations the compelling atmosphere inherent in the process of in-custody interrogation is not necessarily present.

In dealing with statements obtained through interrogation, we do not purport to find all confessions inadmissible. Confessions remain a proper element in law enforcement. Any statement given freely and voluntarily without any compelling influences is, of course, admissible in evidence. The fundamental import of the privilege while an individual is in custody is not whether he is allowed to talk to the police without the benefit of warnings and counsel, but whether he can be interrogated. There is no requirement that police stop a person who enters a police station and states that he wishes to confess to a crime, or a person who calls the police to offer a confession or any other statement he desires to make. Volunteered statements of any kind are not barred by the Fifth Amendment and their admissibility is not affected by our holding today.

* * *

V.

Because of the nature of the problem and because of its recurrent significance in numerous cases, we have to this point discussed the relationship of the Fifth Amendment privilege to police interrogation without specific concentration on the facts of the cases before us. We turn now to these facts to consider the application to these cases of the constitutional principles discussed above. In each instance, we have concluded that statements were obtained from the defendant under circumstances that did not meet constitutional standards for protection of the privilege.

No. 759. Miranda v. Arizona

On March 13, 1963, petitioner, Ernesto Miranda, was arrested at his home and taken in custody to a Phoenix police station. He was there identified by the complaining witness. The police then took him to "Interrogation Room No. 2" of the detective bureau. There he was questioned by two police officers. The officers admitted at trial that Miranda was not advised that he had a right to have an attorney present. Two hours later, the officers emerged from the interrogation room with a written confession signed by Miranda. At the top of the statement was a typed paragraph stating that the confession was made voluntarily, without threats or promises of immunity and "with full knowledge of my legal rights, understanding any statement I make may be used against me."

facts   *

At his trial before a jury, the written confession was admitted into evidence over the objection of defense counsel, and the officers testified to the prior oral confession made by Miranda during the interrogation. Miranda was found guilty of kidnapping and rape. He was sentenced to 20 to 30 years' imprisonment on each count, the sentences to run concurrently. On appeal, the Supreme Court of Arizona held that Miranda's constitutional rights were not violated in obtaining the confession and affirmed the conviction. In reaching its decision, the court emphasized heavily the fact that Miranda did not specifically request counsel.

Rule: right to counsel.

We reverse. From the testimony of the officers and by the admission of respondent, it is clear that Miranda was not in any way apprised of his right to consult with an attorney and to have one present during the interrogation, nor was his right not to be compelled to incriminate himself effectively protected in any other manner. Without these warnings the statements were inadmissible. The mere fact that he signed a statement which contained a typed-in clause stating that he had "full knowledge" of his "legal rights" does not approach the knowing and intelligent waiver required to relinquish constitutional rights.

* * *

[The Court's discussion of the facts of the other cases is omitted. Editors.]

Judgment of Supreme Court of California in No. 584 affirmed.

■ MR. JUSTICE CLARK, dissenting in Nos. 759, 760, and 761, and concurring in the result in No. 584.

* * * Since there is at this time a paucity of information and an almost total lack of empirical knowledge on the practical operation of requirements truly comparable to those announced by the majority, I would be more restrained lest we go too far too fast.

* * *

Custodial interrogation has long been recognized as "undoubtedly an essential tool in effective law enforcement." Haynes v. State of Washington, 373 U.S. 503, 515, 83 S.Ct. 1336, 1344, 10 L.Ed.2d 513 (1963). Recognition of this fact should put us on guard against the promulgation of doctrinaire rules. * * *

The rule prior to today * * * depended upon "a totality of circumstances evidencing an involuntary * * * admission of guilt." * * *

I would continue to follow that rule. Under the "totality of circumstances" rule * * *, I would consider in each case whether the police officer prior to custodial interrogation added the warning that the suspect might have counsel present at the interrogation, and further, that a court would appoint one at his request if he was too poor to employ counsel. In the absence of warnings, the burden would be on the State to prove that counsel was knowingly and intelligently waived or that in the totality of the circumstances, including the failure to give the necessary warnings, the confession was clearly voluntary.

* * *

[The dissenting opinions of Justice Harlan, with whom Justices Stewart and White joined, and of Justice White, with whom Justices Harlan and Stewart joined, are omitted.]

NOTES

1. **Terminology of the Warnings.** How much deviation from the language used by the majority in *Miranda* is permissible in giving suspects *Miranda* warnings? In California v. Prysock, 453 U.S. 355, 101 S.Ct. 2806, 69 L.Ed.2d 696 (1981) (per curiam), the sixteen year old suspect was warned and questioned in the presence of his mother. The officer first told Prysock "you have the right to remain silent," "if you give up your right to remain silent, anything you say can and will be used as evidence against you in a court of law," and "you have the right to talk to a lawyer before you are questioned, have him present with you while you are being questioned, and all during the questioning." He was also told, "you have the right to have a lawyer appointed to represent you at no cost to yourself." This was all tape recorded. There was then a brief off-the-record discussion between the suspect's mother and the officer. The officer later testified that in this discussion, the mother asked if a lawyer would be available later if the suspect did not request one at this time. According to the officer, he responded by saying:

> That he would have an attorney when he went to Court. And that he could have one at this time if he wished one. He could terminate the statement at any time he so desired.

Following the warnings, Prysock consented to questioning without an attorney and admitted the killing. This confession was later used against him in his murder trial, and he was convicted. On appeal, however, the intermediate California appellate court reversed. Emphasizing its view that the rigidity of the *Miranda* requirements affords police clear guidance, the court held Prysock had not been adequately informed that the services of a free attorney were available to him prior to the impending questioning. The Supreme Court reversed. It read the state court as establishing "a flat rule that the content of *Miranda* warnings be a virtual incantation of the precise language contained in the *Miranda* opinion" and holding the warnings here defective because of the order in which they were given. In fact, the Court stressed, "no talismanic incantation" is required to satisfy *Miranda*. The warnings given Prysock adequately conveyed to him that he had a right to an appointed attorney prior to and during questioning. The Court stressed, however, that warnings might be inadequate if the reference to the right to counsel was linked with some future point in time after the police interrogation. It cited with apparent approval United States v. Garcia, 431 F.2d 134 (9th Cir.1970), holding inadequate a statement to the defendant that she could "have an attorney appointed to represent you when you first appear before the U.S. Commissioner or the Court.''

In Duckworth v. Eagan, 492 U.S. 195, 109 S.Ct. 2875, 106 L.Ed.2d 166 (1989), Eagan was given warnings that, in regard to the right to counsel, included:

> You have a right to talk to a lawyer for advice before we ask you any questions, and to have him with you during questioning. You have this right to the advice and presence of a lawyer even if you cannot afford to hire one. We have no way of giving you a lawyer, but one will be appointed for you, if you wish, if and when you go to court. If you wish to answer questions now without a lawyer present, you have the right to stop answering questions at any time. You also have the right to stop answering at any time until you've talked to a lawyer.

By a 5–to–4 vote, the Supreme Court held this complied with *Miranda*. Chief Justice Rehnquist wrote for the Court rejecting Eagan's argument that the "if and when you go to court" phrase rendered the warning confusing and insufficient:

> First, this instruction accurately described the procedure for the appointment of counsel in Indiana. Under Indiana law, counsel is appointed at the defendant's initial appearance in court, and formal charges must be filed at or before that hearing. We think it must be relatively commonplace for a suspect, after receiving *Miranda* warnings, to ask when he will obtain counsel. The "if and and when you go to court" advice simply anticipates that question. Second, *Miranda* does not require that attorneys be producible on call, but only that the suspect be informed, as here, that he has the right to an attorney before and during questioning, and that an attorney would be appointed for him if he could not afford one. The Court in *Miranda* emphasized that it was not suggesting that "each police station must have a 'station house lawyer' present at all times to advise prisoners." If the police cannot provide appointed counsel, *Miranda* requires only that the police not question a suspect unless he waives his right to counsel. Here, [Eagan] did just that.

495 U.S. at 204, 109 S.Ct. at 2880–81, 106 L.Ed.2d at 177–78.

2. **Impeachment Use of Confessions Violating *Miranda*.** The "impeachment exception" to many exclusionary sanctions, discussed in Chapter 1, has been applied to confessions in a manner which distinguishes between the requirements of *Miranda* and voluntariness.

In Harris v. New York, 401 U.S. 222, 91 S.Ct. 643, 28 L.Ed.2d 1 (1971), the majority acknowledged language in *Miranda* could be read as barring the use of a confession obtained in violation of *Miranda* for any purpose. Nevertheless, the Court held a statement obtained after a warning failing to inform the defendant of his right to appointed counsel could be used to impeach the defendant when he took the stand at trial and testified in a manner inconsistent with the statement. "[T]he trustworthiness of the evidence satisfies legal standards," the majority commented, and the confession would undoubtedly aid the jury in evaluating the defendant's credibility as well as determining whether he perjured himself during testimony. Turning to the need to exclude such confessions as a means of deterring violation of the *Miranda* requirements, the majority concluded "sufficient deterrence flows when the evidence in question is made unavailable to the prosecution in its case in chief."

In Oregon v. Hass, 420 U.S. 714, 95 S.Ct. 1215, 43 L.Ed.2d 570 (1975), Hass was arrested and given complete *Miranda* warnings. Although Hass said he wanted to telephone a lawyer, an officer continued to interrogate him without the presence of counsel; he made an incriminating statement. This statement was used for impeachment at trial after Hass took the stand and testified to facts contrary to those in the confession. The Supreme Court found no impropriety in use of the statement at Hass' trial. The dissent contended the case was distinguishable from *Harris*:

> [A]fter *Harris*, police had some incentive for following *Miranda* by warning an accused of his right to remain silent and his right to counsel. If the warnings were given, the accused might still make a statement which could be used in the prosecution's case in chief. [But where the warnings are given and the suspect indicates a desire for counsel], police have almost no incentive for following *Miranda's* requirement that "[i]f the individual states that he wants an attorney, the interrogation must cease until an attorney is present." * * * If the requirement is followed there will almost surely be no statement since the attorney will advise the accused to remain silent. If, however, the requirement is disobeyed, the police may obtain a statement which can be used for impeachment if the accused has the temerity to testify in his own defense.

420 U.S. at 725, 95 S.Ct. at 1222, 43 L.Ed.2d at 579 (Brennan, J., dissenting). Thus the need to exclude the confession to encourage compliance with *Miranda* was greater in the case before the Court than in *Harris*. The majority, in contrast, characterized the possibility of an officer proceeding on the basis suggested by the dissent as "speculative." "If, in a given case," it concluded, "the officer's conduct amounts to an abuse, that case, like those involving coercion or duress, may be taken care of when it arises measured by the traditional standards for evaluating voluntariness and trustworthiness."

In Mincey v. Arizona, 437 U.S. 385, 98 S.Ct. 2408, 57 L.Ed.2d 290 (1978), however, the Court reaffirmed involuntary statements could not be used even for impeachment of a testifying defendant. This is apparently because such statements—unlike the statements in *Harris* and *Hass*—do not satisfy legal standards of trustworthiness.

3. **Use of Suspects' Silence.** A defendant's silence under circumstances in which a reasonable, innocent person would have denied guilt is, generally speaking, admissible to prove the defendant's guilt as a "tacit" confession. See McCormick, Evidence § 161 (5th ed. 1999). *Miranda*, however, imposes some limitations on the admissibility of such silence. In Doyle v. Ohio, 426 U.S. 610, 96 S.Ct. 2240, 49 L.Ed.2d 91 (1976), Doyle was charged with sale of marijuana based on a transaction arranged by one Bonnell, a police informant. None of the narcotics agents who had the transaction under surveillance actually saw the alleged transfer of the marijuana from Doyle to Bonnell. At trial, Doyle took the stand and testified that the arrangement had actually been for Bonnell to sell marijuana to him. On cross examination, the prosecution elicited Doyle's admission that after being arrested and given the *Miranda* warnings he had not told this version of the incident to the arresting officers. Reversing Doyle's conviction, the Supreme Court held that silence after being given the *Miranda* warnings could not be used even for impeachment. Silence after *Miranda* warnings cannot, under *Doyle*, even be used to rebut a defendant's claim of insanity. Wainwright v. Greenfield, 474 U.S. 284, 106 S.Ct. 634, 88 L.Ed.2d 623 (1986).

In Fletcher v. Weir, 455 U.S. 603, 102 S.Ct. 1309, 71 L.Ed.2d 490 (1982) (per curiam), the Court characterized *Doyle* as resting not upon the ambiguity of suspects' silence but the fundamental unfairness of using silence against defendants after they have received governmental assurances that there is a right to remain silent. The Court found no federal constitutional barrier to the use of a defendant's silence after arrest but before *Miranda* warnings, at least where silence was used to impeach the defendant after he took the witness stand at trial and testified to an exculpatory version of the events. Where the *Miranda* warnings were not given, the Court reasoned, no assurances of a right to remain silent were provided and thus there is no unfairness in using the defendants' silence. Whether in such situations a defendant's silence is a sufficiently reliable indicator he lied during direct examination, the Court commented, is a decision each State is entitled to make as a matter of State evidence law policy.

Doyle imposes no federal constitutional bar to the use of *prearrest* silence to impeach a testifying defendant. Jenkins v. Anderson, 447 U.S. 231, 100 S.Ct. 2124, 65 L.Ed.2d 86 (1980). Nor does *Miranda* bar questioning of a testifying defendant concerning inconsistent statements made after arrest and receipt of *Miranda* warnings. Such a defendant has chosen to speak rather than remain silent so there is no impermissible use of silence as prohibited by *Doyle*. Anderson v. Charles, 447 U.S. 404, 100 S.Ct. 2180, 65 L.Ed.2d 222 (1980) (per curiam).

2.   Applicability of *Miranda*

EDITORS' INTRODUCTION: "THRESHOLD" ISSUES AND EXCEPTIONS

Soon after the *Miranda* decision, the Court rejected arguments that its requirements be limited to stationhouse interrogation or at least not applied to custodial questioning conducted in surroundings familiar to the suspect. Orozco v. Texas, 394 U.S. 324, 89 S.Ct. 1095, 22 L.Ed.2d 311 (1969), held *Miranda* applicable to questioning of Orozco in his own bedroom by four officers who entered the bedroom and awoke, arrested, and questioned him.

The *Miranda* opinion itself made clear that the requirements established by the case did not apply to all out-of-court confessions or statements by defendants. Rather, those requirements must be respected only in situations involving both "custody" and "interrogation." When these threshold requirements for the application of *Miranda* are met is addressed in the two subsections that follow. The Court has also considered arguments for exceptions releasing officers from the *Miranda* requirements in situations involving what is at least "technically" custodial interrogation.

Public Safety Exception

A "public safety" exception to the *Miranda* requirements, applicable despite the existence of both custody and interrogation, was adopted and applied in New York v. Quarles, 467 U.S. 649, 104 S.Ct. 2626, 81 L.Ed.2d 550 (1984).

In *Quarles*, a woman approached two New York police officers and reported that she had just been raped by a man who entered a nearby supermarket carrying a gun. Upon arrival at the supermarket, one officer (Kraft) entered the store and the other radioed for assistance. Officer Kraft quickly observed Quarles, who met the woman's description. Apparently upon seeing Officer Kraft, Quarles ran towards the rear of the store. Kraft drew his weapon and pursued Quarles. Although he lost sight of Quarles for several seconds, Officer Kraft soon saw him again and ordered Quarles to stop and place his hands over his head. Several other officers had since arrived. Kraft approached Quarles and, upon frisking him, discovered he was wearing an empty shoulder holster. Quarles was handcuffed. Kraft then, without providing any *Miranda* warnings, asked Quarles where the gun was. Nodding in the direction of some empty cartons, Quarles responded by saying, "The gun is over there." Kraft searched the area and found a loaded .38 caliber revolver. Quarles was then warned under *Miranda* and agreed to answer questions without an attorney present. In response to questions by Kraft, Quarles admitted ownership of the gun and explained how he had acquired it. Before Quarles' trial for criminal possession of a weapon, the trial court considered the admissibility of the revolver, his pre-warning statement, "The gun is over there," and his post-warning admissions. Both the gun and the pre-warning statement were held inadmissible because of Officer Kraft's failure to comply with *Miranda* before asking about the gun's location; the post-warning admissions were excluded as tainted by the preceding *Miranda* violation.

By a five-to-four vote, the Supreme Court reversed. *Miranda* had not been violated, it held, because Officer Kraft's actions came within a "narrow exception" to *Miranda* for situations in which the officer's question is prompted by concern for the public safety. This exception, Justice Rehnquist explained for the Court, is consistent with *Miranda's* rationale. In most situations, the cost of respecting *Miranda's* requirements is the possibility of fewer convictions; this cost is acceptable given the value of the *Miranda* requirements in protecting the underlying right to freedom from compelled self-incrimination. But where in addition compliance with the *Miranda* requirement pose an immediate risk to public safety, the cost becomes unacceptably high:

> We decline to place officers such as Officer Kraft in the untenable position of having to consider, often in a matter of seconds, whether it best serves society for them to ask the necessary questions without the *Miranda* warnings and render whatever probative evidence they uncover inadmissible, or for them to give the warnings in order to preserve the admissibility of evidence they might uncover but possibly damage or destroy their ability to obtain that evidence and neutralize the volatile situation confronting them.

467 U.S. at 657–58, 104 S.Ct. at 2632, 81 L.Ed.2d at 558. On the facts before it, the Court found sufficient risk to public safety. Officer Kraft had reason to believe the gun was somewhere in the store where it might be retrieved by an accomplice of Quarles or discovered by a store employee or customer.

The state court had declined to apply a public safety exception because of its perception that there was no indication that Officer Kraft was actually motivated by a desire to protect himself or the public. This, the Court reasoned, was not controlling:

> [T]he availability of [the] exception does not depend upon the motivation of the individual officer involved. In a kaleidoscopic situation such as the one confronting these officers, where spontaneity rather than adherence to a police manual is necessarily the order of the day, the application of the exception * * * should not be made to depend on *post hoc* findings at a suppression hearing concerning the subjective motivation of the arresting officer.

467 U.S. at 656, 104 S.Ct. at 2631, 81 L.Ed.2d at 557.

The Supreme Court observed it was presented with no claim that Quarles's pre-warning statement was "actually compelled by police conduct which overcame his will to resist." Quarles was free to argue on remand that his statement was "coerced under traditional due process standards." The Court's holding, Justice Rehnquist emphasized, was not a rejection of this argument; he explained, "we merely reject the * * * argument * * * that the statement must be *presumed* compelled because of Officer Kraft's failure to read [Quarles] his *Miranda* warnings." 467 U.S. at 655 n. 5, 104 S.Ct. at 2631 n. 5, 81 L.Ed.2d at 556 n. 5 (emphasis in original).

Routine Booking Question Exception

A plurality of the Court recognized another exception in Pennsylvania v. Muniz, 496 U.S. 582, 110 S.Ct. 2638, 110 L.Ed.2d 528 (1990). After his arrest for drunk-driving, Muniz was taken to the stationhouse. During the ensuing procedure, and without complying with *Miranda*, an officer asked Muniz his name, address, height, weight, eye color, date of birth, and current age. This was videotaped. Justice Brennan, writing for a plurality of four justices, explained why the plurality regarded his answers admissible:

> We agree with amicus United States * * * that Muniz's answers to these * * * questions are * * * admissible because the questions fall within a "routine booking question" exception which exempts from *Miranda's* coverage questions to secure the "biographical data necessary to complete booking or pretrial services." Brief for the United States as Amicus Curiae 12 * * *. The state court found that the first seven questions were "requested for recordkeeping purposes only," and therefore the questions appear reasonably related to the police's administrative concerns. In this context, therefore, the * * * questions * * * fall outside the protections of *Miranda* and the answers thereto need not be suppressed.

495 U.S. at 601–02, 110 S.Ct. at 2650, 110 L.Ed.2d at 552. He added:

> As amicus United States explains, "[r]ecognizing a 'booking exception' to *Miranda* does not mean, of course, that any question asked during the booking process falls within that exception. Without obtaining a waiver of the suspect's *Miranda* rights, the police may not ask questions, even during booking, that are designed to elicit incriminatory admissions." Brief for United States as Amicus Curiae 13.

495 U.S. at 602 n. 14, 110 S.Ct. at 2650 n. 14, 110 L.Ed.2d at 552 n. 14.

Although these exceptions may render *Miranda* inapplicable to some situations, the major limitations on the scope of the decision arise from the requirements of, first, interrogation and, second, custody. The following two subsections address these prerequisites to the application of *Miranda*.

a.   THE REQUIREMENT OF "INTERROGATION"

Unless a suspect in custody is subjected to "interrogation," *Miranda* has no applicability. Thus when a statement is "volunteered" by a suspect, it is admissible despite the failure to comply with *Miranda* requirements.

Rhode Island v. Innis

Supreme Court of the United States, 1980.
446 U.S. 291, 100 S.Ct. 1682, 64 L.Ed.2d 297.

■ Mr. Justice Stewart delivered the opinion of the Court.

* * * The issue in this case is whether the respondent was "interrogated" in violation of the standards promulgated in the *Miranda* opinion.

I.

On the night of January 12, 1975, John Mulvaney, a Providence, R. I., taxicab driver, disappeared after being dispatched to pick up a customer. His body was discovered four days later buried in a shallow grave in Coventry, R. I. He had died from a shotgun blast aimed at the back of his head.

On January 17, 1975, shortly after midnight, the Providence police received a telephone call from Gerald Aubin, also a taxicab driver, who reported that he had just been robbed by a man wielding a sawed-off shotgun. Aubin further reported that he had dropped off his assailant near Rhode Island College in a section of Providence known as Mount Pleasant. While at the Providence police station waiting to give a statement, Aubin noticed a picture of his assailant on a bulletin board. Aubin so informed one of the police officers present. The officer prepared a photo array, and again Aubin identified a picture of the same person. That person was the respondent. Shortly thereafter, the Providence police began a search of the Mount Pleasant area.

At approximately 4:30 a. m. on the same date, Patrolman Lovell, while cruising the streets of Mount Pleasant in a patrol car, spotted the respondent standing in the street facing him. When Patrolman Lovell stopped his car, the respondent walked towards it. Patrolman Lovell then arrested the respondent, who was unarmed, and advised him of his so-called *Miranda* rights. While the two men waited in the patrol car for other police officers to arrive, Patrolman Lovell did not converse with the respondent other than to respond to the latter's request for a cigarette.

Within minutes, Sergeant Sears arrived at the scene of the arrest, and he also gave the respondent the *Miranda* warnings. Immediately thereafter, Captain Leyden and other police officers arrived. Captain Leyden advised the respondent of his *Miranda* rights. The respondent stated that he understood those rights and wanted to speak with a lawyer. Captain Leyden then directed that the respondent be placed in a "caged wagon," a four-door police car with a wire screen mesh between the front and rear seats, and be driven to the central police station. Three officers, Patrolmen Gleckman, Williams, and McKenna, were assigned to accompany the respondent to the central station. They placed the respondent in the vehicle and shut the doors. Captain Leyden then instructed the officers not to question the respondent or intimidate or coerce him in any way. The three officers then entered the vehicle, and it departed.

While en route to the central station, Patrolman Gleckman initiated a conversation with Patrolman McKenna concerning the missing shotgun. As Patrolman Gleckman later testified:

"A. At this point, I was talking back and forth with Patrolman McKenna stating that I frequent this area while on patrol and [that because a school for handicapped children is located nearby,] there's a lot of handicapped children running around in this area, and God forbid one of them might find a weapon with shells and they might hurt themselves.''

Patrolman McKenna apparently shared his fellow officer's concern:

> "A. I more or less concurred with him [Gleckman] that it was a safety factor and that we should, you know, continue to search for the weapon and try to find it.''

While Patrolman Williams said nothing, he overheard the conversation between the two officers:

> "A. He [Gleckman] said it would be too bad if the little—I believe he said girl—would pick up the gun, maybe kill herself.''

The respondent then interrupted the conversation, stating that the officers should turn the car around so he could show them where the gun was located. At this point, Patrolman McKenna radioed back to Captain Leyden that they were returning to the scene of the arrest, and that the respondent would inform them of the location of the gun. At the time the respondent indicated that the officers should turn back, they had traveled no more than a mile, a trip encompassing only a few minutes.

The police vehicle then returned to the scene of the arrest where a search for the shotgun was in progress. There, Captain Leyden again advised the respondent of his *Miranda* rights. The respondent replied that he understood those rights but that he "wanted to get the gun out of the way because of the kids in the area in the school." The respondent then led the police to a nearby field, where he pointed out the shotgun under some rocks by the side of the road.

On March 20, 1975, a grand jury returned an indictment charging the respondent with the kidnapping, robbery, and murder of John Mulvaney. Before trial, the respondent moved to suppress the shotgun and the statements he had made to the police regarding it. After an evidentiary hearing at which the respondent elected not to testify, the trial judge found that the respondent had been "repeatedly and completely advised of his *Miranda* rights." He further found that it was "entirely understandable that [the officers in the police vehicle] would voice their concern [for the safety of the handicapped children] to each other." The judge then concluded that the respondent's decision to inform the police of the location of the shotgun was "a waiver, clearly, and on the basis of the evidence that I have heard, and [*sic*] intelligent waiver, of his [*Miranda*] right to remain silent." Thus, without passing on whether the police officers had in fact "interrogated" the respondent, the trial court sustained the admissibility of the shotgun and testimony related to its discovery. That evidence was later introduced at the respondent's trial, and the jury returned a verdict of guilty on all counts.

* * *

II

* * *

In the present case, the parties are in agreement that the respondent was fully informed of his *Miranda* rights and that he invoked his *Miranda* right to counsel when he told Captain Leyden that he wished to consult with a lawyer. It is also uncontested that the respondent was "in custody" while being transported to the police station.

The issue, therefore, is whether the respondent was "interrogated" by the police officers in violation of the respondent's undisputed right under *Miranda* to remain silent until he had consulted with a lawyer. In resolving this issue, we first define the term "interrogation" under *Miranda* before turning to a consideration of the facts of this case.

A

The starting point for defining "interrogation" in this context is, of course, the Court's *Miranda* opinion. There the Court observed that "[b]y custodial interrogation, we mean *questioning* initiated by law enforcement officers after a person has been taken into custody or otherwise deprived of his freedom of action in any significant way." This passage and other references throughout the opinion to "questioning" might suggest that the *Miranda* rules were to apply only to those police interrogation practices that involve express questioning of a defendant while in custody.

We do not, however, construe the *Miranda* opinion so narrowly. The concern of the Court in *Miranda* was that the "interrogation environment" created by the interplay of interrogation and custody would "subjugate the individual to the will of his examiner" and thereby undermine the privilege against compulsory self-incrimination. The police practices that evoked this concern included several that did not involve express questioning. For example, one of the practices discussed in *Miranda* was the use of lineups in which a coached witness would pick the defendant as the perpetrator. This was designed to establish that the defendant was in fact guilty as a predicate for further interrogation. A variation on this theme discussed in *Miranda* was the so-called "reverse line-up" in which a defendant would be identified by coached witnesses as the perpetrator of a fictitious crime, with the object of inducing him to confess to the actual crime of which he was suspected in order to escape the false prosecution. The Court in *Miranda* also included in its survey of interrogation practices the use of psychological ploys, such as to "posi[t]" "the guilt of the subject," to "minimize the moral seriousness of the offense," and "to cast blame on the victim or on society." It is clear that these techniques of persuasion, no less than express questioning, were thought, in a custodial setting, to amount to interrogation.

This is not to say, however, that all statements obtained by the police after a person has been taken into custody are to be considered the product of interrogation. * * * It is clear * * * that the special procedural safeguards outlined in *Miranda* are required not where a suspect is simply taken into custody, but rather where a suspect in custody is subjected to interrogation. "Interrogation," as conceptualized in the *Miranda* opinion, must reflect a measure of compulsion above and beyond that inherent in custody itself.

We conclude that the *Miranda* safeguards come into play whenever a person in custody is subjected to either express questioning or its functional equivalent. That is to say, the term "interrogation" under *Miranda* refers not only to express questioning, but also to any words or actions on the part of the police (other than those normally attendant to arrest and custody) that the police should know are reasonably likely to elicit an incriminating response from the suspect. The latter portion of this definition focuses primarily upon the perceptions of the suspect, rather than the intent of the police. This focus reflects the fact that the *Miranda* safeguards were designed to vest a suspect in custody with an added measure of protection against coercive police practices, without regard to objective proof of the underlying intent of the police. A practice that the police should know is reasonably likely to evoke an incriminating response from a suspect thus amounts to interrogation.[3] But, since the police surely cannot be held accountable for the unforeseeable results of their words or actions, the definition of interrogation can extend only to words or actions on the part of police officers that they *should have known* were reasonably likely to elicit an incriminating response.[4]

B

Turning to the facts of the present case, we conclude that the respondent was not "interrogated" within the meaning of *Miranda*. It is undisputed that the first prong of the definition of "interrogation" was not satisfied, for the conversation between Patrolmen Gleckman and McKenna included no express questioning of the respondent. Rather, that conversation was, at least in form, nothing more than a dialogue between the two officers to which no response from the respondent was invited.

Moreover, it cannot be fairly concluded that the respondent was subjected to the "functional equivalent" of questioning. It cannot be said, in short, that Patrolmen Gleckman and McKenna should have known that their conversation was reasonably likely to elicit an incriminating response from the respondent. There is nothing in the record to suggest that the officers were aware that the respondent was peculiarly susceptible to an appeal to his conscience concerning the safety of handicapped children. Nor is there anything in the record to suggest that the police knew that the respondent was unusually disoriented or upset at the time of his arrest.[5]

---

3. This is not to say that the intent of the police is irrelevant, for it may well have a bearing on whether the police should have known that their words or actions were reasonably likely to evoke an incriminating response. In particular, where a police practice is designed to elicit an incriminating response from the accused, it is unlikely that the practice will not also be one which the police should have known was reasonably likely to have that effect.

4. Any knowledge the police may have had concerning the unusual susceptibility of a defendant to a particular form of persuasion might be an important factor in determining whether the police should have known that their words or actions were reasonably likely to elicit an incriminating response from the suspect.

5. The record in no way suggests that the officers' remarks were *designed* to elicit a response. It is significant that the trial judge, after hearing the officers' testimony, concluded that it was "entirely understandable that [the officers] would voice their concern [for the safety of the handicapped children] to each other."

The case thus boils down to whether, in the context of a brief conversation, the officers should have known that the respondent would suddenly be moved to make a self-incriminating response. Given the fact that the entire conversation appears to have consisted of no more than a few offhand remarks, we cannot say that the officers should have known that it was reasonably likely that Innis would so respond. This is not a case where the police carried on a lengthy harangue in the presence of the suspect. Nor does the record support the respondent's contention that, under the circumstances, the officers' comments were particularly "evocative." It is our view, therefore, that the respondent was not subjected by the police to words or actions that the police should have known were reasonably likely to elicit an incriminating response from him.

The Rhode Island Supreme Court erred * * * in equating "subtle compulsion" with interrogation. That the officers' comments struck a responsive cord is readily apparent. Thus, it may be said, as the Rhode Island Supreme Court did say, that the respondent was subjected to "subtle compulsion." But that is not the end of the inquiry. It must also be established that a suspect's incriminating response was the product of words or actions on the part of the police that they should have known were reasonably likely to elicit an incriminating response.[6] This was not established in the present case.

* * *

■ MR. JUSTICE STEVENS, dissenting.

* * *

[I]n order to give full protection to a suspect's right to be free from any interrogation at all [after he has invoked his right to cut off questioning], the definition of "interrogation" must include any police statement or conduct that has the same purpose or effect as a direct question. Statements that appear to call for a response from the suspect, as well as those that are designed to do so, should be considered interrogation. By prohibiting only those relatively few statements or actions that a police officer should know are likely to elicit an incriminating response, the Court today accords a suspect considerably less protection. Indeed, * * * this new definition will almost certainly exclude every statement that is not punctuated with a question mark from the concept of "interrogation."

* * *

In any event, I think the Court is clearly wrong in holding, as a matter of law, that Officer Gleckman should not have realized that his statement was likely to elicit an incriminating response. * * *

The Court's assumption that criminal suspects are not susceptible to appeals to conscience is directly contrary to the teachings of police interro-

---

6. By way of example, if the police had done no more than to drive past the site of the concealed weapon while taking the most direct route to the police station, and if the respondent, upon noticing for the first time the proximity of the school for handicapped children, had blurted out that he would show the officers where the gun was located, it could not seriously be argued that this "subtle compulsion" would have constituted "interrogation" within the meaning of the *Miranda* opinion.

gation manuals, which recommend appealing to a suspect's sense of morality as a standard and often successful interrogation technique. Surely the practical experience embodied in such manuals should not be ignored in a case such as this in which the record is devoid of any evidence—one way or the other—as to the susceptibility of suspects in general or of Innis in particular.

Moreover, there is evidence in the record to support the view that Officer Gleckman's statement was intended to elicit a response from Innis. Officer Gleckman, who was not regularly assigned to the caged wagon, was directed by a police captain to ride with respondent to the police station. Although there is a dispute in the testimony, it appears that Gleckman may well have been riding in the back seat with Innis. The record does not explain why, notwithstanding the fact that respondent was handcuffed, unarmed, and had offered no resistance when arrested by an officer acting alone, the captain ordered Officer Gleckman to ride with respondent. It is not inconceivable that two professionally trained police officers concluded that a few well-chosen remarks might induce respondent to disclose the whereabouts of the shotgun. This conclusion becomes even more plausible in light of the emotionally charged words chosen by Officer Gleckman ("God forbid" that a "little girl" should find the gun and hurt herself).

NOTES

1. *Innis* was applied in Arizona v. Mauro, 481 U.S. 520, 107 S.Ct. 1931, 95 L.Ed.2d 458 (1987). Mauro was arrested after he approached authorities, volunteered he had killed his young son, and led authorities to the victim's body. At the stationhouse, he was advised of his *Miranda* rights. He told officers he did not want to make any more statements until his lawyer was present. Questioning then ceased. Meanwhile, Mauro's wife, who had been questioned by other officers, asked to speak to him. After discussion, the officer in charge (Sergeant Allen) permitted this. Mrs. Mauro was taken to the office in which Mauro was held. The couple was told they could speak only if an officer remained present and the officer—Detective Manson—then placed a tape recorder in plain sight. A brief conversation ensued in which Mrs. Mauro expressed despair regarding the situation and Mauro urged his wife not to answer questions until a lawyer was present. At trial, Mauro presented a defense of insanity. The state then in rebuttal sought to prove the conversation between Mauro and his wife to show that Mauro was functioning in a sane fashion. The defense objected that the conversation was the result of "interrogation" conducted in violation of *Miranda* because Mauro had invoked his right to counsel which barred further "interrogation" until a lawyer was present. Nevertheless, the evidence was admitted. By a 5–4 vote, the Supreme Court found no *Miranda* defect. The majority noted some uncertainty in the record as to whether Mauro was given advance notice that his wife would be coming to speak with him. Assuming no notice was provided, however, the Court explained:

> The sole issue * * * is whether the officers' * * * actions rose to the level of interrogation—that is, in the language of *Innis,* whether they were the "functional equivalent" of police interrogation. We think it is clear under both *Miranda* and *Innis* that Mauro was not interrogated. * * * Detective Manson asked Mauro no questions about the crime or his conduct. Nor is it suggested— or supported by any evidence—that Sergeant Allen's decision to allow Mauro's wife to see him was the kind of psychological ploy that properly could be treated as the functional equivalent of interrogation.

There is no evidence that the officers sent Mrs. Mauro in to see her husband for the purpose of eliciting incriminating statements. * * * [T]he weakness of Mauro's claim that he was interrogated is underscored by examining the situation from his perspective. We doubt that a suspect, told by officers that his wife will be allowed to speak to him, would feel that he was being coerced to incriminate himself in any way. * * * Officers do not interrogate a suspect simply by hoping that he will incriminate himself. * * * Mauro was not subjected to compelling influences, psychological ploys, or direct questioning. Thus, his volunteered statements cannot properly be considered the result of police interrogation.

481 U.S. at 527–29, 107 S.Ct. at 1935–37, 95 L.Ed.2d at 467–68. Justice Stevens, joined by Justices Brennan, Marshall and Blackmun, dissented.

2. **Request for Submission to Blood Alcohol Test.** In *Innis,* the Court indicated "interrogation" did not include police words or activity "normally attendant to arrest and custody." In South Dakota v. Neville, 459 U.S. 553, 103 S.Ct. 916, 74 L.Ed.2d 748 (1983), relying on this *Innis* dictum, the Court held that a request a suspect submit to a blood alcohol test is not "interrogation." Justice O'Connor explained for the Court:

> The police inquiry * * * is highly regulated by state law, and is presented in virtually the same words to all suspects. It is similar to a police request to submit to fingerprinting or photography.

459 U.S. at 564 n. 15, 103 S.Ct. at 923 n. 15, 74 L.Ed.2d at 759 n. 15.

b. THE REQUIREMENT OF "CUSTODY"

EDITORS' INTRODUCTION: *MIRANDA'S* CUSTODY PREREQUISITE

The requirement of custody has given rise to more Supreme Court consideration than the requirement of interrogation. In Oregon v. Mathiason, 429 U.S. 492, 97 S.Ct. 711, 50 L.Ed.2d 714 (1977) (per curiam), the Court made clear that the need for custody was firm. *Miranda* would not be applied where custody was lacking, *Mathiason* held, even if the situation presented a "coercive environment" in some sense.

The custody need not be for the offense that is the subject of the questioning. In Mathis v. United States, 391 U.S. 1, 88 S.Ct. 1503, 20 L.Ed.2d 381 (1968), police questioned the suspect while the suspect was in prison serving a sentence for an offense unrelated to that under investigation. Rejecting the argument that *Miranda* applied only to suspects in custody for the offense that was the subject of the interrogation, the majority explained that such a limitation would "[go] against the whole purpose of the *Miranda* decision * * *."

When custody exists has presented a source of continuing controversy. In *Mathiason,* the Court concluded a parolee who appeared at a police station in response to an officer's request for a discussion was not in custody for purposes of *Miranda.* The majority explained, "*Miranda* warnings are required only where there has been such a restriction on a person's freedom as to render him 'in custody.' "

The Court developed and applied the *Mathiason* standard for custody in California v. Beheler, 463 U.S. 1121, 103 S.Ct. 3517, 77 L.Ed.2d 1275 (1983) (per curiam). Beheler himself called police after he and several others attempted to rob a drug dealer and one of the others killed the dealer. He admitted his participation and consented to a search of his backyard; the murder weapon was located there, as he said it would be. That evening, he agreed to accompany officers to the stationhouse. The officers told him he was not under arrest. During a thirty minute interview, he again acknowledged his participation. He was told his statement would be evaluated by the district attorney and he was then permitted to leave. The stationhouse statement was admitted over defense objection at Beheler's trial for aiding and abetting first degree murder. An intermediate California appellate court, however, held admission of the statement violated *Miranda,* reasoning that the prosecution had failed to meet its burden of establishing lack of custody. *Mathiason* was distinguished on several grounds: (a) the interview with Beheler took place soon after the offense, while that with Mathiason occurred 25 days after the crime under investigation; (b) the officers had more information implicating Beheler than had been available against Mathiason at the time of his interview; (c) Beheler had been drinking and was emotionally upset; and (d) Beheler was not a parolee and therefore lacked a parolee's incentive to cooperate with law enforcement officers by voluntarily consenting to an interview.

The Supreme Court reversed. Under *Mathiason,* it explained, "the ultimate inquiry is simply whether there is a 'formal arrest or restraint on freedom of movement' of the degree associated with a formal arrest." Considerations (a) and (b) summarized above, it continued, are irrelevant to this inquiry. Properly framed, the issue presented "is whether *Miranda* warnings are required if the suspect is not placed under arrest, voluntarily comes to the police station, and is allowed to leave unhindered by the police after a brief interview." Since its past decisions clearly directed a negative answer, the Court reversed the decision of the California appellate tribunal.

Similarly, a probationer who appeared at his probation officer's office in response to her request for a meeting with the officer was not in custody under *Mathiason* and *Beheler.* Minnesota v. Murphy, 465 U.S. 420, 104 S.Ct. 1136, 79 L.Ed.2d 409 (1984).

In 1994, the Court returned to the custody problem in Stansbury v. California, 511 U.S. 318, 114 S.Ct. 1526, 128 L.Ed.2d 293 (1994) (per curiam). Officers investigating the rape and murder of a ten year old girl learned that on the day of her death the victim had been seen talking to Stansbury, an ice cream truck driver. At 11:00 p.m., four officers went to Stansbury's trailer home and asked if he would accompany them to the police station to answer some questions. He agreed. During subsequent questioning conducted without *Miranda* warnings, Stansbury made incriminating admissions. The state court held the statement nevertheless admissible, stressing in part that suspicion had not focused on Stansbury until he made the statement. The Supreme Court responded:

> Our decisions make clear that the initial determination of custody depends on the objective circumstances of the interrogation, not on the subjective views harbored by either the interrogating officers or the person being questioned. * * *

> [A] police officer's subjective view that the individual under questioning is a suspect, if undisclosed, does not bear upon the question whether the individual is in custody for purposes of *Miranda.* The

same principle obtains if an officer's undisclosed assessment is that the person being questioned is not a suspect. In either instance, one cannot expect the person under interrogation to probe the officer's innermost thoughts. Save as they are communicated or otherwise manifested to the person being questioned, an officer's evolving but unarticulated suspicions do not affect the objective circumstances of an interrogation or interview, and thus cannot affect the *Miranda* custody inquiry.
* * *

An officer's knowledge or beliefs may bear upon the custody issue if they are conveyed, by word or deed, to the individual being questioned. Those beliefs are relevant only to the extent they would affect how a reasonable person in the position of the individual being questioned would gauge the breadth of his or her " 'freedom of action.' " Even a clear statement from an officer that the person under interrogation is a prime suspect is not, in itself, dispositive of the custody issue, for some suspects are free to come and go until the police decide to make an arrest. The weight and pertinence of any communications regarding the officer's degree of suspicion will depend upon the facts and circumstances of the particular case. In sum, an officer's views concerning the nature of an interrogation, or beliefs concerning the potential culpability of the individual being questioned, may be one among many factors that bear upon the assessment whether that individual was in custody, but only if the officer's views or beliefs were somehow manifested to the individual under interrogation and would have affected how a reasonable person in that position would perceive his or her freedom to leave. (Of course, instances may arise in which the officer's undisclosed views are relevant in testing the credibility of his or her account of what happened during an interrogation; but it is the objective surroundings, and not any undisclosed views, that control the *Miranda* custody inquiry.)

511 U.S. at 523–25, 114 S.Ct. at 1529–30, 128 L.Ed.2d at 298–300. The state court's analysis suggested the court may have regarded the officers' subjective beliefs regarding Stansbury's status "as significant in and of themselves, rather than as relevant only to the extent they influenced the objective conditions surrounding his interrogation." Nevertheless, the parties disagreed on whether the objective facts in the record supported a finding that Stansbury was in custody. Concluding the state court should consider this question in the first instance, the Supreme Court reversed the judgment of the state tribunal and remanded the case "for further proceedings not inconsistent with this opinion."

On remand, the California Supreme Court held that under the analysis directed by the Supreme Court's opinion, the record supported the trial court's finding that Stansbury was not in custody. "[T]he record indicates," the state court concluded, "that a reasonable person in defendant's shoes would not consider that he or she was in custody." It stressed that the officers informed Stansbury he was a possible witness and asked him to come to the station. They invited him to sit in the front seat of their vehicle. Further:

the nature of the interview in this case, which was brief and not accusatory, would not convey to the reasonable person the impression that he or she was in custody, despite the fact that the interview took place in an interview room in the jail area of the police station.

People v. Stansbury, 9 Cal.4th 824, 832, 889 P.2d 588, 592, 38 Cal.Rptr.2d 394, 398 (1995).

Stansbury emphasized suspects' perceptions regarding their ability to break off interactions with police. Nevertheless, the following principal case makes clear that custody does not depend entirely upon whether such a perception exists.

Berkemer v. McCarty

Supreme Court of the United States, 1984.
468 U.S. 420, 104 S.Ct. 3138, 82 L.Ed.2d 317.

■ JUSTICE MARSHALL delivered the opinion of the Court.

This case presents two related questions: First, does our decision in Miranda v. Arizona, 384 U.S. 436, 86 S.Ct. 1602, 16 L.Ed.2d 694 (1966), govern the admissibility of statements made during custodial interrogation by a suspect accused of a misdemeanor traffic offense? Second, does the roadside questioning of a motorist detained pursuant to a traffic stop constitute custodial interrogation for the purposes of the doctrine enunciated in *Miranda?*

[handwritten margin note: does a motor stop questioning require Miranda]

I

A

The parties have stipulated to the essential facts. On the evening of March 31, 1980, Trooper Williams of the Ohio State Highway Patrol observed respondent's car weaving in and out of a lane on Interstate Highway 270. After following the car for two miles, Williams forced respondent to stop and asked him to get out of the vehicle. When respondent complied, Williams noticed that he was having difficulty standing. At that point, "Williams concluded that [respondent] would be charged with a traffic offense and, therefore, his freedom to leave the scene was terminated." However, respondent was not told that he would be taken into custody. Williams then asked respondent to perform a field sobriety test, commonly known as a "balancing test." Respondent could not do so without falling.

While still at the scene of the traffic stop, Williams asked respondent whether he had been using intoxicants. Respondent replied that "he had consumed two beers and had smoked several joints of marijuana a short time before." Respondent's speech was slurred, and Williams had difficulty understanding him. Williams thereupon formally placed respondent under arrest and transported him in the patrol car to the Franklin County Jail.

At the jail, respondent was given an intoxilyzer test to determine the concentration of alcohol in his blood. The test did not detect any alcohol whatsoever in respondent's system. Williams then resumed questioning respondent in order to obtain information for inclusion in the State

Highway Patrol Alcohol Influence Report. Respondent answered affirmatively a question whether he had been drinking. When then asked if he was under the influence of alcohol, he said, "I guess, barely." Williams next asked respondent to indicate on the form whether the marihuana he had smoked had been treated with any chemicals. In the section of the report headed "Remarks," respondent wrote, "No ang[el] dust or PCP in the pot. Rick McCarty."

At no point in this sequence of events did Williams or anyone else tell respondent that he had a right to remain silent, to consult with an attorney, and to have an attorney appointed for him if he could not afford one.

B

Respondent was charged with operating a motor vehicle while under the influence of alcohol and/or drugs * * *. Under Ohio law, that offense is a first-degree misdemeanor and is punishable by fine or imprisonment for up to 6 months. Incarceration for a minimum of 3 days is mandatory.

Respondent moved to exclude the various incriminating statements he had made to Patrolman Williams on the ground that introduction into evidence of those statements would violate the Fifth Amendment insofar as he had not been informed of his constitutional rights prior to his interrogation. When the trial court denied the motion, respondent pleaded "no contest" and was found guilty. He was sentenced to 90 days in jail, 80 of which were suspended, and was fined $300, $100 of which were suspended.

On appeal [in the state courts, respondent's conviction was affirmed.]

Respondent then filed an action for a writ of habeas corpus in the District Court for the Southern District of Ohio. The District Court dismissed the petition * * *.

A divided panel of the Court of Appeals for the Sixth Circuit reversed, holding that "*Miranda* warnings must be given to *all* individuals prior to custodial interrogation, whether the offense investigated be a felony or a misdemeanor traffic offense." * * *

We granted certiorari * * *.

II

* * *

In the years since the decision in *Miranda,* we have frequently reaffirmed the central principle established by that case: if the police take a suspect into custody and then ask him questions without informing him of the rights enumerated above, his responses cannot be introduced into evidence to establish his guilt.

Petitioner asks us to carve an exception out of the foregoing principle. When the police arrest a person for allegedly committing a misdemeanor traffic offense and then ask him questions without telling him his constitutional rights, petitioner argues, his responses should be admissible against him. We cannot agree.

One of the principal advantages of the doctrine that suspects must be given warnings before being interrogated while in custody is the clarity of that rule. * * * The exception to *Miranda* proposed by petitioner would substantially undermine this crucial advantage of the doctrine. The police often are unaware when they arrest a person whether he may have committed a misdemeanor or a felony. * * * It would be unreasonable to expect the police to make guesses as to the nature of the criminal conduct at issue before deciding how they may interrogate the suspect.

* * *

We hold * * * that a person subjected to custodial interrogation is entitled to the benefit of the procedural safeguards enunciated in *Miranda,* regardless of the nature or severity of the offense of which he is suspected or for which he was arrested.

The * * * statements made by respondent at the County Jail were inadmissible. There can be no question that respondent was "in custody" at least as of the moment he was formally placed under arrest and instructed to get into the police car. Because he was not informed of his constitutional rights at that juncture, respondent's subsequent admissions should not have been used against him.

III

To assess the admissibility of the self-incriminating statements made by respondent prior to his formal arrest, we are obliged to address a second issue concerning the scope of our decision in *Miranda:* whether the roadside questioning of a motorist detained pursuant to a routine traffic stop should be considered "custodial interrogation." Respondent urges that it should, on the ground that *Miranda* by its terms applies whenever "a person has been taken into custody *or otherwise deprived of his freedom of action in any significant way.*" Petitioner contends that a holding that every detained motorist must be advised of his rights before being questioned would constitute an unwarranted extension of the *Miranda* doctrine.

It must be acknowledged at the outset that a traffic stop significantly curtails the "freedom of action" of the driver and the passengers, if any, of the detained vehicle. Under the law of most States, it is a crime either to ignore a policeman's signal to stop one's car or, once having stopped, to drive away without permission. Certainly few motorists would feel free either to disobey a directive to pull over or to leave the scene of a traffic stop without being told they might do so. * * *

However, we decline to accord talismanic power to the phrase in the *Miranda* opinion emphasized by respondent. Fidelity to the doctrine announced in *Miranda* requires that it be enforced strictly, but only in those types of situations in which the concerns that powered the decision are implicated. Thus, we must decide whether a traffic stop exerts upon a detained person pressures that sufficiently impair his free exercise of his privilege against self-incrimination to require that he be warned of his constitutional rights.

Two features of an ordinary traffic stop mitigate the danger that a person questioned will be induced "to speak where he would not otherwise do so freely." First, detention of a motorist pursuant to a traffic stop is presumptively temporary and brief. The vast majority of roadside detentions last only a few minutes. A motorist's expectations, when he sees a policeman's light flashing behind him, are that he will be obliged to spend a short period of time answering questions and waiting while the officer checks his license and registration, that he may then be given a citation, but that in the end he most likely will be allowed to continue on his way. In this respect, questioning incident to an ordinary traffic stop is quite different from stationhouse interrogation, which frequently is prolonged, and in which the detainee often is aware that questioning will continue until he provides his interrogators the answers they seek.[7]

Second, circumstances associated with the typical traffic stop are not such that the motorist feels completely at the mercy of the police. To be sure, the aura of authority surrounding an armed, uniformed officer and the knowledge that the officer has some discretion in deciding whether to issue a citation, in combination, exert some pressure on the detainee to respond to questions. But other aspects of the situation substantially offset these forces. Perhaps most importantly, the typical traffic stop is public, at least to some degree. Passersby, on foot or in other cars, witness the interaction of officer and motorist. This exposure to public view both reduces the ability of an unscrupulous policeman to use illegitimate means to elicit self-incriminating statements and diminishes the motorist's fear that, if he does not cooperate, he will be subjected to abuse. The fact that the detained motorist typically is confronted by only one or at most two policemen further mutes his sense of vulnerability. In short, the atmosphere surrounding an ordinary traffic stop is substantially less "police dominated" than that surrounding the kinds of interrogation at issue in *Miranda* itself, and in the subsequent cases in which we have applied *Miranda.*

In both of these respects, the usual traffic stop is more analogous to a so-called "*Terry* stop," see Terry v. Ohio, 392 U.S. 1, 88 S.Ct. 1868, 20 L.Ed.2d 889 (1968), than to a formal arrest. Under the Fourth Amendment, we have held, a policeman who lacks probable cause but whose "observations lead him reasonably to suspect" that a particular person has committed, is committing, or is about to commit a crime, may detain that person briefly in order to "investigate the circumstances that provoke suspicion." "[T]he stop and inquiry must be 'reasonably related in scope to the justification for their initiation.'" Typically, this means that the officer may ask the detainee a moderate number of questions to determine his identity and to try to obtain information confirming or dispelling the officer's suspicions. But the detainee is not obliged to respond. And, unless the detainee's answers provide the officer with probable cause to arrest him, he must then be released. The comparatively nonthreatening character of detentions of this sort explains the absence of any suggestion in our

---

7. The brevity and spontaneity of an ordinary traffic stop also reduces the danger that the driver through subterfuge will be made to incriminate himself. One of the investigative techniques that *Miranda* was designed to guard against was the use by police of various kinds of trickery—such as "Mutt and Jeff" routines—to elicit confessions from suspects. A police officer who stops a suspect on the highway has little chance to develop or implement a plan of this sort.

opinions that *Terry* stops are subject to the dictates of *Miranda*. The similarly noncoercive aspect of ordinary traffic stops prompts us to hold that persons temporarily detained pursuant to such stops are not "in custody" for the purposes of *Miranda*.

Respondent contends that to "exempt" traffic stops from the coverage of *Miranda* will open the way to widespread abuse. Policemen will simply delay formally arresting detained motorists, and will subject them to sustained and intimidating interrogation at the scene of their initial detention. * * * The net result, respondent contends, will be a serious threat to the rights that the *Miranda* doctrine is designed to protect.

We are confident that the state of affairs projected by respondent will not come to pass. It is settled that the safeguards prescribed by *Miranda* become applicable as soon as a suspect's freedom of action is curtailed to a "degree associated with formal arrest." If a motorist who has been detained pursuant to a traffic stop thereafter is subjected to treatment that renders him "in custody" for practical purposes, he will be entitled to the full panoply of protections prescribed by *Miranda*.

Admittedly, our adherence to the doctrine just recounted will mean that the police and lower courts will continue occasionally to have difficulty deciding exactly when a suspect has been taken into custody. Either a rule that *Miranda* applies to all traffic stops or a rule that a suspect need not be advised of his rights until he is formally placed under arrest would provide a clearer, more easily administered line. However, each of these two alternatives has drawbacks that make it unacceptable. The first would substantially impede the enforcement of the nation's traffic laws—by compelling the police either to take the time to warn all detained motorists of their constitutional rights or to forgo use of self-incriminating statements made by those motorists—while doing little to protect citizens' Fifth Amendment rights. The second would enable the police to circumvent the constraints on custodial interrogations established by *Miranda*.

Turning to the case before us, we find nothing in the record that indicates that respondent should have been given *Miranda* warnings at any point prior to the time Trooper Williams placed him under arrest. For the reasons indicated above, we reject the contention that the initial stop of respondent's car, by itself, rendered him "in custody." And respondent has failed to demonstrate that, at any time between the initial stop and the arrest, he was subjected to restraints comparable to those associated with a formal arrest. Only a short period of time elapsed between the stop and the arrest. At no point during that interval was respondent informed that his detention would not be temporary. Although Trooper Williams apparently decided as soon as respondent stepped out of his car that respondent would be taken into custody and charged with a traffic offense, Williams never communicated his intention to respondent. A policeman's unarticulated plan has no bearing on the question whether a suspect was "in custody" at a particular time; the only relevant inquiry is how a reasonable man in the suspect's position would have understood his situation. Nor do other aspects of the interaction of Williams and respondent support the contention that respondent was exposed to "custodial interrogation" at the scene of the stop. From aught that appears in the stipulation of facts, a single police officer asked respondent a modest number of questions and request-ed him to perform a simple balancing test at a location visible to passing motorists. Treatment of this sort cannot fairly be characterized as the functional equivalent of formal arrest.

We conclude, in short, that respondent was not taken into custody for the purposes of *Miranda* until Williams arrested him. Consequently, the statements respondent made prior to that point were admissible against him.

IV

[W]e agree with the Court of Appeals that respondent's postarrest statements should have been suppressed but conclude that respondent's prearrest statements were admissible * * *.   ] *holding*

Accordingly, the judgment of the Court of Appeals is

Affirmed.

NOTES

1. **Modified Warnings for Field Stop Situations.** Insofar as a suspect subjected to a nonarrest detention is not "in custody," *Miranda* is entirely inappli-cable. But are there—or should there be—any requirements for interrogation in such circumstances, other than the apparent demand that any resulting admissions be voluntary? Should, for example, the Court have considered whether a modified version of *Miranda* rights might be required by risks posed to suspects' Fifth Amendment interests in traffic stop situations? Might this be required when nonarrest detention is rather an investigatory field stop concerning a serious offense?

The American Law Institute's Model Code of Pre-Arraignment Procedure proposed the following alternatives to govern questioning during nonarrest stops for investigation:

(5) *Questioning of Suspects.*

(a) *Warnings.* If a law enforcement officer stops any person who he suspects or has reasonable cause to suspect may have committed a crime, the officer shall warn such person as promptly as is reasonable under the circum-stances, and in any case before engaging in any sustained questioning

(i) that such person is not obligated to say anything, and anything he says may be used in evidence against him,

(ii) that within twenty minutes he will be released unless he is arrested.[,]

[(iii) that if he is arrested he will be taken to a police station where he may promptly communicate by telephone with counsel, relatives or friends, and

(iv) that he will not be questioned unless he wishes, and that if he wishes to consult a lawyer or have a lawyer present during questioning, he will not be questioned at this time, and that after being taken to the stationhouse a lawyer will be furnished him prior to questioning if he is unable to obtain one.]

(b) *Limitations on Questioning.* No law enforcement officer shall question a person detained pursuant to the authority of this Section who he suspects or has reasonable cause to suspect may have committed a crime, if such person has indicated in any manner that he does not wish to be questioned, or that he wishes to consult counsel before submitting to any questioning.

A Model Code of Pre-Arraignment Procedure § 110.2 (Official Draft 1975).

2. **Demand for Identifying Information.** In Brown v. Texas, 443 U.S. 47, 99 S.Ct. 2637, 61 L.Ed.2d 357 (1979), Brown was convicted under a Texas statute which made it a criminal offense for a person to refuse to give his name and address to an officer "who has lawfully stopped him and requested the information." The Supreme Court found the officers who stopped Brown had insufficient information to amount to reasonable suspicion Brown was engaged or had engaged in criminal conduct. Under these circumstances, it concluded, Brown could not be punished for refusing to identify himself. The Court specifically noted, however, it was not addressing whether a person could be punished for refusing to identify himself "in the context of a lawful investigatory stop which satisfies Fourth Amendment requirements."

3. THE RIGHT TO PREVENT QUESTIONING

EDITORS' INTRODUCTION: SUSPECTS' RIGHT UNDER *MIRANDA* TO AVOID INTERROGATION

Miranda itself suggested that among the rights of those covered by the opinion is the right to avoid questioning and, perhaps, other efforts by law enforcement officers to persuade suspects to cooperate. The Supreme Court's development of this aspect of *Miranda* is the major post-*Miranda* expansion of the Fifth Amendment law applicable to police interrogation.

The leading post-*Miranda* case is Edwards v. Arizona, 451 U.S. 477, 101 S.Ct. 1880, 68 L.Ed.2d 378 (1981). On January 19, Edwards was arrested on a complaint charging a variety of crimes. He was interrogated by several officers and discussed the possibility of "making a deal." Eventually he said to the interrogating officer, "I want an attorney before making a deal." Questioning ceased and he was taken to a jail cell. The Supreme Court explained what happened next:

> At 9:15 the next morning, two detectives, colleagues of the officer who had interrogated Edwards the previous night, came to the jail and asked to see Edwards. When the detention officer informed Edwards that the detectives wished to speak with him, he replied that he did not want to talk to anyone. The guard told him that "he had" to talk and then took him to meet with the detectives. The officers identified themselves, stated they wanted to talk to him, and informed him of his *Miranda* rights. Edwards was willing to talk, but he first wanted to hear the taped statement of the alleged accomplice who had implicated him. After listening to the tape for several minutes, * * * [h]e * * * implicated himself in the crime.

The Court held that his incriminating statement was inadmissible. It explained:

> *Miranda* itself indicated that the assertion of the right to counsel was a significant event and that once exercised by the accused, "the interrogation must cease until an attorney is present." * * * We reconfirm th[is] view[] and, to lend [it] substance, emphasize that it is inconsistent with *Miranda* and its progeny for the authorities, at their instance, to reinterrogate an accused in custody if he has clearly asserted his right to counsel.

[T]he officers conducting the interrogation on the evening of January 19 ceased interrogation when Edwards requested counsel as he had been advised he had the right to do. * * * [W]ithout making counsel available to Edwards, the police returned to him the next day. This was not at his suggestion or request. Indeed, Edwards informed the detention officer that he did not want to talk to anyone. At the meeting, the detectives told Edwards that they wanted to talk to him and again advised him of his *Miranda* rights. Edwards stated that he would talk, but what prompted this action does not appear. * * * We think it is clear that Edwards was subjected to custodial interrogation on January 20 * * *, and that this occurred at the instance of the authorities. His statement made without having had access to counsel, did not amount to a valid waiver and hence was inadmissible.

451 U.S. at 485–87, 101 S.Ct. at 1883–84, 68 L.Ed.2d at 386–88.

Edwards has been treated as recognizing and implementing a right on the part of those who have invoked their right to counsel not to be interrogated until and unless counsel is present. Neither *Edwards* nor the cases following it distinguished between interrogation in the common sense of that term—questioning aimed at eliciting a self-incriminating admission—and what might usefully be called a "reapproach" to a suspect—an approach to a suspect designed to persuade the suspect to submit to questioning without counsel's presence. Apparently *Edwards* regarded a reapproach in this sense as interrogation barred by the suspect's invocation of the right to counsel. Essentially, then, *Edwards* holds that if a suspect invokes the right to counsel, until the attorney is present the suspect cannot be subjected to either efforts to persuade him to admit guilt (literal interrogation) or attempts to persuade him to submit to such efforts to persuade him to admit guilt (a reapproach not involving literal interrogation).

Rule of Edwards

Edwards Rule Not "Offense Specific"

Edwards' prohibition against further interrogation applies even if officers reapproach the suspect concerning an offense unrelated to that under discussion when the suspect invoked his right to counsel. In this sense, the *Edwards* Fifth Amendment rule—unlike the Sixth Amendment *Edwards*-like rule discussed in part C of this chapter—is not "offense specific."

This was established in Arizona v. Roberson, 486 U.S. 675, 108 S.Ct. 2093, 100 L.Ed.2d 704 (1988). Officers called to the scene of a break-in arrested Roberson for the burglary. This took place on April 16, 1985. After the arresting officer gave him his *Miranda* warnings, Roberson responded that he "wanted a lawyer before answering any questions." The officer noted this in his written report. Three days later, another officer approached Roberson, who was still in custody, regarding a burglary committed on April 15. This officer had not read the arresting officer's report and was unaware Roberson had invoked his right to counsel. After warning Roberson and questioning him, the second officer obtained from Roberson an admission to the April 15 offense. A majority of the Supreme Court held this was inadmissible under *Edwards*. Once a suspect invokes his right to counsel, Justice Stevens reasoned for the Court, *Edwards* bars further interrogation (until a lawyer is provided) even if that subsequent interrogation concerns an offense unrelated to the offense involved in the first interrogation session. Roberson's invocation of his right to counsel during questioning about the April 15 break-in, therefore, barred the second officer from reapproaching him even though that reapproach concerned the separate April 15 offense. The rationale for *Edwards*—that a suspect's invocation of the right to counsel raises a "presumption" that the suspect believes himself incapable of undergoing questioning without the help of an attorney—applies even if the further interrogation concerns a different offense. The rigid *Edwards* rule is justified in order to vigorously discourage police activity creating an especially high risk of an involuntary waiver; the Court found no basis for concluding "that police engaged in separate investigations will be any less eager than police involved in only one inquiry to question a suspect in custody." Suspects like Roberson might have good reason to speak with police about a different offense or at least to learn from police what the new investigation concerns so they can decide whether or not to make a statement, the Court acknowledged. But:

> the suspect, having requested counsel, can determine how to deal with the separate investigations with counsel's advice. Further, even if the police have decided temporarily not to provide counsel, they are free to inform the suspect of the facts of the second investigation as long as such communication does not constitute interrogation.

486 U.S. at 687, 108 S.Ct. at 2101, 100 L.Ed.2d at 717. The second officer's ignorance that Roberson had invoked his right to counsel was of no significance, the Court continued. *Edwards* focuses upon the suspect's state of mind rather than that of the officer. *Miranda* creates a "need to determine whether the suspect has requested counsel." This need exists whether further investigation concerns the same or a different offense or the same or a different interrogator. Failure to honor a request for counsel, the Court concluded, "cannot be justified by the lack of diligence of a particular officer."

Justice Kennedy, joined by the Chief Justice, dissented. When officers reapproach a suspect concerning a separate crime, he reasoned, "the danger of badgering is minimal and insufficient to justify a rigid *per se* rule." Suspects' interests, in this type of situation, are adequately protected by the officers' need to provide the "known and tested warnings" and the prosecution's obligation to prove any waivers were voluntary. When persons are arrested for one offense, it is frequently learned that they are "wanted for questioning" with regard to other offenses. The majority's approach, Justice Kennedy complained, will often bar officers, even those representing a jurisdiction other than the arresting one, from such questioning. "The majority's rule is not necessary to protect the rights of suspects, and it will in many instances deprive our nationwide law enforcement network of a legitimate investigative technique now routinely used to resolve major crimes." 486 U.S. at 688, 108 S.Ct. at 2102, 100 L.Ed.2d at 718 (Kennedy, J., dissenting).

Suspect Initiated Discussion

Edwards described its holding as inapplicable to situations in which "the accused himself initiates further communications, exchanges or conversations with the police." This qualification to the *Edwards* rule was developed in Oregon v. Bradshaw, 462 U.S. 1039, 103 S.Ct. 2830, 77 L.Ed.2d 405 (1983).

Bradshaw was asked to accompany a police officer to the station for further investigation of a traffic accident in which one Reynolds, a minor, had been killed. After being given full *Miranda* warnings, Bradshaw acknowledged furnishing Reynolds with liquor but denied other involvement. He was then placed under arrest for furnishing liquor to a minor and again advised of his *Miranda* rights. A police officer informed him that the officer believed Bradshaw was driving the vehicle in which Reynolds had been killed. After denying this, Bradshaw said, "I do want an attorney before it goes very much further." The officer immediately stopped the conversation.

"Sometime later" officers transported Bradshaw about ten or fifteen miles to a jail. Before or during this trip, Bradshaw asked one of the officers, "Well, what is going to happen to me?" The officer responded, "You do not have to talk to me. You have requested an attorney and I don't want you talking to me unless you so desire because anything you say— because—since you have requested an attorney, you know, it has to be at your own free will." Bradshaw stated he understood. A conversation then took place between Bradshaw and the officer concerning where Bradshaw would be taken and the offense with which he would be charged. The officer suggested Bradshaw take a lie detector test and Bradshaw agreed. The next day, after an officer again read him the *Miranda* rights, Bradshaw took the test. Afterwards, he admitted driving the vehicle and passing out because of intoxication. At his subsequent trial, his post-polygraph test statement was admitted into evidence. A state appellate tribunal, however, held admission of the confession violated *Edwards* and reversed.

Without an opinion of the Court, the Supreme Court found no violation of *Miranda* and *Edwards*. The Court's judgment was announced in an opinion authored by Justice Rehnquist and joined in by three other justices. In this opinion, Justice Rehnquist explained:

> [In *Edwards*,] we held that after the right to counsel had been asserted by an accused, further interrogation of the accused should not take place "unless the accused himself initiates further communication, exchanges, or conversations with the police." This was in effect a prophylactic rule, designed to protect an accused in police custody from being badgered by police officers * * *.
>
> But even if a conversation taking place after the accused had "expressed his desire to deal with the police only through counsel," is initiated by the accused, where reinterrogation follows, the burden remains upon the prosecution to show that subsequent events indicated a waiver of the Fifth Amendment right to have counsel present during the interrogation.

462 U.S. at 1044, 103 S.Ct. at 2834, 77 L.Ed.2d at 411–12. A suspect "initiates" a conversation under *Edwards* only by inquiries which can "be fairly said to represent a desire on the part of an accused to open up a more generalized discussion relating directly or indirectly to the investigation."

Other inquiries, such as requests for water to drink or access to a telephone, are "routine incidents of the custodial relationship" and generally do not amount to an initiation of a conversation within the meaning of *Edwards*.

No violation of the *Edwards* "rule" took place in *Bradshaw*, Justice Rehnquist then concluded:

> Although ambiguous, [Bradshaw's] question in this case as to what was going to happen to him evinced a willingness and a desire for a generalized discussion about the investigation; it was not merely a necessary inquiry arising out of the incidents of the custodial relationship. It could reasonably have been interpreted by the officer as relating generally to the investigation.

462 U.S. at 1045–46, 103 S.Ct. at 2835, 77 L.Ed.2d at 412–13. Progressing to whether the waiver was valid, Justice Rehnquist found no reason to dispute the conclusions of the lower courts that the waiver was voluntary and intelligent. Justice Powell provided the fifth vote to affirm. He did not join Justice Rehnquist's opinion but concurred on the ground the issue should be the voluntariness of Bradshaw's waiver and the record showed the waiver was voluntary.

Justice Marshall, joined by three other members of the Court, dissented. He agreed with Justice Rehnquist that under *Edwards* an accused "initiates" further communication with police only by conduct demonstrating a desire to discuss the subject matter of the investigation. But, he added, this "obviously" means "communication or dialogue *about the subject matter of the criminal investigation.*" (emphasis in original). Turning to the facts before the Court, Justice Marshall construed Bradshaw's inquiry as expressing no more than a desire to find out where the officers were taking him. It did not concern the subject matter of the investigation and therefore did not express a desire to discuss that subject matter. As a result, the officer's actions violated *Edwards' per se* rule and the subsequent confession was inadmissible under *Miranda*.

Effect of Invoking Right to Silence

The *Edwards* rule is limited to situations in which the accused invokes the right to counsel. Six years before *Edwards*, in Michigan v. Mosley, 423 U.S. 96, 96 S.Ct. 321, 46 L.Ed.2d 313 (1975), the Court refused to completely bar officers from reapproaching a suspect who invoked his right to remain silent. *Mosley* explained:

> The issue in this case * * * is whether the conduct of the Detroit police that led to Mosley's incriminating statement did in fact violate the *Miranda* "guidelines," so as to render the statement inadmissible in evidence against Mosley at his trial. Resolution of the question turns almost entirely on the interpretation of a single passage in the *Miranda* opinion * * *:
>
> > Once warnings have been given, the subsequent procedure is clear. If the individual indicates in any manner, at any time prior to or during questioning, that he wishes to remain silent, the interrogation must cease. At this point he has shown that he intends to exercise his Fifth Amendment privilege; any statement

taken after the person invokes his privilege cannot be other than the product of compulsion, subtle or otherwise. Without the right to cut off questioning, the setting of in-custody interrogation operates on the individual to overcome free choice in producing a statement after the privilege has been once invoked.

This passage states that "the interrogation must cease" when the person in custody indicates that "he wishes to remain silent." It does not state under what circumstances, if any, a resumption of questioning is permissible. The passage could be literally read to mean that a person who has invoked his "right to silence" can never again be subjected to custodial interrogation by any police officer at any time or place on any subject. Another possible construction of the passage would characterize "any statement taken after the person invokes his privilege" as "the product of compulsion" and would therefore mandate its exclusion from evidence, even if it were volunteered by the person in custody without any further interrogation whatever. Or the passage could be interpreted to require only the immediate cessation of questioning, and to permit a resumption of interrogation after a momentary respite.

It is evident that any of these possible literal interpretations would lead to absurd and unintended results. To permit the continuation of custodial interrogation after a momentary cessation would clearly frustrate the purposes of *Miranda* by allowing repeated rounds of questioning to undermine the will of the person being questioned. At the other extreme, a blanket prohibition against the taking of voluntary statements or a permanent immunity from further interrogation, regardless of the circumstances, would transform the *Miranda* safeguards into wholly irrational obstacles to legitimate police investigative activity, and deprive suspects of an opportunity to make informed and intelligent assessments of their interests. Clearly, therefore, neither this passage nor any other passage in the *Miranda* opinion can sensibly be read to create a per se proscription of indefinite duration upon any further questioning by any police officer on any subject, once the person in custody has indicated a desire to remain silent.

423 U.S. at 100–03, 96 S.Ct. at 325–26, 46 L.Ed.2d at 316–21. *Edwards* distinguished *Mosley* on the basis that the request made in *Mosley*—"a request to remain silent"—was not the request for counsel that triggers the *Edwards* bar to all further interrogation.

The prosecution may have greater difficulty showing that a suspect effectively waived his rights if the facts show that the suspect was reapproached after invoking the right to silence; this is considered in subsection B(4) of this chapter. But under *Mosley*, a suspect who invokes only the right to silence is protected by no absolute prohibition against officers reapproaching him.

Davis v. United States

Supreme Court of the United States, 1994.
512 U.S. 452, 114 S.Ct. 2350, 129 L.Ed.2d 362.

■ JUSTICE O'CONNOR delivered the opinion of the Court.

In Edwards v. Arizona, 451 U.S. 477, 101 S.Ct. 1880, 68 L.Ed.2d 378 (1981), we held that law enforcement officers must immediately cease questioning a suspect who has clearly asserted his right to have counsel present during custodial interrogation. In this case we decide how law enforcement officers should respond when a suspect makes a reference to counsel that is insufficiently clear to invoke the *Edwards* prohibition on further questioning.

I

Pool brought trouble—not to River City, but to the Charleston Naval Base. Petitioner, a member of the United States Navy, spent the evening of October 2, 1988, shooting pool at a club on the base. Another sailor, Keith Shackleton, lost a game and a $30 wager to petitioner, but Shackleton refused to pay. After the club closed, Shackleton was beaten to death with a pool cue on a loading dock behind the commissary. The body was found early the next morning.

The investigation by the Naval Investigative Service (NIS) gradually focused on petitioner. Investigative agents determined that petitioner was at the club that evening, and that he was absent without authorization from his duty station the next morning. The agents also learned that only privately owned pool cues could be removed from the club premises, and that petitioner owned two cues—one of which had a bloodstain on it. The agents were told by various people that petitioner either had admitted committing the crime or had recounted details that clearly indicated his involvement in the killing.

On November 4, 1988, petitioner was interviewed at the NIS office. As required by military law, the agents advised petitioner that he was a suspect in the killing, that he was not required to make a statement, that any statement could be used against him at a trial by court-martial, and that he was entitled to speak with an attorney and have an attorney present during questioning. Petitioner waived his rights to remain silent and to counsel, both orally and in writing.

About an hour and a half into the interview, petitioner said, "Maybe I should talk to a lawyer." According to the uncontradicted testimony of one of the interviewing agents, the interview then proceeded as follows:

> "[We m]ade it very clear that we're not here to violate his rights, that if he wants a lawyer, then we will stop any kind of questioning with him, that we weren't going to pursue the matter unless we have it clarified is he asking for a lawyer or is he just making a comment about a lawyer, and he said, [']No, I'm not asking for a lawyer,' and then he continued on, and said, 'No, I don't want a lawyer.' "

After a short break, the agents reminded petitioner of his rights to remain silent and to counsel. The interview then continued for another hour, until petitioner said, "I think I want a lawyer before I say anything else." At that point, questioning ceased.

At his general court-martial, petitioner moved to suppress statements made during the November 4 interview. The Military Judge denied the motion * * *. Petitioner was convicted on one specification of unpremeditated murder * * *. The Navy–Marine Corps Court of Military Review affirmed.

The United States Court of Military Appeals granted discretionary review and affirmed. The court recognized that the state and federal courts have developed three different approaches to a suspect's ambiguous or equivocal request for counsel:

> "Some jurisdictions have held that any mention of counsel, however ambiguous, is sufficient to require that all questioning cease. Others have attempted to define a threshold standard of clarity for invoking the right to counsel and have held that comments falling short of the threshold do not invoke the right to counsel. Some jurisdictions ... have held that all interrogation about the offense must immediately cease whenever a suspect mentions counsel, but they allow interrogators to ask narrow questions designed to clarify the earlier statement and the [suspect's] desires respecting counsel."

Applying the third approach, the court held that petitioner's comment was ambiguous, and that the NIS agents properly clarified petitioner's wishes with respect to counsel before continuing questioning him about the offense.

* * *

II

[W]e held in Miranda v. Arizona, 384 U.S. 436, 469473, 86 S.Ct. 1602, 16251627, 16 L.Ed.2d 694 (1966), that a suspect subject to custodial interrogation has the right to consult with an attorney and to have counsel present during questioning, and that the police must explain this right to him before questioning begins. * * * If the suspect effectively waives his right to counsel after receiving the *Miranda* warnings, law enforcement officers are free to question him. But if a suspect requests counsel at any time during the interview, he is not subject to further questioning until a lawyer has been made available or the suspect himself reinitiates conversation. This "second layer of prophylaxis for the *Miranda* right to counsel," is "designed to prevent police from badgering a defendant into waiving his previously asserted *Miranda* rights." * * * "It remains clear, however, that this prohibition on further questioning—like other aspects of *Miranda*is not itself required by the Fifth Amendment's prohibition on coerced confessions, but is instead justified only by reference to its prophylactic purpose." Connecticut v. Barrett, [479 U.S. 523, 528, 107 S.Ct. 828, 832, 93 L.Ed.2d 920 (1987)].

The applicability of the " 'rigid' prophylactic rule" of *Edwards* requires courts to "determine whether the accused *actually invoked* his right to counsel." Smith v. Illinois, [469 U.S. 91, 95, 105 S.Ct. 490, 492 83 L.Ed.2d 488 (1984) (per curiam)] (emphasis added). To avoid difficulties of proof and to provide guidance to officers conducting interrogations, this is an objective inquiry. Invocation of the *Miranda* right to counsel "requires, at a minimum, some statement that can reasonably be construed to be an expression of a desire for the assistance of an attorney." McNeil v. Wisconsin, [501 U.S. 171, 178, 111 S.Ct. 2204, 2209, 115 L.Ed.2d 158

(1991)]. But if a suspect makes a reference to an attorney that is ambiguous or equivocal in that a reasonable officer in light of the circumstances would have understood only that the suspect might be invoking the right to counsel, our precedents do not require the cessation of questioning.

Rather, the suspect must unambiguously request counsel. * * * Although a suspect need not "speak with the discrimination of an Oxford don," he must articulate his desire to have counsel present sufficiently clearly that a reasonable police officer in the circumstances would understand the statement to be a request for an attorney. If the statement fails to meet the requisite level of clarity, *Edwards* does not require that the officers stop questioning the suspect.

We decline petitioner's invitation to extend *Edwards* and require law enforcement officers to cease questioning immediately upon the making of an ambiguous or equivocal reference to an attorney. The rationale underlying *Edwards* is that the police must respect a suspect's wishes regarding his right to have an attorney present during custodial interrogation. But when the officers conducting the questioning reasonably do not know whether or not the suspect wants a lawyer, a rule requiring the immediate cessation of questioning "would transform the *Miranda* safeguards into wholly irrational obstacles to legitimate police investigative activity," because it would needlessly prevent the police from questioning a suspect in the absence of counsel even if the suspect did not wish to have a lawyer present. Nothing in *Edwards* requires the provision of counsel to a suspect who consents to answer questions without the assistance of a lawyer. In *Miranda* itself, we expressly rejected the suggestion "that each police station must have a 'station house lawyer' present at all times to advise prisoners, and held instead that a suspect must be told of his right to have an attorney present and that he may not be questioned after invoking his right to counsel." We also noted that if a suspect is "indecisive in his request for counsel," the officers need not always cease questioning.

We recognize that requiring a clear assertion of the right to counsel might disadvantage some suspects who—because of fear, intimidation, lack of linguistic skills, or a variety of other reasons—will not clearly articulate their right to counsel although they actually want to have a lawyer present. But the primary protection afforded suspects subject to custodial interrogation is the *Miranda* warnings themselves. * * * A suspect who knowingly and voluntarily waives his right to counsel after having that right explained to him has indicated his willingness to deal with the police unassisted. Although *Edwards* provides an additional protection—if a suspect subsequently requests an attorney, questioning must cease—it is one that must be affirmatively invoked by the suspect.

In considering how a suspect must invoke the right to counsel, we must consider the other side of the *Miranda* equation: the need for effective law enforcement. Although the courts ensure compliance with the *Miranda* requirements through the exclusionary rule, it is police officers who must actually decide whether or not they can question a suspect. The *Edwards* rule—questioning must cease if the suspect asks for a lawyer—provides a bright line that can be applied by officers in the real world of investigation and interrogation without unduly hampering the gathering of information. But if we were to require questioning to cease if a suspect makes a statement that might be a request for an attorney, this clarity and ease of application would be lost. Police officers would be forced to make difficult judgment calls about whether the suspect in fact wants a lawyer even though he has not said so, with the threat of suppression if they guess wrong. We therefore hold that, after a knowing and voluntary waiver of the *Miranda* rights, law enforcement officers may continue questioning until and unless the suspect clearly requests an attorney.

Of course, when a suspect makes an ambiguous or equivocal statement it will often be good police practice for the interviewing officers to clarify whether or not he actually wants an attorney. That was the procedure followed by the NIS agents in this case. Clarifying questions help protect the rights of the suspect by ensuring that he gets an attorney if he wants one, and will minimize the chance of a confession being suppressed due to subsequent judicial second-guessing as to the meaning of the suspect's statement regarding counsel. But we decline to adopt a rule requiring officers to ask clarifying questions. If the suspect's statement is not an unambiguous or unequivocal request for counsel, the officers have no obligation to stop questioning him.

* * *

The courts below found that petitioner's remark to the NIS agents "Maybe I should talk to a lawyer" was not a request for counsel, and we see no reason to disturb that conclusion. The NIS agents therefore were not required to stop questioning petitioner, though it was entirely proper for them to clarify whether petitioner in fact wanted a lawyer. Because there is no ground for suppression of petitioner's statements, the judgment of the Court of Military Appeals is

Affirmed.

■ JUSTICE SOUTER, with whom JUSTICE BLACKMUN, JUSTICE STEVENS, and JUSTICE GINSBURG join, concurring in the judgment.

* * *

I agree with the majority that the Constitution does not forbid law enforcement officers to pose questions (like those directed at Davis) aimed solely at clarifying whether a suspect's ambiguous reference to counsel was meant to assert his Fifth Amendment right. Accordingly I concur in the judgment affirming Davis's conviction, resting partly on evidence of statements given after agents ascertained that he did not wish to deal with them through counsel. I cannot, however, join in my colleagues' further conclusion that if the investigators here had been so inclined, they were at liberty to disregard Davis's reference to a lawyer entirely, in accordance with a general rule that interrogators have no legal obligation to discover what a custodial subject meant by an ambiguous statement that could reasonably be understood to express a desire to consult a lawyer. * * * The concerns of fairness and practicality that have long anchored our *Miranda* case law point to a different response: when law enforcement officials "reasonably do not know whether or not the suspect wants a lawyer," they should stop their interrogation and ask him to make his choice clear.

I

A

While the question we address today is an open one, its answer requires coherence with nearly three decades of case law addressing the relationship between police and criminal suspects in custodial interrogation. Throughout that period, two precepts have commanded broad assent: that the *Miranda* safeguards exist " 'to assure that *the individual's right to choose* between speech and silence remains unfettered throughout the interrogation process,' " and that the justification for *Miranda* rules, intended to operate in the real world, "must be consistent with ... practical realities." A rule barring government agents from further interrogation until they determine whether a suspect's ambiguous statement was meant as a request for counsel fulfills both ambitions. It assures that a suspect's choice whether or not to deal with police through counsel will be "scrupulously honored," and it faces both the real-world reasons why misunderstandings arise between suspect and interrogator and the real-world limitations on the capacity of police and trial courts to apply fine distinctions and intricate rules.

B

Tested against the same two principles, the approach the Court adopts does not fare so well. First, as the majority expressly acknowledges, criminal suspects who may (in *Miranda's* words) be "thrust into an unfamiliar atmosphere and run through menacing police interrogation procedures, would seem an odd group to single out for the Court's demand of heightened linguistic care." A substantial percentage of them lack anything like a confident command of the English language; many are "woefully ignorant;" and many more will be sufficiently intimidated by the interrogation process or overwhelmed by the uncertainty of their predicament that the ability to speak assertively will abandon them.[8] * * *

Nor may the standard governing waivers as expressed in these statements be deflected away by drawing a distinction between initial waivers of *Miranda* rights and subsequent decisions to reinvoke them, on the theory that so long as the burden to demonstrate waiver rests on the government, it is only fair to make the suspect shoulder a burden of showing a clear subsequent assertion. *Miranda* itself discredited the legitimacy of any such distinction. The opinion described the object of the warning as being to assure "a continuous opportunity to exercise [the right of silence]." "[C]on-

---

8. Social science confirms what common sense would suggest, that individuals who feel intimidated or powerless are more likely to speak in equivocal or nonstandard terms when no ambiguity or equivocation is meant. See W. O'Barr, Linguistic Evidence: Language, Power, and Strategy in the Courtroom 61–71 (1982). Suspects in police interrogation are strong candidates for these effects. Even while resort by the police to the "third degree" has abated since *Miranda*, the basic forms of psychological pressure applied by police appear to have changed less. Compare, e.g., *Miranda*, supra, 384 U.S., at 449, 86 S.Ct., at 1615 (" '[T]he principal psychological factor contributing to a successful interrogation is privacy' ") (quoting F. Inbau & J. Reid, Criminal Interrogations and Confessions 1 (1962)), with F. Inbau, J. Reid, & J. Buckley, Criminal Interrogation and Confessions 24 (3d ed. 1986) ("The principal psychological factor contributing to a successful interrogation is privacy").

tinuous opportunity" suggests an unvarying one, governed by a common standard of effectiveness. * * *

The Court defends as tolerable the certainty that some poorly expressed requests for counsel will be disregarded on the ground that *Miranda* warnings suffice to alleviate the inherent coercion of the custodial interrogation. But, "[a] once-stated warning, delivered by those who will conduct the interrogation, cannot itself suffice" to "assure that the ... right to choose between silence and speech remains unfettered throughout the interrogation process." * * *

[I]t is easy, amidst the discussion of layers of protection, to lose sight of a real risk in the majority's approach, going close to the core of what the Court has held that the Fifth Amendment provides. The experience of the timid or verbally inept suspect (whose existence the Court acknowledges) may not always closely follow that of the defendant in Edwards v. Arizona (whose purported waiver of his right to counsel, made after having invoked the right, was held ineffective, lest police be tempted to "badge[r]" others like him). * * * When a suspect understands his (expressed) wishes to have been ignored (and by hypothesis, he has said something that an objective listener could "reasonably," although not necessarily, take to be a request), in contravention of the "rights" just read to him by his interrogator, he may well see further objection as futile and confession (true or not) as the only way to end his interrogation.

* * *

The other justifications offered for the "requisite level of clarity" rule are that, whatever its costs, it will further society's strong interest in "effective law enforcement," and maintain the "ease of application," that has long been a concern of our *Miranda* jurisprudence. With respect to the first point, the margin of difference between the clarification approach advocated here and the one the Court adopts is defined by the class of cases in which a suspect, if asked, would make it plain that he meant to request counsel (at which point questioning would cease). While these lost confessions do extract a real price from society, it is one that *Miranda* itself determined should be borne.

As for practical application, while every approach, including the majority's, will involve some "difficult judgment calls,"[9] the rule argued for here would relieve the officer of any responsibility for guessing "whether the suspect in fact wants a lawyer even though he hasn't said so." To the contrary, it would assure that the "judgment call" will be made by the party most competent to resolve the ambiguity, who our case law has always assumed should make it: the individual suspect.

9. In the abstract, nothing may seem more clear than a "clear statement" rule, but in police stations and trial courts the question, "how clear is clear?" is not so readily answered. When a suspect says, "uh, yeah, I'd like to do that" after being told he has a right to a lawyer, has he "clearly asserted" his right? Compare Smith v. Illinois, [469 U.S. 91, 97, 105 S.Ct. 490, 493, 83 L.Ed.2d 488 (1984) (per curiam)] (statement was " 'neither indecisive nor ambiguous' ") (citation omitted), with id., at 101, 105 S.Ct., at 495 496 (REHNQUIST, J., dissenting) (questioning clarity) * * *

As a practical matter, of course, the primary arbiters of "clarity" will be the interrogators themselves, who tend as well to be courts' preferred source in determining the precise words a suspect used. And when an inculpatory statement has been obtained as a result of an unrecorded, incommunicado interrogation, these officers rarely lose "swearing matches" against criminal defendants at suppression hearings.

II

Although I am convinced that the Court has taken the wrong path, I am not persuaded by petitioner's contention, that even ambiguous statements require an end to all police questioning. I recognize that the approach petitioner urges on us can claim some support from our case law, most notably in the "indicates in any manner" language of *Miranda*, and I do not deny that the rule I endorse could be abused by "clarifying" questions that shade subtly into illicitly badgering a suspect who wants counsel. But petitioner's proposal is not entirely in harmony with all the major themes of *Miranda* case law, its virtues and demerits being the reverse images of those that mark the Court's rule. While it is plainly wrong, for example, to continue interrogation when the suspect wants it to stop (and so indicates), the strong bias in favor of individual choice may also be disserved by stopping questioning when a suspect wants it to continue (but where his statement might be understood otherwise). The costs to society of losing confessions would, moreover, be especially hard to bear where the suspect, if asked for his choice, would have chosen to continue. One need not sign the majority's opinion here to agree that resort to the rule petitioner argues for should be had only if experience shows that less drastic means of safeguarding suspects' constitutional rights are not up to the job.

* * *

Our cases are best respected by a rule that when a suspect under custodial interrogation makes an ambiguous statement that might reasonably be understood as expressing a wish that a lawyer be summoned (and questioning cease), interrogators' questions should be confined to verifying whether the individual meant to ask for a lawyer. While there is reason to expect that trial courts will apply today's ruling sensibly (without requiring criminal suspects to speak with the discrimination of an Oxford don) and that interrogators will continue to follow what the Court rightly calls "good police practice" * * *, I believe that the case law under *Miranda* does not allow them to do otherwise.

NOTES

1. **Invoking the *Edwards* Bar to Questioning.** The Supreme Court has held a suspect has a Sixth Amendment right to counsel that applies—among other times—during police interrogation. This right is invoked, the Court has assumed, if a suspect appears in court with counsel representing him. The Sixth Amendment right, unlike the *Miranda–Edwards* right as construed in *Roberson*, is "offense-specific," meaning it only bars officers from approaching the suspect concerning the same offense. This chapter considers these holdings in part C. Action by a defendant

sufficient to invoke the Sixth Amendment right to counsel, however, does not necessarily invoke the *Edwards* rule under *Miranda* and the Fifth Amendment.

In McNeil v. Wisconsin, 501 U.S. 171, 111 S.Ct. 2204, 115 L.Ed.2d 158 (1991), the defendant was arrested for robbery and appeared before a court commissioner who set bail. A public defender represented him at that appearance. A detective later approached McNeil concerning an unrelated burglary and murder. McNeil was warned of his *Miranda* rights and waived them; he then gave a statement incriminating himself in those offenses. The Supreme Court "accepted" that McNeil's appearance before the commissioner with an attorney invoked his Sixth Amendment right to counsel with regard to the robbery. But it held that this action did not invoke McNeil's *Miranda* right to counsel so as to trigger the *Edwards* rule. Justice Scalia explained for the Court:

> [*Edwards*] requires, at a minimum, some statement that can reasonably be construed to be an expression of a desire for the assistance of an attorney *in dealing with custodial interrogation by the police.*

501 U.S. at 178, 111 S.Ct. at 2209, 115 L.Ed.2d at 169 (emphasis in original). Invoking the Sixth Amendment right to counsel concerning an offense for which one has been judicially charged does not suffice. Specifically, and with reference to the facts of *McNeil,* the Court explained, "[r]equesting the assistance of an attorney at a bail hearing does not bear that construction."

The *McNeil* Court also rejected a rule that invoking the Sixth Amendment right to counsel automatically gives the suspect the protection of *Edwards.* Such a rule would impede law enforcement objectives, it reasoned, since suspects are often given counsel in their first formal court appearance.

> Thus * * * most persons in pretrial custody for serious offenses would be *unapproachable* by police officers suspecting them of involvement in other crimes, *even though they have never expressed any unwillingness to be questioned.*

501 U.S. at 181, 111 S.Ct. at 2210, 115 L.Ed.2d at 170 (emphasis in original). The rule would provide only insignificant protection for suspects:

> If a suspect does not wish to communicate with the police except through an attorney, he can simply tell them that when they give him the *Miranda* warnings. There is not the remotest chance that he will feel "badgered" by their asking to talk to him without counsel present, since the subject will not be the charge on which he has already requested counsel's assistance * * * and he will not have rejected uncounseled interrogation on *any* subject before (for in that event *Edwards* would preclude initiation of the interview).

501 U.S. at 180, 111 S.Ct. at 2210, 115 L.Ed.2d at 170.

2. **"Anticipatory" Invocation of the Right to Counsel.** The *McNeil* dissenters suggested the majority's distinction will be nullified by lawyers who, on behalf of their clients, will routinely and at the first court appearance announce that their clients are invoking *Miranda* rights. Responding, Justice Scalia questioned whether these and other "anticipatory" invocations of *Miranda* rights would be effective:

> We have * * * never held that a person can invoke his *Miranda* rights anticipatorily, in a context other than "custodial interrogation"—which a preliminary hearing will not always, or even usually, involve. If the *Miranda* right to counsel can be invoked at a preliminary hearing, it could be argued, there is no logical reason why it could not be invoked by a letter prior to arrest, or indeed even prior to identification as a suspect. Most rights must be asserted when the government seeks to take the action they protect against. The fact

that we have allowed the *Miranda* right to counsel, once asserted, to be effective with respect to future custodial interrogation does not necessarily mean that we will allow it to be asserted initially outside the context of custodial interrogation, with similar future effect.

501 U.S. at 182 n. 3, 111 S.Ct. at 2211 n. 3, 115 L.Ed.2d at 171 n. 3.

3. **Presence of Attorney Required Under *Edwards*.** In Minnick v. Mississippi, 498 U.S. 146, 111 S.Ct. 486, 112 L.Ed.2d 489 (1990), Minnick was interviewed by FBI agents. He told them, "Come back Monday when I have a lawyer." The federal officers ended the interview. Minnick later met with a lawyer appointed to represent him and spoke with that attorney—perhaps by telephone—on several other occasions. A state officer then interviewed Minnick after warning him of his *Miranda* rights; Minnick refused to sign a waiver form but talked with the officer and made incriminating admissions. The state court declined to apply *Edwards*, reasoning that in *Edwards* the Supreme Court indicated that the bar to further interrogation applies only "until counsel has been made available to [the suspect];" the consultations between Minnick and his lawyer established counsel had been "made available." Justice Scalia, joined by the Chief Justice, agreed, arguing that *Edwards* should cease to apply after the initial consultation between the suspect and his attorney:

> The suspect then knows he had an advocate on his side, and that the police will permit him to consult that advocate. He almost certainly also has a heightened awareness (above what the *Miranda* warning itself will provide) of his right to remain silent * * *.

498 U.S. at 162, 111 S.Ct. at 496, 112 L.Ed.2d at 503 (Scalia, J., dissenting).

The *Minnick* majority, however, concluded otherwise. Justice Kennedy explained for the Court:

> [W]e * * * hold that when counsel is requested, interrogation must cease, and officials may not reinstate interrogation without counsel present, whether or not the accused has consulted with his attorney.
>
> We consider our ruling to be an appropriate and necessary application of the *Edwards* rule. A single consultation with an attorney does not remove the suspect from persistent attempts by officials to persuade him to waive his right, or from the coercive pressures that accompany custody and that may increase as custody is prolonged. * * *
>
> The exception proposed * * * would undermine the advantages flowing from *Edwards'* "clear and unequivocal" character. * * * [It] would leave far from certain the sort of consultation required to displace *Edwards*. * * *
>
> [We are also concerned] that the suspect whose counsel is prompt would lose the protection of *Edwards,* while the one whose counsel is dilatory would not. There is more than irony in this rule. There is a strong possibility that it would distort the proper concept of the attorney's duty to the client and set us on a course at odds with what ought to be effective representation.

498 U.S. at 153–55, 111 S.Ct. at 491–92, 112 L.Ed.2d at 498–99.

4.   Waiver of the *Miranda* Rights

EDITORS' INTRODUCTION: WAIVER ISSUES

As *Miranda* makes clear, the constitutionally-required foundation for admissibility of a self-incriminating statement made during custodial interrogation is proof that the defendant "knowingly and intelligently waived his privilege against self-incrimination and [unless a lawyer was present during the interrogation] his right to retained or appointed counsel." The *Miranda* Court clearly believed that counsel's presence when a suspect decides to confess would reduce the difficulty of determining whether that waiver of the right to remain silent was effective. In most cases, however, counsel will not have been present during the interrogation. Consequently, waiver issues have become more prominent in *Miranda* law.

Analysis is helped by distinguishing between the need for the prosecution to prove two different matters. First is that the defendant made a choice that might constitute waiver. Second is that a choice made by the defendant was effective. The two inquiries raise different concerns. What is necessary to prove a choice, for example, is a much different question than what is necessary to prove that a choice was sufficiently voluntary and intelligent and therefore effective.

Burden of Proof. The burden of proof regarding *Miranda* waivers was addressed in Colorado v. Connelly, 479 U.S. 157, 107 S.Ct. 515, 93 L.Ed.2d 473 (1986). The state court had held that the prosecution must establish waivers of the rights to counsel and to remain silent by "clear and convincing evidence." Agreeing that the prosecution bears the burden of proof, the Supreme Court held this burden of proof is by only a preponderance of the evidence. Lego v. Twomey, 404 U.S. 477, 92 S.Ct. 619, 30 L.Ed.2d 618 (1972), the Court noted, established that the prosecution need prove the voluntariness of a confession only by a preponderance of the evidence. "[A] waiver of the auxiliary protections established in *Miranda*," *Connelly* reasoned "should require no higher a burden of proof."

Express Waivers Not Required. No "express" waiver of *Miranda* rights is required; an "implied waiver" is sufficient. The Supreme Court has left somewhat unclear precisely what is required for proof of an implied waiver.

In North Carolina v. Butler, 441 U.S. 369, 99 S.Ct. 1755, 60 L.Ed.2d 286 (1979), the North Carolina Supreme Court was held to have erred in applying a *per se* rule requiring an express waiver. "[A] court may find an intelligent and understanding rejection of counsel in situations where the defendant did not expressly state as much," Justice Stewart explained for the Court. He continued:

> The question is not one of form, but rather whether the defendant in fact knowingly and voluntarily waived the rights delineated in *Miranda*. * * * [M]ere silence is not enough. That does not mean that the defendant's silence, coupled with an understanding of his rights and a course of conduct indicating waiver, may never support a conclusion that a defendant has waived his rights. * * * [I]n at least some cases waiver can be clearly inferred from the actions and words of the person interrogated.

441 U.S. at 373, 99 S.Ct. at 1757, 60 L.Ed.2d at 292.

Distinguishing Different Waivers. Often discussions assume that one waiver or set of waivers is at issue. But often this is not the case. Suppose a suspect, after officers gave her the required warnings, agrees to talk with officers in the absence of an attorney. After two hours of discussion, the suspect makes a self-incriminating admission. Are the suspect's waivers of the right to counsel and the right to silence identical? Clearly not. Her waiver of the right to counsel occurred before interrogation began; her waiver of the right to remain silent occurred only when she made the admission.

This distinction is important because intervening events may bear upon the effectiveness of one waiver but not the other. Suppose, for example, that during a two hour discussion officers inform a suspect that she will not be presented before a judge until the officers have what they regard as a satisfactory statement from her. If the suspect had already waived her right to counsel during interrogation, this threat could not affect the effectiveness of this waiver. (Perhaps, however, her continued willingness to undergo questioning without a lawyer is a continuing waiver of the right to counsel rendered involuntary after the threat was made.) In any case, if, in response to this threat, the suspect decides to give an incriminating statement and thereby waive her right to silence, it is much clearer this waiver was fatally tainted by the threat.

Effectiveness of Waivers: In General. The criteria to be used in determining the effectiveness of *Miranda* waivers were distinguished and to some extent developed in Edwards v. Arizona, 451 U.S. 477, 101 S.Ct. 1880, 68 L.Ed.2d 378 (1981).

Before making his oral confession, given during a custodial interrogation, Edwards insisted he did not want his confession recorded because it could then be used against him in court. The interrogating detectives explained that an unrecorded oral confession could also be used against him. Edwards then made an incriminating statement. Prior to trial, defense counsel moved to suppress the confession on the ground that, despite the detectives' efforts, Edwards did not understand the admissibility of an oral confession and therefore the waiver of his rights was not knowingly made. The trial judge found the confession to have been "voluntary" and denied the motion to suppress. On appeal, the Arizona Supreme Court regarded the applicable standard as that discussed in Schneckloth v. Bustamonte, 412 U.S. 218, 93 S.Ct. 2041, 36 L.Ed.2d 854 (1973) (reprinted in Chapter 5), dealing with the voluntariness of a consent to search. It posed the question as whether, based on the totality of the circumstances, the trial court's conclusions that the defendant's action in confessing was knowing and intelligent and that his will had not been overborne were "clear and manifest error." It found no such error.

The Supreme Court held that the Arizona Supreme Court had not adequately considered whether Edwards had effectively relinquished his right to counsel. Under *Miranda*, it explained, the "voluntariness" of a consent or an admission, on the one hand, and the existence of a knowing and intelligent waiver, on the other, "are discrete inquiries." However sound the state court's conclusion regarding the "voluntariness" of Edwards' confession, the tribunal did not adequately address the *Miranda* waiver issue:

> [W]aivers of counsel must not only be voluntary, but must also constitute a knowing and intelligent relinquishment or abandonment of a known right or privilege * * *. [N]either the trial court nor the

Arizona Supreme Court undertook to focus on whether Edwards understood his right to counsel and intelligently and knowingly relinquished it. It is thus apparent that the decision below misunderstood the requirement for finding a valid waiver of the right to counsel * * *.

451 U.S. at 482–84, 101 S.Ct. at 1883–84, 68 L.Ed.2d at 385–86.

Under *Edwards*, the effectiveness of *Miranda* waivers clearly requires separate consideration of voluntariness and intelligence.

Effectiveness of Waivers: Voluntariness. The prosecution must prove a suspect's *Miranda* waivers were "voluntary." But what does this mean? How does the standard for determining voluntariness in this context compare with the criterion under the due process standard for determining the voluntariness of a confession?

Colorado v. Connelly, 479 U.S. 157, 107 S.Ct. 515, 93 L.Ed.2d 473 (1986), reprinted in part in section A of this chapter on general due process voluntariness, also addressed the voluntariness of *Miranda* waivers. After passing on the admissibility of the Connelly's confessions made before he was placed in custody, the Court assumed that once Officer Anderson handcuffed Connelly *Miranda* became applicable. It then turned to the state court's determination that Connelly had not effectively waived his *Miranda* rights regarding statements he made under custodial interrogation:

> The Supreme Court of Colorado in addressing this question relied on the testimony of the court-appointed psychiatrist to the effect that [Connelly] was not capable of making a "free decision with respect to his constitutional right of silence * * * and his constitutional right to confer with a lawyer before talking to the police."
>
> We think that the Supreme Court of Colorado erred in importing into this area of constitutional law notions of "free will" that have no place there. There is obviously no reason to require more in the way of a "voluntariness" inquiry in the *Miranda* waiver context than in the Fourteenth Amendment confession context. The sole concern of the Fifth Amendment, on which *Miranda* was based, is governmental coercion. * * * The voluntariness of a waiver of this privilege has always depended on the absence of police overreaching, not on "free choice" in any broader sense of the word. * * *
>
> [Connelly] urges this Court to adopt his "free will" rationale, and to find an attempted waiver invalid whenever the defendant feels compelled to waive his rights by reason of any compulsion, even if the compulsion does not flow from the police. But such treatment of the waiver issue would "cut this Court's holding in [*Miranda*] completely loose from its own explicitly stated rationale." *Miranda* protects defendants against government coercion leading them to surrender rights protected by the Fifth Amendment; it goes no further than that. [Connelly's] perception of coercion flowing from the "voice of God," however important or significant such a perception might be in other disciplines, is a matter to which the United States Constitution does not speak.

479 U.S. at 169–71, 107 S.Ct. at 523–24, 93 L.Ed.2d at 486–87.

Effectiveness of Waivers: Intelligence. Edwards made clear that the requirement of an intelligent or knowing waiver is separate from, and requires different proof than, the need for voluntariness.

Perhaps this should have been clear from Tague v. Louisiana, 444 U.S. 469, 100 S.Ct. 652, 62 L.Ed.2d 622 (1980). Tague's confession given during custodial interrogation was offered at his trial for robbery. At a pretrial hearing on the admissibility of the statement, the officer who had taken the confession testified that he had read Tague the *Miranda* rights from a card, that he could not presently remember what those rights were, that he could not recall whether he had asked Tague whether he understood the rights, and that he "couldn't say yes or no" whether he rendered any tests to determine whether Tague was literate or otherwise capable of understanding the rights. The confession was admitted and Tague was convicted. On appeal, the Supreme Court of Louisiana affirmed, reasoning that "absent a clear and readily apparent lack thereof, it can be presumed that a person has capacity to understand [the *Miranda* rights], and the burden is on the one claiming a lack of capacity to show that lack." Without oral argument and in a *per curiam* opinion, the Supreme Court reversed. The Louisiana courts had impermissibly relied upon a presumption that one given the *Miranda* warnings understands the rights involved; such a presumption is inconsistent with the burden placed by *Miranda* on the state to show a knowing and intelligent waiver of the rights. Turning to the facts of the case, the Court continued:

> In this case no evidence at all was introduced to prove that [Tague] knowingly and intelligently waived his rights before making the inculpatory statement. The statement was therefore inadmissible.

441 U.S. at 471, 100 S.Ct. at 653, 62 L.Ed.2d at 625. As *Edwards* reaffirmed the next year, *Tague* held that the prosecution must address and prove that a *Miranda* waiver was intelligent.

But what precisely must a suspect know or understand in order to render intelligent his decisions to forego the assistance of counsel, his right to remain silent, or both? The principal case in this subsection addresses this question.

Suppose a defendant's waiver is "unintelligent," but for reasons not attributable to law enforcement officers' misconduct. *Connelly* made clear a *Miranda* waiver cannot be rendered *involuntary* by the defendant's mental impairment, where there is no law enforcement misconduct. Is it possible, however, that even in the absence of police misconduct, such mental impairment might nevertheless prevent a suspect from adequately understanding his right to counsel and therefore render his decision to relinquish it *unintelligent*?

In *Connelly,* the Supreme Court noted the Colorado Supreme Court's opinion could be read as finding Connelly's waiver invalid "on other grounds." This was apparently a reference to the state court's comment that Connelly's mental impairment had rendered him unable to make an "intelligent" decision. The Colorado court's analysis was influenced by "its mistaken view of 'voluntariness' in the constitutional sense," the *Connelly* majority stated. It thus reversed the state court's judgment "in its entirety," although it commented that on remand the state court was free to reconsider other issues in a manner not inconsistent with the opinion of the Court. Justice Brennan, dissenting, construed the majority's comment as permitting the state court to find that despite the absence of any official compulsion, Connelly's mental illness demonstrated that the prosecution had failed to meet *Miranda's* requirement of a knowing and intelligent waiver.

Scope of Waiver. The scope of effective waivers, especially those of the right to counsel, may raise difficult questions. One such problem was presented by Wyrick v. Fields, 459 U.S. 42, 103 S.Ct. 394, 74 L.Ed.2d 214 (1982). Fields had agreed to a polygraph test and had waived his right to counsel during that procedure. After the examination, the agent who administered the examination told Fields there had been some deceit and asked Fields if he could explain why his answers were bothering him. In the resulting discussion, Fields made incriminating admissions. He argued that neither he nor the lawyer who advised him prior to the waiver anticipated questioning after the examination and, therefore, his waiver of counsel had not extended to such post-examination questioning. Rejecting this contention, the Court explained:

> [I]t would have been unreasonable for Fields and his attorneys to assume that Fields would not be informed of the polygraph readings and asked to explain any unfavorable results. Moreover, Fields had been informed that he could stop the questioning at any time, and could request at any time that his lawyer join him. Merely disconnecting the polygraph equipment could not remove this knowledge from Fields' mind.

459 U.S. 47–48, 103 S.Ct. at 396, 74 L.Ed.2d at 214. Does this mean that the scope of a waiver is not defined by what the defendant actually understood it would cover but rather by what, in the exercise of reasonable care, he should have known it would be treated by police as covering?

Empirical Information on Suspects' Understanding of Miranda. Consideration of whether the Supreme Court has most appropriately formulated *Miranda* waiver law may be facilitated by information concerning what suspects might in actual fact understand as a result of *Miranda* warnings.

Grisso, Juveniles' Capacity to Waive Miranda Rights: An Empirical Analysis, 68 Cal.L.Rev. 1134 (1980), for purposes of comparison with juveniles, studied the results of giving *Miranda* warnings to 203 adult parolees and 57 adults employed in custodial services and university and hospital maintenance crews. He concluded a significant proportion of these adults did not learn the underlying rights from the *Miranda* warnings. 42.3% of the subjects were able accurately to paraphrase all four of the *Miranda* rights after the warning; 57.7% were not. The most commonly misunderstood part of the warning concerned the right to the presence of counsel; 14.6% of the subjects were unable to paraphrase this accurately. In an effort to avoid the effect of facility in verbal expression, Geiss administered a true-false test containing 12 questions to the subjects. 76.5% received a score of 10–12 correct responses; another 18.9% scored 7 to 9 correct answers. But 4.6% of the subjects scored only 5 or 6 correct answers. A further test consisted of questioning the subjects concerning a hypothetical interrogation situation. 89–95% of the subjects recognized the adversarial nature of the interrogation, the role of the subject's lawyer in it, and the lawyers' need for full information concerning the events. But many of the subjects failed to understand the effect which the privilege against self-incrimination would have later in the courtroom. 42.9% believed that they would have to later explain their criminal involvement in court if questioned by the judge. This suggests a significant proportion of *Miranda* waivers may be influenced by the suspects' perception that they will later be compelled to answer questions concerning the situation. Such suspects might reason that since they will have to explain the situation to authorities at some point, they might as well do it during police questioning.

Moran v. Burbine

Supreme Court of the United States, 1986.
475 U.S. 412, 106 S.Ct. 1135, 89 L.Ed.2d 410.

■ JUSTICE O'CONNOR delivered the opinion of the Court.

After being informed of his rights pursuant to Miranda v. Arizona, 384 U.S. 436, 86 S.Ct. 1602, 16 L.Ed.2d 694 (1966), and after executing a series of written waivers, respondent confessed to the murder of a young woman. * * * The question presented is whether either the conduct of the police or respondent's ignorance of the attorney's efforts to reach him taints the validity of the waivers and therefore requires exclusion of the confessions.

I

On the morning of March 3, 1977, Mary Jo Hickey was found unconscious in a factory parking lot in Providence, Rhode Island. Suffering from injuries to her skull apparently inflicted by a metal pipe found at the scene, she was rushed to a nearby hospital. Three weeks later she died from her wounds.

Several months after her death, the Cranston, Rhode Island police arrested respondent and two others in connection with a local burglary. Shortly before the arrest, Detective Ferranti of the Cranston police force had learned from a confidential informant that the man responsible for Ms. Hickey's death lived at a certain address and went by the name of "Butch." Upon discovering that respondent lived at that address and was known by that name, Detective Ferranti informed respondent of his *Miranda* rights. When respondent refused to execute a written waiver, Detective Ferranti spoke separately with the two other suspects arrested on the breaking and entering charge and obtained statements further implicating respondent in Ms. Hickey's murder. At approximately 6:00 p.m., Detective Ferranti telephoned the police in Providence to convey the information he had uncovered. An hour later, three officers from that department arrived at the Cranston headquarters for the purpose of questioning respondent about the murder.

That same evening, at about 7:45 p.m., respondent's sister telephoned the Public Defender's Office to obtain legal assistance for her brother. Her sole concern was the breaking and entering charge, as she was unaware that respondent was then under suspicion for murder. She asked for Richard Casparian who had been scheduled to meet with respondent earlier that afternoon to discuss another charge unrelated to either the break-in or the murder. As soon as the conversation ended, the attorney who took the call attempted to reach Mr. Casparian. When those efforts were unsuccessful, she telephoned Allegra Munson, another Assistant Public Defender, and told her about respondent's arrest and his sister's subsequent request that the office represent him.

At 8:15 p.m., Ms. Munson telephoned the Cranston police station and asked that her call be transferred to the detective division. In the words of the Supreme Court of Rhode Island * * * the conversation proceeded as follows:

> "A male voice responded with the word 'Detectives.' Ms. Munson identified herself and asked if Brian Burbine was being held; the person responded affirmatively. Ms. Munson explained to the person that Burbine was represented by attorney Casparian who was not available; she further stated that she would act as Burbine's legal counsel in the event that the police intended to place him in a lineup or question him. The unidentified person told Ms. Munson that the police would not be questioning Burbine or putting him in a lineup and that they were through with him for the night. Ms. Munson was not informed that the Providence Police were at the Cranston police station or that Burbine was a suspect in Mary's murder."

At all relevant times, respondent was unaware of his sister's efforts to retain counsel and of the fact and contents of Ms. Munson's telephone conversation.

Less than an hour later, the police brought respondent to an interrogation room and conducted the first of a series of interviews concerning the murder. Prior to each session, respondent was informed of his *Miranda* rights, and on three separate occasions he signed a written form acknowledging that he understood his right to the presence of an attorney and explicitly indicating that he "[did] not want an attorney called or appointed for [him]" before he gave a statement. Uncontradicted evidence at the suppression hearing indicated that at least twice during the course of the evening, respondent was left in a room where he had access to a telephone, which he apparently declined to use. Eventually, respondent signed three written statements fully admitting to the murder.

Prior to trial, respondent moved to suppress the statements. The court denied the motion, finding that respondent had received the *Miranda* warnings and had "knowingly, intelligently, and voluntarily waived his privilege against self-incrimination [and] his right to counsel." Rejecting the contrary testimony of the police, the court found that Ms. Munson did telephone the detective bureau on the evening in question, but concluded that "there was no * * * conspiracy or collusion on the part of the Cranston Police Department to secrete this defendant from his attorney." In any event, the court held, the constitutional right to request the presence of an attorney belongs solely to the defendant and may not be asserted by his lawyer. Because the evidence was clear that respondent never asked for the services of an attorney, the telephone call had no

[handwritten margin notes:]
① Sister - attempting to get atty for breaking charges- not aware of murder issue
② Burbine does not want atty signs waiver
- police not aware of sisters efforts

relevance to the validity of the waiver or the admissibility of the statements.

The jury found respondent guilty of murder in the first degree, and he appealed to the Supreme Court of Rhode Island. A divided court rejected his contention that the Fifth and Fourteenth Amendments to the Constitution required the suppression of the inculpatory statements and affirmed the conviction. * * *

After unsuccessfully petitioning the United States District Court for the District of Rhode Island for a writ of habeas corpus, respondent appealed to the Court of Appeals for the First Circuit. That court reversed. * * *

We granted certiorari to decide whether a prearraignment confession preceded by an otherwise valid waiver must be suppressed either because the police misinformed an inquiring attorney about their plans concerning the suspect or because they failed to inform the suspect of the attorney's efforts to reach him. We now reverse.

* * *

II

* * *

Respondent * * * contends * * * that the confessions must be suppressed because the police's failure to inform him of the attorney's telephone call deprived him of information essential to his ability to knowingly waive his Fifth Amendment rights. In the alternative, he suggests that to fully protect the Fifth Amendment values served by *Miranda,* we should extend that decision to condemn the conduct of the Providence police. We address each contention in turn.

A

Echoing the standard first articulated in Johnson v. Zerbst, 304 U.S. 458, 464, 58 S.Ct. 1019, 1023, 82 L.Ed. 1461 (1938), *Miranda* holds that "[t]he defendant may waive effectuation" of the rights conveyed in the warnings "provided the waiver is made voluntarily, knowingly and intelligently." The inquiry has two distinct dimensions. First the relinquishment of the right must have been voluntary in the sense that it was the product of a free and deliberate choice rather than intimidation, coercion or deception. Second, the waiver must have been made with a full awareness both of the nature of the right being abandoned and the consequences of the decision to abandon it. Only if the "totality of the circumstances surrounding the interrogation" reveal both an uncoerced choice and the requisite level of comprehension may a court properly conclude that the *Miranda* rights have been waived.

Under this standard, we have no doubt that respondent validly waived his right to remain silent and to the presence of counsel. The voluntariness of the waiver is not at issue. As the Court of Appeals correctly acknowledged, the record is devoid of any suggestion that police resorted to physical or psychological pressure to elicit the statements. Indeed it appears that it was respondent, and not the police, who spontaneously initiated the conversation that led to the first and most damaging confession. Nor is there any question about respondent's comprehension of the full panoply of rights set out in the *Miranda* warnings and of the potential consequences of a decision to relinquish them. Nonetheless, the Court of Appeals believed that the "[d]eliberate or reckless" conduct of the police, in particular their failure to inform respondent of the telephone call, fatally undermined the validity of the otherwise proper waiver. We find this conclusion untenable as a matter of both logic and precedent.

Events occurring outside of the presence of the suspect and entirely unknown to him surely can have no bearing on the capacity to comprehend and knowingly relinquish a constitutional right. Under the analysis of the Court of Appeals, the same defendant, armed with the same information and confronted with precisely the same police conduct, would have knowingly waived his *Miranda* rights had a lawyer not telephoned the police station to inquire about his status. Nothing in any of our waiver decisions or in our understanding of the essential components of a valid waiver requires so incongruous a result. No doubt the additional information would have been useful to respondent; perhaps even it might have affected his decision to confess. But we have never read the Constitution to require that the police supply a suspect with a flow of information to help him calibrate his self interest in deciding whether to speak or stand by his rights. Once it is determined that a suspect's decision not to rely on his rights was uncoerced, that he at all times knew he could stand mute and request a lawyer, and that he was aware of the state's intention to use his statements to secure a conviction, the analysis is complete and the waiver is valid as a matter of law. The Court of Appeals' conclusion to the contrary was in error.

Rational

Nor do we believe that the level of the police's culpability in failing to inform respondent of the telephone call has any bearing on the validity of the waiver. In light of the state-court findings that there was no "conspiracy or collusion" on the part of the police, we have serious doubts about whether the Court of Appeals was free to conclude that their conduct constituted "deliberate or reckless irresponsibility." But whether intentional or inadvertent, the state of mind of the police is irrelevant to the question of the intelligence and voluntariness of respondent's election to abandon his rights. Although highly inappropriate, even deliberate deception of an attorney could not possibly affect a suspect's decision to waive his *Miranda* rights unless he were at least aware of the incident. Nor was the failure to inform respondent of the telephone call the kind of "trick[ery]" that can vitiate the validity of a waiver. Granting that the "deliberate or reckless" withholding of information is objectionable as a matter of ethics, such conduct is only relevant to the constitutional validity of a waiver if it deprives a defendant of knowledge essential to his ability to understand the nature of his rights and the consequences of abandoning them. Because respondent's voluntary decision to speak was made with full awareness and comprehension of all the information *Miranda* requires the police to convey, the waivers were valid.

B

At oral argument respondent acknowledged that a constitutional rule requiring the police to inform a suspect of an attorney's efforts to reach him would represent a significant extension of our precedents. He contends, however, that the conduct of the Providence police was so inimical to the Fifth Amendment values *Miranda* seeks to protect that we should read that decision to condemn their behavior. Regardless of any issue of waiver, he urges, the Fifth Amendment requires the reversal of a conviction if the police are less than forthright in their dealings with an attorney or if they fail to tell a suspect of a lawyer's unilateral efforts to contact him. Because the proposed modification ignores the underlying purposes of the *Miranda* rules and because we think that the decision as written strikes the proper balance between society's legitimate law enforcement interests and the protection of the defendant's Fifth Amendment rights, we decline the invitation to further extend *Miranda's* reach.

At the outset, while we share respondent's distaste for the deliberate misleading of an officer of the court, reading *Miranda* to forbid police deception of an *attorney* "would cut [the decision] completely loose from its own explicitly stated rationale." As is now well established, "[t]he * * * *Miranda* warnings are 'not themselves rights protected by the Constitution but [are] instead measures to insure that the [suspect's] right against compulsory self-incrimination [is] protected.'" Their objective is not to mold police conduct for its own sake. Nothing in the Constitution vests in us the authority to mandate a code of behavior for state officials wholly unconnected to any federal right or privilege. The purpose of the *Miranda* warnings instead is to dissipate the compulsion inherent in custodial interrogation and, in so doing, guard against abridgement of the suspect's Fifth Amendment rights. Clearly, a rule that focuses on how the police treat an attorney—conduct that has no relevance at all to the degree of compulsion experienced by the defendant during interrogation—would ignore both *Miranda's* mission and its only source of legitimacy.

Nor are we prepared to adopt a rule requiring that the police inform a suspect of an attorney's efforts to reach him. While such a rule might add marginally to *Miranda's* goal of dispelling the compulsion inherent in custodial interrogation, overriding practical considerations counsel against its adoption. As we have stressed on numerous occasions, "[o]ne of the principal advantages" of *Miranda* is the ease and clarity of its application. We have little doubt that the approach urged by respondent and endorsed by the Court of Appeals would have the inevitable consequence of muddying *Miranda's* otherwise relatively clear waters. The legal questions it would spawn are legion: To what extent should the police be held accountable for knowing that the accused has counsel? Is it enough that someone in the station house knows, or must the interrogating officer himself know of counsel's efforts to contact the suspect? Do counsel's efforts to talk to the suspect concerning one criminal investigation trigger the obligation to inform the defendant before interrogation may proceed on a wholly separate matter? We are unwilling to modify *Miranda* in manner that would so clearly undermine the decision's central "virtue of informing police and prosecutors with specificity * * * what they may do in conducting [a] custodial interrogation, and of informing courts under what circumstances statements obtained during such interrogation are not admissible.''

Moreover, problems of clarity to one side, reading *Miranda* to require the police in each instance to inform a suspect of an attorney's efforts to reach him would work a substantial and, we think, inappropriate shift in the subtle balance struck in that decision. Custodial interrogations implicate two competing concerns. On the one hand, ''the need for police questioning as a tool for effective enforcement of criminal laws'' cannot be doubted. Admissions of guilt are more than merely ''desirable''; they are essential to society's compelling interest in finding, convicting and punishing those who violate the law. On the other hand, the Court has recognized that the interrogation process is ''inherently coercive'' and that, as a consequence, there exists a substantial risk that the police will inadvertently traverse the fine line between legitimate efforts to elicit admissions and constitutionally impermissible compulsion. *Miranda* attempted to reconcile these opposing concerns by giving the *defendant* the power to exert some control over the course of the interrogation. Declining to adopt the more extreme position that the actual presence of a lawyer was necessary to dispel the coercion inherent in custodial interrogation, the Court found that the suspect's Fifth Amendment rights could be adequately protected by less intrusive means. Police questioning, often an essential part of the investigatory process, could continue in its traditional form, the Court held, but only if the suspect clearly understood that, at any time, he could bring the proceeding to a halt or, short of that, call in an attorney to give advice and monitor the conduct of his interrogators.

The position urged by respondent would upset this carefully drawn approach in a manner that is both unnecessary for the protection of the Fifth Amendment privilege and injurious to legitimate law enforcement. Because, as *Miranda* holds, full comprehension of the rights to remain silent and request an attorney are sufficient to dispel whatever coercion is inherent in the interrogation process, a rule requiring the police to inform the suspect of an attorney's efforts to contact him would contribute to the protection of the Fifth Amendment privilege only incidentally, if at all. This minimal benefit, however, would come at a substantial cost to society's legitimate and substantial interest in securing admissions of guilt. Indeed, the very premise of the Court of Appeals was not that awareness of Ms. Munson's phone call would have dissipated the coercion of the interrogation room, but that it might have convinced respondent not to speak at all. Because neither the letter nor purposes of *Miranda* require this additional handicap on otherwise permissible investigatory efforts, we are unwilling to expand the *Miranda* rules to require the police to keep the suspect abreast of the status of his legal representation.

We acknowledge that a number of state courts have reached a contrary conclusion. * * * Nothing we say today disables the States from adopting different requirements for the conduct of its employees and officials as a matter of state law. We hold only that the Court of Appeals erred in construing the Fifth Amendment to the Federal Constitution to require the exclusion of respondent's three confessions.

IV

Finally, respondent contends that the conduct of the police was so offensive as to deprive him of the fundamental fairness guaranteed by the Due Process Clause of the Fourteenth Amendment. Focusing primarily on the impropriety of conveying false information to an attorney, he invites us to declare that such behavior should be condemned as violative of canons fundamental to the " 'traditions and conscience of our people.' " Rochin v. California, 342 U.S. 165, 169, 72 S.Ct. 205, 208, 96 L.Ed. 183 (1952). We do not question that on facts more egregious than those presented here police deception might rise to a level of a due process violation. * * * We hold only that, on these facts, the challenged conduct falls short of the kind of misbehavior that so shocks the sensibilities of civilized society as to warrant a federal intrusion into the criminal processes of the States.

We hold therefore that the Court of Appeals erred in finding that the Federal Constitution required the exclusion of the three inculpatory statements. Accordingly, we reverse and remand for proceedings consistent with this opinion.

So ordered.

■ JUSTICE STEVENS, with whom JUSTICE BRENNAN and JUSTICE MARSHALL join, dissenting.

* * *

II

Well-settled principles of law lead inexorably to the conclusion that the failure to inform Burbine of the call from his attorney makes the subsequent waiver of his constitutional rights invalid. * * * [T]his Court has sometimes relied on a case-by-case totality of the circumstances analysis. We have found, however, that some custodial interrogation situations require strict presumptions against the validity of a waiver. *Miranda* established that a waiver is not valid in the absence of certain warnings. * * * In these circumstances, the waiver is invalid as a matter of law * * *. Like the failure to give warnings * * *, police deception of a suspect through omission of information regarding attorney communications greatly exacerbates the inherent problems of incommunicado interrogation and requires a clear principle to safeguard the presumption against the waiver of constitutional rights. As in those situations [involving a failure to warn], the police deception should render a subsequent waiver invalid.

* * *

III

The Court makes the * * * argument that requiring police to inform a suspect of his attorney's communications to and about him is not required because it would upset the careful "balance" of *Miranda*. Despite its earlier notion that the attorney's call is an "outside event" that has "no bearing" on a knowing and intelligent waiver, the majority does acknowledge that information of attorney Munson's call "would have been useful to respondent" and "might have affected his decision to confess." Thus, a rule requiring the police to inform a suspect of an attorney's call would have two predictable effects. It would serve *"Miranda's* goal of dispelling the compulsion inherent in custodial interrogation" and it would disserve the goal of custodial interrogation because it would result in fewer confessions. By a process of balancing these two concerns, the Court finds the benefit to the individual outweighed by the "substantial cost to society's legitimate and substantial interest in securing admissions of guilt."

The Court's balancing approach is profoundly misguided. The cost of suppressing evidence of guilt will always make the value of a procedural safeguard appear "minimal," "marginal," or "incremental." Indeed, the value of any trial at all seems like a "procedural technicality" when balanced against the interest in administering prompt justice to a murderer or a rapist caught redhanded. The individual interest in procedural safeguards that minimize the risk of error is easily discounted when the fact of guilt appears certain beyond doubt.

What is the cost of requiring the police to inform a suspect of his attorney's call? It would decrease the likelihood that custodial interrogation will enable the police to obtain a confession. This is certainly a real cost, but it is the same cost that this Court has repeatedly found necessary to preserve the character of our free society and our rejection of an inquisitorial system. * * *

If the Court's cost benefit analysis were sound, it would justify a repudiation of the right to a warning about counsel itself. There is only a difference in degree between a presumption that advice about the immediate availability of a lawyer would not affect the voluntariness of a decision to confess, and a presumption that every citizen knows that he has a right to remain silent and therefore no warnings of any kind are needed. In either case, the withholding of information serves precisely the same law enforcement interests. And in both cases, the cost can be described as nothing more than an incremental increase in the risk that an individual will make an unintelligent waiver of his rights.

* * *

IV

The Court also argues that a rule requiring the police to inform a suspect of an attorney's efforts to reach him would have an additional cost: it would undermine the "clarity" of the rule of the *Miranda* case. This argument is not supported by any reference to the experience in the States that have adopted such a rule. * * *

* * *

V

At the time attorney Munson made her call to the Cranston Police Station, she was acting as Burbine's attorney. Under ordinary principles of agency law the deliberate deception of Munson was tantamount to deliberate deception of her client. If an attorney makes a mistake in the course of her representation of her client, the client must accept the consequences of that mistake. It is equally clear that when an attorney makes an inquiry on behalf of her client, the client is entitled to a truthful answer. Surely the client must have the same remedy for a false representation to his lawyer that he would have if he were acting *pro se* and had propounded the question himself.

* * *

The possible reach of the Court's opinion is stunning. For the majority seems to suggest that police may deny counsel all access to a client who is being held. * * * [I]t has been widely accepted that police may not simply deny attorneys access to their clients who are in custody. * * * The Court today seems to assume that this view was error—that, from the federal constitutional perspective, the lawyer's access is, as a question from the Court put it in oral argument, merely "a matter of prosecutorial grace."
* * *

VI

The Court devotes precisely five sentences to its conclusion that the police interference in the attorney's representation of Burbine did not violate the Due Process Clause. In the majority's view, the due process analysis is a simple "shock the conscience" test. Finding its conscience troubled, but not shocked, the majority rejects the due process challenge.

* * *

In my judgment, police interference in the attorney-client relationship is the type of governmental misconduct on a matter of central importance to the administration of justice that the Due Process Clause prohibits. Just as the police cannot impliedly promise a suspect that his silence will not be used against him and then proceed to break that promise, so too police cannot tell a suspect's attorney that they will not question the suspect and then proceed to question him. Just as the government cannot conceal from a suspect material and exculpatory evidence, so too the government cannot conceal from a suspect the material fact of his attorney's communication.

* * *

VII

This case turns on a proper appraisal of the role of the lawyer in our society. If a lawyer is seen as a nettlesome obstacle to the pursuit of wrongdoers—as in an inquisitorial society—then the Court's decision today makes a good deal of sense. If a lawyer is seen as an aid to the understanding and protection of constitutional rights—as in an accusatorial society—then today's decision makes no sense at all.

Like the conduct of the police in the Cranston station on the evening of June 29, 1977, the Court's opinion today serves the goal of insuring that the perpetrator of a vile crime is punished. Like the police on that June night as well, however, the Court has trampled on well-established legal principles and flouted the spirit of our accusatorial system of justice.

I respectfully dissent.

NOTES

1. **Knowledge of Subject Matter of Interrogation.** A suspect can apparently effectively waive the *Miranda* rights concerning an interrogation even if that suspect fails to understand the subjects the officers will purse by the interrogation.

In Colorado v. Spring, 479 U.S. 564, 107 S.Ct. 851, 93 L.Ed.2d 954 (1987), an informant told officers of the federal Bureau of Alcohol, Tobacco, and Firearms (ATF) that John Spring was engaged in the transportation of stolen firearms and admitted to the informant he had once shot a companion during a hunting trip in Colorado. The agents set up a "sting" operation in Kansas City, Missouri, and, during a purchase of firearms from Spring, the agents arrested him. Agents advised of his *Miranda* rights at the scene of the arrest. After being taken to the ATF office in Kansas City, he was again advised of his rights and signed a written form stating he understood and waived his rights and he was willing to answer questions and make a statement. After questioning him about the firearms transaction, the ATF agents asked Spring about homicides. He "ducked his head" and mumbled, "I shot another guy once." But when asked specifically about the Colorado killing, he "paused," "ducked his head again," and denied the shooting. The interview ended.

About two months later, Colorado law enforcement officials interviewed Spring while he remained in custody on the federal charges. He was given his *Miranda* warnings and signed another written form indicating he understood his rights and was willing to waive them. When the officers told him they wished to question him about the Colorado homicide, Spring responded that he wanted to "get it off his chest" and confessed to the murder. A written statement was prepared and Springs read, edited and signed it. The Colorado Supreme Court held that admission of Spring's written statement in his trial for the murder violated *Miranda*. His waiver of *Miranda* rights during the interview with ATF agents was not voluntary and intelligent, the state tribunal reasoned, because the agents failed to inform him that the questioning would involve the homicide and such a failure to inform the suspect of the offenses at issue is a factor in evaluating voluntariness and intelligence. His written statement during the later interview with state officers, in turn, was the "fruit" of his earlier and improper interrogation.

The Supreme Court reversed, reasoning in an opinion by Justice Powell that no violation of *Miranda* occurred during the interview of Spring by the ATF agents:

[T]here is no allegation that Spring failed to understand the basic privilege guaranteed by the Fifth Amendment. Nor is there any allegation that he misunderstood the consequences of speaking freely to the law enforcement officials. * * * [T]he trial court was indisputably correct in finding that Spring's waiver was made knowingly and intelligently within the meaning of *Miranda*.

* * *

* * * We have held that a valid waiver does not require that an individual be informed of all information "useful" in making his decision or all information that "might ... affec[t] his decision to confess." Moran v. Burbine, 475 U.S. [412, 422, 106 S.Ct. 1135, 1142, 89 L.Ed.2d 410 (1986)]. * * * [This] additional information could affect only the wisdom of a *Miranda* waiver, not its essentially voluntary and knowing nature. Accordingly, the failure of law enforcement officials to inform Spring of the subject matter of the interrogation could not affect Spring's decision to waive his Fifth Amendment privilege in a constitutionally significant manner.

* * *

[W]e hold that a suspect's awareness of all the possible subjects of questioning in advance of interrogation is not relevant to determining whether the suspect voluntarily, knowingly, and intelligently waived his Fifth Amendment privilege.

479 U.S. at 575–77, 107 S.Ct. at 858–59, 93 L.Ed.2d at 966–68.

2. **Limited or Qualified Waiver.** Can a suspect limit what police officers can do during an interrogation session by qualifying or limiting the waiver? One Supreme Court decision suggests so.

In Connecticut v. Barrett, 479 U.S. 523, 107 S.Ct. 828, 93 L.Ed.2d 920 (1987), Barrett signed an acknowledgment that he had been given the *Miranda* warnings. He then stated to the officers several times that he would not give them any written statement, at least until his lawyer was present. He added, however, that he had "no problem" in talking with them about the incident for which he had been arrested. During the following interrogation sessions, he made oral admissions of involvement in a sexual assault. At trial, testimony concerning these admissions was permitted over defense objection. The state appellate court—emphasizing that requests for counsel are not to be narrowly construed—held that Barrett's response to his *Miranda* warnings invoked his right to counsel and the subsequent conversations resulting in his oral admissions constituted prohibited interrogation without the presence of an attorney. The Supreme Court reversed:

> Barrett's limited requests for counsel * * * were accompanied by affirmative announcements of his willingness to speak with the authorities. The fact that officials took the opportunity provided by Barrett to obtain an oral confession is quite consistent with the Fifth Amendment. *Miranda* gives the defendant a right to choose between speech and silence, and Barrett chose to speak. * * * Here * * * Barrett made clear his intentions, and they were honored by police. To conclude that [Barrett] invoked his right to counsel for all purposes requires not a broad interpretation of an ambiguous statement, but a disregard of the ordinary meaning of [Barrett's] statement.

479 U.S. at 529–30, 107 S.Ct. at 832, 93 L.Ed.2d at 928. Justice Brennan concurred, explaining "a partial waiver of the right to counsel, without more, invariably will be ambiguous." But here, Barrett's partial waiver was accompanied by express waiver of his right to silence, which removed the ambiguity.

3. **Reapproach of Suspect Who Invoked Right to Silence.** A suspect who invokes the right to remain silent raises no bar to being reapproached by officers, as is discussed in subsection B(3) of this chapter. Under Michigan v. Mosley, 423 U.S. 96, 96 S.Ct. 321, 46 L.Ed.2d 313 (1975), however, the fact that the suspect was reapproached after so invoking that right may increase the prosecution's burden of proving that his waivers were effective.

After Mosley was arrested, a Detective Cowie sought to question him about a specific robbery of a White Tower Restaurant. When Mosley said he did not want to answer any questions about the robbery, Cowie ceased the questioning and had Mosley taken to a cell. Several hours later, another officer—Detective Hill—had Mosley brought to an interrogation room for questioning concerning the fatal shooting of one Leroy Williams during a robbery of the 101 Ranch Bar. Hill gave Mosley *Miranda* warnings and Mosley signed a notification form. During the following 15 minute interrogation, Mosley admitted being involved in the slaying. Addressing the prosecution's ability to use that admission in evidence, the Supreme Court first determined that a suspect's invocation of his right to remain silent "can[not] sensibly be read to create a *per se* proscription of indefinite duration upon any further questioning by any police officer on any subject, once the person in custody has indicated a desire to remain silent." It then continued:

We * * * conclude that the admissibility of statements obtained after the person in custody has decided to remain silent depends under *Miranda* on whether his "right to cut off questioning" was "scrupulously honored."

A review of the circumstances leading to Mosley's confession reveals that his "right to cut off questioning" was fully respected in this case. Before his initial interrogation, Mosley was carefully advised that he was under no obligation to answer any questions and could remain silent if he wished. He orally acknowledged that he understood the *Miranda* warnings and then signed a printed notification-of-rights form. When Mosley stated that he did not want to discuss the robberies, Detective Cowie immediately ceased the interrogation and did not try either to resume the questioning or in any way to persuade Mosley to reconsider his position. After an interval of more than two hours, Mosley was questioned by another police officer at another location about an unrelated holdup murder. He was given full and complete *Miranda* warnings at the outset of the second interrogation. He was thus reminded again that he could remain silent and could consult with a lawyer, and was carefully given a full and fair opportunity to exercise these options. The subsequent questioning did not undercut Mosley's previous decision not to answer Detective Cowie's inquiries. Detective Hill did not resume the interrogation about the White Tower Restaurant robbery * * *, but instead focused exclusively on the Leroy Williams homicide, a crime different in nature and in time and place of occurrence from the robberies for which Mosley had been arrested and interrogated by Detective Cowie. Although it is not clear from the record how much Detective Hill knew about the earlier interrogation, his questioning of Mosley about an unrelated homicide was quite consistent with a reasonable interpretation of Mosley's earlier refusal to answer any questions about the robberies.

This is not a case, therefore, where the police failed to honor a decision of a person in custody to cut off questioning, either by refusing to discontinue the interrogation upon request or by persisting in repeated efforts to wear down his resistance and make him change his mind. In contrast to such practices, the police here immediately ceased the interrogation, resumed questioning only after the passage of a significant period of time and the provision of a fresh set of warnings, and restricted the second interrogation to a crime that had not been a subject of the earlier interrogation.

423 U.S. at 104–06, 96 S.Ct. 326–27, 46 L.Ed.2d at 321–22.

4. **Effect of Deception on Effectiveness of Waivers.** What is the effect of police officers' deception before or during interrogation to which *Miranda* applies? The issue was urged in *Spring*, discussed in note 1 above, but the Court held that it was not raised. The ATF agents' failure to inform Spring that he would be questioned about the homicide did not constitute "trickery":

This Court has never held that mere silence by law enforcement officials as to the subject matter of an interrogation is "trickery" sufficient to invalidate a suspect's waiver of *Miranda* rights, and we expressly decline to so hold today.

479 U.S. at 576, 107 S.Ct. at 858, 93 L.Ed.2d at 967. Therefore it was not addressing, the Court noted, the validity of waivers when law enforcement officials made "an affirmative misrepresentation * * * as to the scope of the interrogation * * *."

Miranda itself contains language suggesting that waivers will be rendered ineffective by proof that the defendant "was * * * tricked * * * into [the] waiver." Frazier v. Cupp, discussed in the Editors' Introduction to part A of this chapter, addressed the effect of deception upon due process voluntariness. Although it was decided after *Miranda*, *Frazier* did not acknowledge potential tension between its holding and the discussion in *Miranda*. Perhaps, then, *Frazier's* approach is not necessarily applicable when the issue is the validity of a *Miranda* waiver.

5. **Intoxication.** What effect does a suspect's intoxication have upon the effectiveness of a waiver of the *Miranda* rights? In Berkemer v. McCarty, 468 U.S. 420, 104 S.Ct. 3138, 82 L.Ed.2d 317 (1984), reprinted in subsection B(2)(b) of this chapter, the Court noted:

> [W]e are asked to consider what a State must do in order to demonstrate that a suspect who might have been under the influence of drugs or alcohol when subjected to custodial interrogation nevertheless understood and freely waived his constitutional rights. * * * We prefer to defer resolution of [this matter] to a case in which law enforcement authorities have at least attempted to inform the suspect of rights to which he is indisputably entitled.

468 U.S. at 434 n. 21, 104 S.Ct. at 3147 n. 21, 82 L.Ed.2d at 331 n. 21. In light of *Connelly,* discussed in the Editors' Introduction to this subsection, is intoxication relevant at all in the absence of law enforcement overreaching of some sort?

6. The requirements of an intelligent *Miranda* waiver are also addressed in Oregon v. Elstad, reprinted in the next subsection. Reevaluate what is necessary for a waiver to be effective after considering *Elstad.*

5. "FRUITS" OF AN INADMISSIBLE CONFESSION

Fourth Amendment case law has firmly established that when a defendant shows a violation of his Fourth Amendment rights, Mapp v. Ohio and its progeny require exclusion of what is often called all "fruit of the poisonous tree." This requirement, and various limitations and exceptions that might affect it, were developed in Part B of Chapter 1. The principal case in this subsection, however, establishes that the "fruit of the poisonous tree" rule is not necessarily applicable in some situations in which the poisonous tree is a violation of the Supreme Court's case law dealing with interrogation limitations.

Oregon v. Elstad

Supreme Court of the United States, 1985.
470 U.S. 298, 105 S.Ct. 1285, 84 L.Ed.2d 222.

■ JUSTICE O'CONNOR delivered the opinion of the Court.

Issue

This case requires us to decide whether an initial failure of law enforcement officers to administer the warnings required by Miranda v. Arizona, 384 U.S. 436, 86 S.Ct. 1602, 16 L.Ed.2d 694 (1966), without more, "taints" subsequent admissions made after a suspect has been fully advised of and has waived his *Miranda* rights. * * *

I

In December, 1981, the home of Mr. and Mrs. Gilbert Gross, in the town of Salem, Polk County, Ore., was burglarized. Missing were art objects and furnishings valued at $150,000. A witness to the burglary contacted the Polk County Sheriff's Office, implicating respondent Michael Elstad, an 18-year-old neighbor and friend of the Grosses' teenage son. Thereupon, Officers Burke and McAllister went to the home of respondent Elstad, with a warrant for his arrest. Elstad's mother answered the door.

She led the officers to her son's room where he lay on his bed, clad in shorts and listening to his stereo. The officers asked him to get dressed and to accompany them into the living room. Officer McAllister asked respondent's mother to step into the kitchen, where he explained that they had a warrant for her son's arrest for the burglary of a neighbor's residence. Officer Burke remained with Elstad in the living room. He later testified:

> "I sat down with Mr. Elstad and I asked him if he was aware of why Detective McAllister and myself were there to talk with him. He stated no, he had no idea why we were there. I then asked him if he knew a person by the name of Gross, and he said yes, he did, and also added that he heard that there was a robbery at the Gross house. And at that point I told Mr. Elstad that I felt he was involved in that, and he looked at me and stated, 'Yes, I was there.' "

The officers then escorted Elstad to the back of the patrol car. As they were about to leave for the Polk County Sheriff's office, Elstad's father arrived home and came to the rear of the patrol car. The officers advised him that his son was a suspect in the burglary. Officer Burke testified that Mr. Elstad became quite agitated, opened the rear door of the car and admonished his son: "I told you that you were going to get into trouble. You wouldn't listen to me. You never learn."

Elstad was transported to the Sheriff's headquarters and approximately one hour later, Officers Burke and McAllister joined him in McAllister's office. McAllister then advised respondent for the first time of his *Miranda* rights, reading from a standard card. Respondent indicated he understood his rights, and, having these rights in mind, wished to speak with the officers. Elstad gave a full statement, explaining that he had known that the Gross family was out of town and had been paid to lead several acquaintances to the Gross residence and show them how to gain entry through a defective sliding glass door. The statement was typed, reviewed by respondent, read back to him for correction, initialed and signed by Elstad and both officers. As an afterthought, Elstad added and initialed the sentence, "After leaving the house Robby & I went back to [the] van & Robby handed me a small bag of grass." Respondent concedes that the officers made no threats or promises either at his residence or at the Sheriff's office.

Respondent was charged with first-degree burglary. He was represented at trial by retained counsel. Elstad waived his right to a jury and his case was tried by a Circuit Court Judge. Respondent moved at once to suppress his oral statement and signed confession. He contended that the statement he made in response to questioning at his house "let the cat out of the bag," citing United States v. Bayer, 331 U.S. 532, 67 S.Ct. 1394, 91 L.Ed. 1654 (1947), and tainted the subsequent confession as "fruit of the poisonous tree," citing Wong Sun v. United States, 371 U.S. 471, 83 S.Ct. 407, 9 L.Ed.2d 441 (1963). The judge ruled that the statement, "I was there," had to be excluded because the defendant had not been advised of his *Miranda* rights. The written confession taken after Elstad's arrival at the Sheriff's office, however, was admitted in evidence. The court found:

> "[H]is written statement was given freely, voluntarily and knowingly by the defendant after he had waived his right to remain silent and

have counsel present which waiver was evidenced by the card which the defendant had signed. [It] was not tainted in any way by the previous brief statement between the defendant and the Sheriff's Deputies that had arrested him."

Elstad was found guilty of burglary in the first degree. He received a 5year sentence and was ordered to pay $18,000 in restitution.

Following his conviction, respondent appealed to the Oregon Court of Appeals * * *. The Court of Appeals reversed respondent's conviction, identifying the crucial constitutional inquiry as "whether there was a sufficient break in the stream of events between [the] inadmissible statement and the written confession to insulate the latter statement from the effect of what went before." The Oregon court concluded:

"Regardless of the absence of actual compulsion, the coercive impact of the unconstitutionally obtained statement remains, because in a defendant's mind it has sealed his fate. It is this impact that must be dissipated in order to make a subsequent confession admissible. In determining whether it has been dissipated, lapse of time, and change of place from the original surroundings are the most important considerations."

Because of the brief period separating the two incidents, the "cat was sufficiently out of the bag to exert a coercive impact on [respondent's] later admissions."

The State of Oregon petitioned the Oregon Supreme Court for review, and review was declined. This Court granted certiorari to consider the question whether the Self–Incrimination Clause of the Fifth Amendment requires the suppression of a confession, made after proper *Miranda* warnings and a valid waiver of rights, solely because the police had obtained an earlier voluntary but unwarned admission from the defendant.

II

The arguments advanced in favor of suppression of respondent's written confession rely heavily on metaphor. One metaphor, familiar from the Fourth Amendment context, would require that respondent's confession, regardless of its integrity, voluntariness, and probative value, be suppressed as the "tainted fruit of the poisonous tree" of the *Miranda* violation. A second metaphor questions whether a confession can be truly voluntary once the "cat is out of the bag." Taken out of context, each of these metaphors can be misleading. They should not be used to obscure fundamental differences between the role of the Fourth Amendment exclusionary rule and the function of *Miranda* in guarding against the prosecutorial use of compelled statements as prohibited by the Fifth Amendment. The Oregon court assumed and respondent here contends that a failure to administer *Miranda* warnings necessarily breeds the same consequences as police infringement of a constitutional right, so that evidence uncovered following an unwarned statement must be suppressed as "fruit of the poisonous tree." We believe this view misconstrues the nature of the protections afforded by *Miranda* warnings and therefore misreads the consequences of police failure to supply them.

A

* * *

Respondent's contention that his confession was tainted by the earlier failure of the police to provide *Miranda* warnings and must be excluded as "fruit of the poisonous tree" assumes the existence of a constitutional violation. This figure of speech is drawn from Wong Sun v. United States, in which the Court held that evidence and witnesses discovered as a result of a search in violation of the Fourth Amendment must be excluded from evidence. * * *

But * * * a procedural *Miranda* violation differs in significant respects from violations of the Fourth Amendment, which have traditionally mandated a broad application of the "fruits" doctrine. * * *

The *Miranda* exclusionary rule * * * serves the Fifth Amendment and sweeps more broadly than the Fifth Amendment itself. It may be triggered even in the absence of a Fifth Amendment violation. The Fifth Amendment prohibits use by the prosecution in its case in chief only of *compelled* testimony. Failure to administer *Miranda* warnings creates a presumption of compulsion. Consequently, unwarned statements that are otherwise voluntary within the meaning of the Fifth Amendment must nevertheless be excluded from evidence under *Miranda*. Thus, in the individual case, *Miranda's* preventive medicine provides a remedy even to the defendant who has suffered no identifiable constitutional harm.

But the *Miranda* presumption, though irrebutable for purposes of the prosecution's case in chief, does not require that the statements and their fruits be discarded as inherently tainted. Despite the fact that patently *voluntary* statements taken in violation of *Miranda* must be excluded from the prosecution's case, the presumption of coercion does not bar their use for impeachment purposes on cross-examination. Harris v. New York, 401 U.S. 222, 91 S.Ct. 643, 28 L.Ed.2d 1 (1971). * * *

In Michigan v. Tucker, [417 U.S. 433, 94 S.Ct. 2357, 41 L.Ed.2d 182 (1974)], the Court was asked to extend the *Wong Sun* fruits doctrine to suppress the testimony of a witness for the prosecution whose identity was discovered as the result of a statement taken from the accused without benefit of full *Miranda* warnings. * * * [T]he *Tucker* Court noted that neither the general goal of deterring improper police practices nor the Fifth Amendment goal of assuring trustworthy evidence would be served by suppression of the witness' testimony. The unwarned confession must, of course, be suppressed, but the Court ruled that introduction of the third-party witness' testimony did not violate Tucker's Fifth Amendment rights.

We believe that this reasoning applies with equal force when the alleged "fruit" of a noncoercive *Miranda* violation is neither a witness nor an article of evidence but the accused's own voluntary testimony. As in *Tucker*, the absence of any coercion or improper tactics undercuts the twin rationales—trustworthiness and deterrence—for a broader rule. * * * If errors are made by law enforcement officers in administering the prophylactic *Miranda* procedures, they should not breed the same irremediable consequences as police infringement of the Fifth Amendment itself. It is an unwarranted extension of *Miranda* to hold that a simple failure to administer the warnings, unaccompanied by any actual coercion or other circumstances calculated to undermine the suspect's ability to exercise his free will so taints the investigatory process that a subsequent voluntary and informed waiver is ineffective for some indeterminate period. Though *Miranda* requires that the unwarned admission must be suppressed, the admissibility of any subsequent statement should turn in these circumstances solely on whether it is knowingly and voluntarily made.

B

The Oregon court, however, believed that the unwarned remark compromised the voluntariness of respondent's later confession. It was the court's view that the prior *answer* and not the unwarned questioning impaired respondent's ability to give a valid waiver and that only lapse of time and change of place could dissipate what it termed the "coercive impact" of the inadmissible statement. When a prior statement is actually coerced, the time that passes between confessions, the change in place of interrogations, and the change in identity of the interrogators all bear on whether that coercion has carried over into the second confession. The failure of police to administer *Miranda* warnings does not mean that the statements received have actually been coerced, but only that courts will presume the privilege against compulsory self-incrimination has not been intelligently exercised. Of the courts that have considered whether a properly warned confession must be suppressed because it was preceded by an unwarned but clearly voluntary admission, the majority have explicitly or implicitly recognized that [the] requirement of a break in the stream of events is inapposite. In these circumstances, a careful and thorough administration of *Miranda* warnings serves to cure the condition that rendered the unwarned statement inadmissible. The warning conveys the relevant information and thereafter the suspect's choice whether to exercise his privilege to remain silent should ordinarily be viewed as an "act of free will." Wong Sun v. United States, 371 U.S., at 486, 83 S.Ct., at 416.

The Oregon court nevertheless identified a subtle form of lingering compulsion, the psychological impact of the suspect's conviction that he has let the cat out of the bag and, in so doing, has sealed his own fate. But endowing the psychological effects of *voluntary* unwarned admissions with constitutional implications would, practically speaking, disable the police from obtaining the suspect's informed cooperation even when the official coercion proscribed by the Fifth Amendment played no part in either his warned or unwarned confessions. * * *

This Court has never held that the psychological impact of voluntary disclosure of a guilty secret qualifies as state compulsion or compromises the voluntariness of a subsequent informed waiver. The Oregon court, by adopting this expansive view of Fifth Amendment compulsion, effectively immunizes a suspect who responds to pre-*Miranda* warning questions from the consequences of his subsequent informed waiver of the privilege of remaining silent. This immunity comes at a high cost to legitimate law enforcement activity, while adding little desirable protection to the individual's interest in not being *compelled* to testify against himself. When neither the initial nor the subsequent admission is coerced, little justification exists for permitting the highly probative evidence of a voluntary confession to be irretrievably lost to the factfinder.

There is a vast difference between the direct consequences flowing from coercion of a confession by physical violence or other deliberate means calculated to break the suspect's will and the uncertain consequences of disclosure of a "guilty secret" freely given in response to an unwarned but noncoercive question, as in this case. * * * Certainly, in respondent's case, the causal connection between any psychological disadvantage created by his admission and his ultimate decision to cooperate is speculative and attenuated at best. It is difficult to tell with certainty what motivates a suspect to speak. A suspect's confession may be traced to factors as disparate as "a prearrest event such as a visit with a minister," Dunaway v. New York, [442 U.S. 200, 220, 99 S.Ct. 2248, 2261, 60 L.Ed.2d 824, 841 (1979)] (STEVENS, J., concurring), or an intervening event such as the exchange of words respondent had with his father. We must conclude that, absent deliberately coercive or improper tactics in obtaining the initial statement, the mere fact that a suspect has made an unwarned admission does not warrant a presumption of compulsion. A subsequent administration of *Miranda* warnings to a suspect who has given a voluntary but unwarned statement ordinarily should suffice to remove the conditions that precluded admission of the earlier statement. In such circumstances, the finder of fact may reasonably conclude that the suspect made a rational and intelligent choice whether to waive or invoke his rights.

III

Though belated, the reading of respondent's rights was undeniably complete. McAllister testified that he read the *Miranda* warnings aloud from a printed card and recorded Elstad's responses. There is no question that respondent knowingly and voluntarily waived his right to remain silent before he described his participation in the burglary. It is also beyond dispute that respondent's earlier remark was voluntary, within the meaning of the Fifth Amendment. Neither the environment nor the manner of either "interrogation" was coercive. The initial conversation took place at midday, in the living room area of respondent's own home, with his mother in the kitchen area, a few steps away. Although in retrospect the officers testified that respondent was then in custody, at the time he made his statement he had not been informed that he was under arrest. The arresting officers' testimony indicates that the brief stop in the living room before proceeding to the station house was not to interrogate the suspect but to notify his mother of the reason for his arrest.

The state has conceded the issue of custody and thus we must assume that Burke breached *Miranda* procedures in failing to administer *Miranda* warnings before initiating the discussion in the living room. This breach may have been the result of confusion as to whether the brief exchange qualified as "custodial interrogation" or it may simply have reflected Burke's reluctance to initiate an alarming police procedure before McAllister had spoken with respondent's mother. Whatever the reason for Burke's oversight, the incident had none of the earmarks of coercion. Nor did the officers exploit the unwarned admission to pressure respondent into waiving his right to remain silent.

Respondent, however, has argued that he was unable to give a fully *informed* waiver of his rights because he was unaware that his prior statement could not be used against him. Respondent suggests that Deputy McAllister, to cure this deficiency, should have added an additional warning to those given him at the Sheriff's office. Such a requirement is neither practicable nor constitutionally necessary. In many cases, a breach of *Miranda* procedures may not be identified as such until long after full *Miranda* warnings are administered and a valid confession obtained. The standard *Miranda* warnings explicitly inform the suspect of his right to consult a lawyer before speaking. Police officers are ill equipped to pinch-hit for counsel, construing the murky and difficult questions of when "custody" begins or whether a given unwarned statement will ultimately be held admissible.

This Court has never embraced the theory that a defendant's ignorance of the full consequences of his decisions vitiates their voluntariness. * * * [T]he Court has refused to find that a defendant who confesses, after being falsely told that his codefendant has turned state's evidence, does so involuntarily. Frazier v. Cupp, 394 U.S. 731, 739, 89 S.Ct. 1420, 1424, 22 L.Ed.2d 684 (1969). The Court has also rejected the argument that a defendant's ignorance that a prior coerced confession could not be admitted in evidence compromised the voluntariness of his guilty plea. McMann v. Richardson, [397 U.S. 759, 769, 90 S.Ct. 1441, 1448, 25 L.Ed.2d 763, 772 (1970)]. Likewise, in California v. Beheler, [463 U.S. 1121, 103 S.Ct. 3517, 77 L.Ed.2d 1275 (1983)], the Court declined to accept defendant's contention that, because he was unaware of the potential adverse consequences of statements he made to the police, his participation in the interview was involuntary. Thus we have not held that the *sine qua non* for a knowing and voluntary waiver of the right to remain silent is a full and complete appreciation of all of the consequences flowing from the nature and the quality of the evidence in the case.

IV

When police ask questions of a suspect in custody without administering the required warnings, *Miranda* dictates that the answers received be presumed compelled and that they be excluded from evidence at trial in the State's case in chief. The Court has carefully adhered to this principle, permitting a narrow exception only where pressing public safety concerns demanded. The Court today in no way retreats from the bright line rule of *Miranda*. We do not imply that good faith excuses a failure to administer *Miranda* warnings; nor do we condone inherently coercive police tactics or methods offensive to due process that render the initial admission involuntary and undermine the suspect's will to invoke his rights once they are read to him. A handful of courts has, however, applied our precedents relating to confessions obtained under coercive circumstances to situations involving wholly voluntary admissions, requiring a passage of time or break in events before a second, fully warned statement can be deemed voluntary. Far from establishing a rigid rule, we direct courts to avoid one; there is no warrant for presuming coercive effect where the suspect's initial inculpatory statement, though technically in violation of *Miranda*, was voluntary. The relevant inquiry is whether, in fact, the second statement was also voluntarily made. As in any such inquiry, the finder of fact must examine the surrounding circumstances and the entire course of police conduct with respect to the suspect in evaluating the voluntariness of his statements. The fact that a suspect chooses to speak after being informed of his rights is, of course, highly probative. We find that the dictates of *Miranda* and the goals of the Fifth Amendment proscription against use of compelled testimony are fully satisfied in the circumstances of this case by barring use of the unwarned statement in the case in chief. No further purpose is served by imputing "taint" to subsequent statements obtained pursuant to a voluntary and knowing waiver. We hold today that a suspect who has once responded to unwarned yet uncoercive questioning is not thereby disabled from waiving his rights and confessing after he has been given the requisite *Miranda* warnings.

Rule + Finding

The judgment of the Court of Appeals of Oregon is reversed, and the case is remanded for further proceedings not inconsistent with this opinion.

It is so ordered.

■ JUSTICE BRENNAN, with whom JUSTICE MARSHALL joins, dissenting.

* * *

This Court has had long experience with the problem of confessions obtained after an earlier confession has been illegally secured. Subsequent confessions in these circumstances are not *per se* inadmissible, but the prosecution must demonstrate facts "sufficient to insulate the [subsequent] statement from the effect of all that went before." Clewis v. Texas, 386 U.S. 707, 710, 87 S.Ct. 1338, 1340, 18 L.Ed.2d 423 (1967). * * *

One of the factors that can vitiate the voluntariness of a subsequent confession is the hopeless feeling of an accused that he has nothing to lose by repeating his confession, even where the circumstances that rendered his first confession illegal have been removed. As the Court observed in United States v. Bayer, 331 U.S., at 540, 67 S.Ct., at 1398:

"[A]fter an accused has once let the cat out of the bag by confessing, no matter what the inducement, he is never thereafter free of the psychological and practical disadvantages of having confessed. He can never get the cat back in the bag. The secret is out for good. In such a sense, a later confession always may be looked upon as a fruit of the first."

* * *

Our precedents did not develop in a vacuum. They reflect an understanding of the realities of police interrogation and the everyday experience of lower courts. Expert interrogators, far from dismissing a first admission or confession as creating merely a "speculative and attenuated" disadvantage for a suspect, understand that such revelations frequently lead directly to a full confession. Standard interrogation manuals advise that "[t]he securing of the first admission is the biggest stumbling block. * * * *" A. Aubry & R. Caputo, Criminal Interrogation 290 (3d ed. 1980). If this first admission can be obtained, "there is every reason to expect that the first admission will lead to others, and eventually to the full confession."

> "For some psychological reason which does not have to concern us at this point 'the dam finally breaks as a result of the first leak' with regards to the tough subject. * * * Any structure is only as strong as its weakest component, and total collapse can be anticipated when the weakest part first begins to sag."

* * *

One police practice that courts have frequently encountered involves the withholding of *Miranda* warnings until the end of an interrogation session. Specifically, the police escort a suspect into a room, sit him down and, without explaining his Fifth Amendment rights or obtaining a knowing and voluntary waiver of those rights, interrogate him about his suspected criminal activity. If the police obtain a confession, it is then typed up, the police hand the suspect a pen for his signature, and—just before he signs—the police advise him of his *Miranda* rights and ask him to proceed. Alternatively, the police may call a stenographer in after they have obtained the confession, advise the suspect for the first time of his *Miranda* rights, and ask him to repeat what he has just told them. In such circumstances, the process of giving *Miranda* warnings and obtaining the final confession is " 'merely a formalizing, a setting down almost as a scrivener does, [of] what ha[s] already taken [place].' " People v. Raddatz, 91 Ill.App.2d 425, 430, 235 N.E.2d 353, 356 (1968) (quoting trial court). In such situations, where "it was all over except for reading aloud and explaining the written waiver of the *Miranda* safeguards," courts have time and again concluded that "[t]he giving of the *Miranda* warnings before reducing the product of the day's work to written form could not undo what had been done or make legal what was illegal." People v. Bodner, 75 App.Div.2d 440, 448, 430 N.Y.S.2d 433, 438 (1980).

There are numerous variations on this theme. Police may obtain a confession in violation of *Miranda* and then take a break for lunch or go home for the evening. When questioning is resumed, this time preceded by *Miranda* warnings, the suspect is asked to "clarify" the earlier illegal confession and to provide additional information. Or he is led by one of the interrogators into another room, introduced to another official, and asked to repeat his story. The new officer then gives the *Miranda* warnings and asks the suspect to proceed. Alternatively, the suspect might be questioned by arresting officers "in the field" and without *Miranda* warnings, as was young Elstad in the instant case. After making incriminating admissions or a confession, the suspect is then brought into the stationhouse and either questioned by the same officers again or asked to repeat his earlier statements to another officer.

* * *

I would have thought that the Court, instead of dismissing the "cat out of the bag" presumption out of hand, would have accounted for these practical realities. * * * Expert interrogators and experienced lower-court judges will be startled, to say the least, to learn that the connection between multiple confessions is "speculative" and that a subsequent rendition of *Miranda* warnings "ordinarily" enables the accused in these circumstances to exercise his "free will" and to make "a rational and intelligent choice whether to waive or invoke his rights." * * *

The correct approach, administered for almost 20 years by most courts with no untoward results, is to presume that an admission or confession obtained in violation of *Miranda* taints a subsequent confession unless the prosecution can show that the taint is so attenuated as to justify admission of the subsequent confession. * * *

The Court today refuses to apply the derivative-evidence rule even to the extent necessary to deter objectively unreasonable failures by the authorities to honor a suspect's *Miranda* rights. Incredibly, faced with an obvious violation of *Miranda*, the Court asserts that it will not countenance suppression of a subsequent confession in such circumstances where the authorities have acted "legitimate[ly]" and have not used "improper tactics." One can only respond: whither went *Miranda*?

* * *

I dissent.

■ JUSTICE STEVENS, dissenting.

The Court concludes its opinion with a carefully phrased statement of its holding:

> "We hold today that a suspect who has once responded to unwarned yet uncoercive questioning is not thereby disabled from waiving his rights and confessing after he has been given the requisite *Miranda* warnings."

I find nothing objectionable in such a holding. Moreover, because the Court expressly endorses the "bright line rule of *Miranda*," which conclusively presumes that incriminating statements obtained from a suspect in custody without administering the required warnings are the product of compulsion, and because the Court places so much emphasis on the special facts of this case, I am persuaded that the Court intends its holding to apply only to a narrow category of cases in which the initial questioning of the suspect was made in a totally uncoercive setting and in which the first confession obviously had no influence on the second. I nevertheless dissent because even such a narrowly confined exception is inconsistent with the Court's prior cases, because the attempt to identify its boundaries in future cases will breed confusion and uncertainty in the administration of criminal justice, and because it denigrates the importance of one of the core constitutional rights that protects every American citizen from the kind of tyranny that has flourished in other societies.

* * *

For me, the most disturbing aspect of the Court's opinion is its somewhat opaque characterization of the police misconduct in this case. The Court appears ambivalent on the question whether there was any constitutional violation. This ambivalence is either disingenuous or completely lawless. This Court's power to require state courts to exclude probative self-incriminatory statements rests entirely on the premise that the use of such evidence violates the Federal Constitution. The same constitutional analysis applies whether the custodial interrogation is actually coercive or irrebuttably presumed to be coercive. If the Court does not accept that premise, it must regard the holding in the *Miranda* case itself, as well as all of the Federal jurisprudence that has evolved from that decision, as nothing more than an illegitimate exercise of raw judicial power. If the Court accepts the proposition that respondent's self-incriminatory statement was inadmissible, it must also acknowledge that the Federal Constitution protected him from custodial police interrogation without first being advised of his right to remain silent.

The source of respondent's constitutional protection is the Fifth Amendment's privilege against compelled self-incrimination that is secured against state invasion by the Due Process Clause of the Fourteenth Amendment. Like many other provisions of the Bill of Rights, that provision is merely a procedural safeguard. It is, however, the specific provision that protects all citizens from the kind of custodial interrogation that was once employed by the Star Chamber, by "the Germans of the 1930's and early 1940's," and by some of our own police departments only a few decades ago. Custodial interrogation that violates that provision of the Bill of Rights is a classic example of a violation of a constitutional right.

I respectfully dissent.

6.   LEGISLATIVE "MODIFICATION" OF *MIRANDA*

EDITORS' INTRODUCTION: THE EFFECT OF *MIRANDA*

Despite the outcry following the *Miranda* decision, some evidence suggests its impact was relatively slight. Early research efforts and the problems of such studies are summarized and discussed in The American Law Institute's, A Model Code of Pre-Arraignment Procedure Part II (Study Draft No. 1, 1968). See also Medalie, Zeitz and Alexander, Custodial Police Interrogation in our Nation's Capitol: The Attempt to Implement Miranda, 66 Mich.L.Rev. 1347 (1968).

Project, Interrogations in New Haven: The Impact of Miranda, 76 Yale L.J. 1519 (1965), compared the success of interrogations involving warnings and others in which the suspects received no warnings. Paradoxically, the questioning was *more* successful in those cases in which the subject was warned. The researchers' analysis of the conduct of 81 warned suspects suggested the warning affected the interrogation result for only eight. Three refused to talk; two of these had received advice of counsel. Three others made oral incriminating statements but refused to sign written statements. One admitted his guilt but refused to sign a statement implicating others, and another confessed after consulting an attorney and being advised to do so. The minor impact of the warnings, the study concluded, was not surprising in light of the process observed:

> In the first place, although most interrogations were not intimidating, they were designed to discourage any initiative on the part of the suspect. * * * [T]he warnings * * * were often intoned in a manner designed to minimize or negate their importance and effectiveness. * * * [U]nless the detectives made it absolutely clear what the warn-

ing meant—which they rarely did—most suspects appeared unable to grasp their significance.

Perhaps equally important, almost every person arrested * * * had committed the crime for which he was arrested and knew that the police had evidence of this. When he remained silent, the police would confront him with the evidence. Most suspects apparently felt compelled to give some alibi. Usually they lied and in doing so were caught in their lie. From then on the process was all downhill—from the suspect's point of view. Once a suspect said anything he usually had taken the first step towards incriminating himself.

In addition * * *, the warnings did not have an impact on a number of suspects who, knowing they were guilty, apparently saw no point in denying their guilt. Perhaps previous exposure to the process made them believe silence was futile—several of the defendants we interviewed expressed this belief.

Finally, the warnings had no apparent impact on the behavior of the suspects who seemingly believed they were giving exculpatory statements. * * * Most of those who began by attempting to justify their actions ended by incriminating themselves to some degree.

Id. at 1571–72.

Seeburger and Wettick, *Miranda* in Pittsburgh—A Statistical Study, 29 U.Pitt.L.Rev. 1 (1967), compared cases before and after *Miranda* and produced somewhat different results. The percentage of cases in which suspects made confessions dropped from 54.4% to 37.5% after *Miranda*; in robbery cases, the drop was from 62.4% to 36.7%. The percentage of cases in which confessions were necessary for conviction did not decrease after *Miranda*. Nevertheless, the conviction rate did not drop significantly after *Miranda*. This, the authors suggested, might be explained by grand juries' refusals to indict in the post-*Miranda* cases in which the defendants gave no confessions and in which a confession was essential to conviction, or by the dismissal of these cases at arraignment. Turning to the clearance rate for the crimes studied, the authors concluded the post-*Miranda* clearance rate actually exceeded the pre-*Miranda* rate by a small percentage.

The Seeburger and Wettick study was conducted soon after the *Miranda* decision. It may, then, reflect in part problems of transition as law enforcement adjusted to the new requirements. Certainly the study does not reflect any effects of post-*Miranda* decisions reducing the effect of the seminal case. Nevertheless, some changes seem certain to have occurred after—and perhaps—because of *Miranda*. Gerald Caplan has noted widespread agreement (although no firm evidence) on some matters:

> Before *Miranda*, charges of physical force, questioning in relays, and sustained incommunicado detention were common; after *Miranda*, they became far less frequent.

Caplan, Book Review, 93 Yale L.J. 1375, 1382–83 (1984).

A recent reexamination of the empirical studies conducted on *Miranda* challenged the widespread perception that these studies indicated only minimal results. Cassell, *Miranda's* Social Costs: An Empirical Reassessment, 90 Nw.U.L.Rev. 387 (1966). Professor Cassell contended that "the existing empirical data supports the tentative estimate that *Miranda* has led to lost cases against almost four percent of all criminal suspects in this country who are questioned." A "lost case," he explained, is one in which a confession is needed to convict and, because of *Miranda*, the suspect did not confess. While a lost case is not necessarily one that would have resulted in a conviction, Professor Cassell added, most of the lost cases are probably ones that would have resulted in convictions. Finding that the data permits a "very rough" quantitative estimate of the effect of *Miranda* on plea bargaining, he concluded the decision resulted in more favorable plea bargains in about the same percent of cases. Id. At 445–46.

Turning to the significance of the various *Miranda* requirements, he concluded that advising suspects of their right to remain silent does not appear the critical factor. Instead, he argued, the rules barring questioning explain the results, given that about 20% of suspects invoke their rights and thus cannot be questioned. In the absence of the *Miranda* "cutoff" rules, he indicated, officers could be expected to successfully persuade some of these suspects to make incriminating statements. He also suggested *"Miranda's* greatest cost" is its blocking of searches for new approaches to custodial interrogation that might better reconcile society's need to apprehend offenders and suspects' interest in avoiding coercive questioning. Although *Miranda* purported to invite exploration of alternatives, he argued, the Court's failure to indicate the acceptability of specific alternatives rendered the invitation an empty one.

Professor Cassell acknowledged the drop in the confession rate might be a benefit rather than a cost of *Miranda* if it reflected the results of police inability to use coercive techniques. He concluded, however, that although direct evidence is lacking the indirect indications suggest it is "quite unlikely" that a reduction in police coercion explains the confession rate drop he attributed to *Miranda*. Id., at 478.

Professor Cassell and a colleague themselves conducted a study of the effect of *Miranda* in Salt Lake City, Utah by examining a sample of felony cases presented to the District Attorney for screening and possible prosecution and comparing the results with what they concluded were general pre-*Miranda* facts. Cassell and Hayman, Police Interrogation in the 1990s: An Empirical Study of the Effects of *Miranda*, 43 U.C.L.A.L.Rev. 839 (1966). 21% of the Salt Lake City suspects were not questioned, leading the authors to conclude that questioning rates have declined since *Miranda*. Of those questioned, 83.7% waived their *Miranda* rights, 7.0% requested an attorney, 4.7% invoked their right to silence, and another 4.7% refused to execute a waiver or otherwise invoked their rights. Turning to the productivity of questioning, the study concluded that successful questioning— questioning producing a statement useful to the prosecution—occurred in 33.3% of all the cases and in 42.2% of the cases in which the suspects were questioned. After determining that the available evidence indicated a 55% to 60% success rate in interrogations before *Miranda*, the authors concluded that their data suggested "*Miranda* has hampered law enforcement efforts to obtain incriminating statements." The strength of the evidence police had at the time of the questioning was strongly correlated with the productivity of questioning; questioning was productive in 55.6% of cases in which the available evidence was overwhelming and in only 26.3% of the cases in which it was weak.

Cassell would respond to what he believes to be the current state of affairs by eliminating the right of suspects to counsel during prearraignment interrogation, imposing no requirement of a waiver of rights before interrogation, and eliminating the requirement that interrogation halt upon the suspect's request for counsel or assertion of the right to remain silent. He would require a modified warning telling a suspect he has a right to silence and anything he says can be used as evidence. The suspect would also be told he has a right to be represented when brought before a judge and that the judge will appoint an attorney if necessary. He would add the admonition that the officers are required to bring the suspect before the judge without necessary delay. Balancing this retreat from *Miranda*, he would require the videotaping of all stationhouse interrogations and audiotaping of field custodial interrogations.

Professor Schulhofer responded at length to Professor Cassell in Schulhofer, *Miranda's* Practical Effect: Substantial Benefits and Vanishingly Small Social Costs, 90 Nw.U.L.Rev. 500 (1996). He reevaluated the empirical studies and concluded that *Miranda* has been shown to have resulted in lost convictions "in at most 0.78% of serious criminal cases." Does this suggest *Miranda* has so little impact it is not worth defending? Schulhofer claimed not, reasoning that *Miranda* has changed the nature of interrogation and the basis for suspects' confessing. Modern police questioning, he argued, has become "an elaborate 'confidence game,'"in which the officer dupes the suspect into believing he can help himself by revealing information. As a result:

> [T]oday's suspects typically confess not because of fear of mistreatment but primarily because of misplaced confidence in their own ability to talk their way out of trouble. * * * [C]onfessions are now most the result of persuasion and the suspect's overconfidence, not of pressure and fear.

90 Nw.U.L.Rev. at 561–62. Cassell replied in Cassell, All Benefits, No Costs: The Grand Illusion of Miranda's Defenders, 90 Nw.U.L.Rev. 1084 (1996). See also, Thomas, Plain Talk About the *Miranda* Empirical Debate: A "Steady–State" Theory of Confessions, 43 U.C.L.A. L. Rev. 933 (1996).

Professor Cassell and a colleague have also challenged the conventional wisdom that *Miranda* neither caused nor was followed by a sustained fall in the clearance rate for major offenses. Paul G. Cassell and Richard Fowles, Handcuffing the Cops? A Thirty-year Perspective on *Miranda's* Harmful Effect on law Enforcement, 50 Stan.L.Rev. 1055 (1998). They subjected clearance rate data to regression analysis, and concluded *Miranda* affected clearance rates for robbery, larceny, vehicle theft, and burglary, but not for homicide, rape or assault. Specifically:

> [W]ithout *Miranda*, the number of crimes cleared would have been substantially higher—by as much as 6.6–29.7% for robbery, 6.2–28.9% for burglary, 0.4–11.9% for larceny, and 12.8–45.4% for vehicle theft. * * * As many as 36,000 robberies, 82,000 burglaries, 163,000 larce-

nies, and 78,000 vehicle thefts remain uncleared each year as a result of *Miranda*.

50 Stan.L.Rev. at 1126.

Lawyer-sociologist Richard Leo conducted research of a quite different kind. His results were reported in Leo, Inside the Interrogation Room, 86 J.Crim. & Crim. 266 (1996). Leo observed 122 interrogations of felony suspects in an unidentified city and reviewed sixty videotaped interrogations from two other localities. Of the 175 suspects to whose interrogations *Miranda* applied, 38 (22%) invoked their rights. Leo noted that this is a higher percentage than is assumed by "conventional wisdom." Of the suspects who waived their rights (and who were therefore interrogated), more than three-fourths (76%) made some sort of incriminating statement and about one-third made full confessions. In only four cases, he concluded, did police tactics constitute coercion, and even in these the coercion was psychological rather than physical.

Suspects with felony criminal records, Leo reported, were four times as likely as those with no record to invoke *Miranda* rights. He found no relationship between success of the interrogation and the class, race, or gender of the suspects, victims, or officers, the age of the suspects, the strength of the evidence against the suspects, or the suspect's criminal record. Success of the interrogation was related to the number of tactics officers used and the length of the interrogation—the longer the interrogation and the more tactics used, the more fruitful the interrogation.

Distinguishing among techniques, Leo noted that in almost all cases officers confronted the suspect with existing evidence of his guilt and appealed to his self-interest. In 30% of the cases, officers confronted the suspect with *false* evidence of guilt. Leo found that success tended to be achieved by (1) identifying contradictions in the suspect's denial of involvement; (2) offering a moral justification or psychological excuse for the criminal behavior; (3) praise or flattery; (4) appealing to the suspect's conscience; and (5) appealing to the importance of cooperating with authorities.

Whether a suspect made an incriminating statement or not had a significant effect on the processing of the case. Suspects who made such statements were 20% more likely to be charged, 24% less likely to have charges dismissed, 25% more likely to have their cases resolved by plea bargaining (which meant a conviction in 98% of the cases), and 26% more likely to be convicted.

Leo commented further on the implications of his research in Leo, The Impact of *Miranda* Revisited, 86 J.Crim.L. & Crim. 621 (1996). He suggested compliance with *Miranda* is often a social process orchestrated to predispose suspects towards voluntarily waiving their rights. Leo described the detectives he observed employing three kinds of "subtle psychological strategies." The first was "conditioning," a process in which the officer makes pleasant small talk with the suspect or strikes up a conversation about some point of common interest (such as sports), sometimes while going through the routine booking questions. These practices, Leo concluded, were "intended to disarm the suspect, to lower his anxiety levels, to improve his opinion of the detective, and to create a social psychological setting conducive to both a *Miranda* waiver as well as to subsequent admissions.''

A second strategy—which Leo called ''de-emphasizing''—consisted of downplaying the potential importance of the *Miranda* rights. This was accomplished in either or both of two ways. One consisted of ''blending the *Miranda* warning into the ebb and flow of pre-interrogation conversation by not doing or saying anything unusual when reading the warnings so that the suspect paid no special attention to the admonition.'' The other method of de-emphasizing was to call the suspect's attention to the ''anomalous status'' of the warnings, as by characterizing them as a mere formality required prior to questioning or by suggesting the suspect himself can probably recite them as a result of television viewing.

The third strategy—persuasion—consisted of explicit although often subtle attempts to persuade the suspect to waive the rights. For example, officers sometimes emphasized that the police already had the victim's side of the story and thus suggested that this would become in some sense an ''official'' version unless the suspect talked to the officers. Alternatively, officers sometimes indicated the purpose of the session was to inform the suspect of the evidence against him and what was likely to happen. They would then add that this could be done only if the suspect waived the rights.

Leo suggested the effectiveness of these techniques is more important in explaining why so many suspects waive their *Miranda* rights than other possibilities sometimes offered, such as suggestions that suspects do not actually understand the rights or are impermissibly induced to waive them. These negotiating strategies developed by police to minimize *Miranda's* potential obstacle, he concluded, ''usually remain within the letter of *Miranda*, but frequently they straddle the ambiguous margins of legality.''

Whatever the ''real'' facts, *Miranda* was followed by widespread pressure for some countermeasures to the decision. In 1968, Congress passed legislation—codified as 18 U.S.C.A. § 3501 and reprinted following this Introductory Note—designed ''to offset the harmful effects of the [Supreme] Court decisions'' dealing with the admissibility of confessions, primarily *Miranda*. S.Rep. No. 1097, 90th Cong., 2nd S. (1968), U.S.Code Cong. & Adm.News. Vol. 2, p. 2112, at 2127. Explaining the need for the legislation, the Senate Judiciary Committee stated:

> The committee is convinced * * * that the rigid and inflexible requirements of the majority opinion in the *Miranda* case are unreasonable, unrealistic, and extremely harmful to law enforcement. Instance after instance are documented in the transcript [of the subcommittee hearings] where the most vicious criminals have gone unpunished, even though they had voluntarily confessed their guilt.

Id. at 2132.

Despite the apparent significance of the statute, issues concerning it almost never came before the federal courts until the principal case reprinted in this subsection following the statute. The reason for this drew the ire of one member of the Supreme Court in Davis v. United States, 512

U.S. 452, 457 n. *, 512 U.S. 452, 114 S.Ct. 2350, 2354 n. *, 129 L.Ed.2d 362, 370 note * (1994), reprinted in part in subsection B(3) of this chapter.

In *Davis*, the Court declined the invitation of some amici to consider 18 U.S.C.A. § 3501, explaining that the Government had not relied upon the statute. Justice Scalia concurred in an opinion expressing frustration with the Government's continuing failure to rely on section 3501. "[W]ith limited exceptions," he noted, "the provision has been studiously avoided by every Administration, not only in this court but in the lower courts, since its enactment more than 25 years ago." He then added:

> [T]he refusal to consider arguments not raised is a sound prudential practice, rather than a statutory or constitutional mandate, and there are times when prudence dictates the contrary. As far as I am concerned, such a time will have arrived when a case that comes within the terms of this statute is next presented to us.

* * *

> * * * Section 3501 of Title 18 is a provision of law directed to the courts, reflecting the people's assessment of the proper balance to be struck between concern for persons interrogated in custody and the needs of effective law enforcement. We shirk our duty if we systematically disregard that statutory command simply because the Justice Department systematically declines to remind us of it.

> * * * The point is whether our continuing refusal to consider § 3501 is consistent with the Third Branch's obligation to decide according to the law. I think it is not.

512 U.S. at 464–65, 114 S.Ct. at 2358, 129 L.Ed.2d at 374–5 (Scalia, J., concurring).

OMNIBUS CRIME CONTROL AND SAFE STREETS ACT OF 1968

18 U.S.C.A.

§ 3501. Admissibility of Confessions

(a) In any criminal prosecution brought by the United States or by the District of Columbia, a confession * * * shall be admissible in evidence if it is voluntarily given. Before such confession is received in evidence, the trial judge shall, out of the presence of the jury, determine any issue as to voluntariness. If the trial judge determines that the confession was voluntarily made it shall be admitted in evidence and the trial judge shall permit the jury to hear relevant evidence on the issue of voluntariness and shall instruct the jury to give such weight to the confession as the jury feels it deserves under all the circumstances.

(b) The trial judge in determining the issue of voluntariness shall take into consideration all the circumstances surrounding the giving of the confession, including (1) the time elapsing between arrest and arraignment of the defendant making the confession, if it was made after arrest and before arraignment, (2) whether such defendant knew the nature of the offense with which he was charged or of which he was suspected at the time of making the confession, (3) whether or not such defendant was advised or knew that he was not required to make any statement and that any such statement could be used against him, (4) whether or not such defendant had been advised prior to questioning of his right to the assistance of counsel; and (5) whether or not such defendant was without the assistance of counsel when questioned and when giving such confession.

The presence or absence of any of the abovementioned factors to be taken into consideration by the judge need not be conclusive on the issue of voluntariness of the confession.

* * *

United States v. Dickerson

United States Court of Appeals, Fourth Circuit, 1999.
166 F.3d 667.

■ Before WILLIAMS and MICHAEL, CIRCUIT JUDGES, and KISER, SENIOR UNITED STATES DISTRICT JUDGE FOR THE WESTERN DISTRICT OF VIRGINIA, sitting by designation.

■ WILLIAMS, CIRCUIT JUDGE:[a]

[Defendant Charles T. Dickerson was taken into custody after a witness to a bank robbery reported the license number of the getaway car and that vehicle was traced to him. Without giving Dickerson *Miranda* warnings, federal officers questioned him at length. He gave several statements admitting being the driver but he named Jimmy Rochester as the actual robber. When Rochester was apprehended, he gave a statement naming Dickerson as the driver in a series of eleven bank robberies.

Dickerson moved to suppress both his statement and that of Rochester, arguing that his statement was involuntary and obtained in violation of *Miranda* and that Rochester's statement was the tainted fruit of his statement. The district court held that Dickerson's confession was obtained in violation of *Miranda* and suppressed it. It refused, however, to suppress Rochester's statement, reasoning that fruits of a *Miranda* violation need not be excluded. Although fruits of an involuntary confession must be suppressed, it added, Dickerson's confession was voluntary and hence did not taint Rochester's statement.

The Government exercised its right to take an interlocutory appeal from the order suppressing Dickerson's confession. It did not, however, rely on 18 U.S.C.A. § 3501. In a 1997 unreported case, the Court of Appeals had ordered the Department of Justice to address the effect of the statute on a confession. In response, Attorney General Reno notified Congress that the Department would not defend the constitutionality of § 3501 in the lower federal courts. She acted pursuant to 2 U.S.C.A. § 288k(b), which requires the Department to notify Congress whenever the Department will not defend the constitutionality of a federal statute. The Department also filed a brief in the Court of Appeals taking the same position. It has not,

Handwritten margin note: Dickerson - questioned w/o Miranda - gave name of friend a robber) = Rochester → issue

---

a. Some material from footnotes to the   the text.
original opinion has been incorporated into

however, decided whether in an appropriate case it would ask the United States Supreme Court to overrule or modify *Miranda*.

On the merits of the Government's appeal, the Court of Appeals reasoned that in light of the district court's finding that the confession was voluntary, the court erred in suppressing the confession simply because of a *Miranda* violation if 18 U.S.C.A. § 3501 is constitutionally valid. Thus it turned to that question. Editors.]

* * * Does Congress possess the authority to supersede the irrebuttable presumption created in *Miranda* that any unwarned statement to the police is involuntary, and therefore inadmissible?

* * *

In City of Boerne v. Flores, 521 U.S. 507, 117 S.Ct. 2157, 138 L.Ed.2d 624 (1997), the Court recently held that Congress does not possess the legislative authority to supersede a Supreme Court decision construing the Constitution. See id. 177 S.Ct. at 2172 (refusing to enforce federal statute establishing more narrow test for violation of the Free Exercise Clause than prior test established by Supreme Court). On the other hand, Congress possesses the legislative authority to overrule judicially created rules of evidence and procedure that are not required by the Constitution. See Palermo v. United States, 360 U.S. 343, 345, 348, 79 S.Ct. 1217, 3 L.Ed.2d 1287 (1959) (upholding federal statute establishing more narrow disclosure of *Jenks* material than prior rule established by Supreme Court); see also Carlisle v. United States, 517 U.S. 416, 426, 116 S.Ct. 1460, 134 L.Ed.2d 613 (1996) (noting that the federal courts may formulate rules of evidence and procedure so long as they do not conflict with an Act of Congress); Vance v. Terrazas, 444 U.S. 252, 265, 100 S.Ct. 540, 62 L.Ed.2d 461 (1980) (upholding statute altering the evidentiary standard for expatriation proceedings established by the Supreme Court because prior standard created by the Court was not required by "the Constitution"). In fact, the power of the Supreme Court to prescribe nonconstitutional "rules of procedure and evidence for the federal courts exists only in the absence of a relevant Act of Congress." *Palermo*, 360 U.S. at 353 n. 11, 79 S.Ct. 1217.

Whether Congress has the authority to enact § 3501, therefore, turns on whether the rule set forth by the Supreme Court in *Miranda* is required by the Constitution. If it is, Congress lacked the authority to enact § 3501, and *Miranda* continues to control the admissibility of confessions in federal court. If it is not required by the Constitution, then Congress possesses the authority to supersede *Miranda* legislatively, and § 3501 controls the admissibility of confessions in federal court.

* * *

We begin our analysis * * * with the Supreme Court's decision in *Miranda*. Several passages in Chief Justice Warren's opinion for the Court suggest that the warnings safeguard rights guaranteed by the Constitution. See, e.g., *Miranda*, 384 U.S. at 490 (noting that the privilege against self-incrimination is guaranteed by the Constitution). Surprisingly, the sixty-page opinion does not specifically state the basis for its holding that a statement obtained from a suspect without the warnings would be presumed involuntary. The Court strongly suggested, however, that the basis for the rule was identical to that set forth in [McNabb v. United States, 318 U.S. 332, 63 S.Ct. 608, 87 L.Ed. 819 (1943) (exercising its supervisory power over the federal courts, Supreme Court held that federal courts must exclude all incriminating statements, including voluntary confessions, obtained during an unreasonable delay between a defendant's arrest and initial appearance) and Mallory v. United States, 354 U.S. 449, 77 S.Ct. 1356, 1 L.Ed.2d 1479 (1957) (affirming the holding of *McNabb* under Rule 5(a) of the Federal Rules of Criminal Procedure)]. In particular, just as the "supervisory" rule set forth in *McNabb* and *Mallory* permitted the Court to avoid the constitutional issues associated with federal interrogations, the rule set forth in *Miranda* would allow the Court to avoid the constitutional issues associated with state interrogations.

Although the Court failed to specifically state the basis for its holding in *Miranda*, it did specifically state what the basis was not. At no point does the Court refer to the warnings as constitutional rights. Indeed, the Court acknowledged that the Constitution did not require the warnings, disclaimed any intent to create a "constitutional straightjacket," repeatedly referred to the warnings as "procedural safeguards," and invited Congress and the States "to develop their own safeguards for [protecting] the privilege."

[handwritten marginal note: Miranda – not a constitutional right]

Since deciding *Miranda*, the Supreme Court consistently (and repeatedly) has referred to the warnings as "prophylactic," New York v. Quarles, 467 U.S. 649, 654, 104 S.Ct. 2626, 81 L.Ed.2d 550 (1984), and "not themselves rights protected by the Constitution," Michigan v. Tucker, 417 U.S. 433, 444, 94 S.Ct. 2357, 41 L.Ed.2d 182 (1974); see also Davis v. United States, 512 U.S. 452, 457, 458, 114 S.Ct. 2350, 129 L.Ed.2d 362 (1994) (referring to *Miranda* warnings as "a series of recommended procedural safeguards"); Withrow v. Williams, 507 U.S. 680, 690, 691, 113 S.Ct. 1745, 123 L.Ed.2d 407 (1993) (acknowledging that "*Miranda's* safeguards are not constitutional in character"); Duckworth v. Eagan, 492 U.S. 195, 203, 109 S.Ct. 2875, 106 L.Ed.2d 166 (1989) (noting that the *Miranda* warnings are not required by the Constitution); Connecticut v. Barrett, 479 U.S. 523, 528, 107 S.Ct. 828, 93 L.Ed.2d 920 (1987) (noting that "the *Miranda* Court adopted prophylactic rules designed to insulate the exercise of Fifth Amendment rights"); Oregon v. Elstad, 470 U.S. 298, 306, 105 S.Ct. 1285, 84 L.Ed.2d 222 (1985) (noting that the *Miranda* exclusionary rule "may be triggered even in the absence of a Fifth Amendment violation").

* * *

Of particular importance here, the Court in *Elstad* made the following observation about *Miranda*:

> The *Miranda* exclusionary rule, however, serves the Fifth Amendment and sweeps more broadly than the Fifth Amendment itself. It may be triggered even in the absence of a Fifth Amendment violation. The Fifth Amendment prohibits use by the prosecution in its case in chief only of compelled testimony. Failure to administer *Miranda* warnings creates a presumption of compulsion. Consequently, un-

warned statements that are otherwise voluntary within the meaning of the Fifth Amendment must nevertheless be excluded from evidence under *Miranda*. Thus, in the individual case, *Miranda's* preventive medicine provides a remedy even to the defendant who has suffered no identifiable constitutional harm.

But the *Miranda* presumption, though irrebuttable for purposes of the prosecution's case in chief, does not require that the statements and their fruits be discarded as inherently tainted. Despite the fact that patently voluntary statements taken in violation of *Miranda* must be excluded from the prosecution's case, the presumption of coercion does not bar their use for impeachment purposes on cross-examination.

Id. at 306–07, 105 S.Ct. 1285 (internal footnotes and citations omitted).

In light of the foregoing cases, it is certainly "well established that the failure to deliver *Miranda* warnings is not itself a constitutional violation." United States v. Elie, 111 F.3d 1135, 1142 (4th Cir.1997) (citing Supreme Court cases). As a consequence, the irrebuttable presumption created by the Court in *Miranda* that a confession obtained without the warnings is presumed involuntary is *a fortiori* not required by the Constitution. Accordingly, Congress necessarily possesses the legislative authority to supersede the conclusive presumption created by *Miranda* pursuant to its authority to prescribe the rules of procedure and evidence in the federal courts.

The dissent does not dispute that the applicability of § 3501 turns on whether *Miranda* is a constitutional rule. Even more telling, after considering the merits, the dissent is unable to conclude that *Miranda's* conclusive presumption is, in fact, required by the Constitution. In the end, the dissent poses only the following rhetorical question: "If *Miranda* is not a constitutional rule, why does the Supreme Court continue to apply it in prosecutions arising in state courts." * * * [A]lthough the dissent raises an interesting academic question, the answer to why the Supreme Court applies *Miranda* in prosecutions arising in state courts has no bearing on our conclusion that *Miranda's* conclusive presumption is not required by the Constitution.

It is worth recalling that Congress not only acted in response to the Court's invitation, see *Miranda*, 384 U.S. at 490, 86 S.Ct. 1602 (inviting Congress and the States "to develop their own safeguards for [protecting] the privilege"), but that the Court in *Miranda* had acted in the absence of a relevant Act of Congress. It is well established that the Court's power to prescribe nonconstitutional "rules of procedure and evidence for the federal courts exists only in the absence of a relevant Act of Congress." *Palermo*, 360 U.S. at 353 n. 11, 79 S.Ct. 1217. Thus, just as the Court was free to create an irrebuttable presumption that statements obtained without certain procedural safeguards are involuntary, Congress was free to overrule that judicially created rule.

To be sure, the *Miranda* warnings were meant to safeguard the Fifth Amendment privilege against self-incrimination. Indeed, under § 3501 any statement obtained in violation of the privilege must be suppressed. Thus, we cannot say that Congress's decision to eliminate the irrebuttable presumption created by *Miranda* lessens the protections afforded by the privilege. Indeed, the Court has recognized that *Miranda's* irrebuttable presumption goes beyond what is required to protect the privilege. As a result, even "patently voluntary statements ... must be excluded." *Elstad,* 470 U.S. at 307, 105 S.Ct. 1285. In enacting § 3501, Congress simply recognized the need to offset the harmful effects created by *Miranda's* irrebuttable presumption. No longer will criminals who have voluntarily confessed their crimes be released on mere technicalities.

In addition to recognizing the harmful effects created by *Miranda's* irrebuttable presumption, Congress concluded that the Court's justification for the conclusive presumption that custodial interrogations were inherently coercive and intimidating was simply incorrect as an empirical matter. See S.Rep. No. 901097 (1968), reprinted in 1968 U.S.C.C.A.N. 2112. During the subcommittee hearings, Senator Arlen Specter, then the district attorney of the City of Philadelphia, pointed out

> that the so-called third degree methods deplored by the Supreme Court and cited as a basis for their opinion in *Miranda* is not a correct portrayal of what actually goes on in police stations across the country. While there are isolated cases of police using coercive tactics, this is the exception rather than the rule.

Id. at 2134. Similarly, the final committee report concluded that the basis for the conclusive presumption in *Miranda* was faulty. Id. at 2142 (noting that the "data supporting the [Court's] conclusion of inherent coercion in custodial interrogation were drawn solely from police manuals and texts which may or may not have been followed"); id. at 2134 (noting that "while coercive practices might have been approved 30 years ago, they have no place in modern police techniques"); id. (finding that "the Court overreacted to defense claims that police brutality is widespread").

In sum, Congress, utilizing its superior factfinding ability, concluded that custodial interrogations were not inherently coercive. As Senator Sam Ervin noted at the time § 3501 was enacted:

> A decision of the Supreme Court, if it is based on a factual assumption which is incorrect, may be subject to Congress' power to legislate. The Supreme Court has no right to make ... determinations based on unsound factual assumptions. I don't believe the great majority of law enforcement officers in the United States are such disreputable people that they have to have the criminals protected against them.

Hearings on the Supreme Court Before the Subcomm. on Separation of Powers of the Senate Comm. on the Judiciary, 90th Cong. 25 (1968). Senator Ervin's observation concerning Congress's authority to overrule Supreme Court decisions, whether or not correct as a general matter, is certainly correct when applied to judicially created presumptions. It is well established that a conclusive presumption "should not be applied ... in situations where the generalization is incorrect as an empirical matter." Coleman v. Thompson, 501 U.S. 722, 737, 111 S.Ct. 2546, 115 L.Ed.2d 640 (1991). In fact, "the justification for a conclusive presumption disappears when application of the presumption will not reach the correct result most of the time." According to congressional findings, the basis for *Miranda's* conclusive presumption is incorrect as an empirical matter, and the presumption does not reach the correct result, i.e., suppressing only coerced confessions, most of the time that it is applied. As a result, Congress, pursuant to its authority to prescribe the rules of procedure and evidence in the federal courts, was justified in abandoning the conclusive presumption when it enacted § 3501.

Finally, lest there be any confusion on the matter, nothing in today's opinion provides those in law enforcement with an incentive to stop giving the now familiar *Miranda* warnings. As noted above, those warnings are among the factors a district court should consider when determining whether a confession was voluntarily given. See 18 U.S.C.A. § 3501(b). Indeed, federal courts rarely find confessions obtained in technical compliance with *Miranda* to be involuntary under the Fifth Amendment. Thus, providing the four *Miranda* warnings is still the best way to guarantee a finding of voluntariness.

In the end, and after an exhaustive review of the relevant authority, we are convinced that § 3501 enacted at the invitation of the Supreme Court and pursuant to Congress's unquestioned power to establish the rules of procedure and evidence in the federal courts is constitutional. * * * [W]e find that the admissibility of confessions in federal court is governed by 18 U.S.C.A. § 3501 (West 1985), rather than *Miranda* * * *. Accordingly, the district court's order suppressing the statements Dickerson made * * * is reversed, and the case is remanded for further proceedings.

REVERSED AND REMANDED

■ Michael, Circuit Judge, dissenting * * *:

* * * In pressing § 3501 into the prosecution of a case against the express wishes of the Department of Justice, the majority takes on more than any court should. I therefore respectfully dissent. * * *

* * * The majority holds that § 3501 governs the admissibility of confessions in federal court because *Miranda* is not a constitutional rule. I don't know whether it is or not, but before I had to decide, I would want thoughtful lawyers on both sides to answer one question for me. If *Miranda* is not a constitutional rule, why does the Supreme Court continue to apply it in prosecutions arising in state courts? This question illustrates that the § 3501 issue is so sweeping that we should not be delving into it on our own. In this case, we should follow our usual practice of deciding only the issues raised by the parties.

* * *

NOTES

1.   The Senate Judiciary Committee's report on the bill enacting section 3501 defended the proposal by citing the passage in the *Miranda* majority opinion which encouraged legislative searches "for increasingly effective ways of protecting the rights of the individual while promoting efficient enforcement of our criminal laws." It then concluded:

> The committee feels that it is obvious * * * that the overwhelming weight of judicial opinion in this country is that the voluntariness test does not offend

the Constitution or deprive a defendant of any Constitutional right. No one can predict with any assurance what the Supreme Court might at some future date decide if these provisions are enacted. The committee has concluded that this approach to the balancing of the rights of society and the rights of the individual served us well over the years, that it is constitutional and that Congress should adopt it. After all, the *Miranda* decision itself was by a bare majority of one, and with increasing frequency the Supreme Court has reversed itself. The committee feels that by the time the issue of constitutionality would reach the Supreme Court, the probability rather is that this legislation would be upheld.

S.Rep. No. 1097, supra, at 2138.

2. **Judicially-Supervised Interrogation.** An alternative approach would be to authorize interrogation by or under the supervision of a judicial officer. An early brief for such a procedure was Kauper, Judicial Examination of the Accused—A Remedy for the Third Degree, 30 Mich.L.Rev. 1224 (1932). A "modernized" version of Kauper's proposal was presented in Kamisar, Kauper's "Judicial Examination of the Accused" Forty Years Later—Some Comments on a Remarkable Article, 73 Mich.L.Rev. 15, 23–24, 27, 32 (1974):

1. A person taken into custody because of, or charged with, a crime to which an interrogation relates, may be questioned only in the presence of and under the supervision of a judicial officer.

2. The person shall immediately (that is, as soon as humanly possible) be brought before a judicial officer who shall, before questioning begins, determine the existence of the grounds for detention or arrest.

3. The judicial officer shall give the person the familiar *Miranda* warnings and, in addition, inform him that if he is subsequently prosecuted his refusal to answer any questions will be disclosed at trial.

4. A complete written record shall be kept of the judicial examinations; the information of rights, any waiver thereof, and any questioning shall be recorded upon a sound recording device; and the suspect shall be so informed.

5. The questions shall be asked by police officers or prosecuting attorneys rather than the judicial officer, but only in the presence of the judicial officer, who may intervene to prevent abuse.

Would such a procedure be desirable? Would it be constitutional?

3. **Recording Requirements.** Another reform urged by many is the recording of custodial interrogation and suspects' resulting statements. The Model Code of Pre–Arraignment Procedure, for example, proposed a requirement that sound recordings be made of warnings, waivers, questioning, and statements made in response to questioning. Model Code of Pre–Arraignment Procedure § 130.4(3) (Official Draft 1975). The Alaska Supreme Court has read the state's constitutional due process demand as requiring electronic recording of custodial interrogations. Stephan v. State, 711 P.2d 1156, 1162 (Alaska 1985).

The Minnesota Supreme Court has adopted a recording requirement, but stopped short of mandating suppression of all self-incriminating statements related to noncompliance with this requirement:

[I]n the exercise of our supervisory power to insure the fair administration of justice, we hold that all custodial interrogation including any information about rights, any waiver of those rights, and all questioning shall be electronically recorded where feasible and must be recorded when questioning occurs at a place of detention. If law enforcement officers fail to comply with this recording requirement, any statements the suspect makes in response to the interrogation may be suppressed at trial. The parameters of the exclusionary rule applied to evidence of statements obtained in violation of these requirements must be decided on a case-by-case basis. Following the approach recommended by the drafters of the Model Code of Pre–Arraignment Procedure, suppression will be required of any statements obtained in violation of the recording requirement if the violation is deemed "substantial." This determination is to be made by the trial court after considering all relevant circumstances bearing on substantiality * * *.

State v. Scales, 518 N.W.2d 587, 592 (Minn.1994). Although a recording requirement is often urged on other courts, they have generally refused to impose such a demand. See State v. James, 237 Conn. 390, 431–34, 678 A.2d 1338, 1359–60 (1996). An extensive argument for videotaping is made in Leo, The Impact of *Miranda* Revisited, 86 J.Crim.L. & Crim. 621, 681–92 (1996).

An intermediate Indiana court concluded the Indiana Constitution imposed no duty on law enforcement officers to record custodial interrogations in places of detention. It added, however:

> [A]lthough we impose no legal obligation, we discern few instances in which law enforcement officers would be justified in failing to record custodial interrogations in places of detention. Disputes regarding the circumstances of an interrogation would be minimized, in that a tape recording preserves undisturbed that which the mind may forget. In turn, the judiciary would be relieved of much of the burden of resolving disputes involving differing recollections of events which occurred. Moreover, the recording would serve to protect police officers against false allegations that a confession was not obtained voluntarily. Therefore, in light of the slight inconvenience and expense associated with the recording of custodial interrogations in their entirety, it is strongly recommended, as a matter of sound policy, that law enforcement officers adopt this procedure.
>
> In the absence of an electronic recording of a custodial interrogation in a place of detention, we also note that the following consequences may ensue:
>
> > "[D]efense counsel is entitled to pursue the failure of the police to record a defendant's statements. Counsel may, for example, inquire of a testifying police officer ... whether he or she was aware of the availability of recorders to use during the questioning of suspects. Counsel may argue to a jury and to a judge as factfinder that the failure of the police to record electronically statements made in a place of custody should be considered in deciding the voluntariness of any statement, whether the defendant was properly advised of his rights, and whether any statement attributed to the defendant was made." Commonwealth v. Diaz (1996), 422 Mass. 269, 661 N.E.2d 1326, 1329.

Stoker v. State, 692 N.E.2d 1386, 1390, 1390 n. 11 (Ind.App.1998) (footnote incorporated into text).

C. SIXTH AMENDMENT RIGHT TO COUNSEL

EDITORS' INTRODUCTION: SIXTH AMENDMENT RIGHT TO COUNSEL DURING POLICE QUESTIONING

In a series of cases beginning with Massiah v. United States, 377 U.S. 201, 84 S.Ct. 1199, 12 L.Ed.2d 246 (1964), the Supreme Court held the Sixth Amendment right to counsel applied to law enforcement undercover efforts to elicit self-incriminating statements occurring after the investigation had progressed to a certain point. This is considered further in Chapter 8. In Brewer v. Williams, 430 U.S. 387, 97 S.Ct. 1232, 51 L.Ed.2d 424 (1977), however, the Court held that the Sixth Amendment also applied to overt police interrogations occurring after the case had progressed far enough to trigger the Sixth Amendment. As the principal case in this section makes clear, this holding presented the Court with the difficult task of determining how suspects' rights are affected when their *Miranda* rights are supplemented (or perhaps preempted) by the Sixth Amendment right to counsel.

The Court's application of the Sixth Amendment to overt interrogation raises several other issues. One, of course, is when in this context the Sixth Amendment attaches. Another is the extent to which the Sixth Amendment embodies a prohibition against reapproaching a suspect as is imposed by the Fifth Amendment right to counsel under Edwards v. Arizona, 451 U.S. 477, 101 S.Ct. 1880, 68 L.Ed.2d 378 (1981).

Attachment of the Sixth Amendment. In *Williams,* the Court noted some uncertainty as to when the progress of an investigation triggered the Sixth Amendment but stated it certainly provides its protection "at or after the time that judicial proceedings have been initiated against [a suspect]— 'whether by way of formal charge, preliminary hearing, information or arraignment.' Kirby v. Illinois, [406 U.S. 682, 689, 92 S.Ct. 1877, 1882, 32 L.Ed.2d 411 (1972)]." The Court's citation to *Kirby*, an eyewitness identification decision, indicated attachment of the Sixth Amendment to interrogations poses the same problem raised by application of the provision to lineups and similar law enforcement techniques; this is considered in Chapter 10.

In *Williams,* a magistrate had issued an arrest warrant for Williams. Police took him into custody on that warrant and presented before a judge. Williams was then "committed" to confinement in jail. Thus, the Court held, judicial proceedings had been initiated. In Edwards v. Arizona, 451 U.S. 477, 480 n. 7, 101 S.Ct. 1880, 1882–83 n. 7, 68 L.Ed.2d 378, 383 n. 7 (1981), however, the Court noted but did not reach the prosecution's contention that under Arizona state law adversary judicial proceedings did not begin until the filing of an indictment or information or perhaps at a preliminary hearing if one was held.

Michigan v. Jackson, 475 U.S. 625, 106 S.Ct. 1404, 89 L.Ed.2d 631 (1986), made clear that "arraignment" triggers the Sixth Amendment right. Police questioned Jackson after he was arrested and "arraigned." The State argued that judicial proceedings had not been initiated, but the Court responded, "In view of the clear language in our decisions about the significance of arraignment, the State's argument is untenable."

Unfortunately, *Jackson* did not make clear what the Court meant by the term "arraignment." Apparently, at least in the *Jackson* context, the term refers to the defendant's appearance required by Mich.Comp.Laws Anno. § 764.13:

A peace officer who has arrested a person for an offense without a warrant shall without unnecessary delay take the person arrested before a magistrate of the judicial district in which the offense is charged to have been committed, and shall present to the magistrate a complaint stating the charge against the person arrested.

The Michigan courts have referred to this appearance as an "arraignment." E.g., People v. White, 392 Mich. 404, 424, 221 N.W.2d 357, 366 (1974). In *Williams*, however, the Court quoted language from Powell v. Alabama, 287 U.S. 45, 47, 53 L.Ed. 55, 59, 77 L.Ed. 158 (1932), that used the word "arraignment" in a different sense. Under the Alabama procedure discussed in *Powell*, the arraignment was a postindictment appearance before the trial court at which a defendant entered a plea. This appearance or its equivalent continues to be formally designated the "arraignment" under the procedural law of many jurisdictions. E.g., Fed.R.Crim.P. 10 (arraignment "shall consist of reading the indictment or information to the defendant * * * and calling on him to plead thereto").

Nevertheless, *Jackson* appeared to indicate unequivocally that if police after arrest present a suspect before a magistrate for purposes of a judicial warning and perhaps the setting of bail, judicial proceedings are initiated and the Sixth Amendment attaches.

The Court has refused to move application of the provision to an earlier point. In Moran v. Burbine, 475 U.S. 412, 106 S.Ct. 1135, 89 L.Ed.2d 410 (1986) (reprinted in part in subsection B(4) of this chapter), the defendant argued that Sixth Amendment applied to his interrogation. He acknowledged that "adversary judicial proceedings" had not yet begun, but urged that in some situations at least the Sixth Amendment is triggered before that point. Specifically, he argued the importance of custodial interrogation is such that the Sixth Amendment creates a right to noninterference with an attorney's dealings with a client-suspect if the attorney-client relationship has been formed and custodial interrogation begins. The Supreme Court, however, rejected the proposition that an attorney-client relationship independently triggers the Sixth Amendment right to counsel:

> As a practical matter, it makes little sense to say that the Sixth Amendment right to counsel attaches at different times depending on the fortuity of whether the suspect or his family happened to have retained counsel prior to interrogation. More importantly, the suggestion that the existence of an attorney-client relationship itself triggers the protections of the Sixth Amendment misconceives the underlying purpose of the right to counsel. The Sixth Amendment's intended function is not to wrap a protective cloak around the attorney-client relationship for its own sake any more than it is to protect a suspect from the consequences of his own candor. Its purpose, rather, is to assure than in any "criminal prosecutio[n]," U.S. Const., Amdt. 6, the accused shall not be left to his own devices in facing the " 'prosecutorial forces of organized society.' " Maine v. Moulton, [474 U.S. 159, 169, 106 S.Ct. 477, 484, 88 L.Ed.2d 481 (1985)]. By its very terms, it becomes applicable only when the government's role shifts from investigation to accusation. * * * [L]ooking to the initiation of adversary judicial proceedings, far from being mere formalism, is fundamental to the proper application of the Sixth Amendment right to counsel. * * *

[U]ntil such time as the " 'government has committed itself to prosecute, and ... the adverse positions of the government and defendant have solidified' " the Sixth amendment right to counsel does not attach. [United States v. Gouveia, 467 U.S. 180, 189, 104 S.Ct. 2292, 2298, 81 L.Ed.2d 146 (1984)].

475 U.S. at 430–32, 106 S.Ct. at 1145–46, 89 L.Ed.2d at 427–28.

Application of Edwards *Rule.* In *Jackson,* the Court held the *Edwards* rule as developed in the *Miranda* context, see subsection B(3) of this chapter, also applied in Sixth Amendment situations. This prohibition against reapproach of a suspect who invokes the right to counsel applies somewhat differently where it arises because the suspect has invoked the Sixth Amendment right to counsel.

Police arrested the two defendants in *Jackson* and presented them before a magistrate for "arraignment." At this arraignment they requested that counsel be appointed for them. The records left unclear whether the magistrate first offered to appoint counsel and, if so, in what terms; those records also left uncertain the terms of the defendants' requests for counsel. Later, while the defendants were still in custody, they were approached by police officers, given *Miranda* warnings, and—apparently after agreeing to submit to questioning without counsels' presence—made incriminating statements. A majority of the Supreme Court agreed with the Michigan Supreme Court that the Sixth Amendment required the suppression of these statements. The arraignment caused the defendants' Sixth Amendment right to counsel to attach, so the issue was whether the officers reapproach violated a Sixth Amendment version of the *Edwards* rule. The Sixth Amendment right to counsel includes an *Edwards*-like prohibition against reapproach, because "the Sixth Amendment right to counsel at a postarraignment interrogation requires at least as much protection as does the Fifth Amendment right to counsel at any custodial interrogation." The State argued that the defendants did not trigger this bar to any approach by officers seeking to interrogate the defendants; the defendants could have intended their request for counsel to refer only to counsel for trial and other formal legal purposes and not for purposes of representation during further questioning. But the Court responded:

> [I]t is the State that has the burden of establishing a valid waiver. Doubts must be resolved in favor of protecting the constitutional claim. This settled approach to questions of waiver requires us to give a broad, rather than a narrow, interpretation to a defendant's request for counsel—we presume that the defendant requests the lawyer's services at every critical stage of the prosecution. We thus reject the State's suggestion * * *.

475 U.S. at 633, 106 S.Ct. at 1409, 89 L.Ed.2d at 640. In a footnote, the Court commented further:

> In construing respondents' request for counsel, we do not, of course, suggest that the right to counsel turns on such a request. Rather, we construe the defendant's request for counsel as an extremely important fact in considering the validity of a subsequent waiver in response to police-initiated interrogation.

475 U.S. at 633 n. 6, 106 S.Ct. at 1409 n. 6, 89 L.Ed.2d at 640 n. 6. The Court summarized its holding:

> We * * * hold that, if police initiate interrogation after a defendant's assertion, at an arraignment or similar proceeding, of his right to counsel, any waiver of the defendant's right to counsel for that police-initiated interrogation is invalid.

475 U.S. at 636, 106 S.Ct. at 1411, 89 L.Ed.2d at 642.

But the *Edwards* rule as applied in some Sixth Amendment situations has less impact than it has when applied in *Miranda* contexts. If a suspect invokes the right to counsel during police questioning to which *Miranda* applies, *Edwards* as construed in *Roberson* (discussed in subsection B(3) of this chapter) means that officers cannot reapproach the suspect until a lawyer is present even if the subject of their inquiries is a different offense. In McNeil v. Wisconsin, 501 U.S. 171, 111 S.Ct. 2204, 115 L.Ed.2d 158 (1991), the Supreme Court held that in the Sixth Amendment context *Edwards* was not so broad.

Police arrested McNeil for a West Allis, Wisconsin armed robbery and brought him before a court commissioner on that charge. McNeil was represented by a public defender at this appearance. The commissioner set bail and scheduled a preliminary examination. Subsequently, officers approached McNeil seeking to question him about a robbery-murder committed in Caledonia, Wisconsin. After the officers warned McNeil under *Miranda,* he waived his rights and made several statements admitting participation in the Caledonia crimes. The Supreme Court assumed the Sixth Amendment right to counsel attached by virtue of McNeil's court appearance. It also assumed by appearing with counsel McNeil invoked his Sixth Amendment right with regard to the West Allis robbery. But it rejected McNeil's claim that under *Edwards* and *Roberson* this meant that the officers were barred from reapproaching him concerning the Caledonia crimes.

The Sixth Amendment right to counsel, the *McNeil* majority explained, "is offense-specific." It does not attach until prosecution commences, and its *Edwards* effect is similarly "offense-specific." Thus a suspect's invocation of the Sixth Amendment right to counsel does not bar officers from reapproaching the suspect regarding offenses as to which he does not yet have a Sixth Amendment right to counsel. McNeil "provided the statements at issue here before his Sixth Amendment right to counsel with respect to the Caledonia offenses had been (or could have been) invoked." Therefore, the Sixth Amendment did not bar the use of those statements against him.

* * *

When the Sixth Amendment is triggered, what effect does it have upon the legal status of a suspect undergoing custodial interrogation, above and beyond what is dictated by *Miranda* and the Fifth Amendment? Justice Marshall has suggested waivers of the Sixth Amendment right to counsel should be subjected to greater scrutiny than waivers of *Miranda* rights. A waiver of the former, he urged, should require a greater comprehension of the consequences than a waiver of the latter. See Fields v. Wyrick, 464 U.S.

1020, 1022–23, 104 S.Ct. 556, 557, 78 L.Ed.2d 728, 729 (1983) (Marshall, J., dissenting from denial of certiorari). The following case, to some extent, confronts this general question.

Patterson v. Illinois

Supreme Court of the United States, 1988.
487 U.S. 285, 108 S.Ct. 2389, 101 L.Ed.2d 261.

■ JUSTICE WHITE delivered the opinion of the Court.

In this case, we are called on to determine whether the interrogation of petitioner after his indictment violated his Sixth Amendment right to counsel.

I

Before dawn on August 21, 1983, petitioner and other members of the "Vice Lords" street gang became involved in a fight with members of a rival gang, the "Black Mobsters." Some time after the fight, a former member of the Black Mobsters, James Jackson, went to the home where the Vice Lords had fled. A second fight broke out there, with petitioner and three other Vice Lords beating Jackson severely. The Vice Lords then put Jackson into a car, drove to the end of a nearby street, and left him face down in a puddle of water. Later that morning, police discovered Jackson, dead, where he had been left.

That afternoon, local police officers obtained warrants for the arrest of the Vice Lords, on charges of battery and mob action, in connection with the first fight. One of the gang members who was arrested gave the police a statement concerning the first fight; the statement also implicated several of the Vice Lords (including petitioner) in Jackson's murder. A few hours later, petitioner was apprehended. Petitioner was informed of his rights under Miranda v. Arizona, 384 U.S. 436, 86 S.Ct. 1602, 16 L.Ed.2d 694 (1966), and volunteered to answer questions put to him by the police. Petitioner gave a statement concerning the initial fight between the rival gangs, but denied knowing anything about Jackson's death. Petitioner was held in custody the following day, August 22, as law enforcement authorities completed their investigation of the Jackson murder.

On August 23, a Cook County grand jury indicted petitioner and two other gang members for the murder of James Jackson. Police officer Michael Gresham, who had questioned petitioner earlier, removed him from the lockup where he was being held, and told petitioner that because he had been indicted he was being transferred to the Cook County jail. Petitioner asked Gresham which of the gang members had been charged with Jackson's murder, and upon learning that one particular Vice Lord had been omitted from the indictments, asked: "[W]hy wasn't he indicted, he did everything." Petitioner also began to explain that there was a witness who would support his account of the crime.

At this point, Gresham interrupted petitioner, and handed him a *Miranda* waiver form. The form contained five specific warnings, as suggested by this Court's *Miranda* decision, to make petitioner aware of his right to counsel and of the consequences of any statement he might make to police. Gresham read the warnings aloud, as petitioner read along with him. Petitioner initialed each of the five warnings, and signed the waiver form. Petitioner then gave a lengthy statement to police officers concerning the Jackson murder; petitioner's statement described in detail the role of each of the Vice Lords—including himself—in the murder of James Jackson.

Later that day, petitioner confessed involvement in the murder for a second time. This confession came in an interview with Assistant State's Attorney (ASA) George Smith. At the outset of the interview, Smith reviewed with petitioner the *Miranda* waiver he had previously signed, and petitioner confirmed that he had signed the waiver and understood his rights. Smith went through the waiver procedure once again: reading petitioner his rights, having petitioner initial each one, and sign a waiver form. In addition, Smith informed petitioner that he was a lawyer working with the police investigating the Jackson case. Petitioner then gave another inculpatory statement concerning the crime.

Before trial, petitioner moved to suppress his statements, arguing that they were obtained in a manner at odds with various constitutional guarantees. The trial court denied these motions, and the statements were used against petitioner at his trial. The jury found petitioner guilty of murder, and petitioner was sentenced to a 24–year prison term.

On appeal, petitioner argued that he had not "knowingly and intelligently" waived his Sixth Amendment right to counsel before he gave his uncounseled postindictment confessions. Petitioner contended that the warnings he received, while adequate for the purposes of protecting his *Fifth* Amendment rights as guaranteed by *Miranda,* did not adequately inform him of his *Sixth* Amendment right to counsel. The Illinois Supreme Court, however, rejected, this theory * * *.

II

There can be no doubt that petitioner had the right to have the assistance of counsel at his postindictment interviews with law enforcement authorities. Our cases make it plain that the Sixth Amendment guarantees this right to criminal defendants. Michigan v. Jackson, 475 U.S. 625, 629–630, 106 S.Ct. 1404, 1407–1408, 89 L.Ed.2d 631 (1986); Brewer v. Williams, 430 U.S. 387, 398–401, 97 S.Ct. 1232, 1239–1241, 51 L.Ed.2d 424 (1977); Massiah v. United States, 377 U.S. 201, 205–207, 84 S.Ct. 1199, 1202–1204, 12 L.Ed.2d 246 (1964).[10] Petitioner asserts that the questioning that produced his incriminating statements violated his Sixth Amendment right to counsel in two ways.

---

10. We note as a matter of some significance that petitioner had not retained, or accepted by appointment, a lawyer to represent him at the time he was questioned by authorities. Once an accused has a lawyer, a distinct set of constitutional safeguards aimed at preserving the sanctity of the attorney-client relationship takes effect. See Maine v. Moulton, 474 U.S. 159, 176, 106 S.Ct. 477, 487–88, 88 L.Ed.2d 481 (1985). The State conceded as much at argument.

A

Petitioner's first claim is that because his Sixth Amendment right to counsel arose with his indictment, the police were thereafter barred from initiating a meeting with him. He equates himself with a preindictment suspect who, while being interrogated, asserts his Fifth Amendment right to counsel; under Edwards v. Arizona, 451 U.S. 477, 101 S.Ct. 1880, 68 L.Ed.2d 378 (1981), such a suspect may not be questioned again unless he initiates the meeting.

* * *

At bottom, petitioner's theory cannot be squared with our rationale in *Edwards,* the case he relies on for support. * * * Preserving the integrity of an accused's choice to communicate with police only through counsel is the essence of *Edwards* and its progeny—not barring an accused from making an *initial* election as to whether he will face the State's officers during questioning with the aid of counsel, or go it alone. If an accused "knowingly and intelligently" pursues the latter course, we see no reason why the uncounseled statements he then makes must be excluded at his trial.

Key *

B

Petitioner's principal and more substantial claim is that questioning him without counsel present violated the Sixth Amendment because he did not validly waive his right to have counsel present during the interviews. Since it is clear that after the *Miranda* warnings were given to petitioner, he not only voluntarily answered questions without claiming his right to silence or his right to have a lawyer present to advise him but also executed a written waiver of his right to counsel during questioning, the specific issue posed here is whether this waiver was a "knowing and intelligent" waiver of his Sixth Amendment right.[11] See *Brewer v. Williams,* S.Ct. at 1240–41, 1242; Johnson v. Zerbst, 304 U.S. 458, 464–465, 58 S.Ct. 1019, 1023, 82 L.Ed.2d 1461 (1938).

In the past, this Court has held that a waiver of the Sixth Amendment right to counsel is valid only when it reflects "an intentional relinquishment or abandonment of a known right or privilege." *Johnson v. Zerbst,* supra, at 464, 58 S.Ct. at 1023. In other words, the accused must "kno[w] what he is doing" so that "his choice is made with eyes open." Adams v. United States ex rel. McCann, 317 U.S. 269, 279, 63 S.Ct. 236, 242, 87 L.Ed.2d 268 (1942). In a case arising under the Fifth Amendment, we described this requirement as "a full awareness [of] both the nature of the right being abandoned and the consequences of the decision to abandon it." Moran v. Burbine, 475 U.S. 412, 421, 106 S.Ct. 1135, 1141, 89 L.Ed.2d 410 (1986). Whichever of these formulations is used, the key inquiry in a case such as this one must be: Was the accused, who waived his Sixth Amendment rights during postindictment questioning, made sufficiently aware of his right to have counsel present during the questioning, and of the possible consequences of a decision to forgo the aid of counsel? In this case, we are convinced that by admonishing petitioner with the *Miranda* warn-

Rule

question Issue #2

11.   * * * [T]he voluntariness of petitioner's confession is not before us.

ings, respondent has met this burden and that petitioner's waiver of his right to counsel at the questioning was valid.

First, the *Miranda* warnings given petitioner made him aware of his right to have counsel present during the questioning. By telling petitioner that he had a right to consult with an attorney, to have a lawyer present while he was questioned, and even to have a lawyer appointed for him if he could not afford to retain one on his own, Officer Gresham and ASA Smith conveyed to petitioner the sum and substance of the rights that the Sixth Amendment provided him. * * * There is little more petitioner could have possibly been told in an effort to satisfy this portion of the waiver inquiry.

Second, the *Miranda* warnings also served to make petitioner aware of the consequences of a decision by him to waive his Sixth Amendment rights during postindictment questioning. Petitioner knew that any statement that he made could be used against him in subsequent criminal proceedings. This is the ultimate adverse consequence petitioner could have suffered by virtue of his choice to make uncounseled admissions to the authorities. This warning also sufficed—contrary to petitioner's claim here—to let him know what a lawyer could "do for him" during the postindictment questioning: namely, advise petitioner to refrain from making any such statements. By knowing what could be done with any statements he might make, and therefore, what benefit could be obtained by having the aid of counsel while making such statements, petitioner was essentially informed of the possible consequences of going without counsel during questioning. If petitioner nonetheless lacked "a full and complete appreciation of all of the consequences flowing" from his waiver, it does not defeat the State's showing that the information it provided to him satisfied the constitutional minimum.

Our conclusion is supported by petitioner's inability, in the proceedings before this Court, to articulate with precision what additional information should have been provided to him before he would have been competent to waive his right to counsel. All that petitioner's brief and reply brief suggest is petitioner should have been made aware of his "right under the Sixth Amendment to the broad protection of counsel"—a rather nebulous suggestion—and the "gravity of [his] situation." But surely this latter "requirement" (if it is one) was met when Officer Gresham informed petitioner that he had been formally charged with the murder of James Jackson. Under close questioning on this same point at argument, petitioner likewise failed to suggest any meaningful additional information that he should have been, but was not, provided in advance of his decision to waive his right to counsel. * * *

As a general matter, then, an accused who is admonished with the warnings prescribed by this Court in *Miranda,* has been sufficiently apprised of the nature of his Sixth Amendment rights, and of the consequences of abandoning those rights, so that his waiver on this basis will be considered a knowing and intelligent one.[12]

[handwritten margin note: Why court decided the way it did !]

---

12. This does not mean, of course, that all Sixth Amendment challenges to the conduct of postindictment questioning will fail whenever the challenged practice would pass constitutional muster under *Miranda.* For example, we have permitted a *Miranda* waiv-

C

We consequently reject petitioner's argument, which has some acceptance from courts and commentators, that since "the sixth amendment right [to counsel] is far superior to that of the fifth amendment right" and since "[t]he greater the right the greater the loss from a waiver of that right," waiver of an accused's Sixth Amendment right to counsel should be "more difficult" to effectuate than waiver of a suspect's Fifth Amendment rights. While our cases have recognized a "difference" between the Fifth Amendment and Sixth Amendment rights to counsel, and the "policies" behind these Constitutional guarantees, we have never suggested that one right is "superior" or "greater" than the other, nor is there any support in our cases for the notion that because a Sixth Amendment right may be involved, it is more difficult to waive than the Fifth Amendment counterpart.

Instead, we have taken a more pragmatic approach to the waiver question—asking what purposes a lawyer can serve at the particular stage of the proceedings in question, and what assistance he could provide to an accused at that stage—to determine the scope of the Sixth Amendment right to counsel, and the type of warnings and procedures that should be required before a waiver of that right will be recognized.

At one end of the spectrum, we have concluded there is no Sixth Amendment right to counsel whatsoever at a postindictment photographic display identification, because this procedure is not one at which the accused "require[s] aid in coping with legal problems or assistance in meeting his adversary." At the other extreme, recognizing the enormous importance and role that an attorney plays at a criminal trial, we have imposed the most rigorous restrictions on the information that must be conveyed to a defendant, and the procedures that must be observed, before permitting him to waive his right to counsel at trial. In these extreme cases, and in others that fall between these two poles, we have defined the scope of the right to counsel by a pragmatic assessment of the usefulness of counsel to the accused at the particular proceeding, and the dangers to the accused of proceeding without counsel. An accused's waiver of his right to counsel is "knowing" when he is made aware of these basic facts.

Applying this approach, it is our view that whatever warnings suffice for *Miranda's* purposes will also be sufficient in the context of postindictment questioning. The State's decision to take an additional step and commence formal adversarial proceedings against the accused does not

er to stand where a suspect was not told that his lawyer was trying to reach him during questioning; in the Sixth Amendment context, this waiver would not be valid. See Moran v. Burbine, 475 U.S., at 424, 428, 106 S.Ct. at 1142–43, 1145. Likewise a surreptitious conversion between an undercover police officer and an indicted suspect would not give rise to any *Miranda* violation as long as the "interrogation" was not in a custodial setting; however, once the accused is indicted, such questioning would be prohibited.

Thus, because the Sixth Amendment's protection of the attorney-client relationship—"the right to rely on counsel as a 'medium' between [the accused] and the State"—extends beyond *Miranda's* protection of the Fifth Amendment right to counsel, there will be cases where a waiver which would be valid under *Miranda* will not suffice for Sixth Amendment purposes.

substantially increase the value of counsel to the accused at questioning, or expand the limited purpose that an attorney serves when the accused is questioned by authorities. With respect to this inquiry, we do not discern a substantial difference between the usefulness of a lawyer to a suspect during custodial interrogation, and his value to an accused at postindictment questioning.

Thus, we require a more searching or formal inquiry before permitting an accused to waive his right to counsel at trial than we require for a Sixth Amendment waiver during postindictment questioning—*not* because postindictment questioning is "less important" than a trial (the analysis that petitioner's "hierarchical" approach would suggest)—but because the full "dangers and disadvantages of self-representation," during questioning are less substantial and more obvious to an accused than they are at trial. Because the role of counsel at questioning is relatively simple and limited, we see no problem in having a waiver procedure at that stage which is likewise simple and limited. So long as the accused is made aware of the "dangers and disadvantages of self-representation" during postindictment questioning, by use of the *Miranda* warnings, his waiver of his Sixth Amendment right to counsel at such questioning is "knowing and intelligent."

III

Before confessing to the murder of James Jackson, petitioner was meticulously informed by authorities of his right to counsel, and of the consequences of any choice not to exercise that right. On two separate occasions, petitioner elected to forgo the assistance of counsel, and speak directly to officials concerning his role in the murder. Because we believe that petitioner's waiver of his Sixth Amendment rights was "knowing and intelligent," we find no error in the decision of the trial court to permit petitioner's confessions to be used against him. Consequently, the judgment of the Illinois Supreme Court is

Affirmed.

■ JUSTICE BLACKMUN, dissenting.

I agree with most of what Justice Stevens says in his dissenting opinion. I, however, merely would hold that after formal adversary proceedings against a defendant have been commenced, the Sixth Amendment mandates that the defendant not be " 'subject to further interrogation by the authorities until counsel has been made available to him, unless the accused himself initiates further communication, exchanges, or conversations with the police.' " Michigan v. Jackson, 475 U.S. 625, 626, 106 S.Ct. 1404, 1406, 89 L.Ed.2d 631 (1986), quoting Edwards v. Arizona, 451 U.S. 477, 484–485, 101 S.Ct. 1880, 1884–1885, 68 L.Ed.2d 378 (1981).

* * *

JUSTICE STEVENS, with whom JUSTICE BRENNAN and JUSTICE MARSHALL join, dissenting.

The Court should not condone unethical forms of trial preparation by prosecutors or their investigators. In civil litigation it is improper for a lawyer to communicate with his or her adversary's client without either notice to opposing counsel or the permission of the court. An attempt to obtain evidence for use at trial by going behind the back of one's adversary would be not only a serious breach of professional ethics but also a manifestly unfair form of trial practice. In the criminal context, the same ethical rules apply and, in my opinion, notions of fairness that are at least as demanding should also be enforced.

* * *

The question that this case raises * * * is at what point in the adversary process does it become impermissible for the prosecutor, or his or her agents, to conduct such private interviews with the opposing party? Several alternatives are conceivable: when the trial commences, when the defendant has actually met and accepted representation by his or her appointed counsel, when counsel is appointed, or when the adversary process commences. In my opinion, the Sixth Amendment right to counsel demands that a firm and unequivocal line be drawn at the point at which adversary proceedings commence.

* * *

Today, however * * * the Court backs away from the significance previously attributed to the initiation of formal proceedings. In the majority's view, the purported waiver of counsel in this case is properly equated with that of an unindicted suspect. Yet, * * * important differences separate the two. The return of an indictment, or like instrument, substantially alters the relationship between the state and the accused. Only after a formal accusation has "the government * * * committed itself to prosecute, and only then [have] the adverse positions of government and defendant * * * solidified." Moreover, the return of an indictment also presumably signals the government's conclusion that it has sufficient evidence to establish a prima facie case. As a result, any further interrogation can only be designed to buttress the government's case; authorities are no longer simply attempting " 'to solve a crime.' " Given the significance of the initiation of formal proceedings and the concomitant shift in the relationship between the state and the accused, I think it quite wrong to suggest that *Miranda* warnings—or for that matter, any warnings offered by an adverse party—provide a sufficient basis for permitting the undoubtedly prejudicial—and, in my view, unfair—practice of permitting trained law enforcement personnel and prosecuting attorneys to communicate with as-of-yet unrepresented criminal defendants.

It is well settled that there is a strong presumption against waiver of Sixth Amendment protections. Warnings offered by an opposing party, whether detailed or cursory, simply cannot satisfy this high standard.

The majority premises its conclusion that *Miranda* warnings lay a sufficient basis for accepting a waiver of the right to counsel on the assumption that those warnings make clear to an accused "what a lawyer could 'do for him' during the postindictment questioning: namely, advise [him] to refrain from making any [incriminating] statements." Yet, this is surely a gross understatement of the disadvantage of proceeding without a lawyer and an understatement of what a defendant must understand to make a knowing waiver. The *Miranda* warnings do not, for example, inform the accused that a lawyer might examine the indictment for legal sufficiency before submitting his or her client to interrogation or that a lawyer is likely to be considerably more skillful at negotiating a plea bargain and that such negotiations may be most fruitful if initiated prior to any interrogation. Rather, the warnings do not even go so far as to explain to the accused the nature of the charges pending against him—advice that a court would insist upon before allowing a defendant to enter a guilty plea with or without the presence of an attorney. Without defining precisely the nature of the inquiry required to establish a valid waiver of the Sixth Amendment right to counsel, it must be conceded that at least minimal advice is necessary—the accused must be told of the "dangers and disadvantages of self-representation."

Yet, once it is conceded that certain advice is required and that after indictment the adversary relationship between the state and the accused has solidified, it inescapably follows that a prosecutor may not conduct private interviews with a charged defendant. * * * [T]here are ethical constraints that prevent a prosecutor from giving legal advice to an uncounseled adversary. Thus, neither the prosecutor nor his or her agents can ethically provide the unrepresented defendant with the kind of advice that should precede an evidence-gathering interview after formal proceedings have been commenced. Indeed, in my opinion even the *Miranda* warnings themselves are a species of legal advice that is improper when given by the prosecutor after indictment.

Moreover, there are good reasons why such advice is deemed unethical, reasons that extend to the custodial, postindictment setting with unequaled strength. First, the offering of legal advice may lead an accused to underestimate the prosecuting authorities' true adversary posture. For an incarcerated defendant—in this case, a 17–year–old who had been in custody for 44 hours at the time he was told of the indictment—the assistance of someone to explain why he is being held, the nature of the charges against him, and the extent of his legal rights, may be of such importance as to overcome what is perhaps obvious to most, that the prosecutor is a foe and not a friend. Second, the adversary posture of the parties, which is not fully solidified until formal charges are brought, will inevitably tend to color the advice offered. As hard as a prosecutor might try, I doubt that it is possible for one to wear the hat of an effective advisor to a criminal defendant while at the same time wearing the hat of a law enforcement authority. Finally, regardless of whether or not the accused actually understands the legal and factual issues involved and the state's role as an adversary party, advice offered by a lawyer (or his or her agents) with such an evident conflict of interest cannot help but create a public perception of unfairness and unethical conduct. And as we held earlier this Term, "courts have an independent interest in ensuring that criminal trials are conducted within the ethical standards of the profession and that legal proceedings appear fair to all who observe them." Wheat v. United States, 486 U.S. 153, 160, 108 S.Ct. 1692, 1697, 100 L.Ed.2d 140 (1988). This interest is a factor that may be considered in deciding whether to override a defendant's waiver of his or her Sixth Amendment right to conflict free representation, and likewise, should be considered in determining whether a waiver based on advice offered by the criminal defendant's adversary is ever appropriate.

In sum, without a careful discussion of the pitfalls of proceeding without counsel, the Sixth Amendment right cannot properly be waived. An adversary party, moreover, cannot adequately provide such advice. As a result, once the right to counsel attaches and the adversary relationship between the state and the accused solidifies, a prosecutor cannot conduct a private interview with an accused party without "dilut[ing] the protection afforded by the right to counsel." Although this ground alone is reason enough to never permit such private interviews, the rule also presents the added virtue of drawing a clear and easily identifiable line at the point between the investigatory and adversary stages of a criminal proceeding. Such clarity in definition of constitutional rules that govern criminal proceedings is important to the law enforcement profession as well as to the private citizen. It is true, of course, that the interest in effective law enforcement would benefit from an opportunity to engage in incommunicado questioning of defendants who, for reasons beyond their control, have not been able to receive the legal advice from counsel to which they are constitutionally entitled. But the Court's singleminded concentration on that interest might also lead to the toleration of similar practices at any stage of the trial. I think it clear that such private communications are intolerable not simply during trial, but at any point after adversary proceedings have commenced.

I therefore respectfully dissent.

— dissents says w/o atty cannot know rights + pitfalls if wave right to atty

NOTE

In a footnote, *Patterson* cited Moran v. Burbine, 475 U.S. 412, 428, 106 S.Ct. 1135, 1144, 89 L.Ed.2d 410, 425 (1986) (reprinted in subsection B(4) of this chapter), in which the Court "readily agreed" that once the Sixth Amendment right to counsel attached, "it follows that the police may not interfere with the efforts of a defendant's attorney to act as a 'medium' between [the suspect] and the State' during the interrogation." Burbine's waiver, apparently, would not have been effective if the events had occurred after his Sixth Amendment right to counsel had attached. Why?

CHAPTER 8

UNDERCOVER INVESTIGATIONS

Analysis

EDITORS' INTRODUCTION: UNDERCOVER LAW ENFORCEMENT ACTIVITIES AND SPECIAL CONCERN

Police undercover investigations present a sufficiently unique situation to deserve separate consideration. Such investigations pose unusually difficult problems for legal control of law enforcement conduct. Since undercover activities inherently involve deception, officers' actions may infringe upon subjects' interest in privacy more than do other types of law enforcement investigatory conduct. In addition, however, undercover investigations necessarily involve low visibility decisionmaking. Consequently, decisions whether to conduct such investigations or to use particular investigatory techniques in particular investigations are comparatively less open to scrutiny, evaluation, and control.

Many analyses of undercover investigations—both legal discussions and others—fail to carefully identify the underlying concerns. The risk that undercover investigations will stimulate criminal acts which would not otherwise be committed is, of course, among the considerations. In addition, such investigations may unjustifiably infringe upon subjects' interest in privacy. Deception—or other activities always or sometimes involved in undercover work—may bring a law enforcement agency into public disrepute because some regard these tactics as inherently "wrong" when employed by government agencies. These concerns might be further refined—what the subjects' interest in "privacy" is, for example, obviously could be more carefully developed. Too often, however, discussions fail to make any effort whatsoever to define and evaluate the real underlying concerns.

Perhaps because of this failure to identify and discuss the underlying considerations, the legal situation of undercover investigations and specific techniques used in such investigations is confused. Many doctrines relate to undercover police work but judicial opinions and other discussions often suggest available legal tools are inadequate to deal with problems presented by some undercover police activity. This chapter is divided into sections each focusing upon a doctrine affecting undercover investigations. First, the traditional law of entrapment is presented. Next explored is the Sixth Amendment right to counsel and its effect upon the elicitation and over-hearing by undercover personnel of self-incriminating admissions made by defendants. Finally, the third section addresses the application of the Fourth Amendment's right to be free from unreasonable searches and seizures in this context.

Two categories of undercover law enforcement activities are usefully distinguished. The first involves surveillance by an undercover investigator. Surveillance may be visual observation or involve overhearing communications. It may lead to the officer gaining possession of physical evidence, as where the subject of the surveillance, unaware of the agent's official status, entrusts items to the agent.

Surveillance must be contrasted with the other category of investigation, consisting of the undercover investigator actively stimulating the subject of the investigation to commit an offense at a time and place which make it feasible or easier for law enforcement officers to obtain proof of commission of the offense. L. Tiffany, D. McIntyre and D. Rotenberg, Detection of Crime 273 (1967) and Rotenberg, The Police Detection Practice of Encouragement: Lewis v. United States and Beyond, 4 Hous.L.Rev. 609 (1967), used the phrase "encouragement" to describe this tactic. Dix, Undercover Investigations and Police Rulemaking, 53 Texas L.Rev. 203, 215 (1975), preferred the phrase, "an offer * * * of the opportunity to commit an offense under controlled conditions." Whatever the practice is called, however, it raises considerations different than—or perhaps additional to—those triggered by surveillance. Tactics within both categories involve deception and therefore some possible invasion of the subject's expectation of privacy. The manipulation of the subject involved in encouragement, however, arguably constitutes a significantly greater invasion of that interest. In addition, encouragement creates a greater danger of stimulating the commission of offenses that would not otherwise be committed and of involving police agents in the commission of criminal acts.

A.   ENTRAPMENT

Traditional law has responded to concerns regarding undercover investigations with the doctrine of entrapment. There is, however, some reason to doubt whether entrapment provides an effective incentive for law enforcement to avoid misuse of undercover investigations.

Much dispute regarding entrapment law revolves around whether the controlling standard should be the "subjective" or the "objective" one. The Supreme Court's case law defining the entrapment defense under federal criminal law is a leading model supporting the subjective approach, and in the principal case following the Court adheres to its traditional subjective approach.

United States v. Russell

Supreme Court of the United States, 1973.
411 U.S. 423, 93 S.Ct. 1637, 36 L.Ed.2d 366.

■ MR. JUSTICE REHNQUIST delivered the opinion of the Court.

Respondent Richard Russell was charged in three counts of a five count indictment returned against him and codefendants John and Patrick Connolly. After a jury trial in the District Court, in which his sole defense was entrapment, respondent was convicted on all three counts of having unlawfully manufactured and processed methamphetamine ("speed") and of having unlawfully sold and delivered that drug * * *. He was sentenced to concurrent terms of two years in prison for each offense, the terms to be suspended on the condition that he spend six months in prison and be placed on probation for the following three years. On appeal the United States Court of Appeals for the Ninth Circuit, one judge dissenting, reversed the conviction solely for the reason that an undercover agent supplied an essential chemical for manufacturing the methamphetamine which formed the basis of respondent's conviction. The court concluded that as a matter of law "a defense to a criminal charge may be founded upon an intolerable degree of governmental participation in the criminal enterprise." We granted certiorari, and now reverse that judgment.

There is little dispute concerning the essential facts in this case. On December 7, 1969, Joe Shapiro, an undercover agent for the Federal Bureau of Narcotics and Dangerous Drugs, went to respondent's home on Whidbey Island in the State of Washington where he met with respondent and his two codefendants, John and Patrick Connolly. Shapiro's assignment was to locate a laboratory where it was believed that methamphetamine was being manufactured illicitly. He told the respondent and the Connollys that he represented an organization in the Pacific Northwest that was interested in controlling the manufacture and distribution of methamphetamine. He then made an offer to supply the defendants with the chemical phenyl–2–propanone, an essential ingredient in the manufacture of methamphetamine, in return for one-half of the drug produced. This offer was made on the condition that Agent Shapiro be shown a sample of the drug which they were making and the laboratory where it was being produced.

During the conversation Patrick Connolly revealed that he had been making the drug since May 1969 and since then had produced three pounds of it. John Connolly gave the agent a bag containing a quantity of methamphetamine that he represented as being from "the last batch that we made." Shortly thereafter, Shapiro and Patrick Connolly left respondent's house to view the laboratory which was located in the Connolly house on Whidbey Island. At the house Shapiro observed an empty bottle bearing the chemical label phenyl-2-propanone.

By prearrangement Shapiro returned to the Connolly house on December 9, 1969, to supply 100 grams of propanone and observe the chemical reaction. When he arrived he observed Patrick Connolly and the respondent cutting up pieces of aluminum foil and placing them in a large flask. There was testimony that some of the foil pieces accidentally fell on the floor and were picked up by the respondent and Shapiro and put into the flask.[1] Thereafter Patrick Connolly added all of the necessary chemicals, including the propanone brought by Shapiro, to make two batches of methamphetamine. The manufacturing process having been completed the following morning, Shapiro was given one-half of the drug and respondent kept the remainder. Shapiro offered to buy, and the respondent agreed to sell, part of the remainder for $60.

About a month later Shapiro returned to the Connolly house and met with Patrick Connolly to ask if he was still interested in their "business arrangement." Connolly replied that he was interested but that he had recently obtained two additional bottles of phenyl-2-propanone and would not be finished with them for a couple of days. He provided some additional methamphetamine to Shapiro at that time. Three days later Shapiro returned to the Connolly house with a search warrant and, among other items, seized an empty 500-gram bottle of propanone and a 100-gram bottle, not the one he had provided, that was partially filled with the chemical.

There was testimony at the trial of respondent and Patrick Connolly that phenyl-2-propanone was generally difficult to obtain. At the request of the Bureau of Narcotics and Dangerous Drugs, some chemical supply firms had voluntarily ceased selling the chemical.

At the close of the evidence, and after receiving the District Judge's standard entrapment instruction,[2] the jury found the respondent guilty on all counts charged. On appeal the respondent conceded that the jury could have found him predisposed to commit the offenses, but argued that on the facts presented there was entrapment as a matter of law. The Court of Appeals agreed, although it did not find the District Court had misconstrued or misapplied the traditional standards governing the entrapment defense. Rather, the court in effect expanded the traditional notion of entrapment, which focuses on the predisposition of the defendant, to mandate dismissal of a criminal prosecution whenever the court determines that there has been "an intolerable degree of governmental participation in the criminal enterprise." In this case the court decided that the conduct of the agent in supplying a scarce ingredient essential for the manufacture of a controlled substance established that defense.

---

1. Agent Shapiro did not otherwise participate in the manufacture of the drug or direct any of the work.

2. The District Judge stated the governing law on entrapment as follows: "Where a person has the willingness and the readiness to break the law, the mere fact that the government agent provides what appears to be a favorable opportunity is not entrapment." He then instructed the jury to acquit respondent if it had a "reasonable doubt whether the defendant had the previous intent or purpose to commit the offense * * * and did so only because he was induced or persuaded by some officer or agent of the government." No exception was taken by respondent to this instruction.

This new defense was held to rest on either of two alternative theories. One theory is based on * * * lower court decisions which have found entrapment, regardless of predisposition, whenever the government supplies contraband to the defendants. The second theory, a nonentrapment rationale, is based on a recent Ninth Circuit decision that reversed a conviction because a government investigator was so enmeshed in the criminal activity that the prosecution of the defendants was held to be repugnant to the American criminal justice system. Greene v. United States, 454 F.2d 783 (C.A.9 1971). The court below held that these two rationales constitute the same defense and that only the label distinguishes them. In any event, it held that "[b]oth theories are premised on fundamental concepts of due process and evince the reluctance of the judiciary to countenance 'overzealous law enforcement.' "

This Court first recognized and applied the entrapment defense in Sorrells v. United States, 287 U.S. 435, 53 S.Ct. 210, 77 L.Ed. 413 (1932). In *Sorrells*, a federal prohibition agent visited the defendant while posing as a tourist and engaged him in conversation about their common war experiences. After gaining the defendant's confidence the agent asked for some liquor, was twice refused, but upon asking a third time the defendant finally capitulated, and was subsequently prosecuted for violating the National Prohibition Act.

Chief Justice Hughes, speaking for the Court, held that as a matter of statutory construction the defense of entrapment should have been available to the defendant. Under the theory propounded by the Chief Justice, the entrapment defense prohibits law enforcement officers from instigating criminal acts by persons "otherwise innocent in order to lure them to its commission and to punish them." Thus, the thrust of the entrapment defense was held to focus on the intent or predisposition of the defendant to commit the crime. "[I]f the defendant seeks acquittal by reason of entrapment he cannot complain of an appropriate and searching inquiry into his own conduct and predisposition as bearing upon that issue."

Justice Roberts concurred in the result but was of the view "that courts must be closed to the trial of a crime instigated by the government's own agents." The difference in the view of the majority and the concurring opinions is that in the former the inquiry focuses on the predisposition of the defendant, whereas in the latter the inquiry focuses on whether the government "instigated the crime."

In 1958 the Court again considered the theory underlying the entrapment defense and expressly reaffirmed the view expressed by the *Sorrells* majority. Sherman v. United States, 356 U.S. 369, 78 S.Ct. 819, 2 L.Ed.2d 848 (1958). In *Sherman* the defendant was convicted of selling narcotics to a government informer. As in *Sorrells* it appears that the government agent gained the confidence of the defendant and, despite initial reluctance, the defendant finally acceded to the repeated importunings of the agent to commit the criminal act. On the basis of *Sorrells*, this Court reversed the affirmance of the defendant's conviction.

In affirming the theory underlying *Sorrells*, Chief Justice Warren for the Court, held that "[t]o determine whether entrapment has been established, a line must be drawn between the trap for the unwary innocent and

[handwritten margin note: Entrapment Defined]

[handwritten margin note: trap; innocent v. criminal]

the trap for the unwary criminal." Justice Frankfurter stated in a concurring opinion that he believed Justice Roberts had the better view in *Sorrells* and would have framed the question to be asked in an entrapment defense in terms of "whether the police conduct revealed in the particular case falls below standards * * * for the proper use of governmental power."

In the instant case respondent asks us to reconsider the theory of the entrapment defense as it is set forth in the majority opinions in *Sorrells* and *Sherman*. His principal contention is that the defense should rest on constitutional grounds. He argues that the level of Shapiro's involvement in the manufacture of the methamphetamine was so high that a criminal prosecution for the drug's manufacture violates the fundamental principles of due process. The respondent contends that the same factors that led this Court to apply the exclusionary rule to illegal searches and seizures, and confessions should be considered here. But he would have the Court go further in deterring undesirable official conduct by requiring that any prosecution be barred absolutely because of the police involvement in criminal activity. The analogy is imperfect in any event, for the principal reason behind the adoption of the exclusionary rule was the government's "failure to observe its own laws." * * * [T]he government's conduct here violated no independent constitutional right of the respondent. Nor did Shapiro violate any federal statute or rule or commit any crime in infiltrating the respondent's drug enterprise.

Respondent would overcome this basic weakness in his analogy to the exclusionary rule cases by having the Court adopt a rigid constitutional rule that would preclude any prosecution when it is shown that the criminal conduct would not have been possible had not an undercover agent "supplied an indispensable means to the commission of the crime that could not have been obtained otherwise, through legal or illegal channels." Even if we were to surmount the difficulties attending the notion that due process of law can be embodied in fixed rules, and those attending respondent's particular formulation, the rule he proposes would not appear to be of significant benefit to him. For on the record presented it appears that he cannot fit within the terms of the very rule he proposes.

The record discloses that although the propanone was difficult to obtain it was by no means impossible. The defendants admitted making the drug both before and after those batches made with the propanone supplied by Shapiro. Shapiro testified that he saw an empty bottle labeled phenyl-2-propanone on his first visit to the laboratory on December 7, 1969. And when the laboratory was searched pursuant to a search warrant on January 10, 1970, two additional bottles labeled phenyl-2-propanone were seized. Thus, the facts in the record amply demonstrate that the propanone used in the illicit manufacture of methamphetamine not only *could* have been obtained without the intervention of Shapiro but was in fact obtained by these defendants.

While we may some day be presented with a situation in which the conduct of law enforcement agents is so outrageous that due process principles would absolutely bar the government from invoking judicial processes to obtain a conviction, cf. Rochin v. California, 342 U.S. 165, 72

S.Ct. 205, 96 L.Ed. 183 (1952), the instant case is distinctly not of that breed. Shapiro's contribution of propanone to the criminal enterprise already in process was scarcely objectionable. The chemical is by itself a harmless substance and its possession is legal. While the government may have been seeking to make it more difficult for drug rings, such as that of which respondent was a member, to obtain the chemical, the evidence described above shows that it nonetheless was obtainable. The law enforcement conduct here stops far short of violating that "fundamental fairness, shocking to the universal sense of justice," mandated by the Due Process Clause of the Fifth Amendment.

The illicit manufacture of drugs is not a sporadic, isolated criminal incident, but a continuing, though illegal, business enterprise. In order to obtain convictions for illegally manufacturing drugs, the gathering of evidence of past unlawful conduct frequently proves to be an all but impossible task. Thus in drug-related offenses law enforcement personnel have turned to one of the only practicable means of detection: the infiltration of drug rings and a limited participation in their unlawful present practices. Such infiltration is a recognized and permissible means of apprehension; if that be so, then the supply of some item of value that the drug ring requires must, as a general rule, also be permissible. For an agent will not be taken into the confidence of the illegal entrepreneurs unless he has something of value to offer them. Law enforcement tactics such as this can hardly be said to violate "fundamental fairness" or "shocking to the universal sense of justice."

Respondent also urges, as an alternative to his constitutional argument, that we broaden the nonconstitutional defense of entrapment in order to sustain the judgment of the Court of Appeals. This Court's opinions in Sorrells v. United States, supra, and Sherman v. United States, supra, held that the principal element in the defense of entrapment was the defendant's predisposition to commit the crime. Respondent conceded in the Court of Appeals, as well he might, "that he may have harbored a predisposition to commit the charged offenses." Yet he argues that the jury's refusal to find entrapment under the charge submitted to it by the trial court should be overturned and the views of Justices Roberts and Frankfurter, concurring in *Sorrells* and *Sherman,* respectively, which make the essential element of the defense turn on the type and degree of governmental conduct, be adopted as the law.

We decline to overrule these cases. *Sorrells* is a precedent of long standing that has already been once reexamined in *Sherman* and implicitly there reaffirmed. Since the defense is not of a constitutional dimension, Congress may address itself to the question and adopt any substantive definition of the defense that it may find desirable.

Critics of the rule laid down in *Sorrells* and *Sherman* have suggested that its basis in the implied intent of Congress is largely fictitious, and have pointed to what they conceive to be the anomalous difference between the treatment of a defendant who is solicited by a private individual and one who is entrapped by a government agent. Questions have been likewise raised as to whether "predisposition" can be factually established with the requisite degree of certainty. Arguments such as these, while not devoid of appeal, have been twice previously made to this Court, and twice rejected by it, first in *Sorrells* and then in *Sherman*.

We believe that at least equally cogent criticism has been made of the concurring views in these cases. Commenting in *Sherman* on Justice Roberts' position in *Sorrells* that "although the defendant could claim that the Government had induced him to commit the crime, the Government could not reply by showing that the defendant's criminal conduct was due to his own readiness and not to the persuasion of government agents," Chief Justice Warren quoted the observation of Judge Learned Hand in an earlier stage of that proceeding:

> " 'Indeed, it would seem probable that, if there were no reply [to the claim of inducement], it would be impossible ever to secure convictions of any offences which consist of transactions that are carried on in secret.' "

Nor does it seem particularly desirable for the law to grant complete immunity from prosecution to one who himself planned to commit a crime, and then committed it, simply because government undercover agents subjected him to inducements which might have seduced a hypothetical individual who was not so predisposed. * * *

Several decisions of the United States district courts and courts of appeals have undoubtedly gone beyond this Court's opinions in *Sorrells* and *Sherman* in order to bar prosecutions because of what they thought to be for want of a better term "overzealous law enforcement." But the defense of entrapment enunciated in those opinions was not intended to give the federal judiciary a "chancellor's foot" veto over law enforcement practices of which it did not approve. The execution of the federal laws under our Constitution is confined primarily to the Executive Branch of the Government, subject to applicable constitutional and statutory limitations and to judicially fashioned rules to enforce those limitations. We think that the decision of the Court of Appeals in this case quite unnecessarily introduces an unmanageably subjective standard which is contrary to the holdings of this Court in *Sorrells* and *Sherman*.

Those cases establish that entrapment is a relatively limited defense. It is rooted not in any authority of the Judicial Branch to dismiss prosecutions for what it feels to have been "overzealous law enforcement," but instead in the notion that Congress could not have intended criminal punishment for a defendant who has committed all the elements of a prescribed offense, but who was induced to commit them by the government.

* * *

Respondent's concession in the Court of Appeals that the jury finding as to predisposition was supported by the evidence is, therefore, fatal to his claim of entrapment. He was an active participant in an illegal drug manufacturing enterprise which began before the government agent appeared on the scene, and continued after the government agent had left the scene. He was, in the words of *Sherman, supra,* not an "unwary innocent" but an "unwary criminal." The Court of Appeals was wrong, we believe, when it sought to broaden the principle laid down in *Sorrells* and *Sherman*. Its judgment is therefore reversed.

Reversed.

■ Mr. Justice Stewart, with whom Mr. Justice Brennan and Mr. Justice Marshall join, dissenting.

[handwritten margin note: entrapment = the manufacturing of a crime by defendants]

It is common ground that "[t]he conduct with which the defense of entrapment is concerned is the *manufacturing* of crime by law enforcement officials and their agents." Lopez v. United States, 373 U.S. 427, 434, 83 S.Ct. 1381, 1385, 10 L.Ed.2d 462 (1963). For the Government cannot be permitted to instigate the commission of a criminal offense in order to prosecute someone for committing it. * * * It is to prevent this situation from occurring in the administration of federal criminal justice that the defense of entrapment exists. But the Court has been sharply divided as to the proper basis, scope, and focus of the entrapment defense, and as to whether, in the absence of a conclusive showing, the issue of entrapment is for the judge or the jury to determine.

I.

In Sorrells v. United States, supra, and Sherman v. United States, supra, the Court took what might be called a "subjective" approach to the defense of entrapment. In that view, the defense is predicated on an unexpressed intent of Congress to exclude from its criminal statutes the prosecution and conviction of persons, "otherwise innocent," who have been lured to the commission of the prohibited act through the Government's instigation. * * * The Court today adheres to this approach.

The concurring opinion of Mr. Justice Roberts, joined by Justices Brandeis and Stone, in the *Sorrells* case, and that of Mr. Justice Frankfurter, joined by Justices Douglas, Harlan, and Brennan, in the *Sherman* case, took a different view of the entrapment defense. In their concept, the defense is not grounded on some unexpressed intent of Congress to exclude from punishment under its statutes those otherwise innocent persons tempted into crime by the Government, but rather on the belief that "the methods employed on behalf of the Government to bring about conviction cannot be countenanced." Thus, the focus of this approach is not on the propensities and predisposition of a specific defendant, but on "whether the police conduct revealed in the particular case falls below [the] standards, to which common feelings respond, for the proper use of governmental power." Phrased another way, the question is whether—regardless of the predisposition to crime of the particular defendant involved—the governmental agents have acted in such a way as is likely to instigate or create a criminal offense. Under this approach, the determination of the lawfulness of the Government's conduct must be made—as it is on all questions involving the legality of law enforcement methods—by the trial judge, not the jury.

In my view, this objective approach to entrapment advanced by the concurring opinions in *Sorrells* and *Sherman* is the only one truly consistent with the underlying rationale of the defense. Indeed, the very basis of the entrapment defense itself demands adherence to an approach that focuses on the conduct of the governmental agents, rather than on whether the defendant was "predisposed" or "otherwise innocent." I find it impossible to believe that the purpose of the defense is to effectuate some unexpressed congressional intent to exclude from its criminal statutes persons who committed a prohibited act, but would not have done so except for the Government's inducements. * * *

The purpose of the entrapment defense, then, cannot be to protect persons who are "otherwise innocent." Rather, it must be to prohibit unlawful governmental activity in instigating crime. * * * If that is so, then whether the particular defendant was "predisposed" or "otherwise innocent" is irrelevant; and the important question becomes whether the Government's conduct in inducing the crime was beyond judicial toleration.

Moreover, a test that makes the entrapment defense depend on whether the defendant had the requisite predisposition permits the introduction into evidence of all kinds of hearsay, suspicion, and rumor—all of which would be inadmissible in any other context—in order to prove the defendant's predisposition. It allows the prosecution, in offering such proof, to rely on the defendant's bad reputation or past criminal activities, including even rumored activities of which the prosecution may have insufficient evidence to obtain an indictment, and to present the agent's suspicions as to why they chose to tempt this defendant. This sort of evidence is not only unreliable, as the hearsay rule recognizes; but it is also highly prejudicial, especially if the matter is submitted to the jury, for, despite instructions to the contrary, the jury may well consider such evidence as probative not simply of the defendant's predisposition, but of his guilt of the offense with which he stands charged.

More fundamentally, focusing on the defendant's innocence or predisposition has the direct effect of making what is permissible or impermissible police conduct depend upon the past record and propensities of the particular defendant involved. Stated another way, this subjective test means that the Government is permitted to entrap a person with a criminal record or bad reputation, and then to prosecute him for the manufactured crime, confident that his record or reputation itself will be enough to show that he was predisposed to commit the offense anyway.

* * *

[W]hen the agents' involvement in criminal activities goes beyond the mere offering of such an opportunity and when their conduct is of a kind that could induce or instigate the commission of a crime by one not ready and willing to commit it, then—regardless of the character or propensities of the particular person induced—I think entrapment has occurred. For in that situation, the Government has engaged in the impermissible manufacturing of crime, and the federal courts should bar the prosecution in order to preserve the institutional integrity of the system of federal criminal justice.

II.

In the case before us, I think that the District Court erred in submitting the issue of entrapment to the jury, with instructions to acquit only if it had a reasonable doubt as to the respondent's predisposition to committing the crime. Since, under the objective test of entrapment, predisposition is irrelevant and the issue is to be decided by the trial judge, the Court of Appeals, I believe, would have been justified in reversing the conviction on this basis alone. But since the appellate court did not remand for consideration of the issue by the District Judge under an objective standard, but rather found entrapment as a matter of law and directed that the indictment be dismissed, we must reach the merits of the respondent's entrapment defense.

Since, in my view, it does not matter whether the respondent was predisposed to commit the offense of which he was convicted, the focus must be, rather, on the conduct of the undercover government agent. What the agent did here was to meet with a group of suspected producers of methamphetamine, including the respondent; to request the drug; to offer to supply the chemical phenyl-2-propanone in exchange for one-half of the methamphetamine to be manufactured therewith; and, when that offer was accepted, to provide the needed chemical ingredient, and to purchase some of the drug from the respondent.

It is undisputed that phenyl-2-propanone is an essential ingredient in the manufacture of methamphetamine; that it is not used for any other purpose; and that, while its sale is not illegal, it is difficult to obtain, because a manufacturer's license is needed to purchase it, and because many suppliers, at the request of the Federal Bureau of Narcotics and Dangerous Drugs, do not sell it at all. It is also undisputed that the methamphetamine which the respondent was prosecuted for manufacturing and selling was all produced on December 10, 1969, and that all the phenyl-2-propanone used in the manufacture of that batch of the drug was provided by the government agent. In these circumstances, the agent's undertaking to supply this ingredient to the respondent, thus making it possible for the Government to prosecute him for manufacturing an illicit drug with it, was, I think, precisely the type of governmental conduct that the entrapment defense is meant to prevent.

* * *

I would affirm the judgment of the Court of Appeals.

NOTES

1. **Predisposition Independent of the Undercover Investigation.** The Supreme Court's application of federal entrapment law in Jacobson v. United States, 503 U.S. 540, 112 S.Ct. 1535, 118 L.Ed.2d 174 (1992), may have imposed new demands on undercover activity. Specifically, federal entrapment law may now require the Government to respond to a claim of entrapment by showing the defendant's predisposition was independent of—and perhaps existed before—the undercover investigation.

In 1984, federal postal inspectors examining the records of a California book store found the name of a customer, Keith Jacobson. Jacobson, a Nebraska farmer, had purchased by mail two magazines Bare Boys I and Bare Boys II before federal legislation made criminal receipt through the mail of sexually explicit depictions of children. In January 1985 a postal inspector sent Jacobson a letter purporting to come from the fictitious American Hedonist Society. The letter included a membership application and represented that the Society believed that its members had the "right to read what we desire, the right to discuss similar interests with those who share our philosophy, and finally that we have the right to seek pleasure without restrictions being placed on us by outdated puritan morality." Jacobson joined the organization and returned a sexual attitude questionnaire asking him to rank on a scale of one to four his enjoyment of various sexual materials, one being "really enjoy," two being "enjoy," three being "somewhat enjoy," and four being "do not enjoy." He ranked the entry "[p]re-teen sex" as a two, but indicated he was opposed to pedophilia.

In May 1986, Jacobson was sent a solicitation from a second fictitious consumer research company, "Midlands Data Research," seeking a response from those who "believe in the joys of sex and the complete awareness of those lusty and youthful lads and lasses of the neophite [sic] age." He responded: "Please feel free to send me more information, I am interested in teenage sexuality. Please keep my name confidential." Postal authorities then sent him material purporting to come from another fictitious unit, "Heartland Institute for a New Tomorrow" or HINT. The material explained HINT was "an organization founded to protect and promote sexual freedom and freedom of choice. We believe that arbitrarily imposed legislative sanctions restricting your sexual freedom should be rescinded through the legislative process." A survey was enclosed and in response Jacobson indicated his interest in "[p]reteen sex-homosexual" material was above average, but not high.

A Government "prohibited mail specialist" began writing to Jacobson, using the pseudonym "Carl Long." The letters employed a tactic known as "mirroring," in which the investigator reflects interests expressed by the person under investigation. Jacobson indicated his primary interest was in "male-male items," and elaborated

"As far as my likes are concerned, I like good looking young guys (in their late teens and early 20's) doing their thing together."

After writing two letters, Jacobson discontinued the correspondence.

In March 1987, a second Government agency, the Customs Service, using the fictitious name "Produit Outaouais," mailed Jacobson a brochure advertising photographs of young boys engaging in sex. Petitioner placed an order that was never filled.

The Postal Service then wrote to Jacobson as the "Far Eastern Trading Company Ltd." Its letter began:

"As many of you know, much hysterical nonsense has appeared in the American media concerning 'pornography' and what must be done to stop it from coming across your borders. This brief letter does not allow us to give much comments; however, why is your government spending millions of dollars to exercise international censorship while tons of drugs, which makes yours the world's most crime ridden country are passed through easily."

It continued:

"[W]e have devised a method of getting these to you without prying eyes of U.S. Customs seizing your mail * * *. After consultations with American solicitors, we have been advised that once we have posted our material through your system, it cannot be opened for any inspection without authorization of a judge."

Jacobson responded with a request for more information, and was sent a catalogue. He ordered Boys Who Love Boys, a pornographic magazine depicting young boys engaged in various sexual activities. Postal authorities arranged a controlled delivery of a photocopy of the magazine, and Jacobson was arrested.

Jacobson was prosecuted for violating the Child Protection Act of 1984 by receiving through the mails a visual depiction involving a minor engaged in sexually explicit conduct. At trial, he asserted a defense of entrapment. He testified that, when he received the initial Bare Boys magazines, he was shocked because he expected to receive photographs of young men 18 years or older. A search of Jacobson's home revealed no evidence that Jacobson collected or was actively interested in child pornography. When asked why he placed the order for Boys Who Love Boys, he responded:

> "Well, the statement was made of all the trouble and the hysteria over pornography and I wanted to see what the material was. It didn't describe the—I didn't know for sure what kind of sexual action they were referring to in the Canadian letter * * *."

The jury rejected his defense and convicted him.

The Supreme Court, by a 5 to 4 vote, reversed. Since the Government did not dispute its inducing Jacobson's commission of the offense, the majority explained, it had the burden of proving him predisposed to violate the law before the Government directed its attention to him. It failed to do so:

> [A]lthough he had become predisposed to break the law by May 1987, it is our view that the Government did not prove that this predisposition was independent and not the product of the attention that the Government had directed at [Jacobson] since January 1985.

> The prosecution's evidence of predisposition falls into two categories: evidence developed prior to the Postal Service's mail campaign, and that developed during the course of the investigation. The sole piece of preinvestigation evidence is petitioner's 1984 order and receipt of the Bare Boys magazines. But this is scant if any proof of petitioner's predisposition to commit an illegal act, the criminal character of which a defendant is presumed to know. * * *

> Furthermore, petitioner was acting within the law at the time he received these magazines. * * * Evidence of predisposition to do what once was lawful is not, by itself, sufficient to show predisposition to do what is not illegal, for there is a common understanding that most people obey the law even when they disapprove of it. * * *

> The prosecution's evidence gathered during the investigation also fails to carry the Government's burden. [Jacobson's] responses to the many communications prior to the ultimate criminal act were at most indicative of certain personal inclinations, including a predisposition to view photographs of preteen sex and a willingness to promote a given agenda by supporting lobbying organizations. Even so, [his] responses hardly support an inference that he would commit the crime of receiving child pornography through the mails. * * *

> On the other hand, the strong arguable inference is that, by waving the banner of individual rights and disparaging the legitimacy and constitutionality of efforts to restrict the availability of sexually explicit materials, the Government not only excited petitioner's interest in sexually explicit materials banned by law but also exerted substantial pressure on petitioner to obtain and read such material as part of a fight against censorship and the infringement of individual rights. * * *

> Because * * * the prosecution failed, as a matter of law, to adduce evidence to support the jury verdict that petitioner was predisposed, independent of the

Government's acts and beyond a reasonable doubt, to violate the law by receiving child pornography through the mails, we reverse the Court of Appeals' judgment affirming the conviction of Keith Jacobson.

503 U.S. at 550–54, 112 S.Ct. at 1541–43, 118 L.Ed.2d at 185–86.

The dissenters indicated the majority held "Government conduct may be considered to create a predisposition to commit a crime, even before any Governmental action to induce the commission of the crime." This, they maintained, changed federal entrapment doctrine which has traditionally asked whether the defendant was predisposed before the Government induced the commission of the crime. They predicted the majority's approach would be often relied upon by defendants:

> [A]fter this case, every defendant will claim that something the Government agent did before soliciting the crime "created" a predisposition that was not there before. For example, a bribe taker will claim that the description of the amount of money available was so enticing that it implanted a disposition to accept the bribe later offered. A drug buyer will claim that the description of the drug's purity and effects was so tempting that it created the urge to try it for the first time. In short, the Court's opinion could be read to prohibit the Government from advertising the seductions of criminal activity as part of its sting operation, for fear of creating a predisposition in its suspects. * * *

503 U.S. at 557, 112 S.Ct. at 1545, 118 L.Ed.2d at 190 (O'Connor, J., dissenting).

2. **Requirement of Reasonable Suspicion to Target Suspect for Investigation.** Does *Jacobson*, perhaps in combination with Fourth Amendment law, impose a requirement that officers have reasonable suspicion a person is predisposed to commit an offense before targeting him, perhaps with a view towards offering him an opportunity to commit the offense? The courts have concluded no such requirement exists. United States v. Aibejeris, 28 F.3d 97, 99 (11th Cir.1994); United States v. Harvey, 991 F.2d 981, 989–93 (2d Cir.1993); Commonwealth v. Mance, 539 Pa. 282, 286–89, 652 A.2d 299, 301–02 (1995).

3. **Provision of Contraband for Offense.** The phenyl-2-propanone provided to the defendants by the officer in *Russell* was not contraband, i.e., its possession by persons like the defendants was not itself criminal. Suppose officers provide contraband for use in the commission of an offense?

In Hampton v. United States, 425 U.S. 484, 96 S.Ct. 1646, 48 L.Ed.2d 113 (1976), Hampton and Hutton, a Drug Enforcement Administration informant, sold heroin to federal undercover officers. At his trial for distribution of heroin, Hampton testified Hutton provided the heroin and suggested selling it; other testimony suggested Hampton provided the drug. The defense requested an instruction that Hampton was entitled to acquittal if the jury found the heroin sold supplied to Hampton by a government informer. The instruction was denied, Hampton was convicted, and appeal followed. The Supreme Court, with Justice Stevens not participating, affirmed but without an opinion of the Court. Justice Rehnquist, joined by the Chief Justice and Justice White, concluded *Russell* "ruled out the possibility that the defense of entrapment could ever be based upon governmental misconduct in a case, such as this one, where the predisposition of the defendant to commit the crime was established." He continued:

> The limitations of the Due Process Clause of the Fifth Amendment come into play only when the Government activity in question violates some protected right of the *defendant*. Here, * * * the police, the Government informant, and the defendant acted in concert with one another. * * * If the police engage in illegal activity in concert with a defendant beyond the scope of their duties the remedy lies, not in freeing the equally culpable defendant, but in prosecut-

ing the police under the applicable provisions of state or federal law. But the police conduct here no more deprived defendant of any right secured to him by the United States Constitution than did the police conduct in *Russell* deprive Russell of any rights.

425 U.S. at 490–91, 96 S.Ct. at 1650, 48 L.Ed.2d at 119. Justice Powell, joined by Justice Blackmun, concurred in the judgment. Given that the phenyl-2-propanone in *Russell* was difficult to obtain and useful only in the manufacture of methamphetamine, he found no difference between providing it and providing heroin. *Russell*, he concluded, controlled. Turning to the Due Process argument, he acknowledged "the doctrinal and practical difficulties of delineating limits to police involvement in crimes that do not focus upon predisposition, as Government participation ordinarily will be fully justified in society's 'war with the criminal classes.'" But given that Hampton's Due Process claim could be rejected as controlled by *Russell*, he was unwilling to join the plurality's broad language rejecting such claims in all cases of government involvement in crime.

4. **Expansive Objective "Due Process" Formulations of Entrapment.** The objective approach to entrapment as generally construed provides for the defense only if the officers' conduct violates objective limits designed to discourage law enforcement conduct tending to generate the commission of crime. The Supreme Court of Alaska, for example, defined entrapment under its objective standard as follows:

> [U]nlawful entrapment occurs when a public law enforcement official * * * induces another person to commit * * * an offense by persuasion which would be effective to persuade an average person, other than one who is ready and willing, to commit such an offense.

Grossman v. State, 457 P.2d 226, 229 (Alaska 1969).

Some courts, however, impose more rigorous limits on undercover investigations, often on due process related grounds. The New Mexico Supreme Court, for example, held that defendants are entitled to argue to juries that their situations present entrapment under either a subjective or objective approach. It also recognized a second type of "objective entrapment," based on due process of law as guaranteed by the State Constitution. Under this doctrine, a defendant is entitled to dismissal of the prosecution if the judge determines the law enforcement conduct employed in the investigation so exceeded the standards of proper investigation that the public's confidence in the fair and honorable administration of justice would be shaken by such conduct. State v. Vallejos, 123 N.M. 739, 945 P.2d 957 (1997). It continued:

> In order to provide some benchmarks, we have surveyed the factors and criteria other jurisdictions use when a defendant raises the objective entrapment defense, the outrageous government conduct defense, or the due process defense. We recognize two broad categories of impropriety: unconscionable methods and illegitimate purposes.
>
> * * *
>
> While police may engage in some degree of deception in their efforts to detect certain sorts of crime that are difficult to detect otherwise, police may not employ unconscionable methods in their attempts to ferret out crime. We find the following examples to be helpful as indicia of unconscionability: "coaxing a defendant into a circular transaction;" "[giving defendant] free heroin until he [is] addicted and then play[ing] on [his] addiction to persuade [him] to purchase heroin and cocaine for an undercover police agent;" an extreme plea of desperate illness; an appeal based primarily on sympathy or friendship; an offer of inordinate gain or a promise of excessive profit; persis-

tent solicitation to overcome a defendant's demonstrated hesitancy; the use of brutality or physical or psychological coercion to induce the commission of a crime; an offer to sell drugs to one in a drug rehabilitation program; employment of contingent fee agreements with informants, by which a key witness has "what amounts to a financial stake in criminal convictions;" "unjustified intrusion into citizens' privacy and autonomy;" the inducement of others to engage in violence or the threat of violence against innocent parties; the use of provocateurs sent into political organizations to suggest the commission of crimes; excessive involvement by the police in creating the crime; the "manufacture [of] a crime from whole cloth;" and the " 'engineer[ing] and direct[ion of] the criminal enterprise from start to finish.' "

Police also violate due process when they ensnare a defendant in an operation guided by an illegitimate purpose. "Illegitimate purpose" is not capable of being defined with great precision. However, other courts have described improper purposes in a number of ways. In West Virginia, a court considers whether police have ensnared a defendant "solely for the purpose of generating criminal charges and without any motive to prevent further crime or protect the public at large." The New York Court of Appeals has suggested that due process is violated when "the record reveals simply a desire to obtain a conviction ... [rather than] to prevent further crime or protect the populace."

123 N.M. at 744–45, 945 P.2d at 962–63.

In *Vallejos*, the court found no objective entrapment. Other courts applying similar approaches, however, have found law enforcement conduct impermissible. In Soohoo v. State, 737 So.2d 1108 (Fla.App.1999), for example, the court held the due process prohibition against egregious governmental conduct required dismissal of the charges. Soohoo was charged with purchasing two kilos of cocaine from a confidential informant. The informant, seeking to reduce his sentence for drug offenses, was operating under the loose supervision of an officer. Explaining its conclusion, the court stressed, first, the informant offered to help the defendant sell the cocaine if the defendant would purchase five kilos. Second, the informant responded to the defendant's interest in one kilo by offering a second kilo on credit. In addition, the court emphasized the officer supervising the informant gave him what the court considered too much leeway in structuring the transaction.

Similarly, in State v. Grubb, 319 N.J.Super. 407, 725 A.2d 707 (1999), the appellate court, finding the drug defendant entitled to acquittal under "common law objective entrapment," emphasized the investigating officers had insufficient justification for targeting and investigating the defendant as a criminal suspect. The investigation was triggered when another suspect, who became an informant, reported that he had a deal pending to purchase Clenbuterol from Grubb, but the officers failed to conduct sufficient inquiry to determine that Clenbuterol was not a steroid as the officers suspected. The *Grubb* court also stressed the officers exercised insufficient supervision over the informant.

B.   ELICITATION OF SELF-INCRIMINATING STATEMENTS

EDITORS' INTRODUCTION: APPLICATION OF THE FIFTH AND SIXTH AMENDMENTS TO UNDERCOVER INVESTIGATIONS

The two major federal constitutional limits on law enforcement officers' ability to elicit self-incriminating admissions from suspects are the Fifth Amendment prohibition against compelled self-incrimination, as developed in Miranda v. Arizona, 384 U.S. 436, 86 S.Ct. 1602, 16 L.Ed.2d 694

(1966), and the Sixth Amendment right to counsel. Both doctrines, as they apply to general law enforcement questioning of suspects, are developed in Chapter 7. When self-incriminating admissions are obtained or overheard by undercover officers or informants working as agents of officers, the situation—and the law—is considerably different.

Does an undercover officer passively overhearing self-incriminating admissions made by a suspect engage in action that triggers self-incrimination protection? This was addressed in Hoffa v. United States, 385 U.S. 293, 87 S.Ct. 408, 17 L.Ed.2d 374 (1966), reprinted in part later in this chapter. *Hoffa* considered the argument that testimony by a government informer concerning incriminating admissions made by the defendant in the former's presence violated the defendant's Fifth Amendment privilege against compelled self-incrimination. It was clear that if the informer had disclosed his status he would not have been permitted by the defendant to overhear the conversations. The Court held:

> [A] necessary element of compulsory self-incrimination is some kind of compulsion. * * * [No] claim has been or could be made that [Hoffa's] incriminating statements were the product of any sort of coercion, legal or factual. The * * * conversations * * * were wholly voluntary. For that reason, if for no other, it is clear that no right protected by the Fifth Amendment privilege against compulsory self-incrimination was violated in this case.

384 U.S. at 304, 87 S.Ct. at 414–15, 17 L.Ed.2d at 383.

Does *Miranda* apply when an undercover officer or informant actively persuades a suspect to make incriminating admissions? This was addressed in Illinois v. Perkins, 496 U.S. 292, 110 S.Ct. 2394, 110 L.Ed.2d 243 (1990). Police learned from a former prison acquaintance of Perkins that Perkins had admitted a homicide. Upon locating Perkins in a local jail, police placed the former acquaintance and an undercover officer in the same cellblock. After the former acquaintance introduced them, the officer engaged Perkins in conversations and encouraged Perkins to admit the offense and relate details of its commission. Failure to comply with *Miranda* in this process, the Court held, did not render Perkins's admissions subject to suppression.

> Conversations between suspects and undercover agents do not implicate the concerns underlying *Miranda*. The essential ingredients of a "police-dominated atmosphere" and compulsion are not present when an incarcerated person speaks freely to someone he believes to be a fellow inmate. Coercion is determined from the perspective of the suspect. * * * When a suspect considers himself in the company of cellmates and not officers, the coercive atmosphere is lacking. * * * When the suspect has no reason to think that the listeners have official power over him, it should not be assumed that his words are motivated by the reaction he expects from his listeners. * * *

> *Miranda* forbids coercion, not mere strategic deception by taking advantage of a suspect's misplaced trust in one he supposes to be a fellow prisoner. * * *

496 U.S. at 296–97, 110 S.Ct. at 2397, 110 L.Ed.2d at 251.

As a result of these decisions, federal constitutional regulation of law enforcement conduct in this area is achieved through the Sixth and Fourteenth Amendments right to counsel. The seminal case is Massiah v. United States, 377 U.S. 201, 84 S.Ct. 1199, 12 L.Ed.2d 246 (1964). Massiah, Colson, and others were arrested and indicted for drug offenses; Massiah and Colson were released on bail. Massiah retained a lawyer. Unknown to Massiah, Colson decided to cooperate with the government agents in their continuing investigation, and permitted the installation of a radio transmitter in his car. One evening, Colson and Massiah had a lengthy conversation while sitting in Colson's parked automobile. A federal agent listened over his radio to the conversation, which included several incriminating admissions by Massiah. At Massiah's trial, the agent was permitted to testify as to these admissions. The Supreme Court held this constitutional error:

> We hold that [Massiah] was denied the basic protection of [the Sixth Amendment right to counsel] when there was used against him at his trial evidence of his own incriminating words, which federal agents had deliberately elicited from him after he had been indicted and in the absence of his counsel.

377 U.S. at 206, 84 S.Ct. at 1203, 12 L.Ed.2d at 250. The principal case in this section explores the ramifications of *Massiah*.

United States v. Henry

Supreme Court of the United States, 1980.
447 U.S. 264, 100 S.Ct. 2183, 65 L.Ed.2d 115.

■ MR. CHIEF JUSTICE BURGER delivered the opinion of the Court.

We granted certiorari to consider whether respondent's Sixth Amendment right to the assistance of counsel was violated by the admission at trial of incriminating statements made by respondent to his cellmate, an undisclosed government informant, after indictment and while in custody.

I.

The Janaf Branch of the United Virginia Bank/Seaboard National in Norfolk, Va., was robbed in August 1972. Witnesses saw two men wearing masks and carrying guns enter the bank while a third man waited in the car. No witnesses were able to identify respondent Henry as one of the participants. About an hour after the robbery, the getaway car was discovered. Inside was found a rent receipt signed by one "Allen R. Norris" and a lease, also signed by Norris, for a house in Norfolk. Two men, who were subsequently convicted of participating in the robbery, were arrested at the rented house. Discovered with them were the proceeds of the robbery and the guns and masks used by the gunman.

Government agents traced the rent receipt to Henry; on the basis of this information, Henry was arrested in Atlanta, Ga., in November 1972. Two weeks later he was indicted for armed robbery under 18 U.S.C.A. § 2113(a) and (d). He was held pending trial in the Norfolk City Jail. Counsel was appointed on November 27.

On November 21, 1972, shortly after Henry was incarcerated, government agents working on the Janaf robbery contacted one Nichols, an inmate at the Norfolk City Jail, who for some time prior to this meeting had been engaged to provide confidential information to the Federal Bureau of Investigation as a paid informant. Nichols was then serving a sentence on local forgery charges. The record does not disclose whether the agent contacted Nichols specifically to acquire information about Henry or the Janaf robbery.

Nichols informed the agent that he was housed in the same cellblock with several federal prisoners awaiting trial, including Henry. The agent told him to be alert to any statements made by the federal prisoners, but not to initiate any conversation with or question Henry regarding the bank robbery. In early December, after Nichols had been released from jail, the agent again contacted Nichols, who reported that he and Henry had engaged in conversation and that Henry had told him about the robbery of the Janaf bank. Nichols was paid for furnishing the information.

When Henry was tried in March 1973, an agent of the Federal Bureau of Investigation testified concerning the events surrounding the discovery of the rental slip and the evidence uncovered at the rented house. Other witnesses also connected Henry to the rented house, including the rental agent who positively identified Henry as the "Allen R. Norris" who had rented the house and had taken the rental receipt described earlier. A neighbor testified that prior to the robbery she saw Henry at the rented house with John Luck, one of the two men who had by the time of Henry's trial been convicted for the robbery. In addition, palm prints found on the lease agreement matched those of Henry.

Nichols testified at trial that he had "an opportunity to have some conversations with Mr. Henry while he was in the jail," and that Henry told him that on several occasions he had gone to the Janaf Branch to see which employees opened the vault. Nichols also testified that Henry described to him the details of the robbery and stated that the only evidence connecting him to the robbery was the rental receipt. The jury was not informed that Nichols was a paid government informant.

On the basis of this testimony, Henry was convicted of bank robbery and sentenced to a term of imprisonment of 25 years. On appeal he raised no Sixth Amendment claims. His conviction was affirmed, and his petition to this Court for a writ of certiorari was denied.

On August 28, 1975, Henry moved to vacate his sentence * * *. At this stage, he stated that he had just learned that Nichols was a paid government informant and alleged that he had been intentionally placed in the same cell with Nichols so that Nichols could secure information about the robbery. Thus, Henry contended that the introduction of Nichols' testimony violated his Sixth Amendment right to the assistance of counsel. The District Court denied the motion without a hearing. The Court of Appeals, however, reversed and remanded for an evidentiary inquiry into "whether the witness [Nichols] was acting as a government agent during his interviews with Henry."

On remand, the District Court requested affidavits from the government agents. An affidavit was submitted describing the agent's relationship with Nichols and relating the following conversation:

"I recall telling Nichols at this time to be alert to any statements made by these individuals [the federal prisoners] regarding the charges against them. I specifically recall telling Nichols that he was not to question Henry or these individuals about the charges against them, however, if they engaged him in conversation or talked in front of him, he was requested to pay attention to their statements. I recall telling Nichols not to initiate any conversations with Henry regarding the bank robbery charges against Henry, but that if Henry initiated the conversations with Nichols, I requested Nichols to pay attention to the information furnished by Henry."

The agent's affidavit also stated that he never requested anyone affiliated with the Norfolk City Jail to place Nichols in the same cell with Henry.

The District Court again denied Henry's § 2255 motion, concluding that Nichols' testimony at trial did not violate Henry's Sixth Amendment right to counsel. The Court of Appeals reversed and remanded, holding that the actions of the government impaired the Sixth Amendment rights of the defendant under Massiah v. United States, 377 U.S. 201, 84 S.Ct. 1199, 12 L.Ed.2d 246 (1964). The court noted that Nichols had engaged in conversation with Henry and concluded that if by association, by general conversation, or both, Nichols had developed a relationship of trust and confidence with Henry such that Henry revealed incriminating information, this constituted interference with the right to the assistance of counsel under the Sixth Amendment.

II.

* * *

The question here is whether under the facts of this case, a government agent "deliberately elicited" incriminating statements from Henry within the meaning of *Massiah*. Three factors are important. First, Nichols was acting under instructions as a paid informant for the government; second, Nichols was ostensibly no more than a fellow inmate of Henry; and third, Henry was in custody and under indictment at the time he was engaged in conversation by Nichols.

The Court of Appeals viewed the record as showing that Nichols deliberately used his position to secure incriminating information from Henry when counsel was not present and held that conduct attributable to the government. Nichols had been a paid government informant for more than a year; moreover, the FBI agent was aware that Nichols had access to Henry and would be able to engage him in conversations without arousing Henry's suspicion. The arrangement between Nichols and the agent was on a contingent fee basis; Nichols was to be paid only if he produced useful information. This combination of circumstances is sufficient to support the Court of Appeals' determination. Even if the agent's statement is accepted that he did not intend that Nichols would take affirmative steps to secure incriminating information, he must have known that such propinquity likely would lead to that result.

The Government argues that the federal agents instructed Nichols not to question Henry about the robbery. Yet according to his own testimony, Nichols was not a passive listener; rather, he had "some conversations with Mr. Henry" while he was in jail and Henry's incriminatory statements were "the product of this conversation." * * *

* * *

It is undisputed that Henry was unaware of Nichols' role as a government informant. The Government argues that this Court should apply a less rigorous standard under the Sixth Amendment where the accused is prompted by an undisclosed undercover informant than where the accused is speaking in the hearing of persons he knows to be government officers. That line of argument, however, seeks to infuse Fifth Amendment concerns against compelled self-incrimination into the Sixth Amendment protection of the right to the assistance of counsel. An accused speaking to a known government agent is typically aware that his statements may be used against him. The adversary positions at that stage are well established; the parties are then "arms length" adversaries.

When the accused is in the company of a fellow inmate who is acting by prearrangement as a government agent, the same cannot here be said. Conversation stimulated in such circumstances may elicit information that an accused would not intentionally reveal to persons known to be government agents. Indeed, the *Massiah* Court noted that if the Sixth Amendment "is to have any efficacy it must apply to indirect and surreptitious interrogations as well as those conducted in the jailhouse." The Court pointedly observed that Massiah was more seriously imposed upon because he did not know that his codefendant was a government agent.

Moreover, the concept of a knowing and voluntary waiver of Sixth Amendment rights does not apply in the context of communications with an undisclosed undercover informant acting for the government. In that setting Henry, being unaware that Nichols was a government agent expressly commissioned to secure evidence, cannot be held to have waived his right to the assistance of counsel.

Finally Henry's incarceration at the time he was engaged in conversation by Nichols is also a relevant factor. As a ground for imposing the prophylactic requirements in Miranda v. Arizona, 384 U.S. 436, 467, 86 S.Ct. 1602, 1624, 16 L.Ed.2d 694 (1966), this Court noted the powerful psychological inducements to reach for aid when a person is in confinement. While the concern in *Miranda* was limited to custodial police interrogation, the mere fact of custody imposes pressures on the accused; confinement may bring into play subtle influences that will make him particularly susceptible to the ploys of undercover government agents. The Court of Appeals determined that on this record the incriminating conversations between Henry and Nichols were facilitated by Nichols' conduct and apparent status as a person sharing a common plight. That Nichols had managed to gain the confidence of Henry, as the Court of Appeals determined, is confirmed by Henry's request that Nichols assist him in his escape plans when Nichols was released from confinement.

Under the strictures of the Court's holdings on the exclusion of evidence, we conclude that the Court of Appeals did not err in holding that Henry's statements to Nichols should not have been admitted at trial. By intentionally creating a situation likely to induce Henry to make incriminating statements without the assistance of counsel, the government violated Henry's Sixth Amendment right to counsel. This is not a case where, in Justice Cardozo's words, "the constable blundered," People v. Defore, 242 N.Y. 13, 21, 150 N.E. 585, 587 (1926); rather, it is one where the "constable" planned an impermissible interference with the right to the assistance of counsel.

The judgment of the Court of Appeals for the Fourth Circuit is affirmed.

■ MR. JUSTICE BLACKMUN, with whom MR. JUSTICE WHITE joins, dissenting.

* * *

I.

Massiah mandates exclusion only if a federal agent "deliberately elicited" statements from the accused in the absence of counsel. The word "deliberately" denotes intent. *Massiah* ties this intent to the act of elicitation, that is, to conduct that draws forth a response. Thus *Massiah*, by its own terms, covers only action undertaken with the specific intent to evoke an inculpatory disclosure.

* * *

[W]hile claiming to retain the "deliberately elicited" test, the Court really forges a new test that saps the word "deliberately" of all significance. The Court's extension of *Massiah* would cover even a "negligent" triggering of events resulting in reception of disclosures. This approach, in my view, is unsupported and unwise.

* * *

II.

In my view, the Court not only missteps in forging a new *Massiah* test; it proceeds to misapply the very test it has created. The new test requires a showing that the agent created a situation "likely to induce" the production of incriminatory remarks, and that the informant in fact "prompted" the defendant. Even accepting the most capacious reading of both this language and the facts, I believe that neither prong of the Court's test is satisfied.

A. *"Likely to Induce."* In holding that Coughlin's actions were likely to induce Henry's statements, the Court relies on three facts: a contingent fee arrangement; Henry's assumption that Nichols was just a cellmate; and Henry's incarceration.

* * *

* * * I question whether the existence of a contingent fee arrangement is at all significant. The reasonable conclusion of an informant like Nichols would be that, whatever the arrangement, he would *not* be remunerated if he breached his promise; yet the Court asks us to infer that Coughlin's conversation with Nichols "likely would lead" Nichols to engage in the very conduct which Coughlin told him to avoid.

The Court also emphasizes that Henry was "unaware that Nichols was a government agent." One might properly assign this factor some importance, were it not for Brewer v. Williams, 430 U.S. 387, 97 S.Ct. 1232, 51 L.Ed.2d 424 (1977). In that case, the Court explicitly held that the fact "[t]hat the incriminating statements were elicited surreptitiously in the *Massiah* case, and otherwise here, is *constitutionally irrelevant*." (Emphasis added.) The Court's teeter-tottering with this factor in *Massiah* analysis can only induce confusion.

Finally, the Court notes that Henry was incarcerated when he made his statements to Nichols. The Court's emphasis of the "subtle influences" exerted by custody, however, is itself too subtle for me. This is not a case of a custodial encounter with police, in which the Government's display of power might overcome the free will of the accused. The relationship here was "social" and relaxed. Henry did not suspect that Nichols was connected with the FBI. Moreover, even assuming that "subtle influences" might encourage a detainee to talk about his crime, there are certainly counterbalances of at least equal weight. Since, in jail, "official surveillance has traditionally been the order of the day," and a jailmate has obvious incentives to assist authorities, one may expect a detainee to act with corresponding circumspection. * * *

* * *

B.   *"Prompting."* All Members of the Court agree that Henry's statements were properly admitted if Nichols did not "prompt" him. The record, however, gives no indication that Nichols "stimulated" Henry's remarks with "affirmative steps to secure incriminating information." Certainly the known facts reveal nothing more than "a jailhouse informant who had been instructed to overhear conversations and to engage a criminal defendant in some conversations." The scant record demonstrates only that Nichols "had 'an opportunity to have some conversations with Mr. Henry while he was in the jail.'" "Henry had engaged [Nichols] in conversation," "had requested Nichols' assistance," and "had talked to Nichols about the bank robbery charges against him." Thus, we know only that Nichols and Henry had conversations, hardly a startling development, given their location in the same cellblock in a city jail. We know nothing about the nature of these conversations, particularly whether Nichols subtly or otherwise focused attention on the bank robberies. Indeed, to the extent the record says anything at all, it supports the inference that it was Henry, not Nichols, who "engaged" the other "in some conversations," and who was the moving force behind any mention of the crime. I cannot believe that *Massiah* requires exclusion when a cellmate previously unknown to the defendant and asked only to keep his ears open says: "It's a nice day," and the defendant responds: "It would be nicer if I hadn't robbed that bank."
* * *

■ MR. JUSTICE REHNQUIST, dissenting.

* * *

The doctrinal underpinnings of *Massiah* have been largely left unexplained, and the result in this case, as in *Massiah*, is difficult to reconcile with the traditional notions of the role of an attorney. Here, as in *Massiah*, the accused was not prevented from consulting with his counsel as often as he wished. No meetings between the accused and his counsel were disturbed or spied upon. And preparation for trial was not obstructed. * * *

Once the accused has been made aware of his rights, it is his responsibility to decide whether or not to exercise them. If he voluntarily relinquishes his rights by talking to authorities, or if he decides to disclose incriminating information to someone whom he mistakenly believes will not report it to the authorities, he is normally accountable for his actions and must bear any adverse consequences that result. Such information has not in any sense been obtained because the accused's will has been overborne, nor does it result from any "unfair advantage" that the State has over the accused: the accused is free to keep quiet and to consult with his attorney if he so chooses. In this sense, the decision today and the result in *Massiah* are fundamentally inconsistent with traditional notions of the role of the attorney that underlie the Sixth Amendment right to counsel.

* * *

* * * This Court has never held that an accused is constitutionally protected from his inability to keep quiet, whether or not he has been encouraged by third party citizens to voluntarily make incriminating remarks. I do not think the result should be different merely because the government has encouraged a third party informant to report remarks obtained in this fashion. When an accused voluntarily chooses to make an incriminatory remark in these circumstances, he knowingly assumes the risk that his confidant may be untrustworthy.

* * *

The fact that police carry on undercover activities should not automatically be transmuted because formal criminal proceedings have begun. * * * [T]he mere bringing of formal proceedings does not necessarily mean that an undercover investigation or the need for it has terminated. A person may be arrested on the basis of probable cause arising in the immediate aftermath of an offense and during early stages of investigation, but before the authorities have had an opportunity to investigate fully his connection with the crime. And for the criminal, there is no rigid dichotomy between the time before commencement of former criminal proceedings and the time after such proceedings have begun. Once out on bail the accused remains free to continue his criminal activity, and very well may decide to do so. * * * I would hold that the Government's activity here is merely a continuation of their lawful authority to use covert operations in investigating a criminal case after formal proceedings have commenced.

NOTES

1. **Passive Informants.** If an informant overhears an incriminating admission by a defendant but did not elicit it, does the Sixth Amendment bar the use of this admission? The principal case suggests not, and this has been reaffirmed.

In Kuhlmann v. Wilson, 477 U.S. 436, 106 S.Ct. 2616, 91 L.Ed.2d 364 (1986), Wilson was arrested and arraigned on charges relating to a robbery-murder. He was placed in a cell with prisoner Benny Lee; the cell provided them with a view of the garage at which the crimes were committed. Unknown to Wilson, Lee had entered into an arrangement under which he agreed to listen to Wilson's conversations and report them to police. Lee was instructed not to ask Wilson any questions but to "keep his ears open." Wilson soon told Lee that, although he was present at the robbery and murder, he did not know the perpetrators and was not involved in the crime. According to his later testimony, Lee responded that the story "didn't sound too good" and "things didn't look too good for him." At another point, Lee testified he had told Wilson, "[Y]ou better come up with a better story because that one doesn't sound too cool to me * * *." Several days later, Wilson told Lee another version of the events, admitting guilty participation. At Wilson's state trial, the trial judge found Wilson's admissions to Lee "spontaneous" and "unsolicited" and admitted them. In subsequent federal habeas corpus litigation, the Supreme Court held Wilson entitled to no relief. Acknowledging that it had never expressly addressed whether the Sixth Amendment bars the admission of statements overheard yet not elicited by an informant, the majority resolved the issue:

> [T]he primary concern of the *Massiah* line of decisions is secret interrogation by investigatory techniques that are the equivalent of direct police interrogation. Since "the Sixth Amendment is not violated whenever—by luck or happenstance—the State obtains incriminating statements from the accused after the right to counsel has attached," a defendant does not make out a violation of that right simply by showing that an informant, either through prior arrangement or voluntarily, reported his incriminating statements to the police. Rather, the defendant must demonstrate that the police and their informant took some action, beyond merely listening, that was designed deliberately to elicit incriminating remarks.

477 U.S. at 459, 106 S.Ct. at 2630, 91 L.Ed.2d at 384–85. The record in the case, the majority concluded, did not permit a federal habeas corpus court to find, under this standard, Wilson's Sixth Amendment rights violated.

2. **Target Suspected of Several Crimes.** Special problems are presented when a suspect is believed involved in multiple crimes. If the suspect's Sixth Amendment right to counsel under *Massiah* and *Henry* attaches, may law enforcement officers nevertheless seek to elicit admissions to other offenses under investigation?

In Maine v. Moulton, 474 U.S. 159, 106 S.Ct. 477, 88 L.Ed.2d 481 (1985), both Moulton and one Colson were indicted for theft by receiving stolen property. Colson contacted police; he reported that he had received anonymous threatening telephone calls and that Moulton suggested the two kill Gary Elwell, a state witness. Other witnesses in the case reported to authorities that they had also received threats. The police made and Colson accepted a deal under which he would cooperate with authorities in return for no further charges being brought against him. During later telephone conversations with Colson, Moulton suggested the two meet to plan their defense to the charges. For purposes of this meeting, Colson was equipped with a body wire transmitter to record what was said; according to police testimony, the device was provided for Colson's safety in the event Moulton realized he was cooperating with authorities and to record any further threats to witnesses

Moulton might make. During the conversation, Moulton offered that the plan for killing Elwell would not work. There was extended discussion concerning the falsification of alibis and Colson encouraged Moulton to make a number of incriminating admissions concerning the crime for which he had been indicted. At Moulton's later theft trial, the state successfully offered into evidence those portions of the recorded conversations in which Moulton made admissions concerning the crime charged. One portion of the discussion concerning false alibis was admitted, but no part of the conversation concerning the killing of the witness was offered. Moulton was convicted.

The Supreme Court reversed, reasoning that admission of the conversations violated Moulton's Sixth Amendment rights as developed in *Massiah* and *Henry*. The majority rejected the prosecution's argument that the evidence was admissible because the police activity was legitimately intended to investigate matters other than the theft offense for which Moulton was indicted—the threats to Colson and Moulton's plan to kill Elwell:

> To allow the admission of evidence obtained from the accused in violation of his Sixth Amendment right whenever the police assert an alternative, legitimate reason for their surveillance invites abuse by law enforcement personnel in the form of fabricated investigations and risks the evisceration of the Sixth Amendment right recognized in *Massiah*. * * * Consequently, incriminating statements pertaining to pending charges are inadmissible at the trial of those charges, notwithstanding the fact that the police were also investigating other crimes, if, in obtaining this evidence, the State violated the Sixth Amendment by knowingly circumventing the accused's right to the assistance of counsel.

474 U.S. at 180, 106 S.Ct. at 489, 88 L.Ed.2d at 498–99. Because Moulton's *Massiah* right was violated, the use of the evidence in his theft trial was improper. The Court also offered:

> On the other hand, to exclude evidence pertaining to charges as to which the Sixth Amendment right to counsel had not attached at the time the evidence was obtained, simply because other charges were pending at that time, would unnecessarily frustrate the public's interest in the investigation of criminal activities.

474 U.S. at 180, 106 S.Ct. at 489, 88 L.Ed.2d at 498. It added:

> Incriminating statements pertaining to other crimes, as to which the Sixth Amendment right has not yet attached are, of course, admissible at the trial of those offenses.

474 U.S. at 180 n. 16, 106 S.Ct. at 489 n. 16, 88 L.Ed.2d at 499 n. 16.

C.   UNDERCOVER SURVEILLANCE AS A "SEARCH" (AND RELATED MATTERS)

The Fourth Amendment's prominence in federal constitutional regulation of other aspects of law enforcement investigatory behavior suggests the provision would be appropriate as a means of limiting, but not prohibiting, certain aspects of undercover investigations. This, of course, would be possible only if some or all of the activities of undercover officers and agents constituted "searches" or "seizures" within the meaning of the Fourth Amendment. Whether this is the case is addressed in the principal case in this section.

Hoffa v. United States

Supreme Court of the United States, 1966.
385 U.S. 293, 87 S.Ct. 408, 17 L.Ed.2d 374.

■ MR. JUSTICE STEWART delivered the opinion of the Court.

Over a period of several weeks in the late autumn of 1962 there took place in a federal court in Nashville, Tennessee, a trial by jury in which James Hoffa was charged with violating a provision of the Taft-Hartley Act. That trial, known in the present record as the Test Fleet trial, ended with a hung jury. The petitioners now before us—James Hoffa, Thomas Parks, Larry Campbell, and Ewing King—were tried and convicted in 1964 for endeavoring to bribe members of that jury. The convictions were affirmed by the Court of Appeals. A substantial element in the Government's proof that led to the convictions of these four petitioners was contributed by a witness named Edward Partin, who testified to several incriminating statements which he said petitioners Hoffa and King had made in his presence during the course of the Test Fleet trial. Our grant of certiorari was limited to the single issue of whether the Government's use in this case of evidence supplied by Partin operated to invalidate these convictions.

Issue: ———▷

* * *

The controlling facts can be briefly stated. The Test Fleet trial, in which James Hoffa was the sole individual defendant, was in progress between October 22 and December 23, 1962, in Nashville, Tennessee. James Hoffa was president of the International Brotherhood of Teamsters. During the course of the trial he occupied a three-room suite in the Andrew Jackson Hotel in Nashville. One of his constant companions throughout the trial was the petitioner King, president of the Nashville local of the Teamsters Union. Edward Partin, a resident of Baton Rouge, Louisiana, and a local Teamsters Union official there, made repeated visits to Nashville during the period of the trial. On these visits he frequented the Hoffa hotel suite, and was continually in the company of Hoffa and his associates, including King, in and around the hotel suite, the hotel lobby, the courthouse, and elsewhere in Nashville. During this period Partin made frequent reports to a federal agent named Sheridan concerning conversations he said Hoffa and King had had with him and with each other, disclosing endeavors to bribe members of the Test Fleet jury. Partin's reports and his subsequent testimony at the petitioners' trial unquestionably contributed, directly or indirectly, to the convictions of all four of the petitioners.

Partin's testimony contributed to conviction of Hoffa on bribery of jury members

The chain of circumstances which led Partin to be in Nashville during the Test Fleet trial extended back at least to September of 1962. At that time Partin was in jail in Baton Rouge on a state criminal charge. He was also under a federal indictment for embezzling union funds, and other indictments for state offenses were pending against him. Between that time and Partin's initial visit to Nashville on October 22 he was released on bail on the state criminal charge, and proceedings under the federal indictment were postponed. On October 8, Partin telephoned Hoffa in Washington, D. C., to discuss local union matters and Partin's difficulties with the authorities. In the course of this conversation Partin asked if he could see Hoffa to confer about these problems, and Hoffa acquiesced. Partin again called

Hoffa on October 18 and arranged to meet him in Nashville. During this period Partin also consulted on several occasions with federal law enforcement agents, who told him that Hoffa might attempt to tamper with the Test Fleet jury, and asked him to be on the lookout in Nashville for such attempts and to report to the federal authorities any evidence of wrongdoing that he discovered. Partin agreed to do so.

After the Test Fleet trial was completed, Partin's wife received four monthly installment payments of $300 from government funds, and the state and federal charges against Partin were either dropped or not actively pursued.

[W]e proceed upon the premise that Partin was a government informer from the time he first arrived in Nashville on October 22, and that the Government compensated him for his services as such. It is upon that premise that we consider the constitutional issues presented.

* * *

I.

It is contended that only by violating the petitioner's rights under the Fourth Amendment was Partin able to hear the petitioner's incriminating statements in the hotel suite, and that Partin's testimony was therefore inadmissible * * *. The argument is that Partin's failure to disclose his role as a government informer vitiated the consent that the petitioner gave to Partin's repeated entries into the suite, and that by listening to the petitioner's statements Partin conducted an illegal "search" for verbal evidence.

The preliminary steps of this argument are on solid ground. A hotel room can clearly be the object of Fourth Amendment protection as much as a home or an office. The Fourth Amendment can certainly be violated by guileful as well as by forcible intrusions into a constitutionally protected area. And the protections of the Fourth Amendment are surely not limited to tangibles, but can extend as well to oral statements.

Where the argument falls is in its misapprehension of the fundamental nature and scope of Fourth Amendment protection. What the Fourth Amendment protects is the security a man relies upon when he places himself or his property within a constitutionally protected area, be it his home or his office, his hotel room or his automobile. There he is protected from unwarranted governmental intrusion. And when he puts something in his filing cabinet, in his desk drawer, or in his pocket, he has the right to know it will be secure from an unreasonable search or an unreasonable seizure. * * *

In the present case, however, it is evident that no interest legitimately protected by the Fourth Amendment is involved. It is obvious that the petitioner was not relying on the security of his hotel suite when he made the incriminating statements to Partin or in Partin's presence. Partin did not enter the suite by force or by stealth. He was not a surreptitious eavesdropper. Partin was in the suite by invitation, and every conversation which he heard was either directed to him or knowingly carried on in his presence. The petitioner, in a word, was not relying on the security of the hotel room; he was relying upon his misplaced confidence that Partin would not reveal his wrongdoing. As counsel for the petitioner himself points out, some of the communications with Partin did not take place in the suite at all, but in the "hall of the hotel," in the "Andrew Jackson Hotel lobby," and "at the courthouse."

Neither this Court nor any member of it has ever expressed the view that the Fourth Amendment protects a wrongdoer's misplaced belief that a person to whom he voluntarily confides his wrongdoing will not reveal it. Indeed, the Court unanimously rejected that very contention less than four years ago in Lopez v. United States, 373 U.S. 427, 83 S.Ct. 1381, 10 L.Ed.2d 462. * * * In the words of the dissenting opinion in *Lopez*, "The risk of being overheard by an eavesdropper or betrayed by an informer or deceived as to the identity of one with whom one deals is probably inherent in the conditions of human society. It is the kind of risk we necessarily assume whenever we speak."

Adhering to these views, we hold that no right protected by the Fourth Amendment was violated in the present case.

* * *

IV.

Finally, the petitioner claims that even if there was no violation [of any of his specific federal constitutional rights], the judgment of conviction must nonetheless be reversed. The argument is based upon the Due Process Clause of the Fifth Amendment. The "totality" of the Government's conduct during the Test Fleet trial operated, it is said, to " 'offend those canons of decency and fairness which express the notions of justice of English-speaking peoples even toward those charged with the most heinous offenses' (Rochin v. [People of] California, 342 U.S. 165, 169 [72 S.Ct. 205, 208, 96 L.Ed. 183])."

The argument boils down to a general attack upon the use of a government informer as "a shabby thing in any case," and to the claim that in the circumstances of this particular case the risk that Partin's testimony might be perjurious was very high. Insofar as the general attack upon the use of informers is based upon historic "notions" of "English-speaking peoples," it is without historical foundation. In the words of Judge Learned Hand, "Courts have countenanced the use of informers from time immemorial; in cases of conspiracy, or in other cases when the crime consists of preparing for another crime, it is usually necessary to rely upon them or upon accomplices because the criminals will almost certainly proceed covertly. * * * " United States v. Dennis, 2 Cir., 183 F.2d 201, at 224.

This is not to say that a secret government informer is to the slightest degree more free from all relevant constitutional restrictions than is any other government agent. It *is* to say that the use of secret informers is not *per se* unconstitutional.

The petitioner is quite correct in the contention that Partin, perhaps even more than most informers, may have had motives to lie. But it does not follow that his testimony was untrue, nor does it follow that his testimony was constitutionally inadmissible. The established safeguards of the Anglo-American legal system leave the veracity of a witness to be tested by cross-examination, and the credibility of his testimony to be determined by a properly instructed jury. At the trial of this case, Partin was subjected to rigorous cross-examination, and the extent and nature of his dealings with federal and state authorities were insistently explored. The trial judge instructed the jury, both specifically and generally, with regard to assessing Partin's credibility. The Constitution does not require us to upset the jury's verdict.

Affirmed.

NOTES

1. **Use of Transmitters or Recorders.** If an undercover agent uses electronic devices, does the investigation involve a search? Should it make any difference whether the undercover agent merely records a conversation with the suspect, or causes it to be transmitted for hearing (and perhaps recording) by others?

In United States v. White, 401 U.S. 745, 91 S.Ct. 1122, 28 L.Ed.2d 453 (1971), White was charged with drug transactions with a government informer, Harvey Jackson. Jackson had carried a radio transmitter concealed on his person and nearby government agents listened to the transaction by this means. At trial, Jackson was not available and, over objection, the trial judge permitted the government agents to testify to what they overheard; White was convicted. On appeal, the Court of Appeals read On Lee v. United States, 343 U.S. 747, 72 S.Ct. 967, 96 L.Ed. 1270 (1952), as holding that use of such a transmitting device did not make Jackson's conduct a search. But it further read Katz v. United States, 389 U.S. 347, 88 S.Ct. 507, 19 L.Ed.2d 576 (1967), as overruling *On Lee*. Under *Katz*, it continued, Jackson's activity was a search conducted without a warrant. Therefore the agents' testimony was inadmissible. The Supreme Court reversed. In an opinion announcing the judgment of the Court and joined by three other members of the Court, Justice White relied upon two grounds. First, the Court of Appeals erred in reading *Katz* as overruling *On Lee*:

> If the conduct and revelations of an agent operating without electronic equipment do not invade the defendant's constitutionally justifiable expectations of privacy, neither does a simultaneous recording of the same conversation made by the agent or by others from transmissions received from the agent to whom the defendant is talking and whose trustworthiness the defendant necessarily risks.

401 U.S. at 751, 91 S.Ct. at 1126, 28 L.Ed.2d at 458. Second, under Desist v. United States, 394 U.S. 244, 89 S.Ct. 1030, 22 L.Ed.2d 248 (1969), *Katz* was not to be applied to surveillance which—like that in *On Lee*—took place before the decision in *Katz*. Judged by pre-*Katz* law, i.e., *On Lee*, the facts presented no search.

Justices Harlan, Marshall, and Douglas dissented separately; each expressed the view that *Desist* was wrongly decided and should not be followed. All also took the position that *On Lee* should no longer be regarded as controlling, and that Jackson's activity implicated the Fourth Amendment. Justice Harlan explained:

> The critical question * * * is whether under our system of government, as reflected in the Constitution, we should impose on our citizens the risk of the electronic listener or observer without at least the protection of a warrant requirement.

> This question must, in my view, be answered by assessing the nature of a particular practice and the likely extent of its impact on the individual's sense of security balanced against the utility of the conduct as a technique of law enforcement. * * *
>
> The impact of the practice of third-party bugging must, I think, be considered such as to undermine that confidence and sense of security in dealing with one another that is characteristic of individual relationships between citizens in a free society. It goes beyond the impact on privacy occasioned by the ordinary type of "informer" investigation * * *. The argument of the plurality opinion, to the effect that it is irrelevant whether secrets are revealed by the mere tattletale or the transistor, ignores the differences occasioned by third-party monitoring and recording which insures full and accurate disclosure of all that is said, free of the possibility of error and oversight that inheres in human reporting.

401 U.S. at 786–87, 91 S.Ct. at 1143, 28 L.Ed.2d at 478–79. Overruling *On Lee*, he stressed, would not end third-party monitoring of informants but rather prevent law enforcement officers from engaging in the practice "unless they first had probable cause to suspect an individual of involvement in illegal activities and had tested their version of the facts before a detached judicial officer." Justice Harlan noted that recording of a transaction by an informer-participant (without transmission of it to others) was not at issue. He observed, however, that such a situation might be distinguished on the ground the informer may renege and not provide the recording to the Government; where transmission of the conversation is involved, however, the intrusion involved in providing the government with a documented record of the conversation "is instantaneous."

Justice Marshall expressed the view that in light of *Katz, On Lee* "cannot be considered viable." Justice Douglas' general discussion strongly suggested he would regard either participant recording or transmission as a search.

Justice Brennan concurred in the result on the ground that, under *Desist*, the case was controlled by *On Lee*. But he further offered that in his view "current Fourth Amendment jurisprudence interposes a warrant requirement not only in cases of third-party electronic monitoring * * * but also in cases of electronic recording by a government agent of a face-to-face conversation with a criminal suspect." Justice Black also concurred in the result only. He expressed disagreement with the plurality's reliance upon *Desist* because, in his view, exclusionary rule cases should be applied retroactively. But relying upon his dissent in *Katz*, he took the position that eavesdropping by electronic means cannot constitute a search (i.e., *Katz* was wrongly decided) and therefore Jackson's activities did not constitute a search for Fourth Amendment purposes.

Does *White* settle the issue of transmission of a conversation by an undercover agent? Justices Brennan, Douglas, Marshall and Harlan expressed the view that Jackson's conduct constituted a search under the Fourth Amendment; the four Justices in the plurality were obviously committed to the opposite position. Justice Black's action can be characterized as a refusal to address the effect of *Katz* upon this situation because he regarded *Katz* as wrongly decided.

Despite the Government's apparent victory in *White*, on October 16, 1972, the United States Attorney General issued a memorandum requiring Department of Justice approval for all consensual monitoring of nontelephone conversations by federal departments or agencies. If fewer than 48 hours are available to obtain such approval or if exigent circumstances preclude an effort to secure Department of Justice approval, the head of the department or agency (or someone designated by the head) may authorize the action. In United States v. Caceres, 440 U.S. 741, 99 S.Ct. 1465, 59 L.Ed.2d 733 (1979), the Supreme Court refused to require the exclusion in a federal criminal trial of evidence obtained in violation of Internal Revenue Service regulations adopted pursuant to the Attorney General's memorandum.

2. **Literal "Searches" Conducted by Undercover Officers.** Is the Fourth Amendment applicable if an undercover officer engages in a more traditional "search," as contrasted with the efforts to overhear conversations involved in *Hoffa*? The leading case is Gouled v. United States, 255 U.S. 298, 41 S.Ct. 261, 65 L.Ed. 647 (1921). Army intelligence personnel suspected Gouled of involvement in a scheme to defraud the Government. They discovered an enlisted man assigned to intelligence, Cohen, was a business associate of Gouled and directed him to visit Gouled to see what he could learn. The formal certificate before the Supreme Court stated that Cohen came to Gouled's office during his absence on the pretense of making a friendly call, gained admission to the office, and—in a manner not detailed—found and seized a certain document later admitted at trial. The Solicitor General, however, urged this version of the facts was not supported by the only evidence directly bearing upon the matter, Cohen's own testimony. Cohen testified that Gouled was in his office when he arrived and the two chatted; when Gouled stepped out for a moment, Cohen took the document at issue from the top of Gouled's desk. The Court's opinion stated that Cohen "pretending to make a friendly call upon the defendant gained admission to his office and in his absence * * * seized and carried away" the document. It is not clear whether Gouled, if present at the time of Cohen's visit, was aware of Cohen's status as an army intelligence agent.

The Court held that the manner in which the document was obtained constituted an unreasonable search within the meaning of the Fourth Amendment.

> [W]hether entrance to the home or office of a person suspected of crime be obtained * * * by stealth, or through social acquaintance, or in the guise of a business call, and whether the owner be present or not when [the officer] enters, any search and seizure subsequently and secretly made in his absence falls within the scope of the prohibition of the Fourth Amendment * * *.

255 U.S. at 306, 41 S.Ct. at 264, 65 L.Ed. at 651.

Gouled can be read as holding only that if an undercover officer obtains consent to enter premises or to inspect items through deception, he cannot exceed the scope of that consent. Thus the decision may rest upon the proposition that Cohen's entry into the office, although pursuant to consent obtained by deception, was permissible. When he approached the desk, rummaged through the papers (if he did so), or seized the document, however, he exceeded the scope of that consent and his conduct was no longer supportable on the basis of the consent. It is also possible, however, to read *Gouled* more broadly as imposing or at least suggesting more stringent limitations upon some undercover activities.

CHAPTER 9

GRAND JURY INVESTIGATIVE FUNCTIONS

Analysis

EDITORS' INTRODUCTION: GRAND JURY INVESTIGATIVE POWERS

Grand Jury
Functions
1) screening
2) investigatorial

The grand jury serves two distinct functions. One is a screening function; the grand jury evaluates evidence supporting possible charges and returns an indictment only in those cases in which the evidence amounts to at least probable cause to believe the accused committed the offense. The other is an investigatorial function: the grand jury sometimes develops information that is of value in determining whether grounds for a charge exist and—perhaps incidentally—in proving that charge at the defendant's criminal trial. The second function is the subject of this chapter.

The unique advantage the grand jury has as an investigatorial agency is its subpoena power. Unlike police officers or prosecutors, the grand jury can compel persons, under threat of contempt, to appear, be sworn, and—in absence of a legal privilege—to accurately answer questions. Note, The Grand Jury—Its Investigatory Powers and Limitations, 37 Minn.L.Rev. 586, 606 (1953). See also, Note, The Grand Jury as an Investigatory Body, 74 Harv.L.Rev. 590 (1961). In addition, a grand jury subpoena can direct persons to bring with them papers, documents, or physical items for production to the grand jury. A subpoena directing appearance for oral testimony is often called a subpoena *ad testificandum*, while a subpoena directing the production of items is called a subpoena *duces tecum*. See State ex rel. Pollard v. Criminal Court, 263 Ind. 236, 329 N.E.2d 573 (1975).

Investigatory Role

The grand jury's investigatory role developed out of its function in screening charges. Although the government often presented a proposed criminal charge to the grand jury for consideration, grand juries were traditionally free to act on their own knowledge and return charges on this basis. Costello v. United States, 350 U.S. 359, 362, 76 S.Ct. 406, 408, 100 L.Ed. 397, 402 (1956). Moreover, the grand jury could develop its own information even in the absence of a proposed criminal charge submitted by the government. See Hale v. Henkel, 201 U.S. 43, 26 S.Ct. 370, 50 L.Ed. 652 (1906). The authority to subpoena witnesses and documents developed as an aid in performing the duty to develop information to use in deciding whether to return formal criminal charges. The Supreme Court has commented:

> [T]he grand jury * * * plays an important role in fair and effective law enforcement * * * . Because its task is to inquire into the existence of possible criminal conduct and to return only well-founded indictments, its investigative powers are necessarily broad. "It is a grand inquest, a body with powers of investigation and inquisition, the scope of whose inquiries is not to be limited narrowly by questions of propriety or forecasts of the probable results of the investigation, or by doubts whether any particular individual will be found properly subject to an accused action of crime." Blair v. United States, 250 U.S. 273, 282, 39 S.Ct. 468, 471, 63 L.Ed. 979 (1919). Hence, the grand jury's authority to subpoena witnesses is not only historic * * * but essential to its task.

Branzburg v. Hayes, 408 U.S. 665, 687–88, 92 S.Ct. 2646, 2660, 33 L.Ed.2d 626, 643–44 (1972).

The traditional absence of legal limitations upon the grand jury's inquiries—both their scope and method—is justified on the need for full information, the absence of danger of abuse of the power due in large part to the lay composition of the groups, and the difficulty of imposing such limitations without unduly impeding the work of the bodies. In Costello v. United States, for example, the Court described the grand jury as "a body of laymen, free from technical rules, acting in secret, pledged to indict no one because of prejudice and to free no one because of special favor." Clearly the Court regarded the solemn nature of grand jury service and the absence of a professional or occupational bias in favor of law enforcement as sufficient to prevent abuse of the grand jury's investigatorial powers—at least in light of the disruption and cost entailed in any efforts to regulate those powers by legal means.

Grand Jury Subpoena Power

The grand jury typically has the authority to invoke the subpoena power of the court which called the grand jury into existence. In theory, the grand jury decides whether to compel appearance of a witness and the court determines whether to issue the subpoena. But in practice the situation may be far different:

> [A]lthough like all federal court subpoenas grand jury subpoenas are issued in the name of the district court over the signature of the clerk, they are issued pro forma and in blank to anyone requesting them. The court exercises no prior control whatsoever over their use. * * * [A]lthough grand jury subpoenas are occasionally discussed as if they were instrumentalities of the grand jury, they are in fact almost universally instrumentalities of the United States Attorney's office or

of some other investigative or prosecutorial department of the executive branch.

In re Grand Jury Proceedings, 486 F.2d 85, 90 (3d Cir.1973).

A grand jury may not itself punish an actual or potential witness for failing to respond to the subpoena or for declining to answer questions. Only the court which called the grand jury into existence can exercise contempt power. See 28 U.S.C.A. § 1826. In the federal system, the scenario often develops as follows: A witness appears before the grand jury but refuses to answer questions put. The refusal is brought to the attention of the judge, who considers the witness's reasons, if any, for refusing to answer. The judge then orders the witness to testify. The witness is returned to the grand jury room. If the witness persists in refusing to respond, the matter goes back to the judge and contempt proceedings begin. See Note, Coercive Contempt and the Federal Grand Jury, 79 Colum.L.Rev. 735, 746 n. 83 (1979). In the contempt proceeding, the witness has an opportunity to assert defenses, i.e., any legal reason for declining to answer. 28 U.S.C.A. § 1826(a) provides for contempt sanctions if a witness has refused to comply with a court order "without just cause." If found in contempt, the witness may be confined until s/he is willing to comply. But such confinement cannot, generally, extend beyond the term of the grand jury. Shillitani v. United States, 384 U.S. 364, 86 S.Ct. 1531, 16 L.Ed.2d 622 (1966). A witness found in contempt can also be given a "criminal contempt" penalty, which generally provides no provision for escape from the penalty by complying with the initial order or directive. The Supreme Court indicated in *Shillitani*, however, that the lower federal courts should regard so-called "civil" contempt as the preferred response to an uncooperative witness.

Independence of Grand Jury

Perhaps the major issue in structuring grand jury investigation tools is the extent to which some characteristics of the body render it less susceptible to abuse than other investigatorial agencies. It is traditionally regarded as an independent body, in part because its screening and indictment functions assume such independence; this independence is assumed carry over into its use of the subpoena power for purposes of investigation.

Detractors of the grand jury argue that it is in fact not independent because prosecutors tend to dominate grand juries. Prosecutors are generally given the right to be present during the investigatory stages of the grand jury process, although they may not remain in the chamber for the jury's deliberation and vote on a proposed indictment. E.g., Fed.R.Crim. Pro. 6(d). Although prosecutors have no formal legal power to control the grand jury, they have immense practical authority. Prosecutors generally propose avenues of inquiry, subpoena witnesses, question witnesses when they appear, and advise the grand jurors concerning all matters. One commentator, after noting the "plain fact" of the prosecutor's dominance over the grand jury, concluded:

> The real evil of the grand jury system—its viciousness, if you will—lies not so much in the fact that the grand jury is * * * the prosecutor's alter ego, as it does in our pretensions that it is actually an informed

and independent quasi-judicial organ, a pretension which misrepresents the prosecutor's unilateral action as the product of stately proceedings conducted by judicial standards. Therefore, * * * the grand jury * * * ironically * * * encourages abuses by allowing the prosecuting authority to carry on its work with complete anonymity and with effects greatly magnified by the accompanying judicial rites.

Antell, The Modern Grand Jury: Benighted Supergovernment, 51 A.B.A.J. 153, 156 (1965).

"One Man" Grand Juries

A number of jurisdictions have curious procedures for judicial participation in the investigation of suspected criminal offenses that somewhat resembles the traditional grand jury. These procedures are more streamlined because they provide for inquiry by single judges. See Conn.Gen.Stat. §§ 54–47b–54–47(h) (providing for "investigatory grand jury" that may consist of a single judge); Mich.Con.Law § 767.3. In some jurisdictions, a judge functioning in this capacity is labeled a "special inquiry" judge. See Idaho Code §§ 19.1116–19.1123 (enacted in 1980); Wash.Rev.Code Ann. § 10.27.170; Okla.Stat.Ann. § 21–951 (limited to possible violation of gambling laws). More traditionally, judges operating under such a procedure are referred to as "one man" grand juries. See In re Slattery, 310 Mich. 458, 461, 17 N.W.2d 251, 252 (1945). The judge typically has the power to subpoena witnesses, compel testimony with the contempt power, and grant immunity to witnesses. At the conclusion of the inquiry, the judge may issue a report or direct the apprehension of the suspect (if probable cause is found), but does not appear to have authority to return formal charges. Authority to bring formal charges remains in the traditional grand jury, if the jurisdiction affords defendants the right to grand jury indictment, or in the prosecutor. See State v. Manning, 86 Wn.2d 272, 543 P.2d 632 (1975).

The rationale for this procedure was discussed by the Michigan Supreme Court in In re Colacasides, 379 Mich. 69, 150 N.W.2d 1 (1967):

Experience has demonstrated * * * that regularly constituted law enforcement agencies sometimes are unable effectively and lawfully to enforce the laws, particularly with respect to corrupt conduct by officers of government and conspiratorial criminal activity on an organized and continuing basis. Our experience has also demonstrated that the common-law 23-man grand jury is unwieldy and ineffective for the investigation of such crimes in a modern, industrialized, and mobile society. It has demonstrated also that corruption in government and organized crime are susceptible to discovery and prosecution if the investigative body has the power to compel some participants therein to testify by enforcing attendance of witness by subpoena and granting immunity from prosecution, but police agencies in this country do not possess such extraordinary power. * * * Traditionally in this country, such extraordinary power has been entrusted only to judicial officers. * * *

This dilemma has been resolved * * * by [the] unique one-man grand jury, comprised of a judicial officer who can properly exercise the

subpoena power and the power to grant immunity to compel testimony.
* * *

379 Mich. at 89–90, 150 N.W.2d at 11.

If procedural protections for suspects in police investigations are properly relaxed in traditional grand jury inquiries, is such relaxation also appropriate when the inquiry is conducted by such a one man grand jury or special inquiry judge? A Michigan court read that state's statutes as permitting a witness to have counsel present during questioning by a one man grand jury but not during an appearance before a traditional grand jury. Responding to the argument that this difference violated the equal protection rights of persons appearing before traditional grand juries, the court summarily concluded "the significant differences" between the two types of proceedings justified the different rights to counsel. People v. Blachura, 59 Mich.App. 664, 667, 229 N.W.2d 877, 879 (1975).

* * *

This chapter contains two sections addressing two aspects of the grand jury's investigatory function. The first addresses the subpoena power and the extent to which it is subject to Fourth Amendment requirements placed upon law enforcement investigation. The second considers the applicability of the Fifth Amendment privilege against compelled self-incrimination in this context and more specifically the need to afford grand jury witnesses the procedural incidents of that privilege applying in traditional law enforcement investigations.

In connection with these issues, consider the recommendation of the National Advisory Commission on Criminal Justice Standards and Goals that the subpoena power presently reposing in the grand jury be given to prosecutors. The Commission's proposal would require a prosecutor using the subpoena power to permit the subject's attorney to be present during the questioning, provide an attorney if the subject desires one but is unable to provide any, and warn the subject concerning his rights including the privilege against self-incrimination. This would formally give the subpoena power to those who, in the Commission's judgment, already exercise it as a practical matter. The result, according to the Commission, would be a "workable and efficient alternative to the grand jury in many criminal cases," which could be used "at even less danger to the interests of the subjects, who often are inadequately protected by existing grand jury procedures." National Advisory Commission on Criminal Justice Standards and Goals, Courts 244–45 (1973). In some jurisdictions, prosecutors already have subpoena power under certain circumstances. Del.Code Ann. tit. 29 § 2504(4); Kan.Stat.Ann. § 22–3101(2). Under the Comprehensive Drug Abuse Prevention and Control Act of 1970, the Attorney General has the power to subpoena witnesses, compel testimony, and require the production of records. 21 U.S.C.A. § 876. This authority has been delegated to special agents in charge of the Drug Enforcement Administration. Such agent's exercise of the subpoena power was upheld in United States v. Hossbach, 518 F.Supp. 759 (E.D.Pa.1980).

A.   THE SUBPOENA POWER

A person required by subpoena to appear before a grand jury to testify or participate in the grand jury's investigation could reasonably be regarded as seized within the meaning of the Fourth Amendment. If this is the nature of compelled appearance and participation, the courts would have to consider the circumstances under which such seizures are "reasonable" for Fourth Amendment purposes. The Fourth Amendment significance of grand juries' exercise of the subpoena power is the major issue addressed by the cases in this section.

United States v. Dionisio

Supreme Court of the United States, 1973.
410 U.S. 1, 93 S.Ct. 764, 35 L.Ed.2d 67.

■ MR. JUSTICE STEWART delivered the opinion of the Court.

A special grand jury was convened in the Northern District of Illinois in February 1971, to investigate possible violations of federal criminal statutes relating to gambling. In the course of its investigation the grand jury received in evidence certain voice recordings that had been obtained pursuant to court orders.

The grand jury subpoenaed approximately 20 persons, including the respondent Dionisio, seeking to obtain from them voice exemplars for comparison with the recorded conversations that had been received in evidence. Each witness was advised that he was a potential defendant in a criminal prosecution. Each was asked to examine a transcript of an intercepted conversation, and to go to a nearby office of the United States Attorney to read the transcript into a recording device. The witnesses were advised that they would be allowed to have their attorneys present when they read the transcripts. Dionisio and other witnesses refused to furnish the voice exemplars, asserting that these disclosures would violate their rights under the Fourth and Fifth Amendments.

The Government then filed separate petitions in the United States District Court to compel Dionisio and the other witnesses to furnish the voice exemplars to the grand jury. The petitions stated that the examplars were "essential and necessary" to the grand jury investigation, and that they would "be used solely as a standard of comparison in order to determine whether or not the witness is the person whose voice was intercepted * * * ."

Following a hearing, the district judge rejected the witnesses' constitutional arguments and ordered them to comply with the grand jury's request. He reasoned * * * there would be no Fourth Amendment violation, because the grand jury subpoena did not itself violate the Fourth Amendment, and the order to produce the voice exemplars would involve no unreasonable search and seizure within the proscription of that Amendment * * *. When Dionisio persisted in his refusal to respond to the grand jury's directive, the District Court adjudged him in civil contempt and ordered him committed to custody until he obeyed the court order, or until the expiration of 18 months.

The Court of Appeals for the Seventh Circuit reversed. It * * * concluded that to compel the voice recordings would violate the Fourth Amendment. In the Court's view, the grand jury was "seeking to obtain the voice exemplars of the witnesses by the use of its subpoena powers because probable cause did not exist for their arrest or for some other, less unusual, method of compelling the production of the exemplars." The Court found that the Fourth Amendment applied to grand jury process, and that "under the fourth amendment law enforcement officials may not compel the production of physical evidence absent a showing of the reasonableness of the seizure. * * * "

reversed by court of Appeals

* * *

The Court of Appeals held that the Fourth Amendment required a preliminary showing of reasonableness before a grand jury witness could be compelled to furnish a voice exemplar, and that in this case the proposed "seizures" of the voice exemplars would be unreasonable because of the large number of witnesses summoned by the grand jury and directed to produce such exemplars. We disagree.

The Fourth Amendment guarantees that all people shall be "secure in their persons, houses, papers, and effects, against unreasonable searches and seizures * * *." Any Fourth Amendment violation in the present setting must rest on a lawless governmental intrusion upon the privacy of "persons" rather than on interference with "property relationships or private papers." Schmerber v. California, 384 U.S. 757, 767, 86 S.Ct. 1826, 1833, 16 L.Ed.2d 908. In Terry v. Ohio, 392 U.S. 1, 88 S.Ct. 1868, 20 L.Ed.2d 889, the Court explained the protection afforded to "persons" in terms of the statement in Katz v. United States, 389 U.S. 347, 88 S.Ct. 507, 19 L.Ed.2d 576, that "the Fourth Amendment protects people, not places," and concluded that "wherever an individual may harbor a reasonable 'expectation of privacy,' * * * he is entitled to be free from unreasonable governmental intrusion."

[T]he obtaining of physical evidence from a person involves a potential Fourth Amendment violation at two different levels—the "seizure" of the "person" necessary to bring him into contact with government agents, and the subsequent search for and seizure of the evidence. * * * The constitutionality of the compulsory production of exemplars from a grand jury witness necessarily turns on the same dual inquiry—whether either the initial compulsion of the person to appear before the grand jury, or the subsequent directive to make a voice recording is an unreasonable "seizure" within the meaning of the Fourth Amendment.

It is clear that a subpoena to appear before a grand jury is not a "seizure" in the Fourth Amendment sense, even though that summons may be inconvenient or burdensome. Last Term we again acknowledged what has long been recognized, that "[c]itizens generally are not constitutionally immune from grand jury subpoenas * * *." Branzburg v. Hayes, 408 U.S. 665, 682, 92 S.Ct. 2646, 2656, 33 L.Ed.2d 626.

* * *

[This is] recent reaffirmation[] of the historically grounded obligation of every person to appear and give his evidence before the grand jury. "The personal sacrifice involved is a part of the necessary contribution of the individual to the welfare of the public." Blair v. United States, 250 U.S. 273, 281, 39 S.Ct. 468, 471, 63 L.Ed. 979. And while the duty may be "onerous" at times, it is "necessary to the administration of justice."

The compulsion exerted by a grand jury subpoena differs from the seizure effected by an arrest or even an investigative "stop" in more than civic obligation. For, as Judge Friendly wrote for the Court of Appeals for the Second Circuit:

> "The latter is abrupt, is effected with force or the threat of it and often in demeaning circumstances, and, in the case of arrest, results in a record involving social stigma. A subpoena is served in the same manner as other legal process; it involves no stigma whatever; if the time for appearance is inconvenient, this can generally be altered; and it remains at all times under the control and supervision of a court." United States v. Doe (Schwartz) 457 F.2d 895, 898 (1972).

* * *

This is not to say that a grand jury subpoena is some talisman that dissolves all constitutional protections. The grand jury cannot require a witness to testify against himself. * * * The Fourth Amendment provides protection against a grand jury subpoena *duces tecum* too sweeping in its terms "to be regarded as reasonable." Hale v. Henkel, 201 U.S. 43, 76, 26 S.Ct. 370, 379, 50 L.Ed. 652. And last Term, in the context of a First Amendment claim, we indicated that the Constitution could not tolerate the transformation of the grand jury into an instrument of oppression: "Official harassment of the press undertaken not for purposes of law enforcement but to disrupt a reporter's relationship with his news sources would have no justification. Grand juries are subject to judicial control and subpoenas to motions to quash. We do not expect courts will forget that grand juries must operate within the limits of the First Amendment as well as the Fifth." Branzburg v. Hayes, 408 U.S. 665, 707–708, 92 S.Ct. 2646, 2669–2670, 33 L.Ed.2d 626.

But we are here faced with no such constitutional infirmities in the subpoena to appear before the grand jury or in the order to make the voice recordings. There is * * * no valid Fifth Amendment claim. There was no order to produce private books and papers, and no sweeping subpoena *duces tecum*. And even if *Branzburg* be extended beyond its First Amendment moorings and tied to a more generalized due process concept, there is still no indication in this case of the kind of harassment that was of concern there.

The Court of Appeals found critical significance in the fact that the grand jury had summoned approximately 20 witnesses to furnish voice exemplars. We think that fact is basically irrelevant to the constitutional issues here. The grand jury may have been attempting to identify a number of voices on the tapes in evidence, or it might have summoned the 20 witnesses in an effort to identify one voice. But whatever the case, "[a] grand jury's investigation is not fully carried out until every available clue has been run down and all witnesses examined in every proper way to find if a crime has been committed * * *." United States v. Stone, 2 Cir., 429 F.2d 138, 140. As the Court recalled last Term, "Because its task is to inquire into the existence of possible criminal conduct and to return only well-founded indictments, its investigative powers are necessarily broad." Branzburg v. Hayes, 408 U.S., at 688, 92 S.Ct., at 2659. The grand jury may well find it desirable to call numerous witnesses in the course of an investigation. It does not follow that each witness may resist a subpoena on the ground that too many witnesses have been called. Neither the order to Dionisio to appear, nor the order to make a voice recording was rendered unreasonable by the fact that many others were subjected to the same compulsion.

But the conclusion that Dionisio's compulsory appearance before the grand jury was not an unreasonable "seizure" is the answer to only the first part of the Fourth Amendment inquiry here. Dionisio argues that the grand jury's subsequent directive to make the voice recording was itself an infringement of his rights under the Fourth Amendment. We cannot accept that argument.

 In Katz v. United States, supra, we said that the Fourth Amendment provides no protection for what "a person knowingly exposes to the public, even in his own home or office * * *." The physical characteristics of a person's voice, its tone and manner, as opposed to the content of a specific conversation, are constantly exposed to the public. Like a man's facial characteristics, or handwriting, his voice is repeatedly produced for others to hear. No person can have a reasonable expectation that others will not know the sound of his voice, any more than he can reasonably expect that his face will be a mystery to the world. * * *

Since neither the summons to appear before the grand jury, nor its directive to make a voice recording infringed upon any interest protected by the Fourth Amendment, there was no justification for requiring the grand jury to satisfy even the minimal requirement of "reasonableness" imposed by the Court of Appeals. A grand jury has broad investigative powers to determine whether a crime has been committed and who has committed it. The jurors may act on tips, rumors, evidence offered by the prosecutor, or their own personal knowledge. No grand jury witness is "entitled to set limits to the investigation that the grand jury may conduct." And a sufficient basis for an indictment may only emerge at the end of the investigation when all the evidence has been received.

> "It is impossible to conceive that * * * the examination of witnesses must be stopped until a basis is laid by an indictment formally preferred, when the very object of the examination is to ascertain who shall be indicted." Hale v. Henkel, 201 U.S. 43, 65, 26 S.Ct. 370, 375, 50 L.Ed. 652.

Since Dionisio raised no valid Fourth Amendment claim, there is no more reason to require a preliminary showing of reasonableness here than there would be in the case of any witness who, despite the lack of any constitutional or statutory privilege, declined to answer a question or comply with a grand jury request. Neither the Constitution nor our prior cases justify any such interference with grand jury proceedings.[1]

The Fifth Amendment guarantees that no civilian may be brought to trial for an infamous crime "unless on a presentment or indictment of a Grand Jury." This constitutional guarantee presupposes an investigative body "acting independently of either prosecuting attorney or judge," whose mission is to clear the innocent, no less than to bring to trial those who may be guilty. Any holding that would saddle a grand jury with minitrials and preliminary showings would assuredly impede its investigation and frustrate the public's interest in the fair and expeditious administration of the criminal laws. * * * The grand jury may not always serve its historic role as a protective bulwark standing solidly between the ordinary citizen and an overzealous prosecutor, but if it is even to approach the proper performance of its constitutional mission, it must be free to pursue its investigations unhindered by external influence or supervision so long as it does not trench upon the legitimate rights of any witness called before it.

Since the Court of Appeals found an unreasonable search and seizure where none existed, and imposed a preliminary showing of reasonableness where none was required, its judgment is reversed and this case is remanded to that Court for further proceedings consistent with this opinion.

It is so ordered.

United States v. Mara

Supreme Court of the United States, 1973.
410 U.S. 19, 93 S.Ct. 774, 35 L.Ed.2d 99.

■ MR. JUSTICE STEWART delivered the opinion of the Court.

The respondent, Richard J. Mara, was subpoenaed to appear before the September 1971 Grand Jury in the Northern District of Illinois that was investigating thefts of interstate shipments. On two separate occasions he was directed to produce handwriting and printing exemplars to the grand jury's designated agent. Each time he was advised that he was a potential defendant in the matter under investigation. On both occasions he refused to produce the exemplars.

The Government then petitioned the United States District Court to compel Mara to furnish the handwriting and printing exemplars to the grand jury. * * * The District Judge rejected the respondent's contention that the compelled production of such exemplars would constitute an

1. Mr. Justice Marshall in dissent suggests that a preliminary showing of "reasonableness" is required where the grand jury subpoenas a witness to appear and produce handwriting or voice exemplars, but not when it subpoenas him to appear and testify. Such a distinction finds no support in the Constitution. The dissent argues that there is a potential Fourth Amendment violation in the case of a subpoenaed grand jury witness because of the asserted intrusiveness of the initial subpoena to appear—the possible stigma from a grand jury appearance and the inconvenience of the official restraint. But the initial directive to appear is as intrusive if the witness is called simply to testify as it is if he is summoned to produce physical evidence.

unreasonable search and seizure, and he ordered the respondent to provide them. When the witness continued to refuse to do so, he was adjudged to be in civil contempt and was committed to custody until he obeyed the court order or until the expiration of the grand jury term.

The Court of Appeals for the Seventh Circuit reversed. * * *

We have held today in *Dionisio*, that a grand jury subpoena is not a "seizure" within the meaning of the Fourth Amendment, and further, that that Amendment is not violated by a grand jury directive compelling production of "physical characteristics" which are "constantly exposed to the public." Handwriting, like speech, is repeatedly shown to the public, and there is no more expectation of privacy in the physical characteristics of a person's script than there is in the tone of his voice. * * * Consequently the Government was under no obligation here, any more than in *Dionisio*, to make a preliminary showing of "reasonableness."

Indeed, this case lacks even the aspects of an expansive investigation that the Court of Appeals found significant in *Dionisio*. In that case 20 witnesses were summoned to give exemplars; here there was only one. The specific and narrowly drawn directive requiring the witness to furnish a specimen of his handwriting violated no legitimate Fourth Amendment interest. The District Court was correct, therefore, in ordering the respondent to comply with the grand jury's request.

Accordingly, the judgment of the Court of Appeals is reversed, and this case is remanded to that court for further proceedings consistent with this opinion.

It is so ordered.

■ MR. JUSTICE MARSHALL, dissenting [in both *Dionisio* and *Mara.*]

* * *

The Court concludes that the exemplars sought from the respondents are not protected by the Fourth Amendment because respondents have surrendered their expectation of privacy with respect to voice and handwriting by knowingly exposing these to the public. But even accepting this conclusion, it does not follow that the investigatory seizures of respondents, accomplished through the use of subpoenas ordering them to appear before the grand jury—and thereby necessarily interfering with their personal liberty—are outside the protection of the Fourth Amendment. To the majority, though, "[i]t is clear that a subpoena to appear before a grand jury is not a 'seizure' in the Fourth Amendment sense, even though that summons may be inconvenient or burdensome." With due respect, I find nothing "clear" about so sweeping an assertion.

There can be no question that investigatory seizures effected by the police are subject to the constraints of the Fourth and Fourteenth Amendments. * * * [T]he present cases involve official investigatory seizures which interfere with personal liberty. The Court considers dispositive, however, the fact that the seizures were effected by the grand jury, rather than the police. I cannot agree.

* * *

In the present cases * * * it was not testimony that the grand juries sought from respondents, but physical evidence. The Court glosses over this important distinction from its prior decisions, however, by artificially bifurcating its analysis of what is taking place in these cases—that is, by effectively treating what is done with individuals once they are before the grand jury as irrelevant in determining what safeguards are to govern the procedures by which they are initially compelled to appear. Nonetheless, the fact remains that the historic exception to which the Court resorts is not necessarily as broad as the context in which it is now employed. Hence, I believe that the question we must consider is whether an extension of that exception is warranted, and if so, under what conditions.

* * *

The Court seems to reason that the exception to the Fourth Amendment for grand jury subpoenas directed at persons is justified by the relative unintrusiveness of the grand jury process on an individual's liberty. The Court * * * suggests that arrests or even investigatory "stops" are inimical to personal liberty because they may involve the use of force; they may be carried out in demeaning circumstances; and at least an arrest may yield the social stigma of a record. By contrast, we are told, a grand jury subpoena is a simple legal process, which is served in an unoffensive manner; it results in no stigma; and a convenient time for appearance may always be arranged. The Court would have us believe, in short, that, unlike an arrest or an investigatory "stop," a grand jury subpoena entails little more inconvenience than a visit to an old friend. Common sense and practical experience indicate otherwise.

It may be that service of a grand jury subpoena does not involve the same potential for momentary embarrassment as does an arrest or investigatory "stop." But this difference seems inconsequential in comparison to the substantial stigma which—contrary to the Court's assertion—may result from a grand jury appearance as well as from an arrest or investigatory seizure. Public knowledge that a man has been summoned by a federal grand jury investigating, for instance, organized criminal activity can mean loss of friends, irreparable injury to business, and tremendous pressures on one's family life. Whatever nice legal distinctions may be drawn between police and prosecutor, on the one hand, and the grand jury, on the other, the public often treats an appearance before a grand jury as tantamount to a visit to the station house. Indeed, the former is frequently more damaging than the latter, for a grand jury appearance has an air of far greater gravity than a brief visit "downtown" for a "talk." The Fourth Amendment was placed in our Bill of Rights to protect the individual citizen from such potentially disruptive governmental intrusion into his private life unless conducted reasonably and with sufficient cause.

Nor do I believe that the constitutional problems inherent in such governmental interference with an individual's person are substantially alleviated because one may seek to appear at a "convenient time." * * * No matter how considerate a grand jury may be in arranging for an individual's appearance, the basic fact remains that his liberty has been officially restrained for some period of time. In terms of its effect on the individual, this restraint does not differ meaningfully from the restraint imposed on a suspect compelled to visit the police station house. Thus, the nature of the intrusion on personal liberty caused by a grand jury subpoena cannot, without more, be considered sufficient basis for denying respondents the protection of the Fourth Amendment.

* * *

Thus, the Court's decisions today can serve only to encourage prosecutorial exploitation of the grand jury process, at the expense of both individual liberty and the traditional neutrality of the grand jury. Indeed, by holding that the grand jury's power to subpoena these respondents for the purpose of obtaining exemplars is completely outside the purview of the Fourth Amendment, the Court fails to appreciate the essential difference between real and testimonial evidence in the context of these cases, and thereby hastens the reduction of the grand jury into simply another investigative device of law enforcement officials. By contrast, the Court of Appeals, in proper recognition of these dangers, imposed narrow limitations on the subpoena power of the grand jury which are necessary to guard against unreasonable official interference with individual liberty but which would not impair significantly the traditional investigatory powers of that body.

The Court of Appeals in *Mara* did not impose a requirement that the Government establish probable cause to support a grand jury's request for exemplars. It correctly recognized that "examination of witnesses by a grand jury need not be preceded by a formal charge against a particular individual," since the very purpose of the grand jury process is to ascertain probable cause. * * * [I]t ruled only that the request for physical evidence such as exemplars should be subject to a showing of reasonableness. This "reasonableness" requirement has previously been explained by this Court, albeit in a somewhat different context, to require a showing by the Government that: (1) "the investigation is authorized by Congress"; (2) the investigation "is for a purpose Congress can order"; (3) the evidence sought is "relevant"; and (4) the request is "adequate, but not excessive, for the purposes of the relevant inquiry." See Oklahoma Press Publishing Co. v. Walling, 327 U.S. 186, 209, 66 S.Ct. 494, 506, 90 L.Ed. 614 (1946). This was the interpretation of the "reasonableness" requirement properly adopted by the Court of Appeals. And, in elaborating on the requirement that the request not be "excessive," it added that the Government would bear the burden of showing that it was not conducting "a general fishing expedition under grand jury sponsorship."

These are not burdensome limitations to impose on the grand jury when it seeks to secure physical evidence, such as exemplars, that has traditionally been gathered directly by law enforcement officials. The essence of the requirement would be nothing more than a showing that the evidence sought is relevant to the purpose of the investigation and that the particular grand jury is not the subject of prosecutorial abuse—a showing that the Government should have little difficulty making, unless it is in fact acting improperly. Nor would the requirement interfere with the power of the grand jury to call witnesses before it, to take their testimony, and to ascertain their knowledge concerning criminal activity. It would only discourage prosecutorial abuse of the grand jury process. The "reasonableness" requirement would do no more in the context of these cases than the Constitution compels—protect the citizen from unreasonable and arbitrary governmental interference, and ensure that the broad subpoena powers of the grand jury which the Court now recognizes are not turned into a tool of prosecutorial oppression.

I would therefore affirm the Court of Appeals' decisions reversing the judgments of contempt against respondents and order the cases remanded to the District Court to allow the Government an opportunity to make the requisite showing of "reasonableness" in each case. To do less is to invite the very sort of unreasonable governmental intrusion on individual liberty that the Fourth Amendment was intended to prevent.[2]

NOTES

1. **Nonconstitutional Limits on Grand Jury Subpoena Power.** Statutes and court rules provide limitations upon grand juries' ability to exercise the subpoena power, especially with regard the power to compel the production of documents or items.

Under Federal Rule of Criminal Procedure 17(c), a person served with a subpoena commanding the production of papers or other objects (a subpoena *duces tecum*) may move the court to quash or modify the subpoena on the grounds that "compliance would be unreasonable or oppressive." Application of the provision to grand jury subpoenas was addressed in United States v. R. Enterprises, Inc., 498 U.S. 292, 111 S.Ct. 722, 112 L.Ed.2d 795 (1991). A federal grand jury investigating allegations of interstate transportation of obscene materials issued subpoenas to R. Enterprises and two other companies owned by Martin Rothstein; the subpoenas called for production of records. All three companies moved to quash the subpoenas, primarily on the ground they called for material irrelevant to the grand jury's investigation; the district court denied the motions. The Court of Appeals, however, reversed. In United States v. Nixon, 418 U.S. 683, 94 S.Ct. 3090, 41 L.Ed.2d 1039 (1974), the Supreme Court held that a subpoena calling for production of documents before trial is to be enforced only if the party seeking it shows relevancy, admissibility and specificity. The Court of Appeals in *R. Enterprises* held that these standards were also applicable to grand jury subpoenas *duces tecum* and those issued in the case did not meet the standards.

Nixon =
relevancy

The Supreme Court reversed. Given the function of the grand jury, Justice O'Connor explained, the *Nixon* standards do not apply to grand jury subpoenas. Rule 17(c) imposes a requirement of "reasonableness" on grand jury subpoenas, she continued, and the Court's task was to fashion a standard for reasonableness in the context of grand jury proceedings:

> [T]he law presumes, absent a strong showing to the contrary, that a grand jury acts within the legitimate scope of its authority. Consequently, a grand jury subpoena issued through normal channels is presumed to be reasonable, and the burden of showing unreasonableness must be on the recipient who seeks to avoid compliance. * * * [W]here, as here, a subpoena is challenged on relevancy

2. * * * [A] requirement that the Government establish the "reasonableness" of the request for an exemplar would hardly be so burdensome as the Court suggests. As matters stand, if the suspect resists the request, the Government must seek a judicial order directing that he comply with the request. Thus, a formal judicial proceeding is already necessary. The question whether the request is "reasonable" would simply be one further matter to consider in such a proceeding.

grounds, the motion to quash must be denied unless the district court determines that there is no reasonable possibility that the category of materials the Government seeks will produce information relevant to the general subject of the grand jury's investigation.

498 U.S. at 300–01, 111 S.Ct. at 728, 112 L.Ed.2d at 807–08. The subpoenas at issue were not challenged as too indefinite or calling for overly burdensome production, and consequently the Court did not consider such claims.

A person served with a subpoena may not know the general subject matter of the grand jury's investigation, the Court noted. Therefore, even if such a person has a valid claim to have the subpoena quashed he may not be able to make the showing necessary under the standard set out by the Court. *R. Enterprises, Inc.* did not resolve this difficulty. The Court suggested, however, that in a case where unreasonableness is alleged, the District Court might be justified in requiring the Government to reveal the general subject matter of the investigation before requiring the challenging party to carry its burden of persuasion. To discourage subpoena challenges as a means of achieving discovery, Justice O'Connor added, such disclosure might be required *in camera.* (reviewed by judge)

Turning to the facts of the case, the Court noted all three companies were owned by one person and did business in the same area. One of the three, further, shipped sexually explicit material into the district of concern to the grand jury. From these undisputed facts the District Court could have properly concluded there was a reasonable possibility the records would produce information relevant to the grand jury's investigation into the interstate transportation of obscene material. Thus the District Court correctly denied the motions to quash the subpoenas.

2. **Use of Subpoena For Intrusive Evidence Gathering.** Despite the principal cases, some federal courts have balked at permitting the use of grand jury subpoenas to compel persons to submit to particularly intrusive procedure for developing evidence. One, for example, held that a grand jury subpoena may not be used to compel a person to produce a sample of blood:

> We hold that the United States' decision to seek T.S.'s blood sample with a grand jury subpoena was not an appropriate use of such a subpoena. To allow the United States to use a Rule 17(c) subpoena for this purpose would abrogate T.S.'s Fourth Amendment rights and, thus, transform the subpoena into an instrument by which an illegal search and seizure is effectuated. This is a result clearly not intended under the Federal Rules of Criminal Procedure, the Fourth Amendment, or applicable Supreme Court precedent.

> Therefore, we conclude that the United States must obtain a warrant before we will compel T.S. to comply with the demand for blood samples. To do so, the United States must establish probable cause that T.S.'s blood samples will yield evidence of a crime.

In Re Grand Jury Proceedings, 816 F.Supp. 1196, 1205–06 (W.D.Ky.1993). Another federal court has relied on the same reasoning to bar the Government from using a subpoena to obtain a saliva sample. United States v. Nicolosi, 885 F.Supp. 50 (E.D.N.Y.1995).

In contrast, the court in In re Grand Jury Proceedings (Vickers), 38 F.Supp.2d 159 (D.N.H.1998), employed a more complex analysis for such problems. Even if a suspect's Fourth Amendment rights are implicated by a grand jury subpoena, the *Vickers* court reasoned, the grand jury's independent investigatory function precludes courts from barring the use of a subpoena and requiring the government or the grand jury to obtain a search warrant. Instead, the district court should entertain a motion to quash the subpoena. In ruling on that motion, the court should subject the grand jury's demand to scrutiny, although of a less rigorous type or degree than it would apply to a search warrant application.

A subpoena may seek evidence that is not within Fourth Amendment protection. This is the case with a subpoena that demands the production of fingerprint or hair samples, *Vickers* reasoned, since persons do not have a constitutionally protected privacy interest in their fingerprints or the characteristics of their hair. In such a case, the court should inquire only whether the subpoena describes the evidence sought with sufficient particularity, that evidence is reasonably related to a legitimate aspect of the grand jury's investigation, and complying with the subpoena would impose an unreasonable or oppressive burden on the suspect.

A subpoena may alternatively seek evidence implicating the suspect's Fourth Amendment interests. This is the case, for example, if the subpoena demands the production of saliva samples, since obtaining such samples involves an intrusion compromising the suspect's Fourth Amendment right to bodily integrity. In a case of this sort, *Vickers* indicated, somewhat more rigorous review of an application is required:

> [T]he relevant inquiry is not whether the subpoena is supported by "probable cause." Instead, the court must simply determine whether the subject matter and scope of the subpoena are reasonable under the circumstances, including consideration of the subpoenaed person's constitutional rights.
>
> The following questions are pertinent to that "reasonableness" assessment: (1) Does the subpoena command the production of things relevant to the investigation being pursued by the grand jury?; (2) Does the subpoena specify with sufficient particularity the things being sought?; (3) Is the subpoena sufficiently narrow in scope to be considered reasonable?; (4) Has the subpoena issued for reasons other than to harass the subject?; and (5) Can the subject provide the requested evidence without unnecessary risk of personal harm (e.g., potentially dangerous invasive surgery) and/or personal humiliation (e.g., unnecessary invasion of bodily integrity or dignitary interests)? In short, the court must determine whether protected constitutional values or rights are likely to be unduly burdened or violated if the subpoena is not quashed.

38 F.Supp.2d at 164.

The subpoenas before the *Vickers* court sought, in part, production of saliva samples for a grand jury investigating pipe bombing incidents in Concord, New Hampshire. It evaluated the subpoenas in light of publicly known information and *in camera* review of certain submissions by the government. The court concluded:

> [T]he government has demonstrated that the evidence sought: (1) is plainly relevant to a legitimate and ongoing investigation being conducted by the grand jury; (2) is described with sufficient particularity to notify respondents of precisely what is sought; (3) is not sought to harass respondents or to impose some burden because of their social or political views; (4) could be probative in identifying or eliminating persons who may have participated in, or may have knowledge of or evidence relating to, the crimes under investigation; (5) can be obtained from respondents with very minimal invasion of their bodily integrity (i.e., by simply swabbing the inside of the mouth); and (6) can be obtained with no risk of physical pain, injury, or embarrassment to respondents, and with the most minimal personal inconvenience.

Elements

* * *

On balance, therefore, the court concludes that the grand jury subpoenas at issue are neither "unreasonable" nor otherwise properly subject to an order to quash. The grand jury's justification for issuance and enforcement of those subpoenas is more than adequate to warrant denial of respondents' motion to quash.

38 F.Supp.2d at 167–68.

Some state courts have also developed limits on the grand jury subpoena process, sometimes as a matter of state constitutional law. An Oklahoma court, for example, held that a subpoena for a blood sample should issue only if the grand jury foreman submits to the trial judge an affidavit permitting the judge to find that probable cause exists to believe the sample would result in developing evidence of criminal activity. Woolverton v. Multi–County Grand Jury, 859 P.2d 1112 (Okla. Crim.App.1993). See also, In the Matter of a Grand Jury Investigation, 427 Mass. 221, 692 N.E.2d 56 (1998) (when grand jury subpoena seeks blood sample, Fourth Amendment and state constitution are satisfied if the grand jury is shown to have a reasonable basis for believing resulting tests will significantly aid it in investigating circumstances it has good reason to believe involve crime).

3. **Use of Grand Jury For Trial Preparation.** A few limitations upon the grand jury's investigatory power are widely acknowledged. It is improper for a grand jury to take testimony for purposes of pursuing civil remedies available to the government. United States v. Procter & Gamble Co., 356 U.S. 677, 78 S.Ct. 983, 2 L.Ed.2d 1077 (1958).

Similarly, a grand jury abuses its procedure by using the subpoena power to assist the prosecution in preparing for trial. This was illustrated by State v. Johnson, 287 N.J.Super. 247, 670 A.2d 1100 (1996). Johnson was indicted for murder. In preparing for trial, the prosecutor interviewed Thomas, who acknowledged she had seen Johnson fleeing from the scene of the killing. She added, however, she would not give a sworn statement because she feared retaliation. Soon after, she was brought before a grand jury (other than the indicting one) on a bench warrant and, under oath, she testified she had seen Johnson flee the scene. At trial, she testified she had not seen anyone run from the scene. Her contrary grand jury testimony was then admitted as a prior inconsistent statement. On appeal, Johnson argued the prosecutor had improperly used the grand jury process to prepare for trial:

> Defendants do not argue, nor could they, that a prosecutor must cease all investigatory efforts once an indictment is issued. Similarly, defendants do not argue, nor could they, that a grand jury cannot continue an investigation once an indictment has issued, if the purpose of the investigation is to identify further crimes committed by the indictees or to identify unnamed actors. Defendants contend that Thomas' testimony was not obtained in the course of an investigation of further charges against defendants or others. Rather, they contend that her testimony was obtained solely to prepare for the trial of the pending indictment.
>
> * * * Generally, it is considered appropriate for the government to interrogate witnesses on subjects relevant to a continuing grand jury investigation, even when the evidence received may also relate to a pending indictment.
>
> Use of the grand jury, however, * * * solely to prepare and preserve the testimony of a witness for the trial of a pending indictment is an abuse of the grand jury.
>
> * * * On its face, the transcript suggests that the prosecutor was presenting witnesses to the grand jury as part of an investigation regarding additional charges against defendants, such as [tampering with a witness or retaliation against a witness]. This suggestion, however, is belied by the prosecutor's comments in response to a direct question from the trial judge to explain the purpose of the Thomas testimony. She stated:

It's further investigation, Judge,* * * it's in order to have them for a factfinding trial * * *

The inescapable conclusion from this statement is that Thomas was brought before the grand jury solely to preserve her testimony for trial. The second grand jury panel was not conducting a further investigation concerning the * * * murder or any actions by defendants after the shooting. The use to which the prosecutor put this second grand jury was improper * * *.

827 N.J.Super. at 259–61, 670 A.2d at 1105–07.

4. **Subpoena Directives to Cooperate With Police or Prosecutors.** To what extent can a grand jury subpoena direct a witness not to appear or produce items before the grand jury but rather to cooperate with police or prosecutors?

The issue was addressed in In re John Doe Grand Jury Proceedings, 717 A.2d 1129 (R.I.1998). The subpoenas at issue were served by police officers. Each subpoena asserted by its terms that the officer serving the subpoena was an agent of the grand jury and then directed the documents sought "should be given directly to him." When officers obtained possession of the documents, they were permitted to use them without participation by the grand jury and, in fact, subject to no limits at all. Thus, the documents could be used to bring misdemeanor charges not requiring grand jury approval. Holding the practice unauthorized, the court relied to some extent upon the risk that, under this practice, information would be disclosed in a manner violating grand jury secrecy. But its major basis of decision was considerably broader:

We declare this practice to be well beyond the power of the grand jury and to be potentially abusive to the rights of citizens, resulting in a roving investigating commission that is the very antithesis of the purpose of the grand jury.

* * *

Of greatest concern * * * is the demonstrated abuse of the grand jury subpoena power and the usurping of that power by the state's prosecutors. At oral argument it was disclosed that the Office of the Attorney General utilizes the grand jury for the issuance of subpoenas to obtain evidence concerning matters that are not before the grand jury and may never come before the grand jury. The prosecutor revealed to this Court that approximately 250 subpoenas were issued by the grand juries in Rhode Island for investigations and cases that are not grand jury matters. The state attempts to justify this practice on the grounds of management problems inherent in a procedure that limits grand jury subpoenas to grand jury matters, stating that this would give rise to the need for additional grand juries and staff to handle the increased volume. This practice, however, is simply unlawful and results in a total eradication of the independence of the grand jury and a merger of the identity of the grand jury with the prosecuting arm of the executive branch of government.

We remind the state's prosecutors that the General Assembly has not seen fit to authorize the Office of the Attorney General or the state's police departments to issue subpoenas for criminal investigations. * * * [T]he process issued by the grand jury is the process of the court, not the prosecutor.

Therefore we find ourselves constrained to declare that the grand juries of this state have no authority to appoint agents to recover documents in furtherance of investigations not related to the grand jury. We conclude that the issuance of so-called forthwith subpoenas for the immediate production of documents is more akin to the issuance of a warrant without the intervention of the neutral magistrate and is therefore impermissible. In addition, in circumstances in which a witness seeks to be excused from appearing before the grand jury and voluntarily surrenders records in lieu of a personal appearance, such materials are to be returned to the grand jury forthwith and a record is to be prepared and signed by the witness memorializing the transaction and the fact that the witness voluntarily waived his or her right to a personal appearance and right to contest the subpoena.

717 A.2d at 1138–39.

5. **Self-Incrimination Privilege to Resist Production of Documents.** Grand jury subpoenas *duces tecum* direct the subpoenaed witness to produce documents or other items. Does the Fifth Amendment privilege against compelled self-incrimination justify such a witness in refusing to produce the described documents or items for the grand jury?

Despite language to the contrary in Boyd v. United States, 116 U.S. 616, 634–35, 6 S.Ct. 524, 534, 29 L.Ed.2d 746, 752 (1886), Fisher v. United States, 425 U.S. 391, 96 S.Ct. 1569, 48 L.Ed.2d 39 (1976), held the Fifth Amendment did not protect *the contents* of a document. Any self-incriminating admissions made by putting them in the document occur before the subpoena. Thus, those admissions cannot be compelled by the subpoena. But, Justice White continued for the Court in *Fisher*, compliance with a summons or subpoena for documents may have incriminating and communicative aspects. Compliance with the subpoena may constitute tacit acknowledgments: (1) that the documents described in the subpoena exist and are in the person's possession; and (2) that the produced documents are the ones described and thus constitute an "implicit authentication" of the documents produced. The acknowledged facts may be incriminating. Further, he observed, the act of complying—or the act of production of the documents—is clearly "compelled." But whether particular tacit acknowledgments are both "testimonial" and "incriminating" are questions without categorical answers. Both matters depend upon the facts and circumstances of particular cases or classes of cases.

The Court then turned to tax cases like the ones before the Court in which subpoenas seek from taxpayers' lawyers work papers of the taxpayers' accountants that might incriminate the taxpayers. Justice White first noted the attorney-client privilege permitted the attorneys to resist production if—but only if—the clients could do so. In these cases, however, the client-taxpayers had no right to resist. The Government will already know of the papers' existence and the subjects' access to them; the act of production's confirmation that the documents exist and that the taxpayers have access to them will not significantly add to what the Government knows. Seeking preparation and delivery of the papers by the accountant is not illegal; any testimonial admission to these facts by the act of production, therefore, poses no realistic threat of incriminating the taxpayer. Tacit acknowledgment of the described documents' existence and their possession will not justify noncompliance.

Turning to the danger of implicit authentication by the act of production, *Fisher* noted the taxpayers lacked firsthand knowledge as to the preparation of the documents, could not vouch for their accuracy, and therefore would not be competent to authenticate them. If the documents were eventually offered as evidence of the taxpayers' guilt in a criminal trial, they would not be admissible without authenticating testimony other than evidence the taxpayer produced them in response to the subpoena. "Without more," Justice White reasoned, "responding to the subpoena in the circumstance before us would not appear to represent a substantial threat of self-incrimination." 425 U.S. at 413, 96 S.Ct. at 1582, 48 L.Ed.2d at 57.

A witness was held entitled to resist production of subpoenaed documents in United States v. Doe, 465 U.S. 605, 104 S.Ct. 1237, 79 L.Ed.2d 552 (1984). Grand jury subpoenas issued directing Doe to produce certain records of his businesses. The government conceded these records were or might be incriminating. The district court quashed the subpoenas and the Supreme Court upheld this action.

The facts made a sufficient showing that under *Fisher* the act of producing the documents would involve testimonial self-incrimination. By the act of producing any described documents he had in his possession, Doe would acknowledge—in a testimonial fashion—such documents did exist and they were in his possession. Further, his acknowledgments might relieve the government of the need for other evidence to authenticate those documents should they be offered against Doe in a criminal prosecution. The Court noted the Government was not foreclosed from rebutting this possibility by producing evidence the existence, possession and authentication of the documents were "foregone conclusion[s]," and therefore Doe's act of production would not significantly add to what the Government already knew and had. But no such evidence was produced. Unlike the situation in *Fisher*, the record in *Doe* failed to establish the act of production would have only minimal testimonial value and would not operate to incriminate. As a result, Doe's acts necessary for production of the subpoenaed documents were privileged by the Fifth Amendment. He could not be compelled to produce them.

The *Doe* majority further commented that production of the documents could be compelled if Doe was granted immunity from the use of evidence which might be created by his acts in producing the documents. Immunity as a means of eliminating the risk of "incrimination" is discussed later in this chapter.

B.   QUESTIONING AND THE PRIVILEGE AGAINST COMPELLED SELF-INCRIMINATION

As the Supreme Court's opinion in *Dionisio* recognized, there is universal agreement that the Fifth Amendment privilege against compelled self-incrimination is available to a witness appearing before a grand jury. There is also agreement a witness can, in reliance upon this privilege, decline to answer specific questions put by the jurors or the prosecutor. The major questions concern the extent to which the privilege or sound policy requires that various procedures be followed to implement the right to remain silent. Miranda v. Arizona, presented in Chapter 7, held a suspect undergoing custodial interrogation by police must be afforded the right to the presence of counsel and warnings designed to assure he is aware of the rights to silence and to counsel. Should Fifth Amendment law impose identical or similar requirements when a suspect is interrogated before a grand jury?

There are also additional questions raised by the grand jury process. One who has been taken into custody and questioned by police generally has notice that he or she is a suspect in the investigation, since police do not do this to persons not a target of their investigation. But the grand jury may subpoena witnesses not suspected of criminal involvement, so a person subpoenaed cannot infer from the subpoena that he is a suspect. In light of this lack of notice, does or should one suspected of involvement—a "target"—have the right to be warned of that fact when called to testify before the grand jury?

United States v. Washington

Supreme Court of the United States, 1977.
431 U.S. 181, 97 S.Ct. 1814, 52 L.Ed.2d 238.

■ MR. CHIEF JUSTICE BURGER delivered the opinion of the Court.

The question presented in this case is whether testimony given by a grand jury witness suspected of wrongdoing may be used against him in a later prosecution for a substantive criminal offense when the witness was not informed in advance of his testimony that he was a potential defendant in danger of indictment.

(1)

The facts are not in dispute. Zimmerman and Woodard were driving respondent's van truck when a Washington, D. C., policeman stopped them for a traffic offense. Seeing a motorcycle in the rear of the van which he identified as stolen, the officer arrested both men and impounded respondent's vehicle. When respondent came to reclaim the van, he told police that Zimmerman and Woodard were friends who were driving the van with his permission.

He explained the presence of the stolen motorcycle by saying that while driving the van himself he had stopped to assist an unknown motorcyclist whose machine had broken down. Respondent then allowed the motorcycle to be placed in his van to take it for repairs. Soon after this the van stalled and he walked to a nearby gasoline station to call Zimmerman and Woodard for help, leaving the van with the unknown motorcyclist. After reaching Zimmerman by phone, respondent waited at the gasoline station for his friends, then returned to the spot he had left the van when they failed to appear; by that time the van had disappeared. Respondent said he was not alarmed, assuming his friends had repaired the van and driven it away. Shortly thereafter, Zimmerman and Woodard were arrested with the stolen motorcycle in the van.

Not surprisingly, the officer to whom respondent related this tale was more than a little skeptical; he told respondent he did not believe his story, and advised him not to repeat it in court, "because you're liable to be in trouble if you [do so]." The officer also declined to release the van. Respondent then repeated this story to an Assistant United States Attorney working on the case. The prosecutor, too, was dubious of the account; nevertheless, he released the van to respondent. At the same time, he served respondent with a subpoena to appear before the grand jury investigating the motorcycle theft.

When respondent appeared before the grand jury, the Assistant United States Attorney in charge had not yet decided whether to seek an indictment against him. The prosecutor was aware of respondent's explanation, and was also aware of the possibility that respondent could be indicted by the grand jury for the theft if his story was not believed.

The prosecutor did not advise respondent before his appearance that he might be indicted on a criminal charge in connection with the stolen motorcycle. But respondent, after reciting the usual oath to tell the truth, was given a series of other warnings, as follows:

"Q. * * *

"You have a right to remain silent. You are not required to say anything to us in this Grand Jury at any time or to answer any question.''[3]

"Anything you say can be used against you in Court.

"You have the right to talk to a lawyer for advice before we question you and have him outside the Grand Jury during any questioning.

"If you cannot afford a lawyer and want one a lawyer will be provided for you.

"If you want to answer questions now without a lawyer present you will still have the right to stop answering at any time.

"You also have the right to stop answering at any time until you talk to a lawyer.

"Now, do you understand those rights, sir?

"A. Yes, I do.

"Q. And do you want to answer questions of the Grand Jury in reference to a stolen motorcycle that was found in your truck?

"A. Yes, sir.

"Q. And do you want a lawyer here or outside the Grand Jury room while you answer those questions?

"A. No, I don't think so."

In response to questions, respondent again related his version of how the stolen motorcycle came to be in the rear of his van. Subsequently, the grand jury indicted respondent, Zimmerman, and Woodard for grand larceny and receiving stolen property.

Respondent moved to suppress his testimony and quash the indictment, arguing that it was based on evidence obtained in violation of his Fifth Amendment privilege against compelled self-incrimination. The Superior Court for the District of Columbia suppressed the testimony * * * holding that before the Government could use respondent's grand jury testimony at trial, it had first to demonstrate that respondent had knowingly waived his privilege against compelled self-incrimination. Notwithstanding the comprehensive warnings described earlier, the court found no effective waiver had been made, holding that respondent was not properly advised of his Fifth Amendment rights. The court thought the Constitution required, at a minimum, that

"inquiry be made of the suspect to determine what his educational background is, and what his formal education is and whether or not he understands that this is a constitutional privilege and whether he fully understands the consequences of what might result in the event that

---

3. This was an obvious overstatement of respondent's constitutional rights; the very purpose of the grand jury is to elicit testimony, and it can compel answers, by use of contempt powers, to all except self-incriminating questions.

After the oral warnings, respondent was also handed a card containing all the warnings prescribed by Miranda v. Arizona, 384 U.S. 436, 86 S.Ct. 1602, 16 L.Ed.2d 694 (1966), and a waiver form acknowledging that the witness waived the privilege against compelled self-incrimination. Respondent signed the waiver.

he does waive his constitutional right and in the event that he does make incriminatory statements * * * ."

The court also held that respondent should have been told that his testimony could lead to his indictment by the grand jury before which he was testifying, and could then be used to convict him in a criminal prosecution.

The District of Columbia Court of Appeals affirmed the suppression order. That court also took the position that "the most significant failing of the prosecutor was in not advising [respondent] that he was a potential defendant. Another shortcoming was in the prosecutor's waiting until after administering the oath in the cloister of the grand jury before undertaking to furnish what advice was given."[4]

(2)

The implicit premise of the District of Columbia Court of Appeals' holding is that a grand jury inquiry, like police custodial interrogation, is an "interrogation of persons suspected or accused of crime [that] contains inherently compelling pressures which work to undermine the individual's will to resist and to compel him to speak where he would not otherwise do so freely." Miranda v. Arizona, 384 U.S. 436, 467, 86 S.Ct. 1602, 1624, 16 L.Ed.2d 694 (1966). But this Court has not decided that the grand jury setting presents coercive elements which compel witnesses to incriminate themselves. Nor have we decided whether any Fifth Amendment warnings whatever are constitutionally required for grand jury witnesses; moreover, we have no occasion to decide these matters today, for even assuming that the grand jury setting exerts some pressures on witnesses generally or on those who may later be indicted, the comprehensive warnings respondent received in this case plainly satisfied any possible claim to warnings. Accordingly, respondent's grand jury testimony may properly be used against him in a subsequent trial for theft of the motorcycle.

Although it is well settled that the Fifth Amendment privilege extends to grand jury proceedings, it is also axiomatic that the Amendment does not automatically preclude self-incrimination, whether spontaneous or in response to questions put by government officials. * * * Absent some officially coerced self-accusation, the Fifth Amendment privilege is not violated by even the most damning admissions. Accordingly, unless the record reveals some compulsion, respondent's incriminating testimony cannot conflict with any constitutional guarantees of the privilege.[5]

---

4. Though both courts below found no effective waiver of Fifth Amendment rights, neither court found, and no one suggests here, that respondent's signing of the waiver-of-rights form was involuntary or was made without full appreciation of all the rights of which he was advised. The Government does not challenge, and we do not disturb, the finding that at the time of his grand jury appearance respondent was a potential defendant whose indictment was considered likely by the prosecution.

5. In *Miranda*, the Court saw as inherently coercive any police custodial interrogation conducted by isolating the suspect with police officers; therefore, the Court established a *per se* rule that all incriminating statements made during such interrogation are barred as "compelled." All *Miranda's* safeguards, which are designed to avoid the coercive atmosphere, rest on the overbearing compulsion which the Court thought was

The Constitution does not prohibit every element which influences a criminal suspect to make incriminating admissions. * * * Of course, for many witnesses the grand jury room engenders an atmosphere conducive to truth telling, for it is likely that upon being brought before such a body of neighbors and fellow citizens, and having been placed under a solemn oath to tell the truth, many witnesses will feel obliged to do just that. But it does not offend the guarantees of the Fifth Amendment if in that setting a witness is more likely to tell the truth than in less solemn surroundings. The constitutional guarantee is only that the witness be not *compelled* to give self-incriminating testimony. The test is whether, considering the totality of the circumstances, the free will of the witness was overborne.

totality of circumstances

(3)

After being sworn, respondent was explicitly advised that he had a right to remain silent and that any statements he did make could be used to convict him of crime. It is inconceivable that such a warning would fail to alert him to his right to refuse to answer any question which might incriminate him. This advice also eliminated any possible compulsion to self-incrimination which might otherwise exist. To suggest otherwise is to ignore the record and reality. Indeed, it seems self-evident that one who is told he is free to refuse to answer questions is in a curious posture to later complain that his answers were compelled. Moreover, any possible coercion or unfairness resulting from a witness' misimpression that he must answer truthfully even questions with incriminatory aspects is completely removed by the warnings given here. Even in the presumed psychologically coercive atmosphere of police custodial interrogation, *Miranda* does not require that any additional warnings be given simply because the suspect is a potential defendant; indeed, such suspects are potential defendants more often than not.

Respondent points out that unlike one subject to custodial interrogation, whose arrest should inform him only too clearly that he is a potential criminal defendant, a grand jury witness may well be unaware that he is targeted for possible prosecution. While this may be so in some situations, it is an overdrawn generalization. In any case, events here clearly put respondent on notice that he was a suspect in the motorcycle theft. He knew that the grand jury was investigating that theft and that his involvement was known to the authorities. Respondent was made abundantly aware that his exculpatory version of events had been disbelieved by the police officer, and that his friends, whose innocence his own story supported, were to be prosecuted for the theft. The interview with the prosecutor put him on additional notice that his implausible story was not accepted as true. The warnings he received in the grand jury room served further to alert him to his own potential criminal liability. In sum, by the time he testified respondent knew better than anyone else of his potential defendant status.

However, all of this is largely irrelevant, since we do not understand what constitutional disadvantage a failure to give potential defendant warnings could possibly inflict on a grand jury witness, whether or not he

caused by isolation of a suspect in police custody. * * *

has received other warnings. It is firmly settled that the prospect of being indicted does not entitle a witness to commit perjury, and witnesses who are not grand jury targets are protected from compulsory self-incrimination to the same extent as those who are. Because target witness status neither enlarges nor diminishes the constitutional protection against compelled self-incrimination, potential-defendant warnings add nothing of value to protection of Fifth Amendment rights.

* * *

(4)

Since warnings were given, we are not called upon to decide whether such warnings were constitutionally required. However, the District of Columbia Court of Appeals held that whatever warnings are required are insufficient if given "in the cloister of the grand jury." That court gave no reason for its view that warnings must be given outside the presence of the jury, but respondent now advances two justifications. First, it could be thought that warnings given to respondent before the grand jury came too late, because of the short time to assimilate their significance, and because of the presence of the grand jurors. But respondent does not contend that he did not understand the warnings given here. In any event, it is purely speculative to attribute any such effects to warnings given in the presence of the jury immediately before taking the stand. If anything, the proximity of the warnings to respondent's testimony and the solemnity of the grand jury setting seem likely to increase their effectiveness.

Second, respondent argues that giving the oath in the presence of the grand jury undermines assertion of the Fifth Amendment privilege by placing the witness in fear that the grand jury will infer guilt from invocation of the privilege. But this argument entirely overlooks that the grand jury's historic role is an investigative body; it is not the final arbiter of guilt or innocence. Moreover, it is well settled that invocation of the Fifth Amendment privilege in a grand jury proceeding is not admissible in a criminal trial, where guilt or innocence is actually at stake.

The judgment of the Court of Appeals is reversed, and the cause is remanded for further proceedings not inconsistent with this opinion.

Reversed and remanded.

■ MR. JUSTICE BRENNAN, with whom MR. JUSTICE MARSHALL joins, dissenting.

* * *

I would hold that a failure to warn the witness that he is a potential defendant is fatal to an indictment of him when it is made unmistakably to appear, as here, that the grand jury inquiry became an investigation directed against the witness and was pursued with the purpose of compelling him to give self-incriminating testimony upon which to indict him. I would further hold that without such prior warning and the witness' subsequent voluntary waiver of his privilege, there is such gross encroachment upon the witness' privilege as to render worthless the values protected by it unless the self-incriminating testimony is unavailable to the

Government for use at any trial brought pursuant to even a valid indictment.

NOTES

1. **Perjury Prosecutions.** Insofar as the Fifth Amendment privilege against compelled self-incrimination applies in grand jury proceedings, it provides no license to commit perjury.

In United States v. Wong, 431 U.S. 174, 97 S.Ct. 1823, 52 L.Ed.2d 231 (1977), the defendant was called before a grand jury investigating police corruption. She was warned of her privilege against self-incrimination and then denied giving money to police officers or discussing gambling activities with them. Subsequently, she was indicted for perjury on the basis of these statements, which were false. At a hearing on her motion to dismiss the indictment, she convinced the District Judge that because of her limited command of English she had not understood the warning concerning the Fifth Amendment privilege and, further, had believed she was required to answer all questions. The district judge suppressed her testimony before the grand jury and the Court of Appeals affirmed. A unanimous Supreme Court reversed:

> [T]he Fifth Amendment privilege does not condone perjury. It grants a privilege to remain silent without risking contempt but it "does not endow the person who testifies with a license to commit perjury." * * * The failure to provide a warning of the privilege, in addition to the oath to tell the truth, does not call for a different result.

431 U.S. at 178, 97 S.Ct. at 1825, 52 L.Ed.2d 235. The Court also rejected the argument that the failure to provide an effective warning violated due process requirements of fundamental fairness: "perjury is not a permissible way of objecting to the Government's [unfair or oppressive] questions."

2. **Statutory Rights of Grand Jury Targets.** There is wide variation concerning the rights, if any, a target of a grand jury investigation has under state case law and legislation concerning testimony before the grand jury. The Indiana Code provides:

§ 35–34–2–5 Subpoenas; contents; failure to obey; contempt

* * *

Sec. 5. (a) A subpoena duces tecum or subpoena ad testificandum summoning a witness to appear before the grand jury * * * must contain a statement of the general nature of the grand jury inquiry.

(b) If the subpoena is issued to a target, the subpoena shall also contain a statement informing the target that:

(1) he is a subject of the grand jury investigation;

(2) he has the right to consult with an attorney and to be assisted by an attorney * * *; and

(3) if he cannot afford an attorney, the court impaneling the grand jury will appoint one for him, upon request.

Utah by statute requires a grand jury witness be notified when he appears that he is a "target" ("a person regarding whom the attorney for the state, the special prosecutor, or the grand jury has substantial evidence that links that person to the commission of a crime and who could be indicted or charged with that crime") or a "subject" ("a person whose conduct is within the scope of the grand jury's investigation, [if] that conduct exposes the person to possible criminal prosecution"). Utah St. §§ 77–10a–1, 77–10a–13.

New Mexico statutes require a person who is a target of a grand jury inquiry be advised of that fact and be given an opportunity to testify. N.M.Stat.Ann. § 31–6–11(B). Further, the target is not to be subpoenaed "except where it is found by the prosecuting attorney to be essential to the investigation." N.M.Stat.Ann. § 31–6–12.

3. **Constitutional Right to Counsel.** Under *Miranda*, a suspect has the right to the presence of counsel during custodial police interrogation. As the Supreme Court suggested in *Washington*, the Court has not extended this right to questioning before the grand jury. In United States v. Mandujano, 425 U.S. 564, 96 S.Ct. 1768, 48 L.Ed.2d 212 (1976), the grand jury witness (and subsequent perjury defendant) was informed that if he desired he could have the assistance of counsel, but his lawyer could not be inside the grand jury room. "[T]hat statement," the Supreme Court commented, "was plainly a correct recital of the law." The Court has subsequently, citing *Mandujana,* explained, "A grand jury witness has no constitutional right to have counsel present during the grand jury proceeding, and no decision of this Court has held that a grand jury witness has a right to have her attorney present outside the jury room." Conn and Najera v. Gabbert, 526 U.S. 286, ___, 119 S.Ct. 1292, 1296, 143 L.Ed.2d 399, 400 (1999). It added that it "need not decide today whether * * * a right [to have an attorney present outside the grand jury room] exists."

4. **Statutory Rights to Counsel.** A number of jurisdictions presently provide for at least some grand jury witnesses to have counsel present during questioning. The Colorado statute providing for representation attempts to address a number of potential problems counsel might create:

> Any witness subpoenaed to appear and testify before a grand jury or to produce books, papers, documents, or other objects before such grand jury shall be entitled to assistance of counsel during any such time that such witness is being questioned in the presence of such grand jury, and counsel may be present in the grand jury room with his client during such questioning. However, counsel for the witness shall be permitted only to counsel the witness and shall not make objections, arguments, or address the grand jury. Such counsel may be retained by the witness or may, for any person financially unable to obtain adequate assistance, be appointed * * * . An attorney present in the grand jury room shall take an oath of secrecy. * * *

Colo.Rev.Stat. § 16–5–204(4)(d). Kansas provides by statute that any grand jury witness is entitled to have counsel present and adds:

> (2) Counsel for any witness may be present while the witness is testifying and may interpose objections on behalf of the witness. He shall not be permitted to examine or cross-examine his client or any other witness before the grand jury.

Kan.Stat.Ann. § 23–3009.

The Massachusetts statute, Mass.Rev.Stat. ch. 277, § 14A, specifies further, "no witness may refuse to appear for reason of unavailability of counsel for that witness."

5. **Immunity.** A witness's Fifth Amendment right to decline to respond to questions in the grand jury context as well as in other situations depends upon the answers' "incriminatory" nature. If no danger of incrimination exists, there is no self-incrimination privilege to refuse an answer. The danger of incrimination can be removed by the expiration of the period of limitations for the offenses at issue, an executive pardon for them or—as is more frequently the case—an effective grant of immunity from prosecution. Brown v. Walker, 161 U.S. 591, 16 S.Ct. 644, 40 L.Ed.

819 (1896). In Ullmann v. United States, 350 U.S. 422, 76 S.Ct. 497, 100 L.Ed. 511 (1956), for example, a grand jury witness asserted testifying would result in loss of his job, expulsion from a labor union, ineligibility for a passport and general public opprobrium. Despite a grant of immunity from prosecution, he urged, he had a right to refuse to provide information to a grand jury. Rejecting the argument, the Court stressed that the Fifth Amendment protects only against criminal liability. For a grant of immunity to be effective, it added, "the immunity granted need only remove those sanctions which generate the fear justifying invocation of the privilege * * * ."

The major question presented by grants of immunity is the type of immunity required to render the privilege inapplicable. Specifically, must the immunity be from prosecution for the offenses which the answers concern (so-called "transactional immunity," because the immunity is from criminal prosecution for the transaction concerning which the person is required to testify)? Or, is immunity from the use of the answers (so-called "use immunity") is sufficient? The matter was addressed in Kastigar v. United States, 406 U.S. 441, 92 S.Ct. 1653, 32 L.Ed.2d 212 (1972). Kastigar had been called before a federal grand jury and was granted immunity under 18 U.S.C.A. §§ 6002, 6003. Section 6003 authorizes a federal district judge to issue an order requiring a person to give testimony or provide information if: (a) the person has refused to give testimony or provide information in a proceeding before a court or grand jury of the United States; and (b) the United States attorney requests the order. A person who testifies or provides information under such an order is entitled to certain immunity under Section 6002, which provides as follows:

> Whenever a witness refuses, on the basis of his privilege against self-incrimination, to testify or provide other information in a proceeding before or ancillary to—
>
> (1) a court or grand jury of the United States, * * * .

and the person presiding over the proceeding communicates to the witness an order issued under [Section 6003], the witness may not refuse to comply with the order on the basis of his privilege against self-incrimination; but no testimony or other information compelled under the order (or any information directly or indirectly derived from such testimony or other information) may be used against the witness in any criminal case, except a prosecution for perjury, giving a false statement, or otherwise failing to comply with the order.

Kastigar nevertheless declined to answer the questions and consequently was found in contempt of court. The Supreme Court upheld the contempt citation, concluding the grant of immunity was sufficient and, therefore, Kastigar had no Fifth Amendment basis for refusing to answer:

> The statute's explicit proscription of the use in any criminal case of "testimony or other information compelled under the order (or any information directly or indirectly derived from such testimony or other information)" is consonant with Fifth Amendment standards. We hold that such immunity from use and derivative use is coextensive with the scope of the privilege against self-incrimination, and therefore is sufficient to compel testimony over a claim of the privilege. While a grant of immunity must afford protection commensurate with that afforded by the privilege, it need not be broader. Transactional immunity, which accords full immunity from prosecution for the offense to which the compelled testimony relates, affords the witness considerably broader protection than does the Fifth Amendment privilege. The privilege has never been construed to mean that one who invokes it cannot subsequently be prosecuted. Its sole concern is to afford protection against being "forced to give testimony leading to the infliction of 'penalties affixed to * * * criminal acts.'"

Immunity from the use of compelled testimony, as well as evidence derived directly and indirectly therefrom, affords this protection. It prohibits the prosecutorial authorities from using the compelled testimony in any respect, and it therefore insures that the testimony cannot lead to the infliction of criminal penalties on the witness.

406 U.S. at 453, 92 S.Ct. at 1661, 32 L.Ed.2d at 222.

Kastigar argued that persons compelled to testify who were later prosecuted would experience difficulty in determining whether evidence offered against them was derived from their compelled testimony. In response, the Court held after a grant of use immunity, a prosecuted witness can require the Government to prove its evidence was not derived from compelled testimony. A defendant creates the Government's obligation by demonstrating the prosecution concerns a matter as to which he was compelled to testify under a grant of use immunity. The prosecution then has the burden of showing that its evidence has a legitimate source independent of the compelled testimony and is therefore not tainted by that testimony. Justice Marshall, dissenting, argued the majority's holding fails to sufficiently protect an immunized witness. As a practical matter, a criminal defendant cannot effectively challenge a prosecution claim that evidence offered at trial has a source independent of prior compelled testimony. Only transactional immunity, he concluded, can effectively protect such persons from the use of their testimony and its "fruits."

6. **Immunity and Perjury.** Immunity does not protect against prosecution for or proof of perjury committed during immunized testimony. Applying this position, the Supreme Court has permitted extensive use of compelled testimony in perjury proceedings.

In United States v. Apfelbaum, 445 U.S. 115, 100 S.Ct. 948, 63 L.Ed.2d 250 (1980), Apfelbaum was called before a federal grand jury to testify concerning a suspected robbery and extortion. He invoked his privilege against self-incrimination, was granted immunity under 18 U.S.C.A. § 6002, and testified concerning a number of matters. Subsequently, he was charged with perjury on the basis that during his grand jury testimony he had falsely denied attempting to locate one Harry Brown during December, 1975 and loaning Brown money. At trial, the government introduced over objection portions of Apfelbaum's grand jury testimony other than that charged in the indictment as perjured testimony. This testimony concerned his relationship and discussions with Brown, a trip on another occasion to Florida to visit Brown, and similar matters; the government argued this evidence put the allegedly perjured statements "in context" and proved that Apfelbaum knew they were false. Apfelbaum was convicted. On appeal, he successfully argued the federal statute and the Fifth Amendment prohibited, even in a perjury trial, the use of immunized testimony not specifically the basis for the perjury charge. The Supreme Court reversed the Court of Appeals.

After considering the legislative history of the immunity statute, the Court concluded Congress intended to permit use of both truthful and false statements made during immunized testimony, if use of such statements was permitted by the Fifth Amendment. It then turned to the defendant's argument that the Fifth Amendment prohibited the use of immunized testimony except for the "corpus delicti" or "core" of a perjury charge. The Court of Appeals held that use of defendant's immunized testimony must be limited to that charged as perjury on the following rationale: A grant of immunity must be coextensive with Fifth Amendment protection; this means a defendant must be placed in as near a position as possible to that which he would have occupied had he retained the privilege. The need to prevent perjury requires a narrow exception to this rule permitting the use of perjured testimony in a prosecution for that perjury. But because an immunized witness would not have given the other testimony had he retained the privilege, this other, i.e., nonperjured, testimony must not be used even in a perjury prosecution where it is relevant to guilt. The Supreme Court rejected the Court of Appeals' rationale. It reasoned that for a grant of immunity to provide protection coextensive with that of the privilege, it need not treat the witness as if he had remained silent. As long as the use of immunized testimony is limited to perjury prosecution, the exception is sufficiently narrow. "[W]e hold," the Court concluded, "that neither the statute nor the Fifth Amendment requires that the admissibility of immunized testimony be governed by any different rules than other testimony at a trial for making false statements."

Justices Brennan, Blackmun, and Marshall concurred, preferring to withhold comment on situations not before the Court. Specifically, they expressed reservation concerning the admissibility of immunized testimony in a prosecution for perjury allegedly committed after immunized testimony rather than, as in *Apfelbaum*, during immunized testimony.

CHAPTER 10

EYEWITNESS IDENTIFICATION

Analysis

EDITORS' INTRODUCTION: THE PERSUASIVE POWERS AND RISKS
OF EYEWITNESS IDENTIFICATION

Eyewitnesses testifying at trials that they recall the defendants as the
perpetrators of the charged crimes may, course, be incorrect. This may be
because they are lying or because—despite the confidence with which they
testify—they are actually unable to accurately recall what they observed at
the crime scene. Criminal trial law has long recognized the risk of inaccurate eyewitness testimony. Nevertheless, traditional criminal procedure
trusted triers of fact to evaluate the credibility of eyewitness testimony,
using common sense knowledge as to what testimony is worthy of belief
and what is not. The risks that eyewitnesses are mistaken and that jurors
are ill equipped to evaluate eyewitness testimony's credibility have been the
subject of recent scientific study that may helpfully inform the law in this
area.

"Scientific psychology was in its infancy when articles about mistaken
eyewitness identifications began appearing in the field [in the early
1900s]," Michael R. Leippe, The Case for Expert Testimony About Eyewitness Memory, 1 Psychol. Pub. Pol'y & L. 909 (1995), pointed out. But, he
added, "[a] great upsurge in eyewitness memory research began in the
early 1970s, and much of this research has revealed a disturbingly high
error rate and ever more ways in which eyewitness identifications and

recollections are susceptible to error." A leading researcher and author in this area is Elizabeth F. Loftus, Ph.D., a psychologist. See generally, Elizabeth F. Loftus, Eyewitness Testimony (1979); Elizabeth F. Loftus and James M. Doyle, Eyewitness Testimony: Civil and Criminal (3rd ed. 1997).

The Utah Supreme Court in State v. Long, 721 P.2d 483, 488–90 (Utah 1986), summarized the substance of the basic research:

> The literature is replete with empirical studies documenting the unreliability of eyewitness identification. See generally P. Wall, Eyewitness Identification in Criminal Cases (1965); E. Loftus, Eyewitness Testimony (1979). There is no significant division of opinion on the issue. The studies all lead inexorably to the conclusion that human perception is inexact and that human memory is both limited and fallible. * * *

> [T]he process of perceiving events and remembering them is not as simple or as certain as turning on a camera and recording everything the camera sees on tape or film for later replay. What we perceive and remember is the result of a much more complex process, one that does not occur without involving the whole person, and one that is profoundly affected by who we are and what we bring to the event of perception. See R. Buckhout, Eyewitness Testimony, 15 Jurimetrics J. 171, 179 (1975) (reprinted from 231 Scientific American 23 (Dec. 1974)).

> Research on human memory has consistently shown that failures may occur and inaccuracies creep in at any stage of what is broadly referred to as the "memory process." This process includes the acquisition of information, its storage, and its retrieval and communication to others. These stages have all been extensively studied in recent years, and a wide variety of factors influencing each stage have been identified.

> During the first or acquisition stage, a wide array of factors has been found to affect the accuracy of an individual's perception. Some of these are rather obvious. For example, the circumstances of the observation are critical: the distance of the observer from the event, the length of time available to perceive the event, the amount of light available, and the amount of movement involved. However, perhaps the more important factors affecting the accuracy of one's perception are those factors originating within the observer. One such limitation is the individual's physical condition, including both obvious infirmities as well as such factors as fatigue and drug or alcohol use. Another limitation which can affect perception is the emotional state of the observer. Contrary to much accepted lore, when an observer is experiencing a marked degree of stress, perceptual abilities are known to decrease significantly.

> A far less obvious limitation of great importance arises from the fact that the human brain cannot receive and store all the stimuli simultaneously presented to it. This forces people to be selective in what they perceive of any given event. To accomplish this selective perception successfully, over time each person develops unconscious

strategies for determining what elements of an event are important enough to be selected out for perception. The rest of the stimuli created by the event are ignored by the brain. These unconscious strategies of selective perception work quite well in our day-to-day lives to provide us with only the most commonly useful information, but the strategies may result in the exclusion of information that will later prove important in a court proceeding. For example, the significance of the event to the witness at the time of perception is very important. Thus, people usually remember with some detail and clarity their whereabouts at the time they learned of John F. Kennedy's assassination. Those same people, however, are generally less accurate in their descriptions of people, places, and events encountered only recently in the course of their daily routines. For instance, few of us can remember the color or make of the car that was in front of us at the last traffic signal where we waited for the light to turn green. An everyday situation such as this presents an excellent opportunity to observe, and yet, while such information may be a critical element in a criminal trial, our process of selective perception usually screens out such data completely. To the extent that court proceedings may focus on events that were not of particular importance to the observer at the time they occurred, then, the observer may have absolutely no memory of the facts simply because he or she failed to select the critical information for perception.

Another mechanism we all develop to compensate for our inability to perceive all aspects of an event at once is a series of logical inferences: if we see one thing, we assume, based on our past experience, that we also saw another that ordinarily follows. This way we can "perceive" a whole event in our mind's eye when we have actually seen or heard only portions of it. The implications of this memory strategy for court proceedings are similar to those of selective perception.

Other important factors that affect the accuracy of a viewer's perception, and which are unique to each observer, include the expectations, personal experiences, biases, and prejudices brought by any individual to a given situation. A good example of the effect of preconceptions on the accuracy of perception is the well-documented fact that identifications tend to be more accurate where the person observing and the one being observed are of the same race.

The memory process is also subject to distortion in the second or retention stage, when information that may or may not have been accurately perceived is stored in the memory. Research demonstrates that both the length of time between the witness's experience and the recollection of that experience, and the occurrence of other events in the intervening time period, affect the accuracy and completeness of recall. Just as in the perception stage, where the mind infers what occurred from what was selected for perception, in the retention stage people tend to add extraneous details and to fill in memory gaps over time, thereby unconsciously constructing more detailed, logical, and coherent recollections of their actual experiences. Thus, as eyewitnesses wend their way through the criminal justice process, their reports of what was seen and heard tend to become "more accurate, more complete and less ambiguous" in appearance. * * *

Research has also undermined the common notion that the confidence with which an individual makes an identification is a valid indicator of the accuracy of the recollection. K. Deffenbacher, Eyewitness Accuracy and Confidence: Can We Infer Anything About Their Relationship?, 4 Law and Human Behavior 243 (1980). In fact, the accuracy of an identification is, at times, inversely related to the confidence with which it is made.

Finally, the retrieval stage of the memory process—when the observer recalls the event and communicates that recollection to others—is also fraught with potential for distortion. For example, language imposes limits on the observer. Experience suggests that few individuals have such a mastery of language that they will not have some difficulty in communicating the details and nuances of the original event, and the greater the inadequacy, the greater the likelihood of miscommunication. An entirely independent problem arises when one who has accurately communicated his recollection in a narrative form is then asked questions in an attempt to elicit a more complete picture of the event described. Those asking such questions, by using a variety of subtle and perhaps unconscious questioning techniques, can significantly influence what a witness "remembers" in response to questioning. And as the witness is pressed for more details, his responses become increasingly inaccurate. In addition, research has documented an entirely different set of no less significant problems that relate to the suggestiveness of police lineups, showups, and photo arrays.

Among those factors addressed in the research is "weapon focus"—the tendency of a person exposed to a complex scenario involving—among many other aspects—the display of a weapon to concentrate on the weapon. Weapon focus, the research suggests, reduces the person's ability to accurately recall other details of the situation. See Elizabeth F. Loftus and James M. Doyle, Eyewitness Testimony: Civil and Criminal 29–30 (3rd ed. 1997).

Another factor research suggests may influence identification testimony is "transference"—a phenomenon in which a person observed in one situation is inaccurately recalled as a person seen in a second situation. See Elizabeth F. Loftus and James M. Doyle, at 88–90. Thus a witness who saw a robbery and observed X earlier in the day may unconsciously "transfer" the memory of observing X to the context of the robbery and consequently inaccurately recall X as the robber. Loftus and Doyle indicated such unconscious transference "has been documented in empirical studies." "[I]n any given situation," they added "it is nearly impossible to say definitively that an unconscious transference has occurred, only that it may have occurred."

Can the common sense of jurors and the information they bring to trials be relied upon to enable those jurors to properly evaluate eyewitness identification and thus properly discount testimony of doubtful accuracy? As the *Long* court's discussion indicated, evidence suggests not. Jennifer L.

Devenport, Steven D. Penrod, and Brian L. Cutler, Evaluating Common-sense Evaluations, 3 Psychol. Pub. Pol'y & L. 338, 353 (1997), for example, surveyed the research and concluded:

> [R]esearch * * * has consistently revealed that jurors tend to rely on factors that are not diagnostic of eyewitness accuracy, such as an eyewitness's memory for peripheral details and eyewitness confidence, tend to overestimate eyewitness accuracy, and have difficulty applying their commonsense knowledge of lineup suggestiveness to their verdict decisions.

The results of at least one study, they commented, suggest nearly three out of four mistaken identifications presented to juries may be believed.

Recent technology has give rise to a particularly significant reason to doubt existing mechanisms for testing the credibility of eyewitness identification adequately identify testimony of insufficient reliability. A study commissioned by the National Institute of Justice examined 28 cases in which defendants convicted of serious crimes were later found on the basis of DNA analysis improperly convicted. E. Connors, T. Lundregan, N. Miller and T. McEwen, Convicted by Juries, Exonerated by Science: Case Studies of the Use of DNA Evidence to Establish Innocence After Trial (1996). In all but one case the convictions followed jury trials. Identification testimony was frequently used. All of the 22 nonmurder cases involved victim identification both prior to and during trial; even in the murder cases eyewitness testimony often put the accused in the vicinity of the offense. The eyewitness testimony in these cases was wrong, the study noted, and yet the triers of fact failed to recognize this. These inaccurate convictions make clear the need for improved evaluation of the reliability of eyewitness identification.

A major issue in criminal justice administration, then, is whether the law should respond to this research and, if so, how it should do so.

A. CONSTITUTIONAL ISSUES

EDITORS' INTRODUCTION: THE SUPREME COURT'S EYEWITNESS TRILOGY

In 1967, the United States Supreme Court decided a trilogy of eyewitness identification cases designed to deal constitutionally with some risks of eyewitness identification. These decisions, and the constitutional requirements they established, are considered in the present section. The first two cases, United States v. Wade, 388 U.S. 218, 87 S.Ct. 1926, 18 L.Ed.2d 1149 (1967), and Gilbert v. California, 388 U.S. 263, 87 S.Ct. 1951, 18 L.Ed.2d 1178 (1967), dealt with the right to counsel, the subject of the first subsection following. The third case of the trilogy, Stovall v. Denno, 388 U.S. 293, 87 S.Ct. 1967, 18 L.Ed.2d 1199 (1967), indicated a pretrial identification procedure could be so suggestive that using testimony of the witness who participated in the procedure violated due process of law. This is the subject of the second subsection.

Those cases were decided before the "great upsurge in eyewitness memory research" described by Leippe. Thus there may be reason to reconsider—in light of that research—whether the approach taken in them was appropriate or adequate. Legal requirements other than those mandated by the 1967 trilogy have been suggested as appropriate supplements to the demands of the constitutional requirements. Several of these are considered in Part B of this chapter.

1.   ASSISTANCE OF COUNSEL

Much as the Supreme Court regarded the right to counsel as the appropriate vehicle for dealing with problems raised by law enforcement interrogation techniques, the Court also called that right into play to combat some difficulties with pretrial identification procedures. Consider what the Court anticipated would be the role of counsel in lineups and similar identification procedures. Does the right to counsel mean the right to have counsel at least heard regarding objections to the manner in which an identification procedure is conducted?

In addition, consider the effect of a violation of the right to counsel at a lineup upon the admissibility of later testimony. Specifically, consider the difference between the effect of a violation on in-court identification testimony by the witness and upon testimony as to an identification made by the witness at the lineup.

United States v. Wade

Supreme Court of the United States, 1967.
388 U.S. 218, 87 S.Ct. 1926, 18 L.Ed.2d 1149.

■ MR. JUSTICE BRENNAN delivered the opinion of the Court.

The question here is whether courtroom identifications of an accused at trial are to be excluded from evidence because the accused was exhibited to the witnesses before trial at a postindictment lineup conducted for identification purposes without notice to and in the absence of the accused's appointed counsel.

The federally insured bank in Eustace, Texas, was robbed on September 21, 1964. A man with a small strip of tape on each side of his face entered the bank, pointed a pistol at the female cashier and the vice president, the only persons in the bank at the time, and forced them to fill a pillowcase with the bank's money. The man then drove away with an accomplice who had been waiting in a stolen car outside the bank. On March 23, 1965, an indictment was returned against respondent, Wade, and two others for conspiring to rob the bank, and against Wade and the accomplice for the robbery itself. Wade was arrested on April 2, and counsel was appointed to represent him on April 26. Fifteen days later an FBI agent, without notice to Wade's lawyer, arranged to have the two bank employees observe a lineup made up of Wade and five or six other prisoners and conducted in a courtroom of the local county courthouse. Each person in the line wore strips of tape such as allegedly worn by the robber and upon direction each said something like "put the money in the bag," the words allegedly uttered by the robber. Both bank employees identified Wade in the lineup as the bank robber.

At trial the two employees, when asked on direct examination if the robber was in the courtroom, pointed to Wade. The prior lineup identification was then elicited from both employees on cross-examination. At the close of testimony, Wade's counsel moved for a judgment of acquittal or, alternatively, to strike the bank officials' courtroom identifications on the ground that conduct of the lineup, without notice to and in the absence of his appointed counsel, violated his Fifth Amendment privilege against self-incrimination and his Sixth Amendment right to the assistance of counsel. The motion was denied, and Wade was convicted. The Court of Appeals for the Fifth Circuit reversed the conviction and ordered a new trial at which the in-court identification evidence was to be excluded, holding that, though the lineup * * * held as it was, in the absence of counsel, already chosen to represent appellant, was a violation of his Sixth Amendment rights * * *.

I.

Neither the lineup itself nor anything shown by this record that Wade was required to do in the lineup violated his privilege against self-incrimination. * * * Schmerber v. State of California, 384 U.S. 757, 761, 86 S.Ct. 1826, 1830, 16 L.Ed.2d 908. [This part of the Court's holding is discussed in Chapter 2. Editors.]

* * *

II.

[I]t is urged that the assistance of counsel at the lineup was indispensable to protect Wade's most basic right as a criminal defendant—his right to a fair trial at which the witnesses against him might be meaningfully cross-examined.

The Framers of the Bill of Rights envisaged a broader role for counsel than under the practice then prevailing in England of merely advising his client in "matters of law," and eschewing any responsibility for "matters of fact." * * * This * * * is reflected in the scope given by our decisions to the Sixth Amendment's guarantee to an accused of the assistance of counsel for his defense. When the Bill of Rights was adopted, there were no organized police forces as we know them today. The accused confronted the prosecutor and the witnesses against him, and the evidence was marshaled, largely at the trial itself. In contrast, today's law enforcement machinery involves critical confrontations of the accused by the prosecution at pretrial proceedings where the results might well settle the accused's fate and reduce the trial itself to a mere formality. In recognition of these realities of modern criminal prosecution, our cases have construed the Sixth Amendment guarantee to apply to "critical" stages of the proceedings. The guarantee reads: "In all criminal prosecutions, the accused shall enjoy the right * * * to have the Assistance of Counsel *for his defence.*" (Emphasis supplied.) The plain wording of this guarantee thus encompasses counsel's assistance whenever necessary to assure a meaningful "defence."

[W]e [have] * * * recognized that the period from arraignment to trial was "perhaps the most critical period of the proceedings * * *," during which the accused "requires the guiding hand of counsel * * *," if the guarantee is not to prove an empty right. * * *

* * *

[Our decisions reflect the] principle that in addition to counsel's presence at trial, the accused is guaranteed that he need not stand alone against the State at any stage of the prosecution, formal or informal, in court or out, where counsel's absence might derogate from the accused's right to a fair trial. The security of that right is as much the aim of the right to counsel as it is of the other guarantees of the Sixth Amendment— the right of the accused to a speedy and public trial by an impartial jury, his right to be informed of the nature and cause of the accusation, and his right to be confronted with the witnesses against him and to have compulsory process for obtaining witnesses in his favor. The presence of counsel at such critical confrontations, as at the trial itself, operates to assure that the accused's interests will be protected consistently with our adversary theory of criminal prosecution.

In sum, the principle of [the Sixth Amendment right to counsel] requires that we scrutinize *any* pretrial confrontation of the accused to determine whether the presence of his counsel is necessary to preserve the defendant's basic right to a fair trial as affected by his right meaningfully to cross-examine the witnesses against him and to have effective assistance of counsel at the trial itself. It calls upon us to analyze whether potential substantial prejudice to defendant's rights inheres in the particular confrontation and the ability of counsel to help avoid that prejudice.

III.

The Government characterizes the lineup as a mere preparatory step in the gathering of the prosecution's evidence, not different—for Sixth Amendment purposes—from various other preparatory steps, such as systematized or scientific analyzing of the accused's fingerprints, blood sample, clothing, hair, and the like. We think there are differences which preclude such stages being characterized as critical stages at which the accused has the right to the presence of his counsel. Knowledge of the techniques of science and technology is sufficiently available, and the variables in techniques few enough, that the accused has the opportunity for a meaningful confrontation of the Government's case at trial through the ordinary processes of cross-examination of the Government's expert witnesses and the presentation of the evidence of his own experts. The denial of a right to have his counsel present at such analyses does not therefore violate the Sixth Amendment; they are not critical stages since there is minimal risk that his counsel's absence at such stages might derogate from his right to a fair trial.

IV.

But the confrontation compelled by the State between the accused and the victim or witnesses to a crime to elicit identification evidence is peculiarly riddled with innumerable dangers and variable factors which might seriously, even crucially, derogate from a fair trial. The vagaries of eyewitness identification are well-known; the annals of criminal law are rife with instances of mistaken identification. * * * A major factor contributing to the high incidence of miscarriage of justice from mistaken identification has been the degree of suggestion inherent in the manner in which the prosecution presents the suspect to witnesses for pretrial identification. * * * Suggestion can be created intentionally or unintentionally in many subtle ways. And the dangers for the suspect are particularly grave when the witness' opportunity for observation was insubstantial, and thus his susceptibility to suggestion the greatest.

Moreover, "[i]t is a matter of common experience that, once a witness has picked out the accused at the lineup, he is not likely to go back on his word later on, so that in practice the issue of identity may (in the absence of other relevant evidence) for all practical purposes be determined there and then, before the trial."

The pretrial confrontation for purpose of identification may take the form of a lineup, also known as an "identification parade" or "showup," as in the present case, or presentation of the suspect alone to the witness * * *. It is obvious that risks of suggestion attend either form of confrontation and increase the dangers inhering in eyewitness identification. But as is the case with secret interrogations, there is serious difficulty in depicting what transpires at lineups and other forms of identification confrontations. * * * [T]he defense can seldom reconstruct the manner and mode of lineup identification for judge or jury at trial. Those participating in a lineup with the accused may often be police officers; in any event, the participants' names are rarely recorded or divulged at trial. The impediments to an objective observation are increased when the victim is the witness. Lineups are prevalent in rape and robbery prosecutions and present a particular hazard that a victim's understandable outrage may excite vengeful or spiteful motives. In any event, neither witnesses nor lineup participants are apt to be alert for conditions prejudicial to the suspect. And if they were, it would likely be of scant benefit to the suspect since neither witnesses nor lineup participants are likely to be schooled in the detection of suggestive influences.[1] Improper influences may go undetected by a suspect, guilty or not, who experiences the emotional tension which we might expect in one being confronted with potential accusers. Even when he does observe abuse, if he has a criminal record he may be reluctant to take the stand and open up the admission of prior convictions. Moreover any protestations by the suspect of the fairness of the lineup made at trial are likely to be in vain; the jury's choice is between the accused's unsupported version and that of the police officers present. In short, the accused's inability effectively to reconstruct at trial any unfairness that occurred at the lineup may deprive him of his only opportunity meaningfully to attack the credibility of the witness' courtroom identification.

---

1. An additional impediment to the detection of such influences by participants, including the suspect, is the physical conditions often surrounding the conduct of the lineup. In many, lights shine on the stage in such a way that the suspect cannot see the witness. In some a one-way mirror is used and what is said on the witness' side cannot be heard.

What facts have been disclosed in specific cases about the conduct of pretrial confrontations for identification illustrate both the potential for substantial prejudice to the accused at that stage and the need for its revelation at trial. * * * [S]tate reports, in the course of describing prior identifications admitted as evidence of guilt, reveal numerous instances of suggestive procedures, for example, that all in the lineup but the suspect were known to the identifying witness, that the other participants in a lineup were grossly dissimilar in appearance to the suspect, that only the suspect was required to wear distinctive clothing which the culprit allegedly wore, that the witness is told by the police that they have caught the culprit after which the defendant is brought before the witness alone or is viewed in jail, that the suspect is pointed out before or during a lineup, and that the participants in the lineup are asked to try on an article of clothing which fits only the suspect.

The potential for improper influence is illustrated by the circumstances, insofar as they appear, surrounding the prior identifications in the three cases we decide today. In the present case, [for example,] the testimony of the identifying witnesses elicited on cross-examination revealed that those witnesses were taken to the courthouse and seated in the courtroom to await assembly of the lineup. The courtroom faced on a hallway observable to the witnesses through an open door. The cashier testified that she saw Wade "standing in the hall" within sight of an FBI agent. Five or six other prisoners later appeared in the hall. The vice president testified that he saw a person in the hall in the custody of the agent who "resembled the person that we identified as the one that had entered the bank."

The few cases that have surfaced therefore reveal the existence of a process attended with hazards of serious unfairness to the criminal accused and strongly suggest the plight of the more numerous defendants who are unable to ferret out suggestive influences in the secrecy of the confrontation. We do not assume that these risks are the result of police procedures intentionally designed to prejudice an accused. Rather we assume they derive from the dangers inherent in eyewitness identification and the suggestibility inherent in the context of the pretrial identification. * * *

Insofar as the accused's conviction may rest on a courtroom identification in fact the fruit of a suspect pretrial identification which the accused is helpless to subject to effective scrutiny at trial, the accused is deprived of that right of cross-examination which is an essential safeguard to his right to confront the witnesses against him. And even though cross-examination is a precious safeguard to a fair trial, it cannot be viewed as an absolute assurance of accuracy and reliability. Thus in the present context, where so many variables and pitfalls exist, the first line of defense must be the prevention of unfairness and the lessening of the hazards of eyewitness identification at the lineup itself. The trial which might determine the accused's fate may well not be that in the courtroom but that at the pretrial confrontation, with the State aligned against the accused, the witness the sole jury, and the accused unprotected against the overreaching, intentional or unintentional, and with little or no effective appeal from the judgment there rendered by the witness—"that's the man."

Since it appears that there is grave potential for prejudice, intentional or not, in the pretrial lineup, which may not be capable of reconstruction at trial, and since presence of counsel itself can often avert prejudice and assure a meaningful confrontation at trial, there can be little doubt that for Wade the postindictment lineup was a critical stage of the prosecution at which he was "as much entitled to such aid [of counsel] * * * as at the trial itself." Thus both Wade and his counsel should have been notified of the impending lineup, and counsel's presence should have been a requisite to conduct of the lineup, absent an "intelligent waiver." No substantial countervailing policy considerations have been advanced against the requirement of the presence of counsel. Concern is expressed that the requirement will forestall prompt identifications and result in obstruction of the confrontations. As for the first, we note that in [this] case[ ] * * *, counsel had already been appointed and no argument is made * * * that notice to counsel would have prejudicially delayed the confrontation[ ]. Moreover, we leave open the question whether the presence of substitute counsel might not suffice where notification and presence of the suspect's own counsel would result in prejudicial delay.[2] And to refuse to recognize the right to counsel for fear that counsel will obstruct the course of justice is contrary to the basic assumptions upon which this Court has operated in Sixth Amendment cases. * * * In our view counsel can hardly impede legitimate law enforcement; on the contrary, for the reasons expressed, law enforcement may be assisted by preventing the infiltration of taint in the prosecution's identification evidence.[3] That result cannot help the guilty avoid conviction but can only help assure that the right man has been brought to justice.

Legislative or other regulations, such as those of local police departments, which eliminate the risks of abuse and unintentional suggestion at lineup proceedings and the impediments to meaningful confrontation at trial may also remove the basis for regarding the stage as "critical." But neither Congress nor the federal authorities have seen fit to provide a solution. * * *

V.

We come now to the question whether the denial of Wade's motion to strike the courtroom identification by the bank witnesses at trial because of the absence of his counsel at the lineup required, as the Court of Appeals held, the grant of a new trial at which such evidence is to be excluded. We do not think this disposition can be justified without first giving the Government the opportunity to establish by clear and convincing evidence that the in-court identifications were based upon observations of the suspect other than the lineup identification. Where, as here, the admissibil-

---

2. Although the right to counsel usually means a right to the suspect's own counsel, provision for substitute counsel may be justified on the ground that the substitute counsel's presence may eliminate the hazards which render the lineup a critical stage for the presence of the suspect's *own* counsel.

3. Concern is also expressed that the presence of counsel will force divulgence of the identity of government witnesses whose identity the Government may want to conceal. To the extent that this is a valid or significant state interest there are police practices commonly used to effect concealment, for example, masking the face.

ity of evidence of the lineup identification itself is not involved, a *per se* rule of exclusion of courtroom identification would be unjustified.[4] A rule limited solely to the exclusion of testimony concerning identification at the lineup itself, without regard to admissibility of the courtroom identification, would render the right to counsel an empty one. The lineup is most often used, as in the present case, to crystallize the witnesses' identification of the defendant for future reference. We have already noted that the lineup identification will have that effect. The State may then rest upon the witnesses' unequivocal courtroom identification, and not mention the pretrial identification as part of the State's case at trial. Counsel is then in the predicament in which Wade's counsel found himself—realizing that possible unfairness at the lineup may be the sole means of attack upon the unequivocal courtroom identification, and having to probe in the dark in an attempt to discover and reveal unfairness, while bolstering the government witness' courtroom identification by bringing out and dwelling upon his prior identification. Since counsel's presence at the lineup would equip him to attack not only the lineup identification but the courtroom identification as well, limiting the impact of violation of the right to counsel to exclusion of evidence only of identification at the lineup itself disregards a critical element of that right.

We think it follows that the proper test to be applied in these situations is that quoted in Wong Sun v. United States, 371 U.S. 471, 488, 83 S.Ct. 407, 417, 9 L.Ed.2d 441, " '[W]hether, granting establishment of the primary illegality, the evidence to which instant objection is made has been come at by exploitation of that illegality or instead by means sufficiently distinguishable to be purged of the primary taint.' Maguire, Evidence of Guilt, 221 (1959)." Application of this test in the present context requires consideration of various factors; for example, the prior opportunity to observe the alleged criminal act, the existence of any discrepancy between any prelineup description and the defendant's actual description, any identification prior to lineup of another person, the identification by picture of the defendant prior to the lineup, failure to identify the defendant on a prior occasion, and the lapse of time between the alleged act and the lineup identification. It is also relevant to consider those facts which, despite the absence of counsel, are disclosed concerning the conduct of the lineup.

* * *

On the record now before us we cannot make the determination whether the in-court identifications had an independent origin. This was not an issue at trial, although there is some evidence relevant to a determination. That inquiry is most properly made in the District Court. We therefore think the appropriate procedure to be followed is to vacate the conviction pending a hearing to determine whether the in-court identifications had an independent source, or whether, in any event, the intro-

---

4. We reach a contrary conclusion in Gilbert v. California, [discussed in the notes following this case], as to the admissibility of the witness' testimony that he also identified the accused at the lineup.

duction of the evidence was harmless error, and for the District Court to reinstate the conviction or order a new trial, as may be proper.

The judgment of the Court of Appeals is vacated and the case is remanded to that court with direction to enter a new judgment vacating the conviction and remanding the case to the District Court for further proceedings consistent with this opinion. It is so ordered.

Judgment of Court of Appeals vacated and case remanded with direction.

NOTES

1. In actual fact, no further proceedings took place in the trial court. The case was remanded to the district court which scheduled a hearing. Wade, however, absconded and never appeared. Interview With Weldon Holcomb, Counsel for Wade, May, 1991.

2. **Per Se Rule of Inadmissibility for Testimony Concerning Identification Made at Lineup.** In Gilbert v. California, 388 U.S. 263, 87 S.Ct. 1951, 18 L.Ed.2d 1178 (1967), a companion case to *Wade*, the Court also concluded that a pretrial lineup had been conducted in violation of Gilbert's Sixth Amendment right to counsel. Unlike in *Wade*, however, at trial in *Gilbert* the prosecution solicited from one of the eyewitnesses on direct examination that he had picked Gilbert out of the pretrial lineup. The Supreme Court characterized that testimony as "the direct result of the illegal lineup 'come at by exploitation of [the primary] illegality.' * * *. The State is therefore not entitled to an opportunity to show that testimony had an independent source. Only a *per se* exclusionary rule as to such testimony can be an effective sanction to assure law enforcement authorities will respect the accused's constitutional right to the presence of counsel at the critical lineup."

3. **Attachment of Right to Counsel.** The right to counsel recognized in *Wade* applies only if the identification procedure is conducted after the Sixth Amendment right to counsel attaches. When does this occur?

In Kirby v. Illinois, 406 U.S. 682, 92 S.Ct. 1877, 32 L.Ed.2d 411 (1972), the defendant was arrested and transported to the stationhouse. Shortly thereafter, the robbery victim came to the station where he immediately identified the defendant as one of the men who had robbed him. Kirby was not advised of his right to counsel and no lawyer was present on his behalf. The Supreme Court held the resulting identification evidence was properly admitted because Kirby's right to counsel had not attached:

> The initiation of judicial criminal proceedings is far from a mere formalism. It is the starting point of our whole system of adversary criminal justice. For it is only then that the government has committed itself to prosecute, and only then that the adverse positions of government and defendant have solidified. It is then that a defendant finds himself faced with the prosecutorial forces of organized society, and immersed in the intricacies of substantive and procedural criminal law. It is this point, therefore, that marks the commencement of the "criminal prosecutions" to which alone the explicit guarantees of the Sixth Amendment are applicable.

> * * *

> In this case we are asked to import into a routine police investigation an absolute constitutional guarantee historically and rationally applicable only after the onset of formal prosecutorial proceedings. We decline to do so. * * *

Id. at 689–90, 92 S.Ct. at 1882–83, 32 L.Ed.2d at 418.

Kirby indicated the right to counsel attached at the commencement of judicial criminal proceedings. It failed, however, to identify that point. The lower courts' post-*Wade* assumption that the controlling point was the filing of the formal charge—the indictment or information—was proved erroneous by Moore v. Illinois, 434 U.S. 220, 98 S.Ct. 458, 54 L.Ed.2d 424 (1977). Moore was arrested for a rape. The morning after the arrest, a policeman accompanied the victim to the courtroom where Moore appeared for his preliminary hearing to determine whether there was probable cause to bind him over to the grand jury. At the hearing, Moore was led before the bench and told by the judge he was charged with rape. The judge then called the victim, who had been waiting in the courtroom, to come before the bench. The State's Attorney asked the victim whether she saw her assailant in the courtroom; she pointed at Moore. Moore was not represented by counsel at this appearance and the court did not offer to appoint an attorney. At trial, the victim testified as part of the prosecution's case-in-chief that she had, at the preliminary hearing, identified Moore as the man who raped her and made an in-court identification of Moore as her assailant.

The Supreme Court held that Moore's Sixth Amendment right to counsel applied at the identification made at the hearing. Although the identification confrontation occurred prior to indictment, the Court explained, Moore's Sixth Amendment right to counsel attached because the "prosecution in this case was commenced under Illinois law when the victim's complaint was filed in the court." The State committed itself to prosecute.

Moore also rejected the argument that the right to counsel does not apply to one-on-one identification procedures. Similarly, it refused to exempt from the right to counsel identifications made in the course of judicial proceedings such as the preliminary hearing at issue in the case.

A considerable amount of case law defining the commencement of the prosecution for Sixth Amendment purposes has developed in case law dealing with law enforcement interrogation of suspects. This case law is presented in Section C of Chapter 7. The interrogation case law almost certainly also applies to attachment of the Sixth Amendment for *Wade-Gilbert* purposes.

4. **Photo Showings.** To what extent does the right to counsel apply at investigatory procedures not involving a physical confrontation between the defendant and a potential prosecution witness?

In United States v. Ash, 413 U.S. 300, 93 S.Ct. 2568, 37 L.Ed.2d 619 (1973), the Court held counsel is not required at a photo array showing. Witnesses to a bank robbery were shown five color photographs shortly before trial and long after Ash had been indicted. Finding no violation of the right to counsel, the Court distinguished *Wade* and *Gilbert*. The opportunities for suggestion and the difficulty of reconstructing a suggestive lineup were used in *Wade* only to address whether— assuming a right to counsel at the lineup existed—providing counsel only at trial would be sufficient, the Court explained. Whether the right to counsel attached at the lineup in the first place was determined in *Wade* by the Court's conclusion the lineup constituted a "trial-like confrontation" requiring assistance of counsel to counterbalance any prosecution "overreaching." The critical question, therefore, is whether a photo showing is a "trial-like confrontation" in this sense.

Addressing that question, the Court noted a defendant has no right to be present at the showing of a photo display and most likely will not be present. Thus the showing is not a "trial-like adversary confrontation." There is no possibility that the defendant might be "misled" by his lack of familiarity with the law or overpowered by his professional adversary. Both sides have equal access to witnesses for purposes of showing them photographs. The traditional counterbalance in the American adversary system for the prosecution's ability to interview witnesses and to show them photographs is the equal ability of defense counsel to seek and interview witnesses himself. While counsel's ability to do this does not remove all potential for abuse, "it does remove any inequality in the adversary process itself and thereby fully satisfies the historical spirit of the Sixth Amendment's right to counsel guarantee." The primary safeguard against abuses of pretrial identification, the Court noted, is the ethical responsibility of the prosecutor. "If that safeguard fails, review remains available under the due process standards." The majority then concluded, "We are not persuaded that the risks inherent in the use of photographs are so pernicious that an extraordinary system of safeguards is required."

2.   PROHIBITION AGAINST IMPERMISSIBLY SUGGESTIVE PROCEDURES

EDITORS' INTRODUCTION: THE DUE PROCESS PROHIBITION AGAINST EXCESSIVE SUGGESTIVENESS

The third case of the 1967 identification trilogy, Stovall v. Denno, 388 U.S. 293, 87 S.Ct. 1967, 18 L.Ed.2d 1199 (1967), recognized a due process right to have excluded eyewitness testimony tainted by certain excessively suggestive pretrial procedures.

Stovall involved an attack upon a husband and wife in the kitchen of their home at about midnight, August 23, 1961. The intruder stabbed both; the husband died but the wife, stabbed 11 times, survived. On the basis of evidence found at the scene, Stovall was arrested and arraigned on August 24. The wife underwent surgery on that date for her wounds and there was still substantial question as to whether she would survive. About noon on August 25, Stovall was brought to the wife's hospital room. He was handcuffed to one of five police officers who accompanied him; two prosecutors were also there. Stovall, the only Black in the room, was required to repeat a few words for voice identification; no one could later recall what words he said. After a police officer asked if Stovall "was the man," the wife identified him. At Stovall's later trial, the wife testified that he was the person who assaulted the couple. Stovall was convicted. The Supreme Court held the right to counsel announced in *Wade* and *Gilbert* did not apply retroactively, so the failure to accord Stovall the right to assistance of a lawyer at the confrontation did not entitle him to relief.

Nevertheless, the Court found potential merit in Stovall's alternative claim that "the confrontation conducted in this case was so unnecessarily suggestive and conducive to irreparable mistaken identification that he was denied due process of law." This, the Court commented, "is a recognized ground of attack upon a conviction independent of any right to counsel claim." Whether a violation of due process of law occurred, however, depends upon "the totality of the circumstances" surrounding the confrontation. Stressing the victim's condition made the confrontation "imperative," however, the Court found no due process defect in *Stovall*.

In a number of subsequent cases the Court considered claims that pretrial procedure's suggestiveness rendered witnesses' testimony unavailable to the prosecution as a matter of due process. It has generally found such claims without merit. See Neil v. Biggers, 409 U.S. 188, 93 S.Ct. 375,

34 L.Ed.2d 401 (1972); Coleman v. Alabama, 399 U.S. 1, 90 S.Ct. 1999, 26 L.Ed.2d 387 (1970); Simmons v. United States, 390 U.S. 377, 88 S.Ct. 967, 19 L.Ed.2d 1247 (1968).

Only in Foster v. California, 394 U.S. 440, 89 S.Ct. 1127, 22 L.Ed.2d 402 (1969), did the Court find a violation of the due process standard. Foster was arrested for the late-night robbery of a Western Union office; the only employee present when the two robbers entered was Joseph David, the late-night manager. The following then occurred:

> David was called to the police station to view a lineup. There were three men in the lineup. One was [Foster]. He is a tall man—close to six feet in height. The other men were short—five feet, five or six inches. [Foster] wore a leather jacket which David said was similar to the one he had seen underneath the coveralls worn by the robber. After seeing this lineup, David could not positively identify [Foster] as the robber. He "thought" he was the man, but he was not sure. David then asked to speak to [Foster], and [Foster] was brought into an office and sat across from David at a table. Except for prosecuting officials there was no one else in the room. Even after this one-to-one confrontation David still was uncertain whether [Foster] was one of the robbers: "truthfully—I was not sure," he testified at trial. A week or 10 days later, the police arranged for David to view a second lineup. There were five men in that lineup. [Foster] was the only person in the second lineup who had appeared in the first lineup. This time David was "convinced" [Foster] was the man.

At trial, David identified Foster as one of the robbers and testified to his identification of Foster at the second lineup; Foster was convicted. Finding the suggestive elements in the identification procedure "made it all but inevitable that David would identify [Foster] whether or not he was in fact 'the man,'" the Court concluded the procedure "so undermined the reliability of the eyewitness identification as to violate due process."

Manson v. Brathwaite

Supreme Court of the United States, 1977.
432 U.S. 98, 97 S.Ct. 2243, 53 L.Ed.2d 140.

■ MR. JUSTICE BLACKMUN delivered the opinion of the Court.

This case presents the issue as to whether the Due Process Clause of the Fourteenth Amendment compels the exclusion, in a state criminal trial, apart from any consideration of reliability, of pretrial identification evidence obtained by a police procedure that was both suggestive and unnecessary. This Court's decisions in Stovall v. Denno, 388 U.S. 293, 87 S.Ct. 1967, 18 L.Ed.2d 1199 (1967), and Neil v. Biggers, 409 U.S. 188, 93 S.Ct. 375, 34 L.Ed.2d 401 (1972), are particularly implicated.

I.

Jimmy D. Glover, a fulltime trooper of the Connecticut State Police, in 1970 was assigned to the Narcotics Division in an undercover capacity. On May 5 of that year, about 7:45 p. m., e.d.t., and while there was still daylight, Glover and Henry Alton Brown, an informant, went to an apartment building at 201 Westland, in Hartford, for the purpose of purchasing narcotics from "Dickie Boy" Cicero, a known narcotics dealer. Cicero, it was thought, lived on the third floor of that apartment building. Glover and Brown entered the building, observed by backup Officers D'Onofrio and Gaffey, and proceeded by stairs to the third floor. Glover knocked at the door of one of the two apartments served by the stairway.[5] The area was illuminated by natural light from a window in the third floor hallway. The door was opened 12 to 18 inches in response to the knock. Glover observed a man standing at the door and, behind him, a woman. Brown identified himself. Glover then asked for "two things" of narcotics. The man at the door held out his hand, and Glover gave him two $10 bills. The door closed. Soon the man returned and handed Glover two glassine bags.[6] While the door was open, Glover stood within two feet of the person from whom he made the purchase and observed his face. Five to seven minutes elapsed from the time the door first opened until it closed the second time.

Glover and Brown then left the building. This was about eight minutes after their arrival. Glover drove to headquarters where he described the seller to D'Onofrio and Gaffey. Glover at that time did not know the identity of the seller. He described him as being "a colored man, approximately five feet eleven inches tall, dark complexion, black hair, short Afro style, and having high cheekbones, and of heavy build. He was wearing at the time blue pants and a plaid shirt." D'Onofrio, suspecting from this description that respondent might be the seller, obtained a photograph of respondent from the Records Division of the Hartford Police Department. He left it at Glover's office. D'Onofrio was not acquainted with respondent personally but did know him by sight and had seen him "[s]everal times" prior to May 5. Glover, when alone, viewed the photograph for the first time upon his return to headquarters on May 7; he identified the person shown as the one from whom he had purchased the narcotics.

The toxicological report on the contents of the glassine bags revealed the presence of heroin. The report was dated July 16, 1970.

Respondent was arrested on July 27 while visiting at the apartment of a Mrs. Ramsey on the third floor of 201 Westland. This was the apartment at which the narcotics sale had taken place on May 5.[7]

---

5. It appears that the door on which Glover knocked may not have been that of the Cicero apartment. Petitioner concedes, in any event, that the transaction effected "was with some other person than had been intended."

6. This was Glover's testimony. Brown later was called as a witness for the prosecution. He testified on direct examination that, due to his then use of heroin, he had no clear recollection of the details of the incident. On cross-examination, as in an interview with defense counsel the preceding day, he said that it was a woman who opened the door, received the money, and thereafter produced the narcotics. On redirect, he acknowledged that he was using heroin daily at the time, that he had had some that day, and that there was "an inability to recall and remember events."

7. Respondent testified: "Lots of times I have been there before in that building." He also testified that Mrs. Ramsey was a friend of his wife, that her apartment was the only one in the building he ever visited, and that he and his family, consisting of his wife and five children, did not live there but at 453 Albany Avenue, Hartford.

Respondent was charged, in a two-count information, with possession and sale of heroin * * *. At his trial in January 1971, the photograph from which Glover had identified respondent was received in evidence without objection on the part of the defense. Glover also testified that, although he had not seen respondent in the eight months that had elapsed since the sale, "there [was] no doubt whatsoever" in his mind that the person shown on the photograph was respondent. Glover also made a positive in-court identification without objection.

No explanation was offered by the prosecution for the failure to utilize a photographic array or to conduct a lineup.

Respondent, who took the stand in his own defense, testified that on May 5, the day in question, he had been ill at his Albany Avenue apartment ("a lot of back pains, muscle spasms * * * a bad heart * * * high blood pressure * * * neuralgia in my face, and sinus,") and that at no time on that particular day had he been at 201 Westland. His wife testified that she recalled, after her husband had refreshed her memory, that he was home all day on May 5. Doctor Wesley M. Vietzke, an internist and assistant professor of medicine at the University of Connecticut, testified that respondent had consulted him on April 15, 1970, and that he took a medical history from him, heard his complaints about his back and facial pain, and discovered that he had high blood pressure. The physician found respondent, subjectively, "in great discomfort." Respondent in fact underwent surgery for a herniated disc at L5 and S1 on August 17.

The jury found respondent guilty on both counts of the information. He received a sentence of not less than six nor more than nine years. His conviction was affirmed *per curiam* by the Supreme Court of Connecticut.

Fourteen months later, respondent filed a petition for habeas corpus in the United States District Court for the District of Connecticut. He alleged that the admission of the identification testimony at his state trial deprived him of due process of law to which he was entitled under the Fourteenth Amendment. The District Court * * * dismissed respondent's petition. On appeal, the United States Court of Appeals for the Second Circuit reversed [and ordered relief granted].

In brief summary, the court felt that evidence as to the photograph should have been excluded, regardless of reliability, because the examination of the single photograph was unnecessary and suggestive. And, in the court's view, the evidence was unreliable in any event. We granted certiorari.

* * *

IV.

Petitioner at the outset acknowledges that "the procedure in the instant case was suggestive [because only one photograph was used] and unnecessary" [because there was no emergency or exigent circumstance]. The respondent, in agreement with the Court of Appeals, proposes a *per se* rule of exclusion that he claims is dictated by the demands of the Fourteenth Amendment's guarantee of due process. He rightly observes that this is the first case in which this Court has had occasion to rule upon strictly post-*Stovall* out-of-court identification evidence of the challenged kind.

[In *Biggers*, the victim had identified the defendant at a one-on-one showup conducted before the Supreme Court's decision in *Stovall*. The "central question," *Biggers* indicated, "was whether under the 'totality of the circumstances' the identification was reliable even though the confrontation procedure was suggestive." Since the testimony presented "no substantial likelihood of misidentification," that testimony was properly admitted into evidence. The question now before the Court is whether a stricter standard should be applied where the identification procedure was conducted after the Court's decision in *Stovall*.]

[T]he Courts of Appeals appear to have developed at least two approaches to such evidence. The first, or *per se* approach, employed by the Second Circuit in the present case, focuses on the procedures employed and requires exclusion of the out-of-court identification evidence, without regard to reliability, whenever it has been obtained through unnecessarily suggest[ive] confrontation procedures.[8] The justifications advanced are the elimination of evidence of uncertain reliability, deterrence of the police and prosecutors, and the stated "fair assurance against the awful risks of misidentification."

The second, or more lenient, approach is one that continues to rely on the totality of the circumstances. It permits the admission of the confrontation evidence if, despite the suggestive aspect, the out-of-court identification possesses certain features of reliability. Its adherents feel that the *per se* approach is not mandated by the Due Process Clause of the Fourteenth Amendment. This second approach, in contrast to the other, is ad hoc and serves to limit the societal costs imposed by a sanction that excludes relevant evidence from consideration and evaluation by the trier of fact.

* * *

The respondent here stresses * * * the need for deterrence of improper identification practice, a factor he regards as preeminent. Photographic identification, it is said, continues to be needlessly employed. He notes that the legislative regulation "the Court had hoped [United States v. Wade, 388 U.S. 218, 239, 87 S.Ct. 1926, 1938–1939, 18 L.Ed.2d 1149 (1967),] would engender," has not been forthcoming. He argues that a totality rule cannot be expected to have a significant deterrent impact; only a strict rule of exclusion will have direct and immediate impact on law enforcement agents. Identification evidence is so convincing to the jury that sweeping exclusionary rules are required. Fairness of the trial is threatened by suggestive confrontation evidence, and thus, it is said, an exclusionary rule has an established constitutional predicate.

8. Although the *per se* approach demands the exclusion of testimony concerning unnecessarily suggestive identifications, it does permit the admission of testimony concerning a subsequent identification, including an in-court identification, if the subsequent identification is determined to be reliable. The totality approach, in contrast, is simpler: if the challenged identification is reliable, then testimony as to it and any identification in its wake is admissible.

There are, of course, several interests to be considered and taken into account. The driving force behind United States v. Wade, 388 U.S. 218, 87 S.Ct. 1926, 18 L.Ed.2d 1149 (1967), Gilbert v. California, 388 U.S. 263, 87 S.Ct. 1951, 18 L.Ed.2d 1178 (1967) (right to counsel at a postindictment lineup), and *Stovall*, all decided on the same day, was the Court's concern with the problems of eyewitness identification. Usually the witness must testify about an encounter with a total stranger under circumstances of emergency or emotional stress. The witness' recollection of the stranger can be distorted easily by the circumstances or by later actions of the police. Thus, *Wade* and its companion cases reflect the concern that the jury not hear eyewitness testimony unless that evidence has aspects of reliability. It must be observed that both approaches before us are responsive to this concern. The *per se* rule, however, goes too far since its application automatically and peremptorily, and without consideration of alleviating factors, keeps evidence from the jury that is reliable and relevant.

The second factor is deterrence. Although the *per se* approach has the more significant deterrent effect, the totality approach also has an influence on police behavior. The police will guard against unnecessarily suggestive procedures under the totality rule, as well as the *per se* one, for fear that their actions will lead to the exclusion of identifications as unreliable.

The third factor is the effect on the administration of justice. Here the *per se* approach suffers serious drawbacks. Since it denies the trier reliable evidence, it may result, on occasion, in the guilty going free. Also, because of its rigidity, the *per se* approach may make error by the trial judge more likely than the totality approach. And in those cases in which the admission of identification evidence is error under the *per se* approach but not under the totality approach—cases in which the identification is reliable despite an unnecessarily suggestive identification procedure—reversal is a Draconian sanction.[9] Certainly, inflexible rules of exclusion that may frustrate rather than promote justice have not been viewed recently by this Court with unlimited enthusiasm.

We therefore conclude that reliability is the linchpin in determining the admissibility of identification testimony * * *. The factors to be considered * * * include the opportunity of the witness to view the criminal at the time of the crime, the witness' degree of attention, the accuracy of his prior description of the criminal, the level of certainty demonstrated at the confrontation, and the time between the crime and the confrontation. Against these factors is to be weighed the corrupting effect of the suggestive identification itself.

V.

We turn, then, to the facts of this case and apply the analysis:

9. Unlike a warrantless search, a suggestive preindictment identification procedure does not in itself intrude upon a constitutionally protected interest. Thus, considerations urging the exclusion of evidence deriving from a constitutional violation do not bear on the instant problem.

1. The opportunity to view. Glover testified that for two to three minutes he stood at the apartment door, within two feet of the respondent. The door opened twice, and each time the man stood at the door. The moments passed, the conversation took place, and payment was made. Glover looked directly at his vendor. It was near sunset, to be sure, but the sun had not yet set, so it was not dark or even dusk or twilight. Natural light from outside entered the hallway through a window. There was natural light, as well, from inside the apartment.

2. The degree of attention. Glover was not a casual or passing observer, as is so often the case with eyewitness identification. Trooper Glover was a trained police officer on duty—and specialized and dangerous duty—when he called at the third floor of 201 Westland in Hartford on May 5, 1970. Glover himself was a Negro and unlikely to perceive only general features of "hundreds of Hartford black males," as the Court of Appeals stated. It is true that Glover's duty was that of ferreting out narcotics offenders and that he would be expected in his work to produce results. But it is also true that, as a specially trained, assigned, and experienced officer, he could be expected to pay scrupulous attention to detail, for he knew that subsequently he would have to find and arrest his vendor. In addition, he knew that his claimed observations would be subject later to close scrutiny and examination at any trial.

3. The accuracy of the description. Glover's description was given to D'Onofrio within minutes after the transaction. It included the vendor's race, his height, his build, the color and style of his hair, and the high cheekbone facial feature. It also included clothing the vendor wore. No claim has been made that respondent did not possess the physical characteristics so described. D'Onofrio reacted positively at once. Two days later, when Glover was alone, he viewed the photograph D'Onofrio produced and identified its subject as the narcotics seller.

4. The witness' level of certainty. There is no dispute that the photograph in question was that of respondent. Glover, in response to a question whether the photograph was that of the person from whom he made the purchase, testified: "There is no question whatsoever." This positive assurance was repeated.

5. The time between the crime and the confrontation. Glover's description of his vendor was given to D'Onofrio within minutes of the crime. The photographic identification took place only two days later. We do not have here the passage of weeks or months between the crime and the viewing of the photograph.

These indicators of Glover's ability to make an accurate identification are hardly outweighed by the corrupting effect of the challenged identification itself. Although identifications arising from single-photograph displays may be viewed in general with suspicion, we find in the instant case little pressure on the witness to acquiesce in the suggestion that such a display entails. D'Onofrio had left the photograph at Glover's office and was not present when Glover first viewed it two days after the event. There thus was little urgency and Glover could view the photograph at his leisure. And since Glover examined the photograph alone, there was no coercive pressure to make an identification arising from the presence of another. The identification was made in circumstances allowing care and reflection.

Although it plays no part in our analysis, all this assurance as to the reliability of the identification is hardly undermined by the facts that respondent was arrested in the very apartment where the sale had taken place, and that he acknowledged his frequent visits to that apartment.

Surely, we cannot say that under all the circumstances of this case there is "a very substantial likelihood of irreparable misidentification." Short of that point, such evidence is for the jury to weigh. We are content to rely upon the good sense and judgment of American juries, for evidence with some element of untrustworthiness is customary grist for the jury mill. Juries are not so susceptible that they cannot measure intelligently the weight of identification testimony that has some questionable feature.

Of course, it would have been better had D'Onofrio presented Glover with a photographic array including "so far as practicable * * * a reasonable number of persons similar to any person then suspected whose likeness is included in the array." The use of that procedure would have enhanced the force of the identification at trial and would have avoided the risk that the evidence would be excluded as unreliable. But we are not disposed to view D'Onofrio's failure as one of constitutional dimension to be enforced by a rigorous and unbending exclusionary rule. The defect, if there be one, goes to weight and not to substance. * * *

The judgment of the Court of Appeals is reversed.

It is so ordered.

■ MR. JUSTICE MARSHALL, with whom MR. JUSTICE BRENNAN joins, dissenting.

Today's decision can come as no surprise to those who have been watching the Court dismantle the protections against mistaken eyewitness testimony erected a decade ago * * * .

* * *

[I]n determining the admissibility of the * * * identification in this case, the Court considers two alternatives, a *per se* exclusionary rule and a totality-of-the circumstances approach. The Court weighs three factors in deciding that the totality approach * * * should be applied. In my view, the Court wrongly evaluates the impact of these factors.

First, the Court acknowledges that one of the factors, deterrence of police use of unnecessarily suggestive identification procedures, favors the *per se* rule. Indeed, it does so heavily, for such a rule would make it unquestionably clear to the police they must never use a suggestive procedure when a fairer alternative is available. I have no doubt that conduct would quickly conform to the rule.

Second, the Court gives passing consideration to the dangers of eyewitness identification recognized in the *Wade* trilogy. It concludes, however, that the grave risk of error does not justify adoption of the *per se* approach because that would too often result in exclusion of relevant evidence. In my view, this conclusion totally ignores the lessons of *Wade*. The dangers of mistaken identification are, as *Stovall* held, simply too great to permit unnecessarily suggestive identifications. * * * [T]he Court's opinion today points to [no] contrary empirical evidence. Studies since *Wade* have only reinforced the validity of its assessment of the dangers of identification testimony. While the Court is "content to rely on the good sense and judgment of American juries," the impetus for *Stovall* and *Wade* was repeated miscarriages of justice resulting from juries' willingness to credit inaccurate eyewitness testimony.

Finally, the Court errs in its assessment of the relative impact of the two approaches on the administration of justice. The Court relies most heavily on this factor, finding that "reversal is a Draconian sanction" in cases where the identification is reliable despite an unnecessarily suggestive procedure used to obtain it. Relying on little more than a strong distaste for "inflexible rules of exclusion," the Court rejects the *per se* test. * * *

[I]mpermissibly suggestive identifications are not merely worthless law enforcement tools. They pose a grave threat to society at large in a more direct way than most governmental disobedience of the law. For if the police and the public erroneously conclude, on the basis of an unnecessarily suggestive confrontation, that the right man has been caught and convicted, the real outlaw must still remain at large. Law enforcement has failed in its primary function and has left society unprotected from the depredations of an active criminal.

For these reasons, I conclude that adoption of the *per se* rule would enhance, rather than detract from, the effective administration of justice. In my view, the Court's totality test will allow seriously unreliable and misleading evidence to be put before juries. Equally important, it will allow dangerous criminals to remain on the streets while citizens assume that police action has given them protection. According to my calculus, all three of the factors upon which the Court relies point to acceptance of the *per se* approach.

* * *

Since I [believe that a *per se* approach] should govern this case, but that even if it does not, the facts here reveal a substantial likelihood of misidentification in violation of respondent's right to due process of law, I would affirm the grant of habeas corpus relief. Accordingly, I dissent from the Court's reinstatement of respondent's conviction.

NOTE: INDEPENDENT SOURCE

If a witness identifies a defendant at a pretrial procedure found unconstitutionally suggestive, does the independent source analysis used in the right to counsel cases apply? May the prosecution nevertheless introduce in-court identification testimony if it persuades the judge by clear and convincing evidence that this testimony would have an "independent source"—that is, that the testimony would be untainted by the defective procedure? In Foster v. California, 394 U.S. 440, 89 S.Ct. 1127, 22 L.Ed.2d 402 (1969), discussed in the Editors' Introduction to this section, Justice Black, dissenting, found the Court's case law ambiguous on that point.

Arguably the Court's post-*Foster* cases resolve Justice Black's concern indirectly. *Braithwaite* approved *Biggers'* analysis in which testimony concerning an out-of-court identification made at an impermissibly suggestive procedure is admissible if it presents "no substantial likelihood of misidentification." In contrast, where a case involves an in-court identification by a witness who made an identification of the defendant at an impermissibly suggestive pretrial procedure, the testimony is admissible if it presents "no substantial likelihood of *irreparable* misidentification." Simmons v. United States, 390 U.S. 377, 384, 88 S.Ct. 967, 971, 19 L.Ed.2d 1247, 1253 (1968) (emphasis supplied). This focus upon irreparable misidentification arguably leaves open the possibility that events between an inadmissible out-of-court identification and a later in-court identification might so reduce the risk of unreliability as to make the in-court identification testimony admissible although testimony regarding the out-of-court identification remains inadmissible.

Where the prosecution presents in-court identification testimony by a witness who identified the defendant at a unconstitutionally suggestive pretrial procedure, in other words, the issue is not independent source. Rather, it is whether the unnecessarily suggestive pretrial identification procedure gave rise to a substantial likelihood of *irreparable* misidentification.

B. EVIDENTIARY AND PROCEDURAL SAFEGUARDS AGAINST UNRELIABLE EYEWITNESS TESTIMONY

EDITORS' INTRODUCTION: EXPERT TESTIMONY AND JURY INSTRUCTIONS AS SAFEGUARDS AGAINST MISTAKEN EYEWITNESSES

Critics of the law's traditional assumption that jurors are inclined and able to evaluate the credibility of eyewitness identification testimony have proposed two means of encouraging more critical consideration of the weight given such testimony. One is the admission of expert testimony designed to assist jurors in identifying factors suggesting eyewitness testimony in general, or the testimony of a specific eyewitness in particular, is accurate and reliable. A second is a jury instruction on the credibility of eyewitness testimony and perhaps suggesting to the jurors how they might evaluate a testifying eyewitness's credibility.

Expert Testimony

Most and perhaps all jurisdictions now at least *permit* trial judges to admit expert testimony on this subject. In State v. Schutz, 579 N.W.2d 317 (Iowa 1998), the Iowa Supreme Court concluded Iowa was the only jurisdiction with a blanket prohibition against the use of expert testimony relating to the accuracy of eyewitness identification. Convinced its rule was no longer sound, the court embraced the majority position: "The exclusion of expert testimony is a matter committed to the sound discretion of the trial court and we will reverse only for an abuse of that discretion."

Some argue expert testimony is often or perhaps always unnecessary—since it conveys only what jurors already know from common sense—and unhelpful—since explanation of the mechanisms identified by research "may be of academic interest, but it is of little aid to the jury in judging reliability of the particular eye witness identification before them." *Schutz*, 579 N.W.2d at 321 (Carter, J., dissenting). Lichael R. Leippe, The Case for

Expert Testimony About Eyewitness Memory, 1 Psychol. Pub. Pol'y & L. 909, 922 (1995), however, suggested the strongest objection to the use of expert testimony is its potential for being affirmatively harmful. Such testimony "may prejudice jurors against the eyewitness rather than compel them to carefully apply new knowledge in their own evaluation of the eyewitness may be the strongest objection to such testimony."

Under the general discretionary approach adopted in *Schutz*, appellate courts have been reluctant to hold trial judges who excluded expert testimony abused their discretion in doing so. See United States v. Hall, 165 F.3rd 1095, 1104 (7th Cir.1999) (reaffirming rule that trial court has discretion on expert testimony related to eyewitness identification, and finding no error in excluding testimony in case before the court). Perhaps as a result of the lack of appellate reversals trial judges are too quick to reject such testimony. One appellate court observed in an analagous situation:

> [W]e conclude the trial judge did not abuse his discretion in declining to give the * * * identification instruction.
>
> It deserves mention, however, that the judge * * * was quick, once the Commonwealth objected, to place weight on the circumstance that no Massachusetts case had yet required such an instruction. That is so, but * * * such an instruction ought not to be the target for automatic rejection by * * * a trial judge, or, put another way, a judge should consider a request for such an instruction with a measure of favorable inclination to grant it.

Commonwealth v. Jean–Jacques, 47 Mass.App. 909, 910–11, 712 N.E.2d 1150, 1151–52 (1999).

The hostility of some trial judges to such testimony may be due to their perception that the substance of testimony offered in particular cases renders it unhelpful. Some courts, upholding trial judges' exclusion of expert testimony, have expressed frustration at experts' inability or unwillingness to offer well-based testimony regarding the likelihood that specific eyewitness identification testimony is inaccurate. Experts may even be unwilling to offer opinions concerning the specific factors—which *generally* reduce reliability—affecting the testimony in particular cases. In Jordan v. State, 950 S.W.2d 210, 212 (Tex.App.—Fort Worth 1997, pet. ref'd), for example, the expert—a Dr. Finn—offered to testify to a variety of factors research showed reduced the accuracy of eyewitness identification, such as weapon focus, confabulation, and memory hardening. But, the court noted:

> When asked whether he could testify with any reasonable degree of scientific certainty whether [these] factors * * * influence[d] an identification, Dr. Finn responded: "All I can say, as a scientist, or somebody who talks to scientists, these are processes that operate in normal human processes to a greater or lesser degree. How much they operate in this case, I can't say."

In State v. McClendon, 248 Conn. 572, 587, 730 A.2d 1107, 1115 (1999), the expert testified to several areas of scientific inquiry concerning eyewitness identification. Nevertheless, the court complained, he refused to give an opinion regarding what the scientific inquiries suggested about the specific facts of the case to a "reasonable degree of scientific certainty." He admitted, the court noted critically, "that 'we don't always know what factors are influencing' an eyewitness. He conceded that a controversy existed in the area of the statistical probability of false identification, the one kind of information inaccessible to the average juror."

On the other hand, some courts regard as inappropriate expert testimony concerning specific identifications. In Currie v. Commonwealth, 30 Va.App. 58, 63, 515 S.E.2d 335, 338 (1999), for example, the trial judge admitted some testimony by a defense expert but ruled further: "Defendant's expert will not be allowed to testify as to the specific identification in this case as to its reliability nor as to its validity. Such testimony would usurp the function of the jury to determine the credibility of witnesses."

Experts declining to address the factors influencing particular eyewitnesses may be conscientiously respecting the research's results. Elizabeth F. Loftus and James M. Doyle, Eyewitness Testimony: Civil and Criminal 307 (1997), suggested "the inherently probabalistic nature of psychological knowledge" means that it is questionable whether that knowledge can ever be used "in directly assessing an eyewitness account of a specific event."

If the nature of psychological knowledge means that experts cannot scientifically assess the accuracy of a specific eyewitness's account of a particular event, is the research and expert testimony based on it of insufficient assistance to jurors to justify its use in litigation? Perhaps such testimony will not assist jurors in identifying eyewitness testimony that should be disregarded but rather will make jurors so skeptical of *all* eyewitness identification testimony that they will unjustifiably disregard or discount even reliable testimony of this sort. Leippe, at 912. Whether this result is acceptable or not, of course, depends upon whether the dangers of inaccuracy affect most or at least a sufficient proportion of eyewitness identifications. Many courts assume that the research does not cast doubt upon the traditional assumption that most or nearly all eyewitness identification testimony is accurate and reliable. Thus, the law's objective should be to assist jurors in identifying the very few exceptional situations in which this testimony should be discounted or disregarded. If this assumption is still supportable, the law most likely should not permit use of expert testimony encouraging jurors to discredit all or most eyewitness testimony.

Jury Instructions

Another means by which jurors' ability and inclination to identify and discount unreliable eyewitness identification may be stimulated and facilitated is the giving of a cautionary jury instruction. A typical instruction of this sort, based on a model offered in United States v. Telfaire, 469 F.2d 552 (D.C.Cir.1972) (per curiam), was set out in People v. Ochoa, 19 Cal.4th 353, 425 n. 5, 966 P.2d 442, 486 n. 5, 79 Cal.Rptr.4th 408, 452 n. 5 (1998):

> "Eyewitness testimony has been received in this trial for the purpose of identifying the defendant as the perpetrator of the crimes charged. In determining the weight to be given eyewitness identification testimony, you should consider the believability of the eyewitness as well as other factors which bear upon the accuracy of the witness'

identification of the defendant, including, but not limited to, any of the following:

"The opportunity of the witness to observe the alleged criminal act and the perpetrator of the act;

"The stress, if any, to which the witness was subjected at the time of the observation;

"The witness' ability, following the observation, to provide a description of the perpetrator of the act;

"The extent to which the defendant either fits or does not fit the description of the perpetrator previously given by the witness;

"The cross-racial or ethnic nature of the identification;

"The witness' capacity to make an identification;

"Evidence relating to the witness' ability to identify other alleged perpetrators of the criminal act;

"Whether the witness was able to identify the alleged perpetrator in a photographic or physical lineup;

"The period of time between the alleged criminal act and the witness' identification;

"Whether the witness had prior contacts with the alleged perpetrator;

"The extent to which the witness is either certain or uncertain of the identification;

"Whether the witness' identification is in fact the product of his own recollection;

"Any other evidence relating to the witness' ability to make an identification."

At least one court, persuaded by the research discussed earlier in this chapter, disapproved of any suggestion in such an instruction that the degree of the witness's certainty should be considered as bearing upon the reliability of the witness's identification. See Commonwealth v. Santoli, 424 Mass. 837, 841–45, 680 N.E.2d 1116, 1181–21 (1997).

The Maryland court considered a proposed instruction which "sets forth the factors that the jury should consider in evaluating the identification testimony, advises the jury that identification of the defendant by a single eyewitness is sufficient to convict, informs the jury that the State bears the burden of proof, and cautions the jury to 'examine the identification of the defendant with great care.' " It addressed the variety of views courts have taken:

> The appropriateness of such an instruction is generally unsettled among the various jurisdictions. * * *

> Some courts have suggested that an identification instruction is mandatory if eyewitness testimony is the only evidence of the identity of the criminal actor or if the reliability of the identification testimony

is in doubt. The leading case advocating this approach is United States v. Telfaire, 469 F.2d 552 (D.C.Cir.1972) * * *.

* * *

Proponents of the *Telfaire* approach emphasize that eyewitness identifications are perhaps less reliable than the average juror appreciates, and consider a cautionary instruction necessary to minimize the risk of erroneous convictions. * * *

Other jurisdictions have expressly rejected *Telfaire*-like instructions, however, based on the conclusion that eyewitness identification instructions amount to an impermissible judicial comment on the evidence or places an improper emphasis on eyewitness testimony * * *.

We concur with those courts that have declined to adopt either of the rigid rules on the appropriateness of an identification instruction, and have instead held that the decision as to whether to give such an instruction lies within the sound discretion of the trial court.

Gunning v. State, 347 Md. 332, 340–45, 701 A.2d 374, 378–80 (1997). This view—that trial judges have discretion to give or not give such instructions—is probably the majority approach. See State v. Chinn 85 Ohio St.3d 548, 574–75, 709 N.E.2d 1166, 1187 (1999) (whether to give a *Telfaire* instruction "is a matter committed to the sound discretion of the trial court"). Compare, however, State v. Maestas, 984 P.2d 376 (Utah 1999), in which the Utah Supreme Court reaffirmed its holding in State v. Long, 721 P.2d 483, 488–92 (Utah 1986), that, if requested, a trial court *must* give a cautionary eyewitness identification instruction in every case where identification is a central issue.

Generally, jury instructions on matters such as eyewitness testimony are relatively neutral and simply suggest factors that jurors may consider. Judge Frank H. Easterbrook of the United States Court of Appeals for the Seventh Circuit suggested trial judges might make more vigorous and creative use of jury instructions on such matters rather than relying upon potentially conflicting experts on a case-by-case basis:

[A] judge, recognizing the main conclusions of the scholarly study of memory—that "accuracy of recollection decreases at a geometric rather than arithmetic rate (so passage of time has a highly distorting effect on recollection); accuracy of recollection is not highly correlated with the recollector's confidence; and memory is highly suggestible—people are easily 'reminded' of events that never happened, and having been 'reminded' may thereafter hold the false recollection as tenaciously as they would a true one"—could block a lawyer from arguing that a given witness is sure of his recollection, and therefore is more likely to be right. The judge could inform jurors of the rapid decrease of accurate recollection, and the problem of suggestibility, without encountering the delay and pitfalls of expert testimony. Jurors are more likely to accept that information coming from a judge than from a scholar, whose skills do not lie in the ability to persuade lay jurors (and whose fidgeting on the stand, an unusual place for a genuine scholar, is apt to be misunderstood). Altogether it is much better for judges to incorporate scientific knowledge about the trial process into that process, rather than to make the subject a debatable issue in every case.

United States v. Hall, 165 F.3d 1095, 1120 (7th Cir.1999) (Easterbrook, J., concurring).

* * *

The decision following addresses the need for a jury instruction on a subaspect of eyewitness reliability, and the relationship between expert testimony and propriety of a jury instruction concerning it.

State v. Cromedy

Supreme Court of New Jersey, 1999.
158 N.J. 112, 727 A.2d 457.

■ COLEMAN, J.

* * *

The novel issue presented [in this appeal] is whether a cross-racial identification jury instruction should be required in certain cases. * * *

I

On the night of August 28, 1992, D.S., a white female student then enrolled at Rutgers University in New Brunswick, was watching television in her basement apartment. While she was relaxing on the couch, an African–American male entered the brightly-lit apartment and demanded money from D.S., claiming that he was wanted for murder and that he needed funds to get to New York. After D.S. told the intruder that she had no money, he spotted her purse, rifled through it, and removed money and credit cards.

The intruder then placed his hand on D.S.'s leg, demanded that she be quiet and closed the window blinds. He led her by the arm into the brightly-lit kitchen and ordered her to remove her shorts. The intruder then vaginally penetrated D.S. from behind. Throughout the sexual assault, D.S. was facing the kitchen door with her eyes closed and hand over her mouth to avoid crying loudly.

Once the assault was over, D.S. faced her attacker who, after threatening her again, turned around and left the apartment. At the time of the second threat, D.S. was standing approximately two feet away from her assailant. The attacker made no attempt to conceal his face at any time. D.S. immediately called the New Brunswick Police Department after the intruder left the apartment.

The police dusted for fingerprints and took D.S.'s initial statement. D.S. described her assailant as an African–American male in his late 20's to early 30's, full-faced, about five feet five inches tall, with a medium build, mustache, and unkempt hair. She stated that the intruder was wearing a dirty gray button-down short-sleeved shirt, blue warm-up pants with white and red stripes, and a Giants logo on the left leg. D.S. was then taken to Roosevelt Hospital where rape samples were taken.

The next day, D.S. made a formal statement to the police in which she again described the intruder. Three days later, a composite sketch was drawn by an artist with her assistance. The following day at police headquarters, D.S. was shown many slides and photographs, including a photograph of defendant, in an unsuccessful attempt to identify her assailant.

On April 7, 1993, almost eight months after the crimes were committed, D.S. saw an African–American male across the street from her who she thought was her attacker. She spotted the man while she was standing on the corner of a street in New Brunswick waiting for the light to change. As the two passed on the street, D.S. studied the individual's face and gait. Believing that the man was her attacker, D.S. ran home and telephoned the police, giving them a description of the man she had just seen. Defendant was picked up by the New Brunswick police and taken to headquarters almost immediately.

Within fifteen minutes after seeing defendant on the street, D.S. viewed defendant in a "show-up" from behind a one-way mirror and immediately identified him as the man she had just seen on the street and as her attacker. Defendant was then arrested and, with his consent, saliva and blood samples were taken for scientific analysis.

No forensic evidence linking defendant to the offenses was presented during the trial. The police did not lift any fingerprints belonging to defendant from the apartment. D.S.'s Rape Crisis Intervention Kit, processed by the Middlesex County Rape Crisis Center at Roosevelt Hospital, was submitted to the New Jersey State Police Chemistry Biology Laboratory in Sea Girt for analysis. Testing of the victim's blood revealed that she was a secretor, meaning that she falls within the eighty percent of the population that secretes their blood type in all of their bodily fluids. When defendant's blood and saliva were tested by the same laboratory, it was determined that both the victim and defendant have type "A" blood, but defendant was found to be a non-secretor. That meant that although the rape kit revealed the presence of seminal fluid and spermatozoa, the specimens received from defendant could not be compared with the semen and spermatozoa found on the victim. In other words, the genetic markers found in the semen and spermatozoa could not be said to have come from defendant because he is a non-secretor. On the other hand, the genetic markers were consistent with the victim, who is a secretor.

[D]efense counsel sought a cross-racial identification jury charge. The following language was proposed:

[Y]ou know that the identifying witness is of a different race than the defendant. When a witness who is a member of one race identifies a member who is of another race we say there has been a cross-racial identification. You may consider, if you think it is appropriate to do so, whether the cross-racial nature of the identification has affected the accuracy of the witness's original perception and/or accuracy of a subsequent identification.

In support of that request, defendant cited the June 1992 New Jersey Supreme Court Task Force on Minority Concerns Final Report, 131 N.J.L.J. 1145 (1992) (Task Force Report).

The trial court denied the request * * [and] instead provided the jury with the Model Jury Charge on Identification. The jury convicted defendant * * *. [The conviction was affirmed on appeal to the Appellate Division.]

* * *

II

Defendant argues that the trial court committed reversible error in denying his request for a cross-racial identification charge. He maintains that cross-racial impairment of eyewitnesses "is a scientifically accepted fact," and that the courts of this State can take judicial notice of the fallibility of trans-racial identifications and approve the report of the Task Force that recommended adoption of a cross-racial identification jury charge. Defendant argues that expert testimony is not a necessary factual predicate for such a jury charge. Alternatively, defendant argues that if the Court should require an expert to testify regarding factors that affect the reliability of eyewitness identification, and cross-racial identification specifically, we should remand the case to the trial court to afford him an opportunity to present that evidence.

The State argues that the trial court properly rejected defendant's request for a cross-racial identification charge. The State maintains that there is no consensus within the scientific community that an "own-race" bias exists. The State argues that because some researchers do not know whether cross-racial impairment affects "real life" identifications, and because even some of the scientists who believe that cross-racial impairment does affect identification cannot say what factors influence a person's ability to identify correctly a member of another race, the Court should reject a cross-racial identification charge. Alternatively, the State argues that this Court should not adopt a cross-racial charge until there is general acceptance that cross-racial impairment exists and general agreement on what factors influence a person's ability to correctly identify a member of another race.

A

A cross-racial identification occurs when an eyewitness is asked to identify a person of another race. The reliability of such an identification, though discussed in many cases throughout the country, is an issue of first impression in New Jersey. Because defendant requested a cross-racial identification jury charge, he bore the burden of showing that a reliable basis existed to support the requested charge. Defendant relied on common knowledge, the Task Force Report, and judicial notice to support his request. Rather than calling an expert to testify regarding the factors that may make some cross-racial eyewitness identifications unreliable, defendant maintained that an expert would not aid the jury. In this context, we must decide whether a cross-racial jury instruction should be required where scientific evidence demonstrating the need for a specific instruction has not been presented.

B

For more than forty years, empirical studies concerning the psychological factors affecting eyewitness cross-racial or cross-ethnic identifications have appeared with increasing frequency in professional literature of the behavioral and social sciences. [Some studies] have concluded that eyewitnesses are superior at identifying persons of their own race and have difficulty identifying members of another race. This phenomenon has been dubbed the "own-race" effect or "own-race" bias. Its corollary is that eyewitnesses experience a "cross-racial impairment" when identifying members of another race. Studies have consistently shown that the "own-race effect" is "strongest when white witnesses attempt to recognize black subjects."

Although researchers generally agree that some eyewitnesses exhibit an own-race bias, they disagree about the degree to which own-race bias affects identification. In one study, African–American and white "customers" browsed in a convenience store for a few minutes and then went to the register to pay. Researchers asked the convenience store clerks to identify the "customers" from a photo array. The white clerks were able to identify 53.2% of the white customers but only 40.4% of the African–American subjects. The overall accuracy rate for all participants was only 44.2%. Similar studies have found that own-race bias exists to a lesser degree. A snap-shot of the literature reveals that although many scientists agree that witnesses are better at identifying suspects of their own race, they cannot agree on the extent to which cross-racial impairment affects identification.

* * *

Many studies on cross-racial impairment involve subjects observing photographs for a few seconds. Because the subjects remembered the white faces more often than they recalled the African–American faces, researchers concluded that they were biased towards their own-race. Yet, there is disagreement over whether the results of some of the tests can be generalized to real-world situations in which a victim or witness confronts an assailant face-to-face and experiences the full range of emotions that accompany such a traumatic event.

C

The debate among researchers did not prevent the Supreme Court of the United States, in the famous school desegregation case of Brown v. Board of Education of Topeka, 347 U.S. 483, 494 n. 11, 74 S.Ct. 686, 692 n. 11, 98 L.Ed. 873 (1954), from using behavioral and social sciences to support legal conclusions without requiring that the methodology employed by those scientists have general acceptance in the scientific community. * * * Thus, Brown v. Board of Education is the prototypical example of an appellate court using modern social and behavioral sciences as legislative evidence to support its choice of a rule of law.

In United States v. Telfaire, 469 F.2d 552 (D.C.Cir.1972), Chief Judge Bazelon urged in his concurring opinion that juries be charged on the pitfalls of cross-racial identification. He believed that the cross-racial nature of an identification could affect accuracy in the same way as proximity to the perpetrator and poor lighting conditions. He felt that a meaningful jury instruction would have to apprise jurors of that fact. To achieve that objective, Judge Bazelon proposed the following instruction:

> In this case the identifying witness is of a different race than the defendant. In the experience of many it is more difficult to identify members of a different race than members of one's own. If this is also your own experience, you may consider it in evaluating the witness's testimony. You must also consider, of course, whether there are other factors present in this case which overcome any such difficulty of identification. For example, you may conclude that the witness has had sufficient contacts with members of the defendant's race that he would not have greater difficulty in making a reliable identification.

[Id. at 561 (Bazelon, C.J., concurring).]

Judge Bazelon rejected the notion that instructions on interracial identifications "appeal to racial prejudice." Rather, he believed that an explicit jury instruction would safeguard against improper uses of race by the jury and would delineate the narrow context in which it is appropriate to consider racial differences.

* * *

D

[D]ecisions have been rendered by courts in other jurisdictions. The majority of courts allowing cross-racial identification charges hold that the decision to provide the instruction is a matter within the trial judge's discretion. Omission of such a cautionary instruction has been held to be prejudicial error where identification is the critical or central issue in the case, there is no corroborating evidence, and the circumstances of the case raise doubts concerning the reliability of the identification.

A number of courts have concluded that cross-racial identification simply is not an appropriate topic for jury instruction. Those courts have determined that the cross-racial instruction requires expert guidance, and that cross-examination and summation are adequate safeguards to highlight unreliable identifications.

Other jurisdictions have denied the instruction, finding that the results of empirical studies on cross-racial identification are questionable. See *Telfaire*, supra, 469 F.2d at 561–62 (Leventhal, J., concurring) (rejecting cross-racial instruction because data supporting hypothesis is "meager"). One jurisdiction has even rejected cross-racial identification instructions as improper commentary on "the nature and quality" of the evidence. See State v. Hadrick, 523 A.2d 441, 444 (R.I.1987) (rejecting such instruction in robbery case where victim viewed perpetrator for two to three minutes at close range during robbery and identified him from a line-up).

E

The defense in the present case did not question whether the victim had been sexually assaulted. Rather, the defense asserted that the victim's identification of defendant as the perpetrator was mistaken. It is well-established in this State that when identification is a critical issue in the case, the trial court is obligated to give the jury a discrete and specific instruction that provides appropriate guidelines to focus the jury's attention on how to analyze and consider the trustworthiness of eyewitness identification.

[This] requires that as a part of an identification charge a trial court inform the jury that the State's case relies on an eyewitness identification of the defendant as the perpetrator, and that in weighing the reliability of that identification the jury should consider, among other things, "the capacity or the ability of the witness to make observations or perceptions . . . at the time and under all of the attendant circumstances for seeing that which he says he saw or that which he says he perceived with regard to his identification." What defendant sought through the requested charge in the present case was an instruction that informed the jury that it could consider the fact that the victim made a cross-racial identification as part of the "attendant circumstances" when evaluating the reliability of the eyewitness identification.

The Court-appointed Task Force discussed and debated the issue of the need for a cross-racial and cross-ethnic identification jury instruction for more than five years. That Task Force was comprised of an appellate judge, trial judges, lawyers representing both the prosecution and defense, social scientists, and ordinary citizens. * * * Task Force sessions were conducted in much the same way as legislative committees conduct hearings on proposed legislation. The Task Force consulted a substantial body of professional literature in the behavioral and social sciences concerning the reliability of cross-racial identifications. Except for the view expressed by a county prosecutor, the Task Force was unanimously convinced that a problem exists respecting cross-racial identifications and that the Court should take corrective action. Ultimately, in 1992 the Task Force submitted its final report to the Court in which it recommended, among other things, that the Court develop a special jury charge regarding the unreliability of cross-racial identifications.

The Court referred that recommendation to the Criminal Practice Committee. The Criminal Practice Committee * * * decided against recommending a charge to the Court. Development of a cross-racial charge was deemed to be premature because the issue of admissibility of evidence to support the charge had not been decided by case law. * * *

F

We reject the State's contention that we should not require a cross-racial identification charge before it has been demonstrated that there is substantial agreement in the relevant scientific community that cross-racial recognition impairment is significant enough to support the need for such a charge. This case does not concern the introduction of scientific evidence to attack the reliability of the eyewitness's identification. Defendant's requested jury instruction was not based upon any "scientific, technical, or other specialized knowledge" to assist the jury. He relied instead on ordinary human experience and the legislative-type findings of the Task Force because the basis for his request did not involve a matter that was beyond the ken of the average juror.

This case requires us to focus on the well-established differences between adjudicative or hard evidence, argument, and jury instructions. The hard evidence revealed a cross-racial identification and the circumstances under which that identification was made. The State argued to the jury that the identification was credible based on the evidence. Counsel for defendant, on the other hand, argued that there was a mistaken identification based on the totality of the circumstances. Defendant requested a cross-racial identification jury instruction that would treat the racial character of the eyewitness identification as one of the factors bearing on its reliability in much the same way as lighting and proximity to the perpetrator at the time of the offense.

A national review of the use of cross-racial identification jury instructions reveals that only a small minority of jurisdictions have declined such an instruction because studies finding unreliability in cross-racial identifications lack general acceptance in the relevant scientific community. The majority of jurisdictions that have rejected the instruction did so based on judicial discretion. Those discretionary rulings were influenced by factors such as the nature and quality of the eyewitness identification, the existence of strong corroborating evidence, the fact that the eyewitness had an adequate opportunity to observe the perpetrator, or a combination of those reasons.

[W]e hold that a cross-racial identification, as a subset of eyewitness identification, requires a special jury instruction in an appropriate case.

Indeed, some courtroom observers have commented that the ordinary person's difficulty of "cross-racial recognition is so commonplace as to be the subject of both cliche and joke: 'they all look alike.'" Although laboratory studies concerning the reliability of cross-racial identifications have not been validated in actual courtroom atmospheres, the results of many of those experiments suggest that "decreased accuracy in the recognition of other-race faces is not within the observer's conscious control, and that seriousness of criminal proceedings would not improve accuracy." Moreover, the stress associated with the courtroom atmosphere, based on human experience, is likely to diminish rather than enhance recognition accuracy.

We embrace [an approach] requiring a cross-racial identification charge under the circumstances of this case despite some differences of opinion among the researchers. Notwithstanding those differences, there is an impressive consistency in results showing that problems exist with cross-racial eyewitness identification. We conclude that the empirical data encapsulate much of the ordinary human experience and provide an appropriate frame of reference for requiring a cross-racial identification jury instruction. Under the jurisprudence of this Court, in a prosecution "in which race by definition is a patent factor[, race] must be taken into account to assure a fair trial." State v. Harris, 156 N.J. 122, 235, 716 A.2d 458 (1998) (Handler, J., dissenting).

At the same time, we recognize that unrestricted use of cross-racial identification instructions could be counter-productive. Consequently, care must be taken to insulate criminal trials from base appeals to racial prejudice. An appropriate jury instruction should carefully delineate the context in which the jury is permitted to consider racial differences. The simple fact pattern of a white victim of a violent crime at the hands of a black assailant would not automatically give rise to the need for a cross-racial identification charge. More is required.

A cross-racial instruction should be given only when, as in the present case, identification is a critical issue in the case, and an eyewitness's cross-racial identification is not corroborated by other evidence giving it independent reliability. Here, the eyewitness identification was critical; yet it was not corroborated by any forensic evidence or other eyewitness account. The circumstances of the case raise some doubt concerning the reliability of the victim's identification in that no positive identification was made for nearly eight months despite attempts within the first five days following the commission of the offenses. Under those circumstances, turning over to the jury the vital question of the reliability of that identification without acquainting the jury with the potential risks associated with such identifications could have affected the jurors' ability to evaluate the reliability of the identification. We conclude, therefore, that it was reversible error not to have given an instruction that informed the jury about the possible significance of the cross-racial identification factor, a factor the jury can observe in many cases with its own eyes, in determining the critical issue—the accuracy of the identification.

For the sake of clarity, we repeat that the purpose of a cross-racial instruction is to alert the jury through a cautionary instruction that it should pay close attention to a possible influence of race. Because of the "widely held commonsense view that members of one race have greater difficulty in accurately identifying members of a different race," *Telfaire*, supra, 469 F.2d at 559 (Bazelon, C.J., concurring), expert testimony on this issue would not assist a jury, and for that reason would be inadmissible. We request the Criminal Practice Committee and the Model Jury Charge Committee to revise the current charge on identification to include an appropriate statement on cross-racial eyewitness identification that is consistent with this opinion.

The judgment of the Appellate Division is reversed. The case is remanded to the Law Division for a new trial.

NOTE

Other courts have looked with more favor on expert testimony concerning cross-racial identifications. In Currie v. Commonwealth, 30 Va.App. 58, 65, 515 S.E.2d 335, 339 (1999), for example, the court noted, with apparent approval, that the trial judge permitted an expert "to testify about the mechanical processes of memory and cross-racial identification because these subjects were not within the common knowledge and experience of the jurors."

*

PART TWO

Prosecution and Adjudication

*

603

CHAPTER 11

THE INITIAL APPEARANCE AND DETENTION

Analysis

Under Fed.R.Crim.Proc. 5(a) (reprinted in this Chapter), as well as under similar provisions in virtually all states, a person who is arrested must be "presented" before a judicial officer without substantial delay. Generally, this will be the defendant's first court appearance in connection with the prosecution; hence, it is frequently called the initial appearance. Depending upon local requirements and practice, a "complaint" may have been filed before the defendant's presentation "charging" the defendant with an offense. In felony and potentially in serious misdemeanor prosecutions, this complaint serves only the interim function of formalizing the charge until an indictment or information is filed. In some misdemeanor procedures, however, the complaint is the only formal charge in the case. Frequently, the initial appearance will be before a "lower" court judge who—if the charge is a serious one—lacks jurisdiction to adjudicate the defendant's guilt or innocence. In addition, the initial appearance takes place soon after apprehension. The defendant may not yet be represented by an attorney, or if an attorney is involved, the defendant and counsel may not yet be prepared to address matters relating to the case.

For these reasons, the functions of the initial appearance are quite limited. The defendant will generally be told of the charges and warned of the right to refrain from self-incrimination. Arrangements may be made (or begun) for appointment of counsel if the defendant asserts indigency, pretrial release or detention (see Chapter 12), and for a preliminary hearing (see Chapter 13). The principal case in this Chapter concerns a defendant's right to a judicial determination of "probable cause." This right which may be implemented by expanding the functions of the initial appearance to include the probable cause determination.

FEDERAL RULES OF CRIMINAL PROCEDURE

Rule 5. Initial Appearance Before the Magistrate Judge

(a) **In General.** Except as otherwise provided in this rule, an officer making an arrest under a warrant issued upon a complaint or any person making an arrest without a warrant shall take the arrested person without unnecessary delay before the nearest available federal magistrate judge or, if a federal magistrate judge is not reasonably available, before a state or local judicial officer authorized by 18 U.S.C. § 3041. If a person arrested without a warrant is brought before a magistrate judge, a complaint, satisfying the probable cause requirements of Rule 4(a), shall be promptly filed. When a person, arrested with or without a warrant or given a summons, appears initially before the magistrate judge, the magistrate judge shall proceed in accordance with the applicable subdivisions of this rule. * * *

(b) Misdemeanors and Other Petty Offenses. If the charge against the defendant is a misdemeanor [punishable by not more than one year in prison][a] or other petty offense [punishable by not more than six months' incarceration or a fine of not more than $5,000][b] triable by a United States magistrate judge under 18 U.S.C. § 3401, the magistrate judge shall proceed in accordance with Rule 58.

(c) Offenses not Triable by the United States Magistrate Judge. If the charge against the defendant is not triable by the United States magistrate judge, the defendant shall not be called upon to plead. The magistrate judge shall inform the defendant of the complaint against the defendant and of any affidavit filed therewith, of the defendant's right to retain counsel or to request the assignment of counsel if the defendant is unable to obtain counsel, and of the general circumstances under which the defendant may secure pretrial release. The magistrate judge shall inform the defendant that the defendant is not required to make a statement and that any statement made by the defendant may be used against the defendant. The magistrate judge shall also inform the defendant of the right to a preliminary examination. The magistrate judge shall allow the defendant reasonable time and opportunity to consult counsel and shall detain or conditionally release the defendant as provided by statute or in these rules.

A defendant is entitled to a preliminary examination, unless waived, when charged with any offense, other than a petty offense, which is to be tried by a judge of the district court. If the defendant waives preliminary examination, the magistrate judge shall forthwith hold the defendant to answer in the district court. If the defendant does not waive the preliminary examination, the magistrate judge shall schedule a preliminary examination. Such examination shall be held within a reasonable time but in any event not later than 10 days following the initial appearance if the defendant is in custody and no later than 20 days if the defendant is not in custody, provided, however, that the preliminary examination shall not be held if the defendant is indicted or if an information against the defendant is filed in district court before the date set for the preliminary examination. With the consent of the defendant and upon a showing of good cause, taking into account the public interest in the prompt disposition of criminal cases, time limits specified in this subdivision may be extended one or more times by a federal magistrate judge. In the absence of such consent by the defendant, time limits may be extended by a judge of the United States

---

a.   18 U.S.C. § 1.   **b.**   18 U.S.C. § 1.

only upon a showing that extraordinary circumstances exist and that delay is indispensable to the interests of justice.

Gerstein v. Pugh

Supreme Court of the United States, 1975.
420 U.S. 103, 95 S.Ct. 854, 43 L.Ed.2d 54.

■ MR. JUSTICE POWELL delivered the opinion of the Court.

The issue in this case is whether a person arrested under a prosecutor's information is constitutionally entitled to a judicial determination of probable cause for pretrial restraint of liberty.

I.

In March 1971 respondents Pugh and Henderson were arrested in Dade County, Florida. Each was charged with several offenses under a prosecutor's information. Pugh was denied bail because one of the charges against him carried a potential life sentence, and Henderson remained in custody because he was unable to post a $4,500 bond.

In Florida, indictments are required only for prosecution of capital offenses. Prosecutors may charge all other crimes by information, without a prior preliminary hearing and without obtaining leave of court. Fla.Rule Crim.Proc. 3.140(a). At the time respondents were arrested, a Florida rule seemed to authorize adversary preliminary hearings to test probable cause for detention in all cases. Fla.Rule Crim.Proc. 1.122 (amended 1972). But the Florida courts had held that the filing of an information foreclosed the suspect's right to a preliminary hearing. They had also held that habeas corpus could not be used, except perhaps in exceptional circumstances, to test the probable cause for detention under an information. See Sullivan v. State ex rel. McCrory, 49 So.2d 794, 797 (Fla.1951). The only possible methods for obtaining a judicial determination of probable cause were a special statute allowing a preliminary hearing after 30 days, Fla.Stat.Ann. § 907.045 (1973), and arraignment, which the District Court found was often delayed a month or more after arrest. Pugh v. Rainwater, 332 F.Supp. 1107, 1110 (S.D.Fla.1971). As a result, a person charged by information could be detained for a substantial period solely on the decision of a prosecutor.

Respondents Pugh and Henderson filed a class action against Dade County officials in the Federal District Court claiming a constitutional right to a judicial hearing on the issue of probable cause and requesting declaratory and injunctive relief. Respondents Turner and Faulk, also in custody under informations, subsequently intervened. Petitioner Gerstein, the State Attorney for Dade County, was one of several defendants.

After an initial delay while the Florida legislature considered a bill that would have afforded preliminary hearings to persons charged by information, the District Court granted the relief sought. Pugh v. Rainwater, supra. The court certified the case as a class action under Fed.Rule Civ.Proc. 23(b)(2), and held that the Fourth and Fourteenth Amendments give all arrested persons charged by information a right to a judicial hearing on the question of probable cause. The District Court ordered the Dade County defendants to give the named plaintiffs an immediate preliminary hearing to determine probable cause for further detention. It also ordered them to submit a plan providing preliminary hearings in all cases instituted by information.

The defendants submitted a plan authored by Sheriff E. Wilson Purdy, and the District Court adopted it with modifications. The final order prescribed a detailed post-arrest procedure. 336 F.Supp. 490. Upon arrest the accused would be taken before a magistrate for a "first appearance hearing." The magistrate would explain the charges, advise the accused of his rights, appoint counsel if he was indigent, and proceed with a probable cause determination unless either the prosecutor or the accused was unprepared. If either requested more time, the magistrate would set the date for a "preliminary hearing," to be held within four days if the accused was in custody and within 10 days if he had been released pending trial. The order provided sanctions for failure to hold the hearings at prescribed times. At the "preliminary hearing" the accused would be entitled to counsel, and he would be allowed to confront and cross-examine adverse witnesses, to summon favorable witnesses, and to have a transcript made on request. If the magistrate found no probable cause, the accused would be discharged. He then could not be charged with the same offense by complaint or information, but only by indictment returned within 30 days.

The Court of Appeals for the Fifth Circuit stayed the District Court's order pending appeal, but while the case was awaiting decision, the Dade County judiciary voluntarily adopted a similar procedure of its own. Upon learning of this development, the Court of Appeals remanded the case for specific findings on the constitutionality of the new Dade County system. Before the District Court issued its findings, however, the Florida Supreme Court amended the procedural rules governing preliminary hearings state-wide, and the parties agreed that the District Court should direct its inquiry to the new rules rather than the Dade County procedures.

Under the amended rules every arrested person must be taken before a judicial officer within 24 hours. Fla.Rule Crim.Proc. 3.–130(b). This "first appearance" is similar to the "first appearance hearing" ordered by the District Court in all respects but the crucial one: the magistrate does not make a determination of probable cause. The rule amendments also changed the procedure for preliminary hearings, restricting them to felony charges and codifying the rule that no hearings are available to persons charged by information or indictment. Rule 3.131; see In re Rule 3.131(b), Florida Rules of Criminal Procedure, 289 So.2d 3 (Fla.1974).

In a supplemental opinion the District Court held that the amended rules had not answered the basic constitutional objection, since a defendant charged by information still could be detained pending trial without a judicial determination of probable cause. 355 F.Supp. 1286. Reaffirming its original ruling, the District Court declared that the continuation of this practice was unconstitutional. The Court of Appeals affirmed, 483 F.2d 778, modifying the District Court's decree in minor particulars and suggesting that the form of preliminary hearing provided by the amended Florida rules would be acceptable, as long as it was provided to all defendants in custody pending trial. Id., at 788–789.

State Attorney Gerstein petitioned for review, and we granted certiorari because of the importance of the issue. 414 U.S. 1062, 94 S.Ct. 567, 38 L.Ed.2d 467. We affirm in part and reverse in part.

II.

As framed by the proceedings below, this case presents two issues: whether a person arrested and held for trial on an information is entitled to a judicial determination of probable cause for detention, and if so, whether the adversary hearing ordered by the District Court and approved by the Court of Appeals is required by the Constitution.

a.

Both the standards and procedures for arrest and detention have been derived from the Fourth Amendment and its common-law antecedents. The standard for arrest is probable cause, defined in terms of facts and circumstances "sufficient to warrant a prudent man in believing that the [suspect] had committed or was committing an offense." Beck v. Ohio, 379 U.S. 89, 91, 85 S.Ct. 223, 225, 13 L.Ed.2d 142 (1964). * * *

To implement the Fourth Amendment's protection against unfounded invasions of liberty and privacy, the Court has required that the existence of probable cause be decided by a neutral and detached magistrate whenever possible. The classic statement of this principle appears in Johnson v. United States, 333 U.S. 10, 13–14, 68 S.Ct. 367, 369, 92 L.Ed. 436 (1948):

> "The point of the Fourth Amendment, which often is not grasped by zealous officers, is not that it denies law enforcement the support of the usual inferences which reasonable men draw from evidence. Its protection consists in requiring that those inferences be drawn by a neutral and detached magistrate instead of being judged by the officer engaged in the often competitive enterprise of ferreting out crime."

Maximum protection of individual rights could be assured by requiring a magistrate's review of the factual justification prior to any arrest, but such a requirement would constitute an intolerable handicap for legitimate law enforcement. * * *

Under this practical compromise, a policeman's on-the-scene assessment of probable cause provides legal justification for arresting a person suspected of crime, and for a brief period of detention to take the administrative steps incident to arrest. Once the suspect is in custody, however, the reasons that justify dispensing with the magistrate's neutral judgment evaporate. There no longer is any danger that the suspect will escape or commit further crimes while the police submit their evidence to a magistrate. And, while the State's reasons for taking summary action subside, the suspect's need for a neutral determination of probable cause increases significantly. The consequences of prolonged detention may be more serious than the interference occasioned by arrest. Pretrial confinement may imperil the suspect's job, interrupt his source of income, and impair his family relationships. See R. Goldfarb, Ransom 32–91 (1965); L. Katz,

Justice Is the Crime 51–62 (1972). Even pretrial release may be accompanied by burdensome conditions that effect a significant restraint on liberty. When the stakes are this high, the detached judgment of a neutral magistrate is essential if the Fourth Amendment is to furnish meaningful protection from unfounded interference with liberty. Accordingly, we hold that the Fourth Amendment requires a judicial determination of probable cause as a prerequisite to extended restraint on liberty following arrest.

* * *

B.

Under the Florida procedures challenged here, a person arrested without a warrant and charged by information may be jailed or subjected to other restraints pending trial without any opportunity for a probable cause determination.[1] Petitioner defends this practice on the ground that the prosecutor's decision to file an information is itself a determination of probable cause that furnishes sufficient reason to detain a defendant pending trial. Although a conscientious decision that the evidence warrants prosecution affords a measure of protection against unfounded detention, we do not think prosecutorial judgment standing alone meets the requirements of the Fourth Amendment. Indeed, we think the Court's previous decisions compel disapproval of the Florida procedure. In Albrecht v. United States, 273 U.S. 1, 5, 47 S.Ct. 250, 251, 71 L.Ed. 505 (1927), the Court held that an arrest warrant issued solely upon a United States Attorney's information was invalid because the accompanying affidavits were defective. Although the Court's opinion did not explicitly state that the prosecutor's official oath could not furnish probable cause, that conclusion was implicit in the judgment that the arrest was illegal under the Fourth Amendment.[2] * * *

In holding that the prosecutor's assessment of probable cause is not sufficient alone to justify restraint on liberty pending trial, we do not imply that the accused is entitled to judicial oversight or review of the decision to prosecute. Instead, we adhere to the Court's prior holding that a judicial hearing is not prerequisite to prosecution by information. Nor do we retreat from the established rule that illegal arrest or detention does not void a subsequent conviction. Thus, as the Court of Appeals noted below, although a suspect who is presently detained may challenge the probable cause for that confinement, a conviction will not be vacated on the ground

---

1. A person arrested under a warrant would have received a prior judicial determination of probable cause. Under Fla.Rule Crim.Proc. 3.120, a warrant may be issued upon a sworn complaint that states facts showing that the suspect has committed a crime. The magistrate may also take testimony under oath to determine if there is reasonable ground to believe the complaint is true.

2. By contrast, the Court has held that an indictment, "fair upon its face," and returned by a "properly constituted grand jury" conclusively determines the existence of probable cause and requires issuance of an arrest warrant without further inquiry. Ex parte United States, 287 U.S. 241, 250, 53 S.Ct. 129, 131, 77 L.Ed. 283 (1932). The willingness to let a grand jury's judgment substitute for that of a neutral and detached magistrate is attributable to the grand jury's relationship to the courts and its historical role of protecting individuals from unjust prosecution.

that the defendant was detained pending trial without a determination of probable cause. * * *

III.

Both the District Court and the Court of Appeals held that the determination of probable cause must be accompanied by the full panoply of adversary safeguards—counsel, confrontation, cross-examination, and compulsory process for witnesses. A full preliminary hearing of this sort is modeled after the procedure used in many States to determine whether the evidence justifies going to trial under an information or presenting the case to a grand jury. The standard of proof required of the prosecution is usually referred to as "probable cause," but in some jurisdictions it may approach a prima facie case of guilt. When the hearing takes this form, adversary procedures are customarily employed. The importance of the issue to both the State and the accused justifies the presentation of witnesses and full exploration of their testimony on cross-examination. This kind of hearing also requires appointment of counsel for indigent defendants. And, as the hearing assumes increased importance and the procedures become more complex, the likelihood that it can be held promptly after arrest diminishes.

These adversary safeguards are not essential for the probable cause determination required by the Fourth Amendment. The sole issue is whether there is probable cause for detaining the arrested person pending further proceedings. This issue can be determined reliably without an adversary hearing. The standard is the same as that for arrest.[3] That standard—probable cause to believe the suspect has committed a crime— traditionally has been decided by a magistrate in a nonadversary proceeding on hearsay and written testimony, and the Court has approved these informal modes of proof.

* * *

The use of an informal procedure is justified not only by the lesser consequences of a probable cause determination but also by the nature of the determination itself. It does not require the fine resolution of conflicting evidence that a reasonable-doubt or even a preponderance standard demands, and credibility determinations are seldom crucial in deciding whether the evidence supports a reasonable belief in guilt. See F. Miller, Prosecution: The Decision to Charge a Suspect with a Crime 64–109 (1969). This is not to say that confrontation and cross-examination might not enhance the reliability of probable cause determinations in some cases. In most cases, however, their value would be too slight to justify holding, as a matter of constitutional principle, that these formalities and safeguards

---

3. Because the standards are identical, ordinarily there is no need for further investigation before the probable cause determination can be made.

"Presumably, whomever the police arrest they must arrest on 'probable cause.' It is not the function of the police to arrest, as it were, at large and to use an interrogating process at police headquarters in order to determine whom they should charge before a committing magistrate on 'probable cause.'" Mallory v. United States, 354 U.S. 449, 456, 77 S.Ct. 1356, 1360, 1 L.Ed.2d 1479 (1957).

designed for trial must also be employed in making the Fourth Amendment determination of probable cause.[4]

Because of its limited function and its nonadversary character, the probable cause determination is not a "critical stage" in the prosecution that would require appointed counsel. The Court has identified as "critical stages" those pretrial procedures that would impair defense on the merits if the accused is required to proceed without counsel. Coleman v. Alabama, 399 U.S. 1, 90 S.Ct. 1999, 26 L.Ed.2d 387 (1970); United States v. Wade, 388 U.S. 218, 226–227, 87 S.Ct. 1926, 1931–1932, 18 L.Ed.2d 1149 (1967). In Coleman v. Alabama, where the Court held that a preliminary hearing was a critical stage of an Alabama prosecution, the majority and concurring opinions identified two critical factors that distinguish the Alabama preliminary hearing from the probable cause determination required by the Fourth Amendment. First, under Alabama law the function of the preliminary hearing was to determine whether the evidence justified charging the suspect with an offense. A finding of no probable cause could mean that he would not be tried at all. The Fourth Amendment probable cause determination is addressed only to pretrial custody. To be sure, pretrial custody may affect to some extent the defendant's ability to assist in preparation of his defense, but this does not present the high probability of substantial harm identified as controlling in *Wade* and *Coleman*. Second, Alabama allowed the suspect to confront and cross-examine prosecution witnesses at the preliminary hearing. The Court noted that the suspect's defense on the merits could be compromised if he had no legal assistance for exploring or preserving the witnesses' testimony. This consideration does not apply when the prosecution is not required to produce witnesses for cross-examination.

Although we conclude that the Constitution does not require an adversary determination of probable cause, we recognize that state systems of criminal procedure vary widely. There is no single preferred pretrial procedure, and the nature of the probable cause determination usually will be shaped to accord with a State's pretrial procedure viewed as a whole. While we limit our holding to the precise requirement of the Fourth Amendment, we recognize the desirability of flexibility and experimentation by the States. It may be found desirable, for example, to make the probable cause determination at the suspect's first appearance before a judicial officer,[5] or the determination may be incorporated into the procedure for setting bail or fixing other conditions of pretrial release. In some States, existing procedures may satisfy the requirement of the Fourth Amendment. Others may require only minor adjustment, such as accelera-

---

4. Criminal justice is already overburdened by the volume of cases and the complexities of our system. The processing of misdemeanors, in particular, and the early stages of prosecution generally are marked by delays that can seriously affect the quality of justice. A constitutional doctrine requiring adversary hearings for all persons detained pending trial could exacerbate the problem of pretrial delay.

5. Several States already authorize a determination of probable cause at this stage or immediately thereafter. This Court has interpreted the Federal Rules of Criminal Procedure to require a determination of probable cause at the first appearance. Jaben v. United States, 381 U.S. 214, 218, 85 S.Ct. 1365, 1367, 14 L.Ed.2d 345 (1965); Mallory v. United States, 354 U.S. 449, 454, 77 S.Ct. 1356, 1359, 1 L.Ed.2d 1479 (1957).

tion of existing preliminary hearings. Current proposals for criminal procedure reform suggest other ways of testing probable cause for detention.[6] Whatever procedure a State may adopt, it must provide a fair and reliable determination of probable cause as a condition for any significant pretrial restraint on liberty,[7] and this determination must be made by a judicial officer either before or promptly after arrest.

IV.

We agree with the Court of Appeals that the Fourth Amendment requires a timely judicial determination of probable cause as a prerequisite to detention, and we accordingly affirm that much of the judgment. As we do not agree that the Fourth Amendment requires the adversary hearing outlined in the District Court's decree, we reverse in part and remand to the Court of Appeals for further proceedings consistent with this opinion.

Affirmed in part, reversed in part, and remanded.

■ Mr. Justice Stewart, with whom Mr. Justice Douglas, Mr. Justice Brennan, and Mr. Justice Marshall join, concurring.

I concur in Parts I and II of the Court's opinion, since the Constitution clearly requires at least a timely judicial determination of probable cause as a prerequisite to pretrial detention. Because Florida does not provide all defendants in custody pending trial with a fair and reliable determination

---

6. Under the Uniform Rules of Criminal Procedure (Proposed Final Draft 1974), a person arrested without a warrant is entitled, "without unnecessary delay," to a first appearance before a magistrate and a determination that grounds exist for issuance of an arrest warrant. The determination may be made on affidavits or testimony, in the presence of the accused. Rule 311. Persons who remain in custody for inability to qualify for pretrial release are offered another opportunity for a probable cause determination at the detention hearing, held no more than five days after arrest. This is an adversary hearing, and the parties may summon witnesses, but reliable hearsay evidence may be considered. Rule 344.

The A.L.I. Model Code of Pre-arraignment Procedure (Tent.Draft No. 5, 1972, and Tent.Draft No. 5A, 1973) also provides a first appearance, at which a warrantless arrest must be supported by a reasonably detailed written statement of facts. § 310. The magistrate may make a determination of probable cause to hold the accused, but he is not required to do so and the accused may request an attorney for an "adjourned session" of the first appearance to be held within 2 "court days." At that session, the magistrate makes a determination of probable cause upon a combination of written and live testimony:

"The arrested person may present written and testimonial evidence and arguments for his discharge and the state may present additional written and testimonial evidence and arguments that there is reasonable cause to believe that he has committed the crime of which he is accused. The state's submission may be made by means of affidavits, and no witnesses shall be required to appear unless the court, in the light of the evidence and arguments submitted by the parties, determines that there is a basis for believing that the appearance of one or more witnesses for whom the arrested person seeks subpoenas might lead to a finding that there is no reasonable cause." § 310.2(2) (Tent.Draft No. 5A, 1973).

7. Because the probable cause determination is not a constitutional prerequisite to the charging decision, it is required only for those suspects who suffer restraints on liberty other than the condition that they appear for trial. There are many kinds of pretrial release and many degrees of conditional liberty. We cannot define specifically those that would require a prior probable cause determination, but the key factor is significant restraint on liberty.

of probable cause for their detention, the respondents and the members of the class they represent are entitled to declaratory and injunctive relief.

Having determined that Florida's current pretrial detention procedures are constitutionally inadequate, I think it is unnecessary to go further by way of dicta. In particular, I would not, in the abstract, attempt to specify those procedural protections that constitutionally need *not* be accorded incarcerated suspects awaiting trial.

* * *

NOTES

1.   Under the Court's opinion, is there any reason why a judge could not make the *Gerstein* determination of probable cause by obtaining information over the telephone or by email?

2.   **How quick is "promptly?"** *Gerstein* held that a judicial determination of probable cause must be made "either before or promptly after arrest." The opinion did not, however, define "promptly." In County of Riverside v. McLaughlin, 500 U.S. 44, 111 S.Ct. 1661, 114 L.Ed.2d 49 (1991), the respondent, by federal class action, challenged a practice in Riverside County, California in which persons arrested without a warrant received a judicial determination of probable cause at the arraignment or first appearance before the magistrate. The arraignment occurred within 2 days of arrest, excluding weekends and holidays. Thus, one arrested late in the week might be held as long as 5 days before probable cause was determined by the magistrate; in the case of the Thanksgiving holiday, a 7–day delay was possible. The United States District Court issued an injunction requiring that determinations of probable cause be made within 36 hours of warrantless arrests, absent exigent circumstances. This order was affirmed by the United States Court of Appeals. McLaughlin v. County of Riverside, 888 F.2d 1276 (9th Cir.1989), cert. granted 498 U.S. 808, 111 S.Ct. 40, 112 L.Ed.2d 16 (1990).

The Supreme Court, in an opinion by Justice O'Connor, vacated the judgment of the Court of Appeals. The Ninth Circuit had erroneously interpreted *Gerstein* to require a determination of probable cause as soon as the administrative steps incident to arrest—fingerprinting, photographing, searching—were completed. This did not sufficiently allow for variations in state procedures and in particular did not take into account the need in some states to combine the *Gerstein* determination with the initial appearance before the magistrate. The Court concluded that "a jurisdiction that provides judicial determinations of probable cause within 48 hours of arrest will, as a general matter, comply with the promptness requirement of *Gerstein*." 111 S.Ct. at 1670. A determination may not be prompt, however, even if within the 48 hour guideline if it was delayed unreasonably, such as a delay to gather additional evidence to justify the arrest, a delay motivated by ill will against the arrestee, or a delay for delay's sake. Conversely, if the determination is made later than 48 hours after arrest, the burden is upon the government to justify it by showing "the existence of a bona fide emergency or other extraordinary circumstance." 111 S.Ct. at 1670. The Court made it clear that a desire to combine the probable cause determination with other pretrial proceedings will not justify delay beyond 48 hours, nor will intervening weekends.

Justice Marshall, joined by Justices Blackmun and Stevens, dissented, agreeing with the Court of Appeals that a *Gerstein* determination is required as soon as the administrative steps incident to arrest are completed. Justice Scalia dissented on the ground that any delay beyond 24 hours should create a presumption of unreasonableness requiring governmental rebuttal. This, he believed, was required by the historical common law requirement of prompt presentation to the magistrate following arrest.

3. **What remedy is there for a violation?** In Powell v. Nevada, 511 U.S. 79, 114 S.Ct. 1280, 128 L.Ed.2d 1 (1994), Petitioner was arrested without a warrant and held for four days before being presented to a magistrate. At his trial for murder, a statement made by Petitioner on the fourth day after his arrest was introduced into evidence. The Nevada Supreme Court held that the 48 hour rule of *McLaughlin* did not apply because Petitioner's prosecution began before *McLaughlin* was decided. The Supreme Court vacated that judgment on the ground that *McLaughlin* applies to all cases not yet final when the rule was announced. However, the Court noted Petitioner does not necessarily have to be re-tried because the Nevada Supreme Court had not considered the question what remedy is appropriate for a *McLaughlin* violation, which is a question the Supreme Court has not yet decided.

What remedies would be appropriate? Could they ever include excluding a statement made during a period of detention in violation of *McLaughlin's* requirement of presentment and judicial determination of probable cause within 48 hours?

CHAPTER 12

BAIL AND PREVENTIVE DETENTION

Analysis

EDITORS' INTRODUCTION: THE MONEY BAIL SYSTEM

American pretrial release practice and theory has been dramatically affected by an assumption that exclusive reliance can be placed on so-called money bail. Because the Supreme Court has left unclear the content of the Eighth Amendment as well as its application to the States, bail and pretrial release law has tended to be largely state law. Traditionally, state law—and often state constitutional law—has provided that except for certain suspects charged with crimes carrying the death penalty all defendants are bailable and all have a right to be free from excessive bail. In 1682, Pennsylvania provided by its Constitution that "all Prisoners shall be Bailable by Sufficient Sureties, unless for capital Offenses, where proof is evident or the presumption great." This was widely copied in state constitutions subsequently adopted elsewhere. See Carbone, Seeing Through the Emperor's New Clothes: Rediscovery of Basic Principles in the Administration of Bail, 34 Syracuse L.Rev. 517, 533–34 (1983). Moreover, courts have widely assumed that the sole legitimate function of bail is to provide reasonable assurance that the defendant will appear for trial and that bail must be set only with reference to the amount necessary to achieve this purpose.

The leading case addressing excessive bail is Stack v. Boyle, 342 U.S. 1, 72 S.Ct. 1, 96 L.Ed. 3 (1951). The twelve defendants were charged with conspiracy to advocate the violent overthrow of the United States government and bail was set at $50,000 each. Addressing their claim that this was excessive under the Eighth Amendment, the Supreme Court reasoned:

[T]he modern practice of requiring a bail bond or the deposit of a sum of money subject to forfeiture serves as additional assurance of the presence of an accused. Bail set at a figure higher than an amount reasonably calculated to fulfill this purpose is "excessive" under the Eighth Amendment.

Since the function of bail is limited, the fixing of bail for any individual defendant must be based upon standards relevant to the purpose of assuring the presence of that defendant. The traditional standards as expressed in the Federal Rules of Criminal Procedure [which provide that the amount is to be such as will insure the presence of the defendant "having regard to the nature and circumstances of the offense charged, the weight of the evidence against him, the financial ability of the defendant to give bail and the character of the defendant."] are to be applied in each case to each defendant.

342 U.S. at 5, 72 S.Ct. at 3–4, 96 L.Ed. at 6–7. Turning to the case before it, the Court noted that upon conviction the defendants would be subject to not more than five years' confinement and a fine of not more than $10,000. There was agreement that the $50,000 amount was much higher than was usually set in cases where the crime charged carried similar penalties. The Government urged that the Court consider the likelihood that the defendants owed allegiance to a foreign government and thus would be likely to flee. But the Court responded:

If bail in an amount greater than that usually fixed for serious charges of crimes is required in the case of any of the petitioners, that is a matter to which evidence should be directed in a hearing so that the constitutional rights of each petitioner may be preserved. In the absence of such a showing, we are of the opinion that the fixing of bail before trial in these cases cannot be squared with the statutory and constitutional standards for admission to bail.

342 U.S. at 5, 72 S.Ct. at 4, 96 L.Ed. at 7.

Despite the theory, however, empirical evidence showed that the pretrial release system was working in a manner that raised serious questions. Among the classic published works that influenced the movement toward reform were D. Freed and P. Wald, Bail in the United States: 1964 (1964); R. Goldfarb, Ransom: A Critique of the American Bail System (1965); C. Foote, The Coming Constitutional Crisis in Bail, 113 U.Pa.L.Rev. 959, 1125 (1965). Bail tended to be set, these studies established, largely on the basis of the charged offense, sometimes according to formalized "schedules." As a result, affluent defendants were able to secure release despite realistic concerns regarding the likelihood of their appearance for trial. Indigent defendants, on the other hand, were often detained because of their inability to make bail despite reason to believe they would appear for trial. Moreover, if there was a fear that a suspect would commit additional offenses prior to trial, bail was often set at an amount the suspect would be unable to meet without regard to his likelihood of appearance. Thus pretrial preventive detention was informally accomplished.

Concern also focused upon the impact of extensive pretrial detention of largely indigent defendants. The financial burden on society of maintaining the local jails necessary for this purpose, of course, was a consideration. In addition, the loss of liberty experienced by the defendants themselves was a significant concern. Families were denied the financial and other support that would be provided by the defendant. Evidence that detained suspects were sometimes sentenced to no imprisonment following conviction suggested that the burden upon offenders of awaiting trial sometimes exceeded that of being convicted.

Another important issue was whether pretrial detention tended to affect the outcome of cases. Detained defendants, of course, are less able than their released counterparts to assist counsel in preparing a defense or engaging in investigatory efforts in anticipation of trial. They are less able to make amends with victims and thus encourage the dropping of charges. Detention often results in loss of employment and community contacts, so following conviction a defendant who has been detained pending trial may present a less appealing case for probation or a short period of imprisonment than a convicted defendant who has been in the community pending trial. Whatever the causes, evidence suggested that pretrial detention tended to increase the risk of a defendant being convicted and of receiving a more severe sentence upon conviction. The classic study was Rankin, The Effect of Pretrial Detention, 39 N.Y.U.L.Rev. 641 (1964).

Many of those pushing for reform in the system urged that the problems of the bail system were largely attributable to, or at least increased by, the involvement of professional bondsmen. Such bondsmen agree for a fee—often approximately 10% of the face amount of the bail—to act as surety for the defendant. If the defendant appears as required, the bondsman's obligation is discharged; the defendant, of course, does not receive his fee back. If the defendant does not appear, the bondsman is liable for the face amount of bond, although he might escape or reduce liability by locating the defendant and presenting him to authorities.

In many localities, a defendant's ability to secure pretrial release depended upon his ability to find a bondsman able and willing to become a surety. A bondsman may require, as a condition to acting as surety, that the defendant or his family provide some sort of security to the bondsman. Thus the bondsmen and their practices and policies greatly affected the availability of pretrial release. In Pannell v. United States, 320 F.2d 698, 115 U.S.App.D.C. 379 (D.C.Cir.1963), Judge Skelly Wright commented:

> [T]he professional bondsman system as used in this District is odious. The effect of such a system is that the professional bondsmen hold the keys to the jail in their pockets. They determine for whom they will act as surety—who in their judgment is a good risk. The bad risks, in the bondsmen's judgment, *and the ones who are unable to pay the bondsmen's fees,* remain in jail. The court * * * [is] relegated to the relatively unimportant chore of fixing the amount of bail.

320 F.2d at 699 (Wright, J., concurring) (emphasis in original). During pretrial release, a bondsman could decide for whatever reasons seemed sufficient to him to "get off the risk." He could physically detain the defendant, present him to authorities, and—while the defendant remained incarcerated pending trial—thus escape any further risk of liability. If the defendant failed to appear, the bondsman had the authority to seek him out and take him into custody. Studies suggested that this broad authority of the bondsman was often abused in ways that gave defendants little or no practical recourse.

Involvement of the bondsman complicated the task of implementing the theoretical purpose of bail. Under approaches such as that discussed in Stack v. Boyle, the bailsetting task is to determine the likelihood of the defendant's appearance without regard to bail and then, if that is insufficient, to set bail in an amount that adds a sufficient financial incentive to appear to increase the likelihood of appearance to an acceptable level. But if bail was met by employing a professional bondsman, it was the bondsman who stood to lose by the defendant's nonappearance. This, of course, affected the manner in which even according to theory the bail amount should be determined. Chief Judge David Bazelon commented in *Pannell,* supra:

> It is frequently urged that eligibility for release and the amount of bond are intimately related, because the higher the bail the less "likelihood [there is] of [the defendant] fleeing or going into hiding." This argument presupposes that [a defendant] with higher bail has a more substantial stake and therefore a greater incentive not to flee. This may be true if no professional bondsman is involved. But if one is, it is he and not the court who determines [the defendant's] real stake. Under present practice the bondsman ordinarily makes the decision whether or not to require collateral for the bond. If he does, then [the defendant's] stake may be related to the amount of the bond. If he does not, then [the defendant] has no real financial stake in complying with the conditions of the bond, regardless of the amount, since the fee paid for the bond is not refundable under any circumstances. Hence the court does not decide—or even know—whether a higher bond for a particular applicant means that he has a greater stake.

320 F.2d at 701–02, 115 U.S.App.D.C. 379, 382 (Bazelon, C.J., concurring in part and dissenting in part).

The role of bondsmen in the system can, of course, be defended. They may perform a valuable role for which they are no more than adequately compensated. A bondsman who stands to lose a substantial amount by a defendant's nonappearance may take steps to assure that appearance, as by providing simple reminders when the appearance date approaches. In locating and apprehending defendants who have failed to appear, bondsmen are arguably performing a valuable function upon which overburdened law enforcement agencies cannot afford to spend time. See generally, Goldfarb, supra, at 119–25. On a less formal level, the involvement of a professional bondsman may enable a judge to "share" responsibility for a defendant's release and provide a buffer against any repercussions. The availability of bondsmen may result in the pretrial release of at least some defendants who would not otherwise be released. See Toborg, Bail Bondsmen and Criminal Court, 8 Justice System J. 141, 143–44 (1983).

Reform in the pretrial release system can be divided into two stages. The first, covered in Section A of this Chapter, took place primarily in the 1960's and consisted of modification of the criminal justice system's traditional exclusive reliance upon cash bail and professional bondsmen. The second, addressed in Section B of this Chapter, is currently underway and consists of providing mechanisms for the protection of society from those accused who pose significant dangers of committing further offenses if released pending trial.

A. THE MOVEMENT AWAY FROM MONEY BAIL

During the 1960's, a strong movement developed that emphasized the need for bail decisions to be made individually with regard for the characteristics of particular defendants and for less reliance to be placed on money bail in general and bail bonds, requiring a surety, in particular.

Much of the impetus for these reforms came from programs based upon the Vera Foundation's Manhattan Bail Project begun in 1961. These programs involved personal interviews with arrested defendants, verification of information indicating that the defendants had ties to the community or otherwise suggesting that they would appear for further proceedings, and the recommendation of many of the defendants for release simply upon their own promise to appear for trial—release on their own recognizance, often referred to as "OR" or "ROR." Experience tended to show that those released after such preliminary screening did not fail to appear more significantly than defendants released under traditional bail procedures. Further:

> In order to study the influence of its own recommendations, Vera initiated the project with the use of an experimental control procedure. Out of all defendants believed by the project to be qualified for release, half were in fact recommended to the court, while the other half were placed in a control group, and their recommendations withheld. In the project's first year, 59% of its parole recommendations were followed by the court, compared to only 16% paroled in the control group. In short, recommendations based on facts nearly quadrupled the rate of releases.

> The subsequent case histories of defendants in both groups were thereafter analyzed. They showed that 60% of the recommended parolees had either been acquitted or had their cases dismissed, compared with only 23% of the control group. Moreover, of the 40% who were found guilty out of the parole group, only one out of six was sentenced to prison. In contrast, 96% of those convicted in the control group were sentenced to serve a jail term.

P. Freed and P. Wald, Bail in the United States: 1964, 61–63 (1964).

In terms of the tendency of released defendants to appear, the studies are inconclusive. In contrast to the earliest reports of the Vera Foundation, some studies suggest that a larger percentage of those released on their own recognizance—as compared with those released on money bail—fail to appear for trial. C. Eskridge, Pretrial Release Programming—Issues and Trends (1983), reports on the many studies made and concludes:

> From the data now available, it appears that [pretrial release] programs in general are able to ensure the appearance of an accused individual for the appointed court hearings at least as well as the

traditional money bail system, and probably a bit better due to the screening ability of [pretrial release] programs.

Id., at 99–100.

The reform movement resulted in a number of changes. Some jurisdictions adopted the approach at issue in the principal case in this section. Others opted for increased availability of nonbail release often coupled with a "presumption" that a defendant is appropriate for release on his own recognizance. Perhaps the most influential legislation was the Bail Reform Act of 1966, which provided for release of suspects awaiting trial in federal court. These provisions, as amended by the Bail Reform Act of 1984 (discussed in more detail in the next section) are codified in 18 U.S.C.A. § 3142:

(b) Release on Personal Recognizance or Unsecured Appearance Bond.—The judicial officer shall order the pretrial release of the person on his personal recognizance, or upon execution of an unsecured appearance bond in an amount specified by the court, subject to the condition that the person not commit a Federal, State, or local crime during the period of his release, unless the judicial officer determines that such release will not reasonably assure the appearance of the person as required or will endanger the safety of any other person or the community.

(c) Release on Conditions.—(1) If the judicial officer determines that the release described in subsection (b) will not reasonably assure the appearance of the person as required or will endanger the safety of any other person or the community, he shall order the pretrial release of the person—

(A) subject to the condition that the person not commit a Federal, State, or local crime during the period of release; and

(B) subject to the least restrictive further condition, or combination of conditions, that he determines will reasonably assure the appearance of the person as required and the safety of any other person and the community, which may include the condition that the person—

(i) remain in the custody of a designated person, who agrees to assume supervision and to report any violation of a release condition to the court, if the designated person is able reasonably to assure the judicial officer that the person will appear as required and will not pose a danger to the safety of any other person or the community;

(ii) maintain employment, or, if unemployed, actively seek employment;

(iii) maintain or commence an educational program;

(iv) abide by specified restrictions on his personal associations, place of abode, or travel;

(v) avoid all contact with an alleged victim of the crime and with a potential witness who may testify concerning the offense;

(vi) report on a regular basis to a designated law enforcement agency, pretrial services agency, or other agency;

(vii) comply with a specified curfew;

(viii) refrain from possessing a firearm, destructive device, or other dangerous weapon;

(ix) refrain from excessive use of alcohol, or any use of a narcotic drug or other controlled substance * * * without a prescription by a licensed medical practitioner;

(x) undergo available medical, psychological, or psychiatric treatment, including treatment for drug or alcohol dependency, and remain in a specified institution if required for that purpose;

(xi) execute an agreement to forfeit upon failing to appear as required, property of a sufficient unencumbered value, including money, as is reasonably necessary to assure the appearance of the person as required, and shall provide the court with proof of ownership and the value of the property along with information regarding existing encumbrances as the judicial office may require;

(xii) execute a bail bond with solvent sureties; who will execute an agreement to forfeit in such amount as is reasonably necessary to assure appearance of the person as required and shall provide the court with information regarding the value of the assets and liabilities of the surety if other than an approved surety and the nature and extent of encumbrances against the surety's property; such surety shall have a net worth which shall have sufficient unencumbered value to pay the amount of the bail bond;

(xiii) return to custody for specified hours following release for employment, schooling, or other limited purposes; and

(xiv) satisfy any other condition that is reasonably necessary to assure the appearance of the person as required and to assure the safety of any other person and the community.

(2) The judicial officer may not impose a financial condition that results in the pretrial detention of the person.

(3) The judicial officer may at any time amend his order to impose additional or different conditions of release.

The 1966 statute assumed that the only relevant consideration was the assurance of the defendant's appearance at trial; denial of release on recognizance or on an unsecured bond and the imposition of conditions on release was authorized only upon determinations that this was necessary to assure the defendant's appearance. The 1984 statute provided for consideration of "the safety of any other person and the community." It also added a significant number of conditions that might be imposed upon pretrial release.

Some courts compelled reform on the basis of federal constitutional requirements. In Allen v. Burke, 1981 WL 15186, 29 Crim.L.Rep. (BNA) 2297 (June 4, 1981), award of attorneys' fees upheld, 690 F.2d 376 (4th Cir.1982), affirmed *sub nom.* Pulliam v. Allen, 466 U.S. 522, 104 S.Ct. 1970, 80 L.Ed.2d 565 (1984), for example, the federal district court ruled unconstitutional certain Virginia statutes and the practices under them in Culpepper County which allowed pretrial detention of those arrested for minor offenses:

> This court believes there is a constitutional right not to be jailed solely for failure to make bond on an offense for which no incarceration is authorized by the state. It offends basic notions of fairness to subject a pretrial detainee, clothed with the presumption of innocence, to a greater punishment than he could receive after being found guilty, solely because of inability to pay a money bond. The liberty interest at stake here is an important one. Freedom from bodily restraint and punishment without due process by the state is one of the more basic guarantees of the constitution.

1981 WL 15186, *2.

Other courts have been motivated by a concern that equal protection may be violated by a pretrial release system that offers pretrial liberty only to those with the resources to buy it. Equal protection, then, may bar the pretrial incarceration of an indigent defendant whose appearance for trial could reasonably be assured by other alternatives. See Pugh v. Rainwater, 572 F.2d 1053 (5th Cir.1978) (en banc), vacating 557 F.2d 1189 (5th Cir.1977).

Constitutional considerations may require further refinements in the process. In Van Atta v. Scott, 27 Cal.3d 424, 166 Cal.Rptr. 149, 613 P.2d 210 (1980), the California Supreme Court held that the state and federal requirements of due process imposed certain procedural requirements upon the process of deciding whether to grant a defendant ROR release. At the hearing, the prosecution must bear the burden of proof concerning the defendant's likelihood of appearing at future court proceedings, as to the defendant's record of nonappearances at prior court hearings, and as to the severity of the sentence the defendant faces if convicted. The detainee, however, may be required to bear the burden of producing evidence concerning ties to the community that suggest he will appear. In addition, the court refused to find a constitutional requirement that a statement of reasons be given when OR release is denied.

Schilb v. Kuebel

Supreme Court of the United States, 1971.
404 U.S. 357, 92 S.Ct. 479, 30 L.Ed.2d 502.

■ MR. JUSTICE BLACKMUN delivered the opinion of the Court.

John Schilb, of Belleville, Illinois, was arrested on January 16, 1969, and charged (a) with leaving the scene of an automobile accident and (b) with obstructing traffic. In order to gain his liberty pending trial, and in accord with the Illinois bail statutes hereinafter described, Schilb deposited

$75 in cash with the clerk of the court. This amount was 10% of the aggregate bail fixed on the two charges ($500 on the first and $250 on the second). At his ensuing trial Schilb was acquitted of the charge of leaving the scene, but was convicted of traffic obstruction. When he paid his fine, the amount Schilb had deposited was returned to him decreased, however, by $7.50 retained as "bail bond costs" by the court clerk pursuant to the statute. The amount so retained was 1% of the specified bail and 10% of the amount actually deposited.

Schilb, by this purported state class action against the court clerk, the county, and the county treasurer, attacks the statutory 1% charge on Fourteenth Amendment due process and equal protection grounds. The Circuit Court of St. Clair County upheld the statute and dismissed the complaint. The Supreme Court of Illinois affirmed, with two justices dissenting.

I

The Illinois bail statutes compose Article 110 of the State's Code of Criminal Procedure of 1963, made effective January 1, 1964. This Code complemented Illinois' then new and revised Criminal Code of 1961, made effective January 1, 1962. The work of revision of the theretofore existing statutes was that of a Joint Committee of the Illinois State and Chicago Bar Associations. See 1 Ill.Rev.Stat.1963, p. 1629.

Prior to 1964 the professional bail bondsman system with all its abuses was in full and odorous bloom in Illinois. Under that system the bail bondsman customarily collected the maximum fee (10% of the amount of the bond) permitted by statute, and retained that entire amount even though the accused fully satisfied the conditions of the bond. Payment of this substantial "premium" was required of the good risk as well as of the bad. The results were that a heavy and irretrievable burden fell upon the accused, to the excellent profit of the bondsman, and that professional bondsmen, and not the courts, exercised significant control over the actual workings of the bail system.

One of the stated purposes of the new bail provisions in the 1963 Code was to rectify this offensive situation. The purpose appears to have been accomplished. It is said that the bail bondsman abruptly disappeared in Illinois "due primarily to the success of the ten percent bail deposit provision." Boyle, Bail Under the Judicial Article, 17 De Paul L.Rev. 267, 272 (1968). * * *

II

Article 110 of the 1963 Code, as it read at the time Schilb was arrested and charged, provided that an eligible accused could obtain pretrial release in one of three ways:

(1) Under § 110–2 he may be released on his personal recognizance.

(2) Under § 110–7 he may execute a bail bond and deposit with the clerk cash equal to only 10% of the bail or $25, whichever is the greater. When bail is made in this way and the conditions of the bond have been performed, the clerk returns to the accused 90% of the sum

deposited. The remaining 10% (1% of the bail) is retained by the clerk "as bail bond costs."

(3) Under § 110–8 he may execute a bail bond and secure it by a deposit with the clerk of the full amount of the bail in cash, or in stocks and bonds authorized for trust funds in Illinois, or by unencumbered nonexempt Illinois real estate worth double the amount of the bail. When bail is made in this way and the conditions of the bond have been performed, the clerk returns the deposit of cash or stocks or bonds, or releases the real estate, as the case may be, without charge or retention of any amount.

In each case bail is fixed by a judicial officer. Section 110–5 prescribes factors to be considered in fixing the amount of bail. Under § 110–6 either the State or the defendant may apply to the court for an increase or for a reduction in the amount of bail or for alteration of the bond's conditions.

The choice between § 110–7 and § 110–8 is reserved to the accused.

The thinking and intentions of the Joint Committee revisers are apparent from the Committee's comments * * *[1]

The parties have stipulated that when bail in a particular case is fixed, the judge's "discretion in such respect is not guided by statute, rule of court or any definite, fixed standard; various and divers judges in fact fix the amount of bail for the same types of offenses at various and divers amounts, without relationship as to guilt or innocence of the particular defendant in a criminal charge, and without relationship of the particular offense charged and the bail fixed." They have also stipulated, "The actual cost of administering the provisions of said Sections 110–7 and 110–8 are substantially the same but there may probably be a slightly greater cost in the administration of Section 110–8."

III

The Court more than once has said that state legislative reform by way of classification is not to be invalidated merely because the legislature moves one step at a time. * * *

Bail, of course, is basic to our system of law, and the Eighth Amendment's proscription of excessive bail has been assumed to have application to the States through the Fourteenth Amendment. But we are not at all concerned here with any fundamental right to bail or with any Eighth

---

1. " * * * The provisions of sections 110–7 and 110–8 were designed to severely restrict the activities of professional bail bondsmen and to reduce the cost of liberty to arrested persons awaiting trial. * * * " P. 298.

"The committee realized full well the many arguments advanced in opposition to changing the present system. We were not impressed with any of them. If a person can pay a professional bondsman ten per cent of the bail amount as a fee, he can deposit it with the clerk. At the present time he re-

ceives nothing back from the bondsman if he appears for trial; his ten per cent fee is gone. Under the provisions of [§ 110–7(f)] he gets back ninety per cent of the amount deposited if he appears. The ten per cent of the deposit retained by the county will offset in monetary amount the costs of handling bail bonds (which must be done now anyway), and any loss resulting from the occasional bail jumper where the professional bondsman might now forfeit the amount of the bail. * * * " P. 300.

* * *

Amendment-Fourteenth Amendment question of bail excessiveness. Our concern, instead, is with the 1% cost-retention provision. This smacks of administrative detail and of procedure and is hardly to be classified as a "fundamental" right or as based upon any suspect criterion. The applicable measure, therefore, must be the traditional one: Is the distinction drawn by the statutes invidious and without rational basis?

IV

With this background, we turn to the appellants' primary argument. It is threefold: (1) that the 1% retention charge under § 110–7(f) is imposed on only one segment of the class gaining pretrial release; (2) that it is imposed on the poor and nonaffluent and not on the rich and affluent; and (3) that its imposition with respect to an accused found innocent amounts to a court cost assessed against the not-guilty person.

We are compelled to note preliminarily that the attack on the Illinois bail statutes, in a very distinct sense, is paradoxical. The benefits of the new system, as compared with the old, are conceded. And the appellants recognize that under the pre-1964 system Schilb's particular bail bond cost would have been 10% of his bail, or $75; that this premium price for his pretrial freedom, once paid, was irretrievable; and that, if he could not have raised the $75, he would have been consigned to jail until his trial. Thus, under the old system the cost of Schilb's pretrial freedom was $75, but under the new it was only $7.50. While acknowledging this obvious benefit of the statutory reform, Schilb and his coappellants decry the classification the statutes make and present the usual argument that the legislation must be struck down because it does not reform enough.

A.   It is true that no charge is made to the accused who is released on his personal recognizance. We are advised, however, that this was also true under the old (pre-1964) system and that "Illinois has never charged people out on recognizance." Thus, the burden on the State with respect to a personal recognizance is no more under the new system than what the State had assumed under the old. Also, with a recognizance, there is nothing the State holds for safekeeping, with resulting responsibility and additional paperwork. All this provides a rational basis for distinguishing between the personal recognizance and the deposit situations.

There is also, however, no retention charge to the accused who deposits the full amount of cash bail or securities or real estate. Yet the administrative cost attendant upon the 10% deposit and that upon the full deposit are, by the stipulation, "substantially the same" with, indeed, any higher cost incurred with respect to the full deposit.

This perhaps is a more tenuous distinction, but we cannot conclude that it is constitutionally vulnerable. One who deposits securities or encumbers his real estate precludes the use of that property for other purposes. And one who deposits the full amount of his bail in cash is dispossessed of a productive asset throughout the period of the deposit; presumably, at least, its interim possession by the State accrues to the benefit of the State. Further, the State's protection against the expenses that inevitably are incurred when bail is jumped is greater when 100% cash or securities or real estate is deposited or obligated than when only 10% of the bail amount is advanced. The Joint Committee's and the State Legislature's decision in balancing these opposing considerations in the way that they did cannot be described as lacking in rationality to the point where equal protection considerations require that they be struck down.

* * *

B.   The poor-man-affluent-man argument centers, of course, in Griffin v. Illinois, 351 U.S. 12, 76 S.Ct. 585, 100 L.Ed. 891 (1956), and in the many later cases that "reaffirm allegiance to the basic command that justice be applied equally to all persons." Williams v. Illinois, 399 U.S. 235, 241, 90 S.Ct. 2018, 2022, 26 L.Ed.2d 586 (1970).

In no way do we withdraw today from the *Griffin* principle. That remains steadfast. But it is by no means certain, as the appellants suggest, that the 10% deposit provision under § 110–7 is a provision for the benefit of the poor and the less affluent and that the full-deposit provision of § 110–8 is one for the rich and the more affluent. It should be obvious that the poor man's real hope and avenue for relief is the personal recognizance provision of § 110–2. We do not presume to say, as the appellants in their brief intimate, that § 110–2 is not utilized by Illinois judges and made available for the poor and the less affluent.

Neither is it assured, as the appellants also suggest, that the affluent will take advantage of the full-deposit provision of § 110–8, with no retention charge, and that the less affluent are relegated to the 10% deposit provision of § 110–7 and the 1% retention charge. The record is silent, but the flow indeed may be the other way. The affluent, more aware of and more experienced in the marketplace, may see the advantage, in these days of high interest rates, in retaining the use of 90% of the bail amount. A 5% or greater return on this 90% in a short period of time more than offsets the 1% retention charge. In other words, it is by no means clear that the route of § 110–8 is more attractive to the affluent defendant than the § 110–7 route. The situation, therefore, wholly apart from the fact that appellant Schilb himself has not pleaded indigency, is not one where we may assume that the Illinois plan works to deny relief to the poor man merely because of his poverty.

C.   The court-cost argument is that the person found innocent but already "put to the expense, disgrace and anguish of a trial" is "then assessed a cost for exercising his right to release pending trial." Giaccio v. Pennsylvania, 382 U.S. 399, 86 S.Ct. 518, 15 L.Ed.2d 447 (1966), is cited. *Giaccio* was a holding that an ancient Pennsylvania statute that permitted the jury to impose court costs upon an acquitted defendant, in order to offset the expenses of prosecution, violated the Due Process Clause because of vagueness and the absence of any standards preventing the arbitrary imposition of costs. The Court thus did not reach the merits, although Mr. Justice Stewart and Mr. Justice Fortas, each separately concurring, 382 U.S., at 405, 86 S.Ct., at 522, felt that the very imposition of costs upon an acquitted defendant was violative of due process.

Giaccio is not dispositive precedent for the appellants here. Certainly § 110–7 is not subject to attack for vagueness or for lack of standards. Neither is it a vehicle for the imposition of costs of prosecution as was the

Pennsylvania statute. Instead, § 110–7 authorizes retention of the 1% as "bail bond costs." This is what that description implies, namely, an administrative cost imposed upon all those, guilty and innocent alike, who seek the benefit of § 110–7. This conclusion is supported by the presence of the long-established Illinois rule against the imposition of costs of prosecution upon an acquittal or discharged criminal defendant and by the Illinois court's own determination that the charge under § 110–7(f) is an administrative fee and not a cost of prosecution imposed under Ill.Rev.Stat., c. 38, § 180–3 (1969), only upon the convicted defendant.

* * *

VI

We refrain from nullifying this Illinois statute that, with its companion sections, has brought reform and needed relief to the State's bail system. The judgment of the Supreme Court of Illinois is affirmed.

Affirmed.

■ MR. JUSTICE MARSHALL, concurring.

* * *

In the evolving struggle for meaningful bail reform I cannot find the present Illinois move towards that objective to be unconstitutional.

■ MR. JUSTICE DOUGLAS, dissenting.

* * *

Some costs are the unavoidable consequences of a system of government which is required to proceed against its citizens in a public trial in an adversary proceeding. Yet I see no basis for saying that an accused must bear the costs incurred by the Government in its unsuccessful prosecution of him. * * * I would conclude, with Justices Stewart and Fortas in *Giaccio* [v. Pennsylvania, 382 U.S. 399, 86 S.Ct. 518, 15 L.Ed.2d 447] that [the imposition of costs upon acquitted defendants] violates due process. * * * The costs of administering the bail system occur, by definition, only during the course of criminal prosecutions. They are as much an element of the costs of conducting criminal cases as the prosecutor's salary * * *.

■ MR. JUSTICE STEWART, with whom MR. JUSTICE BRENNAN concurs, dissenting.

* * *

It is clear that not every person accused of a crime is free to choose to be released on his own recognizance. Yet those who are fortunate enough to be so released need pay no costs whatsoever. * * * A[n] * * * attempt to distinguish between those released on their own recognizance and those who deposit 10% turns on the idea that the members of the former class are more "worthy" of the benefit they receive and therefore may rationally be required to pay less. But while the criteria used by judges to determine release on one's own recognizance—e.g., length of residence in the jurisdiction, marital status, employment record, or past criminal record—are obviously relevant to the recognizance decision, they are not rationally related to the decision to impose purely administrative costs, especially when such costs are at least as great for those released on their own recognizance as for those required to post bond. * * * I think the imposition of administrative costs on only one class of persons seeking pretrial release violates the Equal Protection Clause of the Fourteenth Amendment. * * *

NOTES

1. **Court appearance incentives.** Other legal incentives can be created to encourage defendants released before trial to appear and to avoid violating conditions of their release. Many of these are illustrated by federal statutory provisions enacted as part of the Bail Reform Act of 1984. A violation of the conditions of a release order can lead to a revocation of pretrial release; this is considered in the next section. It can also serve as the basis for a prosecution for contempt of court. 18 U.S.C.A. § 3148(c).

Nonappearance can be made a criminal offense. Under 18 U.S.C.A. § 3146, a person released pursuant to the Act commits a criminal offense if he knowingly fails to appear before a court as required by the conditions of his release. Further:

> It is an affirmative defense to a prosecution under this section that uncontrollable circumstances prevented the person from appearing * * *, and that the person did not contribute to the creation of such circumstances in reckless disregard of the requirement that he appear * * *, and that he appeared * * * as soon as such circumstances ceased to exist.

18 U.S.C.A. § 3146(c). The penalty for the offense is determined by the penalty attached to the offense with which the person was charged before release. If the charged offense, for example, was a felony punishable by five to fifteen years of imprisonment, failure to appear is punishable by imprisonment for not more than five years, a fine of not more than $10,000, or both. A term of imprisonment imposed for failure to appear is to be consecutive "to the term of imprisonment for any other offense." 18 U.S.C.A. § 3146(b)(2).

Are these provisions likely to stimulate an appearance by a defendant who is not otherwise motivated to appear?

2. **Deterring the commission of offenses while released.** The Bail Act of 1984 also provides that if a person is convicted of an offense committed while released pursuant to the chapter, he is to receive a penalty in addition to the penalty prescribed for the offense of which he is convicted. If the offense of which he is convicted is a felony, the additional penalty is to be a term of imprisonment of not more than ten years. This additional term of imprisonment is to be consecutive to any other sentence of imprisonment. 18 U.S.C.A. § 3147. Is this likely to cause a released person otherwise inclined to commit an offense to avoid that offense?

3. **Avoiding detention by use of field release citations.** It is often urged that increased use by police of citations in lieu of arrests is a major method of addressing pretrial detention problems, especially in misdemeanor situations. Such a practice avoids the detention in the first place thus eliminating the need for a formal release procedure. It accomplishes the objectives of release more quickly than other methods and, since no additional personnel need be employed, may be less expensive than many alternatives. Provision can be made for officers in the field to issue citations to some persons rather than making a "stationhouse arrest." Further, since there may sometimes be reasons for requiring a stationhouse appearance, provision may also be made for release of other offenders on a citation after their appearance at the police station. See W. Thomas, Bail Reform in America

258 (1976) ("Citations should provide for the release of the majority of misdemeanants and many felony defendants as well.").

4. **Effect of the bail reform movement on the criminal justice system.** In regard to the impact of the reform efforts, M. Feeley, Foreword to R. Flemming, Punishment Before Trial (1982), states:

> This movement has been one of the few clear successes in criminal justice reform during the past two decades. Today throughout the United States arrestees are much more likely to be released than they were twenty-five years ago. Many are now routinely released on their promise to appear. While money bail continues to exist and point up the contradictions inherent in our commitment to equal administration of the law, on average the amounts required are lower than before. No one seriously denies that the bail reform movement has had a significant impact.

Id., at xi. W. Thomas, Bail Reform in America 251–52 (1976) suggests that the major success of the bail reform movement may have been "the education and enlightenment of judges as to the importance of the bail decision, the need to consider individual factors in the setting of bail, and the consequences of pretrial detention."

On the other hand, in only a few jurisdictions have reforms eliminated the participation of professional bondsmen in the pretrial release process. See Toborg, Bailbondsmen and Criminal Courts, 8 Justice System J. 141 (1983).

B.   The Movement for Preventive Pretrial Detention and the Bail Reform Act of 1984

Recent years have seen a growing demand for formal recognition in the pretrial release system of the community's interest in being protected from the commission of crimes by defendants awaiting trial. In a number of jurisdictions, this interest has been accommodated to some extent in pretrial release provisions. But federal legislation has paved the way for explicit and relatively complex provisions for pretrial detention. In 1971, defendants in the District of Columbia were subject to detention under a federal statute applicable only to that jurisdiction. See D.C.Code 1981, § 23–1322. The Bail Reform Act of 1984, however, created a system of preventive detention for the entire federal criminal justice system. Detention of a defendant is authorized, in some situations, as an initial matter, and in others as a consequence of a showing that the defendant has violated the conditions of a pretrial release.

State Provisions for Accommodating Community Protection

State pretrial detention statutes quite often provide for some consideration of the likelihood that a defendant will commit further offenses while on pretrial release. But they differ widely in the showing required and in the significance that is given to it. Some insert the defendant's demonstrated "dangerousness" as a factor to be considered in making pretrial release decisions which, in theory at least, are to turn upon the need to assure the defendant's appearance for trial. Under South Dakota law, for example, whether to release a defendant on unsecured release and what conditions to put upon release are to depend upon what is necessary to assure appearance for trial. S.D. Codified Laws 23A–43–2, 23A–43–3. As a result of a 1980 amendment, however, the factors to be considered in determining what conditions of release to impose now include "the risk that [the defendant] will * * * pose a danger to any person or to the community." Id., at 23A–43–4.

Some jurisdictions authorize the imposition of special conditions of release on defendants identified as posing special risks. Arkansas, for example, authorizes the judicial officer to consider whether "there exists a danger that the defendant will commit a serious crime" and, upon determining that such a risk exists, to impose certain conditions upon the defendant's release. These may include directions that the defendant not go to certain areas, not possess dangerous weapons or engage in certain activities, and a requirement that the defendant report to and remain under the supervision of an officer of the court. Ark.R.Crim.P. 9.3. Upon a showing that a defendant has willfully violated reasonable conditions of release, the release may be "revoke[d]." Id., at 9.5(c).

Other provisions authorize preventive detention as an initial matter. As was noted above, state constitutions have typically provided that defendants charged with crimes carrying the death penalty are not entitled to bail, at least when "the proof is evident or the presumption great." Other state constitutions make further exceptions. The Arizona Constitution, for example, specifies that the following (in addition to those charged with a capital offense) are not bailable:

> 2.   Felony offenses committed when the person charged is already admitted to bail on a separate felony charge and where the proof is evident or the presumption great as to the present charge.

> 3.   Felony offenses if the person charged poses a substantial danger to any other person or the community, if no conditions of release which may be imposed will reasonably assure the safety of the other person or the community and if the proof is evident or the presumption great as to the present charge.

Ariz.R.S. Const. Art. 2, § 22.

The procedures for invoking these provisions differs greatly among jurisdictions. The matter may be entrusted entirely to the discretion of the judge or specific factual matters may have to be proved beyond a reasonable doubt. A specific hearing on the risk posed by the defendant may or may not be required. Limits on the duration of any detention permitted may or may not be imposed. State provisions are thoroughly addressed in B. Gottlieb, The Pretrial Processing of "Dangerous" Defendants: A Comparative Analysis of State Laws (1984). Relevant state laws are digested in B. Gottlieb and P. Rosen, Public Danger as a Factor in Pretrial Release— Digest of State Laws (1985).

Bail Reform Act of 1984: Initial Detention

Under federal legislation, a judicial officer before whom an arrested person is presented may release the person on his personal recognizance or upon an unsecured appearance bond or may release him under one or more conditions. In addition, temporary detention is authorized if the arrestee is determined to be on pretrial release in connection with another offense, probation, or parole, or if the arrestee is determined to be neither a resident nor an alien lawfully admitted for permanent residence and, in either case, the person may flee or pose a danger to any other person or the community. If, after ten days, the appropriate court, parole, probation or immigration official fails to take the person into custody, the person is to be processed in accordance with the standard provisions of the statute. 18 U.S.C.A. § 3142(d).

Most importantly, however, the judicial officer is directed to order the person detained pending trial if, after a detention hearing:

> the judicial officer finds that no conditions or combination of conditions will reasonably assure the appearance of the person as required and the safety of any other person and the community * * *

18 U.S.C.A. § 3142(e). Detention proceedings can, of course, be before the district judge. But a United States magistrate is a judicial officer within the meaning of the statute, and therefore pretrial detention can be ordered by such magistrates. 28 U.S.C.A. § 636(a)(2).

When Detention Hearing Held. Whether a detention hearing needs to be held depends upon the category of the case and who seeks such a hearing. The judicial officer is directed to hold a hearing:

> (1) upon motion of the attorney for the Government, [in a case] that involves—

>> (A) a crime of violence;

>> (B) an offense for which the maximum sentence is life imprisonment or death;

>> (C) an offense for which a maximum term of imprisonment of ten years or more is prescribed in the Controlled Substances Act * * *, the Controlled Substances Import and Export Act * * *, the Maritime Drug Law Enforcement Act * * * or [uses a firearm during specified felonies, conspires to commit certain offenses outside the United States or commits certain acts of terrorism]; or

>> (D) any felony if the person has been convicted of two or more offenses described in subparagraphs (A) through (C) of this paragraph, or two or more State or local offenses that would have been offenses described in subparagraphs (A) through (C) of this paragraph if a circumstance giving rise to Federal jurisdiction had existed, or a combination of such offenses * * *.

18 U.S.C.A. § 3142(f). A hearing is also to be held:

> (2) upon motion of the attorney for the Government or upon the judicial officer's own motion, in a case that involves—

>> (A) a serious risk that the person will flee; or

>> (B) a serious risk that the person will obstruct or attempt to obstruct justice, or threaten, injure, or intimidate, or attempted to threaten, injure, or intimidate a prospective witness or juror.

18 U.S.C.A. § 3142(f). The hearing is to be held immediately upon the person's first appearance before the judicial officer unless a continuance is

sought. Except for good cause, a continuance granted at the request of the defendant cannot exceed five days and a continuance granted at the request of the Government cannot exceed three days. 18 U.S.C.A. § 3142(f).

Procedure At Detention Hearing. With regard to the procedural details of the hearing, the statute provides:

> At the hearing, the person has the right to be represented by counsel, and, if he is financially unable to obtain adequate representation, to have counsel appointed. The person shall be afforded an opportunity to testify, to present witnesses, to cross-examine witnesses who appear at the hearing, and to present information by proffer or otherwise. The rules concerning admissibility of evidence in criminal trials do not apply to the presentation and consideration of information at the hearing. The facts that the judicial officer uses to support a finding * * * that no condition or combination of conditions will reasonably assure the safety of any other person and the community shall be supported by clear and convincing evidence. The person may be detained pending completion of the hearing.

18 U.S.C.A. § 3142(f).

Making of the Detention Decision. In determining whether there are conditions of release that will assure the defendant's appearance and the safety of others and the community, the judicial officer is to take into account available information concerning:

> (1) the nature and circumstances of the offense charged, including whether the offense is a crime of violence or involves a narcotic drug;
>
> (2) the weight of the evidence against the person;
>
> (3) the history and characteristics of the person, including—
>
>> (A) the person's character, physical and mental condition, family ties, employment, financial resources, length of residence in the community, community ties, past conduct, history relating to drug or alcohol abuse, criminal history, and record concerning appearance at court proceedings; and
>>
>> (B) whether, at the time of the current offense or arrest, the person was on probation, or parole, or on other release pending trial, sentencing, appeal, or completion of sentence for an offense under Federal, State, or local law; and
>
> (4) the nature and seriousness of the danger to any person or the community that would be posed by the person's release. In considering the conditions of release * * *, the judicial officer may upon his own motion, or shall upon the motion of the Government, conduct an inquiry into the source of the property to be designated for potential forfeiture or offered as collateral to secure a bond, and shall decline to accept the designation, or the use as collateral, of property that, because of its source, will not reasonably assure the appearance of the person as required.

18 U.S.C.A. § 3142(g).

Presumptions. The making of the detention decision is aided by certain presumptions. In those situations identified above as ones in which a detention hearing is to be held on motion of the Government, 18 U.S.C.A. § 3142(f)(1), a rebuttable presumption arises that no conditions will assure the safety of others and the community if the judge finds:

(1) the person has been convicted of a Federal offense that is described in subsection (f)(1) of this section, or of a State or local offense that would have been an offense described in subsection (f)(1) of this section if a circumstance giving rise to Federal jurisdiction had existed;

(2) the offense described in paragraph (1) of this subsection was committed while the person was on release pending trial for a Federal, State, or local offense; and

(3) a period of not more than five years has elapsed since the date of conviction, or the release of the person from imprisonment, for the offense described in paragraph (1) of this subsection, whichever is later.

In addition, the statute provides further:

Subject to rebuttal by the person, it shall be presumed that no condition or combination of conditions will reasonably assure the appearance of the person as required and the safety of the community if the judicial officer finds that there is probable cause to believe that the person committed an offense for which a maximum term of imprisonment of ten years or more is prescribed in the Controlled Substances Act * * *, the Controlled Substances Import and Export Act * * *, the Maritime Drug Law Enforcement Act * * * or [uses a firearm during specified felonies, conspires to commit certain offenses outside the United States or commits certain acts of terrorism].

18 U.S.C.A. § 3142(e).

Terms of Detention Order. In a detention order, the judicial officer is directed to:

(1) include written findings of fact and a written statement of the reasons for the detention;

(2) direct that the person be committed to the custody of the Attorney General for confinement in a corrections facility separate, to the extent practicable, from persons awaiting or serving sentences or being held in custody pending appeal;

(3) direct that the person be afforded reasonable opportunity for private consultation with counsel; and

(4) direct that, on order of a court of the United States or on request of an attorney for the Government, the person in charge of the corrections facility in which the person is confined deliver the person to a United States marshal for the purpose of an appearance in connection with a court proceeding.

In addition, the statute provides:

The judicial officer may, by subsequent order, permit the temporary release of the person, in the custody of a United States marshal or another appropriate person, to the extent that the judicial officer determines such release to be necessary for the preparation of the person's defense or for another compelling reason.

18 U.S.C.A. § 3142(i).

Review. If a detention order is issued by a magistrate, the defendant may secure review of this by the judge. Review is obtained by filing with the court a motion for revocation or amendment of the order. 18 U.S.C.A. § 3145(b). On the other hand, if a magistrate orders a defendant released, an attorney for the Government may obtain review of this decision by filing with the court a motion for revocation of the order. 18 U.S.C.A. § 3145(a)(1).

Appellate review is also available. A detained defendant may take an interlocutory appeal to the appropriate Court of Appeals from a detention order or a decision denying revocation of a detention order. 18 U.S.C.A. § 3145(c). The Government is also entitled to appeal from an order releasing a defendant or a decision denying a motion to revoke an order granting release. 18 U.S.C.A. §§ 3145(c), 3731.

Bail Reform Act of 1984: Detention Upon Violation of Release Conditions

In contrast with those provisions authorizing preventive detention of a defendant as an initial matter, other provisions of the federal statute address the consequences of a showing that the defendant violated the conditions of a pretrial release. An attorney for the Government may initiate the process by filing a motion with the district court. A warrant may then be issued for the person's arrest and the person is to be brought before a judicial officer. If the officer finds that there are conditions of release that will assure that the person will not flee and will not be dangerous to others or to the community and that the person will abide by these conditions, the officer can again release the defendant and is authorized to amend the conditions of release to impose any additional conditions regarded as necessary.

On the other hand, the appearance may also result in the revocation of release and the person's pretrial detention:

The judicial officer shall enter an order of revocation and detention if, after a hearing, the judicial officer—

(1) finds that there is—

(A) probable cause to believe that the person has committed a Federal, State, or local crime while on release; or

(B) clear and convincing evidence that the person has violated any other condition of his release; and

(2) finds that—

(A) based on the factors set forth in section 3142(g) [discussed above], there is no condition or combination of conditions of release that will assure that the person will not flee or pose a danger to the safety of any other person or the community; or

>   (B) the person is unlikely to abide by any condition or combination of conditions of release.

Again, the judicial officer's task is aided by a presumption:

>   If there is probable cause to believe that, while on release, the person committed a Federal, State, or local felony, a rebuttable presumption arises that no condition or combination of conditions will assure that the person will not pose a danger to the safety of any other person or the community.

18 U.S.C.A. § 3148(b).

United States v. Salerno

Supreme Court of the United States, 1987.
481 U.S. 739, 107 S.Ct. 2095, 95 L.Ed.2d 697.

■ CHIEF JUSTICE REHNQUIST delivered the opinion of the Court.

The Bail Reform Act of 1984 allows a federal court to detain an arrestee pending trial if the government demonstrates by clear and convincing evidence after an adversary hearing that no release conditions "will reasonably assure * * * the safety of any other person and the community." The United States Court of Appeals for the Second Circuit struck down this provision of the Act as facially unconstitutional, because, in that court's words, this type of pretrial detention violates "substantive due process." We granted certiorari because of a conflict among the Courts of Appeals regarding the validity of the Act. We hold that, as against the facial attack mounted by these respondents, the Act fully comports with constitutional requirements. We therefore reverse.

I

Responding to "the alarming problem of crimes committed by persons on release," S.Rep. No. 98–225, p. 3 (1983), U.S.Code Cong. & Admin.News 1984, pp. 3182, 3185, Congress formulated the Bail Reform Act of 1984, 18 U.S.C. § 3141 et seq. (1982 ed., Supp. III), as the solution to a bail crisis in the federal courts. The Act represents the National Legislature's considered response to numerous perceived deficiencies in the federal bail process. By providing for sweeping changes in both the way federal courts consider bail applications and the circumstances under which bail is granted, Congress hoped to "give the courts adequate authority to make release decisions that give appropriate recognition to the danger a person may pose to others if released." S.Rep. No. 98–225, p. 3, U.S.Code Cong. & Admin.News 1984, p. 3185.

To this end, § 3141(a) of the Act requires a judicial officer to determine whether an arrestee shall be detained. Section 3142(e) provides that "[i]f, after a hearing pursuant to the provisions of subsection (f), the judicial officer finds that no condition or combination of conditions will reasonably assure the appearance of the person as required and the safety of any other person and the community, he shall order the detention of the person prior to trial." Section 3142(f) provides the arrestee with a number of procedural safeguards. He may request the presence of counsel at the detention hearing, he may testify and present witnesses in his behalf, as well as proffer evidence, and he may cross-examine other witnesses appearing at the hearing. If the judicial officer finds that no conditions of pretrial release can reasonably assure the safety of other persons and the community, he must state his findings of fact in writing, § 3142(i), and support his conclusion with "clear and convincing evidence," § 3142(f).

The judicial officer is not given unbridled discretion in making the detention determination. Congress has specified the considerations relevant to that decision. These factors include the nature and seriousness of the charges, the substantiality of the government's evidence against the arrestee, the arrestee's background and characteristics, and the nature and seriousness of the danger posed by the suspect's release, § 3142(g). Should a judicial officer order detention, the detainee is entitled to expedited appellate review of the detention order. §§ 3145(b), (c).

Respondents Anthony Salerno and Vincent Cafaro were arrested on March 21, 1986, after being charged in a 29–count indictment alleging various Racketeer Influenced and Corrupt Organizations Act (RICO) violations, mail and wire fraud offenses, extortion, and various criminal gambling violations. The RICO counts alleged 35 acts of racketeering activity, including fraud, extortion, gambling, and conspiracy to commit murder. At respondents' arraignment, the Government moved to have Salerno and Cafaro detained pursuant to § 3142(e), on the ground that no condition of release would assure the safety of the community or any person. The District Court held a hearing at which the Government made a detailed proffer of evidence. The Government's case showed that Salerno was the "boss" of the Genovese Crime Family of La Cosa Nostra and that Cafaro was a "captain" in the Genovese Family. According to the Government's proffer, based in large part on conversations intercepted by a court-ordered wiretap, the two respondents had participated in wide-ranging conspiracies to aid their illegitimate enterprises through violent means. The Government also offered the testimony of two of its trial witnesses, who would assert that Salerno personally participated in two murder conspiracies. Salerno opposed the motion for detention, challenging the credibility of the Government's witnesses. He offered the testimony of several character witnesses as well as a letter from his doctor stating that he was suffering from a serious medical condition. Cafaro presented no evidence at the hearing, but instead characterized the wiretap conversations as merely "tough talk."

The District Court granted the Government's detention motion, concluding that the Government had established by clear and convincing evidence that no condition or combination of conditions of release would ensure the safety of the community or any person:

> "The activities of a criminal organization such as the Genovese Family do not cease with the arrest of its principals and their release on even the most stringent of bail conditions. The illegal businesses, in place for many years, require constant attention and protection, or they will fail. Under these circumstances, this court recognizes a strong

incentive on the part of its leadership to continue business as usual. When business as usual involves threats, beatings, and murder, the present danger such people pose in the community is self-evident." 631 F.Supp. 1364, 1375 (S.D.N.Y.1986).

Respondents appealed, contending that to the extent that the Bail Reform Act permits pretrial detention on the ground that the arrestee is likely to commit future crimes, it is unconstitutional on its face. Over a dissent, the United States Court of Appeals for the Second Circuit agreed. 794 F.2d 64 (1986). Although the court agreed that pretrial detention could be imposed if the defendants were likely to intimidate witnesses or otherwise jeopardize the trial process, it found "§ 3142(e)'s authorization of pretrial detention [on the ground of future dangerousness] repugnant to the concept of substantive due process, which we believe prohibits the total deprivation of liberty simply as a means of preventing future crimes." Id., at 71–72. The court concluded that the Government could not, consistent with due process, detain persons who had not been accused of any crime merely because they were thought to present a danger to the community. Id., at 72, quoting United States v. Melendez–Carrion, 790 F.2d 984, 1000–1001 (C.A.2 1986) (opinion of Newman, J.). It reasoned that our criminal law system holds persons accountable for past actions, not anticipated future actions. Although a court could detain an arrestee who threatened to flee before trial, such detention would be permissible because it would serve the basic objective of a criminal system—bringing the accused to trial. The court distinguished our decision in Gerstein v. Pugh, 420 U.S. 103, 95 S.Ct. 854, 43 L.Ed.2d 54 (1975), in which we upheld police detention pursuant to arrest. The court construed Gerstein as limiting such detention to the " 'administrative steps incident to arrest.' " 794 F.2d, at 74, quoting Gerstein, 420 U.S., at 114, 95 S.Ct. at 863. The Court of Appeals also found our decision in Schall v. Martin, 467 U.S. 253, 104 S.Ct. 2403, 81 L.Ed.2d 207 (1984), upholding postarrest pretrial detention of juveniles, inapposite because juveniles have a lesser interest in liberty than do adults. The dissenting judge concluded that on its face, the Bail Reform Act adequately balanced the Federal Government's compelling interests in public safety against the detainee's liberty interests.

II

A facial challenge to a legislative Act is, of course, the most difficult challenge to mount successfully, since the challenger must establish that no set of circumstances exists under which the Act would be valid. The fact that the Bail Reform Act might operate unconstitutionally under some conceivable set of circumstances is insufficient to render it wholly invalid, since we have not recognized an "overbreadth" doctrine outside the limited context of the First Amendment. We think respondents have failed to shoulder their heavy burden to demonstrate that the Act is "facially" unconstitutional.

Respondents present two grounds for invalidating the Bail Reform Act's provisions permitting pretrial detention on the basis of future dangerousness. First, they rely upon the Court of Appeals' conclusion that the Act exceeds the limitations placed upon the Federal Government by the Due

Process Clause of the Fifth Amendment. Second, they contend that the Act contravenes the Eighth Amendment's proscription against excessive bail. We treat these contentions in turn.

A

The Due Process Clause of the Fifth Amendment provides that "No person shall * * * be deprived of life, liberty, or property, without due process of law. * * * "This Court has held that the Due Process Clause protects individuals against two types of government action. So-called "substantive due process" prevents the government from engaging in conduct that "shocks the conscience." Rochin v. California, 342 U.S. 165, 172, 72 S.Ct. 205, 209, 96 L.Ed. 183 (1952), or interferes with rights "implicit in the concept of ordered liberty," Palko v. Connecticut, 302 U.S. 319, 325–326, 58 S.Ct. 149, 152, 82 L.Ed. 288 (1937). When government action depriving a person of life, liberty, or property survives substantive due process scrutiny, it must still be implemented in a fair manner. Mathews v. Eldridge, 424 U.S. 319, 335, 96 S.Ct. 893, 903, 47 L.Ed.2d 18 (1976). This requirement has traditionally been referred to as "procedural" due process.

Respondents first argue that the Act violates substantive due process because the pretrial detention it authorizes constitutes impermissible punishment before trial. See Bell v. Wolfish, 441 U.S. 520, 535, and n. 16, 99 S.Ct. 1861, 1872, and n. 16, 60 L.Ed.2d 447 (1979). The Government, however, has never argued that pretrial detention could be upheld if it were "punishment." The Court of Appeals assumed that pretrial detention under the Bail Reform Act is regulatory, not penal, and we agree that it is.

As an initial matter, the mere fact that a person is detained does not inexorably lead to the conclusion that the government has imposed punishment. To determine whether a restriction on liberty constitutes impermissible punishment or permissible regulation, we first look to legislative intent. Schall v. Martin, 467 U.S., at 269, 104 S.Ct., at 2412. Unless Congress expressly intended to impose punitive restrictions, the punitive/regulatory distinction turns on " 'whether an alternative purpose to which [the restriction] may rationally be connected is assignable for it, and whether it appears excessive in relation to the alternative purpose assigned [to it].' "Ibid., quoting Kennedy v. Mendoza–Martinez, 372 U.S. 144, 168–169, 83 S.Ct. 554, 567–568, 9 L.Ed.2d 644 (1963).

We conclude that the detention imposed by the Act falls on the regulatory side of the dichotomy. The legislative history of the Bail Reform Act clearly indicates that Congress did not formulate the pretrial detention provisions as punishment for dangerous individuals. Congress instead perceived pretrial detention as a potential solution to a pressing societal problem. There is no doubt that preventing danger to the community is a legitimate regulatory goal.

Nor are the incidents of pretrial detention excessive in relation to the regulatory goal Congress sought to achieve. The Bail Reform Act carefully limits the circumstances under which detention may be sought to the most serious of crimes. See 18 U.S.C. § 3142(f) (detention hearings available if case involves crimes of violence, offenses for which the sentence is life imprisonment or death, serious drug offenses, or certain repeat offenders). The arrestee is entitled to a prompt detention hearing, ibid. and the maximum length of pretrial detention is limited by the stringent time limitations of the Speedy Trial Act.[2] See 18 U.S.C. § 3161 et seq. (1982 ed. and Supp. III). Moreover, as in Schall v. Martin, the conditions of confinement envisioned by the Act "appear to reflect the regulatory purposes relied upon by the government". 467 U.S., at 270, 104 S.Ct., at 2413. As in Schall, the statute at issue here requires that detainees be housed in a "facility separate, to the extent practicable, from persons awaiting or serving sentences or being held in custody pending appeal." 18 U.S.C. § 3142(i)(2). We conclude, therefore, that the pretrial detention contemplated by the Bail Reform Act is regulatory in nature, and does not constitute punishment before trial in violation of the Due Process Clause.

The Court of Appeals nevertheless concluded that "the Due Process Clause prohibits pretrial detention on the ground of danger to the community as a regulatory measure, without regard to the duration of the detention." 794 F.2d, at 71. Respondents characterize the Due Process Clause as erecting an impenetrable "wall" in this area that "no governmental interest—rational, important, compelling or otherwise—may surmount."

We do not think the Clause lays down any such categorical imperative. We have repeatedly held that the government's regulatory interest in community safety can, in appropriate circumstances, outweigh an individual's liberty interest. For example, in times of war or insurrection, when society's interest is at its peak, the government may detain individuals whom the government believes to be dangerous. See Ludecke v. Watkins, 335 U.S. 160, 68 S.Ct. 1429, 92 L.Ed. 1881 (1948) (approving unreviewable Executive power to detain enemy aliens in time of war); Moyer v. Peabody, 212 U.S. 78, 84–85, 29 S.Ct. 235, 236–237, 53 L.Ed. 410 (1909) (rejecting due process claim of individual jailed without probable cause by Governor in time of insurrection). Even outside the exigencies of war, we have found that sufficiently compelling governmental interests can justify detention of dangerous persons. Thus, we have found no absolute constitutional barrier to detention of potentially dangerous resident aliens pending deportation proceedings. Carlson v. Landon, 342 U.S. 524, 537–542, 72 S.Ct. 525, 532–535, 96 L.Ed. 547 (1952); Wong Wing v. United States, 163 U.S. 228, 16 S.Ct. 977, 41 L.Ed. 140 (1896). We have also held that the government may detain mentally unstable individuals who present a danger to the public, Addington v. Texas, 441 U.S. 418, 99 S.Ct. 1804, 60 L.Ed.2d 323 (1979), and dangerous defendants who become incompetent to stand trial, Jackson v. Indiana, 406 U.S. 715, 731–739, 92 S.Ct. 1845, 1854–1858, 32 L.Ed.2d 435 (1972); Greenwood v. United States, 350 U.S. 366, 76 S.Ct. 410, 100 L.Ed. 412 (1956). We have approved of postarrest regulatory detention of juveniles when they present a continuing danger to the community. *Schall v. Martin*, supra. Even competent adults may face substantial liberty restrictions as a result of the operation of our criminal justice system. If the

---

2. We intimate no view as to the point at which detention in a particular case might become excessively prolonged, and therefore punitive, in relation to Congress' regulatory goal.

police suspect an individual of a crime, they may arrest and hold him until a neutral magistrate determines whether probable cause exists. Gerstein v. Pugh, 420 U.S. 103, 95 S.Ct. 854, 43 L.Ed.2d 54 (1975). Finally, respondents concede and the Court of Appeals noted that an arrestee may be incarcerated until trial if he presents a risk of flight, see Bell v. Wolfish, 441 U.S., at 534, 99 S.Ct., at 1871, or a danger to witnesses.

Respondents characterize all of these cases as exceptions to the "general rule" of substantive due process that the government may not detain a person prior to a judgment of guilt in a criminal trial. Such a "general rule" may freely be conceded, but we think that these cases show a sufficient number of exceptions to the rule that the congressional action challenged here can hardly be characterized as totally novel. Given the well-established authority of the government, in special circumstances, to restrain individuals' liberty prior to or even without criminal trial and conviction, we think that the present statute providing for pretrial detention on the basis of dangerousness must be evaluated in precisely the same manner that we evaluated the laws in the cases discussed above.

The government's interest in preventing crime by arrestees is both legitimate and compelling. In *Schall*, supra, we recognized the strength of the State's interest in preventing juvenile crime. This general concern with crime prevention is no less compelling when the suspects are adults. Indeed, "[t]he harm suffered by the victim of a crime is not dependent upon the age of the perpetrator." Schall v. Martin, 467 U.S., at 264–265, 104 S.Ct., at 2410. The Bail Reform Act of 1984 responds to an even more particularized governmental interest than the interest we sustained in *Schall*. The statute we upheld in *Schall* permitted pretrial detention of any juvenile arrested on any charge after a showing that the individual might commit some undefined further crimes. The Bail Reform Act, in contrast, narrowly focuses on a particularly acute problem in which the government interests are overwhelming. The Act operates only on individuals who have been arrested for a specific category of extremely serious offenses. 18 U.S.C. § 3142(f). Congress specifically found that these individuals are far more likely to be responsible for dangerous acts in the community after arrest. See S.Rep. No. 98–225, pp. 6–7. Nor is the Act by any means a scattershot attempt to incapacitate those who are merely suspected of these serious crimes. The government must first of all demonstrate probable cause to believe that the charged crime has been committed by the arrestee, but that is not enough. In a full-blown adversary hearing, the government must convince a neutral decisionmaker by clear and convincing evidence that no conditions of release can reasonably assure the safety of the community or any person. 18 U.S.C. § 3142(f). While the government's general interest in preventing crime is compelling, even this interest is heightened when the government musters convincing proof that the arrestee, already indicted or held to answer for a serious crime, presents a demonstrable danger to the community. Under these narrow circumstances, society's interest in crime prevention is at its greatest.

On the other side of the scale, of course, is the individual's strong interest in liberty. We do not minimize the importance and fundamental nature of this right. But, as our cases hold, this right may, in circumstances where the government's interest is sufficiently weighty, be subordinated to the greater needs of society. We think that Congress' careful delineation of the circumstances under which detention will be permitted satisfies this standard. When the government proves by clear and convincing evidence that an arrestee presents an identified and articulable threat to an individual or the community, we believe that, consistent with the Due Process Clause, a court may disable the arrestee from executing that threat. Under these circumstances, we cannot categorically state that pretrial detention "offends some principle of justice so rooted in the traditions and conscience of our people as to be ranked as fundamental." Snyder v. Massachusetts, 291 U.S. 97, 105, 54 S.Ct. 330, 332, 78 L.Ed. 674 (1934).

Finally, we may dispose briefly of respondents' facial challenge to the procedures of the Bail Reform Act. To sustain them against such a challenge, we need only find them "adequate to authorize the pretrial detention of at least some [persons] charged with crimes." Schall, supra, 467 U.S., at 264, 104 S.Ct., at 2409, whether or not they might be insufficient in some particular circumstances. We think they pass that test. As we stated in Schall, "there is nothing inherently unattainable about a prediction of future criminal conduct." Id., at 278, 104 S.Ct., at 2417; see Jurek v. Texas, 428 U.S. 262, 274, 96 S.Ct. 2950, 2957, 49 L.Ed.2d 929 (1976) (opinion of STEWART, POWELL, and STEVENS, JJ.); id., at 279, 96 S.Ct., at 2959–2960 (WHITE, J., concurring in judgment).

Under the Bail Reform Act, the procedures by which a judicial officer evaluates the likelihood of future dangerousness are specifically designed to further the accuracy of that determination. Detainees have a right to counsel at the detention hearing, 18 U.S.C. § 3142(f). They may testify in their own behalf, present information by proffer or otherwise, and cross-examine witnesses who appear at the hearing. Ibid. The judicial officer charged with the responsibility of determining the appropriateness of detention is guided by statutorily enumerated factors, which include the nature and the circumstances of the charges, the weight of the evidence, the history and characteristics of the putative offender, and the danger of the community, § 3142(g). The government must prove its case by clear and convincing evidence, § 3142(f). Finally, the judicial officer must include written findings of fact and a written statement of reasons for a decision to detain, § 3142(i). The Act's review provisions, § 3145(c), provide for immediate appellate review of the detention decision.

We think these extensive safeguards suffice to repel a facial challenge. The protections are more exacting than those we found sufficient in the juvenile context, see Schall, 467 U.S., at 275–281, 104 S.Ct., at 2415–2418, and they far exceed what we found necessary to effect limited postarrest detention in Gerstein v. Pugh, 420 U.S. 103, 95 S.Ct. 854, 43 L.Ed.2d 54 (1975). Given the legitimate and compelling regulatory purpose of the Act and the procedural protections it offers, we conclude that the Act is not facially invalid under the Due Process Clause of the Fifth Amendment.

B

Respondents also contend that the Bail Reform Act violates the Excessive Bail Clause of the Eighth Amendment. The Court of Appeals did not address this issue because it found that the Act violates the Due Process Clause. We think that the Act survives a challenge founded upon the Eighth Amendment.

The Eighth Amendment addresses pretrial release by providing merely that "Excessive bail shall not be required." This Clause, of course, says nothing about whether bail shall be available at all. Respondents nevertheless contend that this Clause grants them a right to bail calculated solely upon considerations of flight. They rely on Stack v. Boyle, 342 U.S. 1, 5, 72 S.Ct. 1, 3, 96 L.Ed. 3 (1951), in which the Court stated that "Bail set at a figure higher than an amount reasonably calculated [to ensure the defendant's presence at trial] is 'excessive' under the Eighth Amendment." In respondents' view, since the Bail Reform Act allows a court essentially to set bail at an infinite amount for reasons not related to the risk of flight, it violates the Excessive Bail Clause. Respondents concede that the right to bail they have discovered in the Eighth Amendment is not absolute. A court may, for example, refuse bail in capital cases. And, as the Court of Appeals noted and respondents admit, a court may refuse bail when the defendant presents a threat to the judicial process by intimidating witnesses. Brief for Respondents 21–22. Respondents characterize these exceptions as consistent with what they claim to be the sole purpose of bail—to ensure integrity of the judicial process.

While we agree that a primary function of bail is to safeguard the courts' role in adjudicating the guilt or innocence of defendants, we reject the proposition that the Eighth Amendment categorically prohibits the government from pursuing other admittedly compelling interests through regulation of pretrial release. The above quoted dicta in *Stack v. Boyle* is far too slender a reed on which to rest this argument. The Court in *Stack* had no occasion to consider whether the Excessive Bail Clause requires courts to admit all defendants to bail, because the statute before the Court in that case in fact allowed the defendants to be bailed. Thus, the Court had to determine only whether bail, admittedly available in that case, was excessive if set at a sum greater than that necessary to ensure the arrestees' presence at trial.

The holding of *Stack* is illuminated by the Court's holding just four months later in Carlson v. Landon, 342 U.S. 524, 72 S.Ct. 525, 96 L.Ed. 547 (1952). In that case, remarkably similar to the present action, the detainees had been arrested and held without bail pending a determination of deportability. The Attorney General refused to release the individuals, "on the ground that there was reasonable cause to believe that [their] release would be prejudicial to the public interest and *would endanger the welfare and safety of the United States.*" Id., at 529, 72 S.Ct., at 528–529 (emphasis added). The detainees brought the same challenge that respondents bring to us today: the Eighth Amendment required them to be admitted to bail. The Court squarely rejected this proposition:

"The bail clause was lifted with slight changes from the English Bill of Rights Act. In England that clause has never been thought to accord a right to bail in all cases, but merely to provide that bail shall not be excessive in those cases where it is proper to grant bail. When this clause was carried over into our Bill of Rights, nothing was said that indicated any different concept. The Eighth Amendment has not prevented Congress from defining the classes of cases in which bail shall be allowed in this country. Thus, in criminal cases bail is not compulsory where the punishment may be death. Indeed, the very language of the Amendment fails to say all arrests must be bailable." Id., at 545–546, 72 S.Ct., at 536–537 (footnotes omitted).

Carlson v. Landon was a civil case, and we need not decide today whether the Excessive Bail Clause speaks at all to Congress' power to define the classes of criminal arrestees who shall be admitted to bail. For even if we were to conclude that the Eighth Amendment imposes some substantive limitations on the National Legislature's powers in this area, we would still hold that the Bail Reform Act is valid. Nothing in the text of the Bail Clause limits permissible government considerations solely to questions of flight. The only arguable substantive limitation of the Bail Clause is that the government's proposed conditions of release or detention not be "excessive" in light of the perceived evil. Of course, to determine whether the government's response is excessive, we must compare that response against the interest the government seeks to protect by means of that response. Thus, when the government has admitted that its only interest is in preventing flight, bail must be set by a court at a sum designed to ensure that goal, and no more. *Stack v. Boyle,* supra. We believe that when Congress has mandated detention on the basis of a compelling interest other than prevention of flight, as it has here, the Eighth Amendment does not require release on bail.

III

In our society liberty is the norm, and detention prior to trial or without trial is the carefully limited exception. We hold that the provisions for pretrial detention in the Bail Reform Act of 1984 fall within that carefully limited exception. The Act authorizes the detention prior to trial of arrestees charged with serious felonies who are found after an adversary hearing to pose a threat to the safety of individuals or to the community which no condition of release can dispel. The numerous procedural safeguards detailed above must attend this adversary hearing. We are unwilling to say that this congressional determination, based as it is upon that primary concern of every government—a concern for the safety and indeed the lives of its citizens—on its face violates either the Due Process Clause of the Fifth Amendment or the Excessive Bail Clause of the Eighth Amendment.

The judgment of the Court of Appeals is therefore

Reversed.

■ JUSTICE MARSHALL, with whom JUSTICE BRENNAN joins, dissenting [omitted].

■ JUSTICE STEVENS, dissenting [omitted].

NOTES

1. **Applying the 8th Amendment to the States.** In Hunt v. Roth, 648 F.2d 1148 (8th Cir.1981), vacated as moot sub nom. Murphy v. Hunt, 455 U.S. 478, 102

S.Ct. 1181, 71 L.Ed.2d 353 (1982), Hunt had been charged in the Nebraska courts with forcible sexual assault as well as several other nonsexual felonies. He was denied bail under Article 1, Section 9 of the Nebraska Constitution, which provides for denial of bail to persons charged with "sexual offenses involving penetration by force or against the will of the victim, * * * where the proof is evident or the presumption great." He sought habeas corpus and declaratory relief in federal court on the ground that his pretrial detention violated his federal constitutional rights. The district court dismissed his claims but, on appeal, the Eighth Circuit reversed the dismissal of his claim for declaratory relief.

First, the Court of Appeals noted the absence of definitive authority as to whether the Eighth Amendment prohibition against excessive bail is incorporated into the Fourteenth Amendment and thus binding on the states. Noting that bail is basic to America's system of laws and related to the presumption of innocence, the court held that the excessive bail clause is incorporated into the Fourteenth Amendment. 648 F.2d at 1155–56. Second, it rejected the argument that the excessive bail clause does not address when pretrial release may be denied altogether:

> If the eighth amendment has any meaning beyond sheer rhetoric, the constitutional prohibition against excessive bail necessarily implies that unreasonable denial of bail is likewise prohibited. Logic defies any other resolution of the question.

Id. at 1157. Finally, testing the Nebraska provision under this approach, it concluded that the state constitutional section violated the eighth amendment:

> Under the challenged state procedures, bail *must* be denied to every person charged with "sexual offenses involving penetration by force or against the will of the victim" where the "proof is evident or the presumption great." Once the charge is made and it is determined that the proof is evident, no other relevant factor is weighed and no standards relevant to the purpose of assuring the presence of the defendant are considered. No discretion is vested in any judicial officer to grant or to deny bail. * * * [T]here exists a strong argument that bail may be denied without encroaching on constitutional concerns where a judicial officer weighs all the appropriate factors and makes a reasoned judgment that the defendant's past record demonstrates that bail will not reasonably assure his or her appearance or, arguendo, that he or she, because of the overall record and circumstances, poses a threat to the community. The fatal flaw in the Nebraska constitutional amendment is that the state has created an irrebuttable presumption that every individual charged with this particular offense is incapable of assuring his appearance by conditioning it upon reasonable bail or is too dangerous to be granted release. The constitutional protections involved are too fundamental to foreclose by arbitrary state decree. The state may be free to consider the nature of the charge and the degree of proof in granting or denying bail but it cannot give these factors conclusive force. * * *

Id. at 1162–65. (emphasis added) The Supreme Court, however, found that Hunt's conviction mooted his challenge to denial of pretrial bail and vacated the judgment of the Court of Appeals. Murphy v. Hunt, 455 U.S. 478, 102 S.Ct. 1181, 71 L.Ed.2d 353 (1982) (per curiam).

2. **Remedy for violation of the requirement of a prompt detention hearing.** The respondent in United States v. Montalvo–Murillo, 495 U.S. 711, 110 S.Ct. 2072, 109 L.Ed.2d 720 (1990) was arrested on federal drug violations. He was not provided a detention hearing at his first judicial appearance as required by 18 U.S.C.A. § 3142(f). The District Court and Court of Appeals took the position that although respondent should be detained under statutory criteria, he was required to be released because of the failure to comply with the requirement of a prompt

hearing. Respondent was released, fled and was at large at the time of the Supreme Court's decision. The Supreme Court reversed in an opinion by Justice Kennedy. The statute does not require release as a remedy for failure to hold a detention hearing in a timely fashion.

> We find nothing in the statute to justify denying the Government an opportunity to prove that the person is dangerous or a risk of flight once the statutory time for hearing has passed. We do not agree that we should, or can, invent a remedy to satisfy some perceived need to coerce the courts and the Government into complying with the statutory time limits. Magistrates and district judges can be presumed to insist upon compliance with the law without the threat that we must embarrass the system by releasing a suspect certain to flee from justice, as this one did in such a deft and prompt manner. The district court, the court of appeals, and this Court remain open to order immediate release of anyone detained in violation of the statute. Whatever other remedies may exist for detention without a timely hearing or for conduct that is aggravated or intentional, a matter not before us here, we hold that once the Government discovers that the time limits have expired, it may ask for a prompt detention hearing and make its case to detain based upon the requirements set forth in the statute.

495 U.S. at 721, 110 S.Ct. at 2079, 109 L.Ed.2d at 732. Justice Stevens, joined by Justices Brennan and Marshall, dissented.

United States v. Jessup

United States Court of Appeals, First Circuit, 1985.
757 F.2d 378.

■ BREYER, CIRCUIT JUDGE.

This appeal challenges the constitutionality of a provision of the Bail Reform Act of 1984, 18 U.S.C. § 3141 et seq., that requires judicial officers making bail decisions to apply a rebuttable presumption that one charged with a serious drug offense will likely flee before trial. 18 U.S.C. § 3142(e). We find that Congress has acted within the Constitution's prescribed limits in creating this rebuttable presumption and that the magistrate and district court have acted within their lawful authority in applying it, and related statutory provisions, to the appellant Mark Jessup. We affirm the district court's decision to deny him bail and to hold him in custody pending his trial.

I

The Bail Reform Act of 1984 ("the Act") makes it, in one respect, harder and, in another respect, easier for judicial officers to order pretrial detention of those accused of crimes. It makes it harder by specifying explicitly what was implicit in prior law, namely that magistrates and judges cannot impose any "financial condition" that will result in detention. § 3142(c). High money bail cannot be used as a device to keep a defendant in custody before trial. The Act makes detention easier by broadening the category of persons whom the officer can order detained. And, the Act specifies that a judicial officer shall order detention if he finds that no condition or combination of conditions [attaching to release] will reasonably assure the appearance of the person as required and the safety of any other person and the community * * *. § 3142(e). The Act sets forth procedures to be used in applying this standard. It provides a list of factors that the officer is to weigh when doing so § 3142(g); and it creates several "rebuttable presumptions" that the officer is to use when applying the basic standard.

This case concerns one of the "rebuttable presumptions" that the Act creates. It states

Subject to rebuttal by the person, it shall be presumed that no condition or combination of conditions will reasonably assure the appearance of the person as required and the safety of the community if the judicial officer finds that there is probable cause to believe that the person committed an offense for which a maximum term of imprisonment of ten years or more is prescribed in the Controlled Substances Act (21 U.S.C. 801 et seq.) * * *.

§ 3142(e).

The magistrate here used the presumption in deciding to detain appellant Jessup. The magistrate found that Jessup posed a threat to the safety of the community in that, if released, he might continue to commit crimes. The magistrate also found that, if released, there was a substantial risk that Jessup would flee. In particular, the magistrate stated

I am equally of the view that the defendant has not rebutted the presumption that no nonfinancial conditions or combination of nonfinancial conditions of release would reasonably assure his presence. The defendant is charged with a serious crime and the Government's evidence is strong. The defendant has been in this state for only two years; he has no family or relatives living here. In all the circumstances, I do not believe the fact that the defendant is engaged to a Massachusetts resident would deter him from fleeing the jurisdiction in view of the seriousness of the crime charged and the strength of the evidence against him.

Given this alternative basis for the magistrate's decision, we need not consider the Act's "dangerousness" provisions or the magistrate's "dangerousness" finding. It is well established that the government can keep a defendant in custody to secure his presence at trial. See Stack v. Boyle, 342 U.S. 1, 4, 72 S.Ct. 1, 3, 96 L.Ed. 3 (1951) ("The right to release before trial is conditioned upon the accused's giving adequate assurance that he will stand trial and submit to sentence if found guilty."); United States v. Abrahams, 575 F.2d 3, 8 (1st Cir.) (holding that bail may be denied in exceptional circumstances where financial condition of release cannot reasonably assure presence of defendant at trial), cert. denied, 439 U.S. 821, 99 S.Ct. 85, 58 L.Ed.2d 112 (1978). Thus the constitutional issue presented here is whether the government can use the Act's rebuttable presumption in doing so.

II

Before turning to the constitutional question, we must first decide what the rebuttable presumption means. What kind of burden is it designed to impose upon a defendant? Or, to cast the question in terms traditionally used in the law of evidence, does it impose a "burden of persuasion" or only a "burden of production"? See generally C. McCormick, *Evidence* § 342 et seq. (2d ed. 1972). If the former, the alleged drug offender would have to *prove* he would not flee—i.e., he would have to *persuade* the judicial officer on the point. If the latter, he would only have to introduce a certain amount of evidence contrary to the presumed fact; no change in the burden of persuasion is effected. Where the burden of persuasion lies may make a practical difference to a magistrate or judge genuinely uncertain on the basis of what the parties have presented.

The United States Attorney here suggests that Congress meant the presumption to shift the burden of persuasion to the defendant. And he cites a district court case, in support of this view. In two other cases, however, it has been held that Congress did not intend to shift the burden of persuasion to the defendant but intended to impose only a burden of production. We believe the latter interpretation is correct.

Our reasons for believing that the burden of persuasion does not shift include the following. First, we are chary of interpreting ambiguous language to mandate pretrial confinement where evidence before a magistrate is indeterminate. Although pretrial confinement to prevent flight is not punishment, but rather one of various restrictions on the freedom of an accused person aimed at facilitating trial, see Bell v. Wolfish, 441 U.S. 520, 535–39, 99 S.Ct. 1861, 1871–74, 60 L.Ed.2d 447 (1979), it is still a most severe restriction requiring clear cause.

Second, the Senate Judiciary Committee Report explaining the new presumption, while arguably ambiguous, does not suggest that Congress meant to impose a burden of persuasion on the defendant. To understand the relevance of the Report's description, one must realize that § 3142(e) creates not only the drug offender presumptions already mentioned (concerning "flight" and "danger") but it also creates a rebuttable presumption that one previously convicted of having committed a crime while free on bail is sufficiently "dangerous" to warrant detention. The Report describes both of these presumptions in the same place. It says that the object of this last presumption is to shift the burden

> to the defendant *to establish a basis for concluding* that there are conditions of release sufficient to assure that he will not again engage in dangerous criminal activity pending his trial.

S.Rep. No. 225, 98th Cong., 1st Sess. 19 (1983), U.S.Code Cong. & Admin.News 1984, pp. 1, 22 (emphasis added). The position of this sentence in the Report, its language, and the nature of the language of the statutory presumption all suggest that the words "establish a basis for concluding" aptly describe the intended effect of both § 3142(e) presumptions. And, these words do not say that the burden of persuasion shifts to the defendant, nor do they imply that it is up to the defendant to persuade the judicial officer.

Third, a later section in the Act, § 3148(b), establishes another similar presumption, this time in respect to a person who is released on bail (or the equivalent) and *then* commits a crime. The Act requires that such a person be brought back before the magistrate, who will consider whether to revoke his bail and detain him. The Act tells the magistrate that, if he finds probable cause to believe the person committed another crime while on release, he is to presume (subject to rebuttal) that detention is necessary to protect the community from still further crimes. That is to say, the Act applies a rebuttable presumption of "dangerousness." In describing the presumption, the Committee Report states that

> the establishment of probable cause to believe that the defendant has committed a serious crime while on release constitutes compelling evidence that the defendant poses a danger to the community, and, once such probable cause is established, it is appropriate that the burden rest on the defendant *to come forward with evidence* indicating that this conclusion is not warranted in his case.

S.Rep., supra, at 36 (emphasis added), U.S.Code Cong. & Admin.News 1984, p. 39. This language ("come forward with evidence") is traditionally used to suggest a shift in the burden of production, not of persuasion. (Compare, for example, the language used by the congressional Conference Committee which, in preparing the Federal Rules of Evidence, noted that a

> presumption shifts to the party against whom it is directed the burden of *going forward with evidence* to meet or rebut the presumption, but it does not shift to that party the burden of persuasion on the existence of the presumed fact).

Fed.R.Evid. 301, Notes of Conference Committee (emphasis added). The Act then does not impose a burden of persuasion even upon a defendant found likely to have just committed a crime while on bail. It would be anomalous to interpret the Act as imposing such a burden on those who committed such crimes in the past or on those charged with drug offenses, since they, if anything, present less risky cases.

Fourth, an examination of a related section of the Act, § 3143, shows that Congress knew how to create a 'burden of persuasion' when it wanted to do so. Section 3143 creates a presumption that a defendant who has been convicted of a crime may not be released pending his appeal or sentencing unless he shows "by clear and convincing evidence that [he] is not likely to flee or pose a danger to the safety of any other person or the community." § 3143(a), (b). (This provision differs from the Bail Reform Act of 1966, in which even convicted defendants were presumptively entitled to the same opportunity for release on bail as defendants who had not already been convicted. See 18 U.S.C. former § 3148.) The Judiciary Committee Report notes that

> The Committee intends that in overcoming the presumption in favor of detention [in § 3143] *the burden of proof* rests with the defendant.

S.Rep., supra, at 27 (emphasis added), U.S.Code Cong. & Admin.News 1984, p. 30. Congress could have used language similar to that of § 3143, or Report language similar to that just quoted, if it had intended § 3142(e) to impose a similar burden of persuasion. The absence of such language, and the proximity of §§ 3142 and 3143, reinforces our conclusion that § 3142 was meant to impose only a burden of production.

The government's strongest argument to the contrary rests upon two propositions:

> (a) Congress did not intend to create a set of presumptions with little or no practical effect; and

> (b) a 'burden of production' presumption would have little practical effect.

We agree with the first part of the argument: Congress did intend the presumption to have a practical effect. This can be seen in the Report's discussion of the § 3142(e) presumptions, which says that in the circumstances that trigger the presumption (a serious drug offense charge; past commission of a crime on bail), a *"strong probability arises* that no form of conditional release will be adequate." S.Rep., supra, at 19 (emphasis added), U.S.Code Cong. & Admin.News 1984, p. 22. In respect to the § 3148(b) presumption, the Report adds that

> the establishment of probable cause to believe that the defendant has committed a serious crime while on release constitutes *compelling evidence* that the defendant poses a danger to the community.

Id. at 36 (emphasis added), U.S.Code Cong. & Admin.News 1984, p. 39.

We do not agree, however, with the second part of the argument. It is true that, under the prevailing judicial view, a "burden of production" presumption is a "bursting bubble." See C. McCormick, *Evidence* § 345 at 821 (2d ed. 1972) ("bursting bubble" theory is "the most widely followed theory of presumptions in American law"); Legille v. Dann, 544 F.2d 1, 6 (D.C.Cir.1976) (same). Under this theory, the presumption requires the 'presumed against' party to introduce evidence, but, once he does so, the presumption "bursts" and totally disappears, allowing the judge (or jury) to decide the question without reference to the presumption. Since a defendant can always provide the magistrate with *some* reason to believe him a good risk, a "bursting bubble" approach might render the presumption virtually meaningless, contrary to Congress's clear intent.

Nonetheless, Congress does not *have* to make a "bursting bubble" of each "burden of production" presumption. We believe that here it has *not* done so; rather, it has created a "burden of production" presumption that *does* have significant practical impact. That is to say, the Report's language, together with the history of the Act (with its emphasis on the importance of the presumption), indicates to us that Congress meant to impose a "burden of production" presumption, but it did not intend to make that presumption a "bursting bubble."

We are led to this conclusion in part by the strain of legal thought which has marked out a "middle ground" for some presumptions—holding that they neither shift the burden of persuasion nor "burst" once contrary evidence is presented. See Morgan, Instructing the Jury upon Presumptions and Burdens of Proof, 47 Harv.L.Rev. 59, 82–83 (1933); 21 C. Wright & K. Graham, *Federal Practice and Procedure (Evidence)* § 5122 at 566 (noting that while courts pay "lip service" to "bursting bubble" approach, "most of them [have] felt compelled to deviate from the 'bursting bubble' theory at one time or another in order to give greater effect to presumptions"); see generally Hecht & Pinzler, Rebutting Presumptions: Order Out of Chaos, 58 B.U.L.Rev. 527 (1978). Under this view, to remove the presumption entirely from a case once conflicting evidence has been presented could undercut the legislative purpose in creating the presumption (say, an intent to have courts follow the legislature's assessment of probabilities or the furtherance of some other specific public policy). The House Judiciary Committee adopted exactly this sort of "intermediate position" in its Report on Fed.R.Evid. 301. The Committee Report said that the 'bursting bubble' approach gave presumptions "too slight an effect," and proposed a version of Fed.R.Evid. 301 under which presumptions would "not vanish upon the introduction of contradicting evidence" but would remain available "to be considered by the jury." See Fed.R.Evid. 301 and accompanying committee reports; Hearings on Proposed Rules of Evidence Before the Subcommittee on Criminal Justice of the House Comm. on the Judiciary (Supp.), 93d Cong., 1st Sess., ser. 2, at 364 (Comm.Print 1973). A number of courts have also adopted this 'middle ground' view of presumptions. See, e.g., Montgomery County Fire Board v. Fisher, 53 Md.App. 435, 454 A.2d 394, 400 (1983) (statutory presumption that firefighter's heart disease is job related "does not disappear like the bursting bubble upon generation of a jury issue; rather it remains in the case as one of the elements to be considered"); Wright v. State Accident Insurance Fund, 289 Or. 323, 613 P.2d 755, 759–60 (1980) (same presumption) ("If there is opposing evidence, the trier of fact must weigh the evidence, giving the presumption the value of evidence, and determine upon which side the evidence preponderates."); Starr v. Campos, 134 Ariz. 254, 655 P.2d 794, 796 (1982) (jury weighs blood alcohol intoxication presumption along with other evidence); Walker v. Butterworth, 599 F.2d 1074, 1078 (1st Cir.1979) (sanity presumption carries evidentiary value).

The case for a "middle ground" position is particularly strong in this setting of a detention hearing, where the procedures are informal and there is no jury. In such a setting, there is no occasion for the presumption to play its traditional practical role in the judge's decision about whether to direct a verdict (if no evidence is produced) or whether, instead, to send an issue to the jury. In a detention hearing there is no jury. Thus a "bursting bubble" approach would call on the judge (or magistrate) to consider the presumption and then, if it is met with contrary evidence, to erase the presumption from his mind—not a task that is psychologically easy to accomplish.

Moreover, here the Act's history suggests a relatively obvious way to apply this presumption along the lines of the House Judiciary Committee's "intermediate position"—giving it some weight, without shifting the burden of persuasion. Congress investigated a general problem, the problem of drug offenders and flight. After hearing evidence, Congress concluded that "flight to avoid prosecution is particularly high among persons charged with major drug offenses." S.Rep., supra, at 20, U.S.Code Cong. & Admin.News 1984, p. 23. It found that "drug traffickers often have established ties outside the United States * * * [and] have both the resources and foreign contacts to escape to other countries * * *." Id. Congress then wrote its drug offender/flight presumption. These facts suggest that Congress intended magistrates and judges, who typically focus only upon the particular cases before them, to take account of the more general facts that

Congress found. In order to "rebut" the presumption, the defendant must produce some evidence; and the magistrate or judge should then still keep in mind the fact that Congress has found that offenders, as a general rule, pose *special* risks of flight. The magistrate or judge should incorporate that fact and finding among the other special factors that Congress has told him to weigh when making his bail decision. See § 3142(g) (judicial officer shall weigh, among other things, "nature of circumstances of offense," "weight of evidence," "history and characteristics of the person including * * * character, physical and mental condition, family history * * *, past conduct * * *," and so forth). Congress did not precisely describe just how a magistrate will weigh the presumption, along with (or against) other § 3142(g) factors. But the same can be said of each of the several § 3142(g) factors. It is not unusual for Congress to instruct a magistrate or judge conscientiously to weigh several different factors without specifying precise weights for each. See, e.g., Criminal Fine Enforcement Act of 1984, 18 U.S.C. § 3622.

Finally, the most common criticism of the "intermediate position" is that it will confuse a jury; the jury will not understand how to weigh a presumption against direct evidence. See Senate Judiciary Committee Notes on Fed.R.Evid. 301; C. McCormick, *Handbook of the Law of Evidence* § 345 at 825 & n. 60 (1972). This criticism has less weight in the context of a detention hearing, where no jury is involved, and the magistrate or judge is used to the process of weighing several competing factors.

Since the presumption is but one factor among many, its continued consideration by the magistrate does not impose a burden of persuasion upon the defendant. And, since Congress seeks only consideration of the general drug offender/flight problem, the magistrate or judge may still conclude that what is true in general is not true in the particular case before him. He is free to do so, and to release the defendant, as long as the defendant has presented some evidence and the magistrate or judge has evaluated all of the evidence with Congress's view of the general problem in mind. It is worth nothing that the Act requires that all detention orders "include written findings of fact and *a written statement of the reasons for the detention.*" § 3142(i)(1) (emphasis added). Thus, the defendant is protected from a weighing of factors that is arbitrary, or not in keeping with the Act.

In sum, the congressional report language about the presumption's nature and effect, the unsuitability of a "bursting bubble" presumption in an informal, nonjury hearing, and the availability of a "middle way," lead us to reject the government's "burden of persuasion" argument. Insofar as a magistrate or judge previously shared Congress's views about the general nature of the drug offender/flight problem, use of the new presumption might not make much difference. But, insofar as the magistrate or judge did not previously share those views, the presumption will have a significant practical effect. And this, we think, is what Congress intended.

III

We turn now to Jessup's claim that use of the drug offender/flight presumption is unconstitutional because it deprives him of his "liberty

* * * without due process of law." U.S. Constitution, Amendment V. In deciding whether this presumption makes Jessup's bail procedures constitutionally unfair, we shall ask 1) whether the presumption represents a reasonable congressional response to a problem of legitimate legislative concern, and 2) whether the presumption increases the risk of an erroneous deprivation of liberty—i.e., will it likely increase the risk that magistrates will release or detain the wrong people? See Schall v. Martin, ___ U.S. ___, 104 S.Ct. 2403, 2409, 81 L.Ed.2d 207 (1984); Mathews v. Eldridge, 424 U.S. 319, 335, 96 S.Ct. 893, 903, 47 L.Ed.2d 18 (1976) (determining procedural fairness by examining private interests, governmental interests, and risk of error).

The first question must be answered, on the record before us, in the government's favor. The government's interest in securing the appearance of a defendant at trial has been held important enough to warrant pretrial detention where there is a significant risk of flight.

Moreover, Congress held hearings and heard considerable evidence that drug offenders posed a special risk of "flight." It described this evidence, and the problems revealed as follows:

> the Committee received testimony that flight to avoid prosecution is particularly high among persons charged with major drug offenses. Because of the extremely lucrative nature of drug trafficking, and the fact that drug traffickers often have established substantial ties outside the United States from whence most dangerous drugs are imported into the country, these persons have both the resources and foreign contacts to escape to other countries with relative ease in order to avoid prosecution for offenses punishable by lengthy prison sentences. Even the prospect of forfeiture of bond in the hundreds of thousands of dollars has proven to be ineffective in assuring the appearance of major drug traffickers. In view of these factors, the Committee has provided in section 3142(e) that in a case in which there is probable cause to believe that the person has committed a grave drug offense, a rebutable [sic] presumption arises that no condition or combination of conditions will reasonably assure the appearance of the person and the safety of the community.

* * *

> The rationale for the use of financial conditions of release is that the prospect of forfeiture of the amount of a bond or of property used as collateral to secure release is sufficient to deter flight. However, when the proceeds of crime are used to post bond, this rationale no longer holds true. In recent years, there has been an increasing incidence of defendants, particularly those engaged in highly lucrative criminal activities such as drug trafficking, who are able to make extraordinarily high money bonds, posting bail and then fleeing the country. Among such defendants, forfeiture of bond is simply a cost of doing business, and it appears that there is a growing practice of reserving a portion of crime income to cover this cost of avoiding prosecution.

S.Rep., supra, at 20, 23–24 (citations omitted), U.S.Code Cong. & Admin.News 1984, pp. 23, 26, 27. The evidence that was presented in congressional hearings on this subject gave Congress, at the least, a substantial basis for reaching these conclusions. See, e.g., "Bail Reform," Hearings Before the Subcommittee on the Constitution of the Senate Judiciary Committee, 97th Cong., 1st Sess., Sept. 17, Oct. 21, 1981 at 67, 70 (graphs 1, 2) (Comm.Print 1982) (suggesting that in ten districts studied, drug offenders account for about *one-sixth* of all crimes charged but about *one-half* of all bail jumpers). See also sources collected in Appendix B. The drug offender/flight presumption seems a reasonable response to this general problem, requiring that a charged drug offender produce some evidence that he does not present a special risk and then requiring the magistrate to review the matter with Congress's general findings in mind.

Jessup, and a defendant in a related case, United States v. Lepere, No. 85–1012 (1st Cir., argued Feb. 4, 1985), attack the presumption in part by challenging the underlying congressional conclusions—by arguing that the evidence does not show a serious, special drug offender/flight problem. The Supreme Court, however, has cautioned us to give "significant weight" to the "capacity of Congress to amass the stuff of actual experience and cull conclusions from it." Usery v. Turner Elkhorn Mining, 428 U.S. 1, 28, 96 S.Ct. 2882, 2898, 49 L.Ed.2d 752 (1976). We cannot here reevaluate the statistical studies or other evidence presented at congressional hearings. To do so would invite potentially endless, unresolvable scholarly argument. (Statistical assumptions are almost always open to plausible attack.) And, doing so would overlook the fact that factual judgments in Congress (as elsewhere) often rest, less upon the gathering of numbers, than upon instinctive evaluation of the views of those with practical experience in the field—views that may reach the legislative ear both informally and formally. Given Congress's constitutional authority and practical fact-gathering power—a power far greater than that of courts—we are not persuaded that Congress's conclusions concerning the drug offender/flight problem are without substantial basis in fact, or that Congress's solution is unreasonable. And, we conclude that the government's interest in the presumption is a strong and legitimate one.

We also find that the presumption does not significantly increase the risk of an "erroneous deprivation" of liberty. Mathews v. Eldridge, 424 U.S. at 324–25, 96 S.Ct. at 897–98. The presumption shifts the burden of production, not the burden of persuasion. It applies only where there is probable cause to believe a person is guilty of a serious crime. The defendant can provide argument and evidence suggesting that he is not involved in the "highly lucrative" drug operations at the center of congressional concern. The Act further specifically provides a defendant with a hearing at which he

> has the right to be represented by counsel, and, if he is financially unable to obtain adequate representation, to have counsel appointed for him. The person shall be afforded an opportunity to testify, to present witnesses on his own behalf, to cross-examine witnesses who appear at the hearing, and to present information by proffer and otherwise.

§ 3142(f)(2)(B). Although the magistrate will keep the presumption in mind in making a decision, he will do so only as a reminder of

Congress's findings. Given the Act's procedural protections, the fact that the presumption does not shift the burden of persuasion, and the presumption's relation to Congress's factfinding powers, we cannot say that it promotes *less,* rather than *more,* accurate decisionmaking. Given the legitimate governmental interest in securing a defendant's appearance at trial, the presumption's restrictions on the defendant's liberty are constitutionally permissible.

Jessup's strongest argument to the contrary rests upon Leary v. United States, 395 U.S. 6, 89 S.Ct. 1532, 23 L.Ed.2d 57 (1969), which he cites for the proposition that a presumption in a criminal case is invalid unless there is "substantial assurance that the presumed fact is more likely than not to flow from the proved fact on which it is made to depend." Id. at 36, 89 S.Ct. at 1548. No one claims, he adds, that despite money bail and other release conditions, drug offenders are *more likely than not* to run away. We note, however, that the *Leary* Court applied this standard to a presumption in the context of a full blown criminal trial, where the presumption was used to establish an important element of the crime that was charged. Here, on the other hand, we deal with a presumption that is applied to a preliminary hearing, where decisions must be made quickly and where the purpose is not to punish but to increase the likelihood that the trial will go forward. It is well established that the constitutional guarantees at such hearings are less protective of defendants than at trial. * * * The Constitution does not require as great a degree of certainty for charging or for securing the presence at trial of one charged as for convicting that person at a criminal trial. In this context then, the substantial basis of information underlying 'drug offender/flight' conclusions is sufficient to meet the Constitution's requirement of adequate support for a presumption. We reject Jessup's claim that more support is necessary.

We do not consider the government's claim that a still lesser test ("some rational connection," see Usery v. Turner Elkhorn Mining, 428 U.S. at 28, 96 S.Ct. at 2898) is all that the presumptions need satisfy. This lesser standard, applied by the Supreme Court typically in cases involving economic regulation, see id., may be insufficient here, where personal liberty is at stake.

Finally, Jessup contends that the real purpose of the presumption is not to detain those likely to flee but rather to impose extra punishment upon alleged drug offenders. In deciding whether this is, in fact, its purpose, we must ask whether there is "an alternative purpose" with which the presumption is "rationally * * * connected * * * [and to which it is] assignable," and whether the presumption is "excessive in relation to the alternative purpose assigned." Bell v. Wolfish, 441 U.S. 520, 538, 99 S.Ct. 1861, 1873, 60 L.Ed.2d 447 (1979) (quoting Kennedy v. Mendoza–Martinez, 372 U.S. 144, 168–69, 83 S.Ct. 554, 567–68, 9 L.Ed.2d 644 (1963)). Here, the "alternative purpose" is obvious, namely Congress's stated object: preventing pretrial flight. For reasons previously given, the presumption does not impose an excessive burden in respect to this purpose. We find no legal basis for viewing the presumption as imposing "punishment." For these reasons, we believe the presumption, as we have interpreted it, is constitutional.

IV

Assuming the presumption's constitutionality, Jessup still claims his detention is unlawful for several reasons. First, he says that he is not the sort of drug offender (*i.e.,* one with important foreign connections) that Congress had in mind when it created the presumption; therefore, the magistrate should not have applied the presumption to him. The conclusion of this argument, however, does not follow from its premise. The presumption applies to Jessup for he fits within its terms. The Act allows him to present all the special features of his case directly to the magistrate. The less those features resemble the congressional paradigm, the less weight the magistrate will likely give to Congress's concern for flight. The individual characteristics of a case and the precise weight to be given the presumption are matters for a magistrate to take into account within the framework of factors set out in § 3142. In other words, Jessup's argument goes not to the applicability of the presumption but rather to the weight that should properly be accorded it.

Second, Jessup argues that the evidence was insufficient for the magistrate to conclude that "no condition or combination of conditions [attached to release] will reasonably assure * * * [his] appearance as required." § 3142(e). Giving appropriate weight to the scope of the magistrate's power to draw conclusions from the evidence presented, see C. Wright, *Federal Practice and Procedure: Criminal 2d* § 722 at 160 (1982) ("An order concerning release prior to conviction is to be affirmed if it is supported by the proceedings below"),[a] we find the evidence sufficient. On October 29, 1984, the magistrate had before him testimony of a DEA agent, Joseph O'Keefe, and the sworn statement of another DEA agent, Stephen Assarian, that Jessup and a codefendant had met with Assarian to arrange for the sale to Assarian of two kilograms of cocaine. Jessup and the codefendant later met with Assarian to consummate the arrangement, and Jessup showed Assarian the cocaine. Assarian and other DEA agents then arrested Jessup and his codefendant. The magistrate found this evidence adequate to establish 'probable cause' that Jessup committed the drug offense with which he was charged.

The magistrate then considered several factors weighing against release: 1) the offense charged was serious; 2) the offense was within Congress's definition of "dangerous federal offenses"; 3) the weight of the evidence against Jessup was strong (in particular, the evidence suggested to the magistrate that Jessup was a "trusted cohort" of his codefendant, who allegedly had been involved in cocaine dealing for some time); 4) Jessup had no relatives in Massachusetts; 5) Jessup had lived in Massachusetts for only two years; and 6) Jessup had been unemployed for six months before his arrest.

The magistrate also considered several factors weighing in favor of Jessup's release. They included 1) Jessup was engaged to a Massachusetts

---

a. Subsequently, in United States v. O'Brien, 895 F.2d 810 (1st Cir.1990), the court abandoned the "supported by the proceedings below" standard as based on the prior statute and substituted a more intrusive review standard which it characterized as providing "independent review all detention decisions, giving deference to the determination of the district court." 895 F.2d at 814.

resident; 2) Jessup had a job offer (from his codefendant's brother); and 3) Jessup had no prior criminal record. (The United States Attorney has recently brought to our attention information suggesting that Jessup in fact has a prior criminal record; we have, however, conducted our review of the magistrate's decision on the basis of the record before the magistrate, and we have not considered this new information.)

The magistrate initially thought that several conditions, including posting of the $25,000 bond that Jessup's counsel suggested, *might* prove sufficient to guarantee Jessup's appearance. Reserving decision, the magistrate asked counsel to explain the source of the $25,000, see § 3142(g)(4), since Jessup had earlier said that he was indigent. Counsel then responded that Jessup could not raise the $25,000, and that Jessup should be released without the posting of a money bond. At that point, the magistrate concluded that no combination of *non*financial conditions would prove sufficient to assure both Jessup's "appearance" and the "safety of * * * the community."

As previously mentioned, the magistrate's decision rests adequately on the "appearance" ground alone. We believe that the magistrate could reasonably conclude from the facts we have listed that the serious charges, the strong evidence, the lack of Massachusetts connections, the possibility of prior involvement, and the lack of any monetary incentive to return would together create too great a risk of flight. We therefore conclude that the magistrate acted within his lawful powers.

Third, Jessup argues that, since the magistrate would have released him had he been able to post $25,000 bail, he must release him anyway. Otherwise, says Jessup, the magistrate violates the next to last sentence in § 3142(c) which says that

> The judicial officer may not impose a financial condition that results in the pretrial detention of the person.

In a literal sense, Jessup's failure to meet the "financial condition," while a necessary condition for Jessup's detention, is not in fact its relevant cause. Rather, Jessup is confined because *both* 1) he cannot raise the $25,000, *and* 2) no other set of conditions is sufficient to guarantee his appearance. That the quoted sentence from the Act does not foreclose detention in these circumstances is made very clear by the Senate Report, which states

> * * * section 3142(c) provides that a judicial officer may not impose a financial condition of release that results in the pretrial detention of the defendant. The purpose of this provision is to preclude the sub rosa use of money bond to detain dangerous defendants. However, its application does not necessarily require the release of a person who says he is unable to meet a financial condition of release which the judge has determined is the only form of conditional release that will assure the person's future appearance. Thus, for example, if a judicial officer determines that a $50,000 bond is the only means, short of detention, of assuring the appearance of a defendant who poses a serious risk of flight, and the defendant asserts that, despite the judicial officer's finding to the contrary, he cannot meet the bond, the judicial officer may reconsider the amount of the bond. If he still

concludes that the initial amount is reasonable and necessary then it would appear that there is no available condition of release that will assure the defendant's appearance.

S.Rep., supra, at 16, U.S.Code Cong. & Admin.News 1984, p. 19. This Report language is perfectly consistent with the basic purpose of the Act— to detain those who present serious risks of flight or danger *but not* to detain those who simply cannot afford a bail bond. See id. at 9–11.

Fourth, we note Jessup's argument that the $25,000 bond which the magistrate considered setting was constitutionally "excessive." He claims that it was too high because it prevented his release. He has been detained, however, not because he cannot raise the money, but because without the money, the risk of flight is too great. And, as we have previously indicated, it is well established that pretrial detention is constitutionally permissible for such a purpose.

Finally, we have asked ourselves whether it is fair to Jessup to affirm the detention order on the basis of an interpretation of the presumption that the magistrate might not have followed. We now hold that the presumption shifts the burden of production not persuasion and that once the defendant produces evidence, the magistrate will keep in mind Congress's general factual view about special drug offender risks, using it where appropriate along with the factors set out in § 3142(g) to judge the risk of flight in the particular case. Did the magistrate here use the presumption more strongly to Jessup's disadvantage? Having reviewed the magistrate's findings, we think not. The magistrate wrote that Jessup "has not rebutted" the presumption; but he also goes on to consider "all the circumstances" and then states his belief that Jessup would not be deterred from fleeing. Nothing in the record suggests the magistrate believed Jessup had to shoulder a "burden of persuasion" or that his decision turned upon that point. Of course, Jessup remains free to ask the magistrate for reconsideration of his detention order, a fact that allows Jessup a remedy if we have misread the magistrate's decision.

For these reasons, the judgment below is

Affirmed.

NOTES

1. **Release on bail after conviction.** Once a defendant has been convicted, the availability of release has traditionally been more limited than in the pretrial situation. The Supreme Court has held that there is no federal constitutional right to bail after conviction and pending appeal. McKane v. Durston, 153 U.S. 684, 14 S.Ct. 913, 38 L.Ed. 867 (1894). Statutory provisions vary widely. Illinois simply authorizes the court to "order that the original bail stand as bail pending appeal or deny, increase or reduce bail." Ill.—S.H.A. ch. 38, ¶ 110–7(d). New York provides that the factors relevant to pretrial release are also to be applied during appeal, except that instead of considering the weight of the evidence and the likelihood of conviction the court is to consider "the merit or lack of merit of the appeal." New York—McKinney's Crim.Proc.Law § 510.30(2)(a)(vii). Further:

> Where the principal is a defendant-appellant in a pending appeal from a judgment of conviction, the court must also consider the likelihood of ultimate

reversal of the judgment. A determination that the appeal is palpably without merit alone justifies, but does not require, a denial of the application [for bail], regardless of any determination made with respect to [other] factors * * *.

Id. at § 510.30(2)(b). Some provisions are considerably stricter. An Arizona statute provides:

A person shall not be continued at large on bail or be admitted to bail after conviction of a felony offense for which the person has received a sentence of imprisonment except when the * * * court * * * is satisfied upon investigation that the person in custody is in such physical condition that continued confinement would endanger his life.

Ariz.Rev.Stat. § 13–3961.01.

United States v. Miller, 753 F.2d 19 (3d Cir.1985), summarized the applicable provision of the Bail Reform Act of 1984, 18 U.S.C.A. § 3143(b), as follows:

[T]he defendant now has the burden of proving if s/he seeks bail pending appeal [by the defendant and] the court must find:

(1) that the defendant is not likely to flee or pose a danger to the safety of any other person or the community if released;

(2) that the appeal is not for purposes of delay;

(3) that the appeal raises a substantial question of fact or law; and

(4) that if that substantial question is determined favorably to defendant on appeal, that decision is likely to result in reversal or an order for a new trial of all counts on which imprisonment has been imposed.

753 F.2d at 24. Comparing these requirements with those under prior law, i.e., the Bail Reform Act of 1966, the court continued:

Under the new act, after first making the findings as to flight, danger, and delay, a court must determine that the question raised on appeal is a "substantial" one, i.e., it must find that the significant question at issue is one which is either novel, which has not been decided by controlling precedent, or which is fairly doubtful. This represents a marked change in the inquiry into the merits in the context of a bail determination, since the 1966 act only required the court to determine whether the issue was "frivolous" * * *.

Id. at 23.

2. **Post-conviction detention criteria.** The Supreme Court addressed the criteria that may be employed in deciding whether a state prisoner whose conviction has been invalidated by a United States District Court on federal habeas should be detained or released pending appeal by the state in Hilton v. Braunskill, 481 U.S. 770, 107 S.Ct. 2113, 95 L.Ed.2d 724 (1987). The Chief Justice, writing for the Court, identified the criteria:

[T]he possibility of flight should be taken into consideration * * *. We also think that, if the state establishes that there is a risk that the prisoner will pose a danger to the public if released, the court may take that factor into consideration in determining whether or not to enlarge him. The state's interest in continuing custody and rehabilitation pending a final determination of the case on appeal is also a factor to be considered; it will be strongest where the remaining portion of the sentence to be served is long, and weakest where there is little of the sentence remaining to be served.

The interest of the habeas petitioner in release pending appeal, always substantial, will be strongest where the factors mentioned in the preceding

> paragraph are weakest. The balance may depend to a large extent upon determination of the state's prospects of success in its appeal.

481 U.S. at 777, 107 S.Ct. at 2119–20, 95 L.Ed.2d at 733–34. The Court also distinguished the position of the successful habeas petitioner from that of the pretrial detainee:

> [A] successful habeas petitioner is in a considerably less favorable position than a pretrial arrestee * * * to challenge his continued detention pending appeal. Unlike a pretrial arrestee, a state habeas petitioner has been adjudged guilty beyond a reasonable doubt by a judge or jury, and this adjudication of guilt has been upheld by the appellate courts of the state. Although the decision of a district court granting habeas relief will have held that the judgment of conviction is constitutionally infirm, that determination itself may be overturned on appeal before the state must retry the petitioner. This being the case, we do not agree that the Due Process Clause prohibits a court from considering, along with the other factors that we previously described, the dangerousness of a habeas petitioner as part of its decision whether to release the petitioner pending appeal.

481 U.S. at 779, 107 S.Ct. at 2120, 95 L.Ed.2d at 734–35.

CHAPTER 13

DISCRETION TO PROSECUTE

Analysis

Prosecutors exercise very broad discretion in deciding whether to bring formal charges against individuals suspected of crimes. They use this discretion to screen some suspects out of the criminal justice system altogether, to divert others to community programs outside the system, to bargain for information and guilty pleas, and to prosecute some defendants fully. In the day-to-day decision-making process, prosecutors make their decisions relatively free of control, although they may be influenced by the desires and opinions of the public, the police and other government officials.

This Chapter deals with part of the charging process in criminal cases. In felony or other serious cases, the law usually provides for participation in the charging process by agencies outside the office of the public prosecutor—an examining magistrate in a preliminary examination or a body of lay persons assembled into a grand jury, or both. How those agencies function is the subject of the next Chapter. The charging process does not end when the prosecutor has made the initial decisions as to whether to charge, how many charges to bring, and how serious the charges will be. Those initial decisions are constantly reviewed as the case progresses through the courts. The practice of plea bargaining frequently requires the prosecutor to change the initial charging decision in the case in order to induce the defendant to waive trial and enter a plea of guilty. That part of prosecutorial discretion relating directly to plea bargaining is considered in Chapter 22.

This Chapter focuses upon the initial charging decisions made by prosecutors and upon controls, other than the preliminary examination and the grand jury, upon prosecutorial discretion in making those initial decisions.

A. THE PROSECUTOR'S CHARGING DECISIONS

In deciding whether to bring formal charges against a suspect, a prosecutor considers a variety of factors including the strength of the evidence, the suspect's background and characteristics, the costs and benefits of obtaining a conviction and the attitude of the community toward the offense the suspect is believed to have committed. Prosecutors screen a substantial number of suspects out of the criminal justice system. Department of Justice statistics for the years 1974 through 1978 reveal that an average of no more than twenty-five percent of the criminal cases brought to the attention of the 94 United States Attorneys ended in formal prosecution. The rates of prosecution varied greatly from offense to offense. A relatively high percentage of weapons control cases, controlled substance offenses, postal offenses, immigration cases, and cases of fraud against the government are formally prosecuted, while relatively few embezzlement, counterfeiting and forgery cases, escape cases, and stolen property cases end in formal prosecution. Frase, The Decision to File Federal Criminal Charges: A Quantitative Study of Prosecutorial Discretion, 47 U.Chi.L.Rev. 246, 252–53 (1980).

The same study focused on prosecution practices by the United States Attorney for the Northern District of Illinois and on the reasons given when prosecution is declined. In forty-four percent of the cases declined the attorneys cited the minor nature of the offense as a reason for the declination. They cited the availability of state prosecution in twenty-six percent of the cases they declined; insufficiency of the evidence in twenty-two percent of the cases; and the characteristics of the defendant in twenty-one percent. Less frequently cited reasons for declining prosecution included the unavailability of the parties and the adequacy of civil or administrative remedies.

The National Advisory Commission on Criminal Justice Standards in its 1973 Report on Courts advocated open recognition of the "need to halt formal or informal action concerning some individuals who become involved in the criminal justice system." Criteria similar to those discussed above were set out, and a procedure established to encourage their uniform application. Among other things, the Commission recommended that the approval of the prosecutor be obtained before formal proceedings are begun; that the screening decision be made by an experienced prosecutor; that written guidelines should be formulated; that if screening occurs, it should be accompanied by a written statement of reasons.

The Commission recognized the essentially discretionary character of the screening decision but took different positions on whether negative and positive decisions should be subject to judicial review. A decision to prosecute would not be subject to review (except of course on evidence sufficiency grounds), nor would a failure to follow guidelines provide a basis for an attack. A decision not to prosecute would be subject to review at the instance of the police or the private complainant, but the standard for review would be merely whether the decision "was so unreasonable as to constitute an abuse of discretion."

Just as the prosecutor enjoys broad discretion in deciding whether to charge at all, he exercises broad discretion in choosing the specific charges to bring against a defendant. He may decide to charge a defendant suspected of several serious offenses with all those offenses, with only one serious offense, or with a single lesser offense. Courts recognize and accept this exercise of discretion by prosecutors. The Supreme Court has long held "that when an act violates more than one criminal statute, the Government may prosecute under either so long as it does not discriminate against any class of defendants." United States v. Batchelder, 442 U.S. 114, 123–24, 99 S.Ct. 2198, 2204, 60 L.Ed.2d 755, 764 (1979).

In choosing the charge the prosecutor considers many of the same factors he considers in deciding whether to charge at all—the defendant's background, the seriousness of his conduct, the desires of the public, the press, and the victim, and the strength of the evidence. But at this stage the prosecutor considers additional factors as well. He may decide to bring less than the most serious charge the evidence will support because he considers the minimum sentence under that charge too serious in relation to the defendant's conduct. Or the prosecutor may bring less than the most serious charge against a defendant because he believes that a jury would be more likely to convict the defendant on a lesser charge. Prosecutors often agree to bring a lesser charge in return for a defendant's guilty plea.

A prosecutor may also use his discretion to prosecute fully a defendant who, under normal circumstances, would not be charged at all or would be charged with a lesser offense. The decision to charge fully is often made in response to pressures from the police, the press, or the public. If a victim of a crime insists on full prosecution, prosecutors often agree. Prosecutors occasionally bring charges in response to requests from the suspects themselves. For example, in winter months in large cities habitual drunks or vagrants often request housing in the local jail. Some prosecutors oblige them by bringing serious charges against them so that they may be housed and fed for the duration of the cold weather. Prosecutors occasionally charge suspects with violation of statutes that are normally unenforced so that the suspects may be detained while investigation into other offenses proceeds. Finally, prosecutors may bring charges against defendants who were acquitted of previous charges or who received what is perceived as an inadequate sentence on a previous conviction.

In the recent past, it was not uncommon for prosecutors to use the threat of formal prosecution to persuade or compel suspects to comply with conditions set by the prosecutor. This kind of informal alternative to prosecution is being replaced, or at least supplemented, by formal pretrial diversion programs.

Pretrial diversion is the pretrial suspension of formal criminal proceedings against a defendant for a specified period during which he is required to participate in a program that may include supervision, counseling, training, and psychological and medical treatment. If the defendant successfully completes the program, the charges against him may be dismissed. If he fails to complete the program in a satisfactory manner, his case is returned to the system for conventional resolution by plea, trial, or dismissal.

The 1967 report of the President's Commission on Law Enforcement and Administration of Justice, The Challenge of Crime in a Free Society, furnished the original impetus for the development of pretrial diversion programs. The report recommended that procedures be developed to identify and divert to community-based programs those offenders who are in need of treatment and for whom full criminal disposition is not required.

Within one year of this report three pilot programs had been established, and by 1975 cities and counties in at least thirty-five states had programs in operation or in the planning stage. In a number of states, the operation of pretrial diversion programs is regulated by statute or rule.

Most of the statutes set out basic criteria for determining the threshold eligibility of defendants for admission to pretrial diversion programs. These criteria include factors such as the age of the defendant, the crime with which he is charged, and his prior record. In addition, most of the statutes provide that the defendant must waive his right to a speedy trial and his right to be tried within the applicable statute of limitations. Arkansas conditions a defendant's admission to a pretrial diversion program on his pleading guilty.

The statutes typically specify the point in the prosecution process at which an application for admission to pretrial diversion may be initiated. They also specify whether the judge or the prosecutor makes the ultimate decision regarding diversion as well as the procedures the decision maker must follow. Several statutes prescribe procedures by which the defendant may challenge the denial of his application for admission to a program. Provisions for revocation of diversionary status are common to all the statutes, and several statutes establish mandatory procedures for revocation. Most statutes provide for automatic dismissal of charges if a defendant successfully completes his program, but a few provide only that charges *may* be dismissed if a defendant successfully completes his program.

In addition, some of the statutes specifically provide that the defendant has a right to notice of the terms, conditions and consequences of pretrial diversion. A few provide that a defendant has the right to consult his attorney before he consents to participation. Other provisions concern the expungement of the divertee's record, inadmissibility in a later criminal trial of information disclosed during the diversion process, and limits on the duration of diversion.

The benefits of pretrial diversion are, theoretically, various and extensive. Defendants benefit through participation because they avoid the stigma and possible imprisonment that often accompany conviction and they receive needed counseling, training, or treatment. The community benefits because defendants who participate in programs theoretically have a lower rate of recidivism than defendants processed through conventional criminal justice channels. The community benefits also because the cost of diversion is less than that of conventional prosecution. The criminal justice system itself benefits because diversion diminishes the caseloads of courts and prosecutors while permitting them to maintain a degree of control over the conduct of divertees. Thus the resources of the system are available to deal more effectively with serious crimes.

Although the goals and purposes of diversion programs are laudable, the various legal issues created by them have not been fully resolved. The imposition of conditions and supervision on defendants who have not been convicted of crimes raises due process issues. Due process issues also arise in connection with the decisions to admit a defendant to a diversion program or to revoke the diversionary status of a defendant already admitted. Equal protection issues may arise from diversion eligibility requirements and from regional unavailability of diversion. Finally, the allocation of the power to make diversion decisions to either the court or the prosecutor creates separation of powers issues.

Occasionally, a prosecutor agrees with one whom he has charged with a criminal offense to dismiss the criminal charges in exchange for a waiver of any civil claim that may arise from the arrest and prosecution. The First Circuit held all such agreements invalid in Rumery v. Town of Newton, 778 F.2d 66 (1st Cir.1985), rev'd, 480 U.S. 386, 107 S.Ct. 1187, 94 L.Ed.2d 405 (1987), finding them to be inherently coercive to the defendant and finding a risk that criminal charges would be manufactured in defense to potential civil rights claims. The Supreme Court, in an opinion authored by Justice Powell, reversed. Rumery was arrested on witness tampering charges. His attorney negotiated an agreement with the prosecutor that those charges would be dismissed in exchange for Rumery's agreement not to bring civil suit for his arrest and prosecution. Rumery, free on bail, conferred at length with his attorney and signed the agreement. Charges were dismissed. Later, he brought civil suit under 42 U.S.C. § 1983, but the case was dismissed when the agreement was presented as a defense. Although the Supreme Court conceded that an offer of such an agreement could be coercive, this one was not. The idea originated with Rumery's attorney and the agreement was drafted by him. Rumery was not in custody and thought about the matter at length before signing it. Further, the person whom Rumery allegedly intimidated, who had brought sexual assault charges against Rumery's friend, had indicated a strong aversion to testifying in either a criminal or a civil case. The agreement served the important public purpose of saving her from the trauma of testifying, perhaps twice, in court. Justice O'Connor concurred in the judgment, but emphasized that the burden should be upon the government to prove in a civil suit that the release-dismissal agreement was voluntarily signed:

> Many factors may bear on whether a release was voluntary and not the product of overreaching, some of which come readily to mind. The knowledge and experience of the criminal defendant and the circumstances of the execution of the release, including, importantly, whether the defendant was counseled, are clearly relevant. The nature of the criminal charges that are pending is also important, for the greater the charge, the greater the coercive effect. The existence of a legitimate criminal justice objective for obtaining the release will support its validity. And, importantly, the possibility of abuse is clearly mitigated if the release-dismissal agreement is executed under judicial supervision.

480 U.S. at 401–02, 107 S.Ct. at 1197, 94 L.Ed.2d at 421–22. Justice Stevens, joined by Justices Brennan, Marshall and Blackmun, dissented and expressed the view that the prosecutor was placed in a conflict of interest between his public duty to prosecute criminal offenses and his desire to protect the police and municipality from possible civil suit. This conflict should ordinarily result in the invalidation of such release-dismissal agreements.

B.   LIMITS ON PROSECUTORIAL DISCRETION

Although the prosecutor's discretion in making initial charging decisions is substantial, there are some limits upon it. The preliminary examination and the grand jury, the subjects of the next Chapter, are intended to
assure that there is sufficient evidence to bring serious charges and in
practice sometimes also serve to review the wisdom of bringing charges
even when there is sufficient evidence to do so. This section deals with
other controls over prosecutorial discretion. Following a consideration of
whether a prosecutor's *failure* to make an affirmative charging decision is
subject to sanction—or indeed can be reversed, the section focuses mainly
upon whether the decision to charge violated the suspect's right to equal
protection of the laws.

In Peek v. Mitchell, 419 F.2d 575 (6th Cir.1970), plaintiffs sought
injunctive relief against both federal and state prosecuting officials (as well
as other state officials) to compel them to prosecute known civil rights
violators. The court held that separation of powers considerations prevented the court from interfering with federal attorneys' control over criminal
prosecutions, and that state officials were immune from even injunctive
sanctions in the absence of any arbitrary or discriminatory actions.

Are there circumstances in which the refusal of state officials to
initiate criminal proceedings violates the civil rights of the victim of the
offense? In Leeke v. Timmerman, 454 U.S. 83, 102 S.Ct. 69, 70 L.Ed.2d 65
(1981), respondents sought damages for a conspiracy to violate their civil
rights. Respondents were prison inmates who contended that guards used
unnecessary force against them during a prison uprising. They presented
information to a state magistrate in an effort to have arrest warrants
issued for state criminal violations. The magistrate indicated he believed
probable cause for issuance of the warrants existed. As a result of a
meeting of the warden, the legal advisor of the corrections department and
the local prosecutor, the latter requested that the magistrate not issue
warrants. None was issued. Respondents filed a civil rights action and were
awarded damages against the warden and the legal advisor. The Court of
Appeals affirmed the judgment but the Supreme Court reversed. In a per
curiam opinion, the Court reaffirmed the position it had taken in an earlier
case that "a private citizen lacks a judicially cognizable interest in the
prosecution or nonprosecution of another." 454 U.S. at 85–86, 102 S.Ct. at
70, 70 L.Ed.2d at 68. The Court extended this principle to include the
transmittal of information that leads to a decision not to initiate the
criminal process: "Just as respondents were able to present arguments as
to why an arrest warrant should issue, a [prosecutor] must be able to
present arguments as to why an arrest warrant should not issue." 454 U.S.
at 87, 102 S.Ct. at 71, 70 L.Ed.2d at 68. Justice Brennan, joined by Justices
Marshall and Blackmun, dissenting from summary reversal, characterized
the conduct of the petitioners as the "deprivation of [respondents'] constitutional right of access to the courts, assured by the First and Fourteenth
Amendments." 454 U.S. at 89, 102 S.Ct. at 72, 70 L.Ed.2d at 70.

Wayte v. United States

Supreme Court of the United States, 1985.
470 U.S. 598, 105 S.Ct. 1524, 84 L.Ed.2d 547.

■ JUSTICE POWELL delivered the opinion of the Court.

The question presented is whether a passive enforcement policy under which the Government prosecutes only those who report themselves as having violated the law, or who are reported by others, violates the First and Fifth Amendments.

I

On July 2, 1980, pursuant to his authority under § 3 of the Military Selective Service Act, 62 Stat. 605, as amended, 50 U.S.C.App. § 453, the President issued Presidential Proclamation No. 4771, 3 CFR 82 (1981). This proclamation directed male citizens and certain male residents born during 1960 to register with the Selective Service System during the week of July 21, 1980. Petitioner fell within that class but did not register. Instead, he wrote several letters to Government officials, including the President, stating that he had not registered and did not intend to do so.

Petitioner's letters were added to a Selective Service file of young men who advised that they had failed to register or who were reported by others as having failed to register. For reasons we discuss, Selective Service adopted a policy of passive enforcement under which it would investigate and prosecute only the cases of nonregistration contained in this file. In furtherance of this policy, Selective Service sent a letter on June 17, 1981 to each reported violator who had not registered and for whom it had an address. The letter explained the duty to register, stated that Selective Service had information that the person was required to register but had not done so, requested that he either comply with the law by filling out an enclosed registration card or explain why he was not subject to registration, and warned that a violation could result in criminal prosecution and specified penalties. Petitioner received a copy of this letter but did not respond.

On July 20, 1981, Selective Service transmitted to the Department of Justice, for investigation and potential prosecution, the names of petitioner and 133 other young men identified under its passive enforcement system—all of whom had not registered in response to the Service's June letter. At two later dates, it referred the names of 152 more young men similarly identified. After screening out the names of those who appeared not to be in the class required to register, the Department of Justice referred the remaining names to the Federal Bureau of Investigation for additional inquiry and to the United States Attorneys for the districts in which the nonregistrants resided. Petitioner's name was one of those referred.

Pursuant to Department of Justice policy, those referred were not immediately prosecuted. Instead, the appropriate United States Attorney was required to notify identified nonregistrants by registered mail that, unless they registered within a specified time, prosecution would be considered. In addition, an FBI agent was usually sent to interview the nonregistrant before prosecution was instituted. This effort to persuade nonregistrants to change their minds became known as the "beg" policy. Under it, young men who registered late were not prosecuted, while those who never registered were investigated further by the Government. Pursuant to the "beg" policy, the United States Attorney for the Central District of California sent petitioner a letter on October 15, 1981 urging him to register or face possible prosecution. Again petitioner failed to respond.

On December 9, 1981, the Department of Justice instructed all United States Attorneys not to begin seeking indictments against nonregistrants until further notice. On January 7, 1982, the President announced a grace period to afford nonregistrants a further opportunity to register without penalty. This grace period extended until February 28, 1982. Petitioner still did not register.

Over the next few months, the Department decided to begin prosecuting those young men who, despite the grace period and "beg" policy, continued to refuse to register. It recognized that under the passive enforcement system those prosecuted were "liable to be vocal proponents of nonregistration" or persons "with religious or moral objections." Memorandum of March 17, 1982 from Lawrence Lippe, Chief General Litigation and Legal Advice Section, Criminal Division, Department of Justice, to D. Lowell Jensen, Assistant Attorney General, Criminal Division, App. 301. It also recognized that prosecutions would "undoubtedly result in allegations that the [case was] brought in retribution for the nonregistrant's exercise of his first amendment rights." The Department was advised, however, that Selective Service could not develop a more "active" enforcement system for quite some time. Because of this, the Department decided to begin seeking indictments under the passive system without further delay. On May 21, 1982, United States Attorneys were notified to begin prosecution of nonregistrants. On June 28, 1982, FBI agents interviewed petitioner and he continued to refuse to register. Accordingly, on July 22, 1982, an indictment was returned against him for knowingly and willfully failing to register with the Selective Service in violation of sections 3 and 12(a) of the Military Selective Service Act, 62 Stat. 605 and 622, as amended, 50 U.S.C.App. §§ 453 and 462(a). This was one of the first indictments returned against any individual under the passive policy.

II

Petitioner moved to dismiss the indictment on the ground of selective prosecution. He contended that he and the other indicted nonregistrants[1] were "vocal" opponents of the registration program who had been impermissibly targeted (out of an estimated 674,000 nonregistrants) for prosecution on the basis of their exercise of First Amendment rights. After a hearing, the District Court for the Central District of California granted

---

1. The record indicates that only 13 of the 286 young men Selective Service referred to the Department of Justice had been indicted at the time the District Court considered this case. As of March 31, 1984, three more men had been indicted. The approximately 270 not indicted either registered, were found not to be subject to registration requirements, could not be found, or were under continuing investigation. The record does not indicate how many fell into each category.

petitioner's broad request for discovery and directed the Government to produce certain documents and make certain officials available to testify. The Government produced some documents and agreed to make some Government officials available but, citing executive privilege, it withheld other documents and testimony. On October 29, 1982, the District Court ordered the Government to produce the disputed documents and witness. The Government declined to comply and on November 5, 1982 asked the District Court to dismiss the indictment in order to allow an appeal challenging the discovery order. Petitioner asked for dismissal on several grounds, including discriminatory prosecution.

On November 15, 1982, the District Court dismissed the indictment on the ground that the Government had failed to rebut petitioner's prima facie case of selective prosecution. Following precedents of the Court of Appeals for the Ninth Circuit, the District Court found that in order to establish a prima facie case petitioner had to prove that (i) others similarly situated generally had not been prosecuted for conduct similar to petitioner's and (ii) the Government's discriminatory selection was based on impermissible grounds such as race, religion, or exercise of First Amendment rights. 549 F.Supp. 1376, 1380 (C.D.Cal.1982). Petitioner satisfied the first requirement, the District Court held, because he had shown that all those prosecuted were "vocal" nonregistrants[2] and because "[t]he inference is strong that the Government could have located non-vocal non-registrants, but chose not to." The District Court found the second requirement satisfied for three reasons. First, the passive enforcement program was " 'inherently suspect' "because " 'it focuse[d] upon the vocal offender * * * [and was] vulnerable to the charge that those chosen for prosecution [were] being punished for their expression of ideas, a constitutionally protected right.' "Ibid., quoting United States v. Steele, 461 F.2d 1148, 1152 (C.A.9 1972). Second, the Government's awareness that a disproportionate number of vocal nonregistrants would be prosecuted under the passive enforcement system indicated that petitioner was prosecuted because of his exercise of First Amendment rights. Finally, the involvement of high Government officials in the prosecution decisions "strongly suggest[ed] impermissible selective prosecution." The District Court then held that the Government had failed to rebut the prima facie case.

The Court of Appeals reversed. Applying the same test, it found the first requirement satisfied but not the second. The first was satisfied by petitioner's showing that out of the estimated 674,000 nonregistrants the 13 indicted had all been vocal nonregistrants. 710 F.2d 1385, 1387 (C.A.9 1983). As to the second requirement, the Court of Appeals held that petitioner had to show that the Government focused its investigation on him *because of* his protest activities. Petitioner's evidence, however, showed only that the Government was aware that the passive enforcement system would result in prosecutions primarily of two types of men—religious and oral objectors and vocal objectors—and that the Government recognized

---

2. This term is misleading insofar as it suggests that all those indicted had made public statements opposing registration. In some cases, the only statement made by the nonregistrant prior to indictment was his letter to the Government declaring his refusal to register.

that the latter type would probably make claims of selective prosecution. Finding no evidence of impermissible governmental motivation, the court held that the District Court's finding of a prima facie case of selective prosecution was clearly erroneous. The Court of Appeals also found two legitimate explanations for the Government's passive enforcement system: (i) the identities of nonreported nonregistrants were not known, and (ii) nonregistrants who expressed their refusal to register made clear their willful violation of the law.

III

In our criminal justice system, the Government retains "broad discretion" as to whom to prosecute. United States v. Goodwin, 457 U.S. 368, 380, n. 11, 102 S.Ct. 2485, 2492, n. 11, 73 L.Ed.2d 74 (1982); accord, Marshall v. Jerrico, Inc., 446 U.S. 238, 248, 100 S.Ct. 1610, 1616, 64 L.Ed.2d 182 (1980). "[S]o long as the prosecutor has probable cause to believe that the accused committed an offense defined by statute, the decision whether or not to prosecute, and what charge to file or bring before a grand jury, generally rests entirely in his discretion." Bordenkircher v. Hayes, 434 U.S. 357, 364, 98 S.Ct. 663, 668, 54 L.Ed.2d 604 (1978). This broad discretion rests largely on the recognition that the decision to prosecute is particularly ill-suited to judicial review. Such factors as the strength of the case, the prosecution's general deterrence value, the Government's enforcement priorities, and the case's relationship to the Government's overall enforcement plan are not readily susceptible to the kind of analysis the courts are competent to undertake. Judicial supervision in this area, moreover, entails systemic costs of particular concern. Examining the basis of a prosecution delays the criminal proceeding, threatens to chill law enforcement by subjecting the prosecutor's motives and decisionmaking to outside inquiry, and may undermine prosecutorial effectiveness by revealing the Government's enforcement policy. All these are substantial concerns that make the courts properly hesitant to examine the decision whether to prosecute.

As we have noted in a slightly different context, however, although prosecutorial discretion is broad, it is not " 'unfettered.' Selectivity in the enforcement of criminal laws is * * * subject to constitutional constraints." United States v. Batchelder, 442 U.S. 114, 125, 99 S.Ct. 2198, 2205, 60 L.Ed.2d 755 (1979) (footnote omitted). In particular, the decision to prosecute may not be " 'deliberately based upon an unjustifiable standard such as race, religion, or other arbitrary classification,' " Bordenkircher v. Hayes, supra, 434 U.S., at 364, 98 S.Ct., at 668, quoting Oyler v. Boles, 368 U.S. 448, 456, 82 S.Ct. 501, 505, 7 L.Ed.2d 446 (1962), including the exercise of protected statutory and constitutional rights, see United States v. Goodwin, supra, 457 U.S., at 372, 102 S.Ct., at 2488.

It is appropriate to judge selective prosecution claims according to ordinary equal protection standards. See Oyler v. Boles, supra. Under our prior cases, these standards require petitioner to show both that the passive enforcement system had a discriminatory effect and that it was motivated by a discriminatory purpose. Personnel Administrator of Mass. v. Feeney, 442 U.S. 256, 99 S.Ct. 2282, 60 L.Ed.2d 870 (1979); Arlington

Heights v. Metropolitan Housing Development Corp., 429 U.S. 252, 97 S.Ct. 555, 50 L.Ed.2d 450 (1977); Washington v. Davis, 426 U.S. 229, 96 S.Ct. 2040, 48 L.Ed.2d 597 (1976). All petitioner has shown here is that those eventually prosecuted, along with many not prosecuted, reported themselves as having violated the law. He has not shown that the enforcement policy selected nonregistrants for prosecution on the basis of their speech. Indeed, he could not have done so given the way the "beg" policy was carried out. The Government did not prosecute those who reported themselves but later registered. Nor did it prosecute those who protested registration but did not report themselves or were not reported by others. In fact, the Government did not even investigate those who wrote letters to Selective Service criticizing registration unless their letters stated affirmatively that they had refused to comply with the law. The Government, on the other hand, did prosecute people who reported themselves or were reported by others but who did not publicly protest. These facts demonstrate that the Government treated all reported nonregistrants similarly. It did not subject vocal nonregistrants to any special burden. Indeed, those prosecuted in effect selected themselves for prosecution by refusing to register after being reported and warned by the Government.

Even if the passive policy had a discriminatory effect, petitioner has not shown that the Government intended such a result. The evidence he presented demonstrated only that the Government was aware that the passive enforcement policy would result in prosecution of vocal objectors and that they would probably make selective prosecution claims. As we have noted, however, " '[d]iscriminatory purpose' * * * implies more than * * * intent as awareness of consequences. It implies that the decisionmaker * * * selected or reaffirmed a particular course of action at least in part 'because of,' not merely 'in spite of,' its adverse effects upon an identifiable group." Personnel Administrator of Mass. v. Feeney, supra, 442 U.S., at 279, 99 S.Ct., at 2296 (footnotes and citations omitted). In the present case, petitioner has not shown that the Government prosecuted him *because of* his protest activities. Absent such a showing, his claim of selective prosecution fails.

IV

Petitioner also challenges the passive enforcement policy directly on First Amendment grounds. In particular, he claims that "[e]ven though the [Government's passive] enforcement policy did not overtly punish protected speech as such, it inevitably created a content-based regulatory system with a concomitantly disparate, content-based impact on nonregistrants."[3] This

---

3. As an initial matter, we note doubt that petitioner has demonstrated injury to his First Amendment rights. The Government's "beg" policy removed most, if not all, of any burden passive enforcement placed on free expression. Because of this policy, nonregistrants could protest registration and still avoid any danger of prosecution. By simply registering after they had reported themselves to the Selective Service, nonregistrants satisfied their obligation and could thereafter continue to protest registration. No matter how strong their protest, registration immunized them from prosecution. Strictly speaking, then, the passive enforcement system penalized continued violation of the Military Selective Service Act, not speech. The only right it burdened was the asserted "right" not to register, a "right" without foundation either in the Constitution or the history of

Court has held that when, as here, " 'speech' and 'nonspeech' elements are combined in the same course of conduct, a sufficiently important governmental interest in regulating the nonspeech element can justify incidental limitations on First Amendment freedoms." United States v. O'Brien, 391 U.S. 367, 376, 88 S.Ct. 1673, 1678, 20 L.Ed.2d 672 (1968). Government regulation is justified

> "if it is within the constitutional power of the Government; if it furthers an important or substantial governmental interest; if the governmental interest is unrelated to the suppression of free expression; and if the incidental restriction on alleged First Amendment freedoms is no greater than is essential to the furtherance of that interest." Id., at 377, 88 S.Ct., at 1679.

* * *

There can be no doubt that the passive enforcement policy meets the second condition. Few interests can be more compelling than a nation's need to ensure its own security. It is well to remember that freedom as we know it has been suppressed in many countries. Unless a society has the capability and will to defend itself from the aggressions of others, constitutional protections of any sort have little meaning. Recognizing this fact, the Framers listed "provid[ing] for the common defence," U.S. Const., Preamble, as a motivating purpose for the Constitution and granted Congress the power to "provide for the common Defence and general Welfare of the United States," Art. I, § 8, cl. 1. See also The Federalist Nos. 4, 24, and 25. This Court, moreover, has long held that the power "to raise and support armies . . . is broad and sweeping," United States v. O'Brien, supra, 391 U.S., at 377, 88 S.Ct., at 1679; accord Lichter v. United States, 334 U.S. 742, 755–758, 68 S.Ct. 1294, 1301–1303, 92 L.Ed. 1694 (1948); Selective Draft Law Cases, 245 U.S. 366, 38 S.Ct. 159, 62 L.Ed. 349 (1918), and that the "power . . . to classify and conscript manpower for military service is 'beyond question,' " United States v. O'Brien, supra, 391 U.S., at 377, 88 S.Ct., at 1679, quoting Lichter v. United States, supra, 334 U.S., at 756, 68 S.Ct., at 1302; accord Selective Draft Law Cases, supra. With these principles in mind, the three reasons the Government offers in defense of this particular enforcement policy are sufficiently compelling to satisfy the second O'Brien requirement—as to either those who reported themselves or those who were reported by others.

First, by relying on reports of nonregistration, the Government was able to identify and prosecute violators without further delay. Although it still was necessary to investigate those reported to make sure that they were required to register and had not, the Government did not have to search actively for the names of these likely violators. Such a search would have been difficult and costly at that time. Indeed, it would be a costly step in any "active" prosecution system involving thousands of nonregistrants. The passive enforcement program thus promoted prosecutorial efficiency. Second, the letters written to Selective Service provided strong, perhaps

our country. See Selective Draft Law Cases, 245 U.S. 366, 38 S.Ct. 159, 62 L.Ed.2d 349 (1918).

conclusive evidence of the nonregistrant's intent not to comply—one of the elements of the offense. Third, prosecuting visible nonregistrants was thought to be an effective way to promote general deterrence, especially since failing to proceed against publicly known offenders would encourage others to violate the law.

The passive enforcement policy also meets the final requirement of the *O'Brien* test, for it placed no more limitation on speech than was necessary to ensure registration for the national defense. Passive enforcement not only did not subject "vocal" nonregistrants to any special burden, but also was intended to be only an interim enforcement system. Although Selective Service was engaged in developing an active enforcement program when it investigated petitioner, it had by then found no practicable way of obtaining the names and current addresses of likely nonregistrants.[4] Eventually, it obtained them by matching state driver's license records with Social Security files. It took some time, however, to obtain the necessary authorizations and to set up this system. Passive enforcement was the only effective interim solution available to carry out the Government's compelling interest.

We think it important to note as a final matter how far the implications of petitioner's First Amendment argument would extend. Strictly speaking, his argument does not concern passive enforcement but self-reporting. The concerns he identifies would apply to all nonregistrants who report themselves even if the Selective Service engaged only in active enforcement. For example, a nonregistrant who wrote a letter informing Selective Service of his failure to register could, when prosecuted under an active system, claim that the Selective Service was prosecuting him only because of his "protest." Just as in this case, he could have some justification for believing that his letter had focused inquiry upon him. Prosecution in either context would equally "burden" his exercise of First Amendment rights. Under the petitioner's view, then, the Government could not constitutionally prosecute a self-reporter—even in an active enforcement system—unless perhaps it could prove that it would have prosecuted him without his letter. On principle, such a view would allow any criminal to obtain immunity from prosecution simply by reporting himself and claiming that he did so in order to "protest" the law. The First Amendment confers no such immunity from prosecution.

V

We conclude that the Government's passive enforcement system together with its "beg" policy violated neither the First nor Fifth Amendments. Accordingly, we affirm the judgment of the Court of Appeals.

It is so ordered.

■ JUSTICE MARSHALL, with whom JUSTICE BRENNAN joins, dissenting [omitted].

---

4. Selective Service had tried to use Social Security records but found that the addresses there were hopelessly stale. And under the law, 26 U.S.C. § 6103, it could gain no useful access to IRS records—the only other recognized federal source of generally accurate information.

NOTES

1. Suppose the person selected for prosecution presents evidence that his selection was based on protests in a more public manner, for example participation in draft-counseling during the Vietnam War? See United States v. Falk, 479 F.2d 616 (7th Cir.1973).

2. Is it proper to prosecute a person suspected of crime "A" merely because he is believed to have committed crime "B"? See United States v. Choate, 619 F.2d 21 (9th Cir.1980). Would it matter whether the person had previously been convicted of crime "B"?

3. **Disclosure of information to advance a selective prosecution claim.** The Court in United States v. Armstrong, 517 U.S. 456, 116 S.Ct. 1480, 134 L.Ed.2d 687 (1996), addressed the question of what showing must be made of selective prosecution in order to warrant a trial court ordering disclosure of records of prosecutorial decisions as possible evidence to substantiate the claim. The Court, in an opinion by The Chief Justice, addressed the preliminary showing that is needed to advance an equal protection/selective prosecution claim. Respondent had been charged with a "crack" cocaine offense. He sought to show that only African–Americans had been charged with that offense. While respondent presented some evidence that African–Americans had been charged with that offense and that few whites had been charged, he failed to show that the government had declined to charge whites under circumstances in which African–Americans had been charged. The Court held that the absence of such a showing of discrimination among those potential defendants who are "similarly situated" precluded the District Court from ordering the wide-ranging discovery involved in this case.

4. **Charging the same conduct as a felony or a misdemeanor.** Some state courts have found a violation of both their state constitutions and the equal protection clause of the fourteenth amendment when a prosecutor has discretion to charge the same conduct either as a felony or a misdemeanor. See, e.g., Olsen v. Delmore, 48 Wash.2d 545, 295 P.2d 324 (1956). To what extent do cases like *Olsen* survive the *Batchelder* case?

In United States v. Batchelder, 442 U.S. 114, 99 S.Ct. 2198, 60 L.Ed.2d 755 (1979), respondent, a previously convicted felon, was convicted of receiving a firearm that had travelled in interstate commerce. The judge imposed the maximum sentence of five years in prison. The Court of Appeals held that because another statute prohibited precisely the same conduct and provided for a maximum sentence of two years, Congress intended to limit punishment for such conduct to two years. After concluding there was no Congressional intent to limit punishment to the lesser term, Justice Marshall for the Court addressed the constitutional issues raised by the co-existence of the two provisions:

> More importantly, there is no appreciable difference between the discretion a prosecutor exercises when deciding whether to charge under one of two statutes with different elements and the discretion he exercises when choosing one of two statutes with identical elements. In the former situation, once he determines that the proof will support conviction under either statute, his decision is indistinguishable from the one he faces in the latter context. The prosecutor may be influenced by the penalties available upon conviction, but this fact, standing alone, does not give rise to a violation of the Equal Protection or Due Process Clause. (citations omitted) Just as a defendant has no constitutional right to elect which of two applicable federal statutes shall be the basis of his indictment and prosecution neither is he entitled to choose the penalty scheme under which he will be sentenced.

Approaching the problem of prosecutorial discretion from a slightly different perspective, the Court of Appeals postulated that the statutes might impermissibly delegate to the Executive Branch the Legislature's responsibility to fix criminal penalties. We do not agree. The provisions at issue plainly demarcate the range of penalties that prosecutors and judges may seek and impose. In light of that specificity, the power that Congress has delegated to those officials is no broader than the authority they routinely exercise in enforcing the criminal laws. Having informed the courts, prosecutors and defendants of the permissible punishment alternatives available under each Title, Congress has fulfilled its duty.

442 U.S. at 125–26, 99 S.Ct. at 2205, 60 L.Ed.2d at 765–66.

5. **Restrictions on pretrial diversion eligibility.** Several state pretrial diversion statutes limit admission to diversion programs to certain classes of defendants. Several statutes provide that only first offenders or suspects charged with non-violent crimes are eligible for diversion. In Massachusetts only defendants between the ages of seventeen and twenty-one are eligible Mass.Gen.Laws Ann. ch. 276A § 2 (West 1999). In addition, most of the statutes direct the prosecutor or the court to consider various other factors in deciding to admit a defendant to pretrial diversion. These factors include the defendant's background, his attitudes, his family and employment situation, the seriousness of his offense, and his amenability to rehabilitation. Do any of these eligibility requirements create equal protection problems? Should the validity of the requirements be judged by the rational relationship or the compelling state interest test?

In United States v. Smith, 354 A.2d 510 (D.C.App.1976), the court found acceptable the prosecutor's practice of refusing to admit to the informal diversion program any defendant who chose to litigate any issues in his case. In this case the defendant was denied admission to the diversion program after he had moved unsuccessfully for a dismissal of the charges on the ground that the punishment prescribed by the statute for his offense violated the eighth amendment.

In Cleveland v. State, 417 So.2d 653 (Fla.1982), the court held that a pretrial diversion decision is not subject to judicial review:

The state attorney has complete discretion in making the decision to charge and prosecute. In State v. Jogan, 388 So.2d 322 (Fla. 3d DCA 1980), for example, the trial judge dismissed the information against the defendant conditioned on the defendant's enlistment in the military. The district court reversed and remanded holding that the decision to prosecute or nolle prosequi is a pretrial posture vested solely in the state attorney's discretion. The court felt that the state attorney alone had the right to nolle prosequi a defendant conditioned upon his entry into the military. The trial court has great latitude in post-trial proceedings and thus forms the necessary check and balance.

The pretrial diversion is essentially a conditional decision not to prosecute similar to the nolle prosequi situation postulated by *Jogan*. It is a pretrial decision and does not divest the state attorney of the right to institute proceedings if the conditions are not met. The pretrial intervention program is merely an alternative to prosecution and should remain in the prosecutor's discretion. See Commonwealth v. Kindness, 247 Pa.Super. 99, 371 A.2d 1346 (1977). Two factors in the statutory scheme which create the pretrial intervention program support the determination that each party concerned has total discretion to refuse to consent. First, section 944.025(2) requires consent of the administrator of the program, victim, judge, and state attorney, but fails to provide for *any* form of review. In addition, section 944.025(4), Florida Statutes, allows the state attorney to continue prosecution if defendant is not fulfilling his obligations under the program or if the public interest requires. The fact that the state attorney has this discretion to reinstate prosecution is consistent with the view that the pretrial diversion consent by the state attorney is a prosecutorial function.

Finally, defendant's reliance on comparable programs in other states is misplaced. The California program statutorily provides for trial court review. See People v. Superior Court, 11 Cal.3d 59, 520 P.2d 405, 113 Cal.Rptr. 21 (1974). Other programs were created by court rule and are, therefore, subject to court review of the diversion decision. Florida's program was statutorily created and does not expressly provide for judicial review.

We hold that the pretrial diversion decision of the state attorney is prosecutorial in nature and, thus, is not subject to judicial review. * * *

Id. at 654.

6. **Restrictions on termination of pretrial diversion supervision.** Would a prosecutorial decision to terminate diversion be subject to judicial review? In United States v. Hicks, 693 F.2d 32 (5th Cir.1982), the court upheld a speedy trial waiver which was a condition to admission to a pretrial diversion program:

> The government argues that the district court did not have the power to review the decision to terminate appellant from the program. It argues that the court would be participating in the decision to charge. Weaving the argument from the strands of prosecutorial discretion and separation of powers, it seeks to insulate the pretrial diversion program from any and all judicial review.
>
> That would take us too far. The court below, in holding this hearing, was not participating in the decision to charge. The diversion agreement is a contract. The government sought to hold the accused to his side of the bargain, i.e. the waiver of his speedy trial rights. The court was entitled to hear evidence on the violations to make sure that the government had lived up to its side of the bargain.
>
> The court is also charged with the responsibility for safeguarding the constitutional rights of the accused. An apt analogy is the plea bargain. Like pretrial diversion, the plea bargain is an agreement between the prosecutor and the accused. The court has a duty to supervise this process and insure that the defendant's plea is voluntary and that he is informed of his constitutional rights. United States v. Adams, 566 F.2d 962, 966 (5th Cir.1978); Fed.R.Crim.P. 11. In Santobello v. New York, 404 U.S. 257, 92 S.Ct. 495, 30 L.Ed.2d 427 (1971), the Supreme Court dealt with a plea bargain in which the prosecutor failed to keep a commitment regarding sentence recommendation. The court remanded the plea to the state courts for reconsideration. The Court stated
>
>> This phase of the process of criminal justice, and the adjudicative element inherent in accepting a plea of guilty, must be attended by safeguards to insure the defendant what is reasonably due in the circumstances. Those circumstances will vary, but a constant factor is that when a plea rests in any significant degree on a promise or agreement of the prosecutor, so that it can be said to be part of the indictment or consideration, such promise must be fulfilled.
>
> Id. at 263, 92 S.Ct. at 499. While we acknowledge that no "adjudicative element" is present in the pretrial diversion context, we think the analogy sufficiently persuasive to defeat the government's argument that the court lacks jurisdiction to hold a hearing. Our holding is of a limited nature. We do not decide that the court is required to hold a hearing prior to termination of the agreement, with or without request by defendant. We simply hold that in this case the court was entitled to decide whether defendant should be held to his waiver of speedy trial.

Effect of the Agreement and Waiver

The trial court found that the defendant had violated the terms of his agreement. The government presented appellant's probation officer Maples at the hearing. He testified that Hicks violated several conditions of his probation. First, Hicks failed to inform the office when he got a job. Second, Hicks moved without reporting his new address. Third, Maples testified that Hicks used abusive language in the probation office after Maples requested that Hicks not behave rudely in handing in his reports (said to violate the condition requiring Hicks to follow his probation officer's instructions). The findings of fact are not clearly erroneous.[5]

We think that the government is entitled to hold the defendant to strict compliance with the terms of the agreement. It could be argued that the violations here were not substantial. In United States v. Reed, 573 F.2d 1020, 1024 (8th Cir.1978), the court stated

> The decision to revoke probation should not merely be a reflexive reaction to an accumulation of technical violations of the conditions imposed upon the offender. That approach would be inconsistent with and detrimental to the goals of the probation program:
>
>> While presumably it would be inappropriate for a field agent *never* to revoke, the whole thrust of the probation-parole movement is to keep men in the community, working with adjustment problems there, and using revocation only as a last resort when treatment has failed or is about to fail. [Citations omitted]
>
> Rather, probation should be revoked only in those instances in which the offender's behavior demonstrates that he or she "cannot be counted on to avoid antisocial activity." Morrissey v. Brewer, supra, 408 U.S. at 479, 92 S.Ct. at 2599.

See *Lacey,* 661 F.2d at 1022. There are important differences, however, between pretrial diversion and probation. First, the defendant has no right to be placed in the program. The government has given the defendant a benefit in allowing him to forego the burdens attendant upon a criminal prosecution. In exchange, it may properly require strict compliance with the diversion conditions. Second, the standard for violation in *Reed* is promulgated pursuant to the court's supervisory powers of the probation system. See United States v. Feinberg, 631 F.2d 388, 391 (5th Cir.1980). The courts have no similar powers over the pretrial diversion program. Lastly, in probation the government has already

---

5. Our review in this area may be limited. In probation revocation, this court has stated

> The evidence to support a revocation need not establish guilt beyond a reasonable doubt; all that is required is that the evidence of the facts reasonably satisfy the judge that the conduct of the probationer violates the conditions of probation. The district court has broad discretion with regard to the revocation of probation, and its actions will not be disturbed in the absence of a clear showing of an abuse of that discretion.

United States v. Lacey, 661 F.2d 1021, 1022 (5th Cir.1981), cert. denied, 456 U.S. 961, 102 S.Ct. 2036, 72 L.Ed.2d 484 (1982). Of course, probation is court supervised. In reviewing revocations of parole, this court has applied an arbitrary and capricious standard. Thompson v. United States, Federal Prison Industries, 492 F.2d 1082 (5th Cir.1974); Sexton v. United States, 429 F.2d 1300 (5th Cir.1970). Since pretrial diversion is a program administered by the Justice Department, considerations of separation of powers and prosecutorial discretion might mandate an even more limited standard of review. However, this is an issue that this court need not address since no error was committed by whatever standard we review the decision.

obtained a judicial determination of the accused's guilt. Thus, society's interest in convicting the accused has been achieved. Procedural bars to ending probation or parole are more appropriate because the immediate result of probation revocation is imprisonment. In pretrial diversion, there has been no determination of guilt. Strict compliance may be required in order to safeguard the public's interest in seeing criminals punished for their antisocial behavior.

Having upheld the government's decision to terminate Hicks from the program, it follows that Hicks can be held to his waiver of his speedy trial rights.

Id. at 33–35.

CHAPTER 14

THE PRELIMINARY EXAMINATION AND THE GRAND JURY

Analysis

Despite the almost unlimited discretion granted the prosecutor concerning the decision to charge (see Chapter 13), virtually all jurisdictions impose a pretrial screening device in serious cases between the prosecutor's decision to charge and trial on that charge. This may limit the filing of charges, the progress of charges to the trial process, or both. The two major devices used are the preliminary examination or hearing and the grand jury. Both involve scrutiny of the sufficiency of evidence to support actual or proposed charges and sometimes—although perhaps without formal authorization—of the wisdom of bringing the charges.

The preliminary examination, the subject of the first section of this Chapter, is frequently held in a "lower" court that lacks jurisdiction to try the case on its merits. The proceeding is to some extent an adversary one and the presiding judge's function is to determine the existence of "probable cause" to believe the defendant guilty. If probable cause is found to exist, the defendant is "bound over" for further proceedings.

The grand jury also performs a screening function when called upon to consider charges against a particular person. This should be distinguished from the grand jury's investigatory function, addressed in Chapter 9. When the grand jury's screening function is performed, it has the effect of determining the actual charge. If the grand jury finds the evidence sufficient to establish probable cause, it returns an indictment which is filed in the court with jurisdiction over the offense and becomes the charging document in the case.

Among the important questions raised by the variations in preliminary screening devices is the desirable or perhaps constitutionally necessary relationship among the preliminary examination, the process of grand jury indictment, and the bringing of formal charges. The Fifth Amendment to the United States Constitution requires that a prosecution in federal court for an "infamous crime," meaning one for which imprisonment might exceed one year, must be based upon a grand jury indictment. One accused of a serious federal crime, then, has a right before formal charging to screening by a grand jury.

But the federal Constitution imposes few if any requirements upon the states. In Hurtado v. California, 110 U.S. 516, 4 S.Ct. 111, 28 L.Ed. 232 (1884), the Supreme Court held that the Fourteenth Amendment requirement of due process does not require indictment by a grand jury. Stressing the need for federal constitutional requirements to accommodate development in the law, it reasoned:

> [W]e are unable to say that the substitution for ... indictment by a grand jury of the proceeding by information after examination and commitment by a magistrate, certifying to the probable guilt of the defendant, with the right on his part to the aid of counsel, and to the cross-examination of the witnesses produced for the prosecution, is not due process of law. It ... carefully considers and guards the substantial interest of the prisoner.

110 U.S. at 538, 4 S.Ct. at 122, 28 L.Ed. at 239. Later, however, the Court further held that when the information process has been substituted for grand jury indictment, a preliminary examination is not constitutionally required. In Lem Woon v. Oregon, 229 U.S. 586, 33 S.Ct. 783, 57 L.Ed. 1340 (1913), the plaintiff in error urged that due process was violated by his trial and conviction of murder because under Oregon law at the time no preliminary examination or commitment by a magistrate was required for the prosecutor to charge the offense. The Court rejected this, regarding the matter as disposed of by *Hurtado*:

> [S]ince ... the "due process of law" clause does not require the state to adopt the institution and procedure of a grand jury, we are unable to see upon what theory it can be held that an examination, or the opportunity for one, prior to the formal accusation by the district attorney is obligatory upon the states.

229 U.S. at 590, 33 S.Ct. at 784, 57 L.Ed. at 1342. Does this follow? The language from *Hurtado* suggests that the procedure upheld there was an acceptable alternative to grand jury indictment only because it provided for a meaningful "examination and commitment by a magistrate" before charges could be filed.

The absence of significant federal constitutional requirements here, however, does not resolve the questions of local criminal justice policy, which include whether any formal screening of charges should be provided and, if so, how that should be done.

The Uniform Rules of Criminal Procedure suggest a third method of effectuating pretrial screening. Under Rule 481, a defendant is authorized to move in the trial court for a pretrial judgment of acquittal. If the motion appears meritorious on its face, depositions, statements, and other matters are to be produced before the trial court which is then to rule on the motion. If the motion is granted, it constitutes an acquittal except that the prosecution may appeal. Underlying the position of the Uniform Rules is the assumption that neither the preliminary examination nor the grand jury, even if modified, hold adequate promise of being screening devices of maximum effectiveness and efficiency. In considering the following materials, consider also the extent to which the nontraditional alternative suggested in the Uniform Rules might be more appropriate than either of the traditional vehicles utilized for pretrial screening.

A.   THE PRELIMINARY EXAMINATION

The preliminary examination or hearing varies tremendously among American jurisdictions, both in procedure and in function. Perhaps some of this is due to its history. Originally, the examination was a device used for gathering information by taking testimony from witnesses and for restraining the suspect—by committing him to jail or requiring him to post bail—pending prosecution. In this context, it served primarily the interests of the prosecution in assuring the suspect's availability for later formal charges and trial. See Anderson, The Preliminary Hearing—Better Alternatives or More of the Same, 35 Mo.L.Rev. 281, 284 (1970). As concern for the interests of suspects grew, however, the preliminary examination became more significant as a vehicle for requiring the prosecution to make a preliminary showing of the suspect's guilt before the suspect would be put to the deprivation of liberty (or the expense of posting bail) pending the consideration of formal charges by the grand jury. *Id.*, at 285. At this stage, it served primarily as a means of protecting suspects' interest in liberty until formal charges could be brought. Since grand juries were sometimes convened quite infrequently, this was not an insignificant matter. Months could pass between a suspect's arrest and the convening of the next grand jury that might indict him.

In a manner that has not been well documented or studied, the preliminary examination evolved in many jurisdictions into a means of limiting not merely the prosecution's ability to detain the defendant pending formal charges but, in addition, its ability under some circumstances to charge the defendant at all. See C. Whitebread, Criminal Procedure 332 (1980). It is likely that this accompanied the abandonment of grand jury indictment in favor of charging by information. L. Orfield, Criminal Procedure From Arrest to Appeal 52 (1947); Dession, From Indictment to Information—Implications of the Shift, 42 Yale L.J. 163, 170 (1932). As the notes in this section make clear, however, in many jurisdictions today the preliminary examination serves as a device for screening charges as well as for inquiring into the justification for restraint of the suspect. The difference between these two functions is not always drawn and may be of little practical significance today.

In any case, the preliminary examination—perhaps in part because of its flexibility—lends itself to serving other and often informal functions. Where prosecutors have the option of proceeding by either indictment or information and thus of going through one or the other of the traditional screening devices, their responses may be informative on the actual significance of the alternative screening devices. An empirical study addressed the use of preliminary hearings and grand juries in a jurisdiction—Arizona—that permits charges to be brought either by grand jury indictment or by an information filed by the prosecutor. D. Emerson and N. Ames, The Role of the Grand Jury and the Preliminary Hearing in Pretrial Screening (U.S. Dept. of Justice, 1984). The state's two large cities, the report noted, had developed different practices for charging major cases. One relied heavily upon grand jury indictment; the other utilized primarily the information option which, under state law, entitled the defendant to a preliminary hearing. One prosecutor identified those considerations indicating that a preliminary hearing would be desirable from the prosecution's perspective:

— a need existed to have a witness's testimony preserved for possible later use, a process most readily accomplished by having the witness testify at a preliminary hearing;

— confusion and uncertainty existed concerning the events, which might be clarified by witnesses' testimony at a preliminary hearing;

— a need existed to secure an additional identification of the defendant by the victim;

— some doubt existed as to the victim's interest in pursuing the prosecution and the preliminary hearing would serve to confirm that interest; and

— the victim's willingness to testify was in doubt and this could be resolved by determining whether the witness was willing to participate in a preliminary hearing.

Id., at 24.

In the city relying heavily upon non-grand jury charging, only a small percent of cases actually involved a preliminary hearing. This was because the hearing was not held in most cases. *Id.*, at 22. Sometimes this waiver was in return for some specific benefit, such as release on the defendant's own recognizance or some advantageous scheduling. *Id.*, at 26. Where preliminary hearings were held, defendants seldom introduced or offered evidence. Defense counsel explained that they seldom hoped to obtain a finding of no probable cause so that such action was unlikely to be of any help. Further, putting defense witnesses on the stand at this stage might provide the prosecution with information concerning the defense strategy and might make the witness subject to future impeachment should the case go to trial. *Id.*, at 60. But defense counsel often cross examined the prosecution's witnesses, suggesting that the opportunity for informal discovery was often taken. *Id.*, at 59.

The report noted that preliminary hearings in practice tend to serve a variety of functions other than that of screening out cases in which the prosecution has failed to show probable cause. One was to provide the defense with discovery, including an opportunity to probe state witnesses for information that might later serve as the basis for attacking the admissibility of evidence on search and seizure grounds. *Id.*, at 72. In addition, it permitted the preservation of evidence in a form that under local evidence law would permit its use at trial. This was perceived as valuable for several reasons. It often removed any incentive for the defendant or others to harass the witness. When the witness was young and likely to forget the events (or at least some details) before trial, the preserved testimony was likely to be better than the witness' trial testimony. *Id.*, at 73. The transcript of the preliminary hearing also was often valuable in impeaching witnesses who later testified at trial. *Id.*

In addition, the preliminary hearing served as a means of reviewing the conditions of pretrial release. Bail amounts or conditions were sometimes addressed in a more adversary environment than previously. As noted above, defendants' waivers of scheduled preliminary hearings were sometimes rewarded in this context. *Id.*, at 145–46.

The preliminary hearing also served as a means for encouraging plea negotiations, in large part because it constitutes the first formal opportunity for the parties to meet face-to-face. Often, cases scheduled for preliminary hearings were resolved by agreements to plead guilty to misdemeanors in the lower court or to waive the preliminary hearing and to plead guilty to a felony offense in the trial court. *Id.*, at 146.

Comparing the two cities, the report noted that neither practice resulted in formal screening out of a significant number of cases. *Id.*, at 146. Because of the tendency to rely on the testimony of police officers alone in grand jury proceedings and the opportunity for cross examination in preliminary hearings, the study concluded that "the preliminary hearing does appear to be a slightly more rigorous mechanism for determining probable cause." *Id.*, at 148.

FEDERAL RULES OF CRIMINAL PROCEDURE

Rule 5.1 Preliminary Examination

(a) Probable Cause Finding. If from the evidence it appears that there is probable cause to believe that an offense has been committed and that the defendant committed it, the federal magistrate judge shall forthwith hold the defendant to answer in district court. The finding of probable cause may be based upon hearsay evidence in whole or in part. The defendant may cross-examine adverse witnesses and may introduce evidence. Objections to evidence on the ground that it was acquired by unlawful means are not properly made at the preliminary examination. Motions to suppress must be made to the trial court as provided in Rule 12.

(b) Discharge of Defendant. If from the evidence it appears that there is no probable cause to believe that an offense has been committed or that the defendant committed it, the federal magistrate judge shall dismiss the complaint and discharge the defendant. The discharge of the defendant shall not preclude the government from instituting a subsequent prosecution for the same offense.

* * *

Coleman v. Alabama

Supreme Court of the United States, 1970.
399 U.S. 1, 90 S.Ct. 1999, 26 L.Ed.2d 387.

■ MR. JUSTICE BRENNAN announced the judgment of the Court and delivered the following opinion.

* * *

II.

This Court has held that a person accused of crime "requires the guiding hand of counsel at every step in the proceedings against him," Powell v. Alabama, 287 U.S. 45, 69, 53 S.Ct. 55, 64, 77 L.Ed. 158 (1932), and that that constitutional principle is not limited to the presence of counsel at trial. "It is central to that principle that in addition to counsel's presence at trial, the accused is guaranteed that he need not stand alone against the State at any stage of the prosecution, formal or informal, in court or out, where counsel's absence might derogate from the accused's right to a fair trial." United States v. Wade, [388 U.S. 218, 226, 87 S.Ct. 1926, 1932, 18 L.Ed.2d 1149 (1967)]. Accordingly, "the principle of Powell v. Alabama and succeeding cases requires that we scrutinize *any* pretrial confrontation of the accused to determine whether the presence of his counsel is necessary to preserve the defendant's basic right to a fair trial as affected by his right meaningfully to cross-examine the witnesses against him and to have effective assistance of counsel at the trial itself. It calls upon us to analyze whether potential substantial prejudice to defendant's rights inheres in the particular confrontation and the ability of counsel to help avoid that prejudice." Id., at 227, 87 S.Ct. at 1932. Applying this test, the Court has held that "critical stages" include the pretrial type of arraignment where certain rights may be sacrificed or lost, Hamilton v. Alabama, 368 U.S. 52, 54, 82 S.Ct. 157, 158–159, 7 L.Ed.2d 114 (1961), see White v. Maryland, 373 U.S. 59, 83 S.Ct. 1050, 10 L.Ed.2d 193 (1963), and the pretrial lineup, United States v. Wade, supra; Gilbert v. California, supra. Cf. Miranda v. Arizona, 384 U.S. 436, 86 S.Ct. 1602, 16 L.Ed.2d 694 (1966), where the Court held that the privilege against compulsory self-incrimination includes a right to counsel at a pretrial custodial interrogation. See also Massiah v. United States, 377 U.S. 201, 84 S.Ct. 1199, 12 L.Ed.2d 246 (1964).

The preliminary hearing is not a required step in an Alabama prosecution. The prosecutor may seek an indictment directly from the grand jury without a preliminary hearing. The opinion of the Alabama Court of Appeals in this case instructs us that under Alabama law the sole purposes of a preliminary hearing are to determine whether there is sufficient evidence against the accused to warrant presenting his case to the grand jury and if so to fix bail if the offense is bailable. 44 Ala.App., at 433, 211 So.2d 917; 211 So.2d, at 920. See Code of Alabama, Tit. 15, §§ 139, 140, 151. The court continued:

> "At the preliminary hearing ... the accused is not required to advance any defenses, and failure to do so does not preclude him from availing himself of every defense he may have upon the trial of the case. Also Pointer v. State of Texas [380 U.S. 400, 85 S.Ct. 1065, 13 L.Ed.2d 923 (1965)] bars the admission of testimony given at a pretrial proceeding where the accused did not have the benefit of cross-examination by and through counsel. Thus, nothing occurring at the preliminary hearing in the absence of counsel can substantially prejudice the rights of the accused on trial." 44 Ala.App., at 433, 211 So.2d, at 921.

This Court is of course bound by this construction of the governing Alabama law. However, from the fact that in cases where the accused has no lawyer at the hearing the Alabama courts prohibit the State's use at trial of anything that occurred at the hearing, it does not follow that the Alabama preliminary hearing is not a "critical stage" of the State's criminal process. The determination whether the hearing is a "critical stage" requiring the provision of counsel depends, as noted, upon an analysis "whether potential substantial prejudice to defendant's rights inheres in the ... confrontation and the ability of counsel to help avoid that prejudice." United States v. Wade, supra, 388 U.S. at 227, 87 S.Ct. at 1932. Plainly the guiding hand of counsel at the preliminary hearing is essential to protect the indigent accused against an erroneous or improper prosecution. First, the lawyer's skilled examination and cross-examination of witnesses may expose fatal weaknesses in the State's case, that may lead the magistrate to refuse to bind the accused over. Second, in any event, the skilled interrogation of witnesses by an experienced lawyer can fashion a vital impeachment tool for use in cross-examination of the State's witnesses at the trial, or preserve testimony favorable to the accused of a witness who does not appear at the trial. Third, trained counsel can more effectively discover the case the State has against his client and make possible the preparation of a proper defense to meet that case at the trial. Fourth, counsel can also be influential at the preliminary hearing in making effective arguments for the accused on such matters as the necessity for an early psychiatric examination or bail.

The inability of the indigent accused on his own to realize these advantages of a lawyer's assistance compels the conclusion that the Alabama preliminary hearing is a "critical stage" of the State's criminal process at which the accused is "as much entitled to such aid [of counsel] ... as at the trial itself." Powell v. Alabama, supra, 287 U.S. at 57, 53 S.Ct. at 60.

III.

There remains, then, the question of the relief to which petitioners are entitled. The trial transcript indicates that the prohibition against use by the State at trial of anything that occurred at the preliminary hearing was scrupulously observed. Cf. White v. Maryland, supra. But on the record it cannot be said whether or not petitioners were otherwise prejudiced by the absence of counsel at the preliminary hearing. That inquiry in the first instance should more properly be made by the Alabama courts. The test to be applied is whether the denial of counsel at the preliminary hearing was harmless error under Chapman v. California, 386 U.S. 18, 87 S.Ct. 824, 17 L.Ed.2d 705 (1967).

We accordingly vacate the petitioners' convictions and remand the case to the Alabama courts for such proceedings not inconsistent with this opinion as they may deem appropriate to determine whether such denial of counsel was harmless error, and therefore whether the convictions should be reinstated or a new trial ordered.

It is so ordered.

Convictions vacated and case remanded with directions.

* * *

Myers v. Commonwealth

Supreme Judicial Court of Massachusetts, 1973.
363 Mass. 843, 298 N.E.2d 819.

■ TAURO, CHIEF JUSTICE.

This is a petition for a writ of certiorari and related relief brought under G.L. c. 211, § 3, asking the court to exercise its supervisory power "to correct and prevent errors and abuses" in probable cause hearings conducted in the District Courts of the Commonwealth. The petitioner asks us to vacate a finding of probable cause in the Municipal Court of the Roxbury District and remand the case to that court for a new probable cause hearing consistent with the requirements of G.L. c. 276, § 38, which he alleges were violated in his initial preliminary hearing. . . .

The pertinent facts may be summarized briefly. On February 23, 1973, a preliminary examination was held pursuant to G.L. c. 276, § 38, before a judge of the Municipal Court to determine whether there was probable cause to support the prosecution of the petitioner on charges of rape, assault by means of a dangerous weapon, breaking and entering at night, and breaking and entering at night and committing rape of a person lawfully therein. At that probable cause hearing, only the complaining witness was called to testify on behalf of the Commonwealth. At the end of direct examination the petitioner's counsel began his cross-examination of the witness. When the petitioner's counsel questioned the complaining witness about her alleged belief in witchcraft, the judge stated that he had heard enough testimony to find probable cause which made further cross-examination by the petitioner's counsel unnecessary. The petitioner's counsel stated to the court that he wished to complete his cross-examination of the complaining witness, and introduce further evidence in the defendant's behalf. The judge repeated his finding of probable cause and terminated the hearing. The question before us is whether the judge's finding of probable cause before the petitioner had an opportunity to complete cross-examination of the complaining witness and to present relevant testimony and witnesses in his own behalf violated the petitioner's "substantive rights."

1. The rules governing the conduct of preliminary hearings in the Commonwealth are summarily set forth in G.L. c. 276, § 38, "The court or justice before whom a person is taken upon a charge of crime shall, as soon as may be, examine on oath the complainant and the witnesses for the prosecution, in the presence of the defendant, relative to any material matter connected with such charge. . . . *[T]he witnesses for the prisoner, if any, shall be examined on oath, and he may be assisted by counsel in such examination and in the cross examination of the witnesses in support of the prosecution*" (emphasis supplied). The Commonwealth contends that this statute should not be interpreted as granting the defendant an absolute "inflexible" right to cross-examine prosecution witnesses and present testimony in his own behalf at the preliminary hearing because the examining

magistrate has the discretion to find probable cause after listening only to the witnesses for the prosecution. The petitioner argues that c. 276, § 38, grants defendants at such hearings *mandatory* fundamental procedural rights to confront their accusers and present testimony in their own behalf.

The petitioner's construction of the statute is supported by its express mandatory terms ("witnesses for the prisoner if any, *shall* be examined" [emphasis supplied]). "It is difficult to see how language could have been framed which would more clearly and categorically impose an absolute obligation." However, "[t]he word 'shall' as used in statutes ... is not of inflexible signification and not infrequently is construed as permissive or directory in order to effectuate a legislative purpose."

Therefore, the controversy before us as to the proper statutory construction of c. 276, § 38, cannot be resolved without examining the purposes (and procedure) of a probable cause hearing in order to determine which construction of the statute best effectuates those purposes.

2. The judge's chief task at a preliminary hearing is to determine whether the defendant should be bound over for trial in the Superior Court. Defendants are held for trial only if the examining magistrate finds (1) "that a crime has been committed" *and* (2) "that there is probable cause to believe the prisoner guilty." These two requirements are designed to establish an effective bind-over standard which distinguishes between groundless or unsupported charges and meritorious prosecutions. Thus, the preliminary hearing's primary function is to screen out at this early but critical stage of the criminal process those cases that should not go to trial thereby sparing individuals from being held for trial, and from being unjustifiably prosecuted.

The United States Supreme Court recognized the importance of the preliminary hearing's screening function in Coleman v. Alabama, 399 U.S. 1, 90 S.Ct. 1999, 26 L.Ed.2d 387, where the court held that Alabama's preliminary hearing is a "critical stage" of the State's criminal process at which the accused is entitled to the aid of counsel. . . .

Since the examining magistrate's chief task is to determine whether there is sufficient credible evidence to proceed to trial which justifies binding the defendant over, his determination of probable cause to bind over is somewhat analogous in function to the trial court's ruling on a motion for a directed verdict as to whether there is sufficient evidence to send the case to the jury. Unfortunately since this court has never defined the quantum of evidence needed to satisfy probable cause to bind over, some District Court judges have equated probable cause to bind over with probable cause for arrest (and search).

In finding probable cause to arrest, the examining magistrate has determined only that at the time *of the arrest* (or at the time when the warrant for arrest is requested), the "facts and circumstances within ... [the officers'] knowledge and of which they had reasonably trustworthy information were sufficient to warrant a prudent man in believing that the defendant had committed or was committing an offence." Commonwealth v. Stevens, Mass., 283 N.E.2d 673. . . .

... [T]here is a "large difference" between probable cause to arrest [or search] and probable cause to bind over, "and therefore a like difference in the quanta and modes of proof required to establish them." Brinegar v. United States, [338 U.S. 160, 69 S.Ct. 1302, 93 L.Ed. 1879]. A judicial finding of probable cause to arrest validates only the initial decision to arrest the suspect, not the decision made later in the criminal process to hold the defendant for trial. Since many valid arrests are based on reliable hearsay information which could not be introduced at the defendant's trial, probable cause to arrest does not automatically mean that the Commonwealth has sufficient competent legal evidence to justify the costs both to the defendant and to the Commonwealth of a full trial. Therefore the standard of probable cause to bind over must require a greater quantum of legally competent[1] evidence than the probable cause to arrest finding to insure that the preliminary hearing's screening standard is defined in a way that effectuates its purpose.

Since the examining magistrate's determination of the minimum quantum of evidence required to find probable cause to bind over is somewhat analogous in function to the court's ruling on a motion for a directed verdict at trial as to whether there is sufficient evidence to warrant submission of the case to the jury, we have decided to adopt a "directed verdict" rule in defining the minimum quantum of credible evidence necessary to support a bind-over determination. The examining magistrate should view the case as if it were a trial and he were required to rule on whether there is enough credible evidence to send the case to the jury. Thus, the magistrate should dismiss the complaint when, on the evidence presented, a trial court would be bound to acquit as a matter of law. The minimum quantum of evidence required by this bind-over standard is more than that for probable cause for arrest but less than would "prove the defendant's guilt beyond a reasonable doubt."

3.   We must construe G.L. c. 276, § 38, in a manner which effectuates its primary purpose of screening out "an erroneous or improper prosecution," Coleman v. Alabama, 399 U.S. at 9, 90 S.Ct. 1999. ... The Commonwealth's interpretation of the statute fails. ...

The Commonwealth argues that once a prima facie showing of probable cause has been made by prosecution testimony, the examining magistrate can end the hearing before the defendant's attorney has had an opportunity to make a complete cross-examination of the prosecution witness or to present an affirmative defence. We fail to see how such a limited procedure could possibly effectuate the hearing's primary function of screening out cases that should not go to trial. To require such minimal proof of probable cause would render the hearing, in many instances, an

---

1. Since the primary objective of the probable cause hearing is to screen out those cases where the *legally admissible* evidence of the defendant's guilt would be insufficient to warrant submission of the case to a jury if it had gone to trial, the rules of evidence at the preliminary hearing should in general be the same rules that are applicable at the criminal trial. ... Unlike a finding of proba-ble cause for arrest which can be based solely on reliable hearsay testimony, probable cause to hold the defendant for trial must be based on competent testimony which would be admissible at trial. Compare Federal Rule 5.1 Preliminary Examination. If it appears that added exceptions to the hearsay rule are desirable to insure an effective probable cause hearing, specific rules may be developed. ...

empty ritual with a foregone conclusion. If the examining magistrate could simply rest his finding of probable cause on the ipse dixit of the prosecution, there would be little need for defence counsel's presence, let alone the defendant's.

* * *

The primary function of the probable cause hearing of screening out "an erroneous or improper prosecution," Coleman v. Alabama, 399 U.S., supra, at 9, 90 S.Ct. 1999, can only be effectuated by an adversary hearing where the defendant is given a meaningful opportunity to challenge the credibility of the prosecution's witnesses and to raise any affirmative defences he may have. . . .

The facts of the instant case provide an excellent illustration of this point. The only witness at the petitioner's probable cause hearing was the complaining witness who repeated her accusation that the petitioner had raped her. If the petitioner had been afforded his statutory rights, he would have introduced testimony challenging the complaining witness's credibility and supporting his defence of a consensual sexual relationship.[2] The examining magistrate could not have possibly made an informed judgment on the question of whether there was sufficient credible evidence of the defendant's guilt to support a bind over until he had considered all of this evidence.

In some cases, the evidence introduced in behalf of the defendant will do no more than raise a conflict which can best be resolved by a jury at the actual trial where the Commonwealth must prove the defendant's guilt beyond a reasonable doubt. But, in other cases, the evidence elicited by defence counsel on cross-examination or from the testimony of defence witnesses or from other evidence may lead the examining magistrate to disbelieve the prosecution's witnesses and discharge the defendant for lack of probable cause.

* * *

4. In view of our interpretation of the statute, c. 276, § 38, we need not decide the petitioner's contention that the due process requirements of the United States Constitution mandate that the defendant in a probable cause hearing shall have the right to cross-examine prosecution witnesses and present testimony in his own defence. . . .[3]

2. If permitted, the petitioner's counsel would have introduced in evidence a psychiatric evaluation of the prosecutrix which noted that she "has a hysterical neurosis, a condition in which people might make up stories and then half believe them themselves. I would question the veracity of her statements." Defence counsel also wished to introduce a "medical report on the prosecutrix which shows that she received no abdominal injury, no pelvic trauma and that a vaginal discharge test for spermatozoa performed by a physician at the Boston City Hospital the morning of the alleged rape indicated no spermatozoa."

3. Moreover, the Commonwealth's interpretation would permit a procedure that would be subject to serious challenge on equal protection grounds. Past experience indicates that most District Court judges permit defendants (if they so desire) to present testimony in their own behalf at probable cause hearings. The Commonwealth's interpretation of the statute, which gives defendants a right to do so only at the trial court's discretion, would create a situation where

Our analysis of the purposes (and procedure) of the probable cause hearing leads us to conclude that the defendant must be given the opportunity to cross-examine his accusers and present testimony in his own behalf in order to insure that the hearing's vital screening function will be effectuated. Therefore, we hold that c. 276, § 38, grants defendants mandatory statutory rights to cross-examine prosecution witnesses and present testimony in their own behalf *before* the examining magistrate determines whether there is sufficient legally admissible evidence of the defendant's guilt to justify binding him over for trial.

5. The Commonwealth argues in its brief that granting defendants inflexible statutory rights to cross-examine witnesses against them and to present testimony in their own behalf would transform the preliminary hearing into a full-blown trial with disastrous results to a criminal justice system that is already overburdened. However, past experience indicates that trial strategy usually prevents such a result as both the prosecution and the defence wish to withhold as much of their case as possible.

"[N]ormally defense counsel will be more concerned at the preliminary with exploring rather than destroying the prosecution's case. If they were aware of the defects in testimony capable of attack on cross-examination, most lawyers would prefer to save the attack for trial rather than tip their hand at this early stage." Graham & Letwin, 18 U.C.L.A.Law Rev. 916, 926. For the same reasons, defence tactics usually mitigate against putting the defendant on the stand or presenting exculpatory testimony at the preliminary hearing unless defence counsel believes his evidence is compelling enough to overcome the prosecution's case.

In those instances where the defendant does choose to exercise his statutory rights, the examining magistrate at the hearing has the same broad discretion as a trial judge in limiting the scope of cross-examination to relevant issues in dispute. However, the judge at a preliminary hearing should allow reasonable latitude to the scope of the defendant's cross-examination of prosecution witnesses in order to effectuate the ancillary discovery and impeachment functions of the hearing noted in the *Coleman* ... [case]. ...

Since the summary manner in which the petitioner's probable cause hearing was conducted denied the petitioner his statutory right to cross-examine witnesses and present evidence before the issue of probable cause was determined, the petitioner must be given a new preliminary hearing to determine whether there is probable cause to hold him on the charges pending against him. Therefore, ... the original probable cause finding is vacated and the case is remanded to the Municipal Court of the Roxbury District for a new preliminary hearing to be conducted in accordance with the requirements of c. 276, § 38.

So ordered.

some defendants would be afforded a full adversary hearing upon demand while others received summary hearings in which probable cause findings rested on the unchallenged ipse dixit of prosecution witnesses. Certainly, such a discrepancy in the type of probable cause hearing afforded defendants similarly situated would raise a serious constitutional question as to whether those defendants, who received summary hearings, were being denied the equal protection of the law.

NOTES

1. **Admissibility requirements.** Other courts (and legislatures) have disagreed that the bindover decision must be made on admissible evidence. In State v. Morrissey, 295 N.W.2d 307 (N.D.1980), for example, the court reasoned that probable cause in the bindover context has the same meaning as it does in the arrest situation and this meaning demands that hearsay may be relied upon in determining whether it exists. The Colorado court has held that hearsay is admissible, People v. Szloboda, 44 Colo.App. 164, 620 P.2d 36 (1980), but has also held that exclusive reliance on "hearsay-upon-hearsay" in binding a defendant over for trial is not permissible. Maestas v. District Court, 189 Colo. 443, 541 P.2d 889 (1975). See also, State v. Anderson, 612 P.2d 778 (Utah 1980), holding that given the defendant's confrontation rights at a preliminary hearing, it was error to allow the state to present the "testimony" of its main witness by affidavit.

2. **Discovery functions.** The Massachusetts court stated that the scope of cross-examination permitted a defendant at the preliminary hearing should be such as to further the defendant's interest in discovery. But other courts have suggested that discovery is not a permissible basis for defense questions and questioning may be cut off if it proceeds beyond challenging probable cause and into discovery. See Coleman v. Burnett, 155 U.S.App.D.C. 302, 315–17, 477 F.2d 1187, 1200–02 (D.C.Cir.1973). Questioning may also be cut off if it goes beyond what under local standards are the proper issues in the preliminary. See State v. Russo, 101 Wis.2d 206, 303 N.W.2d 846 (1981). A major factor limiting the discovery value of the preliminary hearing is the absence of any requirement that the prosecution produce any particular evidence. The prosecution has almost if not complete discretion as to how to establish probable cause. In People v. Blackman, 91 Ill.App.3d 130, 46 Ill.Dec. 524, 414 N.E.2d 246 (1980), the judge presiding over the preliminary hearing, at the request of the defense, required the state to produce two specific witnesses. Finding this error, the appellate court stressed the state's ability to use hearsay to establish probable cause and its discretion as to what to produce to meet its burden.

3. **Defense witnesses.** Footnote 2 in *Myers,* supra, as well as dicta in *Myers'* text, indicates that in addition to a normal right to cross-examine prosecution witnesses, the suspect would have a similar right to call witnesses of his own. The problem arose in State v. Rud, 359 N.W.2d 573 (Minn.1984). The suspect wished to call his alleged child abuse victims to determine the exact times and locations of the claimed incidents of abuse, so that he could call alibi witnesses. Although it was unnecessary to pass on the general question of the suspect's right to call witnesses, the court held that he could not call the child abuse victims because he did not and could not claim that their testimony would lead directly to dismissal. And see Fed.R.Crim.P. 5.1(a), supra, for the general position.

4. **Defenses.** To what extent, if any, should the judge presiding over a preliminary hearing be concerned with "defensive" matters, such as self-defense, entrapment, etc.? Drawing the line between probable cause and matters that should be left for trial on the merits is not an easy one. See People v. Johnson, 618 P.2d 262 (Colo.1980), a theft prosecution in which a major question was whether the defendant's use of the money at issue was authorized by a contract. The Colorado Supreme Court held that the construction of the contract was a matter for trial on guilt or innocence, not for consideration at the preliminary hearing.

5. **Effect of a finding of no probable cause.** What if the preliminary hearing judge refuses to bind a defendant over? In most jurisdictions, this will not preclude the prosecution from securing an indictment and prosecuting the defendant. People v. Uhlemann, 9 Cal.3d 662, 108 Cal.Rptr. 657, 511 P.2d 609 (1973); People v. Anderson, 92 Ill.App.3d 849, 48 Ill.Dec. 183, 416 N.E.2d 78 (1981). The

effect of a refusal to bind over upon the prosecution's ability to charge the defendant by means of an information is less settled. In State v. Thomas, 529 S.W.2d 379 (Mo.1975) the court adopted what it described as the "prevailing general rule," which permits the state to seek an indictment but not to charge the defendant by information. Jones v. State, 481 P.2d 169 (Okla.Crim.App.1971) held that the preliminary hearing judge's action would be binding upon the prosecution, whether it sought to proceed by indictment or information, unless the prosecution produced additional evidence or established good cause justifying a second preliminary hearing. But some courts have found no bar to a second charge and a second preliminary hearing on that charge. State v. Bloomer, 197 Kan. 668, 421 P.2d 58 (1966); Thomas v. Justice Court, 538 P.2d 42 (Wyo.1975). Other courts have apparently regarded the preliminary hearing judge's decision as binding upon the prosecution, but see no problem in filing charges (and having a second preliminary hearing) before another judge with authority to hold such a hearing. State v. Maki, 291 Minn. 427, 192 N.W.2d 811 (1971); Commonwealth v. Hetherington, 460 Pa. 17, 331 A.2d 205 (1975).

Gilboy, Prosecutors' Discretionary Use of the Grand Jury to Initiate or to Reinitiate Prosecution, 1984 Am.B.Found.Res.J. 1, studying homicide cases actually initiated in Cook County, Illinois, over a 39 month period, found: (a) although re-initiated cases showed a lower rate of conviction, one half of them, nevertheless, resulted in convictions; (b) defendants in re-initiated cases were more likely to demand trials and were more likely to seek bench trials than did defendants with initial probable cause findings. Is it important that in every case which went to the grand jury first the prosecutor's request for an indictment was met, that the re-initiated cases all fell into a group in which there had been a prior no probable cause finding at a preliminary examination, that re-initiation always was before a grand jury, and that no grand jury refused to indict after a no probable cause finding at a preliminary examination? In considering this question, see infra note 6.

A related matter concerns the ability of the preliminary hearing judge to control the charge upon which the defendant is ultimately tried, especially where the prosecutor—following the bindover decision—elects to file an information. In some jurisdictions, a prosecutor who proceeds on an information is limited to the offense for which the defendant was bound over. State v. McCrary, 97 N.M. 306, 639 P.2d 593 (App. 1982). But in others, the preliminary hearing is limited to determining whether there is probable cause to believe that the defendant committed some felony. If this determination is made, the preliminary hearing judge has no authority to bind over on a specific charge. See State ex rel. Thomas v. Crouch, 603 S.W.2d 532 (Mo.1980), appeal dismissed for want of a substantial federal question 451 U.S. 901, 101 S.Ct. 1965, 68 L.Ed.2d 289 (1981) (prosecutor could file capital murder indictment although preliminary hearing judge bound over only for second degree murder). In State v. Hooper, 101 Wis.2d 517, 305 N.W.2d 110 (1981), the court held that once a defendant was bound over at a preliminary hearing, the prosecutor's choice as to a specific charge is subject to attack only for abuse of discretion.

6.   **Choosing a preliminary or grand jury.** The Oregon Supreme Court in State v. Freeland, 295 Or. 367, 667 P.2d 509 (1983), held that although a grant of discretion to the prosecutor to initiate prosecution by information—with its accompanying preliminary—or by indictment, was not per se unconstitutional, the prosecutor's choice must be based on permissible criteria consistently applied in order that similarly situated defendants were offered preliminaries. Greater efficiency and dispatch by using the grand jury was found to be a permissible criterion in State v. Eells, 72 Or.App. 492, 696 P.2d 564 (1985).

In another part of her study, Gilboy, supra, found that the grand jury was initially used in only twenty per cent of the cases and that it was the preferred method for "stronger cases". The reasons given for choosing the grand jury route included avoiding witness intimidation, quickly resolving highly publicized cases, saving court time, and, in some instances, making it more convenient for witnesses. The preliminary examination route was preferred when there was an unusually high risk that a witness would be unavailable at a later stage and to test the strength of the state's case. There was some concern expressed that if the preliminary were used too infrequently, a bill, regularly introduced in the Illinois Legislature to require the preliminary in all cases, would pass.

7. **Post-indictment preliminaries.** In most jurisdictions, a defendant against whom an indictment has been returned has no right to a preliminary hearing. This is based upon the ground that both the indictment process and the preliminary hearing are to determine probable cause and there is no legitimate function served by two such determinations. E.g., United States v. Simon, 510 F.Supp. 232 (E.D.Pa.1981); King v. Venters, 595 S.W.2d 714 (Ky.1980); State *ex rel.* Rowe v. Ferguson, 165 W.Va. 183, 268 S.E.2d 45 (1980). But in State v. Holmes, 388 So.2d 722 (La.1980), the court held that whether to hold a preliminary hearing for an indicted defendant was discretionary with the trial court. And in Hawkins v. Superior Court, 22 Cal.3d 584, 150 Cal.Rptr. 435, 586 P.2d 916 (1978) the California Supreme Court held that the state constitutional requirement of equal protection entitled indicted defendants to a preliminary hearing. After reviewing the benefits which the Supreme Court in Coleman v. Alabama found to flow from the preliminary hearing, the court emphasized the prosecution's control over the alternative grand jury process and reasoned:

> These benefits to the defense which inhere in an adversarial preliminary hearing are either completely denied to a defendant charged in a secret, nonadversarial grand jury proceeding, or ultimately realized by such a defendant only to a limited extent. It cannot be seriously argued that an indicted defendant enjoys a comparable opportunity to discover the state's case and develop evidence because he later obtains a transcript of grand jury proceedings. Such a transcript will invariably reflect only what the prosecutor permits it to reflect; it is certainly no substitute for the possibility of developing further evidence through a probing cross examination of prosecution witnesses—a possibility foreclosed with the denial of an adversarial proceeding. There is no other effective means for the defense to compel the cooperation of a hostile witness; in the unlikely event that all the prosecution witnesses agree to submit to defense interviews, the defense must still incur unnecessary expense and hardship which may be substantial.

22 Cal.3d at 589, 150 Cal.Rptr. at 438, 586 P.2d at 919. By denying indicted defendants access to these advantages which are afforded those charged by information, the court concluded, the state was denying equal protection. Other courts, however, have responded to similar arguments by characterizing these advantages of a preliminary hearing as incidental and unintended side-effects and as of minimal importance given other ways to achieve them. In State ex rel. Rowe v. Ferguson, supra, for example, the court concluded that liberalized discovery for criminal defendants has greatly reduced the importance of the discovery function of the preliminary hearing.

8. **Reform of the California preliminary.** The California preliminary hearing or examination was dramatically changed by an initiative measure—Proposition 115 or the "Crime Victims Justice Reform Act"—adopted in 1990 by the voters of that state. The measure affected both statutory and constitutional provisions. Perhaps the purpose of the changes is best reflected in section 866(b) of the California Penal Code as amended by the measure:

> It is the purpose of a preliminary examination to establish whether there exists probable cause to believe that the defendant has committed a felony. The examination shall not be used for purposes of discovery.

Moreover, the availability of preliminary examinations was reduced by providing in article I, section 14.1 of the California Constitution: "If a felony is prosecuted by indictment, there shall be no postindictment preliminary hearing."

To implement the voters' obvious desire to reduce the impact of preliminary examinations upon crime victims, article I, section 30(b) of the Constitution was amended by Proposition 115 to add the following:

> In order to protect victims and witnesses in criminal cases, hearsay evidence shall be admissible at preliminary hearings, as prescribed by the Legislature or by the people through the initiative process.

This was effectuated by amendment of Section 872(b) of the Penal Code to provide:

> Notwithstanding Section 1200 of the Evidence Code [the hearsay rule], the finding of probable cause may be based in whole or in part upon the sworn testimony of a law enforcement officer relating the statements of declarants made out of court offered for the truth of the matter asserted. Any law enforcement officer testifying as to hearsay statements shall either have five years of law enforcement experience or have completed a training course certified by the Commission on Peace Officer Standards and Training which includes training in the investigation and reporting of cases and testifying at preliminary hearings.

Section 1203 of California's Evidence Code requires that hearsay declarants be made available for cross-examination. The 1990 initiative enacted section 1203.1, which provides:

> Section 1203 is not applicable if the hearsay statement is offered at a preliminary examination, as provided in Section 872 of the Penal Code.

A defendant's right to call witnesses at the preliminary examination was also limited by amendment of Penal Code section 866(a) to provide:

> Upon the request of the prosecuting attorney, the magistrate shall require an offer of proof from the defense as to the testimony expected from [a defense] witness. The magistrate shall not permit the testimony of any defense witness unless the offer of proof discloses to the satisfaction of the magistrate, in his or her discretion, that the testimony of that witness, if believed, would be reasonably likely to establish an affirmative defense, negate an element of a crime charged, or impeach the testimony of a prosecution witness or the statement of a declarant testified to by a prosecution witness.

As the California Supreme Court commented in Whitman v. Superior Court (People), 54 Cal.3d 1063, 2 Cal.Rptr.2d 160, 820 P.2d 262 (1991):

> [Section 866, as amended by the initiative] marks a sharp contrast to this court's previous expansive concept of the preliminary hearing as a discovery and trial preparation device, allowing counsel the opportunity to "fashion" their impeachment tools for use in cross-examination at trial, to preserve testimony favorable to the defense, and to provide the defense "with valuable information about the case against the accused, enhancing its ability to evaluate the desirability of entering a plea or to prepare for trial."

54 Cal.3d at 1081, 2 Cal.Rptr.2d at 170, 820 P.2d at 272, quoting from Hawkins v. Superior Court, 22 Cal.3d 584, 588, 150 Cal.Rptr. 435, 438, 586 P.2d 916, 919 (1978), discussed in note 7, supra.

The California Supreme Court recognized that the enactment of article I, section 14.1 of the California Constitution negated its earlier holding in *Hawkins* that the state Equal Protection Clause gave an indicted felony defendant a right to a preliminary examination. It also held that granting preliminary examinations to only nonindicted defendants does not violate the Equal Protection Clause of the Fourteenth Amendment. Bowens v. Superior Court (People), 1 Cal.4th 36, 2 Cal.Rptr.2d 376, 820 P.2d 600 (1991).

In *Whitman, supra,* the court turned to the effect of the constitutional and statutory provisions permitting hearsay to be used by the prosecution. In *Whitman,* the only witness at the defendant's preliminary examination was a "reader" police officer, that is, an officer with the experience required by section 872(b) but who had no direct, personal knowledge of the offense or the investigation and simply read the report of the investigating officers. The voters' intention, held the court, was not to permit use of this sort of hearsay:

> Properly construed, Proposition 115 does not authorize a finding of probable cause based on the testimony of a noninvestigating officer or "reader" merely reciting the police report of an investigating officer. We believe the probable intent of the framers of the measure was to allow a properly qualified investigating officer to relate out-of-court statements by crime victims or witnesses, including other law enforcement personnel, without requiring the victims' or witnesses' presence in court. The testifying officer, however, must not be a mere reader but must have sufficient knowledge of the crime or the circumstances under which the out-of-court statement was made so as to meaningfully assist the magistrate in assessing the reliability of the statement.

54 Cal.3d at 1072–73, 2 Cal.Rptr.2d at 164–65, 820 P.2d at 266–67.

For a general discussion, see Berend, Proposition 115 Preliminary Hearings: Sacrificing Reliability on the Altar of Expediency, 23 Pac.L.J. 1131 (1992).

B.   THE GRAND JURY

The second major vehicle for pretrial screening is the grand jury. Whether the grand jury can or does perform an acceptable screening function is disputed. Among the concerns that can be raised as to the ability of the grand jury to function effectively are its dependence upon the prosecution for information, investigatory assistance, and legal advice, and the potential difficulty which lay jurors may experience in resolving the sometimes complex legal issues that even probable cause determinations raise. For a vigorous presentation of the view that grand juries are no more than alter egos of prosecutors, see Antell, The Modern Grand Jury: Benighted Supergovernment, 51 A.B.A.J. 153 (1965).

Unless the grand jury is to be abandoned as a pretrial screening tool, however, consideration should be given to the manner in which its function is to be structured. This is the major concern of the present section. In addition, however, attention needs to be paid to the manner in which those requirements imposed will be enforced. Traditionally, this was sought to be accomplished in part by rigidly requiring the prosecution to prove at trial those matters alleged in the indictment and limiting the ability of the prosecution and trial court to change or "amend" an indictment. A defendant's right to indictment, it was reasoned, demanded that he be tried on precisely the charge returned by the grand jury. If amendment of the indictment was permitted, the defendant might be tried and convicted of a version of the offense on which the grand jury never passed.

Modern rules of procedure and proof have strayed away from this approach. The trend was illustrated by United States v. Miller, 471 U.S. 130, 105 S.Ct. 1811, 85 L.Ed.2d 99 (1985). Miller was indicted by a federal grand jury for mail fraud. The indictment alleged that he used the mails to make a fraudulent claim to his insurance company concerning losses allegedly resulting from a burglary. Specifically, the indictment alleged that he fraudulently represented to his insurer that the losses were incurred in a scheme to which he had not consented and that he fraudulently represented the value of the property taken. Under the substantive criminal law, using the mails to obtain insurance proceeds and fraudulently misrepresenting the amount of the loss was sufficient to constitute the crime. At trial, the Government sought unsuccessfully to have struck from the indictment the allegations that Miller consented in advance to the removal of the property and that he misrepresented this in the claim sent through the mails. Its evidence showed that Miller did fraudulently exaggerate the amount of his loss; the Government did not prove his prior consent to the taking of the property and any misrepresentation concerning that. In a sense, there was what has traditionally been called a "variance between the pleading and the proof." The Government's evidence proved the defendant committed the offense charged; it proved that, however, in a way varying from the allegations in the indictment because not all of the allegations made by the grand jury were proved by the trial evidence. The jury convicted Miller. On appeal, the Court of Appeals—taking a traditional approach—held that to permit Miller's conviction on the basis of proof of some but not all of the allegations in the indictment violated his Fifth Amendment right to grand jury indictment. The grand jury, it reasoned, may well have declined to indict him on the theory that the only fraud involved was an exaggeration of the losses incurred. He was convicted of an offense, the Court of Appeals concluded, for which he had not been indicted. 715 F.2d 1360 (9th Cir.1983), modified 728 F.2d 1269 (9th Cir.1984).

The Supreme Court reversed the Court of Appeals and upheld the conviction. It reaffirmed that the right to indictment means that new allegations cannot be added to an indictment except by the grand jury. Moreover, a defendant cannot be convicted on the basis of evidence proving matters not alleged in an indictment. But it rejected the argument that the Fifth Amendment bars convicting a defendant on the basis of facts which constitute the offense but are less than the total facts alleged in the indictment. The Government proved Miller's guilt and it did so by proving only facts alleged in the indictment. It failed to prove some facts alleged in the indictment but these allegations were "in no way essential to the offense on which the jury convicted" and could be regarded as "surplusage" and ignored. 471 U.S. at 145, 105 S.Ct. at 1820, 85 L.Ed.2d at 111.

In *Miller,* is it possible that if the presentation to the grand jury had involved only evidence that Miller had exaggerated the amount of his losses, the grand jury might have refused to indict because of deficiencies in the evidence that the exaggeration was fraudulent or because in its judgment such an exaggeration, even if fraudulent, should not be treated as a serious criminal offense? If so, perhaps the decision in *Miller* reflects the Supreme Court's view that the right to indictment does not include the right to have the grand jury scrutinize the sufficiency of the evidence on each of several alternative ways the accused may have committed the crime. Perhaps it reflects a view that the right to indictment does not include the right to have the grand jury consider, if the evidence establishes probable cause, whether as a matter of prosecutorial judgment charges should be pursued. Or maybe it reflects a view that whatever the content of the Fifth Amendment right to indictment, this right should not be enforced by restricting the Government in its trial proof.

Alleged discrimination in the selection of grand jurors raises issues closely resembling those presented by the petit jury selection process. These issues are therefore considered in Chapter 23 in connection with the right to trial by jury.

Costello v. United States

Supreme Court of the United States, 1956.
350 U.S. 359, 76 S.Ct. 406, 100 L.Ed. 397.

■ MR. JUSTICE BLACK delivered the opinion of the Court.

We granted certiorari in this case to consider a single question: " 'May a defendant be required to stand trial and a conviction be sustained where only hearsay evidence was presented to the grand jury which indicted him?' " 350 U.S. 819, 76 S.Ct. 48.

Petitioner, Frank Costello, was indicted for wilfully attempting to evade payment of income taxes due the United States for the years 1947, 1948 and 1949. The charge was that petitioner falsely and fraudulently reported less income than he and his wife actually received during the taxable years in question. Petitioner promptly filed a motion for inspection of the minutes of the grand jury and for a dismissal of the indictment. His motion was based on an affidavit stating that he was firmly convinced there could have been no legal or competent evidence before the grand jury which indicted him since he had reported all his income and paid all taxes due. The motion was denied. At the trial which followed the Government offered evidence designed to show increases in Costello's net worth in an attempt to prove that he had received more income during the years in question than he had reported. To establish its case the Government called and examined 144 witnesses and introduced 368 exhibits. All of the testimony and documents related to business transactions and expenditures by petitioner and his wife. The prosecution concluded its case by calling three government agents. Their investigations had produced the evidence used against petitioner at the trial. They were allowed to summarize the vast amount of evidence already heard and to introduce computations showing, if correct, that petitioner and his wife had received far greater income than they had reported. We have held such summarizations admissible in a "net worth" case like this. United States v. Johnson, 319 U.S. 503, 63 S.Ct. 1233, 87 L.Ed. 1546.

Counsel for petitioner asked each government witness at the trial whether he had appeared before the grand jury which returned the indictment. This cross-examination developed the fact that the three investigating officers had been the only witnesses before the grand jury. After the Government concluded its case, petitioner again moved to dismiss the indictment on the ground that the only evidence before the grand jury was "hearsay," since the three officers had no firsthand knowledge of the transactions upon which their computations were based. Nevertheless the trial court again refused to dismiss the indictment, and petitioner was convicted. The Court of Appeals affirmed, holding that the indictment was valid even though the sole evidence before the grand jury was hearsay. Petitioner here urges: (1) that an indictment based solely on hearsay evidence violates that part of the Fifth Amendment providing that "No person shall be held to answer for a capital, or otherwise infamous crime, unless on a presentment or indictment of a Grand Jury ..." and (2) that if the Fifth Amendment does not invalidate an indictment based solely on hearsay we should now lay down such a rule for the guidance of federal courts. See McNabb v. United States, 318 U.S. 332, 340–341, 63 S.Ct. 608, 612–613, 87 L.Ed. 819.

The Fifth Amendment provides that federal prosecutions for capital or otherwise infamous crimes must be instituted by presentments or indictments of grand juries. But neither the Fifth Amendment nor any other constitutional provision prescribes the kind of evidence upon which grand juries must act. The grand jury is an English institution, brought to this country by the early colonists and incorporated in the Constitution by the Founders. There is every reason to believe that our constitutional grand jury was intended to operate substantially like its English progenitor. The basic purpose of the English grand jury was to provide a fair method for instituting criminal proceedings against persons believed to have committed crimes. Grand jurors were selected from the body of the people and their work was not hampered by rigid procedural or evidential rules. In fact, grand jurors could act on their own knowledge and were free to make their presentments or indictments on such information as they deemed satisfactory. Despite its broad power to institute criminal proceedings the grand jury grew in popular favor with the years. It acquired an independence in England free from control by the Crown or judges. Its adoption in our Constitution as the sole method for preferring charges in serious criminal cases shows the high place it held as an instrument of justice. And in this country as in England of old the grand jury has convened as a body of laymen, free from technical rules, acting in secret, pledged to indict no one because of prejudice and to free no one because of special favor. As late as 1927 an English historian could say that English grand juries were still free to act on their own knowledge if they pleased to do so. And in 1852 Mr. Justice Nelson on circuit could say "No case has been cited, nor have we been able to find any, furnishing an authority for looking into and revising the judgment of the grand jury upon the evidence, for the purpose of determining whether or not the finding was founded upon sufficient proof...." United States v. Reed, 27 Fed.Cas. pages 727, 738, No. 16,134.

In Holt v. United States, 218 U.S. 245, 31 S.Ct. 2, 4, 54 L.Ed. 1021, this Court had to decide whether an indictment should be quashed because supported in part by incompetent evidence. Aside from the incompetent evidence "there was very little evidence against the accused." The Court refused to hold that such an indictment should be quashed, pointing out that "The abuses of criminal practice would be enhanced if indictments could be upset on such a ground." 218 U.S. at page 248, 31 S.Ct. at page 4. The same thing is true where as here all the evidence before the grand jury was in the nature of "hearsay." If indictments were to be held open to challenge on the ground that there was inadequate or incompetent evidence before the grand jury, the resulting delay would be great indeed. The result of such a rule would be that before trial on the merits a defendant could always insist on a kind of preliminary trial to determine the competency and adequacy of the evidence before the grand jury. This is not required by the Fifth Amendment. An indictment returned by a legally constituted and unbiased grand jury, like an information drawn by the prosecutor, if valid on its face, is enough to call for trial of the charge on the merits. The Fifth Amendment requires nothing more.

Petitioner urges that this Court should exercise its power to supervise the administration of justice in federal courts and establish a rule permitting defendants to challenge indictments on the ground that they are not supported by adequate or competent evidence. No persuasive reasons are advanced for establishing such a rule. It would run counter to the whole history of the grand jury institution, in which laymen conduct their inquiries unfettered by technical rules. Neither justice nor the concept of a fair trial requires such a change. In a trial on the merits, defendants are entitled to a strict observance of all the rules designed to bring about a fair verdict. Defendants are not entitled, however, to a rule which would result in interminable delay but add nothing to the assurance of a fair trial.

Affirmed.

■ MR. JUSTICE CLARK and MR. JUSTICE HARLAN took no part in the consideration or decision of this case.

■ MR. JUSTICE BURTON, concurring.

I agree with the denial of the motion to quash the indictment. In my view, however, this case does not justify the breadth of the declarations made by the Court. I assume that this Court would not preclude an examination of grand-jury action to ascertain the existence of bias or prejudice in an indictment. Likewise, it seems to me that if it is shown that the grand jury had before it no substantial or rationally persuasive evidence upon which to base its indictment, that indictment should be quashed. To hold a person to answer to such an empty indictment for a capital or otherwise infamous federal crime robs the Fifth Amendment of much of its protective value to the private citizen.

* * *

NOTES

1. **Disclosing to the grand jury that testimony is hearsay.** Despite the principal case, some lower federal courts have been disturbed by what they view as excessive reliance upon hearsay before the grand jury. Concern has often focused on

whether the prosecutor deceived the grand jury by not disclosing the hearsay nature of the evidence or otherwise. In response to that concern, the Ninth Circuit has held that deliberate use of perjured testimony before a grand jury by the prosecution constitutes misconduct invalidating the indictment. See United States v. Samango, 607 F.2d 877 (9th Cir.1979). A leading case, United States v. Estepa, 471 F.2d 1132 (2d Cir.1972), involves an indictment returned on the basis of the testimony of a single police officer, who testified concerning a number of incidents in a manner not making clear that he lacked first-hand knowledge of these matters. The Second Circuit noted that it had "previously condemned the casual attitude with respect to the presentation of evidence to a grand jury manifested by the decision of the Assistant United States Attorney to rely on the testimony of the law enforcement officer who knew least, rather than subject the other officers, or himself, to some minor inconvenience...." 471 F.2d at 1135. Summarizing its position, the court stated:

> We have been willing to allow ample ... latitude in the needless use of hearsay, subject to only two provisos—that the prosecutor does not deceive grand jurors as to "the shoddy merchandise they are getting so they can seek something better if they wish," or that the case does not involve "a high probability that with eyewitness rather than hearsay testimony the grand jury would not have indicted."

471 F.2d at 1137. Because the government violated the first of these two provisos, the conviction was reversed and the case remanded with instructions to the District Court to dismiss the indictment without prejudice to the right of the government to seek another indictment.

Other circuits have disapproved of the *Estepa* position. United States v. Barone, 584 F.2d 118, 125 (6th Cir.1978) (court is "not disposed" to follow *Estepa,* but no need to reach issue because no deception of grand jury); United States v. Chanen, 549 F.2d 1306, 1311 (9th Cir.1977). Even in the Second Circuit, *Estepa* has been distinguished where deception was absent. Thus it was found inapplicable in United States v. James, 609 F.2d 36, 49 (2d Cir.1979), cert. denied 445 U.S. 905, 100 S.Ct. 1082, 63 L.Ed.2d 321 (1980), where substantial non-hearsay evidence was presented to the grand jury and the prosecutor told the grand jury that much of the evidence it had received was hearsay and that it could have those witnesses with first-hand knowledge of the matters brought before it if the grand jury wished. In a few jurisdictions, hearsay may not be relied upon by the grand jury. See People v. Jackson, 18 N.Y.2d 516, 277 N.Y.S.2d 263, 223 N.E.2d 790 (1966), holding that a confession of a codefendant implicating the defendant could not be considered by the grand jury.

2. **Illegally-obtained evidence.** Does or should it make any difference that the grand jury considered evidence that would under the Constitution be inadmissible at trial? In United States v. Calandra, 414 U.S. 338, 94 S.Ct. 613, 38 L.Ed.2d 561 (1974) the federal District Court granted Calandra's motion to suppress certain evidence on the ground that it had been seized in violation of Calandra's Fourth Amendment rights. It further ordered that Calandra need not answer questions which it was anticipated would be asked him by a grand jury investigating the matter if those questions were based on the suppressed evidence. Reversing, a majority of the Supreme Court, in an opinion by Justice Powell, explained:

> In deciding whether to extend the exclusionary rule to grand jury proceedings, we must weigh the potential injury to the historic role and functions of the grand jury against the potential benefits of the rule as applied in this context. It is evident that this extension of the exclusionary rule would seriously impede the grand jury. Because the grand jury does not finally adjudicate guilt or innocence, it has traditionally been allowed to pursue its

investigative and accusatorial functions unimpeded by the evidentiary and procedural restrictions applicable to a criminal trial. Permitting witnesses to invoke the exclusionary rule before a grand jury would precipitate adjudication of issues hitherto reserved for the trial on the merits and would delay and disrupt grand jury proceedings. Suppression hearings would halt the orderly progress of an investigation and might necessitate extended litigation of issues only tangentially related to the grand jury's primary objective. The probable result would be "protracted interruptions of grand jury proceedings." Gelbard v. United States, 408 U.S. 41, 70, 92 S.Ct. 2357, 2372, 33 L.Ed.2d 179 (1972) (White, J., concurring), effectively transforming them into preliminary trials on the merits. In some cases the delay might be fatal to the enforcement of the criminal law.... In sum, we believe that allowing a grand jury witness to invoke the exclusionary rule would unduly interfere with the effective and expeditious discharge of the grand jury's duties.

Against this potential damage to the role and functions of the grand jury, we must weigh the benefits to be derived from this proposed extension of the exclusionary rule. Suppression of the use of illegally seized evidence against the search victim in a criminal trial is thought to be an important method of effectuating the Fourth Amendment. But it does not follow that the Fourth Amendment requires adoption of every proposal that might deter police misconduct.

* * *

Any incremental deterrent effect which might be achieved by extending the rule to grand jury proceedings is uncertain at best. Whatever deterrence of police misconduct may result from the exclusion of illegally seized evidence from criminal trials, it is unrealistic to assume that application of the rule to grand jury proceedings would significantly further that goal. Such an extension would deter only police investigation consciously directed toward the discovery of evidence solely for use in a grand jury investigation. The incentive to disregard the requirement of the Fourth Amendment solely to obtain an indictment from a grand jury is substantially negated by the inadmissibility of the illegally seized evidence in a subsequent criminal prosecution of the search victim. For the most part, a prosecutor would be unlikely to request an indictment where a conviction could not be obtained. We therefore decline to embrace a view that would achieve a speculative and undoubtedly minimal advance in the deterrence of police misconduct at the expense of substantially impeding the role of the grand jury.

414 U.S. at 349–52, 94 S.Ct. at 620–22, 38 L.Ed.2d at 572–73. In Gelbard v. United States, supra, the Court held that the statutory exclusionary provision of the federal "wiretap" statute, 18 U.S.C. § 2515, entitled a grand jury witness to decline to answer questions that were the product of electronic surveillance conducted in violation of the statute. But the majority carefully distinguished the issue that would be presented by an effort to challenge an indictment as the product of a violation of the federal statute and noted evidence of Congressional intent to leave undisturbed by the statute the longstanding rule prohibiting attacks on indictments because of presentation of tainted evidence to the indicting grand jury. 408 U.S. at 60, 92 S.Ct. at 2367, 33 L.Ed.2d at 193–94. In re Ellsberg, 446 F.2d 954 (1st Cir.1971) held that the federal statute did not require dismissal of an indictment because the grand jury had considered evidence obtained in violation of the statute. But in State v. Mayes, 284 Md. 625, 399 A.2d 597 (1979) the Maryland court construed a state statute modeled on the federal act as mandating dismissal of an indictment because the grand jury considered evidence obtained in violation of the statute.

3. **Judicial review of indictment for probable cause.** In a few jurisdictions, the trial court is authorized to review the evidence supporting an indictment and to dismiss any indictment found unsupported by sufficient evidence. Colo.Rev. Stat. § 16–5–204(4)(k)(West 1998); N.Y.Crim.Proc.Law §§ 210.20, 210.30 (McKinney 1979). Describing the function of the trial court under the Colorado statute, the Colorado Supreme Court has stated:

> [T]he district court function in conducting the review of the grand jury record . . . is much like the role of the court at a preliminary hearing and . . . the same rule applies in determining the existence or absence of probable cause. The court must draw all inferences in favor of the prosecution and when there is a conflict in the testimony a question of fact exists for determination at trial.

People v. Summers, 197 Colo. 445, 447, 593 P.2d 969, 970 (1979). Bayless, Grand Jury Reform: The Colorado Experience, 67 A.B.A.J. 568, 572 (1981), commenting on practice under the Colorado statute, states that about 10 percent of indictments reviewed under the section have been dismissed. All but one of the dismissals, however, were followed by successful reindictments; in the remaining case, the grand jury had indicted against the recommendation of the prosecutor and no reindictment was sought.

4. **Exculpatory evidence.** Does a prosecutor have a duty to present exculpatory evidence to a grand jury? In Johnson v. Superior Court, 15 Cal.3d 248, 124 Cal.Rptr. 32, 539 P.2d 792 (1975) the California Supreme Court held that "when a district attorney seeking an indictment is aware of evidence reasonably tending to negate guilt, he is obligated . . . to inform the grand jury of its nature and existence, so that the grand jury may exercise its power . . . to order the evidence produced." 15 Cal.3d at 255, 124 Cal.Rptr. at 36, 539 P.2d at 796. But the court relied heavily upon Cal.Penal Code § 939.7, which provides that whenever a grand jury "has reason to believe that other evidence within its reach will explain away the charge, it shall order the evidence to be produced."

The Supreme Court considered federal prosecutors' duty to present exculpatory evidence to grand juries in United States v. Williams, 504 U.S. 36, 112 S.Ct. 1735, 118 L.Ed.2d 352 (1992). The Tenth Circuit had held, pursuant to what it regarded as the federal courts' "supervisory power," that federal prosecutors in possession of "substantial exculpatory evidence" concerning a suspect under consideration by a grand jury had a duty to present that evidence to the grand jury. Finding on the facts of *Williams* that the Government violated this duty and that there was at least a grave doubt as to whether the grand jury's decision to indict Williams was free from substantial influence by this violation, the lower courts required that Williams' indictment be dismissed. The Supreme Court reversed, and disapproved the Tenth Circuit's position. Federal grand juries, Justice Scalia explained for the Court, are "functionally independe[nt]" from the judicial branch, and therefore the federal judiciary has at most very limited supervisory power to fashion rules of procedure for grand jury proceedings. This limited power does not include the authority to promulgate rules that would "reshap[e] the grand jury institution." A rule requiring prosecutors to present exculpatory as well as incriminating evidence to grand juries would "alter the grand jury's historical role, transforming it from an accusatory to an adjudicatory body." The target of a grand jury investigation has no right to tender his "defense" to the grand jury. A grand jury can clearly refuse to hear exculpatory evidence. Federal courts cannot scrutinize the evidentiary support for a grand jury's decision to indict. Imposing upon a prosecutor a legal obligation to present to the grand jury exculpatory evidence in his possession would be incompatible with these aspects of the grand jury. If the courts will not review the evidentiary support for the grand jury's decision, for example, there is no sense in those same courts scrutinizing the prosecutor's presentation to the grand jury.

Moreover, a target could "circumnavigate the system by delivering [his exculpatory evidence] to the prosecutor, whereupon it would have to be passed on to the grand jury * * *." The requirement applied to the case below by the Tenth Circuit, then, was beyond the authority of that court to develop pursuant to its inherent supervisory authority. Williams had not contended, Justice Scalia noted, that the Fifth Amendment itself compelled a rule requiring prosecutorial disclosure of exculpatory evidence to grand juries.

Four members of the Court dissented in an opinion by Justice Stevens. Grand juries, he reasoned, are subject to the control of the courts. The Supreme Court therefore has authority to create and enforce limited rules applicable in grand jury proceedings. Rules prohibiting prosecutorial misconduct are within this authority. Grand juries serve in part to protect citizens against arbitrary and oppressive governmental action. Prohibitions against prosecutorial misconduct—such as misleading grand juries—do not alter the traditional role of grand juries but merely assure their ability to perform one of their traditional functions. The nature of a grand jury proceeding precludes a rule requiring prosecutors to ferret out and present all evidence bearing on a suspect's guilt or innocence.

> But that does not mean that the prosecutor may mislead the grand jury into believing that there is probable cause to indict by withholding clear evidence to the contrary. I thus agree with the Department of Justice that "when a prosecutor conducting a grand jury inquiry is personally aware of substantial evidence which directly negates the guilt of a subject of the investigation, the prosecutor must present or otherwise disclose such evidence to the grand jury before seeking an indictment against such a person." U.S. Dept. of Justice, United States Attorneys' Manual, Title 9, ch. 11, par. 9–11.233, 88 (1988).

504 U.S. at 69–70, 112 S.Ct. at 1754, 118 L.Ed.2d at 379 (Stevens, J., dissenting). To enforce this, he concluded, the federal courts have the power to dismiss indictments because the prosecutor violated this duty.

5. **Target's right to appear before grand jury.** Several jurisdictions, in an apparent effort to improve the screening role of the grand jury, have given persons against whom an indictment is being considered a right to appear before the grand jury. N.M.Stat.Ann. § 31–6–11(B) provides:

> The target shall be notified of his target status and be given an opportunity to testify, if he desires to do so, unless the prosecutor determines that notification may result in flight, endanger other persons, obstruct justice, or the prosecutor is unable with reasonable diligence to notify such person.

This, of course, must be distinguished from the ability of an investigating grand jury to require a target to appear and the rights of such a target when compelled to appear; these are presented in Chapter 9, supra. Would one who is notified of his target status under this section be well-advised to seek an opportunity to appear before the grand jury? Bayless, Grand Jury Reform: The Colorado Experience, 67 A.B.A.J. 568, 570 (1981) notes that voluntary appearances by targets before the grand jury are rare under the Colorado statute.

6. **Record of grand jury proceedings.** Jurisdictions vary widely in regard to the information kept on grand jury proceedings and concerning defendants' access to what information is kept. Rule 6(e)(1) of the Federal Rules of Criminal Procedure provides:

> All proceedings, except when the grand jury is deliberating or voting, shall be recorded stenographically or by an electronic recording device. An unintentional failure of any recording to reproduce all or any portion of the proceeding shall not affect the validity of the prosecution. The recording or reporter's notes or any transcript prepared therefrom shall remain in the custody or control of

the attorney for the government unless otherwise ordered by the court in a particular case.

Grand jurors, government attorneys, court reporters, and others—but not witnesses—are barred by Rule 6(e)(2) from disclosing matters occurring before a grand jury. Rule 6(e)(3)(B)(ii) permits disclosure of matters occurring before a grand jury:

> when permitted by a court at the request of the defendant, upon a showing that grounds may exist for a motion to dismiss the indictment because of matters occurring before the grand jury.

How does a defendant make such a showing without access to the information establishing what happened before the grand jury?

Some jurisdictions not only require that information be compiled but also that it be disclosed to the defense. Rule 12.8 of the Arizona Rules of Criminal Procedure, for example, requires that, within 20 days of the return of an indictment, a transcript of the court reporter's notes of the grand jury proceedings (except the deliberations) and the foreman's record of the votes on indictments be filed with the court and made available to the defense and the prosecution.

7. **Presence of persons who are not witnesses.** Rule 6(d) of the Federal Rules of Criminal Procedure provides that only specified persons, including "the witness under examination" may be present during grand jury proceedings. What legal consequences should ensue from failure to comply with that restriction? In United States v. Mechanik, 475 U.S. 66, 106 S.Ct. 938, 89 L.Ed.2d 50 (1986), two Government witnesses were present while each testified before the grand jury. Despite the exercise of diligence, defendants did not learn of this until after the trial had begun, when the information was disclosed as part of Jencks Act materials. The District Court overruled a motion to dismiss the indictment, but the Court of Appeals reversed on the ground that a violation of Rule 6(d) requires automatic reversal of any subsequent conviction. The Supreme Court, in an opinion authored by Justice Rehnquist, reversed. Expressly offering no opinion as to what the consequences of a violation should be when it is brought to the attention of the trial court before trial begins, the Court concluded that the subsequent convictions of the defendants rendered the violation harmless:

> The error involving Rule 6(d) in these cases had the theoretical potential to affect the grand jury's determination whether to indict these particular defendants for the offenses with which they were charged. But the petit jury's subsequent guilty verdict not only means that there was probable cause to believe that the defendants were guilty as charged, but that they are in fact guilty as charged beyond a reasonable doubt. Measured by the petit jury's verdict, then, any error in the grand jury proceedings connected with the charging decision was harmless beyond a reasonable doubt.

475 U.S. at 70, 106 S.Ct. at 941–42, 89 L.Ed.2d at 56.

Chief Justice Burger concurred on the ground the case should be controlled by Costello v. United States. Is there any practical difference between Justice Burger's position and that of the Court as applied to a violation brought to the attention of the District Court before trial begins?

Justice O'Connor, joined by Justices Brennan and Blackmun, concurred in the judgment on the ground that the test of harm should be whether the violation had a detrimental impact on the grand jury proceedings themselves. She argued that "the remedy of dismissal of the indictment is appropriate if it is established that the violation substantially influenced the grand jury's decision to indict, or if there is grave doubt as to whether it had such effect." 475 U.S. at 78, 106 S.Ct. at 945, 89 L.Ed.2d at 61. The Court's position, she complained, encourages trial courts to delay their rulings on motions to dismiss until after the jury's verdict. If the jury acquits, the question is moot and if it convicts any violation is harmless. Justice Marshall dissented on the ground, among others, that the Court's position renders Rule 6(d) "almost unenforceable."

8. **Prosecutorial misconduct before grand jury.** In Bank of Nova Scotia v. United States, 487 U.S. 250, 108 S.Ct. 2369, 101 L.Ed.2d 228 (1988), the Court considered the standard by which instances of prosecutorial misconduct before the grand jury should be assessed when a motion to dismiss an indictment is presented to the trial court before the trial begins. The indictment in this case was dismissed for various violations of Rule 6 of the Federal Rules of Criminal Procedure. The Court of Appeals reversed the dismissal and the Supreme Court, in an opinion by Justice Kennedy, affirmed. In the context of pretrial motions to dismiss, the Court adopted the standard proposed by Justice O'Connor in her concurring opinion in United States v. Mechanik that dismissal is appropriate "if it is established that the violation substantially influenced the grand jury's decision to indict" or if there is "grave doubt" that the decision to indict was free from the substantial influence of the violation. The Court concluded there was no evidence that the Rule 6 violations had any effect on the grand jury's decision to indict, in short, that the defendant was prejudiced in any fashion by the violations. Justice Marshall dissented, as he had in *Mechanik,* on the ground that "Rule 6 violations can be deterred and redressed effectively only by a *per se* rule of dismissal."

Under the combined effects of *Mechanik* and *Bank of Nova Scotia* what should an appellate court do if a trial court refuses to rule on a motion to dismiss filed before trial and the defendant is convicted at trial?

Petitioner in Midland Asphalt Corp. v. United States, 489 U.S. 794, 109 S.Ct. 1494, 103 L.Ed.2d 879 (1989) moved in the District Court for dismissal of an indictment because of a violation of Rule 6(e) prohibiting public disclosure of matters that occurred before a grand jury. The District Court denied the motion and the Court of Appeals dismissed the appeal on the ground it was interlocutory. The Supreme Court, in an unanimous opinion by Justice Scalia, affirmed the dismissal. The Court rejected the argument that the harmless error doctrine of United States v. Mechanik required provision of an interlocutory appeal since appeal after conviction was effectively eliminated. It also distinguished Abney v. United States in which it had provided for interlocutory appeal from trial court double jeopardy rulings. Finally, it rejected the argument that the Grand Jury Clause of the Fifth Amendment required interlocutory appeal in this situation: "Only a defect so fundamental that it causes the grand jury no longer to be a grand jury, or the indictment no longer to be an indictment, gives rise to the constitutional right not to be tried. An isolated breach of the traditional secrecy requirements does not do so." 489 U.S. at 802, 109 S.Ct. at 1500, 103 L.Ed.2d at 890.

CHAPTER 15

RIGHT TO A SPEEDY TRIAL

Analysis

Delay in administering the criminal justice system is, of course, a matter of major concern. It raises a number of matters of legal significance, some constitutional, others of statutory dimensions. The major—but not the only—federal constitutional provision addressing delay is the Sixth Amendment's speedy trial guarantee, made applicable to the states through the Fourteenth Amendment's Due Process clause. Klopfer v. North Carolina, 386 U.S. 213, 87 S.Ct. 988, 18 L.Ed.2d 1 (1967). Section A of this Chapter addresses the protections given both state and federal court defendants by this provision.

Delay issues have also been addressed by legislation. Congress responded to problems arising in the processing of federal criminal cases with the Federal Speedy Trial Act of 1974. A number of states have enacted similar legislation, some of it modeled in significant ways after the federal act. Section B of this Chapter addresses these statutes by focusing upon the Federal Speedy Trial Act and problems in its implementation.

A. SIXTH AMENDMENT SPEEDY TRIAL GUARANTEE

Barker v. Wingo

Supreme Court of the United States, 1972.
407 U.S. 514, 92 S.Ct. 2182, 33 L.Ed.2d 101.

■ MR. JUSTICE POWELL delivered the opinion of the Court.

Although a speedy trial is guaranteed the accused by the Sixth Amendment to the Constitution, this Court has dealt with that right on infrequent occasions. . . .

. . . [I]n none of these cases have we attempted to set out the criteria by which the speedy trial right is to be judged. 398 U.S., at 40–41, 90 S.Ct. at 1570. This case compels us to make such an attempt.

I.

On July 20, 1958, in Christian County, Kentucky, an elderly couple was beaten to death by intruders wielding an iron tire tool. Two suspects, Silas Manning and Willie Barker, the petitioner, were arrested shortly thereafter. The grand jury indicted them on September 15. Counsel was appointed on September 17, and Barker's trial was set for October 21. The Commonwealth had a stronger case against Manning, and it believed that Barker could not be convicted unless Manning testified against him. Manning was naturally unwilling to incriminate himself. Accordingly, on October 23, the day Silas Manning was brought to trial, the Commonwealth sought and obtained the first of what was to be a series of 16 continuances of Barker's trial. Barker made no objection. By first convicting Manning, the Commonwealth would remove possible problems of self-incrimination and would be able to assure his testimony against Barker.

The Commonwealth encountered more than a few difficulties in its prosecution of Manning. The first trial ended in a hung jury. A second trial resulted in a conviction, but the Kentucky Court of Appeals reversed because of the admission of evidence obtained by an illegal search. Manning v. Commonwealth, 328 S.W.2d 421 (1959). At his third trial, Manning was again convicted, and the Court of Appeals again reversed because the trial court had not granted a change of venue. Manning v. Commonwealth, 346 S.W.2d 755 (1960). A fourth trial resulted in a hung jury. Finally, after five trials, Manning was convicted, in March 1962, of murdering one victim, and after a sixth trial, in December 1962, he was convicted of murdering the other.

The Christian County Circuit Court holds three terms each year—in February, June, and September. Barker's initial trial was to take place in the September term of 1958. The first continuance postponed it until the February 1959 term. The second continuance was granted for one month only. Every term thereafter for as long as the Manning prosecutions were in process, the Commonwealth routinely moved to continue Barker's case to the next term. When the case was continued from the June 1959 term until the following September, Barker, having spent 10 months in jail, obtained his release by posting a $5,000 bond. He thereafter remained free in the community until his trial. Barker made no objection, through his counsel, to the first 11 continuances.

When on February 12, 1962, the Commonwealth moved for the twelfth time to continue the case until the following term, Barker's counsel filed a motion to dismiss the indictment. The motion to dismiss was denied two weeks later, and the Commonwealth's motion for a continuance was granted. The Commonwealth was granted further continuances in June 1962 and September 1962, to which Barker did not object.

In February 1963, the first term of court following Manning's final conviction, the Commonwealth moved to set Barker's trial for March 19. But on the day scheduled for trial, it again moved for a continuance until the June term. It gave as its reason the illness of the ex-sheriff who was the chief investigating officer in the case. To this continuance, Barker objected unsuccessfully.

The witness was still unable to testify in June, and the trial which had been set for June 19, was continued again until the September term over Barker's objection. This time the court announced that the case would be dismissed for lack of prosecution if it were not tried during the next term. The final trial date was set for October 9, 1963. On that date, Barker again moved to dismiss the indictment, and this time specified that his right to a speedy trial had been violated. The motion was denied; the trial commenced with Manning as the chief prosecution witness; Barker was convicted and given a life sentence.

Barker appealed his conviction to the Kentucky Court of Appeals, relying in part on his speedy trial claim. The court affirmed. Barker v. Commonwealth, 385 S.W.2d 671 (1964). In February 1970 Barker petitioned for habeas corpus in the United States District Court for the Western District of Kentucky. Although the District Court rejected the petition without holding a hearing, the court granted petitioner leave to appeal *in forma pauperis* and a certificate of probable cause to appeal. On appeal, the Court of Appeals for the Sixth Circuit affirmed the District Court. 442 F.2d 1141 (1971). It ruled that Barker had waived his speedy trial claim for the entire period before February 1963, the date on which the court believed he had first objected to the delay by filing a motion to dismiss. In this belief the court was mistaken, for the record reveals that the motion was filed in February 1962. The Commonwealth so conceded at oral argument before this Court. The court held further that the remaining period after the date on which Barker first raised his claim and before his trial—which it thought was only eight months but which was actually 20 months—was not unduly long. In addition, the court held that Barker had shown no resulting prejudice, and that the illness of the ex-sheriff was a valid justification for the delay. We granted Barker's petition for certiorari. 404 U.S. 1037, 92 S.Ct. 719, 30 L.Ed.2d 729 (1972).

II.

The right to a speedy trial is generically different from any of the other rights enshrined in the Constitution for the protection of the accused. In addition to the general concern that all accused persons be treated according to decent and fair procedures, there is a societal interest in providing a speedy trial which exists separate from, and at times in opposition to the interests of the accused. The inability of courts to provide a prompt trial has contributed to a large backlog of cases in urban courts which, among other things, enables defendants to negotiate more effectively for pleas of guilty to lesser offenses and otherwise manipulate the system. In addition, persons released on bond for lengthy periods awaiting trial have an opportunity to commit other crimes. It must be of little comfort to the residents of Christian County, Kentucky, to know that Barker was at large on bail for over four years while accused of a vicious and brutal murder of which he was ultimately convicted. Moreover, the longer an accused is free awaiting trial, the more tempting becomes his opportunity to jump bail and escape. Finally, delay between arrest and punishment may have a detrimental effect on rehabilitation.[1]

---

1. "[I]t is desirable that punishment   should follow offence as closely as possible;

If an accused cannot make bail, he is generally confined, as was Barker for 10 months, in a local jail. This contributes to the overcrowding and generally deplorable state of those institutions. Lengthy exposure to these conditions "has a destructive effect on human character and makes the rehabilitation of the individual offender much more difficult." At times the result may even be violent rioting. Finally, lengthy pretrial detention is costly. The cost of maintaining a prisoner in jail varies from $3 to $9 per day, and this amounts to millions across the Nation. In addition, society loses wages which might have been earned, and it must often support families of incarcerated breadwinners.

A second difference between the right to speedy trial and the accused's other constitutional rights is that deprivation of the right may work to the accused's advantage. Delay is not an uncommon defense tactic. As the time between the commission of the crime and trial lengthens, witnesses may become unavailable or their memories may fade. If the witnesses support the prosecution, its case will be weakened, sometimes seriously so. And it is the prosecution which carries the burden of proof. Thus, unlike the right to counsel or the right to be free from compelled self-incrimination, deprivation of the right to speedy trial does not *per se* prejudice the accused's ability to defend himself.

Finally, and perhaps most importantly, the right to speedy trial is a more vague concept than other procedural rights. It is, for example, impossible to determine with precision when the right has been denied. We cannot definitely say how long is too long in a system where justice is supposed to be swift but deliberate. As a consequence, there is no fixed point in the criminal process when the State can put the defendant to the choice of either exercising or waiving the right to a speedy trial. If, for example, the State moves for a 60–day continuance, granting that continuance is not a violation of the right to speedy trial unless the circumstances of the case are such that further delay would endanger the values the right protects. It is impossible to do more than generalize about when those circumstances exist. There is nothing comparable to the point in the process when a defendant exercises or waives his right to counsel or his right to a jury trial. Thus, as we recognized in Beavers v. Haubert, [198 U.S. 77, 25 S.Ct. 573, 49 L.Ed.2d 950 (1905)] any inquiry into a speedy trial claim necessitates a functional analysis of the right in the particular context of the case:

> "The right of a speedy trial is necessarily relative. It is consistent with delays and depends upon circumstances. It secures rights to a defendant. It does not preclude the rights of public justice." 198 U.S., at 87, 25 S.Ct. at 576, 49 L.Ed. 950.

The amorphous quality of the right also leads to the unsatisfactorily severe remedy of dismissal of the indictment when the right has been deprived. This is indeed a serious consequence because it means that a defendant who may be guilty of a serious crime will go free, without having

---

for its impression upon the minds of men is weakened by distance, and, besides, distance adds to the uncertainty of punishment, by affording new chances of escape." J. Bentham, The Theory of Legislation 326 (Ogden ed. 1931).

been tried. Such a remedy is more serious than an exclusionary rule or a reversal for a new trial, but it is the only possible remedy.

III.

Perhaps because the speedy trial right is so slippery, two rigid approaches are urged upon us as ways of eliminating some of the uncertainty which courts experience in protecting the right. The first suggestion is that we hold that the Constitution requires a criminal defendant to be offered a trial within a specified time period. The result of such a ruling would have the virtue of clarifying when the right is infringed and of simplifying courts' application of it. Recognizing this, some legislatures have enacted laws, and some courts have adopted procedural rules which more narrowly define the right. The United States Court of Appeals for the Second Circuit has promulgated rules for the district courts in that Circuit establishing that the government must be ready for trial within six months of the date of arrest, except in unusual circumstances, or the charge will be dismissed. This type of rule is also recommended by the American Bar Association.

But such a result would require this Court to engage in legislative or rulemaking activity, rather than in the adjudicative process to which we should confine our efforts. We do not establish procedural rules for the States, except when mandated by the Constitution. We find no constitutional basis for holding that the speedy trial right can be quantified into a specified number of days or months. The States, of course, are free to prescribe a reasonable period consistent with constitutional standards, but our approach must be less precise.

The second suggested alternative would restrict consideration of the right to those cases in which the accused has demanded a speedy trial. Most States have recognized what is loosely referred to as the "demand rule," although eight States reject it. It is not clear, however, precisely what is meant by that term. Although every federal court of appeals that has considered the question has endorsed some kind of demand rule, some have regarded the rule within the concept of waiver, whereas others have viewed it as a factor to be weighed in assessing whether there has been a deprivation of the speedy trial right. We shall refer to the former approach as the demand-waiver doctrine. The demand-waiver doctrine provides that a defendant waives any consideration of his right to speedy trial for any period prior to which he has not demanded a trial. Under this rigid approach, a prior demand is a necessary condition to the consideration of the speedy trial right. This essentially was the approach the Sixth Circuit took below.

Such an approach, by presuming waiver of a fundamental right from inaction, is inconsistent with this Court's pronouncements on waiver of constitutional rights. The Court has defined waiver as "an intentional relinquishment or abandonment of a known right or privilege." Johnson v. Zerbst, 304 U.S. 458, 464, 58 S.Ct. 1019, 1023, 82 L.Ed. 1461 (1938). Courts should "indulge every reasonable presumption against waiver," Aetna Ins. Co. v. Kennedy, 301 U.S. 389, 393, 57 S.Ct. 809, 812, 81 L.Ed. 1177 (1937), and they should "not presume acquiescence in the loss of fundamental rights," Ohio Bell Tel. Co. v. Public Utilities Comm'n, 301 U.S. 292, 307, 57

S.Ct. 724, 731, 81 L.Ed. 1093 (1937). In Carnley v. Cochran, 369 U.S. 506, 82 S.Ct. 884, 8 L.Ed.2d 70 (1962), we held:

> "Presuming waiver from a silent record is impermissible. The record must show, or there must be an allegation and evidence which show, that an accused was offered counsel but intelligently and understandably rejected the offer. Anything less is not waiver." Id., at 516, 82 S.Ct., at 890.

The Court has ruled similarly with respect to waiver of other rights designed to protect the accused.

In excepting the right to speedy trial from the rule of waiver we have applied to other fundamental rights, courts that have applied the demand-waiver rule have relied on the assumption that delay usually works for the benefit of the accused and on the absence of any readily ascertainable time in the criminal process for a defendant to be given the choice of exercising or waiving his right. But it is not necessarily true that delay benefits the defendant. There are cases in which delay appreciably harms the defendant's ability to defend himself. Moreover, a defendant confined to jail prior to trial is obviously disadvantaged by delay as is a defendant released on bail but unable to lead a normal life because of community suspicion and his own anxiety.

The nature of the speedy trial right does make it impossible to pinpoint a precise time in the process when the right must be asserted or waived, but that fact does not argue for placing the burden of protecting the right solely on defendants. A defendant has no duty to bring himself to trial; the State has that duty as well as the duty of insuring that the trial is consistent with due process. Moreover, for the reasons earlier expressed, society has a particular interest in bringing swift prosecutions, and society's representatives are the ones who should protect that interest.

It is also noteworthy that such a rigid view of the demand-waiver rule places defense counsel in an awkward position. Unless he demands a trial early and often, he is in danger of frustrating his client's right. If counsel is willing to tolerate some delay because he finds it reasonable and helpful in preparing his own case, he may be unable to obtain a speedy trial for his client at the end of that time. Since under the demand-waiver rule no time runs until the demand is made, the government will have whatever time is otherwise reasonable to bring the defendant to trial after a demand has been made. Thus, if the first demand is made three months after arrest in a jurisdiction which prescribes a six-month rule, the prosecution will have a total of nine months—which may be wholly unreasonable under the circumstances. The result in practice is likely to be either an automatic, *pro forma* demand made immediately after appointment of counsel or delays which but for the demand-waiver rule, would not be tolerated. Such a result is not consistent with the interests of defendants, society, or the Constitution.

We reject, therefore, the rule that a defendant who fails to demand a speedy trial forever waives his right. This does not mean, however, that the defendant has no responsibility to assert his right. We think the better rule is that the defendant's assertion of or failure to assert his right to a speedy trial is one of the factors to be considered in an inquiry into the deprivation of the right. Such a formulation avoids the rigidities of the demand-waiver rule and the resulting possible unfairness in its application. It allows the trial court to exercise a judicial discretion based on the circumstances, including due consideration of any applicable formal procedural rule. It would permit, for example, a court to attach a different weight to a situation in which the defendant knowingly fails to object from a situation in which his attorney acquiesces in long delay without adequately informing his client, or from a situation in which no counsel is appointed. It would also allow a court to weigh the frequency and force of the objections as opposed to attaching significant weight to a purely *pro forma* objection.

In ruling that a defendant has some responsibility to assert a speedy trial claim, we do not depart from our holdings in other cases concerning the waiver of fundamental rights, in which we have placed the entire responsibility on the prosecution to show that the claimed waiver was knowingly and voluntarily made. Such cases have involved rights which must be exercised or waived at a specific time or under clearly identifiable circumstances, such as the rights to plead not guilty, to demand a jury trial, to exercise the privilege against self-incrimination, and to have the assistance of counsel. We have shown above that the right to a speedy trial is unique in its uncertainty as to when and under what circumstances it must be asserted or may be deemed waived. But the rule we announce today, which comports with constitutional principles, places the primary burden on the courts and the prosecutors to assure that cases are brought to trial. We hardly need add that if delay is attributable to the defendant, then his waiver may be given effect under standard waiver doctrine, the demand rule aside.

We, therefore, reject both of the inflexible approaches—the fixed-time period because it goes further than the Constitution requires; the demand-waiver rule because it is insensitive to a right which we have deemed fundamental. The approach we accept is a balancing test, in which the conduct of both the prosecution and the defendant are weighed.[2]

IV.

A balancing test necessarily compels courts to approach speedy trial cases on an *ad hoc* basis. We can do little more than identify some of the factors which courts should assess in determining whether a particular defendant has been deprived of his right. Though some might express them in different ways, we identify four such factors: Length of delay, the reason for the delay, the defendant's assertion of his right, and prejudice to the defendant.

The length of the delay is to some extent a triggering mechanism. Until there is some delay which is presumptively prejudicial, there is no necessity for inquiry into the other factors that go into the balance. Nevertheless, because of the imprecision of the right to speedy trial, the length of delay that will provoke such an inquiry is necessarily dependent

---

2. Nothing we have said should be interpreted as disapproving a presumptive rule adopted by a court in the exercise of its supervisory powers which establishes a fixed time period within which cases must normally be brought. . . .

upon the peculiar circumstances of the case.[3] To take but one example, the delay that can be tolerated for an ordinary street crime is considerably less than for a serious, complex conspiracy charge.

Closely related to length of delay is the reason the government assigns to justify the delay. Here, too, different weights should be assigned to different reasons. A deliberate attempt to delay the trial in order to hamper the defense should be weighted heavily against the government.[4] A more neutral reason such as negligence or overcrowded courts should be weighted less heavily but nevertheless should be considered since the ultimate responsibility for such circumstances must rest with the government rather than with the defendant. Finally, a valid reason, such as a missing witness, should serve to justify appropriate delay.

We have already discussed the third factor, the defendant's responsibility to assert his right. Whether and how a defendant asserts his right is closely related to the other factors we have mentioned. The strength of his efforts will be affected by the length of the delay, to some extent by the reason for the delay, and most particularly by the personal prejudice, which is not always readily identifiable, that he experiences. The more serious the deprivation, the more likely a defendant is to complain. The defendant's assertion of his speedy trial right, then, is entitled to strong evidentiary weight in determining whether the defendant is being deprived of the right. We emphasize that failure to assert the right will make it difficult for a defendant to prove that he was denied a speedy trial.

A fourth factor is prejudice to the defendant. Prejudice, of course, should be assessed in the light of the interests of defendants which the speedy trial right was designed to protect. This Court has identified three such interests: (i) to prevent oppressive pretrial incarceration; (ii) to minimize anxiety and concern of the accused; and (iii) to limit the possibility that the defense will be impaired.[5] Of these, the most serious is the last, because the inability of a defendant adequately to prepare his case skews the fairness of the entire system. If witnesses die or disappear during a delay, the prejudice is obvious. There is also prejudice if defense witnesses are unable to recall accurately events of the distant past. Loss of memory, however, is not always reflected in the record because what has been forgotten can rarely be shown.

We have discussed previously the societal disadvantages of lengthy pretrial incarceration, but obviously the disadvantages for the accused who cannot obtain his release are even more serious. The time spent in jail awaiting trial has a detrimental impact on the individual. It often means

---

3. For example, the First Circuit thought a delay of nine months overly long, absent a good reason, in a case that depended on eyewitness testimony. United States v. Butler, 426 F.2d 1275, 1277 (1970).

4. We have indicated on previous occasions that it is improper for the prosecution intentionally to delay "to gain some tactical advantage over [defendants] or to harass them." United States v. Marion, 404 U.S.

307, 325, 92 S.Ct. 455, 466, 30 L.Ed.2d 468 (1971).

5. In Klopfer v. North Carolina, 386 U.S. 213, 221–222, 87 S.Ct. 988, 992–993, 18 L.Ed.2d 1 (1967), we indicated that a defendant awaiting trial on bond might be subjected to public scorn, deprived of employment, and chilled in the exercise of his right to speak for, associate with, and participate in unpopular political causes.

loss of a job; it disrupts family life; and it enforces idleness. Most jails offer little or no recreational or rehabilitative programs. The time spent in jail is simply dead time. Moreover, if a defendant is locked up, he is hindered in his ability to gather evidence, contact witnesses, or otherwise prepare his defense. Imposing those consequences on anyone who has not yet been convicted is serious. It is especially unfortunate to impose them on those persons who are ultimately found to be innocent. Finally, even if an accused is not incarcerated prior to trial, he is still disadvantaged by restraints on his liberty and by living under a cloud of anxiety, suspicion, and often hostility. . . .

We regard none of the four factors identified above as either a necessary or sufficient condition to the finding of a deprivation of the right of speedy trial. Rather, they are related factors and must be considered together with such other circumstances as may be relevant. In sum, these factors have no talismanic qualities; courts must still engage in a difficult and sensitive balancing process. But, because we are dealing with a funda-mental right of the accused, this process must be carried out with full recognition that the accused's interest in a speedy trial is specifically affirmed in the Constitution.

V.

The difficulty of the task of balancing these factors is illustrated by this case, which we consider to be close. It is clear that the length of delay between arrest and trial—well over five years—was extraordinary. Only seven months of that period can be attributed to a strong excuse, the illness of the ex-sheriff who was in charge of the investigation. Perhaps some delay would have been permissible under ordinary circumstances, so that Man-ning could be utilized as a witness in Barker's trial, but more than four years was too long a period, particularly since a good part of that period was attributable to the Commonwealth's failure or inability to try Manning under circumstances that comported with due process.

Two counterbalancing factors, however, outweigh these deficiencies. The first is that prejudice was minimal. Of course, Barker was prejudiced to some extent by living for over four years under a cloud of suspicion and anxiety. Moreover, although he was released on bond for most of the period, he did spend 10 months in jail before trial. But there is no claim that any of Barker's witnesses died or otherwise became unavailable owing to the delay. The trial transcript indicates only two very minor lapses of memory—one on the part of a prosecution witness—which were in no way significant to the outcome.

More important than the absence of serious prejudice, is the fact that Barker did not want a speedy trial. Counsel was appointed for Barker immediately after his indictment and represented him throughout the period. No question is raised as to the competency of such counsel. Despite the fact that counsel had notice of the motions for continuances, the record shows no action whatever taken between October 21, 1958, and February 12, 1962, that could be construed as the assertion of the speedy trial right. On the latter date, in response to another motion for continuance, Barker moved to dismiss the indictment. The record does not show on what ground this motion was based, although it is clear that no alternative motion was made for an immediate trial. Instead the record strongly suggests that while he hoped to take advantage of the delay in which he had acquiesced, and thereby obtain a dismissal of the charges, he definitely did not want to be tried. Counsel conceded as much at oral argument:

> "Your honor, I would concede that Willie Mae Barker probably—I don't know this for a fact—probably did not want to be tried. I don't think any man wants to be tried. And I don't consider this a liability on his behalf. I don't blame him." Tr. of Oral Arg. 39.

The probable reason for Barker's attitude was that he was gambling on Manning's acquittal. The evidence was not very strong against Manning, as the reversals and hung juries suggest, and Barker undoubtedly thought that if Manning were acquitted, he would never be tried. Counsel also conceded this:

> "Now, it's true that the reason for this delay was the Commonwealth of Kentucky's desire to secure the testimony of the accomplice, Silas Manning. And it's true that if Silas Manning were never convicted, Willie Mae Barker would never have been convicted. We concede this." Id., at 15.

That Barker was gambling on Manning's acquittal is also suggested by his failure, following the *pro forma* motion to dismiss filed in February 1962, to object to the Commonwealth's next two motions for continuances. Indeed, it was not until March 1963, after Manning's convictions were final, that Barker, having lost his gamble, began to object to further continuances. At that time, the Commonwealth's excuse was the illness of the ex-sheriff, which Barker has conceded justified the further delay.

We do not hold that there may never be a situation in which an indictment may be dismissed on speedy trial grounds where the defendant has failed to object to continuances. There may be a situation in which the defendant was represented by incompetent counsel, was severely prejudiced, or even cases in which the continuances were granted *ex parte*. But barring extraordinary circumstances, we would be reluctant indeed to rule that a defendant was denied this constitutional right on a record that strongly indicates as does this one, that the defendant did not want a speedy trial. We hold, therefore, that Barker was not deprived of his due process right to a speedy trial.

The judgment of the Court of Appeals is affirmed.

Affirmed.

■ Mr. Justice White, with whom Mr. Justice Brennan joins, concurring.

* * *

[M]any defendants will believe that time is on their side and will prefer to suffer whatever disadvantages delay may entail. But, for those who desire an early trial, these personal factors should prevail if the only countervailing considerations offered by the State are those connected with crowded dockets and prosecutorial case loads. A defendant desiring a speedy trial, therefore, should have it within some reasonable time; and only special circumstances presenting a more pressing public need with respect to the case itself should suffice to justify delay. Only if such special considerations are in the case and if they outweigh the inevitable personal prejudice resulting from delay would it be necessary to consider whether there has been or would be prejudice to the defense at trial. . . .

Of course, cases will differ among themselves as to the allowable time between charge and trial so as to permit prosecution and defense adequately to prepare their case. But unreasonable delay in run-of-the-mill criminal cases cannot be justified by simply asserting that the public resources provided by the State's criminal-justice system are limited and that each case must await its turn. As the Court points out, this approach also subverts the State's own goals in seeking to enforce its criminal laws.

NOTES

1. **When the right to a speedy trial begins.** In United States v. Marion, 404 U.S. 307, 92 S.Ct. 455, 30 L.Ed.2d 468 (1971), the Supreme Court held that the Sixth Amendment's speedy trial protection does not begin until "either a formal indictment or information or else the actual restraints imposed by arrest and holding to answer a criminal charge." 404 U.S. at 320, 92 S.Ct. at 463, 30 L.Ed.2d at 479. Only after arrest or charge, reasoned the Court, does the defendant face the major evils that are the concern of the constitutional provision: loss of liberty, disruption of employment, drain on financial resources, curtailment of associations, public obloquy and anxiety. Earlier delay, the Court acknowledged, may interfere with a defendant's eventual ability to defend himself against criminal charges. But this possibility of prejudice does not warrant extending the protection of the speedy trial clause to pre-charge or pre-arrest situations. The Court did comment that some constitutional protection against pre-arrest or charge delay did exist. "[T]he Government concedes," it noted, "that the Due Process Clause . . . would require dismissal of the indictment if it were shown at trial that the pre-indictment delay in this case caused substantial prejudice to appellees' rights to a fair trial and that the delay was an intentional device to gain tactical advantage over the accused." 404 U.S. at 324, 92 S.Ct. at 465, 30 L.Ed.2d at 481. Since the appellees had relied entirely upon the possibility of prejudice at trial and had made no effort to show either actual prejudice or a delay intended to secure tactical advantage for the Government, the Court found no need to "determine when and in what circumstances actual prejudice resulting from pre-accusation delays requires the dismissal of the prosecution." Id.

2. **Prejudice to the defense.** The question how the fourth *Barker* factor—prejudice to the defense—should be analyzed was addressed by the Court in Doggett v. United States, 505 U.S. 647, 112 S.Ct. 2686, 120 L.Ed.2d 520 (1992). In 1980, Doggett was indicted on a federal drug conspiracy charge. When officers sought to arrest him three weeks later, they were told by his mother that he had left for Colombia four days earlier. The arrest warrant was entered on various law enforcement computer databases, including NCIC, but no further steps of substance were taken to apprehend him. In 1982, Doggett returned to the United States, married, earned a college degree, found a steady job as a computer operations manager, lived openly under his own name, and stayed within the law. In 1988, federal marshals ran a credit check on several thousand persons wanted on arrest warrants and discovered Doggett's whereabouts. He was promptly located and arrested. Doggett filed a motion to dismiss the indictment for speedy trial violation.

The United States District Court denied Doggett's speedy trial claim. He entered a conditional plea of guilty and appealed. The Eleventh Circuit affirmed the conviction. The United States Supreme Court, in an opinion by Justice Souter, reversed.

The length of the delay was well over the presumptively prejudicial one year delay. As to the reason for the delay, the government was negligent in failing to apprehend him at least during the 6 year period when he was living openly under his own name in the United States. As to prompt assertion of the right to a speedy trial, Doggett claimed that he did not know of the indictment until his arrest in 1988 and in the stipulation entered with the guilty plea, the government conceded it had no contradictory information.

As to prejudice from the delay, Doggett was unable to show that his defense was prejudiced from lost exculpatory evidence. However, "excessive delay presumptively compromises the reliability of a trial in ways that neither party can prove or, for that matter, identify." If the government had used diligence in apprehending Doggett, he would have been required to show actual prejudice to prevail. On the other hand, if Doggett could have shown intentional delay by the government to obtain a tactical advantage, no showing of prejudice at all would have been required of him. The delay here was neither, but was negligent. The Court concluded,

> Although negligence is obviously to be weighed more lightly than a deliberate intent to harm the accused's defense, it still falls on the wrong side of the divide between acceptable and unacceptable reasons for delaying a criminal prosecution once it has begun. And such is the nature of the prejudice presumed that the weight we assign to official negligence compounds over time as the presumption of evidentiary prejudice grows. Thus, our toleration of such negligence varies inversely with its protractedness * * * and its consequent threat to the fairness of the accused's trial. Condoning prolonged and unjustifiable delays in prosecution would both penalize many defendants for the state's fault and simply encourage the government to gamble with the interests of criminal suspects assigned a low prosecutorial priority. The Government, indeed, can hardly complain too loudly, for persistent neglect in concluding a criminal prosecution indicates an uncommonly feeble interest in bringing an accused to justice; the more weight the Government attaches to securing a conviction, the harder it will try to get it.

> [T]o warrant granting relief, negligence unaccompanied by particularized trial prejudice must have lasted longer than negligence demonstrably causing such prejudice * * *. When the Government's negligence * * * causes delay six times as long as that generally sufficient to trigger judicial review * * * and when the presumption of prejudice, albeit unspecified, is neither extenuated, as by the defendant's acquiescence, * * * nor persuasively rebutted, the defendant is entitled to relief.

505 U.S. at 657–58, 112 S.Ct. at 2693–94, 120 L.Ed.2d at 531–32. Justice O'Connor, dissenting, characterized the harm to Doggett from the delay as "speculative." She also noted that the delay harmed the Government's ability to discharge its burden of proof. Justice Thomas, joined by The Chief Justice and Justice Scalia, dissented on the ground that the Sixth Amendment guarantee of a speedy trial does not protect against prejudice to the defense.

3. **What counts as delay?** If charges are filed, dismissed, and later reinstated, should the period between the dismissal and reinstatement count in determining whether the constitutional right to a speedy trial has been violated? In United States v. MacDonald, 456 U.S. 1, 102 S.Ct. 1497, 71 L.Ed.2d 696 (1982) the respondent, a military officer, was charged by military authorities with the murder of his wife and two daughters. Six months later, these charges were dismissed. Over five years later, MacDonald was indicted by civilian authorities for the murders and convicted. The Court of Appeals reversed the convictions on the ground his right to

a speedy trial had been violated. The Supreme Court, in an opinion authored by the Chief Justice, reversed. The majority likened the circumstances when charges have been dismissed to those before any charges have been filed. As in United States v. Marion, then, the speedy trial protection has no applicability during that time period: "[T]he Speedy Trial Clause has no application after the Government, acting in good faith, formally drops charges. Any undue delay after charges are dismissed, like any delay before charges are filed, must be scrutinized under the Due Process Clause, not the Speedy Trial Clause." 456 U.S. at 7, 102 S.Ct. at 1501, 71 L.Ed.2d at 703. The majority minimized the role of the speedy trial provision in preventing prejudice to the defense from pre-trial delay:

> The Sixth Amendment right to a speedy trial is ... not primarily intended to prevent prejudice to the defense caused by passage of time; that interest is protected primarily by the Due Process Clause and by statutes of limitations. The speedy trial guarantee is designed to minimize the possibility of lengthy incarceration prior to trial, to reduce the lesser, but nevertheless substantial, impairment of liberty imposed on an accused while released on bail, and to shorten the disruption of life caused by arrest and the presence of unresolved criminal charges.

456 U.S. at 8, 102 S.Ct. at 1502, 71 L.Ed.2d at 704. Justice Marshall, in a dissent joined in by Justices Brennan and Blackmun, argued that the speedy trial provision should be applied during the time charges are dismissed and that under the majority opinion "the government could indefinitely delay a second prosecution for no reason, or even in bad faith, if the defendant is unable to show actual prejudice at trial." 456 U.S. at 21, 102 S.Ct. at 1508, 71 L.Ed.2d at 712. Justice Stevens agreed with the approach of the dissenters but on these facts would not have found the respondent's speedy trial rights had been violated.

4. **Justification for delay.** In United States v. Loud Hawk, 474 U.S. 302, 106 S.Ct. 648, 88 L.Ed.2d 640 (1986), the District Court dismissed the indictment with prejudice, from which the Government appealed. After a delay of over 46 months, during which the appellate and subsequent trial court processes worked their way, respondents stood re-indicted before the District Court, the appellate courts having ruled for the Government. Respondents claimed their re-indictment was vindictive, a position supported as to one respondent and rejected as to others by the District Court. Both sides appealed from this decision, and the Government ultimately prevailed. During pendency of these appeals, respondents were released on their own recognizances. Back again before the District Court, respondents successfully claimed their rights to a speedy trial had been violated and the indictments were dismissed. At this point 90 months had passed from the time of respondents' arrests and initial charges. The Government appealed to the Court of Appeals, this time unsuccessfully. The United States Supreme Court, in an opinion authored by Justice Powell, reversed the decision of the Court of Appeals.

The first round of appeals, during which time respondents were not charged with any offenses, do not count against the Government under *MacDonald* because respondents were not incarcerated or subjected to other substantial restrictions on their liberty during that period. The pendency of appellate processes designed to test the correctness of the trial court's dismissal of charges does not take this case from the effect of *MacDonald*. As to the appeals and cross-appeals on the question of vindictive prosecution, the Court concluded the Government's position was so strong that delay to effectuate its appeal was justified. The respondent's appellate claim as to vindictive prosecution, by contrast, was "so lacking in merit that the time consumed by this appeal should not weigh in support of respondents' speedy trial claim." 475 U.S. at 317, 106 S.Ct. at 657, 88 L.Ed.2d at 655. Justice Marshall, joined by Justices Brennan, Blackmun, and Stevens, dissented.

5. **Persons incarcerated in other cases.** Persons already incarcerated pursuant to a conviction for a different offense present a special problem, which is aggravated when the pending charge and the offense of which the person has been convicted arise in different jurisdictions. In Smith v. Hooey, 393 U.S. 374, 89 S.Ct. 575, 21 L.Ed.2d 607 (1969), the Supreme Court held that the right of speedy trial applied to Texas state charges against Smith, who was serving a sentence in a federal correctional institution. Repeated demands by Smith that he be tried on the state indictment were ignored for six years. Holding that the Sixth Amendment right to speedy trial applied to the case, the Court reasoned:

> [T]his constitutional guarantee has universally been thought essential to protect at least three basic demands of criminal justice in the Anglo–American legal system: "[1] to prevent undue and oppressive incarceration prior to trial, [2] to minimize anxiety and concern accompanying public accusation and [3] to limit the possibilities that long delay will impair the ability of an accused to defend himself." United States v. Ewell, 383 U.S. 116, 120, 86 S.Ct. 773, 776, 15 L.Ed.2d 627. These demands are both aggravated and compounded in the case of an accused who is imprisoned by another jurisdiction.

> At first blush it might appear that a man already in prison under a lawful sentence is hardly in a position to suffer from "undue and oppressive incarceration prior to trial." But the fact is that delay in bringing such a person to trial on a pending charge may ultimately result in as much oppression as is suffered by one who is jailed without bail upon an untried charge. First, the possibility that the defendant already in prison might receive a sentence at least partially concurrent with the one he is serving may be forever lost if trial of the pending charge is postponed. Secondly, under procedures now widely practiced, the duration of his present imprisonment may be increased, and the conditions under which he must serve his sentence greatly worsened, by the pendency of another criminal charge outstanding against him.

> And while it might be argued that a person already in prison would be less likely than others to be affected by "anxiety and concern accompanying public accusation," there is reason to believe that an outstanding untried charge (of which even a convict may, of course, be innocent) can have fully as depressive an effect upon a prisoner as upon a person who is at large. . . .

> Finally, it is self-evident that "the possibilities that long delay will impair the ability of an accused to defend himself" are markedly increased when the accused is incarcerated in another jurisdiction. Confined in a prison, perhaps far from the place where the offense covered by the outstanding charge allegedly took place, his ability to confer with potential defense witnesses, or even to keep track of their whereabouts, is obviously impaired. And, while "evidence and witnesses disappear, memories fade, and events lose their perspective," a man isolated in prison is powerless to exert his own investigative efforts to mitigate these erosive effects of the passage of time.

* * *

> [W]e hold today that the Sixth Amendment right to a speedy trial may not be dispensed with . . . lightly. . . . Upon the petitioner's demand, Texas had a constitutional duty to make a diligent good-faith effort to bring him before the Harris County court for trial.

393 U.S. at 378–83, 89 S.Ct. at 577–79, 21 L.Ed.2d at 611–14. See also Dickey v. Florida, 398 U.S. 30, 90 S.Ct. 1564, 26 L.Ed.2d 26 (1970). If a jurisdiction, despite "diligent, good-faith effort," was unsuccessful in securing a defendant for trial in this context, would delay be excused?

6. **Interstate Agreement on Detainers.** The Sixth Amendment issues discussed by Smith v. Hooey are also dealt with by the Interstate Agreement on Detainers, enacted by the United States and 48 states. Under the Agreement, a prisoner in one member state has a right to be tried by another member state "within one hundred and eighty days after he shall have caused to be delivered" to the state filing the charges a demand for a speedy trial. Failure to observe the time requirement results in dismissal of the charges with prejudice. In Fex v. Michigan, 507 U.S. 43, 113 S.Ct. 1085, 122 L.Ed.2d 406 (1993), the Supreme Court, in an opinion by Justice Scalia, held that the 180 day time period begins to run from the time the demand is received by the court and prosecutor in the State in which the charges had been filed, rather than from the time the prisoner gave the demand to his warden for transmittal. The opinion, based largely on textual analysis, also concluded that the burdens of non-deliverance of the demand or of delay in deliverance under the Court's interpretation were less than the burdens imposed on society should the petitioner's position be adopted. The latter might result in preclusion of prosecution in a case in which the prosecutor had received no timely notice of demand or even no notice at all of demand. Justice Blackmun, joined by Justice Stevens, dissented.

7. **Remedy for violation of speedy trial right.** The appropriate judicial response to a finding that prompt disposition requirements have been violated is a difficult issue. In Strunk v. United States, 412 U.S. 434, 93 S.Ct. 2260, 37 L.Ed.2d 56 (1973), the Court of Appeals had found an unjustified delay of 259 days between indictment and trial, during which time petitioner had been incarcerated serving a sentence on another conviction. But rather than order dismissal of the charge, it remanded the case with directions to the trial court to credit the defendant's sentence for a time equal to the improper delay. The Supreme Court unanimously reversed, commenting:

The Court of Appeals [stated]:

"The remedy for a violation of this constitutional right has traditionally been the dismissal of the indictment or the vacation of the sentence. Perhaps the severity of that remedy has caused courts to be extremely hesitant in finding a failure to afford a speedy trial. Be that as it may, we know of no reason why less drastic relief may not be granted in appropriate cases. Here no question is raised about the sufficiency of evidence showing defendant's guilt, and, as we have said, he makes no claim of having been prejudiced in presenting his defense. In these circumstances, the vacation of the sentence and a dismissal of the indictment would seem inappropriate. Rather, we think the proper remedy is to remand the case to the district court with direction to enter an order instructing the Attorney General to credit the defendant with the period of time elapsing between the return of the indictment and the date of the arraignment. ...." 467 F.2d, at 973.

It is correct, as the Court of Appeals noted, that Barker [v. Wingo, 407 U.S. 514, 92 S.Ct. 2182, 33 L.Ed.2d 101 (1972)] prescribes "flexible" standards based on practical considerations. However, that aspect of the holding in Barker was directed at the process of determining *whether* a denial of speedy trial had occurred; it did not deal with the remedy for denial of this right. By definition, such denial is unlike some of the other guarantees of the Sixth Amendment. For example, failure to afford a public trial, an impartial jury, notice of charges, or compulsory service can ordinarily be cured by providing those guaranteed rights in a new trial. The speedy trial guarantee recognizes that a prolonged delay may subject the accused to an emotional stress that can be presumed to result in the ordinary person from uncertainties in the prospect of facing public trial or of receiving a sentence longer than, or consecutive to, the one he is presently serving—uncertainties that a prompt trial removes. Smith v. Hooey, 393 U.S., at 379, 89 S.Ct., at 577, 578; United States v. Ewell, 383 U.S. 116, 120, 86 S.Ct. 773, 776, 15 L.Ed.2d 627 (1966). We recognize, as the Court did in Smith v. Hooey, that the stress from a delayed trial may be less on a prisoner already confined, whose family ties and employment have been interrupted, but other factors such as the prospect of rehabilitation may also be affected adversely. The remedy chosen by the Court of Appeals does not deal with these difficulties.

The Government's reliance on *Barker* to support the remedy fashioned by the Court of Appeals is further undermined when we examine the Court's opinion in that case as a whole. It is true that *Barker* described dismissal of an indictment for denial of a speedy trial as an "unsatisfactorily severe remedy." Indeed, in practice, "it means that a defendant who may be guilty of a serious crime will go free, without having been tried." 407 U.S., at 522, 92 S.Ct., at 2188, 407 U.S. 514, 33 L.Ed.2d 101. But such severe remedies are not unique in the application of constitutional standards. In light of the policies which underlie the right to a speedy trial, dismissal must remain, as *Barker* noted, "the only possible remedy."

412 U.S. at 438–40, 93 S.Ct. at 2263, 37 L.Ed.2d at 60–61. Was the Court correct in its conclusion that the policies of the right to speedy trial demand that dismissal with prejudice always be the remedy for violation of that right?

B. FEDERAL SPEEDY TRIAL ACT

EDITORS' INTRODUCTION: OUTLINE OF THE STATUTE

Unlike the Court, which refuses to prescribe specific time limitations for the right to a speedy trial, Congress in the Speedy Trial Act, 18 U.S.C.A. §§ 3161–74 (West 1999), requires that an indictment or information be presented within 30 days from arrest or issuance of a summons, with a 30 day extension if no grand jury is in session. If a defendant pleads not guilty he must be brought to trial within 70 days, but not less than 30 days, from the filing date of the information or indictment, or from the date he appeared before a judicial officer of the court in which the charge is pending, whichever date last occurs. In computing this time period, § 3161(h) of the Act specifically excludes any period of delay resulting from: other proceedings concerning the defendant; deferment to allow defendant to demonstrate his good conduct; absence or unavailability of defendant or an essential witness; defendant's mental or physical inability to stand trial; treatment of defendant pursuant to section 2902 of title 28 U.S.C.A. (civil commitment and rehabilitation of narcotics addicts); dismissal of previous information or indictment, upon motion of the attorney for the government, and subsequent filing of charges for the same offense; and a continuance granted by a judge on his findings that the ends of justice will be best served. The time period for a defendant who enters a guilty or nolo contendere plea and who subsequently withdraws it begins when the order for withdrawal of the plea becomes final.

Failure to comply with section 3161 requires dismissal of (1) the charge—if an information or indictment is not filed within the time limit—or (2) the indictment or information—if defendant is not brought to trial within the time limit. Under section 3162, the court has discretion to dismiss the charges with or without prejudice; in doing so, the court considers: "the seriousness of the offense; the facts and circumstances of the case which led to the dismissal; and the impact of a reprosecution on the administration of this chapter and on the administration of justice." 18 U.S.C.A. § 3162(a)(1)(West 1999). But, the right to dismissal is considered waived if the defendant fails to move for dismissal prior to trial or enters a plea of guilty or nolo contendere. Additionally, the Act provides for monetary and disciplinary sanctions against any counsel for the defense or government attorney who: (a) knowingly allows the case to be set for trial without disclosing that a necessary witness would be unavailable for trial; (b) files a frivolous motion solely to delay the proceedings; (c) knowingly gives false information to obtain a continuance; or (d) willfully fails to proceed to trial without justification.

Finally, the Act unequivocally states: "no provision of this chapter shall be interpreted as a bar to any claim of denial of speedy trial as required by amendment VI of the Constitution." 18 U.S.C.A. § 3173(West 1999).

The federal statute and similar state provisions sometimes modeled after it are subject to the objection that they violate federal and state constitutional provisions mandating separation of judicial and legislative powers. In United States v. Howard, 440 F.Supp. 1106 (D.Md.1977), *aff'd on other grounds*, 590 F.2d 564 (4th Cir.1979), for example, the court held that the time within which the judiciary must act on matters *sub curia* is a matter that must remain within the control of the courts. Since the federal statute attempts to interfere with the judiciary's exclusive authority in this area, it is unconstitutional. The same judge again held the statute unconstitutional in United States v. Brainer, 515 F.Supp. 627 (D.Md.1981), rev'd, 691 F.2d 691 (4th Cir.1982). Elaborating on its conclusion, the court stated:

> A major constitutional shortcoming of the Speedy Trial Act is that it diminishes the independence and flexibility of the ... judicial power without adequately taking account of all the interests involved. The right of defendants and society, to assure that criminal trials are achieved as expeditiously as possible is only one area of concern affected by the far-reaching provisions of the Speedy Trial Act. Other societal interests are implicated.... The ability of the criminal justice system to operate effectively and efficiently has been severely impeded by the Speedy Trial Act. Resources are misdirected, unnecessary severances required, cases proceed to trial inadequately prepared, and in some indeterminate number of cases, indictments against guilty persons dismissed.

515 F.Supp. at 637. The Supreme Court of Ohio, however, upheld its state speedy trial statute against similar arguments, primarily on the ground that the statute represented legislative implementation of a constitutional imperative. State v. Pachay, 64 Ohio St.2d 218, 416 N.E.2d 589 (1980).

United States v. Taylor

Supreme Court of the United States, 1988.
487 U.S. 326, 108 S.Ct. 2413, 101 L.Ed.2d 297.

■ JUSTICE BLACKMUN delivered the opinion of the Court.

This case requires us to consider the bounds of a district court's discretion to choose between dismissal with and without prejudice, as a remedy for a violation of the Speedy Trial Act of 1974, as amended, 18 U.S.C. § 3161 et seq. (1982 ed. and Supp. IV) (Act).

I

On July 25, 1984, respondent Larry Lee Taylor was indicted by a federal grand jury on charges of conspiracy to distribute cocaine and possession of 400 grams of cocaine with intent to distribute. His trial was scheduled to commence in the United States District Court for the Western District of Washington in Seattle on November 19, 1984, the day prior to the expiration of the 70–day period within which the Act requires the Government to bring an indicted individual to trial. See 18 U.S.C. § 3161(c)(1). Respondent failed to appear for trial, and a bench warrant was issued for his arrest. On February 5, 1985, respondent was arrested by local police officers in San Mateo County, Cal., on state charges that subsequently were dismissed. Respondent's return to Seattle for his federal trial was delayed for a number of reasons, some related to his being required to testify as a defense witness in a federal narcotics prosecution then pending in San Francisco, and others involving slow processing, the convenience of the United States Marshals service, and what the District Court would later describe as the "lackadaisical" attitude on the part of the Government. On April 24, 1985, while respondent was back in San Francisco to testify at a retrial of the narcotics prosecution, a federal grand jury in Seattle issued a superseding indictment against respondent, adding a failure-to-appear charge based on his nonappearance at the scheduled November 19, 1984, trial.

Upon his return to Seattle, respondent moved to dismiss all charges against him, alleging that the Speedy Trial Act had been violated. The District Court rejected the Government's argument that because respondent had failed to appear for trial, the 70–day speedy trial clock began anew when respondent was arrested on February 5, 1985. After considering the time between respondent's nonappearance on November 19, 1984, and the issuance of the superseding indictment on April 24, 1985, the court determined that the time respondent was at large, or testifying in the San Francisco prosecution, or being held on state charges, as well as some reasonable time for transporting him to Seattle, were excludable under 18 U.S.C. § 3161(h). The District Court concluded, however, that, despite these time exclusions, 15 nonexcludable days had passed, that the clock thus had expired 14 days before the superseding indictment, and that dismissal of the original indictment therefore was mandated. App. to Pet. for Cert. 27a–29a.[6]

---

6. The 15 nonexcludable days included the 6 days between the end of the federal trial in San Francisco at which respondent was testifying and the date on which state charges against respondent were dropped; the 5 additional days after the state charges were dropped that it took the United States Marshals Service to bring respondent before a federal magistrate on the federal bench warrant; and 4 days beyond the 10 days provided for by 18 U.S.C. § 3161(h)(1)(H) that the Marshals Service took to transport respondent back to Seattle.

The District Court found that, although respondent was charged with serious offenses, there was "no excuse for the government's lackadaisical behavior in this case." Id., at 30a. The court observed that some of the Government's explanations for the various nonexcludable delays were inconsistent; that the Marshals Service failed to produce respondent expeditiously when requested to do so by a San Mateo County judge; and that even after the state charges were dropped, respondent was not immediately brought before a federal magistrate on the fugitive warrant. The District Court also noted that after an order issued to bring respondent back to Seattle for trial, the Government responded, but without "dispatch," accommodating the Marshals Service's interest in moving several prisoners at once instead of moving respondent within the time period provided for by the Act. It said:

> "[T]he court concludes that the administration of the [Act] and of justice would be seriously impaired if the court were not to respond sternly to the instant violation. If the government's behavior in this case were to be tacitly condoned by dismissing the indictment without prejudice, then the [Speedy Trial Act] would become a hollow guarantee." Id., at 30a–31a.

The court dismissed the original counts with prejudice to reprosecution.[7]

A divided panel of the United States Court of Appeals for the Ninth Circuit affirmed. 821 F.2d 1377 (1987). The full panel agreed with the District Court's holding that respondent's failure to appear for trial on November 19, 1984, should not restart the speedy trial clock, and confirmed the District Court's calculation of 15 nonexcludable days between respondent's flight and the issuance of the superseding indictment. Id., at 1383–1385.

Applying an abuse of discretion standard, the Court of Appeals reviewed the District Court's discussion of its decision to dismiss the drug charges with prejudice. Characterizing the lower court's purpose as sending "a strong message to the government" that the Act must be "observed," even with respect to recaptured fugitives, the majority concluded: "Under the peculiar circumstances of this case, we see no need to disturb that ruling on appeal. The district court acted within the bounds of its discretion." Id., at 1386.

The third judge concurred with the finding of a Speedy Trial Act violation, but concluded that the District Court abused its discretion in barring reprosecution. After reviewing the chronology and disputing whether, as a factual matter, the Government had failed to act reasonably, he felt that "none of the delay shown in this case—although admittedly nonexcludable under the statute—was of such studied, deliberate, and callous nature as to justify dismissal with prejudice." Id., at 1387.

---

7. The District Court rejected respondent's motion to dismiss the failure-to-appear charge, finding that after subtracting the various time periods held excludable, the Government had not violated the 30–day arrest-to-indictment provision of § 3161(b). See App. to Pet. for Cert. 31a–32a. Respondent eventually entered a plea of guilty to this charge and was sentenced to five years' imprisonment.

On the Government's petition, which suggested that further guidance was needed with respect to the application of the Speedy Trial Act's remedy provision, § 3162, we granted certiorari.

II

A

Neither party has asked this Court to review the lower courts' decision that a violation of the Act actually occurred. And the statute admits no ambiguity in its requirement that when such a violation has been demonstrated, "the information or indictment shall be dismissed on motion of the defendant." § 3162(a)(2). The only question before us, therefore, is whether the District Court abused its discretion under the Act in dismissing the indictment with prejudice rather than permitting reprosecution. In relevant part, the Act's remedy provision, § 3162(a)(2), instructs:

> "If a defendant is not brought to trial within the time limit required by section 3161(c) as extended by 3161(h), the information or indictment shall be dismissed on motion of the defendant. ...In determining whether to dismiss the case with or without prejudice, the court shall consider, among others, each of the following factors: the seriousness of the offense; the facts and circumstances of the case which led to the dismissal; and the impact of a reprosecution on the administration of this chapter and on the administration of justice."

As is plain from this language, courts are not free simply to exercise their equitable powers in fashioning an appropriate remedy, but, in order to proceed under the Act, must consider at least the three specified factors. Because Congress employed somewhat broad and open-ended language, we turn briefly to the legislative history of the Act for some additional indication of how the contemplated choice of remedy should be made.

[After reviewing the Act's legislative history, the Court concluded its thrust was] that the decision to dismiss with or without prejudice was left to the guided discretion of the district court, and that neither remedy was given priority.

B

Consistent with the prevailing view, the Court of Appeals stated that it would review the dismissal with prejudice under an abuse of discretion standard. The court did not, however, articulate what that standard required.

This Court previously has recognized—even with respect to another statute the legislative history of which indicated that courts were to have "wide discretion exercising their equitable powers," 118 Cong.Rec. 7168 (1972), quoted in Albemarle Paper Co. v. Moody, 422 U.S. 405, 421, 95 S.Ct. 2362, 2373, 45 L.Ed.2d 280 (1975)—that "discretionary choices are not left to a court's 'inclination, but to its judgment; and its judgment is to be guided by sound legal principles.' " Id., at 416, 95 S.Ct., at 2371, quoting United States v. Burr, 25 F.Cas. 30, 35 (No. 14692D) (CC Va.1807) (Marshall, C.J.). Thus, a decision calling for the exercise of judicial discretion "hardly means that it is unfettered by meaningful standards or shielded from thorough appellate review." Albemarle Paper Co., 422 U.S., at 416, 95 S.Ct., at 2371.

Whether discretion has been abused depends, of course, on the bounds of that discretion and the principles that guide its exercise. Had Congress merely committed the choice of remedy to the discretion of district courts, without specifying factors to be considered, a district court would be expected to consider "all relevant public and private interest factors," and to balance those factors reasonably. Piper Aircraft Co. v. Reyno, 454 U.S. 235, 257, 102 S.Ct. 252, 266, 70 L.Ed.2d 419 (1981). Appellate review of that determination necessarily would be limited, with the absence of legislatively identified standards or priorities.

In the Speedy Trial Act, however, Congress specifically and clearly instructed that courts *"shall consider,* among others, *each of the following factors,"* § 3162(a)(2) (emphasis added), and thereby put in place meaningful standards to guide appellate review. Although the role of an appellate court is not to substitute its judgment for that of the trial court, review must serve to ensure that the purposes of the Act and the legislative compromise it reflects are given effect. Where, as here, Congress has declared that a decision will be governed by consideration of particular factors, a district court must carefully consider those factors as applied to the particular case and, whatever its decision, clearly articulate their effect in order to permit meaningful appellate review. Only then can an appellate court ascertain whether a district court has ignored or slighted a factor that Congress has deemed pertinent to the choice of remedy, thereby failing to act within the limits prescribed by Congress.

Factual findings of a district court are, of course, entitled to substantial deference and will be reversed only for clear error. Anderson v. Bessemer City, 470 U.S. 564, 105 S.Ct. 1504, 84 L.Ed.2d 518 (1985). A judgment that must be arrived at by considering and applying statutory criteria, however, constitutes the application of law to fact and requires the reviewing court to undertake more substantive scrutiny to ensure that the judgment is supported in terms of the factors identified in the statute. Nevertheless, when the statutory factors are properly considered, and supporting factual findings are not clearly in error, the district court's judgment of how opposing considerations balance should not lightly be disturbed.

III

Because the District Court did not fully explicate its reasons for dismissing with prejudice the substantive drug charges against respondent, we are left to speculate in response to some of the parties' arguments pro and con. Respondent, for example, argues that the District Court may have taken into account the fact that respondent's codefendant had been sentenced on the same charges to three years' imprisonment, and that by dismissing the drug charges but sentencing respondent to five years' imprisonment on the failure-to-appear charge, it would be possible to effect substantial justice while sending at the same time "a strong message" to the Marshals Service and the local United States Attorney. See Tr. of Oral Arg. 29, 32. There are several problems with that line of reasoning, not the least of which is that the District Court did not articulate it. To the extent that respondent is suggesting that his codefendant's 3–year sentence implies that the offenses with which both were charged were not "serious," his argument is directly at odds with the District Court's statement expressly to the contrary: "there is no question that the drug violations with which [respondent] is charged are serious," App. to Pet. for Cert. 30a. We have no reason to doubt the court's conclusion in that regard. Moreover, at the time the District Court decided to dismiss the drug charges against respondent, he had not yet entered a plea to the failure-to-appear charge, so that the court could not be certain that any opportunity would arise to take the drug violations into account in sentencing.[8]

With regard to the second factor that the statute requires a court to consider, that is, the circumstances of the case leading to dismissal, we find it difficult to know what to make of the District Court's characterization of the Government's conduct as "lackadaisical." We do not dispute that a truly neglectful attitude on the part of the Government reasonably could be factored against it in a court's consideration of this issue, but the District Court gave no indication of the foundation for its conclusion. The court's discussion following that statement merely recounted the Speedy Trial Act violations, and chastised the Government for failing to make "any particular show of concern," or to "respon[d] with dispatch." App. to Pet. for Cert. 30a. The District Court did not find that the Government acted in bad faith with respect to respondent; neither did the court discover any pattern of neglect by the local United States Attorney, or evidence of what the Court of Appeals' majority later termed "the government's apparent antipathy toward a recaptured fugitive." 821 F.2d, at 1386; see also Tr. of Oral Arg. 34–35. Any such finding, suggesting something more than an isolated unwitting violation, would clearly have altered the balance. Instead, the extent of the District Court's explanation for its determination that "the second factor, ... tends strongly to support the conclusion that the dismissal must be with prejudice," was that there was "no excuse" for the Government's conduct. App. to Pet. for Cert. 30a.

Then there is the fact of respondent's failure to appear. The Government was prepared to go to trial on the 69th day of the indictment-to-trial period, and it was respondent, not the prosecution, who prevented the trial from going forward in a timely fashion. Respondent argues that he has

---

8. Even more important, respondent had not entered a guilty plea to, or been convicted of, the drug charges. It would have been highly improper—and we shall not presume the District Court assumed such unbridled discretion—to sentence respondent with undue harshness on one count, on the basis of the Court's untested and unsubstantiated assumption of what the facts might have been shown to be with regard to the drug charges, see Tr. of Oral Arg. 29–30, without the sort of inquiry conducted, in another context, under Fed.Rule Crim.Proc. 32. Although we realize it could be tempting to wrap up the "equities" in a single package and, with the best of intentions, effect what could be regarded as an essentially just result, we could not condone an approach that would violate the rights of defendants and misapply the Speedy Trial Act in the hope that the errors would balance out in the end. Contrary to the dissent's suggestion, see post, at 3–4, we do not question here the wisdom of Congress' decision to assess different penalties for failure to appear depending on the severity of the underlying charge. What we cannot countenance is a decision to punish someone more severely than would otherwise have been considered appropriate for the charged offense, solely for the reason that other charges had been dismissed under the Speedy Trial Act.

been charged separately and punished for his failure to appear for trial, that all the time he was at large has been excluded from the speedy trial calculation, and that the District Court therefore was correct in not considering his flight as a factor in deciding whether to bar reprosecution. Respondent also observes that the Court of Appeals held, and the Government does not dispute here, that respondent's failure to appear for a trial scheduled with only one day remaining in the indictment-to-trial period does not restart the full 70–day speedy trial clock. See 821 F.2d, at 1380–1383. That respondent's flight does not restart the clock, however, goes only to whether there has been a violation of the Act, and not to what the appropriate remedy should be. Respondent's culpable conduct and, in particular, his responsibility for the failure to meet the timely trial schedule in the first instance are certainly relevant as "circumstances of the case which led to the dismissal," § 3162(a)(2), and weigh heavily in favor of permitting reprosecution. These factors, however, were considered by neither the District Court nor the Court of Appeals' majority.

Petitioner argues that the District Court failed to consider that the delay caused by the Government's unexcused conduct was brief, and that there was no consequential prejudice to respondent. The length of delay, a measure of the seriousness of the speedy trial violation, in some ways is closely related to the issue of the prejudice to the defendant. The longer the delay, the greater the presumptive or actual prejudice to the defendant, in terms of his ability to prepare for trial or the restrictions on his liberty:

> "[I]nordinate delay between public charge and trial, ... wholly aside from possible prejudice to a defense on the merits, may 'seriously interfere with the defendant's liberty, whether he is free on bail or not, and ... may disrupt his employment, drain his financial resources, curtail his associations, subject him to public obloquy, and create anxiety in him, his family and his friends.' "Barker v. Wingo, 407 U.S. 514, 537, 92 S.Ct. 2182, 2195, 33 L.Ed.2d 101 (1972) (WHITE, J., concurring), quoting United States v. Marion, 404 U.S. 307, 320, 92 S.Ct. 455, 463, 30 L.Ed.2d 468 (1971).

The District Court found the Act's 70–day indictment-to-trial period here was exceeded by 14 nonexcludable days, but made no finding of prejudice. Indeed, the Court of Appeals concluded that the delay, "although not wholly insubstantial, was not so great as to mandate dismissal with prejudice." 821 F.2d, at 1385. That court also found that there was no prejudice to respondent's trial preparation. Ibid. And, as respondent was being held to answer not only for the drug charges but also on a valid bench warrant issued after he did not appear, neither does there seem to have been any additional restrictions or burdens on his liberty as a result of the speedy trial violation.[9] Thus, although the absence of prejudice is not dispositive, in this case it is another consideration in favor of permitting reprosecution.

---

9. We do not decide that as a matter of law there could never be any prejudice to a defendant whose speedy trial rights were violated, but who was also being held on other charges. Because "prejudice" may take many forms, such determinations must be made on a case-by-case basis in the light of the facts.

The District Court's decision to dismiss with prejudice rested largely on its conclusion that the alternative would tacitly condone the Government's behavior, and that a stern response was appropriate in order to vindicate the guarantees of the Speedy Trial Act. We certainly encourage district courts to take seriously their responsibility to consider the "impact of a reprosecution on the administration" of justice and of the Speedy Trial Act, § 3162(a)(2). It is self-evident that dismissal with prejudice always sends a stronger message than dismissal without prejudice, and is more likely to induce salutary changes in procedures, reducing pretrial delays. See Brief for United States 31. Nonetheless, the Act does not require dismissal with prejudice for every violation. Dismissal without prejudice is not a toothless sanction: it forces the Government to obtain a new indictment if it decides to reprosecute, and it exposes the prosecution to dismissal on statute of limitations grounds. Given the burdens borne by the prosecution and the effect of delay on the Government's ability to meet those burdens, substantial delay well may make reprosecution, even if permitted, unlikely. If the greater deterrent effect of barring reprosecution could alone support a decision to dismiss with prejudice, the consideration of the other factors identified in § 3162(a)(2) would be superfluous, and all violations would warrant barring reprosecution.

Perhaps there was more to the District Court's decision than meets the eye. It is always difficult to review a cold appellate record and acquire a full understanding of all the facts, nuances, and attitudes that influence a trial judge's decisionmaking, and we undertake such close review with reluctance. That is why the administration of the Speedy Trial Act and the necessity for thorough appellate review require that a district court carefully express its decision whether or not to bar reprosecution in terms of the guidelines specified by Congress. When the decision whether to bar reprosecution is analyzed in the framework established by the Act, it is evident from the record before us that the District Court abused its discretion in this case. The court did not explain how it factored in the seriousness of the offenses with which respondent stood charged. The District Court relied heavily on its unexplained characterization of the Government conduct as "lackadaisical," while failing to consider other relevant facts and circumstances leading to dismissal. Seemingly ignored were the brevity of the delay and the consequential lack of prejudice to respondent, as well as respondent's own illicit contribution to the delay. At bottom, the District Court appears to have decided to dismiss with prejudice in this case in order to send a strong message to the Government that unexcused delays will not be tolerated. That factor alone, by definition implicated in almost every Speedy Trial Act case, does not suffice to justify barring reprosecution in light of all the other circumstances present.

IV

Ordinarily, a trial court is endowed with great discretion to make decisions concerning trial schedules and to respond to abuse and delay where appropriate. The Speedy Trial Act, however, confines the exercise of that discretion more narrowly, mandating dismissal of the indictment upon violation of precise time limits, and specifying criteria to consider in deciding whether to bar reprosecution. The District Court failed to consider all the factors relevant to the choice of a remedy under the Act. What factors it did rely on were unsupported by factual findings or evidence in the record. We conclude that the District Court abused its discretion under the Act, and that the Court of Appeals erred in holding otherwise. Accordingly, the judgment of the Court of Appeals is reversed.

It is so ordered.

––––––

■ JUSTICE WHITE, concurring.

I join the Court's opinion, agreeing that when a defendant, through deliberate misconduct, interferes with compliance with the Speedy Trial Act and a violation of the Act then occurs, dismissal with prejudice should not be ordered unless the violation is caused by Government conduct that is much more serious than is revealed by this record.

––––––

■ JUSTICE SCALIA, concurring in part [omitted].

––––––

■ JUSTICE STEVENS, with whom JUSTICE BRENNAN and JUSTICE MARSHALL, join, dissenting [omitted].

NOTES

1. **Periods excluded from the statute.** The federal statute permits the trial judge to exclude certain periods of time from consideration in the analysis required by the Act:

(8)(A) Any period of delay resulting from a continuance granted by any judge on his own motion or at the request of the defendant or his counsel or at the request of the attorney for the Government, if the judge granted such continuance on the basis of his findings that the ends of justice served by taking such action outweigh the best interest of the public and the defendant in a speedy trial. No such period of delay resulting from a continuance granted by the court in accordance with this paragraph shall be excludable under this subsection unless the court sets forth, in the record of the case, either orally or in writing, its reasons for finding that the ends of justice served by the granting of such continuance outweigh the best interests of the public and the defendant in a speedy trial.

(B) The factors, among others, which a judge shall consider in determining whether to grant a continuance under subparagraph (A) of this paragraph in any case are as follows:

(i) Whether the failure to grant such a continuance in the proceeding would be likely to make a continuation of such proceeding impossible, or result in a miscarriage of justice.

(ii) Whether the case is so unusual or so complex, due to the number of defendants, the nature of the prosecution, or the existence of novel questions of fact or law, that it is unreasonable to expect adequate preparation for pretrial proceedings or for the trial itself within the time limits established by this section.

(iii) Whether, in a case in which arrest precedes indictment, delay in the filing of the indictment is caused because the arrest occurs at a time such that it is unreasonable to expect return and filing of the indictment within the period specified in section 3161(b), or because the facts upon which the grand jury must base its determination are unusual or complex.

(iv) Whether the failure to grant such a continuance in a case which, taken as a whole, is not so unusual or so complex as to fall within clause (ii), would deny the defendant reasonable time to obtain counsel, would unreasonably deny the defendant or the Government continuity of counsel, or would deny counsel for the defendant or the attorney for the Government the reasonable time necessary for effective preparation, taking into account the exercise of due diligence.

(C) No continuance under paragraph (8)(A) of this subsection shall be granted because of general congestion of the court's calendar, or lack of diligent preparation or failure to obtain available witnesses on the part of the attorney for the Government.

18 U.S.C.A. § 3161(h)(West 1999). Are these provisions so broad that a decision by a District Judge to exclude a given period is virtually unreviewable?

2. **Professional responsibility obligations.** Standard 4–1.2 of the American Bar Association Standards for Criminal Justice states that counsel for defendants should not seek to delay by using procedural devices when there is no legitimate basis for doing so. In a study devoted to counsel's awareness of and compliance with this standard, the conclusion was drawn that because the lawyers interviewed believed their first obligation is to their clients rather than to the court, they frequently ignored the standard and used procedural devices for purposes of delay. See J. Jones, The Compliance of [a Major] Public Defender's Office With The American Bar Association Standards for The Administration of Criminal Justice (undated) (paper on file with the University of Texas School of Law Criminal Justice Project).

CHAPTER 16

COMPETENCY TO STAND TRIAL

Analysis

There is universal agreement that it is a violation of due process as well as the nonconstitutional procedural law of virtually all jurisdictions to try a defendant who is "incompetent." Despite the pervasive federal constitutional aspects of the matter, however, United States Supreme Court caselaw has tended to deal with the procedural aspects of the inquiry into competency and disposition of incompetent defendants rather than with the ultimate question of competency.

What is widely-regarded as the constitutionally-required criteria for evaluating defendants' competency were stated in the per curiam decision in Dusky v. United States, 362 U.S. 402, 80 S.Ct. 788, 4 L.Ed.2d 824 (1960). After accepting the Solicitor General's suggestion that the record failed to support the trial judge's finding of competency, the Court remanded for a new hearing on the matter. It then commented:

> We ... agree with the suggestion of the Solicitor General that it is not enough for the district judge to find that "the defendant [is] oriented to time and place and [has] some recollection of events," but that the "test must be whether he has sufficient present ability to consult with his lawyer with a reasonable degree of rational understanding—and whether he has a rational as well as factual understanding of the proceedings against him."

362 U.S. at 402, 80 S.Ct. at 788–89, 4 L.Ed.2d at 825. Whether this language deserves the prominence it has assumed can be questioned. It is contained in a per curiam decision, handed down before the full constitutional ramifications of competency were developed, and was taken—perhaps uncritically—from a confession of error by the government. Moreover, it arguably contains substantial ambiguity. What is required for a client to consult with his lawyer "with a reasonable degree of rational understanding?" Must the defendant be able to participate effectively in the trial (as by testifying to his version of the events) as well as to discuss them with the attorney? While the so-called *Dusky* standard makes clear that the defendant must "understand" the proceedings as well as be able to consult

with his lawyer, is it clear what "a rational as well as factual" understanding involves?

The Supreme Court has also suggested that the criteria for determining competency may shift depending upon various characteristics of the proceedings. In Westbrook v. Arizona, 384 U.S. 150, 86 S.Ct. 1320, 16 L.Ed.2d 429 (1966), an apparently adequate determination had been made that the defendant was competent to stand trial in a general sense. He had also, however, waived his right to representation by counsel and had undertaken to represent himself. The Court held that a separate inquiry into his competency to waive his constitutional right to the assistance of counsel and to proceed to conduct his own defense might be necessary and remanded for consideration of this question. It did not address what standard should be applied if such an inquiry were found necessary. But in Massey v. Moore, 348 U.S. 105, 108, 75 S.Ct. 145, 147, 99 L.Ed. 135, 138 (1954) the Court had commented, "One might not be insane in the sense of being incapable of standing trial and yet lack the capacity to stand trial without benefit of counsel." On remand in *Westbrook,* the state appellate court directed a further examination of the defendant designed to address, as separate inquiries, his ability to understand the proceedings, his ability to assist in his defense, and his ability "to intelligently and competently waive his constitutional right to the assistance of counsel and conduct his own defense." State v. Westbrook, 101 Ariz. 206, 417 P.2d 530 (1966).

The Court returned to the criteria for determining competency in Godinez v. Moran, 509 U.S. 389, 113 S.Ct. 2680, 125 L.Ed.2d 321 (1993). Godinez shot and killed a bartender and a bar patron and then removed the bar's cash register. Nine days later, he shot and killed his former wife and then shot himself in the abdomen and slit his own wrists. Nevertheless, he survived and was charged with three counts of first degree murder. Two psychiatrists examined him. On the basis of their reports the trial judge found Godinez competent to stand trial. Godinez first pleaded not guilty, but then told the court that he wished to discharge his attorneys, represent himself, and plead guilty. After making a variety of inquiries of him, the court accepted both his waiver of counsel and his plea of guilty. Godinez was subsequently sentenced to death. Several years later, he filed a petition for post-conviction relief in the state court, which held a hearing and determined that he had been competent to represent himself. In subsequent federal habeas litigation, however, the Court of Appeals for the Ninth Circuit held the determinations that Godinez was competent did not adequately protect his federal constitutional rights. *Westbrook,* the court concluded, means that the competency of a defendant who waives counsel or pleads guilty must be determined by a higher standard than *Dusky* directs for assessing the competency of defendants who go to trial. A defendant who waives counsel or pleads guilty is competent, it reasoned, only if he has "the capacity for 'reasoned choice' among the alternatives available to him." Since no determination that Godinez had this capacity was made, his conviction and death sentence were held constitutionally invalid.

The Supreme Court reversed, reasoning that the Ninth Circuit had read too much into *Westbrook.* Justice Thomas explained the Court's position:

[A]ll criminal defendants—not merely those who plead guilty—may be required to make important decisions once criminal proceedings have been initiated. And while the decision to plead guilty is undeniably a profound one, it is no more complicated than the sum total of decisions that a defendant may be called upon to make during the course of a trial. * * * This being so, we can conceive of no basis for demanding a higher level of competence for those defendants who choose to plead guilty. If the *Dusky* standard is adequate for defendants who plead not guilty, it is necessarily adequate for those who plead guilty.

Nor do we think that a defendant who waives his right to the assistance of counsel must be more competent than a defendant who does not, since there is no reason to believe that the decision to waive counsel requires an appreciably higher level of mental functioning than the decision to waive other constitutional rights. * * *

Requiring that a criminal defendant be competent has a modest aim: It seeks to ensure that he has the capacity to understand the proceedings and to assist counsel. While psychiatrists and scholars may find it useful to classify the various kinds and degrees of competence, and while States are free to adopt competency standards that are more elaborate than the *Dusky* formulation, the Due Process Clause does not impose these additional requirements.

509 U.S. at 398–402, 113 S.Ct. at 2686–88, 125 L.Ed.2d at 332–34. *Westbrook,* Justice Thomas commented, simply means that in some cases trial judges are obligated to both inquire into the defendants' competency using the *Dusky* standard and satisfy themselves that the defendants' waivers are both knowing and voluntary.

Justice Blackmun, joined by Justice Stevens, dissented. The competency of defendants such as Godinez, who seek to proceed without counsel, must be determined by a standard that demands that they have the capacity to appreciate their position and to make a rational choice regarding representation, he argued. *Dusky's* test, he concluded, does not assure this:

[T]he standard for competence to stand trial is specifically designed to measure a defendant's ability to "consult with counsel" and to "assist in preparing his defense." A finding that a defendant is competent to stand trial establishes only that he is capable of aiding his attorney in making the critical decisions required at trial or in plea negotiations. The reliability or even relevance of such a finding vanishes when its basic premise—that counsel will be present—ceases to exist. The question is no longer whether the defendant can proceed with an attorney, but whether he can proceed alone and uncounselled. I do not believe we place an excessive burden upon a trial court by requiring it to conduct a specific inquiry into that question at the juncture when a defendant whose competency has already been questioned seeks to waive counsel and represent himself.

509 U.S. at 412–13, 113 S.Ct. at 2693–94, 125 L.Ed.2d at 341 (Blackmun, J., dissenting).

A. THE DUTY TO INQUIRE INTO COMPETENCY

The procedural significance of the due process bar against trying or convicting an incompetent defendant is increased because of the trial judge's duty, established in the principal case of this section, to inquire without request into a defendant's competency under certain circumstances. Consider whether the caselaw provides an adequate standard for use by trial judges in deciding when such an inquiry is necessary. Consider also the type of inquiry required. Is an examination by psychiatrists or other mental health professionals required? Is a full hearing (perhaps before a jury) ever necessary and, if so, when?

Use this case also to apply the *Dusky* standard discussed in the introduction to this Chapter. Do the criteria set out in the Court's language in *Dusky* provide adequate guidance in assessing Robinson's competency? If only the evidence brought to the attention of the judge was available upon further inquiry, should—or must—Robinson be found incompetent to stand trial?

Pate v. Robinson

Supreme Court of the United States, 1966.
383 U.S. 375, 86 S.Ct. 836, 15 L.Ed.2d 815.

■ MR. JUSTICE CLARK delivered the opinion of the Court.

In 1959 respondent Robinson was convicted of the murder of his common-law wife, Flossie May Ward, and was sentenced to imprisonment for life. Being an indigent he was defended by court-appointed counsel. It was conceded at trial that Robinson shot and killed Flossie May, but his counsel claimed that he was insane at the time of the shooting and raised the issue of his incompetence to stand trial. On writ of error to the Supreme Court of Illinois it was asserted that the trial court's rejection of these contentions deprived Robinson of due process of law under the Fourteenth Amendment. His conviction was affirmed, the court finding that no hearing on mental capacity to stand trial had been requested, that the evidence failed to raise sufficient doubt as to his competence to require the trial court to conduct a hearing on its own motion, and further that the evidence did not raise a "reasonable doubt" as to his sanity at the time of the offense. . . .

We have concluded that Robinson was constitutionally entitled to a hearing on the issue of his competence to stand trial. Since we do not think there could be a meaningful hearing on that issue at this late date, we direct that the District Court, after affording the State another opportunity to put Robinson to trial on its charges within a reasonable time, order him discharged. Accordingly, we affirm the decision of the Court of Appeals in this respect, except insofar as it contemplated a hearing in the District Court on Robinson's competence. Our disposition makes it unnecessary to reach the other reasons given by the Court of Appeals for reversal.

I.

The State concedes that the conviction of an accused person while he is legally incompetent violates due process, Bishop v. United States, 350 U.S. 961, 76 S.Ct. 440, 100 L.Ed. 835 (1956), and that state procedures must be adequate to protect this right. It insists, however, that Robinson intelligently waived this issue by his failure to request a hearing on his competence at the trial; and further, that on the basis of the evidence before the trial judge no duty rested upon him to order a hearing *sua sponte*. A determination of these claims necessitates a detailed discussion of the conduct of the trial and the evidence touching upon the question of Robinson's competence at that time.

The uncontradicted testimony of four witnesses called by the defense revealed that Robinson had a long history of disturbed behavior. His mother testified that when he was between seven and eight years of age a brick dropped from a third floor hit Robinson on the head. "He blacked out and the blood run from his head like a faucet." Thereafter "he acted a little peculiar." The blow knocked him "cockeyed" and his mother took him to a specialist "to correct the crossness of his eyes." He also suffered headaches during his childhood, apparently stemming from the same event. His conduct became noticeably erratic about 1946 or 1947 when he was visiting his mother on a furlough from the Army. While Robinson was sitting and talking with a guest, "he jumped up and run to a bar and kicked a hole in the bar and he run up in the front." His mother asked "what on earth was wrong with him and he just stared at [her], and paced the floor with both hands in his pockets." On other occasions he appeared in a daze, with a "glare in his eyes," and would not speak or respond to questions. In 1951, a few years after his discharge from the service, he "lost his mind and was pacing the floor saying something was after him." This incident occurred at the home of his aunt, Helen Calhoun. Disturbed by Robinson's conduct, Mrs. Calhoun called his mother about six o'clock in the morning, and she "went to see about him." Robinson tried to prevent Mrs. Calhoun from opening the door, saying "that someone was going to shoot him or someone was going to come in after him." His mother testified that, after gaining admittance, "I went to him and hugged him to ask him what was wrong and he went to pushing me back, telling me to get back, somebody was going to shoot him, somebody was going to shoot him." Upon being questioned as to Robinson's facial expression at the time, the mother stated that he "had that starey look and seemed to be just a little foamy at the mouth." A policeman was finally called. He put Robinson, his mother and aunt in a cab which drove them to Hines Hospital. On the way Robinson tried to jump from the cab, and upon arrival at the hospital he was so violent that he had to be strapped in a wheel chair. He then was taken in an ambulance to the County Psychopathic Hospital, from which he was transferred to the Kankakee State Hospital. The medical records there recited:

> "The reason for admission: The patient was admitted to this hospital on the 5th day of June, 1952, from the Hines Hospital. Patient began presenting symptoms of mental illness about a year ago at which

time he came to his mother's house. He requested money and when it was refused, he suddenly kicked a hole in her bar.

* * *

"Was drinking and went to the Psychopathic Hospital. He imagined he heard voices, voices of men and women and he also saw things. He saw a little bit of everything. He saw animals, snakes and elephants and this lasted for about two days. He went to Hines. They sent him to the Psychopathic Hospital. The voices threatened him. He imagined someone was outside with a pistol aimed at him. He was very, very scared and he tried to call the police and his aunt then called the police. He thought he was going to be harmed. And he says this all seems very foolish to him now. Patient is friendly and tries to cooperate.

* * *

"He went through an acute toxic episode from which he has some insight. He had been drinking heavily. I am wondering possibly he isn't schizophrenic. I think he has recovered from this condition. I have seen the wife and she is in a pathetic state. I have no objection to giving him a try."

After his release from the state hospital Robinson's irrational episodes became more serious. His grandfather testified that while Robinson was working with him as a painter's assistant, "all at once, he would come down [from the ladder] and walk on out and never say where he is going and whatnot and he would be out two or three hours, and at times he would be in a daze and when he comes out, he comes back just as fresh. He just says he didn't do anything. I noticed that he wasn't at all himself." The grandfather also related that one night when Robinson was staying at his house Robinson and his wife had a "ruckus," which caused his wife to flee to the grandfather's bedroom. Robinson first tried to kick down the door. He then grabbed all of his wife's clothes from their room and threw them out in the yard, intending to set them on fire. Robinson got so unruly that the grandfather called the police to lock him up.

In 1953 Robinson, then separated from his wife, brought their 18-month-old son to Mrs. Calhoun's home and asked permission to stay there for a couple of days. She observed that he was highly nervous, prancing about and staring wildly. While she was at work the next day Robinson shot and killed his son and attempted suicide by shooting himself in the head. It appeared that after Robinson shot his son, he went to a nearby park and tried to take his life again by jumping into a lagoon. By his mother's description, he "was wandering around" the park, and walked up to a policeman and "asked him for a cigarette." It was stipulated that he went to the South Park Station on March 10, 1953, and said that he wanted to confess to a crime. When he removed his hat the police saw that he had shot himself in the head. They took him to the hospital for treatment of his wound.

Robinson served almost four years in prison for killing his son, being released in September 1956. A few months thereafter he began to live with Flossie May Ward at her home. In the summer of 1957 or 1958 Robinson "jumped on" his mother's brother-in-law and "beat him up terrible." She went to the police station and swore out a warrant for his arrest. She described his abnormalities and told the officers that Robinson "seemed to have a disturbed mind." She asked the police "to pick him up so I can have him put away." Later she went back to see why they had not taken him into custody because of "the way he was fighting around in the street, people were beating him up." She made another complaint a month or so before Robinson killed Flossie May Ward. However, no warrant was ever served on him.

The killing occurred about 10:30 p.m. at a small barbecue house where Flossie May Ward worked. At that time there were 10 customers in the restaurant, six of them sitting at the counter. It appears from the record that Robinson entered the restaurant with a gun in his hand. As he approached the counter, Flossie May said, "Don't start nothing tonight." After staring at her for about a minute, he walked to the rear of the room and, with the use of his hand, leaped over the counter. He then rushed back toward the front of the restaurant, past two other employees working behind the counter, and fired once or twice at Flossie May. She jumped over the counter and ran out the front door with Robinson in pursuit. She was found dead on the sidewalk. Robinson never spoke a word during the three-to-four minute episode.

Subsequently Robinson went to the apartment of a friend, Mr. Moore, who summoned the police. When three officers, two in uniform, arrived, Robinson was standing in the hall approximately half way between the elevator and the apartment. Unaware of his identity, the officers walked past him and went to the door of the apartment. Mrs. Moore answered the door and told them that Robinson had left a short time earlier. As the officers turned around they saw Robinson still standing where they had first observed him. Robinson made no attempt to avoid being arrested. When asked his address he gave several evasive answers. He also denied knowing anything about the killing.

Four defense witnesses expressed the opinion that Robinson was insane. In rebuttal the State introduced only a stipulation that Dr. William H. Haines, Director of the Behavior Clinic of the Criminal Court of Cook County would, if present, testify that in his opinion Robinson knew the nature of the charges against him and was able to cooperate with counsel when he examined him two or three months before trial. However, since the stipulation did not include a finding of sanity the prosecutor advised the court that "we should have Dr. Haines' testimony as to his opinion whether this man is sane or insane. It is possible that the man might be insane and know the nature or the charge or be able to cooperate with his counsel. I think it should be in evidence, your Honor, that Dr. Haines' opinion is that this defendant was sane when he was examined." However, the court told the prosecutor, "You have enough in the record now. I don't think you need Dr. Haines." In his summation defense counsel emphasized "our defense is clear. . . . It is as to the sanity of the defendant at the time of the crime and also as to the present time." The court, after closing argument by the defense, found Robinson guilty and sentenced him to prison for his natural life.

II.

The State insists that Robinson deliberately waived the defense of his competence to stand trial by failing to demand a sanity hearing as provided by Illinois law. But it is contradictory to argue that a defendant may be incompetent, and yet knowingly or intelligently "waive" his right to have the court determine his capacity to stand trial. See Taylor v. United States, 282 F.2d 16, 23 (C.A.8th Cir.1960). In any event, the record shows that counsel throughout the proceedings insisted that Robinson's present sanity was very much in issue. He made a point to elicit Mrs. Robinson's opinion of Robinson's "present sanity." And in his argument to the judge, he asserted that Robinson "should be found not guilty and presently insane on the basis of the testimony that we have heard." Moreover, the prosecutor himself suggested at trial that "we should have Dr. Haines' testimony as to his opinion whether this man is sane or insane." With this record we cannot say that Robinson waived the defense of incompetence to stand trial.

We believe that the evidence introduced on Robinson's behalf entitled him to a hearing on this issue. The court's failure to make such inquiry thus deprived Robinson of his constitutional right to a fair trial. See Thomas v. Cunningham, 313 F.2d 934 (C.A.4th Cir.1963). Illinois jealously guards this right. Where the evidence raises a *"bona fide* doubt" as to a defendant's competence to stand trial, the judge on his own motion must impanel a jury and conduct a sanity hearing pursuant to Ill.Rev.Stat., c. 38, § 104–2 (1963). People v. Shrake, 25 Ill.2d 141, 182 N.E.2d 754 (1962). The Supreme Court of Illinois held that the evidence here was not sufficient to require a hearing in light of the mental alertness and understanding displayed in Robinson's "colloquies" with the trial judge. 22 Ill.2d, at 168, 174 N.E.2d, at 823. But this reasoning offers no justification for ignoring the uncontradicted testimony of Robinson's history of pronounced irrational behavior. While Robinson's demeanor at trial might be relevant to the ultimate decision as to his sanity, it cannot be relied upon to dispense with a hearing on that very issue. Cf. Bishop v. United States, 350 U.S. 961, 76 S.Ct. 440, 100 L.Ed. 835 (1956), reversing, 96 U.S.App.D.C. 117, 120, 223 F.2d 582, 585 (1955). Likewise, the stipulation of Dr. Haines' testimony was some evidence of Robinson's ability to assist in his defense. But, as the state prosecutor seemingly admitted, on the facts presented to the trial court it could not properly have been deemed dispositive on the issue of Robinson's competence.

III.

Having determined that Robinson's constitutional rights were abridged by his failure to receive an adequate hearing on his competence to stand trial, we direct that the writ of habeas corpus must issue and Robinson be discharged, unless the State gives him a new trial within a reasonable time. ...It has been pressed upon us that it would be sufficient for the state court to hold a limited hearing as to Robinson's mental competence at the time he was tried in 1959. If he were found competent, the judgment against him would stand. But we have previously emphasized the difficulty of retrospectively determining an accused's competence to stand trial.

Dusky v. United States, 362 U.S. 402, 80 S.Ct. 788, 4 L.Ed.2d 824 (1960). The jury would not be able to observe the subject of their inquiry, and expert witnesses would have to testify solely from information contained in the printed record. That Robinson's hearing would be held six years after the fact aggravates these difficulties. This need for concurrent determination distinguishes the present case from Jackson v. Denno, 378 U.S. 368, 84 S.Ct. 1774, 12 L.Ed.2d 908 (1964), where we held that on remand the State could discharge its constitutional obligation by giving the accused a separate hearing on the voluntariness of his confession.

If the State elects to retry Robinson, it will of course be open to him to raise the question of his competence to stand trial at that time and to request a special hearing thereon. In the event a sufficient doubt exists as to his present competence such a hearing must be held. If found competent to stand trial, Robinson would have the usual defenses available to an accused.

The case is remanded to the District Court for action consistent with this opinion. It is so ordered.

Case remanded to District Court with directions.

■ Mr. Justice Harlan, whom Mr. Justice Black joins, dissenting. [omitted].

NOTES

1. **Duty to inquire mid-trial.** Defendant was charged with participating along with four others in the rape and sexual abuse of his wife. At trial, defendant's wife testified that he would sometimes roll down the stairs when he did not get his way or was worried, that she had initially declined to prosecute because she believed defendant needed psychiatric care, but she had changed her mind after talking with a psychiatrist and following defendant's efforts to choke her to death the Sunday evening prior to trial. On the morning of the second day of trial, defendant's lawyer announced that defendant had shot himself in the abdomen. Could trial proceed without further inquiry into defendant's competence to stand trial? See Drope v. Missouri, 420 U.S. 162, 95 S.Ct. 896, 43 L.Ed.2d 103 (1975) (no).

2. **Rights concerning psychiatric examination.** The inquiry into a defendant's competence to stand trial mandated in some situations by *Robinson* will often involve a psychiatric interview. In Estelle v. Smith, 451 U.S. 454, 101 S.Ct. 1866, 68 L.Ed.2d 359 (1981), the Court stated:

> A criminal defendant, who neither initiates a psychiatric evaluation nor attempts to introduce any psychiatric evidence, may not be compelled to respond to a psychiatrist if his statements can be used against him at a capital sentencing proceeding.

451 U.S. at 468, 101 S.Ct. at 1876, 68 L.Ed.2d at 372. But the Court explained that a defendant who was warned about his Fifth Amendment right not to have interview disclosures so used could voluntarily consent to the interview. And in the absence of consent:

> If, upon being adequately warned, [Smith] had indicated that he would not answer [the psychiatrist's] questions, the validly ordered competency examina-

tion nevertheless could have proceeded upon the condition that the results would be applied solely for that purpose.

451 U.S. at 468, 101 S.Ct. at 1876, 68 L.Ed.2d at 372–73.

Finally, the Court held that failure to notify Smith's already appointed attorney that the psychiatric examination would encompass matters relevant to sentencing denied Smith his Sixth Amendment right to counsel. 451 U.S. at 470–71, 101 S.Ct. at 1877, 68 L.Ed.2d at 374.

In Powell v. Texas, 492 U.S. 680, 109 S.Ct. 3146, 106 L.Ed.2d 551 (1989) (per curiam), the defendant had been interviewed by two psychiatrists who later testified at the sentencing stage of his capital murder trial in support of the prosecution's contention that Powell was dangerous. The state court had concluded that even if the interviews violated Powell's Fifth and Sixth Amendment rights, he had waived the right to object to the testimony by introducing psychiatric testimony in support of an insanity defense at trial. Reversing, the Supreme Court acknowledged some support in its decisions for the proposition that introduction of evidence in support of an insanity defense waives Fifth Amendment objections, at least to the use of testimony offered at the guilt stage of the trial to rebut the defense. But it held that this rationale did not also support a waiver of the Sixth Amendment right with regard to evidence offered on the sentencing issue of dangerousness:

> While it may be unfair to the State to permit the defendant to use psychiatric testimony without allowing the State to rebut that testimony, it certainly is not unfair to require the State to provide counsel with notice before examining the defendant concerning future dangerousness.

492 U.S. at 685, 109 S.Ct. at 3150, 106 L.Ed.2d at 556. Since the psychiatrists had interviewed Powell in violation of his Sixth Amendment right to counsel, the use of their testimony on the dangerousness sentencing issue was impermissible.

3. **Burden of proof.** Constitutional limits upon the allocation and nature of the burden of proof regarding competency to stand trial were addressed in Medina v. California, 505 U.S. 437, 112 S.Ct. 2572, 120 L.Ed.2d 353 (1992). Medina had been charged with first degree murder and defense counsel asked for an inquiry into his competency to stand trial. Under California procedure, the issue was tried to a jury. The jury was instructed that a defendant is presumed competent and that Medina had the burden of proving his incompetency by a preponderance of the evidence. After the jury found Medina competent, trial proceeded, he was convicted, and the death penalty was assessed. Before the Supreme Court, he argued that the California presumption of competency and California's requirement that he prove competency by a preponderance of the evidence offended due process.

The appropriate standard, Justice Kennedy explained for the Court, is that applied in Patterson v. New York, 432 U.S. 197, 97 S.Ct. 2319, 53 L.Ed.2d 281 (1977), discussed on pages 1004–06 of the text. Substantial deference must be given to legislative judgments, and a legislative decision does not violate due process unless it offends a "principle of justice so rooted in the traditions and conscience of our people as to be ranked as fundamental."

Applying that standard, the majority found no due process violation. There is no settled tradition as to the proper allocation of the burden of proof on competency, and "[c]ontemporary practice" of the states and the federal government is varied. Placement of the burden on the defendant does not "transgress[ ] any recognized principle of 'fundamental fairness' in operation." Medina argued that "psychiatry is an inexact science," and placing on him the burden of proof requires that he bear the risk of being required to stand trial as a result of an erroneous finding of competency. Rejecting this, the Court reasoned that defense counsel will often have the best access to information and evidence, even if the defendant's ability to participate is impaired. Justice Kennedy explained:

> The Due Process Clause does not * * * require a State to adopt one procedure over another on the basis that it may produce results more favorable to the accused. * * * [I]t is enough that the State affords the criminal defendant on whose behalf a plea of incompetence is asserted a reasonable opportunity to demonstrate that he is not competent to stand trial.

505 U.S. at 451, 112 S.Ct. at 2580, 120 L.Ed.2d at 367.

Justice Blackmun, joined by Justice Stevens, dissented:

> [T]he Due Process clause does not simply forbid the State from trying and convicting a person who is incompetent. It also demands adequate *anticipatory, protective procedures* to minimize the risk that an incompetent person will be convicted. * * * In my view, [the majority's approach] introduces a systematic and unacceptably high risk that persons will be tried and convicted who are unable to follow or participate in the proceedings determining their fate.

505 U.S. at 458–64, 112 S.Ct. at 2584–87, 120 L.Ed.2d at 371–76. He found three reasons why the majority's reliance upon defense counsel's access to information and evidence was inappropriate:

> First, while the defendant is in custody, the State itself obviously has the most direct, unfettered access to him and is in the best position to observe his behavior. * * *
>
> Second, a competency determination is primarily a medical and psychiatric determination * * * [I]t is the experts and not the lawyers who are credited as the "best-informed," and most able to gauge a defendant's ability to understand and participate in the legal proceedings affecting him.
>
> Third, * * * [defense counsel's] view will likely have no outlet in, or effect on, the competency determination. Unlike the testimony of medical specialists or lay witnesses, the testimony of defense counsel is far more likely to be discounted by the factfinder as self-interested and biased. Defense counsel may also be discouraged in the first place from testifying for fear of abrogating an ethical responsibility or the attorney-client privilege.

505 U.S. at 465–66, 112 S.Ct. at 2588, 120 L.Ed.2d at 376–77.

But in Cooper v. Oklahoma, 517 U.S. 348, 116 S.Ct. 1373, 134 L.Ed.2d 498 (1996), the Court held that due process bars placing upon a defendant the burden of proving he is incompetent by clear and convincing evidence. Common law tradition and the law of most modern jurisdictions, Justice Stevens noted for the Court, require only proof by a preponderance of the evidence. Moreover, the defendant's fundamental right to be tried only while competent outweighs the State's interests:

> For the defendant, the consequences of an erroneous determination of competency are dire. Because he lacks the ability to communicate effectively with counsel, he may be unable to exercise other "rights deemed essential to a fair trial." * * * With the assistance of counsel, the defendant also is called upon to make myriad smaller decisions concerning the course of the defense. The importance of these rights and decisions demonstrates that an erroneous determination of competence threatens a "fundamental component of our criminal justice system."
>
> By comparison to the defendant's interest, the injury to the State of the opposite error—a conclusion that the defendant is incompetent when he is in fact malingering—is modest. To be sure, such an error imposes an expense on the State treasury and frustrates the State's interest in the prompt disposition

of criminal charges. But the error is subject to correction in subsequent proceeding and the State may detain the incompetent defendant * * *.

[W]e perceive no sound basis for allocating to the criminal defendant the large share of the risk which accompanies a clear and convincing evidence standard. * * * While important state interests are unquestionably at stake, * * * the defendant's fundamental right to be tried only while competent outweighs the State's interests in the efficient operation of its criminal justice system.

517 U.S. at 364–67, 116 S.Ct. at 1381–83, 134 L.Ed.2d at 512–14.

B.   PROCESSING OF INCOMPETENT DEFENDANTS

The manner in which a defendant determined incompetent to stand trial may be processed is, of course, a matter of some moment. In part, this is because the matter bears upon issues concerning the competency process. If a defendant found incompetent can, on that basis alone, be detained in a treatment or care facility for a prolonged period of time, perhaps a persuasive argument can be made that even a possibly-incompetent defendant should be able to "waive" inquiry into competency. The principal case in this section develops the federal constitutional limits upon the manner in which the states may deal with defendants incompetent to stand trial.

Jackson v. Indiana

Supreme Court of the United States, 1972.
406 U.S. 715, 92 S.Ct. 1845, 32 L.Ed.2d 435.

■ MR. JUSTICE BLACKMUN delivered the opinion of the Court.

We are here concerned with the constitutionality of certain aspects of Indiana's system for pretrial commitment of one accused of crime.

Petitioner, Theon Jackson, is a mentally defective deaf mute with a mental level of a pre-school child. He cannot read, write, or otherwise communicate except through limited sign language. In May 1968, at age 27, he was charged in the Criminal Court of Marion County, Indiana, with separate robberies of two women. The offenses were alleged to have occurred the preceding July. The first involved property (a purse and its contents) of the value of four dollars. The second concerned five dollars in money. The record sheds no light on these charges since, upon receipt of not guilty pleas from Jackson, the trial court set in motion the Indiana procedures for determining his competency to stand trial. Ind.Ann.Stat. § 9–1706a (Supp.1971), now Ind.Code 35–5–3–2 (1971).

As the statute requires, the court appointed two psychiatrists to examine Jackson. A competency hearing was subsequently held at which petitioner was represented by counsel. The court received the examining doctors' joint written report and oral testimony from them and from a deaf school interpreter through whom they had attempted to communicate with petitioner. The report concluded that Jackson's almost nonexistent communication skill, together with his lack of hearing and his mental deficiency, left him unable to understand the nature of the charges against him or to participate in his defense. One doctor testified that it was extremely unlikely that petitioner could ever learn to read or write and questioned whether petitioner even had the ability to develop any proficiency in sign language. He believed that the interpreter had not been able to communicate with petitioner to any great extent and testified that petitioner's "prognosis appears rather dim." The other doctor testified that even if Jackson were not a deaf mute, he would be incompetent to stand trial, and doubted whether petitioner had sufficient intelligence ever to develop the necessary communication skills. The interpreter testified that Indiana had no facilities that could help someone as badly off as Jackson to learn minimal communication skills.

On this evidence, the trial court found that Jackson "lack[ed] comprehension sufficient to make his defense," § 9–1706a, and ordered him committed to the Indiana Department of Mental Health until such time as that Department should certify to the court that "the defendant is sane."

* * *

Equal Protection

Because the evidence established little likelihood of improvement in petitioner's condition, he argues that commitment under § 9–1706a in his case amounted to a commitment for life. This deprived him of equal protection, he contends, because, absent the criminal charges pending against him, the State would have had to proceed under other statutes generally applicable to all other citizens: either the commitment procedures for feeble-minded persons, or those for mentally ill persons. . . .

In Baxstrom v. Herold, 383 U.S. 107, 86 S.Ct. 760, 15 L.Ed.2d 620 (1966), the Court held that a state prisoner civilly committed at the end of his prison sentence on the finding of a surrogate was denied equal protection when he was deprived of a jury trial that the State made generally available to all other persons civilly committed. Rejecting the State's argument that Baxstrom's conviction and sentence constituted adequate justification for the difference in procedures, the Court said that "there is no conceivable basis for distinguishing the commitment of a person who is nearing the end of a penal term from all other civil commitments." . . . The Court also held that Baxstrom was denied equal protection by commitment to an institution maintained by the state corrections department for "dangerously mentally ill" persons, without a judicial determination of his "dangerous propensities" afforded all others so committed.

If criminal conviction and imposition of sentence are insufficient to justify less procedural and substantive protection against indefinite commitment than that generally available to all others, the mere filing of criminal charges surely cannot suffice. . . .

Respondent argues, however, that because the record fails to establish affirmatively that Jackson will never improve, his commitment "until sane" is not really an indeterminate one. It is only temporary, pending possible change in his condition. Thus, presumably, it cannot be judged against commitments under other state statutes that are truly indeterminate. The State relies on the lack of "exactitude" with which psychiatry can predict the future course of mental illness. . . .

Were the State's factual premise that Jackson's commitment is only temporary a valid one, this might well be a different case. But the record does not support that premise. . . .

We note also that neither the Indiana statute nor state practice make the likelihood of the defendant's improvement a relevant factor. The State did not seek to make any such showing, and the record clearly establishes that the chances of Jackson's ever meeting the competency standards of § 9–1706a are at best minimal, if not nonexistent. The record also rebuts any contention that the commitment could contribute to Jackson's improvement. Jackson's § 9–1706a commitment is permanent in practical effect.

We therefore must turn to the question whether, because of the pendency of the criminal charges which triggered the State's invocation of § 9–1706a, Jackson was deprived of substantial rights to which he would have been entitled under either of the other two state commitment statutes. *Baxstrom* held that the State cannot withhold from a few the procedural protections or the substantive requirements for commitment that are available to all others. In this case commitment procedures under all three statutes appear substantially similar: notice, examination by two doctors, and a full judicial hearing at which the individual is represented by counsel and can cross-examine witnesses and introduce evidence. Under each of the three statutes, the commitment determination is made by the court alone, and appellate review is available.

In contrast, however, what the State must show to commit a defendant under § 9–1706a, and the circumstances under which an individual so committed may be released, are substantially different from the standards under the other two statutes.

Under § 9–1706a, the State needed to show only Jackson's inability to stand trial. We are unable to say that, on the record before us, Indiana could have civilly committed him as mentally ill under § 22–1209 or committed him as feeble-minded under § 22–1907. The former requires at least (1) a showing of mental illness and (2) a showing that the individual is in need of "care, treatment, training or detention." § 22–1201(1). Whether Jackson's mental deficiency would meet the first test is unclear; neither examining physician addressed himself to this. Furthermore, it is problematical whether commitment for "treatment" or "training" would be appropriate since the record establishes that none is available for Jackson's condition at any state institution. The record also fails to establish that Jackson is in need of custodial care or "detention." He has been employed at times, and there is no evidence that the care he long received at home has become inadequate. The statute appears to require an independent showing of dangerousness ("requires . . . detention in the interest of the welfare of such person or . . . others . . . :"). Insofar as it may require such a showing, the pending criminal charges are insufficient to establish it, and no other supporting evidence was introduced. For the same reasons, we cannot say that this record would support a feeble-mindedness commitment under § 22–1907 on the ground that Jackson is "unable properly to care for [himself]." § 22–1801.

More important, an individual committed as feeble-minded is eligible for release when his condition "justifies it," § 22–1814, and an individual civilly committed as mentally ill when the "superintendent or administrator shall discharge such person *or* [when] cured of such illness." § 22–1223 (emphasis supplied). Thus in either case release is appropriate when the individual no longer requires the custodial care or treatment or detention which occasioned the commitment, or when the department of mental health believes release would be in his best interests. The evidence available concerning Jackson's past employment and home care strongly suggests that under these standards he might be eligible for release at almost any time, even if he did not improve. On the other hand, by the terms of his present § 9–1706a commitment, he will not be entitled to release at all absent an unlikely substantial change for the better in his condition.

Baxstrom did not deal with the standard for release, but its rationale is applicable here. The harm to the individual is just as great if the State, without reasonable justification, can apply standards making his commitment a permanent one when standards generally applicable to all others afford him a substantial opportunity for early release.

As we noted above, we cannot conclude that pending criminal charges provide a greater justification for different treatment than conviction and sentence. Consequently, we hold that by subjecting Jackson to a more lenient commitment standard and to a more stringent standard of release than those generally applicable to all others not charged with offenses, and by thus condemning him in effect to permanent institutionalization without the showing required for commitment or the opportunity for release afforded by § 22–1209 or § 22–1907, Indiana deprived petitioner of equal protection of the laws under the Fourteenth Amendment.[1]

---

1. Petitioner also argues that the incompetency commitment deprived him of the right to be assigned to a special "institution for feeble-minded persons" to which he would have been statutorily directed by a § 22–1907 commitment. The State maintains two such institutions. The Indiana Supreme Court thought ..., considering Jackson's condition, his incompetency commitment can still culminate in assignment to a special facility. The State, in argument, went one step further. It contended that in practice the assignment process under all three statutes is identical: the individual is remanded to the central state authority, which assigns him to an appropriate institution regardless of how he was committed.

. . .

Moreover, nothing in the record demonstrates that different or better treatment is available at a special institution than at the general facilities for the mentally ill. We are not faced here, as we were in *Baxstrom,* with

commitment to a distinctly penal or maximum security institution designed for dangerous inmates and not administered by the general state mental health authorities. Therefore, we cannot say that by virtue of his incompetency commitment Jackson has been denied an assignment or appropriate treatment to which those not charged with crimes would generally be entitled.

Similarly, Jackson's incompetency commitment did not deprive him of privileges such as furloughs to which he claims a feeble-mindedness commitment would entitle him. The statutes relate such privileges to particular institutions, not to the method of commitment. Thus patients assigned to the Muscatatuck institution are entitled to furloughs regardless of the statute under which they were committed; and persons committed as feeble-minded would not be entitled to furloughs if assigned to a general mental institution.

Due Process

For reasons closely related to those discussed ... above, we also hold that Indiana's indefinite commitment of a criminal defendant solely on account of his incompetency to stand trial does not square with the Fourteenth Amendment's guarantee of due process.

* * *

The federal statute, 18 U.S.C.A. §§ 4244 to 4246, is not dissimilar to the Indiana law. It provides that a defendant found incompetent to stand trial may be committed "until the accused shall be mentally competent to stand trial or until the pending charges against him are disposed of according to law." § 4246. ...

Since Greenwood [v. United States, 350 U.S. 366, 76 S.Ct. 410, 100 L.Ed. 412 (1956)] federal courts without exception have found improper any straightforward application of §§ 4244 and 4246 to a defendant whose chance of attaining competency to stand trial is slim, thus effecting an indefinite commitment on the grounds of incompetency alone. ...

These decisions have imposed a "rule of reasonableness" upon §§ 4244 and 4246. Without a finding of dangerousness, one committed thereunder can be held only for a "reasonable period of time" necessary to determine whether there is a substantial chance of his attaining the capacity to stand trial in the foreseeable future. If the chances are slight, or if the defendant does not in fact improve, then he must be released or granted a §§ 4247–4248 hearing. Some States appear to commit indefinitely a defendant found incompetent to stand trial until he recovers competency. Other States require a finding of dangerousness to support such a commitment or provide forms of parole. New York has recently enacted legislation mandating release of incompetent defendants charged with misdemeanors after 90 days of commitment, and release and dismissal of charges against those accused of felonies after they have been committed for two-thirds of the maximum potential prison sentence. The practice of automatic commitment with release conditioned solely upon attainment of competence has been decried on both policy and constitutional grounds. Recommendations for changes made by commentators and study committees have included incorporation into pretrial commitment procedures of the equivalent of the federal "rule of reason," a requirement of a finding of dangerousness or of full-scale civil commitment, periodic review by court or mental health administrative personnel of the defendant's condition and progress, and provisions for ultimately dropping charges if the defendant does not improve. One source of this criticism is undoubtedly the empirical data available which tends to show that many defendants committed before trial are never tried, and that those defendants committed pursuant to ordinary civil proceedings are, on the average, released sooner than defendants automatically committed solely on account of their incapacity to stand trial. Related to these statistics are substantial doubts about whether the rationale for pretrial commitment—that care or treatment will aid the accused in attaining competency—is empirically valid given the state of most of our mental institutions. However, very few courts appear to have addressed the problem directly in the state context.

* * *

The States have traditionally exercised broad power to commit persons found to be mentally ill. The substantive limitations on the exercise of this power and the procedures for invoking it vary drastically among the States. The particular fashion in which the power is exercised—for instance, through various forms of civil commitment, defective delinquency laws, sexual psychopath laws, commitment of persons acquitted by reason of insanity—reflects different combinations of distinct bases for commitment sought to be vindicated. The bases that have been articulated include dangerousness to self, dangerousness to others, and the need for care or treatment or training. Considering the number of persons affected, it is perhaps remarkable that the substantive constitutional limitations on this power have not been more frequently litigated.

We need not address these broad questions here. It is clear that Jackson's commitment rests on proceedings that did not purport to bring into play, indeed did not even consider relevant, *any* of the articulated bases for exercise of Indiana's power of indefinite commitment. The state statutes contain at least two alternative methods for invoking this power. But Jackson was not afforded any "formal commitment proceedings addressed to [his] ability to function in society," or to society's interest in his restraint, or to the State's ability to aid him in attaining competency through custodial care or compulsory treatment, the ostensible purpose of the commitment. At the least, due process requires that the nature and duration of commitment bear some reasonable relation to the purpose for which the individual is committed.

We hold, consequently, that a person charged by a State with a criminal offense who is committed solely on account of his incapacity to proceed to trial cannot be held more than the reasonable period of time necessary to determine whether there is a substantial probability that he will attain that capacity in the foreseeable future. If it is determined that this is not the case, then the State must either institute the customary civil commitment proceeding that would be required to commit indefinitely any other citizen, or release the defendant. Furthermore, even if it is determined that the defendant probably soon will be able to stand trial, his continued commitment must be justified by progress toward that goal. In light of differing state facilities and procedures and a lack of evidence in this record, we do not think it appropriate for us to attempt to prescribe arbitrary time limits. We note, however, that petitioner Jackson has now been confined for three and one-half years on a record that sufficiently establishes the lack of a substantial probability that he will ever be able to participate fully in a trial.

These conclusions make it unnecessary for us to reach petitioner's Eighth–Fourteenth Amendment claim.

Disposition of the Charges

Petitioner also urges that fundamental fairness requires that the charges against him now be dismissed. The thrust of his argument is that the record amply establishes his lack of criminal responsibility at the time the crimes are alleged to have been committed. The Indiana court did not discuss this question. Apparently it believed that by reason of Jackson's incompetency commitment the State was entitled to hold the charges pending indefinitely. On this record, Jackson's claim is a substantial one. For a number of reasons, however, we believe the issue is not sufficiently ripe for ultimate decision by us at this time.

A.   Petitioner argues that he has already made out a complete insanity defense. Jackson's criminal responsibility at the time of the alleged offenses, however, is a distinct issue from his competency to stand trial. The competency hearing below was not directed to criminal responsibility, and evidence relevant to it was presented only incidentally. Thus, in any event, we would have to remand for further consideration of Jackson's condition in the light of Indiana's law of criminal responsibility.

B.   Dismissal of charges against an incompetent accused has usually been thought to be justified on grounds not squarely presented here: particularly, the Sixth–Fourteenth Amendment right to a speedy trial, or the denial of due process inherent in holding pending criminal charges indefinitely over the head of one who will never have a chance to prove his innocence. Jackson did not present the Sixth–Fourteenth Amendment issue to the state courts. Nor did the highest state court rule on the due process issue, if indeed it was presented to that court in precisely the above-described form. We think, in light of our holdings [above] that the Indiana courts should have the first opportunity to determine these issues.

C.   Both courts and commentators have noted the desirability of permitting some proceedings to go forward despite the defendant's incompetency. For instance, § 4.06(3) of the Model Penal Code would permit an incompetent accused's attorney to contest any issue "susceptible of fair determination prior to trial and without the personal participation of the defendant." An alternative draft of § 4.06(4) of the Model Penal Code would also permit an evidentiary hearing at which certain defenses, not including lack of criminal responsibility, could be raised by defense counsel on the basis of which the court might quash the indictment. Some States have statutory provisions permitting pretrial motions to be made or even allowing the incompetent defendant a trial at which to establish his innocence, without permitting a conviction. We do not read this Court's previous decisions to preclude the States from allowing at a minimum, an incompetent defendant to raise certain defenses such as insufficiency of the indictment, or make certain pretrial motions, through counsel. Of course, if the Indiana courts conclude that Jackson was almost certainly not capable of criminal responsibility when the offenses were committed, dismissal of the charges might be warranted. But even if this is not the case, Jackson may have other good defenses that could sustain dismissal or acquittal and which might now be asserted. We do not know if Indiana would approve procedures such as those mentioned here, but these possibilities will be open on remand.

Reversed and remanded.

NOTES

1. **Incompetency during initial phases of the case.** What is the proper procedure when a defendant who is allegedly incompetent to stand trial is presented before a magistrate for an initial appearance or a preliminary examination? Compare Flint v. Sater, 374 P.2d 929 (Okla.Crim.App.1962) with State v. McCredden, 33 Wis.2d 661, 148 N.W.2d 33 (1967). In the latter case the court suggested:

> [W]e conclude that the proper procedure to be followed by the circuit court, where a defendant is bound over by the magistrate to determine the issue of insanity, is to hold a hearing to establish whether it is probable that he committed the felony charged in the information. The information should first be filed but no plea thereto should be required. If the defendant is without counsel, counsel should be provided with the right to cross-examine the state's witnesses and to call witnesses on behalf of the defendant. At the conclusion of this hearing a finding should be made on the issue of probable guilt. If this finding is in the affirmative then the court shall proceed to determine the insanity issue. If on the other hand the finding is that the state has failed to prove the probability that the defendant has committed the felony charged in the information, or all the felonies charged if there is more than one, the defendant should be discharged subject to the right of the court to temporarily detain him so as to permit civil proceedings to be instituted ... to determine his mental competency.

33 Wis.2d at 669–70, 148 N.W.2d at 37–38.

2. **Effect of incompetency on pretrial release.** What effect should a defendant's potential incompetency have upon his right to pretrial release? May bail be revoked for purposes of hospitalizing him? Could this be justified if a psychiatric examination could be conducted on an out-patient basis? If a defendant is found incompetent, may bail be revoked or denied on the ground that he is dangerous to others? See United States v. Curry, 410 F.2d 1372 (4th Cir.1969).

3. **Forcing defendants to take medication.** If a defendant is determined to be incompetent to stand trial because of a mental illness, under what circumstances may the defendant be forced to take medication that may sufficiently reduce his symptoms to render him competent to stand trial? Whether federal constitutional considerations limit the states' ability to so medicate incompetent defendants seemed to be at issue in Riggins v. Nevada, 504 U.S. 127, 112 S.Ct. 1810, 118 L.Ed.2d 479 (1992). Riggins, charged with murder, was found incompetent to stand trial and then was treated with Mellaril, a powerful antipsychotic medication. He received 800 milligrams of the drug each day. Riggins was subsequently found to be competent and trial was scheduled. He moved to terminate his treatment with the Mellaril, contending that continued treatment infringed upon his freedom. He also argued that his continued treatment would affect his demeanor and mental state during trial and thus would interfere with his ability to offer an insanity defense, since it would deprive him of the ability to show the jurors his "true mental state." The trial court denied the motion. Riggins was tried, and testified in his own defense. The jury—rejecting his insanity defense—convicted him and set his punishment at death.

The Supreme Court held that even assuming that Riggins' treatment with the Mellaril was "medically appropriate," on the facts of the case this treatment denied Riggins a full and fair trial under Fourteenth Amendment due process. In Washington v. Harper, 494 U.S. 210, 110 S.Ct. 1028, 108 L.Ed.2d 178 (1990), the Court had held that the Fourteenth Amendment's due process clause limits a state's ability to involuntarily treat a prison inmate with antipsychotic drugs because such forcible medication "represents a substantial interference with that person's liberty." 494

U.S. at 229, 110 S.Ct. at 1041, 108 L.Ed.2d at 203. Justice O'Connor explained for the *Riggins* Court:

> Under *Harper*, forcing antipsychotic drugs on a convicted prisoner is impermissible absent a finding of overriding justification and a determination of medical appropriateness. The Fourteenth Amendment affords at least as much protection to persons the State detains for trial. * * * Thus, once Riggins moved to terminate administration of antipsychotic medication, the State became obligated to establish the need for Mellaril and the medical appropriateness of the drug.
>
> Although we have not had occasion to develop substantive standards for judging forced administration of such drugs in the trial or pretrial settings, Nevada certainly would have satisfied due process if the prosecution had demonstrated, and the District Court had found, that treatment with antipsychotic medication was medically appropriate and, considering less intrusive alternatives, essential for sake of Riggins' own safety or the safety of others.... Similarly, the State might have been able to justify medically appropriate, involuntary treatment with the drug by establishing that it could not obtain an adjudication of Riggins' guilt or innocence by using less intrusive means.... We note that during the * * * hearing [in the state court] Riggins did not contend that he had the right to be tried without Mellaril if its discontinuation rendered him incompetent.... The question whether a competent criminal defendant may refuse antipsychotic medication if cessation of medication would render him incompetent at trial is not before us.

504 U.S. at 135–36, 112 S.Ct. at 1815, 118 L.Ed.2d at 489–90.

The trial court had not made the findings that due process required.

> This error may well have impaired the constitutionally protected trial rights Riggins invokes. At the hearing to consider terminating medication, [one expert] suggested that the dosage administered to Riggins * * * could make him "uptight." [Another expert] testified that a patient taking 800 milligrams of Mellaril each day might suffer from drowsiness or confusion. It is clearly possible that such side effects had an impact upon not just Riggins' outward appearance, but also the contents of his testimony on direct or cross examination, his ability to follow the proceedings, or the substance of his communication with counsel.

504 U.S. at 137, 112 S.Ct. at 1816, 118 L.Ed.2d at 490. Requiring Riggins to demonstrate actual prejudice, the Court concluded, would lead to speculation and thus the demonstration of "a strong possibility that Riggins' defense was impaired due to the administration of Mellaril" required that relief be granted. The constitutional error was not "cured" by Riggins' ability at trial to present expert testimony to the jury regarding the effects upon his demeanor of the Mellaril he was taking. This could not have had any impact upon the possibility that the drug affected Riggins' own testimony, his interaction with counsel, or his comprehension. "[A]n unacceptable risk of prejudice remained." 504 U.S. at 138, 112 S.Ct. at 1816, 118 L.Ed.2d at 491.

Justice Kennedy concurred in the judgment of the Court but wrote separately to express his view on the issue not reached by the Court. He reviewed the possible side effects of antipsychotic medications such as the Mellaril administered to Riggins and their possible effects upon defendants at trial. Insofar as the medication inhibits defendants' ability to react and respond to the proceedings and to demonstrate remorse and compassion, he observed, the drug may result in especially acute prejudice during the sentencing stage and in a capital case "may * * * be determinative of whether the offender lives or dies." He then concluded:

In my view elementary protections against state intrusion require the State in every case to make a showing that there is no significant risk that the medication will impair or alter in any material way the defendant's capacity or willingness to react to the testimony at trial or to assist his counsel. Based on my understanding of the medical literature, I have substantial reservations that the State can make that showing. * * *

If the State cannot render the defendant competent without involuntary medication, then it must resort to civil commitment, if appropriate, unless the defendant becomes competent through other means. If the defendant cannot be tried without his behavior and demeanor being affected in this substantial way by involuntary treatment, in my view the Constitution requires that society bear this cost in order to preserve the integrity of the trial process.

504 U.S. at 141–45, 112 S.Ct. at 1818–20, 118 L.Ed.2d at 493–96 (Kennedy, J. concurring in the judgment).

Justice Thomas, joined in part by Justice Scalia, dissented, arguing that Riggins failed to establish that he was actually forced to take the Mellaril and that even if he was forced to take it, he failed to demonstrate that this deprived him of a "fair" trial. 504 U.S. at 147, 112 S.Ct. at 1821, 118 L.Ed.2d at 497.

CHAPTER 17

DISCOVERY AND DISCLOSURE

Analysis

EDITORS' INTRODUCTION: ISSUES UNDER MODERN DISCOVERY PROVISIONS

The rights of the parties to criminal litigation to notice concerning the theories or evidence that will be relied upon by their opponents and to access to statements and physical evidence in the possession of those opponents is a relatively recent development in criminal procedure. Prior to the promulgation of Fed.R.Crim.P. 16 in 1946, no right to such discovery existed in federal litigation; even that early version of Rule 16 conferred only limited disclosure duties. But a strong movement, led judicially by United States Supreme Court Justice Brennan as a (then) member of the New Jersey Supreme Court and by Justice Traynor of the California Supreme Court, has resulted in increasingly broad formal discovery requirements. These requirements are the subject of the present Chapter.

Some discovery rights have developed as a matter of constitutional mandate, but most have their basis in legislation or court rule. Some courts, however, have found an inherent power to compel discovery even in the absence of statutory or rule authority. Thus in United States v. Nobles, 422 U.S. 225, 234–36, 95 S.Ct. 2160, 2168–69, 45 L.Ed.2d 141, 151–52 (1975), the Supreme Court held that the federal judiciary has such inherent power to compel some disclosure, at least during trial, by the defendant as well as by the prosecution.

Various model formulations have been developed, including Fed. R.Crim.P. 16, the Uniform Rules of Criminal Procedure drafted by the Conference of Commissioners on Uniform State Laws, the American Law Institute's Model Code of Pre-arraignment Procedure, the Standards of the National Association of Prosecuting Attorneys, and the National Advisory

Commission's volume on Courts. Perhaps the most influential formulation, however, has been the American Bar Association's Standards Relating to Discovery and Procedure Before Trial (Approved Draft, 1970), revised in 1978, II Standards for Criminal Justice, Standard 11–1.1 et seq. (1980) (the "ABA Standards"). By 1975, 22 states had substantially implemented these Standards through court rule, legislation, or judicial adoption. Robinson, The ABA Standards for Criminal Justice: What They Mean to the Criminal Defense Attorney, 1 Nat.J.Crim.Def. 3 (1975).

Basic Consideration

The ABA Standards, which advocate broad discovery, suggest that such discovery will further the expeditious and fair disposition of criminal charges by encouraging thorough preparation by both sides and by aiding early recognition and disposition of constitutional, collateral, and procedural issues. In addition, discovery is seen as minimizing inequities among similarly situated defendants and as increasing the likelihood that the decision as to which plea to enter will be an informed judgment. See ABA Standards, Standard 1.1. The arguments against discovery were summarized by the Iowa Supreme Court in State v. Eads, 166 N.W.2d 766 (Iowa 1969):

> (1) It would afford the defendant increased opportunity to produce perjured testimony and to fabricate evidence to meet the State's case; (2) witnesses would be subject to bribe, threat and intimidation; (3) since the State cannot compel the defendant to disclose his evidence, disclosure by the State would afford the defendant an unreasonable advantage at trial; and (4) disclosure is unnecessary in any event because of the other sources of information which defendant has under existing law.

166 N.W.2d at 769.

Types of "Discovery"

Discussions concerning discovery generally involve several significantly different procedural matters that can usefully be distinguished. First, discovery may involve notice. Under the Federal Rules of Criminal Procedure, for example, a defendant must give pretrial notice concerning the intention to raise insanity or similar defenses, Fed.R.Crim.P. 12.2, or alibi, Fed.R.Crim.P. 12.1. Uniform Rules of Criminal Procedure 422 would require the prosecution to give the defense notice as to whether any evidence the prosecution intends to use was obtained by search, wiretap, lineup, or voice identification. It also requires notice concerning whether any confession or admission by the defendant, or evidence obtained by use of such confession or admission, will be offered.

A second type of discovery consists of one party's right of access to evidence in the possession of another party. Fed.R.Crim.P. 16(a)(1)(C), for example, gives a defendant the right to "inspect and copy or photograph" certain physical evidence in the possession of the government. A third category consists of a right to have certain items provided by the other party. Fed.R.Crim.P. 16(a)(1)(B) requires that upon request the government furnish the defendant with a copy of the defendant's criminal record.

Finally, a defendant may be obligated to participate in a procedure designed to develop certain evidence. Uniform Rules of Criminal Procedure 434, for example, would require a defendant under some circumstances to participate in a lineup, submit handwriting samples, and similarly cooperate in other nontestimonial procedures.

The timing of discovery must also be considered. As a general rule, a defendant's right to disclosure—especially of the statements of prosecution witnesses—during trial is broader than the right to pretrial access to them. But pretrial access to information may be of substantially greater value in preparing a defense or in deciding to accept an offered plea bargain rather than to mount any defense at all.

Implementation

There are wide variations as to the manner in which discovery is implemented. First, the duty to grant discovery may arise in several ways. A party may have a duty to provide discovery without request; Uniform Rules of Criminal Procedure 422 would impose upon the prosecution the duty to provide the notice discussed above without regard to any request by the defense. Or, the duty may depend upon request; the government's duty to give a defendant access to physical evidence under Fed.R.Crim.P. 16, discussed above, arises only upon defense request. In other situations, the duty arises only upon entry of a court order. The defendant's duty to participate in nontestimonial procedures under Uniform Rules of Criminal Procedure 434, for example, arises only when the court, upon motion by the prosecutor, orders such participation.

If issues arise as to whether discovery requirements have been adequately complied with, provisions are sometimes made for the court to consider certain evidence *in camera,* that is, without the presence of the parties, and to grant relief only if this consideration indicates that discovery is appropriate. Fed.R.Crim.Proc. 16(d)(1). If a party believes that only part of a document or similar item is subject to discovery, some procedures permit the party to excise the other portions of it, perhaps indicating on the copy furnished the opponent that an excision has been made. Uniform Rules of Criminal Procedure 421(b)(4).

A party who believes that otherwise required discovery is, for some special reason, inappropriate in the situation presented is sometimes authorized to apply to the court for an order denying or restricting disclosure or perhaps limiting further dissemination of the information by the party to whom it is disclosed. Fed.R.Crim.P. 16(d)(1), for example, provides:

> Upon a sufficient showing the court may at any time order that the discovery or inspection be denied, restricted, or deferred, or make such other order as is appropriate.

The duty to disclose is generally a continuing duty, so that if information not previously available is later developed the party has a responsibility to communicate it to the opponent. Fed.R.Crim.P. 16(c) provides:

> If, prior to or during trial a party discovers additional evidence or material previously requested or ordered, which is subject to discovery or inspection under this rule, he shall promptly notify the other party

or his attorney or the court of the existence of the additional evidence or material.

Work Product Exception

Work product of the lawyers in the case and perhaps their agents or investigators is often exempted from discovery. Fed.R.Crim.P. 16(a)(2), (b)(2). But there are wide variations as to what constitutes work product. The major question is whether factual information developed by lawyers or investigators is protected from disclosure. ABA Standard 11–2.6(b) limits the work product exception to "legal research" and "records, correspondence, reports or memoranda to the extent that they contain the opinions, theories or conclusions of the prosecuting attorneys or members of his legal staff." Uniform Rules of Criminal Procedure 421(b)(1) contains an identical provision. In United States v. Nobles, 422 U.S. 225, 95 S.Ct. 2160, 45 L.Ed.2d 141 (1975) the Supreme Court found no need to delineate the scope of the work product doctrine as a bar to disclosure at trial and specifically no need to determine whether it protected from disclosure to the government portions of a report by a defense investigator to defense counsel.

Sanctions

Trial judges are generally given broad discretion to fashion appropriate remedies for noncompliance with discovery requirements. Fed.R.Crim.P. 16(d)(2), for example, provides:

> the court may order [a] party to permit the discovery or inspection, grant a continuance, or prohibit the party from introducing evidence not disclosed, or it may enter such other order as it deems just under the circumstances.

Some formulations specifically authorize the trial judge, upon finding prosecutorial noncompliance with discovery requirements, to—among other options—consider dismissal of the prosecution. Uniform Rules of Criminal Procedure 421(e). This drastic remedy may not be favored. In People v. Zamora, 28 Cal.3d 88, 615 P.2d 1361, 167 Cal.Rptr. 573 (1980) defendant asserted excessive force as a defense to a charge of battery upon two police officers; the files concerning these officers, which may have indicated they were violence-prone, had been destroyed. Holding that the appropriate remedy was not dismissal of the charges, the court indicated that the jury should be told of the destruction of the records and that they could infer from this destruction that the records would have shown that the officers were prone to excessive force.

* * *

The Court dealt with the issue of precluding a defense witness from testifying as a discovery sanction in Taylor v. Illinois, 484 U.S. 400, 108 S.Ct. 646, 98 L.Ed.2d 798 (1988). Preparatory to Taylor's trial for attempted murder, his attorney was ordered to disclose to the prosecutor "the names and last known addresses of persons he intends to call as witnesses" as well as any statements they may have given the defense. The names of two defense witnesses were provided pursuant to this order. On the second day of trial, defense counsel sought to amend his witness list to include

Alfred Wormley, explaining to the court that he had not been included earlier because he did not know his whereabouts. The court reserved ruling on the motion until he heard Wormley's testimony. The next day, counsel appeared in court with Wormley, whose testimony was presented to the court outside the presence of the jury as an offer of proof. On cross-examination, Wormley acknowledged that he had been interviewed in his own home by defense counsel the preceding week. The trial court, expressing doubts about the veracity of Wormley's proposed testimony, precluded the defense from calling him to the stand. Following his conviction and its affirmance by the appellate court system, petitioner argued before the United States Supreme Court that precluding a defense witness from testifying as a sanction for a discovery violation was absolutely prohibited by the Compulsory Process Clause of the Sixth Amendment. The Court rejected that position:

> The principle that undergirds the defendant's right to present exculpatory evidence is also the source of essential limitations on the right. The adversary process could not function effectively without adherence to rules of procedure that govern the orderly presentation of facts and arguments to provide each party with a fair opportunity to assemble and submit evidence to contradict or explain the opponent's case. The trial processes would be a shambles if either party had an absolute right to control the time and content of his witnesses' testimony. . . . The State's interest in the orderly conduct of a criminal trial is sufficient to justify the imposition and enforcement of firm, though not always inflexible, rules relating to the identification and presentation of evidence.

484 U.S. at 410–11, 108 S.Ct. at 653, 98 L.Ed.2d at 811–12. The Court also acknowledged that there are sanctions available that are less drastic than witness preclusion, such as granting the State a continuance or a mistrial or even holding the defendant or his attorney in contempt. The Court suggested that the preclusion sanction is appropriate in cases, such as this one, in which the violation is deliberate and engaged in to gain a tactical advantage over the opponent and is also appropriate in situations such as this in which the truthfulness of the proposed testimony of the witness is suspect. Justice Brennan, joined by Justices Marshall and Blackmun, dissented, taking the position that preclusion is permitted by the Compulsory Process Clause only when the defendant was personally involved in the discovery violation.

Informal Practice

Even in those jurisdictions that have limited formal rights of discovery, local practice is often such that defense lawyers are given access to much or all of the prosecution's case in advance. Prosecutors provide such discovery in the belief that such a practice induces the disposition of cases by pleas of guilty because it shows defense counsel the strength of the government's case against his or her client. A major problem with this "open file" practice, however, is that defense lawyers' access to the prosecution's files may depend upon such matters as their experience and personal relationships with prosecuting attorneys. Thus the client of a defense lawyer who finds himself in the unusual situation of being denied access to the prosecution's files may be materially prejudiced because of considerations unrelated to the merits of his case or the interests of the criminal justice system. The absence of formal discovery rights, of course, precludes efforts to seek judicial redress. See Comment, In Search of the Adversary System—The Cooperative Practices of Private Criminal Defense Attorneys, 50 Tex.L.Rev. 60 (1971).

This Chapter considers separately issues raised by prosecutorial disclosure to the defense and defense disclosure to the prosecution. Both areas involve constitutional as well as other considerations.

A. PROSECUTORIAL DISCLOSURE

FEDERAL RULES OF CRIMINAL PROCEDURE

Rule 16. Discovery and Inspection

(a) Disclosure of Evidence by the Government.

(1) Information Subject to Disclosure.

(A) *Statement of Defendant.* Upon request of a defendant the government shall disclose to the defendant and make available for inspection, copying, or photographing: any relevant written or recorded statements made by the defendant, or copies thereof, within the possession, custody or control of the government, the existence of which is known, or by the exercise of due diligence may become known, to the attorney for the government; that portion of any written record containing the substance of any relevant oral statement made by the defendant whether before or after arrest in response to interrogation by any person then known to the defendant to be a government agent; and recorded testimony of the defendant before a grand jury which relates to the offense charged. The government shall also disclose to the defendant the substance of any other relevant oral statement made by the defendant whether before or after arrest in response to interrogation by any person then known by the defendant to be a government agent if the government intends to use that statement at trial. * * *

(B) *Defendant's Prior Record.* Upon request of the defendant, the government shall furnish to the defendant such copy of his prior criminal record, if any, as is within the possession, custody, or control of the government, the existence of which is known, or by the exercise of due diligence may become known, to the attorney for the government.

(C) *Documents and Tangible Objects.* Upon request of the defendant the government shall permit the defendant to inspect and copy or photograph books, papers, documents, photographs, tangible objects, buildings or places, or copies or portions thereof, which are within the possession, custody or control of the government, and which are material to the preparation of his defense or are intended for use by the government as evidence in chief at the trial, or were obtained from or belong to the defendant.

(D) *Reports of Examinations and Tests.* Upon request of a defendant the government shall permit the defendant to inspect and copy or photograph any results or reports of physical or mental examinations, and of scientific tests or experiments, or copies thereof, which are within the possession, custody, or control of the government, the existence of which is known, or by the exercise of due diligence may become known, to the attorney for the government, and which are material to the preparation of the defense or are intended for use by the government as evidence in chief at the trial.

(E) Expert Witnesses. At the defendant's request, the government shall disclose to the defendant a written summary of testimony that the government intends to use under Rules 702 [Testimony by Experts], 703 [Bases of Opinion Testimony by Experts], or 705 [Disclosure of Facts or Data Underlying Expert Opinion] of the Federal Rules of Evidence during its case-in-chief at trial. If the government requests discovery [summary of testimony defendant intends to use under Rules 702, 703 or 705] under subdivision (b)(1)(C)(ii) [when the defendant has given notice of intent to present expert testimony on defendant's mental condition] of this rule and the defendant complies, the government shall, at the defendant's request, disclose to the defendant a written summary of testimony the government intends to use under Rules 702, 703, or 705 as evidence at trial on the issue of the defendant's mental condition. The summary provided under this subdivision shall describe the witnesses' opinions, the bases and the reasons for those opinions, and the witnesses' qualifications.

NOTE

In United States v. Armstrong, 517 U.S. 456, 116 S.Ct. 1480, 134 L.Ed.2d 687 (1996), the Court addressed the question of the scope of a defendant's right to discovery of documents or other tangible objects under Rule 16(a)(1)(C), particularly the meaning of "material to the preparation of his defense". The Court, through The Chief Justice, held that only material that is relevant to defeating the government's case-in-chief is discoverable under this provision. The respondent had requested discovery of prosecutorial records concerning the race of the defendants charged in an effort to make out a claim of selective prosecution. Under the Court's interpretation of Rule 16, he was not entitled to receive such material. Justices Souter, Ginsburg, Breyer and Stevens, all writing separately, disagreed with this holding or emphasized its limited application to selective prosecution claims.

1.   CONSTITUTIONAL OBLIGATIONS

United States v. Bagley

Supreme Court of the United States, 1985.
473 U.S. 667, 105 S.Ct. 3375, 87 L.Ed.2d 481.

■ JUSTICE BLACKMUN announced the judgment of the Court and delivered an opinion of the Court except as to Part III.

In Brady v. Maryland, 373 U.S. 83, 87, 83 S.Ct. 1194, 1196, 10 L.Ed.2d 215 (1963), this Court held that "the suppression by the prosecution of evidence favorable to an accused upon request violates due process where the evidence is material either to guilt or punishment." The issue in the present case concerns the standard of materiality to be applied in determining whether a conviction should be reversed because the prosecutor failed to disclose requested evidence that could have been used to impeach Government witnesses.

I

In October 1977, respondent Hughes Anderson Bagley was indicted in the Western District of Washington on 15 charges of violating federal narcotics and firearms statutes. On November 18, 24 days before trial, respondent filed a discovery motion. The sixth paragraph of that motion requested:

> "The names and addresses of witnesses that the government intends to call at trial. Also the prior criminal records of witnesses, and any deals, promises or inducements made to witnesses in exchange for their testimony." App. 18.[1]

The Government's two principal witnesses at the trial were James F. O'Connor and Donald E. Mitchell. O'Connor and Mitchell were state law-enforcement officers employed by the Milwaukee Railroad as private security guards. Between April and June 1977, they assisted the federal Bureau of Alcohol, Tobacco and Firearms (ATF) in conducting an undercover investigation of respondent.

The Government's response to the discovery motion did not disclose that any "deals, promises or inducements" had been made to O'Connor or Mitchell. In apparent reply to a request in the motion's ninth paragraph for "[c]opies of all Jencks Act material,"[2] the Government produced a series of affidavits that O'Connor and Mitchell had signed between April 12 and May 4, 1977, while the undercover investigation was in progress. These affidavits recounted in detail the undercover dealings that O'Connor and Mitchell were having at the time with respondent. Each affidavit concluded with the statement, "I made this statement freely and voluntarily without any threats or rewards, or promises of reward having been made to me in return for it."

Respondent waived his right to a jury trial and was tried before the court in December 1977. At the trial, O'Connor and Mitchell testified about both the firearms and the narcotics charges. On December 23, the court

---

1. In addition, ¶ 10(b) of the motion requested "[p]romises or representations made to any persons the government intends to call as witnesses at trial, including but not limited to promises of no prosecution, immunity, lesser sentence, etc.," and ¶ 11 requested "[a]ll information which would establish the reliability of the Milwaukee Railroad Employees in this case, whose testimony formed the basis for the search warrant." App. 18–19.

2. The Jencks Act, 18 U.S.C. § 3500, requires the prosecutor to disclose, after direct examination of a Government witness and on the defendant's motion, any statement of the witness in the Government's possession that relates to the subject matter of the witness' testimony.

found respondent guilty on the narcotics charges, but not guilty on the firearms charges.

In mid–1980, respondent filed requests for information pursuant to the Freedom of Information Act and to the Privacy Act of 1974, 5 U.S.C. §§ 552 and 552a. He received in response copies of ATF form contracts that O'Connor and Mitchell had signed on May 3, 1977. Each form was entitled "Contract for Purchase of Information and Payment of Lump Sum Therefor." The printed portion of the form stated that the vendor "will provide" information to ATF and that "upon receipt of such information by the Regional Director, Bureau of Alcohol, Tobacco and Firearms, or his representative, and upon the accomplishment of the objective sought to be obtained by the use of such information to the satisfaction of said Regional Director, the United States will pay to said vendor a sum commensurate with services and information rendered." Each form contained the following typewritten description of services:

> "That he will provide information regarding T–I and other violations committed by Hughes A. Bagley, Jr.; that he will purchase evidence for ATF; that he will cut [*sic*] in an undercover capacity for ATF; that he will assist ATF in gathering of evidence and testify against the violator in federal court."

The figure "$300.00" was handwritten in each form on a line entitled "Sum to Be Paid to Vendor."

Because these contracts had not been disclosed to respondent in response to his pretrial discovery motion,[3] respondent moved under 28 U.S.C. § 2255 to vacate his sentence. He alleged that the Government's failure to disclose the contracts, which he could have used to impeach O'Connor and Mitchell, violated his right to due process under Brady v. Maryland, supra.

The motion came before the same District Judge who had presided at respondent's bench trial. An evidentiary hearing was held before a Magistrate. The Magistrate found that the printed form contracts were blank when O'Connor and Mitchell signed them and were not signed by an ATF representative until after the trial. He also found that on January 4, 1978, following the trial and decision in respondent's case, ATF made payments of $300 to both O'Connor and Mitchell pursuant to the contracts.[4] Although the ATF case agent who dealt with O'Connor and Mitchell testified that these payments were compensation for expenses, the Magistrate found that this characterization was not borne out by the record. There was no documentation for expenses in these amounts; Mitchell testified that his payment was not for expenses, and the ATF forms authorizing the payments treated them as rewards.

---

3. The Assistant United States Attorney who prosecuted respondent stated in stipulated testimony that he had not known that the contracts existed and that he would have furnished them to respondent had he known of them.

4. The Magistrate found, too, that ATF paid O'Connor and Mitchell, respectively, $90 and $80 in April and May 1977 before trial, but concluded that these payments were intended to reimburse O'Connor and Mitchell for expenses, and would not have provided a basis for impeaching O'Connor's and Mitchell's trial testimony. The District Court adopted this finding and conclusion.

The District Court adopted each of the Magistrate's findings except for the last one to the effect that "[n]either O'Connor nor Mitchell expected to receive the payment of $300 or any payment from the United States for their testimony." Instead, the court found that it was "probable" that O'Connor and Mitchell expected to receive compensation, in addition to their expenses, for their assistance, "though perhaps not for their testimony." The District Court also expressly rejected the Magistrate's conclusion that:

> "Because neither witness was promised or expected payment for his testimony, the United States did not withhold, during pretrial discovery, information as to any 'deals, promises or inducements' to these witnesses. Nor did the United States suppress evidence favorable to the defendant, in violation of Brady v. Maryland, 373 U.S. 83, 83 S.Ct. 1194, 10 L.Ed.2d 215 (1963)."

The District Court found beyond a reasonable doubt, however, that had the existence of the agreements been disclosed to it during trial, the disclosure would have had no effect upon its finding that the Government had proved beyond a reasonable doubt that respondent was guilty of the offenses for which he had been convicted. The District Court reasoned: Almost all of the testimony of both witnesses was devoted to the firearms charges in the indictment. Respondent, however, was acquitted on those charges. The testimony of O'Connor and Mitchell concerning the narcotics charges was relatively very brief. On cross-examination, respondent's counsel did not seek to discredit their testimony as to the facts of distribution but rather sought to show that the controlled substances in question came from supplies that had been prescribed for respondent's personal use. The answers of O'Connor and Mitchell to this line of cross-examination tended to be favorable to respondent. Thus, the claimed impeachment evidence would not have been helpful to respondent and would not have affected the outcome of the trial. Accordingly, the District Court denied respondent's motion to vacate his sentence.

The United States Court of Appeals for the Ninth Circuit reversed. Bagley v. Lumpkin, 719 F.2d 1462 (1983). The Court of Appeals began by noting that, according to precedent in the Circuit, prosecutorial failure to respond to a specific *Brady* request is properly analyzed as error, and a resulting conviction must be reversed unless the error is harmless beyond a reasonable doubt. The court noted that the District Judge who had presided over the bench trial concluded beyond a reasonable doubt that disclosure of the ATF agreement would not have affected the outcome. The Court of Appeals, however, stated that it "disagree[d]" with this conclusion. In particular, it disagreed with the Government's—and the District Court's—premise that the testimony of O'Connor and Mitchell was exculpatory on the narcotics charges, and that respondent therefore would not have sought to impeach "his own witness."

The Court of Appeals apparently based its reversal, however, on the theory that the Government's failure to disclose the requested *Brady* information that respondent could have used to conduct an effective cross-examination impaired respondent's right to confront adverse witnesses. The court noted: "In Davis v. Alaska, ... the Supreme Court held that the denial of the 'right of *effective* cross-examination' was ' "constitutional error of the first magnitude" ' requiring automatic reversal." 719 F.2d, at 1464 (quoting Davis v. Alaska, 415 U.S. 308, 318, 94 S.Ct. 1105, 1111, 39 L.Ed.2d 347 (1974)) (emphasis added by Court of Appeals). In the last sentence of its opinion, the Court of Appeals concluded: "we hold that the government's failure to provide requested *Brady* information to Bagley so that he could effectively cross-examine two important government witnesses requires an automatic reversal."

We granted certiorari, 469 U.S. 1016, 105 S.Ct. 427, 83 L.Ed.2d 354 (1984), and we now reverse.

II

The holding in Brady v. Maryland requires disclosure only of evidence that is both favorable to the accused and "material either to guilt or punishment." 373 U.S., at 87, 83 S.Ct. at 1197. See also Moore v. Illinois, 408 U.S. 786, 794–795, 92 S.Ct. 2562, 2567–2568, 33 L.Ed.2d 706, (1972). The Court explained in United States v. Agurs, 427 U.S. 97, 104, 96 S.Ct. 2392, 2398, 49 L.Ed.2d 342 (1976): "A fair analysis of the holding in *Brady* indicates that implicit in the requirement of materiality is a concern that the suppressed evidence might have affected the outcome of the trial." The evidence suppressed in *Brady* would have been admissible only on the issue of punishment and not on the issue of guilt, and therefore could have affected only Brady's sentence and not his conviction. Accordingly, the Court affirmed the lower court's restriction of Brady's new trial to the issue of punishment.

The *Brady* rule is based on the requirement of due process. Its purpose is not to displace the adversary system as the primary means by which truth is uncovered, but to ensure that a miscarriage of justice does not occur. Thus, the prosecutor is not required to deliver his entire file to defense counsel, but only to disclose evidence favorable to the accused that, if suppressed, would deprive the defendant of a fair trial:

> "For unless the omission deprived the defendant of a fair trial, there was no constitutional violation requiring that the verdict be set aside; and absent a constitutional violation, there was no breach of the prosecutor's constitutional duty to disclose. . . .
>
> " . . . But to reiterate a critical point, the prosecutor will not have violated his constitutional duty of disclosure unless his omission is of sufficient significance to result in the denial of the defendant's right to a fair trial." 427 U.S., at 108, 96 S.Ct. at 2400.

In *Brady* and *Agurs,* the prosecutor failed to disclose exculpatory evidence. In the present case, the prosecutor failed to disclose evidence that the defense might have used to impeach the Government's witnesses by showing bias or interest. Impeachment evidence, however, as well as exculpatory evidence, falls within the *Brady* rule. See Giglio v. United States, 405 U.S. 150, 154, 92 S.Ct. 763, 766, 31 L.Ed.2d 104 (1972). Such evidence is "evidence favorable to an accused," *Brady,* 373 U.S. at 87, 83 S.Ct. at 1196, so that, if disclosed and used effectively, it may make the difference between conviction and acquittal. Cf. Napue v. Illinois, 360 U.S.

264, 269, 79 S.Ct. 1173, 1177, 3 L.Ed.2d 1217 (1959) ("The jury's estimate of the truthfulness and reliability of a given witness may well be determinative of guilt or innocence, and it is upon such subtle factors as the possible interest of the witness in testifying falsely that a defendant's life or liberty may depend").

The Court of Appeals treated impeachment evidence as constitutionally different from exculpatory evidence. According to that court, failure to disclose impeachment evidence is "even more egregious" than failure to disclose exculpatory evidence "because it threatens the defendant's right to confront adverse witnesses." 719 F.2d, at 1464. Relying on Davis v. Alaska, 415 U.S. 308, 94 S.Ct. 1105, 39 L.Ed.2d 347 (1974), the Court of Appeals held that the Government's failure to disclose requested impeachment evidence that the defense could use to conduct an effective cross-examination of important prosecution witnesses constitutes " 'constitutional error of the first magnitude' " requiring automatic reversal. 719 F.2d, at 1464 (quoting Davis v. Alaska, supra, at 318, 94 S.Ct. at 1111).

This Court has rejected any such distinction between impeachment evidence and exculpatory evidence. In Giglio v. United States, supra, the Government failed to disclose impeachment evidence similar to the evidence at issue in the present case, that is, a promise made to the key government witness that he would not be prosecuted if he testified for the Government. This Court said:

> "When the 'reliability of a given witness may well be determinative of guilt or innocence,' nondisclosure of evidence affecting credibility falls within the general rule [of *Brady*]. We do not, however, automatically require a new trial whenever 'a combing of the prosecutors' files after the trial has disclosed evidence possibly useful to the defense but not likely to have changed the verdict. . . .' A finding of materiality of the evidence is required under *Brady*. . . . A new trial is required if 'the false testimony could . . . in any reasonable likelihood have affected the judgment of the jury. . . .' " 405 U.S., at 154, 92 S.Ct. at 766 (citations omitted).

Thus, the Court of Appeals' holding is inconsistent with our precedents.

Moreover, the court's reliance on Davis v. Alaska for its "automatic reversal" rule is misplaced. In *Davis,* the defense sought to cross-examine a crucial prosecution witness concerning his probationary status as a juvenile delinquent. The defense intended by this cross-examination to show that the witness might have made a faulty identification of the defendant in order to shift suspicion away from himself or because he feared that his probationary status would be jeopardized if he did not satisfactorily assist the police and prosecutor in obtaining a conviction. Pursuant to a state rule of procedure and a state statute making juvenile adjudications inadmissible, the trial judge prohibited the defense from conducting the cross-examination. This Court reversed the defendant's conviction, ruling that the direct restriction on the scope of cross-examination denied the defendant "the right of effective cross-examination" which "would be constitutional error of the first magnitude and no amount of showing of want of prejudice would cure it. Brookhart v. Janis, 384 U.S. 1, 3, 86 S.Ct. 1245,

1246, 16 L.Ed.2d 314." 415 U.S., at 318, 94 S.Ct. at 1111 (quoting Smith v. Illinois, 390 U.S. 129, 131, 88 S.Ct. 748, 750, 19 L.Ed.2d 956 (1968)).

The present case, in contrast does not involve any direct restriction on the scope of cross-examination. The defense was free to cross-examine the witnesses on any relevant subject, including possible bias or interest resulting from inducements made by the Government. The constitutional error, if any, in this case was the Government's failure to assist the defense by disclosing information that might have been helpful in conducting the cross-examination. As discussed above, such suppression of evidence amounts to a constitutional violation only if it deprives the defendant of a fair trial. Consistent with "our overriding concern with the justice of the finding of guilt," United States v. Agurs, 427 U.S., at 112, 96 S.Ct. at 2401, a constitutional error occurs, and the conviction must be reversed, only if the evidence is material in the sense that its suppression undermines confidence in the outcome of the trial.

III

A

It remains to determine the standard of materiality applicable to the nondisclosed evidence at issue in this case. Our starting point is the framework for evaluating the materiality of *Brady* evidence established in United States v. Agurs. The Court in *Agurs* distinguished three situations involving the discovery, after trial, of information favorable to the accused that had been known to the prosecution but unknown to the defense. The first situation was the prosecutor's knowing use of perjured testimony or, equivalently, the prosecutor's knowing failure to disclose that testimony used to convict the defendant was false. The Court noted the well-established rule that "a conviction obtained by the knowing use of perjured testimony is fundamentally unfair, and must be set aside if there is any reasonable likelihood that the false testimony could have affected the judgment of the jury." 427 U.S., at 103, 96 S.Ct. at 2397 (footnote omitted). Although this rule is stated in terms that treat the knowing use of perjured testimony as error subject to harmless-error review, it may as easily be stated as a materiality standard under which the fact that testimony is perjured is considered material unless failure to disclose it would be harmless beyond a reasonable doubt. The Court in *Agurs* justified this standard of materiality on the ground that the knowing use of perjured testimony involves prosecutorial misconduct and, more importantly, involves "a corruption of the truth-seeking function of the trial process."

At the other extreme is the situation in *Agurs* itself, where the defendant does not make a *Brady* request and the prosecutor fails to disclose certain evidence favorable to the accused. The Court rejected a harmless-error rule in that situation, because under that rule every nondisclosure is treated as error, thus imposing on the prosecutor a constitutional duty to deliver his entire file to defense counsel. At the same time, the Court rejected a standard that would require the defendant to demonstrate that the evidence if disclosed probably would have resulted in acquittal. Id., at 111, 96 S.Ct. at 2401. The Court reasoned: "If the standard applied to the usual motion for a new trial based on newly discovered evidence were the same when the evidence was in the State's possession as when it was found in a neutral source, there would be no special significance to the prosecutor's obligation to serve the cause of justice." Ibid. The standard of materiality applicable in the absence of a specific *Brady* request is therefore stricter than the harmless-error standard but more lenient to the defense than the newly discovered evidence standard.

The third situation identified by the Court in *Agurs* is where the defense makes a specific request and the prosecutor fails to disclose responsive evidence. The Court did not define the standard of materiality applicable in this situation, but suggested that the standard might be more lenient to the defense than in the situation in which the defense makes no request or only a general request. Id., at 106, 96 S.Ct. at 2398. The Court also noted: "When the prosecutor receives a specific and relevant request, the failure to make any response is seldom, if ever, excusable."

The Court has relied on and reformulated the *Agurs* standard for the materiality of undisclosed evidence in two subsequent cases arising outside the *Brady* context. In neither case did the Court's discussion of the *Agurs* standard distinguish among the three situations described in *Agurs*. In United States v. Valenzuela–Bernal, 458 U.S. 858, 874, 102 S.Ct. 3440, 3450, 73 L.Ed.2d 1193 (1982), the Court held that due process is violated when testimony is made unavailable to the defense by Government deportation of witnesses "only if there is a reasonable likelihood that the testimony could have affected the judgment of the trier of fact." And in Strickland v. Washington, 466 U.S. 668, 104 S.Ct. 2052, 80 L.Ed.2d 674 (1984), the Court held that a new trial must be granted when evidence is not introduced because of the incompetence of counsel only if "there is a reasonable probability that, but for counsel's unprofessional errors, the result of the proceeding would have been different." Id., at 694, 104 S.Ct. at 2068. The *Strickland* Court defined a "reasonable probability" as "a probability sufficient to undermine confidence in the outcome."

We find the *Strickland* formulation of the *Agurs* test for materiality sufficiently flexible to cover the "no request," "general request," and "specific request" cases of prosecutorial failure to disclose evidence favorable to the accused: The evidence is material only if there is a reasonable probability that, had the evidence been disclosed to the defense, the result of the proceeding would have been different. A "reasonable probability" is a probability sufficient to undermine confidence in the outcome.

The Government suggests that a materiality standard more favorable to the defendant reasonably might be adopted in specific request cases. The Government notes that an incomplete response to a specific request not only deprives the defense of certain evidence, but has the effect of representing to the defense that the evidence does not exist. In reliance on this misleading representation, the defense might abandon lines of independent investigation, defenses, or trial strategies that it otherwise would have pursued.

We agree that the prosecutor's failure to respond fully to a *Brady* request may impair the adversary process in this manner. And the more specifically the defense requests certain evidence, thus putting the prosecutor on notice of its value, the more reasonable it is for the defense to assume from the nondisclosure that the evidence does not exist, and to make pretrial and trial decisions on the basis of this assumption. This possibility of impairment does not necessitate a different standard of materiality, however, for under the *Strickland* formulation the reviewing court may consider directly any adverse effect that the prosecutor's failure to respond might have had on the preparation or presentation of the defendant's case. The reviewing court should assess the possibility that such effect might have occurred in light of the totality of the circumstances and with an awareness of the difficulty of reconstructing in a post-trial proceeding the course that the defense and the trial would have taken had the defense not been misled by the prosecutor's incomplete response.

B

In the present case, we think that there is a significant likelihood that the prosecutor's response to respondent's discovery motion misleadingly induced defense counsel to believe that O'Connor and Mitchell could not be impeached on the basis of bias or interest arising from inducements offered by the Government. Defense counsel asked the prosecutor to disclose any inducements that had been made to witnesses, and the prosecutor failed to disclose that the possibility of a reward had been held out to O'Connor and Mitchell if the information they supplied led to "the accomplishment of the objective sought to be obtained ... to the satisfaction of [the Government]." This possibility of a reward gave O'Connor and Mitchell a direct, personal stake in respondent's conviction. The fact that the stake was not guaranteed through a promise or binding contract, but was expressly contingent on the Government's satisfaction with the end result, served only to strengthen any incentive to testify falsely in order to secure a conviction. Moreover, the prosecutor disclosed affidavits that stated that O'Connor and Mitchell received no promises of reward in return for providing information in the affidavits implicating respondent in criminal activity. In fact, O'Connor and Mitchell signed the last of these affidavits the very day after they signed the ATF contracts. While petitioner is technically correct that the blank contracts did not constitute a "promise of reward," the natural effect of these affidavits would be misleadingly to induce defense counsel to believe that O'Connor and Mitchell provided the information in the affidavits, and ultimately their testimony at trial re-counting the same information, without any "inducements."

The District Court, nonetheless, found beyond a reasonable doubt that, had the information that the Government held out the possibility of reward to its witnesses been disclosed, the result of the criminal prosecution would not have been different. If this finding were sustained by the Court of Appeals, the information would be immaterial even under the standard of materiality applicable to the prosecutor's knowing use of perjured testimony. Although the express holding of the Court of Appeals was that the nondisclosure in this case required automatic reversal, the Court of Appeals also stated that it "disagreed" with the District Court's finding of harmless error. In particular, the Court of Appeals appears to have disagreed with the factual premise on which this finding expressly was based. The District Court reasoned that O'Connor's and Mitchell's testimony was exculpatory on the narcotics charges. The Court of Appeals, however, concluded, after reviewing the record, that O'Connor's and Mitchell's testimony was in fact inculpatory on those charges. 719 F.2d, at 1464, n. 1. Accordingly, we reverse the judgment of the Court of Appeals and remand the case to that court for a determination whether there is a reasonable probability that, had the inducement offered by the Government to O'Connor and Mitchell been disclosed to the defense, the result of the trial would have been different.

It is so ordered.

■ JUSTICE POWELL took no part in the decision of this case.

■ JUSTICE WHITE, with whom THE CHIEF JUSTICE and JUSTICE REHNQUIST join, concurring in part and concurring in the judgment. [omitted].

■ JUSTICE MARSHALL, with whom JUSTICE BRENNAN joins, dissenting. [omitted].

* * *

■ JUSTICE STEVENS, dissenting.

This case involves a straightforward application of the rule announced in Brady v. Maryland, 373 U.S. 83, 83 S.Ct. 1194, 10 L.Ed.2d 215 (1963), a case involving nondisclosure of material evidence by the prosecution in response to a specific request from the defense. I agree that the Court of Appeals misdescribed that rule, but I respectfully dissent from the Court's unwarranted decision to rewrite the rule itself.

* * *

The question in *Agurs* was whether the *Brady* rule should be *extended*, to cover a case in which there had been neither perjury nor a specific request—that is, whether the prosecution has some constitutional duty to search its files and disclose automatically, or in response to a general request, all evidence that "might have helped the defense, or might have affected the outcome." 427 U.S., at 110, 96 S.Ct. at 2400. Such evidence would, of course, be covered by the *Brady* formulation if it were specifically requested. We noted in *Agurs,* however, that because there had been no specific defense request for the later-discovered evidence, there was no notice to the prosecution that the defense did not already have that evidence or that it considered the evidence to be of particular value. Id., at 106–107, 96 S.Ct. at 2398–2399. Consequently, we stated that in the absence of a request the prosecution has a constitutional duty to volunteer only "obviously exculpatory evidence." Id., at 107. Because this constitutional duty to disclose is *different* from the duty described in *Brady,* it is not surprising that we developed a different standard of materiality in the *Agurs* context. Necessarily describing the "inevitably imprecise" standard in terms appropriate to post-trial review, we held that no constitutional violation occurs in the absence of a specific request unless "the omitted evidence creates a reasonable doubt that did not otherwise exist." Id., at 108, 112, 96 S.Ct. at 2399, 2402.

What the Court ignores with regard to *Agurs* is that its analysis was restricted entirely to the general or no-request context. The "standard of materiality" we fashioned for the purpose of determining whether a prosecutor's failure to *volunteer* exculpatory evidence amounted to constitutional error was and is unnecessary with regard to the two categories of prosecutorial suppression already covered by the *Brady* rule. The specific situation in *Agurs,* as well as the circumstances of United States v. Valenzuela–Burnal, 458 U.S. 858, 102 S.Ct. 3440, 73 L.Ed.2d 1193 (1982) and Strickland v. Washington, 466 U.S. 668, 104 S.Ct. 2052, 80 L.Ed.2d 674 (1984), simply fall "outside the *Brady* context."

But the *Brady* rule itself unquestionably applies to this case, because the Government failed to disclose favorable evidence that was clearly responsive to the defendant's specific request. Bagley's conviction therefore must be set aside if the suppressed evidence was "material"—and it obviously was—and if there is "any reasonable likelihood" that it could have affected the judgment of the trier of fact. . . .

The Court, however, today sets out a reformulation of the *Brady* rule in which I have no such confidence. Even though the prosecution suppressed evidence that was specifically requested, apparently the Court of Appeals may now reverse only if there is a "reasonable probability" that the suppressed evidence "would" have altered "the result of the trial." According to the Court this single rule is "sufficiently flexible" to cover specific as well as general or no-request instances of nondisclosure, because, at least in the view of Justice Blackmun and Justice O'Connor, a reviewing court can "consider directly" under this standard the more threatening effect that nondisclosure in response to a specific defense request will generally have on the truth-seeking function of the adversary process. (Opinion of Justice Blackmun).

I cannot agree. The Court's approach stretches the concept of "materiality" beyond any recognizable scope, transforming it from merely an evidentiary concept as used in *Brady* and *Agurs,* which required that material evidence be admissible and probative of guilt or innocence in the context of a specific request, into a result-focused standard that seems to include an independent weight in favor of affirming convictions despite evidentiary suppression. Evidence favorable to an accused and relevant to the dispositive issue of guilt apparently may still be found not "material," and hence suppressible by prosecutors prior to trial, unless there is a reasonable probability that its use would result in an acquittal. Justice Marshall rightly criticizes the incentives such a standard creates for prosecutors "to gamble, to play the odds, and to take a chance that evidence will later turn out not to have been potentially dispositive."

Moreover, the Court's analysis reduces the significance of deliberate prosecutorial suppression of potentially exculpatory evidence to that merely of one of numerous factors that "may" be considered by a reviewing court. This is not faithful to our statement in *Agurs* that "[w]hen the prosecutor receives a specific and relevant request, the failure to make any response is seldom, if ever, excusable." 427 U.S., at 106, 96 S.Ct. at 2399. Such suppression is far more serious than mere nondisclosure of evidence in which the defense has expressed no particular interest. A reviewing court should attach great significance to silence in the face of a specific request, when responsive evidence is later shown to have been in the Government's possession. Such silence actively misleads in the same way as would an affirmative representation that exculpatory evidence does not exist when, in fact, it does (i.e., perjury)—indeed, the two situations are aptly described as "sides of a single coin." Babcock, Fair Play; Evidence Favorable to An Accused and Effective Assistance of Counsel, 34 Stan.L.Rev. 1133, 1151 (1982).

Accordingly, although I agree that the judgment of the Court of Appeals should be vacated and that the case should be remanded for further proceedings, I disagree with the Court's statement of the correct standard to be applied. I therefore respectfully dissent from the judgment that the case be remanded for determination under the Court's new standard.

NOTES

1. **Is there a duty to preserve evidence?** Are police under a constitutional obligation to preserve evidence that might prove useful to a defendant in the trial of a criminal charge? In California v. Trombetta, 467 U.S. 479, 104 S.Ct. 2528, 81 L.Ed.2d 413 (1984), the respondent was arrested for driving while intoxicated. He provided police with a sample of his breath which was analyzed by an intoxilyzer machine. The readout from the machine was admitted at trial under a presumption of intoxication law. The California Court of Appeal reversed the conviction on the ground it was a violation of due process for the police not to preserve a sample of respondent's breath, using available means, to permit defense testing. The Supreme Court, on petition of the State of California, reversed the Court of Appeal. Justice Marshall, writing for a unanimous Court, noted that the Court has

> never squarely addressed the Government's duty to take affirmative steps to preserve evidence on behalf of criminal defendants. The absence of doctrinal development in this area reflects, in part, the difficulty of developing rules to deal with evidence destroyed through prosecutorial neglect or oversight. Whenever potentially exculpatory evidence is permanently lost, courts face the treacherous task of divining the import of materials whose contents is unknown and, very often, disputed.... Moreover, fashioning remedies for the illegal destruction of evidence can pose troubling choices. In nondisclosure cases, a court can grant the defendant a new trial at which the previously suppressed evidence may be introduced. But, when evidence has been destroyed in violation of the Constitution, the court must choose between barring further prosecution or suppressing ... the State's most probative evidence.

467 U.S. at 486–87, 104 S.Ct. at 2533, 81 L.Ed.2d at 420. Justice Marshall noted that California officials acted in good faith and in accordance with their normal practices. There is no claim of official animus toward the respondent or of a conscious effort to suppress exculpatory evidence.

> Whatever duty the Constitution imposes on the States to preserve evidence, that duty must be limited to evidence that might be expected to play a significant role in the suspect's defense. To meet this standard of constitutional materiality, see United States v. Agurs ..., evidence must both possess an exculpatory value that was apparent before the evidence was destroyed, and also be of such a nature that the defendant would be unable to obtain comparable evidence by other reasonably available means.

467 U.S. at 488–89, 104 S.Ct. at 2534, 81 L.Ed.2d at 422. Finally, Justice Marshall observed that the chances are extremely remote that any preserved breath sample would have been exculpatory.

The Court returned to the issue in Arizona v. Youngblood, 488 U.S. 51, 109 S.Ct. 333, 102 L.Ed.2d 281 (1988). During investigation of a sexual assault upon a ten-year old child, officers collected the victim's clothing, which contained stains made by the assailant's semen, but did not freeze or refrigerate it. At trial, Youngblood's principal defense was that the victim's identification was in error. Expert testimony was introduced that had the victim's clothing been frozen or refrigerated, tests could have been done that would have exonerated Youngblood, assuming he was in fact not the assailant. The state appellate courts held the resulting conviction invalid, but the Supreme Court reversed. The likelihood that the unpreserved evidence would have exonerated the defendant, Chief Justice Rehnquist noted for the Court, was greater in *Youngblood* than in *Trombetta,* but the prosecution had not attempted to make any use of the materials in its own case. Despite this, the Court held that "unless a criminal defendant can show bad faith on the part of the police, failure to preserve potentially useful evidence does not constitute a denial of due process." The requirement of bad faith, it explained,

> both limits the extent of the police's obligation to preserve evidence to reasonable bounds and confines it to that class of cases where the interests of justice most clearly require it, i.e., those cases in which the police themselves by their conduct indicate that the evidence could form a basis for exonerating the defendant.

488 U.S. at 58, 109 S.Ct. at 337, 102 L.Ed.2d at 289. While the officers here may have been negligent, there was "no suggestion" of bad faith. The Court also disapproved a suggestion by the lower court that the police were constitutionally deficient for failing to conduct the tests themselves:

> The situation here is no different than a prosecution for drunk driving that rests on police observation alone; the defendant is free to argue to the finder of fact that a breathalyzer test might have been exculpatory, but the police do not have a constitutional duty to perform any particular tests.

488 U.S. at 59, 109 S.Ct. at 338, 102 L.Ed.2d at 290. Justice Stevens concurred in the judgment, but declined to adopt an absolute requirement of bad faith. 488 U.S. at 59, 109 S.Ct. at 338, 102 L.Ed.2d at 290–91 (Stevens, J., concurring in the judgment). Justice Blackmun, joined by Justices Brennan and Marshall, dissented:

> [W]here no comparable evidence is likely to be available to the defendant, police must preserve physical evidence of a type that they reasonably should know has the potential, if tested, to reveal immutable characteristics of the criminal, and hence to exculpate a defendant charged with the crime.

488 U.S. at 69, 109 S.Ct. at 343, 102 L.Ed.2d at 297 (Blackmun, J., dissenting).

2. **Information in the possession of others.** What information in the possession of persons other than the prosecutors actually trying the case must be disclosed under the Due Process standard? In Giglio v. United States, 405 U.S. 150, 92 S.Ct. 763, 31 L.Ed.2d 104 (1972) certain information concerning a promise made to a witness was in the possession of an Assistant United States Attorney who had been involved in Giglio's prosecution at an early stage. When questioned at trial, the witness denied having been promised anything for his testimony. The Assistant United States Attorney who tried the case was unaware of the promise. Nevertheless, the Supreme Court found a violation of Due Process. A prosecutor's office is an "entity," the Court reasoned, and the lawyers involved in a case have a responsibility to pass along information to lawyers who subsequently assume responsibility for the case.

3. **Timing of disclosure.** When must disclosure required by Due Process occur? In United States v. McPartlin, 595 F.2d 1321 (7th Cir.1979), defendants appealed a conviction on the ground that withholding evidence favorable to them

until the beginning of the trial violated their due process rights under *Brady*. The court stated:

> There is nothing in *Brady* or *Agurs* to require that such disclosures be made before trial, ... Thus, even though evidence might be material or might create a reasonable doubt as to guilt, Due Process, albeit requiring eventual disclosure, does not require that in all instances this disclosure must occur before trial.
>
> The appropriate standard to be applied in a case such as this is whether the disclosure came so late as to prevent the defendant from receiving a fair trial.

595 F.2d at 1346. The court reasoned:

> The concern of *Agurs* and *Brady* is whether the suppression of exculpatory material until after trial requires that a new trial be given so that this evidence may be considered. The Court in *Agurs* characterized the situations to which the *Brady* principles apply as those involving "the discovery, *after trial,* of information which had been known to the prosecution but unknown to the defense." 427 U.S. at 103, 96 S.Ct. at 2397 (emphasis supplied). Indeed the standard developed in *Agurs* can only sensibly be applied to the suppression of evidence throughout the trial: "if the *omitted* evidence creates a reasonable doubt that did not otherwise exist, constitutional error has been committed." Id. at 112, 96 S.Ct. at 2402 (emphasis supplied).

Id. Similar views have been expressed by other circuits.

4. **Materiality.** *Bagley*'s materiality standard was addressed in some detail in Kyles v. Whitley, 514 U.S. 419, 115 S.Ct. 1555, 131 L.Ed.2d 490 (1995). Kyles sought federal habeas corpus relief from his Louisiana conviction and death sentence on the ground that the prosecution had failed to disclose a number of exculpatory matters. Discussing the federal constitutional law to be applied to Kyles' contention, the Court explained:

> Four aspects of materiality under *Bagley* bear emphasis. Although the constitutional duty is triggered by the potential impact of favorable but undisclosed evidence, a showing of materiality does not require demonstration by a preponderance that disclosure of the suppressed evidence would have resulted ultimately in the defendant's acquittal (whether based on the presence of reasonable doubt or acceptance of an explanation for the crime that does not inculpate the defendant). *Bagley's* touchstone of materiality is a "reasonable probability" of a different result, and the adjective is important. The question is not whether the defendant would more likely than not have received a different verdict with the evidence, but whether in its absence he received a fair trial, understood as a trial resulting in a verdict worthy of confidence. A "reasonable probability" of a different result is accordingly shown when the Government's evidentiary suppression "undermines confidence in the outcome of the trial." *Bagley,* 473 U.S., at 678, 105 S.Ct., at 3381.
>
> The second aspect of *Bagley* materiality bearing emphasis here is that it is not a sufficiency of evidence test. A defendant need not demonstrate that after discounting the inculpatory evidence in light of the undisclosed evidence, there would not have been enough left to convict. The possibility of an acquittal on a criminal charge does not imply an insufficient evidentiary basis to convict. One does not show a *Brady* violation by demonstrating that some of the inculpatory evidence should have been excluded, but by showing that the favorable evidence could reasonably be taken to put the whole case in such a different light as to undermine confidence in the verdict.

Third, we note that * * * once a reviewing court applying *Bagley* has found constitutional error there is no need for further harmless-error review. Assuming arguendo that a harmless error enquiry were to apply, a *Bagley* error could not be treated as harmless, since "a reasonable probability that, had the evidence been disclosed to the defense, the result of the proceeding would have been different," necessarily entails the conclusion that the suppression must have had " 'substantial and injurious effect or influence in determining the jury's verdict,' " Brecht v. Abrahamson, 507 U.S. 619, 113 S.Ct. 1710, 1712, 123 L.Ed.2d 353 (1993) [(setting out the standard of harmlessness generally to be applied in habeas cases)], quoting Kotteakos v. United States, 328 U.S. 750, 776, 66 S.Ct. 1239, 1253, 90 L.Ed. 1557 (1946). * * *

The fourth and final aspect of *Bagley* materiality to be stressed here is its definition in terms of suppressed evidence considered collectively, not item-by-item. * * * [T]he Constitution is not violated every time the government fails or chooses not to disclose evidence that might prove helpful to the defense. We have never held that the Constitution demands an open file policy (however such a policy might work out in practice), and the rule in *Bagley* (and, hence, in *Brady*) requires less of the prosecution than the ABA Standards for Criminal Justice, which call generally for prosecutorial disclosures of any evidence tending to exculpate or mitigate.

While the definition of *Bagley* materiality in terms of the cumulative effect of suppression must accordingly be seen as leaving the government with a degree of discretion, it must also be understood as imposing a corresponding burden. On the one side, showing that the prosecution knew of an item of favorable evidence unknown to the defense does not amount to a *Brady* violation, without more. But the prosecution, which alone can know what is undisclosed, must be assigned the consequent responsibility to gauge the likely net effect of all such evidence and make disclosure when the point of "reasonable probability" is reached. This in turn means that the individual prosecutor has a duty to learn of any favorable evidence known to the others acting on the government's behalf in the case, including the police. But whether the prosecutor succeeds or fails in meeting this obligation (whether, that is, a failure to disclose is in good faith or bad faith), the prosecution's responsibility for failing to disclose known, favorable evidence rising to a material level of importance is inescapable.

The State of Louisiana would prefer an even more lenient rule. It pleads that some of the favorable evidence in issue here was not disclosed even to the prosecutor until after trial, and it suggested below that it should not be held accountable under *Bagley* and *Brady* for evidence known only to police investigators and not to the prosecutor. To accommodate the State in this manner would, however, amount to a serious change of course from the *Brady* line of cases. In the State's favor it may be said that no one doubts that police investigators sometimes fail to inform a prosecutor of all they know. But neither is there any serious doubt that "procedures and regulations can be established to carry [the prosecutor's] burden and to insure communication of all relevant information on each case to every lawyer who deals with it." Giglio v. United States, 405 U.S. 150, 154, 92 S.Ct. 763, 766, 31 L.Ed.2d 104 (1972). Since, then, the prosecutor has the means to discharge the government's *Brady* responsibility if he will, any argument for excusing a prosecutor from disclosing what he does not happen to know about boils down to a plea to substitute the police for the prosecutor, and even for the courts themselves, as the final arbiters of the government's obligation to ensure fair trials.

Short of doing that, we were asked at oral argument to raise the threshold of materiality because the *Bagley* standard "makes it difficult ... to know" from the "perspective [of the prosecutor at] trial ... exactly what might become important later on." The State asks for "a certain amount of leeway in making a judgment call" as to the disclosure of any given piece of evidence.

Uncertainty about the degree of further "leeway" that might satisfy the State's request for a "certain amount" of it is the least of the reasons to deny the request. At bottom, what the State fails to recognize is that, with or without more leeway, the prosecution cannot be subject to any disclosure obligation without at some point having the responsibility to determine when it must act. Indeed, even if due process were thought to be violated by every failure to disclose an item of exculpatory or impeachment evidence (leaving harmless error as the government's only fallback), the prosecutor would still be forced to make judgment calls about what would count as favorable evidence, owing to the very fact that the character of a piece of evidence as favorable will often turn on the context of the existing or potential evidentiary record. Since the prosecutor would have to exercise some judgment even if the State were subject to this most stringent disclosure obligation, it is hard to find merit in the State's complaint over the responsibility for judgment under the existing system, which does not tax the prosecutor with error for any failure to disclose, absent a further showing of materiality. Unless, indeed, the adversary system of prosecution is to descend to a gladiatorial level unmitigated by any prosecutorial obligation for the sake of truth, the government simply cannot avoid responsibility for knowing when the suppression of evidence has come to portend such an effect on a trial's outcome as to destroy confidence in its result.

This means, naturally, that a prosecutor anxious about tacking too close to the wind will disclose a favorable piece of evidence. This is as it should be. Such disclosure will serve to justify trust in the prosecutor as "the representative ... of a sovereignty ... whose interest ... in a criminal prosecution is not that it shall win a case, but that justice shall be done." Berger v. United States, 295 U.S. 78, 88, 55 S.Ct. 629, 633, 79 L.Ed. 1314 (1935). And it will tend to preserve the criminal trial, as distinct from the prosecutor's private deliberations, as the chosen forum for ascertaining the truth about criminal accusations. The prudence of the careful prosecutor should not therefore be discouraged.

514 U.S. at 434–40, 115 S.Ct. at 1565–69, 131 L.Ed.2d at 506–10.

In the course of concluding that on the complicated facts before it the nondisclosed information at issue was material under *Bagley,* the Court commented that undisclosed information that would have permitted "the effective impeachment of one eyewitness can call for a new trial even though the attack does not extend directly to others." 514 U.S. at 445, 115 S.Ct. at 1571, 131 L.Ed.2d at 513. This, Justice Scalia observed in dissent, "is the major contribution of today's opinion to *Brady* litigation." "[W]ith our endorsement," he continued, "it will surely be trolled past appellate courts in all future failure to disclose cases." 514 U.S. at 469, 115 S.Ct. at 1582, 131 L.Ed.2d at 528 (Scalia, J., dissenting). He disagreed with the majority's comments on the merits of the matter:

The weakening of one witness's testimony does not weaken the unconnected testimony of another witness; and to entertain the possibility that the jury will give it such an effect is incompatible with the whole idea of a materiality standard, which presumes that the incriminating evidence that would have been destroyed by proper disclosure can be logically separated from the incriminating evidence that would have remained unaffected.

514 U.S. at 469, 115 S.Ct. at 1583, 131 L.Ed.2d at 528.

The Court returned to *Bagley* materiality in Wood v. Bartholomew, 516 U.S. 1, 116 S.Ct. 7, 133 L.Ed.2d 1 (1995)(per curiam). At Bartholomew's state trial for premeditated murder, his brother Rodney testified that Bartholomew had told him before the events that he planned to rob the target laundromat and leave no witnesses. Prosecutors failed to disclose to the defense that before trial Rodney had taken a lie detector test and his negative answers to several questions (had he assisted the defendant in the robbery and had he and the defendant been in laundromat together) indicated deception to the examiner. The federal appeals court considering Bartholomew's request for federal habeas corpus relief had erred, the Supreme Court concluded, in finding that this information was "material" under *Bagley*. Evidence of the result of the test results was itself inadmissible. The lower court's conclusion that defense counsel, had he been given this information, would have discovered admissible evidence indicating innocence was "based on mere speculation, in violation of the standards [the Supreme Court has] established." Bartholomew's contention that had defense counsel been given this information he would have deposed Rodney before trial and thus have been able to more effectively cross-examine Rodney at trial was similarly insufficient; defense counsel sought to minimize his cross-examination of Rodney and unsuccessful efforts in the federal habeas proceeding to use the lie detector results in eliciting contradictions or admissions from Rodney suggest defense counsel would have fared no better before trial. A finding of materiality, the Court stressed, must be based on "more than speculation with slight support * * *." 516 U.S. at 8, 116 S.Ct. at 11, 133 L.Ed.2d at 8.

2. STATUTORY CONSIDERATIONS

Apart from possible constitutional limits, a number of significant issues regarding prosecutorial disclosure exist. Some concern the extent to which it is desirable to provide for such discovery. Other and obviously related ones deal with the construction of statutes and court rules authorizing disclosure. Much of the controversy concerns defense access to the prior statements of prosecution witnesses. This is the subject of the principal case in this subsection.

People v. Bassett

Supreme Court of Illinois, 1974.
56 Ill.2d 285, 307 N.E.2d 359.

■ DAVIS, JUSTICE.

[In the course of a prison riot hostages were taken and three guards killed. Defendants were convicted of murder.]

It is urged that the prosecution had in its possession various statements, made by witnesses for the People, which should have been turned over to the defense in accordance with People v. Wolff (1960), 19 Ill.2d 318, 167 N.E.2d 197. This question is now controlled by Supreme Court Rule 412, which was not effective at the time of this trial.

... Section (a)(i) of Supreme Court Rule 412 provides that upon written motion of defense counsel the State shall disclose to defense counsel the following material and information within its possession and control:

"(i) the names and last known addresses of persons whom the State intends to call as witnesses, together with their relevant written or recorded statements, memoranda containing substantially verbatim reports of their oral statements, and a list of memoranda reporting or summarizing their oral statements. Upon written motion of defense counsel memoranda reporting or summarizing oral statements shall be examined by the court *in camera* and if found to be substantially verbatim reports of oral statements shall be disclosed to defense counsel." 50 Ill.2d R. 412.

Wolff concerned testimony given by a People's witness who testified on cross-examination that he had made a statement to the police, but couldn't recall if it had been written down. Defense counsel then asked if the statement had ever been shown to the witness, the State objected on the ground that defense counsel was assuming the existence of the statement, and the objection was sustained. In *Wolff*, at page 327, 167 N.E.2d at page 201, this court stated:

"... where no privilege exists, and where the relevancy and competency of a statement or report has been established, the trial judge shall order the document delivered directly to the accused for his inspection and use for impeachment purposes. However, if the prosecution claims that any document ordered to be produced contains matter which does not relate to the testimony of the witness sought to be impeached, the trial judge will inspect the document and may, at his discretion, delete unrelated matters before delivery is made to the accused."

The instant case concerns interviews by State personnel with at least 800 to 900 inmates of Menard Penitentiary. The procedure followed according to the prosecuting attorneys, was that notes would be taken on yellow paper during the interview but these would not be verbatim notes. After all the interviews were completed, these notes were transcribed onto white cards, allegedly containing a narrative of what the prosecutor expected to prove by each witness. The prosecution claims that no attempt was made to obtain the signatures of those being interviewed and no such "formal statement" was produced.

It must be conceded that the representatives of the People who conducted these interviews sought to take notes that would be of some use in the preparation and trial of the case; and that when assistant Attorney General Crain or others transcribed these original "rough notes" into "narrative" form on white cards, it was done in such a manner as to make these cards useful at trial. It would seem that these cards would be useless unless they accurately summarized the point the People wished to be proved by any given witness.

There is also testimony that these cards were used in discussing a prospective witness's testimony before trial, and that at the discussion the witness thought he was being told what he had said in his initial interview. He did not say that what was read to him from the card was word for word what he had previously stated, but that it accurately reflected the substance of what he had told the interviewer.

In this case the defense could not prove the existence of the original notes, for they had been destroyed by the prosecution. The defense was then faced with showing that the white cards being used by Crain were verbatim or substantially verbatim copies of the witnesses' earlier remarks. Crain stated repeatedly and strenuously that no verbatim or substantially verbatim statements existed. The truth or falsity of this statement depends upon one's conception of the rationale behind the *Wolff* case and later decisions.

In People v. Sumner (1969), 43 Ill.2d 228, 235, 252 N.E.2d 534, 538, we stated:

> "Curtis's statement should also have been given to the defendant. This court in People v. Wolff, 19 Ill.2d 318, 167 N.E.2d 197, expressly adopted the Federal rule first announced in Jencks v. United States, 353 U.S. 657, 77 S.Ct. 1007, 1 L.Ed.2d 1103, and later made part of a Federal statute (18 U.S.C. sec. 3500) that where the relevancy and competency of a statement or report has been established, and no privilege exists, the trial court, on appropriate demand, shall order the statement or report delivered directly to the accused for his inspection and possible use for impeachment purposes. (19 Ill.2d at 327, 167 N.E.2d 197; see also People v. Cagle, 41 Ill.2d 528, 532, 244 N.E.2d 200.) It was expressly recognized in *Wolff* that once a statement is shown to contain pertinent material, only the defense should be permitted to determine whether it may be useful for impeachment."

This decision precludes the trial court from examining the statement to determine if it is in fact impeaching.

Sumner outlines the proper approach to the problem, and the application of that rationale to the instant case requires that the white cards used by the People's attorneys at trial should have been made available to the defense for impeachment purposes. It must be noted that there may be some problem here in determining what is or is not the substance of the statement by the witness.

The prosecution admittedly had recorded information on white cards of such a nature as to be useful in its examination of the witnesses. The prosecutor had not personally interviewed all of the witnesses, and he could not possibly keep over 800 interviews straight in his mind, even if he had. These cards, by their very nature, had to be a reproduction in one form or another of what the witness said when interviewed earlier. As such, that portion of the material which can fairly be said to be the witness's statement must be turned over to the defense so that they may determine its worth as impeachment material. In the event the prosecutor claims that validly protected work product is also contained in the statement, the trial judge can review the material *in camera* for the limited purpose of excising the work-product material.

The defense here has laid as good a foundation for the admission of this evidence as is possible, and should have been provided the white cards for examination, subject to the People's right to have work product deleted therefrom. The People argue that the destruction of the rough notes taken during interviews of witnesses does not warrant the striking of the witnesses' testimony, absent a showing of bad faith on the part of the State. We agree with that general proposition, but inasmuch as we have held that the white cards should have been made available to the defense, the issue of the destruction of the original rough notes loses its relevance.

■ Underwood, Chief Justice (dissenting):

* * *

If the majority's reason for requiring production of the summaries is that the "yellow sheets" upon which the original "rough notes" were written have been destroyed by the State, it would, in my opinion, be far preferable to simply say so. As matters now stand, Rule 412 and our earlier decisions require statements to be verbatim or substantially so before their production may be ordered; the majority opinion appears to eliminate that requirement. The answers to questions which arise in almost every criminal case ought not to be left by this court in such a confusing state.

NOTES

1. **Witness lists.** Whether pretrial disclosure to the defense of the identities of prosecution witnesses is desirable remains disputed. The model discovery provisions favor disclosure. ABA Standard 11–2.1(a)(1); Uniform Rules of Criminal Procedure 421(a). But Fed.R.Crim.P. 16 does not provide for this. A 1975 proposed revision would have required the government, upon request, to furnish the defense with a written list of witnesses the government intends to call at trial. This was rejected by Congress. Federal Rules of Criminal Procedure Amendments Act of 1975, 89 Stat. 370 (1975). The House Conference Report indicates that concerns regarding discouragement of witnesses and improper contacts designed to influence the testimony of witnesses were responsible for the legislative action. H. Conf. Report No. 94–414, 94th Cong., 1st Sess. (1975), reprinted in [1975] U.S.Code Cong. & Ad.News 713, 716. In capital cases, however, a federal statute requires a prosecutor to provide the defense with a list of prosecution witnesses at least three days before trial. 18 U.S.C.A. § 3432.

2. **Jencks material.** Disclosure of a prosecution witness's statements after the witness has testified is widely regarded as a matter distinguishable from pretrial disclosure and is more generally available. The rule requiring such disclosure is commonly referred to as the Jencks rule, after Jencks v. United States, 353 U.S. 657, 77 S.Ct. 1007, 1 L.Ed.2d 1103 (1957) in which the Court first recognized a right to such disclosure in federal criminal prosecutions. The basic provision governing such disclosure in federal litigation is Rule 26.2 of the Federal Rules of Criminal Procedure:

> (a) Motion for Production. After a witness other than the defendant has testified on direct examination, the court, on motion of a party who did not call the witness, shall order the attorney for the government or the defendant and the defendant's attorney, as the case may be, to produce, for the examination and use of the moving party, any statement of the witness that is in their possession and that relates to the subject matter concerning which the witness has testified.

> (b) Production of Entire Statement. If the entire contents of the statement relate to the subject matter concerning which the witness has testified, the court shall order that the statement be delivered to the moving party.

(c) Production of Excised Statement. If the other party claims that the statement contains privileged information or matter that does not relate to the subject matter concerning which the witness has testified, the court shall order that it be delivered to the court in camera. Upon inspection, the court shall excise the portions of the statement that are privileged or that do not relate to the subject matter concerning which the witness has testified, and shall order that the statement, with such material excised, be delivered to the moving party. Any portion of the statement that is withheld from the defendant over the defendant's objection must be preserved by the attorney for the government, and, if the defendant appeals a conviction, must be made available to the appellate court for the purpose of determining the correctness of the decision to excise the portion of the statement.

(d) Recess for Examination of Statement. Upon delivery of the statement to the moving party, the court, upon application of that party, may recess the proceedings so that counsel may examine the statement and prepare to use it in the proceedings.

(e) Sanction for Failure to Produce Statement. If the other party elects not to comply with an order to deliver a statement to the moving party, the court shall order that the testimony of the witness be stricken from the record and that the trial proceed, or, if it is the attorney for the government who elects not to comply, shall declare a mistrial if required by the interest of justice.

(f) Definition. As used in this rule, a "statement" of a witness means:

(1) a written statement made by the witness that is signed or otherwise adopted or approved by the witness;

(2) a substantially verbatim recital of an oral statement made by the witness that is recorded contemporaneously with the making of the oral statement and that is contained in a stenographic, mechanical, electrical, or other recording or a transcription thereof; or

(3) a statement, however taken or recorded, or a transcription thereof, made by the witness to a grand jury.

(g) Scope of Rule. This rule applies at a suppression hearing conducted under Rule 12, at trial under this rule, and to the extent specified:

(1) in Rule 32(c)(2) at sentencing;

(2) in Rule 32.1(c) at a hearing to revoke or modify probation or supervised release;

(3) in Rule 46(i) at a detention hearing;

(4) in Rule 8 of the Rules Governing Proceedings under 28 U.S.C. § 2255; and

(5) in Rule 5.1 at a preliminary examination.

3. **Police reports.** Should police reports be subject to pretrial discovery? Consider State v. Eads, 166 N.W.2d 766, 769 (Iowa 1969) holding that the trial court abused its discretion in ordering disclosure of such a report. Suppose a police report or similar document quotes directly the words of persons interviewed. Does that make them—or at least portions of them—"statements" of those persons and subject to discovery if the governing court rule or statute makes statements of such persons discoverable? See State v. Latimore, 284 So.2d 423, 425 (Fla.App.1973), holding that "police and other investigation reports *which do not quote [a person whose statement is subject to disclosure] directly and are never signed or shown to that person* are not statements within [the discovery rule] and thus are not subject to discovery thereunder." (emphasis supplied)

B. DISCLOSURE BY THE DEFENSE

EDITORS' INTRODUCTION: DEFENSE DISCLOSURE PROVISIONS

As defendants' rights to discovery from the prosecution increased, a parallel trend developed requiring at least certain discovery by the prosecution from the defendant. Generally, however, even in those jurisdictions that provide for defense disclosure, the prosecution is required to disclose more than it is entitled to obtain from the defense.

Perhaps the most widely-provided form of disclosure required of the defense concerns the intention to raise certain defenses. The federal provisions are typical. Fed.R.Crim.P. 12.1 requires the defense, upon written demand of the government, to provide the government with pretrial written notice of intent to offer a defense of alibi. This notice is to state the specific place or places at which the defendant will claim to have been at the time of the alleged offense and the names and addresses of those witnesses upon whom the defense will rely in an effort to establish this alibi. Fed.R.Crim.P. 12.2 requires the defense, without any demand by the government, to notify the government in writing before trial of the defense intention to rely upon the defense of insanity at trial or to introduce expert testimony bearing upon the issue of whether the defendant had the mental state required for the offense charged.

Some jurisdictions go further. Ariz.R.Crim.P. 15.2(b) requires notice by the defendant of all defenses as to which the defense will introduce evidence at trial, "including but not limited to, alibi, insanity, self-defense, entrapment, impotency, marriage, insufficiency of a prior conviction, mistaken identity, and good character." The notice is to include specification concerning the persons, including the defendant, who will be called as witnesses at trial in support of each defense. The first version of the ABA Standards contained a similar provision. Standards Relating to Discovery and Procedure Before Trial, Standard 3.3 (Approved Draft, 1970). In 1978, however, these were revised to require notice only regarding alibi and defenses involving mental impairments. II Standards for Criminal Justice, Standard 11–3.3 (1980). The commentary suggests some difficulty in interpreting how literally "any defense" in the original formulation was to be taken. In addition, it notes that disclosure should be limited to those defenses that tend to require special preparation by the prosecution or that are likely to generate midtrial delays if pretrial notice is not given. Alibi and insanity, it concludes, are defenses "generally considered" to have these characteristics. Id., at 11.55.

Provision is also sometimes made for prosecution access to physical items in the possession of the defense. Fed.R.Crim.P. 16(b)(1), for example, provides:

(1) Information Subject to Disclosure.

(A) *Documents and Tangible Objects.* If the defendant requests disclosure under subdivision (a)(1)(C) or (D) [providing for inspection and copying of documents, tangible objects, and reports of examinations and tests, see page 758, supra] of this rule, upon compliance with such request of the government, the defendant, on request of the government shall permit the government to inspect and copy or photograph books, papers, documents, photographs, tangible objects, or copies or portions thereof, which are within the possession, custody, or control of the defendant and which the defendant intends to introduce as evidence in chief at the trial.

(B) *Reports of Examinations and Tests.* If the defendant requests disclosure under subdivision (a)(1)(C) or (D) of this rule, upon compliance with such request by the government, the defendant, on request of the government, shall permit the government to inspect and copy or photograph any results or reports of physical or mental examinations and of scientific tests or experiments made in connection with the particular case, or copies thereof, within the possession or control of the defendant, which the defendant intends to introduce as evidence in chief at the trial or which were prepared by a witness whom the defendant intends to call at the trial when the results or reports relate to his testimony.

(C) Expert Witnesses. Under the following circumstances, the defendant shall, at the government's request, disclose to the government a written summary of testimony that the defendant intends to use under Rules 702, 703, or 705 of the Federal Rules of Evidence at trial: (i) if the defendant requests disclosure under subdivision (a)(1)(E) of this rule and the government complies, or (ii) if the defendant has given notice under Rule 12.2(b) of an intent to present expert testimony on the defendant's mental condition. This summary shall describe the witnesses' opinion, the bases and reasons for those opinions, and the witnesses' qualifications.

A major consideration is the extent to which a defendant's duty to disclose or provide access should be conditioned upon the defendant's exercise of his right to discovery against the prosecution. It is, of course, under Fed.R.Crim.P. 16(b)(1), above. The ABA's advisory committee urged unconditional discovery:

> If disclosures to the accused promotes finality, orderliness, and efficiency in prosecution generally, these gains should not depend upon the possible capricious willingness of the accused to make reciprocal discovery. ... Certainly, the usual reasons for denying disclosure to the accused—dangers of "perjury or intimidation of witnesses—are not alleviated by forcing the defendant to make discovery, nor are they heightened by his failure to disclose."

Standards Relating to Discovery and Procedure Before Trial, Commentary to § 1.2, p. 45 (Approved Draft 1970). The first version of the ABA Standards provided for independent discovery. ABA Standards 3.1, 3.2, 3.3 (Approved Draft 1970). In the 1978 revision, defense disclosure of reports or statements which the defense intends to use at trial was made conditional upon the defendant's having invoked his discovery rights, following the pattern of Fed.R.Crim.P. 16(b)(1). No explanation was offered. II Standards for Criminal Justice, Standard 11–3.2 (1980). The Advisory Committee on the Federal Rules noted that making the government's right to discovery conditional may minimize the risk that government discovery will be viewed as an infringement of the defendant's constitutional rights. Committee on Rules of Practice and Procedure of the Judicial Conference of the United States, Preliminary Draft of Proposed Amendments to Rules of Criminal Procedure for the United States District Courts, 48 F.R.D. 546, 607 (1970).

The major—but not only—constitutional concern regarding defense disclosure is whether such requirements violate defendant's privilege against compelled self-incrimination. In Williams v. Florida, 399 U.S. 78, 90 S.Ct. 1893, 26 L.Ed.2d 446 (1970), the Court considered Florida's requirement that a defendant intending to claim alibi give the state pretrial notice of this intention and furnish the prosecution with information as to the place the defendant will claim to have been and with the names and addresses of alibi witnesses the defense plans to use. Nothing in the Fifth Amendment, the Court reasoned, would preclude a trial court from granting a continuance at trial upon the State's request after an alibi witness had testified. Nor would the State be precluded from using this continuance to locate or develop rebuttal evidence and using this when trial continued. The Florida rule, it concluded, did essentially the same thing:

> At most, the rule only compelled petitioner to accelerate the timing of his disclosure, forcing him to divulge at an earlier date information that the petitioner from the beginning planned to divulge at trial. Nothing in the Fifth Amendment entitles a defendant as a matter of constitutional right to await the end of the State's case before announcing the nature of his defense, any more than it entitles him to await the jury's verdict on the State's case-in-chief before deciding whether or not to take the stand himself.

399 U.S. at 85, 90 S.Ct. at 1898, 26 L.Ed.2d at 452. Justice Black, dissenting, argued that a defendant who complied with the requirement and later decided not to present the alibi defense might suffer an infringement of Fifth Amendment interests under the Florida rule:

> Necessarily the defendant will have given the prosecutor the names of persons who may have some knowledge about the defendant himself or his activities. Necessarily the prosecutor will have every incentive to question these persons fully, and in doing so he may discover new leads or evidence. Undoubtedly, there will be situations in which the State will seek to use such information—information it would probably never have obtained but for the defendant's coerced cooperation.

399 U.S. at 110, 90 S.Ct. at 1911, 26 L.Ed.2d at 482. Justice Black's approach had been earlier accepted by the California Supreme Court, which had held that a defendant could not be compelled to disclose prior to trial the names, addresses and expected testimony of defense witnesses. Prudhomme v. Superior Court, 2 Cal.3d 320, 466 P.2d 673, 85 Cal.Rptr. 129 (1970). The California court did, however, indicate that disclosure could be required concerning witnesses who would be produced concerning a particular defense and perhaps other categories of witnesses "from which a court could attempt to determine [disclosure's] incriminating effect." 2 Cal.3d at 326, 466 P.2d at 677, 85 Cal.Rptr. at 133.

The Florida rule at issue in *Williams* required that after defense disclosure of intent to offer an alibi, the State notify the defense of any witnesses it intends to offer in rebuttal to the alibi. In Wardius v. Oregon, 412 U.S. 470, 93 S.Ct. 2208, 37 L.Ed.2d 82 (1973) the Court struck down as violative of Due Process the Oregon notice-of-alibi rule which imposed no such reciprocal duty on the state:

> [I]n the absence of a strong showing of state interests to the contrary, discovery must be a two-way street. The State may not insist that trials be run as a "search for truth" so far as defense witnesses are concerned, while maintaining "poker game" secrecy for its own witnesses. It is fundamentally unfair to require a defendant to divulge the details of his own case while at the same time subjecting him to the hazard of surprise concerning refutation of the very pieces of evidence which he disclosed to the State.

412 U.S. at 475–76, 93 S.Ct. at 2212–13, 37 L.Ed.2d at 88.

In Brooks v. Tennessee, 406 U.S. 605, 92 S.Ct. 1891, 32 L.Ed.2d 358 (1972), the Court held invalid a state statute requiring that if a defendant testifies in his own defense this must be done before any other defense testimony is taken. Emphasizing that a defendant might not be able to assess at the end of the State's case the extent to which his own testimony would be useful or necessary to his defense, the Court held the requirement an impermissible burden on the defendant's privilege against self-incrimination and a violation of the due process right to "the guiding hand of counsel." Would a requirement that the defendant disclose before trial whether or not he will testify in his defense be subject to the same objection?

United States v. Nobles

Supreme Court of the United States, 1975.
422 U.S. 225, 95 S.Ct. 2160, 45 L.Ed.2d 141.

▉ Mr. Justice Powell delivered the opinion of the Court.

In a criminal trial, defense counsel sought to impeach the credibility of key prosecution witnesses by testimony of a defense investigator regarding statements previously obtained from the witnesses by the investigator. The question presented here is whether in these circumstances a federal trial court may compel the defense to reveal the relevant portions of the investigator's report for the prosecution's use in cross-examining him. The U.S. Court of Appeals for the Ninth Circuit concluded that it cannot. 510 F.2d 146. We granted certiorari, 419 U.S. 1119, 95 S.Ct. 801, 42 L.Ed.2d 819 (1975), and now reverse.

I.

Respondent was tried and convicted on charges arising from an armed robbery of a federally insured bank. The only significant evidence linking him to the crime was the identification testimony of two witnesses, a bank teller and a salesman who was in the bank during the robbery. Respondent offered an alibi but, as the Court of Appeals recognized, 510 F.2d, at 150, his strongest defense centered around attempts to discredit these eyewitnesses. Defense efforts to impeach them gave rise to the events that lead to this decision.

In the course of preparing respondent's defense, an investigator for the defense interviewed both witnesses and preserved the essence of those conversations in a written report. When the witnesses testified for the prosecution, respondent's counsel relied on the report in conducting their cross-examination. Counsel asked the bank teller whether he recalled having told the investigator that he had seen only the back of the man he identified as respondent. The witness replied that he did not remember making such a statement. He was allowed, despite defense counsel's initial objection, to refresh his recollection by referring to a portion of the investigator's report. The prosecutor also was allowed to see briefly the relevant portion of the report. The witness thereafter testified that although the report indicated that he told the investigator he had seen only respondent's back, he in fact had seen more than that and continued to insist that respondent was the bank robber.

The other witness acknowledged on cross-examination that he too had spoken to the defense investigator. Respondent's counsel twice inquired whether he told the investigator that "all blacks looked alike" to him, and in each instance the witness denied having made such a statement. The prosecution again sought inspection of the relevant portion of the investigator's report, and respondent's counsel again objected. The court declined to order disclosure at that time, but ruled that it would be required if the investigator testified as to the witnesses' alleged statements from the witness stand. The court further advised that it would examine the investigator's report *in camera* and would excise all reference to matters not relevant to the precise statements at issue.

After the prosecution completed its case, respondent called the investigator as a defense witness. The court reiterated that a copy of the report, inspected and edited *in camera,* would have to be submitted to Government counsel at the completion of the investigator's impeachment testimony. When respondent's counsel stated that he did not intend to produce the report, the court ruled that the investigator would not be allowed to testify about his interviews with the witnesses.

The Court of Appeals for the Ninth Circuit, . . . found that the Fifth Amendment prohibited the disclosure condition imposed in this case. . . . [W]e think the court erred.

* * *

The Court of Appeals concluded that the Fifth Amendment renders criminal discovery "basically a one-way street." 501 F.2d, at 154. Like many generalizations in constitutional law, this one is too broad. The relationship between the accused's Fifth Amendment rights and the prosecution's ability to discover materials at trial must be identified in a more discriminating manner.

The Fifth Amendment privilege against compulsory self-incrimination is an "intimate and personal one," which protects "a private inner sanctum of individual feeling and thought and proscribes state intrusion to exact self-condemnation." Couch v. United States, 409 U.S. 322, 327, 93 S.Ct. 611, 615, 34 L.Ed.2d 548 (1973). As we noted in Couch, 409 U.S., at 328, "the privilege is a *personal* privilege: it adheres basically to the person, not to information that may incriminate him."

In this instance disclosure of the relevant portions of the defense investigator's report would not impinge on the fundamental values protected by the Fifth Amendment. The court's order was limited to statements allegedly made by third parties who were available as witnesses to both the prosecution and the defense. Respondent did not prepare the report, and there is no suggestion that the portions subject to the disclosure order reflected any information that he conveyed to the investigator. The fact that these statements of third parties were elicited by a defense investigator on respondent's behalf does not convert them into respondent's personal communications. Requiring their production from the investigator therefore would not in any sense compel respondent to be a witness against himself or extort communications from him.

We thus conclude that the Fifth Amendment privilege against compulsory self-incrimination, being personal to the defendant, does not extend to the testimony or statements of third parties called as witnesses at trial. The Court of Appeals' reliance on this constitutional guarantee as a bar to the disclosure here ordered was misplaced.

* * *

The court's preclusion sanction was an entirely proper method of assuring compliance with its order. Respondent's argument that this ruling deprived him of the Sixth Amendment rights to compulsory process and cross-examination misconceives the issue. The District Court did not bar the investigator's testimony. It merely prevented respondent from presenting to the jury a partial view of the credibility issue by adducing the investigator's testimony and thereafter refusing to disclose the contemporaneous report that might offer further critical insights. The Sixth Amendment does not confer the right to present testimony free from the legitimate demands of the adversarial system; one cannot invoke the Sixth Amendment as a justification for presenting what might have been a half-truth. Deciding, as we do, that it was within the court's discretion to assure that the jury would hear the full testimony of the investigator rather than a truncated portion favorable to respondent, we think it would be artificial indeed to deprive the court of the power to effectuate that judgment. Nor do we find constitutional significance in the fact that the court in this instance was able to exclude the testimony in advance rather than receive it in evidence and thereafter charge the jury to disregard it when respondent's counsel refused, as he said he would, to produce the report.

NOTES

1. **Notice of defense evidence.** The respondent in Michigan v. Lucas, 500 U.S. 145, 111 S.Ct. 1743, 114 L.Ed.2d 205 (1991) was charged with the rape of his former girlfriend. Under Michigan's rape shield law, evidence of the victim's prior sexual conduct was made inadmissible, subject to an exception for prior sexual acts between the defendant and the victim. For the exception to apply, the defendant

was required to give notice of intent to present such evidence and an offer of proof within 10 days of his arraignment. The trial court would then conduct an in camera hearing to determine whether the proposed evidence would be admitted. Lucas failed to give the statutory notice but wished at trial to introduce his own testimony that he and the victim had had sexual intercourse prior to the incident on trial. The trial court refused to permit this testimony for failure to comply with the rape shield statute. The Michigan Court of Appeals reversed Lucas' conviction on the ground that as applied to prior sexual relations between the defendant and the victim the notice provision serves no useful purpose. The Supreme Court, in an opinion by Justice O'Connor, reversed the Court of Appeals. The Court found that the notice requirement

> permits a prosecutor to interview persons who know the parties and otherwise investigate whether such a prior relationship actually existed. When a prior sexual relationship is conceded, the notice-and-hearing procedure allows a court to determine in advance of trial whether evidence of the relationship "is material to a fact at issue in the case" and whether "its inflammatory or prejudicial nature outweigh[s] its probative value." [Quoting from the Michigan statute.]

500 U.S. at 150, 111 S.Ct. at 1747, 114 L.Ed.2d at 212. Citing United States v. Nobles and Taylor v. Illinois, the Court held that the Michigan Court of Appeals

> erred in adopting a *per se* rule that Michigan's notice-and-hearing requirement violates the Sixth Amendment in all cases where it is used to preclude evidence of past sexual conduct between a rape victim and a defendant. The Sixth Amendment is not so rigid. The notice-and-hearing requirement serves legitimate state interests in protecting against surprise, harassment, and undue delay. Failure to comply with this requirement may in some cases justify even the severe sanction of preclusion.

500 U.S. at 152, 111 S.Ct. at 1748, 114 L.Ed.2d at 214. The Court remanded the case to the Michigan court to determine whether the state statute authorized preclusion and, if so, whether on these particular facts preclusion would violate the Sixth Amendment. Justice Stevens, joined by Justice Marshall, dissented. Justice Blackmun filed a concurring opinion.

2. **Reciprocal discovery in California.** In 1990, California voters approved an initiative measure—the Crime Victims Justice Reform Act or Proposition 115—that made numerous changes in the state's criminal justice system, often thus "overruling" decisions of the California Supreme Court. Among the changes made were modifications of discovery. Article I of the California Constitution was amended to add Section 30, which provides in part:

> (c) In order to provide for fair and speedy trials, discovery in criminal cases shall be reciprocal in nature, as prescribed by the Legislature or by the people through the initiative process.

The initiative measure also added a new Chapter to the Penal Code. This chapter mandates discovery by both the defendant and the prosecution. With regard to disclosure by the defense, Section 1054.3 provides:

> The defendant and his or her attorney shall disclose to the prosecuting attorney:

> (a) The names and addresses of persons, other than the defendant, he or she intends to call as witnesses at trial, together with any relevant written or recorded statements of those persons, or reports of the statements of those persons, including any reports or statements of experts made in connection with the case, and including the results of physical or mental examinations,

scientific tests, experiments, or comparisons which the defendant intends to offer in evidence at the trial.

(b) Any real evidence which the defendant intends to offer in evidence at the trial.

Under section 1054.6, neither the defendant nor the prosecutor is required to disclose any materials or information which are work product as defined in section 2018 of the Code of Civil Procedure. Section 2018(c) defines "work product" as "[a]ny writing that reflects an attorney's impressions, conclusions, opinions, or legal research or theories * * *."

CHAPTER 18

RIGHT TO AN IMPARTIAL TRIAL

Analysis

EDITORS' INTRODUCTION: CHANGE OF VENUE AND OF JUDGE

Defendants and society in general both have an important interest in having "fair" trials, in the sense that the trials result in accurate determinations as to whether there was proof beyond a reasonable doubt of the defendants' guilt. This interest may be endangered by any of a number of circumstances. Among those most frequently claimed, however, are incompetence of the trial judge, bias or partiality of the trial judge or members of the trial jury, consideration by the trial jury or judge of information other than evidence admitted at trial, and the presence of disruptive factors that prevent the judge or jury from carefully and objectively evaluating the sufficiency of the evidence produced by the prosecution to prove guilt. Assuring that trials are not affected by such circumstances is, of course, primarily a nonconstitutional matter of local procedure. But it is also clear that dangers to fairness may violate the general requirement of due process or more specific federal constitutional rights that are, in part at least, designed to assure trial accuracy.

Some of these rights are addressed elsewhere in this book. The prohibition against trying an incompetent defendant, for example, considered in Chapter 16, is in part based upon the fear that a trial conducted without the defendant's participation will result in error. Those aspects of the right to jury trial that involve a defendant's right to a verdict joined by an adequate number of a jury of adequate size and to participate in selecting that jury—addressed in Chapter 23—also, of course, are based in large part upon the need to assure accuracy. The present Chapter presents several additional matters related to the fairness of the trial process.

There are several aspects of nonconstitutional procedure that are designed to deal with the problems raised in the principal case contained in this Chapter. These procedures need to be examined as background for consideration of that case.

Change of Venue

Venue in criminal proceedings generally lies in the locality (often the county) in which the conduct constituting the crime was committed. But American jurisdictions generally have procedures for changing the location of a trial when there is sufficient reason to believe that trial in the locality provided by general venue rules would be "unfair." Uniform Rules of Criminal Procedure Rule 462 is a useful example of such a provision:

Rule 462. [Transfer of Prosecution]

(a) *For Prejudice in the [County].* Upon motion of the defendant [or the prosecuting attorney] conforming to Rule 451, [or upon its own motion,] the court shall transfer the prosecution as to the defendant to another [county] if satisfied that there is a reasonable likelihood that a fair and impartial trial cannot be had in the [county] in which it is pending. The motion may be supported by qualified public opinion surveys or opinion testimony offered by individuals. A showing of actual prejudice is not required. It is not a ground for a denial of the motion that one transfer has already been granted.

(b) *Transfer in Other Cases.* For the convenience of parties or witnesses and in the interest of justice, the court upon motion of the defendant may transfer the prosecution as to him to another [county].

(c) *Disposition.* A motion for transfer made before the jury is impaneled shall be disposed of before impaneling. If a motion for transfer is permitted to be made, or if reconsideration or review of a prior denial is sought, after impaneling, the fact that the jury satisfies legal requirements is not controlling if it appears there is a reasonable likelihood that a fair and impartial trial cannot be had in the [county] in which the prosecution is pending.

(d) *Claim not Precluded.* A claim that a prosecution should have been transferred is not precluded by a waiver of the right to trial by jury or by a failure to exercise all available peremptory challenges.

Unlike some state provisions, the Uniform Rule does not require that a motion for transfer or change of venue be accompanied by sworn statements that a fair trial cannot be had in the locality. It makes optional a provision for motion by the prosecutor, which is part of many state provisions. By requiring that the trial judge determine only that there is a "reasonable likelihood" that a fair trial cannot be had in the locality, the Uniform Rule apparently uses a less restrictive standard than is applied in many jurisdictions, which require a finding that in fact a fair trial cannot be had in the locality.

Change or Substitution of Judge

Local procedures also often provide for proceedings to determine whether the case should be heard before a judge other than the one initially designated to hear it. There is substantial variation among the provisions. The Uniform Rules of Criminal Procedure provide as follows:

Rule 741. [Substitution of Judge]

(a) *On Demand.* A defendant may obtain a substitution of the judge before whom a trial or other proceeding is to be conducted by filing a demand therefor, but if trial has commenced before a judge no demand may be filed as to him. A defendant may not file more than one demand in a case. If there are two or more defendants, a defendant may not file a demand, if another defendant has filed a demand, unless a motion for severance of defendants has been denied. The demand shall be signed by the defendant or his counsel, and shall be filed at least [ten days] before the time set for commencement of trial and at least [three days] before the time set for any other proceeding, but it may be filed within [one day] after the defendant ascertains or should have ascertained the judge who is to preside at the trial or proceeding.

(b) *On Own Motion.* A judge on his own motion may disqualify himself from presiding over a trial or other proceeding.

(c) *For Cause.* A judge may not preside over a trial or other proceeding if upon motion of a party it appears that he is disqualified for a cause provided [by law or by the Code of Judicial Conduct]. The motion to disqualify shall be heard before another judge regularly sitting in the same court or a judge designated by [the appropriate assigning authority], and, unless otherwise ordered by that judge for cause, shall be made at least [ten days] before the time set for commencement of trial and at least [three days] before the time set for any other proceeding, but it may be made within [one day] after the party ascertains or should have ascertained the judge who is to preside at the trial or proceeding.

Probably the major variation among provisions for change of judge is the split as to whether at least one change should be available upon simple request and without inquiry into possible causes, such as bias. The arguments for providing a right to such a change of judge include claims that inquiries into the existence of bias invite delay, detract from the dignity and public image of the courts, strain the relationships between counsel and the judge, and often arouse such resentment that if the effort to establish grounds for disqualification fails the procedure may well assure the impossibility of a fair trial. Moreover, it is claimed, lawyers can be relied upon to use restraint in exercising the right to an automatic change of judge. See Staff Report, Disqualification of Judges for Prejudice or Bias— Common Law Evolution, Current Status, and the Oregon Experience, 48 Ore.L.Rev. 311, 401 (1969). But given the likely basis for a motion for automatic change of judge, perhaps judges will react to such motions much the same as they would react to specified and supported assertions concerning their alleged biases or inadequacies.

Murphy v. Florida

Supreme Court of the United States, 1975.
421 U.S. 794, 95 S.Ct. 2031, 44 L.Ed.2d 589.

■ Mr. Justice Marshall delivered the opinion of the Court.

The question presented by this case is whether the petitioner was denied a fair trial because members of the jury had learned from news accounts about a prior felony conviction or certain facts about the crime with which he was charged. Under the circumstances of this case, we find that petitioner has not been denied due process, and we therefore affirm the judgment below.

I.

Petitioner was convicted in the Dade County, Florida, Criminal Court in 1970 of breaking and entering a home, while armed, with intent to commit robbery, and of assault with intent to commit robbery. The charges stemmed from the January 1968 robbery of a Miami Beach home and petitioner's apprehension, with three others, while fleeing from the scene.

The robbery and petitioner's arrest received extensive press coverage because petitioner had been much in the news before. He had first made himself notorious for his part in the 1964 theft of the Star of India sapphire from a museum in New York. His flamboyant life style made him a continuing subject of press interest; he was generally referred to—at least in the media—as "Murph the Surf."

Before the date set for petitioner's trial on the instant charges, he was indicted on two counts of murder in Broward County, Florida. Thereafter the Dade County court declared petitioner mentally incompetent to stand trial; he was committed to a hospital and the prosecutor *nolle prossed* the robbery indictment. In August 1968 he was indicted by a federal grand jury for conspiring to transport stolen securities in interstate commerce. After petitioner was adjudged competent for trial, he was convicted on one count of murder in Broward County (March 1969) and pleaded guilty to one count of the federal indictment involving stolen securities (December 1969). The indictment for robbery was refiled in August 1969 and came to trial one year later.

The events of 1968 and 1969 drew extensive press coverage. Each new case against petitioner was considered newsworthy, not only in Dade County but elsewhere as well. The record in this case contains scores of articles reporting on petitioner's trials and tribulations during this period; many purportedly relate statements that petitioner or his attorney made to reporters.

Jury selection in the present case began in August 1970. Seventy-eight jurors were questioned. Of these, 30 were excused for miscellaneous personal reasons; 20 were excused peremptorily by the defense or prosecution; 20 were excused by the court as having prejudged petitioner; and the remaining eight served as the jury and two alternates. Petitioner's motions to dismiss the chosen jurors, on the ground that they were aware that he had previously been convicted of either the 1964 Star of India theft or the Broward County murder, were denied, as was his renewed motion for a change of venue based on allegedly prejudicial pretrial publicity.

At trial, petitioner did not testify or put on any evidence; assertedly in protest of the selected jury, he did not cross-examine any of the State's witnesses. He was convicted on both counts, and after an unsuccessful appeal he sought habeas corpus relief in the District Court for the Southern District of Florida.

The District Court denied petitioner relief, D.C.Fla., 363 F.Supp. 1224, and the Court of Appeals for the Fifth Circuit affirmed. 495 F.2d 553 (1974). We granted certiorari, 419 U.S. 1088, 95 S.Ct. 677, 42 L.Ed.2d 680 (1974) in order to resolve the apparent conflict between the decision below and that of the Third Circuit in United States ex rel. Doggett v. Yeager, 472

F.2d 229 (1973), over the applicability of Marshall v. United States, 360 U.S. 310, 79 S.Ct. 1171, 3 L.Ed.2d 1250 (1959), to state criminal proceedings.

II.

The defendant in *Marshall* was convicted of dispensing certain drugs without a prescription. In the course of the trial seven of the jurors were exposed to various news accounts relating that Marshall had previously been convicted of forgery, that he and his wife had been arrested for other narcotics offenses, and that he had for some time practiced medicine without a license. After interviewing the jurors, however, the trial judge denied a motion for a mistrial, relying on the jurors' assurances that they could maintain impartiality in spite of the news articles.

Noting that the jurors had been exposed to information with a high potential for prejudice, this Court reversed the conviction. It did so, however, expressly "[i]n the exercise of [its] supervisory power to formulate and apply proper standards for enforcement of the criminal law in the federal courts," and not as a matter of constitutional compulsion. 360 U.S., at 313, 79 S.Ct. at 1173.

In the face of so clear a statement, it cannot be maintained that *Marshall* was a constitutional ruling now applicable, through the Fourteenth Amendment, to the States. Petitioner argues, nonetheless that more recent decisions of this Court have applied to state cases the principle underlying the *Marshall* decision: that persons who have learned from news sources of a defendant's prior criminal record are presumed to be prejudiced. We cannot agree that *Marshall* has any application beyond the federal courts.

Petitioner relies principally upon Irvin v. Dowd, 366 U.S. 717, 81 S.Ct. 1639, 6 L.Ed.2d 751 (1961), Rideau v. Louisiana, 373 U.S. 723, 83 S.Ct. 1417, 10 L.Ed.2d 663 (1963), Estes v. Texas, 381 U.S. 532, 85 S.Ct. 1628, 14 L.Ed.2d 543 (1965), and Sheppard v. Maxwell, 384 U.S. 333, 86 S.Ct. 1507, 16 L.Ed.2d 600 (1966). In each of these cases, this Court overturned a state court conviction obtained in a trial atmosphere that had been utterly corrupted by press coverage.

In Irvin v. Dowd the rural community in which the trial was held had been subjected to a barrage of inflammatory publicity immediately prior to trial, including information on the defendant's prior convictions, his confession to 24 burglaries and six murders including the one for which he was tried, and his unaccepted offer to plead guilty in order to avoid the death sentence. As a result, eight of the 12 jurors had formed an opinion that the defendant was guilty before the trial began; some went "so far as to say that it would take evidence to overcome their belief" in his guilt. In these circumstances, the Court readily found actual prejudice against the petitioner to a degree that rendered a fair trial impossible.

Prejudice was presumed in the circumstances under which the trials in *Rideau, Estes,* and *Sheppard* were held. In those cases the influence of the news media, either in the community at large or in the courtroom itself, pervaded the proceedings. In *Rideau* the defendant had "confessed" under police interrogation to the murder of which he stood convicted. A 20–minute film of his confession was broadcast three times by a television station in the community where the crime and the trial took place. In reversing, the Court did not examine the *voir dire* for evidence of actual prejudice because it considered the trial under review "but a hollow formality"—the real trial had occurred when tens of thousand of people, in a community of 150,000 had seen and heard the defendant admit his guilt to the cameras.

The trial in *Estes* had been conducted in a circus atmosphere, due in large part to the intrusions of the press, which was allowed to sit within the bar of the court and to overrun it with television equipment. Similarly, *Sheppard* arose from a trial infected not only by a background of extremely inflammatory publicity but also by a courthouse given over to accommodate the public appetite for carnival. The proceedings in these cases were entirely lacking in the solemnity and sobriety to which a defendant is entitled in a system that subscribes to any notion of fairness and rejects the verdict of a mob. They cannot be made to stand for the proposition that juror exposure to information about a state defendant's prior convictions or to news accounts of the crime with which he is charged alone presumptively deprives the defendant of due process. To resolve this case, we must turn, therefore, to any indications in the totality of circumstances that petitioner's trial was not fundamentally fair.

III.

The constitutional standard of fairness requires that a defendant have "a panel of impartial, 'indifferent' jurors." Irvin v. Dowd, supra, 366 U.S., at 722, 81 S.Ct. at 1642. Qualified jurors need not, however, be totally ignorant of the facts and issues involved.

> "To hold that the mere existence of any preconceived notion as to the guilt or innocence of an accused, without more, is sufficient to rebut the presumption of a prospective juror's impartiality would be to establish an impossible standard. It is sufficient if the juror can lay aside his impression or opinion and render a verdict based on the evidence presented in court." Id., at 723, 81 S.Ct. at 1642.

At the same time, the juror's assurances that he is equal to this task cannot be dispositive of the accused's rights, and it remains open to the defendant to demonstrate "the actual existence of such an opinion in the mind of the juror as will raise the presumption of partiality." Ibid.

The *voir dire* in this case indicates no such hostility to petitioner by the jurors who served in his trial as to suggest a partiality that could not be laid aside. Some of the jurors had a vague recollection of the robbery with which petitioner was charged and each had some knowledge of petitioner's past crimes, but none betrayed any belief in the relevance of petitioner's past to the present case. Indeed, four of the six jurors volunteered their views of its irrelevance, and one suggested that people who have been in trouble before are too often singled out for suspicion of each new crime—a predisposition that could only operate in petitioner's favor.

In the entire *voir dire* transcript furnished to us, there is only one colloquy on which petitioner can base even a colorable claim of partiality by a juror. In response to a leading and hypothetical question, presupposing a two-or three-week presentation of evidence against petitioner and his failure to put on any defense, one juror conceded that his prior impression of petitioner would dispose him to convict. We cannot attach great significance to this statement, however, in light of the leading nature of counsel's questions and the juror's other testimony indicating that he had no deep impression of petitioner at all.

The juror testified that he did not keep up with current events and, in fact, had never heard of petitioner until he arrived in the room for prospective jurors where some veniremen were discussing him. He did not know that petitioner was "a convicted jewel thief" even then; it was petitioner's counsel who informed him of this fact. And he volunteered that petitioner's murder conviction, of which he had just heard, would not be relevant to his guilt or innocence in the present case, since "[w]e are not trying him for murder."

Even these indicia of impartiality might be disregarded in a case where the general atmosphere in the community or courtroom is sufficiently inflammatory, but the circumstances surrounding petitioner's trial are not at all of that variety. Petitioner attempts to portray them as inflammatory by reference to the publicity to which the community was exposed. The District Court found, however, that the news articles concerning petitioner had appeared almost entirely during the period between December 1967 and January 1969, the latter date being seven months before the jury in this case was selected. 363 F.Supp., at 1228. They were, moreover, largely factual in nature. Compare Beck v. Washington, 369 U.S. 541, 82 S.Ct. 955, 8 L.Ed.2d 98 (1962), with Sheppard v. Maxwell, supra.

The length to which the trial court must go in order to select jurors who appear to be impartial is another factor relevant in evaluating those jurors' assurances of impartiality. In a community where most veniremen will admit to a disqualifying prejudice, the reliability of the others' protestations may be drawn into question; for it is then more probable that they are part of a community deeply hostile to the accused, and more likely that they may unwittingly have been influenced by it. In Irvin v. Dowd, for example, the Court noted that 90% of those examined on the point were inclined to believe in the accused's guilt, and the court had excused for this cause 268 of the 430 veniremen. In the present case, by contrast, 20 of the 78 persons questioned were excused because they indicated an opinion as to petitioner's guilt. This may indeed be 20 more than would occur in the trial of a totally obscure person, but it by no means suggests a community with sentiment so poisoned against petitioner as to impeach the indifference of jurors who displayed no hostile animus of their own.

In sum, we are unable to conclude, in the circumstances presented in this case, that petitioner did not receive a fair trial. Petitioner has failed to show that the setting of the trial was inherently prejudicial or that the jury selection process of which he complains permits an inference of actual prejudice. The judgment of the Court of Appeals must therefore be affirmed.

■ MR. JUSTICE BRENNAN, dissenting.

I dissent. Irvin v. Dowd, 366 U.S. 717, 81 S.Ct. 1639, 6 L.Ed.2d 751 (1961), requires reversal of this conviction. As in that case, petitioner here was denied a fair trial. The risk that taint of widespread publicity regarding his criminal background, known to all members of the jury, infected the jury's deliberations is apparent, the trial court made no attempt to prevent discussion of the case or petitioner's previous criminal exploits among the prospective jurors, and one juror freely admitted that he was predisposed to convict petitioner.

* * *

Others who ultimately served as jurors revealed similar prejudice toward petitioner on *voir dire*. One juror conceded that it would be difficult, during deliberations, to put out of his mind that petitioner was a convicted criminal. He also admitted that he did not "hold a convicted felon in the same regard as another person who has never been convicted of a felony," and admitted further that he had termed petitioner a "menace."

A third juror testified that she knew from several sources that petitioner was a convicted murderer, and was aware that the community regarded petitioner as a criminal who "should be put away." She disclaimed having a fixed opinion about the result she would reach, but acknowledged that the fact that petitioner was a convicted criminal would probably influence her verdict.

* * *

Still another juror testified that the comments of venire members in discussing the case had made him "sick to [his] stomach." He testified that one venireman had said that petitioner was "thoroughly rotten," and that another had said, "Hang him, he's guilty."

Moreover, the Court ignores the crucial significance of the fact that at no time before or during this daily buildup of prejudice against Murphy did the trial judge instruct the prospective jurors not to discuss the case among themselves. Indeed the trial judge took no steps to insulate the jurors from media coverage of the case or from the many news articles that discussed petitioner's last criminal exploits.

It is of no moment that several jurors ultimately testified that they would try to exclude from their deliberations their knowledge of petitioner's past misdeeds and of his community reputation. *Irvin* held in like circumstances that little weight could be attached to such self-serving protestations. . . .

On the record of this *voir dire*, therefore, the conclusion is to me inescapable that the attitude of the entire venire toward Murphy reflected the "then current community pattern of thought as indicated by the popular news media," id., at 725, 81 S.Ct. at 1644, and was infected with the taint of the view that he was a "criminal" guilty of notorious offenses, including that for which he was on trial. It is a plain case, from a review of the entire *voir dire*, where "the extent and nature of the publicity had caused such a buildup of prejudice that excluding the preconception of guilt from the deliberations would be too difficult for the jury to be honestly found impartial." Bloeth v. Denno, 2 Cir., 313 F.2d 364 (1963). In my view, the denial of a change of venue was therefore prejudicial error, and I would reverse the conviction.

NOTES

1. **Intensity of publicity.** The effects of pretrial publicity on the impartiality of the trial jury was at issue in Patton v. Yount, 467 U.S. 1025, 104 S.Ct. 2885, 81 L.Ed.2d 847 (1984). In 1966, respondent, a high school math teacher, was tried for the murder of an 18–year old female student in a rural Pennsylvania community. Written and oral confessions to the offense were admitted in evidence; he was convicted but the Pennsylvania Supreme Court ordered a new trial because the confessions had been unlawfully obtained. Prior to his second trial in 1970 in the same community, respondent moved for a change of venue, which was denied. Local publicity was intense at the time of the offense, the first trial, the reversal of the conviction and before jury selection in the second trial began. After his conviction in the second trial and after affirmance by state appellate courts, respondent filed a petition for habeas corpus in federal district court claiming prejudicial pretrial publicity. The district court denied relief, but the Third Circuit reversed on the basis of Irvin v. Dowd. The Supreme Court, in an opinion by Justice Powell, reversed:

> [Irvin v. Dowd] held that adverse pretrial publicity can create such a presumption of prejudice in a community that the jurors' claims that they can be impartial should not be believed. ...In *Irvin,* the Court observed that it was during the six or seven months immediately preceding trial that "a barrage of newspaper headlines, articles, cartoons and pictures was unleashed against [the defendant]." ... In this case, the extensive adverse publicity and the community's sense of outrage were at their height prior to Yount's first trial in 1966. The jury selection for Yount's second trial, at issue here, did not occur until four years later, at a time when prejudicial publicity was greatly diminished and community sentiment had softened. In these circumstances, we hold that the trial court did not commit manifest error in finding that the jury as a whole was impartial.

467 U.S. at 1031, 104 S.Ct. at 2889, 81 L.Ed.2d at 854. Justice Marshall did not participate; Justice Stevens, joined by Justice Brennan, dissented.

2. **Questioning panelists about publicity.** The issue in Mu'Min v. Virginia, 500 U.S. 415, 111 S.Ct. 1899, 114 L.Ed.2d 493 (1991) was whether the Sixth and Fourteenth Amendments right to an impartial jury was violated by the refusal of the trial court to question members of the jury panel about the content of pretrial publicity they had acknowledged receiving concerning the case and the defendant. Mu'Min was charged with a murder committed when he escaped from a prison work detail. Publicity was extensive and included the fact that he was already serving a prison sentence for murder, that he had been six times rejected for parole, details of the murder for which he was serving the prison sentence, and indications that he had confessed to the murder with which he was now charged. Twenty-six prospective jurors appeared for voir dire. Sixteen acknowledged they had read or heard about the case. One of the 16 was excused for cause when he stated he could not be impartial in light of the publicity. Further voir dire was conducted in panels of 4 persons. Each person stated that he or she could be impartial and would wait until the entire case was presented before forming an opinion about defendant's guilt or innocence. Defense counsel asked the trial court to question members of the panel who had heard about the case as to the content of the information they had received. The trial court refused this request. Of the 12 persons who were the jury,

8 had read or heard something about the case. Mu'Min was convicted and received the death penalty. The Supreme Court, in an opinion by Chief Justice Rehnquist, held that the trial court's actions did not violate the 6th and 14th Amendments. The Court acknowledged that questioning concerning content would have enabled petitioner to exercise peremptory challenges more intelligently, but refused to make such questions a constitutional requirement because under Ross v. Oklahoma, 487 U.S. 81, 108 S.Ct. 2273, 101 L.Ed.2d 80 (1988) peremptory challenges are not required by the Constitution. Petitioner's reliance on Irvin v. Dowd is misplaced since in that case 8 of 12 jurors had formed an opinion from pretrial publicity as to guilt, while in this case although 8 of 12 had heard of the case none expressed an opinion as to guilt.

> Had the trial court in this case been confronted with the "wave of public passion" engendered by pretrial publicity that occurred in connection with Irvin's trial, the Due Process Clause of the Fourteenth Amendment might well have required more extensive examination of potential jurors than it undertook here. But the showings are not comparable; the cases differ both in the kind of community in which the coverage took place and in the extent of media coverage. Unlike the community involved in *Irvin,* the county in which petitioner was tried, Prince William, had a population in 1988 of 182,537, and this was one of nine murders committed in the county that year. It is a part of the metropolitan Washington statistical area, which has a population of over 3 million, and in which, unfortunately, hundreds of murders are committed each year. In *Irvin,* news accounts included details of the defendant's confessions to 24 burglaries and six murders, including the one for which he was tried, as well as his unaccepted offer to plead guilty in order to avoid the death sentence. They contained numerous opinions as to his guilt, as well as opinions about the appropriate punishment. While news reports about Mu'Min were not favorable, they did not contain the same sort of damaging information. Much of the pretrial publicity was aimed at the Department of Corrections and the criminal justice system in general, criticizing the furlough and work release programs that made this and other crimes possible. Any killing that ultimately results in a charge of capital murder will engender considerable media coverage, and this one may have engendered more than most because of its occurrence during the 1988 Presidential campaign, when a similar crime committed by a Massachusetts inmate became a subject of national debate. But, while the pretrial publicity in this case appears to have been substantial, it was not of the same kind or extent as that found to exist in *Irvin.*

500 U.S. at 429–30, 111 S.Ct. at 1907, 114 L.Ed.2d at 508.

Justice Marshall, joined by Justices Blackmun and Stevens, dissented. Justice Kennedy dissented because "a juror's acknowledgement of exposure to pretrial publicity initiates a duty to assess that individual juror's ability to be impartial." That duty was not discharged in this case:

> The questions were asked of groups, and individual jurors attested to their own impartiality by saying nothing. I would hold * * * that when a juror admits exposure to pretrial publicity about a case, the court must conduct a sufficient colloquy with the individual juror to make an assessment of the juror's ability to be impartial. The trial judge should have substantial discretion in conducting the *voir dire,* but, in my judgment, findings of impartiality must be based on something more than the mere silence of the individual in response to questions asked *en masse.*

500 U.S. at 452, 111 S.Ct. at 1919, 114 L.Ed.2d at 523.

3. **Public access to trial proceedings.** The extent to which some or all of the problems presented in *Murphy* may be attacked by barring the public, the press,

or both from the trial was reduced by Richmond Newspapers, Inc. v. Virginia, 448 U.S. 555, 100 S.Ct. 2814, 65 L.Ed.2d 973 (1980), in which a majority of the Supreme Court concluded that the First Amendment creates a right in the public—and apparently in the representatives of the press—to attend a criminal trial. When and how this might be limited was not addressed; there was no opinion of the Court. In the case, the judge presiding over the state murder trial of one Stevenson, with the agreement of both the defense and the prosecution, closed the trial. Defense counsel specifically voiced concern regarding "difficulty with information between jurors," that information might be published inaccurately and seen by jurors, and that "this is a small community." The trial judge also observed that having people in the courtroom is "distracting to the jury." All members of the court except Justice Powell (who did not participate) and Justice Rehnquist (who dissented) agreed that under the circumstances presented the state trial judge's action was constitutionally unacceptable.

In Globe Newspaper Co. v. Superior Court for the County of Norfolk, 457 U.S. 596, 102 S.Ct. 2613, 73 L.Ed.2d 248 (1982) the appellant newspaper had been excluded from a criminal trial under a Massachusetts statute that had been construed to mandate the exclusion of the public from any trial involving specified sex offenses against persons under the age of 18. The United States Supreme Court, in an opinion by Justice Brennan, relying on *Richmond Newspapers, Inc.*, held that the statute violated the newspaper's First Amendment right of access to the courtroom. The Commonwealth argued that the statute furthered two compelling interests in avoiding the trauma of young persons testifying publicly about intimate events and in encouraging them to come forward to testify in the trial. The Court agreed that the first interest advanced was compelling but denied that it justified a mandatory closure rule, since "the circumstances of the particular case may affect the significance of the interest.... Among the factors to be weighed are the minor victim's age, psychological maturity, and understanding, the nature of the crime, the desires of the victim, and the interests of parents and relatives." 457 U.S. at 608, 102 S.Ct. at 2621, 73 L.Ed.2d at 257–59. As to the second interest advanced, the Court noted that much of the argument could be advanced for all victims of crime and that the statute did not prohibit the press from publishing details of the victim's testimony gained from other sources. The Court noted that "in individual cases, and under appropriate circumstances, the First Amendment does not necessarily stand as a bar to the exclusion from the courtroom of the press and general public during the testimony of minor sex-offense victims." 457 U.S. at 611, n. 27, 102 S.Ct. at 2622, n. 27, 73 L.Ed.2d at 259–60, n. 27.

4. **Public access to pretrial proceedings.** Apparently a trial judge has somewhat more flexibility in closing at least some pretrial proceedings. In Gannett Co., Inc. v. DePasquale, 443 U.S. 368, 99 S.Ct. 2898, 61 L.Ed.2d 608 (1979) the trial judge granted the defense motion that the public and the press be excluded from a pretrial hearing on the admissibility of the defendant's confession. Finding no constitutional error, a majority of the Court stressed that closure was only temporary, since the press and the public were given full opportunity to scrutinize and publicize a transcript of the suppression hearing as soon as the danger of prejudice to the defendant was over. Moreover, the trial judge had considered the interest in the press and the public in having access to the proceedings but—and apparently reasonably, in the view of the majority—concluded that this was outweighed by the defendant's need for a fair trial. 443 U.S. at 392–93, 99 S.Ct. at 2912, 61 L.Ed.2d at 629.

The Court considered the closure of a suppression hearing over defendant's Sixth Amendment public trial objection in Waller v. Georgia, 467 U.S. 39, 104 S.Ct. 2210, 81 L.Ed.2d 31 (1984). Waller was prosecuted for various gambling violations. After the jury was selected, the trial court conducted a hearing on a motion to suppress evidence obtained as a result of a court-ordered wiretap. The State moved to close the hearing to the public on the ground that under Georgia law unnecessary publication of the wiretap fruits might make the evidence inadmissible against others and that the privacy interests of others would be invaded by a public hearing. The trial court closed the hearing which lasted seven days; only two and one-half hours of the hearing were devoted to playing tapes of the intercepted telephone conversations.

The Supreme Court, in an opinion for an unanimous Court authored by Justice Powell, held that the defendant's right to a public trial extended to suppression hearings, as well as to the trial itself. It also held that closure of a suppression hearing over Sixth Amendment objection must meet the First Amendment standards set out in *Press-Enterprise*. The trial court's closure order was unjustified:

> [T]he State's proffer was not specific as to whose privacy interests might be infringed, how they would be infringed, what portions of the tapes might infringe them, and what portion of the evidence consisted of the tapes. ...The court did not consider alternatives to immediate closure of the entire hearing: directing the government to provide more detail about its need for closure, *in camera* if necessary, and closing only those parts of the hearing that jeopardized the interests advanced. As it turned out, of course, the closure was far more extensive than necessary.

467 U.S. at 48–49, 104 S.Ct. at 2216–17, 81 L.Ed.2d at 40. As to remedy, the Court held it was not necessary to award a new trial but instead remanded the case for a new suppression hearing: "A new trial need be held only if a new, public suppression hearing results in the suppression of material evidence not suppressed at the first trial, or in some other material change in the positions of the parties." 467 U.S. at 40, 104 S.Ct. at 2212, 81 L.Ed.2d at 41.

The Court considered the applicability of the First Amendment right of access to criminal proceedings to preliminary hearings in Press–Enterprise Co. v. Superior Court, 478 U.S. 1, 106 S.Ct. 2735, 92 L.Ed.2d 1 (1986). The trial court had, with defendant's consent, closed a preliminary hearing to the press and public. Defendant was charged with 12 counts of murder. The preliminary hearing lasted for 41 days and concluded with a finding of probable cause on all charges. Petitioner attempted unsuccessfully in the California courts to obtain a transcript of the preliminary hearing. The California Supreme Court held there is no First Amendment right of access to preliminary hearings. The United States Supreme Court, in an opinion by Chief Justice Burger, reversed. Preliminary hearings have traditionally been open to the public and in many cases they are the only adversarial proceedings in a case because of the large percentage of pleas of guilty following full preliminaries. When a request for closure of a preliminary is based upon the right of the accused to a fair trial, closure is permissible under the First Amendment

> only if specific findings are made demonstrating that first, there is a substantial probability that the defendant's right to a fair trial will be prejudiced by publicity that closure would prevent and, second, reasonable alternatives to closure cannot adequately protect the defendant's fair trial rights.

478 U.S. at 14, 106 S.Ct. at 2743, 92 L.Ed.2d at 13–14. Because the California Supreme Court failed to apply this standard, its judgment was reversed. Justice Stevens, joined in part by Justice Rehnquist, dissented.

5. **Closing jury selection to the public.** Are there circumstances in which a trial judge would be justified in closing all or parts of jury selection proceedings to the press and public? In Press–Enterprise Company v. Superior Court, 464 U.S. 501, 104 S.Ct. 819, 78 L.Ed.2d 629 (1984), the petitioner newspaper moved that jury selection proceedings in a rape/murder trial be open to the press. The trial court

ruled that only that portion of the proceedings involving a general explanation of the case to the jury panel would be open and that the portion involving individual questioning of members of the panel would be closed. Thus, all but three days of the six week jury selection proceeding was closed. After the jury was selected, the newspaper moved for release of a complete transcript of the proceedings, but this too was denied. The California state courts upheld the trial court but the Supreme Court, in an opinion authored by the Chief Justice, vacated and remanded the case.

The Chief Justice noted that historically criminal trials, including jury selection proceedings, have been open to the public. He characterized criminal trials as having a "presumption of openness" which may be overcome "only by an overriding interest based on findings that closure is essential to preserve higher values and is narrowly tailored to serve that interest." 464 U.S. at 510, 104 S.Ct. at 824, 78 L.Ed.2d at 638. The California courts attempted to justify closure on the ground that it would promote candor by members of the jury panel in responding to the often probing questions by counsel and it was needed to protect the privacy of members of the panel. The Chief found neither argument persuasive. The trial court's closure order was too broad. It did not consider alternatives to the sweeping closure order. When a prospective juror indicates a desire for private discussion of a question, that desire can be accommodated by examining the person *in camera* but on the record with counsel present. The privacy interest of members of the panel cannot justify refusal to release a transcript of the proceedings to the press after the jury has been selected, but in certain circumstances it might justify excising a portion of the transcript or preserving the anonymity of certain members of the panel. The trial court did not make the necessary findings and its order was too broad in light of the arguments advanced in support of it. Justices Blackmun and Stevens concurred in separate opinions. Justice Marshall concurred in the judgment of the Court.

6. **Restricting the contents of published reports.** Another method of dealing with at least some of the problems raised in *Murphy* is to limit dissemination of information by the press, without denying it access to the information. But the acceptability of this approach was limited in Nebraska Press Ass'n v. Stuart, 427 U.S. 539, 96 S.Ct. 2791, 49 L.Ed.2d 683 (1976). The trial judge had issued a so-called "gag order," which—as ultimately modified by the Nebraska Supreme Court—prohibited the reporting of the existence and nature of any confessions or admissions made by the defendant to law enforcement officers, of any confessions or admissions made to any third parties, except members of the press, and of any other facts "strongly implicative" of the defendant. The majority of the court declined to hold that such orders were prohibited under any circumstances, but it examined the justification of the order before it under a presumption of invalidity attaching to prior restraint of the press:

> [W]e must examine the evidence before the trial judge when the order was entered to determine (a) the nature and extent of pretrial news coverage; (b) whether other measures would be likely to mitigate the effect of unrestrained pretrial publicity; and (c) how effectively a restraining order would operate to prevent the threatened danger. The precise terms of the restraining order are also important. We must then consider whether the record supports the entry of a prior restraint on publication, one of the most extraordinary remedies known to our jurisprudence.

427 U.S. at 562, 96 S.Ct. at 2804, 49 L.Ed.2d at 699. Its review of the record led the majority to conclude that there was insufficient evidence that further publicity would so distort the views of potential jurors that twelve satisfactory jurors could not be found. No adequate basis was presented for concluding that means other than pretrial restraint of the press would not sufficiently mitigate the effects of

publicity so as to make the prior restraint unnecessary. Moreover, given the fact that the events took place in a community of 850 persons, the record did not establish with sufficient clarity that the restraining order would in fact serve its intended purpose. That portion of the order prohibiting the reporting of "information strongly implicative of the accused" was held impermissibly vague and broad, and the order was also held fatally broad insofar as it prohibited the reporting of evidence produced at open court at the defendant's preliminary hearing. 427 U.S. at 565–70, 96 S.Ct. at 2804–07, 49 L.Ed.2d at 701–04. Justice Brennan, joined by Justices Stewart and Marshall, concurred in the judgment but urged that prior restraint of the press could never be used to safeguard a defendant's right to a fair trial. 427 U.S. at 604, 96 S.Ct. at 2824, 49 L.Ed.2d at 724.

7.   **Controlling publicity through bar discipline.** The Supreme Court considered the constitutionality under the First Amendment of the use of bar disciplinary rules to restrict attorneys in making pre-trial comments concerning a case in Gentile v. State Bar of Nevada, 501 U.S. 1030, 111 S.Ct. 2720, 115 L.Ed.2d 888 (1991). The Supreme Court of Nevada had promulgated bar disciplinary rule 177 (almost identical to ABA Model Rule of Professional Conduct 3.6) concerning trial publicity:

1.   A lawyer shall not make an extrajudicial statement that a reasonable person would expect to be disseminated by means of public communication if the lawyer knows or reasonably should know that it will have a substantial likelihood of materially prejudicing an adjudicative proceeding.

2.   A statement referred to in subsection 1 ordinarily is likely to have such an effect when it refers to a civil matter triable to a jury, a criminal matter, or any other proceeding that could result in incarceration, and the statement relates to:

(a)   the character, credibility, reputation or criminal record of a party, suspect in a criminal investigation or witness, or the identity of a witness, or the expected testimony of a party or witness;

(b)   in a criminal case or proceeding that could result in incarceration, the possibility of a plea of guilty to the offense or the existence or contents of any confession, admission, or statement given by a defendant or suspect or that person's refusal or failure to make a statement;

(c)   the performance or results of any examination or test or the refusal or failure of a person to submit to an examination or test, or the identity or nature of physical evidence expected to be presented;

(d)   any opinion as to the guilt or innocence of a defendant or suspect in a criminal case or proceeding that could result in incarceration;

(e)   information the lawyer knows or reasonably should know is likely to be inadmissible as evidence in a trial and would if disclosed create a substantial risk of prejudicing an impartial trial; or

(f)   the fact that a defendant has been charged with a crime, unless there is included therein a statement explaining that the charge is merely an accusation and that the defendant is presumed innocent until and unless proven guilty.

3.   Notwithstanding subsection 1 and 2(a-f), a lawyer involved in the investigation or litigation of a matter may state without elaboration:

(a)   the general nature of the claim or defense; * * *

Gentile, a Las Vegas criminal defense attorney, called a press conference shortly after his client was arrested and charged with offenses arising out of four kilograms of cocaine and almost $300,000 in travelers' checks that were missing from a safety deposit box. The box had been used by police in an undercover operation and was part of a business—Western Vault Corporation—owned by petitioner's client. There was extensive local publicity concerning the case before and after the arrest and charge. Petitioner examined the rules of discipline before calling the press conference and refused to answer several questions at the conference on grounds to do so would violate those rules. At the conference petitioner stated that his client was innocent, that the likely thief was a police detective (whom he named) and that others who claimed to be victims of similar losses were rug dealers or convicted money launderers, who were working with police wrongfully to accuse his client. At trial six months later, petitioner's client was acquitted of all charges. The Nevada Bar then brought disciplinary proceedings, which resulted in the Nevada Supreme Court ultimately issuing a private reprimand against petitioner for violation of Rule 177. The United States Supreme Court reversed. The Court held, through Justice Kennedy, that the rules as interpreted by the Nevada Supreme Court, were void for vagueness. Petitioner was misled by the "safe harbor" provision of Rule 177(3)(a) into believing that his conduct at the press conference was protected from bar discipline:

> A lawyer seeking to avail himself of Rule 177(3)'s protection must guess at its contours. The right to explain the "general" nature of the defense without "elaboration" provides insufficient guidance because "general" and "elaboration" are both classic terms of degree. In the context before us, these terms have no settled usage or tradition of interpretation in law. The lawyer has no principle for determining when his remarks pass from the safe harbor of the general to the forbidden sea of the elaborated.

501 U.S. at 1048–49, 111 S.Ct. at 2731, 115 L.Ed.2d at 906–07. Then Justice Kennedy, writing for himself and Justices Marshall, Blackmun and Stevens, concluded that the Rule as applied in this case violated the First Amendment because this is pure political speech and the same standards should be used to determine whether petitioner's speech was protected by the First Amendment as any other person's. While the standard of the rule—"substantial likelihood of materially prejudicing an adjudicative proceeding"—is acceptable under the First Amendment, its application to the facts of this case violated petitioner's First Amendment rights. Chief Justice Rehnquist, writing for the Court, held that lawyers can be held to a lesser standard of First Amendment protection than other persons:

> Lawyers representing clients in pending cases are key participants in the criminal justice system, and the State may demand some adherence to the precepts of that system in regulating their speech as well as their conduct * * *. Because lawyers have special access to information through discovery and client communications, their extrajudicial statements pose a threat to the fairness of a pending proceeding since lawyers' statements are likely to be received as especially authoritative * * *. We agree with the majority of the States that the "substantial likelihood of material prejudice" standard constitutes a constitutionally permissible balance between the First Amendment rights of attorneys in pending cases and the state's interest in fair trials.

501 U.S. at 1074–75, 111 S.Ct. at 2744–45, 115 L.Ed.2d at 923. Chief Justice Rehnquist, writing for himself and for Justices White, Scalia and Souter, concluded that Rule 177 as applied in this case should not be held void for vagueness. Justice O'Connor, while joining in Justice Kennedy's opinion that the Rule was as applied void for vagueness, emphasized her belief that lawyers may be judged by lower First Amendment standards than other persons because "lawyers are officers of the court and, as such, may legitimately be subject to ethical precepts that keep them from engaging in what otherwise might be constitutionally protected speech."

8. **Televising trials.** The Supreme Court's action in Estes v. Texas, discussed in *Murphy,* has been interpreted as a holding that televising a trial is inherently a denial of due process. Estes v. Texas, 381 U.S. 532, 552, 85 S.Ct. 1628, 1637, 14 L.Ed.2d 543, 555 (1965) (Warren, C.J., concurring). But this reading of *Estes* was rejected in Chandler v. Florida, 449 U.S. 560, 101 S.Ct. 802, 66 L.Ed.2d 740 (1981). In *Chandler,* a television camera had covered one afternoon of defendants' trial in state court for conspiracy, grand larceny, and possession of burglary tools. This was done pursuant to recently-revised Canon 3A(7) of the Florida Code of Judicial Conduct, permitting electronic media and still photography coverage of judicial proceedings in accordance with guidelines promulgated by the Florida Supreme Court. Treating the issue as one of first impression, the Court rejected the argument that broadcast coverage is prohibited as a matter of federal constitutional law. The Court noted the danger that coverage may impair the ability of jurors to decide the issue of guilt or innocence uninfluenced by extraneous matters. But the risk of such prejudice, the Court concluded, does not justify an absolute constitutional ban on all broadcast coverage. 449 U.S. at 575, 101 S.Ct. at 810, 66 L.Ed.2d at 752. Turning to the possibility that the coverage of the particular case before it may have constituted a denial of due process, the majority reasoned:

> [A] defendant has the right on review to show that the media's coverage of his case—printed or broadcast—compromised the ability of the jury to judge him fairly. Alternatively, a defendant might show that broadcast coverage of his particular case had an adverse impact on the trial participants sufficient to constitute a denial of due process. Neither showing was made in this case.
>
> To demonstrate prejudice in a specific case a defendant must show something more than juror awareness that the trial is such as to attract the attention of broadcasters. No doubt the presence of a camera in the courtroom made the jurors aware that the trial was thought to be of sufficient interest to the public to warrant coverage. * * * But the appellants have not attempted to show with any specificity that the presence of cameras impaired the ability of the jurors to decide the case on only the evidence before them or that their trial was affected adversely by the impact on any of the participants of the presence of cameras and the prospect of broadcast.

449 U.S. at 581, 101 S.Ct. at 813, 66 L.Ed.2d at 755–56.

9. **Proving juror prejudice.** When a defendant urges that his trial was rendered unfair by the bias of a particular juror, to what extent must the defendant show "actual bias?" In Smith v. Phillips, 455 U.S. 209, 102 S.Ct. 940, 71 L.Ed.2d 78 (1982), Phillips had been convicted of murder and attempted murder in a New York court after a jury trial. He subsequently sought federal habeas corpus relief. Information developed after trial showed that one of the trial jurors, during the trial, applied for and actively pursued employment with the prosecutor's office as an investigator. Phillips urged that this juror's participation in the guilt-determining process deprived him of a fair trial. The federal District Court found insufficient evidence to establish that the juror was actually biased in favor of the prosecution but found "imputed bias" on the ground that an average person in the juror's position would believe that a guilty verdict would improve the consideration given to his employment application. Relief was granted, and this was affirmed on appeal to the United States Court of Appeals for the Second Circuit. The Supreme Court, over the dissent of Justice Marshall joined by Justices Brennan and Stevens, reversed. Rejecting Phillips' argument that actual bias is so difficult to prove that it should not be the standard for determining whether the right to a fair trial has been violated, Justice Rehnquist explained for the Court that "the remedy for allegations of juror partiality is a hearing at which the defendant has the opportunity to prove actual bias." 455 U.S. at 215, 102 S.Ct. at 945, 71 L.Ed.2d at 85. Phillips

was given such a hearing and failed to make the requisite showing of actual bias. Justice O'Connor concurred, but wrote separately to express her understanding that in some circumstances a post-conviction hearing on the existence of actual bias may not be adequate to remedy a claim of juror bias and to suggest that the Court's opinion does not foreclose the use of "implied bias" in such appropriate situations. 455 U.S. at 221, 102 S.Ct. at 948, 71 L.Ed.2d at 89.

10. **Determining juror bias.** The manner in which the trial court handled information about possible juror bias was the subject of Rushen v. Spain, 464 U.S. 114, 104 S.Ct. 453, 78 L.Ed.2d 267 (1983). Respondent was on trial for murder and other offenses. The State attempted to show that the crimes were the product of a conspiracy by the Black Panther Party and that respondent was a member of the Party. During the trial, evidence was introduced that one Pratt, identified as a member of the Black Panther Party, had murdered a Santa Monica woman in 1968. This triggered the memory of juror Fagan that the woman who had been murdered had been a very close friend of hers. She twice approached the trial judge *ex parte* to explain her personal acquaintance with the murder victim and to express the concern that she would cry if evidence of the murder were presented further in the trial. On each occasion, she assured the trial judge that this fact would not affect her disposition of the case. The trial judge did not record these conversations or reveal them to the parties. After respondent was convicted, his attorney learned of these events and a hearing was conducted to determine whether a new trial should be granted. The trial court concluded it should not and this was approved by the California Court of Appeal. On a petition for writ of habeas corpus, a federal District Court concluded that the *ex parte* communications between Ms. Fagan and the trial judge violated the respondent's right to be present during all critical stages of the proceedings and his right to be represented by counsel. This was affirmed by the Ninth Circuit on the ground that an unrecorded *ex parte* communication between a trial judge and juror can never be harmless error.

The Supreme Court without oral argument, reversed the Ninth Circuit. The *per curiam* opinion, citing Smith v. Phillips, concluded that the error of the trial judge was harmless beyond a reasonable doubt and that the post-verdict hearing conducted by the trial court was sufficient to protect the respondent's rights. The Court noted

> There is scarcely a lengthy trial in which one or more jurors does not have occasion to speak to the trial judge about something, whether it relates to a matter of personal comfort or to some aspect of the trial. The lower federal courts' conclusion that an unrecorded *ex parte* communication between trial judge and juror can never be harmless error ignores these day-to-day realities of courtroom life and undermines society's interest in the administration of criminal justice.

464 U.S. at 140, 104 S.Ct. at 466, 78 L.Ed.2d at 273. Justice Stevens concurred in the judgment. He would find that a violation of the right to counsel can never be harmless error but that that right was not violated in this case. Instead, he would characterize the issue involved here as whether the due process right "to notice and an opportunity to be heard in a meaningful manner and at a meaningful time [was violated] by the trial judge's failure to notify the defense of a fact raising a question about a juror's partiality." 464 U.S. at 126, 104 S.Ct. at 460, 78 L.Ed.2d at 278. He concluded that while the trial judge should have promptly notified the defense of the juror communication, failure to do so did not violate due process. Justices Marshall and Blackmun dissented.

11. **Impartial judge.** An impartial trial also includes the right to an "unbiased judge." In Tumey v. Ohio, 273 U.S. 510, 47 S.Ct. 437, 71 L.Ed. 749 (1927), the Court held that a trial before a mayor who personally received fees and costs levied

by him against prohibition law violators violated the Fourteenth Amendment's Due Process Clause. In Dugan v. Ohio, 277 U.S. 61, 48 S.Ct. 439, 72 L.Ed. 784 (1928), however, the Court distinguished *Tumey* on the grounds that (1) in *Dugan* the mayor had only limited executive responsibility and (2) the fines collected went not to the mayor but to the city. Therefore, due process was not denied.

In Ward v. Village of Monroeville, 409 U.S. 57, 93 S.Ct. 80, 34 L.Ed.2d 267 (1972), the mayor had wide executive powers in a municipality a substantial part of whose income was derived from fines imposed by the mayor in ordinance violation and traffic cases. The Court found a violation of due process even though the mayor received no personal benefit, and even though a defendant was entitled to trial de novo as of right. With regard to the latter, the Court said:

> Respondent also argues that any unfairness at the trial level can be corrected on appeal and trial *de novo* in the County Court of Common Pleas. We disagree. This "procedural safeguard" does not guarantee a fair trial in the mayor's court; there is nothing to suggest that the incentive to convict would be diminished by the possibility of reversal on appeal. Nor, in any event, may the State's trial court procedure be deemed constitutionally acceptable simply because the State eventually offers a defendant an impartial adjudication. Petitioner is entitled to a neutral and detached judge in the first instance.

409 U.S. at 61–62, 93 S.Ct. at 83–84, 34 L.Ed.2d at 271. And, in a footnote, the Court added:

> The question presented on this record is the constitutionality of the Mayor's participation in the adjudication and punishment of a defendant in a litigated case where he elects to contest the charges against him. We intimate no view that it would be unconstitutional to permit a mayor or similar official to serve in essentially a ministerial capacity in a traffic or ordinance violation case to accept a free and voluntary plea of guilty or *nolo contendere,* a forfeiture of collateral, or the like.

409 U.S. at 62, 93 S.Ct. at 84, 34 L.Ed.2d at 271.

12. **Judicial impartiality in contempt proceedings.** A defendant's federal constitutional right to an unbiased judge has been most extensively developed in a series of cases involving citation of a defendant or defense lawyer for contempt of court on the basis of conduct during trial. In some situations, at least where the judge does not immediately adjudge the defendant guilty of contempt, due process requires that contempt proceedings be held before a judge other than the one who presided over the trial at which the alleged contempt occurred. This is so where the alleged contempt consists of a highly personal attack upon the judge, as in Mayberry v. Pennsylvania, 400 U.S. 455, 91 S.Ct. 499, 27 L.Ed.2d 532 (1971), where the defendant called the trial judge, among other things, a "fool" and a "dirty tyranical old dog." It is also so where the trial judge is so provoked and embroiled in controversy that either there is actual bias or a sufficient likelihood or appearance of bias. Taylor v. Hayes, 418 U.S. 488, 94 S.Ct. 2697, 41 L.Ed.2d 897 (1974). In *Taylor,* before sentencing the defendant the trial judge made a statement concerning defense counsel, whom he was to hold in contempt. In this statement, he described counsel as not "a lawyer" and as having put on the worst "display" the judge had seen. Further, the judge refused to permit counsel to respond, threatened to gag him, sentenced him to four and one-half years in jail, disbarred him from practice in the court, and denied bond pending appeal. Given this evidence that "marked personal feelings were present on both sides," the Supreme Court held that determination of the contempt charges by the trial judge violated due process. See also, Johnson v. Mississippi, 403 U.S. 212, 91 S.Ct. 1778, 29 L.Ed.2d 423 (1971) (due process violated by trial of contempt charges before trial judge, given affidavits of two lawyers that judge's grand jury charges revealed deep prejudice against civil

rights lawyers, and evidence that immediately before adjudication of contempt judge was losing party in counsel's civil rights suit). The implications of this line of cases are not entirely clear. Given the practical situation, it appears certain that where the trial judge properly cites for contempt immediately after the contemptuous conduct, due process does not require a different judge. But are there constitutional limitations upon the situations in which such immediate action is permissible? To what extent do these cases provide support for the proposition that bias (or the likelihood or appearance of bias) on the part of the judge presiding over a criminal trial on charges other than contempt violates due process? Does it make any difference whether the case is being tried to a jury?

13.   **Judicial recusal.** The Supreme Court addressed the scope of the federal recusal of judges statute in Liteky v. United States, 510 U.S. 540, 114 S.Ct. 1147, 127 L.Ed.2d 474 (1994). Petitioners were charged with destruction of government property, which involved a political protest at a military base. One of the Petitioners had previously been tried before the same judge on a similar charge. Based on the judge's actions in the previous trial, Petitioners made a motion to have the judge recused under 28 U.S.C. § 455(a), which requires a federal judge to "disqualify himself in any proceeding in which his impartiality might reasonably be questioned." The motion was denied and the Petitioners were convicted. The Court of Appeals affirmed on the ground that "matters arising out of the course of judicial proceedings are not a proper basis for recusal." The Supreme Court, in an opinion for the Court by Justice Scalia, affirmed.

The position taken by the Court of Appeals goes too far. A judge can acquire a bias or prejudice from information obtained in judicial proceedings that make him or her unfit to sit further in the case. As to what constitutes a "bias or prejudice,"

> Not all unfavorable disposition towards an individual (or his case) is properly described by those terms. One would not say, for example, that world opinion is biased or prejudiced against Adolf Hitler. The words connote a favorable or unfavorable disposition or opinion that is somehow wrongful or inappropriate, either because it is undeserved, or because it rests upon knowledge that the subject ought not to possess (for example, a criminal juror who has been biased or prejudiced by receipt of inadmissible evidence concerning the defendant's prior criminal activities), or because it is excessive in degree (for example, a criminal juror who is so inflamed by properly admitted evidence of a defendant's prior criminal activities that he will vote guilty regardless of the facts).

510 U.S. at 550, 114 S.Ct. at 1155, 127 L.Ed.2d at 488. As applied to a judge,

> The judge who presides at a trial may, upon completion of the evidence, be exceedingly ill disposed towards the defendant, who has been shown to be a thoroughly reprehensible person. But the judge is not thereby recusable for bias or prejudice, since his knowledge and the opinion it produced were properly and necessarily acquired in the course of the proceedings, and are indeed sometimes (as in a bench trial) necessary to completion of the judge's task. As Judge Jerome Frank pithily put it: "Impartiality is not gullibility. Disinterestedness does not mean child-like innocence. If the judge did not form judgments of the actors in those court-house dramas called trials, he could never render decisions." * * * Also not subject to deprecatory characterization as "bias" or "prejudice" are opinions held by judges as a result of what they learned in earlier proceedings. It has long been regarded as normal and proper for a judge to sit in the same case upon its remand, and to sin in successive trials involving the same defendant.

510 U.S. at 550, 114 S.Ct. at 1155, 127 L.Ed.2d at 488. The reasons invoked by Petitioners—rulings and comments by the judge during the previous trial—are insufficient to require recusal under the statute: "All occurred in the course of

judicial proceedings, and neither (1) relied upon knowledge acquired outside such proceedings nor (2) displayed deepseated and unequivocal antagonism that would render fair judgment impossible." 510 U.S. at 556, 114 S.Ct. at 1158, 127 L.Ed.2d at 491–92. Justice Kennedy, joined by Justices Blackmun, Stevens and Souter, concurred in the judgment and criticized the majority for requiring too great a showing of unfairness in order to mandate recusal.

14. **Right to a law-trained judge.** A defendant's right to a "law-trained" judge was addressed in North v. Russell, 427 U.S. 328, 96 S.Ct. 2709, 49 L.Ed.2d 534 (1976). At issue were the validity of trials conducted by Kentucky nonlawyer judges in police courts located in the state's less populous counties. These courts have jurisdiction over criminal cases punishable by a fine of no more than $500, imprisonment for no longer than twelve months, or both. A defendant convicted in police court, whether on a plea of guilty or after a trial, has a right to appeal to a circuit court, presided over by a lawyer-judge, and a trial *de novo* in that court. North urged that the constitutional right to representation in cases resulting in incarceration would be meaningless without a lawyer-judge to understand the arguments of counsel; the increased complexity of both substantive and procedural criminal law, he further argued, requires that judges be lawyers so as to be able to rule accurately on complicated issues that arise even in some simple misdemeanor cases. The majority of the Court declined to decide whether a defendant could be convicted and imprisoned after a proceeding in which the only trial afforded is conducted by a lay judge. Under Kentucky procedure, a defendant is entitled to a trial *de novo* before a law-trained circuit judge, and by pleading guilty in police court a defendant can in effect bypass the police court and secure an initial trial before the circuit court. This, it concluded, satisfies due process. The majority assumed that Kentucky police court judges inform defendants of their right to representation by counsel (where it applies), of their right to a trial *de novo* in circuit court, and of the procedural steps necessary to secure that trial *de novo*. Justice Stewart, joined by Justice Marshall, dissented, urging that in a trial resulting in imprisonment before a nonlawyer judge the constitutional right to the assistance of counsel becomes a "hollow mockery." He found the majority's reliance upon defendants' right to a trial *de novo* in circuit court unpersuasive because there was no evidence that defendants are informed of this right, implementing it requires multiple court appearances, delay and a financial burden, and a trial *de novo* practice would turn "what should be a solemn court proceeding ... into nothing more than a sham." 427 U.S. at 346, 96 S.Ct. at 2717–18, 49 L.Ed.2d at 545–46.

CHAPTER 19

JOINDER AND SEVERANCE OF CHARGES AND DEFENDANTS

Analysis

The simplest structure for the trial of a criminal case is the trial of a single charge against a single defendant. Many criminal trials fit that model. The laws in most jurisdictions, however, permit the prosecutor to depart from that model, either by bringing a multiplicity of charges or by charging more than one defendant or by both. The rationale for permitting departure from the one charge/one defendant model is to increase the efficiency of the system of adjudication by trial. The danger in such practices is that a defendant's right to a fair trial may be jeopardized because of the multiplicity of charges brought or because he is being tried with one or more codefendants. The laws permitting such proceedings contemplate a two-step structure for determining the scope of the trial: an initial decision whether to join charges and/or defendants in a single proceeding and a decision made by the trial court whether, assuming joinder was authorized by law, one or more of the charges or defendants should be severed from the trial.

The joinder and severance provisions of the Federal Rules of Criminal Procedure provide a useful starting place. Rule 8 provides:

> (a) *Joinder of Offenses.* Two or more offenses may be charged in the same indictment or information in a separate count for each offense if the offenses charged, whether felonies or misdemeanors or both, are of the same or similar character or are based on the same act or transaction or on two or more acts or transactions connected together or constituting parts of a common scheme or plan.

> (b) *Joinder of Defendants.* Two or more defendants may be charged in the same indictment or information if they are alleged to have participated in the same act or transaction or in the same series of acts or transactions constituting an offense or offenses. Such defendants may be charged in one or more counts together or separately and all of the defendants need not be charged in each count.

Rule 13 authorizes the trial court to consolidate two or more indictments or informations for trial "if the offenses, and the defendants if there is more than one, could have been joined in a single indictment or information."

Rule 14 authorizes the trial court to grant relief from prejudicial joinder of charges or defendants:

> If it appears that a defendant or the government is prejudiced by a joinder of offenses or of defendants in an indictment or information or by such joinder for trial together, the court may order an election or separate trials of counts, grant a severance of defendants or provide whatever other relief justice requires. In ruling on a motion by a defendant for severance the court may order the attorney for the government to deliver to the court for inspection *in camera* any statements or confessions made by the defendants which the government intends to introduce in evidence at the trial.

A.   JOINDER AND SEVERANCE OF CHARGES

Under what circumstances is it appropriate to adjudicate more than one criminal charge in the same trial? What gains in efficiency are achieved by permitting multiplicity of charges? What risks to a fair adjudication of guilt or innocence are created by such a procedure? Are there, or should there be, limitations on the number and complexity of charges that can be brought to trial at one time?

Bringing multiple charges against the same defendant, whether in a single proceeding or in sequential proceedings, can raise difficult double jeopardy questions. Those questions are considered in Chapter 20 in context with other double jeopardy issues. In this Section, the limits, if any, that should be placed on multiplicity of charges apart from jeopardy considerations are examined.

United States v. Foutz

United States Court of Appeals, Fourth Circuit, 1976.
540 F.2d 733.

■ WINTER, CIRCUIT JUDGE.

Pembrick Edward Foutz, Jr. was convicted by a jury of twice robbing the Kensington, Maryland, branch of the Bank of Bethesda, in violation of 18 U.S.C.A. §§ 2 and 2113(a), (b), (d), and (f). Although the two robberies took place two and one-half months apart, Foutz was tried for both offenses in one proceeding; his motion for relief from prejudicial joinder under Fed.R.Crim.P. 14 was denied by the district court. On appeal, Foutz argues that the district judge abused his discretion by not granting a severance. He claims that prejudice arose from the fact that the same jury heard evidence of both crimes, whereas had he been tried separately for each robbery, evidence of one offense would not have been admissible at the trial for the other. We agree, and reverse and remand for new, separate trials for each robbery.

I.

On December 30, 1974, a lone black male, armed with a handgun, robbed the Bank of Bethesda at Kensington, Maryland. He entered through the front door, vaulted the tellers' counter at teller position number two, and took money from two tellers' drawers. He left through the same door and walked up a side street. The robber wore a turtleneck sweater pulled up over his mouth and a beret-type hat. Two bank employees testified that Foutz appeared similar to the robber. No fingerprints of Foutz were found at the scene, and the photographs taken by the bank surveillance camera were apparently not helpful in identification. The defense presented as an alibi witness a Washington police cadet who testified with considerable certainty and specificity that Foutz was with her in Washington at the time of the robbery.

On March 13, 1975, the same bank was robbed by a group of three black males. They entered by the front door. One robber, allegedly Foutz, stood near the door holding a handgun on the bank employees. He wore a wide-brimmed hat and may have had on a turtleneck sweater. The other two robbers vaulted the tellers' counter near position number two and took money from several tellers' drawers. All three robbers then escaped down the same side street used by the lone gunman in the previous robbery. There they were observed entering an automobile which was shown to be registered to Foutz. Two bank employees testified that Foutz resembled the robber who stood near the door and held the gun. So far as the record reveals, no fingerprints were found, and apparently the surveillance photographs did not depict the robber alleged to be Foutz. The defense presented an alibi witness who was unable to account for Foutz' whereabouts at the time of the robbery.

Foutz was charged with both robberies in one indictment, as permitted by Fed.R.Crim.P. 8(a), since the offenses were of the "same or similar character." He then made a timely motion for a severance under Rule 14, alleging that he would be prejudiced by a joint trial. The motion was denied. The jury returned a verdict of guilty of both robberies. A motion for a new trial on the grounds of prejudicial joinder was denied. Foutz was sentenced to twenty-five years, imprisonment for each offense, the sentences to run concurrently.

II.

Rule 14 provides that a severance may be granted "[i]f it appears that a defendant or the government is prejudiced by a joinder of offenses...." The granting of a severance under Rule 14 is committed to the discretion of the district court. ...In this case, we believe it was an abuse of that discretion not to grant a severance.

We begin our analysis with Rule 8 which permits joinder under three circumstances: (1) if the offenses "are of the same or similar character"; (2) if they "are based on the same act or transaction"; or (3) if they are based "on two or more acts or transactions connected together or constituting parts of a common scheme or plan.'' In the instant case, joinder was initially permissible only because the offenses were of the same or similar character. When two or more offenses are joined for trial solely on this theory, three sources of prejudice are possible which may justify the granting of a severance under Rule 14: (1) the jury may confuse and cumulate the evidence, and convict the defendant of one or both crimes when it would not convict him of either if it could keep the evidence properly segregated;[1] (2) the defendant may be confounded in presenting defenses, as where he desires to assert his privilege against self-incrimination with respect to one crime but not the other;[2] or (3) the jury may conclude that the defendant is guilty of one crime and then find him guilty of the other because of his criminal disposition. As we view the record, we are concerned here with the latter form of prejudice.

While to the layman's mind a defendant's criminal disposition is logically relevant to his guilt or innocence of a specific crime, the law regards the inference from general to specific criminality so weak, and the danger of prejudice so great, that it attempts to prevent conviction on account of a defendant's bad character. Thus, evidence of "other crimes" which is relevant only to prove a criminal disposition is universally acknowledged to be inadmissible.

One inevitable consequence of a joint trial is that the jury will be aware of evidence of one crime while considering the defendant's guilt or innocence of another. If the rationale of the "other crimes" rule is correct, it would seem that some degree of prejudice is necessarily created by permitting the jury to hear evidence of both crimes.

Although the law does not allow consideration of other crimes as evidence of a defendant's criminal disposition, evidence of other crimes is admissible for certain other purposes because its probative value is then thought to outweigh its prejudicial effect. In those instances where evidence of one crime is admissible at a separate trial for another, it follows that a defendant will not suffer any additional prejudice if the two offenses are tried together.[3]

When offenses are joined under Rule 8 on the ground that they "are based on the same act or transaction or on two or more acts or transactions connected together or constituting parts of a common scheme or plan," it is manifest that evidence of one offense would ordinarily be admissible at a separate trial for the other. When offenses are joined because they "are of

---

1. See Drew v. United States, 118 U.S.App.D.C. 11, 331 F.2d 85, 88 (1964); 1 Wright, Federal Practice and Procedure § 222 at 437.

2. See Cross v. United States, 118 U.S.App.D.C. 324, 335 F.2d 987, 989–90 (1964); 8 Moore's Federal Practice ¶ 14.03 at 14–11 to 14–14.1.

3. This standard does not require that every item of evidence relating to one offense be admissible in a separate trial for the other,

but rather looks in a broader sense to whether the rules relating to "other crimes" evidence have been satisfied. And, at least in the case of non-violent crimes, it is ordinarily the fact of the defendant's having engaged in prior or subsequent criminal conduct that is likely to be damaging in the eyes of the jury rather than the details of its commission. Baker v. United States, 131 U.S.App.D.C. 7, 401 F.2d 958, 975 (1968) (footnote omitted).

the same or similar character," however, admissibility at separate trials is not so clear.

In this case, the government argues that evidence of one bank robbery would have been admissible at a trial for the other in order to prove the identity of the perpetrator, under the so-called "handiwork" or "signature" exception to the other crimes rule. Under this exception, if the prosecution can produce evidence tending to show that the defendant committed the "other crime," and if that crime was committed in a manner so similar to that of the offense for which the defendant is being tried that it is highly probable that the same person committed both crimes, then evidence of the "other crime" is admissible to prove that the defendant committed the offense with which he is charged. The government's proof, especially that showing the use of Foutz' automobile by the robbers, tended to identify Foutz as one of the perpetrators of the second robbery. Thus, if the two robberies were committed in a sufficiently similar manner, evidence of the second robbery would have been admissible at a separate trial for the first, and untoward prejudice could not inhere in joinder.

We do not think that the two robberies were so similar as to warrant the inference that they were perpetrated by the same individual. The same bank was robbed twice; beyond this, the differences between the crimes are more striking than the similarities, and such similarities as do exist "all fit into an obvious tactical pattern which would suggest itself to almost anyone disposed to commit a depredation of this sort." Drew v. United States, 331 F.2d at 93 (robbery of two High's ice cream stores by negroes wearing sunglasses); see United States v. Carter, 154 U.S.App.D.C. 238, 475 F.2d 349 (1973) (two robberies by a man wearing a fur coat and a fur hat; held insufficient similarity).

The first robbery was committed by a single black male; the second by three such persons. In both instances, access to the bank was through the front door, hardly a remarkable congruity. In the first robbery, the gunman vaulted the counter at teller position number two; in the second, the two "bag" men vaulted the counter at the same point. This apparent similarity loses most of its significance, however, because, under the government's theory of the case, Foutz was not one of the men who vaulted the counter in the second robbery, but was stationed near the door with a gun trained on the bank employees. In the first crime, the robber was described as wearing a turtleneck sweater and a beret-type hat; the person claimed to have been Foutz in the second robbery was described as wearing a wide-brimmed hat and perhaps a turtleneck. This possible, limited similarity of apparel is less than compelling. The first robber was last seen walking down a side street; the trio in the second crime fled in a getaway car which had been parked on the same street. Thus as far as the evidence revealed, the locomotive method of escape was different in each case; and use of a side street instead of a main thoroughfare in fleeing the site of a crime is not a uniquely ingenious stroke of criminal artistry.

We conclude that evidence showing that Foutz was one of the perpetrators of the March 13, 1975 robbery would not have been admitted to prove his identity as the perpetrator of the December 30, 1974 crime, had he been tried separately for that offense. We therefore conclude that Foutz was sufficiently prejudiced by the district court's denial of Foutz' motion for severance to constitute that denial an abuse of discretion requiring reversal.[4]

III.

The government urges that any prejudice resulting from the joint trial of the two robberies was cured by the court's limiting instructions which required the jury to consider each offense and the evidence thereof separately. It is said that where the evidence is "simple and distinct," the jury can be trusted to segregate the evidence properly. This position finds some support in the cases. See United States v. Adams, 434 F.2d 756, 758–59 (2 Cir.1970); Drew v. United States, 331 F.2d at 91–92 (dictum); United States v. Lotsch, 102 F.2d 35, 36 (2 Cir.), cert. denied, 307 U.S. 622, 59 S.Ct. 793, 83 L.Ed. 1500 (1939).[5]

While the law often permits the jury to hear evidence admissible for one purpose but not for another, and presumes that the jury will follow a limiting instruction, this practice is justified by practical considerations of trial convenience and expedition. When offenses are initially joined on the ground that they "are of the same or similar character," and evidence of one offense would not be admissible at a separate trial for the other, the saving of time effected by a joint trial is minimal. "Ordinarily, the only time saved by such joinder is the selection of one jury rather than two. Except for character witnesses, the evidence will usually be entirely separate." 8 Moore's Federal Practice ¶ 8.05[2] at 8–19 (footnotes omitted); see 1 Wright, Federal Practice and Procedure § 143 at 318; .... Thus, the only real convenience served by permitting joint trial of unrelated offenses against the wishes of the defendant may be the convenience of the prosecution in securing a conviction.

We therefore reject the government's argument. The reasons for the rule which the government invokes are largely inapplicable and the prejudice to the defendant, arising from the weakness of the government's one case and strength of the other, so marked that we cannot presume that the jury adhered to limiting instructions and properly "segregate[d] [the] evidence into separate intellectual boxes," Bruton v. United States, 391 U.S. 123, 131, 88 S.Ct. 1620, 1625, 20 L.Ed.2d 476 (1968), quoting People v.

---

4. Our conclusion finds support in the ABA Project on Minimum Standards for Criminal Justice, Standards Relating to Joinder and Severance at 291. Section 2.2(a) provides:

Whenever two or more offenses have been joined for trial solely on the ground that they are of the same or similar character, the defendant shall have a right to a severance of the offenses.

See also 8 Moore's Federal Practice ¶ 8.05[2] at 8.22 ("a persuasive argument [has been made] for generally barring joinder of similar offenses, except perhaps where they would be independently admissible as prior similar acts"); 1 Wright, Federal Prac-

tice and Procedure § 143 at 317–18 ("It may fairly be asked, however, whether such joinder should ever be allowed."); ....

5. The "simple and distinct" test articulated in *Drew* may well be an appropriate standard for measuring the danger of prejudice resulting from the jury's confusing and cumulating the evidence. It does not address itself, however, to the graver mischief possible where the jury, while limiting its consideration of the evidence to the crime to which it relates, properly finds the defendant guilty of one crime but considers that finding probative of his guilt of another.

Aranda, 63 Cal.2d 518, 528–29, 47 Cal.Rptr. 353, 359–60, 407 P.2d 265, 271–72.

IV.

Other factors are sometimes said to mitigate the prejudice flowing from joinder of unrelated offenses. In United States v. Clayton, [450 F.2d 16, 19 (1st Cir.1971), cert. denied 405 U.S. 975, 92 S.Ct. 1200, 31 L.Ed.2d 250 (1972)] the First Circuit relied on the fact that the defendant received concurrent sentences (as did Foutz) in upholding the district court's refusal to grant a severance. We are unpersuaded by this reasoning. Even if it could be concluded with the requisite degree of certainty that the defendant would have been convicted of at least one of the offenses in separate trials, conviction of two crimes instead of one may postpone parole eligibility or result in other serious consequences for the defendant. Thus, while concurrent sentencing may ameliorate the prejudicial effect of a joint trial, it cannot cure it completely.

It has also been said that where evidence of *both* crimes is overwhelming, no prejudice inheres in a joint trial. Cf. United States v. Clayton, 450 F.2d at 19 (evidence on both charges "strong"; "this was not an instance where a weak evidentiary case and a strong one were joined in the hope that an overlapping consideration of the evidence would lead to convictions on both"). The rule is inapplicable here.

We have no doubt that the government proved enough of a case against Foutz with respect to the March 13, 1975 robbery based principally on the positive identification of his automobile as the getaway car, to permit, but not require, the jury to find him guilty. In contrast, the only evidence of Foutz' involvement in the December 30, 1974 robbery, aside from its putative similarity to the later crime, was the testimony of two witnesses that Foutz' appearance was "similar" to that of the robber; and opposed to this testimony was an unusually strong alibi. We think it highly probable that a jury ignorant of the second crime and Foutz' alleged participation therein would have acquitted him of the earlier robbery. There is thus a strong likelihood that the jury found Foutz guilty of the second robbery, and then concluded that since he had once robbed the bank, it was plausible that he had done so before. Since we cannot say that the government's case with respect to the March 13, 1975 robbery was indefensible, it is possible that the jury found him guilty of that crime under the rationale that with so much smoke there must be fire. Had the two offenses not been joined for trial, these "spillovers" could not have occurred, and Foutz might well have been acquitted of the first crime; possibly of both.[6]

We thus conclude that Foutz' convictions of both offenses must be reversed and he must be afforded new, separate trials.

* * *

Reversed and Remanded.

---

6. Joinder of similar offenses remains proper where evidence of one crime could be admitted at a separate trial for the other.

NOTES

1. **Harmfulness of misjoinder.** The question whether a misjoinder of offenses can ever be harmless error was presented in United States v. Lane, 474 U.S. 438, 106 S.Ct. 725, 88 L.Ed.2d 814 (1986). James Lane was indicted in count one for mail fraud in connection with the arson of a restaurant, while he and his son, Dennis, were indicted in counts two through four with mail fraud in connection with the arson of a duplex. Respondents unsuccessfully sought severance of count one from the remaining counts on the ground they were misjoined under Rule 8(b). On appeal from conviction on all counts, the Court of Appeals held there was a misjoinder and that it was *per se* harmful and required reversal of the convictions. The Supreme Court, in an opinion authored by Chief Justice Burger, reversed. The Circuits were divided on whether misjoinder can ever be harmless error. The Supreme Court had held in Chapman v. California, 386 U.S. 18, 87 S.Ct. 824, 17 L.Ed.2d 705 (1967) that even errors of constitutional magnitude (which misjoinder is not) can be harmless. Federal Rules of Criminal Procedure Rule 52(a) directs that errors that do not "affect substantial rights shall be disregarded." The Court in *Lane* held that Rule 8(b) misjoinder requires reversal only if it "results in actual prejudice because it 'had substantial and injurious effect or influence in determining the jury's verdict.' " 474 U.S. at 449, 106 S.Ct. at 732, 88 L.Ed.2d at 826. Because of the overwhelming evidence of guilt, the careful limiting instructions of the trial court to the jury and the likelihood that evidence of the count one offense would have been admissible on the question of intent in a separate trial of counts two through four, the misjoinder was harmless. Justices Brennan, Blackmun, Stevens and Marshall dissented.

2. **Defendant's rights to testify and to remain silent.** What should happen when two charges are joined for trial and the defendant expresses a desire to testify in defense of one charge but to remain silent with respect to the other? In Cross v. United States, 335 F.2d 987, 118 U.S.App.D.C. 324 (D.C.Cir.1964) defendant was charged with robbery of a church rectory in Count I of the indictment and with robbery of a tourist home in Count II. The alleged offenses occurred about two months apart. He filed a motion to sever the charges and for a separate trial on each; the trial court denied the motion. At the trial, Cross expressed a desire to testify in his defense of Count II but to remain silent as to Count I. The trial court took the position that he was permitted to take the stand or not but if he elected to testify he could be cross-examined as to both counts. Cross testified:

> His testimony on Count II was that he was a victim and not a cohort of the armed robbers who entered the tourist home behind him. This testimony, which met the Government's case directly, was so convincing that the jury believed it despite the prosecutor's efforts at cross-examination and impeachment. On Count I, however, his denial was plainly evasive and unconvincing. He testified that he had been drinking heavily and did not know his whereabouts at the time of the church robbery. On cross-examination he was open to questioning concerning his generally tawdry way of life and his prior convictions.

335 F.2d at 990, 118 U.S.App.D.C. at 327. The jury acquitted Cross on Count II but returned a verdict of guilty on Count I. On appeal, the District of Columbia Circuit reversed and remanded for a new trial:

> Prejudice may develop when an accused wishes to testify on one but not the other of two joined offenses which are clearly distinct in time, place and evidence. His decision whether to testify will reflect a balancing of several factors with respect to each count: the evidence against him, the availability of defense evidence other than his testimony, the plausibility and substantiality of his testimony, the possible effects of demeanor, impeachment, and cross-

examination. But if the two charges are joined for trial, it is not possible for him to weigh these factors separately as to each count. If he testifies on one count, he runs the risk that any adverse effects will influence the jury's consideration of the other count. Thus he bears the risk on both counts, although he may benefit on only one. Moreover, a defendant's silence on one count would be damaging in the face of his express denial of the other. Thus he may be coerced into testifying on the count upon which he wished to remain silent. It is not necessary to decide whether this invades his constitutional right to remain silent, since we think it constitutes prejudice within the meaning of Rule 14.

. . . Cross had ample reason not to testify on Count I and would not have done so if that count had been tried separately. In a separate trial of that count the jury would not have heard his admissions of prior convictions and unsavory activities; nor would he have been under duress to offer dubious testimony on that count in order to avoid the damaging implication of testifying on only one of the two joined counts. Since the joinder embarrassed and confounded Cross in making his defense, the joinder was prejudicial within the meaning of Rule 14.

335 F.2d at 989–91, 118 U.S.App.D.C. at 326–28.

B.   JOINDER AND SEVERANCE OF DEFENDANTS

This Section focuses upon the considerations that should permit or prohibit the joining together for trial of two or more defendants who are charged with the same offense or with offenses arising out of the same course of conduct. The related problems raised by the representation of two or more jointly charged defendants by the same defense attorney are considered in Chapter 24, "Effective Assistance of Counsel."

Schaffer v. United States

Supreme Court of the United States, 1960.
362 U.S. 511, 80 S.Ct. 945, 4 L.Ed.2d 921.

■ MR. JUSTICE CLARK delivered the opinion of the Court.

Involved here are questions concerning joinder of defendants under Rule 8(b) of the Federal Rules of Criminal Procedure, 18 U.S.C.A. . . . .

The indictment charged transportation in interstate commerce of goods known to have been stolen and having a value in excess of $5,000. It contained three substantive counts. Count 1 charged the two Schaffers (petitioners in No. 111) and the three Stracuzzas (defendants below, who either pleaded guilty or had the charges against them *nolle prossed* at trial) with transporting stolen ladies' and children's wearing apparel from New York to Pennsylvania. Count 2 charged petitioner Marco and the Stracuzzas with a similar movement of stolen goods from New York to West Virginia. Count 3 charged petitioner Karp and the Stracuzzas with like shipments from New York to Massachusetts. The fourth and final count of the indictment charged all of these parties with a conspiracy to commit the substantive offenses charged in the first three counts. The petitioners here were tried on the indictment simultaneously in a single trial. On motion of petitioners for acquittal at the close of the Government's case, the court dismissed the conspiracy count for failure of proof. This motion was denied, however, as to the substantive counts, the court finding that no prejudice would result from the joint trial. Upon submission of the substantive counts to the jury on a detailed charge, each petitioner was found guilty and thereafter fined and sentenced to prison. The Court of Appeals affirmed the convictions, likewise finding that no prejudice existed by reason of the joint trial. 266 F.2d 435. We granted certiorari. 361 U.S. 809, 80 S.Ct. 58, 4 L.Ed.2d 58.

* * *

We first consider the question of joinder of defendants under Rule 8(b) of the Federal Rules of Criminal Procedure. It is clear that the initial joinder of the petitioners was permissible under that Rule, which allows the joinder of defendants "in the same indictment . . . if they are alleged to have participated in the same act or transaction or in the same series of acts or transactions constituting an offense or offenses." It cannot be denied that the petitioners were so charged in the indictment. The problem remaining is whether, after dismissal of the conspiracy count before submission of the cases to the jury, a severance should have been ordered under Rule 14 of the Federal Rules of Criminal Procedure. This Rule requires a separate trial if "it appears that a defendant or the government is prejudiced by a joinder of offenses or of defendants in an indictment or information or by such joinder for trial together. . . . " Under the circumstances here, we think there was no such prejudice.

It is admitted that the three Stracuzzas were the common center of the scheme to transport the stolen goods. The four petitioners here participated in some steps of the transactions in the stolen goods, although each was involved with separate interstate shipments. The separate substantive charges of the indictment employed almost identical language and alleged violations of the same criminal statute during the same period and in the same manner. This made proof of the over-all operation of the scheme competent as to all counts. The variations in the proof related to the specific shipments proven against each petitioner. This proof was related to each petitioner separately and proven as to each by different witnesses. It included entirely separate invoices and other exhibits, all of which were first clearly identified as applying only to a specific petitioner and were so received and shown to the jury under painstaking instructions to that effect. In short, the proof was carefully compartmentalized as to each petitioner. The propriety of the joinder prior to the failure of proof of conspiracy was not assailed. When the Government rested, however, the petitioners filed their motion for dismissal and it was sustained as to the conspiracy count. The petitioners then pressed for acquittal on the remaining counts, and the court decided that the evidence was sufficient on the substantive counts. The case was submitted to the jury on each of these counts, and under a charge which was characterized by petitioners' counsel as being "extremely fair." This charge meticulously set out separately the evidence as to each of the petitioners and admonished the jury that they were "not to take into consideration any proof against one defendant and apply it by inference or otherwise to any other defendant."

Petitioners contend that prejudice would nevertheless be implicit in a continuation of the joint trial after dismissal of the conspiracy count. They say that the resulting prejudice could not be cured by any cautionary instructions, and that therefore the trial judge was left with no discretion. Petitioners overlook, however, that the joinder was authorized under Rule 8(b) and that subsequent severance was controlled by Rule 14, which provides for separate trials where "it appears that a defendant ... is prejudiced ... by such joinder for trial...." It appears that not only was no prejudice shown, but both the trial court and the Court of Appeals affirmatively found that none was present. We cannot say to the contrary on this record. Nor can we fashion a hard-and-fast formula that, when a conspiracy count fails, joinder is error as a matter of law. We do emphasize, however, that, in such a situation, the trial judge has a continuing duty at all stages of the trial to grant a severance if prejudice does appear. And where, as here, the charge which originally justified joinder turns out to lack the support of sufficient evidence, a trial judge should be particularly sensitive to the possibility of such prejudice. However, the petitioners here not only failed to show any prejudice that would call Rule 14 into operation but even failed to request a new trial. Instead they relied entirely on their motions for acquittal. Moreover, the judge was acutely aware of the possibility of prejudice and was strict in his charge—not only as to the testimony the jury was not to consider, but also as to that evidence which was available in the consideration of the guilt of each petitioner separately under the respective substantive counts. The terms of Rule 8(b) having been met and no prejudice under Rule 14 having been shown, there was no misjoinder.

* * *

The judgments are therefore affirmed.

Affirmed.

■ MR. JUSTICE DOUGLAS, with whom THE CHIEF JUSTICE, MR. JUSTICE BLACK, and MR. JUSTICE BRENNAN concur, dissenting.

* * *

... There must somehow be a nexus between the several transactions charged against the several defendants, lest proof of distinct transactions blend to the prejudice of some defendants. The evidence concerning these petitioners was not in any proper sense of the words evidence concerning "the same series of acts or transactions" constituting an offense. The Schaffers had nothing to do with Karp's shipments to Massachusetts nor Marco's shipments to West Virginia; nor did the latter two have anything to do with Schaffers' shipments to Pennsylvania. The only possible connection between these disparate transactions was the fact that each petitioner dealt with the Stracuzzas, who were the brains of these deals. But that was a happenstance which did not make petitioners any the less strangers to each other. The Pennsylvania, Massachusetts, and West Virginia shipments had nothing in common except that they were all from the house of Stracuzza. Yet customers of one shop, engaged in an illegal enterprise, do not become participants "in the same series of acts or transactions," unless somehow or other what each does is connected up with the others or has some relation to them.

It is said that the joinder was proper if participation "in the same series" of transactions was "alleged" in the indictment. Such an allegation, to be sure, saves the indictment from attack at the preliminary stages. Yet once it becomes apparent during the trial that the defendants have not participated "in the same series" of transactions, it would make a mockery of Rule 8(b) to hold that the allegation alone, now known to be false, is enough to continue the joint trial.

. . . It is not enough to say that evidence of the guilt of each of the present petitioners may have been clear. Reasons for severance are founded on the principle that evidence against one person may not be used against a codefendant whose crime is unrelated to the others. Instructions can be given the jury and admonitions can be made explicit that the line between the various defendants must be kept separate. The district judge conscientiously made that effort here. But where, as here, there is no nexus between the several crimes, the mounting proof of the guilt of one is likely to affect another. There is no sure way to protect against it except by separate trials, especially where, as here, the several defendants, though unconnected, commit the crimes charged by dealing with one person, one house, one establishment. By a joint trial of such separate offenses, a subtle bond is likely to be created between the several defendants though they have never met nor acted in unison; prejudice within the meaning of Rule 14 is implicit.

* * *

NOTES

1. **Circumstances mandating severance.** What are some of the circumstances that should require a trial court to sever the cases of defendants joined for trial? Should it be sufficient that one defendant in testifying in his own behalf intends to incriminate a codefendant? See People v. Braune, 363 Ill. 551, 2 N.E.2d 839 (1936). That one defendant chooses to represent himself while the co-defendant is represented by counsel? See United States v. Sacco, 563 F.2d 552 (2d Cir.1977). That one defendant intends to testify while another does not? See United States v. Shuford, 454 F.2d 772 (4th Cir.1971). That the attorney for the testifying defendant intends to comment to the jury on the failure of a codefendant to testify? See De Luna v. United States, 308 F.2d 140 (5th Cir.1962). That one defendant intends to testify as to a joint alibi with a codefendant, an alibi which the co-defendant wishes his attorney to disavow to the jury? See United States v. Gambrill, 449 F.2d 1148, 146 U.S.App.D.C. 72 (D.C.Cir.1971). That one defendant would testify in favor of a co-defendant in a severed trial but intends not to testify in his own trial? See Byrd v. Wainwright, 428 F.2d 1017 (5th Cir.1970). That one defendant has a prior criminal record that will be admissible in evidence while the other does not? See Hardin v. Commonwealth, 437 S.W.2d 931 (Ky.App. 1968). See, generally, Dawson, Joint Trials of Defendants in Criminal Cases: An Analysis of Efficiencies and Prejudices, 77 Mich.L.Rev. 1379 (1979).

2. **Antagonistic defenses.** The Supreme Court considered the issue when severance of defendants is required because of mutually antagonistic defenses in Zafiro v. United States, 506 U.S. 534, 113 S.Ct. 933, 122 L.Ed.2d 317 (1993).

Defendants Garcia and Soto were confronted by government agents while carrying a box up the stairs of an apartment building. They dropped the box and ran into an apartment. The box contained 55 pounds of cocaine. In the apartment, agents found two other persons, Zafiro and Martinez. A search of the apartment revealed a suitcase with 16 pounds of cocaine, a small quantity of heroin and 4 pounds of marijuana. Next to the suitcase was a sack containing over $20,000 in cash. All four were charged with various drug offenses. Each moved for severance from the other defendants. Soto claimed he knew nothing about what was in the box he and Garcia were carrying. Garcia claimed the box belonged to Soto and that Garcia was ignorant of its contents. Zafiro, whose apartment it was, claimed she knew nothing of the drugs in the suitcase, which belonged to her boyfriend, Martinez. Martinez' position was that he was just visiting his girlfriend and had no idea she was involved in distributing drugs. The District Court denied severance and a joint trial resulted in the conviction of each defendant. The Court of Appeals affirmed the convictions over the claim that severance was required because of the nature of the defenses presented at the trial.

The Supreme Court, in an opinion by Justice O'Connor, affirmed. Asserting there is a preference in the federal system for joint trials of defendants who are indicted together, the Court rejected the argument that severance is mandated whenever mutually antagonistic defenses are asserted. Rather,

> a district court should grant a severance under Rule 14 only if there is a serious risk that a joint trial would compromise a specific trial right of one of the defendants, or prevent the jury from making a reliable judgment about guilt or innocence. Such a risk might occur when evidence that the jury should not consider against a defendant and that would not be admissible if a defendant were tried alone is admitted against a codefendant. For example, evidence of a codefendant's wrongdoing in some circumstances erroneously could lead a jury to conclude that a defendant was guilty. When many defendants are tried together in a complex case and they have markedly different degrees of culpability, this risk of prejudice is heightened. Evidence that is probative of a defendant's guilt but technically admissible only against a codefendant also might present a risk of prejudice * * *. Conversely, a defendant might suffer prejudice if essential exculpatory evidence that would be available to a defendant tried alone were unavailable in a joint trial.

506 U.S. at 539, 113 S.Ct. at 938, 122 L.Ed.2d at 325. The Court concluded that the District Court's instructions to the jury to consider each defendant's fate individually were sufficient protection on these facts. Justice Stevens concurred in the judgment, noting that the defenses asserted in this case were not truly mutually antagonistic in that it was possible to believe one defense without also believing that the other defendant was for that reason guilty.

3. **Accusatory confessions.** In Bruton v. United States, 391 U.S. 123, 88 S.Ct. 1620, 20 L.Ed.2d 476 (1968) petitioner was jointly tried with one Evans for armed postal robbery. In the trial, a postal inspector testified that Evans had confessed guilt to him and had named Bruton as his partner in the offense. Evans did not testify and the trial court instructed the jury that it could not consider Evans' confession as evidence against Bruton. The Supreme Court concluded that the procedure employed violated Bruton's right to confrontation of witnesses:

> Not every admission of inadmissible hearsay or other evidence can be considered to be reversible error unavoidable through limiting instructions; instances occur in almost every trial where inadmissible evidence creeps in, usually inadvertently. "A defendant is entitled to a fair trial but not a perfect one." Lutwak v. United States, 344 U.S. 604, 619, 73 S.Ct. 481, 490, 97 L.Ed. 593; see Hopt v. People of Utah, 120 U.S. 430, 438, 7 S.Ct. 614, 617, 30 L.Ed. 708; cf.

Fed.Rule Crim.Proc. 52(a). It is not unreasonable to conclude that in many such cases the jury can and will follow the trial judge's instructions to disregard such information. Nevertheless, ... there are some contexts in which the risk that the jury will not, or cannot, follow instructions is so great, and the consequences of failure so vital to the defendant, that the practical and human limitations of the jury system cannot be ignored. Such a context is presented here, where the powerfully incriminating extrajudicial statements of a co-defendant, who stands accused side-by-side with the defendant, are deliberately spread before the jury in a joint trial. Not only are the incriminations devastating to the defendant but their credibility is inevitably suspect, a fact recognized when accomplices do take the stand and the jury is instructed to weigh their testimony carefully given the recognized motivation to shift blame onto others. The unreliability of such evidence is intolerably compounded when the alleged accomplice, as here, does not testify and cannot be tested by cross-examination. It was against such threats to a fair trial that the Confrontation Clause was directed.

391 U.S. at 135–36, 88 S.Ct. 1627–28, 20 L.Ed.2d at 484–85.

4. **Redacting accusatory confessions.** The Supreme Court considered the validity of editing a co-defendant's confession to eliminate references to the defendant (redaction) in Richardson v. Marsh, 481 U.S. 200, 107 S.Ct. 1702, 95 L.Ed.2d 176 (1987). Marsh was being jointly tried with one Williams for two murders committed during a robbery. Williams had confessed to police, and had stated that Marsh and Martin (a fugitive at the time of trial) had knowingly participated in the offenses with him. Williams' confession was edited by the trial court to eliminate all references not only to Marsh but to the participation by any party in the offense other than Martin. Williams' confession recounted a conversation between Williams and Martin while driving to the scene of the offense with Marsh, in which Martin stated he would kill the victims after the robbery. As so edited, it was introduced in his joint trial with Marsh. Williams did not testify, but Marsh did. She admitted presence at the scene of the offenses, but denied she knew a robbery was to occur, stating she did not hear the conversation in the car between Williams and Martin because she was in the back seat next to a radio speaker. One of the surviving victims testified that Marsh admitted Williams into her home and prevented her and her son from escaping during the robbery. The trial court instructed the jury that it could not consider Williams' confession against Marsh. In federal habeas corpus, the Sixth Circuit held that the redaction was ineffectual because other evidence linked Marsh with the offense and created an unacceptable risk the jury considered the confession in its context as evidence against Marsh in violation of the Confrontation Clause. The Supreme Court, in an opinion authored by Justice Scalia, reversed the Court of Appeals. Because the co-defendant's confession in *Bruton* named Bruton as a participant in the offense, the risk was unacceptable that the jury would be unable to follow the trial court's instruction not to consider it against him.

By contrast, in this case the confession was not incriminating on its face, and became so only when linked with evidence introduced later at trial (the defendant's own testimony).

Where the necessity of such linkage is involved, it is a less valid generalization that the jury will not likely obey the instruction to disregard the evidence. Specific testimony that "the defendant helped me commit the crime" is more vivid than inferential incrimination, and hence more difficult to thrust out of mind. Moreover, with regard to such an explicit statement the only issue is, plain and simply, whether the jury can possibly be expected to forget it in assessing the defendant's guilt; whereas with regard to inferential incrimination the judge's instruction may well be successful in dissuading the jury from entering onto the path of inference in the first place, so that there is no incrimination to forget. In short, while it may not always be simple for the members of a jury to obey the instruction that they disregard an incriminating inference, there does not exist the overwhelming probability of their inability to do so that is the foundation of *Bruton*'s exception to the general rule [that juries follow instructions].

481 U.S. at 208, 107 S.Ct. at 1707–08, 95 L.Ed.2d at 186. The Court held that "the Confrontation Clause is not violated by the admission of a nontestifying codefendant's confession with a proper limiting instruction when, as here, the confession is redacted to eliminate not only the defendant's name, but any references to her existence." 481 U.S. at 211, 107 S.Ct. at 1709, 95 L.Ed.2d at 188. Finally, the Court noted that it expressed "no opinion on the admissibility of a confession in which the defendant's name has been replaced with a symbol or neutral pronoun." 481 U.S. at 211, n. 5, 107 S.Ct. at 1709, n. 5, 95 L.Ed.2d at 188, n. 5. Justice Stevens, joined by Justices Brennan and Marshall, dissented.

The petitioner in Gray v. Maryland, 523 U.S. 185, 118 S.Ct. 1151, 140 L.Ed.2d 294 (1998) was convicted of involuntary manslaughter in a joint trial with one Bell. At the trial, Bell's custodial confession was read which detailed his, Gray's and a deceased third person's role along with unnamed others in the assault and killing of Stacey. Gray's and the other person's names were deleted and replaced with blank spaces or the word "deleted." As read to the jury, part of the confession was as follows:

Question: Who was in the group that beat Stacey?

Answer: Me, deleted, deleted, and a few other guys.

Immediately after the redacted confession was read to the jury, the prosecutor asked the detective "after he gave you that information, you subsequently were able to arrest Mr. Kevin Gray; is that correct?" To which he responded, "That's correct." The written statement admitted into evidence and shown to the jury replaced Gray's and the deceased co-actor's name with "deleted" or a blank space set apart by commas: ", ,". The trial court instructed the jury that the confession was evidence only against Bell, who had not testified. Gray testified and denied participation in the offense. Although the Maryland Court of Appeals reversed the conviction on *Bruton* grounds, the Maryland high court reversed the Court of Appeals. The United States Supreme Court, in an opinion by Justice Breyer, vacated the conviction and remanded, holding that *Bruton* not Richardson v. Marsh controlled this case.

The five-judge majority distinguished *Richardson* on the ground that the confession in that case was redacted to eliminate any reference to Richardson or any other third person at all, while in this case the redaction clearly referenced two other persons, and that the jury would likely decide that Gray was one of the "deleted" persons. The majority opinion provided this explanation of possible jury behavior:

Consider a simplified but typical example, a confession that reads "I, Bob Smith, along with Sam Jones, robbed the bank." To replace the words "Sam Jones" with an obvious blank will not likely fool anyone. A juror somewhat familiar with criminal law would know immediately that the blank, in the phrase "I, Bob Smith, along with , robbed the bank," refers to defendant Jones. A juror who does not know the law and who therefore wonders to whom the blank might refer need only lift his eyes to Jones, sitting at counsel table, to find what will seem the obvious answer, at least if the juror hears the judge's instruction not to consider the confession as evidence against Jones, for that instruction will provide an obvious reason for the blank. A more sophisticated juror, wondering if the blank refers to someone else, might also wonder how, if it did, the prosecutor could argue the confession is reliable, for the prosecutor, after all, has been arguing that Jones, not someone else, helped Smith commit the crime.

523 U.S. at 198, 118 S.Ct. at 1155, 140 L.Ed.2d at 301. Justice Scalia, joined by The Chief Justice, Justice Kennedy and Justice Thomas, dissented on the ground *Richardson* controls this case. Justice Scalia objected to any redaction beyond the obvious deletion of names:

> For inchoate offenses—conspiracy in particular—redaction to delete all references to a confederate would often render the confession nonsensical. If the question was "Who agreed to beat Stacey?", and the answer was "Me and Kevin," we might redact the answer to "Me and [deleted]," or perhaps to "Me and somebody else," but surely not to just "Me"—for that would no longer be a confession to the conspiracy charge, but rather the foundation for an insanity defense. To my knowledge we have never before endorsed—and to my strong belief we should not endorse—the redaction of a statement by some means other than the deletion of certain words, with the fact of the deletion shown. The risk to the integrity of our system (not to mention the increase in its complexity) posed by the approval of such free-lance editing seems to me infinitely greater than the risk posed by the entirely honest reproduction that the Court disapproves.

523 U.S. at 203–04, 118 S.Ct. at 1160, 140 L.Ed.2d at 307–08.

CHAPTER 20

DOUBLE JEOPARDY

Analysis

EDITORS' INTRODUCTION: THE INTERESTS PROTECTED

The Fifth Amendment, after providing that no person is to be held to answer for an infamous crime except on presentation or indictment by a grand jury, continues, "nor shall any person be subject for the same offense to be twice put in jeopardy of life or limb.... " This prohibition against double jeopardy was held binding on the states in Benton v. Maryland, 395 U.S. 784, 89 S.Ct. 2056, 23 L.Ed.2d 707 (1969), overruling Palko v. Connecticut, 302 U.S. 319, 58 S.Ct. 149, 82 L.Ed. 288 (1937):

> The fundamental nature of the guarantee against double jeopardy can hardly be doubted. Its origin can be traced to Greek and Roman times, and it became established in the common law of England long before this Nation's independence. ...Today, every state incorporates some form of the prohibition in its constitution or common law. As this court put it in Green v. United States, 355 U.S. 184, 187–88, 78 S.Ct. 221, 223, 2 L.Ed.2d 199, 204 (1957), "[t]he underlying idea, one that is

deeply ingrained in at least the Anglo–American system of jurisprudence, is that the State with all its resources and power should not be allowed to make repeated attempts to convict an individual for an alleged offense, thereby subjecting him to embarrassment, expense and ordeal and compelling him to live in a continuing state of anxiety and insecurity, as well as enhancing the possibility that even though innocent he may be found guilty."

395 U.S. at 795–96, 89 S.Ct. at 2063, 23 L.Ed.2d at 716–17.

The interests furthered by the prohibition against double jeopardy may be more complex than the language from *Green* indicates. Clearly, the prohibition recognizes and implements an interest in finality. Once put into jeopardy, a defendant has a legitimate interest in having to defend that proceeding but that proceeding only. As the *Green* language suggests, this may be because repeated trials create an unacceptable risk that an innocent defendant will be convicted. But as that same language suggests, this interest seems also to be based upon an independent notion that "fairness" to defendants demands that the government limit itself to one effort to establish a defendant's guilt.

It is also possible that the prohibition protects against multiple punishment. Commentators and courts have traditionally regarded this as an established part of the basis for double jeopardy doctrine. See Westen and Drubel, supra at 84, 106–22. But Whalen v. United States, 445 U.S. 684, 100 S.Ct. 1432, 63 L.Ed.2d 715 (1980), discussed below, suggests that the Court may not regard the prohibition as addressing the propriety of multiple punishment where only a single proceeding is involved.

Double jeopardy issues arise in a variety of procedural contexts. But there are a number of matters sufficiently general to warrant preliminary discussion.

Raising and Resolving Double Jeopardy Issues

Under common law pleading practice, former acquittal and former conviction were pleas in bar and "a mass of learning grew up concerning those pleas both with respect to the manner in which they could be proved and the circumstances under which they were available." L. Orfield, Criminal Procedure from Arrest to Appeal 268 (1947). The procedure for assertion of a claim of former jeopardy differs among jurisdictions under modern law, but the matter is usually one that is to be raised and resolved prior to the trial on the merits. Id. at 306; Fed.R.Crim.Proc., Rule 12. In a number of jurisdictions, however, if a claim of former jeopardy raises a question of fact, this is to be submitted to the jury along with guilt-innocence issues. Kite v. State, 506 P.2d 946 (Okla.Crim.App.1973). Apparently there is no right to a jury determination of such fact issues in the federal courts, and the determination of the merits of a claim of former jeopardy is to be made by the trial judge. United States v. Young, 503 F.2d 1072 (3d Cir.1974).

In Abney v. United States, 431 U.S. 651, 97 S.Ct. 2034, 52 L.Ed.2d 651 (1977), the defendant in a federal criminal prosecution had filed a motion to dismiss on double jeopardy grounds. The District Court denied the motion and Abney sought to take an interlocutory appeal under 28 U.S.C.A. § 1291, which authorizes appeal from all "final decisions" of the district courts. The Supreme Court held that the district court's order denying the motion to dismiss was a final order within the meaning of the statute. It was a complete and—for trial purposes—final rejection of the claim. Moreover, it concerned a claim collateral to, and separable from, the issue of guilt or innocence. Further:

> [T]he rights conferred on a criminal accused by the Double Jeopardy Clause would be significantly undermined if appellate review of double jeopardy claims were postponed until after conviction and sentence. . . . [T]his court has long recognized that the Double Jeopardy Clause protects an individual against more than being subjected to double punishments. It is a guarantee against being twice put to *trial* for the same offense. . . . It thus protects interests wholly unrelated to the propriety of any subsequent conviction. . . . Obviously, these aspects of the guarantee's protections would be lost if the accused were forced to "run the gauntlet" a second time before an appeal could be taken; even if the accused is acquitted, or, if convicted, has his conviction ultimately reversed on double jeopardy grounds, he has still been forced to endure a trial that the Double Jeopardy Clause was designed to prohibit. Consequently, if a criminal defendant is to avoid *exposure* to double jeopardy and thereby enjoy the full protection of the Clause, his double jeopardy challenge to the indictment must be reviewable before that subsequent exposure occurs.

431 U.S. at 660–62, 97 S.Ct. at 2040–41, 52 L.Ed.2d at 660–61 (emphasis in original). Is it possible that inherent in the Double Jeopardy Clause is a right to interlocutory appellate review of a rejection of a double jeopardy claim? In *Abney,* the Court "approached" the question of statutory construction before it with the principle in mind that there is no constitutional right to appeal. 431 U.S. at 656, 97 S.Ct. at 2038, 52 L.Ed.2d at 657–58. Perhaps if a state chooses to make appellate review of double jeopardy claims available to defendants, it is constitutionally necessary that such review be available on an interlocutory basis.

Abney, then, suggests the desirability and perhaps the constitutional necessity of pretrial resolution of double jeopardy claims. In interesting contrast is Illinois v. Vitale, 447 U.S. 410, 100 S.Ct. 2260, 65 L.Ed.2d 228 (1980). An automobile driven by Vitale struck two small children; both died as a result of the accident. At the scene, a traffic citation was issued charging Vitale with failing to reduce speed in violation of § 11–601(a) of the Illinois Vehicle Code, which provides that "[s]peed must be decreased as necessary to avoid colliding with any person. . . . " Vitale was convicted of the violation and a fine of $15 was imposed. The next day, a petition was filed in juvenile court alleging that Vitale "without lawful justification while recklessly driving a motor vehicle" caused the death of the two children killed in the accident, and thereby committed involuntary manslaughter. The relevant part of the Illinois Criminal Code, Ill.Rev.Stat.1973 ch. 38, § 9–3, provided that "[a] person who kills an individual without lawful justification commits involuntary manslaughter if his acts . . . which cause the death are such as are likely to cause death or great bodily harm to some individual, and he performs them recklessly." A motion to dismiss was filed on the ground that the manslaughter prosecution was violative of double jeopardy. The Illinois courts ultimately held that the motion should have been granted because "failing to reduce speed" was a lesser included offense of involuntary manslaughter and the conviction for the former barred prosecution for the latter. In re Vitale, 71 Ill.2d 229, 375 N.E.2d 87, 16 Ill.Dec. 456 (1978).

The Supreme Court reversed and remanded. Justice White, speaking for a majority of the Court, concluded that under Illinois law proof of involuntary manslaughter may not always require proof of failure to slow. The "acts ... likely to cause death or great bodily injury [performed] recklessly," required by the manslaughter statute, might but need not always involve failing to decrease speed to avoid a collision with a person. If, as a matter of Illinois law, a careless failure to slow is *always* a necessary element of involuntary manslaughter, then the *trial* on the manslaughter charge would be barred. But "the mere possibility that the State will seek to rely on [the failure to slow] to establish an element of its manslaughter case would not be sufficient to bar the latter prosecution," the majority concluded. If, however, the State at trial actually proved the failure to slow as a necessary element of its manslaughter charge, or if before trial it conceded that it planned to do so, Vitale's claim of double jeopardy "would be substantial." 447 U.S. at 419–20, 100 S.Ct. at 2266–67, 65 L.Ed.2d at 238.

Justice Stevens, joined by Justices Brennan, Stewart, and Marshall, dissented. He urged that the majority's implication that the State may go to trial before Vitale is entitled to a determination concerning his claim of double jeopardy violates "the vital interest in avoiding a second trial" emphasized in *Abney:*

> If a defendant is entitled to have an appellate court rule on his double jeopardy claim in advance of trial, he is surely entitled to a definitive ruling by the trial court in advance of trial. Since the State has not provided [Vitale] with notice of any basis for the prosecution that does not depend upon proving, for the second time, a careless failure to reduce speed, I would not require [him] to stand trial again.

447 U.S. at 427–28, 100 S.Ct. at 2271, 65 L.Ed.2d at 242–43.

The ramifications of *Vitale* are not clear. Two offenses may have such a relationship that one is a "necessarily included offense" of the other; this relationship exists only if, given the abstract definitions of the two offenses, proof of one always and necessarily involves proof of the other. The *Vitale* dicta indicate that where this relationship exists, a second trial is barred, i.e., a defendant is entitled to a pretrial determination that an asserted claim of double jeopardy is meritorious. But situations where this "necessarily included offense" relationship does not exist may be such that in its proof of one crime the government will in fact rely upon all of the facts used in a prior proceeding to establish guilt of another. In such cases, one of the offenses is an "included offense" of the other, although not a *necessarily* included one. *Vitale* seems to hold that in such situations a defendant's claim of double jeopardy need not be resolved prior to trial unless the government "concedes" that it will rely upon proof of the included offense at trial. Where no such concession is made, a defendant's claim of double jeopardy need not be resolved until during or after trial, when the trial court can determine whether or not the government is relying on proof of the included offense. Is this consistent with the policy interests stressed in *Abney?*

It does not appear that Vitale made any efforts before trial to require the government to specify what evidence it would rely upon in its efforts to prove him guilty of manslaughter. Suppose Vitale had moved for greater specification in the allegations and had urged that such greater specificity was essential to vindicating his interest in having any valid double jeopardy claim determined in his favor before he was required to "run the gauntlet" a second time. Under *Abney,* would he be constitutionally entitled to such greater specificity? As a matter of sound procedural policy, should defendants be entitled to such pretrial specificity of the proof that will be relied upon by the government at trial?

Attachment of Jeopardy

One proceeding does not bar a subsequent prosecution unless jeopardy attached in the first proceeding. Unless jeopardy attached, the disposition of the case cannot conceivably be regarded as an acquittal or a conviction and the absence of a reasonable basis for terminating it will not preclude the government from starting anew. Therefore, it is of major importance to identify the point in a criminal proceeding at which jeopardy attaches. The matter was addressed in Crist v. Bretz, 437 U.S. 28, 98 S.Ct. 2156, 57 L.Ed.2d 24 (1978). Defendants' first prosecution had been terminated after a jury was empaneled and sworn but before any witnesses were called by the state. In a subsequent trial, their double jeopardy objection was overruled on the ground that jeopardy had not attached in the first proceeding. The Supreme Court held this to be constitutional error. The time when jeopardy attaches in a jury trial "serves as the lynchpin for all double jeopardy jurisprudence," the majority noted, and consequently the traditional federal rule—that jeopardy attaches in a jury trial when the jury is empaneled and sworn—is an integral part of the constitutional guarantee against double jeopardy and is binding on the states. 437 U.S. at 38, 98 S.Ct. at 2162, 57 L.Ed.2d at 33. In a bench trial, the federal rule has been that jeopardy attaches when the court begins to hear evidence, i.e., when the first witness is sworn. Serfass v. United States, 420 U.S. 377, 388, 95 S.Ct. 1055, 1062, 43 L.Ed.2d 265, 274 (1975). *Bretz* strongly suggests this rule will be regarded a part of the federal constitutional standard and also binding on the states.

"Separate Sovereignties" Exception

The Supreme Court has repeatedly held that successive prosecutions based on the same conduct are permissible if they are brought by separate and distinct "sovereignties." Whether the first prosecution resulted in acquittal or conviction is apparently of no consequence. Thus trial in a state court does not bar trial in federal court on the basis of the same conduct. Bartkus v. Illinois, 359 U.S. 121, 79 S.Ct. 676, 3 L.Ed.2d 684 (1959); Abbate v. United States, 359 U.S. 187, 79 S.Ct. 666, 3 L.Ed.2d 729

(1959). Conceptually, the Court has reasoned that two offenses are involved, one under the law of each of the two sovereignties, and thus the prohibition against multiple jeopardy for the "same" offense is not violated. See United States v. Wheeler, 435 U.S. 313, 317, 98 S.Ct. 1079, 1082–83, 55 L.Ed.2d 303, 309 (1978). The policy justification for the exception, the Court has stressed, is that each sovereignty has an interest independent of the interest of the other in punishing the conduct. To permit one sovereignty to frustrate the interest of the other by initiating prosecution first would unacceptably deprive the other sovereignty of its right to enforce its own laws. United States v. Wheeler, supra, 435 U.S. at 317–18, 98 S.Ct. at 1083, 55 L.Ed.2d at 309.

A limitation upon the exception is the requirement that the two prosecutions be brought by entities that are in fact separate sovereignties. The federal government and a state government or its subdivision are separate sovereignties. Abbate v. United States, supra. But a state and its municipalities are not, and successive prosecutions by a municipality and then the state itself violates double jeopardy. Waller v. Florida, 397 U.S. 387, 90 S.Ct. 1184, 25 L.Ed.2d 435 (1970). The United States Government and an Indian tribe, however, are separate sovereignties. United States v. Wheeler, supra. Two prosecuting authorities are separate sovereignties under this requirement if the power of each to punish the conduct at issue is "inherent." If one prosecuting authority is merely exercising authority delegated by the other, the two authorities are not separate sovereignties and successive prosecutions are barred. United States v. Wheeler, supra.

In Heath v. Alabama, 474 U.S. 82, 106 S.Ct. 433, 88 L.Ed.2d 387 (1985), the Court applied the doctrine of separate sovereignties to the prosecution of petitioner by Alabama for committing murder during a kidnapping after he had been convicted in Georgia for the same homicide. In an opinion for the Court, Justice O'Connor concluded that Alabama and Georgia were separate sovereignties under the *Wheeler* test and that the same conduct could, therefore, form the basis of a criminal prosecution by each. The petitioner had argued the Court should adopt a balancing test and permit multiple prosecutions in this situation only if "allowing only one entity to exercise jurisdiction over the defendant will interfere with the unvindicated interests of the second entity and that multiple prosecutions therefore are necessary for the satisfaction of the legitimate interests of both entities." 474 U.S. at 92, 106 S.Ct. at 439, 88 L.Ed.2d at 396. The Court rejected this argument:

> A State's interest in vindicating its sovereign authority through enforcement of its laws by definition can never be satisfied by another State's enforcement of *its* own laws. Just as the Federal Government has the right to decide that a state prosecution has not vindicated a violation of the "peace and dignity" of the Federal Government, a State must be entitled to decide that a prosecution by another State has not satisfied its legitimate sovereign interest.

474 U.S. at 93, 106 S.Ct. at 440, 88 L.Ed.2d at 397. Justices Brennan and Marshall dissented.

In 1959, the United States Attorney General acknowledged that the government's ability to prosecute following state proceedings could, if applied indiscriminately and with bad judgment, cause considerable hard-ship. As a result, he promulgated a department policy of bringing federal prosecution after a state trial for the same act or acts only where "the reasons are compelling." Further, no such federal case is to be tried without approval by an Assistant Attorney General, who should bring the case to the attention of the Attorney General before granting approval. See 27 U.S.Law Week 2509 (April 7, 1959). This policy, and the related Justice Department policy of prosecuting together different offenses arising out of the same transaction, came to be known as the "Petite Policy," after Petite v. United States, 361 U.S. 529, 80 S.Ct. 450, 4 L.Ed.2d 490 (1960). In *Petite,* the Supreme Court, at the request of the government, directed dismissal of a federal prosecution which the government determined to have been brought in violation of its policy announced in 1959.

The roles of the courts and the Justice Department in the enforcement of the *Petite* policy were raised in Rinaldi v. United States, 434 U.S. 22, 98 S.Ct. 81, 54 L.Ed.2d 207 (1977). Rinaldi and several companions participat-ed in a plot to rob safe-deposit boxes in a Miami hotel. In February, 1973, they were charged with state offenses based on this activity and, one month later, federal indictments were returned based on the same conduct. In May, Rinaldi was convicted of the state charges and sentenced to six years imprisonment. Nevertheless, the federal prosecution proceeded to trial. Later, it appeared that this was because a Justice Department official (not the appropriate Assistant Attorney General) feared the state conviction would be reversed on appeal. In violation of the *Petite* policy, no approval was obtained from the appropriate Assistant United States Attorney Gener-al; it is not clear whether such approval would have been granted had it been sought. Rinaldi was tried and convicted of the federal charges and received a twelve-year prison term. The government then moved to dismiss the prosecution because of the violation of the *Petite* policy. The motive for this is not entirely clear. On oral argument before the Fifth Circuit, counsel for the government indicated that dismissal was sought at this time because Rinaldi's state conviction had been affirmed by the state's interme-diate appellate court (although it had not yet been considered by the state's highest appellate tribunal) and therefore its integrity was sufficiently assured. But the Solicitor General subsequently took the position that dismissal was sought only because it was discovered at this time by the Assistant Attorney General in charge of enforcement of the *Petite* policy that the prior authorization required by the policy had not been obtained.

The federal district court denied the motion to dismiss. United States v. Washington, 390 F.Supp. 842 (S.D.Fla.1975). This was affirmed on appeal to penalize the government's bad faith attempt to manipulate judicial time and resources through a "capricious, inconsistent application" of the *Petite* policy. In re Washington, 544 F.2d 203 (5th Cir.1976) (en banc). The court commented that it could not understand how Rinaldi might have been unfairly harmed by this, since he was convicted in an apparently fair trial and still retained the right to appeal his conviction. 544 F.2d at 209.

The Supreme Court reversed, and directed dismissal of the case. The majority found that the government's motion to dismiss was made without bad faith, and was not tainted by any bad faith that might have existed earlier in the case. The record was entirely consistent with the Government's argument that the Assistant Attorney General in charge of enforcement of the *Petite* policy was unaware of its violation until shortly before the filing of the motion to dismiss. The purpose of the *Petite* policy is to protect individuals from unfairness associated with needless multiple prosecutions; "the defendant, therefore, should receive the benefit of the policy whenever its application is urged by the government." 434 U.S. at 31, 98 S.Ct. at 86, 54 L.Ed.2d at 215. Turning to the intermediate appellate court's conclusion that denial of the motion for dismissal was justified by the need to deter misconduct by prosecutors, the majority responded, "we fail to see how rewarding those responsible for the *Petite* policy violation with a conviction serves to deter prosecutorial misconduct." 434 U.S. at 31 n. 17, 86 S.Ct. at 86 n. 17, 54 L.Ed.2d at 215 n. 17. If the government were to pursue federal prosecution on the sole basis that the state conviction might fall on appeal, the Court commented, this "would indeed mark a departure from the *Petite* policy." 434 U.S. at 30 n. 16, 98 S.Ct. at 86 n. 16, 54 L.Ed.2d at 214 n. 16.

Suppose the defendant but not the government urges that nonprosecution is dictated by the *Petite* policy? Should a federal trial judge consider what result is dictated by the policy, or should the government's interpretation of the policy be conclusive? In *Rinaldi,* the district judge commented that the federal sentences were more severe than those imposed in the state proceedings, 390 F.Supp. at 844, suggesting that he may have regarded the low penalties in the state proceeding as a "compelling reason", under the *Petite* policy, rendering federal prosecution appropriate. Could the dismissal have been denied on this basis, or is the determination as to the adequacy of the sentence imposed in the state proceeding solely within the prerogative of the government?

Government Appeal

The limits placed by double jeopardy upon the ability of the government to appeal in criminal proceedings presents a number of difficult problems. For many years, the existence of statutory limitations upon such appeals made it unnecessary for the federal courts to reach constitutional questions. But in 1970, Congress amended the Criminal Appeals Act, 18 U.S.C.A. § 3731, so as to authorize government appeals in federal prosecutions wherever this was permitted by the Constitution. See United States v. Wilson, 420 U.S. 332, 337, 95 S.Ct. 1013, 1019, 43 L.Ed.2d 232, 238 (1975). This has required the Court to discuss the impact of the double jeopardy clause upon governmental appeals in a number of post–1970 decisions.

The leading brief for virtually unlimited governmental appeals was authored by Justice Holmes, dissenting in Kepner v. United States, 195 U.S. 100, 134–37, 24 S.Ct. 797, 806–07, 49 L.Ed. 114, 126–28 (1904). A defendant is not placed in jeopardy more than once, he reasoned, as long as both (or all) trials are part of the same cause. The system of appellate review that Justice Holmes' "continuing jeopardy" concept would permit was characterized by the Court in United States v. Wilson, supra, as having "symmetry to recommend it" and as avoiding release of some defendants who have benefited from instructions or evidentiary rulings unduly favorable to them. But the Court rejected it, as it had before, explaining that such a system

> would allow the prosecutor to seek to persuade a second trier of fact of the defendant's guilt after having failed with the first; it would permit him to re-examine the weaknesses in his first presentation in order to strengthen the second; and it would disserve the defendant's legitimate interest in the finality of a verdict of acquittal.

420 U.S. at 352, 95 S.Ct. at 1026, 43 L.Ed.2d at 246–47.

But the Court has also rejected the notion that double jeopardy should bar any appeal from a ruling in favor of the defendant or any termination of the proceeding in the defendant's favor. In *Wilson*, after the jury had returned a verdict of guilty, the trial judge granted a defense motion to dismiss on the ground that the proceedings were brought in violation of the defendant's Due Process rights. In making this determination, the trial judge relied in part upon the evidence produced at trial and apparently upon what this evidence showed concerning the impact of the delay upon the defendant's ability fairly to challenge the government's case. Opposing the government's efforts to appeal the trial judge's ruling, Wilson urged that double jeopardy bars appeal of any order discharging a defendant when that order is based on facts outside of the indictment. The majority in *Wilson* rejected this argument and held that the double jeopardy bar against government appeals applies only when there is a danger of subjecting the defendant to a second trial for the same offense. Explaining, the Court stated:

> Although review of any ruling of law discharging a defendant obviously enhances the likelihood of conviction and subjects him to continuing expense and anxiety, a defendant has no legitimate claim to benefit from an error of law when that error could be corrected without subjecting him to a second trial before a second trier of fact.

420 U.S. at 345, 95 S.Ct. at 1023, 43 L.Ed.2d at 242–43. Where the government could, on appeal, be granted relief without subjecting the defendant to a second trial, double jeopardy is not violated by the appeal. Should the government win on the merits in *Wilson*, the appellate court could simply remand the case with directions to the trial judge to enter judgment on the jury verdict. Since no retrial would be necessary to grant the government relief should it win, appeal by the government is permissible.

Several procedural consequences of this position articulated in *Wilson* are clear from the caselaw. The government may appeal from a ruling made before jeopardy attaches; since no trial has been held, there is no danger of a second trial following a governmental victory on appeal. United States v. Sanford, 429 U.S. 14, 97 S.Ct. 20, 50 L.Ed.2d 17 (1976); Serfass v. United States, 420 U.S. 377, 95 S.Ct. 1055, 43 L.Ed.2d 265 (1975).

If the defendant prevails on appeal in a system with several tiers of appellate tribunals, the government may seek further review of the intermediate court's ruling. The intermediate court can be reversed without subjecting the defendant to a second trial. Forman v. United States, 361

U.S. 416, 80 S.Ct. 481, 4 L.Ed.2d 412 (1960). At least some post-verdict actions by the trial judge can be appealed, because the appellate court can reverse and remand with directions to reinstate the verdict already returned in the previously-held trial. United States v. Morrison, 429 U.S. 1, 97 S.Ct. 24, 50 L.Ed.2d 1 (1976) (government could appeal trial judge's ruling, made after a finding of guilty at a nonjury trial, that the marijuana which was the subject of the charge should be suppressed and that the trial court would "take appropriate action consistent with" this ruling—apparently acquitting the defendant—if the ruling was not appealed or if it was affirmed on appeal); United States v. Wilson, supra.

On the other hand, it is clear that the government cannot appeal from an acquittal. Fong Foo v. United States, 369 U.S. 141, 82 S.Ct. 671, 7 L.Ed.2d 629 (1962) (Court of Appeals erred in granting writ of mandamus ordering trial judge to retry defendants after trial judge had erroneously directed jury to return verdict of acquittal and entered formal judgment of acquittal). In United States v. Martin Linen Supply Co., 430 U.S. 564, 97 S.Ct. 1349, 51 L.Ed.2d 642 (1977), the jury in defendants' criminal contempt trial could not agree on a verdict and was discharged. As was permitted by Rule 29(c) of the Federal Rules of Criminal Procedure, defendants then made a timely motion for judgments of acquittal which was granted by the trial judge. The government sought to appeal; the Supreme Court held that appeal was barred. The judgments entered by the trial court were acquittals "in substance as well as form" 430 U.S. at 572, 97 S.Ct. at 1355, 51 L.Ed.2d at 651, and the application of double jeopardy should not be affected by the timing of the trial judge in entering a judgment of acquittal. 430 U.S. at 575, 97 S.Ct. at 1356, 51 L.Ed.2d at 653. Further, the Court noted:

> a successful governmental appeal reversing the judgments of acquittal would necessitate another trial, or, at least, "further proceedings of some sort, devoted to the resolution of factual issues going to the elements of the offense charged. ..." United States v. Jenkins, 420 U.S. 358, 370, 95 S.Ct. 1006, 1013, 43 L.Ed.2d 250, 259 (1975).

430 U.S. at 570, 97 S.Ct. at 1354, 51 L.Ed.2d at 650.

But some matters remain unclear. May the government appeal from a post-verdict judgment of acquittal where the jury has returned a verdict of guilty? Unlike the situation at issue in *Martin Linen Supply Co.*, such cases would permit the government to be granted relief—an order directing the trial judge to enter judgment of conviction on the jury verdict—without another trial and perhaps even without "further proceedings of some sort, devoted to the resolution of factual issues going to the elements of offenses charged." On the other hand, perhaps an acquittal—as long as it is an acquittal "in substance as well as form"—is insulated from appellate review even if the government could be granted relief without the necessity for a new trial. Consider this in relation to section (A), "Former Acquittal." Another problem is presented by pre-verdict "dismissals" that may or may not involve acquittals on the merits; these are the subject of subsection (C)(2).

In any case, the availability of appellate review seems clearly a separate aspect of double jeopardy law. While this is nowhere spelled out, the decisions strongly suggest that prosecution appeals might be permissible in some situations where double jeopardy would bar the government from simply starting over with a new proceeding. Exactly when the government has—or constitutionally can have—the option of appeal but not of starting prosecution anew is an interesting problem.

———

Because of the interplay among a variety of procedural issues, effective categorization of double jeopardy cases is a difficult task. It is useful, however, to distinguish the decisions according to the outcome in the first proceeding: acquittal, conviction, or termination in some other way—usually by the trial judge's declaration of a mistrial—that involves neither acquittal nor conviction. The first three sections of this chapter follow this distinction.

But in regard to each of these areas, it is important to consider the extent to which the prohibition does or should preclude another trial on a charge related to that on which the first proceeding was held but which is "technically" not for the same crime. In addition, consideration must be given to the extent to which double jeopardy has application to situations in which there have not been multiple proceedings. Among these issues are the limits which the doctrine places upon appeal by the prosecution and upon conviction, punishment, or both for several related offenses in the course of the same prosecution.

The final section of this chapter deals with the limitations the Double Jeopardy Clause places on the ability of the government to pursue both criminal prosecution and civil forfeiture of property used in the commission of the same criminal offense.

A.   FORMER ACQUITTAL

Given the policies underlying the Double Jeopardy provision, a situation involving a previous acquittal presents what is probably the strongest case for rigorous application of the doctrine. Perhaps the most important issue in administering this aspect of Double Jeopardy is defining what constitutes an "acquittal."

Burks v. United States

Supreme Court of the United States, 1978.
437 U.S. 1, 98 S.Ct. 2141, 57 L.Ed.2d 1.

■ MR. CHIEF JUSTICE BURGER delivered the opinion of the Court.

We granted certiorari to resolve the question of whether an accused may be subjected to a second trial when conviction in a prior trial was reversed by an appellate court solely for lack of sufficient evidence to sustain the jury's verdict.

I.

Petitioner Burks was tried in the United States District Court for the crime of robbing a federally insured bank by use of a dangerous weapon, a violation of 18 U.S.C.A. § 2113(d). Burks' principal defense was insanity. To prove this claim petitioner produced three expert witnesses who testified, albeit with differing diagnoses of his mental condition, that he suffered from a mental illness at the time of the robbery, which rendered him substantially incapable of conforming his conduct to the requirements of the law. In rebuttal the Government offered the testimony of two experts, one of whom testified that although petitioner possessed a character disorder, he was not mentally ill. The other prosecution witness acknowledged a character disorder in petitioner, but gave a rather ambiguous answer to the question of whether Burks had been capable of conforming his conduct to the law. Lay witnesses also testified for the Government, expressing their opinion that petitioner appeared to be capable of normal functioning and was sane at the time of the alleged offense.

Before the case was submitted to the jury, the court denied a motion for a judgment of acquittal. The jury found Burks guilty as charged. Thereafter, he filed a timely motion for a new trial, maintaining, among other things, "that the evidence was insufficient to support the verdict." The motion was denied by the District Court, which concluded that petitioner's challenge to the sufficiency of the evidence was "utterly without merit."[1]

On appeal petitioner narrowed the issues by admitting the affirmative factual elements of the charge against him, leaving only his claim concerning criminal responsibility to be resolved. With respect to this point, the Court of Appeals agreed with petitioner's claim that the evidence was insufficient to support the verdict and reversed his conviction. . . .

. . . [T]he Court of Appeals, rather than terminating the case against petitioner, remanded to the District Court "for a determination of whether a directed verdict of acquittal should be entered or a new trial ordered." Indicating that the District Court should choose the appropriate course "from a balancing of the equities," the court explicitly adopted the procedures utilized by the Fifth Circuit in United States v. Bass, 490 F.2d 846, 852–853 (1974), "as a guide" to be used on remand:

> "[W]e reverse and remand the case to the district court where the defendant will be entitled to a directed verdict of acquittal unless the government presents sufficient additional evidence to carry its burden on the issue of defendant's sanity. As we noted earlier, the question of sufficiency of the evidence to make an issue for the jury on the defense of insanity is a question of law to be decided by the trial judge. . . . If the district court sitting without the presence of the jury, is satisfied by the government's presentation, it may order a new trial. . . . Even if the government presents additional evidence, the district judge may refuse to order a new trial if he finds from the record that the prosecution

---

1. Petitioner did not file a post-trial motion for judgment of acquittal, which he was entitled to do under Fed.Rule Crim.Proc. 29(c).

had the opportunity fully to develop its case or in fact did so at the first trial.''

The Court of Appeals assumed it had the power to order this "balancing" remedy by virtue of the fact that Burks had explicitly requested a new trial. . . .

II.

* * *

. . . [At least one proposition emerged from our decisions in this area]: a defendant who *requests* a new trial as one avenue of relief may be required to stand trial again, even when his conviction was reversed due to failure of proof at the first trial. Given that petitioner here appealed from a denial of a motion for a new trial—although he had moved for acquittal during trial—our prior cases would seem to indicate that the Court of Appeals had power to remand on the terms it ordered. To reach a different result will require a departure from those holdings.

III.

It is unquestionably true that the Court of Appeals' decision "represente[d] a resolution, correct or not, of some or all of the factual elements of the offense charged." United States v. Martin Linen Supply Co., 430 U.S. 564, 571, 97 S.Ct. 1349, 1355, 51 L.Ed.2d 642 (1977). By deciding that the government had failed to come forward with sufficient proof of petitioner's capacity to be responsible for criminal acts, that court was clearly saying that Burks' criminal culpability had not been established. If the District Court had so held in the first instance, as the reviewing court said it should have done, a judgment of acquittal would have been entered and, of course petitioner could not be retried for the same offense. Consequently, . . . it should make no difference that the reviewing court, rather than the trial court, determined the evidence to be insufficient. The appellate decision unmistakably meant that the District Court had erred in failing to grant a judgment of acquittal. To hold otherwise would create a purely arbitrary distinction between those in petitioner's position and others who would enjoy the benefit of a correct decision by the District Court.

The Double Jeopardy Clause forbids a second trial for the purpose of affording the prosecution another opportunity to supply evidence which it failed to muster in the first proceeding. This is central to the objective of the prohibition against successive trials. . . .

Nonetheless, . . . our past holdings do not appear consistent with what we believe the Double Jeopardy Clause commands. A close reexamination of those precedents, however, persuades us that they have not properly construed the Clause, and accordingly should no longer be followed.

* * *

[Ball v. United States, 163 U.S. 662, 16 S.Ct. 1192, 41 L.Ed. 300 (1896)] came before the Court twice, the first occasion being on writ of error from federal convictions for murder. On this initial review, those defendants who had been found guilty obtained a reversal of their convictions due to a fatally defective indictment. On remand after appeal, the trial court dismissed the flawed indictment and proceeded to retry the defendants on a new indictment. They were again convicted and the defendants came once more to this Court, arguing that their second trial was barred because of former jeopardy. The Court rejected this plea in a brief statement:

> "[A] defendant, who procures a judgment against him upon an indictment to be set aside, may be tried anew upon the same indictment, or upon another indictment, for the same offence of which he had been convicted." ...

The reversal in *Ball* was therefore based not on insufficiency of evidence, but rather on trial error, i.e., failure to dismiss a faulty indictment. ...

We have no doubt that *Ball* was correct in allowing a new trial to rectify *trial error*. . . .

Various rationales have been advanced to support the policy of allowing retrial to correct trial error, but in our view the most reasonable justification is that advanced in [United States v. Tateo, 377 U.S. 463, 466, 84 S.Ct. 1587, 1589, 12 L.Ed.2d 448, 451 (1964)]:

> "It would be a high price indeed for society to pay were every accused granted immunity from punishment because of any defect sufficient to constitute reversible error in the proceedings leading to conviction."

In short, reversal for trial error, as distinguished from evidentiary insufficiency, does not constitute a decision to the effect that the government has failed to prove its case. As such, it implies nothing with respect to the guilt or innocence of the defendant. Rather, it is a determination that a defendant has been convicted through a judicial process which is defective in some fundamental respect, e.g., incorrect receipt or rejection of evidence, incorrect instructions, or prosecutorial misconduct. When this occurs, the accused has a strong interest in obtaining a fair re-adjudication of his guilt free from error, just as society maintains a valid concern for insuring that the guilty are punished. See Note, Double Jeopardy: A New Trial After Appellate Reversal for Insufficient Evidence, 31 U.Chi.L.Rev. 365, 370 (1964).

The same cannot be said when a defendant's conviction has been overturned due to a failure of proof at trial, in which case the prosecution cannot complain of prejudice, for it has been given one fair opportunity to offer whatever proof it could assemble.[2] Moreover, such an appellate reversal means that the Government's case was so lacking that it should not have even been *submitted* to the jury. Since we necessarily afford absolute finality to a jury's *verdict* of acquittal—no matter how erroneous its decision—it is difficult to conceive how society has any greater interest in retrying a defendant when, on review, it is decided as a matter of law that the jury could not properly have returned a verdict of guilty.

* * *

---

2. It has been suggested, for example, that an appeal from a conviction amounts to a "waiver" of former jeopardy protections ..., or that the appeal somehow continues the jeopardy which attached at the first trial....

In our view it makes no difference that a defendant has sought a new trial as one of his remedies, or even as the sole remedy. It cannot be meaningfully said that a person "waives" his right to a judgment of acquittal by moving for a new trial. ... Since we hold today that the Double Jeopardy Clause precludes a second trial once the reviewing court has found the evidence legally insufficient, the only "just" remedy available for that court is the direction of a judgment of acquittal. To the extent that our prior decisions suggest that by moving for a new trial, a defendant waives his right to a judgment of acquittal on the basis of evidentiary insufficiency those cases are overruled.

Accordingly, the judgment of the Court of Appeals is reversed, and the case remanded for proceedings consistent with this opinion.

Reversed and remanded.

NOTES

1. **Trial judge finding of evidence insufficiency.** Suppose the trial court rather than an appellate tribunal determines that the evidence suggesting guilt is in some sense deficient. Does *Burks* bar another trial of the defendant? The Supreme Court commented on the matter in Hudson v. Louisiana, 450 U.S. 40, 101 S.Ct. 970, 67 L.Ed.2d 30 (1981). Hudson was convicted of murder in a jury trial; after verdict, the trial judge granted a defense motion for a new trial, made on the ground that the jury's verdict was contrary to the evidence. Hudson was retried, the state's evidence included testimony not presented at the first trial, and the jury convicted. Habeas corpus relief was sought in state courts on the basis that the second trial violated Hudson's rights under the Double Jeopardy clause. The Louisiana Supreme Court found no violation of *Burks,* reasoning that the trial judge, in granting a new trial, had found insufficient evidence to support the verdict rather than no evidence. *Burks,* it concluded, is limited to situations "where, *as a matter of law,* a reviewing court has determined that in a prior trial there was *no evidence* of the crime charged or an essential element thereof." State v. Hudson, 373 So.2d 1294 (La. 1979). A unanimous Supreme Court, speaking through Justice Powell, reversed. The record was clear, Justice Powell observed, that the state trial judge granted a new trial because the evidence was legally insufficient to support the verdict. "Nothing in *Burks* suggests ...," he continued, "that double jeopardy protections are violated only when the prosecution has adduced no evidence at all of the crime or an element thereof." 450 U.S. at 43, 101 S.Ct. at 972, 67 L.Ed.2d at 34. The Louisiana Supreme Court had not, Justice Powell commented, found it significant that the trial judge rather than an appellate court made the determination that the evidence was insufficient and the State had not contested this conclusion. 450 U.S. at 44 n. 6, 101 S.Ct. at 973 n. 6, 67 L.Ed.2d at 35 n. 6.

The State had argued that under state law the trial judge had the authority to function as a "13th juror" and in this capacity to grant a new trial because he entertained personal doubts as to the verdict. Further, it urged that the new trial in the case before the Court was granted pursuant to this authority and that *Burks* does not apply to a new trial granted for this reason because the trial judge's action was not based upon a determination that the state failed to meet its burden of proof at trial. The Court rejected this argument on the ground that the record established that the new trial was granted because the trial judge determined that the state failed to prove its case as a matter of law and thus was not acting as a "13th juror." But it continued:

We do not decide whether the Double Jeopardy Clause would have barred Louisiana from retrying [Hudson] if the trial judge had granted a new trial in [his "13th juror"] capacity, for that is not the case before us. We note, however, that *Burks* precludes retrial where the State has failed as a matter of law to prove its case despite a fair opportunity to do so. By definition, a new trial ordered by a trial judge acting as a "13th juror" is not such a case. Thus, nothing in *Burks* precludes retrial in such a case.

450 U.S. at 44 n. 5, 101 S.Ct. at 973 n. 5, 67 L.Ed.2d at 34–35 n. 5.

2. **Appellate court reversal on the weight of the evidence.** In Tibbs v. Florida, 457 U.S. 31, 102 S.Ct. 2211, 72 L.Ed.2d 652 (1982) the Court developed further the distinction suggested by the "13th juror" concept in *Hudson*. Defendant was convicted of murder and rape. On appeal, the Florida Supreme Court found that while the evidence was sufficient under federal standards to support the conviction, the verdict was against "the weight of the evidence." It reversed and remanded for a new trial. On re-prosecution, the Florida Supreme Court held that double jeopardy did not prevent re-prosecution when the reversal was because the verdict was against the weight of the evidence, rather than for evidence insufficiency. The Supreme Court, in an opinion authored by Justice O'Connor, affirmed. The Court advanced the following distinction:

[A] conviction rests upon insufficient evidence when, even after viewing the evidence in the light most favorable to the prosecution, no rational factfinder could have found the defendant guilty beyond a reasonable doubt. A reversal based on the weight of the evidence, on the other hand, draws the appellate court into questions of credibility. The "weight of the evidence" refers to "a determination [by] the trier of fact that a greater amount of credible evidence supports one side of an issue or cause than the other."

457 U.S. at 37, 102 S.Ct. at 2216, 72 L.Ed.2d at 658–59. The Court concluded that "an appellate court's disagreement with the jurors' weighing of the evidence does not require the special deference accorded verdicts of acquittal" which is the justification for the prohibition on re-prosecution following reversal for evidence insufficiency. 457 U.S. at 42, 102 S.Ct. at 2218, 72 L.Ed.2d at 662–63. Justice White, in a dissent joined in by Justices Brennan, Marshall and Blackmun, expressed concern that the Court's position would undermine *Burks* in that appellate courts might be tempted to characterize insufficiency reversals as being because the verdict was against the weight of the evidence to permit re-prosecution.

3. **Appeals resulting in trials *de novo*.** It is quite common in the United States for less serious criminal offenses to be prosecuted under a two-tier system. The first trial is not in a court of record. If the defendant is acquitted, that concludes the prosecution. If the defendant is convicted, he is entitled to appeal to a higher court, but since there is no record "below" the appeal results in a trial *de novo*, that is, in an entirely new trial rather than a review of the correctness of the first trial.

Suppose a defendant is convicted in the first trial of a two-tier system and asserts his right to a trial *de novo*. If he believes that there was insufficient evidence of guilt below, is he entitled to a determination of that issue before proceeding to the trial *de novo*? The respondent in Justices of Boston Municipal Court v. Lydon, 466 U.S. 294, 104 S.Ct. 1805, 80 L.Ed.2d 311 (1984) was charged with possessing burglary implements with intent to steal. Under Massachusetts law, he could insist upon a jury trial and if convicted pursue normal appellate remedies on the record of the trial. He could instead elect a bench trial and if convicted obtain a trial *de novo* before a judge or jury; if convicted in the trial *de novo*, normal appellate remedies would then become available. He chose the latter course of action and was convicted in the first trial, receiving a sentence of two years' imprisonment. After appealing for the trial *de novo*, he was released on his personal recognizance and moved to dismiss the prosecution on the ground there was no evidence introduced in the trial that he intended to steal and that a second trial was barred under *Burks*. This claim was rejected by the trial *de novo* court and by the Massachusetts Supreme Judicial Court. Respondent then sought habeas corpus relief in Federal District Court, which concluded that under *Burks* a second trial was foreclosed if the evidence against respondent at the bench trial was insufficient and that it was. The Court of Appeals affirmed.

The Supreme Court, in an opinion authored by Justice White, reversed. Respondent, like the petitioner Burks, was placed in jeopardy by the trial but, unlike Burks, jeopardy had not terminated at the time respondent demanded the *de novo* court review the sufficiency of the evidence:

> In this case, the Commonwealth is not attempting to impose multiple punishments for a single offense. Nor is it making another attempt to convict Lydon after acquittal. It is satisfied with the results of the bench trial and would have abided the results of a jury trial had Lydon taken that initial course. The conceptual difficulty for Lydon is that he has not been acquitted; he simply maintains that he ought to have been. . . .

> The Double Jeopardy Clause is not an absolute bar to successive trials. The general rule is that the Clause does not bar reprosecution of a defendant whose conviction is overturned on appeal. . . . [I]mplicit in the . . . rule permitting retrial after reversal of a conviction is the concept of "continuing jeopardy. . . . " Interests supporting the continuing jeopardy principle involve fairness to society, lack of finality, and limited waiver. . . . Acquittals, unlike convictions, terminate the initial jeopardy. . . . In *Burks* . . . we recognized that an unreversed determination by a reviewing court that the evidence was legally insufficient likewise served to terminate the initial jeopardy.

> We assume, without deciding, that jeopardy attached at the swearing of the first witness at Lydon's bench trial. The question then is whether jeopardy has now terminated. Lydon's double jeopardy argument requires an affirmative answer to that question, but he fails to identify any stage of the state proceedings that can be held to have terminated jeopardy. Unlike Burks, who could rest his claim upon the appellate court's determination of insufficiency, Lydon is faced with the unreversed determination of the bench-trial judge, contrary to Lydon's assertion, that the prosecution had met its burden of proof.

466 U.S. at 307–09, 104 S.Ct. at 1813–14, 80 L.Ed.2d at 324–25. Does Justice White's position mean that an appellate court has no constitutional obligation to determine whether the evidence below was sufficient? What would have been the status of the case if the *de novo* court judge had determined that the evidence was insufficient?

Justice Brennan, joined by Justice Marshall, concurred in the judgment. Justice O'Connor concurred in the judgment on the ground that respondent, released on personal recognizance, was not in custody and could not, therefore, invoke the habeas jurisdiction of the Federal District Court. Justice Powell, joined by The Chief Justice, concurred in the judgment and in all of the Court's opinion except that part holding that respondent was in custody for federal habeas jurisdiction purposes. Justice Stevens concurred in the judgment in a separate opinion.

4. **The requirement of a termination of proceedings.** The Court considered a related double jeopardy question in Richardson v. United States, 468 U.S. 317, 104 S.Ct. 3081, 82 L.Ed.2d 242 (1984). Petitioner was charged with three counts of federal narcotics violations. At trial, the jury acquitted him of one count but was unable to reach verdicts on the remaining counts. The trial court declared a

mistrial and denied post-trial motions for judgments of acquittal. Before the second trial was scheduled to begin, petitioner moved for dismissal on the grounds there was insufficient evidence in the first trial to submit the case to the jury and that retrial should be barred under *Burks.* The trial court denied the motion and petitioner took an immediate appeal. The Court of Appeals dismissed the appeal on the ground the trial court's order was not a collateral order permitting interlocutory appeal under *Abney.* The Supreme Court, in an opinion by Justice Rehnquist, held that the order was appealable under *Abney.* However, the Court then concluded that the petitioner had no double jeopardy claim to submit to an appellate court in an interlocutory appeal or otherwise. *Burks* held that when an appellate court finds the evidence was insufficient to support a conviction, double jeopardy precludes reprosecution for the same offense. Here, however, no court, trial or appellate, has determined that the government presented insufficient evidence at the first trial. The Court has held since *Perez* and *Logan* that double jeopardy does not preclude reprosecution for the same offense when there was a "manifest necessity" for declaring a mistrial, such as a genuinely hung jury:

> We think that the principles governing our decision in *Burks,* and the principles governing our decisions in the hung jury cases, are readily reconciled when we recognize that the protection of the Double Jeopardy Clause by its terms applies only if there has been some event, such as an acquittal, which terminates the original jeopardy. . . . Since jeopardy attached here when the jury was sworn . . . petitioner's argument necessarily assumes that the judicial declaration of a mistrial was an event which terminated jeopardy in his case and which allowed him to assert a valid claim of double jeopardy.
>
> But this proposition is irreconcilable with cases such as *Perez* and *Logan,* and we hold on the authority of these cases that the failure of a jury to reach a verdict is not an event which terminates jeopardy. . . . The Government, like the defendant, is entitled to resolution of the case by verdict from the jury, and jeopardy does not terminate when the jury is discharged because it is unable to agree. Regardless of the sufficiency of the evidence at petitioner's first trial, he has no valid double jeopardy claim to prevent his retrial.

468 U.S. at 325–26, 104 S.Ct. at 3086, 82 L.Ed.2d at 250–51. Justice Brennan, joined by Justice Marshall, concurred in that part of the Court's opinion holding that an interlocutory appeal is available, but dissented from the remainder of the opinion. He argued that the majority "improperly ignores the realities of the defendant's situation and relies instead on a formalistic concept of 'continuing jeopardy.' " 468 U.S. at 327, 104 S.Ct. at 3087, 82 L.Ed.2d at 252. Justice Stevens dissented on the ground that an interlocutory appeal should not be available in these circumstances.

5. **Jurisdictional deficiencies in proceedings.** Courts have sometimes stated that if the charging instrument in a criminal proceeding is so defective that any conviction on it would necessarily be invalid, an acquittal in that proceeding does not bar a second proceeding. E.g., Thompson v. State, 527 S.W.2d 888 (Tex.Cr.App.1975). This position was rejected as a statement of federal constitutional law in Benton v. Maryland, 395 U.S. 784, 89 S.Ct. 2056, 23 L.Ed.2d 707 (1969). The state urged that Benton's acquittal in the first proceeding did not bar retrial, because the indictment was void and no jeopardy attaches under such a defective indictment. Characterizing the state's position as an effort to use its own error to deprive Benton of the benefit of acquittal, the Court held that the indictment must be viewed as at worst only voidable at the defendant's option. An acquittal on such an indictment cannot, over the defendant's objection, be set aside. 395 U.S. at 796–97, 89 S.Ct. at 2063–64, 23 L.Ed.2d at 717–18.

6. **Appeals from post-verdict judgments of acquittal.** Suppose a jury returns a verdict of guilty and the trial judge then grants a post-verdict motion for judgment of acquittal. See, e.g., Fed.R.Crim.Pro.Rule 29(c). Does—and should—the government have a right to appeal that ruling? Several courts have held that appeal is permitted. United States v. Steed, 646 F.2d 136 (4th Cir.1981); United States v. Dreitzler, 577 F.2d 539 (9th Cir.1978), cert. denied 440 U.S. 921, 99 S.Ct. 1246, 59 L.Ed.2d 473 (1979); United States v. Boyd, 566 F.2d 929 (5th Cir.1978). In United States v. Jenkins, 420 U.S. 358, 365, 95 S.Ct. 1006, 1011, 43 L.Ed.2d 250, 256 (1975), the Court assumed such an appeal would be proper. In United States v. Scott, 437 U.S. 82, 98 S.Ct. 2187, 57 L.Ed.2d 65 (1978), overruling the specific holding of *Jenkins,* the Court noted that post-*Jenkins* decisions never explicitly repudiated this assumption. 437 U.S. at 91 n. 7, 98 S.Ct. at 2193 n. 7, 57 L.Ed.2d at 74 n. 7.

Federal Rules of Criminal Procedure Rule 29(b), as amended in 1994, permits the trial judge to reserve ruling on a motion for judgment of acquittal:

> The court may reserve decision on a motion for judgment of acquittal, proceed with the trial (where the motion is made before the close of all the evidence), submit the case to the jury and decide the motion either before the jury returns a verdict or after it returns a verdict of guilty or is discharged without having returned a verdict. If the court reserves decision, it must decide the motion on the basis of the evidence at the time the ruling was reserved.

7. **What is the same offense for prior acquittal purposes?** Suppose the government sought to prosecute the defendant for a different offense but one that was related in its commission to that of which the defendant was acquitted? What is the criterion for determining whether this second proceeding would be for the "same offense" for double jeopardy purposes? The next section considers the issue in the context of prior convictions and addresses the so-called *"Blockburger* Rule" as a standard for resolving the question of whether two different crimes are the "same" for prior conviction purposes. It has been widely assumed that the same standard applied where the prior proceeding resulted in acquittal. E.g., Sanabria v. United States, 437 U.S. 54, 70 n. 24, 98 S.Ct. 2170, 2182 n. 24, 57 L.Ed.2d 43, 57 n. 24 (1978). After examining this approach as applied to prior conviction situations, consider whether there are any justifications for using a different standard when the first proceeding resulted in acquittal.

A conviction of a lesser included offense constitutes an implied acquittal of the more serious offense for Double Jeopardy purposes. In Green v. United States, 355 U.S. 184, 78 S.Ct. 221, 2 L.Ed.2d 199 (1957), Green was charged with first degree murder but the jury—as the trial judge's instructions permitted—returned a verdict of guilty of second degree murder. Following reversal of this conviction on appeal, Green was retried for first degree murder. Finding this in violation of the prohibition against Double Jeopardy, the Court concluded that the first trial must be given the same effect as would have been required had the jury returned a verdict which expressly read, "We find the defendant not guilty of murder in the first degree but guilty of murder in the second degree." 355 U.S. at 191, 78 S.Ct. at 225, 2 L.Ed.2d at 206.

8. **Jeopardy in non-capital punishment decisions.** When, if ever, is the imposition of a sentence less than the statutory maximum for the crime at issue an "acquittal" of any more severe punishment for Double Jeopardy purposes? Generally, sentencing has not been regarded as having this Double Jeopardy effect. North Carolina v. Pearce, 395 U.S. 711, 89 S.Ct. 2072, 23 L.Ed.2d 656 (1969). The traditional approach was followed and defended in United States v. DiFrancesco, 449 U.S. 117, 101 S.Ct. 426, 66 L.Ed.2d 328 (1980). Following DiFrancesco's conviction for various racketeering offenses, the government sought to have him

sentenced to the special increased term provided by 18 U.S.C.A. § 3575 for "dangerous special offenders." After determining that DiFrancesco was within the statute, the trial judge imposed the special term but made it concurrent with other sentences already imposed. The government sought to appeal on the ground that the decision to make the dangerous offender term concurrent was an abuse of discretion. But the Court of Appeals for the Second Circuit dismissed the appeal as barred by Double Jeopardy. By a 5-to-4 vote, the Supreme Court reversed. Refusing to accord a criminal sentence the same finality and conclusiveness given to an acquittal, Justice Blackmun reasoned for the majority that the considerations underlying the prohibition against Double Jeopardy—the need to avoid undue embarrassment, expense, anxiety and security and the risk of erroneous conviction—do not apply:

> This limited appeal does not involve a retrial or approximate the ordeal of a trial on the basic issue of guilt or innocence. . . . [T]he appeal is to be taken promptly and is essentially on the record of the sentencing court. The defendant, of course, is charged with knowledge of the statute and its appeal provisions, and has no expectation of finality in his sentence until the appeal has expired. To be sure, the appeal may prolong the period of any anxiety that may exist, but it does so only for the finite period provided by the statute. The appeal is no more of an ordeal than any Government appeal . . . from the dismissal of an indictment or information. The defendant's primary concern and anxiety obviously relates to the determination of innocence or guilt, and that already is behind him. The defendant is subjected to no risk of being harassed and then convicted, although innocent. Furthermore, a sentence is characteristically determined in large part on the basis of information, such as the presentence report, developed outside the courtroom. It is purely a judicial determination, and much that goes into it is the result of inquiry that is nonadversarial in nature.

449 U.S. at 136, 101 S.Ct. at 437, 66 L.Ed.2d at 345–46. Justice Brennan, joined by Justices White, Marshall, and Stevens, dissented, urging that imposition of a less-than-maximum sentence be regarded as analogous to acquittal. He characterized the majority's distinction between acquittals and sentences as resting upon a faulty understanding of the import to the defendant of sentencing:

> [M]ost defendants are more concerned with how much time they must spend in prison than with whether their record shows a conviction. . . . [C]learly, the defendant does not breathe a sigh of relief once he has been found guilty. Indeed, an overwhelming number of criminal defendants are willing to enter plea bargains in order to keep their time in prison as brief as possible. Surely, the Court cannot believe . . . that the sentencing phase is merely incidental and that defendants do not suffer acute anxiety. To the convicted defendant, the sentencing phase is certainly as critical as the guilt-innocence phase.

449 U.S. at 149, 101 S.Ct. at 444, 66 L.Ed.2d at 354.

Respondent in Pennsylvania v. Goldhammer, 474 U.S. 28, 106 S.Ct. 353, 88 L.Ed.2d 183 (1985) had been convicted of 56 counts of forgery and 56 counts of theft. He was sentenced to a five year prison sentence on one theft count and to five years' probation on one of the forgery counts. Sentences on the remaining counts were suspended. On appeal he successfully argued that 34 of the theft counts, including the one on which he had received the prison sentence, were barred from prosecution under the statute of limitations. The Commonwealth sought a ruling from the Pennsylvania Supreme Court remanding the case to the trial court for resentencing on the remaining 22 theft counts, but that court refused on the ground to do so would violate double jeopardy. The United States Supreme Court, in a per curiam opinion, reversed on the ground that resentencing in these circumstances was governed by *DiFrancesco* and was not prohibited by the Fifth Amendment.

9. **Jeopardy in capital punishment decisions.** A different approach to capital sentencing was taken, however, in Bullington v. Missouri, 451 U.S. 430, 101 S.Ct. 1852, 68 L.Ed.2d 270 (1981). Under the Missouri capital sentencing procedure, a separate sentencing hearing must be held before the jury which convicted the defendant of capital murder. The jury must determine whether the state has proven any of the ten listed aggravating circumstances beyond a reasonable doubt, whether those aggravating circumstances that have been proven warrant imposition of the death penalty, and whether there are any mitigating circumstances that outweigh the aggravating circumstances. A unanimous decision to impose death is required. Bullington was convicted of capital murder and, after the required sentencing hearing, a sentence of life imprisonment was imposed. A new trial was granted by the trial judge, however, on the basis that exclusion of women from the trial jury violated Bullington's Sixth and Fourteenth Amendment rights. Before the beginning of the second trial, the state announced it would seek the death penalty. The Missouri Supreme Court declined to bar this, concluding that the Double Jeopardy Clause did not preclude imposition of the death penalty should Bullington be convicted of capital murder on the retrial. The Supreme Court reversed. Holding that Double Jeopardy barred the imposition of the death penalty at Bullington's second trial, Justice Blackmun reasoned for the majority that the rationale for the general sentencing rule is that the usual unstructured sentencing proceeding renders it impossible to conclude that a sentence less than the maximum constitutes a decision that the state has failed to prove its case for a more severe penalty. But under a structured sentencing proceeding such as that before the Court, the decision to impose life imprisonment rather than death can reliably be said to reflect a conclusion by the trier of fact that despite a fair opportunity the state has failed to prove its case for imposition of death. Moreover, the reasons for giving an acquittal on guilt or innocence finality apply:

> The "embarrassment, expense and ordeal" and the "anxiety and insecurity" faced by a defendant at the penalty phase of a Missouri capital murder trial surely are at least equivalent to that faced by any defendant at the guilt phase of a criminal trial. The "unacceptably high risk that the [prosecution], with its superior resources, would wear down a defendant," . . . thereby leading to an erroneously imposed death sentence, would exist if the State were to have a further opportunity to convince a jury to impose the ultimate punishment.

451 U.S. at 445, 101 S.Ct. at 1861, 68 L.Ed.2d at 283.

In Arizona v. Rumsey, 467 U.S. 203, 104 S.Ct. 2305, 81 L.Ed.2d 164 (1984), the respondent was convicted of capital murder committed during an armed robbery. Under Arizona law, the trial judge, not the jury, has sentencing authority in capital cases. The trial judge was authorized to impose the death penalty only if after a hearing he found the presence of at least one aggravating circumstance from a statutory list of seven possibilities. The trial judge interpreted the provision defining as an aggravating circumstance committing murder "as consideration for the receipt, or in expectation of the receipt, of anything of pecuniary value" to apply only to murder-for-hire, not to a murder committed during a robbery or theft. Accordingly, a sentence of life imprisonment was imposed. Respondent appealed another point to the Arizona Supreme Court and State filed a cross-appeal. The court denied respondent's claim, but ruled that the trial judge had misconstrued the aggravating circumstance statute—that it did include murder committed during robbery or theft. It remanded the penalty portion of the case for a new hearing. At the new hearing, the trial court imposed the death penalty. Respondent appealed again to the Arizona Supreme Court, this time claiming that imposition of the death penalty violated his right against twice being placed in jeopardy. The court agreed and the State sought and obtained a writ of certiorari from the United States Supreme Court.

The Court, in an opinion by Justice O'Connor, held that *Bullington* was violated by imposition of the death penalty:

> That the sentencer in Arizona is the trial judge rather than the jury does not render the sentencing proceeding any less like a trial. . . . Nor does the availability of appellate review, including reweighing of aggravating and mitigating circumstances, make the appellate process part of a single continuing sentencing proceedings. The Supreme Court of Arizona noted that its role is strictly that of an appellate court, not a trial court. Indeed, no appeal need be taken if life imprisonment is imposed, and the appellate reweighing can work only to the defendant's advantage. . . .

> In making its findings, the trial court relied on a misconstruction of the statute defining the pecuniary gain aggravating circumstances. Reliance on an error of law, however, does not change the double jeopardy effects of a judgment that amounts to an acquittal on the merits. . . .

> [United States v. Wilson, discussed on p. 822 of the Casebook, is not applicable.] By contrast, in respondent's initial capital sentencing, there was only one decisionmaker and only one set of findings of fact, all favorable to respondent. The trial court "acquitted" respondent of the death penalty, and there was no verdict of "guilty" for the appellate court to reinstate.

467 U.S. at 210–12, 104 S.Ct. at 2309–10, 81 L.Ed.2d at 171–72.

Justice Rehnquist, joined by Justice White, dissented:

In no sense can it be meaningfully argued that the State failed to "prove" its case—the existence of at least one aggravating circumstance. It is hard to see how there has been an "implied acquittal" of a statutory aggravating circumstance when the record explicitly establishes the factual basis that such an aggravating circumstance existed. But for the trial judge's erroneous construction of governing state law, the judge would have been required to impose the death penalty.

> If, as a matter of state law, the Arizona Supreme Court had simply corrected the erroneous sentence itself without remanding, there could be no argument that *Bullington* would prevent the imposition of the death sentence. That much was made clear in our decision in United States v. Wilson. . . .

467 U.S. at 214, 104 S.Ct. at 2311, 81 L.Ed.2d at 173.

The Arizona death penalty scheme came under further Supreme Court review in Poland v. Arizona, 476 U.S. 147, 106 S.Ct. 1749, 90 L.Ed.2d 123 (1986). The trial court sentenced petitioners to death for the murders of two Purolator guards committed during a robbery. It found as an aggravating circumstance that the killings were "especially heinous, cruel, or depraved" but found that the pecuniary gain aggravating circumstance in issue in Arizona v. Rumsey was not present because it interpreted that circumstance to require proof of a murder for hire. On appeal, the Arizona Supreme Court reversed and remanded for a new trial for trial error. It also found that the aggravating circumstance that the killings were "heinous, cruel or depraved" was not supported by the evidence. However, it further concluded that the trial court had misunderstood the law in limiting the *Rumsey* circumstance to murders for hire, and that it applies to murder during robbery. It explicitly stated the death penalty could be imposed upon proper proof following a new trial. Following conviction on remand, petitioners were again sentenced to death. The trial court found that both the pecuniary gain and heinous manner circumstances were proved. The Arizona Supreme Court found again the evidence insufficient to support the heinous manner circumstance but sufficient to support that dealing with pecuniary gain. It rejected petitioners' argument that Double Jeopardy precluded imposition of the death penalty in light of the earlier finding of insufficiency to support the heinous manner circumstance. The United States Supreme Court, in an opinion authored by Justice White, affirmed. Unlike in *Rumsey,* at no point did either the trial or appellate courts conclude that the State had failed to prove its case for the death penalty. The Arizona Supreme Court did conclude that the State had failed to prove the heinous manner circumstance, but also found that the trial court had misconstrued the reach of the pecuniary gain circumstance and clearly intended to authorize the death penalty upon appropriate proof during remand. There is a difference between aggravating circumstances and the verdict of death. The death penalty can be imposed by the trial court only if at least one aggravating circumstance is shown and it is not outweighed by any mitigating circumstance. Here, the trial court, unlike in *Rumsey,* concluded that the death penalty was appropriate and the Arizona Supreme Court did not reject that ultimate conclusion:

> The defendant may argue on appeal that the evidence presented at his sentencing hearing was as a matter of law insufficient to support the aggravating circumstances on which his death sentence was based, but the Double Jeopardy Clause does not require the reviewing court, if it sustains that claim, to ignore evidence in the record supporting another aggravating circumstance which the sentencer has erroneously rejected. Such a rule would have the odd and unacceptable result of requiring a reviewing court to enter a death penalty "acquittal" even though that court is of the view that the State has "proved its case."

476 U.S. at 157, 106 S.Ct. at 1756, 90 L.Ed.2d at 133. Justice Marshall, joined by Justices Brennan and Blackmun, dissented.

In Spaziano v. Florida, 468 U.S. 447, 104 S.Ct. 3154, 82 L.Ed.2d 340 (1984), the petitioner was convicted of capital murder. Under Florida law, the trial jury heard evidence relevant to punishment and recommended to the trial court that a sentence of life imprisonment be imposed. The trial court, as authorized by state law, ordered and received a presentence report concerning petitioner. The court then imposed a sentence of death. The Supreme Court, in an opinion by Justice Blackmun, upheld the Florida procedure. The Court concluded there is no Sixth Amendment right to a jury determination of the question of life or death for a person convicted of a capital offense. Since Florida law validly provided that the role of the jury was advisory only, there was no double jeopardy objection to the trial judge imposing a death sentence in the face of a jury recommendation of life.

The petitioner in Schiro v. Farley, 510 U.S. 222, 114 S.Ct. 783, 127 L.Ed.2d 47 (1994) was charged in count one with knowingly killing another, in count two with killing another while committing rape and in count three with killing another while committing deviate conduct. The State sought the death penalty on counts two and three. The jury returned a verdict of guilty on count two and left the remaining verdict sheets blank. Under Indiana law, imposition of the death penalty requires the State to prove at the penalty phase of the proceedings the existence of at least one of nine aggravating circumstances, including that the defendant *intentionally* killed the victim while committing or attempting to commit rape. Although the jury recommended against the death penalty, the trial judge rejected that recommendation on the ground that the aggravating circumstance of intentional killing during rape had been shown. On direct appeals and in federal habeas, Petitioner unsuccessfully argued that the double jeopardy clause prohibited finding in the penalty phase that he had intentionally killed during rape because he had been acquitted of that theory by the jury in the guilt/innocence phase. He also argued the State was collaterally estopped from attempting to show intentional murder as an aggravating circumstance.

The Supreme Court, in an opinion authored by Justice O'Connor, affirmed denial of habeas relief. The Court rejected Petitioner's prior acquittal claim on the ground the guilt/innocence and penalty phases were part of a single trial. It distinguished *Bullington,*

> This case is manifestly different. Neither the prohibition against a successive trial on the issue of guilt, nor the *Bullington* prohibition against a second capital sentencing proceeding, is implicated here—the State did not reprosecute Schiro for intentional murder, nor did it force him to submit to a second death penalty hearing. It simply conducted a single sentencing hearing in the course of a single prosecution. The state is entitled to "one fair opportunity" to prosecute a defendant * * * and that opportunity extends not only to prosecution at the guilt phase, but also to present evidence at an ensuing sentencing proceeding.

510 U.S. at 231, 114 S.Ct. at 790, 127 L.Ed.2d at 58.

The Court refused to decide whether the constitutional principle of collateral estoppel (*Ashe v. Swenson,* later this chapter) could apply to preclude a penalty phase verdict based upon a guilt/innocence phase finding. It concluded that Petitioner had failed to prove the threshold requirement that he had obtained a favorable finding from the jury at guilt innocence on the issue of intentional killing. The three counts were independent of each other; one was not a lesser included offense of another. The jury was not instructed to consider the counts in any particular order. The question of intent to kill was not disputed during the guilt/innocence phase.

10.   **"Acquittals" in non-capital sentencing proceedings.** Does *Bullington* apply to non-capital sentencing proceedings? The petitioner in Monge v. California, 524 U.S. 721, 118 S.Ct. 2246, 141 L.Ed.2d 615, 1998 WL 336328 (1998) was charged with using a minor to sell marijuana, sale or transportation of marijuana and possession of marijuana. The State notified petitioner it would seek to prove two sentence enhancement allegations: that petitioner had a prior conviction for assault and that he had served a prison sentence on that conviction. Under California's three strikes law, proof of those allegations could result in more than doubling the sentence. The petitioner was convicted of all three charges and the trial court in a hearing without a jury found that he had been convicted of an assault and that under California law it was a "serious felony" because a dangerous weapon (a stick) was used in commission of the offense. The court also found he had been imprisoned for that offense. The trial court imposed an eleven year sentence. On appeal, the Court of Appeal reversed on the ground there was no evidence in the record that a dangerous weapon had been used in the assault offense. The court refused to permit the State the opportunity to prove its allegations in a new sentencing hearing on the ground such an opportunity was precluded by the Double Jeopardy Clause under *Bullington.*

The California Supreme Court reversed the Court of Appeals, holding that *Bullington* is confined to capital offense proceedings. The Supreme Court, in an opinion by Justice O'Connor, affirmed. The Court characterized *Bullington* as being an exception to the general rule that double jeopardy principles do not apply to the sentencing phase of cases. That exception was created because of the unique characteristics of capital cases:

> The penalty phase of a capital trial is undertaken to assess the gravity of a particular offense and to determine whether it warrants the ultimate punish-

ment; it is in many respects a continuation of the trial on guilt or innocence of capital murder.

524 U.S. at ___, 118 S.Ct. at 2252, 141 L.Ed.2d at 626. Justice Scalia, joined by Justices Souter and Ginsburg, dissented. He argued that the sentence enhancements in this case are really elements of the offense with which petitioner had been charged and as elements are entitled to Double Jeopardy Clause protection the same as other elements of the offense:

> Suppose that a State repealed all of the violent crimes in its criminal code and replaced them with only one offense, 'knowingly causing injury to another,' bearing a penalty of 30 days in prison, but subject to a series of 'sentencing enhancements' authorizing additional punishment up to life imprisonment or death on the basis of various levels of mens rea, severity of injury, and other surrounding circumstances. Could the state then grant the defendant a jury trial, with requirement of proof beyond a reasonable doubt, solely on the question whether he 'knowingly cause[d] injury to another,' but leave it for the judge to determine by a preponderance of the evidence whether the defendant acted intentionally or accidentally, whether he used a deadly weapon, and whether the victim ultimately died from the injury the defendant inflicted?

524 U.S. at ___, 118 S.Ct. at 2255, 141 L.Ed.2d at 630. Justice Stevens dissented separately on the ground that the preclusion of re-prosecution imposed by Burks v. United States (earlier this chapter) should be applied to the failure to prove that the assault was a serious felony in this case.

11. **What evidence is considered in determining whether there has been a sentencing "acquittal?"** The respondent in Lockhart v. Nelson, 488 U.S. 33, 109 S.Ct. 285, 102 L.Ed.2d 265 (1988), entered a plea of guilty to burglary. The State then introduced evidence of four prior felony convictions. Under Arkansas law, this permitted the imposition of a sentence of between 20 and 40 years. At his sentencing hearing, respondent stated that he believed that one of those convictions had been the subject of a gubernatorial pardon, which would have made that conviction not eligible for use to enhance punishment. When the prosecutor suggested that respondent was confusing a pardon with a commutation of sentence, respondent agreed that was the case. There was, therefore, no defense objection to the admission of that conviction into evidence. After unsuccessful appeals in the state courts, a federal District Court determined that respondent had in fact been pardoned for the prior conviction in question and set aside the sentence. When the State announced its intention to replace the pardoned conviction with another one it had not previously used, the District Court held that double jeopardy principles precluded the State from attempting to resentence respondent as an habitual offender on the burglary charge. The Eighth Circuit affirmed.

The Supreme Court, in an opinion by the Chief Justice, reversed. The majority characterized the question as whether a court should consider all the evidence or only all the admissible evidence in determining whether the evidence at trial was sufficient. It concluded that all the evidence admitted must be considered, including any improperly admitted evidence:

> It is quite clear from our opinion in *Burks* that a reviewing court must consider all of the evidence admitted by the trial court in deciding whether retrial is permissible under the Double Jeopardy Clause—indeed, that was the *ratio decidendi of Burks....* The basis for the *Burks* exception to the general rule [permitting re-trial after appellate reversal] is that a reversal for insufficiency of the evidence should be treated no differently than a trial court's granting a judgment of acquittal at the close of all the evidence. A trial court in passing on such a motion considers all of the evidence it has admitted, and to make the

analogy complete it must be this same quantum of evidence which is considered by the reviewing court.

488 U.S. at 40–42, 109 S.Ct. at 291, 102 L.Ed.2d at 274. The majority further noted that if the respondent had offered evidence at the sentencing hearing of the pardon, "the trial judge would presumably have allowed the prosecutor an opportunity to offer evidence of another prior conviction to support the habitual offender charge." 488 U.S. at 42, 109 S.Ct. at 291, 102 L.Ed.2d at 274. The majority viewed its decision as doing only what the trial judge would have done had the matter been properly raised there.

Justice Marshall, joined by Justices Brennan and Blackmun, dissented:

> If, in seeking to prove Nelson's four prior convictions, the State had offered documented evidence to prove three valid prior convictions and a blank piece of paper to prove a fourth, no one would doubt that Arkansas had produced insufficient evidence and that the Double Jeopardy Clause barred retrial. There is no constitutionally significant difference between that hypothetical and this case.

488 U.S. at 46, 109 S.Ct. at 294, 102 L.Ed.2d at 277. Justice Marshall also argued that whether improperly admitted evidence should be considered in assessing evidence sufficiency might be made to depend upon why the evidence was admissible. Unreliable evidence, such as inadmissible hearsay, might not be counted, while evidence that should have been excluded under a Fourth Amendment exclusionary rule might be counted.

Ashe v. Swenson

Supreme Court of the United States, 1970.
397 U.S. 436, 90 S.Ct. 1189, 25 L.Ed.2d 469.

■ MR. JUSTICE STEWART delivered the opinion of the Court.

In Benton v. Maryland, 395 U.S. 784, 89 S.Ct. 2056, 23 L.Ed.2d 707, the Court held that the Fifth Amendment guarantee against double jeopardy is enforceable against the States through the Fourteenth Amendment. The question in this case is whether the State of Missouri violated that guarantee when it prosecuted the petitioner a second time for armed robbery in the circumstances here presented.

Sometime in the early hours of the morning of January 10, 1960, six men were engaged in a poker game in the basement of the home of John Gladson at Lee's Summit, Missouri. Suddenly three or four masked men, armed with a shotgun and pistols, broke into the basement and robbed each of the poker players of money and various articles of personal property. The robbers—and it has never been clear whether there were three or four of them—then fled in a car belonging to one of the victims of the robbery. Shortly thereafter the stolen car was discovered in a field, and later that morning three men were arrested by a state trooper while they were walking on a highway not far from where the abandoned car had been found. The petitioner was arrested by another officer some distance away.

The four were subsequently charged with seven separate offenses—the armed robbery of each of the six poker players and the theft of the car. In May 1960 the petitioner went to trial on the charge of robbing Donald Knight, one of the participants in the poker game. At the trial the State called Knight and three of his fellow poker players as prosecution witnesses. Each of them described the circumstances of the holdup and itemized his own individual losses. The proof that an armed robbery had occurred and that personal property had been taken from Knight as well as from each of the others was unassailable. The testimony of the four victims in this regard was consistent both internally and with that of the others. But the State's evidence that the petitioner had been one of the robbers was weak. Two of the witnesses thought that there had been only three robbers altogether, and could not identify the petitioner as one of them. Another of the victims, who was the petitioner's uncle by marriage, said that at the "patrol station" he had positively identified each of the other three men accused of the holdup, but could say only that the petitioner's voice "sounded very much like" that of one of the robbers. The fourth participant in the poker game did identify the petitioner, but only by his "size and height, and his actions."

The cross-examination of these witnesses was brief, and it was aimed primarily at exposing the weakness of their identification testimony. Defense counsel made no attempt to question their testimony regarding the holdup itself or their claims as to their losses. Knight testified without contradiction that the robbers had stolen from him his watch, $250 in cash, and about $500 in checks. His billfold, which had been found by the police in the possession of one of the three other men accused of the robbery, was admitted in evidence. The defense offered no testimony and waived final argument.

The trial judge instructed the jury that if it found that the petitioner was one of the participants in the armed robbery, the theft of "any money" from Knight would sustain a conviction. He also instructed the jury that if the petitioner was one of the robbers, he was guilty under the law even if he had not personally robbed Knight. The jury—though not instructed to elaborate upon its verdict—found the petitioner "not guilty due to insufficient evidence."

Six weeks later the petitioner was brought to trial again, this time for the robbery of another participant in the poker game, a man named Roberts. The petitioner filed a motion to dismiss, based on his previous acquittal. The motion was overruled, and the second trial began. The witnesses were for the most part the same, though this time their testimony was substantially stronger on the issue of the petitioner's identity. For example, two witnesses who at the first trial had been wholly unable to identify the petitioner as one of the robbers, now testified that his features, size, and mannerisms matched those of one of their assailants. Another witness who before had identified the petitioner only by his size and actions now also remembered him by the unusual sound of his voice. The State further refined its case at the second trial by declining to call one of the participants in the poker game whose identification testimony at the first trial had been conspicuously negative. The case went to the jury on instructions virtually identical to those given at the first trial. This time the jury found the petitioner guilty, and he was sentenced to a 35-year term in the state penitentiary.

* * *

... The question is ... whether collateral estoppel ... is a part of the Fifth Amendment's guarantee against double jeopardy. ... "Collateral estoppel" is an awkward phrase, but it stands for an extremely important principle in our adversary system of justice. It means simply that when an issue of ultimate fact has once been determined by a valid and final judgment, that issue cannot again be litigated between the same parties in any future lawsuit. Although first developed in civil litigation, collateral estoppel has been an established rule of federal criminal law at least since this Court's decision more than 50 years ago in United States v. Oppenheimer, 242 U.S. 85, 37 S.Ct. 68, 61 L.Ed. 161. ...The federal decisions have made clear that the rule of collateral estoppel in criminal cases is not to be applied with the hypertechnical and archaic approach of a 19th century pleading book, but with realism and rationality. Where a previous judgment of acquittal was based upon a general verdict, as is usually the case, this approach requires a court to "examine the record of a prior proceeding, taking into account the pleadings, evidence, charge, and other relevant matter, and conclude whether a rational jury could have grounded its verdict upon an issue other than that which the defendant seeks to foreclose from consideration." The inquiry "must be set in a practical frame and viewed with an eye to all the circumstances of the proceedings." Sealfon v. United States, 332 U.S. 575, 579, 68 S.Ct. 237, 240. Any test more technically restrictive would, of course, simply amount to a rejection of the rule of collateral estoppel in criminal proceedings, at least in every case where the first judgment was based upon a general verdict of acquittal.

Straightforward application of the federal rule to the present case can lead to but one conclusion. For the record is utterly devoid of any indication that the first jury could rationally have found that an armed robbery had not occurred, or that Knight had not been a victim of that robbery. The single rationally conceivable issue in dispute before the jury was whether the petitioner had been one of the robbers. And the jury by its verdict found that he had not. The federal rule of law, therefore, would make a second prosecution for the robbery of Roberts wholly impermissible.

The ultimate question to be determined, then, in the light of Benton v. Maryland, supra, is whether this established rule of federal law is embodied in the Fifth Amendment guarantee against double jeopardy. We do not hesitate to hold that it is. For whatever else that constitutional guarantee may embrace, it surely protects a man who has been acquitted from having to "run the gantlet" a second time. Green v. United States, 355 U.S. 184, 190, 78 S.Ct. 221, 225, 2 L.Ed.2d 199.

The question is not whether Missouri could validly charge the petitioner with six separate offenses for the robbery of the six poker players. It is not whether he could have received a total of six punishments if he had been convicted in a single trial of robbing the six victims. It is simply whether, after a jury determined by its verdict that the petitioner was not one of the robbers, the State could constitutionally hale him before a new jury to litigate that issue again.

After the first jury had acquitted the petitioner of robbing Knight, Missouri could certainly not have brought him to trial again upon that charge. Once a jury had determined upon conflicting testimony that there was at least a reasonable doubt that the petitioner was one of the robbers, the State could not present the same or different identification evidence in a second prosecution for the robbery of Knight in the hope that a different jury might find that evidence more convincing. The situation is constitutionally no different here, even though the second trial related to another victim of the same robbery. For the name of the victim, in the circumstances of this case, had no bearing whatever upon the issue of whether the petitioner was one of the robbers.

In this case the State in its brief has frankly conceded that following the petitioner's acquittal, it treated the first trial as no more than a dry run for the second prosecution: "No doubt the prosecutor felt the state had a provable case on the first charge and, when he lost, he did what every good attorney would do—he refined his presentation in light of the turn of events at the first trial." But this is precisely what the constitutional guarantee forbids.

The judgment is reversed, and the case is remanded to the Court of Appeals for the Eighth Circuit for further proceedings consistent with this opinion.

It is so ordered.

Reversed and remanded.

■ MR. JUSTICE BRENNAN, whom MR. JUSTICE DOUGLAS and MR. JUSTICE MARSHALL join, concurring [omitted].

■ MR. CHIEF JUSTICE BURGER, dissenting [omitted].

NOTES

1. **Mutuality of collateral estoppel.** In Simpson v. Florida, 403 U.S. 384, 91 S.Ct. 1801, 29 L.Ed.2d 549 (1971) (per curiam), the defendant was acquitted of the robbery of a store manager. This was on retrial; the first trial resulted in a conviction which was overturned on appeal. He was then tried and convicted for the robbery of a customer. The state courts upheld the conviction, reasoning that the conviction in the first trial gave rise to a "double collateral estoppel," which precluded Simpson from contending—for *Ashe* collateral estoppel purposes—that the state failed to prove his identity as the perpetrator of both robberies. The Supreme Court reversed. Rejecting the rationale of the state court's holding, the Court declared that mutuality is not an ingredient of collateral estoppel as embodied in *Ashe*. In Harris v. Washington, 404 U.S. 55, 92 S.Ct. 183, 30 L.Ed.2d 212 (1971) (per curiam), the defendant's acquittal in the first trial followed the trial judge's exclusion of certain evidence offered by the state. He was later convicted of a crime against another victim of the same incident at a trial at which the evidence was admitted. On appeal from this conviction, the state court held that the evidence was properly admitted and collateral estoppel did not apply because the state's evidence had been improperly excluded at the first trial, Harris' identity as the perpetrator had not been "fully litigated," and *Ashe* did not apply. The Supreme Court reversed, holding that *Ashe* governed, "irrespective of whether the jury considered all relevant evidence [in the first proceeding], and irrespective of the good faith of the State in bringing successive prosecutions." 404 U.S. at 56–57, 92 S.Ct. at 184, 30 L.Ed.2d at 215.

2. **Acquittal of the principal and conviction of the accessory.** The Court has assumed that the collateral estoppel aspect of double jeopardy has no application if the second prosecution involves a different defendant than the first. In Standefer v. United States, 447 U.S. 10, 100 S.Ct. 1999, 64 L.Ed.2d 689 (1980), Standefer was charged with aiding and abetting a revenue official in accepting unauthorized compensation. Before Standefer's trial, the alleged principal—the revenue official—was tried and acquitted of the charges against him. Nevertheless, Standefer was tried and convicted. Affirming the conviction, the Court noted, "Nothing in the Double Jeopardy Clause or the Due Process Clause forecloses putting [Standefer] on trial as an aider and abettor simply because another jury has determined that his principal was not guilty of the offenses charged." 447 U.S. at 22 n. 16, 100 S.Ct. at 2007 n. 16, 64 L.Ed.2d at 699 n. 16.

A somewhat related issue was raised in Harris v. Rivera, 454 U.S. 339, 102 S.Ct. 460, 70 L.Ed.2d 530 (1981) (per curiam). Rivera, his wife Cynthia Humdy, and Earl Robinson were jointly tried in a bench trial for a number of offenses related to a robbery incident; the state's evidence showed that Humdy had been apprehended outside of the apartment in which the robbery had taken place and Rivera and Robinson had been found inside the apartment. Robinson testified in his own defense; Rivera and Humdy did not. The trial judge acquitted Robinson of all charges but convicted Rivera and Humdy of robbery, larceny and burglary. In subsequent federal habeas corpus litigation, the Court of Appeals for the Second Circuit held that there was an apparent inconsistency between the trial judge's verdicts acquitting Robinson and convicting Rivera and, in the absence of an adequate explanation for this apparent inconsistency in the record, this inconsistency violated Rivera's federal constitutional rights. The Supreme Court reversed. Rivera noted the Court's decisions finding no defect in inconsistent jury verdicts, but urged that these decisions rested upon the jury's unreviewable power to acquit and were therefore distinguishable. The Court acknowledged that the inconsistencies between the two verdicts may have been the result of consideration of impermissible factors, such as the failure of Rivera to testify at trial. But it noted that there were also other explanations, including the possibility that the judge's observations in the courtroom created reasonable doubt as to Robinson's guilt that the judge might not have been able to articulate in a convincing manner. "We are not persuaded," the Court concluded, "that an apparent inconsistency in a trial judge's verdict gives rise to an inference of irregularity in his finding of guilt that is sufficiently strong to overcome the well-established presumption that the judge adhered to basic rules of procedure." 454 U.S. at 346–47, 102 S.Ct. at 465, 70 L.Ed.2d at 536. It then continued:

> The question that [Rivera] has standing to raise is whether his trial was fairly conducted. . . . Apart from the acquittal of Robinson, this record discloses no constitutional error. Even assuming that this acquittal was logically inconsistent with the conviction of [Rivera], [Rivera], who was found guilty beyond a reasonable doubt after a fair trial, has no constitutional ground to complain that Robinson was acquitted.

454 U.S. at 348, 102 S.Ct. at 465–66, 70 L.Ed.2d at 537.

3. **Inconsistent verdicts.** The Court further addressed the question of inconsistent jury verdicts in United States v. Powell, 469 U.S. 57, 105 S.Ct. 471, 83 L.Ed.2d 461 (1984). Respondent was charged with certain drug offenses and with facilitating through communication facilities those same offenses. The jury acquitted her of the "predicate" drug offenses but found her guilty of the "compound" facilitating offenses. The Ninth Circuit held this necessitated setting aside the convictions for the compound offenses. The Court, in an opinion authored by Justice Rehnquist, reversed:

> [I]nconsistent verdicts—even verdicts that acquit on a predicate offense while convicting on the compound offense—should not necessarily be interpreted as a windfall to the Government at the defendant's expense. It is equally possible that the jury, convinced of guilt, properly reached its conclusion on the compound offense, and then through mistake, compromise, or lenity, arrived at an inconsistent conclusion on the lesser offense. But in such situations the Government has no recourse if it wishes to correct the jury's error; the Government is precluded from appealing or otherwise upsetting such an acquittal by the Constitution's Double Jeopardy Clause.

469 U.S. at 65, 105 S.Ct. at 476–77, 83 L.Ed.2d at 468. The Court also rejected the respondent's argument that principles of collateral estoppel should apply in this situation:

> [T]he argument necessarily assumes that the acquittal on the predicate offense was proper—the one the jury "really meant." This, of course, is not necessarily correct; all we know is that the verdicts are inconsistent. The Government could just as easily—and erroneously—argue that since the jury convicted on the compound offense the evidence on the predicate offense must have been sufficient. The problem is that the same jury reached inconsistent results; once that is established principles of collateral estoppel—which are predicated on the assumption that the jury acted rationally and found certain facts in reaching its verdict—are no longer useful.

469 U.S. at 68, 105 S.Ct. at 478, 83 L.Ed.2d at 470–71.

4. **Other offense evidence and former acquittal.** The petitioner in Dowling v. United States, 493 U.S. 342, 110 S.Ct. 668, 107 L.Ed.2d 708 (1990) was on trial for bank robbery. At that trial, the government was permitted under Rule 404(b) of the Federal Rules of Evidence to introduce the testimony of a witness who claimed that two weeks after the bank robbery Dowling had entered her dwelling and robbed her. This evidence was introduced to assist in proving that Dowling was the perpetrator of the bank robbery. However, Dowling had previously been acquitted of all charges by a jury in the dwelling robbery case. The trial judge instructed the jury in the bank robbery trial that Dowling had been acquitted in the previous case. The jury in the bank robbery trial returned a verdict of guilty. The Court of Appeals upheld the conviction. In the Supreme Court, Dowling made the claim that exclusion of the evidence of the dwelling robbery was required by the collateral estoppel principle of Ashe v. Swenson. The Supreme Court, in an opinion by Justice White, rejected this argument. Collateral estoppel is not applicable because a lower burden of proof is available to the government in showing in the bank robbery trial that Dowling committed the dwelling robbery than was required to convict him of the dwelling robbery. In the bank robbery trial, it did not have to show Dowling's guilt of the dwelling robbery by proof beyond a reasonable doubt; it had only to introduce evidence from which the jury could reasonably conclude that the act occurred and that the defendant was the actor. This is similar to the forfeiture cases discussed in Note 5 supra. Therefore, there is no inconsistency between the jury acquittal in the dwelling robbery case (establishing a reasonable doubt of guilt in that case) and proof by a lower standard of the same conduct in the bank robbery trial. However, Justice White continued, even if the principle of collateral estoppel were applicable, the burden is upon the criminal defendant to prove why the first jury acquitted him. Dowling failed to show that the only rational basis for the dwelling robbery jury's acquittal was a reasonable doubt that Dowling was the robber. Justice Brennan, joined by Justices Marshall and Stevens, dissented.

B. MULTIPLE CONVICTIONS

When the defendant claims a former conviction rather than a former acquittal, it is arguable that somewhat different concerns are raised. Should application of the Double Jeopardy clause be any different in a former conviction situation? Should it make any difference if the "prior" conviction took place in the same prosecution as the conviction which the defendant is seeking to prevent?

Brown v. Ohio

Supreme Court of the United States, 1977.
432 U.S. 161, 97 S.Ct. 2221, 53 L.Ed.2d 187.

■ MR. JUSTICE POWELL delivered the opinion of the Court.

The question in this case is whether the Double Jeopardy Clause of the Fifth Amendment bars prosecution and punishment for the crime of stealing an automobile following prosecution and punishment for the lesser included offense of operating the same vehicle without the owner's consent.

I.

On November 29, 1973, the petitioner, Nathaniel Brown, stole a 1965 Chevrolet from a parking lot in East Cleveland, Ohio. Nine days later, on December 8, 1973, Brown was caught driving the car in Wickliffe, Ohio. The Wickliffe police charged him with "joyriding"—taking or operating the car without the owner's consent—in violation of Ohio Rev.Code § 4549.04(D).[3] The complaint charged that "on or about December 8, 1973, ... Nathaniel H. Brown did unlawfully and purposely take, drive or operate a certain motor vehicle to wit; a 1965 Chevrolet ... without the consent of the owner one Gloria Ingram. ..."Brown pled guilty to this charge and was sentenced to 30 days in jail and a $100 fine.

Upon his release from jail on January 8, 1974, Brown was returned to East Cleveland to face further charges, and on February 5 he was indicted by the Cuyahoga County grand jury. The indictment was in two counts, the first charging the theft of the car "on or about the 29th day of November 1973," in violation of Ohio Rev.Code § 4549.04(A),[4] and the second charging joyriding on the same date in violation of § 4549.04(D). A bill of particulars filed by the prosecuting attorney specified that

"on or about the 29th day of November, 1973, ... Nathaniel Brown unlawfully did steal a Chevrolet motor vehicle, and take, drive or

---

3. Section 4549.04(D) provided at the time: "No person shall purposely take, operate, or keep any motor vehicle without the consent of its owner." A violation was punishable as a misdemeanor. Section 4549.04 was repealed effective January 1, 1974.

4. Section 4549.04(A) provided: "No person shall steal any motor vehicle." A violation was punishable as a felony.

operate such vehicle without the consent of the owner, Gloria Ingram.... "

Brown objected to both counts of the indictment on the basis of former
jeopardy.

On March 18, 1974, at a pretrial hearing in the Cuyahoga County
Court of Common Pleas, Brown pled guilty to the auto theft charge on the
understanding that the court would consider his claim of former jeopardy
on a motion to withdraw the plea.[5] Upon submission of the motion, the
court overruled Brown's double jeopardy objections. The court sentenced
Brown to six months in jail but suspended the sentence and placed Brown
on probation for one year.

The Ohio Court of Appeals affirmed. It held that under Ohio law the
misdemeanor of joyriding was included in the felony of auto theft:

> "Every element of the crime of operating a motor vehicle without the
> consent of the owner is also an element of the crime of auto theft. 'The
> difference between the crime of stealing a motor vehicle, and operating
> a motor vehicle without the consent of the owner is that conviction for
> stealing requires proof of an intent on the part of the thief to
> *permanently* deprive the owner of possession.' ... [T]he crime of
> operating a motor vehicle without the consent of the owner is a lesser
> included offense of auto theft.... "

Although this analysis led the court to agree with Brown that "for purposes
of double jeopardy the two prosecutions involve the same statutory offense," it nonetheless held the second prosecution permissible:

> "The two prosecutions are based on two separate acts of the appellant,
> one which occurred on November 29th and one which occurred on
> December 8th. Since appellant has not shown that both prosecutions
> are based on the same act or transaction, the second prosecution is not
> barred by the double jeopardy clause."

The Ohio Supreme Court denied leave to appeal.

We granted certiorari to consider Brown's double jeopardy claim, 429
U.S. 893 (1976), and we now reverse.

II.

The Double Jeopardy Clause of the Fifth Amendment, applicable to the
States through the Fourteenth, provides that no person shall "be subject
for the same offence to be twice put in jeopardy of life or limb." It has long
been understood that separate statutory crimes need not be identical—
either in constituent elements or in actual proof—in order to be the same
within the meaning of the constitutional prohibition. 1 Bishop's New
Criminal Law § 1051 (1892); Comment, Twice in Jeopardy, 75 Yale L.J.
262, 268–269 (1965). The principal question in this case is whether auto
theft and joyriding, a greater and lesser included offense under Ohio law,
constitute the "same offense" under the Double Jeopardy Clause.

---

5. The joyriding count of the indict-   ment was *nol-prossed*.

The Double Jeopardy Clause "protects against a second prosecution for the same offense after acquittal. It protects against a second prosecution for the same offense after conviction. And it protects against multiple punishments for the same offense." North Carolina v. Pearce, 395 U.S. 711, 717, 89 S.Ct. 2072, 2076, 23 L.Ed.2d 656 (1969). Where consecutive sentences are imposed at a single criminal trial, the role of the constitutional guarantee is limited to assuring that the court does not exceed its legislative authorization by imposing multiple punishments for the same offense. Where successive prosecutions are at stake, the guarantee serves "a constitutional policy of finality for the defendant's benefit." United States v. Jorn, 400 U.S. 470, 479, 91 S.Ct. 547, 554, 27 L.Ed.2d 543 (1971) (plurality opinion). That policy protects the accused from attempts to relitigate the facts underlying a prior acquittal and from attempts to secure additional punishment after a prior conviction and sentence.

The established test for determining whether two offenses are sufficiently distinguishable to permit the imposition of cumulative punishment was stated in Blockburger v. United States, 284 U.S. 299, 304, 52 S.Ct. 180, 182, 76 L.Ed. 306 (1932):

"The applicable rule is that where the same act or transaction constitutes a violation of two distinct statutory provisions, the test to be applied to determine whether there are two offenses or only one, is whether each provision requires proof of a fact which the other does not. . . ."

This test emphasizes the elements of the two crimes. "If each requires proof that the other does not, the *Blockburger* test would be satisfied, notwithstanding a substantial overlap in the proof offered to establish the crimes. . . ." Iannelli v. United States, 420 U.S. 770, 785 n. 17, 95 S.Ct. 1284, 1293, 43 L.Ed.2d 616 (1975).

If two offenses are the same under this test for purposes of barring consecutive sentences at a single trial, they necessarily will be the same for purposes of barring successive prosecutions. Where the judge is forbidden to impose cumulative punishment for two crimes at the end of a single proceeding, the prosecutor is forbidden to strive for the same result in successive proceedings. Unless "each statute requires proof of an additional fact which the other does not," Morey v. Commonwealth, 108 Mass. 433, 434 (1871), the Double Jeopardy Clause prohibits successive prosecutions as well as cumulative punishment.

We are mindful that the Ohio courts "have the final authority to interpret that State's legislation." Garner v. Louisiana, 368 U.S. 157, 169, 82 S.Ct. 248, 254, 7 L.Ed.2d 207 (1961). Here the Ohio Court of Appeals has authoritatively defined the elements of the two Ohio crimes: joyriding consists of taking or operating a vehicle without the owner's consent, and auto theft consists of joyriding with the intent permanently to deprive the owner of possession. Joyriding is the lesser included offense. The prosecutor who has established joyriding need only prove the requisite intent in order to establish auto theft; the prosecutor who has established auto theft necessarily has established joyriding as well.

Applying the *Blockburger* test, we agree with the Ohio Court of Appeals that joyriding and auto theft, as defined by that court, constitute "the same statutory offense" within the meaning of the Double Jeopardy Clause. For it is clearly *not* the case that "each statute requires proof of an additional fact which the other does not." 284 U.S., at 304, 52 S.Ct., at 182. As is invariably true of a greater and lesser included offense, the lesser offense—joyriding—requires no proof beyond that which is required for conviction of the greater—auto theft. The greater offense is therefore by definition the "same" for purposes of double jeopardy as any lesser offense included in it.

This conclusion merely restates what has been this Court's understanding of the Double Jeopardy Clause at least since In re Nielsen was decided in 1889. In that case the Court endorsed the rule that

> "where ... a person has been tried and convicted for a crime which has various incidents included in it, he cannot be a second time tried for one of those incidents without being twice put in jeopardy for the same offence." 131 U.S., at 188, 9 S.Ct., at 675.

Although in this formulation the conviction of the greater precedes the conviction of the lesser, the opinion makes it clear that the sequence is immaterial. ...

III.

After correctly holding that joyriding and auto theft are the same offense under the Double Jeopardy Clause, the Ohio Court of Appeals nevertheless concluded that Nathaniel Brown could be convicted of both crimes because the charges against him focused on different parts of his 9–day joyride. We hold a different view. The Double Jeopardy Clause is not such a fragile guarantee that prosecutors can avoid its limitations by the simple expedient of dividing a single crime into a series of temporal or spatial units. The applicable Ohio statutes, as written and as construed in this case, make the theft and operation of a single car a single offense. Although the Wickliffe and East Cleveland authorities may have had different perspectives on Brown's offense, it was still only one offense under Ohio Law.[6] Accordingly, the specification of different dates in the two charges on which Brown was convicted cannot alter the fact that he was placed twice in jeopardy for the same offense in violation of the Fifth and Fourteenth Amendments.

Reversed.

The concurring opinion of MR. JUSTICE BRENNAN, in which MR. JUSTICE MARSHALL joined, is omitted.

---

6. We would have a different case if the Ohio Legislature had provided that joyriding is a separate offense for each day in which a motor vehicle is operated without the owner's consent. We also would have a different case if in sustaining Brown's second conviction the Ohio courts had construed the joyriding statute to have that effect. We then would have to decide whether the state courts' construction, applied retroactively in this case, was such "an unforeseeable judicial enlargement of a criminal statute" as to violate due process.

The dissenting opinion of MR. JUSTICE BLACKMUN, with whom THE CHIEF JUSTICE and MR. JUSTICE REHNQUIST, joined, is omitted.

NOTES

1. **Greater and lesser offenses.** In Harris v. Oklahoma, 433 U.S. 682, 97 S.Ct. 2912, 53 L.Ed.2d 1054 (1977) (per curiam), Harris had been a participant in a robbery resulting in the shooting death of the victim. He was first convicted of felony murder; in a second trial he was convicted of the robbery. Citing *Brown* but not *Blockburger,* the Court held the robbery conviction invalid. "When as here, conviction of a greater crime, murder, cannot be had without conviction of the lesser crime, robbery with firearms, the Double Jeopardy Clause bars prosecution for the lesser crime after conviction of the greater one." 433 U.S. at 682, 97 S.Ct. at 2913, 53 L.Ed.2d at 1056. But in Jeffers v. United States, 432 U.S. 137, 97 S.Ct. 2207, 53 L.Ed.2d 168 (1977), the Court split 4 to 4 on whether a defendant could be prosecuted for a greater offense after conviction for a lesser included offense where, at the trial for the lesser offense, the defendant had affirmatively sought separate trials on the two offenses.

In Morris v. Mathews, 475 U.S. 237, 106 S.Ct. 1032, 89 L.Ed.2d 187 (1986), respondent entered a plea of guilty to aggravated robbery and received a prison sentence of 7 to 25 years. Later, he was charged with aggravated murder, which under Ohio law was defined as a purposeful killing during flight from aggravated robbery. His contention that jeopardy precluded his prosecution because he had already been convicted of the aggravated robbery alleged in the aggravated murder indictment was overruled. He was convicted of aggravated murder and received a sentence of life imprisonment. The Ohio appellate courts denied relief but the United States Supreme Court remanded for further consideration in light of Illinois v. Vitale. On re-consideration, the Ohio court held that respondent could not be convicted of aggravated murder, but could be convicted of murder and modified the conviction to murder and the sentence to a term of 15 years to life. Being denied further relief on direct appeal, respondent filed a petition for writ of habeas corpus in federal District Court contending he was entitled to an entirely new trial, which was denied. The Sixth Circuit granted relief on the ground that although jeopardy did not bar a conviction for murder, that such a conviction could not stand if there was a "reasonable possibility" that respondent had been prejudiced by being prosecuted for aggravated murder. It found that evidence of the robbery had been admitted in the aggravated murder trial that would not have been admitted in a murder trial and that the jury may have been prejudiced by that evidence. The Supreme Court, in an opinion authored by Justice White, reversed. The Court of Appeals had applied an incorrect standard. The standard, derived from Strickland v. Washington (Casebook chapter 24), should be whether the defendant can "demonstrate a reasonable probability that he would not have been convicted of the non-jeopardy-barred offense absent the presence of the jeopardy-barred offense," that he must show that "but for the improper inclusion of the jeopardy-barred charge, the result of the proceeding probably would have been different." 475 U.S. at 247, 106 S.Ct. at 1038, 89 L.Ed.2d at 197. Respondent has not met that standard. Justice Blackmun, joined by Justice Powell, concurred in the judgment on the ground the Court of Appeals had correctly stated the standard, but that it was incorrect in concluding it had been met on the facts of this case. Justice Marshall, dissenting, agreed with the statement of the standard made by the Court of Appeals, but unlike Justice Blackmun, concluded that the respondent had met the standard. Justice Brennan agreed with Justice Marshall on this point.

2. **Continuing criminal enterprise and target offense.** In Garrett v. U.S., 471 U.S. 773, 105 S.Ct. 2407, 85 L.Ed.2d 764 (1985), Garrett entered a plea of guilty to the offense of importation of marijuana and received a five-year prison sentence. Later, he was indicted for engaging in a continuing criminal enterprise, which requires proof that the defendant in concert with 5 or more others, and occupying a position of organizer, supervisor or other position of management, engaged in a continuing series of felony violations of the law from which he obtained substantial income or resources. One of the three violations alleged against the defendant in this case was the importation of marijuana charge to which he had already plead guilty. His motions to dismiss the continuing criminal enterprise indictment on the ground he had already been convicted of a lesser included offense of that charge were denied by the trial court. He was convicted of engaging in a continuing criminal enterprise and received a sentence of 40 years to run consecutively to the 5 year sentence he had received earlier. The Court of Appeals affirmed the conviction and sentence over double jeopardy claims and the Supreme Court, in an opinion authored by Justice Rehnquist, affirmed.

The first inquiry is to determine whether Congress intended for the offense of continuing criminal enterprise to be separate from any constituent offenses that may be also alleged. The legislative intent is clear that Congress desired the continuing criminal enterprise offense to be separate. Garrett claimed his case is controlled by Brown v. Ohio, but the Court distinguished *Brown* on the ground that some of the conduct alleged against Garrett in the continuing criminal enterprise case had not even occurred at the time of the marijuana importation case:

> Obviously the conduct in which Garrett was charged with engaging in the Florida indictment [for continuing criminal enterprise], when compared with that with which he was charged in the Washington indictment [for importation of marijuana] does not lend itself to the simple analogy of a single course of conduct—stealing a car—comprising a lesser included misdemeanor within a felony. Here the continuing criminal enterprise was alleged to have spanned more than five years; the acts charged in the Washington indictment were alleged to have occurred on single days in 1979 and 1980, respectively. Whenever it was during the five-and-one-half-year period alleged in the indictment that Garrett committed the first of the three predicate offenses required to form the basis for a continuing criminal enterprise prosecution, it could not then have been said with any certainty that he would necessarily go ahead and commit the other violations required to render him liable on a continuing criminal enterprise charge. Every minute that Nathaniel Brown drove or possessed the stolen automobile he was simultaneously committing both the lesser included misdemeanor and the greater felony, but the same simply is not true of Garrett.

471 U.S. at 788–89, 105 S.Ct. at 2416, 85 L.Ed.2d at 777–78. The Court then likened this case to Diaz v. United States, 223 U.S. 442, 32 S.Ct. 250, 56 L.Ed. 500 (1912) in which a defendant plead guilty to assault and after the victim later died was convicted of homicide. The Diaz Court had said, "At the time of the trial for the [assault] the death had not ensued, and not until it did ensue was the homicide committed. Then, and not before, was it possible to put the accused in jeopardy for that offense." Justices Stevens, Brennan and Marshall dissented.

Missouri v. Hunter
Supreme Court of the United States, 1983.
459 U.S. 359, 103 S.Ct. 673, 74 L.Ed.2d 535.

■ CHIEF JUSTICE BURGER delivered the opinion of the court.

We granted certiorari to consider whether the prosecution and conviction of a criminal defendant in a single trial on both a charge of "armed criminal action" and a charge of first degree robbery—the underlying felony—violates the Double Jeopardy Clause of the Fifth Amendment.

I

On the evening of November 24, 1978, respondent and two accomplices entered an A & P supermarket in Kansas City, Missouri. Respondent entered the store manager's office and ordered the manager, at gun point, to open two safes. While the manager was complying with the demands of the robbers, respondent struck him twice with the butt of his revolver. While the robbery was in progress, an employee who drove in front of the store observed the robbery and went to a nearby bank to alert an off-duty police officer. That officer arrived at the front of the store and ordered the three men to stop. Respondent fired a shot at the officer and the officer returned the fire but the trio escaped.

Respondent and his accomplices were apprehended. In addition to being positively identified by the store manager and the police officer at trial and in a line-up, respondent made an oral and written confession which was admitted in evidence. At his trial, respondent offered no direct evidence and was convicted of robbery in the first degree, armed criminal action and assault with malice.

Missouri's statute proscribing robbery in the first degree, Mo.Ann.Stat. App. § 560.120 (Vernon 1979), provides:

> "Every person who shall be convicted of feloniously taking the property of another from his person, or in his presence, and against his will, by violence to his person, or by putting him in fear of some immediate injury to his person; or who shall be convicted of feloniously taking the property of another from the person of his wife, servant, clerk or agent, in charge thereof, and against the will of such wife, servant, clerk or agent by violence to the person of such wife, servant, clerk or agent, or by putting him or her in fear of some immediate injury to his or her person, shall be adjudged guilty of robbery in the first degree."

Mo.Ann.Stat.App. § 560.135 (Vernon 1979) prescribes the punishment for robbery in the first degree and provides in pertinent part:

> "Every person convicted of robbery in the first degree by means of a dangerous and deadly weapon and every person convicted of robbery in the first degree by any other means shall be punished by imprisonment by the division of corrections for not less than five years. . . ."

Mo.Stat.App. § 559.225 (Vernon 1979) proscribes armed criminal action and provides in pertinent part:

> "[A]ny person who commits any felony under the laws of this state by, with, or through the use, assistance, or aid of a dangerous or deadly weapon is also guilty of the crime of armed criminal action and, upon conviction, shall be punished by imprisonment by the division of corrections for a term of not less than three years. The punishment imposed pursuant to this subsection shall be in addition to any punishment provided by law for the crime committed by, with, or

through the use, assistance, or aid of a dangerous or deadly weapon. No person convicted under this subsection shall be eligible for parole, probation, conditional release or suspended imposition or execution of sentence for a period of three calendar years."

Pursuant to these statutes respondent was sentenced to concurrent terms of (a) ten years' imprisonment for the robbery; (b) 15 years for armed criminal action; and (c) to a consecutive term of five years' imprisonment for assault, for a total of 20 years.

On appeal to the Missouri Court of Appeals, respondent claimed that his sentence for both robbery in the first degree and armed criminal action violated the Double Jeopardy Clause of the Fifth Amendment of the United States Constitution made applicable to the states by the Fourteenth Amendment. The Missouri Court of Appeals agreed and reversed respondent's conviction and 15-year sentence for armed criminal action. 622 S.W.2d 374 (1981). The Court of Appeals relied entirely upon the holding of the Missouri Supreme Court opinions in State v. Haggard, 619 S.W.2d 44 (Mo.1981); Sours v. State, 593 S.W.2d 208 (Mo.), vacated sub nom. Missouri v. Sours, 446 U.S. 962, 100 S.Ct. 2935, 64 L.Ed.2d 820 (1980) (*Sours I*); and Sours v. State, 603 S.W.2d 592 (1980), cert. denied, 449 U.S. 1131, 101 S.Ct. 953, 67 L.Ed.2d 118 (1981) (*Sours II*). The State's timely alternative motion for rehearing or transfer to the Missouri Supreme Court was denied by the Court of Appeals on September 15, 1981. The Missouri Supreme Court denied review on November 10, 1981.

We granted certiorari, 456 U.S. 914, 102 S.Ct. 1767, 72 L.Ed.2d 173 (1982), and we vacate and remand.

II

The Missouri Supreme Court first adopted its challenged approach to the Double Jeopardy issue now before us in *Sours I,* supra. In that case, as here, the defendant was convicted and sentenced separately for robbery in the first degree and armed criminal action based on the robbery. The Missouri Supreme Court concluded that under the test announced in Blockburger v. United States, 284 U.S. 299, 52 S.Ct. 180, 76 L.Ed. 306 (1932), armed criminal action and any underlying offense are the "same offense" under the Fifth Amendment's Double Jeopardy Clause. That court acknowledged that the Missouri legislature had expressed its clear intent that a defendant should be subject to conviction and sentence under the armed criminal action statute in addition to any conviction and sentence for the underlying felony. 593 S.W.2d, at 216. The court nevertheless held that the Double Jeopardy Clause "prohibits imposing punishment for both armed criminal action and for the underlying felony." Id., at 223. It then set aside the defendant's conviction for armed criminal action.

When the State sought review here in *Sours I,* we remanded the case for reconsideration in light of our holding in Whalen v. United States, 445 U.S. 684, 100 S.Ct. 1432, 63 L.Ed.2d 715 (1980). Missouri v. Sours, 446 U.S. 962, 100 S.Ct. 2935, 64 L.Ed.2d 820 (1980). On remand, in *Sours II,* supra, the Missouri Supreme Court adhered to its previous ruling that armed criminal action and the underlying felony are the "same offense" and that the Double Jeopardy Clause bars separate punishment of a defendant for each offense, notwithstanding the acknowledged intent of the legislature to impose two separate punishments for the two defined offenses.

Most recently, in State v. Haggard, supra, the Missouri Supreme Court reexamined its decisions in *Sours I,* supra, and *Sours II,* supra, in light of our 1981 holding in Albernaz v. United States, 450 U.S. 333, 101 S.Ct. 1137, 67 L.Ed.2d 275 (1981). The Missouri court, however, remained unpersuaded, stating:

> "Until such time as the Supreme Court of the United States declares clearly and unequivocally that the Double Jeopardy Clause of the Fifth Amendment of the United States Constitution does not apply to the legislative branch of government, we cannot do other than what we perceive to be our duty to refuse to enforce multiple punishments for the same offense arising out of a single transaction." 619 S.W.2d, at 51.

This view manifests a misreading of our cases on the meaning of the Double Jeopardy Clause of the Fifth Amendment; we need hardly go so far as suggested to decide that a legislature constitutionally can prescribe cumulative punishments for violation of its first degree robbery statute and its armed criminal action statute.

III

The Double Jeopardy Clause is cast explicitly in terms of being "twice put in jeopardy." We have consistently interpreted it " 'to protect an individual from being subjected to the hazards of trial and possible conviction more than once for an alleged offense.' " Burks v. United States, 437 U.S. 1, 11, 98 S.Ct. 2141, 2147, 57 L.Ed.2d 1 (1978), quoting Green v. United States, 355 U.S. 184, 187, 78 S.Ct. 221, 223, 2 L.Ed.2d 199 (1957). Because respondent has been subjected to only one trial, it is not contended that his right to be free from multiple trials for the same offense has been violated. Rather, the Missouri court vacated respondent's conviction for armed criminal action because of the statements of this Court that the Double Jeopardy Clause also "protects against multiple punishments for the same offense." North Carolina v. Pearce, 395 U.S. 711, 717, 89 S.Ct. 2072, 2076, 23 L.Ed.2d 656 (1969). Particularly in light of recent precedents of this Court, it is clear that the Missouri Supreme Court has misperceived the nature of the Double Jeopardy Clause's protection against multiple punishments. With respect to cumulative sentences imposed in a single trial, the Double Jeopardy Clause does no more than prevent the sentencing court from prescribing greater punishment than the legislature intended.

In Whalen v. United States, 445 U.S. 684, 100 S.Ct. 1432, 63 L.Ed.2d 715 (1980), we addressed the question whether cumulative punishments for the offenses of rape and of killing the same victim in the perpetration of the crime of rape was contrary to federal statutory and constitutional law. A divided Court relied on Blockburger v. United States, 284 U.S. 299, 52 S.Ct. 180, 76 L.Ed. 306 (1932), in holding that the two statutes in controversy proscribed the "same" offense. The opinion in *Blockburger* stated:

"The applicable rule is that where the same act or transaction constitutes a violation of two distinct statutory provisions, the test to be applied to determine whether there are two offenses or only one, is whether each provision requires proof of a fact which the other does not." 284 U.S., at 304, 52 S.Ct., at 182.

In *Whalen* we also noted that *Blockburger* established a rule of statutory construction in these terms:

"The assumption underlying the rule is that Congress *ordinarily* does not intend to punish the same offense under two different statutes. Accordingly, where two statutory provisions proscribe the 'same offense,' they are construed not to authorize cumulative punishments *in the absence of a clear indication of contrary legislative intent.*" 445 U.S., at 691–692, 100 S.Ct., at 1437–1438 (emphasis added).

We went on to emphasize the qualification on that rule:

"[W]here the offenses are the same . . . cumulative sentences are not permitted, *unless elsewhere specially authorized by Congress.*" Id., at 693, 100 S.Ct., at 1438 (emphasis added).

It is clear, therefore, that the result in *Whalen* turned on the fact that the Court saw no "clear indication of contrary legislative intent." Accordingly, under the rule of statutory construction, we held that cumulative punishment could not be imposed under the two statutes.

In Albernaz v. United States, 450 U.S. 333, 101 S.Ct. 1137, 67 L.Ed.2d 275 (1981), we addressed the issue whether a defendant could be cumulatively punished in a single trial for conspiracy to import marihuana and conspiracy to distribute marihuana. There, in contrast to *Whalen,* we concluded that the two statutes did not proscribe the "same" offense in the sense that " 'each provision requires proof of a fact [that] the other does not.' "450 U.S. 339, 101 S.Ct. at 1142, quoting *Blockburger,* supra, 284 U.S., at 304, 52 S.Ct., at 182. We might well have stopped at that point and upheld the petitioners' cumulative punishments under the challenged statute since cumulative punishment can presumptively be assessed after conviction for two offenses that are not the "same" under *Blockburger.* See, e.g., American Tobacco Co. v. United States, 328 U.S. 781, 66 S.Ct. 1125, 90 L.Ed. 1575 (1946). However, we went on to state that because:

"The *Blockburger* test is a 'rule of statutory construction,' and because it serves as a means of discerning congressional purpose *the rule should not be controlling where, for example, there is a clear indication of contrary legislative intent.*" Albernaz v. United States, supra, 450 U.S., at 340, 101 S.Ct., at 1143 (emphasis added).

We found "[n]othing . . . in the legislative history which . . . discloses an intent contrary to the presumption which should be accorded to these statutes after application of the *Blockburger* test." Ibid. We concluded our discussion of the impact of clear legislative intent on the *Whalen* rule of statutory construction with this language:

[T]he question of what punishments are constitutionally permissible is no different from the question of what punishment the Legislative Branch intended to be imposed. *Where Congress intended, as it did here, to impose multiple punishments, imposition of such sentences does not violate the Constitution.* Id., at 344, 101 S.Ct., at 1145 (emphasis added) (footnote omitted).

Here, the Missouri Supreme Court has construed the two statutes at issue as defining the same crime. In addition, the Missouri Supreme Court has recognized that the legislature intended that punishment for violations of the statutes be cumulative. We are bound to accept the Missouri court's construction of that State's statutes. See O'Brien v. Skinner, 414 U.S. 524, 531, 94 S.Ct. 740, 743, 38 L.Ed.2d 702 (1974). However, we are not bound by the Missouri Supreme Court's legal conclusion that these two statutes violate the Double Jeopardy Clause, and we reject its legal conclusion.

Our analysis and reasoning in *Whalen* and *Albernaz* lead inescapably to the conclusion that simply because two criminal statutes may be construed to proscribe the same conduct under the *Blockburger* test does not mean that the Double Jeopardy Clause precludes the imposition, in a single trial, of cumulative punishments pursuant to those statutes. The rule of statutory construction noted in *Whalen* is not a constitutional rule requiring courts to negate clearly expressed legislative intent. Thus far, we have utilized that rule only to limit a federal court's power to impose convictions and punishments when the will of Congress is not clear. Here, the Missouri Legislature has made its intent crystal clear. Legislatures, not courts, prescribe the scope of punishments.

Where, as here, a legislature specifically authorizes cumulative punishment under two statutes, regardless of whether those two statutes prescribe the "same" conduct under *Blockburger,* a court's task of statutory construction is at an end and the prosecutor may seek and the trial court or jury may impose cumulative punishment under such statutes in a single trial.

Accordingly, the judgment of the Court of Appeals of Missouri, Western District, is vacated and the case is remanded for further proceedings not inconsistent with this opinion.

So ordered.

■ JUSTICE MARSHALL, with whom JUSTICE STEVENS joins, dissenting. [Omitted].

NOTES

1. **Simultaneous trial of multiple offenses.** The respondent in Ohio v. Johnson, 467 U.S. 493, 104 S.Ct. 2536, 81 L.Ed.2d 425 (1984) was charged with murder, involuntary manslaughter, aggravated robbery and grand theft, all arising out of the same occurrence. At his arraignment before the trial court, respondent offered to plead guilty to involuntary manslaughter, which under Ohio law was a lesser included offense of murder, and to theft, which was a lesser included offense of robbery. Over objection by the prosecutor, the trial court accepted the pleas of guilty. It then dismissed the murder and robbery charges on the ground that further prosecution of them would violate respondent's rights under double jeopardy. The Ohio appellate courts affirmed the action of the trial court. The Supreme Court, in an opinion by Justice Rehnquist, reversed.

Respondent's jeopardy interests in avoiding cumulative punishments for the same offense are defined by Missouri v. Hunter. Thus, it is ultimately a question of legislative intent:

> We accept, as we must, the Ohio Supreme Court's determination that the Ohio legislature did not intend cumulative punishment for the two pairs of crimes involved here. But before respondent can ever be punished for the offenses of murder and aggravated robbery he will first have to be found guilty of those offenses. The trial court's dismissal of these more serious charges did more than simply prevent the imposition of cumulative punishments; it halted completely the proceedings that ultimately would have led to a verdict of guilt or innocence on these more serious charges. Presumably the trial court, in the event of a guilty verdict on the more serious offenses, will have to confront the question of cumulative punishments as a matter of state law, but because of that court's ruling preventing even the trial of the more serious offenses that stage of the prosecution was never reached. While the Double Jeopardy Clause may protect a defendant against cumulative punishments for convictions on the same offense, the Clause does not prohibit the State from prosecuting respondent for such multiple offenses in a single prosecution.

467 U.S. at 499–500, 104 S.Ct. at 2541, 81 L.Ed.2d at 433. Respondent also argued that the trial court's action was required by Brown v. Ohio because the guilty pleas constituted prior convictions of lesser included offenses:

> Respondent's argument is apparently based on the assumption that trial proceedings, like amoebae, are capable of being infinitely subdivided, so that a determination of guilt and punishment on one count of a multi-count indictment immediately raises a double jeopardy bar to continued prosecution of any remaining counts that are greater or lesser included offenses of the charge just concluded. We have never held that, and decline to hold it now. ...
>
> No interest of respondent protected by the Double Jeopardy Clause is implicated by continuing prosecution on the remaining charges brought in the indictment. Here respondent offered only to resolve part of the charges against him, while the State objected to disposing of any of the counts against respondent without a trial. Respondent has not been exposed to conviction on the charges to which he pleaded not guilty, nor has the State had the opportunity to marshal its evidence and resources more than once or to hone its presentation of its case through a trial. The acceptance of a guilty plea to lesser included offenses while charges on the greater offenses remain pending, moreover, has none of the implications of an "implied acquittal" which results from a verdict convicting a defendant on lesser included offenses rendered by a jury charged to consider both greater and lesser included offenses.

467 U.S. at 501–02, 104 S.Ct. at 2542, 81 L.Ed.2d at 434. Justice Stevens, joined by Justice Marshall, dissenting, took the position that a conviction based on a plea of guilty has the same legal effect as a conviction based on a jury's verdict and respondent should receive the benefits of prior conviction protection.

2. ***Blockburger* and simultaneous prosecution.** In several cases, the Court addressed the application of the *Blockburger* test to multiple convictions in the same trial. In United States v. Woodward, 469 U.S. 105, 105 S.Ct. 611, 83 L.Ed.2d 518 (1985), the respondent had been convicted of both failing to report he was bringing more than $5,000 into the United States and of willfully making a false statement to a government agency. Both convictions were predicated on the same act: answering "no" to the customs question whether he had more than $5,000 in his possession. The Ninth Circuit had held that *Blockburger,* as a test of Congressional intent, precluded multiple convictions, but the Court, *per curiam,* reversed. Proof of the currency violation does not necessarily include proof of the

false statement violation, since "a traveler who enters the country and passes through customs prepared to answer questions truthfully, but is never asked whether he is carrying over $5,000 in currency, might nonetheless be subject to conviction [under the currency statute but would not have violated the false statement statute]." 469 U.S. at 108, 105 S.Ct. at 612, 83 L.Ed.2d at 521.

In Ball v. United States, 470 U.S. 856, 105 S.Ct. 1668, 84 L.Ed.2d 740 (1985) the petitioner was convicted of being a convicted felon who had received a weapon that had travelled in interstate commerce and of being a convicted felon who had possessed a weapon that had travelled in interstate commerce. Both convictions were based on his possession of the same firearm. The Court, in an opinion authored by the Chief Justice, held that *Blockburger* had been violated because "proof of illegal receipt of a firearm *necessarily* includes proof of illegal possession of that weapon." 470 U.S. at 862, 105 S.Ct. at 1672, 84 L.Ed.2d at 746. Further, the fact that sentences on the two convictions in this case were made to run concurrently does not cure the harm:

> The second conviction, whose concomitant sentence is served concurrently, does not evaporate simply because of the concurrence of the sentence. The separate *conviction,* apart from the concurrent sentence, has potential adverse collateral consequences that may not be ignored. For example, the presence of two convictions on the record may delay the defendant's eligibility for parole or result in an increased sentence under a recidivist statute for a future offense. Moreover, the second conviction may be used to impeach the defendant's credibility and certainly carries the societal stigma accompanying any criminal conviction. ...Thus, the second conviction, even if it results in no greater sentence, is an impermissible punishment.

470 U.S. at 864–65, 105 S.Ct. at 1673, 84 L.Ed.2d at 748. The Court emphasized, however, that the Government is still permitted to charge and seek to prove both violations in the same trial. And the trial court is authorized to submit both charges to the jury. Should the jury return verdicts of guilty on each charge, however, the trial court must then exercise discretion to vacate the conviction on one of the charges and impose sentence on the other.

The Petitioner in Rutledge v. United States, 517 U.S. 292, 116 S.Ct. 1241, 134 L.Ed.2d 419 (1996) was convicted of conspiracy to distribute controlled substances and of conducting a continuing criminal enterprise to distribute controlled substances. The convictions occurred in the same trial and Petitioner received a life sentence without parole for each offense. Sentences were made to run concurrently.

The Second Circuit rejected the claim that the conspiracy offense was a lesser included offense of the continuing criminal enterprise offense, but the Supreme Court, in a unanimous opinion by Justice Stevens, reversed.

The offense of continuing criminal enterprise requires that the defendant act in concert with five or more others with respect to whom the defendant occupies a leadership position. The Court concluded that acting in concert implies an agreement and that in this case the same agreement was being prosecuted as conspiracy and as continuing criminal enterprise. The continuing criminal enterprise offense requires proof of several facts not required under the conspiracy offense, but the reverse is not true. Since the agreement is implicit in the requirement that the defendant act in concert with others, conspiracy requires proof of no fact not required by continuing criminal enterprise. It is, then, a lesser included offense of continuing criminal enterprise.

Therefore, there is a presumption that the Double Jeopardy Clause prohibits convictions for both offenses in the same trial, unless legislative intent can be found to authorize multiple convictions and punishment. There is no suggestion that

Congress intended for a single agreement to be punishable both as a conspiracy and as continuing criminal enterprise. Therefore, the Double Jeopardy Clause prohibits convictions for both offenses.

3.   **Remedy for double jeopardy violation in simultaneous prosecution.** The respondent in Jones v. Thomas, 491 U.S. 376, 109 S.Ct. 2522, 105 L.Ed.2d 322 (1989) was convicted in the same trial of both felony murder and the underlying felony of attempted robbery. He received a 15 year sentence for attempted robbery and a consecutive life sentence for felony murder. After he had served the 15 year sentence, the United States Court of Appeals held that he was entitled to immediate release because the imposition of both sentences violated double jeopardy protections. The Supreme Court, in an opinion by Justice Kennedy, held that gubernatorial commutation of the 15 year sentence to time already served and crediting the time served to the life sentence was adequate to remedy the double jeopardy violation:

> Double jeopardy is an area of the law filled with technical rules, and the protections it affords defendants might at times be perceived as technicalities. This is irrelevant where the ancient and important principles embodied in the Double Jeopardy Clause are implicated ... But neither the Double Jeopardy Clause nor any other constitutional provision exists to provide unjustified windfalls. The Missouri court's alteration of respondent's sentence to a single term for felony murder with credit for time served provided suitable protection of his double jeopardy rights.

491 U.S. at 387, 109 S.Ct. at 2529, 105 L.Ed.2d at 335. Justice Scalia, joined by Justices Stevens, Brennan and Marshall, dissented.

4.   **Prosecution for offense already "used" in sentencing.** Does the Double Jeopardy Clause prohibition against multiple punishments for the same offense prohibit prosecution for an offense the underlying conduct of which has already been taken into account under federal Sentencing Guidelines as "relevant conduct" in the sentence for a previous conviction? The petitioner in Witte v. United States, 515 U.S. 389, 115 S.Ct. 2199, 132 L.Ed.2d 351 (1995) was convicted of a marijuana offense. Conspiracy to commit a cocaine offense was taken into account as relevant conduct by the court in selecting the sentence in the marijuana case. Later, petitioner was indicted for the cocaine offense and interposed a claim of double jeopardy. The District Court upheld the claim but the Fifth Circuit reversed. The Supreme Court, in an opinion by Justice O'Connor, affirmed. It held that consideration of the defendant character at sentencing, as evidenced in part by prior criminal conduct, is not punishment for that conduct but only for the offense for which he is being sentenced. Accordingly, as in the case of repeat offender statutes that enhance punishment for prior criminal convictions, multiple punishment for the same offense does not occur when unadjudicated criminal conduct is taken into account in sentencing for conviction of a different offense. The Sentencing Guidelines further protect against "double counting" by providing for concurrent sentences should the petitioner be found guilty of the cocaine charge, because it was previously taken into account as "relevant conduct" in the marijuana case.

5.   **Using conduct at sentencing for which defendant had been acquitted.** May a United States District Court take into account as relevant conduct at sentencing acts for which the defendant has been tried and acquitted by a jury? The United States Supreme Court, in a *per curiam* reversal of the Ninth Circuit, held in United States v. Watts, 519 U.S. 148, 117 S.Ct. 633, 136 L.Ed.2d 554 (1997) that a District Court may under federal statutory and Sentencing Commission provisions take such acts into account despite the acquittal. As to the Double Jeopardy Clause issue, the Court held that the jury acquittal did not constitute a finding that the defendant did not do the acts charged, but rather constituted only a conclusion that

the government had failed to prove beyond a reasonable doubt that the defendant engaged in the charged conduct. So long as the government subsequently at sentencing proves by a preponderance of the evidence that the defendant did engage in that conduct and that it is relevant to sentencing for an offense for which the defendant stands convicted, there is no Double Jeopardy preclusion to considering the conduct by the sentencing court. Justice Stevens dissented.

United States v. Dixon

Supreme Court of the United States, 1993.
509 U.S. 688, 113 S.Ct. 2849, 125 L.Ed.2d 556.

■ Justice Scalia announced the judgment of the Court and delivered the opinion of the Court with respect to Parts I, II, and IV, and an opinion with respect to Parts III and V, in which Justice Kennedy joins.

In both of these cases, respondents were tried for criminal contempt of court for violating court orders that prohibited them from engaging in conduct that was later the subject of a criminal prosecution. We consider whether the subsequent criminal prosecutions are barred by the Double Jeopardy Clause.

I

Respondent Alvin Dixon was arrested for second-degree murder and was released on bond. Consistent with the District of Columbia's bail law authorizing the judicial officer to impose any condition that "will reasonably assure the appearance of the person for trial or the safety of any other person or the community," D.C.Code Ann. § 23–1321(a) (1989), Dixon's release form specified that he was not to commit "any criminal offense," and warned that any violation of the conditions of release would subject him "to revocation of release, an order of detention, and prosecution for contempt of court." See § 23–1329(a) (authorizing those sanctions).

While awaiting trial, Dixon was arrested and indicted for possession of cocaine with intent to distribute, in violation of D.C.Code Ann. § 33–541(a)(1) (1988). The court issued an order requiring Dixon to show cause why he should not be held in contempt or have the terms of his pretrial release modified. At the show-cause hearing, four police officers testified to facts surrounding the alleged drug offense; Dixon's counsel cross-examined these witnesses and introduced other evidence. The court concluded that the Government had established " 'beyond a reasonable doubt that [Dixon] was in possession of drugs and that those drugs were possessed with the intent to distribute.' " 598 A.2d 724, 728 (D.C.1991). The court therefore found Dixon guilty of criminal contempt under § 23–1329(c), which allows contempt sanctions after expedited proceedings without a jury and "in accordance with principles applicable to proceedings for criminal contempt." For his contempt, Dixon was sentenced to 180 days in jail. D.C.Code § 23–1329(c) (maximum penalty of six months' imprisonment and $1000 fine). He later moved to dismiss the cocaine indictment on double jeopardy grounds; the trial court granted the motion.

Respondent Michael Foster's route to this Court is similar. Based on Foster's alleged physical attacks upon her in the past, Foster's estranged wife Ana obtained a civil protection order (CPO) in Superior Court of the District of Columbia. See D.C.Code Ann. § 16–1005(c) (1989) (CPO may be issued upon a showing of good cause to believe that the subject "has committed or is threatening an intrafamily offense"). The order, to which Foster consented, required that he not " 'molest, assault, or in any manner threaten or physically abuse' " Ana Foster; a separate order, not implicated here, sought to protect her mother. 598 A.2d, at 725–726.

Over the course of eight months, Ana Foster filed three separate motions to have her husband held in contempt for numerous violations of the CPO. Of the 16 alleged episodes, the only charges relevant here are three separate instances of threats (on November 12, 1987, and March 26 and May 17, 1988) and two assaults (on November 6, 1987, and May 21, 1988), in the most serious of which Foster "threw [his wife] down basement stairs, kicking her body[,] . . . pushed her head into the floor causing head injuries, [and Ana Foster] lost consciousness." 598 A.2d, at 726.

After issuing a notice of hearing and ordering Foster to appear, the court held a 3–day bench trial. Counsel for Ana Foster and her mother prosecuted the action; the United States was not represented at trial, although the United States Attorney was apparently aware of the action, as was the court aware of a separate grand jury proceeding on some of the alleged criminal conduct. As to the assault charges, the court stated that Ana Foster would have "to prove as an element, first that there was a Civil Protection Order, and then [that] . . . the assault as defined by the criminal code, in fact occurred." At the close of the plaintiffs' case, the court granted Foster's motion for acquittal on various counts, including the alleged threats on November 12 and May 17. Foster then took the stand and generally denied the allegations. The court found Foster guilty beyond a reasonable doubt of four counts of criminal contempt (three violations of Ana Foster's CPO, and one violation of the CPO obtained by her mother), including the November 6, 1987 and May 21, 1988 assaults, but acquitted him on other counts, including the March 26 alleged threats. He was sentenced to an aggregate 600 days' imprisonment. See § 16–1005(f) (authorizing contempt punishment); Sup.Ct. of D.C. Intrafamily Rules 7(c), 12(e) (maximum punishment of six months' imprisonment and $300 fine).

The United States Attorney's Office later obtained an indictment charging Foster with simple assault on or about November 6, 1987 (Count I, violation of § 22–504); threatening to injure another on or about November 12, 1987, and March 26 and May 17, 1988 (Counts II–IV, violation of § 22–2307); and assault with intent to kill on or about May 21, 1988 (Count V, violation of § 22–501). App. 43–44. Ana Foster was the complainant in all counts; the first and last counts were based on the events for which Foster had been held in contempt, and the other three were based on the alleged events for which Foster was acquitted of contempt. Like Dixon, Foster filed a motion to dismiss, claiming a double jeopardy bar to all counts, and also collateral estoppel as to Counts II–IV. The trial court denied the double-jeopardy claim and did not rule on the collateral-estoppel assertion.

The Government appealed the double jeopardy ruling in *Dixon,* and Foster appealed the trial court's denial of his motion. The District of

Columbia Court of Appeals consolidated the two cases, reheard them en banc, and, relying on our recent decision in Grady v. Corbin, 495 U.S. 508 (1990), ruled that both subsequent prosecutions were barred by the Double Jeopardy Clause. 598 A.2d, at 725. In its petition for certiorari, the Government presented the sole question "[w]hether the Double Jeopardy Clause bars prosecution of a defendant on substantive criminal charges based upon the same conduct for which he previously has been held in criminal contempt of court." We granted certiorari, 503 U.S. 1004 (1992).

II

To place these cases in context, one must understand that they are the consequence of an historically anomalous use of the contempt power. In both *Dixon* and *Foster,* a court issued an order directing a particular individual not to commit criminal offenses. (In Dixon's case, the court incorporated the entire criminal code; in Foster's case, the criminal offense of simple assault.) That could not have occurred at common law, or in the 19th–century American judicial system.

* * *

The Double Jeopardy Clause, whose application to this new context we are called upon to consider, provides that no person shall "be subject for the same offence to be twice put in jeopardy of life or limb." U.S. Const., Amdt. 5. This protection applies both to successive punishments and to successive prosecutions for the same criminal offense. See North Carolina v. Pearce, 395 U.S. 711 (1969). It is well established that criminal contempt, at least the sort enforced through nonsummary proceedings, is "a crime in the ordinary sense." *Bloom,* supra, at 201. Accord, New Orleans v. The Steamship Co., 20 Wall. 387, 392 (1874).

We have held that constitutional protections for criminal defendants other than the double jeopardy provision apply in nonsummary criminal contempt prosecutions just as they do in other criminal prosecutions. See, e.g., Gompers v. Bucks Stove & Range Co., 221 U.S. 418, 444 (1911) (presumption of innocence, proof beyond a reasonable doubt, and guarantee against self-incrimination); Cooke v. United States, 267 U.S. 517, 537 (1925) (notice of charges, assistance of counsel, and right to present a defense); In re Oliver, 333 U.S. 257, 278 (1948) (public trial). We think it obvious, and today hold, that the protection of the Double Jeopardy Clause likewise attaches. Accord, Menna v. New York, 423 U.S. 61 (1975) (*per curiam*); Colombo v. New York, 405 U.S. 9 (1972) (*per curiam*).

In both the multiple punishment and multiple prosecution contexts, this Court has concluded that where the two offenses for which the defendant is punished or tried cannot survive the "same-elements" test, the double jeopardy bar applies. See, e.g., Brown v. Ohio, 432 U.S. 161, 168–169 (1977); Blockburger v. United States, 284 U.S. 299, 304 (1932) (multiple punishment); Gavieres v. United States, 220 U.S. 338, 342 (1911) (successive prosecutions). The same-elements test, sometimes referred to as the *"Blockburger"* test, inquires whether each offense contains an element not contained in the other; if not, they are the "same offence" and double jeopardy bars additional punishment and successive prosecution. In a case such as *Yancy,* for example, in which the contempt prosecution was for disruption of judicial business, the same-elements test would not bar subsequent prosecution for the criminal assault that was part of the disruption, because the contempt offense did not require the element of criminal conduct, and the criminal offense did not require the element of disrupting judicial business.[7]

We recently held in *Grady* that in addition to passing the *Blockburger* test, a subsequent prosecution must satisfy a "same-conduct" test to avoid the double jeopardy bar. The *Grady* test provides that, "if, to establish an essential element of an offense charged in that prosecution, the government will prove conduct that constitutes an offense for which the defendant has already been prosecuted," a second prosecution may not be had.

III

A

The first question before us today is whether *Blockburger* analysis permits subsequent prosecution in this new criminal contempt context, where judicial order has prohibited criminal act. If it does, we must then proceed to consider whether *Grady* also permits it.

We begin with *Dixon.* The statute applicable in Dixon's contempt prosecution provides that "[a] person who has been conditionally released ... and who has violated a condition of release shall be subject to ... prosecution for contempt of court." § 23–1329(a). Obviously, Dixon could not commit an "offence" under this provision until an order setting out conditions was issued. The statute by itself imposes no legal obligation on anyone. Dixon's cocaine possession, although an offense under D.C.Code Ann. § 33–541(a) (1988 and Supp. 1992), was not an offense under § 23–1329 until a judge incorporated the statutory drug offense into his release order.

In this situation, in which the contempt sanction is imposed for violating the order through commission of the incorporated drug offense, the later attempt to prosecute Dixon for the drug offense resembles the situation that produced our judgment of double jeopardy in Harris v. Oklahoma, 433 U.S. 682 (1977) *(per curiam)*. There we held that a subsequent prosecution for robbery with a firearm was barred by the Double Jeopardy Clause, because the defendant had already been tried for felony-murder based on the same underlying felony. We have described our terse *per curiam* in *Harris* as standing for the proposition that, for double jeopardy purposes, "the crime generally described as felony murder" is not "a separate offense distinct from its various elements." Illinois v. Vitale, 447 U.S. 410, 420–421 (1980). Accord, Whalen v. United States, 445 U.S. 684, 694 (1980). So too here, the "crime" of violating a condition of release cannot be abstracted from the "element" of the violated condition. The *Dixon* court order incorporated the entire governing criminal code in the same manner as the *Harris* felony-murder statute incorporated the several

---

7. State v. Yancy, 4 N.C. 133 (1814), it should be noted, involved what is today called summary contempt. We have not held, and do not mean by this example to decide, that the double-jeopardy guarantee applies to such proceedings.

enumerated felonies. Here, as in *Harris*, the underlying substantive criminal offense is "a species of lesser-included offense." *Vitale*, supra, at 420. Accord, *Whalen*, supra.

* * *

* * * Because Dixon's drug offense did not include any element not contained in his previous contempt offense, his subsequent prosecution violates the Double Jeopardy Clause.

The foregoing analysis obviously applies as well to Count I of the indictment against Foster, charging assault in violation of § 22–504, based on the same event that was the subject of his prior contempt conviction for violating the provision of the CPO forbidding him to commit simple assault under § 22–504. The subsequent prosecution for assault fails the *Blockburger* test, and is barred.

B

The remaining four counts in *Foster,* assault with intent to kill (Count V; § 22–501) and threats to injure or kidnap (Counts II–IV; § 22–2307), are not barred under *Blockburger*. As to Count V: Foster's conduct on May 21, 1988 was found to violate the Family Division's order that he not "molest, assault, or in any manner threaten or physically abuse" his wife. At the contempt hearing, the court stated that Ana Foster's attorney, who prosecuted the contempt, would have to prove first, knowledge of a CPO, and second, a willful violation of one of its conditions, here simple assault as defined by the criminal code. On the basis of the same episode, Foster was then indicted for violation of § 22–501, which proscribes assault with intent to kill. Under governing law, that offense requires proof of specific intent to kill; simple assault does not. See Logan v. United States, 483 A.2d 664, 672–673 (D.C.1984). Similarly, the contempt offense required proof of knowledge of the CPO, which assault with intent to kill does not. Applying the *Blockburger* elements test, the result is clear: These crimes were different offenses and the subsequent prosecution did not violate the Double Jeopardy Clause.

Counts II, III, and IV of Foster's indictment are likewise not barred. These charged Foster under § 22–2307 (forbidding anyone to "threate[n] ... to kidnap any person or to injure the person of another or physically damage the property of any person") for his alleged threats on three separate dates. Foster's contempt prosecution included charges that, on the same dates, he violated the CPO provision ordering that he not "in any manner threaten" Ana Foster. Conviction of the contempt required willful violation of the CPO—which conviction under § 22–2307 did not; and conviction under § 22–2307 required that the threat be a threat to kidnap, to inflict bodily injury, or to damage property—which conviction of the contempt (for violating the CPO provision that Foster not "in any manner threaten") did not. Each offense therefore contained a separate element, and the *Blockburger* test for double jeopardy was not met.

IV

Having found that at least some of the counts at issue here are not barred by the *Blockburger* test, we must consider whether they are barred by the new, additional double jeopardy test we announced three Terms ago in *Grady v. Corbin.* They undoubtedly are, since *Grady* prohibits "a subsequent prosecution if, to establish an essential element of an offense charged in that prosecution [here, assault as an element of assault with intent to kill, or threatening as an element of threatening bodily injury], the government will prove conduct that constitutes an offense for which the defendant has already been prosecuted [here, the assault and the threatening, which conduct constituted the offense of violating the CPO]." 495 U.S., at 510.

We have concluded, however, that *Grady* must be overruled. Unlike *Blockburger* analysis, whose definition of what prevents two crimes from being the "same offence," U.S. Const., Amdt. 5, has deep historical roots and has been accepted in numerous precedents of this Court, *Grady* lacks constitutional roots. The "same-conduct" rule it announced is wholly inconsistent with earlier Supreme Court precedent and with the clear common-law understanding of double jeopardy. See, e.g., Gavieres v. United States, 220 U.S., at 345 (in subsequent prosecution, "[w]hile it is true that the conduct of the accused was one and the same, two offenses resulted, each of which had an element not embraced in the other"). We need not discuss the many proofs of these statements, which were set forth at length in the *Grady* dissent. See 495 U.S., at 526 (Scalia, J., dissenting).

* * *

But *Grady* was not only wrong in principle; it has already proved unstable in application. Less than two years after it came down, in United States v. Felix, 503 U.S. 378 (1992), we were forced to recognize a large exception to it. There we concluded that a subsequent prosecution for conspiracy to manufacture, possess, and distribute methamphetamine was not barred by a previous conviction for attempt to manufacture the same substance. We offered as a justification for avoiding a "literal" (i.e., faithful) reading of *Grady* "longstanding authority" to the effect that prosecution for conspiracy is not precluded by prior prosecution for the substantive offense. Of course the very existence of such a large and longstanding "exception" to the *Grady* rule gave cause for concern that the rule was not an accurate expression of the law. This "past practice" excuse is not available to support the ignoring of *Grady* in the present case, since there is no Supreme Court precedent even discussing this fairly new breed of successive prosecution (criminal contempt for violation of a court order prohibiting a crime, followed by prosecution for the crime itself).

A hypothetical based on the facts in *Harris* reinforces the conclusion that *Grady* is a continuing source of confusion and must be overruled. Suppose the State first tries the defendant for felony-murder, based on robbery, and then indicts the defendant for robbery with a firearm in the same incident. Absent *Grady,* our cases provide a clear answer to the double-jeopardy claim in this situation. Under *Blockburger,* the second prosecution is not barred—as it clearly was not barred at common law, as a famous case establishes. In King v. Vandercomb, 2 Leach. 708, 717, 168 Eng.Rep. 455, 460 (K.B.1796), the government abandoned, midtrial, prosecution of defendant for burglary by breaking and entering and stealing goods, because it turned out that no property had been removed on the date of the alleged burglary. The defendant was then prosecuted for burglary by breaking and entering with intent to steal. That second prosecution was allowed, because "these two offences are so distinct in their nature, that evidence of one of them will not support an indictment for the other." Ibid. Accord, English and American cases cited in *Grady*, 495 U.S., at 532–535 (Scalia, J., dissenting).

Having encountered today yet another situation in which the pre-*Grady* understanding of the Double Jeopardy Clause allows a second trial, though the "same-conduct" test would not, we think it time to acknowledge what is now, three years after *Grady*, compellingly clear: the case was a mistake. We do not lightly reconsider a precedent, but, because *Grady* contradicted an "unbroken line of decisions," contained "less than accurate" historical analysis, and has produced "confusion," we do so here. Solorio v. United States, 483 U.S. 435, 439, 442, 450 (1987). Although *stare decisis* is the "preferred course" in constitutional adjudication, "when governing decisions are unworkable or are badly reasoned, 'this Court has never felt constrained to follow precedent.'" Payne v. Tennessee, 501 U.S. 808 (1991) (quoting Smith v. Allwright, 321 U.S. 649, 665 (1944), and collecting examples). We would mock *stare decisis* and only add chaos to our double jeopardy jurisprudence by pretending that *Grady* survives when it does not. We therefore accept the Government's invitation to overrule *Grady*, and Counts II, III, IV, and V of Foster's subsequent prosecution are not barred.[8]

V

Dixon's subsequent prosecution, as well as Count I of Foster's subsequent prosecution, violate the Double Jeopardy Clause.[9] For the reasons set forth in Part IV, the other Counts of Foster's subsequent prosecution do not violate the Double Jeopardy Clause.[10] The judgment of the District of Columbia Court of Appeals is affirmed in part and reversed in part, and the case is remanded for proceedings not inconsistent with this opinion.

It is so ordered.

■ CHIEF JUSTICE REHNQUIST, with whom JUSTICE O'CONNOR and JUSTICE THOMAS join, concurring in part and dissenting in part.

Respondent Alvin Dixon possessed cocaine with intent to distribute it. For that he was held in contempt of court for violating a condition of his bail release. He was later criminally charged for the same conduct with possession with intent to distribute cocaine. Respondent Michael Foster assaulted and threatened his estranged wife. For that he was held in contempt of court for violating a civil protection order entered in a domestic relations proceeding. He was later criminally charged for the same conduct with assault, threatening to injure another, and assault with intent to kill.

---

8. We do not address the motion to dismiss the threat counts based on collateral estoppel, see *Ashe v. Swenson*, supra, because neither lower court ruled on that issue.

9. Justices White, Stevens, and Souter concur in this portion of the judgment.

10. Justice Blackmun concurs only in the judgment with respect to this portion.

The Court today concludes that the Double Jeopardy Clause prohibits the subsequent prosecutions of Foster for assault and Dixon for possession with intent to distribute cocaine, but does not prohibit the subsequent prosecutions of Foster for threatening to injure another or for assault with intent to kill. After finding that at least some of the charges here are not prohibited by the "same-elements" test set out in Blockburger v. United States, 284 U.S. 299, 304 (1932), the Court goes on to consider whether there is a double-jeopardy bar under the "same-conduct" test set out in Grady v. Corbin, 495 U.S. 508, 510 (1990), and determines that there is. However, because the same-conduct test is inconsistent with the text and history of the Double Jeopardy Clause, was a departure from our earlier precedents, and has proven difficult to apply, the Court concludes that *Grady* must be overruled. I do not join Part III of Justice Scalia's opinion because I think that none of the criminal prosecutions in this case were barred under *Blockburger*. I must then confront the expanded version of double jeopardy embodied in *Grady*. For the reasons set forth in the *Grady* dissent, supra, at 526 (Scalia, J., dissenting), and in Part IV of the Court's opinion, I, too, think that *Grady* must be overruled. I therefore join Parts I, II, and IV of the Court's opinion, and write separately to express my disagreement with Justice Scalia's application of *Blockburger* in Part III.

In my view, *Blockburger*'s same-elements test requires us to focus not on the terms of the particular court orders involved, but on the elements of contempt of court in the ordinary sense. Relying on Harris v. Oklahoma, 433 U.S. 682 (1977), a three-paragraph *per curiam* in an unargued case, Justice Scalia concludes otherwise today, and thus incorrectly finds in Part III–A of his opinion that the subsequent prosecutions of Dixon for drug distribution and of Foster for assault violated the Double Jeopardy Clause. In so doing, Justice Scalia rejects the traditional view—shared by every federal court of appeals and state supreme court that addressed the issue prior to *Grady*—that, as a general matter, double jeopardy does not bar a subsequent prosecution based on conduct for which a defendant has been held in criminal contempt. I cannot subscribe to a reading of *Harris* that upsets this previously well-settled principle of law. Because the generic crime of contempt of court has different elements than the substantive criminal charges in this case, I believe that they are separate offenses under *Blockburger*. I would therefore limit *Harris* to the context in which it arose: where the crimes in question are analogous to greater and lesser included offenses. The crimes at issue here bear no such resemblance.

* * *

In sum, I think that the substantive criminal prosecutions in this case, which followed convictions for criminal contempt, did not violate the Double Jeopardy Clause, at least before our decision in *Grady*. Under *Grady*, "the Double Jeopardy Clause bars a subsequent prosecution if, to establish an essential element of an offense charged in that prosecution, the government will prove conduct that constitutes an offense for which the defendant has already been prosecuted." 495 U.S., at 510. As the Court points out, this case undoubtedly falls within that expansive formulation: To secure convictions on the substantive criminal charges in this case, the Government will have to prove conduct that was the basis for the contempt convictions. Forced, then, to confront *Grady,* I join the Court in overruling that decision.

■ JUSTICE WHITE, with whom JUSTICE STEVENS joins, and with whom JUSTICE SOUTER joins as to Part I, concurring in the judgment in part and dissenting in part.

I am convinced that the Double Jeopardy Clause bars prosecution for an offense if the defendant already has been held in contempt for its commission. Therefore, I agree with the Court's conclusion that both Dixon's prosecution for possession with intent to distribute cocaine and Foster's prosecution for simple assault were prohibited. In my view, however, Justice Scalia's opinion gives short shrift to the arguments raised by the United States. I also am uncomfortable with the reasoning underlying this holding, in particular the application of Blockburger v. United States, 284 U.S. 299 (1932), to the facts of this case, a reasoning that betrays an overly technical interpretation of the Constitution. As a result, I concur only in the judgment in Part III–A.

The mischief in Justice Scalia's approach is far more apparent in the second portion of today's decision. Constrained by his narrow reading of the Double Jeopardy Clause, he asserts that the fate of Foster's remaining counts depends on Grady v. Corbin, 495 U.S. 508 (1990), which the Court then chooses to overrule. I do not agree. Resolution of the question presented by Foster's case no more requires reliance on *Grady* than it points to reasons for reversing that decision. Rather, as I construe the Clause, double jeopardy principles compel equal treatment of *all* of Foster's counts. I dissent from the Court's holding to the contrary. Inasmuch as *Grady* has been dragged into this case, however, I agree with Justice Blackmun and Justice Souter that it should not be overruled. From this aspect of the Court's opinion as well, I dissent.

* * *

II

If, as the Court agrees, the Double Jeopardy Clause cannot be ignored in this context, my view is that the subsequent prosecutions in both *Dixon* and *Foster* were impermissible as to *all* counts. I reach this conclusion because the offenses at issue in the contempt proceedings were either identical to, or lesser included offenses of, those charged in the subsequent prosecutions. Justice Scalia's contrary conclusion as to some of Foster's counts, which he reaches by exclusive focus on the formal elements of the relevant crimes, is divorced from the purposes of the constitutional provision he purports to apply. Moreover, the results to which this approach would lead are indefensible.

A

The contempt orders in *Foster* and *Dixon* referred in one case to the District's laws regarding assaults and threats, and, in the other, to the criminal code in its entirety. The prohibitions imposed by the court orders, in other words, duplicated those already in place by virtue of the criminal statutes. Aside from differences in the sanctions inflicted, the distinction between being punished for violation of the criminal laws and being punished for violation of the court orders, therefore, is simply this: Whereas in the former case "the entire population" is subject to prosecution, in the latter such authority extends only to "those particular persons whose legal obligations result from their earlier participation in proceedings before the court." *Young,* 481 U.S., at 800, n. 10. But the *offenses* that are to be sanctioned in either proceeding must be similar, since the contempt orders incorporated, in full or in part, the criminal code.

Thus, in this case, the offense for which Dixon was held in contempt was possession with intent to distribute drugs. Since he previously had been indicted for precisely the same offense, the double jeopardy bar should apply. In Foster's contempt proceeding, he was acquitted with respect to threats allegedly made on November 12, 1987, and March 26 and May 17, 1988. He was found in contempt of court for having committed the following offenses: Assaulting his wife on November 6, 1987, and May 21, 1988, and threatening her on September 17, 1987. 598 A.2d, at 727; App. 42. The subsequent indictment charged Foster with simple assault on November 6, 1987 (Count I); threatening to injure another on or about November 12, 1987, and March 26 and May 17, 1988 (Counts II, III, and IV); and assault with intent to kill on or about May 21, 1988 (Count V). All of the offenses for which Foster was either convicted or acquitted in the contempt proceeding were similar to, or lesser included offenses of, those charged in the subsequent indictment. Because "the Fifth Amendment forbids successive prosecution ... for a greater and lesser included offense," Brown v. Ohio, 432 U.S. 161, 169 (1977); see also *Grafton,* 206 U.S., at 349–351, the second set of trials should be barred in their entirety.

B

Professing strict adherence to *Blockburger's* so-called "same elements" test, see *Blockburger v. United States,* 284 U.S. 299 (1932), Justice Scalia opts for a more circuitous approach. The elements of the crime of contempt, he reasons, in this instance are (1) the existence and knowledge of a court, or CPO; and (2) commission of the underlying substantive offense. Where the criminal conduct that forms the basis of the contempt order is identical to that charged in the subsequent trial, Justice Scalia concludes, *Blockburger* forbids retrial. All elements of Foster's simple assault offense being included in his previous contempt offense, prosecution on that ground is precluded. The same is true of Dixon's drug offense. I agree with this conclusion, though would reach it rather differently: Because in a successive prosecution case the risk is that a person will have to defend himself more than once against the same charge, I would have put to the side the CPO (which, as it were, triggered the court's authority to punish the defendant for acts already punishable under the criminal laws) and compared the substantive offenses of which respondents stood accused in both prosecutions.

The significance of our disaccord is far more manifest where an element is added to the second prosecution. Under Justice Scalia's view, the double jeopardy barrier is then removed because each offense demands proof of an element the other does not: Foster's conviction for contempt requires proof of the existence and knowledge of a CPO, which conviction for assault with intent to kill does not; his conviction for assault with intent to kill requires proof of an intent to kill, which the contempt conviction did not. Finally, though he was acquitted in the contempt proceedings with respect to the alleged November 12, March 26, and May 17 threats, his conviction under the threat charge in the subsequent trial required the additional proof that the threat be to kidnap, to inflict bodily injury, or to damage property. As to these counts, and absent any collateral estoppel problem, Justice Scalia finds that the Constitution does not prohibit retrial.

The distinction drawn by Justice Scalia is predicated on a reading of the Double Jeopardy Clause that is abstracted from the purposes the constitutional provision is designed to promote. To focus on the statutory elements of a crime makes sense where *cumulative* punishment is at stake, for there the aim simply is to uncover legislative intent. The *Blockburger* inquiry, accordingly, serves as a means to determine this intent, as our cases have recognized. See Missouri v. Hunter, 459 U.S., at 368. But, as Justice Souter shows, adherence to legislative will has very little to do with the important interests advanced by double jeopardy safeguards against *successive* prosecutions. The central purpose of the Double Jeopardy Clause being to protect against vexatious multiple prosecutions, see *Hunter*, supra, at 365; United States v. Wilson, 420 U.S., at 343, these interests go well beyond the prevention of unauthorized punishment. The same-elements test is an inadequate safeguard, for it leaves the constitutional guarantee at the mercy of a legislature's decision to modify statutory definitions. Significantly, therefore, this Court has applied an inflexible version of the same-elements test only once, in 1911, in a successive prosecution case, see Gavieres v. United States, 220 U.S. 338 (1911), and has since noted that "[t]he *Blockburger* test is not the only standard for determining whether successive prosecutions impermissibly involve the same offense." *Brown*, 432 U.S., at 166–167, n. 6. Rather, "[e]ven if two offenses are sufficiently different to permit the imposition of consecutive sentences, successive prosecutions will be barred in some circumstances where the second prosecution requires the relitigation of factual issues already resolved by the first." Ibid.

Take the example of Count V in *Foster:* For all intents and purposes, the offense for which he was convicted in the contempt proceeding was his assault against his wife. The majority, its eyes fixed on the rigid elements-test, would have his fate turn on whether his subsequent prosecution charges "simple assault" or "assault with intent to kill." Yet, because the crime of "simple assault" is included within the crime of "assault with intent to kill," the reasons that bar retrial under the first hypothesis are equally present under the second: These include principles of finality, see *United States v. Wilson*, supra, at 343; protecting Foster from "embarrassment" and "expense," Green v. United States, 355 U.S., at 187; and preventing the government from gradually fine-tuning its strategy, thereby minimizing exposure to a mistaken conviction. Id., at 188. See also Tibbs v. Florida, 457 U.S. 31, 41 (1982); Arizona v. Washington, 434 U.S. 497, 503–504 (1978); supra, at 5.

Analysis of the threat charges (Counts II–IV) makes the point more clearly still. In the contempt proceeding, it will be recalled, Foster was acquitted of the—arguably lesser-included—offense of threatening "in any manner." As we have stated,

> "the law attaches particular significance to an acquittal. To permit a second trial after an acquittal, however mistaken the acquittal might have been, would present an unacceptably high risk that the Government, with its vastly superior resources, might wear down the defendant so that 'even though innocent he may be found guilty.'" United States v. Scott, 437 U.S. 82, 91 (1978) (citation omitted).

To allow the government to proceed on the threat counts would present precisely the risk of erroneous conviction the Clause seeks to avoid. That the prosecution had to establish the existence of the CPO in the first trial, in short, does not in any way modify the prejudice potentially caused to a defendant by consecutive trials.

To respond, as the majority appears to do, that concerns relating to the defendant's interests against repeat trials are "unjustified" because prosecutors "have little to gain and much to lose" from bringing successive prosecutions and because "the Government must be deterred from abusive, repeated prosecutions of a single offender for similar offenses by the sheer press of other demands upon prosecutorial and judicial resources," ante, at 21–22, n. 15, is to get things exactly backwards. The majority's prophesies might be correct, and double jeopardy might be a problem that will simply take care of itself. Not so, however, according to the Constitution, whose firm prohibition against double jeopardy cannot be satisfied by wishful thinking.

C

* * *

III

Once it is agreed that the Double Jeopardy Clause applies in this context, the Clause, properly construed, both governs this case and disposes of the distinction between Foster's charges upon which Justice Scalia relies. I therefore see little need to draw *Grady* into this dispute. In any event, the United States itself has not attempted to distinguish between *Dixon* and *Foster* or between the charges of "assault" on the one hand and, on the other, "assault with intent to kill" and "threat to injure another." The issue was not raised before the Court of Appeals or considered by it, and it was neither presented in the petition for certiorari nor briefed by either party. Under these circumstances, it is injudicious to address this matter. See, e.g., Mazer v. Stein, 347 U.S. 201, 206, n. 5 (1954); Adickes v. S.H. Kress & Co., 398 U.S. 144, 147, n. 2 (1970).

The majority nonetheless has chosen to consider *Grady* anew and to overrule it. I agree with Justice Blackmun and Justice Souter that such a course is both unwarranted and unwise. Hence, I dissent from the judgment overruling *Grady*.

IV

Believing that the Double Jeopardy Clause bars Foster's and Dixon's successive prosecutions on all counts, I would affirm the judgment of the District of Columbia Court of Appeals. I concur in the judgment of the Court in Part III–A which holds that Dixon's subsequent prosecution and Count I of Foster's subsequent prosecution were barred. I disagree with Justice Scalia's application of *Blockburger* in Part III–B. From Part IV of the opinion, in which the majority decides to overrule *Grady*, I dissent.

■ JUSTICE BLACKMUN, concurring in the judgment in part and dissenting in part.

I cannot agree that contempt of court is the "same offence" under the Double Jeopardy Clause as either assault with intent to kill or possession of cocaine with intent to distribute it. I write separately to emphasize two interrelated points.

I

I agree with Justice Souter that "the *Blockburger* test is not the exclusive standard for determining whether the rule against successive prosecutions applies in a given case." I also share both his and Justice White's dismay that the Court so cavalierly has overruled a precedent that is barely three years old and that has proved neither unworkable nor unsound. I continue to believe that Grady v. Corbin, 495 U.S. 508 (1990), was correctly decided, and that the Double Jeopardy Clause prohibits a subsequent criminal prosecution where the proof required to convict on the later offense would require proving conduct that constitutes an offense for which a defendant already has been prosecuted.

* * *

II

Contempt is one of the very few mechanisms available to a trial court to vindicate the authority of its orders. I fear that the Court's willingness to overlook the unique interests served by contempt proceedings not only will jeopardize the ability of trial courts to control those defendants under their supervision but will undermine their ability to respond effectively to unmistakable threats to their own authority and to those who have sought the court's protection.

This fact is poignantly stressed by the *amici:*

"[C]ontempt litigators and criminal prosecutors seek to further different interests. A battered woman seeks to enforce her private order to end the violence against her. In contrast, the criminal prosecutor is vindicating *society's* interest in enforcing its criminal law. The two interests are not the same, and to consider the contempt litigator and the criminal prosecutor as one and the same would be to adopt an absurd fiction" (emphasis in original). Brief for Ayuda et al. as *Amici Curiae* 20.

Finally, I cannot so easily distinguish between "summary" and "non-summary" contempt proceedings, for the interests served in both are fundamentally similar. It is as much a "disruption of judicial process" to disobey a judge's conditional release order as it is to disturb a judge's courtroom. And the interests served in vindicating the authority of the court are fundamentally different from those served by the prosecution of violations of the substantive criminal law. Because I believe that neither Dixon nor Foster would be "subject for the same offence to be twice put in jeopardy of life or limb," U.S. Const., Amdt. 5, I would reverse the judgment of the District of Columbia Court of Appeals.

JUSTICE SOUTER, with whom JUSTICE STEVENS joins, concurring in the judgment in part and dissenting in part.

While I agree with the Court as far as it goes in holding that a citation for criminal contempt and an indictment for violating a substantive criminal statute may amount to charges of the "same offence" for purposes of the Double Jeopardy Clause, U.S. Const., Amdt. 5, I cannot join the Court in restricting the Clause's reach and dismembering the protection against successive prosecution that the Constitution was meant to provide. The Court has read our precedents so narrowly as to leave them bereft of the principles animating that protection, and has chosen to overrule the most recent of the relevant cases, Grady v. Corbin, 495 U.S. 508 (1990), decided three years ago. Because I think that Grady was correctly decided, amounting merely to an expression of just those animating principles, and because, even if the decision had been wrong in the first instance, there is no warrant for overruling it now, I respectfully dissent. I join Part I of Justice White's opinion, and I would hold, as he would, both the prosecution of Dixon and the prosecution of Foster under all the counts of the indictment against him to be barred by the Double Jeopardy Clause.

* * *

VIII

Grady simply applied a rule with roots in our cases going back well over 100 years. Nielsen held that the Double Jeopardy Clause bars successive prosecutions for more than one statutory offense where the charges comprise the same act, and Harris, as understood in Vitale, is properly read as standing for the same rule. Overruling Grady alone cannot remove this principle from our constitutional jurisprudence. Only by uprooting the entire sequence of cases, Grady, Vitale, Harris, and Nielsen, could this constitutional principle be undone. Because I would not do that, I would affirm the judgment of the Court of Appeals. I concur in the judgment of the Court in Dixon and with respect to Count I in Foster, but respectfully dissent from the disposition of the case with respect to Counts II–V in Foster.

C. TERMINATION WITHOUT ACQUITTAL OR CONVICTION

EDITORS' INTRODUCTION: DEVELOPMENT OF JEOPARDY
PROTECTION AGAINST ABORTED PROSECUTIONS

English common law double jeopardy doctrine extended a bar to a subsequent trial only if the first trial resulted in either a conviction or acquittal. Early considerations of the Fifth Amendment guarantee of double jeopardy regarded the provision as similarly limited. See Crist v. Bretz, 437 U.S. 28, 33, 98 S.Ct. 2156, 2159, 57 L.Ed.2d 24, 30–31 (1978). In the 19th century, however, state courts began to merge the double jeopardy guarantees in the state and Federal constitutions with a distinguishable common law rule against discharge of a jury without a verdict. See Crist v. Bretz, supra, 437 U.S. at 40–49, 98 S.Ct. at 2163–68, 57 L.Ed.2d at 34–40 (Powell, J., dissenting). By the time of United States v. Perez, 22 U.S. 579, 6 L.Ed. 165, 9 Wheat. 579 (1824), the Court accepted the proposition that a defendant could be placed in jeopardy by a prosecution not culminating in a conviction or acquittal and this has remained an established part of double jeopardy jurisprudence. In Wade v. Hunter, 336 U.S. 684, 69 S.Ct. 834, 93 L.Ed. 974 (1949), this aspect of double jeopardy was referred to as a defendant's "valued right to have his trial completed by a particular tribunal." The policy underlying this expansion of double jeopardy was described by a state court as follows:

> If the judge can arbitrarily discharge and empanel juries until one is obtained that will render such a verdict as the state demands, or the attorney for the prosecution desires, and the only protection against such oppression is that a new trial may be ordered in the court trying him, or by the court of last resort, then of what value is [the] boasted right [to be free of double jeopardy]?

O'Brian v. Commonwealth, 72 Ky. (9 Bush.) 333, 339, 15 Am.Rep. 715, 720 (1873).

In United States v. Scott, 437 U.S. 82, 98 S.Ct. 2187, 57 L.Ed.2d 65 (1978), Justice Rehnquist, speaking for the Court, indicated that defendants' interest in avoiding multiple prosecutions even where no final determination of guilt or innocence had been made in the first proceeding may be raised in two different situations. These differ, he continued, in the nature of the action taken by the trial judge in the first proceeding. One situation exists when the trial judge grants a "mistrial." Mistrials may ordinarily be granted on the motion of either party or by the court on its own motion. In such situations, the trial judge contemplates that another prosecution will be brought, or at least that the government will have the opportunity to bring one. As Illinois v. Sommerville makes clear, however, in some situations the trial judge's expectations cannot constitutionally be fulfilled.

Another situation is presented, Justice Rehnquist asserted in *Scott*, when the trial judge "terminates the proceedings favorably to the defendant on a basis not related to factual guilt or innocence." The granting of a motion for such relief, he continued, "obviously contemplates that the proceedings will terminate then and there in favor of the defendant. The prosecution, if it wishes to reinstate the proceedings in the face of such a ruling, ordinarily must seek reversal of the decision of the trial court." 437 U.S. at 92–94, 98 S.Ct. at 2194–95, 57 L.Ed.2d at 75–76. Discussion of these situations is complicated by variations in terminology used in various jurisdictions. Most frequently these actions are labeled "dismissals." "Dismissal with prejudice" is intended to constitute a bar to subsequent proceedings, at least on the same charge. But trial judges sometimes grant a "dismissal without prejudice," which is clearly intended to permit the prosecution to begin anew its efforts to convict the defendant.

It is clear that the labels used by trial judges will not be conclusive and that trial court actions can, when offered in bar to a subsequent proceeding, be functionally characterized, at least to some extent. In Lee v. United States, 432 U.S. 23, 97 S.Ct. 2141, 53 L.Ed.2d 80 (1977), the defense moved for dismissal of the information on the ground that it failed to allege a necessary element of the offense charged. The trial judge granted the motion. When the state recharged the defendant with sufficient information, the dismissal of the first charge was offered in bar to the second proceeding. Holding that the defendant's plea of former jeopardy was properly rejected, the Supreme Court made clear that it was irrelevant that the trial judge in the first proceeding had labeled his action a "dismissal" of the information. The situation was one in which a mistrial could have been properly granted and was analyzed by the Court as if that was the action taken by the trial judge.

Because the Court in *Scott* clearly indicated that it viewed the situations distinguished in that case as involving different double jeopardy principles, this section divides the material accordingly.

1. MISTRIALS

If a trial judge terminates a trial by declaring a mistrial, it is reasonably certain that the judge anticipates that this action will not bar a second trial on the same indictment or information. Despite this intent, however, double jeopardy bars further proceedings in certain circumstances.

Illinois v. Somerville

Supreme Court of the United States, 1973.
410 U.S. 458, 93 S.Ct. 1066, 35 L.Ed.2d 425.

■ MR. JUSTICE REHNQUIST delivered the opinion of the Court.

We must here decide whether declaration of a mistrial over the defendant's objection, because the trial court concluded that the indictment was insufficient to charge a crime, necessarily prevents a State from subsequently trying the defendant under a valid indictment. We hold that the mistrial met the "manifest necessity" requirement of our cases, since the trial court could reasonably have concluded that the "ends of public justice" would be defeated by having allowed the trial to continue. Therefore, the Double Jeopardy Clause of the Fifth Amendment, made applicable to the States through the Due Process Clause of the Fourteenth Amendment, Benton v. Maryland, 395 U.S. 784, 89 S.Ct. 2056, 23 L.Ed.2d 707 (1969), did not bar retrial under a valid indictment.

I.

On March 19, 1964, respondent was indicted by an Illinois grand jury for the crime of theft. The case was called for trial and a jury impaneled and sworn on November 1, 1965. The following day, before any evidence had been presented, the prosecuting attorney realized that the indictment was fatally deficient under Illinois law because it did not allege that respondent intended to permanently deprive the owner of his property. Under the applicable Illinois criminal statute, such intent is a necessary element of the crime of theft, and failure to allege intent renders the indictment insufficient to charge a crime. But under the Illinois Constitution at that time, an indictment was the sole means by which a criminal proceeding such as this may be commenced against a defendant. Illinois further provides that only formal defects, of which this was not one, may be cured by amendment. The combined operation of these rules of Illinois procedure and substantive law meant that the defect in the indictment was "jurisdictional"; it could not be waived by the defendant's failure to object, and could be asserted on appeal or in a post-conviction proceeding to overturn a final judgment of conviction.

Faced with this situation, the Illinois trial court concluded that further proceedings under this defective indictment would be useless and granted the State's motion for a mistrial. On November 3, the grand jury handed down a second indictment alleging the requisite intent. Respondent was arraigned two weeks after the first trial was aborted, raised a claim of double jeopardy which was overruled, and the second trial commenced shortly thereafter. The jury returned a verdict of guilty, sentence was imposed, and the Illinois courts upheld the conviction. Respondent then sought federal habeas corpus, alleging that the conviction constituted double jeopardy contrary to the prohibition of the Fifth and Fourteenth Amendments. The Seventh Circuit ... held that respondent's petition for habeas corpus should have been granted because ... jeopardy had attached when the jury was impaneled and sworn, and a declaration of mistrial over respondent's objection precluded a retrial under a valid indictment. 447 F.2d 733 (1971). For the reasons stated below, we reverse that judgment.

II.

The fountainhead decision construing the Double Jeopardy Clause in the context of a declaration of a mistrial over a defendant's objection is United States v. Perez, 9 Wheat. 579 (1824). Mr. Justice Story, writing for a unanimous Court, set forth the standards for determining whether a retrial, following a declaration of a mistrial over a defendant's objection, constitutes double jeopardy within the meaning of the Fifth Amendment. In holding that the failure of the jury to agree on a verdict of either acquittal or conviction did not bar retrial of the defendant, Mr. Justice Story wrote:

> "We think, that in all cases of this nature, the law has invested Courts of Justice with the authority to discharge a jury from giving any verdict, whenever, in their opinion, taking all the circumstances into consideration, there is a manifest necessity for the act, or the ends of public justice would otherwise be defeated. They are to exercise a sound discretion on the subject; and it is impossible to define all the circumstances, which would render it proper to interfere. To be sure, the power ought to be used with the greatest caution, under urgent circumstances, and for very plain and obvious causes; and, in capital cases especially, Courts should be extremely careful how they interfere

with any of the chances of life, in favour of the prisoner. But, after all, they have the right to order the discharge; and the security which the public have for the faithful, sound, and conscientious exercise of this discretion, rests, in this, as in other cases, upon the responsibility of the Judges, under their oaths of office." Id., at 580.

This formulation, consistently adhered to by this Court in subsequent decisions, abjures the application of any mechanical formula by which to judge the propriety of declaring a mistrial in the varying and often unique situations arising during the course of a criminal trial. The broad discretion reserved to the trial judge in such circumstances has been consistently reiterated in decisions of this Court. . . .

In reviewing the propriety of the trial judge's exercise of his discretion, this Court, following the counsel of Mr. Justice Story, has scrutinized the action to determine whether, in the context of that particular trial, the declaration of a mistrial was dictated by "manifest necessity" or the "ends of public justice." The interests of the public in seeing that a criminal prosecution proceed to verdict, either of acquittal or conviction, need not be forsaken by the formulation or application of rigid rules that necessarily preclude the vindication of that interest. . . .

In United States v. Perez, supra, and Logan v. United States, 144 U.S. 263, 12 S.Ct. 617, 36 L.Ed. 429 (1892), this Court held that "manifest necessity" justified the discharge of juries unable to reach verdicts, and, therefore, the Double Jeopardy Clause did not bar retrial. In Simmons v. United States, 142 U.S. 148, 12 S.Ct. 171, 35 L.Ed. 968 (1891), a trial judge dismissed the jury, over defendant's objection, because one of the jurors had been acquainted with the defendant, and, therefore, was probably prejudiced against the Government; this Court held that the trial judge properly exercised his power "to prevent the defeat of the ends of public justice." Id., at 154, 12 S.Ct., at 172. In Thompson v. United States, 155 U.S. 271, 15 S.Ct. 73, 39 L.Ed. 146 (1894), a mistrial was declared after the trial judge learned that one of the jurors was disqualified, he having been a member of the grand jury that indicted the defendant. Similarly, in Lovato v. New Mexico, 242 U.S. 199, 37 S.Ct. 107, 61 L.Ed. 244 (1916), the defendant demurred to the indictment, his demurrer was overruled, and a jury sworn. The district attorney, realizing that the defendant had not pleaded to the indictment after the demurrer had been overruled, moved for the discharge of the jury and arraignment of the defendant for pleading; the jury was discharged, the defendant pleaded not guilty, the same jury was again impaneled, and a verdict of guilty rendered. In both of those cases this Court held that the Double Jeopardy Clause did not bar re-prosecution.

While virtually all of the cases turn on the particular facts and thus escape meaningful categorization, . . . it is possible to distill from them a general approach, premised on the "public justice" policy enunciated in United States v. Perez, to situations such as that presented by this case. A trial judge properly exercises his discretion to declare a mistrial if an impartial verdict cannot be reached, or if a verdict of conviction could be reached but would have to be reversed on appeal due to an obvious procedural error in the trial. If an error would make reversal on appeal a certainty, it would not serve "the ends of public justice" to require that the Government proceed with its proof when, if it succeeded before the jury, it would automatically be stripped of that success by an appellate court. This was substantially the situation in both Thompson v. United States, supra, and Lovato v. New Mexico, supra. While the declaration of a mistrial on the basis of a rule or a defective procedure that would lend itself to prosecutorial manipulation would involve an entirely different question, cf. Downum v. United States, [372 U.S. 734, 83 S.Ct. 1033, 10 L.Ed.2d 100 (1963)], such was not the situation in the above cases or in the instant case.

In Downum v. United States, the defendant was charged with six counts of mail theft, and forging and uttering stolen checks. A jury was selected and sworn in the morning, and instructed to return that afternoon. When the jury returned, the Government moved for the discharge of the jury on the ground that a key prosecution witness, for two of the six counts against defendant, was not present. The prosecution knew, prior to the selection and swearing of the jury, that this witness could not be found and had not been served with a subpoena. The trial judge discharged the jury over the defendant's motions to dismiss two counts for failure to prosecute and to continue the other four. This Court, in reversing the convictions on the ground of double jeopardy, emphasized that "[e]ach case must turn on its facts," 372 U.S., at 737, 83 S.Ct., at 1035 and held that the second prosecution constituted double jeopardy, because the absence of the witness and the reason therefor did not there justify, in terms of "manifest necessity," the declaration of a mistrial.

In United States v. Jorn, [400 U.S. 470, 91 S.Ct. 547, 27 L.Ed.2d 543 (1971)], the Government called a taxpayer witness in a prosecution for willfully assisting in the preparation of fraudulent income tax returns. Prior to his testimony, defense counsel suggested he be warned of his constitutional right against compulsory self-incrimination. The trial judge warned him of his rights, and the witness stated that he was willing to testify and that the Internal Revenue Service agent who first contacted him warned him of his rights. The trial judge, however, did not believe the witness' declaration that the IRS had so warned him, and refused to allow him to testify until after he had consulted with an attorney. After learning from the Government that the remaining four witnesses were "similarly situated," and after surmising that they, too, had not been properly informed of their rights, the trial judge declared a mistrial to give the witnesses the opportunity to consult with attorneys. In sustaining a plea in bar of double jeopardy to an attempted second trial of the defendant, the plurality opinion of the Court, emphasizing the importance to the defendant of proceeding before the first jury sworn, concluded:

"It is apparent from the record that no consideration was given to the possibility of a trial continuance; indeed, the trial judge acted so abruptly in discharging the jury that, had the prosecutor been disposed to suggest a continuance, or the defendant to object to the discharge of the jury, there would have been no opportunity to do so. When one examines the circumstances surrounding the discharge of this jury, it seems abundantly apparent that the trial judge made no effort to exercise a sound discretion to assure that, taking all the circumstances into account, there was a manifest necessity for the *sua sponte* declaration of this mistrial. United States v. Perez, 9 Wheat., at 580. Therefore, we must conclude that in the circumstances of this case, appellee's reprosecution would violate the double jeopardy provision of the Fifth Amendment." 400 U.S., at 487, 91 S.Ct., at 558.

III.

* * *

[R]espondent argues that our decision in United States v. Jorn, supra, which respondent interprets as narrowly limiting the circumstances in which a mistrial is manifestly necessary, requires affirmance. Emphasizing the " 'valued right to have his trial completed by a particular tribunal,' " United States v. Jorn, supra, at 484 of 400 U.S., at 557 of 91 S.Ct., . . . respondent contends that the circumstances did not justify depriving him of that right.

* * *

We believe that in light of the State's established rules of criminal procedure, the trial judge's declaration of a mistrial was not an abuse of discretion. . . .

In the instant case, the trial judge terminated the proceeding because a defect was found to exist in the indictment that was, as a matter of Illinois law, not curable by amendment. The Illinois courts have held that even after a judgment of conviction has become final, the defendant may be released on habeas corpus, because the defect in the indictment deprives the trial court of "jurisdiction." The rule prohibiting the amendment of all but formal defects in indictments is designed to implement the State's policy of preserving the right of each defendant to insist that a criminal prosecution against him be commenced by the action of a grand jury. The trial judge was faced with a situation similar to those in *Simmons, Lovato,* and *Thompson,* in which a procedural defect might or would preclude the public from either obtaining an impartial verdict or keeping a verdict of conviction if its evidence persuaded the jury. If a mistrial were constitutionally unavailable in situations such as this, the State's policy could only be implemented by conducting a second trial after verdict and reversal on appeal, thus wasting time, energy, and money for all concerned. Here, the trial judge's action was a rational determination designed to implement a legitimate state policy, with no suggestion that the implementation of that policy in this manner could be manipulated so as to prejudice the defendant. This situation is thus unlike *Downum,* where the mistrial entailed not only a delay for the defendant, but also operated as a post-jeopardy continuance to allow the prosecution an opportunity to strengthen its case. Here, the delay was minimal, and the mistrial was, under Illinois law, the only way in which a defect in the indictment could be corrected. Given the established standard of discretion . . ., we cannot say that the declaration of a mistrial was not required by "manifest necessity" or the "ends of public justice."

* * *

The determination by the trial court to abort a criminal proceeding where jeopardy has attached is not one to be lightly undertaken, since the interest of the defendant in having his fate determined by the jury first impaneled is itself a weighty one. United States v. Jorn, supra. Nor will the lack of demonstrable additional prejudice preclude the defendant's invocation of the double jeopardy bar in the absence of some important countervailing interest of proper judicial administration. Ibid. But where the declaration of a mistrial implements a reasonable state policy and aborts a proceeding that at best would have produced a verdict that could have been upset at will by one of the parties, the defendant's interest in proceeding to verdict is outweighed by the competing and equally legitimate demand for public justice. . . .

Reversed.

■ MR. JUSTICE WHITE, with whom MR. JUSTICE DOUGLAS and MR. JUSTICE BRENNAN join, dissenting.

* * *

There was not, in this case any more than in *Downum* and *Jorn,* "manifest necessity". . . . I cannot find "manifest necessity" for a mistrial to compensate for prosecutorial mistake. . . .

NOTES

1. **Deference to trial judge's assessment of need for mistrial.** At trial, defense counsel in the opening statement, told the jury that it would hear evidence that the state had purposefully withheld evidence from the defense at a preceding trial; there was apparently no basis for believing the state's earlier action intentional. At the state's request and over defense objection, a mistrial was declared. Could another trial be held? See Arizona v. Washington, 434 U.S. 497, 98 S.Ct. 824, 54 L.Ed.2d 717 (1978), permitting another trial and emphasizing that "the highest degree of respect" must be given the trial judge's assessment of the need for terminating the prior proceeding rather than pursuing some other method of dealing with the danger that juror bias may have been created by defense counsel's action. 434 U.S. at 511, 98 S.Ct. at 833, 54 L.Ed.2d at 732.

2. **Defense motion for mistrial.** Suppose defense counsel moves for the mistrial. In United States v. Dinitz, 424 U.S. 600, 96 S.Ct. 1075, 47 L.Ed.2d 267 (1976), Dinitz' lead counsel at his drug trial repeatedly failed to observe the trial judge's limitations on the subject matter of opening statements. The trial judge ejected counsel from the courthouse and offered Dinitz three alternatives: (a) a stay pending appeal of the order ejecting lead counsel; (b) continuation of the trial with Dinitz' other lawyers representing him; or (c) a declaration of mistrial permitting Dinitz to obtain another lead trial counsel. Dinitz moved for a mistrial. At a second proceeding held over his assertion of former jeopardy he was convicted. The Supreme Court affirmed. If a mistrial is declared on defense motion, the Court held, the "manifest necessity" standard need not be met for a second trial to be permissible:

> Even when judicial or prosecutorial error prejudices a defendant's prospects of securing an acquittal, he may nonetheless desire "to go to the first jury and, perhaps, end the dispute then and there with an acquittal." United States v. Jorn, [400 U.S. 470,] 484, 91 S.Ct. [547,] 557, 27 L.Ed.2d [543,] 556 [1971]. Our prior decisions recognize the defendant's right to pursue this course in the

absence of circumstances of manifest necessity requiring a *sua sponte* judicial declaration of mistrial. But it is evident that when judicial or prosecutorial error seriously prejudices a defendant, he may have little interest in completing the trial and obtaining a verdict from the first jury. The defendant may reasonably conclude that a continuation of the tainted proceeding would result in a conviction followed by a lengthy appeal and, if a reversal is secured, by a second prosecution. In such circumstances, a defendant's mistrial request has objectives not unlike the interests served by the Double Jeopardy Clause—the avoidance of the anxiety, expense and delay occasioned by multiple prosecutions. ...The important consideration, for purposes of the Double Jeopardy Clause, is that the defendant retain primary control over the course to be followed in the event of such error.

[To apply the manifest necessity standard to a defense motion for mistrial] undermines rather than furthers the protections of the Double Jeopardy Clause. In the event of severely prejudicial error a defendant might well consider an immediate new trial a preferable alternative to the prospect of a probable conviction followed by an appeal, a reversal of the conviction, and a later retrial. [Application of the manifest necessity standard], in effect, instructs trial judges to reject the most meritorious mistrial motion in the absence of manifest necessity and to require, instead, that the trial proceed to its conclusion despite a legitimate claim of seriously prejudicial error. ...

424 U.S. at 608–10, 96 S.Ct. at 1080–81, 47 L.Ed.2d at 274–76. Even if the trial judge may have overreacted in expelling defense counsel, the Court concluded, there was no evidence that this was done in bad faith to goad Dinitz into requesting a mistrial or to prejudice his prospects for an acquittal. Retrial, therefore, was not prohibited by double jeopardy, even though "manifest necessity" for the mistrial may not have existed.

3. **Prosecutorial misconduct.** The Court in Oregon v. Kennedy, 456 U.S. 667, 102 S.Ct. 2083, 72 L.Ed.2d 416 (1982) addressed the question of when, if ever, double jeopardy bars a re-prosecution when the first trial was terminated by a mistrial at the defendant's behest. Kennedy was being tried for theft of an oriental rug. The State called a rug dealer as an expert witness. On cross-examination, defendant elicited, to show bias, that the witness had once filed a criminal charge against the defendant. On re-direct, the prosecutor asked the witness, "Have you ever done business with the Kennedys?" When the witness responded, "No," the prosecutor asked, "Is that because he is a crook?" The defendant moved for a mistrial, which was granted by the trial court. On re-prosecution, he claimed his double jeopardy rights were infringed. Following conviction, the Oregon Court of Appeals reversed on the ground that the prosecutor had "overreached" in asking the question and that jeopardy barred re-prosecution despite the defendant's motion for mistrial.

The Supreme Court, in an opinion authored by Justice Rehnquist, reversed. The Court acknowledged that language in some of its prior opinions had provided support for the Oregon court's conclusion that jeopardy barred re-prosecution if the motion for mistrial was occasioned by "prosecutorial or judicial overreaching" or when "the error that prompted the mistrial is intended to provoke a mistrial or is motivated by bad faith or undertaken to harass or prejudice the defendant." 456 U.S. at 670, 102 S.Ct. at 2086, 72 L.Ed.2d at 420–21. The Court rejected those formulations of the standard and, instead, opted for limiting the standard to those circumstances in which the prosecutor "intended to provoke the defendant into moving for a mistrial." 456 U.S. at 679, 102 S.Ct. at 2091, 72 L.Ed.2d at 426–27. The Court gave the following as explanation for rejecting the broader standard:

The difficulty with the more general standards which would permit a broader exception than one merely based on intent is that they offer virtually no standards for their application. Every act on the part of a rational prosecutor during a trial is designed to "prejudice" the defendant by placing before the judge or jury evidence leading to a finding of his guilt. Given the complexity of the rules of evidence, it will be a rare trial of any complexity in which some proffered evidence by the prosecutor or by the defendant's attorney will not be found objectionable by the trial court. Most such objections are undoubtedly curable by simply refusing to allow the proffered evidence to be admitted, or in the case of a particular line of inquiry taken by counsel with a witness, by an admonition to desist from a particular line of inquiry.

. . .

By contrast, a standard that examines the intent of the prosecutor, though certainly not entirely free from practical difficulties, is a manageable standard to apply. It merely calls for the court to make a finding of fact. Inferring the existence or nonexistence of intent from objective facts and circumstances is a familiar process in our criminal justice system.

456 U.S. at 674–75, 102 S.Ct. at 2089, 72 L.Ed.2d at 424–25. Justice Stevens, concurring, would have applied an "overreaching" standard but would have concluded that the prosecutor's conduct in this case did not violate that standard.

4. **Hung juries.** The Supreme Court has, as it noted in *Somerville,* found no bar to retrial when the jury in the first proceeding was unable to arrive at a unanimous verdict and consequently a mistrial was declared. The propriety of this position was challenged in Findlater, Retrial After a Hung Jury: The Double Jeopardy Problem, 129 U.Pa.L.Rev. 701 (1981). She stresses that defendants whose first prosecutions result in hung juries "in all probability, have a higher percent of innocents among them than do accuseds in general." Id., at 735. Moreover, the first proceeding terminated for a reason that suggests to the prosecutor the need to make not only an error-free but also more effective and persuasive presentation in the second trial. Consequently, retrials present a significant risk of convictions of innocent defendants.

5. **Opportunity to comment regarding mistrial.** In 1993, the Supreme Court added the following rule to the Federal Rules of Criminal Procedure:

Rule 26.3 Mistrial

Before ordering a mistrial, the court shall provide an opportunity for the government and for each defendant to comment on the propriety of the order, including whether each party consents or objects to a mistrial, and to suggest any alternatives.

The Advisory Committee explained that the rule was in part a response to several recent appellate decisions barring retrial of defendants after mistrials found on appeal to have been the result of precipitous action by district judges, who had failed to solicit the view of the parties as to the need for a mistrial and feasibility of any alternative action. The Committee added:

The Committee regards the Rule as a balanced and modest procedural device which could benefit both the prosecution and the defense. * * * The Rule * * * ensures that the defendant has the opportunity to dissuade a judge from declaring a mistrial in a case where granting one would not be an abuse of discretion, but the defendant believes the prospects for a favorable outcome before that particular court or jury are stronger than they would be at a retrial.

Preliminary Draft of Proposed Amendments, Committee Note to Proposed Rule 26.3, 137 F.R.D. 417, 497 (1991).

2.   Dismissals and Similar Matters

Trial courts sometimes "dismiss" a prosecution, but the precise procedural effect of this action is not always clear. Technically, dismissal renders the indictment or information a nullity and no further prosecution may be had on that charging instrument. But a superseding indictment or information may be obtained charging similar or identical offenses on the basis of the same events. See United States v. Holder, 399 F.Supp. 220, 226 (D.S.D.1975). Where a dismissal occurs after jeopardy has attached, it is quite likely that the trial judge regards the action as precluding the state from beginning anew. But it is often unclear whether this is because the applicable nonconstitutional procedural law attaches this effect to the dismissal or because it is assumed—rightly or wrongly—that double jeopardy requires this result.

United States v. Scott, reprinted in this section, raises the question of when the prosecution may appeal a dismissal or its equivalent and, if it wins, reprosecute the defendant for the same offense. But suppose appeal is unavailable or, for some reason, the prosecution does not wish to use the appeal process. Is it permissible in any cases where appeal would be allowed by double jeopardy for the state simply to begin again at the trial level, hoping perhaps to have a different judge hear the case or to persuade the same judge that the earlier dismissal was inappropriate?

It is important to distinguish from these situations the problem presented by dismissal of a case before jeopardy attaches. Double jeopardy, of course, does not bar prosecution. But there may be nonconstitutional procedural law that makes some such dismissals "with prejudice." In the federal system, a pre-jeopardy dismissal under Fed.R.Crim.P. 48(a) is generally "without prejudice" and the defendant can be reindicted. United States v. Pope, 574 F.2d 320, 327 (6th Cir.1978), cert. denied 439 U.S. 868, 99 S.Ct. 195, 58 L.Ed.2d 179 (1978). But there is authority for the proposition that a trial court may dismiss under the rule "with prejudice" if it finds the situation meriting this. See White v. United States, 377 F.2d 948, 126 U.S.App.D.C. 309 (D.C.Cir.1967). This is a result of nonconstitutional procedural law, however, not double jeopardy.

United States v. Scott

Supreme Court of the United States, 1978.
437 U.S. 82, 98 S.Ct. 2187, 57 L.Ed.2d 65.

■ Mr. Justice Rehnquist delivered the opinion of the Court.

On March 5, 1975, respondent, a member of the police force in Muskegon, Mich., was charged in a three-count indictment with distribution of various narcotics. Both before his trial in the United States District Court for the Western District of Michigan, and twice during the trial, respondent moved to dismiss the two counts of the indictment which concerned transactions that took place during the preceding September, on the ground that his defense had been prejudiced by preindictment delay. At the close of all the evidence, the court granted respondent's motion. Although the court did not explain its reasons for dismissing the second count, it explicitly concluded that respondent had "presented sufficient proof of prejudice with respect to the first count." Pet. for Cert. 8a. The court submitted the third count to the jury which returned a verdict of not guilty.

The Government sought to appeal the dismissals of the first two counts to the United States Court of Appeals for the Sixth Circuit. That court, relying on our opinion in United States v. Jenkins, 420 U.S. 358, 95 S.Ct. 1006, 43 L.Ed.2d 250 (1975), concluded that any further prosecution of respondent was barred by the Double Jeopardy Clause of the Fifth Amendment, and therefore dismissed the appeal. 544 F.2d 903 (1976). The Government has sought review in this Court only with regard to the dismissal of the first count. We granted certiorari to give further consideration to the applicability of the Double Jeopardy Clause to Government appeals from orders granting defense motions to terminate a trial before verdict. We now reverse.

I.

* * *

We ... held in *Jenkins,* supra, 420 U.S., at 370, 95 S.Ct., at 1013, that, whether or not a dismissal of an indictment after jeopardy had attached amounted to an acquittal on the merits, the Government had no right to appeal, because "further proceedings of some sort, devoted to the resolution of factual issues going to the elements of the offense charged, would have been required upon reversal and remand."

If *Jenkins* is a correct statement of the law, the judgment of the Court of Appeals relying on that decision, as it was bound to do, would in all likelihood have to be affirmed. Yet, though our assessment of the history and meaning of the Double Jeopardy Clause in [United States v.] *Wilson* [420 U.S. 332, 95 S.Ct. 1013, 43 L.Ed.2d 232 (1975)], *Jenkins,* and Serfass v. United States, 420 U.S. 377, 95 S.Ct. 1055, 43 L.Ed.2d 265 (1975), occurred only three Terms ago, our vastly increased exposure to the various facets of the Double Jeopardy Clause has now convinced us that *Jenkins* was wrongly decided. It placed an unwarrantedly great emphasis on the defendant's right to have his guilt decided by the first jury empaneled to try him so as to include those cases where the defendant himself seeks to terminate the trial before verdict on grounds unrelated to factual guilt or innocence. We have therefore decided to overrule *Jenkins,* and thus to reverse the judgment of the Court of Appeals in this case.

* * *

IV.

Our decision in *Jenkins* was based upon our perceptions of the underlying purposes of the Double Jeopardy Clause ...:

"The underlying idea, one that is deeply ingrained in at least the Anglo–American system of jurisprudence is that the State with all its resources and power should not be allowed to make repeated attempts to convict an individual for an alleged offense, thereby subjecting him to embarrassment, expense and ordeal and compelling him to live in a continuing state of anxiety and insecurity. ...." *Jenkins,* supra, 420 U.S., at 370, 95 S.Ct., at 1013, quoting *Green* [v. United States, 355 U.S. 184, 187, 78 S.Ct. 221, 223, 2 L.Ed.2d 199 (1957)].

Upon fuller consideration, we are now of the view that this language from *Green,* while entirely appropriate in the circumstances of that opinion, is not a principle which can be expanded to include situations in which the defendant is responsible for the second prosecution. It is quite true that the Government with all its resources and power should not be allowed to make repeated attempts to convict an individual for an alleged offense. This truth is expressed in the three common-law pleas of *autrefois acquit, autrefois convict,* and pardon, which lie at the core of the area protected by the Double Jeopardy Clause. As we have recognized in cases from [United States v.] *Ball* [163 U.S. 662, 16 S.Ct. 1192, 41 L.Ed. 300 (1896)] to Sanabria v. United States [437 U.S. 54, 98 S.Ct. 2170, 57 L.Ed.2d 43 (1978)], a defendant once acquitted may not be again subjected to trial without violating the Double Jeopardy Clause.

But that situation is obviously a far cry from the present case, where the Government was quite willing to continue with its production of evidence to show the defendant guilty before the jury first empaneled to try him, but the defendant elected to seek termination of the trial on grounds unrelated to guilt or innocence. This is scarcely a picture of an all-powerful state relentlessly pursuing a defendant who had either been found not guilty or who had at least insisted on having the issue of guilt submitted to the first trier of fact. It is instead a picture of a defendant who chooses to avoid conviction and imprisonment, not because of his assertion that the Government has failed to make out a case against him, but because of a legal claim that the Government's case against him must fail even though it might satisfy the trier of fact that he was guilty beyond a reasonable doubt.

We have previously noted that "the trial judge's characterization of his own action cannot control the classification of the action." [United States v. Jorn, 400 U.S. 470, 478 n. 7, 91 S.Ct. 547, 554 n. 7, 27 L.Ed.2d 543 (1971)] (opinion of Harlan, J.), citing United States v. Sisson, 399 U.S. 267, 290, 90 S.Ct. 2117, 2129, 26 L.Ed.2d 608 (1970). See also [United States v. Martin Linen Supply Co., 430 U.S. 564, 671, 97 S.Ct. 1349, 1354, 51 L.Ed.2d 642 (1977)]; *Wilson,* 420 U.S. at 336, 95 S.Ct., at 1018. Despite respondent's contentions, an appeal is not barred simply because a ruling in favor of a defendant "is based upon facts outside the face of the indictment," id., at 348, 95 S.Ct., at 1024 or because it "is granted on the ground ... that the defendant simply cannot be convicted of the offense charged," *Lee,* supra, at 30. Rather, a defendant is acquitted only when "the ruling of the judge, whatever its label, actually represents a resolution [in the defendant's favor], correct or not, of some or all of the factual elements of the offense charged." *Martin Linen,* 430 U.S., at 571, 97 S.Ct., at 1355. Where the court, before the jury returns a verdict, enters a judgment of acquittal pursuant to Fed.Rule Crim.Proc. 29, appeal will be barred only when "it is plain that the District Court ... evaluated the Government's evidence and determined that it was legally insufficient to support a conviction." Id., 420 U.S. at 572, 97 S.Ct., at 1355.

Our opinion in *Burks* [v. United States, 437 U.S. 1, 98 S.Ct. 2141, 57 L.Ed.2d 1 (1978)] necessarily holds that there has been a "failure of proof" . . . requiring an acquittal when the Government does not submit sufficient evidence to rebut a defendant's essentially factual defense of insanity, though it may otherwise be entitled to have its case submitted to the jury. The defense of insanity, like the defense of entrapment, arises from "the notion that Congress could not have intended criminal punishment for a defendant who has committed all the elements of a proscribed offense," United States v. Russell, 411 U.S. 423, 435, 93 S.Ct. 1637, 1644, 36 L.Ed.2d 366 (1973), where other facts established to the satisfaction of the trier of fact provide a legally adequate justification for otherwise criminal acts. Such a factual finding does "necessarily establish the criminal defendant's lack of criminal culpability," post, (Brennan, J., dissenting), under the existing law; the fact that "the acquittal may result from erroneous evidentiary rulings or erroneous interpretations of governing legal principles," ibid, affects the accuracy of that determination, but it does not alter its essential character. By contrast, the dismissal of an indictment for preindictment delay represents a legal judgment that a defendant, although criminally culpable, may not be punished because of a supposed constitutional violation.

We think that in a case such as this the defendant, by deliberately choosing to seek termination of the proceedings against him on a basis unrelated to factual guilt or innocence of the offense of which he is accused, suffers no injury cognizable under the Double Jeopardy Clause if the Government is permitted to appeal from such a ruling of the trial court in favor of the defendant. We do not thereby adopt the doctrine of "waiver" of double jeopardy rejected in *Green,* supra. Rather, we conclude that the Double Jeopardy Clause, which guards against Government oppression, does not relieve a defendant from the consequences of his voluntary choice. In *Green,* the question of defendant's factual guilt or innocence of murder in the first degree was actually submitted to the jury as a trier of fact; in the present case, respondent successfully avoided such a submission of the first count of the indictment by persuading the trial court to dismiss it on a basis which did not depend on guilt or innocence. He was thus neither acquitted nor convicted, because he himself successfully undertook to persuade the trial court not to submit the issue of guilt or innocence to the jury which had been empaneled to try him.

The reason for treating a trial aborted on the initiative of the trial judge differently from a trial verdict reversed on appeal, for purposes of double jeopardy, is thus described in *Jorn,* supra, at 484 (opinion of Harlan, J.):

> "[I]n the first situation the defendant has not been deprived of his option to go to the first jury, and, perhaps, end the dispute then and there with an acquittal. On the other hand, where the judge, acting without the defendant's consent, aborts the proceeding, the defendant has been deprived of his 'valued right to have his trial completed by a particular tribunal.' "

We think the same reasoning applies in *pari passu* where the defendant, instead of obtaining a reversal of his conviction on appeal, obtains the termination of the proceedings against him in the trial court without any finding by a court or jury as to his guilt or innocence. He has not been "deprived" of his valued right to go to the first jury; only the public has been deprived of its valued right to "one complete opportunity to convict those who have violated its laws." Arizona v. Washington [434 U.S. 497, 98 S.Ct. 824, 54 L.Ed.2d 717 (1978).] No interest protected by the Double Jeopardy Clause is invaded when the Government is allowed to appeal and seek reversal of such a midtrial termination of the proceedings in a manner favorable to the defendant.[11]

It is obvious from what we have said that we believe we pressed too far in *Jenkins* the concept of the "defendant's valued right to have his trial completed by a particular tribunal." Wade v. Hunter, 336 U.S. 684, 689, 69 S.Ct. 834, 837, 93 L.Ed. 974 (1949). We now conclude that where the defendant himself seeks to have the trial terminated without any submission to either judge or jury as to his guilt or innocence, an appeal by the Government from his successful effort to do so is not barred by 18 U.S.C. § 3731.

* * *

The judgment of the Court of Appeals is therefore reversed, and the cause remanded for further proceedings.

■ MR. JUSTICE BRENNAN, with whom MR. JUSTICE WHITE, MR. JUSTICE MARSHALL, and MR. JUSTICE STEVENS join, dissenting [omitted].

NOTE

Interpreting the meaning of the trial court's decision. In Smalis v. Pennsylvania, 476 U.S. 140, 106 S.Ct. 1745, 90 L.Ed.2d 116 (1986), petitioners, in a jury-waived trial for various arson-related offenses, filed a demurrer at the close of the Commonwealth's case. The trial court granted the demurrer with the comment that there was insufficient evidence to conclude the defendants were guilty beyond a reasonable doubt. The Commonwealth appealed this order and the Superior Court concluded the appeal was barred by jeopardy. The Pennsylvania Supreme Court,

---

11. We should point out that it is entirely possible for a trial court to reconcile the public interest in the Government's right to appeal from an erroneous conclusion of law with the defendant's interest in avoiding a second prosecution. In [United States v. Wilson, 420 U.S. 332, 95 S.Ct. 1013, 43 L.Ed.2d 232 (1975)], the court permitted the case to go to the jury, which returned a verdict of guilt, but it subsequently dismissed the indictment for preindictment delay on the basis of evidence adduced at trial. Most recently in United States v. Ceccolini, [435 U.S. 268, (1978)] we described similar action with approval: "The District Court had sensibly first made its finding on the factual question of guilt or innocence, and then ruled on the motion to suppress; a reversal of these rulings would require no further proceedings in the District Court, but merely a reinstatement of the finding of guilt." . . .

We of course do not suggest that a midtrial dismissal of a prosecution, in response to a defense motion on grounds unrelated to guilt or innocence, is necessarily improper. Such rulings may be necessary to terminate proceedings marred by fundamental error. But where a defendant prevails on such a motion, he takes the risk that an appellate court will reverse the trial court.

relying on United States v. Scott, reversed on the ground that in ruling on a demurrer the trial court does not make a factual determination but rather a ruling of law as to whether "the evidence, if credited by the jury, is legally sufficient to warrant the conclusion that the defendant is guilty beyond a reasonable doubt." It remanded for consideration on the merits. The United States Supreme Court reversed in a unanimous decision. Justice White concluded that the action of the trial court was an acquittal under *Scott* since it was a determination that the Commonwealth's evidence was insufficient to establish factual guilt. That a state may characterize such a decision as a ruling on law rather than a determination of fact makes no difference for jeopardy purposes. Since an appellate ruling in the favor of the Commonwealth would require either a new trial or further proceedings in the trial court devoted to the resolution of factual issues going to the elements of the offense charged, the appeal itself is not permissible.

D. FORFEITURE OF PROPERTY ASSOCIATED WITH THE COMMISSION OF CRIMINAL OFFENSES

United States v. Ursery

Supreme Court of the United States, 1996.
518 U.S. 267, 116 S.Ct. 2135, 135 L.Ed.2d 549.

■ CHIEF JUSTICE REHNQUIST delivered the opinion of the Court.

In separate cases, the United States Court of Appeals for the Sixth Circuit and the United States Court of Appeals for the Ninth Circuit held that the Double Jeopardy Clause prohibits the Government from both punishing a defendant for a criminal offense and forfeiting his property for that same offense in a separate civil proceeding. We consolidated those cases for our review, and now reverse. These civil forfeitures (and civil forfeitures generally), we hold, do not constitute "punishment" for purposes of the Double Jeopardy Clause.

I

No. 95–345: Michigan Police found marijuana growing adjacent to respondent Guy Ursery's house, and discovered marijuana seeds, stems, stalks, and a growlight within the house. The United States instituted civil forfeiture proceedings against the house, alleging that the property was subject to forfeiture under 84 Stat. 1276, as amended, 21 U.S.C. § 881(a)(7) because it had been used for several years to facilitate the unlawful processing and distribution of a controlled substance. Ursery ultimately paid the United States $13,250 to settle the forfeiture claim in full. Shortly before the settlement was consummated, Ursery was indicted for manufacturing marijuana, in violation of § 841(a)(1). A jury found him guilty, and he was sentenced to 63 months in prison.

The Court of Appeals for the Sixth Circuit by a divided vote reversed Ursery's criminal conviction, holding that the conviction violated the Double Jeopardy Clause of the Fifth Amendment of the United States Constitution. 59 F.3d 568 (1995). The court based its conclusion in part upon its belief that our decisions in United States v. Halper, 490 U.S. 435, 109 S.Ct.

1892, 104 L.Ed.2d 487 (1989), and Austin v. United States, 509 U.S. 602, 113 S.Ct. 2801, 125 L.Ed.2d 488 (1993), meant that any civil forfeiture under § 881(a)(7) constitutes punishment for purposes of the Double Jeopardy Clause. Ursery, in the court's view, had therefore been "punished" in the forfeiture proceeding against his property, and could not be subsequently criminally tried for violation of 21 U.S.C. § 841(a)(1).

No. 95–346: Following a jury trial, Charles Wesley Arlt and James Wren were convicted of: conspiracy to aid and abet the manufacture of methamphetamine, in violation of 21 U.S.C. § 846; conspiracy to launder monetary instruments, in violation of 18 U.S.C. § 371; and numerous counts of money laundering, in violation of § 1956. The District Court sentenced Arlt to life in prison and a 10–year term of supervised release, and imposed a fine of $250,000. Wren was sentenced to life imprisonment and a 5–year term of supervised release.

Before the criminal trial had started, the United States had filed a civil in rem complaint against various property seized from, or titled to, Arlt and Wren, or Payback Mines, a corporation controlled by Arlt. The complaint alleged that each piece of property was subject to forfeiture both under 18 U.S.C. § 981(a)(1)(A), which provides that "[a]ny property ... involved in a transaction or attempted transaction in violation of" § 1956 (the money-laundering statute) "is subject to forfeiture to the United States"; and under 21 U.S.C. § 881(a)(6), which provides for the forfeiture of (i) "[a]ll ... things of value furnished or intended to be furnished by any person in exchange for" illegal drugs, (ii) "all proceeds traceable to such an exchange," and (iii) "all moneys, negotiable instruments, and securities used or intended to be used to facilitate" a federal drug felony. The parties agreed to defer litigation of the forfeiture action during the criminal prosecution. More than a year after the conclusion of the criminal trial, the District Court granted the Government's motion for summary judgment in the civil forfeiture proceeding.

Arlt and Wren appealed the decision in the forfeiture action, and the Court of Appeals for the Ninth Circuit reversed, holding that the forfeiture violated the Double Jeopardy Clause. 33 F.3d 1210 (1994). The court's decision was based in part upon the same view as that expressed by the Court of Appeals for the Sixth Circuit in Ursery's case—that our decisions in *Halper,* supra, and *Austin,* supra, meant that, as a categorical matter, forfeitures under § 981(a)(1)(A) and § 881(a)(6) always constitute "punishment."

We granted the Government's petition for certiorari in each of the two cases, and we now reverse. 511 U.S. 767, 114 S.Ct. 1937, 128 L.Ed.2d 767 (1994).

II

The Double Jeopardy Clause provides: "[N]or shall any person be subject for the same offence to be twice put in jeopardy of life or limb." U.S. Const., Amdt. 5. The Clause serves the function of preventing both "successive punishments and ... successive prosecutions." United States v. Dixon, 509 U.S. 688, 696, 113 S.Ct. 2849, 2855, 125 L.Ed.2d 556 (1993), citing North Carolina v. Pearce, 395 U.S. 711, 89 S.Ct. 2072, 23 L.Ed.2d

656 (1969). The protection against multiple punishments prohibits the Government from " 'punishing twice, or attempting a second time to punish criminally for the same offense.' " Witte v. United States, 515 U.S. 389, 395, 115 S.Ct. 2199, 2204, 132 L.Ed.2d 351 (1995)(emphasis omitted), quoting Helvering v. Mitchell, 303 U.S. 391, 399, 58 S.Ct. 630, 633, 82 L.Ed. 917 (1938).

In the decisions that we review, the Courts of Appeals held that the civil forfeitures constituted "punishment," making them subject to the prohibitions of the Double Jeopardy Clause. The Government challenges that characterization of the forfeitures, arguing that the courts were wrong to conclude that civil forfeitures are punitive for double jeopardy purposes.

A

Since the earliest years of this Nation, Congress has authorized the Government to seek parallel in rem civil forfeiture actions and criminal prosecutions based upon the same underlying events. See, e.g., Act of July 31, 1789, ch. 5, § 12, 1 Stat. 39 (goods unloaded at night or without a permit subject to forfeiture and persons unloading subject to criminal prosecution); § 25, id., at 43 (persons convicted of buying or concealing illegally imported goods subject to both monetary fine and in rem forfeiture of the goods); § 34, id., at 46 (imposing criminal penalty and in rem forfeiture where person convicted of relanding goods entitled to drawback); see also The Palmyra, 12 Wheat. 1, 14–15, 6 L.Ed. 531 (1827)("Many cases exist, where there is both a forfeiture in rem and a personal penalty"); cf. Calero–Toledo v. Pearson Yacht Leasing Co., 416 U.S. 663, 683, 94 S.Ct. 2080, 2091–2092, 40 L.Ed.2d 452 (1974)(discussing adoption of forfeiture statutes by early Congresses). And, in a long line of cases, this Court has considered the application of the Double Jeopardy Clause to civil forfeitures, consistently concluding that the Clause does not apply to such actions because they do not impose punishment.

One of the first cases to consider the relationship between the Double Jeopardy Clause and civil forfeiture was Various Items of Personal Property v. United States, 282 U.S. 577, 51 S.Ct. 282, 75 L.Ed. 558 (1931). In Various Items, the Waterloo Distilling Corporation had been ordered to forfeit a distillery, warehouse, and denaturing plant, on the ground that the corporation had conducted its distilling business in violation of federal law. The Government conceded that the corporation had been convicted of criminal violations prior to the initiation of the forfeiture proceeding, and admitted that the criminal conviction had been based upon "the transactions set forth . . . as a basis for the forfeiture." Id., at 579, 51 S.Ct., at 283. Considering the corporation's argument that the forfeiture action violated the Double Jeopardy Clause, this Court unanimously held that the Clause was inapplicable to civil forfeiture actions:

"[This] forfeiture proceeding . . . is in rem. It is the property which is proceeded against, and, by resort to a legal fiction, held guilty and condemned as though it were conscious instead of inanimate and insentient. In a criminal prosecution it is the wrongdoer in person who is proceeded against, convicted, and punished. The forfeiture is no part of the punishment for the criminal offense. The provision of the Fifth Amendment to the

Constitution in respect of double jeopardy does not apply." Id., at 581, 51 S.Ct., at 284 (citations omitted; emphasis added).

In reaching its conclusion, the Court drew a sharp distinction between in rem civil forfeitures and in personam civil penalties such as fines: Though the latter could, in some circumstances, be punitive, the former could not. Ibid. Referring to a case that was decided the same day as Various Items, the Court made its point absolutely clear:

> In United States v. La Franca, [282 U.S.] 568 [51 S.Ct. 278, 75 L.Ed. 551 (1931)], we hold that, under § 5 of the Willis–Campbell Act, a civil action to recover taxes, which in fact are penalties, is punitive in character and barred by a prior conviction of the defendant for a criminal offense involving the same transactions. This, however, is not that case, but a proceeding in rem to forfeit property used in committing an offense.

Id., at 580, 51 S.Ct., at 283.

Had the Court in Various Items found that a civil forfeiture could constitute a "punishment" under the Fifth Amendment, its holding would have been quite remarkable. As that Court recognized, "[a]t common law, in many cases, the right of forfeiture did not attach until the offending person had been convicted and the record of conviction produced." Ibid. In other words, at common law, not only was it the case that a criminal conviction did not bar a civil forfeiture, but, in fact, the civil forfeiture could not be instituted unless a criminal conviction had already been obtained. Though this Court had held that common-law rule inapplicable where the right of forfeiture was "created by statute, in rem, cognizable on the revenue side of the exchequer," The Palmyra, supra, at 14, it never had suggested that the Constitution prohibited for statutory civil forfeiture what was required for common-law civil forfeiture. For the Various Items Court to have held that the forfeiture was prohibited by the prior criminal proceeding would have been directly contrary to the common-law rule, and would have called into question the constitutionality of forfeiture statutes thought constitutional for over a century. See United States v. Curtiss–Wright Export Corp., 299 U.S. 304, 327–328, 57 S.Ct. 216, 224–225, 81 L.Ed. 255 (1936)(Evidence of a longstanding legislative practice "goes a long way in the direction of proving the presence of unassailable grounds for the constitutionality of the practice").

Following its decision in Various Items, the Court did not consider another double jeopardy case involving a civil forfeiture for 40 years. Then, in One Lot Emerald Cut Stones v. United States, 409 U.S. 232, 93 S.Ct. 489, 34 L.Ed.2d 438 (1972)(per curiam), the Court's brief opinion reaffirmed the rule of Various Items. In *Emerald Cut Stones,* after having been acquitted of smuggling jewels into the United States, the owner of the jewels intervened in a proceeding to forfeit them as contraband. We rejected the owner's double jeopardy challenge to the forfeiture, holding that "[i]f for no other reason the forfeiture is not barred by the Double Jeopardy Clause of the Fifth Amendment because it involves neither two criminal trials nor two criminal punishments." 409 U.S., at 235, 93 S.Ct., at 492. Noting that the forfeiture provisions had been codified separately from parallel criminal provisions, the Court determined that the forfeiture clearly was "a civil sanction." Id., at 236, 93 S.Ct., at 492–493. The forfeitures were not criminal punishments because they did not impose a second in personam penalty for the criminal defendant's wrongdoing.

In our most recent decision considering whether a civil forfeiture constitutes punishment under the Double Jeopardy Clause, we again affirmed the rule of Various Items. In United States v. One Assortment of 89 Firearms, 465 U.S. 354, 104 S.Ct. 1099, 79 L.Ed.2d 361 (1984), the owner of the defendant weapons was acquitted of charges of dealing firearms without a license. The Government then brought a forfeiture action against the firearms under 18 U.S.C. § 924(d), alleging that they were used or were intended to be used in violation of federal law.

In another unanimous decision, we held that the forfeiture was not barred by the prior criminal proceeding. We began our analysis by stating the rule for our decision:

"Unless the forfeiture sanction was intended as punishment, so that the proceeding is essentially criminal in character, the Double Jeopardy Clause is not applicable. The question, then, is whether a § 924(d) forfeiture proceeding is intended to be, or by its nature necessarily is, criminal and punitive, or civil and remedial." *89 Firearms,* supra, at 362, 104 S.Ct., at 1105 (citations omitted).

Our inquiry proceeded in two stages. In the first stage, we looked to Congress' intent, and concluded that "Congress designed forfeiture under § 924(d) as a remedial civil sanction." 465 U.S., at 363, 104 S.Ct., at 1105. This conclusion was based upon several findings. First, noting that the forfeiture proceeding was in rem, we found it significant that "actions in rem have traditionally been viewed as civil proceedings, with jurisdiction dependent upon the seizure of a physical object." 89 Firearms, id., at 363, 104 S.Ct., at 1105, citing, Calero–Toledo v. Pearson Yacht Leasing Co., 416 U.S., at 684, 94 S.Ct., at 2092. Second, we found that the forfeiture provision, because it reached both weapons used in violation of federal law and those "intended to be used" in such a manner, reached a broader range of conduct than its criminal analogue. Third, we concluded that the civil forfeiture "further[ed] broad remedial aims," including both "discouraging unregulated commerce in firearms," and "removing from circulation firearms that have been used or intended for use outside regulated channels of commerce." *89 Firearms,* supra, at 364, 104 S.Ct., at 1105–1106.

In the second stage of our analysis, we looked to " 'whether the statutory scheme was so punitive either in purpose or effect as to negate' Congress' intention to establish a civil remedial mechanism," 465 U.S., at 365, 104 S.Ct., at 1106, quoting United States v. Ward, 448 U.S. 242, 248–249, 100 S.Ct. 2636, 2641, 65 L.Ed.2d 742 (1980). Considering several factors that we had used previously in order to determine whether a civil proceeding was so punitive as to require application of the full panoply of constitutional protections required in a criminal trial, see id., at 248, 100 S.Ct., at 2641, we found only one of those factors to be present in the § 924(d) forfeiture. By itself, however, the fact that the behavior proscribed by the forfeiture was already a crime proved insufficient to turn the forfeiture into a punishment subject to the Double Jeopardy Clause. Hence, we found that the petitioner had "failed to establish by the 'clearest proof' that Congress has provided a sanction so punitive as to 'transfor[m] what was clearly intended as a civil remedy into a criminal penalty.'" *89 Firearms,* supra, at 366, 104 S.Ct., at 1107, quoting Rex Trailer Co. v. United States, 350 U.S. 148, 154, 76 S.Ct. 219, 222, 100 L.Ed. 149 (1956). We concluded our decision by restating that civil forfeiture is "not an additional penalty for the commission of a criminal act, but rather is a separate civil sanction, remedial in nature." *89 Firearms,* supra, at 366, 104 S.Ct., at 1107.

B

Our cases reviewing civil forfeitures under the Double Jeopardy Clause adhere to a remarkably consistent theme. Though the two-part analytical construct employed in 89 Firearms was more refined, perhaps, than that we had used over 50 years earlier in Various Items, the conclusion was the same in each case: in rem civil forfeiture is a remedial civil sanction, distinct from potentially punitive in personam civil penalties such as fines, and does not constitute a punishment under the Double Jeopardy Clause. See Gore v. United States, 357 U.S. 386, 392, 78 S.Ct. 1280, 1284, 2 L.Ed.2d 1405 (1958)("In applying a provision like that of double jeopardy, which is rooted in history and is not an evolving concept ... a long course of adjudication in this Court carries impressive authority").

In the case that we currently review, the Court of Appeals for the Ninth Circuit recognized as much, concluding that after *89 Firearms,* "the law was clear that civil forfeitures did not constitute 'punishment' for double jeopardy purposes." 33 F.3d, at 1218. Nevertheless, that court read three of our decisions to have "abandoned" 89 Firearms and the oft-affirmed rule of Various Items. According to the Court of Appeals for the Ninth Circuit, through our decisions in United States v. Halper, 490 U.S. 435, 109 S.Ct. 1892, 104 L.Ed.2d 487 (1989), Austin v. United States, 509 U.S. 602, 113 S.Ct. 2801, 125 L.Ed.2d 488 (1993), and Department of Revenue of Mont. v. Kurth Ranch, 511 U.S. 767, 114 S.Ct. 1937, 128 L.Ed.2d 767 (1994), we "changed [our] collective mind," and "adopted a new test for determining whether a nominally civil sanction constitutes 'punishment' for double jeopardy purposes." 33 F.3d, at 1218–1219. The Court of Appeals for the Sixth Circuit shared the view of the Ninth Circuit, though it did not directly rely upon *Kurth Ranch.* We turn now to consider whether *Halper, Austin,* and *Kurth Ranch* accomplished the radical juris-prudential shift perceived by the Courts of Appeals.

In *Halper,* we considered "whether and under what circumstances a civil penalty may constitute 'punishment' for the purposes of double jeopardy analysis." *Halper,* supra, at 436, 109 S.Ct., at 1895. Based upon his submission of 65 inflated Medicare claims, each of which overcharged the Government by $9, Halper was criminally convicted of 65 counts of violating the false-claims statute, 18 U.S.C. § 287 (1982 ed.), as well as of 16 counts of mail fraud, and was sentenced to two years in prison and fined $5,000. Following that criminal conviction, the Government successfully brought a civil action against Halper under 31 U.S.C. § 3729 (1982 ed. and Supp. II). The District Court hearing the civil action determined that Halper was liable to the Government for over $130,000 under § 3729, which then provided for liability in the amount of $2,000 per violation, double the Government's actual damages, and court costs. The court concluded that imposing the full civil penalty would constitute a second punishment for Halper's already-punished criminal offense, however, and therefore reduced Halper's liability to double the actual damages suffered by the Government and the costs of the civil action. The Government directly appealed that decision to this Court.

This Court agreed with the District Court's analysis. We determined that our precedent had established no absolute and irrebuttable rule that a civil fine cannot be "punishment" under the Double Jeopardy Clause. Though it was well established that "a civil remedy does not rise to the level of 'punishment' merely because Congress provided for civil recovery in excess of the Government's actual damages," we found that our case law did "not foreclose the possibility that in a particular case a civil penalty ... may be so extreme and so divorced from the Government's damages and expenses as to constitute punishment." 490 U.S., at 442, 109 S.Ct., at 1898. Emphasizing the case-specific nature of our inquiry, id., at 448, 109 S.Ct., at 1901–1902, we compared the size of the fine imposed on Halper, $130,000, to the damages actually suffered by the Government as a result of Halper's actions, estimated by the District Court at $585. Noting that the fine was more than 220 times greater than the Government's damages, we agreed with the District Court that "Halper's $130,000 liability is sufficiently disproportionate that the sanction constitutes a second punishment in violation of double jeopardy." Id., at 452, 109 S.Ct., at 1904. We remanded to the District Court so that it could hear evidence regarding the Government's actual damages, and could then reduce Halper's liability to a nonpunitive level. Ibid.

In Austin, we considered whether a civil forfeiture could violate the Excessive Fines Clause of the Eighth Amendment to the Constitution, which provides that "[e]xcessive bail shall not be required, nor excessive fines imposed.... " U.S. Const., Amdt. 8. Aware that Austin had sold two grams of cocaine the previous day, police searched his mobile home and body shop. Their search revealed small amounts of marijuana and cocaine, a handgun, drug paraphernalia, and almost $5,000 in cash. Austin was charged with one count of possessing cocaine with intent to distribute, to which he pleaded guilty. The Government then initiated a civil forfeiture proceeding against Austin's mobile home and auto shop, contending that they had been "used" or were "intended for use" in the commission of a drug offense. See 21 U.S.C. §§ 881(a)(4) and (a)(7). Austin contested the forfeiture on the ground of the Excessive Fines Clause, but the District Court and the Court of Appeals held the forfeiture constitutional.

We limited our review to the question "whether the Excessive Fines Clause of the Eighth Amendment applies to forfeitures of property under 21 U.S.C. §§ 881(a)(4) and (a)(7)." Austin, supra, at 604, 113 S.Ct., at 2803. We began our analysis by rejecting the argument that the Excessive Fines Clause was limited solely to criminal proceedings: The relevant question was not whether a particular proceeding was criminal or civil, we determined, but rather was whether forfeiture under §§ 881(a)(4) and (a)(7) constituted "punishment" for the purposes of the Eighth Amendment.

Austin, supra, at 610, 113 S.Ct., at 2806. In an effort to answer that question, we briefly reviewed the history of civil forfeiture both in this country and in England, see id., at 611–618, 113 S.Ct., at 2806–2810, taking a categorical approach that contrasted sharply with Halper's case-specific approach to determining whether a civil penalty constitutes punishment. Ultimately, we concluded that "forfeiture under [§§ 881(a)(4) and (a)(7)] constitutes 'payment to a sovereign as punishment for some offense,' and, as such, is subject to the limitations of the Eighth Amendment's Excessive Fines Clause." Id., at 622, 113 S.Ct., at 2812.

In Department of Revenue of Mont. v. Kurth Ranch, 511 U.S. 767, 114 S.Ct. 1937, 128 L.Ed.2d 767 (1994), we considered whether a state tax imposed on marijuana was invalid under the Double Jeopardy Clause when the taxpayer had already been criminally convicted of owning the marijuana which was taxed. We first established that the fact that Montana had labeled the civil sanction a "tax" did not end our analysis. We then turned to consider whether the tax was so punitive as to constitute a punishment subject to the Double Jeopardy Clause. Several differences between the marijuana tax imposed by Montana and the typical revenue-raising tax were readily apparent. The Montana tax was unique in that it was conditioned on the commission of a crime and was imposed only after the taxpayer had been arrested: thus, only a person charged with a criminal offense was subject to the tax. We also noted that the taxpayer did not own or possess the taxed marijuana at the time that the tax was imposed. From these differences, we determined that the tax was motivated by a " 'penal and prohibitory intent rather than the gathering of revenue.' " Id., at ___, 114 S.Ct., at 1947. Concluding that the Montana tax proceeding "was the functional equivalent of a successive criminal prosecution," we affirmed the Court of Appeals' judgment barring the tax. Id., at ___, 114 S.Ct., at 1948.

We think that the Court of Appeals for the Sixth Circuit and the Court of Appeals for the Ninth Circuit misread Halper, Austin, and Kurth Ranch. None of those decisions purported to overrule the well-established teaching of Various Items, Emerald Cut Stones, and 89 Firearms. Halper involved not a civil forfeiture, but a civil penalty. That its rule was limited to the latter context is clear from the decision itself, from the historical distinction that we have drawn between civil forfeiture and civil penalties, and from the practical difficulty of applying Halper to a civil forfeiture.

In Halper, we emphasized that our decision was limited to the context of civil penalties: What we announce now is a rule for the rare case, the case such as the one before us, where a fixed-penalty provision subjects a prolific but small-gauge offender to a sanction overwhelmingly disproportionate to the damages he has caused. The rule is one of reason: Where a defendant previously has sustained a criminal penalty and the civil penalty sought in the subsequent proceeding bears no rational relation to the goal of compensating the Government for its loss, but rather appears to qualify as "punishment" in the plain meaning of the word, then the defendant is entitled to an accounting of the Government's damages and costs to determine if the penalty sought in fact constitutes a second punishment. 490 U.S., at 449–450, 109 S.Ct., at 1902.

The narrow focus of Halper followed from the distinction that we have drawn historically between civil forfeiture and civil penalties. Since at least Various Items, we have distinguished civil penalties such as fines from civil forfeiture proceedings that are in rem. While a "civil action to recover . . . penalties, is punitive in character," and much like a criminal prosecution in that "it is the wrongdoer in person who is proceeded against . . . and punished," in an in rem forfeiture proceeding, "it is the property which is proceeded against, and by resort to a legal fiction, held guilty and condemned." Various Items, 282 U.S., at 580–581, 51 S.Ct., at 283–284. Thus, though for Double Jeopardy purposes we have never balanced the value of property forfeited in a particular case against the harm suffered by the Government in that case, we have balanced the size of a particular civil penalty against the Government's harm. See, e.g., Rex Trailer Co. v. United States, 350 U.S. 148, 154, 76 S.Ct. 219, 222–223, 100 L.Ed. 149 (1956)(fines not "so unreasonable or excessive" as to transform a civil remedy into a criminal penalty); United States ex rel. Marcus v. Hess, 317 U.S. 537, 63 S.Ct. 379, 87 L.Ed. 443 (1943)(fine of $315,000 not so disproportionate to Government's harm of $101,500 as to transform the fine into punishment). Indeed, the rule set forth in Halper developed from the teaching of Rex Trailer and Hess. See Halper, supra, at 445–447, 109 S.Ct., at 1900–1901.

It is difficult to see how the rule of Halper could be applied to a civil forfeiture. Civil penalties are designed as a rough form of "liquidated damages" for the harms suffered by the Government as a result of a defendant's conduct. See Rex Trailer, supra, at 153–154, 76 S.Ct., at 222–223. The civil penalty involved in Halper, for example, provided for a fixed monetary penalty for each false claim count on which the defendant was convicted in the criminal proceeding. Whether a "fixed-penalty provision" that seeks to compensate the Government for harm it has suffered is "so extreme" and "so divorced" from the penalty's nonpunitive purpose of compensating the Government as to be a punishment may be determined by balancing the Government's harm against the size of the penalty. Civil forfeitures, in contrast to civil penalties, are designed to do more than simply compensate the Government. Forfeitures serve a variety of purposes, but are designed primarily to confiscate property used in violation of the law, and to require disgorgement of the fruits of illegal conduct. Though it may be possible to quantify the value of the property forfeited, it is virtually impossible to quantify, even approximately, the nonpunitive purposes served by a particular civil forfeiture. Hence, it is practically difficult to determine whether a particular forfeiture bears no rational relationship to the nonpunitive purposes of that forfeiture. Quite simply, the case-by-case balancing test set forth in Halper, in which a court must compare the harm suffered by the Government against the size of the penalty imposed, is inapplicable to civil forfeiture.

We recognized as much in Kurth Ranch. In that case, the Court expressly disclaimed reliance upon Halper, finding that its case-specific approach was impossible to apply outside the context of a fixed civil-penalty provision. Reviewing the Montana marijuana tax, we held that because "tax statutes serve a purpose quite different from civil penalties, . . . Halper's method of determining whether the exaction was remedial or punitive simply does not work in the case of a tax statute." Kurth Ranch, supra, at ___, 114 S.Ct., at 1948 (internal quotation marks omitted); see also id., at ___, 114 S.Ct., at 1949–1950 (REHNQUIST, C.J., dissenting)(Halper inapplicable outside of " 'fixed-penalty provision[s]' "that are meant "to recover the costs incurred by the Government for bringing someone to book for some violation of law"). This is not to say that there is no occasion for analysis of the Government's harm. 89 Firearms makes clear the relevance of an evaluation of the harms alleged. The point is simply that Halper's case-specific approach is inapplicable to civil forfeitures.

In the cases that we review, the Courts of Appeals did not find Halper difficult to apply to civil forfeiture because they concluded that its case-by-case balancing approach had been supplanted in Austin by a categorical approach that found a civil sanction to be punitive if it could not "fairly be said solely to serve a remedial purpose." See Austin, 509 U.S., at 610, 113 S.Ct., at 2806; see also Halper, supra, at 448, 109 S.Ct., at 1901–1902. But Austin, it must be remembered, did not involve the Double Jeopardy Clause at all. Austin was decided solely under the Excessive Fines Clause of the Eighth Amendment, a constitutional provision which we never have understood as parallel to, or even related to, the Double Jeopardy Clause of the Fifth Amendment. The only discussion of the Double Jeopardy Clause contained in Austin appears in a footnote that acknowledges our decisions holding that "[t]he Double Jeopardy Clause has been held not to apply in civil forfeiture proceedings ... where the forfeiture could properly be characterized as remedial." Austin, supra, at 608, n. 4, 113 S.Ct., at 2804, n. 4. And in Austin we expressly recognized and approved our decisions in One Lot Emerald Cut Stones v. United States, 409 U.S. 232, 93 S.Ct. 489, 34 L.Ed.2d 438 (1972), and United States v. One Assortment of 89 Firearms, 465 U.S. 354, 104 S.Ct. 1099, 79 L.Ed.2d 361 (1984). See Austin, supra, at 608, n. 4, 113 S.Ct., at 2804, n. 4.

We acknowledged in Austin that our categorical approach under the Excessive Fines Clause was wholly distinct from the case-by-case approach of Halper, and we explained that the difference in approach was based in a significant difference between the purposes of our analysis under each constitutional provision. See Austin, supra, at 622, n. 14, 113 S.Ct., at 2812, n. 14. It is unnecessary in a case under the Excessive Fines Clause to inquire at a preliminary stage whether the civil sanction imposed in that particular case is totally inconsistent with any remedial goal. Because the second stage of inquiry under the Excessive Fines Clause asks whether the particular sanction in question is so large as to be "excessive," see Austin, 509 U.S., at 622–623, 113 S.Ct., at 2812–2813 (declining to establish criteria for excessiveness), a preliminary-stage inquiry that focused on the disproportionality of a particular sanction would be duplicative of the excessiveness analysis that would follow. See id., at 622, n. 14, 113 S.Ct., at 2812, n. 14 ("[I]t appears to make little practical difference whether the Excessive Fines Clause applies to all forfeitures ... or only to those that cannot be characterized as purely remedial," because the Excessive Fines Clause "prohibits only the imposition of 'excessive' fines, and a fine that serves purely remedial purposes cannot be considered 'excessive' in any event"). Forfeitures effected under 21 U.S.C. §§ 881(a)(4) and (a)(7) are subject to review for excessiveness under the Eighth Amendment after Austin; this does not mean, however, that those forfeitures are so punitive as to constitute punishment for the purposes of double jeopardy. The holding of Austin was limited to the Excessive Fines Clause of the Eighth Amendment, and we decline to import the analysis of Austin into our double jeopardy jurisprudence.

In sum, nothing in *Halper, Kurth Ranch,* or *Austin,* purported to replace our traditional understanding that civil forfeiture does not constitute punishment for the purpose of the Double Jeopardy Clause. Congress long has authorized the Government to bring parallel criminal proceedings and civil forfeiture proceedings, and this Court consistently has found civil forfeitures not to constitute punishment under the Double Jeopardy Clause. It would have been quite remarkable for this Court both to have held unconstitutional a well-established practice, and to have overruled a long line of precedent, without having even suggested that it was doing so. Halper dealt with in personam civil penalties under the Double Jeopardy Clause; Kurth Ranch with a tax proceeding under the Double Jeopardy Clause; and Austin with civil forfeitures under the Excessive Fines Clause. None of those cases dealt with the subject of this case: in rem civil forfeitures for purposes of the Double Jeopardy Clause.

C

We turn now to consider the forfeitures in these cases under the teaching of Various Items, Emerald Cut Stones, and 89 Firearms. Because it provides a useful analytical tool, we conduct our inquiry within the framework of the two-part test used in 89 Firearms. First, we ask whether Congress intended proceedings under 21 U.S.C. § 881, and 18 U.S.C. § 981, to be criminal or civil. Second, we turn to consider whether the proceedings are so punitive in fact as to "persuade us that the forfeiture proceeding[s] may not legitimately be viewed as civil in nature," despite Congress' intent. 89 Firearms, 465 U.S., at 366, 104 S.Ct., at 1107.

There is little doubt that Congress intended these forfeitures to be civil proceedings. As was the case in 89 Firearms, "Congress' intent in this regard is most clearly demonstrated by the procedural mechanisms it established for enforcing forfeitures under the statute[s]." 465 U.S., at 363, 104 S.Ct., at 1105. Both 21 U.S.C. § 881 and 18 U.S.C. § 981, which is entitled "Civil forfeiture," provide that the laws "relating to the seizure, summary and judicial forfeiture, and condemnation of property for violation of the customs laws ... shall apply to seizures and forfeitures incurred" under § 881 and § 981. See 21 U.S.C. § 881(d); 18 U.S.C. § 981(d). Because forfeiture proceedings under the customs laws are in rem, see 19 U.S.C. § 1602 et seq., it is clear that Congress intended that a forfeiture under § 881 or § 981, like the forfeiture reviewed in 89 Firearms, would be a proceeding in rem. Congress specifically structured these forfeitures to be impersonal by targeting the property itself. "In contrast to the in personam nature of criminal actions, actions in rem have traditionally been viewed as civil proceedings, with jurisdiction dependent upon seizure of a physical object." 89 Firearms, 465 U.S., at 363, 104 S.Ct., at 1105, citing Calero–Toledo, 416 U.S., at 684, 94 S.Ct., at 2092.

Other procedural mechanisms governing forfeitures under § 981 and § 881 also indicate that Congress intended such proceedings to be civil.

Forfeitures under either statute are governed by 19 U.S.C. § 1607, which provides that actual notice of the impending forfeiture is unnecessary when the Government cannot identify any party with an interest in the seized article, and by § 1609, which provides that seized property is subject to forfeiture through a summary administrative procedure if no party files a claim to the property. And 19 U.S.C. § 1615, which governs the burden of proof in forfeiture proceedings under § 881 and § 981, provides that once the Government has shown probable cause that the property is subject to forfeiture, then "the burden of proof shall lie upon [the] claimant." In sum, "[b]y creating such distinctly civil procedures for forfeitures under [§ 881 and § 981], Congress has 'indicate[d] clearly that it intended a civil, not a criminal sanction.' "89 Firearms, supra, at 363, 104 S.Ct., at 1105, quoting Helvering v. Mitchell, 303 U.S., at 402, 58 S.Ct., at 634.

Moving to the second stage of our analysis, we find that there is little evidence, much less the " 'clearest proof' "that we require, see 89 Firearms, supra, at 365, 104 S.Ct., at 1106, quoting Ward, 448 U.S., at 249, 100 S.Ct., at 2641–2642, suggesting that forfeiture proceedings under 21 U.S.C. §§ 881(a)(6) and (a)(7), and 18 U.S.C. § 981(a)(1)(A), are so punitive in form and effect as to render them criminal despite Congress' intent to the contrary. The statutes involved in this case are, in most significant respects, indistinguishable from those reviewed, and held not to be punitive, in Various Items, Emerald Cut Stones, and 89 Firearms.

Most significant is that § 981(a)(1)(A), and §§ 881(a)(6) and (a)(7), while perhaps having certain punitive aspects, serve important nonpunitive goals. Title 21 U.S.C. § 881(a)(7), under which Ursery's property was forfeited, provides for the forfeiture of "all real property . . . which is used or intended to be used, in any manner or part, to commit, or to facilitate the commission of" a federal drug felony. Requiring the forfeiture of property used to commit federal narcotics violations encourages property owners to take care in managing their property and ensures that they will not permit that property to be used for illegal purposes. See Bennis v. Michigan, 516 U.S. 442, 450, 116 S.Ct. 994, 1000, 134 L.Ed.2d 68 (1996)("Forfeiture of property prevents illegal uses . . . by imposing an economic penalty, thereby rendering illegal behavior unprofitable"); 89 Firearms, supra, at 364 (forfeiture "discourages unregulated commerce in firearms"); Calero–Toledo, supra, at 687–688, 94 S.Ct., at 2094. In many circumstances, the forfeiture may abate a nuisance. See, e.g., United States v. 141st Street Corp., 911 F.2d 870 (C.A.2 1990)(forfeiting apartment building used to sell crack cocaine); see also Bennis, supra, at ___, 116 S.Ct., at 1000 (affirming application of Michigan statute abating car as a nuisance; forfeiture "prevent[s] further illicit use of" property); cf. 89 Firearms, supra, at 364, 104 S.Ct., at 1106 (forfeiture "remov[ed] from circulation firearms that have been used or intended for use" illegally); Emerald Cut Stones, 409 U.S., at 237, 93 S.Ct., at 493 (forfeiture "prevented forbidden merchandise from circulating in the United States").

The forfeiture of the property claimed by Arlt and Wren took place pursuant to 18 U.S.C. § 981(a)(1)(A), and 21 U.S.C. § 881(a)(6). Section 981(a)(1)(A) provides for the forfeiture of "any property" involved in illegal money-laundering transactions. Section 881(a)(6) provides for the forfeiture of "[a]ll ... things of value furnished or intended to be furnished by any person in exchange for" illegal drugs; "all proceeds traceable to such an exchange"; and "all moneys, negotiable instruments, and securities used or intended to be used to facilitate" a federal drug felony. The same remedial purposes served by § 881(a)(7) are served by § 881(a)(6) and § 981(a)(1)(A). Only one point merits separate discussion. To the extent that § 881(a)(6) applies to "proceeds" of illegal drug activity, it serves the additional nonpunitive goal of ensuring that persons do not profit from their illegal acts.

Other considerations that we have found relevant to the question whether a proceeding is criminal also tend to support a conclusion that § 981(a)(1)(A) and §§ 881(a)(6) and (a)(7) are civil proceedings. See Ward, supra, at 247–248, n. 7, 249, 100 S.Ct., at 2640–2641, n. 7, 2641–2642 (listing relevant factors and noting that they are neither exhaustive nor dispositive). First, in light of our decisions in Various Items, Emerald Cut Stones, and 89 Firearms, and the long tradition of federal statutes providing for a forfeiture proceeding following a criminal prosecution, it is absolutely clear that in rem civil forfeiture has not historically been regarded as punishment, as we have understood that term under the Double Jeopardy Clause. Second, there is no requirement in the statutes that we currently review that the Government demonstrate scienter in order to establish that the property is subject to forfeiture; indeed, the property may be subject to forfeiture even if no party files a claim to it and the Government never shows any connection between the property and a particular person. See 19 U.S.C. § 1609. Though both § 881(a) and § 981(a) contain an "innocent owner" exception, we do not think that such a provision, without more indication of an intent to punish, is relevant to the question whether a statute is punitive under the Double Jeopardy Clause. Third, though both statutes may fairly be said to serve the purpose of deterrence, we long have held that this purpose may serve civil as well as criminal goals. See, e.g., 89 Firearms, supra, at 364, 104 S.Ct., at 1105–1106; Calero–Toledo, supra, at 677–678, 94 S.Ct., at 2088–2089. We recently reaffirmed this conclusion in Bennis v. Michigan, supra, at ___, 116 S.Ct., at 1000, where we held that "forfeiture ... serves a deterrent purpose distinct from any punitive purpose." Finally, though both statutes are tied to criminal activity, as was the case in 89 Firearms, this fact is insufficient to render the statutes punitive. See 89 Firearms, 465 U.S., at 365–366, 104 S.Ct., at 1106–1107. It is well settled that "Congress may impose both a criminal and a civil sanction in respect to the same act or omission," Helvering, 303 U.S., at 399, 58 S.Ct., at 633. By itself, the fact that a forfeiture statute has some connection to a criminal violation is far from the "clearest proof" necessary to show that a proceeding is criminal.

We hold that these in rem civil forfeitures are neither "punishment" nor criminal for purposes of the Double Jeopardy Clause. The judgments of the Court of Appeals for the Sixth Circuit, in No. 95–345, and of the Court of Appeals for the Ninth Circuit, in No. 95–346, are accordingly reversed.

It is so ordered.

■ JUSTICE KENNEDY, concurring.

I join the Court's opinion and add these further observations.

In Austin v. United States, 509 U.S. 602, 619–622, 113 S.Ct. 2801, 2810–2812, 125 L.Ed.2d 488 (1993), we described the civil in rem forfeiture provision of 21 U.S.C. § 881(a)(7) at issue here as punitive. In Libretti v. United States, 516 U.S. 29, 116 S.Ct. 356, 133 L.Ed.2d 271 (1995), we reviewed 21 U.S.C. § 853, which in almost identical terms provides for criminal forfeiture of property involved in or derived from drug crimes. We held that the "fundamental nature of criminal forfeiture" is punishment. 516 U.S. at ___, 116 S.Ct. at 364. Today the Court holds that the civil in rem forfeitures here are not punishment implicating the protections of the Double Jeopardy Clause. Ante, at ___–___. I write to explain why, in my view, our holding is consistent with both Austin and Libretti.

* * *

The key distinction is that the instrumentality-forfeiture statutes are not directed at those who carry out the crimes, but at owners who are culpable for the criminal misuse of the property. See Austin, supra, at 619, 113 S.Ct., at 2810–2811 (statutory "exemptions serve to focus the provisions on the culpability of the owner"). The theory is that the property, whether or not illegal or dangerous in nature, is hazardous in the hands of this owner because either he uses it to commit crimes, or allows others do so. The owner can be held accountable for the misuse of the property. Cf. One 1958 Plymouth Sedan, supra, at 699, 85 S.Ct., at 1250 ("There is nothing even remotely criminal in possessing an automobile. It is only the alleged use to which this particular automobile was put that subjects [the owner] to its possible loss.") The same rationale is at work in the statutory provisions enabling forfeiture of currency "used or intended to be used" to facilitate a criminal offense, § 881(a)(6). See also 18 U.S.C. § 981(a)(1)(A) (property involved in money-laundering transactions or attempts in violation of 18 U.S.C. § 1956). Since the punishment befalls any property holder who cannot claim statutory innocence, whether or not he committed any criminal acts, it is not a punishment for a person's criminal wrongdoing.

Forfeiture, then, punishes an owner by taking property involved in a crime, and it may happen that the owner is also the wrongdoer charged with a criminal offense. But the forfeiture is not a second in personam punishment for the offense, which is all the Double Jeopardy Clause prohibits. See ante, at ___ ("The forfeitures were not criminal punishments because they did not impose a second in personam penalty for the criminal defendant's wrongdoing."); One Lot Emerald Cut Stones v. United States, 409 U.S. 232, 235, 93 S.Ct. 489, 492, 34 L.Ed.2d 438 (1972)(per curiam)("the forfeiture is not barred by the Double Jeopardy Clause of the Fifth Amendment because it involves neither two criminal trials nor two criminal punishments").* * *

■ Justice Scalia, with whom Justice Thomas joins, concurring in the judgment.

In my view, the Double Jeopardy Clause prohibits successive prosecution, not successive punishment. See Department of Revenue of Mont. v. Kurth Ranch, 511 U.S. 767, 796–800, 802–804, 114 S.Ct. 1937, 1955–1957, 1958–1959, 128 L.Ed.2d 767 (1994)(Scalia, J., dissenting). Civil forfeiture proceedings of the sort at issue here are not criminal prosecutions, even under the standard of Kennedy v. Mendoza–Martinez, 372 U.S. 144, 164, 83 S.Ct. 554, 565, 9 L.Ed.2d 644 (1963), and United States v. Ward, 448 U.S. 242, 248–251, 100 S.Ct. 2636, 2641–2643, 65 L.Ed.2d 742 (1980).

■ JUSTICE STEVENS, concurring in the judgment in part and dissenting in part.

The question the Court poses is whether civil forfeitures constitute "punishment" for purposes of the Double Jeopardy Clause. Because the numerous federal statutes authorizing forfeitures cover such a wide variety of situations, it is quite wrong to assume that there is only one answer to that question. For purposes of analysis it is useful to identify three different categories of property that are subject to seizure: proceeds, contraband, and property that has played a part in the commission of a crime. The facts of these two cases illustrate the point.

In No. 95–346 the Government has forfeited $405,089.23 in currency. Those funds are the proceeds of unlawful activity. They are not property that respondents have any right to retain. The forfeiture of such proceeds, like the confiscation of money stolen from a bank, does not punish respondents because it exacts no price in liberty or lawfully derived property from them. I agree that the forfeiture of such proceeds is not punitive and therefore I concur in the Court's disposition of No. 95–346.

None of the property seized in No. 95–345 constituted proceeds of illegal activity. Indeed, the facts of that case reveal a dramatically different situation. Respondent Ursery cultivated marijuana in a heavily wooded area not far from his home in Shiawassee County, Michigan. The illegal substance was consumed by members of his family, but there is no evidence, and no contention by the Government, that he sold any of it to third parties. Acting on the basis of the incorrect assumption that the marijuana plants were on respondent's property, Michigan police officers executed a warrant to search the premises. In his house they found marijuana seeds, stems, stalks, and a growlight. I presume those items were seized, and I have no difficulty concluding that such a seizure does not constitute punishment because respondent had no right to possess contraband. Accordingly, I agree with the Court's opinion insofar as it explains why the forfeiture of contraband does not constitute punishment for double jeopardy purposes.

The critical question presented in No. 95–345 arose, not out of the seizure of contraband by the Michigan police, but rather out of the decision by the United States Attorney to take respondent's home. There is no evidence that the house had been purchased with the proceeds of unlawful activity and the house itself was surely not contraband. Nonetheless, 21 U.S.C. § 881(a)(7) authorized the Government to seek forfeiture of respondent's residence because it had been used to facilitate the manufacture and distribution of marijuana. Respondent was then himself prosecuted for and convicted of manufacturing marijuana. In my opinion none of the reasons supporting the forfeiture of proceeds or contraband provides a sufficient basis for concluding that the confiscation of respondent's home was not punitive.

The Government has advanced four arguments in support of its position that the forfeiture of respondent's home under § 881(a)(7) followed by his prosecution under § 841(a)(1) did not violate the Double Jeopardy Clause: (1) the forfeiture was not punitive; (2) even if punitive, it was not a "jeopardy"; (3) even if both the forfeiture and the prosecution were jeopardizes, they were not based on the same offense under the rule of Blockburger v. United States, 284 U.S. 299, 52 S.Ct. 180, 76 L.Ed. 306 (1932); and (4) in all events, the two cases should be deemed to constitute a single proceeding for double jeopardy purposes. Because the Court addresses only the first of these arguments, I shall begin by explaining why both reason and precedent support the conclusion that the taking of respondent's home was unmistakably punitive in character. I shall then comment on the other three arguments.* * *

The applicability of collateral estoppel and double jeopardy principles to proceedings to forfeit property was the subject of United States v. One Assortment of 89 Firearms, 465 U.S. 354, 104 S.Ct. 1099, 79 L.Ed.2d 361 (1984). One Mulcahey was acquitted of engaging in the business of dealing in firearms without a license. The government then instituted a proceeding seeking forfeiture of the firearms involved under a statute authorizing forfeiture of firearms used or intended to be used in violation of federal law. Mulcahey interposed the defense of collateral estoppel and double jeopardy. The District Court rejected the defense, but the Fourth Circuit reversed, holding both defenses applicable. The Supreme Court, in an opinion authored by the Chief Justice for a unanimous Court, reversed the Court of Appeals.

The burden of proof in the forfeiture was on the government but was only by a preponderance of the evidence. That precluded applicability of the defense of collateral estoppel:

> [A]n acquittal on criminal charges does not prove that the defendant is innocent; it merely proves the existence of a reasonable doubt as to his guilt.... [T]he jury verdict in the criminal action did not negate the possibility that preponderance of the evidence could show that Mulcahey was engaged in an unlawful firearms business. Mulcahey's acquittal ... therefore does not estop the government from proving in a civil proceeding that the firearms should be forfeited.... It is clear that the difference in the relative burdens of proof in the criminal and civil actions precludes the application of the doctrine of collateral estoppel.

465 U.S. at 361, 104 S.Ct. at 1104, 79 L.Ed.2d at 368.

As to Mulcahey's double jeopardy claim, that he had been acquitted of conduct that formed the basis of the forfeiture action, the Chief Justice reasoned that the claim must fail unless the forfeiture proceeding was "essentially criminal in character." That inquiry depends upon whether Congress intended the forfeiture sanction to be criminal and, even if it did not, whether the sanction was so punitive in effect that it should be regarded as criminal. An examination of the legislative history led the Chief Justice to the conclusion that the sanction was intended by Congress to be civil. Congress labeled the forfeiture proceeding a proceeding in rem, not in personam. The forfeiture proceeding plays an important role in furthering the prophylactic purposes of the 1968 gun control legislation by discouraging unregulated commerce in firearms and by removing from circulation firearms that have been used or intended for use outside regulated channels of commerce. Keeping potentially dangerous weapons out of the hands of unlicensed dealers is a goal plainly more remedial than punitive.

465 U.S. at 364, 104 S.Ct. at 1106, 79 L.Ed.2d at 369. As to the effect of the sanction, the fact that the basis for the forfeiture was also made a crime does not resolve the question since "Congress may impose both a criminal and a civil sanction for the same act or omission." Further, the overlap is not complete since the forfeiture sanction included firearms intended for use in violation of the law as well as those in fact so used. Therefore, the forfeiture proceeding is in purpose and effect remedial, not punitive, and double jeopardy does not apply.

NOTE

Civil monetary penalties. In Hudson v. United States, 522 U.S. 93, 118 S.Ct. 488, 139 L.Ed.2d 450 (1997), the Court abandoned the approach it had taken in *Halper* in favor of a more traditional manner of determining multiple punishment double jeopardy questions regarding the relationship between criminal prosecutions and civil monetary penalties. Petitioner was a banker. The United States Department of the Treasury assessed a civil money penalty of $16,000 against him and entered an order of debarment from further employment in the banking business. Later, Hudson was prosecuted for criminal charges arising out of the conduct that gave rise to the money penalties and debarment order. He claimed double jeopardy under *Halper*, which claim was ultimately rejected by the United States Court of Appeals on the ground the monetary penalty was not so disproportional to the proven damages to the government as to render it a punishment under *Halper*. The Supreme Court, in an opinion by The Chief Justice, affirmed the Court of Appeals, but on a much broader ground.

Stating that *Halper* marked the first time the Court had applied the Double Jeopardy Clause to a sanction without determining that it was criminal and that subsequent cases have shown its test to be unworkable, the Court substituted a two-step process to replace the remedial analysis of *Halper*. First, did the legislature intend the sanction to be civil or criminal. In this case, the Court believed the evidence was clear that the Congress intended the monetary penalty and debarment to be civil sanctions. Second, if the legislature intended to create a civil penalty, did it in fact do so. Here the test (which was used by the Court in *Ursery*) is whether there is the "clearest proof" the sanctions are "so punitive in form and effect as to render them criminal despite" legislative intent. In addressing that question, the Court used some of the factors listed in *Kennedy v. Mendoza–Martinez*, 372 U.S. 144, 83 S.Ct. 554, 9 L.Ed.2d 644 (1963), a case involving forfeiture of U.S. citizenship for absence from the country to evade military service. The factors, which are to be used to assess the statute on its face, not as applied, are (1) whether the sanction has historically been regarded as punishment—in this case they have not; (2) whether the sanction involved an affirmative disability or restraint—while petitioner is debarred from further participation in the banking industry, that does not approach imprisonment in severity; (3) whether the sanction comes into play only upon a finding of scienter—neither the monetary penalty nor the debarment require a knowing violation of the law; (4) whether the behavior to which it applies is already a crime—it is here but that is not sufficient to raise a jeopardy bar to multiple proceedings; and (5) whether the operation of the sanction will promote the traditional aims of punishment, retribution and deterrence—the mere presence of a deterrence function does not convert the monetary penalty and debarment into criminal sanctions.

The Chief Justice's opinion was joined in by Justices O'Conner, Scalia, Kennedy, and Thomas. Justice Scalia, joined by Justice Thomas, concurred in the opinion but would go further to hold that protection against multiple punishment is not a purpose of the Double Jeopardy Clause. Justice Souter concurred in the judgment and joined in "much of [the Court's] opinion" but disputed the soundness of the requirement that the criminal nature of the sanction must be established by the "clearest proof." Similarly, Justice Breyer, joined by Justice Ginsburg, concurred in the judgment but did not join the Court's opinion on the requirements of "clearest proof" and that the statute be evaluated only on its face. Justice Stevens, concurring in the judgment, would have applied *Blockburger* to this case rather than use it as a vehicle for re-evaluating *Halper*.

Can you imagine a nominally civil sanction that would be held to be criminal under the factors as they are applied in *Hudson*?

CHAPTER 21

PRETRIAL HEARINGS AND RELATED MATTERS

Analysis

EDITORS' INTRODUCTION: THE PROCEDURAL CONTEXT OF PRETRIAL HEARINGS

There are at least two major considerations that affect provisions governing pretrial motion practice in criminal cases. The first is the federal constitutional right to have certain matters decided by the trial judge out of the presence of the jury, a matter addressed in the principal case in this chapter. This, of course, does not address the need to determine the matter *pretrial;* where the right to have a matter decided by the judge applies, it can be respected by halting trial, sending the jury out of the courtroom, and conducting the required inquiry at that time. The second consideration, however, is the administrative convenience of determining before trial those matters that can be addressed without inquiry into the defendant's guilt or innocence. A procedure that accomplishes this avoids the necessity for trial interruptions and the waste of having jurors and others merely sit idly by while matters other than guilt-or-innocence are being litigated. In addition, pretrial resolution of such matters as the admissibility of crucial evidence may encourage the parties to settle the case—as by entering into a plea agreement—and thus may make a contested trial unnecessary.

Several aspects of what has become known as pretrial motion practice should be explored before the constitutional problems presented by the principal case are addressed.

OBLIGATION TO RAISE MATTERS PRETRIAL

In a large number of jurisdictions, a defendant is, as a general rule, obligated to raise certain matters before trial. For example, Uniform Rules of Criminal Procedure 451(c) provides:

Unless otherwise ordered by the court for cause shown, a party may assert the following only in a pretrial motion . . . :

(1) Defenses and objections based on defects in the institution of the prosecution, other than the lack of jurisdiction of the court over the person or subject matter which can be raised at any time;

915

(2) Defenses and objections based on defects in the [charging instrument];

(3) Requests regarding discovery . . . ;

(4) Requests that potential testimony or other evidence should be suppressed . . . ;

(5) Requests for joinder, dismissal, or severance [under the Rules relating to joinder and severance]; and

(6) Requests for transfer of prosecution. . . .

See also, F.R.Crim.P. 12(f). The Uniform Rules contemplate that a matter may be raised later "for cause shown," and reasonable unawareness of the bases for raising a matter is clearly "cause." But the Uniform Rules, in another section, require the prosecution to provide the defense with pretrial notice of its intention to use certain evidence at trial, including any confession, admission or statement made by the defendant, evidence obtained as a result of any such confession, admission, or statement, a search or seizure, wiretap, or any form of electronic surveillance or eavesdropping, and evidence relating to a lineup, showup, picture or voice identification of the defendant. Uniform Rules of Criminal Procedure 422(a)(1). Such notice, of course, would generally justify requiring matters concerning such evidence to be raised before trial.

DETERMINATION OF MATTERS RAISED BY PRETRIAL MOTION

Uniform Rules of Criminal Procedure 451(e) states what is widely-accepted practice, i.e., that matters raised before trial are to be resolved before trial on the merits, except where the trial judge determines that pretrial resolution of the matter would be "impractical." Issues concerning the Sixth Amendment right to speedy trial, for example, may require consideration of the effect of the delay upon the defense's ability effectively to contest the prosecution's case. A pretrial motion to dismiss on such grounds, then, might reasonably be resolved only after some or all of the evidence bearing upon guilt or innocence has been produced.

APPEAL

If a trial judge resolves a pretrial matter (or any other) in favor of the defendant and the defendant is—perhaps as a result—later acquitted, double jeopardy bars the prosecution from obtaining appellate relief. Despite the general reluctance to provide for interlocutory appeals in criminal cases, therefore, a number of jurisdictions have given the prosecution a limited right to appeal before trial from adverse decisions on pretrial matters. In federal prosecutions, for example, 18 U.S.C.A. § 3731 provides as follows:

An appeal by the United States shall lie to a court of appeals from a decision or order of a district court suppressing or excluding evidence . . ., not made after the defendant has been put in jeopardy and before the verdict or finding on an indictment or information, if the United States attorney certifies to the district court that the appeal is not taken for purposes of delay and that the evidence is a substantial proof of a fact material in the proceeding.

Defendants are usually not authorized to pursue interlocutory appeals, primarily because they have access to appellate courts through an appeal from any conviction that may follow a determination of a pretrial matter. The rule that a guilty plea "forfeits" the right to complain of many matters, however, may sometimes encourage defendants to demand a full trial on the merits only to preserve rulings on pretrial motions as possible errors on appeal. To deal with this situation, some jurisdictions have enacted provisions permitting a defendant who pleads guilty to appeal on the basis of rulings on pretrial matters. N.Y.Criminal Procedure Law § 710.70(2), for example, provides:

> An order finally denying a motion to suppress evidence may be reviewed upon an appeal from an ensuing judgment of conviction notwithstanding the fact that such judgment is entered upon a plea of guilty.

FEDERAL CONSTITUTIONAL RIGHT TO PRETRIAL RESOLUTION OF CERTAIN MATTERS

The due process requirement considered in the principal case in this chapter does not appear to address the right to a *pretrial* resolution of those matters it covers. There is, however, some basis for believing that federal constitutional considerations may, in some limited situations, demand that state procedure provide for resolution before trial of matters by both trial and appellate courts. See Abney v. United States, 431 U.S. 651, 97 S.Ct. 2034, 52 L.Ed.2d 651 (1977), discussed in Chapter 20. In United States v. MacDonald, 435 U.S. 850, 98 S.Ct. 1547, 56 L.Ed.2d 18 (1978), however, the Court held that an order denying a motion to dismiss made on Sixth Amendment speedy trial grounds was not an appealable order under the federal statute, implying, of course, that there is no federal constitutional right to an interlocutory appeal from such an order.

OMNIBUS HEARING PROPOSALS

Among proposals for giving pretrial motion practice more structure, in hopes of increasing efficiency as well as of assuring that all relevant matters are addressed, perhaps the most prominent is the suggestion of the American Bar Association's Project on Standards for Criminal Justice for an "omnibus hearing" in all cases in which a plea of not guilty is entered. A.B.A. Project on Standards for Criminal Justice, Standards Relating to Discovery and Procedure Before Trial §§ 5.2(b), 5.3 (Approved Draft 1970). Motions and similar requests should be made at or before this hearing. At the hearing, the trial court, using "an appropriate check-list form," is to assure that representation and discovery have been provided, rule on motions and other requests for relief or action, and ascertain whether there are any other procedural or constitutional issues which should be considered. Id., at § 5.3(a). Former Supreme Court Justice Tom C. Clark described the objective of the proposal as follows:

The omnibus hearing ... is designed to facilitate the speedy and just disposition of cases. Trials may be eliminated or substantially shortened by the hearing, for prosecutors and defense counsel are encouraged to meet and lay all their cards on the table....

The omnibus hearing is also designed to flush out constitutional issues as well as other questions in dispute and to resolve them before trial rather than in the middle of trial when the jury would have to cool its heels while the matter is settled. By using the omnibus hearing, the issues are considerably sharpened and narrowed when the trial begins, the proceedings are shortened, and the likelihood of a subsequent appeal is reduced.

Clark, The Omnibus Hearing in State and Federal Courts, 59 Cornell L.Rev. 761, 765 (1974). Some reports have indicated less optimism. See e.g., R. Nimmer, The Omnibus Hearing: An Experiment in Relieving Inefficiency, Unfairness and Judicial Delay (1971).

Watkins v. Sowders

Supreme Court of the United States, 1981.
449 U.S. 341, 101 S.Ct. 654, 66 L.Ed.2d 549.

■ JUSTICE STEWART delivered the opinion of the Court.

These cases, consolidated for argument and decision in the Court of Appeals and in this Court, present the question whether a state criminal trial court is constitutionally compelled to conduct a hearing outside the presence of the jury whenever a defendant contends that a witness' identification of him was arrived at improperly.

I.

A.

John Watkins, the petitioner in No. 79–5949, was convicted in a Kentucky court of attempting to rob a Louisville liquor store. On the night of January 11, 1975, four men entered the store, one of whom asked for a pack of cigarettes. Walter Smith, an employee of the store, turned around to get the cigarettes, and one of the men said, "This is a hold-up." Donald Goeing, a part-owner of the store, had been stocking a soft-drink cooler, and when he heard those words, he turned towards the robbers. The man who had spoken thereupon fired two shots at him, one striking him in his arm, the other in the region of his heart. The four men then fled.

That night Smith and Goeing described the gunman to the police. Two days later, the police in the presence of Smith conducted a lineup consisting of three men, one of whom was Watkins. Smith identified Watkins as the gunman. That same day, the police took Watkins to Goeing's hospital bed, and Goeing identified Watkins as the man who had shot him. Watkins was then charged with first-degree robbery and first-degree assault.

At the subsequent trial of Watkins, the prosecution called Smith and Goeing as witnesses. They both identified Watkins as Goeing's assailant but were not asked by the prosecution about the lineup or the showup. Watkins' counsel, however, cross-examined both men at some length about both the lineup and showup. The prosecution then called a police officer. He testified that he had taken Watkins to be identified at the hospital because "at that time there was some question as to whether or not Mr. Goeing was going to survive the incident." Watkins' counsel cross-examined the officer about both the showup and the lineup and through him introduced pictures of the lineup. For the defense, Watkins' counsel called two witnesses who said that they had been in a pool hall with Watkins at the time of the robbery and another witness who said he had been in the liquor store at the time of the robbery and had not seen Watkins. Finally, Watkins himself testified to his innocence.

On appeal, as he had at trial, counsel for Watkins argued that the trial court had a constitutional obligation to conduct a hearing outside the presence of the jury to determine whether the identification evidence was admissible. The Supreme Court of Kentucky rejected that argument. . . . The court [also] found that the identification procedures "fail[ed] to raise any impermissible suggestiveness" and that Watkins "was in no way prejudiced." Watkins v. Kentucky, 565 S.W.2d 630, 631.

Watkins then unsuccessfully sought a writ of habeas corpus in the United States District Court for the Western District of Kentucky.

* * *

The Court of Appeals for the Sixth Circuit affirmed the District Court's judgment and, like the District Court, ruled that a hearing on the admissibility of identification evidence need not be held outside the presence of the jury. Turning to the evidence itself, the court cited Stovall v. Denno, 388 U.S. 293, 87 S.Ct. 1967, 18 L.Ed.2d 1199, as authority for holding that "given the seriousness of the wounds to Donald Goeing, a showup was necessary in this case." Summitt v. Bordenkircher, 608 F.2d 247, 251. The federal appellate court also held that the lineup evidence had been constitutionally admissible at the state trial.

B.

James Summitt, the petitioner in No. 79–5951, was convicted in a Kentucky court of rape. Late on the night of July 20, 1974, the prosecutrix was forced into a car occupied by two men, driven to an isolated location, raped by one of the men, and then returned to her own car. The next day she reported the crime to the police, described the rapist, and looked through 12 volumes of photographs from police files, without identifying the man who had raped her. Two days later she was taken to another police station, where she examined more pictures. A police officer testified at the subsequent trial of Summitt that "after a short time she pointed to the defendant's picture and said, 'This is the man that raped me. There's no doubt about it, this is Jimbo, the man that raped me.' " In addition to the officer, the prosecutrix and her stepfather as witnesses for the prosecution described the prosecutrix's examination of the police photographs, and the prosecutrix testified that Summitt was the man who had raped her. There was extensive cross-examination.

The Supreme Court of Kentucky found "no error in the trial court's refusal to conduct a suppression hearing and no semblance of impermissible suggestiveness in the identification procedure." 550 S.W.2d 548, 550. Summitt then sought a writ of habeas corpus in the United States District Court for the Western District of Kentucky, but that court found no constitutional error. The Court of Appeals, as in the consolidated *Watkins* case, affirmed the judgment of the District Court, 608 F.2d 247.

We granted certiorari to consider the constitutional claim asserted by both petitioners throughout their state and federal court proceedings. 445 U.S. 962, 100 S.Ct. 1312, 63 L.Ed.2d 759.

II.

The issue before us is not, of course, whether a trial court acts prudently in holding a hearing out of the presence of the jury to determine the admissibility of identification evidence. The prudence of such a hearing has been emphasized by many decisions in the Courts of Appeals, most of which have in various ways admonished trial courts to use that procedure. The issue here, rather, is whether such a hearing is required by the Due Process Clause of the Fourteenth Amendment.

In urging an affirmative answer, the petitioners first cite cases holding that a defendant has a right to the presence of his counsel at a post-indictment lineup, e.g., United States v. Wade, 388 U.S. 218, 87 S.Ct. 1926, 18 L.Ed.2d 1149, and that an identification procedure, in the absence of a lineup, may be so defective as to deprive a defendant of due process of law, e.g., Stovall v. Denno, 388 U.S. 293, 87 S.Ct. 1967, 18 L.Ed.2d 1199. The petitioners then analogize their cases to Jackson v. Denno, 378 U.S. 368, 84 S.Ct. 1774, 12 L.Ed.2d 908, in which this Court enunciated a defendant's right "to have a fair hearing and a reliable determination on the issue of voluntariness," id., at 377, 84 S.Ct., at 1781, and in which the Court declared unconstitutional a New York procedure which gave the jury what was in practice unreviewable discretion to decide whether a confession was or was not voluntary.

The petitioners contend that Jackson v. Denno established a *per se* due process right to a hearing outside the presence of the jury whenever a question of the voluntariness of a confession is raised. If such a hearing is required where the voluntariness of a confession is at issue, it follows, the petitioners argue, that a similar hearing must also be required where the propriety of identification procedures has been questioned.

Even if it be assumed that Jackson v. Denno did establish the *per se* rule asserted,[1] the petitioners' argument must fail, because Jackson v. Denno is not analogous to the cases now before us. The Court in *Jackson* did reject the usual presumption that a jury can be relied upon to determine issues according to the trial judge's instructions, but the Court did so because of the peculiar problems the issue of the voluntariness of a

---

1. See Pinto v. Pierce, 389 U.S. 31, 32, 88 S.Ct. 192, 193, 19 L.Ed.2d 31:

"This Court has never ruled that all voluntariness hearings must be held outside the presence of the jury, regardless of the circumstances.... [B]ecause a disputed confession may be found involuntary and inadmissible by the judge, it would seem prudent to hold voluntariness hearings outside the presence of the jury.... In this case, however, the confession was held voluntary and admitted as evidence suitable for consideration by the jury."

confession presents. The Court pointed out that, while an involuntary confession is inadmissible in part because such a confession is likely to be unreliable, it is also inadmissible even if it is true, because of the " 'strongly felt attitude of our society that important human values are sacrificed where an agency of the government, in the course of securing a conviction, wrings a confession out of an accused against his will.' "378 U.S., at 385, 84 S.Ct., at 1785, quoting Blackburn v. Alabama, 361 U.S. 199, 206–207, 80 S.Ct. 274, 279, 4 L.Ed.2d 242. The Court concluded in *Jackson* that a jury "may find it difficult to understand the policy forbidding reliance upon a coerced, but true confession.... Objective consideration of the conflicting evidence concerning the circumstances of the confession becomes difficult and the [jury's] implicit findings become suspect." Id., 378 U.S., at 382, 84 S.Ct., at 1783.

Where identification evidence is at issue, however, no such special considerations justify a departure from the presumption that juries will follow instructions. It is the reliability of identification evidence that primarily determines its admissibility, Manson v. Brathwaite, 432 U.S. 98, 113–114, 97 S.Ct. 2243, 2252, 53 L.Ed.2d 140; United States ex rel. Kirby v. Sturges, 510 F.2d 397, 402–404 (C.A.7 1975) (Stevens, J.). And the proper evaluation of evidence under the instructions of the trial judge is the very task our system must assume juries can perform. Indeed, as the cases before us demonstrate, the *only* duty of a jury in cases in which identification evidence has been admitted will often be to assess the reliability of that evidence. Thus the Court's opinion in Manson v. Brathwaite approvingly quoted Judge Leventhal's statement that,

"'[w]hile identification testimony is significant evidence, such testimony is still only evidence, and, unlike the presence of counsel, is not a factor that goes to the very heart'—the "integrity"—of the adversary process.

"'Counsel can both cross-examine the identification witnesses and argue in summation as to factors causing doubts as to the accuracy of the identification—including reference to both any suggestibility in the identification procedure and any countervailing testimony such as alibi.'" 432 U.S. 98, 114, n. 14, 97 S.Ct. 2243, 2253 n. 14, quoting Clemons v. United States, 133 U.S.App.D.C. 27, 48, 408 F.2d 1230, 1251 (1968) (concurring opinion) (footnote omitted).

The petitioners argue, however, that cross-examination is inadequate in cases such as these. They assert that the presence of the jury deterred their lawyers from cross-examining the witnesses vigorously and fully as to the possible improprieties of the pretrial identifications in these cases. The petitioners point to no specific instances in the trial when their counsel were thus deterred, and the record reveals that the cross-examination on the identity issues was, if not always effective, both active and extended. Nonetheless, the petitioners rely on a passage from United States v. Wade, supra, which referred to

"the predicament in which Wade's counsel found himself—realizing that possible unfairness at the lineup may be the sole means of attack upon the unequivocal courtroom identification, and having to probe in the dark in an attempt to discover and reveal unfairness, while bolstering the government witness' courtroom identification by bringing out and dwelling upon his prior identification." 388 U.S., at 241, 87 S.Ct., at 1939.

The petitioners, however, attribute undue significance to this passage. The "predicament" described in *Wade* was no more than part of the Court's demonstration that, if identification stemming from an improperly conducted lineup was to be excluded, a courtroom identification based on such a lineup logically had to be excluded as well.

A "predicament," if one chooses to call it that, is always presented when a lawyer decides on cross-examination to ask a question that may produce an answer unfavorable to his client. Yet, under our adversary system of justice, cross-examination has always been considered a most effective way to ascertain truth. We decline in these cases to hold that the Due Process Clause of the Fourteenth Amendment inevitably requires the abandonment of the time-honored process of cross-examination as the device best suited to determine the trustworthiness of testimonial evidence.

A judicial determination outside the presence of the jury of the admissibility of identification evidence may often be advisable. In some circumstances, not presented here, such a determination may be constitutionally necessary. But it does not follow that the Constitution requires a *per se* rule compelling such a procedure in every case.

Accordingly, the judgments are

Affirmed.

■ JUSTICE BRENNAN, with whom JUSTICE MARSHALL joins, dissenting.

* * *

Any purported distinction between the instant cases and *Jackson* is plainly specious. In *Jackson,* this Court invalidated a New York State procedure whereby the jury was instructed first to determine the voluntariness of a defendant's confession and then to disregard the confession if it concluded that the confession was involuntary. *Jackson* struck down this practice and required first that the voluntariness of a confession be determined by the judge before its admission in evidence, and second that the jury not be allowed to consider an inadmissible confession. *Jackson* refused to rely on the curative effect of jury instructions where the trial judge had not applied " 'the exclusionary rules before permitting evidence to be submitted to the jury.' " 378 U.S., at 382, n. 10, 84 S.Ct., at 1783, n. 10, quoting Meltzer, Involuntary Confessions: The Allocation of Responsibility Between Judge and Jury, 21 U.Chi.L.Rev. 317, 327 (1954).

For purposes of the instant cases, three factors central to our decision in *Jackson* are apposite. First, *Jackson* stated, as the Court today notes, "that the Fourteenth Amendment forbids the use of involuntary confessions ... because of the probable unreliability of confessions that are obtained in a manner deemed coercive." Second, *Jackson* stated, as the Court today further notes, that involuntary confessions are inadmissible "because of the 'strongly felt attitude of our society that important human values are sacrificed where an agency of the government, in the course of securing a conviction, wrings a confession out of an accused against his will.'" Third, because of the sensitive nature of confession evidence, *Jackson* found that instructions were not adequate to assure that the jury would ignore involuntary confession evidence:

> "Under the New York procedure, the fact of a defendant's confession is solidly implanted in the jury's mind, for it has not only heard the confession, but it has also been instructed to consider and judge its voluntariness and is in position to assess whether it is true or false. If it finds the confession involuntary, does the jury—indeed, can it—then disregard the confession in accordance with its instructions? If there are lingering doubts about the sufficiency of the other evidence, does the jury unconsciously lay them to rest by resort to the confession? Will uncertainty about the sufficiency of the other evidence to prove guilt beyond a reasonable doubt actually result in acquittal when the jury knows the defendant has given a truthful confession?" 378 U.S., at 388, 84 S.Ct., at 1786 (footnote omitted).

Similar considerations plainly require a hearing in the case of identification evidence. First, there can be little doubt that identification evidence is as potentially unreliable as confession evidence. Second, suggestive confrontation procedures which, in the totality of circumstances, create " 'a very substantial likelihood of irreparable misidentification,' "are as impermissible a police practice as the securing of a custodial confession determined, in the totality of the circumstances, to be involuntary. And third, because of the extraordinary impact of much eyewitness identification evidence, juries hearing such evidence will be no more able fully to ignore it upon instruction of the trial judge than will juries hearing confession evidence. To expect a jury to engage in the collective mental gymnastic of segregating and ignoring such testimony upon instruction is utterly unrealistic. The Court's bald assertion, therefore, that jury instructions are adequate to protect the accused, is as untrue for identification evidence as it is for involuntary confessions.

Nor can it be assumed, as the Court has, that cross-examination will protect the accused in this circumstance. That is no more true here than it was in *Jackson,* where the defendant was also allowed to cross-examine on the question of voluntariness. Cross-examination, of course, affects the weight and credibility given by the jury to evidence, but cross-examination is both an ineffective and a wrong tool for purging inadmissible identification evidence from the jurors' minds. It is an ineffective tool because all of the scientific evidence suggests that much eyewitness identification testimony has an unduly powerful effect on jurors. Thus, the jury is likely to give the erroneously admitted evidence substantial weight, however skillful the cross-examination. Cross-examination is also a wrong tool in the sense that jury instructions are the means normally employed to cure the erroneous introduction of evidence. At best, cross-examination might diminish the weight the jury accords to the inadmissible evidence. The likelihood is, however, that the jury would continue to give the improperly admitted evidence substantial weight, even if properly instructed to disregard it.

* * *

In the instant cases, the suggestiveness of the confrontation procedures was clearly shown, and equally clearly cross-examination in front of the jury was inadequate to test the reliability of the evidence because of the undoubted inhibiting effect on cross-examination from fear that rigorous questioning of hostile witnesses would strengthen the eyewitnesses' testimony and impress it upon the jury. In any event, the record is inadequate to decide that petitioners could not have succeeded in foreclosing admission of the evidence if they had been afforded a hearing out of the jury's presence in the first place. Accordingly, I would remand for such further proceedings as are necessary to give these petitioners "a fair hearing and a reliable determination," Jackson v. Denno, supra, 378 U.S., at 377, 84 S.Ct., at 1781, that the identification evidence in each trial was not erroneously admitted.

NOTES

1. **Magistrate-judge relationship in pretrial determinations.** What role should—or must—the trial judge play in resolving issues raised by attacks upon the admissibility of evidence? The Federal Magistrates Act, 28 U.S.C.A. § 631 et seq. authorizes a federal District Judge to designate a magistrate to conduct hearings on motions to suppress evidence and to submit to the judge proposed findings of fact and recommended dispositions of the motions. Any party may file objections. The judge is then to "make a de novo determination" of those portions of the recommendations or proposed findings to which objection has been made. The judge may receive further evidence.

In United States v. Raddatz, 447 U.S. 667, 100 S.Ct. 2406, 65 L.Ed.2d 424 (1980), the defendant filed a motion to suppress his confession, alleging that it was made in return for an agreement that certain federal charges would be dismissed. At a hearing before a magistrate, he testified that such a promise had been made; the federal agents involved in the investigation testified that no such promises had been made. The magistrate submitted a proposed finding that no promise to dismiss charges had been made and a recommendation that the motion be denied. Over the defendant's objections, the District Court accepted the magistrate's recommendation and denied the motion.

The Supreme Court affirmed. The statute, concluded the majority, does not require that the District Court conduct a de novo *hearing* on contested aspects of the magistrate's proposed conclusions. In making the de novo *determination* directed by the statute, the court may rely upon the transcript of the testimony taken before the magistrate. Further, this does not offend due process. Defendants' interests at stake in a suppression hearing are "of a lesser magnitude" than those involved in trial, and the process that is due in the former context is therefore less demanding and elaborate. Finally, since the ultimate decision remains with the District Court, the statute does not offend a defendant's right to a determination of the matter by an Article III judge.

Justice Marshall, joined by Justice Brennan, dissented, urging that due process requires that the District Court conduct an evidentiary hearing whenever there are case-dispositive issues that cannot be resolved on the basis of the record developed in the hearing before the magistrate. Further, where resolution of an issue depends—as it did in the instant case—upon the credibility of the witnesses, the record does not permit resolution of it. In explanation, Justice Marshall urged that resolution of such matters on the basis of an inadequate record creates "an intolerably high risk of error." Further, "as a matter of basic fairness, a person facing the prospect of grievous loss is entitled to relate his version of the facts to the official entrusted with judging its accuracy." 444 U.S. at 696, 100 S.Ct. at 2423, 65 L.Ed.2d at 446. In addition, Justice Marshall regarded the majority's approach as functionally entrusting decision on such matters to magistrates, in violation of defendants' Article III right to a determination of such matters by an Article III judge. Justice Stewart, joined by Justices Brennan and Marshall, dissented on the ground that the Federal Magistrates Act required the result reached by Justice Marshall on constitutional grounds. 447 U.S. at 689–90, 100 S.Ct. at 2419, 65 L.Ed.2d at 441–42. Justice Powell concurred in the majority's reading of the statute as conferring broad discretion on the district courts as to whether or not to rehear evidence in these cases. But he further dissented from the majority's unwillingness to find that in cases such as the one before the court where the outcome of the hearing depends entirely upon an assessment of the credibility of the witnesses that due process requires the court to rehear crucial witnesses. 447 U.S. at 686, 100 S.Ct. at 2418, 65 L.Ed.2d at 440.

2. **Applicability of rules of evidence to admissibility hearings.** Must—and should—the rules of evidence be applied in hearings on the admissibility of evidence challenged on constitutional grounds? In United States v. Matlock, 415 U.S. 164, 94 S.Ct. 988, 39 L.Ed.2d 242 (1974) the government, in an effort to establish that one Gayle Graff had authority to consent to a search of a bedroom, offered testimony that Graff had told officers before the search that she and the defendant occupied the bedroom at issue. The trial judge applied the hearsay rule and excluded the evidence. This was held to have been error. In such hearings, the Court concluded, the rules of evidence applicable in criminal trials do not operate with "full force" and there should be no automatic rule excluding all hearsay. On the facts of the case, there was no doubt that Graff had in fact made the statements. Nothing in the record suggested doubt as to their accuracy. Moreover, they constituted an admission of cohabitation out of wedlock by Graff (a crime in the jurisdiction) and therefore were admissions against her penal interest which carried their own "indicia of reliability." Graff had testified at the hearing and thus was available for cross-examination. Consequently, they should have been admitted and considered by the trial judge. 415 U.S. at 172–77, 94 S.Ct. at 994–96, 39 L.Ed.2d at 250–53. Lower courts have assumed that the rules of evidence do not apply at hearings on motions to suppress. E.g., United States v. Killebrew, 594 F.2d 1103 (6th Cir.1979), cert. denied 442 U.S. 933, 99 S.Ct. 2867, 61 L.Ed.2d 302.

3. **Burden of proof in admissibility hearings.** The burden of proof at hearings on the admissibility of evidence and similar matters is not entirely clear. In Lego v. Twomey, 404 U.S. 477, 92 S.Ct. 619, 30 L.Ed.2d 618 (1972) the Court held that in a hearing on the voluntariness of a confession, the prosecution must establish voluntariness by a preponderance of the evidence. Rejecting the argument that proof beyond a reasonable doubt should be required, the Court noted no indication that admissibility rulings have been unreliable or found "otherwise wanting" because not based on a standard requiring more than proof by a preponderance of the evidence. In Miranda v. Arizona, 384 U.S. 436, 475, 86 S.Ct. 1602, 1628, 16 L.Ed.2d 694, 724 (1966), the Court commented that when a confession is obtained during interrogation without the presence of an attorney, "a heavy burden" is placed on the government to demonstrate a knowing and intelligent waiver of the right to counsel and the privilege against self-incrimination.

In hearings on Fourth Amendment claims, the lower courts have tended to distribute the burden of proof variously, depending upon the specific issue. The defendant, as the moving party, has been held to have the burden of establishing that a "search" within Fourth Amendment meaning took place. United States v. Freeland, 562 F.2d 383 (6th Cir.1977), cert. denied 434 U.S. 957, 98 S.Ct. 484, 54 L.Ed.2d 315 (1977) (defendant had burden of showing sufficient governmental involvement in luggage examination to render it a "search"). Once a warrantless search has been demonstrated, other cases hold, the prosecution has the burden of establishing the "reasonableness" of the search. E.g., United States v. Lee, 541 F.2d 1145 (5th Cir.1976). Where the prosecution's theory is that the defendant consented to the search or seizure, some cases hold, the prosecution has the burden of proving an effective consent. United States v. Williams, 604 F.2d 1102 (8th Cir.1979). Where articulated consent is shown, however, and the defendant claims that it is ineffective because it was procured by fraud or misrepresentations, some cases hold that the defendant has the burden of showing that such fraud or misrepresentations existed. United States v. Meier, 607 F.2d 215 (8th Cir.1979), cert. denied 445 U.S. 966, 100 S.Ct. 1658, 64 L.Ed.2d 243 (1980). In United States v. Matlock, 415 U.S. 164, 177 n. 14, 94 S.Ct. 988, 996 n. 14, 39 L.Ed.2d 242, 253 n. 14 (1974) the Supreme Court found no occasion to consider whether the trial judge had erred in requiring the prosecution to prove a valid consent by the greater weight of the evidence. Where the prosecution claims that despite an unlawful search or seizure challenged evidence is nevertheless admissible because of an exception to the exclusionary rule (such as "dissipation of taint" or "inevitable legitimate discovery"), under other lower court decisions, the prosecution has the burden of proving the factual foundation for its claim. United States v. Brookins, 614 F.2d 1037 (5th Cir.1980).

4. **Trial use of admissibility hearing testimony.** When, if ever, may a defendant's testimony at a hearing out of the presence of the jury be used against the defendant on the trial of guilt or innocence? In Simmons v. United States, 390 U.S. 377, 88 S.Ct. 967, 19 L.Ed.2d 1247 (1968) the defendant was charged with robbery of a bank. Prior to trial, he filed a motion to suppress certain evidence (a gun holster, a sack similar to one used in the robbery, and coin cards and bill wrappers from the robbed bank) which had been seized in a search of a suitcase. In order to establish his "standing" to contest the search of the suitcase, he took the witness stand at the hearing on his motion and testified that the suitcase was similar to one he had owned and that clothing found in the suitcase was his. His motion was overruled; at trial, the government introduced against him his testimony at the suppression hearing, which tended to connect him with the evidence seized in the search. The Court of Appeals affirmed the resulting conviction, but the Supreme Court reversed:

> The rule adopted by the courts below does not merely impose upon a defendant a condition which may deter him from asserting a Fourth Amendment objection—it imposed a condition of a kind to which this Court has always been particularly sensitive. For a defendant who wishes to establish standing must do so at the risk that the words he utters may later be used to incriminate him. Those courts which have allowed the admission of testimony given to establish standing have reasoned that there is no violation of the Fifth Amendment's Self–Incrimination Clause because the testimony was voluntary. ...However, the assumption which underlies this reasoning is that the defendant has a choice: he may refuse to testify and give up the benefit. When this assumption is applied to a situation in which the "benefit" to be gained is that afforded by another provision of the Bill of Rights, an undeniable tension is created. Thus, in this case [the defendant] was obliged either to give up what he believed, with advice of counsel, to be a valid Fourth Amendment claim or, in legal effect, to waive his Fifth Amendment privilege against self-incrimination. In these circumstances, we find it intolerable that one constitutional right should have to be surrendered in order to assert another. We therefore hold that when a defendant testifies in support of a motion to suppress evidence on Fourth Amendment grounds, his testimony may not thereafter be admitted against him at trial on the issue of guilt unless he makes no objection.

390 U.S. at 393–94, 88 S.Ct. at 976, 19 L.Ed.2d at 1258–59. But suppose the defendant had taken the stand and testified at trial that neither the suitcase nor its contents belonged to him? Would his testimony at the motion to suppress have then been admissible to impeach his trial testimony? Consider Harris v. New York, 401 U.S. 222, 91 S.Ct. 643, 28 L.Ed.2d 1 (1971)(holding that a custodial statement that was inadmissible under Miranda v. Arizona in the State's case-in-chief at trial could if trustworthy be admitted on rebuttal to impeach defendant's contradictory testimony).

In United States v. Kahan, 415 U.S. 239, 94 S.Ct. 1179, 39 L.Ed.2d 297 (1974), Kahan, a former immigrations inspector, was charged with improperly receiving gratuities for official acts and with perjury. He requested appointment of an attorney and, at his arraignment, he responded to a direct question as to whether he had funds to employ an attorney by claiming indigency and without disclosing that he had access to and control over four savings accounts in which he had deposited approximately $27,000. At trial, evidence concerning his deposits in these accounts (which exceeded his reported income for the period) was admitted as tending to show that he had improperly received substantial money as charged in the indictment. The government was also permitted to show his statements to the court as to his lack of funds; these were admitted as false exculpatory statements indicating his awareness that the bank deposits were incriminating and as evidence of willfulness in making statements before the grand jury with knowledge of their falsity. He was convicted and the Supreme Court found no constitutional error:

> Even assuming that the *Simmons* principle [can be] appropriately extended to Sixth Amendment claims for appointed counsel . . ., a question which we do not now decide . . ., that principle cannot be applied to protect respondent here. *Simmons* barred the use of pretrial testimony at trial to prove its incriminating content. Here, by contrast, the incriminating component of respondent's pretrial statements derives not from their content, but from respondent's knowledge of their falsity. The truth of the matter was that respondent was not indigent, and did not have a right to appointment of counsel under the Sixth Amendment. We are not dealing, as was the Court in *Simmons,* with what was "believed" by the claimant to be a "valid" constitutional claim. . . . Respondent was not, therefore, faced with the type of intolerable choice *Simmons* sought to relieve. The protective shield of *Simmons* is not to be converted into a license for false representations on the issue of indigency free from the risk that the claimant will be held accountable for his falsehood. Cf. Harris v. New York, 401 U.S. 222, 226, 91 S.Ct. 643, 646, 28 L.Ed.2d 1 (1971).

415 U.S. at 243, 94 S.Ct. at 1181, 39 L.Ed.2d at 301.

5. **Relationship of voluntariness to reliability.** Can a confession be voluntary and unreliable? Is there a constitutional right to present to a jury evidence bearing on the reliability of a confession despite a trial court ruling that the confession is voluntary? In Crane v. Kentucky, 476 U.S. 683, 106 S.Ct. 2142, 90 L.Ed.2d 636 (1986), petitioner's confession was the principal evidence against him in his murder trial. The trial court had heard evidence at a pretrial hearing that the confession had been coerced but found it to have been voluntarily given. The 16–year–old petitioner had testified that he had been detained in a windowless room for a protracted period of time, that he had been surrounded by as many as six police officers during the questioning, that he had repeatedly requested and been denied permission to telephone his mother, and that he had been badgered into making a false confession. Several police officers testified in contradiction. At trial, the defense attempted to present to the jury the same evidence it had presented at the suppression hearing, but the trial court ruled the evidence inadmissible. Petitioner was convicted of murder and his conviction was affirmed by the Kentucky Supreme

Court. The United States Supreme Court, in an opinion authored by Justice O'Connor for a unanimous Court, reversed. Justice O'Connor stated,

> the circumstances surrounding the taking of a confession can be highly relevant to two separate inquiries, one legal and one factual. The manner in which a statement was extracted is, of course, relevant to the purely legal question of its voluntariness, a question most, but not all, States assign to the trial judge alone to resolve. ...But the physical and psychological environment that yielded the confession can also be of substantial relevance to the ultimate factual issue of the defendant's guilt or innocence. Confessions, even those that have been found to be voluntary, are not conclusive of guilt. And, as with any other part of the prosecutor's case, a confession may be shown to be "insufficiently corroborated or otherwise ... unworthy of belief." Lego v. Twomey.... Indeed, stripped of the power to describe to the jury the circumstances that prompted his confession, the defendant is effectively disabled from answering the one question every rational juror needs answered: If the defendant is innocent, why did he previously admit his guilt? Accordingly, regardless of whether the defendant marshaled the same evidence earlier in support of an unsuccessful motion to suppress, and entirely independent of any question of voluntariness, a defendant's case may stand or fall on his ability to convince the jury that the manner in which the confession was obtained casts doubt on its credibility.

476 U.S. at 688–89, 106 S.Ct. at 2145–46, 90 L.Ed.2d at 644. Excluding this evidence under the circumstances of this case deprived the petitioner of his constitutional right to be heard in his own defense.

CHAPTER 22

ADJUDICATION OF GUILT BY PLEA

Analysis

The vast majority of criminal convictions are based upon pleas of guilty and nolo contendere rather than contested proceedings culminating in a finding of guilt by a judge or jury. Probably 90% of convictions for serious offenses are obtained in this manner; if misdemeanors are included, the figure approaches 98%. See Newman, Reshape the Deal, 9 Trial 11 (May/June 1973).

For formal purposes of the criminal justice system, the difference between the guilty plea and the plea of nolo contendere is minimal. Both lead to conviction, and the requirements for entry of a guilty plea generally apply as well to the nolo plea. Technically, the nolo plea is not an admission of guilt but an indication of the defendant's willingness to give up the opportunity to contest the allegation. Therefore, traditionally it could not be used in later civil proceedings against the defendant as an admission. III ABA Standards for Criminal Justice 14–10. Nevertheless, some believe that there are sound reasons for limiting use of the nolo plea. A United States Department of Justice memorandum directs United States Attorneys to oppose entry of a plea of nolo contendere unless the Assistant Attorney General with supervisory responsibility over the subject matter has approved acceptance of the plea. U.S. Department of Justice, Materials Relating to Prosecutorial Discretion, 24 Crim.L.Rptr. 3001, 3006 (Nov. 22, 1978). In explanation, the memorandum quoted a prior departmental directive:

> One of the factors which has tended to breed contempt for federal law enforcement in recent times has been the practice of permitting as a matter of course in many criminal indictments the plea of nolo contendere.... Uncontrolled use of the plea has led to shockingly low sentences and insignificant fines which are no deterrent to crime.... [A] person permitted to plead nolo contendere admits guilt for purposes of imposing punishment for his acts and yet, for all other purposes, and as far as the public is concerned, persists in his denial of wrongdoing. It is no wonder that the public regards consent to such a plea by the Government as an admission that it has only a technical case at most and that the whole proceeding was just a fiasco.

Id. The memo also notes that should the Government later seek civil sanctions against the defendant, use of the nolo plea might require the Government to expend valuable resources in proving the same facts as were at issue in the criminal case. Id. In examining the following materials, consider whether the same requirements should be applied to nolo pleas and pleas of guilty.

The issues concerning guilty pleas are pervasively influenced by the practice of plea bargaining, which is considered in the third section of this chapter. However, attention is initially addressed to two matters presented by all guilty pleas, whether the result of plea bargaining or not. First, the procedure necessary for entry of a plea and judgment of conviction is considered. Second, the effect of the plea upon the defendant's later ability to raise certain procedural issues related to the charge and conviction is explored.

A. ENTRY OF THE PLEA OF GUILTY

EDITORS' INTRODUCTION: STRUCTURES FOR PLEA ACCEPTANCE

The procedural aspects for the acceptance of guilty and *nolo* pleas are increasingly covered by detailed statutory provisions. Many of these statutes are based upon several model formulations. See III American Bar Association Standards for Criminal Justice, Standards 14–1.1 et seq. (the "ABA Standards"); Uniform Rules of Criminal Procedure 444. Federal practice is governed primarily by Fed.R.Crim.P. 11, reprinted in this section. Several aspects of the largely-statutory framework in which pleas are entered require preliminary consideration here. However, a number of federal constitutional concerns are raised by the guilty plea process and convictions based upon pleas. These are the subject of the Supreme Court decisions discussed in this section. Because the major constitutional issues, regarding "voluntariness" for example, are created by plea bargaining, rather than plea acceptance, they are presented primarily in the final section of this chapter.

Entry of the Plea

Several aspects of the procedural requirements often imposed upon the plea acceptance process can be usefully distinguished. First, the trial judge is generally directed by "admonition requirements" to specifically inform the defendant of certain matters before the plea is accepted. Second, the judge may be required to inquire as to certain matters, such as the existence of a plea bargain and any promises that have been made to the defendant. Third, the judge may be required to make certain findings of fact relating to the voluntariness of the offered plea and similar matters before accepting it. This is closely related to the requirement of a "factual basis" for the plea, considered below. Fourth, it may be necessary that a formal record of the proceedings be made. ABA Standard 14–1.7, for example, would require a verbatim record of the proceedings, including the admonitions and the inquiries demanded of the trial judge.

The Supreme Court rigorously applied Rule 11 in McCarthy v. United States, 394 U.S. 459, 89 S.Ct. 1166, 22 L.Ed.2d 418 (1969). McCarthy pleaded guilty to willfully and knowingly attempting to evade federal tax payments. At sentencing, his attorney urged that his failure to pay the taxes had not been deliberate and was the result of negligent bookkeeping during a time when McCarthy had a drinking problem. The trial judge had not complied with Rule 11's requirement that he personally address the defendant and determine that he understand the nature of the charge. The Government argued that since McCarthy stated a desire to plead guilty and was informed of the consequences of his plea, the trial court could assume he understood the charges. Rejecting this, the Court explained:

> We cannot accept this argument which completely ignores the two purposes of Rule 11. . . . First, although the procedure embodied in Rule 11 has not been held to be constitutionally mandated, it is designed to assist the district judge in making the constitutionally required determination that a defendant's guilty plea is truly voluntary. Second, the Rule is intended to produce a complete record at the time the plea is entered of the factors relevant to this voluntariness determination. Thus, the more meticulously the Rule is adhered to, the more it tends to discourage, or at least to enable more expeditious disposition of, the numerous and often frivolous post-conviction attacks on the constitutional validity of guilty pleas.

. . . By personally interrogating the defendant, not only will the judge be better able to ascertain the plea's voluntariness, but he also will develop a more complete record to support his determination in a subsequent post-conviction attack.

These two purposes have their genesis in the nature of a guilty plea. A defendant who enters such a plea simultaneously waives several constitutional rights, including his privilege against compulsory self-incrimination, his right to trial by jury, and his right to confront his accusers. For this waiver to be valid under the Due Process Clause, it must be "an intentional relinquishment or abandonment of a known right or privilege." . . . Consequently, if a defendant's guilty plea is not equally voluntary and knowing, it has been obtained in violation of due process and is therefore void. Moreover, because a guilty plea is an admission of all the elements of a formal criminal charge, it cannot be truly voluntary unless the defendant possesses an understanding of the law in relation to the facts.

Thus, in addition to directing the judge to inquire into the defendant's understanding of the nature of the charge and the consequences of his plea, Rule 11 also requires the judge to satisfy himself that there is a factual basis for the plea. The judge must determine "that the conduct which the defendant admits constitutes the offense charged in the indictment or information or an offense included therein to which the defendant has pleaded guilty." Requiring this examination of the relation between the law and the acts the defendant admits having committed is designed to "protect a defendant who is in the position of pleading voluntarily with an understanding of the nature of the charge but without realizing that his conduct does not actually fall within the charge."

To the extent that the district judge thus exposes the defendant's state of mind on the record through personal interrogation, he not only facilitates his own determination of a guilty plea's voluntariness, but he also facilitates that determination in any subsequent postconviction proceeding based upon a claim that the plea was involuntary. Both of these goals are undermined in proportion to the degree the district judge resorts to "assumptions" not based upon recorded responses to his inquiries. For this reason, we reject the Government's contention that Rule 11 can be complied with although the district judge does not personally inquire whether the defendant understood the nature of the charge.

394 U.S. at 465–67, 89 S.Ct. at 1170–71, 22 L.Ed.2d at 425–26.

The Court continued (in a footnote):

The nature of the inquiry required by Rule 11 must necessarily vary from case to case, and therefore, we do not establish any general guidelines other than those expressed in the Rule itself. As our discussion of the facts in this particular case suggests, however, where the charge encompasses lesser included offenses, personally addressing the defendant as to his understanding of the essential elements of the charge to which he pleads guilty would seem a necessary prerequisite to a determination that he understands the meaning of the charge.

394 U.S. at 467 n. 20, 89 S.Ct. at 1171 n. 20, 22 L.Ed.2d at 426 n. 20. As the cases in this section indicate, a major question in the guilty plea area is the extent, if any, to which the Supreme Court's construction of Rule 11 is also binding on the states as a matter of federal constitutional law. The Court purported to base its decision "solely upon our construction of Rule 11 and ... pursuant to our supervisory power over the lower federal courts" and not to reach any of the constitutional arguments urged by McCarthy. 394 U.S. at 464, 89 S.Ct. at 1169, 22 L.Ed.2d at 424. But the case clearly has constitutional ramifications.

Factual Basis

A number of statutory formulations, including Fed.R.Crim.P. 11(f), require the trial judge to determine that there is a "factual basis" for the plea. This amounts to a requirement that there be some evidence, albeit perhaps not evidence admissible under trial rules, that supports the conclusion that the defendant is in fact guilty. In effect, such a requirement precludes conviction upon the basis of a plea alone. Requiring a factual basis tends to assure that defendants who plead guilty are in fact guilty, thus preventing conviction of the innocent. Requiring a factual basis also assists the court in sentencing (see III Standards for Criminal Justice 14–34), and increases the quality of the contemporaneous record, which discourages later attacks upon the validity of the plea and conviction (or at least eases the task of resolving issues raised in such attacks).

Withdrawal of a Plea

In federal practice, withdrawal of a guilty plea is governed by Fed. R.Crim.P. 32(e):

* * *

> If a motion for withdrawal of a plea of guilty or nolo contendere is made before sentence is imposed [or] imposition of sentence is suspended ... the court may permit withdrawal of the plea upon a showing by the defendant of any fair and just reason. At any later time, a plea may be set aside only on direct appeal or by motion under 28 U.S.C.A. § 2255 [considered in Chapter 26].

The respondent in United States v. Hyde, 520 U.S. 670, 117 S.Ct. 1630, 137 L.Ed.2d 935 (1997) entered pleas of guilty to four counts of an eight count indictment. After appropriate Rule 11 inquiry, the District Court accepted the pleas of guilty but deferred a decision on whether to accept the plea bargain until receipt of the presentence report. Upon re-appearance in court for sentencing, Hyde attempted to withdraw his pleas of guilty, claiming they had been coerced. The District Court, after hearing evidence, concluded they had not been coerced, refused to permit Hyde to withdraw his pleas, and sentenced him in accordance with the plea agreement. The Ninth Circuit reversed on the ground that the absolute right to withdraw a plea for any reason prior to its acceptance by the court is extended to the time a plea bargain is accepted in plea bargained cases because the plea and the bargain are "inextricably bound up together." The Supreme Court, in a unanimous opinion authored by The Chief Justice, held that reading Rule 11 in conjunction with the provisions of Rule 32 require that the defendant show a "fair and just reason" for withdraw of a plea in a circumstance such as this one in which the withdrawal effort is made after the plea is accepted but before the District Court has decided whether to accept the plea agreement.

Later Attack

A conviction resting upon a plea of guilty or nolo contendere can be attacked in several ways. Within the time allotted for appeal, the defendant can seek appellate relief on the ground that the plea was not accepted in compliance with the applicable procedures. United States v. McCarthy, supra. Even if there has been compliance with these requirements, a defendant nevertheless may mount a collateral attack upon the conviction by showing that despite this compliance, the plea was coerced. Fontaine v. United States, 411 U.S. 213, 93 S.Ct. 1461, 36 L.Ed.2d 169 (1973) (per curiam). In *Fontaine,* the defendant stated in open court at the time his plea was accepted that his plea was voluntary. The government urged that this precluded him from later repudiating this statement and attempting to show in collateral attack that his plea was coerced. Rejecting this, the Court explained:

> The objective of Rule 11 of the Federal Rules of Criminal Procedure, of course, is to flush out and resolve all such issues, but like any procedural mechanism, its exercise is neither always perfect nor uniformly invulnerable to subsequent challenge calling for an opportunity to prove the allegations.

411 U.S. at 215, 93 S.Ct. at 1462, 36 L.Ed.2d at 172.

FEDERAL RULES OF CRIMINAL PROCEDURE

Rule 11. Pleas

(a) Alternatives.

(1) In General. A defendant may plead not guilty, guilty, or nolo contendere. If a defendant refuses to plead or if a defendant corporation fails to appear, the court shall enter a plea of not guilty.

(2) Conditional Pleas. With the approval of the court and the consent of the government, a defendant may enter a conditional plea of guilty or nolo contendere, reserving in writing the right, on appeal from the judgment, to review of the adverse determination of any specified pretrial motion. A defendant who prevails on appeal shall be allowed to withdraw the plea.

(b) Nolo Contendere. A defendant may plead nolo contendere only with the consent of the court. Such a plea shall be accepted by the court only after due consideration of the views of the parties and the interest of the public in the effective administration of justice.

(c) Advice to Defendant. Before accepting a plea of guilty or nolo contendere, the court must address the defendant personally in open court and inform the defendant of, and determine that the defendant understands, the following:

(1) the nature of the charge to which the plea is offered, the mandatory minimum penalty provided by law, if any, and the maximum possible penalty provided by law, including the effect of any special parole or supervised release term, the fact that the court is required to consider any applicable sentencing guidelines but may depart from those guidelines under some circumstances, and, when applicable, that the court may also order the defendant to make restitution to any victim of the offense; and

(2) if the defendant is not represented by an attorney, that the defendant has the right to be represented by an attorney at every stage of the proceeding and, if necessary, one will be appointed to represent the defendant; and

(3) that the defendant has the right to plead not guilty or to persist in that plea if it has already been made, the right to be tried by a jury and at that trial the right to the assistance of counsel, the right to confront and cross-examine adverse witnesses, and the right against compelled self-incrimination; and

(4) that if a plea of guilty or nolo contendere is accepted by the court there will not be a further trial of any kind, so that by pleading guilty or nolo contendere the defendant waives the right to a trial; and

(5) if the court intends to question the defendant under oath, on the record, and in the presence of counsel about the offense to which the defendant has pleaded, that the defendant's answers may later be used against the defendant in a prosecution for perjury or false statement; and

(6) the terms of any provision in a plea agreement waiving the right to appeal or to collaterally attack the sentence.[a]

(d) Insuring That the Plea is Voluntary. The court shall not accept a plea of guilty or nolo contendere without first, by addressing the defendant personally in open court, determining that the plea is voluntary and not the result of force or threats or of promises apart from a plea agreement. The court shall also inquire as to whether the defendant's willingness to plead guilty or nolo contendere results from prior discussions between the attorney for the government and the defendant or the defendant's attorney.

a. This subsection was added effective December 1, 1999. The Committee Note states that this addition is made "to reflect the increasing practice of including provisions in plea agreements which require the defendant to waive certain appellate rights. The increased use of such provisions is due in part to the increasing number of direct appeals and collateral reviews challenging sentencing decisions. Given the increased use of such provisions, the Committee believed it was important to insure that first, a complete records exists regarding any waiver provisions, and second, that the waiver was voluntarily and knowingly made by the defendant. Although a number of federal courts have approved the ability of a defendant to enter into such waiver agreements, the Committee takes no position on the underlying validity of such waivers."

(e) Plea Agreement Procedure.

(1) In General. The attorney for the government and the attorney for the defendant or the defendant when acting pro se may engage in discussions with a view toward reaching an agreement that, upon the entering of a plea of guilty or nolo contendere to a charged offense or to a lesser or related offense, the attorney for the government will do any of the following:

(A) move for dismissal of other charges; or

(B) recommend or agree not to oppose the defendant's request for a particular sentence or sentencing range, or that a particular provision of the Sentencing Guidelines, or policy statement, or sentencing factor is or is not applicable to the case. Any such recommendation or request is not binding on the court;[b] or

(C) agree that a specific sentence or sentencing range is the appropriate disposition of the case or that a particular provision of the Sentencing Guidelines, or policy statement, or sentencing factor is or is not applicable to the case. Such a plea agreement is binding on the court once it is accepted by the court.[c]

The court shall not participate in any such discussions.

(2) Notice of Such Agreement. If a plea agreement has been reached by the parties, the court shall, on the record, require the disclosure of the agreement in open court or, on a showing of good cause, in camera, at the time the plea is offered. If the agreement is of the type specified in subdivision (e)(1)(A) or (C), the court may accept or reject the agreement, or may defer its decision as to the acceptance or rejection until there has been an opportunity to consider the presentence report. If the agreement is of the type specified in subdivision (e)(1)(B), the court shall advise the defendant that if the court does not accept the recommendation or request the defendant nevertheless has no right to withdraw the plea.

(3) Acceptance of a Plea Agreement. If the court accepts the plea agreement, the court shall inform the defendant that it will embody in the judgment and sentence the disposition provided for in the plea agreement.

(4) Rejection of a Plea Agreement. If the court rejects the plea agreement, the court shall, on the record, inform the parties of this fact, advise the defendant personally in open court or, on a showing of good cause, in camera, that the court is not bound by the plea agreement, afford the defendant the opportunity to then withdraw the plea, and advise the defendant that if the defendant persists in a guilty plea or plea of nolo contendere the disposition of the case may be less favorable to the defendant than that contemplated by the plea agreement.

(5) Time of Plea Agreement Procedure. Except for good cause shown, notification to the court of the existence of a plea agreement

---

b. This subsection was amended effective December 1, 1999 to include references to the Sentencing Guidelines.

c. This subsection was amended effective December 1, 1999 to include references to the Sentencing Guidelines.

shall be given at the arraignment or at such other time, prior to trial, as may be fixed by the court.

(6) Inadmissibility of Pleas, Plea Discussions, and Related Statements. Except as otherwise provided in this paragraph, evidence of the following is not, in any civil or criminal proceeding, admissible against the defendant who made the plea or was a participant in the plea discussions:

(A) a plea of guilty which was later withdrawn;

(B) a plea of nolo contendere;

(C) any statement made in the course of any proceedings under this rule regarding either of the foregoing pleas; or

(D) any statement made in the course of plea discussions with an attorney for the government which do not result in a plea of guilty or which result in a plea of guilty later withdrawn.

However, such a statement is admissible (i) in any proceeding wherein another statement made in the course of the same plea or plea discussions has been introduced and the statement ought in fairness be considered contemporaneously with it, or (ii) in a criminal proceeding for perjury or false statement if the statement was made by the defendant under oath, on the record, and in the presence of counsel.

(f) Determining Accuracy of Plea. Notwithstanding the acceptance of a plea of guilty, the court should not enter a judgment upon such plea without making such inquiry as shall satisfy it that there is a factual basis for the plea.

(g) Record of Proceedings. A verbatim record of the proceedings at which the defendant enters a plea shall be made and, if there is a plea of guilty or nolo contendere, the record shall include, without limitation, the court's advice to the defendant, the inquiry into the voluntariness of the plea including any plea agreement, and the inquiry into the accuracy of a guilty plea.

(h) Harmless Error. Any variance from the procedures required by this rule which does not affect substantial rights shall be disregarded.

NOTES

1. **Consequences of not complying with Rule 11.** Under what circumstances will a failure to comply with applicable procedural requirements for a guilty plea invalidate the plea (and the conviction) and thus give the defendant the opportunity to go to trial or to again plead guilty, at the defendant's option? In McCarthy v. U.S., 394 U.S. 459, 89 S.Ct. 1166, 22 L.Ed.2d 418 (1969), the Government urged that even if the record showed noncompliance with Fed. R.Crim.P. 11 it was entitled to an opportunity to demonstrate from other parts of the record that the plea was entered voluntarily and with an understanding of the charge. Further, it argued, if this could not be shown, the defendant was entitled to no more than a remand for an evidentiary hearing at which the voluntariness or understanding nature of the plea would be at issue. If at this hearing, the Government argued, it established by evidence outside of the record in the original guilty plea proceeding that the plea was understanding and voluntary, the defen-

dant's conviction should stand. It acknowledged, however, that the Government would have the burden of demonstrating that the plea was understanding and voluntary. The Court rejected this position and held that a defendant who demonstrates on direct appeal that his plea was accepted in violation of Rule 11 is entitled to have the conviction reversed and to plead anew. Explaining, the Court stated:

> From the defendant's perspective, the efficacy of shifting the burden of proof to the Government at a later voluntariness hearing is questionable. In meeting its burden, the Government will undoubtedly rely upon the defendant's statement that he desired to plead guilty and frequently a statement that the plea was not induced by any threats or promises. This prima facie case for voluntariness is likely to be treated as irrebuttable in cases such as this one, where the defendant's reply is limited to his own plaintive allegations that he did not understand the nature of the charge and therefore failed to assert a valid defense or to limit his guilty plea only to a lesser included offense. No matter how true these allegations may be, rarely, if ever, can a defendant corroborate them in a postplea voluntariness hearing.

> Rule 11 is designed to eliminate any need to resort to a later factfinding proceeding "in this highly subjective area." Heiden v. United States, [353 F.2d 53, 55 (9th Cir.1965)]. The Rule "contemplates that disputes as to the understanding of the defendant and the voluntariness of his action are to be eliminated at the outset.... " Ibid. ...There is no adequate substitute for demonstrating in the record at the time the plea is entered the defendant's understanding of the nature of the charge against him.

> . . .

> We thus conclude that prejudice inheres in a failure to comply with Rule 11, for noncompliance deprives the defendant of the Rule's procedural safeguards that are designed to facilitate a more accurate determination of the voluntariness of his plea. ...[This] not only will insure that every accused is afforded those procedural safeguards, but also will help reduce the great waste of judicial resources required to process the frivolous attacks on guilty plea convictions that are encouraged, and are more difficult to dispose of, when the original record is inadequate. It is, therefore, not too much to require that, before sentencing defendants to years of imprisonment, district judges take the few minutes necessary to inform them of their rights and to determine whether they understand the action they are taking.

394 U.S. at 469–72, 89 S.Ct. at 1172–74, 22 L.Ed.2d at 427–28. Suppose, however, a trial judge erroneously understates the maximum prison term to which the defendant could be sentenced upon conviction of the crime to which he is offering to plead guilty. Following conviction, the judge sentences the defendant to a prison term shorter than the term which he mistakenly represented to the defendant as the maximum provided by statute. On appeal, is the defendant entitled to have the conviction reversed and to plead anew?

2. **Challenges in collateral proceedings.** If a convicted defendant seeks relief through collateral attack rather than on direct appeal, a more serious deviation from the procedural requirements for the taking of the plea may be required. In the United States v. Timmreck, 441 U.S. 780, 99 S.Ct. 2085, 60 L.Ed.2d 634 (1979), the defendant pleaded guilty to criminal conspiracy in federal District Court. The judge formally addressed him and complied with Rule 11 of the Federal Rules of Criminal Procedure, except that he failed to inform Timmreck that the applicable statute made a period of at least three years parole mandatory. Timmreck was informed that a sentence of 15 years imprisonment and a fine of $25,000 could be imposed. After accepting the plea, the trial judge sentenced Timmreck to

10 years imprisonment, a special parole term of 5 additional years, and a fine of $5,000. No appeal was taken. Two years later, Timmreck moved to vacate his sentence under 28 U.S.C.A. § 2255 on the ground the trial judge had violated Rule 11 by failing to inform him of the mandatory special parole term. Timmreck's lawyer testified that his normal practice was to inform his clients of the mandatory parole term but he could not recall whether he had given Timmreck this information. The District Court denied Timmreck's motion on the ground that since he received a sentence within the maximum as it was described to him no prejudice was suffered as the result of the violation of Rule 11. On appeal, however, the Court of Appeals ordered relief granted, reasoning that any violation of Rule 11 permits collateral attack upon the resulting conviction. A unanimous Supreme Court reversed. After noting that the violation of Rule 11 was neither constitutional nor jurisdictional, it continued:

> Nor can any claim reasonably be made that the error here resulted in a "complete miscarriage of justice" or in a proceeding "inconsistent with the rudimentary demands of fair procedure." Respondent does not argue that he was actually unaware of the special parole term or that, if he had been properly advised by the trial judge, he would not have pleaded guilty. His only claim is of a technical violation of the rule. That claim could have been raised on direct appeal ... but was not.

441 U.S. at 784, 99 S.Ct. at 2087, 60 L.Ed.2d at 638. Finding it unnecessary to determine whether relief would be available in the context of "other aggravating circumstances," the Court held that a showing of only a failure to comply with the formal requirements of Rule 11 as was made by Timmreck did not entitle him to relief.

Several years later Rule 11(c)(1) was amended, as set out above, to specifically require the court to inform the defendant of "the effect of any special parole term." What is the effect of this amendment on *Timmreck?*

3. **Applicability to property forfeiture.** The petitioner in Libretti v. United States, 516 U.S. 29, 116 S.Ct. 356, 133 L.Ed.2d 271 (1995) entered a plea of guilty to engaging in a continuing criminal enterprise. As part of the plea agreement, he consented to the forfeiture of property of a substantial value that the government believed had been used in, or acquired with the proceeds of, drug transactions. On appeal, Libretti claimed that the criminal forfeiture order was invalid because the District Court had failed to find as required by Rule 11 (f) that there was a factual basis for identifying the property as assets subject to criminal forfeiture. The Court, in an opinion by Justice O'Connor, rejected this claim on the ground that rather than being a criminal offense, "[f]orfeiture is an element of the sentence imposed *following* conviction or, as here, a plea of guilty, and thus falls outside the scope of Rule 11(f)." 516 U.S. at 38–39, 116 S.Ct. at 363, 133 L.Ed.2d at 362.

Boykin v. Alabama

Supreme Court of the United States, 1969.
395 U.S. 238, 89 S.Ct. 1709, 23 L.Ed.2d 274.

■ MR. JUSTICE DOUGLAS delivered the opinion of the Court.

In the Spring of 1966, within the period of a fortnight, a series of armed robberies occurred in Mobile, Alabama. The victims, in each case, were local shopkeepers open at night who were forced by a gunman to hand over money. While robbing one grocery store, the assailant fired his gun once, sending a bullet through a door into the ceiling. A few days earlier in a drugstore, the robber had allowed his gun to discharge in such a way that the bullet, on ricochet from the floor, struck a customer in the leg. Shortly thereafter, a local grand jury indicted petitioner, a 27–year-old Negro, on five counts of common-law robbery—an offense punishable in Alabama by death.

Before the matter came to trial, the court determined that petitioner was indigent and appointed counsel to represent him. Three days later, at his arraignment, petitioner pleaded guilty to all five indictments. So far as the record shows, the judge asked no questions of petitioner concerning his plea, and petitioner did not address the court.

Trial strategy may of course make a plea of guilty seem the desirable course. But the record is wholly silent on that point and throws no light on it.

Alabama provides that when a defendant pleads guilty, "the Court must cause the punishment to be determined by a jury" (except where it is required to be fixed by the court). . . . The jury, upon deliberation, found petitioner guilty and sentenced him severally to die on each of the five indictments.

* * *

It was error, plain on the face of the record, for the trial judge to accept petitioner's guilty plea without an affirmative showing that it was intelligent and voluntary. . . .

A plea of guilty is more than a confession which admits that the accused did various acts; it is itself a conviction; nothing remains but to give judgment and determine punishment. Admissibility of a confession must be based on a "reliable determination on the voluntariness issue which satisfies the constitutional rights of the defendant." Jackson v. Denno, 378 U.S. 368, 387, 84 S.Ct. 1774, 1786, 12 L.Ed.2d 908. The requirement that the prosecution spread on the record the prerequisites of a valid waiver is no constitutional innovation. In Carnley v. Cochran, 369 U.S. 506, 516, 82 S.Ct. 884, 890, 8 L.Ed.2d 70, we dealt with a problem of waiver of the right to counsel, a Sixth Amendment right. We held: "Presuming waiver from a silent record is impermissible. The record must show, or there must be an allegation and evidence which show, that an accused was offered counsel but intelligently and understandingly rejected the offer. Anything less is not waiver."

We think that the same standard must be applied to determining whether a guilty plea is voluntarily made. For, as we have said, a plea of guilty is more than an admission of conduct; it is a conviction. Ignorance, incomprehension, coercion, terror, inducements, subtle or blatant threats might be a perfect cover-up of unconstitutionality. The question of an effective waiver of a federal constitutional right in a proceeding is of course governed by federal standards.

Several federal constitutional rights are involved in a waiver that takes place when a plea of guilty is entered in a state criminal trial. First is the privilege against compulsory self-incrimination guaranteed by the Fifth Amendment and applicable to the States by reason of the Fourteenth.

...Second is the right to trial by jury. Third, is the right to confront one's accusers. ...We cannot presume a waiver of these three important federal rights from a silent record.

What is at stake for an accused facing death or imprisonment demands utmost solicitude of which courts are capable in canvassing the matter with the accused to make sure he has a full understanding of what the plea connotes and of its consequence. When the judge discharges that function, he leaves a record adequate for any review that may be later sought ... and forestalls the spin-off of collateral proceedings that seek to probe murky memories.

* * *

Reversed.

■ Mr. Justice Harlan, whom Mr. Justice Black joins, dissenting.

The Court today holds that petitioner Boykin was denied due process of law, and that his robbery convictions must be reversed outright, solely because "the record [is] inadequate to show that petitioner ... intelligently and knowingly pleaded guilty." ... The Court thus in effect fastens upon the States, as a matter of federal constitutional law, the rigid prophylactic requirements of Rule 11 of the Federal Rules of Criminal Procedure.

* * *

I would hold that petitioner Boykin is not entitled to outright reversal of his conviction simply because of the "inadequacy" of the record pertaining to his guilty plea. Further, I would not vacate the judgment below and remand for a state-court hearing on voluntariness. For even if it is assumed for the sake of argument that petitioner would be entitled to such a hearing if he had alleged that the plea was involuntary, a matter which I find it unnecessary to decide, the fact is that he has never made any such claim. Hence, I consider that petitioner's present arguments relating to his guilty plea entitle him to no federal relief.

NOTES

1. **What must the record show?** Must the record in a guilty plea case show, on its face, that the defendant was informed of his rights to trial by jury, confrontation of accusers, and silence? Compare People v. Jaworski, 387 Mich. 21, 194 N.W.2d 868 (1972) (both logic and language of *Boykin* "require that the defendant must be informed of these three rights, for without knowledge he cannot understandingly waive those rights") with Wilkins v. Erickson, 505 F.2d 761 (9th Cir.1974) ("*Boykin* does not require specific articulation of the ... three rights in a state proceeding").

2. **Proof of the absence of waivers.** The respondent in Parke v. Raley, 506 U.S. 20, 113 S.Ct. 517, 121 L.Ed.2d 391 (1992) challenged the admissibility of prior convictions under a Kentucky recidivist statute on the ground that the record in the prior cases did not show the waivers of constitutional rights required to be shown by *Boykin*. No stenographic record existed of the pleas of guilty upon which the convictions were based. The Sixth Circuit held, on federal habeas, that when no record exists the burden is upon the State to prove the validity of the plea and no presumption of regularity attaches to the judgment. It also held that the State must

make that showing by clear and convincing evidence. The Supreme Court, in an opinion by Justice O'Connor, reversed. The Court noted that with respect to convictions that are several years old, a missing or nonexistent record is "not atypical." Without evidence that governmental misconduct is responsible for the absence of a record, the state is permitted to presume that a conviction was obtained in compliance with *Boykin* based upon a judgment of conviction. Therefore, the burden of producing evidence as to noncompliance with *Boykin* may constitutionally be placed upon the criminal defendant. This is fair since often the criminal defendant has the best access to information concerning the circumstances of the acceptance of the plea. The Court also held that if the state is given the burden of persuasion as to compliance with *Boykin*, the Due Process Clause does not require a higher standard of persuasion than a preponderance of the evidence. Justice Blackmun concurred in the judgment on the understanding that the Kentucky statutory scheme was a sentencing provision only and did not create a separate criminal offense.

3. **Elements of the offense(s) charged.** Will the plea be invalidated as involuntary because the defendant has not been informed of every element of the crime to which he is pleading guilty? In Henderson v. Morgan, 426 U.S. 637, 96 S.Ct. 2253, 49 L.Ed.2d 108 (1976), the Supreme Court overturned a conviction on a plea entered under just such circumstances. The defendant was indicted on a charge of first-degree murder, pleaded guilty to second-degree murder, and was sentenced to imprisonment for 25 years to life. The Court said:

> When he was in seventh grade, respondent was committed to the Rome State School for Mental Defectives where he was classified as "retarded." He was released to become a farm laborer and ultimately went to work on Mrs. Francisco's farm. Following an argument, she threatened to return him to state custody. He then decided to abscond. During the night he entered Mrs. Francisco's bedroom with a knife, intending to collect his earned wages before leaving; she awoke, began to scream, and he stabbed her. He took a small amount of money, fled in her car, and became involved in an accident about 80 miles away. The knife was found in the glove compartment of her car. He was promptly arrested and made a statement to the police. He was then 19 years old and substantially below average intelligence.

> . . .

> Petitioner contends that the District Court applied an unrealistically rigid rule of law. Instead of testing the voluntariness of a plea by determining whether a ritualistic litany of the formal legal elements of an offense was read to the defendant, petitioner argues that the court should examine the totality of the circumstances and determine whether the substance of the charge, as opposed to its technical elements, was conveyed to the accused. We do not disagree with the thrust of petitioner's argument, but we are persuaded that even under the test which he espouses, this judgment finding respondent guilty of second-degree murder was defective.

> We assume, as petitioner argues, that the prosecutor had overwhelming evidence of guilt available. We also accept petitioner's characterization of the competence of respondent's counsel and of the wisdom of their advice to plead guilty to a charge of second-degree murder. Nevertheless, such a plea cannot support a judgment of guilty unless it was voluntary in a constitutional sense. And clearly the plea could not be voluntary in the sense that it constituted an intelligent admission that he committed the offense unless the defendant received "real notice of the true nature of the charge against him, the first and most universally recognized requirement of due process." Smith v. O'Grady, 312 U.S. 329, 334, 61 S.Ct. 572, 574, 85 L.Ed. 859 (1941).

The charge of second-degree murder was never formally made. Had it been made, it necessarily would have included a charge that respondent's assault was "committed with a design to effect the death of the person killed." That element of the offense might have been proved by the objective evidence even if respondent's actual state of mind was consistent with innocence or manslaughter. But even if such a design to effect death would almost inevitably have been inferred from evidence that respondent repeatedly stabbed Mrs. Francisco, it is nevertheless also true that a jury would not have been required to draw that inference. The jury would have been entitled to accept defense counsel's appraisal of the incident as involving only manslaughter in the first degree. Therefore, an admission by respondent that he killed Mrs. Francisco does not necessarily also admit that he was guilty of second-degree murder.

There is nothing in this record that can serve as a substitute for either a finding after trial, or a voluntary admission, that respondent had the requisite intent. Defense counsel did not purport to stipulate to that fact; they did not explain to him that his plea would be an admission of that fact; and he made no factual statement or admission necessarily implying that he had such intent. In these circumstances it is impossible to conclude that his plea to the unexplained charge of second-degree murder was voluntary.

Petitioner argues that affirmance of the Court of Appeals will invite countless collateral attacks on judgments entered on pleas of guilty, since frequently the record will not contain a complete enumeration of the elements of the offense to which an accused person pleads guilty.[1] We think petitioner's fears are exaggerated.

Normally the record contains either an explanation of the charge by the trial judge, or at least a representation by defense counsel that the nature of the offense has been explained to the accused. Moreover, even without such an express representation, it may be appropriate to presume that in most cases defense counsel routinely explain the nature of the offense in sufficient detail to give the accused notice of what he is being asked to admit. This case is unique because the trial judge found as a fact that the element of intent was not explained to respondent. Moreover, respondent's unusually low mental capacity provides a reasonable explanation for counsel's oversight; it also forecloses the conclusion that the error was harmless beyond a reasonable doubt, for it lends at least a modicum of credibility to defense counsel's appraisal of the homicide as a manslaughter rather than a murder.

426 U.S. at 641–47, 96 S.Ct. at 2256–59, 49 L.Ed.2d at 113–16.

B. Effect of a Guilty Plea on Later Assertion of Rights

The fact of a guilty plea greatly limits a defendant's ability to later attack his conviction on the basis of alleged errors, even errors of constitutional dimension. Some issues, however, "survive" a guilty plea and can later be raised on appeal or in collateral attack proceedings. Distinguishing the two types of errors is not an easy task.

1. There is no need in this case to decide whether notice of the true nature, or substance, of a charge always requires a description of every element of the offense; we assume it does not. Nevertheless, intent is such a critical element of the offense of second-degree murder that notice of that element is required.

Some matters are arguably no longer issues because of the effect of a guilty plea upon the procedure that leads to conviction. The prosecution may, for example, have in its possession evidence which, if challenged at trial, the trial court would have to exclude on constitutional or other grounds. If a defendant pleads guilty, however, that evidence may not be introduced at all and therefore a defendant may have no basis for claiming that his conviction rests upon it.

But more importantly, the fact of a plea of guilty or *nolo contendere* may serve to preclude a defendant from raising certain issues whether or not those are procedurally presented given the posture of the trial court proceedings. To some extent, a plea of guilty in state criminal proceedings bars later efforts to assert federal constitutional rights in a federal forum. This was assumed in two of the three cases making up the *Brady* trilogy, presented in the final section of this chapter.

The survival of issues was addressed directly in Tollett v. Henderson, 411 U.S. 258, 93 S.Ct. 1602, 36 L.Ed.2d 235 (1973). Henderson had pleaded guilty to murder in a Tennessee court; he was convicted and sentenced to a term of 99 years in prison. Twenty years later, he sought federal habeas corpus relief, urging that the grand jury which returned the indictment to which he had pled had been selected in a racially discriminatory manner. A majority of the Supreme Court, in an opinion by Justice Rehnquist, held that even if Henderson showed racial discrimination in the selection of the indicting grand jury, he would not, on that basis, be entitled to federal habeas corpus relief:

> [A] guilty plea represents a break in the chain of events which has preceded it in the criminal process. When a criminal defendant has solemnly admitted in open court that he is in fact guilty of the offense with which he is charged, he may not thereafter raise independent claims relating to the deprivation of constitutional rights that occurred prior to the entry of the guilty plea.

411 U.S. at 267, 93 S.Ct. at 1608, 36 L.Ed.2d at 243. As the later cases discussed in this section make clear, however, this is subject to at least some qualification. In addition, it is necessary to distinguish other attacks which a defendant may make. The alleged deprivation of constitutional (or other) rights can be urged to have had such an influence upon the plea as to render the plea itself invalid. Or, the advice of counsel (or lack of either counsel or advice) may be urged as a basis for finding the plea constitutionally infirm. These matters are considered later in this chapter.

Blackledge v. Perry

Supreme Court of the United States, 1974.
417 U.S. 21, 94 S.Ct. 2098, 40 L.Ed.2d 628.

■ Mr. Justice Stewart delivered the opinion of the Court.

While serving a term of imprisonment in a North Carolina penitentiary, the respondent Perry became involved in an altercation with another inmate. A warrant issued, charging Perry with the misdemeanor of assault with a deadly weapon, N.C.Gen.Stat. § 14–33(b)(1) (1969 ed.). Under North

Carolina law, the District Court Division of the General Court of Justice has exclusive jurisdiction for the trial of misdemeanors. N.C.Gen.Stat. § 7A–272. Following a trial without a jury in the District Court of Northampton County, Perry was convicted of this misdemeanor and given a six-month sentence, to be served after completion of the prison term he was then serving.

Perry then filed a notice of appeal to the Northampton County Superior Court. Under North Carolina law, a person convicted in the District Court has a right to a trial *de novo* in the Superior Court. N.C.Gen.Stat. §§ 7A–290, 15–177.1. The right to trial *de novo* is absolute, there being no need for the appellant to allege error in the original proceeding. When an appeal is taken, the statutory scheme provides that the slate is wiped clean; the prior conviction is annulled, and the prosecution and the defense begin anew in the Superior Court.

After the filing of the notice of appeal, but prior to the respondent's appearance for trial *de novo* in the Superior Court, the prosecutor obtained an indictment from a grand jury, charging Perry with the felony of assault with a deadly weapon with intent to kill inflicting serious bodily injury, N.C.Gen.Stat. § 14–32(a) (1969 ed.). The indictment covered the same conduct for which Perry had been tried and convicted in the District Court. Perry entered a plea of guilty to the indictment in the Superior Court, and was sentenced to a term of five to seven years in the penitentiary, to be served concurrently with the identical prison sentence he was then serving.

* * *

[T]he Due Process Clause is not offended by all possibilities of increased punishment upon retrial after appeal, but only by those that pose a realistic likelihood of "vindictiveness." . . . [I]n the situation here the central figure is not the judge or the jury, but the prosecutor. The question is whether the opportunities for vindictiveness in this situation are such as to impel the conclusion that due process of law requires [a bar to the more serious charge.] We conclude that the answer must be in the affirmative.

A prosecutor clearly has a considerable stake in discouraging convicted misdemeanants from appealing and thus obtaining a trial *de novo* in the Superior Court, since such an appeal will clearly require increased expenditures of prosecutorial resources before the defendant's conviction becomes final, and may even result in a formerly convicted defendant going free. And, if the prosecutor has the means readily at hand to discourage such appeals—by "upping the ante" through a felony indictment whenever a convicted misdemeanant pursues his statutory appellate remedy—the State can insure that only the most hardy defendants will brave the hazards of a *de novo* trial.

* * *

A person convicted of an offense is entitled to pursue his statutory right to a trial *de novo*, without apprehension that the State will retaliate by substituting a more serious charge for the original one, thus subjecting him to a significantly increased potential period of incarceration. . . .

The remaining question is whether, because of his guilty plea to the felony charge in the Superior Court, Perry is precluded from raising his constitutional claims in this federal habeas corpus proceeding. In contending that such is the case, the petitioner warden relies chiefly on this Court's decision last Term in Tollett v. Henderson, 411 U.S. 258, 93 S.Ct. 1602, 36 L.Ed.2d 235.

The precise issue presented in *Tollett* was "whether a state prisoner, pleading guilty with the advice of counsel, may later obtain release through federal habeas corpus by proving only that the indictment to which he pleaded was returned by an unconstitutionally selected grand jury." Id., at 260, 93 S.Ct. at 1604. The Court answered that question in the negative. . . .

While the petitioner's reliance upon the *Tollett* opinion is understandable, there is a fundamental distinction between this case and that one. Although the underlying claims presented in *Tollett* and the *Brady* trilogy were of constitutional dimension, none went to the very power of the State to bring the defendant into court to answer the charge brought against him. The defendants in McMann v. Richardson, for example, could surely have been brought to trial without the use of the allegedly coerced confessions, and even a tainted indictment of the sort alleged in *Tollett* could have been "cured" through a new indictment by a properly selected grand jury. In the case at hand, by contrast, the nature of the underlying constitutional infirmity is markedly different. Having chosen originally to proceed on the misdemeanor charges in the District Court, the State of North Carolina was, under the facts of this case, simply precluded by the Due Process Clause from calling upon the respondent to answer to the more serious charge in the Superior Court. Unlike the defendant in *Tollett*, Perry is not complaining of "antecedent constitutional violations" or of a "deprivation of constitutional rights that occurred prior to the entry of the guilty plea." Rather, the right that he asserts and that we today accept is the right not to be hailed into court at all upon the felony charge. The very initiation of the proceedings against him in the Superior Court thus operated to deny him due process of law.

The "practical result" dictated by the Due Process Clause in this case is that North Carolina simply could not permissibly require Perry to answer to the felony charge. That being so, it follows that his guilty plea did not foreclose him from attacking his conviction in the Superior Court proceedings through a federal writ of habeas corpus.

Accordingly, the judgment of the Court of Appeals for the Fourth Circuit is affirmed.

■ MR. JUSTICE REHNQUIST, dissenting.

* * *

II.

. . . I believe this case is governed by cases culminating in Tollett v. Henderson, 411 U.S. 258, 93 S.Ct. 1602, 36 L.Ed.2d 235 (1973). . . . The assertion by the Court that this reasoning is somehow inapplicable here because the claim goes "to the very power of the State to bring the defendant into court to answer the charge brought against him" is little other than a conclusion. Any difference between the issue resolved the other way in Tollett v. Henderson and the issue before us today is at most semantic. But the Court's "test" not only fails to distinguish *Henderson* [*Tollett*]; it also fails to provide any reasoned basis on which to approach such questions as whether a speedy trial claim is merged in a guilty plea. I believe the Court's departure today from the principles of *Henderson* [*Tollett*] and the cases preceding it must be recognized as a potentially major breach in the wall of certainty surrounding guilty pleas for which we have found constitutional sanction in those cases.

There is no indication in this record that respondent's guilty plea was the result of an agreement with the prosecutor. But the Court's basis for distinguishing the *Henderson* [*Tollett*] and *Brady* cases seems so insubstantial as to permit the doctrine of this case to apply to guilty pleas which have been obtained as a result of "plea bargains." In that event it will be not merely the State which stands to lose, but the accused defendant in the position of the respondent as well. Since the great majority of criminal cases are resolved by plea bargaining, defendants as a class have at least as great an interest in the finality of voluntary guilty pleas as do prosecutors. If that finality may be swept aside with the ease exhibited by the Court's approach today, prosecutors will have a reduced incentive to bargain, to the detriment of the many defendants for whom plea bargaining offers the only hope for ameliorating the consequences to them of a serious criminal charge.

* * *

■ Mr. Justice Powell joins in Part II of this opinion.

Menna v. New York

Supreme Court of the United States, 1975.
423 U.S. 61, 96 S.Ct. 241, 46 L.Ed.2d 195.

PER CURIAM.

On November 7, 1968, after being granted immunity, petitioner refused to answer questions put to him before a duly convened Kings County, N.Y., Grand Jury which was investigating a murder conspiracy. On March 18, 1969, petitioner refused to obey a court order to return to testify before the same Grand Jury in connection with the same investigation. On that date, petitioner was adjudicated in contempt of court under Sec. 750 of the New York Judiciary Law for his failure to testify before the Grand Jury; and, on March 21, 1969, after declining an offer to purge his contempt, petitioner was sentenced to a flat 30–day term in civil jail. Petitioner served his sentence.

On June 10, 1970, petitioner was indicted for his refusal to answer questions before the Grand Jury on November 7, 1968. After asserting unsuccessfully that this indictment should be dismissed under the Double Jeopardy Clause of the Fifth Amendment to the United States Constitution, petitioner pleaded guilty to the indictment and was sentenced on his plea.

Petitioner appealed, claiming that the Double Jeopardy Clause precluded the State from haling him into court on the charge to which he had pleaded guilty.[2] The New York Court of Appeals affirmed the conviction, declining to address the double jeopardy claim on the merits. It held, relying, inter alia, on Tollett v. Henderson, 411 U.S. 258, 93 S.Ct. 1602, 36 L.Ed.2d 235 (1973), that the double jeopardy claim had been "waived" by petitioner's counseled plea of guilty.

We reverse. Where the State is precluded by the United States Constitution from haling a defendant into court on a charge, federal law requires that a conviction on that charge be set aside even if the conviction was entered pursuant to a counseled plea of guilty. Blackledge v. Perry, 417 U.S. 21, 30, 94 S.Ct. 2098, 2103, 40 L.Ed.2d 628 (1974).[3] The motion for leave to proceed in forma pauperis and the petition for certiorari are granted, and the case is remanded to the New York Court of Appeals for a determination of petitioner's double jeopardy claim on the merits, a claim on which we express no view.

NOTES

1. **Plead and appeal provisions.** One result of rules such as that applied in Tollett v. Henderson is that a defendant who wishes appellate review of a trial court ruling on matters such as motions to suppress evidence may have to go to trial despite no realistic expectation of any result other than conviction on the crime charged. This has led a number of jurisdictions to give a defendant access to appellate courts on direct appeal despite a plea of guilty, at least for purposes of raising certain issues. New York—McKinney's Crim.Pro.Law § 710.70(2), for example, provides that an order denying a motion to suppress evidence may be reviewed on appeal from a judgment of conviction, "notwithstanding the fact that such judgment of conviction is predicated upon a plea of guilty."

2. **Effect of state plead and appeal provisions on the availability of federal relief.** To what extent would the provisions of Rule 11(a)(2), set out at

2. The State concedes that petitioner's double jeopardy claim is a strong one on the merits. In light of the flat 30–day sentence imposed, the earlier conviction was a criminal conviction ...; and New York law supports the proposition that the earlier conviction was based, at least in part, on the failure to answer questions on November 7, 1968, and was thus for the same crime as the one charged in the instant indictment. ...

3. Neither Tollett v. Henderson, 411 U.S. 258, 93 S.Ct. 1602, 36 L.Ed.2d 235 (1973), nor our earlier cases on which it relied, e.g., Brady v. United States, 397 U.S. 742, 90 S.Ct. 1463, 25 L.Ed.2d 747 (1970), and McMann v. Richardson, 397 U.S. 759, 90 S.Ct. 1441, 25 L.Ed.2d 763 (1970), stand for the proposition that counseled guilty pleas inevitably "waive" all antecedent constitutional violations. If they did so hold, the New York Court of Appeals might be correct. However, in *Tollett* we emphasized that waiv-er was not the basic ingredient of this line of cases,.... The point of these cases is that a counseled plea of guilty is an admission of factual guilt so reliable that, where voluntary and intelligent, it quite validly removes the issue of factual guilt from State's imposition of punishment. A guilty plea, therefore, simply renders irrelevant those constitutional violations not logically inconsistent with the valid establishment of factual guilt and which do not stand in the way of convictions, if factual guilt is validly established. Here, however, the claim is that the State may not convict petitioner no matter how validly his factual guilt is established. The guilty plea, therefore, does not bar the claim.

We do not hold that a double jeopardy claim may never be waived. We simply hold that a plea of guilty to a charge does not waive a claim that—judged on its face—the charge is one which the State may not constitutionally prosecute.

page 930 above, increase the availability of collateral relief? In Lefkowitz v. Newsome, 420 U.S. 283, 95 S.Ct. 886, 43 L.Ed.2d 196 (1975), Newsome, charged in New York state courts, had moved for suppression of certain evidence seized in connection with his arrest. He argued that his arrest was in violation of federal constitutional standards. His motion was denied. He then pleaded guilty and was convicted; on direct appeal, the New York appellate courts affirmed the conviction. Newsome next sought federal habeas corpus relief in federal District Court. This was opposed by the state on the ground that by pleading guilty he had lost the right to review of his constitutional claims through the federal habeas corpus route. The Supreme Court held, however, that in view of New York Crim.Pro.Law § 710.70(2) (discussed in Note 1, supra), Newsome was entitled to pursue federal habeas corpus remedies: "[W]hen state law permits a defendant to plead guilty without forfeiting his right to judicial review of specified constitutional issues, the defendant is not foreclosed from pursuing those constitutional claims in a federal habeas corpus proceeding." 420 U.S. at 293, 95 S.Ct. at 891–92, 43 L.Ed.2d at 204.

3. **Waiver of evidence sufficiency claims.** Respondents in United States v. Broce, 488 U.S. 563, 109 S.Ct. 757, 102 L.Ed.2d 927 (1989) entered pleas of guilty pursuant to an agreement with the government to two counts of conspiracy. Later, in collateral proceedings, they were permitted to show with evidence outside the record in their case that each conspiracy to which they had plead guilty was really part of a single, larger conspiracy. The District Court refused to set aside the convictions on the ground that respondents' pleas of guilty were admissions of the two conspiracies. The Court of Appeals held that under Blackledge v. Perry and Menna v. New York the pleas of guilty did not waive respondents' claim that only one conspiracy existed. The Supreme Court, in an opinion by Justice Kennedy, reversed. *Blackledge* and *Menna* are distinguishable because in them

> the determination that the second indictment could not go forward should have been made by the presiding judge at the time the plea was entered on the basis of the existing record.... The respondents here, in contrast, pleaded guilty to indictments that on their face described separate conspiracies. They cannot prove their claim by relying on those indictments and the existing record. Indeed ... they cannot prove their claim without contradicting those indictments, and that opportunity is foreclosed by the admissions inherent in their guilty pleas.

488 U.S. at 575–76, 109 S.Ct. at 765–66, 102 L.Ed.2d at 938.

C. PLEA BARGAINING

The entire subject of guilty pleas is influenced by the practice of plea bargaining, which is described in the first subsection that follows. Subsequent subsections address specific issues relating to structuring the guilty plea process to accommodate plea bargaining, determination of whether particular pleas offered pursuant to bargains are constitutionally or otherwise "acceptable," and possible abolition of plea bargaining entirely. While relatively few voices have called for efforts to completely abolish plea bargaining, more have suggested restricting the practice. For example, California's passage of "The Victim's Bill of Rights" initiative in 1982 prohibits plea bargaining at the felony trial court level except under specified circumstances. However, most "reform" has involved efforts at open recognition and regulation of the process. Fed.R.Crim.Pro. 11 is an example of this approach.

Plea bargaining takes a variety of forms. But a central question, in addition to the factual voluntariness of a plea entered pursuant to plea bargaining, is the acceptability of a process which results in sentence disparities between those who plead and those who go to trial. Even if it is acceptable for the sentencing judge to reward a guilty plea, it does not necessarily follow, of course, that it is also acceptable for the prosecutor to have the power (perhaps in cooperation with defense counsel) to achieve the same result. This may be a power that is acceptable, if at all, only if judicially exercised. But if it is inappropriate for a sentencing judge to reward a defendant's willingness to plead guilty, it seems to necessarily follow that it is also inappropriate to achieve this same objective by other methods, such as a reduction in charge at the option of the prosecutor.

The issue was addressed by the American Bar Association's Standards for Criminal Justice. The original formulation of those standards, approved in 1968, provided that a sentence in excess of that which would be justified by other purposes of the criminal law should not be imposed because the defendant has chosen to go to trial. Standards Relating to Pleas of Guilty, Standard 1.8(b) (Approved Draft, 1968). It also provided, however, that:

> It is proper for the court to grant charge and sentence concessions to defendants who enter a plea of guilty or nolo contendere when the interest of the public in the effective administration of criminal justice would thereby be served. Among the considerations which are appropriate in determining this question are:
>
> (i) that the defendant by his plea has aided in ensuring the prompt and certain application of correctional measures to him;
>
> * * *
>
> (vi) that the defendant by his plea has aided in avoiding delay (including delay due to crowded dockets) in the disposition of other cases and thereby has increased the probability of prompt and certain application of correctional measures to other offenders.

Id., Standard 1.8(a).

In 1979, however, the American Bar Association approved the following amended version of this standard:

> (a) The fact that a defendant has entered a plea of guilty or nolo contendere should not, by itself alone, be considered by the court as a mitigating factor in imposing sentence. It is proper for the court to grant charge and sentence concessions to defendants who enter a plea of guilty or nolo contendere when consistent with the protection of the public, the gravity of the offense, and the needs of the defendant, and when there is substantial evidence to establish that:
>
> (i) the defendant is genuinely contrite and has shown a willingness to assume responsibility for his or her conduct;
>
> (ii) the concessions will make possible alternative correctional measures which are better adapted to achieving protective, deterrent, or other purposes of correctional treatment, or will prevent undue harm to the defendant from the form of conviction;

(iii) the defendant, by making public trial unnecessary, has demonstrated genuine consideration for the victims of his or her criminal activity, by desiring either to make restitution or to prevent unseemly public scrutiny or embarrassment to them; or

(iv) the defendant has given or offered cooperation when such cooperation has resulted or may result in the successful prosecution of other offenders engaged in equally serious or more serious criminal conduct.

(b) The court should not impose upon a defendant any sentence in excess of that which would be justified by any of the protective, deterrent, or other purposes of the criminal law because the defendant has chosen to require the prosecution to prove guilt at trial rather than to enter a plea of guilty or nolo contendere.

III ABA Standards for Criminal Justice, Standard 14–1.8 (1980). Is there a significant difference between the two versions of the standard? If so, which is the more desirable? Which is most "practical?" Which is most consistent with the various constitutional rights involved? Is some other approach better? Consider the position(s) of the Standards in evaluating the following material.

1.   PRACTICES AND CONTROVERSIES

Newman, Reshape the Deal

9 Trial 11 (1973).*

The Negotiated Plea. Throwing oneself on the mercy of the court is one thing; arranging for charge and sentencing concession ahead of time is, or may be, a more complex and even more controversial issue. When the term "plea bargaining" is used, it rarely refers to simple mercy-of-the-court situations. What is generally meant is a prearraignment "deal" between the prosecution and the defense in which charges are dropped (in spite of sufficient evidence) or where specific sentence promises are made in exchange for the defendant's willingness to plead guilty. There is ample research today to indicate that plea negotiations are common, even routine, in many—perhaps all—jurisdictions in the country.

* * *

Plea Negotiation Practices. While research has shown plea bargaining to be common in courts across the land, there are variations in types of plea-agreements and in the actual procedures followed by prosecutors and defense in different jurisdictions. Part of this variation is the result of differences in criminal codes, especially sentencing provisions, from one place to another. In states with statutorily mandated sentences for certain crimes (20-to-life for armed robbery, for example), the only way a defendant can achieve sentence leniency is to have the charges lowered. In other

* Reprinted from Trial Magazine, 20 Garden St., Cambridge, Mass. (May/June 1973).

places, where indeterminate sentences are common and the judge has wide discretion to choose among types and lengths of sentences regardless of charge, reduction is less important than a pre-plea promise from the prosecutor to "recommend" probation or some other lenient penalty.

The way a typical bargaining session works is as follows: A defendant is apprehended and initially charged with armed robbery, an offense carrying a mandatory minimum prison term of 20 years. Either on his own or through counsel he indicates to the prosecutor a willingness to plead guilty to a lesser crime in order to avoid the mandatory sentence of the higher charge.

In some cases, though actually a settlement process, negotiation can be quite adversary in its own right. The defense counsel may indicate to the prosecutor that he thinks the state has no evidence against his client except possibly a charge of disorderly conduct. The prosecutor in turn may state that he is not only going to push the armed robbery charge but plans to level a special count of being a habitual offender unless the defendant cooperates. Defense counsel then offers to have his client plead guilty to petty larceny with the prosecutor countering by offering to reduce the charge to second degree robbery.

So it goes. Eventually an agreed upon lesser charge—burglary or grand larceny, for example—may result and the defendant will plead guilty, facing at most a substantially reduced prison sentence and at best perhaps probation.

If the defendant wishes to be placed on probation, he may push in negotiation for more than charge reduction. He may also ask the prosecuting attorney to promise that at sentencing the state will "recommend" probation if and when asked by the court. This is a customary (though not universal) practice.

A prosecutor's recommendation of probation is a strong factor in the defendant's favor although a weaker, and also a vigorously sought after promise, is for the prosecutor to make no recommendation at the time of sentencing or to agree "not to oppose" probation if requested by the defendant. After all, the offender knows that should the prosecutor arise at sentencing and recommend a long prison term (perhaps reading prior convictions into the record) it is highly likely that incarceration will result.

Therefore, in most jurisdictions, a preplea sentence promise by the prosecutor is a major concession, even though the district attorney has no official authority to actually impose sentence.

There are other considerations that occasionally arise in plea negotiation depending upon the particular defendant, the crime or crimes charged and the sentencing structure and practices of the jurisdiction in question.

For example, often a person arrested for one crime is subsequently charged with others. It is rare that a burglar is apprehended on his first attempt and, once nabbed, the police may "solve" 20 or 30 separate burglaries, all potential charges against the defendant. Theoretically he could be tried on each count and could receive consecutive sentences. If, for example, he were accused of ten burglaries, tried separately on each and convicted on only half yet got one to three on each (to be served consecutively) he would in effect face a five to fifteen-year sentence. Therefore he may seek to have charges joined into a single accusation, or have some of the counts dismissed if he is willing to plead to one or perhaps two.

Additionally, some offenders may be facing a habitual offender rap, which is normally filed as a separate indictment or information. In exchange for pleading to the crime as charged he may avoid such "supercharging" by the state. Then, too, some defendants are on parole or probation for prior convictions and may negotiate for revocation of the old sentence if the new charge is dismissed or sufficiently reduced.

There is even some "lateral" bargaining, primarily to modify the conviction label without affecting sentence at all. Some defendants are willing to plead guilty to serious crimes such as robbery to avoid conviction of certain sex crimes like rape or sodomy because, while the potential sentence may be longer, the label and its attendant consequences throughout the life of the defendant are considered to be a better deal.

Permutations and combinations of plea agreements are almost endless especially where multiple charges are involved, but the end result is always the same: The defendant is allowed to plead guilty to lesser offenses or receives a preadjudication sentence promise in exchange for his willingness to give up his right to trial.

Why Plea Bargain? Motivations of the guilty defendant in plea bargaining are readily discernible. He wishes to minimize both the sentence which follows conviction and the label which attaches to it. He also usually hopes to avoid publicity, not only for himself, but perhaps to protect his family and friends from likely notoriety if he demands trial. Occasionally he may wish to protect accomplices or confederates by taking the rap himself.

The bargaining motivations of the state are somewhat less readily discernible, though in every instance the bargained plea is much more efficient, cheaper and more certain than a contested case.

There are, however, other more subtle but no less important motivations on the part of the prosecutor and other state officials for engaging in plea negotiation and in fact encouraging it. Some of these are self-seeking, but others rest on a sincere attempt to individualize justice, to build equity into a system that otherwise would be too harsh in certain types of cases.

One of the self-seeking motivations on the part of the state is to avoid challenge not only of the amount of evidence but the ways it was obtained. In spite of all the current controversy about illegal searches, wiretaps, failure to give *Miranda* warnings and the like, such issues are really paramount only in cases where pretrial motions are denied and which go to trial.

A plea of guilty waives almost all defects in the state's case. The way evidence was obtained is never tested. Whether the *Miranda* warning was given or not is irrelevant in the case of the defendant who pleads guilty. The insanity defense, or entrapment, and other important procedural and substantive issues are mooted by the guilty plea.

In short, the guilty plea doesn't refine and hone the law, rather it avoids sticky questions of police practices, prosecutorial trial skills and even the adequacy of legislative sentencing provisions. Furthermore, in most cases the plea satisfies all interested parties. The defendant has his deal; the prosecutor has an assured conviction (for a trial, no matter how carefully prepared, is always an uncertainty given the vagaries of juries), the victim is theoretically satisfied by conviction of the perpetrator and correctional agencies receive an offender who has admitted his guilt. It is always a difficult task for correctional authorities who receive an offender who, though sentenced after a full jury trial, still protests his innocence. How does rehabilitation begin?

At any rate, given the absence of challenge to police methods at one end, and a confessed criminal received in prison at the other, there is more than simple overcrowding behind the state's willingness, to accept the plea. It is not only a quick and efficient way of processing defendants, it is a safe way, for pleading defendants do not rock the boat.

There are, however, a number of other state considerations underlying plea negotiation that are less self-seeking, and perhaps more consistent with a general desire to build equity into our criminal justice system, particularly in regard to sentencing.

It is common practice in many state legislatures (and in Congress as well) for very severe laws to be passed in the heat of anger or at the height of public indignation over what appears to be a serious crime wave. A few years ago about half the states adopted very harsh "sex psychopath" laws. In recent years a number of states have adopted severe sale-of-narcotic laws, mandating life imprisonment or even death to "pushers."

In passing such laws the drafters typically have in mind the worst offenders—the organized criminal or the professional dopefiend who sells heroin to school children or is otherwise the most vicious or professional violator. However, in the day-to-day operation of courts the types of sale-of-narcotics defendants who appear are rarely professional heroin pushers but are more likely to be young men or women who have sold a couple of pills or marijuana cigarettes to friends.

Technically they are guilty of sale of narcotics and in most cases there is little doubt that the evidence held by the state is sufficient to prove the charge. Yet confronted with these cases it is a rare prosecutor or trial judge who wishes to give a mandatory life sentence (sometimes nonparoleable) to an 18–year-old offender whose crime is selling a few reefers to a buddy. On the other hand the district attorney may be unwilling or reluctant to dismiss the case entirely so that the lesser charge of "possession" or some related crime may be offered as a desirable solution.

This motivation pattern for bargaining is an extension of traditional prosecutor's discretion but here instead of dismissing the case the prosecutor in effect sentences the defendant. The reason for this is the nature of criminal law itself. Legislation defining crimes and fixing penalties is necessarily general and broad and if the prosecutor and other court officials are confronted with individual cases which, while they technically fit the same statutory category, are readily distinguishable in terms of the actual harm they have done to victims or to the social order in general they can only achieve individualization of sentences by reducing charges. There are a number of such situations where charge reduction is used to individualize justice without really violating the legislative intent of proceeding against very serious criminals.

In addition to the avoidance of inappropriately excessive mandatory sentences, other motivations which have been identified are:

- reduction to avoid a criminal label which would imply in the public mind that the defendant was guilty of conduct which is really not consistent with the actions that form his criminal violation.

* * *

- where there is a crime involving codefendants of unequal culpability. This is simply a recognition of the prosecutor's discretion to distinguish what the legislatures cannot do; that is, to determine the degree of involvement in a single offense on the part of multiple persons involved in a crime.

An older, sophisticated armed robber who has as a look-out a young, inexperienced, clean-record accomplice may be convicted "on the nose" but his accomplice offered a lesser charge (perhaps attempted robbery or burglary) to balance culpability and consequences. The same thing occurs when there are other mitigating circumstances in the crime, such as the participation of the victim in the criminal activity itself as, for example, in certain forms of confidence games.

- where the therapeutic benefits of alternative sentences can best be achieved by charge reduction or by awarding probation when normally such would not be the case. This is indeed a mercy-of-the-court situation but one which ignores the other administrative advantages of negotiation.

This is an extension of sentencing discretion, with primary concern to place the defendant in the best correctional setting possible which might be precluded if he's convicted on the nose. A mandatory prison term for a good-risk young violator may be more damaging to the community in the long run than if he is given a break on his first sentence.

- reduction to support law enforcement efforts by rewarding informants, state witnesses and the like with lesser charges and sentences. This is sometimes called "trading the little ones for the big ones," but the fact remains that unless differential court leniency is shown major cases cannot be developed.

* * *

The prevailing attitude toward the process (until recently at least) on the part of many, including some appellate courts, is that there is something dirty about plea bargaining, something corruptive or potentially corruptive in negotiating with criminals for punishment less than could be levied if the full force of the law were used. While it is true that from one perspective plea negotiation does act to avoid legislative mandate, and, like the exercise of all administrative discretion, has the *potential* for corruption, another side of the coin is presented by equity decisions, by a conscientious attempt to introduce "justice" into individual cases.

National Advisory Commission on Criminal Justice Standards and Goals

Courts 47–48 (1973).

The Commission ... totally condemns plea bargaining as an institution. ... [I]t has concluded that [plea bargaining] exacts unacceptable costs from all concerned. Perhaps the major cost is that of reduced rationality in the processing of criminal defendants. Whether a defendant is convicted should depend upon the evidence available to convict him, and what disposition is made of a convicted offender should depend upon what action best serves rehabilitative and deterrent needs. The likelihood that these factors will control conviction and disposition is minimized in the inevitable "horsetrading" atmosphere of plea negotiation. Some defendants suffer from the resulting irrationality.

But the public's interest in disposition of cases to serve its interest in protection also suffers. ...

Another major cost involved in plea negotiation is the burden it inevitably places upon the exercise of the rights involved in trial—the rights to jury trial, to confront and cross-examine witnesses, to have the judge or jury convinced of guilt beyond a reasonable doubt, and similar matters. It is inherent in plea negotiation that leniency will be given in return for nonassertion of these rights.

* * *

[I]t is wholly unacceptable to add to [the inevitable costs of trial] the necessity of forfeiting a discount that could otherwise have been obtained. Probably the major individual victim of today's plea bargaining system is the defendant who exercises his right to trial and suffers a substantially more severe sentence than he would have received had he pleaded guilty.

By imposing a penalty upon the exercise of procedural rights in those cases in which there is a reasonable likelihood that the rights will be vindicated, the plea negotiation system creates a significant danger to the innocent. Many of the rights it discourages are rights designed to prevent the conviction of innocent defendants. To the extent these rights are rendered nonoperative by the plea negotiation system, innocent defendants are endangered. ...

NOTES

1. **Impact of defense counsel on plea bargaining.** Some studies have developed evidence that a lawyer's success in the plea bargaining process may depend not only upon the prosecutor's perception of the lawyer's skill and vigor but also upon the existence or nonexistence of a personal relationship between defense counsel and prosecutor. See Dear, Adversary Review: An Experiment in Performance Evaluation, 57 Den.L.J. 401, 416–17 (1980); White, A Proposal for Reform of the Plea Bargaining Process, 119 U.Pa.L.Rev. 439, 448 (1971). A defendant, then, may suffer by comparison with other defendants because of defense counsel's inability or unwillingness to develop such relationships. But does this distinguish plea bargaining from the trial process? Is a lawyer's personality likely to have no effect upon the judge or jury in a contested case?

2. **Pressures on defense counsel to plea bargain.** Alschuler, The Defense Attorney's Role in Plea Bargaining, 84 Yale L.J. 1179 (1975), explores the factors that may render lawyers susceptible to the pressures of the plea bargaining process. Privately-retained lawyers, he notes, often set a single fee at the outset of the case to cover the lawyer's work however the case may proceed. Once the lawyer has collected this fee, the lawyer has a strong financial interest in earning that fee as efficiently as possible. This can often be accomplished by pleading the client guilty. "[T]he guilty-plea system," Alschuler concludes, "subjects even honest and conscientious lawyers to temptations that have no place in a rational system of administering justice." Id., at 1199.

2.   "Voluntariness" of Pleas and Related Matters

a.   BASIC VOLUNTARINESS CONSIDERATIONS

Challenges to the "voluntariness" (and thus the constitutional validity) of a guilty plea are not confined to situations in which the plea is the culmination of plea bargaining. But the effect of plea bargaining upon the validity of guilty pleas presents some of the most significant voluntariness issues. In 1970, the Supreme Court undertook to deal with plea bargaining and its effect upon guilty pleas when those pleas are challenged as violative of federal constitutional standards. Three cases decided together in May of 1970, Brady v. United States, 397 U.S. 742, 90 S.Ct. 1463, 25 L.Ed.2d 747 (1970), McMann v. Richardson, 397 U.S. 759, 90 S.Ct. 1441, 25 L.Ed.2d 763 (1970), and Parker v. North Carolina, 397 U.S. 790, 90 S.Ct. 1458, 25 L.Ed.2d 785 (1970)—the *Brady* trilogy—resulted. These constitute the foundation for federal constitutional doctrine in this area. Some aspects of these cases, of course, have important ramifications for pleas that are not related to plea agreements. For example, the issue of the impact of a coerced confession or other inadmissible "evidence" upon a subsequent plea of guilty, at issue in both *McMann* and *Parker,* can certainly arise in a nonbargain situation.

Brady v. United States

Supreme Court of the United States, 1970.
397 U.S. 742, 90 S.Ct. 1463, 25 L.Ed.2d 747.

■ Mr. Justice White delivered the opinion of the Court.

In 1959, petitioner was charged with kidnaping in violation of 18 U.S.C.A. § 1201(a). Since the indictment charged that the victim of the kidnaping was not liberated unharmed, petitioner faced a maximum penalty of death if the verdict of the jury should so recommend. Petitioner, represented by competent counsel throughout, first elected to plead not guilty. Apparently because the trial judge was unwilling to try the case without a jury, petitioner made no serious attempt to reduce the possibility of a death penalty by waiving a jury trial. Upon learning that his codefendant, who had confessed to the authorities, would plead guilty and be available to testify against him, petitioner changed his plea to guilty. His plea was accepted after the trial judge twice questioned him as to the voluntariness of his plea. Petitioner was sentenced to 50 years' imprisonment, later reduced to 30.

In 1967, petitioner sought relief under 28 U.S.C.A. § 2255, claiming that his plea of guilty was not voluntarily given because § 1201(a) operated to coerce his plea. . . .

After a hearing, the District Court for the District of New Mexico denied relief. . . . The court held that § 1201(a) was constitutional and found that petitioner decided to plead guilty when he learned that his codefendant was going to plead guilty: petitioner pleaded guilty "by reason of other matters and not by reason of the statute" or because of any acts of the trial judge. The court concluded that "the plea was voluntarily and knowingly made."

The Court of Appeals for the Tenth Circuit affirmed, determining that the District Court's findings were supported by substantial evidence and specifically approving the finding that petitioner's plea of guilty was voluntary. 404 F.2d 601 (1968). We granted certiorari, 395 U.S. 976, 89 S.Ct. 2146, 23 L.Ed.2d 764 (1969), to consider the claim that the Court of Appeals was in error in not reaching a contrary result on the authority of this Court's decision in United States v. Jackson, 390 U.S. 570 (1968). We affirm.

I.

In United States v. Jackson, supra, the defendants were indicted under § 1201(a). The District Court dismissed the § 1201(a) count of the indictment, holding the statute unconstitutional because it permitted imposition of the death sentence only upon a jury's recommendation and thereby made the risk of death the price of a jury trial. This Court held the statute valid, except for the death penalty provision; with respect to the latter, the Court agreed with the trial court "that the death penalty provision . . . imposes an impermissible burden upon the exercise of a constitutional right. . . . " 390 U.S., at 572, 88 S.Ct., at 1211. The problem was to determine "whether the Constitution permits the establishment of such a death penalty, applicable only to those defendants who assert the right to contest their guilt before a jury." 390 U.S., at 581, 88 S.Ct., at 1216. The inevitable effect of the provision was said to be to discourage assertion of the Fifth Amendment right not to plead guilty and to deter exercise of the Sixth Amendment right to demand a jury trial. Because the legitimate goal of limiting the death penalty to cases in which a jury recommends it could be achieved without penalizing those defendants who plead not guilty and elect a jury trial, the death penalty provision "needlessly penalize[d] the assertion of a constitutional right," 390 U.S., at 583, 88 S.Ct., at 1217, and was therefore unconstitutional.

Since the "inevitable effect" of the death penalty provision of § 1201(a) was said by the Court to be the needless encouragement of pleas of guilty and waivers of jury trial, Brady contends that *Jackson* requires the invalidation of every plea of guilty entered under that section, at least when the fear of death is shown to have been a factor in the plea. Petitioner, however, has read far too much into the *Jackson* opinion.

The Court made it clear in *Jackson* that it was not holding § 1201(a) inherently coercive of guilty pleas: "the fact that the Federal Kidnaping Act tends to discourage defendants from insisting upon their innocence and demanding trial by jury hardly implies that every defendant who enters a guilty plea to a charge under the Act does so involuntarily.'' 390 U.S., at 583, 88 S.Ct., at 1218.

* * *

Plainly, it seems to us, *Jackson* ruled neither that all pleas of guilty encouraged by the fear of a possible death sentence are involuntary pleas nor that such encouraged pleas are invalid whether involuntary or not. *Jackson* prohibits the imposition of the death penalty under § 1201(a), but that decision neither fashioned a new standard for judging the validity of guilty pleas nor mandated a new application of the test theretofore fashioned by courts and since reiterated that guilty pleas are valid if both ''voluntary'' and ''intelligent.'' See Boykin v. Alabama, 395 U.S. 238, 242, 89 S.Ct. 1709, 1711–1712, 23 L.Ed.2d 274 (1969).

That a guilty plea is a grave and solemn act to be accepted only with care and discernment has long been recognized. Central to the plea and the foundation for entering judgment against the defendant is the defendant's admission in open court that he committed the acts charged in the indictment. He thus stands as a witness against himself and he is shielded by the Fifth Amendment from being compelled to do so—hence the minimum requirement that his plea be the voluntary expression of his own choice. But the plea is more than an admission of past conduct; it is the defendant's consent that judgment of conviction may be entered without a trial—a waiver of his right to trial before a jury or a judge. Waivers of constitutional rights not only must be voluntary but must be knowing, intelligent acts done with sufficient awareness of the relevant circumstances and likely consequences. On neither score was Brady's plea of guilty invalid.

II.

The trial judge in 1959 found the plea voluntary before accepting it; the District Court in 1968, after an evidentiary hearing, found that the plea was voluntarily made; the Court of Appeals specifically approved the finding of voluntariness. We see no reason on this record to disturb the judgment of those courts. Petitioner, advised by competent counsel, tendered his plea after his codefendant, who had already given a confession, determined to plead guilty and became available to testify against petitioner. It was this development which the District Court found to have triggered Brady's guilty plea.

The voluntariness of Brady's plea can be determined only by considering all of the relevant circumstances surrounding it. One of these circumstances was the possibility of a heavier sentence following a guilty verdict after a trial. It may be that Brady, faced with a strong case against him and recognizing that his chances for acquittal were slight, preferred to plead guilty and thus limit the penalty to life imprisonment rather than to elect a jury trial which could result in a death penalty. But even if we assume that Brady would not have pleaded guilty except for the death penalty provision of § 1201(a), this assumption merely identifies the penalty provision as a ''but for'' cause of his plea. That the statute caused the plea in this sense does not necessarily prove that the plea was coerced and invalid as an involuntary act.

The State to some degree encourages pleas of guilty at every important step in the criminal process. For some people, their breach of a State's law is alone sufficient reason for surrendering themselves and accepting punishment. For others, apprehension and charge, both threatening acts by the Government, jar them into admitting their guilt. In still other cases, the post-indictment accumulation of evidence may convince the defendant and his counsel that a trial is not worth the agony and expense to the defendant and his family. All these pleas of guilty are valid in spite of the State's responsibility for some of the factors motivating the pleas; the pleas are no more improperly compelled than is the decision by a defendant at the close of the State's evidence at trial that he must take the stand or face certain conviction.

Of course, the agents of the State may not produce a plea by actual or threatened physical harm or by mental coercion overbearing the will of the defendant. But nothing of the sort is claimed in this case; nor is there evidence that Brady was so gripped by fear of the death penalty or hope of leniency that he did not or could not, with the help of counsel, rationally weigh the advantages of going to trial against the advantages of pleading guilty. Brady's claim is of a different sort: that it violates the Fifth Amendment to influence or encourage a guilty plea by opportunity or promise of leniency and that a guilty plea is coerced and invalid if influenced by the fear of a possibly higher penalty for the crime charged if a conviction is obtained after the State is put to its proof.

Insofar as the voluntariness of his plea is concerned, there is little to differentiate Brady from (1) the defendant, in a jurisdiction where the judge and jury have the same range of sentencing power, who pleads guilty because his lawyer advises him that the judge will very probably be more lenient than the jury; (2) the defendant, in a jurisdiction where the judge alone has sentencing power, who is advised by counsel that the judge is normally more lenient with defendants who plead guilty than with those who go to trial; (3) the defendant who is permitted by prosecutor and judge to plead guilty to a lesser offense included in the offense charged; and (4) the defendant who pleads guilty to certain counts with the understanding that other charges will be dropped. In each of these situations,[4] as in Brady's case, the defendant might never plead guilty absent the possibility or certainty that the plea will result in a lesser penalty than the sentence that could be imposed after a trial and a verdict of guilty. We decline to hold, however, that a guilty plea is compelled and invalid under the Fifth Amendment whenever motivated by the defendant's desire to accept the certainty or probability of a lesser penalty rather than face a wider range of

---

4. We here make no reference to the situation where the prosecutor or judge, or both, deliberately employ their charging and sentencing powers to induce a particular defendant to tender a plea of guilty. In Brady's case there is no claim that the prosecutor threatened prosecution on a charge not justified by the evidence or that the trial judge threatened Brady with a harsher sentence if convicted after trial in order to induce him to plead guilty.

possibilities extending from acquittal to conviction and a higher penalty authorized by law for the crime charged.

The issue we deal with is inherent in the criminal law and its administration because guilty pleas are not constitutionally forbidden, because the criminal law characteristically extends to judge or jury a range of choice in setting the sentence in individual cases, and because both the State and the defendant often find it advantageous to preclude the possibility of the maximum penalty authorized by law. For a defendant who sees slight possibility of acquittal, the advantages of pleading guilty and limiting the probable penalty are obvious—his exposure is reduced, the correctional processes can begin immediately, and the practical burdens of a trial are eliminated. For the State there are also advantages—the more promptly imposed punishment after an admission of guilt may more effectively attain the objectives of punishment; and with the avoidance of trial, scarce judicial and prosecutorial resources are conserved for those cases in which there is a substantial issue of the defendant's guilt or in which there is substantial doubt that the State can sustain its burden of proof. It is this mutuality of advantage which perhaps explains the fact that at present well over three-fourths of the criminal convictions in this country rest on pleas of guilty, a great many of them no doubt motivated at least in part by the hope or assurance of a lesser penalty than might be imposed if there were a guilty verdict after a trial to judge or jury.

Of course, that the prevalence of guilty pleas is explainable does not necessarily validate those pleas or the system which produces them. But we cannot hold that it is unconstitutional for the State to extend a benefit to a defendant who in turn extends a substantial benefit to the State and who demonstrates by his plea that he is ready and willing to admit his crime and to enter the correctional system in a frame of mind which affords hope for success in rehabilitation over a shorter period of time than might otherwise be necessary.

A contrary holding would require the States and Federal Government to forbid guilty pleas altogether, to provide a single invariable penalty for each crime defined by the statutes, or to place the sentencing function in a separate authority having no knowledge of the manner in which the conviction in each case was obtained. In any event, it would be necessary to forbid prosecutors and judges to accept guilty pleas to selected counts, to lesser included offenses, or to reduced charges. The Fifth Amendment does not reach so far.

Bram v. United States, 168 U.S. 532, 18 S.Ct. 183, 42 L.Ed. 568 (1897), held that the admissibility of a confession depended upon whether it was compelled within the meaning of the Fifth Amendment. To be admissible, a confession must be " 'free and voluntary: that is, must not be extracted by any sort of threats or violence, nor obtained by any direct or implied promises, however slight, nor by the exertion of any improper influence.' " 168 U.S., at 542–543, 18 S.Ct., at 187. More recently, Malloy v. Hogan, 378 U.S. 1, 84 S.Ct. 1489, 12 L.Ed.2d 653 (1964), carried forward the *Bram* definition of compulsion in the course of holding applicable to the States the Fifth Amendment privilege against compelled self-incrimination.

Bram is not inconsistent with our holding that Brady's plea was not compelled even though the law promised him a lesser maximum penalty if he did not go to trial. *Bram* dealt with a confession given by a defendant in custody, alone and unrepresented by counsel. In such circumstances, even a mild promise of leniency was deemed sufficient to bar the confession, not because the promise was an illegal act as such, but because defendants at such times are too sensitive to inducement and the possible impact on them too great to ignore and too difficult to assess. But *Bram* and its progeny did not hold that the possibly coercive impact of a promise of leniency could not be dissipated by the presence and advice of counsel, any more than Miranda v. Arizona, 384 U.S. 436, 86 S.Ct. 1602, 16 L.Ed.2d 694 (1966), held that the possibly coercive atmosphere of the police station could not be counteracted by the presence of counsel or other safeguards.

Brady's situation bears no resemblance to Bram's. Brady first pleaded not guilty; prior to changing his plea to guilty he was subjected to no threats or promises in face-to-face encounters with the authorities. He had competent counsel and full opportunity to assess the advantages and disadvantages of a trial as compared with those attending a plea of guilty; there was no hazard of an impulsive and improvident response to a seeming but unreal advantage. His plea of guilty was entered in open court and before a judge obviously sensitive to the requirements of the law with respect to guilty pleas. Brady's plea, unlike Bram's confession, was voluntary.

The standard as to the voluntariness of guilty pleas must be essentially that defined by Judge Tuttle of the Court of Appeals for the Fifth Circuit:

> " '[A] plea of guilty entered by one fully aware of the direct consequences, including the actual value of any commitments made to him by the court, prosecutor, or his own counsel, must stand unless induced by threats (or promises to discontinue improper harassment), misrepresentation (including unfulfilled or unfulfillable promises), or perhaps by promises that are by their nature improper as having no proper relationship to the prosecutor's business (e.g. bribes).' 242 F.2d at page 115."[5]

Under this standard, a plea of guilty is not invalid merely because entered to avoid the possibility of a death penalty.

III.

The record before us also supports the conclusion that Brady's plea was intelligently made. He was advised by competent counsel, he was made aware of the nature of the charge against him, and there was nothing to indicate that he was incompetent or otherwise not in control of his mental faculties; once his confederate had pleaded guilty and became available to testify, he chose to plead guilty, perhaps to ensure that he would face no more than life imprisonment or a term of years. Brady was aware of

---

5. Shelton v. United States, 246 F.2d 571, 572 n. 2 (C.A. 5th Cir.1957) (en banc), rev'd on confession of error on other grounds, 356 U.S. 26, 78 S.Ct. 563, 2 L.Ed.2d 579 (1958).

precisely what he was doing when he admitted that he had kidnapped the victim and had not released her unharmed.

It is true that Brady's counsel advised him that § 1201(a) empowered the jury to impose the death penalty and that nine years later in United States v. Jackson, supra, the Court held that the jury had no such power as long as the judge could impose only a lesser penalty if trial was to the court or there was a plea of guilty. But these facts do not require us to set aside Brady's conviction.

Often the decision to plead guilty is heavily influenced by the defendant's appraisal of the prosecution's case against him and by the apparent likelihood of securing leniency should a guilty plea be offered and accepted. Considerations like these frequently present imponderable questions for which there are no certain answers; judgments may be made that in the light of later events seem improvident, although they were perfectly sensible at the time. The rule that a plea must be intelligently made to be valid does not require that a plea be vulnerable to later attack if the defendant did not correctly assess every relevant factor entering into his decision. A defendant is not entitled to withdraw his plea merely because he discovers long after the plea has been accepted that his calculus misapprehended the quality of the State's case or the likely penalties attached to alternative courses of action. More particularly, absent misrepresentation or other impermissible conduct by state agents, a voluntary plea of guilty intelligently made in the light of the then applicable law does not become vulnerable because later judicial decisions indicate that the plea rested on a faulty premise. A plea of guilty triggered by the expectations of a competently counseled defendant that the State will have a strong case against him is not subject to later attack because the defendant's lawyer correctly advised him with respect to the then existing law as to possible penalties but later pronouncements of the courts, as in this case, hold that the maximum penalty for the crime in question was less than was reasonably assumed at the time the plea was entered.

The fact that Brady did not anticipate United States v. Jackson, supra, does not impugn the truth or reliability of his plea. We find no requirement in the Constitution that a defendant must be permitted to disown his solemn admissions in open court that he committed the act with which he is charged simply because it later develops that the State would have had a weaker case than the defendant had thought or that the maximum penalty then assumed applicable has been held inapplicable in subsequent judicial decisions.

This is not to say that guilty plea convictions hold no hazards for the innocent or that the methods of taking guilty pleas presently employed in this country are necessarily valid in all respects. This mode of conviction is no more foolproof than full trials to the court or to the jury. Accordingly, we take great precautions against unsound results, and we should continue to do so, whether conviction is by plea or by trial. We would have serious doubts about this case if the encouragement of guilty pleas by offers of leniency substantially increased the likelihood that defendants, advised by competent counsel, would falsely condemn themselves. But our view is to the contrary and is based on our expectations that courts will satisfy themselves that pleas of guilty are voluntarily and intelligently made by competent defendants with adequate advice of counsel and that there is nothing to question the accuracy and reliability of the defendants' admissions that they committed the crimes with which they are charged. In the case before us, nothing in the record impeaches Brady's plea or suggests that his admissions in open court were anything but the truth.

Although Brady's plea of guilty may well have been motivated in part by a desire to avoid a possible death penalty, we are convinced that his plea was voluntarily and intelligently made and we have no reason to doubt that his solemn admission of guilt was truthful.

Affirmed.

■ MR. JUSTICE BLACK, while adhering to his belief that United States v. Jackson, 390 U.S. 570, 88 S.Ct. 1209, 20 L.Ed.2d 138 was wrongly decided, concurs in the judgment and in substantially all of the opinion in this case.

* * *

[Mr. Justice Brennan, with whom Mr. Justice Douglas and Mr. Justice Marshall join, dissenting in Parker v. North Carolina, 397 U.S. 790, 90 S.Ct. 1474 (1970), which is omitted, and concurring in the result in Brady v. United States.]

In United States v. Jackson, 390 U.S. 570, 88 S.Ct. 1209, 20 L.Ed.2d 138 (1968), we held that the operative effect of the capital punishment provisions of the Federal Kidnaping Act was unconstitutionally "to discourage assertion of the Fifth Amendment right not to plead guilty and to deter exercise of the Sixth Amendment right to demand a jury trial." 390 U.S., at 581, 88 S.Ct., at 1216. The petitioners in these cases claim that they were the victims of the very vices we condemned in *Jackson*. Yet the Court paradoxically holds that each of the petitioners must be denied relief even if his allegations are substantiated. Indeed, the Court apparently holds that never, except perhaps in highly unrealistic hypothetical situations, will the constitutional defects identified in *Jackson* vitiate a guilty plea.[6] In so holding, the Court seriously undermines the rational underpinnings of *Jackson* and departs broadly from our prior approach to the determination of the voluntariness of guilty pleas and also confessions. This is merely one manifestation of a design to insulate all guilty pleas from subsequent attack no matter what influences induced them. I cannot acquiesce in this

---

6. The precise contours of the Court's theory, developed principally in Brady v. United States, are unclear. The Court initially states that "the possibility of a heavier sentence following a guilty verdict after a trial" is one of the "relevant circumstances" to be taken into account in determining the voluntariness of the guilty plea. ...Subsequently, however, after discussing its notion of voluntariness, the Court concludes that "a plea of guilty is not invalid merely because entered to avoid the possibility of a death penalty." ... Elsewhere the Court states that "there [is no] evidence that Brady was so gripped by fear of the death penalty or hope of leniency that he did not or could not, with the help of counsel, rationally weigh the advantages of going to trial against the advantages of pleading guilty." ... If the latter is what the Court deems to be the criterion of voluntariness, the holding is totally without precedent, for it has never been thought that an individual's mental state must border on temporary insanity before his confession or guilty plea can be found "involuntary."

wholesale retreat from the sound principles to which we have previously adhered.

* * *

There is some intimation in the Court's opinions in the instant cases that, at least with respect to guilty pleas, "involuntariness" covers *only* the narrow class of cases in which the defendant's will has been literally overborne. At other points, however, the Court apparently recognizes that the term "involuntary" has traditionally been applied to situations in which an individual, while perfectly capable of rational choice, has been confronted with factors that the government may not constitutionally inject into the decision-making process. ... [I]t has long been held that certain promises of leniency or threats of harsh treatment by the trial judge or the prosecutor unfairly burden or intrude upon the defendant's decision-making process. Even though the defendant is not necessarily rendered incapable of rational choice, his guilty plea nonetheless may be invalid.

Thus the legal concept of "involuntariness" has not been narrowly confined but refers to a surrender of constitutional rights influenced by considerations that the government cannot properly introduce. The critical question that divides the Court is what constitutes an impermissible factor, or, more narrowly in the context of these cases, whether the threat of the imposition of an unconstitutional death penalty is such a factor.

... [W]e have consistently taken great pains to insulate the accused from the more obvious and oppressive forms of physical coercion. Beyond this, in the analogous area of coerced confessions, for example, it has long been recognized that various psychological devices, some of a very subtle and sophisticated nature, may be employed to induce statements. Such influences have been condemned by this Court. ...

The Court's answer to the stringent criterion of voluntariness imposed by *Bram* and subsequent cases is that the availability of counsel to an accused effectively offsets the illicit influence upon him which threats or promises by the government may impose. Of course, the presence of counsel is a factor to be taken into account in any overall evaluation of the voluntariness of a confession or a guilty plea. However, it hardly follows that the support provided by counsel is sufficient by itself to insulate the accused from the effect of any threat or promise by the government.

It has frequently been held, for example, that a guilty plea induced by threats or promises by the trial judge is invalid because of the risk that the trial judge's impartiality will be compromised and because of the inherently unequal bargaining power of the judge and the accused. The assistance of counsel in this situation, of course, may improve a defendant's bargaining *ability*, but it does not alter the underlying inequality of *power*. Significantly, the Court explicitly refrains from expressing its views on that issue. ...This is an unfortunate omission, for judicial promises of leniency in return for a guilty plea provide a useful analogy to what has occurred in the instant cases. Here, the government has promised the accused, through the legislature, that he will receive a substantially reduced sentence if he pleads guilty. In fact, the legislature has simultaneously threatened the accused with the ultimate penalty—death—if he insists upon a jury trial and promised a penalty no greater than life imprisonment if he pleads guilty.

. . . In any particular case, therefore, the influence of this unconstitutional factor must necessarily be given weight in determining the voluntariness of a plea.

. . . [I]t is perfectly possible that a defendant pleaded guilty for reasons entirely unrelated to the penalty scheme, for example, because his guilt was clear or because he desired to spare himself and his family "the spectacle and expense of protracted courtroom proceedings." 390 U.S., at 584, 88 S.Ct., at 1217. The converse, however, is equally clear: not every defendant who pleaded guilty under the Act did so voluntarily, that is, uninfluenced by the highly coercive character of the penalty scheme. This much is merely the teaching of *Jackson.*

. . . Today the Court appears to distinguish sharply between a guilty plea that has been "encouraged" by the penalty scheme and one that has been entered "involuntarily."

* * *

Of course, whether in a given case the penalty scheme has actually exercised its pernicious influence so as to make a guilty plea involuntary can be decided only by consideration of the factors that actually motivated the defendant to enter his plea. If a particular defendant can demonstrate that the death penalty scheme exercised a significant influence upon his decision to plead guilty, then, under *Jackson,* he is entitled to reversal of the conviction based upon his illicitly produced plea.

* * *

We are dealing here with the legislative imposition of a markedly more severe penalty if a defendant asserts his right to a jury trial and a concomitant legislative promise of leniency if he pleads guilty. This is very different from the give-and-take negotiation common in plea bargaining between the prosecution and defense, which arguably possess relatively equal bargaining power. No such flexibility is built into the capital penalty scheme where the government's harsh terms with respect to punishment are stated in unalterable form.

Furthermore, the legislatively ordained penalty scheme may affect any defendant, even one with respect to whom plea bargaining is wholly inappropriate because his guilt is uncertain. Thus the penalty scheme presents a clear danger that the innocent, or those not clearly guilty, or those who insist upon their innocence, will be induced nevertheless to plead guilty. This hazard necessitates particularly sensitive scrutiny of the voluntariness of guilty pleas entered under this type of death penalty scheme.

The penalty schemes involved here are also distinguishable from most plea bargaining because they involve the imposition of death—the most severe and awesome penalty known to our law. This Court has recognized that capital cases are treated differently in some respects from noncapital cases. We have identified the threat of a death penalty as a factor to be given considerable weight in determining whether a defendant has deliberately waived his constitutional rights.

* * *

Parker comes here after denial of state post-conviction relief. The North Carolina courts have consistently taken the position that United States v. Jackson has no applicability to the former North Carolina capital punishment scheme. Thus, the merits of Parker's contention that his plea was motivated by the unconstitutional death penalty have not been considered by the state courts. I would, therefore, reverse the judgment of the North Carolina Court of Appeals and remand the *Parker* case to that court for proceedings not inconsistent with the principles elaborated herein.

* * *

An independent examination of the record in the instant case [*Brady*] convinces me that the conclusions of the lower courts are not clearly erroneous. Although Brady was aware that he faced a possible death sentence, there is no evidence that this factor alone played a significant role in his decision to enter a guilty plea. Rather, there is considerable evidence, which the District Court credited, that Brady's plea was triggered by the confession and plea decision of his codefendant and not by any substantial fear of the death penalty. Moreover, Brady's position is dependent in large measure upon his own assertions, years after the fact, that his plea was motivated by fear of the death penalty and thus rests largely upon his own credibility. For example, there is no indication, contemporaneous with the entry of the guilty plea, that Brady thought he was innocent and was pleading guilty merely to avoid possible execution. Furthermore, Brady's plea was accepted by a trial judge who manifested some sensitivity to the seriousness of a guilty plea and questioned Brady at length concerning his guilt and the voluntariness of the plea before it was finally accepted.

In view of the foregoing, I concur in the result reached by the Court in the *Brady* case.

NOTES

1. **Effect of illegally-obtained evidence on the validity of a guilty plea.** In both McMann v. Richardson and Parker v. North Carolina, the defendants urged that they had been coerced into giving police confessions and that their guilty pleas were the result of those confessions, i.e., "but for" the illegal coercion exerted upon them and the resulting confessions, they would not have pleaded guilty. A majority of the Court rejected this. Justice White, speaking for the Court in *McMann*, observed that the case did not involve "the situation where the circumstances that coerced the confession have abiding impact and also taint the plea. It is not disputed that in such cases a guilty plea is properly open to challenge." 397 U.S. at 767, 90 S.Ct. at 1447, 25 L.Ed.2d at 771. Emphasizing that the defendants in both cases were represented by counsel at the time they entered their plea, the majority held that a showing of a "but for" relationship between the coercion and the confession, on one hand, and the plea, on the other, was not sufficient. In explanation, Justice White stated in *McMann:*

> For the defendant who considers his confession involuntary and hence unusable against him at a trial, tendering a plea of guilty would seem a most improbable

alternative. The sensible course would be to contest his guilt, prevail on his confession claim at trial, on appeal, or, if necessary, in a collateral proceeding, and win acquittal, however guilty he might be. ... If he nevertheless pleads guilty the plea can hardly be blamed on the confession which in his view was inadmissible evidence and no proper part of the State's case. Since by hypothesis the evidence aside from the confession is weak and the defendant has no reasons of his own to plead, a guilty plea in such circumstances is nothing less than a refusal to present his federal claims to the state court in the first instance—a choice by the defendant to take the benefits, if any, of a plea of guilty and then to pursue his coerced-confession claim in collateral proceedings. Surely later allegations that the confession rendered his plea involuntary would appear incredible, and whether his plain bypass of state remedies was an intelligent act depends on whether he was so incompetently advised by counsel concerning the forum in which he should first present his federal claim that the Constitution will afford him another chance to plead.

A more credible explanation for a plea of guilty by a defendant who would go to trial except for his prior confession is his prediction that the law will permit his admissions to be used against him by the trier of fact. At least the probability of the State's being permitted to use the confession as evidence is sufficient to convince him that the State's case is too strong to contest and that a plea of guilty is the most advantageous course. Nothing in this train of events suggests that the defendant's plea, as distinguished from his confession, is an involuntary act. His later petition for collateral relief asserting that a *coerced* confession induced his plea is at most a claim that the admissibility of his confession was mistakenly assessed and that since he was erroneously advised, either under the then applicable law or under the law later announced, his plea was an unintelligent and voidable act. The Constitution, however, does not render pleas of guilty so vulnerable.

... [T]he decision to plead guilty before the evidence is in frequently involves the making of difficult judgments. All the pertinent facts normally cannot be known unless witnesses are examined and cross-examined in court. Even then the truth will often be in dispute. In the face of unavoidable uncertainty, the defendant and his counsel must make their best judgment as to the weight of the State's case. Counsel must predict how the facts, as he understands them, would be viewed by a court. If proved, would those facts convince a judge or jury of the defendant's guilt? On those facts would evidence seized without a warrant be admissible? Would the trier of fact on those facts find a confession voluntary and admissible? Questions like these cannot be answered with certitude; yet a decision to plead guilty must necessarily rest upon counsel's answers, uncertain as they may be. Waiving trial entails the inherent risk that the good-faith evaluations of a reasonably competent attorney will turn out to be mistaken either as to the facts or as to what a court's judgment might be on given facts.

That a guilty plea must be intelligently made is not a requirement that all advice offered by the defendant's lawyer withstand retrospective examination in a post-conviction hearing. Courts continue to have serious differences among themselves on the admissibility of evidence, both with respect to the proper standard by which the facts are to be judged and with respect to the application of that standard to particular facts. That this Court might hold a defendant's confession inadmissible in evidence, possibly by a divided vote, hardly justifies a conclusion that the defendant's attorney was incompetent or ineffective when he thought the admissibility of the confession sufficiently probable to advise a plea of guilty.

In our view a defendant's plea of guilty based on reasonably competent advice is an intelligent plea not open to attack on the ground that counsel may have misjudged the admissibility of the defendant's confession. Whether a plea of guilty is unintelligent and therefore vulnerable when motivated by a confession erroneously thought admissible in evidence depends as an initial matter, not on whether a court would retrospectively consider counsel's advice to be right or wrong, but on whether that advice was within the range of competence demanded of attorneys in criminal cases.

397 U.S. at 768–71, 90 S.Ct. at 1447–49, 25 L.Ed.2d at 772–73.

2. **Misunderstanding the deal.** The informality of plea bargaining has traditionally given rise to significant problems in determining whether a plea was sufficiently "intelligent" to meet constitutional or other standards. In Huffman v. State, 499 S.W.2d 565 (Mo.App.1973), for example, the defendant pleaded guilty to a reduced charge believing that his sentence would not exceed the two years' imprisonment recommended by the prosecution. No firm promises had been made to him, but he was advised by counsel and the prosecutor that although the judge need not follow the recommendation it was likely that the judge would do so. In denying relief to the defendant, the Missouri court explained:

> In State v. Rose, 440 S.W.2d 441 (Mo.1969), relied upon by appellant, the Missouri Supreme Court distinguished between the sort of things deemed misleading and those which are not when it said that there was a difference between "specific assurances and opinion or speculation based upon general court practice" and that a plea may be withdrawn for a defendant who reasonably relies on the former. . . . In the instant case there were no "positive representations" but only strongly expressed opinions by counsel and the prosecutor, always offered with the *caveat* that the trial court did not have to adopt the prosecutor's recommendation. . . . [A]ppellant had no reasonable basis to believe that a lesser sentence than he ultimately received was assured.

499 S.W.2d at 568. Suppose that defense counsel mistakenly believed that the prosecutor's recommendations would be binding on the court? See People v. Wright, 21 Ill.App.3d 301, 314 N.E.2d 733 (1974) (relief must be granted, because "a motion to withdraw a plea of guilty should be allowed upon a showing of misapprehension of the facts or law or of any misrepresentations by a person having apparent authority."). Suppose defense counsel misrepresents to the defendant that the court has committed itself to a given sentence? See Mosher v. Lavallee, 491 F.2d 1346 (2d Cir.1974) (where plea was stimulated by false statement to defendant by counsel that judge had promised given sentence relief, must be granted because of ineffective assistance of counsel).

Bordenkircher v. Hayes

Supreme Court of the United States, 1978.
434 U.S. 357, 98 S.Ct. 663, 54 L.Ed.2d 604.

■ MR. JUSTICE STEWART delivered the opinion of the Court.

The question in this case is whether the Due Process Clause of the Fourteenth Amendment is violated when a state prosecutor carries out a threat made during plea negotiations to reindict the accused on more serious charges if he does not plead guilty to the offense with which he was originally charged.

I.

The respondent, Paul Lewis Hayes, was indicted by a Fayette County, Ky., grand jury on a charge of uttering a forged instrument in the amount of $88.30, an offense then punishable by a term of two to 10 years in prison. Ky.Rev.Stat. § 434.130 (repealed 1974). After arraignment, Hayes, his retained counsel, and the Commonwealth's attorney met in the presence of the clerk of the court to discuss a possible plea agreement. During these conferences the prosecutor offered to recommend a sentence of five years in prison if Hayes would plead guilty to the indictment. He also said that if Hayes did not plead guilty and "save the court the inconvenience and necessity of a trial," he would return to the grand jury to seek an indictment under the Kentucky Habitual Criminal Act, then Ky.Rev.Stat. § 431.190 (repealed 1975), which would subject Hayes to a mandatory sentence of life imprisonment by reason of his two prior felony convictions. Hayes chose not to plead guilty, and the prosecutor did obtain an indictment charging him under the Habitual Criminal Act. It is not disputed that the recidivist charge was fully justified by the evidence, that the prosecutor was in possession of this evidence at the time of the original indictment, and that Hayes' refusal to plead guilty to the original charge was what led to his indictment under the habitual criminal statute.

A jury found Hayes guilty on the principal charge of uttering a forged instrument and, in a separate proceeding, further found that he had twice before been convicted of felonies. As required by the habitual offender statute, he was sentenced to a life term in the penitentiary. The Kentucky Court of Appeals rejected Hayes' constitutional objections to the enhanced sentence, holding in an unpublished opinion that imprisonment for life with the possibility of parole was constitutionally permissible in light of the previous felonies of which Hayes had been convicted, and that the prosecutor's decision to indict him as an habitual offender was a legitimate use of available leverage in the plea bargaining process.

On Hayes' petition for a federal writ of habeas corpus, the United States District Court for the Eastern District of Kentucky agreed that there had been no constitutional violation in the sentence or the indictment procedure, and denied the writ. The Court of Appeals for the Sixth Circuit reversed the District Court's judgment. . . .

It may be helpful to clarify at the outset the nature of the issue in this case. While the prosecutor did not actually obtain the recidivist indictment until after the plea conferences had ended, his intention to do so was clearly put forth at the outset of the plea negotiations. Hayes was thus fully informed of the true terms of the offer when he made his decision to plead not guilty. This is not a situation, therefore, where the prosecutor without notice brought an additional and more serious charge after plea negotiations relating only to the original indictment had ended with the defendant's insistence on pleading not guilty. As a practical matter, in short, this case would be no different if the grand jury had indicted Hayes as a recidivist from the outset, and the prosecutor had offered to drop that charge as part of the plea bargain.

* * *

This Court held in North Carolina v. Pearce, 395 U.S. 711, 725, 89 S.Ct. 2072, 2080, 23 L.Ed.2d 656, that the Due Process Clause of the Fourteenth Amendment "requires that vindictiveness against a defendant for having successfully attacked his first conviction must play no part in the sentence he receives after a new trial." The same principle was later applied to prohibit a prosecutor from reindicting a convicted misdemeanant on a felony charge after the defendant had invoked an appellate remedy, since in this situation there was also a "realistic likelihood of 'vindictiveness.'" Blackledge v. Perry [417 U.S. 21, at 27, 94 S.Ct. 2098, at 2102] [reprinted at page 907, supra].

In those cases the Court was dealing with the State's unilateral imposition of a penalty upon a defendant who had chosen to exercise a legal right to attack his original conviction—a situation "very different from the give-and-take negotiation common in plea bargaining between the prosecution and the defense, which arguably possess relatively equal bargaining power." The Court has emphasized that the due process violation in cases such as *Pearce* and *Perry* lay not in the possibility that a defendant might be deterred from the exercise of a legal right, but rather in the danger that the State might be retaliating against the accused for lawfully attacking his conviction. See Blackledge v. Perry, supra, 417 U.S., at 26–28, 94 S.Ct., at 2101–02.

To punish a person because he has done what the law plainly allows him to do is a due process violation of the most basic sort, and for an agent of the State to pursue a course of action whose objective is to penalize a person's reliance on his legal rights is "patently unconstitutional." But in the "give-and-take" of plea bargaining, there is no such element of punishment or retaliation so long as the accused is free to accept or reject the prosecution's offer.

Plea bargaining flows from "the mutuality of advantage" to defendants and prosecutors, each with his own reasons for wanting to avoid trial. Defendants advised by competent counsel and protected by other procedural safeguards are presumptively capable of intelligent choice in response to prosecutorial persuasion, and unlikely to be driven to false self-condemnation. Indeed, acceptance of the basic legitimacy of plea bargaining necessarily implies rejection of any notion that a guilty plea is involuntary in a constitutional sense simply because it is the end result of the bargaining process. By hypothesis, the plea may have been induced by promises of a recommendation of a lenient sentence or a reduction of charges, and thus by fear of the possibility of a greater penalty upon conviction after a trial.

While confronting a defendant with the risk of more severe punishment clearly may have a "discouraging effect on the defendant's assertion of his trial rights, the imposition of these difficult choices [is] an inevitable"—and permissible—"attribute of any legitimate system which tolerates and encourages the negotiation of pleas." It follows that, by tolerating and encouraging the negotiation of pleas, this Court has necessarily accepted as constitutionally legitimate the simple reality that the prosecutor's interest at the bargaining table is to persuade the defendant to forego his right to plead not guilty.

It is not disputed here that Hayes was properly chargeable under the recidivist statute, since he had in fact been convicted of two previous felonies. In our system, so long as the prosecutor has probable cause to believe that the accused committed an offense defined by statute, the decision whether or not to prosecute, and what charge to file or bring before a grand jury, generally rests entirely in his discretion.[7] Within the limits set by the legislature's constitutionally valid definition of chargeable offenses, "the conscious exercise of some selectivity in enforcement is not in itself a federal constitutional violation" so long as "the selection was [not] deliberately based upon an unjustifiable standard such as race, religion, or other arbitrary classification." To hold that the prosecutor's desire to induce a guilty plea is an "unjustifiable standard," which, like race or religion, may play no part in his charging decision, would contradict the very premises that underlie the concept of plea bargaining itself. Moreover, a rigid constitutional rule that would prohibit a prosecutor from acting forthrightly in his dealings with the defense could only invite unhealthy subterfuge that would drive the practice of plea bargaining back into the shadows from which it has so recently emerged.

There is no doubt that the breadth of discretion that our country's legal system vests in prosecuting attorneys carries with it the potential for both individual and institutional abuse. And broad though that discretion may be, there are undoubtedly constitutional limits upon its exercise. We hold only that the course of conduct engaged in by the prosecutor in this case, which no more than openly presented the defendant with the unpleasant alternatives of foregoing trial or facing charges on which he was plainly subject to prosecution, did not violate the Due Process Clause of the Fourteenth Amendment.

Accordingly, the judgment of the Court of Appeals is

Reversed.

■ MR. JUSTICE BLACKMUN, with whom MR. JUSTICE BRENNAN and MR. JUSTICE MARSHALL join, dissenting.

Prosecutorial vindictiveness, it seems to me, in the present narrow context, is the fact against which the Due Process Clause ought to protect. I perceive little difference between vindictiveness after what the Court describes ... as the exercise of a "legal right to attack his original conviction," and vindictiveness in the "give-and-take negotiation common in plea bargaining." Prosecutorial vindictiveness in any context is still prosecutorial vindictiveness. The Due Process Clause should protect an accused against it, however it asserts itself. The Court of Appeals rightly so held, and I would affirm the judgment.

It might be argued that it really makes little difference how this case, now that it is here, is decided. The Court's holding gives plea bargaining full sway despite vindictiveness. A contrary result, however, merely would prompt the aggressive prosecutor to bring the greater charge initially in

7. This case does not involve the constitutional implications of a prosecutor's offer during plea bargaining of adverse or lenient treatment for some person *other* than the accused, which might pose a greater danger of inducing a false guilty plea by skewing the assessment of the risks a defendant must consider.

every case, and only thereafter to bargain. The consequences to the accused would still be adverse, for then he would bargain against a greater charge, face the likelihood of increased bail, and run the risk that the court would be less inclined to accept a bargained plea. Nonetheless, it is far preferable to hold the prosecution to the charge it was originally content to bring and to justify in the eyes of its public.[8]

* * *

■ Mr. Justice Powell, dissenting.

Although I agree with much of the Court's opinion, I am not satisfied that the result in this case is just or that the conduct of the plea bargaining met the requirements of due process.

* * *

It seems to me that the question to be asked under the circumstances is whether the prosecutor reasonably might have charged respondent under the Habitual Criminal Act in the first place. The deference that courts properly accord the exercise of a prosecutor's discretion perhaps would foreclose judicial criticism if the prosecutor originally had sought an indictment under that act, as unreasonable as it would have seemed.[9] But here

---

8. That prosecutors, without saying so, may sometimes bring charges more serious than they think appropriate for the ultimate disposition of a case, in order to gain bargaining leverage with a defendant, does not add support to today's decision, for this Court, in its approval of the advantages to be gained from plea negotiations, has never openly sanctioned such deliberate overcharging or taken such a cynical view of the bargaining process. Normally, of course, it is impossible to show that this is what the prosecutor is doing, and the courts necessarily have deferred to the prosecutor's exercise of discretion in initial charging decisions.

Even if overcharging is to be sanctioned, there are strong reasons of fairness why the charges should be presented at the beginning of the bargaining process, rather than as a filliped threat at the end. First, it means that a prosecutor is required to reach a charging decision without any knowledge of the particular defendant's willingness to plead guilty; hence the defendant who truly believes himself to be innocent, and wishes for that reason to go to trial, is not likely to be subject to quite such a devastating gamble since the prosecutor has fixed the incentives for the average case.

Second, it is healthful to keep charging practices visible to the general public, so that political bodies can judge whether the policy being followed is a fair one. Visibility is en-

hanced if the prosecutor is required to lay his cards on the table with an indictment of public record at the beginning of the bargaining process, rather than making use of unrecorded verbal warnings of more serious indictments yet to come.

Finally, I would question whether it is fair to pressure defendants to plead guilty by threat of reindictment on an enhanced charge for the same conduct when the defendant has no way of knowing whether the prosecutor would indeed be entitled to bring him to trial on the enhanced charge. Here, though there is no dispute that respondent met the then current definition of a habitual offender under Kentucky law, it is conceivable that a properly instructed Kentucky grand jury, in response to the same considerations that ultimately moved the Kentucky Legislature to amend the habitual offender statute, would have refused to subject respondent to such an onerous penalty for his forgery charge. There is no indication in the record that, once the new indictment was obtained, respondent was given another chance to plead guilty to the forged check charge in exchange for a five year sentence.

9. The majority suggests … that this case cannot be distinguished from the case where the prosecutor initially obtains an indictment under an enhancement statute and later agrees to drop the enhancement charge in exchange for a guilty plea. I would agree the prosecutor evidently made a reasonable, responsible judgment not to subject an individual to a mandatory life sentence when his only new offense had societal implications as limited as those accompanying the uttering of a single $88 forged check and when the circumstances of his prior convictions confirmed the inappropriateness of applying the habitual criminal statute. I think it may be inferred that the prosecutor himself deemed it unreasonable and not in the public interest to put this defendant in jeopardy of a sentence of life imprisonment.

There may be situations in which a prosecutor would be fully justified in seeking a fresh indictment for a more serious offense. The most plausible justification might be that it would have been reasonable and in the public interest initially to have charged the defendant with the greater offense. In most cases a court could not know why the harsher indictment was sought, and an inquiry into the prosecutor's motive would neither be indicated nor likely to be fruitful. In those cases, I would agree with the majority that the situation would not differ materially from one in which the higher charge was brought at the outset. . . .

But this is not such a case. Here, any inquiry into the prosecutor's purpose is made unnecessary by his candid acknowledgement that he threatened to procure and in fact procured the habitual criminal indictment because of respondent's insistence on exercising his constitutional rights. We have stated in unequivocal terms, that "*Jackson* and *Pearce* are clear and subsequent cases have not diluted their force: if the only objective of a state practice is to discourage the assertion of constitutional rights it is 'patently unconstitutional.'" Chaffin v. Stynchcombe, 412 U.S. 17, 32 n. 20, 93 S.Ct. 1977, 1986, 36 L.Ed.2d 714 (1973). And in Brady v. United States, 397 U.S. 742, 90 S.Ct. 1463, 25 L.Ed.2d 747 (1970), we drew a distinction between the situation there approved and the "situation where the prosecutor or judge, or both, deliberately employ their charging and sentencing powers to induce a particular defendant to tender a plea of guilty." Id., at 751 n. 8, 90 S.Ct., at 1470.

The plea-bargaining process, as recognized by this Court, is essential to the functioning of the criminal-justice system. It normally affords genuine benefits to defendants as well as to society. And if the system is to work effectively, prosecutors must be accorded the widest discretion, within constitutional limits, in conducting bargaining. . . . This is especially true when a defendant is represented by counsel and presumably is fully advised of his rights. Only in the most exceptional case should a court conclude that the scales of the bargaining are so unevenly balanced as to arouse suspicion. In this case, the prosecutor's actions denied respondent due process because their admitted purpose was to discourage and then to penalize with unique severity his exercise of constitutional rights. Implementation of a

---

that these two situations would be alike *only if* it were assumed that the hypothetical prosecutor's decision to charge under the enhancement statute was occasioned not by consideration of the public interest but by a strategy to discourage the defendant from exercising his constitutional rights. In theory, I would condemn both practices. In practice, the hypothetical situation is largely unreviewable. The majority's view confuses the propriety of a particular exercise of prosecutorial discretion with its unreviewability. In the instant case, however, we have no problem of proof.

strategy calculated solely to deter the exercise of constitutional rights is not a constitutionally permissible exercise of discretion. I would affirm the opinion of the Court of Appeals on the facts of this case.

NOTES

1. **Statutory sentencing differentials.** Insofar as United States v. Jackson (discussed in Justice White's *Brady* opinion) prohibits imposition of a more severe penalty under a statutory scheme which penalizes exercise of the right to trial, has it survived the *Brady* trilogy and *Bordenkircher?* In Corbitt v. New Jersey, 439 U.S. 212, 99 S.Ct. 492, 58 L.Ed.2d 466 (1978), Corbitt was charged with first degree murder under New Jersey law. Under the applicable statutory provisions, if he was found guilty by a jury of that offense, a sentence of life imprisonment was mandatory. If a plea of no contest was accepted, however, the trial judge had discretion to sentence him to life imprisonment or to imprisonment for a term not to exceed thirty years. After a jury trial, Corbitt was convicted and received the mandatory sentence of life imprisonment. A majority of the Supreme Court rejected the argument that *Jackson* prohibited this. *Jackson,* Justice White reasoned for the majority, involved the death penalty, which is unique in its severity and irrevocability. Moreover, in *Corbitt* but not in *Jackson* an accused who pleaded not guilty (or no contest) could have received the same sentence as was mandated for conviction on a jury verdict. The choice which Corbitt faced under the New Jersey statutory scheme was not significantly different than the choices posed to the defendant by the prosecutor in *Bordenkircher.* The majority's language, however, leaves open the possibility that some statutory inducements to plead guilty may offend due process. "We hold only that a state may make due allowances for pleas in their sentencing decisions and that New Jersey has not exceeded its powers in this respect by its statutory provision extending the possibility of leniency to those who plead guilty in homicide cases." Further, "[W]e are unconvinced that the New Jersey statutory pattern exerts such a powerful influence to coerce inaccurate guilty pleas that it should be deemed constitutionally suspect." 439 U.S. at 225, 90 S.Ct. at 500, 58 L.Ed.2d at 478.

Justice Stewart, concurring in the judgment, found the distinction between statutory provisions for leniency and plea bargaining significant:

> It seems to me that there is a vast difference between the settlement of litigation through negotiation between counsel for the parties, and a state statute such as is involved in the present case. While a prosecuting attorney, acting as an advocate, necessarily must be able to settle an adversary criminal lawsuit through plea bargaining with his adversary a state legislature has a quite different function to perform. Could a state legislature provide that the penalty for every criminal offense to which a defendant pleads guilty is to be one-half the penalty to be imposed upon a defendant convicted of the same offense after a not guilty plea? I would suppose that such legislation would be clearly unconstitutional under United States v. Jackson.

439 U.S. at 227, 99 S.Ct. at 501–02, 58 L.Ed.2d at 479.

2. **Vindictive prosecution.** Should a "presumption of vindictiveness" apply to invalidate the bringing of more serious charges when a defendant has insisted on asserting rights to a jury trial on lesser charges? In United States v. Goodwin, 457 U.S. 368, 102 S.Ct. 2485, 73 L.Ed.2d 74 (1982), the defendant was charged with several misdemeanor offenses arising out of an assault upon a peace officer. The case was being handled by an attorney on loan from the Justice Department to the United States Attorney's office. Defendant insisted on a trial by jury, which resulted in transfer of the case from the federal Magistrate to the United States District

Court for trial. The case was also transferred to an Assistant United States Attorney for trial. He reviewed the facts and decided to file felony charges. On appeal from felony convictions, defendant contended that the prosecutorial action in this case violated the principles of Blackledge v. Perry. The Court of Appeals reversed the conviction on the ground that although there was no evidence of vindictiveness on the part of the prosecutor, a "presumption of vindictiveness" based on *Blackledge* should be applied in this case. The Supreme Court, in an opinion by Justice Stevens, reversed.

Justice Stevens distinguished *Blackledge* on the ground that it involved a re-trial of a case already tried and that is more likely to evoke prosecutorial vindictive-ness than is assertion of rights before trial by the defendant. Thus, this case is more like Bordenkircher v. Hayes. Since there was no evidence of actual vindictiveness, the reversal of the conviction would have to rest upon a presumption:

> There is good reason to be cautious before adopting an inflexible presump-tion of prosecutorial vindictiveness in a pretrial setting. In the course of preparing a case for trial, the prosecutor may uncover additional information that suggests a basis for further prosecution or he simply may come to realize that information possessed by the State has a broader significance. At this stage of the proceedings, the prosecutor's assessment of the proper extent of prosecu-tion may not have crystallized. In contrast, once a trial begins—and certainly by the time a conviction has been obtained—it is much more likely that the State has discovered and assessed all of the information against an accused and has made a determination, on the basis of that information, of the extent to which he should be prosecuted. Thus, a change in the charging decision made after an initial trial is completed is much more likely to be improperly motivated than is a pretrial decision.

457 U.S. at 381, 102 S.Ct. at 2492–93, 73 L.Ed.2d at 85–86. Justice Brennan, joined by Justice Marshall, dissented.

The Supreme Court applied the presumption of vindictiveness of *Blackledge* in Thigpen v. Roberts, 468 U.S. 27, 104 S.Ct. 2916, 82 L.Ed.2d 23 (1984). Following an accident in which he lost control of his vehicle and collided with another vehicle, killing a passenger in the other vehicle, respondent was charged with reckless driving, driving while his license was revoked, driving on the wrong side of the road and driving while intoxicated. He was convicted of those offenses before a justice of the peace and invoked his right to a trial de novo. While the cases were pending trial de novo he was indicted for involuntary manslaughter arising from the same accident. The State abandoned the misdemeanor charges and respondent was convicted of manslaughter. Ultimately, the Fifth Circuit set aside the manslaughter conviction on the ground it had been obtained in violation of respondent's right against double jeopardy. The Supreme Court, in an opinion by Justice White, affirmed the Court of Appeals on the ground that the manslaughter prosecution was vindictive under *Blackledge* and found it unnecessary to reach the double jeopardy question. The case was squarely controlled by *Blackledge* and the State made no effort to rebut the presumption of vindictiveness, but instead argued the inapplica-bility of that case. Justice Rehnquist dissented on the ground that the conviction was valid under the *Blockburger* test and that *Vitale* does not create a separate test for determining the same offense for jeopardy purposes. Justice O'Connor, joined by Justice Powell, dissented on the ground that jeopardy should be held not to attach to the first proceeding when the defendant has the absolute right to a trial *de novo*.

3. **Vindictive prosecution—interlocutory appeal.** If a defendant raises a question of prosecutorial vindictiveness prior to trial and the trial court rules against the claim, should he be entitled to take an interlocutory appeal on that issue? In United States v. Hollywood Motor Car Co., Inc., 458 U.S. 263, 102 S.Ct.

3081, 73 L.Ed.2d 754 (1982), the Supreme Court, in a per curiam opinion, held there should be no right of interlocutory appeal in that circumstance. Denial of a claim of prosecutorial vindictiveness, unlike a denial of a claim of double jeopardy (see Abney v. United States on p. 844 of Casebook) can be reviewed adequately by the appellate court following a conviction at trial. Any other decision would soon lead to piecemeal litigation:

> [T]here is a superficial plausibility to the contention that any claim, particularly a constitutional claim, that would be dispositive of the entire case if decided favorably to a criminal defendant, should be decided as quickly as possible in the course of the litigation. But if such a principle were to be applied ... the policy against piecemeal appeal in criminal cases would be swallowed by ever-multiplying exceptions.

458 U.S. at 270, 102 S.Ct. at 3085, 73 L.Ed.2d at 760. Justice Blackmun, joined by Justices Brennan and Marshall, dissented.

b.   TRIAL JUDGE PARTICIPATION

Frank v. Blackburn

United States Court of Appeals, Fifth Circuit (en banc), 1980.
646 F.2d 873, modified 646 F.2d 902 (5th Cir.1981).

■ FAY, CIRCUIT JUDGE.

A Louisiana state court jury convicted Jimmy Frank of armed robbery. A Louisiana state court judge sentenced him to thirty-three years in prison. In a petition for habeas corpus, Frank ... attacked the sentence on the ground that the trial judge impermissibly increased the term of confinement because Frank rejected a plea bargain offer and elected to stand trial. ...A majority of the en banc court now finds that no constitutional rights were violated in the conviction and sentencing of Jimmy Frank. ...

* * *

Jimmy Frank contends that because he elected to stand trial rather than plea bargain, his prison sentence on conviction was increased in violation of the fourteenth amendment. Once before the trial and once during a recess in the prosecution's case, the trial judge conducted a plea bargaining session in his chambers. Both the prosecutor and defense counsel participated in these sessions. On both occasions the judge, in response to a request from defense counsel, personally stated that he would sentence Frank to a period of twenty years confinement in return for a plea of guilty. Frank rejected both offers, stood trial, and was convicted by the jury, whereupon the judge imposed a sentence of thirty-three years in prison. Jimmy Frank alleges that the twenty year sentence offered in exchange for a guilty plea was increased by thirteen years after conviction solely to punish him for standing trial. ...

* * *

It should be emphasized that while Rule 11 requires the trial judge to play an active role in insuring that a defendant's guilty plea is voluntary, uncoerced, and made with knowledge of the consequences, the rule specifically prohibits the judge from assuming the role of an active negotiator in the plea bargaining process. See Fed.R.Crim.P. 11(e)(1). This prohibition against judicial participation in plea negotiations avoids the "chilling effect" such participation might have on a defendant's decision to either accept a plea bargain or go to trial. Several valid reasons for keeping the trial judge out of plea discussions have been noted:

> (1) judicial participation in the discussions can create the impression in the mind of the defendant that he would not receive a fair trial were he to go to trial before this judge; (2) judicial participation in the discussions makes it difficult for the judge objectively to determine the voluntariness of the plea when it is offered; (3) judicial participation to the extent of promising a certain sentence is inconsistent with the theory behind the use of the presentence investigation report; and (4) the risk of not going along with the disposition apparently desired by the judge may seem so great to the defendant that he will be induced to plead guilty even if innocent.

American Bar Association Project on Minimum Standards for Criminal Justice, Standards Relating To Pleas of Guilty, Commentary § 3.3(a).

* * *

A state court may not accept a guilty plea unless the defendant enters it voluntarily and with a complete understanding of the nature of the charge and the consequences of his plea. The general voluntary-intelligent standard for plea taking is rooted in the due process clauses of the Constitution and is therefore applicable in both state and federal courts. . . .

Because Rule 11 is not binding on the states, a federal court reviewing a state court plea bargain may only set aside a guilty plea or plea agreement which fails to satisfy due process. If a defendant understands the charges against him, understands the consequences of a guilty plea, and voluntarily chooses to plead guilty, without being coerced to do so, the guilty plea and any concomitant agreement will be upheld on federal review. . . .

* * *

We agree wholeheartedly with Frank's assertion that a defendant cannot be punished *simply* for exercising his constitutional right to stand trial. . . .

* * *

A panel of this court found that the record in this case demonstrated "that the judge lacked reason to increase defendant's sentence over what he proposed in the plea bargaining sessions. . . . With regard to the conduct of the defendant during the course of the robbery and his subsequent arrest, [the] testimony at the preliminary hearing was virtually identical with [the] testimony at trial. Thus, prior to the start of the trial itself, the judge had a virtually complete picture of the events on the night of the robbery." Frank v. Blackburn, 605 F.2d 910, 915 (5th Cir.1979). We find the panel's view of the record too narrow. While the general information in the hands of the judge at the time of plea bargaining may have been the same as at sentencing, we find persuasive the trial judge's assertion that "the Court had more graphic, descriptive and detailed evidence of the crime and the character of the individual at the time of sentencing." ...

* * *

Because the panel opinion placed special emphasis on the trial judge's *personal* involvement in the plea discussions in this case, we note that with respect to the responsibilities of the trial judge, the A.B.A. standards take the position that judicial participation in plea discussions is undesirable. See Pleas of Guilty § 3.3(a). Unlike Fed.R.Crim.P. 11, however, the standards recognize the propriety of procedures which, when requested by the parties and consented to by the trial judge, will also allow a greater degree of certainty when the proposed concessions involve the sentence or the dismissal of other charges before the court. Section 3.3(b) authorizes the trial judge to allow the prosecuting attorney and defense counsel to indicate to him in advance of the plea why they agree that certain concessions would be appropriate. The judge is then permitted to indicate whether he will concur in these concessions if the information in the presentence report is consistent with the representations made to him.

> This procedure, it must be emphasized, does not contemplate participation by the judge in the plea discussions. The judge only becomes involved after the parties have reached agreement, and thus there would appear to be little basis upon which the defendant or counsel could conclude that the judge is attempting to force a certain result upon the parties. Moreover, the judge does not initiate the conference; he is brought into the matter prior to tender of the plea only upon the request of the parties.

Pleas of Guilty, Commentary, § 3.3(b).

In the instant case, there is no record of the actual plea discussions which took place in the trial judge's chambers. The stipulation of the parties suggests, however, that it was defendant's counsel who asked the judge for a sentence proposal; presumably the prosecutor was willing to go along with the judge's proposal. Although we do not wholeheartedly approve of the plea proceedings which took place in the judge's chambers, we do not find the participation in this case to be constitutionally prohibited. ...

* * *

■ HILL, CIRCUIT JUDGE, with whom KRAVITCH, FRANK M. JOHNSON, JR., REAVLEY and THOMAS A. CLARK, CIRCUIT JUDGES, join, dissenting:

* * *

There is good reason for the exclusion of the court from plea bargain negotiation. Plea bargaining has been described as "give-and-take negotiation ... between the prosecution and defense, which arguably possess relatively equal bargaining power." Bordenkircher v. Hayes, 434 U.S. 357, 362, 98 S.Ct. 663, 667, 54 L.Ed.2d 604 (1978), quoting, Parker v. North

Carolina, 397 U.S. 790, 90 S.Ct. 1458, 25 L.Ed.2d 785 (1970) (opinion of Brennan, J.).

Equal bargaining power is essential to constitutionally valid plea bargaining. Indeed, the Supreme Court has stated that "plea bargaining flows from 'the mutuality of advantage' to defendants and prosecutors, each with his own reasons for wanting to avoid trial." Bordenkircher v. Hayes, 434 U.S. at 363, 98 S.Ct. at 668, quoting, Brady v. United States, 397 U.S. 742, 752, 90 S.Ct. 1463, 1471, 25 L.Ed.2d 747 (1970). Unless this mutual advantage exists the system breaks down; bargaining becomes coercion.

Of course, Jimmy Frank went to trial so there is no allegation of a coerced plea.[10] Coercing a plea, however, is only one way in which a trial judge may violate the Constitution by intruding into the plea bargaining process. Here, we are confronted with another. Specifically, we must decide under what circumstances a judge may impose a harsher penalty following conviction when he has previously "proposed" an appropriate sentence in exchange for a plea of guilty. I can come to no other conclusion but that North Carolina v. Pearce, 395 U.S. 711, 89 S.Ct. 2072, 23 L.Ed.2d 656 (1969) should control the outcome.

* * *

Several lessons emerge from [the] cases. First, under a *Pearce* analysis it is not necessary to demonstrate "actual retaliatory motivation." As previously discussed, that would be virtually impossible. Rather, the court should focus on the presence or absence of a "realistic likelihood of vindictiveness." In assessing such a likelihood, the Court has focused on those imposing the second sentence or taking the second action.

* * *

In the instant case the trial judge proposed a sentence of twenty years to defendant's counsel in exchange for a guilty plea. In so doing, he impaired his impartiality. In effect he became a third bargainer with a well-defined position. He had a "personal stake" in the process being resolved his way and therefore a "motivation to engage in self-vindication." Finally, he had an "institutional interest" in imposing punishment through the sentencing process to discourage what he may well have viewed as a meritless trial. In short, the very same indicia of vindictiveness that were present in *Pearce* are present here.

It should be made clear that I am not, as *Pearce* did not, presuming that the trial judge was vindictive. Rather, the "realistic likelihood" that he could have been compels the rule that he must affirmatively state his reasons for imposing a harsher sentence.

* * *

10. The facts of this case do not require us to determine to what extent a trial judge may constitutionally participate in the plea bargaining process. Here, it is enough to say that his participation has triggered the necessity for the constitutional protection announced in North Carolina v. Pearce, 395 U.S. 711, 89 S.Ct. 2072, 23 L.Ed.2d 656 (1969).

■ RUBIN, CIRCUIT JUDGE, with whom RANDALL, CIRCUIT JUDGE, joins, dissenting.

* * *

... A trial judge who joins in sentence bargaining enters the contest with infinitely greater bargaining power than the accused. He is seldom completely neutral: absent public interest in the trial of a particular case, it is in his interest to dispose of cases without trial and, thus, to clear his docket with minimal effort. If he may offer the defendant a deal in return for a guilty plea, and then, when this proffer is rejected, impose a greater sentence, without stated and justifiable reasons, he not only exerts coercive pressure on the accused but affects detrimentally the administration of justice in his court. The criminal defense cogniscenti will quickly learn that, when this judge's proffer is rejected, the defendant, if convicted, will pay a higher price. It is a denial of due process for the judge thus to stain his robes.

NOTES

1. **Acknowledgement of guilt.** On petition for rehearing, the court deleted the following sentence from its discussion concerning the justification for the thirty-three year sentence:

> Even if the trial provided no additional evidence of character, the mere fact that Jimmy Frank refused to acknowledge his guilt and showed no willingness to assume responsibility for his conduct may have led the judge to conclude that this defendant lacked potential for rehabilitation thus justifying the imposition of a greater sentence than that offered in exchange for a guilty plea.

646 F.2d 902 (5th Cir.1981) (on petition for rehearing). Judge Hill observed that the sentence was deleted "presumably ... because the Majority ... concluded that it does not state the law." 646 F.2d at 902 (Hill, J., dissenting).

2. **Right to know of likely sentence differential.** If disparity routinely exists between sentences upon plea or trial, should the defendant have the right to know before making his choice? In United States v. Harris, 635 F.2d 526 (6th Cir.1980), it was disclosed that the probation officer routinely gave a pretrial sentence recommendation to the prosecutor but not to the defense. In *Harris* the prosecutor disclosed to the defense that probation would recommend 3 years on a guilty plea and 5 years on a conviction upon trial. The Court upheld the conviction and sentence since the defendant chose to go to trial despite the sentence recommendation information; and there was no evidence in the record that the District Court was influenced by the pretrial recommendation of the probation officer when it sentenced appellant. As to the practice mentioned, despite its holding, the Court stated:

> Using the probation officer's recommendation to try to persuade the defendant to plead guilty involves the court in the plea bargaining process as the probation office is an arm of the court. While participation of the trial judge in plea negotiations may not amount to a constitutional violation which justifies overturning a guilty plea ..., Rule 11(e)(1), Fed.R.Crim.Pro., forbids the court from participating in plea negotiations. Under Rule 11, the judge's role is limited to acceptance or rejection of the plea agreement after a thorough review of the relevant factors; the judge should not participate in the plea bargaining

process. ...Thus, the judge could not tell the defendant prior to accepting a guilty plea what sentence he would likely give should the plea be accepted. ...

In the present case, the judge himself did not make any representations to the defendant. However, the probation officer who is an arm of the court did so. His recommendation has the weight of the court behind it. If the court puts its imprimatur on a plea offer, the defendant might be coerced into taking it, fearing rejection would mean the imposition of a greater sentence after trial or that he would not get a fair trial before the judge whom he has challenged. ...The trial court must not penalize the defendant for exercising his constitutional right to plead not guilty and go to trial; whether or not the defendant exercises his right to trial must have no bearing on the sentence he receives. ...By having the probation officer recommend one sentence for pleading guilty and another sentence for going to trial, the court will be seen as considering whether or not the defendant exercises his right to trial in determining the sentence and the defendant may well feel pressured to plead guilty....

In the future, ... District Judges should not disclose the probation officer's sentence recommendations to either the defendant or the attorney for the government prior to trial or the acceptance of a guilty or a nolo contendere plea, where the recommendation could in any way affect a defendant's decision to plead guilty or go to trial.

635 F.2d at 528–29.

c.   PLEADING GUILTY WITHOUT ADMITTING GUILT

A plea of guilty usually constitutes an admission by the defendant that he has in fact committed a crime. Acceptance of the plea and sentencing then follow logically from the defendant's admission of guilt. Occasionally, however, a defendant pleads guilty but at the same time claims that he is innocent. In that case, a plea of guilty is patently not an admission of factual guilt, and the judge must decide whether the law allows the acceptance of a guilty plea under these circumstances.

North Carolina v. Alford

Supreme Court of the United States, 1970.
400 U.S. 25, 91 S.Ct. 160, 27 L.Ed.2d 162.

■ MR. JUSTICE WHITE delivered the opinion of the Court.

On December 2, 1963, Alford was indicted for first-degree murder, a capital offense under North Carolina law. The court appointed an attorney to represent him, and this attorney questioned all but one of the various witnesses who appellee said would substantiate his claim of innocence. The witnesses, however, did not support Alford's story but gave statements that strongly indicated his guilt. Faced with strong evidence of guilt and no substantial evidentiary support for the claim of innocence, Alford's attorney recommended that he plead guilty, but left the ultimate decision to Alford himself. The prosecutor agreed to accept a plea of guilty to a charge of second-degree murder, and on December 10, 1963, Alford pleaded guilty to the reduced charge.

Before the plea was finally accepted by the trial court, the court heard the sworn testimony of a police officer who summarized the State's case.

Two other witnesses besides Alford were also heard. Although there was no eyewitness to the crime, the testimony indicated that shortly before the killing Alford took his gun from his house, stated his intention to kill the victim and returned home with the declaration that he had carried out the killing. After the summary presentation of the State's case, Alford took the stand and testified that he had not committed the murder but that he was pleading guilty because he faced the threat of the death penalty if he did not do so. In response to the questions of his counsel, he acknowledged that his counsel had informed him of the difference between second-and first-degree murder and of his rights in case he chose to go to trial. The trial court then asked appellee if, in light of his denial of guilt, he still desired to plead guilty to second-degree murder and appellee answered, "Yes, sir. I plead guilty on—from the circumstances that he [Alford's attorney] told me." After eliciting information about Alford's prior criminal record, which was a long one, the trial court sentenced him to 30 years' imprisonment, the maximum penalty for second-degree murder.

* * *

Ordinarily, a judgment of conviction resting on a plea of guilty is justified by the defendant's admission that he committed the crime charged against him and his consent that judgment be entered without a trial of any kind. The plea usually subsumes both elements, and justifiably so, even though there is no separate, express admission by the defendant that he committed the particular acts claimed to constitute the crime charged in the indictment. Here Alford entered his plea but accompanied it with the statement that he had not shot the victim.

If Alford's statements were to be credited as sincere assertions of his innocence, there obviously existed a factual and legal dispute between him and the State. Without more, it might be argued that the conviction entered on his guilty plea was invalid, since his assertion of innocence negatived any admission of guilt, which, as we observed last Term in *Brady*, is normally "[c]entral to the plea and the foundation for entering judgment against the defendant. . . ."397 U.S. at 748.

In addition to Alford's statement, however, the court had heard an account of the events on the night of the murder, including information from Alford's acquaintances that he had departed from his home with his gun stating his intention to kill and that he had later declared that he had carried out his intention. Nor had Alford wavered in his desire to have the trial court determine his guilt without a jury trial. Although denying the charge against him, he nevertheless preferred the dispute between him and the State to be settled by the judge in the context of a guilty plea proceeding rather than by a formal trial. Thereupon, with the State's telling evidence and Alford's denial before it, the trial court proceeded to convict and sentence Alford for second-degree murder.

State and lower federal courts are divided upon whether a guilty plea can be accepted when it is accompanied by protestations of innocence and hence contains only a waiver of trial but no admission of guilt. . . .

* * *

Implicit in the *nolo contendere* cases is a recognition that the Constitution does not bar imposition of a prison sentence upon an accused who is unwilling expressly to admit his guilt but who, faced with grim alternatives, is willing to waive his trial and accept the sentence.

These cases would be directly in point if Alford had simply insisted on his plea but refused to admit the crime. The fact that his plea was denominated a plea of guilty rather than a plea of *nolo contendere* is of no constitutional significance with respect to the issue now before us, for the Constitution is concerned with the practical consequences, not the formal categorizations of state law. ... Thus, while most pleas of guilty consist of both a waiver of trial and an express admission of guilt, the latter element is not a constitutional requisite to the imposition of criminal penalty. An individual accused of crime may voluntarily, knowingly, and understandingly consent to the imposition of a prison sentence even if he is unwilling or unable to admit his participation in the acts constituting the crime.

Nor can we perceive any material difference between a plea which refuses to admit commission of the criminal act and a plea containing a protestation of innocence when, as in the instant case, a defendant intelligently concludes that his interests require entry of a guilty plea and the record before the judge contains strong evidence of actual guilt. Here the State had a strong case of first-degree murder against Alford. Whether he realized or disbelieved his guilt, he insisted on his plea because in his view he had absolutely nothing to gain by a trial and much to gain by pleading. Because of the overwhelming evidence against him, a trial was precisely what neither Alford nor his attorney desired. Confronted with the choice between a trial for first-degree murder, on the one hand, and a plea of guilty to second-degree murder, on the other, Alford quite reasonably chose the latter and thereby limited the maximum penalty to a 30–year term. When his plea is viewed in light of the evidence against him, which substantially negated his claim of innocence and which further provided a means by which the judge could test whether the plea was being intelligently entered,[11] its validity cannot be seriously questioned. In view of the strong factual basis for the plea demonstrated by the State and Alford's clearly expressed desire to enter it despite his professed belief in his innocence, we hold that the trial judge did not commit constitutional error in accepting it.[12]

---

11. Because of the importance of protecting the innocent and of insuring that guilty pleas are a product of free and intelligent choice, various state and federal court decisions properly caution that pleas coupled with claims of innocence should not be accepted unless there is a factual basis for the plea, ...

In the federal courts, Rule 11 of the Criminal Rules expressly provides that a court "shall not enter a judgment upon a plea of guilty unless it is satisfied that there is a factual basis for the plea."

12. Our holding does not mean that a trial judge must accept every constitutionally valid guilty plea merely because a defendant wishes so to plead. A criminal defendant does not have an absolute right under the Constitution to have his guilty plea accepted by the court, although the States may by statute or otherwise confer such a right. Likewise, the States may bar their courts from accepting guilty pleas from any defendants who assert their innocence. Cf. Fed.Rule Crim.Proc. 11, which gives a trial judge discretion to "refuse to accept a plea of guilty. ..." We need not now delineate the scope of that discretion.

... Alford now argues in effect that the State should not have allowed him this choice but should have insisted on proving him guilty of murder in the first degree. The States in their wisdom may take this course by statute or otherwise and may prohibit the practice of accepting pleas to lesser included offenses under any circumstances. But this is not the mandate of the Fourteenth Amendment and the Bill of Rights. The prohibitions against involuntary or unintelligent pleas should not be relaxed, but neither should an exercise in arid logic render those constitutional guarantees counterproductive and put in jeopardy the very human values they were meant to preserve.

The Court of Appeals for the Fourth Circuit was in error to find Alford's plea of guilty invalid because it was made to avoid the possibility of the death penalty. That court's judgment directing the issuance of the writ of habeas corpus is vacated and the case is remanded to the Court of Appeals for further proceedings consistent with this opinion.

It is so ordered.

[The dissenting opinion of Mr. Justice Brennan, with whom Justices Douglas and Marshall joined, is omitted.]

NOTES

1. **Resistance to *Alford* pleas.** Despite *Alford,* Alschuler, The Defense Attorney's Role in Plea Bargaining, 84 Yale L.J. 1179, 1279–80 (1975), notes, many attorneys refuse to permit clients who deny guilt to plead guilty. In part, this is due to the reluctance of trial judges to accept so-called *Alford* pleas. Public defenders, he observes, appeared to be less willing than private attorneys to permit pleas of this sort, perhaps because public defenders are more vulnerable to post-conviction claims of ineffective assistance of counsel. But even lawyers with policies against *Alford* pleas often report exceptions. Some distinguished between "pro forma" and "bona fide" protestations of innocence, and refused to cooperate in *Alford* pleas only in the case of the latter. In addition, some saw no objection to an *Alford* plea if the client acknowledged the conduct constituting the crime but claimed a defense, such as self-defense, entrapment, or the like. Id., at 1281.

2. **Should there be a right to enter an *Alford* plea?** What, if any, right should a defendant have to enter an *Alford* plea? Alschuler, The Defense Attorney's Role in Plea Bargaining, 84 Yale L.J. 1179, 1301 (1975), points out that *Alford* itself poses no bar to judicial rejection of such pleas. This results, he argues, in some defendants being denied the benefits of a plea because they are unwilling to mouth the "magic words" acknowledging guilt and constitutes unjustified unequal treatment. One possible solution, he notes, is to continue to recognize judicial discretion to refuse such pleas, but to require the judge—if the defendant is ultimately convicted—to impose a sentence no more severe than would have been imposed if the *Alford* plea had been accepted. Id., at 1303–04.

3. ROLE OF THE TRIAL JUDGE IN ACCEPTING OR REJECTING THE PLEA

Once a defendant has decided to plead guilty, whether following plea bargaining or not, a judge must decide whether the plea is legally acceptable. This subsection deals with some of the issues involved in a judge's rejection of a negotiated plea.

United States v. Ammidown

United States Court of Appeals, District of Columbia Circuit, 1973.
497 F.2d 615, 162 U.S.App.D.C. 28.

■ Leventhal, Circuit Judge.

In this unusual case the trial judge rejected a plea bargain struck between the prosecution and the defense on the ground that the public interest required that the defendant be tried on a greater charge. Under the facts presented we hold that the trial judge exceeded his discretion and accordingly reverse.

I.

In a case of extraordinary notoriety, Robert L. Ammidown was charged with first degree murder and conspiracy to commit murder in the death of his wife. Ammidown admitted that a month previous he arranged to have her murdered. . . . At the last minute he changed his mind, ... [A]ccording to his written confession, Ammidown and an associate, Richard Anthony Lee, devised a plan whereby Lee would abduct Mrs. Ammidown and by threat to her life extort a sum of money to be used by Ammidown and Lee to make the down payment for a club on the Eastern Shore of Maryland.

. . .

[A]t the prearranged spot, Lee jumped into Ammidown's car and directed him to drive to the East Capitol Street Bridge, where Lee dragged Mrs. Ammidown from the car and raped her, as planned, to impress Mrs. Ammidown "with the seriousness of the threat."

What then happened was that Lee killed Mrs. Ammidown. Ammidown did not confess to complicity in the murder.

Just prior to trial, the United States Attorney and Ammidown entered into this agreement: Ammidown would plead guilty to second degree murder, and the first degree murder charge would be dismissed. There was no agreement for the prosecutor to recommend sentence less than the maximum, life imprisonment. Ammidown, then aged 49, had no possibility of being even considered for parole for 15 years. Ammidown agreed to testify in the grand jury proceedings and impending trial of Lee, a much younger man, who was believed by the prosecution to be involved in another murder.

The trial judge, however, refused to approve the agreement and accept the lesser plea. With full understanding of the prosecutor's concern with the importance of Ammidown's agreement in connection with its successful prosecution of Lee, the court nonetheless decided that under Rule 11 of the Federal Rules of Criminal Procedure it had the discretion to refuse the plea when it found that the crime was so heinous and the evidence of guilt so overwhelming that the public interest would be ill-served by a judgment of second degree murder, which it referred to as a "tap on the wrist." Appellant then pleaded not guilty to first degree and second degree murder; at trial he was convicted of first degree murder and felony murder and sentenced to two terms of life imprisonment, to run consecutively.

Appellant now asserts that the failure of the trial court to accept his proffered plea of guilty to second degree murder constituted reversible error, and asks this court to remand with instructions to enter a judgment of second degree murder. The Government has decided that it could not in good conscience oppose the appellant; consequently, the position of the trial judge has been ably presented by . . . [counsel].

II.

[Despite the absence of any specific provision in Rule 11, the court concluded that the District Judge did have discretion to reject a plea based upon a bargain agreed to by both the government and the defense. Rule 11 now explicitly provides for this. In developing a foundation for the authority to reject the plea, the court noted that the functional effect of accepting the plea would be to dismiss the charge of first degree murder. Under Fed.R.Crim.P. 48(a), dismissal of an indictment requires leave of the court. Turning to the caselaw concerning the District Court's authority under Rule 48(a), the court noted that some decisions involve situations in which the defendant concurs in the government's motion to dismiss but the court is concerned whether dismissal would adequately protect the public. These decisions, the court concluded, contain some principles useful in addressing the manner in which the discretionary power to reject a bargained plea should be exercised. Editors.]

. . . [I]n the exercise of its responsibility, the court will not be content with a mere conclusory statement by the prosecutor that dismissal is in the public interest, but will require a statement of reasons and underlying factual basis. . . . [T]he court does not have primary responsibility, but rather the role of guarding against abuse of prosecutorial discretion. The rule contemplates exposure of the reasons for dismissal "in order to prevent abuse of the uncontrolled power of dismissal previously enjoyed by prosecutors," and in pursuance of this purpose "to gain the Court's favorable discretion, it should be satisfied that the reasons advanced for the proposed dismissal are substantial."

In this context, it may be helpful to note the considerations, other than protection of defendant, that have been taken into account by courts. If the reason is that the evidence is not sufficient to warrant prosecution, the court recognizes that the responsibility is on the prosecution and is satisfied "if there is a considered judgment," and an application made in good faith, unless it appears that the assigned reason for the dismissal has no basis in fact. In one case, a district court stated that a complete dismissal of charges against an individual, amply supported by the evidence, was not properly grounded in the consideration that the defendant corporation of which he was president would comply with ecology laws. Without commenting on that opinion as such, we note that it expressly recognized that a different consideration applies when the case is not entirely dismissed as to a defendant but he has received a substantial sentence for a phase of the same offense. And of course that is the situation that is involved when there is no dismissal simpliciter, but a plea of guilty to a lesser included offense like second degree murder.

Of particular significance to the case at bar is that even a court which would not accept an unexplained motion for dismissal determined, on reconsideration, that it was satisfied with the prosecutor's subsequent explanation that prejudice would likely be worked upon the Government in another criminal action.

C.

The third element of a plea bargain involving a plea to a lesser included offense, and indeed the most frequent motive behind it, is to circumscribe the judge's discretion in pronouncing sentence. See D. Newman, Conviction 105 (1966). The negotiated plea reduces the upper and lower limits of the range of sentence available to the judge. It is axiomatic that, within the limits imposed by the legislature, imposition of sentence is a matter for discretion of the trial judge. The prosecutor has no role beyond the advisory, and even that is frowned on in the District Court for the District of Columbia. We hesitate to say, therefore, that the United States Attorney and the defendant can by plea manipulate this traditional power of the judge without any recourse by the judge permitting him to forestall gross abuses of prosecutorial discretion.

D.

We have identified that both the District Judge and the United States Attorney have roles in the plea bargaining process. What is required is an effort to harmonize their responsibilities, and to suggest a standard for determining when judicial intervention may be proper.

We start with the presumption that the determination of the United States Attorney is to be followed in the overwhelming number of cases. He alone is in a position to evaluate the government's prosecution resources and the number of cases it is able to prosecute.

Where vigorous prosecution of one case threatens to undermine successful prosecution of another, it has traditionally been the prosecutor who determines which case will be pressed to conclusion, and his decision has been given great deference by the courts.

On the other hand, we do not think Rule 48(a) intends the trial court to serve merely as a rubber stamp for the prosecutor's decision. We agree that "the judge should be satisfied that the agreement adequately protects the public interest". Newman, supra, at 136; The Challenge of Crime in a Free Society: Report of the President's Commission on Law Enforcement & Administration of Justice 118 (1966).

We now state what, in our view, are the appropriate doctrines governing trial judges in considering whether to deny approval either to dismissals of cases outright or to the diluted dismissal—a guilty plea to a lesser included offense.

First, the trial judge must provide a reasoned exercise of discretion in order to justify a departure from the course agreed on by the prosecution and defense. This is not a matter of absolute judicial prerogative. The authority has been granted to the judge to assure protection of the public interest, and this in turn involves one or more of the following components: (a) fairness to the defense, such as protection against harassment; (b) fairness to the prosecution interest, as in avoiding a disposition that does not serve due and legitimate prosecutorial interests; (c) protection of the sentencing authority reserved to the judge. The judge's statement or opinion must identify the particular interest that leads him to require an unwilling defendant and prosecution to go to trial.

We now turn to the content of these components, and begin by passing any discussion of fairness to the defense, since it is not directly involved in the case at bar and it has already been identified in the precedent referred to earlier in this opinion. As to fairness to the prosecution interest, here we have a matter in which the primary responsibility, obviously, is that of the prosecuting attorney. The District Court cannot disapprove of his action on the ground of incompatibility with prosecutive responsibility unless the judge is in effect ruling that the prosecutor has abused his discretion. The requirement of judicial approval entitles the judge to obtain and evaluate the prosecutor's reasons. . . . The judge may withhold approval if he finds that the prosecutor has failed to give consideration to factors that must be given consideration in the public interest, factors such as the deterrent aspects of the criminal law. However, trial judges are not free to withhold approval of guilty pleas on this basis merely because their conception of the public interest differs from that of the prosecuting attorney. The question is not what the judge would do if he were the prosecuting attorney, but whether he can say that the action of the prosecuting attorney is such a departure from sound prosecutorial principle as to mark it an abuse of prosecutorial discretion.

In like vein, we note that a judge is free to condemn the prosecutor's agreement as a trespass on judicial authority only in a blatant and extreme case. In ordinary circumstances, the change in grading of an offense presents no question of the kind of action that is reserved for the judiciary.

Applying these tests to the case at bar, we find the record establishes beyond all doubt that the United States Attorney considered, indeed agonized over, the public interest and concluded that it was best served by assuring a successful prosecution of Lee—"a young man . . . a killer."

* * *

The trial judge was not free to disapprove this assessment by the prosecutor without both stating his reasons and determining that the prosecutor abused his discretion. Neither of these elements appears in the case at bar. The trial judge provided no statement of reasons, and such colloquy as appears indicates that the judge assumed that the correct test was what the judge independently considered best in the public interest.

When we come to the possible ground of intrusion on the sentencing function of the trial judge, we have a consideration that is interdependent of the other. That is to say, a dropping of an offense that might be taken as an intrusion on the judicial function if it were not shown to be related to a prosecutorial purpose takes on an entirely different coloration if it is explained to the judge that there was a prosecutorial purpose, an insufficiency of evidence, a doubt as to the admissibility of certain evidence under exclusionary rules, a need for evidence to bring another felon to justice, or other similar consideration.

III.

Because the trial judge did not provide a statement of reasons based on intrusion on the sentencing authority of the judge, it would be necessary to remand in any event. At the time the judge took the action appealed from, first degree murder was punishable by death, and second degree murder by a maximum of life imprisonment. We need not consider what kind of remand we might have provided if that kind of sentencing disparity were in effect at the present time. For the Supreme Court's decision in Furman v. Georgia, 408 U.S. 238, 92 S.Ct. 2726, 33 L.Ed.2d 346 (1972), has established the unavailability of the death sentence for appellant. We are required to accompany our reversal for lack of requisite findings with a disposition in the interest of justice, that takes into account current conditions.

The situation as it stands today is such that we cannot conceive that if the trial judge were required to provide a current reassessment of the problem in the light of the standards set forth in this opinion, he could justify his rejection of the first degree murder reversal and of the second degree murder plea as reflecting a sentence disparity so blatant as to constitute an intrusion upon the judicial domain. The life sentence is mandatory on a conviction for first degree murder, and discretionary with the court on a conviction for murder in the second degree. Parole is available after a minimum of 20 years in the case of first degree murder, and after a minimum of 15 years in the case of murder in the second degree. The difference is insufficient by itself to warrant judicial rejection of a properly bargained plea of guilty to murder in the second degree on the ground of undue interference with the sentencing domain of the judiciary.

Our duty as a court of appeals calls on us to reverse the action of the trial judge, but we think it only appropriate to accompany our action with an explicit statement that we are fully sensitive to his revulsion concerning this sordid crime. . . . If the decision were for the trial judge alone to make, his sentiment that the interest of justice called for trial on a charge of first degree murder would be conclusive. But our responsibility to apply the law calls on us to take into account both that a decision of the prosecutor was also involved and that substantial reasons undergirded his conclusion that the overriding public interest called for a certainty in the riddance of the hired gun.

For the reasons stated, the judgment and sentence on a conviction of murder in the first degree is vacated and the case remanded with instructions to accept appellant's plea of guilty to second degree murder.

NOTES

1. **Scope of judicial discretion to reject the deal.** Other courts have regarded the standard adopted in *Ammidown* as excessively deferential to the prosecution. In United States v. Bean, 564 F.2d 700 (5th Cir.1977), the court observed that to its knowledge, no other federal circuit had followed *Ammidown* in so drastically limiting the discretion of the judge. The *Bean* court held that in considering offered plea bargains, courts "may be governed by the same broad standards that apply in sentencing." 564 F.2d at 703. Therefore,

A decision that a plea bargain will result in the defendant's receiving too light a sentence under the circumstances of the case is a sound reason for the judge's refusing to accept the agreement. . . . Rule 11 does not compel a judge to impose an inappropriate sentence.

564 F.2d at 704.

2. **Accepting pleas over prosecutor's objection.** Does—or should—a trial court have the authority to permit a defendant to plead guilty to some but not all offenses charged or to a less serious offense than that charged if the prosecutor objects? See Genesee County Prosecutor v. Genesee Circuit Judge, 391 Michigan 115, 215 N.W.2d 145 (1974), holding that no such authority existed under Michigan law. If a trial judge accepts such a plea despite his lack of formal authority to do so, does double jeopardy permit the prosecution to obtain appellate relief and try the defendant on the greater charge (or all of the charges)?

4. THE NECESSITY OF RESPECTING A BARGAIN ONCE MADE

Changed circumstances or simple reconsideration may make a plea bargain less attractive to either the prosecutor or the defendant than it was when the bargain was initially reached. This subsection discusses the consequences of a party's failure to adhere to the agreed-upon bargain.

Santobello v. New York

Supreme Court of the United States, 1971.
404 U.S. 257, 92 S.Ct. 495, 30 L.Ed.2d 427.

■ MR. CHIEF JUSTICE BURGER delivered the opinion of the Court.

We granted certiorari in this case to determine whether the State's failure to keep a commitment concerning the sentence recommendation on a guilty plea required a new trial.

The facts are not in dispute. The State of New York indicted petitioner in 1969 on two felony counts, Promoting Gambling in the First Degree, and Possession of Gambling Records in the First Degree, N.Y. Penal Law, McKinney's Consol.Laws, c. 40, §§ 225.10, 225.20. Petitioner first entered a plea of not guilty to both counts. After negotiations, the Assistant District Attorney in charge of the case agreed to permit petitioner to plead guilty to a lesser-included offense, Possession of Gambling Records in the Second Degree, N.Y.Penal Law § 225.15, conviction of which would carry a maximum prison sentence of one year. The prosecutor agreed to make no recommendation as to the sentence.

On June 16, 1969, petitioner accordingly withdrew his plea of not guilty and entered a plea of guilty to the lesser charge. Petitioner represented to the sentencing judge that the plea was voluntary and that the facts of the case as described by the Assistant District Attorney, were true. The court accepted the plea and set a date for sentencing [which through a series of delays did not occur until January 9, 1970].

* * *

At this appearance, another prosecutor had replaced the prosecutor who had negotiated the plea. The new prosecutor recommended the maximum one-year sentence. In making this recommendation, he cited petitioner's criminal record and alleged links with organized crime. Defense counsel immediately objected on the ground that the State had promised petitioner before the plea was entered that there would be no sentence recommendation by the prosecution. He sought to adjourn the sentence hearing in order to have time to prepare proof of the first prosecutor's promise. The second prosecutor, apparently ignorant of his colleague's commitment, argued that there was nothing in the record to support petitioner's claim of a promise, but the State, in subsequent proceedings, has not contested that such a promise was made.

The sentencing judge ended discussion, with the following statement, quoting extensively from the pre-sentence report:

"Mr. Aronstein [Defense Counsel], I am not at all influenced by what the District Attorney says, so that there is no need to adjourn the sentence, and there is no need to have any testimony. It doesn't make a particle of difference what the District Attorney says he will do, or what he doesn't do.

"I have here, Mr. Aronstein, a probation report. I have here a history of a long, long serious criminal record. I have here a picture of the life history of this man. . . .

" 'He is unamenable to supervision in the community. He is a professional criminal.' This is in quotes. 'And a recidivist. Institutionalization—'; that means, in plain language, just putting him away, 'is the only means of halting his anti-social activities,' and protecting you, your family, me, my family, protecting society. 'Institutionalization.' Plain language, put him behind bars.

"Under the plea, I can only send him to the New York City Correctional Institution for men for one year, which I am hereby doing."

The judge then imposed the maximum sentence of one year.

* * *

This record represents another example of an unfortunate lapse in orderly prosecutorial procedures, in part, no doubt, because of the enormous increase in the workload of the often understaffed prosecutor's offices. The heavy workload may well explain these episodes, but it does not excuse them. The disposition of criminal charges by agreement between the prosecutor and the accused, sometimes loosely called "plea bargaining," is an essential component of the administration of justice. Properly administered, it is to be encouraged. If every criminal charge were subjected to a full-scale trial, the States and the Federal Government would need to multiply by many times the number of judges and court facilities.

Disposition of charges after plea discussions is not only an essential part of the process but a highly desirable part for many reasons. It leads to prompt and largely final disposition of most criminal cases; it avoids much of the corrosive impact of enforced idleness during pre-trial confinement for those who are denied release pending trial; it protects the public from those accused persons who are prone to continue criminal conduct even while on pre-trial release; and, by shortening the time between charge and disposition, it enhances whatever may be the rehabilitative prospects of the guilty when they are ultimately imprisoned.

However, all of these considerations presuppose fairness in securing agreement between an accused and a prosecutor. . . .

This phase of the process of criminal justice, and the adjudicative element inherent in accepting a plea of guilty, must be attended by safeguards to insure the defendant what is reasonably due in the circumstances. Those circumstances will vary, but a constant factor is that when a plea rests in any significant degree on a promise or agreement of the prosecutor, so that it can be said to be part of the inducement or consideration, such promise must be fulfilled.

On this record, petitioner "bargained" and negotiated for a particular plea in order to secure dismissal of more serious charges, but also on condition that no sentence recommendation would be made by the prosecutor. It is now conceded that the promise to abstain from a recommendation was made, and at this stage the prosecution is not in a good position to argue that its inadvertent breach of agreement is immaterial. The staff lawyers in a prosecutor's office have the burden of "letting the left hand know what the right hand is doing" or has done. That the breach of agreement was inadvertent does not lessen its impact.

We need not reach the question whether the sentencing judge would or would not have been influenced had he known all the details of the negotiations for the plea. He stated that the prosecutor's recommendation did not influence him and we have no reason to doubt that. Nevertheless, we conclude that the interests of justice and appropriate recognition of the duties of the prosecution in relation to promises made in the negotiation of pleas of guilty will be best served by remanding the case to the state courts for further consideration. The ultimate relief to which petitioner is entitled we leave to the discretion of the state court, which is in a better position to decide whether the circumstances of this case require only that there be specific performance of the agreement on the plea, in which case petitioner should be resentenced by a different judge, or whether, in the view of the state court, the circumstances require granting the relief sought by petitioner, i.e., the opportunity to withdraw his plea of guilty. We emphasize that this is in no sense to question the fairness of the sentencing judge; the fault here rests on the prosecutor, not on the sentencing judge.

The judgment is vacated and the case is remanded for reconsideration not inconsistent with this opinion.

■ Mr. Justice Marshall, with whom Mr. Justice Brennan and Mr. Justice Stewart join, concurring in part and dissenting in part.

I agree with much of the majority's opinion, but conclude that petitioner must be permitted to withdraw his guilty plea. This is the relief petitioner requested and, on the facts set out by the majority, it is a form of relief to which he is entitled.

* * *

United States v. Benchimol

Supreme Court of the United States, 1985.
471 U.S. 453, 105 S.Ct. 2103, 85 L.Ed.2d 462.

■ PER CURIAM.

In April 1976, respondent pleaded guilty in the United States District Court for the Northern District of California to an information charging him with one count of mail fraud in violation of 18 U.S.C. § 1341. Respondent pleaded pursuant to a plea bargain whereby the Government agreed to recommend probation on condition that restitution be made. The District Court disregarded the recommendation and sentenced respondent to six years of treatment and supervision under the Youth Corrections Act, 18 U.S.C. § 5010(b). He was released on parole after serving 18 months of his sentence, but a warrant for his arrest because of parole violation was issued in 1978, and he was eventually taken into custody on that warrant in October 1981. A few days before his arrest on this warrant, he filed a motion under Federal Rule of Criminal Procedure 32(d) and 28 U.S.C. § 2255 to withdraw his guilty plea or, in the alternative, to have his sentence vacated and be resentenced to the time already served. He claimed that the Government had failed to comply with its part of the plea bargain upon which his guilty plea was based.

The District Court that had received the guilty plea also heard respondent's application for collateral relief, and denied it. The Court of Appeals by a divided vote reversed that judgment, holding that: "[W]hen the government undertakes to recommend a sentence pursuant to a plea bargain, it has the duty to state its recommendation clearly to the sentencing judge and to express the justification for it." 738 F.2d 1001, 1002 (C.A.9 1984). . . . The Court of Appeals had this view of the facts:

> "Benchimol agreed to plead guilty. The government concedes that in exchange for the guilty plea it promised to recommend probation with restitution. However, at the sentencing hearing, the pre-sentence report incorrectly stated that the government would stand silent. Benchimol's counsel informed the court that the government instead recommended probation with restitution. The Assistant United States Attorney then stated: 'That is an accurate representation.' "Ibid.

The Court of Appeals concluded that the Government had breached its plea bargain because, although the Assistant United States Attorney concurred with defense counsel's statement that the Government recommended probation with restitution, it "made no effort to explain its reasons for agreeing to recommend a lenient sentence but rather left an impression with the court of less-than-enthusiastic support for leniency." Ibid.

We think this holding misconceives the effect of the relevant rules and of the applicable case law. Federal Rule of Criminal Procedure 11(e) provides an elaborate formula for the negotiation of plea bargains, which allows the attorney for the Government to agree to move for dismissal of other charges and to agree that a specific sentence is the appropriate disposition of the case. It also authorizes the Government attorney to make a recommendation for a particular sentence, or agree not to oppose the defendant's request for such a sentence, with the understanding that such recommendation or request shall not be binding upon the court.

It may well be that the Government in a particular case might commit itself to "enthusiastically" make a particular recommendation to the Court, and it may be that the Government in a particular case might agree to explain to the Court the reasons for the Government's making a particular recommendation. But respondent does not contend, nor did the Court of Appeals find, that the Government had in fact undertaken to do either of these things here. The Court of Appeals simply held that as a matter of law such an undertaking was to be implied from the Government's agreement to recommend a particular sentence. But our view of Rule 11(e) is that it speaks in terms of what the parties in fact agree to, and does not suggest that such implied-in-law terms as were read into this agreement by the Court of Appeals have any place under the Rule.

The Court of Appeals relied on cases such as United States v. Grandinetti, 564 F.2d 723 (C.A.5 1977), and United States v. Brown, 500 F.2d 375 (C.A.4 1974), for the conclusion it reached with respect to the requirement of "enthusiasm," but it appears to us that in each of these cases the Government attorney appearing personally in court at the time of the plea bargain expressed personal reservations about the agreement to which the Government had committed itself. This is quite a different proposition than an appellate determination from a transcript of the record made many years earlier that the Government attorney had "left an impression with the court of less-than-enthusiastic support for leniency." When the Government agrees pursuant to Rule 11(e) to make a recommendation with respect to sentence, it must carry out its part of the bargain by making the promised recommendation; but even if Rule 11(e) allows bargaining about degrees of enthusiasm, there appears to have been none here.

Rule 11(e) may well contemplate agreement by the Government in a particular case to state to the court its reasons for making the recommendation which it agrees to make. The Government suggests that spreading on the record its reasons for agreement to a plea bargain in a particular case—for example, that it did not wish to devote scarce resources to a trial of this particular defendant, or that it wished to avoid calling the victim as a witness—would frequently harm, rather than help, the defendant's quest for leniency. These may well be reasons why the defendant would not wish to exact such a commitment from the Government, but for purposes of this case it is enough that no such agreement was made in fact. Since Rule 11(e) speaks generally of the plea bargains that the parties make, it was error for the Court of Appeals to imply as a matter of law a term which the parties themselves did not agree upon.

For these reasons, we conclude that there was simply no default on the part of the Government in this case, to say nothing of a default remediable on collateral attack under 28 U.S.C. § 2255 or under Federal Rule of Criminal Procedure 32(d), as in effect before August 1, 1983. See Hill v. United States, 368 U.S. 424, 428, 82 S.Ct. 468, 471, 7 L.Ed.2d 417 (1962). The petition for certiorari is accordingly granted, and the judgment of the Court of Appeals is

Reversed. [The concurring opinion of JUSTICE STEVENS, and the dissenting opinion of JUSTICE BRENNAN with JUSTICE MARSHALL are omitted.]

NOTES

1. **Prosecutor's statements at sentencing.** Defendant agrees to plead guilty to one of several charges. In return, the prosecution agrees to dismiss other charges and to give no recommendation to the court as to sentencing or disposition of the case. In the presentence report, the probation officer recommends a suspended sentence and supervised probation. At the hearing on sentencing, the following exchange takes place:

> (The Court): Now, does the State want to say anything with regard to this disposition?

> (Mr. Howard [the prosecutor]): No, Your Honor. I agreed as part of our plea bargaining that I would not in this case make a recommendation to this Court. I would just state that I am not in full compliance with the recommendation of the Probation Officer, but I have not gone into it that fully.

Defendant is sentenced to five years' imprisonment. Was *Santobello* violated? See Miller v. State, 272 Md. 249, 322 A.2d 527 (1974) (over dissent, holding yes). Would *Benchimol* alter this result?

> Suppose that, at the sentencing hearing, the prosecutor makes the recommendation for three years as provided in the plea agreement. The following exchange then occurs:

> THE COURT: Why?

> PROSECUTOR: Well, Your Honor, that was part of the plea bargaining.

> THE COURT: Not because you believe in it?

> PROSECUTOR: Well, Your Honor, I do have some problems with that, anyhow, but that is the way I understand it.

Has *Santobello* been violated? See United States v. Brown, 500 F.2d 375 (4th Cir.1974), holding (over dissent) yes on the ground that "the consideration which induced defendant's guilty plea was not simply the prospect of a formal recitation of a possible sentence but rather the promise [of] ... sound advice, expressed with some degree of advocacy, of a government officer familiar both with the defendant and with his record and cognizant of his public duty as a prosecutor ... ". 500 F.2d at 377. Would *Benchimol* change this conclusion?

2. **Is an agreement binding before the plea is entered?** Once the prosecutor and defense attorney have arrived at a plea bargain, does the constitution preclude the prosecutor from reneging on the deal before the plea is entered? In Mabry v. Johnson, 467 U.S. 504, 104 S.Ct. 2543, 81 L.Ed.2d 437 (1984), respondent was serving a 21 year prison sentence for burglary. He was charged with murder. The prosecutor offered to recommend a sentence of 21 years to run concurrently with the burglary sentence in exchange for a plea of guilty to the murder. The defense attorney, after consulting with his client, communicated to the prosecutor that the offer was accepted. The prosecutor then informed defense counsel that he had mistakenly made the offer; he proposed instead to recommend a sentence of 21 years to be served consecutively to the burglary sentence in exchange for a plea of guilty. Defendant ultimately accepted this offer and plead guilty to the murder charge; he received a sentence of 21 years to be served consecutively to the burglary sentence. The Court of Appeals in federal habeas corpus proceedings set aside the murder conviction on the ground that defendant's due process rights had been violated by the prosecutor's withdrawal of his offer after it had been accepted

by the defense. The Supreme Court, in a unanimous opinion by Justice Stevens, reversed the Court of Appeals. Justice Stevens observed that "a plea bargain standing alone is without constitutional significance; in itself it is a mere executory agreement which, until embodied in the judgment of a court, does not deprive an accused of liberty or any other constitutionally protected interest." 467 U.S. at 507, 104 S.Ct. at 2546, 81 L.Ed.2d at 442. Justice Stevens then distinguished *Santobello:*

> Respondent's plea was in no sense induced by the prosecutor's withdrawn offer; unlike Santobello, who pleaded guilty thinking he had bargained for a specific prosecutorial sentencing recommendation which was not ultimately made, at the time respondent pleaded guilty he knew the prosecution would recommend a 21–year consecutive sentence ... [H]e pleaded guilty with the advice of competent counsel and with full awareness of the consequences—he knew that the prosecutor would recommend and that the judge could impose the sentence now under attack. Respondent's plea was thus in no sense the product of governmental deception; it rested on no "unfulfilled promises" and fully satisfied the test for voluntariness and intelligence.

467 U.S. at 510, 104 S.Ct. at 2548, 81 L.Ed.2d at 444. There was no evidence respondent had detrimentally relied upon the first plea agreement.

3. **Prosecutor's withdrawal of consent.** If the sentencing court decides to impose a lesser punishment than the agreement contemplates, should the prosecution be permitted to withdraw consent to the guilty plea? In People v. Farrar, 52 N.Y.2d 302, 437 N.Y.S.2d 961, 419 N.E.2d 864 (1981), the court characterized this opportunity as the counterpart of the defendant's right to withdraw the plea if the trial judge decides to impose a more severe sentence and held that the prosecution should have the opportunity:

> However justified the court's unwillingness to impose the negotiated sentence, fairness dictates that [the prosecution's option to withdraw consent] be left open. Of course, this is not to say that the People's application must be granted in all cases, for, among other things, prejudice to a defendant following a plea may prevent restoration to *status quo ante* and render vacatur of the plea inappropriate. Absent defendant's showing of such prejudice or other circumstances militating against vacatur, however, relief to the People would be proper.

52 N.Y.2d at 308, 437 N.Y.S.2d at 963, 419 N.E.2d at 866.

5. **Statements made during or after negotiation.** Under what, if any, circumstances are confessions made during plea negotiations later admissible? In Hutto v. Ross, 429 U.S. 28, 97 S.Ct. 202, 50 L.Ed.2d 194 (1976), the defendant and the prosecution had arrived at an agreement pursuant to which the defendant would plead guilty and the prosecution would recommend a fifteen year sentence with ten years suspended. When the prosecutor inquired concerning the defendant's willingness to make a statement concerning the crimes, defense counsel advised the defendant that the bargain did not require any such statement. Nevertheless, the defendant made a statement confessing to the offenses charged. Later, after the defendant withdrew from the agreement and demanded jury trial, this statement was introduced against him and he was convicted. The Supreme Court found no constitutional defect in the proceedings. Framing the issue as "whether a confession is *per se* inadmissible in a criminal trial because it was made subsequent to an agreed upon plea bargain that did not call for such a confession", it concluded:

> The existence of the bargain may well have entered into respondent's decision to give a statement, but counsel made it clear to respondent that he could enforce the terms of the plea bargain whether or not he confessed. The confession thus does not appear to have been the result of "any direct or

implied promises" or any coercion on the part of the prosecution, and was not involuntary.

429 U.S. at 30, 97 S.Ct. 203–04, 50 L.Ed.2d at 194. The Court specifically noted that the case did not involve the admissibility of statements made during the plea negotiation process. 429 U.S. at 30 n. 3, 97 S.Ct. at 203 n. 3, 50 L.Ed.2d at 197 n. 3.

6. **Waiving confidentiality of statements made during plea negotiations.** Federal Rules of Criminal Procedure 11(e)(6) provides that evidence of "any statement made in the course of plea discussions with an attorney for the government which do not result in a plea of guilty" are inadmissible in evidence. Can the defendant agree with the prosecutor to waive that exclusion as to statements that might be used to impeach later testimony in the event of a trial?

The respondent in United States v. Mezzanatto, 513 U.S. 196, 115 S.Ct. 797, 130 L.Ed.2d 697 (1995) made incriminatory statements during plea discussions with a prosecutor concerning his role in a drug distribution scheme. Before discussions began, he agreed to waive the protections of Rule 11(e) as to any statements he might make that could be used to impeach contradictory trial testimony. Plea discussions concluded without an agreement and the case went to trial. The government was permitted to impeach respondent's trial testimony with prior inconsistent statements he had made during the aborted plea discussions. The Ninth Circuit, viewing the exclusion as non-waivable, reversed the conviction. The Supreme Court, in an opinion by Justice Thomas, reversed the Ninth Circuit and reinstated the conviction.

The Court found nothing in the Rule to rebut the general presumption that legal rights can be waived by their intended beneficiary. Accordingly, it announced the rule that "absent some affirmative indication that the agreement was entered into unknowingly or involuntarily, an agreement to waive the exclusionary provisions of the plea-statement Rules is valid and enforceable." 513 U.S. at 210, 115 S.Ct. at 806, 130 L.Ed.2d at 710.

Justice Ginsburg concurred with the observation that an agreement to permit statements made during plea discussions to be admitted during the Government's case-in-chief might be dealt with differently on the ground admission would be inconsistent with Congress's intent to promote plea bargaining by the exclusionary provision.

7. **Remedies for post-plea entry agreement breach by defendant.** What remedies are available to the government when the defendant repudiates a plea bargain after he has pled guilty and been sentenced in accordance with its terms? The respondent in Ricketts v. Adamson, 483 U.S. 1, 107 S.Ct. 2680, 97 L.Ed.2d 1 (1987), was charged with first degree murder. As part of a plea agreement, he promised to testify against two others charged with the same offense in exchange for being permitted to plead guilty to second degree murder and receiving a negotiated prison sentence. He pled guilty, testified against the others, and was sentenced to the term he had negotiated. An appellate court reversed the convictions of the others and remanded for a new trial. Respondent refused to testify again against the others, taking the position that this contingency was not covered by the plea agreement. The State of Arizona obtained an order vacating the second degree murder conviction and sentence and re-instating the charge of first degree murder. Respondent was convicted under that charge and given the death penalty. His claim that this procedure was prohibited by the double jeopardy clause was accepted by the United States Court of Appeals, but the Supreme Court, in an opinion by Justice White, reversed. Respondent's interpretation of the plea agreement is untenable in view of his promise to "testify fully and completely in any Court, State or Federal, when requested by proper authorities against any and all parties involved in the murder of Don Bolles." The Court rejected the argument

that reinstatement of first degree murder charges was precluded because respondent had not explicitly waived double jeopardy protections in the plea agreement:

> The terms of the agreement could not be clearer: in the event of respondent's breach occasioned by a refusal to testify, the parties would be returned to the *status quo ante,* in which case respondent would have *no* double jeopardy defense to waive. And, an agreement specifying that charges may be *reinstated* given certain circumstances is, at least under the provisions of this plea agreement, *precisely* equivalent to an agreement waiving a double jeopardy defense.

483 U.S. at 10, 107 S.Ct. at 2685–86, 97 L.Ed.2d at 11–12. Justice Brennan, joined by Justices Marshall, Blackmun and Stevens, dissented.

5. EFFORTS TO ABOLISH PLEA BARGAINING

The National Advisory Commission on Criminal Justice Standards and Goals recommendation that plea bargaining should be prohibited no later than 1978 has not been followed nationwide. Some efforts to bar plea bargaining have been undertaken, however, and these provide some basis for believing that the traditional skepticism concerning the practicality of positions such as that of the Commission may be unwarranted.

Parnas and Atkins, Abolishing Plea Bargaining: A Proposal, 14 Crim. L.Bull. 101, 110–14 (1978), review reform efforts in the federal Southern District of California, Multnomah County, Oregon, and Maricopa County, Arizona and report conclusions somewhat similar to those in the report on the Alaska efforts, infra. But compare Callan, An Experience in Justice Without Plea Negotiation, 13 L. & Soc. 327 (1979), reporting on the practice in El Paso, Texas, and providing some support for those who fear that elimination of plea bargaining will produce a disruptive increase in contested cases. The state-wide experience in Alaska is discussed in RUBENSTEIN AND CLARK, CONCLUSIONS, in THE OFFICIAL PROHIBITION OF PLEA BARGAINING ON THE DISPOSITION OF FELONY CASES IN ALASKA CRIMINAL COURTS 219–29 (ALASKA JUDICIAL COUNCIL, 1978). The study concluded that there was considerable change in the system of plea bargaining as a result.

Parnas and Atkins, Abolishing Plea Bargaining: A Proposal, 14 Crim. L.Bull. 101 (1978), suggest that if plea bargaining is to be eliminated, the key to a workable system will be the appropriateness of the charge. Given the importance of the charging decision in a system without plea bargaining, they conclude that "there must be a control on [charging] beyond the district attorney's good faith and adherence to established criteria." Id., at 119. They propose a charge setting hearing before a judge. After considering the prosecutor's recommendation (which would carry great weight) and informally considering information concerning the matter, the judge would select an appropriate charge that would be binding during the remainder of the prosecution. If new information became available, a subsequent hearing to modify the charge might be granted under "exceptional circumstances." Id., at 119–20.

CALIFORNIA PENAL CODE (1982)

§ 1192.7. **[Limitation of plea bargaining.]** (a) Plea bargaining in any case in which the indictment or information charges any serious felony or any offense of driving while under the influence of alcohol, drugs, narcotics, or any other intoxicating substance, or any combination thereof, is prohibited, unless there is insufficient evidence to prove the people's case, or testimony of a material witness cannot be obtained, or a reduction or dismissal would not result in a substantial change in sentence.

(b) As used in this section "plea bargaining" means any bargaining, negotiation, or discussion between a criminal defendant, or his or her counsel, and a prosecuting attorney or judge, whereby the defendant agrees to plead guilty or nolo contendere, in exchange for any promises, commitments, concessions, assurances, or consideration by the prosecuting attorney or judge relating to any charge against the defendant or to the sentencing of the defendant.

(c) As used in this section "serious felony" means any of the following: (1) Murder or voluntary manslaughter; (2) mayhem; (3) rape; (4) sodomy by force, violence, duress, menace, or threat of great bodily harm; (5) oral copulation by force, violence, duress, menace, or threat of great bodily harm; (6) lewd acts on a child under the age of 14 years; (7) any felony punishable by death or imprisonment in the state prison for life; (8) any other felony in which the defendant inflicts great bodily injury on any person, other than an accomplice, or any felony in which the defendant uses a firearm; (9) attempted murder; (10) assault with intent to commit rape or robbery; (11) assault with a deadly weapon or instrument on a peace officer; (12) assault by a life prisoner on a noninmate; (13) assault with a deadly weapon by an inmate; (14) arson; (15) exploding a destructive device or any explosive with intent to injure; (16) exploding a destructive device or any explosive causing great bodily injury; (17) exploding a destructive device or any explosive with intent to murder; (18) burglary of a residence; (19) robbery; (20) kidnapping; (21) taking of a hostage by an inmate of a state prison; (22) attempt to commit a felony punishable by death or imprisonment in the state prison for life; (23) any felony in which the defendant personally used a dangerous or deadly weapon; (24) selling, furnishing, administering or providing heroin, cocaine, or phencyclidine (PCP) to a minor, (25) any attempt to commit a crime listed in this subdivision other than an assault.

(d) The provisions of this section shall not be amended by the Legislature except by statute passed in each house by rollcall vote entered in the journal two-thirds of the membership concurring, or by a statute that becomes effective only when approved by the electors.

NOTES

1. **The California provision in practice.** The California Penal Code provision has been construed in practice as permitting substantial plea bargaining. The prohibition applies to those cases—but only to those cases, it is urged—in which an indictment or information has been filed that "charges" one of the specified offenses. Felonies are often charged by information rather than indictment. A preliminary charge in the form of a complaint is filed in a lower court. No information is filed in the superior court—the court with general trial jurisdiction—unless a preliminary hearing has been held in the lower court or the defendant has waived this hearing. Substantial plea bargaining occurs during these early steps and

before an information is filed in superior court charging the offense. Is this consistent with the spirit which moved California voters to approve § 1192.7 by initiative in 1982?

2.   For an extensive explication of alternatives to plea bargaining, see Alschuler, Implementing the Criminal Defendant's Right to Trial: Alternatives to the Plea Bargaining System, 50 U.Chi.L.Rev. 931 (1983).

CHAPTER 23

ADJUDICATION OF GUILT OR INNOCENCE BY TRIAL

Analysis

This Chapter considers very selectively some of the issues raised by the criminal trial as a method of adjudication of guilt or innocence. Four clusters of federal constitutional issues are discussed: the requirement of proof beyond a reasonable doubt, the right to trial by jury, the rights to confrontation, cross-examination and compulsory process, and the privilege against self-incrimination. The right to the effective assistance of counsel at trial is considered in Chapter 24.

A.   PROOF BEYOND A REASONABLE DOUBT

In In re Winship, 397 U.S. 358, 90 S.Ct. 1068, 25 L.Ed.2d 368 (1970), the Court held that the "beyond a reasonable doubt standard" was required in Juvenile Court at the trial stage of serious juvenile delinquency cases by Fourteenth Amendment Due Process. Also in that opinion, the Court made explicit for the first time that that standard was constitutionally mandated in adult criminal trials:

The requirement that guilt of a criminal charge be established by proof beyond a reasonable doubt dates at least from our early years as a Nation. The "demand for a higher degree of persuasion in criminal cases was recurrently expressed from ancient times, [though] its crystallization into the formula 'beyond a reasonable doubt' seems to have occurred as late as 1798. It is now accepted in common law jurisdictions as the measure of persuasion by which the prosecution must convince the trier of all the essential elements of guilt." C. McCormick, Evidence § 321, pp. 681–682 (1954); see also 9 J. Wigmore, Evidence, § 2497 (3d ed. 1940). Although virtually unanimous adherence to the reasonable-doubt standard in common-law jurisdictions may not conclusively establish it as a requirement of due process, such adherence does "reflect a profound judgment about the way in which law should be enforced and justice administered." Duncan v. Louisiana, 391 U.S. 145, 155, 88 S.Ct. 1444, 1451, 20 L.Ed.2d 491 (1968).

Expressions in many opinions of this Court indicate that it has long been assumed that proof of a criminal charge beyond a reasonable doubt is constitutionally required. ...Mr. Justice Frankfurter stated that "[i]t is the duty of the Government to establish ... guilt beyond a reasonable doubt. This notion—basic in our law and rightly one of the boasts of a free society—is a requirement and a safeguard of due process of law in the historic, procedural content of 'due process.'" Leland v. Oregon, supra, 343 U.S., at 802–803, 72 S.Ct., at 1009 (dissenting opinion). In a similar vein, the Court said in Brinegar v. United States, supra, 338 U.S., at 174, 69 S.Ct., at 1310, that "[g]uilt in a criminal case must be proved beyond a reasonable doubt and by evidence confined to that which long experience in the common-law tradition, to some extent embodied in the Constitution, has crystallized into rules of evidence consistent with that standard. These rules are historically grounded rights of our system, developed to safeguard men from dubious and unjust convictions, with resulting forfeitures of life, liberty and property." Davis v. United States, supra, 160 U.S., at 488, 16 S.Ct., at 358 stated that the requirement is implicit in "constitutions ... [which] recognize the fundamental principles that are deemed essential for the protection of life and liberty." In *Davis* a murder conviction was reversed because the trial judge instructed the jury that it was their duty to convict when the evidence was equally balanced regarding the sanity of the accused. This Court said: "On the contrary, he is entitled to an acquittal of the specific crime charged, if upon all the evidence, there is reasonable doubt whether he was capable in law of committing crime. ...No man should be deprived of his life under the forms of law unless the jurors who try him are able, upon their consciences, to say that the evidence before them ... is sufficient to show beyond a reasonable doubt the existence of every fact necessary to constitute the crime charged." Id., at 484, 493, 16 S.Ct., at 357, 360.

The reasonable-doubt standard plays a vital role in the American scheme of criminal procedure. It is a prime instrument for reducing the risk of convictions resting on factual error. The standard provides concrete substance for the presumption of innocence—that bedrock "axiomatic and elementary" principle whose "enforcement lies at the foundation of the administration of our criminal law." Coffin v. United States, supra, 156 U.S., at 453, 15 S.Ct., at 403. As the dissenters in the New York Court of Appeals observed, and we agree, "a person accused of a crime ... would be at a severe disadvantage, a disadvantage amounting to a lack of fundamental fairness, if he could be adjudged guilty and imprisoned for years on the strength of the same evidence as would suffice in a civil case." 24 N.Y.2d, at 205, 299 N.Y.S.2d, at 422, 247 N.E.2d, at 259.

The requirement of proof beyond a reasonable doubt has this vital role in our criminal procedure for cogent reasons. The accused during a criminal prosecution has at stake interest of immense importance, both because of the possibility that he may lose his liberty upon conviction and because of the certainty that he would be stigmatized by the conviction. Accordingly, a society that values the good name and freedom of every individual should not condemn a man for commission of a crime when there is reasonable doubt about his guilt. As we said in Speiser v. Randall, supra, 357 U.S., at 525–526, 78 S.Ct., at 1342: "There is always in litigation a margin of error, representing error in factfinding, which both parties must take into account. Where one party has at stake an interest of transcending value—as a criminal defendant his liberty—this margin of error is reduced as to him by the process of placing on the other party the burden of ... persuading the factfinder at the conclusion of the trial of his guilt beyond a reasonable doubt. Due process commands that no man shall lose his liberty unless the Government has borne the burden of ... convincing the factfinder of his guilt." To this end, the reasonable-doubt standard is indispensable, for it "impresses on the trier of fact the necessity of reaching a subjective state of certitude of the facts in issue." Dorsen & Rezneck, In Re Gault and the Future of Juvenile Law, 1 Family Law Quarterly, No. 4, pp. 1, 26 (1967).

Moreover, use of the reasonable-doubt standard is indispensable to command the respect and confidence of the community in applications of the criminal law. It is critical that the moral force of the criminal law not be diluted by a standard of proof that leaves people in doubt whether innocent men are being condemned. It is also important in our free society that every individual going about his ordinary affairs have confidence that his government cannot adjudge him guilty of a criminal offense without convincing a proper factfinder of his guilt with utmost certainty.

Lest there remain any doubt about the constitutional stature of the reasonable-doubt standard, we explicitly hold that the Due Process Clause protects the accused against conviction except upon proof beyond a reasonable doubt of every fact necessary to constitute the crime with which he is charged.

397 U.S. at 361–64, 90 S.Ct. at 1071–73, 25 L.Ed.2d at 373–75. This section explores the ramifications of *Winship,* including those affecting the substantive definition of criminal offenses as well as others of a more procedural nature.

Mullaney v. Wilbur

Supreme Court of the United States, 1975.
421 U.S. 684, 95 S.Ct. 1881, 44 L.Ed.2d 508.

■ Mr. Justice Powell delivered the opinion of the Court.

The State of Maine requires a defendant charged with murder to prove [by a "fair preponderance"] that he acted "in the heat of passion on sudden provocation" in order to reduce the homicide to manslaughter. We must decide whether this rule comports with the due process requirement, as defined in In re Winship, 397 U.S. 358, 364, 90 S.Ct. 1068, 1072, 25 L.Ed.2d 368 (1970), that the prosecution prove beyond a reasonable doubt every fact necessary to constitute the crime charged.

I.

* * *

[T]he jury found respondent guilty of murder.

Respondent appealed to the Maine Supreme Judicial Court, arguing that he had been denied due process because he was required to negate the element of malice aforethought by proving that he had acted in the heat of passion on sudden provocation. . . .

The Maine Supreme Judicial Court rejected this contention. . . .

Respondent next successfully petitioned for a writ of habeas corpus in federal district court. . . .

The Court of Appeals for the First Circuit affirmed . . .

* * *

Because of the importance of the issues presented, we . . . granted certiorari. . . . We now affirm.

* * *

III.

* * *

A.

Our analysis may be illuminated if this issue is placed in historical context.

* * *

[A]t common law the burden of proving heat of passion on sudden provocation appears to have rested on the defendant.

... [T]he large majority of States ... now require the prosecution to prove the absence of the heat of passion on sudden provocation beyond a reasonable doubt. See LaFave & Austin, Criminal Law 539–540 (1972).

This historical review establishes two important points. First, the fact at issue here—the presence or absence of the heat of passion on sudden provocation—has been, almost from the inception of the common law of homicide, the single most important factor in determining the degree of culpability attaching to an unlawful homicide. And, second, the clear trend has been toward requiring the prosecution to bear the ultimate burden of proving this fact. ...

B.

Petitioners, the warden of the Maine Prison and the State of Maine, argue that despite these considerations *Winship* should not be extended to the present case. They note that as a formal matter the absence of the heat of passion on sudden provocation is not a "fact necessary to constitute the *crime* "of felonious homicide in Maine. In re Winship, 397 U.S., at 364, 90 S.Ct., at 1073 (emphasis supplied). This distinction is relevant, according to petitioners, because in *Winship* the facts at issue were essential to establish criminality in the first instance whereas the fact in question here does not come into play until the jury already has determined that the defendant is guilty and may be punished at least for manslaughter. In this situation, petitioners maintain, the defendant's critical interests in liberty and reputation are no longer of paramount concern since, irrespective of the presence or absence of the heat of passion on sudden provocation, he is likely to lose his liberty and certain to be stigmatized. In short, petitioners would limit *Winship* to those facts which, if not proved, would wholly exonerate the defendant.

This analysis fails to recognize that the criminal law of Maine, like that of other jurisdictions, is concerned not only with guilt or innocence in the abstract but also with the degree of criminal culpability. Maine has chosen to distinguish those who kill in the heat of passion from those who kill in the absence of this factor. Because the former are less "blameworth[y]," they are subject to substantially less severe penalties. By drawing this distinction, while refusing to require the prosecution to establish beyond a reasonable doubt the fact upon which it turns, Maine denigrates the interests found critical in *Winship*.

The safeguards of due process are not rendered unavailing simply because a determination may already have been reached that would stigmatize the defendant and that might lead to a significant impairment of personal liberty. The fact remains that the consequences resulting from a verdict of murder, as compared with a verdict of manslaughter, differ significantly. ...

Moreover, if *Winship* were limited to those facts that constitute a crime as defined by state law, a State could undermine many of the interests that decision sought to protect without effecting any substantive change in its law. It would only be necessary to redefine the elements that comprise different crimes, characterizing them as factors that bear solely on the extent of punishment.[1] . . .

Winship is concerned with substance rather than this kind of formalism.[2] The rationale of that case requires an analysis that looks to the "operation and effect of the law as applied and enforced by the state," and to the interests of both the State and the defendant as affected by the allocation of the burden of proof.

* * *

These interests are implicated to a greater degree in this case than they were in *Winship* itself. Petitioner there faced an 18–month sentence, with a maximum possible extension of an additional four and one-half years, 397 U.S., at 360, 90 S.Ct., at 1070, whereas respondent here faces a differential in sentencing ranging from a nominal fine to a mandatory life sentence. Both the stigma to the defendant and the community's confidence in the administration of the criminal law are also of greater consequence in this case, since the adjudication of delinquency involved in *Winship* was "benevolent" in intention, seeking to provide "a generously conceived program of compassionate treatment." In re Winship, 397 U.S., at 376, 90 S.Ct., at 1079 (Burger, C.J., dissenting).

Not only are the interests underlying *Winship* implicated to a greater degree in this case, but in one respect the protection afforded those interests is less here. In *Winship* the ultimate burden of persuasion remained with the prosecution, although the standard had been reduced to proof by a fair preponderance of the evidence. In this case, by contrast, the State has affirmatively shifted the burden of proof to the defendant. The result, in a case such as this one where the defendant is required to prove the critical fact in dispute, is to increase further the likelihood of an erroneous murder conviction. Such a result directly contravenes the principle articulated in Speiser v. Randall, 357 U.S. 513, 525–526, 78 S.Ct. 1332, 1342, 2 L.Ed.2d 1460 (1958):

> "[W]here one party has at stake an interest of transcending value—as a criminal defendant his liberty—th[e] margin of error is reduced as to him by the process of placing on the [prosecution] the burden . . . of persuading the factfinder at the conclusion of the trial. . . . "

* * *

1. Many States impose different statutory sentences on different degrees of assault. If *Winship* were limited to a State's definition of the elements of a crime, these States could define all assaults as a single offense and then require the defendant to disprove the elements of aggravation—e.g., intent to kill or intent to rob. But see State v. Ferris, 249 A.2d 523 (Me.1969) (prosecution must prove elements of aggravation in criminal assault case by proof beyond a reasonable doubt).

2. Indeed, in *Winship* itself the Court invalidated the burden of proof in a juvenile delinquency proceeding even though delinquency was not formally considered a "crime" under state law. 397 U.S. at 365–366, 90 S.Ct. at 1073–1074, id., at 373–374, 90 S.Ct. at 1077–1078 (Harlan, J., concurring).

C.

* * *

Nor is the requirement of proving a negative unique in our system of criminal jurisprudence.[3] Maine itself requires the prosecution to prove the absence of self-defense beyond a reasonable doubt. See State v. Millett, 273 A.2d 504 (1971).[4] Satisfying this burden imposes an obligation that, in all practical effect, is identical to the burden involved in negating the heat of passion on sudden provocation. Thus, we discern no unique hardship on the prosecution that would justify requiring the defendant to carry the burden of proving a fact so critical to criminal culpability.[5]

IV.

Maine law requires a defendant to establish by a preponderance of the evidence that he acted in the heat of passion on sudden provocation in order to reduce murder to manslaughter. Under this burden of proof a defendant can be given a life sentence when the evidence indicates that it is *as likely as not* that he deserves a significantly lesser sentence. This is an intolerable result in a society where, to paraphrase Mr. Justice Harlan, it is far worse to sentence one guilty only of manslaughter as a murderer than to sentence a murderer for the lesser crime of manslaughter. In re Winship, 397 U.S., at 372, 90 S.Ct., at 1076 (concurring opinion). We therefore hold

---

3. ... Many States do require the defendant to show that there is "some evidence" indicating that he acted in the heat of passion before requiring the prosecution to negate this element by proving the absence of passion beyond a reasonable doubt. Nothing in this opinion is intended to affect that requirement.

4. In *Millett* the Maine Supreme Judicial Court adopted the "majority rule" regarding proof of self-defense. The burden of producing "some evidence" on this issue rests with the defendant, but the ultimate burden of persuasion by proof beyond a reasonable doubt remains on the prosecution.

5. This conclusion is supported by consideration of a related line of cases. Generally in a criminal case the prosecution bears both the production burden and the persuasion burden. In some instances, however, it is aided by a presumption, see Davis v. United States, 160 U.S. 469, 16 S.Ct. 353, 40 L.Ed. 499 (1895) (presumption of sanity), or a permissible inference, see United States v. Gainey, 380 U.S. 63, 85 S.Ct. 754, 13 L.Ed.2d 658 (1965) (inference of knowledge from presence at an illegal still). These procedural devices require (in the case of a presumption) or permit (in the case of an inference) the trier of fact to conclude that the prosecution has met its burden of proof with respect to

the presumed or inferred fact by having satisfactorily established other facts. Thus, in effect they require the defendant to present some evidence contesting the otherwise presumed or inferred fact. See Barnes v. United States, 412 U.S. 837, 846 n. 11, 93 S.Ct. 2357, 37 L.Ed.2d 380 (1973). Since they shift the production burden to the defendant, these devices must satisfy certain due process requirements. See e.g., Barnes v. United States, supra; Turner v. United States, 396 U.S. 398, 90 S.Ct. 642, 24 L.Ed.2d 610 (1970).

In each of these cases, however, the ultimate burden of persuasion by proof beyond a reasonable doubt remained on the prosecution. See, e.g., Barnes v. United States, 412 U.S., at 845 n. 9, 93 S.Ct., at 2362; Davis v. United States, 160 U.S., at 484–488, 16 S.Ct., at 356–358. Shifting the burden of persuasion to the defendant obviously places an even greater strain upon him since he no longer need only present some evidence with respect to the fact at issue; he must affirmatively establish that fact. Accordingly, the Due Process Clause demands more exacting standards before the State may require a defendant to bear this ultimate burden of persuasion. See generally Ashford & Risinger, Presumptions, Assumptions and Due Process in Criminal Cases: A Theoretical Overview, 79 Yale L.J. 165 (1969).

that the Due Process Clause requires the prosecution to prove beyond a reasonable doubt the absence of the heat of passion on sudden provocation when the issue is properly presented in a homicide case. Accordingly, the judgment below is affirmed.

Affirmed.

■ MR. JUSTICE REHNQUIST, with whom THE CHIEF JUSTICE joins, concurring.

* * *

I agree with the Court that In re Winship, 397 U.S. 358, 90 S.Ct. 1068, 25 L.Ed.2d 368 (1970), does require that the prosecution prove beyond a reasonable doubt every element which constitutes the crime charged against a defendant. I see no inconsistency between that holding and the holding of Leland v. Oregon, 343 U.S. 790, 72 S.Ct. 1002, 96 L.Ed. 1302 (1952). In the latter case this Court held that there was no constitutional requirement that the State shoulder the burden of proving the sanity of the defendant.

The Court noted in *Leland* that the issue of insanity as a defense to a criminal charge was considered by the jury only after it had found that all elements of the offense, including the *mens rea* if any required by state law, had been proven beyond a reasonable doubt. Id., at 792, 795, 72 S.Ct., at 1004–1005. Although as the state court's instructions in *Leland* recognized, id., at 794–795, 72 S.Ct., at 1005–1006, evidence relevant to insanity as defined by state law may also be relevant to whether the required *mens rea* was present, the existence or nonexistence of legal insanity bears no necessary relationship to the existence or nonexistence of the required mental elements of the crime. For this reason, Oregon's placement of the burden of proof on insanity on Leland, unlike Maine's redefinition of homicide in the instant case, did not effect an unconstitutional shift in the State's traditional burden of proof beyond a reasonable doubt of all necessary elements of the offense. Id., at 795, 72 S.Ct., at 1005. . . . Having once met that rigorous burden of proof that, for example, in a case such as this, the defendant not only killed a fellow human being, but did it with malice aforethought, the State could quite consistently with such a constitutional principle conclude that a defendant who sought to establish the defense of insanity, and thereby escape any punishment whatever for a heinous crime, should bear the laboring oar on such an issue.

NOTES

1. **Re-defining offense elements.** The significance of *Mullaney* may have been affected by Patterson v. New York, 432 U.S. 197, 97 S.Ct. 2319, 53 L.Ed.2d 281 (1977). Patterson had been charged with murder under a New York statute defining the crime as causing the death of another with the intent of causing the death of that person or a third individual. But under other provisions of the state's homicide statutes, if a defendant established, by a preponderance of the evidence, that an intentional killing was committed "under the influence of extreme emotional disturbance," he is to be convicted only of manslaughter. In an opinion by Justice White, a majority of the Supreme Court held that the New York scheme did not violate *Mullaney*. The New York scheme, the Court reasoned, was unlike the Maine

statute in that it did not presume any element of the offense of murder (i.e., lack of provocation) and place the burden on the defendant to rebut that presumption. The absence of extreme emotional disturbance is not an element of murder and therefore Leland v. Oregon (discussed in *Mullaney*) did not bar the state from placing the burden of proof on the defendant. Addressing the broader ramifications of the case, Justice White continued, "We ... decline to adopt as a constitutional imperative, operative countrywide, that a State must disprove beyond a reasonable doubt every fact constituting any and all affirmative defenses related to the culpability of an accused." 432 U.S. at 210, 97 S.Ct. at 2327, 53 L.Ed.2d at 292. The Court acknowledged that some language in *Mullaney* might be read as requiring the prosecution to prove beyond a reasonable doubt any fact affecting the degree of criminal culpability. "The Court," Justice White commented, "did not intend *Mullaney* to have such far-reaching effect." 432 U.S. 215 n. 15, 97 S.Ct. at 2329 n. 15, 53 L.Ed.2d at 295 n. 15.

In Martin v. Ohio, 480 U.S. 228, 107 S.Ct. 1098, 94 L.Ed.2d 267 (1987), the defendant was convicted of aggravated murder in a trial in which she raised a claim of self-defense. Ohio law defined aggravated murder as a killing committed purposely and with prior calculation and design. It placed the burden upon the state to prove each element of aggravated murder beyond a reasonable doubt. Under Ohio law, self-defense was classified as an affirmative defense. The burden of producing evidence of self-defense was placed on the defendant and, once produced, the burden of persuasion was upon the defendant to prove self-defense by a preponderance of the evidence. The United States Supreme Court, in an opinion authored by Justice White, rejected the argument that the Ohio scheme violated *Mullaney*. Instead, it came within *Patterson:*

> The State did not exceed its authority in defining the crime of murder as purposely causing the death of another with prior calculation or design. It did not seek to shift to Martin the burden of proving any of those elements, and the jury's verdict reflects that none of her self-defense evidence raised a reasonable doubt about the state's proof that she purposefully killed with prior calculation and design. She nevertheless had the opportunity under state law and the instructions given to justify the killing and show herself to be blameless by proving that she acted in self-defense. The jury thought she had failed to do so, and Ohio is as entitled to punish Martin as one guilty of murder as New York was to punish Patterson.

480 U.S. at 233, 107 S.Ct. at 1102, 94 L.Ed.2d at 274. The Court noted that nothing in the trial court's instructions prevented the jury from using the evidence offered on self-defense to assist it in deciding whether the State carried its burden of proving that the killing was committed with prior calculation and design. Further, although only two states, Ohio and South Carolina, place the burden of persuasion on the defendant in cases of self-defense, the question of constitutionality "is not answered by cataloging the practices of other States. We are no more convinced that the Ohio practice of requiring self-defense to be proved by the defendant is unconstitutional than we are that the Constitution requires the prosecution to prove the sanity of a defendant who pleads not guilty by reason of insanity." 480 U.S. at 236, 107 S.Ct. at 1103, 94 L.Ed.2d at 276. Justice Powell, joined by Justices Brennan, Marshall, and Blackmun, dissented.

2. **Offense element or sentence enhancer?** In McMillan v. Pennsylvania, 477 U.S. 79, 106 S.Ct. 2411, 91 L.Ed.2d 67 (1986), the petitioners had been sentenced under a statutory scheme that required a minimum sentence of 5 years upon conviction of specified offenses if it is shown by a preponderance of the evidence at a sentencing hearing that the offender "visibly possessed a firearm" during the commission of the offense. The Pennsylvania Supreme Court rejected the

argument that permitting proof by a preponderance violated *Mullaney*. The United States Supreme Court, in an opinion by Justice Rehnquist, affirmed. *Mullaney,* as explicated in *Patterson,* does suggest there are certain constitutional minimum restrictions on the ability of the states to define the elements of criminal offenses to avoid the requirement that each be proved beyond a reasonable doubt, but this case does not reach those limits. While Pennsylvania could have made visible possession of a firearm an element of various other offenses, and would have been required to comply with *Mullaney* had it done so, instead

> [i]t simply took one factor that has always been considered by sentencing courts to bear on punishment—the instrumentality used in committing a violent felony—and dictated the precise weight to be given that factor if the instrumentality is a firearm. Pennsylvania's decision to do so has not transformed against its will a sentencing factor into an "element" of some hypothetical "offense."

477 U.S. at 89–90, 106 S.Ct. at 2418, 91 L.Ed.2d at 78–79. The Court also rejected the arguments that due process requires that there be proof by clear and convincing evidence and that there is a right to trial by jury on the question whether petitioners visibly possessed a firearm during the offense. Justice Stevens, dissenting, distinguished between the aggravating circumstances at issue in this case and ·the mitigating circumstances at issue in *Patterson.* He argued that,

> a state legislature may not dispense with the requirement of proof beyond a reasonable doubt for conduct that it targets for severe criminal penalties. Because the Pennsylvania statute challenged in this case describes conduct that the Pennsylvania legislature obviously intended to prohibit, and because it mandates lengthy incarceration for the same, I believe that the conduct so described is an element of the criminal offense to which the proof beyond a reasonable doubt requirement applies.

477 U.S. at 96, 106 S.Ct. at 2421, 91 L.Ed.2d at 83. Justice Stevens argued that we can rely upon the political process to guard against overzealous use of mitigating or exculpating circumstances to avoid the effects of *Mullaney.* For example, a legislature would not make it a criminal offense to be in a bank subject to an affirmative defense to be proved by the defendant that he was not robbing it. Justice Marshall, joined by Justices Brennan and Blackmun, dissenting, agreed with much of Justice Stevens' opinion but disapproved of his distinction between aggravating and mitigating circumstances and of his willingness to rely upon democratic processes to protect against *Mullaney*-abuse in the latter circumstance.

The petitioner in Jones v. United States, 526 U.S. 227, 119 S.Ct. 1215, 143 L.Ed.2d 311 (1999) was convicted under the federal carjacking statute, which made it a federal crime to steal a motor vehicle by use of a firearm. The offense was punishable by not more then 15 years imprisonment, but if serious bodily injury resulted by not more than 25 years and if death resulted by any number of years up to life. Jones was simply charged with committing carjacking with no allegation of serious bodily injury or death. After his conviction, the District Court, based on information about injuries to the victim contained in the presentence investigation report, imposed a sentence of 25 years. The Supreme Court, in an opinion by Justice Souter, held that the serious bodily injury must be plead and proved at trial to authorize the 25 year sentence since the fact is an element of the offense, not merely a sentence enhancement fact. The Court distinguished McMillan v. Pennsylvania on the ground that the provision in that case merely required the imposition of a minimum sentence upon showing of the enhancement fact and did not attempt to increase the maximum punishment otherwise authorized for the offense. The Court also distinguished Almendarez–Torres v. United States [Chapter 25 of this Supplement] on the ground of the history of treatment of prior convictions as a sentencing factor, not an element of a subsequent offense.

Finally, Justice Souter noted for the Court that adopting the position that the fact of serious bodily injury is merely a sentence enhancer would place the statute in constitutional jeopardy under due process and jury trial provisions, which is a further reason for interpreting it to create an element of the offense instead. Justice Stevens concurred on the ground that the due process and jury trial provisions of the Constitution forbid making serious bodily injury a sentence enhancement. Justice Scalia concurred on the ground that to do so would violate the right to trial by jury. Justice Kennedy, joined by The Chief Justice and Justices O'Connor and Breyer, dissented.

3. **Evidence sufficiency review as a constitutional requirement.** *Winship* has clearly directed increased attention at the sufficiency of the evidence to support a state conviction. Earlier, in Thompson v. City of Louisville, 362 U.S. 199, 80 S.Ct. 624, 4 L.Ed.2d 654 (1960), the Court held that a state conviction violated Due Process when there was "no evidence whatever" in the record supporting the finding of guilt. But in Jackson v. Virginia, 443 U.S. 307, 99 S.Ct. 2781, 61 L.Ed.2d 560 (1979), the Court held that in light of *Winship* greater scrutiny of the sufficiency of the evidence was warranted:

> After *Winship* the critical inquiry on review of the sufficiency of the evidence to support a criminal conviction must be not simply to determine whether the jury was properly instructed, but to determine whether the record evidence could reasonably support a finding of guilt beyond a reasonable doubt. But this inquiry does not require a court to "ask itself whether *it* believes that the evidence at the trial established guilt beyond a reasonable doubt." Instead, the relevant question is whether, after viewing the evidence in the light most favorable to the prosecution, *any* rational trier of fact could have found the essential elements of the crime beyond a reasonable doubt.

443 U.S. at 318–19, 99 S.Ct. at 2788–89, 61 L.Ed.2d at 573. On the facts of the case before it, the Court found sufficient circumstantial evidence that the petitioner acted with premeditation in killing the deceased to support the conviction.

4. **Burdens of production and persuasion.** Jury instructions may raise constitutional issues by classifying and allocating the burdens of going forward with the evidence and of proof. In Henderson v. Kibbe, 431 U.S. 145, 97 S.Ct. 1730, 52 L.Ed.2d 203 (1977), the defendant was charged with second degree murder. Prosecution evidence showed that he had abducted the highly-intoxicated victim, robbed him, and left him abandoned—without his glasses or warm clothing—on a rural, unlighted road. Another driver, traveling in excess of the posted speed limit, subsequently struck the victim and killed him. The controlling statute provided for liability of a defendant if, "under circumstances evincing a depraved indifference to human life, he recklessly engages in conduct which creates a grave risk of death to another person, and thereby causes the death of another person". Although there was substantial argument over whether the cause of the victim's death was the defendant's conduct or that of the driver, no instructions concerning the meaning of the statutory language—"thereby causes the death of another person"—were requested or given. Kibbe was convicted, but in later federal habeas corpus litigation the Second Circuit held that the failure to instruct the jury on causation created a high risk that the jury had not made a finding that the prosecution had proven causation by proof beyond a reasonable doubt. Consequently, the conviction violated In re Winship. The Supreme Court reversed, noting that a convicted person's burden of establishing that an erroneous instruction renders the conviction subject to collateral attack is especially heavy when no request for the instruction was made in the trial court. Although an instruction on causation would not have been cumulative of the instruction defining recklessness, the Court concluded, it was logical to assume that an instruction on causation would not have affected the

jury verdict. Would such an instruction have been constitutionally necessary had Kibbe specifically and vigorously demanded it at trial?

In Sandstrom v. Montana, 442 U.S. 510, 99 S.Ct. 2450, 61 L.Ed.2d 39 (1979), the petitioner was convicted of the offense of deliberate murder, which required proof that he intentionally caused the death of another. Petitioner had confessed to killing the victim but contended it was not done intentionally, and relied upon the testimony of mental health experts in support of his contention. Over his objection, the trial court instructed the jury without further elaboration that the "law presumes that a person intends the ordinary consequences of his voluntary acts." A unanimous Supreme Court held that the instruction violated the petitioner's rights under *Winship*. Proceeding on the basis that the relevant question is how a reasonable jury might understand such an instruction, the Court suggested four possible interpretations that it might have been given: as merely a permissible inference; as a statement that the burden of producing "some evidence" is upon the defendant but that the ultimate burden of persuasion remains upon the prosecution; as a statement that the burden of persuasion is upon the defendant; and as a conclusive presumption or rule of law that must control its deliberations on that issue. Since either of the latter two interpretations would violate petitioner's rights under *Winship* and since it cannot be said the jury did not employ one of them in reaching its verdict, the conviction was reversed.

In Francis v. Franklin, 471 U.S. 307, 105 S.Ct. 1965, 85 L.Ed.2d 344 (1985), Justice Brennan, for a 5–4 Court, found a denial of due process even when the *Sandstrom* instruction explicitly informed the jury that the presumption of intent was rebuttable and the entire jury charge contained several general instructions concerning the presumption of innocence and the States burden of proof beyond a reasonable doubt:

* * *

The analysis is straightforward. "The threshold inquiry in ascertaining the constitutional analysis applicable to this kind of jury instruction is to determine the nature of the presumption it describes." *Winship*, 442 U.S., at 514, 99 S.Ct., at 2454. The court must determine whether the challenged portion of the instruction creates a mandatory presumption . . . or merely a permissive inference . . .

Mandatory presumptions must be measured against the standards of *Winship* as elucidated in *Sandstrom*. Such presumptions violate the Due Process Clause if they relieve the State of the burden of persuasion on an element of an offense. . . .[6] A permissive inference does not relieve the State of its burden of persuasion because it still requires the State to convince the jury that the suggested conclusion should be inferred based on the predicate facts proven. Such inferences do not necessarily implicate the concerns of *Sandstrom*. A permissive inference violates the Due Process Clause only if the suggested conclusion is not one that reason and common sense justify in light of the proven facts before the jury. . . .

Analysis must focus initially on the specific language challenged, but the inquiry does not end there. If a specific portion of the jury charge, considered in isolation, could reasonably have been understood as creating a presumption that relieves the State of its burden of persuasion on an element of an offense, the potentially offending words must be considered in the context of the charge

---

6. We are not required to decide in this case whether a mandatory presumption that shifts only a burden of production to the defendant is consistent with the Due Process Clause, and we express no opinion on that question.

as a whole. Other instructions might explain the particular infirm language to the extent that a reasonable juror could not have considered the charge to have created an unconstitutional presumption. ...This analysis "requires careful attention to the words actually spoken to the jury ..., for whether a defendant has been accorded his constitutional rights depends upon the way in which a reasonable juror could have interpreted the instruction." *Sandstrom, supra,* 442 U.S., at 514, 99 S.Ct., at 2454.

* * *

As we explained in *Sandstrom,* general instructions on the State's burden of persuasion and the defendant's presumption of innocence are not "rhetorically inconsistent with a conclusive or burden-shifting presumption," because "[t]he jury could have interpreted the two sets of instructions as indicating that the presumption was a means by which proof beyond a reasonable doubt as to intent could be satisfied." 442 U.S., at 518–519, n. 7, 99 S.Ct., at 2456, n. 7.

* * *

Language that merely contradicts and does not explain a constitutionally infirm instruction will not suffice to absolve the infirmity. A reviewing court has no way of knowing which of the two irreconcilable instructions the jurors applied in reaching their verdict.[7]

471 U.S. at 313–22, 105 S.Ct. at 1971–75, 85 L.Ed.2d at 353–58.

5. **Harmless error.** When, if ever, may an instruction of the type condemned by *Sandstrom* and *Franklin* be considered harmless error?

In Rose v. Clark, 478 U.S. 570, 106 S.Ct. 3101, 92 L.Ed.2d 460 (1986), the trial court instructed the jury that malice is an element of murder and that all homicides are presumed to be malicious in the absence of evidence which would rebut that presumption. Respondent was found guilty of first-degree murder for one killing and of second-degree murder for the other. On federal habeas corpus, the District Court held that the trial court's instruction violated *Sandstrom.* This was affirmed by the Court of Appeals, which also held that the error could not be regarded as harmless because respondent had contested the issue of malice at the trial. The Supreme Court, in an opinion by Justice Powell, vacated and remanded. The Court concluded that the harmless error standard of Chapman v. California, discussed infra, applies. It made the generalization that

> if the defendant had counsel and was tried by an impartial adjudicator, there is a strong presumption that any other errors that may have occurred are subject to harmless error analysis. The thrust of the many constitutional rules governing the conduct of criminal trials is to ensure that those trials lead to fair and correct judgments. Where a reviewing court can find that the record developed at trial establishes guilt beyond a reasonable doubt, the interest in fairness had been satisfied and the judgment should be affirmed. As we have repeatedly

---

7. The Court today holds that contradictory instructions as to intent—one of which imparts to the jury an unconstitutional understanding of the allocation of burdens of persuasion—create a reasonable likelihood that a juror understood the instructions in an unconstitutional manner, unless other language in the charge *explains* the infirm language sufficiently to eliminate this possibility. If such a reasonable possibility of an unconstitutional understanding exists, "we have no way of knowing that [the defendant] was not convicted on the basis of the unconstitutional instruction." *Sandstrom,* 442 U.S., at 526, 99 S.Ct., at 2460. For this reason, it has been settled law since Stromburg v. California, 283 U.S. 359, 51 S.Ct. 532, 75 L.Ed. 1117 (1931), that when there exists a reasonable possibility that the jury relied on an unconstitutional understanding of the law in reaching a guilty verdict, that verdict must be set aside.

stated, "the Constitution entitles a criminal defendant to a fair trial, not a perfect one."

478 U.S. at 579, 106 S.Ct. at 3106, 92 L.Ed.2d at 471. Because the Court of Appeals did not consider whether the error here was harmless under *Chapman* the case was remanded with instructions to do so.

The Court further discussed harmless error in the context of burden-shifting jury instructions in Yates v. Evatt, 500 U.S. 391, 111 S.Ct. 1884, 114 L.Ed.2d 432 (1991). In Yates' murder trial, the court instructed the jury on the definition of murder, which included "malice" as an element. It further instructed the jury that malice is implied or presumed (1) from the willful, deliberate and intentional doing of an unlawful act and (2) from the use of a deadly weapon. The state supreme court found that these were mandatory presumptions, although rebuttable ones, and were, therefore, unconstitutional under *Sandstrom* and *Francis*. However, it found them to be harmless errors. The Supreme Court, in an opinion by Justice Souter, reversed. It established an approach to analyzing whether burden-shifting instructions were harmless under Chapman v. California (Casebook p. 1236) test of whether it appears "beyond a reasonable doubt that the error complained of did not contribute to the verdict obtained." The ultimate question is whether the "error [was] unimportant in relation to everything else the jury considered on the issue in question, as revealed by the record." The first step is to ask what evidence, based on the instructions and the record, the jury must have considered in reaching its verdict. The second step is to weigh the probative force of that evidence against the probative force of the invalid presumption. The standard is

> whether the force of the evidence presumably considered by the jury in accordance with the instructions is so overwhelming as to leave it beyond a reasonable doubt that the verdict resting on that evidence would have been the same in the absence of the presumption. It is only when the effect of the presumption is comparatively minimal to this degree that it can be said, in *Chapman's* words, that the presumption did not contribute to the verdict rendered.

500 U.S. at 405, 111 S.Ct. at 1893–94, 114 L.Ed.2d at 449. It then analyzed the evidence in light of that standard and concluded it could not find the errors harmless.

6.   **Commenting on presumption of innocence.** Jury instructions play an important part in implementing or hindering the presumption of innocence, i.e. the requirement of proof beyond a reasonable doubt. What happens when the prosecution makes derogatory comments about the presumption of innocence and the court then refuses to give a jury instruction on the presumption?

Taylor v. Kentucky, 436 U.S. 478, 98 S.Ct. 1930, 56 L.Ed.2d 468 (1978), was a state prosecution for robbery. The only prosecution witness was the victim, who identified Taylor as the robber; Taylor testified to an alibi. In the opening statement, the prosecutor observed that the complaining witness had taken out a warrant against Taylor and that the grand jury had indicted Taylor. In the closing statement, the prosecutor stated that Taylor, "like any other defendant who's ever been tried who's in the penitentiary or in the reformatory today," had the presumption of innocence, and in the course of argument declared that "[o]ne of the first things defendants do after they rip someone off, they get rid of the evidence." Defense counsel asked the trial judge to instruct the jury that "[t]he law presumes a defendant to be innocent of a crime" and that the indictment, which had been read to the jury, was not evidence to be considered against the defendant. The trial judge refused these requests but did instruct the jury that the state had the burden of proving Taylor's guilt beyond a reasonable doubt. The Supreme Court reversed, finding that on the facts of Taylor's case due process was violated by the trial judge's refusal of the requested instruction on the presumption of innocence. Without holding that the prosecutor's comments and argument were reversible error or even improper, the Court found that they were relevant to the issue before it. The comments during opening argument invited the jury to draw inferences of guilt from the fact of arrest and indictment. The references during closing argument to Taylor's status as a defendant implied that all defendants are guilty and invited the jury to consider this in determining his guilt or innocence of the crime charged.

Consequently, the refusal of the requested instructions on presumption of innocence deprived Taylor of a fair trial.

However, in Kentucky v. Whorton, 441 U.S. 786, 99 S.Ct. 2088, 60 L.Ed.2d 640 (1979) (per curiam), where the Kentucky Supreme Court had held that failure to give the presumption of innocence instruction automatically required reversal of the respondent's conviction under *Taylor,* the Supreme Court reversed on the ground that *Taylor* should not be given such an expansive interpretation:

> [T]he failure to give a requested instruction on the presumption of innocence does not in and of itself violate the Constitution. Under *Taylor,* such a failure must be evaluated in light of the totality of the circumstances— including all the instructions to the jury, the arguments of counsel, whether the weight of the evidence was overwhelming, and other relevant factors—to determine whether the defendant received a constitutionally fair trial.

441 U.S. at 789, 99 S.Ct. at 2090, 60 L.Ed.2d at 643. Mr. Justice Stewart, joined by Justices Brennan and Marshall, dissented on the ground that failure to give the instruction upon request is always constitutional error. They would have vacated the judgment for consideration of whether the error was harmless. Compare Coffin v. United States, 156 U.S. 432, 460–61, 15 S.Ct. 394, 405–06, 39 L.Ed. 481, 493–94 (1895), holding that in federal criminal trials it is reversible error to refuse a request for a proper instruction on the presumption of innocence.

7. **Defining proof beyond a reasonable doubt.** Trial courts sometimes attempt to define reasonable doubt in jury instructions mandating use of the constitutional standard of proof beyond a reasonable doubt. In Cage v. Louisiana, 498 U.S. 39, 111 S.Ct. 328, 112 L.Ed.2d 339 (1990), the trial court had included the following in the jury instructions concerning the meaning of reasonable doubt:

> "This doubt, however, must be a reasonable one; that is one that is founded upon a real tangible substantial basis and not upon mere caprice and conjecture. *It must be such doubt as would give rise to a grave uncertainty,* raised in your mind by reasons on the unsatisfactory character of the evidence or lack thereof. A reasonable doubt is not a mere possible doubt. *It is an actual substantial doubt.* It is a doubt that a reasonable man can seriously entertain. What is required is not an absolute or mathematical certainty, but a *moral certainty.*"

498 U.S. at 40, 111 S.Ct. at 329, 112 L.Ed.2d at 342 (alteration in original). The Supreme Court, per curiam, found this instruction violated In re Winship,

> The charge * * * equated a reasonable doubt with a "grave uncertainty" and an "actual substantial doubt," and stated that what was required was a "moral certainty" that the defendant was guilty. It is plain to us that the words "substantial" and "grave," as they are commonly understood, suggest a higher degree of doubt than is required for acquittal under the reasonable doubt standard. When those statements are then considered with the reference to "moral certainty," rather than evidentiary certainty, it becomes clear that a reasonable juror could have interpreted the instruction to allow a finding of guilt based on a degree of proof below that required by the Due Process Clause.

498 U.S. at 41, 111 S.Ct. at 329–30, 112 L.Ed.2d at 342. What definition of reasonable doubt could a trial court give that would satisfy Due Process? Should a trial court refrain from giving the jury any definition at all? Is the trial court constitutionally required to give a definition? Is "proof beyond a reasonable doubt" a concept the jury can be expected to understand without elaboration?

The Court in Victor v. Nebraska, 511 U.S. 1, 114 S.Ct. 1239, 127 L.Ed.2d 583 (1994), in an opinion by Justice O'Connor, held that the instructions in that case and in Sandoval v. California did not violate due process. The instruction in Sandoval v. California defined reasonable doubt by using the words "moral evidence" and "moral certainty." Victor challenged the instruction in his case for using the terms "substantial doubt" and "strong probabilities" in defining the burden of proof. Unlike in Cage v. Louisiana, the Court concluded here that " 'taken as a whole, the instructions correctly conveyed the concept of reasonable doubt to the jury.' * * * There is no reasonable likelihood that the jurors who determined petitioners' guilt applied the instructions in a way that violated the Constitution." 511 U.S. at 22–23, 114 S.Ct. at 1251, 127 L.Ed.2d at 601.

A jury instruction on reasonable doubt that violates *Cage* cannot be harmless error, the Court held in Sullivan v. Louisiana, 508 U.S. 275, 113 S.Ct. 2078, 124 L.Ed.2d 182 (1993). The Fifth Amendment requirement of proof beyond a reasonable doubt and the Sixth Amendment requirement of a jury verdict are interrelated, Justice Scalia reasoned for the Court, and a verdict returned by a jury inaccurately instructed on reasonable doubt does not meet the Sixth Amendment jury trial requirement. As applied to harmless error situations, the Sixth Amendment jury trial guarantee demands that a reviewing court inquire as to what if any effect the error had upon the verdict actually returned in the case. It does not permit an inquiry into what effect the error might have upon some "reasonable" jury. If under *Cage* a jury has been misinstructed on the prosecution's burden of proof, all of the jury's findings are vitiated. There is, therefore, no verdict to use in a harmless error analysis.

> There being no jury verdict of guilty-beyond-a-reasonable-doubt, the question whether the *same* verdict of guilty-beyond-a-reasonable-doubt would have been rendered absent the constitutional error is utterly meaningless. There is no *object*, so to speak, upon which harmless-error scrutiny can operate. The most an appellate court can conclude is that a jury *would surely have found* [the defendant] guilty beyond a reasonable doubt—not that the jury's actual finding of guilty beyond a reasonable doubt *would surely not have been different* absent the constitutional error. That is not enough.

508 U.S. at 280, 113 S.Ct. at 2082, 124 L.Ed.2d at 189–90. Alternatively, the Court reasoned, the right to a jury verdict of guilty beyond a reasonable doubt is "a 'basic protectio[n]' whose precise effects are unmeasurable." Therefore, an instruction that violates this right is one of the "structural defects in the constitution of the trial mechanism, which defy analysis by 'harmless error' standards." Under Arizona v. Fulminante, 499 U.S. 279, 111 S.Ct. 1246, 113 L.Ed.2d 302 (1991), such defects cannot be harmless error.

8. **Witness credibility instructions.** Jury instructions pertaining to the credibility of witnesses also affect the burden of proof. In Cool v. United States, 409 U.S. 100, 93 S.Ct. 354, 34 L.Ed.2d 335 (1972), it was held constitutional error to instruct jurors that they should disregard the testimony of an alleged accomplice (called by the defense) unless they were convinced it was true beyond a reasonable doubt. Given the heavy reliance upon the testimony by the defense, the Court commented, the effect of the instruction was to shift to the defendant the burden of proving innocence by proof beyond a reasonable doubt. In Cupp v. Naughten, 414 U.S. 141, 94 S.Ct. 396, 38 L.Ed.2d 368 (1973), several eyewitnesses identified the

defendant as the perpetrator of the robbery charged and the defense produced no witnesses. In addition to instructing the jury on the prosecution's burden of proof, the trial judge told them:

> "Every witness is presumed to speak the truth. This presumption may be overcome by the manner in which the witness testifies, by the nature of his or her testimony, by evidence affecting his or her character, interest, or motives, by contradictory evidence, or by a presumption."

414 U.S. at 142, 94 S.Ct. at 398, 38 L.Ed.2d at 371. This was held not to invalidate the conviction.

9. **Trying defendant in jail clothes.** Other aspects of the conduct of a trial may also infringe upon the right to have the prosecution prove guilt beyond a reasonable doubt. In Estelle v. Williams, 425 U.S. 501, 96 S.Ct. 1691, 48 L.Ed.2d 126 (1976), the Court assumed that compelling a defendant to appear at trial in jail clothing would violate the right:

> [T]he accused's condition implicit in such distinctive, identifiable attire may affect a juror's judgment. The defendant's clothing is so likely to be a continuing influence throughout the trial that, not unlike placing a jury in the custody of deputy sheriffs who were also witnesses for the prosecution, an unacceptable risk is presented of impermissible factors coming into play.

> * * *

> That it may be more convenient for jail administrators ... provides no justification for the practice.

425 U.S. at 504–05, 96 S.Ct. at 1693, 48 L.Ed.2d at 131. But it also noted that in some situations a defendant might prefer to stand trial in jail garments, hoping by this to elicit sympathy from the jury. The constitutional prohibition, therefore, is against compelling a defendant to stand trial in identifiable prison clothing. Since the respondent in *Williams* had not objected before the trial judge to the unavailability of street clothing, the Court concluded, there was no showing of the compulsion necessary to establish a constitutional violation.

B.   RIGHT TO A TRIAL BY JURY

Historically, the right to trial by jury has been one of the unique attributes of adjudication of guilt or innocence by trial rather than plea. But implementation of that right in the modern context involves several complex problems. It is necessary to determine whether the right exists in all criminal prosecutions and, if not, where the line is to be drawn. Limits upon the composition of the jury must be defined. Finally, the appropriate size and vote required for a determination of guilt or innocence must be determined. These matters are the subject of this Section.

The Sixth Amendment right to jury trial and the Fifth Amendment right to proof beyond a reasonable doubt are "interrelated." Sullivan v. Louisiana, 508 U.S. 275, 278, 113 S.Ct. 2078, 2081, 124 L.Ed.2d 182, 188 (1993). Together, "these provisions require criminal convictions to rest upon a jury determination that the defendant is guilty of every element of the crime with which he is charged, beyond a reasonable doubt." United States v. Gaudin, 515 U.S. 506, 518, 115 S.Ct. 2310, 2313, 132 L.Ed.2d 444, 449 (1995). *Gaudin* presented the question whether there is an exception to this general rule for the materiality of the allegedly false statement in a perjury prosecution. At Gaudin's trial for making false statements on federal loan documents, the trial judge instructed the jury that the Government was required to prove that the alleged false statements were material but he added:

> [t]he issue of materiality ... is not submitted to you for your decision but rather is a matter for the decision of the court. You are instructed that the statements charged in the indictment are material statements.

Finding that this was error, the Court considered and rejected the Government's contention that case law indicating that materiality is a matter for the court rather than the jury created or reflected an exception to the general Fifth and Sixth Amendment rule:

> [W]e find nothing like a consistent historical tradition supporting the proposition that the element of materiality in perjury prosecutions is to be decided by the judge. Since that proposition is contrary to the uniform general understanding (and we think the only understanding consistent with principle) that the Fifth and Sixth Amendments require conviction by a jury of all elements of the crime, we must reject those cases that have embraced it. Though uniform postratification practice can shed light upon the meaning of an ambiguous constitutional provision, the practice here is not uniform, and the core meaning of the constitutional guarantees is unambiguous.

515 U.S. at 518–19, 115 S.Ct. at 2317–18, 132 L.Ed.2d at 455.

1.   PROSECUTIONS TO WHICH THE RIGHT APPLIES

The Sixth Amendment grants the right to trial by jury to defendants in "all criminal prosecutions." The right to a jury in state criminal proceedings, however, is not specifically provided for in the Federal Constitution. The following case deals with that issue.

Duncan v. Louisiana

Supreme Court of the United States, 1968.
391 U.S. 145, 88 S.Ct. 1444, 20 L.Ed.2d 491.

■ MR. JUSTICE WHITE delivered the opinion of the Court.

Appellant, Gary Duncan, was convicted of simple battery.... Under Louisiana law simple battery is a misdemeanor, punishable by a maximum of two years' imprisonment and a $300 fine. Appellant sought trial by jury, but because the Louisiana Constitution grants jury trials only in cases in which capital punishment or imprisonment at hard labor may be imposed, the trial judge denied the request. Appellant was convicted and sentenced to serve 60 days in the parish prison and pay a fine of $150. Appellant sought review in the Supreme Court of Louisiana, asserting that the denial of jury trial violated rights guaranteed to him by the United States Constitution. The Supreme Court, finding "[n]o error of law in the ruling complained of," denied appellant a writ of certiorari. Pursuant to 28 U.S.C.A. § 1257(2) appellant sought review in this Court, alleging that the Sixth and Fourteenth Amendments to the United States Constitution secure the right to jury trial in state criminal prosecutions where a sentence as long as two years may be imposed. . . .

Appellant was 19 years of age when tried. While driving on Highway 23 in Plaquemines Parish on October 18, 1966, he saw two younger cousins engaged in a conversation by the side of the road with four white boys. Knowing his cousins, Negroes who had recently transferred to a formerly all-white high school, had reported the occurrence of racial incidents at the school, Duncan stopped the car, got out, and approached the six boys. At trial the white boys and a white onlooker testified, as did appellant and his cousins. The testimony was in dispute on many points, but the witnesses agreed that appellant and the white boys spoke to each other, that appellant encouraged his cousins to break off the encounter and enter his car and that appellant was about to enter the car himself for the purpose of driving away with his cousins. The whites testified that just before getting in the car appellant slapped Herman Landry, one of the white boys, on the elbow. The Negroes testified that appellant had not slapped Landry, but had merely touched him. The trial judge concluded that the State had proved beyond a reasonable doubt that Duncan had committed simple battery, and found him guilty.

I.

The Fourteenth Amendment denies the States the power to "deprive any person of life, liberty, or property, without due process of law." In resolving conflicting claims concerning the meaning of this spacious language, the Court has looked increasingly to the Bill of Rights for guidance; many of the rights guaranteed by the first eight Amendments to the Constitution have been held to be protected against state action by the Due Process Clause of the Fourteenth Amendment. . . .

The test for determining whether a right extended by the Fifth and Sixth Amendments with respect to federal criminal proceedings is also protected against state action by the Fourteenth Amendment has been phrased in a variety of ways in the opinions of this Court. The question has been asked whether a right is among those " 'fundamental principles of liberty and justice which lie at the base of all our civil and political institutions,' "; whether it is "basic in our system of jurisprudence,"; and whether it is "a fundamental right, essential to a fair trial". The claim before us is that the right to trial by jury guaranteed by the Sixth Amendment meets these tests. The position of Louisiana, on the other hand, is that the Constitution imposes upon the States no duty to give a jury trial in any criminal case, regardless of the seriousness of the crime or the size of the punishment which may be imposed. Because we believe that trial by jury in criminal cases is fundamental to the American scheme of justice, we hold that the Fourteenth Amendment guarantees a right of jury trial in all criminal cases which—were they to be tried in a federal court—would come within the Sixth Amendment's guarantee. Since we consider the appeal before us to be such a case, we hold that the Constitution was violated when appellant's demand for jury trial was refused.

The history of trial by jury in criminal cases has been frequently told. It is sufficient for present purposes to say that by the time our Constitution was written, jury trial in criminal cases had been in existence in England for several centuries and carried impressive credentials traced by many to Magna Carta.

* * *

Jury trial came to America with English colonists, and received strong support from them. Royal interference with the jury trial was deeply resented. Among the resolutions adopted by the First Congress of the American Colonies (the Stamp Act Congress) on October 19, 1765—resolutions deemed by their authors to state "the most essential rights and liberties of the colonists"—was the declaration:

"That trial by jury is the inherent and invaluable right of every British subject in these colonies." . . .

The Constitution itself, in Art. III, § 2, commanded:

"The Trial of all Crimes, except Cases of Impeachment, shall be by Jury; and such Trial shall be held in the State where the said Crimes shall have been committed."

Objections to the Constitution because of the absence of a bill of rights were met by the immediate submission and adoption of the Bill of Rights. Included was the Sixth Amendment which, among other things provided:

"In all criminal prosecutions, the accused shall enjoy the right to a speedy and public trial, by an impartial jury of the State and district wherein the crime shall have been committed."

The constitutions adopted by the original States guaranteed jury trial. Also, the constitution of every State entering the Union thereafter in one form or another protected the right to jury trial in criminal cases.

* * *

Jury trial continues to receive strong support. The laws of every State guarantee a right to jury trial in serious criminal cases; no State has dispensed with it; nor are there significant movements underway to do so. Indeed, the three most recent state constitutional revisions, in Maryland, Michigan, and New York, carefully preserved the right of the accused to have the judgment of a jury when tried for a serious crime.

* * *

The guarantees of jury trial in the Federal and State Constitutions reflect a profound judgment about the way in which law should be enforced and justice administered. A right to jury trial is granted to criminal defendants in order to prevent oppression by the Government. Those who wrote our constitutions knew from history and experience that it was necessary to protect against unfounded criminal charges brought to eliminate enemies and against judges too responsive to the voice of higher authority. The framers of the constitutions strove to create an independent judiciary but insisted upon further protection against arbitrary action. Providing an accused with the right to be tried by a jury of his peers gave him an inestimable safeguard against the corrupt or overzealous prosecutor and against the compliant, biased, or eccentric judge. If the defendant preferred the common-sense judgment of a jury to the more tutored but perhaps less sympathetic reaction of the single judge, he was to have it. Beyond this, the jury trial provisions in the Federal and State Constitutions reflect a fundamental decision about the exercise of official power—a reluctance to entrust plenary powers over the life and liberty of the citizen to one judge or to a group of judges. Fear of unchecked power, so typical of our State and Federal Governments in other respects, found expression in the criminal law in this insistence upon community participation in the determination of guilt or innocence. The deep commitment of the Nation to the right of jury trial in serious criminal cases as a defense against arbitrary law enforcement qualifies for protection under the Due Process Clause of the Fourteenth Amendment, and must therefore be respected by the States.

Of course jury trial has "its weaknesses and the potential for misuse." We are aware of the long debate, especially in this century, among those who write about the administration of justice, as to the wisdom of permitting untrained laymen to determine the facts in civil and criminal proceedings. Although the debate has been intense, with powerful voices on either side most of the controversy has centered on the jury in civil cases. Indeed, some of the severest critics of civil juries acknowledge that the arguments for criminal juries are much stronger. In addition, at the heart of the dispute have been express or implicit assertions that juries are incapable of adequately understanding evidence or determining issues of fact, and that they are unpredictable, quixotic, and little better than a roll of dice. Yet, the most recent and exhaustive study of the jury in criminal cases concluded that juries do understand the evidence and come to sound conclusions in most of the cases presented to them and that when juries differ with the result at which the judge would have arrived, it is usually because they are serving some of the very purposes for which they were created and for which they are now employed.[a]

The State of Louisiana urges that holding that the Fourteenth Amendment assures a right to jury trial will cast doubt on the integrity of every trial conducted without a jury. Plainly, this is not the import of our holding. Our conclusion is that in the American States, as in the federal judicial system, a general grant of jury trial for serious offenses is a fundamental right, essential for preventing miscarriages of justice and for assuring that fair trials are provided for all defendants. We would not assert, however, that every criminal trial—or any particular trial—held before a judge alone is unfair or that a defendant may never be as fairly treated by a judge as he would be by a jury. Thus we hold no constitutional doubts about the practices, common in both federal and state courts, of accepting waivers of jury trial and prosecuting petty crimes without extending a right to jury trial. However, the fact is that in most places more trials for serious crimes are to juries than to a court alone; a great many defendants prefer the judgment of a jury to that of a court. Even where defendants are satisfied with bench trials, the right to a jury trial very

a. H. Kalven, Jr. & H. Zeisel, The American Jury 4, n. 24 (1966).

likely serves its intended purpose of making judicial or prosecutorial unfairness less likely.

* * *

II

Louisiana's final contention is that even if it must grant jury trials in serious criminal cases, the conviction before us is valid and constitutional because here the petitioner was tried for simple battery and was sentenced to only 60 days in the parish prison. We are not persuaded. It is doubtless true that there is a category of petty crimes or offenses which is not subject to the Sixth Amendment jury trial provision and should not be subject to the Fourteenth Amendment jury trial requirement here applied to the States. Crimes carrying possible penalties up to six months do not require a jury trial if they otherwise qualify as petty offenses, Cheff v. Schnackenberg, 384 U.S. 373, 86 S.Ct. 1523, 16 L.Ed.2d 629 (1966). But the penalty authorized for a particular crime is of major relevance in determining whether it is serious or not and may in itself, if severe enough, subject the trial to the mandates of the Sixth Amendment. District of Columbia v. Clawans, 300 U.S. 617, 57 S.Ct. 660, 81 L.Ed. 843 (1937). The penalty authorized by the law of the locality may be taken "as a gauge of its social and ethical judgments," 300 U.S., at 628, 81 L.Ed. at 848, of the crime in question. In *Clawans* the defendant was jailed for 60 days, but it was the 90-day authorized punishment on which the Court focused in determining that the offense was not one for which the Constitution assured trial by jury. In the case before us the Legislature of Louisiana has made simple battery a criminal offense punishable by imprisonment for up to two years and a fine. The question, then, is whether a crime carrying such a penalty is an offense which Louisiana may insist on trying without a jury.

We think not. So-called petty offenses were tried without juries both in England and in the Colonies and have always been held to be exempt from the otherwise comprehensive language of the Sixth Amendment's jury trial provisions. There is no substantial evidence that the Framers intended to depart from this established common-law practice, and the possible consequences to defendants from convictions for petty offenses have been thought insufficient to outweigh the benefits to efficient law enforcement and simplified judicial administration resulting from the availability of speedy and inexpensive nonjury adjudications. These same considerations compel the same result under the Fourteenth Amendment. Of course the boundaries of the petty offense category have always been ill-defined, if not ambulatory. . . .

In determining whether the length of the authorized prison term or the seriousness of other punishment is enough in itself to require a jury trial, we are counseled by District of Columbia v. Clawans, supra, to refer to objective criteria, chiefly the existing laws and practices in the Nation. In the federal system, petty offenses are defined as those punishable by no more than six months in prison and a $500 fine. In 49 of the 50 States crimes subject to trial without a jury, which occasionally include simple battery, are punishable by no more than one year in jail. Moreover, in the late 18th century in America crimes triable without a jury were for the most part punishable by no more than a six-month prison term, although there appear to have been exceptions to this rule. We need not, however, settle in this case the exact location of the line between petty offenses and serious crimes. It is sufficient for our purposes to hold that a crime punishable by two years in prison is, based on past and contemporary standards in this country, a serious crime and not a petty offense.[8] Consequently, appellant was entitled to a jury trial and it was error to deny it.

The judgment below is reversed and the case is remanded for proceedings not inconsistent with this opinion.

NOTES

1. **Defining a "serious" offense.** The line between "serious" and "petty" offenses, left unsettled in *Duncan,* was drawn in Baldwin v. New York, 399 U.S. 66, 90 S.Ct. 1886, 26 L.Ed.2d 437 (1970). Baldwin, after unsuccessfully petitioning for a jury trial, was convicted of "jostling" (a misdemeanor designed to deal with pickpocketing) and sentenced to the maximum term allowable, one year. On appeal, he challenged the constitutionality of his conviction under the New York statute, which prohibited jury trials in the New York City Criminal Court where he was tried. The Supreme Court reversed. Justice White, in a plurality opinion joined by Justices Brennan and Marshall, concluded that "no offense can be deemed 'petty' for purposes of the right to trial by jury where imprisonment for more than six months is authorized." 399 U.S. at 69, 90 S.Ct. at 1888, 26 L.Ed.2d at 440. Responding to the concurring opinion of Justice Black, joined by Justice Douglas, which argued that the Sixth Amendment guarantees, much as its language suggests, a jury trial "in all criminal prosecutions," Justice White continued:

> One who is threatened with the possibility of imprisonment for six months may find little difference between the potential consequences which face him, and the consequences which faced appellant here. Indeed, the prospect of imprisonment for however short a time will seldom be viewed by the accused as a trivial or "petty" matter and may well result in quite serious repercussions affecting his career and his reputation. Where the accused cannot possibly face more than six months imprisonment, we have held that these disadvantages, onerous though they may be, may be outweighed by the benefits which result from speedy and inexpensive nonjury adjudications. We cannot, however, conclude that these administrative conveniences, in light of the practices which now exist in every one of the 50 States as well as in the federal courts, can similarly

---

8. It is argued that Cheff v. Schnackenberg, 384 U.S. 373, 86 S.Ct. 1523, 16 L.Ed.2d 629 (1966), interpreted the Sixth Amendment as meaning that to the extent that the length of punishment is a relevant criterion in distinguishing between serious crimes and petty offenses, the critical factor is not the length of sentence authorized but the length of the penalty actually imposed. In our view that case does not reach the situation where a legislative judgment as to the seriousness of the crime is imbedded in the statute in the form of an express authorization to impose a heavy penalty for the crime in question. *Cheff* involved criminal contempt, an offense applied to a wide range of conduct including conduct not so serious as to require jury trial absent a long sentence. In addition criminal contempt is unique in that legislative bodies frequently authorize punishment without stating the extent of the penalty which can be imposed. The contempt statute under which Cheff was prosecuted, 18 U.S.C.A. § 401, treated the extent of punishment as a matter to be determined by the forum court. It is therefore understandable that this Court in *Cheff* seized upon the penalty actually imposed as the best evidence of the seriousness of the offense for which Cheff was tried.

justify denying an accused the important right to trial by jury where the possible penalty exceeds six months' imprisonment.

399 U.S. at 73–74, 90 S.Ct. at 1890–91, 26 L.Ed.2d at 443.

The Supreme Court returned to the task of drawing a line to define the right to a trial by jury in Blanton v. City of North Las Vegas, 489 U.S. 538, 109 S.Ct. 1289, 103 L.Ed.2d 550 (1989). Petitioner was charged with driving under the influence of alcohol, which under Nevada law carried a maximum statutory penalty of 6 months' imprisonment and a $1,000 fine. One convicted of that offense would also automatically have his motor vehicle operator's license suspended for 90 days and would be required to attend at his own expense an alcohol education course. As an alternative to imprisonment, the trial court could order a person convicted of this offense to perform 48 hours of work for the community while dressed in "distinctive garb" which identifies him as a DUI offender. Petitioner claims that the combination of these penalties made the offense a non-petty one that carried with it the right of trial by jury. Justice Marshall, writing for a unanimous Court, disagreed:

> Although we did not hold in *Baldwin* that an offense carrying a maximum prison term of six months or less automatically qualifies as a "petty" offense, and decline to do so today, we do find it appropriate to presume for purposes of the Sixth Amendment that society views such an offense as "petty." A defendant is entitled to jury trial in such circumstances only if he can demonstrate that any additional statutory penalties, viewed in conjunction with the maximum authorized period of incarceration, are so severe that they clearly reflect a legislative determination that the offense in question is a "serious" one. This standard, albeit somewhat imprecise, should ensure the availability of a jury trial in the rare situation where a legislature packs an offense it deems "serious" with onerous penalties that nonetheless "do not puncture the 6–month incarceration line."

489 U.S. at 543, 109 S.Ct. at 1293, 103 L.Ed.2d at 556–57. The Court then examined the full package of penalties for the offense and concluded it remained a petty offense for Sixth Amendment purposes.

The offense at issue in United States v. Nachtigal, 507 U.S. 1, 113 S.Ct. 1072, 122 L.Ed.2d 374 (1993)(per curiam) was driving under the influence and carried a maximum punishment of six months' imprisonment and a $5,000 fine. Alternatively, the court could impose probation not to exceed five years and to impose numerous conditions to the probation. Under *Blanton*, the Supreme Court held, this was a petty offense for which jury trial was not available. The maximum term of imprisonment—six months—creates a presumption that the offense is a petty one and the additional penalties "are not sufficiently severe to overcome this presumption." The fine could be $4,000 greater than was permissible in *Blanton*, but that was not controlling. Nor was the probation alternative:

> Like a monetary penalty, the liberty infringement caused by a term of probation is far less intrusive than incarceration. The discretionary probation conditions do not alter this conclusion; while they obviously entail a greater infringement on liberty than probation without attendant conditions, they do not approximate the severe loss of liberty caused by imprisonment for more than six months.

507 U.S. at 5, 113 S.Ct. at 1074, 122 L.Ed.2d at 380.

Petitioner in Lewis v. United States, 518 U.S. 322, 116 S.Ct. 2163, 135 L.Ed.2d 590 (1996), a postal worker, was charged with two counts of obstructing the mail. Each count carried a possible sentence of not more than six months. The federal magistrate denied petitioner's request for a jury trial on the ground each count charged but a petty offense and stated that the total sentence on both counts would not in this case exceed six months. The United States Supreme Court, in an opinion by Justice O'Connor, approved. The nature of the offense is determined by each offense, not by the possible consecutive sentences that could be imposed. The government could have charged each count in a separate charging instrument and cumulative sentences following separate non-jury trials could have been imposed. Since there was no deprivation of the right to a jury trial, the effect of the magistrate's statement limiting liability to six months total punishment was not reached. Justice Kennedy, joined by Justice Breyer, concurred in the judgment on the ground that ordinarily a jury trial right should attach in this circumstance but that since the magistrate voluntarily limited petitioner's liability to a term not to exceed six months, the Sixth Amendment was not violated in this particular case. Justice Stevens, joined by Justice Ginsburg, dissented.

2. **Juvenile proceedings.** In McKeiver v. Pennsylvania, 403 U.S. 528, 91 S.Ct. 1976, 29 L.Ed.2d 647 (1971), the Supreme Court held that the due process clause of the Fourteenth Amendment does not provide a right to trial by jury in state juvenile court delinquency proceedings despite the fact that a juvenile could be deprived of liberty for years. In a separate opinion Justice Brennan stressed the need for a state to provide some alternate procedure such as public access to the hearing to provide due process protection to a juvenile "from oppression by the Government."

2. COMPOSITION OF THE JURY

All potential jurors, as determined by the governing law, constitute the jury pool. Those called from the pool for possible selection to a petit jury are termed the jury venire (or panel). Voir dire is the questioning of venirepersons, by defense counsel, the prosecutor, and/or the court itself, to select the petit jury. If the pool or venire is not drawn from a fair cross section of the community, i.e., if certain "cognizable" groups are excluded, successful constitutional attack may result. Although the petit jury itself need not consist of a fair cross section of the community, successful constitutional attack may be made if peremptory challenges are exercised in a discriminatory manner.

Powers v. Ohio

Supreme Court of the United States, 1991
499 U.S. 400, 111 S.Ct. 1364, 113 L.Ed.2d 411

■ JUSTICE KENNEDY delivered the opinion of the Court.

Jury service is an exercise of responsible citizenship by all members of the community, including those who otherwise might not have the opportunity to contribute to our civic life. Congress recognized this over a century ago in the Civil Rights Act of 1875, which made it a criminal offense to exclude persons from jury service on account of their race. See 18 U.S.C. § 243. In a trilogy of cases decided soon after enactment of this prohibition, our Court confirmed the validity of the statute, as well as the broader constitutional imperative of race neutrality in jury selection. In the many times we have confronted the issue since those cases, we have not questioned the premise that racial discrimination in the qualification or selection of jurors offends the dignity of persons and the integrity of the courts. Despite the clarity of these commands to eliminate the taint of racial discrimination in the administration of justice, allegations of bias in the jury selection process persist. In this case, petitioner alleges race discrimination in the prosecution's use of peremptory challenges. Invoking the Equal Protection Clause and federal statutory law, and relying upon well-established principles of standing, we hold that a criminal defendant may object to race-based exclusions of jurors effected through peremptory challenges whether or not the defendant and the excluded juror share the same races.

I

Petitioner Larry Joe Powers, a white man, was indicted in Franklin County, Ohio, on two counts of aggravated murder and one count of attempted aggravated murder. Each count also included a separate allegation that petitioner had a firearm while committing the offense. Powers pleaded not guilty and invoked his right to a jury trial.

In the jury selection process, Powers objected when the prosecutor exercised his first peremptory challenge to remove a black venireperson. Powers requested the trial court to compel the prosecutor to explain, on the record, his reasons for excluding a black person. The trial court denied the request and excused the juror. The State proceeded to use nine more peremptory challenges, six of which removed black venirepersons from the jury. Each time the prosecution challenged a black prospective juror, Powers renewed his objections, citing our decision in Batson v. Kentucky, 476 U.S. 79, 106 S.Ct. 1712, 90 L.Ed.2d 69 (1986). His objections were overruled. The record does not indicate that race was somehow implicated in the crime or the trial; nor does it reveal whether any black persons sat on petitioner's petit jury or if any of the nine jurors petitioner excused by peremptory challenges were black persons.

The empaneled jury convicted Powers on counts of murder, aggravated murder, and attempted aggravated murder, each with the firearm specifications, and the trial court sentenced him to a term of imprisonment of 53 years to life. Powers appealed his conviction to the Ohio Court of Appeals, contending that the prosecutor's discriminatory use of peremptories violated the Sixth Amendment's guarantee of a fair cross section in his petit jury, the Fourteenth Amendment's Equal Protection Clause, and Article I, §§ 10 and 16, of the Ohio Constitution. Powers contended that his own race was irrelevant to the right to object to the prosecution's peremptory challenges. The Court of Appeals affirmed the conviction, and the Supreme Court of Ohio dismissed Powers' appeal on the ground that it presented no substantial constitutional question.

Petitioner sought review before us, renewing his Sixth Amendment fair cross section and Fourteenth Amendment equal protection claims. While the petition for certiorari was pending, we decided Holland v. Illinois, 493 U.S. 474, 110 S.Ct. 803, 107 L.Ed.2d 905 (1990). In Holland it was alleged the prosecution had used its peremptory challenges to exclude from the jury members of a race other than the defendant's. We held the Sixth Amendment did not restrict the exclusion of a racial group at the peremptory challenge stage. Five members of the Court there said a defendant might be able to make the objection on equal protection grounds. After our decision in Holland, we granted Powers' petition for certiorari limited to the question whether, based on the Equal Protection Clause, a white defendant may object to the prosecution's peremptory challenges of black venirepersons. 493 U.S. 1068, 110 S.Ct. 1109, 107 L.Ed.2d 1017 (1990). We now reverse and remand.

II

For over a century, this Court has been unyielding in its position that a defendant is denied equal protection of the laws when tried before a jury from which members of his or her race have been excluded by the State's purposeful conduct. "The Equal Protection Clause guarantees the defendant that the State will not exclude members of his race from the jury venire on account of race, Strauder, [100 U.S.,] at 305 [25 L.Ed. 664], or on the false assumption that members of his race as a group are not qualified to serve as jurors, see Norris v. Alabama, 294 U.S. 587, 599 [55 S.Ct. 579, 584, 79 L.Ed. 1074] (1935); Neal v. Delaware, 103 U.S. 370, 397 [26 L.Ed. 567] (1880)." Batson, supra, 476 U.S., at 86, 106 S.Ct., at 1717 (footnote omitted). Although a defendant has no right to a "petit jury composed in whole or in part of persons of [the defendant's] own race," Strauder, 100 U.S., at 305, 25 L.Ed. 664, he or she does have the right to be tried by a jury whose members are selected by nondiscriminatory criteria.

We confronted the use of peremptory challenges as a device to exclude jurors because of their race for the first time in Swain v. Alabama, 380 U.S. 202, 85 S.Ct. 824, 13 L.Ed.2d 759 (1965). Swain involved a challenge to the so-called struck jury system, a procedure designed to allow both the prosecution and the defense a maximum number of peremptory challenges. The venire in noncapital cases started with about 35 potential jurors, from which the defense and the prosecution alternated with strikes until a petit panel of 12 jurors remained. The defendant in Swain, who was himself black, alleged that the prosecutor had used the struck jury system and its numerous peremptory challenges for the purpose of excluding black persons from his petit jury. In finding that no constitutional harm was alleged, the Court in Swain sought to reconcile the command of racial neutrality in jury selection with the utility, and the tradition, of peremptory challenges. The Court declined to permit an equal protection claim premised on a pattern of jury strikes in a particular case, but acknowledged that proof of systematic exclusion of black persons through the use of peremptories over a period of time might establish an equal protection violation. Id., at 222–228, 85 S.Ct., at 836–840.

We returned to the problem of a prosecutor's discriminatory use of peremptory challenges in Batson v. Kentucky. There, we considered a situation similar to the one before us today, but with one exception: Batson, the defendant who complained that black persons were being excluded from his petit jury, was himself black. During the voir dire examination of the venire for Batson's trial, the prosecutor used his peremptory challenges to strike all four black persons on the venire, resulting in a petit jury composed only of white persons. Batson's counsel moved without success to discharge the jury before it was empaneled on the ground that the prosecutor's removal of black venirepersons violated his rights under the Sixth and Fourteenth Amendments. Relying upon the Equal Protection Clause alone, we overruled Swain to the extent it foreclosed objections to the discriminatory use of peremptories in the course of a specific trial. 476 U.S., at 90–93, 106 S.Ct., at 1719–1721. In Batson we held that a defendant can raise an equal protection challenge to the use of peremptories at his own trial by showing that the prosecutor used them for the purpose of excluding members of the defendant's race. Id., at 96, 106 S.Ct., at 1722.

The State contends that our holding in the case now before us must be limited to the circumstances prevailing in Batson and that in equal protection analysis the race of the objecting defendant constitutes a relevant precondition for a Batson challenge. Because Powers is white, the State argues, he cannot object to the exclusion of black prospective jurors. This limitation on a defendant's right to object conforms neither with our accepted rules of standing to raise a constitutional claim nor with the substantive guarantees of the Equal Protection Clause and the policies underlying federal statutory law.

In Batson, we spoke of the harm caused when a defendant is tried by a tribunal from which members of his own race have been excluded. But we did not limit our discussion in Batson to that one aspect of the harm caused by the violation. Batson "was designed 'to serve multiple ends,'" only one of which was to protect individual defendants from discrimination in the selection of jurors. Allen v. Hardy, 478 U.S. 255, 259, 106 S.Ct. 2878, 2880, 92 L.Ed.2d 199 (1986) (per curiam) (quoting Brown v. Louisiana, 447 U.S. 323, 329, 100 S.Ct. 2214, 2220, 65 L.Ed.2d 159 (1980)). Batson recognized that a prosecutor's discriminatory use of peremptory challenges harms the excluded jurors and the community at large. 476 U.S., at 87, 106 S.Ct., at 1718.

The opportunity for ordinary citizens to participate in the administration of justice has long been recognized as one of the principal justifications for retaining the jury system. See Duncan v. Louisiana, 391 U.S. 145, 147–158, 88 S.Ct. 1444, 1446–1452, 20 L.Ed.2d 491 (1968). In Balzac v. Porto Rico, 258 U.S. 298, 42 S.Ct. 343, 66 L.Ed. 627 (1922), Chief Justice Taft wrote for the Court:

> "The jury system postulates a conscious duty of participation in the machinery of justice.... One of its greatest benefits is in the security it gives the people that they, as jurors actual or possible, being part of the judicial system of the country can prevent its arbitrary use or abuse." Id., at 310, 42 S.Ct., at 347.

And, over 150 years ago, Alexis de Tocqueville remarked:

> "[T]he institution of the jury raises the people itself, or at least a class of citizens, to the bench of judicial authority [and] invests the people, or that class of citizens, with the direction of society.

> . . . . .

> " ... The jury ... invests each citizen with a kind of magistracy; it makes them all feel the duties which they are bound to discharge towards society; and the part which they take in the Government. By

obliging men to turn their attention to affairs which are not exclusively their own, it rubs off that individual egotism which is the rust of society.

. . . . .

"I do not know whether the jury is useful to those who are in litigation; but I am certain it is highly beneficial to those who decide the litigation; and I look upon it as one of the most efficacious means for the education of the people which society can employ." 1 Democracy in America 334–337 (Schocken 1st ed. 1961).

Jury service preserves the democratic element of the law, as it guards the rights of the parties and ensures continued acceptance of the laws by all of the people. See Green v. United States, 356 U.S. 165, 215, 78 S.Ct. 632, 659, 2 L.Ed.2d 672 (1958) (Black, J., dissenting). It "affords ordinary citizens a valuable opportunity to participate in a process of government, an experience fostering, one hopes, a respect for law." Duncan, supra, 391 U.S., at 187, 88 S.Ct., at 1469 (Harlan, J., dissenting). Indeed, with the exception of voting, for most citizens the honor and privilege of jury duty is their most significant opportunity to participate in the democratic process.

While States may prescribe relevant qualifications for their jurors, see Carter v. Jury Comm'n of Greene County, 396 U.S. 320, 332, 90 S.Ct. 518, 524, 24 L.Ed.2d 549 (1970), a member of the community may not be excluded from jury service on account of his or her race. "Whether jury service be deemed a right, a privilege, or a duty, the State may no more extend it to some of its citizens and deny it to others on racial grounds than it may invidiously discriminate in the offering and withholding of the elective franchise." Carter, supra, 396 U.S., at 330, 90 S.Ct., at 523. Over a century ago, we recognized that:

"The very fact that [members of a particular race] are singled out and expressly denied . . . all right to participate in the administration of the law, as jurors, because of their color, though they are citizens, and may be in other respects fully qualified, is practically a brand upon them, affixed by the law, an assertion of their inferiority, and a stimulant to that race prejudice which is an impediment to securing to individuals of the race that equal justice which the law aims to secure to all others." Strauder, supra, 100 U.S., at 308.

Discrimination in the jury selection process is the subject of a federal criminal prohibition, and has been since Congress enacted the Civil Rights Act of 1875. The prohibition has been codified at 18 U.S.C. § 243, which provides:

"No citizen possessing all other qualifications which are or may be prescribed by law shall be disqualified for service as grand or petit juror in any court of the United States, or of any State on account of race, color, or previous condition of servitude; and whoever, being an officer or other person charged with any duty in the selection or summoning of jurors, excludes or fails to summon any citizen for such cause, shall be fined not more than $5,000."

In Peters v. Kiff, 407 U.S. 493, 92 S.Ct. 2163, 33 L.Ed.2d 83 (1972), Justice White spoke of "the strong statutory policy of § 243, which reflects the central concern of the Fourteenth Amendment." Id., at 507, 92 S.Ct., at 2170 (opinion concurring in judgment). The Court permitted a white defendant to challenge the systematic exclusion of black persons from grand and petit juries. While Peters did not produce a single majority opinion, six of the Justices agreed that racial discrimination in the jury selection process cannot be tolerated and that the race of the defendant has no relevance to his or her standing to raise the claim.

Racial discrimination in the selection of jurors in the context of an individual trial violates these same prohibitions. A State "may not draw up its jury lists pursuant to neutral procedures but then resort to discrimination at 'other stages in the selection process.'" Batson, 476 U.S., at 88, 106 S.Ct., at 1718 (quoting Avery v. Georgia, 345 U.S. 559, 562, 73 S.Ct. 891, 892, 97 L.Ed. 1244 (1953)). We so held in Batson, and reaffirmed that holding in Holland. See 493 U.S., at 479, 110 S.Ct., at 806–807. In Holland, the Court held that a defendant could not rely on the Sixth Amendment to object to the exclusion of members of any distinctive group at the peremptory challenge stage. We noted that the peremptory challenge procedure has acceptance in our legal tradition. See id., at 481, 110 S.Ct., at 808. On this reasoning we declined to permit an objection to the peremptory challenge of a juror on racial grounds as a Sixth Amendment matter. As the Holland Court made explicit, however, racial exclusion of prospective jurors violates the overriding command of the Equal Protection Clause, and "race-based exclusion is no more permissible at the individual petit jury stage than at the venire stage." Id., at 479, 110 S.Ct., at 807.

We hold that the Equal Protection Clause prohibits a prosecutor from using the State's peremptory challenges to exclude otherwise qualified and unbiased persons from the petit jury solely by reason of their race, a practice that forecloses a significant opportunity to participate in civic life. An individual juror does not have a right to sit on any particular petit jury, but he or she does possess the right not to be excluded from one on account of race.

It is suggested that no particular stigma or dishonor results if a prosecutor uses the raw fact of skin color to determine the objectivity or qualifications of a juror. We do not believe a victim of the classification would endorse this view; the assumption that no stigma or dishonor attaches contravenes accepted equal protection principles. Race cannot be a proxy for determining juror bias or competence. "A person's race simply 'is unrelated to his fitness as a juror.'" Batson, supra, 476 U.S., at 87, 106 S.Ct., at 1718 (quoting Thiel v. Southern Pacific Co., supra, 328 U.S., at 227, 66 S.Ct., at 989 (Frankfurter, J., dissenting)). We may not accept as a defense to racial discrimination the very stereotype the law condemns.

We reject as well the view that race-based peremptory challenges survive equal protection scrutiny because members of all races are subject to like treatment, which is to say that white jurors are subject to the same risk of peremptory challenges based on race as are all other jurors. The suggestion that racial classifications may survive when visited upon all persons is no more authoritative today than the case which advanced the theorem, Plessy v. Ferguson, 163 U.S. 537, 16 S.Ct. 1138, 41 L.Ed. 256 (1896). This idea has no place in our modern equal protection jurisprudence. It is axiomatic that racial classifications do not become legitimate on the assumption that all persons suffer them in equal degree. Loving v. Virginia, 388 U.S. 1, 87 S.Ct. 1817, 18 L.Ed.2d 1010 (1967).

III

We must consider whether a criminal defendant has standing to raise the equal protection rights of a juror excluded from service in violation of these principles. In the ordinary course, a litigant must assert his or her own legal rights and interests, and cannot rest a claim to relief on the legal rights or interests of third parties. Department of Labor v. Triplett, 494 U.S. 715, 720, 110 S.Ct. 1428, 1431, 108 L.Ed.2d 701 (1990); Singleton v. Wulff, 428 U.S. 106, 96 S.Ct. 2868, 49 L.Ed.2d 826 (1976). This fundamental restriction on our authority admits of certain, limited exceptions. We have recognized the right of litigants to bring actions on behalf of third parties, provided three important criteria are satisfied: The litigant must have suffered an "injury in fact," thus giving him or her a "sufficiently concrete interest" in the outcome of the issue in dispute, id., at 112, 96 S.Ct., at 2873; the litigant must have a close relation to the third party, id., at 113–114, 96 S.Ct., at 2873–2874; and there must exist some hindrance to the third party's ability to protect his or her own interests. Id., at 115–116, 96 S.Ct., at 2874–2875. These criteria have been satisfied in cases where we have permitted criminal defendants to challenge their convictions by raising the rights of third parties. See, e.g., Eisenstadt v. Baird, 405 U.S. 438, 92 S.Ct. 1029, 31 L.Ed.2d 349 (1972); Griswold v. Connecticut, 381 U.S. 479, 85 S.Ct. 1678, 14 L.Ed.2d 510 (1965); see also McGowan v. Maryland, 366 U.S. 420, 81 S.Ct. 1101, 6 L.Ed.2d 393 (1961). By similar reasoning, we have permitted litigants to raise third-party rights in order to prevent possible future prosecution. See, e.g., Doe v. Bolton, 410 U.S. 179, 93 S.Ct. 739, 35 L.Ed.2d 201 (1973).

The discriminatory use of peremptory challenges by the prosecution causes a criminal defendant cognizable injury, and the defendant has a concrete interest in challenging the practice. See Allen v. Hardy, 478 U.S., at 259, 106 S.Ct., at 2880 (recognizing a defendant's interest in "neutral jury selection procedures"). This is not because the individual jurors dismissed by the prosecution may have been predisposed to favor the defendant; if that were true, the jurors might have been excused for cause. Rather, it is because racial discrimination in the selection of jurors "casts doubt on the integrity of the judicial process," Rose v. Mitchell, 443 U.S. 545, 556, 99 S.Ct. 2993, 3000, 61 L.Ed.2d 739 (1979), and places the fairness of a criminal proceeding in doubt.

The jury acts as a vital check against the wrongful exercise of power by the State and its prosecutors. Batson, 476 U.S., at 86, 106 S.Ct., at 1717. The intrusion of racial discrimination into the jury selection process damages both the fact and the perception of this guarantee. "Jury selection is the primary means by which a court may enforce a defendant's right to be tried by a jury free from ethnic, racial, or political prejudice, Rosales–Lopez v. United States, 451 U.S. 182, 188 [101 S.Ct. 1629, 1634, 68 L.Ed.2d 22]

(1981); Ham v. South Carolina, 409 U.S. 524 [93 S.Ct. 848, 35 L.Ed.2d 46] (1973); Dennis v. United States, 339 U.S. 162 [70 S.Ct. 519, 94 L.Ed. 734] (1950), or predisposition about the defendant's culpability, Irvin v. Dowd, 366 U.S. 717 [81 S.Ct. 1639, 6 L.Ed.2d 751] (1961)." Gomez v. United States, 490 U.S. 858, 873, 109 S.Ct. 2237, 2246–2247, 104 L.Ed.2d 923 (1989). Active discrimination by a prosecutor during this process condones violations of the United States Constitution within the very institution entrusted with its enforcement, and so invites cynicism respecting the jury's neutrality and its obligation to adhere to the law. The cynicism may be aggravated if race is implicated in the trial, either in a direct way as with an alleged racial motivation of the defendant or a victim, or in some more subtle manner as by casting doubt upon the credibility or dignity of a witness, or even upon the standing or due regard of an attorney who appears in the cause.

Unlike the instances where a defendant seeks to object to the introduction of evidence obtained illegally from a third party, see, e.g., United States v. Payner, 447 U.S. 727, 100 S.Ct. 2439, 65 L.Ed.2d 468 (1980), here petitioner alleges that the primary constitutional violation occurred during the trial itself. A prosecutor's wrongful exclusion of a juror by a race-based peremptory challenge is a constitutional violation committed in open court at the outset of the proceedings. The overt wrong, often apparent to the entire jury panel, casts doubt over the obligation of the parties, the jury, and indeed the court to adhere to the law throughout the trial of the cause. The voir dire phase of the trial represents the "jurors' first introduction to the substantive factual and legal issues in a case." Gomez, supra, 490 U.S., at 874, 109 S.Ct., at 2247. The influence of the voir dire process may persist through the whole course of the trial proceedings. Ibid. If the defendant has no right to object to the prosecutor's improper exclusion of jurors, and if the trial court has no duty to make a prompt inquiry when the defendant shows, by adequate grounds, a likelihood of impropriety in the exercise of a challenge, there arise legitimate doubts that the jury has been chosen by proper means. The composition of the trier of fact itself is called in question, and the irregularity may pervade all the proceedings that follow.

The purpose of the jury system is to impress upon the criminal defendant and the community as a whole that a verdict of conviction or acquittal is given in accordance with the law by persons who are fair. The verdict will not be accepted or understood in these terms if the jury is chosen by unlawful means at the outset. Upon these considerations, we find that a criminal defendant suffers a real injury when the prosecutor excludes jurors at his or her own trial on account of race.

We noted in Singleton that in certain circumstances "the relationship between the litigant and the third party may be such that the former is fully, or very nearly, as effective a proponent of the right as the latter." 428 U.S., at 115, 96 S.Ct., at 2874. Here, the relation between petitioner and the excluded jurors is as close as, if not closer than, those we have recognized to convey third-party standing in our prior cases. See, e.g., Griswold v. Connecticut, supra (Planned Parenthood official and a licensed physician can raise the constitutional rights of contraceptive users with whom they had professional relationships); Craig, supra (licensed beer vendor has standing to raise the equal protection claim of a male customer challenging a statutory scheme prohibiting the sale of beer to males under the age of 21 and to females under the age of 18); Department of Labor v. Triplett, 494 U.S. 715, 110 S.Ct. 1428, 108 L.Ed.2d 701 (1990) (attorney may challenge an attorney's fees restriction by asserting the due process rights of the client). Voir dire permits a party to establish a relation, if not a bond of trust, with the jurors. This relation continues throughout the entire trial and may in some cases extend to the sentencing as well.

Both the excluded juror and the criminal defendant have a common interest in eliminating racial discrimination from the courtroom. A venireperson excluded from jury service because of race suffers a profound personal humiliation heightened by its public character. The rejected juror may lose confidence in the court and its verdicts, as may the defendant if his or her objections cannot be heard. This congruence of interests makes it necessary and appropriate for the defendant to raise the rights of the juror. And, there can be no doubt that petitioner will be a motivated, effective advocate for the excluded venirepersons' rights. Petitioner has much at stake in proving that his jury was improperly constituted due to an equal protection violation, for we have recognized that discrimination in the jury selection process may lead to the reversal of a conviction. See Batson, 476 U.S., at 100, 106 S.Ct., at 1725; Vasquez v. Hillery, 474 U.S. 254, 264, 106 S.Ct. 617, 623, 88 L.Ed.2d 598 (1986); Rose v. Mitchell, 443 U.S., at 551, 99 S.Ct., at 2997–2998; Cassell v. Texas, 339 U.S. 282, 70 S.Ct. 629, 94 L.Ed. 839 (1950). Thus, " 'there seems little loss in terms of effective advocacy from allowing [the assertion of this claim] by' the present jus tertii champion." Craig, supra, 429 U.S., at 194, 97 S.Ct., at 455 (quoting Singleton, 428 U.S., at 118, 96 S.Ct., at 2876).

The final inquiry in our third-party standing analysis involves the likelihood and ability of the third parties, the excluded venirepersons, to assert their own rights. See Singleton, supra, at 115–116, 96 S.Ct., at 2874–2875. We have held that individual jurors subjected to racial exclusion have the legal right to bring suit on their own behalf. Carter, 396 U.S., at 329–330, 90 S.Ct., at 523–524. As a practical matter, however, these challenges are rare. See Alschuler, The Supreme Court and the Jury: Voir Dire, Peremptory Challenges, and the Review of Jury Verdicts, 56 U.Chi.L.Rev. 153, 193–195 (1989). Indeed, it took nearly a century after the Fourteenth Amendment and the Civil Rights Act of 1875 came into being for the first such case to reach this Court. See Carter, supra, at 320, 90 S.Ct., at 518.

The barriers to a suit by an excluded juror are daunting. Potential jurors are not parties to the jury selection process and have no opportunity to be heard at the time of their exclusion. Nor can excluded jurors easily obtain declaratory or injunctive relief when discrimination occurs through an individual prosecutor's exercise of peremptory challenges. Unlike a challenge to systematic practices of the jury clerk and commissioners such as we considered in Carter, it would be difficult for an individual juror to show a likelihood that discrimination against him at the voir dire stage will recur. See Los Angeles v. Lyons, 461 U.S. 95, 105–110, 103 S.Ct. 1660, 1666–1670, 75 L.Ed.2d 675 (1983). And, there exist considerable practical barriers to suit by the excluded juror because of the small financial stake involved and the economic burdens of litigation. See Vasquez, supra, 474 U.S., at 262, n. 5, 106 S.Ct., at 623, n. 5; Rose v. Mitchell, supra, 443 U.S., at 558, 99 S.Ct., at 3001. The reality is that a juror dismissed because of race probably will leave the courtroom possessing little incentive to set in motion the arduous process needed to vindicate his own rights. See Barrows v. Jackson, 346 U.S. 249, 257, 73 S.Ct. 1031, 1035, 97 L.Ed. 1586 (1953).

We conclude that a defendant in a criminal case can raise the third-party equal protection claims of jurors excluded by the prosecution because of their race. In so doing, we once again decline "to reverse a course of decisions of long standing directed against racial discrimination in the administration of justice." Cassell v. Texas, supra, 339 U.S., at 290, 70 S.Ct., at 633 (Frankfurter, J., concurring in judgment). To bar petitioner's claim because his race differs from that of the excluded jurors would be to condone the arbitrary exclusion of citizens from the duty, honor, and privilege of jury service. In Holland and Batson, we spoke of the significant role peremptory challenges play in our trial procedures, but we noted also that the utility of the peremptory challenge system must be accommodated to the command of racial neutrality. Holland, 493 U.S., at 486–487, 110 S.Ct., at 810–811; Batson, supra, 476 U.S., at 98–99, 106 S.Ct., at 1723–1724.

The Fourteenth Amendment's mandate that race discrimination be eliminated from all official acts and proceedings of the State is most compelling in the judicial system. Rose v. Mitchell, supra, 443 U.S., at 555, 99 S.Ct., at 2999–3000. We have held, for example, that prosecutorial discretion cannot be exercised on the basis of race, Wayte v. United States, 470 U.S. 598, 608, 105 S.Ct. 1524, 1531, 84 L.Ed.2d 547 (1985), and that, where racial bias is likely to influence a jury, an inquiry must be made into such bias. Ristaino v. Ross, 424 U.S. 589, 596, 96 S.Ct. 1017, 1021, 47 L.Ed.2d 258 (1976); see also Turner v. Murray, 476 U.S. 28, 106 S.Ct. 1683, 90 L.Ed.2d 27 (1986). The statutory prohibition on discrimination in the selection of jurors, 18 U.S.C. § 243, enacted pursuant to the Fourteenth Amendment's Enabling Clause, makes race neutrality in jury selection a visible, and inevitable, measure of the judicial system's own commitment to the commands of the Constitution. The courts are under an affirmative duty to enforce the strong statutory and constitutional policies embodied in that prohibition. See Peters v. Kiff, 407 U.S., at 507, 92 S.Ct., at 2170–2171 (WHITE, J., concurring in judgment); see also id., at 505, 92 S.Ct., at 2169–2170 (opinion of MARSHALL, J.).

The emphasis in Batson on racial identity between the defendant and the excused prospective juror is not inconsistent with our holding today that race is irrelevant to a defendant's standing to object to the discriminatory use of peremptory challenges. Racial identity between the defendant and the excused person might in some cases be the explanation for the prosecution's adoption of the forbidden stereotype, and if the alleged race bias takes this form, it may provide one of the easier cases to establish both a prima facie case and a conclusive showing that wrongful discrimination has occurred. But to say that the race of the defendant may be relevant to discerning bias in some cases does not mean that it will be a factor in others, for race prejudice stems from various causes and may manifest itself in different forms.

It remains for the trial courts to develop rules, without unnecessary disruption of the jury selection process, to permit legitimate and well-founded objections to the use of peremptory challenges as a mask for race prejudice. In this case, the State concedes that, if we find the petitioner has standing to object to the prosecution's use of the peremptory challenges, the case should be remanded. We find that petitioner does have standing. The judgment is reversed, and the case is remanded for further proceedings not inconsistent with our opinion.

It is so ordered.

■ Justice Scalia, with whom the Chief Justice joins, dissenting [omitted].

NOTES

1. **Civil suits.** Does *Batson* apply to civil suits between private parties? Petitioner in Edmonson v. Leesville Concrete Co., 500 U.S. 614, 111 S.Ct. 2077, 114 L.Ed.2d 660 (1991), a black construction worker, sued for injuries suffered on the work site. During jury selection, Leesville used 2 of its 3 peremptory challenges to remove blacks from the panel. The jury consisted of 11 whites and one black. The District Court rejected petitioner's *Batson* claim on the ground that decision applied only in criminal cases. The Supreme Court, in an opinion by Justice Kennedy, held that under Powers v. Ohio race-based use of strikes violates the excluded persons' equal protection rights. Although Leesville is a private party, its use of strikes was state action because strikes are authorized by law and can be used only in a court proceeding. The case was remanded for a determination whether petitioner had made a prima facie case of racial discrimination in the defendant's use of strikes. Justice O'Connor, joined by Chief Justice Rehnquist and Justice Scalia, dissented on the ground that the defendant's use of strikes did not constitute state action. Justice Scalia dissented separately, with the observation that the decision

> will not necessarily be a net help rather than hindrance to minority litigants in obtaining racially diverse juries. In criminal cases, *Batson v. Kentucky* already prevents the *prosecution* from using race-based strikes. The effect of today's decision (which logically must apply to criminal prosecutions) will be to prevent the *defendant* from doing so—so that the minority defendant can no longer seek to prevent an all-white jury, or to seat as many jurors of his own race as possible. To be sure, it is ordinarily more difficult to *prove* race-based strikes of white jurors, but defense counsel can generally be relied upon to do what we say the Constitution requires. So in criminal cases, today's decision represents a net loss to the minority litigant.

500 U.S. at 644, 111 S.Ct. at 2095, 114 L.Ed.2d at 689.

2. **Defense strikes.** *Batson* was held to apply to peremptory challenges by criminal defendants in Georgia v. McCollum, 505 U.S. 42, 112 S.Ct. 2348, 120 L.Ed.2d 33 (1992). The State filed a motion requesting an order from the trial court to preclude Respondent, who is white, from using strikes to eliminate African-Americans from his criminal jury in a trial in which the victims were African-American. The trial court denied this motion and the Georgia Supreme Court affirmed in an interlocutory appeal. The Supreme Court, in an opinion by Justice Blackmun, reversed and held that *Batson* applies to strikes used by criminal defendants:

"Be it at the hands of the State or the defense," if a court allows jurors to be excluded because of group bias, "[it] is [a] willing participant in a scheme that could only undermine the very foundation of our system of justice—our citizens' confidence in it." Just as public confidence in criminal justice is undermined by a conviction in a trial where racial discrimination has occurred in jury selection, so is public confidence undermined where a defendant, assisted by racially discriminatory peremptory strikes, obtains an acquittal.

505 U.S. at 49–50, 112 S.Ct. at 2354, 120 L.Ed.2d at 45. The Court then sought to distinguish cases in which criminal defendants have been held to have a constitutional right to question potential jurors about racial attitudes:

[A] defendant has the right to an impartial jury that can view him without racial animus, which so long has distorted our system of criminal justice. We have, accordingly, held that there should be a mechanism for removing those on the venire whom the defendant has specific reason to believe would be incapable of confronting and suppressing their racism. See Ham v. South Carolina, 409 U.S. 524, 526–527, 93 S.Ct. 848, 35 L.Ed.2d 46 (1973) * * *.

But there is a distinction between exercising a peremptory challenge to discriminate invidiously against jurors on account of race and exercising a peremptory challenge to remove an individual juror who harbors racial prejudice. This Court firmly has rejected the view that assumptions of partiality based on race provide a legitimate basis for disqualifying a person as an impartial juror.

505 U.S. at 58–59, 112 S.Ct. at 2358–59, 120 L.Ed.2d at 51. Justice Thomas concurred in the judgment with the comment, "I am certain that black criminal defendants will rue the day that this court ventured down this road that inexorably will lead to the elimination of peremptory strikes." 505 U.S. at 60, 112 S.Ct. at 2359–60, 120 L.Ed.2d at 52. Justice O'Connor dissented on the ground that there is no state action when a criminal defendant exercises a peremptory challenge.

3. **Gender-based strikes.** Does Batson apply to strikes based on gender? Petitioner in J.E.B. v. Alabama ex rel. T.B., 511 U.S. 127, 114 S.Ct. 1419, 128 L.Ed.2d 89 (1994) was the respondent in a paternity suit. The State used 9 of its 10 strikes to remove men from the jury panel, while Petitioner used 9 of his 10 strikes to remove women from the panel. The jury was composed entirely of women. Petitioner was adjudicated the father of the child and ordered to pay support. Before the Supreme Court, he claimed that the State's use of its strikes violated equal protection of the laws. The Court, in an opinion by Justice Blackmun, held that the State's use of strikes to remove men from the jury panel violated equal protection of the laws:

Discrimination in jury selection, whether based on race or on gender, causes harm to the litigants, the community, and the individual jurors who are wrongfully excluded from participation in the judicial process. The litigants are harmed by the risk that the prejudice which motivated the discriminatory selection of the jury will infect the entire proceedings * * *. The community is harmed by the State's participation in the perpetuation of invidious group stereotypes and the inevitable loss of confidence in our judicial system that state-sanctioned discrimination in the courtroom engenders.

511 U.S. at 140, 114 S.Ct. at 1427, 128 L.Ed.2d at 104. Justice O'Connor, concurring, would limit the equal protection principle to actions by the government. Justice Scalia, joined by The Chief Justice and Justice Thomas, dissented.

4. **Procedures for implementing *Batson*.** In Batson v. Kentucky, 476 U.S. 79, 106 S.Ct. 1712, 90 L.Ed.2d 69 (1986), Justice Powell established the following procedures for litigating *Batson* claims at the trial level:

[A] defendant may establish a prima facie case of purposeful discrimination in selection of the petit jury solely on evidence concerning the prosecutor's exercise of peremptory challenges at the defendant's trial. To establish such a case, the defendant first must show that he is a member of a cognizable racial group, and that the prosecutor has exercised peremptory challenges to remove from the venire members of the defendant's race. Second, the defendant is entitled to rely on the fact, as to which there can be no dispute, that peremptory challenges constitute a jury selection practice that permits "those to discriminate who are of a mind to discriminate." Finally, the defendant must show that these facts and any other relevant circumstances raise an inference that the prosecutor used that practice to exclude the veniremen from the petit jury on account of their race. This combination of factors in the empanelling of the petit jury, as in the selection of the venire, raises the necessary inference of purposeful discrimination.

In deciding whether the defendant has made the requisite showing, the trial court should consider all relevant circumstances. For example, a "pattern" of strikes against black jurors included in the particular venire might give rise to an inference of discrimination. Similarly, the prosecutor's questions and statements during *voir dire* examination and in exercising his challenges may support or refute an inference of discriminatory purpose. These examples are merely illustrative. We have confidence that trial judges, experienced in supervising *voir dire,* will be able to decide if the circumstances concerning the prosecutor's use of peremptory challenges creates a prima facie case of discrimination against black jurors.

Once the defendant makes a prima facie showing, the burden shifts to the State to come forward with a neutral explanation for challenging black jurors. Though this requirement imposes a limitation in some cases on the full peremptory character of the historic challenge, we emphasize that the prosecutor's explanation need not rise to the level justifying exercise of a challenge for cause. But the prosecutor may not rebut the defendant's prima facie case of discrimination by stating merely that he challenged jurors of the defendant's race on the assumption—or his intuitive judgment—that they would be partial to the defendant because of their shared race. Just as the Equal Protection Clause forbids the States to exclude black persons from the venire on the assumption that blacks as a group are unqualified to serve as jurors, so it forbids the States to strike black veniremen on the assumption that they will be biased in a particular case simply because the defendant is black. The core guarantee of equal protection, ensuring citizens that their State will not discriminate on account of race, would be meaningless were we to approve the exclusion of jurors on the basis of such assumptions, which arise solely from the jurors' race. Nor may the prosecutor rebut the defendant's case merely by denying that he had a discriminatory motive or "affirming his good faith in individual selections." If these general assertions were accepted as rebutting a defendant's prima facie case, the Equal Protection Clause "would be but a vain and illusory requirement." The prosecutor therefore must articulate a neutral explanation related to the particular case to be tried. The trial court then will have the duty to determine if the defendant has established purposeful discrimination.

476 U.S. at 96–98, 106 S.Ct. at 1723–24, 90 L.Ed.2d at 87–89.

5. **Language as a race-neutral reason.** In Hernandez v. New York, 500 U.S. 352, 111 S.Ct. 1859, 114 L.Ed.2d 395 (1991), the Court addressed the question what showing must be made to justify the use of peremptory challenges on racial groups. Hernandez, identified in the Supreme Court's opinion as a "Latino," was on

trial for attempted murder. The prosecutor used four peremptory challenges to exclude Latino potential jurors. A *Batson* claim was made with respect to two of those panel members. The prosecutor, without waiting for the trial court to rule on whether a *prima facie* showing had been made, volunteered that the reason he struck those two was that he was not persuaded they would be able to accept the official interpretation of Spanish language testimony because they were bilingual. This was based on their responses to that question on *voir dire* and their demeanor while responding. He added that since the defendant, victims, and all the civilian witnesses were Latino, he had no reason to exclude Latinos from the jury. The trial court found no *Batson* violation, which was upheld by the New York appellate courts on direct appeal from Hernandez' conviction. The United States Supreme Court, in a plurality opinion authored by Justice Kennedy and joined in by The Chief Justice and Justices White and Souter, affirmed. Because the prosecutor volunteered an explanation for his strikes, the question whether defendant had made a prima facie case of discrimination became moot. The prosecutor's neutral explanation—one based on something other than the race of the juror—was that

> the challenges rested neither on the intention to exclude Latino or bilingual jurors, nor on stereotypical assumptions about Latinos or bilinguals. The prosecutor's articulated basis for these challenges divided potential jurors into two classes: those whose conduct during *voir dire* would persuade him they might have difficulty in accepting the translator's rendition of Spanish-language testimony and those potential jurors who gave no such reason for doubt. Each category would include both Latinos and non-Latinos. While the prosecutor's criterion might well result in the disproportionate removal of prospective Latino jurors, that disproportionate impact does not turn the prosecutor's actions into a *per se* violation of the Equal Protection Clause.

500 U.S. at 361, 111 S.Ct. at 1867, 114 L.Ed.2d at 407. Once the prosecutor offered race-neutral explanations, the trial court was required to find whether the defendant had established purposeful discrimination. An appellate court can set aside such a finding only if it is clearly erroneous. Justice O'Connor, joined by Justice Scalia, concurred in the judgment, commenting,

> if, as in this case, the trial court believes the prosecutor's nonracial justification, and that finding is not clearly erroneous, that is the end of the matter. *Batson* does not require that a prosecutor justify a jury strike at the level of a for-cause challenge. It also does not require that the justification be unrelated to race. *Batson* requires only that the prosecutor's reason for striking a juror not *be* the juror's race.

500 U.S. at 375, 111 S.Ct. at 1875, 114 L.Ed.2d at 416. Justice Stevens, joined by Justice Marshall and in part by Justice Blackmun, dissented.

6. **Prosecutor's race-neutral explanation.** The Court refined somewhat the procedural steps in the trial litigation of a *Batson* claim in its *per curiam* opinion in Purkett v. Elem, 514 U.S. 765, 115 S.Ct. 1769, 131 L.Ed.2d 834 (1995). After the prosecutor struck two African–American panelists, respondent made a *Batson* objection. The prosecutor explained the strike of one panelist because he had long unkempt hair, a mustache and a goatee type beard. He explained striking the second panelist because he also had a mustache and goatee type beard. He added that those were the only members of the panel with facial hair. Further, the second panelist had once been the victim of a robbery with a sawed-off shotgun and the prosecutor expressed concern that he would not therefore regard the unarmed robbery being tried as robbery. The trial court overruled the *Batson* objection. On federal habeas following conviction, the Eighth Circuit found the trial court had not complied with *Batson* because the prosecutor's statement did not explain how the

objectionable features would affect each person's ability to perform duties as a juror in the case.

The Supreme Court reversed. *Batson* claims require a three step procedure in the trial court: (1) a prima facie case of discrimination by the claimant, (2) a neutral explanation for the strike in question by the party exercising the challenged strike, and (3) a showing of purposeful discrimination by the claimant. The Court of Appeals erroneously combined steps (2) and (3). Step (2) merely requires that the explanation be non-discriminatory. It does not require that the explanation must relate to trial strategy. Once a non-discriminatory explanation is provided, then the burden shifts to the *Batson* claimant to show purposeful discrimination. So long as the step (2) explanation is race-neutral, it doesn't matter that it is "silly or superstitious." Such an explanation may fail, but only at step (3) and only as part of the conclusion that the claimant has shown purposeful discrimination.

7. **Abolish peremptory challenges?** Although concurring in the reversal of the conviction in *Batson,* Justice Marshall stated:

> The decision today will not end the racial discrimination that peremptories inject into the jury-selection process. That goal can be accomplished only by eliminating peremptory challenges entirely.

* * *

Evidentiary analysis similar to that set out by the Court has been adopted as a matter of state law in States including Massachusetts and California. Cases from those jurisdictions illustrate the limitations of the approach. First, defendants cannot attack the discriminatory use of peremptory challenges at all unless the challenges are so flagrant as to establish a prima facie case. This means, in those States, that where only one or two black jurors survive the challenges for cause, the prosecutor need have no compunction about striking them from the jury because of their race. See Commonwealth v. Robinson, 382 Mass. 189, 195, 415 N.E.2d 805, 809–810 (1981) (no prima facie case of discrimination where defendant is black, prospective jurors include three blacks and one Puerto Rican, and prosecutor excludes one for cause and strikes the remainder peremptorily, producing all-white jury); People v. Rousseau, 129 Cal.App.3d 526, 536–537, 179 Cal.Rptr. 892, 897–898 (1982) (no prima facie case where prosecutor peremptorily strikes only two blacks on jury panel). Prosecutors are left free to discriminate against blacks in jury selection provided that they hold that discrimination to an "acceptable" level.

Second, when a defendant can establish a prima facie case, trial courts face the difficult burden of assessing prosecutors' motives. See King v. County of Nassau, 581 F.Supp. 493, 501–502 (E.D.N.Y.1984). Any prosecutor can easily assert facially neutral reasons for striking a juror, and trial courts are ill-equipped to second-guess those reasons. How is the court to treat a prosecutor's statement that he struck a juror because the juror had a son about the same age as defendant, see People v. Hall, 35 Cal.3d 161, 197 Cal.Rptr. 71, 672 P.2d 854 (1983), or seemed "uncommunicative," King, supra, at 498, or "never cracked a smile" and, therefore "did not possess the sensitivities necessary to realistically look at the issues and decide the facts in this case," Hall, supra, at 165, 197 Cal.Rptr. at 73, 672 P.2d, at 856? If such easily generated explanations are sufficient to discharge the prosecutor's obligation to justify his strikes on nonracial grounds, then the protection erected by the Court today may be illusory.

Nor is outright prevarication by prosecutors the only danger here. "[I]t is even possible that an attorney may lie to himself in an effort to convince himself that his motives are legal." King, supra, at 502. A prosecutor's own conscious or unconscious racism may lead him easily to the conclusion that a prospective black juror is "sullen," or "distant," a characterization that would not have come to his mind if a white juror had acted identically. A judge's own conscious or unconscious racism may lead him to accept such an explanation as well supported. As Justice Rehnquist concedes, prosecutors' peremptories are based on their "seat-of-the-pants instincts" as to how particular jurors will vote. Yet "seat-of-the-pants instincts" may often be just another term for racial prejudice. . . .

The inherent potential of peremptory challenges to distort the jury process by permitting the exclusion of jurors on racial grounds should ideally lead the Court to ban them entirely from the criminal justice system. . . .

Some authors have suggested that the courts should ban prosecutors' peremptories entirely, but should zealously guard the defendant's peremptory as "essential to the fairness of trial by jury," and "one of the most important of the rights secured to the accused." I would not find that an acceptable solution. Our criminal justice system "requires not only freedom from any bias against the accused, but also from any prejudice against his prosecution. Between him and the state the scales are to be evenly held." We can maintain that balance, not by permitting both prosecutor and defendant to engage in racial discrimination in jury selection, but by banning the use of peremptory challenges by prosecutors and by allowing the States to eliminate the defendant's peremptory as well.

476 U.S. at 102–08, 106 S.Ct. at 1726–29, 90 L.Ed.2d at 92–95 . .

8. **Systematic exclusion.** Prior to *Batson*, in the only Supreme Court opinion on the issue, Swain v. Alabama, 380 U.S. 202, 85 S.Ct. 824, 13 L.Ed.2d 759 (1965), the court found no violation of equal protection in a prosecutor's use of peremptory challenges to strike Blacks from the defendant's trial jury. Dictum concurred in by four Justices implied that a meritorious claim might be stated "when the prosecutor in a county, in case after case, whatever the circumstances, whatever the crime and whoever the defendant or the victim may be," removed every Black from every petit jury. 380 U.S. at 223, 85 S.Ct. at 837, 13 L.Ed.2d at 774.

9. **Statistical proof of systematic exclusion.** Systematic exclusion of cognizable groups from the jury venire has traditionally been proved by a showing of a statistical difference in the per cent of the group in the population and the per cent of the group on the venire. In Whitus v. Georgia, 385 U.S. 545, 87 S.Ct. 643, 17 L.Ed.2d 599 (1967), for example, it was shown that 27.1% of the taxpayers in the county and 42.6% of males over 21 in the county were Black. Of 33 prospective grand jurors drawn, 3 were Black; only one Black actually served on the grand jury. A venire of 90 persons was selected for the petit jury to try the defendants; only seven of these were Blacks, and no Black was actually accepted on the petit jury. Further, there was a showing that the jury lists had been made up from an earlier list compiled from tax returns which indicated clearly the taxpayer's race. This, the Court held, "constituted a prima facie case of purposeful discrimination" which was not overcome by testimony of the jury commissioners that no one was included or excluded from the list because of race.

In People v. Harris, 36 Cal.3d 36, 201 Cal.Rptr. 782, 679 P.2d 433 (1984), the California Supreme Court found that the defendant had made a prima facie showing of the systematic exclusion of Blacks and Hispanics from jury venires when voter registration lists were used as the sole source of the venires. The defendant had furnished statistics showing that significant percentages of Blacks and Hispanics did not register to vote, and thus were not included in jury venire selection.

10. **Permitting women to opt out of jury service.** In Duren v. Missouri, 439 U.S. 357, 99 S.Ct. 664, 58 L.Ed.2d 579 (1979), Duren had been convicted of murder and assault in a state court sitting in Jackson County, Missouri. Under Missouri law, any woman who requested not to serve was exempted from jury duty. Practice in Jackson County was to excuse any woman who failed to appear for jury service on the appointed day. Census figures indicated that 54% of the adult inhabitants of Jackson County were women; during the period in which Duren's jury was selected, only 14.5% of the persons on the jury venires were women. The Supreme Court reversed, reasoning that the above evidence established a prima facie violation of the Constitution's fair-cross-section requirement and that on the record the state had not justified this by showing that "a significant state interest [was] manifestly and primarily advanced by those aspects of the jury selection process [that resulted in the underrepresentation of women]." It explained:

> We recognize that a State may have an important interest in assuring that those members of the family responsible for the care of children are available to do so. An exemption appropriately tailored to this interest would, we think, survive a fair-cross-section challenge.

439 U.S. at 369, 99 S.Ct. at 671, 58 L.Ed.2d at 590. But the exemption provided by Missouri was not appropriately tailored to this interest.

What would be the holding under *Duren* if exfelons were excluded from serving as jurors by state law? Resident aliens? See Rubio v. Superior Court, 24 Cal.3d 93, 154 Cal.Rptr. 734, 593 P.2d 595 (1979) in which the court held that neither were "cognizable groups within the meaning of the representative cross-section rule."

11. **Exclusions from grand juries.** The prohibition against intentional exclusion of identifiable groups from the petit jury venire has also been enforced in the grand jury context. In Castaneda v. Partida, 430 U.S. 482, 97 S.Ct. 1272, 51 L.Ed.2d 498 (1977), the Court held that the petitioner had made a *prima facie* showing of discrimination against Mexican–Americans in the grand jury selection process. Since the state had made no effort to refute this showing, respondent's conviction had to fall.

The appropriateness of the remedy of reversal of a criminal conviction when discriminatory selection of grand jurors has been shown was the subject of the Court's decision in Vasquez v. Hillery, 474 U.S. 254, 106 S.Ct. 617, 88 L.Ed.2d 598 (1986). A majority of the Court rejected the argument that any deficiency in the selection of grand jurors was rendered harmless in light of respondent's conviction in an error-free trial.

The Court has also addressed the question of racial and gender discrimination in the selection of federal grand jury foremen in Hobby v. United States, 468 U.S. 339, 104 S.Ct. 3093, 82 L.Ed.2d 260 (1984). However, finding the functions of the federal grand jury foreman to be ministerial and clerical in nature, the Court stated that:

> [T]he role of the foreman of a federal grand jury is not so significant to the administration of justice that discrimination in the appointment of that office impugns the fundamental fairness of the process itself so as to undermine the integrity of the indictment.

468 U.S. at 345, 104 S.Ct. at 3097–98, 82 L.Ed.2d at 266.

However, the result might be different if the foreman had the power to veto an indictment as in Rose v. Mitchell, 443 U.S. 545, 99 S.Ct. 2993, 61 L.Ed.2d 739 (1979), although the Court concluded that a prima facie case of racial discrimination in foremen selection had not been established, even if none had been selected in 20 years.

Rose was further distinguished in *Hobby* because the defendants in *Rose* brought their claim as a denial of equal protection of the laws, whereas *Hobby* based his claim on fundamental fairness under the due process clause:

> *Rose* involved a claim brought by two Negro defendants under the Equal Protection Clause. As members of the class allegedly excluded from service as grand jury foremen, the *Rose* defendants had suffered the injuries of stigmatization and prejudice associated with racial discrimination. . . . Petitioner [a white male], however, has alleged only that the exclusion of women and Negroes from the position of grand jury foremen violates his right to fundamental fairness under the Due Process Clause. . . . [D]iscrimination in the selection of federal grand jury foremen cannot be said to have a significant impact upon the due process interests of criminal defendants. Thus, the nature of petitioner's alleged injury and the constitutional basis of his claim distinguish his circumstances from those of the defendants in *Rose.*

468 U.S. at 347, 104 S.Ct. at 3098, 82 L.Ed.2d at 267–68. Justice Marshall, joined by Justices Brennan and Stevens, dissented.

The Supreme Court in Campbell v. Louisiana, 523 U.S. 392, 118 S.Ct. 1419, 140 L.Ed.2d 551 (1998) held that the standing of a white person to challenge under the Equal Protection Clause discrimination against African Americans recognized by Powers v. Ohio in the context of trial jury formation applies also to the selection of grand jurors. Under Louisiana procedure, the trial judge selects the grand jury foreperson before the balance of the jurors are selected; the foreperson is a full voting member of the grand jury. Petitioner showed that in over 15 years in the Parish in issue no African American had ever served as grand jury foreperson, although twenty percent of the registered voters in the Parish are African American. The Court in an opinion by Justice Kennedy held that the same considerations that led the Court in *Powers* to extend standing also applied in the grand jury context. Justice Thomas, joined by Justice Scalia, dissented from the holding giving standing to the petitioner.

12. **Intentional inclusion of identifiable groups.** To what, if any, extent is the intentional *inclusion* of members of an identifiable group in jury venires permissible? See Brooks v. Beto, 366 F.2d 1 (5th Cir.1966), *cert. denied* 386 U.S. 975, 87 S.Ct. 1169, 18 L.Ed.2d 135 (1967), approving—in the circumstances of the case—the intentional inclusion of Blacks in the grand jury which indicted Brooks.

3. THE JURY SIZE AND AGREEMENT REQUIRED

Juries traditionally have consisted of twelve jurors, and unanimity has been required for a verdict. But neither of these features was explicitly included in the United States Constitution, and both eventually came under close scrutiny. After an historical inquiry into the size and unanimity requirements, a fragmented Supreme Court rejected the argument that these commonly accepted notions are constitutionally required, as indicated in the materials in this Section.

Apodaca v. Oregon

Supreme Court of the United States, 1972.
406 U.S. 404, 92 S.Ct. 1628, 32 L.Ed.2d 184.

■ MR. JUSTICE WHITE announced the judgment of the Court in an opinion in which THE CHIEF JUSTICE, MR. JUSTICE BLACKMUN, and MR. JUSTICE REHNQUIST joined.

Robert Apodaca, Henry Morgan Cooper, Jr., and James Arnold Madden were convicted respectively of assault with a deadly weapon, burglary in a dwelling, and grand larceny before separate Oregon juries, all of which returned less than unanimous verdicts. The vote in the cases of Apodaca and Madden, was 11–1, while the vote in the case of Cooper was 10–2, the minimum requisite vote under Oregon law for sustaining a conviction. After convictions had been affirmed by the Oregon Court of Appeals, and review had been denied by the Supreme Court of Oregon, all three sought review in this Court upon a claim that conviction of crime by a less than unanimous jury violates the right to trial by jury in criminal cases specified by the Sixth Amendment and made applicable to the States by the Fourteenth. We granted certiorari to consider this claim, which we now find to be without merit.

In Williams v. Florida, 399 U.S. 78, 90 S.Ct. 1893, 26 L.Ed.2d 446 (1970), we had occasion to consider a related issue: whether the Sixth Amendment's right to trial by jury requires that all juries consist of 12 men. After considering the history of the 12–man requirement and the functions it performs in contemporary society, we concluded that it was not of constitutional stature. [In explanation, the Court said in Williams:

> . . . [The] essential feature of a jury obviously lies in the interposition between the accused and his accuser of the common-sense judgment of a group of laymen, and in the community participation and shared responsibility which results from that group's determination of guilt or innocence. The performance of this role is not a function of the particular number of the body which makes up the jury. To be sure, the number should probably be large enough to promote group deliberation, free from outside attempts at intimidation, and to provide a fair possibility for obtaining a representative cross section of the community. But we find little reason to think that these goals are in any meaningful sense less likely to be achieved when the jury numbers six, than when it numbers 12—particularly if the requirement of unanimity is retained. And, certainly the reliability of the jury as a factfinder hardly seems likely to be a function of its size.

> It might be suggested that the 12–man jury gives a defendant a greater advantage since he has more "chances" of finding a juror who will insist on acquittal and thus prevent conviction. But the advantage might just as easily belong to the State, which also needs only one juror out of twelve insisting on guilt to prevent acquittal. What few experiments have occurred—usually in the civil area—indicate that there is no discernible difference between the results reached by the two different-sized juries. In short, neither currently available evidence nor theory suggests that the 12–man jury is necessarily more advantageous to the defendant than a jury composed of fewer members.

399 U.S. at 100–01, 90 S.Ct. at 1906–07, 26 L.Ed.2d at 460–61. Editors.] We reach the same conclusion today with regard to the requirement of unanimity.

I.

Like the requirement that juries consist of 12 men, the requirement of unanimity arose during the Middle Ages and had become an accepted feature of the common-law jury by the 18th century. But, as we observed in *Williams,* "the relevant constitutional history, casts considerable doubt on the easy assumption ... that if a given feature existed in a jury at common law in 1789, then it was necessarily preserved in the Constitution." Id., at 92–93. The most salient fact in the scanty history of the Sixth Amendment, which we reviewed in full in *Williams,* is that, as it was introduced by James Madison in the House of Representatives, the proposed Amendment provided for trial

> "by an impartial jury of the freeholders of the vicinage, with the requisite of unanimity for conviction, of the right of challenge, and other accustomed requisites. ..." 1 Annuals of Cong. 435 (1789).

Although it passed the House with little alteration, this proposal ran into considerable opposition in the Senate,.... [T]he Amendment that ultimately emerged ... provided only for trial

> "by an impartial jury of the State and district wherein the crime shall have been committed, which district shall have been previously ascertained by law. ..."

As we observed in *Williams,* one can draw conflicting inferences from this legislative history. One possible inference is that Congress eliminated references to unanimity and to the other "accustomed requisites" of the jury because those requisites were thought already to be implicit in the very concept of jury. A contrary explanation, which we found in *Williams* to be the more plausible, is that the deletion was intended to have some substantive effect. See 399 U.S., at 96–97, 90 S.Ct., at 1903, 1904. Surely one fact that is absolutely clear from this history is that, after a proposal had been made to specify precisely which of the common-law requisites of the jury were to be preserved by the Constitution, the Framers explicitly rejected the proposal and instead left such specification to the future. As in *Williams,* we must accordingly consider what is meant by the concept "jury" and determine whether a feature commonly associated with it is constitutionally required. And, as in *Williams,* our inability to divine "the intent of the Framers" when they eliminated references to the "accustomed requisites" requires that in determining what is meant by a jury we must turn to other than purely historical considerations.

II.

Our inquiry must focus upon the function served by the jury in contemporary society. As we said in *Duncan,* the purpose of trial by jury is to prevent oppression by the Government by providing a "safeguard against the corrupt or overzealous prosecutor and against the compliant, biased, or eccentric judge." Duncan v. Louisiana, supra, 391 U.S. at 156, 88 S.Ct. at 1451. "Given this purpose, the essential feature of a jury obviously lies in the interposition between the accused and his accuser of the commonsense judgment of a group of laymen. ..."Williams v. Florida, supra, 399 U.S. at 100, 90 S.Ct. at 1906. A requirement of unanimity, however, does not materially contribute to the exercise of this commonsense judgment. As we said in *Williams,* a jury will come to such a judgment as long as it consists of a group of laymen representative of a cross section of the community who have the duty and the opportunity to deliberate, free from outside attempts at intimidation, on the question of a defendant's guilt. In terms of this function we perceive no difference between juries required to act unanimously and those permitted to convict or acquit by votes of 10 to two or 11 to one. Requiring unanimity would obviously produce hung juries in some situations where nonunanimous juries will convict or acquit.[9] But in either case, the interest of the defendant in having the judgment of his peers interposed between himself and the officers of the State who prosecute and judge him is equally well served.

III.

Petitioners nevertheless argue that unanimity serves other purposes constitutionally essential to the continued operation of the jury system. Their principal contention is that a Sixth Amendment "jury trial" made mandatory on the States by virtue of the Due Process Clause of the Fourteenth Amendment, Duncan v. Louisiana, supra, should be held to require a unanimous jury verdict in order to give substance to the reasonable doubt standard otherwise mandated by the Due Process Clause. See In re Winship, 397 U.S. 358, 363–364 (1970).

We are quite sure, however, that the Sixth Amendment itself has never been held to require proof beyond a reasonable doubt in criminal cases. The reasonable doubt standard developed separately from both the jury trial and the unanimous verdict. As the Court noted in the *Winship* case, the rule requiring proof of crime beyond a reasonable doubt did not crystallize in this country until after the Constitution was adopted. And in that case, which held such a burden of proof to be constitutionally required, the Court purported to draw no support from the Sixth Amendment.

* * *

IV.

Petitioners also cite quite accurately a long line of decisions of this Court upholding the principle that the Fourteenth Amendment requires jury panels to reflect a cross section of the community. They then contend that unanimity is a necessary precondition for effective application of the cross section requirement, because a rule permitting less than unanimous verdicts will make it possible for convictions to occur without the acquiescence of minority elements within the community.

There are two flaws in this argument. One is petitioners' assumption that every distinct voice in the community has a right to be represented on every jury and a right to prevent conviction of a defendant in any case. All that the Constitution forbids, however, is systematic exclusion of identifiable segments of the community from jury panels and from the juries ultimately drawn from those panels; a defendant may not, for example, challenge the makeup of a jury merely because no members of his race are

---

9. The most complete statistical study of jury behavior has come to the conclusion that when juries are required to be unanimous, "the probability that an acquittal mi- nority will hang the jury is about as great as that a guilty minority will hang it." H. Kalven & H. Zeisel, The American Jury 461 (1966).

on the jury, but must prove that his race has been systematically excluded. No group, in short, has the right to block convictions; it has only the right to participate in the overall legal processes by which criminal guilt and innocence are determined.

We also cannot accept petitioners' second assumption—that minority groups, even when they are represented on a jury, will not adequately represent the viewpoint of those groups simply because they may be outvoted in the final result. They will be present during all deliberations, and their views will be heard. We cannot assume that the majority of the jury will refuse to weigh the evidence and reach a decision upon rational grounds, just as it must now do in order to obtain unanimous verdicts, or that a majority will deprive a man of his liberty on the basis of prejudice when a minority is presenting a reasonable argument in favor of acquittal. We simply find no proof for the notion that a majority will disregard its instructions and cast its votes for guilt or innocence based on prejudice rather than the evidence.

We accordingly affirm the judgment of the Court of Appeals of Oregon.

It is so ordered.

Judgment affirmed.

■ MR. JUSTICE BLACKMUN, concurring.

I join the Court's opinion and judgment.... I add only the comment, which should be obvious and should not need saying, that in so doing I do not imply that I regard a State's split verdict system as a wise one. My vote means only that I cannot conclude that the system is constitutionally offensive. Were I a legislator, I would disfavor it as a matter of policy. Our task here, however, is not to pursue and strike down what happens to impress us as undesirable legislative policy.

I do not hesitate to say, either, that a system employing a 7–5 standard, rather than a 9–3 or 75% minimum, would afford me great difficulty. As Mr. Justice White points out "a substantial majority of the jury" are to be convinced. That is all that is before us in each of these cases.

■ MR. JUSTICE POWELL, concurring....

* * *

I concur in the plurality opinion ... insofar as it concludes that a defendant in a state court may constitutionally be convicted by less than a unanimous verdict, but I am not in accord with a major premise upon which that judgment is based. Its premise is that the concept of jury trial, as applicable to the States under the Fourteenth Amendment, must be identical in every detail to the concept required in federal courts by the Sixth Amendment. I do not think that all of the elements of jury trial within the meaning of the Sixth Amendment are necessarily embodied in or incorporated into the Due Process Clause of the Fourteenth Amendment. ...

In an unbroken line of cases reaching back into the late 1800's, the Justices of this Court have recognized, virtually without dissent, that unanimity is one of the indispensable features of *federal* jury trial. In these cases, the Court has presumed that unanimous verdicts are essential in federal jury trials, not because unanimity is necessarily fundamental to the function performed by the jury, but because that result is mandated by history. The reasoning which runs throughout this Court's Sixth Amendment precedents is that, in amending the Constitution to guarantee the right to jury trial, the Framers desired to preserve the jury safeguard as it was known to them at common law. At the time the Bill of Rights was adopted, unanimity had long been established as one of the attributes of a jury conviction at common law. It therefore seems to me, in accord both with history and precedent, that the Sixth Amendment requires a unanimous jury verdict to convict in a federal criminal trial.

But it is the Fourteenth Amendment, rather than the Sixth, which imposes upon the States the requirement that they provide jury trials to those accused of serious crimes. ...

The question, therefore, which should be addressed in this case is whether unanimity is in fact so fundamental to the essentials of jury trial that this particular requirement of the Sixth Amendment is necessarily binding on the States under the Due Process Clause of the Fourteenth Amendment.

* * *

■ MR. JUSTICE DOUGLAS, with whom MR. JUSTICE BRENNAN and MR. JUSTICE MARSHALL concur, dissenting.

* * *

I.

... [I]n cases dealing with juries it had always been assumed that a unanimous jury was required. Today the bases of those cases are discarded and two centuries of American history are shunted aside.

The result of today's decision is anomalous: though unanimous jury decisions are not required in state trials, they are constitutionally required in federal prosecutions. How can that be possible when both decisions stem from the Sixth Amendment?

* * *

II.

The plurality approves a procedure which diminishes the reliability of a jury. First, it eliminates the circumstances in which a minority of jurors (a) could have rationally persuaded the entire jury to acquit, or (b) while unable to persuade the majority to acquit, nonetheless could have convinced them to convict only on a lesser-included offense. Second, it permits prosecutors in Oregon and Louisiana to enjoy a conviction-acquittal ratio substantially greater than that ordinarily returned by unanimous juries.

The diminution of verdict reliability flows from the fact that nonunanimous juries need not debate and deliberate as fully as must unanimous juries. As soon as the requisite majority is attained, further consideration is not required either by Oregon or by Louisiana even though the dissident jurors might, if given the chance, be able to convince the majority. Such persuasion does in fact occasionally occur in States where the unanimous requirement applies: "In roughly one case in ten, the minority eventually succeeds in reversing an initial majority, and these may be cases of special importance."[10] One explanation for this phenomenon is that because jurors are often not permitted to take notes and because they have imperfect memories, the forensic process of forcing jurors to defend their conflicting recollections and conclusions flushes out many nuances which otherwise would go overlooked. This collective effort to piece together the puzzle of historical truth, however, is cut short as soon as the requisite majority is reached in Oregon and Louisiana. Indeed, if a necessary majority is immediately obtained, then no deliberation at all is required in these States. (There is a suggestion that this may have happened in the 10–2 verdict rendered in only 41 minutes in Apodaca's case.) To be sure, in jurisdictions other than these two States, initial majorities normally prevail in the end, but about a tenth of the time the rough and tumble of the juryroom operates to reverse completely their preliminary perception of guilt or innocence. The Court now extracts from the juryroom this automatic check against hasty factfinding by relieving jurors of the duty to hear out fully the dissenters.

It is said that there is no evidence that majority jurors will refuse to listen to dissenters whose votes are unneeded for conviction. Yet human experience teaches that polite and academic conversation is no substitute for the earnest and robust argument necessary to reach unanimity. As mentioned earlier, in Apodaca's case, whatever courtesy dialogue transpired could not have lasted more than 41 minutes. I fail to understand why the Court should lift from the States the burden of justifying so radical a departure from an accepted and applauded tradition and instead demand that these defendants document with empirical evidence what has always been thought to be too obvious for further study.

To be sure in Williams v. Florida, 399 U.S. 78, 88, 90 S.Ct. 1893, 1899, 26 L.Ed.2d 446, we held that a State could provide a jury less than 12 in number in criminal trial. We said "What few experiments have occurred— usually in the civil area—indicate that there is no discernible difference between the results reached by the two different-sized juries. In short, neither currently available evidence nor theory suggests that the 12–man jury is necessarily more advantageous to the defendant than a jury composed of fewer members." Id., at 101–102, 90 S.Ct. at 1906.

That rationale of *Williams* can have no application here. *Williams* requires that the change be neither more nor less advantageous to either the State or the defendant. It is said that such a showing is satisfied here since a 3:9 (Louisiana) or 2:10 (Oregon) verdict will result in acquittal. Yet experience shows that the less than unanimous jury overwhelmingly favors the States.

Moreover, even where an initial majority wins the dissent over to its side, the ultimate result in unanimous jury States may nonetheless reflect

10. H. Kalven & H. Zeisel, The American Jury 490 (1966). See also The American   Jury: Notes For an English Controversy, 48 Chi. B.Rec. 195 (1967).

the reservations of uncertain jurors. I refer to many compromise verdicts on lesser-included offenses and lesser sentences. Thus, even though a minority may not be forceful enough to carry the day, their doubts may nonetheless cause a majority to exercise caution. Obviously, however, in Oregon and Louisiana, dissident jurors will not have the opportunity through full deliberation to temper the opposing faction's degree of certainty of guilt.

The new rule also has an impact on cases in which a unanimous jury would have neither voted to acquit nor to convict, but would have deadlocked. In unanimous jury States, this occurs about 5.6% of the time. Of these deadlocked juries, Kalven and Zeisel say that 56% contain either one, two, or three dissenters. In these latter cases, the majorities favor the prosecution 44% (of the 56%) but the defendant only 12% (of the 56%).[11] Thus, by eliminating these deadlocks, Louisiana wins 44 cases for every 12 that it loses, obtaining in this band of outcomes a substantially more favorable conviction ratio (3.67) than the unanimous jury ratio of slightly less than two guilty verdicts for every acquittal. H. Kalven & H. Zeisel, The American Jury 461, 488 (Table 159) (1966). By eliminating the one and two dissenting juror cases, Oregon does even better, gaining 4.25 convictions for every acquittal. While the statutes on their face deceptively appear to be neutral, the use of the nonunanimous jury stacks the truth-determining process against the accused. Thus, we take one step more away from the accusatorial system that has been our proud boast.

It is my belief that a unanimous jury is necessary if the great barricade known as proof beyond a reasonable doubt is to be maintained. ...

Today the Court approves a nine to three verdict. Would the Court relax the standard of reasonable doubt still further by resorting to eight to four verdicts or even a majority rule? Moreover, in light of today's holdings and that of Williams v. Florida, in the future would it invalidate three to two or even two to one convictions?

Is the next step the elimination of the presumption of innocence?

[The dissenting opinions of Mr. Justice Brennan (joined by Mr. Justice Marshall), Mr. Justice Stewart (joined by Mr. Justice Brennan and Mr. Justice Marshall), and Mr. Justice Marshall (joined by Mr. Justice Brennan) are omitted.]

NOTES

1. **But not one juror fewer than six.** In Ballew v. Georgia, 435 U.S. 223, 98 S.Ct. 1029, 55 L.Ed.2d 234 (1978), the Court concluded:

11. The American Jury, at 460, n. 3.

Last Vote of Deadlocked Juries

Vote for Conviction	Per Cent
11:1	24
10:2	10
9:3	10
8:4	6
7:5	13
6:6	13
5:7	8
4:8	4
3:9	4
2:10	8
1:11	–
	100%

Number of Juries in Sample—48.

[T]he purpose and functioning of the jury in a criminal trial is seriously impaired, and to a constitutional degree, by a reduction in size to below six members. . . . [T]he assembled data raise substantial doubt about the reliability and appropriate representation of panels smaller than six. Because of the fundamental importance of the jury trial to the American system of criminal justice, any further reduction that promotes inaccurate and possibly biased decisionmaking, that causes untoward differences in verdicts, and that prevents juries from truly representing their communities, attains constitutional significance.

435 U.S. at 239, 98 S.Ct. at 1038–39, 55 L.Ed.2d at 246. In addition, the Court commented that reduction of jury size from six to five would result in only minimal savings in court time and financial costs.

2. **Six person juries must be unanimous.** In Burch v. Louisiana, 441 U.S. 130, 99 S.Ct. 1623, 60 L.Ed.2d 96 (1979), the Court, in an opinion by Justice Rehnquist, declared:

[M]uch the same reasons that led us in *Ballew* to decide that use of a five-member jury threatened the fairness of the proceeding and the proper role of the jury, lead us to conclude now that conviction for a nonpetty offense by only five members of a six-person jury presents a similar threat to preservation of the substance of the jury trial guarantee and justifies our requiring verdicts rendered by six-person juries to be unanimous. . . .

[footnote 11: We, of course, intimate no view as to the constitutionality of nonunanimous verdicts rendered by juries comprised of more than six members.]

441 U.S. at 138 & n. 11, 99 S.Ct. at 1627–28 & n. 11, 60 L.Ed.2d at 103–04 & n. 11.

3. **Reducing size of juries after trial begins.** Rule 23(b) of the Federal Rules of Criminal Procedure provides:

Juries shall be of 12 but at any time before verdict the parties may stipulate in writing with the approval of the court that the jury shall consist of any number less than 12 or that a valid verdict may be returned by a jury of less than 12 should the court find it necessary to excuse one or more jurors for any just cause after trial commences. Even absent such stipulation, if the court finds it necessary to excuse a juror for just cause after the jury has retired to consider its verdict, in the discretion of the court a valid verdict may be returned by the remaining 11 jurors.

4. **Unanimity.** Rule 31 of the Federal Rules of Criminal Procedure provides that verdicts of federal juries in criminal cases must be unanimous.

5. **Agreement on a single legal theory of guilt.** Must the jury agree on a single legal theory of an offense when more than one have been charged and submitted to it? In Schad v. Arizona, 501 U.S. 624, 111 S.Ct. 2491, 115 L.Ed.2d 555 (1991), petitioner was charged with first-degree murder by premeditated killing and by killing in perpetration of robbery. There was evidence in support of each theory. The jury was instructed to return a verdict of not guilty, guilty of first-degree murder, or guilty of the lesser included offense of second degree murder, but was not required to agree upon which theory of first degree murder it found proved. The jury returned a verdict of guilty of first degree murder and the death sentence was imposed. Petitioner's contention that this procedure violated the Due Process Clause was rejected by the Court. In a plurality opinion by Justice Souter, joined by The Chief Justice and Justices O'Connor and Kennedy, the issue was characterized as whether under Arizona law first-degree murder is a single crime or whether premeditated murder and felony murder are separate crimes. Acknowledging that "nothing in our history suggests that the Due Process Clause would permit a State

to convict anyone under a charge of 'Crime' so generic that any combination of jury findings of embezzlement, reckless driving, murder, burglary, tax evasion, or littering, for example, would suffice for conviction," this is not such a case. The Arizona court has determined that there is only one offense of first-degree murder and the Supreme Court is not free to take a different view of Arizona law; the only question is whether the view taken by the Arizona court is constitutional. Both premeditated killing and felony-murder are simply different forms of *mens rea*. Historically, each has simply been a different way of defining the same criminal offense. Finally, felony murder can be regarded as the moral equivalent of premeditated killing. Justice Scalia, concurring, placed emphasis upon the historical roots of the Arizona practice:

> Submitting killing in the course of a robbery and premeditated killing to the jury under a single charge is not some novel composite that can be subjected to the indignity of "fundamental fairness" review. It was the norm when this country was founded, was the norm when the Fourteenth Amendment was adopted in 1868, and remains the norm today. Unless we are here to invent a Constitution rather than enforce one, it is impossible that a practice as old as the common law and still in existence in the vast majority of States does not provide that process which is "due."

501 U.S. at 651, 111 S.Ct. at 2507, 115 L.Ed.2d at 577–78. Justice White, joined by Justices Marshall, Blackmun and Stevens, dissenting, took issue with the plurality's characterization of the two legal theories as simply alternative *mens rea* for the offense of first degree murder:

> [I]t is entirely possible that half of the jury believed the defendant was guilty of premeditated murder and not guilty of felony murder/robbery, while half believed exactly the reverse.... [T]he plurality affirms this conviction without knowing that even a single element of either of the ways for proving first-degree murder, except the fact of a killing, has been found by a majority of the jury, let alone found unanimously by the jury as required by Arizona law. A defendant charged with first-degree murder is at least entitled to a verdict— something petitioner did not get in this case as long as the possibility exists that no more than six jurors voted for any one element of first-degree murder, except the fact of a killing.

501 U.S. at 655, 111 S.Ct. at 2509, 115 L.Ed.2d at 580.

The Court was asked in Richardson v. United States, 526 U.S. 813, 119 S.Ct. 1707, 143 L.Ed.2d 985 (1999) whether a jury is required to agree unanimously on each violation of federal drug law necessary to support the charge of a continuing criminal enterprise brought by the Government. Distinguishing Schad v. Arizona, the Court in an opinion by Justice Breyer held that unanimous agreement on each supporting violation (although not on each one alleged, since an excess might be alleged) was required. Each violation alleged is an element of the continuing criminal enterprise offense and a sufficient minimum number must be proved (assumed in the opinion to be three) to the unanimous agreement of the jury as to each. The violations here are criminal offenses, unlike the means alleged in *Schad* to commit the criminal offense of first degree murder.

6. **Evidence sufficiency when alternative legal theories are presented to the jury.** What should happen when theories are presented to a jury in the alternative, a general verdict of guilty is returned, and the evidence is insufficient to support one of those theories? Petitioner in Griffin v. United States, 502 U.S. 46, 112 S.Ct. 466, 116 L.Ed.2d 371 (1991) was charged with conspiracy to defraud the United States Government. Two objects of the conspiracy were charged: defrauding the Internal Revenue Service and defrauding the Drug Enforcement Administration. The jury was instructed to return a verdict of guilty if it found that petitioner

participated in either of the two objects of the conspiracy. The jury returned a general verdict of guilty. The Government conceded there was insufficient evidence that petitioner conspired to defraud the DEA. The Supreme Court, in an opinion by Justice Scalia, held that the verdict could stand despite the insufficiency of evidence.

The Court distinguished prior cases in which the theories submitted were based upon constitutionally protected conduct or in which the theories were not authorized by law. Evidence insufficiency is different:

> Jurors are not generally equipped to determine whether a particular theory of conviction submitted to them is contrary to law—whether, for example, the action in question is protected by the Constitution, is time barred, or fails to come within the statutory definition of the crime. When, therefore, jurors have been left the option of relying upon a legally inadequate theory, there is no reason to think that their own intelligence and expertise will save them from that error. Quite the opposite is true, however, when they have been left the option of relying upon a factually inadequate theory, since jurors *are* well equipped to analyze the evidence.

502 U.S. at 59, 112 S.Ct. at 474, 116 L.Ed.2d at 382–83.

C. CONFRONTATION, CROSS-EXAMINATION AND COMPULSORY PROCESS TO OBTAIN WITNESSES

The Sixth Amendment provides, in part, that, "in all criminal prosecutions, the accused shall enjoy the right . . . to be confronted with the witnesses against him [and the right] to have compulsory process for obtaining witnesses in his favor. . . . " The Fourteenth Amendment imposes upon the states both the requirement that the accused be afforded confrontation rights, Pointer v. Texas, 380 U.S. 400, 85 S.Ct. 1065, 13 L.Ed.2d 923 (1965), and compulsory process, Washington v. Texas, 388 U.S. 14, 87 S.Ct. 1920, 18 L.Ed.2d 1019 (1967). Despite the concise language of the constitutional provision, however, the rights have broad implications. In Faretta v. California, 422 U.S. 806, 95 S.Ct. 2525, 45 L.Ed.2d 562 (1975) the Court observed:

> The rights to notice, confrontation, and compulsory process, when taken together, guarantee that a criminal charge may be answered in a manner now considered fundamental to the fair administration of American justice—through the calling and interrogation of favorable witnesses, and the orderly introduction of evidence. In short, the [Sixth] Amendment constitutionalizes the right in an adversary criminal trial to make a defense as we know it.

422 U.S. at 818, 95 S.Ct. at 2532–33, 45 L.Ed.2d at 572.

1. CONFRONTATION

Recently the Court has addressed a series of confrontation clause issues involving the tension between providing "a defense as we know it" and protecting victims of child abuse from traditional aspects of that defense.

In Coy v. Iowa, 487 U.S. 1012, 108 S.Ct. 2798, 101 L.Ed.2d 857 (1988), appellant was convicted of sex offenses against two 13 year old girls. At his trial, under authority of a state statute authorizing testimony in such cases by closed circuit television or from behind a screen, they testified behind a screen that enabled appellant to hear them and see them dimly but which prevented them from seeing him. The United States Supreme Court, in an opinion by Justice Scalia, concluded this procedure violated the Confrontation Clause:

> The perception that confrontation is essential to fairness has persisted over the centuries because there is much truth to it. A witness "may feel quite differently when he has to repeat his story looking at the man whom he will harm greatly by distorting or mistaking the facts. He can now understand what sort of human being that man is.... " It is always more difficult to tell a lie about a person "to his face" than "behind his back." In the former context, even if the lie is told, it will often be told less convincingly. The Confrontation Clause does not, of course, compel the witness to fix his eyes upon the defendant; he may studiously look elsewhere, but the trier of fact will draw its own conclusions. Thus the right to face-to-face confrontation serves much the same purposes as a less explicit component of the Confrontation Clause that we have had more frequent occasion to discuss—the right to cross-examine the accuser; both "ensur[e] the integrity of the fact-finding process.... " The State can hardly gainsay the profound effect upon a witness of standing in the presence of the person the witness accuses, since that is the very phenomenon it relies upon to establish the potential "trauma" that allegedly justified the extraordinary procedure in the present case. That face-to-face presence may, unfortunately, upset the truthful rape victim or abused child; but by the same token it may confound and undo the false accuser, or reveal the child coached by a malevolent adult. It is a truism that constitutional protections have costs.

487 U.S. at 1019–20, 108 S.Ct. at 2802, 101 L.Ed.2d at 866. The Court remanded the case for a determination whether the violation of appellant's confrontation rights was harmless beyond a reasonable doubt "on the basis of the remaining evidence." Justice O'Connor, joined by Justice White, concurred to emphasize that while the Confrontation Clause was violated by the procedures employed in this case, its command is not absolute. In a case in which there was a specific finding of necessity, supported by the evidence, she would permit a trial procedure that employed something other than face-to-face confrontation.

Another child abuse case two years after *Coy*, provided Justice O'Connor that opportunity. This time Justice Scalia dissented. That case, Maryland v. Craig, is the principal case in this section, which together with the notes provides an examination of the general parameters of these Sixth Amendment rights.

Maryland v. Craig

Supreme Court of the United States, 1990.
497 U.S. 836, 110 S.Ct. 3157, 111 L.Ed.2d 666.

■ JUSTICE O'CONNOR delivered the opinion of the Court.

This case requires us to decide whether the Confrontation Clause of the Sixth Amendment categorically prohibits a child witness in a child abuse case from testifying against a defendant at trial, outside the defendant's physical presence, by one-way closed circuit television.

I

In October 1986, a Howard County grand jury charged respondent, Sandra Ann Craig, with child abuse, first and second degree sexual offenses, perverted sexual practice, assault, and battery. The named victim in each count was Brooke Etze, a six-year-old child who, from August 1984 to June 1986, had attended a kindergarten and prekindergarten center owned and operated by Craig.

In March 1987, before the case went to trial, the State sought to invoke a Maryland statutory procedure that permits a judge to receive, by one-way closed circuit television, the testimony of a child witness who is alleged to be a victim of child abuse. To invoke the procedure, the trial judge must first "determin[e] that testimony by the child victim in the courtroom will result in the child suffering serious emotional distress such that the child cannot reasonably communicate." Md.Cts. & Jud.Proc.Code Ann. § 9–102(a)(1)(ii) (1989). Once the procedure is invoked, the child witness, prosecutor, and defense counsel withdraw to a separate room; the judge, jury, and defendant remain in the courtroom. The child witness is then examined and cross-examined in the separate room, while a video monitor records and displays the witness' testimony to those in the courtroom. During this time the witness cannot see the defendant. The defendant remains in electronic communication with defense counsel, and objections may be made and ruled on as if the witness were testifying in the courtroom.

In support of its motion invoking the one-way closed circuit television procedure, the State presented expert testimony that Brooke, as well as a number of other children who were alleged to have been sexually abused by Craig, would suffer "serious emotional distress such that [they could not] reasonably communicate," § 9–102(a)(1)(ii), if required to testify in the courtroom. ...Craig objected to the use of the procedure on Confrontation Clause grounds, but the trial court rejected that contention, concluding that although the statute "take[s] away the right of the defendant to be face to face with his or her accuser," the defendant retains the "essence of the right of confrontation," including the right to observe, cross-examine, and have the jury view the demeanor of the witness. ...The trial court further found that, "based upon the evidence presented ... the testimony of each of these children in a courtroom will result in each child suffering serious emotional distress ... such that each of these children cannot reasonably communicate." Id., at 66. The trial court then found Brooke and three other children competent to testify and accordingly permitted them to testify against Craig via the one-way closed circuit television procedure. The jury convicted Craig on all counts, ...

The Court of Appeals of Maryland reversed and remanded for a new trial. 316 Md. 551, 560 A.2d 1120 (1989). The Court of Appeals rejected Craig's argument that the Confrontation Clause requires in all cases a face-to-face courtroom encounter between the accused and his accusers, ... but concluded: ... that, "as [it] read *Coy* [v. Iowa, 487 U.S. 1012, 108 S.Ct. 2798, 101 L.Ed.2d 857 (1988)], the showing made by the State was insufficient to reach the high threshold required by that case before § 9–102 may be invoked." Id. 316 Md., at 554–555, 560 A.2d, at 1121 (footnote omitted).

We granted certiorari to resolve the important Confrontation Clause issues raised by this case. 493 U.S. ___, 110 S.Ct. 834, 107 L.Ed.2d 830 (1990).

II

The Confrontation Clause of the Sixth Amendment, made applicable to the States through the Fourteenth Amendment, provides: "In all criminal prosecutions, the accused shall enjoy the right ... to be confronted with the witnesses against him."

We observed in *Coy v. Iowa* that "the Confrontation Clause guarantees the defendant a face-to-face meeting with witnesses appearing before the trier of fact." 487 U.S., at 1016, 108 S.Ct., at 2800 (citing Kentucky v. Stincer), 482 U.S. 730, 748, 749–750, 107 S.Ct. 2658, 2668–2669, 2669, 96 L.Ed.2d 631 (1987) ... This interpretation derives not only from the literal text of the Clause, but also from our understanding of its historical roots.

We have never held, however, that the Confrontation Clause guarantees criminal defendants the *absolute* right to a face-to-face meeting with witnesses against them at trial. Indeed, in *Coy v. Iowa,* we expressly "le[ft] for another day ... the question whether any exceptions exist" to the "irreducible literal meaning of the Clause: 'a right to *meet face to face* all those who appear and give evidence at trial.'" 487 U.S., at 1021, 108 S.Ct. at 2802–2803.... The procedure challenged in *Coy* involved the placement of a screen that prevented two child witnesses in a child abuse case from seeing the defendant as they testified against him at trial. See 487 U.S., at 1014–1015, 108 S.Ct., at 2799–2800. In holding that the use of this procedure violated the defendant's right to confront witnesses against him, we suggested that any exception to the right "would surely be allowed only when necessary to further an important public policy"—i.e., only upon a showing of something more than the generalized, "legislatively imposed presumption of trauma" underlying the statute at issue in that case. Id., at 1021, 108 S.Ct. at 2802–2803; see also id., at 1025, 108 S.Ct., at 2804 (concurring opinion). We concluded that "[s]ince there ha[d] been no individualized findings that these particular witnesses needed special protection, the judgment [in the case before us] could not be sustained by any conceivable exception." Id., at 1021, 108 S.Ct., at 2802–2803. Because the trial court in this case made individualized findings that each of the child witnesses needed special protection, this case requires us to decide the question reserved in *Coy.*

The central concern of the Confrontation Clause is to ensure the reliability of the evidence against a criminal defendant by subjecting it to rigorous testing in the context of an adversary proceeding before the trier of fact. The word "confront," after all, also means a clashing of forces of ideas, thus carrying with it the notion of adversariness. As we noted in our earliest case interpreting the Clause:

"The primary object of the constitutional provision in question was to prevent depositions or *ex parte* affidavits, such as were sometimes admitted in civil cases, being used against the prisoner in lieu of a personal examination and cross-examination of the witness in which the accused has an opportunity, not only of testing the recollection and sifting the conscience of the witness, but of compelling him to stand face to face with the jury in order that they may look at him, and judge by his demeanor upon the stand and the manner in which he gives his testimony whether he is worthy of belief." [Mattox v. United States, 156 U.S. 237, 242–43, 15 S.Ct. 337, 339–40, 39 L.Ed. 409 (1895).]

As this description indicates, the right guaranteed by the Confrontation Clause includes not only a "personal examination," id., at 242, 15 S.Ct., at 339, but also "(1) insures that the witness will give his statements under oath—thus impressing him with the seriousness of the matter and guarding against the lie by the possibility of a penalty for perjury; (2) forces the witness to submit to cross-examination, the 'greatest legal engine ever invented for the discovery of truth'; [and] (3) permits the jury that is to decide the defendant's fate to observe the demeanor of the witness in making his statement, thus aiding the jury in assessing his credibility." [California v. Green, 399 U.S. 149, 158, 90 S.Ct. 1930, 1935, 26 L.Ed.2d 489 (1970).]

The combined effect of these elements of confrontation—physical presence, oath, cross-examination, and observation of demeanor by the trier of fact—serves the purposes of the Confrontation Clause by ensuring that evidence admitted against an accused is reliable and subject to the rigorous adversarial testing that is the norm of Anglo–American criminal proceedings. . . .

We have recognized, for example, that face-to-face confrontation enhances the accuracy of factfinding by reducing the risk that a witness will wrongfully implicate an innocent person. See *Coy,* 487 U.S., at 1019–1020, 108 S.Ct., at 2802 ("It is always more difficult to tell a lie about a person 'to his face' than 'behind his back.' . . . That face-to-face presence may, unfortunately, upset the truthful rape victim or abused child; but by the same token it may confound and undo the false accuser, or reveal the child coached by a malevolent adult") . . . We have also noted the strong symbolic purpose served by requiring adverse witnesses at trial to testify in the accused's presence. See *Coy,* supra, 487 U.S., at 1017, 108 S.Ct., at 2800 ("[T]here is something deep in human nature that regards face-to-face confrontation between accused and accuser as 'essential to a fair trial in a criminal prosecution'") (quoting Pointer v. Texas, 380 U.S. 400, 404, 85 S.Ct. 1065, 1068, 13 L.Ed.2d 923 (1965)).

Although face-to-face confrontation forms "the core of the values furthered by the Confrontation Clause," *Green,* supra, 399 U.S., at 157, 90 S.Ct., at 1934, we have nevertheless recognized that it is not the *sine qua non* of the confrontation right. See Delaware v. Fensterer, 474 U.S. 15, 22, 106 S.Ct. 292, 295, 88 L.Ed.2d 15 (1985) (per curiam) ("[T]he Confrontation Clause is generally satisfied when the defense is given a full and fair opportunity to probe and expose [testimonial] infirmities [such as forgetfulness, confusion, or evasion] through cross-examination, thereby calling to the attention of the factfinder the reasons for giving scant weight to the witness' testimony") ... see also *Stincer,* supra, 482 U.S. at 739–744, 107 S.Ct., at 2664 (confrontation right not violated by exclusion of defendant from competency hearing of child witnesses, where defendant had opportunity for full and effective cross-examination at trial); ...

For this reason, we have never insisted on an actual face-to-face encounter at trial in *every* instance in which testimony is admitted against a defendant. Instead, we have repeatedly held that the Clause permits, where necessary, the admission of certain hearsay statements against a defendant despite the defendant's inability to confront the declarant at trial. ...In *Mattox,* for example, we held that the testimony of a government witness at a former trial against the defendant, where the witness was fully cross-examined but had died after the first trial, was admissible in evidence against the defendant at his second trial. See 156 U.S., at 240–244, 15 S.Ct., at 338–340. We explained:

> "There is doubtless reason for saying that ... if notes of [the witness's] testimony are permitted to be read, [the defendant] is deprived of the advantage of that personal presence of the witness before the jury which the law has designed for his protection. But general rules of law of this kind, however beneficent in their operation and valuable to the accused, must occasionally give way to considerations of public policy and the necessities of the case. To say that a criminal, after having once been convicted by the testimony of a certain witness, should go scot free simply because death has closed the mouth of that witness, would be carrying his constitutional protection to an unwarrantable extent. The law in its wisdom declares that the rights of the public shall not be wholly sacrificed in order that an incidental benefit may be preserved to the accused." Id., at 243, 15 S.Ct., at 339–340.

We have accordingly stated that a literal reading of the Confrontation Clause would "abrogate virtually every hearsay exception, a result long rejected as unintended and too extreme." [Ohio v. Roberts, 448 U.S. 56, 63, 100 S.Ct. 2531, 2537, 65 L.Ed.2d 597 (1980).] Thus, in certain narrow circumstances, "competing interests, if 'closely examined,' may warrant dispensing with confrontation at trial." Id., at 64, 100 S.Ct., at 2538 (quoting Chambers v. Mississippi, 410 U.S. 284, 295, 93 S.Ct. 1038, 1045, 35 L.Ed.2d 297 (1973), and citing *Mattox,* supra). We have recently held, for example, that hearsay statements of nontestifying co-conspirators may be admitted against a defendant despite the lack of any face-to-face encounter with the accused. See Bourjaily v. United States, 483 U.S. 171, 107 S.Ct. 2775, 97 L.Ed.2d 144 (1987); United States v. Inadi, 475 U.S. 387, 106 S.Ct. 1121, 89 L.Ed.2d 390 (1986). Given our hearsay cases, the word "confront," as used in the Confrontation Clause, cannot simply mean face-to-face confrontation, for the Clause would then, contrary to our cases, prohibit the admission of any accusatory hearsay statement made by an absent declarant—a declarant who is undoubtedly as much a "witness against" a defendant as one who actually testifies at trial.

In sum, our precedents establish that "the Confrontation Clause reflects a *preference* for face-to-face confrontation at trial," *Roberts,* supra, 448 U.S., at 63, 100 S.Ct., at 2537 (emphasis added; footnote omitted), a preference that "must occasionally give way to considerations of public policy and the necessities of the case," *Mattox,* supra, 156 U.S., at 243, 15 S.Ct., at 339–340. "[W]e have attempted to harmonize the goal of the Clause—placing limits on the kind of evidence that may be received against a defendant—with a societal interest in accurate factfinding, which may require consideration of out-of-court statements." *Bourjaily*, supra, 483 U.S., at 182, 107 S.Ct., at 2782. We have accordingly interpreted the Confrontation Clause in a manner sensitive to its purposes and sensitive to the necessities of trial and the adversary process. ...Thus, though we reaffirm the importance of face-to-face confrontation with witnesses appearing at trial, we cannot say that such confrontation is an indispensable element of the Sixth Amendment's guarantee of the right to confront one's accusers. ...

This interpretation of the Confrontation Clause is consistent with our cases holding that other Sixth Amendment rights must also be interpreted in the context of the necessities of trial and the adversary process. See, e.g., Illinois v. Allen, 397 U.S. 337, 342–343, 90 S.Ct. 1057, 1060, 25 L.Ed.2d 353 (1970) (right to be present at trial not violated where trial judge removed defendant for disruptive behavior); ... Taylor v. United States, 484 U.S. 400, 410–416, 108 S.Ct. 646, 653–656, 98 L.Ed.2d 798 (1988) (right to compulsory process not violated where trial judge precluded testimony of a surprise defense witness); Perry v. Leeke, 488 U.S. 272, 280–285, 109 S.Ct. 594, ___, 102 L.Ed.2d 624 (1989) (right to effective assistance of counsel not violated where trial judge prevented testifying defendant from conferring with counsel during a short break in testimony). We see no reason to treat the face-to-face component of the confrontation right any differently, and indeed we think it would be anomalous to do so.

That the face-to-face confrontation requirement is not absolute does not, of course, mean that it may easily be dispensed with. As we suggested in *Coy,* our precedents confirm that a defendant's right to confront accusatory witnesses may be satisfied absent a physical, face-to-face confrontation at trial only where denial of such confrontation is necessary to further an important public policy and only where the reliability of the testimony is otherwise assured. See *Coy,* 487 U.S., at 1021, 108 S.Ct., at 2802–2803....

III

Maryland's statutory procedure, when invoked, prevents a child witness from seeing the defendant as he or she testifies against the defendant at trial. We find it significant, however, that Maryland's procedure preserves all of the other elements of the confrontation right: the child witness must be competent to testify and must testify under oath; the defendant retains full opportunity for contemporaneous cross-examination; and the judge, jury, and defendant are able to view (albeit by video monitor) the demeanor (and body) of the witness as he or she testifies. Although we are mindful of the many subtle effects face-to-face confrontation may have on an adversary criminal proceeding, the presence of these other elements of confrontation—oath, cross-examination, and observation of the witness' demeanor—adequately ensures that the testimony is both reliable and subject to rigorous adversarial testing in a manner functionally equivalent to that accorded live, in-person testimony. These safeguards of reliability and adversariness render the use of such a procedure a far cry from the undisputed prohibition of the Confrontation Clause: trial by *ex parte* affidavit or inquisition, see *Mattox,* 156 U.S., at 242, 15 S.Ct., at 389; see also *Green,* 399 U.S., at 179, 90 S.Ct., at 1946 (Harlan, J., concurring) ("[T]he Confrontation Clause was meant to constitutionalize a barrier against flagrant abuses, trials by anonymous accusers, and absentee witnesses"). Rather, we think these elements of effective confrontation not only permit a defendant to "confound and undo the false accuser, or reveal the child coached by a malevolent adult," *Coy,* 487 U.S., at 1020, 108 S.Ct., at 2802, but may well aid a defendant in eliciting favorable testimony from the child witness. Indeed, to the extent the child witness' testimony may be said to be technically given out-of-court (though we do not so hold), these assurances of reliability and adversariness are far greater than those required for admission of hearsay testimony under the Confrontation Clause. . . . We are therefore confident that use of the one-way closed-circuit television procedure, where necessary to further an important state interest, does not impinge upon the truth-seeking or symbolic purposes of the Confrontation Clause.

The critical inquiry in this case, therefore, is whether use of the procedure is necessary to further an important state interest. The State contends that it has a substantial interest in protecting children who are allegedly victims of child abuse from the trauma of testifying against the alleged perpetrator and that its statutory procedure for receiving testimony from such witnesses is necessary to further that interest.

We have of course recognized that a State's interest in "the protection of minor victims of sex crimes from further trauma and embarrassment" is a "compelling" one. . . . "[W]e have sustained legislation aimed at protecting the physical and emotional well-being of youth even when the laws have operated in the sensitive area of constitutionally protected rights." [New York v. Ferber, 458 U.S. 747, 756–757, 102 S.Ct. 3348, 3354, 73 L.Ed.2d 1113 (1982).] In *Globe Newspaper,* for example, we held that a State's interest in the physical and psychological well-being of a minor victim was sufficiently weighty to justify depriving the press and public of their constitutional right to attend criminal trials, where the trial court makes a case-specific finding that closure of the trial is necessary to protect the welfare of the minor. [Globe Newspaper Co. v. Superior Court, 457 U.S. 596, 608–609, 102 S.Ct. 2613, 2620–2621, 73 L.Ed.2d 248 (1982).] This Term, in Osborne v. Ohio, 495 U.S. ___, 110 S.Ct. 1691, 109 L.Ed.2d 98 (1990), we upheld a state statute that proscribed the possession and viewing of child pornography, reaffirming that " '[i]t is evident beyond the need for elaboration that a State's interest in "safeguarding the physical and psychological well-being of a minor" is "compelling." ' " . . .

We likewise conclude today that a State's interest in the physical and psychological well-being of child abuse victims may be sufficiently important to outweigh, at least in some cases, a defendant's right to face his or her accusers in court. That a significant majority of States has enacted statutes to protect child witnesses from the trauma of giving testimony in child abuse cases attests to the widespread belief in the importance of such a public policy. ...Thirty-seven States, for example, permit the use of videotaped testimony of sexually abused children; 24 States have authorized the use of one-way closed circuit television testimony in child abuse cases; and 8 States authorize the use of a two-way system in which the child-witness is permitted to see the courtroom and the defendant on a video monitor and in which the jury and judge is permitted to view the child during the testimony.

The statute at issue in this case, for example, was specifically intended "to safeguard the physical and psychological well-being of child victims by avoiding, or at least minimizing, the emotional trauma produced by testifying." Wildermuth v. State, 310 Md. 496, 518, 530 A.2d 275, 286 (1987). The *Wildermuth* court noted:

> " ... This would both protect the child and enhance the public interest by encouraging effective prosecution of the alleged abuser." Id., at 517, 530 A.2d, at 285.

Given the State's traditional and " 'transcendent interest in protecting the welfare of children,' " [Ginsberg v. New York, 390 U.S. 629, 640, 88 S.Ct. 1274, 1281, 20 L.Ed.2d 195 (1968)] and buttressed by the growing body of academic literature documenting the psychological trauma suffered by child abuse victims who must testify in court, ... we will not second-guess the considered judgment of the Maryland Legislature regarding the importance of its interest in protecting child abuse victims from the emotional trauma of testifying. Accordingly, we hold that, if the State makes an adequate showing of necessity, the state interest in protecting child witnesses from the trauma of testifying in a child abuse case is sufficiently important to justify the use of a special procedure that permits a child witness in such cases to testify at trial against a defendant in the absence of face-to-face confrontation with the defendant.

The requisite finding of necessity must of course be a case-specific one: the trial court must hear evidence and determine whether use of the one-way closed circuit television procedure is necessary to protect the welfare of the particular child witness who seeks to testify. ...The trial court must also find that the child witness would be traumatized, not by the courtroom generally, but by the presence of the defendant. ...Denial of face-to-face confrontation is not needed to further the state interest in protecting the child witness from trauma unless it is the presence of the defendant that causes the trauma. In other words, if the state interest were merely the interest in protecting child witnesses from courtroom trauma generally, denial of face-to-face confrontation would be unnecessary because the child could be permitted to testify in less intimidating surroundings, albeit with the defendant present. Finally, the trial court must find that the emotional distress suffered by the child witness in the presence of the defendant is more than *de minimis,* i.e., more than "mere nervousness or excitement or some reluctance to testify," *Wildermuth,* 310 Md., at 524, 530 A.2d, at 289; see also State v. Mannion, 19 Utah 505, 511–512, 57 P. 542, 543–544 (1899). We need not decide the minimum showing of emotional trauma required for use of the special procedure, however, because the Maryland statute, which requires a determination that the child witness will suffer "serious emotional distress such that the child cannot reasonably communicate," § 9–102(a)(1)(ii), clearly suffices to meet constitutional standards.

To be sure, face-to-face confrontation may be said to cause trauma for the very purpose of eliciting truth, cf. *Coy, supra*, 487 U.S., at 1019–1020, 108 S.Ct., at 2802–03, but we think that the use of Maryland's special procedure, where necessary to further the important state interest in preventing trauma to child witnesses in child abuse cases, adequately ensures the accuracy of the testimony and preserves the adversary nature of the trial. . . . Indeed, where face-to-face confrontation causes significant emotional distress in a child witness, there is evidence that such confrontation would in fact *disserve* the Confrontation Clause's truth-seeking goal. See, e.g., *Coy, supra*, 487 U.S., at 1032, 108 S.Ct., at 2809 (Blackmun, J., dissenting) (face-to-face confrontation "may so overwhelm the child as to prevent the possibility of effective testimony, thereby undermining the truth-finding function of the trial itself") . . .

In sum, we conclude that where necessary to protect a child witness from trauma that would be caused by testifying in the physical presence of the defendant, at least where such trauma would impair the child's ability to communicate, the Confrontation Clause does not prohibit use of a procedure that, despite the absence of face-to-face confrontation, ensures the reliability of the evidence by subjecting it to rigorous adversarial testing and thereby preserves the essence of effective confrontation. Because there is no dispute that the child witnesses in this case testified under oath, were subject to full cross-examination, and were able to be observed by the judge, jury, and defendant as they testified, we conclude that, to the extent that a proper finding of necessity has been made, the admission of such testimony would be consonant with the Confrontation Clause.

IV

The Maryland Court of Appeals held, as we do today, that although face-to-face confrontation is not an absolute constitutional requirement, it may be abridged only where there is a " 'case-specific finding of necessity.' " 316 Md., at 564, 560 A.2d, at 1126 (quoting *Coy, supra*, 487 U.S., at 1025, 108 S.Ct., at 2805 (concurring opinion)). Given this latter requirement, the Court of Appeals reasoned that "[t]he question of whether a child is unavailable to testify . . . should not be asked in terms of inability to testify in the ordinary courtroom setting, but in the much narrower terms of the witness's inability to testify in the presence of the accused." 316 Md., at 564, 560 A.2d, at 1126 (footnote omitted). "[T]he determinative inquiry required to preclude face-to-face confrontation is the effect of the presence of the defendant on the witness or the witness's testimony." Id., at 565, 560 A.2d, at 1127. The Court of Appeals accordingly concluded that, as a prerequisite to use of the § 9–102 procedure, the Confrontation Clause requires the trial court to make a specific finding that testimony by the child in the courtroom *in the presence of the defendant* would result in the child suffering serious emotional distress such that the child could not reasonably communicate. Id., at 566, 560 A.2d, at 1127. This conclusion, of course, is consistent with our holding today.

In addition, however, the Court of Appeals interpreted our decision in *Coy* to impose two subsidiary requirements. First, the court held that "§ 9–102 ordinarily cannot be invoked unless the child witness initially is questioned (either in or outside the courtroom) in the defendant's presence." Id., at 566, 560 A.2d, at 1127; see also *Wildermuth*, 310 Md., at 523–524, 530 A.2d, at 289 (personal observation by the judge should be the rule rather than the exception). Second, the court asserted that, before using the one-way television procedure, a trial judge must determine whether a child would suffer "severe emotional distress" if he or she were to testify by *two*-way closed circuit television. 316 Md., at 567, 560 A.2d, at 1128.

Reviewing the evidence presented to the trial court in support of the finding required under § 9–102(a)(1)(ii), the Court of Appeals determined that "the finding of necessity required to limit the defendant's right of confrontation through invocation of § 9–102 ... was not made here." Id., at 570–571, 560 A.2d, at 1129. ...

* * *

The Court of Appeals appears to have rested its conclusion at least in part on the trial court's failure to observe the children's behavior in the defendant's presence and its failure to explore less restrictive alternatives to the use of the one-way closed circuit television procedure. See id., at 568–571, 560 A.2d, at 1128–1129. Although we think such evidentiary requirements could strengthen the grounds for use of protective measures, we decline to establish, as a matter of federal constitutional law, any such categorical evidentiary prerequisites for the use of the one-way television procedure. The trial court in this case, for example, could well have found, on the basis of the expert testimony before it, that testimony by the child witnesses in the courtroom in the defendant's presence "will result in [each] child suffering serious emotional distress such that the child cannot reasonably communicate," § 9–102(a)(1)(ii). See id., at 568–569, 560 A.2d, at 1128–1129; see also App. 22–25, 39, 41, 43, 44–45, 54–57. So long as a trial court makes such a case-specific finding of necessity, the Confrontation Clause does not prohibit a State from using a one-way closed circuit television procedure for the receipt of testimony by a child witness in a child abuse case. Because the Court of Appeals held that the trial court had not made the requisite finding of necessity under its interpretation of "the high threshold required by [*Coy*] before § 9–102 may be invoked," 316 Md., at 554–555, 560 A.2d, at 1121 (footnote omitted), we cannot be certain whether the Court of Appeals would reach the same conclusion in light of the legal standard we establish today. We therefore vacate the judgment of the Court of Appeals of Maryland and remand the case for further proceedings not inconsistent with this opinion.

It is so ordered.

■ JUSTICE SCALIA, with whom JUSTICE BRENNAN, JUSTICE MARSHALL, and JUSTICE STEVENS join, dissenting.

Seldom has this Court failed so conspicuously to sustain a categorical guarantee of the Constitution against the tide of prevailing current opinion.

The Sixth Amendment provides, with unmistakable clarity, that "[i]n all criminal prosecutions, the accused shall enjoy the right ... to be confronted with the witnesses against him." The purpose of enshrining this protection in the Constitution was to assure that none of the many policy interests from time to time pursued by statutory law could overcome a defendant's right to face his or her accusers in court. ...

Because of this subordination of explicit constitutional text to currently favored public policy, the following scene can be played out in an American courtroom for the first time in two centuries: A father whose young daughter has been given over to the exclusive custody of his estranged wife, or a mother whose young son has been taken into custody by the State's child welfare department, is sentenced to prison for sexual abuse on the basis of testimony by a child the parent has not seen or spoken to for many months; and the guilty verdict is rendered without giving the parent so much as the opportunity to sit in the presence of the child, and to ask, personally or through counsel, "it is really not true, is it, that I—your father (or mother) whom you see before you—did these terrible things?" Perhaps that is a procedure today's society desires; perhaps (though I doubt it) it is even a fair procedure; but it is assuredly not a procedure permitted by the Constitution.

Because the text of the Sixth Amendment is clear, and because the Constitution is meant to protect against, rather than conform to, current "widespread belief," I respectfully dissent.

I

... It is wrong because the Confrontation Clause does not guarantee reliable evidence; it guarantees specific trial procedures that were thought to assure reliable evidence, undeniably among which was "face-to-face" confrontation. Whatever else it may mean in addition, the defendant's constitutional right "to be confronted with the witnesses against him" means, always and everywhere, at least what it explicitly says: the " 'right to meet face to face all those who appear and give evidence at trial.' " Coy v. Iowa, 487 U.S. 1012, 1016, 108 S.Ct. 2798, 2800, 101 L.Ed.2d 857 (1988), quoting California v. Green, 399 U.S. 149, 175, 90 S.Ct. 1930, 1943–44, 26 L.Ed.2d 489 (1970) (Harlan, J. concurring).

The Court supports its antitextual conclusion by cobbling together scraps of dicta from various cases that have no bearing here. It will suffice to discuss one of them, since they are all of a kind: Quoting Ohio v. Roberts, 448 U.S. 56, 63, 100 S.Ct. 2531, 2537, 65 L.Ed.2d 597 (1980), the Court says that "[i]n sum, our precedents establish that 'the Confrontation Clause reflects a *preference* for face-to-face confrontation at trial,' " ante, (emphasis added by the Court). But *Roberts,* and all the other "precedents" the Court enlists to prove the implausible, dealt with the *implications* of the Confrontation Clause, and not its literal, unavoidable text. When *Roberts* said that the Clause merely "reflects a preference for face-to-face confrontation at trial," what it had in mind as the nonpreferred alternative was not (as the Court implies) the appearance of a witness at trial without confronting the defendant. That has been, until today, not merely "nonpreferred" but utterly unheard-of. What *Roberts* had in mind was the receipt of *other-than-first-hand testimony* from witnesses at trial—that is, witnesses' recounting of hearsay statements by absent parties who, *since they did not appear at trial,* did not have to endure face-to-face confrontation. Rejecting that, I agree, was merely giving effect to an evident constitutional preference; there are, after all, many exceptions to the Confrontation Clause's hearsay rule. But that the defendant should be confronted by the witnesses who appear at trial is not a preference "reflected" by the Confrontation Clause; it is a constitutional right unqualifiedly guaranteed.

The Court claims that its interpretation of the Confrontation Clause "is consistent with our cases holding that other Sixth Amendment rights must also be interpreted in the context of the necessities of trial and the adversary process." Ante, at 3165–3166. I disagree. It is true enough that the "necessities of trial and the adversary process" limit the *manner* in which Sixth Amendment rights may be exercised, and limit the *scope* of Sixth Amendment guarantees to the extent that scope is textually indeterminate. Thus (to describe the cases the Court cites): The right to confront is not the right to confront in a manner that disrupts the trial. Illinois v. Allen, 397 U.S. 337, 90 S.Ct. 1057, 25 L.Ed.2d 353 (1970). The right "to have compulsory process for obtaining witnesses" is not the right to call witnesses in a manner that violates fair and orderly procedures. Taylor v. Illinois, 484 U.S. 400, 108 S.Ct. 646, 98 L.Ed.2d 798 (1988). The scope of the right "to have the assistance of counsel" does not include consultation with counsel at all times during the trial. Perry v. Leeke, 488 U.S. 272, 109 S.Ct. 594, 102 L.Ed.2d 624 (1989). The scope of the right to cross-examine does not include access to the State's investigative files. Pennsylvania v. Ritchie, 480 U.S. 39, 107 S.Ct. 989, 94 L.Ed.2d 40 (1987). But we are not talking here about denying expansive scope to a Sixth Amendment provision whose scope for the purpose at issue is textually unclear; "to confront" plainly means to encounter face-to-face, whatever else it may mean in addition. And we are not talking about the manner of arranging that face-to-face encounter, but about whether it shall occur at all. The "necessities of trial and the adversary process" are irrelevant here, since they cannot alter the constitutional text.

II

Much of the Court's opinion consists of applying to this case the mode of analysis we have used in the admission of hearsay evidence. The Sixth Amendment does not literally contain a prohibition upon such evidence, since it guarantees the defendant only the right to confront "the witnesses against him." ... The phrase obviously refers to those who give testimony against the defendant at trial. We have nonetheless found implicit in the Confrontation Clause some limitation upon hearsay evidence, since otherwise the Government could subvert the confrontation right by putting on witnesses who know nothing except what an absent declarant said. And in determining the scope of that implicit limitation, we have focused upon whether the reliability of the hearsay statements (which are not *expressly* excluded by the Confrontation Clause) "is otherwise assured." Ante. The same test cannot be applied, however, to permit what is explicitly forbidden by the constitutional text; there is simply no room for interpretation with regard to "the irreducible literal meaning of the Clause." *Coy,* supra, 487 U.S., at 1020–1021, 108 S.Ct., at 2803.

Some of the Court's analysis seems to suggest that the children's testimony here was itself hearsay of the sort permissible under our Confrontation Clause cases. ..."In the usual case ..., the prosecution must either produce or demonstrate the unavailability of, the declarant whose statement it wishes to use against the defendant." Ohio v. Roberts, 448 U.S., at 65, 100 S.Ct., at 2538. We have permitted a few exceptions to this general rule—e.g., for co-conspirators' statements, whose effect cannot be replicated by live testimony because they "derive [their] significance from the circumstances in which [they were] made," United States v. Inadi, 475 U.S. 387, 395, 106 S.Ct. 1121, 1126, 89 L.Ed.2d 390 (1986). "Live" closed-circuit television testimony, however—if it can be called hearsay at all—is surely an example of hearsay as "a weaker substitute for live testimony," id., at 394, 106 S.Ct., at 1126, which can be employed only when the genuine article is unavailable. "When two versions of the same evidence are available, longstanding principles of the law of hearsay, applicable as well to Confrontation Clause analysis, favor the better evidence." Ibid. ...

The Court's test today requires unavailability only in the sense that the child is unable to testify in the presence of the defendant. That cannot possibly be the relevant sense. If unconfronted testimony is admissible hearsay when the witness is unable to confront the defendant, then presumably there are other categories of admissible hearsay consisting of unsworn testimony when the witness is unable to risk perjury, uncross-examined testimony when the witness is unable to undergo hostile questioning, etc. California v. Green, 399 U.S. 149, 90 S.Ct. 1930, 26 L.Ed.2d 489 (1970), is not precedent for such a silly system. That case held that the Confrontation Clause does not bar admission of prior testimony when the declarant is sworn as a witness but refuses to answer. But in *Green,* as in most cases of refusal, we could not know *why* the declarant refused to testify. Here, by contrast, we know that it is precisely because the child is unwilling to testify in the presence of the defendant. That unwillingness cannot be a valid excuse under the Confrontation Clause, whose very object is to place the witness under the sometimes hostile glare of the defendant. ...To say that a defendant loses his right to confront a witness when that would cause the witness not to testify is rather like saying that the defendant loses his right to counsel when counsel would save him, or his right to subpoena witnesses when they would exculpate him, or his right not to give testimony against himself when that would prove him guilty.

III

The Court characterizes the State's interest which "outweigh[s]" the explicit text of the Constitution as an "interest in the physical and psychological well-being of child abuse victims," ante, at 3167, an "interest in protecting" such victims "from the emotional trauma of testifying," ante, at 3169. That is not so. A child who meets the Maryland statute's requirement of suffering such "serious emotional distress" from confrontation that he "cannot reasonably communicate" would seem entirely safe. Why would a prosecutor want to call a witness who cannot reasonably communicate? And if he did, it would be the State's own fault. Protection of the child's interest—as far as the Confrontation Clause is concerned[12]—is entirely within Maryland's control. The State's interest here is in fact no more and no less than what the State's interest always is when it seeks to get a class of evidence admitted in criminal proceedings: more convictions of guilty defendants. That is not an unworthy interest, but it should not be dressed up as a humanitarian one.

And the interest on the other side is also what it usually is when the State seeks to get a new class of evidence admitted: fewer convictions of innocent defendants—specifically, in the present context, innocent defendants accused of particularly heinous crimes. The "special" reasons that exist for suspending one of the usual guarantees of reliability in the case of children's testimony are perhaps matched by "special" reasons for being particularly insistent upon it in the case of children's testimony. Some studies show that children are substantially more vulnerable to suggestion than adults, and often unable to separate recollected fantasy (or suggestion) from reality. ...The injustice their erroneous testimony can produce is evidenced by the tragic Scott County investigations of 1983–1984, which disrupted the lives of many (as far as we know) innocent people in the small town of Jordan, Minnesota. At one stage those investigations were pursuing allegations by at least eight children of multiple murders, but the prosecutions actually initiated charged only sexual abuse. Specifically, 24 adults were charged with molesting 37 children. In the course of the investigations, 25 children were placed in foster homes. Of the 24 indicted defendants, one pleaded guilty, two were acquitted at trial, and the charges against the remaining 21 were voluntarily dismissed. ...There is no doubt that some sexual abuse took place in Jordan; but there is no reason to believe it was as widespread as charged. A report by the Minnesota Attorney General's office, based on inquiries conducted by the Minnesota Bureau of Criminal Apprehension and the Federal Bureau of Investigation, concluded that there was an "absence of credible testimony and [a] lack of significant corroboration" to support reinstitution of sex-abuse charges, and "no credible evidence of murders." H. Humphrey, report on Scott County Investigation 8, 7 (1985). ...The value of the confrontation right in guarding against a child's distorted or coerced recollections is dramatically evident with respect to one of the misguided investigative techniques the report cited: some children were told by their foster parents that reunion with their real parents would be hastened by "admission" of their parents' abuse. Id., at 9. Is it difficult to imagine how unconvincing such a testimonial admission might be to a jury that witnessed the child's delight at seeing his parents in the courtroom? Or how devastating it might be if, pursuant to a psychiatric evaluation that "trauma would impair the child's ability to communicate" in front of his parents, the child were permitted to tell his story to the jury on closed-circuit television?

12. A different situation would be presented if the defendant sought to call the child. In that event, the State's refusal to compel the child to appear, or its insistence upon a procedure such as that set forth in the Maryland statute as a condition of its compelling him to do so, would call into question—initially, at least, and perhaps exclusively—the scope of the defendant's Sixth Amendment right "to have compulsory process for obtaining witnesses in his favor."

In the last analysis, however, this debate is not an appropriate one. I have no need to defend the value of confrontation, because the Court has no authority to question it. It is not within our charge to speculate that, "where face-to-face confrontation causes significant emotional distress in a child witness," confrontation might "in fact *disserve* the Confrontation Clause's truth-seeking goal." Ante. If so, that is a defect in the Constitution—which should be amended by the procedures provided for such an eventuality, but cannot be corrected by judicial pronouncement that it is archaic, contrary to "widespread belief" and thus null and void. For good or bad, the Sixth Amendment requires confrontation, and we are not at liberty to ignore it. . . .

The Court today has applied "interest-balancing" analysis where the text of the Constitution simply does not permit it. We are not free to conduct a cost-benefit analysis of clear and explicit constitutional guarantees, and then to adjust their meaning to comport with our findings. The Court has convincingly proved that the Maryland procedure serves a valid interest, and gives the defendant virtually everything the Confrontation Clause guarantees (everything, that is, except confrontation). I am persuaded, therefore, that the Maryland procedure is virtually constitutional. Since it is not, however, actually constitutional I would affirm the judgment of the Maryland Court of Appeals reversing the judgment of conviction.

NOTES

1. **Accusatory confessions.** In Bruton v. United States, 391 U.S. 123, 88 S.Ct. 1620, 20 L.Ed.2d 476, (1968), there was a joint trial of the petitioner and a codefendant upon a charge of armed postal robbery. A postal inspector testified that the codefendant, Evans, had confessed to him that Evans and the petitioner had committed the robbery. This evidence was, concededly, wholly inadmissible against the petitioner. Evans did not testify. Although the trial judge instructed the jury to disregard the evidence of Evans' confession in considering the question of the petitioner's guilt, the Supreme Court reversed the petitioner's conviction. The primary focus of the Court's opinion in *Bruton* was upon the issue of whether the jury in the circumstances presented could reasonably be expected to have followed the trial judge's instructions. The Court found that the risk of prejudice in petitioner's case was unacceptable when "the powerfully incriminating extrajudicial statements of a codefendant, who stands accused side-by-side with the defendant, are deliberately spread before the jury in a joint trial." 391 U.S. at 135–36, 88 S.Ct. at 1628, 20 L.Ed.2d 485. Accordingly, the Court held that "in the context of a joint trial we cannot accept limiting instructions as an adequate substitute for petitioner's constitutional right of cross-examination." 391 U.S. at 137, 88 S.Ct. at 1628, 20 L.Ed.2d at 485.

2. **Interlocking confessions.** Lee v. Illinois, 476 U.S. 530, 106 S.Ct. 2056, 90 L.Ed.2d 514 (1986) also involved a co-defendant's confession. Lee and her boyfriend, Thomas, were jointly tried for two murders. Lee had confessed to police that after her boyfriend had killed one of the persons she confronted the other, her aunt, who brandished a knife, whereupon Lee stabbed her to death. Thomas' confession was similar to Lee's but added that they had earlier planned both killings. Both were tried before the court without a jury, and neither testified. Both confessions were introduced into evidence. Lee took the position that, in accordance with her confession, she had nothing to do with the death of the second person and that with respect to her aunt's death, it was either self-defense or at least voluntary man-

slaughter upon a sudden provocation. The trial court rejected all these contentions, basing his conclusions explicitly upon the accusations in Thomas' statement as to Lee's knowledge and behavior. She was convicted of two counts of murder and upon appeal the Illinois Court of Appeals affirmed on the ground that her confession and Thomas' were so similar—"interlocking"—that her right of confrontation was not violated by the use against her of Thomas' statements. The United States Supreme Court, in an opinion by Justice Brennan, reversed. The basic Confrontation Clause principle is that "when one person accuses another of a crime under circumstances in which the declarant stands to gain by inculpating another, the accusation is presumptively suspect and must be subjected to the scrutiny of cross-examination." 476 U.S. at 541, 106 S.Ct. at 2062, 90 L.Ed.2d at 526. The fact that the confessions "interlock" at certain points does not change the situation:

> [A] codefendant's confession is presumptively unreliable as to the passages detailing the defendant's conduct or culpability because those passages may well be the product of the codefendant's desire to shift or spread blame, curry favor, avenge himself, or divert attention to another. If those portions of the codefendant's purportedly "interlocking" statement which bear to any significant degree on the defendant's participation in the crime are not thoroughly substantiated by the defendant's own confession, the admission of the statement poses too serious a threat to the accuracy of the verdict to be countenanced by the Sixth Amendment.

476 U.S. at 545, 106 S.Ct. at 2064, 90 L.Ed.2d at 529. The Court concluded that there were not sufficient indicia of reliability from the circumstances surrounding the making of the confession or its "interlocking" character to overcome the presumption against admission. Justice Blackmun, joined by Chief Justice Burger, Justice Powell and Justice Rehnquist, dissented on the ground that there were indicia of reliability of Thomas' statement, primarily that his statement was adverse to his own penal interest. Indeed, his own statement tended to incriminate himself more than did the statement of Lee. Further, there was corroboration for the statement, principally Lee's confession. Although Lee's confession was not identical to Thomas', it did not contradict it either, that is, Lee in her statement did not deny that the planning activity recounted in Thomas' statement occurred.

The Court again addressed the question of interlocking confessions in Cruz v. New York, 481 U.S. 186, 107 S.Ct. 1714, 95 L.Ed.2d 162 (1987). Eulogio Cruz and his brother, Benjamin, were on trial for killing a person during a gas station robbery. At the trial, Benjamin's videotaped confession was admitted, which incriminated Eulogio as well as himself. A state's witness testified that both Eulogio and Benjamin confessed to him before they were apprehended that they had killed the gas station attendant. This testimony was impeached by evidence that the witness believed that Eulogio and Benjamin had killed his brother and thus presented his testimony in revenge. The trial court instructed the jury that neither defendant's confession could be used against the other. Eulogio's conviction was affirmed by the New York Court of Appeals, but the United States Supreme Court, in an opinion by Justice Scalia, reversed. The Court rejected the reasoning of previous plurality opinions that the devastating effects of a codefendant's confession, as condemned by *Bruton*, see note 1, are not present when the defendant has also confessed, the so-called interlocking confessions exception to *Bruton:*

> "[I]nterlocking" bears a positively inverse relationship to devastation. A codefendant's confession will be relatively harmless if the incriminating story it tells is different from that which the defendant himself is alleged to have told, but enormously damaging if it confirms, in all essential respects, the defendant's alleged confession. It might be otherwise if the defendant were *standing by* his confession, in which case it could be said that the codefendant's confession does

no more than support the defendant's very own case. But in the real world of criminal litigation, the defendant is seeking to *avoid* his confession—on the ground that it was not accurately reported, or that it was not really true when made.... Quite obviously, what the "interlocking" nature of the codefendant's confession pertains to is not its *harmfulness* but rather its *reliability:* If it confirms essentially the same facts as the defendant's own confession it is more likely to be true. Its reliability, however, may be relevant to whether the confession should (despite the lack of opportunity for cross-examination) be *admitted as evidence* against the defendant, ... but cannot conceivably be relevant to whether, assuming it cannot be admitted, the jury is likely to obey the instruction to disregard it, or the jury's failure to obey is likely to be inconsequential. The law cannot command respect if such an inexplicable exception to a supposed constitutional imperative is adopted. Having decided *Bruton,* we must face the honest consequences of what it holds.

481 U.S. at 192–93, 107 S.Ct. at 1718–19, 95 L.Ed.2d at 171. The Court held that

> where a nontestifying codefendant's confession incriminating the defendant is not directly admissible against the defendant, ... the Confrontation Clause bars its admission at their joint trial, even if the jury is instructed not to consider it against the defendant, and even if the defendant's own confession is admitted against him. Of course, the defendant's confession may be considered at trial in assessing whether his codefendant's statements are supported by sufficient "indicia of reliability" to be directly admissible against him [under Lee v. Illinois] and may be considered on appeal in assessing whether any Confrontation Clause violation was harmless.

481 U.S. at 193–94, 107 S.Ct. at 1719, 95 L.Ed.2d at 172. Justice White, joined by The Chief Justice, and Justices Powell and O'Connor, dissented.

3. **Testimony at a prior hearing.** In Ohio v. Roberts, 448 U.S. 56, 100 S.Ct. 2531, 65 L.Ed.2d 597 (1980), Roberts was arrested for forgery of a check in the name of Bernard Isaacs. At his preliminary examination, he called as a defense witness Anita Isaacs, daughter of the complainant, in an effort to show that she had given him the checkbook with the assurance that it was permissible for him to use it. She denied doing so. Roberts was indicted and his case was set for trial on four different dates. Anita failed to respond to the court's subpoena on each occasion. On the fifth try, the case was presented to a jury and Roberts testified that he had been given permission by Anita to use the checkbook. In rebuttal, the state was permitted to read a transcript of Anita's preliminary examination testimony to the jury over respondent's objection that his rights of confrontation were being violated. Anita's mother testified at the trial that Anita had run away from home shortly after the preliminary examination and she did not know her whereabouts. The Ohio Supreme Court reversed the conviction on the ground that Roberts' confrontation rights were violated. The Supreme Court, by a vote of 6–3, reversed. Justice Blackmun's opinion for the Court attempted to distill from the Court's earlier decisions a standard for determining when admission of hearsay violates the Sixth Amendment:

> [W]hen a hearsay declarant is not present for cross-examination at trial, the Confrontation Clause normally requires a showing that he is unavailable. Even then, his statement is admissible only if it bears adequate "indicia of reliability." Reliability can be inferred without more in a case where the evidence falls within a firmly rooted hearsay exception. In other cases, the evidence must be excluded, at least absent a showing of particularized guarantees of trustworthiness.

448 U.S. at 66, 100 S.Ct. at 2539, 65 L.Ed.2d at 608. Here, the Court concluded that Anita's testimony fell within the traditional hearsay exception for testimony at a

prior hearing. Since defense counsel had subjected her to the equivalent of full cross examination, the Court found no need to consider whether the mere unexercised opportunity for cross examination (or *de minimis* questioning) at the prior hearing would suffice. Since the case came within a "firmly rooted hearsay exception," no particularized search for "indicia of reliability" was necessary. Moreover, the evidence of the state's efforts to locate Anita and the absence of knowledge concerning her location sufficed to establish unavailability. Justice Brennan, joined by Justices Marshall and Stevens, dissented on the ground that the state had failed to adequately follow up certain leads to Anita's location and therefore had not made an adequate showing of unavailability.

4. **Statements of a co-conspirator.** In United States v. Inadi, 475 U.S. 387, 106 S.Ct. 1121, 89 L.Ed.2d 390 (1986), respondent was convicted of drug conspiracy in a trial in which the recorded statements of a co-conspirator were admitted into evidence over his objection that the Confrontation Clause as interpreted in Ohio v. Roberts required a showing of unavailability of the declarant as a predicate to admission. The Court of Appeals reversed the conviction on that ground but the United States Supreme Court, in an opinion by Justice Powell, reversed the Court of Appeals. *Roberts* dealt with the admissibility of prior testimony and the requirement of unavailability of the witness is a traditional and sound requirement for that category of evidence for if the witness is available then the jury ought to hear his testimony from the witness stand. With respect to co-conspirator's statements, however, their evidentiary value derives from the fact that they are made in furtherance of the conspiracy:

> When the Government—as here—offers the statement of one drug dealer to another in furtherance of an illegal conspiracy, the statement often will derive its significance from the circumstances in which it was made. Conspirators are likely to speak differently when talking to each other in furtherance of their illegal aims than when testifying on the witness stand.

475 U.S. at 395, 106 S.Ct. at 1126, 89 L.Ed.2d at 398. Justice Marshall, joined by Justice Brennan, dissented.

5. **Statements to a physician by a child.** In a companion case to Maryland v. Craig, also involving child abuse, Idaho v. Wright, 497 U.S. 805, 110 S.Ct. 3139, 111 L.Ed.2d 638 (1990), the Court considered whether there were sufficient indicia of reliability in hearsay statements offered by the examining physician. Respondent Wright was charged with sexual abuse of her two daughters, 5½ and 2½ years old. Dr. Jambura, an experienced pediatrician, found physical evidence of sexual abuse. At trial, the judge determined the younger girl was not capable of communicating to the jury. The judge then admitted Dr. Jambura's testimony concerning statements the child had made in an interview with him. This ruling was based on Idaho's "residual hearsay exception" under which hearsay was admissible despite witness availability so long as it met a three-part test for trustworthiness: (A) offered as evidence of a material fact; (B) more probative than any other evidence which can be procured through reasonable efforts; and (C) in the interests of justice. Respondent was convicted on both counts. She appealed the conviction involving the younger daughter. The Idaho Supreme Court reversed, finding Dr. Jambura's testimony inadmissible because his interview technique lacked adequate procedural safeguards: the interview was not recorded; the doctor asked "blatantly leading questions"; and he had "a preconceived idea of what the child should be disclosing."

The United States Supreme Court in an opinion by Justice O'Connor affirmed. The Court assumed for purposes of the opinion that the child was an "unavailable witness" and proceeded to the "indicia of reliability" test from Ohio v. Roberts, supra. Because no "firmly rooted hearsay exception" applied, the inquiry focused on the other *Roberts* alternative—whether the statements were supported by "a showing of particularized guarantees of trustworthiness." In holding that this requirement was not met, the Court held:

> We think the "particularized guarantees of trustworthiness" required for admission under the Confrontation Clause must [like the firmly rooted hearsay exceptions] be drawn from the totality of circumstances that surround the making of the statement ... [And likewise the] evidence admitted ... must ... be so trustworthy that adversarial testing would add little to its reliability ... Thus, unless an affirmative reason, arising from the circumstances in which the statement was made, provides a basis for rebutting the presumption that a hearsay statement is not worthy of reliance at trial, the Confrontation Clause requires exclusion of the out-of-court statement.

497 U.S. at 820–21, 110 S.Ct. at 3149–50, 111 L.Ed.2d at 655–56.

The Court announced that consideration of corroborating evidence for this analysis would improperly bootstrap and frustrate the rule that the hearsay be so reliable as to render cross-examination "of marginal utility." The majority concluded that corroboration more properly would go to harmless error analysis if at all. The Court concluded:

> Of the factors the trial court found relevant, only two relate to circumstances surrounding the making of the statements: whether the child had a motive to "make up a story of this nature," and whether, given the child's age, the statements are of the type "that one would expect a child to fabricate." ... The other factors ... such as the ... physical evidence of abuse, the opportunity of the respondent to commit the offense, and the older daughter's corroborating identification ... are irrelevant ...

> We think the Supreme Court of Idaho properly focused on the presumptive unreliability of the out-of-court statements and on the suggestive manner in which Dr. Jambura conducted the interview. Viewing the totality of the circumstances ... we agree with the court below that the State has failed to show that the younger daughter's incriminating statements to the pediatrician possessed sufficient "particularized guarantees of trustworthiness" under the Confrontation Clause to overcome that presumption.

497 U.S. at 826–27, 110 S.Ct. at 3152–53, 111 L.Ed.2d at 659–60.

Justice Kennedy, joined by the Chief Justice and Justices White and Blackmun, dissented:

> The Court's apparent misgivings about the weight to be given corroborating evidence may or may not be correct, but those misgivings do not justify wholesale elimination of this evidence from consideration, in derogation of an overwhelming judicial and legislative consensus to the contrary.

497 U.S. at 829–30, 110 S.Ct. at 3154, 111 L.Ed.2d at 661–62.

Justice Kennedy insisted that "[t]he Court in *Lee* was unanimous in its recognition of corroboration as a legitimate indicator of reliability ... "and that the Court in *Cruz* had unequivocally rejected the suggestion that corroboration goes more to harmless error than to reliability when it said:

> "Quite obviously, what the 'interlocking' nature of the codefendant's confession pertains to is not its *harmfulness* but rather its *reliability*: If it confirms essentially the same facts as the defendant's own confession it is more likely to be true." Cruz v. New York, 481 U.S. 186, 192, 1j07 S.Ct. 1714, 1719, 95 L.Ed.2d 162 (1987) (emphasis in original).

497 U.S. at 832, 110 S.Ct. at 3155, 111 L.Ed.2d at 6630.

6. **Outcry evidence.** The Petitioner in White v. Illinois, 502 U.S. 346, 112 S.Ct. 736, 116 L.Ed.2d 848 (1992) was seen exiting the bedroom of a four-year old girl by her babysitter who was awakened by the girl's screams. The babysitter recognized the petitioner as a friend of the girl's mother. The girl told the babysitter that petitioner had engaged in sexual contact with her. About 30 minutes later, she told her mother the same story and about 45 minutes after the alleged assault, she told the same story to a police officer. About 4 hours after the alleged assault she told the same story first to a nurse and then to a doctor at a local hospital.

Statements by the babysitter, mother, police officer, nurse and doctor were admitted into evidence over hearsay and confrontation objections. The girl was called as a witness but did not testify. Petitioner was convicted of various offenses. The Supreme Court, in an opinion by The Chief Justice, affirmed the convictions.

The Court rejected as coming too late in history the *amicus curiae* arguments of the United States Government that the Confrontation Clause should be restricted to efforts to prove criminal charges by ex parte affidavits, that is, "where the circumstances surrounding the out-of-court statement's utterance suggest that the statement has been made for the principal purpose of accusing or incriminating the defendant." In this case, the girl's statements to her babysitter, mother and the police officer came within the traditional exception to the hearsay rule for spontaneous declarations while the last two statements came within the traditional exception for statements made in the course of receiving medical treatment:

> A statement that has been offered in a moment of excitement—without the opportunity to reflect on the consequences of one's exclamation—may justifiably carry more weight with a trier of fact than a similar statement offered in the relative calm of the courtroom. Similarly, a statement made in the course of procuring medical services, where the declarant knows that a false statement may cause misdiagnosis or mistreatment, carries special guarantees of credibility that a trier of fact may not think replicated by courtroom testimony.

502 U.S. at 356, 112 S.Ct. at 742–43, 116 L.Ed.2d at 859. The Court concluded that "where proffered hearsay has sufficient guarantees of reliability to come within a firmly rooted exception to the hearsay rule, the Confrontation Clause is satisfied." 502 U.S. at 356, 112 S.Ct. at 743, 116 L.Ed.2d at 859.

Contrary to petitioner's contention, the Court said that Coy v. Iowa and Maryland v. Craig do not require any showing of necessity for the statements at issue to be admitted in this case. Those cases "involved only the question of what *in-court* procedures are constitutionally required to guarantee a defendant's confrontation right once a witness is testifying. Such a question is quite separate from that of what requirements the Confrontation Clause imposes as a predicate for the introduction of out-of-court declarations." 502 U.S. at 358, 112 S.Ct. at 743–44, 116 L.Ed.2d at 860.

Justice Thomas, joined by Justice Scalia, concurred in the judgment. He would hold that

> the Confrontation Clause is implicated by extrajudicial statements only insofar as they are contained in formalized testimonial materials, such as affidavits, depositions, prior testimony, or confessions. It was this discrete category of testimonial materials that was historically abused by prosecutors as a means to depriving criminal defendants of the benefit of the adversary process, and under this approach, the Confrontation Clause would not be construed to extend beyond the historical evil to which it was directed.

502 U.S. at 365, 112 S.Ct. at 747, 116 L.Ed.2d at 865.

7. **Right of defendant to be present during trial.** Included within a defendant's right of confrontation is the right to be present in the courtroom. Under what circumstances can a constitutionally-valid conviction result from a trial which the defendant declines to attend? In Taylor v. United States, 414 U.S. 17, 94 S.Ct. 194, 38 L.Ed.2d 174 (1973) (per curiam), the defendant Taylor, after a noon recess, failed to return to his trial for sale of cocaine. Relying upon the then-effective provisions of Fed.R.Crim.P. 43, that in a noncapital case "the defendant's voluntary absence after the trial has been commenced in his presence shall not prevent continuing the trial to and including the return of the verdict," the trial judge directed the trial to continue. The jury was admonished that no inference of guilt could be drawn from his absence; it returned a verdict of guilty. After being arrested, Taylor was sentenced. He challenged his conviction on the ground that it violated his Sixth Amendment right to confront witnesses. The Supreme Court found no merit in the challenge. Rule 43, it noted, reflects a long-recognized rule that voluntary absence from a trial operates as a waiver of the right to be present and permits the court to proceed as if the defendant were present. Taylor never challenged the voluntariness of his absence; both the trial court and the lower appellate court had concluded that his absence was voluntary. Taylor, however, urged that he could lose his Sixth Amendment confrontation right only by a waiver constituting an intentional relinquishment of a known right, and that no such waiver could be found in the absence of evidence that he knew or had been expressly warned that trial would continue if he were to be absent. The Court rejected this, noting that Taylor was questioned at sentencing about his flight and never contended that he was unaware that if he fled the trial would continue. Further, the Court reasoned:

> The right at issue is the right to be present, and the question becomes whether that right was effectively waived by [Taylor's] voluntary absence.
>
> It is wholly incredible to suggest that [Taylor] ... entertained any doubts about his right to be present at every stage of the trial. It seems equally incredible to us, as it did to the Court of Appeals, "that a defendant who flees from a courtroom in the midst of a trial—where judge, jury, witnesses and lawyers are present and ready to continue—would not know that as a consequence the trial could continue in his absence."

414 U.S. at 20, 94 S.Ct. at 196, 38 L.Ed.2d at 177–78. Does this mean that if, on the facts of another case, a trial judge was convinced that a defendant tried *in absentia* under the rule was actually unaware that trial would continue in his absence, the continuation of that trial was in violation of the defendant's Sixth Amendment rights?

The relevant portions of Rule 43 of the Federal Rules of Criminal Procedure now provide:

> (a) Presence Required. The defendant shall be present at the arraignment, at the time of the plea, at every stage of the trial including the impaneling of the jury and the return of the verdict, and at the imposition of sentence, except as otherwise provided by this rule.
>
> (b) Continued Presence Not Required. The further progress of the trial to and including the return of the verdict, and the imposition of sentence, will not be prevented and the defendant will be considered to have waived the right to be present whenever a defendant, initially present at trial, or having pleaded guilty or nolo contendere,
>
> > (1) is voluntarily absent after the trial has commenced (whether or not the defendant has been informed by the court of the obligation to remain during the trial),

(2) in a noncapital case, is voluntarily absent at the imposition of sentence, or

(3) after being warned by the court that disruptive conduct will cause the removal of the defendant from the courtroom, persists in conduct which is such as to justify exclusion from the courtroom.

Whether a defendant's failure to appear at trial for reasons of financial hardship amounts to a knowing and intelligent waiver of the right to be present is "primarily a factual issue" for the trial court, noted the Supreme Court in a per curiam dismissal of a writ of certiorari in Tacon v. Arizona, 410 U.S. 351, 352, 35 S.Ct. 998, 999, 35 L.Ed.2d 346, 348 (1973).

8. **Right to be present when trial begins.** Whether a federal criminal trial can begin under Rule 43 if the accused does not appear was presented in Crosby v. United States, 506 U.S. 255, 113 S.Ct. 748, 122 L.Ed.2d 25 (1993). Crosby failed to appear for trial, although his attorney and three codefendants were present. After several days of searching failed to turn him up, the district judge began trial without him. He was convicted. Six months later he was apprehended in another state and brought back to the trial court for sentencing. Under Rule 43, the Supreme Court ruled, the trial court erred in beginning Crosby's trial without him present. "The language, history, and logic of Rule 43," it reasoned, "support a straightforward interpretation that prohibits the trial *in absentia* of a defendant who is not present at the beginning of trial." In explanation, Justice Blackmun offered for the Court:

[W]e do not find the distinction between pretrial and midtrial flight so far-fetched as to convince us that Rule 43 cannot mean what it says. As a general matter, the costs of suspending a proceeding already under way will be greater than the cost of postponing a trial not yet begun. If a clear line is to be drawn marking the point at which the costs of delay are likely to outweigh the interests of the defendant and society in having the defendant present, the commencement of trial is at least a plausible place at which to draw that line . . . .

There are additional practical reasons for distinguishing between flight before and flight during a trial. * * * [T]he Rule treats midtrial flight as a knowing and voluntary waiver of the right to be present. Whether or not the right constitutionally may be waived in other circumstances—and we express no opinion here on that subject—the defendant's initial presence serves to assure that any waiver is indeed knowing. "Since the notion that trial may be commenced in absentia still seems to shock most lawyers, it would hardly seem appropriate to impute knowledge that this will occur to their clients." Starkey, Trial in Absentia, 54 N.Y.St.B.J. 30, 34, n. 28 (1982). It is unlikely, on the other hand, " 'that a defendant who flees from a courtroom in the midst of a trial—where judge, jury, witnesses and lawyers are present and ready to continue—would not know that as a consequence the trial could continue in his absence.' " Taylor v. United States, 414 U.S. 17, 20, 94 S.Ct. 194, 196, 38 L.Ed.2d 174 (1973), quoting from Chief Judge Coffin's opinion, 478 F.2d 689, 691 (C.A.1 1973), for the Court of Appeals in that case. Moreover, a rule that allows an ongoing trial to continue when a defendant disappears deprives the defendant of the option of gambling on an acquittal knowing that he can terminate the trial if it seems that the verdict will go against him—an option that might otherwise appear preferable to the costly, perhaps unnecessary, path of becoming a fugitive from the outset.

506 U.S. at 261–62, 113 S.Ct. at 752–53, 122 L.Ed.2d at 32. Having thus resolved the case, the Court emphasized that it was not reaching Crosby's claim that his trial *in absentia* was prohibited by the United States Constitution. 506 U.S. at 262, 113 S.Ct. at 753, 122 L.Ed.2d at 33.

10. **Presence during capital trials.** Is the Sixth Amendment rule any different in capital cases? Should it be? Does the Constitution protect a defendant from being convicted in absentia in a capital case? Even if his absence is voluntary? In Drope v. Missouri, 420 U.S. 162, 182, 95 S.Ct. 896, 909, 43 L.Ed.2d 103, 119 (1975), the Court was able to side-step this issue where defendant inflicted a gunshot wound upon himself, and thus was absent during a portion of his trial for an offense for which death was a possible penalty.

11. **Conferences in chambers.** The Court expanded further on the extent of a defendant's right to be present at all stages of his criminal trial in United States v. Gagnon, 470 U.S. 522, 105 S.Ct. 1482, 84 L.Ed.2d 486 (1985). Gagnon and three other respondents were jointly being tried for drug offenses when a juror contacted the trial judge to express concern over Gagnon's sketching portraits of the jurors "because of what could happen afterwards." The trial judge interviewed the juror in chambers with Gagnon's attorney and a court reporter. She explained that Gagnon was an artist and that the portraits had been confiscated. She also determined that the juror was not prejudiced by the sketching and the trial proceeded without objection by any of the respondents as to the interviewing of the juror with only Gagnon's counsel present. On appeal from convictions, however, each respondent claimed that rights to an impartial jury and to presence under Rule 43 had been violated by the in chambers examination. The Ninth Circuit reversed the convictions under Rule 43 and the due process clause of the Fifth Amendment. The Supreme Court, in a *per curiam* opinion, reversed. While the Court acknowledged that due process includes a right to presence even when a witness is not being confronted under the Sixth Amendment, it disposed of the claim with the comment that due process is not violated by an ex parte conversation between a trial judge and a juror and that "the defense has no constitutional right to be present at every interaction between a judge and a juror, nor is there a constitutional right to have a court reporter transcribe every such communication." The Court also held that the respondents had waived any claim they might have under Rule 43 to presence "at every stage of the trial. . . ." because they knew about the proposed conference with the juror in chambers and failed to assert a right to be present.

12. **Ejection for disruptive conduct.** The right to be present may also be lost by disruptive conduct in the courtroom, as was recognized in Illinois v. Allen, 397 U.S. 337, 90 S.Ct. 1057, 25 L.Ed.2d 353 (1970). Allen had been ejected from his trial for robbery after he interrupted the proceedings, tore up a file, and threatened the judge. He was permitted to return but was again removed when he repeated his disruptive conduct. In later federal habeas corpus proceedings attacking the resulting conviction, the Court of Appeals held that Allen's absolute right to be present had been violated. The Supreme Court reversed:

> [W]e explicitly hold ... that a defendant can lose his right to be present at trial if, after he has been warned by the judge that he will be removed if he continues his disruptive behavior, he nevertheless insists on conducting himself in a manner so disorderly, disruptive, and disrespectful of the court that his trial cannot be carried on with him in the courtroom. Once lost, the right to be present can, of course, be reclaimed as soon as the defendant is willing to conduct himself consistently with the decorum and respect inherent in the concept of courts and judicial proceedings.

It is essential to the proper administration of criminal justice that dignity, order, and decorum be the hallmarks of all court proceedings in our country.

The flagrant disregard in the courtroom of elementary standards of proper conduct should not and cannot be tolerated. We believe trial judges confronted with disruptive, contumacious, stubbornly defiant defendants must be given sufficient discretion to meet the circumstances of each case. No one formula for maintaining the appropriate courtroom atmosphere will be best in all situations. We think there are at least three constitutionally permissible ways for a trial judge to handle an obstreperous defendant like Allen: (1) bind and gag him, thereby keeping him present; (2) cite him for contempt; (3) take him out of the courtroom until he promises to conduct himself properly.

397 U.S. at 343–44, 90 S.Ct. at 1060–61, 25 L.Ed.2d at 359. Addressing the exercise of the discretion it recognized in the trial judge, the Court continued:

Trying a defendant for a crime while he sits bound and gagged before the judge and jury would to an extent comply with that part of the Sixth Amendment's purposes that accords the defendant an opportunity to confront the witnesses at the trial. But even to contemplate such a technique, much less see it, arouses a feeling that no person should be tried while shackled and gagged except as a last resort. Not only is it possible that the sight of shackles and gags might have a significant effect on the jury's feelings about the defendant, but the use of this technique is itself something of an affront to the very dignity and decorum of judicial proceedings that the judge is seeking to uphold. Moreover, one of the defendant's primary advantages of being present at the trial, his ability to communicate with his counsel, is greatly reduced when the defendant is in a condition of total physical restraint. It is in part because of these inherent disadvantages and limitations in this method of dealing with disorderly defendants that we decline to hold with the Court of Appeals that a defendant cannot under any possible circumstances be deprived of his right to be present at trial. However, in some situations which we need not attempt to foresee, binding and gagging might possibly be the fairest and most reasonable way to handle a defendant who acts as Allen did here.

* * *

[C]iting or threatening to cite a contumacious defendant for criminal contempt might in itself be sufficient to make a defendant stop interrupting a trial. If so, the problem would be solved easily, and the defendant could remain in the courtroom. Of course, if the defendant is determined to prevent *any* trial, then a court in attempting to try the defendant for contempt is still confronted with the identical dilemma that the Illinois court faced in this case. And criminal contempt has obvious limitations as a sanction when the defendant is charged with a crime so serious that a very severe sentence such as death or life imprisonment is likely to be imposed. In such a case the defendant might not be affected by a mere contempt sentence when he ultimately faces a far more serious sanction. Nevertheless, the contempt remedy should be borne in mind by a judge in the circumstances of this case.

Another aspect of the contempt remedy is the judge's power, when exercised consistently with state and federal law, to imprison an unruly defendant such as Allen for civil contempt and discontinue the trial until such time as the defendant promises to behave himself. This procedure is consistent with the defendant's right to be present at trial, and yet it avoids the serious shortcomings of the use of shackles and gags. It must be recognized, however, that a defendant might conceivably, as a matter of calculated strategy, elect to spend a prolonged period in confinement for contempt in the hope that adverse witnesses might be unavailable after a lapse of time. A court must guard against allowing a defendant to profit from his own wrong in this way.

397 U.S. at 344–45, 90 S.Ct. at 1061–62, 25 L.Ed.2d at 359–60.

2. CROSS–EXAMINATION AND COMPULSORY PROCESS TO OBTAIN WITNESSES

As the opinions in the previous section indicate, confrontation and cross-examination are interrelated. Indeed a major purpose behind the right of confrontation is cross-examination. In addition, the Sixth Amendment explicitly provides that the accused is "to have compulsory process for obtaining witnesses in his favor." The principal case in this section combines all of these procedural rights.

Chambers v. Mississippi

Supreme Court of the United States, 1973.
410 U.S. 284, 93 S.Ct. 1038, 35 L.Ed.2d 297.

■ MR. JUSTICE POWELL delivered the opinion of the Court.

Petitioner, Leon Chambers, was tried by a jury in a Mississippi trial court and convicted of murdering a policeman. The jury assessed punishment at life imprisonment and the Mississippi Supreme Court affirmed, one justice dissenting. ...Subsequently the petition for certiorari was granted to consider whether petitioner's trial was conducted in accord with principles of due process under the Fourteenth Amendment. We conclude that it was not.

* * *

II.

Chambers filed a pretrial motion requesting the court to order McDonald to appear. Chambers also sought a ruling at that time that, if the State chose not to call McDonald itself, he be allowed to call him as an adverse witness. Attached to the motion were copies of McDonald's sworn confession and of the transcript of his preliminary hearing at which he repudiated that confession. The trial court granted the motion requiring McDonald to appear but reserved ruling on the adverse witness motion. At trial, after the State failed to put McDonald on the stand, Chambers called McDonald, laid a predicate for the introduction of his sworn out-of-court confession, had it admitted into evidence, and read it to the jury. The State, upon cross-examination, elicited from McDonald the fact that he had rejected his prior confession. McDonald further testified, as he had at the preliminary hearing, that he did not shoot Liberty, and that he confessed to the crime only on the promise of Reverend Stokes that he would not go to jail and would share in a sizable tort recovery from the town. He also retold his own story of his actions on the evening of the shooting....

At the conclusion of the State's cross-examination, Chambers renewed his motion to examine McDonald as an adverse witness. The trial court denied the motion, stating: "He may be hostile, but he is not adverse in the sense of the word, so your request will be overruled." On appeal, the State Supreme Court upheld the trial court's ruling, finding that "McDonald's testimony was not adverse to appellant" because "[n]owhere did he point the finger at Chambers."

Defeated in his attempt to challenge directly McDonald's renunciation of his prior confession, Chambers sought to introduce the testimony of the three witnesses to whom McDonald had admitted that he shot the officer. The first of these, Sam Hardin, would have testified that, on the night of the shooting, he spent the late evening hours with McDonald at a friend's house after their return from the hospital and that, while driving McDonald home later that night, McDonald stated that he shot Liberty. The State objected to the admission of this testimony on the ground that it was hearsay. The trial court sustained the objection.

Berkley Turner, the friend with whom McDonald said he was drinking beer when the shooting occurred, was then called to testify. In the jury's presence, and without objection, he testified that he had not been in the cafe that Saturday and had not had any beers with McDonald. The jury was then excused. In the absence of the jury, Turner recounted his conversations with McDonald while they were riding with James Williams to take Chambers to the hospital. When asked whether McDonald said anything regarding the shooting of Liberty, Turner testified that McDonald told him that he "shot him." Turner further stated that one week later, when he met McDonald at a friend's house, McDonald reminded him of their prior conversation and urged Turner not to "mess him up." Petitioner argued to the court that, especially where there was other proof in the case that was corroborative of these out-of-court statements, Turner's testimony as to McDonald's self-incriminating remarks should have been admitted as an exception to the hearsay rule. Again, the trial court sustained the State's objection.

The third witness, Albert Carter, was McDonald's neighbor. They had been friends for about 25 years. Although Carter had not been in Woodville on the evening of the shooting, he stated that he learned about it the next morning from McDonald. That same day he and McDonald walked out to a well near McDonald's house and there McDonald told him that he was the one who shot Officer Liberty. Carter testified that McDonald also told him that he had disposed of the .22–caliber revolver later that night. He further testified that several weeks after the shooting he accompanied McDonald to Natchez where McDonald purchased another .22 pistol to replace the one he had discarded. The jury was not allowed to hear Carter's testimony. Chambers urged that these statements were admissible, the State objected, and the court sustained the objection. On appeal, the State Supreme Court approved the lower court's exclusion of these witnesses' testimony on hearsay grounds. 252 So.2d, at 220.

In sum, then, this was Chambers' predicament. As a consequence of the combination of Mississippi's "party witness" or "voucher" rule and its hearsay rule, he was unable either to cross-examine McDonald or to present witnesses in his own behalf who would have discredited McDonald's repudiation and demonstrated his complicity. Chambers had, however, chipped away at the fringes of McDonald's story by introducing admissible testimony from other sources indicating that he had not been seen in the cafe where he says he was when the shooting started, that he had not been having beer with Turner, and that he possessed a .22 pistol at the time of the crime. But all that remained from McDonald's own testimony was a single written confession countered by an arguably acceptable renunciation. Chambers' defense was far less persuasive than it might have been had he been given an opportunity to subject McDonald's statements to cross-examination or had the other confessions been admitted.

III.

The right of an accused in a criminal trial to due process is, in essence, the right to a fair opportunity to defend against the State's accusations. The rights to confront and cross-examine witnesses and to call witnesses in one's own behalf have long been recognized as essential to due process. ...

A.

Chambers was denied an opportunity to subject McDonald's damning repudiation and alibi to cross-examination. He was not allowed to test the witness' recollection, to probe into the details of his alibi, or to "sift" his conscience so that the jury might judge for itself whether McDonald's testimony was worthy of belief. The right of cross-examination is more than a desirable rule of trial procedure. It is implicit in the constitutional right of confrontation, and helps assure the "accuracy of the truth-determining process." Dutton v. Evans, 400 U.S. 74, 89, 91 S.Ct. 210, 220, 27 L.Ed.2d 213 (1970).... Of course, the right to confront and to cross-examine is not absolute and may, in appropriate cases, bow to accommodate other legitimate interests in the criminal trial process. But its denial or significant diminution calls into question the ultimate "integrity of the fact-finding process" and requires that the competing interest be closely examined.

* * *

The argument that McDonald's testimony was not "adverse" to, or "against," Chambers is not convincing. The State's proof at trial excluded the theory that more than one person participated in the shooting of Liberty. To the extent that McDonald's sworn confession tended to incriminate him, it tended also to exculpate Chambers. And, in the circumstances of this case, McDonald's retraction inculpated Chambers to the same extent that it exculpated McDonald. It can hardly be disputed that McDonald's testimony was in fact seriously adverse to Chambers. The availability of the right to confront and to cross-examine those who give damaging testimony against the accused has never been held to depend on whether the witness was initially put on the stand by the accused or by the State. We reject the notion that a right of such substance in the criminal process may be governed by that technicality or by any narrow and unrealistic definition of the word "against." The "voucher" rule, as applied in this case, plainly interfered with Chambers' right to defend against the State's charges.

B.

We need not decide, however, whether this error alone would occasion reversal since Chambers' claimed denial of due process rests on the ultimate impact of that error when viewed in conjunction with the trial court's refusal to permit him to call other witnesses. The trial court refused to allow him to introduce the testimony of Hardin, Turner and Carter. Each would have testified to the statements purportedly made by Mc-Donald, on three separate occasions shortly after the crime, naming himself as the murderer. The State Supreme Court approved the exclusion of this evidence on the ground that it was hearsay.

The hearsay rule, which has long been recognized and respected by virtually every State, is based on experience and grounded in the notion that untrustworthy evidence should not be presented to the triers of fact. Out-of-court statements are traditionally excluded because they lack the conventional indicia of reliability: they are usually not made under oath or other circumstances that impress the speaker with the solemnity of his statements; the declarant's word is not subject to cross-examination; and he is not available in order that his demeanor and credibility may be assessed by the jury. California v. Green, 399 U.S. 149, 158, 90 S.Ct. 1930, 1935, 26 L.Ed.2d 489 (1970). . . .

* * *

The hearsay statements involved in this case were originally made and subsequently offered at trial under circumstances that provided considerable assurance of their reliability. First, each of McDonald's confessions was made spontaneously to a close acquaintance shortly after the murder had occurred. Second, each one was corroborated by some other evidence in the case—McDonald's sworn confession, the testimony of an eyewitness to the shooting, the testimony that McDonald was seen with a gun immediately after the shooting, and proof of his prior ownership of a .22–caliber revolver and subsequent purchase of a new weapon. The sheer number of independent confessions provided additional corroboration for each. Third, whatever may be the parameters of the penal-interest rationale[13] each confession here was in a very real sense self-incriminatory and unquestionably against interest. McDonald stood to benefit nothing by disclosing his role in the shooting to any of his three friends and he must have been aware of the possibility that disclosure would lead to criminal prosecution. Indeed, after telling Turner of his involvement, he subsequently urged Turner not to "mess him up." Finally, if there was any question about the truthfulness of the extrajudicial statements, McDonald was present in the courtroom and had been under oath. He could have been cross-examined by the State, and his demeanor and responses weighed by the jury. See California v. Green, 399 U.S. 149, 90 S.Ct. 1930, 26 L.Ed.2d 489 (1970). The availability of McDonald significantly distinguishes this case from the prior Mississippi

---

13. The Mississippi case which refused to adopt a hearsay exception for declarations against penal interest concerned an out-of-court declarant who purportedly stated that he had committed the murder with which his brother had been charged. The Mississippi Supreme Court believed that the declarant may have been motivated by a desire to free his brother rather than by any compulsion of guilt. The Court also noted that the declarant had fled, was unavailable for cross-examination, and may well have known at the time he made the statement that he would not suffer for it. Brown v. State, 99 Miss. 719, 55 So. 961 (1911). There is, in the present case, no such basis for doubting McDonald's statements. See Note, 43 Miss.L.J. 122, 127–129 (1972).

precedent, Brown v. State, supra, and from the *Donnelly*-type situation, since in both cases the declarant was unavailable at the time of trial.[14]

Few rights are more fundamental than that of an accused to present witnesses in his own defense. In the exercise of this right, the accused, as is required of the State, must comply with established rules of procedure and evidence designed to assure both fairness and reliability in the ascertainment of guilt and innocence. Although perhaps no rule of evidence has been more respected or more frequently applied in jury trials than that applicable to the exclusion of hearsay, exceptions tailored to allow the introduction of evidence which in fact is likely to be trustworthy have long existed. The testimony rejected by the trial court here bore persuasive assurances of trustworthiness and thus was well within the basic rationale of the exception for declarations against interest. That testimony also was critical to Chambers' defense. In these circumstances, where constitutional rights directly affecting the ascertainment of guilt are implicated, the hearsay rule may not be applied mechanistically to defeat the ends of justice.

We conclude that the exclusion of this critical evidence, coupled with the State's refusal to permit Chambers to cross-examine McDonald, denied him a trial in accord with traditional and fundamental standards of due process. In reaching this judgment we establish no new principles of constitutional law. Nor does our holding signal any diminution in the respect traditionally accorded to the States in the establishment and implementation of their own criminal trial rules and procedures. Rather, we hold quite simply that under the facts and circumstances of this case the rulings of the trial court deprived Chambers of a fair trial.

The judgment is reversed and the case is remanded to the Supreme Court of Mississippi for further proceedings not inconsistent with this opinion.

It is so ordered.

Reversed and remanded.

NOTES

1. **Governmental restrictions on cross-examination for bias.** The Sixth Amendment restricts the states' ability to place limits upon the nature and extent

---

14. McDonald's presence also deprives the State's argument for retention of the penal-interest rule of much of its force. In claiming that "[t]o change the rule would work a travesty of justice," the State posited the following hypothetical:

"If the rule were changed, A could be charged with the crime; B could tell C and D that he committed the crime; *B could go into hiding* and at A's trial C and D would testify as to B's admission of guilt; A could be acquitted and B would return to stand trial; B could then provide several witnesses to testify as to his whereabouts at the time of the crime.

The testimony of those witnesses along with A's statement that he really committed the crime would result in B's acquittal. A would be barred from further prosecution because of the protection against double jeopardy. No one could be convicted of perjury as A did not testify at his first trial, B did not lie under oath, and C and D were truthful in their testimony." Respondent's Brief, at 7 n. 3 (emphasis supplied).

Obviously, "B's" absence at trial is critical to the success of the justice-subverting ploy.

of cross-examination. In Davis v. Alaska, 415 U.S. 308, 94 S.Ct. 1105, 39 L.Ed.2d 347 (1974), the Supreme Court reversed a conviction in a case where the trial court had barred defense cross-examination of a witness to show that he was on juvenile probation which could be revoked unless he assisted the state. Because "the exposure of a witness' motivation in testifying is a proper and important function of the constitutionally protected right of cross-examination," 415 U.S. at 316, 94 S.Ct. at 1110, 39 L.Ed.2d at 354, the Supreme Court concluded that this right is "paramount to the State's policy of protecting a juvenile offender." 415 U.S. at 319, 94 S.Ct. at 1112, 39 L.Ed. at 355.

However, a violation of the defendant's right to confront and cross-examine witnesses may be harmless error. In Delaware v. Van Arsdall, 475 U.S. 673, 106 S.Ct. 1431, 89 L.Ed.2d 674 (1986), the defendant, on trial for murder, was prohibited from cross-examining a State's witness to elicit evidence of bias arising out of a prior plea bargaining arrangement. The Supreme Court reversed the conviction:

> [A] criminal defendant states a violation of the Confrontation Clause by showing that he was prohibited from engaging in otherwise appropriate cross-examination designed to show a prototypical form of bias on the part of the witness, and thereby "to expose to the jury the facts from which jurors ... could appropriately draw inferences relating to the reliability of the witness." Davis v. Alaska. Respondent has met that burden here: A reasonable jury might have received a significantly different impression of [the witness'] credibility had respondent's counsel been permitted to pursue his proposed line of cross-examination.

475 U.S. at 680, 106 S.Ct. at 1436, 89 L.Ed.2d at 684. But the Court remanded the case for harmless error analysis under Chapman v. California (discussed in Chapter 26):

> The correct inquiry is whether, assuming that the damaging potential of the cross-examination were fully realized, a reviewing court might nonetheless say that the error was harmless beyond a reasonable doubt. Whether such an error is harmless in a particular case depends upon a host of factors ... includ[ing] the importance of the witness' testimony in the prosecution's case, whether the testimony was cumulative, the presence or absence of evidence corroborating or contradicting the testimony of the witness on material points, the extent of cross-examination otherwise permitted, and, of course, the overall strength of the prosecution's case.

475 U.S. at 684, 106 S.Ct. at 1438, 89 L.Ed.2d at 686–87.

The petitioner in Olden v. Kentucky, 488 U.S. 227, 109 S.Ct. 480, 102 L.Ed.2d 513 (1988) was convicted of forcible sodomy on the basis of the testimony of the complaining witness, Matthews, whose testimony was corroborated by one Russell, who had seen her exiting the car of petitioner's co-defendant, Harris, the night in question. Petitioner's defense was consent. On cross-examination, he attempted to show that at the time of the alleged offense the complaining witness and Russell, although married to others, were having an affair with each other and that at the time of trial they were living with each other. Thus, petitioner's theory was that when Russell saw the complainant exit the co-defendant's car, she fabricated the rape charge to avoid jeopardizing her relationship with Russell. The trial court refused to admit this evidence on the ground that since the complainant was white and Russell and petitioner were black the evidence would be more prejudicial to the State than probative for the defense. The Kentucky Court of Appeals affirmed the conviction, but the Supreme Court reversed in a per curiam opinion. The Court concluded that the trial court violated the right to confrontation and that the error was not harmless:

Here, Matthews' testimony was central, indeed crucial, to the prosecution's case. Her story, which was directly contradicted by that of petitioner and Harris, was corroborated only by the largely derivative testimony of Russell, whose impartiality would also have been somewhat impugned by revelation of his relationship with Matthews. Finally ... the State's case against petitioner was far from overwhelming. In sum, considering the relevant *Van Arsdall* factors within the context of this case, we find it impossible to conclude "beyond a reasonable doubt" that the restriction on petitioner's right to confrontation was harmless.

488 U.S. at 233, 109 S.Ct. at 484, 102 L.Ed.2d at 520–21.

2.   **Pretrial discovery of investigatory files for cross-examination.** The defendant in Pennsylvania v. Ritchie, 480 U.S. 39, 107 S.Ct. 989, 94 L.Ed.2d 40 (1987) was prosecuted for sexual abuse of his 13–year–old child. He demanded and was refused pretrial discovery of the file maintained by the governmental agency that investigated the child abuse case against him. State law made that material privileged, but defendant claimed that under Davis v. Alaska that privilege had to yield to his right of confrontation, a position accepted by the Pennsylvania Supreme Court. A plurality of the United States Supreme Court rejected that interpretation of *Davis:*

The Pennsylvania Supreme Court apparently interpreted our decision in *Davis* to mean that a statutory privilege cannot be maintained when a defendant asserts a need, prior to trial, for the protected information that might be used at trial to impeach or otherwise undermine a witness' testimony....

If we were to accept this broad interpretation of *Davis,* the effect would be to transform the Confrontation Clause into a constitutionally-compelled rule of pretrial discovery. Nothing in the case law supports such a view. The opinions of this Court show that the right of confrontation is a *trial* right, designed to prevent improper restrictions on the types of questions that defense counsel may ask during cross-examination. The ability to question adverse witnesses, however, does not include the power to require the pretrial disclosure of any and all information that might be useful in contradicting unfavorable testimony.

480 U.S. at 52–53, 107 S.Ct. at 998–99, 94 L.Ed.2d at 54. The Court also rejected defendant's claim that the right of compulsory process requires disclosure of the file to enable the defense to identify and subpoena possible favorable witnesses. The Court held that such a claim should be analyzed under the due process standards of the Brady v. Maryland line of cases (supra) rather than under the compulsory process clause of the Sixth Amendment. Applying those standards, the Court decided that the Pennsylvania court was incorrect in holding that Ritchie's attorney had the right to examine the file to determine whether it contained useful material because that would interfere with the confidentiality interests that were recognized by state law. Further, it held that defendant's interests would be fully protected by requiring the trial court to examine the entire file *in camera* and to disclose to the attorneys information that is material under the *Brady* line of cases.

3.   **Compulsory production of witnesses.** As *Chambers* makes clear, the Sixth Amendment also protects an accused's right to produce testimony. The leading case developing this aspect of the provision is Washington v. Texas, 388 U.S. 14, 87 S.Ct. 1920, 18 L.Ed.2d 1019 (1967). Washington was charged with murder and the state's evidence indicated that either Washington or one Fuller fired the fatal shot. Fuller had already been convicted of murder on the basis of the shooting. Washington sought to call Fuller to testify that Washington tried to persuade Fuller to leave the scene before the killing and ran off before Fuller fired the fatal shot. Fuller's testimony was excluded pursuant to a Texas statute which provided that

persons charged or convicted as coparticipants in a crime could not testify for one another. Reviewing Washington's conviction, the Supreme Court noted that the effect of the state statute was not to refuse to compel the attendance of Washington's witness but to bar his testimony whether he was present or not. "We are thus called upon to decide," it stated, "whether the Sixth Amendment guarantees a defendant the right under any circumstances to put his witnesses on the stand, as well as the right to compel their attendance in court." 388 U.S. at 19, 87 S.Ct. at 1923, 18 L.Ed.2d at 1023. The Texas statute, it observed, was a remnant of a common law rule that disqualified many witnesses, including codefendants, from testifying on the basis of interest. This rule was based on the fear that if codefendants were permitted to testify for each other, each would lie in an effort to exonerate his companion. The Court noted that under the Texas statute accused accomplices can be called as witnesses by the prosecution and by the defense after acquittal at their own trials. In both situations, it reasoned, the accomplice has a significant incentive to commit perjury, perhaps greater than in the situations in which his testimony is barred under the statute. The Texas statute, therefore, arbitrarily selected a class of witnesses whose testimony would be unavailable to criminal defendants, and this violated the Sixth Amendment:

> [Washington] was denied his right to have compulsory process for obtaining witnesses in his favor because the State arbitrarily denied him the right to put on the stand a witness who was physically and mentally capable of testifying to events that he had personally observed, and whose testimony would have been relevant and material to the defense. The Framers of the Constitution did not intend to commit the futile act of giving to a defendant the right to secure the attendance of witnesses whose testimony he had no right to use.

388 U.S. at 23, 87 S.Ct. at 1925, 18 L.Ed.2d at 1025.

What result if the government deports a potential witness for the defense in connection with the same criminal activity that led to the defendant's arrest? In United States v. Valenzuela–Bernal, 458 U.S. 858, 102 S.Ct. 3440, 73 L.Ed.2d 1193 (1982), the Supreme Court concluded, in an opinion by Justice Rehnquist: "The mere fact that the Government deports such [illegal alien] witness is not sufficient to establish a violation of the Compulsory Process Clause of the Sixth Amendment or the Due Process Clause of the Fourteenth Amendment. A violation of these provisions requires some showing that the evidence lost would be both material and favorable to the defense." 458 U.S. at 872–73, 102 S.Ct. at 3449, 73 L.Ed.2d at 1206.

4. **Hypnotically-enhanced testimony by defendant.** Petitioner in Rock v. Arkansas, 483 U.S. 44, 107 S.Ct. 2704, 97 L.Ed.2d 37 (1987), was charged with the shooting death of her husband. She told police she acted in self-defense and gave a sketchy version of the events leading to the killing. As part of defense preparation for trial, she was placed under hypnosis and questioned about the events. For the first time, she recalled that her finger was on the hammer of the handgun, not the trigger, and that the weapon had discharged when her husband grabbed her arm. Later defense-ordered examination of the handgun showed that it was defective and was prone to fire when hit or dropped without the trigger's being pulled. The trial court prohibited the petitioner from testifying to any facts she recalled as a result of the hypnosis but she was permitted to testify as to her pre-hypnotic recall, which did not include the placement of the weapon in her hand or her husband's grabbing her arm. Her conviction for manslaughter over her interposed claim of self-defense was affirmed by the Arkansas Supreme Court in an opinion which prohibited any use of hypnotically-induced testimony. The United States Supreme Court, in an opinion by Justice Blackmun, vacated that decision. The Court found that a defendant's right to testify is based on the due process, compulsory process and self-incrimination clauses. Further, "restrictions of a defendant's right to testify may

not be arbitrary or disproportionate to the purposes they are designed to serve. In applying its evidentiary rules a State must evaluate whether the interests served by a rule justify the limitation imposed on the defendant's constitutional right to testify." 483 U.S. at 55–56, 107 S.Ct. at 2711, 97 L.Ed.2d at 49. Justice Blackmun then reviewed the current status of hypnosis and the risk of inaccuracy it poses:

> Hypnosis by trained physicians or psychologists has been recognized as a valid therapeutic technique since 1958,.... The use of hypnosis in criminal investigations, however, is controversial, and the current medical and legal view of its appropriate role is unsettled.

* * *

> The inaccuracies the process introduces can be reduced, although perhaps not eliminated, by the use of procedural safeguards. ...

> The more traditional means of assessing accuracy of testimony also remain applicable in the case of a previously hypnotized defendant. Certain information recalled as a result of hypnosis may be verified as highly accurate by corroborating evidence. Cross-examination, even in the face of a confident defendant, is an effective tool for revealing inconsistencies. Moreover, a jury can be educated to the risks of hypnosis through expert testimony and cautionary instructions....

> We are not now prepared to endorse without qualifications the use of hypnosis as an investigative tool; ... But [the state] has not shown that hypnotically enhanced testimony is always so untrustworthy and so immune to the traditional means of evaluating credibility that it should disable a defendant from presenting her version of the events for which she is on trial.

483 U.S. at 58–61, 107 S.Ct. at 2712–14, 97 L.Ed.2d at 51–52. The Chief Justice, joined by Justices White, O'Connor and Scalia, dissented on the ground that "until there is a much more general consensus on the use of hypnosis than there is now, the Constitution does not warrant this Court's mandating its own view of how to deal with the issue." 483 U.S. at 65, 107 S.Ct. at 2716, 97 L.Ed.2d at 55.

D.   EXERCISE AT TRIAL OF THE PRIVILEGE AGAINST COMPELLED SELF-INCRIMINATION

The essence of the Fifth Amendment's self-incrimination clause—"No person shall be ... compelled in any criminal case to be a witness against himself.... "—is obviously that during a criminal trial the prosecution cannot call the defendant as a witness. But the constitutional privilege has much greater ramifications, some of which are developed in this Section. First, the inferences that can be drawn from a defendant's failure to testify are explored. Second, attention is turned to a defendant's ability to waive the privilege by testifying in his own behalf and the ramifications of a decision to so waive the privilege.

1.   COMMENT UPON AND INFERENCES FROM THE FAILURE TO TESTIFY

There are many reasons why a defendant might choose not to testify at the trial. The decision, to testify or not, is personal to the defendant. But certainly the silence of the one whose conduct is under scrutiny may cause jurors to draw inferences about the defendant's failure to testify. Accordingly, defense counsel's strategy and advice on this decision is often very problematic. At issue in the following case is what instruction, if any, should be given a jury under these circumstances.

Carter v. Kentucky

Supreme Court of the United States, 1981.
450 U.S. 288, 101 S.Ct. 1112, 67 L.Ed.2d 241.

■ JUSTICE STEWART delivered the opinion of the Court.

* * *

The petitioner was ... indicted for third-degree burglary of Young's Hardware Store. The indictment also charged him with being a persistent felony offender,.... The prosecutor's opening statement recounted the evidence expected to be introduced against the petitioner. The opening statement of defense counsel began as follows:

> "Let me tell you a little bit about how this system works. If you listened to Mr. Ruff [the prosecutor] you are probably ready to put Lonnie Joe in the penitentiary. He read you a ... true bill that was issued by the Grand Jury. ...[T]he defendant is ... not allowed to present any of his testimony before this group of people. The only thing that the Grand Jury hears is the prosecution's proof.... I suppose that most of you would issue a true bill if Mr. Ruff told you what he has just told you and you didn't have a chance to hear what the defendant had to say for himself. Now, that is just completely contrary to our system of law. A man, as the Judge has already told you, ... is innocent until ... proved guilty.... "

The prosecution rested after calling Officers Ellison, Davis, another officer, and the owner of Young's Hardware Store.

* * *

... [T]he petitioner's counsel advised the court that there would be no testimony introduced on behalf of the defense.[15] He then requested that the following instruction be given to the jury:

> "The defendant is not compelled to testify and the fact that he does not cannot be used as an inference of guilt and should not prejudice him in any way."

The trial court refused the request.

The prosecutor began his summation by stating that he intended to review the evidence "that we were privileged to hear,".... The prosecutor continued that if there was a reasonable explanation why the petitioner ran when he saw the police, it was "not in the record."[16]

15. Defense counsel summarized his private conversation with his client for the record, observing "that the advice of counsel to Mr. Carter was that in plain terms he was between a rock and hard place.... " If the petitioner testified he would be impeached and "if he didn't testify the jury, ... would probably use that against him."

16. Defense counsel began his closing argument as follows:

The jury found the petitioner guilty, recommending a sentence of two years. The recidivist phase of the trial followed. The prosecutor presented evidence of the previous felony convictions that had been listed in the indictment. The defense presented no evidence, and the jury found the petitioner guilty as a persistent offender, sentencing him to the maximum term of 20 years in prison.

Upon appeal, the Kentucky Supreme Court rejected the argument that the Fifth and Fourteenth Amendments to the United States Constitution require that a criminal trial judge give the jury an instruction such as was requested here. ... [17]

* * *

[This] Court had held that the Fifth Amendment command that no person "shall be compelled in any criminal case to be a witness against himself" is applicable against the States through the Fourteenth Amendment. Malloy v. Hogan, 378 U.S. 1, 84 S.Ct. 1489, 12 L.Ed.2d 653. In *Griffin,* the Court considered the question whether it is a violation of the Fifth and Fourteenth Amendments to invite a jury in a state criminal trial to draw an unfavorable inference from a defendant's failure to testify. Griffin v. California, 380 U.S. 609, 85 S.Ct. 1229, 14 L.Ed.2d 106. The trial judge had there instructed the jury "that a defendant has a constitutional right not to testify," and that the defendant's exercise of that right "does not create a presumption of guilt or by itself warrant an inference of guilt" nor "relieve the prosecution of any of its burden of proof." But the instruction additionally permitted the jury to "take that failure into consideration as tending to indicate the truth of [the State's] evidence and as indicating that among the inferences that may be reasonably drawn therefrom those unfavorable to the defendant are the more probable." Id., at 610, 85 S.Ct., at 1230.

This Court set aside Griffin's conviction because "the Fifth Amendment ... forbids either comment by the prosecution on the accused's silence or instructions by the Court that such silence is evidence of guilt." Id., at 615, 85 S.Ct., at 1233.[18] It condemned adverse comment on a defendant's failure to testify as reminiscent of the "inquisitorial system of criminal justice," and concluded that such comment effected a court-

---

"Ladies and Gentlemen of the jury, I am sure you all right now are wondering well what has happened? Why didn't Mr. Carter take the stand and testify? Let me tell you. The judge just read to you that the man is presumed innocent and that it is up to the prosecution to prove him guilty beyond a reasonable doubt. He doesn't have to take the stand in his own behalf. He doesn't have to do anything."

17. Kentucky is one of at least five States that prohibit giving such an instruction to the jury. Others are Minnesota, ... Nevada, Oklahoma and Wyoming. A few States have a statutory requirement that

such an instruction be given to the jury unless the defendant objects. See, e.g., Conn. Gen.Stat.Ann. § 54–84 (West 1958). The majority of the States, by judicial pronouncement, require that a defense request for such a jury instruction be honored. See, e.g., Woodard v. State, 234 Ga. 901, 218 S.E.2d 629.

18. The Court in the *Griffin* case expressly reserved decision "on whether an accused can require ... that the jury be instructed that his silence be disregarded." 380 U.S., at 615, n. 6, 85 S.Ct., at 1233, n. 6.

imposed penalty upon the defendant that was unacceptable because "[i]t cuts down on the privilege by making its assertion costly."

The Court returned to a consideration of the Fifth Amendment and jury instructions in Lakeside v. Oregon, 435 U.S. 333, 98 S.Ct. 1091, 55 L.Ed.2d 319, where the question was whether the giving of a "no-inference" instruction over defense objection violates the Constitution. Despite trial counsel's complaint that his strategy was to avoid any mention of his client's failure to testify, a no inference instruction[19] was given by the trial judge. The petitioner contended that when a trial judge in any way draws the jury's attention to a defendant's failure to testify, unless the defendant acquiesces, the court invades the defendant's privilege against compulsory self-incrimination. This argument was rejected.

The *Lakeside* Court reasoned that the Fifth and Fourteenth Amendments bar only *adverse* comment on a defendant's failure to testify, and that "a judge's instruction that the jury must draw *no* adverse inferences of any kind from the defendant's exercise of his privilege not to testify is 'comment' of an entirely different order." 435 U.S., at 339, 98 S.Ct., at 1094. The purpose of such an instruction, the Court stated, "is to remove from the jury's deliberations any influence of unspoken adverse inferences," and "cannot provide the pressure on a defendant found impermissible in *Griffin*." Ibid.

The Court observed in *Lakeside* that the petitioner's argument there rested on "two very doubtful assumptions:"

First, that the jurors have not noticed that the defendant did not testify and will not, therefore, draw adverse inferences on their own. Second, that the jurors will totally disregard the instruction, and affirmatively give weight to what they have been told not to consider at all. Federal constitutional law cannot rest on speculative assumptions so dubious as these." 435 U.S., at 340, 98 S.Ct., at 1095 (footnote omitted).

Finally, the Court stressed that "the very purpose" of a jury instruction is to direct the jurors' attention to important legal concepts "that must not be misunderstood, such as reasonable doubt and burden of proof," and emphasized that instruction "in the meaning of the privilege against compulsory self-incrimination is no different." Ibid.

* * *

... The principles enunciated in our cases construing this privilege,[20] against both statutory and constitutional backdrops, lead unmistakably to

---

19. The *Lakewood* trial judge gave the following instruction to the jury:

"Under the laws of this State a defendant has the option to take the witness stand in his or her own behalf. If a defendant chooses not to testify, such a circumstance gives rise to no inference or presumption against the defendant, and this must not be considered by you in determining the question of guilt or in-

nocence." 435 U.S., at 335, 98 S.Ct., at 1092.

20. The Court has recognized that there are many reasons unrelated to guilt or innocence for declining to testify:

"It is not every one who can safely venture on the witness stand though entirely innocent of the charge against him. Excessive timidity, nervousness when facing others and attempting to explain the conclusion that the Fifth Amendment requires that a criminal trial judge must give a "no adverse inference" jury instruction when requested by a defendant to do so.

* * *

The *Griffin* case stands for the proposition that a defendant must pay no court-imposed price for the exercise of his constitutional privilege not to testify. The penalty was exacted in *Griffin* by adverse comment on the defendant's silence; the penalty may be just as severe when there is no adverse comment, but when the jury is left to roam at large with only its untutored instincts to guide it, to draw from the defendant's silence broad inferences of guilt. Even without adverse comment, the members of a jury, unless instructed otherwise, may well draw adverse inferences from a defendant's silence.[21]

The significance of a cautionary instruction was forcefully acknowledged in *Lakeside*, where the Court found no constitutional error even when a no-inference instruction was given over a defendant's objection. The salutary purpose of the instruction, "to remove from the jury's deliberations any influence of unspoken adverse inferences," was deemed so important that it there outweighed the defendant's own preferred tactics.[22]

* * *

A trial judge has a powerful tool at his disposal to protect the constitutional privilege—the jury instruction—and he has an affirmative constitutional obligation to use that tool when a defendant seeks its employment. No judge can prevent jurors from speculating about why a defendant stands mute in the face of a criminal accusation, but a judge can,

transactions of a suspicious character, and offences charged against him, will often confuse and embarrass him to such a degree as to increase rather than remove prejudices against him. It is not every one, however honest, who would, therefore, willingly be placed on the witness stand." Wilson v. United States, 149 U.S. 60, 66, 13 S.Ct. 765, 766, 37 L.Ed. 650.

Other reasons include the fear of impeachment by prior convictions (the petitioner's fear in the present case), or by other damaging information not necessarily relevant to the charge being tried, *Griffin*, 380 U.S., at 615, 85 S.Ct., at 1233, and reluctance to "incriminate others whom [defendants] either love or fear," *Lakeside*, 435 U.S., at 344, n. 2, 98 S.Ct., at 1097, n. 2 (dissenting opinion).

21. Indeed, the dissenting opinion in *Griffin* suggested that more harm may flow from the lack of guidance to the jury on the meaning of the Fifth Amendment privilege

than from reasonable comment upon the exercise of that privilege. With specific reference to decisions from Kentucky and one other State, the dissenters observed that "[w]ithout limiting instructions, the danger exists that the inferences drawn by the jury may be unfairly broad." The Court in *Griffin* indicated no disagreement with this view.

22. It has been almost universally thought that juries notice a defendant's failure to testify. "[T]he jury will of course realize this quite evident fact, even though the choice goes unmentioned.... [It is] a fact inescapably impressed on the jury's consciousness." *Griffin*, 380 U.S., at 621, 622, 85 S.Ct., at 1237 (dissenting opinion). In *Lakeside* the Court cited an acknowledged authority's statement that "[t]he layman's natural first suggestion would probably be that the resort to privilege in each instance is a clear confession of crime." 435 U.S., at 340, n. 10, 85 S.Ct., at 1095, n. 10, quoting 8 Wigmore, Evidence § 2272, p. 426 (McNaughton rev. ed. 1961).

and must, if requested to do so, use the unique power of the jury instruction to reduce that speculation to a minimum.[23]

The only state interest advanced by Kentucky in refusing a request for such a jury instruction is protection of the defendant: "the requested 'no inference' instruction ... would have been direct comment by the court and would have emphasized the fact that the accused had not testified in his own behalf." Green v. Commonwealth, Ky., 488 S.W.2d 339–341. This purported justification was specifically rejected in the *Lakeside* case, where the Court noted that "[i]t would be strange indeed to conclude that this cautionary instruction violates the very constitutional provision it is intended to protect." 435 U.S., at 339, 98 S.Ct., at 1094.

* * *

While it is arguable that a refusal to give an instruction similar to the one that was requested here can never be harmless, we decline to reach the issue, because it was not presented to or considered by the Supreme Court of Kentucky.

... [T]he failure to limit the jurors' speculation on the meaning of that silence, when the defendant makes a timely request that a prophylactic instruction be given, exacts an impermissible toll on the full and free exercise of the privilege. Accordingly, we hold that a state trial judge has the constitutional obligation, upon proper request, to minimize the danger that the jury will give evidentiary weight to a defendant's failure to testify.

For the reasons stated, the judgment is reversed, and the case is remanded to the Supreme Court of Kentucky for further proceedings not inconsistent with this opinion.

It is so ordered.

■ JUSTICE POWELL, concurring.

* * *

The one person who usually knows most about the critical facts is the accused. For reasons deeply rooted in the history we share with England, the Bill of Rights included the self-incrimination Clause, which enables a defendant in a criminal trial to elect to make no contribution to the factfinding process. But nothing in the Clause requires that jurors not draw logical inferences when a defendant chooses not to explain incriminating circumstances. Jurors have been instructed that the defendant is presumed to be innocent and that this presumption can be overridden only by evidence beyond a reasonable doubt. California Chief Justice Traynor commented that judges and prosecutors should be able to explain that "a jury [may] draw unfavorable inferences from the defendant's failure to explain or refute evidence when he could reasonably be expected to do so. Such comment would not be evidence and would do no more than make clear to the jury the extent of its freedom in drawing inferences." Traynor,

---

23. The importance of a no-inference instruction is underscored by a recent national public opinion survey conducted for the National Center for State Courts, revealing that 37% of those interviewed believed that it is the responsibility of the accused to prove his innocence. 64 ABAJ 653 (1978).

The Devils of Due Process in Criminal Detection, Detention, and Trial, 33 U.Chi.L.Rev. 657, 677 (1966).

I therefore would have joined JUSTICES STEWART and WHITE in dissent in *Griffin*. But *Griffin* is now the law, and based on that case the present petitioner was entitled to the jury instruction that he requested. I therefore join the opinion of the Court.

■ JUSTICE STEVENS, with whom JUSTICE BRENNAN joins, concurring.

While I join the Court's opinion, I add this comment to emphasize that today's holding is limited to cases in which the defendant has requested that the jury be instructed not to draw an inference of guilt from the defendant's failure to testify. I remain convinced that the question whether such an instruction should be given in any specific case—like the question whether the defendant should testify on his own behalf—should be answered by the defendant and his lawyer, not by the State.

NOTES

1. **Comment on failure to testify in response to defense argument.** Defense counsel in United States v. Robinson, 485 U.S. 25, 108 S.Ct. 864, 99 L.Ed.2d 23 (1988) had argued to the jury that the government had breached its duty to play fair in its handling of his client's mail fraud case in that his client had not been given the opportunity to explain the charges. After a conference at the bench in which the trial court stated that he interpreted counsel's argument to refer to his client's opportunity to testify at trial as well as to offer explanations during the investigatory stage of the case, the prosecutor was permitted in rebuttal argument to state that the defendant "could have taken the stand and explained it to you, anything he wanted to." Defense counsel did not dispute the trial court's characterization of his argument or object to the prosecutor's argument. The Court of Appeals reversed the conviction on the grounds that Griffin v. California had been violated.

The United States Supreme Court, in an opinion authored by The Chief Justice, reversed. While defense counsel's argument was ambiguous as it appears in the printed record, the trial court in the bench conference interpreted it to refer to the defendant's opportunity to testify at trial as well as to his opportunity to explain his position to investigators. Since defense counsel did not dispute that characterization with the trial court and did not object to the prosecutor's argument, the Court accepted the trial court's interpretation of the defense argument. *Griffin* does not control this case:

> "[The] central purpose of a criminal trial is to decide the factual question of the defendant's guilt or innocence".... To this end it is important that both the defendant and the prosecutor have the opportunity to meet fairly the evidence and arguments of one another.... It is one thing to hold, as we did in *Griffin*, that the prosecutor may not treat a defendant's exercise of his right to remain silent at trial as substantive evidence of guilt; it is quite another to urge, as defendant does here, that the same reasoning would forbid the prosecutor from fairly responding to an argument of the defendant by adverting to that silence.

485 U.S. at 33–34, 108 S.Ct. at 869–70, 99 L.Ed.2d at 32. Justice Marshall, joined by Justice Brennan, dissented on the ground that the Court's departure from the "bright-line rules of *Griffin* . . . is unsettling and unwarranted." Justice Blackmun, concurring in part and dissenting in part, expressed concern with whether the

Supreme Court had properly formulated a plain error doctrine to guide lower courts reviewing cases of unobjected to error.

2. **Self-incriminatory acts of production.** The potential breadth of the self incrimination protection as well as its limitations are exemplified by its attempted application under the unusual facts of Baltimore City Dept. of Social Serv. v. Bouknight, 493 U.S. 549, 110 S.Ct. 900, 107 L.Ed.2d 992 (1990). In *Bouknight,* a juvenile court ordered a child, whose whereabouts were unexplained and subject to a homicide investigation, taken from his mother's custody and placed in foster care. The court cited the mother, Bouknight, for contempt and directed that she be imprisoned until she purged herself of contempt by either producing her son, Maurice, or revealing to the court his exact whereabouts. Bouknight argued that the juvenile court's order violated her privilege against self incrimination.

Justice O'Connor, writing for the majority, stated that the act of producing the child might be testimonial in nature, operating as an "implicit communication of control over Maurice at the moment of production," but:

> The possibility that a production order will compel testimonial assertions that may prove incriminating does not, in all contexts, justify invoking the privilege to resist production ... Even assuming that this limited testimonial assertion is sufficiently incriminating and "sufficiently testimonial," ... Bouknight may not invoke the privilege to resist the production order because she has assumed custodial duties related to production and because production is required as part of a noncriminal regulatory regime.

493 U.S. at 555–56, 110 S.Ct. at 905, 107 L.Ed.2d at 1000.

The Court cited its authority in Shapiro v. United States, 335 U.S. 1, 68 S.Ct. 1375, 92 L.Ed. 1787 (1948) (required records exception to Fifth Amendment privilege); In re Harris, 221 U.S. 274, 279, 31 S.Ct. 557, 55 L.Ed. 732 (1911) (Fifth Amendment not applicable to surrender of property (account books) which defendant was no longer entitled to keep); and California v. Byers, 402 U.S. 424, 91 S.Ct. 1535, 29 L.Ed.2d 9 (1971) (ability to invoke the privilege may be greatly diminished when invocation would interfere with the effective operation of a generally applicable civil regulatory requirement directed at the public at large—privilege not applicable to drivers involved in accidents who are required by statute to stop and provide their names and addresses). According to the Court, by agreeing to the terms of an initial protective order, Bouknight had impliedly agreed to "permit inspection" of Maurice who, like certain books and public records, was the object of legitimate State regulatory interests. The Court also noted that the juvenile court's demand for production of the child did not single out the parent as a person suspected of criminal activity, but merely promoted concern for the child's safety. The Court suggested that some limitations might be placed upon the State's power to use Bouknight's "testimony" in a future criminal proceeding, but declined to rule on that issue.

Justice Marshall, in a dissent joined by Justice Brennan, observed that because Bouknight could face criminal abuse and neglect or even homicide charges, the threat of self incrimination was more significant than the majority recognized. Justice Marshall also took exception to the Court's analogies. A mother is not similar to a custodian of records, he argued. And the child custody statute employed in this case was, unlike the hit and run statute in *Byers,* linked to a related criminal statute (covering child abuse).

2. WAIVER

In a variety of situations, defendant faces the hard choice of whether to testify. The choice is hard because some advantages are given up by testifying. For example, if a defense motion for acquittal at the end of the Government's case is denied, the defendant must decide whether to stand on his motion or put up a defense—which may include his taking the stand—with the unintended but possible result that the Government's case may be strengthened sufficiently to justify a guilty verdict. In addition, a defendant who takes the stand may be impeached by highly prejudicial evidence that would not otherwise be admissible, including some kinds of unconstitutionally obtained evidence.

Of immediate concern here is the extent to which a defendant who chooses to testify in his own defense waives his privilege against self-incrimination.

United States v. Hearst

United States Court of Appeals, Ninth Circuit, 1977.
563 F.2d 1331.

■ Before Browning, Trask, and Wallance, Circuit Judges.

Per Curiam:

Appellant was tried under a two-count indictment charging her with armed robbery of a San Francisco bank [the Hibernia Bank].... The government introduced photographs and testimony descriptive of appellant's role in the robbery. Appellant raised the defense of duress, contending her co-participants[, members of the Symbionese Liberation Army, who had kidnapped her,] compelled her to engage in the criminal activity. [To rebut this defense, the government was permitted to introduce evidence tending to show that appellant voluntarily participated in various revolutionary activities of her captors. Some of this evidence tended to show that appellant fired with an automatic weapon upon a clerk at Mel's Sporting Goods when the clerk attempted to arrest two of appellant's captors—Bill and Emily Harris—for shoplifting. Editors.] The jury found appellant guilty. . . .

Appellant argues that the trial judge erred . . . in ruling on appellant's privilege against self-incrimination. . . .

During the trial appellant elected to testify in her own behalf. She described in exhaustive detail the events immediately following her kidnapping of February 4, 1974. These included physical and sexual abuses by members of the Symbionese Liberation Army (SLA), extensive interrogations, forced tape recordings and written communications designed to convince her family that she had become a revolutionary, and training in guerrilla welfare. She next described how the SLA compelled her under threat of death to participate in the robbery of the Hibernia Bank on April 15, 1974, and to identify herself by reading a revolutionary speech. She explained that by the time the group moved to Los Angeles, the SLA had convinced her that they would kill her if she tried to escape and that the Federal Bureau of Investigation also desired to murder her. Appellant added that the SLA required her to make various post-robbery admissions about her voluntary role in the crime.

Appellant's story continued by describing her participation one month after the robbery in the disturbance at Mel's Sporting Goods Store. She claimed that her reaction in firing at the store resulted from fear of the SLA, as did her admission to Thomas Matthews of complicity in the bank robbery. She then told how she, the Harrises, and Jack Scott traveled from Los Angeles to Berkeley, then to New York, to Pennsylvania, and finally to Las Vegas in September of 1974. Again, she emphasized that she was an unwilling companion of the group. After mentioning her arrival in Las Vegas, her testimony jumped a year to the time of her arrest in San Francisco on September 18, 1975.

On cross-examination, appellant refused to answer most questions concerning the period between her arrival in Las Vegas and her arrest in San Francisco.[24] In response to questions about her activities, residences, and association with other suspected members of the SLA during this year, she invoked the Fifth Amendment privilege against self-incrimination 42 times.

Prior to government questioning, appellant had moved for an order limiting the scope of the cross-examination so as to avoid the necessity of invoking the Fifth Amendment in response to questions implicating her in other crimes for which she was not on trial. Finding that appellant had waived her privilege against self-incrimination as to all relevant matters by testifying in her own behalf, the court denied this motion and allowed the government to ask her questions which resulted in her assertion of the Fifth Amendment. United States v. Hearst, 412 F.Supp. 885 (N.D.Cal. 1976). Appellant now offers five separate grounds for finding that the court committed reversible error in making this ruling.

1. The Fifth Amendment provides that "[n]o person ... shall be compelled in any criminal case to be a witness against himself." But it is also true, as the trial court stressed, that a defendant who testifies in his own behalf waives his privilege against self-incrimination with respect to the relevant matters covered by his direct testimony and subjects himself to cross-examination by the government. Brown v. United States, 356 U.S. 148, 154–55, 78 S.Ct. 622, 2 L.Ed.2d 589 (1958). Appellant contends that she "did not voluntarily waive her Fifth Amendment privilege by testifying because her testimony was compelled by the introduction of certain evidence, i.e., post-crime conduct, which was challenged as inadmissible and highly prejudicial." Reply Brief for Appellant at 7. She pleads that she was caught between the "rock and the whirlpool" when forced to decide whether to testify or allow the evidence to stand unrebutted.

The validity of this argument depends largely on appellant's assumption that evidence of her post-robbery behavior was admitted erroneously, and that she had no choice but to respond to this inadmissible evidence. We

---

24. Appellant did answer some of the government's questions about her activities during this period, but she refused to answer questions which she or her counsel perceived as incriminating. Thus, she answered questions about the membership of James Kilgore, Stephen Soliah, and Cathleen Soliah in a subversive organization, the New World Liberation Front. R.T. 1826–27. However, she refused to discuss her relationship with these individuals. She also discussed her August 12, 1975 visit to a dermatologist. R.T. 1827–29.

have concluded previously, however, that the trial court determined correctly that this evidence was relevant and admissible. Thus, appellant's attempt to compare her situation to that involved in Harrison v. United States, 392 U.S. 219, 88 S.Ct. 2008, 20 L.Ed.2d 1047 (1968), where the defendant had to testify in order to overcome the impact of prior confessions which had been illegally obtained and introduced, is unconvincing. In the present case, neither the trial court nor we found that any illegal, inadmissible evidence forced appellant to testify.

Appellant also suggests it is sufficient that she *thought* she was being compelled to testify in response to the admission of evidence which she *perceived* as prejudicial, inadmissible, and damaging to her defense. We refuse to hold that a defendant's subjective impressions of what he is "forced" to do during his trial are enough to render his testimony involuntary. A defendant often will view evidence as incriminating and inadmissible, and feel that he must take the witness stand in order to save his case. This is an inherent feature of our criminal justice system, however:

> The defendant in a criminal trial is frequently forced to testify himself and to call other witnesses in an effort to reduce the risk of conviction. When he presents his witnesses, he must reveal their identity and submit them to cross-examination which in itself may prove incriminating or which may furnish the State with leads to incriminating rebuttal evidence. That the defendant faces such a dilemma demanding a choice between complete silence and presenting a defense has never been thought an invasion of the privilege against compelled self-incrimination.

Williams v. Florida, 399 U.S. 78, 83–84, 90 S.Ct. 1893, 1897, 26 L.Ed.2d 446 (1970). In *Williams,* the Supreme Court found that the defendant had a free choice between giving notice of his alibi defense, as required by a Florida statute, and refraining from presenting this defense. Similarly, in our case, we find that appellant freely elected to testify in her own behalf.

2. Appellant also argues that she did not waive her privilege against self-incrimination because her testimony was limited to the collateral issue of the voluntariness of certain statements (i.e., the admissions of willing participation in the bank robbery) made by her and introduced into evidence over her objection. She contends that since her testimony did not address the merits of the case, the government should not have been allowed to ask questions which attempted to prove her guilt. She refers us to Calloway v. Wainwright, 409 F.2d 59, 66 (5th Cir.), cert. denied, 395 U.S. 909, 89 S.Ct. 1752, 23 L.Ed.2d 222 (1969), which stated: "[t]hat appellant took the stand for the sole purpose of testifying upon the credibility of the voluntariness of his [earlier] confession should not be taken as a complete waiver of his constitutional privilege against self-incrimination."

Appellant's assumption about the nature of her testimony is completely erroneous. The central theme of her lengthy testimony was that from the moment of her kidnapping to the time of her arrest she was an unwilling victim of the SLA who acted under continual threats of death. She tried to show, not merely that she made her admissions involuntarily, but that she acted under duress in robbing the Hibernia Bank, firing at the sporting goods store, and traveling with the Harrises for over one year. She disputed the main element of the government's case: that she had the necessary criminal intent when she participated in the bank robbery. Thus, her reliance on *Calloway* is misplaced, for that case dealt with the much narrower situation in which a defendant takes the witness stand solely to deny the voluntariness of his confession. Calloway v. Wainwright, supra, 409 F.2d at 66.

3. Appellant next claims that even if she did waive her privilege against self-incrimination by testifying in her own behalf, the waiver did not extend to the period between her arrival in Las Vegas and her arrest in San Francisco. She argues that since she did not testify concerning her activities during this "lost year," the government had no right or reason to ask any questions about it. She would confine the proper scope of cross-examination to the events which she specifically discussed during her direct testimony.

We find that appellant misinterprets the controlling case law on waiver and the permissible limits of the cross-examination of a testifying defendant. The Supreme Court has stated that when a defendant takes the witness stand, "his credibility may be impeached and his testimony assailed like that of any other witness, and the breadth of his waiver is determined by the scope of relevant cross-examination." Brown v. United States, supra, 356 U.S. at 154–55, 78 S.Ct. at 626. "[A] defendant who takes the stand in his own behalf cannot then claim the privilege against cross-examination on matters reasonably related to the subject matter of his direct examination." McGautha v. California, 402 U.S. 183, 215, 91 S.Ct. 1454, 1471, 28 L.Ed.2d 711 (1971). This rule is premised on basic goals of fairness and ascertainment of the truth:

> The witness himself, certainly if he is a party, determines the area of disclosure and therefore of inquiry. Such witness has the choice, after weighing the advantage of the privilege against self-incrimination against the advantage of putting forward his version of the facts and his reliability as a witness, not to testify at all. He cannot reasonably claim that the Fifth Amendment gives him not only this choice but, if he elects to testify, an immunity from cross-examination on the matters he has himself put in dispute.

Brown v. United States, supra, 356 U.S. at 155–56, 78 S.Ct. at 627. Nowhere in this rule is there even a suggestion that the waiver and the permissible cross-examination are to be determined by what the defendant actually discussed during his direct testimony. Rather, the focus is on whether the government's questions are "reasonably related" to the subjects covered by the defendant's testimony.

Applying this principle to the present case, we conclude that the trial court did not abuse its broad discretion, . . . in allowing the government to ask questions about the year which appellant failed to cover in her direct testimony. As we have already concluded, appellant's testimony was not limited to disputing the voluntariness of her post-robbery admissions. Instead, she attempted to show that from her kidnapping until her arrest she acted exactly as her captors directed.[25] She tried to persuade the jury

---

25. Appellant's counsel, Mr. Bailey, indicated very directly his desire to show that appellant had been threatened, abused, and coerced by the SLA for almost two years.

that her post-robbery conduct and feelings of fear, dependence, and obedience proved that she had also acted involuntarily and without criminal intent in robbing the Hibernia Bank.

We agree with the trial court's conclusion that appellant's testimony placed in issue her behavior during the entire period from abduction to arrest, and gave the government a right to question her about the "lost year." See United States v. Hearst, supra, 412 F.Supp. at 887. Although appellant did not discuss this year, the natural inference from her other testimony, if believed, was that she had acted involuntarily during this period. Having offered selective evidence of the nature of her behavior for the whole period, appellant had no valid objection to the government's attempt to show that her conduct during the omitted year belied her story and proved that she was a willing member of the SLA. Since appellant's direct testimony raised an issue about the nature of her conduct during the entire one and one-half years prior to her arrest, the government's questions about her activities, associations, and residences during the interim year were more than "reasonably related" to the subject matter of her prior testimony. That answers to these questions might have implicated appellant in crimes for which she was not on trial had no bearing on the questions' relevancy or relationship to her direct testimony.

4.   Appellant argues that even if she had no right to refuse to answer the government's questions, the court erred in allowing the prosecution to continue to ask questions which it knew would elicit repeated assertions of the privilege against self-incrimination. We find that appellant's authorities do not support her proposition. Her cases involve situations in which the government or the defendant questioned a witness or a co-defendant, knowing that a valid, unwaived Fifth Amendment privilege would be asserted. . . . She fails to offer support relating to the very different problem, present in our case, in which the government attempts to cross-examine a witness-defendant who has previously waived his privilege against self-incrimination.

In determining whether it is improper for the government to ask a defendant questions which will result in an assertion of the privilege against self-incrimination, the central consideration is whether the defendant has waived his privilege as to the propounded questions. When a witness or a defendant has a valid Fifth Amendment privilege, government questions designed to elicit this privilege present to the jury information that is misleading, irrelevant to the issue of the witness's or the defendant's credibility, and not subject to examination by defense counsel. . . . Therefore, we do not allow this form of questioning.

But when a defendant has voluntarily waived his Fifth Amendment privilege by testifying in his own behalf, the rationale for prohibiting privilege-invoking queries on cross-examination does not apply. The defen-

---

When he sought to gain admission into evidence of a portion of her testimony, he stated: "She has been threatened by them [the Harrises] for two years, Your Honor." R.T. 1416. He termed her testimony "a rebuttal to the notion that Mr. Browning [the United States Attorney] wishes to sell this jury that she had no actual fear of the Harrises." R.T. 1418.

dant has chosen to make an issue of his credibility; he has elected to take his case to the jury in the most direct fashion. The government, accordingly, has a right to challenge the defendant's story on cross-examination. ...The government may impeach the defendant by developing inconsistencies in his testimony; the government may also successfully impeach him by asking questions which he refuses to answer. If the refusals could not be put before the jury, the defendant would have the unusual and grossly unfair ability to insulate himself from challenges merely by declining to answer embarrassing questions. He alone could control the presentation of evidence to the jury.

Our view finds support in decisions construing the propriety of judicial and prosecutorial comment upon a defendant's refusal to testify. Griffin v. California, 380 U.S. 609, 615, 85 S.Ct. 1229, 14 L.Ed.2d 106 (1965), held that neither the government nor the court may comment on an accused's exercise of his Fifth Amendment privilege by refusing to testify. But it has long been established that comment is allowed when a defendant fails to explain evidence against him after first waiving his privilege by taking the witness stand. Caminetti v. United States, 242 U.S. 470, 492–95, 37 S.Ct. 192, 61 L.Ed. 442 (1917).[26] Since the offering of questions designed to elicit invocations of the Fifth Amendment is really only a form of comment upon the defendant's failure to testify, intended to present to the jury the government's interpretation of his credibility, we believe that the rule of *Caminetti* should apply to the present case.

We have concluded that appellant waived her privilege against self-incrimination with respect to her activities during the interval between her arrival in Las Vegas and her arrest in San Francisco. Therefore, it was permissible for the government to ask questions about this period, even though they led to 42 assertions of the Fifth Amendment.

* * *

NOTES

1. **Privileges of defendants and witnesses.** McCormick on Evidence distinguishes two "branches" of the privilege against compelled self-incrimination: the privilege of an accused in a criminal proceeding and the privilege of a witness:

> A criminal accused ordinarily need not affirmatively "invoke" his privilege, as he is even entitled not to be called as a witness at all. A non-accused who appears as a witness, in contrast, will ordinarily invoke the privilege as a response to particular questions asked on direct or cross-examination.

1 Kenneth S. Broun, et al., McCormick on Evidence § 118 (5th ed. 1999). There is a similar difference in regard to when persons in the two statuses have "waived" the privilege. A witness "waives" the privilege only by actually disclosing incriminating information such that further testimony would not significantly increase the risk of incrimination. Id. § 134. But, as the principal case holds, an accused waives the privilege by testifying in his own behalf. Id. § 129.

---

26. The indication in Brown v. United States, supra, 356 U.S. at 154–55, 78 S.Ct. 622, that a defendant retains a privilege against self-incrimination as to subjects not related to his direct testimony suggests that the prosecution may not comment upon the defendant's silence on matters beyond the scope of his direct examination.

2.   **Scope of cross-examination.** The scope of permitted cross-examination varies from jurisdiction to jurisdiction. At one end of the spectrum stands the English rule, also in force in a number of American states, which permits the cross-examiner to ask about any facts relevant to any issue in the case. At the opposite end stand the federal and most state courts: Cross-examination is limited to matters brought out on direct. Not surprisingly, there are in between positions. The one sub-rule shared by all jurisdictions is that cross-examination conducted solely to impeach is not restricted to matters brought out on direct.

The question of importance at this point is not the relative merits of those rules, but whether the federal constitutional rights of a defendant in one state ought to vary from the rights of a defendant in another state according to the accident of which cross-examination rule the state has. One writer has advanced the position that as a practical matter, the limited scope of the federal cross-examination rule leaves "a portion of the privilege intact." He then argues, from the reasoning in cases like Malloy v. Hogan, that the first, fourth and sixth amendment protections should be the same in scope whether the action complained of was that of the federal or a state government, that the waiver by taking the stand might well be limited in scope to that which would occur in a federal case. See Note, 45 N.C.L.Rev. 1030 (1967).

3.   **Using inadmissible evidence to cross-examine.** A defendant who testifies in his own behalf also loses the right to have certain evidence totally excluded because of the way in which it was obtained. Thus a confession elicited in violation of Miranda v. Arizona, 384 U.S. 436, 86 S.Ct. 1602, 16 L.Ed.2d 694 (1966), can be used for otherwise permissible impeachment of a testifying defendant, Harris v. New York, 401 U.S. 222, 91 S.Ct. 643, 28 L.Ed.2d 1 (1971), as may evidence obtained in an unreasonable search or seizure, United States v. Havens, 446 U.S. 620, 100 S.Ct. 1912, 64 L.Ed.2d 559 (1980). Coercion in obtaining a confession, however, casts doubt upon the confession's reliability and thus precludes its use even for impeachment. Mincey v. Arizona, 437 U.S. 385, 98 S.Ct. 2408, 57 L.Ed.2d 290 (1978). In *Havens,* the Court also held that the prosecution could use otherwise inadmissible evidence to impeach statements made by a testifying defendant during cross examination as well as in the course of direct examination, as long as those statements made during cross examination were "reasonably suggested by the defendant's direct examination." 446 U.S. at 627, 100 S.Ct. at 1917, 64 L.Ed.2d at 566. The Court explained:

> We have repeatedly insisted that when defendants testify, they must testify truthfully or suffer the consequences. This is true even though a defendant is compelled to testify against his will. It is essential, therefore, to the proper functioning of the adversary system that when a defendant takes the stand, the government be permitted proper and effective cross-examination in an attempt to elicit the truth. The defendant's obligation to testify truthfully is fully binding on him when he is cross-examined. His privilege against self-incrimination does not shield him from proper questioning. He would unquestionably be subject to a perjury prosecution if he knowingly lies on cross-examination. In terms of impeaching a defendant's seemingly false statements with his prior inconsistent utterances or with other reliable evidence available to the government, we see no difference of constitutional magnitude between the defendant's statements on direct examination and his answers to questions put to him on cross-examination that are plainly within the scope of the defendant's direct examination. Without this opportunity, the normal function of cross-examination would be severely impeded.

446 U.S. at 626–27, 100 S.Ct. at 1916–17, 64 L.Ed.2d at 565–66.

CHAPTER 24

Effective Assistance of Counsel

Analysis

The major traditional issue in applying the Sixth Amendment's right to representation by counsel has been the prosecutions to which it applies. Betts v. Brady, 316 U.S. 455, 62 S.Ct. 1252, 86 L.Ed. 1595 (1942), held that failure to appoint counsel for an indigent defendant in a state felony prosecution violated the right to counsel only if, considering all the circumstances, the absence of representation was a denial of fundamental fairness. This approach was abandoned in Gideon v. Wainwright, 372 U.S. 335, 83 S.Ct. 792, 9 L.Ed.2d 799 (1963), in which the Supreme Court held that all indigent state defendants charged with serious crimes are entitled to state-provided representation. The Court reasoned that "in our adversary system of criminal justice, any person haled into court, who is too poor to hire a lawyer, cannot be assured of a fair trial unless counsel is provided for him." 372 U.S. at 344, 83 S.Ct. at 796, 9 L.Ed.2d at 805. Argersinger v. Hamlin, 407 U.S. 25, 92 S.Ct. 2006, 32 L.Ed.2d 530 (1972), held that an indigent defendant tried and convicted of the misdemeanor of carrying a concealed weapon and sentenced to 90 days in jail was denied the right to counsel when he made no waiver of the right to representation and no lawyer was provided at state expense. But in Scott v. Illinois, 440 U.S. 367, 99 S.Ct. 1158, 59 L.Ed.2d 383 (1979), the Court declined to require state-provided representation for indigent defendants charged with misdemeanors carrying possible jail sentences but whose actual sentence did not include a period of confinement. In explaining the holding that the Sixth and Fourteenth Amendments require only that no indigent defendant be sentenced to a term of imprisonment unless the state has offered access to appointed counsel, Justice Rehnquist stated:

> [A]ctual imprisonment as the line defining the constitutional right to appointment of counsel ... has proved reasonably workable, whereas any extension would create confusion and impose unpredictable, but substantial costs on 50 quite diverse States.

440 U.S. at 373, 99 S.Ct. at 1162, 59 L.Ed.2d at 389. Flexibility in the *Argersinger-Scott* standard appeared in Middendorf v. Henry, 425 U.S. 25, 96 S.Ct. 1281, 47 L.Ed.2d 556 (1976), where the Court held that given the unique characteristics of the military community, a military summary court-martial is not a "criminal proceeding" within the meaning of the Sixth Amendment. Consequently, imposition of thirty days' confinement at hard labor upon a soldier by such a proceeding, without providing access to representation, did not violate the Sixth Amendment.

The two major issues presented by the Sixth and Fourteenth Amendments' right to representation are developed in the two sections of this Chapter. First, the requirement that counsel be effective is explored. Second, defendants' right to self-representation and the related matter of waiver of this right and the right to representation by counsel is presented.

A.   THE RIGHT TO HAVE COUNSEL BE "EFFECTIVE"

There has long been general agreement that the right to counsel involves the right to have counsel actually perform effectively. However, there had been widespread disagreement concerning the standard that must be applied to determine whether the performance of counsel was so deficient as to deny the defendant the Sixth and Fourteenth Amendments' right to representation. As late as 1978 Justice White chastised the Court for failing to grant certiorari to address the issue in Maryland v. Marzullo, 435 U.S. 1011, 98 S.Ct. 1885, 56 L.Ed.2d 394 (1978).

A number of lower courts had traditionally distinguished between retained and publicly provided lawyers for purposes of Sixth Amendment analysis. But this approach was apparently rejected by the Supreme Court in Cuyler v. Sullivan, 446 U.S. 335, 100 S.Ct. 1708, 64 L.Ed.2d 333 (1980). Responding to the argument that a conflict of interest on the part of Sullivan's retained counsel did not violate the Sixth Amendment because the conduct of such an attorney involved no state action, the Court explained:

> A proper respect for the Sixth Amendment disarms [the] contention that defendants who retain their own lawyers are entitled to less protection than defendants for whom the State appoints counsel. . . . Since the State's conduct of a criminal trial itself implicates the State in the defendant's conviction, we see no basis for drawing a distinction between retained and appointed counsel that would deny equal justice to defendants who must choose their own lawyers.

446 U.S. at 344–45, 100 S.Ct. at 1716, 64 L.Ed.2d at 344.

United States v. Cronic

Supreme Court of the United States, 1984.
466 U.S. 648, 104 S.Ct. 2039, 80 L.Ed.2d 657.

■ JUSTICE STEVENS delivered the opinion of the Court.

Respondent and two associates were indicted on mail fraud charges. ...Shortly before the scheduled trial date, respondent's retained counsel withdrew. The court appointed a young lawyer with a real estate practice to represent respondent, but allowed him only 25 days for pretrial preparation, even though it had taken the Government over four and one-half years to investigate the case and it had reviewed thousands of documents during that investigation. The two codefendants agreed to testify for the Government; respondent was convicted on 11 of the 13 counts in the indictment and received a 25–year sentence.

The Court of Appeals reversed the conviction because it concluded that respondent did not "have the Assistance of Counsel for his defence" that is guaranteed by the Sixth Amendment to the Constitution. This conclusion was not supported by a determination that respondent's trial counsel had made any specified errors, that his actual performance had prejudiced the defense, or that he failed to exercise "the skill, judgment, and diligence of a reasonably competent defense attorney"; instead the conclusion rested on the premise that no such showing is necessary "when circumstances hamper a given lawyer's preparation of a defendant's case." The question presented by the Government's petition for certiorari is whether the Court of Appeals has correctly interpreted the Sixth Amendment.

I

The indictment alleged a "check kiting" scheme. At the direction of respondent, his codefendant Cummings opened a bank account in the name of Skyproof Manufacturing, Inc. (Skyproof), at a bank in Tampa, Florida, and codefendant Merritt opened two accounts, one in his own name and one in the name of Skyproof, at banks in Norman, Oklahoma. ...By "kiting" insufficient funds checks between the banks in those two cities, defendants allegedly created false or inflated balances in the accounts. ...

At trial the Government proved that Skyproof's checks were issued and deposited at the times and places, and in the amounts, described in the indictment. Having made plea bargains with defendants Cummings and Merritt, who had actually handled the issuance and delivery of the relevant written instruments, the Government proved through their testimony that respondent had conceived and directed the entire scheme, ...

After the District Court ruled that a prior conviction could be used to impeach his testimony, respondent decided not to testify. Counsel put on no defense. By cross-examination of Government witnesses, however, he established that Skyproof was not merely a sham, but actually was an operating company with a significant cash flow, though its revenues were not sufficient to justify as large a "float" as the record disclosed. Cross-examination also established the absence of written evidence that respondent had any control over Skyproof, or personally participated in the withdrawals or deposits.

The four-day jury trial ended on July 17, 1980, and respondent was sentenced on August 28, 1980. His counsel perfected a timely appeal, which was docketed on September 11, 1980. Two months later respondent filed a motion to substitute a new attorney in the Court of Appeals, and also filed a motion in the District Court seeking to vacate his conviction on the ground that he had newly discovered evidence . . . and . . . he also challenged the competence of his trial counsel.[1] The District Court refused to entertain the motion while the appeal was pending. . . .

The Court of Appeals reversed the conviction because it inferred that respondent's constitutional right to the effective assistance of counsel had been violated. That inference was based on its use of five criteria: "(1) [T]he time afforded for investigation and preparation; (2) the experience of counsel; (3) the gravity of the charge; (4) the complexity of possible defenses; and (5) the accessibility of witnesses to counsel." United States v. Cronic, 675 F.2d 1126, 1129 (C.A.10 1982) (quoting United States v. Golub, 638 F.2d 185, 189 (C.A.10 1980)). Under the test employed by the Court of Appeals, reversal is required even if the lawyer's actual performance was flawless. By utilizing this inferential approach, the Court of Appeals erred.

II

An accused's right to be represented by counsel is a fundamental component of our criminal justice system. Lawyers in criminal cases "are necessities, not luxuries." Their presence is essential because they are the means through which the other rights of the person on trial are secured. Without counsel, the right to a trial itself would be "of little avail," as this Court has recognized repeatedly. "Of all the rights that an accused person has, the right to be represented by counsel is by far the most precious, for it affects his ability to assert any other right he may have."

The special value of the right to the assistance of counsel explains why "[i]t has long been recognized that the right to counsel is the right to the effective assistance of counsel." McMann v. Richardson, 397 U.S. 759, 771, n. 14, 90 S.Ct. 1441, 1449, 25 L.Ed.2d 763 (1970). The text of the Sixth Amendment itself suggests as much. The amendment requires not merely the provision counsel to the accused, but "Assistance," which is to be "for his defence." Thus, "the core purpose of the counsel guarantee was to assure 'Assistance' at trial, when the accused was confronted with both the intricacies of the law and the advocacy of the prosecutor." United States v. Ash, 413 U.S. 300, 309, 93 S.Ct. 2568, 2573, 37 L.Ed.2d 619 (1973). If no actual "Assistance" "for" the accused's "defence" is provided, then the constitutional guarantee has been violated. To hold otherwise

> "could convert the appointment of counsel into nothing more than a formal compliance with the Constitution's requirement that an accused be given the assistance of counsel. The Constitution's guarantee of assistance of counsel cannot be satisfied by mere formal appointment." Avery v. Alabama, 308 U.S. 444, 446, 60 S.Ct. 321, 322, 84 L.Ed. 377 (1940) (footnote omitted).

Thus, in *McMann* the Court indicated that the accused is entitled to "a reasonably competent attorney," 397 U.S., at 770, 90 S.Ct., at 1448, whose advice is "within the range of competence demanded of attorneys in

---

1. During trial, in response to questions from the bench, respondent expressed his satisfaction with counsel's performance. However, in his motion for new trial, respondent attacked counsel's performance and explained his prior praise of counsel through an affidavit of a psychologist who indicated that he had advised respondent to praise trial counsel in order to ameliorate the lawyer's apparent lack of self-confidence.

criminal cases." In Cuyler v. Sullivan, 446 U.S. 335, 100 S.Ct. 1708, 64 L.Ed.2d 333 (1980), we held that the Constitution guarantees an accused "adequate legal assistance." And in Engle v. Isaac, 456 U.S. 107, 102 S.Ct. 1558, 71 L.Ed.2d 783 (1982), the Court referred to the criminal defendant's constitutional guarantee of "a fair trial and a competent attorney."

The substance of the Constitution's guarantee of the effective assistance of counsel is illuminated by reference to its underlying purpose. "Truth," Lord Eldon said, "is best discovered by powerful statements on both sides of the question." This dictum describes the unique strength of our system of criminal justice. "The very premise of our adversary system of criminal justice is that partisan advocacy on both sides of a case will best promote the ultimate objective that the guilty be convicted and the innocent go free." Herring v. New York, 422 U.S. 853, 862, 95 S.Ct. 2550, 2555, 45 L.Ed.2d 593 (1975). It is that "very premise" that underlies and gives meaning to the Sixth Amendment. It "is meant to assure fairness in the adversary criminal process." United States v. Morrison, 449 U.S. 361, 364, 101 S.Ct. 665, 667, 66 L.Ed.2d 564 (1981). Unless the accused receives the effective assistance of counsel, "a serious risk of error infects the trial itself." Cuyler v. Sullivan, 446 U.S., at 343, 100 S.Ct., at 1715.

Thus, the adversarial process protected by the Sixth Amendment requires that the accused have "counsel acting in the role of an advocate," Anders v. California, 386 U.S. 738, 743, 87 S.Ct. 1396, 1399, 18 L.Ed.2d 493 (1967). The right to the effective assistance of counsel is thus the right of the accused to require the prosecution's case to survive the crucible of meaningful adversarial testing. When a true adversarial criminal trial has been conducted—even if defense counsel may have made demonstrable errors—the kind of testing envisioned by the Sixth Amendment has occurred. But if the process loses its character as a confrontation between adversaries, the constitutional guarantee is violated. As Judge Wyzanski has written: "While a criminal trial is not a game in which the participants are expected to enter the ring with a near match in skills, neither is it a sacrifice of unarmed prisoners to gladiators." United States ex rel. Williams v. Twomey, 510 F.2d 634, 640 (CA7), cert. denied, 423 U.S. 876, 96 S.Ct. 148, 46 L.Ed.2d 109 (1975).[2]

III

While the Court of Appeals purported to apply a standard of reasonable competence, it did not indicate that there had been an actual breakdown of the adversarial process during the trial of this case. Instead it concluded that the circumstances surrounding the representation of respondent mandated an inference that counsel was unable to discharge his duties.

---

2. Thus, the appropriate inquiry focuses on the adversarial process, not on the accused's relationship with his lawyer as such. If counsel is a reasonably effective advocate, he meets constitutional standards irrespective of his client's evaluation of his performance. See Jones v. Barnes, 463 U.S. [475], 103 S.Ct. 3308, 77 L.Ed.2d 987 (1983); Morris v. Slappy, 461 U.S. 1, 103 S.Ct. 1610, 75 L.Ed.2d 610 (1983). It is for this reason that we attach no weight to either respondent's expression of satisfaction with counsel's performance at the time of his trial, or to his later expression of dissatisfaction.

In our evaluation of that conclusion, we begin by recognizing that the right to the effective assistance of counsel is recognized not for its own sake, but because of the effect it has on the ability of the accused to receive a fair trial. Absent some effect of challenged conduct on the reliability of the trial process, the Sixth Amendment guarantee is generally not implicated. ...Moreover, because we presume that the lawyer is competent to provide the guiding hand that the defendant needs, ...the burden rests on the accused to demonstrate a constitutional violation. There are, however, circumstances that are so likely to prejudice the accused that the cost of litigating their effect in a particular case is unjustified.

Most obvious, of course, is the complete denial of counsel. The presumption that counsel's assistance is essential requires us to conclude that a trial is unfair if the accused is denied counsel at a critical stage of his trial. Similarly, if counsel entirely fails to subject the prosecution's case to meaningful adversarial testing, then there has been a denial of Sixth Amendment rights that makes the adversary process itself presumptively unreliable. No specific showing of prejudice was required in Davis v. Alaska, 415 U.S. 308, 94 S.Ct. 1105, 39 L.Ed.2d 347 (1974) because the petitioner had been "denied the right of effective cross-examination" which " 'would be constitutional error of the first magnitude and no amount of showing of want of prejudice would cure it.' " Id., at 318, 94 S.Ct., at 1111 (citing Smith v. Illinois, 390 U.S. 129, 131, 88 S.Ct. 748, 749, 19 L.Ed.2d 956 (1968), and Brookhart v. Janis, 384 U.S. 1, 3, 86 S.Ct. 1245, 1246, 16 L.Ed.2d 314 (1966)).

Circumstances of that magnitude may be present on some occasions when although counsel is available to assist the accused during trial, the likelihood that any lawyer, even a fully competent one, could provide effective assistance is so small that a presumption of prejudice is appropriate without inquiry into the actual conduct of the trial. Powell v. Alabama, 287 U.S. 45, 53 S.Ct. 55, 77 L.Ed. 158 (1932), was such a case.

The defendants had been indicted for a highly publicized capital offense. Six days before trial, the trial judge appointed "all the members of the bar" for purposes of arraignment. "Whether they would represent the defendants thereafter if no counsel appeared in their behalf, was a matter of speculation only, or, as the judge indicated, of mere anticipation on the part of the court." Id., 287 U.S., at 56, 53 S.Ct., at 59. On the day of trial, a lawyer from Tennessee appeared on behalf of persons "interested" in the defendants, but stated that he had not had an opportunity to prepare the case or to familiarize himself with local procedure, and therefore was unwilling to represent the defendants on such short notice. The problem was resolved when the court decided that the Tennessee lawyer would represent the defendants, with whatever help the local bar could provide.

> "The defendants, young, ignorant, illiterate, surrounded by hostile sentiment, haled back and forth under guard of soldiers, charged with an atrocious crime regarded with special horror in the community where they were to be tried, were thus put in peril of their lives within a few moments after counsel for the first time charged with any degree of responsibility began to represent them." Id., at 58–59, 53 S.Ct., at 60.

This Court held that "such designation of counsel as was attempted here was either so indefinite or so close upon the trial as to amount to a denial of effective and substantial aid in that regard." Id., at 53, 53 S.Ct., at 58. The Court did not examine the actual performance of counsel at trial, but instead concluded that under these circumstances the likelihood that counsel could have performed as an effective adversary was so remote as to have made the trial inherently unfair. *Powell* was thus a case in which the surrounding circumstances made it so unlikely that any lawyer could provide effective assistance that ineffectiveness was properly presumed without inquiry into actual performance at trial.

But every refusal to postpone a criminal trial will not give rise to such a presumption. In Avery v. Alabama, 308 U.S. 444, 60 S.Ct. 321, 84 L.Ed. 377 (1940), counsel was appointed in a capital case only three days before trial, and the trial court denied counsel's request for additional time to prepare. Nevertheless, the Court held that since evidence and witnesses were easily accessible to defense counsel, the circumstances did not make it unreasonable to expect that counsel could adequately prepare for trial during that period of time. Similarly, in Chambers v. Maroney, 399 U.S. 42, 90 S.Ct. 1975, 26 L.Ed.2d 419 (1970), the Court refused "to fashion a *per se* rule requiring reversal of every conviction following tardy appointment of counsel." Thus, only when surrounding circumstances justify a presumption of ineffectiveness can a Sixth Amendment claim be sufficient without inquiry into counsel's actual performance at trial.[3]

The Court of Appeals did not find that respondent was denied the presence of counsel at a critical stage of the prosecution. Nor did it find, based on the actual conduct of the trial, that there was a breakdown in the adversarial process that would justify a presumption that respondent's conviction was insufficiently reliable to satisfy the Constitution. The dispositive question in this case therefore is whether the circumstances surrounding respondent's representation—and in particular the five criteria identified by the Court of Appeals—justified such a presumption.

---

3. The Government suggests that a presumption of prejudice is justified when counsel is subject to "external constraints" on his performance. In this case the Court of Appeals identified an "external" constraint— the District Court's decision to give counsel only 25 days to prepare for trial. The fact that the accused can attribute a deficiency in his representation to a source external to trial counsel does not make it any more or less likely that he received the type of trial envisioned by the Sixth Amendment, nor does it justify reversal of his conviction absent an actual effect on the trial process or the likelihood of such an effect. Cf. United States v. Agurs, 427 U.S. 97, 110, 96 S.Ct. 2392, 2400, 49 L.Ed.2d 342 (1976) (prosecutorial misconduct should be evaluated not on the basis of culpability but by its effect on the fairness of the trial). That is made clear by *Chambers* and *Avery*. Both cases involved "external constraints" on counsel in the form of court-imposed limitations on the length of pretrial preparation, yet in neither did the Court presume that the "constraint" had an effect on the fairness of the trial. In fact, only last Term we made it clear that with respect to a trial court's refusal to grant the defense additional time to prepare for trial, an "external constraint" on counsel, great deference must be shown to trial courts, because of the scheduling problems they face. See Morris v. Slappy, 461 U.S. 1, 11, 103 S.Ct. 1610, 1616, 75 L.Ed.2d 610 (1983). Conversely, we have presumed prejudice when counsel labors under an actual conflict of interest, despite the fact that the constraints on counsel in that context are entirely self-imposed. See Cuyler v. Sullivan, 446 U.S. 335, 100 S.Ct. 1708, 64 L.Ed.2d 333 (1980).

IV

The five factors listed in the Court of Appeals' opinion are relevant to an evaluation of a lawyer's effectiveness in a particular case, but neither separately nor in combination do they provide a basis for concluding that competent counsel was not able to provide this respondent with the guiding hand that the Constitution guarantees.

Respondent places special stress on the disparity between the duration of the Government's investigation and the period the District Court allowed to newly appointed counsel for trial preparation. . . .

Neither the period of time that the Government spent investigating the case, nor the number of documents that its agents reviewed during that investigation, is necessarily relevant to the question whether a competent lawyer could prepare to defend the case in 25 days. The Government's task of finding and assembling admissible evidence that will carry its burden of proving guilt beyond a reasonable doubt is entirely different from the defendant's task in preparing to deny or rebut a criminal charge. Of course, in some cases the rebuttal may be equally burdensome and time consuming, but there is no necessary correlation between the two. In this case, the time devoted by the Government to the assembly, organization, and summarization of the thousands of written records evidencing the two streams of checks flowing between the banks in Florida and Oklahoma unquestionably simplified the work of defense counsel in identifying and understanding the basic character of the defendants' scheme. When a series of repetitious transactions fit into a single mold, the number of written exhibits that are needed to define the pattern may be unrelated to the time that is needed to understand it.

The significance of counsel's preparation time is further reduced by the nature of the charges against respondent. Most of the Government's case consisted merely of establishing the transactions between the two banks. A competent attorney would have no reason to question the authenticity, accuracy or relevance of this evidence—there could be no dispute that these transactions actually occurred. As respondent appears to recognize, the only *bona fide* jury issue open to competent defense counsel on these facts was whether respondent acted with intent to defraud. When there is no reason to dispute the underlying historical facts, the period of 25 days to consider the question whether those facts justify an inference of criminal intent is not so short that it even arguably justifies a presumption that no lawyer could provide the respondent with the effective assistance of counsel required by the Constitution.

That conclusion is not undermined by the fact that respondent's lawyer was young, that his principal practice was in real estate, or that this was his first jury trial. Every experienced criminal defense attorney once tried his first criminal case. Moreover, a lawyer's experience with real estate transactions might be more useful in preparing to try a criminal case involving financial transactions than would prior experience in handling, for example, armed robbery prosecutions. The character of a particular lawyer's experience may shed light in an evaluation of his actual performance, but it does not justify a presumption of ineffectiveness in the absence of such an evaluation.

The three other criteria—the gravity of the charge, the complexity of the case, and the accessibility of witnesses—are all matters that may affect what a reasonably competent attorney could be expected to have done under the circumstances, but none identifies circumstances that in themselves make it unlikely that respondent received the effective assistance of counsel.

V

This case is not one in which the surrounding circumstances make it unlikely that the defendant could have received the effective assistance of counsel. The criteria used by the Court of Appeals do not demonstrate that counsel failed to function in any meaningful sense as the Government's adversary. Respondent can therefore make out a claim of ineffective assistance only by pointing to specific errors made by trial counsel. In this Court, respondent's present counsel argues that the record would support such an attack, but we leave that claim—as well as the other alleged trial errors raised by respondent which were not passed upon by the Court of Appeals—for the consideration of the Court of Appeals on remand.

The judgment is reversed and the case is remanded for further proceedings consistent with this opinion.

It is so ordered.

■ JUSTICE MARSHALL concurs in the judgment.

NOTES

1. **External constraints on effectiveness.** A number of aspects of trial procedure have been scrutinized and sometimes condemned on the basis of government interference with the right to counsel. In Ferguson v. Georgia, 365 U.S. 570, 81 S.Ct. 756, 5 L.Ed.2d 783 (1961), for example, Georgia procedure permitted a defendant to make an unsworn statement—but no more—before the jury. Because this denied a defendant the right to have his attorney question him before the jury to elicit his version of the events, the Court found the procedure a denial of the right to "the guiding hand of counsel as is guaranteed by due process." In Brooks v. Tennessee, 406 U.S. 605, 92 S.Ct. 1891, 32 L.Ed.2d 358 (1972), a Tennessee requirement that a defendant who wishes to testify in his own behalf do so before any other defense witness testifies was found to suffer the same defect. By Herring v. New York, 422 U.S. 853, 95 S.Ct. 2550, 45 L.Ed.2d 593 (1975), the Court stated, "The right to the assistance of counsel has . . . been given a meaning that ensures to the defense in a criminal trial the opportunity to participate fully and fairly in the adversary factfinding process." 422 U.S. at 858, 95 S.Ct. at 2553, 45 L.Ed.2d at 598. In *Herring,* the Court held that complete denial to defense counsel of any opportunity, in a bench trial, to make closing or summary argument violated the right to counsel. "[N]o aspect of . . . advocacy could be more important than the opportunity finally to marshall the evidence for each side before submission of the case to judgment." 422 U.S. at 862, 95 S.Ct. at 2555, 45 L.Ed.2d at 600. Geders v. United States, 425 U.S. 80, 96 S.Ct. 1330, 47 L.Ed.2d 592 (1976) involved a trial judge's order that during a 17–hour overnight recess, between the defendant's testimony on direct and his cross examination the next day, the defendant not consult with his attorney "about anything." Stressing the existence of alternative methods of dealing with the potential problem of "coaching" a witness, the Supreme Court found the defendant's Sixth Amendment right infringed. But the trend was re-

versed in Lakeside v. Oregon, 435 U.S. 333, 98 S.Ct. 1091, 55 L.Ed.2d 319 (1978). After losing his argument that an instruction to the jury that no inference could be drawn from the defendant's failure to testify violated his Fifth Amendment rights, Lakeside urged that the instruction interfered with defense counsel's strategy and thus violated the right to counsel. Rejecting this "ingenious" argument, the Court reasoned that the Sixth Amendment has never been read as giving defense counsel the right to veto otherwise permissible actions of a trial judge. "To hold otherwise," it continued, "would mean that the constitutional right to counsel would be implicated in almost every wholly permissible ruling of a trial judge, if it is made over the objection of the defendant's lawyer." 435 U.S. at 341, 98 S.Ct. at 1096, 55 L.Ed.2d at 326.

In Morris v. Slappy, 461 U.S. 1, 103 S.Ct. 1610, 75 L.Ed.2d 610 (1983) defendant, charged with several felonies, was assigned a deputy public defender to represent him. A week before trial that attorney was hospitalized for emergency surgery and another deputy public defender was assigned to the case. Respondent made several requests for a continuance of his trial to permit the hospitalized defender to represent him. The trial court refused the motions for continuances on the assurance of the replacement that he was prepared to try the case. The United States Court of Appeals found that the trial court's action denied respondent's Sixth Amendment right to counsel because it denied respondent "a meaningful attorney-client relationship." The Court, in an opinion by the Chief Justice, reversed:

> The Court of Appeals' conclusion that the Sixth Amendment right to counsel "would be without substance if it did not include the right to a *meaningful attorney-client relationship,*" . . . is without basis in the law. . . . No court could possibly guarantee that a defendant will develop the kind of rapport with his attorney—privately retained or provided by the public—that the Court of Appeals thought part of the Sixth Amendment guarantee of counsel. Accordingly, we reject the claim that the Sixth Amendment guarantees a "meaningful relationship" between an accused and his counsel.

461 U.S. at 13–14, 103 S.Ct. at 1617, 75 L.Ed.2d at 621.

The Court returned to the issue raised in *Geders,* supra, in Perry v. Leeke, 488 U.S. 272, 109 S.Ct. 594, 102 L.Ed.2d 624 (1989). The Court held that an order prohibiting contact between defendant and his attorney during a fifteen minute recess between defendant's direct and cross-examination did not violate the right to counsel. The Court surmised that only the defendant's impending cross-examination would be discussed during such a break, whereas during the overnight recess in *Geders* a variety of matters not involving testimony could be expected to be discussed.

> [W]hen he assumes the role of a witness, the rules that generally apply to other witnesses . . . are generally applicable to him as well.

* * *

> [I]t is simply an empirical predicate of our system of adversary rather than inquisitorial justice that cross-examination of a witness who is uncounseled between direct examination and cross-examination is more likely to lead to discovery of truth.

488 U.S. at 282, 109 S.Ct. at 600–01, 102 L.Ed.2d at 634–35.

2. **Forfeiture of assets intended as attorney's fees.** Federal drug and racketeering statutes permit forfeiture to the government of all property derived from illegal activities. Do the Fifth and Sixth Amendments place restrictions upon forfeitures of property used or intended to be used by an accused to pay the legal fees of defense counsel? In Caplin & Drysdale, Chartered v. United States, 491 U.S.

617, 109 S.Ct. 2646, 105 L.Ed.2d 528 (1989), one Reckmeyer was charged with drug offenses. After conviction, an order was entered forfeiting specified assets to the government. Petitioner, a law firm representing Reckmeyer, intervened to claim $17,000 of those funds for legal fees. The Supreme Court, in an opinion by The Chief Justice, held that the forfeiture statutes were not intended by Congress to exempt attorneys' fees from their reach. As to the claim that the Sixth Amendment prohibits such a forfeiture, the Court said

> Whatever the full extent of the Sixth Amendment's protection of one's right to retain counsel of his choosing, that protection does not go beyond "the individual's right to spend his own money to obtain the advice and assistance of ...counsel." A defendant has no Sixth Amendment right to spend another person's money for services rendered by an attorney, even if those funds are the only way that that defendant will be able to retain the attorney of his choice. A robbery suspect, for example, has no Sixth Amendment right to use funds he has stolen from a bank to retain an attorney to defend him if he is apprehended. The money, though in his possession, is not rightfully his; the government does not violate the Sixth Amendment if it seizes the robbery proceeds, and refuses to permit the defendant to use them to pay for his defense.

491 U.S. at 626, 109 S.Ct. at 2652–53, 105 L.Ed.2d at 541–42. As to petitioner's Fifth Amendment claim, that this use of the forfeiture statute would upset the balance of forces between the accused and his accuser, because a prosecutor could use the forfeiture provisions deliberately to deprive the defendant of the opportunity to retain especially effective counsel, the Court responded that

> The Constitution does not forbid the imposition of an otherwise permissible criminal sanction, such as forfeiture, merely because in some cases prosecutors may abuse the processes available to them, e.g., by attempting to impose them on persons who should not be subjected to that punishment.... Cases involving particular abuses can be dealt with individually by the lower courts, when (and if) any such cases arise.

491 U.S. at 634–35, 109 S.Ct. at 2657, 105 L.Ed.2d at 547. Justice Blackmun, joined by Justices Brennan, Marshall and Stevens, dissented.

In the companion case of United States v. Monsanto, 491 U.S. 600, 109 S.Ct. 2657, 105 L.Ed.2d 512 (1989), the Court held that a trial court may enter a pretrial order freezing assets based on a finding of probable cause that the assets are forfeitable and that such an order can reach assets intended by the defendant to pay his attorney.

Strickland v. Washington

Supreme Court of the United States, 1984.
466 U.S. 668, 104 S.Ct. 2052, 80 L.Ed.2d 674.

■ JUSTICE O'CONNOR delivered the opinion of the Court.

This case requires us to consider the proper standards for judging a criminal defendant's contention that the Constitution requires a conviction or death sentence to be set aside because counsel's assistance at the trial or sentencing was ineffective.

I

A

During a ten-day period in September 1976, respondent planned and committed three groups of crimes, which included three brutal stabbing murders, torture, kidnapping, severe assaults, attempted murders, attempted extortion, and theft. After his two accomplices were arrested, respondent surrendered to police and voluntarily gave a lengthy statement confessing to the third of the criminal episodes. The State of Florida indicted respondent for kidnapping and murder and appointed an experienced criminal lawyer to represent him.

Counsel actively pursued pretrial motions and discovery. He cut his efforts short, however, and he experienced a sense of hopelessness about the case, when he learned that, against his specific advice, respondent had also confessed to the first two murders. By the date set for trial, respondent was subject to indictment for three counts of first degree murder and multiple counts of robbery, kidnapping for ransom, breaking and entering and assault, attempted murder, and conspiracy to commit robbery. Respondent waived his right to a jury trial, again acting against counsel's advice, and pleaded guilty to all charges, including the three capital murder charges.

In the plea colloquy, respondent told the trial judge that, although he had committed a string of burglaries, he had no significant prior criminal record and that at the time of his criminal spree he was under extreme stress caused by his inability to support his family. He also stated, however, that he accepted responsibility for the crimes. The trial judge told respondent that he had "a great deal of respect for people who are willing to step forward and admit their responsibility" but that he was making no statement at all about his likely sentencing decision.

Counsel advised respondent to invoke his right under Florida law to an advisory jury at his capital sentencing hearing. Respondent rejected the advice and waived the right. He chose instead to be sentenced by the trial judge without a jury recommendation.

In preparing for the sentencing hearing, counsel spoke with respondent about his background. He also spoke on the telephone with respondent's wife and mother, though he did not follow up on the one unsuccessful effort to meet with them. He did not otherwise seek out character witnesses for respondent. Nor did he request a psychiatric examination, since his conversations with his client gave no indication that respondent had psychological problems.

Counsel decided not to present and hence not to look further for evidence concerning respondent's character and emotional state. That decision reflected trial counsel's sense of hopelessness about overcoming the evidentiary effect of respondent's confessions to the gruesome crimes. It also reflected the judgment that it was advisable to rely on the plea colloquy for evidence about respondent's background and about his claim of emotional stress: the plea colloquy communicated sufficient information about these subjects, and by foregoing the opportunity to present new evidence on these subjects, counsel prevented the State from cross-examining respondent on his claim and from putting on psychiatric evidence of its own.

Counsel also excluded from the sentencing hearing other evidence he thought was potentially damaging. He successfully moved to exclude respondent's "rap sheet." Because he judged that a presentence report might prove more detrimental than helpful, as it would have included respondent's criminal history and thereby undermined the claim of no significant history of criminal activity, he did not request that one be prepared.

At the sentencing hearing, counsel's strategy was based primarily on the trial judge's remarks at the plea colloquy as well as on his reputation as a sentencing judge who thought it important for a convicted defendant to own up to his crime. Counsel argued that respondent's remorse and acceptance of responsibility justified sparing him from the death penalty. Counsel also argued that respondent had no history of criminal activity and that respondent committed the crimes under extreme mental or emotional disturbance, thus coming within the statutory list of mitigating circumstances. He further argued that respondent should be spared death because he had surrendered, confessed, and offered to testify against a co-defendant and because respondent was fundamentally a good person who had briefly gone badly wrong in extremely stressful circumstances. The State put on evidence and witnesses largely for the purpose of describing the details of the crimes. Counsel did not cross-examine the medical experts who testified about the manner of death of respondent's victims.

The trial judge found several aggravating circumstances with respect to each of the three murders. He found that all three murders were especially heinous, atrocious, and cruel, all involving repeated stabbings. All three murders were committed in the course of at least one other dangerous and violent felony, and since all involved robbery, the murders were for pecuniary gain. All three murders were committed to avoid arrest for the accompanying crimes and to hinder law enforcement. In the course of one of the murders, respondent knowingly subjected numerous persons to a grave risk of death by deliberately stabbing and shooting the murder victim's sisters-in-law, who sustained severe—in one case, ultimately fatal—injuries.

With respect to mitigating circumstances, the trial judge made the same findings for all three capital murders. First, although there was no admitted evidence of prior convictions, respondent had stated that he had engaged in a course of stealing. In any case, even if respondent had no significant history of criminal activity, the aggravating circumstances "would still clearly far outweigh" that mitigating factor. Second, the judge found that, during all three crimes, respondent was not suffering from extreme mental or emotional disturbance and could appreciate the criminality of his acts. Third, none of the victims was a participant in, or consented to, respondent's conduct. Fourth, respondent's participation in the crimes was neither minor nor the result of duress or domination by an accomplice. Finally, respondent's age (26) could not be considered a factor in mitigation, especially when viewed in light of respondent's planning of the crimes and disposition of the proceeds of the various accompanying thefts.

In short, the trial judge found numerous aggravating circumstances and no (or a single comparatively insignificant) mitigating circumstance. With respect to each of the three convictions for capital murder, the trial judge concluded: "A careful consideration of all matters presented to the court impels the conclusion that there are insufficient mitigating circumstances ...to outweigh the aggravating circumstances. ..." See Washington v. State, 362 So.2d 658, 663–664 (Fla.1978), cert. denied, 441 U.S. 937, 99 S.Ct. 2063, 60 L.Ed.2d 666 (1979) (quoting trial court findings). He therefore sentenced respondent to death on each of the three counts of murder and to prison terms for the other crimes. The Florida Supreme Court upheld the convictions and sentences on direct appeal.

B

Respondent subsequently sought collateral relief in state court on numerous grounds, among them that counsel had rendered ineffective assistance at the sentencing proceeding. Respondent challenged counsel's assistance in six respects. He asserted that counsel was ineffective because he failed to move for a continuance to prepare for sentencing, to request a psychiatric report, to investigate and present character witnesses, to seek a presentence investigation report, to present meaningful arguments to the sentencing judge, and to investigate the medical examiner's reports or cross-examine the medical experts. In support of the claim, respondent submitted fourteen affidavits from friends, neighbors, and relatives stating that they would have testified if asked to do so. He also submitted one psychiatric report and one psychological report stating that respondent, though not under the influence of extreme mental or emotional disturbance, was "chronically frustrated and depressed because of his economic dilemma" at the time of his crimes.

The trial court denied relief without an evidentiary hearing, finding that the record evidence conclusively showed that the ineffectiveness claim was meritless. ...

* * *

The Florida Supreme Court affirmed the denial of relief. Washington v. State, 397 So.2d 285 (Fla.1981). ...

C

...[T]he United States District Court for the Southern District of Florida ...denied the petition for a writ of habeas corpus.

On appeal, a panel of the United States Court of Appeals for the Fifth Circuit affirmed in part, vacated in part, and remanded ...The panel decision was itself vacated when ...the Eleventh Circuit, decided to rehear the case en banc. 679 F.2d 23 (1982). The full Court of Appeals developed its own framework for analyzing ineffective assistance claims and reversed the judgment of the District Court and remanded the case for new factfinding under the newly announced standards. 693 F.2d 1243 (1982).

* * *

D

Petitioners, who are officials of the State of Florida, filed a petition for a writ of certiorari seeking review of the decision of the Court of Appeals. ...

In assessing attorney performance, all the Federal Courts of Appeals and all but a few state courts have now adopted the "reasonably effective assistance" standard in one formulation or another. ...Yet this Court has not had occasion squarely to decide whether that is the proper standard. With respect to the prejudice that a defendant must show from deficient attorney performance, the lower courts have adopted tests that purport to differ in more than formulation. ...

For these reasons, we granted certiorari to consider the standards by which to judge a contention that the Constitution requires that a criminal judgment be overturned because of the actual ineffective assistance of counsel. ...

II

* * *

...Government violates the right to effective assistance when it interferes in certain ways with the ability of counsel to make independent decisions about how to conduct the defense. See, e.g., Geders v. United States, 425 U.S. 80, 96 S.Ct. 1330, 47 L.Ed.2d 592 (1976) (bar on attorney-client consultation during overnight recess); Herring v. New York, 422 U.S. 853, 95 S.Ct. 2550, 45 L.Ed.2d 593 (1975) (bar on summation at bench trial); Brooks v. Tennessee, 406 U.S. 605, 612–613, 92 S.Ct. 1891, 1895, 32 L.Ed.2d 358 (1972) (requirement that defendant be first defense witness); Ferguson v. Georgia, 365 U.S. 570, 593–596, 81 S.Ct. 756, 768–770, 5 L.Ed.2d 783 (1961) (bar on direct examination of defendant). Counsel, however, can also deprive a defendant of the right to effective assistance, simply by failing to render "adequate legal assistance," Cuyler v. Sullivan, supra, 446 U.S., at 344, 100 S.Ct., at 1716. Id., at 345–350, 100 S.Ct., at 1716–1719 (actual conflict of interest adversely affecting lawyer's performance renders assistance ineffective).

The Court has not elaborated on the meaning of the constitutional requirement of effective assistance in the latter class of cases—that is, those presenting claims of "actual ineffectiveness." In giving meaning to the requirement, however, we must take its purpose—to ensure a fair trial—as the guide. The benchmark for judging any claim of ineffectiveness must be whether counsel's conduct so undermined the proper functioning of the adversarial process that the trial cannot be relied on as having produced a just result.

The same principle applies to a capital sentencing proceeding such as that provided by Florida law. We need not consider the role of counsel in an ordinary sentencing, which may involve informal proceedings and standardless discretion in the sentencer, and hence may require a different approach to the definition of constitutionally effective assistance. A capital sentencing proceeding like the one involved in this case, however, is sufficiently like a trial in its adversarial format and in the existence of standards for decision, ...that counsel's role in the proceeding is comparable to counsel's role at trial—to ensure that the adversarial testing process works to produce a just result under the standards governing decision. For purposes of describing counsel's duties, therefore, Florida's capital sentencing proceeding need not be distinguished from an ordinary trial.

III

A convicted defendant's claim that counsel's assistance was so defective as to require reversal of a conviction or death sentence has two components. First, the defendant must show that counsel's performance was deficient. This requires showing that counsel made errors so serious that counsel was not functioning as the "counsel" guaranteed the defendant by the Sixth Amendment. Second, the defendant must show that the deficient performance prejudiced the defense. This requires showing that counsel's errors were so serious as to deprive the defendant of a fair trial, a trial whose result is reliable. Unless a defendant makes both showings, it cannot be said that the conviction or death sentence resulted from a breakdown in the adversary process that renders the result unreliable.

A

As all the Federal Courts of Appeals have now held, the proper standard for attorney performance is that of reasonably effective assistance. The Court indirectly recognized as much when it stated in McMann v. Richardson, supra, 397 U.S., at 770, 771, 90 S.Ct., at 1448, 1449, that a guilty plea cannot be attacked as based on inadequate legal advice unless counsel was not "a reasonably competent attorney" and the advice was not "within the range of competence demanded of attorneys in criminal cases." When a convicted defendant complains of the ineffectiveness of counsel's assistance, the defendant must show that counsel's representation fell below an objective standard of reasonableness.

More specific guidelines are not appropriate. The Sixth Amendment refers simply to "counsel," not specifying particular requirements of effective assistance. It relies instead on the legal profession's maintenance of standards sufficient to justify the law's presumption that counsel will fulfill the role in the adversary process that the Amendment envisions. The proper measure of attorney performance remains simply reasonableness under prevailing professional norms.

Representation of a criminal defendant entails certain basic duties. Counsel's function is to assist the defendant, and hence counsel owes the client a duty of loyalty, a duty to avoid conflicts of interest. From counsel's function as assistant to the defendant derive the overarching duty to advocate the defendant's cause and the more particular duties to consult with the defendant on important decisions and to keep the defendant informed of important developments in the course of the prosecution. Counsel also has a duty to bring to bear such skill and knowledge as will render the trial a reliable adversarial testing process.

These basic duties neither exhaustively define the obligations of counsel nor form a checklist for judicial evaluation of attorney performance. In any case presenting an ineffectiveness claim, the performance inquiry must be whether counsel's assistance was reasonable considering all the circumstances. Prevailing norms of practice as reflected in American Bar Association standards and the like, e.g., ABA Standards for Criminal Justice 4–1.1

to 4–8.6 (2d ed. 1980) ("The Defense Function"), are guides to determining what is reasonable, but they are only guides. No particular set of detailed rules for counsel's conduct can satisfactorily take account of the variety of circumstances faced by defense counsel or the range of legitimate decisions regarding how best to represent a criminal defendant. Any such set of rules would interfere with the constitutionally protected independence of counsel and restrict the wide latitude counsel must have in making tactical decisions. Indeed, the existence of detailed guidelines for representation could distract counsel from the overriding mission of vigorous advocacy of the defendant's cause. Moreover, the purpose of the effective assistance guarantee of the Sixth Amendment is not to improve the quality of legal representation, although that is a goal of considerable importance to the legal system. The purpose is simply to ensure that criminal defendants receive a fair trial.

Judicial scrutiny of counsel's performance must be highly deferential. It is all too tempting for a defendant to second-guess counsel's assistance after conviction or adverse sentence, and it is all too easy for a court, examining counsel's defense after it has proved unsuccessful, to conclude that a particular act or omission of counsel was unreasonable. A fair assessment of attorney performance requires that every effort be made to eliminate the distorting effects of hindsight, to reconstruct the circumstances of counsel's challenged conduct, and to evaluate the conduct from counsel's perspective at the time. Because of the difficulties inherent in making the evaluation, a court must indulge a strong presumption that counsel's conduct falls within the wide range of reasonable professional assistance; that is, the defendant must overcome the presumption that, under the circumstances, the challenged action "might be considered sound trial strategy." There are countless ways to provide effective assistance in any given case. Even the best criminal defense attorneys would not defend a particular client in the same way.

The availability of intrusive post-trial inquiry into attorney performance or of detailed guidelines for its evaluation would encourage the proliferation of ineffectiveness challenges. Criminal trials resolved unfavorably to the defendant would increasingly come to be followed by a second trial, this one of counsel's unsuccessful defense. Counsel's performance and even willingness to serve could be adversely affected. Intensive scrutiny of counsel and rigid requirements for acceptable assistance could dampen the ardor and impair the independence of defense counsel, discourage the acceptance of assigned cases, and undermine the trust between attorney and client.

Thus, a court deciding an actual ineffectiveness claim must judge the reasonableness of counsel's challenged conduct on the facts of the particular case, viewed as of the time of counsel's conduct. A convicted defendant making a claim of ineffective assistance must identify the acts or omissions of counsel that are alleged not to have been the result of reasonable professional judgment. The court must then determine whether, in light of all the circumstances, the identified acts or omissions were outside the wide range of professionally competent assistance. In making that determination, the court should keep in mind that counsel's function, as elaborated in prevailing professional norms, is to make the adversarial testing process work in the particular case. At the same time, the court should recognize that counsel is strongly presumed to have rendered adequate assistance and made all significant decisions in the exercise of reasonable professional judgment.

These standards require no special amplification in order to define counsel's duty to investigate, the duty at issue in this case. As the Court of Appeals concluded, strategic choices made after thorough investigation of law and facts relevant to plausible options are virtually unchallengeable; and strategic choices made after less than complete investigation are reasonable precisely to the extent that reasonable professional judgments support the limitations on investigation. In other words, counsel has a duty to make reasonable investigations or to make a reasonable decision that makes particular investigations unnecessary. In any ineffectiveness case, a particular decision not to investigate must be directly assessed for reasonableness in all the circumstances, applying a heavy measure of deference to counsel's judgments.

The reasonableness of counsel's actions may be determined or substantially influenced by the defendant's own statements or actions. Counsel's actions are usually based, quite properly, on informed strategic choices made by the defendant and on information supplied by the defendant. In particular, what investigation decisions are reasonable depends critically on such information. For example, when the facts that support a certain potential line of defense are generally known to counsel because of what the defendant has said, the need for further investigation may be considerably diminished or eliminated altogether. And when a defendant has given counsel reason to believe that pursuing certain investigations would be fruitless or even harmful, counsel's failure to pursue those investigations may not later be challenged as unreasonable. In short, inquiry into counsel's conversations with the defendant may be critical to a proper assessment of counsel's investigation decisions, just as it may be critical to a proper assessment of counsel's other litigation decisions.

B

An error by counsel, even if professionally unreasonable, does not warrant setting aside the judgment of a criminal proceeding if the error had no effect on the judgment. The purpose of the Sixth Amendment guarantee of counsel is to ensure that a defendant has the assistance necessary to justify reliance on the outcome of the proceeding. Accordingly, any deficiencies in counsel's performance must be prejudicial to the defense in order to constitute ineffective assistance under the Constitution.

In certain Sixth Amendment contexts, prejudice is presumed. Actual or constructive denial of the assistance of counsel altogether is legally presumed to result in prejudice. So are various kinds of state interference with counsel's assistance. Prejudice in these circumstances is so likely that case by case inquiry into prejudice is not worth the cost. Moreover, such circumstances involve impairments of the Sixth Amendment right that are easy to identify and, for that reason and because the prosecution is directly responsible, easy for the government to prevent.

One type of actual ineffectiveness claim warrants a similar, though more limited, presumption of prejudice. In Cuyler v. Sullivan, 446 U.S., at 345–350, 90 S.Ct., at 1716–1719, the Court held that prejudice is presumed when counsel is burdened by an actual conflict of interest. In those circumstances, counsel breaches the duty of loyalty, perhaps the most basic of counsel's duties. Moreover, it is difficult to measure the precise effect on the defense of representation corrupted by conflicting interests. Given the obligation of counsel to avoid conflicts of interest and the ability of trial courts to make early inquiry in certain situations likely to give rise to conflicts, see, e.g., Fed.Rule Crim.Proc. 44(c), it is reasonable for the criminal justice system to maintain a fairly rigid rule of presumed prejudice for conflicts of interest. Even so, the rule is not quite the *per se* rule of prejudice that exists for the Sixth Amendment claims mentioned above. Prejudice is presumed only if the defendant demonstrates that counsel "actively represented conflicting interests" and "that an actual conflict of interest adversely affected his lawyer's performance."

Conflict of interest claims aside, actual ineffectiveness claims alleging a deficiency in attorney performance are subject to a general requirement that the defendant affirmatively prove prejudice. The government is not responsible for, and hence not able to prevent, attorney errors that will result in reversal of a conviction or sentence. Attorney errors come in an infinite variety and are as likely to be utterly harmless in a particular case as they are to be prejudicial. They cannot be classified according to likelihood of causing prejudice. Nor can they be defined with sufficient precision to inform defense attorneys correctly just what conduct to avoid. Representation is an art, and an act or omission that is unprofessional in one case may be sound or even brilliant in another. Even if a defendant shows that particular errors of counsel were unreasonable, therefore, the defendant must show that they actually had an adverse effect on the defense.

It is not enough for the defendant to show that the errors had some conceivable effect on the outcome of the proceeding. Virtually every act or omission of counsel would meet that test, and not every error that conceivably could have influenced the outcome undermines the reliability of the result of the proceeding. Respondent suggests requiring a showing that the errors "impaired the presentation of the defense." That standard, however, provides no workable principle. Since any error, if it is indeed an error, "impairs" the presentation of the defense, the proposed standard is inadequate because it provides no way of deciding what impairments are sufficiently serious to warrant setting aside the outcome of the proceeding.

On the other hand, we believe that a defendant need not show that counsel's deficient conduct more likely than not altered the outcome in the case. This outcome-determinative standard has several strengths. It defines the relevant inquiry in a way familiar to courts, though the inquiry, as is inevitable, is anything but precise. The standard also reflects the profound importance of finality in criminal proceedings. Moreover, it comports with the widely used standard for assessing motions for new trial based on newly discovered evidence. Nevertheless, the standard is not quite appropriate.

Even when the specified attorney error results in the omission of certain evidence, the newly discovered evidence standard is not an apt source from which to draw a prejudice standard for ineffectiveness claims. The high standard for newly discovered evidence claims presupposes that all the essential elements of a presumptively accurate and fair proceeding were present in the proceeding whose result is challenged. An ineffective assistance claim asserts the absence of one of the crucial assurances that the result of the proceeding is reliable, so finality concerns are somewhat weaker and the appropriate standard of prejudice should be somewhat lower. The result of a proceeding can be rendered unreliable, and hence the proceeding itself unfair, even if the errors of counsel cannot be shown by a preponderance of the evidence to have determined the outcome.

Accordingly, the appropriate test for prejudice finds its roots in the test for materiality of exculpatory information not disclosed to the defense by the prosecution, United States v. Agurs, 427 U.S., at 104, 112–113, 96 S.Ct., at 2397, 2401–2402, and in the test for materiality of testimony made unavailable to the defense by Government deportation of a witness, United States v. Valenzuela–Bernal, 458 U.S., at 872–874, 102 S.Ct., at 3449–3450. The defendant must show that there is a reasonable probability that, but for counsel's unprofessional errors, the result of the proceeding would have been different. A reasonable probability is a probability sufficient to undermine confidence in the outcome.

* * *

The governing legal standard plays a critical role in defining the question to be asked in assessing the prejudice from counsel's errors. When a defendant challenges a conviction, the question is whether there is a reasonable probability that, absent the errors, the factfinder would have had a reasonable doubt respecting guilt. When a defendant challenges a death sentence such as the one at issue in this case, the question is whether there is a reasonable probability that, absent the errors, the sentencer—including an appellate court, to the extent it independently reweighs the evidence—would have concluded that the balance of aggravating and mitigating circumstances did not warrant death.

* * *

IV

. . .Although those principles should guide the process of decision, the ultimate focus of inquiry must be on the fundamental fairness of the proceeding whose result is being challenged. In every case the court should be concerned with whether, despite the strong presumption of reliability, the result of the particular proceeding is unreliable because of a breakdown in the adversarial process that our system counts on to produce just results.

To the extent that this has already been the guiding inquiry in the lower courts, the standards articulated today do not require reconsideration of ineffectiveness claims rejected under different standards. . . .In particular, the minor differences in the lower court's precise formulations of the performance standard are insignificant: the different formulations are mere variations of the overarching reasonableness standard. . . .

Although we have discussed the performance component of an ineffectiveness claim prior to the prejudice component, there is no reason for a court deciding an ineffective assistance claim to approach the inquiry in the same order or even to address both components of the inquiry if the defendant makes an insufficient showing on one. In particular, a court need not determine whether counsel's performance was deficient before examining the prejudice suffered by the defendant as a result of the alleged deficiencies. The object of an ineffectiveness claim is not to grade counsel's performance. If it is easier to dispose of an ineffectiveness claim on the ground of lack of sufficient prejudice, which we expect will often be so, that course should be followed. Courts should strive to ensure that ineffectiveness claims not become so burdensome to defense counsel that the entire criminal justice system suffers as a result.

The principles governing ineffectiveness claims should apply in federal collateral proceedings as they do on direct appeal or in motions for a new trial.

* * *

V

Having articulated general standards for judging ineffectiveness claims, we think it useful to apply those standards to the facts of this case in order to illustrate the meaning of the general principles. . . .

Application of the governing principles is not difficult in this case. The facts as described above make clear that the conduct of respondent's counsel at and before respondent's sentencing proceeding cannot be found unreasonable. They also make clear that, even assuming the challenged conduct of counsel was unreasonable, respondent suffered insufficient prejudice to warrant setting aside his death sentence.

With respect to the performance component, the record shows that respondent's counsel made a strategic choice to argue for the extreme emotional distress mitigating circumstance and to rely as fully as possible on respondent's acceptance of responsibility for his crimes. Although counsel understandably felt hopeless about respondent's prospects, nothing in the record indicates, as one possible reading of the District Court's opinion suggests, that counsel's sense of hopelessness distorted his professional judgment. Counsel's strategy choice was well within the range of professionally reasonable judgments, and the decision not to seek more character or psychological evidence than was already in hand was likewise reasonable.

The trial judge's views on the importance of owning up to one's crimes were well known to counsel. The aggravating circumstances were utterly overwhelming. Trial counsel could reasonably surmise from his conversations with respondent that character and psychological evidence would be of little help. Respondent had already been able to mention at the plea colloquy the substance of what there was to know about his financial and emotional troubles. Restricting testimony on respondent's character to what had come in at the plea colloquy ensured that contrary character and psychological evidence and respondent's criminal history, which counsel had successfully moved to exclude, would not come in. On these facts, there can be little question, even without application of the presumption of adequate performance, that trial counsel's defense, though unsuccessful, was the result of reasonable professional judgment.

With respect to the prejudice component, the lack of merit of respondent's claim is even more stark. The evidence that respondent says his trial counsel should have offered at the sentencing hearing would barely have altered the sentencing profile presented to the sentencing judge. As the state courts and District Court found, at most this evidence shows that numerous people who knew respondent thought he was generally a good person and that a psychiatrist and a psychologist believed he was under considerable emotional stress that did not rise to the level of extreme disturbance. Given the overwhelming aggravating factors, there is no reasonable probability that the omitted evidence would have changed the conclusion that the aggravating circumstances outweighed the mitigating circumstances and, hence, the sentence imposed. Indeed, admission of the evidence respondent now offers might even have been harmful to his case: his "rap sheet" would probably have been admitted into evidence, and the psychological reports would have directly contradicted respondent's claim that the mitigating circumstances of extreme emotional disturbance applied to his case.

* * *

Failure to make the required showing of either deficient performance or sufficient prejudice defeats the ineffectiveness claim. Here there is a double failure. More generally, respondent has made no showing that the justice of his sentence was rendered unreliable by a breakdown in the adversary process caused by deficiencies in counsel's assistance. Respondent's sentencing proceeding was not fundamentally unfair.

We conclude, therefore, that the District Court properly declined to issue a writ of habeas corpus. The judgment of the Court of Appeals is accordingly reversed.

■ JUSTICE BRENNAN, concurring in part and dissenting in part [omitted].

■ JUSTICE MARSHALL, dissenting.

* * *

My objection to the performance standard adopted by the Court is that it is so malleable that, in practice, it will either have no grip at all or will yield excessive variation in the manner in which the Sixth Amendment is interpreted and applied by different courts. To tell lawyers and the lower courts that counsel for a criminal defendant must behave "reasonably" and must act like "a reasonably competent attorney," is to tell them almost nothing. In essence, the majority has instructed judges called upon to assess claims of ineffective assistance of counsel to advert to their own intuitions regarding what constitutes "professional" representation, and has discouraged them from trying to develop more detailed standards governing the performance of defense counsel. In my view, the Court has thereby not only abdicated its own responsibility to interpret the Constitution, but also impaired the ability of the lower courts to exercise theirs.

* * *

...It is an unfortunate but undeniable fact that a person of means, by selecting a lawyer and paying him enough to ensure he prepares thoroughly, usually can obtain better representation than that available to an indigent defendant, who must rely on appointed counsel, who, in turn, has limited time and resources to devote to a given case. Is a "reasonably competent attorney" a reasonably competent adequately paid retained lawyer or a reasonably competent appointed attorney? It is also a fact that the quality of representation available to ordinary defendants in different parts of the country varies significantly. Should the standard of performance mandated by the Sixth Amendment vary by locale? The majority offers no clues as to the proper responses to these questions.

* * *

...I agree that counsel must be afforded "wide latitude" when making "tactical decisions" regarding trial strategy, but many aspects of the job of a criminal defense attorney are more amenable to judicial oversight. For example, much of the work involved in preparing for a trial, applying for bail, conferring with one's client, making timely objections to significant, arguably erroneous rulings of the trial judge, and filing a notice of appeal if there are colorable grounds therefor could profitably be made the subject of uniform standards.

* * *

I object to the prejudice standard adopted by the Court for two independent reasons. First, ...The difficulties of estimating prejudice after the fact are exacerbated by the possibility that evidence of injury to the defendant may be missing from the record precisely because of the incompetence of defense counsel. [I]t seems to me senseless to impose on a defendant whose lawyer has been shown to have been incompetent the burden of demonstrating prejudice.

Second and more fundamentally, the assumption on which the Court's holding rests is that the only purpose of the constitutional guarantee of effective assistance of counsel is to reduce the chance that innocent persons will be convicted. In my view, the guarantee also functions to ensure that convictions are obtained only through fundamentally fair procedures. The majority contends that the Sixth Amendment is not violated when a manifestly guilty defendant is convicted after a trial in which he was represented by a manifestly ineffective attorney. I cannot agree. Every defendant is entitled to a trial in which his interests are vigorously and conscientiously advocated by an able lawyer. A proceeding in which the defendant does not receive meaningful assistance in meeting the forces of the state does not, in my opinion, constitute due process.

In Chapman v. California, 386 U.S. 18, 23, 87 S.Ct. 824, 827, 17 L.Ed.2d 705 (1967), we acknowledged that certain constitutional rights are "so basic to a fair trial that their infraction can never be treated as harmless error." Among these rights is "the right to the assistance of counsel at trial." Id., at 23, n. 8, 87 S.Ct., at 827, n. 8; see Gideon v. Wainwright, 372 U.S. 335, 83 S.Ct. 792, 9 L.Ed.2d 799 (1963). In my view, the right to *effective* assistance of counsel is entailed by the right to counsel, and abridgment of the former is equivalent to abridgment of the latter. I would thus hold that a showing that the performance of a defendant's lawyer departed from constitutionally prescribed standards requires a new trial regardless of whether the defendant suffered demonstrable prejudice thereby.

* * *

NOTES

1.   **Proving prejudice.** Justice Stevens, in his opinion in *Cronic,* supra, stated that some circumstances so clearly indicate a denial of effective assistance of counsel and are so likely to prejudice the defendant that no specific showing of prejudice is required. The most obvious example is complete denial of counsel. Yet in some instances counsel may be present but render such minimal assistance that prejudice will be presumed.

However, the fact that defense counsel suffered from a rare sleep disorder, causing him to occasionally doze off during trial for as much as 30 seconds each time, did not result in reversal in a 1984 California federal district court case. The defendant was unable to specify exactly how many or when the naps occurred. He said he awakened counsel quickly because his snoring was embarrassing. Following an evidentiary hearing on effectiveness of counsel, Judge Garcia, explicitly applying *Strickland,* refused to grant a retrial because the defendant had failed to prove that his defense was prejudiced by counsel's conduct. Sacramento Bee, Nov. 7, 1984, at B1.

Strickland's test was developed—perhaps only for very unusual situations—in Lockhart v. Fretwell, 506 U.S. 364, 113 S.Ct. 838, 122 L.Ed.2d 180 (1993). In 1985, upon proof that he killed the victim in the course of a robbery, Fretwell was convicted of capital felony murder in an Arkansas court. At the penalty stage, the State sought the death penalty and argued that the facts showed two aggravating circumstances: (a) that the murder was committed for pecuniary gain; and (b) that the murder was committed to facilitate Fretwell's escape. Shortly before the trial, the Eighth Circuit Court of Appeals had held in Collins v. Lockhart, 754 F.2d 258 (8th Cir.), cert. denied, 474 U.S. 1013, 106 S.Ct. 546, 88 L.Ed.2d 475 (1985) that a death sentence in a felony murder case was unconstitutional if it was based upon an aggravating factor that duplicated an underlying element of the felony. Fretwell's lawyer did not object to the trial judge's submission to the jury of the first aggravating circumstance urged by the State, even though reliance upon it was almost certainly contrary to *Collins.* The jury found the first aggravating circumstance to have been proved and sentenced Fretwell to death.

In later federal habeas corpus proceedings, Fretwell argued that he had been denied the effective assistance of counsel because defense counsel had not raised *Collins* in connection with the sentencing proceeding. By this time, however, *Collins* had been overruled as inconsistent with an intervening decision of the Supreme Court. Thus Fretwell challenged his counsel's performance on the basis of counsel's failure to raise an argument that was "good law" at the time of trial but at the time of his attack was recognized as without ultimate legal merit. The lower federal courts granted Fretwell relief. Counsel's failure to invoke *Collins* constituted deficient performance under *Strickland.* If counsel had invoked *Collins,* the trial judge would not have permitted the State to rely upon their first proffered aggravating circumstance, the jury would not have found the other circumstance shown by the evidence, and the jury would not have sentenced Fretwell to death. Thus Fretwell had established prejudice under *Strickland*.

The Supreme Court reversed, concluding that the lower federal courts had erred in finding that Fretwell showed prejudice. Defendants are afforded the Sixth Amendment right to counsel, Chief Justice Rehnquist explained for the majority, to protect their right to a fair—that is, reliable—trial. *Strickland's* test reflects this concern with reliability.

> Thus, an analysis focusing solely on mere outcome determination, without attention to whether the result of the proceeding was fundamentally unfair or unreliable, is defective. To set aside a conviction or sentence solely because the outcome would have been different but for counsel's error may grant the defendant a windfall to which the law does not entitle him.
>
> *   *   *
>
> The result of the sentencing proceeding in the present case was neither unfair nor unreliable.

506 U.S. at 369–71, 113 S.Ct. at 842–43, 122 L.Ed.2d at 189–90.

Under *Strickland*, the Court agreed, whether counsel performed acceptably is to be viewed as of the time of the conduct challenged. Whether a defendant was prejudiced, however, is not to be determined under such a "rule of contemporary assessment." If counsel's ineffectiveness does not deprive a defendant of any substantive or procedural right to which the law—as it is later or ultimately known to be—entitles the defendant, no unreliability or unfairness results and there has been no prejudice. Since Fretwell is now known not to have been entitled to have the trial judge follow *Collins*, he suffered no prejudice from counsel's deficiency in failing to argue *Collins*. 506 U.S. at 371, 113 S.Ct. at 844, 122 L.Ed.2d at 191.

Justice O'Connor concurred to suggest that the Court's holding will affect only the unusual situations where defendants attempt "to demonstrate prejudice based on considerations that, as a matter of law, ought not inform the inquiry." In the vast majority of cases, she added, the Court's decision will have no effect on the prejudice inquiry under *Strickland*. 506 U.S. at 373, 113 S.Ct. at 845, 122 L.Ed.2d at 192 (O'Connor, J., concurring).

Justice Stevens, joined by Justice Blackmun, dissented, arguing that ineffective assistance of counsel claims should be evaluated under the law as it stood at the time of trial:

> Hindsight has no place in a Sixth Amendment jurisprudence that focuses, quite rightly, on protecting the adversarial balance at trial. * * * [A]s it happened, counsel's failure to object came at a time when it signified a breakdown in the adversarial process. A *post hoc* vision of what would have been the case years later has no bearing on the force of this showing.

506 U.S. at 381, 113 S.Ct. at 849, 122 L.Ed.2d at 197 (Stevens, J., dissenting).

2. **Advice by counsel.** The Supreme Court applied Strickland v. Washington to advice by counsel at the plea-bargaining stage in Hill v. Lockhart, 474 U.S. 52, 106 S.Ct. 366, 88 L.Ed.2d 203 (1985). The Court, through Justice Rehnquist, stated:

> In the present case the claimed error of counsel is erroneous advice as to eligibility for parole under the sentence agreed to in the plea bargain. We find it unnecessary to determine whether there may be circumstances under which erroneous advice by counsel as to parole eligibility may be deemed constitutionally ineffective assistance of counsel, because in the present case we conclude that petitioner's allegations are insufficient to satisfy the *Strickland v. Wash-*

ington requirement of "prejudice." Petitioner did not allege in his habeas petition that, had counsel correctly informed him about his parole eligibility date, he would have pleaded not guilty and insisted on going to trial. He alleged no special circumstances that might support the conclusion that he placed particular emphasis on his parole eligibility in deciding whether or not to plead guilty. Indeed, petitioner's mistaken belief that he would become eligible for parole after serving one-third of his sentence would seem to have affected not only his calculation of the time he likely would serve if sentenced pursuant to the proposed plea agreement, but also his calculation of the time he likely would serve if he went to trial and were convicted.

Because petitioner in this case failed to allege the kind of "prejudice" necessary to satisfy the second half of the *Strickland v. Washington* test, the District Court did not err in declining to hold a hearing on petitioner's ineffective assistance of counsel claim.

474 U.S. at 60, 106 S.Ct. at 371, 88 L.Ed.2d at 211. Justice White, joined by Justice Stevens, concurred in the judgment on the ground petitioner had not alleged his attorney knew of the prior conviction which altered his parole eligibility period but failed to advise petitioner of the correct parole eligibility term despite that knowledge.

3. **Duty not to tolerate perjury.** A lawyer's duty when he knows or suspects that a client or witness will testify falsely may involve more than ethical considerations. Those decisions may lead to claims of ineffective assistance of counsel.

In State v. Lee, 142 Ariz. 210, 689 P.2d 153 (1984), defense counsel gave in to his client's demand that he call two witnesses whose testimony defense counsel believed would be perjurious. Counsel let the witnesses give narrative accounts on the stand. He then told the judge in chambers that he believed the witnesses were lying; but after much "mental wrestling" he believed that he could not interfere with the defendant's constitutional right to present testimony on his own behalf. Under the circumstances, he felt his ethical duty required waiver of closing argument. The defendant was then convicted and received the maximum sentence.

The Arizona Supreme Court found ineffective assistance of counsel under the *Strickland* test, holding that the first prong of the test, deficient performance of counsel, had been met and remanding for a determination of prejudice. Counsel should have either refused to call the witnesses (as this was a tactical choice to be left to the attorney), or made a closing argument omitting any reference to the perjured testimony.

In Nix v. Whiteside, 475 U.S. 157, 106 S.Ct. 988, 89 L.Ed.2d 123 (1986), the defense attorney feared that the defendant himself intended to give perjured testimony. After stating in earlier interviews that he failed to see a gun in the hand of the victim, Whiteside told his attorney immediately before trial that he then recalled seeing something "metallic" in the victim's hand and commented, "If I don't say I saw a gun I'm dead." His attorney informed Whiteside that he would not allow him to commit perjury, that if he did so he would inform the trial court, would withdraw from the case and would be allowed to impeach that testimony. Whiteside testified without mentioning the metallic object and was convicted. Writing for the Court, Chief Justice Burger stated that the attorney's conduct in this case was not ineffective assistance under *Strickland*. Justice Burger reviewed the various bar association statements of professional responsibility and concluded,

Considering [the defense attorney's] representation of respondent in light of these accepted norms of professional conduct, we discern no failure to adhere to reasonable professional standards that would in any sense make out a deprivation of the Sixth Amendment right to counsel. Whether [the attorney's] conduct is seen as a successful attempt to dissuade his client from committing the crime of perjury, or whether seen as a "threat" to withdraw from representation and disclose the illegal scheme, [his] representation of Whiteside falls well within accepted standards of professional conduct and the range of reasonable professional conduct acceptable under *Strickland*.

475 U.S. at 171, 106 S.Ct. at 996, 89 L.Ed.2d at 137. The Court also held that as a matter of law respondent could not have been prejudiced under *Strickland* because his attorney kept him from committing perjury. Justice Brennan concurred in the judgment but characterized Justice Burger's "essay regarding what constitutes the correct response to a criminal client's suggestion that he will perjure himself" as "pure discourse without force of law." 475 U.S. at 177, 106 S.Ct. at 999, 89 L.Ed.2d at 141. Justice Blackmun, joined by Justices Brennan, Marshall and Stevens, concurring in the judgment, found that Whiteside had failed to show prejudice under *Strickland* and would not have reached the question of whether counsel's conduct was in some manner deficient. Justice Stevens, concurring in the judgment, commented on the difficulties facing trial counsel in this situation:

> A lawyer's certainty that a change in his client's recollection is a harbinger of intended perjury—as well as judicial review of such apparent certainty—should be tempered by the realization that, after reflection, the most honest witness may recall (or sincerely believe he recalls) details that he previously overlooked. Similarly, the post-trial review of a lawyer's pretrial threat to expose perjury that had not yet been committed—and, indeed, may have been prevented by the threat—is by no means the same as review of the way in which such a threat may actually have been carried out. Thus, one can be convinced—as I am—that this lawyer's actions were a proper way to provide his client with effective representation without confronting the much more difficult questions of what a lawyer must, should, or may do after his client has given testimony that the lawyer does not believe.

475 U.S. at 190–91, 106 S.Ct. at 1006, 89 L.Ed.2d at 150.

4. **Joint representation.** Joint representation—representation of several co-defendants by a single lawyer (or possibly, by a single law firm), Burger v. Kemp, 483 U.S. 776, 107 S.Ct. 3114, 97 L.Ed.2d 638 (1987)—raises special Sixth Amendment problems. It has long been clear that while joint representation is not a *per se* violation of each defendant's right to counsel, joint representation by one lawyer of codefendants whose interests conflict *may* violate that right. Glasser v. United States, 315 U.S. 60, 62 S.Ct. 457, 86 L.Ed. 680 (1942).

In Cuyler v. Sullivan, 446 U.S. 335, 100 S.Ct. 1708, 64 L.Ed.2d 333 (1980), the Court reasoned:

> In order to establish a violation of the Sixth Amendment, a defendant who raised no objection at trial must demonstrate that an actual conflict of interest adversely affected his lawyer's performance. ... [A] defendant who shows that a conflict of interests actually affected the adequacy of his representation need not demonstrate prejudice in order to obtain relief. But until a defendant shows that his counsel actively represented conflicting interest, he has not established the constitutional predicate for this claim of ineffective assistance.

446 U.S. at 348–50, 100 S.Ct. at 1718–19, 64 L.Ed.2d at 346–47. In Glasser v. United States, supra, the Court found a conflict of interests shown by evidence that counsel failed to cross-examine a critical Government witness and to challenge arguably inadmissible evidence because of a desire to diminish the jury's perception of the guilt of Glasser's co-defendant.

Fed.R.Crim.P. 44 provides:

Rule 44. Right to and Assignment of Counsel

* * *

(c) *Joint Representation.* Whenever two or more defendants have been jointly charged pursuant to Rule 8(b) or have been joined for trial pursuant to Rule 13, and are represented by the same retained or assigned counsel or by retained or assigned counsel who are associated in the practice of law, the court shall promptly inquire with respect to such joint representation and shall personally advise each defendant of his right to the effective assistance of counsel, including separate representation. Unless it appears that there is good cause to believe no conflict of interest is likely to arise, the court shall take such measures as may be appropriate to protect each defendant's right to counsel.

5. **Conflicts created by fee arrangements.** Wood v. Georgia, 450 U.S. 261, 101 S.Ct. 1097, 67 L.Ed.2d 220 (1981), involved another type of conflict of interests. When a criminal defendant is represented by a lawyer hired and paid by a third party, there are inherent dangers that are increased when the third party is the operator of the alleged criminal enterprise. In such a case, involving the prosecution of adult bookstore employees, the Court stated:

> One risk is that the lawyer will prevent his client from obtaining leniency by preventing the client from offering testimony against his former employer or from taking other actions contrary to the employer's interest. Another kind of risk is present where . . . the party paying the fees may have had a long-range interest in establishing a legal precedent and could do so only if the interests of the defendants themselves were sacrificed.

450 U.S. at 269–70, 101 S.Ct. at 1102–03, 67 L.Ed.2d at 229.

6. **Civil liability for ineffective assistance.** To what extent is a suit for damages against a defense attorney who has rendered ineffective assistance a useful method of setting and enforcing professional standards? Such cases are relatively rare. In Ferri v. Ackerman, 444 U.S. 193, 100 S.Ct. 402, 62 L.Ed.2d 355 (1979), an attorney appointed by a federal judge to represent an indigent defendant in a federal criminal prosecution was sued for malpractice in state court. Lower courts had sustained the attorney's claim that under federal law he was entitled to absolute immunity from suit, but the Supreme Court reversed on the ground that the role of the defense attorney is such that there is no need for conferring upon him the same immunity that is given to judges and prosecutors. Thus, the door to potential liability—and the setting of standards—was opened; however, in Polk County v. Dodson, 454 U.S. 312, 102 S.Ct. 445, 70 L.Ed.2d 509 (1981), the federal courthouse door was closed to some such cases. Respondent had sued his former state public defender in federal court in a civil rights action under 42 U.S.C.A. § 1983. The Supreme Court, in an opinion by Justice Powell, held that the public defender was not acting under color of state law and, therefore, could not be sued under Section 1983. The Court stressed that the duties of the public defender or appointed attorney are the same as privately-retained counsel and that those duties do not involve serving the public except as a by-product of participation on behalf of the client in the adversary process:

> Within the context of our legal system, the duties of a defense lawyer are those of a personal counselor and advocate. . . .[The adversary system] posits that a defense lawyer best serves the public, not by acting on behalf of the State or in concert with it, but rather by advancing "the undivided interests of his client." This is essentially a private function, traditionally filled by retained counsel, for which state office and authority are not needed.

454 U.S. at 318–19, 102 S.Ct. at 450, 70 L.Ed.2d at 516–17.

7. **Expert and investigative assistance for counsel.** To what extent should, or must, an indigent be entitled to public funding for expert and investigational assistance? Statutory provision for such aid is quite frequent. 18 U.S.C.A. § 3006A, "Adequate Representation of Defendants ...", provides:

(e) Services Other Than Counsel.

(1) Upon request.—Counsel for a person who is financially unable to obtain investigative, expert, or other services necessary for adequate representation may request them in an ex parte application. Upon finding, after appropriate inquiry in an ex parte proceeding, that the services are necessary and that the person is financially unable to obtain them, the court, or the United States magistrate if the services are required in connection with a matter over which he has jurisdiction, shall authorize counsel to obtain the services.

(2) Without prior request.—(A) Counsel appointed under this section may obtain, subject to later review, investigative, expert, and other services without prior authorization if necessary for adequate representation. Except as provided in subparagraph (B) of this paragraph, the total cost of services obtained without prior authorization may not exceed $300 and expenses reasonably incurred.

(B) The court, or the United States magistrate (if the services were rendered in a case disposed of entirely before the United States magistrate), may, in the interest of justice, and upon the finding that timely procurement of necessary services could not await prior authorization, approve payment for such services after they have been obtained, even if the cost of such services exceeds $300.

(3) Maximum amounts.—Compensation to be paid to a person for services rendered by him to a person under this subsection, or to be paid to an organization for services rendered by an employee thereof, shall not exceed $1,000, exclusive of reimbursement for expenses reasonably incurred, unless payment in excess of that limit is certified by the court, or by the United States magistrate if the services were rendered in connection with a case disposed of entirely before him, as necessary to provide fair compensation for services of an unusual character or duration, and the amount of the excess payment is approved by the chief judge of the circuit. The chief judge of the circuit may delegate such approval authority to an active circuit judge.

(4) Disclosure of fees.—The amounts paid under this subsection for services in any case shall be made available to the public.

The standard for determining whether requested assistance is "necessary" under these statutes, however, is not entirely clear. In United States v. Bass, 477 F.2d 723, 725 (9th Cir.1973), quoted with approval in United States v. Sims, 617 F.2d 1371, 1375 (9th Cir.1980), the court held:

The statute requires the district judge to authorize defense services when the defense attorney makes a timely request in circumstances in which a reasonable attorney would engage such services for a client having the independent financial means to pay for them.

But defendants have frequently experienced great difficulty convincing appellate courts that a trial court's refusal to authorize expenditures under these statutes is reversible error. In *Sims,* for example, the court noted that even an erroneous refusal to appoint the requested expert on eyewitness testimony would require reversal only if the defendant showed prejudice.

But in a few cases failure to provide assistance to counsel has been held reversible error on constitutional grounds. [T]he Supreme Court found a deprivation of due process and reversed a death sentence in Ake v. Oklahoma, 470 U.S. 68, 105 S.Ct. 1087, 84 L.Ed.2d 53 (1985). Justice Marshall wrote:

> This Court has long recognized that when a State brings its judicial power to bear on an indigent defendant in a criminal proceeding, it must take steps to assure that the defendant has a fair opportunity to present his defense. This elementary principle, grounded in significant part on the Fourteenth Amendment's due process guarantee of fundamental fairness, derives from the belief that justice cannot be equal where, simply as a result of his poverty, a defendant is denied the opportunity to participate meaningfully in a judicial proceeding in which his liberty is at stake.

> * * *

> Meaningful access to justice has been the consistent theme of these cases. We recognized long ago that mere access to the courthouse doors does not by itself assure a proper functioning of the adversary process, and that a criminal trial is fundamentally unfair if the State proceeds against an indigent defendant without making certain that he has access to the raw materials integral to the building of an effective defense. Thus, while the Court has not held that a State must purchase for the indigent defendant all the assistance that his wealthier counterpart might buy, see Ross v. Moffitt, 417 U.S. 600, 94 S.Ct. 2437, 41 L.Ed.2d 341 (1974), it has often reaffirmed that fundamental fairness entitles indigent defendants to "an adequate opportunity to present their claims fairly within the adversary system," id., at 612, 94 S.Ct., at 2444. To implement this principle, we have focused on identifying the "basic tools of an adequate defense or appeal," Britt v. North Carolina, 404 U.S. 226, 227, 92 S.Ct. 431, 433, 30 L.Ed.2d 400 (1971), and we have required that such tools be provided to those defendants who cannot afford to pay for them.

> * * *

> Three factors are relevant to this determination. The first is the private interest that will be affected by the action of the State. The second is the governmental interest that will be affected if the safeguard is to be provided. The third is the probable value of the additional or substitute procedural safeguards that are sought, and the risk of an erroneous deprivation of the affected interest if those safeguards are not provided.

> * * *

> We therefore hold that when a defendant demonstrates to the trial judge that his sanity at the time of the offense is to be a significant factor at trial, the State must, at a minimum, assure the defendant access to a competent psychiatrist who will conduct an appropriate examination and assist in evaluation, preparation, and presentation of the defense. This is not to say, of course, that the indigent defendant has a constitutional right to choose a psychiatrist of his personal liking or to receive funds to hire his own. Our concern is that the indigent defendant have access to a competent psychiatrist for the purpose we have discussed, and as in the case of the provision of counsel we leave to the State the decision on how to implement this right.

470 U.S. at 76–83, 105 S.Ct. at 1092–96, 84 L.Ed.2d at 61–66.

B.   Self-Representation and Waiver of Sixth Amendment Rights

The constitutional right to counsel is not so absolute that it cannot be waived. Most instances in which courts have confronted the issue have involved indigents, but it is clear that non-indigents have the same right to waive counsel. As a practical matter, some non-indigents may try to waive counsel merely because they do not choose to spend money for representation. This may be done simply because the non-indigent intends to plead guilty and if so it approximates a "pure waiver" situation. In addition, both indigents and non-indigents may also try to waive counsel because (1) they wish to stand trial, and believe that some unusual features of their cases can best be brought out if they have full control over the conduct of that trial, or (2) they have a general distrust of the bar, or (3) they are less concerned about the result of their cases than they are about using the court as a forum for exposure of political views.

These three situations represent a combination of the waiver problem with the problem of whether there is a right to act for one's self; if there is, whether it is statutory or constitutional in dimension; whether it must be asserted at any particular time; and under what circumstances it can be limited or lost. Whether the cases in this section dealing with self-representation by indigents are fully applicable to efforts of non-indigents to represent themselves should be considered.

The test for waiver of counsel most often stated is found in Johnson v. Zerbst, 304 U.S. 458, 58 S.Ct. 1019, 82 L.Ed. 1461 (1938). It requires that the waiver be intelligent and competent, a standard which must be particularized by the facts and circumstances of the case, " ... including the background, experience, and conduct of the accused." 304 U.S. at 464, 59 S.Ct. at 1023, 82 L.Ed. at 1466.

In Von Moltke v. Gillies, 332 U.S. 708, 68 S.Ct. 316, 92 L.Ed. 309 (1948), Mr. Justice Black laid down a more exacting standard:

We have said: "The constitutional right of an accused to be represented by counsel invokes, of itself, the protection of a trial court, in which the accused—whose life or liberty is at stake—is without counsel. This protecting duty imposes the serious and weighty responsibility upon the trial judge of determining whether there is an intelligent and competent waiver by the accused." To discharge this duty properly in light of the strong presumption against waiver of the constitutional right to counsel, a judge must investigate as long and as thoroughly as the circumstances of the case before him demand. The fact that an accused may tell him that he is informed of his right to counsel and desires to waive this right does not automatically end the judge's responsibility. To be valid such waiver must be made with an apprehension of the nature of the charges, the statutory offenses included within them, the range of allowable punishments thereunder, possible defenses to the charges and circumstances in mitigation thereof, and all other facts essential to a broad understanding of the whole matter. A judge can make certain that an accused's professed waiver of counsel is understandingly and wisely made only from a penetrating and comprehensive examination of all the circumstances under which such a plea is tendered.

This case graphically illustrates that a mere routine inquiry—the asking of several standard questions followed by the signing of a standard written waiver of counsel—may leave a judge entirely unaware of the facts essential to an informed decision that an accused has executed a valid waiver of his right to counsel.

332 U.S. at 723–24, 68 S.Ct. at 323, 92 L.Ed. at 320–21 (plurality opinion).

Ascertaining the validity of purported waivers of Sixth Amendment rights is further complicated by the principal case in this section, which establishes a constitutional right to self-representation. To the extent that a defendant must select either representation by counsel (and, if indigent, by court-provided counsel) or self-representation, is the process better conceptualized as one of "choice" rather than "waiver?" If so, does this make any difference?

Faretta v. California

Supreme Court of the United States, 1975.
422 U.S. 806, 95 S.Ct. 2525, 45 L.Ed.2d 562.

■ MR. JUSTICE STEWART delivered the opinion of the Court.

The Sixth and Fourteenth Amendments of our Constitution guarantee that a person brought to trial in any state or federal court must be afforded the right to the assistance of counsel before he can be validly convicted and punished by imprisonment. This clear constitutional rule has emerged from a series of cases decided here over the last 50 years. The question before us now is whether a defendant in a state criminal trial has a constitutional right to proceed *without* counsel when he voluntarily and intelligently elects to do so. Stated another way, the question is whether a State may constitutionally hail a person into its criminal courts and there force a lawyer upon him, even when he insists that he wants to conduct his own defense. It is not an easy question, but we have concluded that a State may not constitutionally do so.

I.

Anthony Faretta was charged with grand theft in an information filed in the Superior Court of Los Angeles County, California. At the arraignment, the Superior Court Judge assigned to preside at the trial appointed the public defender to represent Faretta. Well before the date of trial, however, Faretta requested that he be permitted to represent himself. Questioning by the judge revealed that Faretta had once represented himself in a criminal prosecution, that he had a high school education, and that he did not want to be represented by the public defender because he believed that that office was "very loaded down with . . . a heavy case load." The judge responded that he believed Faretta was "making a mistake" and emphasized that in further proceedings Faretta would receive no special favors. Nevertheless, after establishing that Faretta wanted to represent himself and did not want a lawyer, the judge, in a "preliminary ruling," accepted Faretta's waiver of the assistance of counsel. The judge indicated, however, that he might reverse this ruling if it later appeared that Faretta was unable adequately to represent himself.

Several weeks thereafter, but still prior to trial, the judge *sua sponte* held a hearing to inquire into Faretta's ability to conduct his own defense, and questioned him specifically about both the hearsay rule and the state law governing the challenge of potential jurors.[4] After consideration of

"THE COURT: In the Faretta matter, I brought you back down here to do some reconsideration as to whether or not you should continue to represent yourself.

"How have you been getting along on your research?

"THE DEFENDANT: Not bad, your Honor.

"Last night I put in the mail a 995 motion and it should be with the Clerk within the next day or two.

"THE COURT: Have you been preparing yourself for the intricacies of the trial of the matter?

"THE DEFENDANT: Well, your Honor, I was hoping that the case could possibly be disposed of on the 995.

"Mrs. Ayers informed me yesterday that it was the Court's policy to hear the pretrial motions at the time of trial. If possible, your Honor, I would like a date set as soon as the Court deems adequate after they receive the motion, sometime before trial.

"THE COURT: Let's see how you have been doing on your research.

"How many exceptions are there to the hearsay rule?

"THE DEFENDANT: Well, the hearsay rule would, I guess, be called the best evidence rule, your Honor. And there are several exceptions in case law, but in actual statutory law, I don't feel there is none.

"THE COURT: What are the challenges to the jury for cause?

"THE DEFENDANT: Well, there is twelve peremptory challenges.

"THE COURT: And how many for cause?

"THE DEFENDANT: Well, as many as the Court deems valid.

"THE COURT: And what are they? What are the grounds for challenging a juror for cause?

"THE DEFENDANT: Well, numerous grounds to challenge a witness—I mean, a juror, your Honor, one being the juror is perhaps suffered, was a victim of the same type of offense, might be prejudice toward the defendant. Any substantial

ground that might make the juror prejudice toward the defendant.

"THE COURT: Anything else?

"THE DEFENDANT: Well, a relative perhaps of the victim.

"THE COURT: Have you taken a look at that code section to see what it is?

"THE DEFENDANT: Challenge a juror?

"THE COURT: Yes.

"THE DEFENDANT: Yes, your Honor. I have done—

"THE COURT: What is the code section?

"THE DEFENDANT: On voir diring a jury, your Honor?

"THE COURT: Yes.

"THE DEFENDANT: I am not aware of the section right offhand.

"THE COURT: What code is it in?

"THE DEFENDANT: Well, the research I have done on challenging would be in Witkins Jurisprudence.

"THE COURT: Have you looked at any of the codes to see where these various things are taken up?

"THE DEFENDANT: No, your Honor, I haven't.

"THE COURT: Have you looked in any of the California Codes with reference to trial procedure?

"THE DEFENDANT: Yes, your Honor.

"THE COURT: What codes?

"THE DEFENDANT: I have done extensive research in the Penal Code, your Honor, and the Civil Code.

"THE COURT: If you have done extensive research into it, then tell me about it.

"THE DEFENDANT: On empaneling a jury, your Honor?

"THE COURT: Yes.

"THE DEFENDANT: Well, the District Attorney and the defendant, defense counsel, has both the right to 12 peremptory challenges of a jury. These 12 challenges are undisputable. Any reason that the defense or prosecution should feel that a juror would be inadequate to try the case or to rule on a case, they may then discharge that juror.

Faretta's answers, and observation of his demeanor, the judge ruled that Faretta had not made an intelligent and knowing waiver of his right to the assistance of counsel, and also ruled that Faretta had no constitutional right to conduct his own defense. The judge accordingly reversed his earlier ruling permitting self-representation and again appointed the public defender to represent Faretta. Faretta's subsequent request for leave to act as cocounsel was rejected, as were his efforts to make certain motions on his own behalf. Throughout the subsequent trial, the judge required that Faretta's defense be conducted only through the appointed lawyer from the public defender's office. At the conclusion of the trial, the jury found Faretta guilty as charged, and the judge sentenced him to prison.

The California Court of Appeal, relying upon a then recent California Supreme Court decision that had expressly decided the issue, affirmed the trial judge's ruling that Faretta had no federal or state constitutional right to represent himself. Accordingly, the appellate court affirmed Faretta's conviction. A petition for rehearing was denied without opinion, and the California Supreme Court denied review.[5] We granted certiorari. 415 U.S. 975, 94 S.Ct. 1559, 39 L.Ed.2d 870.

II.

In the federal courts, the right of self-representation has been protected by statute since the beginnings of our Nation. Section 35 of the Judiciary Act of 1789, 1 Stat. 73, 92 ... The right is currently codified in 28 U.S.C.A. § 1654.

With few exceptions, each of the several States also accords a defendant the right to represent himself in any criminal case. The constitutions of 36 States explicitly confer that right.[6] Moreover, many state courts have expressed the view that the right is also supported by the Constitution of the United States.

This Court has more than once indicated the same view. In Adams v. United States ex rel. McCann, 317 U.S. 269, 279, 63 S.Ct. 236, 241, 87 L.Ed. 268, the Court ... did recognize, albeit in dictum, an affirmative right of self-representation:

"But if there is a valid challenge due to grounds of prejudice or some other grounds, that these aren't considered in the 12 peremptory challenges. There are numerous and the defendant, the defense and the prosecution both have the right to make any inquiry to the jury as to their feelings toward the case."

5. The California courts' conclusion that Faretta had no constitutional right to represent himself was made in the context of the following not unusual rules of California criminal procedure: An indigent criminal defendant has no right to appointed counsel of his choice. ... The appointed counsel manages the lawsuit and has the final say in all but a few matters of trial strategy. ...A California conviction will not be reversed on grounds of ineffective assistance of counsel except in the extreme case where the quality of representation was so poor as to render the trial a "farce and a sham."

6. Some States grant the accused the right to be heard, or to defend, in person *and* by counsel . . . . .

Others grant the right to defend in person *or* by counsel. . . .

Still others provide the accused the right to defend either by himself, by counsel, or both. . . .

"The right to assistance of counsel and the *correlative right to dispense with a lawyer's help* are not legal formalisms. They rest on considerations that go to the substance of an accused's position before the law. . . .

"What were contrived as protections for the accused should not be turned into fetters. . . . To deny an accused a choice of procedure in circumstances where he, though a layman, is as capable as any lawyer of making an intelligent choice, is to impair the worth of great Constitutional safeguards by treating them as empty verbalisms.

" . . . When the administration of the criminal law . . . is hedged about as it is by the Constitutional safeguards for the protection of an accused, to deny him in the exercise of his free choice the right to dispense with some of these safeguards . . . is to imprison a man in his privileges and call it the Constitution." Id., at 279–280, 63 S.Ct., at 241–242 (emphasis added).

* * *

The United States Courts of Appeals have repeatedly held that the right of self-representation is protected by the Bill of Rights. . . .

This Court's past recognition of the right of self-representation, the federal court authority holding the right to be of constitutional dimension, and the state constitutions pointing to the right's fundamental nature form a consensus not easily ignored. "[T]he fact that a path is a beaten one," Mr. Justice Jackson once observed, "is a persuasive reason for following it." We confront here a nearly universal conviction, on the part of our people as well as our courts, that forcing a lawyer upon an unwilling defendant is contrary to his basic right to defend himself if he truly wants to do so.

III.

This consensus is soundly premised. The right of self-representation finds support in the structure of the Sixth Amendment as well as in the English and colonial jurisprudence from which the Amendment emerged.

A.

The Sixth Amendment includes a compact statement of the rights necessary to a full defense:

"In all criminal prosecutions, the accused shall enjoy the right . . . to be informed of the nature and cause of the accusation; to be confronted with the witnesses against him; to have compulsory process for obtaining witnesses in his favor, and to have the Assistance of Counsel for his defence."

* * *

The Sixth Amendment does not provide merely that a defense shall be made for the accused; it grants to the accused personally the right to make his defense. It is the accused, not counsel, who must be "informed of the nature and cause of the accusation," who must be "confronted with witnesses against him," and who must be accorded "compulsory process for obtaining witnesses in his favor." Although not stated in the Amendment in so many words, the right to self-representation—to make one's own defense personally—is thus necessarily implied by the structure of the Amendment. The right to defend is given directly to the accused; for it is he who suffers the consequences if the defense fails.

The counsel provision supplements this design. It speaks of the "assistance" of counsel, and an assistant, however expert, is still an assistant. The language and spirit of the Sixth Amendment contemplate that counsel like the other defense tools guaranteed by the Amendment, shall be an aid to a willing defendant—not an organ of the State interposed between an unwilling defendant and his right to defend himself personally. To thrust counsel upon the accused, against his considered wish, thus violates the logic of the Amendment. In such a case, counsel is not an assistant, but a master; and the right to make a defense is stripped of the personal character upon which the Amendment insists. It is true that when a defendant chooses to have a lawyer manage and present his case, law and tradition may allocate to the counsel the power to make binding decisions of trial strategy in many areas. . . . This allocation can only be justified, however, by the defendant's consent, at the outset, to accept counsel as his representative. An unwanted counsel "represents" the defendant only through a tenuous and unacceptable legal fiction. Unless the accused has acquiesced in such representation, the defense presented is not the defense guaranteed him by the Constitution, for, in a very real sense, it is not his defense.

B.

The Sixth Amendment, when naturally read, thus implies a right of self-representation. This reading is reinforced by the Amendment's roots in English legal history.

In the long history of British criminal jurisprudence, there was only one tribunal that ever adopted a practice of forcing counsel upon an unwilling defendant in a criminal proceeding. The tribunal was the Star Chamber. That curious institution, which flourished in the late 16th and early 17th centuries, was of mixed executive and judicial character, and characteristically departed from common-law traditions. . . .

The Star Chamber was swept away in 1641 by the revolutionary fervor of the Long Parliament. The notion of obligatory counsel disappeared with it.

By the common law of that time, it was not representation by counsel but self-representation that was the practice in prosecutions for serious crime. At one time, every litigant was required to "appear before the court in his own person and conduct his own cause in his own words." While a right to counsel developed early in civil cases and in cases of misdemeanor, a prohibition against the assistance of counsel continued for centuries in prosecutions for felony or treason. Thus, in the 16th and 17th centuries the accused felon or traitor stood alone, with neither counsel nor the benefit of other rights—to notice, confrontation and compulsory process—that we now associate with a genuinely fair adversary proceeding. The trial was merely a "long argument between the prisoner and the counsel for the

Crown." As harsh as this now seems, at least "the prisoner was allowed to make what statements he liked. . . . Obviously this public oral trial presented many more opportunities to a prisoner than the secret enquiry based on written depositions, which, on the continent had taken the place of a trial. . . ."

With the Treason Act of 1695, there began a long and important era of reform in English criminal procedure. The 1695 statute granted to the accused traitor the rights to a copy of the indictment, to have his witnesses testify under oath, and "to make . . . full defense, by counsel learned in the law." It also provided for court appointment of counsel, *but only if the accused so desired.* Thus, as new rights developed, the accused retained his established right "to make what statements he liked." The right to counsel was viewed as guaranteeing a choice between representation by counsel and the traditional practice of self-representation. The ban on counsel in felony cases, which had been substantially eroded in the courts, was finally eliminated by statute in 1836. In more recent years, Parliament has provided for court appointment of counsel in serious criminal cases, but only at the accused's request. At no point in this process of reform in England was counsel ever forced upon the defendant. . . .

C.

In the American colonies the insistence upon a right of self-representation was, if anything, more fervent than in England.

The colonists brought with them an appreciation of the virtues of self-reliance and a traditional distrust of lawyers. When the Colonies were first settled, "the lawyer was synonymous with the cringing Attorneys–General and Solicitors–General of the Crown and the arbitrary Justices of the King's Court, all bent on the conviction of those who opposed the King's prerogatives, and twisting the law to secure convictions." This prejudice gained strength in the colonies where "distrust of lawyers became an institution." Several Colonies prohibited pleading for hire in the 17th century. The prejudice persisted into the 18th century as "the lower classes came to identify lawyers with the upper class." The years of Revolution and Confederation saw an upsurge of anti-lawyer sentiment, a "sudden revival, after the War of the Revolution of the old dislike and distrust of lawyers as a class." In the heat of these sentiments the Constitution was forged.

This is not to say that the Colonies were slow to recognize the value of counsel in criminal cases. Colonial judges soon departed from ancient English practice and allowed accused felons the aid of counsel for their defense. At the same time, however, the basic right of self-representation was never questioned. We have found no instance where a colonial court required a defendant in a criminal case to accept as his representative an unwanted lawyer. Indeed, even where counsel was permitted, the general practice continued to be self-representation.

The right of self-representation was guaranteed in many colonial charters and declarations of rights. These early documents establish that the "right to counsel" meant to the colonists a right to choose between pleading through a lawyer and representing oneself. After the Declaration of Independence, the right of self-representation, along with other rights basic to the making of a defense, entered the new state constitutions in wholesale fashion. The right to counsel was clearly thought to supplement the primary right of the accused to defend himself, utilizing his personal rights to notice, confrontation and compulsory process. And when the Colonies or newly independent States provided by statute rather than by constitution for court appointment of counsel in criminal cases, they also meticulously preserved the right of the accused to defend himself personally.

The recognition of the right of self-representation was not limited to the state lawmakers. As we have noted, § 35 of the Judiciary Act of 1789, signed one day before the Sixth Amendment was proposed, guaranteed in the federal courts the right of all parties "to plead and manage their own cause personally or by the assistance of . . . counsel." See 1 Stat. 92 (1789) as amended, 28 U.S.C.A. § 1654 (1970). . . . No State or Colony had ever forced counsel upon an accused; no spokesman had ever suggested that such a practice would be tolerable, much less advisable. If anyone had thought that the Sixth Amendment, as drafted, failed to protect the long-respected right of self-representation, there would undoubtedly have been some debate or comment on the issue. But there was none.

In sum, there is no evidence that the colonists and the Framers ever doubted the right of self-representation, or imagined that this right might be considered inferior to the right of assistance of counsel. To the contrary, the colonists and the Framers, as well as their English ancestors, always conceived of the right to counsel as an "assistance" for the accused, to be used at his option, in defending himself. The Framers selected in the Sixth Amendment a form of words that necessarily implies the right of self-representation. That conclusion is supported by centuries of consistent history.

IV.

There can be no blinking the fact that the right of an accused to conduct his own defense seems to cut against the grain of this Court's decisions holding that the Constitution requires that no accused can be convicted and imprisoned unless he has been accorded the right to the assistance of counsel. See Powell v. Alabama, 287 U.S. 45, 53 S.Ct. 55, 77 L.Ed. 158; Johnson v. Zerbst, 304 U.S. 458, 58 S.Ct. 1019, 82 L.Ed. 1461; Gideon v. Wainwright, 372 U.S. 335, 83 S.Ct. 792, 9 L.Ed.2d 799; Argersinger v. Hamlin, 407 U.S. 25, 92 S.Ct. 2006, 32 L.Ed.2d 530. For it is surely true that the basic thesis of those decisions is that the help of a lawyer is essential to assure the defendant a fair trial. And a strong argument can surely be made that the whole thrust of those decisions must inevitably lead to the conclusion that a State may constitutionally impose a lawyer upon even an unwilling defendant.

But it is one thing to hold that every defendant, rich or poor, has the right to the assistance of counsel, and quite another to say that a State may compel a defendant to accept a lawyer he does not want. The value of state-appointed counsel was not unappreciated by the Founders, yet the notion of compulsory counsel was utterly foreign to them. And whatever else may be said of those who wrote the Bill of Rights, surely there can be no doubt that they understood the inestimable worth of free choice.

It is undeniable that in most criminal prosecutions defendants could better defend with counsel's guidance than by their own unskilled efforts. But where the defendant will not voluntarily accept representation by counsel, the potential advantage of a lawyer's training and experience can be realized, if at all, only imperfectly. To force a lawyer on a defendant can only lead him to believe that the law contrives against him. Moreover, it is not inconceivable that in some rare instances, the defendant might in fact present his case more effectively by conducting his own defense. Personal liberties are not rooted in the law of averages. The right to defend is personal. The defendant, and not his lawyer or the State, will bear the personal consequence of a conviction. It is the defendant, therefore, who must be free personally to decide whether in his particular case counsel is to his advantage. And although he may conduct his own defense ultimately to his own detriment, his choice must be honored out of "that respect for the individual which is the lifeblood of the law." Illinois v. Allen, 397 U.S. 337, 350–351, 90 S.Ct. 1057, 1064, 25 L.Ed.2d 353 (concurring opinion of Brennan, J.).[7]

V.

When an accused manages his own defense, he relinquishes, as a purely factual matter, many of the traditional benefits associated with the right to counsel. For this reason, in order to represent himself, the accused must "knowingly and intelligently" forego those relinquished benefits. Johnson v. Zerbst, 304 U.S. 458, 464–465, 58 S.Ct. 1019, 1023, 82 L.Ed. 1461. . . . Although a defendant need not himself have the skill and experience of a lawyer in order competently and intelligently to choose self-representation, he should be made aware of the dangers and disadvantages of self-representation, so that the record will establish that "he knows what he is doing and his choice is made with eyes open." Adams v. United States ex rel. McCann, 317 U.S. 269, 270, 63 S.Ct. 236, 242, 87 L.Ed. 268.

Here, weeks before trial, Faretta clearly and unequivocally declared to the trial judge that he wanted to represent himself and did not want counsel. The record affirmatively shows that Faretta was literate, competent, and understanding, and that he was voluntarily exercising his in-

---

7. We are told that many criminal defendants representing themselves may use the courtroom for deliberate disruption of their trials. But the right of self-representation has been recognized from our beginnings by federal law and by most of the States, and no such result has thereby occurred. Moreover, the trial judge may terminate self-representation by a defendant who deliberately engages in serious and obstructionist misconduct. See Illinois v. Allen, 397 U.S. 337, 90 S.Ct. 1057, 25 L.Ed.2d 353. Of course, a State may—even over objection by the accused—appoint a "standby counsel" to aid the accused if and when the accused requests help, and to be available to represent the accused in the event that termination of the defendant's self-representation is necessary. See United States v. Dougherty, 154 U.S.App. D.C. 76, 473 F.2d 1113, 1124–1126.

The right of self-representation is not a license to abuse the dignity of the courtroom. Neither is it a license not to comply with relevant rules of procedural and substantive law. Thus, whatever else may or may not be open to him on appeal, a defendant who elects to represent himself cannot thereafter complain that the quality of his own defense amounted to a denial of "effective assistance of counsel."

formed free will. The trial judge had warned Faretta that he thought it was a mistake not to accept the assistance of counsel, and that Faretta would be required to follow all the "ground rules" of trial procedure. We need make no assessment of how well or poorly Faretta had mastered the intricacies of the hearsay rule and the California code provisions that govern challenges of potential jurors on *voir dire.* For his technical legal knowledge, as such, was not relevant to an assessment of his knowing exercise of the right to defend himself.

In forcing Faretta, under these circumstances, to accept against his will a state-appointed public defender, the California courts deprived him of his constitutional right to conduct his own defense. Accordingly, the judgment before us is vacated, and the case is remanded for further proceedings not inconsistent with this opinion.

It is so ordered.

■ Mr. Chief Justice Burger, with whom Mr. Justice Blackmun and Mr. Justice Rehnquist join, dissenting.

...[T]here is nothing desirable or useful in permitting every accused person, even the most uneducated and inexperienced, to insist upon conducting his own defense to criminal charges. Moreover, there is no constitutional basis for the Court's holding and it can only add to the problems of an already malfunctioning criminal justice system. I therefore dissent.

...Its ultimate assertion that such a right is tucked between the lines of the Sixth Amendment is contradicted by the Amendment's language and its consistent judicial interpretation. ...[T]his Court's decisions have consistently included the right to counsel as an integral part of the bundle making up the larger "right to a defense as we know it." ...[I]n all but an extraordinarily small number of cases an accused will lose whatever defense he may have if he undertakes to conduct the trial himself.

* * *

In short, both the "spirit and the logic" of the Sixth Amendment are that every person accused of crime shall receive the fullest possible defense; in the vast majority of cases this command can be honored only by means of the expressly-guaranteed right to counsel, and the trial judge is in the best position to determine whether the accused is capable of conducting his defense. True freedom of choice and society's interest in seeing that justice is achieved can be vindicated only if the trial court retains discretion to reject any attempted waiver of counsel and insist that the accused be tried according to the Constitution. This discretion is as critical an element of basic fairness as a trial judge's discretion to decline to accept a plea of guilty. See Santobello v. New York, 404 U.S. 257, 262, 92 S.Ct. 495, 498–499, 30 L.Ed.2d 427 (1971).

[The dissent further argued that the judge and prosecutor are charged with the duty of insuring that justice, "in the broadest sense of that term," is achieved in every criminal trial, and that objective is ill-served "when an easy conviction is obtained due to the defendant's ill-advised decision to waive counsel."

The dissenters also argued that the majority's assumption that the accused who has elected to defend himself will not be heard to complain of it later ignores the role of appellate review, with the result that "many expensive and good-faith prosecutions will be nullified on appeal for reasons that trial courts are now deprived of the power to prevent." Editors.]

[Justice Blackmun's separate dissent, in which the Chief Justice and Justice Rehnquist joined, is omitted.]

NOTE

Standby counsel. In *Faretta,* the majority said in a footnote that "a State may—even over objection by the accused—appoint a 'standby counsel' to aid the accused if and when the accused requests help." Is it always impermissible, as the language from *Faretta* suggests, for standby counsel to interject himself into a trial without a request from the defendant? The Court dealt with this question in McKaskle v. Wiggins, 465 U.S. 168, 104 S.Ct. 944, 79 L.Ed.2d 122 (1984). Wiggins was permitted by the trial court to represent himself, but two standby attorneys were appointed to assist him. At various points in the trial, one or the other of the standby attorneys participated in the proceedings without specific invitation by Wiggins. Sometimes Wiggins approved of the participation and sometimes he did not. At some points in the trial, standby counsel participated at the specific request of Wiggins. Wiggins was convicted and, after exhausting state remedies, filed a federal petition for writ of habeas corpus claiming that the uninvited participation by standby counsel in his trial deprived him of his right to pro se representation under *Faretta.* The Fifth Circuit held for Wiggins on the ground that standby counsel is "to be seen, but not heard" unless and to the extent specifically requested by the *pro se* defendant. Wiggins v. Estelle, 681 F.2d 266 (5th Cir.1982). The Supreme Court granted the State of Texas' petition for writ of certiorari and, in an opinion authored by Justice O'Connor, reversed.

The Court specifically rejected the position of the Fifth Circuit. Instead, it adopted a two part test: a defendant's right of *pro se* representation is not violated if he maintains actual control over the defense and if counsel's participation does not destroy the jury's perception that the defendant is representing himself:

> First, the *pro se* defendant is entitled to preserve actual control over the case he chooses to present to the jury. This is the core of the *Faretta* right. If standby counsel's participation over the defendant's objection effectively allows counsel to make or substantially interfere with any significant tactical decisions, or to control the questioning of witnesses, or to speak *instead* of the defendant on any matter of importance, the *Faretta* right is eroded.

> Second, participation by standby counsel without the defendant's consent should not be allowed to destroy the jury's perception that the defendant is representing himself. The defendant's appearance in the status of one conducting his own defense is important in a criminal trial, since the right to appear *pro se* exists to affirm the accused's individual dignity and autonomy. . . . From the jury's perspective, the message conveyed by the defense may depend as much on the messenger as on the message itself. From the defendant's own point of view, the right to appear *pro se* can lose much of its importance if only the lawyers in the courtroom know that the right is being exercised.

465 U.S. at 178–79, 104 S.Ct. at 951, 79 L.Ed.2d at 133–34. The Court then examined counsel's uninvited participation in those portions of the trial that occurred outside the presence or hearing of the jury. It found no violation of the actual control standard, since Wiggins was given ample opportunity to participate in

all matters under discussion, the trial court repeatedly informed Wiggins that his tactical decisions, not those of standby counsel, would control, and in all instances of conflict the wishes of Wiggins were honored.

The Court characterized counsel's participation in front of the jury as "more problematic." At times, Wiggins invited counsel to participate in front of the jury, at times counsel participated without specific invitation and Wiggins appeared to approve, and at times Wiggins specifically disapproved of counsel's uninvited participation. The Court thought Wiggins' various positions were significant:

> *Faretta* does not require a trial judge to permit "hybrid" representation of the type Wiggins was actually allowed. But if a defendant is given the opportunity and elects to have counsel appear before the court or jury, his complaints concerning counsel's subsequent unsolicited participation lose much of their force. A defendant does not have a constitutional right to choreograph special appearances by counsel. Once a *pro se* defendant invites or agrees to any substantial participation by counsel, subsequent appearances by counsel must be presumed to be with the defendant's acquiescence, at least until the defendant expressly and unambiguously renews his request that standby counsel be silenced.

465 U.S. at 183, 104 S.Ct. at 953, 79 L.Ed.2d at 136.

The Court isolated standby counsel's role in assisting the defendant in understanding trial procedure and to achieve his own goals, such as by showing him how to get testimony or objects admitted into evidence, and explicitly approved of that role without any requirement of invitation by the defendant: "Participation by counsel to steer a defendant through the basic procedures of trial is permissible even in the unlikely event that it somewhat undermines the *pro se* defendant's appearance of control over his own defense." 465 U.S. at 184, 104 S.Ct. at 954, 79 L.Ed.2d at 137. Counsel's other unsolicited activities in front of the jury, while not "a model for future trials," were not so extensive as to undermine the jury's perception that Wiggins was representing himself.

Justice White, joined by Justices Brennan and Marshall, dissenting, criticized the majority for providing inadequate guidance to lower courts on the question of when standby counsel has gone too far. The dissent concluded that the actions of standby counsel in this case,

> distracted Wiggins and usurped his prerogatives, altered the tenor of the defense, disrupted the trial, undermined Wiggins' perception that he controlled his own fate, induced a belief—most assuredly unfounded, but sincerely held nevertheless—that "the law contrive[d] against him," and undoubtedly reduced Wiggins' credibility and prejudiced him in the eyes of the jury.

465 U.S. at 195–96, 104 S.Ct. at 960, 79 L.Ed.2d at 144.

CHAPTER 25

SENTENCING

Analysis

1143

Sentencing in a narrow sense is that stage of the criminal justice process involving decisions about what to do initially with convicted criminal offenders. Later decisions may also be involved, of course, and may be made by a variety of decisionmakers, including parole authorities. In a broader sense, however, the entire criminal justice process has sentencing implications for the suspect or defendant even if he is not prosecuted or convicted. Thus pre-trial diversion can be regarded as essentially a "sentencing" decision made at a very early stage of the process, sometimes by the police.

Sentencing in both senses has been the subject of a great deal of recent concern and law revision. Perhaps the most controversial recent development is the federal Sentencing Reform Act of 1984, considered at several places in this chapter. See Breyer, "The Federal Sentencing Guidelines and the Key Compromises Upon Which They Rest," 17 Hofstra L.Rev. 1 (1988); and von Hirsch, "Federal Sentencing Guidelines: The United States and Canadian Schemes Compared," IV Occasional Papers From The Center for Research in Crime and Justice at N.Y.U. School of Law (1988).

This chapter is an introduction to the major legal issues that touch upon sentencing. It lists the goals that might be pursued in the sentencing process, describes the manner in which the sentencing process might be structured, and explores several procedural issues concerning the carrying out of the sentencing task. The chapter then provides an introduction to some alternatives and supplements to sentences of imprisonment.

A.   Sentencing Goals

Underlying the sentencing process are various ideas of what sentencing might accomplish. These ideas have given rise to several commonly recognized philosophies which can be applied in sentencing tasks. Some are complementary; some are mutually exclusive. One or more of these philosophies is implicit in every sentencing decision, including legislative decisions as to how to structure sentencing systems.

BURNS AND MATTINA, SENTENCING 1–5 (1978)*

JUDICIAL PHILOSOPHIES OF SENTENCING

Judges . . . will necessarily be expressing their personal philosophy of the ends of the criminal law, whether they realize it or not. . . .

. . . [W]e can identify four basic ends which a sentencing judge may consider.

I. Deterrence:

Deterrence . . . is customarily looked at from two perspectives. One, commonly referred to as "specific" or "individual" deterrence, rests on the notion that the sentence imposed will deter the individual defendant from repetition of the behavior that brought him before the court in the first instance. . . .

The second perspective is that of "general" deterrence. This rests on the notion that by the sentence imposed on an individual defendant, and by communication of that sentence to others who might commit similar crimes, the latter will forego their projected criminal behavior out of fear they will suffer the same or similar sentence.

* * *

. . . One may argue . . . that general deterrence is more class-specific than crime-specific.

Consideration of the effectiveness of general deterrence also requires an evaluation of the means and extent of communicating sentencing information to the group of persons sought to be deterred. . . .

* * *

[I]f the criminal behavior involved is impulsive, tends to occur in the presence of high emotion and with little time for reflection (as, for example, most family homicides), the general deterrent rationale for sentencing may not apply or may apply only minimally. By contrast, where the criminal behavior is carefully planned and carried out over an extended period (such as certain criminal frauds, embezzlement, and the like), the very fact of a period for reflection by the criminal ought to make the general deterrent purpose more available.

II. Separation:

. . . This end is sometimes referred to as incapacitation or neutralization. Normally, separation is considered appropriate in the case of crimes that involve a grave risk to the personal peace and safety of members of the community. . . . The separation rationale assumes that the conduct in these crimes is so serious and the chance of repetition so great that the judge, acting for society, must conclude that protection of the public is the primary objective. . . . In a sense, imposition of a death sentence is based in part upon separation rationale.

---

* Published by The National Judicial   Reno, Nevada.
College located at The University of Nevada,

Even apart from homicides, in most jurisdictions armed robbery, rape, serious physical assault, residential burglary, and other similar crimes, carry lengthy maximum sentences. In these cases there has been an initial legislative determination that persons who commit such acts should be separated (or considered for separation) from society through imprisonment for a lengthy period of time. . . .

III. Rehabilitation:

. . . [I]f rehabilitation is the prime consideration, total confinement in a large central prison is rare . . .

Customarily, rehabilitation is . . . [the goal of] probation, either with no confinement involved or with a limited period of partial confinement. Partial confinement (a limited period of time in a county jail, work release, or other community treatment center) coupled with probation will usually be selected in cases where the judge believes that the primary goal of the sentence is to promote rehabilitation of the defendant. . . .

IV. Retribution:

The fourth major purpose of sentencing is frequently referred to as retribution (sometimes "punishment;" sometimes "vengeance"). . . . This notion incorporates a basic human feeling. . . . If law lacks a sanction, the argument runs, no reason exists for the law-abiding to obey the law when they see that those who violate it do not have to "pay." . . . The criminal offender has acted in violation of societal rules and must be "punished" in order that he or she receives "just deserts." This ingrained concept of punishment or retribution is the product of thousands of years of history, culture, tradition, religion and other societal forces.

To be valid as a principle of sentencing, retribution must be proportional. . . . Initially, the legislature, by fixing a maximum (e.g., five years for car theft) expresses societal estimation of the maximum retribution to be demanded. Thereafter, it is for the sentencing judge to decide how much the offender ought to "pay" in a given case, where retribution is either the primary, or a significant goal.

V. The Choice of Sentence:

. . . Frequently, the judge is faced with the dilemma of knowing that if he imposes a particular type of sentence to achieve one purpose, he thereby frustrates the likelihood of achieving another. . . .

B. Structuring the Sentencing System

The major issues presented by the need for a sentencing system are the amount of discretion that should exist and, to the extent that discretion is appropriate, upon whom the authority to exercise it should be conferred, and how it should be exercised and controlled. A partial historical perspective was provided by Chief Justice Burger in United States v. Grayson, 438 U.S. 41, 98 S.Ct. 2610, 57 L.Ed.2d 582 (1978):

In the early days of the Republic, when imprisonment had only recently emerged as an alternative to the death penalty, confinement in public stocks, or whipping in the town square, the period of incarceration was generally prescribed with specificity by the legislature. Each crime had its defined punishment. ... The "excessive rigidity of the [mandatory or fixed sentence] system" soon gave way in some jurisdictions, however, to a scheme permitting the sentencing judge— or jury—to consider aggravating and mitigating circumstances surrounding an offense, and, on that basis, to select a sentence within a *range* defined by the legislature. Tappan, Sentencing Under the Model Penal Code, 23 Law & Contemp.Prob. 528, 529 (1958). Nevertheless, the focus remained on the crime: Each particular offense was to be punished in proportion to the social harm caused by it and according to the offender's culpability. ... The purpose of incarceration remained, primarily, retribution and punishment.

Approximately a century ago, a reform movement asserting that the purpose of incarceration, and therefore the guiding consideration in sentencing, should be rehabilitation of the offender, dramatically altered the approach to sentencing. A fundamental proposal of this movement was a flexible sentencing system permitting judges and correctional personnel, particularly the latter, to set the release date of prisoners according to informed judgments concerning their potential for, or actual, rehabilitation and their likely recidivism. Indeed, the most extreme formulations of the emerging rehabilitation model, with its "reformatory sentence," posited that "convicts [regardless of the nature of their crime] can never be rightfully imprisoned except upon proof that it is unsafe for themselves and for society to leave them free, and when confined can never be rightfully released until they show themselves fit for membership in a free community." Lewis, The Indeterminate Sentence, 9 Yale L.J. 17, 27 (1899).

This extreme formulation, although influential, was not adopted unmodified by any jurisdiction. ... "The influences of legalism and realism were powerful enough ... to prevent the enactment of this form of indeterminate sentencing. Concern for personal liberty, skepticism concerning administrative decisions about prisoner reformation and readiness for release, insistence upon the preservation of some measure of deterrent emphasis, and other such factors, undoubtedly, led, instead, to a system—indeed, a complex of systems—in which maximum terms were generally employed." Id., at 530. ... To an unspecified degree, the sentencing judge is obligated to make his decision on the basis, among others, of predictions regarding the convicted defendant's potential, or lack of potential, for rehabilitation.

Indeterminate sentencing under the rehabilitation model presented sentencing judges with a serious practical problem: how rationally to make the required predictions so as to avoid capricious and arbitrary sentences, which the newly conferred and broad discretion placed within the realm of possibility. ...

438 U.S. at 45–48, 98 S.Ct. at 2613–14, 57 L.Ed.2d at 586–88. Obviously, parole authorities were presented with similar problems in exercising their role in traditional indeterminate sentencing.

Whether this discretion in sentencing judges and parole authorities is desirable and can be adequately regulated is, of course, a major concern. This section first addresses the nature of this sentencing discretion and then turns to its regulation by relatively traditional legal devices. Attention is then directed to recent proposals and reforms that substantially reduce and further structure the exercise of discretion in sentencing and release from imprisonment.

1.   THE PROBLEM OF DISCRETION IN SENTENCING

The indeterminate sentencing structure described by Chief Justice Burger in *Grayson* provides for substantial discretion in the sentencing judge and/or parole boards. Indeed, this discretion is seen as a major attribute of that structure. But is it reasonable to expect that this discretion will be exercised wisely? Effectively? Are legal controls on it desirable? Are they feasible? The present subsection places these issues in the judicial sentencing context existing prior to current reform efforts.

Frankel, Lawlessness in Sentencing
41 Cincinnati Law Review 1, 4–10 (1972).

The common form of criminal penalty provision confers upon the sentencing judge an enormous range of choice. . . .

The statutes granting such powers characteristically say nothing about the factors to be weighed in moving to either end of the spectrum or to some place between. . . . Even the most basic sentencing principles are not prescribed or stated with persuasive authority. There is, to be sure, a familiar litany in the literature of sentencing "purposes": retribution, deterrence ("special" and "general"), "denunciation," incapacitation, rehabilitation. Nothing tells us, however, when or whether any of these several goals are to be sought, or how to resolve such evident conflicts as that likely to arise in the effort to punish and rehabilitate all at once. . . .

. . . [W]e have no structure of rules, or even guidelines, affecting other elements arguably pertinent to the nature or severity of the sentence. Should it be a mitigating factor that the defendant is being sentenced upon a plea of guilty rather than a verdict against him? Should it count in his favor that he spared the public "trouble" and expense by waiving a jury? Should the sentence be more severe because the judge is convinced that the defendant perjured himself on the witness stand? Should churchgoing be considered to reflect favorably? Consistently with the first amendment, should it be considered at all? What factors should be assessed—and where, if anywhere, are comparisons to be sought—in gauging the relative seriousness of the specific offense and offender as against the spectrum of offenses by others in the same legal category? The list of such questions could be lengthened. Each is capable of being answered, and is answered by sentencing judges, in contradictory or conflicting, or at least differing, ways. There is no controlling requirement that any particular view be followed on any such subject by the sentencing judge.

With the delegation of power so unchanneled, it is surely no overstatement to say that "the new penology has resulted in vesting in judges and parole and probation agencies the greatest degree of uncontrolled power over the liberty of human beings that one can find in the legal system." The process would be totally unruly even if judges were superbly and uniformly trained for the solemn work of sentencing. As everyone knows, however, they are not trained at all. . . .

Viewed as a group, the people who enter upon service as trial judges are somewhat elderly, more experienced than most lawyers in litigation, almost totally unencumbered by learning or experience relevant to sentencing, and inclined by temperament and circumstance toward the major orthodoxies. Nothing they studied in law school touched our subject more than remotely. Probably a large majority had no contact, or trivial contact, with criminal proceedings of any kind during their years of practice. Those who had such exposure worked preponderantly on the prosecution side. Whether or not this produces a troublesome bias, the best that can be said is that prosecutors tend generally either to refrain altogether from taking positions on sentencing or to deal with the subject at a bargaining level somewhat removed from the plane of penological ideals.

Thus qualified, the new judge may be discovered within days or weeks fashioning judgments of imprisonment for long years. No training, formal or informal, precedes the first of these awesome pronouncements. Such formal and intentional education, other than from the job itself, as may happen along the way is likely to be fleeting, random, anecdotal, and essentially trivial. Shop talk with fellow judges—at least in my experience on a court where the judges are numerous, convivial, and likely to talk shop in the court lunchroom and other gathering places—rarely lights on problems of sentencing. Because the sentence is not appealable except on rare and extraordinary grounds, there is little occasion for the kind of relatively organized reflection instigated by the reading of advance sheets. The experienced trial judge, then, is one who has imposed many sentences, improving, we would hope, from a course of solitary brooding and conversations with probation officers, consulting in the end himself as the final authority, and perhaps sinking deeper each year the footings of premises that have never been tested by detached scrutiny or by open debate.

Given the sure combination of substantially unbounded discretion and decision-makers unrestrained by shared professional standards, it is not astonishing that the commonplace worry in any discussion of sentencing concerns "disparity." The factual basis for the worry is clear and huge; nobody doubts that essentially similar people in large numbers receive widely divergent sentences for essentially similar or identical crimes. The causes of the problem are equally clear: judges vary widely in their explicit views and "principles" affecting sentencing; they vary, too, in the accidents of birth and biography generating the guilts, the fears, and the rages that affect almost all of us at times and in ways we often cannot know. The judge who reports there is no surge of emotion when he imposes a stiff sentence is likely to be mistaken, unperceptive, or a person of alarmingly flat affect. It is unnecessary, though not irrelevant, to frighten ourselves with the statistical probability and direct personal knowledge that some percentage of judges may be psychotic. It is disturbing enough that a charged encounter like the sentencing proceeding, while it is the gravest of legal matters, should turn so arbitrarily upon the variegated passions and prejudices of individual judges.

* * *

But at least in one critical respect our training, our habits, and our accomplishments ought to be pertinent: we are taught and qualified to seek and formulate rules—that is, law. We are steeped in a tradition of hostility to unruliness, the condition we condemn when we denounce the arbitrary and the capricious. If we have not followed the tradition in sentencing, it may be because the effort is hopeless. Or it may be that we have not tried hard enough despite all the professions of concern. I join with many others in the belief that a much nearer approach to law and order in sentencing is possible as well as desirable.

* * *

There is no ... requirement [to give reasons] in the announcement of a prison sentence. Sometimes judges give reasons anyway, or reveal in colloquy the springs of their action. The explanations or revelations sometimes disclose reasoning so perverse or mistaken that the sentence, normally unreviewable, must be invalidated on appeal. Most trial judges (to my impressionistic and conversational knowledge, at least) say little or nothing, certainly far less than a connected "explanation" or rationale of the sentence. Many, aware of their unreviewable powers, and sharing a common aversion to being reversed, are perhaps motivated by the view (not unknown on trial benches) that there is safety in silence. It is likely that the judge, not expected to explain, has never organized a full and coherent explanation even for himself. Some judges use the occasion of sentencing to flaunt or justify themselves by moral pronunciamentos and excoriations of the defendant. This has no relation to the serious and substantial idea that the community's "denunciation" is a—possibly the—chief aim of sentencing. It is, in any event, not kin to the reasoned decisions for which judges are commissioned.

The judge's failure to explain is part of a more pervasive silence that makes sentencing and its sequelae so much a shadowland of doubt, ignorance, and fragmented responsibility. ...

2. CONTROLLING SENTENCING DISCRETION BY APPELLATE REVIEW

If the existence of substantial discretion in the sentencing judge is in fact a matter of serious concern, one response is to attempt to regulate that discretion by traditional means such as appellate review. This subsection addresses such efforts, first by judicial review of a sentencing judges' consideration of specific matters, and, second, by judicial review of the final sentence imposed by the sentencing judge.

a. APPELLATE REVIEW OF SENTENCING CONSIDERATIONS

Among the legal controls that might be placed upon sentencing discretion is review of a sentencing judge's decision to consider certain information in imposing sentence. The principal case deals with the appropriateness of consideration in sentencing of what the judge believes was the defendant's false trial testimony. If it is determined that at least in some circumstances certain factors should not be considered, it is then necessary to consider whether judicial review of the sentencing decision is an effective method of preventing their consideration.

United States v. Grayson

Supreme Court of the United States, 1978.
438 U.S. 41, 98 S.Ct. 2610, 57 L.Ed.2d 582.

■ Mr. Chief Justice Burger delivered the opinion of the Court.

We granted certiorari to review a holding of the Court of Appeals that it was improper for a sentencing judge, in fixing the sentence within the statutory limits, to give consideration to the defendant's false testimony observed by the judge during the trial.

In August 1975, respondent Grayson was confined in a federal prison camp under a conviction for distributing a controlled substance. ...[H]e escaped but was apprehended....He was indicted for prison escape....

Grayson testified in his own defense. ...

Grayson's version of the facts was contradicted by the Government's rebuttal evidence and by cross-examination on crucial aspects of his story.
...

The jury returned a guilty verdict, whereupon the District Judge ordered the United States Probation Office to prepare a presentence report. At the sentencing hearing, the judge stated:

> "I'm going to give my reasons for sentencing in this case with clarity, because one of the reasons may well be considered by a Court of Appeals to be impermissible; and although I could come into this Court Room and sentence this Defendant to a five-year prison term without any explanation at all, I think it is fair that I give the reasons so that if the Court of Appeals feels that one of the reasons which I am about to enunciate is an improper consideration for a trial judge, then the Court will be in a position to reverse this court and send the case back for resentencing.

> "In my view a prison sentence is indicated, and the sentence that the Court is going to impose is to deter you, Mr. Grayson, and others who are similarly situated. Secondly, *it is my view that your defense was a complete fabrication without the slightest merit whatsoever. I feel it is proper for me to consider that fact in the sentencing, and I will do so.*" (Emphasis added.)

He then sentenced Grayson to a term of two years' imprisonment, consecutive to his unexpired sentence.

On appeal, a divided panel of the Court of Appeals for the Third Circuit directed that Grayson's sentence be vacated and that he be resentenced by the District Court without consideration of false testimony. . . .

We granted certiorari to resolve conflicts between holdings of the Courts of Appeals. . . . We reverse.

* * *

A defendant's truthfulness or mendacity while testifying on his own behalf, almost without exception, has been deemed probative of his attitudes toward society and prospects for rehabilitation and hence relevant to sentencing. . . . Judge Marvin Frankel's analysis for the Second Circuit is persuasive:

"The effort to appraise 'character' is, to be sure, a parlous one, and not necessarily an enterprise for which judges are notably equipped by prior training. Yet it is in our existing scheme of sentencing one clue to the rational exercise of discretion. If the notion of 'repentence' is out of fashion today, the fact remains that a manipulative defiance of the law is not a cheerful datum for the prognosis a sentencing judge undertakes. . . . Impressions about an individual being sentenced—the likelihood that he will transgress no more, the hope that he may respond to rehabilitative efforts to assist with a lawful future career, the degree to which he does or does not deem himself at war with his society—are, for better or worse, central factors to be appraised under our theory of 'individualized' sentencing. The theory has its critics. While it lasts, however, a fact like the defendant's readiness to lie under oath before the judge who will sentence him would seem to be among the more precise and concrete of the available indicia." United States v. Hendrix, 505 F.2d 1233, 1236 (1974).

Only one Circuit has directly rejected the probative value of the defendant's false testimony in his own defense. In Scott v. United States, 135 U.S.App.D.C. 377, 382, 419 F.2d 264, 269 (1969), the court argued that

"the peculiar pressures placed upon a defendant threatened with jail and the stigma of conviction make his willingness to deny the crime an unpromising test of his prospects for rehabilitation if guilty. It is indeed unlikely that many men who commit serious offenses would balk on principle from lying in their own defense. The guilty man may quite sincerely repent his crime but yet, driven by the urge to remain free, may protest his innocence in a court of law."

. . . The *Scott* rationale rests not only on the realism of the psychological pressures on a defendant in the dock—which we can grant—but also on a deterministic view of human conduct that is inconsistent with the underlying precepts of our criminal justice system. A "universal and persistent" foundation stone in our system of law, and particularly in our approach to punishment, sentencing and incarceration, is the "belief in freedom of the human will and a consequent ability and duty of the normal individual to choose between good and evil." Morissette v. United States, 342 U.S. 246, 250, 72 S.Ct. 240, 243, 96 L.Ed. 288 (1952). . . . Given that long accepted view of the "ability and duty of the normal individual to choose," we must conclude that the defendant's readiness to lie under oath—especially when, as here, the trial court finds the lie to be flagrant—may be deemed probative of his prospects for rehabilitation.

* * *

...The right guaranteed by law to a defendant is narrowly the right to testify truthfully in accordance with the oath—unless we are to say that the oath is mere ritual without meaning. This view of the right involved is confirmed by the unquestioned constitutionality of perjury statutes, which punish those who willfully give false testimony. ...Further support for this is found in an important limitation on a defendant's right to the assistance of counsel: Counsel ethically cannot assist his client in presenting what the attorney has reason to believe is false testimony. ...Assuming, *arguendo*, that the sentencing judge's consideration of defendants' untruthfulness in testifying has any chilling effect on a defendant's decision to testify falsely, that effect is entirely permissible. There is no protected right to commit perjury.

...Nothing we say today requires a sentencing judge to enhance, in some wooden or reflex fashion, the sentences of all defendants whose testimony is deemed false. Rather, we are reaffirming the authority of a sentencing judge to evaluate carefully a defendant's testimony on the stand, determine—with a consciousness of the frailty of human judgment— whether that testimony contained willful and material falsehoods, and, if so, assess in light of all the other knowledge gained about the defendant the meaning of that conduct with respect to his prospects for rehabilitation and restoration to a useful place in society. Awareness of such a process realistically cannot be deemed to affect the decision of an accused but unconvicted defendant to testify truthfully in his own behalf.

Accordingly, we reverse the judgment of the Court of Appeals and remand for reinstatement of the sentence of the District Court.

Reversed and remanded.

■ MR. JUSTICE STEWART, with whom MR. JUSTICE BRENNAN and MR. JUSTICE MARSHALL join, dissenting.

The Court begins its consideration of this case with the assumption that the respondent gave false testimony at his trial. But there has been no determination that his testimony was false. This respondent was given a greater sentence than he would otherwise have received—how much greater we have no way of knowing—solely because a single judge *thought* that he had not testified truthfully. In essence, the Court holds today that *whenever* a defendant testifies in his own behalf and is found guilty, he opens himself to the possibility of an enhanced sentence. Such a sentence is nothing more nor less than a penalty imposed on the defendant's exercise of his constitutional and statutory rights to plead not guilty and to testify in his own behalf.

* * *

NOTES

1. **Accepting responsibility as a sentencing criterion.** Section 3C1.1 of the Federal Sentencing Guidelines provides an increased penalty if the defendant

has "willfully impeded or obstructed, or attempted to impede or obstruct the administration of justice during the investigation or prosecution...." The Commentary to that section lists "testifying untruthfully" as conduct which "may provide a basis for applying this adjustment." However, section 3E1.1 provides for a reduction in penalty if "the defendant clearly demonstrates a recognition and affirmative acceptance of personal responsibility for the offense...."

In United States v. Gonzalez, 897 F.2d 1018 (9th Cir.1990), a United States Court of Appeals rejected Fifth and Sixth Amendment challenges to application of section 3E1.1. Gonzales argued that the reduction in sentence for acceptance of responsibility was effectively unavailable to those defendants who exercise their right to have a jury trial instead of pleading guilty, unless they also sacrifice their Fifth Amendment privilege against self-incrimination. The court agreed that a defendant who protests innocence throughout trial may have difficulty in later accepting responsibility for the crime "without appearing to contradict his previous stance." But this difficulty does not encourage perjury in violation of the Fifth Amendment; and the Sixth Amendment right to a jury trial is not sacrificed by the provision because a defendant "may manifest sincere contrition despite the exercise of his right to go to trial—as when he goes to trial to assert and preserve issues unrelated to factual guilt...." 897 F.2d at 1021.

2.   **Perjurious testimony.** United States v. Dunnigan, 507 U.S. 87, 113 S.Ct. 1111, 122 L.Ed.2d 445 (1993) raised the question of increasing punishment under the Sentencing Guidelines because the trial judge believed the defendant committed perjury in her trial testimony. Five witnesses testified for the Government as to defendant's involvement in cocaine trafficking. Defendant testified on her own behalf and denied any involvement. Following conviction, the trial judge increased the punishment under § C1.1 of the Guidelines because he believed she committed perjury at trial. The Court of Appeals set aside the sentence, distinguishing United States v. Grayson (Casebook p. 1147) on the ground that Grayson was based on the greater need for rehabilitation demonstrated by a defendant's committing perjury, while the Sentencing Guidelines base enhancement on punishment considerations. Also, the Court of Appeals believed that Grayson did not support the rigid enhancement imposed by the Guidelines.

The Supreme Court, in an opinion by Justice Kennedy for a unanimous Court, reversed. Grayson did not state that rehabilitation is the only justification for increasing a sentence because the defendant committed perjury. There are other considerations:

> [A]   defendant who commits a crime and then perjures herself in an unlawful attempt to avoid responsibility is more threatening to society and less deserving of leniency than a defendant who does not so defy the trial process. The perjuring defendant's willingness to frustrate judicial proceedings to avoid criminal liability suggests the need for incapacitation and retribution is heightened as compared with the defendant charged with the same crime who allows judicial proceedings to progress without resorting to perjury.

507 U.S. at 97–98, 113 S.Ct. at 1118, 122 L.Ed.2d at 455. Just because a defendant testifies in his own defense and is convicted does not mean his testimony was perjurious:

> [A]n accused may give inaccurate testimony due to confusion, mistake or faulty memory. In other instances, an accused may testify to matters such as lack of capacity, insanity, duress or self-defense. Her testimony may be truthful, but the jury may nonetheless find the testimony insufficient to excuse criminal liability or prove lack of intent. For these reasons, if a defendant objects to a sentence enhancement resulting from her trial testimony, a district court must review the evidence and make independent findings necessary to establish a

willful impediment to or obstruction of justice, or an attempt to do the same
* * *.

507 U.S. at 95, 113 S.Ct. at 1117, 122 L.Ed.2d at 454.

3. **Refusing to cooperate with law enforcement authorities.** That cooperation with the police may result in a more lenient sentence for the criminal defendant is well established. But should a refusal to cooperate be considered in imposing a harsher sentence than would otherwise be the case? In Roberts v. United States, 445 U.S. 552, 100 S.Ct. 1358, 63 L.Ed.2d 622 (1980), the defendant had confessed his involvement in a conspiracy to distribute heroin but refused to name other dealers in his community in exchange for a favorable disposition of his case. The District Court imposed consecutive rather than concurrent terms and gave as one of its reasons the defendant's refusal to name names. Upholding consideration of this factor as proper, the Supreme Court observed that "gross indifference to the duty to report known criminal behavior remains a badge of irresponsible citizenship" and that the defendant had "rejected an 'obligation of community life' that should be recognized before rehabilitation can begin." It brushed aside the defendant's claim that his refusal was motivated by fear of retaliation and self-incrimination because these explanations were never offered to the sentencing court.

4. **Right to remain silent at sentencing.** Does a defendant who enters a plea of guilty waive his right to remain silent at the sentencing phase of the case? The defendant in Mitchell v. United States, 526 U.S. 314, 119 S.Ct. 1307, 143 L.Ed.2d 424 (1999) entered a plea of guilty to four drug distribution counts, the punishment for which depended upon the quantity of drugs she distributed and could have been as short as one year or as long as life. She reserved her right to contest at sentencing the amount of drugs she distributed. At sentencing, there was testimony from accomplices as to the amount of drugs she normally distributed over a period of time as part of the conspiracy. Based upon that testimony, the District Court concluded it was required to impose a sentence of at least ten years and imposed a ten year sentence. At sentencing, the court stated that he "held it against" the defendant that she did not testify at sentencing to minimize the quantity of drugs she distributed. The Court of Appeals upheld the sentence but the Supreme Court, in an opinion by Justice Kennedy, reversed. The Court held that neither the entry of a plea of guilty nor the colloquy that accompanies such a plea is a waiver of the defendant's right not to incriminate herself at sentencing. Justice Kennedy commented that accepting the Government's contrary position would mean

> prosecutors could indict without specifying the quantity of drugs involved, obtain a guilty plea, and then put the defendant on the stand at sentencing to fill in the drug quantity. The result would be to enlist the defendant as an instrument in his or her own condemnation, undermining the long tradition and vital principle that criminal proceedings rely on accusations proved by the Government, not on inquisitions conducted to enhance its own prosecutorial power.

526 U.S. at ___, 119 S.Ct. at 1313.

The Court also ruled that the Fifth Amendment prohibits the trial court from drawing an adverse inference from the defendant's silence at sentencing:

> The concerns which mandate the rule against negative inferences at a criminal trial apply with equal force at sentencing. Without question, the stakes are high: Here, the inference drawn by the District Court from petitioner's silence may have resulted in decades of added imprisonment. The Government often has a motive to demand a severe sentence, so the central purpose of the

privilege—to protect a defendant from being the unwilling instrument of his or her own condemnation—remains of vital importance.

526 U.S. at ___, 119 S.Ct. at 1315. Justice Scalia, joined by The Chief Justice and Justices O'Connor and Thomas, dissented, taking the position that the defendant still retained a privilege against self-incrimination at sentencing but that the Fifth Amendment was not violated by the District Court drawing an adverse inference from her assertion of that right. Justice Thomas, dissenting separately, called for a re-examination of Griffin v. California and its progeny, which established the no adverse inference rule for the guilt/innocence phase of trials.

5. **Imposing a more severe sentence following appellate reversal.** In North Carolina v. Pearce, 395 U.S. 711, 89 S.Ct. 2072, 23 L.Ed.2d 656 (1969), the Supreme Court held:

> Neither the double jeopardy provision nor the Equal Protection Clause imposes an absolute bar to a more severe sentence upon reconviction [following reversal of a conviction on appeal]. A trial judge is not constitutionally precluded, in other words, from imposing a new sentence, whether greater or less than the original sentence, in the light of events subsequent to the first trial that may have thrown new light upon defendant's "life, health, habits, conduct, and mental and moral propensities." Williams v. New York, 337 U.S. 241, 245, 69 S.Ct. 1079, 1082, 93 L.Ed. 1337 (1949). Such information may come to the judge's attention from evidence adduced at the second trial itself, from a new presentence investigation, from the defendant's prison record, or possibly from other sources. The freedom of a sentencing judge to consider the defendant's conduct subsequent to the first conviction in imposing a new sentence is no more than consonant with the principle, fully approved in Williams v. New York, supra, that a State may adopt the "prevalent modern philosophy of penology that the punishment should fit the offender and not merely the crime." . . .

395 U.S. at 723, 89 S.Ct. at 2079–80, 23 L.Ed.2d at 668.

The Court, however, went on to state:

> This Court has never held that the States are required to establish avenues of appellate review, but it is now fundamental that, once established, these avenues must be kept free of unreasoned distinctions that can only impede open and equal access to the courts. . . .

> Due process of law, then, requires that vindictiveness against a defendant for having successfully attacked his first conviction must play no part in the sentence he receives after a new trial. And since the fear of such vindictiveness may unconstitutionally deter a defendant's exercise of the right to appeal or collaterally attack his first conviction, due process also requires that a defendant be freed of apprehension of such a retaliatory motivation on the part of the sentencing judge.

> In order to assure the absence of such a motivation, we have concluded that whenever a judge imposes a more severe sentence upon a defendant after a new trial, the reasons for his doing so must affirmatively appear. Those reasons must be based upon objective information concerning identifiable conduct on the part of the defendant occurring after the time of the original sentencing proceeding. And the factual data upon which the increased sentence is based must be made part of the record, so that the constitutional legitimacy of the increased sentence may be fully reviewed on appeal.

395 U.S. at 724–26, 89 S.Ct. at 2080–81, 23 L.Ed.2d at 669–70.

In Wasman v. United States, 468 U.S. 559, 104 S.Ct. 3217, 82 L.Ed.2d 424 (1984), the Court considered the question whether *Pearce* was violated. Petitioner had been convicted of a criminal offense and received a sentence of six months' imprisonment to be followed by three years' probation. At the time of sentencing, petitioner had another charge pending against him. The sentencing judge stated he did not take the pending charge into account in fixing the sentence. Petitioner appealed his conviction and received a new trial. In the meantime, he was convicted on the pending charge and received two years' probation. Upon re-conviction for the first offense, the same trial judge sentenced petitioner to two years' imprisonment, stating he was taking into account the conviction which occurred between the first and second trials of the case. The Supreme Court, in an opinion by The Chief Justice, held these events did not violate *Pearce:*

> Consideration of a criminal conviction obtained in the interim between an original sentencing and a sentencing after retrial is manifestly legitimate. This amply rebuts any presumption of vindictiveness. Here, the trial judge's justification is plain even from the record of petitioner's first sentencing proceeding; the judge informed the parties that, although he did not consider pending *charges* when sentencing a defendant, he always took into account prior criminal *convictions.* This, of course, was proper; indeed, failure to do so would have been inappropriate.

468 U.S. at 569–70, 104 S.Ct. at 3224, 82 L.Ed.2d at 434.

6. **Imposing a more severe sentence following trial court granting of a new trial.** In Texas v. McCullough, 475 U.S. 134, 106 S.Ct. 976, 89 L.Ed.2d 104 (1986), the respondent was convicted of murder and sentenced by the jury to 20 years' imprisonment. He filed a motion for new trial on the basis of prosecutorial misconduct, which was granted by the trial judge. In the second trial, respondent elected to be sentenced by the trial judge. He was again convicted of murder and the trial judge sentenced him to 50 years' imprisonment. The trial judge justified the sentence on the ground that two witnesses had testified during the second trial who had not testified during the first and had stated that respondent, rather than his accomplice, had slashed the throat of the victim, and that during the second trial the trial judge learned for the first time that respondent had been released from prison only four months before the offense was committed. The trial judge also stated that had she been the sentencer after the first trial she would have imposed more than the 20 years assessed by the jury. The Texas appellate courts set aside the sentence on the ground it violated North Carolina v. Pearce, but the Supreme Court in an opinion authored by Chief Justice Burger reversed.

The majority concluded that because the trial judge, rather than an appellate court, set aside the first conviction there should be no presumption that she acted vindictively in selecting the second sentence. The majority also concluded that the presumption is inapplicable because a different sentencer was involved in the second trial than the first—that there can be no claim she imposed a harsher sentence after the first conviction was set aside than she imposed before. The majority also concluded that if the presumption of vindictiveness of *Pearce* were applicable, it was sufficiently rebutted in this case. *Pearce* was not intended to restrict the sentencer to taking into account conduct of the defendant that occurred after the first conviction was set aside. Rather, it permits consideration of any objective information justifying the increased sentence. The trial testimony of the two new witnesses and the new information about McCullough's criminal history amply rebut any presumption of vindictiveness that might be present. Justice Brennan concurred in the judgment on the ground that the *Pearce* presumption should not apply here where it was the trial judge herself who granted the new trial. Justice Marshall, joined by Justices Blackmun and Stevens, dissented.

7. **Change from plea to trial following reversal.** Should it make a difference under North Carolina v. Pearce if the conviction that was set aside was based on a plea of guilty while the second conviction was based on a trial? In Alabama v. Smith, 490 U.S. 794, 109 S.Ct. 2201, 104 L.Ed.2d 865 (1989), respondent was charged with burglary, rape and sodomy. He plead guilty to burglary and rape and the State dismissed the sodomy charge. He was sentenced to 30 years' imprisonment on each offense to run concurrently. Later, he succeeded in vacating the pleas on the ground the trial court had improperly admonished him. The sodomy charge was reinstated and respondent went to trial on all three charges. He was convicted of all three and the same trial judge who presided at the first trial imposed concurrent life sentences on the burglary and sodomy convictions and a consecutive 150 year sentence on the rape conviction. The Supreme Court, in an opinion by The Chief Justice, held this sequence of events did not violate North Carolina v. Pearce. Information was presented during the trial of the case, not presented when the guilty pleas were accepted, that respondent repeatedly raped and sodomized the victim at knife point for over an hour in her own bedroom next to the bedroom where her three small children were sleeping. The Court concluded

> that when a greater penalty is imposed after trial than was imposed after a prior guilty plea, the increase in sentence is not more likely than not attributable to the vindictiveness on the part of the sentencing judge. Even when the same judge imposes both sentences, the relevant sentencing information available to the judge after the plea will usually be considerably less than that available after a trial. ... [I]n the course of the proof at trial the judge may gather a fuller appreciation of the nature and extent of the crimes charged. The defendant's conduct during trial may give the judge insights into his moral character and suitability for rehabilitation.... Finally, after trial, the factors that may have indicated leniency as consideration for the guilty plea are no longer present.

490 U.S. at 801, 109 S.Ct. at 2205–06, 104 L.Ed.2d at 873–74. Justice Marshall dissented on the ground that any increase in punishment following re-conviction is a violation of double jeopardy guarantees. What implications, if any, does the majority's reasoning have on the appropriateness of post plea bargain sentences?

b.   APPELLATE REVIEW OF THE SENTENCES IMPOSED

Sentencing discretion might also be controlled or regulated by judicial review of the sentence ultimately imposed. The National Academy of Science commented that "in virtually all common law jurisdictions except the United States, appellate review of sentences has been the principal method used to develop principles for and achieve consistency in sentencing." National Academy of Science Panel on Sentencing Research, I Research on Sentencing: The Search for Reform 141 (1983). Over half of American jurisdictions permit appellate review of sentences that are within statutory limits. IV American Bar Association Standards for Criminal Justice 20.7 (1980). The standards for review, however, vary tremendously and are often quite limited. Some jurisdictions authorize modification by the appellate court of sentences simply found to be "excessive." But in others no relief is available on appeal unless the sentence is found "manifestly excessive," "clearly erroneous," or an "abuse of discretion." See Zalman, Appellate Review of Sentences and the Antinomy of Law Reform, 1983 Det.C.L.Rev. 1513, 1513–14.

As the principal case in this subsection indicates, appellate review can also be accomplished as a matter of federal constitutional law.

Can appellate review be realistically accomplished, given that the appellate courts do not have first hand opportunities to observe witnesses and the defendant himself? If appellate review is provided, what standard of review should be used? Are the criteria applied in the principal case appropriate?

Solem v. Helm

Supreme Court of the United States, 1983.
463 U.S. 277, 103 S.Ct. 3001, 77 L.Ed.2d 637.

■ JUSTICE POWELL delivered the opinion of the Court.

The issue presented is whether the Eighth Amendment proscribes a life sentence without possibility of parole for a seventh nonviolent felony.

I

By 1975 the State of South Dakota had convicted respondent Jerry Helm of six nonviolent felonies. In 1964, 1966, and 1969 Helm was convicted of third-degree burglary. In 1972 he was convicted of obtaining money under false pretenses. In 1973 he was convicted of grand larceny. And in 1975 he was convicted of third-offense driving while intoxicated. . . . [A]lcohol was a contributing factor in each case.

In 1979 Helm was charged with uttering a "no account" check for $100. . . . Helm pleaded guilty.

Ordinarily the maximum punishment for uttering a "no account" check would have been five years imprisonment in the state penitentiary and a $5,000 fine. . . . As a result of his criminal record, however, Helm was subject to South Dakota's recidivist statute:

> "When a defendant has been convicted of at least three prior convictions [*sic*] in addition to the principal felony, the sentence for the principal felony shall be enhanced to the sentence for a Class 1 felony."
> . . .

The maximum penalty for a "Class 1 felony" was life imprisonment in the state penitentiary and a $25,000 fine. . . . Moreover, South Dakota law explicitly provides that parole is unavailable: . . .

Immediately after accepting Helm's guilty plea, the South Dakota Circuit Court sentenced Helm to life imprisonment. . . . The court explained:

> " 'I think you certainly earned this sentence and certainly proven that you're an habitual criminal and the record would indicate that you're beyond rehabilitation and that the only prudent thing to do is to lock you up for the rest of your natural life, so you won't have further victims of your crimes, just be coming back before Courts. You'll have plenty of time to think this one over.' " . . .

The South Dakota Supreme Court, in a 3–2 decision, affirmed the sentence despite Helm's argument that it violated the Eighth Amendment.

* * *

In November 1981, Helm sought habeas relief in the United States District Court for the District of South Dakota. Helm argued, among other things, that his sentence constituted cruel and unusual punishment under the Eighth and Fourteenth Amendments. Although the District Court recognized that the sentence was harsh, it concluded that this Court's recent decision in Rummel v. Estelle, 445 U.S. 263, 100 S.Ct. 1133, 63 L.Ed.2d 382 (1980), was dispositive. It therefore denied the writ.

The United States Court of Appeals for the Eighth Circuit reversed. 684 F.2d 582 (1982). The Court of Appeals noted that Rummel v. Estelle was distinguishable. Helm's sentence of life without parole was qualitatively different from Rummel's life sentence with the prospect of parole because South Dakota has rejected rehabilitation as a goal of the criminal justice system. The Court of Appeals examined the nature of Helm's offenses, the nature of his sentence, and the sentence he could have received in other States for the same offense. It concluded, on the basis of this examination, that Helm's sentence was "grossly disproportionate to the nature of the offense." 684 F.2d, at 587. It therefore directed the District Court to issue the writ unless the State resentenced Helm. Ibid.

We granted certiorari to consider the Eighth Amendment question presented by this case. 459 U.S. 986, 103 S.Ct. 339, 74 L.Ed.2d 381 (1982). We now affirm.

II

The Eighth Amendment declares: "Excessive bail shall not be required, nor excessive fines imposed, nor cruel and unusual punishments inflicted." The final clause prohibits not only barbaric punishments, but also sentences that are disproportionate to the crime committed.

A

The principle that a punishment should be proportionate to the crime is deeply rooted and frequently repeated in common-law jurisprudence. ...

* * *

B

The constitutional principle of proportionality has been recognized explicitly in this Court for almost a century. In the leading case of Weems v. United States, 217 U.S. 349, 30 S.Ct. 544, 54 L.Ed. 793 (1910), the defendant had been convicted of falsifying a public document and sentenced to 15 years of "cadena temporal," a form of imprisonment that included hard labor in chains and permanent civil disabilities. ...The Court endorsed the principle of proportionality as a constitutional standard, see, e.g., id., at 372–373, 30 S.Ct., at 551, and determined that the sentence before it was "cruel in its excess of imprisonment," id., at 377, 30 S.Ct., at 553, as well as in its shackles and restrictions.

The Court next applied the principle to invalidate a criminal sentence in Robinson v. California, 370 U.S. 660, 82 S.Ct. 1417, 8 L.Ed.2d 758 (1962). A 90–day sentence was found to be excessive for the crime of being " 'addicted to the use of narcotics.' …Even one day in prison would be a cruel and unusual punishment for the 'crime' of having a common cold." Ibid.

Most recently, the Court has applied the principle of proportionality to hold capital punishment excessive in certain circumstances. Enmund v. Florida, 458 U.S. 782, 102 S.Ct. 3368, 73 L.Ed.2d 1140 (1982) (death penalty excessive for felony murder when defendant did not take life, attempt to take life, or intend that a life be taken or that lethal force be used); Coker v. Georgia, 433 U.S. 584, 592, 97 S.Ct. 2861, 2866, 53 L.Ed.2d 982 (1977) (plurality opinion) ("sentence of death is grossly disproportionate and excessive punishment for the crime of rape"); id., at 601, 97 S.Ct., at 2870 (Powell, J., concurring in the judgment in part and dissenting in part) ("ordinarily death is disproportionate punishment for the crime of raping an adult woman"). …

C

* * *

…It is true that the "penalty of death differs from all other forms of criminal punishment, not in degree but in kind." Furman v. Georgia, 408 U.S. 238, 306, 92 S.Ct. 2726, 2760, 33 L.Ed.2d 346 (1972) (Stewart, J., concurring). As a result, "our decisions [in] capital cases are of limited assistance in deciding the constitutionality of the punishment" in a noncapital case. Rummel v. Estelle, 445 U.S., at 272, 100 S.Ct., at 1138. We agree, therefore, that, "[o]utside the context of capital punishment, *successful* challenges to the proportionality of particular sentences [will be] exceedingly rare," ibid. (emphasis added); see Hutto v. Davis, 454 U.S., at 374, 102 S.Ct., at 705. This does not mean, however, that proportionality analysis is entirely inapplicable in noncapital cases.

In sum, we hold as a matter of principle that a criminal sentence must be proportionate to the crime for which the defendant has been convicted. Reviewing courts, of course, should grant substantial deference to the broad authority that legislatures necessarily possess in determining the types and limits of punishments for crimes, as well as to the discretion that trial courts possess in sentencing convicted criminals. But no penalty is *per se* constitutional. As the Court noted in Robinson v. California, 370 U.S., at 667, 82 S.Ct., at 1420, a single day in prison may be unconstitutional in some circumstances.

III

A

When sentences are reviewed under the Eighth Amendment, courts should be guided by objective factors that our cases have recognized. First, we look to the gravity of the offense and the harshness of the penalty. …

Second, it may be helpful to compare the sentences imposed on other criminals in the same jurisdiction. If more serious crimes are subject to the same penalty, or to less serious penalties, that is some indication that the punishment at issue may be excessive. . . .

Third, courts may find it useful to compare the sentences imposed for commission of the same crime in other jurisdictions. . . .

* * *

B

Application of these factors assumes that courts are competent to judge the gravity of an offense, at least on a relative scale. . . . Comparisons can be made in light of the harm caused or threatened to the victim or society, and the culpability of the offender. . . . For example, as the criminal laws make clear, nonviolent crimes are less serious than crimes marked by violence or the threat of violence. . . .

There are other accepted principles that courts may apply in measuring the harm caused or threatened to the victim or society. The absolute magnitude of the crime may be relevant. Stealing a million dollars is viewed as more serious than stealing a hundred dollars—a point recognized in statutes distinguishing petty theft from grand theft. . . . Few would dispute that a lesser included offense should not be punished more severely than the greater offense. . . . It also is generally recognized that attempts are less serious than completed crimes. . . . Similarly, an accessory after the fact should not be subject to a higher penalty than the principal.

Turning to the culpability of the offender, there are again clear distinctions that courts may recognize and apply. In *Enmund* the Court looked at the petitioner's lack of intent to kill in determining that he was less culpable than his accomplices. Most would agree that negligent conduct is less serious than intentional conduct. . . . A court, of course, is entitled to look at a defendant's motive in committing a crime. Thus a murder may be viewed as more serious when committed pursuant to a contract. . . .

This list is by no means exhaustive. It simply illustrates that there are generally accepted criteria for comparing the severity of different crimes on a broad scale, despite the difficulties courts face in attempting to draw distinctions between similar crimes.

C

Application of the factors that we identify also assumes that courts are able to compare different sentences. This assumption, too, is justified. The easiest comparison, of course, is between capital punishment and noncapital punishments, for the death penalty is different from other punishments in kind rather than degree. For sentences of imprisonment, the problem is not so much one of ordering, but one of line-drawing. It is clear that a 25–year sentence generally is more severe than a 15–year sentence, but in most cases it would be difficult to decide that the former violates the Eighth Amendment while the latter does not. Decisions of this kind, although troubling, are not unique to this area. . . .

* * *

IV

It remains to apply the analytical framework established by our prior decisions to the case before us. We first consider the relevant criteria, viewing Helm's sentence as life imprisonment without possibility of parole. We then consider the State's argument that the possibility of commutation is sufficient to save an otherwise unconstitutional sentence.

A

Helm's crime was "one of the most passive felonies a person could commit." State v. Helm, 287 N.W.2d, at 501 (Henderson, J., dissenting). It involved neither violence nor threat of violence to any person. The $100 face value of Helm's "no account" check was not trivial, but neither was it a large amount. One hundred dollars was less than half the amount South Dakota required for a felonious theft. It is easy to see why such a crime is viewed by society as among the less serious offenses. . . .

Helm, of course, was not charged simply with uttering a "no account" check, but also with being an habitual offender.[1] And a State is justified in punishing a recidivist more severely than it punishes a first offender. Helm's status, however, cannot be considered in the abstract. His prior offenses, although classified as felonies, were all relatively minor. All were nonviolent and none was a crime against a person. Indeed, there was no minimum amount in either the burglary or the false pretenses statutes, and the minimum amount covered by the grand larceny statute was fairly small.

Helm's present sentence is life imprisonment without possibility of parole. Barring executive clemency, . . ., Helm will spend the rest of his life in the state penitentiary. This sentence is far more severe than the life sentence we considered in Rummel v. Estelle. Rummel was likely to have been eligible for parole within 12 years of his initial confinement, a fact on which the Court relied heavily. . . . Helm's sentence is the most severe punishment that the State could have imposed on any criminal for any crime. Only capital punishment, a penalty not authorized in South Dakota when Helm was sentenced, exceeds it.

* * *

In sum, there were a handful of crimes that were necessarily punished by life imprisonment: murder, and, on a second or third offense, treason, first degree manslaughter, first degree arson, and kidnapping. There was a larger group for which life imprisonment was authorized in the discretion of the sentencing judge, including: treason, first degree manslaughter, first degree arson, and kidnapping; attempted murder, placing an explosive device on an aircraft, and first degree rape on a second or third offense; and any felony after three prior offenses. Finally, there was a large group of

---

1. Helm, who was 36 years old when he was sentenced, is not a professional criminal. The record indicates an addiction to alcohol, and a consequent difficulty in holding a job. His record involves no instance of violence of any kind. Incarcerating him for life without possibility of parole is unlikely to advance the goals of our criminal justice system in any substantial way. Neither Helm nor the State will have an incentive to pursue clearly needed treatment for his alcohol problem, or any other program of rehabilitation.

very serious offenses for which life imprisonment was not authorized, including a third offense of heroin dealing or aggravated assault.

Criminals committing any of these offenses ordinarily would be thought more deserving of punishment than one uttering a "no account" check—even when the bad-check writer had already committed six minor felonies. Moreover, there is no indication in the record that any habitual offender other than Helm has ever been given the maximum sentence on the basis of comparable crimes. It is more likely that the possibility of life imprisonment under § 22-7-8 generally is reserved for criminals such as fourth-time heroin dealers, while habitual bad-check writers receive more lenient treatment.[2] In any event, Helm has been treated in the same manner as, or more severely than, criminals who have committed far more serious crimes.

Finally, we compare the sentences imposed for commission of the same crime in other jurisdictions. . . . it is clear that Helm could not have received such a severe sentence in 48 of the 50 States. . . . even under Nevada law, a life sentence without possibility of parole is merely authorized in these circumstances. See Nev.Rev.Stat. § 207.010(2) (1981). We are not advised that any defendant such as Helm, whose prior offenses were so minor, actually has received the maximum penalty in Nevada. It appears that Helm was treated more severely than he would have been in any other State.

B

The State argues that the present case is essentially the same as Rummel v. Estelle, for the possibility of parole in that case is matched by the possibility of executive clemency here. The State reasons that the Governor could commute Helm's sentence to a term of years. We conclude, however, that the South Dakota commutation system is fundamentally different from the parole system that was before us in *Rummel.*

As a matter of law, parole and commutation are different concepts, despite some surface similarities. Parole is a regular part of the rehabilitative process. Assuming good behavior, it is the normal expectation in the vast majority of cases. The law generally specifies when a prisoner will be eligible to be considered for parole, and details the standards and procedures applicable at that time. . . . Thus it is possible to predict, at least to some extent, when parole might be granted. Commutation, on the other hand, is an *ad hoc* exercise of executive clemency. A Governor may commute a sentence at any time for any reason without reference to any standards.

* * *

2. The State contends that § 22-7-8 is more lenient than the Texas habitual offender statute in *Rummel,* for life imprisonment under § 22-7-8 is discretionary rather than mandatory. Brief for Petitioner 22. Helm, however, has challenged only his own sentence. No one suggests that § 22-7-8 may not be applied constitutionally to fourth-time heroin dealers or other violent criminals. Thus we do not question the legislature's judgment. Unlike in *Rummel,* a lesser sentence here could have been entirely consistent with both the statute and the Eighth Amendment. See Note, Disproportionality in Sentences of Imprisonment, 79 Colum.L.Rev. 1119, 1160 (1979).

The Texas and South Dakota systems in particular are very different. In *Rummel,* the Court did not rely simply on the existence of some system of parole. Rather it looked to the provisions of the system presented, . . . Thus Rummel . . . could have expected to become eligible, in the normal course of events, in only 12 years.

In South Dakota commutation is more difficult to obtain than parole. . . . In fact, no life sentence has been commuted in over eight years, . . . while parole—where authorized—has been granted regularly during that period, ... Furthermore, even if Helm's sentence were commuted, he merely would be eligible to be considered for parole. Not only is there no guarantee that he would be paroled, but the South Dakota parole system is far more stringent than the one before us in *Rummel.* . . .[3]

The possibility of commutation is nothing more than a hope for "an *ad hoc* exercise of clemency." It is little different from the possibility of executive clemency that exists in every case in which a defendant challenges his sentence under the Eighth Amendment. Recognition of such a bare possibility would make judicial review under the Eighth Amendment meaningless.

V

The Constitution requires us to examine Helm's sentence to determine if it is proportionate to his crime. Applying objective criteria, we find that Helm has received the penultimate sentence for relatively minor criminal conduct. He has been treated more harshly than other criminals in the State who have committed more serious crimes. He has been treated more harshly than he would have been in any other jurisdiction, with the possible exception of a single State. We conclude that his sentence is significantly disproportionate to his crime, and is therefore prohibited by the Eighth Amendment. The judgment of the Court of Appeals is accordingly

Affirmed.

■ CHIEF JUSTICE BURGER, with whom JUSTICE WHITE, JUSTICE REHNQUIST, and JUSTICE O'CONNOR join, dissenting.

The controlling law governing this case is crystal clear, but today the Court blithely discards any concept of *stare decisis,* trespasses gravely on the authority of the States, and distorts the concept of proportionality of punishment by tearing it from its moorings in capital cases. Only two Terms ago, we held in Rummel v. Estelle, 445 U.S. 263, 100 S.Ct. 1133, 63 L.Ed.2d 382 (1980), that a life sentence imposed after only a *third* nonviolent felony conviction did not constitute cruel and unusual punishment under the Eighth Amendment. Today, the Court ignores its recent precedent and holds that a life sentence imposed after a *seventh* felony convic-

---

3. Assume, for example, that in 1979 the Governor had commuted Helm's sentence to a term of 40 years (his approximate life expectancy). Even if Helm were a model prisoner, he would not have been eligible for parole until he had served over 21 years— more than twice the *Rummel* minimum. And this comparison is generous to South Dakota's position. If Rummel had been sentenced to 40 years rather than life, he could have been eligible for parole in less than 7 years.

tion constitutes cruel and unusual punishment under the Eighth Amendment. Moreover, I reject the fiction that all Helm's crimes were innocuous or nonviolent. Among his felonies were three burglaries and a third conviction for drunk driving. By comparison Rummel was a relatively "model citizen." Although today's holding cannot rationally be reconciled with *Rummel,* the Court does not purport to overrule *Rummel.* I therefore dissent.

I

A

...What the Court means is that a sentence is unconstitutional if it is more severe than five justices think appropriate. In short, all sentences of imprisonment are subject to appellate scrutiny....

* * *

...This analysis is completely at odds with the reasoning of our recent holding in *Rummel,* in which, of course, Justice Powell dissented.

B

The facts in *Rummel* bear repeating. Rummel was convicted in 1964 of fraudulent use of a credit card; in 1969, he was convicted of passing a forged check; finally, in 1973 Rummel was charged with obtaining money by false pretenses, which is also a felony under Texas law. These three offenses were indeed nonviolent. Under Texas' recidivist statute, which provides for a mandatory life sentence upon conviction for a third felony, the trial judge imposed a life sentence as he was obliged to do after the jury returned a verdict of guilty of felony theft.

Rummel, in this Court, advanced precisely the same arguments that respondent advances here; we rejected those arguments notwithstanding that his case was stronger than respondent's. The test in *Rummel* which we rejected would have required us to determine on an abstract moral scale whether Rummel had received his "just desserts" for his crimes. We declined that invitation; today the Court accepts it. Will the Court now recall Rummel's case so five justices will not be parties to "disproportionate" criminal justice?

...[E]ven a cursory review of our cases shows that this type of proportionality review has been carried out only in a very limited category of cases, and never before in a case involving solely a sentence of imprisonment. ...

* * *

...In language quoted incompletely by the Court, ante, at 3009, n. 14, the *Rummel* Court stated:

> "Given the *unique nature* of the punishments considered in *Weems* and in the death penalty cases, one could argue without fear of contradiction by any decision of this Court that for crimes concededly classified and classifiable as felonies, that is, as punishable by significant terms of imprisonment in a state penitentiary, the *length of the*

sentence actually imposed is purely a matter of legislative prerogative." 445 U.S., at 274, 100 S.Ct., at 1139. (Emphasis added.)

Five Justices joined this clear and precise limiting language.

...[T]he *Rummel* Court emphasized that drawing lines between different sentences of imprisonment would thrust the Court inevitably "into the basic line-drawing process that is pre-eminently the province of the legislature" and produce judgments that were no more than the visceral reactions of individual Justices. Ibid.

The *Rummel* Court categorically rejected the very analysis adopted by the Court today. ...

First, it rejected the distinctions Rummel tried to draw between violent and nonviolent offenses, noting that "the absence of violence does not always affect the strength of society's interest in deterring a particular crime or in punishing a particular individual." Ibid. Similarly, distinctions based on the amount of money stolen are purely "subjective" matters of line drawing. Id., at 275–276, 100 S.Ct., at 1140.

Second, the Court squarely rejected Rummel's attempt to compare his sentence with the sentence he would have received in other States—an argument that the Court today accepts. The *Rummel* Court explained that such comparisons are flawed for several reasons. ...Perhaps most important, such comparisons trample on fundamental concepts of federalism. Different states surely may view particular crimes as more or less severe than other states. Stealing a horse in Texas may have different consequences and warrant different punishment than stealing a horse in Rhode Island or Washington, D.C. ...

Finally, we flatly rejected Rummel's suggestion that we measure his sentence against the sentences imposed by Texas for other crimes: ...

Rather, we held that the severity of punishment to be accorded different crimes was peculiarly a matter of legislative policy. Ibid.

In short, *Rummel* held that the length of a sentence of imprisonment is a matter of legislative discretion; this is so particularly for recidivist statutes. I simply cannot understand how the Court can square *Rummel* with its holding that "a criminal sentence must be proportionate to the crime for which the defendant has been convicted."[4]

If there were any doubts as to the meaning of *Rummel,* they were laid to rest last Term in Hutto v. Davis, 454 U.S. 370, 102 S.Ct. 703, 70 L.Ed.2d 556 (1982) *(per curiam).* There a United States District Court held that a 40-year sentence for the possession of nine ounces of marijuana violated the Eighth Amendment. The District Court applied almost exactly the same analysis adopted today by the Court. ...

...We reversed in a brief *per curiam* opinion, holding that *Rummel* had disapproved each of the "objective" factors on which the District Court

---

4. Although Rummel v. Estelle, 445 U.S. 263, 274, n. 11, 100 S.Ct. 1133, 1139, n. 11, 63 L.Ed.2d 382 (1980), conceded that "a proportionality principle [might] come into play ...if a legislature made overtime parking a felony punishable by life imprisonment," the majority has not suggested that respondent's crimes are comparable to overtime parking. Respondent's seven felonies are far more severe than Rummel's three.

and *en banc* Court of Appeals purported to rely. 454 U.S., at 373, 102 S.Ct., at 704. It was therefore clear error for the District Court to have been guided by these factors, which, paradoxically, the Court adopts today.

...*Hutto* makes crystal clear that under *Rummel* it is error for appellate courts to second-guess legislatures as to whether a given sentence of imprisonment is excessive in relation to the crime, as the Court does today.

...While the doctrine of *stare decisis* does not absolutely bind the Court to its prior opinions, a decent regard for the orderly development of the law and the administration of justice requires that directly controlling cases be either followed or candidly overruled.[5] Especially is this so with respect to two key holdings only three years old.

II

Although historians and scholars have disagreed about the Framers' original intentions, the more common view seems to be that the Framers viewed the Cruel and Unusual Punishments Clause as prohibiting the kind of torture meted out during the reign of the Stuarts. Moreover, it is clear that until 1892, over 100 years after the ratification of the Bill of Rights, not a single Justice of this Court even asserted the doctrine adopted for the first time by the Court today. The prevailing view up to now has been that the Eighth Amendment reaches only the *mode* of punishment and not the length of a sentence of imprisonment. In light of this history, it is disingenuous for the Court blandly to assert that "[t]he constitutional principle of proportionality has been recognized explicitly in this Court for almost a century." That statement seriously distorts history and our cases.

* * *

By asserting the power to review sentences of imprisonment for excessiveness the Court launches into uncharted and unchartable waters. Today it holds that a sentence of life imprisonment, without the possibility of parole, is excessive punishment for a seventh allegedly "nonviolent" felony. How about the eighth "nonviolent" felony? The ninth? The twelfth? Suppose one offense was a simple assault? Or selling liquor to a minor? Or

---

5. I do not read the Court's opinion as arguing that respondent's sentence of life imprisonment without possibility of parole is so different from Rummel's sentence of life imprisonment with the possibility of parole as to permit it to apply the proportionality review used in the death penalty cases, e.g., Coker v. Georgia, 433 U.S. 584, 97 S.Ct. 2861, 53 L.Ed.2d 982 (1977), to the former although not the latter. Nor would such an argument be tenable. As was noted in Woodson v. North Carolina, 428 U.S. 280, 305, 96 S.Ct. 2978, 2991, 49 L.Ed.2d 944 (1976) (opinion of Justice Stewart, Justice Powell, and Justice Stevens),

"[T]he penalty of death is qualitatively different from a sentence of imprison-ment. Death, in its finality, differs more from life imprisonment than a 100–year prison term differs from one of only a year or two. Because of that qualitative difference, there is a corresponding difference in the need for reliability in the determination that death is the appropriate punishment in a specific case."

The greater need for reliability in death penalty cases cannot support a distinction between a sentence of life imprisonment with possibility of parole and a sentence of life imprisonment without possibility of parole, especially when an executive commutation is permitted as in South Dakota.

statutory rape? Or price-fixing? The permutations are endless and the Court's opinion is bankrupt of realistic guiding principles. Instead, it casually lists several allegedly "objective" factors and arbitrarily asserts that they show respondent's sentence to be "significantly disproportionate" to his crimes. Must all these factors be present in order to hold a sentence excessive under the Eighth Amendment? How are they to be weighed against each other? Suppose several States punish severely a crime that the Court views as trivial or petty? I can see no limiting principle in the Court's holding.

There is a real risk that this holding will flood the appellate courts with cases in which equally arbitrary lines must be drawn. It is no answer to say that appellate courts must review criminal convictions in any event; up to now, that review has been on the validity of the judgment, not the sentence. The vast majority of criminal cases are disposed of by pleas of guilty, and ordinarily there is no appellate review in such cases. To require appellate review of all sentences of imprisonment—as the Court's opinion necessarily does—will "administer the *coupe de grace* to the courts of appeal as we know them." H. Friendly, Federal Jurisdiction: A General View 36 (1973). This is judicial usurpation with a vengeance; Congress has pondered for decades the concept of appellate review of sentences and has hesitated to act.

* * *

NOTES

1. **Cruel and unusual punishment for drug possession.** The Supreme Court re-visited the Solem v. Helm issue in Harmelin v. Michigan, 501 U.S. 957, 111 S.Ct. 2680, 115 L.Ed.2d 836 (1991). Petitioner was convicted of possessing 672 grams of cocaine and sentenced to a mandatory term of life imprisonment without possibility of parole. He contended the sentence violated Eighth Amendment because it was disproportionate to the crime and because it was mandatory. The Supreme Court upheld petitioner's sentence and in doing so delivered five different opinions. Justice Scalia announced the judgment of the Court and delivered an opinion. In Part V of that opinion, joined by Chief Justice Rehnquist and Justices O'Connor, Kennedy and Souter, the Court rejects the argument that the sentence in this case was cruel and unusual because it was mandatory and, therefore, precluded the sentencer from taking mitigating circumstances into account. "Severe, mandatory penalties may be cruel, but they are not unusual in the constitutional sense, having been employed in various forms throughout our Nation's history." It is true that a requirement of individualization of sentence has been imposed in death penalty cases but there is a "qualitative difference between death and all other penalties."

It is true that petitioner's sentence is unique in that it is the second most severe known to the law; but life imprisonment *with* possibility of parole is also unique in that it is the third most severe. And if petitioner's sentence forecloses some "flexible techniques" for later reducing his sentence, * * * it does not foreclose all of them, since there remain the possibilities of retroactive legislative reduction and executive clemency. In some cases, moreover, there will be negligible difference between life without parole and other sentences of imprisonment—for example, a life sentence with eligibility for parole after 20 years, or even a lengthy term sentence without eligibility, given to a 65–year–old man.

> But even where the difference is the greatest, it cannot be compared with death.

501 U.S. at 996, 111 S.Ct. at 2702, 115 L.Ed.2d at 865. Justice Scalia, writing for himself and Chief Justice Rehnquist, contended that the Eighth Amendment does not prescribe a constitutional requirement of proportionality of penalty to offense and argued that *Solem* should be overruled. Justice Kennedy, joined by Justices O'Connor and Souter, rejected Justice Scalia's view of the Eighth Amendment and contended that *"stare decisis* counsels our adherence to the narrow proportionality principle that has existed in our Eighth Amendment jurisprudence for 80 years." He then compared the seriousness of petitioner's offense with that of Solem. The cocaine possessed in this case would produce between 32,500 and 65,000 doses. Petitioner's "crime threatened to cause grave harm to society:"

> Studies * * * demonstrate a direct nexus between illegal drugs and crimes of violence * * *. 57 percent of a national sample of males arrested in 1989 for homicide tested positive for illegal drugs * * *. The comparable statistics for assault, robbery, and weapons arrests were 55, 73 and 63 percent, respectively * * *. In Detroit, Michigan in 1988, 68 percent of a sample of male arrestees and 81 percent of a sample of female arrestees tested positive for illegal drugs * * *. And last year an estimated 60 percent of the homicides in Detroit were drug-related, primarily cocaine-related.

501 U.S. at 1003, 111 S.Ct. at 2706, 115 L.Ed.2d at 870. Since petitioner's punishment is not disproportionate to his offense, there is no need to perform an analysis comparing his sentence to those imposed on others. As to the mandatory feature of the Michigan sentencing scheme,

> The scheme provides clear notice of the severe consequences that attach to possession of drugs in wholesale amounts, thereby giving force to one of the first purposes of criminal law—deterrence. In this sense, the Michigan scheme may be as fair, if not more so, than other sentencing systems in which the sentencer's discretion or the complexity of the scheme obscures the possible sanction for a crime, resulting in a shock to the offender who learns the severity of his sentence only after he commits the crime.

501 U.S. at 1008, 111 S.Ct. at 2708, 115 L.Ed.2d at 873.

Justice White, joined by Justices Blackmun and Stevens, dissented, emphasizing the fact that this was petitioner's first criminal conviction. Examining the case in light of the factors in *Solem,* he would have found the sentence to violate the Eighth Amendment. Justice Marshall agreed with Justice White's opinion, except that portion asserting that the Eighth Amendment does not proscribe the death penalty. Justice Stevens, joined by Justice Blackmun, also agreed with Justice White's opinion but added that life without parole cannot purport to serve a rehabilitative purpose and that "no jurisdiction except Michigan has concluded that the offense belongs in a category where reform and rehabilitation are considered totally unattainable."

2. **Capital cases.** The argument that federal constitutional considerations require "proportionality review" of a somewhat different sort in death penalty cases was rejected in Pulley v. Harris, 465 U.S. 37, 104 S.Ct. 871, 79 L.Ed.2d 29 (1984). Because under then-prevailing capital sentencing schemes the death penalty was being imposed discriminatorily, wantonly and freakishly, and infrequently, the Court in Furman v. Georgia, 408 U.S. 238, 92 S.Ct. 2726, 33 L.Ed.2d 346 (1972), held that any given death sentence was cruel and unusual within the meaning of the Eighth Amendment. In 1976, however, the Court upheld death penalties imposed under several procedures developed after *Furman.* Gregg v. Georgia, 428 U.S. 153, 96 S.Ct. 2909, 49 L.Ed.2d 859 (1976); Proffitt v. Florida, 428 U.S. 242, 96

S.Ct. 2960, 49 L.Ed.2d 913 (1976); Jurek v. Texas, 428 U.S. 262, 96 S.Ct. 2950, 49 L.Ed.2d 929 (1976). In *Harris,* the argument was made that a capital sentencing scheme sufficiently assures against arbitrary application of the death penalty to meet *Furman's* Eighth Amendment standards only if the scheme requires that an appellate court consider whether the death penalty is unacceptable in each case because it is disproportionate to the punishment imposed upon others convicted of the same or similar offenses.

But the Court found "no basis in our cases for holding that comparative proportionality review by an appellate court is required in every case in which the death penalty is imposed and the defendant requests it." 465 U.S. at 50–51, 104 S.Ct. at 879, 79 L.Ed.2d at 40. Assuming that some capital sentencing schemes might be so lacking in checks on arbitrariness that comparative proportionality review would be necessary to meet constitutional requirements, the majority concluded that the California sentencing scheme was not of that sort. Whether or not to impose the death penalty is addressed only if the defendant is convicted of first degree murder and the jury finds that the state has proven at least one "special circumstance." At a penalty hearing, additional evidence is taken and the jury is given a list of factors relevant to the sentencing decision. The jury is to determine whether life imprisonment or death is to be imposed. If death is imposed, the trial judge reviews the matter and makes an independent determination as to whether the "weight of the evidence" supports the jury's determination. Reasons for the judge's conclusions are to be placed in the record. Appeal is automatic and the appellate court must consider whether the evidence relied upon by the trial judge is sufficient. Despite the absence of a requirement that the appellate tribunal engage in proportionality review, the Court concluded, the California procedure—on its face—cannot be said to contain constitutionally insufficient protection against the defects found in *Furman.* 465 U.S. at 53, 104 S.Ct. at 881, 79 L.Ed.2d at 42.

3. **Effectiveness of appellate review of sentences.** Generally speaking, the evaluations of appellate review of sentences have not been overwhelmingly favorable. A major concern has been that appellate tribunals are so reluctant to override sentencing judges' discretionary decisions that review is seldom meaningful. One commentator who reviewed thirty years of appellate review of sentences in Arizona concluded:

> Despite the incorporation into the formal legal framework of an authorization for appellate supervision of the sentencing process, the participants in the process (the appellate judges as well as the trial bench and bar) rejected the underlying assumptions of the proposal: (a) that scientific sentencing was possible; (b) that a body of relatively precise rules for the conduct of judicial sentencing could be developed; and (c) that the appellate judiciary was the appropriate agency to supervise reform of the sentencing process. Given the failure of the participants to accept the underlying assumptions, the attempt to achieve reform by revision of the legal framework was destined to fail from the beginning.

Dix, Judicial Review of Sentences: Implications for Individual Disposition, 1969 Law and the Social Order 369, 405. See also, Zeisel and Diamond, Search for Sentencing Equality: Sentence Review in Massachusetts and Connecticut, 4 Am.Bar Foundation Research J. 881 (1977).

3. REDUCING DISCRETION BY "DETERMINATE" SENTENCING

Another response to what might be perceived as the serious problems posed by discretion under traditional "indeterminate" sentencing schemes is, of course, to alter the basic structure of the sentencing process. Many jurisdictions have undertaken to do this. Among them is 1984 legislation dramatically altering the sentencing and correctional process in the federal criminal justice system.

a. STATE REFORMS

Hussey and Lagoy, The Impact of Determinate Sentencing Structures

17 Criminal Law Bulletin 197–203 (1981).*

The intensity of recent intellectual and legislative activity relative to the sentencing of criminal offenders suggests that a broad and fundamental change in sentencing policy—and perhaps even in underlying ideologies of criminal justice—is taking place. Frustrated by the criminal justice system's inability to rehabilitate criminals, sentencing reformers of many types, including radical criminologists, more traditional academicians, blue-ribbon commissions, and the federal judiciary, have endorsed proposals for broad-brush changes in criminal sentencing which focus on the crime committed rather than the rehabilitative needs of the criminal. . . .

Since the turn of the century, most jurisdictions at each level of government have embraced the rehabilitative ideal, a criminological theory which perceives crime as a pathology and has as its objective the effecting of a cure in the afflicted offender. The rehabilitative ideal was expressed in the use of indeterminate sentencing systems and parole. Indeterminate sentences are perhaps best described as a . . . process involving discretionary legislative, judicial, and administrative decisions. Characteristically, the legislature established broad ranges of prison time for each offense or class of offense within which convicted criminals could be sentenced. The potential ranges increased according to the severity of the particular offense. The actual determination of sentence within these ranges was the province of the judge who was required to select both a minimum term, which had to be served, and a maximum term. The portion of the term to be served in excess of the minimum term, and which could extend until the maximum was served, was left to the parole board or other administrative body which made its decision ostensibly based on the perceived rehabilitation of the offender.

Now, in several states the indeterminate sentence, with its wide ranges of minimum and maximum sentences, has been replaced by sentences which, theoretically at least, are much more specific in nature. As testimony to the extent of this shift, it was recently reported that seven states had altered radically their sentencing systems "resulting in more predictable and definite lengths of prison terms." There is little doubt that legislative bodies which have altered their sentencing structures have done so with the objectives of limiting discretion in sentencing both at the judicial and administrative level, decreasing disparity of sentences among similar offenders who have committed similar offenses, and increasing the overall definiteness or determinacy of prison terms.

* * *

The first criminal code that appeared to bring greater determinacy to sentencing was enacted in Maine in 1976. The passage of Maine's new code brought to fruition sentencing reform efforts begun in the 1960s, before most literature on determinate sentencing appeared. Maine's sentencing code resulted in two notable features. First, sentences to incarceration were for a specific number of years and, essentially, could be reduced only through the operation of good time. Second, Maine abolished not only the parole board but also post-sentence supervision for offenders sentenced under the new code. It did not follow the prescription for presumptive sentences . . .; nor was there any formal mechanism for the consideration of aggravating and mitigating factors. Furthermore, the code provided for only maximum sentences for the five classes of crime; no minimums were specified. . . .

The second state to implement reform was California, and it chose to adopt a presumptive sentencing system. Under that approach, felony offenses, except for murder, were placed into one of four classes of crime and for each class three terms were specified: a presumptive term which was to be imposed absent aggravating or mitigating circumstances, a lower term which could be selected if mitigating factors predominated, and an upper term which could be imposed in cases in which aggravating factors were predominant. Offenders are released at the expiration of their term, less good time earned which may range up to four months per year or a 33 percent reduction. Once released, offenders serve a three-year ''parole'' period. Inasmuch as the power to release from prison does not lie with a parole board and the three-year parole period does not fall within a maximum term, the parole period might more legitimately be seen as a post-incarceration ''add-on.'' However, the California code still labels this as a parole period.

Indiana followed California in implementing what has been called a hybrid approach to determinate sentencing. Indiana adopted the mechanics of presumptive sentencing but also specified very wide ranges for sentences in mitigation and aggravation. For example, in California the sentencing range for rape is three to eight years,[a] while in Indiana it is six to fifty years. These potentially long sentences can be greatly modified by the provision of good time which ranges between zero good time and day-for-day good time, amounting to a 50 percent reduction in sentence. An offender is released on parole at the completion of the determinate term (reduced by good time) and undergoes parole supervision for the remainder of the term. The offender, however, must be discharged after one year if parole has not been revoked.

Illinois was the last of the ''pioneer'' states to adopt determinate sentencing. Illinois does not specify presumptive sentences but does define

a. In order to reduce disparity, under California's Determinate Sentence Law *as originally enacted*, all sentence ranges were 2 years. For example, rape was 3, 4, or 5 years before any enhancements.

a range for various crime classes within which a determinate sentence must be selected. Offenders are released at the expiration of sentence and must serve one, two, or three years on parole. The length of the parole period is related to the class of crime committed. As in each of the other determinate sentencing states, good time may reduce a term of incarceration up to 50 percent (day-for-day good time).

NOTES

1. **Formal sentencing criteria.** California's Determinate Sentence law required, for the first time, "rules providing criteria for the consideration of the trial judge at the time of sentencing." Cal.Pen.Code § 1170.3. Criteria for selecting one of three base prison terms possible for most California crimes are set out here. Among the other rules promulgated are those for enhancing base terms and imposing consecutive terms. Factors to be considered for the crucial probation decision are set out in that section, infra.

CALIFORNIA JUDICIAL COUNCIL, SENTENCING RULES FOR THE SUPERIOR COURTS (1990)

Rule 421. Circumstances in Aggravation [Upper Term]

Circumstances in aggravation include:

(a) Facts relating to the crime, including the fact that:

(1) The crime involved great violence, great bodily harm, threat of great bodily harm, or other acts disclosing a high degree of cruelty, viciousness or callousness, whether or not charged or chargeable as an enhancement under section 12022.7.

(2) The defendant was armed with or used a weapon at the time of the commission of the crime, whether or not charged or chargeable as an enhancement under section 12022 or 12022.5.

(3) The victim was particularly vulnerable.

(4) The crime involved multiple victims.

(5) The defendant induced others to participate in the commission of the crime or occupied a position of leadership or dominance of other participants in its commission.

(6) The defendant threatened witnesses, unlawfully prevented or dissuaded witnesses from testifying, suborned perjury, or in any other way illegally interfered with the judicial process.

(7) The defendant was convicted of other crimes for which consecutive sentences could have been imposed but for which concurrent sentences are being imposed.

(8) The planning, sophistication or professionalism with which the crime was carried out, or other facts, indicate premeditation.

(9) The defendant used or involved minors in the commission of the crime.

(10) The crime involved an attempted or actual taking or damage of great monetary value, whether or not charged or chargeable as an enhancement under section 12022.6.

(11) The crime involved a large quantity of contraband.

(12) The defendant took advantage of a position of trust or confidence to commit the offense.

(b) Facts relating to the defendant, including the fact that:

(1) He has engaged in a pattern of violent conduct which indicates a serious danger to society.

(2) The defendant's prior convictions as an adult or adjudications of commission of crimes as a juvenile are numerous or of increasing seriousness.

(3) The defendant has served prior prison terms whether or not charged or chargeable as an enhancement under section 667.5.

(4) The defendant was on probation or parole when he committed the crime.

(5) The defendant's prior performance on probation or parole was unsatisfactory.

Rule 423. Circumstances in Mitigation [Lower Term]

Circumstances in mitigation include:

(a) Facts relating to the crime, including the fact that:

(1) The defendant was a passive participant or played a minor role in the crime.

(2) The victim was an initiator, willing participant, aggressor or provoker of the incident.

(3) The crime was committed because of an unusual circumstance, such as great provocation, which is unlikely to recur.

(4) The defendant participated in the crime under circumstances of coercion or duress, or his conduct was partially excusable for some other reason not amounting to a defense.

(5) A defendant with no apparent predisposition to do so was induced by others to participate in the crime.

(6) The defendant exercised caution to avoid harm to persons or damage to property, or the amounts of money or property taken were deliberately small, or no harm was done or threatened against the victim.

(7) The defendant believed he had a claim or right to the property taken, or for other reasons mistakenly believed his conduct was legal.

(8) The defendant was motivated by a desire to provide necessities for his family or himself.

(b) Facts relating to the defendant, including the fact that:

(1) He has no prior record or an insignificant record of criminal conduct considering the recency and frequency of prior crimes.

(2) The defendant was suffering from a mental or physical condition that significantly reduced his culpability for the crime.

(3) The defendant voluntarily acknowledged wrongdoing prior to arrest or at an early stage of the criminal process.

(4) The defendant is ineligible for probation and but for that ineligibility would have been granted probation.

(5) The defendant made restitution to the victim.

(6) The defendant's prior performance on probation or parole was good.

2. **Abolishing parole.** Also consider the following approach to sentencing disparity embodied in Section 1170 of the West's Ann. California Penal Code:

(a)(1) The Legislature finds and declares that the purpose of imprisonment for crime is punishment. This purpose is best served by terms proportionate to the seriousness of the offense with provision for uniformity in the sentences of offenders committing the same offense under similar circumstances. The Legislature further finds and declares that the elimination of disparity and the provision of uniformity of sentences can best be achieved by determinate sentences fixed by statute in proportion to the seriousness of the offense as determined by the Legislature to be imposed by the court with specified discretion.

* * *

(d) When a defendant ...has been sentenced to be imprisoned in the state prison and has been committed to the custody of the Director of Corrections, the court may, within 120 days of the date of commitment on its own motion, or at any time upon the recommendation of the Director of Corrections or the Board of Prison Terms, recall the sentence and commitment previously ordered and resentence the defendant in the same manner as if he had not previously been sentenced, provided the new sentence, if any, is no greater than the initial sentence. The resentence under this subdivision shall apply the sentencing rules of the Judicial Council so as to eliminate disparity of sentences and to promote uniformity of sentencing. Credit shall be given for time served.

* * *

(f)(1) Within one year after the commencement of the term of imprisonment, the Board of Prison Terms shall review the sentence to determine whether the sentence is disparate in comparison with the sentences to be imposed in similar cases. If the Board of Prison Terms determines that the sentence is disparate, the board shall notify the judge, the district attorney, the defense attorney, the defendant, and the Judicial Council. The notification shall include a statement of the reasons for finding the sentence disparate.

Within 120 days of receipt of this information, the sentencing court shall schedule a hearing and may recall the sentence and commitment previously ordered and resentence the defendant in the same manner as if the defendant had not been sentenced previously, provided the new sentence is no greater than the initial sentence. In resentencing under this subdivision the court shall apply the sentencing rules of the Judicial Council and shall consider the information provided by the Board of Prison Terms.

3. **Sentencing grids.** Many jurisdictions adopted systems involving sentencing commissions. Minnesota, for example, created a sentencing commission and directed it to develop guidelines. Minn.Stat.Ann. § 244.09. Its guideline development resulted in the following grid:

CRIMINAL HISTORY SCORE

SEVERITY LEVELS OF CONVICTION OFFENSE		0	1	2	3	4	5	6 or more
Unauthorized Use of Motor Vehicle Possession of Marijuana	I	12*	12*	12*	13	15	17	19 18-20
Theft Related Crimes ($250-$2500) Aggravated Forgery ($250-$2500)	II	12*	12*	13	15	17	19	21 20-22
Theft Crimes ($250-$2500)	III	12*	13	15	17	19 18-20	22 21-23	25 24-26
Nonresidential Burglary Theft Crimes (over $2500)	IV	12*	15	18	21	25 24-26	32 30-34	41 37-45
Residential Burglary Simple Robbery	V	18	23	27	30 29-31	38 36-40	46 43-49	54 50-58
Criminal Sexual Conduct. 2nd Degree (a) & (b)	VI	21	26	30	34 33-35	44 42-46	54 50-58	65 60-70
Aggravated Robbery	VII	24 23-25	32 30-34	41 38-44	49 45-53	65 60-70	81 75-87	97 90-104
Criminal Sexual Conduct 1st Degree Assault. 1st Degree	VIII	43 41-45	54 50-58	65 60-70	76 71-81	95 89-101	113 106-120	132 124-140
Murder. 3rd Degree Murder. 2nd Degree (felony murder)	IX	105 102-108	119 116-122	127 124-130	149 143-155	176 168-184	205 195-215	230 218-242
Murder. 2nd Degree (with intent)	X	120 116-124	140 133-147	162 153-171	203 192-214	243 231-255	284 270-298	324 309-339

The guideline sentence (expressed in months) is found by determining the offense severity and criminal history score and then looking to the grid cell in the appropriate row and column. Cells below the heavy black line contain sentences of imprisonment in a state prison system; cells above the line refer to probated sentences. First degree murder carries a mandatory life sentence and is exempted from the guidelines.

A number of rules govern the calculation of a defendant's criminal history score. For each prior felony conviction, one point is assigned. One additional point is assigned if the defendant was on probation or parole, jailed or imprisoned, or released pending sentence at the time the offense was committed. One "unit" is assigned for each misdemeanor conviction, unless the misdemeanor was a "gross" or serious one, in which case two units are assigned; four "units" equal one point. A further point is assigned if the defendant committed two offenses as a juvenile (after his sixteenth birthday) that would have been felonies if committed by an adult.

b. FEDERAL REFORM: THE SENTENCING REFORM ACT OF 1984

The Sentencing Reform Act of 1984, Chapter II of the Comprehensive Crime Control Act of 1984 and codified primarily as 18 U.S.C.A. §§ 3551–

3580, dramatically changed the framework for sentencing persons convicted of criminal offenses in federal courts. Its progress through Congress was lengthy and troubled. It finally became effective November 1, 1987. But court challenges to many of its provisions are numerous and ongoing. For example, prior to the decision in the principal case, which follows, "158 U.S. district courts had ruled that the guidelines were unconstitutional, while 116 others had upheld them. Two U.S. Circuit Courts of Appeals were also in conflict—the 9th Circuit striking the guidelines down, by a 2–to–1 vote, and the 3rd Circuit upholding them, also by a 2–to–1 vote." 20 Crim.J.Newsletter No. 3, February 1, 1989, p. 1.

The principal case is the first to be decided by the Supreme Court. It provides an outline of some of the main points of the Act while addressing the constitutionality of the Sentencing Commission created by the Act. More detailed descriptions and other provisions of the statute are presented elsewhere in this chapter.

Mistretta v. United States

Supreme Court of the United States, 1989.
488 U.S. 361, 109 S.Ct. 647, 102 L.Ed.2d 714.

■ JUSTICE BLACKMUN delivered the opinion of the Court.

In this litigation, we granted certiorari before judgment in the United States Court of Appeals for the Eighth Circuit in order to consider the constitutionality of the Sentencing Guidelines promulgated by the United States Sentencing Commission. The Commission is a body created under the Sentencing Reform Act of 1984, as amended (Act), 18 U.S.C. § 3551 et seq. (1982 ed., Supp. IV), and 28 U.S.C. §§ 991–998 (1982 ed., Supp. IV). The United States District Court for the Western District of Missouri ruled that the Guidelines were constitutional. United States v. Johnson, 682 F.Supp. 1033 (W.D.Mo.1988).

I

A

Background

For almost a century, the Federal Government employed in criminal cases a system of indeterminate sentencing. Statutes specified the penalties for crimes but nearly always gave the sentencing judge wide discretion to decide whether the offender should be incarcerated and for how long, whether he should be fined and how much, and whether some lesser restraint, such as probation, should be imposed instead of imprisonment or fine. This indeterminate-sentencing system was supplemented by the utilization of parole, by which an offender was returned to society under the "guidance and control" of a parole officer.

Both indeterminate sentencing and parole were based on concepts of the offender's possible, indeed probable, rehabilitation, a view that it was realistic to attempt to rehabilitate the inmate and thereby to minimize the risk that he would resume criminal activity upon his return to society. It obviously required the judge and the parole officer to make their respective sentencing and release decisions upon their own assessments of the offender's amendability to rehabilitation. As a result, the court and the officer were in positions to exercise, and usually did exercise, very broad discretion. This led almost inevitably to the conclusion on the part of a reviewing court that the sentencing judge "sees more and senses more" than the appellate court; thus, the judge enjoyed the "superiority of his nether position," for that court's determination as to what sentence was appropriate met with virtually unconditional deference on appeal. The decision whether to parole was also "predictive and discretionary." The correction official possessed almost absolute discretion over the parole decision.

Historically, federal sentencing—the function of determining the scope and extent of punishment—never has been thought to be assigned by the Constitution to the exclusive jurisdiction of any one of the three Branches of government. Congress, of course, has the power to fix the sentence for a federal crime, and the scope of judicial discretion with respect to a sentence is subject to congressional control. Congress early abandoned fixed-sentence rigidity, however, and put in place a system of ranges within which the sentencer could choose the precise punishment. Congress delegated almost unfettered discretion to the sentencing judge to determine what the sentence should be within the customarily wide range so selected. This broad discretion was further enhanced by the power later granted the judge to suspend the sentence and by the resulting growth of an elaborate probation system. Also, with the advent of parole, Congress moved toward a "three-way sharing" of sentencing responsibility by granting correction personnel in the Executive Branch the discretion to release a prisoner before the expiration of the sentence imposed by the judge. Thus, under the indeterminate-sentence system, Congress defined the maximum, the judge imposed a sentence within the statutory range (which it usually could replace with probation), and the Executive Branch's parole official eventually determined the actual duration of imprisonment. . . .

Serious disparities in sentences, however, were common. Rehabilitation as a sound penalogical theory came to be questioned and, in any event, was regarded by some as an unattainable goal for most cases. See N. Morris, The Future of Imprisonment, 24–43 (1974); F. Allen, The Decline of the Rehabilitative Ideal (1981). . . .

. . . Congress had wrestled with the problem for more than a decade when, in 1984, it enacted the sweeping reforms that are at issue here.

* * *

Before settling on a mandatory-guideline system, Congress considered other competing proposals for sentencing reform. It rejected strict determinate sentencing because it concluded that a guideline system would be successful in reducing sentence disparities while retaining the flexibility needed to adjust for unanticipated factors arising in a particular case. . . . The Judiciary Committee rejected a proposal that would have made the sentencing guidelines only advisory. . . .

B

The Act

The Act, as adopted, revises the old sentencing process in several ways:

1.   It rejects imprisonment as a means of promoting rehabilitation, 28 U.S.C. § 994(k), and it states that punishment should serve retributive, educational, deterrent, and incapacitative goals, 18 U.S.C. § 3553(a)(2).

2.   It consolidates the power that had been exercised by the sentencing judge and the Parole Commission to decide what punishment an offender should suffer. This is done by creating the United States Sentencing Commission, directing that Commission to devise guidelines to be used for sentencing, and prospectively abolishing the Parole Commission. 28 U.S.C. §§ 991, 994, and 995(a)(1).

3.   It makes all sentences basically determinate. A prisoner is to be released at the completion of his sentence reduced only by any credit earned by good behavior while in custody. 18 U.S.C. §§ 3624(a) and (b).

4.   It makes the Sentencing Commission's guidelines binding on the courts, although it preserves for the judge the discretion to depart from the guideline applicable to a particular case if the judge finds an aggravating or mitigating factor present that the Commission did not adequately consider when formulating guidelines. §§ 3553(a) and (b). The Act also requires the court to state its reasons for the sentence imposed and to give "the specific reason" for imposing a sentence different from that described in the guideline. § 3553(c).

5.   It authorizes limited appellate review of the sentence. It permits a defendant to appeal a sentence that is above the defined range, and it permits the Government to appeal a sentence that is below that range. It also permits either side to appeal an incorrect application of the guideline. §§ 3742(a) and (b).

* * *

C

The Sentencing Commission

The Commission is established "as an independent commission in the judicial branch of the United States." § 991(a). It has seven voting members (one of whom is the Chairman) appointed by the President "by and with the advice and consent of the Senate." "At least three of the members shall be Federal judges selected after considering a list of six judges recommended to the President by the Judicial Conference of the United States." Ibid. No more than four members of the Commission shall be members of the same political party. The Attorney General, or his designee, is an ex officio nonvoting member. The Chairman and other members of the Commission are subject to removal by the President "only for neglect of duty or malfeasance in office or for other good cause shown." § 991(a). Except for initial staggering of terms, a voting member serves for six years and may not serve more than two full terms. §§ 992(a) and (b).

D

The Responsibilities of the Commission

In addition to the duty the Commission has to promulgate determinative-sentence guidelines, it is under an obligation periodically to "review and revise" the guidelines. § 994(o). It is to "consult with authorities on, and individual and institutional representatives of, various aspects of the Federal criminal justice system." Ibid. It must report to Congress "any amendments of the guidelines." § 994(p). It is to make recommendations to Congress whether the grades or maximum penalties should be modified. § 994(r). It must submit to Congress at least annually an analysis of the operation of the guidelines. § 994(w). It is to issue "general policy statements" regarding their application. § 994(a)(2). And it has the power to "establish general policies . . . as are necessary to carry out the purposes" of the legislation, § 995(a)(1); to "monitor the performance of probation officers" with respect to the guidelines, § 995(a)(9); to "devise and conduct periodic training programs of instruction in sentencing techniques for judicial and probation personnel" and others, § 995(a)(18); and to "perform such other functions as are required to permit Federal courts to meet their responsibilities" as to sentencing, § 995(a)(22).

We note, in passing, that the monitoring function is not without its burden. Every year, with respect to each of more than 40,000 sentences, the federal courts must forward, and the Commission must review, the presentence report, the guideline worksheets, the tribunal's sentencing statement, and any written plea agreement.

II

This Litigation

On Dec. 10, 1987, John M. Mistretta (petitioner) and another were indicted in the United States District Court for the Western District of Missouri on three counts centering in a cocaine sale. Mistretta moved to have the promulgated Guidelines ruled unconstitutional on the grounds that the Sentencing Commission was constituted in violation of the established doctrine of separation of powers, and that Congress delegated excessive authority to the Commission to structure the Guidelines. As has been noted, the District Court was not persuaded by these contentions.

The District Court rejected petitioner's delegation argument on the ground that, despite the language of the statute, the Sentencing Commission "should be judicially characterized as having Executive Branch status," and that the Guidelines are similar to substantive rules promulgated by other agencies. The court also rejected petitioner's claim that the Act is unconstitutional because it requires Article III federal judges to serve on the Commission. . . .

Petitioner then pleaded guilty to the first count of his indictment (conspiracy and agreement to distribute cocaine, in violation of 21 U.S.C. §§ 846 and 841(b)(1)(B)). The Government thereupon moved to dismiss the remaining counts. That motion was granted. Petitioner was sentenced under the Guidelines to 18 months' imprisonment, to be followed by a 3–

year term of supervised release. The court also imposed a $1,000 fine and a $50 special assessment.

Petitioner filed a notice of appeal to the Eighth Circuit, but both petitioner and the United States, pursuant to this Court's Rule 18, petitioned for certiorari before judgment. Because of the "imperative public importance" of the issue, as prescribed by the Rule, and because of the disarray among the Federal District Courts, we granted those petitions.

III

Delegation of Power

Petitioner argues that in delegating the power to promulgate sentencing guidelines for every federal criminal offense to an independent Sentencing Commission, Congress has granted the Commission excessive legislative discretion in violation of the constitutionally based nondelegation doctrine. We do not agree.

The nondelegation doctrine is rooted in the principle of separation of powers that underlies our tripartite system of government. The Constitution provides that "[a]ll legislative Powers herein granted shall be vested in a Congress of the United States," U.S. Const., Art. I, § 1, and we long have insisted that "the integrity and maintenance of the system of government ordained by the Constitution," mandate that Congress generally cannot delegate its legislative power to another Branch. Field v. Clark, 143 U.S. 649, 692, 12 S.Ct. 495, 504, 36 L.Ed. 294 (1892). We also have recognized, however, that the separation-of-powers principle, and the non-delegation doctrine in particular, do not prevent Congress from obtaining the assistance of its coordinate Branches. . . .

. . .Accordingly, this Court has deemed it "constitutionally sufficient if Congress clearly delineates the general policy, the public agency which is to apply it, and the boundaries of this delegated authority." American Power & Light Co. v. SEC, 329 U.S. 90, 105, 67 S.Ct. 133, 142, 91 L.Ed. 103 (1946).

* * *

In light of our approval of these broad delegations, we harbor no doubt that Congress' delegation of authority to the Sentencing Commission is sufficiently specific and detailed to meet constitutional requirements. Congress charged the Commission with three goals: to "assure the meeting of the purposes of sentencing as set forth" in the Act; to "provide certainty and fairness in meeting the purposes of sentencing, avoiding unwarranted sentencing disparities among defendants with similar records . . . while maintaining sufficient flexibility to permit individualized sentences," where appropriate; and to "reflect to the extent practicable, advancement in knowledge of human behavior as it relates to the criminal justice process." 28 U.S.C. § 991(b)(1). Congress further specified four "purposes" of sentencing that the Commission must pursue in carrying out its mandate: "to reflect the seriousness of the offense, to promote respect for the law, and to provide just punishment for the offense"; "to afford adequate deterrence to criminal conduct"; "to protect the public from further crimes of the defendant"; and "to provide the defendant with needed ...correctional treatment." 18 U.S.C. § 3553(a)(2).

In addition, Congress prescribed the specific tool—the guidelines system—for the Commission to use in regulating sentencing. More particularly, Congress directed the Commission to develop a system of "sentencing ranges" applicable "for each category of offense involving each category of defendant." 28 U.S.C. § 994(b).[6] Congress instructed the Commission that these sentencing ranges must be consistent with pertinent provisions of Title 18 of the United States Code and could not include sentences in excess of the statutory maximum. Congress also required that for sentences of imprisonment, "the maximum of the range established for such a term shall not exceed the minimum of that range by more than the greater of 25 percent or 6 months, except that, if the minimum term of the range is 30 years or more, the maximum may be life imprisonment." § 994(b)(2). Moreover, Congress directed the Commission to use current average sentences "as a starting point" for its structuring of the sentencing ranges. § 994(m).

To guide the Commission in its formulation of offense categories, Congress directed it to consider seven factors: the grade of the offense; the aggravating and mitigating circumstances of the crime; the nature and degree of the harm caused by the crime; the community view of the gravity of the offense; the public concern generated by the crime; the deterrent effect that a particular sentence may have on others; and the current incidence of the offense. § 994(c)(1)–(7). Congress set forth 11 factors for the Commission to consider in establishing categories of defendants. These include the offender's age, education, vocational skills, mental and emotional condition, physical condition (including drug dependence), previous employment record, family ties and responsibilities, community ties, role in the offense, criminal history, and degree of dependence upon crime for a livelihood. § 994(d)(1)–(11). Congress also prohibited the Commission from considering the "race, sex, national origin, creed, and socio-economic status of offenders," § 994(d), and instructed that the guidelines should reflect the "general inappropriateness" of considering certain other factors, such as current unemployment, that might serve as proxies for forbidden factors, § 994(e).

In addition to these overarching constraints, Congress provided even more detailed guidance to the Commission about categories of offenses and offender characteristics. Congress directed that guidelines require a term of confinement at or near the statutory maximum for certain crimes of

---

6. Congress mandated that the guidelines include:

   "(A) a determination whether to impose a sentence to probation, a fine, or a term of imprisonment;

   "(B) a determination as to the appropriate amount of a fine or the appropriate length of a term of probation or a term of imprisonment;

   "(C) a determination whether a sentence to a term of imprisonment should include a requirement that the defendant be placed on a term of supervised release after imprisonment, and, if so, the appropriate length of such a term; and

   "(D) a determination whether multiple sentences to terms of imprisonment should be ordered to run concurrently or consecutively." 28 U.S.C. § 994(a)(1).

violence and for drug offenses, particularly when committed by recidivists. § 994(h). Congress further directed that the Commission assure a substantial term of imprisonment for an offense constituting a third felony conviction, for a career felon, for one convicted of a managerial role in a racketeering enterprise, for a crime of violence by an offender on release from a prior felony conviction, and for an offense involving a substantial quantity of narcotics. § 994(i). Congress also instructed "that the guidelines reflect . . . the general appropriateness of imposing a term of imprisonment" for a crime of violence that resulted in serious bodily injury. On the other hand, Congress directed that guidelines reflect the general inappropriateness of imposing a sentence of imprisonment "in cases in which the defendant is a first offender who has not been convicted of a crime of violence or an otherwise serious offense." § 994(j). Congress also enumerated various aggravating and mitigating circumstances, such as, respectively, multiple offenses or substantial assistance to the Government, to be reflected in the guidelines. §§ 994(*l*) and (n). In other words, although Congress granted the Commission substantial discretion in formulating guidelines, in actuality it legislated a full hierarchy of punishment—from near maximum imprisonment, to substantial imprisonment, to some imprisonment, to alternatives—and stipulated the most important offense and offender characteristics to place defendants within these categories.

We cannot dispute petitioner's contention that the Commission enjoys significant discretion in formulating guidelines. The Commission does have discretionary authority to determine the relative severity of federal crimes and to assess the relative weight of the offender characteristics that Congress listed for the Commission to consider. See §§ 994(c) and (d) (Commission instructed to consider enumerated factors as it deems them to be relevant). The Commission also has significant discretion to determine which crimes have been punished too leniently, and which too severely. § 994(m). Congress has called upon the Commission to exercise its judgment about which types of crimes and which types of criminals are to be considered similar for the purposes of sentencing.[7]

* * *

Developing proportionate penalties for hundreds of different crimes by a virtually limitless array of offenders is precisely the sort of intricate,

---

7. Petitioner argues that the excessive breadth of Congress' delegation to the Commission is particularly apparent in the Commission's considering whether to "reinstate" the death penalty for some or all of those crimes for which capital punishment is still authorized in the Federal Criminal Code. Whether, in fact, the Act confers upon the Commission the power to develop guidelines and procedures to bring current death penalty provisions into line with decisions of this Court is a matter of intense debate between the Executive Branch and some members of Congress, including the Chairman of the Senate Judiciary Committee. We assume, without deciding, that the Commission was assigned the power to effectuate the death penalty provisions of the Criminal Code. That the Commission may have this authority (but has not exercised it) does not affect our analysis. Congress did not authorize the Commission to enact a federal death penalty for any offense. As for every other offense within the Commission's jurisdiction, the Commission could include the death penalty within the guidelines only if that punishment was authorized in the first instance by Congress and only if such inclusion comported with the substantial guidance Congress gave the Commission in fulfilling its assignments. Justice Brennan does not join this footnote.

labor-intensive task for which delegation to an expert body is especially appropriate. Although Congress has delegated significant discretion to the Commission to draw judgments from its analysis of existing sentencing practice and alternative sentencing models, "Congress is not confined to that method of executing its policy which involves the least possible delegation of discretion to administrative officers." Yakus v. United States, 321 U.S., at 425–426, 64 S.Ct., at 668. We have no doubt that in the hands of the Commission "the criteria which Congress has supplied are wholly adequate for carrying out the general policy and purpose" of the Act. Sunshine Coal Co. v. Adkins, 310 U.S. 381, 398, 60 S.Ct. 907, 915, 84 L.Ed. 1263 (1940).

IV

Separation of Powers

Having determined that Congress has set forth sufficient standards for the exercise of the Commission's delegated authority, we turn to Mistretta's claim that the Act violates the constitutional principle of separation of powers.

* * *

In sum, since substantive judgment in the field of sentencing has been and remains appropriate to the Judicial Branch, and the methodology of rulemaking has been and remains appropriate to that Branch, Congress' considered decision to combine these functions in an independent Sentencing Commission and to locate that Commission within the Judicial Branch does not violate the principle of separation of powers.

* * *

V

We conclude that in creating the Sentencing Commission—an unusual hybrid in structure and authority—Congress neither delegated excessive legislative power nor upset the constitutionally mandated balance of powers among the coordinate Branches. The Constitution's structural protections do not prohibit Congress from delegating to an expert body located within the Judicial Branch the intricate task of formulating sentencing guidelines consistent with such significant statutory direction as is present here. Nor does our system of checked and balanced authority prohibit Congress from calling upon the accumulated wisdom and experience of the Judicial Branch in creating policy on a matter uniquely within the ken of judges. Accordingly, we hold that the Act is constitutional.

The judgment of the United States District Court for the Western District of Missouri is affirmed.

It is so ordered.

■ JUSTICE SCALIA, dissenting [omitted].

NOTES

1. **Congressional directives.** In the legislation, Congress has provided a number of additional directives concerning the substance of the guidelines that the

Commission is to develop. 28 U.S.C.A. § 994(b)–(m). For example, the Commission is directed to assure that the guidelines will specify a sentence to "a substantial term of imprisonment" for categories of defendants in which the defendant has a history of two or more prior felony convictions for offenses committed on different occasions. 28 U.S.C.A. § 944(i)(1).

In addition, the Commission is to promulgate general policy statements regarding application of the guidelines and other aspects of sentencing or sentencing implementation.

2. **Statutory sentencing criteria.** The legislation directs the court, in selecting a sentence, to consider:

(1) the nature and circumstances of the offense and the history and characteristics of the defendant;

(2) the need for the sentence imposed—

(A) to reflect the seriousness of the offense, to promote respect for the law, and to provide just punishment for the offense;

(B) to afford adequate deterrence to criminal conduct;

(C) to protect the public from further crimes of the defendant; and

(D) to provide the defendant with needed education or vocational training, medical care, or other correctional treatment in the most effective manner;

(3) the kinds of sentences available;

(4) the kinds of sentences and the sentencing range established for the applicable category of offense committed by the applicable category of defendant as set forth in the guidelines that are issued by the Sentencing Commission . . .;

(5) any pertinent policy statement issued by the Sentencing Commission . . .;

(6) the need to avoid unwarranted sentence disparities among defendants with similar records who have been found guilty of similar conduct; and

(7) the need to provide restitution to any victims of the offense.

18 U.S.C.A. § 3553(a). The sentence is to be "sufficient, but not greater than necessary, to comply with the purposes set forth in paragraph (2). . . ." Id.

With regard to the Sentencing Commission's guidelines, the statute provides:

The court shall impose a sentence of the kind and within the range, [of the guidelines issued by the Sentencing Commission] unless the court finds that an aggravating or mitigating circumstance exists that was not adequately taken into consideration by the Sentencing Commission in formulating the guidelines and that should result in a sentence different from that described.

18 U.S.C.A. § 3553(b).

At the time of sentencing, the court "shall state in open court the reasons for the imposition of the particular sentence. . . ." 18 U.S.C.A. § 3553(c). If the sentence is not of the kind, or outside the range, provided for in the Commission's guidelines, the court is also to state the specific reason for the imposition of a sentence different from that indicated by the guidelines. Id.

3. **Elimination of parole.** The legislation abolishes parole as it has traditionally been administered in the federal system and in many states. A convicted defendant sentenced to imprisonment is to be released on the expiration of his sentence, less any time credited to him for "satisfactory behavior." 18 U.S.C.A.

§ 3624(a). Within 15 days of the end of each year of a prison term, a defendant is to receive—in addition to credit for time actually served—credit for 54 more days unless the Bureau of Prisons determines that during the year the defendant has not satisfactorily complied with institutional disciplinary regulations. Once such additional time has been credited to a defendant, it "vests" and cannot be withdrawn for later misbehavior. 18 U.S.C.A. § 3624(b). This, of course, means that a defendant's actual release date is no longer determined as a discretionary matter by a parole authority.

Nevertheless, a defendant may not, upon completion of his term of imprisonment, be entitled to absolute discharge. A sentencing court is authorized to impose upon a convicted defendant, in addition to a term of imprisonment, a requirement that the defendant be placed on a term of "supervised release" after imprisonment. 18 U.S.C.A. § 3583. The length of the term of supervised release which the court is authorized to impose ranges from one to five years, depending upon the crime of which the defendant has been convicted. Conditions may be imposed upon this release. If a term of supervised release has been imposed by the sentencing court, the defendant—upon release from imprisonment—is to be supervised by a probation officer "to the degree warranted by the conditions specified by the sentencing court." 18 U.S.C.A. § 3624(e). The term of supervised release is subject to revocation upon a showing by a preponderance of the evidence that the defendant has violated its terms. No credit for time served on supervised release will be given upon revocation. 18 U.S.C.A. § 3583(e)(3).

During service of a term of imprisonment, efforts are to be made to prepare the prisoner for transition from prison to community life. The Bureau of Prisons is directed "to the extent practicable" to assure that a prisoner spends a portion of the last part of his term of imprisonment "under conditions that will afford the prisoner a reasonable opportunity to adjust to and prepare for his re-entry into the community." 18 U.S.C.A. § 3624(c).

4. **Appellate review.** A defendant is authorized to appeal from a sentence on the ground that it was imposed in violation of law or as a result of an incorrect application of the Sentencing Commission's guidelines, or that it was greater than is provided for in the guidelines or in a plea agreement. 18 U.S.C.A. §§ 3742(a) and 3742(c)(1). The Government may appeal on similar grounds, although its case would, of course, be based on the proposition that the sentence was less severe than that provided for in the guidelines. 18 U.S.C.A. §§ 3742(b) and 3742(c)(2).

The Court of Appeals is to "give due regard to the opportunity of the district court to judge the credibility of the witnesses." It is to accept the findings of fact by the district court unless they are clearly erroneous. 18 U.S.C.A. § 3742(d). The appellate tribunal is authorized to remand a case for either the imposition of a lesser or more severe sentence or for further sentencing proceedings. It is also permitted to itself impose a lesser or greater sentence. 18 U.S.C.A. § 3742(e).

The Government in Koon v. United States, 518 U.S. 81, 116 S.Ct. 2035, 135 L.Ed.2d 392 (1996) argued that appellate courts should apply a *de novo* review to sentences to determine there compliance with the guidelines. The Supreme Court, in an opinion by Justice Kennedy, rejected this contention. An appellate court must in most instances grant deference to the district court's sentencing findings:

> That the district court retains much of its traditional discretion does not mean appellate review is an empty exercise. Congress directed courts of appeals to "give due deference to the district court's application of the guidelines to the facts." 18 U.S.C. § 3742(e)(4). The deference that is due depends on the nature of the question presented. The district court may be owed no deference, for instance, when the claim on appeal is that it made some sort of mathematical error in applying the Guidelines; under these circumstances, the appellate court

will be in as good a position to consider the question as the district court was in the first instance.

A district court's decision to depart from the Guidelines, by contrast, will in most cases be due substantial deference, for it embodies the traditional exercise of discretion by a sentencing court.

518 U.S. at 98, 116 S.Ct. at 2046, 135 L.Ed.2d at 412–13.

Koon involved the federal prosecution to Los Angeles police officers for violating the civil rights of Rodney King by beating him after stopping him during a high-speed chase. The incident was videotaped by a by-stander. Defendants had previously been tried and acquitted in state court. They were then tried and convicted of civil rights violations in federal court. The federal district court determined that the offense level was 27, which would have yielded a sentence of 70 to 87 months. However, the court granted a five-level downward departure because it determined that King's wrongful conduct contributed significantly to provoking the offense. It also granted a three-level downward departure because defendants were particularly likely to be the object of abuse in prison, would be terminated from their jobs as police officers, had been significantly burdened by having to defend successive state and federal prosecutions for the same conduct, and were unlikely to recidivate. Thus, it concluded the modified offense level was 19, which resulted in a sentence range of 30 to 37 months. The district court imposed a 30 year sentence.

The Supreme Court held that the district court did not abuse its discretion in departing five levels because of King's misconduct. With respect to the three-level departure, the Court concluded that the sole issue is whether the Sentencing Commission has proscribed the use of any particular sentencing factor. "If the answer to the question is no—as it will be most of the time—the sentencing court must determine whether the factor, as occurring in the particular circumstances, takes the case outside the heartland of the applicable Guideline." 518 U.S. at 109, 116 S.Ct. at 2051, 135 L.Ed.2d at 419. The defendants' career loss was inappropriately used to justify departure because the nature of a civil rights act violation—an intentional violation of another's civil rights—means that loss of public employment would not be unusual as a consequence of being convicted of such an offense. The unlikelihood of recidivism was also inappropriately taken into account because that was already taken into account in the criminal history portion of the matrix. The susceptibility to abuse in prison was based on the notoriousness of this offense and was, therefore, sufficiently unusual to justify downward departure. Finally, the successive state and federal prosecutions were sufficiently unusually burdensome to justify downward departure.

5. **Downward departures for substantial assistance to the government.** Federal law authorizes a District Court to impose a sentence below a statutory or guidelines minimum if the Government has filed a motion stating the defendant has provided substantial assistance in the investigation or prosecution of another person. The petitioner in Wade v. United States, 504 U.S. 181, 112 S.Ct. 1840, 118 L.Ed.2d 524 (1992) pleaded guilty to an offense that carried a 10 year minimum sentence. At sentencing he asked the District Court to impose a sentence less than 10 years on the ground he had provided substantial assistance. The District Court refused, taking the position it lacked that power without a motion from the Government. The United States Supreme Court, in an opinion for a unanimous Court by Justice Souter, upheld this decision. A District Court lacks power to impose a sentence lower than a statutory minimum or the minimum provided by guidelines unless the Government has filed a substantial assistance motion or unless the defendant can show that its failure to do so was based upon an unconstitutional motive, such as race or religion. This is the same standard that governs judicial review of prosecutorial charging decisions. Wade made no claim of

unconstitutional motive. Wade also did not claim that the Government's failure to file a substantial assistance motion was a breach of a plea agreement.

6. **Sentencing Commission policy statements and commentaries.** In addition to guidelines, the United States Sentencing Commission publishes policy statements and commentaries. What weight should courts give to those "lesser" declarations from the Commission? In Williams v. United States, 503 U.S. 193, 112 S.Ct. 1112, 117 L.Ed.2d 341 (1992), the petitioner was convicted of possession of a firearm by a convicted felon. The District Court imposed a longer sentence than normally authorized by the sentencing guidelines on the basis of the petitioner's arrest record. While such action was not specifically prohibited by guidelines, it was done contrary to a policy statement that records of arrests for unadjudicated offenses can not be taken into account in this manner. The Supreme Court, in an opinion by Justice O'Connor, held that "[w]here ... a policy statement prohibits a district court from taking a specified action, the statement is an authoritative guide to the meaning of the applicable guideline. An error in interpreting such a policy statement could lead to an incorrect determination that a departure was appropriate." 503 U.S. at 201, 112 S.Ct. at 1119, 117 L.Ed.2d at 353. The Court vacated sentence and remanded for a determination whether the sentence was a result of the "error in interpreting" the policy statement or of authorized considerations in the case. Justice White, joined by Justice Kennedy, dissented.

The weight to be given to Commission commentaries was considered by the Court in Stinson v. United States, 508 U.S. 36, 113 S.Ct. 1913, 123 L.Ed.2d 598 (1993). Petitioner was also convicted of possession of a firearm by a convicted felon. The District Court sentenced him as a career offender based on a finding that the offense of possession of a firearm by a convicted felon is a "crime of violence" justifying that upward departure. Later, the Commission promulgated a commentary to the guidelines stating explicitly that possession of a firearm by a convicted felon is not a crime of violence under the career offender guidelines. The Supreme Court, in a unanimous opinion by Justice Kennedy, held that guidelines should be given a weight akin to an administrative agency's interpretation of its own legislative rules. "[P]rovided an agency's interpretation of its own regulations does not violate the Constitution or a federal statute, it must be given 'controlling weight unless it is plainly erroneous or inconsistent with the regulation.' " 508 U.S. at 45, 113 S.Ct. at 1919, 123 L.Ed.2d at 608. The Court also addressed the relationship between amendments in the commentary, as occurred in this case, and prior inconsistent appellate court interpretations of the underlying guideline:

> Although amendments to guidelines provisions are one method of incorporating revisions, another method open to the Commission is amendment of the commentary, if the guideline which the commentary interprets will bear the construction. Amended commentary is binding on the federal courts even though it is not reviewed by Congress, and prior judicial constructions of a particular guideline cannot prevent the Commission from adopting a conflicting interpretation that satisfies the standard we set forth today.

508 U.S. at 46, 113 S.Ct. at 1919, 123 L.Ed.2d at 608–09. The Court remanded the case to the Court of Appeals for it to determine what effect, if any, the amended commentary should be given in petitioner's case.

C. PROCEDURAL ISSUES IN SENTENCING

Traditionally the procedures employed in gathering information and making the initial decision as to sentence have been comparatively informal. A sentencing hearing may be held at which witnesses are placed under oath and testimony and evidence is taken. But the procedure may be far less formal. The sentencing judge may obtain information in many ways. Suggestions and arguments are frequently offered by counsel for both sides and perhaps the defendant as well. Letters and phone calls may also have been the source of information to the judge from the probation officer, an examining psychiatrist, or other interested party. Most commonly, however, the court's probation officer will have been directed to conduct an investigation into the circumstances of the offense and the defendant's background. The written product, often made available to the judge before the hearing, is usually called the presentence report (or presentence investigation report [PSI]). The dominance of guilty pleas and the trend toward determinate sentencing have resulted in increased attention upon the sentencing process. This subsection considers some of the practices and issues concerning information used in sentencing and the parts played at this stage by opposing counsel.

1.   DEVELOPMENT OF SENTENCING INFORMATION

Presentence reports play an integral part in sentencing and correctional decisions in the federal system and in many states. Therefore, the data contained in these reports is vital. This subsection focuses upon the content of the report, disclosure and challenge of these contents, and the manner in which the data is collected, presented and used.

Fennell and Hall, Due Process at Sentencing: An Empirical and Legal Analysis of the Disclosure of Presentence Reports in Federal Courts

93 Harvard L.Rev. 1613, 1627–30 (1980).

C.   *Importance of the Presentence Report*

The presentence report serves two essential functions in the sentencing process. First, because an overwhelming majority of defendants plead guilty and therefore forgo trial, the report often substitutes for the trial itself as a mechanism through which facts are found in a criminal case. In those cases, the report provides the sentencing judge with his only knowledge of the offense and the defendant, other than the minimal facts necessary to support the acceptance of a guilty plea.[8] . . .

---

8.   . . . In several districts, the report also plays an important role in the plea bargaining process. For example, in one district the probation office initiates the investigation prior to arraignment. After the report is completed, the probation office recommendation for disposition is voted on at a staff meeting, with each probation officer and the chief judge casting one vote. The resulting recommendation and the information from the investigation are conveyed to the Assistant United States Attorney on the case. He uses these as the basis for his negotiations with the defense attorney. If he strays too far from the recommendation, the judge will refuse to accept the negotiated sentence. After negotiations, the defendant is arraigned—and in this district, 95% of the defendants plead guilty at arraignment.

A second district has a presentence conference that includes a magistrate, prosecutor, and defense attorney. The magistrate is supplied with the probation office recommendation and copies of the report's prior-record section. He gives the

After sentencing, the presentence report continues to function as the central document in the correctional process. If the defendant is placed on probation, the report helps the probation officer determine an appropriate treatment program and level of supervision. If incarceration is necessary, the report is used in determining both the proper institution and the defendant's classification within the institution. The report also plays a crucial role in parole decisions and in aiding parole supervision when the defendant returns to the community. . . .

D. *Problems Associated with the Presentence Report*

The principal problem inherent in the use of the presentence report is its potential for introducing inaccurate or misleading information into the sentencing decision. Because of the report's importance in the sentencing and later correctional processes, any misinformation or misleading statements it contains often have a multiple impact—affecting not only the severity of the sentence, but also the offender's classification in prison, his ability to obtain furloughs and work release, and the likelihood of his early parole. . . .

The opportunity for inclusion of misinformation is particularly acute after the guilty plea, when the probation officer engages in a new investigation of the offense without the use of traditional adversarial and evidentiary safeguards for ensuring fairness and accuracy. Similarly, when a probation officer attempts to determine whether an offender was represented by counsel at a conviction,[9] a significant possibility of error exists because the recordkeeping practices of local courts are often inadequate.

Misleading information in the presentence report, in the form of subtle distortions resulting from incompleteness, innuendo, or ambiguity, can also adversely affect the defendant's treatment. For example, one presentence report stated that a sex offender "had a knife" when he committed the offense; the knife proved to be merely a pocketknife that the defendant customarily carried but did not use in the commission of the crime. Computerized data may often be deceptive in that information is often transmitted in the form of a categorical, often pejorative, label such as "major drug supplier" or "organized crime member." Without further substantiation, the reliability of these labels cannot be tested. Even clinical information, though valuable in portraying the defendant's character and criminal motivation, has a tendency both to categorize the individual and to negate the impact of equally important, but less authoritative, data. Moreover, clinical evaluations are generally unverifiable without knowledge of the expert's credentials and the basis for his assessment of the defendant.

prior-record section to the attorneys but retains the recommendation. Negotiations then commence. In the past, the magistrate acted as a referee, nodding his head when the attorneys got "warm" and grimacing when they strayed too far from the recommended sentence. Now, because of concern over the implications of this practice for judicial participation in plea bargaining, the magistrate presides silently over the proceeding and gives no indication of the court's position.

9. It is unconstitutional for uncounseled convictions to be used as the basis for imposing sentence. United States v. Tucker, 404 U.S. 443, 447–49 (1972).

Concerns such as these led to the eventual amendment of rule 32(c)(3) to require disclosure of the presentence report and to permit the defendant to comment upon it. The policy of the new rule, as stated in the Advisory Committee Note, is that "[t]he best way of insuring accuracy is disclosure with an opportunity for the defendant and counsel to point out to the court information thought to be inaccurate, incomplete, or otherwise misleading."

* * *

FEDERAL RULES OF CRIMINAL PROCEDURE RULE 32 SENTENCE AND JUDGMENT

* * *

(c) Presentence Investigation.

(1) When Made. A probation officer shall make a presentence investigation and report to the court before the imposition of sentence unless the court finds that there is in the record information sufficient to enable the meaningful exercise of sentencing authority pursuant to 18 U.S.C. 3553, and the court explains this finding on the record.

Except with the written consent of the defendant, the report shall not be submitted to the court or its contents disclosed to anyone unless the defendant has pleaded guilty or nolo contendere or has been found guilty.

(2) Report. The report of the presentence investigation shall contain—

(A) information about the history and characteristics of the defendant, including prior criminal record, if any, financial condition, and any circumstances affecting the defendant's behavior that may be helpful in imposing sentence or in the correctional treatment of the defendant.

(B) the classification of the offense and of the defendant under the categories established by the Sentencing Commission . . .; the kinds of sentence and the sentencing range suggested for such a category of offense committed by such a category of defendant as set forth in the guidelines issued by the Sentencing Commission . . .; and an explanation by the probation officer of any factors that may indicate that a sentence of a different kind or of a different length than one within the applicable guideline would be more appropriate under all the circumstances;

(C) any pertinent policy statement issued by the Sentencing Commission . . .;

(D) verified information stated in a nonargumentative style containing an assessment of the financial, social, psychological, and medical impact upon, and cost to, any individual against whom the offense has been committed;

(E) unless the court orders otherwise, information concerning the nature and extent of nonprison programs and resources available for the defendant; and

(F) such other information as may be required by the court.

(3) Disclosure.

(A) At least 10 days before imposing sentence, unless this minimum period is waived by the defendant, the court shall provide the defendant and the defendant's counsel with a copy of the report of the presentence investigation including the information required by subdivision (c)(2) and not including any final recommendation as to sentence, and not to the extent that in the opinion of the court the report contains diagnostic opinions which if disclosed, might seriously disrupt a program of rehabilitation; or sources of information obtained upon a promise of confidentiality; or any other information which, if disclosed, might result in harm, physical or otherwise, to the defendant or other persons. The court shall afford the defendant and his counsel an opportunity to comment on the report and, in the discretion of the court, to introduce testimony or other information relating to any alleged factual inaccuracy contained in it.

(B) If the court is of the view that there is information in the presentence report which should not be disclosed under subdivision (c)(3)(A) of this rule, the court in lieu of making the report or part thereof available shall state orally or in writing a summary of the factual information contained therein to be relied on in determining sentence, and shall give the defendant and the defendant's counsel an opportunity to comment thereon. The statement may be made to the parties in camera.

(C) Any material which may be disclosed to the defendant and the defendant's counsel shall be disclosed to the attorney for the government.

(D) If the comments of the defendant and the defendant's counsel or testimony or other information introduced by them allege any factual inaccuracy in the presentence investigation report or the summary of the report or part thereof, the court shall, as to each matter controverted, make (i) a finding as to the allegation, or (ii) a determination that no such finding is necessary because the matter controverted will not be taken into account in sentencing. A written record of such findings and determinations shall be appended to and accompany any copy of the presentence investigation report thereafter made available to the Bureau of Prisons.

* * *

Gardner v. Florida

Supreme Court of the United States, 1977.
430 U.S. 349, 97 S.Ct. 1197, 51 L.Ed.2d 393.

■ MR. JUSTICE STEVENS announced the judgment of the Court and delivered an opinion, in which MR. JUSTICE STEWART and MR. JUSTICE POWELL joined.

Petitioner was convicted of first-degree murder and sentenced to death. When the trial judge imposed the death sentence he stated that he was relying in part on information in a presentence investigation report. Portions of the report were not disclosed to counsel for the parties. Without reviewing the confidential portion of the presentence report, the Supreme Court of Florida, over the dissent of two justices, affirmed the death sentence. 313 So.2d 675 (1975). We conclude that this procedure does not satisfy the constitutional command that no person shall be deprived of life without due process of law.

I.

On June 30, 1973, the petitioner assaulted his wife with a blunt instrument, causing her death. On January 10, 1974, after a trial in the Circuit Court of Citrus County, Fla., a jury found him guilty of first-degree murder.

The separate sentencing hearing required by Florida law in capital cases was held later on the same day. The State merely introduced two photographs of the decedent, otherwise relying on the trial testimony. That testimony, if credited, was sufficient to support a finding of one of the statutory aggravating circumstances, that the felony committed by petitioner "was especially heinous, atrocious, or cruel."

In mitigation petitioner testified that he had consumed a vast quantity of alcohol during a day-long drinking spree which preceded the crime, and professed to have almost no recollection of the assault itself. His testimony, if credited, was sufficient to support a finding of at least one of the statutory mitigating circumstances.[10]

After hearing this evidence the jury was instructed to determine by a majority vote (1) whether the State had proved one of the aggravating circumstances defined by statute, (2) whether mitigating circumstances outweighed any such aggravating circumstance, and (3) based on that determination, whether the defendant should be sentenced to life or death.

After the jury retired to deliberate, the judge announced that he was going to order a presentence investigation of petitioner. Twenty-five minutes later the jury returned its advisory verdict. It expressly found that the mitigating circumstances outweighed the aggravating circumstances and advised the court to impose a life sentence.

The presentence investigation report was completed by the Florida Parole and Probation Commission on January 28, 1974. On January 30, 1974, the trial judge entered findings of fact and a judgment sentencing petitioner to death. His ultimate finding was that the felony "was especially heinous, atrocious or cruel; and that such aggravating circumstances outweighs the mitigating circumstance, to-wit: none." As a preface to that ultimate finding, he recited that his conclusion was based on the evidence presented at both stages of the bifurcated proceeding, the arguments of counsel, and his review of "the factual information contained in said presentence investigation."

---

10. The statute provides, in part:

"(6) Mitigating circumstances.—Mitigating circumstances shall be the following:

"(b) The capital felony was committed while the defendant was under the influence of extreme mental or emotional disturbance.

"(f) The capacity of the defendant to appreciate the criminality of his conduct or to conform his conduct to the requirements of law was substantially impaired." Fla.Stat.Ann. §§ 921.141(6)(b), (f) (Supp.1976).

* * *

There is no dispute about the fact that the presentence investigation report contained a confidential portion which was not disclosed to defense counsel. Although the judge noted in his findings of fact that the State and petitioner's counsel had been given "a copy of that portion [of the report] to which they are entitled," counsel made no request to examine the full report or to be apprised of the contents of the confidential portion. The trial judge did not comment on the contents of the confidential portion. His findings do not indicate that there was anything of special importance in the undisclosed portion, or that there was any reason other than customary practice for not disclosing the entire report to the parties.

* * *

II.

The State places its primary reliance on this Court's landmark decision in Williams v. New York, 337 U.S. 241, 69 S.Ct. 1079, 93 L.Ed. 1337 [(1949)]. In that case, as in this, the trial judge rejected the jury's recommendation of mercy and imposed the death sentence in reliance, at least in part, on material contained in a report prepared by the court's probation department. The New York Court of Appeals had affirmed the sentence, rejecting the contention that it was a denial of due process to rely on information supplied by witnesses whom the accused could neither confront nor cross-examine.

This Court referred to appellant's claim as a "narrow contention," id., at 243, 69 S.Ct., at 1081, and characterized the case as one which

"presents a serious and difficult question ... relat[ing] to the rules of evidence applicable to the manner in which a judge may obtain information to guide him in the imposition of sentence upon an already convicted defendant." Id., at 244, 69 S.Ct., at 1082.

The conviction and sentence were affirmed, over the dissent of two Justices.

Mr. Justice Black's opinion for the Court persuasively reasons why material developed in a presentence investigation may be useful to a sentencing judge, and why it may not be unfair to a defendant to rely on such information even if it would not be admissible in a normal adversary proceeding in open court. We consider the relevance of that reasoning to this case in Part III of this opinion. Preliminarily, however, we note two comments by Mr. Justice Black that make it clear that the *holding* of *Williams* is not directly applicable to this case.

It is first significant that in *Williams* the material facts concerning the defendant's background which were contained in the presentence report were described in detail by the trial judge in open court. Referring to this material, Mr. Justice Black noted:

"The accuracy of the statements made by the judge as to appellant's background and past practices was not challenged by appellant or his counsel, nor was the judge asked to disregard any of them or to afford appellant a chance to refute or discredit any of them by cross-examination or otherwise." Ibid.

In contrast, in the case before us, the trial judge did not state on the record the substance of any information in the confidential portion of the presentence report that he might have considered material. There was, accordingly, no similar opportunity for petitioner's counsel to challenge the accuracy or materiality of any such information.

It is also significant that Mr. Justice Black's opinion recognized that the passage of time justifies a re-examination of capital-sentencing procedures. As he pointed out:

> "This whole country has traveled far from the period in which the death sentence was an automatic and commonplace result of convictions—even for offenses today deemed trivial." Id., at 247–248, 69 S.Ct., at 1083.

Since that sentence was written almost 30 years ago, this Court has acknowledged its obligation to re-examine capital-sentencing procedures against evolving standards of procedural fairness in a civilized society.

III.

In 1949, when the *Williams* case was decided, no significant constitutional difference between the death penalty and lesser punishments for crime had been expressly recognized by this Court. At that time the Court assumed that after a defendant was convicted of a capital offense, like any other offense, a trial judge had complete discretion to impose any sentence within the limits prescribed by the legislature. As long as the judge stayed within those limits, his sentencing discretion was essentially unreviewable and the possibility of error was remote, if, indeed, it existed at all. In the intervening years there have been two constitutional developments which require us to scrutinize a State's capital-sentencing procedures more closely than was necessary in 1949.

First, five Members of the Court have now expressly recognized that death is a different kind of punishment from any other which may be imposed in this country. ...From the point of view of the defendant, it is different in both its severity and its finality. From the point of view of society, the action of the sovereign in taking the life of one of its citizens also differs dramatically from any other legitimate state action. It is of vital importance to the defendant and to the community that any decision to impose the death sentence be, and appear to be, based on reason rather than caprice or emotion.

Second, it is now clear that the sentencing process, as well as the trial itself, must satisfy the requirements of the Due Process Clause. Even though the defendant has no substantive right to a particular sentence within the range authorized by statute, the sentencing is a critical stage of the criminal proceeding at which he is entitled to the effective assistance of counsel. Mempa v. Rhay, 389 U.S. 128, 88 S.Ct. 254, 19 L.Ed.2d 336; Specht v. Patterson, 386 U.S. 605, 87 S.Ct. 1209, 18 L.Ed.2d 326. The defendant has a legitimate interest in the character of the procedure which leads to the imposition of sentence even if he may have no right to object to a particular result of the sentencing process. ...[11]

---

11. The fact that due process applies does not, of course, implicate the entire panoply of criminal trial procedural rights. "Once it is determined that due process applies, the question remains what pro-

In the light of these developments we consider the justifications offered by the State for a capital-sentencing procedure which permits a trial judge to impose the death sentence on the basis of confidential information which is not disclosed to the defendant or his counsel.

The State first argues that an assurance of confidentiality to potential sources of information is essential to enable investigators to obtain relevant but sensitive disclosures from persons unwilling to comment publicly about a defendant's background or character. The availability of such information, it is argued, provides the person who prepares the report with greater detail on which to base a sentencing recommendation and, in turn, provides the judge with a better basis for his sentencing decision. But consideration must be given to the quality, as well as the quantity, of the information on which the sentencing judge may rely. Assurances of secrecy are conducive to the transmission of confidences which may bear no closer relation to fact than the average rumor or item of gossip, and may imply a pledge not to attempt independent verification of the information received. The risk that some of the information accepted in confidence may be erroneous, or may be misinterpreted, by the investigator or by the sentencing judge, is manifest.

If, as the State argues, it is important to use such information in the sentencing process, we must assume that in some cases it will be decisive in the judge's choice between a life sentence and a death sentence. If it tends to tip the scales in favor of life, presumably the information would be favorable and there would be no reason why it should not be disclosed. On the other hand, if it is the basis for a death sentence, the interest in reliability plainly outweighs the State's interest in preserving the availability of comparable information in other cases.

The State also suggests that full disclosure of the presentence report will unnecessarily delay the proceeding. We think the likelihood of significant delay is overstated because we must presume that reports prepared by professional probation officers, as the Florida procedure requires, are generally reliable. In those cases in which the accuracy of a report is contested, the trial judge can avoid delay by disregarding the disputed material. Or if the disputed matter is of critical importance, the time invested in ascertaining the truth would surely be well spent if it makes the difference between life and death.

The State further urges that full disclosure of presentence reports, which often include psychiatric and psychological evaluations, will occasionally disrupt the process of rehabilitation. The argument, if valid, would hardly justify withholding the report from defense counsel. Moreover, whatever force that argument may have in non-capital cases, it has abso-

cess is due. It has been said so often by this Court and others as not to require citation of authority that due process is flexible and calls for such procedural protections as the particular situation demands. ...Its flexibility is in its scope once it has been determined that some process is due; it is a recognition that not all situations calling for procedural safeguards call for the same kind of procedure." Morrissey v. Brewer, 408 U.S. 471, 481, 92 S.Ct. 2593, 2600, 33 L.Ed.2d 484.

lutely no merit in a case in which the judge has decided to sentence the defendant to death. Indeed, the extinction of all possibility of rehabilitation is one of the aspects of the death sentence that makes it different in kind from any other sentence a State may legitimately impose.

Finally, Florida argues that trial judges can be trusted to exercise their discretion in a responsible manner, even though they may base their decisions on secret information. However acceptable that argument might have been before Furman v. Georgia, it is now clearly foreclosed. Moreover, the argument rests on the erroneous premise that the participation of counsel is superfluous to the process of evaluating the relevance and significance of aggravating and mitigating facts. Our belief that debate between adversaries is often essential to the truth-seeking function of trials requires us also to recognize the importance of giving counsel an opportunity to comment on facts which may influence the sentencing decision in capital cases.

* * *

We conclude that petitioner was denied due process of law when the death sentence was imposed, at least in part, on the basis of information which he had no opportunity to deny or explain.

IV.

There remains only the question of what disposition is now proper. Petitioner's conviction, of course, is not tainted by the error in the sentencing procedure. The State argues that we should merely remand the case to the Florida Supreme Court with directions to have the entire presentence report made a part of the record to enable that court to complete its reviewing function. That procedure, however, could not fully correct the error. For it is possible that full disclosure, followed by explanation or argument by defense counsel, would have caused the trial judge to accept the jury's advisory verdict. Accordingly, the death sentence is vacated, and the case is remanded to the Florida Supreme Court with directions to order further proceedings at the trial court level not inconsistent with this opinion.

Vacated and remanded.

■ THE CHIEF JUSTICE concurs in the judgment.

[The opinions of Justice White and Justice Blackmun, concurring in the judgment, the separate opinion of Justice Brennan, and the dissenting opinions of Justice Marshall and Justice Rehnquist, are omitted].

NOTES

1. **Defense access to report.** In United States v. Rone, 743 F.2d 1169 (7th Cir.1984), the Seventh Circuit held that the district court's failure to assure defendant access to his presentence report at a reasonable time before the sentencing hearing required vacation of sentence and remand for new sentencing. In reaching this decision, the court stated that all defendants have a due process right to a fair sentencing procedure which includes the right to be sentenced on the basis of accurate information, but that the trial court at the sentencing hearing need

directly ask defendant only three questions: whether he has had an opportunity to read the presentence report; whether defendant and defense counsel have discussed the report; and whether defendant wishes to challenge any facts in the report. A sentence must be set aside, the court said, where defendant can demonstrate that false information formed part of the basis for the sentence.

2. **Constitutionality of using presentence reports.** In Williams v. New York, 337 U.S. 241, 69 S.Ct. 1079, 93 L.Ed. 1337 (1949), distinguished in *Gardner,* supra, on the issue of nondisclosure, the Court also held that the Due Process Clause of the Fourteenth Amendment did not require a judge to have hearings and to give a convicted person an opportunity to participate in those hearings when he came to determine the sentence to be imposed. Justice Black stated:

> Under the practice of individualizing punishments, investigational techniques have been given an important role. Probation workers making reports of their investigations have not been trained to prosecute but to aid offenders. Their reports have been given a high value by conscientious judges who want to sentence persons on the best available information rather than on guesswork and inadequate information. To deprive sentencing judges of this kind of information would undermine modern penological procedural policies that have been cautiously adopted throughout the nation after careful consideration and experimentation. We must recognize that most of the information now relied upon by judges to guide them in the intelligent imposition of sentences would be unavailable if information were restricted to that given in open court by witnesses subject to cross-examination. And the modern probation report draws on information concerning every aspect of a defendant's life. The type and extent of this information make totally impractical if not impossible open court testimony with cross-examination. Such a procedure could endlessly delay criminal administration in a retrial of collateral issues. . . .

337 U.S. at 249–50, 69 S.Ct. at 1084, 93 L.Ed. at 1343.

How viable is *Williams* after *Gardner?*

3. **Required findings of fact.** Specht v. Patterson, 386 U.S. 605, 87 S.Ct. 1209, 18 L.Ed.2d 326 (1967), had earlier distinguished *Williams* in a different kind of sentencing situation.

Mr. Justice Douglas delivered the opinion of the Court.

> The question is whether the rule of the *Williams* case applies to this Colorado case where petitioner, having been convicted for indecent liberties under one Colorado statute that carries a maximum sentence of 10 years . . . but not sentenced under it, may be sentenced under the Sex Offenders Act . . . for an indeterminate term of from one day to life without notice and full hearing. The Colorado Supreme Court approved the procedure, ... The case is here on a petition for certiorari. . . .

> * * *

> We adhere to Williams v. People of State of New York, supra; but we decline the invitation to extend it to this radically different situation. . . . We hold that the requirements of due process were not satisfied here. . . .

> The Sex Offenders Act does not make the commission of a specified crime the basis for sentencing. It makes one conviction the basis for commencing another proceeding under another Act to determine whether a person constitutes a threat of bodily harm to the public, or is an habitual offender and mentally ill. That is a new finding of fact . . . that was not an ingredient of the offense charged. The punishment under the second Act is criminal punishment

even though it is designed not so much as retribution as it is to keep individuals from inflicting future harm. . . .

. . . Under Colorado's criminal procedure, here challenged, the invocation of the Sex Offenders Act means the making of a new charge leading to criminal punishment. The case is not unlike those under recidivist statutes where an habitual criminal issue is "a distinct issue" . . . on which a defendant "must receive reasonable notice and an opportunity to be heard." . . . Due process, in other words, requires that he be present with counsel, have an opportunity to be heard, be confronted with witnesses against him, have the right to cross-examine, and to offer evidence of his own. And there must be findings adequate to make meaningful any appeal that is allowed. . . . None of these procedural safeguards we have mentioned is present under Colorado's Sex Offenders Act. We therefore hold that it is deficient in due process as measured by the requirements of the Fourteenth Amendment. . . .

386 U.S. at 607–11, 87 S.Ct. at 1211–13, 18 L.Ed.2d at 328–31.

4.   **Freedom of Information Act.** In United States Department of Justice v. Julian, 486 U.S. 1, 108 S.Ct. 1606, 100 L.Ed.2d 1 (1988), the Court was faced with the question of whether an inmate could compel disclosure of his presentence investigation report under the Freedom of Information Act from the Bureau of Prisons or the Parole Commission. The Court, through The Chief Justice, held that disclosure was required by the Freedom of Information Act, subject to the same three restrictions of Federal Rules of Criminal Procedure Rule 32(c)(3)(A) [supra] for diagnostic opinions, confidential sources of information, or harmful material.

2.   DEFENSE COUNSEL'S ROLE

In most cases the guilt-innocence question is resolved by the defendants' pleas of guilty. If defense counsel has little opportunity to challenge the prosecution's ability to prove the defendant guilty, counsel's primary opportunity to serve the defendant involves sentencing. How this might best be done is addressed in this subsection. Various ethical dilemmas in defense counsel's sentencing role are also touched upon.

Mempa v. Rhay

Supreme Court of the United States, 1967.
389 U.S. 128, 88 S.Ct. 254, 19 L.Ed.2d 336.

■ MR. JUSTICE MARSHALL delivered the opinion of the Court.

These consolidated cases raise the question of the extent of the right to counsel at the time of sentencing where the sentencing has been deferred subject to probation.

Petitioner Jerry Douglas Mempa was convicted in the Spokane County Superior Court on June 17, 1959, of the offense of "joyriding," Wash.Rev. Code § 9.54.020. This conviction was based on his plea of guilty entered with the advice of court-appointed counsel. He was then placed on probation for two years on the condition, *inter alia,* that he first spend 30 days in the county jail, and the imposition of sentence was deferred pursuant to Wash.Rev.Code §§ 9.95.200, 9.95.210.

About four months later the Spokane County prosecuting attorney moved to have petitioner's probation revoked on the ground that he had been involved in a burglary on September 15, 1959. A hearing was held in the Spokane County Superior Court on October 23, 1959. Petitioner Mempa, who was 17 years old at the time, was accompanied to the hearing by his stepfather. He was not represented by counsel and was not asked whether he wished to have counsel appointed for him. Nor was any inquiry made concerning the appointed counsel who had previously represented him.

At the hearing Mempa was asked if it was true that he had been involved in the alleged burglary and he answered in the affirmative. A probation officer testified without cross-examination that according to his information petitioner had been involved in the burglary and had previously denied participation in it. Without asking petitioner if he had anything to say or any evidence to supply, the court immediately entered an order revoking petitioner's probation and then sentenced him to 10 years in the penitentiary, but stated that it would recommend to the parole board that Mempa be required to serve only a year.

* * *

In 1948 this Court held in Townsend v. Burke, 334 U.S. 736, 68 S.Ct. 1252, 92 L.Ed. 1690, that the absence of counsel during sentencing after a plea of guilty coupled with "assumptions concerning his criminal record which were materially untrue" deprived the defendant in that case of due process. Mr. Justice Jackson there stated in conclusion, "In this case, counsel might not have changed the sentence, but he could have taken steps to see that the conviction and sentence were not predicated on misinformation or misreading of court records, a requirement of fair play which absence of counsel withheld from this prisoner." . . .

. . . Townsend v. Burke, supra, illustrates the critical nature of sentencing in a criminal case and might well be considered to support by itself a holding that the right to counsel applies at sentencing. . . .

. . . It is true that sentencing in Washington offers fewer opportunities for the exercise of judicial discretion than in many other jurisdictions. Obviously to the extent . . . recommendations [by the judge to the Parole Board which determines the length of imprisonment] are influential in determining the resulting sentence, the necessity for the aid of counsel in marshaling the facts, introducing evidence of mitigating circumstances and in general aiding and assisting the defendant to present his case as to sentence is apparent.

Even more important . . . is the fact that certain legal rights may be lost if not exercised at this stage. For one, . . . absence of counsel . . . might well result in loss of the right to appeal. While ordinarily appeals from a plea of guilty are less frequent than those following a trial on the merits, the incidence of improperly obtained guilty pleas is not so slight as to be capable of being characterized as *de minimis.* . . .

Likewise the Washington statutes provide that a plea of guilty can be withdrawn at any time prior to the imposition of sentence . . . if the trial judge in his discretion finds that the ends of justice will be served. . . . An uncounseled defendant might very likely be unaware of this opportunity.

The two foregoing factors assume increased significance when it is considered that, as happened in these two cases, the eventual imposition of sentence on the prior plea of guilty is based on the alleged commission of offenses for which the accused is never tried.

In sum, we do not question the authority of the State of Washington to provide for a deferred sentencing procedure coupled with its probation provisions. Indeed, it appears to be an enlightened step forward. All we decide here is that a lawyer must be afforded at this proceeding whether it be labeled a revocation of probation or a deferred sentencing. We assume that counsel appointed for the purpose of the trial or guilty plea would not be unduly burdened by being requested to follow through at the deferred sentencing stage of the proceeding.

NOTES

1. **Functions of counsel.** While discussing the important functions counsel could have performed in the Washington probation revocation proceedings, was it by oversight that Mr. Justice Marshall failed to mention the functions of counsel (1) in litigating the issue whether probation was violated and, (2) if the trial court concluded it was, in representing his client in an attempt to persuade the judge to exercise his discretion not to revoke probation? How do these functions of counsel compare in importance with those discussed in the opinion?

2. **Right to hearing and counsel.** In Gagnon v. Scarpelli, 411 U.S. 778, 93 S.Ct. 1756, 36 L.Ed.2d 656 (1973), the case presented "the related questions whether a previously sentenced probationer [unlike *Mempa*] is entitled to a hearing when his probation is revoked and, if so, whether he is entitled to be represented by appointed counsel at such a hearing." The court stated:

> Probation revocation, like parole revocation, is not a stage of a criminal prosecution, but does result in a loss of liberty. Accordingly, we hold that a probationer, like a parolee, is entitled to a preliminary and a final revocation hearing, under the conditions specified in Morrissey v. Brewer, [408 U.S. 471, 92 S.Ct. 2593, 33 L.Ed.2d 484 (1972)].

> * * *

> The second, and more difficult, question posed by this case is whether an indigent probationer or parolee has a due process right to be represented by appointed counsel at these hearings. In answering that question, we draw heavily on the opinion in *Morrissey*.

> * * *

> At the preliminary hearing, a probationer or parolee is entitled to notice of the alleged violations of probation or parole, an opportunity to appear and to present evidence in his own behalf, a conditional right to confront adverse witnesses, an independent decisionmaker, and a written report of the hearing. ...The final hearing is a less summary one because the decision under consideration is the ultimate decision to revoke rather than a mere determination of probable cause, but the "minimum requirements of due process" include very similar elements:

>> "(a) written notice of the claimed violations of [probation or] parole; (b) disclosure to the [probationer or] parolee of evidence against him; (c) opportunity to be heard in person and to present witnesses and documentary evidence; (d) the right to confront and cross-examine adverse witnesses

(unless the hearing officer specifically finds good cause for not allowing confrontation); (e) a 'neutral and detached' hearing body such as a traditional parole board, members of which need not be judicial officers or lawyers; and (f) a written statement by the fact-finders as to the evidence relied on and reasons for revoking [probation or] parole." Morrissey v. Brewer, supra, 408 U.S., at 489, 92 S.Ct., at 2604.

These requirements in themselves serve as substantial protection against ill-considered revocation, ...[but] may in some circumstances depend on the use of skills which the probationer or parolee is unlikely to possess.

...We think, ...that the decision as to the need for counsel must be made on a case-by-case basis in the exercise of a sound discretion by the state authority charged with responsibility for administering the probation and parole system. Although the presence and participation of counsel will probably be both undesirable and constitutionally unnecessary in most revocation hearings, there will remain certain cases in which fundamental fairness—the touchstone of due process—will require that the State provide at its expense counsel for indigent probationers or parolees.

* * *

Presumptively, it may be said that counsel should be provided in cases where, after being informed of his right to request counsel, the probationer or parolee makes such a request, based on a timely and colorable claim (i) that he has not committed the alleged violation of the conditions upon which he is at liberty; or (ii) that, even if the violation is a matter of public record or is uncontested, there are substantial reasons which justified or mitigated the violation and make revocation inappropriate and that the reasons are complex or otherwise difficult to develop or present. In passing on a request for the appointment of counsel, the responsible agency also should consider, especially in doubtful cases, whether the probationer appears to be capable of speaking effectively for himself. In every case in which a request for counsel at a preliminary or final hearing is refused, the grounds for refusal should be stated succinctly in the record.

411 U.S. at 782–91, 93 S.Ct. at 1759–64, 36 L.Ed.2d at 661–67.

3. **Sentencing functions before the sentencing hearing.** According to Kuh, Defense Counsel's Role in Sentencing, 14 Criminal Law Bulletin 433 (1978), counsel's role begins at the first client meeting with information gathering and advice on the subsequent attitude and conduct of the defendant. The possibility of a preplea investigation and social report to provide an early sentence reading is the next step, followed by counsel's discreet but protective presence at the presentence investigation, examination of the presentence report, defense sentencing memorandum, and in-court statement. See also Feit, "Before Sentence is Pronounced ...": A Guide to Defense Counsel on the Exercise of his Post–Conviction Responsibilities, 9 Criminal Law Bulletin 140 (1973), which provides a sentencing checklist.

4. **Defense advocacy strategies at sentencing.** Commentary, ABA Standards Relating to Sentencing Alternatives and Procedures, Approved Draft (1968), § 5.3 states:

[T]he lawyer should ...assume the same position of advocacy that is his duty at the trial. While the lawyer is indeed obligated at trial to make for the defendant the "best possible defense," there are obvious limits which in concrete cases require the lawyer on the spot to draw some tough ethical lines. The "best possible defense," for example, clearly does not include the knowing use of perjured testimony: while this may be "best" from the point of view of the client, the lawyer owes a much larger duty to the court and to the system not to participate in such a scheme. By analogy, there will be limits to the representations that the lawyer can and should make on the sentencing issue. The lawyer should not be expected to argue probation for a rape-murder by a sixth offender by submitting that his record is clean and the offense only minor. At the same time, such a defendant—to the same extent that he deserves "the best possible defense" on guilt, and for the same reasons—deserves the best possible statement of his point of view at the sentencing proceeding. In concrete terms, what this means is that the defense attorney must make a judgment about what sentences are realistically possible, and use the facts at his disposal to do the best he can for the interests of his client.

* * *

Just as the lawyer would not think of pleading him guilty without consultation, he should not ignore the wishes of the client at the sentencing stage. In extreme cases, this may force the attorney to the conclusion that he cannot in conscience pursue the course demanded of him by his client. The difficulty of this position is paralleled by the possibility of its occurrence at the guilt stage as well. The point, in other words, is that the relationship of lawyer to client should not be very much different just because of the arrival of a different stage of the proceeding. And it should be recognized by the lawyer that for many convicted defendants, the sentence will be the most important and the only really difficult issue in the case.

An explanation by the lawyer of the sentencing alternatives and their consequences can also serve a collateral purpose. As was observed in a slightly different context:

> [T]he actual consequences of any sentence for a defendant and his family are usually more complex than expressed by the recitation of statutory sentencing provisions. In some instances there are civil consequences of conviction, such as loss of a license, which are not usually mentioned by the court. Some sentences, for certain sex offenders for example, are predicated on the existence of treatment facilities while in other situations no specific therapy is provided. The nature of imprisonment, the conditions of probation, eligibility for release, and the consequences of these for himself and for his family are all primary concerns of the defendant. In practice, these matters are explained to the defendant by his defense counsel, if they are explained at all. Neither the judge nor the prosecutor usually feels called upon to go into specific, individual consequences of conviction and sentencing; they rely on counsel to relate these details to his client and to his client's family.

Newman, Conviction: The Determination of Guilt or Innocence without Trial 209 (1966).

A defendant who understands what is happening to him is much more likely to respond favorably to the ultimate sentence which is imposed. There is thus a significant correctional objective served by leaving the client with the impression that he has been fairly dealt with. It takes very little effort by the lawyer to convince the average client that he has been railroaded.

There is also a third objective which can be served by a conference between an informed lawyer and his client. That the lawyer can play a significant role in the rehabilitation of his client is often lost in the zeal to procure an expedient sentence. The attorney should not so readily assume that the "best deal" for the client is the lightest possible sentence. There may well be particular correctional services available which will better suit his long-run needs. The lawyer should be aware of these possibilities, and be prepared to recommend their consideration to his client.

* * *

In addition to the fact that the defendant normally must desire such a . . . disposition in order for it to work, the lawyer can find himself in an embarrassing position if his client openly disagrees with a recommendation to the court on his behalf. Most importantly, however, it is not the lawyer's function to decide what is the best disposition for his client. The lawyer is a representative and an advisor, and when he suggests that a . . . disposition is desirable he ought to be doing so with the consent of his client.

A more "collaborative" or "educational" role for defense counsel at sentencing is put forward by Judge Cooper in the context of a real case. Cooper, United States v. Unterman: The Role of Counsel at Sentencing, 13 Criminal Law Bulletin 101 (1977).

Also see Dash, The Defense Lawyers Role At The Sentencing Stage of a Criminal Case, 54 F.R.D. 315 (1972), for a more detailed consideration of the complex ethical issues involved.

3. PROSECUTOR'S ROLE

The prosecutor's role at sentencing is the subject of broad disagreement, even among prosecutors themselves. The following survey provides the range of possibilities and their rationales.

Teitelbaum, The Prosecutor's Role in the Sentencing Process: A National Survey

1 American Journal of Criminal Law 75 (1972).

[T]he vast majority of district attorney's offices do participate in the sentencing process in some fashion. Though a significant minority of offices indicate that as a general policy they abstain from participation, some do intervene in the case of certain major crimes.

The majority of offices taking part in the sentencing process participate in three distinct ways: (1) the prosecutor presents arguments concerning the nature and severity of the crime and the criminal history of the defendant; (2) the prosecutor expresses his position concerning the desirability of an award of probation; and (3) the prosecutor makes a specific sentence recommendation. The next largest group of offices employs only method (3), and the third largest group makes use solely of method (1).

* * *

The survey inquired into the philosophy of the offices that take part in the sentencing process. . . . A slight plurality selected what might be called a "quasi-judicial" position—the prosecutor should recommend exactly the same sentence that he would impose were he the judge. The others favored what might be called an "advocate" philosophy: the job of the prosecutor is to suggest aggravating factors to counterbalance the mitigating factors presented by the defense. . . .

The twenty-six offices that do not participate in the sentencing process are scattered throughout the nation with no regional or geographical pattern. A number of these offices maintained that it would be improper for prosecutors to tender sentence recommendations to the court and they suggested a number of reasons for this view. Most pointed out that the court has the assistance of a probation department or similar agency to assist it in determining the appropriate sentence; they also suggested that sentence determination is a judicial prerogative which should not be lightly invaded. The most startling comment came from Canton, Ohio: sentence recommendations by the prosecutor would "inhibit the system, develop difficulties between the court and the district attorney's office, and make plea bargaining more difficult."

* * *

Most of the offices that usually abstain from the sentencing process abandon that policy in certain cases. . . . The sorts of crime that cause prosecutors to abandon their usual policy of nonparticipation in the sentencing process cover a wide range of activity.

The most frequently listed exception came in cases involving organized crime. Only three other exceptions were listed by more than one office: sex crimes involving children, assaults on police officers, and cases involving defendants with no serious prior record who had cooperated with the police.

* * *

Most district attorney's offices expend the energy to formulate sentence recommendations, yet how often do the courts follow this advice? A plurality of the offices participating in the sentencing process believe that their recommendations are followed "almost all the time." A substantial percentage, however, believe that the courts accept their sentence recommendations only "more than half the time." A small percentage of offices report that their recommendations are followed "less than half the time."

Neither the presence of a probation department nor a difference in prosecutorial philosophy substantially affects the prosecutor's self-perceived success in persuading the court to concur with his recommendations. District attorneys in jurisdictions with a probation office and those with a preference for the "advocate theory" of sentencing see their proposals followed slightly less often than do other prosecutors.

* * *

Prosecutorial sentence recommendations do provide the court with additional information for the decision-making process. Certainly an abundant informational input contributes to thoughtful deliberation; however, rational results depend not merely on quantity of information but also on its relevance. The ultimate question then becomes: Do prosecutorial sentence recommendations provide information helpful to a judge trying to determine an appropriate sentence?

Those district attorney's offices that do make sentence recommendations justify their practice by claiming (in order of importance) that their sentence recommendations provide the court with (1) a law enforcement viewpoint regarding the appropriate sentence, (2) the victim's viewpoint concerning the appropriate sentence, (3) pressure necessary to restrain some judges' propensity for leniency, and (4) information based on greater experience than many judges themselves have had.

* * *

The survey reveals that most district attorney's offices actively take part in the sentencing process. Though prosecutors generally believe that their participation contributes to the effectiveness of the criminal justice system, the value of their contribution remains questionable. . . .

No evidence suggests that the quality of justice suffers in those areas where the prosecutor refrains from actively participating in the sentencing process. . . .

D.   ALTERNATIVES OR SUPPLEMENTS TO INCARCERATION

Despite record rates of incarceration, a high level of public concern about crime continues. Overcrowded institutions, many thus subject to constitutional challenge, are the result. Given these circumstances, there is an urgent need for dispositions or penalties that may be imposed as alternatives to any incarceration or, in some situations at least, in addition. The present section describes some of these alternatives or supplements—probation, fines, and restitution. It also deals with methods of extending periods of incarceration by civil commitment proceedings or by recidivist statutes.

1.   PROBATION

A defendant sentenced to probation is placed under the supervision of a probation officer and must comply with various conditions of probation. Upon a showing that the defendant has violated these conditions, the sentencing court is generally authorized—but not required—to "revoke" the probation and sentence the defendant to a term of incarceration.

Initially, probation was reserved largely for offenders who had committed relatively minor crimes. But in 1973, the National Advisory Commission on Criminal Justice Standards and Goals stated:

> The Commission believes that the most hopeful move towards effective corrections is to continue and strengthen the trend away from confining people in institutions and towards supervising them in the community. . . . The thrust of the Commission's *Report on Corrections* is that probation, which is now the largest community-based program, will become the standard sentence in criminal cases, with confinement retained chiefly for those offenders who cannot safely be supervised in the community.

* * *

There are compelling reasons to continue the move away from institutions. First, State institutions consume more than three-fourths of all expenditures for corrections while dealing with less than one-third of all offenders. Second, as a whole they do not deal with those offenders effectively. There is no evidence that prisons reduce the amount of crime.

A National Strategy to Reduce Crime 121 (1973).

But, as the material in this subsection indicates, there was substantial later concern that probation may be overused. Insofar as it is used, there is also concern that the heavier caseloads may result in offenders being actually given little supervision.

Among the major issues raised by the availability of probation are the circumstances in which it is desirable, the conditions which can or should be imposed upon it, and when revocation is appropriate. These are addressed in the present subsection.

NATIONAL ADVISORY COMMISSION ON CRIMINAL JUSTICE STANDARDS AND GOALS, CORRECTIONS 150 (1973)

Standard 5.2 Sentencing the Nondangerous Offender

Criteria should be established for sentencing offenders. Such criteria should include:

1. A requirement that the least drastic sentencing alternative be imposed that is consistent with public safety. The court should impose the first of the following alternatives that will reasonably protect the public safety:

    a. Unconditional release.

    b. Conditional release.

    c. A fine.

    d. Release under supervision in the community.

    e. Sentence to a halfway house or other residential facility located in the community.

    f. Sentence to partial confinement with liberty to work or participate in training or education during all but leisure time.

    g. Total confinement in a correctional facility.

2. A provision against the use of confinement as an appropriate disposition unless affirmative justification is shown on the record. Factors that would justify confinement may include:

    a. There is undue risk that the offender will commit another crime if not confined.

    b. The offender is in need of correctional services that can be provided effectively only in an institutional setting, and such services are reasonably available.

    c. Any other alternative will depreciate the seriousness of the offense.

3. Weighting of the following in favor of withholding a disposition of incarceration:

a. The offender's criminal conduct neither caused nor actually threatened serious harm.

b. The offender did not contemplate or intend that his criminal conduct would cause or threaten serious harm.

c. The offender acted under strong provocation.

d. There were substantial grounds tending to excuse or justify the offender's criminal conduct, though failing to establish defense.

e. The offender had led a law-abiding life for a substantial period of time before commission of the present crime.

f. The offender is likely to respond affirmatively to probationary or other community supervision.

g. The victim of the crime induced or facilitated its commission.

h. The offender has made or will make restitution or reparation to the victim of his crime for the damage or injury which was sustained.

i. The offender's conduct was the result of circumstances unlikely to recur.

j. The character, history, and attitudes of the offender indicate that he is unlikely to commit another crime.

k. Imprisonment of the offender would entail undue hardship to dependents.

l. The offender is elderly or in poor health.

m. The correctional programs within the institutions to which the offender would be sent are inappropriate to his particular needs or would not likely be of benefit to him.

CALIFORNIA JUDICIAL COUNCIL, SENTENCING RULES FOR THE SUPERIOR COURTS (1990)

Rule 414. Criteria Affecting Probation

Criteria affecting the decision to grant or deny probation include:

(a) Statutory provisions authorizing, limiting or prohibiting the grant of probation.

(b) The likelihood that if not imprisoned the defendant will be a danger to others.

(c) Facts relating to the crime, including:

(1) The nature, seriousness and circumstances of the crime.

(2) The vulnerability of the victim and the degree of harm or loss to the victim.

(3) Whether the defendant was armed with or used a weapon.

(4) Whether the defendant inflicted bodily injury.

(5) Whether the defendant planned the commission of the crime, whether he instigated it or was solicited by others to participate, and whether he was an active or passive participant.

(6) Whether the crime was committed because of an unusual circumstance, such as great provocation, which is unlikely to recur.

(7) Whether the manner in which the crime was carried out demonstrated criminal sophistication or professionalism on the part of the defendant.

(8) Whether the defendant took advantage of a position of trust or confidence to commit the crime.

(d) Facts relating to the defendant, including:

(1) Prior record of criminal conduct, including the recency and frequency of prior crimes, age at which first convicted as an adult or adjudicated to have committed a crime as a juvenile, age at which first confined for prior crimes, and whether the record indicates a pattern of regular or increasingly serious criminal conduct.

(2) Prior performance on probation or parole and present probation or parole status.

(3) Willingness and ability to comply with the terms of probation.

(4) Age, education, health, mental faculties, and family background and ties.

(5) Employment history, military service history, and financial condition.

(6) Danger of addiction to or abuse of alcohol, narcotics, dangerous drugs, or other mood or consciousness-altering substances.

(7) The likely effect of imprisonment on the defendant and his dependents.

(8) The possible effects on the defendant's life of a felony record.

(9) Whether the defendant is remorseful.

(10) Whether a financially able defendant refuses to make restitution to the victim.

18 U.S.C.A.

§ 3563.   Conditions of Probation

(a) Mandatory Conditions.—The court shall provide, as an explicit condition of a sentence of probation—

(1) for a felony, a misdemeanor, or an infraction, that the defendant not commit another Federal, State, or local crime during the term of probation;

(2) for a felony, that the defendant also abide by at least one condition set forth in subsection (b)(2), (b)(3), or (b)(13), unless the court finds on the record that extraordinary circumstances exist that would make such a condition plainly unreasonable, in which event the court shall impose one or more of the other conditions set forth under subsection (b); and

(3) for a felony, a misdemeanor, or an infraction, that the defendant not possess illegal controlled substances.

If the court has imposed and ordered execution of a fine and placed the defendant on probation, payment of the fine or adherence to the court-established installment schedule shall be a condition of the probation.

(b) Discretionary Conditions.—The court may provide, as further conditions of a sentence of probation, to the extent that such conditions are reasonably related to the factors set forth in section 3553(a)(1) and (a)(2) and to the extent that such conditions involve only such deprivations of liberty or property as are reasonably necessary for the purposes indicated in section 3553(a)(2), that the defendant—

(1) support his dependents and meet other family responsibilities;

(2) pay a fine . . . ;

(3) make restitution to a victim of the offense . . . ;

(4) give [notice and explanation] to the victims of [fraud] . . . ;

(5) work conscientiously at suitable employment or pursue conscientiously a course of study or vocational training that will equip him for suitable employment;

(6) refrain, in the case of an individual, from engaging in a specified occupation, business, or profession bearing a reasonably direct relationship to the conduct constituting the offense, or engage in such a specified occupation, business, or profession only to a stated degree or under stated circumstances;

(7) refrain from frequenting specified kinds of places or from associating unnecessarily with specified persons;

(8) refrain from excessive use of alcohol, or any use of a narcotic drug or other controlled substance, as defined in section 102 of the Controlled Substances Act (21 U.S.C. 802), without a prescription by a licensed medical practitioner;

(9) refrain from possessing a firearm, destructive device, or other dangerous weapon;

(10) undergo available medical, psychiatric, or psychological treatment, including treatment for drug or alcohol dependency, as specified by the court, and remain in a specified institution if required for that purpose;

(11) remain in the custody of the Bureau of Prisons during nights, weekends, or other intervals of time, totaling no more than the lesser of one year or the term of imprisonment authorized for the offense in section 3581(b), during the first year of the term of probation;

(12) reside at, or participate in the program of, a community corrections facility . . . for all or part of the term of probation;

(13) work in community service as directed by the court;

(14) reside in a specified place or area, or refrain from residing in a specified place or area;

(15) remain within the jurisdiction of the court, unless granted permission to leave by the court or a probation officer;

(16) report to a probation officer as directed by the court or the probation officer;

(17) permit a probation officer to visit him at his home or elsewhere as specified by the court;

(18) answer inquiries by a probation officer and notify the probation officer promptly of any change in address or employment;

(19) notify the probation officer promptly if arrested or questioned by a law enforcement officer;

(20) remain at his place of residence during nonworking hours and, if the court finds it appropriate, that compliance with this condition be monitored by telephonic or electronic signaling devices, except that a condition under this paragraph may be imposed only as an alternative to incarceration; or

(21) satisfy such other conditions as the court may impose.

(c) Modifications of Conditions.—The court may modify, reduce, or enlarge the conditions of a sentence of probation at any time ...

(d) Written Statement of Conditions.—The court shall direct that the probation officer provide the defendant with a written statement that sets forth all the conditions to which the sentence is subject, and that is sufficiently clear and specific to serve as a guide for the defendant's conduct and for such supervision as is required.

NOTES

1. **Validity of probation conditions.** When a defendant is eligible for probation, judges have almost limitless discretion in setting probation conditions. People v. Lent, 15 Cal.3d 481, 541 P.2d 545, 124 Cal.Rptr. 905 (1975), set forth the traditional circumstances in which a probation condition will be found invalid:

> The Legislature has placed in trial judges a broad discretion in the sentencing process, including the determination as to whether probation is appropriate and, if so, the conditions thereof. A condition of probation will not be held invalid unless it "(1) has no relationship to the crime of which the offender was convicted, (2) relates to conduct which is not in itself criminal, and (3) requires or forbids conduct which is not reasonably related to future criminality...." (People v. Dominguez (1967) 256 Cal.App.2d 623, 627, 64 Cal.Rptr. 290, 293.) Conversely, a condition of probation which requires or forbids conduct which is not itself criminal is valid if, that conduct is reasonably related to the crime of which the defendant was convicted or to future criminality.

15 Cal.3d at 486, 541 P.2d at 548, 124 Cal.Rptr. at 908.

2. **Relationship of condition to crime.** In People v. Higgins, 22 Mich.App. 479, 177 N.W.2d 716 (1970), the defendant pleaded guilty to burglary. He was placed on probation. In addition to the usual conditions of probation, the court imposed a special condition stating: "No varsity or professional basketball during probation unless permitted by the Court." A state statute authorized the trial court to impose "such other lawful conditions of probation ... as the circumstances of the

case may require or warrant, or as in its judgment may be meet and proper." The defendant was a college basketball player "of no small ability" and was in school on an athletic scholarship which he would lose if he were not permitted to play. Although seven months after defendant was placed on probation the trial judge permitted him to play varsity ball, the appellate court held the special condition was invalid:

> The trial judge stated no reason for the restriction, nor have the people explained how this restriction might be related to the defendant's rehabilitation. On the other hand, the defendant has persuasively shown that the restriction on playing basketball is more likely to impede than to promote his rehabilitation. As no rational reason has been suggested in justification and as it appears that the restriction is more likely to impede rehabilitation than promote it, we conclude that it is not a 'lawful provision' within the meaning of the statute.

22 Mich.App. at 482, 177 N.W.2d at 718. The dissenting judge commented: "It is not for an appellate court to . . . try to second guess the rehabilitation efforts of the trial judge. In fact, from what has been disclosed, the efforts of the trial judge have been successful. The defendant, to the knowledge of this writer, has in fact lived up to all the conditions of probation and may now realize that his former behavior will not lead to the type of career which he hopes to pursue at the end of his educational endeavors." 22 Mich.App. at 482, 177 N.W.2d at 719.

3. **Searches of probationers.** "Searches" of the property of convicted persons who have been placed on probation were held subject to significantly relaxed Fourth Amendment standards in Griffin v. Wisconsin, 483 U.S. 868, 107 S.Ct. 3164, 97 L.Ed.2d 709 (1987). Probation officials received "information" from a police detective that "there were or might be" guns in Griffin's apartment. A Wisconsin administrative regulation permits a probation officer to search a probationer's home without a search warrant if there are "reasonable grounds" to believe that contraband is in the home and a probation department supervisor approves the search. Pursuant to this regulation, Griffin's apartment was searched and a handgun found. The demands of a state's probation system, Justice Scalia reasoned for the 5 person majority, include effective supervision. "The search of Griffin's home satisfied the demands of the Fourth Amendment because it was carried out pursuant to a regulation that itself satisfies the Fourth Amendment's reasonableness requirement . . . [This] is a 'special need' of the State permitting a degree of impingement upon privacy that would not be constitutional if applied to the public at large." 483 U.S. at 873–75, 107 S.Ct. at 3168–69, 97 L.Ed.2d at 718. See Chapter 5.

In a much earlier case, an otherwise illegal search was held to be permissible where the person searched was a probationer subject to the following conditions: "submit his person, place of residence, vehicle, to search and seizure at any time of the day or night, with or without a search warrant, whenever requested to do so by the Probation Officer or any law enforcement officer." People v. Mason, 5 Cal.3d 759, 97 Cal.Rptr. 302, 488 P.2d 630 (1971), *cert. denied* 405 U.S. 1016, 92 S.Ct. 1289, 31 L.Ed.2d 478 (1972).

4. **Jail as a probation condition.** Although a jail term may be the court's complete sentence, jail time is also frequently ordered as a condition of misdemeanor or felony probation. A probationary period of incarceration and non-incarceration is sometimes referred to as a split sentence.

5. **Restitution.** Payment of restitution is a very common condition of probation. (See also the section on restitution infra.) There is no doubt that the willingness and ability of the defendant to make restitution payments is a factor weighing heavily in his favor in being placed on probation in the first place. To the

extent that financial ability to make restitution (or pay other court orders) influences the decision to grant or deny probation is the probation system in violation of equal protection of the laws? When practicable, some courts regularly require probationers to pay the costs of prosecution and probation supervision as a condition of probation and some courts require the probationer to pay a fee to his court-appointed counsel.

6. **Reimbursement for the costs of appointed counsel.** In Fuller v. Oregon, 417 U.S. 40, 94 S.Ct. 2116, 40 L.Ed.2d 642 (1974), the Supreme Court held that a state may impose, as a condition of probation or as part of the sentence of a convicted person, the repayment of the cost of state-appointed defense counsel. Such a condition is permissible only if the convicted person is or will be able to pay the costs. Repayment is "quite clearly directed only at those convicted defendants who are indigent at the time of the criminal proceedings against them, but who subsequently gain the ability to pay the expenses of legal representation." 417 U.S. at 45, 94 S.Ct. at 2121, 40 L.Ed.2d at 647.

7. **Support of dependents.** If the probationer has a history of failure to support his family, the court is very likely to require payment of family support as a condition of probation; the order often requires the probationer to make periodic payments to the probation department which in turn pays his dependents. The frequency with which financial orders are made conditions of probation and the very substantial role which collecting payments from probationers plays in the supervision process has led to criticism of the probation system as a glorified collection agency.

Black v. Romano

Supreme Court of the United States, 1985.
471 U.S. 606, 105 S.Ct. 2254, 85 L.Ed.2d 636.

■ JUSTICE O'CONNOR delivered the opinion of the Court.

In this case we consider whether the Due Process Clause of the Fourteenth Amendment generally requires a sentencing court to indicate that it has considered alternatives to incarceration before revoking probation. After a hearing, a state judge found that respondent had violated his probation conditions by committing a felony shortly after his original prison sentences were suspended. The judge revoked probation and ordered respondent to begin serving the previously imposed sentences. Nearly six years later, the District Court for the Eastern District of Missouri held that respondent had been denied due process because the record of the revocation hearing did not expressly indicate that the state judge had considered alternatives to imprisonment. The District Court granted a writ of habeas corpus and ordered respondent unconditionally released from custody. . . . The Court of Appeals for the Eighth Circuit affirmed. . . . We granted certiorari, . . . and we now reverse.

I

On November 15, 1976, respondent Nicholas Romano pleaded guilty in the Circuit Court of Laclede County, State of Missouri, to two counts of transferring and selling a controlled substance. . . . Romano's attorney urged the court to order probation. He argued that the offenses had not involved any victim, that Romano had no previous felony convictions, and that, except for running a stop sign, he had not violated the law after his arrest on the controlled substance charges. . . . Both the Probation Department and the prosecutor opposed probation. . . . The trial judge nonetheless concluded that probation was appropriate because the underlying charges did not involve an offense against the person. . . .

The judge imposed concurrent sentences of twenty years on each count, suspended execution of the sentences, and placed Romano on probation for five years. . . . The trial judge observed that Romano appeared to "have an uphill run on this probation," . . . given the presentence report and the fact that his "past track record [was] not too good." . . . The trial judge warned that if any of the conditions of probation were violated, he would revoke probation and order Romano imprisoned under the terms of the suspended sentence. . . . Only two months after being placed on probation, Romano was arrested for leaving the scene of an automobile accident. . . . he was charged with . . . a felony punishable by up to five years' imprisonment. . . .

On July 18, 1977, the judge who had sentenced Romano on the controlled substance charges held a probation revocation hearing. Several witnesses gave testimony. . . . Romano offered no explanation of his involvement in the accident. Instead, his counsel challenged the credibility of the witnesses, argued that the evidence did not justify a finding that Romano had violated his probation conditions, and requested the court to continue the defendant's probation. . . . Neither Romano nor his two lawyers otherwise proposed or requested alternatives to incarceration. The judge found that Romano had violated his probation conditions by leaving the scene of an accident, revoked probation, and ordered execution of the previously imposed sentence. . . . Although the judge prepared a memorandum of his findings, . . . he did not expressly indicate that he had considered alternatives to revoking probation. On October 12, 1977, the State filed an amended information reducing the charges arising from the automobile accident to the misdemeanor of reckless and careless driving. . . . Romano was convicted on the reduced charges and ordered to pay a $100 fine. . . .

Romano was incarcerated in state prison following the revocation of his probation. . . .

II

The Due Process Clause of the Fourteenth Amendment imposes procedural and substantive limits on the revocation of the conditional liberty created by probation. . . .

A

In identifying the procedural requirements of due process, we have observed that the decision to revoke probation typically involves two distinct components: (1) a retrospective factual question whether the probationer has violated a condition of probation; and (2) a discretionary determination by the sentencing authority whether violation of a condition warrants revocation of probation. . . . Probationers have an obvious interest in retaining their conditional liberty, and the State also has an interest in assuring that revocation proceedings are based on accurate findings of fact and, where appropriate, the informed exercise of discretion. . . . Our previous cases have sought to accommodate these interests while avoiding the imposition of rigid requirements that would threaten the informal nature of probation revocation proceedings or interfere with exercise of discretion by the sentencing authority.

... One point relevant to the present case is immediately evident from a review of the minimum procedures set forth in some detail in *Gagnon* and *Morrissey:* the specified procedures do not include an express statement by the factfinder that alternatives to incarceration were considered and rejected.

... Where such discretion [to order incarceration] exists, however, the parolee or probationer is entitled to an opportunity to show not only that he did not violate the conditions, but also that there was a justifiable excuse for any violation or that revocation is not the appropriate disposition. ... This Court has not held that a defendant who is afforded these opportunities is also entitled to an explicit statement by the factfinder explaining why alternatives to incarceration were not selected.

We do not question the desirability of considering possible alternatives to imprisonment before probation is revoked. ... Nonetheless, incarceration for violation of a probation condition is not constitutionally limited to circumstances where that sanction represents the only means of promoting the State's interest in punishment and deterrence. The decision to revoke probation is generally predictive and subjective in nature, *Gagnon,* 411 U.S., at 787, 93 S.Ct., at 1762, and the fairness guaranteed by due process does not require a reviewing court to second-guess the factfinder's discretionary decision as to the appropriate sanction. Accordingly, our precedents have sought to preserve the flexible, informal nature of the revocation hearing, which does not require the full panoply of procedural safeguards associated with a criminal trial. ... We believe that a general requirement that the factfinder elaborate upon the reasons for a course not taken would unduly burden the revocation proceeding without significantly advancing the interests of the probationer. ...

The procedures already afforded by *Gagnon* and *Morrissey* protect the defendant against revocation of probation in a constitutionally unfair manner. ... Cf. Douglas v. Buder, 412 U.S. 430, 93 S.Ct. 2199, 37 L.Ed.2d 52 (1973) (per curiam) (revocation invalid under Due Process Clause where there was no evidentiary support for finding that probation conditions were violated). ...

B

The Court's decision in Bearden v. Georgia [461 U.S. 660, 103 S.Ct. 2064, 76 L.Ed.2d 221 (1983)] recognized that in certain circumstances, fundamental fairness requires consideration of alternatives to incarceration prior to the revocation of probation. Where a fine or restitution is imposed as a condition of probation, and "the probationer has made all reasonable efforts to pay ... yet cannot do so through no fault of his own, it is fundamentally unfair to revoke probation automatically without considering whether adequate alternative methods of punishing the defendant are available." 461 U.S., at 668–669, 103 S.Ct., at 2070, 2071 ... *Bearden* acknowledged this Court's sensitivity to the treatment of indigents in our criminal justice system . . .

We need not decide today whether concerns for fundamental fairness would preclude the automatic revocation of probation in circumstances other than those involved in *Bearden*. . . . Under Missouri law, the determination to revoke probation was at the discretion of the trial judge, who was obligated to make independent findings and conclusions apart from any recommendation of the probation officer. . . . We must presume that the state judge followed Missouri law and, without expressly so declaring, recognized his discretionary power to either revoke or continue probation. . . .

III

. . . Romano does not dispute that he had a full opportunity to present mitigating factors to the sentencing judge and to propose alternatives to incarceration. The procedures required by the Due Process Clause of the Fourteenth Amendment were afforded in this case, even though the state judge did not explain on the record his consideration and rejection of alternatives to incarceration.

As a substantive ground for challenging the action of the state court, Romano argues that because the offense of leaving the scene of an accident was unrelated to his prior conviction for the controlled substance offenses, revocation of his probation was arbitrary and contrary to due process. This argument also lacks merit. The revocation of probation did not rest on a relatively innocuous violation of the terms and conditions of probation, but instead resulted from a finding that Romano had committed a felony involving injury to another person only two months after receiving his suspended sentence. The Fourteenth Amendment assuredly does not bar a State from revoking probation merely because the new offense is unrelated to the original offense. Nor is our conclusion in this regard affected by the fact that after the revocation proceeding, the charges arising from the automobile accident were reduced to reckless and careless driving.

. . . The judgment of the Court of Appeals is reversed.

It is so ordered.

■ JUSTICE POWELL took no part in the consideration or decision of this case.

■ JUSTICE MARSHALL, with whom JUSTICE BRENNAN joins, concurring. [Omitted.]

* * *

Petersilia, Turner, Kahan, and Peterson

GRANTING FELONS PROBATION V–XIII (1985)

Summary

* * *

Although the data used in our study are limited to California, we believe our findings have significance for other states as well. California's probation system is the largest in the nation, was once regarded as the most innovative, and has suffered the most severe budget cuts. Consequently, its experiences should prove instructive to other states.

* * *

Major Findings and Conclusions

In our opinion, felons granted probation present a serious threat to public safety. During the 40–month follow-up period of our study, 65 percent of the probationers in our subsample were rearrested, 51 percent were reconvicted, 18 percent were reconvicted of serious violent crimes, and 34 percent were reincarcerated. Moreover, 75 percent of the official charges filed against our subsample involved burglary/theft, robbery, and other violent crimes—the crimes most threatening to public safety.

The performance of felony probationers raises questions about the sentencing criteria the courts use in the prison/probation decision. There is a high correlation between sentencing to prison and offenders' "basic factors" (i.e., having two or more conviction counts, having two or more prior convictions, being on parole or probation at the time of arrest, being drug addicts, being armed, using a weapon, or seriously injuring the victim). For all offenses except assault, offenders having three or more of these characteristics had an 80 percent probability of going to prison in California, regardless of the type of crime of which they were currently convicted. The factors identified by our statistical models as significant in the prison/probation decision are quite consistent with those that the California Penal Code (Sec. 1203) states should be weighed prior to granting probation in felony cases.

After controlling for these basic factors, we performed analyses to determine whether the manner in which the case was officially processed by the courts made a difference in the prison/probation decision. The analyses revealed that having a private attorney could reduce a defendant's chances of imprisonment for all six offenses. For drugs and forgery cases, whether the defendant was represented by a public or court-appointed attorney was not significant. For all six of the crimes we considered, obtaining pretrial release lessened the probability of going to prison, whereas going to trial (except for forgery) increased that probability. . . .

. . . These data suggest that many offenders who are granted felony probation are indistinguishable in terms of their crimes or criminal record from those who are imprisoned.

. . . In our subsample, 78 percent of those who were granted probation when our models predicted imprisonment were eventually rearrested. The recidivism rate for felons for whom our model had predicted a probation sentence was considerably lower—55 percent.

These findings indicate that the factors specified by law as appropriate considerations in the prison/probation decision appear, in practice, to strongly influence that decision. Moreover, these indicators probably should be used more consistently in sentencing, since they are also related to probationer recidivism. However, our findings also suggest that, *given the information now routinely provided to the court,* the ability to predict which felons will succeed on probation probably cannot be vastly improved.

To determine which factors were associated with rearrests, reconvictions, and reconvictions for violent crime, we created a hierarchy of levels of information similar to the hierarchy the court uses in the prison/probation decision. Through regression analysis, we found that the following factors predicted recidivism: type of conviction crime (property offenders recidivated most often); number of prior juvenile and adult convictions (the greater the number, the greater the recidivism); income at arrest (some income was associated with lower recidivism); and whether the offender was living with spouse and/or children (if yes, recidivism was lower). After controlling for these factors, we found no effects for factors such as drug abuse, prior probation revocations, or education level.

But how accurately were we able to predict which offenders would recidivate and which would not? ...We predicted subsequent convictions with 64 percent accuracy, and violent crime convictions with 71 percent accuracy.

* * *

...Sixty-three percent of those recommended for probation in the PSI report were subsequently rearrested, as compared with 67 percent of those recommended for prison. ...[V]ery few adults convicted of felonies in Los Angeles and Alameda counties are good candidates for probation, as it is now administered.

We believe that the criminal justice system needs an alternative, intermediate form of punishment for those offenders who are too antisocial for the relative freedom that probation now offers, but not so seriously criminal as to require imprisonment. A sanction is needed that would impose intensive surveillance, coupled with substantial community service and restitution. It should be structured to satisfy public demands that the punishment fit the crime, to show criminals that crime really does not pay, and to control potential recidivists.

What might such a sentencing alternative look like, and how could the courts identify appropriate candidates? Several states have experimental programs in place which indicate that an intensive surveillance program (ISP) should have intensive monitoring and supervision; real constraints on movement and action; employment; added requirements of community service, education, counseling, and therapy programs; and mechanisms for immediately punishing probationers who commit infractions. Early evaluations of programs in New York and Wisconsin offer hope that intensive surveillance may reduce the recidivism rates of high-risk offenders.

We believe that ISPs will be one of the most significant criminal justice experiments in the next decade. If ISPs prove successful, they will restore probation's credibility and reduce imprisonment rates without increasing crime. Most important, they may offer the prospect of rehabilitating some of the offenders who participate.

* * *

2. FINES

Fines, of course, serve to impose upon an offender a financial penalty payable to the government. When does a fine serve legitimate sentencing purposes? What considerations might militate against the imposition of a fine? What limits exist—or should exist—upon imposition or enforcement of a fine? These issues are addressed in the present subsection.

AMERICAN LAW INSTITUTE, MODEL PENAL CODE AND COMMENTARIES (Official Draft and Revised Comments) 1985*

Section 7.02 Criteria for Imposing Fines.

(1) The Court shall not sentence a defendant only to pay a fine, when any other disposition is authorized by law, unless having regard to the nature and circumstances of the crime and to the history and character of the defendant, it is of the opinion that the fine alone suffices for protection of the public.

(2) The Court shall not sentence a defendant to pay a fine in addition to a sentence of imprisonment or probation unless:

(a) the defendant has derived a pecuniary gain from the crime; or

(b) the Court is of opinion that a fine is specially adapted to deterrence of the crime involved or to the correction of the offender.

(3) The Court shall not sentence a defendant to pay a fine unless:

(a) the defendant is or will be able to pay the fine; and

(b) the fine will not prevent the defendant from making restitution or reparation to the victim of the crime.

(4) In determining the amount and method of payment of a fine, the Court shall take into account the financial resources of the defendant and the nature of the burden that its payment will impose.

18 U.S.C.A.

§ 3572. Imposition of a sentence of fine and related matters

(a) **Factors to be considered.**—In determining whether to impose a fine, and the amount, time for payment, and method of payment of fine, the court shall consider, in addition to the factors set forth in section 3553(a)—

(1) the defendant's income, earning capacity, and financial resources;

(2) the burden that the fine will impose upon the defendant, any person who is financially dependent on the defendant, or any other person (including a government) that would be responsible for the welfare of any person financially dependent on the defendant, relative to the burden that alternative punishments would impose;

(3) any pecuniary loss inflicted upon others as a result of the offense;

(4) whether restitution is ordered or made and the amount of such restitution;

(5) the need to deprive the defendant of illegally obtained gains from the offense;

(6) the expected costs to the government of any imprisonment, supervised release, or probation component of the sentence;

(7) whether the defendant can pass on to consumers or other persons the expense of the fine; and

(8) if the defendant is an organization, the size of the organization and any measure taken by the organization to discipline any officer, director, employee, or agent of the organization responsible for the offense and to prevent a recurrence of such an offense.

(b) **Fine not to impair ability to make restitution.**—If, as a result of a conviction, the defendant has the obligation to make restitution to a victim of the offense, the court shall impose a fine or other monetary penalty only to the extent that such fine or penalty will not impair the ability of the defendant to make restitution.

NOTES

1. **Use of fines in Europe.** Harris and Dunbaugh, Premise for a Sensible Sentencing Debate: Giving Up Imprisonment, 7 Hofstra L.R. 417, 451–2 (1979):

> Motivated by the strong belief that imprisonment should be used only as a last resort and then only in small increments, Dutch sentencing practices rely heavily on fines, even for serious offenses. In 1975, fines constituted 43.4% of all penalties imposed for serious offenses. An additional 20.7% of the penalties consisted of fines combined with suspended incarcerative sentences.

> Use of money fines as a criminal penalty could be expanded considerably in the United States. Fines could be graded according to ability to pay; in addition, installment payments could be permitted and other nonincarcerative penalties instituted if payment is not made. The Swedish "day fine" system offers a model worth emulating. The theory underlying the day-fine system is that "a monetary penalty should be equally burdensome for both rich and poor." The amount of a fine is based on (1) the seriousness of the offense and (2) the offender's financial resources. Offense severity is ranked on a scale of "day fines" from 1 to 120. The offender's financial worth is reduced to a per diem income, generally formulated at one-tenth of one percent of annual income. For example, drunk driving might be assigned a value of 50 "day fines." An offender earning $20,000, would have a per diem figure of $20. Thus, the penalty set for this offender would be 50 multiplied by $20 or $1000. For an offender who earned $10,000 annually, the penalty would be half as much.

> Although imprisonment for unpaid fines is possible in Sweden, strenuous efforts are made to avoid it. By considering ability to pay, allowing extensions of time and installment payments, and enforcing payment, the number of persons actually imprisoned for nonpayment is kept between 100 and 200 persons per year. Given that about 250,000 persons are punished with fines each year, nonincarcerative methods of enforcement clearly predominate.

2. **Imprisonment for failure to pay fines.** Under what circumstances may a state imprison an indigent criminal defendant for failure to pay a fine?

In Williams v. Illinois, 399 U.S. 235, 90 S.Ct. 2018, 26 L.Ed.2d 586 (1970), the defendant was given the maximum sentence for petty theft provided by state law: one year imprisonment and a $500 fine. The judgment directed that if the fine and court costs had not been paid by the time the year was up, defendant was to remain in jail to "work it off" at the rate of $5 per day. The result was to permit imprisonment of indigent defendants beyond the statutory maximum. Calling this practice impermissible discrimination based on ability to pay, the Court vacated the judgment on Equal Protection grounds.

In Tate v. Short, 401 U.S. 395, 91 S.Ct. 668, 28 L.Ed.2d 130 (1971), the petitioner was imprisoned because he was unable due to indigency to pay $425 in accumulated traffic fines. Under state law, the offenses of which Tate was convicted were punishable by fine only. The Court held that Tate's imprisonment was unconstitutional under Williams v. Illinois. Justice Brennan, writing in the Court's opinion of alternative methods of enforcing payment of fines, such as permitting payment in installments, concluded with this statement: "Nor is our decision to be understood as precluding imprisonment as an enforcement method when alternative means are unsuccessful despite the defendant's reasonable efforts to satisfy the fines by those means; the determination of the constitutionality of imprisonment in that circumstance must await the presentation of a concrete case." Id. at 400–01, 91 S.Ct. at 672, 28 L.Ed.2d at 134.

In Wood v. Georgia, 450 U.S. 261, 101 S.Ct. 1097, 67 L.Ed.2d 220 (1981), the Court was faced with the issue of whether *Tate* would govern a situation where the defendant's probation was revoked and jail ordered when monthly fine installments were not paid. However, the court vacated and remanded on other grounds.

As pointed out in *Romano,* supra, the court surveyed another ramification of the defendant's failure to pay a fine in Bearden v. Georgia, 461 U.S. 660, 103 S.Ct. 2064, 76 L.Ed.2d 221 (1983). There, the defendant was sentenced to probation on the condition that he pay a $500 fine. The defendant paid $200, but then was laid off his job and could not find other employment. Consequently the defendant did not pay the fine on time. The court held that the trial court had erred in automatically revoking probation because of failure to pay the fine. Before revocation for failure to pay a fine, a court must determine that the probationer has not made "sufficient bona fide efforts to pay or that adequate alternative forms of punishment [do] not exist." 461 U.S. at 662, 103 S.Ct. at 2067, 76 L.Ed.2d at 226.

3.   RESTITUTION

Most criminal sanctions do little to address the plight of the victim of the crime. Restitution is an exception. When a court orders restitution, the defendant is ordered to give the victim either money, property, or services as reparation for personal or property damages caused by the crime. In the past, American courts made little use of restitution. Almost incidentally, restitution was sometimes directed as a condition of probation. But recent emphasis upon the rights of crime victims has resulted in increased attention being paid to restitution. This subsection illustrates how restitution functions as a sentence and some of the problems caused by the quasi-criminal nature of restitutionary damages.

18 U.S.C.A.

§ 3663.   Order of restitution

(a)(1)(A) The court, when sentencing a defendant convicted of an offense . . . may order, in addition to or, in the case of a misdemeanor, in lieu of any other penalty authorized by law, that the defendant make restitution to any victim of such offense, or if the victim is deceased, to the victim's estate. The court may also order, if agreed to by the parties in a plea agreement, restitution to persons other than the victim of the offense.

(B)(i) The court, in determining whether to order restitution under this section, shall consider—

(I) the amount of the loss sustained by each victim as a result of the offense; and

(II) the financial resources of the defendant, the financial needs and earning ability of the defendant and the defendant's dependents, and such other factors as the court deems appropriate.

(ii) To the extent that the court determines that the complication and prolongation of the sentencing process resulting from the fashioning of an order of restitution under this section outweighs the need to provide restitution to any victims, the court may decline to make such an order.

(2) For the purposes of this section, the term "victim" means a person directly and proximately harmed as a result of the commission of an offense for which restitution may be ordered including, in the case of an offense that involves as an element a scheme, conspiracy, or pattern of criminal activity, any person directly harmed by the defendant's criminal conduct in the course of the scheme, conspiracy, or pattern. In the case of a victim who is under 18 years of age, incompetent, incapacitated, or deceased, the legal guardian of the victim or representative of the victim's estate, another family member, or

any other person appointed as suitable by the court, may assume the victim's rights under this section, but in no event shall the defendant be named as such representative or guardian.

(3) The court may also order restitution in any criminal case to the extent agreed to by the parties in a plea agreement.

(b) The order may require that such defendant—

(1) in the case of an offense resulting in damage to or loss or destruction of property of a victim of the offense—

(A) return the property to the owner of the property or someone designated by the owner; or

(B) if return of the property under subparagraph (A) is impossible, impractical, or inadequate, pay an amount equal to the greater of—

(i) the value of the property on the date of the damage, loss, or destruction, or

(ii) the value of the property on the date of sentencing, less the value (as of the date the property is returned) of any part of the property that is returned;

(2) in the case of an offense resulting in bodily injury to a victim including an offense under chapter 109A or chapter 110—

(A) pay an amount equal to the cost of necessary medical and related professional services and devices relating to physical, psychiatric, and psychological care, including nonmedical care and treatment rendered in accordance with a method of healing recognized by the law of the place of treatment;

(B) pay an amount equal to the cost of necessary physical and occupational therapy and rehabilitation; and

(C) reimburse the victim for income lost by such victim as a result of such offense;

(3) in the case of an offense resulting in bodily injury also results in the death of a victim, pay an amount equal to the cost of necessary funeral and related services;

(4) in any case, reimburse the victim for lost income and necessary child care, transportation, and other expenses related to participation in the investigation or prosecution of the offense or attendance at proceedings related to the offense; and

(5) in any case, if the victim (or if the victim is deceased, the victim's estate) consents, make restitution in services in lieu of money, or make restitution to a person or organization designated by the victim or the estate.

(c)(1) Notwithstanding any other provision of law (but subject to the provisions of subsections (a)(1)(B)(i)(II) and (ii)), when sentencing a defendant convicted of an offense described in section 401, 408(a), 409, 416, 420, or 422(a) of the Controlled Substances Act (§ 21 U.S.C. 841, § 848(a), § 849, § 856, § 861, § 863), in which there is no identifiable victim, the court may order that the defendant make restitution in accordance with this subsection.

(2)(A) An order of restitution under this subsection shall be based on the amount of public harm caused by the offense, as determined by the court in accordance with guidelines promulgated by the United States Sentencing Commission.

(B) In no case shall the amount of restitution ordered under this subsection exceed the amount of the fine ordered for the offense charged in the case.

(3) Restitution under this subsection shall be distributed as follows:

(A) 65 percent of the total amount of restitution shall be paid to the State entity designated to administer crime victim assistance in the State in which the crime occurred.

(B) 35 percent of the total amount of restitution shall be paid to the State entity designated to receive Federal substance abuse block grant funds.

(4) The court shall not make an award under this subsection if it appears likely that such award would interfere with a forfeiture under chapter 46 or chapter 96 of this title or under the Controlled Substances Act (21 U.S.C. 801 et seq.).

(5) Notwithstanding section 3612(c) or any other provision of law, a penalty assessment under section 3013 or a fine under subchapter C of

chapter 227 shall take precedence over an order of restitution under this subsection.

(6) Requests for community restitution under this subsection may be considered in all plea agreements negotiated by the United States.

(7)(A) The United States Sentencing Commission shall promulgate guidelines to assist courts in determining the amount of restitution that may be ordered under this subsection.

(B) No restitution shall be ordered under this subsection until such time as the Sentencing Commission promulgates guidelines pursuant to this paragraph.

(d) An order of restitution made pursuant to this section shall be issued and enforced in accordance with section 3664.

§ 3664. Procedure for issuance and enforcement of order of restitution

(a) For orders of restitution under this title, the court shall order the probation officer to obtain and include in its presentence report, or in a separate report, as the court may direct, information sufficient for the court to exercise its discretion in fashioning a restitution order. The report shall include, to the extent practicable, a complete accounting of the losses to each victim, any restitution owed pursuant to a plea agreement, and information relating to the economic circumstances of each defendant. If the number or identity of victims cannot be reasonably ascertained, or other circumstances exist that make this requirement clearly impracticable, the probation officer shall so inform the court.

(b) The court shall disclose to both the defendant and the attorney for the Government all portions of the presentence or other report pertaining to the matters described in subsection (a) of this section.

(c) The provisions of this chapter, chapter 227, and Rule 32(c) of the Federal Rules of Criminal Procedure shall be the only rules applicable to proceedings under this section.

(d)(1) Upon the request of the probation officer, but not later than 60 days prior to the date initially set for sentencing, the attorney for the Government, after consulting, to the extent practicable, with all identified victims, shall promptly provide the probation officer with a listing of the amounts subject to restitution.

(2) The probation officer shall, prior to submitting the presentence report under subsection (a), to the extent practicable—

(A) provide notice to all identified victims of—

(i) the offense or offenses of which the defendant was convicted;

(ii) the amounts subject to restitution submitted to the probation officer;

(iii) the opportunity of the victim to submit information to the probation officer concerning the amount of the victim's losses;

(iv) the scheduled date, time, and place of the sentencing hearing;

(v) the availability of a lien in favor of the victim pursuant to subsection (m)(1)(B); and

(vi) the opportunity of the victim to file with the probation officer a separate affidavit relating to the amount of the victim's losses subject to restitution; and

(B) provide the victim with an affidavit form to submit pursuant to subparagraph (A)(vi).

(3) Each defendant shall prepare and file with the probation officer an affidavit fully describing the financial resources of the defendant, including a complete listing of all assets owned or controlled by the defendant as of the date on which the defendant was arrested, the financial needs and earning ability of the defendant and the defendant's dependents, and such other information that the court requires relating to such other factors as the court deems appropriate.

(4) After reviewing the report of the probation officer, the court may require additional documentation or hear testimony. The privacy of any records filed, or testimony heard, pursuant to this section shall be maintained to the greatest extent possible, and such records may be filed or testimony heard in camera.

(5) If the victim's losses are not ascertainable by the date that is 10 days prior to sentencing, the attorney for the Government or the probation officer shall so inform the court, and the court shall set a date for the final determination of the victim's losses, not to exceed 90 days after sentencing. If the victim subsequently discovers further losses, the victim shall have 60 days after discovery of those losses in which to petition the court for an amended restitution order. Such order may be granted only upon a showing of good cause for the failure to include such losses in the initial claim for restitutionary relief.

(6) The court may refer any issue arising in connection with a proposed order of restitution to a magistrate judge or special master for proposed findings of fact and recommendations as to disposition, subject to a de novo determination of the issue by the court.

(e) Any dispute as to the proper amount or type of restitution shall be resolved by the court by the preponderance of the evidence. The burden of demonstrating the amount of the loss sustained by a victim as a result of the offense shall be on the attorney for the Government. The burden of demonstrating the financial resources of the defendant and the financial needs of the defendant's dependents, shall be on the defendant. The burden of demonstrating such other matters as the court deems appropriate shall be upon the party designated by the court as justice requires.

(f)(1)(A) In each order of restitution, the court shall order restitution to each victim in the full amount of each victim's losses as determined by the court and without consideration of the economic circumstances of the defendant.

(B) In no case shall the fact that a victim has received or is entitled to receive compensation with respect to a loss from insurance or any other source be considered in determining the amount of restitution.

(2) Upon determination of the amount of restitution owed to each victim, the court shall, pursuant to section 3572, specify in the restitution order the manner in which, and the schedule according to which, the restitution is to be paid, in consideration of—

(A) the financial resources and other assets of the defendant, including whether any of these assets are jointly controlled;

(B) projected earnings and other income of the defendant; and

(C) any financial obligations of the defendant; including obligations to dependents.

(3)(A) A restitution order may direct the defendant to make a single, lump-sum payment, partial payments at specified intervals, in-kind payments, or a combination of payments at specified intervals and in-kind payments.

(B) A restitution order may direct the defendant to make nominal periodic payments if the court finds from facts on the record that the economic circumstances of the defendant do not allow the payment of any amount of a restitution order, and do not allow for the payment of the full amount of a restitution order in the foreseeable future under any reasonable schedule of payments.

(4) An in-kind payment described in paragraph (3) may be in the form of—

(A) return of property;

(B) replacement of property; or

(C) if the victim agrees, services rendered to the victim or a person or organization other than the victim.

(g)(1) No victim shall be required to participate in any phase of a restitution order.

(2) A victim may at any time assign the victim's interest in restitution payments to the Crime Victims Fund in the Treasury without in any way impairing the obligation of the defendant to make such payments.

(h) If the court finds that more than 1 defendant has contributed to the loss of a victim, the court may make each defendant liable for payment of the full amount of restitution or may apportion liability among the defendants to reflect the level of contribution to the victim's loss and economic circumstances of each defendant.

(i) If the court finds that more than 1 victim has sustained a loss requiring restitution by a defendant, the court may provide for a different payment schedule for each victim based on the type and amount of each victim's loss and accounting for the economic circumstances of each victim. In any case in which the United States is a victim, the court shall ensure that all other victims receive full restitution before the United States receives any restitution.

(j)(1) If a victim has received compensation from insurance or any other source with respect to a loss, the court shall order that restitution be paid to the person who provided or is obligated to provide the compensation, but the restitution order shall provide that all restitution of victims required by the order be paid to the victims before any restitution is paid to such a provider of compensation.

(2) Any amount paid to a victim under an order of restitution shall be reduced by any amount later recovered as compensatory damages for the same loss by the victim in—

(A) any Federal civil proceeding; and

(B) any State civil proceeding, to the extent provided by the law of the State.

(k) A restitution order shall provide that the defendant shall notify the court and the Attorney General of any material change in the defendant's economic circumstances that might affect the defendant's ability to pay restitution. The court may also accept notification of a material change in the defendant's economic circumstances from the United States or from the victim. The Attorney General shall certify to the court that the victim or victims owed restitution by the defendant have been notified of the change in circumstances. Upon receipt of the notification, the court may, on its own motion, or the motion of any party, including the victim, adjust the payment schedule, or require immediate payment in full, as the interests of justice require.

(*l*) A conviction of a defendant for an offense involving the act giving rise to an order of restitution shall estop the defendant from denying the essential allegations of that offense in any subsequent Federal civil proceeding or State civil proceeding, to the extent consistent with State law, brought by the victim.

(m)(1)(A)(i) An order of restitution may be enforced by the United States in the manner provided for in subchapter C of chapter 227 and subchapter B of chapter 229 of this title; or

(ii) by all other available and reasonable means.

(B) At the request of a victim named in a restitution order, the clerk of the court shall issue an abstract of judgment certifying that a judgment has been entered in favor of such victim in the amount specified in the restitution order. Upon registering, recording, docketing, or indexing such abstract in accordance with the rules and requirements relating to judgments of the court of the State where the district court is located, the abstract of judgment shall be a lien on the property of the defendant located in such State in the same manner and to the same extent and under the same conditions as a judgment of a court of general jurisdiction in that State.

(2) An order of in-kind restitution in the form of services shall be enforced by the probation officer.

(n) If a person obligated to provide restitution, or pay a fine, receives substantial resources from any source, including inheritance, settlement, or other judgment, during a period of incarceration, such person shall be required to apply the value of such resources to any restitution or fine still owed.

* * *

Hughey v. United States

Supreme Court of the United States, 1990.
495 U.S. 411, 110 S.Ct. 1979, 109 L.Ed.2d 408.

■ JUSTICE MARSHALL delivered the opinion of the Court.

The restitution provisions of the Victim and Witness Protection Act of 1982 (VWPA), 18 U.S.C. §§ 3579, 3580 (1982 ed. and Supp. IV), authorize federal courts, when sentencing defendants convicted of certain offenses, to order, "in addition to or in lieu of any other penalty authorized by law, that the defendant make restitution to any victim of such offense." 18 U.S.C. § 3579(a)(1) (1982 ed., Supp. IV). We must decide whether these provisions allow a court to order a defendant who is charged with multiple offenses but who is convicted of only one offense to make restitution for losses related to the other alleged offenses. We hold that the language and structure of the Act make plain Congress' intent to authorize an award of restitution only for the loss caused by the specific conduct that is the basis of the offense of conviction.[12]

I

In 1986, petitioner Frasiel L. Hughey was indicted for three counts of theft by a United States Postal Service employee and three counts of use of unauthorized credit cards. Petitioner pleaded guilty to count four of the indictment in exchange for the Government's agreement to dismiss the remaining counts and to forgo prosecution "for any other offense arising in the Western District of Texas as part of the scheme alleged in the indictment." App. 7. Count four charged "[t]hat on or about October 18, 1985, . . . [petitioner] did knowingly and with intent to defraud use an unauthorized [MBank Mastercard credit card] issued to Hershey Godfrey, . . . and by such conduct did obtain things of value aggregating more than $1,000. . . ." Id., at 5. During the plea proceeding and as part of the factual basis of petitioner's plea, the Government proffered evidence that petitioner had stolen not only Godfrey's card, but also at least fifteen other cards. Id., at 10. Petitioner's counsel informed the court at that time that petitioner's plea was confined to the allegations in count four and that petitioner did "not mak[e] admissions to anything other than the facts pertaining to count four." Id., at 11.

After the plea hearing but before sentencing, the Government notified petitioner that it would propose that he be ordered to pay restitution of $147,646.89. The Government calculated that figure by adding the losses of several financial institutions, including MBank, that resulted from petitioner's alleged theft and use of approximately 30 credit cards. Petitioner objected to the proposed restitution order on the ground that the proposed figure was unauthorized because it "exceed[ed] the losses of any victims of the offense of which the Defendant was convicted." Id., at 13. The Government then submitted a revised restitution figure of $90,431, the total of

---

12. The restitution provisions in effect at the time of petitioner's sentencing were recodified, effective November 1, 1987, pursuant to the Sentencing Reform Act of 1984, 98 Stat.1987. Thus, 18 U.S.C. § 3579 now appears as 18 U.S.C. § 3663, and 18 U.S.C. § 3580 appears as 18 U.S.C. § 3664. We will refer to the provisions as they were codified at the time of petitioner's sentencing in April 1987. See 18 U.S.C. §§ 3579–3580 (1982 ed.).

MBank's losses relating to petitioner's alleged theft and use of 21 cards from various MBank cardholders. Petitioner countered that the appropriate restitution figure should be $10,412, the losses MBank sustained as a result of all unauthorized uses of the Godfrey credit card identified in the count for which he was convicted.

The District Court ordered petitioner to make restitution to MBank in the amount of $90,431. Id., at 78. Petitioner moved to reduce and correct his sentence under Federal Rule of Criminal Procedure 35, arguing that the District Court had exceeded its authority in ordering restitution for offenses other than the offense of conviction. The District Court denied the motion. Id., at 82–85. The Court of Appeals for the Fifth Circuit affirmed, holding that "VWPA permits a court to require restitution beyond that amount involved in the offense of conviction when there is a significant connection between the crime of conviction and similar actions justifying restitution." 877 F.2d 1256, 1264 (1989).

The courts of appeals have reached varying conclusions regarding a court's ability under VWPA to require an offender to pay restitution for acts other than those underlying the offense of conviction. We granted certiorari to resolve this split in authority. 493 U.S. ___, 110 S.Ct. 716, 107 L.Ed.2d 736 (1990).

II

A

As in all cases involving statutory interpretation, we look first to the language of the statute itself. . . . Given that the ordinary meaning of "restitution" is restoring someone to a position he occupied before a particular event, see, e.g., Webster's Third New International Dictionary 1936 (1986); Black's Law Dictionary 1180 (5th ed. 1979), the repeated focus in § 3579 on the offense of which the defendant was convicted suggests strongly that restitution as authorized by the statute is intended to compensate victims only for losses caused by the conduct underlying the offense of conviction.

The Government argues, however, that § 3579 answers only the question of who may receive restitution and offers no guidance as to how much restitution a court may order the defendant to pay. In the Government's view, § 3579(a) indicates merely that to receive restitution, a victim must be a victim of the offense of conviction. Once such a victim is identified, the Government maintains, the amount of restitution is calculated in accordance with 18 U.S.C. § 3580(a) (1982 ed.), which provides:

> "The court, in determining whether to order restitution under section 3579 of this title and the amount of such restitution, shall consider the amount of the loss sustained by any victim as a result of the offense, the financial resources of the defendant, the financial needs and earning ability of the defendant and the defendant's dependents, and such other factors as the court deems appropriate."

Specifically, the Government contends that the catchall phrase of § 3580(a), which directs courts to consider "such other factors as the court deems appropriate," authorizes courts to include in their restitution calculus losses resulting from offenses other than the offense of conviction.

The Government's reading of §§ 3579 and 3580 is unconvincing. . . .

. . . The Government's argument ignores this Court's commitment to "giving effect to the meaning and placement of the words chosen by Congress." Adams Fruit Co. v. Barrett, 494 U.S. ___, ___, 110 S.Ct. 1384, 1388, 108 L.Ed.2d 585 (1990). . . .

. . . Indeed, had Congress intended to permit a victim to recover for losses stemming from all conduct attributable to the defendant, including conduct unrelated to the offense of conviction, Congress would likely have chosen language other than "the offense," which refers without question to the offense of conviction. . . .

The remaining considerations preceding the catchall phrase also are designed to limit, rather than to expand, the scope of any order of restitution. These factors—"the financial resources of the defendant" and "the financial needs and earning ability of the defendant's dependents"— provide grounds for awarding less than full restitution under the statute. Congress plainly did not intend that wealthy defendants pay more in "restitution" than otherwise warranted because they have significant financial resources, nor did it intend a defendant's dependents to be forced to bear the burden of a restitution obligation because they have great "earning ability." In light of the principle of *ejusdem generis*—that a general statutory term should be understood in light of the specific terms that surround it—the catchall phrase should not be read to introduce into the restitution calculus losses that would expand a defendant's liability beyond the offense of conviction. . . .

B

The Government endeavors to buttress its interpretation of the statute by invoking the expansive declaration of purpose accompanying VWPA, see, e.g., § 2(b)(2), note following 18 U.S.C. § 1512 (one purpose of the Act is "to ensure that the Federal Government does all that is possible within limits of available resources to assist victims . . . without infringing on the constitutional rights of the defendant"), and by referring to portions of the legislative history that reflect Congress' goal of ensuring "that Federal crime victims receive the fullest possible restitution from criminal wrongdoers," 128 Cong.Rec. 27391 (Oct. 1, 1982) (remarks of Rep. Rodino). The Government also emphasizes policy considerations that purportedly support court-ordered restitution for acts outside the offense of conviction. Without such authority, the Government insists, in many cases courts cannot compensate victims for the full losses they suffered as a result of a defendant's conduct. The potential for undercompensation is heightened by prosecutorial discretion in charging a defendant, the argument goes, because prosecutors often frame their indictments with a view to success at trial rather than to a victim's interest in full compensation. See, e.g., United States v. Hill, 798 F.2d 402, 405 (C.A.10 1986). Finally, the Government maintains that the extensive practice of plea bargaining would, as a practical matter, wholly undermine victims' ability to recover fully for their losses because prosecutors often drop charges of which a defendant may be guilty in exchange for a plea to one or more of the other charges. See, e.g., United States v. Berrios, 869 F.2d 25, 30 (C.A.2 1989).

These concerns are not insignificant ones, but neither are they unique to the issue of victim compensation. If a prosecutor chooses to charge fewer than the maximum possible number of crimes, the potential recovery of victims of crime is undoubtedly limited, but so too is the potential sentence that may be imposed on a defendant. And although a plea agreement does operate to limit the acts for which a court may order the defendant to pay restitution, it also ensures that restitution will be ordered as to the count or counts to which the defendant pleads guilty pursuant to the agreement. The essence of a plea agreement is that both the prosecution and the defense make concessions to avoid potential losses. Nothing in the statute suggests that Congress intended to exempt victims of crime from the effects of such a bargaining process.

C

...Even were the statutory language regarding the scope of a court's authority to order restitution ambiguous, longstanding principles of lenity, which demand resolution of ambiguities in criminal statutes in favor of the defendant, ...preclude our resolution of the ambiguity against petitioner on the basis of general declarations of policy in the statute and legislative history.

III

The plain language of VWPA makes clear that the District Court's restitution order in this case was unauthorized. Petitioner pleaded guilty only to the charge that he fraudulently used the credit card of Hershey Godfrey. Because the restitution order encompassed losses stemming from alleged fraudulent uses of cards issued to persons other than Godfrey, such portions of the order are invalid. Accordingly, the decision of the Court of Appeals is reversed and the case is remanded for further proceedings consistent with this opinion.

It is so ordered.

NOTES

1. **Civil or criminal sanction?** A sentence of restitution resembles an award of damages in a civil action. This has led to some confusion in the federal courts about whether restitution is a criminal or civil penalty. In United States v. Welden, 568 F.Supp. 516 (N.D.Ala.1983), the court found the federal restitution provisions unconstitutional. The Act, said the court, "turns a restitution order into a civil judgment", 568 F.Supp. at 534, because it provides for civil enforcement and collateral estoppel. The Act failed to provide the defendant with a civil jury to determine the amount of restitution, and thus violated the defendant's Seventh Amendment right to a jury in a suit at common law. The Act was also said to run afoul of equal protection and due process.

Welden was reversed on appeal in United States v. Satterfield, 743 F.2d 827 (11th Cir.1984). The Court of Appeals said that " ...Congress made clear in both the language of the statute and its accompanying legislative history that victim restitution would be imposed as a criminal, rather than civil, penalty."

743 F.2d at 836. Since the restitution or sentencing hearing is not a civil action at common law, there is no Seventh Amendment right to a jury. A similar conclusion was reached in United States v. Brown, 744 F.2d 905 (2d Cir.1984).

2. **Determining a restitution amount.** The amount of restitution is often determined by reference to the presentence report, which under Fed.R.Crim.P. 32(c)(2)(D) includes a victim impact statement. The presentence report draws on various sources, many of which constitute hearsay, to present a comprehensive background for sentencing. One court has ruled that the presentence report alone does not meet the government's burden of proof as to the extent of the victim's injuries. United States v. Watchman, 749 F.2d 616 (10th Cir.1984).

3. **Inability to pay restitution.** What happens if the defendant is unable to pay the restitution ordered? This question was treated briefly in dicta in *Satterfield,* supra. The court reasoned that, since restitution automatically becomes a condition of probation or parole, *Bearden,* supra, should apply. Therefore, before deciding to revoke probation or parole for failure to pay restitution, the court should consider " . . . whether the defendant has made a bona fide effort to pay; and if he has done so and still cannot comply, whether alternative measures of punishment are available." 743 F.2d at 842. What is the remedy for failure to pay restitution when restitution is ordered independent of probation?

4. **Restitution orders when there are multiple defendants.** The nuances of restitution by multiple defendants under the federal provisions have not yet been fully explored. One case, United States v. Wyzynski, 581 F.Supp. 1550 (E.D.Penn. 1984), refused to reduce one defendant's restitutionary sentence to the same level as his co-defendant. The defendant claimed that he was less culpable than his co-defendant; he cooperated with the authorities while his co-defendant did not; and he was unemployed; yet he had been ordered to pay $25,000 restitution while his co-defendant was ordered to pay only $10,000. In refusing to reduce the restitution order, the court pointed out that the appropriate amount of restitution does not depend upon the relative culpabilities of the defendants, rather, the amount of restitution is calculated to make the victim whole.

4. Involuntary Commitment of "Sexual Predators"

Kansas v. Hendricks

Supreme Court of the United States, 1997.
521 U.S. 346, 117 S.Ct. 2072, 138 L.Ed.2d 501.

■ JUSTICE THOMAS delivered the opinion of the Court.

In 1994, Kansas enacted the Sexually Violent Predator Act, which establishes procedures for the civil commitment of persons who, due to a "mental abnormality" or a "personality disorder," are likely to engage in "predatory acts of sexual violence." Kan. Stat. Ann. § 59–29a01 et seq. (1994). The State invoked the Act for the first time to commit Leroy Hendricks, an inmate who had a long history of sexually molesting children, and who was scheduled for release from prison shortly after the Act became law. Hendricks challenged his commitment on, inter alia, "substantive" due process, double jeopardy, and ex post facto grounds. The Kansas Supreme Court invalidated the Act, holding that its pre-commitment condition of a "mental abnormality" did not satisfy what the court perceived to be the "substantive" due process requirement that involuntary civil commitment must be predicated on a finding of "mental illness." In re

Hendricks, 259 Kan. 246, 261, 912 P.2d 129, 138 (1996). The State of Kansas petitioned for certiorari. Hendricks subsequently filed a cross-petition in which he reasserted his federal double jeopardy and ex post facto claims. We granted certiorari on both the petition and the cross-petition, 518 U.S. 1004, 116 S.Ct. 2522, 135 L.Ed.2d 1047 (1996), and now reverse the judgment below.

I

A

The Kansas Legislature enacted the Sexually Violent Predator Act (Act) in 1994 to grapple with the problem of managing repeat sexual offenders. Although Kansas already had a statute addressing the involuntary commitment of those defined as "mentally ill," the legislature determined that existing civil commitment procedures were inadequate to confront the risks presented by "sexually violent predators." In the Act's preamble, the legislature explained:

> "[A] small but extremely dangerous group of sexually violent predators exist who do not have a mental disease or defect that renders them appropriate for involuntary treatment pursuant to the [general involuntary civil commitment statute]. . . . In contrast to persons appropriate for civil commitment under the [general involuntary civil commitment statute], sexually violent predators generally have anti-social personality features which are unamenable to existing mental illness treatment modalities and those features render them likely to engage in sexually violent behavior. The legislature further finds that sexually violent predators' likelihood of engaging in repeat acts of predatory sexual violence is high. The existing involuntary commitment procedure . . . is inadequate to address the risk these sexually violent predators pose to society. The legislature further finds that the prognosis for rehabilitating sexually violent predators in a prison setting is poor, the treatment needs of this population are very long term and the treatment modalities for this population are very different than the traditional treatment modalities for people appropriate for commitment under the [general involuntary civil commitment statute]." Kan. Stat. Ann. § 59–29a01 (1994).

As a result, the Legislature found it necessary to establish "a civil commitment procedure for the long-term care and treatment of the sexually violent predator." Ibid. The Act defined a "sexually violent predator" as:

> "any person who has been convicted of or charged with a sexually violent offense and who suffers from a mental abnormality or personality disorder which makes the person likely to engage in the predatory acts of sexual violence."

§ 59–29a02(a).

A "mental abnormality" was defined, in turn, as a "congenital or acquired condition affecting the emotional or volitional capacity which predisposes the person to commit sexually violent offenses in a degree constituting such person a menace to the health and safety of others." § 59–29a02(b).

As originally structured, the Act's civil commitment procedures pertained to: (1) a presently confined person who, like Hendricks, "has been convicted of a sexually violent offense" and is scheduled for release; (2) a person who has been "charged with a sexually violent offense" but has been found incompetent to stand trial; (3) a person who has been found "not guilty by reason of insanity of a sexually violent offense"; and (4) a person found "not guilty" of a sexually violent offense because of a mental disease or defect. § 59–29a03(a), § 22–3221 (1995).

The initial version of the Act, as applied to a currently confined person such as Hendricks, was designed to initiate a specific series of procedures. The custodial agency was required to notify the local prosecutor 60 days before the anticipated release of a person who might have met the Act's criteria. § 59–29a03. The prosecutor was then obligated, within 45 days, to decide whether to file a petition in state court seeking the person's involuntary commitment. § 59–29a04. If such a petition were filed, the court was to determine whether "probable cause" existed to support a finding that the person was a "sexually violent predator" and thus eligible for civil commitment. Upon such a determination, transfer of the individual to a secure facility for professional evaluation would occur. § 59–29a05. After that evaluation, a trial would be held to determine beyond a reasonable doubt whether the individual was a sexually violent predator. If that determination were made, the person would then be transferred to the custody of the Secretary of Social and Rehabilitation Services (Secretary) for "control, care and treatment until such time as the person's mental abnormality or personality disorder has so changed that the person is safe to be at large." § 59–29a07(a).

In addition to placing the burden of proof upon the State, the Act afforded the individual a number of other procedural safeguards. In the case of an indigent person, the State was required to provide, at public expense, the assistance of counsel and an examination by mental health care professionals. § 59–29a06. The individual also received the right to present and cross-examine witnesses, and the opportunity to review documentary evidence presented by the State. § 59–29a07.

Once an individual was confined, the Act required that "[t]he involuntary detention or commitment . . . shall conform to constitutional requirements for care and treatment." § 59–29a09. Confined persons were afforded three different avenues of review: First, the committing court was obligated to conduct an annual review to determine whether continued detention was warranted. § 59–29a08. Second, the Secretary was permitted, at any time, to decide that the confined individual's condition had so changed that release was appropriate, and could then authorize the person to petition for release. § 59–29a10. Finally, even without the Secretary's permission, the confined person could at any time file a release petition. § 59–29a11. If the court found that the State could no longer satisfy its burden under the initial commitment standard, the individual would be freed from confinement.

B

In 1984, Hendricks was convicted of taking "indecent liberties" with two 13–year-old boys. After serving nearly 10 years of his sentence, he was slated for release to a halfway house. Shortly before his scheduled release, however, the State filed a petition in state court seeking Hendricks' civil confinement as a sexually violent predator. On August 19, 1994, Hendricks appeared before the court with counsel and moved to dismiss the petition on the grounds that the Act violated various federal constitutional provisions. Although the court reserved ruling on the Act's constitutionality, it concluded that there was probable cause to support a finding that Hendricks was a sexually violent predator, and therefore ordered that he be evaluated at the Larned State Security Hospital.

Hendricks subsequently requested a jury trial to determine whether he qualified as a sexually violent predator. During that trial, Hendricks' own testimony revealed a chilling history of repeated child sexual molestation and abuse, beginning in 1955 when he exposed his genitals to two young girls. At that time, he pleaded guilty to indecent exposure. Then, in 1957, he was convicted of lewdness involving a young girl and received a brief jail sentence. In 1960, he molested two young boys while he worked for a carnival. After serving two years in prison for that offense, he was paroled, only to be rearrested for molesting a 7–year-old girl. Attempts were made to treat him for his sexual deviance, and in 1965 he was considered "safe to be at large," and was discharged from a state psychiatric hospital. App. 139–144.

Shortly thereafter, however, Hendricks sexually assaulted another young boy and girl—he performed oral sex on the 8–year-old girl and fondled the 11–year-old boy. He was again imprisoned in 1967, but refused to participate in a sex offender treatment program, and thus remained incarcerated until his parole in 1972. Diagnosed as a pedophile, Hendricks entered into, but then abandoned, a treatment program. He testified that despite having received professional help for his pedophilia, he continued to harbor sexual desires for children. Indeed, soon after his 1972 parole, Hendricks began to abuse his own stepdaughter and stepson. He forced the children to engage in sexual activity with him over a period of approximately four years. Then, as noted above, Hendricks was convicted of "taking indecent liberties" with two adolescent boys after he attempted to fondle them. As a result of that conviction, he was once again imprisoned, and was serving that sentence when he reached his conditional release date in September 1994.

Hendricks admitted that he had repeatedly abused children whenever he was not confined. He explained that when he "get[s] stressed out," he "can't control the urge" to molest children. Id., 172. Although Hendricks recognized that his behavior harms children, and he hoped he would not sexually molest children again, he stated that the only sure way he could keep from sexually abusing children in the future was "to die." Id., at 190. Hendricks readily agreed with the state physician's diagnosis that he suffers from pedophilia and that he is not cured of the condition; indeed, he told the physician that "treatment is bull——." Id., at 153, 190.

The jury unanimously found beyond a reasonable doubt that Hendricks was a sexually violent predator. The trial court subsequently determined, as a matter of state law, that pedophilia qualifies as a "mental abnormality" as defined by the Act, and thus ordered Hendricks committed to the Secretary's custody.

Hendricks appealed, claiming, among other things, that application of the Act to him violated the Federal Constitution's Due Process, Double Jeopardy, and Ex Post Facto Clauses. The Kansas Supreme Court accepted Hendricks' due process claim. In re Hendricks, 259 Kan., at 261, 912 P.2d, at 138. The court declared that in order to commit a person involuntarily in a civil proceeding, a State is required by "substantive" due process to prove by clear and convincing evidence that the person is both (1) mentally ill, and (2) a danger to himself or to others. Id., at 259, 912 P.2d, at 137. The court then determined that the Act's definition of "mental abnormality" did not satisfy what it perceived to be this Court's "mental illness" requirement in the civil commitment context. As a result, the court held that "the Act violates Hendricks' substantive due process rights." Id., at 261, 912 P.2d, at 138.

The majority did not address Hendricks' ex post facto or double jeopardy claims. The dissent, however, considered each of Hendricks' constitutional arguments and rejected them. Id., at 264–294, 912 P.2d, at 140–156 (Larson, J., dissenting).

II

A

Kansas argues that the Act's definition of "mental abnormality" satisfies "substantive" due process requirements. We agree. Although freedom from physical restraint "has always been at the core of the liberty protected by the Due Process Clause from arbitrary governmental action," Foucha v. Louisiana, 504 U.S. 71, 80, 112 S.Ct. 1780, 1785, 118 L.Ed.2d 437 (1992), that liberty interest is not absolute. The Court has recognized that an individual's constitutionally protected interest in avoiding physical restraint may be overridden even in the civil context:

> "[T]he liberty secured by the Constitution of the United States to every person within its jurisdiction does not import an absolute right in each person to be, at all times and in all circumstances, wholly free from restraint. There are manifold restraints to which every person is necessarily subject for the common good. On any other basis organized society could not exist with safety to its members."

Jacobson v. Massachusetts, 197 U.S. 11, 26, 25 S.Ct. 358, 361, 49 L.Ed. 643 (1905).

Accordingly, States have in certain narrow circumstances provided for the forcible civil detainment of people who are unable to control their behavior and who thereby pose a danger to the public health and safety. See, e.g., 1788 N.Y. Laws, ch. 31 (Feb. 9, 1788) (permitting confinement of the "furiously mad"); see also A. Deutsch, The Mentally Ill in America (1949) (tracing history of civil commitment in the 18th and 19th centuries); G. Grob, Mental Institutions in America: Social Policy to 1875 (1973) (discussing colonial and early American civil commitment statutes). We have consistently upheld such involuntary commitment statutes provided the confinement takes place pursuant to proper procedures and evidentiary standards. See Foucha, supra, at 80, 112 S.Ct., at 1785–1786; Addington v. Texas, 441 U.S. 418, 426–427, 99 S.Ct. 1804, 1809–1810, 60 L.Ed.2d 323 (1979). It thus cannot be said that the involuntary civil confinement of a limited subclass of dangerous persons is contrary to our understanding of ordered liberty. Cf. id., at 426, 99 S.Ct., at 1809–1810.

The challenged Act unambiguously requires a finding of dangerousness either to one's self or to others as a prerequisite to involuntary confinement. Commitment proceedings can be initiated only when a person "has been convicted of or charged with a sexually violent offense," and "suffers from a mental abnormality or personality disorder which makes the person likely to engage in the predatory acts of sexual violence." Kan. Stat. Ann. § 59–29a02(a) (1994). The statute thus requires proof of more than a mere predisposition to violence; rather, it requires evidence of past sexually violent behavior and a present mental condition that creates a likelihood of such conduct in the future if the person is not incapacitated. As we have recognized, "[p]revious instances of violent behavior are an important indicator of future violent tendencies." Heller v. Doe, 509 U.S. 312, 323, 113 S.Ct. 2637, 2644, 125 L.Ed.2d 257 (1993); see also Schall v. Martin, 467 U.S. 253, 278, 104 S.Ct. 2403, 2417, 81 L.Ed.2d 207 (1984) (explaining that "from a legal point of view there is nothing inherently unattainable about a prediction of future criminal conduct").

A finding of dangerousness, standing alone, is ordinarily not a sufficient ground upon which to justify indefinite involuntary commitment. We have sustained civil commitment statutes when they have coupled proof of dangerousness with the proof of some additional factor, such as a "mental illness" or "mental abnormality." See, e.g., Heller, supra, 314–315, 113 S.Ct., at 2639–2640 (Kentucky statute permitting commitment of "mentally retarded" or "mentally ill" and dangerous individual); Allen v. Illinois, 478 U.S. 364, 366, 106 S.Ct. 2988, 2990–2991, 92 L.Ed.2d 296 (1986) (Illinois statute permitting commitment of "mentally ill" and dangerous individual); Minnesota ex rel. Pearson v. Probate Court of Ramsey Cty., 309 U.S. 270, 271–272, 60 S.Ct. 523, 524–525, 84 L.Ed. 744 (1940) (Minnesota statute permitting commitment of dangerous individual with "psychopathic personality"). These added statutory requirements serve to limit involuntary civil confinement to those who suffer from a volitional impairment rendering them dangerous beyond their control. The Kansas Act is plainly of a kind with these other civil commitment statutes: It requires a finding of future dangerousness, and then links that finding to the existence of a "mental abnormality" or "personality disorder" that makes it difficult, if not impossible, for the person to control his dangerous behavior. Kan. Stat. Ann. § 59–29a02(b) (1994). The precommitment requirement of a "mental abnormality" or "personality disorder" is consistent with the requirements of these other statutes that we have upheld in that it narrows the class of persons eligible for confinement to those who are unable to control their dangerousness.

Hendricks nonetheless argues that our earlier cases dictate a finding of "mental illness" as a prerequisite for civil commitment, citing Foucha, and Addington. He then asserts that a "mental abnormality" is not equivalent to a "mental illness" because it is a term coined by the Kansas Legislature, rather than by the psychiatric community. Contrary to Hendricks' assertion, the term "mental illness" is devoid of any talismanic significance. Not only do "psychiatrists disagree widely and frequently on what constitutes mental illness," Ake v. Oklahoma, 470 U.S. 68, 81, 105 S.Ct. 1087, 1095, 84 L.Ed.2d 53 (1985), but the Court itself has used a variety of expressions to describe the mental condition of those properly subject to civil confinement. See, e.g., Addington, 441 U.S., at 425–426, 99 S.Ct., at 1808–1810 (using the terms "emotionally disturbed" and "mentally ill"); Jackson, 406 U.S., at 732, 737, 92 S.Ct., at 1855, 1857–1858 (using the terms "incompetency" and "insanity"); cf. Foucha, 504 U.S., at 88, 112 S.Ct., at 1789–1790 (O'CONNOR, J., concurring in part and concurring in judgment) (acknowledging State's authority to commit a person when there is "some medical justification for doing so").

Indeed, we have never required State legislatures to adopt any particular nomenclature in drafting civil commitment statutes. Rather, we have traditionally left to legislators the task of defining terms of a medical nature that have legal significance. Cf. Jones v. United States, 463 U.S. 354, 365, n. 13, 103 S.Ct. 3043, 3050, n. 13, 77 L.Ed.2d 694 (1983). As a consequence, the States have, over the years, developed numerous specialized terms to define mental health concepts. Often, those definitions do not fit precisely with the definitions employed by the medical community. The legal definitions of "insanity" and "competency," for example, vary substantially from their psychiatric counterparts. See, e.g., Gerard, The Usefulness of the Medical Model to the Legal System, 39 Rutgers L.Rev. 377, 391–394 (1987) (discussing differing purposes of legal system and the medical profession in recognizing mental illness). Legal definitions, however, which must "take into account such issues as individual responsibility ...and competency," need not mirror those advanced by the medical profession. American Psychiatric Association, Diagnostic and Statistical Manual of Mental Disorders xxiii, xxvii (4th ed. 1994).

To the extent that the civil commitment statutes we have considered set forth criteria relating to an individual's inability to control his dangerousness, the Kansas Act sets forth comparable criteria and Hendricks' condition doubtless satisfies those criteria. The mental health professionals who evaluated Hendricks diagnosed him as suffering from pedophilia, a condition the psychiatric profession itself classifies as a serious mental disorder. See, e.g., id., at 524–525, 527–528; 1 American Psychiatric Association, Treatments of Psychiatric Disorders, 617–633 (1989); Abel & Rouleau, Male Sex Offenders, in Handbook of Outpatient Treatment of Adults 271 (M. Thase, B. Edelstein, & M. Hersen, eds. 1990). Hendricks even conceded that, when he becomes "stressed out," he cannot "control the urge" to molest children. App. 172. This admitted lack of volitional control, coupled with a prediction of future dangerousness, adequately distinguishes Hendricks from other dangerous persons who are perhaps more properly dealt with exclusively through criminal proceedings. Hendricks' diagnosis as a pedophile, which qualifies as a "mental abnormality" under the Act, thus plainly suffices for due process purposes.

B

We granted Hendricks' cross-petition to determine whether the Act violates the Constitution's double jeopardy prohibition or its ban on ex post facto lawmaking. The thrust of Hendricks' argument is that the Act establishes criminal proceedings; hence confinement under it necessarily constitutes punishment. He contends that where, as here, newly enacted "punishment" is predicated upon past conduct for which he has already been convicted and forced to serve a prison sentence, the Constitution's Double Jeopardy and Ex Post Facto Clauses are violated. We are unpersuaded by Hendricks' argument that Kansas has established criminal proceedings.

The categorization of a particular proceeding as civil or criminal "is first of all a question of statutory construction." Allen, 478 U.S., at 368, 106 S.Ct., at 2992. We must initially ascertain whether the legislature meant the statute to establish "civil" proceedings. If so, we ordinarily defer to the legislature's stated intent. Here, Kansas' objective to create a civil proceeding is evidenced by its placement of the Sexually Violent Predator Act within the Kansas probate code, instead of the criminal code, as well as its description of the Act as creating a "civil commitment procedure." Kan. Stat. Ann., Article 29 (1994) ("Care and Treatment for Mentally Ill Persons"), § 59–29a01 (emphasis added). Nothing on the face of the statute suggests that the legislature sought to create anything other than a civil commitment scheme designed to protect the public from harm.

Although we recognize that a "civil label is not always dispositive," Allen, supra, at 369, 106 S.Ct., at 2992, we will reject the legislature's manifest intent only where a party challenging the statute provides "the clearest proof" that "the statutory scheme [is] so punitive either in purpose or effect as to negate [the State's] intention" to deem it "civil." United States v. Ward, 448 U.S. 242, 248–249, 100 S.Ct. 2636, 2641, 65 L.Ed.2d 742 (1980). In those limited circumstances, we will consider the statute to have established criminal proceedings for constitutional purposes. Hendricks, however, has failed to satisfy this heavy burden.

As a threshold matter, commitment under the Act does not implicate either of the two primary objectives of criminal punishment: retribution or deterrence. The Act's purpose is not retributive because it does not affix culpability for prior criminal conduct. Instead, such conduct is used solely for evidentiary purposes, either to demonstrate that a "mental abnormality" exists or to support a finding of future dangerousness. We have previously concluded that an Illinois statute was nonpunitive even though it was triggered by the commission of a sexual assault, explaining that evidence of the prior criminal conduct was "received not to punish past misdeeds, but primarily to show the accused's mental condition and to predict future behavior." Allen, supra, at 371, 106 S.Ct., at 2993. In addition, the Kansas Act does not make a criminal conviction a prerequisite for commitment—persons absolved of criminal responsibility may nonetheless be subject to confinement under the Act. See Kan. Stat. Ann. § 59–29a03(a) (1994). An absence of the necessary criminal responsibility suggests that the State is not seeking retribution for a past misdeed. Thus, the fact that the Act may be "tied to criminal activity" is "insufficient to render the statut[e] punitive." United States v. Ursery, 518 U.S. 267, 291, 116 S.Ct. 2135, 2149, 135 L.Ed.2d 549 (1996).

Moreover, unlike a criminal statute, no finding of scienter is required to commit an individual who is found to be a sexually violent predator; instead, the commitment determination is made based on a "mental abnormality" or "personality disorder" rather than on one's criminal intent. The existence of a scienter requirement is customarily an important element in distinguishing criminal from civil statutes. See Kennedy v. Mendoza–Martinez, 372 U.S. 144, 168, 83 S.Ct. 554, 567–568, 9 L.Ed.2d 644 (1963). The absence of such a requirement here is evidence that confinement under the statute is not intended to be retributive.

Nor can it be said that the legislature intended the Act to function as a deterrent. Those persons committed under the Act are, by definition, suffering from a "mental abnormality" or a "personality disorder" that prevents them from exercising adequate control over their behavior. Such persons are therefore unlikely to be deterred by the threat of confinement. And the conditions surrounding that confinement do not suggest a punitive purpose on the State's part. The State has represented that an individual confined under the Act is not subject to the more restrictive conditions placed on state prisoners, but instead experiences essentially the same conditions as any involuntarily committed patient in the state mental institution. App. 50–56, 59–60. Because none of the parties argues that people institutionalized under the Kansas general civil commitment statute are subject to punitive conditions, even though they may be involuntarily confined, it is difficult to conclude that persons confined under this Act are being "punished."

Although the civil commitment scheme at issue here does involve an affirmative restraint, "the mere fact that a person is detained does not inexorably lead to the conclusion that the government has imposed punishment." United States v. Salerno, 481 U.S. 739, 746, 107 S.Ct. 2095, 2101, 95 L.Ed.2d 697 (1987). The State may take measures to restrict the freedom of the dangerously mentally ill. This is a legitimate non-punitive governmental objective and has been historically so regarded. Cf. id., at 747, 107 S.Ct., at 2101–2102. The Court has, in fact, cited the confinement of "mentally unstable individuals who present a danger to the public" as one classic example of nonpunitive detention. Id., at 748–749, 107 S.Ct., at 2102–2103. If detention for the purpose of protecting the community from harm necessarily constituted punishment, then all involuntary civil commitments would have to be considered punishment. But we have never so held.

Hendricks focuses on his confinement's potentially indefinite duration as evidence of the State's punitive intent. That focus, however, is misplaced. Far from any punitive objective, the confinement's duration is instead linked to the stated purposes of the commitment, namely, to hold the person until his mental abnormality no longer causes him to be a threat to others. Cf. Jones, 463 U.S., at 368, 103 S.Ct., at 3051–3052 (noting with approval that "because it is impossible to predict how long it will take for any given individual to recover [from insanity]—or indeed whether he will ever recover—Congress has chosen ...to leave the length of commitment indeterminate, subject to periodic review of the patients's suitability for release"). If, at any time, the confined person is adjudged "safe to be at large," he is statutorily entitled to immediate release. Kan. Stat. Ann. § 59–29a07 (1994).

Furthermore, commitment under the Act is only potentially indefinite. The maximum amount of time an individual can be incapacitated pursuant to a single judicial proceeding is one year. § 59–29a08. If Kansas seeks to continue the detention beyond that year, a court must once again determine beyond a reasonable doubt that the detainee satisfies the same standards as required for the initial confinement. Ibid. This requirement again demonstrates that Kansas does not intend an individual committed pursuant to the Act to remain confined any longer than he suffers from a mental abnormality rendering him unable to control his dangerousness.

Hendricks next contends that the State's use of procedural safeguards traditionally found in criminal trials makes the proceedings here criminal rather than civil. In Allen, we confronted a similar argument. There, the petitioner "place[d] great reliance on the fact that proceedings under the Act are accompanied by procedural safeguards usually found in criminal trials" to argue that the proceedings were civil in name only. 478 U.S., at 371, 106 S.Ct., at 2993. We rejected that argument, however, explaining that the State's decision "to provide some of the safeguards applicable in criminal trials cannot itself turn these proceedings into criminal prosecutions." Id., at 372, 106 S.Ct., at 2993. The numerous procedural and evidentiary protections afforded here demonstrate that the Kansas Legislature has taken great care to confine only a narrow class of particularly dangerous individuals, and then only after meeting the strictest procedural standards. That Kansas chose to afford such procedural protections does not transform a civil commitment proceeding into a criminal prosecution.

Finally, Hendricks argues that the Act is necessarily punitive because it fails to offer any legitimate "treatment." Without such treatment, Hendricks asserts, confinement under the Act amounts to little more than disguised punishment. Hendricks' argument assumes that treatment for his condition is available, but that the State has failed (or refused) to provide it. The Kansas Supreme Court, however, apparently rejected this assumption, explaining:

> "It is clear that the overriding concern of the legislature is to continue the segregation of sexually violent offenders from the public. Treatment with the goal of reintegrating them into society is incidental, at best. The record reflects that treatment for sexually violent predators is all but nonexistent. The legislature concedes that sexually violent predators are not amenable to treatment under [the existing Kansas involuntary commitment statute]. If there is nothing to treat under [that statute], then there is no mental illness. In that light, the provisions of the Act for treatment appear somewhat disingenuous."

259 Kan., at 258, 912 P.2d, at 136.

It is possible to read this passage as a determination that Hendricks' condition was untreatable under the existing Kansas civil commitment statute, and thus the Act's sole purpose was incapacitation. Absent a treatable mental illness, the Kansas court concluded, Hendricks could not be detained against his will.

Accepting the Kansas court's apparent determination that treatment is not possible for this category of individuals does not obligate us to adopt its legal conclusions. We have already observed that, under the appropriate circumstances and when accompanied by proper procedures, incapacitation may be a legitimate end of the civil law. See Allen, supra, at 373, 106 S.Ct., at 2994; Salerno, 481 U.S., at 748–749, 107 S.Ct., at 2102–2103. Accordingly, the Kansas court's determination that the Act's "overriding concern" was the continued "segregation of sexually violent offenders" is consistent with our conclusion that the Act establishes civil proceedings, 259 Kan., at 258, 912 P.2d, at 136, especially when that concern is coupled with the State's ancillary goal of providing treatment to those offenders, if such is possible. While we have upheld state civil commitment statutes that aim both to incapacitate and to treat, see Allen, supra, we have never held that the Constitution prevents a State from civilly detaining those for whom no treatment is available, but who nevertheless pose a danger to others. A State could hardly be seen as furthering a "punitive" purpose by involuntarily confining persons afflicted with an untreatable, highly contagious disease. Accord Compagnie Francaise de Navigation a Vapeur v. Louisiana Bd. of Health, 186 U.S. 380, 22 S.Ct. 811, 46 L.Ed. 1209 (1902) (permitting involuntary quarantine of persons suffering from communicable diseases). Similarly, it would be of little value to require treatment as a precondition for civil confinement of the dangerously insane when no acceptable treatment existed. To conclude otherwise would obligate a State to release certain confined individuals who were both mentally ill and dangerous simply because they could not be successfully treated for their afflictions. Cf. Greenwood v. United States, 350 U.S. 366, 375, 76 S.Ct. 410, 415, 100 L.Ed. 412 (1956) ("The fact that at present there may be little likelihood of recovery does not defeat federal power to make this initial commitment of the petitioner"); O'Connor v. Donaldson, 422 U.S. 563, 584, 95 S.Ct. 2486, 2498, 45 L.Ed.2d 396 (1975) (Burger, C. J., concurring) ("[I]t remains a stubborn fact that there are many forms of mental illness which are not understood, some which are untreatable in the sense that no effective therapy has yet been discovered for them, and that rates of 'cure' are generally low").

Alternatively, the Kansas Supreme Court's opinion can be read to conclude that Hendricks' condition is treatable, but that treatment was not the State's "overriding concern," and that no treatment was being provided (at least at the time Hendricks was committed). 259 Kan., at 258, 912 P.2d, at 136. See also ibid. ("It is clear that the primary objective of the Act is to continue incarceration and not to provide treatment"). Even if we accept this determination that the provision of treatment was not the Kansas Legislature's "overriding" or "primary" purpose in passing the Act, this does not rule out the possibility that an ancillary purpose of the Act was to provide treatment, and it does not require us to conclude that the Act is punitive. Indeed, critical language in the Act itself demonstrates that the Secretary of Social and Rehabilitation Services, under whose custody sexually violent predators are committed, has an obligation to provide treatment to individuals like Hendricks. § 59–29a07(a) ("If the court or jury determines that the person is a sexually violent predator, the person shall be committed to the custody of the secretary of social and rehabilitation services for control, care and treatment until such time as the person's mental abnormality or personality disorder has so changed that the person is safe to be at large" (emphasis added)). Other of the Act's sections echo this obligation to provide treatment for committed persons. See, e.g., § 59–29a01 (establishing civil commitment procedure "for the long-term care and treatment of the sexually violent predator"); § 59–29a09 (requiring the confinement to "conform to constitutional requirements for care and treatment"). Thus, as in Allen, "the State has a statutory obligation to provide 'care and treatment for [persons adjudged sexually dangerous] designed to effect recovery,'" 478 U.S., at 369, 106 S.Ct., at 2992 (quoting Ill.Rev.Stat., ch. 38, ¶ 105–8 (1985)), and we may therefore conclude that "the State has ...provided for the treatment of those it commits." 478 U.S., at 370, 106 S.Ct., at 2992.

Although the treatment program initially offered Hendricks may have seemed somewhat meager, it must be remembered that he was the first person committed under the Act. That the State did not have all of its treatment procedures in place is thus not surprising. What is significant, however, is that Hendricks was placed under the supervision of the Kansas Department of Health and Social and Rehabilitative Services, housed in a unit segregated from the general prison population and operated not by employees of the Department of Corrections, but by other trained individuals. And, before this Court, Kansas declared "[a]bsolutely" that persons committed under the Act are now receiving in the neighborhood of "31.5 hours of treatment per week." Tr. of Oral Arg. 14–15, 16.[13]

Where the State has "disavowed any punitive intent"; limited confinement to a small segment of particularly dangerous individuals; provided strict procedural safeguards; directed that confined persons be segregated from the general prison population and afforded the same status as others who have been civilly committed; recommended treatment if such is possible; and permitted immediate release upon a showing that the individual is no longer dangerous or mentally impaired, we cannot say that it acted with punitive intent. We therefore hold that the Act does not establish criminal proceedings and that involuntary confinement pursuant to the Act is not punitive. Our conclusion that the Act is nonpunitive thus removes an essential prerequisite for both Hendricks' double jeopardy and ex post facto claims.

1

The Double Jeopardy Clause provides: "[N]or shall any person be subject for the same offence to be twice put in jeopardy of life or limb." Although generally understood to preclude a second prosecution for the

---

13. Indeed, we have been informed that an August 28, 1995, hearing on Hendricks' petition for state habeas corpus relief, the trial court, over admittedly conflicting testimony, ruled that: "[T]he allegation that no treatment is being provided to any of the petitioners or other persons committed to the program designated as a sexual predator treatment program is not true. I find that they are receiving treatment." App. 453–454. Thus, to the extent that treatment is available for Hendricks' condition, the State now appears to be providing it. By furnishing such treatment, the Kansas Legislature has indicated that treatment, if possible, is at least an ancillary goal of the Act, which easily satisfies any test for determining that the Act is not punitive.

same offense, the Court has also interpreted this prohibition to prevent the State from "punishing twice, or attempting a second time to punish criminally, for the same offense." Witte v. United States, 515 U.S. 389, 396, 115 S.Ct. 2199, 2204, 132 L.Ed.2d 351 (1995) (emphasis and internal quotation marks omitted). Hendricks argues that, as applied to him, the Act violates double jeopardy principles because his confinement under the Act, imposed after a conviction and a term of incarceration, amounted to both a second prosecution and a second punishment for the same offense. We disagree.

Because we have determined that the Kansas Act is civil in nature, initiation of its commitment proceedings does not constitute a second prosecution. Cf. Jones v. United States, 463 U.S. 354, 103 S.Ct. 3043, 77 L.Ed.2d 694 (1983) (permitting involuntary civil commitment after verdict of not guilty by reason of insanity). Moreover, as commitment under the Act is not tantamount to "punishment," Hendricks' involuntary detention does not violate the Double Jeopardy Clause, even though that confinement may follow a prison term. Indeed, in Baxstrom v. Herold, 383 U.S. 107, 86 S.Ct. 760, 15 L.Ed.2d 620 (1966), we expressly recognized that civil commitment could follow the expiration of a prison term without offending double jeopardy principles. We reasoned that "there is no conceivable basis for distinguishing the commitment of a person who is nearing the end of a penal term from all other civil commitments." Id., at 111–112, 86 S.Ct., at 763. If an individual otherwise meets the requirements for involuntary civil commitment, the State is under no obligation to release that individual simply because the detention would follow a period of incarceration.

Hendricks also argues that even if the Act survives the "multiple punishments" test, it nevertheless fails the "same elements" test of Blockburger v. United States, 284 U.S. 299, 52 S.Ct. 180, 76 L.Ed. 306 (1932). Under Blockburger, "where the same act or transaction constitutes a violation of two distinct statutory provisions, the test to be applied to determine whether there are two offenses or only one, is whether each provision requires proof of a fact which the other does not." Id., at 304, 52 S.Ct., at 182. The Blockburger test, however, simply does not apply outside of the successive prosecution context. A proceeding under the Act does not define an "offense," the elements of which can be compared to the elements of an offense for which the person may previously have been convicted. Nor does the Act make the commission of a specified "offense" the basis for invoking the commitment proceedings. Instead, it uses a prior conviction (or previously charged conduct) for evidentiary purposes to determine whether a person suffers from a "mental abnormality" or "personality disorder" and also poses a threat to the public. Accordingly, we are unpersuaded by Hendricks' novel application of the Blockburger test and conclude that the Act does not violate the Double Jeopardy Clause.

2

Hendricks' ex post facto claim is similarly flawed. The Ex Post Facto Clause, which " 'forbids the application of any new punitive measure to a crime already consummated,' " has been interpreted to pertain exclusively to penal statutes. California Dept. of Corrections v. Morales, 514 U.S. 499,

505, 115 S.Ct. 1597, 1601, 131 L.Ed.2d 588 (1995) (quoting Lindsey v. Washington, 301 U.S. 397, 401, 57 S.Ct. 797, 799, 81 L.Ed. 1182 (1937)). As we have previously determined, the Act does not impose punishment; thus, its application does not raise ex post facto concerns. Moreover, the Act clearly does not have retroactive effect. Rather, the Act permits involuntary confinement based upon a determination that the person currently both suffers from a "mental abnormality" or "personality disorder" and is likely to pose a future danger to the public. To the extent that past behavior is taken into account, it is used, as noted above, solely for evidentiary purposes. Because the Act does not criminalize conduct legal before its enactment, nor deprive Hendricks of any defense that was available to him at the time of his crimes, the Act does not violate the Ex Post Facto Clause.

III

We hold that the Kansas Sexually Violent Predator Act comports with due process requirements and neither runs afoul of double jeopardy principles nor constitutes an exercise in impermissible ex post facto lawmaking. Accordingly, the judgment of the Kansas Supreme Court is reversed.

It is so ordered.

■ JUSTICE KENNEDY, concurring.

I join the opinion of the Court in full and add these additional comments.

Though other issues were argued to us, as the case has matured it turns on whether the Kansas statute is an ex post facto law. A law enacted after commission of the offense and which punishes the offense by extending the term of confinement is a textbook example of an ex post facto law. If the object or purpose of the Kansas law had been to provide treatment but the treatment provisions were adopted as a sham or mere pretext, there would have been an indication of the forbidden purpose to punish. The Court's opinion gives a full and complete explanation why an ex post facto challenge based on this contention cannot succeed in the case before us. All this, however, concerns Hendricks alone. My brief, further comment is to caution against dangers inherent when a civil confinement law is used in conjunction with the criminal process, whether or not the law is given retroactive application.

On the record before us, the Kansas civil statute conforms to our precedents. If, however, civil confinement were to become a mechanism for retribution or general deterrence, or if it were shown that mental abnormality is too imprecise a category to offer a solid basis for concluding that civil detention is justified, our precedents would not suffice to validate it.

■ JUSTICE BREYER, with whom JUSTICES STEVENS and SOUTER join, and with whom JUSTICE GINSBURG joins as to Parts II and III, dissenting.

* * *

II

Kansas' 1994 Act violates the Federal Constitution's prohibition of "any . . . ex post facto Law" if it "inflicts" upon Hendricks "a greater punishment" than did the law "annexed to" his "crime[s]" when he "committed" those crimes in 1984. Calder v. Bull, 3 Dall. 386, 390, 1 L.Ed. 648 (1798) (opinion of Chase, J.); U.S. Const., Art. I, § 10. The majority agrees that the Clause " 'forbids the application of any new punitive measure to a crime already consummated.' " California Dept. of Corrections v. Morales, 514 U.S. 499, 504, 115 S.Ct. 1597, 1601, 131 L.Ed.2d 588 (1995) (citation omitted; emphasis added). Ante, at ___. But it finds the Act is not "punitive." With respect to that basic question, I disagree with the majority.

* * *

III

To find that the confinement the Act imposes upon Hendricks is "punishment" is to find a violation of the Ex Post Facto Clause. Kansas does not deny that the 1994 Act changed the legal consequences that attached to Hendricks' earlier crimes, and in a way that significantly "disadvantage[d] the offender," Weaver v. Graham, 450 U.S. 24, 29, 101 S.Ct. 960, 964, 67 L.Ed.2d 17 (1981). See Brief for Respondent State of Kansas 37–39.

To find a violation of that Clause here, however, is not to hold that the Clause prevents Kansas, or other States, from enacting dangerous sexual offender statutes. A statute that operates prospectively, for example, does not offend the Ex Post Facto Clause. Weaver, 450 U.S., supra, at 29, 101 S.Ct., at 964–965. Neither does it offend the Ex Post Facto Clause for a State to sentence offenders to the fully authorized sentence, to seek consecutive, rather than concurrent, sentences, or to invoke recidivism statutes to lengthen imprisonment. Moreover, a statute that operates retroactively, like Kansas' statute, nonetheless does not offend the Clause if the confinement that it imposes is not punishment—if, that is to say, the legislature does not simply add a later criminal punishment to an earlier one. Ibid.

The statutory provisions before us do amount to punishment primarily because, as I have said, the legislature did not tailor the statute to fit the nonpunitive civil aim of treatment, which it concedes exists in Hendricks' case. The Clause in these circumstances does not stand as an obstacle to achieving important protections for the public's safety; rather it provides an assurance that, where so significant a restriction of an individual's basic freedoms is at issue, a State cannot cut corners. Rather, the legislature must hew to the Constitution's liberty-protecting line. See The Federalist, No. 78, p. 466 (C. Rossiter ed. 1961) (A. Hamilton).

I therefore would affirm the judgment below.

5. ENHANCED PUNISHMENT UNDER RECIDIVIST PROVISIONS

Almendarez-Torres v. United States

Supreme Court of the United States, 1998.
523 U.S. 224, 118 S.Ct. 1219, 140 L.Ed.2d 350.

■ JUSTICE BREYER delivered the opinion of the Court.

Subsection (a) of 8 U.S.C. § 1326 defines a crime. It forbids an alien who once was deported to return to the United States without special permission, and it authorizes a prison term of up to, but no more than, two years. Subsection (b)(2) of the same section authorizes a prison term of up to, but no more than, 20 years for "any alien described" in subsection (a), if the initial "deportation was subsequent to a conviction for commission of an aggravated felony." § 1326(b)(2). The question before us is whether this latter provision defines a separate crime or simply authorizes an enhanced penalty. If the former, i.e., if it constitutes a separate crime, then the Government must write an indictment that mentions the additional element, namely a prior aggravated felony conviction. If the latter, i.e., if the provision simply authorizes an enhanced sentence when an offender also has an earlier conviction, then the indictment need not mention that fact, for the fact of an earlier conviction is not an element of the present crime.

We conclude that the subsection is a penalty provision, which simply authorizes a court to increase the sentence for a recidivist. It does not define a separate crime. Consequently, neither the statute nor the Constitution require the Government to charge the factor that it mentions, an earlier conviction, in the indictment.

I

In September 1995, a federal grand jury returned an indictment charging petitioner, Hugo Almendarez–Torres, with having been "found in the United States ...after being deported" without the "permission and consent of the Attorney General" in "violation of ...Section 1326." App. 3. In December 1995, Almendarez–Torres entered a plea of guilty. At a hearing, before the District Court accepted his plea, Almendarez–Torres admitted that he had been deported, that he had later unlawfully returned to the United States, and that the earlier deportation had taken place "pursuant to" three earlier "convictions" for aggravated felonies. Id., at 10–14.

In March 1996, the District Court held a sentencing hearing. Almendarez–Torres pointed out that an indictment must set forth all the elements of a crime. See Hamling v. United States, 418 U.S. 87, 117, 94 S.Ct. 2887, 2907–2908, 41 L.Ed.2d 590 (1974). He added that his indictment had not mentioned his earlier aggravated felony convictions. And he argued that, consequently, the court could not sentence him to more than two years imprisonment, the maximum authorized for an offender without an earlier conviction. The District Court rejected this argument. It found applicable a Sentencing Guideline range of 77 to 96 months, see United States Sentencing Commission, Guidelines Manual § 2L1.2; ch. 5, pt. A (sentencing table) (Nov. 1995) (USSG), and it imposed a sentence of 85 months' imprisonment. App. 17.

On appeal the Fifth Circuit also rejected petitioner's argument. 113 F.3d 515 (1996). Like seven other Circuits, it has held that subsection (b)(2) is a penalty provision which simply permits a sentencing judge to impose a higher sentence when the unlawfully returning alien also has a record of prior convictions....The Ninth Circuit, however, has reached the opposite conclusion. . . .We granted certiorari to resolve this difference among the Circuits.

II

An indictment must set forth each element of the crime that it charges. Hamling v. United States, supra, at 117, 94 S.Ct., at 2907–2908. But it need not set forth factors relevant only to the sentencing of an offender found guilty of the charged crime. Within limits, see McMillan v. Pennsylvania, 477 U.S. 79, 84–91, 106 S.Ct. 2411, 2415–2419, 91 L.Ed.2d 67 (1986), the question of which factors are which is normally a matter for Congress. See Staples v. United States, 511 U.S. 600, 604, 114 S.Ct. 1793, 1796, 128 L.Ed.2d 608 (1994) (definition of a criminal offense entrusted to the legislature, " 'particularly in the case of federal crimes, which are solely creatures of statute' ") (quoting Liparota v. United States, 471 U.S. 419, 424, 105 S.Ct. 2084, 2087, 85 L.Ed.2d 434 (1985)). We therefore look to the statute before us and ask what Congress intended. Did it intend the factor that the statute mentions, the prior aggravated felony conviction, to help define a separate crime? Or did it intend the presence of an earlier conviction as a sentencing factor, a factor that a sentencing court might use to increase punishment? In answering this question, we look to the statute's language, structure, subject matter, context, and history—factors that typically help courts determine a statute's objectives and thereby illuminate its text. See, e.g., United States v. Wells, 519 U.S. 482, ___, 117 S.Ct. 921, ___, 137 L.Ed.2d 107 (1997); Garrett v. United States, 471 U.S. 773, 779, 105 S.Ct. 2407, 2411–2412, 85 L.Ed.2d 764 (1985).

The directly relevant portions of the statute as it existed at the time of petitioner's conviction included subsection (a), which Congress had enacted in 1952, and subsection (b), which Congress added in 1988. See 8 U.S.C. § 1326 (1952 ed.) (as enacted June 27, 1952, § 276, 66 Stat. 229); 8 U.S.C. § 1326 (1988 ed.) (reflecting amendments made by § 7345(a), 102 Stat. 4471). We print those portions of text below:

"§ 1326. Reentry of deported alien; criminal penalties for reentry of certain deported aliens.

"(a) Subject to subsection (b) of this section, any alien who—

"(1) has been . . .deported . . . , and thereafter

"(2) enters . . . , or is at any time found in, the United States [without the Attorney General's consent or the legal equivalent], "shall be fined under title 18, or imprisoned not more than 2 years, or both.

"(b) Notwithstanding subsection (a) of this section, in the case of any alien described in such subsection—

"(1) whose deportation was subsequent to a conviction for commission of [certain misdemeanors], or a felony (other than an aggravated felony), such alien shall be fined under title 18, imprisoned not more than 10 years, or both; or

"(2) whose deportation was subsequent to a conviction for commission of an aggravated felony, such alien shall be fined under such title, imprisoned not more than 20 years, or both." 8 U.S.C. § 1326.

[In Sections A and B of Part II, the Court concluded that Congress intended its amendment to be a sentencing provision, not an element of the offense.]

III

Invoking several of the Court's precedents, petitioner claims that the Constitution requires Congress to treat recidivism as an element of the offense—irrespective of Congress' contrary intent. Moreover, petitioner says, that requirement carries with it three subsidiary requirements that the Constitution mandates in respect to ordinary, legislatively intended, elements of crimes. The indictment must state the "element." See, e.g., Hamling v. United States, 418 U.S., at 117, 94 S.Ct., at 2907–2908. The Government must prove that "element" to a jury. See, e.g., Duncan v. Louisiana, 391 U.S. 145, 149, 88 S.Ct. 1444, 1447, 20 L.Ed.2d 491 (1968). And the Government must prove the "element" beyond a reasonable doubt. See, e.g., Patterson v. New York, 432 U.S. 197, 210, 97 S.Ct. 2319, 2327, 53 L.Ed.2d 281 (1977). We cannot find sufficient support, however, in our precedents or elsewhere, for petitioner's claim.

This Court has explicitly held that the Constitution's Due Process Clause "protects the accused against conviction except upon proof beyond a reasonable doubt of every fact necessary to constitute the crime with which he is charged." In re Winship, 397 U.S. 358, 364, 90 S.Ct. 1068, 1073, 25 L.Ed.2d 368 (1970). But Winship, the case in which the Court set forth this proposition of constitutional law, does not decide this case. It said that the Constitution entitles juveniles, like adults, to the benefit of proof beyond a reasonable doubt in respect to the elements of the crime. It did not consider whether, or when, the Constitution requires the Government to treat a particular fact as an element, i.e., as a "fact necessary to constitute the crime," even where the crime-defining statute does not do so.

Mullaney v. Wilbur, 421 U.S. 684, 95 S.Ct. 1881, 44 L.Ed.2d 508 (1975), provides petitioner with stronger support. The Court there struck down a state homicide statute under which the State presumed that all homicides were committed with "malice," punishable by life imprisonment, unless the defendant proved that he had acted in the heat of passion. Id., at 688, 95 S.Ct., at 1884. The Court wrote that "if Winship were limited to those facts that constitute a crime as defined by state law, a State could undermine many of the interests that decision sought to protect" just by redefining "the elements that constitut[ed] different crimes, characterizing them as factors that bear solely on the extent of punishment." Id., at 698, 95 S.Ct., at 1889. It simultaneously held that the prosecution must establish "beyond a reasonable doubt" the nonexistence of "heat of passion"— the fact that, under the State's statutory scheme, distinguished a homicide punishable by a life sentence from a homicide punishable by a maximum of 20 years. Id., at 704, 95 S.Ct., at 1892. Read literally, this language, we concede, suggests that Congress cannot permit judges to increase a sentence in light of recidivism, or any other factor, not set forth in an indictment and proved to a jury beyond a reasonable doubt.

This Court's later case, Patterson v. New York, supra, however, makes absolutely clear that such a reading of Mullaney is wrong. The Court, in Patterson, pointed out that the State in Mullaney made the critical fact— the absence of "heat of passion"—not simply a potential sentencing factor, but also a critical part of the definition of "malice aforethought," which was itself in turn "part of" the statute's definition of "homicide," the crime in question. Patterson, 432 U.S., at 215–216, 97 S.Ct., at 2329–2330. (The Maine Supreme Court, in defining the crime, had said that "malice" was "presumed" unless "rebutted" by the defendant's showing of "heat of passion." Id., at 216, 97 S.Ct., at 2330.) The Court found this circumstance extremely important. It said that Mullaney had considered (and held "impermissible") the shifting of a burden of proof "with respect to a fact which the State deems so important that it must be either proved or presumed." 432 U.S., at 215, 97 S.Ct., at 2329 (emphasis added). And the Court then held that similar burden-shifting was permissible with respect to New York's homicide-related sentencing factor "extreme emotional disturbance." Id., at 205–206, 97 S.Ct., at 2324–2325. That factor was not a factor that the state statute had deemed "so important" in relation to the crime that it must be either "proved or presumed." Id., 205–206, 215, 97 S.Ct., at 2324–2325, 2329.

The upshot is that Mullaney's language, if read literally, suggests that the Constitution requires that most, if not all, sentencing factors be treated as elements. But Patterson suggests the exact opposite, namely that the Constitution requires scarcely any sentencing factors to be treated in that way. The cases, taken together, cannot significantly help the petitioner, for the statute here involves a sentencing factor—the prior commission of an aggravated felony—that is neither "presumed" to be present, nor need be "proved" to be present, in order to prove the commission of the relevant crime. See 8 U.S.C. § 1326(a) (defining offense elements). Indeed, as we have said, it involves one of the most frequently found factors that effects sentencing—recidivism.

Nor does Specht v. Patterson, 386 U.S. 605, 87 S.Ct. 1209, 18 L.Ed.2d 326 (1967), which petitioner cites, provide significant additional help, for Specht was decided before Patterson (indeed before Winship); it did not consider the kind of matter here at issue; and, as this Court later noted, the Colorado defendant in Specht was "confronted with 'a radically different situation' from the usual sentencing proceeding." McMillan v. Pennsylvania, 477 U.S., at 89, 106 S.Ct., at 2417. At most, petitioner might read all these cases, taken together, for the broad proposition that sometimes the Constitution does require (though sometimes it does not require) the State to treat a sentencing factor as an element. But we do not see how they can help petitioner more than that.

We turn then to the case upon which petitioner must primarily rely, McMillan v. Pennsylvania, supra. The Court there considered a Pennsylvania statute that set forth a sentencing factor—"visibly possessing a firearm"—the presence of which required the judge to impose a minimum prison term of five years. The Court held that the Constitution did not require the State to treat the factor as an element of the crime. In so holding, the Court said that the State's "link[ing] the 'severity of punishment' to 'the presence or absence of an identified fact' " did not automatically make of that fact an "element." 477 U.S., at 84, 106 S.Ct., at 2415 (quoting Patterson v. New York, supra, at 214, 97 S.Ct., at 2329). It said, citing Patterson, that "the state legislature's definition of the elements of the offense is usually dispositive." 477 U.S., at 85, 106 S.Ct., at 2415. It said that it would not "define precisely the constitutional limits" of a legislature's power to define the elements of an offense. Id., at 86, 106 S.Ct., at 2416. And it held that, whatever those limits might be, the State had not exceeded them. Ibid. Petitioner must therefore concede that "firearm possession" (in respect to a mandatory minimum sentence) does not violate those limits. And he must argue that, nonetheless, "recidivism" (in respect to an authorized maximum) does violate those limits.

In assessing petitioner's claim, we have examined McMillan to determine the various features of the case upon which the Court's conclusion arguably turned. The McMillan Court pointed out: (1) that the statute plainly "does not transgress the limits expressly set out in Patterson," id., at 86, 106 S.Ct., at 2416; (2) that the defendant (unlike Mullaney 's defendant) did not face " 'a differential in sentencing ranging from a nominal fine to a mandatory life sentence,' " 477 U.S., at 87, 106 S.Ct., at 2417 (quoting Mullaney, 421 U.S., at 700, 95 S.Ct., at 1890); (3) that the statute did not "alte[r] the maximum penalty for the crime" but "operates solely to limit the sentencing court's discretion in selecting a penalty within the range already available to it," 477 U.S., at 87–88, 106 S.Ct., at 2417; (4) that the statute did not "creat[e] a separate offense calling for a separate penalty," id., at 88, 106 S.Ct., at 2417; and (5) that the statute gave "no impression of having been tailored to permit the visible possession finding to be a tail which wags the dog of the substantive offense," but, to the contrary, "simply took one factor that has always been considered by sentencing courts to bear on punishment . . .and dictated the precise weight to be given that factor," id., at 88, 89–90, 106 S.Ct., at 2417, 2418.

This case resembles McMillan in respect to most of these factors. But it is different in respect to the third factor, for it does "alte[r] the maximum penalty for the crime," 477 U.S., at 87, 106 S.Ct., at 2417; and, it also creates a wider range of appropriate punishments than did the statute in McMillan. We nonetheless conclude that these differences do not change the constitutional outcome for several basic reasons.

First, the sentencing factor at issue here—recidivism—is a traditional, if not the most traditional, basis for a sentencing court's increasing an offender's sentence. See, e.g., Parke v. Raley, 506 U.S. 20, 26, 113 S.Ct. 517, 521–522, 121 L.Ed.2d 391 (1992) (Recidivism laws "have a long tradition in this country that dates back to colonial times" and currently are in effect in all 50 States); U.S. Dept. of Justice, Office of Justice Programs, Statutes Requiring the Use of Criminal History Record Information 17–41 (June 1991) (50–state survey); USSG §§ 4A1.1, 4A1.2 (Nov. 1997) (requiring sentencing court to consider defendant's prior record in every case). Consistent with this tradition, the Court said long ago that a State need not allege a defendant's prior conviction in the indictment or information which alleges the elements of an underlying crime, even though the conviction was "necessary to bring the case within the statute." Graham v. West

Virginia, 224 U.S. 616, 624, 32 S.Ct. 583, 585–86, 56 L.Ed. 917 (1912). That conclusion followed, the Court said, from "the distinct nature of the issue," and the fact that recidivism "does not relate to the commission of the offense, but goes to the punishment only, and therefore . . . may be subsequently decided." Id., at 629, 32 S.Ct., at 588 (emphasis added). The Court has not deviated from this view. See Oyler v. Boles, 368 U.S. 448, 452, 82 S.Ct. 501, 503–504, 7 L.Ed.2d 446 (1962) (due process does not require advance notice that trial for substantive offense will be followed by accusation that the defendant is an habitual offender); Parke, supra, at 27, 113 S.Ct., at 522 ("[A] charge under a recidivism statute does not state a separate offense, but goes to punishment only"). And, as we said before, infra, at 5–6, Congress, reflecting this tradition, has never, to our knowledge, made a defendant's recidivism an element of an offense where the conduct proscribed is otherwise unlawful. See United States v. Jackson, 824 F.2d 21, 25, and n. 6 (C.A.D.C.1987) (R. Ginsburg, J.) (referring to fact that few, if any, federal statutes make "prior criminal convictions . . . elements of another criminal offense to be proved before the jury"). Although these precedents do not foreclose petitioner's claim (because, for example, the state statute at issue in Graham and Oyler provided for a jury determination of disputed prior convictions), to hold that the Constitution requires that recidivism be deemed an "element" of petitioner's offense would mark an abrupt departure from a longstanding tradition of treating recidivism as "go[ing] to the punishment only." Graham, supra, at 629, 32 S.Ct., at 587–588.

Second, the major difference between this case and McMillan consists of the circumstance that the sentencing factor at issue here (the prior conviction) triggers an increase in the maximum permissive sentence, while the sentencing factor at issue in McMillan triggered a mandatory minimum sentence. Yet that difference—between a permissive maximum and a mandatory minimum—does not systematically, or normally, work to the disadvantage of a criminal defendant. To the contrary, a statutory minimum binds a sentencing judge; a statutory maximum does not. A mandatory minimum can, as Justice STEVENS dissenting in McMillan pointed out, "mandate a minimum sentence of imprisonment more than twice as severe as the maximum the trial judge would otherwise have imposed." McMillan, supra, at 95, 106 S.Ct., at 2421. It can eliminate a sentencing judge's discretion in its entirety. See, e.g., 18 U.S.C. § 2241(c) (authorizing maximum term of life imprisonment for sexual abuse of children; mandating life imprisonment for second offense). And it can produce unfairly disproportionate impacts on certain kinds of offenders. See United States Sentencing Commission, Mandatory Minimum Penalties in the Federal Criminal Justice System 26–34 (Aug. 1991) (discussing "tariff" and "cliff" effects of mandatory minimums). In sum, the risk of unfairness to a particular defendant is no less, and may well be greater, when a mandatory minimum sentence, rather than a permissive maximum sentence, is at issue.

Although McMillan pointed to a difference between mandatory minimums and higher authorized maximums, it neither, "rested its judgment" on that difference, nor "rejected" the above analysis, as the dissent contends, post, at 1236. Rather, McMillan said that the petitioners' argument in that case would have had "more *superficial* appeal" if the sentencing fact "exposed them to greater or additional punishment." 477 U.S., at 88, 106 S.Ct., at 2417 (emphasis added). For the reasons just given, and in light of the particular sentencing factor at issue in this case—recidivism— we should take McMillan's statement to mean no more that it said, and therefore not to make a determinative difference here.

Third, the statute's broad permissive sentencing range does not itself create significantly greater unfairness. Judges (and parole boards) have typically exercised their discretion within broad statutory ranges. See, e.g., supra, at 1224, 1226 (statutory examples); National Institute of Justice, Sentencing Reform in the United States (Aug. 1985) (survey of sentencing laws in the 50 States); L. Friedman, Crime and Punishment in American History 159–163 (1993) (history of indeterminate sentencing). And the Sentencing Guidelines have recently sought to channel that discretion using "sentencing factors" which no one here claims that the Constitution thereby makes "elements" of a crime.

Finally, the remaining McMillan factors support the conclusion that Congress has the constitutional power to treat the feature before us—prior conviction of an aggravated felony—as a sentencing factor for this particular offense (illegal entry after deportation). The relevant statutory provisions do not change a pre-existing definition of a well-established crime, nor is there any more reason here, than in McMillan, to think Congress intended to "evade" the Constitution, either by "presuming" guilt or "restructuring" the elements of an offense. Cf. McMillan, supra, at 86–87, 89–90, 106 S.Ct., at 2416–2417, 2417–2418.

For these reasons, we cannot find in McMillan (a case holding that the Constitution permits a legislature to require a longer sentence for gun possession) significant support for the proposition that the Constitution forbids a legislature to authorize a longer sentence for recidivism.

Petitioner makes two basic additional arguments in response. He points to what he calls a different "tradition"—that of courts having treated recidivism as an element of the related crime. See, e.g., Massey v. United States, 281 F. 293, 297–298 (C.A.8 1922); Singer v. United States, 278 F. 415, 420 (C.A.3 1922); People v. Sickles, 156 N.Y. 541, 51 N.E. 288, 289 (N.Y.1898); see also post, at 9–10 (citing authority). We do not find this claim convincing, however, for any such tradition is not uniform. See Spencer v. Texas, 385 U.S., at 566, 87 S.Ct., at 654–55 ("The method for determining prior convictions . . . varies between jurisdictions affording a jury trial on this issue . . . and those leaving that question to the court"); Note, Recidivist Procedures, 40 N.Y.U.L.Rev. 332, 347 (1965) (as of 1965, eight States' recidivism statutes provide for determination of prior convictions by judge, not jury). Nor does it appear modern. Compare State v. Thorne, 129 Wash.2d 736, 776–784, 921 P.2d 514, 533–538 (1996) (upholding state recidivism law against federal constitutional challenge) with State v. Furth, 5 Wash.2d 1, 11–19, 104 P.2d 925, 930–933 (1940). And it nowhere (to our knowledge) rested upon a federal constitutional guarantee. See, e.g., Massey v. United States, supra, at 297 (applying federal law, noting jury determination of prior offense applied "unless the statute designates a different mode of procedure").

Petitioner also argues, in essence, that this Court should simply adopt a rule that any significant increase in a statutory maximum sentence would trigger a Constitutional "elements" requirement. We have explained why we believe the Constitution, as interpreted in McMillan and earlier cases, does not impose that requirement. We add that such a rule would seem anomalous in light of existing case law that permits a judge, rather than a jury, to determine the existence of factors that can make a defendant eligible for the death penalty, a punishment far more severe than that faced by petitioner here. See Walton v. Arizona, 497 U.S. 639, 647, 110 S.Ct. 3047, 3053–3054, 111 L.Ed.2d 511 (1990) (rejecting capital defendant's argument that every finding of fact underlying death sentence must be made by a jury); Hildwin v. Florida, 490 U.S. 638, 640–641, 109 S.Ct. 2055, 2056–2057, 104 L.Ed.2d 728 (1989) (per curiam) (judge may impose death penalty based on his finding of aggravating factor because such factor is not element of offense to be determined by jury); Spaziano v. Florida, 468 U.S. 447, 465, 104 S.Ct. 3154, 3164–3165, 82 L.Ed.2d 340 (1984) (same). And we would also find it difficult to reconcile any such rule with our precedent holding that the sentencing-related circumstances of recidivism are not part of the definition of the offense for double jeopardy purposes. Graham, 224 U.S., at 623–624, 32 S.Ct., at 585–586.

For these reasons, we reject petitioner's constitutional claim that his recidivism must be treated as an element of his offense.

IV

We mention one final point. Petitioner makes no separate, subsidiary, standard of proof claims with respect to his sentencing, perhaps because he admitted his recidivism at the time he pleaded guilty and would therefore find it difficult to show that the standard of proof could have made a difference to his case. Accordingly, we express no view on whether some heightened standard of proof might apply to sentencing determinations which bear significantly on the severity of sentence. Cf. United States v. Watts, 519 U.S. 148, ___ and n. 2, 117 S.Ct. 633, 637–638 and n. 2, 136 L.Ed.2d 554 (1997) (per curiam) (acknowledging, but not resolving, "divergence of opinion among the Circuits" as to proper standard for determining the existence of "relevant conduct" that would lead to an increase in sentence).

The judgment of the Court of Appeals is

Affirmed.

■ JUSTICE SCALIA, with whom JUSTICE STEVENS, JUSTICE SOUTER, and JUSTICE GINSBURG join, dissenting.

Because Hugo Roman Almendarez–Torres illegally re-entered the United States after having been convicted of an aggravated felony, he was subject to a maximum possible sentence of 20 years imprisonment. See 8 U.S.C. § 1326(b)(2). Had he not been convicted of that felony, he would have been subject to a maximum of only two years. See 8 U.S.C. § 1326(a). The Court today holds that § 1326(b)(2) does not set forth a separate offense, and that conviction of a prior felony is merely a sentencing enhancement for the offense set forth in § 1326(a). This causes the Court to confront the difficult question whether the Constitution requires a fact which substantially increases the maximum permissible punishment for a crime to be treated as an element of that crime—to be charged in the indictment, and found beyond a reasonable doubt by a jury. Until the Court said so, it was far from obvious that the answer to this question was no; on the basis of our prior law, in fact, the answer was considerably doubtful.

In all our prior cases bearing upon the issue, however, we confronted a criminal statute or state-court criminal ruling that unambiguously relieved the prosecution of the burden of proving a critical fact to the jury beyond a reasonable doubt. In McMillan v. Pennsylvania, 477 U.S. 79, 106 S.Ct. 2411, 91 L.Ed.2d 67 (1986), the statute provided that " 'visibl[e] possess[ion][of] a firearm' " " 'shall not be an element of the crime[,]' " but shall be determined at sentencing by " '[t]he court . . . by a preponderance of the evidence,' " id., at 81, n. 1, 106 S.Ct., at 2413, n. 1 (quoting 42 Pa. Cons.Stat. § 9712 (1982)). In In re Winship, 397 U.S. 358, 90 S.Ct. 1068, 25 L.Ed.2d 368 (1970), it provided that determinations of criminal action in juvenile cases " 'must be based on a preponderance of the evidence,' " id., at 360, 90 S.Ct., at 1070 (quoting N.Y. Family Court Act § 744(b)). In Patterson v. New York, 432 U.S. 197, 97 S.Ct. 2319, 53 L.Ed.2d 281 (1977), the statute provided that extreme emotional disturbance " 'is an affirmative defense,' " id., at 198, n. 2, 97 S.Ct., at 2321, n. 2 (quoting N.Y. Penal Law § 125.25 (McKinney 1975)). And in Mullaney v. Wilbur, 421 U.S. 684, 95 S.Ct. 1881, 44 L.Ed.2d 508 (1975), Maine's highest court had held that in murder cases malice aforethought was presumed and had to be negated by the defendant, id., at 689, 95 S.Ct., at 1884–1885 (citing State v. Lafferty, 309 A.2d 647 (1973)).

In contrast to the provisions involved in these cases, 8 U.S.C. § 1326 does not, on its face, place the constitutional issue before us: it does not say that subsection (b)(2) is merely a sentencing enhancement. The text of the statute supports, if it does not indeed demand, the conclusion that subsection (b)(2) is a separate offense that includes the violation described in subsection (a) but adds the additional element of prior felony conviction. I therefore do not reach the difficult constitutional issue in this case because I adopt, as I think our cases require, that reasonable interpretation of § 1326 which avoids the problem. Illegal re-entry simpliciter (§ 1326(a)) and illegal reentry after conviction of an aggravated felony (§ 1326(b)(2)) are separate criminal offenses. Prior conviction of an aggravated felony being an element of the latter offense, it must be charged in the indictment. Since it was not, petitioner's sentence must be set aside.

[The balance of Justice Scalia's dissenting opinion is omitted.]

CHAPTER 26

APPEAL AND COLLATERAL ATTACK

Analysis

This final chapter follows up the prior materials about trial court proceedings with an introduction to some general principles governing post-trial proceedings. There are some post-trial matters that have already been addressed in this book. Chapter 22 covered two. One is the extent to which failure to comply with procedural requirements for the taking of guilty pleas justifies disturbing a conviction on appeal or in collateral proceedings. The other is the degree to which various other issues continue to exist despite a guilty plea, allowing them to be addressed on collateral attack. In addition, Chapter 25 addressed appellate review of sentences.

In order to conceptualize post-trial proceedings in a practical manner, this chapter distinguishes post-trial proceedings that involve direct appeal from those that consist of so-called "collateral" attacks upon a conviction or sentence. But first, the 1990 Report of the Federal Courts Study Committee, which immediately follows, highlights the tension between providing for post-conviction relief and court congestion.

A. THE CONTEXT: TENSION BETWEEN APPELLATE CASELOAD AND POST CONVICTION REMEDIES

REPORT OF THE FEDERAL COURTS STUDY COMMITTEE, 109–110
(APRIL 2, 1990)

Chapter 6

Dealing with the Appellate Caseload Crisis

However people may view other aspects of the federal judiciary, few deny that its appellate courts are in a "crisis of volume" that has transformed them from the institutions they were even a generation ago. Further and more fundamental change to the appellate courts would seem to be inevitable unless there is a halt to the climb in appellate workload. While it is impossible to read the future, we see little reason to anticipate such a halt.

If growth continues, the nation must ask how further changes in the appellate courts will occur. Will they be insidious and unplanned; will oral argument and reasoned opinions simply fade away, for example? Or will Congress and the courts fashion new structures and procedures specifically designed to preserve the hallmarks of our judiciary? Those hallmarks include that the judges do much of their own work, grant oral argument in cases that need it, decide cases with sufficient thought, and produce opinions in cases of precedential importance with the care they deserve, including independent, constructive insight and criticism from judges on the court and the panel other than the judge writing the opinion. These conditions are essential to a carefully crafted case law. Modern society requires no less.

Today's federal appellate courts have been able to provide these conditions only through increases in productivity that seem to be approaching their limit. Further attempts to raise productivity by the most commonly suggested and employed means, such as increases in staff and reducing opportunity for oral argument, could threaten the integrity of the process.
. . .

. . . The crisis is caused partly by an increase in district court cases but mainly by a heightened proclivity to appeal district court terminations. In 1945, litigants appealed about one of every forty district court terminations; they now appeal about one in eight. As a result, appellate filings have risen nearly fifteen-fold. . . . The number of appellate judges, however, has increased since 1945 by a factor of less than three, from 59 to 168. Consequently, the caseload per judge has multiplied by nearly six over the same period. . . .

To date, the courts of appeals have managed to avoid the worst effects of this growth. There has been no systemic breakdown in the quality of the courts' work. . . . But the appellate courts have avoided major deterioration only by pushing productivity to maximum levels and by adopting truncated procedures that probably have reached the limits of their utility without compromising the quality of the process.

The appellate caseload explosion, moreover, threatens not only the courts of appeals as we know them. It also threatens the Supreme Court's role as the enunciator of national law. The Court is unable to give full review to more than about 150 cases per year. As court of appeals decisions increase in number, there is a corresponding decline in the percentage of those decisions that the Supreme Court reviews, thus making the thirteen intermediate appellate courts more and more the nation's courts of last resort. . . .

B. APPEAL

EDITORS' INTRODUCTION: STRUCTURES FOR DIRECT APPEAL

Statutes and court rules governing criminal procedure generally provide for convicted defendants to have access to one or more appellate tribunals to review actions by the trial court that contributed to the conviction. In the federal system, for example, a defendant convicted in federal District Court may appeal, as a matter of right, to the appropriate United States Court of Appeals. 28 U.S.C.A. § 1291. If denied relief at this level, the defendant may seek further review by the United States Supreme Court by application for a writ of certiorari. 28 U.S.C.A. § 1254. The Supreme Court's rules indicate that it will exercise its discretion to review a decision only where "special and important reasons" exist. Among the reasons suggesting that the Court will review a Court of Appeals decision are a split among the Court of Appeals on the issue involved, the presentation of an important and undecided question of federal law that should be settled, and determination of a federal question by the Court of Appeals in a way conflicting with Supreme Court precedent. Sup.Ct.R. 17.

Although the Supreme Court has never held that federal constitutional considerations require states to provide convicted defendants with appellate review, see Abney v. United States, 431 U.S. 651, 656, 97 S.Ct. 2034, 2038, 52 L.Ed.2d 651, 657–58 (1977), the states have generally provided for appeals from convictions. A large number of states have patterned appellate review after the federal system, with only limited (if any) review as of right beyond the first of several levels of appellate courts. Appeal by a defendant from an intermediate Court of Appeals to the state's highest court is generally discretionary. In cases involving a penalty of death or life imprisonment, appeal is often directly to the state's highest court.

A state criminal defendant can seek review by the United States Supreme Court of a decision of the highest court of the state to which he has access under state law. This review is by means of application for the writ of certiorari. See 28 U.S.C.A. § 1257. The Supreme Court has indicated that it will exercise its discretionary authority to review state court decisions on certiorari pursuant to the same sort of guidelines used to determine whether to review decisions of the United States Courts of Appeal. Sup.Ct.R. 17.

Appellate review is generally "on the record." This means that the reviewing court considers only the formal record compiled in the trial court. This record consists of the original papers and exhibits (including physical or "real" evidence) filed in the trial court, a transcription of the proceedings (usually a typed version of the court reporter's notes), and a copy of the trial court's docket entries related to the case. See Fed.R.App.Pro. 10. The reviewing court considers claims that the trial court erred in the proceeding. Generally, an appellate court will consider only matters that were brought to the attention of the trial court. But certain types of errors will be reviewed even if raised for the first time on appeal. Fed.R.Crim.P. 52(b) ("Plain errors" or "defects affecting substantial rights" may be considered on appeal even though not called to attention of trial court). Appellate relief to the defendant, if it is granted, may take any of a number of forms, depending upon the defect found in the trial proceeding and the procedural posture of the matter. For example, the appellate court may direct that the trial court hold a new trial, dismiss the charges, or enter judgment of acquittal for the defendant.

But certain errors, even if established, may be too insubstantial to warrant any relief at all. Thus F.R.Crim.P. 52(a), titled "Harmless Error," directs that on appeal "any error, defect, irregularity, or variance which does not affect substantial rights shall be disregarded." In ruling upon a contention that an error of federal constitutional dimensions is "harmless," i.e., does not require granting relief, the Supreme Court has directed that an especially stringent standard be used. In Chapman v. California, 386 U.S. 18, 87 S.Ct. 824, 17 L.Ed.2d 705 (1967), the Court observed that some federal constitutional errors may well be of such a nature as to preclude a finding that they are harmless. It held, however, that comments upon the defendant's failure to testify at trial could be regarded as harmless, but only if the prosecution convinced the appellate court beyond a reasonable doubt that the comments "did not contribute to the . . . convictions." 386 U.S. at 26, 87 S.Ct. at 829, 17 L.Ed.2d at 711.

The United States Supreme Court held in Brecht v. Abrahamson, 507 U.S. 619, 113 S.Ct. 1710, 123 L.Ed.2d 353 (1993) that when review is obtained in federal habeas corpus proceedings the proper harmless error standard is the less onerous one of Kotteakos v. United States, 328 U.S. 750, 66 S.Ct. 1239, 90 L.Ed. 1557 (1946)—whether the constitutional violation "had substantial and injurious effect or influence in determining the jury's verdict"—rather than the *Chapman* standard that is applied on direct appeal.

Provisions are also made—albeit less frequently—for the prosecution to have access to appellate review. Considerations of Double Jeopardy limit the ability of an appellate court to give the prosecution relief; these matters are considered in detail in Chapter 20. The 1970 revision of the applicable federal statute, 18 U.S.C.A. § 3731, has been construed as intended to permit the Government to appeal in any situation where appeal is not barred by Double Jeopardy. See United States v. Wilson, 420 U.S. 332, 337–39, 95 S.Ct. 1013, 1018–19, 43 L.Ed.2d 232, 238–39 (1975). As a general rule, interlocutory appeals have not been favorably regarded in criminal litigation. But some provisions for such appeals exist, especially in situations where only such a procedure can enable the prosecution to be given access to appellate review without violation of defendants' Double Jeopardy rights. Interlocutory appeals by the prosecution from rulings on pretrial motions are considered in Chapter 21, and by the defense on a claim of former jeopardy in Chapter 20. That no general federal constitutional right to interlocutory appeals exists, however, was strongly suggested by United States v. MacDonald, 435 U.S. 850, 98 S.Ct. 1547, 56 L.Ed.2d 18 (1978), involving a speedy trial claim, suggests, however, that there is no general federal constitutional right to interlocutory appeals.

Ross v. Moffitt

Supreme Court of the United States, 1974.
417 U.S. 600, 94 S.Ct. 2437, 41 L.Ed.2d 341.

■ MR. JUSTICE REHNQUIST delivered the opinion of the Court.

I.

* * *

[In federal habeas corpus litigation, the Fourth Circuit Court of Appeals held that respondent's federal constitutional rights had been violated by the refusal of North Carolina to provide him with court-appointed counsel in seeking discretionary review by the state and U.S. Supreme courts. Editors.]

II.

This Court, in the past 20 years, has given extensive consideration to the rights of indigent persons on appeal. In Griffin v. Illinois, 351 U.S. 12, 76 S.Ct. 585, 100 L.Ed. 891 (1956), the first of the pertinent cases, the Court had before it an Illinois rule allowing a convicted criminal defendant to present claims of trial error to the Supreme Court of Illinois only if he procured a transcript of the testimony adduced at his trial. No exception was made for the indigent defendant, and thus one who was unable to pay the cost of obtaining such a transcript was precluded from obtaining appellate review of asserted trial error. ... The Court in *Griffin* held that this discrimination violated the Fourteenth Amendment.

Succeeding cases invalidated similar financial barriers to the appellate process, at the same time reaffirming the traditional principle that a State is not obliged to provide any appeal at all for criminal defendants. ...

The decisions ... stand for the proposition that a State cannot arbitrarily cut off appeal rights for indigents while leaving open avenues of appeal for more affluent persons. In Douglas v. California, 372 U.S. 353, 83 S.Ct. 814, 9 L.Ed.2d 811 (1963), however, ... the Court departed somewhat from the limited doctrine of the transcript and fee cases and undertook an examination of whether an indigent's access to the appellate system was adequate. The Court in *Douglas* concluded that a State does not fulfill its responsibility toward indigent defendants merely by waiving its own requirements that a convicted defendant procure a transcript or pay a fee in order to appeal, and held that the State must go further and provide counsel for the indigent on his first appeal as of right. It is this decision we are asked to extend today.

* * *

The precise rationale for the *Griffin* and *Douglas* lines of cases has never been explicitly stated, some support being derived from the Equal Protection Clause of the Fourteenth Amendment, and some from the Due Process Clause of that Amendment. Neither Clause by itself provides an entirely satisfactory basis for the result reached, each depending on a different inquiry which emphasizes the different factors. "Due process" emphasizes fairness between the State and the individual dealing with the State, regardless of how other individuals in the same situation may be treated. "Equal protection," on the other hand, emphasizes disparity in treatment by a State between classes of individuals whose situations are arguably indistinguishable. We will address these issues separately in the succeeding sections.

III.

* * *

We do not believe that the Due Process Clause requires North Carolina to provide respondent with counsel on his discretionary appeal to the State Supreme Court. At the trial stage of a criminal proceeding, the right of an indigent defendant to counsel is fundamental and binding upon the States by virtue of the Sixth and Fourteenth Amendments. Gideon v. Wainwright, 372 U.S. 335, 83 S.Ct. 792, 9 L.Ed.2d 799 (1963). But there are significant differences between the trial and appellate stages of a criminal proceeding. The purpose of the trial stage from the State's point of view is to convert a criminal defendant from a person presumed innocent to one found guilty beyond a reasonable doubt. To accomplish this purpose, the State employs a prosecuting attorney who presents evidence to the court, challenges any witnesses offered by the defendant, argues rulings of the court, and makes direct arguments to the court and jury seeking to persuade them of the defendant's guilt. Under these circumstances "reason and reflection require us to recognize that in our adversary system of criminal justice, any person haled into court, who is too poor to hire a lawyer, cannot be assured a fair trial unless counsel is provided for him." Id., at 344, 83 S.Ct., at 796.

By contrast, it is ordinarily the defendant, rather than the State, who initiates the appellate process, seeking not to fend off the efforts of the State's prosecutor but rather to overturn a finding of guilt made by a judge or a jury below. The defendant needs an attorney on appeal not as a shield to protect him against being "haled into court" by the State and stripped of his presumption of innocence, but rather as a sword to upset the prior determination of guilt. This difference is significant for, while no one would agree that the State may simply dispense with the trial stage of proceedings without a criminal defendant's consent, it is clear that the State need not provide any appeal at all. McKane v. Durston, 153 U.S. 684, 14 S.Ct. 913, 38 L.Ed. 867 (1894). The fact that an appeal *has* been provided does not automatically mean that a State then acts unfairly by refusing to provide counsel to indigent defendants at every stage of the way. Douglas v. California, supra. Unfairness results only if indigents are singled out by the State and denied meaningful access to the appellate system because of their poverty. That question is more profitably considered under an equal protection analysis.

IV.

* * *

In this case we do not believe that the Equal Protection Clause, when interpreted in the context of these cases, requires North Carolina to provide free counsel for indigent defendants seeking to take discretionary appeals to the North Carolina Supreme Court, or to file petitions for certiorari in this Court.

* * *

The facts show that respondent ... received the benefit of counsel in examining the record of his trial and in preparing an appellate brief on his behalf for the state Court of Appeals. Thus, prior to his seeking discretionary review in the State Supreme Court, his claims had "once been presented by a lawyer and passed upon by an appellate court." Douglas v. California, 372 U.S., at 356, 83 S.Ct., at 816. We do not believe that it can be said, therefore, that a defendant in respondent's circumstances is denied meaningful access to the North Carolina Supreme Court simply because the State does not appoint counsel to aid him in seeking review in that court. At that stage he will have, at the very least, a transcript or other record of trial proceedings, a brief on his behalf in the Court of Appeals setting forth his claims of error, and in many cases an opinion by the Court of Appeals disposing of his case. These materials, supplemented by whatever submission respondent may make *pro se,* would appear to provide the Supreme Court of North Carolina with an adequate basis for its decision to grant or deny review.

V.

Much of the discussion in the preceding section is equally relevant to the question of whether a State must provide counsel for a defendant seeking review of his conviction in this Court. ...

* * *

Reversed.

■ Mr. Justice Douglas, with whom Mr. Justice Brennan and Mr. Justice Marshall concur, dissenting.

* * *

NOTES

1. **Effective assistance in first appeal of right.** Although a defendant does not have a right to counsel on a discretionary appeal under *Ross,* the Supreme Court has found a due process right to the effective assistance of counsel on the defendant's first appeal as of right. In Evitts v. Lucey, 469 U.S. 387, 105 S.Ct. 830, 83 L.Ed.2d 821 (1985), defendant's appeal had been dismissed by the Kentucky Court of Appeals when his counsel failed to file the required statement of appeal:

[N]ominal representation on an appeal as of right—like nominal representation at trial—does not suffice to render the proceedings constitutionally adequate; a party whose counsel is unable to provide effective representation is in no better position than one who has no counsel at all.

469 U.S. at 396, 105 S.Ct. at 836, 83 L.Ed.2d at 830.

Chief Justice Burger and Justice Rehnquist vigorously dissented, Chief Justice Burger on the grounds that the decision "adds another barrier to finality and one that offers no real contribution to fairer justice." 469 U.S. at 406, 105 S.Ct. at 841, 83 L.Ed.2d at 836.

2. **Ineffective assistance is discretionary review proceedings.** The respondent in Wainwright v. Torna, 455 U.S. 586, 102 S.Ct. 1300, 71 L.Ed.2d 475 (1982) was represented at trial and on appeal by retained counsel. After losing his state appeal, his attorney agreed to present a petition for discretionary review to the Florida Supreme Court. Because of a mistake by a secretary in the attorney's office, the petition was filed one day late. The Florida court dismissed it because it was untimely filed. In federal habeas, an out-of-time appeal was ordered on the ground respondent did not receive the effective assistance of counsel. The Supreme Court reversed in a per curiam opinion. The majority concluded that since under Ross v. Moffitt, supra, there was no Sixth Amendment right to counsel to petition for discretionary review before the state supreme court, there could be no ineffective assistance of counsel either. Further, there was no due process violation since the fault lay with retained counsel, not the state. Justice Marshall, dissenting, took the position that

> when a defendant can show that he reasonably relied on his attorney's promise to seek discretionary review, due process requires the State to consider his application, even when the application is untimely. To deny the right to seek discretionary review simply because of counsel's error is fundamentally unfair. Requiring the state courts to consider untimely applications when a defendant can show that he reasonably relied on his counsel will not impose a heavy burden. The State is not required to grant the application; it is simply barred from dismissing the application on the ground that it was not timely filed.

455 U.S. at 589, 102 S.Ct. at 1302, 71 L.Ed.2d at 479. If Justice Marshall's position were adopted and applied elsewhere in the criminal process, what effect would it have on numerous time requirements in the process?

3. **Is counsel obliged to brief all claims?** In Jones v. Barnes, 463 U.S. 745, 103 S.Ct. 3308, 77 L.Ed.2d 987 (1983), respondent wished his appointed counsel to present on appeal certain claims but counsel refused to do so, concentrating instead on other claims he believed had more merit. After his conviction was affirmed on direct appeal, respondent obtained federal relief on the ground that his attorney appointed for appeal had rendered ineffective assistance and denied respondent the equal protection of the laws. The Supreme Court, in an opinion by the Chief Justice, reversed. The lower federal court had granted relief on the basis of Anders v. California, 386 U.S. 738, 87 S.Ct. 1396, 18 L.Ed.2d 493 (1967), in which the Court had held that appointed counsel who determines that an appeal is frivolous is not permitted simply to refuse to brief and argue the case. He is required to present to the appellate court a brief referring to anything in the record that might arguably support the appeal no matter what counsel's professional opinion of the merits of those claims may be. The Chief Justice distinguished Anders on the ground that "experienced advocates since time beyond memory have emphasized the importance of winnowing out weaker arguments on appeal and focusing on one central issue if possible, or at most on a few key issues." 463 U.S. at 751–52, 103 S.Ct. at 3313, 77 L.Ed.2d at 994. Indeed, the Chief Justice concluded that Anders supported the Court's decision in this case:

Anders recognized that the role of the advocate "requires that he support his client's appeal to the best of his ability." ... Here the appointed counsel did just that. For judges to second-guess reasonable professional judgments and impose on appointed counsel a duty to raise every "colorable" claim suggested by a client would disserve the very goal of vigorous and effective advocacy that underlies *Anders*.

463 U.S. at 754, 103 S.Ct. at 3314, 77 L.Ed.2d at 995. Justice Brennan, joined by Justice Marshall, dissented, taking the position that *Anders* and Faretta v. California, (Chapter 24) require counsel on appeal to honor the wishes of his client as to which nonfrivolous issues to pursue:

I cannot accept the notion that lawyers are one of the punishments a person receives merely for being accused of a crime. Clients, if they wish, are capable of making informed judgments about which issues to appeal, and when they exercise that prerogative their choices should be respected unless they would require lawyers to violate their consciences, the law, or their duties to the court.

463 U.S. at 764, 103 S.Ct. at 3319, 77 L.Ed.2d at 1001–02.

The Court further considered the obligations of an attorney appointed for appeal in McCoy v. Court of Appeals of Wisconsin, 486 U.S. 429, 108 S.Ct. 1895, 100 L.Ed.2d 440 (1988). The Wisconsin Supreme Court had adopted a rule requiring an appointed attorney who concludes that an appeal lacks arguable merit to file a brief that complies with *Anders* and that also contains a "discussion of why the issue lacks merit." Counsel for appellant concluded that the appeal lacked merit and filed a brief complying with *Anders*. He specifically refused to comply with the rule requiring a discussion of why the issue lacked merit on the grounds such a requirement was contrary to *Anders*, and that compliance would violate his client's right to counsel and would be unethical conduct. The Court of Appeals ordered the appellant's brief stricken and that a brief complying with the rule be filed. Appellant filed an original action in the Wisconsin Supreme Court seeking a declaration that its rule was unconstitutional. When the Wisconsin Supreme Court upheld its rule, he appealed to the United States Supreme Court. The Court, in an opinion by Justice Stevens, affirmed the Wisconsin Supreme Court. The Court noted that the basis of appellant's claim is that the rule discriminates against the indigent. It observed that an attorney, whether appointed or retained, is under an ethical obligation to refuse to proceed with a frivolous appeal. To the extent the rule requires counsel to inform an appellate court of law contrary to the arguments he is making, it places no obligation on counsel that the rules of legal ethics do not already impose. To the extent the rule requires counsel to disclose to the appellate court his thinking about why the appeal lacks merit, the rule furthers, rather than frustrates, the interests advanced in *Anders*:

Because counsel may discover previously unrecognized aspects of the law in the process of preparing a written explanation for his or her conclusion, the discussion requirement provides an additional safeguard against mistaken conclusions by counsel that the strongest arguments he or she can find are frivolous. Just like the references to favorable aspects of the record required by *Anders*, the discussion requirement may forestall some motions to withdraw and will assist the court in passing on the soundness of the lawyer's conclusion that the appeal is frivolous.

486 U.S. at 442, 108 S.Ct. at 1904, 100 L.Ed.2d at 456. Justice Brennan, joined by Justices Marshall and Blackmun, dissented on the ground that the Wisconsin requirement is inconsistent with counsel's obligations as advocate for his client.

The United States Supreme Court in Pennsylvania v. Finley, 481 U.S. 551, 107 S.Ct. 1990, 95 L.Ed.2d 539 (1987), rejected the position that the United States Constitution requires that the procedural steps set out in *Anders* must be followed when appointed counsel concludes that other state post-conviction proceedings are frivolous. All that is required is for counsel to satisfy the appointing court that he should be permitted to withdraw from the appointment because there are no meritorious grounds of relief to present.

4. **Frivolous certiorari petitions.** In a series of decisions, the Court has issued orders prospectively denying *in forma pauperis* status to pro se litigants who have repeatedly filed frivolous petitions in the United States Supreme Court. See In re McDonald, 489 U.S. 180, 109 S.Ct. 993, 103 L.Ed.2d 158 (1989) (73 filings with the Supreme Court since 1971); In re Sindram, 498 U.S. 177, 111 S.Ct. 596, 112 L.Ed.2d 599 (1991) (24 filings with Supreme Court during October 1990 Term); In re Demos, 500 U.S. 16, 111 S.Ct. 1569, 114 L.Ed.2d 20 (1991) (32 filings with the Supreme Court since 1988). These cases culminated in an order amending Rule 39 of the Rules of the Supreme Court of the United States to add Rule 39.8:

> If satisfied that a petition for a writ of certiorari, jurisdictional statement, or petition for an extraordinary writ, as the case may be, is frivolous or malicious, the Court may deny a motion for leave to proceed *in forma pauperis*.

In re Amendment to Rule 39, 500 U.S. 13, 111 S.Ct. 1572, 114 L.Ed.2d 15 (1991). Justice Stevens, joined by Justice Blackmun, dissented. Justice Marshall dissented with the comment,

> This Court once had a great tradition: "All men and women are entitled to their day in Court." That guarantee has now been conditioned on monetary worth. It now will read: "All men and women are entitled to their day in Court only if they have the *means* and the *money.*"

500 U.S. at 15, 111 S.Ct. at 1573–74, 114 L.Ed.2d at 18. A denial of *in forma pauperis* status has the effect of requiring the payment of a $300 filing fee and the costs of printing the documents filed.

In In re Anderson, 511 U.S. 364, 114 S.Ct. 1606, 128 L.Ed.2d 332 (1994), the Court, per curiam, invoked Rule 39.8 with respect to the filing of petitions for extraordinary writs. Since the abuse had been limited principally to extraordinary writs, the Court restricted the Rule 39.8 action to extraordinary writs. Justice Stevens, joined by Justice Blackmun, dissented.

5. **Effect of escape on appeal.** In some circumstances, a convicted defendant may lose an otherwise available right of appeal by escaping from custody. In Ortega–Rodriguez v. United States, 507 U.S. 234, 113 S.Ct. 1199, 122 L.Ed.2d 581 (1993), the Supreme Court recounted that it has since 1876 approved of federal courts dismissing appeals of defendants who are fugitives from justice during the pendency of their appeals and has upheld state provisions for dismissal of appeals under similar circumstances. Dismissal is justified in part because any judgments affirming the convictions would be unenforceable. Further, flight or escape can properly be viewed as tantamount to waiver or abandonment of the pending appeal. Dismissal discourages escapes. It also promotes efficient and dignified appellate processes. 507 U.S. at 240–42, 113 S.Ct. at 1203–05, 122 L.Ed.2d at 591–93.

Ortega–Rodriguez, however, had fled after conviction but before sentencing. He was sentenced *in absentia*. Nearly a year later, he was apprehended. The district court granted his motion for resentencing and sentenced him to a somewhat less severe sentence than that imposed while he was a fugitive. When he sought to appeal, the Government moved to dismiss the appeal because he had been a fugitive after his conviction; the Court of Appeals granted the motion. Reversing by a 5–to–4 vote, the Supreme Court held that a federal appellate court cannot dismiss an appeal because the defendant was a fugitive before the appellate process began, unless the appellate court concludes that the defendant's flight significantly interfered with the appellate process.

Such defendants pose no risk that appellate courts' judgments cannot be enforced, Justice Stevens explained for the majority. Nor do they generally interfere with the orderly and efficient operation of the appellate process or affront the dignity of the appellate court. District courts are better equipped to fashion appropriate penalties for escape of defendants while the cases are before those courts; thus dismissal of appeals is not sufficiently necessary to deter pre-appeal escapes. 507 U.S. at 242–49, 113 S.Ct. at 1205–08, 122 L.Ed.2d at 594–97. Dismissal of an appeal is appropriate, however, if on the facts of a particular case an appellate court finds that a defendant's pre-appeal escape actually and substantially interfered with the appellate process. This might occur, for example, if escape prevented the defendant's appeal from being joined with that of his codefendants for expeditious decision together. 507 U.S. at 250, 113 S.Ct. at 1209, 122 L.Ed.2d at 597–98.

Chief Justice Rehnquist, joined by three other justices, argued that dismissal in pre-appeal escape cases was justified as a general rule. Defendants who escape pose a threat to the orderly operation of the appellate process and flout the authority of the judicial process of which the appellate court is an integral part. Moreover, dismissals serve the important interest of discouraging escapes. 507 U.S. at 253–257, 113 S.Ct. at 1211–13, 122 L.Ed.2d at 599–603 (Rehnquist, C.J., dissenting).

Whether *Ortega–Rodriguez* portended federal constitutional limits on fugitive dismissal rules was raised in Goeke v. Branch, 514 U.S. 115, 115 S.Ct. 1275, 131 L.Ed.2d 152 (1995) (per curiam). Branch, a defendant in a Missouri prosecution, had escaped after conviction but before sentencing. She was quickly captured and sentenced. The state appellate court dismissed her attempted appeal based on Missouri's fugitive dismissal rule. Branch sought federal habeas corpus relief and the Eighth Circuit held she was entitled to it. Due process, it reasoned, bars a state from applying a fugitive dismissal rule in a case where the appellant's escape did not delay appellate proceedings, inconvenience the appellate court, or otherwise affect the appellate process. The United States Supreme Court reversed on the ground that any federal constitutional rule barring a state from enforcing its fugitive dismissal rule would be a new rule not enforceable in a federal habeas corpus proceeding. Rejecting Branch's argument that the rule applied by the Eighth Circuit was not a new rule, the Court found no basis for the intermediate court's position in existing or well-settled authority. In *Ortega–Rodriguez,* the Court acknowledged, it had stated "that absent some adverse effect of pre-appeal flight on the appellate process, 'the defendant's former fugitive status may well lack the kind of connection to the appellate process that would justify an appellate sanction of dismissal.' " Nevertheless, the Court explained in *Goeke,* the rationale for *Ortega–Rodriguez* was limited to the Court's supervisory powers and thus did not suggest that dismissal of a fugitive's appeal implicated constitutional principles.

> As we explained in Allen v. Georgia, [166 U.S. 138, 140, 17 S.Ct. 525, 526, 41 L.Ed. 949 (1897)], where the Court upheld against constitutional attack the dismissal of the petition of a fugitive whose appeal was pending, "if the Supreme Court of a State has acted in consonance with the constitutional laws of a State and its own procedures, it could only be in very exceptional circumstances that this court would feel justified in saying that there had been a failure of due legal process. We might ourselves have pursued a different course in this case, but that is not the test." The Eighth Circuit converted a rule for the administration of the federal courts into a constitutional one.

514 U.S. at 120, 115 S.Ct. at 1278, 131 L.Ed.2d at 159. The Court emphasized, however, that it was not reaching the merits of Branch's contention that due

process prohibits dismissal of appeals for escapes that do not affect the appellate process.

6. **Retroactive application of new rules.** When a major change or "clarification" in the law is made by judicial decision, should the new law be applied retroactively to cases investigated or litigated before the decision? The Supreme Court's approach to this question of retroactivity was summarized by Justice Brennan:

> It is by now uncontroverted that "the Constitution neither prohibits nor requires retrospective effect." [Linkletter v. Walker, 381 U.S. 618, 629, 85 S.Ct. 1731, 1737, 14 L.Ed.2d 601 (1965).] ...[T]hat decision firmly settled that "in appropriate cases the Court may in the interest of justice make the rule prospective ...where the exigencies of the situation require such an application." Id., at 628, 85 S.Ct., at 1737; Johnson v. New Jersey, 384 U.S. 719, 726–727, 86 S.Ct. 1772, 1777, 16 L.Ed.2d 882 (1966).
>
> Similarly, it is clear that resolution of the question of retroactivity does not automatically turn on the particular provision of the Constitution on which the new prescription is based. "Each constitutional rule of criminal procedure has its own distinct functions, its own background of precedent, and its own impact on the administration of justice, and the way in which these factors combine must inevitably vary with the dictate involved." Id., at 728, 86 S.Ct., at 1778. Accordingly, the test consistently employed by the Court to decide whether a new constitutional doctrine should be applied retroactively contemplates the consideration of three criteria: "(a) the purpose to be served by the new standards, (b) the extent of the reliance by law enforcement authorities on the old standards, and (c) the effect on the administration of justice of a retroactive application of the new standards." Stovall v. Denno, 388 U.S. 293, 297, 87 S.Ct. 1967, 1970, 18 L.Ed.2d 1199 (1967).
>
> Moreover, our decisions establish that "[f]oremost among these factors is the purpose to be served by the new constitutional rule," Desist v. United States, 394 U.S. 244, 249, 89 S.Ct. 1030, 1033, 22 L.Ed.2d 248 (1969), and that we will give controlling significance to the measure of reliance and the impact on the administration of justice "only when the purpose of the rule in question [does] not clearly favor either retroactivity or prospectivity." Id., at 251, 89 S.Ct., at 1035. "Where the major purpose of new constitutional doctrine is to overcome an aspect of the criminal trial that substantially impairs its truth-finding function and so raises serious questions about the accuracy of guilty verdicts in past trials, the new rule has been given complete retroactive effect. Neither good-faith reliance by state or federal authorities on prior constitutional law or accepted practice, nor severe impact on the administration of justice has sufficed to require prospective application in these circumstances." Williams v. United States, 401 U.S. 646, 653, 91 S.Ct. 1148, 1152, 28 L.Ed.2d 388 (1971) (plurality opinion of White, J.).
>
> Finally, we have recognized that the extent to which the purpose of a new constitutional rule requires its retroactive application "is necessarily a matter of degree." Johnson v. New Jersey, supra, 384 U.S., at 729, 86 S.Ct., at 1778. Constitutional protections are frequently fashioned to serve multiple ends; while a new standard may marginally implicate the reliability and integrity of the factfinding process, it may have been designed primarily to foster other, equally fundamental values in our system of jurisprudence. Not every rule that "tends incidentally" to avoid unfairness at trial must be accorded retroactive effect. So, too, additional safeguards may already exist that minimize the likelihood of past injustices. In short, "[t]he extent to which a condemned practice infects the integrity of the truth-determining process at trial is a

'question of probabilities.' " Stovall v. Denno, supra, 388 U.S., at 298, 87 S.Ct., at 1970 (quoting Johnson v. New Jersey, supra, 384 U.S., at 729, 86 S.Ct., at 1778). And only when an assessment of those probabilities indicates that the condemned practice casts doubt upon the reliability of the determinations of guilt in past criminal cases must the new procedural rule be applied retroactively.

Brown v. Louisiana, 447 U.S. 323, 327–29, 100 S.Ct. 2214, 2219–20, 65 L.Ed.2d 159, 165–66 (1980).

The Court has been especially reluctant to give retroactive effect to holdings which affect police conduct where such prior conduct had cast no doubt on the accuracy of the convictions or where there was a likelihood of widespread reliance on earlier decisions of the Court. For example, the Court declined to give retroactive effect to the holding in Mapp v. Ohio, 367 U.S. 643, 81 S.Ct. 1684, 6 L.Ed.2d 1081 (1961) (application of exclusionary rule in state courts to evidence obtained in unreasonable search and seizure) in Linkletter v. Walker, supra; Katz v. United States, 389 U.S. 347, 88 S.Ct. 507, 19 L.Ed.2d 576 (1967) (eavesdropping on a private conversation with no physical trespass was a "search" under the Fourth Amendment) in Desist v. United States, supra; or to United States v. Wade, 388 U.S. 218, 87 S.Ct. 1296, 18 L.Ed.2d 1149 (1967) (right to appointed counsel at certain pretrial lineups) in Stovall v. Denno, supra.

Certain holdings relating to the trial process have also been denied retroactivity, such as: Griffin v. California, 380 U.S. 609, 85 S.Ct. 1229, 14 L.Ed.2d 106 (1965) (comment on defendant's failure to testify violates Fifth Amendment) in Tehan v. United States ex rel. Shott, 382 U.S. 406, 86 S.Ct. 459, 15 L.Ed.2d 453 (1966); and cases involving the right to jury trial and the procedures for jury selection (see Daniel v. Louisiana, 420 U.S. 31, 95 S.Ct. 704, 42 L.Ed.2d 790 (1975), DeStefano v. Woods, 392 U.S. 631, 88 S.Ct. 2093, 20 L.Ed.2d 1308 (1968), and Griffith v. Kentucky, 479 U.S. 314, 107 S.Ct. 708, 93 L.Ed.2d 649 (1987).)

On the other hand, the direct and "substantial" relationship between the due process requirement of proof beyond a reasonable doubt and trial accuracy has persuaded the Court to give retroactive effect to its rulings in: Barber v. Page, 390 U.S. 719, 88 S.Ct. 1318, 20 L.Ed.2d 255 (1968) (use of witness' preliminary hearing testimony at trial violates Confrontation Clause unless State has made good faith effort to secure the witness' presence) in Berger v. California, 393 U.S. 314, 89 S.Ct. 540, 21 L.Ed.2d 508 (1969); and Burch v. Louisiana, 441 U.S. 130, 99 S.Ct. 1623, 60 L.Ed.2d 96 (1979) (due process requirement of unanimity in 6–member juries) in Brown v. Louisiana, supra.

In United States v. Johnson, 457 U.S. 537, 102 S.Ct. 2579, 73 L.Ed.2d 202 (1982), the Court adopted a new approach to retroactivity: (1) When an opinion "merely has applied settled precedents to a new and different factual situation" no question of retroactivity is presented since the law has not been altered in any material way. (2) If the opinion is a "clear break with the past" it is to be applied prospectively. (3) Only if the new rule is to the effect that the trial court lacked authority to convict or punish a criminal defendant in the first place, for example, a double jeopardy ruling, is the new rule applied retroactively. In this case the Court concluded that the rule of Payton v. New York (prohibiting warrantless, nonconsensual entry into suspect's home to make routine felony arrest) did not fall into the first, second, or third category and therefore should be applied neither solely prospectively nor fully retroactively. Instead it should be applied to all cases pending on direct review at the time the rule was announced.

In Griffith v. Kentucky, supra, the Court rejected that portion of *Johnson* which mandated prospectivity for "clear break" decisions. Denying retroactive application of such decisions to petitioners on direct review when the decision is announced would improperly depart from the principle that the Court applies current law to cases on direct review and would treat petitioners unequally solely on the fortuity of which case reaches the Court first. "We therefore hold that a new rule for the conduct of criminal prosecution is to be applied ...to all cases, state or federal, pending on direct review or not yet final, with no exception for cases in which the new rule constitutes a 'clear break' with the past." 479 U.S. at 328, 107 S.Ct. at 716, 93 L.Ed.2d at 661. Justice White, joined by The Chief Justice and Justice O'Connor, dissented.

5. **Retroactivity a new rule and the stage of proceedings of the case in which application is sought.** The retroactive application of a new rule of criminal procedure also depends on when it is advanced during the pendency of petitioner's case. Cases on this issue are summarized by Justice Kennedy for the majority in Saffle v. Parks, 494 U.S. 484, 110 S.Ct. 1257, 108 L.Ed.2d 415(1990):

> In Penry v. Lynaugh, 492 U.S. ___, 109 S.Ct. 2934, 106 L.Ed.2d 256 (1989), we held that a new rule of constitutional law will not be applied in cases on collateral review unless the rule comes within one of two narrow exceptions. This limitation on the proper exercise of habeas corpus jurisdiction applies to capital and noncapital cases. See id., at ___, 109 S.Ct. at ___. ...

* * *

> In *Teague,* we defined a new rule as a rule that "breaks new ground," "imposes a new obligation on the States or the Federal Government," or was not "*dictated* by precedent existing at the time the defendant's conviction became final." *Teague,* supra, 489 U.S., at 301, 109 S.Ct., at 1070 (emphasis in original). The explicit overruling of an earlier holding no doubt creates a new rule; it is more difficult, however, to determine whether we announce a new rule when a decision extends the reasoning of our prior cases. As we recognized in Butler v. McKellar, ___ U.S. ___, ___-___, 110 S.Ct. 1212, 1216–1217, [108] L.Ed.2d ___ (1990), the question must be answered by reference to the underlying purposes of the habeas writ. Foremost among these is ensuring that state courts conduct criminal proceedings in accordance with the Constitution as interpreted at the time of the proceedings. See ibid. " '[T]he threat of habeas serves as a necessary additional incentive for trial and appellate courts throughout the land to conduct their proceedings in a manner consistent with established constitutional standards. In order to perform this deterrence function, ...the habeas court need only apply the constitutional standards that prevailed at the time the original proceedings took place.' " *Teague,* supra, 489 U.S., at 306, 109 S.Ct., at 1073 (quoting Desist v. United States), 394 U.S. 244, 262–263, 89 S.Ct. 1030, 1040–1041, 22 L.Ed.2d 248 (1969) (Harlan, J., dissenting). ..."The 'new rule' principle therefore validates reasonable, good-faith interpretations of existing precedents made by state courts even though they are shown to be contrary to later decisions." Butler, supra, ___ U.S., at ___, 110 S.Ct., at 1217. ...

* * *

> ...The first exception permits the retroactive application of a new rule if the rule places a class of private conduct beyond the power of the State to proscribe, see *Teague,* 489 U.S., at 311, 109 S.Ct., at 1075, or addresses a "substantive categorical guarante[e] accorded by the Constitution," such as a rule "prohibiting a certain category of punishment for a class of defendants because of their status or offense." *Penry,* 492 U.S., at ___, 109 S.Ct., at 2953. ...The second exception is for "watershed rules of criminal procedure" implicating the fundamental fairness and accuracy of the criminal proceeding. See *Teague,* supra, 489 U.S., at 311, 109 S.Ct., at 1075; *Butler,* supra, ___ U.S., at

___-___, 110 S.Ct., at 1218. . . . Although the precise contours of this exception may be difficult to discern, we have usually cited Gideon v. Wainwright, 372 U.S. 335, 83 S.Ct. 792, 9 L.Ed.2d 799 (1963), holding that a defendant has the right to be represented by counsel in all criminal trials for serious offenses, to illustrate the type of rule coming within the exception. . . .

494 U.S. at 486–95, 110 S.Ct. at 1259–64.

In O'Dell v. Netherland, 521 U.S. 151, 117 S.Ct. 1969, 138 L.Ed.2d 351 (1997) the Court held that the rule in Simmons v. South Carolina, 512 U.S. 154, 114 S.Ct. 2187, 129 L.Ed.2d 133 (1994) that a jury in a capital case must be informed if its life sentence verdict alternative is without possibility of parole when dangerousness is argued is a "new rule" which will not be applied to cases that were final when *Simmons* was decided.

C. COLLATERAL ATTACK

EDITORS' INTRODUCTION: STRUCTURES FOR COLLATERAL ATTACK

A collateral attack upon a conviction is an effort to seek relief in a proceeding other than that in which the judgment of conviction was rendered. Thus it is distinguishable from appeal or review by writ of certiorari, both of which are continuations of the original prosecution.

Collateral attacks are different from appeal remedies in at least two important ways. First, they are not subject to stringent time limitations as are appeals. Therefore, a convicted person who has failed to pursue an appeal within the time provided is likely to find collateral attack the only available avenue of further litigation. Second, unlike appeals, collateral attack proceedings are not "on the record" made at the original trial. Therefore, a convicted person may have the opportunity to introduce evidence which was, for whatever reason, not introduced at the original trial proceedings.

A person convicted in a federal District Court can pursue collateral attack only in the federal judicial system. Following a conviction in state court, however, a person may generally seek such relief in state courts, federal courts, or both. Federal and state procedures require separate consideration.

State Procedures

The United States Supreme Court has never held that the states are required by federal constitutional demands to provide persons convicted in their courts with a means for mounting collateral attacks upon those convictions. But as the United States Supreme Court began to develop state defendants' federal constitutional rights and to open federal courts to state defendants' attacks, the states began to develop their own procedures in order to avoid having federal tribunals preempt the area. The tendency was to use familiar vehicles, especially the old common law writs of habeas corpus and, to a lesser extent, coram nobis. Habeas corpus means literally, "you have the body," and was a traditional method of requiring one person holding another in custody to justify that custody. Because of its breadth, the writ was (and still is) used for a variety of purposes other than collateral attacks upon criminal convictions.

Dissatisfaction with procedural problems and technicalities involved in the common law writs led a number of jurisdictions to adopt, by legislation or court rule, fairly comprehensive procedures for postconviction attacks as an alternative to these writs. A major characteristic of many of these procedures is the requirement that the convicted person seek collateral relief in the convicting court rather than in a court with jurisdiction over the geographical area in which the person happens to be confined.

Federal Procedures

Prior to 1948, persons convicted in federal court could attack their convictions collaterally through the use of the writ of habeas corpus. In that year, however, Congress enacted what is now 28 U.S.C.A. § 2255 [infra] providing for collateral attack by a "motion to vacate sentence" filed in the convicting court. Although Article 1, § 9 of the United States Constitution prohibits the suspension of habeas corpus except in situations involving rebellion or invasion, the section 2255 procedure has, for all practical purposes, superseded the writ.

Brown v. Allen, 344 U.S. 443, 73 S.Ct. 397, 97 L.Ed. 469 (1953), made clear that federal constitutional claims of state prisoners are cognizable in federal habeas corpus, that the federal courts are not bound by any disposition of the federal claim that may have been made in state court, and that federal courts may inquire into factual matters related to a state prisoner's federal claim even if those facts were purportedly resolved in the state litigation. The prevailing practice is for a state prisoner to apply for the writ to a federal District Court judge. The judge's action on the application may be appealed by either party to the appropriate Court of Appeals as a matter of right, and the decision of the Court of Appeals is subject to review by the Supreme Court as in other cases.

In Sumner v. Mata, 449 U.S. 539, 101 S.Ct. 764, 66 L.Ed.2d 722 (1981), the Court noted that the enactment of § 2254(d), which follows was intended to alleviate some of the friction between state and federal courts caused by federal courts "refinding" facts related to state defendants' federal constitutional claims. To assure enforcement of Congress' mandate that federal habeas courts not reject state court findings on the basis of the usual "preponderance of the evidence" standard, the Court held that a federal habeas court granting a state prisoner relief on grounds which include rejecting state courts' findings of fact "should include in its opinion . . . the reasoning which led it to conclude that any of the first seven factors [specified in § 2254(d)] were present, or the reasoning which led it to conclude that the state finding was 'not fairly supported by the record.' "449 U.S. at 551, 101 S.Ct. at 771, 66 L.Ed.2d at 734.

Another issue with significant federalism implications that is presented by the availability of federal habeas corpus relief is the effect that should or must be given to a state prisoner's failure, during state litigation, to follow state procedures for implementation of federal constitutional rights. This is presented in the principal case in this section.

Federal Habeas Corpus Statutes
(amended as part of the Antiterrorism
and Effective Death Penalty Act of 1996)

28 U.S.C.A. § 2254.   State custody; remedies in Federal courts

(a) The Supreme Court, a Justice thereof, a circuit judge, or a district court shall entertain an application for a writ of habeas corpus in behalf of a person in custody pursuant to the judgment of a State court only on the ground that he is in custody in violation of the Constitution or laws or treaties of the United States.

(b) (1) An application for a writ of habeas corpus on behalf of a person in custody pursuant to the judgment of a State court shall not be granted unless it appears that—

(A) the applicant has exhausted the remedies available in the courts of the State; or

(B) (i) there is an absence of available State corrective process; or

(ii) circumstances exist that render such process ineffective to protect the rights of the applicant.

(2) An application for a writ of habeas corpus may be denied on the merits, notwithstanding the failure of the applicant to exhaust the remedies available in the courts of the State.

(3) A State shall not be deemed to have waived the exhaustion requirement or be estopped from reliance upon the requirement unless the State, through counsel, expressly waives the requirement.

(c) An applicant shall not be deemed to have exhausted the remedies available in the courts of the State, within the meaning of this section, if he has the right under the law of the State to raise, by any available procedure, the question presented.

(d) An application for a writ of habeas corpus on behalf of a person in custody pursuant to the judgment of a State court shall not be granted with respect to any claim that was adjudicated on the merits in State court proceedings unless the adjudication of the claim—

(1) resulted in a decision that was contrary to, or involved an unreasonable application of, clearly established Federal law, as determined by the Supreme Court of the United States; or

(2) resulted in a decision that was based on an unreasonable determination of the facts in light of the evidence presented in the State court proceeding.

(e) (1) In a proceeding instituted by an application for a writ of habeas corpus by a person in custody pursuant to the judgment of a State court, a determination of a factual issue made by a State court shall be presumed to be correct. The applicant shall have the burden of rebutting the presumption of correctness by clear and convincing evidence.

(2) If the applicant has failed to develop the factual basis of a claim in State court proceedings, the court shall not hold an evidentiary hearing on the claim unless the applicant shows that—

(A) the claim relies on—

(i) a new rule of constitutional law, made retroactive to cases on collateral review by the Supreme Court, that was previously unavailable; or

(ii) a factual predicate that could not have been previously discovered through the exercise of due diligence; and

(B) the facts underlying the claim would be sufficient to establish by clear and convincing evidence that but for constitutional error, no reasonable factfinder would have found the applicant guilty of the underlying offense.

(f) If the applicant challenges the sufficiency of the evidence adduced in such State court proceeding to support the State court's determination of a factual issue made therein, the applicant, if able, shall produce that part of the record pertinent to a determination of the sufficiency of the evidence to support such determination. If the applicant, because of indigency or other reason is unable to produce such part of the record, then the State shall produce such part of the record and the Federal court shall direct the State to do so by order directed to an appropriate State official. If the State cannot provide such pertinent part of the record, then the court shall determine under the existing facts and circumstances what weight shall be given to the State court's factual determination.

(g) A copy of the official records of the State court, duly certified by the clerk of such court to be a true and correct copy of a finding, judicial opinion, or other reliable written indicia showing such a factual determination by the State court shall be admissible in the Federal court proceeding.

(h) Except as provided in section 408 of the Controlled Substances Act, in all proceedings brought under this section, and any subsequent proceedings on review, the court may appoint counsel for an applicant who is or becomes financially unable to afford counsel, except as provided by a rule promulgated by the Supreme Court pursuant to statutory authority. Appointment of counsel under this section shall be governed by section 3006A of title 18.

(i) The ineffectiveness or incompetence of counsel during Federal or State collateral post-conviction proceedings shall not be a ground for relief in a proceeding arising under section 2254.

28 U.S.C.A. § 2255. Federal custody; remedies on motion attacking sentence

A prisoner in custody under sentence of a court established by Act of Congress claiming the right to be released upon the ground that the sentence was imposed in violation of the Constitution or laws of the United States, or that the court was without jurisdiction to impose such sentence, or that the sentence was in excess of the maximum authorized by law, or is otherwise subject to collateral attack, may move the court which imposed the sentence to vacate, set aside or correct the sentence.

Unless the motion and the files and records of the case conclusively show that the prisoner is entitled to no relief, the court shall cause notice thereof to be served upon the United States attorney, grant a prompt hearing thereon, determine the issues and make findings of fact and conclusions of law with respect thereto. If the court finds that the judgment was rendered without jurisdiction, or that the sentence imposed was not authorized by law or otherwise open to collateral attack, or that there has been such a denial or infringement of the constitutional rights of the prisoner as to render the judgment vulnerable to collateral attack, the court shall vacate and set the judgment aside and shall discharge the prisoner or resentence him or grant a new trial or correct the sentence as may appear appropriate.

A court may entertain and determine such motion without requiring the production of the prisoner at the hearing.

An appeal may be taken to the court of appeals from the order entered on the motion as from a final judgment on application for a writ of habeas corpus.

An application for a writ of habeas corpus in behalf of a prisoner who is authorized to apply for relief by motion pursuant to this section, shall not be entertained if it appears that the applicant has failed to apply for relief, by motion, to the court which sentenced him, or that such court has denied him relief, unless it also appears that the remedy by motion is inadequate or ineffective to test the legality of his detention.

A 1–year period of limitation shall apply to a motion under this section. The limitation period shall run from the latest of—

(1) the date on which the judgment of conviction becomes final;

(2) the date on which the impediment to making a motion created by governmental action in violation of the Constitution or laws of the United States is removed, if the movant was prevented from making a motion by such governmental action;

(3) the date on which the right asserted was initially recognized by the Supreme Court, if that right has been newly recognized by the Supreme Court and made retroactively applicable to cases on collateral review; or

(4) the date on which the facts supporting the claim or claims presented could have been discovered through the exercise of due diligence.

Except as provided in section 408 of the Controlled Substances Act, in all proceedings brought under this section, and any subsequent proceedings on review, the court may appoint counsel, except as provided by a rule promulgated by the Supreme Court pursuant to statutory authority. Appointment of counsel under this section shall be governed by section 3006A of title 18.

A second or successive motion must be certified as provided in section 2244 by a panel of the appropriate court of appeals to contain—

(1) newly discovered evidence that, if proven and viewed in light of the evidence as a whole, would be sufficient to establish by clear and convincing evidence that no reasonable factfinder would have found the movant guilty of the offense; or

(2) a new rule of constitutional law, made retroactive to cases on collateral review by the Supreme Court, that was previously unavailable.

NOTES

1. **Retroactivity of 1996 amendments.** In Lindh v. Murphy, 521 U.S. 320, 117 S.Ct. 2059, 138 L.Ed.2d 481 (1997) the Court, in a 5 to 4 opinion by Justice Souter, held that the standards of Section 2254(d), as amended in 1996, do not apply to federal habeas applications pending on April 24, 1996, the date of enactment.

2. **Exhaustion of state remedies.** The Supreme Court held in O'Sullivan v. Boerckel, 526 U.S. 838, 119 S.Ct. 1728, 144 L.Ed.2d 1 (1999) that the requirement of exhaustion of state remedies in 28 U.S.C. § 2254(b) means that an applicant must present the federal claim to the highest available court of the state even if that court's review is discretionary with it. In this case, the respondent had not included certain federal claims in a petition for discretionary review to the Illinois Supreme Court from a decision of the Illinois Court of Appeals. Thus, he did not exhaust his state remedies and is precluded from raising those issues in federal habeas.

3. **The requirement of custody.** Collateral attacks are available only to persons who are "in custody" as a result of the convictions sought to be attacked. This is specifically provided in the federal statutes, 28 U.S.C.A. §§ 2254, 2255, and is probably a jurisdictional requirement of the traditional writ of habeas corpus. See L. Yackle, Postconviction Remedies § 43 (1981). But the concept of "custody" has been broadly construed. In Jones v. Cunningham, 371 U.S. 236, 83 S.Ct. 373, 9 L.Ed.2d 285 (1963), the Supreme Court held that a state prisoner who had been released on parole was, given the limitations upon the freedom of a parolee, still "in custody" for purposes of federal habeas corpus. A related issue arises if the petitioner is in custody at the time when relief is applied for but is released before a final adjudication of the issues is reached. In Carafas v. LaVallee, 391 U.S. 234, 88 S.Ct. 1556, 20 L.Ed.2d 554 (1968), the Court held that release of a state prisoner would not render his petition for federal habeas corpus moot as long as there were collateral consequences of the conviction which would be affected by a final determination of the issues raised by the petition.

In Maleng v. Cook, 490 U.S. 488, 109 S.Ct. 1923, 104 L.Ed.2d 540 (1989) was a federal prisoner who had been convicted in state court in 1958, but had fully served that sentence. He later received a state court sentence that was enhanced by the earlier state court conviction, but he will not begin serving that sentence until he is released from federal custody. He challenged the 1958 conviction in federal District Court. The District Court dismissed on the ground he was not in custody under the 1958 conviction. The Ninth Circuit reversed and the Supreme Court, in a per curiam opinion, affirmed. The Supreme Court held that he was not in custody under the 1958 conviction because he had fully served that sentence. However, he was in custody under the yet-to-be-begun state sentence because he was in federal custody subject to a detainer filed by the state authorities. Therefore, he was "in custody" for federal habeas purposes, however, the court declined to decide the extent to which he might challenge the 1958 conviction itself.

How should the "in custody" requirement be employed when the petitioner has received consecutive prison sentences? The petitioner in Garlotte v. Fordice, 515 U.S. 39, 115 S.Ct. 1948, 132 L.Ed.2d 36 (1995) received a three year prison sentence on a marijuana charge and two life sentences of murder charges. The life sentences were imposed consecutively to the three year sentence. After serving the three year sentence, but while still incarcerated on the life sentences, petitioner filed a federal habeas petition challenging the validity of the three year sentence. The District Court denied the petition on the merits, but the Fifth Circuit dismissed the petition on the ground he was no longer in custody under the three year sentence. The Supreme Court, in an opinion by Justice Ginsburg, reversed. In Peyton v. Rowe, 391 U.S. 54, 88 S.Ct. 1549, 20 L.Ed.2d 426 (1968), the Court had held that a state prisoner is "in custody" with respect to a consecutive sentence that he had not yet started serving. This case is *Peyton* in reverse. The key feature in this case is that the three year sentence, although already served, continues to postpone petitioner's parole eligibility date on the two life sentences. Since successful challenge of that sentence would advance petitioner's parole eligibility date, he is still in custody under that sentence.

4. **Issues that can be raised.** What issues can be raised in collateral attacks? In early cases, the United States Supreme Court held that only those defects in the proceedings that deprived the trial court of jurisdiction could be considered on habeas corpus. E.g., Ex parte Watkins, 28 U.S. (3 Pet.) 193, 7 L.Ed. 650 (1830). In Waley v. Johnston, 316 U.S. 101, 62 S.Ct. 964, 86 L.Ed. 1302 (1942), however, the Court rejected this jurisdictional standard and held that any issue of federal constitutional dimensions could be raised by federal habeas corpus. But this is no longer strictly accurate. In Stone v. Powell, 428 U.S. 465, 96 S.Ct. 3037, 49 L.Ed.2d 1067 (1976), the Court held that a state prisoner is not entitled to federal habeas corpus relief on the basis that evidence obtained in violation of his Fourth Amendment right to be free from unreasonable searches and seizures was introduced at his trial, unless the prisoner also shows that he was denied a full and fair opportunity to litigate his Fourth Amendment claim in state courts. The majority carefully characterized the exclusionary rule which it held could not be enforced in federal habeas proceedings as "a judicially created remedy rather than a personal constitutional right" and emphasized that its decision "is *not* concerned with the scope of the habeas corpus statute as authority for litigating constitutional claims generally." 428 U.S. at 495 n. 37, 96 S.Ct. at 3053 n. 37, 49 L.Ed.2d at 1088 n. 37.

The reach of Stone v. Powell was discussed in Rose v. Mitchell, 443 U.S. 545, 99 S.Ct. 2993, 61 L.Ed.2d 739 (1979), involving a claim of racial discrimination in the selection of a grand jury foreman. A majority of the Court concluded that the defendant had not established a *prima facie* case that such discrimination took place. But in addition, five members of the Court, in an opinion written by Justice Blackmun, rejected the argument—advanced by Justice Powell in dissent—that Stone v. Powell barred a state defendant from raising claims of the sort at issue in federal habeas corpus proceedings. First, Mitchell's claim included allegations that the state judiciary had violated the Fourteenth Amendment; thus the state judiciary could not be relied upon to provide the "full and fair hearing" such a claim requires and a federal forum remains necessary. Second, the claim was of a violation of "the direct command of the Fourteenth Amendment," rather than a judicially created remedy as in *Stone*. Moreover, state judges may, because of their closeness to the alleged problem, be unable to evaluate discrimination claims adequately and thus federal review is likely to produce "great" educative and deterrent effects. Since states remain free to reindict and reconvict defendants who obtain relief in federal proceedings, the costs of federal intervention are less. Finally, the constitutional interests at stake in a claim of racial discrimination involve "fundamental values of our society and our legal system" and are therefore substantially more compelling than those raised in *Stone*. 443 U.S. at 561–64, 99 S.Ct. at 3003–04, 61 L.Ed.2d at 752–55.

In Kimmelman v. Morrison, 477 U.S. 365, 106 S.Ct. 2574, 91 L.Ed.2d 305 (1986), writing for the Court, Justice Brennan held that the failure of trial defense counsel to request pretrial discovery from the State and, therefore, to move to suppress evidence prior to trial as required by New Jersey law, constituted inadequate performance under the first part of the standard of Strickland v. Washington (see chapter 24). He concluded that the Sixth Amendment claim is distinct, although related to, the Fourth Amendment claim barred by Stone v. Powell:

> Although a meritorious Fourth Amendment issue is necessary to the success of a Sixth Amendment claim like respondent's, a good Fourth Amendment claim alone will not earn a prisoner federal habeas relief.

> Only those habeas petitioners who can prove under *Strickland* that they have been denied a fair trial by the gross incompetence of their attorneys will be granted the writ and will be entitled to retrial without the challenged evidence.

477 U.S. at 382, 106 S.Ct. at 2586–87, 91 L.Ed.2d at 324. The Court refused the invitation of the respondent to rule that the record reflected prejudice under *Strickland* and affirmed the decision of the Court of Appeals remanding for that issue. Justice Powell, joined by Chief Justice Burger and Justice Rehnquist, concurred in the judgment on the ground that an error of counsel that results in reliable evidence not being excluded from the trial can never constitute prejudice under the *Strickland* standard because

> the harm suffered by respondent in this case is not the denial of a fair and reliable adjudication of his guilt, but rather the absence of a windfall.

477 U.S. at 396, 106 S.Ct. at 2594, 91 L.Ed.2d at 333.

In Withrow v. Williams, 507 U.S. 680, 113 S.Ct. 1745, 123 L.Ed.2d 407 (1993), by a 5-to-4 vote, the Court held that the *Stone* approach would not be applied when a state defendant sought federal habeas corpus on grounds that a confession obtained in violation of Miranda v. Arizona, 384 U.S. 436, 86 S.Ct. 1602, 16 L.Ed.2d 694 (1966) had been used to convict him. The reasons for not applying *Stone's* approach to *Miranda* claims, Justice Souter explained for the majority, rest in part upon differences between a state defendant's right under Mapp v. Ohio, 367 U.S. 643, 81 S.Ct. 1684, 6 L.Ed.2d 1081 (1961) to have evidence obtained in violation of the Fourth Amendment excluded from trial and *Miranda. Mapp* created no personal constitutional right; *Miranda's* requirements, in contrast, safeguard defendants' Fifth Amendment privilege against self-incrimination, "a fundamental *trial* right." *Mapp* protects privacy rights divorced from the correct ascertainment of guilt in criminal trials. *Miranda,* on the other hand "serves to guard against 'the use of unreliable statements at trial' ""[b]y bracing against 'the possibility of unreliable statements in every instance of in-custody interrogation[.]' "

Most importantly, Justice Souter continued, state prisoners barred from raising *Miranda* claims in federal habeas corpus would simply convert those claims into due process claims that involuntary confessions had been used. Federal courts' workload would not be lightened by limiting habeas petitioners' ability to raise *Miranda* claims; federal judges would simply be confronted with due process involuntariness rather than *Miranda* claims. Nor would this change in the form of claims made by state prisoners go far towards reducing tensions between the state and federal judicial systems. "[E]liminating review of *Miranda* claims," Justice Souter concluded, "would not significantly benefit the federal courts in their exercise of habeas jurisdiction, or advance the cause of federalism in any substantial way." 507 U.S. at 693, 113 S.Ct. at 1754, 123 L.Ed.2d at 420. The Chief Justice and Justices O'Connor, Scalia and Thomas dissented. Justice O'Connor explained that when a case is on collateral review, the "marginal" benefits of applying *Miranda* are outweighed by the costs of undercutting finality of state conviction, aggravating tension between state and federal courts, and sometimes requiring reversal of guilty persons' convictions when the passage of time makes reprosecutions impossible.

5. **Claims of evidence insufficiency.** In contrast to *Stone's* reduction of the issues cognizable in federal habeas corpus is Jackson v. Virginia, 443 U.S. 307, 99 S.Ct. 2781, 61 L.Ed.2d 560 (1979), holding that a state prisoner is entitled, in federal habeas corpus proceedings, to some scrutiny by the federal court of the sufficiency of the evidence showing his guilt. The United States Constitution prohibits conviction of a state defendant except upon proof of guilt beyond a reasonable doubt, In re Winship, 397 U.S. 358, 90 S.Ct. 1068, 25 L.Ed.2d 368 (1970), and when a state conviction is challenged in federal habeas corpus proceedings the federal court has a duty to assess the historic facts necessary to determine whether a federal constitutional right was violated. But in performing this task in the context of sufficiency of the evidence, the majority continued, the federal habeas judge should not ask whether he himself believes that the evidence produced at trial established guilt beyond a reasonable doubt:

> Instead, the relevant question is whether, after viewing the evidence in the light most favorable to the prosecution, any rational trier of fact could have found the essential elements of the crime beyond a reasonable doubt.

443 U.S. at 319, 99 S.Ct. at 2789, 61 L.Ed.2d at 573.

6. **Nonconstitutional claims.** There is authority for the proposition that under some collateral attack schemes nonconstitutional errors of limited sorts may be asserted. Sunal v. Large, 332 U.S. 174, 67 S.Ct. 1588, 91 L.Ed. 1982 (1947), is widely read as indicating that a person convicted in federal court cannot use section 2255 as the vehicle for asserting all matters that, if raised on direct appeal, would constitute reversible error. But in Davis v. United States, 417 U.S. 333, 94 S.Ct. 2298, 41 L.Ed.2d 109 (1974), the Supreme Court, noting that section 2255 refers to prisoners claiming their sentences to have been imposed "in violation of the Constitution *or laws* of the United States," refused to limit section 2255 to constitutional claims. Cautioning that "not . . . every asserted error of law can be raised on a § 2255 motion," the Court held that the appropriate inquiry to determine whether an issue could be raised in a motion to vacate sentence under section 2255 is:

> whether the claimed error of law was "a fundamental defect which inherently results in a complete miscarriage of justice," and whether "[i]t . . . present[s] exceptional circumstances where the need for the remedy afforded by the writ of *habeas corpus* is apparent."

417 U.S. at 346, 94 S.Ct. at 2305, 41 L.Ed.2d at 119.

7. **Claims of innocence.** Is a claim that a person sentenced to death is innocent of the offense for which he was sentenced independently cognizable on federal habeas corpus? The petitioner in Herrera v. Collins, 506 U.S. 390, 113 S.Ct. 853, 122 L.Ed.2d 203 (1993) was convicted of the capital murder of a police officer and was sentenced to death. Later, he plead guilty to the related killing of another police officer. His conviction and sentence were upheld on direct appeal and on state and federal habeas. Under Texas law, motions for new trial based on newly discovered evidence can be made only within 30 days of sentencing. Ten years after his conviction, petitioner urged in state habeas that he was actually innocent of the murders and produced three affidavits from relatives that his now-deceased brother committed the killings. The Supreme Court, in an opinion by The Chief Justice, held that a claim of actual innocence by a state prisoner is not cognizable on federal habeas corpus,

> [I]n state criminal proceedings the trial is the paramount event for determining the guilt or innocence of the defendant. Federal habeas review of state convictions has traditionally been limited to claims of constitutional violations occurring in the course of the underlying state criminal proceedings * * *. History

shows that the traditional remedy for claims of innocence based on new evidence, discovered too late in the day to file a new trial motion, has been executive clemency.

506 U.S. at 416, 113 S.Ct. at 869, 122 L.Ed.2d at 203. The Court acknowledged "for the sake of argument in deciding this case" that "a truly persuasive demonstration of 'actual innocence' made after trial would render the execution of a defendant unconstitutional" but then asserted that the facts in *Herrera* fell far short of such a demonstration. Justice O'Connor, joined by Justice Kennedy, concurred while expressing doubt about the wisdom of the Court's dictum about a truly persuasive demonstration of actual innocence. She then examined all of the evidence in the case, including the affidavits attesting to petitioner's innocence, and concluded that it shows his guilt "overwhelmingly." Justice Scalia, joined by Justice Thomas, concurred with the observation that "[t]here is no basis * * * for finding in the Constitution a right to demand judicial consideration of newly discovered evidence of innocence brought forward after conviction." Justice White concurred on the explicit assumption that the position expressed in argument by the Court that relief would be granted on a persuasive showing of actual innocence would ultimately prevail. Justice Blackmun, joined in part by Justices Stevens and Souter, dissented and would have remanded the case to District Court to give petitioner an opportunity to prove his innocence.

Wainwright v. Sykes

Supreme Court of the United States, 1977.
433 U.S. 72, 97 S.Ct. 2497, 53 L.Ed.2d 594.

■ MR. JUSTICE REHNQUIST delivered the opinion of the Court.

[Respondent Sykes was convicted of murder in a Florida trial court. A confession made by him during police interrogation was offered by the prosecution, no objection was raised by the defense, and it was admitted. Sykes appealed his conviction but no challenge to the propriety of the admission of the confession was made. Then, in state post-conviction proceedings, he urged that his confession had been obtained in violation of Miranda v. Arizona, 384 U.S. 436, 86 S.Ct. 1602, 16 L.Ed.2d 694 (1966), and its use in his prosecution invalidated his conviction. The state courts rejected this claim, apparently on the ground that the state's "contemporaneous objection" rule barred his claim. Under this rule, a failure to object to evidence at the time of its offer by the prosecution precludes a defendant from later complaining of admission of the evidence. He then sought federal habeas corpus relief, and the lower federal courts ruled in his favor. Editors.]

* * *

The simple legal question before the Court calls for a construction of the language of 28 U.S.C.A. § 2254(a), which provides that the federal courts shall entertain an application for a writ of habeas corpus "in behalf of a person in custody pursuant to the judgment of a state court only on the ground that he is in custody in violation of the Constitution or laws or treaties of the United States." . . .

[I]t is a well-established principle of federalism that a state decision resting on an adequate foundation of state substantive law is immune from review in the federal courts. The application of this principle in federal habeas corpus proceedings [has resulted in controversy concerning] ...the reviewability of federal claims which the state court had declined to pass on because not presented in the manner prescribed by its *procedural* rules. ...

In Fay v. Noia, [372 U.S. 391, 83 S.Ct. 822, 9 L.Ed.2d 837 (1963)], respondent Noia sought federal habeas to review a claim that his state-court conviction had resulted from the introduction of a coerced confession in violation of the Fifth Amendment to the United States Constitution. While the convictions of his two codefendants were reversed on that ground in collateral proceedings following their appeals, Noia did not appeal and the New York courts ruled that his subsequent *coram nobis* action was barred on account of that failure. This Court held that petitioner was nonetheless entitled to raise the claim in federal habeas....

As a matter of comity but not of federal power, the Court acknowledged "a limited discretion in the federal judge to deny relief ...to an applicant who had deliberately by-passed the orderly procedure of the state courts and in so doing has forfeited his state court remedies." Id., at 438, 83 S.Ct., at 848. In so stating, the Court made clear that the waiver must be knowing and actual—" 'an intentional relinquishment or abandonment of a known right or privilege.' " Johnson v. Zerbst, 304 U.S., at 464, 83 S.Ct., at 862. ...

A decade later we decided Davis v. United States, [411 U.S. 233, 93 S.Ct. 1577, 36 L.Ed.2d 216 (1973)], in which ...we concluded that review of the [federal prisoner's] claim should be barred on habeas, as on direct appeal, absent a showing of cause for the noncompliance and some showing of actual prejudice resulting from the alleged constitutional violation.

Last Term, in Francis v. Henderson, [425 U.S. 536, 96 S.Ct. 1708, 48 L.Ed.2d 149 (1976)], the rule of *Davis* was applied to the parallel case of a state procedural requirement....As applied to the federal petitions of state convicts, the *Davis* cause-and-prejudice standard was thus incorporated directly into the body of law governing the availability of federal habeas corpus review.

* * *

We thus come to the crux of this case. Shall the rule of Francis v. Henderson, supra, barring federal habeas review absent a showing of "cause" and "prejudice" attendant to a state procedural waiver, be applied to a waived objection to the admission of a confession at trial? We answer that question in the affirmative.

...We leave open for resolution in future decisions the precise definition of the "cause"-and-"prejudice" standard, and note here only that it is narrower than the standard set forth in dicta in Fay v. Noia, 372 U.S. 391, 83 S.Ct. 822, 9 L.Ed.2d 837 (1963), which would make federal habeas review generally available to state convicts absent a knowing and deliberate waiver of the federal constitutional contention. It is the sweeping language of Fay v. Noia, going far beyond the facts of the case eliciting it, which we today reject.[1]

* * *

1. We have no occasion today to consid-   er the *Fay* rule as applied to the facts there

We think that the rule of Fay v. Noia, broadly stated, may encourage "sandbagging" on the part of defense lawyers, who may take their chances on a verdict of not guilty in a state trial court with the intent to raise their constitutional claims in a federal habeas court if their initial gamble does not pay off. The refusal of federal habeas courts to honor contemporaneous-objection rules may also make state courts themselves less stringent in their enforcement. Under the rule of Fay v. Noia, state appellate courts know that a federal constitutional issue raised for the first time in the proceeding before them may well be decided in any event by a federal *habeas* tribunal. Thus, their choice is between addressing the issue notwithstanding the petitioner's failure to timely object, or else face the prospect that the federal habeas court will decide the question without the benefit of their views.

The failure of the federal habeas courts generally to require compliance with a contemporaneous-objection rule tends to detract from the perception of the trial of a criminal case in state court as a decisive and portentous event. . . .

There is nothing in the Constitution or in the language of § 2254 which requires that the state trial on the issue of guilt or innocence be devoted largely to the testimony of fact witnesses directed to the elements of the state crime, while only later will there occur in a federal habeas hearing a full airing of the federal constitutional claims which were not raised in the state proceedings. If a criminal defendant thinks that an action of the state trial court is about to deprive him of a federal constitutional right there is every reason for his following state procedure in making known his objection.

The "cause"-and-"prejudice" exception of the *Francis* rule will afford an adequate guarantee, we think, that the rule will not prevent a federal habeas court from adjudicating for the first time the federal constitutional claim of a defendant who in the absence of such an adjudication will be the victim of a miscarriage of justice. Whatever precise content may be given those terms by later cases, we feel confident in holding without further elaboration that they do not exist here. Respondent has advanced no explanation whatever for his failure to object at trial,[2] and, as the proceeding unfolded, the trial judge is certainly not to be faulted for failing to question the admission of the confession himself. The other evidence of guilt presented at trial, moreover, was substantial to a degree that would negate any possibility of actual prejudice resulting to the respondent from the admission of his inculpatory statement.

We accordingly conclude that the judgment of the Court of Appeals for the Fifth Circuit must be reversed, and the cause remanded to the United

confronting the Court. Whether the *Francis* rule should preclude federal habeas review of claims not made in accordance with state procedure where the criminal defendant has surrendered, other than for reasons of tactical advantage, the right to have all of his claims of trial error considered by a state appellate court, we leave for another day.

2. In Henry v. Mississippi, [379 U.S. 443, 451, 85 S.Ct. 564, 569, 13 L.Ed.2d 408 (1965)] the Court noted that decisions of counsel relating to trial strategy, even when made without the consultation of the defendant, would bar direct federal review of claims thereby forgone, except where "the circumstances are exceptional."

States District Court for the Middle District of Florida with instructions to dismiss respondent's petition for a writ of habeas corpus.

It is so ordered.

[JUSTICE WHITE concurred in the judgment. The separate concurrences of CHIEF JUSTICE BURGER and JUSTICE STEVENS are omitted.]

■ MR. JUSTICE BRENNAN, with whom MR. JUSTICE MARSHALL joins, dissenting.

* * *

[A]ny realistic system of federal habeas corpus jurisdiction must be premised on the reality that the ordinary procedural default is born of the inadvertence, negligence, inexperience, or incompetence of trial counsel. The case under consideration today is typical. The Court makes no effort to identify a tactical motive for the failure of Sykes' attorney to challenge the admissibility or reliability of a highly inculpatory statement. ...[A]ny realistic reading of the record demonstrates that we are faced here with a lawyer's simple error.

Fay's answer to this is plain: the bypass test simply refuses to credit what is essentially a lawyer's mistake as a forfeiture of constitutional rights. I persist in the belief that the interests of Sykes and the State of Florida are best rationalized by adherence to this test....

Florida, of course, can point to a variety of legitimate interests in seeking allegiance to its reasonable procedural requirements, the contemporaneous-objection rule included.

* * *

Punishing a lawyer's unintentional errors by closing the federal courthouse door to his client is both a senseless and misdirected method of deterring the slighting of state rules. It is senseless because unplanned and unintentional action of any kind generally is not subject to deterrence; and, to the extent that it is hoped that a threatened sanction addressed to the defense will induce greater care and caution on the part of trial lawyers, thereby forestalling negligent conduct or error, the potential loss of all valuable state remedies would be sufficient to this end. And it is a misdirected sanction because even if the penalization of incompetence or carelessness will encourage more thorough legal training and trial preparation, the habeas applicant, as opposed to his lawyer, hardly is the proper recipient of such a penalty. Especially, with fundamental constitutional rights at stake, no fictional relationship of principal-agent or the like can justify holding the criminal defendant accountable for the naked errors of his attorney. This is especially true when so many indigent defendants are without any realistic choice in selecting who ultimately represents them at trial. Indeed, if responsibility for error must be apportioned between the parties, it is the State, through its attorney's admissions and certification policies, that is more fairly held to blame for the fact that practicing lawyers too often are ill-prepared or ill-equipped to act carefully and knowledgeably when faced with decisions governed by state procedural requirements.

* * *

In short, I believe that the demands of our criminal justice system warrant visiting the mistakes of a trial attorney on the head of a habeas corpus applicant only when we are convinced that the lawyer actually exercised his expertise and judgment in his client's service, and with his client's knowing and intelligent participation where possible. This, of course, is the precise system of habeas review established by Fay v. Noia.

* * *

NOTES

1. **Cause.** In Engle v. Isaac, 456 U.S. 107, 102 S.Ct. 1558, 71 L.Ed.2d 783 (1982) the Court further explained the meaning of "cause" for failure to comply with state requirements of contemporaneous objection. The respondents were convicted of murder in a trial in which the trial court instructed the jury that the burden of persuasion on the issue of self-defense rested with them. They made no objection to this instruction; it conformed to long-standing Ohio law on the subject. After the trials, the Supreme Court decided Mullaney v. Wilbur (page 1000, supra) in which it held that under some circumstances due process of law is violated when the state seeks to place the burden of persuasion on the defendant in a criminal case. Respondents urged that objection would have been futile since Ohio law on the subject was firmly established against their position and they further argued that they should not be held to have anticipated the Court's decision in *Mullaney.* Writing for the majority, Justice O'Connor stated:

> [T]he futility of presenting an objection to the state courts cannot alone constitute cause for a failure to object at trial. If a defendant perceives a constitutional claim and believes it may find favor in the federal courts, he may not bypass the state courts simply because he thinks they will be unsympathetic to the claim.

* * *

> We need not decide whether the novelty of a constitutional claim ever establishes cause for a failure to object. We might hesitate to adopt a rule that would require trial counsel either to exercise extraordinary vision or to object to every aspect of the proceedings in the hope that some aspect might mask a latent constitutional claim.

456 U.S. at 130–32, 102 S.Ct. at 1572–73, 71 L.Ed.2d at 802. The Court noted that In re Winship (Chapter 23) decided over 4 years before the respondents' trials, could have been used by trial counsel to construct a constitutional claim concerning the burden of persuasion instruction. Some lower courts had decided that *Winship* required the State to shoulder the burden of persuasion for certain defenses:

> Where the basis of a constitutional claim is available, and other defense counsel have perceived and litigated that claim, the demands of comity and finality counsel against labelling alleged unawareness of the objection as cause for a procedural default.

456 U.S. at 134, 102 S.Ct. at 1574, 71 L.Ed.2d at 804.

Two years later the Court in Reed v. Ross, 468 U.S. 1, 104 S.Ct. 2901, 82 L.Ed.2d 1 (1984), addressed the issue. Respondent was tried in state court for murder. The trial court instructed the jury in accordance with long-standing state law that if the jury found that respondent killed intentionally, the burden shifted to him to show self-defense or that he killed in the heat of passion. The trial antedated the Supreme Court's decision in the Winship case. Ultimately, the Fourth Circuit set aside respondent's conviction on the ground the trial court's instruction violated Mullaney v. Wilbur, which the Supreme Court had earlier held to be fully retroactive. The Court of Appeals excused the failure of respondent to make this claim in the trial court on the ground that at that time the claim would have been novel. The Supreme Court, in an opinion by Justice Brennan, affirmed. If counsel had "no reasonable basis" upon which to formulate a constitutional question, that is cause for failure to assert it in a timely fashion:

> Counsel's failure to raise a claim for which there was no reasonable basis in existing law does not seriously implicate any of the concerns that might otherwise require deference to a State's procedural bar. Just as it is reasonable to assume that a competent lawyer will fail to perceive the possibility of raising such a claim, it is also reasonable to assume that a court will similarly fail to appreciate the claim. It is in the nature of our legal system that legal concepts, including constitutional concepts, develop slowly, finding partial acceptance in some courts while meeting rejection in others. Despite the fact that a constitutional concept may ultimately enjoy general acceptance, as the *Mullaney* issue currently does, when the concept is in its embryonic stage, it will, by hypothesis, be rejected by most courts. Consequently, a rule requiring a defendant to raise a truly novel issue is not likely to serve any functional purpose.

468 U.S. at 15, 104 S.Ct. at 2910, 82 L.Ed.2d at 14. Justice Powell concurred; Justice Rehnquist, joined by The Chief Justice and Justices Blackmun and O'Connor, dissented.

In United States v. Frady, 456 U.S. 152, 102 S.Ct. 1584, 71 L.Ed.2d 816 (1982) the Court had also explicated the cause and prejudice standards of Wainwright v. Sykes. Frady was convicted of first degree murder after a jury trial in a United States District Court in the District of Columbia. After his conviction was affirmed on appeal, he filed a petition for post-conviction relief as a federal prisoner under 28 U.S.C.A. § 2255. He contended that the trial court had erroneously instructed the jury in such a way that it was permitted to presume the presence of the element of malice from certain circumstances of the case. Cases decided after Frady's trial and appeal had established that the instructions given were erroneous. Frady's counsel had not objected to the instructions at trial. The Court of Appeals for the District of Columbia Circuit granted post-conviction relief, basing its decision in part on the ground that failure to object at the trial came within the ambit of the "plain error" standard of Rule 52(b) of the Federal Rules of Criminal Procedure. The Supreme Court, in an opinion authored by Justice O'Connor, reversed. It found that the plain error standard was inappropriate for application in a § 2255 proceeding, as opposed to a direct appeal, on the ground that the governmental interest in finality outweighs the defendant's interest in raising a question in a post-conviction proceeding after time for appeal has expired or the appeal has been unsuccessfully taken:

> [T]he Court of Appeals accorded no significance whatever to the existence of a final judgment perfected by appeal. Once the defendant's chance to appeal has been waived or exhausted ...we are entitled to presume he stands fairly and finally convicted, especially when, as here, he already has had a fair opportunity to present his federal claims to a federal forum. Our trial and appellate procedures are not so unreliable that we may not afford their completed operation any binding effect beyond the next in a series of endless post-conviction collateral attacks.

456 U.S. at 165–66, 102 S.Ct. at 1592–93, 71 L.Ed.2d at 828. The majority concluded that the cause and prejudice requirements of Wainwright v. Sykes apply in the § 2255 proceeding. The majority also concluded that whether there may have been "cause" for failure to object at trial, there was no actual prejudice from the erroneous instruction in this case because of the overwhelming evidence of actual malice introduced in the trial.

2. **Cause in an appeal.** The Supreme Court dealt with the question of the meaning of the requirement of cause for procedural defaults in the appeal of criminal convictions raised upon federal habeas corpus in Murray v. Carrier, 477 U.S. 478, 106 S.Ct. 2639, 91 L.Ed.2d 397 (1986). Justice O'Connor held that so long as there is no claim of ineffective assistance of counsel the type of mistake made by counsel has no bearing on whether the cause requirement of Wainwright v. Sykes has been met. Of course, a claim of ineffective assistance can be made in federal habeas, but the petitioner must exhaust state remedies before doing so. Justice O'Connor did recognize an exception to the requirement of a showing of cause for procedural default "in an extraordinary case, where a constitutional violation has probably resulted in the conviction of one who is actually innocent...." 477 U.S. at 496, 106 S.Ct. at 2649, 91 L.Ed.2d at 413. Justice Brennan, joined by Justice Marshall, dissented. Similarly, see also Smith v. Murray, 477 U.S. 527, 106 S.Ct. 2661, 91 L.Ed.2d 434 (1986) in which Justice Stevens, joined by Justices Marshall, Blackmun and Brennan, dissented.

The matter was again considered in Dugger v. Adams, 489 U.S. 401, 109 S.Ct. 1211, 103 L.Ed.2d 435 (1989). Adams argued that where the error concerns capital sentencing an "innocent" defendant is one who does not deserve the death penalty. Rejecting this, the *Adams* majority noted the difficulty of defining defendants who are "actually innocent" of death penalties. But it relied primarily upon its conclusion that the circumstances failed to show that the erroneous jury instruction concerning sentencing responsibilities resulted in a "fundamental miscarriage of justice." 489 U.S. at 410 n. 6, 109 S.Ct. at 1217–18 n. 6, 103 L.Ed.2d at 446 n. 6.

3. **Identifying the basis for state court decision.** In Harris v. Reed, 489 U.S. 255, 109 S.Ct. 1038, 103 L.Ed.2d 308 (1989), a state procedural default to raising a federal constitutional claim does not bar consideration of a claim for federal habeas corpus relief unless the last state court rendering a judgment in the case " 'clearly and expressly' states that its judgment rests on a state procedural bar."

4. **Failing to appeal in state court.** The petitioner in Coleman v. Thompson, 501 U.S. 722, 111 S.Ct. 2546, 115 L.Ed.2d 640 (1991) was convicted in a Virginia state court of murder and given the death penalty. On direct appeal, the Virginia Supreme Court affirmed the conviction and sentence. Coleman then filed a petition for habeas corpus in the state trial court, alleging various additional federal constitutional grounds for relief. The state trial court conducted a two-day evidentiary hearing and denied all relief. Thirty-three days later, Coleman's attorney filed notice of appeal from that decision to the Virginia Supreme Court. On motion of the Commonwealth, that court dismissed the appeal because notice of appeal had not been given within 30 days of the habeas decision. Coleman then filed a petition for habeas corpus in the United States District Court, making the federal claims he had made in his direct appeal and state habeas proceedings. The District Court ruled that Coleman had procedurally defaulted the claims that had been made only in the state habeas proceeding by failing to file a timely notice of appeal; it also considered all the claims on the merits and denied them. This decision was affirmed by the United States Court of Appeals. The Supreme Court, in an opinion by Justice O'Connor, held that Coleman had procedurally defaulted those claims by filing notice of appeal 3 days late. Under the rule of Fay v. Noia, a procedural default

cannot be found except upon a showing petitioner waived the state remedy by deliberately bypassing it and there was no contention the late notice of appeal was deliberate. However, the Court reasoned subsequent cases, primarily Wainwright v. Sykes signal a change in emphasis from *Fay:*

> In all cases in which a state prisoner has defaulted his federal claims in state court pursuant to an independent and adequate state procedural rule, federal habeas review of the claims is barred unless the prisoner can demonstrate cause for the default and actual prejudice as a result of the alleged violation of federal law, or demonstrate that failure to consider the claims will result in a fundamental miscarriage of justice. *Fay* was based on a conception of federal/state relations that undervalued the importance of state procedural rules. The several cases after *Fay* that applied the cause and prejudice standard to a variety of state procedural defaults represent a different view. We now recognize the important interest in finality served by state procedural rules, and the significant harm to the States that results from the failure of federal courts to respect them.

501 U.S. at 750, 111 S.Ct. at 2565, 115 L.Ed.2d at 669. Coleman argued that his counsel was ineffective in filing notice of appeal late and that should be regarded as cause for excusing the procedural default. The Court rejected that argument,

> There is no constitutional right to an attorney in state post-conviction proceedings. Pennsylvania v. Finley, 481 U.S. 551, 107 S.Ct. 1990, 95 L.Ed.2d 539 (1987); Murray v. Giarratano, 492 U.S. 1, 109 S.Ct. 2765, 106 L.Ed.2d 1 (1989) * * *. Consequently, a petitioner cannot claim constitutionally ineffective assistance of counsel in such proceedings * * *. Coleman contends that it was his attorney's error that led to the late filing of his state habeas appeal. This error cannot be constitutionally ineffective, therefore Coleman must "bear the risk of attorney error that results in a procedural default."

501 U.S. at 752, 111 S.Ct. at 2566, 115 L.Ed.2d at 671. Justice Blackmun, joined by Justices Marshall and Stevens, dissented.

In a related opinion, Ylst v. Nunnemaker, 501 U.S. 797, 111 S.Ct. 2590, 115 L.Ed.2d 706 (1991), the Court dealt with the requirement of Harris v. Reed that a state procedural default requires an express statement of reliance on state law as applied to unexplained, memorandum decisions of state courts. Nunnemaker was convicted in a California state court of murder. The California Court of Appeals affirmed his conviction, rejecting a *Miranda* claim on the ground respondent had not raised it in the trial court. The California Supreme Court denied discretionary review. A state habeas petition was denied without opinion, as was a similar petition in the Court of Appeals. Finally, an original state habeas petition was denied by the California Supreme Court by memorandum decision that cited two cases not here relevant. Respondent filed a federal habeas petition alleging the *Miranda* violation, which was rejected by the United States District Court on the ground of state procedural default. The United States Court of Appeals reversed this decision under Harris v. Reed on the ground that since the California Supreme Court decision was not explicitly based on state grounds, it could not be said the decision was not based on federal grounds rather than state procedural requirements. The United States Supreme Court, in an opinion by Justice Scalia, reversed:

> The * * * question presented by the present case * * * is how federal courts in habeas proceedings are to determine whether an unexplained order (by which we mean an order whose text or accompanying opinion does not disclose the reason for the judgment) rests primarily on federal law. The question is not an easy one * * *.

The problem we face arises * * * because many formulary orders are not meant to convey *anything* as to the reason for the decision. Attributing a reason is therefore both difficult and artificial. We think that the attribution necessary for federal habeas purposes can be facilitated, and sound results more often assured, by applying the following presumption: where there has been one reasoned state judgment rejecting a federal claim, later unexplained orders upholding that judgment or rejecting the same claim rest upon the same ground. If an earlier opinion "fairly appear[s] to rest primarily upon federal law," * * * we will presume that no procedural default has been invoked by a subsequent unexplained order that leaves the judgment or its consequences in place. Similarly where, as here, the last reasoned opinion on the claim explicitly imposes a procedural default, we will presume that a later decision rejecting the claim did not silently disregard that bar and consider the merits.

501 U.S. at 802–03, 111 S.Ct. at 2594, 115 L.Ed.2d at 716–17. While the presumption is rebuttable, it is not rebutted here. Therefore, the memorandum decision of the California Supreme Court did not alter the procedural default ruling of the earlier California Court of Appeals decision and federal habeas relief is barred under Coleman v. Thompson unless respondent can on remand establish cause and prejudice. Justice Blackmun, joined by Justices Marshall and Stevens, dissented.

5. **Total exhaustion.** As 28 U.S.C.A. § 2254(b) makes clear, a state defendant who seeks federal habeas corpus relief must ordinarily exhaust any available state procedure for raising the issue the defendant seeks to raise in the federal forum. This was affirmed in Duckworth v. Serrano, 454 U.S. 1, 102 S.Ct. 18, 70 L.Ed.2d 1 (1981) (per curiam) and in Rose v. Lundy, 455 U.S. 509, 102 S.Ct. 1198, 71 L.Ed.2d 379 (1982), the Court adopted what it termed a requirement of "total exhaustion." A habeas application must be dismissed if it contains any claims which had not been presented to state courts first. This requirement:

will encourage state prisoners to seek full relief first from the state courts, thus giving those courts the first opportunity to review all claims of constitutional error. As the number of prisoners who exhaust all of their federal claims increases, state courts may become increasingly familiar with and hospitable toward federal constitutional issues. ...Equally as important, federal claims that have been fully exhausted in state courts will more often be accompanied by a complete factual record to aid the federal courts in their review.

455 U.S. at 518–19, 102 S.Ct. at 1203–04, 71 L.Ed.2d at 388. Justice O'Connor then advanced the proposition, concurred in by only three other justices, that a prisoner faced with the dismissal of his application because it contains unexhausted claims could amend it to eliminate those claims but if that course of action is taken "the prisoner would risk forfeiting his unexhausted claims in federal court" under the doctrine of abuse of the writ of habeas corpus by presenting piecemeal claims to the courts. 455 U.S. at 519, 102 S.Ct. at 1204, 71 L.Ed.2d at 389.

In Anderson v. Harless, 459 U.S. 4, 103 S.Ct. 276, 74 L.Ed.2d 3 (1982) the Court further dealt with the requirement of exhaustion of state remedies. Respondent was convicted of murder in a trial in which the jury was instructed in such a way that the burden of persuasion may have been shifted in violation of Sandstrom v. Montana, 442 U.S. 510, 99 S.Ct. 2450, 61 L.Ed.2d 39 (1979). However in state appeals, Respondent simply cited a state case that had dealt with the impropriety of such an instruction under state law. A petition for writ of habeas corpus in federal court was granted and affirmed on appeal. The Supreme Court reversed in a per curiam opinion. The Court noted that "it is not enough that all the facts necessary to support the federal claim were before the state courts ...or that a somewhat similar state-law claim was made. ...[T]he habeas petitioner must have 'fairly presented' to the state courts the 'substance' of his federal habeas corpus claim."

459 U.S. at 6, 103 S.Ct. at 277, 74 L.Ed.2d at 7. See also Castille v. Peoples, 489 U.S. 346, 109 S.Ct. 1056, 103 L.Ed.2d 380 (1989).

6. **State forfeiture of exhaustion claim.** Is the requirement of exhaustion of state remedies waived if the state fails to raise it before the United States District Court? The petitioner in Granberry v. Greer, 481 U.S. 129, 107 S.Ct. 1671, 95 L.Ed.2d 119 (1987), an Illinois prisoner, lost in the District Court on a motion to dismiss for failure to state a claim. He appealed to the Seventh Circuit, where the State of Illinois, for the first time, raised his failure to exhaust state remedies. The Court of Appeals rejected petitioner's argument that the State had waived the exhaustion requirement by failure to raise it before the District Court and, without reaching the merits, remanded the case for dismissal without prejudice. The United States Supreme Court, in an unusual unanimous opinion authored by Justice Stevens, reversed:

> How an appellate court ought to handle a nonexhausted habeas petition when the State has not raised this objection in the district court is a question that might be answered in three different ways. We might treat the State's silence on the matter as a procedural default precluding the State from raising the issue on appeal. At the other extreme, we might treat nonexhaustion as an inflexible bar to consideration of the merits of the petition by the federal court, and therefore require that a petition be dismissed when it appears that there has been a failure to exhaust. Or, third, we might adopt an intermediate approach and direct the courts of appeals to exercise discretion in each case to decide whether the administration of justice would be better served by insisting on exhaustion or by reaching the merits of the petition forthwith.

481 U.S. at 131, 107 S.Ct. at 1673, 95 L.Ed.2d at 123. The Court had previously decided that failure to exhaust does not deprive an appellate court of jurisdiction to consider the federal claim on its merits. Adopting the second position would encourage the state to withhold its exhaustion defense until after a determination on the merits by the District Court, which is "unwise." Eschewing both extremes, the Court adopted the "intermediate approach" and illustrated some of the considerations that should guide courts of appeals in exercising their discretion:

> If . . . the case presents an issue on which an unresolved question of fact or of state law might have an important bearing, both comity and judicial efficiency may make it appropriate for the court to insist on complete exhaustion to make sure that it may ultimately review the issue on a fully informed basis. On the other hand, if it is perfectly clear that the applicant does not raise even a colorable federal claim, the interests of the petitioner, the warden, the state attorney general, the state courts, and the federal courts will all be well served even if the State fails to raise the exhaustion defense, [if] the district court denies the habeas petition, and the court of appeals affirmed the judgment of the district court forthwith.

> Conversely, if a full trial has been held in the district court and it is evident that a miscarriage of justice has occurred, it may also be appropriate for the court of appeals to hold that the nonexhaustion defense has been waived in order to avoid unnecessary delay in granting relief that is plainly warranted.

481 U.S. at 134–35, 107 S.Ct. at 1675–76, 95 L.Ed.2d at 125–26.

7. **Writ abuse.** The subject of abuse of the writ of habeas corpus was addressed in McCleskey v. Zant, 499 U.S. 467, 111 S.Ct. 1454, 113 L.Ed.2d 517 (1991). McCleskey was convicted of murder in a Georgia state court and given the death penalty. After losing appeals, he filed a state habeas corpus petition in which, among other grounds of relief, he claimed a custodial statement had been obtained in violation of Massiah v. United States. Relief was denied. He filed his first federal

habeas petition, in which he made several claims, but not the Massiah claim. Relief was ultimately denied, as was relief on a second state habeas petition. McCleskey then filed his second federal habeas petition, alleging seven grounds of relief, including the Massiah claim missing from the first federal habeas petition. The United States District Court granted relief based on the Massiah claim. It also rejected an argument by the State that McCleskey had abused the federal writ by finding that he had not deliberately abandoned his Massiah claim by failing to raise it in the first federal petition. The United States Court of Appeals reversed the District Court, finding that McCleskey had deliberately abandoned the Massiah claim.

The United States Supreme Court, in an opinion by Justice Kennedy, affirmed the Court of Appeals. It held that a showing of deliberate abandonment was not required for abuse of the writ, that "the same standard [Wainwright v. Sykes] used to determine whether to excuse state procedural defaults should govern the determination of inexcusable neglect in the abuse of the writ context." 499 U.S. at 490, 111 S.Ct. at 1468, 113 L.Ed.2d at 542. The Court then attempted to define a process for resolving questions of writ abuse under this standard:

> When a prisoner files a second or subsequent application, the government bears the burden of pleading abuse of the writ. The government satisfies this burden if, with clarity and particularity, it notes petitioner's prior writ history, identifies the claims that appear for the first time, and alleges that petitioner has abused the writ. The burden to disprove abuse then becomes petitioner's. To excuse his failure to raise the claim earlier, he must show cause for failing to raise it and prejudice therefrom as those concepts have been defined in our procedural default decisions. The petitioner's opportunity to meet the burden of cause and prejudice will not include an evidentiary hearing if the district court determines as a matter of law that petitioner cannot satisfy the standard. If petitioner cannot show cause, the failure to raise the claim in an earlier petition may nonetheless be excused if he or she can show that a fundamental miscarriage of justice would result from a failure to entertain the claim.

499 U.S. at 494–95, 111 S.Ct. at 1470, 113 L.Ed.2d at 545. Finally, the Court concluded that "the requirement of cause * * * is based on the principle that petitioner must conduct a reasonable and diligent investigation aimed at including all relevant claims and grounds for relief in the first federal habeas petition." 499 U.S. at 498, 111 S.Ct. at 1472, 113 L.Ed.2d at 547. Justice Marshall, joined by Justices Blackmun and Stevens, dissented.

Felker v. Turpin

Supreme Court of the United States, 1996.
518 U.S. 651, 116 S.Ct. 2333, 135 L.Ed.2d 827.

■ Chief Justice Rehnquist delivered the opinion of the Court.

Title I of the Antiterrorism and Effective Death Penalty Act of 1996 (Act) works substantial changes to chapter 153 of Title 28 of the United States Code, which authorizes federal courts to grant the writ of habeas corpus. Pub.L. 104–132, 110 Stat. 1217. We hold that the Act does not preclude this Court from entertaining an application for habeas corpus relief, although it does affect the standards governing the granting of such relief. We also conclude that the availability of such relief in this Court obviates any claim by petitioner under the Exceptions Clause of Article III,

§ 2, of the Constitution, and that the operative provisions of the Act do not violate the Suspension Clause of the Constitution, Art. I, § 9.

I

On a night in 1976, petitioner approached Jane W. in his car as she got out of hers. Claiming to be lost and looking for a party nearby, he used a series of deceptions to induce Jane to accompany him to his trailer home in town. Petitioner forcibly subdued her, raped her, and sodomized her. Jane pleaded with petitioner to let her go, but he said he could not because she would notify the police. She escaped later, when petitioner fell asleep. Jane notified the police, and petitioner was eventually convicted of aggravated sodomy and sentenced to 12 years' imprisonment.

Petitioner was paroled four years later. On November 23, 1981, he met Joy Ludlam, a cocktail waitress, at the lounge where she worked. She was interested in changing jobs, and petitioner used a series of deceptions involving offering her a job at "The Leather Shoppe," a business he owned, to induce her to visit him the next day. The last time Joy was seen alive was the evening of the next day. Her dead body was discovered two weeks later in a creek. Forensic analysis established that she had been beaten, raped, and sodomized, and that she had been strangled to death before being left in the creek. Investigators discovered hair resembling petitioner's on Joy's body and clothes, hair resembling Joy's in petitioner's bedroom, and clothing fibers like those in Joy's coat in the hatchback of petitioner's car. One of petitioner's neighbors reported seeing Joy's car at petitioner's house the day she disappeared. A jury convicted petitioner of murder, rape, aggravated sodomy, and false imprisonment. Petitioner was sentenced to death on the murder charge. The Georgia Supreme Court affirmed petitioner's conviction and death sentence, Felker v. State, 252 Ga. 351, 314 S.E.2d 621, and we denied certiorari, 469 U.S. 873, 105 S.Ct. 229, 83 L.Ed.2d 158 (1984). A state trial court denied collateral relief, the Georgia Supreme Court declined to issue a certificate of probable cause to appeal the denial, and we again denied certiorari. Felker v. Zant, 502 U.S. 1064, 112 S.Ct. 950, 117 L.Ed.2d 118 (1992).

Petitioner then filed a petition for a writ of habeas corpus in the United States District Court for the Middle District of Georgia, alleging that (1) the State's evidence was insufficient to convict him; (2) the State withheld exculpatory evidence, in violation of Brady v. Maryland, 373 U.S. 83, 83 S.Ct. 1194, 10 L.Ed.2d 215 (1963); (3) petitioner's counsel rendered ineffective assistance at sentencing; (4) the State improperly used hypnosis to refresh a witness' memory; and (5) the State violated double jeopardy and collateral estoppel principles by using petitioner's crime against Jane W. as evidence at petitioner's trial for crimes against Joy Ludlam. The District Court denied the petition. The United States Court of Appeals for the Eleventh Circuit affirmed, 52 F.3d 907, extended on denial of petition for rehearing, 62 F.3d 342 (1995), and we denied certiorari, 516 U.S. 1133 (1996).

The State scheduled petitioner's execution for the period May 2–9, 1996. On April 29, 1996, petitioner filed a second petition for state collateral relief. The state trial court denied this petition May 1, and the Georgia Supreme Court denied certiorari May 2.

On April 24, 1996, the President signed the Act into law. Title I of this Act contained a series of amendments to existing federal habeas corpus law. The provisions of the Act pertinent to this case concern second or successive habeas corpus applications by state prisoners. Subsections 106(b)(1) and (b)(2) specify the conditions under which claims in second or successive applications must be dismissed, amending 28 U.S.C. § 2244(b) to read:

> (1) A claim presented in a second or successive habeas corpus application under section 2254 that was presented in a prior application shall be dismissed.

> (2) A claim presented in a second or successive habeas corpus application under section 2254 that was not presented in a prior application shall be dismissed unless—

>> (A) the applicant shows that the claim relies on a new rule of constitutional law, made retroactive to cases on collateral review by the Supreme Court, that was previously unavailable; or

>> (B)(i) the factual predicate for the claim could not have been discovered previously through the exercise of due diligence; and

>> (ii) the facts underlying the claim, if proven and viewed in light of the evidence as a whole, would be sufficient to establish by clear and convincing evidence that, but for constitutional error, no reasonable factfinder would have found the applicant guilty of the underlying offense.

110 Stat. 1220–1221.

Subsection 106(b)(3) creates a "gatekeeping" mechanism for the consideration of second or successive applications in district court. The prospective applicant must file in the court of appeals a motion for leave to file a second or successive habeas application in the district court. § 106(b)(3)(A). A three-judge panel has 30 days to determine whether "the application makes a prima facie showing that the application satisfies the requirements of" § 106(b). § 106(b)(3)(C); see §§ 106(b)(3)(B), (D). Section 106(b)(3)(E) specifies that "[t]he grant or denial of an authorization by a court of appeals to file a second or successive application shall not be appealable and shall not be the subject of a petition for rehearing or for a writ of certiorari."

On May 2, 1996, petitioner filed in the United States Court of Appeals for the Eleventh Circuit a motion for stay of execution and a motion for leave to file a second or successive federal habeas corpus petition under § 2254. Petitioner sought to raise two claims in his second petition, the first being that the state trial court violated due process by equating guilt "beyond a reasonable doubt" with "moral certainty" of guilt in voir dire and jury instructions. See Cage v. Louisiana, 498 U.S. 39, 111 S.Ct. 328, 112 L.Ed.2d 339 (1990). He also alleged that qualified experts, reviewing the forensic evidence after his conviction, had established that Joy must have died during a period when petitioner was under police surveillance for Joy's disappearance and thus had a valid alibi. He claimed that the testimony of the State's forensic expert at trial was suspect because he is not a licensed physician, and that the new expert testimony so discredited the State's testimony at trial that petitioner had a colorable claim of factual innocence.

The Court of Appeals denied both motions the day they were filed, concluding that petitioner's claims had not been presented in his first habeas petition, that they did not meet the standards of § 106(b)(2) of the Act, and that they would not have satisfied pre-Act standards for obtaining review on the merits of second or successive claims. 83 F.3d 1303 (C.A.11 1996). Petitioner filed in this Court a pleading styled a "Petition for Writ of Habeas Corpus, for Appellate or Certiorari Review of the Decision of the United States Circuit Court for the Eleventh Circuit, and for Stay of Execution." On May 3, we granted petitioner's stay application and petition for certiorari. We ordered briefing on the extent to which the provisions of Title I of the Act apply to a petition for habeas corpus filed in this Court, whether application of the Act suspended the writ of habeas corpus in this case, and whether Title I of the Act, especially § 106(b)(3)(E), constitutes an unconstitutional restriction on the jurisdiction of this Court. 517 U.S. 1182 (1996).

II

We first consider to what extent the provisions of Title I of the Act apply to petitions for habeas corpus filed as original matters in this Court pursuant to 28 U.S.C. §§ 2241 and 2254. We conclude that although the Act does impose new conditions on our authority to grant relief, it does not deprive this Court of jurisdiction to entertain original habeas petitions.

A

Section 106(b)(3)(E) of the Act prevents this Court from reviewing a court of appeals order denying leave to file a second habeas petition by appeal or by writ of certiorari. More than a century ago, we considered whether a statute barring review by appeal of the judgment of a circuit court in a habeas case also deprived this Court of power to entertain an original habeas petition. Ex parte Yerger, 8 Wall. 85, 19 L.Ed. 332 (1869). We consider the same question here with respect to § 106(b)(3)(E).

Yerger's holding is best understood in the light of the availability of habeas corpus review at that time. Section 14 of the Judiciary Act of 1789 authorized all federal courts, including this Court, to grant the writ of habeas corpus, when prisoners were "in custody, under or by colour of the authority of the United States, or [were] committed for trial before some court of the same." Act of Sept. 24, 1789, ch. 20, § 14, 1 Stat. 82. Congress greatly expanded the scope of federal habeas corpus in 1867, authorizing federal courts to grant the writ, "in addition to the authority already conferred by law," "in all cases where any person may be restrained of his or her liberty in violation of the constitution, or of any treaty or law of the United States." Act of Feb. 5, 1867, ch. 28, 14 Stat. 385. Before the Act of 1867, the only instances in which a federal court could issue the writ to produce a state prisoner were if the prisoner was "necessary to be brought into court to testify," Act of Sept. 24, 1789, ch. 20, § 14, 1 Stat. 82, was "committed . . . for any act done . . . in pursuance of a law of the United States," Act of Mar. 2, 1833, ch. 57, § 7, 4 Stat. 634–635, or was a "subjec[t] or citize[n] of a foreign State, and domiciled therein," and held under state law, Act of Aug. 29, 1842, ch. 257, 5 Stat. 539–540.

The Act of 1867 also expanded our statutory appellate jurisdiction to authorize appeals to this Court from the final decision of any circuit court on a habeas petition. 14 Stat. 386. This enactment changed the result of *Barry v. Mercein*, 5 How. 103, 12 L.Ed. 70 (1847), in which we had held that the Judiciary Act of 1789 did not authorize this Court to conduct appellate review of circuit court habeas decisions. However, in 1868, Congress revoked the appellate jurisdiction it had given in 1867, repealing "so much of the [Act of 1867] as authorizes an appeal from the judgment of the circuit court to the Supreme Court of the United States." Act of Mar. 27, 1868, ch. 34, § 2, 15 Stat. 44.

In *Yerger*, we considered whether the Act of 1868 deprived us not only of power to hear an appeal from a inferior court's decision on a habeas petition, but also of power to entertain a habeas petition to this Court under § 14 of the Act of 1789. We concluded that the 1868 Act did not affect our power to entertain such habeas petitions. We explained that the 1868 Act's text addressed only jurisdiction over appeals conferred under the Act of 1867, not habeas jurisdiction conferred under the Acts of 1789 and 1867. We rejected the suggestion that the Act of 1867 had repealed our habeas power by implication. *Yerger*, 8 Wall., at 105, 19 L.Ed. 332. Repeals by implication are not favored, we said, and the continued exercise of original habeas jurisdiction was not "repugnant" to a prohibition on review by appeal of circuit court habeas judgments. Ibid.

Turning to the present case, we conclude that Title I of the Act has not repealed our authority to entertain original habeas petitions, for reasons similar to those stated in *Yerger*. No provision of Title I mentions our authority to entertain original habeas petitions; in contrast, § 103 amends the Federal Rules of Appellate Procedure to bar consideration of original habeas petitions in the courts of appeals. Although § 106(b)(3)(E) precludes us from reviewing, by appeal or petition for certiorari, a judgment on an application for leave to file a second habeas petition in district court, it makes no mention of our authority to hear habeas petitions filed as original matters in this Court. As we declined to find a repeal of § 14 of the Judiciary Act of 1789 as applied to this Court by implication then, we decline to find a similar repeal of § 2241 of Title 28—its descendant, n. 1, supra—by implication now.

This conclusion obviates one of the constitutional challenges raised. The critical language of Article III, § 2, of the Constitution provides that, apart from several classes of cases specifically enumerated in this Court's original jurisdiction, "[i]n all the other Cases . . . the supreme Court shall have appellate Jurisdiction, both as to Law and Fact, with such Exceptions, and under such Regulations as the Congress shall make." Previous decisions construing this clause have said that while our appellate powers "are given by the constitution," "they are limited and regulated by the [Judiciary Act of 1789], and by such other acts as have been passed on the subject." *Durousseau v. United States*, 6 Cranch 307, 314, 3 L.Ed. 232 (1810); see also United States v. More, 3 Cranch 159, 172–173, 2 L.Ed. 397 (1805). The Act does remove our authority to entertain an appeal or a petition for a writ of certiorari to review a decision of a court of appeals exercising its "gatekeeping" function over a second petition. But since it does not repeal our authority to entertain a petition for habeas corpus, there can be no plausible argument that the Act has deprived this Court of appellate jurisdiction in violation of Article III, § 2.

B

We consider next how Title I affects the requirements a state prisoner must satisfy to show he is entitled to a writ of habeas corpus from this Court. Title I of the Act has changed the standards governing our consideration of habeas petitions by imposing new requirements for the granting of relief to state prisoners. Our authority to grant habeas relief to state prisoners is limited by § 2254, which specifies the conditions under which such relief may be granted to "a person in custody pursuant to the judgment of a State court." § 2254(a). Several sections of the Act impose new requirements for the granting of relief under this section, and they therefore inform our authority to grant such relief as well.

Section 106(b) of the Act addresses second or successive habeas petitions. Section 106(b)(3)'s "gatekeeping" system for second petitions does not apply to our consideration of habeas petitions because it applies to applications "filed in the district court." § 106(b)(3)(A). There is no such limitation, however, on the restrictions on repetitive and new claims imposed by subsections 106(b)(1) and (2). These restrictions apply without qualification to any "second or successive habeas corpus application under section 2254." §§ 106(b)(1), (2). Whether or not we are bound by these restrictions, they certainly inform our consideration of original habeas petitions.

III

Next, we consider whether the Act suspends the writ of habeas corpus in violation of Article I, § 9, clause 2, of the Constitution. This clause provides that "[t]he Privilege of the Writ of Habeas Corpus shall not be suspended, unless when in Cases of Rebellion or Invasion the public Safety may require it."

The writ of habeas corpus known to the Framers was quite different from that which exists today. As we explained previously, the first Congress made the writ of habeas corpus available only to prisoners confined under the authority of the United States, not under state authority. Supra, at 6–7; see Ex parte Dorr, 3 How. 103, 11 L.Ed. 514 (1844). The class of judicial actions reviewable by the writ was more restricted as well. In Ex parte Watkins, 3 Pet. 193, 7 L.Ed. 650 (1830), we denied a petition for a writ of habeas corpus from a prisoner "detained in prison by virtue of the judgment of a court, which court possesses general and final jurisdiction in criminal cases." Id., at 202. Reviewing the English common law which informed American courts' understanding of the scope of the writ, we held that "[t]he judgment of the circuit court in a criminal case is of itself evidence of its own legality," and that we could not "usurp that power by the instrumentality of the writ of habeas corpus." Id., at 207.

It was not until 1867 that Congress made the writ generally available in "all cases where any person may be restrained of his or her liberty in violation of the constitution, or of any treaty or law of the United States." Supra, at 6. And it was not until well into this century that this Court interpreted that provision to allow a final judgment of conviction in a state court to be collaterally attacked on habeas. See, e.g., Waley v. Johnston, 316 U.S. 101, 62 S.Ct. 964, 86 L.Ed. 1302 (1942); Brown v. Allen, 344 U.S. 443 (1953). But we assume, for purposes of decision here, that the Suspension Clause of the Constitution refers to the writ as it exists today, rather than as it existed in 1789. See Swain v. Pressley, 430 U.S. 372, 97 S.Ct. 1224, 51 L.Ed.2d 411 (1977); id., at 385 (Burger, C.J., concurring).

The Act requires a habeas petitioner to obtain leave from the court of appeals before filing a second habeas petition in the district court. But this requirement simply transfers from the district court to the court of appeals a screening function which would previously have been performed by the district court as required by 28 U.S.C. § 2254 Rule 9(b). The Act also codifies some of the pre-existing limits on successive petitions, and further restricts the availability of relief to habeas petitioners. But we have long recognized that "the power to award the writ by any of the courts of the United States, must be given by written law," Ex parte Bollman, 4 Cranch 75, 94, 2 L.Ed. 554 (1807), and we have likewise recognized that judgments about the proper scope of the writ are "normally for Congress to make." Lonchar v. Thomas, 517 U.S. 314, ___ (slip op., at 8).

The new restrictions on successive petitions constitute a modified res judicata rule, a restraint on what is called in habeas corpus practice "abuse of the writ." In McCleskey v. Zant, 499 U.S. 467, 111 S.Ct. 1454, 113 L.Ed.2d 517 (1991), we said that "the doctrine of abuse of the writ refers to a complex and evolving body of equitable principles informed and controlled by historical usage, statutory developments, and judicial decisions." Id., at 489. The added restrictions which the Act places on second habeas petitions are well within the compass of this evolutionary process, and we hold that they do not amount to a "suspension" of the writ contrary to Article I, § 9.

IV

We have answered the questions presented by the petition for certiorari in this case, and we now dispose of the petition for an original writ of habeas corpus. Our Rule 20.4(a) delineates the standards under which we grant such writs:

A petition seeking the issuance of a writ of habeas corpus shall comply with the requirements of 28 U.S.C. §§ 2241 and 2242, and in particular with the provision in the last paragraph of § 2242 requiring a statement of the "reasons for not making application to the district court of the district in which the applicant is held." If the relief sought is from the judgment of a state court, the petition shall set forth specifically how and wherein the petitioner has exhausted available remedies in the state courts or otherwise comes within the provisions of 28 U.S.C. § 2254(b). To justify the granting of a writ of habeas corpus, the petitioner must show exceptional circumstances warranting the exercise of the Court's discretionary powers and must show that adequate relief cannot be obtained in any other form or from any other court. These writs are rarely granted.

Reviewing petitioner's claims here, they do not materially differ from numerous other claims made by successive habeas petitioners which we have had occasion to review on stay applications to this Court. Neither of them satisfies the requirements of the relevant provisions of the Act, let alone the requirement that there be "exceptional circumstances" justifying the issuance of the writ.

* * *

The petition for writ of certiorari is dismissed for want of jurisdiction. The petition for an original writ of habeas corpus is denied. It is so ordered.

■ JUSTICE STEVENS, with whom JUSTICE SOUTER and JUSTICE BREYER join, concurring [omitted].

■ JUSTICE SOUTER, with whom JUSTICE STEVENS and JUSTICE BREYER join, concurring [omitted].

*

INDEX

References are to Pages